St. James Encyclopedia of Popular Culture

Second Edition

St. James Encyclopedia of Popular Culture

Second Edition

VOLUME 4

NIA–STY

Thomas Riggs

EDITOR

ST. JAMES PRESS

A part of Gale, Cengage Learning

Detroit • New York • San Francisco • New Haven, Conn • Waterville, Maine • London

St. James Encyclopedia of Popular Culture

Thomas J. Riggs, Editor

Product Manager: Douglas Dentino

Project Editor: Carol A. Schwartz

Editorial: Laura Avery; Dana Barnes; Erin Bealmear; Shawn Corridor; Matthew Derda; Jason Everett; Dana Ferguson; Jennifer Greve; Kristy Harper; Kristin Hart; Alan Hedblad; Andrea Henderson; Monica Hubbard; Jeff Hunter; Victor Ibarra; Reed Kalso; Kristin Key; Debra Kirby; Laurie Malashanko; Kim McGrath; Chelsea Merchan; Kathy Nemeh; Scot Peacock; Jennifer Wisinski

Rights Acquisition and Management: Christine Myaskovsky

Composition: Gary Leach

Manufacturing: Wendy Blurton

Imaging: John Watkins

Product Design: Kristine Julien

LIBRARY OF CONGRESS CATALOGING-IN-PUBLICATION DATA

St. James encyclopedia of popular culture / Thomas Riggs, editor ; with an introduction by Jim Cullen. -- 2nd edition.
p. cm. --
Includes bibliographical references and index.
ISBN 978-1-55862-847-2 (set) -- ISBN 978-1-55862-848-9 (vol. 1) -- ISBN 978-1-55862-849-6 (vol. 2) -- ISBN 978-1-55862-850-2 (vol. 3) -- ISBN 978-1-55862-851-9 (vol. 4) -- ISBN 978-1-55862-852-6 (vol. 5) -- ISBN 978-1-55862-853-3 (ebook)
1. United States--Civilization--20th century--Encyclopedias. 2. United States--Civilization--21st century--Encyclopedias. 3. Popular culture--United States--History--20th century--Encyclopedias. 4. Popular culture--United States--History--21st century--Encyclopedias. I. Riggs, Thomas, 1963- II. Title: Saint James encyclopedia of popular culture.

E169.1.J3 2013
973.9--dc23 2012049921

Gale, a part of Cengage Learning
27500 Drake Rd.
Farmington Hills, MI, 48331-3535

ISBN-13: 978-1-55862-847-2 (set) ISBN-10: 1-55862-847-9 (set)
ISBN-13: 978-1-55862-848-9 (vol. 1) ISBN-10: 1-55862-848-7 (vol. 1)
ISBN-13: 978-1-55862-849-6 (vol. 2) ISBN-10: 1-55862-849-5 (vol. 2)
ISBN-13: 978-1-55862-850-2 (vol. 3) ISBN-10: 1-55862-850-9 (vol. 3)
ISBN-13: 978-1-55862-851-9 (vol. 4) ISBN-10: 1-55862-851-7 (vol. 4)
ISBN-13: 978-1-55862-852-6 (vol. 5) ISBN-10: 1-55862-852-5 (vol. 5)

This title is also available as an e-book.
ISBN-13: 978-1-55862-853-3 ISBN-10: 55862-853-3
Contact your Gale, a part of Cengage Learning, sales representative for ordering information.

Printed in China
1 2 3 4 5 6 7 17 16 15 14 13

Contents

List of Entries

B

C

G

M

VOLUME 5

S *continued*

T

U

V

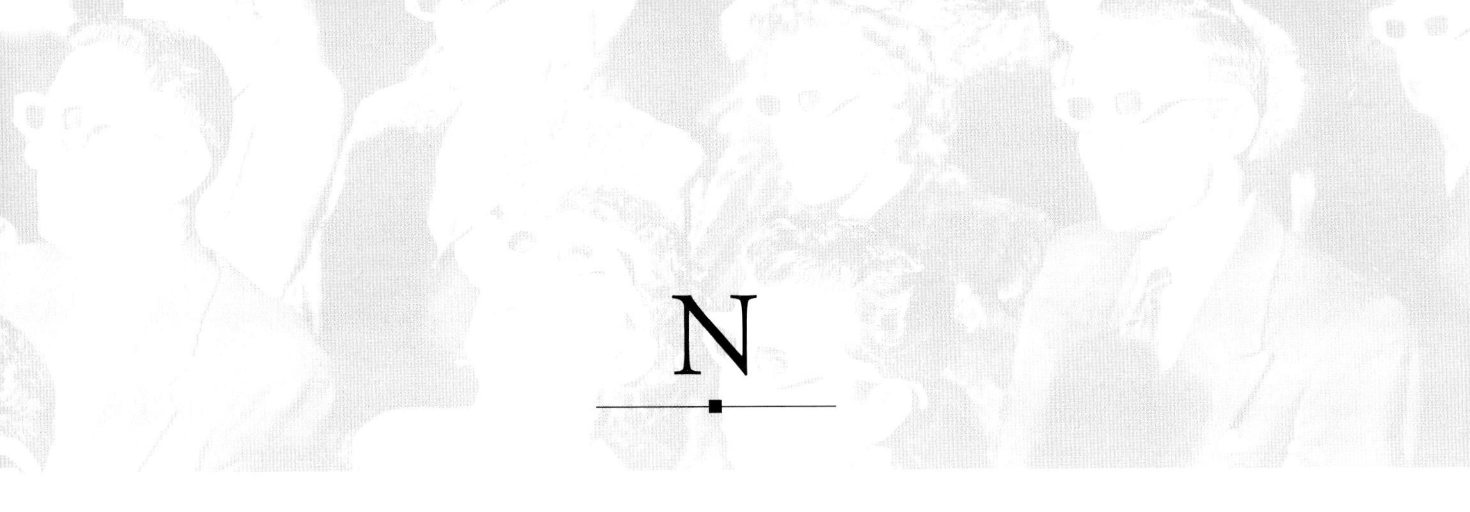

N

Niagara Falls

Heart-shaped bathtubs and romantic overlooks define the contemporary vision of the greatest waterfall of North America. Linked with romantic honeymooning, Niagara Falls has become a tourist mecca that happens to contain an awesome natural wonder. The wonder of the falls has attracted visitors to this site for hundreds of years; however, the onlookers' interest has been enhanced by a host of attractions. With their natural grandeur, the falls have impressed business developers looking for sources of power and exhibitionists looking for a wondrous thrill.

Many Americans refer to Niagara Falls as the first scenic wonder of North America. In fact, the falls attracted native people to the area for many years. Settlers converted the site into a primitive tourist destination, complete with dangerous catwalks leading out into the falls' mists. As the early republic strained to find ways of defining itself and impressing Europeans, many Americans of the early 1800s turned to natural wonders or oddities. Chief among such icons, Niagara Falls rapidly became one of the nation's first attractions.

Some European Americans gazed at the crashing falls and saw unrealized profit, water-powered milling quickly took shape above the falls. The awesome force of the water offered entrepreneurs a bit of a free-for-all as they pursued power generation. This avenue of progress continued to be developed in haphazard fashion throughout the nineteenth century. The tourist industry also turned more intrusive during the mid-1800s, leading to the haphazard construction of hotels and motels, as well as roads and bridges to access them.

Such developments so close to the nation's preeminent natural wonder spurred a new type of reaction among Americans, and the falls became one of the first focuses of American preservationists. Initially, outraged tourists bypassed the industrialized Niagara for more pristine or peaceful resorts. However, beginning in 1870, socially conservative, highly cultured reformers came to Niagara's aid. Led by Frederick Law Olmsted, the leader of American landscape architecture and planning, the preservationists sought to secure lands adjacent to the falls on both the American and Canadian sides. By 1887 the Niagara Preservation Movement had secured these lands, and New York established a state reservation at the site in 1885. Soon the preservationists realized that they also needed to prohibit development upriver from the falls, but the state was resistant. The "Free Niagara" movement continued through the early 1900s.

In tandem with its appeal as a majestic natural wonder, Niagara has consistently appealed to American culture's fascination with the bizarre. The feature films *Niagara* (1953) and *Superman* (1978) were partly filmed near the falls, and H. G. Wells was so impressed with the electrical dynamos in place after 1900 that he made the falls an important part of some of his science fiction. This became a fairly familiar characteristic of sci fi stories, including *Flash Gordon*, which used the falls as the unique place on Earth from which to achieve interplanetary travel. A number of individuals have "shot," or ridden over, the falls since 1901—some successful, some not—in vehicles ranging from barrels and balls to, more recently, a jet ski.

Brian Black

SEE ALSO: *Environmentalism;* Flash Gordon*; Jet Skis; Leisure Time; National Parks; Protest Groups; Science Fiction Publishing; Superman.*

BIBLIOGRAPHY

Irwin, William R. *The New Niagara*. University Park, PA: Penn State University Press, 1996.

McGreevy, Patrick Vincent. *Imagining Niagara*. Amherst: University of Massachusetts Press, 1994.

McKinsey, Elizabeth. *Niagara Falls: Icon of the American Sublime*. New York: Cambridge University Press, 1985.

Strand, Ginger, Gail. *Inventing Niagara*. New York: Simon & Schuster, 2008.

Nichols, Mike, and Elaine May

Along with Lenny Bruce and other satirists who emerged during the late 1950s and early 1960s, the team of Mike Nichols (1931–) and Elaine May (1932–) made a major impact on the development of modern American comedy. Nichols and May first encountered each together in the Hyde Park neighborhood surrounding the University of Chicago in the early 1950s. The daughter of a Yiddish actor who had grown up in the world of theater, May had married, conceived a child, divorced her husband and then briefly studied acting before she hitchhiked to Hyde Park. Nichols, born Michael Igor Peschkowsky, immigrated to the United States with his family in order to escape the Nazis in 1939. He enrolled at the University of Chicago in 1950 as a premed student, but he was eventually drawn into the world of theater.

The two precocious iconoclasts began working together in 1955 as members of the Compass Players, an improvisational theater troupe that took root in Hyde Park's offbeat, bohemian cultural scene. From the beginning, the uncommon rapport these young, quick-witted performers enjoyed together enabled them to improvise innovative parodies of popular culture, mock interviews, and satiric dialogues with ease. Together with another young performer who would later make his mark on the early 1960s satire revival, Shelley Berman, Nichols and May acquired reputations as sassy, irreverent clowns—satiric renegades who, with their quick wit and native intelligence, devastated the lifestyles, hypocrisies, and mores of suburban WASPs and of modern, middle-class males in particular.

Following the disintegration of the Compass Players in early 1957, Nichols and May began honing much of their material into a duo nightclub act. Signed by an ambitious and savvy manager named Jack Rollins (who would soon manage the career of another up-and-coming comedic performer, Woody Allen), Nichols and May appeared at New York clubs such as the Blue Angel and the Village Vanguard before getting booked on *The Jack Paar Show*, *The Steve Allen Plymouth Show*, and NBC-TV's *Omnibus*. It was on the latter program, aired in January 1958, that Nichols and May performed "Dawn of Love"—a propless set piece developed at the Compass that featured a teenage boy desperately attempting to make it with his date in the back seat of an automobile.

The acclaim this televised scene brought Nichols and May was considerable, and almost immediately the pair became show business celebrities. Over the next several years, Nichols and May appeared on dozens of television programs and specials, performed weekly segments for NBC Radio's *Monitor*, enjoyed a successful run on Broadway, produced several popular comedy albums, and even improvised material for Narragansett Beer television commercials.

For many Americans who saw or heard them perform, Nichols and May brought a startlingly new, fresh, and "sophisticated" approach to comedy. Eschewing traditional male/female patter, they created timely and occasionally daring satires of psychoanalysis, show business, contemporary sexual mores, the PTA (parent-teacher association), and many other subjects dealing with suburban, middle-class life. Audiences and critics marveled at the pair's sharp, incisive social satire and the way they were able to riff together onstage like two nimble jazz musicians. Respected theater critic Robert Brustein spoke for many of Nichols and May's admirers when he gushed over the pair's ability to "employ extraordinary powers of observation to locate the clichés of conventional middle-class life. Nichols and May," he continued, "are the voice of the outraged intelligence in a world given over to false piety, cloying sentiment, and institutionalized stupidity." Like many other American satirists who rose to prominence in the early 1960s, Nichols and May were identified with and absorbed into the orbit of well-educated, sophisticated Kennedy-era liberals.

Shortly after performing at the legendary 1962 Madison Square Garden birthday party for President John F. Kennedy—an avowed fan of the period's "liberal satire"—Nichols and May decided to pursue individual careers. While May continued to experiment with several edgy satirical ventures in the mid-1960s, Nichols teamed with playwright Neil Simon on several Broadway blockbusters, including *Barefoot in the Park* and *The Odd Couple*. Established as a star stage director, Nichols was given the opportunity to direct a screen adaptation of Edward Albee's *Who's Afraid of Virginia Woolf?* A string of later successes in moviemaking—most notably his direction of the 1967 film *The Graduate*—and in stage productions have distinguished Nichols as a significant contributor to modern American popular culture. May followed Nichols's footsteps into the film business but never achieved comparable success or influence.

Since breaking up as an improvisational duo in 1962, Nichols and May performed jointly at the inauguration gala of President Jimmy Carter and at a one-night-only performance on Broadway sixteen years later. They later teamed up on two 1990s film comedies directed by Nichols, *The Birdcage* (1996) and *Primary Colors* (1998).

Stephen Kercher

SEE ALSO: *Allen, Steve; Allen, Woody; Broadway; Bruce, Lenny;* The Graduate*;* The Odd Couple*;* Omnibus*; Paar, Jack; Simon, Neil; Television.*

BIBLIOGRAPHY

Coleman, Janet. *The Compass: The Improvisational Theatre That Revolutionized American Comedy*. Chicago: University of Chicago Press, 1990.

Kercher, Stephen. *Revel with a Cause: Liberal Satire in Postwar America*. Chicago: University of Chicago Press, 2006.

Nachman, Gerald. *Seriously Funny: The Rebel Comedians of the 1950s and 1960s*. New York: Back Stage Books, 2004.

Nicholson, Jack *(1937–)*

Oscar-winning actor Jack Nicholson rose to fame in the 1970s with a series of critically acclaimed roles as hard-living men down on their luck. Now in his seventies, the actor is still active on the big screen and remains a fixture at the home games of the National Basketball Association's Los Angeles Lakers.

EARLY CAREER

Born in New York City on April 22, 1937, John Joseph ("Jack") Nicholson moved to Hollywood, California, in the 1950s. He worked in the mailroom at Metro-Goldwyn-Mayer during the day and pursued his acting dreams at night, appearing in local plays and taking acting classes. His first film role came in 1958 when Roger Corman cast him as the lead in *The Cry Baby Killer*, in which Nicholson depicts a juvenile delinquent who, thinking he has committed murder, takes several hostages. Nicholson made the character into a strangely appealing, oddball young man with an unpredictable violent streak, a portrait he would recapitulate in many of his early films. He went on to do several other movies with Corman, most notably appearing in *Little Shop of Horrors* (1960) as a masochistic patient who asks his dentist to hold off on the Novocain because "it dulls the senses."

By the mid-1960s Nicholson was working steadily in "B" movies and had a recurring role on the television serial *Dr. Kildare*, starring Richard Chamberlain. He also wrote a number of screenplays, including *The Trip*, a Peter Fonda vehicle illustrating the mind-expanding benefits of LSD on a straight-laced television executive, and *Head*, a psychedelic flick centered on the band the Monkees and featuring Frank Zappa, Annette Funicello, and Victor Mature.

EASY RIDER AND THE 1970s

Nicholson's breakout role came in 1969, when Rip Torn dropped out of Fonda and Dennis Hopper's edgy motorcycle-

and-drugs film *Easy Rider* (1969). Nicholson garnered his first Oscar nomination for his portrayal of George Hanson, the hard-drinking lawyer fleeing the rat race who joins Fonda and Hopper's characters for a leg of their cross-country jaunt. *Easy Rider*, a brash portrait of countercultural rebellion and hedonism, resonated with the public.

Nicholson's next film, *Five Easy Pieces* (1970), examines the downside of dropping out and turning on. He stars as Bobby Eroica Dupea, an angry oilrig worker haunted by his past as a musical prodigy in a family of musicians. Nicholson received his second Academy Award nomination for this role and, thus, found himself a sought-after Hollywood actor. He went on to appear in more than a dozen movies in the 1970s, including *Carnal Knowledge* (1971); *The Last Detail* (1973); and *Chinatown* (1974), Roman Polanski's modern noir tale in which Nicholson plays a jaded Sam Spade–type who gets caught up in a political broil over land and water rights and is hoodwinked by a beautiful woman. His signature performance of the 1970s was in Milos Forman's acclaimed film adaptation of Ken Kesey's *One Flew over the Cuckoo's Nest* (1975). Nicholson won the Academy Award for Best Actor as Korean War vet and rebellious mental ward patient Randel P. McMurphy.

***Jack Nicholson in* The Shining.** *Jack Nicholson delivered a memorable performance as an author driven to madness in* The Shining. WARNER BROS/THE KOBAL COLLECTION.

THE 1980s AND 1990s

Nicholson began the 1980s with the lead role in Stanley Kubrick's *The Shining* (1980), based on the Stephen King novel of the same name. As Jack Torrance, a writer who brings his wife (Shelley Duvall) and young son to stay in a deserted and haunted hotel, only to be slowly driven mad by the evil spirit of the grounds, Nicholson paints a vivid portrait of ordinary frustrations taken to a psychotic extreme. Over the rest of the decade, the actor made a series of high-profile films, including a remake of *The Postman Always Rings Twice* (1981), *Reds* (1981), the tearjerker *Terms of Endearment* (1983), *Prizzi's Honor* (1985), *The Witches of Eastwick* (1987), and *Ironweed* (1987). He received Oscar nominations for his roles in *Reds*, *Prizzi's Honor*, and *Ironweed* and won Best Supporting Actor for his portrayal of former astronaut Garrett Breedlove in *Terms of Endearment*.

At the end of the decade, Nicholson's trademark grin turned surrealistic when he immortalized the arch-villain the Joker in Tim Burton's blockbuster production *Batman* (1989). He worked steadily through the 1990s, earning another Oscar nomination for his role as Colonel Nathan R. Jessup in *A Few Good Men* (1992) and the Best Actor award for his role as Melvin Udall in *As Good as It Gets* (1997).

THE 2000s AND PERSONAL LIFE

Nicholson started off the new century with a bang, earning an Oscar nomination for his star turn in *About Schmidt* (2002), the morose tale of a retired actuary struggling with his wife's death. After that, however, he took on far fewer roles, most notably a persistent therapist in the Adam Sandler vehicle *Anger Management* (2003), an older man who falls for his young girlfriend's mother in *Something's Gotta Give* (2003), an Irish gangster in director Martin Scorsese's *The Departed* (2006), and a dying man trying to fulfill his list of final wishes in *The Bucket List* (2007).

Nicholson's love life off the screen has also generated a buzz over the course of his career. While never married and known as somewhat of a playboy, Nicholson has had a number of long-term romantic relationships with actresses. Between 1973 and 1989, he was involved with Anjelica Huston, but the two broke up when Nicholson had an affair with Rebecca Broussard. Nicholson has two children with Broussard, a daughter with Sandra Knight, and a daughter with Winnie Hollman. He is known for dating much younger women, such as Broussard, Bebe Buell, and Lara Flynn Boyle.

Jenny Ludwig

SEE ALSO: *Academy Awards; "B" Movies; Batman; Celebrity; Celebrity Couples;* Chinatown*; Corman, Roger;* Easy Rider*; Funicello, Annette; Hollywood; Kesey, Ken; King, Stephen; Kubrick, Stanley; The Los Angeles Lakers; The Monkees;* One Flew over the Cuckoo's Nest*; Scorsese, Martin; Zappa, Frank.*

BIBLIOGRAPHY

Crane, Robert ,and Christopher Fryer. *Jack Nicholson: The Early Years*. Lexington: University Press of Kentucky, 2012.

McDougal, Dennis. *Five Easy Decades: How Jack Nicholson Became the Biggest Movie Star in Modern Times*. New York: John Wiley & Sons, 2008.

McGilligan, Patrick. *Jack's Life: A Biography of Jack Nicholson*. New York: W. W. Norton, 1995.

Nickelback

Nickelback is a Canadian rock band that is often labeled "post-grunge" in recognition of its roots in the Seattle, Washington, grunge era of the early 1990s. The group began as a cover band, the Village Idiots, in the small Alberta town of Hanna. In its earliest incarnation, the group consisted of lead singer and guitarist Chad Kroeger; his brother, bassist Mike Kroeger; their childhood friend, guitarist Ryan Peake; and cousin Brandon Kroeger as drummer. Moving to Vancouver, the band changed their name to Nickelback and released two albums in 1996: the extended-play *Hesher* and the full-length *Curb*. Soon after, Brandon left and was replaced briefly by Mitch Guindon and then by Ryan Vikedal. It was not until the band's second album, *The State* (widely released in 1999–2000) that the group gained significant recognition.

Nickelback received the Juno Award for Best New Group in 2001, and its popularity continued to increase over the next ten years. In December 2009 *Billboard* named Nickelback "Group of the Decade," noting the band's impact on the music community and its album sales of more than thirty million. Despite the band's commercial success, it has been criticized for the derivative quality of its work and for betraying the rawness of its grunge roots with pop-accented offerings.

Silver Side Up (2001), the band's third album, included "How You Remind Me," the most-played song of 2002. Seven years later *Billboard* named "How You Remind Me" the decade's top rock song. The album sold more than ten million copies worldwide, reaching the top of the sales charts in Canada, the United Kingdom, Austria, South Africa, Ireland, Australia, and New Zealand. "Someday," the lead song off *The Long Road* (2003), Nickelback's fourth album, was mocked for its similarity to mega-hit "How You Remind Me," and the *Boston Phoenix*, an alternative weekly newspaper, branded Nickelback "the worst band in the history of music." Allmusic.com was only slightly less harsh, calling them "unspeakably awful." However, music consumers, undeterred by such criticism, bought more than five million copies of the album. The awards kept coming too. Nickelback captured the Best Group and Fan Choice awards at the 2004 Junos.

Vikedal left the band after *The Long Road*, and Canadian drummer Daniel Adair, formerly of 3 Doors Down, joined the group as drummer. Nickelback's next album, 2005's *All the Right Reason*, remained on the Billboard Top 30 for more than two years and sold more than seven million copies in the United States alone. The album featured a guest appearance by legendary country rock band ZZ Top's guitarist, Billy Gibbons, who had a solo on "Follow You Home" and contributed backup vocals for "Rockstar." The latter was another big hit for the band, as was the music video, which featured a galaxy of stars lip-syncing lyrics, including Gibbons, hockey player Wayne Gretzky, NASCAR driver Dale Earnhardt Jr., actress Eliza Dushku, and singers and musicians Gene Simmons, Jerry Cantrell, Nelly Furtado, and Ted Nugent. The song itself generated considerable debate, as critics could not decide whether the lyrics satirized the excesses of the rock-star lifestyle or offered a self-analytical narrative.

The success of *The Long Road* attracted the attention of songwriter and accomplished rock producer Mutt Lange. Lange coproduced the band's sixth studio album, *Dark Horse* (2008), which became a multiplatinum seller. It debuted in the number one spot on Canadian sales charts and in the top five in the United States, Australia, New Zealand, the United Kingdom, Germany, Austria, and Switzerland. Six hits from the album helped it win Album of the Year and Nickelback Group of the Year at the 2009 Juno Awards.

Almost three years after the release of *Dark Horse*, the group's seventh studio album, *Here and Now*, was released on November 21, 2011. The album debuted at number two on the Billboard U.S. 200. Critical reactions were mixed. *Entertainment Weekly* gave it a *C*, saying that the band sounded bored, and *Billboard* labeled it a "well-crafted brand of meat 'n potatoes hard rock." *Atlanta Music Guide* advised against expecting too much of the lyrics.

Some people did not expect much from the band generally. When fans of the Detroit Lions learned that Nickelback was scheduled to perform the socially conscious "When We Stand Together" at halftime during the Detroit Lions–Green Bay Packers game on Thanksgiving Day, they protested vehemently. An online petition calling for Nickelback to be replaced in the halftime show charged that the performance would be a betrayal of Detroit's rich musical heritage. The petition was signed by 55,000 people. Although the critical attacks may continue unabated, so do Nickelback's successes. With more than fifty million albums sold as of 2011 and a string of Top 10 hits in mainstream rock, alternative rock, and adult Top 40, the band has proved its endurance and consistency—qualities rock bands that have won greater critical praise have failed to emulate.

Wylene Rholetter

SEE ALSO: *Facebook; The Green Bay Packers; Gretzky, Wayne; Grunge; National Football League (NFL); Pop Music; Rock and Roll; Top 40; ZZ Top.*

BIBLIOGRAPHY

Binelli, Mark. "New Faces: Nickelback." *Rolling Stone*, November 23, 2000, 53.

Leahey, Andrew. "Biography: Nickelback." AllMusic.com. Accessed February 2012. Available from http://www.allmusic.com/artist/nickelback-p410589/biography

LePage, Mark. "Why Nickelback Is the World's Most Hated Band." *Montreal Gazette*, April 3, 2010.

Mansfield, Brian. "Nickelback Is Living in the Diversity of *Here and Now*." *USA Today*, November 22, 2011.

Nickelodeons

Although nickelodeons did not show the first moving pictures, which had been appearing as part of the entertainment offered at vaudeville shows since the 1890s, they represented the first efforts to create a new venue in which moving pictures would be shown as the featured attraction. Also known as storefront theaters, nickelodeons experienced their heyday from about 1903 to 1915.

Named for *nickel*, the price of admission, and *odeon*, the Greek word for theater, nickelodeons offered the first affordable mass entertainment for lower-income urban people, and hence became wildly popular during the first decades of the twentieth century. As businesses, they were more affordable to run than the ubiquitous penny arcades that featured hand-cranked "peep show" moving pictures (of usually quite wholesome subjects)

Nickelodeon. *Barkers and ticket takers pose outside the entrance of a nickelodeon theater in 1905.* AMERICAN STOCK/GETTY IMAGES.

that could only accommodate one viewer at a time at each machine. The rise of the nickelodeon marked a transition away from penny arcades and vaudeville shows; they were the first institutions to treat the moving picture as a credible and viable form of entertainment in its own right.

Harry Davis, a Pittsburgh businessman, is said to have coined the term *nickelodeon* in 1904 when he converted a store into a theater, made its interior luxurious, and added a piano as musical accompaniment for the silent footage. His venture was so successful that similar theaters began springing up all over the country, and by 1908 there were between 8,000 and 10,000 nickelodeons nationwide. Other early entrepreneurs included men who would become future movie moguls, such as Marcus Loew, Adolph Zukor, the Warner brothers, and William Fox. Locating their businesses in working-class urban districts, these men catered to workers' needs for leisure activities while acknowledging their lack of free time and spending money. Most vaudeville shows, which took place in special theaters uptown, cost at least 25 cents and were therefore economically and culturally prohibitive to the typical laborer. Going to the nickelodeon, in contrast, was cheap and required no advance tickets, reserved seating, formal clothing, or special decorum.

The first nickel theaters were located in central business districts, but the majority sat on secondary streets near immigrant and working-class residential areas, where storefronts could be easily converted into suitable spaces. The fronts were recessed up to six feet in order to create outside vestibules that housed a box office and gave patrons a place to wait. These exteriors, often embellished with bright paint, tin or stucco facades, movie posters, lurid signs, and thousands of electric lights, helped draw people in. In addition, owners often used live barkers to shout the latest attractions to passersby. The interiors were spartan in contrast, furnished with rows of simple wooden folding chairs (seating capacity at first ranged from 50 to 299 and later reached 600), a canvas screen, and papered-over windows and doorways. The projection booth, located in the rear of the theater, was merely a small box, six feet square, with enough room to house the projector and the projectionist, who cranked the film by hand. For about $200 in equipment, an owner could be in business—because these storefront theaters were not considered "real" theaters, licenses cost much less than those for "legitimate" theaters.

The typical nickelodeon show ran about thirty minutes and was usually composed of three 10-minute reels and an illustrated song or lecture in between. The shows sometimes ran 24 hours a day, and the programs were usually changed daily to encourage a constant turnover. People flocked to nickelodeons because of the freedom allowed within the sites themselves in addition to the films they showed. To satisfy the need for novelty, movie producers turned out thousands of these one-reel films, which took their plots from current events, Shakespearean plays, operas, novels, and even the Bible. Edwin S. Porter's *The Great Train Robbery* of 1903, which featured the attack on a telegraph operator, the escape of bandits with the engine, their pursuit and capture, and Western dance hall scenes, was the first "blockbuster" story film, and it inspired many imitations. Other popular features borrowed from the realities of working-class life included such titles as *The Eviction*, *The Ex-Convict*, *A Desperate Encounter*, and *She Won't Pay Her Rent*. Audiences, however, were perhaps most impressed by their exposure to images they had never seen before. Film footage of sights such as Niagara Falls and train travel appealed to their appetite for wonder and their desire to see what they could not normally see, or afford to see, at vaudeville acts.

Besides exposing people to the latest technological wonders of motion pictures, nickelodeons were key social venues. They provided immigrants with their first non-work exposure to American culture. More respectable than dance halls, cheap cafes, and amusement parks, they were also considered safe and acceptable places for working women to go in the early evenings and on weekends, providing one of their few refuges away from life at home. Also known as the "academy of the workingman," the "workingman's college," and the "true theater of the people," the nickelodeon was additionally a viable place of entertainment for the working-class man, either alone or with his family.

Because of their popularity with lower-income people, nickelodeons drew the critical attention of Progressive Era reformers, who saw them as seedy, dangerous places that were as deleterious as cheap vaudeville, prize fights, honkytonks, and similar forms of entertainment. Reformers believed that working-class people were not educated enough to watch these films critically and that they lacked the intellect to read into and resist the temptations presented (it is estimated that by 1910, one out of five nickelodeon films showed characters thinking about or actually engaging in criminal activity).

The perceived threats of nickelodeons to children drew the most attention of reformers, especially because turn-of-the-century children comprised between one-fourth and one-half of all nickelodeon audiences. Jane Addams even criticized them as "houses of dreams" that encouraged dangerous flights of fancy for youngsters. But these places continued to be key social centers for working-class children, who often got rowdy after the lights went down, sang along with the illustrated music, shouted at the images projected on the screen, and sometimes exchanged sexual favors in the darkened back rows. The efforts of reformers and anti-vice crusaders around 1908 and 1909 led to the first censorship drives, which historian David Nasaw defined as "'class' legislation aimed at the working people and immigrants who owned, operated, and patronized the nickel theaters." In 1909 the National Board of Censorship was formed as a response to pressures to monitor the content of nickelodeon films.

Reform efforts led to the gradual demise of the nickelodeon. By the early 1910s the film industry itself was engaged in self-censorship, meaning that novel and interesting films free of "harmful" images were that much more difficult to create. In addition, operators now had to spend more money to maintain the interior space of their businesses. Because entrances were blocked off, theaters presented real and dangerous fire hazards to the crowds within. In addition, the air—foul and fetid from never being circulated or replenished—was thought to cause various diseases. Fire safety ordinances and new building codes made it more costly to operate storefront theaters.

In addition to these external factors, changes were being made in the films themselves. As time went by, the movies got longer and demonstrated a greater variety of subject content, including dramatic, historical, and narrative stories, comedies, mysteries, scenic pictures, and those featuring "personalities." By the mid-1910s, businessmen catering to the upper classes saw the financial potential of motion pictures and built their own, much more lavish, movie "palaces" that brought in a finer trade of people and served as the precursors to standard movie theaters.

The nickelodeon, for its relatively short lifetime, was the first viable form of mass entertainment for the poor in America. It was an institution that gave workers a place to go in their leisure hours and exposed them to various aspects of American culture. Most importantly, the nickelodeon instilled in young Americans a love of movies and motion picture entertainment that sparked and sustained an important twentieth-century industry and cultural institution.

Wendy Woloson

SEE ALSO: *Addams, Jane;* The Great Train Robbery*; Leisure Time; Movie Palaces; Niagara Falls; Silent Movies; Vaudeville.*

BIBLIOGRAPHY

Herzog, Charlotte. "The Nickelodeon Phase (1903–c. 1917)." *Marquee* 13 (1981), 5–11.

Keim, Norman O. *Our Movie Houses.* Syracuse, NY: Syracuse University Press, 2008.

Nasaw, David. *Going Out: The Rise and Fall of Public Amusements.* New York: BasicBooks, 1993.

Sklar, Robert. *Movie-Made America: A Cultural History of American Movies.* New York: Vintage Books, 1994.

Wagenknecht, Edward. *The Movies in the Age of Innocence.* Norman, : University of Oklahoma Press, 1962.

Nicklaus, Jack *(1940–)*

In the world of men's professional golf, no one has been more successful than Jack Nicklaus, the "Golden Bear." Winner of eighteen major championships, Nicklaus played a major part in the development of the Professional Golfers' Association (PGA) Tour. His name has been cemented in twentieth-century golf history, not only as the best professional golfer to ever play the game but also as one of golf's leading ambassadors.

Born on January 21, 1940, in Columbus, Ohio, Nicklaus began playing golf at age ten and won his first tournament, the Scioto Club Juvenile Trophy, that same year. His training progressed quickly under the tutelage of golf professional Jack Grout at the Scioto Country Club in Columbus, and he rose among the Ohio amateur ranks, winning the Ohio Junior Championship in 1953, 1954, and 1955 and the Ohio Open Championship in 1956. He played in his first U.S. Amateur Championship in 1955 in Richmond, Virginia, where he lost in the first round.

From 1957 to 1961 Nicklaus attended The Ohio State University, where he played for the Buckeyes and enrolled in a pre-pharmacy program. He met his future wife, Barbara Jean Bash, as a student, and the couple married on July 23, 1960. He had much success at Ohio State, winning a number of collegiate tournaments. His first major victory came at the Broadmoor Golf Club in Colorado in 1959, where he won his first U.S. Amateur Championship. Two years later he won his second, at the Pebble Beach Golf Links in California, which convinced him to give up his amateur status later that year.

As a rookie professional golfer, success came rapidly to Nicklaus. He won the U.S. Open at Oakmont Country Club in Pennsylvania in a famous play-off against Arnold Palmer and won four more PGA tournament events in his first year, earning him the title Rookie of the Year in 1962. He captured his first victory in the Masters Golf Tournament in Augusta, Georgia, in 1963, which was also the year he won his first PGA championship. He earned his first British Open title in 1966 in Muirfield, Scotland, making him the winner of each of the four major golf championships by the age of twenty-six.

As the dominant golfer of his time, Nicklaus became known for his aggressive play and prodigious drive. During the 1960s, he won thirty tournaments, and his success continued into the 1970s, when he won thirty-eight tournaments. The golf world was stunned in 1986 when, at age 46, he won the Masters for a record sixth time. His dominance slowly declined in the 1980s, when he won only five tournaments. He began playing in the Senior PGA Tour in 1990 and won ten tour events before retiring from competitive golf in 2005.

As one of golf's most prolific champions, he set several PGA Tour records, including the most major championships (eighteen), most U.S. Open wins (four), and most Masters wins (six). In all he won seventy-three PGA Tour events and nineteen international or unofficial tournaments. He was named PGA Player of the Year five times and has parlayed his success into profitable business ventures such as golf course design and golf club manufacturing. He also operates a popular golf instruction school and has produced many instructional videos and books. His influence on the game as a teacher and ambassador of the sport has earned him the title "Golfer of the Century" or "Golfer of the Millennium" in almost every major golf publication in the world.

Jay Parrent

SEE ALSO: *Golf; The Masters Golf Tournament; Palmer, Arnold.*

BIBLIOGRAPHY

Moritz, Charles, ed. *Current Biography Yearbook 1962.* New York: H. W. Wilson, 1963.

Nicklaus, Jack. *Golf My Way: The Instructional Classic, Revised and Updated.* New York: Simon and Schuster, 2005.

Nicklaus, Jack, and Herbert Warren Wind. *The Greatest Game of All: My Life in Golf.* New York: Simon and Schuster, 1969.

Nicklaus, Jack, and Ken Bowden. *On and Off the Fairway: A Pictorial Autobiography.* New York: Simon and Schuster, 1978.

Nicklaus, Jack, and Ken Bowden. *My Story.* New York: Simon and Schuster, 1997.

Night of the Living Dead

In October 1968 a low-budget horror film titled *Night of the Living Dead*, directed and cowritten by the independent film-

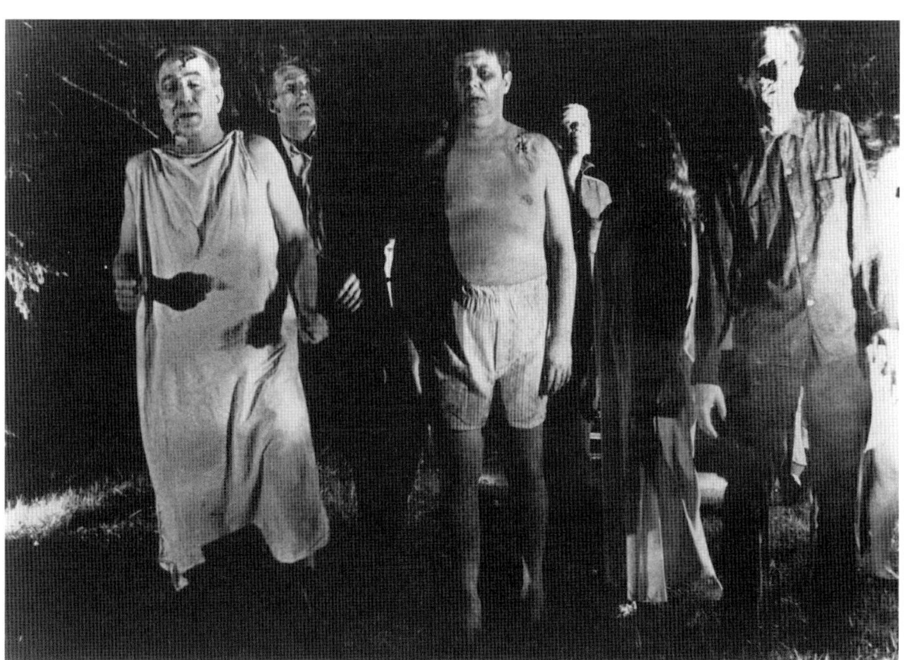

Night of the Living Dead. *Zombies seek human flesh in* Night of the Living Dead. IMAGE TEN/ THE KOBAL COLLECTION.

maker George Romero, opened in Pittsburgh, Pennsylvania, far from Hollywood and the mainstream cinema. Shot in the Pennsylvania countryside using mostly amateur actors and boasting ludicrously low production values, Romero's short black-and-white film nevertheless managed to leave its first viewers disturbed, even traumatized, through its unflinching depiction of bloody violence and cannibalism. The film set a new standard for intense screen horror—a standard the Hollywood industry took notice of and appropriated for its own increasingly graphic product in the late 1960s and early 1970s. Decades later the film is considered a classic. Recognized for its cultural significance, the film was placed in the National Film Registry in 1999 by the Library of Congress.

A CULT CLASSIC IS BORN

The story line of *Night of the Living Dead*, originally titled at various development stages as "Night of Anubis" or "The Night of Flesh Eaters," is deceptively simple and even derivative. Romero always admitted that his primary inspiration for the screenplay was the novel *I Am Legend* (1954) by Richard Matheson, about the last surviving human on earth battling vampires created by a plague. Another obvious influence, in regard to the explicit gore and cannibalism, is EC horror comics. In many ways, *Night of the Living Dead* at first seems little more than a rehash of 1950s science fiction clichés. A space probe has apparently brought back to earth an unknown form of radiation that has reanimated the corpses of the recently dead. (Other possible explanations for the plague were discarded from the final cut of the film.) What gives the film its taboo-shattering resonance is what Romero does next with his scenario. The shambling, mindless zombies are motivated by one primal drive: to consume the flesh of the living.

The plot, then, centers on the futile efforts of a small group of people, thrown together by circumstance, to fend off a zombie onslaught upon an isolated Pennsylvania farmhouse. The protagonists of the film are ill equipped to handle the crisis, and Romero makes it clear early on that they are doomed. Barbara, after witnessing in the film's opening sequence the murder of her brother Johnny by one of the zombies, is nearly catatonic and is finally devoured by a group of zombies, among which is her dead brother. Tom and Judy, two sympathetic young lovers, are unexpectedly killed in a truck explosion during an abortive escape attempt. The zombie feast upon their charred remains is the film's most horrific scene. Harry and Helen, an older married couple, are unable to stop their bickering and quarreling even as their daughter Karen lies dying of a zombie bite.

Ben, the narrative's ostensible hero, is engaged in a power struggle with Harry for control of the group's ever-worsening fortunes. The group's defenses, both physical and psychological, crumble one by one, and the final zombie attack on the farmhouse forces Ben, the single remaining survivor, to lock himself in the cellar (ironically the one part of the household that the cowardly Harry had claimed for his own) and cower until daylight. The film ends on a truly nihilistic note as Ben, spared the grisly fate of the others, is fatally shot by a member of a sheriff's posse who believes him to be a zombie.

Romero's artistic breakthrough as an independent filmmaker also demonstrated that movies need not originate from within the California film industry to achieve public and critical recognition. *Night of the Living Dead* was financed by Romero and nine associates, who put up $600 apiece to form a company called Image Ten. The film was shot on weekends and at night over seven months and ultimately cost approximately $115,000. Romero showed the finished film to two distributors, Columbia and American International Pictures (AIP), which rejected it. The Walter Reade company, initially hesitant, finally decided to buy the film and place it in drive-ins around the country.

At first it seemed as if the film might be condemned to a short run of drive-in obscurity before final extinction. However, public word of mouth about the film's graphic violence and relentlessly paced horror, combined with high-profile, savage critical denunciations in the pages of *Reader's Digest* (penned by the film critic Roger Ebert), the *New York Times*, and *Variety*, brought the film to the attention of many who might not have otherwise heard of it. When *Night of the Living Dead* went overseas in 1968, French and British critics in the pages of *Cahiers du Cinema* and *Sight and Sound*, respectively, were quick to praise the film as one of the year's best. The American critic Rex Reed was also an early proponent of the film.

SEQUELS AND REMAKES

In 1969 the Museum of Modern Art chose Romero's film as a notable first feature. Walter Reade was encouraged enough by this kind of recognition to bring back *Night of the Living Dead* into New York theaters, most famously the Waverly, for midnight showings. During the early 1970s the film achieved "cult" status, and pirated copies quickly found their way to cities and television stations across the world. Because of copyright problems with Walter Reade, Romero's Image Ten company received little of the many millions of dollars the film was now grossing. Since the early 1970s, however, Romero has achieved great measures of financial compensation and public and critical recognition, with the release of five "Dead" sequels: *Dawn of the Dead* (1978) *Day of the Dead* (1985), *Land of the Dead* (2005), *Diary of the Dead* (2007), and *Survival of the Dead* (2009).

Night of the Living Dead has been remade and revised several times. A remake, *Night of the Living Dead* (1990), was directed by Romero's special-effects collaborator Tom Savini, with the blessing of Romero. Another remake unconnected to Romero, *Night of the Living Dead 3-D* (2006), was directed by Jeff Broadstreet. Romero's original cowriter, John Russo, teamed with the writer-director Dan O'Bannon for *Return of the Living Dead* (1985), an alternative satirical continuation of the series that resulted in four sequels. Russo also "revised" the original *Night* by adding several new scenes and inserting a different soundtrack for *Night of the Living Dead: 30th Anniversary Edition* (1999). Other revisions of the original released over the years have involved colorization and conversion to 3-D.

Though Romero did not invent the American "gore" film genre—that distinction belongs primarily to Herschell Gordon Lewis, director of, among others, *Blood Feast* (1963)—he demonstrated unequivocally that excellence in filmmaking can legitimate even the most disreputable genres and their trappings. Critics have praised Romero for daring to cast a black actor as Ben, the hero. They have argued that Ben's shooting by the white mob of hunters is an indirect allusion to America's shameful history of racist lynching. The critics have also identified the mass of featureless zombies as the silent majority of middle-class Americans. The film, released in one of the most violent years of one of America's most violent decades, captures perfectly the mood of the time—its nihilism, its anxiety over mob action, its radicalism and reactionary conservatism, its domestic wartime paranoia, its body-count newscasts, and its unspoken fear of radiation and nuclear war.

Philip L. Simpson

SEE ALSO: *Cult Films; EC Comics; Horror Movies; The* New York Times*;* Reader's Digest*;* Variety.

BIBLIOGRAPHY

Gagne, Paul R. *The Zombies That Ate Pittsburgh: The Films of George A. Romero*. New York: Dodd, Mead, 1987.

McCarty, John. *The Modern Horror Film*. Secaucus, NJ: Carol Publishing, 1990.

Paffenroth, Kim. *Gospel of the Living Dead: George Romero's Visions of Hell on Earth*. Waco, TX: Baylor University Press, 2006.

Russell, Jamie. *Book of the Dead: The Complete History of Zombie Cinema*. Goldaming, UK: FAB Press, 2005.

Russo, John. *The Complete "Night of the Living Dead" Filmbook*. Pittsburgh, PA: Imagine, 1985.

Samuels, Stuart. *Midnight Movies*. New York: Collier, 1983.

Nightline

The ABC television news program *Nightline* developed out of the widespread need to see in-depth news coverage of the Iranian Hostage Crisis on a nightly basis. In a strange twist, the event that caused so much frustration and anger on the part of Americans created a television show that routinely gave guests, sitting in different parts of the globe, the opportunity to talk to one another. Often these discussions were among people who otherwise would never have met. In addition to exploiting new satellite technologies, *Nightline* expanded network news coverage into the late-night time slot. This allowed the program to dispense with conventional news techniques, such as edited interviews and prepared questions. In retrospect, the appearance of *Nightline* was improbable. The show that emerged from the 1979 hostage crisis began with future-anchor Ted Koppel thinking, "This story's gonna die." Needless to say, neither the story nor *Nightline* did.

Roone Arledge, the man in charge of the lowest-rated network newscast, wanted to expand news coverage past the dinner hour, something the more prestigious news divisions were having trouble effecting. Arledge suggested the unthinkable: he wanted to follow the local 11 p.m. newscasts with a news program, competing directly with Johnny Carson's *Tonight Show*. Carson's talk show held an unbreakable monopoly on the late-night slot at the time, and people tuned in to his opening monologues with unfailing regularity. Undaunted, Arledge produced sporadic, one-time news specials for late-night viewers on such subjects as the death of Elvis Presley and the signing of the Panama Canal Treaty.

Arledge initially covered the hostage crisis like the other topics, treating it as a news item that people might be interested in seeing more of than what the evening news had presented. Originally hosted by anchor Frank Reynolds, the November 8, 1979, show, called "America Held Hostage," heard from correspondents stationed from every possible angle of the story: Tehran, the White House, Capitol Hill, and the State Department. Like Koppel, many Americans did not perceive the hostage crisis to have the marks of a long-lasting conflict. By contrast, the images being broadcast from Iran became increasingly hostile, showing blindfolded American embassy workers and anti-American demonstrations in Tehran that included the burning of the American flag and other effigies.

ENTER TED KOPPEL

Americans soon became united in searching for ways to respond to the Iranians, and Arledge, sensing this, wanted to air a follow-up special. When the show's second installment finally aired, the phrase "Day 11" was attached to the title of "America Held Hostage." The marking of time in the title became a symbol of the national vigil that lasted until the crisis was resolved, and it continued to point out on a nightly basis that President Jimmy Carter had not been able to free the hostages. Arledge got his late-night time slot, but "journalism was only part of it," write Koppel and Kyle Gibson in *"Nightline": History in the Making and the Making of Television*. "This was the seizing of 11:30." With a resolution to the crisis nowhere in sight, Reynolds returned to his evening news duties, and the search was on for a replacement. After top news anchors declined the opportunity, Koppel, a diplomatic correspondent who had covered the American civil rights movement, Latin America, and the Vietnam War, became the show's final integral piece.

Nightline represents the geopolitical version of Edward R. Murrow's broadcast of the split-screen view of the Brooklyn and Golden Gate bridges. The ability to bring together people from halfway around the world, who might not otherwise speak to each other, was used to great advantage. In a ploy that Koppel later described as "a little bit shameless," *Nightline* ambushed the Iranian charge d'affaires, Ali Agah, by neglecting to inform him that he would be appearing with Dorothea Morefield, the wife of one of the American captives. The Iranian diplomat soon found himself backtracking in response to Morefield's questions about why Iran was impeding communications between the hostages and their families. For many viewers it was a satisfying episode, but the length of the crisis made their satisfaction brief.

Koppel's no-nonsense attitude created the effect that he was an advocate for the viewer who challenged evasive politicians to answer the questions posed. Some viewers watched *Nightline* as much out of the desire to see Koppel make someone squirm as much as from any desire to become informed. Koppel once told then-governor of Arizona Evan Mecham, "I tell you what. . . . Let's play by my rules for a moment, let's go back to the question that I asked you initially." He admonished Soviet commentator Vitali Kobesh: "When I come on your program I'll answer your questions; now you're on my program. . . . You answer mine, all right?" When baseball executive Al Campanis suggested that blacks had inferior management skills, Koppel replied, "That really sounds like garbage, if you'll forgive me for saying so."

As much as *Nightline* was Koppel's show, the program was not immune to being used as a public relations vehicle by prominent figures. Public figures who were in trouble often used *Nightline*'s live format because they knew the live broadcast afforded them the chance to present their side of the story. Failed Bill Clinton nominee Lani Guinier, who once appeared in a desperate attempt to save her nomination, remarked that *Nightline* had "a moment of emotional intimacy" that no newspaper was capable of delivering. This quality led *Nightline* to score major journalistic coups throughout the 1980s: Senator Gary

Hart after his extramarital affair; televangelist Jim Bakker following the PTL (Praise the Lord) scandal; and UN Secretary Kurt Waldheim hopelessly trying to minimize his Nazi past.

Through its willingness to exert the journalistic clout that it had begun to acquire, *Nightline* continued to demonstrate an ability to produce groundbreaking television into the late 1990s. Producing the first face-to-face debate between Israeli and Palestinian leaders was the most improbable result of the show that had begun so improbably. After wrangling with both sides just to get them to appear on the same stage together, the show had to ensure that result by building a 3-foot-high wall in between the two panels. The image of Koppel in a Jerusalem theater, straddling the wall because of Middle Eastern differences, became one of those immediate and succinct metaphors that television effectively communicates.

CHANGING OF THE GUARD

Koppel left *Nightline* in November 2005. The general feeling was that the show *was* Koppel and could not survive without him. There was much talk about the fact that ABC had unsuccessfully tried to woo David Letterman away from CBS and considered moving Jimmy Kimmel up to the 11:35 p.m. spot, which belonged to *Nightline*. Surprisingly, the show thrived. Martin Bashir, Cynthia McFadden, and Terry Moran were hired as coanchors. The format was changed to handle three topics instead of one, and it returned to the live format that had made it successful in the beginning. Ratings climbed, and the show challenged and sometimes topped the ratings of Letterman and Conan O'Brien, who had replaced Jay Leno on the *Tonight Show* on NBC. In 2010 Bashir left ABC to take a job with rival NBC News, and Bill Weir was named as the new cohost. By that time, *Nightline* was recording a 3.8 million audience show, right behind Leno, who had reclaimed his *Tonight Show* slot.

Daryl Umberger

SEE ALSO: *Arledge, Roone; Carson, Johnny; Civil Rights Movement; Leno, Jay; Letterman, David; Live Television; Murrow, Edward R.; O'Brien, Conan; Presley, Elvis; Television;* The Tonight Show*; Vietnam.*

BIBLIOGRAPHY

Carter, Bill. "*Nightline* Is Thriving in Late Nights." *New York Times*, July 27, 2009.

Dorfman, Herbert. "The Seizing of 11:30 P.M." *New Leader*, June 3, 1996, 18–19.

Koppel, Ted, and Kyle Gibson. *"Nightline": History in the Making and the Making of Television.* New York: Times Books, 1996.

Kurtz, Howard. "The Night Stalker." *Columbia Journalism Review*, May/June 1996, 65–68.

Timberg, Bernard M. *Television Talk: A History of the TV Talk Show.* Austin: University of Texas Press, 2002.

Nike

The emergence of the Nike sports apparel corporation in the latter part of the twentieth century mirrored the skyrocketing popularity of spectator sports, professional and big-time college athletes, and personal athletic activity. Nike fueled a great deal of this demand, particularly by employing athletes as product spokespeople and infusing the world of sports with vast amounts of capital. Moreover, by becoming a bone fide cultural icon, "the swoosh," as the corporation's symbol is referred to, has become one of the most ubiquitous product emblems in American life, possibly second only to that of Coca-Cola.

A MAN AND AN IDEA

Nike began in 1962 when Phil Knight took an idea he had proposed in his MBA thesis at Stanford and made it a reality. His paper theorized that well-merchandised shoes from Japan could end Germany's domination of the U.S. athletic shoe market. After completing his degree, Knight met in Japan with the Onitsuka Tiger Company, a manufacturer of quality athletic shoes, and convinced it of the merit of tapping into the U.S. market. When the Tiger representatives asked which company he represented, Knight spontaneously created the name Blue Ribbon Sports, the forerunner of Nike.

Knight and his wife financed the endeavor with their own money, as well as an investment of $500 from Bill Bowerman, Knight's former track coach at the University of Oregon. With Bowerman reshaping the Tiger products using designs he conjured himself, Blue Ribbon Sports began producing its own products in 1971. In six years revenues climbed from $8,000 to $1.96 million. Legal wrangling with Tiger led to the dissolution of Blue Ribbon Sports and the birth of Nike, the debut of which took place at the 1972 Olympic Trials in Eugene, Oregon. By 1979 Nike claimed 50 percent of the U.S. running shoe market.

From the start Nike pushed the similarity between contemporary sport and ancient warfare: Nike the shoe was intended to inspire athletes just as Nike the Greek goddess had inspired Greek warriors on history's earliest battlefields. With such imagery, the corporation's name suggests the added importance of sports in contemporary life. Nike may be more responsible than any other entity for the rapid commercialization of sport in the late twentieth century. The sneaker, a fairly rudimentary article of clothing prior to the 1970s, became a way for the fan and athlete to unite and raise the role of sports in American life to new levels.

In terms of sales, Nike is one of the most successful companies in the world. Shoes form the core of the business, which reached its apex in the late 1980s through the mid-1990s. The company held about 30 percent of the U.S. market in 1995, far outdistancing the 20 percent of its nearest rival, Reebok. Overseas revenues also rose steadily, reaching nearly $2 billion by 1995, about 40 percent of the company's overall total. At this point, the company broadened into all types of sports apparel and equipment and actually saw its power diminish.

SOARING WITH AIR JORDAN

One of Nike's most memorable ad campaigns screams: "It's the shoes!" As opposing athletes tried to explain the exceptional skills of Michael Jordan, the basketball legend who became a Nike spokesman in 1984, this was the only explanation they could find. Conveniently for Nike, this explanation also helped to make Air Jordans the shoe that formed a link between fans and their stars. Millions of fans purchased a pair of Air Jordans in hopes that the shoes would give them a piece of Jordan's rare athletic gifts.

As evidenced by the Air Jordan ad campaign, Nike commodified sports in a way not previously seen. The core of this restructuring revolved around using athletes to represent products to the public in carefully crafted advertisements. Athletes became characters to be packaged with products that somehow reflected their actual or contrived personal details. With such "product tie-ins," sporting events now often appear as stages on which corporations such as Nike orchestrate "product placement," a term for noticeably positioning name-brand products in feature films and such. For example, it is common for football's Super Bowl, or other significant sporting events, to be tied to the introduction of new ads, each attempting to outdo the others or to continue an ongoing narrative with the viewing public. Such efforts are aimed at reinforcing a bond between performer/athlete and fan/viewer that ultimately benefits corporations such as Nike.

These changes have helped to transform sports into a big-time business for athletes and their agents. Agents are tasked with delivering lucrative endorsement opportunities from companies such as Nike to their clients. Nike has proved to be visionary in defining this process by creating associations with young athletes that transcend their team affiliations. Upon turning professional, major athletes often garner contracts to wear and represent certain apparel lines. Nike now has thousands of athletes in the fold worldwide, including three-quarters of the players in the National Basketball Association (NBA), more than half of the Major League Baseball and National Football League (NFL) players, and athletes at hundreds of universities. In addition to imitating the moves of their favorite athletes, youngsters often copy their apparel choices. This tendency has been fostered, if not altogether manufactured, by Nike's effort to give athletes personal characteristics in the marketplace.

The most famous of the branded sports personalities was Jordan, the prototypical modern athlete. Jordan was signed to represent Nike prior to his emergence in the 1980s and 1990s as the best basketball player ever, and as both he and Nike rose to prominence, the line was blurred between his public image and real-life personality. His work with Nike created a formula that has made athletes such as golfer Tiger Woods, basketball player LeBron James, tennis player Raphael Nadal, and countless others into icons who have transcended their respective sports.

NIKE'S DAMAGED IMAGE

In the late 1990s, with most of Nike's shoes being made in Indonesia, Vietnam, and China, the company's manufacturing was linked to the exploitation of child labor abroad. Exposé articles in 1998 revealed that Nike plants forced workers into a substandard, "sweatshop" environment and often employed younger workers. It was a public relations nightmare for Nike—many Americans came to view Nike as a symbol of unethical big corporations and greed.

Nike survived the sweatshop episode, and in the early 2010s it has expanded well beyond the realm of shoes. In addition to having retail stores all over the world, Nike is active in many forms of media, including amusement parks and film. The company also has many competitors in what now is a multibillion-dollar industry. It is a far cry from the 1980s, when Nike was the pioneer that took the relatively insignificant industry of sneakers to unimaginable heights within American popular culture.

Brian Black

SEE ALSO: *Basketball; Consumerism; James, LeBron; Jordan, Michael; National Basketball Association (NBA); Woods, Tiger.*

BIBLIOGRAPHY

Becklund, Laurie, and J. B. Strasser. *Swoosh: The Unauthorized Story of Nike and the Men Who Played There.* New York: HarperBusiness, 1993.

Collins, David R. *Philip Knight: Running with Nike.* Ada, OK: Garrett Educational Corporation, 1991.

Frisch, Aaron. *The Story of Nike.* North Mankato, MN: Smart Apple Media, 2004.

Goldman, Robert, and Stephen Papson. *Nike Culture: The Sign of the Swoosh.* London; Thousand Oaks, CA: Sage Publications, 1998.

Greenberg, Keith Elliot, and Dick Smolinski. *Bill Bowerman & Phil Knight: Building the Nike Empire.* Woodbridge, CT: Blackbird Press, 1994.

Hollister, Geoff. *Out of Nowhere: The Inside Story of How Nike Marketed the Culture of Running.* Maidenhead, UK: Meyer & Meyer Sports, 2008.

Katz, Donald R. *Just Do It: The Nike Spirit in the Corporate World.* New York: Random House, 1994.

LaFeber, Walter. *Michael Jordan and the New Global Capitalism.* New York: Norton, 1999.

9/11

The morning of September 11, 2001, dawned clear in New York City. It appeared to be an ordinary day until 8:46 a.m., when American Airlines flight 11, flying from Boston to Los Angeles, plunged into the North Tower of the World Trade Center. Almost immediately, the scene was transmitted around the country via television. The most common reaction was disbelief, and many people assumed it was the result of an accident. All doubt evaporated when United Airlines flight 175, also flying from Boston to Los Angeles, struck the South Tower at 9:03 a.m. The 110-story Twin Towers contained offices, restaurants, and stores, where some 50,000 workers from around the world were employed. As events unfolded over the next few hours, the world learned that the planes had been hijacked by suicide bombers working for al-Qaeda, a globally recognized Islamic terrorist organization. Almost 3,000 people died at the Twin Towers, but thousands more were saved.

Even as events continued to unfold in New York, a third plane crashed into the Pentagon in Washington, D.C., killing 189 people. An attack on a fourth target was circumvented by the courage and quick thinking of passengers and crew who prevented United Airlines flight 93 from reaching the capital by crashing it into the ground in Shanksville, Pennsylvania.

For most Americans, September 11 became a defining moment in their lives. Nonstop television coverage became one of the most important elements in that experience. Regular programming was suspended on many channels, and channels worldwide covered unfolding events. Eighty million Americans turned to television for coverage of the disaster that night, and most continued to watch for days. The events of 9/11 produced a rise in patriotism and unity that had not been seen in the United States since December 7, 1941, when the Japanese attacked Pearl Harbor. After 9/11, the sense that safety and normalcy had been lost permeated the country, as airport security became a major focus of national security, and the war on terror, legitimized by the USA Patriot Act of 2001, signaled major changes in the rights to due process and civil liberties that had long been taken for granted.

THE TWIN TOWERS

Arriving at the scene of destruction, New York firefighters quickly decided that rescue rather than firefighting should be the focus of efforts. The call had come in at shift change, and those going off duty answered the call along with on-duty personnel. As many as 60 percent of firefighters who arrived at the World Trade Center were off duty. Poor internal and external communication, coupled with a lack of cooperation with members of the New York Police Department (NYPD), proved to be disastrous. The chaos inside the towers was heightened by the fact that, for safety reasons, doors to the roof were kept locked. Many of those who climbed upward became trapped when the call for evacuation of the North Tower was issued just before 9 a.m. A second announcement informed workers and rescuers that the danger had passed. Thus, when the second plane hit, some workers had begun climbing upward rather than continuing on their way out of the building.

At 9:59 a.m., the South Tower collapsed, burying thousands in wreckage and debris. Firefighters on upper floors of the North Tower did not know about the collapse and thus did not evacuate the building. When electricity was lost, many people were trapped inside elevators in the North Tower, which also collapsed at 10:28 a.m. At the end of the horrible day, 343 firefighters were dead, leaving behind 244 widows and 606 children who had lost a parent.

The NYPD also proved to be instrumental in rescue efforts, but their losses were much lighter than those of the New York Fire Department (NYFD) because superior communication allowed them to evacuate when ordered to do so. Nevertheless, the NYPD lost twenty-three members on 9/11. The Port Authority, the first rescue workers to arrive on the scene, lost thirty-seven workers.

In the days following the attacks, rescue workers labored for twelve- to sixteen-hour shifts removing 1,506,124 tons of debris, much of it toxic, by hand from what became known as "Ground Zero," "Hallowed Ground," or "The Pile." In addition to rescue workers assigned to duty, off-duty personnel, retired workers, and volunteers from all over the United States participated in cleanup duty. Many rescue workers paid a heavy price, as a high rate of illness and death proliferated among them in the years following.

THE PENTAGON

Just as the Twin Towers were a symbol of American economic might, the Pentagon was a symbol of American military might. At 9:37 a.m., terrorists rammed American Airlines flight 77, bound from the nation's capital to Los Angeles, into the Pentagon. The five sides of the Pentagon are composed of Rings A through E, and the attack sliced through Rings E, D, and C and partially damaged B. Ceilings tumbled down, and walls and floors crumbled. Black smoke filled the area as thousands of workers and visitors fled the building. Fatalities included the sixty-four people aboard the plane, seventy civilians, and fifty-five military personnel. Evacuation at the Pentagon was much smoother than that at the Twin Towers because of better emergency preparedness and greater cooperation among rescue workers.

The government went into emergency mode immediately. The White House was evacuated, and security was tightened. Military personnel were placed on full alert. Air travel was suspended except for military planes. President George W. Bush was criticized for remaining in Sarasota, Florida, where he was speaking at an elementary school. He was subsequently sequestered at a safe location in Louisiana before arriving in Washington at 7 p.m. that night.

FLIGHT 93

A fourth hijacked plane left Newark, New Jersey, on its way to San Francisco. The hijackers herded the passengers to the rear of the plane but did not stop them from using cell phones. From calls to family and friends, they learned about what had happened in New York and Washington. Todd Beamer, a thirty-two-year-old software salesman, called for help rather than scaring his pregnant wife. Beamer contacted Lisa Jefferson, a GTE Airfone operator. Jefferson's meticulous notes, along with the plane's recorder, provided detailed information about what happened aboard United flight 93, where passengers and crew devised a plan to prevent the plane from launching a fourth attack.

Jefferson heard Beamer shout, "Okay, let's roll!" just before passengers and crew used a food cart as a battering ram and wielded knives, forks, and boiling water to gain control of the plane. At 10:03 a.m., the plane plowed into a deserted field in the small town of Shanksville, Pennsylvania, at a 45-degree angle at a speed of more than 583 miles per hour. Thirty-three passengers, seven crew members, and the four hijackers were killed. The plane had been only twenty minutes away from Washington, D.C.

9/11 IN BOOKS AND MOVIES

The events of 9/11 have continued to exert a major impact on American popular culture through books, movies, songs, and television. The handling of 9/11 has crossed all genres and subgenres. Many treatments have been controversial, and they have portrayed 9/11 from a range of perspectives. There has been considerable praise for nonfiction books about 9/11, and treatments have surfaced across all academic disciplines. However, it is generally accepted that the definitive fiction work on the subject has yet to be written.

Some of the best efforts have come from journalists such as Steve Coll (*Ghost Wars*, 2004), George Packer (*The Assassins' Gate*, 2005), Tom Ricks (*Fiasco*, 2006), and Rajiv Chandrasekaran (*Imperial Life in the Emerald City*, 2006). Other well-received works include John Updike's *Terrorist* (2006), Martin Amis's *The Second Plane* (2008), Don DeLillo's *Falling Man* (2007), Ken Kalfus's *A Disorder Peculiar to the Country* (2006), Benjamin Kunkel's *Indecision* (2005), Jay McInerney's *The Good Life* (2006), Claire Messud's *The Emperor's Children* (2006), Jonathon Safran Foer's *Extremely Loud & Incredibly Close* (2005), and Lynne Sharon Schwartz's *The Writing on the Wall* (2005).

In films, Oliver Stone's *World Trade Center* (2006) focuses on experiences of two transit workers caught in the aftermath of the collapse of the Twin Towers. Michael Moore's *Fahrenheit 9/11* (2004) taps into mounting cynicism about the Bush administration's war on terror. In 2006 Paul Greengrass's *United 93* and Peter Markle's *Flight 93* honored those who went down in Pennsylvania. Julia Loktev's *Day Night Day Night* deals with homegrown terrorism. Even comedian Adam Sandler entered the fray with *Reign over Me* (2007), in which he portrays a 9/11 widower. *Imperial Life in the Emerald City* was adapted for film as *Green Zone* (2010) with Matt Damon, and *Extremely Loud & Incredibly Close* (2012) was turned into a Tom Hanks vehicle. Kathryn Bigelow (*The Hurt Locker*) is working on a film about the death of Osama bin Laden, slated for release in 2012.

9/11 IN MUSIC AND TV

The music world responded to 9/11 with a plethora of offerings that ranged from reworking existing songs to devoting entire albums to the event and its aftermath. Tributes to the victims of 9/11 such as "America, a Tribute to Heroes, the Concert for New York City," and "United We Stand" produced additional 9/11 collections. Artists from rock to country to rap released memorials and commentaries. Enrique Iglesias's "Hero," remixed with 9/11 accounts, became an instant hit in 2001. Artists such as Paul McCartney focused on democratic ideals ("Freedom," 2001). Neil Young sings "Let's Roll" (2002) from the perspective of Flight 93's Todd Beamer, and Melissa Etheridge pays tribute to fellow passenger Mark Bingham in "Tuesday Morning" (2004). Trace Adkins's "Welcome to Hell" tells of the nineteen hijackers meeting with the devil.

One of the most controversial songs is Toby Keith's "Courtesy of the Red, White, and Blue (The Angry American)," a 2002 pro-military anthem. Slayers' "Jihad" (2006) also proved to be controversial, chronicling events from the perspective of the hijackers. New Jersey native Bruce Springsteen's "The Rising" (2002) is considered the definitive 9/11 anthem, with lyrics about a firefighter climbing the stairs of the Twin Towers as well as personal reactions to the event.

No other medium has been more closely associated with 9/11 than television, and coverage has been plentiful in the years following the attacks. In addition to news reports, specials, and documentaries, television shows and movies have addressed 9/11 from a range of perspectives. Regular shows have dealt with 9/11 almost since it happened. *Ally McBeal*'s "Nine One One," which aired December 10, 2001, presents a heartfelt tribute to the victims of 9/11 and their families, culminating with Josh Groban singing "To Where You Are" about the loss of a loved one. The New York firefighting drama *Rescue Me*, the political drama *The West Wing*, and *CSI: NY* contained numerous references to 9/11.

Television movies also provided vast opportunities for dealing with 9/11-related themes. *Dirty War* (2004) chronicles the devastation of terrorists loose in a large city. *The Path to 9/11* (2006) addresses ways the attacks might have been averted, and *The Hamburg Cell* (2004) offers a fictionalized portrait of the hijackers. One of the first documentaries was the Naudet brothers' *9/11* (2002), which uses actual footage that the French filmmakers captured on 9/11.

In 2011, the tenth anniversary of 9/11 produced a score of new television offerings that included Steven Spielberg's *Rising: Rebuilding Ground Zero*, a six-hour documentary about reconstruction efforts on the site of the Twin Towers. Other offerings included the Smithsonian channel's *9/11: Day That Changed the World*, National Geographic's *Inside 9/11: War on America* and *George W. Bush: The 9/11 Interview*, Showtime's *Rebirth*, NBC's *Children of 9/11*, and A&E's *102 Minutes That Changed America*.

In the years following 9/11, a number of planned attacks have been circumvented, including an attack on a Christmas tree lighting ceremony, an attack on New York's transit system, a shoe bomber aboard a transatlantic flight, and explosives aboard a Detroit, Michigan–bound plane. The masterminds of 9/11 have mostly been eliminated or arrested. Although many people experienced a sense of closure with the death of al-Qaeda leader bin Laden at the hands of Navy SEALS on May 1, 2011, most Americans understand that the threat to American security did not die with the wars in Afghanistan and Iraq or the death of bin Laden.

Elizabeth Rholetter Purdy

SEE ALSO: *Air Travel;* Ally McBeal*; Cable TV; Country Music; Damon, Matt; Hanks, Tom; Live Television; Made-for-Television Movies; McCartney, Paul; Moore, Michael;* National Geographic*; Pop Music; Rap; Rock and Roll; Spielberg, Steven; Springsteen, Bruce; Stone, Oliver; Television; War in Afghanistan;* The West Wing*; World Trade Center; Young, Neil.*

BIBLIOGRAPHY

Brill, Steven. *After: How America Confronted the September 12 Era*. New York: Simon & Schuster, 2003.

Dixon, Wheeler Winston, ed. *Film and Television after 9/11*. Carbondale: Southern Illinois University Press, 2004.

Golway, Terry. *So Others Might Live: A History of New York's Bravest*. New York: Basic Books, 2002.

Griffin, David Ray. *The 9/11 Commission Report: Omissions and Distortions*. Northampton, MA: Olive Branch Press, 2005.

Griffin, David Ray. *The New Pearl Harbor Revisited: 9/11, the Cover-up, and the Exposé*. Northampton, MA: Olive Branch Press, 2008.

Heller, Dana, ed. *The Selling of 9/11: How a National Tragedy Became a Commodity*. New York: Palgrave Macmillan, 2005.

Henshall, Ian. *9/11: The New Evidence*. New York: Carroll and Graf, 2007.

Knott, Stephen F. *Rush to Judgment: George W. Bush, the War on Terror, and His Critics*. Lawrence: University Press of Kansas, 2012.

Lardner, James, and Thomas Reppetto. *NYPD: A City and Its Police*. New York: Henry Holt, 2000.

Longman, Jere. *Among the Heroes: United Flight 93 and the Passengers and Crew Who Fought Back*. New York: HarperCollins, 2002.

Marrs, Jim. *The Terror Conspiracy: Deception, 9/11, and the Loss of Liberty*. New York: Disinformation, 2006.

Moore, Michael. *The Official Fahrenheit 9/11 Reader*. New York: Simon & Schuster, 2004.

National Commission on Terrorist Attacks upon the United States. *The 9/11 Commission Report*. New York: Norton, 2004.

Ridgeway, James. *The 5 Unanswered Questions about 9/11: What the 9/11 Commission Report Failed to Tell Us*. New York: Seven Stories Press, 2005.

Takacs, Stacy. *Terrorism TV: Popular Entertainment in Post-9/11 America*. Lawrence: University of Kansas Press, 2012.

19 Kids and Counting

SEE: *The Duggar Family.*

1968 Mexico City Summer Olympic Games

Few who witnessed Tommie Smith's and John Carlos's black power salute on the medal stand on October 16, 1968, following their gold- and bronze-medal performances in the 200 meters at the Mexico City Olympic Games, could remain neutral about the sentiments behind their protest. Fewer still could challenge the symbolic significance of their action. Nor was it possible to explain their stance as the actions of isolated extremists, for although they provided the most public protest of those games, their action articulated a political sentiment that was widespread among African American athletes competing for the United States. Smith and Carlos—in stocking feet, wearing black beads and black scarves, with their black-gloved fists raised over their heads as the American national anthem was played—used the biggest stage in sports to air grievances about racial injustice in the United States.

The Mexico City Olympics had arrived during a transitional period in the American civil rights movement. Although the movement had achieved important success in gaining legal protections for African Americans, particularly in dismantling "Jim Crow" laws mandating segregation in the southern states, the movement had been less successful in ameliorating economic disparity between whites and blacks. Frustrated with white America's lack of commitment to change, many younger African Americans, especially men, increasingly supported the more militant black power wing of the movement, turning away from older leaders who had emphasized alliances with white liberals.

U.S. Athletes Raise Fists at 1968 Mexico City Olympics. Tommie Smith, center, and John Carlos, right, raise their gloved fists while on the medal stand in what has become an enduring image of the 1968 Olympic Games. AFP/STRINGER/GETTY IMAGES.

These changes were reflected within the sports world. Led by Harry Edwards, a sociologist at San Jose State University in the late 1960s, a group of fifty to sixty African American athletes representing several sports, particularly track and field, formed the Olympic Project for Human Rights, an organization that hoped to use its visibility within the sports world for political action. Reflecting prejudices even among individuals fighting against bigotry, however, membership was limited to men. Although members of the project rejected a suggestion that they boycott the Mexico City Games in protest, some athletes resolved to take individual action. The assassination of civil rights leader Dr. Martin Luther King in April 1968 only heightened tensions in the months leading up to the games, as did attempts by the white Olympic leadership to allow South Africa in the games, despite that nation's policy of racial apartheid.

These Olympic Games saw tremendous performances by African American athletes, as many resolved to make their statements through competition. African American athletes won ten golds and set seven world records in track and field. Several black athletes, including heavyweight boxer George Foreman, also won gold medals in other sports.

As a result of their silent protest, Smith and Carlos were stripped of their medals, becoming the only athletes to be punished in that way for political reasons by the U.S. Olympic Committee. (Silver medalist Peter Norman of Australia, a white athlete who also participated in the protest, was severely reprimanded by his national sports federation as well.) Their protest highlighted the relationship between race, politics, and sports in their era, much as Jesse Owens's victories in the 1936 Berlin Games had done for his.

John Smolenski

SEE ALSO: *Civil Rights Movement; King, Martin Luther, Jr.; Olympics; Owens, Jesse.*

BIBLIOGRAPHY

Espy, Richard. *The Politics of the Olympic Games.* Berkeley: University of California Press, 1979.

Guttmann, Allen. *The Olympics: A History of the Modern Games.* Urbana: University of Illinois Press, 1992.

Hoffer, Richard. *Something in the Air: American Passion and Defiance in the 1968 Mexico City Olympics.* New York: Free Press, 2009.

Moore, Kenny. "A Courageous Stand: In '68, Olympians Tommie Smith and John Carlos Raised Their Fists for Racial Justice." *Sports Illustrated,* August 5, 1991.

Moore, Kenny. "The Eye of the Storm: The Lives of the U.S. Olympians Who Protested Racism in 1968 Were Changed Forever." *Sports Illustrated,* August 12, 1991.

1980 U.S. Olympic Hockey Team

Before the 1980 Winter Olympics in Lake Placid, New York, the United States Olympic hockey team was not expected to compete for a medal. After all, their pool included powerhouses such as Sweden and Czechoslovakia, while the other pool included the Soviet Union and Finland. Only the top two teams from each pool would advance to the medal round, so the United States team faced long odds. But by the time the fortnight had ended, the U.S. team had pulled off one of the greatest upsets in hockey history by defeating the Russians in the semifinals and winning the gold medal after defeating Finland 4-2 in the final game.

The victory inspired a national celebration. After a year of disappointment and disaster, from the Iran hostage crisis to the Soviet invasion of Afghanistan (a result of which was the boycott by the United States of the summer Olympics in Moscow), Americans were looking for something to cheer for. High inflation and unemployment plagued the country, and President Jimmy Carter's policies were often met with scorn and derision.

After defeating the Russians for the right to play for the gold medal, the U.S. team retreated to its locker room and attempted to sing "God Bless America"—though many could not remember all the words. Euphoria swept through the country. The audience at Radio City Music Hall erupted into cheers during an performance when the Finland score was announced. A nationally televised NBA game between the Kansas City Kings and Milwaukee Bucks was interrupted for a second rendition of "The Star-Spangled Banner."

U.S. Hockey's "Miracle on Ice." *Members of the U.S. Olympic hockey team celebrate their "miracle on ice" victory over the Soviet Union on February 22, 1980, in Lake Placid, New York.* FOCUS ON SPORT/CONTRIBUTOR/GETTY IMAGES SPORT/GETTY IMAGES.

Prior to 1980, the United States had formed its Olympic hockey teams hastily and then expected them to be competitive in the tournament. But more often than not the U.S. teams struggled against European squads that had played together for months. In 1980, however, the plan was different. Led by University of Minnesota coach Herb Brooks, the U.S. team spent six months in training and played 61 games before the Olympics. At the same time, Brooks installed a European-type system, emphasizing puck control instead of the dump-and-chase style favored in the past. Those preparations appeared to be all for naught just before the tournament, as the Soviet squad routed the U.S. team 10-3 on the eve of the tournament. Brooks commented after the game that a loss like that was not necessarily bad, since it might prevent overconfidence in his team.

The U.S. team would find out quickly if it had a chance for a medal, because its first two contests were against Sweden and Czechoslovakia. In that first contest, the U.S. managed a 2-2 tie, scoring with only 27 seconds left. A huge upset followed two days later as the host team routed the Czechs 7-3. With those two tough contests out of the way, the U.S. had a good chance to advance to the medal round. Their next three opponents—Norway, Romania, and West Germany—were not as strong. The host team took care of business, winning all three contests with relative ease to advance to the medal round. Both the United States and Sweden had 4-0-1 records in pool play, but the Swedes were the top seed because of goal differential. That fact forced the United States to face the same Soviet squad that had annihilated them only two weeks earlier.

The Soviets controlled play throughout much of the game, outshooting the Americans 39-16. Going into the third period, the United States trailed the four-time defending champs 3-2. However, two U.S. goals scored only 90 seconds apart propelled the Americans to the improbable win. Mark Johnson and Mike Eruzione became forever etched in American Olympic history with their goals. AABC broadcaster Al Michaels's postwin words became famous: "Do you believe in miracles? YES!"

It must be remembered, though, that the victory over the Soviets did not win the Americans the gold medal. The United States still had to beat Finland in order to take home the gold. The contest was televised live in the United States, despite its early Sunday morning start (11 a.m. local time, 8 a.m. West Coast time). If the United States had lost this game, they actually would have finished third, and the hated Russians would still have won by virtue of their win over Sweden. Things looked bleak going into the final period, as the United States trailed 2-1. The never-say-die American team did not quit, however, and with three third-period goals, they won the gold medal in a 4-2 triumph.

Since that improbable win, the United States hockey team has failed to earn a medal. Even in 1998 in Nagano, Japan, with NHL players participating for the first time, the Americans could not corral a medal, though they earned distinction for the damage they caused to their hotel rooms following raucous parties.

D. Byron Painter

SEE ALSO: *Hockey; Olympics.*

BIBLIOGRAPHY

Clendinen, Dudley. "U.S. Hockey Victory Stirs National Celebration." *New York Times*, February 25, 1980, C1–C4.

Coffey, Wayne R. *1980 U.S. Hockey Team.* Woodbridge, CT: Blackbirch Press, 1993.

Eskenazi, Gerald. "U.S. Hockey Squad Captures Gold Medal." *New York Times*. February 25, 1980, C1–C4.

Eskenazi, Gerald. "U.S. Defeats Soviet Squad in Olympic Hockey by 4-3." *New York Times*, February 23, 1998, A1, A16.

Naughton, Jim. "Russia Routs U.S. in Hockey by 10-3." *New York Times*. February 10, 1980, E1, E4.

Powers, John, and Arthur C. Kaminsky. *One Goal: A Chronicle of the 1980 U.S. Olympic Hockey Team.* New York: Harper & Row, 1984.

Sarantakes, Nicholas Evan. *Dropping the Torch: Jimmy Carter, the Olympic Boycott, and the Cold War.* New York: Cambridge University Press, 2011.

Wallechinsky, David. *The Complete Book of the Olympics.* Boston: Little, Brown, 1991.

Nirvana

Rarely does a single album make a massive impact on music and popular culture, but Nirvana's *Nevermind*—released in the fall of 1991—did just that. Nirvana brought the sound and fury of punk rock to the American mainstream about fifteen years after it initially broke, temporarily changing the course of popular music in the process. Fusing punk's speed and energy with the metal heaviness of the 1970s, Nirvana popularized what would later be labeled grunge, making loud and abrasive guitar rock one of the biggest money-making genres of the 1990s. Within one year of *Nevermind*'s success, MTV (Music Television) went from being dominated by lightweight dance-pop and hair metal acts to being monopolized by guitar-wielding, long-haired quasi-punk rockers. Furthermore, in the early 1990s grunge fashion became popular, with numerous fashion stores imitating the flannel thrift-store shirts and ripped jeans worn by Nirvana members. The group's two-and-a-half-year reign over popular music ended tragically, however, when leader Kurt Cobain committed suicide in April 1994.

Nirvana. *The members of Nirvana, from left, Kurt Cobain, Dave Grohl, and Krist Novoselic, perform on stage in 1993.* JEFF KRAVITZ/ CONTRIBUTOR/FILMMAGIC, INC/GETTY IMAGES.

For those who did not have their ear to the American underground music scene of the 1980s, Nirvana's sound may have come as a shock. The group was, however, more representative of a musical tradition than an aberration. Formed in 1987, core members Cobain (1967–1994) and Krist Novoselic (1965–) were directly inspired by American underground music played by bands such as the Minutemen, Big Black, Black Flag, the Melvins, and Sonic Youth. This Aberdeen, Washington, band soon was signed to the ultrahip Seattle label Sub Pop, which specialized in the type of heavy punk meets 1970s metal music that Nirvana played at the time. After an initial single, the band recorded their first album, *Bleach*, for $600; it went on to be a moderate underground success, picking up a considerable amount of critical acclaim along the way. Still, in 1990 the band was considered to be nothing more than just another pretty good band on an independent label.

MAINSTREAM POPULARITY

After Nirvana resurfaced in 1991 on a major label, DGC, the group had both a new drummer, Dave Grohl (1969–), and considerably improved songs—creating catchier, albeit no less loud, music. "Smells like Teen Spirit" was perhaps their most likable song, and when it was released in the fall of 1991, it steadily climbed the charts and its video quickly became a staple on MTV. With little push from Nirvana's record company, *Nevermind* went to the top of the *Billboard* album charts by early 1992, unseating such superstars as U2, Garth Brooks, Michael Jackson, and MC Hammer. Even though there was a precedent for what Nirvana was doing, the American mainstream reacted to it as being the newest, biggest thing in music. Major record labels began signing relatively unknown bands (Stone Temple Pilots, L7, Pearl Jam, Helmet) that fit the newly dubbed alternative genre, as well as older artists such as Circle Jerks, Jesus Lizard, and the Butthole Surfers.

Always a punk idealist, Cobain often did his best to alienate many of the new members of his audience, whom he referred to as the ones "who used to beat me up in school." The desire to drive away this segment of his audience began with Cobain planting an open-mouthed kiss on Novoselic on *Saturday Night Live* and culminated in the recording of *In Utero* (1993). Feeling like *Nevermind* was too slick, the band hired veteran underground engineer Steve Albini to produce an extremely abrasive follow-up to their multiplatinum major label debut. But Cobain's plan backfired, and *In Utero* went to the top of the *Billboard* album charts again, primarily because Cobain had not buried his songwriting gifts and, furthermore, because the landscape of popular music had changed dramatically since *Nevermind* was released. In two years, mainstream listeners' ears had been hardened by endless streams of Nirvana-clone bands, making even the extremely dissonant sounds of *In Utero*'s "Scentless Apprentice" and "Very Ape" palatable.

GROWING DISCONTENT

Growing increasingly discontent with his role as a big rock star, Cobain became more depressed—a feeling that was fueled by his heroin use. He and his wife, musician Courtney Love, developed drug-related problems, which fell under mounting scrutiny by the mainstream press. In addition, Nirvana repeatedly took criticism from the underground music community for selling out. (After buying a new Lexus, for instance, Cobain took so much flack from his peers that he returned the car to the dealership and took back his old Volvo from the pre-*Nevermind* days.) For reasons that will never be fully known, Cobain took his own life on April 5, 1994, in the room above his Seattle home's garage. When his body was found on April 8, it was a major media event, and thousands publicly mourned, including Love, who recorded an infamous eulogy/rant in which she read parts of her husband's suicide note—punctuated by her own grief-stricken asides.

Love's group, Hole, had already recorded *Live through This*, and it was coincidentally released shortly after Cobain's suicide. It went on to become a critical and commercial success. Nirvana drummer Grohl formed the extremely popular Foo Fighters, while bassist Novoselic concentrated on forming political action committees that lobbied against anticensorship laws. In early 1998 Novoselic's band, Sweet 75, released its poorly selling debut, which had not even surpassed *Bleach*'s sales of 35,000 months after its release.

In 2011 Nirvana launched a two-year traveling exhibit in order to give fans a chance to view personal artifacts from the band's career. The exhibit included such items as the first guitar that Cobain ever smashed on stage, his signature yellow cardigan, handwritten lyrics to their songs, and a score of personal items. Worldwide, Nirvana sold more than 50 million albums. Despite legal battles with Love over Cobain's copyrights, Nirvana released *Nirvana* (2002), *Silver: The Best of Box* (2005), and *Icon* (2010). They also released two box sets: *With the Lights Out* (2004) and *Nevermind: The Singles* (2011). The impact of Nirvana continued to grow. In 2005 the Library of Congress included *Nevermind* on its list of the world's most significant recordings. The group's influence on young recording artists such as Kelly Clarkson, Taylor Swift, and Katy Perry guaranteed that the group would not be forgotten. In a *Rolling Stone* article published in 2011, Jody Rosen muses that Nirvana "may be the greatest power trio ever."

Kembrew McLeod

SEE ALSO: *Alternative Rock; Brooks, Garth; Grunge; Heavy Metal; Jackson, Michael; Love, Courtney; MTV; Pearl Jam; Perry, Katy; Punk;* Saturday Night Live*; Swift, Taylor; U2.*

BIBLIOGRAPHY

Arnold, Gina. *Route 666: On the Road to Nirvana*. New York: St. Martin's Press, 1993.

Azerrad, Michael. *Come As You Are: The Story of Nirvana*. New York: Doubleday, 1994.

Browne, David. "Inside the Massive New Nirvana Exhibit." *Rolling Stone*, April 28, 2011.

Rosen, Jody. "A Jampacked Box Set Dusts Off the Myth of Nirvana's Masterpiece." *Rolling Stone*, September 29, 2011.

Nixon, Agnes *(1927–)*

Agnes Nixon is the most influential writer in daytime television, credited with introducing social issues and moral seriousness to the soap opera. She served an apprenticeship with the creator of the genre, Irna Phillips, developing dialogue for the radio serial *Woman in White*. After writing anthology dramas and working on inaugural story lines for *Search for Tomorrow*, she worked again with Phillips on *As the World Turns*. During the early sixties she became head writer of another Phillips creation, *The*

Guiding Light, where she had the heroine, Bert Bauer, undergo treatment for uterine cancer.

In 1968 Nixon created her first series, *One Life to Live*, conceiving a multicultural community of many ethnic groups, a major departure from the traditional WASP universe of the soaps. In 1970 she produced her most personal series, *All My Children*, in which she tackled the Vietnam War, abortion, and drug addiction. For *All My Children* she crystallized one of the genre's most enduring archetypes, the bitch goddess, as embodied in Susan Lucci's Erica Kane. Erica was not only a soap icon, but, like all of Nixon's characters, a three-dimensional individual who grew over time. In the early 1980s Nixon created the prime-time miniseries *The Manions of America* and the serial *Loving* with Douglas Marland. She was the first woman and writer to receive the prestigious Trustee's Award from the National Academy of Television Arts & Sciences.

Nixon has worked in daytime television for more than sixty years, and the entire industry was saddened when two of her beloved series were cancelled: *All My Children* in 2011 and *One Life to Live* in 2012.

Ron Simon

SEE ALSO: *Abortion;* All My Children*;* As the World Turns*;* Guiding Light*; Phillips, Irna;* Search for Tomorrow*; Soap Operas; Television; Vietnam.*

BIBLIOGRAPHY

Allen, Robert. *Speaking of Soap Operas*. Chapel Hill: University of North Carolina Press, 1985.

The Museum of Television & Radio. *Worlds without End: The Art and History of the Soap Opera*. New York: Abrams, 1997.

Schemering, Christopher. *The Soap Opera Encyclopedia*. New York: Ballantine Books, 1985.

Townley, R. "She Introduced a Stranger to the World of Soaps (Agnes Nixon, Creator of Several Soap Operas)." *TV Guide*, May 3, 1975, 12–16.

Warner, Gary. *"All My Children": The Complete Family Scrapbook*. Los Angeles: General Publishing Group, 1994.

Noloesca, La Chata *(1903–1979)*

La Chata Noloesca was the most famous and celebrated vaudevillian on the Hispanic theatrical circuits of the United States and northern Mexico. For more than four decades, she sang, danced, and acted on stage and screen, principally drawing her material from Mexican American working-class culture and performing for the Hispanic working classes in Los Angeles; Chicago; New York; Tampa, Florida; Havana, and San Juan.

La Chata Noloesca was born Beatriz Escalona Pérez on August 20, 1903, in San Antonio, Texas, to impoverished Mexican immigrants. Her schooling was minimal, and she began working at an early age, selling food and drink to passengers on trains that stopped in San Antonio. Her sharp observations of street life and her acute ear for the nuances of Spanish working-class dialect were likely nurtured during these years of daily contact with the masses of Mexican immigrants and Mexican Americans in transit at the train station.

Her life as a theatrical artist began in 1920, when she was discovered while working as an usherette and box-office cashier at the Teatro Nacional, the most important theater house in Texas at that time. She was recruited by Hermanos Areu, a Spanish-Cuban song and dance troupe, after they spotted her on the Nacional stage competing in a beautiful-legs contest, a promotional event run by a hosiery company. She won the contest as well as a place in the Areu troupe. She made her debut with the Areus that same year in El Paso (she later married José Areu) and went on to star in everything from melodrama to vaudeville.

Over the course of the 1920s, she developed and perfected her comic persona of La Chata Noloesca (Noloesca is a scrambled version of her last name, Escalona)—the streetwise maid, a *peladita*, or underdog character, who maintained a spicy and satirical banter that was not above touching taboo subjects and improvising monologues on topical themes. So successful did the Areus become with La Chata Noloesca on board, that they were able to rent their own theater in Los Angeles and serve as the impresarios for the numerous Hispanic companies touring to that city during the 1920s. Noloesca became the main draw for the mainly working-class, immigrant audiences of Los Angeles during these years.

By 1930 Noloesca had divorced Areu, split from the Areus, and formed her own company, Atracciones Noloesca, which mainly consisted of young women recruited in her hometown of San Antonio. During the Great Depression she continued to tour the Southwest and northern Mexico, but as Mexicans voluntarily and involuntarily returned to their homeland during the economic crisis, audiences dwindled. Theater owners could no longer afford live performances in their houses, and many switched to the more lucrative showing of movies that were now offered with Spanish soundtracks. In response Noloesca decided to set out for venues where the Hispanic community was growing, not decreasing; this meant heading out for cities that were drawing Puerto Rican immigrants, such as New York and Chicago.

In 1938 she reformed her company with local San Antonio talent under the name of Compañía Mexicana and set out to weather the Depression by performing at points east: Tampa, Chicago, and New York, as well as Puerto Rico and Havana. Noloesca's novel idea was to bring to the Puerto Ricans, Cubans, and other ethnic Hispanics her brand of Mexican vaudeville, music, folklore, and humor. In 1941 the company set down roots in New York for a stretch of nine years, during which time it was a mainstay on the Hispanic vaudeville circuit made up of the Teatro Hispano, Teatro Puerto Rico, Teatro Triboro, and 53rd Street Theater.

In 1950 Noloesca returned to her beloved San Antonio for her retirement but nevertheless performed periodically for special community events until her death in 1979. She was survived by her daughter, Belia Areu, a singer and vaudevillian in her own right who had come up in Noloesca's companies.

Nicolás Kanellos

SEE ALSO: *The Great Depression; Vaudeville.*

BIBLIOGRAPHY

Kanellos, Nicolás. *History of Hispanic Theater in the United States: Origins to 1940*. Austin: University of Texas Press, 1990.

Ramirez, Elizabeth C. *Chicanas/Latinas in American Theatre: A History of Performance.* Bloomington: Indiana University Press, 2000.

Norris, Frank *(1870–1902)*

Native Chicagoan Frank Norris is best known as one of the leading lights of American literary naturalism. Having studied art in Paris for a year before attending the University of California, Berkeley, and then Harvard, Norris worked as a reporter and critic for a number of newspapers and magazines in San Francisco and New York. After moving to New York in 1898, he published seven novels and two short story collections in quick succession. *Moran of the Lady Letty* (1898), *Blix* (1899), and *A Man's Woman* (1900) were standard "New Woman" adventure novels, largely forgotten during the twentieth century. *Vandover and the Brute* (published posthumously in 1914) and *McTeague* (1899), on the other hand, were Norris's classic Zolaesque studies of human degeneration. *The Octopus* (1901) and *The Pit* (1903), his last two novels before his untimely death from peritonitis in 1902, were both contributions to his ambitious Epic of the Wheat trilogy.

Bennett Lovett-Graff

SEE ALSO: *The Great Depression; Muckraking; Sinclair, Upton.*

BIBLIOGRAPHY

Hochman, Barbara. *The Art of Frank Norris, Storyteller.* Columbia: University of Missouri Press, 1988.

Hussman, Lawrence E. *Harbingers of a Century: The Novels of Frank Norris.* New York: Peter Lang, 1999.

McElrath, Joseph R. *Frank Norris Revisited.* Boston: Twayne, 1992.

McElrath, Joseph R., and Douglas K. Burgess. *The Apprenticeship Writings of Frank Norris: 1896–1898.* Philadelphia: American Philosophical Society, 1996.

McElrath, Joseph R., and S. Jesse Crisler. *Frank Norris: A Life.* Urbana: University of Illinois, 2006.

North by Northwest

When screenwriter Ernest Lehman was assigned to work for Alfred Hitchcock, he told the famed "master of suspense," I'd like to write "the Hitchcock picture to end all Hitchcock pictures." The result, released in 1959, was *North by Northwest*, and although—fortunately—it did not end all Hitchcock pictures, it did seem to offer a summation of the best of the director's work up to that time. Starring Cary Grant in a fast-paced thriller of mistaken identity and Cold War intrigue, *North by Northwest* had it all: glamour, mystery, wit, hairbreadth escapes, macabre humor, romance, and a breakneck cross-country chase culminating in a literally cliff-hanging climax atop the Mount Rushmore

North by Northwest. *Cary Grant as Roger Thornhill runs from an approaching biplane in an iconic scene from Alfred Hitchcock's* North by Northwest. SILVER SCREEN COLLECTION/CONTRIBUTOR/ MOVIEPIX/GETTY IMAGES.

monument. It was in this film that Hitchcock inserted one of his most famous set pieces: Grant, alone near a seemingly deserted cornfield, suddenly being stalked and strafed by a crop-dusting airplane. A big hit movie, *North by Northwest* represents a turning point for Hitchcock and remains a pinnacle of the romantic-spy-chase genre that he virtually originated.

DEVELOPING THE HITCHCOCK FORMULA

Before *North by Northwest*, Hitchcock gained fame with a series of romantic espionage thrillers, including *The Man Who Knew Too Much* (1934), *The 39 Steps* (1935), and *The Lady Vanishes* (1938). In *The 39 Steps*, the leading man (Robert Donat) is mistakenly accused of murder, causing him to flee both the police and the spies who are the true killers. The chase carries the hero all over Scotland, handcuffed to blond Madeleine Carroll, with whom he is forced to have a relationship characterized by equal parts distrust and sexual attraction. All of this is played out and filmed in a style of high comedy, which actually serves to emphasize the excitement and suspense—the "Hitchcock touch."

Once Hitchcock had established himself in Hollywood in the late 1930s, he wasted no time extending the genre he had created, directing such successful pictures as *Foreign Correspondent* (with Joel McCrea) in 1940 and *Saboteur* (with Robert Cummings) in 1942. Both are regarded as classic Hitchcock thrillers, but at the time the director was disappointed that his reputation was not big enough to secure the services of the most important stars (he had wanted Gary Cooper for *Foreign Correspondent*).

By the 1950s this was no longer a problem for Hitchcock. As one of the top directors in town, he could employ such first-rank actors as James Stewart and Grant—and he preferred such casting because he felt the audience could most readily identify with a big star and empathize with him during the scenes where he's placed in jeopardy. With *North by Northwest*, Hitchcock's only film at MGM (Metro-Goldwyn-Mayer), he once more had the services of Grant—and also the opportunity to improve upon his best work. As Hitchcock later explained to François Truffaut, audiences were terrified by the climax of *Saboteur*, in which hero Cummings tries to save a spy who is dangling from the Statue of Liberty—but they would have been twice as frightened if it had been the hero, not the spy, who was hanging on for dear life. With his new film, Hitchcock made sure that Grant and his leading lady (Eva Marie Saint) were both hanging by Grant's manicured fingernails atop the Mount Rushmore monument.

The story line with which Lehman and Hitchcock manipulated their stars into this precarious position was an improbable cross-country labyrinth of spy versus spy and love versus betrayal, all spinning out from the fateful moment when jaded Madison Avenue executive Roger Thornhill (Grant) is mistaken for a mysterious Mr. Kaplan by the henchmen of spy-master Phillip Vandamm (James Mason, at his slyly sinister best). The spies kidnap Thornhill, interrogate him for secrets (which, of course, he does not possess), and attempt to kill him. Though Thornhill manages to survive this ordeal, his troubles are only beginning.

Unable to convince the authorities—or even his own mother—that he was attacked, Thornhill investigates the mystery, only to find himself mistakenly accused of murdering an ambassador at the United Nations. Now, in the tradition of *39 Steps*, with the spies and the police after him, Thornhill flees west by train, befriended—or is he?—en route by beautiful blond Eve Kendall (Saint), who hides him in her state room. Thornhill's perils continue to pile up as he makes his way across the country in search of the real Mr. Kaplan. What the audience learns before Thornhill is that there is no Mr. Kaplan—he's an imaginary agent created as a decoy by real U.S. agents.

MACGUFFINS, MUSIC, AND MASTERFUL ACTING

If all of this begins to sound confusing or farfetched, that is part of the point. If ever a director made a film with a twinkle in his eye, Hitchcock is that director, and *North by Northwest* is that film. (He claimed that he'd intended to call the picture *The Man in Lincoln's Nose* and include a scene of Grant in the giant nostril having a sneezing fit. The actual title is, inconsequentially, a reference to Hamlet's madness.) Hitchcock always claimed that logic was a quality a filmmaker should be willing to sacrifice if it would allow for a great scene or a great shot, and *North by Northwest* is filled with such scenes and shots. (In truth, the plotting of the picture, improbable though it may be, is worked out ingeniously.) Hitchcock also claimed that in a thriller, the revelation of the secret being sought—"the MacGuffin," as he called it—was totally irrelevant to the story; for Hitchcock, the fun was in the chase. Consequently, he took delight in the airport sequence where government operative Leo G. Carroll finally explains the mystery to Grant—and his words are drowned off the soundtrack by airplane engines.

For his original screenplay, titled *The Sweet Smell of Success*, Lehman was nominated for an Academy Award (as were the film's editor and art directors). Bernard Herrmann, Hitchcock's favorite composer in the 1950s, concocted an exciting musical score. The main title was in the form of a fandango—symbolizing, according to Herrmann, "the crazy dance about to take place between Cary Grant and the world." For the film's most famous scene, the attack of the crop-dusting airplane, Herrmann wisely refrained from providing any music, realizing it would only distract from the sonic impact of the ever-approaching plane and the firing of its machine gun. Ironically, the following year, Hitchcock would request that Herrmann leave the shower murder in *Psycho* similarly unscored. Herrmann, of course, disregarded this instruction, and when Hitchcock saw the scene with Herrmann's now-famous attacking violins on the soundtrack, the director apologized for having made "an improper suggestion."

Grant contributed one of his most expert performances as the unlikely Thornhill, suavely romancing Saint's Eve while being pursued by a world of spies. *North by Northwest* proved a triumph for both its star and its director, a cinematic high-water mark that remains much admired and much imitated in films, including *Charade* (1963) and *Silver Streak* (1976). The second James Bond feature, *From Russia with Love* (1963), boasts an exciting helicopter sequence not unlike Hitchcock's crop-dusting scene. From that point on, however, the Bond films would start going their own way, creating the genre of outrageously gimmick-stuffed espionage thrillers.

After his horror film one-two punch of *Psycho* (1960) and *The Birds* (1963), Hitchcock would go on to make films such as *Marnie* (1964) and *Topaz* (1969), which called to mind such erotic espionage thrillers of the 1940s as *Notorious* (1946). But never again did Hitchcock attempt another flat-out, action/chase thriller in the manner of his 1930s hits.

North by Northwest has proven itself a film with staying power. In 2009 Warner Brothers released a fiftieth-anniversary edition on both DVD and Blu-ray. And as of 2012 the film had a 100 percent approval rating on the film review website Rotten Tomatoes.

Preston Neal Jones

SEE ALSO: *Academy Awards; Celebrity; Cold War; Cooper, Gary; Grant, Cary; Hitchcock, Alfred; Hollywood; Horror Movies; James Bond Films; McCrea, Joel; MGM (Metro-Goldwyn-Mayer); Mount Rushmore; Movie Stars;* Psycho; *Stewart, Jimmy.*

BIBLIOGRAPHY

Lehman, Ernest. *North by Northwest.* New York: Viking Press, 1972.

McGilligan, Patrick. *Alfred Hitchcock: A Life in Darkness and Light.* New York: Harper, 2003.

Rubin, Steven Jay. *The Complete James Bond Movie Encyclopedia.* Chicago: Contemporary Books, 1990.

Northern Exposure

Airing first in 1990, comedy-drama series *Northern Exposure* brought an engaging and eccentric vision of small-town Alaskan life to television viewers. Its utopian portrait of a simpler existence reflected an early 1990s concern with scaling down from the yuppie excesses of the 1980s.

Set in the fictional town of Cicely, the series begins with the arrival of Dr. Joel Fleischman (Rob Morrow), a native New Yorker, and it hinges upon the initial contrast and growing affinity between the urbane doctor and the quirky, close-knit local populace. Created by *St. Elsewhere*'s Joshua Brand and John Falsey, the series combined savvy artistic and literary references with off-beat story lines. *Northern Exposure* picked up a loyal audience, along with six Emmys in the second of its six seasons. The series ended in 1996, its demise hastened by Morrow's departure.

James Lyons

SEE ALSO: *Emmy Awards;* St. Elsewhere.

BIBLIOGRAPHY

Chunovic, Louis. *The* Northern Exposure *Book.* New York: Citadel Press, 1995.

Thompson, Robert J. *Television's Second Golden Age: From* Hill Street Blues *to* ER. New York: Continuum, 1996.

Weiner, Ellis. *Letters from Cicely.* New York: Pocket Books, 1992.

Novak, Kim *(1933–)*

Critics have never been kind to Kim Novak. They often (and wrongly) have dismissed her as a typical star manufactured by the studio system or as one of the many cinema's goddesses gifted with plenty of sex appeal but little acting talent. Directors have not been too kind either. Richard Quine, allegedly paying her a compliment, declared she had "the proverbial quality of the lady in the parlor and the whore in the bedroom." An embittered Henry Hathaway remembered resigning as director of *Of Human Bondage* (1964), which he had originally planned to film with Marilyn Monroe, because of Novak: "They made it with Stupid—what's her name—Kim Novak. . . . I worked one day with her and quit." And yet, although briefly, audiences loved her passionately and were most receptive to her peculiar appeal as an actress, responding to it with 3,500 fan letters per week.

Born Marilyn Pauline Novak, Kim Novak's star began to shine when Rita Hayworth's started to fade. In the early 1950s Harry Cohn, the head of Columbia Pictures, decided to create another sex goddess to replace Hayworth, and his choice fell on the young model Novak. She was cast as a femme fatale in *Pushover* (1954) by Quine, and her first starring performance is already remarkable for that peculiar mixture of destructive sex appeal and extreme vulnerability that would later inform her role in Alfred Hitchcock's *Vertigo* (1958). In 1955 she starred in two of that year's biggest hits: the sexy comedy *Picnic* by Joshua Logan and the controversial *Man with the Golden Arm* by Otto Preminger. In both movies, Novak plays characters who are only superficially weak and who refuse to be appreciated only as sex objects. Her slow-motion jitterbug dance with the sexy hobo William Holden in *Picnic* (1955) ranks as one of the most sensual scenes of the 1950s.

Kim Novak. *Kim Novak's sex symbol image proved to be both an advantage and a hindrance in her movie career.* SILVER SCREEN COLLECTION/GETTY IMAGES.

TRUSTING HER INSTINCTS

By the end of 1956, Novak was being paid at least $300,000 per film, and a poll commissioned by *Box Office* magazine voted her the most popular star in the United States. Meanwhile, she developed a reputation for being "difficult" to work with. George Sidney, who directed Novak and Tyrone Power in *The Eddy Duchin Story* (1956), listed her as evidence of that "hopeless poison that gets into actresses when they become big stars." But Novak began to make it clear that she was unwilling to conform to the cliché of the brainless sex goddess that Cohn had thought she would fit so well. Interviewed in 1998 on the occasion of the release of the restored copy of *Vertigo*, Novak declared that instead of the label "difficult" she preferred "impudent": "I had views, or rather, instincts—like animals do. I trusted my instincts and wanted to be true to myself, so a director had to convince me of something else."

When Vera Miles became pregnant, Alfred Hitchcock replaced her with Novak for the role of Madeline Elster/Judy Barton in *Vertigo*. One of the central motifs of the movie is Madeline's, and then Judy's, ability to make the quasi-Pygmalion character Scottie Ferguson, played by Jimmy Stewart, fall in love with the beautiful image he has created for himself. Novak displays a remarkable ability to sustain the ambiguity and tension between sensuality and vulnerability, between what seems to be and what is implied in her character. When the restored copy of the movie was rereleased, Novak claimed she saw the Stewart character as a variation on Cohn, who had created an actress he thought had no quality: "Cohn wasn't interested in me as a woman. He didn't think I had anything to offer . . . he just didn't see you. He looked beyond you . . . to where the audiences were."

During the 1960s and 1970s, Novak made a series of wrong choices. She was either miscast in movies that did no justice to her abilities (*The Amorous Adventures of Moll Flanders*, 1965; *Satan's Triangle*, 1975; *White Buffalo*, 1977) or that received poor distribution (*The Legend of Lylah Claire*, 1968). By the end of the 1970s, after marrying her veterinarian, she decided to be less active as an actress. She appeared in a supporting role in David Hemmings's *Just a Gigolo* (1979), where she seduces David Bowie over the body of her dead husband, and she joined the all-star cast of the rather bland Agatha Christie mystery *The Mirror Crack'd* (1980). In both movies Novak's performances are interesting for her subtle irony at the self-parodying of her own former image of sex goddess.

After appearing in the miniseries *Malibu* (1983) and in the extremely popular prime-time soap opera *Falcon's Crest* (1986), she made a major comeback to cinema, giving very fine performances in Tony Palmer's *The Children* (1990) and in Mike Figgis's *Liebestraum* (1991). Both movies offered her complex roles. In the former she is a refined widow, courted by a man promising affection who ultimately abandons her, whereas in the latter she plays a tormented woman dying of cancer coming to terms with her own past. Both performances show Novak's maturity as an actress, one who, as the character of Madge Owens in *Picnic* says, gets tired of simply being told she is beautiful. For once, a former sex goddess who did not turn to drugs, alcohol, or suicide escapes from her past image.

Luca Prono

SEE ALSO: *Bowie, David; Christie, Agatha; Hayworth, Rita; Hitchcock, Alfred; Holden, William; Monroe, Marilyn; Preminger, Otto; Sex Symbol; Stewart, Jimmy; Studio System;* Vertigo.

BIBLIOGRAPHY

Barnett, Vincent. "Dualling for Judy: The Concept of the Double in the Films of Kim Novak." *Film History* 19, no. 1 (2007): 86–101.

Brown, Peter Harry. *Kim Novak—Reluctant Goddess*. New York: St. Martin's Press, 1986.

Byars, Jackie. "The Prime of Miss Kim Novak: Struggling over the Feminine in the Star Image." In *The Other Fifties: Interrogating Midcentury American Icons*, ed. Joel Foreman, 197–223. Urbana: University of Illinois Press, 1997.

Humphries, Patrick. *The Films of Alfred Hitchcock*. New York: Portland House, 1986.

Kashner, Sam, and Jennifer MacNair. *The Bad & The Beautiful: Hollywood in the Fifties*. New York: W. W. Norton, 2003.

Kleno, Larry. *Kim Novak on Camera*. San Diego, CA: A. S. Barnes, 1980.

Parish, James Robert, and Don E. Stanke. *The Glamour Girls*. New Rochelle, NY: Arlington House, 1975.

Shipman, David. *The Great Movie Stars: The International Years*, vol. 2. London: Warner Books, 1993.

Nureyev, Rudolf *(1938–1993)*

Perhaps the first Russian male ballet dancer to become a worldwide superstar since Vaslav Nijinsky, Rudolf Nureyev completely redefined the place of men in classical ballet. A moody, bigoted egomaniac who routinely revised ballets to give himself larger roles, Nureyev was nonetheless an electrifying performer.

Nureyev gained fame as a soloist with the Leningrad Kirov Ballet (now Mariinsky Ballet) in his home country. In 1961, while on tour in Europe, however, he generated spectacular publicity when he defected from the Soviet Union. His celebrated partnership with Margot Fonteyn, a prima ballerina with Britain's Royal Ballet who was more than twice his age and poised to retire when they began dancing together, completely revitalized her career. From 1983 to 1989, as the artistic director of the Paris Opéra Ballet, Nureyev promoted a new generation of dancers and revived the world's oldest ballet company, making it one of the finest contemporary ballet troupes. Passionately devoted to performing, he continued to dance almost until his death from AIDS in 1993.

Jeffrey Escoffier

SEE ALSO: *AIDS; Ballet; Fonteyn, Margot.*

BIBLIOGRAPHY

Kavanagh, Julie. *Rudolf Nureyev: The Life*. New York: Pantheon Books, 2007.

The Royal Ballet with Rudolf Nureyev and Margot Fonteyn in Romeo and Juliet. Film. Directed by Paul Czinner. West Long Branch, NJ: Kultur International Films, 1966.

Stuart, Otis. *Perpetual Motion: The Public and Private Lives of Rudolf Nureyev*. New York: Simon, 1995.

Nylon

A synthetic thermoplastic material, nylon was first introduced commercially by E. I. du Pont de Nemours and Company (also called DuPont) in the form of toothbrush bristles in 1938. The process of condensation polymerization, by which nylon and the synthetic rubber neoprene are made, was discovered by Wallace Carothers, a chemist working for DuPont in the 1930s. The name "nylon" itself was originally a trademark of DuPont, but the material is now produced in many different forms, all of which belong to the chemical group known as polyamides. Although these nylons have different characteristics and can be used in different ways, they all share the same basic qualities.

In general, nylon is useful because it is a light, strong, hard-wearing material that is resistant to corrosive chemicals, can be easily molded when heated, and can be colored with pigments. Nylon is also remarkably cheap and easy to manufacture. As a result, a huge variety of different uses have been found for it, and nylon is present in almost all areas of life. For example, it appears in the form of woven fabrics, thread, and rope, and as plastic sheets, moldings, and netting. Because it is resistant to wear, nylon is also used as an alternative to conventional steel bearings and gears and as insulation in electrical equipment.

Within two years of the introduction of the first nylon toothbrushes, nylon was being spun as a multifilament yarn to make hosiery. Because they were more durable than silk, nylon stockings were highly sought after when they first appeared in 1940. This was particularly true in Europe during World War II, when gifts of nylons made American servicemen as popular with local women as Hershey's chocolate made them with children. More crucially, nylon parachutes were lighter and more reliable than silk versions, and in military slang a parachute descent became known as a "nylon letdown."

In the 1960s and 1970s nylon was at the height of its popularity as a fabric material, perhaps because of its longevity and the fact that clothes made from colored nylon do not fade with washing. Because of their tendency to generate static electricity, however, nylon fabrics are not always comfortable to wear, and as dye and detergent technologies have improved, nylon's popularity has decreased. Since the 1990s nylon fabrics have most often been found in waterproof outer clothing and hosiery. The material has also had an effect on modern health-care, because nylon surgical sutures, splints, braces, and many other medical items are cheap, and easy to sterilize and keep clean.

Shopping for Nylon Stockings. *Crowds of women shopping for nylon stockings at Gimbal's department store in 1947.* SAM SHERE/ TIME & LIFE PICTURES/GETTY IMAGES.

The versatility of nylon as a material means that—aside from the multifilament yarns used in clothing and the monofilaments used as bristles—nylon can also be molded into solid objects of many different sizes and shapes. Because of its resilience, nylon is a good material for making objects that need to resist wear and tear, such as plastic containers, stationary items, floor coverings, and bearings. Nylon bearings are particularly useful in extreme conditions, where lubrication is impractical or where the bearing is exposed to water. Nylon can also be formed into objects that hold pressure, such as bicycle tires, inflated balls, certain pump cylinders, and valves. The invention of nylon, and the plastics technologies that followed, made possible the cheap mass production of high-quality consumer objects, from children's toys and kitchen utensils to computers, cameras, televisions, and sound systems.

Despite his remarkable discovery, and despite receiving more than fifty other patents, the inventor of nylon, Wallace Carothers, was an unhappy man who suffered from severe depression and alcoholism. Although nylon revolutionized life in the late twentieth century, Carothers did not live to enjoy the benefits of his work. He committed suicide in 1937, not long before those first bristles went into production.

Chris Routledge

SEE ALSO: *Advertising; World War II.*

BIBLIOGRAPHY

Gaines, Ann. *Wallace Carothers and the Story of du Pont Nylon.* Bear, DE: Mitchell Lane, 2002.

Hermes, Matthew E. *Enough for One Lifetime: Wallace Carothers, Inventor of Nylon.* History of Modern Chemical Sciences Series. Washington, DC: American Chemical Society, 1996.

Kohan, Melvin I. *The Nylon Plastics Handbook.* Cincinnati, OH: Hanser and Gardner, 1995.

NYPD Blue

Premiering on September 21, 1993, *NYPD Blue* was one of the most critically acclaimed series ever and among the most controversial shows television had seen in years. Even before the first program aired, word had leaked out regarding its use of language and presentation of partial nudity. Although critics across the country praised its style and content, the show caused controversy among ABC's affiliates, fifty-seven of whom had declined to carry the program by the time the first episode aired. Perhaps because of the immense publicity it generated, this gritty police drama managed to rank nineteenth in the ratings and garnered a record twenty-seven Emmy nominations during its first year. In its second season, *NYPD Blue* won the Emmy for Outstanding Dramatic Series and became the seventh-highest-rated program in the country. Amid a whirlwind of controversy and debate, cocreators Steven Bochco and David Milch had managed, during a period of conservative programming, to launch what some have referred to as the first "R-rated" television series.

NYPD Blue's rare combination of critical acclaim, controversy, and mass appeal was familiar terrain for Bochco, who had also produced *Hill Street Blues* (1981–1987) and *Cop Rock* (1990). Like other Bochco programs, *NYPD Blue* used an ensemble cast led by *Blues* veterans Dennis Franz and David Caruso. Franz became a fixture at the Emmy Awards, winning Outstanding Lead Actor in a Drama Series three of the show's first four years. Meanwhile, Caruso, who appeared partially nude in multiple episodes, became a popular star and generated new controversy when he demanded higher pay. Eventually, and quite publicly, Caruso left the show. Rather than slipping in the ratings, however, the program again benefited from the controversy and became even more popular with the addition of *LA Law* veteran Jimmy Smits, who took over as Franz's partner. In addition to Franz, who played detective Andy Sipowicz, and Smits's character Bobby Simone, other cast members included Emmy winner Kim Delaney, James McDaniel, Rick Schroder (who replaced Smits in 1998), and Nicholas Turturro.

In the middle of the first decade of the 2000s *NYPD Blue* became embroiled in further controversy over its nudity when the Parents' Television Council (PTC) criticized the show for the use of obscenities, holding it accountable for the general increase in profanity and violence on prime-time television. In 2003 the PTC filed a complaint with the FCC over the use of obscene language. Although that case was dismissed, the FCC fined ABC $1.4 million for the 2003 episode "Nude Awakening," citing scenes of "adult sexual nudity." A court battle ensued, and finally on January 4, 2011, the U.S. Court of Appeals for the Second Circuit rejected the fine.

The success of *NYPD Blue* can be linked in part to its realistic depiction of police work and the complex and conflicting impact that regular exposure to crime has upon these committed, yet flawed, individuals. The program consistently used crimes, investigative processes, and character interactions to explore complex ethical and contemporary social conditions related to class, gender, and race. Like the hit *Hill Street Blues*, *NYPD Blue* managed to be thought provoking, entertaining, and moving whether it was dealing with the mundane activities of day-to-day life or the disturbing events that detectives might experience in New York City.

NYPD Blue won numerous Emmy Awards, Screen Actors Guild Awards, and Satellite Awards before it went off the air in 2005. The final episode, which depicts previous squad leader Lieutenant Bale handing over the reins to Sipowicz, aired on March 1, 2005.

James Friedman

SEE ALSO: *Bochco, Steven; Emmy Awards;* Hill Street Blues*; Smits, Jimmy; Television.*

BIBLIOGRAPHY

Thompson, Robert J. *Television's Second Golden Age.* New York: Continuum, 1996.

Vest, Jason P. *"The Wire," "Deadwood," "Homicide," and "NYPD Blue": Violence Is Power.* Santa Barbara, CA: ABC-CLIO, LLC, 2011.

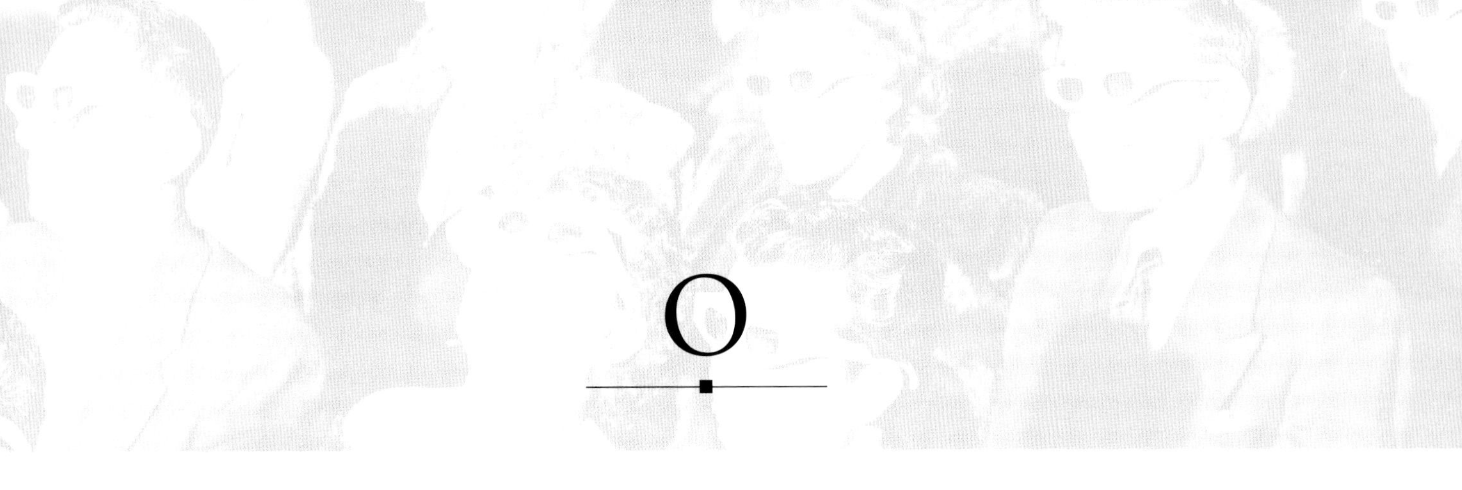

The Oakland Raiders

The Oakland Raiders, a professional football franchise based in California, operates under the motto "Commitment to Excellence." Yet turmoil has been as much a hallmark of the team's history as high-quality play. Established in 1960 from the ruins of a Minneapolis franchise, the Raiders were one of the stalwart clubs of the now-defunct American Football League. From 1963 through 2011, they were run by Al Davis, a maverick who instilled a pirate ethic in his silver-and-black-clad players as well as a high-powered passing offense under quarterback Daryle Lamonica that led the team to the Super Bowl in 1968—a contest they lost.

In 1969 the team hired coach John Madden, who led them to an incredible ten winning seasons in a row. The Raiders won their first world championship under Madden in 1977. The stars of that era included tough, hard-hitting defensive players such as Jim Otto, Gene Upshaw, Art Shell (who later coached the team), Ted Hendricks, and Willie Brown. The offensive side had quarterback Ken "the Snake" Stabler, wide receiver Fred Biletnikoff, and kicker George Blanda (who played more seasons—twenty-six—than any other player in NFL history). In 1981 head coach Tom Flores (a former Raiders quarterback) led the team to another Super Bowl victory. In 1982, in defiance of a National Football League lawsuit, Davis moved the club to Los Angeles, where it remained for thirteen years. World champions again in 1984, the Raiders moved back to Oakland in 1995, where, at the end of the twentieth century, they continued to rank among the league's roughest, most penalized teams.

The Raiders performed dismally in 1996 and 1997. In 1998 Davis hired hot-shot young coach Jon Gruden, who improved the team from 8–8 records his first two years to two consecutive division titles. However, Gruden's feeling that he was underpaid led to his leaving Oakland for the Tampa Bay Buccaneers. During the 2002 season, the Raiders had new coach Bill Callahan and a high-powered offense with quarterback Rich Gannon and receivers Jerry Rice and Tim Brown, which carried them all the way to the Super Bowl. Ironically, the Raiders lost to Gruden's Bucs in the championship game.

Since that bitter defeat, the team has experienced almost continuous turmoil and disappointment. From 2003 through 2011 the team had seven consecutive losing seasons, followed by two seasons with 8–8 records. Even more telling, the Raiders had six different head coaches, as Davis hired and fired people with abandon. Davis also became known for interfering too much with the running of the team and making poor decisions. For instance, the team failed in its attempt to develop a franchise quarterback. In 2007 the Raiders selected quarterback JaMarcus Russell of Louisiana State as the number one pick of the NFL draft, which proved to be one of the most costly mistakes in NFL history. The franchise was forced to release Russell after three seasons and only twenty-five starts with seven wins. They had paid the failed quarterback more than $30 million. Davis passed away in October 2011, and team ownership passed to his family. Observers around the league wondered what that change would mean for the troubled franchise.

Robert E. Schnakenberg

SEE ALSO: *Madden, John; National Football League (NFL); Professional Football; Rice, Jerry; Sports Heroes; Super Bowl.*

BIBLIOGRAPHY

Ribowsky, Mark. *Slick: The Silver and Black Life of Al Davis.* New York: Macmillan, 1991.

Richmond, Peter. *Badasses: The Legend of Snake, Foo, Dr. Death, and John Madden's Oakland Raiders.* New York: HarperCollins, 2010.

Travers, Steven. *The Good, the Bad, & the Ugly: Oakland Raiders: Heart-Pounding, Jaw-Dropping, and Gut-Wrenching Moments from Oakland Raiders History.* Chicago: Triumph Books, 2008.

Oates, Joyce Carol *(1938–)*

One of the most prolific contemporary American authors, Joyce Carol Oates writes short stories, novels, nonfiction, plays, poetry, screenplays, essays, and articles. She composes mysteries under two pseudonyms, Rosamond Smith and Lauren Kelly, and she has also branched into the teen and children's markets. Her works have been included numerous times in compilations such as *The Best American Short Stories*, The O. Henry Awards anthology, The Pushcart Prize anthology, and *The Year's Best Fantasy and Horror.* She won the National Book Award in 1970 for the novel *them,* and three of her novels, including *Blonde* (2000), have been nominated for Pulitzer Prizes. Oates has also won and been shortlisted for countless other literary awards.

Called her best book by several reviewers, *Blonde* is a fictional, historical account of Marilyn Monroe's personal life. The longest of Oates's novels, the book posits that Monroe was assassinated. It was adapted to television in 2001, but the movie was seen by many as a departure from the text. In 2001 *We Were the Mulvaneys* (1996) was selected for Oprah's Book Club and was later adapted into an Emmy-nominated television movie.

The *New York Times* best seller *Gravedigger's Daughter* was published in 2007 and is a fictional account of Oates's own family history. "Where Are You Going, Where Have You Been," a story about a teenage girl who is pursued by an older and seemingly dangerous man, is one of the most anthologized stories of the twentieth century and is read frequently in literature classes around the United States.

Oates has taught creative writing at Princeton University since 1978 and has been recognized as a distinguished professor for her continued work there. Her writing receives continuous critical attention, and though she is alternately praised for the quality of her work and criticized for being too prolific, too dark, or too violent, she has earned a permanent place on many reading lists and has ensured her continuing influence on American fiction.

Adrienne Furness

SEE ALSO: *Best Sellers; Emmy Awards; Made-for-Television Movies; Monroe, Marilyn; The* New York Times*; Oprah's Book Club; Teenagers; Television; Winfrey, Oprah.*

BIBLIOGRAPHY

Johnson, Greg. *Invisible Writer: A Biography of Joyce Carol Oates.* New York: Dutton, 1998.

"Joyce Carol Oates." Contemporary Authors Online. Detroit, MI: Gale, 2011.

Milazzo, Lee, ed. *Conversations with Joyce Carol Oates.* Jackson: University Press of Mississippi, 1989.

Obama, Barack *(1961–)*

On November 4, 2008, the United States of America elected its first African American president: Barack Obama. Although the young Democrat from Illinois had served in the U.S. Senate for only three years prior to his 2008 campaign, Obama's profound skill as an orator, success in using social media, and overall appearance as the embodiment of "change" for a nation craving new direction won him a decisive victory over Republican candidate John McCain. Buoyed by his positive proclamations of "hope" and "change," Obama rode a wave of incredible enthusiasm into office, receiving a 68 percent approval rating in the first Gallup poll following his inauguration on January 20, 2009.

However, after the initial fervor for this fresh-faced senator subsided, Obama's first term in office drove public opinion in divergent directions. Some of the more liberal members of Obama's base expressed disappointment that his approach to governance was not more hard-nosed in executing progressive legislation. By contrast, many of Obama's centrist supporters came to question whether his vision of a more bipartisan political climate was within his power to implement, as fierce polarization continued to characterize American politics throughout his term. Conservatives, unsurprisingly critical of Obama and his policies, often vilified the new president, calling him un-American and a socialist. Some even questioned the validity of his birth certificate, accusing him of being a Muslim not born on American soil.

Though Obama certainly still had his champions at the close of his first term—in *Washington Monthly* Paul Glastris called Obama's legislative accomplishments "stunning," saying he had "gotten more done in three years than any president in decades"—on the eve of the 2012 presidential election, it remained to be seen whether Obama could win a second term.

EARLY LIFE AND CAREER

Barack Hussein Obama was born on August 4, 1961, in Honolulu, Hawaii, the son of Ann Dunham, a white, eighteen-year-old American from Kansas, and Barack Obama Sr., a native of Kenya and the first African student to attend the University of Hawaii. The couple divorced when Obama was only two, and Dunham remarried in 1966 and moved the family to Indonesia for four years. Obama returned to Honolulu in 1971, where he spent the majority of his youth growing up in a single-parent home. He enrolled at Occidental College in Los Angeles in 1979 and transferred to Columbia University in New York City two years later. After graduating from college, he spent a short time living in Chicago before enrolling in Harvard Law School at the age of twenty-eight. There, he became the first African American president of the *Harvard Law Review* and graduated magna cum laude in 1991.

Before graduating, Obama made the fateful decision to accept a summer internship at the Chicago law firm of Sidley & Austin, where Michelle Robinson was assigned to mentor him. A young associate at the firm, she had worked her way from a modest upbringing on the South Side of Chicago to graduate from Harvard Law. Obama and Robinson quickly discovered their shared passion for social justice and were married in 1992, settling in Chicago's Hyde Park neighborhood. At the time, Obama was teaching constitutional law at the University of Chicago and had yet to launch his political career. One year after publishing a memoir titled *Dreams from My Father* in 1995, Obama was elected to the Illinois state senate.

On July 27, 2004, after just under a decade as a state senator, Obama gave a rousing keynote address at the Democratic National Convention (DNC) in Boston, vaulting him into the national spotlight. In his book *Obama: From Promise to Power,* David Mendell recalls walking with Obama and his entourage through Boston on the way to the DNC, asking the state senator how he felt about impressing the bigwigs of the Democratic party. Without breaking stride, Obama replied, "I'm LeBron, baby, I can play on this level. I got some game." The comparison to NBA superstar LeBron James was bold but not unwarranted. On November 2 of the same year, Obama was elected to represent Illinois in the U.S. Senate.

2008 PRESIDENTIAL PRIMARIES

Following Obama's 2004 DNC speech and subsequent election to the U.S. Senate, his public visibility progressed apace. Inspired by his address in Boston, Eli Attie, the chief speechwriter for Al Gore during his 2000 campaign and a writer and producer for the hit TV show *The West Wing,* based *West Wing* character Matt Santos (a presidential candidate, no less) on Obama. Attie's characterization proved prescient, as on February 10, 2007, Obama announced his candidacy for the presidency of the United States. He released another book on the eve of his presidential candidacy: *The Audacity of Hope.* This book—a more explicitly political biography that established the central tenets of Obama's campaign—was an instant best seller.

Obama's campaign needed more than the boon from a best seller in order for him to beat his chief opponent in the

Democratic primaries: Hillary Clinton. With six years in the Senate and eight in the White House as first lady, Clinton's experience eclipsed the young Obama's by several orders of magnitude. Her campaign strategies and finances were also more strongly established at the onset of the primary campaign, and with the political character and clout of former President Bill Clinton as a wild card on her side, her position as the potential Democratic nominee appeared to be all but unassailable in the spring of 2007.

That appearance proved misleading. Obama's campaign harnessed the growing momentum of social media—combined with the candidate's magnetic, charismatic persona—to slingshot him into a position where his prominence and political capital rivaled Clinton's. When Obama won the Iowa Democratic caucuses on January 3, 2008, it was not only a red flag to Hillary's campaign but also a sign of his success at using online resources to garner support. From YouTube to Twitter, Facebook to texting, Obama's success in building a grassroots base through social media was unprecedented, and in the aftermath of his eventual victory, multiple commentators would come to call this online grassroots success the "Obama effect." Still, even after the sea change signaled in Iowa, the campaign between Clinton and Obama was protracted and hard fought; it was not until June 3, after a seventeen-month battle, that Obama finally won enough delegates to secure his nomination as the official Democratic candidate in 2008.

CONTROVERSY AND CLINTON'S CONCESSION

In mid-March 2008, Obama's nomination had looked to be anything but automatic, as a furor over comments made by Jeremiah Wright, Obama's longtime pastor at Trinity United Church of Christ in Chicago, threatened to jeopardize his campaign. As a member of Trinity Church, Obama had maintained a close relationship with Wright for more than two decades. Indeed, the pastor had officiated at the Obamas' wedding, and he had baptized their daughters, Malia and Sasha. Obama's association with Wright became a sensational news story on March 13 when ABC News brought out excerpts from Wright's sermons, including a clip where he said, "God damn America." The comment was cast as an insinuation that America deserved the 9/11 terrorist attacks.

Initially, Obama attempted to diffuse the fracas, telling ABC that Wright was "like an old uncle who says things I don't always agree with." He then addressed the situation head on, foregrounding—and attempting to prove historical context for—Wright's comments in "A More Perfect Union," a nationally televised speech delivered in Pennsylvania on March 18, in which Obama spoke with remarkable candor about issues of racial resentment and mistrust for both whites and blacks in America. Although the speech was widely hailed as an act of political bravery that broke long-standing silences in the national conversation about race, it was not enough to quench the firestorm surrounding Wright. By early June, the political pressure proved too much, and though Obama said he made the decision "with sadness," he and Michelle publicly quit their membership in Trinity Church, citing "the divisive statements of Reverend Wright, which sharply conflict with our own views."

In addition to continued pressure about Wright's sermons, Obama drew criticism for comments he had made suggesting the nation's dire economic situation led some people to "cling to guns or religion." Although he claimed the remark was intended to be empathetic, conservatives seized on it as evidence of his elitism and inability to share their values. In a debate with Hillary Clinton in Pennsylvania, Obama attempted to clarify his comments, saying, "The point I was making was that when people feel like Washington's not listening to them, when they're promised year after year, decade after decade, that their economic situation is going to change and it doesn't, then, politically, they end up focusing on those things that are constant, like religion." Although the statement lingered as an unfortunate gaffe, Obama built an unbeatable advantage over his Democratic rival, and on June 7, 2008, Clinton conceded, officially endorsing Obama. Although most political scientists acknowledge that Obama is a talented politician, many also note that Clinton was at a distinct disadvantage in the primary because of her gender and the lingering fallout from her husband's sexual escapades with Monica Lewinsky.

OBAMA VS. McCAIN

After being the underdog against Clinton, initial poll results showed Obama ahead of Republican Senator John McCain of Arizona. Although the numbers fluctuated, the combination of powerful rhetoric and great grassroots organization continued to propel Obama toward the presidency. Obama's ability to electrify crowds with his aspirational oratory and charismatic yet calm demeanor drew comparisons to previous iconic presidents, including Ronald Reagan; John F. Kennedy; and, perhaps most frequently, his fellow Illinoisan Abraham Lincoln. With Obama's own rhetorical flourish mustered behind campaign slogans such as "Hope," "Change," and "Yes We Can," his campaign successfully cast him as an irrepressibly positive "can-do" candidate with the vision to create a better future and a better America.

By the end of the 2008 campaign, the image of Obama gazing optimistically toward the horizon was enshrined in the national consciousness, not by the Obama campaign itself but by guerrilla street artist Shepard Fairey. While the campaign was certainly adept at harnessing the power of online networking, it was Fairey's *Hope* poster that became an Internet sensation. Fairey's initial printing of 350 posters became instant collector's items, while the digital image went viral and became universally recognized as a hallmark of Obama's youthful, populist appeal.

In the final Gallup poll prior to the election, Obama enjoyed an eleven-point lead. The writing was on the wall. When Americans went to the polls on November 4, 2008, 52.9 percent of them voted for Obama, giving him a decisive victory, with 365 votes in the Electoral College over McCain's 173. America had elected its first African American president. On that night, in Grant Park in Chicago, Obama came to the podium to deliver his victory speech. As he was greeted by cheers and chants of "Yes, we can," he proclaimed in his opening line, "If there is anyone out there who still doubts that America is a place where all things are possible, who still wonders if the dream of our founders is alive in our time, who still questions the power of our democracy, tonight is your answer."

ECONOMIC STIMULUS

Upon his inauguration into office on January 20, 2009, Obama faced a daunting set of challenges, the perilous state of the economy foremost among them. At the time he took office, the U.S. economy was losing an average of 750,000 jobs per month, and experts were calling it the worst financial crisis since the Great Depression. Wasting little time, on February 17, President

Obama signed into law the American Recovery and Reinvestment Act of 2009, a multibillion-dollar stimulus package aimed at jump-starting the economy through government spending. Whereas many economists and political commentators credit Obama's stimulus as having averted what could have been an even more catastrophic crisis, Obama's conservative opponents considered his plan weak at best and counterproductive at worst. Appearing on *Glenn Beck*, trend forecaster Gerald Celente went so far as to call Obama's 2009 economic stimulus package "fascism light." There could be no doubt about the swiftness of Obama's action in attempting to save the economy, but the questions surrounding its long-term success or failure remained open for years to come.

One aspect of Obama's economic bailout, however, was quickly deemed an overwhelming success. His deal with American automakers—including his stipulation that General Motors CEO Rick Wagoner must step down in order for the company to secure billions in federal aid—was seen as a decisive move to save the industry from imminent collapse. In 2010 *Washington Post* business columnist Steven Pearlstein observed that "a year later, the auto bailout is an unqualified success." Although Obama's auto industry stimulus still had its critics, the rapid shift from losses to profits for Detroit's automakers was broadly regarded as a credit to Obama's bailout. In 2012 one of the early cornerstones of Obama's campaign for reelection was his perceived success in revitalizing an industry that not only provides hundreds of thousands of domestic jobs but also has stood for more than a century as a symbol of American innovation and prosperity.

HEALTH CARE REFORM

President Obama's Reinvestment Act of 2009 proved politically divisive, but his health care reform in 2010 was a veritable fault line in Washington. Initially enacted as the Patient Protection and Affordable Care Act on March 23, 2010, and subsequently amended as the Health Care and Education Reconciliation Act of 2010, the reform bill was signed into law on March 30. Making good on his 2008 campaign promise to establish universal health care coverage in the United States, the reform allows young adults to stay on their parents' health coverage until the age of twenty-six, and it bars insurance companies from denying children coverage for preexisting conditions and from dropping anyone's coverage upon their getting sick. Although the reform was seen by many as a vast improvement, many conservatives derided "Obamacare"—initially a term used pejoratively by critics but subsequently adopted by those on both sides of the reform—as "socialist," suggesting that it violated the principles of individual freedom by mandating the purchase of health insurance. Heading into the 2012 presidential election, Obama counted health care reform among the signature accomplishments of his first term. It survived an initial challenge when the Supreme Court ruled the legislation constitutional in 2012.

BP OIL SPILL

Less than a month after "Obamacare" was enacted, the Obama administration was confronted by the worst environmental disaster in decades. On April 20, 2010, British Petroleum's Deepwater Horizon drilling rig exploded in the Gulf of Mexico, killing eleven workers and releasing millions of gallons of oil into the Gulf for the next three months as BP clambered to cap the oil well. On May 21 President Obama issued an executive order establishing a special congressional commission on the BP spill and on offshore drilling in general. In June he met with BP officials to ensure that the company create a multibillion-dollar fund dedicated to stopping the ongoing spill. Despite Obama's efforts, the resulting spill was the worst in U.S. history, producing an oil slick that could be seen from space. Although the commission established by Obama ultimately found fault with BP for cutting costs at the expense of safety measures, the commission also initially criticized the Obama administration, charging that they were "either not fully competent" or "not fully candid with the American people about the scope of the problem."

OBAMA AND THE MILITARY

Obama inherited foreign wars in both Iraq and Afghanistan when he arrived in office in 2009. After pledging to strengthen the U.S. force in Afghanistan by 30,000 in December 2009, Obama demonstrated muscle as commander in chief just six months later, when he demanded the resignation of General Stanley McChrystal, the leader of those newly bolstered forces. McChrystal and a number of his aides were quoted in a July 2010 *Rolling Stone* article by reporter Michael Hastings criticizing a number of members of the Obama administration—with the most notable slight being on Vice President Joe Biden. Despite McChrystal calling Biden with a preemptive apology for the article, the comments were widely seen as having crossed an inviolable political line, and Obama replaced McChrystal with General David Petraeus.

The president's troop increases in Afghanistan seemed ironic to some, as they were announced on the eve of his accepting the 2009 Nobel Peace Prize for his commitment to nuclear nonproliferation and improving U.S. relations with the Muslim world. In February 2009, however, when Obama promised to withdraw the last combat forces from Iraq within eighteen months, he seemed to be acting more in concord with the accolade. Although some of Obama's liberal supporters were disillusioned by Obama's prosecution of the Afghan war, he nonetheless made good on his pledge in Iraq, as the final combat forces withdrew from the country on August 19, 2010. A transitional force of several thousand troops remained for more than a year, but on December 18, 2011, the last U.S. soldier left Iraq.

Perhaps the most defining military moment of Obama's term occurred on May 1, 2011. After spending the evening joking at the White House Correspondents' Association dinner, Obama secretly repaired to the Situation Room to oversee a Navy SEAL operation being conducted in Pakistan. The most elite military unit in America descended on a compound in Abbottabad, and after a brief firefight with the al-Qaeda militants inside, the mission's main target—Osama bin Laden, elusive architect of the 9/11 attacks—was dead. Obama appeared on television later that evening, and the announcement of the mission's outcome sparked an outpouring of patriotic sentiment in a series of spontaneous public celebrations across the United States.

Less than three months before the final troops left Iraq, Obama made another, more symbolic, military withdrawal: repealing the military's "Don't Ask Don't Tell" policy. Having been in place since 1993, DADT had prohibited openly gay, lesbian, or bisexual Americans from serving in the military. After signing the Repeal Act in July, on September 20, 2011, Obama saw the official end of the U.S. military's ban on openly gay service members.

"THE AGE OF OBAMA"

The era after the election of the first African American to the presidency of the United States—an age presaged almost forty years to the day by Robert Kennedy's prediction amid the Freedom Rides in 1968—has become broadly referred to as "The Age of Obama." The precise meaning and import of this epoch, however, are far from clear. That Obama's election was a watershed date—indeed it was a tearful, "at last" moment for millions, in America and abroad—is clear. Still, although some might suggest that Obama's election was a panacea for race relations in America, incidents of racial polarization persist and prove difficult to mediate, even for a leader as adept as Obama. One such incident occurred in 2009, when Henry Louis "Skip" Gates Jr., a prominent African American Harvard professor, was arrested when police officers believed he was breaking and entering into a home in Cambridge, Massachusetts (the house he was entering was his own). Obama added fuel to the media fire when he said that the Cambridge police had acted "stupidly" that night, but he quickly compensated for this slip with a brilliantly effective peace-making summit between Gates and the arresting officer—over beers at a picnic table on the White House lawn.

In *The Persistence of the Color Line*, Harvard law professor Randall Kennedy reflects on Obama's election as, for some, the perceived harbinger of a supposedly "postracial America." Although Kennedy suggests that the "symbolic power" of Obama's election "has irrevocably changed the imagination of America," he also counsels "caution in interpreting his election as the ultimate racial breakthrough." In November 2012, Obama leveraged both the symbolic capital his election had accrued and the legislative and foreign policy achievements of his first term to prevail over his Republican opponent, Mitt Romney, in a hard-fought battle.

Elliott J. Niblock

SEE ALSO: *Automobile; Beck, Glenn; Best Sellers; Freedom Rides; James, LeBron; 9/11;* Rolling Stone*; Social Media; Television; War in Afghanistan;* The West Wing.

BIBLIOGRAPHY

Asim, Jabari. *What Obama Means . . . For Our Culture, Our Politics, Our Future*. New York: HarperCollins, 2009.

Broder, John M. "Report Slams Administration for Underestimating Gulf Spill." *New York Times*, October 6, 2010, A20.

Harfoush, Rahaf. *Yes We Did: An Inside Look at How Social Media Built the Obama Brand*. Berkeley, CA: New Riders, 2009.

Hastings, Michael. "The Runaway General: The *Rolling Stone* Profile of Stanley McChrystal That Changed History." *Rolling Stone*. Accessed June 2012. Available from http://www.rollingstone.com/politics/news/the-runaway-general-20100622

Kennedy, Randall. *The Persistence of the Color Line: Racial Politics and the Obama Presidency*. New York: Pantheon Books, 2011.

Mansfield, Stephen. *The Faith of Barack Obama*. Nashville, TN: Thomas Nelson, 2008.

Mendell, David. *Obama: From Promise to Power*. New York: HarperCollins, 2007.

Obama, Barack. *Dreams from My Father: A Story of Race and Inheritance*. New York: Times Books, 1995.

Obama, Barack. *The Audacity of Hope: Thoughts on Reclaiming the American Dream*. New York: Random House, 2006.

Parks, Gregory S., and Matthew W. Hughley. *The Obamas and a (Post) Racial America*. New York: Oxford University Press, 2011.

Powell, Michael. "Following Months of Criticism, Obama Quits His Church." *New York Times*. Accessed June 2012. Available from http://www.nytimes.com/2008/06/01/us/politics/01obama.html?_r=1&l&lex=1212552000&en=4f275b18627314ec&ei=5087%0A

Ross, Brian. "Obama's Pastor: God Damn America, U.S. to Blame for 9/11." ABC News. Accessed June 2012. Available from http://abcnews.go.com/Blotter/story?id=4443788#.T82vz8g-dyl

Objectivism/Ayn Rand

Few philosophers or philosophies can claim the public recognition and "fan" following of Ayn Rand (1905–1982) and her philosophy, objectivism. Rand argued that reality is an "objective absolute"; that reason, informed by the senses, is the only way of perceiving reality; that rational self-interest is the only moral position; and that *laissez-faire* capitalism, uncontrolled by governments, is the ideal economic system. Espoused in several novels and in countless essays and speeches, Rand's objectivism glorifies heroic individuals pursuing their goals utterly free of the fetters that society, especially government, would place upon them.

Though Rand's written works have always been extremely popular, it was the movie of her novel *The Fountainhead* (1949), starring Gary Cooper, that made her a kind of intellectual celebrity. Rand and her philosophy attained a cult stature among college students, not least because her works narrate the process by which a person can articulate a principled rejection of the social mores in which they were raised. In the twenty-first century, particularly in the wake of the 2008 financial crisis, Rand's ideas again gained traction among Republican and "Tea Party" supporters in the United States, who favor small or minimal government and "personal responsibility" over business legislation, welfare programs, and government assistance.

EARLY LIFE

Rand was born Alisa Rosenbaum in 1905 in St. Petersburg, Russia. Her father's pharmacy was confiscated by Bolshevik authorities after the Russian Revolution. The anti-Semitism of the czarist regime and the anticapitalism of the communist regime did not seem to have endeared her to government intervention in private affairs, and she opposed it throughout her political life. She studied history at the University of Petrograd and left for the United States to be a writer. In America, she took the first name Ayn (rhymes with *line*) and the last name Rand (naming herself after her typewriter) and ended up in Hollywood, where she worked as a movie extra and as an employee of RKO's wardrobe department. In Hollywood, she met and married writer Frank O'Connor.

Rand worked her way up to writing scripts for Hollywood and Broadway, moving to New York in 1934. She published her first novel—an anticommunist work called *We the Living*—in

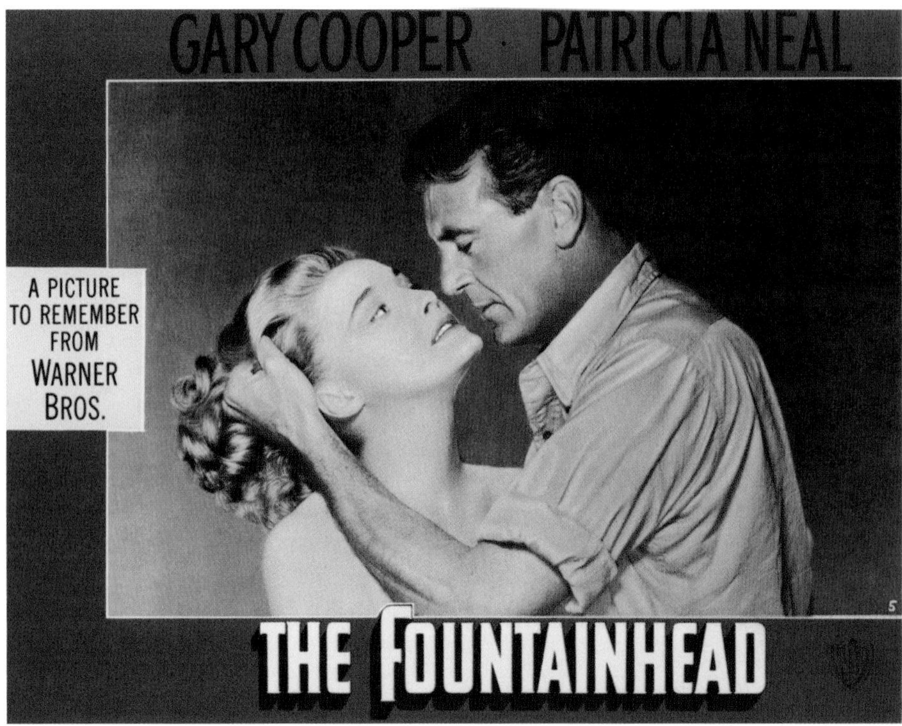

The Fountainhead *Movie Poster.* *Any Rand's novel* The Fountainhead *was made into a film in 1949 starring Gary Cooper and Patricia Neal.* © CINEMAPHOTO/CORBIS.

1936. This was followed in 1938 by *Anthem*, a story set in a totalitarian society that attempts to destroy individuality.

In 1943 Rand published *The Fountainhead*, the story of a young architect named Howard Roark (a character apparently modeled on Frank Lloyd Wright). Roark insists on pursuing his own vision of architecture, which brings him into conflict with his teachers, his customers, and the government and into the arms of the heroine (whom he rapes in a scene that is denounced in Susan Brownmiller's 1975 book *Against Our Will*). The novel's portrayal of heroic individualism seems to have hit a chord with American readers, who put the novel on the best-seller list for two years after it came out. By the 1980s the book had sold more than 4.5 million copies. The movie version of the novel, released in 1949 with Cooper in the lead role, helped make a hero out of Roark and began attracting adherents to Rand's philosophy.

After *The Fountainhead*, Rand became fairly well known. She was a friendly witness before the House Committee on Un-American Activities when it was investigating communism in Hollywood. She also acquired many followers, one of whom, a young man named Nathaniel Branden, helped her publicize her ideas. Branden became an important figure in the objectivist movement she founded and eventually became her lover. But Rand's fame was not fully secure until 1957, when she published her most famous novel, *Atlas Shrugged*.

ATLAS SHRUGGED

At more than 1,000 pages long, *Atlas Shrugged* is best described as a dramatization of Rand's philosophy. The title's reference to Atlas (whose broad shoulders, according to the ancient Greeks, held up the world) alludes to the independent, self-sustaining, "productive" members of society, many of whom in the novel move to a secret outpost where they can live in freedom without the government taxing and confiscating the fruits of their labor. By taking themselves out of the jurisdiction of the government, the freedom fighters are basically going on strike, refusing to collaborate with an oppressive state. The characters are not so much fully fleshed-out individuals as they are embodiments of Rand's philosophy, and they have ample opportunity to give speeches outlining their (i.e., Rand's) principles. The most prominent of these speeches, hero John Galt's speech, is perhaps the best single statement of the objectivist creed.

The influence of *Atlas Shrugged* is difficult to overstate. In 1991 it was voted the second most popular book after the Bible in a survey of Book-of-the-Month Club members. Despite widespread academic criticism of her work, Rand has received increasing interest from scholars since her death in 1982. Since 1999 the *Journal of Ayn Rand Studies* has published twice-yearly editions of peer-reviewed articles about Rand, but many of the organizations devoted to promoting her work, including the Ayn Rand Institute, founded in 1985, have remained controversial in academia, where Rand's reputation as a philosopher remains problematic.

Although conservatives often denounce government welfare programs, Rand was opposed to any form of "altruism," whether public or private. In fact, altruism was something of a dirty word in Rand's writing. Also, in contrast to traditional conservative values, Rand was both an atheist and pro-choice. Whittaker Chambers, writing in the leading conservative magazine of the time, *National Review*, denounced *Atlas Shrugged*, saying, "I find it a remarkably silly book. It is certainly a bumptious one. Its story is preposterous." Most other reviews were also hostile, focusing on the writing style. But despite the critics, *Atlas Shrugged* was, and still is, a very popular novel. Politically, it is probably fair to say that *Atlas Shrugged* proved an inspiration to libertarians, especially the young. A three-part film adaptation of the novel, of which the first part was released in 2011, suggests the book had become an inspiration again, although the film itself was not a critical success.

Though Rand endorsed libertarian individualism, she insisted that her associates define individualism in her terms. If someone adopted an interpretation of individualism different from hers, that person was generally unwelcome in Rand's circle. Rand's relationship with her more committed followers (they called themselves "the Collective," with self-conscious irony) was similar to the relationship between a prophetess and her worshippers.

With the help of Branden (who collaborated with her until they broke up in 1968), Rand propagated her objectivist views through lectures (especially speeches to college students), a newsletter, a newspaper column, and philosophical books. The theme was always the same: the heroic individual versus the collective, which was usually the state. She praised Canadian doctors who went on strike against socialized medicine. She denounced both racism (a collectivist philosophy) and the Civil Rights Bill of 1964 (she saw it as a gross violation of property rights). She spoke of the importance of "self-esteem," meaning a justifiable pride in one's accomplishments. Self-esteem was deemed a necessary defense against altruists who wanted individuals to give up their liberty or property for the sake of an alleged greater good, even in the form of taxes.

FAMOUS RAND SUPPORTERS

Rand has inspired some important public figures. One of her fans was Supreme Court Justice Clarence Thomas. Another Rand disciple who later rose to high position was Alan Greenspan, who, as chairman of the Federal Reserve, presided over the 2008 banking crisis, which was caused, in part, by lax regulation of the financial industry and a reliance on free markets. While he was a budding economist and Wall Street analyst in the 1950s and 1960s, Greenspan was a member of Rand's inner circle. Former British Prime Minister Margaret Thatcher and tennis star Billie Jean King were also followers of Rand's philosophy. In the early twenty-first century, Rand had many devotees in the U.S. government. Republicans such as Allen West, Mick Mulvaney, and House Speaker John Boehner, among others, all espoused Randian ideas for reducing government intervention in markets to set businesses free.

Rand died in 1982. Her intellectual legacy is claimed by the Ayn Rand Institute, founded in 1985 and run by her follower (and legal heir) Leonard Peikoff; by the breakaway organization the Atlas Society, founded by philosopher David Kelley in 1990; and by the Anthem Society, founded in 2001 by historian John McCaskey. The BB&T Corporation offers grants to Rand scholars.

Eric Longley

SEE ALSO: *Cooper, Gary; King, Billie Jean; McCarthyism; The Tea Party.*

BIBLIOGRAPHY

Ayn Rand Institute. Accessed March 2012. Available from http://www.aynrand.org/

Bradford, R. W. "Alan Greenspan—Cultist? The Fascinating Personal History of Mr. Pinstripe." *American Enterprise*, September/October 1997, 31–33.

Branden, Barbara. *The Passion of Ayn Rand*. Garden City, NY: Doubleday, 1986.

Branden, Nathaniel, and Barbara Branden. *Who Is Ayn Rand?: An Analysis of the Novels of Ayn Rand*. New York: Random House, 1962.

Branden, Nathaniel, and Ayn Rand. *My Years with Ayn Rand*. San Francisco: Jossey-Bass, 1999.

Brownmiller, Susan. *Against Our Will: Men, Women, and Rape*. New York: Simon & Schuster, 1975.

Burns, Jennifer. *Goddess of the Market: Ayn Rand and the American Right*. New York: Oxford University Press, 2009.

Chambers, Whittaker. "Big Sister Is Watching You." *National Review*, December 28, 1957.

Gladstein, Mimi Reisel. *The Ayn Rand Companion*. Westport, CT: Greenwood Press, 1984.

McDonald, Marci. "Fighting over Ayn Rand: A Radical Invidividualist's Followers Can't Get Along." *U.S. News and World Report*, March 9, 1998, 54–57.

O'Neill, William. *With Charity toward None: An Analysis of Ayn Rand's Philosophy*. New York: Philosophical Library, 1971.

Paxton, Michael. *Ayn Rand: A Sense of Life; The Companion Book*. Layton, UT: Gibbs Smith, 1998.

Pierpont, Claudia Roth. "Twilight of the Goddess." *New Yorker*, July 24, 1995, 10–81.

Rand, Ayn. *For the New Intellectual: The Philosophy of Ayn Rand*. New York: New American Library, 1961.

Rand, Ayn. *Letters of Ayn Rand*, ed. Michael S. Berliner. New York: Dutton, 1995.

Rand, Ayn, and Nathaniel Branden. *The Virtue of Selfishness: A New Concept of Egoism*. New York: New American Library, 1964.

Rand, Ayn; David Harriman; and Leonard Peikoff. *Journals of Ayn Rand*. New York: Dutton, 1997.

Sciabarra, Chris Matthew. *Ayn Rand: The Russian Radical*. State College: Pennsylvania State University Press, 1995.

Walker, Jeff. *The Ayn Rand Cult*. Chicago: Open Court, 1999.

O'Brien, Conan *(1963–)*

A well-known late-night talk show host and comedy writer, Conan O'Brien gained further notoriety in his 2009 battle with NBC over hosting *The Tonight Show*. Although O'Brien often plays, as he told the *Boston Globe*'s Don Aucoin in 2003, "the character of [a] self-important, deluded fool," in reality he is anything but. President of the *National Lampoon* for two years during college, he got his start drawing cartoons and writing humor pieces. His former *Lampoon* colleagues describe him as a person with "keen powers of observation, a killer range of spot-on impressions, and a genuine interest in everyone he meets." After graduating from Harvard in 1985, O'Brien and former classmate Greg Daniels wrote for the HBO comedy *Not Necessarily the News* (1985–1987). Then Lorne Michaels hired him to write for *Saturday Night Live* (1987–1991), and O'Brien won an Emmy for his sketches in 1989. He also wrote and produced several seasons of *The Simpsons* (1991–1993).

LATE NIGHT

When David Letterman announced he was moving to CBS in 1993, O'Brien was chosen to be the replacement host of NBC's *Late Night* show. This was his chance to move from behind the writer's desk and perform. Despite his success as a comedy writer, he was an unknown to much of the public and the late-night circuit, and his first attempts were shaky. The press proclaimed him a disaster, and NBC threatened to cancel his show. Tom Shales of the *Washington Post* called O'Brien "the host who should never have come." O'Brien responded to the criticism with his classic self-effacing wit. When a *New York Times* reporter asked O'Brien what it felt like "to be getting this job as a relative unknown," O'Brien responded, "Sir, I am a complete unknown."

However, after a year and a half, he had a fan base of young adults. He brought an infectious enthusiasm to the *Late Night* show, ushering in his own brand of comedy. As Aucoin notes, "O'Brien uses his monologues and sketches to bridge the gap between the one-liner and the knockabout farce, marrying his writer's sensibility with his love of physical comedy to create a show in which, in his words, 'anything can come to life at any time.' That means comedy that is both silly and smart." This spontaneity and unconventional humor attracted about 2.5 million viewers, and O'Brien hosted the *Late Night* show for sixteen years (1993–2009).

THE TONIGHT SHOW

In 2004 Jay Leno announced that he would resign from *The Tonight Show* in five years, and NBC chose O'Brien to replace him. A mainstay of late-night television since 1954, the program had previously been hosted by Steve Allen, Jack Paar, and Johnny Carson. Carson maintained his role for thirty years before Leno. O'Brien was very aware Carson's influence on show, but he also wanted to make his own mark. Unfortunately, his ratings were not as strong as Leno's had been, so NBC decided to schedule Leno's new show at 11:35 p.m. and move *The Tonight Show*to 12:05 a.m. O'Brien refused to go along with this. *The Tonight Show* had always aired at 11:35, and he insisted on honoring Carson's memory by keeping the show at its original time slot.

O'Brien and the network could not reach an agreement, so he quit after only seven months. Due to contractual obligations with NBC, O'Brien was legally barred from appearing on television until May 2010. He embarked on a thirty-two-city tour, calling it the "Legally Prohibited from Being Funny on Television Tour." O'Brien spent most of the tour ridiculing NBC and making jokes about the eight stages of grief. His young-adult fan base supported him by booing whenever he mentioned the network. The tour also featured guest appearances by other comedians, such as Jon Stewart and Stephen Colbert. Some critics wondered if O'Brien was justified in his protest, seeing as he had received a $32.5 million settlement from NBC. Alessandra Stanley pointed out in the *New York Times*, "Mr. O'Brien didn't attract a large enough following to prevail. Show business is usually a meritocracy, but nobody ever said it was fair, let alone honorable."

TEAM COCO

The TBS network noticed all of the media attention and offered O'Brien his own show, titled *Conan*. He initially turned down the offer when he learned that, in order to make room for *Conan*, George Lopez's talk show would be moved further into the evening. When Lopez personally called O'Brien and gave his blessing, O'Brien accepted. *Conan* first aired on November 8, 2010, and in February 2012 was renewed through 2014.

O'Brien had help getting back and staying on the air thanks to the support of his young fans, who dubbed themselves "Team Coco." At one point Team Coco's Twitter account had more than five million viewers, many of whom created and signed online petitions in support of O'Brien. They were largely responsible for TBS's initial offer and the renewal of the *Conan* show despite its lackluster ratings. Public support for new television shows that networks want to drop is nothing new. However, this was the first time social media such as Twitter and Facebook were used to such a focused degree to support an entertainment figure.

Vanessa Grigoriadis analyzed O'Brien's popularity in a *New York Entertainment* article, writing, "There's something oddly unprofessional and ad hoc—an imaginary giant squid, for example—to O'Brien's show. He's as much of a nervous Nellie as Jack Paar, but he draws our attention to it, constantly poking fun at himself." It's this self-deprecating humor and charm that kept his fans rooting for him and continues to attract new fans.

Daniel Coffey

SEE ALSO: *Allen, Steve; Cable TV; Carson, Johnny; Colbert, Stephen; Emmy Awards; Facebook; Leno, Jay; Letterman, David; Lopez, George;* National Lampoon*; Paar, Jack;* Saturday Night Live*;* The Simpsons*; Social Media; Stand-Up Comedy; Stewart, Jon; Television;* The Tonight Show*; Twitter.*

BIBLIOGRAPHY

Aucoin, Don. "Understanding Conan." *Boston Globe*, August 31, 2003.

Barzilay, Julie R. "The Conan We Knew." *Harvard Crimson*, May 27, 2010.

Carter, Bill. "NBC Wants Leno Back in Old Slot." *New York Times*, January 7, 2010.

Collins, Scott. "Conan Renewed Thanks to Fans." *Los Angeles Times*, February 23, 2012.

Grigoriadis, Vanessa. "Conan on the Couch." *New York Magazine*, September 26, 2005.

Stanley, Alessandra. "Slings, Arrows, Self-Pity. What a Kidder!" *New York Times*, June 2, 2010.

O'Brien, Tim *(1946–)*

Best known for his fictional portrayal of the Vietnam War, Tim O'Brien is an American novelist and short-story writer who has been compared to Ernest Hemingway, Stephen Crane, and Joseph Heller. In *Going after Cacciato* (1978) and *The Things They Carried* (1990), the novels that established his reputation, O'Brien explores the horrors and ambiguities of war in a style that is eloquent, precise, and highly evocative. An intensely passionate writer, O'Brien has attempted to move beyond the tag of "war writer" by composing works that reveal the ways in which love and civilian life can resemble war. In his novel *In the Lake of the Woods* (1994), which portrays a defeated politician struggling with a secret past and imperiled marriage, O'Brien brings the fear and torment of Vietnam to the Minnesota wilderness.

In *July, July* (2004), the author takes a different perspective, chronicling the disillusionment of a group of Darton Hall alumni who return for their thirtieth reunion in the summer of 1999. Reviewers disagree on O'Brien's message in this novel. A reviewer for *Publisher's Weekly* sees the characters as sympathetic former friends who, despite their middle-aged disillusionment with the world around them, retain a deep sense of camaraderie and love for one another. Contrarily a *Booklist* reviewer sees them as shallow and narcissistic individuals who have lost the political consciousness of their youth. In 1999 O'Brien began teaching creative writing at Southwestern Texas State University.

James Schiff

SEE ALSO: *Hemingway, Ernest; Vietnam.*

BIBLIOGRAPHY

Herzog, Tobey C. *Tim O'Brien.* New York: Twayne, 1997.

Kaplan, Stephen. *Understanding Tim O'Brien.* Columbia: University of South Carolina Press, 1995.

Ochs, Phil *(1940–1976)*

A contemporary of Bob Dylan and Joan Baez, Phil Ochs achieved modest success as a singer-songwriter during the mid-1960s. After receiving a standing ovation at the Newport Folk Festival in 1963, he was signed by Elektra Records. Ochs was a fervent activist who yearned for stardom. He gained recognition for his topical songs about subjects such as civil rights and the Vietnam War. As a protest singer in the era of the urban folk revival, he was often overshadowed by Dylan. In the late 1960s his interest in politics remained strong even as his compositions became more personal. Bothered by political events and his inability to write commercially successful songs, Ochs suffered from severe depression in the last years of his life. His career essentially ended in the early 1970s, and in 1976 he hung himself.

Anna Hunt Graves

SEE ALSO: *Baez, Joan; Civil Rights Movement; Depression; Dylan, Bob; Folk Music; Newport Jazz and Folk Festivals; Protest Groups; Suicide; Vietnam.*

BIBLIOGRAPHY

Cohen, David. *Phil Ochs: A Bio-bibliography.* Westport, CT: Greenwood Press, 1999.

Eliot, Marc. *Phil Ochs: Death of a Rebel.* New York: Franklin Watts, 1989.

Schumacher, Michael *There but for Fortune: The Life of Phil Ochs.* New York: Hyperion, 1996.

O'Connor, Flannery *(1925–1964)*

The name Flannery O'Connor is synonymous with southern literature. Her characters are good country people and lowly misfits who speak with rich southern accents, and no matter how misguided their actions, they are never beyond redemption. In an essay titled "The Catholic Novelist in the South," O'Connor, an orthodox Catholic, wrote that the "two circumstances that have given character to [her] own writing have been those of being Southern and being Catholic." Her remarkable fictional landscape—a "Christ-haunted" place, as she put it, filled with backwoods preachers, mad prophets, and moonshine visionaries—signifies the intimate relationship that exists between O'Connor's art and the dynamics of the southern culture that brought her art to life.

Born in Savannah, Georgia, on March 25, 1925, O'Connor was the only child of Regina Cline and Edward Francis O'Connor Jr. She was raised in her mother's family home in Milledgeville, Georgia, and later moved to a dairy farm in Andalusia, Georgia, where she lived with her mother. In 1951, after leaving Georgia to study at the fabled Iowa Writers' Workshop at the University of Iowa, she was diagnosed with lupus erythematosus, the disease that caused her untimely death at age thirty-nine.

In a letter to a friend, O'Connor wrote, "Sickness is more instructive than a long trip to Europe." She further described her illness as "one of life's blessings." The blessing was that the disease brought her home to her native Georgia and to the landscape where she recreated the language and often bizarre and grotesque characters of her fiction. Addressing her Georgia homecoming—one strikingly similar to that of Asbury in her short story "The Enduring Chill"—O'Connor told fellow southern author Cecil Dawkins that she had always thought the "life of [her] writing depended on . . . staying away" and that she would have persisted in that delusion had she "not got very ill and had to come home. The best of my writing has been done here."

O'Connor's body of work, though scant, generates the kind of critical attention that places her among notable figures in southern literature such as William Faulkner, Eudora Welty Walker Percy, Truman Capote, and Tennessee Williams. Her canon is composed of two novels, *Wise Blood* (1952) and *The Violent Bear It Away* (1960); two collections of short stories, *A Good Man Is Hard to Find* (1955) and *Everything That Rises Must Converge* (1965); and a collection of essays, *Mystery and Manners* (1969). The essays—including "Some Aspects of the Grotesque in Southern Fiction," "The Fiction Writer and His Country," "Catholic Novelists and Their Readers," "The Catholic Novelist in the Protestant South," and "The Teaching of Literature"—address the issues with which O'Connor was most concerned. *The Flannery O'Connor Bulletin* is devoted solely to O'Connor scholarship, and books about O'Connor's life and work continue to proliferate.

Sue Walker

SEE ALSO: *Capote, Truman; Faulkner, William; Williams, Tennessee.*

BIBLIOGRAPHY

Brinkmeyer, Robert H., Jr. *The Art and Vision of Flannery O'Connor.* Baton Rouge: Louisiana State University Press, 1989.

Coles, Robert. *Flannery O'Connor's South.* Baton Rouge: Louisiana State University Press, 1980.

Fitzgerald, Sally, ed. *The Habit of Being: The Letters of Flannery O'Connor. New York: Farrar, Straus & Giroux, 1979.*

Gooch, Brad. *Flannery: A Life of Flannery O'Connor.* New York: Little, Brown: 2009.

Johansen, Ruthann Knechel. *The Narrative Secret of Flannery O'Connor.* Tuscaloosa: University of Alabama Press, 1994.

McCullen, Joanne Halleran. *Writing against God: Language as Message in the Literature of Flannery O'Connor.* Macon, GA: Mercer University Press, 1996.

Prown, Katherine Hemple. *Revising Flanner O'Connor.* Charlottesville: University Press of Virginia, 2001.

Spivey, Ted R. *Flannery O'Connor: The Woman, the Thinker, the Visionary.* Macon, GA: Mercer University Press, 1995.

Octomom *(1975–)*

"Octomom" is the nickname given by the media to American Nadya Suleman when she gave birth to octuplets on January 26, 2009. Suleman had six boys and two girls via cesarean section. They were only the second set of octuplets ever born alive in the United States, and the first set in which all of the babies survived. The birth of Suleman's octuplets received international attention; shined a spotlight on the practice of assisted reproductive technology (ART); and ignited much controversy that touched on matters of individual rights, societal rights, parental responsibility, medical ethics, reproductive choice, and the nature of fame and celebrity.

When the public first heard about the octuplets, wonderment quickly turned to concern and scorn when it was learned that Suleman was an unemployed, single mother who already had six children, all of whom, like the octuplets, were conceived via in vitro fertilization (IVF) with a donor's sperm. She had used disability payments from a previous injury to pay for all of the costly IVF procedures.

Public outcry grew over whether or not Suleman was making responsible parenting choices or even had the right to bear children given her financial situation and marital status. It was these factors that turned public sentiment largely against her, as they constituted the only major differences between her circumstances and those of other large families that tend to be more revered by media, such as the fundamentalist Christian Duggar family of Arkansas or even the family of actress Angelina Jolie. Many wondered how Suleman planned to provide for her fourteen children, as there was no job she could realistically get that would still allow her to take care of her children or to pay for their care. She appeared to lack a support system, as she was single, and her own parents disapproved of her choices. Some were worried that taxpayers would end up paying to support her, causing public condemnation to the extent that there were calls for the children to be removed from Suleman's custody. Suleman and her family even received death threats.

Many people were also disturbed as to why Suleman's fertility doctor, Michael Kamrava, would transfer so many embryos at once to Suleman. The guidelines of the American Society for Reproductive Medicine (ASRM) specify that for a woman under the age of thirty-five, no more than one or two embryos should be transferred at any one time in order to avoid multiple births, which tends to be riskier for both the mother and the babies. Out of fear that they would be otherwise discarded, Suleman had twelve frozen embryos transferred, all of which were left over from her earlier IVF procedures. After this revelation, the Medical Board of California revoked Kamrava's medical license, and the ASRM revoked his membership.

Further public conversation about ART and ethics was prompted by the revelation that Suleman had declined selective reduction. National discussions focused on what it really means to be pro-choice or pro-life within the context of the Octomom. Suleman chose to become pregnant and to have many children, and some wondered if she should have had the right to make those choices. Questions were raised as to whether medical personnel should have an ethical obligation to screen patients seeking IVF for factors such as financial stability, mental condition, and fitness for parenthood. Yet others pointed out that people who are capable of conceiving naturally do not have to meet any standards or obtain permission before conceiving. Discussion also focused on whether the number of viable embryos implanted at any one time should be regulated by law, especially because the risks of multiple births and health problems increase with multiple embryos.

Finally, the birth of the octuplets caused an examination of the nature of celebrity in U.S. society. Many wondered if Suleman's pregnancy was an attempt to achieve fame. In a society obsessed with "reality" entertainment, hers is a story that would certainly garner attention—and it did. Suleman's parenting, life choices, and mental state were scrutinized and judged by the public. She denied accusations that she was exploiting her children to be in the media spotlight, but she also made decisions that made her intentions questionable, such as agreeing to let her family be filmed for television and for interviews. Suleman's life seems to symbolize particular specters for the American public, awakening latent fears concerning independent women, single mothers, and public assistance recipients (although Suleman denied that she and her family have ever been on public assistance, this fact is contested). Society's reaction to her, therefore, has been both vicious and visceral, with a degree of schadenfreude, and the fascination for her is not likely to abate any time in the near future.

Sarah McHone-Chase

SEE ALSO: *Celebrity; Jolie, Angelina; Media Feeding Frenzies.*

BIBLIOGRAPHY

Bowe, John. "The Octomom and Her Babies Prepare for Prime Time." *New York Times Magazine.* Accessed December 8, 2011. Available from http://www.nytimes.com/2009/11/15/magazine/15octomom-t.html

Otto, Sheila, and Winifred J. Ellenchild Pinch. "Ethical Dimensions in the Case of the 'Octomom': Two Perspectives." *Pediatric Nursing* 35, no. 6 (2009): 389–392.

The Odd Couple

Can two divorced men share an apartment without driving each other crazy? That was the question that fueled a play, a movie, and a classic sitcom. Neil Simon's 1965 play *The Odd Couple* and the subsequent 1968 movie—starring Walter Matthau as sloppy sportswriter Oscar Madison and Jack Lemmon as fastidious photographer Felix Unger (Art Carney had the role on Broadway)—spawned a popular and well-written television series that ran on ABC from 1970 to 1975.

In the television series, Oscar was played by Jack Klugman (who had taken over the role from Matthau on Broadway), Felix was played by Tony Randall, and the spirit of the play remained intact. Oscar is a happily divorced New Yorker who thinks of ketchup as "tomato wine" and who sleeps with his wardrobe and his meals. Felix, still pining away for his ex-wife, is a neat freak, constantly spraying air freshener in Oscar's direction and reheating gourmet meals for which Oscar was late. They are the definition of opposites: Felix loves opera and classical music, and Oscar prefers gambling; Oscar gruffly throws stuff on the floor, Felix picks it up, complaining; Oscar smokes cigars and eats junk food despite his ulcer, and Felix has constant sinus trouble but otherwise takes compulsively excellent care of himself. The point of the show was that despite their vast differences, these two guys cared about each other and were friends when it counted.

The only other regular who stayed on through the whole run of the series was Al Molinaro, who played dim-witted police officer and poker buddy Murray the Cop. Other poker buddies included Speed (Garry Walberg), Roy (Ryan McDonald), and Vinnie (Larry Gelman). Elinor Donahue played Felix's girlfriend, Miriam, from 1972 to 1975. Klugman's real-life wife, Brett Somers (a regular on the television game show *Match Game* in the 1970s), played Oscar's acerbic ex-wife, Blanche. Janis Hansen played Felix's long-suffering ex-wife, Gloria, whose name had been Frances in the play and movie. The series borrowed flighty British neighbors the Pigeon sisters from the play and movie for the first season. Because the roommates were somewhat in the New York media, *The Odd Couple* could justify guest stars playing themselves, such as Bobby Riggs, Billie Jean King, David Steinberg, Monty Hall, Allen Ludden, Roy Clark, Howard Cosell, Richard Dawson, and Deacon Jones.

Forever linked to their roles now, Randall and Klugman were not everyone's first choices. ABC did want Tony Randall, but the network also fancied Mickey Rooney for Oscar. The producers wanted Art Carney and Martin Balsam. Garry Marshall and Sheldon Keller served as executive producers for the series. Marshall, who created *Happy Days* (1974–1984) and its spin-offs and directed *Pretty Woman* (1990), also wrote several episodes. His sister, Penny, who went on to direct *Big* (1988) and *A League of Their Own* (1992), played Oscar's nebbishy secretary Myrna from 1973 to 1975 (Garry had a cameo in one episode, as did Rob Reiner, Penny's then husband).

Though the series wrapped up cleanly with Gloria and Felix finally remarrying, the Odd Couple formula was often repeated. From 1975 to 1977 a cartoon called *The Oddball Couple* ran on ABC Saturday mornings. It featured Fleabag, a sloppy dog, and Spiffy, a neat cat, as reporters who shared an office. Simon updated his durable play in the mid-1980s to support female versions of his characters; it starred Sally Struthers as Florence Unger and Rita Moreno as Olive Madison. From 1982 to 1983 ABC tried to cash in again with *The New Odd Couple*, which borrowed scripts from the original series but cast black actors. Ron Glass, of *Barney Miller* fame, played Felix, and Demond Wilson, from *Sanford and Son*, played Oscar. Felix's ex-wife went back to being called Frances. It did not take long for that show's producer to admit that seven out of the first thirteen episodes of *The New Odd Couple* had been recycled from its predecessor.

Felix and Oscar informed every subsequent role Randall and Klugman played. Randall had his own show, *The Tony Randall Show*, from 1976 to 1978, in which he played a stuffy widowed Philadelphia Superior Court judge. Klugman and Walberg were reunited in the television drama *Quincy, M.E.* (1976–1983) in which Klugman played the gruff but lovable titular medical examiner (who was never given a first name) who helped solve the murders of the bodies he autopsied, and Walberg played police liaison Lieutenant Frank Monahan.

In 1993 Randall, Klugman, Walberg, and Marshall returned for *The Odd Couple: Together Again*, a two-hour CBS television movie. Klugman was recovering from throat cancer, and in the movie Felix moves back in with Oscar, who was recovering from throat cancer surgery. Randall and Klugman also revived another Neil Simon play—*The Sunshine Boys*—on Broadway late in the 1990s. Matthau and Lemmon reunited in 1998 in *Neil Simon's Odd Couple II*. They also did a few other Odd Couple-esque buddy films together in the 1990s, such as *Grumpy Old Men* (1993) and *Out to Sea* (1997). The original *Odd Couple* series was rerun in the 1990s on Nick at Nite and Comedy Central.

The term *odd couple* goes beyond the pop culture scope and has taken on a life of its own, being used by snappy headline writers to describe any unlikely pair of opposites who are working together or merely get along, much like *The Odd Couple* continues to get along with audiences of all ages.

Karen Lurie

SEE ALSO: Barney Miller*; Cosell, Howard;* Happy Days*; King, Billie Jean;* A League of Their Own*; Marshall, Garry; Moreno, Rita; Riggs, Bobby;* Sanford and Son*; Simon, Neil.*

BIBLIOGRAPHY

Brooks, Tim, and Earle Marsh. *The Complete Directory to Prime Time Network and Cable TV Shows 1946–Present*. New York: Ballantine Books, 1999.

McNeil, Alex. *Total Television*. New York: Penguin, 1996.

Simon, Neil. *The Odd Couple*. Random House, 1966.

O'Donnell, Rosie *(1962–)*

Stand-up comic Rosie O'Donnell transformed the definition of "talk show" with her syndicated debut in 1996. Rather than falling into the trap of sensationalized fisticuffs and searing emotionalism à la Jerry Springer and Jenny Jones, O'Donnell created *The Rosie O'Donnell Show*, which featured a set as comfortable as one's own living room with a host as familiar as one's best friend. Her starstruck reaction to her guests often mirrored that of her viewers, and her ease with guests and audiences alike created an atmosphere of having a few friends over to visit. O'Donnell has often confessed that she does not sing well. Yet she sang often and loud, and the viewers loved it—and her.

Despite being a celebrity in the spotlight, O'Donnell refuses to apologize for her weight and has become a positive role model for females of all sizes and ages. The adjective most often used to describe her is "real." O'Donnell is openly gay and avidly political, and Jay Nordlinger of *National Review* has called her the "celebrity who most inflames the Right."

In 2002, after six years of being the "Queen of Nice," O'Donnell walked away from her award-winning talk show, announcing that she intended to spend more time with her children. She also became embroiled in an acrimonious lawsuit when she walked away from *Rosie* magazine (formerly *McCall's*) after disagreements over content. O'Donnell subsequently began

Rosie O'Donnell. After getting her start in show business as a stand-up comic, Rosie O'Donnell continues her work as an actress, talk-show host, and an advocate for gay and lesbian causes. TAYLOR HILL/CONTRIBUTOR/WIREIMAGE/GETTY IMAGES.

moving aggressively away from her former image. In 2002 she published a painfully honest memoir, *Find Me*, and followed it up with *Celebrity Detox: The Fame Game* (2007), a critical assessment of life as a celebrity. During a yearlong stint on *The View* (2006–2007), O'Donnell carried on public feuds with a conservative cohost and with business mogul Donald Trump. Later, her talk show for Sirius XM Radio allowed her to express her own views without restriction. By late 2010 O'Donnell was back on television with *The Rosie Show* on OWN, Oprah Winfrey's network, and was again garnering accolades.

EARLY LIFE

O'Donnell was born and raised in Commack, New York, on Long Island, and her early years were typically middle class and suburban. Her Irish Catholic father was an electrical engineer, and her mother was the president of the Parent Teacher Association. The middle of five children, O'Donnell reveled in her tightly knit family. This typical suburban lifestyle ended abruptly when her mother was diagnosed with what was believed to be pancreatic cancer in 1972—O'Donnell has since said that she believes her mother died of breast cancer. Edward O'Donnell chose to hide the seriousness of his wife's illness, telling the children that she had hepatitis.

The O'Donnell offspring were caught unprepared when their mother died at the age of thirty-six. Roseann O'Donnell was buried on her daughter Rosie's eleventh birthday. Either believing that he was helping his children or blinded by his own grief, her father refused to let the children openly grieve for their mother or to attend her funeral. When her father turned to alcohol to ease his pain, O'Donnell, by all accounts, was left to mother her four siblings.

While she was nurtured by both teachers and neighbors, O'Donnell turned to the fantasy world of movies and television to give her the family life that she needed; she particularly liked stories in which families regenerated themselves after the loss of a parent. Her favorite fantasy parents were the Von Trapps from *The Sound of Music* (1965), the Bradfords from *Eight Is Enough* (1977–1981), and the Bradys from *The Brady Bunch* (1969–1974). O'Donnell's mother's death became the defining point of her life, leaving her with the certainty that she, too, would die at a young age. She has frequently said that she associated being thin with being sick. Eating was, therefore, a way to avoid illness and, ultimately, death.

Despite the problems with her home life, O'Donnell did well at school. She was popular with her classmates and was named homecoming queen, prom queen, and senior class president. She was also an athlete and continues to be interested in sports. Even as a teenager, O'Donnell understood that humor brought her the attention she craved. This recognition of her ambition and talent led her to become a stand-up comic at the age of sixteen. She won recognition for her abilities on *Star Search* (1983–1995) on five separate occasions. This exposure paved the way for her stint as Nell Carter's neighbor on *Gimme a Break!* (1986–1987) and her hosting of VH-1's *Stand-up Spotlight* (1988–1991).

PERSONAL AND PROFESSIONAL SUCCESS

By the time O'Donnell appeared in *A League of Their Own* (1992), she had won a loyal following. She cemented her popularity with supporting roles in *Sleepless in Seattle* (1993), *Another Stakeout* (1993), *Car 54, Where Are You?* (1994), *The Flintstones* (1994), *Now and Then* (1995), and *Beautiful Girls* (1996). Realizing her lifelong ambition to star on Broadway, she spent a year playing Rizzo in *Grease!* in 1994. The following year, O'Donnell decided that it was time for a new direction in her life. She had recently adopted a son, Parker Jaren, and wanted to spend more time with him than her movie career allowed. She pitched a show idea to Disney, but the studio was not interested. Fortunately for O'Donnell's fans, Warner Brothers proved to have more foresight and signed her to a contract.

The Rosie O'Donnell Show was born, providing a breath of much-needed fresh air amid the tawdry sensationalism of daytime television. O'Donnell adopted a daughter, Chelsea Belle, in 1997 and a second son, Blake Christopher, in 1999. Her partner, Kelli Carpenter, gave birth to O'Donnell's fourth child, Vivienne Rose, in 2002. After ten years together and a San Francisco marriage, the couple split in 2007. O'Donnell has insisted that despite rumors to the contrary, the children remain with her. She subsequently became involved in a relationship with Tracy Kachtick-Anders, an artist and mother of six, but the relationship was short-lived. O'Donnell announced in late 2011 that she is engaged to Michelle Rounds, a corporate headhunter.

O'Donnell continued to act in movies during breaks from her talk show, playing a nanny in *Harriet the Spy* (1996) and a nun in *Wide Awake* (1998), and providing the voice of Terk in

Disney's *Tarzan* (1999); negotiations to star in a television movie about the life of comedienne Totie Fields have been ongoing

Throughout the late 1990s, O'Donnell won popular and critical acclaim. She won a Daytime Emmy for Best Talk Show Host in 1997 and tied with Oprah Winfrey for that honor in 1998. *The Rosie O'Donnell Show* won an Emmy each year between 1999 and 2002. O'Donnell almost singlehandedly rejuvenated the theater industry with her championship of Broadway, serving as host for the Tony Awards in 1997, 1998, and 2000. She also hosted the Grammy Awards in 2000. In 2007, during her brief stint as moderator on *The View*, that show was also nominated for a Daytime Emmy.

WIDE-RANGING ROLES

O'Donnell's departure from starring in a daily talk show gave her more freedom to pursue other projects. When she wanted to convince Boy George that she was hip enough to produce his risqué *Taboo* on Broadway, she adopted a punk haircut and style. O'Donnell and Carpenter won both praise and criticism for introducing a series of cruises for gay families. In 2006 *All Aboard! Rosie's Family Cruise* highlighted the inaugural cruise on HBO. O'Donnell also won acclaim for *A Family Is a Family Is a Family* (2010), a documentary about different kinds of American families. The show, which aired on HBO, combined brief live-action segments with cartoons, songs, and interviews with children talking about their families.

O'Donnell continued to prove that her talents were not limited to hosting talk shows and stand-up comedy, taking on the recurring role of Dawn Budge on *Nip/Tuck* (2006–2008) and guest starring in television shows that included *Spin City* (1997 and 2001), *Third Watch* (2000), *The Practice* (2000), *Will & Grace* (2002), *Little Britain* (2008), *Judging Amy* (2003), *Curb Your Enthusiasm* (2005–2011), *Drop Dead Diva* (2009–2010), and *Web Therapy* (2011). She received critical acclaim for two television movies made in the first decade of the twenty-first century. In 2005 she starred in Anjelica Huston's *Riding on the Bus with My Sister*, which told the story of Judge Beth Simon and her developmentally disabled sister. The second was Yves Simoneau's *America* (2009), which dealt with a young boy growing up and out of the foster care system; O'Donnell won a Prism Award for her role as Dr. Maureen Brennan. She also appeared in television specials, including *Christmas in Rockefeller Center* (2008).

O'Donnell's film work during this period was limited to providing the voice of Octopus Masseuse in *The Flintstones in Viva Rock Vegas* (2000), taking on an uncredited role in *Hedwig and the Angry Inch* (2001), and participating in a number of documentaries. She returned to Broadway in *Seussical* (2001), *Fiddler on the Roof* (2005), and *Love, Loss, and What I Wore* (2009). Despite her continued claim to lack musical talent, she followed up *A Rosie Christmas* (1999) with a second album, *Another Rosie Christmas*, the following year.

ONGOING CONTRIBUTIONS

O'Donnell's love of children has been well documented. Her youthful spirit was on display when she hosted the *Kid's Choice Awards* for Nickelodeon from 1996 to 2003. Sales of her book *Kids Are Punny* and the Rosie O'Doll by Tyco generated at least $1 million for her For All Kids Foundation. When Scope named her one of the least kissable celebrities, O'Donnell won her revenge by negotiating a deal with Listerine, whereby the company donated $1,000 to her foundation every time she kissed a guest on her show.

O'Donnell combined her love of children and Broadway by creating Rosie's Broadway Kids Foundation to provide training and opportunities for young actors, singers, and dancers. She released *Kids Are Punny 2* in 1998. Her third family-oriented book, *Crafty U: 100 Easy Projects the Whole Family Can Enjoy All Year Long*, was released in 2008. In late 2011 O'Donnell announced plans to provide homes for children who were orphaned by the devastating earthquake in Haiti.

Nearing age fifty, O'Donnell created *The Rosie Show*, which she says is influenced by Dick Cavett, Carol Burnett, and Craig Ferguson. As host, she seems at once more comfortable with herself and determined to prove that she is not hiding who she really is. During each show, following a brief question/answer session with the audience, O'Donnell settles into interviewing only one or two guests per episode. Her guests have ranged from comedic greats Bob Newhart and Phyllis Diller to actors Russell Brand and Kevin Bacon. Interviews are interspersed with music, short games, and human interest stories. Once dubbed the "Queen of Nice" by *Newsweek*, O'Donnell continues to demonstrate that "nice" girls do win—and that they do not have to fit a restricted image of femininity to do so.

Elizabeth Rholetter Purdy

SEE ALSO: *Boy George;* The Brady Bunch*; Broadway; Burnett, Carol;* Car 54, Where Are You?*; Cavett, Dick; Daytime Talk Shows; Diller, Phyllis; Emmy Awards;* Fiddler on the Roof*;* The Flintstones*; Grammy Awards; Hollywood; Jones, Jennifer;* A League of Their Own*;* McCall's Magazine*; Newhart, Bob;* The Sound of Music*; Springer, Jerry; Tony Awards;* The View*;* Will & Grace*; Winfrey, Oprah.*

BIBLIOGRAPHY

Altman, Sheryl. "Everything's Coming up Rosie." *Biography*, October 1998, 32–39.

Bianco, Robert. "*A Family Is a Family Is a Family*: A Rosie O'Donnell Celebration." *USA Today*, January 28, 2010.

Goodman, Gloria. *The Life and Humor of Rosie O'Donnell: A Biography*. New York: William Morrow, 1998.

Nordlinger, Jay. "Rosie O'Donnell, Political Activist." *National Review* 52, no. 11 (2000).

O'Donnell, Rosie. *Find Me.*New York: Warner Books, 2002.

O'Donnell, Rosie. *Celebrity Detox: The Fame Game.*New York: Grand Central Publishing, 2007.

Oldenburg, Ann. "Rosie's Back in the Talk Game." *USA Today*, October 10, 2011.

Parish, James Robert. *Rosie: Rosie O'Donnell Biography*. New York: Carroll and Graf, 1997.

Spreng, Patrick. *Everything Rosie: The Ultimate Guide for Rosie O'Donnell Fans*. Secaucus, NJ: Carol Publishing Group, 1998.

The Office

The Office is a mockumentary television comedy series, based on a British predecessor of the same name, that aired on NBC beginning in 2005. The original program, created by Ricky Gervais and Stephen Merchant, was filmed in a documentary style and starred Gervais as the manager of a small paper distributor in the small, post-industrial borough of Slough, in Berkshire, England. Though only lasting two seasons, the series enjoyed great success and international acclaim, winning two British Comedy Awards in 2002 and, more amazingly, becoming the first British comedy ever awarded a Golden Globe in 2004. The American adaptation, executive produced by Gervais, premiered on March 24, 2005, and ran for an abbreviated first season of only six episodes, replacing another series midseason. Like its British predecessor, the U.S. show depicts a group of coworkers employed at a small paper distributor, this time located in Scranton, Pennsylvania.

The program is filmed in documentary style, using a single camera that the characters are aware of and often play to. Unlike a traditional sitcom, *The Office* has no laugh track, and though it is scripted, many of the cast members draw on a background in improvisational comedy to deviate from their lines. During the first few seasons, the documentary style was adhered to very strictly: if a single camera could not easily (or logically) follow a character or characters to a location on the set, the scene would not be filmed. Though the show gradually widened its focus to incorporate other styles and formats, the documentary remained a vital element throughout its evolution.

The Office began its eighth season in the United States in September 2011, despite the departure of lead actor Steve Carell, who portrayed branch/regional manager Michael Scott. Other key characters include Dwight Schrute (Rainn Wilson), Jim Halpert (John Krasinski), Pam Beesly (Jenna Fischer), Ryan Howard (B. J. Novak), Angela Martin (Angela Kinsey), Oscar Martinez (Oscar Nuñez), Kelly Kapoor (Mindy Kaling), and Andy Bernard (Ed Helms), who took over as office manager after Scott's departure. Off-camera, Novak and Kaling are also executive producers and frequent contributing writers for the show.

Two story arcs anchored the series from its premiere in 2005. The first involves the misadventures of office manager Michael Scott, who wants to be both boss and close friend to his employees. As a manager, Michael is almost completely incompetent; he frequently commits unwitting social faux pas, often to the discomfort or detriment of his employees. But over the course of the series he displays a surprising generosity of spirit, genuinely wishing to help his employees professionally and personally. His personal life also became fodder for the program, with several episodes depicting his (largely unsuccessful) attempts to find a romantic partner. Producers brought closure to this story line for Carell's departure from the show in 2011, having Scott relocate to Colorado with his fiancée Holly Flax, a recurring character from previous seasons.

The second main story line involves Pam and Jim. At the start of the series Pam is the office receptionist and is engaged to warehouse employee Roy Anderson. Jim is clearly in love with Pam, and it is insinuated that Pam returns his affections. Although Pam and Roy's wedding is called off near the end of season two, Pam and Jim do not begin dating until later in the series. Many episodes are propelled by the romantic tension between Jim and Pam, encouraging viewers to speculate about their future together. At the start of season four, it is revealed that the two have been secretly dating for some time, and in season six they are wed. By the middle of season eight, in 2012, the couple have two children together.

In addition to the U.S. version, *The Office* was adapted for German, French, French-Canadian, Chilean, Israeli, Swedish, and Chinese audiences. The German version, *Stromberg*, took place at an insurance agency; its only reference to the British version was an "inspired by" credit, but the stylistic influence is unmistakable. Most other international versions are set in paper or office supply sales offices, and many had short runs akin to the original two-season British version.

For much of its run, the U.S. *Office* was the highest rated among NBC's prime-time scripted programs. But after the departure of Carell toward the end of season seven, viewership dropped dramatically, with the show suffering much lower ratings in the middle of season eight. Despite declining interest, in May 2012 NBC renewed *The Office* for a ninth and final season.

Jeff Merro

SEE ALSO: *Carell, Steve; Gervais, Ricky; Mockumentaries; Sitcom; Television.*

BIBLIOGRAPHY

Carter, Bill; Stuart Elliott; and Brian Stelter. "Comedies Lead the Way for the Next TV Season." *New York Times*, May 14, 2012.

Osborn, Michael. "The Office: A Decade around the World." *BBC*, July 8, 2011.

Stanley, Alessandra. "An American-Style 'Office' with a Boss from Heck." *New York Times*, March 24, 2005.

Timms, Dominic. "U.S. Version of *The Office* Scores Ratings Victory." *Guardian Unlimited*, March 29, 2005.

"The Office." Official NBC website. Accessed June 2012. Available from http://www.nbc.com/the-office/

O'Keeffe, Georgia *(1887–1986)*

One of America's most important artists, and certainly its most renowned female artist, Georgia O'Keeffe was among the first generation of American modernists. She translated a love of nature and a feeling for form into some of the most advanced paintings and drawings of the twentieth century.

EARLY INFLUENCES

Born in Sun Prairie, Wisconsin, into a family of farmers, O'Keeffe decided to be an artist at the age of ten. She studied at the Art Institute of Chicago in 1905–1906 and, after her move to New York the following year, at the Art Students League under William Merritt Chase and Kenyon Cox. Chase was an important American impressionist who encouraged O'Keeffe's love of landscape. She was more stylistically influenced, however, by Arthur Wesley Dow at Columbia University. Dow had studied with the postimpressionist Paul Gauguin and greatly admired Japanese art. O'Keeffe was moved by Dow's orientalizing landscapes, arranged simply in flat, saturated color.

Alfred Stieglitz, the most passionate promoter of art photography and modern art in America at this time, exhibited O'Keeffe's remarkably advanced watercolors—without her permission—in 1916. Stieglitz's gallery 291, named for its Fifth Avenue address, also hosted her first solo exhibition the following year. Along with artists such as John Marin, Marsden Hartley, and Max Weber, O'Keeffe became one of the artists in Stieglitz's stable of talented modernists. The young painter (age thirty-seven) and the older photographer/impresario (age sixty) were married in 1924. Their long, fitful relationship has never ceased to intrigue the public. In 2009 Lifetime Television produced a biopic of the couple with Joan Allen as O'Keeffe and Jeremy Irons as Stieglitz.

In 1912 O'Keeffe had accepted a position as supervisor of art in the public schools in Amarillo, Texas. The landscape and light there inspired her to create some radically reductive abstractions. A series of watercolors and charcoal drawings she made at this time—for example, *Light Coming on the Plains III* (1917, Amon Carter Museum, Fort Worth, Texas)—is among the most abstract art made in the twentieth century.

A NEW APPROACH TO ABSTRACT

Throughout the 1920s, O'Keeffe painted the sharp architectural forms of Manhattan and the soft landscapes around Lake George, in the foothills of the Adirondacks. Though she often said that she was "not a joiner," her works of the 1920s shared affinities with contemporary painting. The art of Charles Sheeler, Charles Demuth, and other "precisionists" consisted of precisely rendered architectural forms, industrial landscapes, and machine subjects. Although O'Keeffe depicted cavernous city streets and painted in crisp forms, her touch was never quite as dry as theirs. Moreover, she eschewed specifically industrial subjects in favor of more natural ones.

Georgia O'Keeffe. *Georgia O'Keeffe was an innovative modernist who was able capture abstract forms in nature in her paintings.* JOE MUNROE/CONTRIBUTOR/ARCHIVE PHOTOS/GETTY IMAGES.

In 1924 she began painting her renowned series of large-scale flowers—viewed closely and filling the entire canvas. At once realistic and abstract, these works often reveal explicit vaginal shapes, as in *Black Iris III* (1926, Metropolitan Museum of Art, New York). Though the artist vehemently denied any sexual readings of these works, they may safely be said to express a generalized feminine principle.

Wintering in New York and summering in the west, O'Keeffe made annual visits to New Mexico beginning in 1929. That summer she stayed in Taos, where she painted *Black Cross, New Mexico* (1929, Art Institute of Chicago). Explaining their appearance in her art, she recalled, "I saw the crosses so often—and often in unexpected places—like a thin dark veil of the Catholic Church spread over the New Mexico landscape."

Three years after Stieglitz's death, in 1946, she moved to remote Abiquiu, New Mexico, to a ruined adobe called Ghost Ranch. Here she spent the last four decades of her life. On intimate terms with the land, and ever sensitive to the shapes of things, O'Keeffe began collecting the bones she found in the desert. One is featured in *Cow's Skull—Red, White, and Blue* (1931–1936, Metropolitan Museum of Art, New York). In 2006, a species of dinosaur was named for the artist, *Effigia okeeffeae* ("O'Keeffe's Ghost"), from specimens originally quarried near Ghost Ranch in the late 1940s. Characteristically, she denied that the bones that appear in her art reflected a personal preoccupation with death.

LATER YEARS

In 1953, when O'Keeffe was in her middle sixties, she traveled throughout Europe. Six years later she took a three-month trip around the world by air, and in 1960 she visited the Far East. The experience of flying was an epiphany for O'Keeffe; she was entranced by the topography below and cloud formations seen from the air. Her works of this period reflect this new visual preoccupation—for example, *Sky above Clouds IV* (1965, Art Institute of Chicago), a mural measuring 8 by 24 feet, which was painted for a major retrospective exhibition of her work in 1966.

As attested by photographs that show her determined face, her svelte body, and her hair tightly pulled back, O'Keeffe's last years saw no decline in energy or creativity. Extending her range of artistic expression, she took up pottery in the last decade of her life. And in 1976 she produced a lavishly illustrated self-titled autobiography. On the occasion of her ninetieth birthday, the National Gallery in Washington, D.C., hosted a tribute to her.

Although her greatest contribution to avant-garde art occurred in the years between 1915 and 1920, O'Keeffe had in subsequent decades come to embody the notion of the uncompromising artist and is regarded as the very icon of the independent woman.

Mark B. Pohlad

SEE ALSO: *Abstract Expressionism; Feminism; Metropolitan Museum of Art; Modernism.*

BIBLIOGRAPHY

Benke, Britta. *Georgia O'Keeffe, 1887–1986: Flowers in the Desert.* Cologne, Germany: Benedikt Taschen, 1995.

Castro, Jan Garden. *The Art and Life of Georgia O'Keeffe.* New York: Crown Trade Paperbacks, 1995.

Cowart, Jack, and Juan Hamilton. *Georgia O'Keeffe: Art and Letters.* New York: Graphic Society, 1987.

Eldredge, Charles C. *Georgia O'Keeffe: American and Modern.* New Haven: Yale University Press, 1993.

Greenough, Sarah, ed. *My Faraway One: Selected Letters of Georgia O'Keeffe and Alfred Stieglitz: Volume One, 1915–1933.* New Haven, CT: Yale University Press, 2011.

Hassrick, Peter H., ed. *The Georgia O'Keeffe Museum.* New York: Abrams and Georgia O'Keeffe Museum, 1997.

Lisle, Laurie. *Portrait of an Artist: A Biography of Georgia O'Keeffe.* New York: Washington Square Press, 1997.

Oklahoma!

The musical *Oklahoma!* was the first collaboration between composer Richard Rodgers (1902–1979) and lyricist-librettist Oscar Hammerstein II (1895–1960), both of whom already had extensive careers in show business behind them. *Oklahoma!* was based on the play *Green Grow the Lilacs* by Lynn Riggs, first produced by the Theatre Guild in New York in 1931. The work took a radically new approach to musical theater on several fronts. The story of ordinary people and rural life during the Oklahoma land rush was an unusual subject at that time. The libretto follows the play closely, breaking with the conventional placement of song and dance elements. The choreography by Agnes de Mille synthesizes ballet and American vernacular dance, and a "dream ballet" advances the story. Hammerstein's libretto and lyrics celebrate the hardy, optimistic spirit of the American West during the bleakest years of World War II.

Oklahoma! became a runaway hit show and won a Pulitzer Prize for Drama in 1944. Many of the young actors and dancers in the opening production went on to stellar careers. Since the initial run, touring companies have presented the musical around the world, and revivals have been frequent. *Oklahoma!* proved to be only the first of a series of artistically and financially successful musicals by Rodgers and Hammerstein, but none of their works has influenced the development of musical theater more than this one.

Oklahoma! takes place at the turn of the twentieth century between the Oklahoma land rushes in 1889 and 1893 and statehood in 1907. Curley, a cowhand, and Jud Fry, a farmhand, are in love with Laurey. She is in love with Curley, but after an argument with him Laurey agrees to go to a dance with Jud Fry, whom she secretly fears. At the dance Curley puts up his entire belongings to buy Laurey's box lunch. She and Curley admit their love for each other and are married. After the wedding Jud fights with Curley and is killed with his own knife during the struggle. Laurey's Aunt Eller engineers a trial at the scene, and Curley is acquitted, enabling the young couple to begin married life happily. A second, more comic subplot involves man-crazy Ado Annie; her true love cowboy, Will Parker; and her temporary interest, peddler Ali Hakim. Like Laurey and Curley, Ado Annie and Will work out their problems and settle down to married life.

RODGERS AND HAMMERSTEIN

The happy combination of events that produced *Oklahoma!* began with the 1940 revival of *Green Grow the Lilacs* by the Westport Country Playhouse in Westport, Connecticut. The playhouse was owned by Lawrence Langer and his wife, Armina Marshall, who were also partners in the Theatre Guild, a theater-management group active in New York since 1918. Another partner in the distinguished Theatre Guild was Theresa Helburn. After seeing the Riggs play revival in Westport with square dances choreographed by Gene Kelly, Helburn thought it would make a good musical theater production.

Later in the summer of 1940, Rodgers saw the play and told Langer and Helburn that he agreed the musical theater adaptation was a promising idea. Rodgers was still working with his first partner, Lorenz Hart, in 1940; their shows *Pal Joey* (1940) and *By Jupiter* (1942) had yet to open. Hart had struggled with alcoholism for years, and although he continued to write inspired lyrics, his working habits had become erratic. Rodgers, however, was determined to continue collaborating with Hart as long as possible, and he asked Hart to join the *Oklahoma!* project. Hart refused, feeling that Riggs's play did not provide good musical theater material. Rodgers turned to Hammerstein for *Oklahoma!* Hammerstein knew the play and was eager to write the book and lyrics.

Oklahoma! opened at the St. James Theatre in New York on March 31, 1943, remaining on Broadway for a remarkable 2,212 performances. The reviews after opening night in New York were dazzling. A *New York Times* review noted, "Wonderful is the nearest adjective, for this excursion of the Guild combines a fresh and infectious gaiety, a charm of manner, beautiful acting, singing and dancing, and a score by Richard Rodgers that doesn't do any harm, either, since it is one of his best."

The next morning the box office was in pandemonium, and performances quickly sold out for the foreseeable future. But no accolade could have meant more to Rodgers than that of his former partner, Hart. In *Musical Stages*, Rodgers remembers the traditional postshow gathering at Sardi's when a grinning Hart threw his arms around him and said, "Dick, I've never had a better evening in my life! This show will be around 20 years from now!" Max Wilk's *OK! The Story of Oklahoma!* quotes lyricist and librettist Alan Jay Lerner, who said, "A musical in the twenties and the thirties had no dramatic validity and the wit was the lyric writer's, never the characters'. Oscar Hammerstein, on the other hand, was very much a dramatic writer, and with *Oklahoma!* he and Dick Rodgers radically changed the course of the musical theater. The musical comedy became a play."

POPULAR SONGS

A remarkable number of popular songs came from *Oklahoma!*, especially when compared to earlier shows. Except for the monumental *Show Boat* (1927) by Jerome Kern and Hammerstein, most musicals of the 1920s and 1930s contained one or two memorable songs. *Oklahoma!* gave birth to several: "Oh, What a Beautiful Mornin'"; "The Surrey with the Fringe on Top"; "Kansas City"; "I Cain't Say No"; "People Will Say We're in Love"; and, of course, "Oklahoma," the energetic title song that caused the musical's original title *Away We Go!* to be changed. Songs from the show became overnight smashes: "People Will Say We're in Love" was the top radio song of 1943, and the cast recorded the first original-cast recording of a

Broadway show, beginning a practice that continues in the 2010s. Since 1943 the original cast album has almost never gone out of print as 78s, LPs, cassette tapes, and compact discs.

Writing his autobiography *Musical Stages* in 1975, Rodgers theorized about what made Oklahoma such an extraordinary work. "When a show works perfectly, it's because all the individual parts complement each other and fit together. No single element overshadows any other. . . . That's what made *Oklahoma!* work. All the components dovetailed. There was nothing extraneous or foreign, nothing that pushed itself into the spotlight yelling 'Look at me!'"

Critics and audiences continue to agree with Rodgers about *Oklahoma!*'s significance. In 1993 the U.S. Postal Service acknowledged its place in American cultural history with a stamp commemorating the show's fiftieth anniversary. In 1998 Australian actor Hugh Jackman starred in a London stage revival of *Oklahoma!* Directed by Trevor Nunn and choreographed by Susan Stroman, the revival was well received. A film version of the London performance was produced in 1999. A Broadway revival of the musical, also run by Nunn and Stroman but featuring a different cast, began at the George Gershwin Theatre in 2002 and ran for a year. It was nominated for a number of Tony Awards. The popularity of the musical led to countless revivals, including a 2006 performance in Japan by an all-female cast and a 2010 revival in Washington, D.C., that garnered strong reviews.

Ann Sears

SEE ALSO: *Broadway; The Musical; Rodgers and Hammerstein; Rodgers and Hart.*

BIBLIOGRAPHY

Carter, Tim. Oklahoma!: *The Making of an American Musical.* New Haven, CT: Yale University Press, 2007.

De Mille, Agnes. *Dance to the Piper.* New York: Da Capo, 1980.

Riggs, Lynn. *Green Grow the Lilacs.* Norman, CT: The Easton Press, 1991.

Rodgers, Richard. *Musical Stages: An Autobiography.* New York: Da Capo Press, 1995.

Rodgers, Richard, and Oscar Hammerstein. *Six Plays.* New York: Random House, 1953.

Wilk, Max. *OK! The Story of* Oklahoma! New York: Grove Press, 1993.

Old Navy

If the Gap was the Cinderella among clothing retailers in the affluent 1980s, its down-market offshoot Old Navy enjoyed a comparable fairy-tale existence in the belt-tightened 1990s. The brainchild of Gap CEO Millard "Mickey" Drexler, the store began as an attempt to reel in customers put off by the Gap's prices but too hip to buy clothes at Wal-Mart. By relying on attractive packaging, quirky promotions, and the pioneering use of headsets by customer service personnel, Old Navy succeeded in making cheap threads seem cool. Even the Gap's pseudo hipsters were won over by a series of campy television commercials featuring such entertainment industry fossils as Barbara Eden and Eartha Kitt, alongside an adorable pooch named Magic and the campaign's icon, weirdly fascinating fashion doyenne Carrie Donovan. The company continued to grow in the new century and in 2011 reported annual sales of more than $5 billion.

Robert E. Schnakenberg

SEE ALSO: *Advertising; Consumerism; The Gap; Wal-Mart.*

BIBLIOGRAPHY

Caminiti, Susan. "Will Old Navy Fill the Gap?" *Fortune*, March 18, 1996.

Kaufman, Leslie. "Downscale Moves Up." *Newsweek*, July 27, 1998.

Oliphant, Pat *(1935–)*

With a career spanning multiple decades of American politics, popular political artist Pat Oliphant serves as a role model for a generation of political and editorial cartoonists. He was deemed the "most influential editorial cartoonist now working" by the *New York Times* and credited by fellow Pulitzer Prize–winning editorial cartoonist Mike Luckovich with "creating modern-day political cartoons." At the height of his career, Oliphant's work appeared in about 375 newspapers, four days a week. By the early twenty-first century, the frequency had been reduced to three times a week.

Oliphant grew up in Adelaide, South Australia, the son of a cartographer for Australia's Ministry of Lands. According to Oliphant, art was an early interest. He was drawing constantly by the age of five and spent a couple of years in art school following high school. In 1953 he joined the *Adelaide News* as a copy boy and "press artist" charged with drawing weather maps. Two years later he became the editorial cartoonist for the *Adelaide Advertiser*, a job that combined his love for art with an interest in political cartoons fostered by his father.

In 1964 he immigrated to the United States to escape what he described as a stifling, oppressive editorial environment. As he put it, "In 10 years cartooning there, I couldn't get anything controversial in the paper. To get anything done I had to leave." An artistic artifact of his days of dealing with conservative, intrusive Australian editors is his alter ego, the miniature penguin Punk, who still expresses his subversiveness by delivering the final word from the corners of his cartoons. Oliphant explained that the editors may not have realized that he was "trying to subvert their system and say something in my own words. But the bird became very popular and became a regular element of my cartoons."

DRAWING AMERICA

Just one example of the way Punk adds an extra element of humor to Oliphant's cartoons can be illustrated through a 1972 drawing published upon the death of President Harry Truman. The drawing pokes fun at Truman's well-known forthrightness by portraying a confrontation between Truman and St. Peter at the gates of heaven: As Truman tosses a harp over his shoulder with grumpy indignation, St. Peter leans back toward his assistant with an expression of weary resignation to ask, "See what you can do about digging up a piano" (a reference to Truman's hobby of playing the piano). In the bottom left-hand corner, Puck warns an angel, "And you just better like his playing!"

Within a year of his arrival in the United States, Oliphant was a nationally syndicated editorial cartoonist working at the *Denver Post*. He moved to the *Washington Star* in 1975, remaining there until it folded in 1981. Since then, unlike most syndicated cartoonists, Oliphant has not been affiliated with a single newspaper. Instead he works directly for the Universal Press Syndicate.

ACCLAIM AND CONTROVERSY

A curator who coordinated a 1998 exhibition of Oliphant's work at the Library of Congress characterized him as a "fine artist who happens to be a cartoonist rather than a cartoonist who happens to be a fine artist." In addition to his syndicated panels, Oliphant produces political sculptures (wax busts and bronze sculptures), abstract oil paintings, lithography, and monotypes. In 1998 a collection of his sculptures of seven American presidents was featured in a national traveling exhibition. The tour included a bust of President Gerald Ford with a quizzical expression on his face and a small plastic bandage on his head and a bronze of President George H. W. Bush playing horseshoes that one critic described as "a large almost insect-like figure . . . all thinned-out arms, torso, and legs."

Oliphant's self-described artistic routine involves spending his mornings drawing cartoons and his afternoons painting, sculpting, and printmaking. Although largely self-taught, he took three years of drawing classes in the 1980s at the Corcoran School of Art in Washington, D.C. He has also traveled to New York City monthly to participate in a drawing group that works with live models. Among his artistic idols are painter Edgar Degas, English cartoonist Ronald Searle, and French artist and political cartoonist Honoré Daumier.

Among his many awards, Oliphant holds a Pulitzer Prize, awarded in 1967. The account of how he won it is a testament to his bluntness and honesty. He recounted his prizewinning strategy as follows: He sought out a book of past Pulitzer winners and noted that they were all "very jingoistic sorts of cartoons." Using that book as a guide, he found one "very patriotic jingoistic cartoon" that he had done earlier in the year and included it among his entries. The cartoon portrays North Vietnamese leader Ho Chi Minh carrying the corpse of a Viet Cong soldier, with a caption that reads, "They won't get us to the conference table . . . will they?" The committee selected it as their winner. Another infamous tale reveals a self-proclaimed tendency to vote for politicians he despises because they provide the most material for his cartoons. Confirming this old story in a 1998 interview, Oliphant explained, "Of course I voted for Reagan, who would want to draw Walter Mondale for four years?"

Throughout Oliphant's career, he has demonstrated no fear of offending individuals or groups through his inimitable cartoons. In early 2004 the *Boston Globe* ran an Oliphant cartoon in which he poked fun at Mel Gibson's recently released *The Passion of the Christ*. The cartoon depicted a large nun wielding a ruler and wearing an evil smile along with a small and bloody boy who had obviously just been beaten. Oliphant's caption read, "In his early school days, little Mel Gibson gets beaten to a bloody pulp by Sister Dolorosa Excruciata of the Little Sisters of the Holy Agony, and an idea is born." Among Boston Catholics, there was much outrage. Offended readers viewed the cartoon not as a satiric poke at Gibson and the violence portrayed in the movie but as an attack on nuns. There were a number of subscriptions canceled, and the controversy spread outside Boston to other Catholics. Writing for the *National Journal*, William Powers suggested that such reactions are responsible for the fact that newspapers in America are "dying a long, slow death" that is similar to that of dinosaurs, "but more pathetic." Political cartoonists who must constantly be afraid of offending one group or another are unable to react to the political scene as they see it. Oliphant, however, remains undaunted.

Courtney Bennett

SEE ALSO: *Comics; Gibson, Mel;* The Passion of the Christ; *Reagan, Ronald.*

BIBLIOGRAPHY

Hess, Stephen, and Northrop, Sandy. *Drawn & Quartered: The History of American Political Cartoons*. Montgomery, AL: Elliott & Clark, 1996.

Oliphant, Pat. *Oliphant: The New World Order in Drawing and Sculpture: 1983–1993*. Kansas City, MO: Andrews McMeel, 1994.

Oliphant, Pat, and Wendy Wick Reaves. *Oliphant's Presidents: Twenty-Five Years of Caricature*. Kansas City, MO: Andrews McMeel, 1990.

Oliphant, Pat; Katz, H.; and Day, S. *Oliphant's Anthem: Pat Oliphant at the Library of Congress*. Kansas City, MO: Andrews McMeel, 1998.

Powers, William. "Be Not Wicked." *National Journal*, March 13, 2004.

Protzman, F. "Mr. Sharp Pen; Library of Congress Shows Oliphant's Work." *Washington Post*, May 17, 1998.

Silverman, Jonathan, and Rader, Dean. *The World Is a Text: Writing, Reading, and Thinking about Visual and Popular Culture*, 3rd ed. New York: Prentice-Hall, 2008.

Olivier, Laurence *(1907–1989)*

Hailed as the greatest actor of his time, Laurence Olivier reflected the twentieth-century definition of the consummate actor. He starred in hundreds of roles onstage and on screen; was fundamental in establishing Great Britain's Royal National Theatre; and wrote *On Acting*, one of acting's most influential texts. In addition, he was a successful director, writer, and producer, credited as the first to bring William Shakespeare to the silver screen. Olivier's persona on and off the stage led to his widespread acceptance as one of the finest actors and most popular personalities the world has known.

Laurence Kerr Olivier was born to a family of churchmen and schoolmasters in the town of Dorking, Surrey, England. His father was a parson. Much of Olivier's life would be shaped by the death of his mother, Agnes Louise Crookenden, who died of cancer in 1920. He would later write of his mother, "I've been looking for her ever since." His father encouraged him to be an actor, and by age nine he was playing Brutus in *Julius Caesar* and, at age eleven, Maria in *Twelfth Night* at All Saints School. He enrolled in the Central School of Speech Training and Dramatic Art in 1924. It was there that his passion for creating roles through the use of makeup took root. Olivier rejected method-acting techniques, preferring a character-driven acting style. "I discovered the protective shelter of nose putty and enjoyed a pleasurable sense of relief and relaxation when some character part called for a sculptural addition to my face," he

Laurence Olivier. *Laurence Olivier plays the title role in 1944's* Henry V. ITV GLOBAL/THE KOBAL COLLECTION.

wrote in 1982 in *Confessions of an Actor*, "affording me the shelter of an alien character and enabling me to avoid anything so embarrassing as self-representation."

Olivier's professional stage-acting career spanned almost five decades, beginning with an engagement with the Lena Ashwell Players in 1925 and concluding in 1973 at the Royal National Theatre. During that time he acted in and directed many of the classics of the stage. Following his stint with the Lena Ashwell Players, he was a member of Birmingham Repertory Theatre Company (1926–1928) and Old Vic Company (1937–1949) and was the director of the National Theatre Company from 1962 to 1973. His most memorable stage performance was as Othello in the National Theatre Company's 1964 production of the Shakespeare masterpiece. In *On Acting*, Olivier writes, "I am Othello. . . . He belongs to no one else; he belongs to me. When I sigh, he sighs. When I laugh, he laughs. When I cry, he cries."

Olivier's first foray into film came in 1930, but his first major success was in William Wyler's *Wuthering Heights* in 1939. Despite his roles in popular films of the time, his greatest success was his film adaptation of Shakespeare's *Henry V* (1944), which he produced, directed, and starred in. The success of the picture led to his Academy Award–winning film *Hamlet* (1948) and *Richard III* (1955). As the first director/producer to successfully bring Shakespeare to the screen, he reintroduced mainstream culture to the bard's works and led to a revitalization of the classics in the modern age. Olivier would perform many more Shakespearean roles in film and television, including *Othello* (1965) and *King Lear* (1983).

Olivier married three times: to actress Jill Esmond in 1930, to actress Vivien Leigh in 1940, and to actress Joan Plowright in 1961. He fathered two sons and two daughters. He would later say that Plowright filled the place left so long empty by the death of his mother. During the last years of his life, Olivier played roles that were considered beneath him, and he was plagued by a series of painful illnesses. His poor health forced his retirement in 1986, although he came back for one last appearance, in 1989's *War Requiem*. He wrote two revealing books before his death: *Confessions of an Actor* (1982) and *On Acting*. Olivier was buried in Westminster Abbey beside the Shakespeare Memorial and the graves of King Henry V and Henry Irving.

Few personalities have made an impression on the world as did that of Sir Laurence Olivier. He left an indelible mark on the world of theater, film, and television. His legacy has inspired directors such as Franco Zeffirelli and Kenneth Branagh to bring Shakespeare's plays to contemporary film audiences. On the 100th anniversary of his birth, the *Guardian*'s theater critic Michael Billington wrote, "While Olivier in some ways belongs to another age, I'd argue that, as an actor, he was the first of the moderns and his legacy is still visible today." Branagh portrayed Olivier in the 2011 film *My Week with Marilyn* and said afterward that the film left him wanting "to jump in and be as brave, and courageous, and as artistically adventurous as Olivier was." It is clear that Olivier's presence still haunts, and influences, contemporary culture. Perhaps director Richard Eyre put it best when he said, "We shall never see his like again."

Michael Najjar

SEE ALSO: *Academy Awards; Cancer; Celebrity; Hollywood; Movie Stars.*

BIBLIOGRAPHY

Feinberg, Scott. *Kenneth Branagh on Playing Laurence Olivier in "My Week with Marilyn,"* December 9, 2011. Accessed

December 2011. Available from http://scottfeinberg.com/kenneth-branagh-on-playing-laurence-olivier-in-my-week-with-marilyn-audio

Holden, Anthony. *Olivier*. London: Weidenfeld and Nicolson, 1988.

Lewis, Roger. *The Real Life of Laurence Olivier*. London: Century, 1996.

Olivier, Laurence. *Confessions of an Actor*. London: Weidenfeld and Nicolson, 1982.

Olivier, Laurence. *On Acting*. London: Weidenfeld and Nicolson, 1986.

Olivier, Richard. *Melting the Stone: A Journey around My Father*. Woodstock, CT: Spring Publications, 1996.

Olivier, Richard, and Joan Olivier. *Olivier at Work: The National Years*, ed. Lyn Haill. London: Nick Hern Books, 1989.

Olmos, Edward James *(1947–)*

A 1988 issue of *Time* magazine described Edward James Olmos as "not only possibly the best Hispanic-American actor of his generation, but one of the best performers working today." Olmos, however, did not have Hollywood success and greatness served to him on a platter. Born and raised in the poor, working-class Boyle Heights section of East Los Angeles, at a young age Olmos avoided drugs and gangs by throwing himself into baseball; it was only at baseball games that he saw his father. By his late teens, it wasn't baseball that beckoned, but rock and roll. After graduating from Montebello High School, a long-haired Olmos became the lead vocalist for the band Eddie James and the Pacific Ocean while earning an associate degree in sociology at a junior college. He then transferred to California State University, Los Angeles, to study acting. He appeared in several small productions around Los Angeles and eventually landed bit parts on *Kojak* and *Hawaii Five-O*.

In 1975 Olmos landed a nonspeaking part in the low-budget movie *Aloha, Bobby and Rose*, which was followed by a starring role in the successful independent Chicano feature *Alambrista!* (1977). Thanks to much hard work and a Tony Award nomination for his role as *El Pachuco* in the Broadway production of Luis Valdez's musical *Zoot Suit* (1978), doors began to open. In 1982 he appeared as the Mexican Asian detective in Ridley Scott's blockbuster *Blade Runner*, and two years later he became known to television audiences as Lieutenant Martin Castillo of *Miami Vice*—a role that won him an Emmy.

In 1989 Olmos was nominated for an Academy Award for his role as Jaime Escalante, the inspirational East Los Angeles barrio math teacher in the widely acclaimed film *Stand and Deliver* (1988). He also received critical praise for his acting in *Mi Familia* (1995), *Selena* (1997), and *The Disappearance of Garcia Lorca* (1997). On the acclaimed television drama *American Family* (2002), he starred as the patriarch of a Latino family living in Los Angeles. From 2003 to 2009 Olmos played Commander William Adama on the science fiction show *Battlestar Galactica*, which *Time* magazine called the best show on television in 2005. He also directed *Battlestar Galactica: The Plan*, a made-for-TV prequel to the series that aired in 2010. Among his peers Olmos is respected for his talent as well as his dedication to perfecting his roles. For example, he spent hours studying the tape-recorded speech patterns of the real-life Escalante and gained an estimated twenty pounds to resemble him.

While Olmos is a working actor willing to play anyone from a Greek to an American Indian steelworker, he is actively committed to portraying characters in stories about Chicano lives, culture, and history. He formed his own production company to produce such films as *The Ballad of Gregorio Cortez* (1982)—the true story of a Tejano farmer (played by Olmos) brutally victimized by the Texas Rangers in the early part of the twentieth century—and *American Me* (1992), a powerful cautionary tale of Chicano gang life for which Olmos served as producer, director, and star.

Olmos's commitment to the Chicano community extends beyond his work in film. Understanding the importance of promoting positive Chicano male role models, he regularly visits and gives lectures on crime and education at public schools, hospitals, American Indian reservations, libraries, prisons, and colleges across the country. After the Rodney King riots in April 1992, Olmos was out with a broom helping to clean up the streets. Actor and activist, Edward James Olmos has offered disenfranchised members of society a vision of life's possibilities.

Frederick Luis Aldama

SEE ALSO: Stand and Deliver.

BIBLIOGRAPHY

Martinez, Elizabeth Coonrod. *Edward James Olmos: Mexican American Actor*. Brookfield, CT: Millbrook Press, 1994.

Poniewozik, James. "Best of 2005: Television." *Time*, December 16, 2005.

Olsen, Tillie *(1912–2007)*

Short-story writer Tillie Olsen has given voice to populations that have traditionally been under- or unrepresented in literature, particularly working-class women. Influenced by her socialist parents, Olsen joined the Young Communist League in 1931 and embarked on a career of political activism. She began writing the pre–Depression era novel *Yonnondio* when she was nineteen. In 1934 she published part of the first chapter as "The Iron Throat" in the *Partisan Review*. After having to put the novel aside, she rediscovered it in 1973. As this lapse indicates, Olsen's artistic career suffered interruptions, primarily from the exigencies of motherhood and poverty. She poignantly reflected on the gender politics of her forced sabbatical in *Silences* (1978).

A fellowship to Stanford University enabled her to resume writing in 1957, when she began a collection of short fiction, *Tell Me a Riddle* (1961). The title piece earned the O. Henry Award for the year's outstanding short story. In addition to writing, Olsen played a prominent role in rediscovering previously unheralded women authors, including Rebecca Harding Davis, Charlotte Perkins Gilman, and Agnes Smedley. Olson died on January 1, 2007.

Bryan Garman

SEE ALSO: *Communism; Feminism; The Great Depression.*

BIBLIOGRAPHY

Coiner, Constance. *Better Red: The Writing and Resistance of Tillie Olsen and Meridel Le Sueur*. New York: Oxford University Press, 1995.

Orr, Elaine Neil. *Tillie Olsen and a Feminist Spiritual Vision*. Jackson: University Press of Mississippi, 2009.

Olympics

The athlete is among the most compelling of popular culture heroes. Throughout history, the athlete—a uniquely human manifestation of beauty, valor, and physical prowess—has frequently been said to symbolize the best of an individual culture. Over the course of the twentieth century and into the twenty-first, the modern Olympics have provided the greatest international stage for the creation of the athlete hero. In two-week competitions featuring men and women from around the world, Olympians come together in a gathering of the best athletes from each country.

Hosted every two years by a different country, the Olympic Games allow the world to turn its attention not only to the individual competitors but also to the host nation, which invariably puts on a display of its artistic, cultural, and often political puissance. With the advent of television, the Olympics have become a global media event—a conscious stage for the creation of history. Peopled with heroes and villains, royalty and the common person, the Olympics have become one of the world's most anticipated rituals—a drama of victory, defeat, joy, and tragedy that captures the global imagination as perhaps no other event in contemporary society can.

THE ANCIENT OLYMPICS

The modern Olympic Games, first held in Athens in 1896, were inspired by the ancient Olympic Festivals, which took place in the sacred sanctuary of Olympia on the Greek mainland every four years from 776 BCE until they were banned in 394 CE. As both athletic and religious pageants, the Olympics were revered throughout Greece as essential displays of athleticism, beauty, and physical perfection. Attended by poets, writers, and artists, who lauded the athlete-heroes in paintings and in poetry, the ancient Olympic Festival became the most important of all Greek festivities.

The ancient Olympics lasted only five days and included chariot races, horse racing, the pentathlon, foot races, wrestling, and boxing as well as two days of religious ceremonies and sacrifices. To compete in the ancient Olympics was the highest honor to which a Greek man could aspire. Victors were crowned with a wreath of olive branches and were assured fame and wealth—and often immortality—for, in the ancient Olympics, there were no second prizes, only winners.

Closing Ceremonies at 2008 Beijing Olympics. *Athletes and performers fill the stadium floor during the closing ceremony of the 2008 Olympic Games in Beijing, China.* SACRAMENTO BEE/CONTRIBUTOR/MCCLATCHY-TRIBUNE/GETTY IMAGES.

Throughout the city-states of ancient Greece, young men prepared for the Games in schools and clubs dedicated to training athletes. In order to qualify to compete in the Games themselves, athletes had to undergo strict training and testing, so as to ensure the absolute purity of the competitors. The Olympic festival was an all-male domain; women could neither compete nor observe the competitions on threat of death. So sacred were the Olympics that wars were known to cease during the festival. However, by the third century CE, the widespread influence of Christianity had begun to undermine the influence of the Olympics, and by 394 CE the games were banned. But their legacy, as captured in literature and art, would remain alive and ultimately captivate the imagination of a generation of young athletes almost 1,500 years later.

REVIVING THE OLYMPIC IDEAL

In the mid-nineteenth century—after hundreds of years of societal indifference to sports—athletic activities once again assumed a place of prominence in Europe and America. Scientists promoted sporting activities for the health and well-being of humankind, and sporting clubs became popular gathering places for the upper classes. During the 1880s a young Frenchman named Baron Pierre de Coubertin undertook a study of the impact of sports on society. As noted in *Chronicle of the Olympics*, de Coubertin "became convinced that exercise had to be the basis of sensible education." He was "convinced that equal opportunity for all participants was a prerequisite for these competitions." De Coubertin's amateur ideal in his new "religion of sport" reached its apotheosis in his dream of reviving the ancient Olympic games. His idea met with little enthusiasm initially, but the persistent Frenchman recruited sport enthusiasts from Europe and the Americas and finally succeeded in organizing the first modern Olympic Games in Athens in 1896.

One hundred years later, in 1996, Juan Antonio Samaranch, president of the International Olympic Committee, wrote, "When Coubertin established the International Olympic Committee in 1894 in Paris, his goal was to encourage a better understanding among nations through the linking of sport, education, art, and culture." The first Olympic Games were not particularly well organized, as amateur athletes from Europe and the Americas gathered in Athens for the first "international sporting competition"—most of them having arrived in Greece under their own steam. Approximately 200 men from fourteen countries competed in nine events; however, most of the participants were Greek. Winners were awarded an olive branch, a certificate, and a silver medal; the next two runners-up received a laurel sprig along with a copper medal. Despite the fact that the participants were mostly Greek, the United States won more medals than any other country. The Greeks, however, were triumphant in the most symbolic event of the first Olympiad—the recreation of the ancient Greek run by a messenger following the Battle of Marathon. A shepherd named Spiridon Louis won the 26-mile race and was hailed as a national hero.

Greece hoped to host all of the Olympic games, as it had done in the past. But political unrest made that impossible. Thus, in 1900, the Games were brought to de Coubertin's homeland and held in Paris. Public interest in the event, however, was almost nonexistent because the Olympiad was merely a part of the World's Fair taking place in the city. Four years later, the Games traveled to the United States, where they were also subsumed by the World's Fair in St. Louis, Missouri. St. Louis marked the first time athletes paraded in an opening ceremony, and winners were awarded gold, silver, and bronze medals. Still, it wasn't until 1908, when the Olympics were staged as an event in their own right in London, that the public really began to take notice.

SHAPING THE MODERN OLYMPICS

Four years later the Fifth Olympiad would become the model upon which future Games were based. Held in Stockholm and featuring athletes from all the continents of the world, the brilliantly organized two-week event included 2,547 athletes from twenty-eight countries. Women were now competing as well, and the opening day parade was a truly international pageant. From the Stockholm Olympics emerged the first global sports hero—Jim Thorpe, a Native American from Oklahoma, won both the pentathlon and the decathlon. Another star for the American team was swimmer Duke Kahanamoku, descended from the Hawaiian royal family, who would go on to popularize surfing around the world.

The modern Olympic Games had finally caught on, but World War I prevented the 1916 Olympiad. When the games resumed in Antwerp in 1920, the spirit of reconciliation that enveloped Europe transformed the Games into a symbolic spectacle. At the opening ceremony doves were released, and one competitor took the Olympic oath on behalf of all his fellow athletes, pledging to participate in the Games "in the true spirit of sportsmanship." A new Olympic flag was also introduced. The white banner, which featured five interlocking colored circles, symbolized the unity of the five continents. The star of the Games was Finnish runner Paavo Nurmi, who took home four medals—three gold and one silver.

Throughout the first twenty-four years of the modern Olympics, various sports were added, such as diving, rowing, yachting, and cycling, whereas others such as tug-of-war, cricket, and lacrosse were discontinued. Over time, various sports would come and go, but the major events would remain: track and field, gymnastics, swimming and diving, wrestling, boxing, weightlifting, sailing and rowing, and equestrian events.

During the first quarter century of the Olympics, athletes who participated in winter sports were largely excluded. In 1920 ice-skating and ice hockey were included in the Antwerp Games, but a movement was afoot to create a separate Winter Olympics. In 1924 an International Winter Sports Week was held in Chamonix, France, but it wasn't until four years later in St. Moritz that the first official Winter Games took place. During the mid-1920s France seemed to hold the monopoly on the Olympics, as the Summer Games of 1924 were once again held in Paris. There, handsome American swimmer Johnny Weissmuller won four medals and would later parlay his status as Olympic champion into a Hollywood movie career. Because the crux of the Olympics was to promote amateur sports, the 1924 Games would be the last to include tennis; the sport was later reintroduced in Seoul in 1988.

In 1928 the Winter Games officially captured the public imagination as fifteen-year-old Sonja Henie captured the first of her three gold medals in ice-skating. She, too, would eventually find her way to Hollywood through her Olympic fame. The 1928 Amsterdam Summer Games introduced another symbolic Olympic act—the lighting of the Olympic flame brought from Greece. And, finally, women were allowed to compete in track-and-field events. Four years later, in 1932, the Games would return to the United States for the first time in twenty-eight years, with the Winter Games in Lake Placid, New York, and the Summer Games in Los Angeles, California. Among the stars of the Los Angeles Games was a woman who would go on to become one of the world's first professional female athletes, the inimitable Babe Didrikson.

POLITICS SHAPE THE OLYMPICS

Four years later both the Winter and Summer Olympics of 1936 were held in Germany, where Adolf Hitler and the Nazi Party used the Games as a showcase for their new regime. Politics entered the Olympics with a vengeance when German emigrants living in the United States tried to force a boycott of the Games. Although their efforts failed, the IOC felt compelled to step in and demand that Jewish athletes not be excluded from German teams. In the Summer Games Hitler staged an immense spectacle glorifying the Aryan race. Ironically, the star of the Games was an African American athlete named Jesse Owens, who—to Hitler's ire—won four gold medals in track and field.

Although the IOC had done its best to ensure that politics did not interfere with sports, World War II prevented the staging of another Olympics until 1948, when athletes from around the world once again met in St. Moritz for the Winter Games and in London for the Summer Games. Both Germany and Japan were prevented from competing in these first postwar Games.

In the years following World War II, the Olympics gradually grew in size and spectacle. Having lived through the tragedy of a global conflict, athletes and fans alike warmed to the idea of a peacetime gathering of nations. As if to exemplify this desire, a truly international collection of men and women rose to stardom through the ensuing games, from Czechoslovakia's brilliant distance runner, Emil Zápotek, to America's world-class ice-skater, Dick Button, and unmatched decathlete, Bob Mathias, to Australian swimming phenomenon, Dawn Fraser. But the biggest change in the makeup of the Olympic Games was the emergence of the powerhouse teams from the Soviet bloc, whose athletes would dominate the Games for almost forty years. Their presence would guarantee the often-unwelcome shadow of politics that would cloud the Games for years to come.

During the 1960s television brought increasingly global audiences to the Olympics, quickly making stars out of winners, losers, and charismatic participants—even if only for Andy Warhol's proverbial fifteen minutes. Wilma Rudolph, who had overcome polio to become the top woman sprinter in the 1960 Games in Rome, soon became a household name in America, as did boxers Cassius Clay (soon to become Muhammad Ali), Joe Frazier, and George Foreman. Certain sports seemed to gain in popularity as television allowed them to be viewed to their best effect for the first time. Downhill skiing was one such sport whose stars, such as Jean-Claude Killy of France, gained international fame. But television also created a new arena for political exploitation, and the Mexico City Olympics of 1968 became as famous for the high-altitude record set there by long jumper Bob Beamon as for the black-gloved fists raised on the winners' podium by African American sprinters Tommie Smith and John Carlos in salute of "Black Power." But it wasn't until the 1972 Summer Games in Munich that politics would virtually succeed in completely dominating sports.

Although the 1972 Olympics created huge stars, such as swimmer Mark Spitz, winner of seven gold medals, and nineteen-year-old Soviet gymnast Lyudmila Turishcheva, who catapulted women's gymnastics into the Olympic spotlight almost single-handedly, the Munich Games will undoubtedly be most remembered for the tragic kidnapping and killing of members of the Israeli team by Arab terrorists. In ensuing Games politics seemed to creep into public consciousness more and more, particularly as Cold War tensions between the United States and the Soviet Union heightened. The 1980 Winter Games were capped off with the patriotic fervor surrounding the upset of the Soviet ice hockey team by an inexperienced American squad. Six months later the United States boycotted the Moscow Games to protest the Soviet invasion of Afghanistan. Four years later the Soviet bloc countries would retaliate by boycotting the Los Angeles Games.

COMMERCIALIZING THE GAMES

As television audiences for the Olympics swelled around the world, the media latched on to the sports that seemed to garner the best ratings. Women's gymnastics continued to grow in popularity, assuring young stars such as fourteen-year-old Romanian phenom Nadia Comaneci, American Mary Lou Retton, and the brilliant Soviet squads plenty of air time. Track and field continued in popularity, with Edwin Moses, Carl Lewis, Florence Griffith Joyner, and Jackie Joyner-Kersee garnering fame and fortune from their Olympic wins. In the Winter Games ice-skating continued to be the ratings winner, with winners such as Britain's Jayne Torvill and Christopher Dean; America's Scott Hamilton, Brian Boitano, and Kristi Yamaguchi; Germany's Katarina Witt; and Japan's Midori Ito finding that Olympic gold guaranteed them lucrative professional careers.

But, in fact, the line between amateur and professional athletics was becoming blurrier every year, and in 1981 the term "Olympic amateur" was stricken from the Olympic Charter, allowing each individual sports association to decide athletic eligibility for the Games. This new ruling seemed to open the door for a new kind of Olympiad, and in 1992 the American basketball team was dubbed "The Dream Team" when it featured stars from the NBA instead of amateur athletes. Since then other professional athletes have begun to compete, including tennis and hockey players.

Despite these changes or, as the media would claim, because of them, the Olympics continues to attract ever-larger television audiences, eager to watch the drama of the Games unfold every four years. From the ever-grander spectacle of the Opening of the Games, which provide each host country the opportunity to show off their cultural contributions to the world, to the dramatic human stories that inevitably unfold at each Olympiad, the Games are ready-made for the media. In fact, the Winter and Summer Games are no longer held during the same year so that television audiences can recover from the Olympic media saturation over a two-year period. Nonetheless, new stars continue to emerge, many of whom parlay their Olympic glory into professional opportunities and endorsements. Although ice-skaters such as Tara Lipinski and Ilya Kulik, track stars such as Michael Johnson, and downhill skiers such as Alberto Tomba and Picabo Street remain among the most popular Olympic athletes, the Games inevitably produce heroes in a variety of sports, from diver Greg Louganis to swimmer Janet Evans to freestyle mogul skier Johnny Mosely. Record-breaking performances frequently catapult athletes to worldwide fame. American swimmer Michael Phelps, who won an unprecedented eight gold medals in 2008, gained instant celebrity and a number of lucrative endorsement deals.

In the latter part of the twentieth century, the Olympics began to add new sports that appealed to younger audiences—events that emerged from the world of high-risk extreme sports. Short-track speed skating and freestyle skiing debuted in 1992, and snowboarding first appeared in the 1998 Olympics. In summer sports, mountain biking first became part of the Olympics in 1996, and motocross racing debuted in 2008. These highly popular sports contributed their share of medal-winning celebrities, such as snowboarder Shaun White (popularly known as "the Flying Tomato" because of his red hair) and short-track skater Apolo Anton Ohno.

Because the modern Olympics have become an international media event, they are inevitably subject to the pendulum swings of modern politics. From the bombing in Atlanta in 1996 to the scandal of the Salt Lake City Organizing Committee for the 2002 Winter Games, the Olympics continue to be rocked by controversy and confusion. Every year American television audiences complain about the escalating commercialization of the games and the increasingly jingoistic coverage by the networks. But each year audiences continue to come back for more. In the current media-saturated age, when so much of what the public views and reads is filled with tragedy and despair, sports in general and particularly the Olympics, which still remain largely free from the money controversies swirling around professional athletics, continue to attract audiences who crave the rare, unscripted moments of heroism, athletic prowess, physical beauty, and acts of bravery that can still be said to exemplify the best of the human condition.

Victoria Price

SEE ALSO: *Advertising; Ali, Muhammad; Boxing; Cold War; Didrikson, Babe; Dream Team; Foreman, George; Frazier, Joe; Gymnastics; Hockey; Hollywood; Johnson, Michael; Joyner, Florence Griffith; Joyner-Kersee, Jackie; Mountain Biking; Multiculturalism; National Basketball Association (NBA); Owens, Jesse; Parades; Phelps, Michael; Skating; Snowboarding; Spitz, Mark; Sports Heroes; Television; Tennis; Thorpe, Jim; Warhol, Andy; Weissmuller, Johnny; White, Shaun; World War I; World War II; World's Fairs.*

BIBLIOGRAPHY

Chronicle of the Olympics. London: Dorling Kindersley, 1998.

Guttmann, Allen. *The Olympics: A History of the Modern Games.* Urbana: University of Illinois Press, 1992.

"Olympics through Time." Foundation of the Hellenic World. Accessed March 2012. Available from http://olympics.fhw.gr

Pound, Richard W. *Inside the Olympics: A Behind-the-Scenes Look at the Politics, the Scandals, and the Glory of the Games.* Hoboken, NJ: Wiley, 2006.

Wels, Susan. *The Olympic Spirit: 100 Years of the Games.* Del Mar, CA: Tehabi Books, 1995.

Omnibus

Produced and funded by the Radio and Television Workshop of the Ford Foundation under the direction of Robert Saudek, *Omnibus* introduced Sunday afternoon and evening commercial television audiences to a wide variety of programs of cultural distinction. Hosted by Alistair Cooke, the British Broadcasting Corporation's American correspondent, the ninety-minute *Omnibus* was carried by the CBS network from 1952 to 1956; by ABC from 1956 to 1957; and by NBC from 1957 to 1959. NBC continued *Omnibus* on an irregular basis during the 1960–1961 season, and ABC revived it briefly in 1980.

Notable segments included James Agee's *Abraham Lincoln—The Early Years,* which appeared in installments during the 1952–1953 season; Orson Welles's television debut in *King Lear* in 1953; and concerts conducted by Leonard Bernstein during the 1954–1956 seasons. *Omnibus* helped establish an elite audience for programming later carried by the Public Broadcasting Service.

Paul Ashdown

SEE ALSO: *Bernstein, Leonard; Public Television (PBS); Welles, Orson.*

BIBLIOGRAPHY

Bergreen, Laurence. *James Agee: A Life.* New York: E. P. Dutton, 1984.

Clarke, Nick. *Alistair Cooke: A Biography.* New York: Arcade Publishers, 1999.

McNeil, Alex. *Total Television: A Comprehensive Guide to Programming from 1948 to the Present.* New York: Penguin Books, 1991.

On the Road

Jack Kerouac's 1957 novel is a mostly autobiographical travelogue of cross-country trips that Kerouac took during the late 1940s. *On the Road*'s characters are thinly disguised Beat luminaries, including Allen Ginsberg and William S. Burroughs. Kerouac himself acts as narrator Sal Paradise, who reflects the American fascination with road travel. Indeed, the attraction of taking to the road is expressed throughout American literature, popular culture, and twentieth-century life. Upon its release, *On the Road* fostered an alternative view of American life, preceding the counterculture of the 1960s; this unintended effect was partially responsible for Kerouac's reclusiveness during his later years.

The book covers four road trips, mainly between New York and San Francisco, with several stops in Denver and detours into Chicago, New Orleans, Virginia, and Mexico. The catalyst for the book was Neal Cassady, a mutual friend of Kerouac's and Ginsberg's, whose character is named Dean Moriarty. A fast-talking, charismatic womanizer from Denver, Cassady had a love of joyriding in stolen cars, which earned him a trip through Denver's reform schools. In *On the Road,* Sal idolizes Dean (as Kerouac idolized Cassady) as a swaggering, cowboylike man of action, describing Dean's criminality as "a wild yea-saying overburst of American joy; it was Western, the west wind, an ode from the Plains."

Kerouac's book sparked controversy by featuring the underside of American life in the 1950s: frenetic travel, hit-and-run romances, bop jazz, liquor, marijuana, all-night diners, and hitchhiking. The book begins with Sal, the novelist-to-be, who lives with his aunt in New Jersey, traveling to Denver to see Dean. This journey initiates a series of cross-country trips via car, bus, and hitchhiking. One memorable sequence finds Dean and Sal traveling east from Denver to Chicago in a Cadillac they are hired to drive. The pair make the trip in seventeen hours, leaving the car in sorry shape when they finally arrive in Chicago.

ON A ROLL

The actual writing of the book provided *On the Road* with a built-in legend. Kerouac loved promoting the story of how, in 1951, he wrote the book in three weeks, typing continuously onto a 120-foot roll of teletype paper while on Benzedrine. Although the story is true, Kerouac actually began *On the Road* in November 1948, producing several versions before the completion of his manuscript in 1951. According to Douglas Brinkley in the *Atlantic Monthly*, the teletype roll was "the outcome of a fastidious process of outlining, chapter drafting, and trimming—begun long before April of 1951."

The impetus for the continuous roll developed out of Kerouac's dissatisfaction with his early manuscripts. In excerpted diaries published in the *Atlantic Monthly*, Kerouac writes, "All along I've felt 'Road' was not enough for a full-scale effort of my feelings in prose: too thin, too hung up on unimportant characters, too unfeeling. I have the feelings but not the proper vehicle as yet." In other words, conventional prose failed to capture the exhilaration that Kerouac felt for the open road.

In 1950 he experienced an epiphany after receiving a letter from Cassady that some scholars call "The Joan Letter." A 1,000-word rambling confessional, Cassady's letter describes his visit to his hospitalized girlfriend, Joan, after her suicide attempt, including a sexual episode that requires his escape by climbing out of a window. Neal's autobiographical style "convinced Kerouac that the best way to write his own novel," writes biographer Ann Charters in *Kerouac*, "was to tell the story of his trips cross-country with Cassady as if he were writing a letter to a friend, using first-person narration." Kerouac soon outlined his style in the "Essentials of Spontaneous Prose," which were guidelines for a form that reflected the improvisational fluidity of a jazz musician: "Blow as deep as you want—write as deeply, fish as far down as you want . . . then reader cannot fail to receive telepathic shock and meaning."

CRITICS AND FANS

Published on September 5, 1957, with a second printing scheduled fifteen days later, the book was on the best-seller list for five weeks late that year. By the 1990s its sales had reached three million copies. *On the Road*'s auspicious reception was deceptive; Kerouac would later be savaged by reviewers. Upon its release *On the Road* was heralded by the *New York Times* as "an authentic work of art," but the following Sunday, in its regular review section, the newspaper panned it. Kerouac was attacked for his aesthetic philosophy: Truman Capote quipped that Kerouac's fiction was not writing but typing. Other reviewers were scandalized by the book's spotlight on characters who were drifters and misfits. The *Washington Post* dismissed *On the Road* as a chronicle of "the frantic fringe," while *Time* magazine vilified the book for its "degeneracy."

Although literature's self-appointed guardians viewed *On the Road* as a barbarian storming the gates of literature's manor, they ignored the book's deep connection to uniquely American themes. "Whenever spring comes to New York," wrote Kerouac in his misunderstood book, "I can't stand the suggestions of the land that come blowing over the river from New Jersey and I've got to go. So I went." *On the Road* recalls the Mississippi travels of Mark Twain's Tom Sawyer and Huck Finn and the fascination with the road in the poetry of Walt Whitman.

Kerouac became a precursor to the writers of the 1960s and 1970s—such as Norman Mailer, Hunter S. Thompson, and Tom Wolfe—who were active participants in the stories they covered. By the 1990s reviewers began to favorably reappraise *On the Road:* "Kerouac's work represents the most extensive experiment in language and literary form undertaken by an American writer of his generation," declared the *New York Times* in 1995. For many readers, however, the emotional response to *On the Road* will always remain foremost in their judgment. According to Charters, "No book has ever caught the feel of speeding down the broad highway in a new car, the mindless joyousness of 'joyriding' like *On the Road.*"

Daryl Umberger

SEE ALSO: *The Beat Generation; Burroughs, William S.; Capote, Truman; Ginsberg, Allen; Mailer, Norman; Thompson, Hunter S.; Twain, Mark; Wolfe, Tom.*

BIBLIOGRAPHY

Brinkley, Douglas. "In the Kerouac Archive." *Atlantic Monthly*, November 1998, 49–76.

Birkerts, Sven. "Off the Road." *New Republic*, April 24, 1995, 43–45.

Charters, Ann. *Kerouac: A Biography*. San Francisco: Straight Arrow Books, 1973.

Douglas, Ann. "On the Road Again" (review). *The Portable Jack Kerouac*, ed. Ann Charters. *New York Times*, April 9, 1995, sec. 7, 2.

Kerouac, Jack. *On the Road*. New York: New American Library, 1957.

Kerouac, Jack. "Essentials of Spontaneous Prose." *The Portable Beat Reader*, ed. Ann Charters. New York: Penguin Books, 1992.

Suiter, John. *Poets on the Peaks: Gary Snyder, Philip Whalen & Jack Kerouac in the Cascades*. New York: Counterpoint Press, 2002.

On the Waterfront

On the Waterfront (1954), a riveting drama of labor union corruption on the New York City docks, was directed by Elia Kazan and won eight Academy Awards; it has been a classic of the American cinema for more than half a century. Reasons for its enduring appeal include a taut script by Budd Schulberg, magnetic performances by an all-star cast featuring Marlon Brando, a compelling score by Leonard Bernstein, stark black-and-white photography by Boris Kaufman, and above all transcendent themes that resonate across the decades with the American experience.

The film tells the story of Terry Malloy (Brando), a dock worker and former prize fighter, who turns against the union's mob leaders, including his brother Charlie (Rod Steiger) and union boss John Friendly (Lee J. Cobb), by testifying in a federal Crime Commission investigation. Terry's inner moral struggle is inspired by the love of a good woman, Edie Doyle (Eva Marie

On the Waterfront. *Marlon Brando won an Oscar for his portrayal of ex-boxer Terry Malloy in the 1954 film* On The Waterfront. JOHN KOBAL FOUNDATION/CONTRIBUTOR/MOVIEPIX/GETTY IMAGES.

Saint), with encouragement from Father Barry (Karl Malden), who is modeled on crusading waterfront priest Father John Corrigan.

Brando brings complexity to his portrayal of the confused prize fighter, striving for decency and dignity despite pressure from his brother to keep silent about the union's criminal activities. The Oscar-winning performance is one of Brando's most memorable, conveying the subtle emotions of a simple man enmeshed by irresistible forces.

CULTURAL CONTEXT

The movie reflects the historical conditions of the 1950s in subject matter and theme. Author Budd Schulberg (*What Makes Sammy Run*) based the screenplay on a newspaper exposé of labor conditions on the New York waterfront. Men jostled for work every morning in the infamous "shape up," forming a horseshoe around foremen and vying for favors. This degrading system thrived on nepotism and violence. *On the Waterfront*'s realistic subject matter, captured by moody black-and-white photography and a score with harsh jazz elements, places the film in an emergent realist genre of filmmaking that was turning away from the light musicals and romantic comedies of the 1930s and 1940s to dramas about social problems, including Kazan's earlier treatments of anti-Semitism (*Gentleman's Agreement*, 1947) and racism (*Pinky*, 1949).

The film's theme rationalizes Kazan's appearance as a friendly witness before the House Committee on Un-American Activities (HUAC). Kazan renounced his involvement in the Communist Party and gave up the names of Hollywood "fellow travelers." The hearings reflected a fierce ideological struggle: a political movement that had held enormous intellectual appeal during the hard times of the Depression came under suspicion due to Cold War fears about Communist Russian aggression and nuclear proliferation. The HUAC inquisition ruined careers, divided friends, and sent ten well-known directors and writers to prison for refusing to cooperate. Malloy, in the words of Peter Biskind, "is the informer as hero." Terry's renunciation of his union "family," personified by his brother Charlie, valorizes Kazan's decision (also that of Schulberg) as the film sorts through issues of loyalty to family and friends versus duty to one's country—silence versus informing.

The film remains a favorite long after waterfront corruption and the HUAC investigations have faded from fans' minds, because it captures cultural concerns that transcend 1954 realities. In addition to the perennial dilemmas people confront in negotiating issues of personal versus national loyalty and silence versus honesty, the story embodies the heroic American vision of the good individual struggling against dehumanizing civilization, moral redemption, the Cain and Abel parable, and the frustration of personal failure when confronted with the forces of mass society.

PLOT SUMMARY

Terry is a hero in the American tradition of rugged individualism, exemplified by the cowboy who rides into town, fights the outlaws, saves corrupt society from itself, and then rides off into the sunset. After testifying against the mob, Terry reclaims his job in a dramatic fight. He takes a beating from mob goons and then dispatches Friendly into the river. Terry restores order to the longshore community as he, battered like a crucified Jesus, leads the men back to work at the urging of Father Barry. It is an ambiguous ending, critics have argued, as the huge warehouse doors close on Terry's back, suggesting entrapment in the processes of mass society as much as triumphant resolution.

Terry's decision to testify exacts a high price. He nearly loses the love of Edie when he reveals he played an unwitting role in the mob murder of her brother, Joey, who is killed to prevent his appearance before the Crime Commission. The plot creates a situation where "informing on criminal associates is the only honorable course of action for a just man," Biskind writes, and it is the only way that Terry can redeem himself in his own eyes and in those of Edie and his fellow dock workers.

Terry also pays for his choice when the mob kills his brother, Charlie, a variation on the ancient Cain and Abel theme. This exploration of fraternal conflict provides the set piece of the movie. In a scene filmed in the tight confines of the backseat of a car that allows no escape, Terry and Charlie come to grips with their relationship with virtuoso performances by Brando and Steiger. Terry condemns Charlie for asking him to throw a fight, ending his chance at the title. Hemmed in by the imposing forces of corrupt civilization and family pressure, Terry settles for "a couple of bucks and a one-way ticket to Palookaville. It was you, Charlie. You was my brother. You should have looked out for me instead of making me take them dives for the short end money."

When Charlie demurs, Terry continues with the words that are most closely identified with the film: "You don't understand! I could've been a contender. I could've had class and been somebody." As spoken by Brando, the words have become a hackneyed cultural emblem of the film yet remain a poignant cry of the little guy overwhelmed by the forces of family and mass society. They also express a cultural excuse for stifled ambition and dreams gone sour that places blame outside the self. Terry's words remain as timely and apt as when they first impressed audiences in 1954.

E. M. I. Sefcovic

SEE ALSO: *Academy Awards; Bernstein, Leonard; Brando, Marlon; Communism; Labor Unions.*

BIBLIOGRAPHY

Anderson, Lindsay. "The Last Sequence of 'On the Waterfront.'" *Sight and Sound* 24, no. 3 (1955): 127–130.

Biskind, Peter. "The Politics of Power in 'On the Waterfront.'" *Film Quarterly* 29, no. 1 (1975): 25–38.

Kael, Pauline. "The Glamour of Delinquency." *I Lost It at the Movies*. Boston: Little, Brown, 1965.

Kitses, Jim. "Elia Kazan: A Structural Analysis." *Cinema* 7, no. 3 (1972–1973): 25–36.

Maland, Charles J. "'On the Waterfront' (1954): Film and the Dilemmas of American Liberalism in the McCarthy Era." *American Studies in Scandinavia* 14, no. 2 (1982), 107–127.

"*On the Waterfront:* A Defence and Some Letters." *Sight and Sound* 24, no. 4 (1955): 214–216.

Schulberg, Budd. *What Makes Sammy Run?*. New York: Vintage Books, 1990.

Stead, Peter. "The Post-War Age of Anxiety." *Film and Working Class*. London: Routledge, 1989.

Walker, John, ed. *Halliwell's Film and Video Guide 1998*. New York: Harper Perennial, 1997.

Onassis, Jacqueline Lee Bouvier Kennedy *(1929–1994)*

Jacqueline Lee Bouvier Kennedy Onassis, wife of President John F. Kennedy, captivated the world as she evolved from political wife to widow to pop-culture icon and became famous in her own right as Jackie O. Jacqueline was complex, creative, elegant, intelligent, and ambitious, qualities that endeared her to many and that ensured her a place among twentieth-century American celebrities.

Jacqueline was born to wealthy parents, John (Black Jack) Vernou Bouvier III and Janet Lee, in Southampton, New York, on July 28, 1929. Her parents divorced in 1940, but her mother married wealthy Hugh Dudley Auchincloss, which permitted Jacqueline and her sister, Lee, to live on in wealth and privilege. In 1947 she was dubbed "debutante of the year" and was the toast of East Coast society. She was educated at Vassar College, studied one year in France at the University of Grenoble and the Sorbonne, and graduated with a BA from George Washington University.

Jacqueline met John F. Kennedy in 1951 while working as a photographer for the *Washington Times Herald*. They married September 12, 1953, at St. Mary's Church in Newport, Rhode Island. She was a dutiful but stylish political wife whose celebrity status began when she became First Lady.

Jacqueline's White House days are remembered for her efforts at restoration and her impact on foreign dignitaries. In 1962 she gave a televised tour of the progress of restoring the White House. As First Lady she presented herself with an image of grace and charm. She set fashion trends, most notably with the little pillbox hats she wore during her White House days. A favorite of artists among many genres, she was written into songs, discotheques were named for her, and Andy Warhol painted her portrait in a famous pop-art series.

Jacqueline led the nation through the grief of President Kennedy's assassination with incredible composure and with an astute eye to history. She stood by in a bloodstained suit as President Lyndon Johnson was sworn in on November 22, 1963. She planned the funeral pageantry; she appeared as a widow, dressed in black, with her children by her side. As a final tribute, she requested the eternal flame that burns at President Kennedy's grave site.

Interestingly, *Camelot*, the 1960 musical based on King Arthur and his court, influenced Jacqueline and the Kennedy presidency. In 1995 the John F. Kennedy Library in Boston released the secret "Camelot Papers," notes from Jacqueline's interview with author Theodore H. White a week after President Kennedy was assassinated. William Langley of the *Sunday Telegraph* reports that Jacqueline worked to identify Kennedy's 1,000-day administration of youth and good fortune with *Camelot*.

Jacqueline transformed from the fairy-tale widow of a fallen president into a global celebrity after her marriage to Aristotle Onassis, the Greek shipping tycoon, in 1968. When Onassis died in 1975, she went to court to get the $26 million that she said he would will her. She later found a companion in a third wealthy individual, diamond merchant Maurice Tempelsman, who was married. Tempelsman quadrupled her fortune to an estimated $200 million.

Jacqueline was a good mother to her children: Caroline, born November 27, 1957, and John Jr., born November 25, 1960. John Jr. died in July 1999 when a plane he was piloting crashed. A third child, Patrick Bouvier, was born on August 7, 1963, and the nation mourned with her when he died two days later. Jacqueline developed an identity apart from Kennedy and Onassis when she began a career as a book editor, first at Viking Press in 1975 and later at Doubleday in 1978. A wealthy woman, she did not have to work, and yet she held her job at Doubleday until her death. Jacqueline died of non-Hodgkin's lymphoma at the age of sixty-four on May 19, 1994.

Jacqueline was a firm believer in her right to privacy, but her fame coincided with a tremendous growth of media that made her personal struggle for seclusion more difficult; more than twenty-five unauthorized biographies have been written about her. In death, as in life, Jacqueline cherished her privacy. She left behind 1964 audio recordings of her interviews with Arthur Schlesinger Jr. about her life with Kennedy. The tapes were sealed for fifty years, but after forty-seven years, in 2011, Caroline released them in conjunction with the fiftieth anniversary of the Kennedy administration. The interviews she gave to William Manchester for his book, *The Death of a President*, she had sealed for 100 years, until 2067. Although she remains a private person, her historical sense of ceremony and dignity not only helped preserve a young assassinated president in the nation's memory but also reserved for her a place in American history.

Rosemarie Skaine

SEE ALSO: Camelot; *Celebrity; Debutantes; Kennedy Assassination.*

BIBLIOGRAPHY

Andersen, Christopher P. *Jack and Jackie: Portrait of an American Marriage.* New York: William Morrow, 1996.

Bond, Alma H. *Jackie O: On the Couch: Inside the Mind and Life of Jackie Kennedy Onassis.* Baltimore, MD: Bancroft Press, 2011.

Heymann, C. David. *A Woman Named Jackie.* New York: L. Stuart, 1989.

Kelley, Kitty. *Jackie Oh!* Secaucus, NJ: L. Stuart, 1978.

Kennedy, Caroline, ed. *The Best Loved Poems of Jacqueline Kennedy-Onassis.* New York: Hyperion, 2001.

Kennedy, Caroline, and Michael Beschloss. *Jacqueline Kennedy: Historic Conversations on Life with John F. Kennedy.* New York: Hyperion, 2011.

Klein, Edward. *All Too Human: The Love Story of Jack and Jackie Kennedy.* New York: Pocket Books, Simon & Schuster, 1996.

Langley, William. "How Grief of Jackie Gave Birth to Camelot Revealed: Interview That Launched JFK Legend." *Sunday Telegraph,* May 28, 1995, 26.

Raatma, Lucia. *Jacqueline Kennedy.* North Mankato, MN: Coughlan Publishing, 2011.

Robinson, John. "Jacqueline Onassis Is Dead; Cancer Claims Her at Age 64; Children at Side." *Boston Globe,* May 20, 1994.

One Day at a Time

American television producer Norman Lear's situation comedy *One Day at a Time* (1975–1984) explores the life of a liberated divorcée who takes back her maiden name and finds success without a husband. Ann Romano (Bonnie Franklin) marries too young, divorces her husband, and takes her two teenage daughters, who keep their father's name, from suburban Logansport to a tiny apartment in the big city of Indianapolis. The older daughter, seventeen-year-old Julie (Mackenzie Phillips), is stubborn, headstrong, and impetuous. Her sister, fifteen-year-old wisecracking Barbara (Valerie Bertinelli), is basically a good girl. The girls have all the dating and school problems of most teenagers but live with only one parent, the feisty Ann, who has gone from her parents' to her husband's house and is now finally on her own.

Though developed by Lear, *One Day at a Time* was created by Allan Manings and Whitney Blake, who had been a regular on the TV series *Hazel.* Originally called *All about Us,* the show became almost notorious for the casting of pert, freckle-faced, redhead Franklin as a hot-tempered Italian woman. Like all Lear comedies, *One Day at a Time* tackles serious contemporary issues. The show focuses on these issues and how they play out in an unconventional family structure.

Many episodes focus on Ann's, Julie's, and Barbara's relationships with men. For example, the building superintendent, mustachioed Dwayne Schneider (Pat Harrington Jr.), who fancies himself Don Juan with a passkey, soon develops a strong platonic relationship with Ann and becomes a sort of uncle to the kids. Ann's romantic life also features predominantly. First she dates her divorce lawyer, a younger man named David Kane (Richard Masur). She later incorporates partner and lover Nick Handris (Ron Rifkin) and his ten-year-old son, Alex (Glenn Scarpelli), into her life. Nick soon leaves the show, and—in one of the more contrived plot twists—Ann raises Alex even though his real mother is still alive.

As youths, Julie runs away with her boyfriend, and Barbara tries to shed her good-girl image by running off with a platonic friend. As the series continued, Bertinelli's character made her a teen star at a time when actresses Jodie Foster and Tatum O'Neal also played all-American tomboys. In 1981, when Bertinelli married rock musician Eddie Van Halen, CBS tried to keep it a secret, worrying that it would tarnish "Barbara's" image as the little sister or girlfriend everyone wanted. But on the show Barbara soon grows old enough to marry dental student Mark Royer (Boyd Gaines).

After the series ended, Bertinelli enjoyed success making made-for-television movies and became a miniseries regular. Phillips, daughter of the 1960s folk rock group the Mamas and the Papas leader John Phillips, developed chronic drug problems that forced *One Day at a Time*'s writers the unenviable job of coming up with reasons for the now-skeletal and bug-eyed Julie to leave and return, culminating toward the end of the series with the character abandoning her husband Max (Michael Lembeck) and infant daughter.

One Day at a Time held a unique position in television as one of the first shows to feature a mother who has chosen to be single. Ann is not widowed, and her ex-husband, Ed (the occasionally seen Joseph Campanella), is not an adultering lout. Ann and Ed simply did not have a happy marriage. Ann was also TV's first prominent "Ms." One of Ann's bosses makes a big deal out of calling her "M.S. Romano," and the television audience identified with the down-home woman trying to lead a successful life sans partner. Ann's coworker—and later business partner—Francine Webster (Shelley Fabares) represents a more strident version of a liberated woman. Unlike Ann, Francine is calculating, manipulative, and sexual.

One Day at a Time did not conclude with a cancellation; it was ended when Franklin and Bertinelli decided not to return for another season. By the last season, Ann becomes a successful advertising executive, remarries (her son-in-law Mark's father), and moves to London after receiving a great job offer. Julie is gone, and Barbara and her husband are starting a new life.

Karen Lurie

SEE ALSO: *Divorce; Foster, Jodie; Lear, Norman; The Mamas and the Papas; Sitcom; Television; Van Halen.*

BIBLIOGRAPHY

Brooks, Tim, and Earle Marsh. *The Complete Directory to Prime Time Network and Cable TV Shows 1946–Present.* New York: Ballantine Books, 1995.

Campbell, Sean. *The Sitcoms of Norman Lear.* Jefferson, NC: McFarland, 2007.

McNeil, Alex. *Total Television: The Comprehensive Guide to Programming from 1948 to the Present.* New York: Penguin, 1996.

One Flew over the Cuckoo's Nest

Ken Kesey's first and best-known novel, *One Flew over the Cuckoo's Nest* (1962), the story of an unlikely redeemer who triumphs over the authoritarian "Combine" run by Big Nurse Ratched, became the credo of an entire generation of rebels; in the decades that followed, it continued to command the interest of new generations of readers with its comedic virtuosity.

THE INSPIRATION FOR *CUCKOO'S NEST*

The novel's genesis seems to confirm Kesey's belief that life is a form of art. As a graduate student at Stanford University in the late 1950s, Kesey learned from a fellow student about experiments with "psychomimetic" drugs at the Veteran's Hospital in Menlo Park and volunteered to be a paid subject. Kesey—by his own admission in *Kesey's Garage Sale* (1973) "a jock, never even been drunk but that one night in my frat house before my wedding"—began taking government-administered LSD and other hallucinogens. When the original drug experiments ended, Kesey accepted a job as night attendant on the psychiatric unit at Menlo Park, where his access to the patients' medicines and the long stretches of time between ward checks led him to abandon his novel-in-progress about San Francisco's North Beach and to undertake a new work, about the plight of asylum inmates who defiantly assert their humanity against overwhelming forces.

Kesey claimed that peyote was the inspiration for the character of Chief Bromden, whose highly subjective and often hallucinatory first-person narration gives *Cuckoo's Nest* its metaphoric richness, its peculiar horror, and ultimately its emotional force. Chief, a hulking giant who survived not only the horrors of World War II but also the asylum's 200 or more electroshock therapy treatments, has been emasculated and dehumanized by Big Nurse and the Combine. Reduced to an object of ridicule by the orderlies, who call him Chief Broom, Chief withdraws into a voluntary muteness. Only with the help of the newly admitted con man Randle Patrick ("Mack") McMurphy, who draws all of the inmates into his game of wits with Big Nurse, is Chief able to find his way back from "the fog," rediscover his manhood, and ultimately escape the hospital's confines to return to the world of nature he had left behind.

McMurphy is like the Grail Knight who restores life to the wasteland; his eccentric behavior brings laughter to the ward and serves as a liberating countertherapy to Ratched's regimen of silence and fear, just as the friendly touch of his big hand, the opposite of Ratched's icy mothering, helps the men to regain their potency. In the asylum and on a day-long fishing trip, Mack forces them to appreciate the importance of solidarity and to exercise their new strength. Ratched, of course, recognizes the radical threat to her authority that McMurphy poses; in an act of symbolic castration, she arranges to have him lobotomized. But McMurphy's self-sacrifice only further empowers the inmates, who rebel against her tyranny and ultimately break out—or sign themselves out—of the hospital, leaving her powerless over them.

CUCKOO'S NEST ON THE BIG SCREEN

Recognizing the tremendous cinematic potential of such a popular novel, actor Kirk Douglas bought the rights from Kesey in 1962 for $18,000. Douglas, who had played McMurphy in Dale Wasserman's theatrical adaptation of *Cuckoo's Nest* (which ran briefly and unsuccessfully in late 1963 at the Cort Theatre in New York), originally intended to recreate the role on film himself. After numerous delays, however, he turned the rights over to his son, Michael Douglas, who co-produced the film with Saul Zaentz in 1975. Directed by Milos Forman and starring Jack Nicholson as McMurphy and Louise Fletcher as Ratched, with Brad Dourif (Billy Bibbit), Sydney Lassick (Cheswick), Scatman Crothers (Turkle), and Danny DeVito (Martini) in supporting roles, the film proved to be a commercial and critical success, sweeping all four of the major Academy Awards—best picture, best director, best actor, and best actress—as well as winning the Oscar for best screenplay adapted from another medium. Remarkably, it was the first film since *It Happened One Night* (1934) to win the "Big Four" awards.

Kesey, originally hired to write the screenplay and then fired, successfully sued over the use of his name in the final version. He was particularly displeased with the handling of the character of Chief. Unlike the producers, who wanted a realistic depiction of institutional life (even to the point of casting a real psychiatrist as Dr. Spivey and several inmates as patients in minor roles), Kesey felt that the film needed Bromden's hallucinatory point of view. Indeed, contrary to Kesey's vision, the film's Bromden (Will Sampson) appears as a figure of lesser importance than McMurphy, and the Combine is never mentioned at all. Similarly, on film Ratched is far less monstrous than her counterpart in the novel; an attractive woman (albeit with a hairstyle suggesting two devil's horns) who is contemporary in age to McMurphy, she loses much of her mythic stature and at times seems more misguided than malicious and machinelike.

Forman's departures from the novel, however, are often as artistic as they are original. By moving some of the novel's ward scenes outdoors, he establishes a keen visual contrast between the claustrophobia of the institution and the freedom just beyond its walls. And his recurring use of windows, including the dark television set that reflects the inmates' mounting insubordination, heightens the impact of Chief's escape at the film's end. Above all, Nicholson's brilliant depiction of McMurphy brings Kesey's manic, mythic hero to life.

Barbara Tepa Lupack

SEE ALSO: *Academy Awards; Kesey, Ken; Nicholson, Jack.*

BIBLIOGRAPHY

Christensen, Mark. *Acid Christ: Ken Kesey, LSD and the Politics of Ecstasy*. Tucson, AZ: Schaffner Press, 2010.

Leeds, Barry H. *Ken Kesey*. New York: Ungar, 1981.

Lupack, Barbara Tepa. *Insanity as Redemption in Contemporary American Fiction: Inmates Running the Asylum*. Gainesville: University Press of Florida, 1995.

Porter, M. Gilbert. *The Art of Grit: Ken Kesey's Fiction*. Columbia: University of Missouri Press, 1982.

Pratt, John C., ed. *One Flew over the Cuckoo's Nest: Text and Criticism*. New York: Viking, 1973.

Tanner, Stephen L. *Ken Kesey*. Boston: Twayne, 1983.

One Man's Family

One Man's Family (1932–1959) was the granddaddy of a radio broadcasting genre that decades later was dubbed the "prime-time soap." It was also arguably its era's most realistic portrayal of American family life. True, the fictional Barbour family saw its share of psychotic maniacs, international intrigue, and even a case of amnesia as the years passed, but even the silliest plots were enacted with a sense of depth and history that eluded most of the series' contemporaries. Writer-director Carlton E. Morse remained the series' guiding hand for its entire twenty-seven-year run; the same actors portrayed the key roles for years, even decades. And the stories they enacted faced head-on the realities of the day: war, death, the changing roles of gender, and generational transitions. The result was a series whose integrity, consistency, and sense of reality left it unparalleled in the history of broadcasting.

Patriarch Henry Barbour was, even in middle age, a curmudgeon: conservative, bullheaded, frequently wrong but never in doubt. Henry's wife, Fanny, suffered his tirades and flights of fancy, frequently with an exasperated cry of "That man!" Henry had no shortage of complaints; his own children seemed determined—if not destined—to make his life miserable. Eldest son Paul, a pilot, had been crippled in action in World War I; his ambivalence bordered on a bitterness that his father would not abide. Hazel, the oldest Barbour daughter, was cut straight from her mother's cloth: a sensible, straitlaced girl who seemed particularly stodgy in comparison with the other Barbour daughter, Claudia, who along with twin brother, Cliff, made up the least well-adjusted segment of the Barbour household. Cliff was a free spirit whose lack of ambition drove his father to distraction; Claudia was a spitfire, an uninhibited rebel whose antics led to trouble even in the series' opening episode on April 29, 1932. The youngest Barbour was Jack, a high-spirited teen when the series began.

The series was first broadcast weekly from San Francisco to a limited network of NBC's West Coast affiliates. The series struck an immediate chord, proving so popular that it soon attracted a sponsor and was picked up for the full NBC network. Production moved to Los Angeles at mid-decade, and by 1940 *One Man's Family* stood near the top of the weekly ratings chart, its audience share approaching those of Jack Benny and Bob Hope. The series' fans, meanwhile, were unusually loyal—and outspoken; a 1935 sponsorship deal with a cigarette company was quickly nixed when listeners protested against their wholesome family drama being bankrolled by such a nasty product.

The serial proceeded in top form as the Great Depression gave way to World War II, its huge audience following every Barbour trial and tribulation: romances, marriages, pregnancies, and the sudden deaths of many of the Barbour children's spouses. The family was also known for its fertility—Hazel gave birth to twins early in the series; some years later, Jack's wife, Betty, bore a set of triplets. The series suffered its share of wartime loss. When actress Kathleen Wilson (Claudia) got married and left the series in 1943, Morse shocked his audience by making the character a casualty of war: Claudia and two of her children were sent to the bottom of the ocean when Nazis torpedoed their ocean liner. Claudia's husband was also killed in action.

Actress Winifred Wolfe (who played Paul's adopted daughter Teddy) left in 1945, also to get married; her character was written out and eventually became an army nurse. When actor Page Gilman entered the service, his character, Jack, followed suit. For much of the war, Jack appeared periodically whenever Gilman was on leave; actor and character disappeared completely when Gilman shipped out for the Pacific in May 1945. Jack's good-bye to his family stands arguably as not only the finest episode of this series, but possibly the most wrenching, true-to-life, dramatic radio presentation of the entire war.

By 1945 the series was an institution. Gilman's Jack returned from the service, and the Claudia character returned, too—from the dead—and was portrayed by actress Barbara Fuller, with the explanation that Claudia had survived her ocean ordeal and had spent two years in a Nazi concentration camp. When longtime sponsor Standard Brands abruptly dropped the series in early 1949, 75,000 fans flooded NBC with letters begging the network to keep the Barbours on the air, and NBC decided to continue running the show; Miles Laboratories picked it up in 1950. That June, in a risky but successful move, the series ended its eighteen-year weekly run and shifted into a nightly fifteen-minute format that within a year dominated its time period.

With the aging of the original children—and the unexpected death of actor Barton Yarborough (Cliff) in December 1951—the second generation of Barbours moved to the forefront of the narrative: the trials of Joan, Pinky, Hank, Penelope, and Teddy carried the series through much of its final decade. The show moved to an afternoon time slot in July 1955. NBC unexpectedly canceled the series in 1959, so abruptly that the cast had already recorded what turned out to be the show's final episodes. The show simply ended in mid-story on May 8, 1959.

Chris Chandler

SEE ALSO: *Benny, Jack; The Great Depression; Hope, Bob; Morse, Carlton E.; Radio; Radio Drama; Soap Operas; World War I; World War II.*

BIBLIOGRAPHY

Dunning, John. *On the Air: The Encyclopedia of Old-Time Radio*. New York: Oxford University Press, 1998.

Morse, Carlton E. *The "One Man's Family" Album*. Woodside, CA: Seven Stones Press, 1988.

Starr, Kevin. *The Dream Endures: California Enters the 1940s*. New York: Oxford University Press, 2002.

O'Neal, Shaquille *(1972–)*

At the close of the twentieth century, celebrities began to be used in the multimedia marketing of products. Shaquille O'Neal, or "Shaq," was one of the pioneers in this area. A star basketball player for the Orlando Magic and the Los Angeles Lakers, O'Neal quickly branched out into motion pictures and popular music. He also attached his name to children's toys, video game cameos, clothing, and basketball shoes. A star of the court, television, radio, music video, and screen, O'Neal's 7-foot presence has been felt across the commercial spectrum, epitomizing changes in the sports industry.

EARLY YEARS

On March 6, 1972, Shaquille Rashaun O'Neal was born in Newark, New Jersey. His biological father left the family, and O'Neal's mother and stepfather, a U.S. Army sergeant, raised O'Neal in Germany, New Jersey, and Georgia before settling in

San Antonio, Texas, offering an abundance of food and discipline along the way. After high school in Texas, O'Neal set off to Louisiana State University (LSU) and stardom. After his freshman year in college, he thundered into national prominence. He was named national player of the year by AP and UPI in 1991 and was a unanimous first team All-American in 1991 and 1992. His size and power sometimes drew three defenders, leaving teammates unguarded. But even with O'Neal, LSU was unable to go far in the NCAA championship tournament.

O'Neal left college after his junior year and was the first pick of the fledgling expansion-team Orlando Magic, then in its third year, in the 1992 National Basketball Association (NBA) draft. He had an instant impact in the league and was the 1993 NBA Rookie of the Year, averaging 23.4 points per game and 13.9 rebounds per game. At 7 feet, 1 inch and 300 pounds, O'Neal's size, strength, and athleticism were unmatched, and his trademark "Shaq Attaq" was a dunk few players could stop. His greatest weakness, however, was his free-throw shooting, thus many teams would foul him in order to keep his offense contained. Off the court, O'Neal pursued a rap career and in 1993 released his first rap album *Shaq Diesel*, which went double platinum despite lack of critical acclaim.

Shaquille O'Neal. *Shaquille O'Neal signs copies of his autobiography* Shaq Uncut *at a bookstore in 2011.* VALLERY JEAN/ CONTRIBUTOR/FILMMAGIC/GETTY IMAGES.

The following year the Magic drafted Anfernee "Penny" Hardaway, and the Shaq-Penny combination got the team to the play-offs for the first time. The two would also team up off court, playing basketball players in the Nick Nolte film *Blue Chips* (1994). In 1995 the Magic made the play-offs again and won the Eastern Conference to reach the NBA finals, but they were then swept (4–0) by Hakeem Olajuwon and the Houston Rockets. Throughout his time with Orlando, O'Neal repeatedly made the All-Star team, and his star continued to rise. As a member of the so-called Dream Team in 1996, he helped the team win Olympic gold. Many critics, however, did not consider him one of basketball's great players. When he was named to the NBA's Fifty Greatest Players after his fourth year in the NBA, many critics questioned his worthiness. Yet his basketball abilities were surely more credible than his acting skills; his role as a rapping genie in 1996's *Kazaam* was a box-office flop. O'Neal's follow-up appearance in *Steel* (1997) was equally unimpressive.

THE MOVE TO L.A.

When O'Neal's contract with Orlando expired, he attracted the largest NBA contract in history. He rejected a larger offer from Orlando and signed with the Los Angeles Lakers for $120 million. O'Neal's decision was based partially on the allure of the Lakers' championship tradition and partially by the close proximity to Hollywood. Whatever additional millions Orlando offered could not be matched by the prospects of show business. O'Neal's move to Los Angeles reflected the evolving merger of sports with other entertainment industries. By becoming a Laker, O'Neal hoped to cash in on his larger-than-life (and larger-than-court) status. He had many product endorsement deals, as well as his own clothing line. His debut with the Lakers coincided with the release of his third rap album, featuring a collaboration with the Notorious B.I.G., who was killed four months later.

O'Neal's salary, unthinkable only ten years earlier, showed the value of a marquee name: a player of O'Neal's status had the power to drive television ratings, ticket prices, "luxury box" seating sales, corporate sponsorships, and even public financing of arenas. Although quality players were perceived as valuable by any team, none drew as much attention as a quality player with a name-brand persona. Where city rivalries and team names once clashed, a new merchandising ethic promoted a contest of star players. For example, what was once advertised as a game between Los Angeles and New York became a battle between Shaq and Patrick Ewing. More than ever before, profit became the name of the game, and profit became linked to charismatic players. In the new era of player as product, O'Neal was at center stage.

Kobe Bryant joined O'Neal on the Lakers in 1996. At the time Bryant was eighteen years old and had just graduated from Lower Merion High School, a private academy in the Philadelphia area. In their first year together, the Lakers won fifty-six games and made the play-offs, advancing to the second round before being eliminated by the Utah Jazz. The following season was similarly frustrating with a solid season ending in a third round play-off loss to the Jazz. A third consecutive play-off appearance the next year ended in a second-round loss to the San Antonio Spurs.

O'Neal and the Lakers' fortunes began to change in 1999 when Phil Jackson accepted the job as the Lakers' new head coach. Instituting the triangle offense that had worked so well in Chicago, Jackson immediately brought O'Neal's play to another level. O'Neal won the regular season MVP, finishing first in scoring, second in rebounds, and third in blocked shots. Play-off success came as well. The Lakers won three consecutive championships in 2000, 2001, and 2002; O'Neal was named MVP of the finals all three years. In 2000 he also fulfilled a promise to his mother, finally finishing his BA at LSU.

LATER CAREER

Things were not going as well in the locker room as on the court, however, and O'Neal and Bryant's off-court feuding began to affect team chemistry. The 2003 and 2004 seasons were rocky due to O'Neal's lingering toe injury as the team missed the finals in 2003 and lost the championship to the Pistons in 2004. When Jackson left the team, O'Neal did as well, and he promised his new team, the Miami Heat, a championship. He was not able to fulfill that promise during his first two seasons, but after Pat Riley arrived as coach and forced O'Neal to play fewer minutes throughout the regular season, the Heat won the championship in 2006, O'Neal's fourth title in seven seasons.

Off the court, O'Neal was planning for the future, receiving an MBA from the University of Phoenix in 2005. He was also the subject of a reality show on ESPN that year, *Shaquille*, which followed him throughout the season. O'Neal went on to produce *Shaq's Big Challenge* (2007), where he helped Florida kids lose weight and exercise.

On the basketball court, however, O'Neal began to struggle with injuries, ending his streak of All-Star appearances, and his next several seasons were disappointing as he moved from team to team in a series of trades. He spent two seasons with Phoenix, one with Cleveland, and one with Boston before retiring on June 1, 2011, at age thirty-nine. He was an All-Star in fifteen of his nineteen total seasons and finished his career at fifth all-time for points scored and field goals, seventh all-time for blocks, and twelfth all-time for rebounds.

POST-BASKETBALL CELEBRITY LIFE

In July 2011 O'Neal announced that he had signed a multiyear deal as an analyst for TNT, joining fellow NBA veteran Charles Barkley on *Inside the NBA*. In addition to his ESPN duties, he hosted awards shows, directed PSA commercials, served as a reserve police officer, supported charities such as Nothing but Net's fight against malaria, and tried to bring an NBA team (back) to New Jersey after the Nets moved to Brooklyn. O'Neal also began pursuing his Doctor of Education degree in human resource development at Barry University in Miami. He published his autobiography, *Shaq Uncut* (2011), in which he discusses his basketball career, Riley's campaign against O'Neal's body fat levels, and his beef with Bryant. In the memoir O'Neal accepts blame for the dissolution of his seven-year marriage to Shaunie Nelson.

Dylan Clark

SEE ALSO: *Barkley, Charles; Basketball; The Boston Celtics; The Chicago Bulls; ESPN; Hip-Hop; The Los Angeles Lakers; National Basketball Association (NBA); National Collegiate Athletic Association (NCAA); Reality Television; Riley, Pat; Sports Heroes.*

BIBLIOGRAPHY

Gorman, Jerry; Kirk Calhoun; and Skip Rozin. *The Name of the Game: The Business of Sports*. New York: John Wiley & Sons, 1994.

Lupica, Mike. *Mad as Hell*. New York: G. P. Putnam, 1996.

O'Neal, Shaquille, and Jackie MacMullan. *Shaq Uncut: My Story*. New York: Grand Central, 2011.

Smith, Eric L. "Negotiating the Deals." *Black Enterprise*, July 1995, 94.

O'Neill, Eugene *(1888–1953)*

Four times the winner of a Pulitzer Prize and the Nobel laureate for Literature in 1936, New York–born Eugene O'Neill is a towering, groundbreaking figure in American dramatic literature. The son of actor James O'Neill and a drug-addicted mother, he recorded his tormented upbringing in a dysfunctional family with lacerating honesty in his autobiographical play *Long Day's Journey into Night*. The work allows for a tour de force of acting and is often revived on both sides of the Atlantic and beyond. O'Neill ordered it withheld from production for fifty years, but in 1956 his widow released the play to Jose Quintero and it received its first staging in New York.

O'Neill traveled the globe aboard tramp steamers, and his experiences formed the basis for several of his plays. Many of them are extremely long—running typically four or five hours on stage—and tend to feature marathon monologues and profound themes touching on the human condition. A number have been filmed, but the only popular success among these was *Anna Christie* (1930), the film in which Greta Garbo first spoke on screen.

Robyn Karney

SEE ALSO: *Broadway; Garbo, Greta.*

BIBLIOGRAPHY

Gelb, Arthur, and Barbara Gelb. *O'Neill*. New York: Harper, 1962.

Griffiths, Trevor R., and Carol Woddis. *Bloomsbury Theatre Guide*. London: Bloomsbury Publishing, 1988.

Krasner, David. *A Companion to Twentieth-Century American Drama*. Malden, MA: Blackwell Publishing, 2005.

Sheaffer, Louis. *O'Neill, Son and Artist*. London: Elek Books, 1974.

The Onion

Those who prefer their facts straight will want to know that the *Onion* was founded in 1988 as a satirical newspaper by University of Wisconsin juniors Tim Keck and Chris Johnson. According to Keck and Johnson, the name for the paper was suggested to them by Johnson's uncle when he saw the pair eating onion sandwiches. Maybe this is true, maybe not. People are not encouraged to take anything that comes from the *Onion* franchise at face value. For example, the "official" company history states that German immigrant Friedrich Siegfried Zweibel (*zweibel* is German for "onion") founded the newspaper in 1756 with the name *Mercantile Onion* because those were the only English words he knew. Friedrich ran the paper for 140 years until his death in 1896, at which point his twenty-year-old great-grandson, T. Herman Zweibel, took over as editor, holding the post until he left the earth in 2001. T. Herman currently serves as publisher emeritus.

The Onion. *Copies of the print version of* The Onion *are stacked in a news rack in San Francisco, California.* JUSTIN SULLIVAN/GETTY IMAGES.

ONION ROOTS

The Onion began as a weekly print publication that targeted the local student population and gradually acquired a loyal readership in cities such as Madison and Milwaukee in Wisconsin and Chicago. In 1996, with the launch of its website, the *Onion* reached a national audience and has continued to grow through the early part of the twenty-first century. In 2010 it partnered with the *Wisconsin State Journal*, the *Austin American-Statesman*, the *St. Paul Pioneer Press*, and the *Denver Post*, each of which manages local distribution of the paper in its respective area. As of 2012 the paper was distributed for free in more than ten US cities and Toronto. The print edition has failed, however, in several major American markets, including Los Angeles, San Francisco, and Philadelphia, due to an inability to raise advertising revenue. It is also likely that the success of the website, which is updated daily and draws more than 7.5 million unique visitors and forty million page views per month, makes the print edition less relevant.

The Onion franchise also includes radio spots, mobile apps, and a host of books archiving old material. The most notable of these is *Our Dumb Century* (1999), the *Onion*'s first bound volume, which offers a comical retrospective of the previous century compiled on pages that are laid out like a newspaper. A headline from Monday, January 1, 1900, for example, reads, "Death-by-Corset Rates Stabilize at One in Six."

In 2007 the *Onion* began broadcasting video news segments from its website that parodied the coverage on twenty-four-hour news networks such as Fox News and CNN. The venture, called the *Onion News Network*, eventually grew into a full twenty-two-minute mock news show that aired for two seasons on the Independent Film Channel before being cancelled in March 2012. In one memorable segment from *Onion News Network*, a fictional New Hampshire congressman, Gregory White, holds a news conference to offer a preemptive apology for an assignation he has scheduled for later that afternoon with "two poor, deaf teenage runaways." *The Onion* also publishes the *A.V. Club*, a separate paper and website offering serious reviews of visual art, music, and books. *The Onion* has garnered a number of prestigious accolades over the years, including a Peabody Award in 2009 for the quality of its mock video broadcasts. *Time* magazine has called its website the funniest on the Internet.

A UNIQUE BRAND OF SATIRE

The Onion ridicules politicians and debunks bloated figures and polarizing organizations in American society in much the same way that television shows such as *Saturday Night Live*, *The Daily Show with Jon Stewart*, and *The Colbert Report* do. However, the *Onion* differs from these programs in some important ways. First, unlike its contemporaries, the *Onion* relies almost exclusively on fabricated stories rather than lampooning actual people and events. Whereas *Saturday Night Live* satirized the Bill Clinton/Monica Lewinsky affair by having overweight comic actor John Goodman play Linda Tripp, the secretary who exposed the illicit union, on a lunch date with Lewinsky, the aforementioned Gregory White is a fictitious character whose news conference never actually happened. Furthermore, the *Onion* parodies the news sources themselves as much as the people and organizations featured in its reports. In addition to being a dig on lecherous politicians, the White sketch parodies the many occasions when credible news sources give public figures a venue for reading hollow, false-sounding apologies that have obviously been written by their staffs. The real joke is that everyone present at the news conference, including the soon-to-be betrayed wife, is acting so solemnly.

Several *Onion* stories have been mistaken for authentic news coverage. In February 2012, for example, Louisiana congressman John Fleming issued a press release criticizing Planned Parenthood after he fell for the article "Planned Parenthood Opens $8 Billion Abortionplex." In 2009 two Bangladeshi newspapers republished portions of an *Onion* story that reported Neil Armstrong's admission that the 1969 moon landing never happened.

Writers at the *Onion* have not shied away from insulting the parent company either. When *Onion* executives announced in 2011 that they were moving the main office from New York to Chicago, the writing staff expressed its very real displeasure in—how else?—a satirical article penned by none other than T. Herman Zweibel, with the headline, "I'm Moving This Miserable Periodical to the Yukon." In it, Zweibel excoriates his staffers by calling them "some pansy-sniffing modern types," and he shows no sympathy for the lives they have established in New York. CEO Steve Hannah took the writers' barbs in stride, noting, "If you want to work at *The Onion*, you have to be willing to be part of the joke."

Sarah Roggio

SEE ALSO: *Cable TV; Colbert, Stephen; The Internet;* Saturday Night Live*; Stewart, Jon; Television.*

BIBLIOGRAPHY

"Congressman Offers Preemptive Apology for Extramarital Affair." *The Onion*. Accessed June 2012. Available from http://www.theonion.com/video/congressman-offers-preemptive-apology-for-extramar,14316/

Hudson, John. "*The Onion*'s Bumpy Ride to Chicago." *The Atlantic Wire*. Accessed June 2012. Available from http://www.theatlanticwire.com/business/2012/03/onions-bumpy-ride-chicago/50149/

Kafka, Peter. "No Joke: *The Onion* Wins One of Journalism's Biggest Awards." *All Things D*. Accessed June 2012. Available from http://allthingsd.com/20090401/no-joke-the-onion-wins-one-of-journalisms-biggest-awards/

Stableford, Dylan. "Remembering *The Onion*'s 9/11 Issue: 'Everyone Thought This Would Be Our Last Issue in Print.'" *The Cutline*. Accessed May 2012. Available from http://news.yahoo.com/blogs/cutline/remembering-onion-9-11-issue-everyone-thought-last-162024809.html

Online Dating

As of 2012 there were an estimated 1,500 dating websites in the United States and thousands more around the world. Though they vary widely, all of them try to harness the expansive reach of the Internet to make finding a compatible date more efficient. Newspaper personal ads, matchmaking agencies, and other dat-

Online Dating. *Match.com is one of several dating websites available to people looking to meet a mate.* DIGITALLIFE/ALAMY.

ing services have long offered people the opportunity to reach outside their social circles for romantic partners. But with an estimated twenty million people visiting dating websites per month, online dating greatly expands users' networks of potential partners, instantly connecting them to countless new, unknown people seeking marriage, romance, a casual good time, or someone with a shared sexual fetish.

The vast increase in choice that comes with online dating does not necessarily translate into an increase in lasting connections, however. In fact, dating websites open the distinct possibility that users will get lost in a sea of unfamiliar people—or even unwittingly encounter someone unsavory. Dating websites have sought means of combating these risks: after a Match.com user accused someone she met on the website of sexual assault, the site began to screen members against sex offender registries. Numerous private companies also offer comprehensive background checks of potential dates.

To increase the compatibility of their members upfront, some websites narrow their group of users by catering to specific groups of people, such as farmers, the elderly, Christians, or even singles with sexually transmitted diseases. These niche websites have proliferated as more people have turned to online dating. The most popular dating websites, however, appeal to a general audience. Some of these, such as Match.com and eHarmony, charge members to use their services; others, such as PlentyofFish and OkCupid, are free.

Users of dating websites typically create profiles as they would on a social networking website such as Facebook and design these profiles to tell other users about themselves and to indicate what they are seeking in a partner. A profile might, for example, indicate that the user works for a nonprofit organization, loves chicken tacos, and seeks someone who is unafraid of commitment and interested in foreign movies. Users can then search through other members' profiles, send them messages, and seek dates.

Dating websites do not simply leave their members to blindly search by themselves for suitors. The role of the dating website is to sift through its many members, match compatible users, and facilitate communication that will lead to further interaction offline. To do so websites elicit information about users and use that data to find potential pairings. Most dating websites require members to fill out lengthy, in-depth questionnaires. The average member of OkCupid, for example, answers at least 300 questions ranging from general preferences to specific desires. Some websites also track what users do online in order to create a more accurate picture of their preferences.

Many dating websites rely on complex algorithms to synthesize vast amounts of personal information in an attempt to identify the variables of taste, personality, and preference that account for successful romantic relationships. This is, of course, a complex task. The most popular dating website, Match.com, for example, uses an algorithm with 1,500 variables. Some websites, such as OkCupid, analyze members' answers to questions, compare those answers to the answers of other members, and then express their compatibility as a percentage. Other websites simply suggest that members consider particular profiles.

With their emphasis on data collection and mathematical analysis, it has been said that dating websites seek a means of quantifying love. Although it is difficult to know how accurate their formulas really are, researchers have found evidence that dating websites do lead to a substantial number of successful long-term relationships. According to a study conducted by a Stanford University sociologist, 21 percent of heterosexual and 61 percent of same-sex couples formed between 2007 and 2009 met online. Match.com commissioned a study that found online dating is the third most common way for people seeking romance to meet and that one in six new marriages is the result of a match made online.

The successes of dating websites has boosted their popularity. According to a study conducted by the Pew Research Center's Internet & American Life Project, 74 percent of Americans who use the Internet and are looking for partners have used the Internet to "further their romantic interests." New developments in online dating even allow users to employ avatars to meet and interact in virtual environments, thereby making it increasingly possible that people will someday be able to perform all the functions of dating over the Internet.

Ted McDermott

SEE ALSO: *Chatting; Facebook; The Internet; Online Shopping; Safe Sex.*

BIBLIOGRAPHY

Epstein, Robert. "The Truth about Online Dating." *Scientific American*, January 30, 2007.

Finkel, Eli J.; Paul W. Eastwick; et al. "Online Dating: A Critical Analysis from the Perspective of Psychological Science." *Psychological Science in the Public Interest* 13, no. 1 (2012): 3–66.

Lawsson, Helene M., and Kira Leck. "Dynamics of Internet Dating." *Social Science Computer Review* 24, no .2 (2006): 189–208.

Madrigal, Alexis. "Take the Data out of Dating." *Atlantic Monthly*, December 2010, 30.

Paumgarten, Nick. "Looking for Someone." *New Yorker*, July 4, 2011.

Online Gaming

Online games are video games played over the Internet. The first online video games appeared in the 1970s and were played on small networks of computers housed at universities. Most of the first online gamers were computer scientists and students, and early games such as *Empire* and *Maze Wars* were basic first-person shooters and flight simulators, in which the gamer experienced the action from the perspective of a marksman or a pilot. As the Internet became available to the public at large, online gaming expanded beyond college campuses and smaller computer networks, and attracted people from all demographics, including very young boys and girls and middle-aged men and women. The games also became more varied and more sophisticated, involving multiple players inhabiting a wide range of characters and participating in a virtual universe that was often very similar to the actual universe.

Islands of Kesmai, which debuted in 1985, is considered the first commercially available multiplayer online role-playing game. Though its interface was dependent on text-based graphics and play was relatively simple, *Islands of Kesmai* included a number of features that became standard fare for the radically more complex and realistic games that have been developed since it appeared. Users created a character and navigated that character through a virtual world, encountering the characters of other users and completing quests. All of this was done using a text-based interface, meaning its world was mapped, described, and navigated with the characters available on a keyboard.

Text-based games such as *Islands of Kesmai* that can be played by multiple people at once are known as MUDs. MUD is an acronym that commonly stands for Multi-User Dungeon. Though games of this genre continue to be developed and played, they have largely given way to far more sophisticated MMOGs, or massively multiplayer online games. Many of these games were initially played exclusively on computers, but they are now also available on Internet-enabled video game consoles and even, increasingly, on smartphones. A wide variety of games fall under the rubric of MMOGs. There are massively multiplayer first-person shooters, racing games, and social games.

A vast majority of the games, such as the popular *World of Warcraft*, are role-playing games; these are referred to as massively multiplayer online role-playing games (MMORPGs). According to the protocols of *World of Warcraft*, players first choose a side, either the Alliance, who are the good guys, or the Horde, who are evil. Next the gamer chooses a race: troll, dwarf, human, or orc, among other options. Then the player gives the character a name, alters its appearance, and enters the universe of the game. It is an animated place that can be explored with simple keystrokes—press "W" to move forward; press "A" to turn left. When the gamer approaches another character a box of text appears on screen. The character offers the gamer's character, or avatar, a quest and a reward for completing it. The avatar fights enemies, enters cities, joins guilds, earns money, and chats with other characters. The gamer can live in this world for an inexhaustible amount of time without reaching the game's end. It exists on some ten million computers around the world, and it is a fantastically complex place. The game can support thousands of users at once. It has been known to be highly addictive, and users must pay to play, either by subscribing to the game or by paying for minutes.

Though they vary in setting and various other features, contemporary online games require the user to choose a role and navigate the perils of a fantastic universe. Because of their size, complexity, and interactivity, these games function less like games, which are meant to be played and won, and more like places, which offer the user a physically consistent, inexhaustible, and interactive world for their character to live in. The designers of these games have been very successful at creating the kinds of places where users can—and do—perform many of the functions of being alive, including forming friendships, exchanging money, settling conflicts, and driving cars. These functions even leak into the real world. Characters and virtual items are auctioned off on eBay for real money—at least $10 million worth a year.

Online gamers are known for their depth of involvement in these worlds. In his book *Synthetic Worlds*, scholar Edward Castronova reports that typical players spend between twenty and thirty hours a week living in the worlds of these games and that a fifth of players consider the world of their chosen game their "'real' place of residence," rather than Earth. For Castronova the huge amounts of time and money (in excess of a billion dollars a year) people spend in these virtual worlds is illustrative of the ways in which computers are becoming "realms of existence" that are as "real" as real life.

Although players of MMORPGs such as *World of Warcraft* are a huge and committed group, many people's experience with online gaming comes in the form of free browser and social networking games. According to data from 2012, fifty-six million people a day play games on the Facebook website alone. Some of these games incorporate Facebook's social networking characteristics into a course of play that requires the user to perform virtual tasks that are analogous to real-world ones. FarmVille, for example, requires users to manage a virtual farm. They have to plow and irrigate fields, plant and harvest crops, and raise and sell livestock. Other games, such as Bubble Shooter, are more like early arcade video games and only ask users to solve basic, repetitive, two-dimensional puzzles. With their various levels of complexity, online games offer people ways to connect and to get lost alone in the Internet's synthetic realms.

Ted McDermott

SEE ALSO: *Computer Games; eBay; Facebook; The Internet; Smartphones; Social Media; Video Games.*

BIBLIOGRAPHY

"Infographic: A Massive History of Multiplayer Online Gaming." *PC Magazine Online*, August 11, 2011.

Castronova, Edward. *Synthetic Worlds: The Business and Culture of Online Games*. Chicago: University of Chicago Press, 2005.

Online Shopping

In November and December 2011, people spent $37.2 billion shopping online. This marked a 15 percent increase from the year before and is indicative of the rapid and accelerating growth in the popularity of online shopping, which has steadily been gaining market share since 2000. Though online retailers are a fairly new entrant in the market, their success has been astonishing, and the development of new mobile technologies has only made them stronger.

AUCTION AND WAREHOUSE MODELS

Amazon and eBay were among the earliest online retailers; both set up shop in the mid-1990s just as the Internet was making its way into popular culture. eBay harnessed the power of the Internet to revive, and revolutionize, a largely lost form of shopping: haggling in bazaars and markets. Before the mid-nineteenth century products did not come with price tags, and the cost of nearly everything was bargained and negotiated between buyer and seller. eBay brought back this model: instead of bringing their wares to an actual market, for a small fee a person could announce the sale of an item or set of items and wait to hear from interested buyers who frequented the website looking for a good deal. None of the merchandise on eBay was priced, and everything was auctioned off.

eBay's success spawned imitators, and it seemed that the company's auction model would become the standard for online shopping. The website Priceline, for example, allowed users to name their own prices for airline tickets, car rentals, and hotel rooms. The website then searched for a company that would offer the requested service for the proposed bid. With the actor William Shatner as its spokesman, the company was initially successful at offering travel services; it later diversified into selling everything from groceries to gas.

Whereas the auction system remains popular in some sectors—sales of used cars, for example—its initial promise has faded for a variety of reasons. As buyers became more familiar with online auctions, they became better at manipulating the eventual purchase prices for goods through practices such as sniping, or bidding at the last possible moment. Sniping eventually reduced the number of bids and kept prices down. For their part, sellers also became savvier about researching and knowing the real value of a product, thereby making prices more accurate and bargains less likely. But according to *Wired* journalist James Surowiecki, "The biggest factor in the decline of the auction may simply be that the novelty of bidding wore off." While eBay and Priceline remain in business, both have found ways to incorporate more traditional, if modified, fixed-price systems like that of eBay's early competitor, Amazon.

Amazon began as a bookstore but has expanded to sell a wide variety of products, ranging from movies and music to pet supplies and household appliances. Rather than attempt to upend traditional retail as eBay did, Amazon set out to reconcile the benefits of shopping at traditional brick-and-mortar stores with the Internet's potential to reduce overhead and reach a much larger customer base. Because its marketplace was entirely online, Amazon did not have to buy or lease storefronts, did not have to staff or stock traditional bookstore spaces, and was not confined by the physical limitations of four walls and a roof. As a result, its cost to operate was drastically reduced and its inventory could be drastically expanded. After creating an easy-to-use Web interface and building a reputation for fast and reliable delivery, Amazon became the model for the online shopping experience.

ACCESSIBILITY AND EVOLUTION

In addition to transforming the way established retailers sell their products, the Internet has made it feasible for individual crafters and artisans to reach a much broader audience for their wares. Sites such as Etsy, for example, allow makers of handmade goods, collectors of vintage apparel, and other small-scale sellers to connect with buyers without having to commit to the infrastructure of maintaining their own websites, much less paying rent, hiring employees, and doing everything else that is required to establish a retail outlet. Similar online retailers include 1000 Markets, DaWanda, and ArtFire.

The reduction of cost and increase of choice are at the heart of the popularity of online shopping, but the Internet has also facilitated other important innovations in the consumer experience. Whereas consumers previously relied on salespeople and advertisements for product information, shopping websites have reinvented the ways in which products are reviewed and recommended. Many websites, including Amazon, use computers to analyze consumers' buying and viewing histories in order to make recommendations for future purchases.

Consumers themselves have a more integrated role in online shopping: they write and read product reviews by and for other consumers The ability to access more and different information about products has significantly affected the way people shop. According to a Nielsen survey, consumers rely heavily on their peers' opinions when buying something online. This is especially true of high-tech products. When buying consumer electronics, 57 percent of the survey's respondents said they consider peer and expert product reviews prior to making a purchase.

A growing segment of online shopping involves the purchase of downloadable products, such as songs, books, and other forms of media. As more and more virtual items become available in virtual outlets such as the iTunes Store and as people become increasingly accustomed to using the Internet to make common purchases such as groceries, online shopping is expected to continue its growth. The research firm Forrester has estimated that Internet sales in America and Europe will continue to grow by 10 percent annually and will reach $279 billion per year by 2015. And downloads will not be the only products that drive this growth: the popularization of nascent 3-D printing technology, which quickly and easily makes physical objects from digital files, will eliminate the hassle and cost of shipping and reinvent the way people consume goods.

LIMITATIONS

Despite the many advantages to shopping on the Internet, there are major limitations imposed by the virtual marketplace. Information shared online is always susceptible to manipulation. Some companies have been caught exploiting users' trust by fraudulently posing as customers or paying customers to post falsely positive reviews. The website TripAdvisor, for example, has become the source of so many misleading reviews that it has been banned by the Advertising Standards Authority from calling itself truthful. Another source of online shopping fraud is theft of credit card information, though websites have developed sophisticated ways of encrypting transactions and credit card companies have created programs to analyze consumer purchasing patterns and to identify suspicious transactions. Services such as PayPal offer another layer of security by acting as an intermediary and eliminating the need to share financial information with a seller.

Online shopping is also limited by the Internet's inability to let consumers touch, test, or try out products before purchase. Other negatives of online shopping include the cost of having items shipped from distant warehouses and the inconvenience of having to ship back unsatisfactory purchases.

These constraints have led to new forms of hybrid consumerism. The advent and popularization of smartphones is changing online shopping. The most common use is research, which typically is conducted while in a store. Mobile access to the Internet means access not only to shopping websites but also to apps that can scan bar codes and QR codes and immediately provide product information. Although only 22 percent of smartphone shoppers make online purchases using their phones, that number is growing, especially in urban areas where consumers and retailers have more readily embraced the potential of this technology. On the cutting edge of this innovation are digital wallets, which allow consumers to use their phone as a credit card. According to the Nielsen study, 71 percent of smartphone app users are interested in adopting this method of payment.

Ted McDermott

SEE ALSO: *Advertising; Amazon.com; Apple Computer; Craigslist; eBay; E-Readers; The Internet; iPod / iTunes; MP3; Online Dating; Online Gaming; Smartphones.*

BIBLIOGRAPHY

Cai, Yi, and Brenda J. Cude. "Online Shopping." In *Handbook of Consumer Finance Research, Part II*, ed. Jing Jian Xiao. New York: Springer Science+Business Media, 2008.

Fernie, John, ed. "Online Shopping." *International Journal of Retail and Distribution Management* 33, no. 2 (2005): 100–181.

Surowiecki, James. "Going, Going Gone: Who Killed the Internet Auction?" *Wired*, May 17, 2011.

Op Art

A writer for *Time* magazine coined the term *Op Art* in a 1964 article describing an upcoming exhibit at the Museum of Modern Art in New York. The popular show, titled "The Responsive Eye," featured works by artists such as Victor Vasarely, Bridget Riley, and Richard Anuszkiewicz, who, beginning in the late 1950s and 1960s, created paintings and graphic designs featuring optical illusions. With machinelike precision, Op artists painted swirling lines and checkered grids that effectively played with the way people see, seeming to flicker and vibrate, heave and billow, and change color. Op works were extolled in the popular press as refreshingly neat and mechanical; they appeared scientific and were popular with a post–World War II American public consumed with lust for gadgetry, modern appliances, and atomic power.

Op Art started mainly as a reaction to the high spiritualism of prevalent postwar movements such as Abstract Expressionism and Action Painting. Whereas abstractionists and action painters attempted to express the inner world of their emotions and philosophical yearnings on their canvases, Op artists joined a wider cultural movement to demystify the creative process and recapture it from an increasingly elite class of artists and scholars. Therefore, Op artists made a direct appeal to the spectator; they relied upon viewers' eyes to complete their works by physiologically dissolving and expanding the space between lines, mixing colors, and generating afterimages. "There must be no more productions exclusively for: the cultivated eye, the sensitive eye, the intellectual eye . . . " wrote the Groupe de Recherche in their 1964 Op manifesto. "THE HUMAN EYE is our point of departure." The fact that during the1960s advertisers and fashion designers lifted Op paintings for use on billboards, T-shirts, bathing suits, and dresses, for instance, only served to bolster proud assertions that Op was art for the masses.

SCIENTIFIC INFLUENCE

Unlike Pop Art, which similarly aimed at closing the gap between art and life, Op Art attracted attention mostly because of its scientific character. Indeed, in the cultural climate fostered by the Cold War during the 1950s, many may have viewed Op Art, with its foreign language manifestos and proletarian sympathies, as a threatening import from the European Left. During the age of the space race, however, anything couched in science and technology carried cachet. Op Art not only appeared computer-generated but was also partially a product of well-known seminars taught at Harvard and Yale by scientist-painters including Josef Albers. In fact, in 1965 *Yale Scientific Magazine* devoted an entire issue to Op Art, claiming that the movement served "as an example of the interrelationship of science and the humanities in the modern world."

In its own way, the psychedelic movement of the 1960s also championed Op Art. Timothy Leary's widely imitated "celebrations" at the Village Theater on Second Avenue in New York included Op designs in multimedia shows intended to simulate drug-induced experiences. Popular and commercial psychedelic art that erupted out of San Francisco at that time similarly incorporated Op designs. Concert posters, comic strips, album covers, and concert stage sets inspired by hippie guru Ken Kesey's "Acid Tests" regularly borrowed Op's radial images and distorted checkerboards for use alongside Day-Glo Pop Art images and art nouveau lettering.

OP ART FASHION

Outside the Ivy League and beyond the world of the psychedelic underground, Op thrived as fashion design. A 1965 *Vogue* magazine cover featured a model's face overprinted with an Op pattern, and *Harper's Bazaar* celebrated a new line of dotted and checkered dresses perfect for social occasions in the "Op scene." It was the borrowings of the fashion industry that finally provoked British artist Bridget Riley to rail against the way her art was being "vulgarized" and to sue an American clothing manufacturer for using one of her paintings as a dress pattern.

Predictably, the same qualities that made Op popular with news magazines and fashion reporters made it vulnerable to attacks in the art world. Many critics dismissed Op Art as trendy kitsch—as mere gimmickry devoid of serious content. Others, however, highlighted the movement's ties to venerated investigations in optics conducted by the Impressionists and painters such as Georges Seurat, Paul Signac, and Piet Mondrian. In addition to Riley, Albers, Vasarely, and Anuszkiewicz, the most famous Op artists include Jesús-Rafael Soto and Julio Le Parc.

The first decade of the 2000s saw a resurgence of interest in the Op Art movement, and a number of retrospective exhibits were held around the world. These included shows in New York City; Frankfurt, Germany; and Wellington, New Zealand.

John Tomasic

SEE ALSO: Harper's*; Leary, Timothy; Pop Art; Psychedelia;* Time*;* Vogue.

BIBLIOGRAPHY

Alloway, Lawrence. *Topics in American Art since 1945*. New York: Norton, 1975.

Barrett, Cyril. *An Introduction to Optical Art*. New York: Dutton, 1971.

Houston, Joe, and Dave Hickey. *Optic Nerve: Perceptual Art of the 1960s*. London: Merrell Publishers, 2007.

"Op Art: Pictures That Attack the Eye." *Time*, October 23, 1964.

Parola, Rene. *Optical Art: Theory and Practice*. New York: Van Nostrand Reinhold, 1969.

Sandler, Irving. *American Art of the 1960s*. New York: Harper, 1988.

Seitz, William. *Art in the Age of Aquarius 1955–1970*. Washington, DC: Smithsonian, 1992.

Yale Scientific Magazine, November 1965.

Opportunity

Opportunity magazine was published from 1923 to 1949 by the National Urban League (at first as a monthly, later as a quarterly). Founded in 1911, the National Urban League hoped to document the urban conditions of African Americans who, in the wake of World War I, increasingly migrated north from the southern United States. The publication's title came from the National Urban League's slogan, "Not Alms but Opportunity." Charles S. Johnson served as its first editor for five and a half years; Elmer A. Carter took over in 1928. The magazine published both sociological reporting on conditions of African American life and poetry and literature written by young black writers.

Opportunity reached its highest reputation and widest circulation in the late 1920s (what one member of the National Urban League called its "Golden Era"). Published out of New York City during a time when Harlem, New York, was becoming a predominantly black neighborhood, the magazine became a central part of the "Harlem Renaissance." This literary movement of black writers of poetry and fiction created what Alain Locke (who wrote major pieces of literary criticism for *Opportunity* on a regular basis) called "the New Negro." Writing about the distinct but inherently American experiences of black citizens, these writers expressed pride in their people's accomplishments.

As editor of *Opportunity* during the 1920s, Johnson played a central role in the Harlem Renaissance. He was something of a "sidelines activist"—playing the role of a behind-the-scenes agent, a connection maker, and an entrepreneur. As Langston Hughes (the author of the poem "The Weary Blues," which originally appeared in *Opportunity*) put it, Johnson "did more to encourage and develop Negro writers during the 1920s than anyone else in America." He did this by publishing numerous young black writers in the pages of *Opportunity* at a time when they had very few venues.

Beyond publishing young African American writers, Johnson used the pages of *Opportunity* to publicize his awards system for good literature and poetry. Finding financial sponsorship from wealthy black businessmen such as Casper Holstein and supportive white writers such as Carl Van Vechten, Johnson granted prize money to black writers. These included Zora Neale Hurston and Countee Cullen, who went on to greater fame. At celebration dinners that Johnson put together and *Opportunity* sponsored, young black writers were given a chance to network with major book and magazine publishers, furthering the promotion of black writers to a wider audience. Johnson sincerely believed that this sort of promotion would improve race relations in America. Announcing a story competition in the September 1924 issue of *Opportunity*, Johnson explained that African Americans could force "the interest and kindred feeling of the rest of the world by sheer force of the humanness and beauty of [their] own story."

Alongside this literary expression, Johnson published essays by a variety of social workers and sociologists with titles such as "How Minimum Standards of Life May Be Attained," "Helping Negro Workers to Purchase Homes," "Tuberculosis and Environment," and "The Need for Health Education among Negroes." In fact, Johnson seemed less enamored with literature and more with the sort of sociological positivism he had been schooled in by University of Chicago sociologist Robert Park. *Opportunity* documented the living conditions of black Americans in northern cities (this included some of the earliest works by the sociologist E. Franklin Frazier) and the social work efforts to improve their conditions.

After Johnson left *Opportunity* for Fisk University in 1928, the magazine continued to stress socioeconomic analysis of northern, urban African Americans. Though he never stopped publishing stories and poems, Carter, Johnson's successor, "directed his attention to the sociological and economic aspects of the Negro's relation to American life," as one early historian of the publication put it. The magazine focused on working conditions of African Americans during the Great Depression—and their precarious relationship with America's labor unions. Then it focused on the Fair Employment Practice Committee during the 1940s and the general fight for racial equality that occurred during and immediately after World War II.

Opportunity accomplished a great deal for a publication with a small circulation. In every possible way, it promoted the work of black writers and documented the lives of a growing number of African Americans in northern cities.

Kevin Mattson

SEE ALSO: *Cullen, Countee; The Great Depression; Harlem Renaissance; Hughes, Langston; Hurston, Zora Neale; Van Vechten, Carl; World War I; World War II.*

BIBLIOGRAPHY

Baldwin, William. "Well Done." *Opportunity*, Winter 1949, 3–7.

Gilpin, Patrick. "Charles S. Johnson: Entrepreneur of the Harlem Renaissance." In *The Harlem Renaissance Remembered*, ed. Arna Bontemps. New York: Dodd, Mead, 1972.

Ikonne, Chidi. "*Opportunity* and Black Literature, 1923–1933." *Phylon* 40 (1979): 86–93.

Robbins, Richard. *Sidelines Activist: Charles S. Johnson and the Struggle for Civil Rights*. Jackson: University Press of Mississippi, 1996.

Weiss, Nancy. *The National Urban League, 1910–1940*. New York: Oxford University Press, 1974.

Wintz, Cary D., and Paul Finkelman. *Encyclopedia of the Harlem Renaissance*. New York: Routledge, 2004.

The Oprah Winfrey Show

SEE: *Oprah's Book Club; Winfrey, Oprah.*

Oprah's Book Club

Oprah's Book Club was launched on the September 17, 1996, broadcast of the Oprah Winfrey's top-rated daily talk show when she encouraged her viewers to read one of her personal favorites, Jacqueline Mitchard's *The Deep End of the Ocean*, in preparation for a future on-air discussion of the book. Winfrey then began regularly assigning titles to her audience and inviting their authors to appear on the show in a book-club-discussion setting. Viewers who established membership in the club through Winfrey's website were entitled to a purchase discount, provided with online study guides, and invited to participate in interactive message boards and the establishment of local book clubs. In total, Winfrey recommended seventy books throughout the fifteen-year history of the club, which was dissolved when *The Oprah Winfrey Show* went off the air on May 25, 2011.

With a television fan base estimated at anywhere between fifteen and twenty million viewers and a developing multimedia empire, Winfrey held enormous sway over public opinion, the so-called "Oprah Effect." Oprah's Book Club quickly became, in the words of Chris Lehmann in a 2001 article in *American Prospect*, "the most powerful market force in American publishing." The books Winfrey recommended instantly went to the top of the best-seller lists. Sight unseen, booksellers ordered hundreds of thousands of copies of books stamped with the iconic "O" book club sticker, and publishers followed suit by immediately requesting substantially increased print runs. The success generated for some books was so great they went on to be adapted for film, including Mitchard's *The Deep End of the Ocean*, Bernhard Schlink's *The Reader*, and Cormac McCarthy's *The Road*.

From its inception, Oprah's Book Club was both praised and damned in the press. She was credited with making readers of millions of nonreaders and with confounding pundits who had predicted the club's failure in the digital era. But she was also skewered for submitting the books to on-air discussions that channeled into the self-help psychology that informed her show, encouraging emotional identification and catharsis rather than critical thinking. Her reputation for endorsing "touchy-feely" books so bothered author Jonathan Franzen that he publicly expressed reservations following his September 2001 selection for his novel *The Corrections*. In various interviews, Franzen stated that he did not want a corporate logo detracting from the literary merits of his creation and that his novel was not a good fit for Winfrey's audience, implying both that he wanted to reach a male demographic and that Oprah's mostly female audience was accustomed to reading for entertainment rather than intellectual stimulation. Winfrey was so incensed by Franzen's remarks that she revoked her invitation to have him appear on her show, but the logo stayed.

Winfrey suspended the book club for several months following the Franzen affair, citing time constraints. The revamped club started again in 2003, with the focus shifted to the classics, including novels by John Steinbeck, Leo Tolstoy, and William Faulkner. In September 2005 her first new contemporary pick since the hiatus, James Frey's *A Million Little Pieces*, unleashed what was to be the biggest controversy surrounding the club in its history. Billed as a memoir of Frey's life as an alcoholic and addict, *A Million Little Pieces* skyrocketed Frey to fame after Oprah's nod of approval. But the media hype also resulted in increased scrutiny of Frey's story, and a scandal of international proportion erupted when Frey was accused of fabricating whole episodes about his criminal record and time spent in jail and in treatment.

Oprah initially defended Frey but finally felt compelled to confront both him and his Doubleday publisher, Nan Talese, on her January 26, 2006, program. Frey confessed to lying, and Talese admitted that she had never bothered to check the veracity of the book. David Carr of the *New York Times* wrote, "Both Mr. Frey and Ms. Talese were snapped in two like dry winter twigs." Doubleday, in fact, went on to offer refunds for buyers of *A Million Little Pieces*.

The number of annual book club selections decreased over the next several years, and the club appeared to lose some of its momentum. Still, its landmark influence on the way books were read and marketed in the United States is attested by a large body of scholarship on such aspects of its operation as Winfrey's selection criteria, her targeted audience, the suggested modes for book interpretation, and the rise of book clubs across the country. James Harker and Cecilia Konchar Farr write in their 2008 introduction to *The Oprah Affect*, "Oprah's Book Club has officially crossed over; it is now an academic, as well as a cultural, phenomenon."

Janet Mullane

SEE ALSO: *Best Sellers; Daytime Talk Shows; Fake Memoirs; Faulkner, William; Steinbeck, John; Television; Winfrey, Oprah.*

BIBLIOGRAPHY

Carr, David. "How Oprah Trumped Truthiness." *New York Times*, January 30, 2006.

Harker, James, and Cecilia Konchar Farr, eds. *The Oprah Affect: Critical Essays on Oprah's Book Club*. Albany, NY: SUNY, 2008.

Harris, Jennifer, and Elwood Watson, eds. *The Oprah Phenomenon*. Lexington: University Press of Kentucky, 2007.

Lehmann, Chris. "Literati: The Oprah Wars." *American Prospect*, November 20, 2001.

Rooney, Kathleen. *Reading with Oprah: The Book Club That Changed America*. Fayetteville: The University of Arkansas Press, 2005.

Orbison, Roy *(1936–1988)*

Introduced by Elvis Presley in 1976 as "quite simply, the greatest singer in the world," Roy Orbison—with his lush, dramatic orchestral songs and near-operatic voice—helped expand the sonic and emotional limitations of pop music. His most influential material came from his work during the early to mid-1960s, and his songs "Only the Lonely," "Running Scared," "It's Over," "Down the Line," "Cryin'," and "In Dreams," among others, would support his career for decades. Although Orbison's stage show would remain essentially the same from the mid-1960s until his death in 1988, he insisted that he didn't tire of repeatedly singing the same songs. "Gracious, no, because I've worked a lifetime to do a show of just my own material," Orbison told *Radio Two*, according to Alan Clayson in his biography *Only the Lonely*.

Orbison credited the lasting impact of his music to a certain innocence in his songs. He noted in *The Face* that "God has a way of giving you the lyric and the melody and, if it stands up over the years, that adolescence, that innocence helps to keep its intentions pure. That innocence is the big ingredient that keeps my songs alive, that makes them stand tall," according to Clayson.

SMALL-TOWN COUNTRY ROOTS

Born in Vernon, Texas, to a musical family (his father played Jimmie Rodgers songs and his uncle was a blues artist), Orbison made his performing debut at age eight and was soon regularly playing on local radio stations. In high school he formed the Wink Westerners, which played mostly western swing music, and when Orbison went off to college at North Texas State College, he rechristened the group the Teen Kings. While in college the group recorded a raucous rockabilly tune called "Ooby Dooby," which eventually caught the attention of Sun Records

Roy Orbison. *Roy Orbison wears his trademark black clothes and dark sunglasses at a performance in 1985.* PAUL NATKIN/CONTRIBUTOR/WIREIMAGE/GETTY IMAGES.

owner Sam Phillips, who rereleased it to become a mild hit in 1956. On the heels of his first hit, Orbison cut a number of sides for Sun during the mid- to late 1950s, and although his career as a minor rockabilly star was booming, he grew increasingly tired of this music and the energetic stage presence it required.

By the late 1950s Orbison had severed his ties with Phillips and Sun and had moved to Nashville, Tennessee, to write songs for the country music publishing powerhouse Acuff-Rose. The ballad "Claudette," written about his wife, became a hit for the Everly Brothers. Interested in returning to his own singing career, Orbison—with the help of Wesley Rose—signed with Fred Foster at the newly opened Monument in 1959 and the same year released "Uptown," which rose high enough on Billboard's pop chart to suggest that Orbison could maintain a career as a singer.

By 1960, with the release of "Only the Lonely," Orbison had embraced what would become his unique presence in pop music. With this song, he exercised his vocal range and introduced audiences to the power of his voice, which Clayson noted would stretch to "an impossible six octaves." Duane Eddy commented, according to Clayson, that "when you thought he'd sung as high as he possibly could, he would effortlessly go higher and finish up with a big finish and it was wonderful." "Only the Lonely" soon hit number two on the Hot 100 in the United States and topped the charts in both Australia and Great Britain.

Although Orbison had already been dying his hair black for years, he soon incorporated what would become his trademark black attire and sunglasses into his stage act. He dropped his hip-shaking stage acrobatics in favor of a much more emotionally composed vocal style and austere stage presence. Deciding to let his voice stand on its own, Orbison would remain almost motionless onstage.

A NEW KIND OF ROCK STAR

Orbison's voice opened pop music to manly emotions. About his song "Cryin'," Orbison told *New Musical Express* that "I wanted to show that the act of crying for a man—and that record came out in a real 'macho' era when any sign of sensitivity was really frowned on—was a good thing and not some weak . . . defect almost," according to Clayson. With the operatic quality of his voice and his soulful singing, Orbison successfully maintained a strong sense of masculinity in dramatic melodies. His use of falsetto and his ability to quickly switch to a vulnerable delivery lent to the emotional buildup in songs such as "Blue Bayou," "I'm Hurtin'," and "Pretty Woman."

After the success of "Pretty Woman," Orbison signed with Metro-Goldwyn-Mayer (MGM) for a contract estimated at more than $1 million. And soon the emotions Orbison displayed in his songs became tragically real when his wife, Claudette, died in a motorcycle accident in 1966 and again when two of his three children died in a fire in 1968. Orbison found happiness again in 1969 when he married Barbara Wellhoener-Jakobs, a German woman he had met while on tour. The couple had another two children, and Orbison returned to performing.

Throughout the 1970s and early 1980s, Orbison continued to tour the world. His stage presence won over audiences for years. He received a standing ovation when he toured in the United Kingdom with the Beatles in 1963 and later charmed adolescent audiences when on tour with the Eagles in the early 1980s. By 1980 Orbison's duet with Emmylou Harris of "That Lovin' You Feelin' Again" won the pair a Grammy Award for Best Country Performance by a Duo or Group. Although Orbison is often associated with countrified pop music, his duet with Harris was the only time he ever made the country charts. Once produced by the influential Chet Atkins and backed by musicians of the "Nashville sound," Orbison was Nashville's first major pop success.

Even though—as Bruce Springsteen noted at Orbison's induction into the Rock and Roll Hall of Fame—"no one sings like Roy Orbison," many artists have enjoyed the rewards of recording Orbison's songs and trying to mimic his vocal style. Springsteen borrowed much from Orbison for his *Thunder Road* album; John Lennon noted that he'd tried to write a "Roy Orbison song" with "Please Please Me"; Linda Ronstadt sold more of her 1977 version of "Blue Bayou" than Orbison sold of his original; and by the early 1980s, when the music charts were filled with nostalgic reissues or revivals of 1960s songs, heavy metal band Van Halen reached number twelve with a version of "Pretty Woman" in 1982. John Cougar recorded the same song in 1986.

A LASTING INFLUENCE

Orbison's career was given an unconventional boost in 1986 when movie director David Lynch featured "In Dreams" during a brutal scene in *Blue Velvet*. During the scene the Dennis Hopper character sadistically had another character beaten; the dark quality of "In Dreams" perfectly fit the sinister montage-like cinematography that is Lynch's trademark. In 1987 Orbison was inducted into the Rock and Roll Hall of Fame at its second ceremony by Springsteen. Orbison's achievement was honored with a tribute concert at the Coconut Grove night club in Los Angeles. "A Black and White Night," as it was called, featured Orbison playing alongside such musical fans as Springsteen, Elvis Costello, Jackson Browne, Tom Waits, Bonnie Raitt, and k.d. lang. Orbison soon found himself in the company of Bob Dylan, Tom Petty, Jeff Lynne, and George Harrison, which resulted in the release of the big-selling *The Traveling Wilburys* collaborative album.

By 1988 Orbison's career was regaining momentum—he recorded a hit single, "You Got It," and completed an album with songs and production by Costello, U2's Bono and The Edge, and Lynne—but before that record was released he died at home of a heart attack on December 6, 1988. *Mystery Girl*, his posthumous comeback album, became the highest-charting album of his career, eventually going platinum.

Orbison's tremendous influence on modern music did not end with his death. His widow, Barbara, worked hard to keep his legacy alive, managing Orbison Enterprises, Orbison Records, Roy Orbison Music, and the Still Working Music Group and even releasing, in 2009, a Pretty Woman perfume. In 2008 Barbara and son Roy Jr. released a comprehensive four-CD box set of all 107 of Orbison's recordings, beginning with the 1956 recording of "Ooby Dooby" and ending with a haunting version of "It's Over," taped just two days before the artist's death. *Roy Orbison: The Soul of Rock and Roll* was acclaimed by critics as an important part of American musical history.

In 2011 the music industry rallied to celebrate Orbison's seventy-fifth birthday year with a variety of tributes, including a display of memorabilia at the Grammy museum in Los Angeles. Other acknowledgements included a special CD release by national coffee giant Starbucks; an Orby Records tribute album featuring a number of musicians covering Orbison songs; and special Roy Orbison selections on popular rock music video games Rock Band 3, Guitar Hero, and Sing Star. Most significant, perhaps, was the release of the *Monument Singles Collection*, a two-CD anthology of all of the songs Orbison recorded on the Monument label between 1959 and 1966. This historic compilation includes both Orbison's hits and lesser-known recordings from the very beginning of his rising career. To ensure authenticity, producers sought out the original monaural recordings to create CDs that recreate as closely as possible Orbison's unique sound in those early years.

Though Orbison is identified with an elemental simplicity that was the heart of early rock and roll, his legacy has kept up with the technological times. There is a Roy Orbison YouTube channel and a Roy Orbison presence on MySpace and Facebook. In the early 2000s, a Roy Orbison website was launched, which featured, along with information about Orbison recordings and history, a "six degrees of separation" game in which fans could enter the name of any musician and find his or her connection to Orbison—a twenty-first-century method of proving Orbison's deeply felt influence on American music. In 2008 "Pretty Woman" was added to the Library of Congress National Recording Registry, marking it as a song of significant national importance.

Kembrew McLeod

SEE ALSO: *Atkins, Chet; The Beatles;* Blue Velvet; *Browne, Jackson; Costello, Elvis; Dylan, Bob; The Everly Brothers; Hopper, Dennis; lang, k.d.; Lennon, John; Lynch, David; Pop Music; Presley, Elvis; Raitt, Bonnie; Rock and Roll; Rodgers, Jimmie; Springsteen, Bruce; Top 40; Van Halen; Waits, Tom.*

BIBLIOGRAPHY

Amburn, Ellis. *Dark Star: The Roy Orbison Story*. London: Hodder and Stoughton, 1991.

Clayson, Alan. *Only the Lonely*. New York: St. Martin's Press, 1989.

Lehman, Peter. *Roy Orbison: The Invention of an Alternative Rock Masculinity*. Philadelphia: Temple University Press, 2003.

Robins, Wayne. "A Monumental Talent." *Billboard*, April 23, 2011, 23.

Roy Orbison. Accessed April 2012. Available from http://www.royorbison.com

O'Reilly, Bill *(1949–)*

Political commentator Bill O'Reilly hosts America's most-watched cable news program, *The O'Reilly Factor* on the Fox News Channel. With his acerbic, flamboyant style, O'Reilly is as well known to his foes as he is to his fans. Though most of those enemies are on the political left, O'Reilly, who describes himself as a political independent, is far from an orthodox conservative. Above all, the former *Inside Edition* host and veteran journalist is a consummate entertainer, whose on-air style and catchphrases (for example, his description of his show as "the no-spin zone") are etched into the popular consciousness. O'Reilly, who hosted *The Radio Factor* from 2002 to 2009, is also the author of numerous books, many of them major best sellers.

William James O'Reilly Jr. was born in New York City on September 10, 1949, to William J. and Winifred Angela Drake O'Reilly. Though O'Reilly has described his background as working class, his detractors dispute this claim, citing the fact that his father worked as a currency accountant for an oil company, hardly a working-class profession. In any case, the family moved to the decidedly blue-collar community of Levittown on Long Island, New York, in 1951. O'Reilly and his sister, Janet, attended Catholic parochial schools, but he opted for a public high school because most of his friends went there.

After graduating in 1967, O'Reilly enrolled at Marist College, from which he received a BA in history in 1971. Though he played semiprofessional baseball as a pitcher, after college O'Reilly worked as a high school English and history teacher in Miami, Florida. In 1973 he enrolled at Boston University, where he earned an MA in broadcast journalism. During the years that followed, he worked variously as a reporter, an anchor, and a weatherman for TV stations in cities around the country.

Having earned two local Emmys, O'Reilly caught the attention of CBS News, which made him a network correspondent in 1982. Four years later, his eulogy at a correspondent's funeral so impressed ABC News president Roone Arledge that the latter hired him. O'Reilly spent the next few years reporting for a number of ABC News shows before leaving to become anchor of the news/gossip program *Inside Edition* in 1989. He remained there until 1995, when he entered the master's program in public administration at Harvard's John F. Kennedy School of Government, earning a degree the following year. Also in 1996, he married Maureen E. McPhilmy, a public relations executive, with whom he later had a daughter and a son.

With the launch of the Fox News Channel in October 1996, O'Reilly returned to television as host of a show originally called *The O'Reilly Report*. In 1998 the program got a new name, based on the observation that the host put his personal stamp, "the O'Reilly factor," on any story he reported. Over the years that followed, *The O'Reilly Factor* won and held the position of number one cable news program, and O'Reilly became widely recognized for his aggressive, hard-hitting (and, in the view of some, pompous) style. Comedian Stephen Colbert based an entire show on him, satirizing *The O'Reilly Factor* with his *Colbert Report*.

In a more serious vein, detractors on the left consistently attacked O'Reilly's positions and persona, and he even managed to rile conservatives by parting ways with them on issues such as gun control. More potentially damaging than any political controversy was a sexual harassment lawsuit brought by former *O'Reilly Factor* producer Andrea Mackris in October 2004. O'Reilly and Mackris settled out of court later that month. O'Reilly has had public disagreements with a number of celebrities, including Whoopi Goldberg and Joy Behar, who stormed off the set of *The View* in October 2010 in protest of his statement that "Muslims killed us on 9/11."

In May 2002 Fox News Radio launched *The Radio Factor*, a syndicated talk show with O'Reilly as host. By the time he stepped down in February 2009, citing the pressures of his workload, his was the number two program in its time slot, behind only Rush Limbaugh's show. As of February 2012, O'Reilly had published ten books, most of which were best sellers and several of which had hit number one on the *New York Times* nonfiction list.

Judson Knight

SEE ALSO: *Arledge, Roone; Best Sellers; Cable TV; Colbert, Stephen; Fox News Channel; Goldberg, Whoopi; Limbaugh, Rush; 9/11; Political Correctness; Radio; Tabloid Television; Talk Radio; Television;* The View.

BIBLIOGRAPHY

Bill O'Reilly Official Home on the Web. Accessed May 23, 2012. Available from http://www.billoreilly.com

Biography in Context. "Newsmakers." Detroit, MI: Gale, 2001.

Fox News. "The O'Reilly Factor." Accessed May 23, 2012. Available from http://www.foxnews.com/topics/the-oreilly-factor-with-bill-oreilly.htm

O'Reilly, Bill. *The No-Spin Zone: Confrontations with the Powerful and Famous in America*. New York: Random House, 2001.

O'Reilly, Bill. *A Bold, Fresh Piece of Humanity*. New York: Broadway Books, 2008.

O'Reilly, Bill. *Killing Lincoln*. New York: Henry Holt, 2011.

Organic Food

During the decades of the 1970s and 1980s, the growing need for environmental reform pervaded the popular consciousness, influencing policy makers and ordinary Americans alike. Many people began to seek out ways to incorporate ecologically responsible decisions into their daily lives and to reduce their negative impact on the world around them. Many stores found that these "green" consumers would support products created with an environmental consciousness. In an ironic twist in this era of mass consumption, massive retail enterprises, such as Wal-mart, sought to make themselves more palatable to green consumers.

As ecological awareness became a more widely accepted part of American culture, many people began to include at least minimal consideration of the environment in their decisions about what to buy, what to eat, and what leisure activities to pursue. This cultural foundation would serve as a critical tool as humans began to wrestle with large-scale environmental problems such as food production. After 1970, environmental or "green" thinking influenced many American ideas about food, including the increasing popularity of organic food.

Starting with communes and other small-scale, anti-big-agriculture efforts in the late 1960s, organics in the early twenty-first century have become part of a popular movement that includes categories such as "slow food" and efforts to buy locally produced agriculture. Even First Lady Michelle Obama has focused Americans' attention on such ideas: first by installing an organic garden at the White House in 2009, and second by initiating the call for school lunch regulations across the nation to begin to factor in organic and local products. From their beginnings as roadside farm stand fare, organics have become mainstream thanks to green consumerism.

As a more organized movement, the slow food movement began in Italy in 1986 when Carlo Petrini protested the opening of a McDonald's—the symbol of "fast" food—in Rome. The movement was first known as "Arcigola" and was designed to resist fast food. In the 2010s, the object has expanded to not only combat fast food but also help preserve traditional plants, seeds, animals, and farming practices, in addition to the cultural cuisine associated with these traditions. The movement includes more than 80,000 members and is active in more than fifty countries.

The objectives of the slow food movement are preserving and celebrating local culinary traditions, forming and maintaining seed banks to preserve local heirloom varieties, supporting small-scale production and processing, and educating people about the qualities of good food and the risks of fast food and agribusiness. As the movement stands in the 2010s, each slow food chapter is responsible for promoting local farmers, flavors, and culinary artisans through programs such as farmers' markets and taste workshops. The slow food movement also lobbies to include organic farming concerns in agricultural policies and to limit funding of genetically modified organisms (GMOs) and agrochemical use. In addition, the movement works with primary and secondary school students creating school gardens, educating the students about nutrition, and perpetuating the skills of farming.

As a cultural movement in the United States, organics received considerable attention following the 2006 publication of Michael Pollan's best-selling book *The Omnivore's Dilemma*. Tapping into the nascent interest of highly educated, environmentally conscious consumers, Pollan turned the paradigm of 1950s-style mass consumption on its head. His basic principles of eating locally and simply turned into a franchise of guidebooks, including *Omnivore's Dilemma: Young Readers Edi-*

tion (2009), *In Defense of Food* (2008), and *Food Rules: An Eater's Manual* (2009). This work also inspired a 2009 pseudo-documentary film that won wide viewership, *Food Inc.*

Critics of the slow food movement claim it is elitist. They also suggest that the movement is disparaging of cheaper, alternative methods of food processing and preparation, methods that are important to lower-income people and families. The slow food movement counters these critiques by suggesting that they support local production and preparation because ultimately these processes are less expensive—they do not necessitate long-haul transportation or energy and chemical use. According to the slow food movement, most food travels long distances, necessitating the use of substantial amounts of fuel and preservatives and other additives. The movement notes that the so-called cheaper alternatives do not accurately reflect their true costs due to government subsidies, which keep transportation and other costs artificially low.

Overall, green consumerism and organic agriculture in particular have woven an alternative ethic into American consumerism. As a cultural creation of modern environmentalism, green culture marks a grassroots effort by individuals to protect not only cultural heritage but also regional diversity and biodiversity. By supporting local, small farms and organics, the movement works to preserve each regional ecosystem and the culture that has developed over generations of living within each ecosystem.

Brian Black

SEE ALSO: *Consumerism; Environmentalism; Farmers' Markets; Fast Food; Foodies; Gourmet Grocery Stores.*

BIBLIOGRAPHY

Petrini, Carlo. *Slow Food Nation: Why Our Food Should Be Good, Clean, and Fair.* New York: Rizzoli Ex Libris, 2007.

Pollan, Michael. *The Omnivore's Dilemma: A Natural History of Four Meals.* New York: Penguin, 2006.

Rodale, Maria. *Organic Manifesto: How Organic Farming Can Heal Our Planet, Feed the World, and Keep Us Safe.* New York: Rodale, 2010.

Schlosser, Eric. *Fast Food Nation: The Dark Side of the All-American Meal.* Boston: Houghton Mifflin, 2001.

The Organization Man

William H. Whyte's popular psychology best seller of the mid-1950s outlined a contemporary figure who captured many fears about the nature of the American individual in an age of increasing rationalization. *The Organization Man* (1956) showed the white-collar employee as increasingly shaped by his employer's demands: focused on advancement through the firm, he became narrow, conformist, and unwilling to innovate. This figure's fear of original thought and his lifestyle (situated in rationalized suburbs and marked by consumption rather than community) seemed to contravene the contemporary American values of competitive individualism. Whyte's work was simplistic and deterministic, but it influenced the broad discussion of conformity and its risks in the 1950s.

Kyle Smith

SEE ALSO: *The Fifties; Popular Psychology.*

BIBLIOGRAPHY

Pells, Richard H. *The Liberal Mind in a Conservative Age: American Intellectuals in the 1940s and 1950s.* New York: Harper & Row, 1985.

Ross, Andrew. *No Respect: Intellectuals & Popular Culture.* London: Routledge, 1989.

Whyte, William H. *The Organization Man.* New York: Simon and Schuster, 1956.

Whyte, William H., and Albert LaFarge. *The Essential William H. Whyte.* New York: Fordham University Press, 2000.

Original Dixieland Jass (Jazz) Band

The Original Dixieland Jass Band initiated the jazz revolution when Columbia Records released the band's first recordings in April 1917. Composed of white New Orleans musicians and led by Nick LaRocca, the band has often been maligned by jazz purists. When compared to King Oliver's Creole Jazz Band with Louis Armstrong or to any of Armstrong's own groups, the Original Dixieland Jass Band does suffer. The music it played, however, was fresh and bright when compared with the popular music of the day, and the musicians in the group were more than competent in their performance.

Frank A. Salamone

SEE ALSO: *Armstrong, Lance; Armstrong, Louis; Dixieland; Jazz; New Orleans Rhythm and Blues.*

BIBLIOGRAPHY

Brunn, Harry O. *The Story of the Original Dixieland Jazz Band.* New York: Da Capo Press, 1977.

Martin, Henry, and Keith Waters. *Jazz: The First 100 Years.* Belmont, CA: Wadsworth, 2002.

Williams, Martin. *Jazz Masters of New Orleans.* New York: Da Capo Press, 1978.

Orman, Suze *(1951–)*

Best-selling author, motivational speaker, and television personality Suze Orman has helped millions of Americans understand personal finance since the late 1990s. A veteran in the financial planning business, Orman has been featured as an authority on managing personal finances by many media outlets and has become a household name. She is best known for offering inspirational and practical advice and for discussing the psychology behind fiscal decisions to help her viewers change their attitudes about money and its place in their lives. Fans have applauded her ability to make complex business concepts more accessible to nonexperts, while critics claim that she oversimplifies financial issues and that her advice is nothing more than common sense.

Susan Lynn Orman was born in Chicago on June 5, 1951, to working-class parents. She got a job at a delicatessen when she was thirteen and continued to work as a waitress through high school and college. In 1980, after she earned a degree in social work from the University of Illinois, Orman borrowed $50,000 to start her own restaurant. When she invested the money with Merrill Lynch, a broker convinced her to buy options even though Orman had said she wanted a more reliable investment. Buying options is a risky strategy, and Orman lost all her money within three months of investing it.

Having studied the financial markets by reading the *Wall Street Journal* and watching *Wall Street Week* on PBS, Orman applied for a broker position at Merrill Lynch because she needed the money to pay back her debt. In an industry where few women worked, Orman says she got the job because the manager was trying to fill a quota. After completing Merrill Lynch's training program, she became a successful account executive, recruiting blue-collar workers as clients while her coworkers concentrated on wealthy patrons. She simultaneously sued Merrill Lynch for her investment loss and settled with the company out of court.

In 1983 Orman was hired by Prudential Bache Securities as vice president of investments and worked there until 1987 when she founded the Suze Orman Financial Group. She compiled the lessons she had learned about money into the advice book *You've Earned It, Don't Lose It* (1994). Orman has said that her goal in writing the book was to "bring personal finance to people who used to have no interest in the subject," an idea that seemed to have shaped her career. The book quickly sold out on home shopping television network QVC and helped Orman gain public recognition.

Orman's next book, *The 9 Steps to Financial Freedom* (1997), sold more than three million copies and became the basis for a popular PBS television special, *Money Class*, featuring Orman. She was then recruited by a PBS affiliate to host a pledge season segment, which helped raise more than $2.3 million. Orman's career got a huge boost with a 1998 invitation to appear on *The Oprah Winfrey Show* (1986–2011). After gaining exposure on *Oprah* and other talk shows, Orman reached the *New York Times* best-seller list with *The Courage to Be Rich* (1999).

Critics have cited Orman's overly simplistic solutions and questionable spending habits as reasons people should be wary of her financial advice. They have also questioned some of her sponsors, such as Lending Tree, and her branded prepaid debit card, which offers consumers the advantage of loading money on the card with no option of running up a negative balance. There are quite a few fees associated with the card, and some financial advisers have said that using a debit card associated with one's checking or savings account is a more financially savvy option. Chuck Jaffe wrote in his column for *Market Watch*, "[Orman] has big commercial relationships that aren't always disclosed and shouldn't be ignored. . . . The standard for most journalists is to avoid conflicts entirely, not to embrace the relationships and explain away the appearance of a problem."

Orman has written, coproduced, and hosted six PBS specials, which have won two Emmy Awards. Her books include *The Money Book for the Young, Fabulous, and Broke* (2005), *Women and Money* (2007), and *The Money Class* (2011). She has also written a money advice column for Winfrey's magazine *O*. In 2010 *Forbes* magazine listed Orman among the 100 most powerful women in the world. In January 2012 her show, *America's Money Class with Suze Orman*, premiered on Winfrey's television network, OWN. Defying long-held conventions in the financial sector, Orman has blended the power of positive thinking with practical financial solutions, along the way becoming the personal finance guru for many Americans.

Jill Clever

SEE ALSO: *Cable TV; Daytime Talk Shows; Emmy Awards; Home Shopping Network/QVC; Public Television (PBS); The* Wall Street Journal*; Winfrey, Oprah.*

BIBLIOGRAPHY

Orman, Suze. *The 9 Steps to Financial Freedom*. New York: Crown, 1997.

Orman, Suze. *The Courage to Be Rich*. New York: Riverhead Books, 1999.

Orman, Suze. *The Money Class: Learn to Create Your New American Dream*. New York: Speigel & Grau, 2011.

"Suze Orman." In *Current Biography*. New York: H.W. Wilson, 2003.

O'Rourke, P. J. *(1947–)*

In 1998 satirist P. J. O'Rourke announced his intention to write a memoir. The most serious problem with this idea, he wrote, is "that I haven't really done much. But I don't feel this should stand in my way. O. J. Simpson wrote a memoir, and the jury said he hadn't done anything at all." A sharp social critic, O'Rourke is one of the most loved—or hated—literary figures of the twentieth century.

EARLY LIFE AND CAREER

Patrick Jake O'Rourke grew up in Toledo, Ohio. He went to the state university in Miami, Ohio (where he majored in English), and then to Johns Hopkins. He became a strong leftist, which caused some distress to his Republican grandmother. He says that he informed his grandmother that he was a Maoist, prompting the reply, "just so long as you're not a Democrat."

From 1969 to 1971 O'Rourke worked for an underground Baltimore, Maryland, newspaper titled *Harry*. He then moved to New York and later told the magazine *New York* that he came to the city to "write experimental, deeply incomprehensible novels." Instead he went to work for another underground publication, the East Village *Other*, after which he joined the humor magazine *National Lampoon*. He rose through the ranks, becoming a junior editor in 1973 and editor-in-chief in 1978.

O'Rourke left *National Lampoon* in 1981 and worked in Hollywood for a brief time as a scriptwriter. He eventually returned to New York, working freelance and acting as the foreign affairs editor for *Rolling Stone*. He left the magazine in 2000 but writes frequently for other magazines, including the *Atlantic Monthly*, *Vanity Fair*, *Esquire*, *Harper's*, and the *American Spectator*. As evidence of his political acumen, O'Rourke became an H. L. Mencken research fellow at the Cato Institute, a libertarian think tank.

O'Rourke appears frequently on the humorous NPR quiz show *Wait, Wait . . . Don't Tell Me* and has published seventeen books since 1974, including both original works and reprints of his journalistic efforts. Both *Parliament of Whores* (1991), a conservative critique of the American system of government, and *Give War a Chance* (2003), a collection of essays that semi-facetiously links liberalism with evil, reached number one on the *New York Times* best sellers list. Recent books include *Driving Like Crazy* (2009), *Don't Vote!—It Just Encourages the Bastards* (2010), and *Holidays in Heck* (2011).

POLITICAL VIEWS

O'Rourke's political views have evolved since his days as a young Maoist in the 1960s. By the late 1990s he wrote as a Libertarian Republican. "You know," he said in a 1993 speech at the Cato Institute, "if government were a product, selling it would be illegal." O'Rourke explained in a 1995 article why he shared the conservative faith in individualism: "Under collectivism . . . individual decision making is replaced by the political process. Suddenly the system that elected the prom queen at your high school is in charge of your whole life."

Despite his association with the conservative movement, O'Rourke disassociates himself from the more puritanical conservatives. In 1994, over drinks with a reporter from the Toronto alternative newspaper *eye*, O'Rourke said, "I would be incredibly hypocritical if I were to say that I was in favor of the sort of morality that is put forward by some elements of the right wing: never sleep with anybody but your wife, . . . never get a divorce, never touch drugs and, more to the point this evening, never touch booze! Forget it!"

THE LIGHTER SIDE

A look at O'Rourke's publications shows that he can discuss both high politics and less exalted matters. In his satirical etiquette book *Modern Manners*, he includes a section on the etiquette of drug use, especially the use of cocaine: "Cocaine is bad for the health. And this is why it's never bad manners to go off alone and fire some 'nose Nikes' and not share them with anyone else. . . . When offered someone else's cocaine, you should Electrolux as much as possible for their sake." An article by O'Rourke that originally appeared in *National Lampoon*, and which he included in his book *Republican Party Reptile*, is called "How to Drive Fast on Drugs While Getting Your Wing-Wang Squeezed and Not Spill Your Drink." Indeed, the article lives up to its title: "Most people like to drive on speed or cocaine with plenty of whiskey mixed in. This gives you the confidence you want and need for plowing through red lights and passing trucks on the right."

O'Rourke somehow manages to combine this kind of style with serious political commentary. Discussing the savings and loan scandal, he deplores what he sees as the incompetence of the government investigators who might have prevented the mess: "Federal bank regulators . . . had to clean their room and mow the lawn before they were allowed to go regulate banks." Commenting on allegedly anti-American attitudes in the Jordanian Rotary Club, O'Rourke imagines a meeting of that organization: "Okay, fellows, any member who hasn't drunk the blood of an infidel dog since the last meeting has to stand on his chair and sing 'I'm a Little Teapot.'" It is exactly this kind of "call-'em-as-you-see-'em" critique that has brought O'Rourke fame—or infamy—in his attempts to entertain and educate Americans in the latter half of the twentieth century and into the new millennium.

Eric Longley

SEE ALSO: *Alternative Press;* Atlantic Monthly*; Best Sellers; Cocaine/Crack;* Esquire*;* Harper's*; Hollywood; Mencken, H. L.;* National Lampoon*; The* New York Times*; Radio;* Rolling Stone*; Simpson, O. J.;* Vanity Fair.

BIBLIOGRAPHY

Burrill, William. "On the Way to Hell with P. J. O'Rourke." *eye*, October 20, 1994.

Ickes, Bob. "White Mischief." *New York*, December 21–28, 1992, 126–127.

O'Rourke, P. J. "Up Ulster Way." *National Lampoon: This Side of Parodies*. New York: Warner Paperback Library, 1974.

O'Rourke, P. J. *Republican Party Reptile*. New York: Atlantic Monthly Press, 1987.

O'Rourke, P. J. "Putting the Moi Back in Memoir." *New York Times Book Review*, March 1, 1998.

O'Rourke, P. J. *Modern Manners: An Etiquette Book for Rude People*. New York: Atlantic Monthly Press, 1989.

O'Rourke, P. J. *Parliament of Whores*. New York: Atlantic Monthly Press, 1991.

O'Rourke, P. J. *Give War a Chance: Eyewitness Accounts of Mankind's Struggle against Tyranny, Injustice and Alcohol-Free Beer*. New York: Atlantic Monthly Press, 1992.

O'Rourke, P. J. *Age and Guile Beat Youth, Innocence and a Bad Haircut: Twenty-Five Years of P. J. O'Rourke*. New York: Atlantic Monthly Press, 1995.

O'Rourke, P. J. *The Enemies List*. New York: Atlantic Monthly Press, 1996.

Safire, Paul. "Animal House Meets Church Lady." *American Prospect*, March 1996, 50–52.

Orr, Bobby *(1948–)*

Before Wayne Gretzky took over the ice in the 1980s, three names topped the lists of the greatest hockey players: Gordie Howe, Bobby Hull, and Bobby Orr. Bobby Orr's name is indelibly linked with the Boston Bruins as their legendary number 4. With 915 career points in the National Hockey League (NHL), including 270 career goals and 645 career assists, this defenseman revolutionized hockey by being highly efficient on the offensive end.

Born on March 20, 1948, in the small town of Parry Sound in Ontario, Canada, Robert Gordon Orr, the third child of Arva Steele and amateur athlete Douglas Orr, was named after a paternal grandfather who had been a professional soccer player in Ireland. At the age of four, Bobby began skating and playing "shinny," which was a training game for stick handling, dodging, passing, and controlling the puck. From the age of five he played hockey in the Minor Squirt Hockey League, and he became the Most Valuable Player in the Pee-Wee Division at age nine while dazzling fans with a particularly fast spin on his skates. He was quickly considered a natural defenseman, although he was also feared an offensive threat.

In 1960, playing in a tournament with the Parry Sound Bantam All-Stars, Orr made a profound impression on a scout for the Boston Bruins. At thirteen, while still attending school, he signed a contract card with the Bruins to play for their affiliated Junior A League team the Oshawa Generals. In a team of much older players Orr was noted for his precise interceptions and dazzling rushes up ice. He played four all-star seasons with the Generals and won the league MVP.

BOSTON BLUELINER

In 1966, when Orr signed a $50,000 contract for two years with the Bruins, with a $25,000 signing bonus, his contract played a part in changing the NHL pay structure. Assigned number 27 when he first signed, he quickly switched to his now-famous number 4. His first goal against the Montreal Canadiens at Boston Garden on October 23 marked the beginning of a career during which, while he was a blueliner, he twice won the Art Ross Trophy as the league's scoring leader in 1970 and 1975.

Orr won the Calder Trophy as top rookie for the 1966–67 season and, beginning with the 1967–68 season, won the James Norris Trophy for the NHL's top defenseman for a record eight years in a row. He was also a perennial choice for the NHL All-Star Team for those same eight straight seasons. During his best season with the Bruins, in 1970–1971, he had 37 goals and 102 assists for 139 points. From 1969 to 1975, he established a record for defensemen with regular 100-point seasons. *Sports Illustrated* named him "Sportsman of the Year" in 1970.

Bobby Orr. *Legendary Boston Bruins defenseman Bobby Orr waves to fans prior to Game Four of the 2011 NHL Stanley Cup Finals.* BRIAN BABINEAU/CONTRIBUTOR/NATIONAL HOCKEY LEAGUE/NHLI/GETTY IMAGES.

STANLEY CUP CHAMPIONS

Although his individual brilliance is undisputed, Bobby Orr won the heart of Boston fans because he was the ultimate team player. He led a team of perennial also-rans to the top of the NHL. With his speed, grace, precision, and recklessness he led the Bruins to their first Stanley Cup in twenty-nine years. His best-known goal occurred in overtime of the fourth game of the Stanley Cup Finals on May 10, 1970, when a photographer captured him diving through the air as if he could fly. The photo is perhaps the most famous in hockey.

Although the 1970–71 Stanley Cup went to the Montreal Canadiens, the 1971–1972 Finals saw the Cup back in Boston, with Orr winning the Conn Smythe Trophy (playoff MVP) for the second time after having scored his second Stanley Cup-clinching goal. In 1976 he played, despite extreme pain, in the historic Canada Cup series against the Soviets, again winning the Outstanding Player award as Team Canada defeated the Soviets.

In 1976, wanting to prove to himself he could still play despite numerous knee surgeries, he signed with the Chicago Blackhawks for $3 million over five years, but he was able to play only twenty-six games. At age thirty, he hung up his skates. On January 9, 1979, Orr's number 4 was lifted to the rafters at Boston Garden. In 1979 he was the youngest player, at age thirty-one, elected to the Hockey Hall of Fame. A newspaper chose him in 1989 as the most representative Boston athlete.

Human qualities won Orr the enduring respect of fans and other players alike. In his retirement, Orr became a sports agent beginning in 1996. In 2000 he merged his agency with another, and the company became incorporated as Orr Hockey Group in 2002. He also has devoted his spare time to doing charity work throughout New England. Although his contracts with the Bruins paved the way for the higher pay scales of NHL stars, he never agreed to a heavy commercial use of his name and accomplishments.

Henri Paratte

SEE ALSO: *Boston Garden; Gretzky, Wayne; Hockey; Howe, Gordie; Hull, Bobby; National Hockey League (NHL).*

BIBLIOGRAPHY

Brunt, Stephen. *Searching for Bobby Orr.* Chicago: Triumph Books, 2006.

Fischler, Stan. *Bobby Orr and the Big, Bad Bruins.* New York: Dodd, Mead, 1969.

Hirschberg, Albert. *Bobby Orr: Fire on Ice.* New York: Putnam, 1975.

Liss, Howard. *Bobby Orr: Lightning on Ice.* Champaign, IL: Garrard Publishing, 1975.

Neely, Cam, Bobby Orr, et al. *Hockey for Everybody: Cam Neely's Guide to the Red-Hot Game on Ice.* Worcester, MA: Chandler House Press, 1998.

Smith, Jay H. *Hockey's Legend, Bobby Orr.* Mankato, MN: Creative Education, 1977.

The Osborne Brothers

Kentucky natives Bobby (1931–) and Sonny (1937–) Osborne made their mark on bluegrass and country music by combining innovative, jazzy instrumental work on the mandolin and banjo, respectively, with precise and powerful harmony singing. According to bluegrass historian Neil Rosenberg, "Bobby Osborne made a major contribution to bluegrass mandolin lead playing. . . . [M]ost bluegrass mandolin players play breaks like Bobby pioneered in the '50s."

Intent on finding steady work before country audiences, they were dogged by controversy in bluegrass circles over their use of country instrumentation (drums, pedal steel guitar, strings) and electric amplification in the 1960s and 1970s. (They would remove all amplification from their act in 1991.) The brothers achieved enduring popularity by creating a vocal style that emphasized Bobby's clear, high voice, placing two harmony parts underneath his leads; known as "high lead," this form of arrangement found widespread use by female singers in country and bluegrass.

The Brothers would become the first bluegrass band to perform for a college audience when they played at Antioch College in Ohio in 1960, and they were the first bluegrass band to play at the White House when they played for President Richard Nixon in 1973. Though it was only a modest commercial success when released, their 1967 recording of "Rocky Top" has since become one of the most recorded song in bluegrass music history. "Rocky Top" was named the state song of Tennessee in 1982, and a decade leader their arrangement of "Kentucky" was named that state's official song. In 1994 the brothers were inducted into the International Bluegrass Hall of Honor. When Sonny left the group for health reasons in 2004, the Osborne Brothers disbanded, although their music lives on with the annual Osborne Brothers festival held in Hyden, Kentucky, and in the music of Bobby's new band, Bobby Osborne & the Rocky Top X-Press.

Jon Weisberger

SEE ALSO: *Bluegrass; Country Music.*

BIBLIOGRAPHY

Artis, Bob. *Bluegrass: From the Lonesome Wail of a Mountain Love Song to the Hammering Drive of the Scruggs-Style Banjo, the Story of an American Musical Tradition.* New York: Hawthorn Books, 1975.

Rosenberg, Neil V., and Goldsmith, Thomas, eds. *The Bluegrass Reader.* Urbana: University of Illinois Press, 2004.

Osbourne, Ozzy *(1948–)*

With his image as a dangerously extreme rock musician, Ozzy Osbourne helped create the heavy metal genre and became one of the most outrageous performers of the 1980s. He first came to prominence as the lead vocalist for the British hard-rock group Black Sabbath from 1969 to 1978. Throughout his career, his music has consistently focused on alienation and nonconformity, from "Paranoid" (1970), one of Black Sabbath's biggest hits, to his solo song "Mama, I'm Coming Home" (1991).

As a master of overwrought stage performances, Osbourne showed other acts how to transform hard rock into theater, especially during his years with Black Sabbath, which employed pseudo-religious images such as upside-down crosses and pentagrams. He advocated the notion that a rock hero should be a troubled, alienated outcast. Of all of his contemporaries, his rebellion against church, family, and convention seems most extreme and genuine. He was simultaneously one of the most despised, censored, and idolized musical figures of the 1980s.

HUMBLE BEGINNINGS

John Michael Osbourne was born to a blue-collar family in Birmingham, England. He dabbled in vocal music in his early years while working in local steel mills and engaging in petty thievery. During a prison term, he tattooed the word "OZZY" onto his knuckles. His band, Earth, formed with Tony Iommi, Terry "Geezer" Butler, and Bill Ward, had some local success in the late 1960s, but it was after changing the band's name to Black Sabbath, a reference to the 1963 Italian horror film starring Boris Karloff, that the foursome recorded its first album and toured outside of Britain. Black Sabbath played blues hooks under muddy distortion, topping their often-disturbing sound with Osbourne's wavering nasal vocals.

Sabbath's first manager is reported to have said, "Black Sabbath makes Led Zeppelin look like a kindergarten house band." *Paranoid*, Black Sabbath's 1970 album, caught the attention of American record executives and catapulted Osbourne and his bandmates to world-class status. As he described it, "When we hit America we were the wild bunch. We bought dope and f—ed anything that moved." Black Sabbath's behavior did nothing to alienate audiences of the time, and their star rose steadily. The band produced hit after hit—its 1973 album *Sabbath Bloody Sabbath* was its fifth platinum-selling U.S. release.

GOING SOLO

Osbourne's addiction problems led to constant fights with Iommi, who fired Osbourne in 1979 at the height of the band's popularity. Osbourne, however, attributed his departure to his bouts with depression, the death of his father in 1977, and a sense that Black Sabbath were "losing their edge." Sabbath replaced him with Ronnie James Dio, and Osbourne struck out on his own. As a solo performer, Osbourne helped to hasten the development of the heavy metal genre. He capitalized on his reputation as a troubled soul with album titles such as *Diary of a Madman* (1981), *Speak of the Devil* (1982), and *The Ultimate Sin* (1986). A verse of his 1980 hit "Crazy Train" sums up Osbourne during this time: "Mental wounds not healing, life's a bitter shame / I'm going off the rails on a crazy train." Osbourne's dark songs became targets of the Religious Right and other groups concerned about the bad influence of rock music. He was sued more than once for the negative effects of his 1980 song "Suicide Solution," which Osbourne claimed was really about the ill effects of alcoholism.

Osbourne spent the 1980s developing a personal mythology that placed him on the gothic fringe of heavy metal. He threw raw meat into the crowd at concerts; was arrested for urinating on the Alamo; bit the head off of a dove in a record company's office; and, in his most publicized antic, allegedly bit the head off of a bat onstage. His stage performances were celebrated for their mania, and his personal life was equally chaotic. After he met Sharon Arden, who would become his second wife and his manager, he began to clean up his addiction problems. However, his *Diary of a Madman* tour in 1982 was beset by tragedy when the guitarist in his band, Randy Rhoads, died in bizarre plane crash. The plane had reportedly been making low passes over Osbourne's tour bus.

A KINDER, GENTLER OZZY

Finally sober, Osbourne released *No More Tears* in 1991. It was intended to be his last album before retirement, but it achieved crossover success, and one of its singles, "I Don't Want to Change the World," earned Osbourne his first Grammy. Thus, he decided to continue recording. While releasing solo efforts throughout the 1990s, Osbourne, his wife, and their son Jack also decided to become tour organizers, establishing an annual summer heavy metal festival called Ozzfest in 1996.

In 2002 the Osbourne family became famous with its MTV reality show *The Osbournes*, featuring Ozzy, Sharon, Jack, and daughter Kelly. Another daughter, Aimee, declined to appear. During the show's run from 2002 to 2005, Ozzy had his first-ever number one single in the UK (a duet with Kelly called "Changes," which was originally recorded by Black Sabbath) and a serious ATV accident in which he broke his collarbone, eight ribs, and some vertebrae and required emergency surgery. *The Osbournes* won the Emmy in 2002 for Outstanding Reality Program and, based on the show's success, the family was invited to host the 2003 American Music Awards. In 2005 Ozzy was inducted into the UK Music Hall of Fame, both as a solo artist and as a member of Black Sabbath and to the Rock and Roll Hall of Fame in the United States in 2006.

In 2009 Fox Entertainment announced the Osbournes would be leading their own prime-time variety show, *Osbournes Reloaded*; however many Fox affiliates chose to preempt the program, and only a shortened version of the premiere episode was ever aired in the United States. Osbourne released his tenth studio album, *Scream*, in 2010, which reached number four on the Billboard 200 chart. The first single, "Let Me Hear You Scream," debuted nationally on an episode of *CSI: New York*. In 2011 the satellite radio provider SiriusXM gave Osbourne his own 24/7 music channel, called Boneyard.

In addition to continuing his music career, Osbourne has become a best-selling author, publishing a memoir titled *I Am Ozzy* (2009) and *Trust Me, I'm Dr. Ozzy: Advice from Rock's Ultimate Survivor* (2011), a collection of his tongue-in-cheek health-advice columns that were previously printed in the *Sunday Times* and *Rolling Stone*. Both books were best sellers, providing further proof that the one-time bad boy of rock and roll had become a mainstream success.

Colby Vargas

SEE ALSO: *Black Sabbath;* CSI*; Emmy Awards; Heavy Metal; Led Zeppelin; MTV; Radio; Reality Television; Religious Right; Rock and Roll; Satellite Radio; Television; Top 40.*

BIBLIOGRAPHY

Osbourne, Ozzy. *The Best of Ozzy Osbourne*. New York: Hal Leonard, 1993.

Osbourne, Ozzy, and Chris Ayres. *I Am Ozzy*. New York: Grand Central Publishing, 2009.

Osbourne, Sharon. *Sharon Osbourne Extreme: My Autobiography*. New York: Springboard Press, 2006.

Rosen, Steven. *Wheels of Confusion: The Story of Black Sabbath*. New York: Music Sales, 1996.

Wylde, Zack, and Eric Hendrikx. *Bringing Metal to the Children: The Complete Berzerker's Guide to World Domination*. New York: William Morrow, 2012.

The Osbournes

While ordinary people were dominating reality television shows such as *Survivor* (2000–), *Big Brother* (2000–), and *American Idol* (2002–), at the turn of the twenty-first century, *The Osbournes*, starring Ozzy Osbourne, the former lead singer of the English heavy metal band Black Sabbath, and his family, proved that this emerging genre could also be hospitable to celebrities, especially those needing a career boost. *The Osbournes* premiered on March 2002 on MTV, becoming an immediate media sensation. This outrageous hybrid of family sitcom, heavy metal nostalgia, and Beverly Hills luxury generated the cable channel's highest rating to date and paved the way for its reality makeover with such series as *Punk'd* (2003–2007) and *Jersey Shore* (2009–).

In many ways *The Osbournes* was a reality television update of 1950s suburban comedies, such as *Father Knows Best* (1954–1960) and *Leave It to Beaver* (1957–1963). Like those shows, *The Osbournes* depicts the struggles and compromises of a nuclear family. The patriarch of the Osbourne brood was one of the most unlikely dads in television history: the iconic lead singer of a legendary British heavy metal band. Years of touring and substance abuse had left Osbourne dazed, but he revealed himself to be a loving parent. His shrewd manager and wife, Sharon, whose smarts and business savvy kept the family living in luxury, came into her own as a celebrity during the series run.

As in a typical sitcom, the show's kids spent the series searching for their own identity. Daughter Kelly is a gloomy pink-haired teenager, hoping to make it into show business as a singer. Her younger brother, Jack, is rebellious and likes to party. The oldest sibling, Aimee, refused to be on the show. During the run of the show, Sharon also took in a boy, Robert Marcato, after his mother died of cancer.

Also like a typical sitcom, *The Osbournes* features everyday occurrences. For example, Ozzy worries when Kelly goes out on the town, telling her, "Don't drink, don't do drugs, and if you have sex, wear a condom." The Osbournes battle their neighbors over loud music, and viewers learn that even the self-proclaimed "Prince of Darkness" has to clean up after family pets, just like everyone else.

The family also experienced some dark moments during the show. Sharon battled colon cancer, and Ozzy crashed an all-terrain vehicle and spent several weeks in a hospital. In the final episode, Dr. Phil McGraw, host of the talk show *Dr. Phil* (2003–), visits the Osbournes, examining the issues that affected the family.

Few reality shows were able to compete with *The Osbournes* in terms of national impact. In a review for the *New York Times*, critic Caryn James was amazed by "how fast the family has become an institution." *The Osbournes* received the Emmy Award for Outstanding Reality Show for its first season, and it went on to air for a total of four seasons, ending in 2005. In 2009 the family hosted a variety series called *Osbournes Reloaded* for the Fox television network, but it was canceled after just one episode.

Ron Simon

SEE ALSO: American Idol*; Black Sabbath; Cancer; Emmy Awards;* Father Knows Best*;* Leave It to Beaver*; McGraw, Dr. Phil;*

MTV; Osbourne, Ozzy; Punk'd*; Reality Television;* Survivor*; Television.*

BIBLIOGRAPHY

James, Caryn. "*The Osbournes* Return, Still Weird and Warm." *New York Times*, November 26, 2002.

Osbourne, Ozzy, and Chris Ayres. *I Am Ozzy*. New York: Grand Central Publishing, 2011.

Osbourne, Sharon. *Sharon Osbourne Extreme: My Autobiography*. New York: Springboard Press, 2006.

The Oscars

SEE: *Academy Awards.*

Ouija Boards

The mysterious Ouija board has long epitomized the fear and curiosity people feel toward the unknown. Noted as being used by Pythagoras as early as 540 BCE, ouija boards came to more popular attention in the nineteenth century when they were played as parlor games. To use a ouija board, one or more people place their fingers lightly on the indicator, which moves across the wooden board, seemingly involuntarily, from letter to letter, making words or sentences. The messages created during the game have been described as links to the spiritual world and/or the subconsciousness of the players.

Ouija Board. *Ouija board users rest their hands on the indicator, awaiting a message from beyond.* JAMES PORTER/ALAMY.

The modern ouija board was invented to ease the process of what believers thought of as communicating with the beyond. Its predecessors included the "automatic writing" of nineteenth-century French spiritualist M. Planchette and the system of raps (one for no, two for yes) devised by the Fox sisters of New York state, who were among the first to hold séances with the dead. In 1891 Charles Kennard set up the Kennard Novelty Company to market the ouija board that he, E. C. Reiche, and Elijah Bond had designed. Their flat wooden board was inscribed with two arches, one of letters and one of numbers, with "Yes" and "No" options on either side. The board had an indicator (called a planchette) that floated mysteriously across the board to spell out words when users lightly placed their fingers on it. Throughout the years various methods of communication have been devised for the boards, including automatic writing, drawing, and musical notation.

In 1892 William Fuld purchased the company and renamed it the Ouija Novelty Company. It was Fuld who explained the name *Ouija* as the combination of the French and German words for *yes*. After he died in 1927, the company remained a family operation until 1966, when Parker Brothers bought the business.

Studying ouija boards in 1914, William F. Barrett of the American Society for Psychical Research declared that after "reviewing the results as a whole, I am convinced of their supernatural character, and that we have here an exhibition of some intelligent discarnate agency, mingling with the personality of one or more of the sitters and guiding their muscular movements." In addition to those who viewed the ouija board as a medium for receiving messages from other worlds, others suggested that the boards were a medium for the subconscious of an individual or a group to say things that they would not voice out loud. After World War I and the Spanish flu epidemic caused the deaths of hundreds of thousands, spiritualism became very popular and so did ouija boards. National newspapers ran regular columns devoted to the subject of ouija boards.

Mrs. John H. Curran is perhaps the most noted ouija board user. A woman of limited education and travel, she nevertheless created texts of quality by using the ouija board. Her books, *The Sorry Tale: A Story of the Time of Christ* (1917), *Hope Trueblood* (1918), and *The Pot upon the Wheel* (1921), listed the spirit Patience Worth as the imputed author and Mrs. Curran as the communicator.

In the 1970s ouija boards played a role in frightening urban legends and graphic horror films, including *The Exorcist* (1973), which linked them to evil spirits and demon possession. At this time, moral and religious objections to ouija boards increased. The dangerous connotations of ouija boards spurred some users to incorporate ritual elements into the use of the boards, including reciting Psalm 23 and opening and closing each session with blessings. In the 2000s ouija boards continue to be viewed either as dangerous links to the occult or as amusing games. Yet the devices continued their hold on the popular imagination. The use of a ouija board was a plot device in the hit movie *Paranormal Activity* (2007), and versions of ouija boards can be found online.

Nickianne Moody

SEE ALSO: *Board Games;* The Exorcist*; Monopoly; Parker Brothers; Psychics.*

BIBLIOGRAPHY

Cornelius, J. Edward. *Aleister Crowley and the Ouija Board.* Port Townsend, WA: Feral House, 2005.

Covina, Gina. *The Ouija Book.* New York: Simon & Schuster, 1979.

Gruss, Edmond C. *The Ouija Board: A Doorway to the Occult.* Phillipsburg, NJ: P&R Publishing, 1994.

Hunt, Stoker. *Ouija: The Most Dangerous Game.* New York: Barnes and Noble, 1985.

Stadtmauer, Saul A. *Visions of the Future: Magic Boards.* New York: Contemporary Perspectives, 1977.

Our Gang

Children acting like children—making mischief and finding themselves in goofy predicaments as they play with their pals—has been a foundation for endless and ageless humor. This is precisely what producer Hal Roach had in mind when he began making his *Our Gang* comedies in 1922. In these films a hard-scrabble conglomeration of boys and girls come together to amuse themselves and their audiences with prankishness and frivolity. The series was astoundingly successful, and over the next twenty-two years 221 ten- and twenty-minute-long *Our Gang* comedies were produced, with Roach reenergizing the series by adding carefully selected replacements as his pint-sized stars outgrew their roles.

Our Gang comedies were not completely original, having evolved from a series of "Sunshine Sammy" shorts produced by Roach in 1921 and 1922 and featuring Ernie "Sunshine Sammy" Morrison, a black child actor. Back in the 1920s the majority of silent comedy shorts emphasized visual humor and pratfalls over plotlines; indeed, many comic one- and two-reelers were surreal affairs in which a zany star moved from one unrelated predicament to the next. *Our Gang* films were different in that they were more story driven, with the humor a byproduct of the everyday situations in which the children found themselves.

ACTOR CHARACTERISTICS

While seeking out the right mix of youngsters to star in the series, Roach emphasized character types over acting ability or experience. He was searching for children who were naturally funny, either because of their physical appearance or the manner in which they interacted among their peers or around adults, rather than those who could become characters on cue. His aim was to milk laughs from their instinctive behavior. At the same

Our Gang *Stars.* *Some of the child stars of the* Our Gang *serial comedies pose together around 1930.* IMAGNO/CONTRIBUTOR/HULTON ARCHIVE/GETTY IMAGES.

time, Roach wanted his *Our Gang* kids to be resourceful and tenacious. These were youngsters who needed no adults to show them how to enjoy themselves. In fact, Mickey Rooney, then at the beginning of his long Hollywood career, unsuccessfully auditioned for *Our Gang* in the late 1920s. It was Roach's belief that, even at his young age, Rooney was too affected to fit into the series.

The naturalness of the *Our Gang* kids could also be contrasted to the popular child stars of the day, including Jackie Coogan and Shirley Temple, who were tug-at-your-heartstrings adorable, starring in classics of children's literature or other material artificially contrived for the cinema. The *Our Gang* comedies were not set in faraway locales; indeed, the most exotic spots in which the youngsters found themselves were junkyards, ball fields, or makeshift backyard stages. They were not depicted as orphans to be teamed with an adult as Coogan was teamed with Chaplin's Little Tramp in *The Kid*; neither were they polished miniature belters and hoofers who, like Temple, could wow one and all while vocalizing "On the Good Ship Lollipop" and tap dancing with Bill "Bojangles" Robinson.

While Coogan played *Oliver Twist* (1922), *Little Robinson Crusoe* (1924), and *A Boy of Flanders* (1924) and Temple starred in *Baby Take a Bow* (1934), *Susannah of the Mounties* (1939), and *Little Miss Broadway* (1938), the *Our Gang* titles were much more akin to a child's real life: *Circus Fever* (1925), *Ask Grandma (1925), Helping Grandma (1931), Shootin' Injuns* (1925), *Your Own Back Yard (1925), Buried Treasure* (1925), *Telling Whoppers* (1926), *Baby Brother* (1927), *Rainy Days* (1928), *Wiggle Your Ears* (1929), *Fly My Kite* (1931), *Bedtime Worries* (1933), *Mama's Little Pirate* (1934), *The Awful Tooth* (1938), *Hide and Shriek* (1938), and *Practical Jokers* (1938). Quite a few emphasized the trials of education: *School Begins* (1928), *Readin' and Writin'* (1932), *Playin' Hookey* (1928), *Fish Hooky* (1933), *Spooky Hooky* (1936), *Bored of Education* (1936), *Time Out for Lessons* (1939), and *Teacher's Beau.* Others spotlighted pets: *Love My Dog* (1927); *Cat, Dog & Co.* (1929); *Pups Is Pups* (1930); *Dogs Is Dogs* (1931); *The Pooch* (1932); and *Dog Days* (1925).

THE CHILD ACTORS

The series debut was titled, appropriately enough, *Our Gang.* The original members were a mix of types: cute and lovable Mary Kornman; pretty Peggy Cartwright; freckle-faced Mickey Daniels, a true (albeit vulnerable) leader of boys, girls, and pets; devilish Jackie Condon; good-looking, rough-and-tough Jackie Davis; roguish yet cheerful Ernie "Sunshine Sammy" Morrison himself, who at age eleven was the eldest in the group; and its littlest member, one-year-old Allen Clayton "Farina" Hoskins, who would be featured in 105 *Our Gang* comedies—more than any of his fellow players. The first of the *Our Gang* pets was a mule named Dinah; the most famous came to be Pete the Pup, a bulldog with a black circle painted around his right eye. Added to the group early on were such diverse types as fat Joe Cobb and all-American handsome Johnny Downs.

As the years passed and these kids outgrew their roles, they were replaced by other pubescent performers. Jackie Cooper (who was six and seven years old when he appeared in fifteen *Our Gang* films) was a rare casting exception in that he was a showbiz veteran who had been performing on-screen since age three. He later enjoyed an impressive (albeit brief) career as a junior Hollywood superstar, earning an Academy Award nomination in 1930 for his performance in *Skippy.* Other casting selections were more in the original *Our Gang* mold. Norman "Chubby" Chaney was a clone of Joe Cobb, while Jean Darling and Darla Hood were pretty-girl replacements. Engaging little Bobby "Wheezer" Hutchins fit in nicely, as did Dorothy De-Borba, Scotty Beckett, Eugene "Porky" Lee, and Tommy "Butch" Bond. Another *Our Gang* performer started out billed as Mickey Gubitosi. He eventually changed his name to Bobby Blake and grew up to be Robert Blake, Emmy Award–winning star of the hit television series *Baretta.*

The most renowned and beloved of the kids, however, were a quartet of 1930s series headliners: Matthew "Stymie" Beard and William Henry "Buckwheat" Thomas (both captivating "Farina" successors); freckle-faced, creaky-voiced Carl "Alfalfa" Switzer; and pudgy, irrepressible George "Spanky" McFarland, arguably the most popular of all *Our Gang* actors. These youngsters are the best known in the early twenty-first century, because the most enduring *Our Gang* comedies came during their years with the series and their films were talkies—the first nonsilent *Our Gang* film was *Small Talk,* released in 1929—and are more likely to be screened on television. (Because ownership of the name *Our Gang* was held by Metro-Goldwyn-Mayer (MGM), the series was renamed *The Little Rascals* when it first came to TV in 1955.)

One other special feature of the *Our Gang* films is that their casts were integrated—"Sunshine Sammy," "Farina," "Buckwheat," and "Stymie" were black—and all the children were allowed to act funny in equal measure. Back in the 1920s, 1930s, and 1940s, African American characters in Hollywood movies were commonly and demeaningly stereotyped as lower-class types, mammies and maids, train porters, and janitors who usually fractured the English language. In *Our Gang* films, children were children, whether black or white.

In 1938 the changing economics of the movie business resulted in a sharp decrease in the production of comedy shorts. That year Roach sold his rights to the series to MGM, and the quality of *Our Gang* films sharply declined. Of the 221 films in the series, a fair share from all periods was bound to be lackluster. Still, the series was loaded with what film historians and *Our Gang* experts Leonard Maltin and Richard W. Bann have called "imperishable comedy classics, full of heart and warmth." All those are from the 1930s. "If *Our Gang* had made only a dozen films like *Dogs Is Dogs, Mama's Little Pirate, Hi-Neighbor!, Free Wheeling, The Kid from Borneo, Teacher's Pet, Bedtime Worries, Divot Diggers, Our Gang Follies of 1938, Glove Taps, Fly My Kite* and *Pups Is Pups,*" note Maltin and Bann, "the series would be worthy of comparison with the best short films of Chaplin, Keaton, Laurel & Hardy, W.C. Fields, and anyone else who's come before or since, in theaters or on television."

AFTER THE SHOW

Only a couple of *Our Gang* alumni eventually went on to thriving careers in show business. Blake won his stardom only after being booted out of high school and embracing drugs and alcohol. After his career as a child performer waned, Cooper endured a rough period as a young actor before becoming a television sitcom star, director, and executive producer. Blake and Cooper were the glaring exceptions. After leaving the series, quite a few of the kids made some additional films or worked in vaudeville and on radio and television, only then to drift out of the industry. Meanwhile, the careers of others ended at the conclusion of their series stints.

Condon went on to become an accountant at Rockwell International, and Cobb also worked there. Daniels was a construction engineer, Hoskins worked with the mentally disabled, and Davis became a doctor. Thomas worked as a lab technician, and McFarland toiled at a variety of odd jobs, eventually becoming a sales executive. The lives of other "Our Gangers" were brief and tragic. Hutchins served in the army during World War II and then became an air cadet. He was twenty years old when he was killed during an instructional drill just after the war's end. Chaney became much more than plump. As an adolescent, his weight ballooned to 300 pounds. He was afflicted with a glandular disorder and died at age eighteen.

Sadly, the plights and fates of several *Our Gang* graduates reflect upon the often disastrous lives led by child stars who are unable to adjust to normal life away from the spotlight. Beard quit high school and ended up a heroin addict and petty criminal who did not rehabilitate himself until the 1960s. While featured in small parts in quite a few high-prestige Hollywood features of the 1930s and 1940s, including *Going My Way* (1944), *It's a Wonderful Life* (1946), *State of the Union* (1948), *A Letter to Three Wives* (1949), and *Pat and Mike* (1952), Switzer was no longer a leading light, and he was just thirty-one when he was killed by a former business partner in a dispute over a $50 debt. While still a teenager, Beckett began leading a tumultuous life that was characterized by frequent lawbreaking. He died at age thirty-eight of a fatal beating.

Ironically, Roach, the comic genius behind *Our Gang*, outlived most of his youthful actors. He died in 1992 at the age of 100.

Rob Edelman

SEE ALSO: *Chaplin, Charlie; Fields, W. C.; Hollywood;* It's a Wonderful Life*; Keaton, Buster; Laurel and Hardy; Screwball Comedies; Television; Temple, Shirley.*

BIBLIOGRAPHY

Bond, Tommy "Butch," and Ron Genini. *Darn Right It's Butch: Memories of Our Gang, The Little Rascals.* Wayne, PA: Morgin Press, 1994.

Maltin, Leonard. *The Great Movie Shorts.* New York: Crown Publishers, 1972.

Maltin, Leonard, and Richard W. Bann. *Our Gang: The Life and Times of the Little Rascals.* New York: Crown Publishers, 1977.

The Outer Limits

From 1963 to 1965 *The Outer Limits* was the gold standard of television science fiction. The hour-long series, broadcast weekly by ABC, adopted the anthology format of earlier series such as *The Twilight Zone* and *Tales of Tomorrow*. *Outer Limits* distinguished itself from these seminal programs with its high production values and its emphasis on "hard" science concepts and themes. "What is all this experimentation and exploration getting us?" the series seemed to ask time and time again, with the standard answer being a kick in the chops from a large mutated alien.

Outer Limits was the brainchild of two men. Producers Leslie Stevens and Joseph Stefano both came with theatrical and feature film backgrounds. Stevens had written the script for *The Left-Handed Gun*, a 1958 Western starring a young Paul Newman. Stefano had enjoyed even more success, penning the screenplay for Alfred Hitchcock's classic *Psycho* in 1960. The pair teamed up in 1962 to begin work on Stevens's idea for a sci-fi anthology series, originally titled *Please Stand By*.

After a year of work, *Please Stand By* germinated into *The Outer Limits*. A pilot was sold to ABC, and the series premiered on the network on September 16, 1963. In some ways, it was a typical sci-fi genre show. Like *The Twilight Zone*, the stand-alone stories were bracketed by narration. Voice-over specialist Vic Perrin supplied the all-knowing "Control Voice" for these segments, reminding viewers that "there is nothing wrong with your television set." The program's startling visual effects were light years beyond any show of its time, evidence of the care and thinking lavished on the series by its creators. As the playlets unfolded, television watchers of the early 1960s were introduced to a number of performers who would go on to become household names on other series, including Martin Landau, William Shatner, and Robert Culp.

The Outer Limits is remembered primarily for its elaborately realized monsters—or "bears" as they were known in production parlance. Notable entries in this derby of horrors included "The Zanti Misfits," a race of antlike extraterrestrials; a hissing lizard-like creature in "Fun and Games"; and the amphibious beasts of "Tourist Attraction." A crack team of production specialists, including professional monster performer Janos Prohaska, was brought in to bring these exotic creatures to life.

When *The Outer Limits* wasn't shocking the bejesus out of viewers, it could also generate terror in subtler, more suggestive ways. Episodes such as "The Man Who Was Never Born," about an earth inhabitant of the far future who returns to the present day to kill his own father and thus prevent a worldwide plague, featured little of the pyrotechnics customary to the "bear" installments. Another classic episode, "The Hundred Days of the Dragon," involved the replacement of an American presidential aspirant by a double created by the Chinese—a plot strongly reminiscent of the feature film *The Manchurian Candidate* (1962).

These atypical stories were among the series' finest, but they became increasingly rare as low ratings forced network executives to ratchet up the monster content. By the show's second season, a "bear a week" policy had been put in place—albeit with budget cuts that compelled the supplanting of intricately designed creatures with cheaply constructed puppets. Leslie Stevens and Joseph Stefano left the show altogether, and though a number of classic episodes were filmed—"Demon with a Glass Hand" by veteran fantasist Harlan Ellison is a notable standout—the quality of the show slipped precipitously. The axe of cancellation fell in January 1965.

The Outer Limits never lost its core fan following, however. Reruns of the show continued in syndication, introducing it to a whole new generation of viewers. From 1995 to 2002 the Showtime cable network revived *The Outer Limits* using the same sci-fi anthology format but largely foregoing the "monster of the week" approach. Stefano himself returned to contribute scripts for the new show. Directorial chores went to the usual sci-fi veterans, as well as such "outside-the-box" choices as *Beverly Hills, 90210* heartthrob Jason Priestley, *SCTV* alum Catherine O'Hara, and blaxploitation pioneer Melvin van Peebles. The series spawned the development of an *Outer Limits* feature film by the Trilogy Entertainment Group for MGM (Metro-Goldwyn-Mayer).

Robert E. Schnakenberg

SEE ALSO: Beverly Hills, 90210; *Ellison, Harlan; Hitchcock, Alfred;* The Manchurian Candidate; *MGM (Metro-Goldwyn-Mayer); Newman, Paul;* Psycho; *Television;* The Twilight Zone.

BIBLIOGRAPHY

Abbott, Jon. *Irwin Allen Television Productions, 1964–1970.* Jefferson, NC: McFarland, 2006.

Schow, David J., and Jeffrey Frentzen. *The Outer Limits: The Official Companion.* New York: Ace Science Fiction Books, 1986.

Outing

Unlike most other identity variables, homosexuality is invisible. Western culture may have developed a complex and elaborate range of codes by which people identify homosexuality—from voice (lisps) and gestures (limp wrists) to hairstyles and clothing (gay male flamboyance, lesbian dungarees)—but these remain only suggestions. The codes are transient and could, indeed, be adopted by anyone. This means that homosexuality can easily remain hidden and that its revelation can truly come as a shock. *Outing* is the activity of exposing someone's homosexuality; the shifting forms it has taken over the twentieth century are indicative of changing attitudes toward sexuality.

FORCED IN THE CLOSET

Given that lesbians and gay men have endured a history of persecution due to their sexual orientation, the ability to "hide" homosexuality is a useful survival tool. Over the course of the twentieth century, homosexuality has been culturally conceptualized variously as an illness, as "unnatural," and as a moral weakness. Such widespread views, with their core notion of homosexuals as "lesser" individuals, have led to bullying and acts of violence against individual lesbians and gay men. They also enable the reputations and statuses of individuals to be instantly tarnished; accusations of homosexuality supposedly expose inferiority. Outing can thus be employed as a political smearing device. For example, Senator Joseph McCarthy's attempts in the 1950s to uncover all subversive anti-American activities took the form of witch hunts for communist sympathizers. This included homosexuals; McCarthy conflated homosexuality with communism in his paranoid drive to expunge political and moral minorities from the United States.

It is difficult to think outside the dominant (negative) conceptualizations of homosexuality because they have been (and remain) so prevalent. The birth of the gay rights movement in the late 1960s, however, proposed an alternative—a positive conception of homosexuality. Lesbians and gay men claimed that they were "glad to be gay." "Gay is good," proclaimed sloganeers, while lesbians and gay men outed themselves to publicly demonstrate that they were not degenerates and that, in fact, they were little different from "normal" heterosexuals. (Historically, there had previously been more minor attempts to garner acceptance for homosexuals, such as the efforts of the American "Mattachine Society" of the 1950s; the scale of organization, among other factors, prevented success.) Again, this form of outing has a political dimension. For the gay rights movement, as with other civil rights movements, the personal was/is political, and outing oneself was a way of expressing solidarity with other, similar, marginalized individuals. Although a risky process, outing oneself enabled participation in a burgeoning lesbian and gay community.

Despite the best efforts of the gay rights movement, homosexuality has continued to be widely conceived of in a negative way. Thus, even as individuals continue to find group solidarity in coming out, particular groups (the political right and conservative Christians, particularly) still out homosexuals to imply their inferiority. The gay rights cause has not been helped by the emergence of the AIDS epidemic. The spread of the virus that causes AIDS was initially highly concentrated among gay men and particular black minorities and was thus sometimes seen as (perhaps divine) judgment exacted upon the marginalized. AIDS often manifests through cancerous facial scarring and thyroid problems, altering facial appearance; suddenly, the invisible homosexuality of gay men was readable in physical symptoms.

OUTING AS A POLITICAL STATEMENT

Following the Stonewall riots of 1969 and the expansion of the gay rights movement over the following decade, the late 1980s and early 1990s saw an additional twist added to the history of outing: the formation of a more radical group of gay rights activists. "Queer" activism, as it became known, believed that the perspective of the 1970s gay rights movement had been too assimilationist; that is, it was looking for acceptance by the heterosexual mainstream. With a chant of "we're here, we're queer, get used to it," queer activists loudly proclaimed their difference from, rather than similarity to, heterosexuals. The underlying drive, however, was similar—to reduce the stigma against sexual minorities.

For queer activists, reducing this stigma involved outing themselves but also, notably, public figures. This included individuals seen as hypocritical, such as priests and politicians who publicly preached against what they performed in private, but it could also include media celebrities. The argument mustered was that if all "hidden" homosexuals were outed, the widespread prevalence of homosexuality would be recognized and the stigma would be removed. Such tactics have been harshly criticized by those who believe that outing by others is never acceptable behavior. Even within the gay community, there is a good deal of controversy over the ethics of outing. Whereas a federal district judge held in 2004 that calling someone gay does not constitute slander or libel, the label may be devastating to individuals who choose to remain closeted and to those who are erroneously labeled as homosexual.

This imposed form of outing carries problematic moral, ethical, and conceptual implications. For many people, the outing of oneself should be a personal decision, not one forced upon them by a group of activists with a particular political agenda. Perhaps more problematically, outing serves to reproduce rigid sexuality boundaries—one is either gay, straight, or bisexual—whereas a great deal of evidence would seem to suggest that sexuality is a much more fluid variable. In the 1990s, then, it became clear that the differences between queer activists, tabloid journalists, and religious/political groups, all of whom out people for particular reasons, were more complex and confused than they were only twenty years previously.

On August 5, 1990, the *San Francisco Chronicle* announced that Hollywood stars were becoming petrified over being outed. After the gay press had initiated the practice in 1989, the tabloids had picked it up. It soon spread to mainstream media. By the early twenty-first century, the list of celebrities who had been outed or who had outed themselves had grown to include entertainers Rosie O'Donnell, Neil Patrick Harris, Cynthia Nixon, Jane Lynch, Portia de Rossi, Meredith Baxter, Wanda Sykes, and Sara Gilbert. Some revelations of homosexuality, such as announcements by singing sensations Lance Bass and Ricky Martin, caused major ripples, but in general most people applauded these celebrities for acknowledging who they really were and for serving as positive role models for young gays and lesbians. Openness about one's sexual orientation had become common enough, in fact, that outing was no longer much of an issue. In more conservative circles, however, the acknowledgment that one is gay can be seen as career suicide. As a result, gospel singer Ray Boltz and country singer Chely Wright spent their lives trying to hide who they were before going public with their homosexuality. Politicians continued to be among the most vulnerable gays, and many have become the butt of jokes for hiding their sexual orientation.

Glyn Davis

SEE ALSO: *Gay Liberation Movement; Gay Men; Lesbianism; Martin, Ricky; McCarthyism; O'Donnell, Rosie; Stonewall Rebellion; Sykes, Wanda.*

BIBLIOGRAPHY

Marech, Rona. "Activists Consider Ethics, Efficacy of Outing." *San Francisco Chronicle*, November 14, 2004.

Gross, Larry. *Contested Closets: The Politics and Ethics of Outing.* Minneapolis: University of Minnesota Press, 1993.

Johansson, Warren, and William A. Percy. *Outing: Shattering the Conspiracy of Silence.* New York: Haworth Press, 1994.

McLaren, Angus. *Sexual Blackmail: A Modern History.* Cambridge, MA: Harvard University Press, 2002.

Murphy, Timothy F., ed. *Gay Ethics: Controversies in Outing, Civil Rights, and Sexual Science.* New York: Haworth Press, 1994.

Signorile, Michelangelo. *Queer in America: Sex, the Media, and the Closets of Power.* New York: Random House, 1993.

Signorile, Michelangelo. *Hitting Hard.* New York: Carroll & Graf, 2005.

The Outline of History

British author H. G. Wells is probably best known today for his forays into science fiction. Indeed, many consider him the father of modern science fiction, and the influence of his novels—such as *The Time Machine* (1895), *The War of the Worlds* (1898), *The Invisible Man* (1897), and *The Island of Doctor Moreau* (1896)—can be seen throughout the genre. But Wells was no mere writer of fantastic tales. In fact, science fiction made up but a fraction of his more than eighty published books. Wells also worked within the traditional forms of the novel and wrote extensive nonfiction, often with a sociological bent. Of all his work, none had the impact of *The Outline of History*. This massive project was first published serially in 1919, and as a single volume in September 1920, to critical and popular acclaim, initially selling an astonishing two million copies. Besides being one of the most popular histories ever written, the book was groundbreaking, a new kind of history text, arguing for a holistic look at history with a nod to the necessary subjectivity of such a project. Wells acknowledged that history was what the historian made of it, and his own interests manifested themselves as he regarded the history of humanity as a story of inevitable change and progress toward world unification.

Wells's own life certainly shaped the views that would manifest themselves in *The Outline of History*. He was born in 1866 in Bromley, Kent, into a lower-middle-class family that, in 1880, would experience financial collapse, dropping into poverty. Wells experienced firsthand the economic struggles of those trying merely to survive. He continued in school, however, eventually working briefly as an apprentice draper. After quitting his apprenticeship and returning to school, Wells had his break in 1884—a scholarship to the Normal School of Science in South Kensington. There he came under the tutelage of T. H. Huxley, and it was during this time that he was introduced to the Socialist party. After earning his degree in zoology, Wells published his first book, *A Text-book of Biology*.

The impact of the natural sciences and socialist thought is visible throughout Wells's work, informing both his fiction and his nonfiction. Ultimately, divergent works such as *The Time Machine* and *The Outline of History* explore the same territory, examining the way humankind has evolved or will evolve. In writing *The Outline of History*, Wells had definite agendas. He claimed that the book was an attempt to explain the truth about human nature, arguing that that nature was one of change; humankind, in other words, had been gradually evolving toward a greater social state. For Wells the evolution toward global unity was to be applauded, but he was aware that although change must by nature occur, there was nothing dictating that such change would be positive. *The Outline of History* thus served as a cautionary tale that not only demonstrated how humanity had advanced, but also highlighted historical figures and institutions that resisted this change. On these grounds Wells encouraged education, elevated sound philosophy and literature, and discouraged sexual licentiousness (in print, if not in person).

Yet Wells was not content to state his ideas and let the public sort them out. Instead, he enlisted the aid of the numerous experts through which *The Outline of History* passed to contribute footnotes to the work, sometimes complementary, sometimes argumentative. The footnotes made clear to the reader that the work was not intended as the final word on history, but only the beginning of the conversation. They also suggested the "interpretability" and mutability of historical thought. And the footnotes were not the only standout feature of *The Outline of History*. Illustrations and charts filled the book and, stylistically, it demonstrated Wells's wit and accessibility.

H. G. Wells did not strictly consider himself a historian. Thus, it is understandable that, though critically acclaimed within the field, *The Outline of History* was largely intended for a lay audience, as evidenced by its readability and Wells's own insistence on the importance of knowledge to the common people. Previously, history texts of this scope had been largely academic, but now history had entered the popular realm. The success of the book surprised and pleased Wells; understandably, it became his own dearest achievement and one on which he would continue to work. Subsequent editions were published with additions and modifications by the author into the 1940s. *The Outline of History* also spawned other works. An abbreviated version of the book, *A Short History of the World*, sold nearly as well, whereas two companion books, *The Science of Life* (written with Julian Huxley and H. G.'s son G. P.) and *The Work, Wealth and Happiness of Mankind*, failed to perform as expected.

Despite these failures and the fact that *The Outline of History* is not nearly so widely disseminated in the 2010s, the impact of Wells's most ambitious project has been profound. The work is still considered by many to be one of the great books of the twentieth century and one of the finest overviews of human history. Most importantly, perhaps, Wells's dream of educating the masses has largely been fulfilled, and *The Outline of History* deserves much of the credit for dragging the field of history away from the exclusive grasp of experts and scholars and into the public forum.

Marc Oxoby

SEE ALSO: War of the Worlds.

BIBLIOGRAPHY

Foot, Michael. *H. G.: The History of Mr. Wells*. Washington, DC: Counterpoint, 1995.

Kemp, Peter. *H. G. Wells and the Culminating Ape*. New York: St. Martin's Press, 1996.

Murray, Brian. *H. G. Wells*. New York: Continuum, 1990.

Reed, John R. *The Natural History of H. G. Wells*. Athens: Ohio University Press, 1982.

Ross, William T. *H. G. Wells's World Reborn: The Outline of History and Its Companions*. Cranbury, NJ: Associated University Presses, 2002.

Owens, Buck *(1929–2006)*

Challenging Nashville country music conventions, the Bakersfield-based Buck Owens helped put his California town on the musical map. He shunned the background singing and orchestral fluff that dominated country music in the late 1950s and early 1960s, preferring a spare, twangy, rock-influenced sound. Along with Bakersfield native Merle Haggard, Owens helped popularize a more "authentic" version of country music known as the Bakersfield Sound. Their style better reflected the country music played in bars and honky-tonks throughout the United States. Despite Owens's great musical influence—he made a big impression on such artists as Gram Parsons, and his song "Act Naturally" was covered by the Beatles—he is most commonly remembered as a television personality from the country comedy variety show *Hee-Haw*, on which he appeared from its inception in 1969 until 1986.

Owens was born in Sherman, Texas. In the 1930s his family moved to Mesa, Arizona, where he met and later married country singer Bonnie Campbell; the couple had two sons. Owens moved his family to Bakersfield, where he began playing music around town. Although it was semidepressed, the town provided a slight relief for the many people escaping the 1930s midwestern Dust Bowl. Bars proliferated as a distraction from the bleak conditions of the surrounding area. Owens once claimed that Bakersfield's music was actually a reaction to those desperate conditions, providing a welcome escape. In defining the Bakersfield Sound, he emphasized the elements that got live crowds most excited: loud, twangy electric guitar laid atop a rock-and-roll backbeat and bouncy bass. He developed the style during his days playing guitar with Bill Woods's Orange Blossom Playboys at one of Bakersfield's more popular clubs, the Black Board. His signature technique is evident in his first hit, "Under Your Spell Again" (1959) and in his number one hits, "Act Naturally" (1963) and "I've Got a Tiger by the Tail" (1964).

Owens's success helped add variety to country music of the 1960s: his more edgy sound provided a counterbalance to the string-laden recordings being produced in Nashville at the time. He used his commercial success to open the doors for Haggard, who quickly went on to match Owens's sales and artistic influence. Owens also used his newfound clout to branch out, and by the late 1960s he owned a television production company, a significant amount of real estate, numerous radio stations, a management company, and a booking agency; he became a Bakersfield music giant both behind and in front of the scene.

In 1969 *Hee-Haw* made its debut, initially as a summer replacement show. It gained enormous popularity, however, and brought Owens, who regularly hosted and appeared on the show through the mid-1980s, even greater celebrity. Despite his popularity on *Hee-Haw*, Owens virtually disappeared from the music scene by the mid-1970s—partially because of a self-imposed exile from which he only rarely emerged. He played a few live dates and occasionally recorded a live album or duet. Owens and Emmylou Harris's "Play Together Again, Again" was a highlight of 1979. Owens died of a heart attack on March 25, 2006, a few hours after playing at his Bakersfield restaurant and club, the Crystal Palace.

Kembrew McLeod

SEE ALSO: *The Beatles; Country Music; The Great Depression; Haggard, Merle;* Hee Haw*; Radio; Rock and Roll; Television.*

BIBLIOGRAPHY

Carr, Patrick, ed. *Illustrated History of Country Music*. New York: Random House/Times Books, 1995.

Dawidoff, Nicholas. *In the Country of Country: A Journey to the Roots of American Music*. New York: Vintage, 1998.

Sisk, Eileen. *Buck Owens: The Biography*. Chicago: Chicago Review Press, 2010.

Owens, Jesse *(1913–1980)*

J. C. "Jesse" Owens is best remembered for participating in the 1936 Olympics in Berlin, where he won four gold medals in track and field as part of the U.S. team. His success as a black athlete was an affront to the Nazi doctrine of Aryan supremacy, and German chancellor Adolf Hitler refused to congratulate him on the feat, leaving the stadium before the awards ceremony began. The politics of Owens's Olympic achievement, as much as the achievement itself, have sealed his place in history.

His victories at "Hitler's" Olympics highlighted a clear division within pre–World War II Europe but had ambiguous implications for domestic U.S. politics. In the year before his triumph in Berlin, white mobs lynched nearly two dozen black Americans, and Harlem witnessed its worst racial rioting since

Jesse Owens at 1936 Olympics. *Jesse Owens flies through the air during the long jump event at the 1936 Olympic Games in Berlin, Germany, where he won four gold medals.* CENTRAL PRESS/STRINGER/HULTON ARCHIVE/GETTY IMAGES.

1919. Although Owens received widespread public acclaim on his return from Germany, including a ticker tape parade in New York, the White House did not acknowledge his performance through any official channels. Despite the racial climate in the United States—which would later segregate black soldiers in the fight against Aryan supremacy—Owens was hailed as a living symbol of American freedom and democracy. Scholars have compared the complex political implications of his achievement to those of the victory of Joe Louis, the black American boxer, over Max Schmeling, "Hitler's heavyweight."

Like Louis, Owens was the son of Alabama sharecroppers. He was nine when his family moved to Cleveland, Ohio. His athletic prowess was already evident in junior high school, where he established the first in a remarkable series of performances that extended his records in long jump and broad jump. He later joined The Ohio State University's track team and on May 25, 1935, set three world records, in the 220-yard sprint, 220-yard low hurdles, and long jump. He also tied the record for the 100-yard sprint.

He retained a high profile in the years after his retirement from competitive athletics and became an influential figure in American sports administration. In 1950 he was named top track performer in a poll of American sportswriters, and in 1955, as an ambassador of sports, he represented the United States in a goodwill tour of India, Malaysia, Singapore, and the Philippines. In 1956 he was President Dwight D. Eisenhower's personal representative at the Olympics in Melbourne, Australia, and in 1976 President Gerald Ford presented him with the highest U.S. civilian honor, the Presidential Medal of Freedom. Owens died four years later, and in 1990 President George H. W. Bush presented the Congressional Gold Medal to his widow, Ruth.

David Holloway

SEE ALSO: *Louis, Joe; Olympics; World War II.*

BIBLIOGRAPHY

Baker, William Joseph. *Jesse Owens: An American Life*. New York: Free Press, 1986.

Owens, Jesse, and Paul Neimark. *Jesse: A Spiritual Autobiography*. Plainfield, NJ: Logos International, 1978.

Riess, Steven A. *Major Problems in American Sport History: Documents and Essays*. Boston, MA: Houghton Mifflin, 1997.

Sanford, William R., and Carl R. Green. *Jesse Owens*. New York: Crestwood House, 1992.

Streissguth, Thomas. *Jesse Owens*. Minneapolis, MN: Lerner Publications, 2006.

Oxford Bags

In 1924 Oxford (and Cambridge) students, reacting to a ban on knickers in university classrooms, began wearing wide trousers, 25 inches around at the knee and 22 inches around the bottom, slipped over their knickers. These capacious pants, which came in a variety of colors that included pale green and lavender, as well as traditional black, navy, beige, and gray, became an immediate fad in America, where they were known as Oxford bags. Illustrator John Held's collegiate caricatures featured undergraduates in vast pants cavorting and doing the Charleston with girls in short skirts. Wanamaker's department store in New York advertised the pants at $20 a pair in the spring of 1925, and *Men's Wear* reported on their presence in San Francisco and on the University of California campus in the fall of 1925. Even for those not enthralled by the outlandish width of the Oxford bags, young men's pants were loose and roomy through the 1930s. Many on American campuses enjoyed genuine or spurious Oxford pedigree—Oxford cloth shirts, Oxfords (shoes), Oxford gold eyeglass frames, and Oxford bags—these last as much a fad as goldfish swallowing.

The trend died out after the 1930s, but the fashion of wide pants for both males and females again became widespread during the bell-bottom craze of the 1970s. The trend resurfaced in the 1990s and continued into the twenty-first century with young males sporting wide-legged jeans.

Richard Martin

SEE ALSO: *College Fads; Flappers; Retro Fashion.*

BIBLIOGRAPHY

Schoeffler, O. E., and William Gale. *Esquire's Encyclopedia of 20th Century Men's Fashions*. New York: McGraw-Hill, 1973.

Oz, Dr. *(1960–)*

Dr. Mehmet Oz is a respected cardiothoracic surgeon who became a popular television star in the first decade of the 2000s. He offers health and medical advice on the Emmy-winning program, *The Doctor Oz Show*. The child of Turkish parents, Oz is renowned for his energy and for making patients feel comfortable discussing sensitive, potentially embarrassing health concerns. He has performed surgeries, authored books and magazine columns, and regularly appeared on Oprah Winfrey's radio talk show while working on his television show. In his article "Dr. Does-It-All" for the *New York Times*, Frank Bruni writes, "Part of what propels [Oz] is the voice and example of his father, who grew up poor in Turkey during the Depression and, according to Oz, could not afford to slack off for even a second on his path to his own career as a cardiothoracic surgeon."

Perhaps because Americans visited their own doctors less and less or had no physician at all during the 2000s, doctors began making appearances on news and information programs. Networks hired their own doctors to discuss everything from the latest in cancer treatments to the death of Michael Jackson. The growth of "lifestyle" television, a genre that provides viewers with information on how to live, look, eat, or work, also led to a need for more medical professionals to offer advice on nutrition, preventative care, and exercise. Oz became the poster child for this trend.

Dr. Oz. *Dr. Mehmet Oz parlayed his popularity as one of Oprah Winfrey's frequent guests into his own self-titled talk show in 2009.* AP IMAGES.

After receiving an undergraduate degree at Harvard, Oz earned a dual MBA/MD at the University of Pennsylvania. He worked at the New York Presbyterian Hospital/Columbia University Medical Center, eventually becoming vice chair and professor of surgery. After marrying actress and movie producer Lisa Lemole in 1985, he became interested in Eastern medicine and alternative care and founded the Complementary Care Center at Columbia Presbyterian. The center combined Western medicine with more alternative treatments. This sparked the attention of the media in 1995. A year later his involvement in the surgery of Frank Torre, brother of then-Yankees manager Joe Torre, led to several television appearances. He appeared as a medical expert on ABC, CNN, and Winfrey's talk show in 2011.

In 2003, with the help of his wife, he developed his first television show. His former college roommate was the chairman of Discovery Health Network when Lisa pitched the series *Second Opinion with Dr. Oz*. The thirteen-episode show aired in 2003. The first topic Oz chose was obesity, and he invited Winfrey to be a guest and discuss her weight-loss struggles.

In addition to his work on *Second Opinion*, Oz became a regular guest on *The Oprah Winfrey Show*, appearing fifty-five times. He wore his operating scrubs instead of a suit and often brought preserved organs to further explain the inner workings of the body to the audience. Winfrey dubbed him "America's Doctor." As she told the *New York Times*, "When he made it O.K. to talk about the shape of a good poop, I knew he could talk about anything. He always found ways to make the human body endlessly fascinating."

Oz considered his television appearances an extension of his work as a heart surgeon. As a doctor he only saw people after their bad health choices brought them to his office instead of earlier when he could help change their behavior. This was also part of his mission with his book series, *You*, written with his business partner, Dr. Michael Roizen of the Cleveland Clinic. The *New York Times* best-selling series includes *You: The Owner's Manual*, *You: On a Diet*, and *You: The Smart Patient*. In addition, Oz has written more than 400 other publications, including medical journal articles and a column for *Time*.

Handsome, telegenic, and an excellent communicator, Oz was primed by Winfrey's team for his own show. Following *Dr. Phil*, the syndicated daily *The Doctor Oz Show* was the second from Winfrey's Harpo Productions, debuting September 14, 2009. On the show he presents medical and health information, including fitness and diet, often using props to explain medical conditions. It became an instant hit with an audience of about 3.5 million viewers. He won an Emmy for Outstanding Talk Show Host in 2010 and again in 2011, tying that year with Regis Philbin and Kelly Ripa. The show itself also won the 2011 Emmy for Outstanding Talk Show/Informative.

Oz's career has led to media success for his family. Lisa has a show on Winfrey's satellite radio network and her own *Us* books. His oldest daughter, Daphne, turned her *Dorm Room Diet* book, with a forward from her dad, into a hosting spot on ABC's *The Chew*, a daily show about food and cooking.

The Doctor Oz Show has drawn its own controversy, presenting alternative health gurus and tangling with the FDA over the levels of arsenic in apple juice. When some doctors scoffed at the light treatment of topics, Oz turned the tables and invited them to appear. His multiple appearances on *The Oprah Winfrey Show* taught him valuable lessons that he applies to his own show. As he wrote in the Huffington Post, "What I learned most poignantly on *The Oprah Show* was that I did not need to fix everything, especially difficult for a doctor. What many people really crave is to be heard and validated. Then we can disrupt their beliefs as we break their patterns on our way to helping out."

Michele Lellouche

SEE ALSO: *Best Sellers; Cancer; CNN; Daytime Talk Shows; Dieting; Emmy Awards; The Huffington Post; Ivy League; Jackson, Michael; McGraw, Dr. Phil; The* New York Times*; Radio; Satellite Radio; Syndication; Television;* Time*; Winfrey, Oprah.*

BIBLIOGRAPHY

Brown, Chip. "The Experiments of Dr. Oz." *New York Times*, July 30, 1995.

Bruni, Frank. "Dr. Does-It-All." *New York Times*, April 16, 2010.

"Mehmet Oz, MD." Accessed May 2012. Available from http://www.doctoroz.com/bios/mehmet-oz-md

Oz, Dr. Mehmet. "What I Learned on *The Oprah Show*." Huffington Post, May 9 2009.

P

Paar, Jack *(1918–2004)*

When Jack Paar was chosen to host NBC's faltering *Tonight Show* in July 1957, the program had been reduced to two sponsors and was carried by only sixty-two network stations. Within eighteen months the antics of the witty, unpredictable Paar had brought a total of 115 stations onboard, and the show, renamed *The Jack Paar Tonight Show*, had full sponsorship. Paar's unique style would both establish the popularity of talk shows and set the standard for all future television hosts.

Born in Canton, Ohio, on May 1, 1918, Paar dropped out of high school to work as a radio announcer for stations in Indianapolis, Indiana; Youngstown, Ohio; Cleveland, Ohio; Pittsburgh; Pennsylvania; and Buffalo, New York. Working for the army special services during World War II, he entertained enlisted men with irreverent gibes at the military brass. He appeared in three movies in the early 1950s: *Walk Softly, Stranger* (1950), *Love Nest* (1951), and *Down among the Sheltering Palms* (1953). During the same period he hosted two television game shows, *Bank on the Stars* (1953–1954) and *Up to Paar* (1952), which led to a contract as host of *The Morning Show* (1954), an attempt by CBS to compete with *Today* (1952–) on NBC. However, none of these programs would ever bring him the amount of success he enjoyed with the *Tonight Show*.

Temperamental, spontaneous, and at times brilliantly incisive, Paar brought drama to the art of late-night conversation with such semiregular guests as Washington hostess Elsa Maxwell, Cliff Arquette (who played the character Charlie Weaver), Joey Bishop, Hans Conried, Peggy Cass, Zsa Zsa Gabor, Hermione Gingold, Buddy Hackett, Florence Henderson, Betty White, and Oscar Levant. Levant, a classical pianist with an acid tongue, is remembered for such barbs as "Zsa Zsa has discovered the secret of perpetual middle age" and his nomination of Elizabeth Taylor for the "Other Woman of the Year Award." There were also more serious guests. During the 1960 presidential campaign, John F. Kennedy and Richard Nixon made separate appearances on Paar's show.

In addition to conversing with his guests, Paar featured comic sketches and frequently visited the audience for interviews. On one memorable occasion, Cary Grant was seated in the audience as a surprise to Paar, who pretended not to recognize the international film star while interviewing a little old lady from out of town sitting beside him. Paar's orchestra leader, José Melis, liked to play a "telephone game," improvising melodies based on the last four digits of an audience member's telephone number. In another popular routine Paar showed baby pictures on the screen while supplying humorous captions.

CONTROVERSY

Although he professed to dislike controversy, Paar was continually involved in it, carrying on much-publicized feuds with such celebrities as Steve Allen, Dorothy Kilgallen, Walter Winchell, and Ed Sullivan. Many of the feuds started with a remark made on the show. Paar said, for example, that Winchell's "high, hysterical voice" came from "wearing too tight underwear." The feuds were never easy to quell. Paar's friend and mentor, Jack Benny, finally had to step in to moderate the Paar-Sullivan conflict. But the most famous controversy occurred on February 11, 1960, when an angry Paar walked onstage and began to berate NBC executives for censoring a joke from the previous night's taped show. He then told the audience he was tired of being the center of controversy and bid them an emotional farewell, leaving an astonished Hugh Downs to carry on the show.

Paar returned a month later, but his controversial days had not ended. In September 1961 he took Peggy Cass and a camera crew to Germany to report on the Berlin Wall, which had been erected a month earlier. Paar arranged for a detachment of American troops to be shown in the background of his televised scenes near the Brandenburg Gate. The incident led to a Defense Department inquiry, and the press raked Paar over the coals for the militaristic overtones of his broadcast. He maintained that his visit had actually eased East-West tensions. A short time later he announced he would be leaving the show the following spring, and this time he kept his word. His last show aired on March 29, 1962, and dozens of celebrities dropped by or sent tapes to wish him an affectionate farewell.

After his much publicized departure from *The Jack Paar Tonight Show*, he became the owner of Mount Washington TV Inc., broadcasting from WMTW TV and FM in Portland and Poland Springs, Maine. From 1962 to 1965 he hosted *The Jack Paar Program*, a weekly prime-time variety show, and he also produced some prime-time travel documentaries. He attempted a late-night comeback in 1973 called *Jack Paar Tonight*, but it only lasted eleven months, and he was said to have regretted the attempt later. His last television appearance was as a guest on a CNBC talk show hosted by his friend Charles Grodin in 1997. Paar published four autobiographical humorous books: *I Kid You Not* (1960), *My Saber Is Bent* (1961), *Three on a Toothbrush* (1965), and *P.S. Jack Paar: An Entertainment* (1983). In 1997 PBS featured Paar as the subject of an American Masters documentary *Jack Paar: As I Was Saying*, so named after his famous opening line after a month-long absence from *The Tonight Show*.

Paar's health declined in later years, and although he recovered from quadruple bypass surgery in 1999, he then suffered a stroke in 2003. He died on January 27, 2004, at the age of eighty-five. A few months later the American Masters documentary was released as *Jack Paar: Smart Television*, a DVD compilation, along with celebrity interviews and clips, and is included in the box set *The Jack Paar Collection*, which primarily features clips from *The Jack Paar Program*.

Benjamin Griffith

SEE ALSO: *Allen, Steve; Celebrity; Daytime Talk Shows; Downs, Hugh; Grant, Cary; Hackett, Buddy; Movie Stars; Public Television (PBS); Radio; Sullivan, Ed; Taylor, Elizabeth; Television;* The Tonight Show*; White, Betty; Winchell, Walter; World War II.*

BIBLIOGRAPHY

Brooks, Tim, and Earle Marsh. *The Complete Directory to Prime Time Network TV Shows: 1946–Present.* New York, Ballantine, 1981.

Galanoy, Terry. *Tonight*! Garden City, NJ: Doubleday, 1972.

McNeil, Alex. *Total Television: A Comprehensive Guide to Programming from 1948 to the Present.* New York: Penguin, 1991.

Metz, Robert. *The Tonight Show.* New York: Playboy Press, 1980.

Pachucos

Pachucos were Latino street rebels of the 1940s who innovated a style and attitude that expressed their defiance of mainstream America. Dressed to kill in zoot suits and adorned with pompadour haircuts, they hung out on the streets of East Los Angeles, speaking their own language and asserting their difference from everyone around them. They were the first subcultural group to exhibit their rebellion by display—through their clothing and behavior on the street. Their unique brand of defiance opened up an avenue of rebellion that was later followed by youth cultures in genres such as rock and roll.

The pachucos were second-generation Mexican American youths who lived in the barrios of East Los Angeles during the years of World War II. They were branded "delinquents" by the Los Angeles Police Department and held responsible for the wave of juvenile crime sweeping the city at the time. Pachucos also incurred the wrath of their Mexican elders by their "degenerate" behavior of draft dodging and marijuana smoking and their foppish attention to clothes.

The style they sported was the zoot suit: a long drape jacket that reached to the knees and high-waisted trousers that were baggy on the leg but tapered at the ankle. The suit was worn with a very long key chain and often a crucifix or a medallion over the tie. The hairdo that went with the look was the pompadour, a relatively long hair cut for men, worn greased into a quiff at the front and combed into a duck's tail at the back. In their hair the pachucos kept their *fileros* (flick knives), the thickness of the hair style providing a secure hiding place for weapons. Distinctive tattoos, such as the Virgin of Guadalupe, where also part of the pachuco look. Their female counterparts, the pachucas, had their own dress code, which consisted of short, tight skirts; flimsy blouses; dramatic makeup; and longer pompadour hairdos.

The word *pachuco* is of uncertain origin but is believed to be derived from Pachuca, a town in east-central Mexico. The pachucos spoke a hybrid slang called Calo, derived from the gypsy tongue. The word *Chicano*—a politicized term of self-definition for Mexican Americans—is itself a Calo word. Music was also an important ingredient in the scene, and much of the pachuco lifestyle revolved around the dance halls where they would dance and listen to swing bands. A bandleader called Don Tosti had a hit with a song called "Pachuco Boogie," a big-band number with lyrics in Calo.

The Sleepy Lagoon Case in 1942 brought the pachucos into the national limelight, when thirteen Mexican American youths were convicted on varying charges, including first-degree murder, for the killing of José Díaz. The trial took place at a time when William Randolph Hearst's Los Angeles newspapers were running incendiary stories about gang violence. The image of the pachuco circulated by these papers was that of a bloodthirsty killer spurred on by the ancestral Aztec desire to let blood. Two years later these convictions were reversed by an appeal court, largely due to the efforts of the Sleepy Lagoon Defense Committee, which featured public figures as illustrious as Orson Welles and Rita Hayworth. Luis Valdez's 1981 film *Zoot Suit*, an adaptation of the stage musical, gives a part-fact, part-fiction account of the case from the perspective of Henry Reyna, the leader of the convicted gang of pachucos.

The pachucos' brush with controversy, however, did not end there. In early June 1943, disturbances broke out in East Los Angeles. Mobs of sailors and marines began scouring the streets in taxis looking for zoot-suited pachucos to beat up, supposedly in retaliation for attacks on their number by pachucos. If no candidates could be found, the servicemen would storm into movie theaters and drag out any young males they perceived to be pachucos, stripping them of their zoot suits and cutting their pompadours. Eyewitness accounts report the attacks as unprovoked and, furthermore, were actively encouraged by crowds of observing civilians.

At a time when national obedience was highly prized, "pachuquismo"—or the pachuco style—was the total contradiction of military discipline, order, measure, and effort. The pachucos cultivated a manner of languid detachment and were not perceived to have a good work ethic. They performed their defiance through their clothes, openly inviting hostile attention. The Mexican poet Octavio Paz described the pachuco as a "sinister clown" who courted the hunter by decking himself out as his prey.

The pachuco look was taken up by the mainstream and emerged in the 1950s greaser style. Within marginal groups, the pachucos served as inspirational icons for the Chicano civil rights movement that fomented in the late 1960s. As the first Mexican Americans to forge a position for themselves in opposition both to the American mainstream and their traditional Mexican backgrounds, the pachucos were the first Mexican Americans to self-consciously style and define themselves on exactly their own terms.

In the late 1990s renewed interest in swing music brought "pachuquismo" back into vogue. The 1994 film *The Mask*, starring Jim Carrey, characterized the pachuco as the outrageous transformation of the wimpish bank clerk protagonist for the rebellious, maverick, and magical qualities that the style evokes.

Quixotic, sinister, and theatrical, the pachuco is continually evoked as one of the mythic figures of American popular culture.

Candida Taylor

SEE ALSO: *Retro Fashion; Swing Dancing; Zoot Suit.*

BIBLIOGRAPHY

Cosgrove, Stuart. "The Zoot Suit and Style Warfare." In *Zoot Suits and Second-Hand Dresses: An Anthology of Fashion and Music*, ed. Angela McRobbie. Boston: Unwin Hyman, 1988.

Mazón, Mauricio. *The Zoot-Suit Riots: The Psychology of Symbolic Annihilation*. Austin: University of Texas Press, 1984.

Muñoz, Carlos, Jr. *Youth, Identity, Power: The Chicano Movement*. New York: Verso, 1989.

Paz, Octavio. *The Labyrinth of Solitude*. London: Penguin, 1990.

Peiss, Kathy. *Zoot Suit: The Enigmatic Career of an Extreme Style*. Philadelphia: University of Pennsylvania Press, 2011.

Pacino, Al *(1940–)*

When director Francis Ford Coppola's film masterpiece *The Godfather* was released in 1972, Al Pacino galvanized filmgoers with his brooding, dark good looks and masterfully controlled performance as a Mafia leader. Pacino, already an award-winning stage actor, virtually established a new level of screen intensity, winning an Oscar nomination and launching an international career as a major film star. The film depicts a significant passing of power when the ailing Vito Corleone (Marlon Brando) makes his son Michael (Pacino) the new "godfather." Because both Brando (a film icon) and Pacino (relatively unknown in films) were method actors, many critics and filmgoers saw a parallel symbolic passing of influence from one generation of actors to another. For box-office reasons Brando was designated "the star," but Pacino, with his aura of low-key sensuality, compelling screen presence, and underlying explosiveness, not only held his ground on-screen with Brando but mesmerized audiences.

Pacino is especially effective at changing his facial expressions and altering the volume of his voice, dialect, and speech patterns. But he is best known for using his eyes, which in any one film can be tender and loving, cold and penetrating, full of rage or melancholy, confused, imploring, or cloudy and distant, changing from one look to another in an instant. He is capable of generating an icy heat, of exuding a physical energy while standing perfectly still. Although relatively short of build, he has a compelling presence and body language that increase his physical stature.

Pacino always seemed determined to become an actor. Although poor, from an early age he regularly watched movies,

Al Pacino. *Al Pacino, right, dances with Gabrielle Anwar in the famous tango scene from 1992's* Scent of a Woman. **UNIVERSAL/THE KOBAL COLLECTION.**

afterward reenacting the major roles. He also was excited by and continues to love the stage. Because of family finances he had to quit school early and worked at various jobs; after some acting classes he began to get theater parts. In 1966 the Actors Studio accepted him; two years later he won an Obie Award. His first Tony Award came in 1969, and in that same year he made an effective screen debut with a bit part in *Me, Natalie*. Those performances led to his first leading role in a film at age thirty-one—*The Panic in Needle Park* (1971).

THE GODFATHER

Pacino's performance in *The Godfather* forever changed filmgoers' image of gang lords, and the film completely transcended the traditional gangster picture. The uneducated, raised-in-poverty, loud, brutal Edward G. Robinson/James Cagney "tough guy" persona of the past was replaced by Pacino's educated, soft-spoken, unobtrusively wealthy, self-controlled characterization. In this film and in *The Godfather, Part II* (1974), for which he was nominated for a Best Actor Oscar and Golden Globe, Pacino chillingly portrays the metamorphosis of the basically decent Michael—idealistic, patriotic, and gentle—into an austere, steely eyed, implacably heartless tyrant, deadly to anyone who defies him. His portrayal of Michael's obsessive self-control is so effective that his rare displays of temper jar the audience. Pacino shows the gradual erosion of humanity in Michael by infrequent but extreme changes in character intensity and subtle alterations in manner, speech, posture, and facial muscles, as well as in his deep, expressive eyes. Writer Jimmy Breslin has said that Pacino "dominates *The Godfather* with a creeping sense of tyranny." Many years later, in *The Godfather, Part III* (1990), Pacino again assumed the role of Michael Corleone, now an aging, ill, demoralized, and ultimately tragic figure. Breslin described Pacino well: "The [*Godfather*] movies unleashed a new force, raw and fearless in his willingness to allow the intrusion of a camera into the soul of a man."

In the 1970s Pacino starred in five film hits, each role garnering him an Oscar nomination: the first two *Godfather* portrayals; an incorruptible, volcanic hippie cop in *Serpico* (1973); a sexually confused would-be bank robber in *Dog Day Afternoon* (1975); and an idealistic, angry lawyer in *And Justice for All* (1979). In the 1980s he chose far-ranging and unusual scripts but did not have any major hits. Although the movie was not a huge success upon release, Pacino's role as Cuban drug lord Tony Montana in Brian De Palma's 1983 *Scarface* would prove his most iconic role outside of the *Godfather* films. He remained among the most popular film stars, but his box-office success was shrinking. Then, in 1989 he played a hard-drinking, lonely-hearts police detective having a steamy affair with a possible murderess in *Sea of Love*. The reviews were mostly good, and many heralded his "comeback." Most filmgoers do not know that in those two decades, Pacino also was performing onstage in works by playwrights as diverse as Tennessee Williams, William Shakespeare, Bertolt Brecht, and David Mamet; he won another Tony Award (1977, for Best Actor) for David Rabe's *The Basic Training of Pavlo Hummel*.

PLAYING THE PART

Pacino films made in the 1990s were successful because—with few exceptions, such as the comically hammy *Dick Tracy* (1990)—Pacino returned to the persona/roles that his fans wanted and expected: the intense, focused, explosive, emotionally disconnected antihero on either side of the law. Successful performances included the haunting and haunted Godfather in *The Godfather, Part III*; the sharklike real estate "closer" in *Glengarry Glen Ross* (1992); the ferociously bitter blind man in *Scent of a Woman* (1992); the charismatic wheeler-dealer mayor in *City Hall* (1996); and the declining "goodfella" in *Donnie Brasco* (1997). *Looking for Richard*, a 1996 pseudo-documentary Pacino produced, directed, and starred in, shows a cast and crew during parts of the rehearsals, discussions, and stage production of Shakespeare's *Richard III*. This unusual and enlightening film makes Shakespeare's gripping drama more accessible to a broader audience.

Pacino continued to bounce between stage and screen in the twenty-first century, winning a Golden Globe and an Emmy in 2004 for his performance in the HBO miniseries *Angels in America*. In 2011 he was nominated for a Tony for Best Performance by a Leading Actor as Shylock in a Shakespeare in the Park production of *The Merchant of Venice*. His film career stalled with a series of poorly received films, such as 2008's *Righteous Kill*, costarring Robert De Niro, and the box-office bombs/critical flops *Gigli* (2003) and *S1mOne* (2002). Although the decade was not filled with success, it was filled with honors, as Pacino received lifetime achievement awards from the Golden Globes in 2001 and American Film Institute in 2007. He returned to HBO in 2010, starring as suicide doctor Jack Kevorkian in *You Don't Know Jack* and won his fourth Golden Globe and second Emmy. He stepped behind the camera once again, directing *Wilde Salome*, which premiered at the 2011 Venice International Film Festival.

In the sentiments of *Entertainment Weekly* writer Ty Burr, Pacino is "[the best] fusion of Method acting and charisma since the young Brando." He has become an elder statesman of Hollywood; his versatility, integrity, and dedication to his craft are admired and respected by critics, fans, and peers. Eminent film director Sidney Lumet has said that "every star evokes a sense of danger, something unmanageable." Pacino is a star; in the best sense, he has become the "godfather" of acting. While this might be true of an older generation of film fans, to younger fans it is Pacino as Scarface yelling "say hello to my little friend" that keeps his star shining, both on film and in the millions of Scarface T-shirts that sport his image.

Jaye Cohen

SEE ALSO: *Academy Awards; Brando, Marlon; Broadway; Cable TV; Cagney, James; De Niro, Robert; Dick Tracy; Emmy Awards;* Entertainment Weekly*;* The Godfather*; Hollywood; Mamet, David; Movie Stars; Robinson, Edward G.; Tony Awards; Williams, Tennessee.*

BIBLIOGRAPHY

Grobel, Lawrence. *Al Pacino in Conversation with Lawrence Grobel*. New York: Simon Spotlight Entertainment, 2006.

Lebo, Harlan. *"The Godfather" Legacy*. New York: Fireside, 1997.

Maltin, Leonard, ed. *Leonard Maltin's Movie Encyclopedia*. New York: Dutton, 1994.

Schoell, William. *The Films of Al Pacino*. Secaucus, NJ: Citadel Press/Carol Publishing Group, 1995.

Yule, Andrew. *Life on the Wire: The Life and Art of Al Pacino*. New York: Donald I. Fine, 1991.

Pac-Man

Pac-Man is the one of the longest-running and most successful video game franchises of all time. Since its release in Japan in 1980 by Namco, it has become one of the most recognizable video game designs, leading to an animated television show, merchandise, and multiple versions of the game on different gaming platforms.

Initially, the game was launched in Japan as Puckman. As the legend goes, Tohru Iwatani, the game's creator, was staring at his pizza with two slices missing and came up with the Pac-Man character. When it was licensed for distribution in the United States by Midway, they changed the name to Pac-Man, and the craze began. Although most video games at that time were produced for a male audience, Pac-Man appealed to both genders. "Pac-Man was created as a 'cute' game with both good and bad characters that were colorful and endearing," explained Kenji Hisatsune, president, CEO, and COO of Namco Networks America Inc.

The idea was simple. Direct the lead character, the Pac-Man, through a maze. It "eats" small pellets while avoiding four ghosts (Inky, Blinky, Pinky, and Clyde), who can kill it. The Pac-Man must consume all the pellets and also the four "power pellets," which allow it to eat the ghosts before heading to the next level of the game. The four ghosts were also designed with separate personalities. Pinky, for example, is speedy, and Inky is bashful. In the Japanese version of the game, the character personalities are less flattering. Otoboke, who is Clyde in the American version, is described as "stupid" in the Japanese version of the game.

Pac-Man does not have a plot, unlike the action-oriented games at the time. It was conceived with no ending. Theoretically, players could keep going all day, provided they could progress through the levels without being caught by the ghosts. However, a software glitch in the original arcade game meant that after 255 levels, the next level had a split screen, where half the maze was obscured with random symbols. Because it is impossible to win that level, this ends the game. Several people have recorded perfect scores of 3,333,360 points. There have been rumors of people having passed the split screen and scoring higher than perfect, but no documented case has been proven.

The game's design and sound effects became iconic of the 1980s. The simplistic tune repeats, mimicking the repetition of the game as players level up. It can be operated with only a joystick, and CNN's Larry Frum wrote, "Some speculated that Pac-Man became popular in bars in part because gamers needed only one hand to play and could hold a drink in the other."

By the 1990s Pac-Man had earned more than $2.5 billion in quarters. It has been consistently published in multiple platforms since its release. In 1981 a Ms. Pac-Man game was released in America. It was not designed by Namco but was sold to Midway, the American distributor, without Namco's permission. It became as popular as the original and offered more mazes and faster game play. Namco sued over this unauthorized game; eventually a legal deal was made, and Ms. Pac-Man became an authorized sequel. At a later date Namco severed ties with Midway after Midway released further unauthorized spin-offs such as Junior Pac-Man, Baby Pac-Man, and Professor Pac-Man.

The popular culture effect of the game was immediate. A Pac-Man Hanna-Barbera cartoon aired from 1982 to 1984 on ABC. There was also a slew of merchandise, including T-shirts, toys, and pasta. The 1981 song "Pac-Man Fever" by Buckner & Garcia made it into the number nine slot of the Billboard Hot 100.

The game became synonymous with the decade of its release, but its popularity transcends the 1980s. When it hit its thirtieth anniversary, it was still going strong. "I think there's a high nostalgia value with Pac-Man," said Sean Mylett, senior marketing manager for Namco. "I think Pac-Man is a game where people really remember being younger and pumping quarters and quarters into machines."

Kim Keeline

SEE ALSO: *Mario Brothers; Saturday Morning Cartoons; Video Games; Wii; Xbox Kinect.*

BIBLIOGRAPHY

Greene, David. "Blasts from the Past: The Art of Video Games." National Public Radio. Accessed May 2012. Available from http://www.npr.org/2012/04/29/151605949/blasts-from-the-past-the-art-of-video-games

Kent, Steven. *The Ultimate History of Video Games: From Pong to Pokémon and Beyond—The Story behind the Craze That Touched Our Lives and Changed the World.* Roseville, CA: Prima, 2001.

Melissinos, Chris, and Patrick O'Rourke. *The Art of Video Games: From Pac-Man to Mass Effect.* New York: Welcome Books, 2012.

Morris, Chris. "Pac-Man Turns 25: A Pizza Dinner Yields a Cultural Phenomenon and Millions of Dollars in Quarters." *CNN/Money*, May 10, 2005.

Vargas, Jose Antonio. "Still Love at First Bite." *Washington Post*, June 22, 2005.

Paglia, Camille *(1947–)*

Following the release of her provocative book *Sexual Personae* in 1990, Camille Paglia, a professor of liberal arts at the University of Pennsylvania, established herself as an internationally recognized and highly controversial public intellectual. She is known for being nonconformist in her approach to intellectual life and for her unique methods of communicating her uncommon and sometimes unpopular viewpoints.

Born April 2, 1947, in Endicott, New York, to parents Pasquale and Lydia Anne (Colapietro) Paglia, she was raised in Syracuse, New York, where she attended public school. Her academic training continued on a traditional path: she earned a BA from SUNY Binghamton in 1968, a master's degree in philosophy from Yale University in 1971, and a PhD in English in 1974, also from Yale. Her teaching career began at Binghamton University in Bennington, Vermont, where she was a faculty member in the literature and language department until 1980. Before arriving at Philadelphia's University of the Arts in 1984, she held various fellowships and was a visiting lecturer at both Wesleyan and Yale.

ACADEMIC WRITING

Although Paglia is an accomplished scholar, nonacademic influences are instrumental to her work. In her writing, she often identifies herself as a "daughter of the sixties," and the decade's progressive politics are evident in her work. In addition, she was greatly influenced by her Italian American heritage, using her cultural experience to shape her feminist analyses. She argues that women should view the world as a Darwinian battle for survival. Paglia began to learn such lessons as a child, she writes in *Vamps & Tramps* (1994), when she "was fed wild black mushrooms, tart dandelion greens, spiny artichokes, and tangy olives flecked with red pepper flakes . . . life lessons in the sour and prickly."

Sprinkling her prose with such observations, Paglia broke many of the conventions of academic publishing in ways that both thrilled and angered readers. *Sexual Personae*, the scholarly tome that launched her into the public spotlight, is a study of art, social ideas, and sexuality in the Western world. In it, she argues that great art derives from tensions between "Dionysian lust" and "Apollonian rationality," and she makes her argument with salacious discussions of John Keats and Emily Dickinson, attacking "sanctimonious P.C. intellectuals" and the "weakness of those who cry date rape." The best-selling book, which combined standard research with highly abstract philosophies, became controversial for three reasons. First, it espoused a belief in the pagan origins of human sexuality. Second, the book's approach to feminism directly opposed most of the feminist establishment, including institutionalized feminism on American campuses. Third, the format of the book grated on those who rejected her idiosyncratic style of academic argument.

An instant academic celebrity, Paglia was drawn into national controversies over date rape, sexual harassment, censorship, political correctness, poststructuralism, and the role of television, among others. In 1992 she published *Sex, Art, and American Culture*, a collection of essays that chronicled her engagement with these thorny cultural issues; her second book of essays, *Vamps & Tramps*, addressed similar themes. The main essay in *Vamps & Tramps*, titled "No Law in the Arena: A Pagan Theory of Sexuality," systematically presents Paglia's libertarian views on rape, abortion, sexual harassment, prostitution, strippers, pornography, homosexuality, pedophilia, and transvestitism. She writes, "Vamps and tramps are the seasoned symbols of tough-cookie feminism, my answer to the smug self-satisfaction and crass materialism of yuppie feminism." Unlike other feminists—who she claims were focused on victimization—Paglia argues that "women will never succeed at the level or in the numbers they deserve until they get over their genteel reluctance to take abuse in the attack and counterattack of territorial warfare."

PUBLIC IMAGE AND NOTORIETY

These and other remarks earned Paglia a reputation as an "antifeminist." Not surprisingly, this stance contributed to her notoriety, and Paglia appeared on a variety of television shows such as CBS's *60 Minutes* (1992) and *Think Tank* on PBS (1995), where she displayed her combative style of discourse. She was featured in or contributed to many of the leading periodicals of the day, including *Playboy*, *Vanity Fair*, *New Republic*, the *New York Times*, *Time*, *Rolling Stone*, the *New York Times Book Review*, and *Harper's Magazine*. In 1991 Paglia even graced the cover of *Village Voice* with the headline "Counterfeit Feminism, Wanted for Intellectual Fraud."

Paglia may be one of the most misunderstood thinkers of the twentieth century. Not unlike earlier radicals, her innovation was in employing unique methods for making her arguments against the status quo. As she explained, "Although I wasn't a follower per se of . . . Allen Ginsberg or Marshall McLuhan . . . those radical thinkers broke through the conventions of tradition and allowed us of the Sixties to find our own voices . . . which is what I wish to do for students of the 1990s." Her aggressive conduct befit this goal. In *Vamps & Tramps* she writes, "I espouse offensiveness for its own sake as a tool of attack against received opinion and unexamined assumptions." Given that she claims her highest ideals are free speech and free thought, this approach corresponds with her philosophy.

Her critics from the feminist establishment notwithstanding, many found her approach liberating. She received a series of stellar reviews for her books, was nominated for a National Book Critics' Circle Award in 1991, and has a number of followers in the academic world. In 1997 she became a columnist for the online magazine *Salon* and in 1998 published a book about Alfred Hitchcock's classic film *The Birds* at the behest of the British Film Institute. In 2005 she published an anthology and commentary on forty-three short poems, ranging from William Shakespeare to Joni Mitchell, titled *Break, Blow, Burn*. Only time will tell whether Paglia achieved her goal of helping students of the 1990s find their own voices. There can be no doubt that she found hers.

Julie Scelfo

SEE ALSO: *Feminism; Ginsberg, Allen;* Harper's*; Hitchcock, Alfred; McLuhan, Marshall; Mitchell, Joni;* New Republic*; The* New York Times*;* Playboy*; Public Television (PBS);* Rolling Stone*;* 60 Minutes*; Television;* Time*;* Vanity Fair.

BIBLIOGRAPHY

Clark, VèVè; Shirley Nelson Garner; Margaret Higonnet; et al, eds. *Antifeminism in the Academy*. New York: Routledge, 1996.

Female Misbehavior. Directed by Monika Treut. New York: First Run Features, 1992. Videocassette (VHS).

hooks, bell. "Camille Paglia: *Black* Pagan or White Colonizer." In *Outlaw Culture: Resisting Representations*. Boston: South End Press, 1994.

Kregloe, K., and J. Caputi. "Supermodels of Lesbian Chic." In *Cross Purposes: Lesbians, Feminists, and the Limits of Alliance*, ed. Dana Heller. Bloomington: Indiana University Press, 1997.

Kumar, Mina. "Katha Pollitt on Women and Feminism." *Sojourner* 20, no. 9, (1995).

Paglia, Camille. *Sexual Personae: Art and Decadence from Nefertiti to Emily Dickinson*. New Haven, CT: Yale University Press, 1990.

Paglia, Camille. *Sex, Art, and American Culture: Essays*. New York: Vintage, 1992.

Paglia, Camille. *Vamps & Tramps: New Essays*. New York: Vintage, 1994.

Paige, Satchel *(1899?–1982)*

In an era when American major-league sports were a white man's game, African American player Leroy "Satchel" Paige achieved legendary fame as Negro League baseball's undisputed star and standard bearer. In a career spanning three decades, the lanky, limber, right-handed pitcher hurled a reputed 2,500 games, won nearly 2,000, and came to symbolize the untapped potential of black professional athletes. He later followed Jackie Robinson (1919–1972) and Larry Doby (1923–2003) into the major leagues as one of baseball's first African American players and solidified his reputation among the game's most talented performers. Joe DiMaggio (1914–1999), facing a Paige well past his prime, praised him as "the best and fastest pitcher I've ever faced."

Controversy has surrounded the issue of Paige's age throughout his career, and his date of birth has been placed as early as December 18, 1899, and as late as July 7, 1906. By 1930 the young Alabaman had earned a reputation as a bright young star in Negro League baseball. He joined Gus Greenlee's Pittsburgh Crawfords in 1931 for an extraordinary $250 a month, and for the next several years he teamed up with catcher Josh Gibson (1911–1947) to form the dominant battery in black baseball. His performance with the Crawfords quickly demonstrated that he was worth his salary. In 1933 he won twenty-one games in a row and ended the season with a 31–4 record, racking up a professional record of sixty-two straight scoreless innings in the process; in 1935 he pitched on twenty-nine consecutive days. Paige later led the Kansas City Monarchs to five pennants, earning both the nickname "iron man" for his stamina and a reputation as the most respected—as well as one

Satchel Paige. *Satchel Paige capped his long and storied baseball with a stint as a coach for the Atlanta Braves in the late 1960s.* LOU REQUENA/CONTRIBUTOR/MAJOR LEAGUE BASEBALL/GETTY IMAGES.

of the most talented—figures in Negro League baseball. He also played before sell-out crowds in the Caribbean and Central and South America.

It was Paige's success in exhibition play against white athletes, however, that helped earn him nationwide renown. On barnstorming tours against white pitching aces Dizzy Dean (1911–1974) in the 1930s and Bob Feller (1918–2010) in the early 1940s, Paige proved that he could stand toe to toe with the best players that white baseball had to offer. He struck out the game's leading right-handed hitter, Rogers Hornsby (1896–1963), five times in one game and, in another exhibition match, struck out twenty-two big leaguers including future Hall of Famers Hack Wilson (1900–1948) and Babe Herman (1903–1987). His 1–0 victory in thirteen innings over Dean in 1934 is still widely touted as the greatest pitching performance of all time.

When Brooklyn Dodgers general manager Branch Rickey (1881–1965) determined to break Major League Baseball's color barrier during the mid-1940s, Paige's name was circulated widely as a possible candidate. The veteran's age proved to be an obstacle, however, and the role fell to Paige's Kansas City Monarchs teammate Jackie Robinson. By the time Robinson entered the National League in 1947, Paige—well into his forties—appeared to be too old for the majors. His high salary demands did little to help his prospects. Although a nationally recognized figure, Paige seemed destined to follow fellow veteran Negro League stars Gibson, Cool Papa Bell (1903–1991), and Judy Johnson (1890–1989) into obscurity.

Bill Veeck (1914–1986), the owner of the Cleveland Indians, considered purchasing Paige's contract in 1947 but abandoned the plan for fear his efforts would be misinterpreted as a publicity stunt. In 1948, however, Veeck's team was in a tight four-way pennant race, and the young executive found himself desperately in need of pitching. Scouting reports suggested that Paige was the best player available. Veeck signed Paige to the Indians, generating one of the most vocal outcries in the history of professional sports. J. G. Taylor Spink of the *Sporting News* typified Veeck's detractors with the observation that "to sign a hurler at Paige's age is to demean the standards of baseball in the big circuits. . . . If Satchel were white, he would not have drawn a second thought from Veeck." Veeck's reply became legend: "If Satch were white, of course he would have been in the majors twenty-five years earlier and the question would not have been before the house."

On July 9, 1948, Paige made his major-league debut in Cleveland to a cheering crowd of 34,780 fans—the majority of whom had come to the ballpark to see the Negro League star play. In an unprecedented frenzy, press photographers ran onto the field to photograph his warm-up pitches. The forty-something Paige then stunned his audience with two scoreless innings. By the middle of August, he became, in historian Jules Tygiel's words, "the most discussed performer in baseball." He finished the 1948 season with a 6–1 record and 2.48 earned run average, and the Indians went on to win the American League pennant.

Paige later pitched for the St. Louis Browns, and at the age of fifty-nine he threw three scoreless innings for the Kansas City Athletics. He ended his major-league stint with a modest 28–31 record and a 3.29 earned run average. Yet throughout his career, Paige continued to be one of baseball's most popular attractions. Author A. S. "Doc" Young estimated that on one occasion, one in six black residents of Cleveland came out to watch "Ol'

Satch" perform. After retirement, Paige coached for the Atlanta Braves in 1968. He died in 1982 in Kansas City, Missouri.

During a time when many whites disparaged the abilities of black athletes, Paige's perennial feats served as a powerful symbol to the critics of segregated sports. Along with track star Jesse Owens (1913–1980) and boxer Joe Louis (1914–1981), he became one of the leading African American celebrities of the preintegration era and a unifying, morale-boosting figure in the black community. Sports critic Tom Meany wrote in the *Sporting News* that Paige's major-league debut proved to be an event "far more interesting than was the news when Branch Rickey broke baseball's color line." Paige's celebrity and talent helped pave the way for pioneers Robinson and Doby. Moreover, he may have been the best pitcher ever to play professional baseball. Quite appropriately, when the Baseball Hall of Fame formed a Committee on Negro Leagues in 1971, Satchel Paige was the first man elected to the shrine in Cooperstown.

Jacob Appel

SEE ALSO: *Baseball; Negro Leagues; Robinson, Jackie.*

BIBLIOGRAPHY

Bruce, Janet. *The Kansas City Monarchs: Champions of Black Baseball.* Lawrence: University Press of Kansas, 1985.

Holway, John. *Voices from the Great Black Baseball Leagues.* New York: Dodd, Mead, 1975.

Paige, Leroy (Satchel), and David Lipman. *Maybe I'll Pitch Forever.* Garden City, NY: Doubleday, 1962.

Peterson, Robert. *Only the Ball Was White.* Englewood Cliffs, NJ: Prentice Hall, 1970.

Ribowsky, Mark. *Don't Look Back: Satchel Paige and the Shadows of Baseball.* New York: Simon & Schuster, 1994.

Tygiel, Jules. *Baseball's Great Experiment.* New York: Oxford University Press, 1997.

Young, A. S. *Great Negro Baseball Stars and How They Made the Major Leagues.* New York: A. S. Barnes, 1953.

Paley, Grace *(1922–2007)*

Grace Paley was known as much for her feminism and social activism as for her writing. With the publication in 1959 of the first of four short-story collections, *The Little Disturbances of Man: Stories of Men and Women at Love*, Paley, at the age of thirty-seven, made an immediate impact on the literary scene. Throughout her life, she published only three other volumes of short stories: *Enormous Changes at the Last Minute* (1974), *Later the Same Day* (1985), and *Collected Stories* (1994, rereleased in 2007). She published one book of essays: *Just as I Thought* (1998). In all of her works, she allowed conversation to carry the story along, and readers were charmed by a voice that was startlingly original yet as familiar as an overheard conversation on a city bus.

Paley's work clearly reflected her own experience as a child of the Jewish Bronx, a young wife and mother staked out with the kids in Greenwich Village's Washington Square Park, and an activist involved in many of the important political movements of her time. In 2000 she published *Begin Again: Collected Poems*, in which she gathered together all the pieces of her life, relishing her time as mother and grandmother as well as time spent in literary pursuits and social activism. Paley left New York for Vermont and was poet laureate of the state from 2003 until her death in 2007. That same year, *Here and Somewhere Else*, a collection of stories written by Paley and her husband, writer Robert Nichols, was published.

Sue Russell

SEE ALSO: *Feminism; Greenwich Village.*

BIBLIOGRAPHY

Arcana, Judith. *Grace Paley's Life Stories: A Literary Biography.* Urbana: University of Illinois, 1993.

Bach, Gerhard, and Hall, Blaine H., eds. *Conversations with Grace Paley.* Jackson: University Press of Mississippi, 1997.

Paley, Grace. *New and Collected Poems.* Gardiner, ME: Tilbury House, 1992.

Paley, Grace. *The Collected Stories.* New York: Farrar Straus Giroux, 1994.

Paley, Grace. *Just as I Thought.* New York: Farrar Straus Giroux, 1998.

Paley, Grace, and Nichols, Robert. *Here and Somewhere Else.* New York: Feminist Press at the City University of New York, 2007.

Paley, William S. *(1901–1990)*

For more than fifty years, CBS and William S. Paley were synonymous. In 1927 Paley was involved with the formation of the Columbia Broadcasting System, and in 1928 his family purchased the company. The network grew quickly under Paley's leadership. Within six years the upstart challenger to the National Broadcasting Company (NBC) had almost 100 affiliate stations, nearly equal to NBC's total. By 1940 CBS was being recognized as the leader in the broadcasting field, in large part because of balanced mass entertainment and highly respected reportage, first in radio and later in television.

Reporters/broadcasters hired by Paley included Edward R. Murrow, Eric Sevareid, William L. Shirer, Howard K. Smith, and Walter Cronkite. Paley was still serving as chair of the board of directors in 1990, the year he died, and under his leadership CBS remained the leading network well into the 1980s.

Lloyd Chiasson Jr.

SEE ALSO: *Cronkite, Walter; Murrow, Edward R.; Shirer, William L.; Television.*

BIBLIOGRAPHY

Barnouw, Erik. *Tube of Plenty: The Evolution of American Television.* New York: Oxford University Press, 1982.

Bliss, Edward, Jr. *Now the News: The Story of Broadcast Journalism.* New York: Columbia University Press, 1991.

Emery, Michael, and Edwin Emery. *The Press and America: An Interpretive History of the Mass Media*, 7th ed. Englewood Cliffs, NJ: Prentice Hall, 1992.

Ghiglione, Loren. *CBS's Don Hollenbeck: An Honest Reporter in the Age of McCarthyism.* New York: Columbia University Press, 2008.

Weaver, Pat. *The Best Seat in the House: The Golden Years in Radio and Television.* New York: Knopf, 1994.

Palin, Sarah *(1964–)*

When Senator John McCain announced the selection of Alaska governor Sarah Palin as his running mate in August 2008, she became one of the most polarizing figures in twenty-first-century American politics. The first Republican woman nominated for the vice presidency, Palin was loudly vilified by opponents across the political spectrum but just as ardently championed by her supporters. Brought on to McCain's campaign to woo women voters, Palin espoused beliefs in gun rights and limited federal government while decrying abortion and same-sex marriage with unwavering, almost defiant, conviction. A proud hockey mom, she attempted to court middle-class women by commiserating with their busy lives and to satiate conservatives by appealing to traditional gender roles.

Although her supporters hailed her tenacity, Palin's unwillingness to acknowledge political gray areas soured her to many, including gay rights groups, environmentalists, and immigration advocates. She even raised concerns among conservatives, such as columnists David Brooks and George F. Will, who saw her lack of experience and off-the-cuff responses as political liabilities. During and after the election, the former governor became the subject of lighthearted parodies and tasteless, misogynistic attacks as she proved to be uninformed on many issues.

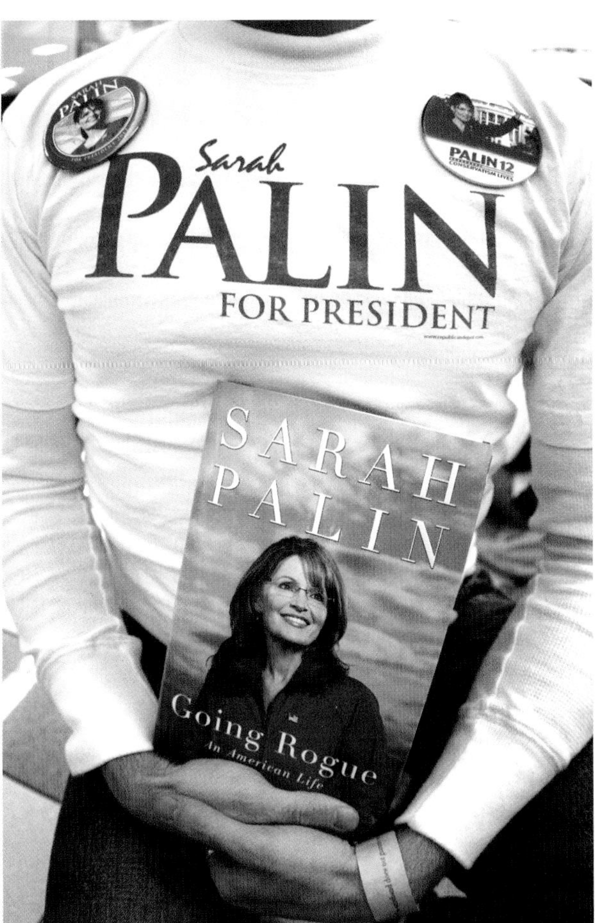

Sarah Palin Fan at Book Signing. *A Sarah Palin supporter waits in line to meet the former vice presidential candidate at a book signing in Grand Rapids, Michigan, in 2009.* BILL PUGLIANO/GETTY IMAGES.

EARLY LIFE AND CAREER

Sarah Louise Heath, born in Sandpoint, Idaho, on February 11, 1964, is the third of four children born to Charles R. and Sarah Sheeran Heath. Charles was a science teacher and track coach, and Sarah was a school secretary. The Heaths moved to Skagway, Alaska, when daughter Sarah was a baby, settling in Wasilla in 1972. At Wasilla High School, Sarah played basketball, ran track, and dated Todd Palin. After graduating in 1982, she enrolled at the University of Hawaii at Hilo.

Between 1982 and 1987 she transferred schools six times, eventually earning a BA in communications from the University of Idaho in 1987. She won the Miss Wasilla beauty pageant in 1984 and placed third in the Miss Alaska contest. After graduating college, she worked as a TV sportscaster, and on August 29, 1988, she and Todd eloped. The first of their five children, son Track, was born in 1989, followed by a daughter, Bristol, in 1990. Over the next decade she had two more children, Willow in 1994 and Piper in 2001.

Palin won election to the Wasilla City Council in 1992, and in 1996 she defeated the incumbent to become mayor of Wasilla. After reelection in 1999, she emerged as a prime candidate for U.S. Senator Frank Murkowski's vacated seat. Palin had helped him become governor of Alaska, but he appointed his daughter Lisa to his vacated seat instead, making Palin chairperson of the Alaska Oil and Gas Conservation Commission. Palin later resigned that post, alleging ethics violations by Randy Ruedrich, a fellow commission member and chairman of the state's Republican party. She then joined forces with a Democratic legislator in a successful effort to force the resignation of state attorney general Gregg Renkes, whom she charged with conflicts of interest. Her charges ran deep, suggesting that Ruedrich had provided oil companies with sensitive information and that his holdings in KFx Inc. precluded him from negotiating a deal for coal exports between the state and the company.

GOVERNORSHIP

The political capital she gained while pursuing the ethics violations helped bolster her 2006 gubernatorial campaign. Saying she wanted to remove cronyism from politics, she defeated Murkowski in the Republican primary and won the general election against former Democratic governor Tony Knowles, becoming Alaska's first female governor and its youngest ever. An enormously popular governor, she emphasized ethics and often found herself at odds with the state's Republican establishment. Particularly notable was her effort to force longtime Republican U.S. Senator Ted Stevens to disclose information regarding a federal investigation into his finances.

During her campaign, she had supported efforts to obtain federal funds for the Gravina Island Bridge, a multimillion-dollar project that became notorious nationwide as the Bridge to Nowhere, a symbol of runaway government spending. As governor, however, she reversed her position and canceled the project. The move enamored her to critics of earmarks, but many questioned why Alaska did not return the funds for the bridge to the federal government. Palin argued that Alaskans should be permitted to decide how to best spend the money, and she directed the funds to other transportation projects, including an access road on Gravina Island.

In April 2008 she had her fifth and last child, Trig, who was diagnosed with Down syndrome while in the womb. Her pregnancy was mired in controversy. Claims that Trig was in fact Bristol's son flew from all directions, including from Alaska Senate president Lyda Green, who suggested that Palin had not shown any physical signs of pregnancy. Other detractors accused her of adopting the baby to promote her pro-life persona. Supporters saw the decision not to abort the baby as evidence of her staunch antiabortion stance.

NOMINATION FOR VICE PRESIDENT

On August 29, 2008, Palin's twentieth wedding anniversary, McCain announced he had selected her as his running mate. She was the first Alaskan and the second woman to be listed on the presidential ticket of a major party. Because she had little name recognition outside of her home state, the choice surprised many. Although she provoked scorn on the Left and caused many on the Right to question McCain's decision-making skills, her down-to-earth demeanor, good looks, and maverick persona rejuvenated a stagnant political base. She was immediately popular with a considerable portion of the voting public who hoped the anonymous politician from small-town America could succeed on the public stage.

Her folksy way of speaking, fundamentalist Christian beliefs, and political conservatism made her anathema among educated liberal voters. Media outlets poured over her political and personal past. A report surfaced that she had fired public safety commissioner Walt Monegan because he had refused to fire state trooper and Palin's ex-brother-in-law Mike Wooten, who had been in a custody feud with her sister. The Alaska legislature conducted an investigation and ultimately cleared her of all charges, but doubts lingered about her ability to objectively administer her office. To make matters worse, her flip-flop on the Bridge to Nowhere resurfaced in the headlines, as did a report that the Republican National Committee had spent $150,000 on clothing, hairstyling, and makeup for her family.

Palin's first major TV interviews did little to help her image. When ABC News anchor Charles Gibson asked her about the Bush Doctrine of acting preemptively against nations deemed security threats, she appeared perplexed. Later, when CBS News anchor Katie Couric asked her what periodicals she reads, the candidate answered, "Most of them." When pressed further, she avoided naming a specific publication, leading many to conjecture that she did not read any periodicals. Her poll numbers plummeted, and some Republicans suggested she resign. Supporters charged the mainstream media with elitism, claiming that her interviewers were mocking traditional, conservative values by portraying her as a backward outsider.

PARODIES, JOKES, AND PORN

Early in her candidacy, Palin, with her distinctive appearance and phrases such as "You betcha," became the target of satire. Most notable were comedian Tina Fey's frequent impersonations of Palin on *Saturday Night Live* (1975–). The candidate even participated in the joke, appearing on the show during the 2008 campaign. After a backstage scene in which she interacted with Left-leaning actor Alec Baldwin, Palin appeared in the show's "Weekend Update" segment. Actress Amy Poehler performed a rap song that lampooned Palin's statement that she could "see Russia . . . from Alaska," and Palin danced in her chair, laughing as a moose was brought onstage.

However, she was much less amused when late-night talk show host David Letterman joked in June 2009 about daughter Bristol being "knocked up" again (Palin's daughter had made headlines the previous year when she announced that she was pregnant at age seventeen). After Republicans organized boycotts of his show, Letterman apologized, stating that the joke was beyond flawed. Other comedians made fun of her son Trig's Down syndrome. On a February 2010 episode of *Family Guy* (1999–), a character with Down's stated that her mother was the former governor of Alaska.

During the campaign, Palin also was the subject of a porn film, *Who's Nailin' Paylin?* Released on Election Day 2008, the film featured Lisa Ann as Serra Paylin, a brainless politician of voracious sexual appetite. Claims of sexism ran rampant when *Newsweek* magazine ran a cover photo of Palin wearing running shorts for its November 2009 issue.

CONTROVERSY, TABLOIDS, AND REALITY TELEVISION

After losing her White House bid to U.S. Senator Barack Obama and his running mate Joe Biden, Palin's nationwide notoriety and the many negative stories about her in the media affected her popularity in Alaska. Her approval rating as governor began to decline. Citing the $2.5 million the state had spent defending her against what she called "frivolous" ethics charges, she resigned as governor on July 26, 2009. She made headlines again in August when she used the phrase "death panel" on her Facebook page to describe a provision in pending federal health care legislation. The expression set off a firestorm of reaction, and the provision mandating that physicians provide Medicare recipients with end-of-life counseling was removed from the legislation.

In 2009 she published a memoir, *Going Rogue: An American Life*, which she promoted in a widely publicized interview with talk show host Oprah Winfrey. The book sold more than one million copies in its first two weeks, and the Associated Press detailed eleven reporters to scrutinize it for errors. *Going Rouge: Sarah Palin: An American Nightmare*, a collection of essays by Palin detractors, was published on the same day as Palin's memoir, setting off a string of anti-Palin books ranging from screeds and collections of gaffes to more substantive material such as *The Rogue: Searching for the Real Sarah Palin* (2011) by veteran journalist Joe McGinniss. (While researching his book, McGinniss rented a house next to the Palins' in Wasilla.)

Palin also debuted a TLC network reality show, *Sarah Palin's Alaska* (2010–2011), produced by Mark Burnett, known for producing the hit reality competition *Survivor* (2000–). The premiere of Palin's show set a TLC record of five million viewers. The same year, she began providing political commentary for the Fox News Channel and became one of the primary proponents of the Tea Party movement. Speaking at an inaugural convention on February 6, 2010, she endorsed extremist Tea Party candidates for the midterm elections, including U.S. Senate candidate Christine O'Donnell, opening rifts between her and the Republican establishment. At the end of 2010 Palin released a second book, *America by Heart*.

She continued to make headlines in 2011, including after the January 8 shooting of U.S. Representative Gabrielle Giffords, when opponents decried the use of a graphic on the Sarah PAC website that showed crosshairs over Gifford's district. Although she pulled the graphic after Giffords was shot, Palin's comparison of the criticisms to "blood libel" only heightened the controversy. During a May northeastern bus tour, she also commented that Paul Revere "warned the British that they weren't going to be taking away our arms, by ringing those bells" and firing "warning shots." Commentators castigated her for her poor knowledge of U.S. history; however, several historians stated that there was some truth to her statement, though it was poorly worded. Although she hinted at the possibility of a 2012 presidential bid, she eventually announced that she would not seek the nomination. On March 10, 2012, the cable TV network HBO presented a feature film, *Game Change*, based on the book of the same name, which documents the 2008 Republican campaign.

Judson Knight

SEE ALSO: *Abortion; Baldwin, Alec; Beauty Queens; Cable TV;* Family Guy*; Fey, Tina; Gay and Lesbian Marriage; Letterman, David; Made-for-Television Movies; Obama, Barack; Pornography; Reality Television;* Saturday Night Live*; Sex Scandals; Tabloid Television; Tabloids; The Tea Party; Television; Will, George F.; Winfrey, Oprah.*

BIBLIOGRAPHY

Carroll, Susan J., and Richard L. Fox, eds. *Gender and Elections: Shaping the Future of American Politics*. New York: Cambridge University Press, 2010.

Kim, Richard, and Betsy Reed, eds. *Going Rouge: Sarah Palin: An American Nightmare*. Deerfield Beach, FL: Health Communications, 2009.

McGinniss, Joe. *The Rogue: Searching for the Real Sarah Palin*. New York: Crown, 2011.

Palin, Sarah. *America by Heart: Reflections on Family, Faith, and Flag*. New York: Harper, 2010.

Palin, Sarah. *Going Rogue: An American Life*. New York: Harper, 2009.

Weiner, Rachel. "Sarah Palin Faced Trig Rumors from the Start." *Washington Post*, June 11, 2011.

Palmer, Arnold *(1929–)*

Modern professional golf began its rise to popularity with the emergence of Arnold Palmer in 1955. As the son of a club professional from Latrobe, Pennsylvania, Palmer learned the game as a child. He won the U.S. Golf Association Amateur Championship in 1954 before entering the professional ranks and dominating in the early 1960s. He won the Masters four times (1958, 1960, 1962, and 1964), the British Open back-to-back in 1961 and 1962, and the U.S. Open in 1960. Palmer won the Seniors Championship, his first event on the Senior PGA Tour, in 1980, and he won the U.S. Seniors Open in 1981.

Palmer was one of the earliest golfers to use his success on the golf course to attract lucrative endorsement and business deals. Legions of fans, known as "Arnie's Army," followed Palmer weekly on the professional tour, and he was responsible for introducing the game to millions.

Jay Parrent

SEE ALSO: *Golf; The Masters Golf Tournament; Nicklaus, Jack.*

BIBLIOGRAPHY

McCormack, Mark H. *Arnie: The Evolution of a Legend*. New York: Simon and Schuster, 1967.

Palmer, Arnold, and William Barry Furlong. *Go for Broke: My Philosophy of Winning Golf.* New York: Simon and Schuster, 1973.

Sampson, Curt. *The Eternal Summer: Palmer, Nicklaus, and Hogan in 1960, Golf's Golden Year*. New York, Villard: 2009.

Palmer, Jim *(1945–)*

From 1965 to 1984, Jim Palmer was among baseball's most successful pitchers, winning three Cy Young Awards for a team that won six pennants. Palmer achieved stardom at the age of twenty when the right-hander shut out the Dodgers on the way to a Baltimore Orioles sweep in the 1966 World Series. An injury kept Palmer out of baseball for nearly two years, but in 1969 he was able to come back and establish himself as one of the game's premier pitchers, winning 268 games in a career that spanned nineteen years. Despite the team's success, throughout his career Palmer shared a stormy relationship with manager Earl Weaver.

When his baseball pitching days ended in 1984, the handsome Palmer embarked on a new career as a pitchman for Jockey shorts. Advertising posters in which he modeled underwear could be seen in Europe and Asia in addition to the United States. He also appeared in television advertisements for The Money Store and various health products. In 1990 Palmer was inducted into the Baseball Hall of Fame in his first year of eligibility. He has remained involved in baseball as a color commentator, first on network TV and later working in the broadcast booth for the Orioles.

Kevin O'Connor

SEE ALSO: *Advertising; Baseball; Sports Heroes.*

BIBLIOGRAPHY

Cohen, Joel H. *Jim Palmer: Great Comeback Competitor*. New York: Putnam, 1978.

Palmer, Jim, and Jim Dale. *Together We Were Eleven Foot Nine: The Twenty-Year Friendship of Hall of Fame Pitcher Jim Palmer and Orioles Manager Earl Weaver*. Kansas City, MO: Andrews and McMeel, 1996.

Shaughnessy, Dan, and Grossfeld, Stan. *Fenway: A Biography in Words and Pictures*. Boston: Houghton Mifflin, 2007.

Pants for Women

As the proverbial question of who "wears the pants" in a relationship suggests, the history of women's pants says as much

Marlene Dietrich Makes Pants Fashionable. *When diva film star Marlene Dietrich appeared in slacks with flared bottoms in her debut film* Morocco *in 1930, she signaled the emergence of women's pants from sportswear to high fashion.* EUGENE ROBERT RICHEE/CONTRIBUTOR/MOVIEPIX/GETTY IMAGES.

about the evolution of twentieth-century gender roles as it does about the capricious swings of the fashion pendulum. Pants for women emerged from the burgeoning nineteenth-century feminist movement, which demanded a change from Victorian dresses to a more practical costume that permitted women to engage in activities beyond those traditionally assigned to the female domestic sphere. Ironically, pants for women achieved widespread social acceptance only when the fashion industry convinced women that pants were a necessary part of a well-dressed woman's wardrobe.

The first feminine garments approximating pants were bloomers—a full skirt reaching just below the knee with full-cut trousers underneath. Named for their chief advocate, feminist Amelia Jenks Bloomer, the outfit liberated women from heavy skirts, whalebone corsets, petticoats, bustles, and padding. In spite of the unprecedented mobility bloomers permitted, they were seen as too radical, and the fashion never spread beyond a small group. The bloomers' association with the suffrage movement stigmatized its wearers, and as an article in the September 1851 issue of *Godey's Lady's Book* hypothesized, bloomers did not take because most women would not wear what did not originate in fashionable Paris.

BEGINNING OF ACCEPTANCE

Though unsuccessful themselves, bloomers influenced the design of the popular feminine bicycling costume of the 1880s and 1890s, which consisted of a pair of knee-length, very baggy knickerbockers with a split skirt and stockings worn beneath. These bicycle bloomers marked the first concession made by the fashion industry toward enabling women's participation in skirt-prohibitive activities. Formerly, as with the original bloomers, an activity was deemed immodest and unladylike if it could not be performed in a skirt. Although some criticized bicycling for this reason, most women showed no inclination to give up cycling, and the craze for bicycle bloomers raged for the next two decades.

As the somber mood of World War I replaced the frivolity of the Gay Nineties, women replaced men in the factories as the latter headed for battlefields. At work, when skirts proved too cumbersome, women wore trousers or overalls, though this practice was much criticized. Women worked in the fields, too, sometimes wearing overalls, as noted by L. M. Montgomery in her book *Rilla of Ingleside* (1921), a fictional account with autobiographical overtones that depicts life on Canada's Prince Edward Island during World War I. In the novel some young women wear pants as they work, whereas the older women working beside them remain in their skirts because pants are still considered indecent or shocking. It is clear, however, that those women who wore pants during World War I did so for reasons of practicality and not of fashion.

By the 1920s the boyish look had become fashionable, and women began exposing their arms and legs, flattening their chests, and bobbing their hair. Even though women had won the vote, they were still restricted in other areas, and pants remained taboo except in the realm of sports. Here, ease of movement somewhat dictated fashion. And so the ski costume, a knitted tunic over knitted trousers that fit into ankle-high ski boots, was created. Riding outfits similar to those worn by men became popular, and women wore the loose trousers of "lounge pajamas" on the beach.

When diva film star Marlene Dietrich appeared in slacks in her U.S. debut film *Morocco* in 1930, she signaled the emergence of women's pants from sportswear to high fashion. Wearing them both in films and private life, she popularized pants for women. For summer wear, shorts and beach slacks were stylish, and pants were worn regularly with short-sleeved knit tops. Women's pants had gained such importance by 1939 that in the November issue of *Vogue* the magazine advised, "Your wardrobe is not complete without a pair or two of the superbly tailored slacks of 1939."

During World War II fashion followed the needs of the war. Clothing was simple, sensible, and, in some cases, rationed. In England the Board of Trade specified the maximum amount of cloth and buttons that could be used in women's slacks. Needing to fill jobs left vacant by men at the front, the government began using such images as "Rosie the Riveter"—who was shown once on a 1943 cover of the *Saturday Evening Post* as muscular and wearing coveralls—to convince women that it was their patriotic duty to return to factory work; this time they wore their dungarees without looks askance.

CULTURAL NECESSITY

In 1947, after the austerity of the war years, Christian Dior introduced his lush New Look, reverting to full skirts and soft femininity. Women's pants, however, were by then an acknowledged fact, and the 1950s brought many innovations to casual wear. Women wore a variety of slacks, ranging from tight-fitting to loose and comfortable, worn with all types of blouses. Following the post–World War II baby boom, the 1950s ushered in the cult of youth and the creation of a market division specifically for teenage fashions. Girls wore capri pants, stretch pants with stirrups, and Bermuda shorts.

These innovations set the stage for "unisex" fashions, which were developed in the 1960s. Both men and women wore blue jeans, "hipsters," and close-fitting pants with zip-fly fronts. The spirit of this latest association of pants with social and sexual liberation can be seen in Alice Walker's novel *The Color Purple* (1982), in which the social victory of the heroine culminates in her opening of a unisex jeans shop. In addition to jeans, pant suits became popular with women in fabrics ranging from PVC and lurex to velvet and satin.

Since the 1960s women's pants have run the gamut of trends from the bellbottoms of the 1970s and the skin-tight jeans of the 1980s to the return of bellbottoms and tight jeans in the 1990s. The fashion, however, is not yet entirely divorced from its controversial beginnings. Only in the 1990s did the issue over whether women should wear pants in the workplace cool, aided by the phenomenon of "business casual" days and "dress-down Fridays."

In 2001 the publication of Ann Brashares's novel *The Sisterhood of the Traveling Pants* served to illustrate the importance of women's pants within popular culture and to highlight the fact that pants have become essential elements in the female wardrobe. A coming-of-age story about female bonding, the book focuses on four young girls (Tibby, Lena, Carmen, and Bridget) who, while searching for the "perfect" pants, find a pair of jeans that magically fits each of them. The pants also act as a good luck charm for the wearer. Separated by the dictates of summer schedules, the pants are mailed to each girl in turn, playing an important part in her evolving life and maturity. Brashares published *The Second Summer of the Sisterhood* in 2003 and *Girls in Pants* in 2006. The first novel was made into a movie starring Amber Tamblyn as Tibby, Alexis Bledel as Lena, America Ferrera as Carmen, and Blake Lively as Bridget. A film sequel based on the second book, *Sisterhood of the Traveling Pants 2*, was released in 2008.

Sandra Sherman

SEE ALSO: *Baby Boomers; Bellbottoms; Casual Friday; Dietrich, Marlene; Feminism; The Fifties; Jeans; New Look; Retro Fashion; The* Saturday Evening Post; *Teenagers;* Vogue; *Walker, Alice; World War I; World War II.*

BIBLIOGRAPHY

Adams, J. Donald. *Naked We Came: A More or Less Lighthearted Look at the Past, Present, and Future of Clothes.* New York: Holt, Rinehart, and Winston, 1967.

De Fircks, Tatiana. *History of Costume and Style.* Melbourne: Pitman Publishing, 1992.

Fifty Years of Fashion: Documented Sketches and Text from the Costume Library of Women's Wear Daily. New York: Fairchild Publications, 1950.

Smith, Catherine, and Cynthia Greig. *Women in Pants: Manly Maidens, Cowgirls, and Other Renegades.* New York: H. N. Abrams, 2003.

Tyrrell, Anne V. *Changing Trends in Fashion: Patterns of the Twentieth Century 1900–1970.* London: B. T. Batsford, 1986.

Pantyhose

In 1937 the invention of spinnable nylon made sheer, durable stockings affordable for the average woman, but in the 1960s pantyhose—a convenient one-piece garment consisting of nylon-spandex stretchable stockings and underpants—made traditional stockings practically obsolete. Supermodel Twiggy popularized pantyhose when she stepped out on a runway in a miniskirt in 1965. Soon afterward, pantyhose, which come in a wide range of colors, styles, and prices (starting at about $3.50 per pair and going up to about $40), became an indispensable part of virtually every woman's working or fashion wardrobe.

Emotionally appealing to women and sexually appealing to men, pantyhose became a staple product in the global economy, having created a competitive, multibillion-dollar market. During the 1990s, however, their popularity began to fall as business casual dress spread in the workplace. Increasingly, women chose to go out with bare legs, especially during warm-weather months, and the decline in pantyhose sales continued into the early twenty-first century. Sales spiked somewhat in 2011 with the news that Kate Middleton—the fashion-conscious bride of Britain's Prince William—preferred to wear stockings, but it was unclear if the royal-inspired trend would continue.

John R. Deitrick

SEE ALSO: *Casual Friday; Nylon; Twiggy.*

BIBLIOGRAPHY

Bruce, Katherine. "The Missionary of Pantyhose." *Forbes*, December 15, 1997, 116.

Fasel, Penny Proddow. "Stocking Smarts." *In Style*, September 1998, 131.

Paperbacks

When Pocket Books introduced the paperback to American consumers in 1939, book publishing changed forever. Paperbacks did more than make books affordable to a mass audience: they made books available to readers who did not live near bookstores. They helped popularize genre fiction. They turned otherwise obscure writers into best-selling authors, and they ensured a lasting existence for hardback books that went into paperback.

EUROPEAN ORIGINS

Although there were many earlier attempts to publish books with paper covers, the modern paperback book can be traced to Tauchnitz Books, a German publisher that began issuing paperbound books in 1841. Tauchnitz published English-language editions of American and English books, primarily in non-English-speaking European countries, under the assumption that there were enough American and British expatriates as well as Europeans fluent in English to establish a market for inexpensive English-language books. Tauchnitz attempted to publish only the best literature and voluntarily paid royalties to its English and American writers at a time when most European publishers did not, so it was both flattering and financially rewarding to be chosen for publication by Tauchnitz. Perhaps what is most striking about Tauchnitz books is their complete lack of color or decoration; in contrast with American paperbacks, Tauchnitz book covers carried no illustration, only bearing the title and author in black letters against an off-white background.

For ninety years Tauchnitz had the European paperback market to itself. Its primary competitor, Albatross, emerged in 1931. Albatross was founded by German and English publishers; the name *Albatross* was chosen because that word is the same in nearly every major European language and, therefore, would need no translation. Albatross brought one major innovation to the paperback market: it color-coded its books so that readers could determine the book's subject matter merely by glancing at the cover. Blue books were love stories, red books were crime novels, and so forth. In 1934 Albatross bought out Tauchnitz, and the two houses continued to publish until the outbreak of World War II. Meanwhile, an English paperback publisher, Penguin, largely adopted Albatross's systematic approach for its own publications, using a penguin as its company logo and color-coding its books. All Penguin paperbacks were orange, blue, or green until the 1990s.

POCKET BOOKS

Robert de Graff brought the paperback to America in 1939. De Graff had worked in book publishing for fourteen years and was convinced that there was a market for inexpensive books in the United States. He said he got the idea of selling books for twenty-five cents when he was driving to work one day, stopped to pay a quarter at a tollbooth, and realized, "Nobody misses a quarter." He named his new company Pocket Books because the books were small enough to fit into one's pants pocket; at 6.5 inches high and 4.25 inches wide, the books were .25 inch shorter than paperbacks.

De Graff faced two key obstacles in the development and marketing of the paperback book. He solved the problem of keeping the price to twenty-five cents by lowering author royalty rates and by using cheaper paper, which is why the paperback has always had a reputation of being "cheaper" than the hardback book, in terms of quality as well as price. The second problem was a lack of cooperation from book publishers, which were reluctant to sell paperback rights to Pocket Books, fearing that potentials buyers would wait and buy the less expensive version. To prove that paperbacks would not harm the sales of hardback books, de Graff arranged for a test marketing in Texas of Dale Carnegie's *How to Win Friends and Influence People.* When the paperback sold well and sales of the hardback book remained steady, publishers realized that the two formats could coexist. Eventually it became standard practice to delay the release of a paperback edition for a year or more after the hardback was published.

Pocket Books was launched in June 1939. Ten titles were published, with a print run of approximately10,000 copies per title. The selected titles ranged from classics such as *The Way of All Flesh* to popular literature such as Agatha Christie's *The Murder of Roger Ackroyd.* The initial print run sold out in one week, the first indication de Graff had that his new company might be a big success. By the end of the year Pocket Books had sold 1.5 million books.

The success of the new paperback format can be attributed to many factors. Before the books were printed, de Graff had the edges of the paper dyed red, so that they stood out on a book rack. He had also insisted that his books be grouped by subject matter rather than simply divided into fiction and nonfiction, so that a person looking for one specific mystery novel, for example, might see several such novels grouped together and buy two or more. He even insisted that the company's recognizable trademark/mascot, a kangaroo named Gertrude (kangaroos have pockets), had a great deal to do with the company's success.

But the most important factor in the success of Pocket Books was distribution. De Graff had managed to have his paperbacks sold in many more stores than hardback books; one estimate was that there were forty stores carrying paperbacks for every one carrying hardbacks in the United States. Pocket Books were not just available in bookstores; they could be purchased in grocery stores, pharmacies, and candy stores; at bus stations, airports, and train terminals; through Sears Roebuck and Spiegel catalogs—all at a price of twenty-five cents. De Graff transformed books into impulse purchases, like candy bars or packs of gum.

THE WAR YEARS

The success of Pocket Books did not go unnoticed by the publishing industry, and several competitors emerged in 1941. The most successful was Avon Books, which imitated the Pocket Books format slavishly. Avon adopted the same dimensions as Pocket Books, dyed its pages red on the edge, used a bust of Shakespeare as a trademark, and originally called its products Avon Pocket-Size Books. Pocket Books sued; eventually Avon dropped the term *Pocket-Size* from its cover but retained the logo, the red-trimmed pages, and the size.

When America entered World War II, it became difficult for Pocket Books and Avon to obtain enough paper to meet the demand for paperbacks, and the war did substantial damage to the industry—at least in the short term. In the long term, it might have been the best thing that ever happened to paperbacks.

During the war, Avon, Pocket Books, and Penguin printed military editions under the auspices of the Council on Books in Wartime, a government organization. These books were given free to servicemen and women during the war. Military editions were a different size and shape than regular paperbacks; wider than they were tall, approximately 5.5 inches across but only 3.75 inches high, the books could easily be slid into a shirt pocket if a soldier under attack suddenly had to put the book away. Military editions were extremely popular with American GIs and helped create a strong market for paperbacks in postwar America; not only did most of the returning soldiers who had read military editions overseas continue to buy and read paperback books, but many also recommended them to their family and friends.

In 1943 two more publishers entered the paperback market: Dell and Popular Library. Both companies were founded by magazine publishers and therefore were even more attuned to the popular tastes of the American public than was Pocket Books. Dell's most noteworthy contribution to the paperback format was the "map book"—on the back cover of many Dell paperbacks was a map of the setting of the novel to help readers who might otherwise get confused.

Bantam Books, like Avon, closely followed the Pocket Books model of red pages, small size, and mascot, a bantam rooster in this case. Bantam was founded in 1945 by Ian Ballantine, a former Penguin editor who went on to found another company, Ballantine, in 1952. New American Library, also founded by former Penguin editors, was established in 1948. Its

Signet and Mentor imprints soon developed a reputation as the most literary paperbacks, publishing William Faulkner and D. H. Lawrence, among others.

PRESTIGIOUS PAPERBACKS, RACY NOVELS

The paperback industry changed again in 1950 with the founding of Fawcett Books, certainly the most influential publisher of paperbacks since Pocket Books and arguably the most important publisher in the history of the paperback. Like Dell and Popular Library, Fawcett had published magazines before entering the paperback market and had in fact distributed paperbacks for other companies along with its magazines. Fawcett wanted to enter into paperback publishing but was contractually bound from producing paperback reprints of hardcover books. So Fawcett by necessity created the key market innovation of the paperback industry—the paperback original.

Fawcett's Gold Medal line published brand-new novels. This was particularly appealing to customers at the time; many publishers changed the titles of books when putting them into paperback so that buyers frequently got home with books they had already read, but Gold Medal novels guaranteed that would not happen. Each Gold Medal book concluded with this phrase: "The End of an Original Gold Medal Novel. The Gold Medal Seal on this book means it has never been published as a book before. To select an original book that you have not already read, look for the Gold Medal seal."

Fawcett attracted better authors than might have been expected from a paperback house: Kurt Vonnegut, John D. MacDonald, Jim Thompson, and Lawrence Block are among the authors who published early works with Gold Medal. The company paid $1,000 upon delivery of a manuscript, which meant writers did not have to wait to collect royalties; they also received a bonus if the book was reprinted. Fawcett also had a genuinely talented editor, Knox Burger, heading up its paperback line. Gold Medal targeted male readers; its books were mostly crime and Western novels with titles such as *Second-Hand Nude* or *River Girl*, and its covers were lewd and lurid even by the standards of the paperback industry. It was also very successful and inspired a host of imitators.

Dell quickly introduced its line of first edition paperbacks, and other paperback houses started issuing original novels. New publishers appeared as well, including some that were more disreputable than the older publishers and willing to go even further than Fawcett in using sex and violence to attract a male audience. Paperback houses such as Midwood and Beeline produced hundreds of sexually explicit novels, not quite softcore pornography, in the 1960s. The paperback original boosted sales of softcover books so much that publishers in the early twenty-first century refer to the "paperback boom" of the 1950s. Ironically, the success of its Gold Medal line eventually led Fawcett to create a reprint line, Crest; the company has published Gold Medal books very infrequently since the early 1980s.

The overtly sexual nature of many of the paperbacks published in the early 1950s eventually resulted in the threat of censorship. In 1952 the House of Representatives Select Committee on Current Pornographic Materials began an investigation of the paperback book industry. One representative referred to the three S's of paperbacks: "sex, sadism, and the smoking gun." Gold Medal was under particular scrutiny by the committee, due in part to the lesbian novels the company published. The committee never made any official move to censor books, but the industry did begin to restrict the sexual content of paperbacks, with many books actually recalled and reissued with new covers. Furthermore, censorship attempts occurred at state and local levels throughout the 1950s.

GENRE NOVELS AND MOVIE NOVELIZATIONS

Few major paperback publishers emerged after Fawcett. Ace, founded in 1952, added its own market innovation with the double novel—after completing an Ace paperback, readers could turn it over and find another entire (though usually very brief) novel. Harlequin, a Canadian publisher founded in 1949, began publishing its highly successful line of romance books in 1964.

In 1969 Pinnacle was founded by former publishers of 1950s "adult" paperbacks. Pinnacle specialized in the series novel, books with recurring characters that even included numbers on each new installment so that customers could easily collect an entire series. Pinnacle's most successful characters were the Executioner and the Destroyer; the former was a Vietnam veteran turned vigilante, and the latter was a former police officer who worked for a secret government agency. The series novel dominated the 1970s, with Westerns, military adventures, and martial arts stories being particularly popular. In the 1970s DAW Books became the first paperback house to specialize in one genre; founded by respected editor and author Donald A. Wollheim, the company published science fiction only.

Other trends developed in the 1970s and 1980s. The relative speed with which a paperback could be published resulted in the "instant" book, a quickly produced volume that discusses a current political or social event. The O. J. Simpson trial, Operation Desert Shield, and the Monica Lewinsky scandal all generated instant books, and there have been instant biographies of stars whose fame seemed destined to be short-lived, such as the Spice Girls and Vanilla Ice. A novelization is a book that is based upon a movie or television program rather than the other way around. Novelizations of all sorts of TV shows and motion pictures were common in the 1970s, and at least one, the novel version of *Jaws 2*, actually achieved best seller status. By the 1980s novelizations in the science fiction genre were most common, and hundreds of *Doctor Who* and *Star Trek* novels have been written, many featuring original adventures of the characters.

A CHANGING INDUSTRY

The trade paperback, also called the quality paperback and the oversized paperback, has been in existence at least since 1953, when Doubleday introduced its series of Anchor Books, but has enjoyed its greatest success since the 1980s. Trade paperbacks are substantially larger than regular paperback books, now referred to as "mass market" books. They are almost as large as a standard hardcover book and cost about half as much. Trade paperbacks seem to have a cachet of respectability that regular paperback novels were never able to acquire.

In the 1990s consolidation of publishers left only a handful of companies producing most of the paperback books in America. Prices have risen considerably from de Graff's 25 cents, and $6 and $7 paperbacks are standard. A great emphasis, especially among mass market publishers, is placed on "category fiction"—novels that can be placed into easily identifiable genres, such as science fiction, Westerns, courtroom thrillers, or historical novels. There are fewer original novels published in paperback.

The paperback book has played an enormous role in the development of literature in contemporary America. Authors as disparate as J. R. R. Tolkien, Benjamin Spock, Louis L'Amour, and Mickey Spillane all reached mass audiences through the paperback medium. The paperback has been a ubiquitous part of American life; since the first Pocket Books appeared in 1939, almost anybody in America, living anywhere, has been able to walk into a local store and find a wire rack filled with paperback books.

Technological developments of the early 2000s, however, may spell the end of the paperback book—or at least its sharp decline. Consumers began to buy electronic book readers on which to read downloaded e-books. Both the devices and digital books caught on quickly. Amazon, the online bookselling giant, announced in 2010 that its e-book sales had surpassed those of hardbacks; the following year, it announced that e-book sales had also surpassed paperbacks—a milestone that occurred more quickly than expected. Publishing industry experts remain unsure whether print and e-books will be able to coexist or if digital offerings will bring about the demise of printed books.

Randall Clark

SEE ALSO: *Amazon.com; Carnegie, Dale; Christie, Agatha; Dime Novels;* Doctor Who*; Faulkner, William; Graphic Novels;* Jaws*; L'Amour, Louis; Lewinsky, Monica; MacDonald, John D.; Romance Novels; Science Fiction Publishing; Sears Roebuck Catalogue; Simpson, O. J.; Simpson Trial; The Spice Girls; Spillane, Mickey; Spock, Dr. Benjamin;* Star Trek*; Tolkien, J. R. R.; Vanilla Ice; Vonnegut, Kurt, Jr.; The Western; World War II.*

BIBLIOGRAPHY

Bonn, Thomas. *Under Cover.* New York: Penguin, 1982.

Bonn, Thomas. *Heavy Traffic & High Culture.* Carbondale: Southern Illinois Press, 1989.

Darnton, Robert. *The Case for Books: Past, Present, and Future.* New York: PublicAffairs, 2010.

Davis, Kenneth. *Two-Bit Culture.* Boston: Houghton Mifflin, 1984.

O'Brien, Geoffrey. *Hardboiled America.* New York: Van Nostrand Reinhold, 1981.

Petersen, Clarence. *The Bantam Story: Twenty-Five Years of Paperback Publishing.* New York: Bantam, 1970.

Server, Lee. *Over My Dead Body.* San Francisco: Chronicle, 1994.

Thompson, John B. *Merchants of Culture.* Cambridge, UK: Polity Press, 2010.

Parades

Whether they are held to demonstrate military might, to advertise public events and holidays, or simply to entertain, parades are part of the community experience and probably have been since human beings first gathered together in a social order. As far back as 3000 BCE there are records of religious processions and parades. From a New York ticker tape parade to a ragtag local procession, a parade is a kind of social narrative, as symbols and tableaux approach and pass by, telling cheering spectators a sort of story about their society.

PARADE EVOLUTION

The first public parades were likely military or political in origin, as armies and rulers found that a huge demonstration of power was an effective way to intimidate opposition forces and to muster support. Patriotism, that nationalistic pride so important to those who rule nations and those who make war, is still an important product of military and political pageants. Religious institutions also used parades to gain power and solidify connections with the populace. The public welcomed such parades, both as a diversion from workday life and because, for a moment, the powerful were within reach of the common people. Less enthusiastic were the conquered people forced to watch the victors flaunt their triumph down the main streets of vanquished towns.

Other early parades were connected with fairs, festivals, and athletic competitions and offered opportunities for people to gather, socialize, and exchange information. In medieval Italy, *carreros*, or carts, were painted with historical scenes and brought out at parade times as a sort of rolling history exhibit. Circus parades were often the most anticipated public events in small towns in earlier centuries. Part flamboyant spectacle and part advertisement for the show, the brightly painted wagons and

Macy's Thanksgiving Day Parade. *The Macy's Thanksgiving Day Parade in New York City is a traditional event that marks the start of the holiday season.* DOUG KANTER/AFP/GETTY IMAGES.

exotic performers and animals of the circus parade were greeted with enthusiasm by the working people in small, usually quiet towns. As long ago as the ancient Greek Olympics, athletic events have also featured festive processions. From the Gator Bowl Parade in Florida to the Tournament of Roses Parade in California, cities and towns from coast to coast continue to host parades in conjunction with big sporting events, especially football games.

More modern parades have tended to fall into the same categories, augmented by modern excesses. The military parade is still a standby, whether it honors veterans of past wars or celebrates victory in a new one. The end of World War II was cause for hundreds of parades nationwide, but later wars evoked more complicated emotions. Veterans of the undeclared conflicts in Korea and Vietnam, for example, complained that their homecomings went unfeted, because most Americans were merely glad to put the controversy and discomfort behind them.

In a sort of backlash effect, subsequent public and government organizations seemed almost embarrassingly determined to honor troops. In the next major U.S. conflict, the Persian Gulf War of 1991, the spate of parades celebrating the returning troops lasted longer than the forty-three-day war itself. Following the first Gulf War, U.S. wars once again became mired in controversy and complication, as it became hard to distinguish when simultaneous wars in Afghanistan (beginning 2001) and Iraq (2003–2011) were actually over. When President Barack Obama ordered the withdrawal of troops from Iraq in 2011, there was little public acknowledgement until two men in St. Louis, Missouri, organized a parade in January 2012. Other cities soon followed suit, arranging parades for returning troops.

REASONS FOR PARADES

Religion has always been a major inspiration for a parade, and many major U.S. parades are at least nominally religious. Mardi Gras parades, major events in New Orleans, Louisiana, and other cities in the South, celebrate the last feast before the beginning of Lent. In practice, Mardi Gras has always been an occasion for revelry and debauchery—and endless parades. In New Orleans, where the first Mardi Gras celebration was held in 1837, social groups called krewes sponsor dozens of balls and parades. The krewes offer visibility to many groups who are otherwise marginalized. There are black and Jewish krewes, and, since 1958, gay krewes. All are welcomed and celebrated in the spirit of Mardi Gras, and all compete to have the most artistic and ostentatious parade floats.

The feast of St. Patrick also offers an excuse for a parade in many U.S. cities. In New York City, the nation's largest St. Patrick's Day parade drew 200,000 marchers and almost two million spectators in 2011. Though it is on one hand a raucous revel, a St. Patrick's Day parade also often has a subtle political agenda of Irish nationalism. Unlike Mardi Gras parades, however, St. Patrick's Day parades have often sought to prevent the inclusion of marginalized groups; many have banned contingents of gay Irish marchers, for example.

As in circus parades, advertising continues to be a motivating factor for holding parades. Since 1924 the famous Macy's Thanksgiving Day parade in New York City has been an extravagant advertising mechanism, in which companies pay hundreds of thousands of dollars to display helium-filled toys and logos before millions of spectators. Many other companies are catching on to the parade as a marketing tool, hiring specialized companies to plan and execute their parades to maximum effect.

Gay Pride Day offers an example of the political evolution of a parade. With the beginning of the gay liberation movement in the 1970s, Gay Pride marches started as demonstrations, often angry and challenging, demanding gay rights. As the movement progressed and gays began to feel more strength and solidarity in their communities, the event evolved into a celebratory parade, complete with elaborate floats, commercial advertisements, and glad-handing politicians seeking votes. Though some gays bemoan this change from protest to festivity, others see it as a sign of progress and social acceptance.

Tina Gianoulis

SEE ALSO: *College Football; Gay Liberation Movement; Gulf Wars; Macy's; Mardi Gras; Olympics; Vietnam; War in Afghanistan; World War II.*

BIBLIOGRAPHY

Davis, Susan G. *Parades and Power: Street Theatre in Nineteenth-Century Philadelphia.* Philadelphia: Temple University Press, 1986.

Ryan, Mary. "The American Parade: Representations of the Nineteenth Century Social Order." *The New Cultural History*, ed. Lynn Hunt. Berkeley: University of California Press, 1989.

Salter, Jim. "St. Louis Parade Is First to Welcome Home Iraq War Veterans." *Washington Post*, January 29, 2012.

Sussman, Mark. "Celebrating the New World Order: Festival and War in New York." *Drama Review* 39, no. 2 (1995): 147.

Paretsky, Sara *(1947–)*

In creating the character of the feminist Chicago detective V. I. Warshawski, author Sara Paretsky paved the way for a new category of female detectives within the mystery genre. Angered at the treatment of female mystery writers, who were too often unrewarded and underappreciated, Paretsky helped to create Sisters in Crime in 1986. This group has consistently worked to garner awards for female mystery writers, promote more reviews of mysteries by women, and improve the image of women in mystery novels. Sisters in Crime celebrated its twenty-fifth anniversary in 2011. By that time, its worldwide membership included forty-eight chapters and some three thousand members.

Paretsky, who was born in Iowa and grew up in Lawrence, Kansas, was influenced in her choice of career by her mother, a children's librarian at the Lawrence Public Library. Young Sara began writing at the age of five. As an adult Paretsky worked as a dishwasher, secretary, market manager, and freelance writer before publishing her first V. I. Warshawski mystery, *Indemnity Only*, in 1982. In this her first novel, Paretsky combined her love of writing with her experience in the insurance industry to create a realistic, feminist detective who dealt with real problems on her own terms.

Victoria Warshawski, who prefers to be called V. I. or Vic, is described as being 5 feet 8 inches tall and weighing 140 pounds, with dark brown hair and green eyes. She loves Black Label whiskey, red wine, and pasta. V. I. is ferociously loyal to her friends and tenacious when solving crimes. Although she is frequently assisted in her endeavors by her friend Dr. Lotty Herschel and downstairs neighbor Mr. Conteras, V. I. primarily applies her own intelligence and physical abilities to solve cases. In 2012, Paretsky published her fifteenth mystery featuring Warshawski, *Breakdown*. Paretsky also edited *Women on the Case* (1997), a collection of short stories with female protagonists.

In the Warshawski series, Paretsky has succeeded in her goal of creating a female detective who combats the stereotypes of women prevalent in fiction before 1980. In her wake, other mystery writers, such as Dorothy Cannell (the Ellie Haskell series) and Selma Eichler (the Desiree Shapiro series), challenged the traditional mode of women in mysteries throughout the 1980s and 1990s. Within the mystery genre, major female characters now include black, Jewish, lesbian, sixty-plus, and divorced protagonists.

BEYOND WARSHAWSKI

In 1998 Sara Paretsky turned her attention to writing a novel that dealt with the lives of women in a broader context than was possible with the V. I. Warshawski series. *Ghost Country* features a group of women from distinctly different backgrounds who come together in Chicago's underground network of streets and tunnels and become involved with exploring their own identities and their relationship to the world around them. Paretsky returned to her roots in 2008 with *Bleeding Kansas*, a novel dealing with religion and politics among contemporary farming families.

Paretsky became increasingly political in the wake of the September 11 attacks and is a vocal advocate for the rights of library patrons. She addresses both post-9/11 violations of civil liberties and McCarthyism in the V. I. Warshawski mystery *Blacklist* (2003).

Sara Paretsky, a mother and grandmother, lives in Chicago with her husband, physicist Courtenay Wright, and her golden retriever, Cordhu. She was named *Ms.* magazine's Woman of the Year in 1987, was awarded the Mark Twain Award by the Society for the Study of Midwestern Literature, and won a Silver Dagger award for *Blood Shot*. In all her novels, Paretsky addresses traditional perceptions regarding the role of women in American society. She published her memoirs, *Writing in the Age of Silence*, in 2007.

Elizabeth Rholetter Purdy

SEE ALSO: *Detective Fiction; Feminism; McCarthyism; 9/11.*

BIBLIOGRAPHY

Kaminsky, Stuart M. *Behind the Mystery: Top Mystery Writers*. Cohasset, MA: Hot House Press, 2005.

Paretsky, Sara. *Blood Shot*. New York: Dell Books, 1988.

Paretsky, Sara. *Ghost Country*. New York: Delacorte, 1998.

Paretsky, Sara. *Indemnity Only*. New York: Dell Books, 1991.

Paretsky, Sara. *Writing in an Age of Silence*. New York: Verso, 2007.

Reddy, Maureen T., ed. *Sisters in Crime: Feminism and the Crime Novel*. New York: Continuum, 1988.

Swanson, Jean, and Dean Jones. *By a Woman's Hand: A Guide to Mystery Fiction by Women*. New York: Berkley Books, 1994.

Trosky, Susan M., ed. *Contemporary Authors: A Bio-Bibliographical Guide to Current Writers in Fiction, General Nonfiction, Poetry, Journalism, Drama, Motion Pictures, Television, and Other Fields*. Vol. 129. Detroit, MI: Gale Research, 1990.

Parker, Charlie *(1920–1955)*

When alto saxophonist Charlie "Bird" Parker died at the age of thirty-four from the effects of drug and alcohol addiction and hard living, graffiti appeared on walls and sidewalks all over New York City proclaiming "Bird Lives!" The grief-stricken graffiti artists were more prescient than they could have imagined. One of the premier jazz artists in history, Parker made a contribution to American music that continues to be strongly felt more than half a century after his own life was cut short.

First reckoned as a major influence in jazz when he helped develop the bebop style while playing in Harlem, New York, clubs in the 1940s, his style is still widely imitated not only by saxophone players but also by jazz musicians on every instrument and even by scat singers. A master improviser whose command of theme and counterpoint has been compared by some critics to Johann Sebastian Bach, Parker was not only a victim of his addictions but also of the contradictions of being a brilliant black musician in the racist United States of the 1940s and 1950s.

Charlie Parker. *The music that Charlie Parker created in his short, turbulent life remains relevant to jazz fans today.* MICHAEL OCHS ARCHIVES/STRINGER/GETTY IMAGES.

A BORN MUSICIAN

Charles Christopher Parker Jr. was born in Kansas City, Kansas. His father, a singer and dancer who also worked as a Pullman chef for the railroad, left the family when Parker was quite young. Parker was raised by his mother, who doted on her chubby, affectionate, only child. His hearty appetite, especially his love for chicken, may have given rise to his lifelong nickname "Yardbird," or "Bird." When he was eleven, Parker bought his first alto sax, inspired by listening to Rudy Vallee on the radio. By the age of fifteen he had left school to become a professional musician, playing at clubs in the lively Kansas City, Missouri, jazz district. Within a year, through a family friend, he became addicted to morphine.

While developing his music in Kansas City jazz clubs, Parker married a local girl at age sixteen, and by the time he was eighteen he was a father. A year later, in 1939, he asked his wife's permission to leave. He felt that he needed to go to New York to develop his music. Playing with several well-known big bands as well as in the Harlem jam sessions where the direction of jazz evolved, Parker developed a formidable reputation as a saxophone soloist. Modern studies of Parker's recorded music show that he never repeated an improvisation, no matter how often he played the same piece of music.

It was while playing in Harlem with trumpet player Dizzy Gillespie that Parker helped develop the innovative flexible rhythm patterns that became known as bebop, or bop. The bebop sound worked better in small combos rather than big bands, and Parker and Gillespie worked together for many years, coleading small jazz groups. From the big bands Parker had learned the delicate art of blending with other instruments while leading them through inventive riffs and motifs. In the five-piece combos and jamming with such greats as Thelonious Monk and Max Roach, he learned to expand on the rhythmic inventions and dynamic phrasing that would revolutionize jazz.

STRUGGLES

Parker was always a man of contradictions. His warm personality and transcendent horn improvisations made him a revered character in the jazz community, whereas his ruthless ambition and flamboyant disregard for authority often caused both peers and employers to be wary of him. In the 1920s and 1930s, white America's view of the African American experience usually came from minstrel shows featuring white (or even black) actors in blackface. With the rise of the Jazz Age, white audiences thronged to hear black musicians playing the blues and jazz they had developed. Parker was deeply angry and defiant about the contradictions of being famous and black, privileged and oppressed. As a leader in jazz, one of the most American and one of the most truly African American art forms, Parker constantly rebelled against the power structures in the music business.

Unfortunately, his rebellion was often self-destructive, and he became known as a difficult musician. In 1946, after being found naked in his hotel lobby and setting a mattress on fire, he was sent to jail and then to a state mental hospital for six months. Even when he returned to his career, he continued to have problems bowing to authority. In 1949 the famous Birdland Club, named in honor of Parker, opened in Harlem, but in 1954 he was fired, no longer allowed to play there because of his unpredictable behavior.

Parker died in 1955 of complications from pneumonia, but his impact on jazz was immense, and it continues to affect not only how jazz is played but also how it is listened to. From the time of his death into the twenty-first century, other artists have paid tribute to Parker's genius. Jazz pianist Lennie Tristano first played his "Requiem" in memory of Parker at a benefit for Parker's family shortly after his death, and dozens of others have followed with tribute songs and albums, including Rolling Stones drummer Charlie Watts in 1992 and jazz drummer Roy Hanes in 2001. The rock band Sparks' 1994 album *Gratuitous Sax and Senseless Violins* includes the song "When I Kiss You (I Hear Charlie Parker Playing)." Since 1992 the annual Charlie Parker Jazz Festival in Harlem has showcased innovative jazz musicians.

Parker's life has also been documented on film. Actor/director Clint Eastwood made a movie about Parker's life called *Bird*, which was released in 1988. Many of Parker's fans complained that it stereotyped the sax player by focusing on his addictions and showing his life through the eyes of his fourth wife, a white woman, and other white characters. Ken Burns's 2001 documentary *Jazz* includes a section titled "Dedicated to Chaos" about Bird and other bebop musicians, and in 2005 Tony Followell directed *The Charlie Parker Story* for British television.

Perhaps the best way to understand Parker is simply to listen to his music. New mixes of his recordings are continually released, and jazz fans wait for them enthusiastically. YouTube and other online video sites have made original vinyl recordings and even rare live film footage of Parker's performances widely available. It is in these recordings, as well as in the music of thousands of subsequent musicians and singers influenced by Parker's style, that Bird truly lives.

Tina Gianoulis

SEE ALSO: *Big Bands; Blues; Burns, Ken; Eastwood, Clint; Gillespie, Dizzy; Graffiti; Jazz; The Rolling Stones; YouTube.*

BIBLIOGRAPHY

"Charlie Parker Jazz Festival Celebrates Legendary Musician Uptown and Downtown." *DNA Info.com Manhattan Local News*. Accessed February 29, 2012. Available from http://www.dnainfo.com/20110824/harlem/charlie-parker-jazz-festival-celebrates-legendary-musician-uptown-downtown#ixzz1np93Wv6A

Crouch, Stanley. "Birdland: Charlie Parker, Clint Eastwood, and America." *New Republic* 200, no. 8 (1989): 25.

Giddins, Gary. *Celebrating Bird*. New York: Da Capo Press, 1999.

Remnick, David. "Bird-Watcher." *New Yorker* 84, no. 14 (2008): 58.

Woideck, Carl. *Charlie Parker: His Life and Music*. Ann Arbor: University of Michigan Press, 1998.

Parker, Dorothy *(1893–1967)*

American poet and short-story writer Dorothy Parker was the leading light and most scathing wit of the notorious Algonquin Round Table—a collection of literary notables who defined the intellectual tastes of New York City in the 1920s and 1930s. She is most often remembered for short verses such as "Men seldom make passes at girls who wear glasses." Her wisecracks ("I require only three things of a man. He must be handsome, ruthless and stupid.") and acerbic critiques ("This is not a novel to be tossed aside lightly. It should be thrown with great force.") filled the gossip columns of the New York press, gained her a national following, and helped establish the "magazine culture" of the period.

Barry Morris

SEE ALSO: *The Big Apple; The Twenties.*

BIBLIOGRAPHY

Meade, Marion. *Dorothy Parker: What Fresh Hell Is This?* New York: Penguin, 1989.

Parker, Dorothy, and Barry Day. *Dorothy Parker: In Her Own Words.* Lanham, MD: Taylor Trade Publishing, 2004.

The Portable Dorothy Parker. New York: Penguin, 1976.

Parker Brothers

Parker Brothers is best known for producing *Monopoly*, arguably the most famous board game of all. In 1883 a sixteen-year-old named George S. Parker of Salem, Massachusetts, invented *The Game of Banking*. After two companies rejected the game, he decided to market it himself. With his profits, he established the George S. Parker Company. He later invited his brothers to join, and the company officially became Parker Brothers. The company enjoyed success alongside its rival Milton Bradley (also located in Massachusetts). Parker Brothers' biggest success came in the 1930s with *Monopoly*, which brought the company revenues of a million dollars by 1936.

Over the years Parker Brothers produced many other popular games, such as *Clue* and *Trivial Pursuit*. In 1968 General Mills bought the company; it was spun off as Kenner-Parker two years later, and in 1991 it was acquired by Hasbro, the second-leading toy producer (after Mattel). Hasbro continues to release updated versions of classic Parker Brothers games such as *Boggle*, *Guesstures*, *Pictionary*, and *Sorry!* In addition to modernized versions of *Monopoly*, the company has achieved considerable financial success with themed editions of *Trivial Pursuit* and *Clue* that use popular culture icons such as Harry Potter to draw in a new generation of consumers.

Robin Lent

SEE ALSO: *Board Games; Harry Potter; Milton Bradley; Monopoly; Trivial Pursuit.*

BIBLIOGRAPHY

Orbanes, Philip. *The Game Makers: The Story of Parker Brothers from Tiddledy Winks to Trivial Pursuit.* Boston: Harvard Business School Press, 2004.

Parker Brothers. *Ninety Years of Fun, 1883–1973: The History of Parker Brothers.* Salem, MA: Parker Brothers, 1973.

Wojahn, Ellen. *Playing by Different Rules.* New York: AMACON, 1998.

Parks, Rosa *(1913–2005)*

One of the most prominent African American women in history, Rosa Parks is regarded as the person who sparked the twentieth-century civil rights movement in the United States. On December 1, 1955, in Montgomery, Alabama, a white bus driver told Parks to stand and give her seat to a white man. She was already seated in the "Negro" section at the back of the bus, and she refused to relinquish her seat. The bus driver responded by calling the police, who arrested Parks and took her to jail. The act changed the lives of African Americans, especially in the South, as well as the course of American history.

Rosa Lee McCauley was born on February 4, 1913, in Tuskegee, Alabama, to a carpenter father and a schoolteacher mother. Both her grandparents had been born into slavery. When Rosa was eleven, her mother sent her to a private school in Montgomery. Attending a summer institute at Highlander Folk School in Tennessee changed her life. The integrated institution was renowned for producing social activists, and she would become one of them.

In 1932 McCauley married Raymond Parks, a barber, and the couple settled in Montgomery. She found work as a seamstress for the Montgomery Ward department store and served as the secretary of the local chapter of the National Association for the Advancement of Colored People (NAACP), which she joined in 1943. Parks organized the NAACP Youth Council in Montgomery and sat on the national committee to vindicate the Scottsboro Boys, nine black teenagers who had been wrongfully accused of raping two white women in Alabama.

All over the United States the NAACP was gaining momentum in its quest for civil rights for African Americans, especially after the 1954 *Brown v. Board of Education* decision ended legal segregation in schools. Parks was well known in Montgomery and had gained respect for her many activities prior to the bus boycott, including failed attempts to vote.

The Montgomery bus system was notorious for racial discrimination beyond enforcing segregation policies. For example, African American riders were forced to enter buses through the front door to pay their fare, exit, and reenter

Rosa Parks and Al Gore. *Rosa Parks, left, with Vice President Al Gore, displays her Congressional Gold Medal, the highest civilian award given by the U.S. Congress, in 1999.* AP IMAGES.

through the rear door. Sometimes drivers left the stop before black passengers could reenter the bus; this had happened to Parks. The same driver who had the forty-three-year-old arrested had driven off on Parks twelve years earlier, an incident she had not forgotten.

Parks was by no means the first person to be arrested for refusing to give up her seat. In fact, someone had been jailed the week before for the same offense. What made Parks unique was her standing in the African American community. Montgomery civil rights leaders knew she would be an ideal person to support their fight for integration in the court system. On December 5, 1955, the court found her guilty and fined her $14. The stage was set for an extended lawsuit, as well as a battle of wills in the form of the Montgomery Bus Boycott. The boycott was organized by the new Montgomery Improvement Association (MIA) and brought the young MIA leader Martin Luther King Jr. to national prominence. It lasted for 380 days, ending only with a U.S. Supreme Court order in November 1956 that banned bus segregation.

In 1957 Parks and her husband, fired from their jobs and victims of harassment, moved to Detroit, Michigan, where Parks took a job with local U.S. Congressmen John Conyers. She worked for Conyers in his Detroit office for twenty-five years. In 1995, in her eighties, she gave a rousing speech at the Million Man March in Washington, D.C. Parks continued her social activism throughout her life. She and Raymond, who died in 1977, founded the Institute for Self-Development to train African American youth to take leadership roles in their community.

Parks received numerous tributes and awards in her lifetime. In 1987 she was honored at the John F. Kennedy Center for the Performing Arts in Washington, D.C. She received the Congressional Gold Medal and the Presidential Medal of Freedom, the two top governmental honors for civilians in the United States. The Southern Christian Leadership Conference sponsors the annual Rosa Parks Freedom Award.

In October 2005, at ninety-two, Parks died of natural causes in her Detroit apartment. She became the first American not associated with government to lie in state at the Capitol, where as many as 50,000 people filed by her casket. President George W. Bush ordered that flags fly at half-staff in Parks's honor on the day of her funeral, which took place on October 30 in Detroit. Many accolades have been bestowed on Parks since her death. Public sites and monuments across the country have been dedicated to the civil rights pioneer, including a statue of her in the U.S. Capitol's National Statuary Hall.

Scott Stabler

SEE ALSO: *Civil Disobedience; Civil Rights Movement; King, Martin Luther, Jr.; Million Man March.*

BIBLIOGRAPHY

Abdul-Jabbar, Kareem, and Alan Steinberg. *Black Profiles in Courage: A Legacy of African-American Achievement.* New York: William and Morrow, 1996.

Brinkley, Douglas. *Rosa Parks.* New York: Penguin, 2005.

Hanson, Joyce Ann. *Rosa Parks: A Biography.* Santa Barbara, CA: Greenwood, 2011.

Metcalf, George R. *Black Profiles.* New York, McGraw-Hill, 1968.

Parks, Rosa, and James Haskins. *My Story.* New York: Dial Books, 1992.

Parks, Rosa, and Gregory J. Reed. *Quiet Strength: The Faith, the Hope, and the Heart of a Woman Who Changed a Nation.* Grand Rapids, MI: Zondervan Publishing House, 1994.

Parks, Rosa, and Gregory J. Reed. *Dear Mrs. Parks: A Dialogue with Today's Youth.* New York: Lee and Low Books, 1996.

Parrish, Maxfield *(1870–1966)*

Maxfield Parrish was one of the most popular and prolific American artists of the twentieth century. In his long career he produced paintings, illustrations for books and magazines, advertisements, posters, and murals. Although many of his paintings initially give the impression of a meticulous devotion to realism, he actually had a highly individual approach to color and lighting, and many of his most famous illustrations depict giants, dragons, genies, centaurs, mythical kingdoms, and enchanted palaces. Observers of Parrish's work point out that what he really did was rearrange and improve on reality.

Parrish was born in Philadelphia. His father was a landscape painter and etcher. Parrish initially intended to be an architect but soon shifted to illustration. By the mid-1890s he started getting work designing magazine covers. His first was for *Harper's Weekly.* In 1897 Parrish illustrated his first book, *Mother Goose in Prose* by L. Frank Baum, who was still a few years away from creating Oz. Soon Parrish was specializing in children's books, and over the next decade or so he provided imaginative pictures for *The Golden Age* and *Dream Days* by Kenneth Grahame, *Poems of Childhood* by Eugene Field, *A Wonder Book and Tanglewood Tales* by Nathaniel Hawthorne, and *The Arabian Nights* edited by Kate Douglas Wiggin and Nora A. Smith.

From the mid-1890s into the 1930s, Parrish was in high demand as a magazine artist. He turned out numerous covers for *Century Magazine, Life, Harper's Bazaar,* and *Collier's.* His work also appeared in *Scribner's, McClure's, Ladies' Home Journal,* and *St. Nicholas.* In addition to magazine work, Parrish illustrated advertisements for companies such as Jell-O, Wanamaker's (a department store), Oneida, H-O Company (Hornby's Oats), Columbia Bicycle, Royal Baking Powder, and Swift's Premium Ham. Often he made use of fantasy and fairy-tale elements in these pictures, using knights in armor, fantastic palaces, jesters, kings, princesses, dwarfs, goddesses, and nursery rhyme characters.

Probably the most financially rewarding for Parrish were color reproductions of his paintings that were sold by distributors such as House of Art. *Daybreak,* issued in 1923, has the distinction of being the best-selling art print of all time. During the 1920s and 1930s, copies of the work could be seen framed and hanging in many a parlor and living room around the United States. The painting shows a colonnade in the foreground with a young woman in Grecian robes reclining on the ground while a nude girl bends over her as dawn tints everything pink. There are leafy branches dangling overhead and misty mountains in the distance. The model for the reclining figure was the granddaughter of William Jennings Bryan, a well-known American lawyer and politician, and the naked little girl was Parrish's daughter. Parrish always worked from photographs that he took himself, except when depicting monsters, elves, and the like. He projected the photo onto his drawing or painting surface and then traced it in with pencil.

Another very successful print was *Stars*, which shows a naked young woman sitting on a rock and gazing contentedly up at the night sky. Parrish painted it a few years after *Daybreak*, using a photo of his daughter Jean. Parrish's favorite model was Susan Lewin. Originally the housekeeper for Parrish and his family at their Vermont home, The Oaks, Lewin can be seen in several of his paintings, including *Sleeping Beauty*.

In addition to paintings, Parrish created several murals. The most famous is *Old King Cole*, painted in 1906 for the Hotel Knickerbocker (later the St. Regis) in New York. He also painted *The Pied Piper* for the Palace Hotel in San Francisco and *Sing a Song of Sixpence* for the Sherman House hotel in Chicago. His most ambitious undertaking was a series of eighteen murals, each over 10 feet high, painted for the offices of the *Saturday Evening Post* in Philadelphia. Parrish worked from 1911 to 1913 on the project.

From the mid-1930s onward Parrish concentrated almost exclusively on landscapes. They include farmhouses, old mills, and small town churches and exhibit the artist's meticulous rendering and his fascination with the effects of light. He stopped painting in 1960, at the age of ninety. In 1965 the Metropolitan Museum of Art in New York finally took notice of him and purchased one of his fantasy paintings, *The Errant Pan*. Parrish died the following year.

Ron Goulart

SEE ALSO: *Baum, L. Frank;* Harper's*; Jell-O; Metropolitan Museum of Art; The* Saturday Evening Post.

BIBLIOGRAPHY

Cutler, Lawrence S., and Judy Goffman Cutler. *Maxfield Parrish: A Retrospective*. San Francisco: Pomegranate Books, 1995.

Ludwig, Coy. *Maxfield Parrish*. New York: Watson-Guptill Publications, 1973.

Wagner, Margaret E. *Maxfield Parrish & the Illustrators of the Golden Age*. San Francisco: Pomegranate, 2000.

Partner Swapping

SEE: *Swinging.*

Parton, Dolly *(1946–)*

Dolly Parton is a country singer, songwriter, movie actress, businesswoman, children's author, and media personality, and yet none of these labels—neither singly or collectively—capture the paradox that is Dolly. Her public image is near caricature: big blond hair, little-girl voice, and a bust measurement that defies belief. But both her autobiographical lyrics and her multimillion-dollar empire, Dolly Parton Enterprises, testify to the substance beneath the image.

THE STUFF OF LEGEND

Parton's life story is the stuff of which American legends are made. Born the fourth of twelve children in a log cabin in Sevier County, Tennessee, she was delivered by a doctor who was paid with a sack of corn meal milled from corn grown by her then tenant father. The country cliché of humble beginnings where material things were scarce but love and faith were plentiful has been captured in some of her best-known songs, including "My Tennessee Mountain Home." But in the skilled hands of this talented songwriter, the cliché acquired an unexpected freshness and power. For example "Coat of Many Colors," the title cut from her 1971 album (RCA Victor), recalls an actual incident from Parton's life. The coat her mother made her from scraps of material becomes an object of ridicule when she wears it to school; her mother assuages her pain by reminding her that the coat was made with love. Parton later revealed in interviews that the episode, which she still found hurtful, fired her ambition to become a star. It also gave her a country classic and the material for her first children's book, *Coat of Many Colors*.

Musical ability was not rare in the family of Avie Lee and Lee Parton. Seven of their twelve children would someday work as professional musicians, but Parton's talent was exceptional even among so talented a group. She began singing before she was two years old and was writing songs on her homemade guitar before she was seven. By the age of ten she was singing

Dolly Parton. *Dolly Parton has successfully partnered her glamorous image with her skill as a songwriter, performer, and businesswoman to build a successful and diverse entertainment career.* MICHAEL PUTLAND/GETTY IMAGES.

on a Knoxville, Tennessee, radio station, and in 1957 she recorded her song "Puppy Love" for Gold Band, a small record label. A local celebrity by the time she reached high school, Parton dreamed of Grand Ole Opry stardom. She left for Nashville, Tennessee, immediately after her high school graduation.

Three years later she had her first charting record, "Dumb Blonde" (Monument); that same year she became Porter Wagoner's "girl singer," appearing regularly on his syndicated television show. Enormously successful as duet partners, Parton and Wagoner had fourteen Top 10 hits and were twice named the Country Music Association's duo of the year. Parton, however, wanted to be known as more than Wagoner's duet partner. She signed with RCA in 1968 and became a Grand Ole Opry member in 1969. Successes such as "Joshua," number one on country charts in 1970, gave her the courage to strike out on her own, and she left Wagoner in 1974, though she recorded duets with him through 1980.

Recognition as a solo artist was immediate and impressive. The awards began to stack up: the Country Music Association (CMA) named her Female Vocalist of the Year in 1975 and 1976, and she received a Grammy for Best Female Country Vocal Performance in 1978 and Entertainer of the Year awards from both the Academy of Country Music and the CMA in 1977 and 1978, respectively. As she began appearing on television specials and talk shows, her fan base increased. Parton's dreams were growing larger.

BREAKING THE RULES

Parton came under attack within the country music community when it became clear that her plans were not limited to success in a single field. She was not the first country music star to explore different avenues of entertainment, but her independence and ambition were viewed as ingratitude by many in the industry, which was still a man's world. Her switch to Los Angeles management and the firing of her family band made it clear that Parton would ignore critics and chart her own course.

Her film debut in *9 to 5* (1980) proved that she could succeed in other media. The million-selling *Trio* album, a 1987 collaboration with Emmylou Harris and Linda Ronstadt, offered further evidence of Parton's range. The irony was that whatever the medium or the message, she remained her inimitable self. Roger Ebert praised her natural acting ability, but Parton perhaps came nearer the truth when she explained that she only played herself. Both Doralee Rhodes (*9 to 5*) and Truvy Jones (*Steel Magnolias*), her two most acclaimed characterizations, are essentially Parton, warm, vulnerable, strong, funny, and as southern as grits and barbecue.

The best metaphor for Dolly Parton may be found in the history of one of her songs. Parton admitted that she wrote "I Will Always Love You" for Wagoner in an effort to express her reasons for leaving him. She first recorded the song in 1973; a year later it was number one on the country charts. She recorded it again in 1982 and repeated her success. When Whitney Houston recorded it a decade later for the soundtrack of her first film, *The Bodyguard*, it was number one on the pop charts for fourteen weeks. Parton recorded it once again, this time as a duet with Vince Gill, and again it was a hit. Like "I Will Always Love You," Parton continued to appear in new guises even as she remained unmistakably Dolly. "I enjoy being able to make fun of myself and join in when other people are making jokes. I don't *ever* take that personal because I know exactly who I am," Parton asserted in a 1998 Country Music Television interview.

Parton became fodder for clever comics in 1986 when she signed on as a partner in a Smokey Mountain theme park to which she gave her name, but in the early 2010s Dollywood is a flourishing multimillion-dollar business and ranks as the twenty-fourth most popular theme park in the United States. Her business empire continued to expand after Dollywood. She is a co-owner of The Dollywood Company, which, in addition to the theme park, operates a dinner theater; Dolly Parton's Dixie Stampede with venues in Branson, Missouri, and Myrtle Beach, South Carolina; and the waterpark Dollywood's Splash Country, also in Pigeon Forge.

STILL SINGING AFTER ALL THESE YEARS

But her business empire takes second place to her music. When radio relegated Parton to blasts-from-the-past airtime, she returned to her roots and released three bluegrass albums on a small label, a decision that garnered critical praise and gained her a seventh Grammy for *The Grass Is Blue* (1999). A Lifetime Achievement Award in 2011 increased the number to eight. With five decades in the music business, she proved she was unafraid of new challenges, writing music and lyrics for *9 to 5: The Musical*, which opened on Broadway in April 2009. It was nominated for four Tony Awards and for fifteen Drama Desk Awards, the most received by a production in a single year. Parton also won an LA Critics Award for the tryout run of the musical.

At an age when most members of her generation are settling into retirement, Parton shows no signs of slowing down. The literacy project she launched in her home county in East Tennessee in 1996 has become an international program with nearly forty million books mailed to children in the United States, Canada, and the United Kingdom. She has released two albums on her own Dolly label: *Backwoods Barbie* (2008), which charted at two on the country charts and seventeen on pop charts, and *Better Day* (2011), for which she toured in the United States, Europe, and Australia. She lent her voice and music to the Canadian coming-of-age dramedy *The Year Dolly Parton Was My Mom* and costarred with Queen Latifah in the gospel music movie *Joyful Noise* (2012).

With more than 100 million records sold and more than seventy albums to her credit, Parton is the top female country performer of all time based on album chart performance, and with forty-one Top 10 albums, her record places her ahead of all other country artists. In the 1990s and first decade of the 2000s she added a host of honors to her already impressive résumé: in 1999 she received country music's highest honor, induction into the Country Music Hall of Fame, and two years later she was inducted into the National Academy of Popular Music/Songwriters Hall of Fame. In 2004 she was presented with the Living Legend Medal by the U.S. Library of Congress for her contributions to the cultural heritage of the United States, and the following year she received the National Medal of Arts, the highest honor given by the U.S. government for excellence in the arts.

On December 3, 2006, Parton received the Kennedy Center Honors from the John F. Kennedy Center for the Performing Arts for her lifetime of contributions to the arts. However, Parton considers a bronze sculpture on the courthouse lawn in Sevierville "the greatest honor" because it represents the esteem of people who were there when she started writing and singing the songs that moved her from the Smoky Mountains to the pinnacle of her profession.

Wylene Rholetter

SEE ALSO: *Amusement Parks; Bluegrass; Broadway; Celebrity; Country Music; Daytime Talk Shows; Gospel Music; Grammy Awards;* Grand Ole Opry; *Hollywood; Houston, Whitney; Movie Stars; The Musical; Pop Music; Queen Latifah; Radio; Siskel and Ebert; Syndication; Television; Tony Awards; Top 40.*

BIBLIOGRAPHY

Bufwack, Mary A., and Robert K. Oermann. *Finding Her Voice: The Saga of Women in Country Music*. New York: Crown, 1993.

Dunn, Jancee. "Women Who Rock: Dolly Parton—She's the Lady, the Tramp and the Queen." *Rolling Stone*, October 2003, 53–56.

Gallo, Phil. "6 Questions with Dolly Parton." *Billboard*, July 2011.

James, Otis. *Dolly Parton*. New York: Quick Fox, 1978.

Miller, Stephen. *Smart Blonde: Dolly Parton*. London: Omnibus, 2009.

Nash, Alanna. *Dolly*. Los Angeles: Reed, 1978.

Nash, Alanna. *Dolly: My Life and Other Unfinished Business*. New York: HarperCollins, 1994.

The Partridge Family

From 1970 to 1974, a time when most kids swore by the adage "Don't trust anyone over thirty," ABC aired *The Partridge Family*, an extremely popular sitcom featuring a mom who went on tour with her kids in a band. The hit show was loosely based on the late-1960s folk-music family, the Cowsills.

The Partridge Family (one of two 1970s sitcoms about a big family and a perky blond mom; *The Brady Bunch* [1969–1974] was the other) starred Oscar winner and musical theater staple Shirley Jones as Shirley Partridge, the widowed matriarch whose kids started jamming in an impromptu session in the garage of their suburban California home. They asked her to join them, and it sounded groovy. They recorded the song "I Think I Love You," and to everyone's surprise, a record company bought it, it became a smash hit, and a band was born.

And what's a family band without a manager and reluctant father-figure? Enter fast-talking, child-hating, stewardess-dating Reuben Kincaid (Dave Madden), perpetual foil for ten-year-old con artist, Danny Partridge (Danny Bonaduce). The rest of the family included Suzanne Crough as five-year-old Tracy; Jeremy Gelbwaks (1970–1971) and then Brian Forster (1971–1974) as seven-year-old Chris; Susan Dey as fifteen-year-old Laurie; and Jones's stepson, David Cassidy, as seventeen-year-old Keith.

The Partridge Family toured around the country in a psychedelically painted school bus (with the astoundingly unhip "Careful, Nervous Mother Driving" on the back). The show focused on their exploits on the road and in their California hometown and their attempt to have normal family lives and be pop stars at the same time. Every show wrapped up in time for a song, during which the Partridges were usually wearing matching burgundy velvet pantsuits with white ruffled shirts.

Like the Monkees before them, the Partridge Family TV band was heavily cross-promoted in the music business, and "I Think I Love You" sold more than four million copies. Unlike the Monkees, they had no musical pretensions as a band. None of them were professional musicians, and Cassidy and Jones were the only ones providing actual vocals in recordings and on the show. It didn't take a musical genius to figure out that if Cassidy was the lead male vocalist, preteen Bonaduce was (impossibly) singing the baritone harmony parts.

The Partridge Family made a huge teen idol out of the androgynous Cassidy, who toured solo to throngs of screaming adolescent girls. His fans were so rabid that one actually asked for one of the gallstones he'd passed as a keepsake. After failing at solo television, he found he was a powerful draw in Las Vegas in the 1990s.

Despite his heartthrob status, Cassidy actually didn't carry the show. That responsibility fell to impish, red-headed, smart-aleck Bonaduce. The precocious Bonaduce had the comic timing of an old master. Unfortunately, as he got older and was told he wasn't cute anymore, he went the way of many a child actor—into a drug haze, punctuated with appearances on *The Love Boat* (1977–1986) and *Fantasy Island* (1977–1984). His antics included an arrest in 1990 in Daytona Beach, Florida, for attempting to buy cocaine; a year later he was charged with assaulting a transvestite prostitute in Phoenix. He has since had success as a radio disc jockey.

The saga of a slightly hipper than Mrs. Cleaver mom and family couldn't hold up; ratings of *The Partridge Family* started to sag in 1973, when it was moved from Friday night to Saturday night, up against *All in the Family* (1968–1979) and *Emergency* (1972–1979). The 1974–1975 season included an ABC Saturday morning cartoon version called the *Partridge Family 2200 AD*, which, for some reason, put the family in space. Dey, Bonaduce, Forster, Crough, and Madden provided their voices.

Young viewers in the early 1970s inexplicably felt the need to "choose" between *The Brady Bunch* (which some saw as even more implausible) and *The Partridge Family*. In the end, both shows were representative of the happy, mindless nature of many 1970s sitcoms.

Karen Lurie

SEE ALSO: All in the Family*;* The Brady Bunch*; Cassidy, David;* Fantasy Island*;* The Love Boat*; The Monkees; Sitcom; Television.*

BIBLIOGRAPHY

Allis, Tim. "By the Way . . . Whatever Happened to the Other Partridge Kids?" *People Weekly*, November 1, 1993, 73.

Appelo, Tim. "C'mon, Get Happy . . . Fear and Loathing on the Partridge Family Bus." *Entertainment Weekly*, July 29, 1994, 52.

Cunneff, Tom. "Spinning off His Partridge Past, Danny Bonaduce Rocks Philly as a Raunchy Midnight Deejay." *People Weekly*, February 27, 1989, 97.

Gliatto, Tom. "Picks and Pans Main: Tube." *People Weekly*, July 12, 1993, 11.

Green, Joey. *The Partridge Family Album*. Foreword by Shirley Jones. New York: HarperPerennial, 1994.

The Passion of the Christ

Few films in motion picture history have attracted as much attention or incited as much controversy as director Mel Gibson's

2004 blockbuster, *The Passion of the Christ*. Revered by some and reviled by others, the film sparked dissenting opinions concerning its graphic depiction of violence and suffering, as well as its inclusion of content regarded by some as anti-Semitic. Questions also arose over one of the sources used by Gibson, and there were debates about the film's historical and biblical accuracy. Even the unusual marketing approach, focused particularly on gaining support from evangelical churches, drew both criticism and praise.

Nevertheless, Gibson's *The Passion of the Christ*—which uses Latin, Hebrew, and Aramaic for its spoken dialogue—is acknowledged by many critics as an exceptional creative achievement. The film tells a powerful, often shocking visual story that begins with Jesus praying in the Garden of Gethsemane and ends with a glimpse of his resurrection. In between Jesus is betrayed, convicted, tortured, and executed. There are also occasional flashbacks to scenes from his childhood and ministry. Although Gibson's public statements about the scriptural basis of the film were sometimes contradictory, he acknowledged that his primary goal was to create an intense emotional experience for the audience.

When the film opened, enthusiastic churches and religious organizations gave away free tickets, provided transportation, and held discussions. By contrast, however, some Christian groups disagreed with the film's emphasis on suffering rather than salvation, and concerns were raised by Christians and Jews alike over negative depictions of Jewish characters. A wide variety of opinions and interpretations appeared in magazine articles and books, ranging from pro-and-con discussions to devotional commentaries, outraged critiques, and testimonial tributes.

As if all that were not enough, Gibson's star status and colorful personality attracted curious audiences to the film—so it was not surprising that *The Passion of the Christ* set box-office records. At the end of 2004 it was the highest-grossing R-rated film ever made and also topped the all-time list of non-English-language films. A theatrical rerelease in 2005 did not fare well, however, and neither DVD sales nor television audiences went on to match the film's original success.

Cynthia Giles

SEE ALSO: *Blockbusters; Celebrity; Gibson, Mel; Leisure Time; Movie Stars; Television.*

BIBLIOGRAPHY

Beal, Timothy K, and Tod Linafelt. *Mel Gibson's Bible: Religion, Popular Culture, and "The Passion of the Christ."* Chicago: University of Chicago Press, 2006.

Fredriksen, Paula. *On "The Passion of the Christ": Exploring the Issues Raised by the Controversial Movie.* Berkeley: University of California Press, 2006.

Patinkin, Mandy *(1952–)*

Known for his work on Broadway, film, and television, Mandy Patinkin is one of the most versatile performers working in the entertainment industry. The three principal roles he created on Broadway—Che Guevara in Andrew Lloyd Webber's *Evita* (1979), George Seurat in Stephen Sondheim's *Sunday in the Park with George* (1984), and Archibald Craven in Lucy Simon's *The Secret Garden* (1991)—all received critical praise. Film credits include *Ragtime* (1981), *Yentl* (1983), *The Princess Bride* (1987), and *Dick Tracy* (1990).

In the mid-1990s, Patinkin starred in the television series *Chicago Hope*, for which he won an Emmy Award in 1995. His character in *Chicago Hope*, Dr. Jeffrey Geiger, provided the opportunity for Patinkin to showcase his vocal abilities for television audiences. He also appeared as FBI profiler Jason Gideon on the television series *Criminal Minds*, a part he played during the show's first two seasons (2005–2007). In 2011 he joined the cast of the Showtime series *Homeland* as Saul Berenson, Middle East Division chief of the CIA.

Patinkin has recorded a number of solo albums, including *Mandy Patinkin* (1989), *Dress Casual* (1990), *Oscar and Steve* (1995), and the entirely Yiddish *Mamaloshen* (1998).

William A. Everett

SEE ALSO: *Broadway; Dick Tracy; FBI (Federal Bureau of Investigation); Lloyd Webber, Andrew; The Musical; Sondheim, Stephen; Television.*

BIBLIOGRAPHY

Zadan, Craig. *Sondheim & Company.* New York: Da Capo, 1994.

Patrick, Danica *(1982–)*

American auto racer Danica Patrick became famous in 2005 when she joined Rahal Letterman Racing (as of 2011, Rahal Letterman Lanigan Racing) to compete in that year's Indycar championship. Later that year she became only the fourth woman to compete in the iconic Indianapolis 500 race and was the first to lead it. She eventually finished fourth, the highest-ever placing for a woman at the time, and was named Rookie of the Year. After finishing twelfth in the drivers' standings for 2005, she won the same accolade for the season as a whole.

Patrick began racing go-karts in her home state of Wisconsin in 1992, when she was ten years old. At the age of sixteen she moved to England, to race in the Formula Ford series, often considered a proving ground for upcoming drivers in Formula 1. She moved back to the United States in 2002 and quickly established herself in the Indy Racing League (IRL). After the successes of her first season, Patrick continued to make progress, regularly qualifying and finishing inside the top ten. In 2007 she joined Andretti Green Racing (as of late 2009, Andretti Autosport), and in 2008 she became the first woman to win a race in American open-wheel racing, placing first at the Indy Japan 300 at Motegi, Japan, following the reunification of the IRL and Champ Car series.

Patrick raced in additional IndyCar championships, but despite finishing third in the Indianapolis 500 in 2009, she acquired a reputation for crashing. Furthermore, when she complained about the poor performance of her car in 2010, she was booed by fans at that year's race. In 2011, the year in which 2005 champion Dan Wheldon was killed in a crash at Las Vegas, Patrick finished tenth for the season overall. In 2012 she moved to the Nationwide NASCAR series, where she has raced part time since 2010.

Patrick is part of a gradual rise in the number of female racing drivers, and her successes have helped with their acceptance in a male-dominated sport. Her critics argue that her appearance in 2008's *Sports Illustrated* swimsuit issue and her other modeling appearances, in particular for Victoria's Secret, do not help the cause of women who want to be taken seriously as competitors.

Chris Routledge

SEE ALSO: *Automobile; Indianapolis 500; Letterman, David;* Sports Illustrated*; Stock-Car Racing; Victoria's Secret.*

BIBLIOGRAPHY

Caldwell, Dave. "As Patrick's Star Rises, I.R.L. Is along for Ride." *New York Times*, May 31, 2005.

Danica Patrick Official Website. Accessed April 2012. Available from http://www.danicaracing.com/

Weintraub, Robert. "Queen for a Day." *Slate*, April 21, 2008.

Patton

Patton, one of the most critically acclaimed films of the 1970s, opened with George C. Scott as U.S. general George S. Patton, addressing the audience in front of a giant American flag. His speech combined inspiration with profanity: "Now I want you to remember, that no bastard ever won a war by giving his life for his country. He won it by making the other poor dumb bastard die for his country."

Based on Omar Bradley's memoirs, *Patton* presented an unflinching look at the volatile general during the European battles of World War II. General Patton was given to poetic, occasionally vulgar evocations of the duty of soldiers in the heat of battle, claiming that he had been a warrior during past lives ("The Carthaginians were proud and brave but they couldn't hold. They were massacred. Arab women stripped them of their swords and their tunics and lances. The soldiers laid naked in the sun. Two thousand years ago. I was here"). To his military colleagues, Patton was a brilliant strategist but emotionally unstable. His instability reached critical mass when, in a fit of rage, he slapped a wounded soldier.

The box-office success of the film surprised many 1970 moviegoers. Hollywood had been inundated with World War II movies since the 1940s, and a movie about the toughest American general seemed a risky commercial proposition during the unpopular Vietnam War; the extensive profanity of the screenplay was also unprecedented for a major studio release in 1970. But director Franklin J. Schaffner, screenwriters Francis Ford Coppola and Edward North, and star Scott crafted a compelling, sophisticated movie that satisfied both conservative and liberal audiences. In *5001 Nights at the Movies*, critic Pauline Kael observes that Patton's character "is what people who believe in military values can see as the true military hero—the red-blooded American who loves to fight and whose crude talk is straight talk. He is also what people who despise militarism can see as the worst kind of red-blooded American mystical maniac; for them, Patton can be the symbolic proof of the madness of the whole military complex."

The outstanding cast included Karl Malden as Omar Bradley and Michael Bates as Field Marshal Montgomery. *Patton* won seven Academy Awards in 1970, including one for best picture. Scott won a well-deserved Oscar for best actor, but he publicly rejected the award (the first such rejection in history), saying he did not wish to compete against fellow actors. Scott had already portrayed a war-mongering general (Buck Turgidson) in Stanley Kubrick's landmark 1964 comedy *Dr. Strangelove*, but his performance in *Patton* was more nuanced and sympathetic and caught the pathos in Patton's gradual loss of control; indeed, it became his signature role. Scott reprised his role in a 1986 made-for-television movie, *The Last Days of Patton*.

One of the most prominent fans of the film was President Richard Nixon, who reportedly watched *Patton* over and over prior to announcing the expansion of the Vietnam War into Cambodia in April 1970. Coppola and North won an Oscar for their screenplay, and on the strength of *Patton*'s success, Coppola was able to green-light his next project—directing*The Godfather* (1972).

Andrew Milner

SEE ALSO: *Academy Awards;* Dr. Strangelove or: How I Learned to Stop Worrying and Love the Bomb*;* The Godfather*; Scott, George C.; Vietnam; War Movies; World War II.*

BIBLIOGRAPHY

Biskind, Peter. *Easy Riders, Raging Bulls: How the Sex, Drugs and Rock 'n' Roll Generation Saved Hollywood*. New York: Simon & Schuster, 1998.

Kael, Pauline. *5001 Nights at the Movies*. New York: Holt, 1991.

Lazare, Aaron. *On Apology*. New York: Oxford University Press, 2004.

Paul, Les *(1915–2009)*

An influential guitarist and recording artist, Les Paul fundamentally changed the way in which popular music was produced. Among many other innovations, he developed the first successful techniques of multitracking and the eight-track tape recorder, which led directly to modern recording technology.

EARLY YEARS

Lester Polsfuss was born in Waukesha, Wisconsin, on June 9, 1915. He began playing harmonica at the age of eight, performing at every opportunity. By age twelve he was a sidewalk musician, playing for tips. Over the next few years he taught himself guitar and formed his first band in 1929.

At age seventeen Polsfuss dropped out of high school and became a full-time professional musician. Over the next six years he performed in a bewildering number of radio and personal appearances under several different stage names and in a variety of smaller and larger acts. Somewhere along the line he changed his name to the more easily remembered Les Paul. About the same time, he became intrigued by jazz music, especially during a long stay in Chicago in the mid-1930s, and he gradually changed from a hot country picker to a jazz stylist. Soon he gained recognition in the music world as a superior guitarist.

Although Paul did not invent the electric guitar, he made major improvements in the area of electronic amplification. He was fascinated by the technical aspects of amplifying and recording sound, often building his own pickups and speaker arrangements, as well as consulting with engineers to produce equipment to his specifications. (The eight-track tape recorder of the late 1950s was developed under this sort of symbiotic relationship with an electronics engineer.) Paul created a major innovation in guitar construction and design with his one-of-a-kind "Log," the world's first solid-body guitar, and he was the first to put two pickups on an electric guitar, now a standard feature.

In 1938 Paul and his sidemen went to New York, quickly landing jobs with Fred Waring and the Pennsylvanians, a prestigious radio and dance orchestra. During his three years in Waring's outfit, Paul gained something of a national following and continued to mature both as a musician and as a technological experimenter. Always a perfectionist and driven by ambition, Paul tired of his relatively small place in Waring's musical empire and once more went out on his own in 1941.

RECORDING, INVENTING, PERFORMING

It was a wise move. After a year or two of frequent job changes, Paul found his niche in wartime Hollywood. He performed regularly on the NBC radio network, eventually playing on records with Bing Crosby. The added exposure greatly helped his career. During this time in California, Paul continued his experiments in recording technology. Using a homemade lathe, he produced high-quality wax recordings with several generations of overlapped musical tracks. Paul succeeded in this where others had failed—due more to his obsessive perfectionism and drive than from any new technological breakthrough. He used

Les Paul. *Les Paul made an impact on the music industry as both a performer and as an inventor.* MICHAEL OCHS ARCHIVES/GETTY IMAGES.

this technique to record several separate guitar tracks on one song. His recordings from this point on all used some variation of multitracking, giving his work a unique sound.

In 1947 Paul became romantically involved with Iris Colleen Summers (1924–1977), a young country singer in Southern California. His first marriage was failing, and he would soon marry Summers. Before this, however, she frequently accompanied him on tour. During a road trip in January 1948, with Summers at the wheel of Paul's Buick, they were in a major automobile accident. Summers was only slightly injured, but Paul suffered numerous broken bones. His right elbow was essentially destroyed, and doctors were seriously considering amputating the arm. Paul refused to let the operation be performed; when his elbow had to be fused into an immobile solid mass, he directed his surgeons to place it at a roughly 90-degree angle to facilitate his guitar playing.

RECORDING STARDOM, GUITAR FAME

After months of recuperation, Paul reentered show business. He created a new act with Summers—a gifted singer and guitarist—whom he renamed Mary Ford. In 1949 Paul and Ford made numerous records and toured at a frantic pace. Their recordings made use of Paul's multitracking to feature many simultaneous guitar and vocal lines, and their work became very popular. Later in the year they were married.

The duo recorded for Capitol Records, for which they produced numerous singles and best-selling albums over the next decade. Paul and Ford were among the most popular and successful musical performers in the world, and Paul masterminded their professional and private lives in a domineering manner. They were sought by radio and television, producing daily programs for the former and a short weekly show for the latter during the early 1950s.

In 1951 Paul was approached by the Gibson guitar company, who sought his endorsement for their new solid-body guitar—based on his Log design—which would become one of the most popular electric guitars in existence. This, along with his innovative use of guitar as a solo instrument, helped Paul become known as the "Father of the Electric Guitar"—the first so-called guitar hero of pop music. Partially in response to his popularization of guitar, a new wave of music arose by the mid-1950s: rock and roll, which had roots in rhythm and blues and country. Paul and Ford were among the many older performers who vanished from the Hit Parade. Their last major hit was "Hummingbird" in 1955. In 1958 the duo moved to Columbia Records but had no more success there. In 1964 Ford and Paul were divorced, and Ford died in 1977.

RETURN TO THE SPOTLIGHT

Paul spent the 1960s in relative obscurity, focusing mainly on developing new musical innovations and recovering from surgery for a broken eardrum. He returned to recording in the 1970s, however, putting out two albums of instrumental duets with country star Chet Atkins—one of which won a Grammy—as well as releasing his next invention, the echo-repeat device, known as the Les Paulverizer. By the late 1970s Paul began to receive some of the credit he deserved for his innovations in popular music. A 1980 documentary film, *The Wizard of Waukesha*, helped promote a comeback. The following year he underwent a quintuple bypass and was told by his doctor that he needed to keep playing to keep himself alive. Paul took the advice to heart, despite also struggling with arthritis in his fingers, and in 1983 he started a long-term weekly performance at Fat Tuesday's, a New York night club that soon became highly popular with music business insiders. His Monday night shows moved to the Iridium Jazz Club in 1995 and would continue until his death in 2009.

In 1988 Paul was inducted into the Rock and Roll Hall of Fame, in the category of "Early Influences." His technological advances continued to receive recognition, and in 1991 the TEC Foundation for Excellence in Audio and the National Association of Music Merchants (NAMM) established the annual Les Paul Award, honoring musicians who are innovators in the creative application of audio technology. In 1995 Paul formed the Les Paul Foundation, an organization that gives study grants in various fields of music (electronic, mechanical, aural) as well as funding medical research on hearing impairment. The Iridium continues to donate 20 percent of their Monday night ticket sales to the foundation.

In 2005 Paul celebrated his ninetieth birthday by releasing an album *American Made, World Played* featuring guest appearances from guitar heroes such as Eric Clapton, Keith Richards, and Jeff Beck, among others. The album won two Grammy Awards. Paul was elected to the National Inventors Hall of Fame that same year and is one of only a few musical artists who has a permanent stand-alone exhibition in the Rock and Roll Hall of Fame. Paul died in 2009 due to complications from pneumonia.

On June 9, 2011, to celebrate what would have been Paul's ninety-sixth birthday, the Google interactive doodle for the day was an interactive, playable guitar on which users could record a thirty-second snippet. The doodle proved so popular that Google kept it up an extra day, and recordings by numerous musical superstars were posted around the Internet. The Les Paul Trio continues to host Monday nights at the Iridium, joined weekly by superstar musical guests.

David Lonergan

SEE ALSO: *Atkins, Chet; Automobile; Celebrity; Clapton, Eric; Country Music; Crosby, Bing; Divorce; Eight-Track Tape; Electric Guitar; Google; Grammy Awards; Harmonica Bands; Hollywood; The Internet; Jazz; Pop Music; Radio; Rhythm and Blues; Rock and Roll; Television; World War II.*

BIBLIOGRAPHY

Clarke, Donald, ed. *The Penguin Encyclopedia of Popular Music.* New York: Viking, 1989.

Shaughnessy, Mary Alice. *Les Paul: An American Original.* New York: William Morrow, 1993.

Slonimsky, Nicolas, ed. *Baker's Biographical Dictionary of Musicians*, 8th ed. New York: Macmillan, 1992.

Paulsen, Pat *(1927–1997)*

Performing perhaps the longest parody skit in history, comic Pat Paulsen ran for president five times between 1968 and 1996. A performer and comedy writer with progressive, rabble-rousing political leanings, Paulsen ran on a satirical platform, which—though relentlessly silly—drew serious attention to the real lack of choices in the American political arena. Paulsen often said he represented the citizen who wanted to vote for 'none of the above.'

Paulsen was born in South Bend, Washington, and raised in Point Bonita, California. He majored in forestry at City College in San Francisco, but his career as a ranger was derailed when he joined the Ric-Y-Tic Players performing troupe. He was performing and working odd jobs as a Fuller Brush salesman and a gypsum miner when he was discovered in the mid-1960s by Tom and Dick Smothers. The Smothers Brothers, quirky comics who did leftist political comedy interspersed with droll dialogue and farcical antics, hired Paulsen as a writer for their new weekly television show on CBS.

Paulsen spent three years on *The Smothers Brothers Comedy Hour*, writing satirical songs and much of the political comedy that kept the show in a constant battle with the CBS censors. He also participated in sketches and performed his own monologues, always with his trademark deadpan expression and loopy, off-the-wall sensibility. In 1968 he won an Emmy for his work on the show.

It was Tom and Dick Smothers who first suggested Paulsen run for president in the highly contentious 1968 election. Paulsen reportedly responded, "Why not? I can't dance." Paulsen began his tradition of pointing out the ludicrous contradictions in American politics then, running as a candidate of the Straight Talkin' American Government Party, or STAG Party. He opposed sex education ("Let kids learn it where we did—in the gutter.") and promised to fight poverty ("by shooting four hundred beggars a week"). His mock campaign was so successful that he went on television to remind people not to really vote for him. Even so he got 200,000 votes in the 1968 election.

The Smothers Brothers Show was taken off the air in 1970, at least partly because of its continued volatile political content. Paulsen had a short stint on his own network show on ABC in 1970, and when that failed, he moved to Cloverdale, California, where he and his second wife bought a 500-acre farm and started a winery.

Paulsen's life continued to provide fodder for comedy and for the hangdog expression he always wore. Even at the winery he expressed his comedic sensibility—one of his basic wines was called Refrigerator White and came with Paulsen's mournful face on the label. The winery also entertained visitors with the satirical Pat Paulsen Museum. Even thus trading on his fame, the winery was not a successful business, and Paulsen was soon drowning in debt and back-tax penalties. Even his lucky moments were dogged by disaster. His third marriage ended in divorce when he caught his wife embezzling hundreds of thousands of dollars from him, and once while on a comedy tour in Reno, Nevada, when he won a $300,000 jackpot on a quarter slot machine, the IRS stepped in to claim $285,000 of it. By 1986 Paulsen was forced to sell the winery and go back on the road with his comedy.

Through it all Paulsen kept his sense of the ridiculous. He continued to perform, both his comedy act and theatrical roles, and he campaigned for president every four years. Beginning in 1972 his name actually appeared on the ballot. For the baby boomers who had nurtured their rebellious politics each week watching the Smothers Brothers, Paulsen was a comforting and irreverent reminder that rebellion still existed even in the complacent 1980s and the cynical 1990s. Paulsen last ran in 1996 under the campaign slogan, "United we sit."

A ubiquitous participant in American political history and popular culture during the latter third of the twentieth century, Paulsen died in 1997 in Tijuana, Mexico, where he was receiving alternative medical treatments for cancer.

Tina Gianoulis

SEE ALSO: *Baby Boomers; Cancer; Divorce; Emmy Awards; Gambling; Safe Sex; The Smothers Brothers; Stand-up Comedy; Television.*

BIBLIOGRAPHY

Gray, Jonathan; Jeffrey P. Jones; and Ethan Thompson. *Satire TV: Politics and Comedy in the Post-network Era.* New York: NYU Press, 2009.

Paulsen, Pat. *How to Wage a Successful Campaign for the Presidency.* Los Angeles: Nash Publishing, 1972.

Sanz, Cynthia, and Dan Knapp. "Stalked by Tax Woes, Pat Paulsen Tries to Keep His Whine Sparkling." *People,* November 19, 1990, 173.

Paypal

SEE: *eBay.*

Payton, Walter *(1954–1999)*

Walter Payton is considered one of the greatest running backs in the history of American professional football. Born in Columbia, Mississippi, on July 25, 1954, Payton attended Jackson State University, where he set a college football record for points scored and earned his degree in special education. Although he left his mark on college football, it was in the National Football League (NFL) that he secured his astonishing reputation.

Drafted by the Chicago Bears in 1975, Payton showed phenomenal talents that had an immediate impact on the team. He led the National Football Conference (NFC) in rushing in 1976, the same year that he made the Pro Bowl team for what would be the first of nine times. In addition to his talents as a running back, Payton was a gifted receiver and team leader, and he was elected the NFL's Most Valuable Player in 1977 and again in 1985. In 1984 he became football's all-time rushing leader when he broke the record previously held by Jim Brown. After many years of toiling with mediocre rosters, Payton and his Bears finally played in the Super Bowl in 1986, demolishing the New England Patriots in one of the biggest routs in Super Bowl history.

When Payton retired after the 1987 season, he was the NFL's career leader in rushing yards (16,726), rushing touchdowns (110), and total yards gained (21,264). He also held the record for most rushing yards gained in a single game (275), and he had passed for more than 300 yards and eight touchdowns. All of Payton's records have since been broken by other players, but that does not lessen his accomplishments. Payton was elected to the Pro Football Hall of Fame in 1993 and to the College Football Hall of Fame in 1996.

While his statistics and on-field accomplishments rank Payton as one of the greatest athletes in the history of professional football, it was his off-field accomplishments that truly set him apart from his contemporaries. His nickname, "Sweetness," not only described his ability as an athlete but was also an accurate comment on his personality. His charm and understated demeanor made him one of the most endearing of sports personalities, and he quickly became a favorite among the fans. He never had a negative word to say about his opponents or his city, and his overwhelming love for the game of football was obvious to everybody.

By the end of the 1990s, Payton had been long and constantly dedicated to charity work, particularly causes involving inner-city children and special education. He recognized his position as a role model for youngsters, and he made enormous efforts to provide a positive image for them to emulate. In 1988 he helped to start the Halas/Payton Foundation to help the inner-city youth of Chicago. His dedication, integrity, and generosity made him one of the most admired men in the history of professional sports, and his name has become inextricably linked to the city of Chicago.

Ironically for a player famous for never having suffered a serious injury during his career, Payton died at the young age of forty-five. In 1999 he announced at a news conference that he had a rare liver condition and needed a transplant to live. Payton went on a waiting list, but his condition deteriorated, and he died on November 1 of that year. After his death it was revealed that the condition was cancer of the bile duct. The year of Payton's passing, the NFL renamed its Man of the Year Award the Walter Payton Man of the Year Award to honor his legacy as a humanitarian.

In 2011 a controversial new biography written by Jeff Pearlman claimed that Payton wasn't as sweet as his image—that in fact he had battled depression, suicidal thoughts, and addiction to painkillers. The tell-all further alleged that Payton had a longtime mistress. Many of Payton's former teammates and coach Mike Ditka expressed anger that the author would sling mud on the reputation of a man who could no longer defend himself. One teammate, Kevin Butler, offered a defense of his own, pointing out that recent research into the brain showed that the constant pounding inflicted by football gave a plausible explanation for many of the problems Pearlman claimed Payton had. In spite of the brief flurry of negative publicity, it remained certain that Chicagoans—and avid football fans around the country—would retain their love and gratitude for the man they had known as Sweetness.

Geoff Peterson

SEE ALSO: *Brown, Jim; The Chicago Bears; College Football; Ditka, Mike; National Football League (NFL); Professional Football; Sports Heroes; Super Bowl.*

BIBLIOGRAPHY

Koslow, Philip. *Walter Payton.* New York: Chelsea House, 1995.

Payton, Connie; Jarrett Payton; Brittney Payton; et al. *Payton.* New York: Rugged Land, 2005.

Payton, Walter, and Don Yaeger. *Never Die Easy: The Autobiography of Walter Payton.* New York: Villard, 2000.

Pearlman, Jeff. *Sweetness: The Enigmatic Life of Walter Payton.* New York: Gotham, 2011.

Whittingham, Richard. *The Bears: A 75-Year Celebration.* Dallas, TX: Taylor Publishing, 1994.

Peale, Norman Vincent *(1898–1993)*

A long and happy life, national acclaim, professional satisfactions, and accumulating wealth seemed to attest to the success of Norman Vincent Peale's blend of New Thought, psychotherapy, optimism, and Protestant Christianity. The phrase "positive thinking" became part of the national vocabulary, as Peale's books repeatedly topped the best-seller lists. Although Pealeism, as his thought came to be known, exactly suited the American post–World War II mood, it also became the object of angry attack from academic theologians for two decades. Along with televangelists Billy Graham and Catholic bishop Fulton J. Sheen, Peale became one of the best-known American clergymen of his time. His books constituted the greatest commercial success of religion in the mid-twentieth century, and his concepts, though no longer labeled as "Pealeism," linger on in the optimism and mind-control techniques of the New Age.

EARLY MINISTERING

Peale was born in Bowersville, Ohio, the son of a Methodist preacher who had given up a medical practice to answer a higher call. After some hesitation, young Peale accepted ordination in the Methodist ministry, studying theology at Boston University and serving churches in Rhode Island, New York, and New Jersey. Congregations grew and flourished under his care. In 1930 he married Loretta Ruth Stafford, who would become a full partner in his national media ministry.

In 1932 Peale was persuaded to accept appointment to the historic Marble Collegiate Church in New York City, founded by the Dutch in 1628 and reputed to be the oldest Protestant church in continuous use in North America. This appointment necessitated his transfer from Methodist to Dutch Reformed affiliation—which caused no crisis of conscience for Peale, because denominational identity meant little to him. Under Peale's direction, church attendance grew. He was soon preaching to a packed house every Sunday at Marble Collegiate Church and acting as a spiritual minister to U.S. presidents.

His calling, however, could never be limited to one congregation, no matter how enormously it expanded. His publications and lectures became central to his national ministry. Peale's best-known self-help book, *The Power of Positive Thinking* (1952), was one of the best-selling books of the decade. It remained at the top of the *New York Times* best-seller list for three years. Other organs of ministry included his monthly pastoral magazine, *Guideposts*; an inspirational book club; the American Foundation of Religion and Psychiatry, emanating from his church's counseling center; and the Foundation for Christian Living, operated by his wife with the aim of disseminating Peale's sermons through booklets and recordings. Radio appearances were also frequent, and the *Reader's Digest* was the perfect forum for Pealeism.

Peale became increasingly well known as a motivational speaker, and his message was consistent: The American dream was real, and the Protestant work ethic made one virtuous, wise, and prosperous. Material pleasures were not contrary to Christian piety, and personal goals were realizable. With the power of positive thought working, a person need not fear any defeat. Good mental and physical health were possible, and the goal of life seemed to be contentment, even joy.

APPLIED CHRISTIANITY

There was much of New England transcendentalism in Peale's thought, and he gratefully acknowledged his debt to American transcendentalist Ralph Waldo Emerson. There was also much of New Thought in Peale's spirituality. He would have agreed frequently with Christian Science founder Mary Baker Eddy, though they did not speak the same theological language. He further learned from both Sigmund Freud and Carl Jung, though he never penetrated the depths of the human psyche or engaged in speculation about psychological archetypes. Most of all, he never discovered the murky underground passages of the human soul; most serious theologians agreed he had a deficient sense of sin.

But within modest limits, Peale's thought was energizing; his self-applied therapy seemed to work, and people enjoyed reading his books, which made few intellectual demands and abounded in homey anecdotes of folks who became millionaires or successes in their professions. His biblical quotations were invariably sunny ones.

Peale described his therapeutic system as "applied Christianity, a simple yet scientific system of practical techniques of successful living that works." His techniques of spiritual healing, derived from his personal experiences and a variety of other sources and ultimately, he claimed, traceable to the Gospels, involved silent meditation, positive affirmation, creative visualization, and biblical quotations used almost as mantras. When he talked about getting into "time synchronization" with the Almighty by listening to the sounds of the earth, he sounded suspiciously pantheistic.

CONTROVERSY AND CRITICISM

A Republican and a personal friend of Dwight D. Eisenhower and Richard M. Nixon, Peale ventured unsteadily into political controversy during the 1960 presidential campaign of John F. Kennedy. Much to his later embarrassment, he lent his name to a statement issued by a group of religious leaders opposing Kennedy on the basis of the politics of the Roman Catholic Church and its record of church-state relations. Peale certainly did not harbor any personal anti-Catholic prejudice. He maintained cordial relations with Bishop Sheen and other Catholic dignitaries, including Catholic author and *Reader's Digest* editor C. Fulton Oursler, who called Peale "my Protestant pastor."

To the end of his career, Peale's critics were harsh in their attacks. They found his thinking simplistic, even heretical in its confusion of historic Christianity with American materialism and doctrines of self-reliance and worldly success. Critics found Peale's optimism at variance with reality in a century that had witnessed history's two bloodiest wars, the Holocaust, and the advent of nuclear weapons. Peale's own sons attending seminary were forced to listen to their professor's tirades against "Pealeism," and his wife especially found the attacks a savagery against a gentle man. It might be supposed that Peale himself, who became wealthy from the sale of his books, would have laughed all the way to the bank. On the contrary, he was deeply wounded and even considered dropping out of the ministry. His own brand of positive thinking eventually won over; he forgave his critics, outliving them all, and dying with his optimism unshaken.

Allene Phy-Olsen

SEE ALSO: *Eddy, Mary Baker; Freud, Sigmund; Graham, Billy; New Age Spirituality; Popular Psychology;* Reader's Digest*; Televangelism.*

BIBLIOGRAPHY

George, Carol V. R. *God's Salesman: Norman Vincent Peale and the Power of Positive Thinking.* New York: Oxford University Press, 1993.

Meyer, Donald B. *The Positive Thinkers: Religion as Pop Psychology from Mary Baker Eddy to Oral Roberts.* New York: Pantheon Books, 1980.

Occhiogrosso, Peter. *The Joy of Sects: A Spirited Guide to the World's Religious Traditions.* New York: Doubleday, 1996.

Peale, Norman Vincent. *The True Joy of Positive Living: An Autobiography.* New York: William Morrow, 1984.

Peale, Norman Vincent. *The Power of Positive Thinking.* New York: Fireside/Simon & Schuster, 2003.

Phy-Olsen, Allene. *The Bible and Popular Culture in America.* Minneapolis, MN: Fortress Press, 1985.

Peanuts

Charles Schulz's famous comic strip, *Peanuts*, premiered on October 2, 1950, in only seven U.S. newspapers. It was originally marketed for its flexible size and format: four squares that allowed papers to run the strip horizontally, vertically, or in two rows. United Features Syndicate chose the title—a title, Schulz said in *Charlie Brown, Snoopy and Me*, he never liked. Sales of the strip climbed slowly at first, but by 1960 it appeared in more than 400 newspapers worldwide. In 1984 *The Guinness Book of Records* listed *Peanuts* as the world's most widely syndicated comic strip, and by its fortieth anniversary in 1990, the strip was running in more than 2,000 newspapers in dozens of countries. Through the years, the *Peanuts* characters have appeared in print, animated specials, and even onstage, making them some of the most popular cartoon characters of the twentieth century.

UNLIKELY LEADING MAN

Charlie Brown, Schulz's main character, first appeared in a panel cartoon called *L'il Folks* that Schulz sold to a St. Paul, Minnesota, newspaper in 1947. Charlie Brown was not named until the first *Peanuts* strip, in which he quickly took the lead role. The things that people fear will happen to them are the types of things that do happen to Charlie Brown: he cannot fly a kite, his baseball team never wins, he receives no valentines on Valentine's Day, and he gets rocks instead of candy on Halloween. Faced with depression and the torment of his peers, Charlie Brown is friendly and kind, and he displays a plucky spirit. People empathize with his perseverance in the face of life's unfairness.

Snoopy, Charlie Brown's exuberant beagle, acts as Charlie Brown's foil. Snoopy is relentlessly happy and confident, and he does not let being a dog get in the way of his ambitions. He imagines himself as a writer, a World War I flying ace, an attorney, and the impressive Joe Cool. He plays hockey and baseball, and like any dog, he enjoys eating, sleeping, and picking on the neighbor's cat. He is a quirky character who embodies childlike qualities more than the actual children do in the strip. Snoopy is everything Charlie Brown is not, and Snoopy may even exceed his owner's popularity.

The neighborhood children are not quite as depressed as Charlie Brown, but they all have their own insecurities and vulnerabilities. Lucy Van Pelt, Charlie Brown's next-door

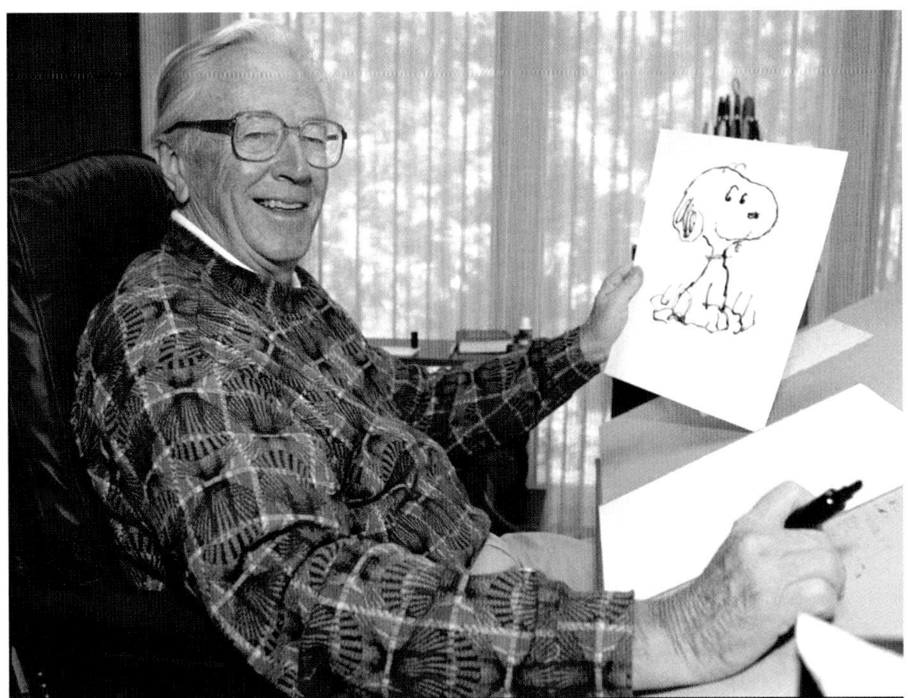

Peanuts *Creator Charles Schulz.* *The late cartoonist Charles Schulz holds a drawing of his comic strip character "Snoopy" in 1995.* © BEN MARGOT/AP PHOTOS.

neighbor, is a bossy fussbudget. She is loud and mean-spirited, and she is best known for annually coaxing Charlie Brown into kicking the football she has every intention of pulling away at the last minute. Seemingly invulnerable, she has a crush on the musical Schroeder and continually suffers his insults just to be around him. Lucy's younger brother, Linus, carries a security blanket in spite of the criticism of his sister and grandmother. Charlie Brown's little sister, Sally, worries constantly about her schoolwork. The other neighborhood children are much the same, worrying about school, unrequited crushes, and sports—typical childhood worries. Children and adults alike see themselves and their own insecurities in these characters.

The *Peanuts* characters, however, are not typical children. In some ways they are among the first realistic children in comics: they torment each other and play games, much as other children do. However, the *Peanuts* characters are more serious and intelligent than the average child. Lucy says she would like real estate for Christmas, Linus can philosophize about life's problems while sucking his thumb, and Schroeder's hero is Beethoven. They quote the Bible, have impressive vocabularies, and have a high degree of independence. Adults only appear off-panel, and rarely at that.

The characters tend to be a bit less fun-loving than real children: when they laugh, they laugh at each other's misfortunes and foibles. As Schulz himself says in *Charlie Brown, Snoopy and Me*, "Pleasant things are not really funny. You cannot create humor out of happiness." The *Peanuts* characters have enough childlike qualities to keep children interested, but much of it is adult humor.

A MULTIMEDIA SENSATION

The successful transition of *Peanuts* into other media is another element that has helped maintain and expand the strip's popularity. The first animated television special, *A Charlie Brown Christmas*, premiered on December 9, 1965, and drew 50 percent of the U.S. viewing audience. It won an Emmy Award and a Peabody Award and continues to be rerun annually. Other *Peanuts* animated specials have received Emmys, including *A Charlie Brown Thanksgiving* and *You're a Good Sport, Charlie Brown*.The specials had a huge impact when they first aired, drawing large audiences and reactions. After the premieres of the *Peanuts* animated Halloween and Valentine's Day specials, hundreds of people sent Schulz candy and valentines to give to Charlie Brown. On December 11, 1969, the first of several *Peanuts* animated feature films premiered at Radio City Music Hall. The shows and movies continue to be popular, and new specials have appeared even after Schulz's death in 2000.

A musical based on the strip, *You're a Good Man, Charlie Brown*, opened off-Broadway on March 7, 1967. The show has been a favorite of regional and school groups in the years since, and a 1999 revival of the musical on Broadway garnered two Tony Awards. Other authors have also used *Peanuts* comics as springboards for their own work. Therapist Abraham J. Twerski chose *Peanuts* comics to illustrate psychological concepts in his book, *When Do the Good Things Start*. In *The Gospel According to Peanuts* and *Short Meditations on the Bible and Peanuts*, Robert L. Short uses the cartoons to highlight lessons in Christian living. The universal appeal of Schulz's characters has led the strip to appear in more than twenty languages in more than seventy-five countries.

Peanuts was also the first aggressively merchandized strip, paving a path to profitability that has become a standard in the field. It began with plastic dolls in 1958, expanded to Hallmark greeting cards in 1960, and then exploded into the characters appearing on countless items such as stickers, pajamas, sheets, and lunch boxes. The *Peanuts* gang has endorsed Metropolitan Life Insurance, Chex Party Mix, and the U.S. National Park Foundation. Schulz himself exercised a great deal of control over the merchandizing of his characters during his lifetime, vetoing any item he felt did not fit the values and spirit of his work. He became a rich man through this effort, ultimately being listed in *Forbes* magazine's list of the ten wealthiest entertainers in 1989 and being inducted to the Licensing Industry Merchandisers' Association Hall of Fame in 1994.

The popularity and relevance of *Peanuts* have created a feedback loop that has kept the strip in the public eye. In the late 1960s, Snoopy was adopted as the official emblem of the National Aeronautics and Space Administration (NASA) for outstanding achievement within the organization. In 1969 the Apollo 10 Lunar Expedition nicknamed their command module "Charlie Brown" and the lunar module "Snoopy," and astronaut John Young transmitted a picture of Snoopy back to Earth during the mission's fourth telecast.

In 1974, when Hank Aaron was approaching Babe Ruth's home run record, Schulz read about people sending Aaron hate mail, angry that a black man was challenging the record. Schulz addressed this in a series of cartoons recounting Snoopy's trials and tribulations as he approaches the home run record. Schulz even commemorated the fiftieth anniversary of D-Day in his strip. *Peanuts* characters have appeared on the covers of *Time*, *Life*, *Newsweek*, *Woman's Day*, the *Saturday Review*, and *TV Guide*.

AWARDS AND RECOGNITION

Schulz prided himself on not rerunning strips and produced original dailies until failing health forced him to stop. His last original weekday comic was published on January 3, 2000, and his last original Sunday strip was published on February 13, 2000, just hours after his death on February 12. Schulz was highly regarded as a comic artist and received numerous awards and honors for his work. The National Cartoonist's Society awarded him their prestigious Reuben Award in 1955 and again in 1964.

In 1962 Schulz won the National Cartoonist Society's "Best Humor Strip of the Year" Award. In 1978 he received the "Cartoonist of the Year" Award from the International Pavilion of Humor of Montreal. In 1990 the Smithsonian's National Museum of American History presented "This Is Your Childhood Charlie Brown—Children in American Culture, 1945–1970," and in 1996 Schulz received a star on the Hollywood Walk of Fame. Schulz was repeatedly recognized for his professionalism, his intelligence, and for the quality of his output, and he experienced a popularity not enjoyed by many cartoonists.

Years after his death, Schulz and *Peanuts* remain relevant. The strips rerun in syndication in newspapers all over the world. In 2002, the Charles M. Schulz Museum and Research Center opened in Santa Rosa, California. Though Schulz was not overly enthusiastic about a museum showcasing his work, his friends and family were, and instrumental in its creation were Schulz's wife; his attorney, Edwin Anderson; and cartoon historian Mark Cohen.

In 2007 David Michaelis brought Schulz himself back into the spotlight with his book *Schulz and Peanuts: A Biography*, in which the writer asserts that Schulz's characters are highly autobiographical and that even after becoming successful, the cartoonist spent most of his life mired in insecurity, anger, pettiness, and self-absorption. The book sold well and was reviewed widely, getting attention for its negative portrait of Schulz. It also prompted several members of Schulz's family, who were interviewed for the book, to publicly criticize the veracity of the portrait. Beverly Gherman brought Schulz's life to child audiences in her well-reviewed 2010 biography, *Sparky: The Life and Art of Charles Schulz*. And in 2012 new life was infused into the *Peanuts* gang with the launch of a new comic-book series by kaboom! Studios. The monthly series paired artwork by Schulz with new stories and new art.

In his book *When Do the Good Things Start*, Twerski says, "The lovable characters created by Schulz do more than amuse; they depict important psychological principles in a manner so deceptively simple that it masks the force of their impact." Indeed, *Peanuts* raised a new standard for what could be done in comic art. The sharpness and wit displayed in such comics as Bill Watterson's *Calvin and Hobbes* and Gary Larson's *The Far Side* come from this tradition, the belief that comics can have more meaning than a simple laugh. The *Peanuts* characters are some of the most popular in the genre: Charlie Brown, Snoopy, Lucy, Linus, and the other characters are easily recognized by most Americans and by many people throughout the world, and their popularity shows no signs of flagging.

Adrienne Furness

SEE ALSO: Calvin and Hobbes*; Comics; Emmy Awards;* The Far Side*; Guaraldi, Vince; Television.*

BIBLIOGRAPHY

Boxer, Sarah. "Charles M. Schulz, 'Peanuts' Creator, Dies at 77." *New York Times*, February 14, 2000.

Johnson, Rheta Grimsley. *Good Grief: The Story of Charles M. Schulz*. New York: Pharos Books, 1989.

Mendelson, Lee, and Charles M. Schulz. *Happy Birthday, Charlie Brown*. New York: Random House, 1979.

Michaelis, David. *Schulz and "Peanuts": A Biography*. New York: HarperCollins Publishers, 2007.

Schulz, Charles M., and R. Smith Kiliper. *Charlie Brown, Snoopy and Me*. Garden City, NY: Doubleday, 1980.

Short, Robert L. *The Gospel According to "Peanuts."* Richmond, VA: Westminster John Knox Press, 1965.

Short, Robert L. *Short Meditations on the Bible and "Peanuts."* Louisville, KY: Westminster John Knox Press, 1990.

Twerski, Abraham J. *When Do the Good Things Start?* New York: Topper Books, 1988.

Pearl, Minnie *(1912–1996)*

Country music's first comedian, Minnie Pearl entertained Grand Ole Opry audiences for more than half a century. Her gingham dress, white stockings, and straw hat complete with $1.98 price tag dangling from it made her a figure recognized wherever country music was heard. Ploughboys and presidents responded to her contagious grin, her homespun humor, and her exuberant greeting. So familiar was her image that upon her death in March 1996, commentators, columnists, and cartoonists alike pictured her entering the pearly gates with her trademark, "Howdee! I'm just so proud to be here."

Sarah Ophelia Colley Cannon never planned to become a country comic. The sheltered, youngest daughter of conventionally conservative southern parents and a product of Ward-Belmont, a Tennessee finishing school, she dreamed of becoming a fine dramatic actress; she said she planned "to out-Bernhardt Bernhardt."

The character "Minnie Pearl" evolved from young Ophelia's years working for the Sewell Production Company, an Atlanta-based touring theater company that sent young women directors to stage productions throughout the small-town and rural South. What began as a collection of stories culled from her touring experience gradually developed into a country character that Ophelia used to sell the Sewell productions. She named the character Minnie Pearl, choosing common country names that were familiar to her audiences. When Ophelia earned her first job, it was not as a Sewell director but as Minnie Pearl. She later added the costume to her act, which she performed for the Pilots Club Convention in Aiken, South Carolina, in 1939; Ophelia Cannon had acquired an alter ego. That performance, the comedian later revealed, was the first time that she "became the character."

A year after the Aiken appearance, Minnie Pearl debuted on the Grand Ole Opry in a three-minute spot at 11:05 p.m., a time chosen so that if Minnie flopped, the affected audience would be as small as possible. Far from failing, however, Minnie received several hundred fan letters and an offer to become a regular at the Opry. For the next fifty-one years, Minnie, with her tales of Brother, Uncle Nabob, Aunt Ambrosy, and other inhabitants of Grinder's Switch (a name Cannon borrowed from an abandoned loading switch in Hickman County, Tennessee) captured the affections of Opry audiences and others far from Nashville, including standing-room-only audiences at Carnegie Hall. An early indication that Minnie was on her way to becoming an American icon came in 1948 when Alben Barkley, Harry Truman's vice president, began his first official address to the nation with the words "well, as Minnie Pearl would say, I'm just so *proud* to be here!"

Minnie, with her hillbilly naïveté and her inexhaustible search for a "feller," may seem an incongruous figure as a pioneer for women's equality, but she opened doors in the country music business that other women eagerly walked through. She headlined in an era when the only women around were "girl singers" in clearly subordinate roles. Aside from being the first female member of the Grand Ole Opry, Minnie was also one of the first women to be elected to the Country Music Hall of Fame (1975) as well as the National Comedy Hall of Fame (1994).

The woman who auditioned for Nashville radio station WSM knowing nothing about country music became one of the most beloved figures in the country music industry. Initially befriended by Roy Acuff—already an established star when Minnie Pearl came to the Opry—she in turn befriended generations of newcomers, including Chet Atkins and Hank Williams. The esteem in which younger entertainers held her is evident. Dwight Yoakam, who managed to alienate himself from many in the industry, sent fifty dozen roses for Minnie's fiftieth anniversary celebration on the Grand Ole Opry. And both pop-contemporary Christian music star Amy Grant and country music sensation Garth Brooks named daughters after her.

The same generosity that endeared her to the country music community led her to work for humanitarian causes. As a cancer survivor, Minnie worked tirelessly for the American Cancer Society. Her efforts were recognized in 1987 by President Ronald Reagan, who presented her with the Cancer Society's Courage Award. In 1988 she became the first recipient of the Nashville Network/Music City News humanitarian award, which bears her name. A stroke in 1991 forced her to retire, but her presence continued to be felt in the country music community, where good wishes for Miss Minnie were standard fare on award shows. Her husband, Henry Cannon, represented her on tribute shows she could only watch. She died on March 4, 1996.

Minnie ended her 1980 autobiography by wishing for her readers a Grinder's Switch. "Grinder's Switch," she wrote, "is a state of mind—a place where there is no illness, no war, no unhappiness, no political unrest, no tears." Perhaps it was her ability to evoke such a place that endeared her to fans and peers alike. She allowed her audience to inhabit a space where eccentricities were tolerated, humor was barbless, and laughter was easy. The Minnie Pearl Cancer Foundation to which Minnie lent her stage name in 1992 continues to honor the generosity and compassion of the comedian through its work.

Wylene Rholetter

SEE ALSO: *Atkins, Chet; Broadway; Brooks, Garth; Cancer; Carnegie Hall; Country Music; Feminism;* Grand Ole Opry; *Grant, Amy; Reagan, Ronald; Stand-up Comedy; Williams, Hank, Sr.; Yoakam, Dwight.*

BIBLIOGRAPHY

Country Music Hall of Fame and Museum. *The Encyclopedia of Country Music: The Ultimate Guide to the Music*, ed. Paul Kingsbury. Oxford University Press: 2004.

Escott, Colin, and Brenda Colladay. *The Grand Ole Opry: The Making of an American Icon.* New York: Hatchette Digital, 2006.

Minnie, Pearl, and Dew Joan. *Minnie Pearl: An Autobiography.* New York: Simon & Schuster, 1980.

Tassin, Myron, and Jerry Henderson. *Fifty Years at the Grand Ole Opry.* Gretna, LA: Pelican, 1975.

Pearl Jam

When grunge music exploded into mainstream popular culture in the early 1990s, Pearl Jam, along with fellow Seattle band Nirvana, filled column inches and topped the Billboard charts. Although Nirvana's *Nevermind* (1991) generated an immediate media frenzy, Pearl Jam's more orthodox blues-rock album, *Ten*, released almost simultaneously, eventually overtook *Nevermind* in sales and became one of the best-selling pop albums of the 1990s. The video for the group's breakthrough single, "Jeremy," won four MTV Video Music Awards and created a coherent narrative to match lead singer Eddie Vedder's typically elusive lyrics. The music and video epitomized the pain and anger that flow through many of Pearl Jam's early songs. The band's energy helped to recharge rock and roll, which after the late 1980s was slipping in both market share and musical relevance.

EARLY YEARS

Pearl Jam was formed in 1991 by bass guitarist Jeff Ament and rhythm guitarist Stone Gossard. Together with Vedder, Mike McCready (guitar), and drummer Dave Krusen (later replaced by Dave Abbruzzese and then Jack Irons), the band began recording under the name Mookie Blaylock, after the New Jersey Nets basketball star. After Blaylock objected, they changed their name to Pearl Jam (allegedly after a jam containing peyote made by Vedder's great-grandmother Pearl). Their debut album, *Ten*, combined a hard guitar-rock sound with anthemic choruses, slow pop melodies, and Vedder's vocal gyrations, telling stories of suicide and childhood neglect.

If Nirvana's *Nevermind* was a punk-infused incendiary aimed at classic rock, Pearl Jam's *Ten* was a more mainstream-sounding attack on the established order. Both albums were instrumental in positioning grunge, or what became known as the Seattle sound (fellow alternative bands Soundgarden and Alice in Chains also hailed from the city), as the dominant MTV aesthetic of the early 1990s. However, Pearl Jam's more commercial approach prompted Nirvana's lead singer Kurt Cobain in 1993 to call them a "corporate, alternative, cock-rock crossover," charging the group with "jumping on the alternative bandwagon."

Pearl Jam's next album, *Vs.* (1993), was much rawer and harder. The group refused to support the release with videos, singles, or a major tour. (Vedder appeared on the front cover of *Time* magazine in October 1993 despite his refusal to be interviewed for the accompanying article.) Still the album sold more than five million copies and topped the Billboard charts.

REJECTION OF MAINSTREAM ROCK

In 1994 the band took a stand against ticketing agency Ticketmaster, alleging that the company had a monopoly over distribution in U.S. arenas and stadiums. The group asked the Department of Justice to investigate the agency on antitrust charges, and members Ament and Gossard testified before a congressional committee. Although the Justice Department dropped the investigation in July 1995, Pearl Jam gained praise in many quarters for opposing a stadium system that in some ways mirrored the mainstream rock aesthetic they had increasingly rejected.

The band's third album, *Vitalogy* (1994), stripped away the grunge sound in favor of a diverse collection of influences, including folk and reggae. One standout, the Grammy Award–winning track "Spin the Black Circle," is an homage to vinyl records. So great was the group's desire to reestablish grassroots credibility after the tremendous media hype they had received that Pearl Jam released the album on vinyl before other, more accessible formats. The release reflected Vedder's musings in light of Cobain's suicide, an event that had intensified scrutiny on the Pearl Jam vocalist.

The group increasingly shirked the limelight, moving further away from the grunge sound that had helped generate their fame. A fourth album, *No Code* (1996), employed Indian drones, psychedelic rock, folk, and punk, only occasionally returning to a high-energy rock sound. Similarly, *Yield* (1998) combined Vedder's existential musings and an eclectic range of musical instruments. It included a track showing the influence of Pakistani qawwali star Nusrat Fateh Ali Khan, with whom Vedder collaborated for the soundtrack to *Dead Man Walking* (1995).

Music critics were less than receptive to Pearl Jam's attempts to redefine themselves; yet the demise of grunge and the group's diminished but still significant fan base suited the new direction. Their stated wish was to sustain a lengthy and credible musical career in line with those they admired, such as folk legend Bob Dylan; the Who's lead guitarist Pete Townshend; and singer-songwriter Neil Young, with whom they collaborated on Young's 1995 *Mirror Ball.*

INDEPENDENT RELEASES

Having long allowed fans to make amateur recordings of their shows, Pearl Jam began an official bootleg program in 2000, releasing a live recording of each of their seventy-two shows on their *Binaural* (2000) tour. The band has continued the program for almost every tour since, releasing many of the recordings on their website. Before splitting with Epic Records in 2003, they released 2002's *Riot Act.*

In a one-off deal with J Records, the group released a self-titled eighth studio album, often referred to as the "Avocado Album" by fans because of the photograph on its cover. The release debuted at number two on the Billboard 200, and many critics saw it as a return to Pearl Jam's hard-hitting original sound. Although the cover art received mixed reviews, the album was considered a comeback hit, outselling *Riot Act.*

The band continued to tour but took a break from recording. Vedder penned a Golden Globe–winning solo album, *Into the Wild* (2007), the soundtrack to writer-director Sean Penn's film adaptation of Jon Krakauer's book. In 2009 Pearl Jam made a surprising move when they announced their new self-released album, *Backspacer*, would be distributed in partnership with the Target Corporation. Fans and critics accused the band of selling out, but according to Ament, Target was the only retailer willing to share distribution rights with independent music stores and with the band's voracious fan club, the Ten Club. Also, under the deal, Pearl Jam would own the rights to its master recordings. The album became the band's first number one Billboard hit in thirteen years.

Pearl Jam marked their twentieth anniversary in 2011 with much fanfare, including a career-spanning documentary directed by longtime friend Cameron Crowe (the group appeared alongside actor Matt Dillon as the fictional band Citizen Dick in Crowe's second film *Singles* [1992]). The two-hour *Pearl Jam Twenty* (2011) contains unreleased interviews with band members combed from more than 1,200 hours of archival footage. A two-disc, twenty-nine-song soundtrack of live cuts and rarities curated by Crowe accompanied the film's release. The band celebrated the anniversary with a two-day concert festival in East Troy, Wisconsin, which featured popular rock acts the Strokes and Queens of the Stone Age and Soundgarden's lead singer Chris Cornell.

James Lyons

SEE ALSO: *Blues; Dylan, Bob; Folk Music; Grunge; Indie Music; Long-Playing Record; MTV; Nirvana; Pop Music; Punk; Rock and Roll; Stadium Concerts;* Time; *Top 40; Videos; The Who; Young, Neil.*

BIBLIOGRAPHY

Clarke, Malcolm. *Pearl Jam and Eddie Vedder: None Too Fragile.* London: Plexus, 1998.

Humphrey, Clark. *Loser: The Real Seattle Music Story.* Portland, OR: Feral House, 1995.

Morrell, Brad. *Pearl Jam: The Illustrated Biography.* New York: Omnibus, 1993.

Neeley, Kim. *Five against One.* New York: Penguin, 1998.

Pearl Jam. *Pearl Jam Twenty.* New York: Simon & Schuster, 2011.

Wall, Mick. *Pearl Jam.* London: Sidgwick & Jackson, 1994.

Peck, Gregory *(1916–2003)*

The last of the classic leading men from Hollywood's golden age, Gregory Peck became a star during the 1940s when a spinal injury prevented him from joining the armed forces during World War II. With many of its male stars in uniform, Hollywood turned to the tall, dark, and handsome Peck, who soon made a name for himself playing men of moral fortitude and great dignity. A five-time Academy Award nominee and an Oscar winner for Best Actor for his turn as Atticus Finch in the classic *To Kill a Mockingbird* (1962), Peck was a versatile actor who was able to take on a wide range of roles, including those depicting the darker side of humanity. A tireless supporter of the film industry, Peck served on almost every major film and arts council. But Hollywood's dedicated elder statesman is best remembered as the actor who became a pop culture icon by unflinchingly showing America both the best and the worst about itself.

EARLY LIFE AND CAREER

Eldred Gregory Peck was born in the beach town of La Jolla, California, and was the son of the town's only pharmacist. Peck's parents divorced when he was five, but the boy continued to live in the seaside resort community with his mother and grandmother until age ten, when he was sent to St. John's Military Academy in Los Angeles. Upon graduating from the academy after ninth grade, Peck moved in with his father in San Diego, where the teenager attended San Diego High School. The handsome 6-foot, 2-inch young man was an average student who enjoyed being on the rowing team, but because his father wanted him to become a doctor, Peck studied at San Diego State University before transferring to study medicine at the University of California, Berkeley. There he quickly realized that he was more interested in literature than in medicine and, as an English major, he fell in with an artistic crowd and was soon persuaded to audition for a production of *Moby Dick.* Cast as Captain Ahab, Peck so fell in love with the theater that shortly before graduation he dropped out of school and caught a train for New York City.

Arriving in New York in 1939, Peck found work as a barker at the New York World's Fair, before auditioning for Sanford Meisner's famed Neighborhood Playhouse. While studying there with renowned dancer Martha Graham, he suffered the severe back injury that kept him out of the war. He gradually began to find acting work in stock companies around the East Coast before being "discovered" by distinguished director Guthrie McClintic, who regularly began to use the handsome young leading man in his productions. Peck made his Broadway debut in McClintic's 1942 production of an Emlyn Williams wartime drama. The young actor received excellent reviews and soon found regular work on Broadway. But not long thereafter, Hollywood, whose ranks of leading men had been depleted by the war, came calling.

HOLLYWOOD CAREER

Because of the paucity of available actors, the talented Peck was immediately cast in prime leading roles, working with some of Hollywood's best directors—from John Stahl in *The Keys of the Kingdom* (1944) to Alfred Hitchcock in *Spellbound* (1945); and from King Vidor in *Duel in the Sun* (1946) to Elia Kazan in *Gentleman's Agreement* (1947). Overnight the versatile actor became a star, garnering four Academy Award nominations in five years. Despite becoming a famous movie actor, Peck continued to devote himself to the theater, cofounding the prestigious La Jolla Playhouse in his hometown with fellow actors Dorothy McGuire and Mel Ferrer.

Although the gifted Peck could play a wide range of characters, as Baseline's *Encyclopedia of Film* notes, it was "as an authority figure of quiet dignity and uncompromising single-mindedness" that audiences seemed to love Peck best—in such films, for example, as *The Yearling* (1946), *The Gunfighter* (1950), and *The Man in the Gray Flannel Suit* (1956). Throughout the 1950s his popularity only seemed to grow. He was a popular leading man opposite such "A"-list actresses as Audrey Hepburn, Jean Simmons, and Lauren Bacall, even as he topped the list of Hollywood's favorite action heroes in war films such as *Pork Chop Hill* (1959) and *The Guns of Navarone* (1961). But the apex of his career came in 1962, when he was cast in the role that earned him cinematic immortality. Playing a morally courageous lawyer and single father of two children in a small southern town who defends a black man accused of rape, Peck turned in a superb performance as Atticus Finch, epitomizing his appeal as an actor. *To Kill a Mockingbird*, which has become a screen classic, won three Academy Awards, including Peck's win for Best Actor.

He continued to work in films throughout the 1960s and into the 1990s, but only a few of his later movies, such as *The Omen* (1976) and *The Boys from Brazil* (1978), were particularly notable. Peck, however, found an outlet for his creative energies as a founder of the prestigious American Film Institute, a three-time president of the Academy of Motion Picture Arts and Sciences, and a member of the National Council for the Arts. He died on June 12, 2003, at the age of eighty-seven, leaving a legacy as one of Hollywood's most popular actors, having managed to meld life and art in creating an honorable career playing some of film's most honorable men.

Victoria Price

SEE ALSO: *Academy Awards; Bacall, Lauren; Broadway; Graham, Martha; Hepburn, Audrey; Hitchcock, Alfred; Hollywood;* To Kill a Mockingbird*; World War II; World's Fairs.*

BIBLIOGRAPHY

Everitt, David. "A Bushel of Peck." *Entertainment Weekly*, March 1998, 95–96.

Fishgall, Gary, and the Editors of Baseline. *Gregory Peck: A Biography*. New York: Scribner, 2002.

Monaco, James, and the Editors of Baseline. *The Encyclopedia of Film*. New York: Perigee, 1991.

Peep Shows

Peep shows, featuring videotaped or live performances of sexual activity, were once commonplace in urban downtowns across America. With the passage of time and emerging technology, however, they have become rare or have evolved into fundamentally new forms. Peep shows developed on the heels of several hundred years of interest in optical principles; the construction of novel, very small spaces; and apparent human fascination with the particulars of these settings. The history of peep shows might even be much older. Certainly, examples of small private meal cubicles (often associated with licentious behavior), buskers and tented tableaus, and traveling entertainers with all manners of portable containers offering the entrepreneur control and the consumer a sense of security are mentioned across continents and ages. Twenty-first century manifestations exhibit the presence of several particular circumstances: new and cheap materials, changes in public mores and the ability to regulate human behavior, and rapid changes and improvements in technology. The most recent iteration of what might be considered peep show presentations involves pay-for-view access to webcam broadcasts via home computers.

As science became the pastime of leisured gentlemen in the 1700s and through the early quarter of the 1800s (when a transition began to move science into the hands of specialists and societies), experiments with amusing outcomes were very popular. Thus the camera obscura (a closed device ranging in size from a large box to a reasonable-sized room) and the related camera lucida both entertained and fostered further work with the phenomena of sight. Literally a "dark chamber," the camera obscura allowed the projection of images, often pornographic, onto a wall, through the agency of the physics of light, a tiny hole, and a willing actor. Meanwhile, the participants inside could act along.

EXPANSION OF THE HOSPITALITY INDUSTRY

At about the same time, the expanding notion of a hospitality industry allowed commercial eateries and inns to flourish in growing commercial centers. Tiny, secluded chambers away from the restaurant's main hall provided privacy for a range of adult hanky-panky. By the mid-1800s the commingling of the commercial provision of secure, intimate chambers and the development of a number of ways to "play" reproductions of titillating forms of entertainment reliably and cheaply offered lucrative opportunities. The early "secure chamber" still exists as the so-called private room at contemporary full-service striptease clubs and, indeed, in a slightly changed form at many present-day peep shows. In addition, as web-provided commercial pornography became available, a number of the sites offered a service whereby the consumer's suggestion was acted out. Finally, after the turn of the twenty-first century, webcam hostesses again provided direct access to peep-show-like performances on websites expressly devoted to this task.

Zoetropes, stereoscopes, crankable flip-card devices, and early movie loops tumbled off the inventor's and manufacturer's conveyor belt from the mid- to late 1800s. Burgeoning city growth and the accompanying cash economy of the factory system virtually guaranteed the lush development of adult entertainment neighborhoods chock-a-block with cafés, dance halls (where prostitutes were often to be found), taverns, theaters, and so on. Well before the assault of Reform Movement "do gooders" in urban centers after the Civil War, the peep show devices made good sense to entrepreneurs. Images could be loaded to suit the consumer; for example, if the nudes were of brown-skinned women, one could deny prurient intent and ride the rage for exotic exploration. Bars would advertise new "shows" and have underemployed day workers hand out tokens. Tokens would work the peep shows, and, lured to the tavern, the viewer would buy drinks.

By the time of the Great Depression, movies were commonplace and, through market pressure, cheap. It was hard for a penny peep show to compete with a nickel or dime movie. One result of such competition was a tendency to show increasingly risqué content, but what happened more regularly was that peep shows failed at the competition. By the 1960s or so, the peep show machines that still existed were largely curiosities. The sexual revolution stimulated two related but separate updates of the peep show idea.

At first, small booths with a lock, a seat, and a roll of paper towels were made available for individual viewing of 8mm or 16mm stag loops or for access to a usually circular "stage" with living performers. Innovation was rapid and, with the development of cheap video cameras, duplicators, and players—or, in live-action settings, willing responses to the consumer's varied tastes—peep shows became an enormously profitable industry. In the privacy of the secure booth, patrons could view recorded pornography while sitting passively or masturbating, as they preferred. Peep shows featuring live-performance booths functioned in several ways, but generally once the patron locked the entry/exit door, feeding tokens or coins to a slot dropped and kept lowered a partition at the front. Depending on the particular business, patrons could tip fully or partially nude "models" to act out their directions and requests. In some cases the patron could fondle the performers.

As was the case throughout the history of these secure settings for one or two people, it was commonplace for patrons to hire a loitering sex professional to enter the booth and carry out this or that commercial sexual transaction. Because it was far easier for most regions to regulate prostitution than to regulate the vague, poorly defined activity of viewing live or filmed sexual display, this activity was carefully controlled by the management.

DIGITAL PEEP SHOWS

At the end of the twentieth century, widespread downtown cleanup campaigns; the explosive growth in availability of inexpensive, technically high-quality pornographic videos and appropriate home viewing units; and a growing fear of crime combined to make the traditional peep show businesses less profitable. Much investment capital was wooed elsewhere. Occasional peep show settings continue to exist, because of nostalgia or novelty. In addition, some peep show businesses have evolved to accommodate particular customer wishes, such as conversation. In the meantime, interactive websites have been quick to embrace the proliferation of home computers and inexpensive video telecommunication to create innovative responses to the demand for peep-show-like entertainment.

Dr. Jon Griffin Donlon

SEE ALSO: *Dance Halls; The Great Depression; The Internet; Pornography; Sexual Revolution; Strip Joints/Striptease.*

BIBLIOGRAPHY

Balzer, Richard. *Peepshows: A Visual History.* New York: Harry N. Abrams, 1998.

Pee-wee's Playhouse

Despite the taint of scandal, *Pee-wee's Playhouse*, a live-action Saturday morning children's television show, stands as one of the creative examples of successful children's programming. First airing in 1986, the show starred actor and stand-up comedian Paul Reubens as Pee-wee Herman and featured the multicultural playhouse gang, talking puppets, a robot, and occasional celebrity guests. Despite its time slot, *Pee-wee's Playhouse* appealed to adults as well as to their children, as Pee-wee led viewers through inventive educational activities that did not condescend to young audiences and held enough double entendres to keep adults laughing.

When Reubens was arrested in the summer of 1991 on an indecent exposure charge, CBS pulled the five remaining episodes from its schedule and canceled the series entirely. The scandal and CBS's subsequent action sparked intense public debate and nearly ruined the actor's career. As resilient as his alter ego, however, Reubens refused to give up on the idea of reviving Pee-wee, and in 2010 he premiered *The Pee-wee Herman Show*, with many of Pee-wee's playhouse friends, onstage in Los Angeles and New York.

Pee-Wee's Playhouse. *Paul Reubens as Pee-Wee Herman poses on his beloved bike in a scene from* Pee-Wee's Playhouse *in 1986.* CBS PHOTO ARCHIVE/CONTRIBUTOR/GETTY IMAGES.

PEE-WEE IS BORN

Reubens conceived of his Pee-wee character at the Groundlings Theater in Los Angeles in 1980 and introduced him to audiences in a sketch that became the basis for the 1981 HBO special *The Pee-wee Herman Show.* The actor claims he took the first name from a toy harmonica with the word *Pee Wee* printed on its side, while the character's last name was borrowed from a disliked childhood acquaintance. Audiences appreciated Pee-wee's obnoxious attitude and silly humor.

In 1985 Reubens starred in the summer film *Pee-wee's Big Adventure.* The movie cost about $6 million to make and earned nearly $50 million, becoming a sleeper summer hit. The main character, Pee-wee Herman, was a hyperactive man dressed like a boy in a tight-fitting, gray, glen plaid suit with a perky red bow tie. Although Reubens always maintained in interviews that Pee-wee was male, some critics thought that Pee-wee's effeminate body language and mincing manner made the character's gender, not to mention his sexuality, ambivalent at best.

DEVELOPMENT OF TELEVISION SHOW

CBS executives liked the character so much that they invited Reubens to develop a children's television show based on Pee-wee Herman. While the network laid down some ground rules (no toilet paper sticking to Pee-wee's shoe as he emerged from the playhouse bathroom, for instance), Reubens basically had carte blanche in developing *Pee-wee's Playhouse.* Compared to the other Saturday morning television shows, *Pee-wee's Playhouse*—part *Captain Kangaroo* and part sophisticated performance art—was a breath of fresh, wacky air. Whereas *Sesame Street* was the undisputed leader in children's programming for its seamless blend of education and puppet magic, *Pee-wee's Playhouse* stood out as a smart, creative show among the formulaic animation typically pitched to smaller viewers on weekend mornings, and its sharply ironic goofiness attracted adult viewers as well.

From the show's carnivalesque score written by former Devo member Mark Mothersbaugh to its visually stimulating set design that mixed vintage decor with plastic toys, *Pee-wee's Playhouse* distinguished itself through sheer difference. This difference was essential to the message that Reubens wanted his character and the show to project to kids. "I'm just trying to illustrate that it's okay to be different—not that it's good, not that it's bad, but that it's all right. I'm trying to tell kids to have a good time and to encourage them to be creative and to question things," Reubens told an interviewer in *Rolling Stone* during the program's first season.

SHOW TECHNIQUES AND THEMES

Gary Panter's art direction and the program's title design and sound mixing were all recognized with Emmy Awards throughout the program's five-year run. At a time when many children's shows were experimenting with new effects in computer animation, *Pee-wee's Playhouse* was using seemingly outdated techniques such as stop-motion photography to set itself apart. The program also made use of Claymation designed by Aardman Animations in Bristol, England, the company that brought to life the beloved Wallace and Gromit characters.

Each episode of *Pee-wee's Playhouse* began with a wild ride through its opening graphics accompanied by a zany theme song. Viewers would learn the day's secret word and were instructed to "scream real loud" every time a character on the show said the word, which was given to Pee-wee by his robot friend, Conky. Although the episodes were guided by Pee-wee's childlike stream of consciousness, each show revolved around a loosely structured narrative dilemma, such as Pee-wee's winning a Hawaiian dinner for two and having to decide which playhouse friend to invite along. The plots embodied basic values such as loyalty, honesty, and sharing. Helping Pee-wee to have fun and negotiate personal dilemmas were show regulars such as the glamorous Miss Yvonne (Lynne Stewart), curmudgeonly Kap'n Karl (Phil Hartman), sneaky neighbor Mrs. Steve (Shirley Stoler), and amiable Cowboy Curtis (Laurence Fishburne).

Although many critics faltered in trying to categorize *Pee-wee's Playhouse,* all agreed that its fast pace and frenetic energy made it a natural for children, whose nonlinear thought patterns and short attention spans were matched by Pee-wee's near-manic behavior. Critic Jack Barth described the program's quick-moving visuals in a 1986 article in *Film Comment* as "a fast-paced technologically updated Ernie Kovacs in color." Pee-wee's snarky innocence was also a large part of the show's appeal, and it was Pee-wee, not Reubens, who received a star on the Hollywood Walk of Fame and an invitation to host *Saturday Night Live.*

SCANDAL ERUPTS

Given its action-packed innovation, *Pee-wee's Playhouse* was an exhausting show to produce, and by 1989 Reubens decided not to renew his contract with CBS. Instead, he spent the next year working overtime to produce two years' worth of episodes so that he could fulfill his contract to the network and retire the character for good. In the summer of 1991, having completed production on the final episodes, Reubens was visiting family in Sarasota, Florida, when he was arrested in an adult theater for indecent exposure, touching off a media scandal. CBS abruptly canceled the remaining episodes of *Pee-wee's Playhouse,* and Reubens spent months trying to resuscitate his career while parents tried to explain to their children what had happened to their favorite television character.

Reubens's career did continue, although not with the same prescandal promise of success. A skilled character actor, he took roles in films such as *Batman Returns* and *Buffy the Vampire Slayer* (both 1992), as well as on television shows such as the CBS sitcom *Murphy Brown,* on which he had recurring role from 1995 to 1997.

Though episodes of *Pee-wee's Playhouse* had been packaged as a set and released for home video rental in the early 1990s and the Fox Family Channel began rerunning the show in the fall of 1998, it was almost twenty years before the memory of scandal had dimmed enough for Reubens to revive Pee-wee. During that time the bow-tied nerd had only appeared once—on the 2007 Spike TV's *Guys Choice* awards show. In 2010 Pee-wee made another appearance on *The Jay Leno Show,* this time publicizing his new *Pee-wee Herman Show* at Club Nokia in Los Angeles. The show, a revival of the playhouse world, including Chairry, Clocky, Mr. Window, and the rest of the gang, played successfully in Los Angeles and on Broadway before being made into a TV movie in 2011.

Alison Macor

SEE ALSO: *Batman; Broadway;* Buffy the Vampire Slayer*;* Captain Kangaroo*; Devo; Emmy Awards; Hollywood; Kovacs,*

Ernie; Murphy Brown*;* Rolling Stone*; Saturday Morning Cartoons;* Saturday Night Live*;* Sesame Street*; Sex Scandals; Sitcom; Stand-up Comedy; Television.*

BIBLIOGRAPHY

Barth, Jack. "Pee-wee TV." *Film Comment* 22, no. 6 (1986): 78–79.

Carpenter, Cassie. "Playhouse Bound." *Back Stage*, January 14, 2010, 8.

Doty, Alexander. "The Sissy Boy, the Fat Ladies, and the Dykes: Queerness and/as Gender in Pee-wee's World." In *Male Trouble*, ed. Constance Penley and Sharon Willis. Minneapolis: University of Minnesota Press, 1993.

Gaines, Caseen. *Inside "Pee-wee's Playhouse": The Untold, Unauthorized, and Unpredictable Story of a Pop Phenomenon.* Toronto: ECW, 2011.

Gertler, T. "The Pee-wee Perplex." *Rolling Stone*, February 12, 1987, 36–40.

Jenkins, Henry. "Going Bonkers!: Children, Play, and Pee-wee." In *Male Trouble*, ed. Constance Penley and Sharon Willis. Minneapolis: University of Minnesota Press, 1993.

McNeil, Alex. "Pee-wee's Playhouse." In *Total Television: The Comprehensive Guide to Programming from 1948 to the Present.* New York: Penguin Books, 1996.

Wilkinson, Peter. "Who Killed Pee-wee Herman?" *Rolling Stone*, October 3, 1991, 36–42.

Pelé *(1940–)*

Pelé, born Edson Arantes do Nascimento on October 23, 1940, in a small village in the Brazilian state of Minas Gerais, is recognized as the greatest, and most popular, soccer player the world has ever seen. Pelé played professional soccer for Santos Football Club in Brazil from 1956 to 1974. Between 1958 and 1970 he played in four World Cup finals, distinguishing himself as the only person to have won three World Cups as a player and scoring an astonishing 1,281 goals in 1,363 professional games. In April 1975 the New York Cosmos of the North American Soccer League signed Pelé in an attempt to popularize the sport in the United States. Although thousands came to see him play in New York, only a minority of the American public saw or appreciated his unique skills.

Pelé retired from soccer in 1977 and was chosen Athlete of the Century by the International Olympic Committee in 1999 and Soccer Player of the Century by the governing body of world soccer, the Federation Internationale de Football Associations (FIFA), in 2000. In his retirement Pelé has acted as an ambassador for the United Nations and for UNICEF.

John F. Lyons

SEE ALSO: *Leisure Time; Soccer; Sports Heroes; World Cup.*

BIBLIOGRAPHY

Murray, Bill. *Football: A History of the World Game.* London: Scholar Press, 1994.

Pelé. *Pelé: The Autobiography.* London: Simon & Schuster, 2006.

"Pelé (Edson Arantes do Nascimento): The King of Football." Federation Internationale de Football Associations. Accessed March 2012. Available from www.fifa.com/classicfootball/players/player=63869/index.html

Penn, Irving *(1917–2009)*

Irving Penn began his photographic career with *Vogue* magazine in 1943. Rejecting the ornate, theatrical style of fashion photography that dominated the market at the time, he produced simple, powerful images that revolutionized the discipline. Penn's subsequent work falls into a variety of categories: fashion, portraits, still lifes, nudes, travel photos, ethnographic studies, and street photography. In his advertising work, his straightforward manner of focusing on the subject while stripping away superfluous elements is especially apparent, as in the photos he took for a series of product-centered Clinique advertisements.

Penn died in his New York City home on October 7, 2009, but his photographs—especially his portraits of influential individuals, including actors, artists, politicians, and writers—continue to serve as a record of cultural, economic, and political trends during his life.

Jennifer Jankauskas

SEE ALSO: *Advertising;* Vogue.

BIBLIOGRAPHY

Penn, Irving. *Passage: A Work Record.* New York: Alfred A. Knopf, 1991.

Westerbeck, Colin, ed. *Irving Penn, A Career in Photography.* Chicago: Art Institute of Chicago and Bulfinch Press/Little, Brown, 1997.

Penthouse

Penthouse, billed as "the international magazine for men," became a household name along with its main competitor, Hugh Hefner's *Playboy*, during the sexual revolution in the 1960s and 1970s. Following the 1953 debut of *Playboy*, Bob Guccione rightly sensed that men might prefer to see a bit more "flesh" than was being offered in Hefner's magazine. In 1965 Guccione launched the London-based *Penthouse*, which featured slightly racier pictorials as well as investigative stories.

BUILDING THE *PENTHOUSE* EMPIRE

In 1969 *Penthouse* was moved to the United States, where it expanded into a publishing dynasty that included *Forum* (launched in 1975), *Penthouse Letters* (1981), and several non-erotic ventures, such as *Omni*, *Compute* (1979), and *Longevity* (1989). Although *Penthouse* (a subsidiary of General Media Publishing) continued to grow and diversify over the next three decades, the company remained privately owned by Guccione and his companion, Kathy Keeton. It was something of a mom-and-pop operation that was staffed by several members of Guccione's family. Working from the nine-story mansion he shared with Keeton on Manhattan's Upper East Side, Guccione became known for his gold chains and lavish lifestyle.

Guccione's enterprise experienced anything but smooth sailing during the 1980s. Throughout the Ronald Reagan era,

Penthouse was ravaged by attacks from Christian-based groups such as the National Federation for Decency. One of the more damaging campaigns came in 1986, when United States Attorney General Edwin Meese and the eleven-member Commission on Pornography sought to intimidate retailers by publishing a blacklist of pornography distributors. Sending its warning on Justice Department stationery, the commission advised several large booksellers and retail chains that they would be named. Bowing to the pressure, Southland Corporation, the parent company of 7-Eleven convenience stores, announced that it would no longer sell either *Penthouse* or *Playboy* in its 4,500 outlets. By the end of the campaign, some 20,000 retail and convenience stores had been dissuaded from carrying the adult titles.

Penthouse retaliated, along with *Playboy* and the American Booksellers Association, by filing a lawsuit against the commission that charged it with violating the First Amendment. Although a federal district court eventually forced the commission to retract its letter, the plaintiffs were denied financial relief. (In a strange footnote, Meese was later reported to have said that he did not consider either *Playboy* or *Penthouse* to be obscene.)

Penthouse's legal battles throughout the 1980s and 1990s cost it millions of dollars, but another problem developed that was even more threatening to the magazine: videocassette distributors, who boasted that some 10 percent of their sales were in the category of erotica. "People are simply reading less," noted Guccione. "They're into other media."

A LONG, STEADY DECLINE

Starting in the 1980s, *Penthouse* experienced a steady decline in circulation, never again reaching its high of 4.7 million readers in 1979. By 1987 the magazine's circulation had fallen to three million; by 1995 it was just over one million. That same year, the magazine lost money for the first time in its history. *Playboy*'s numbers were also steadily declining, though they remained slightly higher than *Penthouse*'s.

To recoup profits, Guccione's team experimented with a range of strategies, including a cover story on celibacy as "the new hot lifestyle." It also launched three new ventures in the 1980s: *Spin*, a music magazine to be run by Bob Guccione Jr.; *New Look*, which survived less than six months; and the unexpected *Nuclear, Biological and Chemical Defense Technology*, which was geared toward defense industry personnel.

Penthouse found itself under First Amendment siege again in 1990, this time by the American Family Association, a Christian group that planned to picket 400 Waldenbooks and Kmart stores for carrying *Penthouse* and *Playboy*. In response to the threat, Ed Morrow, president of the American Booksellers Association, and Harry Hoffman, president and CEO of Waldenbooks, took out advertising space in twenty-eight daily papers in which readers were asked to respond by "voting" for freedom of expression. The campaign was a success: Within seven days, more than 50,000 Americans returned ballots in support of First Amendment rights. In contrast, fewer than 100 picketers showed up for the American Family Association's planned protests.

In 1992 *Penthouse* faced yet another challenge, from the United States Navy, which found the distribution and sale of adult magazines on naval bases to be inconsistent with rules and regulations concerning sexual harassment and human dignity. Guccione responded rhetorically, asking, "How do you put a man in uniform, teach him to kill, expose him to images of war and all sorts of inhumanity, and in the same breath tell him he is not sanctioned to buy a magazine that shows people making love?" This, however, was a battle that *Penthouse* would lose. In 1996 President Bill Clinton signed the Military Honor and Decency Act, which states that "the Secretary of Defense may not permit the sale or rental of sexually explicit material on property under the jurisdiction of the Department of Defense." Although Guccione won an appeal , the decision was overturned in a 1998 Supreme Court ruling that held that a military base is not a public forum.

TRYING TO HANG ON

So as not to be left behind in the technology age, *Penthouse* went online in 1995 and quickly became one of the twenty-five most frequently visited websites. The magazine also found something of a new niche in the early 1990s with unauthorized celebrity sex photos. During this period, it won court battles to publish explicit photos of Tonya Harding (sold to the magazine by her ex-husband, Jeff Gillooly), Paula Jones (also obtained from a former boyfriend), and Pamela Anderson Lee and her husband Tommy Lee.

In 1995 *Penthouse* received additional publicity from an unlikely source when the Unabomber (later revealed to be Theodore Kaczynski) named the magazine as his third choice—after the *New York Times* and *Washington Post*—for publication of his manuscript advocating an antitechnology revolution. Guccione offered the terrorist—who had been linked to sixteen bombings since 1978—an unedited monthly column in return for his agreement not to strike again. The offer was nullified, of course, by Kaczynski's subsequent capture in 1996.

Competitive forces continued to eat away at *Penthouse*'s readership, and in August 2003 the magazine filed for bankruptcy. That same year, Guccione was forced to resign. In 2010 Guccione died at age seventy-nine. Peter Bloch, who became *Penthouse*'s editor in 1983, once claimed that Guccione's publication, unlike *Playboy*, had never been ashamed to portray explicit sexuality in its pages. Indeed, *Penthouse* broke barriers, said Bloch, by being "the first to show full frontal nudity." The magazine ventured a step further into carnality in 1997, announcing that it would no longer shy away from depicting copulation. And in January 2011 *Penthouse* gave new ammunition to conservative crusaders by launching a 3-D pornography channel.

Kristal Brent Zook

SEE ALSO: *Hefner, Hugh;* Playboy*; Pornography; Sex Scandals; Sexual Revolution.*

BIBLIOGRAPHY

Flora, Paul. *Penthouse.* New York: Abrams, 1978.

Reese, Diane. "Penthouse: When Sex Doesn't Sell." *Folio,* January 1987.

Slade, Joseph W. *Pornography and Sexual Representation: A Reference Guide.* Vol. 3. Westport, CT: Greenwood, 2000.

The Wonderful World of Penthouse Sex: Radical Sex in the Establishment. New York: Penthouse Press, 1975.

People

When Time Inc. launched *People* magazine in 1974, the leading afternoon talk show, *Donahue*, was bringing considered debate about important issues into the nation's living rooms, and the leading national daily newspaper, the *Wall Street Journal*, was delivering serious news directly to the nation's doorsteps. *People* defined the personality-driven style that paved the way for confessional, emotional—often exhibitionistic—television talk shows such as *The Oprah Winfrey Show* in the 1980s and, later, the *Jerry Springer Show*. *People*'s reliance on images rather than insightful text anticipated *USA Today*'s visual, less wordy approach to news in the 1980s and subsequent ascendance to the top position among daily newspapers in the United States. Striving to capture the intimate and everyday lives of celebrities and the occasionally astonishing lives of everyday people, *People* further disintegrated the line between entertainment and news, bringing the personal into the public space.

LAUNCH

People focused on what made public figures seem more like regular people and what made regular people noteworthy. Instead of reporting the great public triumphs of public figures, the magazine covered common personal problems such as divorce or addiction, along with stories of how individuals overcame their woes to attain their oft-reported triumphs. This novel formula was described as "extraordinary people doing ordinary things and ordinary people doing extraordinary things." *People*'s appearance on the media landscape was consistent with changes in the way Americans had begun to perceive public figures. This new way of recording everyday people's lives was very much in line with what Leo Braudy, the author of *The Frenzy of Renown: Fame and Its History*, describes as a new social order, in which the media places the spotlight on how people overcome their problems.

Years before *People*, fanzines had been trading in gossip and intimate stories about celebrities, relating their favorite recipes, likes and dislikes, or how they relaxed at home. And tabloids such as the *National Enquirer* had long reported on celebrity gossip and the freakish events that happened to everyday people. But fanzines and tabloids were not published by Time Inc., a respected journalistic institution. *People* was designed, graphically and editorially, to look conventional, respectable, and mainstream. Whereas the tabloids and fanzines historically made no pretenses of "respectability," *People* treated the reporting of intimate information about stars and everyday people as a perfectly legitimate undertaking. The magazine also expanded the boundaries of celebrity beyond the movie, television, and music stars of the fanzines and the freaks of the tabloids to include religious leaders, business people, fashion designers, models, athletes, and politicians.

People drew on the conventions of television, adopting its visual treatment to news and working within strict constraints of space. By the 1970s news was being treated more and more as entertainment, as dramatized in the 1976 film *Network*. This was evidenced by the signing of Barbara Walters as an *ABC Nightly News* coanchor for a record-setting $1 million. *People* treated news as another branch of entertainment, but it also reported celebrity gossip and stories as valid news. *Life* had already shown that a magazine could be a collection of pictures narrated by text. However, where traditional print journalism allowed one or more images to stand alone to tell a dramatic story, *People* adopted television's visual language, displaying a blizzard of images, none standing dramatically alone.

FINDING A NICHE

The first national weekly magazine to be launched since *Sports Illustrated* twenty years earlier, *People* became profitable within eighteen months. However, the news establishment was not as receptive as the average consumer. Said William Safire in the *New York Times*, "*People* fails on the tawdry terms it has chosen." Tom Donnelly of the *Washington Post* declared, "It will tax none but the shortest attention spans and it is so undemanding that it can be read while the TV commercials are on. . . . It is the reading equivalent of those 'convenience foods.'" *People* was represented no better in popular culture. To indicate that a character in the movie *The Big Chill* had completely sold out his 1960s idealism, he is shown lamenting his life as a writer for *People*, where, he complains, the length of his articles are constrained by the length of time readers spend in the bathroom.

Initially, the magazine was not sold by subscription and the cover was crucial in generating copy sales. Editor Richard Solley developed a set of rules for magazine covers based on experience with sales figures:

Young is better than old.

Pretty is better than ugly.

Rich is better than poor.

TV is better than music.

Music is better than movies.

Movies are better than sports.

Anything is better than politics.

And nothing is better than the celebrity dead.

Experience proved that covers showing women sold more copies than did those with men. In the magazine's first twenty-five years, Princess Diana, Elizabeth Taylor, Sarah Ferguson, John Travolta, and Madonna were among the most frequent cover subjects. Tribute issues always boosted sales, and best-selling covers included tributes to John Lennon, Princess Grace of Monaco, and Princess Diana, soon after their deaths.

People examined anything and everything through the lens of personalities. Every story was anchored to a person or group of people and generally concerned the more intimate details of their lives. This approach of covering the personality more than the event began to filter into other media properties. This was reflected in the rise of "softer" shows such as *The Oprah Winfrey Show* and in the launch of *USA Today*. While *People* was wielding its influence on the field of publishing, Rupert Murdoch extended his reach from Europe to the United States and launched the supermarket tabloid, leading to a proliferation of tabloid shows such as *A Current Affair*. Other television shows of the 1980s and 1990s, including *Entertainment Tonight* and *Access Hollywood*, helped to further blur the line between news and entertainment.

STAYING POWER

A number of magazines unabashedly imitated *People*, including *Us*. *People* changed the mainstream, "serious" media, and in the 1980s and 1990s most newspapers developed a "style" or "people" section to report on celebrity news and human interest.

These newspapers became more and more inclined to report on rumor, stars, and scandal in their news sections. Newsweeklies such as *Time* and *Newsweek* also increased their coverage of celebrities and personalities. When, in 1997, sportscaster Marv Albert pled guilty to minor sex crimes committed in private, off the job, the respected paper of record, the *New York Times*, reported it as front-page news.

The influence of *People* stretches to the dozens of new outlets for celebrity gossip and intimate confession in its wake. It continues to affect the legitimization of personality journalism in the mainstream press and the introduction of the intimate and personal into the public realm. *People* is the emblem of American celebrity culture and its public intimacy.

By 1999 *People* had become Time Inc.'s biggest moneymaker. The magazine celebrated itself that same year with a 340-page twenty-fifth anniversary issue. By that time *People* was selling 3.6 million copies a week and generating $626 million in annual advertising revenues. In the twenty-first century, its readership includes a wide segment of the American population, though the majority of its readers are females between the ages of eighteen and thirty-four (38 percent). The magazine also has considerable appeal for females aged forty-five to fifty-nine (28 percent), and editors sometimes have to tread a fine line in choosing covers that appeal to both groups. Because covers attract casual buyers and catch eyes at supermarkets and newsstands, they continue to be the most important factor in selling the magazine.

In 2009 the issue that outsold every other was the January 23 issue celebrating the inauguration of Barack Obama. Ironically, the second best seller was the bikini-clad photograph of Valerie Bertinelli, who had recently lost 50 pounds. Bertinelli, who as of 2012 plays Melanie Moretti in *Hot in Cleveland*, is best known for her role as teenager Barbara Cooper in *One Day at a Time* (1975–1984). Princess Diana, who was known as "the People's Princess," still holds the record for appearing on the most covers of *People* (fifty-seven).

Steven Kotok

SEE ALSO: *Advertising; Albert, Marv; Celebrity; Celebrity Couples; Confession Magazines; Daytime Talk Shows; Diana, Princess of Wales; Divorce; Donahue, Phil;* Entertainment Tonight*; Fan Magazines; Lennon, John;* Life*; Madonna; Movie Stars;* The National Enquirer*; The* New York Times*;* Newsweek*; Obama, Barack;* One Day at a Time*; Pulp Magazines;* Sports Illustrated*; Springer, Jerry; Tabloid Television; Tabloids; Taylor, Elizabeth; Television; Travolta, John;* USA Today*; The* Wall Street Journal*; Walters, Barbara; The* Washington Post*; Winfrey, Oprah.*

BIBLIOGRAPHY

Braudy, Leo. *The Frenzy of Renown: Fame and Its History*. New York: Oxford University Press, 1986.

Hamblin, Dora Jane. *That Was the Life: The Upstairs Downstairs behind-the-Doors Story of America's Favorite Magazine*. New York: W. W. Norton, 1977.

Kessler, Judy. *Inside "People": The Stories behind the Stories*. New York: Villard Books, 1994.

Krajicek, David J. *Scooped!: Media Miss Real Story on Crime While Chasing Sex, Sleaze, and Celebrities*. New York: Columbia University Press, 1998.

"*People* Magazine at 25: It's a Certified Cash Cow." *Sarasota Herald Tribune*, March 6, 1999.

Schickel, Richard. *Intimate Strangers: The Culture of Celebrity*. Garden City, NJ: Doubleday, 1985.

Stolley, Richard B, ed. *"People Weekly" Celebrates People: The Best of 20 Unforgettable Years*. New York: People Weekly Books, 1994.

Winerip, Michael. "*People* Magazine Still Has a Bikini Body." *New York Times*, May 24, 2009.

The Peppermint Lounge

The Peppermint Lounge, or the "Pep," a midtown biker bar on West 45th Street between Sixth and Seventh avenues in New York City, was established in 1958. It was the site where rock and roll and youth culture crossed generational and social boundaries.

A brief mention by American gossip columnist Cholly Knickerbocker (Igor Cassini) in September 1961 in the *Journal-American* made the tiny club a mecca for society types and celebrities. Judy Garland, Noel Coward, Elsa Maxwell, Greta Garbo, and the Duke and Duchess of Bedford mingled with a young crowd, many of them New Jerseyites. They twisted to the music of the house band, Joey Dee and the Starliters, who shortly thereafter had a number one record with *Peppermint Twist–Part I* and starred in a movie, *Hey, Let's Twist!*. Extensive media coverage reignited the twist dance craze and made it an international phenomenon.

Louis Scheeder

SEE ALSO: *Garbo, Greta; Garland, Judy; Rock and Roll.*

BIBLIOGRAPHY

Carpozi, George. *Let's Twist!*. New York: Pyramid Books, 1962.

Dawson, Jim. *The Twist: The Story of the Song and Dance That Changed the World*. Boston: Faber & Faber, 1995.

Lucchese, John A. *Joey Dee and the Story of the Twist*. New York: MacFadden, 1962.

Pepsi-Cola

The beverage that evolved into Pepsi-Cola originated in the early 1890s in the North Carolina drugstore of Caleb Bradham. Patterned after other soft drinks and patent medicines of the time, the concoction was initially known as "Brad's Drink." In 1893 the name of the drink was changed to Pepsi-Cola, and a few years later the Pepsi-Cola company was formed. Like industry leader Coca-Cola, the drink was largely made of sugar and water. Combining the sugar and water with other oils and extracts unique to Pepsi gave it a citrusy flavor and aroma.

Unlike Coca-Cola, Pepsi did not find success quickly. Instead, the beverage struggled to challenge Coca-Cola for dominance in the nearly century-long "Cola War." Through much of its history Pepsi often found itself playing the role of David to Coca-Cola's Goliath. In the early years of the twentieth century, however, it did not appear as if the beverage would be around long enough to challenge anyone.

STRUGGLING FOR SUCCESS

Through a combination of poor business decisions, limited distribution, and less than insightful marketing, Pepsi spent many of its early years on the fringes of the soft drink industry. By the early 1930s the company that manufactured the beverage had gone bankrupt twice, and rights to manufacture the drink were held by a man who was employed in the candy industry. Charles Guth of Loft Incorporated, attracted to Pepsi only after Coca-Cola refused to grant price concessions on the sale of Coke in his drugstores, resurrected the beverage in 1932. Guth's early fortunes with Pepsi were no better than those of his predecessors, and he was nearly forced into bankruptcy. At one point Guth attempted to sell the rights of Pepsi to Coca-Cola. Assuming that the drink would soon disappear of its own accord, Coke officials refused, allowing Guth—to their lasting regret—to continue to manufacture the drink.

Desperate for any means to sell Pepsi, Guth was persuaded to sell the drink in used beer bottles that were 12 ounces in size. Because the bottle was twice the size of the normal 6-ounce soft drink, he marketed Pepsi at ten cents per bottle, twice the price of the 6-ounce beverage. Sales of the new, larger Pepsi continued to lag, and the drink's future appeared dim—until Guth hit upon a marketing scheme that forever changed the face of the soft drink industry. In a move that spoke more of desperation than marketing savvy, Guth decided to sell the 12-ounce Pepsi for just five cents per bottle. In Depression-era America, the "Twice as Much for a Nickel Too" campaign was a success. Within six months of the start of the marketing campaign, sales of Pepsi had grown tremendously, and it was soon on its way to prosperity. However, due to some extralegal measures he had used to acquire Pepsi-Cola, Guth was forced out of the company and its future.

ADVERTISING STRATEGIES

Despite its growing success, Pepsi manufacturers did not have the advertising capital of industry leader Coca-Cola. Therefore, they were forced to invest in nontraditional sources of advertising. The company seized upon the new medium of radio, and the attributes of Pepsi were soon being hailed in the nation's first musical jingle. The Pepsi jingle not only spurred interest in the drink, but it also revolutionized radio advertisements. Pepsi was also promoted through art shows, skywriting, and comic strips. Sales of Pepsi continued to grow until limitations on the drink's ingredients were imposed during World War II.

During World War II sales of Pepsi, although substantial, paled in comparison to those of Coca-Cola. After the war ended, Pepsi's identification with youth, labor, and minorities—as well as being seen as the "poor man's drink"—limited the drink's mass appeal. The identification with value that had served Pepsi well during the Depression and war years was less suited for the growing middle class that was looking for prosperity and material comforts. Accordingly, Pepsi's advertising began to target new American suburban markets and stress its connection to modernity and glamour. Whereas Coke was marketed as a product of nostalgia, Pepsi highlighted its appropriateness for the future. In doing so, its advertising largely identified it as a youth product.

Slogans such as "Now it's Pepsi for those who think young," and "Come Alive, You're in the Pepsi Generation," made Pepsi appealing to the youth market. In the 1960s Pepsi began to cement its reputation as the drink for the younger market. It consistently targeted young people, labeling them the "Pepsi Generation," a slogan that would go beyond advertising into popular jargon. In the 1980s social critics labeled eighteen- to thirty-year-olds as "Generation X" as well as the "Pepsi Generation."

Since the 1960s Pepsi has promoted itself as the drink of both the present and the future. Even though many industry observers claimed that the taste of Pepsi caused Coke to change its formula, Pepsi still does not challenge the status of Coke. Though it has been the underdog to Coca-Cola throughout the century, its existence as an alternative to Coke has helped fuel the "Cola War," to the delight of consumers.

THE NEXT GENERATION

The early twenty-first century has failed to build upon Pepsi's successes of the latter half of the twentieth century. The new millennium ushered in a period of management problems and failed marketing strategies that led some of its critics to assert that the company had lost its direction. A good deal of the negative publicity focused on design guru Peter Arnell's failed redesign of Pepsi-Cola product Tropicana orange juice, leading the company to pull the new packaging after a mere seven weeks. In 2010 Pepsi bowed out of advertising at the Super Bowl, choosing to concentrate on its Refresh Project, which designated $20 million to innovative consumers. Unfortunately, the project has been marred by charges of cheating and accusations that Pepsi shuts out competition for grant money by channeling grants to major nonprofits. A major blow came in 2011, when, for the first time in decades, Pepsi dropped out of the number two spot in the soft drink industry, with Diet Coke claiming the coveted spot.

Jason Chambers

SEE ALSO: *Advertising; Coca-Cola; Consumerism; The Great Depression; Radio; World War II.*

BIBLIOGRAPHY

Capparell, Stephanie. *The Real Pepsi Challenge: The Inspirational Story of Breaking the Color Barrier in American Business.* New York: The Free Press, 2007.

Dietz, Lawrence. *Soda Pop: The History, Advertising, Art, and Memorabilia of Soft Drinks in America.* New York: Simon & Schuster, 1973.

Enrico, Roger, and Jesse Kornbluth. *The Other Guy Blinked: How Pepsi Won the Cola Wars.* New York: Bantam, 1986.

Haig, Matt. *Brand Failures.* Sterling, VA: Kogan Page Limited, 2003.

Louis, J. C., and Harvey Z. Yazijian. *The Cola Wars.* New York: Everest House, 1980.

Martin, Milward. *Twelve Full Ounces.* New York: Holt, Rinehart, and Winston, 1962.

Stoddard, Bob. *Pepsi: 100 Years.* Los Angeles: General Publishing Group, 1997.

Zmuda, Natalie. "How Pepsi Blinked, Fell Behind Diet Coke." *Advertising Age*, March 21, 2011.

Percy Jackson

Percy Jackson is the main character in Rick Riordan's best-selling middle-grade fantasy series *Percy Jackson and the*

Olympians. First introduced in *The Lightning Thief* (2005), Percy is a good-natured sixth grader who has attention deficit hyperactivity disorder (ADHD), dyslexia, and a knack for inadvertently causing trouble. Within a few chapters, he has been attacked by monsters, has gotten kicked out of yet another school, and has learned that the father he has never met is the Greek god Poseidon. Desperate to keep him safe, Percy's mother brings him to Camp Half-Blood, a sleepaway camp, safe space, and training ground for demigods.

The Lightning Thief quickly found an enthusiastic audience. Readers desperate for the next book in J. K. Rowling's Harry Potter series found a similarly fast-paced and action-oriented plot; a relatable underdog protagonist; and themes exploring the strength of friendship and love in relation to anger, jealousy, and a lust for power. Many readers found Riordan's portrayal of ADHD and dyslexia refreshing, as both are common and adaptive among demigods in his novels: ADHD makes them better fighters, and dyslexia makes it easier for them to read ancient Greek.

Riordan's characters are all from single-parent or blended families, and his take on absentee parents is realistic while avoiding melodrama—something largely and oddly missing from popular literature for this age group in an era in which divorce is commonplace. Adults in general are presented as multidimensional characters dealing with their own struggles—one of the reasons the series has so many adult fans. The books are also infused with humor, much of which comes from Percy himself, who narrates the novels in a voice that is wry, sometimes overconfident, sometimes unsure, and always winning.

Subsequent books in the series include *The Sea of Monsters* (2006), *The Titan's Curse* (2007), *The Battle of the Labyrinth* (2008), and *The Last Olympian* (2009). The publication of each volume became a successively larger event, and by 2010 fifteen million copies of books in the series were in print. Percy grows a year older as he tackles the quests in each book, and his larger mission becomes protecting himself and his fellow demigods while attempting to save the world from Kronos, the once-vanquished father of Zeus, who is working his way back to power, intent on destroying Western civilization. Percy is joined in his quest by his best friend, Grover, a satyr with a fondness for coffee, and by antagonist-turned-love-interest Annabeth, a daughter of Athena. Percy's other allies and foes include Chiron; Medusa; Hera; Dionysus; and his half-brother, a Cyclops named Tyson.

The success of the Percy Jackson books has made author Rick Riordan something of a celebrity. A former middle-school teacher and a father, he began writing the stories to amuse a son who struggled with reading but loved the Greek myths. Books in the series have been adapted into audiobooks and translated into multiple languages. The year 2010 saw the release of a graphic novel adaptation of *The Lightning Thief* as well as a film version directed and produced by Chris Columbus. Spin-off books include *The Demigod Files* (2009) and *The Ultimate Guide* (2010).

In 2010 Riordan published the first of the *Kane Chronicles*, a middle-grade fantasy series focused on Egyptian mythology, and that same year he published the first in his *Heroes of Olympus* series, which extends the world of Percy Jackson with a new generation of demigods. Riordan has also been a driving force behind Scholastic's popular *39 Clues* series. With a strong backlist, multiple adaptations, and several new best-selling series, he is poised to remain a presence in the middle-grade fiction market for years to come.

Like the Harry Potter series, *Percy Jackson and the Olympians* attracts multiple audiences: hardcore fantasy readers, those who typically do not read fantasy, and a large number of adult readers. The fast pace, action, humor, and positive portrayal of learning disabilities in the series have made it a favorite among traditionally reluctant readers. The success of the series has added energy to the fantasy boom started by Harry Potter and has ultimately helped make fantasy a more mainstream genre.

The series has also rekindled interest in Greek mythology, paving the way for the publication of a number of new collections and adaptations of the Greek myths for middle-grade readers, such as George O'Connor's *Olympians* graphic novel series and Joan Holub and Suzanne Williams's *Goddess Girls* series. It also brought new attention to Kate McMullan's *Myth-o-Mania* series and the classic *D'Aulaires' Book of Greek Myths* (1961). Riordan's contribution of a series that transcends its genre in a way that is both intelligent and highly engaging will continue to impact publishing and has earned *Percy Jackson and the Olympians* a solid place in the fantasy cannon.

Adrienne Furness

SEE ALSO: *Best Sellers; Divorce; Graphic Novels; Harry Potter.*

BIBLIOGRAPHY

Devereaux, Elizabeth. "The Gods Must Be Crazy." *New York Times*, May 28, 2009.

Hynes, James. "It's All Greek to Him." *Texas Monthly*, October, 2010, 54–56.

Larson, Jeanette. "Talking with Rick Riordan." *Book Links*, May 2009, 18.

Performance Art

Performance art followed the Happenings and action art of the 1960s and came of age in the 1970s. The concept behind performance art has been linked historically to the Russian "living newspaper" groups of the 1920s that performed selections of political events and breaking news in streets, factories, clubs, and colleges. Performance art has been referred to as possessing postmodernist qualities; thus, it tends to be discussed in contrast to modernist art, such as painting and sculpture as well as modernist and avant-garde theater, for its interrogation of language, signs, and visual codes. Unlike most traditional arts and theater, the actual presence, control, and guidance of the artist who conceives the piece is central to performance art. Whereas modernist and avant-garde theatrical performers in the late nineteenth and early twentieth centuries saw their work as part of a new movement in acting, performance artists generally sprang from non-theatrical backgrounds, utilizing the act of performance to convey diverse meanings and create a new type of communication.

PERFORMANCE ART BASICS

Though the term *performance* has been vaguely defined, the performance art piece typically exists in one time and space for spectators. Unlike other artists, performance artists are in direct contact with their audiences. And unlike a finished painting or sculpture, performance art is not static—it varies from circumstance to circumstance. Commonly, performance artists draw from a wide range of media to create their art, and they choose meaningful durations of time and locations to perform it. Some observers have suggested that the rise of performance art signaled a shunning of the hierarchical art world and its production of esoteric pieces for a wealthy clientele. Others believe that many artists turned to performance art as a matter of professional necessity—it was a way to enter the art world in a time of diminishing opportunities in painting and sculpture. Performance art offers opportunities to more than just traditional artists. Because it does not make creating a masterpiece the ultimate goal—instead it encourages a blurring between disciplines—performance art accommodates the work of the nonexpert or non-virtuoso.

Performance art has been generally associated with the technology of production and the process as opposed to the finished product. The idea triumphs over the finished piece, and the visual communication of ideas and actions are privileged over pictorial values. The emphasis is on the role, as well as the presence (body), of the artist.

TRACING THE INFLUENCE OF JOHN CAGE

The work of music composer John Cage served as a precursor to performance art, as he challenged many established boundaries in the United States and Europe in the 1950s and early 1960s. Cage's work involved the concept of "silence," which he believed traditional art could not convey or embody. Cage's silent pieces were scored musical performances lasting for a specified duration of time and in which no musical instrument was played. Through these pieces, Cage attempted to convey an absence of empty space or time. His pieces were a compilation of the sounds in any given environment that would be suppressed by predetermined parameters of other works of music.

Cage was opposed to notions of fixity or "real" qualities with respect to art. He wanted to deflect attention from ideas of an "object" and focus instead on art's continual state of becoming. For Cage, the introduction of the concept of silence signified the dissolution of the formal integrity and authority traditionally claimed by the art object or piece of music. In addition, Cage's work included the viewer or listener in the process. By mingling notions of art and nonart, it allowed the spectator a hand in the creation of the piece.

THE WORK OF VITO ACCONCI

The poet Vito Acconci became a performance artist when he felt art had reached a stage in which it needed to transcend its standard location on the page or museum wall. Acconci's "body art" of the early 1970s can be said to reveal the ideology behind the historical and cultural construction of the human body. In a 1971 video piece called *Waterways*, Acconci lets his mouth fill with saliva until it spills into his cupped hands. In *Rubbing Piece* (1970), a performance piece that takes place in a restaurant, he rubs the same spot on his arm until a sore appears. Both of these pieces emphasize the time it takes the body to perform an action. Acconci also produced a short film, *Hand to Mouth* (1970), in which he puts his hand in his mouth and pushes it down his throat until he chokes.

In 1970 Acconci performed a piece in which he ran in place for two hours, pressed up against a painted wall, and left the wall stained with sweat and parts of his body covered in paint. His 1971 film *Conversions* explores issues of gender, as he uses a variety of tactics to try to change his body from male to female, including burning the hair off of his chest and assuming poses in front of the camera in which his penis is strategically hidden. The failure to produce a polished image of a female body for the camera is very much the point of this film. In his "body art" pieces, Acconci emphasized the degree to which the body's normal functions and productions must be suppressed in order for it to be represented as a natural part of an orderly society. Through his work, Acconci drew attention to society's discomfort and anxiety about notions such as sexuality and uncleanliness.

LIVING ART

Performance art often intervenes in a physical or social reality and is situational. For example, in 1977 at the Bologna Art Fair, performance artists Ulay and Marina Abramovic stood face to face on each side of the doorway to a Bologna museum, causing patrons to pass through the narrow space between the artists' bodies as they entered. The scene was relayed via video camera to a screen in the main gallery of the museum. The performance piece was designed to counter the definition of traditional theater, which creates a set time, place, and space, and attempts to recreate it over and over. This particular performance aimed to expose the hierarchical structure between an art product, the institution surrounding the product, and the consumer of the product.

In another performance art piece, *one year performance: 26 Sept. '81—26 Sept. '82*, artist Teh-ching Hsieh lived on the streets of New York City for an entire year without going into a building for shelter. Hsieh illustrated the ways in which traditional modes of art interpretation are often deconstructed in performance art, as the value of the art does not reside in aesthetic characteristics but rather in the artist's actions. In this case, interpretation involves considering how and why an action is done. Questions of time and place are also foregrounded.

CHANGING WITH THE TIMES

Performance art of the late 1980s and 1990s has been characterized as quieter and perhaps less optimistic than the form in its earlier stages, with a focus on issues of cultural diversity, spatial politics, and notions of all types of borders and border crossings. For example, as a result of the collapse of a ten-year period of economic prosperity, in the 1990s in London performance art began to appear in the spatial ruins of the economic boom, such as empty factories, warehouses, and office buildings. Along the same lines, adverse conditions with respect to economic, political, gender, and race relations were addressed in the semi-autobiographical performance pieces of such well-known artists as Guillermo Gomez-Peña, Annie Sprinkle, Karen Finley, and Spalding Gray. Radical transformations in city spaces, film, music, video, and television in the 1980s and 1990s forced artists to create new contexts for their work: inclusion of new cultural forms, rather than exclusion, became the rule. In the face of the continued institutionalization of art and culture and prolonged funding crises for independent artists, club-style events emerged in the United Kingdom and the United States. These events provided an affordable venue for artists, created a more informal relationship between performance artists and audience members, and incorporated new trends in music and club culture into the performances.

By the late twentieth century, performance artists were beginning to use computers, calling on software such as Microsoft PowerPoint to add validity to their work. Performers such as Marina Abramovic continued to exhibit great versatility. In the spring of 2010, New York's Museum of Modern Art hosted a retrospective of Abramovic's work, *Marina Abramovic: The Artist Is Present*, in which she sat in the museum's atrium each day from before opening until after closing, totaling 736 hours and 30 minutes of immobility. Visitors to the museum were invited to sit opposite her. Elsewhere, her sound pieces, videos, photographs, and collaborations with Uwe Laysiepen (Ulay) were featured. The highly publicized exhibit was proof of performance art's assimilation into mainstream American culture and served as testimony to its continued importance in the development of new art forms.

Kristi M. Wilson

SEE ALSO: *Modernism; Postmodernism.*

BIBLIOGRAPHY

Auslander, Philip. *From Acting to Performance: Essays in Modernism and Postmodernism.* New York: Routledge, 1997.

Battcock, Gregory, and Robert Nickas. *The Art of Performance: A Critical Anthology.* New York: E. P. Dutton, 1984.

Bronson, A. A., and Peggy Gale. *Performance by Artists.* Toronto: Art Metropole, 1979.

Burnham, Linda Frye, and Steve Durland, eds. *The Citizen Artist: 20 Years of Art in the Public Arena.* New York: Critical Press, 1998.

Childs, Nicky, and Jeni Walwin, eds. *A Split Second of Paradise: Live Art, Installation and Performance.* New York: Rivers Oram Press, 1998.

Dupuy, Jean, ed. *Collective Consciousness: Art Performances in the Seventies.* New York: Performance Arts Journal Publication, 1980.

Heathfield, Adrian, ed. *Live: Art and Performance.* New York: Routledge, 2004.

Hill, Leslie, and Helen Paris. *The Guerilla Guide to Performance Art.* London: Continuum, 2004.

Hoffman, Jens, and Joan Jonas. *Art Works: Perform.* New York: Thames and Hudson, 2005.

Kaye, Nick. *Art into Theatre: Performance, Interviews and Documents.* Amsterdam: Harwood Academic, 1996.

Kostelanetz, Richard. *On Innovative Performance(s): Three Decades of Recollections of Alternative Theater.* Jefferson, NC: McFarland, 1994.

Lacy, Suzanne. *Leaving Art: Writings on Performance, Politics and Publics 1974–2007.* Durham, NC: Duke University Press, 2010.

Mars, Tanya, and Johanna Householder, eds. *Caught in the Act: An Anthology of Performance Art by Canadian Women.* Toronto: YYZ, 2004.

Otfinoski, Steven. *African Americans in the Performing Arts: A to Z of African Americans.* New York: Facts On File, 2010.

Yoshimoto, Midori. *Into Performance: Japanese Women Artists in New York.* New Brunswick, NJ: Rutgers University Press, 2005.

Perot, Ross *(1930–)*

Maverick businessman Ross Perot turned U.S. politics upside down in 1992 when he mounted one of the most effective independent campaigns for president in history. Although he was ultimately unsuccessful, his bid threatened to derail the hopes of Republican incumbent George H. W. Bush and Democratic challenger Bill Clinton, who ultimately won the election.

Henry Ross Perot was born on June 27, 1930, in Texarkana, Texas. He learned his distinct worldview of self-reliance and ambition as an Eagle Scout and later as a U.S. Naval officer. He married Margot Birmingham in 1956; they would eventually have five children. After several years as a computer salesman for IBM (International Business Machines), Perot founded Electronic Data Systems Corporation (EDS) with $1,000 in 1962. His shrewd dealing and ability to land lucrative government contracts made EDS a major player and Perot a billionaire in a few short years.

EARLY CONTROVERSIES

Long before he ever ran for elected office, Perot courted controversy several times. He was seen by some as an apologist for Richard Nixon's administration, holding televised town hall meetings in 1969 that, according to Perot biographer Todd Mason, gave implicit support to Nixon. Nevertheless, Perot's interest in U.S. prisoners of war (POWs) in Vietnam tended to strain his relationship with Republican administrations. In 1969 he tried to deliver Christmas gifts, food, and medicine to the POWs, and in 1986 and 1987 he strongly criticized the U.S. Defense Department and the administration of President Ronald Reagan, accusing them of covering up information that POWs remained in Vietnam.

Perot achieved a reputation as a folk hero and a certain amount of notoriety in 1978, when two of his employees were imprisoned by Iranians who demanded that EDS design a new computer system for Iran. Perot, who made a point of hiring Vietnam veterans, recruited several talented members of his staff to rescue the pair. The tale of the recovery was told in Ken Follett's 1983 nonfiction novel *On Wings of Eagles* and adapted as a television movie starring Richard Crenna as Perot.

BUILDING FROM THE GROUND UP

Perot gained more attention on February 20, 1992, when he announced on the *Larry King Live* talk show that he would run for president if volunteers could get him on the ballot in all fifty states. Within days his Texas offices were swamped with hundreds of thousands of phone calls from volunteers offering to help with the campaign. The following weeks and months were a flurry of activity as word of Perot's intentions spread and volunteers across the country joined the effort to get him on the ballot. The nationwide volunteer effort would eventually coalesce into a new political party, known as the Reform Party (formed 1995), and also demonstrated the potential power of a grassroots political campaign.

Perot's greatest edge may have been sheer luck. The political scene in 1992 was perfect for a third-party candidate to enter. Voters were fed up with what they perceived as politics as usual in Washington, D.C.: Republicans and Democrats in discord, pointing fingers and spreading blame without really solving any problems. Perot appealed to the large segment of the

Ross Perot. *Ross Perot's presidential run in 1992 was the most effective third-party bid in American history.* BILL CLARK/CONTRIBUTOR/CQ-ROLL CALL GROUP/GETTY IMAGES.

population who identified with neither Democrats nor Republicans and resented being forced to choose between the two.

Perot energized the U.S. citizens who were disgusted with politics in general. Cynical voters who had long ago given up any hope of finding candidates who would stand up for what they believed in suddenly found someone they could believe in. Even those who disagreed with Perot's political stance—and one of the main criticisms leveled at him was that he often appeared to have no real stance—could not deny that he had a powerful personal charisma and rarely allowed himself to be bullied. In addition, many voters were leery of the influence of special-interest money in campaigns. Perot's pledge to pay his own campaign expenses greatly heartened those who feared that politicians were increasingly for sale.

Despite such grassroots support, Perot had a difficult time being taken seriously by much of the mainstream media. With his short stature, squeaky voice, and large ears, he was rich fodder for late-night comedians and editorial cartoonists. Perot was one of comedian Dana Carvey's best-known impressions on *Saturday Night Live*. Furthermore, Perot always did and said exactly what he thought was best, a trait that tended to both endear and infuriate his followers. In 1990 biographer Mason wrote these oddly prescient words, which perfectly describe the difficulty many had envisioning Perot as president: "[Perot] realizes that his low tolerance for frustration rules out politics. . . . He continues to decline invitations to run for president. He doesn't have the patience to deal with the inanities of public office. He can't compromise. He sees bureaucracy as maddeningly slow and ineffective at its best, and wrongheaded and corrupt at its worst."

CAMPAIGN STRATEGY

As a presidential candidate, Perot had an advantage in the mercurial nature of public opinion, which was unusually difficult to predict in 1992. The previous year had been historic, marking the fall of communism and an enormously popular conflict in the Persian Gulf. Bush's approval ratings hovered above 90 percent for months after the war, but an economic recession hurt his ratings in 1992. Clinton understood the public's unrest and ran on a theme summed up by his motto, "It's the economy, stupid."

Perot also campaigned on an economic platform and took the bold step of validating the worst fears people had about the economy. Speaking plainly, Perot told the U.S. public that everything was messed up; that the government had squandered their money; and that, if the country continued on the same course, things would only get worse. He also made a special point of bringing up the nation's $4 trillion debt—a number so large it almost defied description—and which he insisted must be paid sooner or later.

Perot ran an unorthodox campaign, eschewing large staffs and often ignoring the advice of his experienced campaign strategists, Hamilton Jordan and Ed Rollins. He used television as a campaign medium in manners very unlike anything that had been done in major races of the past. He avoided paid advertisements, preferring to appear on the free media: talk shows, morning news shows, and *Larry King Live*. The differences in his approach to campaigning, his bitter-medicine campaign speeches, and his outsider status struck a chord with many voters early in the summer. At the campaign's peak Perot ranked ahead of Clinton and Bush in many voter polls, including one in June, which reported that 37 percent of the voting population intended to vote for Perot.

QUITTING AND REENTERING THE RACE

On July 16 Perot made a surprise announcement, stating that he believed that the revitalized Democratic Party was the right choice to lead the nation. Furthermore, according to Perot, the close three-way race would end up throwing the election into the House of Representatives, so he had decided to drop out of the race entirely. The reaction of Perot's followers covered the gamut from complete shock to anger. Most felt betrayed. Supporters and critics alike wondered if Perot's entire campaign had been a rich man's game, a diversion played out with millions of pawns until he had quit when the going got rough. By October, after weeks of speculation, Perot returned to the race, claiming that he was not satisfied that Bush or Clinton were really willing to fix the severe problems with the economy. After quitting once already, Perot had an uphill battle on his hands to regain his credibility.

His biggest advertising effort came late in the campaign, when he purchased half-hour blocks of time on major networks to present his campaign infomercials. The infomercials were charming, low-budget affairs. For the most part they featured Perot speaking in an office, using his distinctive folksy humor and illustrating economic issues with a pointer. "Let's take a little time to figure out what's happened to the engine (of the American economy)," Perot said in one characteristically homespun analogy. "Let's raise the hood and go to work." Once again he flew in the face of conventional political wisdom and managed to come out on top. "The ruling political wisdom was that a single 'talking head' was the most boring thing in television and would drive viewers away rather than attract them," writes Robert D. Loevy in *The Flawed Path to the Presidency 1992*. Instead, Perot's infomercials attracted large audiences and praise from voters.

Unlike many politicians Perot ignored negative campaigning almost altogether, even as he painted a drastic picture of the economy. His speeches, advertisements, and infomercials often avoided attacking his opponents by name, which was another popular move. He also made a strong impression during the presidential debates with Bush and Clinton; many observers felt that he was the real winner of the first and third debates and that he held his own in the second.

RACE RESULTS

Despite the popularity of Perot's approach, he was not wholeheartedly embraced. Many of his most devoted followers and volunteers felt betrayed by his quitting; they had put their lives on hold for his campaign, and he had failed them by bailing out for reasons that never became quite clear. In addition, negative reports emerged that his management style was dictatorial and autocratic and that he maintained absolute control over his company and employees. There were also those who questioned the wisdom of his choice of running mate, retired Vice Admiral James Stockdale. The choice of Stockdale, who had been the highest-ranking prisoner of war during the Vietnam conflict, was in character for Perot because of his respect for Vietnam veterans and former POWs. Nevertheless, Stockdale seemed a bit out of touch to some and tended to turn away those whose support for Perot was wavering.

Shortly before the election, Perot harmed his campaign by revealing that he had initially quit the campaign based on information he had that a Republican dirty tricks committee was planning to sabotage his daughter's wedding. He never offered any evidence to support this allegation, and it gave much ammunition to his detractors, who painted him as a conspiracy-theorizing, paranoid eccentric. Ultimately, Perot lost the election, garnering 18.9 percent of the popular vote and no electoral votes.

LIFE AFTER 1992

After losing the presidential race in 1992, Perot remained in the public eye, speaking out against the North American Free Trade Agreement (NAFTA) and airing his concerns about the rising national debt. In 1996 he participated in the presidential race as the official candidate for the Reform Party, which he had helped found in 1995. After losing the second election, he largely withdrew from the political arena. His involvement with the Reform Party was contentious in the intervening years, in part because of criticism that his interests in the party were only selfish. After years of silence regarding political issues, Perot reemerged before the heated 2008 election to publicly decry Arizona senator John McCain and endorse Massachusetts representative Mitt Romney as the Republican presidential nominee.

By energizing voters in the 1992 election, Perot was tapping into a larger zeitgeist that had infused U.S. politics nearly since the country was founded. Select politicians in history, such as orator William Jennings Bryan and U.S. Senator Robert La Follette, had ridden the reform wave to varying degrees of success. Although Perot's campaigns were ultimately unsuccessful, he left a strong populist legacy and a reminder to both parties that a two-party system was not the unassailable fortress many believed it to be. This legacy found new champions in the Tea Party movement of the late 2000s. His populist message spoke to many U.S. citizens, who showed their appreciation through various honors and awards, many of which came from veteran's organizations and from Perot's fellow Texans.

Perot's extraordinarily high poll numbers early in 1992 and his garnering of 18.9 percent of the final vote, one of the highest ever for an independent candidacy, sent a clear message to Washington that voters no longer considered a third party an irrational choice. His presence and influence reminded Republicans and Democrats alike that the two-party system could not be taken for granted.

Paul F. P. Pogue

SEE ALSO: *Follett, Ken; IBM (International Business Machines); King, Larry; Reagan, Ronald;* Saturday Night Live*; The Tea Party; Vietnam.*

BIBLIOGRAPHY

Black, Gordon S., and Benjamin D. Black. *The Politics of American Discontent: How a New Party Can Make Democracy Work Again.* New York: Wiley, 1994.

Dye, Thomas R., and L. Harmon Zeigler. *The Irony of Democracy: An Uncommon Introduction to American Politics.* Boston: Wadsworth Cengage Learning, 2009.

Follett, Ken. *On Wings of Eagles.* New York: New American Library, 1984.

Loevy, Robert D. *The Flawed Path to the Presidency 1992: Unfairness and Inequality in the Presidential Selection Process.* Albany: State University of New York Press, 1995.

Mason, Todd. *Perot: An Unauthorized Biography*. Homewood, IL: Dow Jones-Irwin, 1990.

Pomper, Gerald M., ed. *The Election of 1992: Reports and Interpretations*. Chatham, NJ: Chatham House Publishers, 1993.

Perry, Katy *(1984–)*

Singer and bubblegum pop starlet Katy Perry began her career incongruously in the world of Christian rock but soon switched to mainstream pop. An energetic performer, the singer-songwriter has racked up two platinum albums before the age of thirty and is beloved by fans and the media alike for her sassy, friendly outlook and the emotional generosity of her songs and interviews.

Born on October 25, 1984, in Santa Barbara, California, Katheryn Elizabeth Hudson was raised in a strict Christian household with two pastors as parents. As a child, she joined the church choir and became obsessed with singing, explaining that, as a middle child, she especially enjoyed the attention she received from performing. Her parents, she later recalled, forbade what she called "secular" culture in their home, and her early musical influences came from the church and from the gospel tradition. The precocious and energetic teenager convinced her parents to allow her to pursue a singing career at the age of fifteen and moved to Nashville, Tennessee, releasing a self-titled Christian rock-gospel album under the name Katy Hudson when she was only seventeen.

Although this record floundered, Hudson (later performing under the name Katy Perry) was determined to jump-start her musical career. She earned her GED and moved to Los Angeles (while still seventeen) to collaborate with Glen Ballard (the producer behind Alanis Morissette and Christina Aguilera). After an early period of struggle, performing in clubs around the city, fame came rapidly to Perry, who was signed to Capitol Records in 2007. She offered the single "Ur So Gay" as a free download from her MySpace account later that year. Receiving attention for its catchy, hip lyrics and rhythms, the song went viral. Her second single, "I Kissed a Girl," which appeared in an episode of the WB hit series *Gossip Girl*, rocketed up the charts. While the song, with lyrics saying "I kissed a girl and I liked it," was controversial for its lesbian undertones, Perry herself matter of factly explained the relative innocence of the lyrics, telling the *Toronto Star*:

> It's a song about curiosity. The fact of the matter is that girls smell much better than boys; we all know this. We're beautiful creatures, we've started wars, we've ended wars. Girl hangouts are very touchy: we have slumber parties, we have sleepovers, we choreograph dance numbers in our pyjamas. And there's nothing perverted about that. It's just really sweet and innocent, and if Scarlett Johansson wanted to kiss me, I'm not sure I would say no.

In 2008 Perry released her first full-length album, *One of the Boys*, which includes both "Ur So Gay" and "I Kissed a Girl." The album was an instant success, going platinum within weeks and earning Perry a nomination for a Grammy Award for Best Female Pop Vocal Performance in 2009 for "I Kissed a Girl." As Perry's album sales began to rise, she spent the summer of 2008 traveling with the Vans Warped Tour. She became known for her sweetly sexy sartorial choices; her high-energy persona; and her brightly colored, peppy live shows.

Perry released her second album, *Teenage Dream*, in 2010. The singer described the album as giving fans "the full spectrum . . . you're getting the sugary sweet, but you're also getting the 'Oh my goodness, she had to sit down for a minute and let some things off her chest.'" Bubbly, upbeat songs like the title track and "California Gurls" made this sophomore album an equally big hit, earning Perry four Grammy nominations, including one for Album of the Year in 2011. That same year she was awarded the Video of the Year award at the MTV Video Music Awards.

Perry has received numerous other awards, including the MTV Artist of the Year award for 2011, eight People's Choice Awards, and four Teen Choice Awards. She makes frequent television appearances, on talk shows as well as on such shows as *American Idol* and *Who Wants to Be a Millionaire*. She has also taken some small acting parts, including a lauded cameo as Zoey's dim-witted cousin Honey on the sitcom *How I Met Your Mother*. Perry has provided voices for a number of animated characters, including that of Smurfette in the 2011 film *The Smurfs*.

A fan and media favorite, Perry has appeared on nearly twenty magazine covers, and her personal life is avidly followed by the media. After being linked romantically with Gym Class Heroes' frontman Travis McCoy in 2008 and early 2009, she began dating British actor and comedian Russell Brand in late 2009. After a very public, whirlwind courtship, the two married with relative discretion in India, on October 23, 2010. In 2012, after sixteen months of marriage, the couple divorced.

Favoring a playful style, Perry usually wears bright red lipstick that contrasts with her pale skin and dark eyes and sports brightly colored clothing and accessories, right down to a series of brightly colored guitars. Onstage and off, her outfits sometimes push the boundaries of conventional good taste—her naturally dark hair has been dyed not just blond and red but a number of candy-colored shades, and she once wore a light-up dress to a ball at the Metropolitan Museum Costume Institute—but are invariably young, cute, and sexy. She herself describes her fashion choices as "Lucille Ball meets Bob Mackie. . . . I want everyone to get the joke but I want them to think about it for a minute." Perry, who fronted a marketing campaign with Steve Madden shoes and introduced her own line of perfume, Purr by Katy Perry, in October 2010, has spoken about her desire to design her own line of clothing and accessories in the future.

Jenny Ludwig

SEE ALSO: *Aguilera, Christina;* American Idol*; Ball, Lucille; Contemporary Christian Music; Divorce; Gospel Music; Grammy Awards; Morissette, Alanis; MTV; Pop Music; Rock and Roll; Top 40;* Who Wants to Be a Millionaire.

BIBLIOGRAPHY

Govan, Chloe. *Katy Perry: A Life of Fireworks*. New York: Omnibus Press, 2011.

Montgomery, Alice. *Katy Perry: The Unofficial Biography*. New York: Penguin, 2011.

Perry, Tyler *(1969–)*

A self-taught creative artist and a savvy entrepreneur, Tyler Perry consistently writes, produces, and stars in top-grossing works for the stage, film, and television. His work predominantly appeals to middle-aged African American Christian women, though it has received much criticism from other groups. Despite negative reviews, Perry has had an undeniable impact on the African American theater, film, and television industries and a track record of making commercially successful films. As of 2011 his films had grossed more than $500 million.

Born Emmitt R. Perry Jr. in New Orleans, Louisiana, Perry grew up in an economically depressed yet culturally rich African American neighborhood. His domineering and abusive father, Emmitt Perry Sr., often drank and whipped him. Young Tyler was also sexually molested by several abusers. To distance himself from his father, Perry changed his first name from Emmitt to Tyler at age sixteen. He sought solace from his troubled home life in church. His mother sang in the choir, and no matter what they suffered at home, they went to church every Sunday morning.

Nonetheless, the stigma, denial, and repression of Perry's physical and sexual abuse lingered into his adult life. An episode of *The Oprah Winfrey Show* (1986–2011) in which the host encouraged victims of child abuse to write about their experiences as therapy, first inspired him to write. With no formal training, he began writing letters to himself, forming the basis for his first play, *I Know I've Been Changed* (1992). The title comes from the gospel song "Lord I Know I've Been Changed" (gospel music plays an important part in many of Perry's works).

He debuted the play in a rented Atlanta, Georgia, theater with $12,000 that he had saved. It bombed. After several revisions, he launched the play again at the House of Blues, and this time it was a success. His next play, *I Can Do Bad All by Myself* (1999), called for a leading lady that Perry had fashioned after his mother, Maxine; his Aunt Mayola; and other mature, strong black women he knew as a child. The character's name is Mable Simmons, though she is known as Madea, a contraction of *mother dear*, a common moniker in the South. The 6-foot, 5-inch Perry chose to play the grumpy, matronly, silver-haired mother by dressing in drag and a padded fat suit.

In Madea, Perry found his defining role and spawned a cottage industry. His plays target the urban black theater circuit, originally known as the Chitlin' Circuit, which features black performers, musicians, and actors who play for black audiences. Perry's do-it-yourself ethic and fidelity to his core audience served him well as he transitioned from the stage to film. He used his own financing ($5.5 million) to produce his first movie, *Diary of a Mad Black Woman* (2005), after Hollywood denied him funding. The film grossed more than $21 million during its opening weekend and has since grossed more than $50 million worldwide. LionsGate Entertainment now coproduces and distributes Perry's films, though he retains full copyright ownership and regularly places his name in front of his films' titles.

In 2006 he premiered a pilot for a ten-episode sitcom called *House of Payne* on the TBS network. The show was a success, and the network offered him $200 million for an additional 100 episodes. The TV series *Meet the Browns* (2008–2011) and *For Better or Worse* (2011–) followed. Perry used his success to establish a production studio featuring five sound stages, a gym, and a chapel on 30 acres in Atlanta, making him the first African American to own his own television studio. Through the company, he produces movies and employs many black actors and movie personnel. He also has branched out into other projects and roles, including executive producing the hit movie *Precious* (2009) and writing the best-selling book *Don't Make a Black Woman Take off Her Earrings: Madea's Uninhibited Commentaries on Love and Life* (2006).

Although he has a devoted audience of moviegoers, many film critics loathe him, perhaps because his work reaches out to audiences that Hollywood has historically neglected, such as Christian women who value family and God. He attempted to broaden his audience with *The Family That Preys* (2008) but realized limited success. Critics—and even some filmmakers, such as director Spike Lee—ruthlessly assail his imagery as "coonery" and "buffoonery." In *Brainwashed: Challenging the Myth of Black Inferiority* (2010), author Tom Burrell contends that some of Perry's images are egregious and that the writer's popularity preys on blacks' appetite for seeing themselves as dysfunctional or incompetent. Winfrey has defended Perry's work, stating that his character Madea is a celebration of strong black women.

Willie R. Collins

SEE ALSO: *Best Sellers; Hollywood; Lee, Spike; Sitcom; Television; Winfrey, Oprah.*

BIBLIOGRAPHY

Burrell, Tom. *Brainwashed: Challenging the Myth of Black Inferiority.* New York: Smiley Books, 2010.

Genzlinger, Neil. "Tyler Perry's *I Can Do Bad All by Myself.*" *New York Times*, September 12, 2009.

Gordon, Ed. "Spike Lee Blasts a Hole into Tyler Perry." *Root*, June 1, 2009.

Hutson, Darralynn. "Tyler Perry Decoded: The Deals, the Brand, the Influence." *Black Enterprise*, March 21, 2011.

Johnson, Todd. "Ad Exec Tom Burrell Says America Has Been 'Brainwashed' about Blacks." *Griot*, February 12, 2010.

Perry Mason

America's favorite crime-solving lawyer, Perry Mason, was a character created by lawyer-turned-author Erle Stanley Gardner (1889–1970). Eventually featured in more than eighty popular books, Gardner's creation had a modest success in films and radio but proved a sensation on television.

Mason's first appearance came in *The Case of the Velvet Claws* (1933), but it was not until subsequent volumes that Gardner allowed Mason to spend much time in court. The mixture of legalistic detail with the time-honored whodunit format was a winning combination, but one which Warner Brothers failed to capture in its series of six films (1934–1937); there was also a brief radio series in 1943. Determined not to repeat Hollywood's mistakes, Gardner formed his own production company and oversaw the creation of the *Perry Mason* series, which debuted on CBS in 1957 and ran until 1966.

Cold War viewers who had been exposed to the Army-McCarthy Hearings quickly warmed to this invincible knight who invariably ferreted out the enemy within. With undertones of film noir, each episode led to a gripping conclusion of almost ritualistic predictability: Mason's courtroom theatrics and cross examination elicited a sudden confession from the person who had committed the murder for which Mason's client was on trial. This weekly morality play made a television star out of movie villain Raymond Burr, sparked public awareness of America's legal system, and led to countless other courtroom drama series on the tube. The Burr-Mason combo proved so popular that, after starring in the *Ironside* series as the wheelchair-bound detective, the actor reprised his most famous role in *Perry Mason Returns* (1985), the first in a sequence of ninety-minute made-for-television movies, which ended only with Burr's death in 1993.

Preston Neal Jones

SEE ALSO: *Burr, Raymond; Cold War.*

BIBLIOGRAPHY

Collins, Max Allan, and John Javna. *The Best of Crime and Detective TV:* Perry Mason *to* Hill Street Blues, *the* Rockford Files *to* Murder She Wrote. New York: Harmony Books, 1988.

Hughes, Dorothy B. *Erle Stanley Gardner: The Case of the Real Perry Mason.* New York: Morrow, 1978.

Kelleher, Brian, and Diana Merrill. *The* Perry Mason *TV Show Book.* New York: St. Martin's Press, 1987.

Leitch, Thomas M. *Perry Mason.* Detroit, MI: Wayne State University Press, 2005.

Personal Watercraft

SEE: *Jet Skis.*

Pet Rocks

Pet Rocks were among the most popular gifts of 1975, and the name has become synonymous with ridiculous fads. The brainchild of Gary Dahl, a California advertising man, the Pet Rock—actually rosarita beach stones that Dahl bought for one cent each and sold for $2 wholesale—was a hit at a gift show in San Francisco in August 1975. By Christmas of that year, Dahl had sold two and a half tons of Pet Rocks, or one million rocks, and had become a millionaire. The Pet Rock was packaged in a cardboard "pet" carrying case and came with the *Pet Rock Training Manual.*

Dahl rocketed to fame, appearing on *The Tonight Show* twice. Immediately after Christmas in 1975, the market for Pet Rocks dried up. A year later Dahl donated his remaining inventory of 100,000 Pet Rocks to needy children. His next attempt to sell nothing for something, the Official Sand Breeding Kit in 1976, was a flop. In 2009, riding a wave of 1970s nostalgia, I-Star Entertainment reintroduced the Pet Rock to the marketplace.

Jeff Merron

SEE ALSO: *Consumerism.*

BIBLIOGRAPHY

Epting, Chris *Pet Rocks, Puka Shells, and Pong: An Illustrated History of 1970s.* Solana Beach, CA: Santa Monica Press, 2012.

Peter, Paul, and Mary

Peter, Paul, and Mary (PP&M) came together in Greenwich Village in 1961. Noel Paul Stookey (1937–) was working as a stand-up comic when he met Mary Travers (1936–2009). They formed a folksinging duo, but soon they were approached by Albert Grossman, producer for the Kingston Trio. He united them with Peter Yarrow (1938–), who had played at the 1959 Newport Folk Festival. Grossman debuted PP&M at the Bitter End coffeehouse, where the magic of their beautiful harmonies and the skillful, subtle interaction of their two guitars captivated audiences. Soon PP&M were touring the country, bringing their positive vibes to young, hip audiences.

EARLY MUSIC

PP&M embraced many strains of folk music: political songs, love songs, traditional ballads, spirituals, humor, and children's songs. All these elements were featured on their first album, *Peter, Paul and Mary* (1962), which occupied the *Billboard* Top 10 for ten months. Their biggest single of the year was Pete Seeger's "If I Had a Hammer." Their second album, *Moving* (1963), introduced their hit "Puff, the Magic Dragon" and the Woody Guthrie song, "This Land Is Your Land." Their third album, *In the Wind* (1963), included three songs by Bob Dylan, notably "Blowin' in the Wind," which reached the number two spot on the charts and even featured a poem by Dylan on the back

Peter, Paul, and Mary. *Paul Stooker, Mary Travers, and Peter Yarrow of the folk group Peter, Paul, and Mary had hits in the 1960s with "Puff, the Magic Dragon," Woody Guthrie's "This Land Is Your Land," and Bob Dylan's "Blowin' in the Wind."* MICHAEL OCHS ARCHIVES/GETTY IMAGES.

cover, thereby introducing their friend and inspiration to a wider audience. Their fourth production, *Peter, Paul and Mary in Concert* (1964) was a double album with plenty of original material, including Paul's comedy routines.

A Song Will Rise and *See What Tomorrow Brings* (both 1965) offered more of the PP&M magic but little in the way of development at a time when the rest of the music world was in a state of exciting flux. They acknowledged this on the back cover of *See What Tomorrow Brings*, noting that the "Beatles have gone folk, Bob Dylan has gone pop," but PP&M chose to stick to their roots.

With *Album* (1966), PP&M began to experiment with more instrumentation and a harder sound. Mike Bloomfield, Paul Butterfield, and Al Kooper played on some tracks. "Norman Normal," with its electric guitar, proved to be their hardest rock song, with supercilious lyrics criticizing the "average" man, in imitation of the Beatles' "Nowhere Man." On *Album 1700* (1967) they continued to experiment with other instruments but were more at home singing about rock rather than imitating it: "I Dig Rock and Roll Music" is a classic commentary upon the music scene, praising the Mamas and Papas, the Beatles, and other bands who were influenced by folk and, in turn, enriched folk music.

Their next album, *Late Again* (1968), was another fine performance but still showed little development. Perhaps running out of ideas, PP&M then recorded a collection of children's songs, with the embarrassing title *Peter, Paul and Mommy* (1969). This is easily their worst album of the 1960s. The inclusion of "Puff" and "It's Raining," both of which had appeared on earlier studio albums as well as on the live album, made *Mommy* all the more regrettable. The album, however, is valuable for the inclusion of two excellent songs, the folk ballad "Leatherwing Bat" and Gilbert and Sullivan's "I Have a Song to Sing, O!" These two beautiful performances, mercifully appearing back to back, make the album worth having. Also in 1968, the group's version of John Denver's "Leaving on a Jet Plane" made it to number one on the charts.

BEYOND THE '70s

In 1970 PP&M split to pursue solo projects. Peter and Mary continued their political activism, while Paul converted to Christianity. Their solo albums tended to fall in with the "singer/songwriter" trend that emerged in the early 1970s. The many charms that had made the original trio so spellbinding were nowhere to be found on the solo albums. Special mention, however, should go to Paul's timeless classic "The Wedding Song (There Is Love)." In 1978 Peter invited Paul and Mary to join him for an antinuclear benefit concert, and the album *Reunion* (1978) soon followed. This, too, lacked the quiet magic of their earlier folk tunes: there seemed to be no going back. Thereafter they produced an album every few years and appeared frequently on PBS membership drives. Highlights from the reunion period include *A Holiday Celebration* (1988), which found the trio once again drawing on traditional material, and *Lifelines* (1995), which featured an impressive gathering of the "folk family," including Pete Seeger, Judy Collins, and Richie Havens.

PP&M were often objects of ridicule for their smiley, sunshiny image. Their covers usually showed them skipping down a country lane arm in arm. This led even the Beatles (who also had a clean-cut image in the early days) to call them "Pizza, Pooh and Magpie." Unfortunately PP&M are often remembered by this G-rated image and dismissed as superficial family entertainment. Some wondered whether they were genuine folk musicians or mere popularizers like the Kingston Trio. Folk purists found them too polished and wholesome, lacking the earthy ruggedness of Dylan or Guthrie. It should be remembered, however, that many of their lyrics dealt frankly and realistically with adult themes such as infidelity, loneliness, death, and the sorrows of growing old. Furthermore, PP&M proved their commitment to folk ideals time and again in many benefit concerts, demonstrations, and marches for civil rights and other causes.

Not least among PP&M's legacy is the recruitment of fans into other kinds of folk music, both contemporary and traditional. Besides introducing Dylan and Gordon Lightfoot to the genre, they brought Guthrie and Seeger and introduced traditional ballads to a new generation, bridging two eras of folk music when rock was stagnant. Half the fun of spending time with the "folk family" lies in recognizing different versions of songs, sometimes with different lyrics, arrangements, or titles. Anyone well versed in PP&M and folk rock will experience a shock of recognition when listening to the *Anthology of American Folk Music* (1952), a collection of recordings from the 1920s and 1930s that often contain the nucleus of songs popularized in the 1960s. For many people, the winding, dusty road back to that winding, dusty anthology begins with Peter, Paul, and Mary.

Throughout their career, Peter, Paul, and Mary brought joy to generations of Americans. They also won five Grammys and had thirteen Top 40 hits. Eight of their albums went gold, and another five went platinum. During the early years of the twenty-first century, Peter, Paul, and Mary continued to perform, averaging forty concerts a year. Peter spent his time away from the group in demonstrations, benefits, and campaigns, or performing with his daughter Bethany. Paul became involved in technology, opening a multimedia company and running the group's website. Mary spent time with her family while battling leukemia.

The group had a stellar year in 2004, simultaneously releasing *Carry It On*, a four-CD box set with a bonus DVD featuring live performances from their career, and *In These Times*, an album of all-new Peter, Paul, and Mary material. PBS also aired a special featuring the group's work that same year. In 2006 Peter, Paul, and Mary received a Lifetime Achievement Award from the Songwriters Hall of Fame. Three years later Mary lost her battle with leukemia, leaving behind a legacy that has transcended the folk genre to become not only part of American musical history but also an iconic element in American popular culture.

Douglas Cooke

SEE ALSO: *The Beatles; Compact Discs; Denver, John; Dylan, Bob; Folk Music; Greenwich Village; Guthrie, Woody; The Internet; The Kingston Trio; The Mamas and the Papas; Newport Jazz and Folk Festivals; Public Television (PBS); Rock and Roll; Seeger, Pete; Stand-up Comedy; Top 40.*

BIBLIOGRAPHY

Ruhlmann, William. "Peter, Paul, and Mary: A Song to Sing All over This Land." *Goldmine*, April 12, 1996, 20–50, 62–82, 142–50.

Slobin, Mark. *Folk Music: A Very Short Introduction*. New York: Oxford University Press, 2011.

Winkler, Allan M. *To Everything There Is a Season: Pete Seeger and the Power of Song*. New York: Oxford University Press, 2009.

Peters, Bernadette *(1948–)*

Bernadette Peters is a most distinctive Broadway singer. Her voice encompasses all facets of vocal technique—she can sing with a small, pinched sound; a full-bodied belt sound; or anywhere between the two, depending on the dramatic needs of the song. Peters made her stage debut at age eleven in a revival of *The Most Happy Fella*. Her principal Broadway roles include Dot in *Sunday in the Park with George* (1984), Emma in *Song and Dance* (1985), the Witch in *Into the Woods* (1987), Marsha in *The Goodbye Girl* (1993), Annie Oakley in *Annie Get Your Gun* (1999 revival), Mama Rose in *Gypsy* (2003 revival), Desiree Armfeldt in *A Little Night Music* (2009 revival; she replaced Catherine Zeta-Jones in 2010 and dazzled audiences and critics with her rendition of "Send in the Clowns"), and Sally in *Follies* (2011 revival).

Peters won Tony Awards for her performances in *Song and Dance* and *Annie Get Your Gun*. Her musical film credits include *Pennies from Heaven* (1981), for which she won a Golden Globe Award, and *Annie* (1982). She provided singing voices for the animated *Beauty and the Beast 2: The Enchanted Christmas* (1997) and *Anastasia* (1997). Her tremendous talent and vocal ability have earned her the well-deserved reputation as one of the finest musical theater performers of the century.

William A. Everett

SEE ALSO: *Animated Films;* Annie*;* Annie Get Your Gun*; Broadway; The Musical.*

BIBLIOGRAPHY

Gans, Andrew. "Bernadette's Back."*Playbill* 11, no. 10 (1993): 41–43.

Zadan, Craig. *Sondheim & Company*. New York: Da Capo, 1994.

Pets

For thousands of years, people have kept and cared for domesticated animals, often developing strong emotional ties with their pets and regarding them as members of the family. While once important for the services they provided—including rodent control, hunting, and guarding—pets have become even more popular as companions. Noting that relationships between people seem to be less reliable and more complicated, veterinarian Aaron Katcher described the appeal of pets, explaining that animals offer "a much less complex and difficult relationship." Pets have made an impact on more than just their owners, however. Stories of pets' heroism, hilarious escapades, and loyal companionship abound throughout popular media.

ANIMAL STORIES

The dramatic heroism and unbreakable devotion of some animals is reflected in literature. In such stories as *The Incredible Journey* (1961), loyal pets brave the Canadian wilderness to find their families; Wilbur, a pig, wins the heart of a small farming community in *Charlotte's Web* (1952); and when Odysseus returns home in *The Odyssey*, it is his dog, Argus, who alone recognizes him.

Animal stories have proven to be potent material for Hollywood movies. In 1957 *Old Yeller* broke the hearts of American movie audiences with the story of a dog who lost his own life in order to save that of a boy. The little dog Benji used cunning intelligence to solve crimes in the 1970s. The 1980s and 1990s saw a virtual explosion of live and animated films starring pets. Hooch slobbers his way through a murder mystery with Tom Hanks in *Turner & Hooch* (1989). The true story of the Siberian husky Balto, who in 1925 carried the diphtheria serum more than 670 miles, from Nenana to Nome, Alaska, became a moving animated film in 1995. And hits such as *Beethoven, 101 Dalmatians*, and *Babe* scored at the box office with stories of animal ingenuity.

Since the golden age of television, pets have entertained audiences. *Lassie*, one of television's longest-running dramas, kept people tuned in for twenty years beginning in the 1950s while the loyal dog saved people, solved mysteries, and generally loved its owner. In lesser roles, animals have added insight and comic relief to the tensions in human life. Both Murray, who drinks out of the toilet in *Mad about You*, and Eddie, who

Barbara Bush and Dogs. *Barbara Bush sits with dogs Millie and Ranger outside the White House in 1991.* JENNIFER LAW/AFP/GETTY IMAGES.

won't stay off the furniture in *Frasier*, angered and amused humans by exposing the triviality of common annoyances. Vincent, the yellow Labrador on *Lost*, endured adventures every bit as rigorous as did his human companions. Even Data from *Star Trek: The Next Generation* kept Spot the cat as a companion in his quarters because the pet made him feel more human.

Beginning in the 1970s, pets dominated the world of animated cartoons. In 1976 cat and bird duo Sylvester and Tweety Pie began a long-running cartoon showcasing their antics. Comic-born Snoopy entertained audiences with fascinating stories of his imaginary world, and *Garfield* comically revealed the intelligence of animals and the foibles of humans. On PBS, *Clifford the Big Red Dog* entertained young children with stories of a giant pet.

Even in the comics, stories of pets inspire and excite. In *For Better or Worse*, Farley saved April from drowning and then died from exhaustion. Little Orphan Annie's dog, Sandy, stays loyally by her side. Hobbes, Calvin's real pet hamster, provides amusing comments about the young boy's adventures with his stuffed Tiger in *Calvin and Hobbes*.

WHITE HOUSE PETS

Americans have been fascinated by the pets who occupy the White House. Richard Nixon talked about his dog Checkers in a speech that saved his place on the Dwight D. Eisenhower ticket. Barbara Bush helped the cocker spaniel Millie write a best-selling book in 1990 about what it's like to be the president's best friend. The coverage of President Bill Clinton's decision to adopt a dog in 1997 overshadowed major news events. The White House received so many letters concerning the first pets that Hillary Rodham Clinton compiled *Dear Socks, Dear Buddy: Kids' Letters to the First Pets* to share American children's interesting questions about the Clintons' cat and dog. During the 2008 presidential campaign, candidate Barack Obama promised his daughters a dog after the election was over, a pledge that was later fulfilled by the arrival of a Portuguese Water Dog named Bo at the White House. The presence of pets in the White House has become such a part of American life that it would be hard for many Americans to imagine a petless president.

The twentieth century was truly a remarkable one for pets, famous or not. Despite the fact that they can be dirty, expensive, and demanding, pets reside in nearly half of all Western European and North American homes. Many people consider their pets to be surrogate children. In 1993 alone Americans spent $17 billion on food, veterinary bills, leashes, apparel, toys, and other accessories and services for their pets. By 2009 that amount of money had skyrocketed to $43 billion—in spite of the fact that the United States was in the midst of the worst recession it had experienced since the Great Depression. The influence of pets in popular media surely encouraged many people to become pet owners, and it is clear that anyone wishing to understand pet-human relationships need watch only an episode or two of *Lassie* to find the answer.

Angela O'Neal

SEE ALSO: Calvin and Hobbes; *Comics;* Frasier; *The Great Depression; Hanks, Tom; Hollywood; Lassie; Little Orphan Annie;* Lost; *Obama, Barack;* Peanuts; Star Trek: The Next Generation; *Television; Tweety Pie and Sylvester.*

BIBLIOGRAPHY

Comfort, David. *The First Pet History of the World.* New York: Simon & Schuster, 1994.

Fogle, Bruce, ed. *Interrelationships between People and Pets.* Springfield, IL: Charles C. Thomas, 1981.

Fogle, Bruce. *Pets and Their People.* New York: Viking Press, 1983.

Katcher, Aaron Honori, and Alan M. Beck, eds. *New Perspectives on Our Lives with Companion Animals.* Philadelphia: University of Pennsylvania Press, 1983.

Rice, Berkeley. *The Other End of the Leash: The American Way with Pets.* Boston: Little, Brown, 1968.

Schaffer, Michael. *One Nation under Dog: Adventure in the New World of Prozac-Popping Puppies, Dog-Park Politics, and Organic Pet Food.* New York: Henry Holt, 2009.

Petting

Though the term *petting* may seem quaintly archaic in the sexually frank modern era, it reveals a lot about sexual attitudes in the earlier part of the century in which it was coined. Describing pre-intercourse sexual acts or foreplay, the word *petting* manages to capture both the innocence and the euphemistic repression identified with the 1950s and early 1960s.

This post–World War II period, which is loosely referred to as "the fifties," was characterized by coded and metaphorical references to sex, one of the most common being a baseball metaphor. There are regional differences in the meanings of the bases, but one common definition describes first base as passionate kissing, second base as touching the (girl's) breasts, third base as touching the (girl's) genitals with the (boy's) hands, and home base as intercourse.

Likewise, the definitions of *necking* and *petting* have been a subject of intense debate, especially among those engaged in these activities, but necking is generally described to be passionate physical contact occurring above the neck, while petting comprises attention to the parts of the body below the neck. The social meaning of petting and other forms of introductory sexuality is explored in Obie Benz's documentary film, *Heavy Petting* (1989), which juxtaposes representations of sex in the media of the 1950s with sex education materials of the time and the reminiscences of celebrities who came of age then. One such representation came from Evelyn Duvall, author of a much-used sex education guide of the 1950s, *Facts of Life and Love for Teen-Agers*, who defines petting as "the caressing of other more sensitive parts of the body in a crescendo of sexual stimulation." She also warns, "These forces are often very strong and insistent. Once released, they tend to press for completion."

This, then, is the true "fifties" meaning of petting, the unleashing of forces within the body that may then spiral out of control. This idea encapsulates decades of fear of sex, which has its roots, for both sexes, in religious notions of mortal sin and—for young men—perhaps a latent fear of women. Almost all of the sexual metaphors of the era describe heterosexual sex in which the male is the aggressor and the woman is the defender. The very word *petting* implies a passive recipient, a "pet" receiving attention from a "petter."

If the feelings aroused by petting were to get out of control, they could lead to the most feared result of all—pregnancy out of wedlock, with the attendant stigma that might bring harsh social condemnation, even ostracism, and possibly lead to suicide. That situation had its own euphemism: "getting in trouble." Sex was viewed as a dangerous force, a threat to young people, to society, to civilization itself. Because boys were largely viewed as slaves to their raging libidos, it was up to girls to control the sexual urge. Most sex education of the time revolved around the general theme of the girl simply declining all sexual advances.

Though this was the conventional morality of the 1950s and early 1960s, it had not always been that way. F. Scott Fitzgerald had described ribald "petting parties" in the 1920s, and, in fact, conventional morality often had little to do with people's actual experience even in the 1950s. The Kinsey Report on women's sexuality, released in August 1953, scandalized the conservative society of the time with its statistics compiled from interviews with women. Kinsey reported that ninety-nine out of 100 of female interviewees born between 1910 and 1929 had petted by age thirty-five. In the same age group, one-third of the unmarried women were no longer virgins by age twenty-five, and a sizable percentage of those had had several sexual partners. There was so little awareness about women's sexuality at mid-century that these figures were surprising.

Kinsey's statistics challenged the notion that women were by nature less sexual creatures than men. It was not women's nature, but the will of 1950s society, that demanded sexual repression. Interestingly, many girls found they preferred the partially permitted petting to the totally forbidden intercourse for purely sexual reasons. Petting was focused on the female body and often led to orgasm for young women, whereas the self-involved male fumblings of early intercourse seldom did.

The sexual revolution of the late 1960s and 1970s brought an openness about sexuality that made the concept of petting seem almost obsolete, as heterosexual sex outside of marriage became more socially accepted among teenagers and young adults. However, by the 1980s the AIDS epidemic reinforced the dangers of "going all the way." As fear of the disease, transmitted by the exchange of intimate bodily fluids, rose, petting was frequently promoted as a safe alternative to intercourse.

Overt sexuality in the early 2010s is a staple of film, television, advertising, and fashion. In reaction to this, a conservative, often religion-based abstinence movement arose, encouraging young people to refrain from sex until marriage. This idea was popularized by the best-selling *Twilight* series of young adult novels by Stephenie Meyer, in which a teenage girl and her vampire boyfriend must abstain from sex for her safety. Some proponents of abstinence include petting among prohibited behaviors, but for many, necking and petting have once again become a way to place safe limits on sexuality.

Tina Gianoulis

SEE ALSO: *Advertising; AIDS; Best Sellers; The Fifties; Fitzgerald, F. Scott; Kinsey, Dr. Alfred C.; Safe Sex; Sexual Revolution; Television;* Twilight; *World War II.*

BIBLIOGRAPHY

Landers, Ann. *Ann Landers Talks to Teen-Agers about Sex.* Upper Saddle River, NJ: Prentice Hall, 1963.

Mukherjea, Ananya. "Team Bella: Fans Navigating Desire, Security, and Feminism." In *Theorizing "Twilight": Critical Essays on What's at Stake in a Post-Vampire World*, ed. Maggie Parke and Natalie Wilson. Jefferson, NC: McFarland, 2011.

Petersen, James R. "*Playboy*'s History of the Sexual Revolution: Something Cool (Part IV, 1950–1959)." *Playboy*, February 1998, 72.

Petty, Richard *(1937–)*

Known throughout the stock-car racing world as "King Richard," Richard Lee Petty garnered an extraordinary record of 200 wins in events sanctioned by the National Association of Stock Car Auto Racing (NASCAR). After thirty-four years of success in the sport, he retired in 1992 with a record 700 Top 10 finishes and an astonishing seven Winston Cup Series championships, based on annual point totals. Finishing in the money nearly every time he raced, he earned a career total of $7,757,964. He was widely sought after for commercial endorsements, and his fans voted him the most popular Winston Cup Series driver of the year nine times.

THE GOLDEN AGE

The 1964 through 1979 seasons, when Petty won his seven Winston Cup Series championships, were to many fans the golden age of stock-car racing. In the 1967 season he won ten consecutive races—one of his many records that are unlikely to be broken—and came in first in several races where the odds were stacked against him. In one race in Nashville, Tennessee,

Richard Petty. *Richard Petty celebrates in victory lane after winning the 1974 Daytona 500.* ISC ARCHIVES/GETTY IMAGES.

he was leading when a tire blew out, causing him to smash against the fence. He managed to drive his car to the pits, and his crew changed the tires and hammered on the sheet metal to straighten it. While he waited, he dropped from first place to ten laps behind. "It looked awful," he said of the car. But by the time the race was three-fourths over, he was in fifth place, and with the leaders falling out one by one, he eventually won.

The same year, Petty won his fifty-fifth race, replacing his father, Lee, as the NASCAR driver with the most victories. After the 1958 and 1959 seasons, Lee, a NASCAR pioneer and three-time winner of the Winston Cup, became the first back-to-back winner of the trophy. Lee and Richard were the first in what became a dynasty of champion stock-car race drivers, which by the late 1990s included Richard's son, Kyle, and grandson Adam.

During stock-car racing's golden age, Petty faced fierce competition from some of the top drivers in NASCAR history. David Pearson and Cale Yarborough each were three-time Winston Cup winners. Petty called Pearson "a better pure driver than I am, and probably the best ever." Pearson opined that Petty "drives smart and hard. . . . You have to respect his record, which is the best ever." Assessing Yarborough, Richard called him a "tremendous competitor, but he runs so close to the ragged edge he'll spin cars more often than most good drivers." Yarborough said, at the midpoint of Petty's career, "The thing that sets Richard apart is his dedication to stock-car racing. He's been at it a long time, he knows it as well as anyone, and he works just as hard at it today as he did ten years ago."

THE PETTY DYNASTY

Darlington Raceway in South Carolina, called the granddaddy of stock-car tracks, was the scene of some bad racing luck for Petty, including his most dramatic accident, which occurred in 1970. Coming out of the fourth turn, he lost control of his car, struck a concrete wall, and skidded sideways into the main stretch before becoming airborne, tumbling end over end, and crashing into the pit wall in front of the main stands. Fans were hushed with horror as they saw an unconscious Petty hanging out of his upturned car. After being rescued by pit crewmen, he was carried off on a stretcher. When the track announcer finally spread the good news that Petty had suffered no more than a dislocated shoulder and a few cuts and bruises, fans gave a standing ovation. After the Darlington incident, Petty helped create the window net that is now mandatory to keep drivers inside their cars during rollovers.

Petty has argued that athleticism is required in the sport of stock-car racing, stating that the "race driver has to have the reflexes, eyesight, strength, and stamina of any athlete." He pointed out that "driving in tight traffic, speeding up and slowing down at just the right times, passing and being passed, there isn't a time your reflexes aren't important." Eyesight is as important for a race driver as for a baseball hitter, he says, and physical strength is needed to "wrestle a car that weighs three to four thousand pounds for three to five hours." Stamina is vital to compete at a high level for hours in a "roasting hot" car, with no breaks other than the fifteen seconds or so during pit stops.

After winning his 200th race in 1984, Petty continued to compete throughout the 1980s. Although his career was slowing as he passed the torch to his son, Kyle, his winnings were higher than ever due to NASCAR's growing popularity, which he had helped build through his friendliness and willingness to spend hours signing autographs. After surviving another near-fatal crash at Daytona Beach, Florida, in 1988, he announced that he would retire once he had made what he called a final "fan appreciation tour" in 1992.

Although he stopped racing, he continued to run the family's racing team, Petty Enterprises, which had been fielding drivers for decades, and the Richard Petty Driving Experience, which gives amateurs the chance to drive a stock car on a NASCAR track. In 1998 his grandson Adam began a racing career, becoming the fourth generation of the Petty dynasty. In 2000 Adam's career ended in tragedy when he died in a crash while training. Several years later Petty Enterprises merged with Gillett Evernham Motorsports, also owned by Petty, and in 2004 the Petty family founded Victory Junction Gang Camp for seriously or chronically ill children as a memorial to Adam.

Petty's legendary status, jovial personality, and signature style—sunglasses and a cowboy hat—have earned him cameo appearances in movies such as *Speed Zone!* (1989), starring comic actor John Candy, and *Days of Thunder* (1990), starring actor Tom Cruise. In *Swing Vote* (2008) Petty rides shotgun while Kevin Costner (as Bud) drives Petty's famous Number 43 stock car. He also played a small but significant role in Pixar's Oscar-nominated animated film *Cars* (2006), performing the voice of Strip Weathers ("The King"), whose "Petty blue" exterior is an homage to Petty's 1970 Plymouth Superbird. (The scene in which The King crashes is intended as a re-creation of Petty's near-fatal crash at the Daytona 500 in 1988.) In 2010 Petty sealed his legacy as a racing legend by becoming an original member of the NASCAR Hall of Fame.

Benjamin Griffith

SEE ALSO: *Animated Films; Costner, Kevin; Cruise, Tom; Daytona 500; Stock-Car Racing.*

BIBLIOGRAPHY

Bledsoe, Jerry. *The World's Number One, Flat-Out, All-Time Great, Stock Car Racing Book.* Garden City, NY: Doubleday, 1975.

Howell, Mark D. *From Moonshine to Madison Avenue: A Cultural History of the NASCAR Winston Cup Series.* Bowling Green, OH: Bowling Green State University Popular Press, 1997.

Libby, Bill, and Richard Petty. *"King Richard": The Richard Petty Story.* Garden City, NY: Doubleday, 1977.

Vehorn, Frank. *A Farewell to the King: A Personal Look Back at the Career of Richard Petty, Stock Car Racing's Winningest and Most Popular Driver.* Asheboro, NC: Down Home Press, 1992.

Peyton Place

Few imaginary cities are as well known as Peyton Place, and perhaps only Metropolis and Gotham City can rival it for success in a variety of media. The fictitious New England village has been the setting of two novels, two motion pictures, one primetime television series, one daytime drama, and two made-for-television movies—all this from a book written by a New Hampshire homemaker with little formal education.

Grace Metalious published *Peyton Place* in 1956. It was the first novel for Metalious, who was thirty-two at the time, a homemaker with three children and a high school education. Metalious had lived in New Hampshire her entire life, and it is widely assumed that she based her novel on her experiences growing up. *Peyton Place* is set in the late 1930s and early 1940s. The primary character is Allison MacKenzie, a teenager whose mother, Constance, owns a dress store. Constance claims to be widowed, but eventually it is revealed that she never married Allison's father. Other major characters in the novel are Betty Anderson, Allison's beautiful and flirtatious classmate; Rodney Harrington, a spoiled rich youth; Selena Cross, Allison's best friend, who comes from an impoverished family; and the new school principal, Michael Rossi. The novel interweaves many stories as it reveals the dirty secrets of many of the townspeople, particularly Allison's illegitimacy and Selena's rape by her stepfather, whom she murders.

Authors had explored the seamy side of small-town America before, particularly John O'Hara in his Gibbsville stories and Henry Bellamann in *King's Row* (1940), but the fact that Metalious was a woman and a New Englander made *Peyton Place* more shocking. Critics were not kind to the novel—the *New Yorker* complained that its characters lead "humorless, ungenerous lives," and the *New York Herald Tribune* commented that "the book reads like a tabloid version of life in a small town." Nevertheless, *Peyton Place* was an enormously popular success, the third-best-selling novel in 1956 and the second in 1957. By 1965 it had become the best-selling novel in U.S. history, although it was eventually surpassed by *To Kill a Mockingbird* (1960), *The Godfather* (1969), and *The Exorcist* (1971). Metalious was sued in 1958 by her hometown's high school principal, who claimed she had based one of the novel's characters on him; the case was settled out of court. She wrote a sequel, *Return to Peyton Place* (1959), and several other less notable books, but died due to complications from alcoholism in 1964.

Hollywood immediately recognized the potential of Metalious's novel. *Peyton Place* the motion picture was released in 1957. Lana Turner starred as Constance MacKenzie, and her casting against type generated a great deal of publicity for the movie, which was the highest-grossing film of that year. The film received nine Academy Award nominations, including Best Picture, Best Director, and Best Adapted Screenplay. Turner received a Best Actress nomination, and Diane Varsi and Hope Lange, who played Allison MacKenzie and Selena Cross, respectively, each received a nomination for Best Supporting Actress. The sequel, *Return to Peyton Place*, was released in 1961.

Peyton Place reappeared in 1964 as a television series on ABC. Because it was one of the first prime-time soap operas, new episodes of *Peyton Place* were broadcast twice a week, and three times a week from 1965 to 1967, when the series was at the height of its popularity. The television version of *Peyton Place* is best remembered for making stars of Mia Farrow, who portrayed Allison MacKenzie, and Ryan O'Neal, who portrayed Rodney Harrington. The series was canceled in 1969, but it paved the way for subsequent primetime soaps such as *Dallas* (1978–1991) and *Knot's Landing* (1979–1993).

A daytime drama, *Return to Peyton Place*, ran on NBC from 1972 to 1974. In 1977 the television movie *Murder in Peyton Place* reunited most of the television series cast except Farrow and O'Neal, whose successful film careers kept them from making television appearances. The movie explained the absence of Allison and Rodney by explaining they had been killed, hence the film's title. Another television movie, *Peyton Place: The Next Generation* (1985), also brought back many of the television show's cast members and introduced new characters as well in the hopes of inspiring a television series, but such a program never materialized.

Peyton Place has become a permanent part of American culture. The name itself is synonymous with deceit and vice. When Jeannie C. Reilly sang in "Harper Valley PTA" "Well, this is just a little Peyton Place and you're all Harper Valley hypocrites," all America knew exactly what she meant. And when the Warner Brothers network launched its primetime soap *Savannah* (1996–1997), it seemed almost inevitable that its sluttiest character would be named Peyton.

Randall Clark

SEE ALSO: *Best Sellers;* Dallas*;* The Exorcist*;* The Godfather*;* Knots Landing*; Made-for-Television Movies; Metalious, Grace; Television;* To Kill a Mockingbird*; Turner, Lana.*

BIBLIOGRAPHY

Metalious, George, and June O'Shea. *The Girl from Peyton Place: A Biography of Grace Metalious.* New York: Dell, 1965.

Metalious, Grace. *Peyton Place.* New York: Messner, 1956.

Toth, Emily. *Inside Peyton Place: The Life of Grace Metalious.* Garden City, NY: Doubleday, 1981.

Valentino, Lou. *The Films of Lana Turner.* Secaucus, NJ: Citadel, 1976.

Pfeiffer, Michelle *(1958–)*

A three-time Oscar nominee, actress Michelle Pfeiffer also holds the distinction of being the only actress to be cited in *People* magazine as one of the "50 Most Beautiful People in the World" six times. Whereas her looks have always gotten her parts, she has captivated audiences with her ability to portray both serious and comedic characters. She has received critical acclaim for such films as *Dangerous Liaisons* (1988) and starred in box office successes such as *Dangerous Minds* (1995) and *What Lies Beneath*—yet rarely have her critical successes also been box office ones.

RISE TO FAME

Born in Santa Ana, California, in 1958, Michelle Pfeiffer was the second of four children. Pfeiffer has said that she did not consider herself pretty and that she was often bigger than all of the other girls. Nevertheless, encouraged by a high school teacher who told her that she had some talent, Pfeiffer studied acting. Upon graduating from high school, she studied court reporting at a junior college while working as a supermarket checker. After learning that talent scouts were often judges at beauty pageants, Pfeiffer entered and won the 1978 Miss Orange County beauty pageant, and with it, an agent, who got her a part on an episode of *Fantasy Island.* The next year she landed her first regular role in a TV series as a character simply known as "the Bombshell" in ABC's short-lived *Delta House* (1979), an *Animal House* derivation.

Pfeiffer's first starring role was in the feature film *Grease II*—the highly anticipated 1982 sequel to the box office hit. Though this film failed at the box office, Pfeiffer was praised by

Michelle Pfeiffer. Michelle Pfeiffer attends the premiere of New Year's Eve *in 2011.* DIMITRIOS KAMBOURIS/STAFF/WIREIMAGE/ GETTY IMAGES.

critics for her performance as Al Pacino's drug-addicted wife in the box office hit *Scarface* (1983). This led to what many consider her breakthrough role, playing one of the women romanced by devilish Jack Nicholson in the 1987 hit *The Witches of Eastwick*. Her dramatic portrayal of Madame De Tourvel, the tortured object of John Malkovich's sexual treachery in *Dangerous Liaisons* (1988), won Pfeiffer her first Oscar nomination as Best Supporting Actress. But it was her subsequent role as sexy but world-weary lounge singer Susie Diamond in *The Fabulous Baker Boys* (1989) that brought Pfeiffer her greatest success: she earned a second Oscar nomination and won six major acting awards, including those from the New York Film Critics Circle, the National Board of Review, and the Golden Globes.

Pfeiffer was further acclaimed for her turn as the tormented Selina Kyle/Catwoman in *Batman Returns* (1992), for which she did some of her own stunts. She won her third Oscar nomination—her second for Best Actress—for the little-seen 1992 film *Love Field*, a character study of a 1960s Dallas housewife who travels by bus to John F. Kennedy's funeral. Pfeiffer also played the part of the mysterious Countess Olenska, who abandons her philandering husband and falls in love with Newland Archer (Daniel Day-Lewis)—though they are forced to live a platonic relationship due to the repressive society of 1870s New York—in Martin Scorsese's prestigious period piece *Age of Innocence* (1993).

WIDE-RANGING WORK

Pfeiffer produced *Dangerous Minds* through her company Via Rosa. A critical disaster but a box office hit, the film was the first on which Pfeiffer acted as executive producer. Based on the true story of Lou Ann Johnson, an ex-Marine turned inner-city English teacher, the film cost approximately $24 million and grossed more than $175 million worldwide. This was followed by a role in *Up Close and Personal* (1996) opposite Robert Redford in the story of a journalist inspired by Jessica Savitch. Then she tried her hand at romantic comedy opposite George Clooney in *One Fine Day* (1996).

The string of films that followed were largely unmemorable: *To Gillian on Her 37th Birthday* (1996), *A Thousand Acres* (1997)—from Jane Smiley's Pulitzer Prize–winning novel—and *The Story of Us* (1999) with Bruce Willis. In 2000 Pfeiffer starred in *What Lies Beneath* with Harrison Ford as a happily married woman whose life begins to unravel due a series of supernatural encounters that lead her to believe that her husband may be involved in infidelity and murder. The film was a major hit and was followed by Pfeiffer's critically acclaimed turn as a twisted murderess in *White Oleander* (2002).

After taking a four-year hiatus to spend time with her family, Pfeiffer resurfaced in the film version of the Broadway musical *Hairspray* (2007), singing and dancing as Velma Von Tussle, a vain mother and repressive television station manager who refuses to integrate her teen dance show. Pfeiffer received a star on the Hollywood Walk of Fame that same year. Pfeiffer received critical acclaim for the period piece adaptation of Colette's tragic novel *Chéri* (2009), about the tortured relationship between an aging courtesan and her impetuous younger lover. In 2012 director Tim Burton cast Pfeiffer as the imperious matriarch Elizabeth Collins Stoddard in his feature film version of *Dark Shadows*, based on the immensely popular "supernatural soap opera" of the late 1960s.

Once married to *thirtysomething*'s Peter Horton, Pfeiffer later married writer-producer David E. Kelley (*Chicago Hope*, *Picket Fences*, *Ally McBeal*), *Harry's Law*). The couple has one adopted daughter and one son. Since she started her family in the early 1990s, Pfeiffer has limited her roles based on time spent away from her children. She has always considered the level of nudity involved in a role, calling herself "the biggest prude in the industry," and her interest level in a role. As a result she has become known for turning down roles in some major movies, including the leads in *Pretty Woman* (1990), *Basic Instinct* (1992), and *Thelma and Louise* (1991). Pfeiffer has stated that her main criterion for accepting a role is having a strong connection with the character. Pfeiffer also contends that despite reviews to the contrary, she has not improved as an actress since *Grease II*, but rather that the quality of material she is offered has gotten higher.

Rick Moody

SEE ALSO: *Academy Awards;* Ally McBeal; Animal House*; Batman; Broadway; Clooney, George;* Fantasy Island*; Hollywood; Kelley, David E.; Nicholson, Jack; Pacino, Al;* People*; Redford, Robert; Scorsese, Martin; Television.*

BIBLIOGRAPHY

Crowther, Bruce. *Michelle Pfeiffer: A Biography*. London: R. Hale, 1994.

Tierney, Tom. *Glamorous Movie Stars of the Eighties Paper Dolls.* Mineola, NY: Dover, 2002.

The Phantom of the Opera

The Phantom of the Opera, seen by more than 130 million people around the world, is one of the most successful pieces of entertainment of all time. The musical premiered at Her Majesty's Theatre in London in 1986, and in 2011 it was still playing there, celebrating its twenty-fifth anniversary. In 1988 the show opened at the Majestic Theater in New York, and in 2011 it was still running there as well. *The Phantom of the Opera* became Broadway's longest-running show in history in 2006 when it overtook the record set by the musical *Cats* (1982).

With music by Andrew Lloyd Webber and lyrics by Charles Hart, *The Phantom of the Opera* is based on the 1911 novel of the same name by French author Gaston Leroux. It is the story of a disfigured, masked man who lives below the Paris Opera House in France. Called the Phantom by the troupe that performs in the opera house, the masked man is in love with Christine Daaé, a beautiful young soprano with a magnificent voice. The Phantom teaches Christine how to sing properly and secures for her the lead role in his opera, *Don Juan Triumphant*, by terrorizing everyone who opposes him, including Raoul, Christine's true love. At the end, the Phantom kidnaps Christine, but when she kisses him without being repulsed by his physical appearance, he disappears and leaves her to be with Raoul.

Since its premiere, *The Phantom of the Opera* has been produced in 145 cities in twenty-seven countries around the world. The original London cast included Michael Crawford as the mysterious Phantom, Sarah Brightman (Lloyd Webber's wife) as Christine, and Steve Barton as Raoul. The show's director was Harold Prince, whose imaginative and impressive staging captivated audiences on both sides of the Atlantic.

Lauded by audiences and critics alike, *The Phantom of the Opera* has received more than fifty major theater awards. England's version of the Tony Awards is the Olivier Awards, and *The Phantom* won two: Musical of the Year and Outstanding Performance in a Musical (for Crawford). In the United States *The Phantom of the Opera* received ten Tony Award nominations and won seven, including Best Musical, Best Actor (for Crawford), and Best Director (for Prince).

The Phantom of the Opera is representative of two dominant trends in musicals of the 1980s: the sung-through musical and the megamusical. The sung-through musical is a show in which spoken dialogue is minimalized and generally replaced by operatic recitative (speech singing). A megamusical is a show in which sets, costumes, and special effects are as important to the dramatic narrative as are the traditional coupling of music and words. Every aspect of the work is meant to dazzle the audience.

Among the show's hauntingly beautiful songs are "Think of Me," "The Phantom of the Opera," "Angel of Music," "All I Ask of You," "The Music of the Night," "Masquerade," "Prima Donna," "Wishing You Were Somehow Here Again," and "The Point of No Return." The music is decidedly operatic in style, as befits the story. Rock elements permeate much of the score, whether in a hard style as in the title number or in a gentler vein as in "All I Ask of You." Lloyd Webber recreated the atmosphere of nineteenth-century operatic Paris and made it accessible to audiences of the twentieth and twenty-first centuries.

Spectacular visual effects accompany the music. Most memorable is the chandelier, which lights up and slowly rises from the stage to the ceiling above the audience during the overture. It suddenly comes crashing down just before intermission, and in the blackened theater it seems like it is falling into the audience. Almost as fantastic is the Phantom navigating his boat on the lake underneath the opera house, surrounded by fog.

The Phantom of the Opera had two significant reinterpretations in the early 2000s. A lavish film adaptation starring Emmy Rossum, Gerard Butler, Patrick Wilson, Minnie Driver, and Miranda Richardson appeared in 2004. Directed by Joel Schumacher, the film includes "Learn to Be Lonely," a new song by Lloyd Webber. In 2006 a ninety-five-minute version, *Phantom—The Las Vegas Spectacular*, opened in a custom-built theater at the Venetian Casino, Hotel & Resort in Las Vegas. The *Las Vegas Review-Journal*, Nevada's largest newspaper, named it the Best Show in Las Vegas for 2011.

William A. Everett

SEE ALSO: *Academy Awards; Broadway;* Cats*; Las Vegas; Lloyd Webber, Andrew; The Musical; Prince, Hal; Tony Awards.*

BIBLIOGRAPHY

Everett, William A. "The Mega-Musical as Transcultural Phenomenon." In *The New Europe at the Crossroads*, ed. Ursula E. Beitter. Baltimore, MD: Lang, 1999.

Perry, George C. *The Complete Phantom of the Opera*. New York: Holt, 1991.

Richmond, Keith. *The Musicals of Andrew Lloyd Webber.* London: Virgin, 1995.

Snelson, John. *Andrew Lloyd Webber*. New Haven, CT: Yale University Press, 2009.

Sternfeld, Jessica. *The Megamusical.* Bloomington: Indiana University Press, 2006.

Phelps, Michael *(1985–)*

Swimming champion Michael Phelps is best known for winning fourteen gold medals by the close of the 2008 Summer Olympic Games, more than any other Olympic athlete in history. Born the youngest of three children on June 30, 1985, in Baltimore, Maryland, Phelps is the son of a middle school teacher and a state trooper. When his parents divorced in 1994, the young swimmer, just nine at the time, and his sisters went to live with their mother, gradually losing contact with their father. Older sisters Hillary and Whitney were strong swimmers, and Whitney almost made the U.S. Olympic team in 1996.

Phelps began swimming competitively at age seven and set his first national record when he was ten. Frequently taken to task in grammar school for not being able to sit still, Phelps was diagnosed with ADHD around the time of his parents' divorce. Although swimming helped him channel his energy, it was not until he began working with coach Bob Bowman at the North Baltimore Aquatic Center that the young swimmer tapped his potential. After a string of national age-group records, the fifteen-year-old Phelps earned a spot on the U.S. swim team for the 2000 Summer Olympics in Sydney, Australia, becoming the youngest male athlete to compete in the Olympics in sixty-eight years. Although he did not win any medals, he took fifth place in the 200-meter butterfly, and at the end of the Sydney games, he ranked seventh in the world in that event.

In the 2001 Phillips 66 National Championships, Phelps broke a world record in the 200-meter butterfly, only to break his own record several months later at the World Championships in Fukuoka, Japan. His star continued to rise as he won in multiple events and broke world records at the 2002 U.S. Nationals and Pan Pacific Championships. At the 2003 U.S. Spring National Championships, Phelps became the first swimmer to win races in three different strokes at one national event. At the 2003 World Championships, he medaled in six events, breaking five world records. At the U.S. Summer Nationals, he won five titles, becoming the first male athlete to complete this feat in a single competition.

Phelps signed a multimillion-dollar contract with Speedo in 2003, and soon other companies, such as Visa and AT&T, followed suit, making the swimmer a fully sponsored, professional athlete by age eighteen. At the 2004 Summer Olympics, he qualified for six individual events, setting new world records and winning six gold and two bronze medals. He displayed great team spirit by conceding his spot in the 400-meter medley to teammate Ian Crocker, allowing Crocker one final chance at Olympic gold. After the 2004 Olympics, Phelps joined several teammates on a national tour called Swim with the Stars.

However, Phelps's fortunes quickly took a sour turn. In 2004 he was arrested for DUI and underage drinking after being pulled over for running a stop sign. He was sentenced to eighteen months' probation, slapped with a $250 fine, and made to do community service by speaking at local schools about alcohol abuse. The negative press did not deter him. Bowman told the Edge Foundation in 2008, "One of the things I call Michael is the motivation machine. Bad moods, good moods, he channels everything for gain." At the 2005 World Championships and the 2006 Pan Pacific Championships, Phelps continued to break records and win gold medals.

At the 2007 World Championships in Melbourne, Phelps broke his hero Ian Thorpe's record of six gold medals. Phelps won seven events, setting new world records in five of them and provoking media speculation that he would beat U.S. swimmer Mark Spitz's record of seven Olympic gold medals, set in 1972. Speedo offered Phelps a $1 million bonus if he beat Spitz's record at the upcoming games in Beijing, China. The swimmer not only won eight golds, breaking Spitz's record, but he also broke U.S. speed skater Eric Heiden's record for most individual golds in a single Olympiad.

After his triumph in Beijing, Phelps used his bonus money from Speedo to start the Michael Phelps Foundation, which promotes healthy lifestyles among young swimmers. However, less than a year later, photos of the swimmer allegedly smoking marijuana from a bong surfaced in a British tabloid. Although he was not prosecuted for the incident, he was suspended from competing for three months, lost his sponsorship from the Kellogg Company, and made the cover of *High Times* magazine.

At the 2009 World Championships, Phelps lost his first race in four years, in the 200-meter freestyle to German Paul Biedermann, who was wearing an Arena X-Glide full-body suit. The suit, which gave Biedermann added buoyancy, became a source of controversy throughout the games. Phelps's coach threatened to pull him from international competitions, and as of October 1, 2009, the suits were banned from international competitions. Phelps continued winning gold at the 2010 Pan Pacific Championships and at the 2011 World Championships.

Ron Horton

SEE ALSO: *Divorce; Marijuana; Olympics; Spitz, Mark; Sports Heroes; Swimming Pools.*

BIBLIOGRAPHY

Crouse, Karen. "Phelps Apologizes for Marijuana Pipe Photo." *New York Times*, February 2, 2009, D8(L).

Edge Foundation. "Michael Phelps ADHD Is Not an Attention Deficit." Edge Foundation Blog. Accessed May 2012. Available from http://www.edgefoundation.org/blog/2008/08/15/michael-phelpss-adhd-is-not-an-attention-deficit/

Phelps, Michael, and Alan Abrahamson. *No Limits: The Will to Succeed.* New York: Free Press, 2009.

Phelps, Michael, and Brian Cazeneuve. *Beneath the Surface.* Champaign, IL: Sports Publishing, 2008.

The Philadelphia Story

The Philadelphia Story (1940) is an Academy Award–winning comedy directed by George Cukor. In the film, socialite Tracy Lord (Katharine Hepburn) is about to marry George Kittredge (John Howard), when her first husband, C. K. Dexter Haven (Cary Grant), arrives with two gossip magazine reporters (Jimmy Stewart, who won an Academy Award for best actor for the role, and Ruth Hussey). Tracy suddenly cannot decide whether she should marry George, Dexter, or Mike, the magazine reporter. Donald Ogden Stewart's witty, Academy Award–winning script, derived from a stage play by Philip Barry, satirizes the divisions between classes and argues that people should have sympathy for the flaws of others.

Christian L. Pyle

SEE ALSO: *Academy Awards; Cukor, George; Grant, Cary; Hepburn, Katharine; Stewart, Jimmy.*

BIBLIOGRAPHY

Barry, Philip. *The Philadelphia Story: A Comedy in Three Acts.* New York: Coward-McCann, 1939.

Long, Robert Emmet. *George Cukor: Interviews.* Jackson: University Press of Mississippi, 2001.

Philco Television Playhouse

One of the most distinguished live anthology series in television history, NBC's *Philco Television Playhouse* is best remembered for nurturing talent to create original television productions. Producer Fred Coe assembled one of television's most illustrious writing teams, including Paddy Chayefsky, Horton Foote, Tad Mosel, and Gore Vidal. When the series debuted on October 3, 1948, it was produced in conjunction with the Actors' Equity Association and specialized in Broadway adaptations, including *Dinner at Eight* with Peggy Wood; *Cyrano de Bergerac* starring Jose Ferrer; and *Counsellor-at-Law*, Paul Muni's TV debut. A year later *Philco* worked with the Book-of-the-Month Club to present dramatizations of noteworthy novels, including *Sense and Sensibility* in 1950 with Cloris Leachman.

Beginning in the early 1950s, Coe instructed his writers to create intimate dramas for the small screen. What resulted were such acclaimed teleplays as Chayefsky's *Marty* with Rod Steiger (1953); Foote's *A Trip to Bountiful* with Lillian Gish (1955); and Vidal's *The Death of Billy the Kid* with Paul Newman (1955), all of which were later made into films. Goodyear became an alternating sponsor of Coe's *Playhouse* in 1951, and, in all, more than 250 live dramas were produced over eight seasons.

Ron Simon

SEE ALSO: *Book-of-the-Month Club; Broadway; Chayefsky, Paddy; Gish, Lillian; Leachman, Cloris; Muni, Paul; Newman, Paul; Television; Vidal, Gore.*

BIBLIOGRAPHY

Considine, Shaun. *Mad as Hell: The Life and Work of Paddy Chayefsky*. New York: Random House, 1994.

Krampner, Jon. *The Man in the Shadows: Fred Coe and the Golden Age of Television*. New Brunswick, NJ: Rutgers University Press, 1997.

Rodman, Ronald W. *Tuning In: American Narrative Television Music*. New York: Oxford University Press, 2010.

Phillips, Irna *(1901–1973)*

A pioneering radio writer, Irna Phillips created arguably the first soap opera, *Painted Dreams* in 1930. She then spent the next forty years as the creative force behind such radio shows as *Today's Children* (1933–1938, 1943–1950), *Road of Life* (1937–1959), and *Woman in White* (1938–1942, 1944–1948). *The Guiding Light* debuted on radio (1937–1956) before moving to television (1952–2009). Her other daytime television shows included *As the World Turns* (1956–2010) and *Another World* (1964–1999).

Phillips was among the first soap opera writers to focus on professional characters—doctors, nurses, and lawyers. She also developed the cliff-hanger, which ended each episode of her shows. Phillips mentored soap opera writers Agnes Nixon, perhaps best known as the creator of television's *All My Children* (1970–2011) and *One Life to Live* (1968–), and William J. Bell, the creative force behind *The Young and the Restless* (1973–) and *The Bold and the Beautiful* (1987–).

Chris Chandler

SEE ALSO: All My Children*;* Another World*;* As the World Turns*;* Guiding Light*; Radio; Radio Drama; Soap Operas; Television;* The Young and the Restless.

BIBLIOGRAPHY

Dunning, John. *On the Air: The Encyclopedia of Old-Time Radio*. New York: Oxford University Press, 1998.

Sterling, Christopher H., and Michael C. Keith. *Encyclopedia of Radio*. New York: Fitzroy Dearborn, 2004.

Phone Sex

Computerization and the deregulation of the telephone industry in the United States and Europe in the 1980s made it possible for companies to provide a wide variety of services over the telephone, including banking, insurance, and mail-order shopping. The telephone also became a major source of income for the sex industry, which is often at the forefront of technological innovation and ready to exploit new business opportunities. The mostly male callers to premium-rate "fantasy lines" pay by credit card to engage in sexually stimulating and anonymous role-playing over the telephone. Some commentators suggest that the fear of AIDS contributed to the popularity of phone sex calls to "900" numbers—so called because they are normally assigned the prefix 900 in lieu of an area code. In the twenty-first century phone sex lines have largely been superseded by online forms of live pornography, chatrooms, and individual operators with their own webpages, but the industry remains an extremely lucrative one.

Opinion is divided over whether it is the customer or the operator who is being exploited in the phone sex "relationship," but when interviewed many operators (also known as "call-doers" or "fantasy makers") describe what they do as an ordinary job. Many of the companies that provide phone sex services are run by women, and many women in the industry claim that the life is liberating. It allows them to work from home or to look after children; some phone sex workers report that they are glad to be able to dress the way they want or that the job frees them to work at other things. For others phone sex is an alternative to prostitution.

That is not to suggest, of course, that there are no downsides to life in this industry. Writer Amy Flowers—who worked for four months as a phone sex operator in the 1990s—points to low pay, insecurity, and exposure to abuse as factors that make such employment a bad experience. In her book *The Fantasy Factory: An Insider's View of the Phone Sex Industry*, she criticizes the role of phone sex companies in American society, suggesting that they are not selling sex so much as the fantasy of human intimacy. For many of the men on the other end of the line, phone sex is an addiction. They spend thousands of dollars on credit cards and run up debts that destroy marriages and break up families.

Traditionally, phone sex companies have provided two basic forms of service: the prerecorded message, accessed by the caller making choices through the telephone keypad, and access to live operators, who specialize in performing particular identities and fantasies. On the Internet, such services were first augmented and then almost entirely replaced by online chat services, including video chat. Phone sex services are mostly advertised on adult TV channels and online. Pornographic magazines are also popular places to advertise sex chat services, though they are in terminal decline, placing phone sex somewhere in between the unreality of the magazine and the physical risks of prostitution. Many U.S. fantasy makers are around thirty years of age and describe themselves as white and middle class. Similarly, most of the callers are middle-class, white, heterosexual males. A small number of lines cater to heterosexual women. In the late 1990s there emerged a lucrative gay and cross-gender market, which has flourished online.

In the 1990s, prerecorded messages were the cheapest and most lucrative services, sometimes generating revenue by credit-card subscription, but primarily making money by keeping the caller on the premium-rate line for as long as possible. Premium rate lines fell out of favor when they became associated with fraud but also because credit card processing allows operators to check the age and identity of the caller. Credit card verification also makes it more difficult for callers to deny making the call, either through embarrassment at being found out or regret at having to pay the bill. Although they can be seen as an audio equivalent of pornographic stories, prerecorded adult telephone messages differ significantly from written forms of pornography in that they address the caller directly and involve him or her in a secret, personal conversation. This illusion of privacy is achieved despite the fact that the brief messages are played continuously and can be accessed by many thousands of callers at the same time.

The illusion of involving the caller in personal contact is created still more effectively on the more expensive live fantasy lines. Live fantasy makers can respond to the caller's requirements, adjusting their stated identity, occupation, and the story they tell as they go along. Operators are trained to begin the call by presenting themselves as the ideal woman before moving on to various stereotypes, such as lesbian, coed, housewife, or teen. Operators take pride in being able to take on whatever identity the caller demands, to the extent that African American roles are often successfully played by European American women, and the few male operators are able to disguise their voices enough to convince callers that they are talking to a woman. Many regard their work as a form of theater or performance art and describe themselves with titles such as "fantasy artist." One operator, interviewed by Kira Hall in the mid-1990s, described herself as a storyteller and claimed to have improved her work by studying the techniques of Garrison Keillor.

Phone sex is not always part of a transaction between paying customers and service providers. Many couples use phone sex to enjoy intimacy over long distances, including erotic SMS text messaging or "sexting." Phone sex has also featured as a plot device in movies, including *Get Carter* (1971), and TV shows such as *Sex and the City* (1998–2004).

By adopting stereotyped identities, professional phone sex operators can protect themselves from much of the racist, sexist, and personal abuse directed at them by callers, but they also help to perpetuate racist, sexist, or antisocial perceptions. Hall acknowledges that whereas European Americans are often successful in playing the role of African American women, African American women themselves are sometimes rejected by clients for not being "realistic" enough. The anonymity of the phone sex lines allows the participants on both sides to be whoever they choose to be, an anonymity that is largely removed in online sex chat, especially when it involves video. Though it continues to exist and remains a significant part of the adult entertainment industry, the brief heyday of commercial phone sex was between the 1980s and the late 1990s. Since the arrival of widespread high-speed Internet services, phone sex lines have diversified to websites and video chat, but traditional phone sex chat remains a multimillion-dollar industry.

Chris Routledge

SEE ALSO: *Advertising; AIDS; Consumerism; Divorce; Gay Men; Keillor, Garrison; Leisure Time; Lesbianism; Pornography; Safe Sex; Strip Joints/Striptease; Telephone.*

BIBLIOGRAPHY

Flowers, Amy. *The Fantasy Factory: An Insider's View of the Phone Sex Industry.* Philadelphia: University of Pennsylvania Press, 1998.

Goldstein, Harry. "The Dial-ectic of Desire: For Women at the Other End of the Phone Sex Line, Some Fantasies Ring Painfully True." *Utne Reader*, March/April 1991, 32–33.

Hall, Kira, and Mary Bucholtz, eds. "Lip Service on the Fantasy Lines." In *Gender Articulated: Language and the Socially Constructed Self.* London: Routledge, 1995.

Leigh, Jennifer. "Phone Sex Industry: Still Alive and Well in the U.S." Socyberty. Accessed January 25, 2012. Available from http://socyberty.com/sexuality/phone-sex-industry-still-alive-and-well-in-the-us/2/

Weatherall, Ann. *Gender, Language and Discourse.* New York: Routledge, 2002.

Phonograph

Thomas Edison's invention of the phonograph in 1877 opened up a world of recorded sound and created one of the great entertainment industries. The phonograph made it possible to reproduce sounds at will, and the machine eventually emerged as a critical step in the mechanization of leisure time. The first talking machine, the phonograph was an entertainment technology encased in a piece of furniture. Its acceptance into millions of homes made it an important forerunner of the radio and television sets that became the centers of home entertainment in the twentieth century.

Edison Phonograph. *Thomas A. Edison poses with his favorite invention, the tinfoil phonograph, in 1877.* AP IMAGES.

The technology of sound recording was conceived as an accessory to the telephone. Alexander Graham Bell's invention was aimed primarily at businesspeople, and it followed that once a message was transmitted, there should be a device to make a permanent record of it. Edison was heavily involved in improving all aspects of Bell's telephone, and he stumbled upon the principles of acoustic sound recording in the fall of 1877. He found that the sound vibrations of his voice were strong enough to power a stylus to cut a signal into a revolving sheet of tinfoil. Even members of his own laboratory staff were surprised to hear a faint reproduction of his voice when the tinfoil was rerun under the stylus.

Edison was only one of many inventors and scientists experimenting in telephony, and in the years after his famous invention of 1877, several important improvements were made to his phonograph: wax cylinders were used instead of sheets of tinfoil, spring motors replaced hand-powered cranks, and a disc format for the recording medium was developed. The latter was the work of the inventor Emile Berliner, who called his machine the gramophone. Both phonographs and gramophones were based on the same technology; only the format of the record was different. Two large business organizations were founded on each format, and the competition between cylinder and disc lasted until the late 1920s when Edison phased out the production of cylinders. Despite the demise of the cylinder-playing phonograph, Americans continued to call their talking machines "phonographs" whereas Europeans called theirs "gramophones," regardless of make or format.

AN ENTERTAINING INVENTION

Acoustic sound recording technology was as yet too primitive to be adopted by businesspeople; subsequently, the only commercial applications were found in entertainment. First people paid to hear their own voices, and then they paid to listen to music. The demand for prerecorded cylinders and discs was so great that the manufacturers of talking machines moved into studio recording and the mass production of records. They recorded all types of popular music—patriotic band music, sentimental Irish and German ballads for immigrants, bawdy songs and the ethnic humor of vaudeville, and selections from opera and classical music.

As mass production techniques were applied to the manufacture of talking machines, more customers had to be found to maintain sales levels, so more types of music were recorded. By 1914 the manufacturers of talking machines had recorded the music of every immigrant group in the United States—including those from Asia—and had delved into the nostalgic antebellum past to recycle the music of the minstrel show, the "coon" songs that made fun of the slaves.

It was not until the 1920s that the manufacturers discovered two groups of customers that would sustain their business for much of the century: African Americans and rural folk. In 1920 the Okeh record company discovered the enormous untapped market of black urban consumers with the phenomenal sales of "Crazy Blues," sung by Mamie Smith. This began the craze for blues and jazz records in the 1920s that prompted the author F. Scott Fitzgerald to label the decade "the Jazz Age." In 1927 RCA sent Ralph Peer to the South to record local music. He recruited, among others, Jimmie Rodgers and the Carter family to sing for the recording machine and enshrined them as the pioneers of country music. During the Great Depression, when sales of records dried up, the demand for "hick discs" sold in general stores or by mail order was an important source of income for record companies.

The introduction of radio and electronic recording in the 1920s dramatically extended the capabilities of sound recording and reproduction but did little to change the role of the phonograph in popular culture. Nearly every household in the United States had a talking machine and a collection of records in the living room as a source of entertainment. Radio initially cut into sales of phonographs, but over time, the two learned to coexist; radio depended on recorded sound as a primary source of programming, and the phonograph companies found that radio was a good way to introduce new recordings to a national audience. The industry of recorded sound survived the Great Depression, and by the 1940s recordings of swing music were selling in the millions of units.

Recorded sound defined popular music in the twentieth century, and the record companies determined how it was categorized. Rock and roll bridged the gap between country music for the white audience and rhythm and blues for African Americans in the late 1950s. The musical tastes of the Baby Boom Generation, born after World War II, drove the industry of recorded sound in the 1960s and 1970s, as rock and roll on vinyl 45-rpm discs was gradually supplanted by art rock and psychedelic rock recorded on long-playing discs.

RECEDING INTO HISTORY

Although generations of users had learned how to place a needle on a revolving disc and ignore the scratches and pops as it traveled along the groove, the phonograph still suffered from short playing times and a lack of recording capability. Magnetic tape recording proved to be the solution to these problems, and the introduction of the first tape cassettes in the 1960s signaled the beginning of the decline for the phonograph. During the 1970s sales of the Philips compact audio cassette equaled those of phonograph records, and a tape recorder became an essential part of the home entertainment center.

A new form of sound recording based on digital encoding was introduced in the 1980s. The compact disc offered virtually noiseless recordings, ease of operation, and much longer recording times. In the 1990s the advent of MP3 technology further pushed the phonograph into the background. Phonograph records disappeared from retail stores, and it seemed as if the end had come for a technology that was now more than 100 years old. Yet many music lovers refused to throw away their phonographs, and the manufacture of needles and record players continued into the twenty-first century.

Andre Millard

SEE ALSO: *Cassette Tape; Compact Discs; Edison, Thomas Alva; MP3.*

BIBLIOGRAPHY

Eisenberg, Evan. *Recording Angel: Music, Records and Culture from Aristotle to Zappa*. London: Picador, 1987.

Frow, George L., and Albert F. Sefl. *The Edison Cylinder Phonograph: A Detailed Account of the Entertainment Models until 1929*. Sevenoaks, Kent, United Kingdom: Frow, 1978.

Huber, David Miles, and Robert E. Runstein. *Modern Recording Techniques*. Boston: Focal Press, 2001.

Koenigsberg, Allen. *The Patent History of the Phonograph,*

1877–1912: A Source Book. Brooklyn, NY: APM Press, 1990.

Millard, Andre J. *America on Record: A History of Recorded Sound.* New York: Cambridge University Press, 1995.

Photoplay

The editors of *Photoplay,* Julian Johnson and James Quirk, established one of the most popular fan magazines of the early twentieth century. By 1918 the editors could boast a circulation figure of 204,434. The basic format of *Photoplay* set a precedent for almost all other movie magazines that followed. It catered largely to the public's craving for information about their favorite stars and for reviews of new motion picture releases. A color picture of a movie star, drawn specially for the magazine, appeared on the cover of each issue. Such original artwork distinguished *Photoplay* from other fan magazines and made the covers collectors' items.

Inside the magazine, following a few pages of advertisements and the table of contents, was a section of about ten to fifteen pages of photographs of actors and actresses. The key to this layout was a proper balance between pictures and text. And the text could vary between long articles on screen personalities such as D. W. Griffith and the Gish sisters, Lillian and Dorothy, and short opinion pieces written by the editors.

Johnson, the first editor appointed by magazine Vice President Quirk, started a column called "Close-Ups" in which he commented on the state of the moving picture world. He advanced the notion that a better educated public would lead to better films. In order to make this endeavor seem serious, Johnson and Quirk worked to convince their readers that movies were indeed an art form. For example, when Geraldine Farrar, an opera singer of high repute, crossed over into the movies, Johnson remarked that "the triumph of active photography" was complete. "Let us never hear again the snivel that photodrama is a minor art, or not an art at all." Active photography, he believed, was "destined to raise the art standard of the world by bringing every art, every land and every interpretative genius to every man's door."

Many of *Photoplay*'s contributors, including respected critics Terry Ramsaye and Burns Mantle, published extended pieces on the history of the film industry (Ramsaye) and critiques on movies (Mantle), illustrating that they could be considered serious fun. In a series of editorials that praised the democratic nature of movies, Quirk seemed to exemplify the spirit of a new cultural criticism.

Photoplay performed a double service: it catered to the fan's appreciation of movies as entertainment and as an escape while also treating the photoplay and its audience with a respect normally reserved for elite patrons of fine arts. As other periodicals that were devoted solely to expert evaluation of film emerged, *Photoplay* settled into a role that accentuated stars over everything else. Photo essays, for example, became the staple of the magazine's success. Fans could browse through pictures of movie stars in and out of their screen roles. Mary Pickford and Douglas Fairbanks—two megastars of the silent era—received considerable coverage on their estate in California known as Pickfair. By the 1940s *Photoplay* was providing the "pin-ups" that teenagers and young adults prized for their collections of Hollywood's stars and starlets.

A second feature that bolstered *Photoplay*'s coverage of stars was the gossip column. Quirk reportedly hired a young woman named Adela Rogers St. John to begin a regular column that commented (and speculated) on the lives of the famous. This feature grew into an industry—a rumor mill—all its own. Generations of readers were entertained by the gossip of notable insiders such as Hedda Hopper, Sheilah Graham, Dorothy Kigallen, and Louella Parsons, one of the most powerful voices (and ears) of them all. The most valuable currency in the gossip trade was rumors of love—whether illicit, broken, triangular, or innocent. *Photoplay* readers had a chance to hear about Charlie Chaplin's marriages and divorces; Rudolph Valentino's mysterious love life; and, in another generation, the public love affairs of Lana Turner, Clark Gable, Errol Flynn, and many others.

Photoplay merged with another fan magazine—*Movie Mirror*—in 1941 and changed again in 1977 when the name became *Photoplay and TV Mirror.*

Ray Haberski Jr.

SEE ALSO: *Chaplin, Charlie; Fairbanks, Douglas, Sr.; Fan Magazines; Flynn, Errol; Gable, Clark; Gish, Dorothy; Gish, Lillian; Gossip Columns; Griffith, D. W.; Pickford, Mary; Turner, Lana; Valentino, Rudolph.*

BIBLIOGRAPHY

Gelman, Barbara, ed. *Photoplay Treasury.* New York: Crown Publishers, 1972.

Jowett, Garth. *Film: The Democratic Art.* Boston: Little, Brown, 1976.

Koszarski, Richard. *An Evening's Entertainment: The Age of the Silent Feature Picture, 1915–1928.* Berkeley: University of California Press, 1990.

Levine, Lawrence. *Highbrow/Lowbrow: The Emergence of Cultural Hierarchy in America.* Cambridge: Harvard University Press, 1988.

Slide, Anthony. *Inside the Hollywood Fan Magazine: A History of Star Makers, Fabricators, and Gossip Mongers.* Jackson: University Press of Mississippi, 2010.

Physique Pictorial

SEE: *Athletic Model Guild.*

Picasso, Pablo *(1881–1973)*

Pablo Picasso was one of the most versatile, prolific, and influential artists of the twentieth century. His widely reported lifestyle, his wealth and womanizing, and his meticulously documented method of working are legendary; his face has become a mythic symbol of the artist for millions around the world. Likewise, his immediately recognizable paintings, sculptures, and ceramics epitomize modern art. Reproductions of Picasso and his works decorate everything from neck ties and coffee cups to flatware and umbrellas. Protean, bold, a daring experimentalist, and a technical master, Picasso stands as the indisputable genius of twentieth-century art.

Artworks as commodities reaches its most dizzying heights in the case of Picasso. His paintings, etchings, pottery, sketches—indeed, anything he scribbled upon—brought small fortunes even as he produced them. For those who cannot afford an original, an endless supply of reproductions and imitations exist. By the early 1950s Picasso transcended the need for money, because "whatever he wishes to own, he can acquire by drawing it," according to art writer and novelist John Berger in his book *The Success and Failure of Picasso.*

The explanation for this incredible reality lay in the technological advances of the twentieth century and in the ability of Picasso to harness them for an unprecedented experiment in self-promotion. In this, as in so much of his work, Picasso created the model that would generate endless variations. Celebrities of all sorts continue to take cues from his life. He invited expert photographer friends into his studio to capture his eccentric and expansive lifestyle. He constantly reworked stories of his creative influences and accomplishments for sympathetic writers. He painted with specially designed inks before a film crew for the popular 1956 movie *The Mystery of Picasso,* a setting tailor-made to showcase his particular artistic style. The film presents Picasso in all his glory: not meticulous or painterly, but dynamic and mercurial, as if he were a channel through which some greater force spoke. In fact, his own story is one of his masterpieces. His life is the archetypal tale of modern genius, inspiring countless fictional and real-life imitations.

Born Pablo Ruiz y Picasso in Málaga, Spain, Picasso attended the School of Fine Arts in Barcelona when he was fourteen years old. He exhibited his works at the Els Quatre Gats gallery five years later. He moved from Barcelona to Paris in 1904 and spent the next decade or so living impoverished on the streets of Montmartre, meeting interesting women and enjoying the easy camaraderie of the so-called Picasso Gang of soon-to-be-great men.

In 1906 sister and brother collectors Gertrude and Leo Stein and art dealer Daniel-Henry Kahnweiler began to buy Picasso's paintings. In 1919 the artist moved forever away from his famously bohemian lodgings to a lavish apartment in one of the most fashionable quarters of Paris. Soon he was a millionaire and one of the first superstar celebrities of the modern era. He was hounded by the press, which he courted and castigated in ritual fashion. He was the subject of tell-all best sellers written by his beautiful ex-lovers Fernande Olivier and Françoise Gilot. His family and friends made a cottage industry of his life. In the face of all this, he hid behind the curtain of his wealth, retreating to a series of fenced-off villas in the south of France. Estranged from his family and surrounded finally by more sycophants and curiosity seekers than friends, Picasso nevertheless remained vital and prolific until his death.

It is a testament to the extraordinary power of the modern celebrity-making industry that Picasso's persona came to overshadow his art, for Picasso created unrivalled masterpieces in several of modernism's widely diverse and rapidly changing styles. The sentimental works of his Blue Period and Rose Period remain popular favorites, perhaps in part because they seem to conform to reality. The distorted figures of his later work are less immediately appealing, with their characteristic sideways noses, uneven torsos, and twisted limbs. Yet these works, inspired in part by African sculpture, freed Picasso from the vanishing-point perspective and naturalistic figuration of traditional European art.

After completing his great masterwork of that era, *Les Demoiselles d'Avignon* (1907), Picasso, together with Georges Braque, turned toward cubism, where many angles of a figure are portrayed at once, where the constantly varying perspectives of reality constitute the actual subject of the painting. Picasso's antiwar works also represent the standard of the genre. In 1937 Picasso completed *Guernica* (1937), an enormous painting depicting in ferocious allegory the aerial bombing of a Basque town during the Spanish Civil War. *Guernica* contains many of the images that mark Picasso's body of work, including a gored and dying horse, an ominous monster bull, and the upraised arms of a powerless victim.

John Tomasic

SEE ALSO: *Modernism.*

BIBLIOGRAPHY

Berger, John. *The Success and Failure of Picasso.* New York: Penguin, 1965.

Gilot, Francoise, and Carlton Lake. *Life with Picasso.* New York: Doubleday, 1989.

Malraux, André. *Picasso's Mask.* New York: Holt, Rinehart and Winston, 1976.

O'Brian, Patrick. *Picasso: A Biography.* New York: Putnam, 1976.

Richardson, John. *A Life of Picasso,* 2 vols. New York: Random House, 1991 and 1996.

Rubin, William, ed. *Pablo Picasso: A Retrospective.* New York: Museum of Modern Art, 1980.

Stassinopoulos, Arianna. *Picasso: Creator and Destroyer.* New York: Simon & Schuster, 1988.

Stein, Gertrude. *Picasso.* New York: Beacon Press, 1959.

Walther, Ingo F. *Pablo Picasso.* Cologne, Germany: Taschen, 2000.

Pickford, Mary *(1893–1979)*

Touted as the first female movie mogul, "America's Sweetheart" Mary Pickford is best remembered for the sticky-sweet Pollyanna image she cultivated in her films of the 1910s and 1920s. The childlike innocence and eternal optimism of her star persona have become somewhat cliché, obscuring the fact that Pickford was one of the most popular international screen icons of her day. Biographer Scott Eyman contends that "she defined her era, roughly 1910–1925, as surely as Marilyn Monroe defined hers."

Born Gladys Smith in Toronto, Ontario, Canada, in 1893, she grew into one of the most powerful figures of early Hollywood. This power was secured in 1919 when she formed the independent studio United Artists with Douglas Fairbanks, Charlie Chaplin, and D. W. Griffith. Her stature was reinforced a year later when she entered into a highly celebrated marriage with Fairbanks. One of the most salient aspects of Pickford's career is the dichotomy between naive "Little Mary" and the liberated, sophisticated businesswoman that structured her persona. In later life, the star lamented that her public never allowed her to grow up.

Starting her career in 1898 at the age of five, Pickford began acting in an effort to help support her mother, Charlotte, and two siblings, Jack and Lottie, after her father's death. She made her Broadway debut at the age of fourteen in David Belas-

Mary Pickford. *Mary Pickford poses in her wedding dress at her marriage to Douglas Fairbanks in 1920.* GENERAL PHOTOGRAPHIC AGENCY/STRINGER/HULTON ARCHIVE/GETTY IMAGES.

co's *The Warrens of Virginia* and subsequently signed a film contract with Griffith's Biograph Studio. By 1914 Pickford had made dozens of films, including *In the Bishop's Carriage* (1913), *Cinderella* (1914), and *Rags* (1914). Though her name and off-screen personality were unknown to her audiences, she realized that she was one of the major reasons that her films brought in extraordinary box-office receipts, and, on that basis, she continually renegotiated for higher salaries through the 1910s. Adolph Zukor, then head of Famous Players Film Company, grumbled that "it often took longer to make one of Mary's contracts than it did to make one of Mary's pictures." With Zukor, Pickford made a number of high-grossing films, including one of her best-remembered silent films, *Tess of the Storm Country* (1914), which the producer later claimed saved Famous Players from bankruptcy.

PICKFORD'S "FIRSTS"

Pickford's involvement in early Hollywood includes a range of contributions. In addition to being one of the first actors to recognize the economic and social power of film stardom, she achieved many technological "firsts" (albeit some of which are self-proclaimed). For example, Pickford alleged that she conceived of the film "close-up" on the set of her picture *Friends* (1912) when she encouraged cameraman Billy Bitzer to move his camera in toward her face—she reapplied her makeup to further facilitate the innovation. She also helped invent the low-level (hazy) lighting that would become a staple of silent, black-and-white films. Hollywood biographer Cari Beauchamp argues in her 1997 book that Pickford's collaborations with screenwriter Frances Marion significantly shaped the storytelling structures that have become classical tradition and that these women's mutual contribution to early cinema cannot be overestimated.

PEAK OF POWER

In 1916 Pickford gained a great deal of creative autonomy by signing a contract with Zukor that afforded her the Pickford Film Corporation, her own production unit, and allowed her films to be distributed separately through Paramount's Artcraft. With her newfound agency, Pickford starred in some of her more memorable roles, including *The Poor Little Rich Girl* (1917), *Rebecca of Sunnybrook Farm* (1917), and *Stella Maris* (1918). In the latter film she plays both the wealthy, sheltered title character and a working-class, homely orphan, impressing critics with her theatrical talents and wowing audiences with her willingness to dress down for the camera. Around this time a distribution contract with First National increased Pickford's power even further. The deal, unprecedented for a female star, meant that she would choose her own scripts, develop them, and be able to exercise final cut.

However, it was Pickford's organization of United Artists with Fairbanks, Chaplin, and Griffith in 1919 that cemented her position in film history. These four figures considered themselves artists whose creative potential was being squashed by the studio economy. By forming an independent studio, they could engage in a hands-on approach to the development, production, distribution, and eventually exhibition of their films without interference from "above." Their actions provoked the exasperated proclamation (and now infamous quotation) from the president of Metro Pictures that "the lunatics have taken charge of the asylum." Despite such skepticism, the founders of United Artists fared quite well for more than a decade, with Pickford proving to be one of the company's more capable leaders. In *Doug and Mary and Others*, Allene Talmey writes that Pickford had a great deal more business sense than her counterpart, Fairbanks, and that she deserved the title "mental arithmetic Mary."

Pollyanna (1920) was one of Pickford's first United Artists films. The story of an orphan who sees the bright side of every adversity, *Pollyanna* drew on the most charming and endearing qualities of Pickford's persona. The actress, however, evidenced some disdain for the blind optimism of the character in her autobiography, writing, "If reincarnation should prove to be true, and I had to come back as one of my roles, I suppose some avenging fate would return me to earth as Pollyanna—the 'glad girl.'"

Pickford's aura of childish naïveté seemed particularly well-suited to audiences of her time. As support of this, her films of the 1920s consistently garnered huge dollar amounts at the box office except for those in which she attempted more mature characters (*Rosita* in 1923 and *Dorothy Vernon of Haddon Hall* in 1924). Film critic C. A. LeJeune explains the phenomenon, remarking that the star's films were "made yesterday for today rather than today for tomorrow." In a historical period of great social upheaval related to industrialization, first-wave feminism, and World War I, Pickford reassured audiences with her blend of nostalgic sentimentality and an optimistic eye toward the future. Moviegoers of the early part of the twentieth century felt strongly that she was "one of them," a regular person who understood life's difficulties and had summoned the strength to triumph over her hardships.

DOUGLAS FAIRBANKS SR.

Pickford's 1920 marriage to Douglas Fairbanks has been celebrated as one of the first Hollywood "fairy-tale" marriages. The stars had spent a great deal of time together on the Liberty Bond tour during World War I, so much so that fans were speculating that the two would marry even though they had yet to divorce their respective spouses. At the time, Pickford was married to film star Owen Moore, though the two basically had been separated since the honeymoon. Sensationalistic newspaper reports stirred up the situation and nearly led to scandal after claiming less than stellar conduct from the parties involved. Scandal was averted again later when word leaked to the public that Pickford had supposedly lied under oath about her residency status in order to obtain a divorce from Moore.

But Fairbanks and Pickford's marriage that spring was received warmly by their fans. It seemed only appropriate that "the Glad Girl" and "the Smile Guy" should come together. While the couple enjoyed an international honeymoon, swamped by massive public attention and mob hysteria, *Photoplay* issued a definitive judgment in a one-page telegram that read, "ALL IS FORGIVEN. PLEASE COME HOME." Eventually, they did return home to an estate named Pickfair, which boasted fountains, ponds, stables, a swimming pool, a tennis court, a gymnasium, and a home movie theater. Their estate became a favorite destination for European royalty, and they were often referred to as American royalty themselves. Accounts that have emerged since Pickford's death suggest that she suffered from Fairbanks's jealousy and possessiveness, but the precedent they set as Hollywood's premiere star couple is powerful nonetheless.

FALTERING CAREER

Pickford won an Academy Award for her performance in *Coquette* (1929), but her popularity had already begun to slip. Her attempts at adult characters found little success, and her 1928 decision to cut off the long curls that had been her signature earned scorn. For her last film, she chose *Secrets* (1933), a remake of a Gloria Swanson movie that she had initiated two years earlier. Her discontent with the project had led her to burn the 1931 print, which was one-third complete. In the version that made it to the screen, Pickford plays Mary Carlton from early womanhood to retirement. Her character is forced to confront her husband's adultery and try to rebuild her marriage after the ensuing scandal. (At the time, Pickford's own marriage was headed for divorce because of Fairbanks's infidelity.) Predictably, reviewers admired the star in the early part of the picture, when she played a young Mary, but they disliked her as an older woman. Pickford's last film performed decently in theaters, but it signified a disheartening denouement.

Pickford tried her hand at a producing career; however, she lacked the cachet and industry intuition that had proven so beneficial for the early films in which she had starred. *One Rainy Day Afternoon* (1936), *The Gay Desperado* (1936), and director Douglas Sirk's *Sleep, My Love* (1948) failed to launch her as a producer. In the late 1940s she came close to starring as the faded silent-screen actress Norma Desmond in *Sunset Boulevard* (1950). In 1953 she and Chaplin sold United Artists. Pickford, who had exclusive rights to all her original prints, allowed friend and film preservationist Matty Kemp to create a custodial space for them by forming the Mary Pickford Film Corporation, which eventually led to a retrospective of her work in 1971.

As for her personal life, the "Queen of Hollywood" married *My Best Girl* (1927) costar Charles "Buddy" Rogers in 1937 (she had divorced Fairbanks in 1936) and remained his wife until her death in 1979. As her career declined, so did her optimistic outlook. In Pickford's later years, she began to be viewed as a rigid relic of the Victorian era. She became increasingly reclusive, withdrawing into Pickfair and, many say, resorting to alcohol as a salve for her poor spirits. According to her niece Gwynne Ruppe Pickford, the star came home from a Paris retrospective of her films in 1965 and announced that "she had worked hard all her life since she was five . . . and she would not get up out of bed or leave the house again, except to go to the hospital."

Christina Lane

SEE ALSO: *Celebrity Couples; Chaplin, Charlie; Fairbanks, Douglas, Sr.; Griffith, D. W.; Hollywood; Silent Movies;* Sunset Boulevard*; United Artists.*

BIBLIOGRAPHY

Balio, Tino. *United Artists: The Company Built by the Stars.* Madison: University of Wisconsin Press, 1976.

Beauchamp, Cari. *Without Lying Down: Frances Marion and the Powerful Women of Early Hollywood.* New York: Scribner, 1997.

Carey, Gary. *Doug and Mary: A Biography of Douglas Fairbanks and Mary Pickford.* New York: Dutton, 1977.

DeCordova, Richard. *Picture Personalities: The Emergence of the Star System in Early America.* Chicago: University of Illinois Press, 1990.

Eyman, Scott. *Mary Pickford: America's Sweetheart.* New York: Donald I. Fine, 1990.

Herndon, Booten. *Mary Pickford and Douglas Fairbanks: The Most Popular Couple the World Has Ever Known.* New York: Norton, 1977.

Pickford, Mary. *Sunshine and Shadow: An Autobiography.* New York: Doubleday, 1955.

Talmey, Allene. *Doug and Mary and Others.* New York: Macy-Masius, 1927.

Thompson, Kristin. *Herr Lubitsch Goes to Hollywood: German and American Film after World War I.* Amsterdam: University Press, 2005.

Whitfield, Eileen. *Pickford: The Woman Who Made Hollywood.* Lexington: University of Kentucky Press, 1997.

Windeler, Robert. *Sweetheart: The Story of Mary Pickford.* New York: Praeger, 1973.

The Pill

In 1968 a popular writer ranked the Pill's importance with the discovery of fire, among other things. Twenty-five years later, the Pill was still in the news, with the *Economist*, the leading British weekly, listing it as one of the seven wonders of the modern world. In the early twenty-first century, more than ten million women in the United States used oral contraceptives, "the Pill," as birth control. During the 1950s Margaret Sanger, a nurse and feminist who championed birth control education and methods for women, played a pivotal role in finding research funding for the development of the birth control pill.

Shortly after chemist Carl Djerassi first synthesized the Pill, its widespread use helped to catalyze the sexual revolution of the 1960s, a time when people were exploring "free love"—sex with multiple partners, without traditional commitment. Because the Pill's accuracy rate in preventing pregnancy is almost 100 percent, it offered an opportunity, before AIDS, for people to be sexually adventurous without the fear of unplanned pregnancies. "The commercial availability of birth control pill in the early 1960s permitted women far greater reproductive choice, created a new set of ethical and religious questions, encouraged feminism, changed the dynamics of women's health care, and forever altered gender relations," asserts Elizabeth Siegel Watkins in *On the Pill, A Social History of Oral Contraceptives, 1950–1970*. The Pill liberated women's sexual views considerably, making them feel more in control of their bodies, as America was just coming out of the puritanical tyranny of the 1950s, when sex was still confined to the nuptial bed.

The 1960s was a landmark decade, when America questioned conventional ideas about marriage, family, and sex. People continue to look on that period with nostalgia, whether they lived through it or not. The 1960s and 1970s combined student protests and the peace movement with the counterculture and oral contraceptives, to help create a climate where people felt freer about sex. Capitalism was challenged by such New Left writers as Herbert Marcuse and William Reich, who argued that it demanded self-restraint and compulsive work, which were contrary to any liberated sexual expression. Sexuality was also becoming more political, and with the new freedom and ease that the Pill offered, relations between men and women, among other things, were starting to shift.

Introduced at a time of social reforms, such as the civil rights and gay and lesbian movements and environmental and peace movements, the impact of the Pill is intertwined with these social changes. The social controversy surrounding the Pill stems from some critics asserting that it encouraged promiscuity. Some analysts think the sexual mentality of the 1960s, which continued well after the decade, has caused devastating consequences for society. "It's woven its way into every single fabric of our society and has literally almost destroyed us," according to Dr. Joe McIlhaney Jr., president of the Medical Institute for Sexual Health. In Kristine Vick's CBN report, "The Sexual Revolution Thirty Years Later," Dr. McIlhaney noted the abundance of sexually transmitted diseases (against which the Pill does not safeguard), nonmarital pregnancies, and abortions since the advent of the sexual revolution. Attitudes among the sexes were conflicted because although the Pill took the burden of unwanted pregnancy off women, it put the responsibility of contraception entirely on them. The sudden, widespread acceptance and use of the Pill caused men to often expect and assume that a woman would "go on the Pill" when a couple began a sexual relationship. The Pill did make preventing pregnancy seem simple and easy, but it is not entirely innocuous, having various side effects ranging in severity, in addition to causing women to gamble with their hormone levels.

SIDE EFFECTS AND CONTROVERSY

The Pill works by stopping ovaries from releasing an egg each month, making the mucus in the cervix thicker, so it is harder for sperm to travel into it, and thinning the lining of the uterus, so it is more difficult for a fertilized egg to attach itself. It interferes with a woman's normal cycle of ovulation by creating a hormone imbalance (pills contain estrogen and progestin; progesterone blocks ovulation) that mimics pregnancy. Many women have no problems with it, but there are common, diminishing side effects, among them nausea, bloating, and changes in skin. Although rare, there are more serious side effects, which include severe headaches, visual changes, blood clots, and/or heart attacks.

On the plus side, the Pill has been shown to reduce the risk of ovarian cancer and endometrial cancer, to help clear up acne, to ease symptoms of premenstrual syndrome, and to relieve endometriosis and polycystic ovarian syndrome. Many studies have been done to determine if it contributes to breast cancer, but the most recent thinking is that it does not. In 2011 a study found that 14 percent of users took the Pill for noncontraceptive purposes and more than half of users rely on the Pill, at least in part, for purposes other than preventing pregnancy.

In 2012 the Pill made the news again as the center of a firestorm of controversy. One of the provisions of President Barack Obama's 2009 health care law mandated that health insurers must offer birth control coverage to women. Catholic leaders and employers objected to the requirement on the grounds that their religious beliefs oppose the use of birth control. In response, the president offered the compromise that such employers would not have to pay for the coverage but that insurers must still provide it.

Catholics and conservatives rejected the compromise, and a congressional hearing was held to see if the requirement violated the constitutionally protected freedom of religion. Many people denounced the hearing itself, however, because only male religious leaders were allowed to testify. A proposed female witness, a law student who intended to testify about noncontraceptive uses of the Pill, was refused, and in the weeks following, a heated debate played out in the media. Conservatives continued to denounce government interference in matters of conscience, while many liberals labeled the entire sequence of events as "a war on religion."

The controversy demonstrated that even though many people had assumed that the Pill was a long-accepted part of American life, one part of society remained bitterly opposed to it and was willing to fight to limit its use. From the heat that the controversy generated, it looked like battles over contraception were going to join the abortion wars as a contentious but ever-present part of American politics.

Sharon Yablon

SEE ALSO: *AIDS; Civil Rights Movement; Gay Liberation Movement; Obama, Barack.*

BIBLIOGRAPHY

Djerassi, Carl. *The Pill, Pygmy Chimps, and Degas' Horse/The Remarkable Autobiography of the Award-Winning Scientist Who Synthesized the Birth Control Pill.* New York, Basic Books, 1992.

Juhn, Greg. *Understanding the Pill: A Consumer's Guide to Oral Contraceptives.* New York: Pharmaceutical Products Press, 1994.

May, Elaine Tyler. *America and the Pill: A History of Promise, Peril, and Liberation.* New York: Basic Books, 2010.

Sigel, Roberta S. *Ambition and Accommodation: How Women View Gender Relations*. Chicago: University of Chicago Press, 1996.

Vick, Kristine. "The Sexual Revolution Thirty Years Later." Accessed April 2012. Available from http://www.cbn.org/news/stories/980212b.asp

Watkins, Elizabeth Siegel. *On the Pill: A Social History of Oral Contraceptives*. Baltimore, MD: Johns Hopkins University Press, 1998.

Watts, Alan. *Summer of Love: The Spirituality and Consciousness of the 1960s*. n.p.: Electronic University, 1998.

Pink *(1979–)*

Pink (born Alecia Beth Moore) burst on the pop scene in 2000 with her shocking pink hair and a tattooed, pierced, punkette attitude to match. Her debut solo album, *Can't Take Me Home*, featured poppy R&B hooks and went double platinum, catapulting the singer to stardom.

Pink's career soared further with her 2001 remake of Patti LaBelle's disco hit "Lady Marmalade," which also featured R&B divas Christina Aguilera, Mya, and Lil' Kim. The song held fast at number one on the Billboard Hot 100 for five weeks and went on to win a Grammy Award for Best Pop Collaboration with Vocals in 2002.

R&B seemed a natural fit for the singer, who grew up listening to the likes of Aretha Franklin and Dionne Warwick; however, Pink was determined to set herself apart from the era's other pretty, young female singers. The outspoken star—who cites Madonna and Janis Joplin as musical and career influences—battled music executives for more creative control on her second album. The result, 2001's *M!ssundaztood*, features edgier music with rock and blues influences.

On her personal website Pink explains, "*M!ssundaztood* was my 'coming-out party.' I knew I was capable of more. The world had no idea who I was or what I was made of. . . . But I had a lot to say, and so I didn't want others to be speaking for me."

Pink's new direction paid off: the album sold nearly ten million copies and inspired up-and-coming artists such as Katy Perry, Ke$ha, and Lady Gaga to mix raw sound and emotion with rock-centered dance beats. Even Pink's contemporaries such as Christina Aguilera were compelled to add more substance to their music. This influence prompted *Los Angeles Times* music critic Ann Powers in 2010 to name Pink "the most trailblazing artist from the famous teen pop class of circa 1999."

Pink has garnered other accolades. *Billboard* magazine named her the number one pop artist of the decade in 2009, and *Forbes* listed her as the twenty-seventh most powerful celebrity in the world in 2010. Pink also has also won several Grammy Awards and MTV Video Music Awards.

Kerri Kennedy

SEE ALSO: *Aguilera, Christina; Alternative Rock; Franklin, Aretha; Grammy Awards; Joplin, Janis; Lady Gaga; Madonna; MTV; Perry, Katy; Pop Music; Punk; Rhythm and Blues.*

BIBLIOGRAPHY

Hilburn, Robert. "Her Colors Don't Run." *Los Angeles Times*, November 9, 2003.

Pink: The Official Pink Site. Accessed May 23, 2012. Available from http://www.pinkspage.com

Powers, Ann. "The Many Shades of Pink—So Far." *Los Angeles Times*, December 21, 2010.

Pink Floyd

Formed in London in 1965 and named for Georgia bluesmen Pink Anderson and Floyd Council, Pink Floyd performed music that marked the pinnacle of the psychedelic rock scene in the late 1960s. After the departure of drugged-out frontman Syd Barrett in 1968, bassist Roger Waters took charge and penned a string of meditations on madness and the perils of stardom that proved to be wildly popular, including *Dark Side of the Moon* (1973) and *The Wall* (1979). Floyd's expansive and atmospheric sound, combined with over-the-top special effects, attracted sellout crowds to stadiums across America. The group disbanded in 1983 but was reformed in 1987 under guitarist David Gilmour's leadership and without Waters. Pink Floyd was inducted into the Rock and Roll Hall of Fame in 1996.

The final live performance of the entire group was in 2005 at a Live 8 concert in London's Hyde Park. In 2008 keyboardist Richard Wright died of cancer. The three surviving members of the band (Gilmour, Waters, and drummer Nick Mason) reunited for one night only in 2011 during Waters's solo tour.

David B. Welky

SEE ALSO: *LSD; Psychedelia; Rock and Roll; Stadium Concerts.*

BIBLIOGRAPHY

Dallas, Karl. *Bricks in the Wall*. London: Baton Press, 1987.

Schaffner, Nicholas. *Saucerful of Secrets: The Pink Floyd Odyssey*. New York: Delta, 1992.

Shea, Stuart. *Pink Floyd FAQ: Everything Left to Know . . . and More!* New York: Backbeat Books, 2009.

Pinsky, Dr. Drew *(1958–)*

Popular psychiatrist and media personality Dr. Drew Pinsky is widely known for his role in radio and television programs devoted to matters of sexuality and addiction. He first came to fame in the early 1980s, before he had finished medical school, as host of *Loveline* on KROQ-FM in Los Angeles. He went on to cohost a televised version of the show on MTV in the late 1990s. A series of reality and self-help programs, most notably *Celebrity Rehab with Dr. Drew*, followed in the 2000s. Pinsky, who has been in private practice in the Los Angeles area since the late 1980s, has served as physician to a variety of celebrities.

David Drew Pinsky, born in Pasadena, California, on September 4, 1958, is the son of physician Morton Pinsky and homemaker Helene Stanton Pinsky. Going on house calls with his father convinced him to become a doctor, and in 1976, after graduating from Polytechnic High School in Pasadena—where

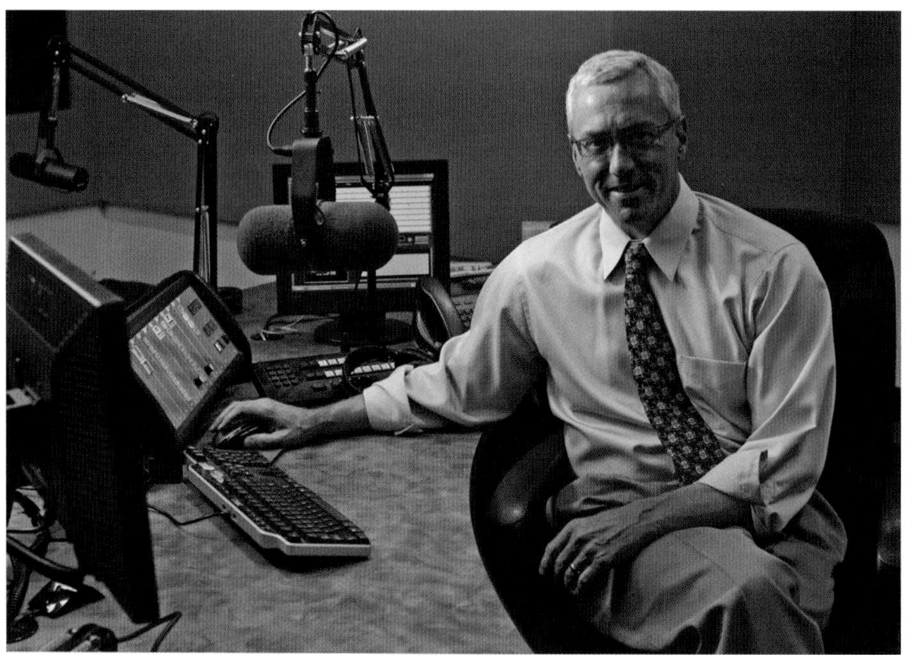

Dr. Drew Pinsky. *Dr. Drew Pinsky poses at the studio from which he broadcasts his popular radio show in 2008.* AP IMAGES.

he was captain of the football team and student-body president—Pinsky enrolled at Amherst College in Massachusetts as a biology major. He went on to the University of Southern California (USC) School of Medicine, where he earned an MD in 1984.

Also in 1984, Pinsky began his residency in internal medicine at the USC County Hospital. He later became chief resident at Huntington Memorial Hospital in Pasadena, launched his private practice, and joined the staff of Pasadena's Las Encinas Hospital as program medical director of the chemical dependency unit in the early 1990s. Pinsky married Susan Sailer on July 20, 1991, and the following year the couple had triplets.

DEBUTS ON *LOVELINE*

Pinsky began his career in electronic media as a fourth-year medical student, when KROQ's Jim "Poorman" Trenton and "Swedish" Egil Aalvik began featuring him on their new show, *Loveline.* Launched in 1983 *Loveline* aired late on Sunday nights and addressed issues of relationships, sex, and health through a call-in advice format. Pinsky began making regular appearances as a volunteer medical consultant in a segment called "Ask a Surgeon," and by the early 1990s he was serving as cohost with Trenton. The show went from one to five nights a week in 1992 and in 1995 became nationally syndicated.

The following year saw the launch of the MTV version, hosted by Pinsky and Adam Carolla. Chosen by Pinsky himself, Carolla had a humorous, offhand manner that contrasted favorably with Pinsky's necessarily more clinical approach, and the show soon became a big hit with its young audience. The unlikely pair of hosts, who were later joined by Diane Farr in order to provide a female perspective, fielded a variety of questions, and virtually no topic was off limits. They did a nationwide *Loveline* tour in 1998, visiting college campuses and taking questions from students that were neither taped nor broadcast.

The TV show ran until 2000, but the radio version continued. Carolla stepped down in November 2005, but Pinsky remained as cohost of the program, which as of January 2012 was still going strong. As it neared the end of its third decade, the show's format remained much the same as always, with listeners calling in to discuss issues of sexuality, addiction, and (occasionally) matters of general health.

A VARIETY OF VENTURES

Named clinical assistant professor of pediatrics at Los Angeles Children's Hospital in 2000, Pinsky went on to become clinical professor of psychiatry at the Keck School of Medicine at USC in 2004. He also expanded his media presence. However, not all of his ventures around the turn of the twenty-first century would prove to be successes. Pinsky's website, DrDrew.com, launched in 1999 but soon faltered and had to be sold, and his syndicated talk show *Men Are from Mars, Women Are from Venus* did not outlast the 2001 TV season. He enjoyed better fortune as an author, publishing his first work, *The Dr. Drew and Adam Book: A Survival Guide to Life and Love* (with Carolla and Marshall Fine) in 1998. This was followed in 2003 with *Cracked: Life on the Edge in a Rehab Clinic* and in 2004 with *When Painkillers Become Dangerous: What Everyone Needs to Know about OxyContin and Other Prescription Drugs,* by Pinsky and a number of other physicians.

After a stint as "health and human relations" expert on the reality TV show *Big Brother* in 2000, Pinsky hosted two limited series on Discovery Health Channel. *Strictly Sex with Dr. Drew,* which ran in 2005, was followed in 2006 by *Strictly Dr. Drew,* a more general program on health topics that included obesity, pain, and "embarrassing personal matters" such as snoring and flatulence. His greatest TV success since *Loveline* came in January 2008, when *Celebrity Rehab with Dr. Drew* debuted on VH1.

CELEBRITY REHAB AND MORE

Celebrity Rehab, for which Pinsky is host, executive producer, and lead medical specialist, is a reality program in which a group of celebrities undergoes a twenty-one-day treatment program for drug and alcohol addiction at the Pasadena Recovery Center. Participants are filmed twenty-four hours a day and, in addition to receiving a treatment program valued at more than $50,000, are paid for their involvement.

The show, which ran its fifth season in 2011, has included a number of notable figures, many of whom have experienced highly publicized bouts with addiction and its consequences, both legal and personal, including Rodney King, Dennis Rodman, Tawny Kitaen, Gary Busey, Heidi Fleiss, and Tom Sizemore. The program has spawned two VH1 spin-offs, *Celebrity Rehab Presents Sober House* (2009), which followed participants as they attempted to lead sober lives, and *Sex Rehab with Dr. Drew* (2009), in which Pinsky and his staff treated celebrities with sexual addictions.

Pinsky formed Dr. Drew Productions in 2010 and in April 2011 became host of a new show, *Dr. Drew*, a current affairs program on HLN. He also launched *Lifechangers* on the CW Daytime in September 2011. Pinsky has made numerous appearances on other television programs, ranging from *Today* and *Larry King Live* to *Hollywood Squares* and *Space Ghost Coast to Coast*.

Judson Knight

SEE ALSO: *Celebrity; Daytime Talk Shows;* Hollywood Squares*; The Internet; King, Larry; King, Rodney; Leisure Time; MTV; Radio; Reality Television; Rodman, Dennis; Syndication; Television;* Today.

BIBLIOGRAPHY

Jesella, Kara. "Detox for the Camera. Doctor's Order!" *New York Times*, February 3, 2008.

Pinsky, Dr. Drew. *Cracked: Putting Broken Lives Together Again*. New York: Regan Books, 2003.

Pinsky, Dr. Drew; Adam Carolla; and Marshall Fine. *The Dr. Drew and Adam Book: A Survival Guide to Life and Love*. New York: Dell, 1998.

Pinsky, Dr. Drew, and S. Mark Young. *The Mirror Effect: How Celebrity Narcissism Is Seducing America*. New York: HarperCollins, 2009.

The Pin-Up

The term *pin-up* gets its name from the act of display that it encourages. Consequently, it might apply to any mass-produced and widely distributed image. Within popular culture, however, the term has historically been used to identify a narrow category of pictures referring to glossy portraits of Hollywood stars or *Playboy*'s monthly centerfolds. With an even tighter focus, the word *pin-up* is usually reserved for pictures of pretty girls wearing skimpy bathing suits, exotic lingerie, or sometimes even less.

Although sexy, such images are rarely considered obscene—even by the most puritanical viewer. The term's most evocative use recalls the drawn, painted, or photographed representations of idealized, all-American femininity produced in the decades surrounding World War II. Although the pin-up has obvious precursors in naughty French postcards from the turn of the twentieth century and later variants such as the annual *Sports Illustrated* swimsuit issue, the form is exemplified by the odd balance of eroticism, innocence, healthiness, and patriotism found in commercial images of women produced between the 1920s and 1960s.

In 1972 popular leading man Burt Reynolds paved the way for the male pin-up when he posed nearly nude as a centerfold for the women's magazine *Cosmopolitan*. In its contemporary incarnation, pin-up describes a photograph of a male or female celebrity that is pinned to the wall by adolescents of either sex. Such photographs are rarely explicitly sexual in nature.

HISTORY

Viewed within a larger frame, the pin-up is a species of portrait yanked off the walls of exclusive galleries and museums and posted in ordinary gas stations and pool halls. Generated by the development and proliferation of inexpensive processes of photography, lithography, and color printing, the pin-up contributed to more democratic—and perhaps inevitably more vulgar—understandings of celebrity, voyeurism, consumption, and eroticism, closing the gap in taste and appreciation between classical nudes and burlesque showgirls. Early professional photographers such as Nadar in France and Napoleon Sarony in New York specialized in the celebrity portrait, redefining the concept of fame through the mass production and distribution of commercial publicity stills. Although pictures of prominent theatrical performers were common by the turn of the twentieth century, the pin-up thrived as a component of the film industry, as talented photographers such as Clarence Sinclair Bull, George Hurrell, Eugene Robert Richee, and Ted Allen were exclusively employed by the Hollywood studios to idealize their most precious commodities, the movie stars. Much of the residual glamour of Hollywood's golden age certainly derives from the striking black-and-white images these photographers produced of screen celebrities such as Jean Harlow, Louise Brooks, Greta Garbo, and Joan Crawford.

Preceding the Hollywood dream factory, commercial illustrators and graphic artists such as Charles Dana Gibson and Howard Chandler Christy had already glorified the American girl in the pages of such popular illustrated magazines as *Life* and *Collier's*. The cleanly etched "Gibson Girl" first appeared in 1887 and proceeded to define the modern ideal of femininity that eventually coalesced as the flapper of the Jazz Age. From the 1920s onward, popular magazine, calendar, and advertising artists such as Antonio Vargas, Gil Elvgren, Earl Moran, Zoe Mozert, and George Petty produced hundreds of "cheesecake" images of sleek, flawless, all-American femininity marked by the "tease" of blowing skirts and sheer fabric rather than by explicit nude display.

By World War II the Vargas girl and Hollywood pin-ups such as Betty Grable and Rita Hayworth had come to represent not only American femininity but also the very values American soldiers were defending. The erotic titillation of pin-ups was thus effectively linked to patriotic sentiment and memories of the home front. With five million copies in print, the most popular image of this period was Grable's famous bathing suit pose (photographed by Frank Powolny in 1943), which was distributed to American soldiers around the globe. As the French

Bettie Page Pin-Up. *Bettie Page remains a cult icon for her risqué 1950s-era pin-up photos.* ARCHIVE PHOTOS/STRINGER/GETTY IMAGES.

film critic André Bazin later recognized, "A wartime product created for the benefit of the American soldiers swarming to a long exile at the four corners of the world, the pin-up girl soon became an industrial product, subject to well-fixed norms and as stable in quality as peanut butter or chewing gum."

In the 1960s, the fascination with celebrity and the prominence of television, movies, and rock and roll gave birth to the celebrity pin-up that is still ubiquitous. A plethora of magazines were devoted to feeding the desire to know more about celebrities, and some focused entirely on providing pin-ups. The October 1962 issue of *Pin-Up*, for instance, offered photographs of actresses Haley Mills, Sandra Dee, Connie Stevens, and Annette Funicello for young boys, and singers Elvis Presley and Paul Anka and actors Troy Donahue and Warren Beatty for young girls. By the 1970s and 1980s these earlier idols had been replaced by Bobby Sherman, David Cassidy, Molly Ringwald, and Emilio Estevez.

NUDITY AND PRURIENCE

After the war the classic, scantily clad pin-up continued to thrive until an underground tradition was brought into the mainstream in 1953 by Hugh Hefner's *Playboy* magazine, which provided an entire "Playboy philosophy" of robust, healthy heterosexuality to justify its monthly inclusion of a nude Playmate at the heart of each issue. *Playboy* redefined the pin-up by shifting the earlier period's emphasis on long legs to an all-but-exclusive fascination with large breasts. Eventually, with the appearance of pubic hair and further investigations of all the classic pin-up had (barely) concealed, *Playboy* and other men's magazines left little to the once-necessary erotic imagination. The concept of "tease" that had crucially defined the voyeur's relation to earlier pin-ups now seemed rather prim. At the very least, the presumably long-standing function of the pin-up as an aid to self-arousal could no longer be denied. Still, against the widespread competition of explicit pornography in the mainstream market by the 1970s, *Playboy* held its relatively demure ground, maintaining an airbrushed glamour ignored by the more gynecological perspectives provided in subsequent magazines, such as Bob Guccione's *Penthouse* and Larry Flynt's *Hustler*.

Playboy, by publishing an early nude photograph of Hollywood star Marilyn Monroe, had collapsed the distinction between "innocent" sexiness in mainstream "leg art" and a more surreptitious tradition of straightforward sexual imagery. But for specialized tastes, alternatives to the Vargas girl and Hefner's Playmates were also available. Although fetishistic photographs had been produced in Europe at an early stage in the medium's development, the U.S. mail-order market for "kinky" images did not develop until much later.

In the late 1940s Irving Klaw and his sister, Paula—the owners of Movie Star News, a New York shop that sold Hollywood movie stills—began producing their own photographs of women in fetish gear and bondage poses to satisfy the requests of customers with particular tastes. Among Klaw's models, a young woman with jet-black bangs named Betty (or Bettie) Page quickly became a customer favorite, and decades after she disappeared from sight, Page became a cult icon among comic-book fans and collectors of 1950s kitsch, perhaps because she so effectively summarized the cultural contradictions of the postwar period: Page, like most pin-ups, was a pretty, girl-next-door type, but she also wore stiletto heels and leather bondage gear. In retrospect, Page seems the ideal pin-up of a period that produced both the McCarthy witch hunts and the Kinsey Reports on human sexuality.

Another specialized market for pin-ups was also first addressed in Europe, where the photographs of nude boys taken by Baron Wilhelm von Gloeden in the Sicilian village of Taormina around the turn of the twentieth century circulated among homosexual collectors. In the United States a number of studios mirroring Klaw's Movie Star News marketed their images to homosexual consumers. Because the period demanded secrecy and obfuscation, pin-ups of nude or loin-clothed young men were commonly sold to physique or muscle-building enthusiasts, but the erotic component of images produced by "beefcake" pioneers such as Bruce of Los Angeles (Bruce Harry Bellas); Chicago's Kris Studios; and most notably Bob Mizer's Athletic Model Guild, through its regular catalog *Physique Pictorial*, was never completely underground.

Although the pin-up has commonly been assumed to be a form depicting women for an audience of heterosexual males, the homosexual tradition of pin-ups has a lengthy history as well: in fact, one of the young artists who regularly contributed his drawings to *Physique Pictorial*, Tom of Finland, eventually emerged as the gay Vargas, exaggerating the features of his muscular young men just as the earlier artist idealized his female figures. Recuperated and celebrated in later decades, the "physique" photographs of the postwar period, like Page's bondage pictures, revise simple and nostalgic stereotypes of the era's conservative values and sexual inhibitions.

The legacy of the classic Hollywood pin-up survives in the work of such contemporary celebrity photographers as Matthew Rolston, Annie Liebovitz, Bruce Weber, and Herb Ritts, whose subjects are as likely to be rock musicians or supermodels as movie stars. Posters of attractive women in bathing suits or underwear, from Farrah Fawcett or Madonna to Katy Perry, have also never disappeared from adolescent bedroom walls. But the classic pin-up, save for a thriving network of nostalgic collectors, seems to have succumbed to, on the one hand, feminism's largely effective redefinition of women as social beings rather than simply sexual objects and, on the other hand, the increased availability of hard-core pornography, whose blatant meanings no longer encourage the slightly muted eroticism essential to the classic pin-up.

In 2006 the film *The Notorious Bettie Page*, starring Gretchen Mol as the pin-up who became known as "Pin-Up Queen of the Universe," was released to mixed reviews. Although most critics felt the film did not go far enough in examining the history of the 1950s, Peter Travers of *Rolling Stone* found it "subversively funny" and applauded director Mary Harron's taking "an ax[e] to male vanity and greed." In the movie Page has been asked to appear before a Senate investigating committee examining the impact of pornography on adolescents, and the film uses that hearing as its setting. Her life is recounted in flashbacks that include a gang rape, a failed acting career, a pattern of rampant exploitation, and a religious conversion.

Corey K. Creekmur

SEE ALSO: *Advertising; Anka, Paul; Army-McCarthy Hearings; Athletic Model Guild; Beatty, Warren; Burlesque; Celebrity; Comic Books;* Cosmopolitan*; Crawford, Joan; Fan Magazines; Fawcett, Farrah; Feminism; Flappers; Garbo, Greta; Gas Stations; Gay and Lesbian Press; Gay Men; Gibson Girl; Grable, Betty; Harlow, Jean; Hayworth, Rita; Hefner, Hugh; Hollywood;* Hustler*; Kinsey, Dr. Alfred C.; Leibovitz, Annie;* Life*; Madonna; Monroe, Marilyn; Movie Stars;* Penthouse*;* Playboy*; Pornography; Postcards; Presley, Elvis; Pulp Magazines; Reynolds, Burt; Rock and Roll;* Rolling Stone*;* Sports Illustrated*; Television; Tom of Finland; World War II.*

BIBLIOGRAPHY

Bazin, André. "Entomology of the Pin-Up Girl." *What Is Cinema?* Vol. 2. Berkeley: University of California Press, 1971.

Buszek, Maria Elena. *Pin-Up Grrrls: Feminism, Sexuality, Popular Culture.* Durham, NC: Duke University Press, 2006.

Fahey, David, and Linda Rich. *Masters of Starlight: Photographers in Hollywood.* New York: Ballantine Books, 1987.

Gabor, Mark. *The Pin-Up: A Modest History.* New York: Universe Books, 1972.

Hooven, F. Valentine, III. *Beefcake: The Muscle Magazines of America 1950–1970.* Cologne: Taschen, 1995.

Martignette, Charles G., and Louis K. Meisel. *The Great American Pin-Up.* Cologne: Taschen, 1996.

Moore, Ryan. *Sells Like Teen Spirit: Music, Youth Culture, and Social Crisis.* New York: New York University Press, 2010.

Smilby, Francis. *Stolen Sweets: The Cover Girls of Yesteryear, Their Elegance, Charm, and Sex Appeal.* New York: Playboy Press, 1981.

Travers, Peter. "The Notorious Bettie Page." *Rolling Stone*, April 4, 2006.

Waugh, Thomas. *Hard to Imagine: Gay Male Eroticism in Photography and Film from Their Beginnings to Stonewall.* New York: Columbia University Press, 1996.

Piper, "Rowdy" Roddy *(1954–)*

One of professional wrestling's hottest renegades and all-time great interviews, "Rowdy" Roddy Piper was a headliner for more than twenty-five years. Piper, whose real name is Roderick George Toombs, was born in Glasgow, Scotland, but spent most of his early years in Canada. He was a Golden Gloves boxer who began his wrestling career at the age of fifteen. Piper headlined cards in California and the Pacific Northwest throughout the 1970s. While wrestling in Georgia in the early 1980s, he received national attention through exposure on Ted Turner's WTBS Superstation. In a "sport" that receives much criticism for its "authenticity" (or lack thereof), Piper fashioned himself as one of the twentieth century's more prominent television personas.

Piper's ability to rile a crowd and "draw heat" almost cost him his life in 1982 when a fan stabbed him. His subsequent turn into a good guy was a classic wrestling angle. In *Wrestling to Rasslin'*, Gerald W. Morton and George M. O'Brien describe the transformation: "the drama finally played itself out on television when one of his [Piper's] hired assassins, Don Muraco, suddenly attacked the commentator Gordon Solie. Seeing Solie hurt, Piper unleashed his Scottish fury on Muraco. In the week that followed, like Achilles avenging Patroklas, he slaughtered villain after villain." Piper's character went from lunatic villain to a classic hero: standing tall, standing alone, and standing up for right. It is the same character he would play throughout his wrestling career and in most of his film and television work.

WORLD WRESTLING FEDERATION CAREER

Piper was one of the first wrestlers signed in 1984 as part of Vince McMahon's national expansion of the World Wrestling Federation (WWF), although at first Piper was brought in only as a manager and personality. His manic style shone through in an interview segment called "Piper's Pit," where he would interview other "heel" wrestlers. Famous Piper Pits include Piper interviewing himself on a split screen and attacking Jimmy "SuperFly" Snuka with a coconut. Entering the ring to a chorus of bagpipe music, Piper became the most hated wrestler due to his penchant for sneak attacks, low blows, and devastating verbal put-downs.

After his feud with Snuka, Piper became new WWF champion Hulk Hogan's number one rival. It was Piper who started the feud and the "rock 'n' wrestling connection" by smacking Captain Lou Albano over the head during a broadcast on MTV that featured pop singer Cyndi Lauper. The feud escalated with Lauper's involvement, leading to "the brawl to settle it all" between Hogan and Piper. Rather than settle anything, this match, which was broadcast live on MTV, set a cable ratings record at the time and served as a precursor to *Wrestlemania I*, the first successful nationwide wrestling show. Teaming with Paul "Mr. Wonderful" Orndorff, Piper squared off in the main event against Hogan and television star Mr. T. The celebrity-laden event put wrestling back on the popular culture landscape. Piper continued the feud with Hogan, as well as with Mr. T, whom he battled in a boxing match at *Wrestlemania II*. Piper's features on NBC's *Saturday Night's Main Events* demonstrated a charisma that soon caught the attention of Hollywood.

PIPER HEADS TO HOLLYWOOD

Piper left wrestling after winning a "retirement match" at *Wrestlemania III*. He started off strong in movies such as *Body Slam* (1987), in which he more or less played himself, and in *Hell Comes to Frogtown* (1987), playing the only virile man left in the world. His biggest role, however, was in John Carpenter's *They Live* (1988). Considered a cult classic, Piper stars as Nada, a homeless man who stumbles upon an alien takeover. In Carpenter's vision, yuppies and Reaganites are an alien force as they bombard citizens with subliminal messages to consume and obey. The film's cult following certainly comes from Piper's performance, which was described by *Entertainment Weekly* as "scenery chewing," and from the fight scene that Piper claimed was the "longest fight scene ever." He also claims to have ad-libbed the film's most famous line: "I have come here to chew bubble gum and kick ass, and I'm all out of bubble gum."

STEROID SCANDAL AND LATER CAREER

Like many other WWF wrestlers, Piper found himself in the middle of the steroid scandal in 1994 when shipments of illegal steroids to Piper from an indicted doctor were entered into court as evidence. He weathered that storm and continued to work part time with the WWF, wrestling, commentating, or playing the role of WWF commissioner while keeping a career in Hollywood. In 1996 Piper unexpectedly left the WWF and showed up in World Championship Wrestling (WCW) to rekindle his feud with Hogan. During their interviews, Piper reminded Hogan that fans only "loved you because they hated me." Piper's match with Hogan at the 1996 Starrcade pay-per-view event was the company's most successful to date. Piper would remain in WCW until 2000 but also kept busy in Hollywood with roles in direct-to-video movies.

Piper's 2002 autobiography seemed to take aim at wrestling promoters, but by 2003 he was back working for WWF, once again feuding with Hogan. In 2005 he was inducted into the WWF Hall of Fame. Piper continues to appear sporadically on WWF (now WWE) television shows and pay-per-view events, including a 2009 match at Wrestlemania XXV that involved actor Mickey Rourke. Although a fan favorite since returning to WWE, his two-year run as the lead heel made him a crossover celebrity. He was, true to the cliché, the man the fans loved to hate.

Patrick Jones

SEE ALSO: *Boxing; Cult Films;* Entertainment Weekly*; Hogan, Hulk; Hollywood; Lauper, Cyndi; MTV; Television; Turner, Ted; World Wrestling Federation; Yuppies.*

BIBLIOGRAPHY

Lentz, Harris M. *Biographical Dictionary of Professional Wrestling*. Jefferson, NC: McFarland, 1997.

Morton, Gerald, and George M. O'Brien. *Wrestling to Rasslin': Ancient Sport to American Spectacle*. Bowling Green, OH: Bowling Green State University Press, 1985.

Piper, Roddy, and Robert Picarello. *In the Pit with Piper*. New York: Berkley Boulevard Books, 2002.

Pippen, Scottie *(1965–)*

Scottie Pippen is considered one of the greatest all-around players in the history of the National Basketball Association (NBA). Born September 25, 1965, in Hamburg, Arkansas, Pippen was one of twelve children. His road to stardom began at the University of Central Arkansas, which was anything but a collegiate basketball power. He was a walk-on player (meaning he had not been offered a scholarship) and received financial aid for also being the team manager. As a senior, he averaged 23.6 points per game and ten rebounds and become known for his versatility.

Pippen was drafted fifth in the 1987 draft by the Seattle SuperSonics but was traded to the Chicago Bulls just a few weeks later. After some growing pains, Pippen came into his own with the Bulls. He and Michael Jordan were the cornerstones in the team's run of six NBA titles in the 1990s. During Jordan's temporary retirement from basketball, spanning the entire 1993–1994 season and most of 1994–1995, Pippen was the focal point of the Bulls. In the 1994–1995 season, he became just the second player in NBA history to lead his team in points, rebounds, assists, steals, and blocks.

After the Bulls' sixth championship in 1998, Jordan retired again and Pippen was traded to the Houston Rockets, with whom he spent one season before signing with the Portland Trail Blazers. The Trail Blazers made it to the playoffs in each of Pippen's four seasons with them, but he became increasingly plagued by injuries. He played his final NBA season, 2003–2004, with the Bulls, helping them reach the playoffs for the first time since he and Jordan had departed.

Pippen's NBA achievements were numerous: he was a seven-time All-Star, an eight-time member of the All-Defensive First Team, and the Most Valuable Player of the 1994 All-Star Game. In 1996 the NBA named him one of its fifty greatest players of all time. Furthermore, Pippen won two gold medals in the Olympics (1992 and 1996). Since retiring as a player, he has served as an analyst for ESPN and ABC, as well as an assistant coach for the Los Angeles Lakers and the Bulls. In 2010 he was inducted into the Naismith Memorial Basketball Hall of Fame.

Jay Parrent

SEE ALSO: *Basketball; The Chicago Bulls; ESPN; Jordan, Michael; National Basketball Association (NBA); Olympics; Sports Heroes.*

BIBLIOGRAPHY

Bjarkman, Peter C. *Sports Great Scottie Pippen.* Springfield, NJ: Enslow Publishing, 1996.

Graham, Judith, ed. *Current Biography Yearbook 1994.* New York: H.W. Wilson, 1994.

Pippen, Delois Billings. *The Manager Who Became a Superstar: The Story of Scottie Pippen.* New York: Vantage Press, 1994.

Pippen, Scottie, and Greg Brown. *Reach Higher.* Dallas, TX: Taylor Publishing, 1996.

Pirates of the Caribbean

Film critics did not expect great things from *Pirates of the Caribbean: The Curse of the Black Pearl* before its release in spring 2003. The last in a series of lackluster films inspired by rides at Disney theme parks, the film revived a genre many considered tired and overworked—the pirate swashbuckler. However, lead actor Johnny Depp's quirky portrayal of bad-boy pirate Captain Jack Sparrow delighted audiences and turned *Pirates of the Caribbean* into a surprise hit and Sparrow into a cultural icon. The movie spawned three highly successful sequels and inspired fashion designs, video games, action figures, and product tie-ins, becoming one of the best-known film franchises in the world.

DEVELOPMENT

During the late 1990s and early 2000s, in an effort to promote its theme parks, Disney Studios made several films based on famous rides. Most of these, such as Peter Hastings's *The Country Bears* (2002) and Rob Minkoff's *The Haunted Mansion* (2003), were easily forgotten box-office flops, and most critics expected the Disney homage to its Pirates of the Caribbean ride to be the same. Pirate films were popular in the mid-1900s, but for decades audiences had been unimpressed by swashbucklers. However, director Gore Verbinski, who had made the comedy *Mouse Hunt* (1997) and the horror film *The Ring* (2002), and writers Terry Rossio and Ted Elliot, who had received an Academy Award nomination for writing the animated hit *Shrek* (2001), determined to create a different kind of pirate movie. They developed an original plot that revolved around a reverse treasure hunt and added elements of the supernatural, tons of special effects, and a pair of steadfast lovers (Elizabeth Swann and Will Turner, played by Keira Knightley and Orlando Bloom) who must overcome daunting odds to be together.

Into this mix they threw a dashing pirate captain, Jack Sparrow, played by Depp, a versatile actor known for his unconventional characterizations. Though the part was written as a standard adventure protagonist, Depp immediately understood that Sparrow was not meant to be a stereotypical pirate hero. He has said in interviews that he based his portrayal on a combination of rock guitarist Keith Richards of the Rolling Stones and amorous Gallic cartoon skunk Pepé le Pew, and he turned Sparrow into a sort of pirate rock star—campy, cocky, and constantly inebriated.

Johnny Depp as Captain Jack Sparrow. *Johnny Depp hams it up as Captain Jack Sparrow in the popular* Pirates of the Caribbean *movie franchise.* WALT DISNEY/THE KOBAL COLLECTION.

Many of the other actors are appealing in their roles, such as Geoffrey Rush as the villainous Captain Barbossa, Bloom as the stalwart Turner, and Knightley as the audacious heroine Swann, knocking out an assailant while quipping, "You like pain? Try wearing a corset!" But Depp steals the show, turning the manly pirate stereotype on its head with his mincing, sloshy portrayal of Sparrow, drawling lines like, "Shoot him! And cut out his tongue! Then shoot his tongue!" Depp's Sparrow also has a unique physical appearance, with long beaded dreadlocks and a beard braided into two narrow strands. Dark kohl eyeliner reinforces the glam-rock look, and a liberal sprinkling of gold teeth adds a reminder that pirate life is gritty and rough. Sparrow's layered outfits of flowing shirts, scarves, vests, medallions, and soft boots inspired fashion designs for both men and women.

SUCCESS AND CRITICISM

Between Depp's inspired characterization and the film's elaborate special effects, *Pirates of the Caribbean: The Curse of the Black Pearl* was an instant hit with audiences. The film earned more than $70 million during its first week of release and grossed $654 million worldwide. Two sequels were in the works almost immediately. *Pirates of the Caribbean: Dead Man's Chest* (2006) grossed a record $135.6 million during its first weekend and went on to earn more than $1 billion worldwide. *Pirates of the Caribbean: At World's End* (2007) followed with respectable though not record-breaking earnings. After a four-year hiatus, *Pirates of the Caribbean: On Stranger Tides* (2011) was released, grossing more than $1 billion around the world.

All of the *Pirates of the Caribbean* films were special-effects blockbusters with elements of the ghost story interwoven with fantasy, comedy, and romance. The plot of the first film focuses on a grisly ancient curse that turns a pirate crew to skeletons by moonlight. The second two revolve around Davy Jones, depicted as half-man, half-seafood, who lives at the bottom of the ocean and makes devilish deals with drowning sailors, and the fourth involves a race to find the fountain of youth. Knightley and Bloom dropped out of the franchise by the fourth film, and Sparrow takes center stage supported by Penelope Cruz and Ian McShane.

Although critics continued to find fault with the films, the influence of *Pirates of the Caribbean* was widely felt. The soundtrack of *Pirates of the Caribbean: Curse of the Black Pearl* reached number six on the Billboard soundtrack chart in 2003. In 2006 Disney revamped its Pirates of the Caribbean attraction to include Captain Jack Sparrow. Pirates of the Caribbean video and online games were introduced, and novelizations of the films and other adventures of Sparrow and his friends were published. Mars candies marketed special "Pirate Pearls" white chocolate M&Ms. Pirate Halloween costumes became more popular than ever, and in 2006, at the height of *Pirates of the Caribbean: Dead Man's Chest*'s popularity, Jack Sparrow outfits outsold all other Halloween costumes.

Tina Gianoulis

SEE ALSO: *Academy Awards; Bruckheimer, Jerry; Depp, Johnny; Disney (Walt Disney Company); The Rolling Stones;* Shrek; *Toys; Video Games.*

BIBLIOGRAPHY

George, Lianne. "Rock the Plank: Captain Jack Sparrow Is One of the Most Unexpected, Enduring Fashion Icons of the Past Decade. But What on Earth Is He Wearing?" *Maclean's* 120, no. 23 (2007): 60.

Lally, Kevin. "See Worthy: Gore Verbinski Commandeers *Pirates of the Caribbean.*" *Film Journal International* 106, no. 6 (2003): 10.

Rottenberg, Josh. "The Rough Seas of the Upcoming *Pirates of the Caribbean* Films." *Entertainment Weekly*, July 14, 2006, 36.

Singer, Michael. *Bring Me That Horizon: The Making of "Pirates of the Caribbean."* New York: Disney Editions, 2007.

Smith, Sean. "A Pirate's Life: He Wasn't Looking for Superstardom, So Superstardom Came Looking for Him." *Newsweek*, June 26, 2006, 42.

Surrell, Jason. *"Pirates of the Caribbean": From the Magic Kingdom to the Movies.* New York: Disney Editions, 2005.

Pitt, Brad *(1963–)*

Brad Pitt had only fourteen minutes of screen time in the 1991 Ridley Scott film *Thelma & Louise*, but his portrayal of the raffish cowboy J. D. riveted audiences and caused critics to hail him as the new James Dean. Since that first breakout role, Pitt has become a Hollywood superstar, in demand by directors as a skilled actor and followed by paparazzi for a glimpse into his glamorous personal life. In the midst of the media hype and idolatry, Pitt has worked to overcome his pretty-boy image and build a serious career. He has also worked to use the rewards of his celebrity responsibility with substantial philanthropic enterprises in such devastated areas as Africa and post–Hurricane Katrina New Orleans, Louisiana.

William Bradley Pitt comes by his devilish southern charm authentically. Born in 1963 in Shawnee, Oklahoma, and raised in Springfield, Missouri, in the heart of the Ozarks, Pitt was one of three children of staunchly religious Baptist parents. His mother, Jane, was a family counselor, and his father, Bill, managed a trucking company. Pitt studied journalism and advertising at the University of Missouri but began to desire to see the world beyond his Ozark home. He left school just two credits short of graduating and drove to Hollywood in pursuit of an acting career. In California he worked a variety of odd jobs while taking acting classes, and by the late 1980s he had begun to get small roles in films and on television shows.

EARLY ROLES

Pitt had appeared in uncredited roles in several films and in episodes of such television shows as the soap opera *Another World* on NBC, *Dallas* on CBS, and *21 Jump Street* on Fox when he was cast in a small but pivotal role in the 1991 female buddy adventure film *Thelma & Louise*. Pitt's performance as the charming rogue who steals the heroines' money launched his career as a sexy leading man. His next important film, *A River Runs through It* (1992), directed by Robert Redford, proved Pitt had the acting skill to carry a leading role and prompted comparisons to Redford himself, another handsome actor who had proven that he had depth as well as charm.

Although his status as a heartthrob seemed secure, Pitt purposely backed away from his handsome image, choosing his next films carefully and changing his look to avoid being typecast in shallow "hunk" roles. In 1993 he grew his hair out to play a serial killer in *Kalifornia*, directed by Dominic Sena. He followed another acclaimed romantic role in the pioneer epic *Legends of the Fall* (1994), directed by Edward Zwick, by cutting his own hair to play a manic mental patient in the futuristic *12 Monkeys* (1995), directed by Terry Gilliam. Unable entirely to escape the focus on his looks (he was named *People* magazine's "Sexiest Man Alive" in 1995 and 2000), Pitt began to be taken seriously as an actor as well. He continued to alternate glamorous Hollywood blockbusters such as *Interview with the Vampire* (1994), directed by Neil Jordan, and *Ocean's Eleven* (2001), directed by Steven Soderbergh, with more controversial independent efforts such as *Fight Club* (1999), directed by David Fincher, and *Inglourious Basterds* (2009).

PERSONAL LIFE

Perhaps because of Pitt's large base of fans infatuated with his boyish good looks and chiseled physique, his love life has always been as widely publicized as his professional accomplishments. During his early career, he was paired with the actresses Robin Givens, Jill Schoelen, and Juliette Lewis. In 1994 he began a relationship with Gwyneth Paltrow when they were both working in the Fincher police thriller *Se7en*. The two became engaged before breaking up in 1997. In 1998 Pitt became involved with Jennifer Aniston, star of the NBC ensemble sitcom *Friends*, and the two married in 2000. In spite of numerous articles and interviews portraying the couple as having the ideal Hollywood marriage, their relationship ended in 2005 when Pitt began a relationship with Angelina Jolie, his costar in the Doug Liman film *Mr. & Mrs. Smith*, a spy movie about a bored married couple who, unbeknownst to each other, are both hired assassins.

Pitt's betrayal of Aniston and their fairy-tale marriage outraged many fans, but most quickly became smitten with "Brangelina," as the couple was dubbed. Their relationship became so celebrated that it boosted both their careers into superstardom. Jolie had made headlines in 2002 when she adopted a Cambodian baby she named Maddox. In the summer of 2005, Pitt accompanied Jolie to Ethiopia, where she adopted her second child, Zahara. Pitt adopted both children, whose last names became Jolie-Pitt. The couple adopted another child, Pax, from Vietnam, and had three biological children—Shiloh, Knox, and Vivienne. To forestall the paparazzi, who followed their every move, Pitt and Jolie sold the right to photograph their children to the American and British fan magazines *People* and *Hello!*, donating the proceeds to charity. Although for many years the pair declined to marry, saying that they would not do so until marriage became legal for gay couples, they announced their engagement in 2012.

From the beginning of his high-profile career, Pitt has keenly felt that with celebrity comes responsibility. He has launched a number of philanthropic enterprises to bring aid to disadvantaged areas from Africa to the Ozarks. The most ambitious of these efforts has been the Make It Right Foundation. The organization works to help rebuild the Lower Ninth Ward neighborhood in New Orleans, which was devastated by Hurricane Katrina in 2005. Pitt fell in love with the rich culture and relaxed warmth of New Orleans in 1994, when he filmed *Interview with the Vampire* there, and he was horrified at governmental failures to protect the poorest citizens of the city before and after the hurricane. Through his foundation, which he started with a $5 million pledge, he has helped rebuild the city's most damaged neighborhoods using sustainable designs and green energy systems such as solar panels.

Tina Gianoulis

SEE ALSO: Another World; *Celebrity; Celebrity Couples;* Dallas; *Divorce;* Fight Club; *Hollywood; Hurricane Katrina; Jolie, Angelina;* People; *Redford, Robert; Soap Operas; Soderbergh, Steven; Television.*

BIBLIOGRAPHY

Bennetts, Leslie. "Aspects of Brad." *Vanity Fair*, June 2004.

Kaplan, James. "Brad Pitt's Transformation." *Entertainment Weekly*, November 6, 1992.

Make It Right Foundation. Accessed May 2012. Available from http://makeitrightnola.org/

Mundy, Chris. "Slippin' around on the Road with Brad Pitt." *Rolling Stone*, December 1, 1994, 92.

Robb. Brian J. *Brad Pitt: The Rise to Stardom*. London: Plexus, 2002.

The Pittsburgh Steelers

The Pittsburgh Steelers are regarded as the most successful professional football franchise of the 1970s, the decade when the sport became a major spectator pastime in the United States thanks to increased live television coverage and the growing momentum of the annual Super Bowl. As millions of American fans were getting hooked on weekly football telecasts in the 1970s, the Steelers won four Super Bowl titles, becoming a sort of touchstone that represented pro football at its best. The team has remained a consistent playoff contender in the decades since and has captured two more championships, giving it a record six Super Bowl victories.

DIFFICULT EARLY YEARS

The Steelers were founded in July 1933 by Arthur J. Rooney, who used $2,500 he had won at the racetrack to purchase a football team. The team was known as the Pirates until 1940, when Rooney changed the name to reflect Pittsburgh's steelmaking heritage. Rooney's first obstacle was to circumvent Pennsylvania's blue laws, which did not allow professional sporting events on Sundays; he did so with several clever maneuvers, including inviting high police officials to be his guests at the team's first game. The Steelers lacked any major honors until 1972, when the team captured its first division title. Despite the team's lack of success from the 1930s until the 1970s, Rooney remained dedicated to the team and maintained a constant presence at games and other events with his ever-present cigar.

Although its initial record was poor, the team did have a number of star performers, including running backs Johnny "Blood" McNally and Bill Dudley, and quarterback Bobby Layne. In the late 1930s Rooney signed Colorado University star Byron "Whizzer" White for nearly $16,000, making him the highest-paid player in professional football. White played only one season for Pittsburgh. Later, in the 1960s, he was appointed by President Kennedy as a Supreme Court justice.

The Steelers started to gain a small measure of respectability in the 1950s and 1960s, but the team's turnaround really began in 1969 with the arrival of Chuck Noll as head coach. Noll had started his career as a defensive assistant and then coached the Baltimore Colts from 1966 to 1968. At the same time, Dan Rooney, Arthur's eldest son, began to assume greater control over the team. Noll and Rooney assembled a group of outstanding players, including defensive tackle Joe Greene, quarterback Terry Bradshaw, running back Franco Harris, and wide receivers Lynn Swann and John Stallworth. The hallmark of the Steelers' success in the 1970s was its defense, which earned the nickname the "Steel Curtain" for its ability to prevent opposing offenses from gaining yardage.

MAKING A DYNASTY

The team's turnaround after Noll's arrival was gradual, as the Steelers won only one game during his first season. However, by 1972 the team went 11–3 and won its first division title. The team reached its first Super Bowl in 1975, beating the Minnesota Vikings by a score of 16–6. Running back Harris, who set a Super Bowl record 158 rushing yards on thirty-four carries, was named Most Valuable Player. The following year, the Steelers returned to the Super Bowl and defeated the Dallas Cowboys 21–17, with wide receiver Swann earning MVP honors.

In 1978 the Steelers once again beat Dallas in the championship game, 35–31, and returned to defeat Los Angeles 31–19 in the 1979 Super Bowl, becoming the first team ever to win back-to-back Super Bowls on two separate occasions. Quarterback Bradshaw was the MVP in both games, setting records for most career touchdowns (nine) and passing yards (932) in the Super Bowl. These honors were a vindication of sorts for Bradshaw, who had initially struggled under high expectations after coming to the team as the first player selected in the 1970 draft. Bradshaw, who came from a rural background and played for an unheralded program at Louisiana State University, suffered from a lack of support and had to endure fans and commentators who habitually questioned his intelligence.

In 1980 the Steelers' dominance came to an end when the team suffered a devastating array of injuries and missed the playoffs for the first time since 1972. Gradually, many of the team's stalwarts of the 1970s retired. Noll retired as coach after the 1991 season, having served one of the longest head coaching tenures in league history. Bill Cowher succeeded Noll as coach, and the Steelers once again became a perennial playoff team. Cowher hired Dick LeBeau as defensive coordinator; LeBeau developed a punishing defense that depended on blitzes to pressure the quarterback and disrupt the passing game. Under Cowher, the team reached Super Bowl XXX in 1996, only to lose to Dallas 27–17 in its first trip to the championship game since 1979.

A NEW ERA

The team's fortunes began to improve with the arrival of some impressive new talent. In 1998 the Steelers drafted wide receiver Hines Ward, who went on to become the team's all-time leader in receptions, receiving yards, and receiving touchdowns. In 2004 the Steelers drafted quarterback Ben Roethlisberger, who shocked the league by leading his team to an unheard-of 15–1 regular-season record in his rookie year. On the defensive side, the team had hard-hitting players in safety Troy Polamalu and linebacker James Harrison. The team returned to the Super Bowl in 2006 and defeated the Seattle Seahawks. After the following season, Cowher stepped down as head coach.

The Rooneys hired Mike Tomlin, a thirty-four-year-old defensive coordinator, as their next head coach. In his second year as coach he led the team back to the championship, in which the Steelers defeated the Arizona Cardinals. This victory made Tomlin the youngest coach ever to win a Super Bowl and Pittsburgh the team with the most championships. The team again played in Super Bowl XLV in 2011 but lost to the Green Bay Packers.

Jason George

SEE ALSO: *Bradshaw, Terry; The Dallas Cowboys; Gambling; The Green Bay Packers; Steel Curtain; Super Bowl; Swann, Lynn; Television.*

BIBLIOGRAPHY

Chastain, Bill. *Steel Dynasty: The Team That Changed the NFL.* Chicago: Triumph Books, 2005.

Didinger, Ray. *Pittsburgh Steelers.* New York: Macmillan, 1974.

Mendelson, Abby. *The Pittsburgh Steelers: The Official Team History*, 4th ed. Lanham, MD: Taylor Trade Publishing, 2011.

Sahadi, Lou. *Super Steelers: The Making of a Dynasty.* New York: Times Books, 1980.

Pizza

Pizza is a popular dish in America that consists of a baked crust, typically between 12 and 20 inches in diameter, topped with a combination of tomato sauce, vegetables, meats, and melted cheese. The overwhelming popularity of pizza in America is mainly a result of its convenience, versatility, and association with pleasure, communal eating, and informality. In cities and suburbs, it is easy to grab a slice for lunch if one's time is limited. It can be made with an almost endless combination of ingredients depending on the whims of the consumer (in the first decade of the 2000s pepperoni was the most preferred topping in the United States), with thick, thin, or stuffed crusts. It can be delivered to one's home and eaten in front of the television set or consumed in a restaurant. It can be the homogenized product of a national chain operation or a unique pie from a local mom-and-pop establishment.

ORIGIN AND DEVELOPMENT

Originally an open-face tomato pie, pizza began as a simple, cheap, and popular "workingman's food" in Italy. Although the dish had been baked since ancient times, the term *pizza* (meaning "to pluck") started appearing in Italian dictionaries in the 1850s. The quintessential pizza is said to have been created by a baker, Raffaele Esposito of Naples, for the 1889 visit of the reigning king and queen of Italy. Inspired by patriotism, Esposito incorporated Italy's national colors into his creation—tomatoes for red, mozzarella cheese for white, and basil for green—establishing the basic ingredients for the pizza. At the turn of the twentieth century Italian immigrants brought pizza to the United States, and Gennaro (or Giovanni, depending on the account) Lombardi opened the first pizzeria in 1905 in New York City's Little Italy. Other Italians (many trained by Lombardi) quickly opened their own shops, baking their pizzas in coal- or wood-burning brick ovens.

By the 1930s and 1940s people running small local shops were making and selling pizzas in towns all across the country,

Pizza. The overwhelming popularity of pizza in America developed mainly due to its convenience, versatility, and its association with pleasure, communal eating, and informality. MICHAEL ONISIFOROU/SHUTTERSTOCK.COM.

enabled in part by new gas-heated ovens that made the baking safer, more efficient, and more reliable. Despite the improvements in technology, the real accelerator in making pizza a national fad came with the return of soldiers who had developed a taste for the pizza of Naples during World War II. As a food of relative simplicity, pizza allowed for many ethnic and regional variations, making it a foodstuff readily able to please most Americans. Traditional Italian pizzas were round and had thin crusts, whereas Sicilian versions were square with thick, chewy crusts. Chicago was known for its deep-dish style, while midwesterners in general preferred pizza pies with thin crusts and spicy sauce, and Northeasterners opted for thick-crust pizzas with a lot of sauce, extra cheese, and less meat. New Haven was known for its clam pie; California for its thin crusts, gourmet toppings, and unusual combinations.

Although some pizzerias were sit-down restaurants that also served other Italian cuisine, the most successful businesses, founded in the later decades of the twentieth century, specialized in take-out and delivery service, making pizza a very mobile food that suited Americans' growing preference for home delivery of convenience meals. Delivery service combined convenience and the desire for choice: people could call up a nearby pizza shop, place an order selecting as many "pies" with as many different toppings as they liked, and have the food delivered to their door within the hour.

As such, pizza enjoyed a reputation for being a casual food meant for informal occasions and indeed came to define these occasions. People commonly ate slices of pizza with their hands, right out of the boxes they were delivered in, foregoing plates and eating utensils. Popular with all age groups and ethnicities, pizzas were generally associated with children and teenagers, becoming familiar staples at parties and other casual gatherings in college dorm rooms and private homes, around the television, and especially during media events such as the Super Bowl. Specific occasions, called pizza parties, were even organized around the food.

GROWING POPULARITY

The American love for pizza has given rise to many successful national chains. Shakey's, the first pizza franchise, began in 1954 in Sacramento, California. Pizzeria Uno, an Italian restaurant specializing in deep-dish Chicago-style pizzas, opened in 1943 and has expanded to more than 150 restaurants nationally. Pizza Hut, a pizza restaurant founded in 1958, grew to more than 11,000 stores and made $10 billion in sales by its fiftieth anniversary. Domino's, offering delivery-only service (and promising its pizzas would reach one's doorstep within thirty minutes or the pizza was free), was started in 1960 and enjoyed global retail sales of more than $6 billion in 2010.

The growth of the American appetite for pizza has also sparked the development of frozen pizzas that can be cooked at home. Rose and Jim Totino began one of the most successful frozen pizza enterprises in 1962; Totino's was quickly joined by other brands such as Red Baron, Celeste PizzaForOne, and Stouffer's. In addition, other make-at-home pizza products were successful, including Ragu pizza sauce in a jar, Boboli ready-made pizza crust, and Robin Hood pizza dough mix.

In 2005 a pizza delivery association reported that more than 11.5 million pizzas were sold daily, making pizza a $30 billion industry. In that same year more than 62,000 pizzerias were operating in the United States, many characterized by familiar red-and-white checkered tablecloths. Recent decades have seen such a proliferation of pizza that anything topped with tomato sauce and cheese is called "pizza," including pizza bagels, pizza

English muffins, and pizza burgers. Many snack foods, such as tortilla chips and snack crackers, also come in pizza-flavored varieties.

Wendy Woloson

SEE ALSO: *Fast Food; Super Bowl; World War II.*

BIBLIOGRAPHY

Asimov, Eric. "New York Pizza, the Real Thing, Makes a Comeback." *New York Times*, June 10, 1998.

Gabaccia, Donna R. *We Are What We Eat: Ethnic Food and the Making of Americans.* Cambridge, MA: Harvard University Press, 1998.

Gay, Kathlyn, and Martin K. Gay. *Encyclopedia of North American Eating & Drinking Traditions, Customs, & Rituals.* Santa Barbara, CA: ABC-CLIO, 1996.

Hanson, Gayles M. B. "Square, Stuffed, Thin, Frozen, Americans Just Adore Pizza." *Insight on the News* 12, no. 25 (1996), 42.

Helstosky, Carol. *Pizza: A Global History.* London: Reaktion Books, 2008.

A Place in the Sun

A Place in the Sun (1951) was the second film adaptation of Theodore Dreiser's novel *An American Tragedy*, based on a 1906 murder case in upstate New York. Director George Stevens won an Oscar for the movie, which deemphasized the novel's focus on class and social justice, instead bringing the romantic angle to the story's center. Montgomery Clift starred as George Eastman, a small-town factory foreman who cannot bring himself to break off an affair with his equally poor lover (Shelley Winters), even after falling for a wealthy socialite (Elizabeth Taylor). When George's lover becomes pregnant, he contemplates murder. After he decides not to go through with the killing, she drowns and he is accused of her murder.

As the film's star, the naturalistic Clift delivered a sympathetic performance, in addition to several passionate love scenes with Taylor (in one of her first adult roles). Winters proved a formidable actress in her role as Clift's passive-aggressive ex-lover. The film was both a critical and box-office hit, and legendary comedic actor Charlie Chaplin stated he considered it the best movie in Hollywood history.

Andrew Milner

SEE ALSO: *Clift, Montgomery; Dreiser, Theodore; Taylor, Elizabeth.*

BIBLIOGRAPHY

Brandon, Craig. *Murder in the Adirondacks: An American Tragedy Revisited.* Utica, NY: North Country Books, 1986.

LaGuardia, Robert. *Monty: A Biography of Montgomery Clift.* New York: Arbor House, 1977.

Peary, Danny. *Guide for the Film Fanatic.* New York: Simon & Schuster, 1986.

Reid, John Howard. *Success in the Cinema: Money-Making Movies and Critics' Choices.* Raleigh, NC: Lulu, 2006.

Planet of the Apes

Planet of the Apes, directed by Franklin Schaffner and released in 1968, was almost singlehandedly responsible for elevating cinema's science fiction genre from the traditional "B" movie slot to the lavish and expensive blockbuster art form. Based on Pierre Boulle's novel *La Planète des singes* (1963), the film portrays misanthropic George Taylor (Charlton Heston) and his fellow astronauts' deep-space mission to find other forms of life. These voyagers program the ship's computers to wake them from their hibernation 2,000 years in the future, when they expect to be light-years from Earth; having traveled at the speed of light, the astronauts do not age during the journey.

Upon awakening, the crew guides the spaceship to a remote, seemingly barren planet. Soon, however, they encounter a race of reasoning and talking apes with a complex aristocratic civilization, as well as a rogue group of primate-like humans with whom the apes are at war. The ape leader, Dr. Zaius (Maurice Evans), is horrified by Taylor's arrival and demands his death, but two apes, Cornelius (Roddy McDowall) and Zira (Kim Hunter), risk their lives to protect Taylor. In the process of saving Taylor's life, they also uncover the damning secret of the planet's history.

Previous science fiction films such as *The Man from Planet X* (1951) and *The Day the Earth Stood Still* (1951) were big box-office hits despite their shoddy low-budget depictions of futuristic worlds and beings. *Planet of the Apes*, with its expensive makeup and costumes, demonstrated to Hollywood studios the economic viability of big-budget science fiction fare. Over the following three decades a host of similar futuristic blockbusters were produced. By the late 1990s the big-budget science fiction film had become one of the most popular styles of filmmaking and one of the surest returns on studio investment.

Planet of the Apes was such a cultural phenomenon that it spawned four sequels—*Beneath the Planet of the Apes* (1970), *Escape from the Planet of the Apes* (1971), *Conquest of the Planet of the Apes* (1972), and *Battle for the Planet of the Apes* (1973)—as well as a live action series (1974) and an animated television series (1975–1976). In addition, the film occasioned its own merchandising line, allowing children of the 1970s to own *Planet of the Apes* action figures and lunch boxes. The film's cultural resonance continued into the 1980s and 1990s. Greenpeace, for instance, seized upon the image of Taylor kneeling before the fallen Statue of Liberty as the basis for a series of antinuclear posters. White supremacists have embraced *Planet of the Apes* as well, reading the film's ape dominance as a coded warning against increased racial tolerance.

In 2001 Tim Burton directed a remake of *Planet of the Apes*, reinterpreting the novel and using cutting-edge visual technology to present space travel and the ape planet. Despite the dazzling special effects, the film was a flop. Not so with 20th Century Fox's 2011 return to the *Planet of the Apes* franchise, *Rise of the Planet of the Apes*. Starring James Franco, this film tells the story of a genetically altered chimpanzee, Caesar (Andy Serkis), who leads a rebellion of apes on Earth. Fox announced that the film, a box-office hit, would be the first in a new series based on Boulle's novel.

Scott Tribble

SEE ALSO: The Day the Earth Stood Still; *Heston, Charlton; Hollywood; Science Fiction Publishing; White Supremacists.*

BIBLIOGRAPHY

Greene, Eric. *"Planet of the Apes" as American Myth: Race and Politics in the Films and Television Series.* Jefferson, NC: McFarland, 1996.

Kim, Erwin. *Franklin J. Schaffner.* Metuchen, NJ: Scarecrow Press, 1985.

Pohl, Frederick, and Frederick Pohl IV. *Science Fiction: Studies in Film.* New York: Ace Books, 1981.

Plastic

Plastic (from the Greek word *plassein*, meaning "to mold or shape a soft substance") was originally invented as a substitute for natural resources. It has become a material in its own right, no longer simulating organic substances but instead being used to create entirely new products—everything from tableware to car bodies to artificial hearts. More than any other material, plastic changed life in America even as it came to symbolize a particularly artificial and superficial culture that is concerned more with appearances than substance and more with imitation than reality. In the popular vernacular, *plastic* took on a pejora-

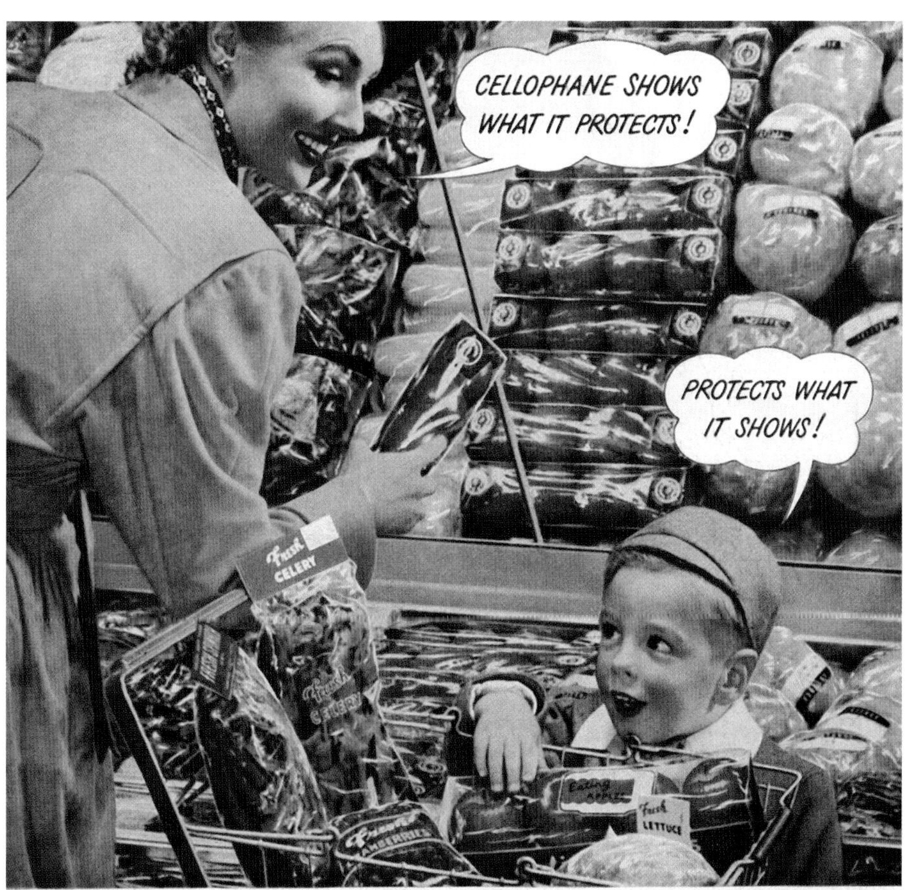

Cellophane. *A 1947 advertisement from DuPont cellophane touts it as ideal for packaging and protecting produce.* APIC/GETTY IMAGES.

tive connotation early on, to mean false or fake or disingenuous. Early Hollywood starlets were called "celluloid women," and in 1962 Ken Kesey used the phrase "her fixed plastic smile" in his writing. In an ironic statement on the condition of the culture, a character in the movie *The Graduate* confided these words of advice to Dustin Hoffman's character: "I just want to say one word to you, Ben. Just one word. Plastics."

BEGINNINGS

Celluloid, a derivative of cellulose and the first material with some properties of modern plastic, was invented in 1869 by John Wesley Hyatt, a man in search of a substitute for the ivory used in billiard balls. Although celluloid was never successfully put to this recreational purpose, it did become a viable replacement for coral, marble, bone, and ivory and was used to make piano keys, collars, cuffs, novelties, combs, and brushes. Celluloid democratized a host of consumer goods by offering a less expensive but equally functional substitute for rare materials. In addition, it reflected the growing desire and willingness of people to harness the products of nature and control them for their own interests, a practice that was expressed most often in the burgeoning industrial ethic.

Celluloid found many applications beyond domestic ones. In the 1920s it was used as transparent sheeting in rear windows and windshields of automobiles. Cellulose acetate, a nonflammable version of celluloid, could be shaped through injection molding into a variety of objects, from adding machine keys and knife handles to bobbins and eyeglass frames. The use of celluloid that affected American culture on the grandest scale was its application in the photography and movie industries. George Eastman revolutionized photography by improving upon a gelatin-coated flexible celluloid film in 1889, which enabled photographers to snap pictures without the encumbrance of a large apparatus and a dark room. This new portable photographic technique proved extremely popular at the turn of the twentieth century, and sales of film soared.

Thomas Edison ordered film from Eastman to use in his Kinetoscope and showed the first films in American cities in 1894. Celluloid moving pictures took the power of cultural reproduction away from the academy and took its products out of museums, exposing them to masses of people. As historian Stephen Fenichell points out in *Plastic: The Making of a Synthetic Century*, "Celluloid film succeeded in raising the first plastic's cultural profile from a medium of mere mimicry into a priceless repository of human memory."

BAKELITE

Because it was derived from cellulose, celluloid had its roots in nature. By contrast, Bakelite was the first chemically synthetic plastic; it was invented in 1907 by Leo H. Baekeland, who is known as "the father of plastics." Bakelite, "the material of a thousand uses," was marketed not as a substitute for natural materials but as an innovative material in its own right. A major advantage of Bakelite over hard rubber and other materials was its ability to conform to the exact details of a mold. It found ready applications in the power industry as electrical insulators, but its formation into pipe stems, billiard balls, buttons, knife handles, radios, telephones, cigarette holders, jewelry, pens, and even airplane propellers indicated the degree to which Americans were willing to accept wholly new materials on their own terms rather than as nature's substitutes.

Indeed, Bakelite was *the* material of the Art Deco 1920s. Industrial designer Henry Dreyfuss used the plastic in his redesign of the Bell telephone, creating its quintessential shape by combining the ear and mouthpiece into a single handset, giving the entire object a streamlined silhouette. Raymond Loewy improved on the design of a mimeograph machine in 1929 by adding a Bakelite shell that concealed its inner workings, creating an artful yet utilitarian object for the office. Walter Dorwin Teague used brown Bakelite in 1934 for the body of the "Baby Brownie" camera he designed for Kodak; it was so popular that four million of them sold in the first year—in the depths of the Depression.

The success of Bakelite and the subsequent popularity of other types of plastic, including many that were much more colorful and versatile than celluloid and Bakelite, moved America from the machine age into the plastic age. *Plastic* became a household word between the world wars and came to be a popularly understood symbol of modernity. As with all new things, however, the increasing intrusion of plastic items into people's lives was met with widespread ambivalence.

Plastic at once enabled people to escape the forces and often limited resources of nature and threatened an abrupt disjunction with past materials and manufacturing processes. During the 1920s and 1930s the world of plastic was a hopeful and stable one, bright and unthreatened by rust and decay. By the late 1930s and 1940s conservative utopians looked upon plastic as a substance that promised social stability by replacing scarcity with abundance and enabling many more people to own consumer goods. By the 1960s and 1970s environmentalists had become worried about the glut of plastic materials, especially throwaway food containers, disposable diapers, and plastic bags that were clogging landfills and littering the landscape.

CELLOPHANE AND RAYON

Social utopianism, in part, led to the popularity of plastic products such as cellophane, a French invention that DuPont purchased the rights to in the 1920s. The first American products wrapped in cellophane, Whitman's chocolates, were soon followed by cigarette packs that were promoted as fresh if wrapped in sheets of this crisp, clear plastic. During the rest of the decade, everything seemed to be wrapped in cellophane—from sheets and towels to tires and pianos. Cellophane offered a new sensibility based on ideas of cleanliness and sterility. People wanted to see the products they were buying, but they also wanted to be assured of their purity and freshness. Lucite and Plexiglas, more substantial forms of clear plastic that also tapped into this popular ethos, entered the market in the 1930s.

Cellophane also made things glamorous, immediately conferring a kind of sparkle and sex appeal to the most mundane objects. Cole Porter's 1934 song "You're the Top" exclaimed, "You're the purple light of a summer night in Spain / You're the National Gallery / You're Garbo's salary / You're cellophane!" Aside from heightening the fetishized aspects of consumer goods, the thin plastic film had practical uses. In 1930 Richard Drew, an engineer at 3M (then the Minnesota Mining and Manufacturing Company), devised a way to coat cellophane with pressure-sensitive adhesive, coming up with "Scotch" tape, an enduring modern convenience. Cellophane was also used as the lens for gas masks in World War I and World War II and served as an ideal semipermeable membrane for dialysis machines. In a 1940 poll, the most beautiful words in English were identified as *mother*, *memory*, and *cellophane*.

Rayon, or viscose, was a fabric made out of cellulose fibers, which gave it an attractive sheen and silken luster. Elsa Schiaparelli, an avant-garde designer, incorporated this prosaic material into her fashions, immediately making luxury more affordable with her draped, form-fitting outfits. Sales of rayon underwear increased fivefold between 1925 and 1928; by the mid-1930s, about 85 percent of all American dresses had rayon content, thus moving synthetics into the realm formerly monopolized by such organic materials as cotton, wool, silk, and linen. People were even willing to put plastics intimately close to their bodies ("wrap themselves in plastic," as an acidulous Ralph Nader sneered in the 1970s).

VINYL AND NYLON

Polyvinyl chloride (also known as PVC and more commonly called vinyl) was developed into a workable material in 1926 by Waldo Semon. He found that it was water-resistant and fireproof and that it could be molded and extruded into any number of forms. Semon used his new invention to make things such as shower curtains, raincoats, ship's upholstery, and color-coded electrical wires. A related synthetic, polyethylene, was used to coat coaxial cable, an innovation that enabled high-speed telecommunications and revolutionized the methods by which people communicated with one another.

Nylon, which had been primarily used for toothbrush bristles before World War II, was one of plastic's best success stories. Silk was expensive and was not durable enough for wartime needs. In addition, most silk imports came from Japan, an unreliable supplier by the late 1930s. Invented by DuPont chemist Wallace Carothers, nylon was the first truly artificial fiber that could be woven.

Even though nylon stockings (generally called "nylons") were more expensive than their silk precursors, women bought them en masse in the hope that they were more durable (they were, but only slightly); women also loved the sheerness of nylons, a welcome change from the opacity of silk stockings. Like the cellophane sheaths that enhanced and glamorized the products they wrapped, nylons functioned similarly for the women who wore them: they were seen as naughty but sexy. May 15, 1940, known as "N-day," marked the beginning of national sales of nylon stockings. They proved so popular that all five million pairs had been sold by day's end.

During World War II plastics reverted to their original purposes as replacements for scarce natural materials, and nylon was no exception. It was made into glider towropes, parachutes, and cords for synthetic rubber tires, among other things. As a result, women had to give up their beloved nylons; many sported the "bare-legged" look to signify their patriotism, often painting a line down the backs of their legs to simulate the stocking seam—even in its absence, nylon was very much a cultural presence.

Other plastics that figured into the war effort included Naugahyde, a form of vinyl used to upholster military vehicles and furniture; bubbled windshields of Plexiglas that replaced glass in cockpits, allowing pilots to survey their surroundings without visual interference; phenolic resin, a relative of Bakelite, which substituted for steel as a viable helmet liner; and Teflon, whose durability and slipperiness made it ideal for coating the valves and gaskets used in uranium processing and testing at the Manhattan Project. The success of plastic during the war convinced the American public of its worth and value—people could trust it because it had helped the Allies win the war. As Fenichell states, "If before the war plastic's image had been defined by frivolity, trumpery, and above all, a sleazy pretense at luxury, by the time Teflon was enlisted in the atomic bomb effort, plastic materials had matured under fire."

POSTWAR USES

By the late 1940s plastic was firmly rooted in the material life of all Americans, especially in the domestic sphere. Tupperware, made from polyethylene, was a brand of housewares developed by Earl S. Tupper in 1942. Even before the war's end, Tupperware and its home sales method of marketing and distribution, which combined entrepreneurialism with domestic duties, had enjoyed large success among suburban housewives. Tupperware exploited the very flexibility of plastics, producing tumblers, bowls, tableware, and resealable containers that were durable yet soft. It was also strangely organic, appearing in many forms and in colors such as pink, blue, orange, yellow, and green pastels.

Dacron, another form of polyester, was invented by DuPont chemist Hale Charch; DuPont began production of Dacron in 1953, weaving it into fabric to make clothing. Even though it melted, easily pilled, and caused static cling, such fabrics were used in drip-dry suits that were machine washable and did not require dry cleaning.

Vinyl experienced similar postwar popularity. Naugahyde, a cheaper and tougher substitute for leather, was used to upholster recliners such as La-Z-Boys and Barcaloungers and came to symbolize a durable manliness in material form. In 1946 RCA marketed the first vinyl phonograph records, which performed better than earlier versions made from brittle shellac. These were further improved in 1949 with more grooves pressed into the vinyl, thus producing the first long-playing record album. Saran Wrap, a vinyl film, could stick to itself and was therefore used to provide airtight protection; it found use as a kind of disposable Tupperware, covering food either under refrigeration or being transported.

It was only after the war that some plastics that had been around for decades came into their own, especially for domestic use. The durable but slick Teflon, for example, which was invented in 1938 by Roy Plunkett, had unique qualities that made its application to normal life difficult at best. Teflon did not burn, freeze, or conduct electricity. As the original space-age material, it was used in space exploration and as an industrial lubricant. But it was not until Teflon was applied to create nonstick cookware that it gained a foothold in popular culture.

Formica had a similar history. Invented in 1913 by Westinghouse engineers Daniel J. O'Connor and Harold A. Faber, this cousin to Bakelite was used in institutional settings as an easily cleaned, durable, heat-resistant table surface most apt for hotels, diners, and soda fountains. Because Formica sheets could be manufactured with any number of designs, the material was frequently used to simulate natural surfaces such as wood grain or marble. After the war it appeared as a popular surface for items such as kitchen tables. Fenichell argues that while utilitarian, Formica also "provided a blank screen for the unconscious projection of a prime fifties anxiety: the atom bomb. . . . Formica provided protection against internal and external attack, eternally vigilant in its struggle to wipe clean the past."

TOYS AND FADS

The exuberance expressed in postwar America as it reveled in its material abundance was most clearly seen in plastic objects.

Children were surrounded by plastic toys, from educational Legos to quirky Silly Putty and faddish Hula-Hoops and Frisbees. Adult versions of these novelties included pink flamingo or elfin lawn ornaments. Velcro ("velvet hook"), perfected in 1957, was inspired by the sticking power of the cocklebur in nature. Pieces of Velcro stuck together could be easily peeled apart from each other but required considerable strength to pull the pieces sideways.

The Houston Astrodome, complete with Lucite sky and Astroturf grass, was an almost wholly plasticized environment. The creation of Disneyland and other similar fantasy places during this time symbolized America's willingness to settle for the artificial rather than the real and to prefer the human-made world of plasticized fakery over that of nature. This comfort with the unreal had by the 1980s and 1990s emerged in a postmodern culture of simulacra that accepted not only artificial replicas of nature but also replicas of the replicas.

The 1960s pop aesthetic, influenced by modernity, space flight, and the interrelationships of human and machine, embraced the colors, textures, and forms of plastic, highlighting its materiality. Inflatable furniture, vinyl go-go boots, and plastic bubble helmets all enjoyed great popularity. Paco Rabanne connected hard plastic pieces to each other with metal rings, creating chain mail–like dresses, vests, and pieces of jewelry. Betsey Johnson designed an entire line of see-through clothing made out of cellophane. Conceptual artist Christo made it his trademark to wrap buildings and landscapes—including part of the Australian coast—in plastic fabrics to celebrate the beauty of synthetic materials as juxtaposed against the natural landscape.

ENVIRONMENTAL CONCERNS

By the 1970s any clinging romance between people and plastic had disappeared. In this decade, the links between plastics and cancer became clearer, even to the plastics industry, which found that its toxic fumes threatened the health of industrial workers. The wholesale disposability of convenient plastic goods that ranged from contact lenses to drinking cups to diapers was seen to pose acute environmental hazards. Many forms of plastic did not biodegrade, making them a polluter of seashores and a threat to marine life. In the late 1980s an anti-Styrofoam campaign finally succeeded in pressuring McDonald's into finding a more ecologically sound alternative to its Styrofoam sandwich containers and coffee cups.

Around this same time, doctors diagnosed a new malady variously called "environmental illness," "twentieth century disease," or "sick building syndrome," which caused some people to develop oversensitivity to the toxic environment around them. Concurrently, the first artificial heart made of plastic, the Jarvik-7, was successfully implanted in Barney Clark, underscoring the fact that plastic no longer existed only in the external world but could become a literal part of people.

Consumers debated the relative merits of plastic and paper bags in grocery stores with little consensus. Twenty-first century consumers are generally given a choice between paper and plastic bags. Many stores also sell low-priced reusable cloth bags that customers can bring with them each time they shop.

The disposal of plastic continues to be a major problem for Americans. In the 1970s mariners began noticing a large island of garbage in the Pacific Ocean. It was not until 1997, however, that the Great Pacific Garbage Patch came to public notice. The garbage island has grown to twice the size of the United States. The debris is caught up in a vortex caused by ocean currents and stretches from California to Hawaii; 90 percent of the garbage island is composed of plastic items such as bottles, cups, bags, and packing materials.

The United Nations has estimated that 80 percent of all such garbage deposited in the world's oceans originated on land. All it takes is for the wind to pick up loose garbage and carry it out to sea. Ships also contribute to the size of the garbage island, depositing 639,000 items overboard each day. While environmentalists have attempted to carry the plastic away one boatload at a time, experts say the only solution is to prevent further plastic from making its way to the garbage islands that are now found in many countries of the world.

CONTINUING DEVELOPMENTS

Scientists continue to discover new uses for plastic. The American Chemistry Council has announced that plastic could conceivably solve American energy needs. The 29 million tons of plastic deposited in dumps in 2008 alone could be converted into fuel for six million vehicles or into energy for 5.2 million homes. Plastic is also being used in developing countries. Some 10,000 homes in the Philippines are now being lit through clean energy developed by scientists at the Massachusetts Institute of Technology.

The simple apparatus used in Philippine homes is composed of a soft drink bottle filled with water and a few drops of bleach to prevent algae from forming. The container is then placed up to the halfway point inside a small hole cut in the roof, and the area surrounding it is sealed. During the day, the sun heats the water and lights up the home. No cheap method has yet been invented to allow the storage of energy, so the homes go dark once the sun sets. Such innovative techniques may be the answer to using ubiquitous plastic without allowing it to destroy the environment.

Plastic has entered Americans' material lives to such a degree that extrication from that reliance on simulated products seems impossible without seriously impacting the standard of living. The material has become so "naturalized" that it often seems more real, tangible, and honest than nature itself. It permeates every aspect of daily life, even to the extent that many consumer transactions are carried out via credit cards that are generically referred to as "plastic."

As a descriptive term applied to people, *plastic* has come to reflect the larger trends in American culture that have blurred the distinction between animate beings and the inanimate goods that surround them. Ronald Reagan enjoyed notoriety as the "Teflon president" because nothing terrible that happened during his time in office stuck to his reputation. In an attempt at beautification, large numbers of women and men turn to plastic surgery to alter noses and brows and to dispense with wrinkles and fat. They have been accused of emulating their idealized plastic counterparts, Barbie and Ken, whose sleek plastic figures represent a seemingly unreachable goal to millions of Americans who are dissatisfied with their appearance. In a little over a century, the plastic ethos has embraced not only the versatile material but also the lifestyle and mindset that accompanied it, turning America into a prefabricated, simulated environment filled with people hungry for bright surfaces devoid of decay.

Wendy Woloson

SEE ALSO: *Brownie Cameras; Cigarettes; Consumerism; Disney (Walt Disney Company); Edison, Thomas Alva; Environmen-*

talism; Frisbee; Hula Hoop; Kesey, Ken; Kodak; La-Z-Boy Loungers; Legos; Long-Playing Record; McDonald's; Nader, Ralph; Nylon; Porter, Cole; Telephone; Tupperware; World War I; World War II.

BIBLIOGRAPHY

Blomberg, Lindsey E. "The Great Pacific Garbage Patch." *Environmental Magazine*, May/June 2011.

Fenichell, Stephen. *Plastic: The Making of a Synthetic Century.* New York: HarperBusiness, 1996.

Friedel, Robert. *Pioneer Plastic: The Making and Selling of Celluloid.* Madison: University of Wisconsin Press, 1983.

Katz, Sylvia. *Plastics: Common Objects, Classic Designs.* New York: Harry N. Abrams, 1984.

McBride, Samantha. *Recycling Reconsidered: The Present Failure and Future Promise of Environmental Action in the United States.* Cambridge, MA: MIT Press, 2012.

McKenzie-Mohr, Doug; Nancy R. Lee; P Wesley Schultz; et al. *Social Marketing to Protect the Environment: What Works.* Thousand Oaks, CA: Sage, 2012.

Meikle, Jeffrey L. *American Plastic: A Cultural History.* New Brunswick, NJ: Rutgers University Press, 1995.

Mossman, Susan, ed. *Early Plastics: Perspectives, 1850–1950.* London: Leicester University Press, 1997.

"Plastic Bottles Light Homes." *Current Science*, February 24, 2012, 12.

Slater, Dashka. "The Next Big Thing." *Sierra*, March/April 2012.

Plastic Surgery

Plastic surgery has traditionally been defined as a surgical procedure involving repair of skin defects and deformities, the removal of skin tumors, or body-part reconstruction. Increasingly, however, this medical specialty is being used for cosmetic purposes such as face-lifts or reshaping, the removal of fatty tissue, wrinkle reduction, breast and penile enlargement or reduction, and even the permanent application of makeup. Technological advances and changing cultural mores have continually broadened the scope of plastic surgery such that it is now primarily equated with cosmetic or aesthetic surgery. The emphasis on youth and attractiveness that is prevalent in American culture has led many Americans to undergo plastic surgery in order to boost self-esteem or improve workplace competitiveness.

Surgery may well be the oldest branch of medicine, but many centuries passed before modern methods, including plastic surgery, were commonly available. Precise knowledge of the body was necessary before anesthesia could be understood, and methods of controlling hemorrhage and postoperative infection were also essential before complex surgery could be undertaken. There is evidence to suggest, however, that surgery could have been an ancient practice. One Indian text dating from the fourth century BCE includes an extended section on surgery, though it is unknown whether the procedures described were actually practiced.

Direct accounts of a plastic surgery performed in Poona in 1793 do exist, and the British physicians who witnessed the procedure described the "Hindu method" as far superior to comparable North American and European techniques, which suggests that plastic surgery had been performed in India for perhaps centuries. Interestingly, the procedure was a rhinoplasty involving skin grafts and reconstruction for a man whose nose had been amputated as punishment for adultery. Because this method of punishment was common, it may have served as impetus for the development of early plastic surgery. Other records indicate that syphilis, which reached epidemic proportions during European colonial expansion, may also have facilitated advances in surgical techniques that attempted to repair the disease's grotesque manifestations. The first recorded face-lift was performed in Berlin in 1901.

RECONSTRUCTIVE SURGERY FOR WAR WOUNDS

Innovations in reconstructive surgery continued through the nineteenth century and, at least in America, interest in cosmetic surgery was already rising. Yet most medical historians designate World War I as the dramatic beginning of modern plastic surgery. The war resulted in unprecedented devastation and death but also in thousands of mutilating facial injuries. The horror inspired physician Harold Gillies to establish a plastic surgery unit in the south of England, where he personally attended approximately 2,000 cases of facial trauma, handling both the patient's medical needs and appearance with equal sensitivity. In America three military hospitals were specifically designated as plastic surgery units to treat soldiers disfigured in battle. By 1941 the American Board of Plastic Surgery had been certified as a primary specialty board by the American Medical Association.

THE SHIFT TO COSMETIC SURGERY

By the 1960s evolving attitudes about beauty began to change the course of plastic surgery, and cosmetic rather than reconstructive procedures began to dominate the field. In the intervening decades, many new techniques emerged to reduce or reverse the effects of aging, including dermabrasion to remove acne scarring, collagen injection to fill out the lips or sunken skin, and blepharoplasty to eliminate bags under the eye. Rhinoplasty, or the "nose job"—which reached its height of popularity in the 1960s and 1970s—had declined in popularity by the end of the twentieth century.

As plastic surgery has become a common cultural phenomenon, critics have grown increasingly vocal. Some view it as radical conformity to artificial standards of beauty perpetuated by mass media, and its most strident opponents have been particularly concerned that women have aesthetic operations more often than men and that even adolescent girls sometimes elect to have plastic surgery. Nonetheless each year more cosmetic procedures are performed than ever before, and many plastic surgery patients attest to the psychological benefits of feeling younger, thinner, and more attractive. Perhaps the most notable, if ambiguous, commentary on cosmetic surgery has been offered by the French performance artist Orlan, who explores standards of beauty by undergoing repeated plastic surgery procedures.

The early years of the twenty-first century were marked by a lengthy recession, but even during that period rates of plastic surgery continued to rise. In a 2011 article for *Newsweek*, Rebecca Dana points out that even as Americans spent less on food (3.8 percent), housing (2 percent), clothing (1.4 percent), and entertainment (7 percent), they continued to lay out money for plastic surgery. Rates for breast augmentation rose by 1.3 percent, rates for liposuction climbed by 5.1 percent, and rates of eyelid surgery increased by 8.1 percent. The field of butt lifts saw the biggest increase (24.4 percent). Contrary to popular belief, most people who have plastic surgery for cosmetic reasons are not wealthy. According to a 2009 study by the American Society for Aesthetic Plastic Surgery, a third of patients make less than $30,000 a year, and 70 percent have incomes lower than $60,000. A number of companies exist for the sole purpose of financing plastic surgeries.

Perhaps no single individual comes closer to illustrating the length to which some people are prepared to go to change their appearance than reality star Heidi Montag, who underwent ten separate procedures in a single day in 2010. Those procedures included chin reduction, a brow lift, a butt lift, a nose job, and modification of a previous breast augmentation. Plastic surgery patients run the gamut from children to the elderly, suggesting that dissatisfaction with personal appearance may not be limited to those who use cosmetic plastic surgery as a substitute for the fountain of youth.

Michele S. Shauf

SEE ALSO: *Botox; Breast Implants; Celebrity; Consumerism;* The Hills*; Hollywood;* Newsweek*; Performance Art; Reality Television; World War I.*

BIBLIOGRAPHY

Berry, Bonnie. *Beauty Bias: Discrimination and Social Power.* Westport, CT: Praeger Publications, 2007.

Camp, John. *Plastic Surgery: The Kindest Cut.* New York: Henry Holt, 1989.

Dana, Rebecca. "All I Want for Christmas Is a Brand-New Face." *Newsweek*, December 19, 2011.

Haiken, Elizabeth. *Venus Envy: A History of Cosmetic Surgery.* Baltimore, MD: Johns Hopkins University Press, 1997.

Perrett, David. *In Your Face: The New Science of Human Attraction.* New York: Palgrave Macmillan, 2010.

Porter, Roy. *The Greatest Benefit to Mankind: A Medical History of Humanity.* New York: W. W. Norton, 1997.

Rutkow, Ira M. *American Surgery: An Illustrated History.* Philadelphia: Lippincott-Raven, 1998.

Wangensteen, Owen H., and Sarah D. Wangensteen. *The Rise of Surgery: From Empiric Craft to Scientific Discipline.* Minneapolis: University of Minnesota Press, 1978.

Weatherford, M. Lisa. *Reconstructive and Cosmetic Surgery Sourcebook: Basic Consumer Health Information on Cosmetic and Reconstructive Plastic Surgery.* Detroit, MI: Omnigraphics, 2001.

Plath, Sylvia *(1932–1963)*

Author Sylvia Plath's association with death and madness stemmed from her confessional poetry; her novel *The Bell Jar*; the facts of her life; and, most of all, from the cult of readers—many of them teenage girls—that formed after her suicide. Plath's stormy marriage to poet Ted Hughes was a matter for the literary tabloids, and her work was taken up by scholars as evidence of a troubled soul oppressed by sexist times. Her poems—most particularly those published posthumously in *Ariel* (1965)—are an enduring proof of her very real talent.

Plath was born in Boston on October 27, 1932. Her father, a college professor and expert on bees, died when she was eight. She was a good student, and she published her first short story in the magazine *Seventeen* when she was just a teenager. In 1951 Plath entered Smith College on a scholarship. She already had an impressive list of publications, and while at Smith she wrote more than 400 poems. She spent some time in New York as a "guest editor" at *Mademoiselle*; when she returned home, she attempted suicide by swallowing sleeping pills. Afterward, she received electroconvulsive therapy and psychotherapy in a mental hospital. (Plath used much of this experience for her autobiographical novel *The Bell Jar*, published pseudonymously in England in 1963 under the name Victoria Lucas. Plath's mother, Aurelia, successfully fought against the book's release in the United States until 1970.)

MARRIAGE AND POETRY

Plath graduated from Smith in 1955. She won a Fulbright scholarship to study at Cambridge, England, where she met Hughes. The story of their tempestuous first meeting is now mythic in literary circles: he stole her hair band; she bit his cheek. They were married in 1956. The next year, Plath attended Robert Lowell's poetry class at Boston University, where she met the poet Anne Sexton; together, Plath, Hughes, and Sexton would come to be considered the foci of the intensely personal "confessional school" of poetry. In 1959 Plath and Hughes moved back to England. The following year, when she

Sylvia Plath. *Sylvia Plath committed suicide in 1963 after a long struggle with depression.* © BETTMANN/CORBIS.

was twenty-eight, her first book of poetry, *The Colossus and Other Poems*, was published.

Plath and Hughes separated in 1962, when he left her for another woman. Plath spent that winter with their two children, Frieda and Nicholas, in a small London flat, waking up at 4 a.m. in order to write before the children arose. This was a very productive period for her; she wrote almost a poem a day. However, all was not well. Plath became severely depressed and, on February 11, 1963, just days after the publication of *The Bell Jar*, she committed suicide by placing her head in the oven with the gas turned on, poisoning herself with carbon monoxide.

Hughes became Plath's literary executor. He brought her collection of poetry, *Ariel*, to publication in 1965. Among the "scorching" poems in *Ariel* is Plath's most famous poem, "Daddy," along with "Death and Co." and "Lady Lazarus" ("Dying / Is an art, like everything else. / I do it exceptionally well. / I do it so it feels like hell. / I do it so it feels real. / I guess you could say I've a call.") Other posthumous publications included 1971's *Crossing the Water* and *Winter Trees* and, in 1981, *The Collected Poems*, edited by Hughes, which won the Pulitzer Prize for poetry.

A SILENCED WOMAN

For feminist scholars, Plath was a talented, brilliant woman done wrong by men and the times. It has been suggested that her life would have unfolded in a different way had she lived in a later era—that she was a victim of the 1950s ideal of woman as housewife and mother, wedged into a domestic role inappropriate for someone with her skills. Sexton and Plath are usually mentioned in the same literary breath—both were women, were confessional poets, and committed suicide. Sexton's poem "Sylvia's Death" discusses their mutual preoccupation with the subjects of death and desire.

After her death, Plath achieved iconic status as a "madwoman" poet. For some cultural critics, she was the epitome of the silenced woman. Hughes had total control over her literary estate and may have exerted that control to protect his own image; he destroyed at least one journal and censored many other pieces. Many Plath fans had a deep hatred for Hughes, calling him a betrayer, even a murderer. Although her gravestone was inscribed "Sylvia Plath Hughes," it has been repeatedly defaced to read just "Sylvia Plath."

Diane Middlebrook's *Her Husband: Hughes and Plath* (2003) is an extended look at the marriage, and Kate Moses's novel *Wintering: A Novel of Sylvia Plath* (2003) is a fictional account of it. Other books have sprung up around Plath's marriage and suicide, including Jillian Becker's *Giving Up: The Last Days of Sylvia Plath* (2003) and Yehuda Koren and Eilat Negev's *Lover of Unreason: Assia Wevill, Sylvia Plath's Rival and Ted Hughes's Doomed Love* (2007). In 2003 Gwyneth Paltrow played the title role in *Sylvia*, a major motion picture about Plath's life.

Many years after her death, Plath remains a literary presence. In 1996 *About Sylvia: Poems* was published, containing works by Diane Ackerman, John Berryman, Rachel Hadas, Robert Lowell, Sexton, and Richard Wilbur. Hughes, British poet laureate, broke his silence on Plath soon before his own death in 1998 with the publication of *Birthday Letters*, a collection of poems about their relationship. In 2000 Plath's unabridged journals were published in a single volume of 768 pages, and in 2004 HarperCollins published a "restored edition" of *Ariel*, reordering the poems according to Plath's original manuscript and including a foreword by Frieda Hughes. In 2012 Plath was one of ten poets featured by the U.S. Postal Service in its commemorative "Twentieth-Century Poets" set of stamps.

Jessy Randall

SEE ALSO: *Depression; Feminism;* Seventeen*; Suicide.*

BIBLIOGRAPHY

Alexander, Paul. *Rough Magic: A Biography of Sylvia Plath.* New York: Viking, 1991.

Kirk, Connie Ann. *Sylvia Plath: A Biography.* Westport, CT: Greenwood Press, 2004.

Plath, Aurelia Schober, ed. *Letters Home: Correspondence, 1950–1963 (by Sylvia Plath).* New York: Harper & Row, 1975.

Rose, Jacqueline. *The Haunting of Sylvia Plath.* Cambridge, MA: Harvard University Press, 1992.

Stevenson, Anne. *Bitter Fame: A Life of Sylvia Plath.* Boston: Houghton Mifflin, 1989.

Platoon

Oliver Stone's *Platoon* (1986), a critically acclaimed Hollywood film about the Vietnam War, was the first in its category to be directed by a combatant in that most divisive of U.S. wars. The film, which cost $6 million to make, grossed more than $160 million and won four Oscars, including those for best film and best director. Like his cinematic alter ego, Chris Taylor (played by Charlie Sheen), Stone abandoned a wealthy family and an Ivy League education for a chance to fight in Vietnam. His grandfather had fought in World War I and his father in World War II. When, in 1967, Stone was stationed near the Cambodian border, he felt that he had made a terrible mistake. The pressure of battle caused him to behave erratically, once shooting at an old man's feet (as Chris does in the film) and once attacking the Viet Cong with such extreme ferocity that he was awarded a Bronze Star. Stone also received a Purple Heart with an Oak Leaf Cluster for his injuries.

During his second week in Vietnam, his platoon encountered a group of Viet Cong. In the ensuing battle, he was wounded in the back of the neck; the arm of the soldier next to him was blown off. Stone's injury was deemed a flesh wound, and he soon returned to combat. His war experiences helped make *Platoon* an especially valuable vehicle for conveying the immediacy and brutality of armed conflict. He has said that most soldiers fell into one of two camps, as shown in the film: the lifers, juicers (drinkers), and unintelligent whites in one and the progressive, hippie, dope-smokers—who wanted only to survive the war with some integrity intact—in the other. Stone fell in with this second group.

After being wounded again, he was transferred to the platoon where he met Juan Angel Elias, the inspiration for Sergeant Elias (Willem Dafoe) in the movie. The part-Spanish, part-Apache, compassionate Elias proved to Stone that someone could be both a good soldier and a decent human being. Stone also met a facially scarred officer who served as the inspiration for the character of Sergeant Barnes—the best soldier Stone had ever met but also an angry loner obsessed with killing and getting even.

Platoon *Movie Poster*. *Oliver Stone based* Platoon *on his own experiences as a soldier in Vietnam.* **ORION/THE KOBAL COLLECTION.**

Platoon is remembered for its authentic and unbiased portrayal of combat. The only Hollywood Vietnam War movie released during the war was *The Green Berets* (1968), a John Wayne and propaganda vehicle partly financed by the U.S. government. The film was said to be so inaccurate that the last scene of the sun setting in the east seemed appropriate. Critics have described *Rambo: First Blood* (1982) and *Missing in Action* (1984) as using the conflict to convey soldiers' fantasies of war. *The Deer Hunter* (1978) and *Apocalypse Now* (1979) condemn war in general rather than this particular war, whereas *Platoon* immediately drops the viewer into a jungle so thick that the idea of technological superiority becomes meaningless. Its closely observed details earned the movie the reputation of being true-to-life. Stone has said that the film shows "what combat is really like, and what war really means. . . . I hope a lot of kids who see *Platoon* will think twice. Maybe they won't make the same mistake I made."

Bob Sullivan

SEE ALSO: *Academy Awards;* Apocalypse Now; The Deer Hunter; *Hollywood; Movie Stars; Rambo; Vietnam; War Movies; Wayne, John.*

BIBLIOGRAPHY

Beaver, Frank. *Oliver Stone: Wakeup Cinema.* New York: Twayne Publishers, 1994.

Kagan, Norman. *The Cinema of Oliver Stone.* New York: Continuum Publishing, 1995.

Kunz, Don, ed. *The Films of Oliver Stone.* Lanham, MD: Scarecrow Press, 1997.

Mackey-Kallis, Susan. *Oliver Stone's America: "Dreaming the Myth Outwards."* Boulder, CO: Westview Press, 1996.

Riordan, James. *Stone: The Controversies, Excesses, and Exploits of a Radical Filmmaker.* New York: Hyperion, 1995.

Salewicz, Chris. *Oliver Stone: The Making of His Movies.* New York: Thunder's Mouth Press, 1998.

Stone, Oliver, and Charles L. P. Silet *Oliver Stone: Interviews.* Jackson: University Press of Mississippi, 2001.

Playboy

In the 1950s the frigid, puritanical tradition that had dominated American sexual mores for centuries began to thaw. The heat came from two principal sources: One was Dr. Alfred C. Kinsey, who conducted the first scientific research on the sexual practices of Americans. The other was Hugh Hefner and his magazine, *Playboy.*

HEFNER'S VISION

Before creating *Playboy* in 1953, Hugh Marston Hefner had not achieved much success in life. After attending college and joining the army, he returned to his native Chicago and married his high school sweetheart. Failing as a freelance cartoonist, he worked in the promotion departments of several magazines, including *Esquire,* the premier men's magazine of its day. But when *Esquire* moved its headquarters to New York City, it did not invite Hefner to come along. Frustrated and somewhat desperate, the twenty-seven-year-old borrowed a few thousand dollars from relatives and friends and prepared to launch the magazine that had been his dream for years.

The new magazine was nearly called *Stag Party,* featuring a drawing of an urbane-looking buck in a smoking jacket. But there was already a magazine devoted to hunting called *Stag,* and its publisher threatened to sue if Hefner used the name. Thus, at the last minute, the magazine was rechristened *Playboy,* with the horny deer transformed into a sophisticated-looking rabbit—a name and image that would eventually became known throughout the world.

The first issue appeared in December 1953. So uncertain of success was Hefner that he left his name off the editorial masthead and declined to put a date on the magazine's cover. The former decision would allow him to avoid associating his name with a flop; the latter would make the issue marketable beyond the month of its publication.

But he need not have worried. Although he would have welcomed the sale of 30,000 copies, the first issue sold more than 54,000—helped, no doubt, by a centerfold photo of a nude Marilyn Monroe, one of America's most popular actresses. She had posed for the picture years earlier, while unknown and in need of money. Hefner bought the rights to the photo for $500.

From that point, *Playboy* and its publisher were on their way up. Within a year, the magazine had a circulation of about 100,000, a figure that would eventually reach several million. The magazine catered to the educated urban man who either was affluent and sophisticated or wished to see himself that way. In short, the typical *Playboy* reader was a young man not unlike Hefner himself.

ARTICLES AND FEATURES

As *Playboy* matured, it took on certain features that would eventually help to define it, both within the publishing world and in American culture. These characteristics included profiles of upscale consumer goods such as sports cars, stereo equipment, and elegant clothing. There also were articles on fine food, good wine, and sophisticated cocktails—and the best places to find them all.

The magazine also ran fiction and nonfiction by well-known writers. Hefner wanted to compete for *Esquire*'s audience and knew that having legitimate authors writing for him meant he could defend *Playboy* as more than a mere skin magazine. At first his resources were so limited that he was forced to rely on work in the public domain, such as Arthur Conan Doyle's Sherlock Holmes stories.

But the magazine's success soon brought in enough money to purchase original fiction from such notables as Ernest Hemingway, Ray Bradbury, Irwin Shaw, and Gore Vidal. Not surprisingly, one of *Playboy*'s favorite writers was Ian Fleming, whose James Bond character embodied many of the fantasies dear to the magazine's readership. The suave secret agent made his first *Playboy* appearance in March 1960. Thereafter, until Fleming's death in 1964, the magazine serialized each new Bond novel.

The *Playboy* Interview was another addition greeted with enthusiasm by readers. Beginning with the September 1962 issue, the magazine featured long interviews with prominent figures. The subjects included actors, athletes, and sex symbols, but there were surprising choices such as black activist Malcolm X, Cuban prime minister Fidel Castro, German theologian Albert Schweitzer, Palestinian leader Yasir Arafat, and presidential candidate Jimmy Carter (who created a flap by admitting in the magazine that he sometimes lusted after women in his heart).

PLAYMATES AND THE PLAYBOY LIFESTYLE

From the beginning, naked ladies were a mainstay of the magazine. Each issue usually offered readers three pictorials, one of which occupied the center of the magazine and included a folded miniposter of the Playmate of the Month. Hefner's conception of the young model who occupied the centerfold and its surrounding pages has become an American cultural cliché: beautiful but not glamorous, she would be, in his words, "the girl next door." The famous Monroe centerfold notwithstanding, the Playmate would not be a celebrity (those would appear elsewhere in the magazine), and the photos of her would show her in her daily life—at home, at school, or in a restaurant having lunch. The message to the male reader was, this girl is real and accessible—her perfect skin, hair, and measurements notwithstanding.

Other pictorials featured a montage of young women grouped around themes that might be educational ("The Girls of the West Coast Conference"), geographical ("The Girls of Australia"), or occupational ("The Girls of Radio"). Sometimes a pictorial featured a single model who happened to work in an occupation popular in male sexual fantasies. Thus, photo layouts were devoted to female police officers, firefighters, or stockbrokers. Although Monroe's appearance in *Playboy* was not her decision, many well-known women have voluntarily graced the magazine's pages, including model Brigitte Bardot; singers Madonna, LaToya Jackson, and Nancy Sinatra; and actresses Drew Barrymore, Farrah Fawcett, Lindsay Lohan, Jayne Mansfield, Kim Novak, Sharon Stone, and Raquel Welch.

The *Playboy* formula was hugely successful, drawing increasing numbers of readers and advertising dollars throughout the 1950s, 1960s, and 1970s. Hefner spent some of the revenue on a lavish lifestyle, including the Playboy Mansion in Chicago; the Playboy Mansion West in Los Angeles; and a luxury, full-sized jet named the Big Bunny. However much of his money went into building what became known as the Playboy empire. Its components included a chain of Playboy clubs (best known for their scantily clad waitresses, called bunnies), followed by resort hotels and then casinos in Great Britain and Atlantic City, New Jersey. The empire also had a book publishing division, a music division, and a film production company. All of it made money—for a time.

COMPETITION AND OPPOSITION

The 1980s were not kind to the Hefner's empire. It faced competition on the magazine front from such rivals as *Penthouse* and *Hustler*. Both were more explicitly erotic than the wholesome-by-comparison *Playboy*, although they took different approaches. *Penthouse* strove for the same sophistication as *Playboy*, but with a European accent, whereas raunchy *Hustler* was blatantly lowbrow.

The new magazines were not the worst of Hefner's problems. Although he had faced opposition from religious groups in the past, none had been sufficiently well organized to be troublesome. The rise of archconservative televangelists such as Jerry Falwell and Jimmy Swaggart in the 1980s, and the founding of political-religious organizations such as Falwell's Moral Majority and reverend Pat Robertson's Christian Coalition, fomented outrage over pornography. Many feminists, who otherwise had little in common with fundamentalist Christians, found common ground on the issue of smut and its supposed danger to women. Following the 1980 election, social conservatives had allies in Washington, including in the White House. President Ronald Reagan courted the Christian right by establishing the Meese Commission on Pornography, and attorney general Edwin Meese, assembling a panel that heavily favored social and religious conservatism, set out to expose the harmful effects of pornography on U.S. society.

If the political climate of the 1980s was unfavorable to *Playboy*, the economic one was even more so. Playboy Enterprises lost its gaming license in Great Britain for violating gambling regulations, causing the New Jersey Gaming Commission to reconsider the Playboy Hotel and Casino's license in Atlantic City. The Playboy clubs, considered daring in the 1960s, were almost quaint two decades later. Club membership declined greatly and financial losses followed. Further, advertising in the magazine, the flagship institution of the empire, was down 60 percent since 1970. Clearly, drastic change was in order if *Playboy* were to survive.

LEADERSHIP AND THE DIGITAL AGE

Appropriately for an empire founded on the female form, the answer to Hefner's woes was his adult daughter, Christie. She agreed to serve as chief executive officer of Playboy Enterprises while her father enjoyed semiretirement at Playboy Mansion West (although he retained the majority share of company stock). Working with experienced financial managers, Christie sold off the clubs and resorts, as well as other drains on revenue (including her father's jet). She recognized the potential of the emerging video market and soon began profitably producing soft-core adult videos, CD-ROMs, and cable television shows. As the new millennium approached, Playboy was again in the black, with its magazine (subscribers numbering in the millions) bringing in about half of all revenue.

The twenty-first century posed new challenges for *Playboy*, however, as Americans increasingly found an abundance of free content on the Internet. Subscriptions for magazines of all types began to plummet. By 2008 *Playboy*'s circulation had dropped to 2.7 million, and Playboy Enterprises reported slumping sales and a 22 percent drop in revenues. In December 2008 Christie stepped down from her position as CEO, although she denied that her decision had anything to do with Playboy's financial difficulties.

Revenues continued to fall in 2009 and 2010, and the company posted losses in both years in spite of trying to cut costs. In early 2011 Hefner reached a deal to buy out whatever shares of Playboy Enterprises he did not own, thus returning the company to private ownership. "The brand still resonates today as clearly as at any time in its 57-year history," he remarked. It remains to be seen whether *Playboy*'s colorful history and name recognition will be enough to help it thrive in the digital age.

Justin Gustainis

SEE ALSO: *Atlantic City; Bradbury, Ray; Cable TV;* Esquire; *Fawcett, Farrah; Feminism; The Fifties; Fleming, Ian; Gambling; Hefner, Hugh; Hemingway, Ernest;* Hustler; *The Internet; Kinsey, Dr. Alfred C.; Lohan, Lindsay; Madonna; Mansfield, Jayne; Monroe, Marilyn; Moral Majority; Novak, Kim;* Penthouse; Playgirl; *Pornography; Reagan, Ronald; Robertson, Pat; Sex Symbol; Swaggart, Jimmy; Televangelism; Vidal, Gore; Videos.*

BIBLIOGRAPHY

Edgren, Gretchen, and Hugh Hefner. *The "Playboy" Book: Forty Years.* Santa Monica, CA: General Publishing Group, 1998.

Miller, Russell. *Bunny: The Real Story of "Playboy."* New York: Holt, Rinehart & Winston, 1985.

Watts, Steven. *Mr. "Playboy": Hugh Hefner and the American Dream.* Hoboken, NJ: John Wiley & Sons, 2008.

Weyr, Thomas. *Reaching for Paradise: The "Playboy" Vision of America.* New York: NYT Books, 1978.

Playgirl

Appearing on newsstands in June 1973, *Playgirl* magazine was the first women's magazine to focus on men. *Playgirl*, first published by Douglas Lambert and edited by Marin Scott Milam, was intended as a female counterpart to the men's magazine *Playboy*, although *Cosmopolitan*, led by editor-in-chief Helen Gurley Brown, was first to feature a nude male centerfold. Whereas *Cosmopolitan* pushed at the fringes of women's magazines, *Playgirl* went over the line in its effort to bring a newly blossomed feminism to the realm of popular reading material. It desired to offer women "the good life" in the same way *Playboy* did by encompassing the music, books, cars, and women that its male readers wanted.

By the late 1990s *Playgirl* boasted a circulation of more than 500,000, nowhere near the much larger figures of *Cosmopolitan* or *Playboy*. Perhaps this was because *Playgirl* always had trouble deciding what kind of magazine it wanted to be. Its fiction, at times featuring such notable authors as Joyce Carol Oates and Margaret Atwood, rarely rose higher than romance novels or confession magazines, whereas *Playboy* often featured the top writers of the day and interviews with prominent figures such as British prime minister Margaret Thatcher, secretary of state Henry Kissinger, actor Warren Beatty, and actress Jane Fonda, to name a few. While aspiring to emulate *Playboy*, in its early years *Playgirl* periodically featured silly centerfolds such as actor Rip Torn and Benji the dog. Even on the nudity question, it wavered between the extremes of full frontal and none at all.

Playgirl's lack of identity reflected that American women were struggling to find and assert their identity during the 1970s and 1980s. Women were divided on such issues as whether they should work outside the home and whether a working mother could properly care for her family. Another reason for the magazine's lack of focus was its publishing history. Whereas the image of *Playboy* boss Hugh Hefner offered men a vision of what the ultimate playboy looked like, *Playgirl*'s original publisher was a man. Competitors *Cosmopolitan* and *Ms.* were headed by strong feminists who could commit themselves to the message they were proclaiming in the pages of their magazines.

In 1986 Drake Publishers bought *Playgirl* and relocated to New York. It believed that women didn't want to see nude men, preferring traditional images of handsome men that they could fantasize about. This romanticized view of women's sexuality didn't go over well with the readers, and the change lasted less than a year before the full frontal nudity was back.

Further, *Playgirl* ignored a vocal part of the women's movement that decried the objectification of women in such magazines as *Playboy* and *Penthouse*. Many men and women argued that sexualizing women led to violent crimes such as rape and that men's magazines objectified not only women but men as well. Whereas many women's groups called for reform in men's magazines, *Playgirl* was pushing for what many considered equal depravity rather than equal rights, ostensibly weakening the argument for fair treatment of women.

Despite its rocky history, *Playgirl* earned a reputation for listening to what its readers wanted. When the first issue came out, actor and centerfold Lyle Waggoner was featured in a cross-legged pose. Readers complained that the magazine hadn't gone far enough, and the next issue featured a fully revealed actor George Maharis. In 1986 it was the readers' responses to the withdrawal of nudity that convinced Drake Publishers to reintroduce male nudity in the magazine. In the last years of the twentieth century, *Playgirl* remained the only women's magazine that regularly featured nude men. Deciding at last to be the only erotic magazine for women, *Playgirl*, in the words of its historical overview, now serves "to legitimize female sexuality and introduce women to the same provocative features and photographs men [have] been enjoying for years." Although it may not have presented the fully fleshed-out vision of "the good life" that *Playboy* inspired, the magazine has remained for many women the authority on female sexuality.

Scandal hit the publication in 2000 when the Federal Trade Commission charged that *Playgirl*'s website was illegally charging thousands of consumers for services that had been advertised as free and charging others who had never visited the website. Its new publisher, Crescent, had to pay $30 million to settle the charges and post bond before selling services on the Internet again. Crescent, later renamed Blue Horizon Media, continued to publish *Playgirl* and other pornographic magazines.

Like so many other publications in the 2000s, *Playgirl* began to struggle with rising costs, reduced ad revenues, and declining subscriptions. In 2008 the magazine announced it would cease print operations the following year and would have a presence only online. In 2010 the magazine brought back a print version with a photo shoot of Levi Johnston, the former fiancé of vice presidential candidate Sarah Palin's daughter.

Cheryl A. Smith

SEE ALSO: *Beatty, Warren;* Cosmopolitan*; Feminism; Fonda, Jane; Hefner, Hugh; The Internet;* Ms.*; Oates, Joyce Carol; Palin, Sarah;* Penthouse*;* Playboy*; Pornography; Sexual Revolution.*

BIBLIOGRAPHY

Brooks, Gary R., and Lenore Walker. *The Centerfold Syndrome: How Men Can Overcome Objectification and Achieve Intimacy with Women.* San Francisco: Jossey-Bass, 1995.

Chancer, Lynn S. *Reconcilable Differences: Confronting Beauty, Pornography, and the Future of Feminism.* Los Angeles: University of California Press, 1998.

Dines, Gail; Robert Jensen; and Ann Russo. *Pornography: The Production and Consumption of Inequality.* New York: Routledge, 1998.

McElroy, Wendy. *XXX: A Woman's Right to Pornography.* New York: St. Martin's Press, 1997.

Strossen, Nadine. *Defending Pornography: Free Speech, Sex, and the Fight for Women's Rights.* New York: Anchor, 1996.

Weitzer, Ronald. *Sex for Sale: Prostitution, Pornography, and the Sex Industry.* New York: Routledge, 2009.

Playhouse 90

Considered by many to be the most ambitious of the anthology dramas to emerge during the golden age of television (a period lasting from about 1949 to 1960, during which original dramas were produced for live television), *Playhouse 90* was voted the greatest television series of all time in a 1970 *Variety* magazine poll of television editors. Appearing Thursday nights on CBS from 1956 to 1959, the program presented ninety-minute dramas, many of which were telecast live. Like other anthology dramas of the era, *Playhouse 90* was a fertile ground for quality performances and an opportunity for writers and directors to showcase dramatic talents for a national audience. During its four-year run, the program launched careers, lured those working in the movies or on the stage to television, and allowed actors the opportunity to take chances performing roles that they otherwise might not have been offered.

Playhouse 90 began on October 4, 1956, with the episode "Forbidden Area," starring Charlton Heston, Tab Hunter, and Vincent Price. The second episode was writer Rod Serling's classic "Requiem for a Heavyweight," which won three Emmy Awards: Best Single Program of the Year, Best Teleplay Writing for One Hour or More for Serling's script, and Best Single Performance by an Actor for Jack Palance. Other *Playhouse 90* stars included Johnny Carson (in his first dramatic television role), Errol Flynn, Kim Hunter, Paul Newman (in his last dramatic television role), Joanne Woodward, Cliff Robertson, Jack Lemmon, Claude Rains, Burt Reynolds, and Robert Redford.

Among the memorable episodes from the series are "For Whom the Bell Tolls," "Judgment at Nuremberg," "The Male Animal," "The Days of Wine and Roses," and novelist Joseph Conrad's "The Heart of Darkness." *Playhouse 90* was recognized with six Emmys for its first season: the three for "Requiem for a Heavyweight," plus Best New Program Series, Best Direction One Hour or More, and Best Art Direction One Hour or More. It went on to win five Emmys for its second season and one Emmy each for its third and final seasons. In its final season of production, *Playhouse 90* was limited to seventeen episodes and specials as it alternated with the variety show *The Big Party* in its time slot.

James Friedman

SEE ALSO: *Carson, Johnny; Emmy Awards; Flynn, Errol; Heston, Charlton; Hunter, Tab; Newman, Paul; Price, Vincent; Rains, Claude; Redford, Robert; Reynolds, Burt; Serling, Rod; Television;* Variety.

BIBLIOGRAPHY

Brooks, Tim, and Earle F. Marsh. *The Complete Directory to Prime Time Network and Cable TV Shows, 1946–Present*, 9th ed. New York: Ballantine, 2007.

McMahon, Ed, with David Fisher. *When Television Was Young: The Inside Story with Memories by Legends of the Small Screen.* Nashville, TN: Thomas Nelson, 2007.

Pocket Books

SEE: *Paperbacks.*

Pogo

Eventually a very political possum, Walt Kelly's Pogo was first seen in the early 1940s in a comic book. By the time he moved into the funny papers in 1948, he was not only considerably cuter but also much more socially aware. A success, albeit a controversial one, from almost the start of his newspaper days, Pogo soon branched out into a series of popular soft-cover reprint books. As the strip progressed, Kelly took increasing interest, and delight, in poking fun at many of the biggest political targets of the day—including Senator Joe McCarthy, Lyndon Johnson, Nikita Khrushchev, Spiro Agnew, and J. Edgar Hoover—which was sometimes a risky sort of satire in which to indulge, especially in the social climate of the 1950s.

Born in Philadelphia and raised in Bridgeport, Connecticut, Kelly had always yearned to be a cartoonist. In the mid-1930s he went West to work for the Disney organization. Along with hundreds of other artists, the young Kelly worked on such

Walt Kelly and Pogo. *Walt Kelly creates a drawing of Pogo at the 1956 Democratic National Convention.* NBC/NBC NEWSWIRE/ GETTY IMAGES.

animated features as *Snow White and the Seven Dwarfs* (1937), *Pinocchio* (1940), and *Dumbo* (1941). After leaving Disney in 1941, Kelly returned East and was soon gainfully employed in the comic-book business. By then he had become an excellent cartoonist; it was logical that he would find work with *Animal Comics* and *Fairy Tale Parade.*

In 1942 Kelly invented *Pogo* as a backup feature for *Animal Comics,* a magazine wherein the designated star was supposed to be the venerable rabbit gentleman Uncle Wiggily. A very scruffy and too-realistic-looking possum at the start, Pogo soon improved in appearance and eventually came to be the leading character in the feature. Among his swamp companions were the turtle Churchy LaFemme, Porky Pine, Howland Owl, and Albert the Alligator, a likeable ne'er-do-well who smoked cigars and possessed a mind overflowing with sly schemes—a goodly portion of which involved food.

By 1948 Kelly was working as staff artist and chief political cartoonist for the short-lived *New York Star,* which was more or less the successor to the liberal newspaper *PM.* On October 4 of that year, *Pogo* began as a daily comic strip exclusively in the pages of the *New York Star.* When the paper ceased publication three months later, Kelly's swamp denizens were temporarily without a home. The strip, however, was picked up for syndication that May, and it immediately began to gather a sizeable client list. Although he had liberal political views, Kelly was at heart a comedian, and he also included considerable slapstick, burlesque, puns, and uncontrolled nonsense in his saga of Okefenokee Swamp. In addition to outrageous continuities, mixed frequently with political satire, Kelly was especially fond of having his characters sing somewhat garbled versions of traditional songs. No Christmas, for example, went by without a heartfelt rendering of "Deck Us All with Boston Charlie."

Aware that Kelly's views on such topics as Senator McCarthy, the Ku Klux Klan, and the John Birch Society did not sit especially well with some of their subscribing editors, his syndicate suggested that he prepare a few alternative strips to run in place of an offensive one. Kelly went along with this, creating what he called his "bunny rabbit strips." These featured none of the *Pogo* regulars but instead a bunch of cute little rabbits enacting very tame and quiet gags. Kelly produced at least two dozen of these, and some of them must have been run far more than once.

Because of failing health in his final years, Kelly had to rely on assistants to turn out his strip. After he died in 1973, *Pogo* went on until 1975, written and drawn by others and controlled by his heirs. Early in 1989 the *Los Angeles Times Syndicate* attempted to resurrect Pogo, Albert, and the rest of the gang. A brand-new version of the strip, titled *Walt Kelly's Pogo,* was launched, with art by Neal Sternecky and scripts by Larry Doyle. This version, which concentrated mostly on whimsy and not social comment, was not particularly successful. By 1992 both members of the creative team had departed, and Kelly's daughter Carolyn was drawing it while his son Peter oversaw the writing. *Pogo* closed up shop for the second time soon after.

Ron Goulart

SEE ALSO: *Comic Books; Comics; Disney (Walt Disney Company); Hoover, J. Edgar; John Birch Society; Ku Klux Klan; McCarthyism;* Snow White and the Seven Dwarfs.

BIBLIOGRAPHY

Goulart, Ron. *The Great Comic Book Artists.* New York: St. Martin's Press, 1986.

Goulart, Ron. *Comic Book Culture: An Illustrated History.* Portland, OR: Collectors Press, 2000.

Horn, Maurice. *100 Years of American Newspaper Comics: An Illustrated Encyclopedia.* New York: Gramercy Books, 1996.

Kelly, Selby, and Bill Crouch, eds. *The Best of Pogo.* New York: Simon & Schuster, 1982.

Kelly, Walt. *Ten Ever-Lovin' Blue-Eyed Years with Pogo, 1949–1959.* New York: Simon & Schuster, 1959.

The Pointer Sisters

Popular music audiences in the late twentieth century had never seen anything quite like the Pointer Sisters. Throughout their career, the sisters maintained their substantial popularity and defied categorization as no other female group had. They took risks and expanded the scope of women in music. Their strong, self-aware style came through no matter what style of music they performed, reflecting the changing image of women in 1970s and 1980s America.

Born in Oakland, California, sisters Ruth (1946–), Anita (1948–), Bonnie (1950–), and June (1953–2006) Pointer had a strict upbringing. Their parents were ministers in the West Oakland Church of God, and for many years church singing was their only form of public performance. Eventually, Bonnie and June began entertaining in San Francisco clubs as a duo. Anita later joined them, and in 1971 they officially became the Pointer Sisters, signing with manager Bill Graham.

For the next few years, they sang backing vocals for a number of popular 1970s recording artists. Their strong singing skills brought them to the attention of Atlantic Records, which signed them. Their first few singles, in the rhythm-and-blues style, were unsuccessful, but the sisters persevered. Ruth quit her job to join the act, and the quartet left Atlantic to join ABC's Blue Thumb label.

Their self-titled debut album immediately brought them national recognition. The songs moved seamlessly from jazz to rhythm and blues and showcased the Pointer Sisters' dynamic range, powerful soul-shouting lungs, fierce scat-singing technique, and distinctive vocal blend. They dressed in World War II–era clothes, evoking positive comparisons with the 1940s vocal group the Andrews Sisters. The group performed at Nashville's Grand Ole Opry—becoming the first African American women to do so—and in 1974 became the first pop act to perform at the San Francisco Opera House.

The subjects of a 1974 PBS documentary, the sisters did not restrict themselves to R&B for long. Bonnie and Anita wrote a country song called "Fairytale," which fared well on the pop charts and won them a Grammy Award in 1974 for Best Country Single of the Year. However, emotional and financial hardships divided the sisters. Bonnie decided to be a solo recording artist and left in 1977 to sign with Motown Records. She found minimal success, and the remaining trio struggled with their declining record sales and image as a nostalgia group. The sisters knew they needed to change if they were to keep making successful records.

Ruth, Anita, and June signed with Planet Records in 1978, and with producer Richard Perry's help, they launched a stream of Top 10 pop records that solidified their place in contemporary music history. The new and improved Pointer Sisters no longer donned period fashions; instead, they sported the latest trends. Always known for their energetic performances, they seemed to dance faster, jump higher, and sing stronger than they ever had. Four Top 10 hits in a row made the Pointers a household name by the mid-1980s.

Other groups may have been content to stay with a single formula, as the girl groups of the 1960s had done, but the Pointer Sisters seemed intent on breaking the mold. Their cover of rocker Bruce Springsteen's "Fire" earned them status as a quasi-rock group, though their soulful pop song "He's So Shy" seemed to resist the rock label. Another hit, "Slow Hand," highlighted the strong R&B flavor of their voices, whereas "Jump" showed they could deliver pop music with a steady punch. The nature of their lyrics and melodies—world-wise, sexy, and high spirited—captured their independent, energetic personalities.

The advent of MTV and the group's appearance in a number of music videos and television specials helped advertise their new image. The title of one of their biggest hits, "I'm So Excited," evoked their new party attitude and self-determination. Revitalized by their renewed public image and exploration of new styles, the sisters developed a model that other female artists could emulate and expand upon.

At the end of the 1980s, the group took a break. They occasionally made television appearances, but it was not until the mid-1990s that they again stepped into the spotlight. This time they turned their attention to Broadway, starring in a revival of *Ain't Misbehavin'*—the hugely successful 1930s musical revue about the Harlem Renaissance. The group saw another surge of popularity in Europe in the first decade of the 2000s after performing in the annual festival Night of the Proms in 2002. Although June died in 2006, the group continued to perform, often with children and grandchildren of the original four sisters. Boasting a career of sweet musical surprises, the Pointer Sisters and their powerful voices will not easily be forgotten.

Brian Granger

SEE ALSO: *The Andrews Sisters; Broadway; Country Music; Girl Groups; Graham, Bill; Grammy Awards;* Grand Ole Opry; *Harlem Renaissance; Jazz; Motown; MTV; Pop Music; Public Television (PBS); Retro Fashion; Rhythm and Blues; Rock and Roll; Soul Music; Springsteen, Bruce; Television; World War II.*

BIBLIOGRAPHY

O'Brien, Lucy. *She Bop: The Definitive History of Women in Rock, Pop and Soul.* New York: Penguin Books, 1995.

Romanowski, Patricia, and Holly George-Warren, eds. *The New Rolling Stone Encyclopedia of Rock & Roll.* New York: Rolling Stone Press, 1995.

Poitier, Sidney *(1927–)*

As one of the first African American actors to consistently appear in serious dramatic roles in American films, Sidney Poitier is acknowledged as a major catalyst for Hollywood offering more substantive roles to black performers. In 1992 the American Film Institute paid tribute to Poitier, with Denzel Washington referring to him as "a source of pride for many African Americans," and James Earl Jones saying that Poitier has "played a great role in the life of our country."

FROM POVERTY TO STARDOM

Although he was born in Miami, Florida, Poitier grew up on his family's farm in the Bahamas. Poitier has said that, despite being a poor man, his father—a tomato farmer—was never a man of self-pity. "Every time I took a part, from the first part, from the first day, I always said to myself, 'This must reflect well on his name,'" Poitier said. The family moved from the tiny village of Cat Island to Nassau, the Bahamian capitol, when Poitier was eleven years old. It was at that age that he became captivated with the cinema after watching a Western drama unfold on the screen.

After serving in the U.S. Army in the early 1940s, Poitier worked as a dishwasher and janitor until he landed a backstage position with the American Negro Theater. Because his West Indian accent was difficult for many Americans to understand, he developed a more professional voice by listening to radio commercials and imitating the announcers. After he perfected his voice, he was cast in several American Negro Theater productions during the 1940s, including *Days of Our Youth, Lysistrata, Anna Lucasta*, and *A Raisin in the Sun*. Poitier understudied for actor-singer Harry Belafonte in *Days of Our Youth*, and he impressed critics with his work in *Lysistrata*, despite being so nervous on the play's opening night that he delivered the wrong lines and ran off the stage.

Poitier's film career began in 1950 in the feature *No Way Out*, in which he played a doctor tormented by the racist brother of a man whose life he could not save. He worked steadily throughout the 1950s, most notably in the South African story *Cry, the Beloved Country*; the urban classroom drama *The*

Sidney Poitier. *Sidney Poitier starred as Det. Virgil Tibbs in* In the Heat of the Night *in 1967.* **MIRISCH/UNITED ARTISTS/THE KOBAL COLLECTION.**

Blackboard Jungle; and Stanley Kramer's *The Defiant Ones*, in which Poitier and Tony Curtis play prison escapees whose mutual struggle help them gain respect for each other despite their racial divisions.

In the 1960s Poitier produced his most impressive body of work, which simultaneously helped to reduce the barriers faced by African American actors and to dispel racial stereotypes on the screen. He appeared in the 1961 film adaptation of the play *A Raisin in the Sun*, in which he played the role he had created on the Broadway stage in 1959. Following that film, Poitier accepted the role of an American serviceman in Germany in the 1963 production *Lilies of the Field*, which earned him the Best Actor Academy Award. He was the first African American actor to receive this honor.

BREAKING DOWN RACIAL BARRIERS

Throughout the 1960s Poitier continued to break down racial barriers in American film. In 1967 he played a charismatic schoolteacher in *To Sir, with Love*, and that same year he costarred with Rod Steiger in the film *In the Heat of the Night*. In the latter role, Poitier played Virgil Tibbs, an African American detective from the North who helps solve a murder in a small southern town with the assistance of a racist police chief. Poitier's role as Tibbs spawned two sequels and a television series, although he did not appear in the TV project. The actor concluded the watershed year of 1967 by working with Spencer Tracy and Katharine Hepburn in the film *Guess Who's Coming to Dinner*—an important work because it was Hollywood's first interracial love story that did not end in tragedy.

Poitier has acknowledged that he suited the needs of filmmakers during this period who wanted to deliver an antiracist message. "I was a pretty good actor," he said. "I believed in brotherhood, in a free society. I hated racism, segregation. And I was a symbol against those things." However, his involvement in civil rights was more than just symbolic: the actor participated in demonstrations led by Martin Luther King Jr. in Montgomery, Alabama, and Memphis, Tennessee.

In 1972 Poitier costarred with Belafonte in the revisionist Western *Buck and the Preacher*. On this picture he made his debut as a film director when the original director resigned because of creative differences. Although Poitier and Belafonte wanted Columbia Pictures to hire another director, studio officials liked some of Poitier's footage so much that they asked him to finish the film himself. His other directorial credits include *A Warm December* (1973), *Uptown Saturday Night* (1974), *Let's Do It Again* (1975), *A Piece of the Action* (1977), *Stir Crazy* (1980), *Hanky Panky* (1982), *Fast Forward* (1985), and *Ghost Dad* (1990).

LATER CAREER

In the 1980s Poitier took only a handful of film roles, primarily *Shoot to Kill* and *Little Nikita*, both action thrillers released in 1988. However, the 1990s produced an upswing in his film activity, starting with playing Supreme Court Justice Thurgood Marshall in the television film *Separate but Equal*. In 1992 he returned to the big screen, costarring with Robert Redford, River Phoenix, and Dan Aykroyd in the espionage comedy-drama *Sneakers*. That same year the American Film Institute presented him with a Lifetime Achievement Award, with the veteran actor humbly remarking in his acceptance speech: "I enter my golden years with nothing profound to say and no advice to leave, but I thank you for paying me this great honor while I still have hair, and my stomach still has not obscured my view of my shoetops." In 1995 Poitier returned to television for a role in the Western drama *Children of the Dust*. In 2009 he received another prestigious honor when President Barack Obama awarded him a Medal of Freedom, the highest civilian honor in the United States.

With more than thirty film credits to his name, coupled with his work as a director and civil rights activist, Poitier emerged from a childhood of poverty to attain the status of an American icon. Actor Michael Moriarty summed up what Poitier represents both on and off the screen by saying, "You see a face that you've grown up with and admired, someone who was . . . a symbol of strength and persistence and grace. And then you find out that in the everyday . . . work of doing movies, he is everything he symbolizes on screen."

Dennis Russell

SEE ALSO: *Academy Awards; Aykroyd, Dan; Belafonte, Harry;* The Blackboard Jungle*; Broadway; Civil Rights Movement; Hepburn, Katharine; Hollywood; King, Martin Luther, Jr.; Obama, Barack; Redford, Robert; Tracy, Spencer; Washington, Denzel.*

BIBLIOGRAPHY

Hoffman, William. *Sidney*. New York: Lyle Stuart, 1971.

Keyser, Lester J., and André Ruszkowski. *The Cinema of Sidney Poitier*. San Diego, CA: A. S. Barnes, 1980.

Marill, Alvin H. *The Films of Sidney Poitier*. Secaucus, NJ: Citadel Press, 1978.

Poitier, Sydney. *This Life*. New York: Alfred A. Knopf, 1980.

Poitier, Sydney. *The Measure of a Man: A Spiritual Autobiography*. New York: HarperSanFrancisco, 2007.

Poitier, Sydney. *Life beyond Measure: Letters to My Great-Grandaughter*. New York: HarperLuxe, 2008.

Pokémon

First a Japanese video game for the handheld Nintendo Gameboy system in 1996, Pokémon has grown into a worldwide phenomenon. Hundreds of species of the collectible characters have been portrayed in television, movies, and video games and have been reproduced as toys, as costumes, and even in a card game. The different venues allow children, usually boys or girls between four and fourteen, to define the Pokémon universe by using their imaginations.

The first Pokémon movie premiered in the United States in November 1999 as the number one box-office draw. So many students called in sick on the Wednesday that it debuted, the phenomenon became known as the Pokémon flu. Pokémon trading cards became so highly prized that some schools banned them, and a nine-year-old in New York even stabbed a classmate during a dispute about the cards. By 2001 the cute, loveable characters of Pokémon had generated more than $8 billion in revenues.

Japanese entertainment exports gained widespread popularity with American children during the 1980s, when Japanese companies debuted the Sony Walkman portable audio cassette player, Transformers robot action figures, and scores of video games. In the 1990s Japanese anime became popular in America, as did the Japanese children's television series *Mighty Morphin Power Rangers* (1993–1996), which spawned a number of spin-offs, movies, and products. Pokémon combined the popular elements of anime and Japanese technology, quickly becoming a hit with children worldwide.

Pokémon's developer, Satoshi Tajiri, spent six years on the project, sometimes working in twenty-four-hour stretches. By the time he finished, the Gameboy had been losing some of its appeal. Nevertheless, Nintendo released Tajiri's game, and an animated series, *Pokémon* (1997–2002), also was released. However, the franchise suffered a major setback in December 1997 when 700 Japanese children simultaneously experienced seizures while watching an attack sequence. The show was shut down so producers could rework the animation techniques, and Warner Brothers purchased the revised show for American audiences.

Different versions of the original Nintendo game have been released, increasing the marketability of the franchise. Initially, in order to complete *Pokémon Red*, *Pokémon Blue*, and *Pokémon Yellow*, players had to link different Gameboys together. Other versions include *Pokémon Gold*, *Pokémon Diamond*, and *Pokémon Pearl*. As Nintendo introduced new gaming systems, the company debuted Pokémon games for the Nintendo DS handheld system and the Nintendo Wii wireless system.

Not everyone has received Pokémon enthusiastically, however. Some conservatives have labeled it "satanic." Perceiving the various mystic and psychic powers as tied to the occult, some critics cautioned that the violence and the various characters' abilities to conjure elements and assume serpentlike forms evidenced their anti-Christian message; however, the Vatican endorsed the game, stating that it provided essential imaginative play and promoted friendship. Nevertheless, Pokémon has continued to attract new generations of fans. When *Pokémon Black* and *Pokémon White* were released on March 6, 2011—fifteen years after the first Pokémon game hit shelves—retailers sold more than one million of the games in a single day.

Elizabeth Rholetter Purdy

SEE ALSO: *Animated Films; Gameboy; Television; Toys; Transformers; Video Games; Walkman.*

BIBLIOGRAPHY

Allison, Anne. "Portable Monsters and Commodity Cuteness: Pokémon as Japan's New Global Power." *Postcolonial Studies* 6, no. 3 (2003): 381–395.

Chua-Eaon, Howard; Tim Larimer; Lisa McLaughlin; et al. "Beware of the Poke Mania." *Time*, November 29, 1999, 80–84.

Tobin, Joseph, ed. *Pickachu's Global Adventure*. Durham, NC: Duke University Press, 2004.

Polio

Throughout most of human history, polio has caused paralysis and death. Often found in wet areas, the virus is most acute in cities during summer months. The virus inflames nerves in the brain and spinal cord, causing paralysis. It can be passed through contact with contaminated feces or oral secretion. Throughout the nineteenth and early twentieth centuries, paralytic poliomyelitis was perhaps the most feared disease in the nation. In 1950 alone, 33,300 people were stricken. In its widespread impact and public awareness, polio bears a striking resemblance to more contemporary diseases such as AIDS.

President Franklin Delano Roosevelt, who had been struck by a form of polio in 1921 and left unable to use his legs, declared a "War on Polio," and developing a vaccine became a national priority in the 1930s. Although he took an active role in getting the leg braces, iron lungs, and other hardware for polio treatment to all communities in the 1930s, Roosevelt went to great lengths to limit public awareness of his own affliction. Although there are more than 35,000 still photographs of FDR at the Presidential Library, only two show him seated in his wheelchair. Through his own experience Roosevelt seemed to understand that rehabilitation of the polio patient was a social problem with medical aspects, not a medical problem with social aspects. Speaking to a group at the Warm Springs, Georgia, rehabilitation center, FDR said: "The important point is that people all over the country know about what we are doing and are following our example in their own communities." Iron lungs and rural retreats became well-known possibilities for those suffering from polio, but FDR sought to reduce their stigma.

Roosevelt sought to raise funds for polio victims throughout his presidency. In 1937 he helped create the National Foundation for Infantile Paralysis, which offered financial assistance to families with polio victims. The foundation also helped to establish treatment centers in many American communities, whereas previously polio victims had been shunned to remote facilities. Further donations were made to a less medical and more popular organization, the March of Dimes, also created in 1937. In 1938 the two organizations collected $1.8 million; by 1945 they collected $18.9 million. Treatment was only one use of the funds: these donations combined with government funding to initiate the pursuit of a vaccine. Controlling the virus became one of the first examples of the federal government's involvement in Americans' expectations for a safer standard of living. In essence the public began to look toward the federal government to ensure a healthy environment. Public awareness campaigns made the virus and its modes of transmission part of the American popular culture through 1950.

With federal funds assisting the search, vaccines became available in the early 1960s. The most well known was created by Jonas Salk. The Salk vaccine enabled most of the industrialized world to defeat the polio virus, creating a significant economic effect: it is said that the polio vaccine pays for itself every three weeks. By the end of the twentieth century, 97 percent of all children had been administered a polio vaccine. The scourge of early twentieth-century polio in America and its control became indicative of the nation's ability to solve social and medical problems with increasing technology.

Brian Black

SEE ALSO: *AIDS.*

BIBLIOGRAPHY

Daniel, Thomas M., ed. *Polio.* Rochester, NY: University of Rochester Press, 1997.

Oshinsky, David. *Polio.* New York: Oxford University Press, 2006.

Silver, Julie. *Polio Voices.* New York: Praeger, 2007.

Smith, Jane S. *A Paralyzing Fear: The Triumph over Polio in America.* New York: TV Books, 1998.

Political Bosses

Political bosses are professional politicians who control political machines in cities, counties, or states in ostensibly democratic regimes. Bosses first emerged in the United States in the early 1800s, when masses of newly franchised, inexperienced voters provided bosses with opportunities for regimentation, mobilization, and manipulation. Each subsequent expansion of the franchise to new classes of voters and each new wave of immigrants allowed bosses to strengthen their political power base.

Each individual political boss is a leader within the political machine hierarchy. Little bosses and big bosses are connected in a feudal hierarchy, each with a fiefdom to be exploited, and each bound to the other by mutual self-interest and personal loyalty. The boss is accountable for his actions to no one outside the machine.

HOW THE BOSSES REIGN

The principal methods used by the boss to gain control over voting blocs are patronage (the power to appoint persons to formal positions of power in the government); spoils (the power to distribute tangible rewards, including government contracts for goods and services, tax favoritism, formal and informal exemptions from legal enforcement and prosecution, and the issuance of government permits); the politics of recognition, especially the rapid integration of newly arrived immigrant groups and minority groups into the political system; and the nomination of a balanced electoral ticket in which all supporters of the machine are represented.

Bosses secure the public and electoral support of extended families, gangs, business organizations, neighborhoods, ethnic groups, and immigrant groups through patronage, graft, and the granting or withholding of favors, including government services, government welfare benefits, and social and economic benefits provided by the machine itself. Machine-provided benefits include membership in social clubs, gift baskets for the needy, and make-work employment for unemployed machine supporters.

The political machine is an interdependent community bound together through the boss. Various class, race, and ethnic groups are united by the common political objectives of seizing control of government and using government to secure advantages for the constituent groups within the machine. The machine is a vehicle for class, race, and ethnic cooperation and integration and the distribution of economic, social, and political benefits across all social groups. Membership in the machine is an achieved status, earned through demonstrated service to the machine. The machine recruits political outsiders into the

"Boss" Tweed Cartoon. *A political cartoon by Thomas Nast depicts "Boss" Tweed with a money bag for a head to illustrate Tammany Hall corruption in 1871.* KEAN COLLECTION/GETTY IMAGES.

political system, provides rapid political and social advancement for members of immigrant and minority groups, and helps mainstream and empower groups and individuals previously outside the acting political community.

In jurisdictions where political machines are active, the informal political power of the machine replaces the legal authority of government officials. Bosses typically put their personal self-interest and the machine's self-interest above the interests of political parties, government institutions, and the public. Bosses use their power over politics and government to accumulate personal wealth and social status and to demand deference from leaders of nonpolitical institutions, including businesses, churches, charities, community groups, and criminal organizations. Bosses practice politics for personal profit.

During the course of building the machine, bosses often form mutual-support alliances with corrupt business and criminal elements. These alliances, the conspiracy upon which they are based, and the scintillating lawlessness inherent in reciprocation of power and influence, undermine popular respect for politics and for machine-supported public officials. The resulting scandals and public outrage are the central themes for many novels, films, and television programs, especially police dramatic series. Feelings of helplessness in confronting an overpowering machine also leads to public withdrawal from politics and to political apathy.

Efforts at political reform during the Progressive Era in the late nineteenth and early twentieth centuries—including the civil service system; party primary elections; the multiplication of elected offices, especially in the state and local executive branches; the rotation, staggering, and shortening of elected terms of office; and introduction of the Australian ballot—merely strengthened the power of the boss. First, the reforms further complicated politics, making amateur political leaders less able to compete with the bosses. Second, the diffusion and legal limitations of official authority increased the need and opportunity for unofficial, efficient authority to emerge. Attempts to solve the problem of bossism merely increased the opportunities for bosses to flourish.

FAMOUS BOSSES

Famous bosses include William W. "Boss" Tweed and George Washington Plunkitt, leaders of Tammany Hall, a fraternal aid, charitable, and political organization that controlled the New York City Democratic Party and city politics from 1798 until Tweed's fraud conviction in 1872. Boss Tom Pendergast ran the Kansas City, Missouri, machine throughout the 1930s, paving city streets and rivers and giving Harry Truman his start before being sent to jail on tax evasion charges late in the decade. Mayor Richard J. Daley controlled the Chicago machine during the mid-twentieth century.

Most American cities and states succumbed to the power of similar bosses and political machines at one time or another. There is no distinctive personality type, life history, or other measurable criteria to distinguish a boss from a legitimate political leader. "Bossism" is defined subjectively. Edward J. Flynn, an early twentieth-century New York machine politician and author of *You're the Boss*, writes that it is only the leader one does not like who is a boss and the political organization one does not support that is a machine. Throughout U.S. history, writers, journalists, and political opponents have readily found evidence of bossism in the political leaders they dislike.

Gordon Neal Diem

SEE ALSO: *Mafia/Organized Crime; Royko, Mike.*

BIBLIOGRAPHY

Callow, Alexander B. *The Tweed Ring.* New York: Oxford University Press, 1966.

Croly, Herbert David. *Progressive Democracy.* New York: Macmillan, 1914.

Erie, Steven P. *Rainbow's End: Irish-Americans and the Dilemmas of Urban Machine Politics, 1840–1985.* Berkeley: University of California Press, 19890

Fadely, James, P. *Thomas Taggart: Public Servant, Political Boss, 1856–1929.* Indianapolis: Indiana Historical Society, 1997.

Flynn, E. J. *You're the Boss.* New York: Viking Press, 1949.

Menard, Orville D. *Political Bossism in Mid-America: Tom Dennison's Omaha, 1900–1933.* Lanham, MD: University Press of America, 1989.

Royko, Mike. *Boss: Richard J. Daley of Chicago.* New York: Dutton, 1971.

Steinberg, Alfred. *The Bosses.* New York: Macmillan, 1972.

Trounstine, Jessica. *Political Monopolies in American Cities: The Rise and Fall of Bosses and Reformers.* Chicago: University of Chicago Press, 2008.

Van Devander, Charles W. *The Big Bosses.* New York: Howell, Soskin, 1944.

Zink, Harold. *City Bosses in the United States; A Study of Twenty Municipal Bosses.* Durham, NC: Duke University Press, 1930.

Political Correctness

The social and cultural phenomenon known as political correctness emerged on American college campuses during the 1980s and became a part of the larger cultural scene in the 1990s. Political correctness was neither a social movement nor a coherent political platform but rather a tendency among governing bodies, especially in academic institutions, to police the spoken, written, or implied beliefs of those with whom they disagreed. Organizations and individuals behaved in a politically correct, or PC, manner when they attempted to restrict the rights of others to espouse opposing beliefs or to use offensive language. To its critics, primarily conservatives, political correctness was censorship, pure and simple; to its proponents, primarily liberals, it was an attempt to create a protective environment that is welcoming of diversity.

The historical origins of the term *political correctness* are unclear but telling. Some trace the origins of political correctness to Chinese communist leader Mao Tse-tung, who debated the origins of correct ideas in his *Little Red Book* in the 1960s. The term was used even earlier, however, when in 1793 a U.S. Supreme Court justice wrote in an opinion, "This is not politically correct." In Russia in the 1930s, Stalinists used the phrase to evoke a "sense of historical certitude," and Leninists used the phrase to describe those steadfast in their party affiliations. The phrase was used in the 1960s to describe people who altered their manners and beliefs to fit the prevailing political movements.

But the meaning of *political correctness* at the end of the twentieth century had its beginnings in the 1980s, when conservative campus activists began using the phrase to describe the liberal movement to increase multicultural, gay, and feminist studies and to impose codes of conduct that would eliminate behaviors deemed racist, sexist, homophobic, or otherwise unacceptable. *Political correctness* was thus a pejorative term used by conservatives to describe what they perceived as an attempt to undermine their values.

POLITICAL ORIGINS

Whatever its origins, it is clear that political correctness was born of political power and exerted by socially or politically powerful blocs attempting to establish norms for behavior and speech. When those politically powerful groups first emerged on college campuses in the 1980s, they were largely identified with the generation of academics who had come of age in the 1960s and had recently acquired enough power, through tenure or academic leadership, to enact their agenda. Under the banner of a celebration of American multiculturalism, politically correct academics encouraged the study of feminism, homosexuality, and ethnicity, all in an attempt to give oppressed groups a stronger voice in society. Politically correct theorists proposed that oppressive white males of European descent had dominated American history for long enough and that it was time to value the contributions of other social and cultural groups.

IMPACT

The concrete impact of political correctness on college campuses came in the creation of codes of conduct and the establishment of courses and departments dedicated to the study of previously marginalized topics. Codes of conduct took many forms across college campuses. Speech and harassment codes punished verbal or physical conduct (epithets, slurs, graphic materials, etc.) that offended an individual or group of individuals.

Whereas most such codes were inherently reasonable (how could one favor date rape?), critics claimed that they were used to silence the opinions of conservative white males and that they were enforced, often without regard to due process, by governing bodies eager to serve the needs of the so-called oppressed minorities. As politically correct ideals were mandated, open and honest debate declined. Students and faculty feared being labeled incorrect and faced serious punishment if they violated broadly defined and sometimes subjective speech codes. Although conduct codes were created with good intentions, many students and faculty felt the codes limited academic freedom and the constitutional rights to freedom of speech and assembly.

Multicultural studies were intended to make higher education more demographically and culturally inclusive. Feminist and homosexual studies followed the multicultural movement and quickly became established in college curricula. Supporters of political correctness claimed that they were attempting to broaden the canons of classical texts and studies by including works by women and minority groups. Conservatives and traditionalists argued that politically correct professors required students to read inferior writings at the expense of the classics. Stanford University, for one, engaged in a very public and divisive debate over which books to include in its curriculum in the late 1980s. This, in part, prompted Allan Bloom to write his polemic on cultural literacy, *The Closing of the American Mind* (1987).

Political correctness did not descend on campuses overnight, nor did it change college curriculums without a fight. As they began to perceive the ill effects of political correctness, social and political conservatives and liberal proponents of free expression began to articulate their opposition to the changing political atmosphere. Opponents of political correctness decried the inclusion of what they deemed inferior subject matter into the curriculum, charged that politically correct professors were intimidating students into expressing only politically correct beliefs, and hailed the crackdown on anything politically incorrect as a new kind of McCarthyism. These fights were soon carried out in public debates, in articles and books, and on talk shows, thus bringing political correctness to the attention of mainstream culture.

Many governmental organizations soon found themselves facing similar issues to those debated on college campuses in the 1980s as they attempted to define how they would deal with such issues as gays in the workplace and the military, sexual harassment, and hate crimes. On both a state and a national level, legislatures argued over whether to adjust laws to extend special protections to women, homosexuals, and minorities. The passage of the Americans with Disabilities Act in 1990, the backlash against any form of sexual harassment that followed the Clarence Thomas–Anita Hill Senate Hearings in 1991, and the passage of hate crime legislation all seemed to indicate that political correctness had found its way into American law.

Perhaps the most pervasive impact of political correctness on American culture came with regard to language. In an effort to show no disrespect for anyone, promoters of political correctness largely succeeded in reducing the number of offensive or inaccurate names used to refer to people. For example, descendants of historically oppressed groups are now called "Native Americans" instead of "Indians" and "African Americans" instead of "negroes." (But descendants of groups that are predominantly of European origin, such as Italians, Germans, and Irish, did not receive new classifications.)

Euphemistic language emerged as a means to prevent offending the sensitivities of others. Examples include using the term *sanitation engineer* instead of *garbage man* and *firefighter* instead of *fireman*. The mentally retarded or physically handicapped became *challenged*. It also became politically correct behavior to recycle, to oppose wearing fur, and to accept homosexuality as an "alternative lifestyle." Though such language became the source of frequent jokes (short people, for example, became known as *vertically challenged*), its impact was far reaching.

By the late 1990s open public discussion of political correctness had largely ended, in large part because it had been naturalized into the cultural landscape but also in response to criticism from figures on both ends of the political spectrum. Liberal commentators abandoned the term en masse, viewing it as a tool of the Right for minimizing or unfairly dismissing real social reforms that had measurable impacts on the day-to-day lives of American citizens. Conservatives in turn backed away from the term when it began to be used in describing the ideological rigidity of the neoconservative movement.

To its credit, political correctness helped create a new politeness and sensitivity to differences among American cultural groups; however, by pointing out the differences and mandating codes of behavior, it also heightened hostilities between opposing political sides and contributed to the culture wars of the late twentieth and early twenty-first centuries.

Debra Lucas Muscoreil

SEE ALSO: *Anita Hill–Clarence Thomas Senate Hearings; Feminism; Free Speech Movement; Gay Liberation Movement; McCarthyism; Multiculturalism; 9/11; Obama, Barack; Sexual Harassment.*

BIBLIOGRAPHY

Berman, Paul, ed. *Debating P.C.: The Controversy over Political Correctness on College Campuses.* New York: Dell, 1992.

Clark, Charles S. *Academic Politics.* Washington, DC: Congressional Quarterly Press, 1996.

Darnovsky, Marcy; Barbara Epstein; and Richard Flacks, eds. *Cultural Politics and Social Movements.* Philadelphia: Temple University Press, 1995.

Dickman, Howard, ed. *The Imperiled Academy.* New Brunswick, NJ: Transaction, 1993.

D'Souza, Dinesh. *Illiberal Education: The Politics of Race and Sex on Campus.* New York: Free Press, 1991.

Gitlin, Todd. *The Twilight of Common Dreams.* New York: Holt, 1995.

Hentoff, Nat. *Free Speech for Me—but Not for Thee.* New York: HarperCollins, 1992.

Hughes, Geoffrey. *Political Correctness: A History of Semantics and Culture.* Malden, MA: Wiley-Blackwell, 2010.

Ravitch, Diane. *The Language Police: How Pressure Groups Restrict What Students Learn.* New York: Knopf, 2003.

Sacks, David O., and Peter A. Thiel. *The Diversity Myth: Multiculturalism and the Politics of Intolerance at Stanford.* Oakland, CA: Independent Institute, 1995.

Schwartz, Howard S. *Society against Itself: Political Correctness and Organizational Self-Destruction.* London: Karnac Books, 2010.

Wilson, John. *The Myth of Political Correctness: The Conservative Attack on Higher Education.* Durham, NC: Duke University Press, 1995.

Pollock, Jackson *(1912–1956)*

Artist Jackson Pollock's "action painting" technique, combined with his aggressive, sometimes violent personality, elevated him to legendary status among American painters and also made him into a stereotype of the modern artist. His gestural works and technique of flinging and dripping paint over canvas had their inspiration in an exploration of the painting process and stemmed from his association with surrealist artists. Pollock used his abstract expressionist art as a means to reconcile the unconscious with the creative act of painting.

Pollock once referenced the act of painting as a source of magic. Art critic Harold Rosenberg picked up on this thought and termed the style "action painting." The technique redefined pictorial space by doing away with any differentiation between the foreground and the background. Pollock's work stunned the art world when it was first presented at the Betty Parsons New York Gallery in 1949. His action paintings became the cornerstone of the abstract expressionist art movement.

Paul Jackson Pollock, born in Cody, Wyoming, on January 28, 1912, spent his early years in the American Southwest, specifically Arizona and California, where he developed an interest in mysticism and mythology. This fascination resurfaced after he studied with American Regionalist painter Thomas Hart Benton at the Art Students League in New York from 1930 to 1932. Pollock's imagery began to contrast sharply with the realism of Benton; Pollock was interested in the intangible expressions of emotions as subject matter. Pollock's exposure to the work of Mexican muralists Diego Rivera and Clement Orozco during his tenure with the Works Projects Administration Federal Art Project in 1935 reinforced his interest in metaphysical ideas. Pollock also became obsessed with large-scale images. In the 1940s he began creating canvases that were more than 16 feet long.

Before Pollock developed his action painting technique, his work in the early 1940s related to the influence of Wassily Kandinsky and Pablo Picasso and to the automatic gestural painting practiced by many surrealists. Pollock's earliest images contained loose, gestural figurative forms. The gesture of the painting overtook the subjects beginning in 1947. Soon, recognizable imagery became obliterated by tangles of lines and shapes formed by dripped and poured paint. The movement and layers of the paint intermingled, flattening the plane and often seeming to continue beyond the edges of the canvas. Large-scale works such as *Lavender Mist* (1950) and *Full Fathom Five* (1947) were the culmination of this style and became some of Pollock's best-known and most successful pieces.

Pollock claimed every drip and line was deliberate; he refuted the idea of chance or accident as part of his creative process. Art critic Clement Greenberg, who was familiar with Pollock's work, encouraged the artist to continue with his unique technique. Greenberg's favorable reviews and his backing of the New York School, with Pollock at the center, led to an exciting period in art history. The abstract expressionists, including Pollock, Mark Rothko, Willem De Kooning, Robert Motherwell, and Franz Kline, in addition to Pollock's wife, artist Lee Krasner, helped make New York the center of the art world. There, artists produced exciting works that defined the idea of avant-garde art.

A return to figurative imagery in Pollock's work after 1950, seen in works such as *Number 27* (1950) and *Easter and the Totem* (1953), still incorporated the philosophy of applying paint purely for its expressive qualities. Yet Pollock did not have as much success with these later images as he did with his earlier non-figurative paintings. This lack of success fueled a problem with alcoholism that began to consume Pollock. Moreover, his marriage was disintegrating, and Pollock's life rapidly spiraled downward, culminating in a fatal automobile accident in 1956.

During his short life, Pollock was a prolific and original artist. His paintings had a profound impact on an art community that was ready for reinvention. Pollock and the New York School revitalized the American art scene while filling New York City with a raw, artistic excitement—the discovery of a new way of producing and thinking about art. Pollock and his action paintings were pivotal to abstract expressionism as a movement. Often parodied, Pollock remains a legendary figure representing modernity in art. In 2006 his painting *Number 5, 1948* was sold for a reported $140 million, the highest recorded price for a painting at that time. *Pollock*, a movie about his life starring Ed Harris, was released in 2000.

Jennifer Jankauskas

SEE ALSO: *Abstract Expressionism; Conceptual Art; Picasso, Pablo; Rivera, Diego; Works Progress Administration (WPA) Murals.*

BIBLIOGRAPHY

Emmerling, Leonard. *Jackson Pollock.* Cologne, Germany: Taschen, 2009.

Landau, Ellen G. *Jackson Pollock.* New York: Abrams, 2010.

Naifeh, Steven W., and Gregory White Smith. *Jackson Pollock: An American Saga.* New York: C. N. Potter, 1989.

O'Connor, Francis V., ed. *Pollock: A Catalogue Raisonné of Paintings, Drawings, and Other Works.* 4 volumes. New Haven, CT: Yale University Press, 1978.

O'Hara, Frank. *Jackson Pollock.* New York: G. Braziller, 1959.

Potter, Jeffrey. *To a Violent Grave: An Oral Biography of Jackson Pollock.* New York: G. P. Putnam's Sons, 1985.

Ratcliff, Carter. *The Fate of a Gesture: Jackson Pollock and Post-War American Art.* New York: Farrar, Straus, Giroux, 1996.

Robertson, Bryan. *Jackson Pollock.* New York: Harry N. Abrams, 1960.

Solomon, Deborah. *Jackson Pollock: A Biography.* New York: Simon and Schuster, 1987.

Polyester

The Frankenstein's monster of fabrics, polyester was the wonder fiber of postwar Europe and America and the fashion rage of the superfueled 1970s. Dismissed and disavowed by the cognoscenti in the 1980s, it seemed on the verge of extinction until modern science resurrected it in the form of polar fleece. In the twenty-first century, clothing manufacturers have found new and diverse uses for the fiber, proving yet again polyester's staying power as a staple of American fashion.

Perhaps no synthetic compound has influenced the style of an era quite like polyester. The fiber originated in a European laboratory as the invention of two chemists working at the Calico Printers Association in England. It was not the first synthetic fiber: rayon and nylon had been in use for years as sportswear and stockings, respectively. But when chemists J. T. Dickson and J. R. Whinfield hit upon a way to spin petrochemical molecules into threads, they created a fiber that was light years ahead of its time in terms of versatility and utility. DuPont, a chemical manufacturer, sensed the commercial potential of the new invention and purchased the patents for it in 1950. Within three years polyester was being produced in mass quantities.

Polyester's principal virtue is its plasticity. Natural fibers such as cotton or wool cannot be reengineered, but a synthetic fabric such as polyester can be custom designed to produce different aesthetics. With advances in technology, new polyester blends were concocted to simulate the look and feel of natural fabrics. Because polyester is naturally permanently pressed, the need for irons and ironing boards is greatly reduced. DuPont coined the term *wash-and-wear* to describe the wondrous properties of its new synthetic.

Throughout the 1960s polyester was sold to the public as the avatar of a new era of space-age convenience in clothing. Ads for "perma-prest" and double-knit items began dotting the pages of such barometers of public taste as the *New York Times* and the Sears catalog. In the 1970s polyester pantsuits, leisure suits, and garishly colored knit shirts stormed into fashion as the fabric attained a hipster cachet among suburban moderns. Poly-blend sport shirts and flared slacks seemed the perfect attire for weekend barbecues and trips to the singles bar. Demand for the wonder fiber became so great by 1974 that manufacturers had difficulty filling orders.

So the question is, what ultimately killed polyester? There is no easy answer. For one thing, there was the problem of ubiquity. By the late 1970s polyester fashion had become so absorbed into the mainstream that it lost all claim on fashionable taste. Furthermore, with so much polyester on the market—and so much of it cheaply constructed—the fabric's inherent weaknesses became apparent. Polyester does not breathe the way cotton does, and the resultant tendency toward sweatiness gave the fabric a disagreeable, down-market connotation. The excesses of disco, epitomized by actor John Travolta's egregious white polyester suit in the 1977 film *Saturday Night Fever*, seemed to put the final nail in the wonder fabric's coffin.

For almost two decades, polyester languished in popular disrepute. Occasionally used in blends to make clothes less expensive, the fiber was all but shunned as emblematic of poor taste. Camp film director John Waters even titled his 1981 celebration of tackiness *Polyester*. In the mid-1990s, however, the miracle fiber began to make a comeback in the form of polar fleece. Best known as Polartec, the fabric was marketed in the

Polyester Fashions. *Two women model polyester pant suit styles in 1970.* © BETTMANN/CORBIS.

form of sweaters, leggings, hats, and mittens by hip winter-wear outfitters such as Patagonia and Lands' End. Once again polyester's utility was the major selling point. (Polar fleece is lightweight and does not absorb as much water as other fabrics, making it a perfect lining for outerwear.)

As it had in the 1950s, utility begat fashionability. By 1998 top designers such as Donna Karan and Tommy Hilfiger were integrating polar fleece into their clothing lines. Perhaps it was too early to declare polyester completely rehabilitated, but the popularity of winter sports and the rise of casual chic seemed to assure the continued marketability of polar fleece into the new millennium.

Polyester's flexibility was evident in the surprising uses clothing manufacturers found for it in the first decade of the 2000s. New lightweight, paper-thin versions of the wonder fiber began to be used for athletic wear, and the fabric once denigrated for its inability to breathe became popular for its ability to stretch, to protect against wind, and to quickly dry—all at a cost less than that of cotton. Still, the fabric's most remarkable attribute seems to be its resilience to the vagaries of American culture.

Robert E. Schnakenberg

SEE ALSO: *Disco; Karan, Donna; LSD; Nylon; Retro Fashion;* Saturday Night Fever*; Singles Bars; Travolta, John; Waters, John.*

BIBLIOGRAPHY

Scheirs, John, and Timothy E. Long. *Modern Polyesters: Chemistry and Technology of Polyesters and Copolyesters.* Hoboken, NJ: John Wiley and Sons, 2003.

Smith, Matthew Boyd. *Polyester: The Indestructible Fashion.* Atglen, PA: Schiffer, 1998.

Stern, Jane, and Michael Stern. *The Encyclopedia of Bad Taste.* New York: HarperCollins, 1990.

Pop, Iggy *(1947–)*

As the vocalist and leader of the rock band the Stooges in the late 1960s and early 1970s, Iggy Pop helped popularize a new style of music that was loud, raw, and deceptively simple. As a result, Iggy and the Stooges were an important influence on the punk and grunge movements. Though he and the members of the Stooges went their separate ways in the 1970s, Pop never disappeared from the music scene. He cultivated his solo career and reunited with the Stooges in 2003. The band continues to tour and perform live shows.

BIRTH OF THE STOOGES

Pop, born James Osterberg, originally planned to be a blues drummer and moved from his home in Ann Arbor, Michigan, to Chicago to learn the music firsthand. Although he sometimes sat in with established musicians, he came to realize that the best he could do was to parrot their riffs, which he believed was exactly what most prominent white blues bands were doing. Deciding to create a type of simple yet powerful music based on his own experiences, he contacted Ron and Scott Asheton, whom he knew from high school, and their neighbor, Dave Alexander. They formed a band, which was first known as the Psychedelic Stooges.

Shortly afterward, he began calling himself Iggy Pop and established an onstage persona that was designed to shock audiences. Pop would sometimes perform with his head and eyebrows shaved, wearing a maternity dress, but as his reputation spread and his drug problems worsened, his antics escalated accordingly. Pop lacerated himself onstage, picked fights with members of motorcycle gangs who had come to heckle the band, and routinely dove from the stage to crawl at the feet of audience members. On one infamous occasion, he even vomited into the crowd before a show. Although the Stooges never achieved commercial success, their music and performances set the stage for the punk movement of the late 1970s and 1980s, and a number of groups explicitly acknowledged a debt to Iggy and the Stooges. The Ramones cited the band as one of their favorites, and the Sex Pistols released a version of "No Fun."

Whereas Pop may have to some extent cultivated the persona of an idiot, the image was far from the reality—he was even class valedictorian in high school. The Stooges soon collected a number of equally intelligent and musically savvy supporters. Jazz trumpeter Miles Davis counted himself as a fan, and although David Bowie was moving toward a heavily produced, complex form of rock that seemed the antithesis of the Stooges, he also praised them. John Cale, then with the Velvet Underground and formerly with La Monte Young's avant-garde ensemble the Dream Syndicate, produced their first release in 1969.

That self-titled album drew no shortage of detractors who claimed that the band was little more than a bunch of amateurs whose popularity rested entirely on Pop's antics. Although the music seemed basic, its vigor attracted a following. A number of bands attempted to imitate the Stooges' seemingly elementary sound, but few came anywhere near the power and intensity of songs like "I Wanna Be Your Dog." After releasing *Funhouse* in 1970, the band took a four-year hiatus from the studio that was due in part to their increasing drug abuse and, later, to Pop's departure for England to work with Bowie. Bowie produced the band's final album, *Raw Power,* in 1974. Songs such as "Gimme Danger" and "Search and Destroy" showed that the Stooges had lost none of their edge, although critics complained that Bowie's production effectively sanitized the band's sound. The Stooges broke up shortly afterward.

SOLO CAREER

Pop's solo work for the rest of the 1970s was more restrained. Still, songs such as "Lust for Life" and "The Passenger" garnered some praise, and Bowie enjoyed a hit single with "China Girl," a song he had cowritten with Pop. In fact, "Lust for Life" enjoyed remarkable longevity; it was featured on the soundtracks to the films *Trainspotting* (1996) and *Basquiat* (1996), as well as in television commercials, including a long-running set of ads for Royal Caribbean Cruise Line. The irony of the commercial popularity of the song was that the lyrics celebrated heroin use.

Pop continued his solo efforts in the 1980s and 1990s and firmly established himself as a rock icon. His album releases in the 1980s, including *Blah Blah Blah* (1986), produced by Bowie, and *Brick by Brick* (1990), produced by Don Was, were more commercial in sound yet also reflected a more mature musical sense. In the 1990s Pop also turned to acting. He appeared in John Waters's *Cry Baby* (1990) and Jim Jarmusch's *Dead Man* (1995) and even appeared in a number of episodes of the family-oriented television series *The Adventures of Pete & Pete*, which aired on Nickelodeon in the mid-1990s. In 2007 Pop was a regular cast member of the animated series *Lil' Bush: Resident of the United States*. The show aired on Comedy Central.

Though it would be impossible to classify Pop as mainstream, he did begin to reach a larger audience with his increased visibility: not only was he the voice behind "Lust for Life," but he also appeared in several television commercials in the first decade of the 2000s, including one for French telephone company SFR and another for British insurance company Swiftcover.com.

In 2003 Pop released *Skull Ring*, on which he reunited with Ron and Scott Asheton of the Stooges. The reformed band then recorded *The Weirdness* in 2007 and went on tour. In 2010 *Raw Power* was reissued under the Sony Legacy label. It included the original recordings along with bonuses such as live recordings from the band's tour.

Iggy Pop is proof that rock legends can live on. Though he turned sixty in 2007, he has shown no indication of slowing down and continues to perform shirtless and with unbridled energy. Pop and the Stooges even appeared on the popular television show *American Idol* (2002–), where his gyrating hips made even judge and pop star Jennifer Lopez blush.

Bill Freind

SEE ALSO: American Idol*; Blues; Bowie, David; Davis, Miles; Grunge; Lopez, Jennifer; Punk; The Ramones; Rock and Roll; The Sex Pistols; The Velvet Underground; Waters, John.*

BIBLIOGRAPHY

"Iggy and the Stooges Music."Accessed February 2012. Available from http://www.iggyandthestoogesmusic.com

McNeil, Legs, and Gillian McCain. *Please Kill Me: The Uncensored Oral History of Punk*. New York: Grove Press, 1996.

Mead, Rebecca. "Torso." *New Yorker*, August 9, 2010, 23.

Pop, Iggy. *I Need More*. Los Angeles: 2.13.61 Publications, 1997.

Tutton, Mark. "Iggy Pop: A Lust for Life." *CNN*. Accessed February 2012. Available from http://edition.cnn.com/2008/TRAVEL/12/03/iggy.biog

Trynka, Paul. *Iggy Pop: Open up and Bleed*. New York: Broadway Books, 2007.

Pop Art

Pop Art developed in the turbulent cultural milieu of the early 1960s as a response to the brooding intellectual and emotional aspects of abstract expressionism. Originally a British movement of the mid-1950s, in American hands Pop Art became a commentary on the mass-production culture and the banality of everyday life. Artists such as Andy Warhol, Roy Lichtenstein, and Claes Oldenburg utilized the images and production techniques of daily American life in a consumer society, transforming them into objects that were neither wholly real nor wholly art. In the process, they strove to make viewers aware of the extent to which advertising and the production/consumption cycle had come to dominate their lives.

ORIGINS AND CHARACTERISTICS

The term *Pop Art* seems to have originated from two sources: from British artist Richard Hamilton's 1956 collage picture *Just What Is It that Makes Today's Homes So Different, So Appealing?*, that features a bodybuilder holding a gigantic Tootsie Pop sucker; and as a descriptor of an art that highlighted popular everyday objects. The latter definition is more relevant. Pop Art was filled with images of consumer products, rendered in styles derived from advertisements or familiar images. The subject matter, as an early critic described it, was "the twentieth-century communications network of which we are all a part." Pop artists borrowed heavily from the slick, flashy, cliché-ridden advertising industry to depict the objects that were a part of American consumerism. Subjects were rendered in a simple, flat manner that emphasized the thinness of the canvas. Strong, bright colors were favored, and the image was centralized within the pictorial space. All of this was in direct contrast to the work of the abstract expressionists, who created formless, nonobjective art that grappled with existential questions of meaning.

MAJOR FIGURES

The most successful pop artists adopted these techniques in different ways. Roy Lichtenstein used the style of comic strips—bright colors, single scenes, Ben Day dots, and dialogue balloons. He depicted a world of prepackaged emotions (parallel to consumer products) and gender stereotypes. The women in Lichtenstein's paintings are concerned with love and marriage, as in the romance comics; the men inhabit the war comic world of violence and death. In the mid-1960s Lichtenstein also drew from art history within his comic strip style, integrating such genres as Cubism and Abstract Expressionism. His work thus shifted from a critique of the banal world of everyday America to a commentary on the secularization of high culture.

James Rosenquist's referent was the billboard. A former sign painter, Rosenquist painted on huge canvases a succession of seemingly random fragmented images. For example, his most famous painting, *F-111* (1965), features a military jet, a young girl beneath a missile-shaped hair dryer, and close-ups of spaghetti and an automobile tire. Rosenquist described his work in these words: "I treat the billboard image as it is. I paint it as a reproduction of other things. I try to get as far away from it as possible."

This retreat from the thing itself into the image of the thing was most evident in the work of Pop Art's most famous practitioner, Andy Warhol, whose Campbell's Soup cans, Brillo pad boxes, and Coca-Cola bottles epitomized the tension between high art and popular culture. Rather than stacking actual Brillo boxes, he made his own—at a studio appropriately called The Factory—and thus demonstrated a preference for the representation over the original. Perhaps this approach was most cogently demonstrated in Warhol's *The Marilyn Diptych* (1962), which reduces the late actress to a single repeated image that exemplified Hollywood's commodification of the individual. This detachment from the real thing became a desensitization or anesthetization in Warhol's images of automobile crashes and electric chairs. The banality of the every day had spilled over into people's emotional lives, numbing them to the real feeling that should naturally arise in the face of violence or tragedy. Warhol, like other Pop artists, used the mass-production techniques of advertising. His particular favorite was the silkscreen, which he used to repeat identical images across a canvas.

Claes Oldenburg transformed common consumer products into sculptures. In 1961 he turned his New York studio, which occupied a converted shop front, into what he called *The Store*. He lined the space with his plaster recreations of food items and consumer goods. Visitors who purchased his work, such as a plaster soda can, were thus recreating the activity of a traditional store. Oldenburg succeeded in treating the gallery as a pseudo marketplace, underscoring the producer/consumer aspect of the artist/patron relationship. Later, he created huge soft sculptures—foam-filled images of everyday items that sag and droop, like the human body, under the effects of gravity.

LEGACY

Perhaps the greatest legacy of Pop Art was the union of art and popular culture. Pop Art expressed the idea that the American common stock of shared cultural knowledge no longer came from high-culture sources such as literature or mythology, or from religion, but rather from television, movies, and advertisements. Although increasingly fewer Americans in the late twentieth century were familiar with great poetic works, for example, nearly all could recite a good line from a popular movie or a clichéd phrase from a television advertisement. Pop artists sought to reflect this increasing banality by blurring the distinction between art and consumption.

After the heyday of Pop Art, the public no longer could be sure whether a Coca-Cola bottle was an object, a work of art, or both. In Pop Art and commercial advertising the image became more important than the thing. In the end, Pop Art may have been, as the poet and critic Frank O'Hara called it, merely a "put on." Nevertheless, it was important in that it facilitated the examination of the effects of consumerism on human thought, emotion, and creativity.

Dale Allen Gyure

SEE ALSO: *Abstract Expressionism; Advertising; Billboards; Coca-Cola; Comics; Consumerism; Lichtenstein, Roy; Monroe, Marilyn; Television; Warhol, Andy.*

BIBLIOGRAPHY

Alloway, Lawrence. *American Pop Art*. New York: Collier Books, 1974.

Francis, Mark, ed. *Pop*. New York: Phaidon, 2010.

Livingstone, Mario, ed. *Pop Art*. London: Royal Academy of Arts, 1991.

Mahsun, Carol Anne Runyon, ed. *Pop Art: The Critical Dialogue*. Ann Arbor, MI: UMI Research Press, 1989.

Mamiya, Christin J. *Pop Art and Consumer Culture: American Super Market*. Austin: University of Texas Press, 1992.

Pop Music

While there has always been "popular" music in the United States, and all forms of music are popular with certain audiences, the term *pop music* generally denotes forms of music that are nonclassical, very mainstream, intended for very wide audiences, and often controlled by the giants of the music business: sheet music publishers in the early decades of the twentieth century and recording companies after 1930. Whereas these companies often produced a great variety of music, their need for profits mandated a constant search for the "next big thing"; the next great artist or style of music whose popularity would generate big record sales. Thus fueled by the profit motive, companies sought to reach the widest markets possible. And although the large companies did produce music targeted at markets considered "marginal," such as the African American population, they tended to focus on music that was unchallenging, unthreatening, and palatable across the spectrum of listeners.

THE EARLY DOMINANCE OF CROONERS

The focus on palatable, tuneful, and unchallenging music did not necessarily mean music of poor quality. Crooners such as Bing Crosby, Frank Sinatra, Doris Day, and Tony Bennett, along with jazz and big-band performers such as Ella Fitzgerald and Nat King Cole, dominated the popular music charts during the 1940s and early 1950s. They also produced some of the finest pop vocal music ever recorded, often composed by the accepted masters of the popular genre such as the Gershwins, Cole Porter, Jerome Kern, Irving Berlin, and Harold Arlen, whose best-known songs have become standards of the repertoire—the classics of light, romantic, and/or witty music.

Prior to the rise of rock and roll in the mid-1950s, this style of music *was* American pop music, and it appealed to white Americans and listeners in other English-speaking countries of all ages and classes. The music was easy to produce, and the recording companies knew what material to look for. With the rise of rock and roll, however, things changed. The large companies that defined the pop music field began finding it increasingly difficult to control or predict the course of pop music, and the "next big thing" became harder and harder to find with any regularity. Thus, after 1955, the pop music field fragmented and, by the end of the twentieth century, that fragmentation had become so great that the term *pop music* became very difficult to define.

This fragmentation was the result of numerous factors. First, although the major record companies such as Columbia, RCA, Decca, and Capitol dominated the pop vocal field during the 1940s and 1950s, they were not the only companies in the music business. Small, independent labels such as Chess, King, Specialty, and Sun were busy recording and selling more marginal or specialized music—blues, rhythm and blues, country and western, ethnic, folk, gospel, and so on. What they were doing was tapping into the diverse musical landscape that existed in the United States.

Occasionally, one of these small independents would have a major hit. Chess had huge successes in the mid- and late 1950s with such early rock-and-roll greats as Chuck Berry and Bo Diddley. Sun was the first to record Elvis Presley, whose amalgamation of country, blues, and rhythm-and-blues styles hit the charts in the mid-1950s. These successes not only challenged the commercial success of the major labels, but they also shattered the homogeneity of the pop music field. How could Berry and Bennett both be singing pop music? The answer was that they were not. After the rise of rock and roll, new styles challenged the primacy of pop music dominated by white crooners.

This rupture in the landscape of popular music set off a scramble by the large companies to keep up with the changes. For a brief period, from about 1955 to 1958, they were unable to do so alone. RCA succeeded for a time by buying Presley's contract from Sun, adopting an "if you can't beat 'em, join 'em" approach, but Presley's experience at RCA was indicative of the entire approach the major labels took to pop music: co-optation. Compared to the raw power of his early Sun recordings, his output on RCA was a rapid devolution into the pop crooner formula. It was the only form the major labels understood. Thus, while Presley scored some rock-and-roll hits on RCA ("Hound Dog" [1956], "Jailhouse Rock" [1957]), at the same time he was being reshaped into the pop crooner mold, recording such songs as "Love Me Tender" (1956) and "Treat Me Nice" (1957). By the mid-1970s, Presley was recording the same songs as Frank Sinatra, notably "My Way."

OVERLAPPING STYLES

By 1958 the major companies had regained much of their position through the process of co-opting many of the more marginal subgenres of American music. If a record became a hit in one of these more marginal markets, the major labels found someone to record the same song in a way that was palatable to white middle-America. Thus, while black America heard an original like Little Richard singing "Tutti Frutti" in 1955, white America heard Pat Boone's watered-down version the next year. These major labels also followed the tried-and-true formula that had worked during the crooner era of relying on professional songwriters to write material for young singers. Pop music during the 1958 to 1963 period, therefore, was dominated by teen idols and young vocal groups singing professionally written songs, many composed out of New York's Brill Building songwriting center. This was a system the major labels understood, one controlled by professional producers using professional songwriters and studio musicians. Although some great music came out of this era, it largely conformed to the major pop requirements, producing unthreatening, easy-to-listen-to music with mass appeal.

The pop music genre fragmented further after the arrival of the Beatles in 1964. Since the dominance achieved by rock and roll by the late 1950s, the line between rock and pop has never again been clear. The Beatles were simultaneously great rock and great pop artists, and they dominated the pop charts throughout the 1960s. "Yesterday" was undeniably in the pop mold (1965); "Revolution" (1968) was clearly rock. Pop music in the 1960s could include both the 1965 Rolling Stones song "(I Can't Get No) Satisfaction" and Dionne Warwick singing the Burt Bacharach/Hal David song "Walk on By" (1963). With this degree of variety, the meaning of the term *pop music* was becoming increasingly hazy, yet the term endures as a loose description of a wide variety of musical styles and trends. And, whereas earlier periods in pop music can be described as homogeneous (the "crooner" era, the "Brill Building sound," etc.), the pop field after the mid-1960s came to encompass a wide variety of overlapping styles in various stages of waxing or waning. New styles often emerged from regional, ethnic, racial, gender-specific, or other musical communities, or they arose due to the influence of one particular artist or group. After 1964, no one style could be called *pop music* to the exclusion of all others. This fact reflected the diversity of the record-buying public, now exposed to such a wide variety of music that many were not content listening only to one style.

GROUNDBREAKERS AND IMITATORS

However, these developments did not mean the extinction of older pop styles. Crooners such as Sinatra and Bennett enjoyed great commercial success in the 1960s and 1970s. The professional songwriting tradition lived on in the work of Bacharach and others, and traditional practices in the pop music industry continued. As each new trend emerged, major record companies rushed to take advantage of it. For example, after the emergence of the Beatles, record companies promoted a host of Beatles knock-offs, and almost any band from Liverpool, England, the Beatles' hometown, could get a record contract after 1964. Numerous American groups were also developed and promoted to capitalize on the music and image of the Beatles. Some, such as the Knickerbockers and their 1965 song "Lies," were direct rip-offs of the Beatles sound; others, such as the Monkees, aimed to emulate the Beatles in both looks and sound.

When the Beatles recorded their psychedelic masterpiece *Sergeant Pepper's Lonely Hearts Club Band* album in 1967, they set off another round of imitators, beginning with the Rolling Stones' *Their Satanic Majesties Request* later that year. After 1967 the Beatles moved on from psychedelic music, but their influence meshed with the rising San Francisco psychedelic sound that produced such groups as the Grateful Dead and Jefferson Airplane, both of which used drug imagery in their music. These groups might have been too much for the broad range of American pop music listeners, but the pop music field was still able to profit from the sound. Following the old tradition of watering down a musical form, music producers presented Top 40 radio listeners with the Mamas and Papas' "California Dreaming" (1965) and Scott McKenzie singing "San Francisco (Be Sure to Wear Flowers in Your Hair)" in 1967.

This trend of co-opting more marginal musical forms and making them palatable to broad audiences remained strong in the late 1960s. The decade was a period when several of popular music's most innovative artists were making ground-breaking records, some of which made the pop music charts, but they shared the charts with much lighter fare. In addition to trying to co-opt other sounds, large corporate record companies tried to manufacture their own groups for the preteen and teen market, which, increasingly, had been left behind by psychedelia and other, harsher, forms of rock music. With such groups as the Monkees, the Partridge Family, and the cartoon group the Archies, companies could make light, pop fare that was extremely palatable to this young market. These groups were promoted with their own television shows, and the Monkees and David Cassidy from the Partridge Family became teen idols. This practice was not a new one: Earlier teen idols had been similarly "manufactured," and the trend continued in later decades with such singers and groups as Shaun Cassidy, Andy Gibb, Leif Garrett, Menudo, New Edition, N'Sync, Hannah Montana, and others.

A PROLIFERATION OF SOUNDS

In the 1970s the variety of styles considered part of the broad pop music mainstream increased. They included the singer-songwriter tradition, hard rock, southern rock, the California sound, disco, glam rock, stadium rock, heavy metal, and others. All entered the pop field at various points. The most significant of these trends were the singer-songwriter tradition, the California sound, and disco. The light sound of the singer-songwriter tradition was especially suited to pop music and brought huge hits for artists such as Carole King, James Taylor, Joni Mitchell, Cat Stevens, Paul Simon, Randy Newman, and John Denver during the decade. All sang introspective songs, often using mostly acoustic instruments that were perfect for the pop sound. Some listeners could find deep meaning in the lyrics of the songs, but these songs were also extremely radio-friendly—soft and often very hummable.

Carole King's *Tapestry* album (1971) sold more than ten million copies and remained on the charts for almost six years;

John Denver was all over the airwaves in the 1970s with such songs as "Rocky Mountain High" (1972) and "Sunshine on My Shoulders" (1973). The singer-songwriter tradition meshed well with the California sound that emerged in the early 1970s. Led by such groups and singers as America, the Eagles, Linda Ronstadt, and Jackson Browne, the California sound was often easygoing, acoustically oriented music that reflected the laid-back atmosphere of Southern California. The Eagles' songs "Peaceful Easy Feeling" and "Take It Easy" (both released in 1972) spoke for themselves.

The singer-songwriter tradition and the California sound were largely eclipsed in the late 1970s—as was much of popular music—by disco. Disco music, with its thumping, repetitive dance beat and electronic sound, was greeted with great enthusiasm by many; for others, it was considered the death of pop music. Disco music was dance music, and as such it was part of a much larger club scene rather than simply music for listening. Disco grew, like much of pop music, from the culture of black America, particularly the smooth black urban pop of the early 1970s. Some commentators trace elements of it to dance clubs in Manhattan, in particular to the city's gay culture.

Whatever its precise origins, the style reached the pop charts in the mid-1970s with Donna Summer's "Love to Love You Baby" (1975) KC & the Sunshine Band's "Get Down Tonight" (also 1975), and others. But the genre exploded in popularity when the film *Saturday Night Fever*, starring John Travolta as a disco-dancing Brooklyn teenager, was released in 1977. Its soundtrack album, featuring the Bee Gees' new disco sound, became one of the most successful records in pop music history. After this success, everyone from the Beach Boys to Rod Stewart to the Rolling Stones jumped on the disco bandwagon for a time. Disco's heyday was short-lived, ending with the 1970s, but its influence continued in the 1980s and beyond.

THE 1980s AND 1990s

Pop music's purview widened even further in the 1980s and 1990s, encompassing both old and new trends and styles. The vocal tradition, although far removed from its crooner days, continued with such major solo vocal divas as Whitney Houston, Mariah Carey, Celine Dion, and Madonna. Whereas most of these singers stayed with predictable and comfortable material, Madonna was unique among them and achieved great success with her meld of disco, pop, and R&B and often outrageous looks and controversial material. The teen-idol tradition remained alive and well, but now many of the teen idols were young women, such as Debbie Gibson, Tiffany, and the Spice Girls, who offered soft pop to an eager preteen market. Similar to earlier decades, this was also an era of great solo stars such as Billy Joel, Michael Jackson, and Elton John, all of whose songs topped the charts in the 1980s and drew huge crowds for their stadium concerts. Jackson's 1982 album *Thriller* was one of the best-selling albums of all time, crossing over between pop, disco, and rhythm and blues.

A new trend in the early 1980s was what has been called a "second British Invasion" (the first being the Beatles-led invasion of the early 1960s). Coming out of the influential but less widely popular new wave movement of the late 1970s, groups and artists such as Duran Duran, the Eurythmics, Culture Club, U2, Adam Ant, Wham!, and others were significant to the decade. Many relied on synthesizers and drum machines that gave their sound a widely popular electronic feel. There was also a strong fashion consciousness to many of these bands, which—as always in pop and rock—was integral to their image. The visual aspects of this music were heightened by the rise of cable television's MTV, which launched in 1981 and played specially produced music videos of new bands. MTV's increasing influence proved a powerful force in music during the 1980s and 1990s.

A TIME OF "ATEMPORALITY"

Pop music continued to absorb other, more marginal, musical styles. Rap music, a product of black urban youth culture in the 1980s, was one such style. While rap still maintains its authenticity in the hands of many artists, mainstream pop music gradually adopted some of its conventions in diluted form with such performers as MC Hammer and Vanilla Ice, both of whom achieved brief periods of popularity.

Another important trend in the late 1980s and into the 1990s was the rise of "alternative" music. Originally, alternative music was the harder-edged, guitar-based "grunge" sound that emerged out of Seattle with such bands as Nirvana and Pearl Jam. But the alternative label could just as easily be applied to somewhat older, influential bands such as R.E.M. and the B-52s. The style was broadened during the 1990s to include a whole host of new bands that challenged the bland pop music that was occupying the official pop charts. Groups such as Nirvana, Pearl Jam, and Stone Temple Pilots provided a fresh alternative to mainstream fare such as Phil Collins, Michael Bolton, and Whitney Houston. The alternative genre saw the rise of a new influx of female talent, including the somewhat harder-edged Alanis Morrissette and Joan Osborne. As in many of the trends absorbed by pop, the term *alternative* widened to such a degree that it had become virtually meaningless by the late 1990s. With the great success achieved by these and other bands, the question "alternative to what?" had become a hard one to answer.

As a whole, pop music was much more diverse by the late 1990s than at any other period in its history, and a wide variety of performers and genres could be grouped under its broad umbrella. This trend continued into the early 2000s. In a July 15, 2011, *New York Times* article, music critic Simon Reynolds borrowed a concept from fiction writers William Gibson and Bruce Sterling called *atemporality* to describe contemporary pop music. Atemporality is the absence of features that can distinguish contemporary style from other periods, and Reynolds sees it as a defining characteristic of pop music in the first decades of the 2000s. He cited the diversity of available musical styles, such as the rhythm-and-blues-influenced singing of Adele, the soul-music roots of Cee Lo Green, the Madonna-like sounds of Lady Gaga, and the continuing popularity of hip-hop. Analysts believe one reason for the survival and ongoing influence of so many past musical styles is the Internet, which made decades of musical history available for young musicians to draw upon as their artistic inspiration.

Although that variety certainly proved refreshing to many people, it has perpetuated the problem of defining pop music. However, there are some general characteristics of pop music that have remained fairly constant. First, whereas pop music is an inclusive genre that draws from a wide variety of styles, it often does so by co-opting them, taking unique musical forms and watering them down for mass consumption. While unique performers and artists continue to find success, the pop charts are often crowded with lesser talents enjoying their ride on the current trends. Second, pop music is primarily commercially driven. All recorded music has its commercial imperatives, but in pop music the drive for commercial success dominates, and this focus often leads to less than original music, centered on the lowest common denominator.

Third, the style of pop music is fundamentally dictated by trends, and no one in the music industry knows what the next big trend will be. When a trend emerges, often because of a particularly innovative artist or group, a host of imitators follow close on their heels. The originators often move on to new areas, the wave of imitators eventually crashes, and the search for the new begins all over again. Thus, for better or worse, pop music is an ever-changing phenomenon in American popular culture.

Timothy Berg

SEE ALSO: *The Beach Boys; The Beatles; The Bee Gees; Bennett, Tony; Berlin, Irving; Berry, Chuck; Boone, Pat; The Brill Building; British Invasion; Browne, Jackson; Carey, Mariah; Cassidy, David; Cole, Nat King; Country Music; Crosby, Bing; Day, Doris; Denver, John; Diddley, Bo; Disco; Fitzgerald, Ella; Folk Music; Gospel Music; The Grateful Dead; Grunge; Heavy Metal; Hip-Hop; Houston, Whitney; Jackson, Michael; Jazz; Jefferson Airplane/Starship; John, Elton; Kern, Jerome; King, Carole; Lady Gaga; Little Richard; Madonna; The Mamas and the Papas; Mitchell, Joni; The Monkees; MTV; Nirvana;* The Partridge Family*; Pearl Jam; Porter, Cole; Presley, Elvis; Rap; R.E.M.; Rhythm and Blues; Rock and Roll; The Rolling Stones;* Saturday Night Fever*; Simon, Paul; Sinatra, Frank; Soul Music; The Spice Girls; Stadium Concerts; Summer, Donna; Sun Records; Taylor, James; Travolta, John; U2; Vanilla Ice.*

BIBLIOGRAPHY

Breithaupt, Don, and Jeff Breithaupt. *Precious and Few: Pop Music of the Early '70s.* New York: St. Martin's Press, 1996.

Clarke, Donald, ed. *The Penguin Encyclopedia of Popular Music.* London: Viking, 1989.

Gregory, Hugh. *A Century of Pop: A Hundred Years of Music That Changed the World.* New York: Acapella Publishers, 1998.

Have a Nice Decade: The '70s Pop Culture Box. Rhino Records, 1998, 7 compact discs.

Miller, Jim, ed. *The Rolling Stone Illustrated History of Rock & Roll.* New York: Rolling Stone Press, 1980.

Reynolds, Simon. *Retromania: Pop Culture's Addiction to Its Own Past.* New York: Faber & Faber, 2011.

Whitburn, Joel. *Joel Whitburn's Top Pop Singles 1955–1996: Chart Data Compiled from Billboard's Pop Singles Charts, 1955–1996*, 8th ed. Menomonee Falls, WI: Record Research, 1997.

The Pope

Within the Roman Catholic Church, the pope serves a dual role as both the Bishop of Rome and the spiritual and symbolic leader of the church as a whole. According to Catholic doctrine, the pope is the ultimate arbiter of church tradition and, in specific cases, his teachings are recognized as infallible in matters of faith and morals. As the global personification of Catholicism, the institution of the papacy has exerted a strong influence on American religion, culture, and politics, shaping not only how Catholics express their religious beliefs but how they have been viewed by their Protestant neighbors.

Historically, Catholicism in general and the papacy in particular sparked periodic attacks by "nativist" Protestants who saw newly arriving Catholic immigrants as detrimental or dangerous to American society. In the nineteenth century this resulted in several riots in northern cities and the burning of Catholic churches, schools, and convents. Both evangelical Protestant leaders and the popular press condemned Catholic immigrants as soldiers or spies for Rome who were undermining the Protestant character of the nation. Although tensions between Catholics and Protestants cooled in the twentieth century, the pope remained a polarizing figure. Although protestants still did not accept "papal authority," the perceived rise of secularism in the United States provided a chance for Catholics and Protestants to cooperate, and many saw the Pope as a figurehead who gave voice to common moral concerns.

PREJUDICE

The crux of the nativist argument was that individuals, particularly newly arrived immigrants, could not be spiritually committed to the pope and remain politically loyal to the American government. One of the most outspoken proponents of this line of thinking was the early twentieth-century writer and agrarian populist Tom Watson. He insisted that several Catholic groups in America, including parish priests, the Knights of Columbus, and religious orders such as Jesuits, were actually the pope's secret warriors. Their goal, Watson claimed, was to overthrow the American republic and enthrone the pope as supreme ruler over the United States.

The same themes were articulated by the prominent anti-Catholic journal *The Menace*, which both warned of a papal coup and blamed Catholic corruption for the failure of progressive political reforms. *The Menace* was founded in 1911, and within four years it boasted a circulation in excess of 500,000.

Pope Benedict XVI. *Pope Benedict XVI was elevated to the papacy in 2005 after the death of Pope John Paul II.* POOL/POOL/GETTY IMAGES NEWS/GETTY IMAGES.

The journal also spawned a host of imitators in rural towns. Tensions with Germany and the onset of World War I brought a halt to *The Menace* and ushered in a lull in anti-Catholicism in general. In the 1920s and for the next several decades thereafter, Catholics were exposed to renewed attacks, largely from the Ku Klux Klan. Catholics were one of many groups singled out as "un-American" by the Klan, which became an increasingly powerful and political organization. Jack Chick, a devout evangelical, began releasing hate literature disguised as comics in the 1970s. Chick's comics played on many stereotypes and suggested that the Vatican had created Islam as a means to eradicate competing Christian groups. Similarly, he suggested that the Vatican was responsible for the KKK and established it as a Protestant group in order to discredit them in the public's mind.

American Catholics' own understanding of the papacy has often been ambiguous. On the one hand, Catholic prayer, ritual, and iconography centers on the pope. On the other hand, American Catholics frequently reinterpret, or even ignore, papal demands that seem out of place in American life. During the first decade of the twentieth century, Pope Leo XIII and Pius X routinely condemned Catholic leaders for cooperating with Protestants in providing public schooling for Catholic children, involving the laity in parish affairs, and doing ecumenical work with other Christian denominations. By labeling these offenses "Americanism," the popes insisted that Americans had broken from longstanding Catholic traditions and needed to bring their behavior in line with the rest of the Catholic world.

Yet on several levels, the breach between America and Rome increased over the next several decades, particularly in the liturgical movement of the 1930s and 1940s, which sought to reform the traditional Latin Mass long before it was altered by the dictates of the Second Vatican Council in the 1960s. Thus, American Catholics were caught in a paradoxical bind, criticized by their religious leaders for being too American and denounced by journalists and politicians as not being American enough.

POLITICS

America's uneasiness toward Catholicism often has had deep political implications. "No Popery" and "Immigrants Out" became synonymous slogans in the political battle for immigration restrictions in the 1920s. In fact, the immigration quotas adopted in 1924 were designed explicitly to exclude large numbers of immigrants from the southern and eastern regions of Europe, whose religious beliefs and ethnic stock were deemed inferior to those of Protestant Americans. In 1928 Al Smith, the Catholic governor of New York, encountered similar resentment when he ran for president. Although he won the Democratic nomination, Smith was defeated by Herbert Hoover in the general election largely because of assumptions that he would bring "popery" into public schools and undermine the Protestant character of the nation.

In 1960 John F. Kennedy faced similar opposition in his presidential campaign against Richard Nixon. Kennedy, a Catholic who was a Democratic senator from Massachusetts, was heavily influenced by the anti-Catholic propaganda surrounding his candidacy. He often downplayed his connections to Rome, insisting that he "wore his religion lightly" and that the Constitution, not papal dogma, would dictate his political decisions. In the Senate, Kennedy voted against using federal funds to subsidize parochial schools and opposed the appointment of an American ambassador to the Vatican. Although both moves led to sharp reprisal in the Catholic press, Kennedy's political record demonstrated to many Protestant voters that Catholicism was not enough to disqualify a candidate from office. Some conservative critics, however, still felt that Kennedy's election was part of a papal plot aimed at subjecting Americans to Roman rule. Overall, Catholics cheered Kennedy's election not simply as a political victory but as a symbol of prosperity and success in the face of adversity and bigotry.

PAPAL INFLUENCE

According to Catholic doctrine, when a reigning pope dies, a new one is chosen by the College of Cardinals, a group of high-ranking church officials serving throughout the world. Although the papacy as an abstract symbol has played a pivotal role in shaping America's politics and culture, the actions of certain individual popes have also attracted attention in the United States among Catholics and non-Catholics alike. One example is Pius X (1835–1914), who reigned from 1903 to 1914 and was the only twentieth-century pope to be declared a saint. Pius X seriously offended many Americans by refusing to receive Theodore Roosevelt during his visit to the Vatican because the former president had gone to a Methodist congregation earlier on his trip.

A more significant example of the papacy's role in American culture is the decision by Pope John XXIII (1881–1963), who reigned from 1958 to 1963, to call the Second Vatican Council. Convened from 1962 to 1965, the council enacted rules that transformed Catholic services and increased communication and dialogue with other religions. More importantly, however, Vatican II sought to modernize Catholicism by signaling a new willingness to participate in and minister to an increasingly complex world. In light of this, the Second Vatican Council extended a symbolic hand to Protestants, referring to them as "separated brethren." Perhaps the gesture was a strategic move, but its effect was not lost on Protestants, who, in the Catholic Church's eyes, were officially no longer heretics.

Yet for many Catholics, John XXIII's successor, Paul VI (1897–1978), did much to undo the enthusiasm and liberalism generated by Vatican II. In 1968 Paul VI issued an encyclical (papal ruling) known as *Humanae Vitae* that denounced all forms of artificial birth control. The ruling was rejected by 90 percent of American Catholics, as well as several of his own advisers. While he upheld the rulings of Vatican II, Paul VI represented a conservative shift in Catholic leadership that continued through the late twentieth century.

POPE JOHN PAUL II

This was particularly apparent in the papacy of John Paul II (1920–2005), formerly the Archbishop of Krakôw and the first non-Italian pope elected in more than 400 years. While previous popes had remained in relative isolation within the Vatican, John Paul II was a world traveler who became known for his charisma and dramatic speaking voice. Although he was criticized in America and abroad for his condemnation of abortion, birth control, homosexuality, and women's ordination, John Paul II increasingly brought Catholicism into the public eye. He was the twentieth century's longest-living pope, as well as one of its most prolific and outspoken. His conservative theology caused many late-twentieth-century Americans to view the papacy not as an institution bent on national domination, as was feared in earlier decades, but as either a guardian of traditional morality or as a model of leadership that had become increasingly out of touch with the modern world. In 1990 Pope John Paul II advised the Catholic community to avoid attending Madonna's "Like a Virgin" tour. In spite of his popularity, the church's slow actions concerning sexual abuse committed by priests caused many to view the church as a conspiratorial epicenter. In 1992 pop singer Sinead O'Connor took advantage of her appearance on NBC's *Saturday Night Live* to protest the pope's role in the cover-ups by ripping up a photo on live television. Surprisingly, Madonna criticized her actions.

In 2003 John Paul II came out strongly against the American war in Iraq, saying, "War is not always inevitable. It is always a defeat for humanity." Many Americans, both Catholics and non-Catholics, agreed with his assessment. John Paul II died on April 2, 2005. On April 19 of that year, Benedict XVI was elected as the 265th Roman Catholic pope.

POPE BENEDICT XVI

Benedict XVI's papacy has been riddled with scandals, both old and new. The scandal involving the sex abuse of children by Catholic priests had been going on for decades before he became pope, and he had been involved with efforts to prevent new cases from occurring. He is credited with banishing Reverend Marcial Maciel Degollado, one of the most notorious abusers, to a life of penance in exile. As pope, however, Benedict XVI became the target of concentrated demands for modern accountability of the Catholic Church. In September 2010 two British writers, Christopher Hitchens and Richard Dawkins, sought to have the pope arrested during his visit to Britain, demanding that he be charged with crimes against humanity for the church's mishandling of the sex-abuse cases.

Early in 2012, a scandal that became known as "Vatileaks" arose when a series of confidential Vatican documents began appearing in the Italian press. The general feeling was that the leaks were the result of both personal and political vendettas. Secrets unearthed in the documents included letters from various sources expressing concern about financial corruption within the Vatican, accusations that the "Vatican bank" (the Institute for Works of Religion) was transferring euros to foreign banks to avoid Italian oversight of church funds, and suspicions that the new money-laundering law passed by the Vatican had intentionally contained a loophole that prevented offenses committed before the law took effect on April 1, 2011, from coming to trial.

Benedict XVI has continued to espouse conservative policies, frequently criticizing cultural practices in the United States. In 2012, in the midst of the ongoing battle over same-sex marriage, Benedict XVI told a group of American bishops visiting the Vatican that gay marriage was inherently wrong and advised the bishops to exhort American Catholics to refrain from premarital sex.

Justin Nordstrom

SEE ALSO: *Abortion; Gay and Lesbian Marriage; The Pill; Religious Right; Sex Scandals.*

BIBLIOGRAPHY

Allen, John L., Jr. "Puccini Meets Watergate in 'Vatileaks' Scandal." *National Catholic Reporter*, March 2, 2012.

Alvarez, David J. *The Pope's Soldiers: A Military History of the Modern Vatican*. Lawrence: University Press of Kansas, 2011.

Bentley, James. *God's Representatives: The Eight Twentieth-Century Popes*. London: Constable, 1997.

Dolan, Jay P. *The American Catholic Experience: A History from Colonial Times to the Present*. Notre Dame, IN: University of Notre Dame Press, 1992.

Duffy, Eamon. *Saints and Sinners: A History of the Pope*. New Haven, CT: Yale Nota Bene, 2006.

Fuchs, Lawrence H. *John F. Kennedy and American Catholicism*. New York: Meredith Press, 1967.

Hingham, John. *Strangers in the Land: Patterns of American Nativism 1860–1925*. New Brunswick, NJ: Rutgers University Press, 1988.

Israely, Jeff, and Howard Chua-Eoan. "The Trial of Benedict XVI." *Time*, June 7, 2010.

Kelly, J. N. D., and Michael J. Walsh. *A Dictionary of Popes*. New York: Oxford University Press, 2011.

Simpson, Peter L. P. "Transcending Justice: Pope John Paul II and Just War." *Journal of Religious Ethics*, June 2011.

Popeil, Ron *(1935–)*

Inventor and marketer Ron Popeil, cofounder of Ronco, became a fixture of television in the 1960s and 1970s with products such as the Veg-O-Matic, Pocket Fisherman, and Mr. Microphone, and in the 1990s he pioneered the thirty-minute infomercial. Parodied by Dan Aykroyd, "Weird Al" Yankovic, and many others, Popeil and his flamboyant marketing style are cultural touchstones. He did not coin the phrase "But wait, there's more"—most likely the creation of state fair auctioneers in the mid-twentieth century—but it has become inextricably linked with Popeil, the consummate pitchman.

Born on May 3, 1935, in New York City, Popeil (pronounced "poe-PEEL") had an unhappy childhood. His parents—Julia and Samuel J. Popeil, an inventor and salesman—divorced when he was a small child, and he and his older brother Jerry were sent to boarding school. Later they went to live with their grandparents in Florida, but their grandfather proved to be a harsh disciplinarian. At the age of sixteen Popeil moved to Chicago to live with his father.

His father had established Popeil Brothers, which manufactured and sold inventions for the home. Popeil went to work selling the company's wares at a flea market and soon discovered that he had a knack for sales. He eventually began selling products at the flagship store of Woolworth's, and by his late teens he was earning $1,000 a week at a time when $500 a month was a good salary.

During the mid-1950s Popeil spent a year at the University of Illinois, where he met Mel Korey, with whom he formed Ronco in 1964. Despite his great success in direct sales, Popeil realized that he could reach far more people through television and, for just $500, made a sixty-second commercial at WFLA-TV in Tampa, Florida. This proved to be a wise move: in 1964 Ronco's sales were $200,000, and four years later this number had burgeoned to more than $8 million. The products that made possible this enormous growth mostly had "O-Matic" names, among them the Chop-, Dial-, Veg-, and Mince-O-Matic. Ronco went public in 1969, and Popeil became a multimillionaire.

The company grew throughout the 1970s, and its commercials became recognizable enough to spawn Aykroyd's "Bass-O-Matic" parody on *Saturday Night Live*. But in 1984 Ronco's bank called in the company's loans, which Ronco could not cover. The bank auctioned off the company, with the result that Popeil himself bought Ronco for $2 million.

Also in 1984 the Federal Communications Commission changed its guidelines, making possible the thirty-minute infomercial. During the early 1990s Popeil emerged as a master of the format, which he used to market the Electric Food Dehydrator and the Showtime Rotisserie. In 2005 he sold Ronco but continued to serve as its spokesman. It is estimated that during his career Popeil has sold $1 billion worth of products.

Popeil has four daughters, and he and his fourth wife, Robin, live in Beverly Hills, California. He is the cousin of actress and singer Ashley Tisdale.

Judson Knight

SEE ALSO: *Advertising; Aykroyd, Dan; Dime Stores/Woolworth's; Mays, Billy;* Saturday Night Live*; Television; Yankovic, "Weird Al."*

BIBLIOGRAPHY

Dow, Sheila, and Jaime E. Noce, eds. *Business Leader Profiles for Students*, vol. 2. Detroit, MI: Gale, 2002.

Popeil, Ron, and Jefferson Graham. *The Salesman of the Century: Inventing, Marketing and Selling on TV: How I Did It and How You Can Too!* New York: Delacorte, 1995.

Samuelson, Timothy. *But Wait! There's More! The Irresistible Appeal and Spiel of Ronco and Popeil.* New York: Rizzoli, 2002.

Popeye

Seagoing superhero Popeye was first seen in 1929 in E. C. Segar's comic strip *Thimble Theatre*. The strip, which dispensed cockeyed mock-adventure continuities, had been running since King Features Syndicate introduced it in 1919. Segar, however, did not get around to inventing his tough, spinach-eating sailor until almost ten years later. Already onboard the cartoon were the quintessentially thin Olive Oyl and her diminutive and entrepreneurial brother Castor Oyl, and J. Wellington Wimpy, whose fondness for hamburgers knew no bounds. By 1931 the two-fisted Popeye had become the undisputed star of the comic strip, and the title changed to *Thimble Theatre Starring Popeye*.

Never a master cartoonist, Segar compensated for his lack of drawing ability with a gift for audacious comedy. In his long, rambling, comic continuities, he kidded serious adventure narratives, as well as current political and social activities at home and abroad. He frequently made fun of the newspaper business and the cartooning profession. In one early 1930s sequence, he showed an artists' bullpen where a group of interchangeable cartoonists spoke nothing but exclamations such as "Zowie," "Zam," and "Bonk" and drew strips with such titles as *Zip the Dip* and *Boop the Doop*.

A longtime science fiction buff, Segar frequently built stories around strange creatures and odd inventions. Among the eccentrics who frequented *Thimble Theatre* were Alice the Goon; the Sea Hag; the tough café owner Roughhouse; the mystical critter known as Eugene the Jeep; and Popeye's foster child, Swee'pea. Popeye was a firm believer that might made right, and a sock in the snoot was his frequent negotiating tool. As the strip progressed, Popeye's powers continued to increase until he was bulletproof and incredibly strong, almost foreshadowing Superman—although the squint-eyed sailor was not nearly as serious. Eventually Segar revealed that it was spinach, usually consumed straight from the can, that gave Popeye his incredible abilities.

Popeye also proved a successful merchandising figure. In addition to being reprinted in comic books and Big Little Books, he inspired windup toys, toy musical instruments, pull toys, and puppets. According to toy expert Richard O'Brien, "the two most popular comic strip toy characters of the 1930s were Popeye and Buck Rogers." Popeye's image appeared on every sort of product from canned goods to toothbrushes.

In 1933 King Features licensed Max Fleischer Studios to produce a series of animated cartoon shorts. Though not especially faithful to Segar's strip, the cartoons were box-office hits and continued to be produced for more than twenty-four years. Later they became a staple of children's television. The annual revenue from the salty seaman's subsidiary rights eventually reached the millions. Popeye's oft-repeated pragmatic statement "I yam what I yam" was widely quoted during his heyday—as were such Wimpyisms as "I would gladly pay you Tuesday for a hamburger today," "Let's you and him fight," and "Come up to my house for a duck dinner—you bring the ducks."

After Segar died of leukemia in 1938 at the age of forty-four, King Features replaced him with bullpen artist Doc Winner. King then brought in cartoonist Bill Zaboly and writer Tom Sims. Although Zaboly was a better cartoonist than either of his predecessors, Sims never duplicated the eccentric nonsense and oddly paced adventures that Segar had concocted. During the early 1950s writer and magazine gag cartoonist Ralph Stein was brought in to work with Zaboly, and in 1958 Bud Sagendorf took over the writing and drawing, a job he had sought for twenty years while working on art assignments for King Features. He had been Segar's assistant in the 1930s, starting the job while in high school.

In the mid-1980s onetime underground cartoonist Bobby London assumed the daily strip. In the 2010s *Thimble Theatre* runs in a handful of papers around the world. The daily strip consists of reprints of Sagendorf's material; only the Sunday page, drawn by Hy Eisman, offers new material. In 2004, the seventy-fifth anniversary of Popeye's creation, Fox Primetime televised a new special, *Popeye's Voyage—The Quest for Pappy*, the first time computer-generated imagery (CGI) had been used to animate Segar's characters.

Ron Goulart

SEE ALSO: *Animated Films; Big Little Books; Buck Rogers; CGI; Comics; Saturday Morning Cartoons; Superman; Television; Toys.*

BIBLIOGRAPHY

Marschall, Richard. *America's Great Comic Strip Artists.* New York: Abbeville Press, 1989.

O'Brien, Richard. *The Story of American Toys.* New York: Artabras, 1990.

Sagendorf, Bud, and Craig Yoe. *Popeye: The Great Comic Book*

Tales of Bud Sagendorf. San Diego: IDW Publishing, 2011.
Segar, E. C. *Popeye.* Seattle, WA: Fantagraphics Books, 2006.

Popsicles

Popsicles, a confection made of fruit-flavored liquid frozen on a stick, are a classic American treat. The ancestor of the Popsicle, the Hokey-Pokey, appeared in the 1870s, sold by the Ross and Robbins company. In 1924 Frank Epperson, a powdered lemonade vendor from California, patented a more fully realized version of the product, which he originally named the Epsicle. He then sold his patent to the Joe Lowe Corporation, which became Popsicle Industries.

The chief Popsicle flavors were grape, orange, and cherry. Later variations of the product included the Creamsicle, Fudgsicle, Twin Pop, and Bomb Pop, which helped keep neighborhood ice cream trucks such as Skippy and Good Humor in business. What made the Popsicle line distinctive was the inclusion of a flat wooden stick that allowed the frozen confections to be eaten like lollipops. Consumers saved these sticks to use for craft projects, making everything from baskets and boxes to lamp bases. In the 2010s Popsicle sold around two billion ice pops each year.

Wendy Woloson

SEE ALSO: *Ice Cream Cone.*

BIBLIOGRAPHY

Dickson, Paul. *The Great American Ice Cream Book.* New York: Atheneum, 1972.

Popular Mechanics

Since 1902 *Popular Mechanics* has been published as a monthly magazine that describes the wonders of twentieth-century technology for the lay reader in a "gee-whiz" style, with do-it-yourself home-workshop projects thrown in for good measure. Debuting just a year before the Wright Brothers' flight at Kitty Hawk, when automobiles and motion pictures were still recent innovations, *Popular Mechanics* has chronicled the breakthroughs of the most productive century in the history of science and mechanics. The periodical made its appearance in Chicago in January 1902 as *Popular Mechanics* and did not become *Popular Mechanics Magazine* until 1913, by which time it had already absorbed another small technical publication by the name of *Technical World.* Its readership grew from only five subscribers in 1902, plus a few readers paying five cents a copy at the newsstand, to a worldwide circulation of 1,428,356 by 1998. In 1947 a Spanish-language edition (*Mecanica Popular*) was produced, along with several other foreign-language editions in French, Danish, and Swedish.

EARLY DAYS UNDER FOUNDER HENRY HAVEN WINDSOR SR.

The story of its founding tells as much about American ingenuity as its content. *Popular Mechanics Magazine* was founded by Henry Haven Windsor Sr., a former city editor of the Marshalltown, Iowa, newspaper and the son of an Iowa minister. A strong advocate of science and mechanics, Windsor saw the need for a periodical that could present clearly written technical material to the average man (*Popular Mechanics* continued its focus on a male readership into the 1990s). Prior to his work as founder and editor of *Popular Mechanics*, Windsor had worked for the Chicago City Railway Company in the 1880s. There he started a trade magazine, the *Street Railway Review*, which he edited from 1892 to 1901. Researching articles for the *Review*, Windsor once spent six months disguised as an operator of an old-fashioned grip car so he could acquire firsthand understanding of the problems of operators.

Windsor brought this same passion for mechanical detail and technical know-how to *Popular Mechanics.* Initially he wrote every article and sold every advertisement for the fledgling sixteen-page weekly, which by 1904 had grown to one hundred pages. Its rapid growth in both size and circulation was testimony to Windsor's vision for the magazine and his ability to tap into a previously unrecognized market. After Windsor died in 1924, the magazine remained under the control and editorship of the Windsor family through several generations. It became part of the Hearst Corporation in the mid-1950s.

Although developments in science and technology spawned other successful publications, such as the earlier *Popular Science*

Popular Mechanics *1956.* *A 1956 issue of* Popular Mechanics *includes an article on rocket technology, a common topic for the times.* APIC/GETTY IMAGES.

Monthly (1872) and *Mechanics Illustrated* (1928), followed by *Science Digest*, *Popular Homecraft*, *Popular Electronics*, and others, none gained the wide appeal of *Popular Mechanics Magazine*. During World War II the magazine was popular among American GIs, who sometimes wrote letters home to request that family members respond to job-training advertisements for them, in anticipation of their return to civilian life. With its practical, down-to-earth, hands-on advice; its focus on "how-to" articles; its clear writing and copious illustrations, the periodical's success lay in its narrow focus, appealing directly to the independent, do-it-yourself reader. With its slogan, "Written So You Can Understand It," *Popular Mechanics* strove to appeal to the general, nonacademic reader who wanted to read about new "modern" advances during the golden years of American science and technology. The publication was also famous during these years for its classified ads section, which offered hundreds of money-making schemes every month, ranging from home locksmithing equipment to furniture building kits to such "untechnical" pursuits as songwriting, stuffing envelopes, and selling patent medicine nostrums.

CONTENT DEVELOPMENT IN LATER YEARS

Especially from the 1930s through the 1950s, *Popular Mechanics* anticipated developments in astronautics by publishing futuristic articles that offered hints about the evolution of rocket science and space exploration, some of which were dismissed as speculative "Buck Rogers" fiction but that were later proven to have been prescient. During the 1970s, when the omnipotence of science and technology began to fade in the minds of some Americans, the magazine and others like it were criticized by environmentalists and others for advancing a worldview based on technological domination of the planet and the exploitation of nonrenewable resources. In the 1980s *Popular Mechanics* devoted many pages to covering new developments in consumer electronics and personal computers. By the end of the 1990s the magazine was featuring such articles as "Half Man, Half Machine: New Breakthroughs in Bionics Perfect Battery-Powered Eyes, Ears, Limbs and Muscles," as well as buyers' guides to new cars and trucks, new lawn mowers, and gardening tools. These articles reflected perspectives of the late twentieth century, with awareness of current breakthroughs in medical technology as well as attention to consumer information.

Since its beginnings, a distinctive feature of *Popular Mechanics* has been its emphasis on "descriptive illustration." As Roland E. Wolseley points out in *Understanding Magazines*, Henry Windsor issued a policy statement when he founded the publication: "Most magazines use illustrated articles. We do not. We use described pictures." At the end of the 1990s, articles in *Popular Mechanics* remained profusely illustrated with detailed analyses of machine parts and step-by-step procedures for everything from replacing roof shingles to performing periodic washing machine maintenance.

In the late 1990s Joe Oldham was editor-in-chief of *Popular Mechanics Magazine*, which by then had its own website, called "PM. Zone," and a television version of *Popular Mechanics for Kids*. Offering a detailed chronicle of mechanical and technological innovation throughout the twentieth century, the magazine was as familiar to working- and middle-class Americans as *Harper's Weekly*, with its illustrated coverage of the Civil War, had been to those of the nineteenth century.

During the first decades of the twenty-first century, *Popular Mechanics* continued to adjust itself to changes within the culture, offering readers digital options in addition to its traditional print version of the journal. These included an iPad digital edition, smart phone apps, blogs, videos on its website, and a free newsletter. The journal maintained its traditional focus on automotive care, science, technology, home improvement, and outdoor recreation. In the first and second decades of the millennium, the magazine published its traditional "DIY," or "do-it-yourself," projects with an appeal to working- and middle-class audiences, particularly targeting men. Articles published in 2011 included "How to Brew Beer," "100 Skills Every Man Should Know," and "Build Your Own Garden Shed from PM (Popular Mechanics) Plans." Its steadfast focus on practical, hands-on advice and information, along with its embrace of new technologies, helped to expand its circulation. The publication had by then become part of Hearst Communication, Inc., and maintained itself as part of the Hearst Men's Network.

Lolly Ockerstrom

SEE ALSO: *Advertising; Automobile; Blogging; Buck Rogers; DIY/Home Improvement; Environmentalism;* Harper's; *iPad; Lawn Care/Gardening; Smart Phones; World War II.*

BIBLIOGRAPHY

Mott, Frank Luther. *A History of American Magazines, 1885–1905*. Cambridge, MA: Harvard University Press, 1957.

Peterson, Theodore Bernard. *Magazines in the Twentieth Century*. Urbana: University of Illinois Press, 1956.

Wolseley, Roland E. *Understanding Magazines*, 2nd ed. Ames: Iowa State University Press, 1969.

Popular Psychology

Popular psychology springs from the search for inspiration and self-improvement in a secular form. This search accounted for some of the success of the eighteenth-century best seller *Poor Richard's Almanack*, through which Benjamin Franklin conveyed proverbs and aphorisms about human nature along with weather reports and other practical information. By the time psychology emerged as a discipline in the 1880s and 1890s, the United States already had a sizable reading public that readily consumed literature on self-improvement and the "gospel of success," and there was also a strong market for spiritualism and mental healing. Books and articles of popular psychology merged easily into two streams, one secular and the other metaphysical, because they aimed to provide an understanding of the mind's workings that could be used either for practical self-improvement or for more mystical psychic explorations.

It is clear that many of the same problems and goals of contemporary Americans were already well articulated in the early decades of the twentieth century. Then, as now, the quest for inner reserves of power and tranquility, for methods of maximizing energy and efficiency, and for solutions to vexatious emotional problems has fueled the engine of popular psychology. Yet there are discernible phases and eras of popular psychology, which reflect significant changes in American society and culture.

RELIGION, RELAXATION, AND EFFICIENCY

Although psychology detached itself from religion when it became an academic discipline, popular psychology maintained a fairly close relationship with the religious lives of Americans. This connection was visible from the start. William James, the most influential of all American psychologists, believed in mesmerism, the practice of inducing a trance in order to open the mind of the subject to extrasensory perceptions and healing forces. Mesmerism in America yielded a very popular mind-cure philosophy that predisposed Americans to consider psychology a means for tapping unconscious psychic forces for the general betterment of the person.

The phenomenal 1897 best seller *In Tune with the Infinite* by Ralph Waldo Trine exemplified this "transcendentalist" strain of American popular thought. Until the appearance of the not dissimilar *Power of Positive Thinking* (1952) by Norman Vincent Peale, Trine's book was the best-selling inspirational book of the twentieth century. In it, the author offers his readers peace of mind through a meditative, ecumenical approach for achieving psychic oneness with God. Though not a book of psychology, *In Tune with the Infinite* draws on the concept of the unconscious as a deep spiritual reservoir. Trine urges the reader "to come into the full realization of your own awakened interior powers": "There is a mystic force that transcends the powers of the intellect and likewise of the body. There are certain faculties that we have that are not a part of the active, thinking mind. . . . Through them we have intuitions, impulses, leadings, that instead of being merely the occasional, *should be the normal and habitual*."

As formally trained psychologists, neurologists, and psychiatrists entered the fray of popular literature, they often seemed to be saying much the same thing, but in a secular form and with titles that were less ethereal, more "scientific," or simply more dull. *Directing Mental Energy* (1927) by Francis Aveling, for example, a book whose jacket carries the supertitle "The Business of Thinking," aims to help readers "economize" their mental and emotional energy so as to lead more productive and satisfying lives. "The successful man or woman of today," the book's promotional copy reads, "must know how to organize every ounce of energy to meet the pressure of our complicated existence."

Efficiency in the use of one's inner resources and relaxation of an overtaxed body and mind were common themes of psychological self-help books, all of which were based on the premise that Americans were coping with a complex and nerve-wracking civilization. The words *nervous* and *nerves* frequently appeared in the titles of this literature. Some of the most popular books of the 1920s, 1930s, and 1940s were neurologist Abraham Myerson's *The Nervous Housewife* (1920), psychiatrist Josephine Jackson's *Outwitting Our Nerves* (1921), and psychiatrist David Harold Fink's *Release from Nervous Tension* (1943). These authors aimed to help their readers cope with anxiety, insomnia, exhaustion, boredom, and depression, problems that were linked to the peculiar demands of America's fast-paced, competitive, work-oriented, and technologically driven society.

JOSEPH JASTROW

The genesis of popular psychology can be observed partly through the career of Joseph Jastrow, the first person to receive a Ph.D. in psychology in the United States and a pioneer of the discipline. Born in Warsaw, Poland, in 1863 and raised in Philadelphia, Jastrow was the son of a prominent rabbi and Talmud scholar. Studying with Charles S. Peirce and G. Stanley Hall, he completed his Ph.D. in psychology at Johns Hopkins in 1886 and went on to the University of Wisconsin, where he set up one of the nation's first and best psychology laboratories. At the Chicago World's Fair of 1893, Jastrow and Hugo Munsterberg, a pioneer of applied psychology, made the first big public demonstration of modern psychology. The two men set up an apparatus to measure various mental responses and distributed an explanatory pamphlet. For a nominal fee, visitors tried out the testing laboratory and learned something about their mental characteristics.

From the beginning of his career, Jastrow regularly wrote on psychological topics for magazines, but his fame as a popular psychologist was rooted in the 1920s and 1930s, when he wrote syndicated newspaper advice columns based on psychology. These became the basis of two popular books, *Keeping Mentally Fit* (1928) and *Piloting Your Life* (1930). Jastrow also hosted a radio program on this subject for NBC from 1935 to 1938. His writing and speaking encompassed all aspects of the field and offer a glimpse of the prevailing attitudes toward psychology at the time. Jastrow authored a book, *The House That Freud Built* (1932), for the general public on the theories of Freud but was not a Freudian himself. Like many psychologists, as opposed to psychoanalysts, Jastrow preferred to discuss the facts produced by tests of perception and cognition rather than to wander into grand theories of childhood sexuality.

JASTROW'S PSYCHOLOGY

One of the purposes Jastrow set for himself, and one that typified books of psychology for laypeople, was to puncture myths and weigh generalizations with data. Are bright children weaklings? Do school leaders make good? Are city children brighter?—these were the sort of questions being answered by citing the latest studies of aptitude and achievement. A second goal of Jastrow's work was simply to explain psychological categories that had come into vogue, such as "complex" and "repression," and to give an explanation of such everyday phenomena as absentmindedness, fatigue, anxiety over dreams, and sexual self-consciousness.

The most obvious defect of these "genres" of popular psychology, even in the hands of an eminent scholar such as Jastrow, was their tendency to degenerate into glibness and conviviality. For example, in *Keeping Mentally Fit* Jastrow answered one young woman's appeal for advice about her "sex-consciousness" with the jest that men cannot really understand the way women think about sex: "A man can have only the man's sense of this sex relation, and he sees nothing in other men to get excited about. He isn't blind to the fact that women find men attractive, and he tries to see some compliment in it to himself; he doesn't get much farther than recognizing it as an amiable weakness of women."

By far the overriding theme of Jastrow's psychology, and of many of his contemporaries, was the need for emotional self-control and proper social adjustment to one's work, community, and family. The mental hygiene movement of the Progressive Era and the 1920s emphasized bodily integrity through exercise and diet, emotional integrity through relaxation, and mental integrity through proper self-assessment and concentration on one's tasks. Americans were dedicated enough to an optimistic philosophy of efficiency and advancement, both personal and social, that they managed to transform even Freudianism in their own image, deleting its atheism and pessimism and making it another program for social betterment.

Freud's notion of sublimation, whereby unruly impulses were applied to productive endeavors, was easily compatible with the psychology of usefulness. Whereas child psychology underscored the value of giving children freedom to express themselves, particularly through constructive play, Jastrow's generation nonetheless emphasized the dangers of the self-indulgent personality type. "For efficiency and happiness we must have emotional control," advised the 1929 book *The Healthy Mind: Mental Hygiene for Adults*, edited by Henry Elkind:

> The angry man cannot think clearly; the man in fear of losing his job does poor work. . . . The infant, a complete tyrant, absolutely selfish, is a model exhibition of anger, or fear and of most of the undesirable emotions. He has to learn control of his responses through social pressure. That is the object of modern education—the comfortable adjustment of the individual to his surroundings.

POSTWAR PSYCHOLOGICAL TRENDS

Popular psychology entered a second phase of popularity in the 1940s, catalyzed by World War II. As had happened in World War I, the reality of war-related mental disorders—"psychoneuroses," as they were known—stimulated great public interest in the workings of the mind and their effect on the soul. Sympathetic to the plight of GIs who returned home troubled by insomnia, nightmares, nervousness, and malaise, the American public showed not only a heightened interest in psychology but also a greater appreciation of its usefulness for normal people experiencing temporary or occasional problems. Popular magazines ran feature stories candidly conveying the emotional effects of war on fighting men and approving the soldiers' need to express their emotions by crying when necessary. Psychologist Abraham Sperling began his 1946 book *Psychology for the Millions* by discussing this new phenomenon: "The model of courageous behavior is no longer portrayed by a stoic, tight-lipped, muscle-bound he-man. . . . The supposed hard-bitten soldier bares his soul and is that much better off for it." *Psychology for the Millions*, in its praise of the new emotional openness of Americans, reflected the rising sophistication about psychology and the more exuberant self-expression that characterized American society beginning in the 1920s.

The psychology boom of the 1940s was perhaps most obvious in its penetration of religious inspirational literature. The postwar therapeutic age was heralded in 1946 by an immensely popular book on psychology that was written not by a psychologist but by a clergyman, Rabbi Joshua Loth Liebman. The book, *Peace of Mind*, sold 1.5 million copies in a few years, preaching a new creed in which an optimistic neo-Freudian psychology, based on the work of Karen Horney and Alfred Adler, teamed up with religion to help Americans overcome angst and personal problems en route to spiritual fulfillment. Liebman believed in the power of modern psychotherapy to cure ills that had befuddled traditional religion, and in this belief he was joined by two of the most influential Protestant ministers of the century, Harry Emerson Fosdick and Norman Vincent Peale.

FOSDICK AND PEALE

Fosdick and Peale had begun to introduce psychology into their pastoral counseling in the 1930s, and along with Liebman, they helped disseminate it to millions of people in the 1940s and 1950s. It was significant that both were members of the clergy, for their audience included many people who might not otherwise have considered psychology a legitimate resource. Fosdick's *On Being a Real Person* (1943) was based on actual cases of people who came for pastoral counseling. The book, Fosdick hoped, would describe the "familiar mental and emotional maladies" of ordinary people, "their alibis and rationalizations, their ingenious, unconscious tricks of evasion and escape, their handling of fear, anxiety, guilt, and humiliation, their compensations and sublimations also, and the positive faiths and resources from which I have seen help come."

Peale, the best-selling inspirational writer of the century, collaborated with a psychiatrist for the popular 1950 book *The Art of Real Happiness*, which, following the lead of Liebman's *Peace of Mind*, showed how psychological insight and religious guidance could solve personal problems. Like Fosdick, Peale discusses real cases, frankly presenting stories of guilt and neurosis induced by repressed sexuality and repressed anger, as well as family harmony ruined by alcoholism, and inundating his readers with uplifting accounts of people overcoming obstacles through prayerful concentration. Peale's 1948 *A Guide to Confident Living*, which went through thirty-five printings in seven years, was promoted as a "book of workable spiritual prescriptions [that] used the principles of religion and modern psychiatry to bring practical help and new hope to millions of readers."

DRAWING ON NEW INFLUENCES

In the 1960s and 1970s Peale's blend of Christianity and psychology found a competitor in a "countercultural" mélange of Eastern meditation, consciousness-raising, and humanistic and Gestalt psychology. Instead of concentrating on the Book of Psalms and the Gospel, some Americans strove for a "Zen mind" and "peak experiences." The venerable American belief in the great hidden capacities of the mind, in a subconsciousness in which the mental and the spiritual could be unified, transformed from "the power of positive thinking" to "transcendental meditation." Peale's positive thinking was supposed to produce public success, not just peace of mind. The meditationist trend of the 1960s and 1970s, however, rejected social convention and focused intensely on the state of the mind. At its most extreme, this trend was personified by psychologist Timothy Leary.

Leary's idiosyncratic career started with the prestigious job of directing the Kaiser Foundation Hospital of Oakland, California. Swept up by the current of the times and by experiments with hallucinogenic drugs, Leary quit his practice to preach to American youth about a new drug-based psycho-spiritual creed: "Turn on, tune in, drop out." The college-oriented youth culture produced wide-ranging demands for a new psychology of insight and growth, whether through the fiction of Hermann Hesse's *Journey to the East* (1964) or *Siddhartha* (first published in the United States in 1951), Richard Bach's quirky best seller *Jonathan Livingston Seagull* (1970), the lectures and writings of Zen disseminator Alan Watts, or the holistic and growth-oriented theories of Gestalt and humanistic psychology. Gestalt therapists introduced the "holistic" theory into American awareness, and the founders of humanistic psychology, especially Abraham Maslow, purveyed the concepts of "self-actualization" and "peak experiences." These ideas gained currency fairly rapidly in the 1960s and 1970s because they conformed to the era's optimistic, almost utopian, expectations of human growth and potential.

In the 1980s and 1990s popular psychology took another turn, this time back toward religion and physiology, both of which were predominant interests at the start of the twentieth century. M. Scott Peck, a psychiatrist with a strong Christian orientation, wrote one of the biggest best sellers of the late twentieth century. *The Road Less Traveled: A New Psychology of Love, Traditional Values and Spiritual Growth* first appeared in 1978 and stayed on the *New York Times* nonfiction best-seller list until the early 1990s. Peck merged psychoanalytic and humanistic insights with a strong commitment to lasting relationships of marriage and family. Turning away from the idealization of the self that was apparent in the popular psychology of the 1960s, he insisted that to love another person required emotional self-discipline, an ability to subordinate one's immediate gratification to the spiritual needs of another.

These decades also saw another type of traditionalist return to biology. After several generations dominated by environmentalist approaches, psychologists reasserted the importance of biochemical processes in the brain. Peter D. Kramer's *Listening to Prozac* (1993) was the most popular exposition of the new evidence for physical sources of depression, one that mirrored and stimulated the sudden popularity of Prozac and other antidepressants. Public fascination with the neurology of the brain surfaced in the 1980s with Oliver Sacks's *The Man Who Mistook His Wife for a Hat and Other Clinical Tales* (1985), which detailed case histories of people whose relationships and identities were derailed by discrete forms of brain damage or dysfunction.

RELATIONSHIPS AND RECOVERY

The close of the twentieth century also witnessed a flowering of psychology books on interpersonal communication between men and women, such as John Gray's *Men Are from Mars, Women Are from Venus* (1992), and Deborah Tannen's *That's Not What I Meant!* (1986) and *You Just Don't Understand!* (1990). Counterpoised to the emphasis on biological roots of behavior, these books emphasize the social and cultural bases of gender differences in language. Interpersonal communication—"getting along with others"—had long been an interest of American popular psychology, although these books show a new sensitivity to the role of gender differences.

There was, however, one completely new development that has defined much of contemporary American popular psychology. This is the literature of "recovery"—meaning recovery from addictions. Rooted in the twelve-step program of Alcoholics Anonymous (AA), a unique American organization founded in the 1930s, the concept of addiction expanded in the 1980s to include not only substance abuse—alcohol and drugs—but also other kinds of deeply ingrained, habitual behavior ranging from temper tantrums to sexual obsessiveness. Although the addiction idea has undoubtedly been stretched too far, the AA model for coping with seriously troubled people has proved magnetic.

Merging with the newly popular idea of "dysfunctional families," the AA model of recovery produced a separate psychotherapeutic literature that counsels individuals on how to maintain their own dignity while involved with "out-of-control" friends and family members. The twelve-step idea is grounded in a nonsectarian monotheistic creed and therefore represents a unique fusion of self-help and religion. As addicts came increasingly into the domain of psychiatric rehabilitation centers during and after the 1960s, the grassroots AA approach was adapted by psychiatrists such as Abraham Twerski. Founder of a rehabilitation center in Pennsylvania, Twerski, a Hasidic rabbi, wrote a number of popular books on recovery in the 1980s and 1990s. Like Peck, he blended traditional religious values with therapeutic insights.

The existence of celebrity psychologists made a comeback in the first decade of the 2000s, spurred by popular television shows and twenty-four-hour news coverage, which used psychologists as guest experts. Perhaps the epitome of this phenomenon is Dr. Phil McGraw, a psychologist who first gained national attention in the late 1990s by appearing regularly on *The Oprah Winfrey Show*. Dr. Phil, as he is commonly known, launched his own program in 2002 and has become well loved for his blunt, practical approach, which claims to offer real solutions rather than psychobabble or in-depth psychotherapy. The new millennium has brought American popular psychology full circle with intense public interest in psychological healing.

Andrew R. Heinze

SEE ALSO: *Brothers, Dr. Joyce; Depression; Freud, Sigmund; Leary, Timothy; McGraw, Dr. Phil; Peale, Norman Vincent; Prozac; Psychedelia; Twelve-Step Programs; Winfrey, Oprah; World War I; World War II; World's Fairs.*

BIBLIOGRAPHY

Aveling, Francis. *Directing Mental Energy*. New York: George H. Doran, 1927.

Cordón, Luis A. *Popular Psychology: An Encyclopedia*. Westport, CT: Greenwood, 2005.

Elkind, Henry. *The Healthy Mind: Mental Hygiene for Adults*. New York: Greenberg, 1929.

Fosdick, Harry Emerson. *On Being a Real Person*. New York: Harper & Bros., 1943.

Fuller, Robert C. *Americans and the Unconscious*. New York: Oxford University Press, 1986.

Hale, Nathan G. *The Rise and Crisis of Psychoanalysis in the United States: Freud and the Americans, 1917–1985*. New York: Oxford University Press, 1995.

Holifield, E. Brooks. *A History of Pastoral Care in America: From Salvation to Self-Realization*. Nashville, TN: Abingdon Press, 1983.

Jastrow, Joseph. *Keeping Mentally Fit*. Garden City, NY: Garden City Publishing, 1928.

Meyer, Donald B. *The Positive Thinkers: A Study of the American Quest for Health, Wealth and Personal Power from Mary Baker Eddy to Norman Vincent Peale*. New York: Doubleday, 1965.

Peale, Norman Vincent. *A Guide to Confident Living*. New York: Prentice Hall, 1948.

Rieff, Philip. *The Triumph of the Therapeutic: Uses of Faith after Freud*. New York: Harper and Row, 1966.

Sperling, Abraham Paul. *Psychology for the Millions*. New York: Frederick Fell, 1946.

Trine, Ralph Waldo. *In Tune with the Infinite*. New York: Dodd, Mead, 1897.

Pop-Up Restaurants

Pop-up, or temporary restaurants, are fully functional restaurants established in nonfixed locations for brief periods of time. Most pop-ups rely on a good location, solid financing, well-known chefs, seasoned staff, and aggressive marketing tactics to draw customers. They may be set up almost anywhere, including private homes, closed restaurants, empty warehouses, or virtually any vacant area imaginable. If no kitchens are on site, food carts or pods are imported. These restaurants advertise their locale and their hours through social media sites such as Facebook and Twitter or through blogs, such as the one devoted to pop-up restaurants by TasteTV, that are devoted to keeping patrons up to date. This type of dining venue became popular in major metropolitan areas such as New York, San Francisco, and London in the first decade of the 2000s. London's *Independent* explains in a June 4, 2009, review that the lure of pop-ups is "a return to real eating, when dining out was a social event worth dressing up for and getting excited about, and food was about fresh, seasonal ingredients cooked well but without gimmickry."

One of the most famous pop-up ventures is the New York City–based Guerrilla Culinary Brigade, established in 2010 by veteran hospitality marketer Alan Philips, a regular contributor to famed Zagat restaurant guides, and professional caterer Jason Apfelbaum, whose clients include Google, Audi, Dreamworks, and NBC. On its website the Guerrilla Culinary Brigade promises "one-of-a-kind, memorable culinary and social moments" that are the result of what the group somewhat mysteriously refers to as a combination of "underground culinary tactics along with extraordinary imagination, the element of surprise, and astonishing mobility." The Brigade staged a number of successful pop-up experiences in Lower Manhattan, including a four-night extravaganza called The Hunger, which took place in the Yard at the Soho Grand Hotel and featured the cooking of *Top Chef* contestant Camille Becerra.

Pop-ups also grant new, less-experienced chefs an opportunity to showcase their skills without the risk and expense of opening a standard restaurant. Such events typically feature innovative cuisine in a fresh, transitory environment, and if done properly, allow the creators to ply their trade in a way that ensures maximum gain and minimal loss, a ratio seldom achieved in the full-fledged restaurant experience. Young chefs often hold these events to showcase their talent in the hope of securing funding for permanent restaurants.

This concept of creating a dining experience out of thin air has inspired several television shows, including *Restaurant Impossible*, where Chef Robert Irvine seeks out failing restaurants to infiltrate and revamp in a two-day period on a $10,000 budget. Other food-oriented TV shows such as *Top Chef* and *MasterChef* put inexperienced professional and home chefs in similar situations, where they are forced to create fresh cuisine in a fixed amount of time for the sake of competition.

Ron Horton

SEE ALSO: *Celebrity Chefs; Facebook; Foodies; Google; Social Media;* Top Chef; *Twitter.*

BIBLIOGRAPHY

"Everyone Back to Mine: Pop-Up Restaurants in Private Homes Are the Latest Foodie Fad." *Independent* (London), June 4, 2009.

Miller, Laurel. "Pop-Up Restaurants: Dining for a New Decade." Gadling. Accessed May 2012. Available from http://www.gadling.com/2011/04/28/pop-up-restaurants-dining-for-a-new-decade/

Pornography

Sweeping technological change has ushered in revolutionary change in the way human beings create, distribute, and consume pornography. Part of that revolution may be seen to have largely resolved the century-long debate about the role of pornography in American society. Despite years of social crusades and legal and political wrangling, America remained, in the early twenty-first century, deeply conflicted about how to handle the "problem" posed by the existence of pornography, which *Webster's International Dictionary* defines as "the depiction of erotic behavior (as in pictures or writing) intended to cause sexual excitement." To some, any mention or depiction of human sexuality is pornographic and should be censored; to others, no depiction of human sexuality, no matter how "perverse," should be forbidden to adults (with the exception of child pornography, which no one defends). Supreme Court Justice Potter Stewart's enigmatic 1964 statement on pornography perhaps best captured the opinion of most Americans concerning pornography: in his comment regarding *Jacobellis v. Ohio*, Stewart acknowledged that while he couldn't define pornography precisely, "I know it when I see it."

ONLY FOR THE WEALTHY

Pornography—long a luxury product for the wealthy—has always existed in the United States, undergoing several important changes ending in the late twentieth century. Up until the middle part of the 1800s, the costs of production and widely imposed social, religious, and cultural prohibitions against pornographic materials kept such materials largely hidden. Early pornography was considered either literary or artistic, and such materials tended to circulate among the literate and well-to-do, who tended not to worry about their corrupting effects. Several factors combined to put pornography into the hands of the growing working and lower classes that, according to their social "betters," were unable to fend off pornography's corrupting influence.

Technology, chiefly the invention of cheap printing and great improvements in transportation, allowed inexpensive sexually explicit images to be made available to the masses. This was piggy-backed on the emergence of mass merchandizing and the use of sales catalogs, sometimes with overly graphic sections that aided in distribution. Next, the invention and spread of arcade devices and eventually the cinema brought the display of human sexuality to ever-larger markets. After that, the revolution of VCRs and commercial exploitation of video rental and ownership brought pornographic viewing to the domestic setting. Finally, the explosive availability and growth of home computers (and access to the Internet) both made it easy and secure to view pornography and, at the same time, destroyed the traditional means of profiting from its creation and sale.

THE SPREAD OF PORNOGRAPHY

America's legal and social relationship with pornography is easily traced. The vastly increased immigration of non-Protestant peoples and the concentration of the working class in urban centers in the late nineteenth century, combined with the expansion of printing operations and the rise in sex trades in cities, all helped to alarm the middle-class Protestant Americans concerned with their lack of control over the direction of American culture. By the turn of the century, a number of forms of pornography became widely available, including French postcards featuring pictures of nude women; flip books (small, multipage booklets that revealed an "animated" sex act as the pages flipped by); and, by 1904, the first calendar featuring scantily clad women. As such materials became available to an emerging urban "underclass" no longer willing to subscribe to the moral dictates of a moralizing middle- and upper-class Protestant establishment, pornography emerged as a problem that required the attention of reformers and the arbitration of lawyers.

The last half of the nineteenth century saw the growth of numerous reform movements in the United States (as in other industrializing nations). Reform groups, typically led by middle-class Protestant women, worked hard to improve the quality of life for urban workers swarming in their crowded warrens. Especially during the Progressive Era, reform-minded activists sought safe workplaces and humane work hours, especially for children; improved educational opportunity; and the suppression of "dissipating" pastimes such as gaming, festive drinking, and what was called at the time "whoring." The reformers sought to change notions of women's clothing, duties, and rights and lobbied for women's suffrage. Through the good agency of these reformers, school attendance was mandated; parks were established; and drinking hours, human sexual interaction, and hunting seasons were under strict schedules.

PORNOGRAPHY AND THE LAW

Whereas social reformers, claiming that the consumption of pornography did individual or social harm, sought to remove or criminalize the forums in which pornography might circulate, prosecutors and lawyers struggled to define what exactly was meant by terms such as *obscenity* and *pornography*. For years, U.S. obscenity law (which covered pornography) relied on the English case *Regina v. Hicklin* (1868), which overtly supported class, race, and sex divisions. It stated that obscenity be determined by "whether . . . [its] tendency . . . [was] to deprave and corrupt those whose minds [were] open to such immoral influences, and into whose hands a publication of this sort may fall." This benchmark thus assumed that a small group of morally superior people were capable of setting the standards of what was obscene for their social inferiors. Such a standard may have made sense within a rigidly defined social and class structure, but it ran counter to the very freedoms on which the American democracy was based, savaged the First Amendment, and abridged both the letter and spirit of the Constitution as a whole. Technically, it was so unnecessarily broad that even academic or scientific discussion about almost any sexual topic could be suppressed. Supreme Court Justice Felix Frankfurter once opined that the case tended to "reduce the adult population . . . to reading what is fit for children."

The first major case that aimed to clarify the legal standing of pornography was the now famous *Roth v. United States*. The 1957 ruling attempted to establish a uniform and constant standard for determining obscenity. As the result of the case, a three-part test was developed to determine whether what was under examination did, in fact, have a realistic tendency to excite lust or lustful thought and thus should be censored. According to *Roth*, the key to dissemination was "whether to the average person, applying contemporary community standards, the dominant theme of the material taken as a whole appeals to prurient interest." Despite the best efforts of the Court, the ambiguity concerning the terms *dominant theme, community standards*, and *prurient interest* meant that the issue was far from being resolved.

Subsequent rulings added to the *Roth* decision. In *Jacobellis v. Ohio* (1964), the Supreme Court added another requirement to the legal definition by declaring that to be pornographic the material must be "utterly without redeeming social value." Publishers of such magazines as *Playboy* and its many (and often more raunchy) imitators learned that as long as they published articles with some redeeming value, their work as a whole, though it contained images of nudity, would not be deemed pornographic. But the legal resolution of just such a case—*Miller v. California* (1973)—brought about the most elaborate ruling on obscenity yet issued by the Supreme Court. In addition to the *Roth* language, *Miller* offered as a standard that the work in question "depicts or describes in a patently offensive way . . . sexual conduct specifically defined by the applicable law" and "that a reasonable person would find that the work, taken as a whole, lacks serious literary, artistic, political, and scientific value." Chief Justice Warren Burger further clarified the ruling by explaining that the Court meant only to restrict hard-core materials from constitutional protection.

The *Miller* ruling, together with the ongoing sexual revolution that had begun in the 1960s and that generally increased the nation's tolerance for sexual material, meant that most pornographic works (excluding child pornography) were now extended First Amendment protections and that pornographers could safely produce and distribute their works.

PORNOGRAPHY AND MEDIA

The major forums for pornography produced in the twentieth century were magazines and films. The first pornographic magazines appeared in the United States and England during the Victorian era, and an odd pulp called *Captain Billy's Whiz Bang* published French postcards in its pages in the early 1920s, but it wasn't until the publication of *Esquire* in 1933 that a mass-market magazine began to offer pictures of scantily clad women. *Esquire*'s Varga and Petty girls wore only the briefest and flimsiest of clothes, but they were meant to be respectable. *Playboy* trumped *Esquire* when, beginning in 1953, it began to publish nude photographs of wholesome American girls next door. *Playboy* opened the door for the "girlie" magazine in America, and such imitators as *Penthouse*, *Oui*, *Dude*, *Gent*, and others soon followed. The raunchiest of the girlie magazines, and the only one to truly push the now-loosened definitions of obscenity, was Larry Flynt's *Hustler*.

The presentation of nudity on film also has a long history. Early silent films, including D. W. Griffith's *Intolerance* (1916), sometimes presented brief flickers of nudity, and imported stag films showed much more. But the motion picture Production Code administered by Will Hays successfully barred any mention or depiction of sexuality in major motion pictures for several decades beginning in the 1930s. Truly pornographic films, first imported and then domestically produced, first caught on in the 1960s, where they were shown in adult theaters and in the homes of those with a movie projector. With the advent of the VCR, the pornographic video industry boomed—410 million adult videos were rented in 1991 alone, according to one study. Moreover, images once considered pornographic were by the 1980s and 1990s a regular feature in popular films and even on television.

The widespread availability of pornography beginning in the late 1960s and early 1970s reinvigorated the opponents of pornography. Concerned with whether pornography indeed promoted social problems, the U.S. Congress in 1967 formed the National Commission on Obscenity and Pornography to study the problem. The commission's 1970 findings stated that, according to available data, regulating pornography and obscenity was not a matter of national importance. Further, it recommended that "federal, state, and local legislation prohibiting the sale, exhibition and distribution of sexual materials to consenting adults should be repealed," except in the cases of child pornography. Seventeen of the nineteen commission members concluded that "empirical research designed to clarify the question has found no evidence to date that exposure to explicit sexual material plays a significant role in the causation of delinquent or criminal behavior among youth or adults."

THE MEESE COMMISSION

The findings of the commission, which had been appointed by then-President Lyndon Johnson, enraged President Richard Nixon, who denounced the commission as "morally bankrupt." Other conservatives followed suit, and the commission's findings were largely disregarded and led to no new legislation. Under the even more socially conservative administration of Ronald Reagan in the 1980s, another commission was established to study the "scourge" of pornography. Attorney General Edwin Meese's commission set out to study the effects of pornography on the American people and, according to *Pornography: Debating the Issues* author Ted Gottfried, "to figure out ways to stop it from spreading without stepping on rights guaranteed by the Constitution." The highly publicized commission findings charged that exposure to pornography led to "antisocial acts of sexual violence" and to other "non-violent forms of discrimination against . . . women," among other evils.

The diametrically opposed findings of these two government commissions made one thing clear: after almost three decades of research, no consistent body of empirical data published in English corroborated the idea that mainstream pornography causes any particular harm or damage to the normal consumer or citizen. Nor, it might be noted, does much data support the contrary theory that pornography acts as a sort of catharsis, that its presence creates a "safety valve" in a stressful society. The absence of any conclusive data on the social effects of pornography at the time meant that the battles over pornography would be based not on reason and science but on emotion and politics. On one side of the debate were those who decried the devastation pornography visited on families and women; on the other side were those who warned of the even greater devastation that censorship caused to civil society. The debate raged on, with no clear winners in spite of an accumulation of weight in the research, often abetted by the improved tools of social science represented by personal computers and access to the Internet.

Though they led to only one piece of significant legislation (the Child Protection and Obscenity Enforcement Act of 1988), the Meese Commission's findings energized an array of right-wing activists; pressured the Southland Corporation (owner of the 7-Eleven convenience store chain) to pull *Playboy* and *Penthouse* magazine from its shelves; and encouraged Senator Jesse Helms of North Carolina, who led an attack on the National Endowment for the Arts for its alleged sponsorship of pornographic art, notably the work of Robert Mapplethorpe and Andres Serrano. Perhaps the most surprising ally of the anti-pornography forces in the 1980s was a vocal group of what came to be known as anti-pornography feminists.

FEMINIST VIEWS

Women Against Pornography founding member Andrea Dworkin announced her group's agenda to audiences in the late 1970s when she declared that "pornography exists because men despise women, and men despise women in part because pornography exists." Anti-pornography feminists (including the group Feminists Fighting Pornography) found a potent ally in University of Michigan law professor Catharine MacKinnon, who led the campaign to establish new legislation to suppress pornography (though such laws were largely unsuccessful). Other leading feminists, including Nadine Strossen and Betty Friedan (whose own *The Feminine Mystique* had once been labeled obscene), fought very publicly against what they depicted as the forces of censorship, pure and simple. The issue thus revealed sharp divides within the feminist movement, divides that mirrored those in the public at large.

Decades later, sound research seems to refute these claims. In his 1990 essay in the *Journal of Sex Research*, Larry Baron, looking for an association between the circulation of pornographic magazines and women's equality, in fact found an inverse relationship, contrary to his hypothesis. His results, based on information from the fifty United States, found higher incidence of gender equality correlated with higher circulation rates of pornography. Similarly, both Luis Garcia's essay in the *Journal of Sex Research* and Cynthia Gentry's in *Deviant Behavior* found that an assumed relationship between consumption of pornography and a "less liberal attitude to women" failed. No causal or correlational relationship between rape and mainstream pornography was found.

PORNOGRAPHY AND THE INTERNET

The rise of the Internet in the 1990s added new fuel to the debate over pornography. With all that the Internet could do, the thing that it seemed to do best in the 1990s was provide ready access to a vast trove of visual pornography. Some studies claimed that as much as 30 percent of the material available via the Internet was pornographic in nature. To be sure, the porn was out there: vast archives of still photography, much of it hard core, were available with the click of a mouse; much of it was available free of charge, and still more for a fee. By the late 1990s technology had made possible the transmission of video clips as well. The most troubling element of Internet pornography was its ease of access. Without special filters to screen out adult content, any child could easily stumble upon material that no parent would deem permissible. Politicians responded to the problem of "cyberporn" in 1996 with the creation of the Communications Decency Act, which prohibited the transmission of material deemed "indecent" over computer networks. The bill attracted the immediate attention of civil liberties groups and was soon found to be unconstitutional. At the end of the twentieth century, politicians, parents, and public librarians still struggled to figure out a way to restrict the access of minors to pornography over the Internet without infringing upon the rights of adults.

Concerns about the enormous convenience of accessing pornography via the Internet with home computers did not seem to pan out as the century turned. Indeed, the difficulty of monetizing pornography went a long way toward destabilizing the commercial industry. At the same time, research indicated that the incidence of rape went down with expanded access to the Internet and its facile delivery of pornography. Furthermore, there was no predicted increase in sexual crime, including rape, as access to pornography became easier.

THE TWENTY-FIRST CENTURY

Data failed to support any claim of social harm associated with pornography, but that did not diminish the zeal certain individuals felt toward even mild sexual display. In 2010 Virginia's Attorney General Ken Cuccinelli attempted a bowdlerizing of Virginia's Great Seal of the Commonwealth, which is a two-sided device of classic design from 1776. One side (depicted on the state flag) shows Virtus, or the Roman God of Virtue, standing in victory over the male figure, Tyranny, groveling on the ground in uncrowned defeat; below him is the motto *Sic Semper Tyrannis*—Thus Always to Tyrants. Unfortunately, being classical, the pose was too risqué for Cuccinelli, who requested that alternative lapel pins featuring a coy Virtus be made. Years earlier, in 2002, U.S. Attorney General John Ashcroft demanded that heavy drapes be installed because of the so-called nude statues at the U.S. Justice Department.

In 2004 the half-second flash of Janet Jackson's "wardrobe malfunction" at Super Bowl XXXVIII exposed CBS to fines reported to be more than $500,000. Moreover, according to one report, it led to an immediate crackdown and widespread debate on perceived indecency in broadcasting, as well as an increase in Federal Communications Commission (FCC) fines levied for indecency violations, from less than $50,000 per incident to $325,000.

Throughout the last century, Americans have grappled with the problem of pornography. This struggle has illuminated one of the central dramas of the American experience—the struggle between individual freedom and social control—and revealed a prudery that international observers have often found amusing. The agonizing struggle over pornography gives no indication of abating. It has largely supported the rights of adult Americans to have access to sexually explicit materials. Nonetheless, conservative zealots, progressive feminists, and concerned parents alike wonder at the social costs of such freedom of access. Pornography is probably a social phenomenon that will remain the target of unabated debate.

Dr. John Griffin Donlon

SEE ALSO: Esquire*; Feminism; Griffith, D. W.; Hefner, Hugh;* Hustler*; The Internet; Jackson, Janet; Mapplethorpe, Robert;* Penthouse*;* Playboy*;* Playgirl*; Reagan, Ronald; Super Bowl.*

BIBLIOGRAPHY

Arcand, Bernard. *The Jaguar and the Anteater: Pornography and Degree Zero*. London: Verso, 1993.

Baron, Larry. "Pornography and Gender Equality: An Empirical Analysis. " *Journal of Sex Research* 27, (1990): 363–380.

Christensen, F. M. *Pornography: The Other Side*. New York: Praeger, 1990.

Donlon, J. G. "Strippers: Pandering to Patriarchy or Subverting Bourgeois Authority?" *Popular Culture Review* 8, no. 1 (1996): 75–82.

Dworkin, Andrea. *Pornography: Men Possessing Women*. New York: Putnam, 1981.

Garcia, Luis. "Exposure to Pornography and Attitudes about Women: A Correlational Study." *Journal of Sex Research* 22 (1986): 378–385.

Gentry, Cynthia. "Pornography and Rape: An Empirical Analysis. " *Deviant Behavior* 12, no. 3 (1991): 277–288.

Gertzman, Jay A. *Bookleggers and Smuthounds: The Trade in Erotica, 1920–1940*. Philadelphia: University of Pennsylvania Press, 1999.

Gottfried, Ted. *Pornography: Debating the Issues*. Springfield, NJ: Enslow Publishers, 1997.

Hyde, H. Montgomery. *A History of Pornography*. New York: Farrar, Straus & Giroux, 1965.

Kendrick, Walter. *The Secret Museum: Pornography in Modern Culture*. New York: Viking, 1987.

Kipnis, Laura. *Bound and Gagged: Pornography and the Politics of Fantasy in America*. New York: Grove Press, 1996.

MacKinnon, Catharine A., and Andrea Dworkin. *In Harm's Way: The Pornography Civil Rights Hearings*. Cambridge, MA: Harvard University Press, 1997.

McElroy, Wendy. *XXX: A Woman's Right to Pornography*. New York: St. Martin's Press, 1995.

Nielsen, Alan. *The Great Victorian Sacrilege: Preachers, Politics and the Passion, 1879–1884*. Jefferson, NC: McFarland, 1991.

Stoller, Robert J. *Porn: Myths for the Twentieth Century*. New Haven, CT: Yale University Press, 1991.

Strossen, Nadine. *Defending Pornography: Free Speech, Sex, and the Fight for Women's Rights*. New York: Scribner, 1995.

Porter, Cole *(1891–1964)*

Cole Porter was one of the most important creators of musicals from the 1920s to the 1950s. He was one of those rare Broadway composers who wrote both lyrics and music. His impressive list of Broadway shows include *Anything Goes* (1934), *Kiss Me, Kate* (1948), and *Can-Can* (1953). Porter also wrote songs for films such as *Rosalie* (1937) and *High Society* (1956). He enjoyed the luxurious lifestyle, and his affluent upbringing is reflected in the wit and sophistication of both his music and his lyrics.

Cole Porter was born on June 9, 1891, in Peru, Indiana, with a proverbial silver spoon in his mouth; his grandfather was a multimillionaire. Music was important to the young Cole, and he was already publishing songs at age eleven. He continued writing songs and playing piano while a prelaw student at Yale University. He earned a bachelor's degree in 1913, but law school at Harvard did not fit well with Porter's interests, and he changed his studies to music. This greatly concerned his family, which was fearful that the heir to the family fortune would not have formal training in business acumen.

A devoted Francophile, Porter spent a great deal of time in Paris, where he maintained a lavish apartment. He studied in Paris with French composer Vincent d'Indy, and Parisian locales appeared frequently in his shows. Porter's first show, *See America First* (1916), opened and closed almost immediately. His second show, the revue *Hitchy-Koo* (1920), was as disastrous as its predecessor. Despite these early failures, Porter nevertheless continued to pursue a career as a composer. His first successful song, "Let's Do It," appeared in the musical comedy *Paris* (1928). In this song, Porter's penchant for double entendre is readily apparent. Two moderately successful shows, *Fifty Million Frenchmen* and *Wake Up and Dream*, appeared in 1929. During the early 1930s he had hit songs with "Love for Sale" from *The New Yorkery* (1930) and "Night and Day" from *The Gay Divorce* (1932).

FIRST HIT SHOW

Although he had produced a number of hit songs by the mid-1930s, Porter still had not written a successful show. *Anything Goes* (1934) changed that, playing 420 performances in its initial Broadway run. The plot involves mistaken identity aboard a ship. The play's colorful list of characters includes Reno Sweeney, an ex-evangelist turned nightclub singer; Billy Crocker, a stowaway; Hope Harcourt, a debutante; and Moon-Face Mooney, Public Enemy No. 13. Songs such as "Anything Goes," "You're the Top," "I Get a Kick out of You," and "Blow, Gabriel, Blow" garnered lavish praise for the show and its creator. Ethel Merman, William Gaxton, and Victor Moore starred in the original production.

Porter's success continued through the 1930s with several important musicals. *Jubilee* (1935), inspired by the Silver Jubilee of Britain's King George V and Queen Mary, concerns a royal family that was able to live incognito. Songs include "Just One of Those Things," "Begin the Beguine," and "Why Shouldn't I?" *Red, Hot and Blue!* (1936), a political satire, starred Jimmy Durante, Ethel Merman, and Bob Hope. "It's De-Lovely," one of Porter's greatest songs, was introduced in this show. Another political spoof, *Leave It to Me!* (1938), is best remembered as the show in which Mary Martin made her Broadway debut. She sang her one solo number, "My Heart Belongs to Daddy" (the lyrics of which are replete with double entendres), while doing a striptease atop a steamer trunk and surrounded by fur-clad chorus boys. *DuBarry Was a Lady* (1939), the fifth-longest-running musical of the decade, starred Bert Lahr and Merman, who introduced the immortal duet "Friendship."

Cole Porter. *Many of the songs that Cole Porter wrote for his Broadway and movie musicals have become American standards.* MICHAEL OCHS ARCHIVES/STRINGER/MICHAEL OCHS ARCHIVES/ GETTY IMAGES.

Porter was an avid equestrian. In 1937 he suffered a serious riding accident from which he never would completely recover, despite more than two dozen operations and several years in a wheelchair. His right leg, which was crushed in the accident, had to be amputated in 1958. From 1937 to 1958, despite intense, constant pain, Porter continued to write successful musical comedies filled with notable songs.

HITS OF THE 1940S

Porter's shows from the 1940s included *Panama Hattie* (1940), *Let's Face It!* (1941), *Mexican Hayride* (1944), and *Kiss Me, Kate* (1948). *Kiss Me, Kate*, his most successful Broadway show, takes place onstage and backstage during rehearsals for a musical version of Shakespeare's *The Taming of the Shrew*. The book by Samuel and Bella Spewack blurs the distinction between the lives of the characters as actors and nonactors. The cavalcade of hit songs includes "Another Op'nin', Another Show"; "Why Can't You Behave?"; "Wunderbar"; "So in Love"; "I Hate Men"; "Where Is the Life That Late I Led?"; and "Brush Up Your Shakespeare." The show starred Alfred Drake and Patricia Morison. Howard Keel and Kathryn Grayson played the lead roles in the 1953 film version.

During the 1950s Porter continued to compose successful musicals. *Can-Can* (1953) epitomizes Porter's love for the French capital. Songs include "C'est Magnifique" and "I Love Paris." Lido, the French actress who played the lead role, introduced the world to "I Love Paris." It was Gwen Verdon, however, performing an Apache dance and the sensuous "Garden of Eden" ballet, who received the greatest accolades. *Silk Stockings* (1955) was Porter's last show and his sixth to be set in France. The spy plot spawned songs such as "Paris Loves Lovers," "All of You," and "Silk Stockings." The 1957 film version featured Fred Astaire and Cyd Charisse.

Porter also maintained an active career in Hollywood. Twelve of his Broadway shows were made into films, and he wrote songs for numerous other motion pictures. Significant film songs include "I've Got You Under My Skin" from *Born to Dance* (1936), "Rosalie" and "In the Still of the Night" from *Rosalie* (1937), "Be a Clown" from *The Pirate* (1948), and "True Love" from *High Society* (1956).

Porter was one of the most important creators of musicals during the middle part of the century. His sophisticated use of double entendre and his love for the city of Paris inspired his greatest work. His ability to create both sophisticated words and chic music made his songs stand out from those of many of his contemporaries.

William A. Everett

SEE ALSO: *Astaire, Fred, and Ginger Rogers; Broadway; Hope, Bob; The Musical.*

BIBLIOGRAPHY

Citron, Stephen. *Noel and Cole: The Sophisticates*. New York: Oxford University Press, 1993.

Eels, George. *The Life That Late He Led*. New York: G. P. Putnam's Sons, 1967.

Howard, Jean. *Travels with Cole Porter*. New York: Abrams, 1991.

Kimball, Robert, ed. *The Complete Lyrics of Cole Porter*. New York: Vintage Books, 1984.

McBrien, William. *Cole Porter: A Biography*. New York: Knopf, 1998.

Morella, Joe. *Genius and Lust: The Creativity and Sexuality of Cole Porter and Noel Coward*. New York: Carroll & Graf, 1995.

Porter, Cole; Robert Kimball; and Richard M. Sudhalter. *You're the Top: Cole Porter in the 1930s*. Indianapolis: Indiana Historical Society, 1992.

Schwartz, Charles. *Cole Porter: A Biography*. New York: Dial Press, 1977.

Postcards

Perhaps no communications medium exemplifies twentieth-century popular culture more accurately than the unpretentious postcard. This simple message-bearer had tremendous public appeal during the final decades of the 1800s, and although it seemed to have reached a peak in popularity during the first twenty years of the twentieth century, more than a decade into the new millennium the postcard's symbolic power and presence show little sign of giving way to e-mail or other potential electronic replacements. In fact, in 2008 the United Kingdom reported an increase in postcard sales. Readily available at any tourist destination along the way, at interstate truck stops, or in the revolving racks at local downtown shops, postcards are an icon of a culture in a hurry. Taped to refrigerator doors or tacked to office bulletin boards, they have become commonplace signals that someone one knows is off traveling. Expressions such as "wish you were here" have become popular parlance ushered into common vocabulary by virtue of being oft utilized on postcards.

The postcard has a fascinating and well-documented history. Before the idea of a graphic face became popular, plain cards were used for brief correspondence during the mid-nineteenth century. The concept was officially recognized at the 1865 General Postal conference in Karlsruhe, Germany, and four years later the first card published by a government postal agency was issued by the Austrian-Hungary monarchy. It was a plain card with a printed stamp. In the United States, a federal law passed by Congress on May 19, 1898, authorized Private Mailing Cards, with one side exclusively for the address. This allowed the other side of the card to be used for a picture or drawing. Prior to 1907, one whole side of a picture postcard was reserved for the address, leaving the only place for a written note to be across the picture itself. But in 1907 another law permitted a divided back, one half for the address and the other for the message.

PICTURE POSTCARDS

With the sanctioning of a graphical front to the postcard by government postal agencies, picture postcards soon became very

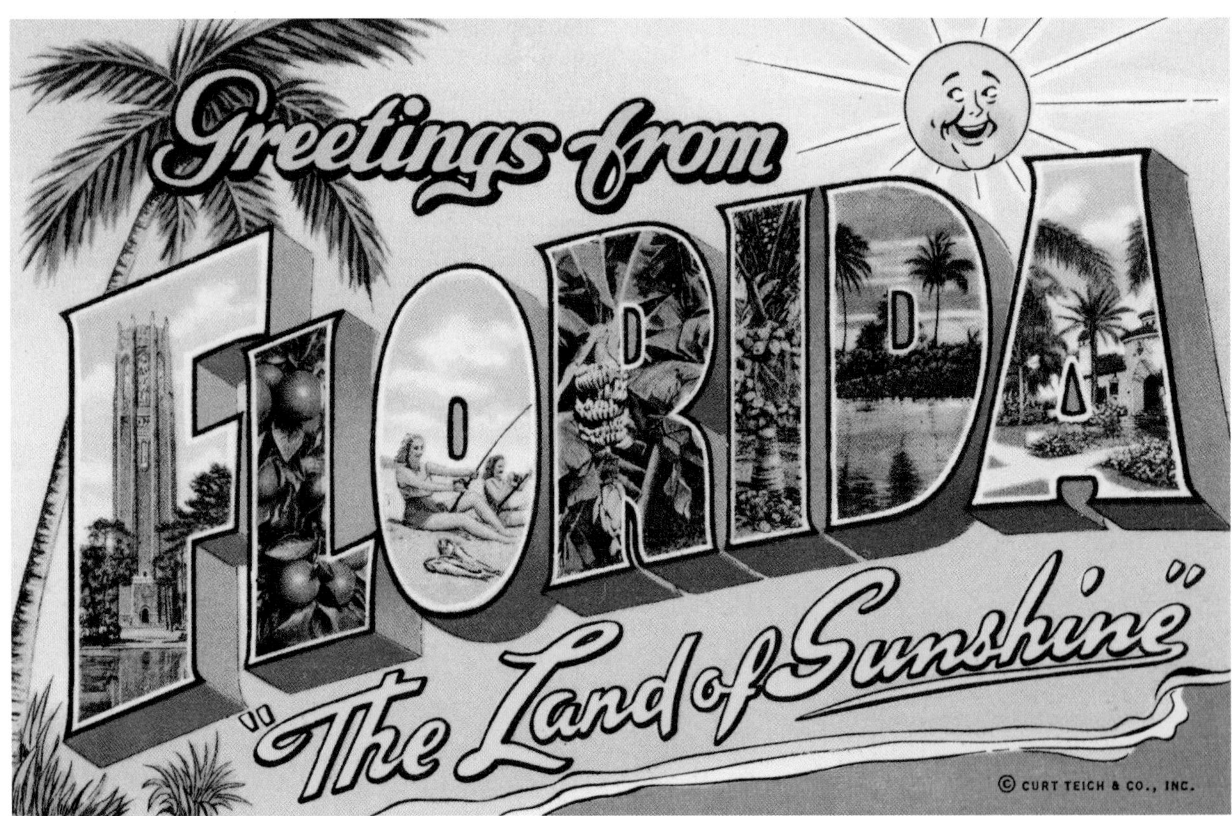

Florida Postcard. *A Florida postcard from the early 1940s illustrates the many tourist attractions the state has to offer.* LCDM UNIVERSAL HISTORY ARCHIVE/GETTY IMAGES.

popular. This was encouraged by advances in printing and photography allowing mass production. Also, Rural Free Delivery was instituted in 1898, stimulating personal use of the mail system for spontaneous correspondence. People could always find the time to scribble a short note on the back of a postcard and seemed to enjoy sending these pictures to each other. It has been estimated that more than a billion postcards were produced in the United States during the decade preceding World War I. Such volume suggests a significant retail commodity for many commercial establishments, and marketing strategies took advantage of postcard popularity. In *The Book of Postcard Collecting*, Thomas Range reports that "the familiar revolving wire rack for the display of cards has been attributed to one E. I. Dail, who patented this product in 1908." After 1915 the use of postcards declined somewhat, partly due to the war but also because the telephone and the automobile were creating a revolution in communications and transport connectivity.

In the late 1990s a revival of postcard popularity began in the United States, both for currently published offerings as a means of quick communication and for the collecting of postcards from the past. Collecting postcards became very popular during the height of their production just after the turn of the twentieth century. Postcards lend themselves to collecting because of their generally uniform size and ease of storage. Postcard collectors clubs first formed during the 1940s and remain a major storehouse of information and research. In the early twenty-first century the widespread use of computers provided a new way to keep the hobby alive; many collectors went online to find other enthusiasts around the world with whom they could exchange mailed postcards.

DELTIOLOGY

There exists a recognized field of study for postcards, which probably began as the popularity of sending postcards declined. As related by Marian Klamkin in the book *Picture Postcards*, "Randall Rhoades of Ashland, Ohio, coined a word in the early 1930s that became the accepted description of the study of picture postcards. 'Deltiology,' taken from the Greek word, deltion, meaning a small picture or card." In the 2010s numerous newsletters and magazines are devoted to the hobby. Many postcard collectors concentrate on various themes: railroad stations, city and town bird's-eye views, steamships, and other symbols of technological progress. These subjects often represent the spirit of the age, what seems or had seemed important to us at the time. Natural disasters commonly became topics for postcards, perhaps going along with what Hal Morgan and Andreas Brown, in their book *Prairie Fires and Paper Moons*, term an "emphasis on the minor events in out-of-the-way places." Of course, whatever the subject, there was always an imbedded discourse within the image portrayed. And this hidden message continues in the postcards of the twenty-first century, especially for those cards with the "wish you were here" scenery.

Here are the glossy images of lakes, waterfalls, rugged mountains, or bucolic rural scenery. That the picture postcard is produced and designed to be sent through the mail is itself an act of reinforcement for popular perceptions of place, and as such, the lowly postcard can offer insight into both past and present geographies. The record they leave behind is indelible and unmistakable. Postcards represent a sequential snapshot of both the landscape's and society's changes over time. Not only do postcards impart information about trends and cultural shifts but have themselves been used as vehicles for diffusion of new ideas and styles of artistic expression. Their use in commercial advertising likewise has a long history. The hobby of collecting postcards has resulted in additional value being imparted to them. Ultimately, however, postcards are fun to send and fun to receive and therefore show little sign of disappearing from popular culture.

Robert Kuhlken

SEE ALSO: *E-mail; World War I.*

BIBLIOGRAPHY

Carline, Richard. *Pictures in the Post: The Story of the Picture Postcard and Its Place in the History of Popular Art.* Philadelphia: Deltiologists of America, 1972.

Fanelli, Giovanni, and Ezio Godoli. *Art Nouveau Postcards.* New York: Rizzoli, 1987.

Klamkin, Marian. *Picture Postcards.* New York: Dodd, Mead, 1974.

Mashburn, J. L. *The Postcard Price Guide: A Comprehensive Reference*, 4th ed. Enka, NC: Colonial House, 2001.

Morgan, Hal, and Andreas Brown. *Prairie Fires and Paper Moons: The American Photographic Postcard, 1900–1920.* Boston: David R. Godine, 1981.

Range, Thomas. *The Book of Postcard Collecting.* New York: Dutton, 1980.

Ryan, Dorothy, and George Miller. *Picture Postcards in the United States, 1893–1918.* New York: Clarkson N. Potter, 1982.

Staff, Frank. *The Picture Postcard and Its Origins.* New York: F. A. Praeger, 1966.

The Postman Always Rings Twice

The Postman Always Rings Twice (1934), the controversial best seller by James M. Cain (1892–1977), is an erotic and violent story about a waitress and a drifter who kill the woman's well-heeled, unattractive older husband. Cain's work is central to the hard-boiled literary tradition. In this genre, an amoral hero often falls victim to his sexual attraction to a femme fatale. Obsessive love is at the heart of much of Cain's writing, making it eminently adaptable to film noir—a cinematic genre in which amorality, violence, and malevolent fate hang over psychologically realistic, morally ambiguous characters.

Cain's novel has been adapted four times to the screen: as *Ossessione* in 1943 (directed by Luchino Visconti); under its original title in 1946 (directed by Tay Garnett and starring Lana Turner and John Garfield) and in 1981 (directed by Bob Rafelson and starring Jessica Lange and Jack Nicholson); and as *Kiss Me a Killer* in 1991 (directed by Marcus DeLeon).

Jeannette Sloniowski

SEE ALSO: *Best Sellers; Detective Fiction; Film Noir; Garfield, John; Nicholson, Jack; Turner, Lana.*

BIBLIOGRAPHY

Biesen, Sheri Chinen. "Raising Cain with the Censors, Again: *The Postman Always Rings Twice.*" *Literature Film Quarterly* 28, no. 1: 41–48.

Cain, James M. *The Postman Always Rings Twice*. New York: Vintage, 1992.

Dyer, Richard. "Four Films of Lana Turner." *MOVIE* 25, Winter (1977–1978): 30–52.

Orr, Christopher. "Cain, Naturalism and Noir." *Film Criticism* 25, no. 1: 47–64.

Porfirio, Robert G. "Whatever Happened to Film Noir? *The Postman Always Rings Twice*." *Literature/Film Quarterly* 13, no. 2, 1985: 101–111.

Silver, Alain, and Elizabeth Ward, eds. *Film Noir: An Encyclopedic Reference to the American Style*. Woodstock, NY: Overlook Press, 1992.

Silver, Alain, and James Ursini. *Film Noir Reader 4: The Crucial Films and Themes*. New York: Proscenium Publishers, 2004.

Postmodernism

The term *postmodernism* signifies the variety of responses in art, science, and philosophy to the cultural changes brought about in the historical wake of World War II. Although it is difficult to pinpoint an exact date when postmodernism began, most theorists and critics acknowledge that Albert Toynbee's *A Study of History* (1947) and Bernard Rosenberg's *Mass Culture* (1957) ushered in the first systematic attempts to describe the noticeable break from the first half of the twentieth century. Whereas the artistic and intellectual responses in the first half of the century could be viewed as an adherence to modernist principles that relied upon universal notions of beauty, truth, and justice, postmodern visions reject notions of universal ideals, focusing instead on the multiplicity of perspectives that help generate an understanding of the world. In the broadest sense, postmodernism can be seen as a robust skepticism that challenges explanations that attempt to subsume experience under some universal authority, and, instead, postmodernism offers a counternarrative that privileges experience over abstract principles.

The numerous political and social movements circling around issues concerning civil rights, gay rights, and feminism, coupled with the political horrors revealed through Nazism, communism, fascism, and capitalism, gave rise to multidisciplinary approaches to account for the way people perceive the world. Many postmodern intellectuals challenged the binary oppositions that remained latent in Western thought such as male/female, culture/nature, self/other, white/black, straight/gay, imperial/colonial. Highlighting the various relations of power in each binary relationship, postmodernists interrogated the dualisms in order to reveal the subtle ways in which the relationships crafted an individual's knowledge and perception of the world. By privileging the individual, postmodern thought countered holistic visions of the world with highly contextualized and particularized expressions of reality.

As such, postmodern thought is highly difficult to categorize, because no systematic vision can offer an adequate representation of its projects, claims, and ideas. The disparate voices of Jean François Lyotard, Jaques Derrida, Homi Bhabha, Julia Kristeva, Judith Butler, Edward Said, Slavoj Zizek, Fredric Jameson, Gayatri Spivak, and Hélène Cixous each offered articulations that provided for a plurality of voices, permitting for a fluid and dynamic reconfiguring of individual experience. That is, by pushing up against the prevalent cultural narratives, they proceeded to reveal the various ruptures, breaks, inconsistencies, and contradictions within the dominant culture. Individual expressions were vastly reinterpreted through artists such as Don DeLillo, Thomas Pynchon, Ralph Ellison, Maxine Hong Kingston, Jackson Pollock, Andy Warhol, Carolee Schneemann, Cindy Sherman, Alice Aycock, Robert Venturi, Joyce Kozloff, Richard Haas, Brian Eno, David Byrne, and John Zorn.

VISUAL ARTISTS

Unsurprisingly, perhaps, architecture offered the first reinterpretation of physical space. Robert Venturi announced a move away from the functionalist modernist aesthetic in 1966 when he published his book *Complexity and Contradiction in Architecture*. In his book, Venturi argues that ornamentation is necessary in architecture since it reflected and communicated the variety of contemporary life. One of his most famous buildings, the Vanna Venturi House (1962–1964), juxtaposed a variety of influences and styles so that the contradictions remain evident rather than resolved. In typical postmodernist fashion, the house includes a wide array of ornamentation, including a pitched roof and decorative arch. The inside of the house evidences an eclectic array of design systems as it incorporates a spiral staircase and chimney to offset the main room on the second floor.

As architecture flourished through the 1970s and 1980s, postmodern expressions spread across the globe. Buildings and public spaces took on a much more sculptural element than their modernist predecessors, continually borrowing and reinterpreting elements from earlier periods and placing them in new contexts. Richard Haas's mural on the Boston Architectural Center (1977) at once celebrates an historical rendering but introduces a playful collage of the building's evolution. Michael Graves embellishes his Portland Building (1982) with a variety of materials and colors, contrasting with the steel and glass used in traditional business buildings. Moving into larger scales, artists and architects began collaborating on public spaces. Jackie Ferrara and Paul Friedberg's *Garden Courtyard* (1989) in Atlanta, Georgia, injects curious moments of individuality within the complex walkways and platforms. Multicolored tiles cross the granite at varying angles and spaces, suggesting that the space never reaches closure. In many ways, postmodern architecture attempted to combat the stark facades of modernism by including moments in which the artist expressed him or herself.

Much like their modernist predecessors, the visual arts—including painting, sculpture, collage, and performance art—encompassed multiple artistic movements. At times competing and complementary, the various movements transcended decades, being simultaneously challenged and incorporated into the multitude of styles, including abstract expressionism, minimalism, pop art, conceptual art, and performance art. A fundamental point of departure for many of the postmodern artists was to erase the divide between high art and so called low art. By assembling a series of competing logics and symbols, visual artists were able to express the foundational element of fragmentation inherent in postmodernism's projects.

Perhaps the most famous abstract expressionist, Jackson Pollock, illustrated the infinite series of interpretations when he reconceived the process of making art. His revolutionary technique involved removing the canvas from the easel and placing it on the floor. From here, Pollock incorporated a variety of techniques, including splattering, dripping, brushing, and drawing. His famous numbered series (1948–1953) served as a new way to view painting, not as a means of excavating meaning but as a means to translate the very act of painting. Heavily influenced by existentialism, Pollock's art mimicked the transient nature of time and space, not only by allowing the viewer to experience the process but also by extending the paintings to the very margins of the canvas, erasing its sense of boundaries. Pollock's style influenced a host of artists, including Mark Rothko, Willem de Kooning, and Barnett Newman.

Following the abstract expressionists, Robert Rauschenberg provided a bridge to pop art. His "Combines" featured found objects, trash, and taxidermy, effectively incorporating sculptural elements into his paintings. His famous *Canyon* (1959) proposes to include fabric, a stuffed eagle, buttons, and a mirror that he happened to come across. Unlike the surrealists and Dadaists, Rauschenberg did not set out to find objects or juxtapose a seemingly random set of images as expressions of the unconscious; rather, he attempted to erase the gap between life and art by collaging spontaneous elements from everyday experience. His use of objects such as the stuffed eagle and candy wrappers would be further exploited by pop artists such as Warhol, Richard Hamilton, and Roy Lichtenstein. Pop art glorified the everyday, parodying icon rich symbols such as Campbell's Tomato Soup, comic strips, and Tootsie Pops. Mimicking the increasingly prevalent advertisements, pop art called attention to consumer projects but also, in ways, served to glorify them as idealized images of contemporary culture.

Pop art's commercial and critical success opened the door for other forms of art. Already highly expressive, performance art challenged many of the preconceived notions of what is art. Premised on the claim that capitalism had commodified experience, performance artists used the concept of a spontaneous event to resist the commodification process, because the performance was tied to a direct experience between the artist and audience. Generally the performance occurred only once and sought to disrupt normal theatrical conventions by doing away with linear narratives, traditional characters, and settings. Notably, performance art took on political tones by questioning social norms involving gender and sexuality as well as attempting to unshackle experience from consumer society through satire and parody. Schools such as fluxus and situationists merged dance, spoken-word, music, and theater into dynamic pieces that commented on social inequities. Schneemann, for example, not only openly questioned traditional artistic conventions but also revolted against the dominant masculine ethos that permeated much of contemporary art. Her piece *Interior Scroll* (1975) offered a profound criticism of masculine based aesthetics that ignored the body as a means of expression.

Along the same lines, conceptual artists attempted to unhinge the entire realm of museums and galleries. Arguing that art is increasingly commodified, conceptual artists such as Yves Klein and Joseph Kosuth mocked museum settings. Klein's *Void* (1957) was ostensibly an empty room, whereas Kosuth's *One and Three Hammers* included a hammer, a photograph of a hammer, and definition of "hammer." As artists challenged the ontological category of art, they progressively opened up new means of expression. No longer was art confined to the gallery; rather, it now took place in warehouses, on street corners, involving the body and a variety of materials. Stemming from pop art's explosion, traditionally low-brow art forms such as graffiti and comic books became legitimate realms of artistic expression.

NOVELISTS AND POETS

Postmodern writers have perhaps one of the more complicated relationships with postmodern aesthetics. As an attitude, postmodernism represented a profound shift away from modernism's adherence to form and certainty. Employing a variety of tropes such as pastiche, irony, and metafiction, postmodern writers continually revamped the art of storytelling, playwriting, and poetry. Blending genres and motifs from the other arts, novels, plays, and poems challenged their conceptual core. Like the other artists of the period, novelists and poets inherited a rich theoretical framework from existentialism, poststructuralism, deconstruction, and feminism; however, writers were still bound by the written word. Some critics point to Samuel Beckett's later work as providing the intellectual gap between high modernisms infatuation with language and postmodernism's lament over the inadequacy of language.

One of the better known icons of postmodernism emerged from the Beats. Writing in the 1950s, Jack Kerouac, Allen Ginsberg, and William S. Burroughs offered scathing critiques of postwar America. Blaming consumerism for the rampant decay of individuality and artistic expression, Ginsberg's *Howl* (1956) and Kerouac's *On the Road* (1957) painted vivid pictures of nonconformity. Whereas both writers openly challenged traditional structures and played with anticipation, Burroughs emerges as one of the quintessential postmodern writers. Known for his cutup style, Burroughs pieces together a variety of genres, including detective novels, manifesto, and memoir, into *Naked Lunch*. The fractured narrative, drug-addicted and untrustworthy narrator, repetitive prose, and lack of temporal progression rest as prototypical attributes in postmodern writing. Some, such as Donald Barthelme, used motives employed by conceptual artists. Like Klein, pages of Barthelme's *Snow White* (1967) remain blank or have chapters designed like *Mad Libs*, where the reader can insert an adjective or noun.

Thomas Pynchon, possibly the most vexing novelist, attempted to subvert narrative structure through a series of labyrinthine plots in *The Crying of Lot 49* (1966) and *Gravity's Rainbow* (1973), but he also formulates a critique that lies beneath myriad pop culture references to comic books, pop music, and commodities. In the *Woman Warrior* (1975), Maxine Hong Kingston openly challenges genres as she weaves together magical realist elements with embellished personal details that serve to construct a cross-generational historical narrative that seemingly opens more questions than it seeks to answer.

The Columbian novelist Gabriel García Márquez created hybrid worlds through magical realism. His novels, such as *Love in the Time of Cholera* (1985), incorporate supernatural elements such as ghosts and premonitions that disrupt seemingly normal, everyday activities. Indian writers such as Salman Rushdie and Bharati Mukherjee adopted a similar aesthetic to Márquez. Rushdie's controversial *The Satanic Verses* uses dream sequences, devils and physical transformations to highlight ongoing struggles with diasporic communities that find themselves lost between two cultures. Mukherjee's *The Holder of the World* (1993) plays with elements of time travel and virtual reality as she offers a retelling of *The Scarlet Letter*, challenging the prestige of the Western canon while attempting to resituate colonized people within the academy. Don DeLillo's *White Noise* (1985) overtly situates itself within a media-saturated environment, calling into question individual perceptions of reality. Throughout the decades, postmodern fiction has incorporated a variety of elements as it seeks to manipulate its contemporary environment with the unenviable task of making sense of it.

Postmodern poetry evolved in a similar manner to prose. The canonical tradition of poetry had long been challenged, but experimental poets such as the Beats, Black Mountain School, and language poets explored new forms that allowed for a broader expression of the self as opposed to the limitations imposed by traditional rhyme, meter, and stanzas. Free-verse provided poets with an "organic" means to organize their thoughts as they used seemingly arbitrary line breaks, spacing, and page layouts. Feminist and African American poets assailed the canon, portraying it as a means to silence minority voices. The manipulated poetic forms mirrored the desire for individual voices to be heard. Adrienne Rich's *Snapshots of a Daughter-in-Law* (1963), for example, focused more on exploration and dialog than in expressing moments of truth. Gwendolyn Brooks employed a variety of everyday speech patterns to paint vivid pictures of contemporary black life. Her later collected works such as *Blacks* (1987) reinvigorated her earlier themes by incorporating elements of jazz and hip-hop to present a culture that had its own historical evolution.

Other writers, such as John Ashbery and Elizabeth Bishop, attempted to be less political; however, their poetics pursued ways in which individual expressions could be made manifest within the larger world. Focusing on language and images, Bishop and Ashbery offered narratives that combined everyday experience with poetics. Bishop's "In the Waiting Room" (1976) offers a fairly commonplace description of waiting for her aunt at the dentist's office, but the world opened up by images in *Geographic III* challenge the narrator's identity. Similarly, Ashbery's poems experiment with everyday speech patterns and cultural references. Written as a prose poem, "The Lonedale Operator" (1984) chronicles the narrator's psychological development via a series of memories associated with movies and actors.

FILM AND MUSIC

Film proved to be one of the most illustrative and innovative modes of expression of postmodernist aesthetics. Unlike modernist film, which called attention to the medium and illustrated its ability to thoroughly capture reality or to offer up celebrations of the individual genius, postmodernist film attempts to play with the medium by offering multiple narratives, transcending time and space, and challenging the distinction between the audience and film. Like the novel, postmodern films typically parody a variety of styles, incorporating elements of drama, action, comedy, noir, pornography, and horror into one single film. *Blade Runner* (1982) represents the paradigmatic postmodern film. Based on Philip K. Dick's *Do Androids Dream of Electric Sheep?* the film offers up a dystopian world in which robotic replicants are juxtaposed against human beings. Overrun by megacorporations and shadowed by police, the movie explores the hyperreality of contemporary, global capitalism.

Films such as Quentin Tarantino's *Pulp Fiction* (1994) situate the viewer in a world that is close to contemporary; however, the stylized costumes and music appeal to an earlier era. In addition, Tarantino's merging of time lines as well as cross-generational pop cultural references leave the audience virtually in limbo. Other movies, such as *Memento* (2000), exploit the twisting of temporal elements as the protagonist is forced to piece together his life through a series of polaroids and post-it notes. The film operates in reverse, illustrating the limits of linear storytelling. Postmodernism's infatuation with metafiction is apparent in *Adaptation* (2002), which hinges upon the writing of a book about orchids. In the end, the movie parodies itself, becoming a movie about thieves, murder, and sex—everything the protagonist wishes his book would avoid.

Music provided postmodern artists with a variety of tools. Composers such as John Cage and John Zorn attempted to circumvent traditional classical music through avant-garde techniques. Arguably Cage's most infamous piece, *4'33"* (1952) instructs the performers to not play. Cage hoped that the sounds of the environment would fill the silence left by the musicians and challenge commonly held boundaries between performer and audience since it is largely the sounds of the audience that are heard during the performance. Zorn blends a variety of musical styles, including jazz and Japanese music, in a jump-cut style, similar to collage artists. His work with *Naked City*, for example, fused jazz, punk rock, and heavy metal into quick-changing compositions.

Postmodern music's more foundational shift is perhaps evidenced by the numerous popular artists who participated in its aesthetic. Pops musicians such as David Bowie, the Talking Heads, Michael Jackson, and Madonna incorporated an eclectic array of musical genres into their compositions. The sampling and mash-up techniques of hip-hop and dance music challenged the melody-based structure of music, focusing on rhythm and improvisation.

In spite of its popular mystique and its self-proclaimed challenges to the dominant sociopolitical structures, postmodernism has also been highly criticized for its apparent celebration of the new. In his highly influential book, *Postmodernism, or, the Cultural Logic of Late Capitalism* (1991), Fredric Jameson argues that postmodernism unwittingly plays out the same cultural structures it wishes to contest. Juxtaposition, pastiche, and sampling served to remove the cultural elements from their historical context, erasing any connection between the artistic expression and its world. In a complex analysis, he reasons that while postmodern art attempted to offer counter narratives it merely articulated the same logic of capitalism by subsuming a variety of disparate parts under a new abstract principle or expression.

Josh Harteis

SEE ALSO: *Advertising; Consumerism; Jackson, Michael; Madonna; Modernism; Warhol, Andy.*

BIBLIOGRAPHY

Baudrillard, Jean. *America*. London: Verso, 1988.

Connor, Steven. *Postmodernist Culture: An Introduction to Theories of the Contemporary*. Oxford, UK: Blackwell, 1997.

Derrida, Jacques. "Différance." In *Margins of Philosophy*, tr. Allan Bass. Chicago: University of Chicago Press, 1982.

Jameson, Fredric. *Postmodernism, or, the Cultural Logic of Late Capitalism*. Durham: Duke University Press, 1991.

Lyotard, Jean François. *The Postmodern Condition: A Report on Knowledge*, tr. Geoff Bennington and Brian Massumi. Minneapolis: University of Minnesota Press, 1984.

Natoli, Joseph P., and Linda Hutcheon, eds. *A Postmodern Reader*. Albany, NY: State University of New York Press, 1993.

PostSecret.com

In November 2004, Maryland businessman Frank Warren initiated what he believed would be a small community art project. He distributed 3,000 postcards on the streets of Washington,

D.C., inviting recipients to confess a secret and mail the postcard back to him. The results of his experiment stunned him and led to the creation of a website, five published books, and museum exhibits curated by Warren, all showcasing anonymous confessions and revealing the pervasiveness of an intense human need to be seen and understood—even if only by strangers.

Warren only received around 100 of his original postcards back, but just when he thought his project had ended, he began to receive other postcards, created by the individuals who sent them from all over the country. He soon started a blog he named PostSecret.com, on which he posted the secrets that kept pouring in. Reading the secrets soon became as popular as sending them—by 2005 *Advertising Age* named PostSecret.com among its ten top blogs, and by 2008 Warren was receiving more than 1,000 postcards a week, and video secrets could be uploaded. Secrets varied from the humorous, "I only date girls with pretty feet," to the guilty, "I only love two of my children," and senders often decorate their postcards elaborately with appropriate artwork.

While Warren was surprised by the outpouring of secrets to his blog, he also felt he had tapped into a basic human need for self-revelation. He continued to require the use of postcards rather than enabling typed-in confessions because he believed that the process of creating the cards aided in the sense of unburdening. Warren also felt a sense of responsibility to those who confided in him. When many of the revealed secrets involved threats of suicide, PostSecret became involved in various suicide prevention projects, including raising more than $150,000 for 1800SUICIDE and joining with other groups to sponsor the launch of IMAlive, an online crisis counseling service that provides support through instant messaging.

Warren believes that his secret-sharing blog has created a meaningful virtual community and has said that "PostSecret helps us kind of tap into that heroism and frailty and extraordinary nature of our inner lives that we don't always get a chance to share and communicate." This was borne out in 2010 when an undocumented resident's painful confession that she or he might jump off San Francisco's Golden Gate Bridge led a concerned reader to establish a "Please don't jump" Facebook page and prompted others to leave encouraging notes on the bridge in hopes of preventing the suicide.

Tina Gianoulis

SEE ALSO: *Facebook; Golden Gate Bridge; The Internet; Postcards; Social Media; Suicide.*

BIBLIOGRAPHY

Bhargava, Rohit. "How Curation Could Save the Internet." *Communication World* 29, no. 1 (2012): 20.

Carlin, Flora. "The Decline and Fall of the Private Self." *Psychology Today* 40, no. 3 (2007): 82.

Molter, Jennifer L. "The PostSecret Project." *Studies in Art Education* 52, no. 4 (2011): 342.

Warren, Frank. *A Lifetime of Secrets: A PostSecret Book.* New York: William Morrow, 2007.

Potter, Dennis *(1935–1994)*

Screenwriter Dennis Potter was one of the most significant and innovative dramatists in the history of British television. From 1965 until his death in 1994, he created an oeuvre of haunting intensity and personal vision that ranks with the greatest achievements in any popular art form. His best-known works among international audiences, *Pennies from Heaven* (1978) and *The Singing Detective* (1986), are strikingly original miniseries that use the television narrative form to journey into an inner, psychological reality. Both series and many of his other dramas, including *Moonlight on the Highway* (1969), *Cream in My Coffee* (1980), and *Karaoke* (produced posthumously in 1996), share a fascination with popular culture and nonnaturalistically employ songs to reveal repressed emotions. Although he wrote such films as *Dreamchild* (1985) and *Track 29* (1988), he considered television "the most democratic medium" and used all his creative powers to open up its artistic possibilities. His work has had a major influence on such American film and television writers as Steven Bochco, Alan Ball, and Charlie Kaufman.

Ron Simon

SEE ALSO: *Bochco, Steven; Television.*

BIBLIOGRAPHY

Carpenter, Humphrey. *Dennis Potter: The Authorized Biography.* London: Faber & Faber, 1998.

Cook, John R. *Dennis Potter: A Life on Screen.* Manchester, UK: Manchester University Press, 1995.

Fuller, Graham, ed. *Potter on Potter.* London: Faber & Faber, 1993.

Gilbert, W. Stephen. *Fight & Kick & Bite: The Life and Work of Dennis Potter.* London: Hodder & Stroughton, 1995.

Museum of Television and Radio. *The Television of Dennis Potter.* New York: Author, 1991.

Potter, Dennis. *Seeing the Blossoms: Two Interviews and a Lecture.* London: Faber & Faber, 1994.

Powell, Dick *(1904–1963)*

American pop singer and bandleader Dick Powell rose to fame as the perennial youthful star of backstage musical films during the 1930s. He appeared as the lead opposite actresses such as Ruby Keeler and Joan Blondell in a string of films, including *42nd Street*, *Footlight Parade*, and *Gold Diggers of 1933* (all 1933). He also starred in the musical comedies *Gold Diggers of 1935* (1935), *Thanks a Million* (1935), *Gold Diggers of 1937* (1936), *On the Avenue* (1937), and *Star Spangled Rhythm* (1942). Powell later eschewed his clean-cut image and began to aspire to nonsinging, dramatic roles, appearing in films such as *Murder, My Sweet* (1944) and *The Bad and the Beautiful* (1952). He also directed several films. In the 1950s he ventured into television, both as an actor and as a producer. Powell was married to Blondell from 1936 to 1944 and wed actress June Allyson in 1945.

William A. Everett

SEE ALSO: 42nd Street*; The Musical; Pop Music; Television.*

BIBLIOGRAPHY

Carpozi, George. *The Magnificent Entertainers.* New York: Manor Books, 1978.

McNeil, W. K., and Louis Hatchett. *The Dick Powell Bio-Discography: November 14, 1904–January 2, 1963.* Portland, OR: Joyce Record Club, 2000.

Thomas, Tony. *The Dick Powell Story.* Burbank, CA: Riverwood Press, 1993.

Powell, William *(1892–1984)*

Actor William Powell, who lived to the age of ninety-two, retired from the screen in 1955 after making ninety-four films, beginning with the role of Moriarty in the 1922 silent version of *Sherlock Holmes* (1922) starring John Barrymore. He was never more than a supporting player, generally playing a villain of some kind or another during the 1920s, until his accomplished performance in a featured role in Josef von Sternberg's *The Last Command* (1928) brought him attention. The development of sound in movies, which ruined the career of many a silent star unable to deliver lines, gradually elevated Powell to stardom as the quintessential screen sophisticate of the glamorous 1930s—immaculately tailored, impeccably spoken, witty, occasionally attractively caddish, and sometimes cynical. He was as much the perfect embodiment of the type as Gary Cooper was the archetypal emblem of honor or Clark Gable the prototype of brash and unbridled masculinity. With later change in styles and trends, Powell was in danger of sharing the obscurity of many of his forgotten films. He escaped such a fate thanks to *The Thin Man* (1934), which has defined his image ever since, despite the fact that the "thin man" of the title was not Powell but some mysterious stranger.

The debonair, urbane, and amusing Powell persona that brightened the lives of moviegoers during the Great Depression was famously blended into the perfect screen incarnation of Dashiell Hammett's cocktail-sipping sophisticate-cum-detective Nick Charles, who, with his wife Nora (Myrna Loy) and their dog, Asta, beguiled audiences in *The Thin Man* with such hugely profitable results for MGM (Metro-Goldwyn-Mayer) that five more Thin Man films followed, ending with the inferior *Song of the Thin Man* (1947). Powell and the glamorous Loy, both needing a bit of a career boost, found it together when director W. S. Van Dyke paired them in *Manhattan Melodrama* (1934), Powell's first film for MGM. *Manhattan Melodrama* was followed by *The Thin Man,* in which the stars joyously impersonated a couple to whom marriage was clearly an equal and thoroughly enjoyable partnership—an innovative concept for the time. Powell and Loy were also teamed in *Evelyn Prentice* (1934), a melodrama of adultery and blackmail, and in the screwy comedy *Double Wedding* (1937), but their portrayal of Nick and Nora made them perhaps the most successful star team of the 1930s—after Fred Astaire and Ginger Rogers. As film historian David Thomson puts it in *A Biographical Dictionary of the Cinema,* "The match was perfect: two slender sophisticates, smiling haughtily at each other through a mist of wisecracks."

EARLY CAREER

William H. Powell was born in Pittsburgh, Pennsylvania, on July 29, 1892. His father was an accountant who intended that the younger Powell should go into the law. Instead he became an avid playgoer who fell in love with the theater at an early age and dropped out of the University of Kansas to pursue a stage

William Powell. *William Powell, left, plays a scene with Henry Fonda and Jack Lemmon in the 1955 film* Mister Roberts. WARNER BROS/THE KOBAL COLLECTION.

career in New York. He studied at the American Academy of Dramatic Arts (with such talented classmates as Edward G. Robinson and Joseph Schildkraut) and, after a couple of years of struggle, began to find work in vaudeville and stock and on Broadway starting in 1912. Powell worked steadily but without particular distinction until 1920, when his performance in the play *Spanish Love* brought him some notice and led to the beginning of his film career. By then he had honed his craft through years of stage performances.

Powell was under contract with Paramount from 1924 to 1931, during which time he made *The Last Command* and *The Dragnet* (1928) for von Sternberg and made the transition to sound, appearing in *Interference* (1928), a drama whose only distinction lay in being the studio's first all-talkie. In 1929, however, he was cast as S. S. Van Dine's gentleman detective Philo Vance in *The Canary Murder Case*, establishing the image that grew familiar to audiences and paved the way for Nick Charles. He played Vance in three more films (the last at Warner Brothers), was paired with Kay Francis in two movies, and made two comedies—*Man of the World* and *Ladies' Man*—with Carole Lombard in 1931. That same year Powell ended his fifteen-year marriage to Eileen Wilson and married Lombard (the union lasted two years).

The actor's professional union with Paramount also faltered, and along with Kay Francis, he left the studio for Warner Brothers, which revived his pairing with Francis in *One Way Passage* (1932), in which he played a condemned criminal, she the doomed object of his affections. In addition his fourth Vance outing, *The Kennel Murder Case* (1933), directed by Michael Curtiz, Powell made *The Key* (1934) for the same director, but Warner Brothers proved no more satisfactory than Paramount, and he departed the studio.

En route to Columbia, he was intercepted by Van Dyke and MGM for *Manhattan Melodrama* (1934)—the movie John Dillinger saw just before he was gunned down by the FBI—and was put under contract with the studio for which his talents would be best employed. Powell's next film with Loy was *The Thin Man*, breezily directed by W. S. ("One-Take Woody") Van Dyke. Powell earned an Oscar nomination, and more importantly, the movie set the tone for many of his romantic comedies to follow. "Few images so succinctly convey the essence of thirties comedy," asserted critic Tom Shales, "as a scene from . . . *The Thin Man* in which Powell's Nick Charles, reclining on the couch, shoots the ornaments off a Christmas tree with the new gun his wife has given him."

HEIGHT OF STARDOM

As one of the brightest lights at MGM, Powell brought his impeccable flair to such comedy-dramas as *Reckless* (1935) with Jean Harlow; *Libeled Lady* (1936) with Harlow, Loy, and Spencer Tracy; and the biographical extravaganza *The Great Ziegfeld* (1936)—Powell played the title role—which won the Best Picture Oscar. (He again played impresario Florenz Ziegfeld in *The Ziegfeld Follies* in 1946). On loan to Universal, he costarred with ex-wife Lombard in one of the most exemplary of screwball comedies, *My Man Godfrey* (1936), and earned his second Oscar nomination.

Ever the gentleman in life as well as art, Powell insisted that Lombard be cast, explaining, "Just because we couldn't live together doesn't mean we shouldn't work together." As film columnist Robert Osborne commented, "For a man with such a perpetual twinkle in his eye, always seemingly in good humor, his personal life was surrounded with a surprising number of tragedies." Among these were the sudden death in 1937 of Jean Harlow, Powell's fiancée, with whom he was deeply in love; the bout with cancer that kept the actor off the screen for almost two years and hastened his retirement; and the suicide of his son from his first marriage. In 1940 Diana Lewis became Powell's third wife, a union that lasted until his death.

As Powell got older, he effected a smooth transition to character parts, chiefly by giving an Oscar-nominated and New York Critics' Circle Award–winning performance in the plum role of the elder Clarence Day in *Life with Father* (1947) opposite Irene Dunne. Onstage, Day's pronouncements were peppered with profanity; denied these choice words for the film version, Powell put so much persuasive power into his tirades that the epithets were never missed. The way in which Powell bypassed the censors by making "Oh Gad!" sound as profane as "Oh God!" was a true lesson in the actor's craft. He made *The Senator Was Indiscreet*, a political satire, that same year, and played half the title role in a wistful, rueful fantasy, *Mr. Peabody and the Mermaid.*

Powell, who had begun his film career in the days of the silent movies, continued working into the era of CinemaScope, essaying a key part in *How to Marry a Millionaire* (1953) with Marilyn Monroe and Lauren Bacall. He bowed out as Doc in the film version of *Mister Roberts* (1955) opposite Henry Fonda, giving a performance every bit as expert as his Nick Charles or his Ziegfeld. The three-time Oscar nominee, resting on his laurels as one of the legends of Hollywood's golden era, passed away at age ninety-two in his Palm Springs, California, home.

Preston Neal Jones

SEE ALSO: *Academy Awards; Astaire, Fred, and Ginger Rogers; Bacall, Lauren; Barrymore, John; Broadway; Celebrity; Dunne, Irene; Fonda, Henry; The Great Depression; Hammett, Dashiell; Harlow, Jean; Hollywood; Lombard, Carole; Loy, Myrna; Monroe, Marilyn; Robinson, Edward G.; Tracy, Spencer; Van Dine, S. S.; Vaudeville; von Sternberg, Josef;* The Ziegfeld Follies.

BIBLIOGRAPHY

Baxt, George. *The William Powell and Myrna Loy Murder Case.* New York: St. Martin's Press, 1996.

Bryant, Roger. *William Powell: The Life and Films.* Jefferson, NC: McFarland, 2006.

Francisco, Charles. *Gentleman: The William Powell Story.* New York: St. Martin's Press, 1985.

Morella, Joe, and Epstein, Edward Z. *Gable & Lombard & Powell & Harlow.* New York: Dell, 1975.

Parish, James Robert. *The Debonairs.* New Rochelle, NY: Arlington House, 1975.

Quirk, Lawrence J. *The Complete Films of William Powell.* Secaucus, NJ: Citadel Press, 1986.

Thomson, David. *A Biographical Dictionary of the Cinema.* New York: Alfred A. Knopf, 1994.

Prang, Louis *(1824–1909)*

Founder of one of America's best-known art education publishers and art supply firms, Louis Prang immigrated to Boston from Prussia in 1850. Initially a wood engraver, he became a lithographer, making prints to decorate the homes of New England's growing middle class. He also made labels for manufactured goods, campaign maps for families of Civil War soldiers, and America's first Christmas cards.

In 1870 a Massachusetts law mandated art instruction in the public schools to meet a burgeoning demand for commercial artists. Prang and Company seized on this new market with drawing cards for imitation in the classroom, art textbooks, the Prang Solids (geometric forms to be drawn by the student), paints, crayons, and drawing papers. Although the "art labor" movement receded by the turn of the twentieth century, Prang's firm continued to manufacture art supplies into the 1990s as a subsidiary of the American Crayon Company.

Nick Humez

SEE ALSO: *Greeting Cards.*

BIBLIOGRAPHY

Barnhill, Georgia B.; Diana Korzenik; and Caroline Stoat, eds. *The Cultivation of Artists in Nineteenth-Century America.* Worcester, MA: American Antiquarian Society, 1997.

Freeman, Larry. *Louis Prang: Color Lithographer.* Watkins Glen, NY: Century House, 1971.

Korzenik, Diana. *Drawn to Art: A Nineteenth-Century American Dream.* Hanover, NH: University Press of New England, 1985.

McClinton, Katharine Morrison. *The Chromolithographs of Louis Prang.* New York: Clarkson and Potter, 1973.

Prater, Dave

SEE: *Sam and Dave.*

Preminger, Otto *(1905–1986)*

During his career, Austrian-born director and actor Otto Preminger worked equally hard at his films and his public persona. Over the years he cultivated his identity as an independent producer-director par excellence who refused to submit to the studio system or restrictive production codes and who could fire a star such as Lana Turner, originally cast for Lee Remick's role in *Anatomy of a Murder* (1959), because she refused to wear the pair of trousers he had selected for her. The following statement is as typical of his persona as courtroom scenes are of his movies: "I say what I like because it is completely my picture, an independent picture. I am the producer, the director, the casting director, it's all my decision." This self-consciously iconoclastic and autocratic character endeared him in the 1950s and 1960s to the French critics and directors of *Cahiers du Cinéma* as well as to auteur-theorists such as Andrew Sarris and others writing for magazines such as *Movie* and the *Village Voice.*

FIRST FILMS

Preminger's career can be divided into three periods. After immigrating to the United States in 1936, he signed a contract with Twentieth Century Fox, where he had several conflicts with producer Darryl F. Zanuck. Along with his first hit *Laura* (1944), Preminger's most interesting works of this period are a series of film noirs shot during the late 1940s and early 1950s: *Whirlpool* (1949), *Where the Sidewalk Ends* (1950), *The Thirteenth Letter* (1951), and *Angel Face* (1952). Preminger was always quite reluctant to talk about these movies and emphasized instead his conflicts with Zanuck, thus adding to his reputation as a rebel against big-studio rules.

INDEPENDENT PRODUCER-DIRECTOR

The Moon Is Blue (1953) marked the beginning of Preminger's career as an independent producer-director, and it was his first movie to be released without Motion Picture Association of America (MPAA) approval because of his refusal to cut dialogue containing sexual innuendo. With his newly gained independence from the major studios, Preminger started a successful series of grand-scale movies that focused on, at least superficially, scandalous topics such as drug addiction (*The Man with the Golden Arm*, 1955), rape (*Anatomy of a Murder*, 1959), communism and homosexuality (*Advise & Consent*, 1962), and institutions such as the U.S. Army (*The Court Martial of Billy Mitchell*, 1955, and *In Harm's Way*, 1965) and the Catholic Church (*The Cardinal*, 1963). His iconoclastic persona notwithstanding, Preminger's use of these and other controversial topics was essentially conservative and embedded in the conformist ideology of the 1950s and early 1960s.

A recurring theme of Preminger's rather diverse and eclectic movies of this period is the quest for truth through an apparently objective and scientific "anatomy" whose results, in the end, turn out to be more ambiguous than expected. This quest is embodied by the numerous courtroom scenes in Preminger's films and is usually carried out by solitary male heroes such as General Billy Mitchell (Gary Cooper) in *The Court Martial of Billy Mitchell* and lawyer Paul Biegler (Jimmy Stewart) in *Anatomy of a Murder.*

As in the case of *The Moon Is Blue*, *The Man with the Golden Arm* (1956) was released without the MPAA seal of approval because of its subject. Nelson Algren's novel of defeat in the Chicago slums is turned by Preminger into a success story starring Frank Sinatra as the ultimate self-made man: by the end of the movie Sinatra's Frankie Machine gets rid of his addiction and his hysterical wife Zosh (Eleanor Parker), leaves the slums together with his new supportive girlfriend Molly (Kim Novak), and becomes a musician with the help of American big business. The movie was a great box-office hit, and people queued to see the taboo topic of drugs on the big screen for the first time. Yet, according to Jackie Byars in *All That Hollywood Allows*, what they saw was a movie that is radical only on its surface, having at its base "a very conservative championing of the family, of aspirations to upward mobility, and of traditional gender definitions."

Just as *The Man with the Golden Arm* was perhaps the first mainstream movie to portray drug addiction, *Advise & Consent* (1962) was one of the first to explicitly treat the topic of homosexuality. The movie ultimately influenced the fate of many cinematic gay characters as well as their popular perception: tormented by their sexuality, gays have little choice but to die.

In *Advise & Consent*, a story of political intrigues and scandals, Senator Brigham Anderson (Don Murray) is appointed chair of the committee investigating the communist past of Senator Robert Leffingwell (Henry Fonda), who has just been designated secretary of state. Anderson is blackmailed by Leffingwell's supporters because of a gay affair he had while he was in the army. The movie clearly contrasts the cozy domestic space of Anderson's heterosexual household—filled with a beautiful, supportive wife and a cute daughter—with the squalor of the New York gay neighborhood where Anderson travels to meet his former lover, Ray. The landlord who first receives Anderson is the very antithesis of his wife. He is ugly and obese; homosexuality is conceived in terms of both moral and physical corruption. In the last instance, as Vito Russo points out in *The Celluloid Closet*, Anderson kills himself "not because he is being blackmailed in Washington, but because he has gone to New York and found people with whom he has something in common, and he is so repulsed he sees no alternative to the straight razor."

LATER WORKS

Preminger's final phase, which includes movies continuing his analysis of contemporary society (race relations in the South in *Hurry Sundown*, 1967, and Palestinian terrorism in *Rosebud*, 1975) and others striving for new directions (the slapstick farce *Skidoo*, 1968), was marked by critical and commercial disappointments. In spite of Preminger's self-appointed role as freedom fighter, Dwight MacDonald in *On Movies* suggests that perhaps no other director was more skilled than he "at giving the appearance of dealing with large 'controversial' themes in a bold way without making the tactical error of doing so."

Luca Prono

SEE ALSO: *Cooper, Gary; The Fifties; Film Noir; McCarthyism; Novak, Kim; Sinatra, Frank; Stewart, Jimmy; Studio System; Turner, Lana; Zanuck, Darryl F.*

BIBLIOGRAPHY

Byars, Jackie. *All That Hollywood Allows: Re-Reading Gender in 1950s Melodrama.* Chapel Hill: University of North Carolina Press, 1991.

Hirsch, Foster. *Otto Preminger: The Man Who Would Be King.* New York: Alfred A. Knopf, 2007.

MacDonald, Dwight. *On Movies.* New York: Da Capo Press, 1981.

Phillips, Gene D. *Exiles in Hollywood: Major European Film Directors in America* Bethlehem, PA: Lehigh University, 1998.

Pratley, Gerald. *The Cinema of Otto Preminger.* New York: A. S. Barnes, 1971.

Preminger, Otto. *Preminger: An Autobiography.* Garden City, NY: Doubleday, 1977.

Russo, Vito. *The Celluloid Closet: Homosexuality in the Movies.* New York: Harper & Row, 1981.

Preppy

The word *preppy* (also spelled *preppie*) derives from *preparatory* and refers to someone who attends or has attended a college preparatory secondary school. In actual use, preppy implies a wide variety of assumptions about the class, style, and values of such a person. Preppy can be used as a noun ("she dresses like a preppy") or an adjective ("I'm not interested in your preppy friends"). It can be congratulatory or condescending, though its use is usually humorous and to some degree derisive.

Though preppy was long in use among high school and college students, the word first gained wide national exposure in Erich Segal's 1970 romantic novel *Love Story* and the movie that was made from it. Set on the Harvard University campus, the novel describes the relationship between working-class Radcliffe student Jenny Cavilleri and blueblood Harvard jock Oliver Barrett. Jenny's personality is characterized by salty language, a blue-collar chip on her shoulder, and her hostile references to Oliver as "preppy." The word *preppy* entered the national vocabulary at that point in its most common usage—an antagonistic epithet for the elite, used by those who are not in the upper classes.

In 1980 Lisa Birnbach published *The Official Preppy Handbook*, a tongue-in-cheek look at the very real characteristics, quirks, and foibles of the privileged classes. She focuses her not-altogether-unloving mockery on the "old money" upper-crust society of the East Coast, the alumni of such schools as Choate, Groton, Exeter, and Andover. By poking fun at their "Chip and Muffy" nicknames and their expensive-shoes-without-socks pseudo-casual style, Birnbach shined a revealing light on the quietly rich. Her book inspired imitators, including some that were more overtly hostile to her subject, such as Ralph Schoenstein's *The I-Hate-Preppies Handbook: A Guide for the Rest of Us.*

Part fashion, part breeding, and part attitude, preppiness denotes both wealth and privilege, pomposity and dissipation. The hostility with which the epithet *preppy* is often hurled casts doubt on the reality behind the U.S. myth of the classless society. Since the 1980s the term *preppy* has been used regularly in the press, sometimes interchangeably with *yuppie*, though yuppie does not carry the East Coast blueblood connotation that preppy does. One of the most memorable outbreaks of preppy in the headlines occurred in the fall of 1986, after Jennifer Levin was strangled in New York's Central Park by Robert Chambers. Levin and Chambers were both members of Manhattan's high-society prep-school elite, and Levin's death was immediately dubbed "The Preppy Murder" in newspapers across the country, giving credibility to the axiom that a particular form of public outrage is reserved for the misdeeds of those who have "all of the advantages."

By the early years of the twenty-first century, postmodern irony began to give a new twist to the preppy epithet, as websites and blogs with titles such as *Preppy Must Have* and *The Preppy Princess* reclaimed the term with humorous self-deprecation. In 2010 Birnbach, along with collaborator Chip Kidd, followed up her iconic preppy guide with *True Prep: It's a Whole New Old World*, and in 2011 Jeffrey Banks, Doria De La Chapelle, and Lilly Pulitzer published *Preppy: Cultivating Ivy Style*, a historical exploration of preppy culture.

Films such as Wes Anderson's 2001 *The Royal Tenenbaums* introduced a kind of dysfunctional chic by showcasing the foibles of old money families. In 2011 designer Tommy Hilfiger capitalized on this quirky image to update the preppy style with an advertising campaign titled "The Hilfigers," which presented an ethnically mixed, eccentric fictional preppy family, much like the Tenenbaums. Terms such as *preppy grunge* and *post preppy* illustrate this updated preppy sensibility in the fashion world.

Though the working classes may have their revenge on preppies in the press and in film, it is the preppies who continue to triumph. With elite boarding schools becoming almost as expensive as private colleges, the prep-school education is more out of reach than ever for working people. Preppies may be targets of fun and ridicule, but grown-up preppies become the power elite who perhaps see themselves safely insulated from the impact of jokes made at their expense.

Tina Gianoulis

SEE ALSO: *Central Park;* Fortune*; Yuppies.*

BIBLIOGRAPHY

Banks, Jeffery; Doria De La Chapelle; and Lilly Pulitzer. *Preppy: Cultivating Ivy Style.* New York: Rizzoli, 2011.

Birnbach, Lisa. *The Official Preppy Handbook.* New York: Workman Publishing, 1980.

Birnbach, Lisa, and Chip Kidd. *True Prep: It's a Whole New Old World.* New York: Alfred A. Knopf, 2010.

Flippin, Royce. *Save an Alligator, Shoot a Preppie: A Terrorist Guide.* New York: A&W Visual Library, 1981.

Schoenstein, Ralph. *The I-Hate-Preppies Handbook: A Guide for the Rest of Us.* New York: Simon & Schuster, 1981.

Presley, Elvis *(1935–1977)*

It is no accident that Elvis Presley's rise to fame in the 1950s was in tandem with the rise of rock and roll, for the man and the music are indelibly linked. Though not the first rock-and-roll star, Presley was the most prominent prophet of the pioneering musical form. Moreover, with his daringly unique style, delivery, and sound, he symbolized the cultural shakeup that rumbled throughout the era. As the Pulitzer Prize–winning journalist and social historian David Halberstam proclaimed, "In cultural terms, [Elvis's] coming was nothing less than the start of a revolution."

Presley himself was as complex and as conflicted as the decade he has come to represent. Though shy and beguilingly sweet offstage, his early onstage persona was swaggering, even leering, with performances marked by frenzied bumping and grinding and seemingly gravity-defying bolts, leaps, and slides. To the sexually repressed young people of the day, he was an emblem of rebellious liberation. To the terrified adult establishment, parents especially, he was initially viewed as the devil incarnate. At the time, no one could have predicted that rock and roll would last or that Presley's stardom would not only endure but also grow to mythic proportions following his death in 1977.

A CHILDHOOD OF MUSICAL DIVERSITY

Known the world over by his first name, the American legend had decidedly humble beginnings. Elvis Aaron Presley was born on January 8, 1935, in a two-room shack in Tupelo, Mississippi, following the stillborn birth of twin brother Jesse Garon. The attending country doctor had to collect his $15 fee through welfare. Scions of large sharecropping families, Presley's parents were poor and uneducated. But Vernon and Gladys Presley indulged their precocious, towheaded son, and Gladys went on to become a pivotal force in his early career. In fact, Presley was so devoted to her that he has often been depicted as a "mama's boy."

Drawn to music from early childhood, Presley was initially exposed to the gospel music that was inherent to the Deep South and the Pentecostal church he attended in Tupelo. His musical horizons expanded in 1948 when he moved with his family to Memphis, Tennessee. Beale Street, home of the blues, was within walking distance of Lauderdale Courts, the public housing project that became home to the Presleys. Roadhouses were venues for hillbilly bands and cowboy singers. Churches and meeting halls echoed with spirituals. Local airwaves were also diverse. In defiance of the times, Presley avidly listened to so-called race stations, which played the music of African American artists for their primarily African American audience.

It was during high school that Presley began experimenting with his looks and dress style. At a time when others his age were wearing plaid shirts and blue jeans, he favored flashy "pimp"-type clothing. Colors not ordinarily worn by the era's males, including pink, were a Presley fashion favorite. His hairstyle was equally distinct. Though crew cuts were the rage, he wore his dark blond hair slicked back with rose oil. That "greaser" look would go on to become a "cool" statement in films and on television. But Presley was far from popular at school. Most students recoiled from the young man with the

Elvis Presley. *Elvis Presley performs in 1975 in the midst of a career resurgence that included a long-term stint in Las Vegas and tours of arenas around the country.* **FOTOS INTERNATIONAL/ CONTRIBUTOR/ARCHIVE PHOTOS/GETTY IMAGES.**

greasy-looking hair and the acne. His shyness, thick Mississippi accent, and a tendency to stutter, further hampered his status among both classmates and teachers, who were taken aback when he performed in a student show during his senior year. Most were unaware that he sang. But in fact, Presley was consumed by both music and ambition.

AN ELECTRIC PERFORMER

It was a July 1953 vanity recording, made just six weeks after high school graduation, that led to his introduction to Sun Records founder Sam Phillips. The blues-loving Phillips was known for recording "colored" artists, such as B. B. King, Bobby "Blue Bland, and Big Ma Rainey. But what he was searching for, he used to say, was "a white man who can sing like a Negro." He sensed that Presley, with his wide-ranging voice, might be that person. Presley was working as a truck driver when Phillips teamed him with guitarist Scotty Moore and bass player Bill Black. Their potent chemistry resulted in a sped-up, rhythmically charged version of "That's All Right (Mama)," their first Sun recording. Popular local disc jockey Dewey Phillips, no relation to Sam, played the song multiple times on the night of July 10, 1954. Later that month, as an extra added attraction at a local "hillbilly hoe-down," Presley subconsciously exhibited the gyrating body movements that he would eventually make a trademark.

For the next year and a half, Presley and musicians Moore and Black, who were now Sun Records artists, went on an extended road trip. Traveling throughout east and west Texas, Arkansas, and Louisiana, they played high school auditoriums, Future Farmers of America halls, and backwater honky-tonks. One show found Presley performing atop a flatbed truck parked at the second base of a baseball diamond. As his regional celebrity grew, disc jockeys and promoters alternately labeled him "the hillbilly cat," the "Memphis flash," a "bebop Western star," and even a "folk music fireball." But if his music was difficult to label, there was unanimity that Presley was one of a kind. Recalling the sensational impact of the early Presley, country music singer Bob Luman once related:

> This cat came out in red pants and a green coat and a pink shirt and socks, and he had this sneer on his face and he stood behind the mike for five minutes, I'll bet, before he made a move. Then he hit his guitar a lick, and he broke two strings. . . . So there he was, these two strings dangling, and he hadn't done anything yet, and these high school girls were screaming and fainting and running up to the stage, and then he started to move his hips real slow like he had a thing for his guitar. That was Elvis Presley when he was about 19, playing Kilgore, Texas. He made chills run up my back, man, like when your hair starts grabbing at your collar.

Radio was a pivotal force in Presley's early career. Via the popular *Louisiana Hayride* radio show, his music reached listeners in thirteen states. His sensual, electric performances increasingly drew young women. When he wrapped an act in Jacksonville, Florida, by drawling "Girls, I'll see y'all backstage," hundreds of female attendees took him at his word. The May 1955 incident marked the first riot of his career.

ROCKETING TO STARDOM

His ascendancy caught the attention of manager-promoter Colonel Tom Parker. The former carnival man had received his honorary "Colonel" title in the 1940s, from hillbilly singer-turned-Louisiana governor Jimmie Davis. As shrewd as he was colorful, the Colonel was managing the *Grand Ole Opry*'s Hank Snow when he first heard about the young man from Memphis. He signed Presley to a contract in late summer 1955 and then promptly negotiated the singer's move from the regional Sun Records to the nationally prominent RCA Records.

Even before the move to RCA, Presley proved surprisingly astute about stardom and its demands. From his own office in Memphis, he saw to it that fan mail was answered and photo requests were filled. Aware that he was becoming the music world's equivalent of James Dean and Marlon Brando, the image-savvy Presley refused to smile for a *Parade* magazine photographer during a late 1955 session, explaining, "I know that you can't be sexy if you smile. You can't be a rebel if you grin." After asking if he could pose himself, Presley casually stripped off his shirt and stared soulfully at the lens.

A momentous year for Presley, 1956 saw his first RCA single, "Heartbreak Hotel," top the charts and become his first gold record. His first album, *Elvis Presley*, likewise went gold. "Don't Be Cruel" and "Hound Dog" were Top 10 hits. Television appearances followed, along with a lucrative film contract and, in a triumphant homecoming, several now-legendary performances at the Tupelo fairgrounds. Presley's name and likeness also adorned a myriad of products, ranging from charm bracelets to stuffed hound dogs. During their first fifteen months on the shelves, Presley merchandise accounted for $40 million in sales.

There was, after all, a new and burgeoning market: the American teenager. The country's approximately 13 million teenagers had annual earnings, including allowances, of more than $7 billion. Teen paychecks, the emergence of the 45 rpm record, and the popularity of the jukebox were integral to Presley's meteoric rise.

But not everyone applauded his pervasive presence. Originally it was "race" artists, such as Fats Domino, Little Richard, and Chuck Berry, who spread the startling sound called rock and roll, which merged elements of gospel, rockabilly, and rhythm and blues. When white artists performed the music, it became more accessible. As performed by Presley, it became a volatile force. Denounced from pulpits, as well as by educators, the music was targeted for suppression by communities from coast to coast. As moral indignation grew, Presley became a whipping boy. The national boiling point followed his sexually charged performance of "Hound Dog" on *The Milton Berle Show*. Critics railed, calling him "lewd," "obscene," and "suggestive." A reprieve came with his third and final appearance on America's premiere variety show, *The Ed Sullivan Show*. Following Presley's performance of January 1957, the respected host assured his audience that Presley was a "real decent, fine boy."

FROM THE ARMY TO HOLLYWOOD

Fame brought changes to Presley's personal life. He moved his family into their new home, the Memphis estate named Graceland. He indulged in cosmetic alterations, including capped teeth, a nose job, and skin treatments. He dyed his hair black, in the belief that black hair made a subject more striking for the cameras.

The inveterate moviegoer had dreamed of becoming a serious actor. But producers did not want Presley to dramatically emote; they wanted him to sing. Thus, anachronistic musical numbers found their way into Presley's 1956 film debut, the bittersweet Civil War romance, *Love Me Tender*, for which he was critically reviled. He fared better in 1957 with the back-to-back, somewhat autobiographical entries *Loving You* and *Jailhouse Rock*. The latter is significant for his surly performance and the stunning title song musical sequence. His follow-up film, the gritty *King Creole*, boasted his most promising work. Then came his induction into the U.S. Army.

The Memphis Selective Service Commission's 1958 decision to draft Presley prompted congratulatory letters from parents, along with death threats from teenage girls. For many in the former group, his haircut by U.S. Army barbers was a powerful and welcome sign that a rebellious era was ending.

The military stint proved significant for Presley. While stationed in Germany he began seriously popping barbiturates in an effort to keep longer hours. In the wake of his mother's death, which left him devastated, he formed a close relationship with the fourteen-year-old daughter of an Air Force captain. He later had the teenage Priscilla Beaulieu brought to Memphis, to surreptitiously live at Graceland.

Returning from the service in 1960, Presley headed to Hollywood, where he and his entourage became renowned for their womanizing and wild parties. Presley's inner circle, which came to be known as the Memphis Mafia, provided a buffer for the star, who increasingly kept his private life private.

His first post-Army film, the formulaic *G.I. Blues*, triggered a series of lightweight romantic musicals set against exotic settings, costarring myriad pretty girls. Presley cynically referred to them as "travelogues." Still, films such as *Blue Hawaii* and *Fun in Acapulco* were huge moneymakers. And he found his match, in talent and charisma, opposite real-life romantic interest Ann-Margret in the 1964 film *Viva Las Vegas*.

Musically, the post-Army Presley concentrated on ballads. Signifying his shift from rock and roll was "Are You Lonesome Tonight?" as well as "It's Now or Never," which featured Presley in a crooning mode. There were also frothy songs from his movies and religious entries, including "Crying in the Chapel." To young people, it appeared that Presley was stagnating. He himself worried that he was being eclipsed by the "British invasion." In desperation, he agreed to star in an NBC-TV special. The resulting *Elvis*, which aired in December 1968, stands as one of the great show business comebacks. Looking slim and sexy, clad in tight-fitting black leather, Presley performed before a live audience in jam session style. When he returned to TV five years later, Presley was likewise a mesmerizing figure, in white jumpsuit and an American eagle-emblazoned cape. *Elvis: Aloha from Hawaii—Via Satellite* was beamed to countries around the world, to a record-breaking audience of as many as 1.5 billion.

THE DANGERS OF EXCESS

Enshrined as "the King," the Presley of the early 1970s was the top headliner of Las Vegas, where he was under contract to the Hilton International Hotel. He also played to sold-out crowds in concert arenas across the country. With the revitalization of his career came a tone of playful self-mockery, as evidenced by the inclusion of Richard Strauss's monumental "Also Sprach Zarathustra" as the opening music for his concerts.

But Presley's professional triumphs were marred by escalating personal woes. His relationship with Beaulieu (the two having married in May 1967) unraveled shortly after the 1968 birth of daughter Lisa Marie. The couple divorced in 1973. His health also suffered. From late 1973 until his death, Presley was in and out of hospitals, "officially" for treatment of pneumonia, exhaustion, and other ailments. In truth he was battling a long-term dependence on prescription drugs, as well as weight problems. During 1975 and 1976 his performances were increasingly erratic. One Las Vegas engagement was canceled when he collapsed, in tears, onstage.

Despite the warning signs, the world was stunned when forty-two-year-old Presley died at his Graceland home on August 16, 1977. President Jimmy Carter observed his passing with a statement saluting the man who symbolized America's "vitality, rebelliousness, and good humor." An estimated 80,000 people lined the streets of Memphis to watch the funeral procession.

Coincidentally, Presley died shortly after the publication of *Elvis: What Happened?*, a lurid exposé penned by former aides. The dark side of his life consequently became fodder for tabloid writers and biographers. Among them was Albert Goldman, whose 1981 book *Elvis* is infamous for its cruel tone. Because of the tell-alls, some Presley associates, including personal physician Dr. George Nichopolous and Mafia members, became familiar names. And there was heightened skepticism over the exact cause of Presley's death. When he died his system contained traces of ten different drugs, including morphine and codeine. But the medical examiner determined that "hypertensive heart disease" had caused the death. Autopsy results were reexamined in 1994, and it was concluded that Presley had died of a heart attack. Yet drugs and gluttony certainly contributed to his downward spiral. Presley stands as a preeminent example of the dangers of excess.

THE LEGEND ENDURES

Presley, however, also personifies the American dream. He ranks as a preeminent musical influence of the twentieth century. At the time of his death, he had sold more than 500 million records. His vast catalog—encompassing blues, rockabilly, country, gospel, rock and roll, and more—is unsurpassed. In revolutionizing popular music, he spawned countless imitators, including the pompadoured rock and rollers who climbed the charts in his aftermath, and he influenced generations of performers and musicians, professionally and personally.

With his penchant for pink Cadillacs, jewel-encrusted rings, and other audacious trappings, Presley embodied the concept of the superstar as conspicuous consumer. By cleverly reinventing himself to suit changing times and tastes, he set a pattern since emulated by rock stars ranging from Elton John to Michael Jackson, from Madonna to Courtney Love. But unlike his successors, his varying images went beyond promotional angles to become cultural benchmarks. When the U.S. Postal Service issued a twenty-nine cent Presley stamp in 1993, the public voted for the image to illustrate the young 1950s-era Elvis. Within the merchandising arena, Elvises of all eras abound, on products ranging from alarm clocks to dolls, from designer ties to doormats. Closely guarding the name, likeness, and image of the entertainer is Elvis Presley Enterprises, Inc., a multimillion dollar business that was largely owned by Presley's daughter, Lisa Marie Presley, until 2005, when a majority interest in the company was sold to media mogul Robert Sillerman. It was Lisa Marie's mother, Priscilla Presley, who salvaged the Presley estate, which was mismanaged during Presley's lifetime due to business dealings balanced in favor of Colonel Parker. The empire's crown jewel is Graceland, which is visited annually by some 750,000 people, making it the second most-toured residence following the White House. Because of the enduring popularity of his music and Elvis-themed merchandise and performances, Presley consistently ranks as one of the top-earning deceased celebrities. In 2011 he placed second on that list, annually published by *Forbes*.

Presley was himself a visitor to the White House, albeit an uninvited one, when he showed up in December 1970 and asked to be part of the country's war on drugs. Unaware of the rock star's own drug dependency, President Richard M. Nixon made Presley an honorary narcotics agent. Their meeting, one of the oddest political summits ever, typified the surreal, unsurpassed nature of Presley's stardom. That bizarre quality continued into the 1990s, as personified by Elvis cults, Elvis "sightings," Elvis impersonators, and even Lisa Marie Presley's brief marriage to pop superstar Michael Jackson.

So rife is the Elvis Presley influence that the mere mention of certain foods, such as the fried peanut butter and banana sandwich, a Presley favorite, summon up his memory. Certain clothing attire, including blue suede shoes, immediately suggest Presley. He is the subject of a thriving cottage publishing industry, has been scrutinized in movies and TV shows, and even shows up as a "character" in movies and on TV. His appeal spans all social strata. Not only is he studied and analyzed in universities, but also, he remains a frequent tabloid subject. The Presley concert closing announcement, that "Elvis has left the building!" has even become part of the lexicon. But Presley has not really left. He lives in the collective conscience. In the parlance of Presley fans, Elvis is eternal.

Pat H. Broeske

SEE ALSO: *Berle, Milton; Berry, Chuck; Bland, Bobby "Blue"; Blues; Brando, Marlon; British Invasion; Consumerism; Country Music; Dean, James; Disc Jockeys; Domino, Fats; The Draft; Folk Music; Gospel Music; Graceland;* Grand Ole Opry*; Hollywood; Jackson, Michael; Jeans; John, Elton; King, B. B.; Las Vegas; Little Richard; Love, Courtney; Madonna; Mafia/Organized Crime; The Musical; Pop Music; Rainey, Gertrude "Ma"; Rhythm and Blues; Rock and Roll; Sullivan, Ed; Sun Records; Tabloids.*

BIBLIOGRAPHY

Brown, Peter Harry, and Pat H. Broeske. *Down at the End of Lonely Street: The Life and Death of Elvis Presley.* New York: Dutton, 1997.

"Elvis—A Different Kind of Idol." *Life*, August 27, 1956, 101–109.

Goldman, Albert. *Elvis.* New York: Avon, 1981.

Guralnick, Peter. *Careless Love: The Unmaking of Elvis Presley.* Boston: Little, Brown, 1999.

Guralnick, Peter. *Last Train to Memphis: The Rise of Elvis Presley.* Boston: Little, Brown, 1994.

Halberstam, David. *The Fifties.* New York: Villard Books, 1993.

Klein, George, and Chuck Crisafulli. *Elvis: My Best Man; Radio Days, Rock 'n' Roll Nights, and My Lifelong Friendship with Elvis Presley.* New York: Crown, 2010.

Shearer, Lloyd. "I Remember Elvis." *Parade*, January 29, 1978, 4–9.

Torgoff, Martin, ed. *The Complete Elvis.* New York: Delilah Books, 1982.

West, Red; Sonny West; and Dave Hebler, as told to Steve Dunleavy. *Elvis: What Happened?* New York: Ballantine Books, 1977.

Price, Reynolds *(1933–2011)*

Southern novelist and man of letters Reynolds Price became a distinguished figure in American literature after the 1962 publication of his first novel, *A Long and Happy Life.* With a distinct prose style and rich narrative voice rooted in the language and rhythms of his native North Carolina, he depicted a world of rural familiarity. His characters struggle with personal desires while trying to answer to family duties. His many works include novels, short stories, plays, poems, essays, translations, and memoirs. The most notable include the novels *Kate Vaiden* (1986) and *The Surface of Earth* (1975) and the cancer memoir *A Whole New Life* (1994), which chronicled Price's battle against spinal cancer.

Price also collaborated on songs with singer/songwriter James Taylor and broadcast personal commentaries on National Public Radio's *All Things Considered* from 1996 to 2002. He contributed stories, poems, and articles to a number of publications, including the *New Yorker* and *Esquire.* His final published work was the memoir *Ardent Spirits: Leaving Home, Coming Back*, which was published in 2009. A graduate of Duke University and a Rhodes scholar, Price taught in the English Department at Duke from 1958 until his death in 2011.

James Schiff

SEE ALSO: *Cancer; Esquire; The* New Yorker*; Radio; Taylor, James.*

BIBLIOGRAPHY

Humphries, Jefferson, ed. *Conversations with Reynolds Price.* Jackson: University Press of Mississippi, 1991.

Kimball, Sue Laslie, and Lynn Veach Sadler, eds. *Reynolds Price: From "A Long and Happy Life" to "Good Hearts."* Fayetteville, NC: Methodist College Press, 1989.

Rooke, Constance. *Reynolds Price.* Boston: Twayne, 1983.

Schiff, James. *Understanding Reynolds Price.* Columbia: University of South Carolina Press, 1996.

Schiff, James A., ed. *Critical Essays on Reynolds Price.* New York: G. K. Hall, 1998.

Price, Vincent *(1911–1993)*

A veteran of theater, film, radio, and television, Vincent Leonard Price Jr. had a fifty-five-year acting career that ran the gamut from classic film noir to "B" movies. In particular he is known for his Gothic horror movies, which he made with good humor and ghoulish glee. Before the dawn of late-twentieth-century slasher films, the mellifluous and debonair Price reigned as Hollywood's master of the macabre. With his distinctive voice, handsome demeanor, and tongue-in-cheek approach to Gothic films, as he liked to call them, he brought style and fun to the horror genre. Generations of film fans have reveled in his ability to send audiences on a hilarious horror romp before scaring them to the core.

Although his style was English, Price hailed from Middle America. The youngest child of a successful candy manufacturer, he lived comfortably among the social elite of St. Louis, Missouri. The son and brother of Yale graduates, Price graduated from Yale with a degree in English and art history. He went on to pursue his passion for art history at the prestigious Courtauld Institute in London.

A longtime theater and movie buff, he auditioned for a bit part at London's Gate Theatre on a dare and was cast in the role of a Chicago policeman. Bitten by the acting bug, he won the coveted role of Prince Albert in *Victoria Regina* (1934). When Broadway producer Gilbert Miller bought the play as a vehicle for actress Helen Hayes, Price returned to New York and made his Broadway debut in 1936. For two years he appeared nightly in the hottest play on Broadway. Regarded as a matinee idol, the handsome 6-foot-4-inch actor eventually struck out on his own and found roles at director Orson Welles's Mercury Theatre.

In 1938 Price signed with Universal Pictures, where he was groomed to be a leading man. But after a disappointing screen debut in a light comedy, he was cast in second and third leads for four years. In 1941 he returned to Broadway to star in *Angel Street* (1938) as a sadistic villain. The play became Broadway's longest-running melodrama for several decades (and later a hit movie, *Gaslight* [1944]). Having discovered his penchant for playing evildoers, Price returned to Hollywood in 1942 to join the strong stable of actors at Twentieth Century Fox.

During the 1940s he appeared in such screen classics as *Laura* (1944) and *The Song of Bernadette* (1943) before starring in *Dragonwyck* (1946). Cast as a despotic, drug-addicted, murdering landowner, he won rave reviews. But it was not until the 1953 3-D horror classic *House of Wax* (1953) that he catapulted to horror-movie fame. The genre had a resurgence of public interest during the 1950s, helping make two of Price's next films cult classics: *House on Haunted Hill* (1959) and *The Tingler* (1959). The master showman of horror, William Castle, directed both movies.

Price's next decade of work would establish him as the undisputed king of horror. He starred in American International Pictures' cycle of films based on the work of horror writer Edgar Allan Poe. Shot in fifteen days on a ridiculously low budget, director Roger Corman's *House of Usher* (1960) marked a tour de force performance for Price, who played the tormented Roderick Usher. The film was both critically acclaimed and financially successful. Price and Corman made five more Poe films together, from the lighthearted *Tales of Terror* (1962) to the surreal *The Masque of the Red Death* (1964). *The Raven* (1963), a delectable comedy that united Price with fellow horror stars Boris Karloff and Peter Lorre, became an audience favorite and a staple of late-night television.

Price's tongue-in-cheek approach delighted his fans, as did his willingness to spoof himself in popular TV shows such as *The Brady Bunch* (1969–1974) and *Batman* (1966–1968), where he appeared as the villainous Egghead. To counteract his horror persona, he assembled and sold the Vincent Price art collection for Sears Roebuck & Company and wrote several gourmet cookbooks. Cultured and intelligent, he was often referred to as Hollywood's Renaissance man.

During the early 1970s, Price continued to make horror classics such as *The Abominable Dr. Phibes* (1971). But he soon grew discouraged as the genre changed from Gothic tales to slasher films. He decided to return to his roots in the theater, spending almost a decade touring the globe with his one-man show about writer Oscar Wilde, *Diversions and Delights* (1978). In the mid-1980s, he reached a new generation when pop music icon Michael Jackson asked the seventy-two-year-old actor to rap for the mega-hit "Thriller." In 1987 Price played his first nonhorror role in decades in the acclaimed film *The Whales of August* (1987), starring actresses Bette Davis and Lillian Gish.

Price's final role would come through another memorable partnership. In 1982 a young animator at Disney named Tim Burton made a short film about a boy who wanted to grow up to be Price. Burton approached Price about narrating the film, and the actor agreed. Price and Burton became friends, and eight years later Burton gave the ailing actor his cinematic swan song as the kindhearted inventor in *Edward Scissorhands* (1990). Price died at age eighty-two in 1993.

Victoria Price

SEE ALSO: *Batman;* The Brady Bunch*; Broadway; Corman, Roger; Davis, Bette; Disney (Walt Disney Company); Gish, Lillian; Hollywood; Horror Movies; Jackson, Michael; Karloff, Boris; Lorre, Peter; Radio; Rap; Sears Roebuck Catalogue; Slasher Movies; Television; Welles, Orson.*

BIBLIOGRAPHY

Meikle, Denis. *Vincent Price: The Art of Fear.* London: Reynolds & Hearn, 2003.

Price, Victoria. *Vincent Price: A Daughter's Biography.* New York: St. Martin's Press, 1999.

Price, Vincent. *I Like What I Know.* New York: Doubleday, 1959.

Williams, Lucy Chase. *The Complete Films of Vincent Price.* Secaucus, NJ: Citadel Press, 1995.

The Price Is Right

The Price Is Right, the longest-running game show in television history, is a proving ground of consumer shrewdness that could one day serve as an artifact of capitalist frenzy. As it entered its seventh decade on the air during the 2010s, the program continued to entrance millions of American shut-ins, homemakers, and truant school children. The venerable show made its debut on NBC in November 1956, with Bill Cullen as host. In its early days the program had a rigid format centered on contestants guessing the prices of various consumer items. This incarnation ran until 1965, when it was canceled and seemed consigned to TV oblivion.

But it came back in 1972 with a new host, genial former *Truth or Consequences* emcee Bob Barker. He would remain with *The Price Is Right* until 2007, logging more man-hours on network television than any other person in history. Under his stewardship, the show took on a looser format with a bevy of price-guessing games, some with complicated rules that bewildered contestants. In the Clock Game, for example, a contestant would receive thirty seconds to guess the prices of two prizes. Barker would tell the contestant only whether the

The Price Is Right. *Bob Barker leads an excited contestant through a game on* The Price Is Right *in 1978.* CBS PHOTO ARCHIVE/GETTY IMAGES.

prices he or she guessed were higher or lower than the actual retail price, and the guessing game would continue until the contestant hit on the exact price. At the end of every show was the Showcase Showdown, in which the show's two most successful contestants competed for expensive prizes such as trips, cars, and furniture.

A number of staple features gave *The Price Is Right* a distinctive look and sound. Announcer Johnny Olson became famous for his booming exhortation to contestants to "Come on down!" (Spokesman Rod Roddy succeeded Olson after Olson's death in 1985.) Viewers also came to recognize Barker's Beauties, an ever-changing company of leggy models who presented the prizes. Almost as intriguing were the show's frantic contestants and onstage mishaps, such as a woman losing her tube top while running down to the stage after her name was called and a refrigerator that nearly toppled over onto a contestant.

Perhaps the most unusual aspect of the show's long television run was the bizarre behavior of its well-tanned host and star. A onetime karate student of action hero Chuck Norris, Barker seemed the epitome of blow-dried, hair-dyed emcee cool. But off the set he often courted controversy. An ardent animal rights activist, he enraged the producers of the Miss USA Pageant in 1988 when he stopped hosting the show to protest the awarding of furs to contestants. The next year, in response to ads he had run in *Variety* accusing the American Humane Association of negligence and incompetence, the organization, which monitors the treatment of animals in show business, slapped the host with a $10 million suit for libel, slander, and invasion of privacy.

Litigation against Barker also reached into his personal life. In 1994 Dian Parkinson, a former *Price Is Right* model, sued the eighty-year-old Barker for sexually harassing her during their years together on the show. According to the suit, Parkinson claimed that Barker frequently called her to his dressing room; told her, "Daddy's bored"; and forced her to perform oral sex on him. The case was eventually dropped.

Such shenanigans might have been the kiss of death for any other game show host but Barker. Even after he stopped dyeing his trademark coiffure (with network approval) in 1987, the new, silver-maned Barker gave no indication of slowing down. In June 2007, after winning nineteen Daytime Entertainment Emmy Awards during his thirty-five years with the show, Barker retired, later publishing a memoir about his years on air titled *Priceless Memories*. He was succeeded as host by comedian and comic actor Drew Carey, whose first episode aired in October 2007. Vastly different from the suave Barker, Carey and his famously dorky persona launched a new era for the show, drawing viewers with his empathetic humor and on-air dialogue about weight loss.

Robert E. Schnakenberg

SEE ALSO: *Consumerism; Emmy Awards; Game Shows; Hairstyles; Sex Scandals; Television;* Variety.

BIBLIOGRAPHY

Barker, Bob, and Digby Diehl. *Priceless Memories*. New York: Center Street, 2009.

Schwartz, David; Steve Ryan; and Fred Wostbrock. *The Encyclopedia of TV Game Shows*. New York: Facts On File, 1995.

Smith, Lucinda. "Speaking up for 'Abused' Animals, Bob Barker Is Hit with a Lawsuit." *People*, September 18, 1989.

Pride, Charley *(1938–)*

Singer Charley Pride has the distinction of being the only African American musician to have a career entirely in country music, a musical genre dominated by white performers. His string of hits that began in the mid-1960s and continued for nearly twenty years broke the color line in country music, even though no other black performers followed Pride's lead. His smooth voice and country-pop sound carried him to success despite his record company's initial fears that he would not be accepted by the country music establishment, or its fans, because of his race.

Born in 1938 to a sharecropping family on a cotton farm in Sledge, Mississippi, Pride crossed racial lines early in life, preferring to listen to white country music rather than delta blues or other black musical forms. He bought his first guitar from the Sears Roebuck catalog at the age of fourteen with money he earned picking cotton and began to teach himself country songs he heard on the radio. When he was seventeen, he left home to play baseball with the Negro American League, where he played with the Detroit Eagles and later the Memphis Red Sox. He served for two years in the army and returned to baseball after his discharge, joining the Los Angeles Angels. He tried to break into the major leagues with both the California Angels and the New York Mets, but he missed the cut both times.

His short career in professional baseball over, Pride went to work part time as a semipro baseball player and as a smelter for the Anaconda Mining Company in Helena, Montana. He also sang in a local nightclub, where he was heard one night by country singer Red Sovine, who was impressed by Pride's voice and singing style. Sovine encouraged him to go to Nashville, Tennessee, the birthplace of country music. Pride did, and while unsuccessful at first, he was eventually heard by country guitarist and producer Chet Atkins, who was also in charge of RCA Records' Nashville division. Atkins signed Pride to a record deal in 1966.

Pride's first single, "The Snakes Crawl at Night," was issued without any publicity photos, fearing that southern disc jockeys would not play a country record by a black artist. "The Snakes Crawl at Night" and Pride's next song, "Before I Met You," were modest successes. His first major hit was "Just Between You and Me," released at the end of 1966. In early 1967 Pride became the first black artist to appear on the *Grand Ole Opry* since harmonica player DeFord Bailey in 1925.

From 1969 to 1971 Pride had five number one singles: "All I Have to Offer You (Is Me)," "I'd Rather Love You," "Is Anybody Goin' to San Antone," "Wonder Could I Live There Anymore," and "I'm So Afraid of Losing You Again." His biggest chart successes came in 1971 with "Kiss an Angel Good Mornin'" and "I'm Just Me." These songs not only topped the country charts but also crossed over onto the pop charts, providing compelling evidence of Pride's wide appeal among a variety of audiences and establishing him as a major star in mainstream country music. His acceptance by country music fans eliminated any fears that a black artist could not succeed in country music. Next to Elvis Presley, Pride was RCA's best-selling artist.

Pride maintained his consistent country-pop style throughout the 1970s and 1980s, refusing to follow newer trends in country music. His adherence to his trademark sound led him to leave RCA in 1986, unhappy that the record label was spending less time promoting established artists, like himself, in order to focus on newcomers. In the 1990s he continued to record, occasionally forming duets with younger performers, such as Travis Tritt, and he maintained an active concert schedule.

Throughout his career, Pride received three Grammy Awards and sixteen Academy of Country Music Awards, including the Pioneer Award in 1993 in recognition of his groundbreaking achievements in country music. He was inducted into the Country Music Hall of Fame and Museum in 2000, and in 2008 he received the Mississippi Governor's Award for Excellence in the Arts in Lifetime Achievement.

Timothy Berg

SEE ALSO: *Atkins, Chet; Country Music; Grammy Awards;* Grand Ole Opry; *Negro Leagues; The New York Mets; Pop Music; Presley, Elvis; Sears Roebuck Catalogue.*

BIBLIOGRAPHY

The Country Music Foundation, eds. *Country: The Music and the Musicians.* New York: Abbeville Press, 1994.

Kingsbury, Paul. *The Encyclopedia of Country Music: The Ultimate Guide to Music.* New York: Oxford University Press, 2004.

Malone, Bill C. *Country Music, U.S.A.: A Fifty-Year History,* rev. ed. Austin: University of Texas Press, 1985.

Pride, Charley. *The Essential Charley Pride.* RCA Nashville/Legacy, 1997, 2 compact discs.

Pride, Charley, and Jim Henderson. *Pride: The Charley Pride Story.* New York: Quill, 1994.

Stambler, Irwin, and Grelun Landon. *Country Music: The Encyclopedia.* New York: St. Martin's, 1997.

Prince *(1958–)*

An exciting live performer and a prolific singer-songwriter, Prince resists easy categorization because of his uncanny ability to transcend genres in music and image. Often a misunderstood and controversial entertainer, he emerged on the music scene in 1977 to eventually record a staggering twenty albums in just twenty years. In the 1990s he staged a bitter and highly publicized dispute with his record company, Warner Brothers, over the nature of his contract. Ultimately, the artist changed his name to a symbol in an attempt to regain creative control over his career, then changed it back again once he had achieved independence. Prince attained the peak of his critical and commercial success in the early 1980s, but by the first decade of the 2000s he had become a musical entrepreneur, continuing to tour regularly while maintaining a legion of fans in the United States and abroad.

DEVELOPING A UNIQUE STYLE

Prince Rogers Nelson was born in Minneapolis, Minnesota, on June 7, 1958, to Mattie Shaw and John Nelson, a local musician. In his formative years during the 1960s and 1970s, Prince honed his skills on a number of different instruments and immersed himself in the music of artists who would eventually influence his sound: Carlos Santana, Joni Mitchell, Curtis Mayfield, Stevie Wonder, Sly and the Family Stone, and Jimi Hendrix. Drawing from this rich legacy, by the late 1970s Prince had helped invent what became known as the Minneapolis Sound: a blend of horns, guitars, and electronic synthesizers supported by a steady, bouncing rhythm.

Although Prince has often been classified as a rock musician, his work is much more complex, fusing elements from rhythm and blues, pop, rock, funk, punk, and country. He also boasts a wide-ranging vocal ability that includes a growling baritone, a full tenor sound, an elegant falsetto, and a piercing shriek. The multifaceted nature of Prince's music and singing have helped earn him a broad and diverse audience throughout his career, allowing him to cross over the racial boundaries that tended to dominate the music scene before his arrival.

In April 1978 Prince released his first album, *For You*, playing most of the instruments and overdubbing his voice to heightened effect. While the recording was a modest success, his next release, *Prince* (1979), reached platinum status and produced the hit singles "I Feel for You" and "I Wanna Be Your Lover." The two albums that followed, *Dirty Mind* (1980) and *Controversy* (1981), were highly influenced by 1980s new wave and punk music. The latter album is aptly named: with each release, Prince became increasingly controversial for his explicit lyrics that engaged sexual themes, including oral sex, incest, and sadomasochism.

Prince's outrageous sense of style also proved to be attention grabbing. Possessing a small, short frame and a full mane of hair, he showed an affinity for lacy, frilly, and often suggestive clothing. His rare appearances in media interviews were awkward and self-effacing; yet on stage, he was carnal and exhibitionistic in a way audiences had not witnessed before. Along with his musical peers Boy George and Michael Jackson, Prince helped establish a sense of masculinity in the 1980s that owed a major debt to the images of such popular rock stars as David Bowie, Iggy Pop, and Mick Jagger. In Prince's world, men could wear makeup and women's clothes and still maintain a diverse and supportive fan base.

Prince. *Prince performs in the United Kingdom in 2011.* NEIL LUPIN/CONTRIBUTOR/REDFERNS/GETTY IMAGES.

BECOMING A SUPERSTAR

Prince rose to superstar standing with the release of his next two groundbreaking albums: *1999* (1982), a double-album set featuring several hit singles, including "Little Red Corvette" and the infectious, prophetic title track, and *Purple Rain* (1984), which brought about the defining moment of Prince's career. The album functioned as a soundtrack for his first film, also titled *Purple Rain.* Directed on a modest budget by Albert Magnoli (who later became Prince's manager), the semiautobiographical film presented Prince as the Kid, a struggling rock singer tormented by his dysfunctional relationships with women and his father.

Unexpectedly, *Purple Rain* became the most commercially and critically successful rock film since the Beatles' *A Hard Day's Night* (1964). The soundtrack spawned a series of number one and Top 10 singles on the pop charts, including "Let's Go Crazy" and "When Doves Cry." The album ultimately earned Prince three Grammy Awards, while the title track garnered him a 1985 Academy Award for Best Original Song. The unprecedented success of the black-cast film also prepared the way for Spike Lee's groundbreaking independent film, *She's Gotta Have It* (1986), which in turn helped catalyze a new wave of black filmmaking in the 1980s and 1990s.

Although Prince never again attained the commercial visibility of the year in which he released *Purple Rain*, he followed that work with a series of sophisticated and critically praised albums on his own record label, Paisley Park. These included *Around the World in a Day* (1985), which sold more than two million copies and featured the hit single "Raspberry Beret," and *Parade* (1986), which served as the soundtrack for his next film, the disastrous *Under the Cherry Moon.*

After disbanding his backup group the Revolution, Prince released a double-album set, *Sign o' the Times* (1987), which generated a concert film the same year. The melodic complexity and musical diversity of *Sign o' the Times* helped establish Prince as a "true" artist in many critical circles. His next release, *Lovesexy* (1988), was complemented by a lavish international tour. The album received attention mostly for its controversial cover, on which Prince appeared fully nude, his loin area strategically covered. He also composed the soundtrack music for two films: Tim Burton's hugely successful *Batman* (1989) and his own film vehicle, *Graffiti Bridge* (1990), a project that failed miserably at the box office.

During the height of his fame in the 1980s, Prince was linked in the media to a string of glamorous female performers, including Vanity, Appolonia, Sheena Easton, and Kim Basinger. He also helped bring a number of artists to visibility, among them Morris Day, Tevin Campbell, Sheila E, and Carmen Electra. In the 1990s he used his formidable talent to produce albums and songs for legendary but largely forgotten rhythm-and-blues and funk artists such as Mavis Staples and George Clinton.

SURVIVING ARTISTIC STRUGGLES

In October 1991 Prince released an album titled *Diamonds and Pearls*, featuring his newly formed backup band, the New Power Generation. Although the recording was a commercial success, Prince's mix of rap, rhythm and blues, and funk styles no longer came across as fresh or original in the changing popular music scene of the 1990s. According to his biographer, Liz Jones, the artist seemed to be "chasing trends rather than creating them." Moreover, Prince's androgyny was no match for the powerfully abrasive images of masculinity that had gained appeal in popular culture in the early 1990s through gangsta rap and black films.

In 1993 Prince's behind-the-scenes battle with Warner Brothers—the record label that had represented him since his debut—came to public attention. In August 1992 he had signed a deal with the company that promised him $100 million for six albums, with a $10 million advance. In order to recoup funds spent on Prince in the latter half of the 1980s and into the 1990s, Warner Brothers released a double-album set of his greatest hits in 1993 over the singer's objections. In 1994 the company closed his struggling Paisley Park label. In response, Prince refused to release newly composed music, choosing instead to provide Warner with prerecorded and often lesser material from his vault of more than 500 unreleased songs.

Prince's attempt to resist Warner Brothers had far-reaching effects on his audience and his critics, who longed to hear the musical quality that had defined his early career. As part of his rebellion, in 1993 Prince had changed his name to a symbol that combined the generic signs for male and female. His new non-name alienated the singer from many of his fans, who were obliged to refer to him as The Artist Formerly Known as Prince or The Artist. In September 1995 he released a new album, *The Gold Experience*, under the new symbol. Eventually, the recording went gold, spawning one hit single, "The Most Beautiful Girl in the World." Partly because of poor management, however, he found himself deeply in debt at the end of year. As a result he was forced to close several of the entrepreneurial ventures he had launched since the 1980s, including his Miami nightclub, Glam Slam, and his merchandise shops in Minneapolis and London.

In 1996, after the commercially and critically disastrous release of the album *Chaos and Disorder*, The Artist Formerly Known as Prince and Warner Brothers reached a mutual agreement to terminate their contractual agreement. The Artist then signed with EMI and released a CD collection titled *Emancipation*. The recording contained new material and covers of songs made famous by artists as diverse as Bonnie Raitt and the Stylistics. A celebration of both his relationship with his new wife, Mayte Garcia, and his hard-won independence from Warner Brothers, the album rose to number eleven on Billboard's pop album chart and number six on the rhythm-and-blues charts. His next album, *Crystal Ball*, was released in 1998. That same year he further developed his independent label by writing, producing, and distributing material for R&B icons Chaka Khan and Larry Graham of Sly and the Family Stone.

ATTEMPTING A COMEBACK

Although The Artist continued to be known as an innovator in popular music, he was not able to sustain the commercial success of his early career in the 1990s, partly because of the rise of rap and other changes in popular music. In 1999 he began to use the name Prince again and released *Rave Un2 the Joy Fantastic* on the Arista label. The album—a collaboration with Sheryl Crow, Chuck D, and other artists—did not fare well. Prince also experienced personal difficulties. He and his wife, Mayte, lost their newborn son to a rare disease, and the tragedy took a toll on their marriage. They divorced in 2000. Prince's second marriage, to Manuela Testolini, lasted from 2001 to 2006.

Prince made something of a comeback in the first decade of the 2000s. His 2004 album *Musicology* sold well, received two Grammy Awards, and spawned a successful concert tour. He was inducted into the Rock and Roll Hall of Fame that year. His next recording, *3121* (2006), received mediocre reviews. In 2007 he performed during the halftime show of Super Bowl XLI.

Prince's ups and downs in the new millennium cannot reduce the powerful influence of his devotion to live instrumentation and musical virtuosity on an entire generation of artists of the 1990s, including rhythm-and-blues performers D'Angelo and Maxwell. He also helped to establish a crossover scene in popular music, in which black singers were no longer limited to certain musical styles and became increasingly able to cross racial boundaries. Always ahead of his time, Prince's ambiguous, gender-bending image helped usher in a new, ostentatious style in popular culture and worked to transform the perception of black masculinity in U.S. society. No matter what name he goes by, Prince is a truly American superstar.

Jason King

SEE ALSO: *Academy Awards; Batman; The Beatles; Bowie, David; Boy George; Chuck D; Clinton, George; Country Music; Crow, Sheryl; Funk; Gangsta Rap; Grammy Awards; Hendrix, Jimi; Jackson, Michael; Mayfield, Curtis; Mitchell, Joni; New Wave Music; Pop, Iggy; Pop Music; Punk; Raitt, Bonnie; Rap; Rhythm and Blues; Rock and Roll; Santana; Sly and the Family Stone; Super Bowl; Wonder, Stevie.*

BIBLIOGRAPHY

Bream, Jon. *Prince: Inside the Purple Reign*. New York: Collier Macmillan, 1984.

Hill, Dave. *Prince: A Pop Life*. London: Faber & Faber, 1989.

Jones, Liz. *Purple Reign: The Artist Formerly Known as Prince*. Secaucus, NJ: Carol Publishing Group, 1998.

Ro, Ronin. *Prince: Inside the Music and the Masks*. New York: St. Martin's Press, 2011.

Prince, Hal *(1928–)*

Harold "Hal" S. Prince revolutionized the American musical in the twentieth century. His resistance to the acting and singing conventions of early twentieth-century musical theater, his refusal to construct musicals as star vehicles, and his use of filmic staging techniques make him one of the world's most original and innovative directors. From his first production, *The Pajama Game* (1954), which cost $170,000, to his 2006 production of *Phantom—The Las Vegas Spectacular*, which rang in at $75 million, Prince has known his share of artistic and financial successes as well as failures. *New York Times* critic David Richards described Prince as "the undisputed master of the Broadway musical."

EARLY EXPOSURE TO THE THEATER

Although not from a theatrical family, Prince was constantly exposed to the theater as a young boy. "Mine was a family addicted to theatre, and still there was no effort to encourage me to work in it nor discourage me, and at no time was there any to push me into finance. So I didn't have to resist something I *would* have resisted." Prince was born into what he called a "privileged upper-middle-, lower-rich-class" German-Jewish family in New York City on January 30, 1928. He was exposed to many of the greatest productions and actors of the time, including Orson Welles's *Julius Caesar* and Burgess Meredith's *Winterset*. In 1944 he graduated from the Franklin School, a private preparatory school, which was also his grandfather's alma mater.

He attended the University of Pennsylvania, where he was a member of the Penn Players. Along with his work in the theater, he founded and managed the campus radio station and wrote, acted in, and directed weekly play adaptations. He enrolled in a liberal arts program with a concentration on English, psychology, philosophy, and history. After graduating in 1948, he wrote plays and sent them to New York producers. After sending one script to ABC-TV, he was referred to the television production office of George Abbott in New York City. There he offered to work "on spec" and, by the end of the month, was earning $25 a week.

Prince worked on all aspects of Abbott's productions, including an original program titled *The Hugh Martin Show*. After Abbott's production company disbanded, Prince was hired by Abbott's production stage manager, Robert E. Griffith. Prince was stage manager for Broadway revues such as *Touch and Go* and *Tickets, Please*. In 1950 he was drafted into the army and stationed in Stuttgart, Germany, for two years as an anti-aircraft artillery gunner. There he spent many evenings visiting a nightclub called Maxim's, which would later become the muse for his hit musical *Cabaret*. Prince was discharged in October 1952. He immediately returned to work with Abbott and Griffith on several more hit musicals and began to learn the craft of directing from Abbott. Their production of Leonard Bernstein's *Wonderful Town* ran 500 performances, inspiring Griffith and Prince to become a producing team. Prince directed his first play, *The Pajama Game*, at the age of twenty-six. The following years led to a string of successes for the Griffith-Prince team, including *Damn Yankees* (1955) and *New Girl in Town* (1957).

PRINCE COMES INTO HIS OWN

Prince's career became much more prominent after 1957 due to two major factors: his collaboration with composer/lyricist Stephen Sondheim and his ability to create his own directorial style free from the influences of George Abbott. His first major success was coproducing the Leonard Bernstein–Sondheim musical *West Side Story* (1957). Biographer Carol Ilson notes that Prince, "having learned his trade well through his working experiences with Abbott, Robbins, Bernstein, Laurents and Sondheim, would emerge with a unique vision of his own for the American Musical Theatre." He would go on to collaborate with Sondheim on many more breakthrough productions: *Company* (1970), *Follies* (1971), *A Little Night Music* (1973), *Pacific Overtures* (1976), *Sweeney Todd* (1979), *Merrily We Roll Along* (1981), and *Bounce* (2003). Prince described their partnership as "creative abrasion," combining Sondheim's shy, introverted nature with his own gregariousness. Summarizing the relationship with Prince, Sondheim's website states, "one of the most successful partnerships on Broadway ended with back-to-back bombs [*Merrily We Roll Along* and *Bounce*]. Not exactly the way they would have wanted to go out."

In the 1980s Prince had a string of box-office and critical failures, including the musicals *A Doll's Life* (1982), *Grind* (1985), and *Roza* (1986). He has said of those six years, "no matter what I did, it could not please critics or audiences. . . . During that period, I thought maybe I'd ceased to be able to create something that people want to see." His career rebounded following a series of successful collaborations with British composer/lyricist Sir Andrew Lloyd Webber. Their productions of *Evita* (1978) and *The Phantom of the Opera* (1986) were international successes. In the following years, Prince directed operas, dramas, and musicals, yet none were as successful as his stagings of *Kiss of the Spider Woman* (1993), *Show Boat* (1994), and *Parade* (1998).

Few directors can claim to have revolutionized the theater as much as Prince. His career, spanning the golden age of Broadway to the postmodern theater, has been one of incredible success and failure. He set the standard for the musical art form, and his productions are known worldwide for their innovative stagings, astounding effects, and impact on the popular theater. Prince has said, "I want to leave a mark, to do something of artistic value." Judging from the lasting impact of his work, he has managed to do both.

Michael Najjar

SEE ALSO: *Bernstein, Leonard; Broadway; Lloyd Webber, Andrew; The Musical;* The Phantom of the Opera*;* Show Boat*; Sondheim, Stephen; Welles, Orson;* West Side Story.

BIBLIOGRAPHY

Adams, Cindy. "Prince among Men." *New York Post*, April 3, 2012.

Bartow, Arthur. "Harold S. Prince." *The Director's Voice: Twenty-One Interviews*. New York: Theatre Communications Group, 1988.

Hirsch, Foster. *Harold Prince and the American Musical Theatre: Expanded Edition*. Cambridge, MA: Cambridge University Press, 2005.

Ilson, Carol. *Harold Prince: From "Pajama Game" to "Phantom of the Opera."* Ann Arbor, MI: UMI Research Press, 1989.

Prince, Hal. *Contradictions: Notes on Twenty-Six Years in the Theatre*. New York: Dodd, Mead, 1974.

Richards, David. "Theater Review: Show Boat; Classic Music with a Change in Focus." *New York Times*, October 3, 1994.

Silva, Cristina. "'Phantom' Show in Vegas to Close after 6 Years." *Washington Times*, January 12, 2012

Sondheim, Stephen. *Finishing the Hat: Collected Lyrics (1954–1981) with Attendant Comments, Principles, Heresies, Grudges, Whines and Anecdotes*. New York: Alfred A. Knopf, 2010.

Sondheim, Stephen. *Look, I Made a Hat*. New York: Alfred A. Knopf, 2011.

"Stephen Sondheim." Accessed May 2012. Available from http://sondheimonsondheim.com

Princess Diana

SEE: *Diana, Princess of Wales.*

Prinze, Freddie *(1954–1977)*

Comedian Freddie Prinze is one of only a handful of Latin Americans to earn national prominence as a popular entertainer. Prinze was born in Washington Heights, a multiethnic neighborhood on New York City's Upper West Side. His father was a Hungarian immigrant of German descent who worked as a tool-and-die maker; his mother was a Puerto Rican immigrant who worked in a factory. Playing on the name "Nuyorican," which is how many Puerto Ricans living in New York identify themselves, Prinze called himself a "Hungarican."

USING HUMOR TO FIT IN

Prinze not only came from a diverse ethnic background but a varied religious one as well. His father was part Jewish, his mother Catholic, but they chose to send him to a Lutheran elementary school. On Sundays he attended Catholic mass. "All was confusing," he told *Rolling Stone* in 1975, "until I found I could crack up the priest [by] doing Martin Luther." Prinze was also overweight when he was a young boy, which further heightened his anxiety about his "mixed" identity. "I fitted in nowhere," he continued. "I wasn't true spic, true Jew, true anything. I was a miserable fat schmuck kid with glasses and asthma." Like many comedians, Prinze used humor to cope with the traumas of his childhood. "I started doing half-hour routines in the boys' room, just winging it. Guys cut class to catch the act. It was, 'What time's Freddie playing the toilet today?'" His comedic talents paid off, as he was selected to attend the prestigious Performing Arts High School in New York.

Although Prinze did not officially graduate from the school, after his professional successes school administrators awarded him a certificate of graduation. The young comedian skipped many of his morning classes, most commonly economics, because he often worked as late as 3 a.m. in comedy clubs perfecting his routine. One of his favorite spots was the Improvisation on West Forty-Fourth Street, a place where aspiring comics could try out their material on receptive audiences.

AN "OBSERVATION COMIC"

Prinze called himself an "observation comic," and his routines often included impressions of ethnic minorities and film stars such as Marlon Brando. One of his most famous impressions was of his Puerto Rican apartment building superintendent, who, when asked to fix a problem in the building, would say with a thick accent: "Eez not mai yob." The line soon became a national catchphrase. His comedy also had a political edge that was poignant and raw. This is perhaps best illustrated by his line about Christopher Columbus: "Queen Isabelle gives him all the money, three boats, and he's wearing a red suit, a big hat, and a feather—that's a pimp." Prinze's comic wit, based in the tradition of street humor pioneered by such comics as Lenny Bruce and Richard Pryor, landed him a number of television appearances, including *The Tonight Show* in 1973.

Prinze's performance on *The Tonight Show* was a major success and signaled the start of his television career. Indeed, Jimmie Komack, a television producer, liked what he saw in Prinze's routine and cast him to play the part of Chico Rodriquez, a wisecracking Mexican American, in a situation comedy called *Chico and the Man* (1974–1978). The series also starred veteran actor Jack Albertson, who played "the Man," a crusty old-timer who owned a rundown garage in a East Los Angeles barrio. In the tradition of situation comedies such as *All in the Family* and *Sanford and Son*, most of the plots involved ethnic conflicts between Chico, who worked in the garage, and the Man, who was the only Caucasian living in the mostly Latino neighborhood. "Latin music sounds like Montovani getting mugged," the Man says to Chico in one episode. Chico would often respond to the old-timer's bigoted statements with the line, "Looking good," which also became a national catch phrase.

Chico and the Man faced criticism from the Los Angeles Mexican American community, who protested the use of Prinze, a New York Puerto Rican, to play a Los Angeles Mexican American. Citing dialect and accent differences—and the fact that network television rarely employed Mexican actors—Mexican American groups picketed NBC's Burbank studios. Prinze responded with his usual irreverent humor: "If I can't play a Chicano because I'm Puerto Rican, then God's really gonna be mad when he finds out Charlton Heston played Moses." Fearful of the bad publicity, the network and producers of the show changed the character of Chico into a half Puerto Rican and half Mexican who was brought up in New York City. The shift in the character's ethnic identity apparently did not bother the audiences, as *Chico and the Man* never slipped below sixth place in the Nielsen ratings while Prinze was its star.

COPING WITH DEPRESSION

Prinze had a difficult time adjusting to his success. Indeed, friends reported that the comic turned to drugs to cope with the pressures of fame. "Freddie was into a lot of drugs," comedian Jimmy Walker told the *New York Times*, "not heroin, as far as I know, but coke and a lot of Ludes. The drug thing was a big part of Freddie's life. It completely messed him up." During this period he also experienced many personal problems. His wife of fifteen months, Katherine Elaine Cochran, filed for divorce. They had a ten-month-old son, Freddie Jr., whom Prinze adored. He was also engaged in a lawsuit with one of his business associates. The totality of these events depressed the young comic.

On January 28, 1977, after a night of phone calls to his secretary, psychiatrist, mother, and estranged wife, Prinze shot himself in the head in front of his business manager. He was rushed to the hospital, where he was put on life support but pronounced dead the next day. He was twenty-two years old. A note found in his apartment read: "I can't take any more. It's all my fault. There is no one to blame but me." According to the *New York Times*, Prinze had previously threatened suicide in front of many of his friends and associates, often by holding a gun to his head and pulling the trigger while the safety was on. It is not known whether the young comedian actually intended to kill himself that night or just feign shooting himself as he had done in the past, but it is clear that he was extremely depressed.

The death of Freddie Prinze is an American success story turned tragedy. His streetwise insight and raw wit are surely missed, perhaps most by the Puerto Rican American community who has yet to see another politically minded Puerto Rican comedian grab national attention. "I am ee-noyed there is no

Puerto Rican astronaut," Prinze told *Rolling Stone* in an exaggerated Spanish accent. "Thee bigots think we will blow thee horn all the way to thee moon, play thee radio, stick our heads out thee window and whistle . . . and then, on thee moon, the white astronaut says, 'Bring in the Rocks now,' and we reply, 'Eez not mai yob, man!'"

Daniel Bernardi

SEE ALSO: *Bruce, Lenny; Depression; Pryor, Richard; Stand-up Comedy; Suicide;* The Tonight Show.

BIBLIOGRAPHY

Beltrán, Mary. *Latina/o Stars in U.S. Eyes: The Making and Meanings of Film and TV Stardom.* Urbana: University of Illinois Press, 2009.

Burke, Tom. "The Undiluted South Bronx Truth about Freddie Prinze." *Rolling Stone*, January 30, 1975, 38–43.

Edelman, Rosemary. "'Pobrito,' It Ain't Easy Being a Star." *TV Guide*, February 15, 1975, 20–22.

Kasindorf, Jeanie. "'If I Was Bitter, I Wouldn't Have Chosen Comedy.'" *New York Times*, February 9, 1975, D27.

Nordheimer, Jon. "Freddie Prinze, 22, Dies after Shooting." *New York Times*, January 30, 1977, 19.

Pruetzel, Maria, and John Andrews Barbour. *The Freddie Prinze Story.* Kalamazoo, MI: Master's Press, 1978.

Seiler, Michael. "Freddie Prinze: He Didn't Believe in Himself: Friends Reflect on Comedian's Childhood, Sudden Rise to Success and His Death." *New York Times*, March 1, 1977, C1.

The Prisoner

The British television series *The Prisoner* aired in the United States during the summer of 1968, setting a standard for imagination and existential vagary that later American shows, such as *Twin Peaks* (1990–1991) and *Lost* (2004–2010), aspired to match.

The brainchild of actor/writer Patrick McGoohan, *The Prisoner* chronicles the travails of prisoner Number Six (played by McGoohan), an unwilling "resident" of what appears to be a sleepy British resort village. Under constant surveillance and thwarted in his repeated attempts to escape, Number Six may (or may not) be John Drake, the spy hero of *Secret Agent* (1964–1966), another television series in which McGoohan had also starred. The fact that the events in each episode had no particular explanation was part of *The Prisoner*'s visionary charm. The program's deep plots touched on themes of conformity, rebellion, and free will over the course of only seventeen increasingly bizarre episodes. In the end, Number Six managed to turn the tables on his captors and escape from the village. Or did he?

Robert E. Schnakenberg

SEE ALSO: Lost*; Television;* Twin Peaks.

BIBLIOGRAPHY

Short, Sue. *Cult Telefantasy Series: A Critical Analysis of* The Prisoner, Twin Peaks, The X-Files, Buffy the Vampire Slayer, Lost, Heroes, Doctor Who *and* Star Trek. Jefferson, NC: McFarland, 2011.

White, Matthew, and Jaffer Ali. *The Official* Prisoner *Companion.* New York: Warner Books, 1988.

The Producers

The quintessential tribute to political incorrectness, *The Producers* was a 1968 film spoof of Broadway, revived in 2001 as a Broadway musical send-up of Broadway musicals, then once again made into a new movie in 2006. Billing itself as an "equal opportunity offender," *The Producers* in all its incarnations mocks the theater community, Nazi Germany, gay people, and old women with such outrageous ribaldry that audiences are left gasping in disbelieving laughter.

The Producers is the brainchild of producer, director, and comic actor Mel Brooks. Brooks honed his slapstick skills as a stand-up comic in vacation resorts in New York's Catskill Mountains, then wrote for early television programs such as Sid Caesar's *Your Show of Shows. The Producers* was his first film, and Brooks, as writer, lyricist, and director, seemed determined to prove that no subject was off-limits to his sharp, satiric wit.

In *The Producers*, Max Bialystock, an unprincipled theatrical producer teams up with Leo Bloom, a timid accountant, to steal money by getting his Broadway investors (a collection of "little old ladies") to back a sure flop. They pick the worst, most offensive play they can find, a musical homage called *Springtime for Hitler*, but their plans are foiled when, in the hands of a campy drag queen director, the show is a hit. Max and Leo go to jail, but they emerge victorious with another hit musical, *Prisoners of Love*.

Though some in the audience, especially women and gays, who are the butt of shameless stereotypes in the films and play, were less than amused, many critic and viewers loved *The Producers* as theatrical satire at its best. The 1968 film, which starred Zero Mostel and Gene Wilder, won an Academy Award for Best Screenplay for Brooks, and the Broadway revival, starring Nathan Lane and Matthew Broderick, won twelve Tony Awards. In 2005 the Lane/Broderick *Producers* was again made into a film, directed by Susan Stroman, who had staged the Broadway play, but the modern movie was not as well received by critics as the first film and the stage version had been.

Tina Gianoulis

SEE ALSO: *Academy Awards; Borscht Belt; Broadway; Brooks, Mel; Caesar, Sid; Gay Men; Stand-up Comedy;* Your Show of Shows.

BIBLIOGRAPHY

Brooks, Mel, and Tom Meehan. "*The Producers*: How We Did It." New York: Hyperion, 2001.

Eger, Henrik. "Location, Location, Location: How Theatre Critics Construct and Deconstruct *The Producers* in Berlin and in Philadelphia." All About Jewish Theater. Accessed May 23, 2012. Available from http://www.jewish-theatre.com/visitor/article_display.aspx?articleID=3276

Jones, Chris. "*The Producers*." *Variety*, February 26, 2001, 51.

Professional Football

Mention *professional football* to the average American sports fan, and they will automatically assume you are referring to the National Football League (NFL). The most lucrative sports league in history, the NFL boasts annual revenues in excess of $9 billion, a sum fueled by massive stadium attendance figures, highly profitable television contracts, and countless merchandising deals. By the end of the twentieth century, the NFL had surpassed Major League Baseball (MLB) in both earnings and popularity, causing many to believe that professional football had become America's real national pastime.

Even with the NFL's dominance over virtually every inch of the professional football landscape, however, rival leagues have formed from time to time over the years, as bold entrepreneurs have attempted to cash in on the sport's broad appeal. In some instances, these leagues have posed a real threat to the NFL's hegemony. In the 1940s the upstart All-American Football Conference (AAFC), bolstered by a group of wealthy owners willing to pay for talent, began drawing top players away from the NFL. Although the AAFC eventually disbanded, three of its marquee franchises (Cleveland Browns, San Francisco 49ers, and Baltimore Colts) joined the NFL, where they quickly joined the ranks of the league's elite teams. The rapid rise of the American Football League (AFL) in the 1960s, culminating with the New York Jets' stunning upset victory over the Baltimore Colts in Super Bowl III, ultimately compelled to NFL to pursue a merger agreement with the rival league.

WORLD FOOTBALL AND THE USFL

Other attempts to compete against the NFL juggernaut have ended in failure. Since the 1970s a number of alternative professional football leagues have formed, each positioning themselves as a direct challenge to the NFL's near-monopoly control over talent and media coverage. The next significant attempt to smash the NFL's supremacy came in 1973, with the formation of the World Football League (WFL). The WFL was the brainchild of Gary L. Davidson, an attorney and entrepreneur. Davidson had unique experience in challenging the American sports establishment, having played a role in founding both the American Basketball Association (ABA), a successful rival to the National Basketball Association (NBA), as well as the World Hockey Association (WHA), which offered an alternative to the National Hockey League (NHL). Undaunted by the NFL's enormous popularity and financial resources, Davidson recruited a pool of prominent sports owners to help jump-start the new league. Intent on creating a faster, more high-scoring version of the game, the WFL proposed a number of new rules that made it easier for offenses to get into the end zone. The new league was also ambitious in its geographical scope, at one point discussing the possibility of establishing franchises in Tokyo, Rome, and Mexico City.

The WFL officially launched in July 1974. In the beginning, the league appeared poised for surprising success. Capitalizing on a training camp strike that threatened to curtail the 1974 NFL season, the WFL reported impressive crowds in its opening week; nearly 60,000 fans turned out to see the Jacksonville Sharks defeat the New York Stars, while the Philadelphia Bell filled more than 55,000 seats for its home opener. Elvis Presley even made an appearance at an WFL contest, watching the Memphis Southmen defeat the Detroit Wheels alongside a crowd of more than 30,000.

While these early numbers seemed promising, the league's popularity soon proved to be a mirage. In August 1974 it emerged that both Philadelphia and Jacksonville had significantly inflated their attendance figures. The Sharks had given away nearly 44,000 tickets to its season opener, while only 20,000 of the 120,000 fans who attended the Bell's first two home games had actually paid for their seats. The league's credibility crisis was soon accompanied by organizational issues. On September 24, the Detroit Wheels declared bankruptcy; that same day, New York Stars owner Robert J. Schmertz sold his franchise to Upton Bell, who relocated the team to Charlotte, North Carolina. Though the league did manage to host a 1974 World Bowl, by 1975 it became overwhelmed by financial struggles, and it ceased to exist only twelve games into its second season.

The next bid to dethrone the NFL came in 1982, when another football labor dispute led to the formation of the United States Football League (USFL). The new league originally positioned itself as an outlet for football fans during the NFL offseason, with a schedule running from March to July. From the beginning, the USFL enjoyed significant financial backing and boasted such high-profile owners as real estate magnate Donald Trump. Soon after its formation, the league scored a publicity coup when it signed major television deals with ABC and the newly formed ESPN cable sports network, worth a combined $24 million. The USFL gained even greater credibility in 1983, when it managed to entice Herschel Walker—star running back at the University of Georgia and a Heisman Trophy winner—to ink a three-year contract with the New Jersey Generals. The fact that Walker was willing to spurn the NFL, where he was poised to become a top draft pick, was considered a major accomplishment for the new league. With the Walker signing, USFL founder David F. Dixon told *Ebony* in June 1983 that "not even the dumbest human being could ruin this league."

Indeed, the USFL enjoyed some success during its first two seasons. Walker quickly fulfilled his promise as the league's first legitimate superstar, rushing for 1,812 yards and seventeen touchdowns in his rookie season. The league also earned recognition for incorporating several new rules, including the use of instant replay to review calls on the field, the introduction of the two-point conversion as an alternative to the extra point after touchdowns, and the implementation of a salary cap—all three of which would later be adopted by the NFL. By 1984 the USFL was able to lure several highly touted college recruits away from the NFL, including quarterbacks Jim Kelly and Steve Young and defensive end Reggie White.

Although Dixon strove to build the new league gradually, and in a fiscally responsible manner, a number of USFL officials resisted the founder's long-term vision. In 1984 a group of owners led by Trump lobbied to begin playing a fall schedule, in order to compete directly against the NFL. The USFL eventually filed an antitrust suit in 1986, claiming that the NFL exerted monopoly control over television broadcasts, thereby stifling competition. The USFL technically won its case, but the presiding judge ultimately decided that the league had suffered primarily from its own poor business planning; in the end, the USFL was awarded $1 in damages. Deeply in debt and saddled with legal fees, it disbanded a short time later.

OTHER PROFESSIONAL LEAGUES

Some professional football leagues have managed to thrive by establishing their own unique identities and appealing to different fan bases. Founded in 1958, the Canadian Football League (CFL) has emerged as one of the premier professional sports associations in Canada, second only to professional hockey in popularity. The league consists of eight teams in two divisions, East and West, that compete each year for a chance to win the Grey Cup. A number of players who later starred in the NFL, including Joe Theismann and Warren Moon, launched their professional football careers in Canada.

In the United States, alternative professional football leagues have found success by introducing a radically different style of game than that offered by the NFL. Originally inspired by indoor soccer, arena football was first invented in 1981 by NFL executive Jim Foster, who wanted to develop a faster, more offense-oriented style of the game. His concept came to fruition in 1987, with the official launch of the Arena Football League (AFL). Played indoors, AFL contests take place on 50-yard fields, with the approximate dimensions of an NHL arena. Over the next two decades, the AFL grew rapidly, establishing franchises in cities throughout the United States, signing television contracts, and promoting itself as the "50-Yard Indoor War." To NFL fans, arena football remains best known as the league where quarterback Kurt Warner began his professional career before joining the NFL and leading the St. Louis Rams to a Super Bowl title in 2001. Although the original AFL disbanded in 2008, the league was resuscitated two years later.

Another organization with strong ties to the NFL was NFL Europe. Founded in 1990 as the World League of American Football (WLAF), the European league aimed to promote the game of American football to a broader international audience, while also serving as a developmental league for potential NFL prospects. The league existed in various incarnations, including the World League (1995–1998), NFL Europe (1998–2007), and NFL Europa (2007), before finally disbanding in 2007. By contrast, the ill-conceived XFL, founded in 2001 by wrestling impresario Vince McMahon as a "smashmouth" alternative to the NFL, lasted only one season before going out of business. Formed in 2009, the more modest United Football League (UFL) consists of only four teams, which played anywhere between four and eight regular season games during its first three seasons. In 2007 the All-American Football League attempted to launch a spring version of the sport, although it ceased operations a year later. In November 2011 a group of former executives from the USFL, XFL, and NFL began to develop plans to launch the Spring Professional Football League, with the aim of debuting in 2013.

Stephen Meyer

SEE ALSO: *Bradshaw, Terry; Brady, Tom; Brown, Jim; Brown, Paul; Butkus, Dick; The Chicago Bears; College Football; The Dallas Cowboys; Ditka, Mike; ESPN; Gifford, Frank; The Great Depression; The Green Bay Packers; Halas, George "Papa Bear"; Ivy League; Landry, Tom; Live Television; Lombardi, Vince;* Monday Night Football*; Montana, Joe; Namath, Joe; National Football League (NFL); The Oakland Raiders; Olympics; Payton, Walter; The Pittsburgh Steelers; Presley, Elvis; Radio; Rice, Grantland; Rice, Jerry; Robeson, Paul; Rockne, Knute; Sanders, Barry; Simpson, O. J.; Sports Heroes; Starr, Bart; Staubach, Roger; Super Bowl; Television; Thorpe, Jim; Unitas, Johnny; World Series; World War II.*

BIBLIOGRAPHY

Byrne, Jim. *The $1 League: The Rise and Fall of the USFL.* New York: Prentice-Hall Press, 1986.

Chad, Norman. "Credit ESPN for Arena Football." *Washington Post,* July 3, 1987.

Davidson, Gary, and Bill Libby. *Breaking the Game Wide-Open.* New York: Atheneum, 1974.

Forrest, Brett. *Long Bomb: How the XFL Became TV's Biggest Fiasco.* New York: Crown, 2002.

Theismann, Joe, and Brian Tarcy. *The Complete Idiot's Guide to Football.* Indianapolis, IN: Alpha, 2001.

"The USFL: A Whole New Ball Game." *Ebony,* June 1983.

Prohibition

Prohibition, which lasted from 1919 to 1933, was an attempt to eliminate consumption of alcoholic beverages in the United States. Instead it created a host of bootleggers, flappers, and speakeasies; widespread crime in American cities; and corruption within enforcement agencies. The Prohibition era began in January 1919, by which time two-thirds of U.S. states had ratified the Eighteenth Amendment, making the manufacture, sale, and transport of alcoholic beverages illegal. The widely accepted Volstead Act, enacted in October 1919, provided for enforcement of the new law. The legislation marked the first and only time in American history that a constitutional amendment was enacted to limit rights rather than to protect them.

BEGINNINGS

Although nationwide prohibition officially began on January 29, 1920, the effort to ban alcohol had been ongoing for a century. In the 1820s temperance movements campaigned to reduce alcohol consumption to prevent men from drinking away their wages or from going home drunk and abusing their families. In 1838 Massachusetts became the first state to enact prohibition laws, by banning the sale of spirits in containers less than 15 gallons. However, the law was repealed two years later. In the 1850s several states enacted prohibition laws, but support for the laws declined during the Civil War. States maintained jurisdiction over prohibition laws from 1880 to 1914.

The Prohibition Party, formed in 1869, revitalized the temperance movement, and the battle to eliminate alcohol consumption spread. Other reformers such as ministers, physicians, devout middle-class Protestants, and the Woman's Christian Temperance Union were the driving forces behind the movement. Reformers believed that drinking caused numerous social dilemmas, blaming alcohol for poverty, moral decay, and domestic abuse. Physicians argued that alcohol caused health problems, and political reformers saw taverns as corrupt establishments. Employers in the newly industrialized society believed that employees who drank alcohol were lazy; unproductive; and prone to sickness, absenteeism, and on-the-job accidents.

EFFECTS

Although Prohibition initially reduced the amount of alcohol consumed in the United States, it caused an increase in crime and produced a new breed of outlaw. Millions of otherwise law-abiding citizens became criminals because they purchased beer, wine, and spirits. Gangsters, enticed by enormous profits from distributing and manufacturing alcohol, battled for business and

Prohibition. *Two men pour out the contents of barrels of confiscated moonshine in Chicago, Illinois, during Prohibition.* CHICAGO HISTORY MUSEUM/CONTRIBUTOR/ARCHIVE PHOTOS/GETTY IMAGES.

settled market disputes with guns. The bootlegger became an American icon as smuggled liquor came across Canadian waterways, off the Atlantic and Pacific coasts, and up from the Caribbean Sea. Bootleggers also manufactured alcohol in makeshift distilleries or bathtubs, giving homemade spirits the nickname bathtub gin. However, such liquor was often poor in quality and constituted a health hazard.

Drinking patterns changed as sales of hard liquor rose. Because bootleggers found it easier to transport and distribute hard liquor, beer became less popular. Drinking became fashionable, and speakeasies, or illegal drinking establishments, proliferated. By 1927 there were 30,000 speakeasies selling illegal alcohol in New York, many more than the number of legal establishments that had existed before Prohibition. Although it was considered immoral for women to frequent saloons, the flappers of the Prohibition Era, sporting bobbed hair and beaded dresses, rebelled by becoming speakeasy fixtures. Part of the attraction for flappers and their friends was jazz, which was sweeping the United States, giving the decade its monikers the Jazz Age and the Roaring Twenties.

BACKLASH AND REPEAL

Anti-prohibitionists argued that prohibition encouraged crime and widespread disrespect for the law. The dramatic increase in crime overwhelmed the criminal justice system. Citizens lost respect for the system, and corruption within enforcement agencies thrived. Although some enforcement agents took bribes, others could not be bought. Enforcement varied widely between states, with agents cracking down harder in areas where the prohibition movement was strongest. Lawmakers thought getting tougher on alcohol crimes would improve matters, so they increased penalties for the sale of one drink to five years in prison and thousands of dollars in fines.

Little changed as federal prisons operated at more than 150 percent of capacity, enforcement budgets increased, and more cops were put on the beat. Enacted while American men were fighting in World War I, the prohibition movement was considered largely a women's effort. Upon returning home, the soldiers put pressure on lawmakers to repeal the ban. Support further declined during the Great Depression as many reasoned that ending Prohibition would create jobs in alcohol manufacturing and distribution. In 1932 the Democratic Party endorsed a repeal of Prohibition, and Democratic presidential candidate Franklin D. Roosevelt won by a large margin.

Roosevelt carried through on his promise. In February 1933 Congress proposed the Twenty-First Amendment to repeal Prohibition. The states quickly ratified it, and national prohibition ended on December 5, 1933, making the Eighteenth Amendment the only amendment to be repealed in U.S. history. Although a few states maintained prohibition after the enactment of the Twenty-First Amendment, by 1966 all states had overturned prohibition laws.

LEGACY

After Prohibition ended, local government officials created liquor control laws. County governments in some areas passed laws banning the manufacture and sale of alcohol within their borders. Although the number of these so-called dry counties has drastically decreased since the 1960s, around 18,000 Americans still live in such areas. In other counties, the sale of alcohol is banned only on Sundays. In Mississippi, which imposed prohibition in 1918 and was the first state to ratify the Eighteenth Amendment, laws still ban the transport of alcohol across a dry-county line.

Most Americans believe that the failure of Prohibition shows that banning the manufacture and sale of alcohol creates a massive crime wave. However, some contemporary analysis suggests that by imposing taxes and strictly regulating alcohol sales between 1919 and 1933, the government could have curtailed the social problems associated with alcohol without giving rise to organized crime. Prohibition continues to be a popular topic in American media. In 2010 the HBO television network presented the twenty-four-episode series *Boardwalk Empire*, which chronicles the life of Nucky Thompson (played by actor Steve Buscemi), the gangster/politician who ruled Atlantic City, New Jersey, during the Prohibition era. The show won multiple awards, including a Grammy Award for Best Soundtrack. In 2011 PBS aired the miniseries *Prohibition* by documentarians Ken Burns and Lynn Novick, detailing the lives of Americans during the period that turned street gangs into crime syndicates and ordinary people into wanted criminals.

Debra Lucas Muscoreil

SEE ALSO: *Atlantic City; Flappers; Grammy Awards; The Great Depression; Jazz; Mafia/Organized Crime; Public Television (PBS); Television; The Twenties; World War I.*

BIBLIOGRAPHY

Gray, Mike. *Drug Crazy: How We Got into This Mess and How We Can Get Out*. New York: Random House, 1998.

Kyvig, David E. *Repealing National Prohibition*. Kent, OH: Kent State University Press, 2000.

Okrent, Daniel. *Last Call: The Rise and Fall of Prohibition*. New York: Scribner, 2011.

Peck, Garrett. *The Prohibition Hangover: Alcohol in America from Demon Rum to Cult Cabernet*. New Brunswick, NJ: Rutgers University Press, 2009.

Rumbarger, John J. *Profits, Power and Prohibition: Alcohol Reform and the Industrializing of America, 1800–1930*. Albany: State University of New York Press, 1989.

Sinclair, Andrew. *Era of Excess: A Social History of the Prohibition Movement*. New York: Harper and Row, 1964.

Prom

Every spring, millions of teenagers across the United States take part in a quintessentially American rite of passage known as the high school prom. Experienced by rich and poor, black and white, Jewish and Catholic, Californians and Virginians, prom night is arguably the most widely shared of all modern American rituals. Certainly, it is one of the most talked about. Though the exact format varies, a traditional prom involves high school students in tuxedos and gowns coming together for a formal dinner-dance. Corsages, limousines, favors, photographers, and postprom festivities are all standard extras. Depending on the location of the school and the age of the participants, proms are held either in school gyms and cafeterias or in hotels, country clubs, and banquet halls. Freshman, sophomore, and junior proms tend to be less extravagant rehearsals for the all-important senior prom, the final social gathering of a graduating class.

HISTORICAL ROOTS

Though popular historical imagination, influenced by such films as *Back to the Future* (1985) and *Grease* (1978), remembers proms as a product of the 1950s, they in fact long predate that legendary era of bobby socks and drive-ins. In Philadelphia, home to many of the nation's oldest public, private, and parochial schools, proms first emerged in the 1920s and rapidly replaced "senior play and dance" evenings as the high school social events of the year. By the 1930s proms were commonplace, their rise in popularity linked to several interwoven factors, including ongoing urbanization and industrialization; the expansion of secondary education; the rise of "youth culture"; and, stemming from all of the above, the mass dissemination of prom stories.

Tales about the glories and mishaps of prom night were first published in the pages of high school magazines, which were then exchanged among educational institutions throughout the nation. Early twentieth-century student journalists were extremely zealous about this new event and appear to have regarded prom attendance as an essential marker of good citizenship. "If You Don't Like This," quipped the headline of a 1931 article on the merits of prom night, "Go Back to Where You Came From." There is evidence to suggest that these early proms served an important unifying function, especially in city schools filled with first- and second-generation immigrants from around the world. Certainly then, as now, prom night was constructed as having been synonymous with "Americanness."

Prom night quickly became a hot topic for the writers of popular dramas and romance novels. From 1934 onward a whole series of prom plays, short stories, and novels went to press. The 1930s also saw the publication of the first-ever prom guidebook, penned by Marietta Abell and Agnes Anderson. Writing in the midst of the Great Depression, the authors hailed the prom as a potential money-saver but admonished readers that "no one should think of planning and arranging for any one of the proms suggested in less than four weeks." To millennial readers, both statements seem laughably ironic. Modern proms cost individual students anywhere from $200 to $2,000, are planned a year in advance, and call on the expertise and services of a vast array of party professionals. Proms in the early twenty-first century are very big business.

The exact ritual antecedents of prom night are difficult to trace, as proms draw on a number of earlier cultural traditions. To many observers, the prom resembles a democratic version of the elite debutante ball, which is in turn a version of the aristocratic ritual of presenting young ladies at the royal courts of Europe. Proms are also closely related to the cotillions and college dances of the mid- to late nineteenth century, where formal dress and terpsichorean skill were essential and the practice of giving out party favors was popularized. Important regional differences existed though. In the Deep South, where religious intolerance of dancing determined the shape and form of early-twentieth-century youthful pleasures, proms were literally promenades, during which young ladies would take short and keenly supervised walks around the block with male escorts.

CUSTOMS AND CONTROVERSIES

Throughout their history, proms have most obviously resembled weddings in both their ritual form and function. Weddings and proms share an emphasis on heterosexual pairing that is reinforced through parallel iconography and corresponding rites of exchange and remembrance. Prom couples often look—from the gown to the tux, flowers, limo, and location—like a young bride and groom. Their night together is subject to many of the same acts of ritual celebration and sanctification. Families gather to send the young couple off, photographs are taken, and flowers and keepsakes are exchanged. Late-twentieth-century prom couples also often share a postritual "honeymoon." Indeed, for many teens, these postprom trips are now more eagerly anticipated than the prom itself.

Prom night's emphasis on heterosexual dating has, since the early 1980s, been a subject of public controversy. Several lawsuits have arisen at schools where students who wanted to attend solo or who wanted to attend with a same sex partner were barred. Aaron Fricke's *Reflections of a Rock Lobster* offers an autobiographical account of his legal battle to take his male partner to his senior prom in 1980. A similar battle waged by lesbian student Constance McMillen in Mississippi made national headlines in 2010. In the twenty-first century, many public schools have been forced to relax their boy-girl dating rules, and many teenagers have come to regard prom night less as a night of romance and more as a night to have fun as a group. Meanwhile, since the late 1980s, lesbian, gay, and bisexual teenagers who want to celebrate with a date and who live in major cities in the United States have had the option of attending "gay proms" that provide a safe and friendly environment in which these teens can celebrate. Prom traditions, however, prevail, particularly in parochial schools. In Philadelphia, Catholic schools continue to insist that prom night be a heterosexual affair and they continue to bar both single teens and same-sex couples.

Prom night has also been involved in debates about racial discrimination. In 1994 an Alabama student challenged her school's policy barring interracial prom dating. Meanwhile, at schools around the nation that are de jure desegregated, de facto segregation within the student body often leads to heated disputes over music selection for prom night.

At all schools, the greatest ongoing prom battle concerns drug use. Prom night is mythically a night for letting go and experimenting, but a series of tragedies, most involving drunk driving, have led teachers, parents, and students across the nation to campaign against prom night's infamous excesses. Some schools have experimented with random breath tests, and many lock students inside their prom venues to prevent furtive drinking. Preprom safety awareness programs are commonplace, and all schools enforce tough penalties for students involved in prom night drug use. Eager to distance themselves from inappropriate symbolism, most school boards have also now banned the giving of glasses as prom favors. Savvy promware manufacturers have responded quickly; they now fill their ever-popular champagne, wine, and beer glasses with brightly colored wax and market them as "candles."

Perhaps the most famous prom controversy occurred in 1997 when an eighteen-year-old New Jersey senior gave birth at her prom. According to prosecutors, she then suffocated the infant and returned to the dance floor. She was sentenced to fifteen years for aggravated manslaughter. Her case stands as a vivid reminder that prom night is not always as sweet and innocent an event as popular mythology would have us believe. Students make remarkable sacrifices on prom night, and though these are usually financial, they can also be academic, emotional, and physical.

PROMS IN POPULAR CULTURE

At its best, prom night offers adolescents a unique opportunity to dress up, go out with their peers, and celebrate their high school achievements. Many find the excitement, camaraderie, and grandeur of it all profoundly enjoyable and memorable. At its worst, prom night diverts students' attention away from their academic studies and breeds unhealthy and superficial competition between peers at an age when self-esteem is notoriously fragile. Certainly, this is the angle exploited by filmmakers in classic prom movies such as *Carrie* (1976), *Prom Night* (1980), *Pretty in Pink* (1986), and *She's All That* (1999).

Prom night is as much a controversy as it is a national pastime; few if any rituals are so widely shared, and few are subject to as much hope or hype. Proms are featured in magazines and movies, talk shows and tabloids, soap operas and songs. They make millions of dollars for the numerous industries that have grown up around them, and, for all the talk of declining traditions, proms show no sign of waning in popularity. In fact, in 2011 it was estimated that the prom industry was worth $4 billion. For better or worse, prom night is a part of American popular culture that is very much here to stay.

Felicity H. Paxton

SEE ALSO: Back to the Future*; Bobby Socks; Drive-In Theater; The Great Depression; Teenagers.*

BIBLIOGRAPHY

Abell, Marietta, and Agnes Anderson. *"The Junior-Senior Prom": Complete Practical Suggestions for Staging the Junior-Senior Prom.* Minneapolis, MN: Northwestern Press, 1936.

Best, Amy L. *Prom Night: Youth, Schools, and Popular Culture.* New York: Routledge, 2000.

Fricke, Aaron. *Reflections of a Rock Lobster: A Story about Growing up Gay.* Boston: Alyson Publications, 1981.

Myrick, Susan. "Whatever Became of the Prom Party?" *Georgia Review* 22, no. 3 (1968), 354–359.

Promise Keepers

Public gatherings promoting spiritual revivalism have been a distinctive feature of American religious life since the frontier camp meetings of the early nineteenth century. During the 1990s a new and controversial expression of this tradition of public revivalism emerged in the activities of the Promise Keepers, a Christian men's organization devoted to restoring conservative family values to American society. Through large outdoor rallies, often held in football stadiums and drawing tens of thousands of participants at a time, the Promise Keepers spread their message of male responsibility and family leadership to millions of American men. The group's name derives from its members' pledge to maintain an active Christian life, to build strong families and marriages, to seek moral and ethical purity, and to associate with other men who have made the same commitments. The Promise Keepers' insistence on male leadership of the family has produced considerable opposition among feminists, who see the group as a threat to women's equality. Moderates and liberals have also criticized the group for its conservative stance on politically charged social issues such as abortion and gay rights. The controversies surrounding the Promise Keepers reflect the ongoing conflict between religious tradition and secular trends within American culture.

The Promise Keepers movement was founded in 1990 by Bill McCartney, a former football coach at the University of Colorado. It began as a local fellowship led by McCartney and other members of the Vineyard Church, a conservative, charismatic group with a strong emphasis on evangelism. By stressing discipline and male bonding, the organization provided support for members trying to lead an exemplary Christian life. The group's leaders also sought to extend its message of religious renewal across denominational boundaries and so began staging large public rallies to attract new members. Centering on sermons, hymns, prayer, and mutual support, these exclusively male rallies attracted several million participants during the 1990s and helped to spread the movement across the United States. The Promise Keepers' largest and most widely publicized rally, held on October 4, 1997, attracted 700,000 men to the Mall in Washington, D.C. Through the success of their public rallies, the Promise Keepers also established a network of thousands of local support groups, led by specially trained leaders, or "key men," whose members monitored one another's observance of the organization's principles.

To its supporters, drawn largely from conservative Protestant churches, the Promise Keepers represented a necessary response to moral decay and the decline of the American family. The organization found many critics, however, among feminists, political moderates and liberals, and mainstream religious leaders. The Promise Keepers' emphasis on the need for male-headed households struck many as an antiquated commitment to patriarchal families and an attack on women's rights. Critics also faulted the group for its ties to the new Religious Right and that movement's conservative social agenda. The Promise Keepers denied the existence of such ties, but McCartney himself was a featured speaker at meetings of the militant antiabortion group Operation Rescue, and he publicly supported a Colorado constitutional amendment limiting the legal recourse available to homosexuals subjected to discrimination in housing or employment. Critics also challenged the Promise Keepers' avowed commitment to racial reconciliation, arguing that the group did little to support concrete efforts to promote political, social, or economic equality for racial minorities.

By the late 1990s, attendance at the Promise Keepers' rallies had begun to decline, and financial difficulties led the organization to reduce the size of its paid staff and the scope of its activities. The organization continued to function in a reduced capacity in the early twenty-first century by holding much smaller, less-publicized conferences. Some observers believe that one reason for its decline was that it focused a spotlight on men's needs, and when local churches started to develop men's ministries, few men felt the need to go to Promise Keepers events. Another reason, perhaps, was that people became disillusioned after the public revelation that during the very time McCartney was building up Promise Keepers and telling other men how to be good husbands, he had neglected his own wife, who was depressed and nearly suicidal after learning of her husband's past infidelity.

For whatever reason, the press loss interest in Promise Keepers shortly after its 1997 high point, and the organization never again wielded such national influence. During its initial period of growth, however, it had a significant impact on American society by sustaining the resurgence of religious conservatism that had started in the 1970s. In its concern with male responsibility and authority, the Promise Keepers movement also focused attention on the persisting differences of opinion within American society regarding gender roles and family structure, decades after the start of the women's movement.

Roger W. Stump

SEE ALSO: *Abortion; Evangelism; Feminism; Gay Liberation Movement.*

BIBLIOGRAPHY

Abraham, Ken. *Who Are the Promise Keepers?* New York: Doubleday, 1997.

Bartkowski, John P. *The Promise Keepers: Servants, Soldiers, and Godly Men.* Piscataway, NJ: Rutgers University Press, 2004.

Kintz, Linda. *Between Jesus and the Market: The Emotions That Matter in Right-Wing America.* Durham, NC: Duke University Press, 1997.

Protest Groups

Protest groups are groups of people who have united to collectively object to a policy or course of action taken by an authority, such as a federal or state government. U.S. history is replete with examples of protest groups and their efforts. One early protest group was made up of colonists who objected to British tax policies. This group organized a protest that later became known as the Boston Tea Party. Members of the group, disguised as Native Americans, secretly boarded British ships docked in Boston Harbor and dumped their shipments of tea into the water.

It was not until the 1960s, however, that protesting in America became part of the popular culture. The still relatively new medium of television brought the strife and turmoil of the Vietnam War and the civil rights movement into the living rooms of all Americans. Since that turbulent era, sit-ins, marches, demonstrations, and boycotts have become common protest tactics practiced by various groups attempting to gain legitimacy in the eyes of the public. By the early twenty-first century the introduction of social media greatly aided protest groups in their efforts to spread their message and increase their ranks.

The nineteenth century witnessed the birth of several important protest groups in the United States. The abolitionists sought the immediate and uncompensated end of slavery. Antislavery groups were present as far back as the colonial era, but most had not advocated complete freedom or equality for blacks. For example, the American Colonization Society, which began in 1817, attempted to solve America's race problem by shipping willing blacks back to Africa.

In 1831 New England publisher and radical abolitionist William Lloyd Garrison condemned this gradual approach to ending slavery and called for immediate emancipation. Supporters of this position included prominent ministers and other activists in the northern states, and they flooded the country with antislavery literature. At first, they sought to convince slave owners that slavery was a sin and attempted to secure voluntary emancipation. Later, they turned to political action and were potent enough to produce two political parties: the Liberty Party in the early 1840s and the Free-Soil Party in the late 1840s.

Also during the antebellum era, the women's suffrage movement began. Women had always been kept politically and legally subordinate to men; they could not own property, make wills, vote, attend college, or retain wages they had earned. As women became active in various reform activities and social crusades, they began to seek equality. The official beginning of this women's movement dates from an 1848 meeting at Seneca Falls, New York, where a women's right to vote was pronounced as a national goal. Under the leadership of Elizabeth Cady Stanton, Lucy Stone, Julia Ward Howe, and Susan B. Anthony, a variety of women's protest groups championed this cause for the next generation. Some states passed suffrage laws, but it was not until the passage of the Nineteenth Amendment in 1919 that women gained the right to vote nationally.

MORE GROUPS, DIFFERENT ISSUES

The late nineteenth century saw the rise of two predominant protest groups: farmers and labor activists. Associations of farmers organized in the Midwest after the Civil War. Railroad abuses and high shipping rates compelled American farmers to seek regulatory legislation. In addition, overproduction, resulting from the introduction of sophisticated farm machinery, brought a decline in the price of crops. Farmers and farm protest groups sought to redress these problems with federal regulations. Rural protest groups included the National Grange, the Farmer's Alliances, the National Farmers Union, and various political coalitions, such as the Greenback Party and the Populist Party.

In that same period, industrial laborers began to protest their working conditions. The rapid rise of industrialization after the Civil War stimulated the growth of labor unions at the local, state, and national levels. Unions and labor organizations sought to alleviate dangerous and unhealthy working conditions and to resolve problems concerning pensions, disability pay, and child labor. Leading labor protest groups included the Knights of Labor, the National Labor Union, the American Federation of Labor, the Molly Maguires, the Industrial Workers of the World, and the Congress of Industrial Organizations.

The contemporary American view of protests unquestionably emanated from two mid-twentieth-century issues: civil rights and the Vietnam War. During the 1950s blacks began to challenge segregation in the South. Leading groups included the National Association for the Advancement of Colored People (NAACP), the Congress of Racial Equality (CORE), and the Southern Christian Leadership Conference (SCLC).

Southern blacks used a variety of protest tactics, such as boycotts, sit-ins, and marches, in their attempts to achieve racial equality and end segregation. Perhaps the most famous protest is the Montgomery Bus Boycott of 1955 and 1956. Black community leaders organized the boycott in response to the arrest and conviction of African American Rosa Parks, who refused to move to the back of a segregated bus in Montgomery, Alabama. The boycott was a huge success, creating a serious financial threat to the bus company and leading to the Supreme Court decision that the segregation law was unconstitutional.

In the early 1960s black college students throughout the South passively sat at segregated department store lunch counters in order to force integration. Often, these students were attacked by local whites and carried off to jail for this "illegal" practice. In 1961 CORE and the Student Nonviolent Coordinating Committee (SNCC) organized a group of Freedom Riders in an attempt to further integrate bus systems in the South; the Freedom Riders embarked on a long bus ride through the South. In Alabama they were beaten by white hoodlums and their bus was bombed. The federal government finally dispatched marshals to protect the Freedom Riders, although they were ultimately arrested and sent to jail.

The largest demonstration during the civil rights era took place in Washington, D.C., in August 1963. Civil rights groups organized the March on Washington to pressure the federal government to support the civil rights of African Americans. More than 250,000 people gathered and heard civil rights leader Martin Luther King Jr. give his "I Have a Dream" speech. African American protest groups continued to organize throughout the 1960s, using sit-ins, boycotts, marches, and voter registration drives in their efforts to gain equality in the South and in the nation as a whole.

VIETNAM AND THE FEMINIST MOVEMENT

The Vietnam War also provided fuel for major protests during the 1960s. A peace movement had long existed in the United States, largely based upon Quaker and Unitarian beliefs. Whereas protest groups were active during many of America's wars, they failed to gain popular support until the Cold War era. The escalating nuclear arms race brought about groups such as the National Committee for a Sane Nuclear Policy (SANE), Women Strike for Peace (WSP), and the Student Peace Union (SPU). The SPU not only wanted to stop the production of nuclear weapons but also sought to restructure society on a more equitable basis. But the SPU never became an effective student interest group and faded away by 1964; its banner was taken up by the more active and successful Students for a Democratic Society (SDS).

SDS, centered on college campuses, published the Port Huron Statement in 1962, expressing its disillusionment with the American military-industrial-academic establishment. SDS cited the uncertainty of life in Cold War America and the degradation of African Americans in the South as examples of social and cultural drift and called for a revolution of sorts among American youth. Throughout the first years of its existence, SDS focused on domestic concerns. But in 1965, when the United States began bombing North Vietnam, SDS and other student protest groups began focusing on the war. In February and March 1965 SDS organized a series of "teach-ins," modeled after earlier civil rights seminars. These teach-ins sought to educate large segments of the student population about both the moral and political foundations of America's Vietnam involvement.

As the Vietnam War escalated, the antiwar protests became more raucous. In 1968 protestors occupied the administration building at Columbia University; police used force to evict them. Raids on draft boards in Baltimore, Maryland; Milwaukee, Wisconsin; and Chicago soon followed, as activists smeared blood on records and shredded files. In May 1970 Ohio National Guardsmen fired on a group of antiwar protestors at Kent State University, killing four and wounding nine.

As the Vietnam War became more unpopular in the early 1970s, antiwar sentiment and protest began to gain popular acceptance. During the next three decades, protests became a normal reaction to what were believed to be zealous excesses of power by government and other institutions. After the 1960s other groups attempted to repeat their predecessors' protest tactics, but most met with less success. In the 1970s environmental activists registered their concerns over the ravaging effects of industrial pollution. The environmental movement was led by older, conservation organizations, such as the Sierra Club and the Wilderness Society, as well as several new protests groups. Greenpeace, founded in 1971, protested nuclear testing and campaigned to save whales, other ocean animals, and rain forests around the world. Established in 1980, Earth First! was a more militant group committed to direct action and the sabotage of projects harmful to the environment.

The feminist movement came to fruition during the 1970s, spawning hundreds of new protest groups and advancing radical ideas regarding women's role in society. The National Organization for Women (NOW) advanced three demands: equality for women in employment and education; child-care centers throughout the nation; and women's control over their own reproduction, including a woman's right to abortion. Women's protest actions ranged from lobbying Congress to more direct action.

NEW ISSUES EMERGE

The 1980s and 1990s saw a change in protest and activism. Since the 1950s, protest groups in the United States had come from the left of the political spectrum. But the 1980s saw a political and social counterrevolution—probably in response to the rapid upheaval and perceived cultural permissiveness of the 1960s. Conservatives found a voice through the Moral Majority, founded in 1979, while the Christian Coalition advanced its views with more religious fervor. Conservatives also used journals and research institutions (think tanks) to advance their message. These included publications such as the *National Review* edited by William F. Buckley Jr. and institutions such as the American Enterprise Institute and the Heritage Foundation.

A vigorous antiabortion protest movement also became a part of the conservative resurgence. Liberal groups remained active in the 1980s and 1990s but with much less political support than earlier decades. A nuclear freeze movement, gays and lesbians, and AIDS activists were all active, but the focus of protest continued to change and new issues evolved.

In the early twenty-first century several important protest movements emerged. The politically conservative and libertarian Tea Party movement began in early 2009, calling for reduced government, lower taxes, reduction of the national debt, and an original interpretation of the U.S. Constitution. Although the Tea Party denied a link to any specific political party, research shows that Tea Party members were predominantly older, white conservatives with Republican Party connections and Christian evangelical religious roots. As a protest movement, the Tea Party held some conventional demonstrations but also used other media outlets to distribute its message, such as blogs and talk radio.

Another important protest movement of the early twenty-first century was Occupy Wall Street (OWS). Unconventional in its methods, OWS was a grassroots movement that occupied public spaces in American cities to make the public aware of the influence of money in the United States. OWS began on September 17, 2011, in Liberty Square in Manhattan's Financial District and spread to more than 100 cities in the United States and more than 1,500 cities around the world. Its message centered on the corrosive power of major banks and multinational corporations over the democratic process, as well as the role of Wall Street in creating an economic collapse that caused the greatest recession in generations.

OWS did not have a leader, and it was organized using a nonbinding, consensus-based, collective-decision-making tool known as a "people's assembly." The phrase "We Are the 99%" became the political slogan of OWS, and it referred to the concentration of wealth that exists among the top 1 percent of income earners in the United States compared to everyone else. Paul Taylor, executive vice president of the Pew Research Center, told National Public Radio (NPR) that the slogan is "arguably the most successful slogan since 'Hell no, we won't go,' going back to the Vietnam era." According to Taylor, majorities of Democrats, Independents, and Republicans see the income gap as a cause of friction in the United States.

The most critical innovations in modern protests have been technological. Portable devices, such as cell phones and digital cameras, allow protestors to record minute details of their exploits. Social media networks, such as Twitter and Facebook, and blogs allow protest groups to announce their views and complaints to the world. In totalitarian nations where a free press does not exist, social media and cell phones give protest groups a way of reporting happenings to the world, despite government attempts to stop the free flow of information.

David E. Woodard

SEE ALSO: *AIDS; Buckley, William F., Jr.; Civil Rights Movement; Cold War; Environmentalism; Facebook; Feminism; Freedom Rides; Greenpeace; Kent State Massacre; King, Martin Luther, Jr.; March on Washington; Moral Majority; National Organization for Women (NOW); Parks, Rosa; Student Demonstrations; Students for a Democratic Society (SDS); The Tea Party; Twitter; Vietnam.*

BIBLIOGRAPHY

Chen, Gwendolyn. *Occupy Wall Street: Social Networking and the Arab Spring.* London: Pearce Heart Group, 2011.

Council on Foreign Relations. *The New Arab Revolt: What Happened, What It Means, and What Comes Next.* New York: CFR/Foreign Affairs, 2011.

Flexner, Eleanor. *Century of Struggle: The Women's Rights Movement in the United States.* New York: Atheneum, 1973.

Garrow, David. *Bearing the Cross: Martin Luther King, Jr., and the Southern Christian Leadership Conference.* New York: Vintage Books, 1986.

Goldman, Eric. *Rendezvous with Destiny: A History of Modern Reform.* New York: Vintage Books, 1955.

Goodwyn, Lawrence. *The Populist Moment: A Short History of the Agrarian Revolt in America.* New York: Oxford University Press, 1978.

Morris, Aldon. *The Origins of the Civil Rights Movement: Black Communities Organizing for Change.* New York: The Free Press, 1984.

Skocpol, Theda, and Vanessa Williamson. *The Tea Party and the Making of Republican Conservatism.* New York: Oxford University Press, 2012.

Van Gelder, Sarah. *This Changes Everything: Occupy Wall Street and the 99% Movement.* San Francisco: Berrett-Koehler Publishers, 2011.

Walters, Ronald. *American Reformers, 1815–1860.* New York: Hill and Wang, 1978.

Wells, Tom. *The War Within: America's Battle over Vietnam.* New York: Henry Holt, 1996.

Zandt, Deanna. *Share This! How You Will Change the World with Social Networking.* San Francisco: Berrett-Koehler Publishers, 2010.

Zernike, Kate. *Boiling Mad: Inside Tea Party America.* New York: Times Books, 2010.

Prozac

Perhaps more than any prescription medication in history, Prozac has had a profound impact not only on the patients who have taken it but also on the very practice of psychiatry and on popular conceptions of mood and personality. Within three years of its 1987 release, Prozac (fluoxetine hydrochloride) had become the drug most prescribed by psychiatrists in the United States; by 1994 it was the second best-selling drug of any kind in the world, with a reported one billion prescriptions written per month. In *A History of Psychiatry: From the Era of the Asylum to the Age of Prozac*, Edward Shorter describes Prozac as the household word of the 1990s; in 1994 *Newsweek* proclaimed that Prozac had attained the familiarity of Kleenex and the social status of spring water.

The drug has been the subject of numerous television programs, magazine articles, and psychology and self-help books. According to Elizabeth Wurtzel in her 1994 best seller, *Prozac Nation*, Prozac has come to represent the angst and antidote of a generation. With millions of people taking Prozac each year, and its benefits being touted in the media and discussed at cocktail parties, this new-generation antidepressant has contributed to the destigmatization of mental illness.

Released in December 1987 by the Eli Lilly Company, Prozac was the first in a new class of antidepressant medications: selective serotonin reuptake inhibitors (SSRI). SSRIs are "designer drugs," highly potent chemical compounds that selectively affect a single biological process and, by extension, target a highly specified physiological function. In the case of Prozac (and the other SSRIs, such as Zoloft and Paxil), the target is the brain's reuptake of the neurotransmitter serotonin (5-HT), which is involved in the regulation of mood. By increasing the levels of serotonin available to the brain, Prozac has been found to enhance not only mood but also energy, assertiveness, and optimism; it also treats anxiety, panic attacks, social discomfort, rejection sensitivity, and obsessive thoughts. Thus the effect of Prozac goes beyond the relief of clinical depression: it ultimately improves one's self-concept.

ANTIDEPRESSANTS BEFORE PROZAC

Although earlier antidepressants such as tricyclics and monoamine oxidase inhibitors (MAOIs) were effective in controlling depressive symptoms, they were less selective in their action, making them cumbersome to use and difficult to monitor. Tricyclics, which are highly effective in controlling "classical" depression—characterized by insomnia, loss of appetite, low mood, and low energy—also interfere with the neurotransmitter acetylcholine, triggering side effects associated with the "flight or fight" response: rapid heart rate, sweating, dry mouth, constipation, and urinary retention. The MAOIs, which effectively alleviate the "nonclassical" depressions that are not helped by tricyclics, are not as "dirty" but are more problematic because of their potentially fatal interactions with many foods.

In clinical trials Prozac has proven to be as effective in treating classical depression as the tricyclics and, for many patients, even more effective in alleviating nonclassical depression than MAOIs. Because its action is so specific, Prozac is difficult to overdose on, and overdose typically does not pose major risk of death. Most significantly Prozac is "clean": it works without the sedative effects, weight gain, and dangerous interactions associated with the other antidepressant medications. Its tendencies to increase energy and decrease appetite are both highly desirable and supremely marketable traits that have contributed much to its popularity.

SAFETY CONCERNS

Despite the clinical evidence supporting Prozac's marketing as a safe drug that is virtually free of side effects, its initial release was marred by sensational reports of patients "going crazy" on Prozac: some purportedly becoming suicidal for the first time, others claiming to experience episodes of violent behaviors—including murder—triggered by the medication. In 1989 an attorney filed a series of lawsuits against Eli Lilly following an incident in which a man who had taken Prozac (along with several other medications), killed eight people, wounded twelve, and then killed himself. This story was featured on *Donahue* (in a show provocatively titled "Prozac—Medication That Makes You Kill"). A similar story was featured on *Larry King Live* in 1991, but neither case held up in court. In the end the claims that Prozac created dangerous behavior in patients who previously had no history of suicide or violence subsided for lack of evidence to the contrary. Sensational headlines soon gave way to a general acceptance of Prozac as a drug safe enough for patients with severe depression and "clean" enough to appeal to a more general public seeking relief from mild dysphoria.

The use of medication to enhance personality in the absence of significant mental illness, which Peter Kramer has labeled "cosmetic pharmacology," has produced an economic boon for drug manufacturers while raising a red flag for naturalists and ethicists. Although *Time* lauded the use of Prozac for personality improvement as "a medical breakthrough," other sources have decried the use of pharmaceuticals to enhance socially desirable traits as a triumph of consumer culture over rational science and an alarming example of social Darwinism. Those concerned about the ethical implications argue that, by enabling people who are not clinically depressed to brighten their moods and improve their personalities, Prozac may contribute to a lowering of society's cultural tolerance for pessimism, grief, and other manifestations of dysphoria. On the other hand, some have argued that a positive by-product of the widespread popularity of Prozac may be a narrowing of the gap between the so-called "normal" population and the "mentally ill."

The use of Prozac had declined by the early twenty-first century, but it continued to be the most commonly prescribed medicine of its kind. In the first five months of 2004, physicians wrote more than forty million prescriptions for Prozac. Many physicians are concerned that the drug is being overused. The only federally approved use of Prozac is for the treatment of depression and Obsessive Compulsive Disorder (OCD). However, doctors continue to prescribe Prozac (or, more commonly, generic fluoxetine, which largely replaced brand-name Prozac after its release in 2001) for various conditions that include seasonal affective disorder, eating disorders, obesity, anxiety, phobias, panic disorders, and even migraine and premenstrual syndrome.

After decades of use, researchers have developed a detailed history of Prozac use, and critics warn that taking the drug is not without risk. Common side effects include insomnia, nausea, nervousness, and uncontrolled body movements. Less common are mania, hypomania, and seizures resulting from central nervous system overstimulation. Regardless of these side effects, Prozac is seen as a cure-all by many Americans, and Eli Lilly's campaign of direct-to-consumer advertising feeds that hunger for the perfect drug.

Ava Rose

SEE ALSO: *Advertising; Best Sellers; Depression; Donahue, Phil; King, Larry;* Newsweek*; Suicide; Television;* Time.

BIBLIOGRAPHY

"The Culture of Prozac." *Newsweek*, February 7, 1994, 41.

Elfenbein, Debra, ed. *Living with Prozac.* San Francisco: Harper, 1995.

Elliott, Carl, and Tod Chambers. *Prozac as a Way of Life.* Chapel Hill: University of North Carolina Press, 2004.

Fenter, Virginia L. "Concerns about Prozac and Direct-to-Consumer Advertising of Prescription Drugs." *International Journal of Risk and Safety in Medicine* 18, no. 1 (2006).

Kramer, Peter. *Listening to Prozac.* New York: Viking, 1993.

Lewis, Bradley. *Moving beyond Prozac, DSM, and the New Psychiatry: The Birth of Postpsychiatry.* Ann Arbor: University of Michigan Press, 2006.

Metzel, Jonathan. *Prozac on the Couch: Prescribing Gender in the Era of Wonder Drugs.* Durham, NC: Duke University Press, 2003.

"The Personality Pill." *Time*, October 11, 1993, 53.

Shorter, Edward. *A History of Psychiatry: From the Era of the Asylum to the Age of Prozac.* New York: John Wiley & Sons, 1997.

Wurtzel, Elizabeth. *Prozac Nation.* Boston: Houghton Mifflin, 1994.

Pryor, Richard *(1940–2005)*

In the 1970s and 1980s, Richard Pryor was one of America's top comedians, creating a daring new brand of comedy by transforming African American culture into a form of hilarious performance art. Pryor called upon both personal and social tragedy for his comic material, tackling such thorny subject matter as racism, urban violence, and drug addiction while lacing his irreverent stage appearances with adult language and humor. Indeed, Pryor's comedy invariably contained an undercurrent of deep personal anguish; Bill Cosby once summed up the element of tragedy in Pryor's life and work by saying, "For Richard, the line between comedy and tragedy is as fine as you can paint it." In addition to producing a string of popular comedy albums, Pryor enjoyed a long film and television career, appearing in numerous comedic and dramatic roles. Although his career was ultimately cut short by multiple sclerosis, his groundbreaking style has exerted a powerful influence on later generations of comedians, shaping the work of such African American stars as Eddie Murphy, Keenen Ivory Wayans, and Dave Chappelle.

ROUGH UPBRINGING

Born in Peoria, Illinois, in 1940 to a single mother, Pryor was raised in his grandmother's brothel, where his mother worked as a prostitute. His parents, LeRoy and Gertrude Pryor, married when he was three years old, but the marriage soon failed. Pryor continued to live with his grandmother, who administered beatings on a regular basis. While in school, the comedian was often in trouble with the law. At age eleven he got his first taste of show business when he was cast in a community theater performance by a teacher who also allowed him to entertain fellow students with his comedic antics. Many years later, Pryor gave that teacher an Emmy Award that the comedian had won for writing a Lily Tomlin special.

Trouble continued to plague Pryor in high school when he was expelled for hitting a teacher. After deciding not to return

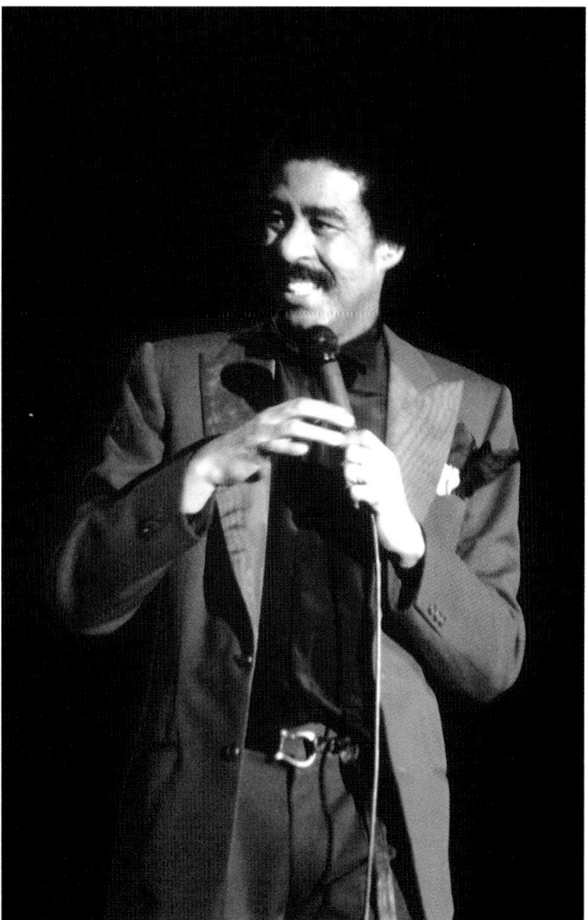

***Richard Pryor in* Live on Şunset Strip.** *Richard Pryor performs in the hit concert film* Live on Sunset Strip. **RASTAR PICTURES/ THE KOBAL COLLECTION.**

to school, he worked in a meatpacking house and then joined the U.S. Army in 1958. While serving a two-year hitch in West Germany, Pryor clashed with his superiors. In 1960 he returned to Peoria, married the first of five wives (he was married twice to two of his wives), and fathered his second child, Richard Pryor Jr. His first child, Renee, had been born four years earlier.

Pryor's first professional break came when a popular African American nightclub in Peoria let him perform stand-up on stage. By the early 1960s he was performing regularly on a comedy circuit that included East St. Louis, Missouri, and Youngstown and Pittsburgh, Pennsylvania. In 1963 he moved to New York City, performing an act highly influenced by his comedic heroes, Cosby and Dick Gregory. Pryor made his television debut in 1964 on the series *On Broadway Tonight* (1964–1965). Soon thereafter, he appeared on *The Ed Sullivan Show* (1948–1971) and the *The Merv Griffin Show* (1962–1986). By the mid-1960s Pryor had moved to Los Angeles and landed small parts in such films as *The Green Berets* (1968) and *Wild in the Streets* (1968). During this time he continued playing live shows, primarily in Las Vegas showrooms, where he dropped the Cosby-influenced act and developed his own raw, raucous stage persona.

COMEDY LEGEND

By the late 1960s Pryor's career was in high gear while his personal life was in chaos: a cocaine habit; clashes with Las Vegas management, landlords, and hotel clerks; a battery lawsuit by one of his wives; and an Internal Revenue Service audit for failure to pay taxes between 1967 and 1970. After lying low in the counterculture community in Berkeley, California, for several years, he emerged in 1972 with a new stand-up act and a supporting role in the film *Lady Sings the Blues*. In 1976 he starred in *The Bingo Long Traveling All-Stars & Motor Kings* and costarred with Gene Wilder in the hit comedy-suspense film *Silver Streak*, which grossed more than $50 million. Also in the 1970s two of Pryor's comedy albums went platinum, and the 1979 movie *Richard Pryor: Live! in Concert* was acclaimed by critics as the comedian's crowning achievement. In the film, the characters portrayed by Pryor include winos, junkies, prostitutes, street fighters, blue-collar drunks, and pool hustlers—all denizens of the underbelly of the American Dream.

During the course of this success, Pryor's life continued on its erratic path, as he suffered a heart attack in 1978 and was divorced after a violent New Year's Eve incident that ended with Pryor riddling his wife's car with bullets. By 1980 he was freebasing cocaine, which apparently precipitated the June 9, 1980, incident in which Pryor caught on fire, suffering severe injuries to half his body. Once again calling upon material from his own life, Pryor parodied the accident, his drug use, and his stay in the hospital in his 1982 concert movie *Richard Pryor: Live on the Sunset Strip*. A year later he joined a drug rehabilitation program and worked with other addicts to overcome his problems. In 1985 Pryor cowrote, directed, and starred in the autobiographical movie *Jo Jo Dancer, Your Life Is Calling*, playing a comedian reliving his life following a near-fatal accident. Other 1980s films featuring Pryor included *The Toy* (1982), *Brewster's Millions* (1985), *See No Evil, Hear No Evil* (1989), and *Harlem Nights* (1989).

Pryor was diagnosed with multiple sclerosis in 1986, and his later films show him in a weakened condition. In spite of his deteriorating health, he continued to work over the course of the next decade. In 1991 he appeared in *Another You*, and he also had a small role in David Lynch's 1997 film *Lost Highway*. In his later years he lived a reclusive life in his Bel Air, California, home, almost unable to walk and seeing only a small group of friends. Pryor died of a heart attack on December 10, 2005, in Los Angeles. Writing in the *Washington Post* days after Pryor's death, Eugene Robinson asserted that the comedian was "an artist, not a journalist; he exaggerated, flattened, telescoped, stretched and technicolored ordinary reality until it told a heightened truth." The end result, Robinson suggested, was a portrait of Pryor himself: "foolish, human, perceptive, painfully honest."

Dennis Russell

SEE ALSO: *Chappelle, Dave; Cosby, Bill; Emmy Awards; Gregory, Dick; Griffin, Merv; Lynch, David; Murphy, Eddie; Stand-up Comedy; Sullivan, Ed; Tomlin, Lily; The Wayans Family.*

BIBLIOGRAPHY

Haskins, James. *Richard Pryor: A Man and His Madness.* New York: Beaufort Books, 1984.

Pryor, Richard, and Todd Gold. *Pryor Convictions and Other Life Sentences.* New York: Pantheon, 1995.

Robbins, Fred, and David Ragan. *Richard Pryor: This Cat's Got 9 Lives!* New York: Delilah Books, 1982.

Robinson, Eugene. "Richard Pryor: Preacher of Truth." *Washington Post,* December 13, 2005.

Watkins, Mel. "Richard Pryor, Who Turned Humor of the Streets into Social Satire, Dies at 65." *New York Times,* December 12, 2005.

Williams, John A., and Dennis A. Williams. *If I Stop I'll Die: The Comedy and Tragedy of Richard Pryor.* New York: Thunder's Mouth Press, 1991.

Psychedelia

The word *psychedelic* entered the English language in 1957, courtesy of British psychologist Humphrey Osmond. In a paper he was presenting at a conference of the New York Academy of Sciences, Osmond described his own experiences with mind-altering chemicals, such as LSD and mescaline. Dissatisfied with the judgmental terms that his profession typically used to describe such drugs, Osmond came up with *psychedelic* as a more neutral descriptor, and the name stuck.

Psychedelic drugs remained in the cultural background, the sole province of discreet, professional, scientific research, until 1963. That year, it became widely known that two Harvard psychology professors, Timothy Leary and Richard Alpert, were giving controlled doses of LSD to graduate student volunteer subjects. Leary and Alpert were engaged in legitimate research, and the LSD (short for lysergic acid diethylamide) had been obtained legally and with government permission. Harvard deemed the project irresponsible, however, and fired both men on the grounds of unprofessional conduct.

Freed from the constraints of academia, Leary became a vocal advocate of the use of LSD to expand human consciousness. He was perhaps best known for his pithy admonition to young people: "Tune in, turn on, drop out." By the middle of the decade, many had heard of Leary's advice—and quite a few had taken it. LSD and other psychedelic drugs, such as psilocybin and peyote, came to occupy a prominent place in the youth culture that developed in the 1960s and continued into the 1970s.

One of the focal points for what became known as the counterculture was San Francisco, especially the city's Haight-Ashbury district. An area of traditionally low rent and bohemian lifestyle, "the Haight" attracted many young people who were in search of new experiences, whether chemical, sexual, or social. Although they sometimes referred to themselves as "flower children" or even "freaks," many adults began to use the term *hippie*, a word that eventually grew so imprecise that it was often used to refer to anyone who looked, dressed, or acted unconventionally.

MUSIC, BOOKS, AND ART

An important aspect of the scene was the music, especially the variety that became known as psychedelic music or acid rock—so named because listening to it could supposedly simulate the experience of a hallucinogenic "trip" without the use of chemicals. Psychedelic music was characterized by extremely high volume, deliberate electronic distortion, the use of synthesizers, extended instrumental improvisations or jams, and the addition of Eastern instruments, such as the sitar, to the traditional rock instrument repertoire. The accompanying lyrics tended to emphasize mysticism or drug references. Some of the more successful acid rock bands included Jefferson Airplane, Iron Butterfly, Quicksilver Messenger Service, the Grateful Dead, and the British bands Pink Floyd and Led Zeppelin. Other musical groups, while not usually identified as psychedelic, sometimes recorded songs that fit the mold—such as the Beatles' "Lucy in the Sky with Diamonds," Strawberry Alarm Clock's "Incense and Peppermints," and the Jimi Hendrix Experience's "Purple Haze." Scottish folk singer Donovan had a hit record with "Mellow Yellow," which extolled the mind-altering properties of dried banana peels.

Nor was any other aspect of 1960s and 1970s culture left untouched by psychedelia. The publishing world produced such books as Aldous Huxley's *The Doors of Perception* (1954) and Carlos Castaneda's three-volume *Teachings of Don Juan* (1968)—the former a paean to the mind-expending aspects of hallucinogens, the latter an account of the author's initiation, at the hands of a Yacqui Indian guru, into the mystical dimensions of peyote.

Films were also quick to cash in on the psychedelic scene. In 1967 Roger Corman, a director best known for his series of horror movies based on the works of Edgar Allan Poe, brought *The Trip*, starring Peter Fonda, to audiences. A year later, the Beatles' animated film *Yellow Submarine* was released. Its kaleidoscopic imagery and outrageous use of color hinted at, for some, the surreal experience of an LSD trip.

The world of art was also affected. Psychedelic artists employed glaringly bright colors and unusual shapes to evoke the visual experience that came from the use of mind-altering drugs. The work of Isaac Abrams is notable in this regard, and some of Andy Warhol's paintings also show a psychedelic influence. A number of illustrators also adopted the psychedelic style, especially for display on concert posters and the covers of record albums. Some of the better-known work was produced by R. Crumb and Rick Griffin, but the most successful of the psychedelic illustrators was Peter Max. Born in Germany, Max lived for a time in China and Israel before coming to the United States to study art. He had achieved modest success as an illustrator by the mid-1960s, but in 1967 his career really began to take off. Max's bold, colorful designs graced products from posters to shirts to clocks to lamps. In 1968 his posters alone sold more than one million copies.

By the mid-1970s the psychedelic era was over, its LSD and acid rock replaced by cocaine and disco. Although a brief attempt at revival took place in the late 1990s, it was no more than an exercise in nostalgia. Occasionally, psychedelic influences still pop up, as in the solo music released by rock musician Noel Gallagher after 2009, but such efforts seem to be isolated to individuals rather than heralding a new cultural movement. The psychedelic era was a product of its time, and, for better or worse, that time is unlikely to come again.

Justin Gustainis

SEE ALSO: *The Beatles; Castaneda, Carlos; Cocaine/Crack; Corman, Roger; Crumb, Robert; Disco; Donovan; The Grateful Dead; Haight-Ashbury; Hendrix, Jimi; Hippies; Jefferson Airplane/Starship; Leary, Timothy; Led Zeppelin; LSD; Max, Peter; Pink Floyd; Warhol, Andy.*

BIBLIOGRAPHY

Henke, James; Parke Puterbaugh; Charles Perry, et al. *I Want to Take You Higher: The Psychedelic Era, 1965–1969.* San Francisco: Chronicle Books, 1997.

Hicks, Michael. *Sixties Rock: Garage, Psychedelic, and Other Satisfactions.* Urbana: University of Illinois Press, 2000.

Stevens, Jay. *Storming Heaven: LSD and the American Dream.* New York: Atlantic Monthly Press, 1987.

Watts, W. David, Jr. *The Psychedelic Experience: A Sociological Study.* Beverly Hills, CA: Sage Publications, 1971.

Psychics

Psychics as clairvoyants, fortune-tellers, and earth-bound connections to the spirit world can be traced back thousands of years and as far away as ancient Egypt. As an element of American popular culture in the twenty-first century, a psychic reading is as close as the Internet or a 1-900 phone call, though some who claim to be more serious clairvoyants scorn these pay-by-the-minute fortune-tellers as charlatans.

NINETEENTH CENTURY

The psychic movement in the United States followed closely on the tails of the Mesmeric and Spiritualist movements of the nineteenth century. Austrian doctor Franz Antoine Mesmer (1734–1815) captured followers' attention with his reports of psychic phenomenon such as "thought transference, clairvoyance and 'eyeless vision'" in subjects who came to be referred to as "mesmerized." Mesmer's popularity opened the door for acceptance of the spiritualist movement by acknowledging the concepts of clairvoyance and communication with the dead. The mesmeric trance, as it had come to be known, led naturally to the idea of the mediumistic trance, the core of the spiritualist movement.

In 1848 Margaret Fox and her sister from Hydesville, New York, produced spirit "rappings" in response to questions from the audience. They moved to Rochester, New York, where they grew in popularity until their fame as mediums had spread across the Atlantic. Several imitators followed the Fox sisters, with varying routines: ESP (extrasensory perception), table levitation or "turning," spirit-induced writing, and speaking in a spirit's voice while in trance, later referred to as channeling. Spiritualism gained such popularity—even First Lady Jane (Mrs. Franklin) Pierce was an adherent—that many churches and societies were born of the movement. Incidentally, Fox later confessed to producing the "rapping" noises through her joints.

Connecting the spiritualist movement with religion did little to shelter the movement from accusations of fraud. In 1882 Sir William Barrett (1844–1925), Henry Sidgwick (1838–1900), and F. W. H. Meyers (1843–1901) founded the Society for Psychical Research (SPR) to scientifically investigate claims of psychic phenomena. The SPR made very few strides toward proving psychic manifestations and instead uncovered myriad fraudulent activities, including those of the famed Russian psychic, Madame Helena Petrovna Blavatsky.

TWENTIETH CENTURY

Interest in psychics waxed and waned throughout the twentieth century. In the United States two psychics in particular had a strong hold on the popular imagination: Edgar Cayce and Jeane Dixon. Edgar Cayce (1877–1945), known as America's "sleeping prophet," had a remarkable talent for learning clairvoyantly in his sleep and for diagnosing ailments and describing an appropriate treatment while from a trancelike state. Consistently, doctors confirmed the diagnoses and the treatments were effective. Cayce's individual "health readings" eventually turned into predictions of life events, not only for individual clients but also for the country and the world at large. Cayce successfully predicted the 1929 Wall Street crash, America's involvement in World War II, the defeat of the Axis powers in 1945, and the collapse of Soviet communism. Cayce also predicted a number of worldwide geological upheavals, many of which simply did not occur.

By allegedly predicting the assassination of John F. Kennedy in 1963, Dixon (1918–1997) became something of a media sensation, though she had won the confidence of followers from an early age. She served as a consultant to Presidents Roosevelt and Truman and Britain's Winston Churchill. Dixon successfully predicted the assassination of Gandhi, the suicide of Marilyn Monroe, and the assassinations of Robert Kennedy and Martin Luther King Jr. Despite her success, however, she began to discredit herself by publicly showcasing her talents and authoring a syndicated horoscope column with worldwide distribution. Her annual "predictions," most of which did not materialize, became a prominent feature in supermarket-tabloid newspapers.

The pop-culture psychic of the 1990s emerged on the crest of New Age metaphysics, Hollywood hype, and a good TV infomercial. For a $3.99-per-minute phone call, the psychics at singer Dionne Warwick's Psychic Friends Network could be consulted about love, money, careers, and even weight loss. In person, a look into the future can cost between $45 and $200. It is estimated that psychic hotlines gross approximately $1 billion per year. Psychic Friends Network fell prey to poor business decisions and filed for bankruptcy in 1998. In 2004 the network won a lawsuit against MCI claiming that the phone company cost it revenues by billing improperly and cutting off calls prematurely. Despite Psychic Friends Network's decline, other companies continued to offer the services of telephone psychics into the 2000s, and in 2011 Psychic Friends Network announced that it was starting business again.

Investigative journalists have uncovered evidence that some psychic hotlines do not employ psychics at all but hire unemployed actors or housewives who offer their consultations from prepared scripts. In spite of such efforts to debunk the work of psychics, many Americans continued to believe in the paranormal. A 2005 Gallup poll reported that 41 percent of Americans believe in ESP and 26 percent believe in clairvoyance.

The psychics of the 2010s are a far cry from the joint-rapping Fox sisters of the early psychic movement. Every large city, and some smaller ones, have their share of storefront "gypsy fortune-tellers," and many ethnic groups have their own psychic traditions, such as the "roots" healers in black and Caribbean communities or the psychics in U.S. Chinatowns that are regularly consulted for advice on business or romantic decisions. Others are more media savvy, with their 1-900 numbers and websites. Most, it appears, are seasoned entertainers, though they are far shrewder businesspeople then their early counterparts, with technology clearly on their side. The evolution of the psychic from early charlatan to telephone fortune-teller is proof positive of two basic tenets of human existence: humankind will always have a burning desire to know what the future holds, and nothing, absolutely nothing, can escape commercialization—not even the paranormal.

Nadine-Rae Leavell

SEE ALSO: *Communism; Hollywood; Kennedy Assassination; King, Martin Luther, Jr.; Monroe, Marilyn; New Age Spirituality; Tabloids; World War II.*

BIBLIOGRAPHY

Bodine, Michael. *Growing Up Psychic: From Skeptic to Believer.* Woodbury, MN: Llewellyn Publications, 2010.

Cavendish, Richard, ed. *Man, Myth and Magic: The Illustrated Encyclopedia of Mythology, Religion and the Unknown*, rev. ed. New York: Marshall Cavendish, 1994.

Guiley, Rosemary Ellen. *Harper's Encyclopedia of Mystical & Paranormal Experience.* San Francisco: HarperSanFrancisco, 1991.

Melton, J. Gordon, and Leslie A. Shepard, eds. *Encyclopedia of Occultism and Parapsychology*, 4th ed. Detroit, MI: Gale Research, 1996.

Poinsot, M. C. *The Encyclopedia of Occult Sciences.* Detroit, MI: Gale Research, 1972.

Psycho

Most famous for the much-loved and much-parodied shower scene, Alfred Hitchcock's 1960 film thriller *Psycho* was shot on a shoestring budget of $800,000 by the crew of the director's television show. This black-and-white classic was a carefully crafted work of cinema that also upped the ante on movie mayhem. The staggering box-office success of *Psycho*—it has earned more than $40 million to date—inspired, and continues to encourage, a host of imitators who are still pushing the envelope on cinema bloodshed but rarely with the artistry displayed by Hitchcock. As is true of Hitchcock in general, *Psy-*

cho is a favorite with film theorists and cultural critics more generally and has been the basis of innumerable academic theses addressing everything from Norman Bates's psychology to the film's subversion of the norms of domesticity to its revelation of the violence that lay beneath the calm perfection of 1950s America.

The plot of *Psycho* was based on mystery/fantasy/science fiction writer Robert Bloch's 1959 novel *Psycho*, itself loosely derived from the real-life story of murderer Ed Gein. In the book, lonely motel keeper Norman Bates and his mother are the sole proprietors of the Bates Motel, a now-seedy establishment patronized by Mary Crane, a young office worker who has impulsively stolen $40,000 of her boss's money. After a chat with Norman in which he discusses his apparently unbalanced mother ("I think perhaps all of us go a little crazy at times"), Mary resolves to return the loot before anyone knows it's missing. But Mary, fated not to leave the Bates Motel alive, is brutally cut down in her shower by a butcher knife wielded by someone with "the face of a crazy old woman." Mary's sister initiates an investigation into her disappearance, which, after more murder and mystery, eventually reveals that Norman killed his mother as a youth and has now become a homicidal split personality of Norman/Mother.

It was screenwriter Joseph Stefano who decided to open the story with Marion (the Mary of the novel) instead of Norman and his mother. Because the film's narrative was told from the victim's point of view, engaging the audience's sympathy, viewers were shocked when she died less than halfway through. Hitchcock cast well-known actress Janet Leigh as Marion and, to make Norman seem sympathetic, chose Anthony Perkins, portrayer of sensitive men in such 1950s films as *Friendly Persuasion* (1956) and *Fear Strikes Out* (1957), to play Norman. After the release of *Psycho*, public perception of Perkins was irrevocably altered, leading to a career full of "weird" roles including reprises of Norman in several much-belated sequels.

Shooting on *Psycho* was generally swift, but a week was lavished on the shower murder sequence. Working from a storyboard by title designer Saul Bass, Hitchcock shot the death scene from many different angles, which, edited into a rapid montage and underscored by the piercing strings of Bernard Herrmann's music, shocked the audience viscerally.

The shock ending was advertised through Hitchcock's tongue-in-cheek ad campaign—"Don't give away the ending—it's the only one we have!"—and dramatic integrity was ensured by the stricture against seating anyone after the film had begun. Although Hitchcock maintained that the film was a black-humored joke, not to be taken seriously, there was no denying its impact on the moviegoers who flocked to the film in great numbers and subsequently swore off taking showers. (Among those claiming still to be afraid of showers: Janet Leigh.) *Psycho* proved to be the capstone of Hitchcock's career, earning him one of his few Oscar nominations.

Compared to the host of horrors that have followed in its wake, from the *Friday the 13th* series to *Scream* and its imitators, *Psycho* was circumspect in its handling of gore. Hitchcock deliberately chose not to show a knife actually entering Marion's torso but rather to achieve his effects through montage. The monochromatic cinematography he used not only suited the eerie, haunted-house mood but also avoided a Technicolor bloodbath: the blood seen spattering in the shower sequence was actually chocolate syrup.

The granddaddy of all slasher films, *Psycho* also generated its own franchise, though none of the remakes or sequels have had anywhere near the success of the original. In *Psycho II* (1983), *Psycho III* (1986), and *Psycho IV: The Beginning* (1990), Perkins reprised his role as Norman as well as directed *Psycho III*. On the other hand, Perkins refused to play Norman in the 1987 television movie *Bates Motel*, which was originally intended as a pilot episode for a television series, and the movie was panned. In 1998 director Gus Van Sant produced a color remake of *Psycho*. An homage to Hitchcock, the film is essentially a shot-by-shot remake of the original, modeling the earlier director's every camera movement and directional shot.

Preston Neal Jones

SEE ALSO: *Academy Awards; Cable TV;* Friday the 13th*; Hitchcock, Alfred; Hollywood; Horror Movies; Made-for-Television Movies; Movie Stars;* Scream*; Slasher Movies; Television.*

BIBLIOGRAPHY

Bloch, Robert. *Psycho.* New York: Simon & Schuster, 1959.

Bogdanovich, Peter. *Who the Devil Made It?* New York: Ballantine, 1998.

Gottlieb, Sidney, ed. *Hitchcock on Hitchcock.* Berkeley: University of California Press, 1997.

Leigh, Janet. *"Psycho": Behind the Scenes of the Classic Thriller.* New York: Harmony Books, 1995.

Smith, Steven C. *A Heart at Fire's Center: The Life and Music of Bernard Herrmann.* Berkeley: University of California Press, 1991.

Spoto, Donald. *The Dark Side of Genius: The Life of Alfred Hitchcock.* Boston: Little, Brown, 1983.

Taylor, John Russell. *Hitch: The Life and Times of Alfred Hitchcock.* New York: Pantheon (Random House), 1978.

Truffaut, François *Hitchcock.* New York: Simon & Schuster, 1984.

Wells, Amanda Sheahan. *"Psycho": Director Alfred Hitchcock.* London: York Press, 2001.

PTA/PTO (Parent Teacher Association/ Organization)

Parent Teacher Associations or Organizations are voluntary groups that forge mutually cooperative relationships between parents and public schools. The umbrella organization of these local groups is the National Parent Teacher Association, which claims affiliation with 27,000 local groups and more than five million members. Its mission statement advocates speaking out on behalf of children and youth in schools, assisting parents in their child-rearing responsibilities, and encouraging parental involvement in schools. Originally called the National Congress of Mothers, it was formed during the 1890s by Alice McLellan Birney and Phoebe Apperson Hearst, the latter a member by marriage of the prominent Hearst newspaper dynasty.

The name of the original national organization reflects its historical context. During the late nineteenth century women were expected to focus on nurturing and raising children. Most Americans believed these crucial activities took place solely in the domestic sphere and the private home. What women such as Birney did was to extend the traditional role of female nurturing to a realm outside the home and into the arena of public advocacy and activity. This new organization both confirmed the special—some would say subordinate—role of women in raising children while extending it to what Settlement House Movement leader Jane Addams once called "social housekeeping." This early group viewed parenting as a specialized activity in need of education and training.

Not surprisingly, the National Congress of Mothers also reflected the spirit of the Progressive Era in American history (roughly 1890–1917), during which time the organization changed its name to the National Congress of Mothers and Parent Teacher Associations. These years saw an increasing number of middle-class Americans dedicate themselves to reforming the inhumane excesses of industrial capitalism. Perhaps the most famous leader of this movement was President Theodore Roosevelt, who played a major role in the National Congress by serving as a speaker at its conventions. Taking up Roosevelt's call for social and political reform, the National Congress threw itself into numerous Progressive Era causes, including the abolition of child labor, the reform of the juvenile court system, and the passage of the Pure Food Bill in 1906. In addition, the organization helped promote John Dewey's child-centered schooling methods that became known as "progressive education."

During the Progressive Era the National Congress carved out its particular concern in the midst of other school reform movements. According to Louise Montgomery, a Chicago educator at the turn of the twentieth century, the proliferation of the public school system brought with it new challenges because it divorced the traditional activities of education from the home. She argued, "The parent has been strangely silent, surrendering his child to the school system with a curious, unquestioning faith." Parent Teacher Associations were meant to challenge this sort of passivity on the part of parents. Members of the organization believed ordinary citizens had a fundamental role to play in America's civic and public life.

Though the original idealism of the groups declined after the Progressive Era, the goals remained the same at the turn of the century, with the National PTA maintaining its role as the nation's biggest child-advocacy organization. The PTA continued to involve parents in decision making about local schools and to make child welfare its central focus. Among the contemporary issues important to the PTA in the early twenty-first century were developing and implementing common core educational standards, educating parents about Internet safety practices, providing resources for military families, preventing bullying, and offering grants to support arts education.

One of the biggest challenges facing the PTA is recruiting a larger percentage of parents to participate in the organization. In many families, both parents work outside the home, leaving little time to volunteer for school activities. Strategies to deal with the volunteer shortage include improving communication by using the latest tools such as e-mail, encouraging parents that even a small investment of time can make a difference, and seeking to increase male membership in the PTA. Like so many long-standing American institutions, the PTA will have to adapt to the demands of fast-paced contemporary life in order to thrive in the twenty-first century.

Kevin Mattson

SEE ALSO: *Addams, Jane; Hearst, William Randolph.*

BIBLIOGRAPHY

Cremin, Lawrence Arthur. *The Transformation of the School: Progressivism in American Education, 1876–1957.* New York: Vintage Books, 1961.

Cutright, Melitta J. *The National PTA Talks to Parents.* New York: Doubleday, 1989.

Henderson, Anne T. *Beyond the Bake Sale: The Essential Guide to Family/School Partnerships.* New York: New Press, 2007.

Swap, Susan McAllister. *Developing Home-School Partnerships.* New York: Teachers College, 1993.

Public Enemy

Public Enemy burst onto the hip-hop scene in 1987 with their debut album *Yo! Bum Rush the Show.* Articulating a militant black nationalism over a heavy bass line and driving rhythms, the group marked out a new space in the emerging rap genre. They soon attracted attention with their uncompromising lyrics, which advocated bringing down the white power structure that had oppressed blacks for so long. Their twin tactics of visibility and militancy soon marked them as a threat to the Establishment, and they were hailed as the "Black Panthers of rap."

The members of Public Enemy have gone beyond making rap music. Fronted by Chuck D (Carlton Ridenhour), who calls himself a prophet of rage, they pronounced themselves the "Black CNN" early on. Hailing from Long Island, New York, Chuck D is the son of ex-1960s activists who proclaims that his mission is to champion the cause of the African American underclass. He locates himself in the tradition of such black orators as Jesse Jackson and Martin Luther King Jr. Chuck D distinguishes himself from his rap predecessors by a conspicuous lack of macho clichés and empty boasts. Instead, he raps intelligently and unrelentingly about African American history while his sidekick, Flavor Flav (William Drayton), urges him on. Meanwhile, former member DJ Terminator X (Norman Rogers) fused the revolutionary teachings of Malcolm X, Kwame Toure, Louis Farrakhan, and King with the beats of L. L. Cool J. and Run-DMC. Public Enemy's emphasis on education over machismo situates them in a rap tradition initiated by the Last Poets, and they have served as a blueprint for other rappers. Paris, KRS-One, Basehead, the Disposable Heroes of Hip-Hoprisy, and Kool Moe Dee soon followed Public Enemy's lead in establishing the new genre of "hardcore" rap that fused edification with entertainment.

Visibility is key to Public Enemy's strategy. Their logo, a silhouetted figure between the crosshairs of a gun sight, indicates both that they are targets of society at large and that society is their target. The figure represents the black man in America, a perceived menace to an establishment bent on excluding him. Many of Public Enemy's fans wear the logo on their shirts. Flavor Flav sports a huge stopped alarm clock as a reminder that we should "know what time it is"; it caricatures a consumer society that privileges expensive watches although, as far as social reform goes, time has stopped. Public Enemy were originally backed onstage by Professor Griff (Richard Griffin) and his Security of the First World (S1W) posse—toting Uzis and wearing paramilitary uniforms—whose image was aimed at subverting existing power relations.

Public Enemy. *Chuck D, left, and Flava Flav of Public Enemy brought issues of African American history and oppression into rap music.* JEFF KRAVITZ/CONTRIBUTOR/FILMMAGIC, INC/GETTY IMAGES.

Public Enemy's second album, *It Takes a Nation of Millions to Hold Us Back* (1988), extended their campaign to uproot the status quo with such tracks as "Bring the Noise" and "Rebel without a Pause." "Black Steel in the Hour of Chaos" opposes the military draft as a principle of black defiance, whereas "Louder Than a Bomb" accuses the Central Intelligence Agency of assassinating King and Malcolm X. "Fight the Power," on the group's next album, debunks such American icons as Elvis Presley and John Wayne; the track was Motown Records' biggest-selling twelve-inch album and has been described as a prototype of what rap music can achieve. By turning platinum, producing provocative videos, and attracting a vast multiracial audience, Public Enemy set the trend and standards to which rap could aspire.

Accusations of anti-Semitism, however, nearly destroyed the group in 1989. Professor Griff, Public Enemy's "minister of information" and a member of Louis Farrakhan's Nation of Islam, stated that Jews were responsible "for the majority of wickedness that goes on across the globe." Chuck D fired Griff (who later formed his own group) and replied to the media criticism with *Fear of a Black Planet* (1990). By combining news clips with music and recreating media broadcasts about the group, Public Enemy attempted to fight back, depicting themselves as the victims of a system committed to destroying them. Griff later met with a Holocaust awareness organization, and after a lively discussion, he admitted that he had been wrong in his remarks.

Public Enemy has since made several more albums, includ-ing*Apocalypse '91* (1991), *Greatest Misses* (1992), *Muse Sick-n-Hour Mess Age* (1994), *He Got Game* (1998), *New Whirl Order* (2005), and *Beats and Places* (2006). Chuck D took a break from the group to make a solo album titled *The Autobiography of Mistachuck* (1996). Singles such as "Shut 'Em Down" (1991), "Give It Up" (1994), and "I Stand Accused" (1994) continued in the groove of hard-line, myth-breaking militancy. One of the group's more recent efforts, *How You Sell Soul to a Soulless People Who Sold Their Soul???* (2007), received good reviews and was named by *Rolling Stone* critic Robert Christgau as one of the best albums of that year.

Public Enemy not only raised consciousness among their black following but also attracted a significant body of white fans; this allowed them to establish an influence beyond the confines of inner-city ghettos and to sell a substantial number of records. Their popularity among white middle-class fans drew a sizeable following to the rap genre in general, greatly benefitting groups such as NWA and other "gangsta" rappers. The new consumer bloc undoubtedly helped rap to cross over into the mainstream music industry. By the late 1990s hip-hop singles often reached number one in the charts, selling more than half a million copies each.

Public Enemy's militancy shifted rap from the party-style swaggering of "electro" toward a more politically conscious music, setting a trend and spawning a host of imitators. By attracting a broad, multiracial following, the group has ensured a wider audience for its vocalization of the problems of blacks in America.

Nathan Abrams

SEE ALSO: *Black Panthers; Chuck D; The Draft; Gangsta Rap; Hip-Hop; Jackson, Jesse; King, Martin Luther, Jr.; L. L. Cool J.; Malcolm X; Presley, Elvis; Rap;* Rolling Stone*; Run-DMC; Wayne, John.*

BIBLIOGRAPHY

Abrams, Nathan. "Antonio's B-Boys: Rap, Rappers, and Gramsci's Intellectuals." *Popular Music and Society* 19, no. 4 (1995): 1–18.

Fernando, S. H., Jr. *The New Beats: Exploring the Music Culture and Attitudes of Hip-Hop*. Edinburgh, UK: Payback Press, 1995.

Myrie, Russell. *Don't Rhyme for the Sake of Riddlin': The Authorized Story of Public Enemy*. New York: Grove Press, 2010.

Nelson, Havelock, and Michael A. Gonzales. *Bring the Noise: A Guide to Rap Music and Hip-Hop*. New York: Harmony Books, 1991.

Toop, David. *Rap Attack 2: African Rap to Global Hip Hop*. London: Serpent's Tail, 1991.

Public Libraries

Of all of its public institutions, perhaps America's most enduring are its libraries. U.S. libraries arose out of the democratic belief in an informed public, enlightened civic discourse, social and intellectual advancement, and participation in the democratic process. Libraries became part of America's commitment to equal opportunity in education and freedom of thought and expression. Though libraries have existed for almost as long as records have been kept, libraries as public institutions are rather recent, and the idea of using public funds for libraries had to first overcome considerable opposition. In 1854 the Boston Public Library opened, becoming the first American library to be supported by general taxation. Public libraries became products of the nineteenth century due to the influences of the Industrial Revolution, urban growth, and the accumulation of private and public wealth.

The traditional structure of the public library is based on service, education, democracy, intellectual freedom, and the preservation of the record of civilization. For more than 150 years, the mission of public libraries has been to collect, organize, preserve, and provide free and equal access to information, knowledge, and entertainment in different media formats. By following this mission, libraries fostered a level playing field for all Americans to access information free of charge while providing community enhancement, lifelong learning, recreation, literacy, and personal advancement. America's public library system has been highly revered and copied in countries throughout the world.

Though public libraries enjoy an image of well-organized houses of information, it was not always this way. Early public libraries lacked standards of service, adequate acquisition funds, proper cataloging, and professional librarians. To ameliorate the problems in libraries, library leaders resolved at an 1876 librarian conference to professionalize their occupation. Soon an accelerated library movement started. Librarians founded the American Library Association and began developing methods and systems for organizing information. Among the methodologies created was the Dewey Decimal Classification system, created by Melvil Dewey in 1876 for cataloging materials. Dewey went on to establish the first professional school for librarianship at Columbia University in 1887, an idea that had grown to fifty-eight accredited schools by 2010.

PRIVATE AND PUBLIC FUNDING

Whereas standardization, organization methodologies, and the professionalization of librarians made public libraries more service oriented and accessible, private funding provided the boost needed to reach out to many more underserved communities and neighborhoods. Steel magnate Andrew Carnegie gave more than $41 million to erect 1,679 public library buildings in 1,412 communities between 1890 and 1919. Many of these libraries are still in use in the 2010s. Carnegie's level of philanthropy was unmatched until 1997 when once again America's richest man chose the library as the object of his giving. Bill Gates, through the Bill and Melinda Gates Foundation, gave two $200 million grants directed at providing digital technology, "ensuring that if you can get to a public library, you can reach the Internet." In the current environment, more than 99 percent of public libraries provide Internet access.

In addition to philanthropic gifts, federal programs and grants have assisted the local tax base of library budgets. During the 1930s Franklin Delano Roosevelt's Works Progress Administration (WPA) built 140 new libraries and repaired many existing ones. Later, the Library Services Act of 1956 and the Library Services and Construction Act of 1964–65 provided federal dollars for library construction. In 1996 the Institute of Museum and Library Services, an independent agency of the government, was established to work with state and local organizations to sustain heritage, culture, and knowledge; enhance learning and innovation; and support professional development.

Funds provided for libraries produced some significant results. The 188 public libraries in 1876 grew to more than 16,600 by 2010. Studies show that in 2007 two-thirds of Americans had a library card, libraries were visited approximately 1.4 billion times, and 7.9 million items were charged out. A number of studies have shown the return on investment in library services to be between $4 and $5 for each tax dollar spent, and public library per capita spending averaged $36.36 in fiscal year 2008. Public libraries have been criticized as an institution serving primarily the middle class, yet the library's strength lies in its democratic nature, providing equal and free access across ethnic, economic, and cultural lines, including servicing many immigrants. Public libraries are focused on local communities and are governed by trustees made up of community members.

TECHNOLOGICAL ADVANCES

Libraries and librarianship evolved radically in the latter half of the twentieth century and into the twenty-first century, based largely on new forms of information technology. The technology allowed new ways to create, store, organize, and distribute information and provide other services. Public expectations of the role of libraries increased, and librarians responded by offering, for example, training in new communication technologies; providing Internet access and wireless connections; making available remote access to the library's catalog, databases, and other information; and staffing online ask-a-librarian reference services. Librarians view online services as community outreach, a time-honored service from the early horse-drawn book wagons to the modern bookmobile. Libraries began to reach out by providing reference services delivered by mail, telephone, e-mail, and online chat and texting.

Though libraries maintain a strong virtual presence, there is still a need for libraries as a physical space. Individuals visit libraries for many reasons; for example, to browse collections, receive assistance in resume development and job searching, gather information for particular needs, and gather in meeting rooms. Most libraries engage the community by offering activities and seminars for children, adolescents, and adults.

In addition to adjusting to rapidly changing technology, libraries have faced other challenges. They have tried to keep up with changing demographics, especially in serving multiethnic and multiracial populations. Librarians have consistently stood against censorship in all its forms. They have fought to keep the "fair use" and "first sale" clauses in the copyright laws that allow libraries to loan materials and duplicate copyrighted material after certain criteria are met. Libraries have been challenged by competition from online book sales, book superstores, and the Internet. This competition makes it easy and convenient to find information, order books, and download reading material, bypassing a key library role. Libraries compete for limited public dollars, and many library systems have been forced to downsize by closing branches and cutting services, staff, and hours of operation.

Despite the challenges, it is clear that communities still want libraries. Local libraries are viewed as an important education resource, and they often enter into quality-of-life measures of a community. People want libraries to provide free access, serve the disadvantaged, and offer activities and programs. Libraries remain one of the best investments a community can make.

Byron Anderson

SEE ALSO: *E-Readers; The Internet; Leisure Time; Works Progress Administration (WPA) Murals.*

BIBLIOGRAPHY

Garrison, Dee. *Apostles of Culture: The Public Librarian and American Society, 1876–1920.* New York: Free Press, 1979.

Jones, Plummer Alston. *Libraries, Immigrants, and the American Experience.* Westport, CT: Green Wood Press, 1999.

"The State of America's Libraries. A Report from the American Library Association." Accessed April 2012. Available from http://www.ala.org/news/mediapresscenter/americaslibraries

Van Slyck, Abigail Ayres. *Free to All: Carnegie Libraries & American Culture, 1890–1920.* Chicago: University of Chicago Press, 1995.

Public Television (PBS)

With its dedication to the high ideals of presenting the finest in drama, music, children's programs, and political debate, public television has proved a significant cultural force in an America in which broadcasting is largely driven by commercial considerations, often to the detriment of quality. Public television was at least partially born in reaction to Federal Communications Commission (FCC) Chairman Newton Minow's famous comment that by 1961 American commercial television had become "a vast wasteland." (In 1978 Minow became chairman of PBS.) Building on its 1950s roots in educational television (ETV), public (or noncommercial) television has attained considerable popular success as a formidable, if vulnerable, alternative to the increasingly trivial and commercial-saturated programming of network television. However, that success has not been achieved without problems, internal conflicts, political opposition, and funding setbacks.

EARLY HISTORY

Public and educational television dates back to the first public radio broadcasts from universities and scientific laboratories. The first radio broadcast of any kind originated from the University of Wisconsin in 1919. Over the course of the ensuing decade, other universities followed suit, forming electronic extension services. Early audiences were scattered and limited to those who owned crystal sets.

Although the first television programs were broadcast in the late 1930s, World War II curtailed industry development. By 1945, however, the FCC had set aside thirteen channels for commercial television; by 1949 one million television receivers were in use across the United States. During the FCC's four-year freeze on station licenses (1948–1952) a movement began among educators intent on lobbying for noncommercial channels dedicated to education. In 1952, after its historic Sixth Report and Order, the FCC reserved 242 channels for noncommercial TV, and the Educational Television and Radio Center (ETRC) was established in Ann Arbor, Michigan, with a grant from the Ford Foundation's Fund for Adult Education. The center secured and distributed programs for the emerging system, as well as renting them out to schools and other public institutions.

In 1958 the ETRC moved to New York, where it became National Educational Television (NET), again chiefly supported by the Ford Foundation. NET soon revised the limited classroom approach to educational TV and shifted to providing a broader range of cultural, public affairs, documentary, and children's programming. It laid the groundwork for expansion into network status and for educational TV's eventual redesignation as public TV. NET lives on in the spirit and call letters of WNET, New York City's Channel 13 public television station, which is still active in producing original programming for public television.

Public television thus evolved directly out of educational television, a difficult rite of passage because ETV began as a collection of autonomous stations, each serving in various ways the cause of education but with no overriding administrative/creative policy. PBS's noncommercial status was another stumbling block because it was totally financed by federal and state funding and increasingly by voluntary contributions from local viewers and grants from foundations and corporations. The fact that public TV was born after commercial network television was firmly entrenched in the American mind was another obstacle to its development.

CONFLICTS AND IDENTITY

When the ETV system was redefined as public television by the Public Broadcasting Act of 1967, some internal confusion remained as a result of the diversity of the original educational TV system in spite of the fact that ideals for noncommercial TV had been clarified in the Carnegie Commission Report of that same year. Some stations clung to their original ETV agendas, while others were reluctant to surrender their autonomy to the national system. Regional and political differences further complicated PBS's development and contributed to the factionalism of its first decades.

Despite internal and organizational conflicts, the avowed overall purpose of public television from the start was to make a dedicated attempt to free the television medium from the tyranny of the marketplace and to address the ideal of quality rather than mass appeal and commercial profit. In theory, it also marked an attempt to realize the humanistic, social, and intellectual potential of the mass television medium and to provide a varied menu of cultural, informational, educational, and innovative programming. These ideals were first voiced in the Carnegie Commission Report of 1967, *Public Television: A Program for Action*. The report was the result of a two-year study of educational TV by a prestigious fifteen-member commission composed of educators, businesspeople, producers, and artists. A second Carnegie Commission, also funded by the Carnegie Corporation, was formed in 1977 to examine the history of the first decade of public television.

Public television has been called "a name without a concept," but the system has nonetheless consistently managed to build an audience and a profile while competing positively with the commercial system, and sometimes even influencing it. By the 1970s PBS ratings were on the rise due to a flowering of a variety of excellent, well-produced original shows. These shows ranged from sitcoms and children's programs to documentary series about the arts and classical music. Programs included *The Adams Chronicles*, *Great Performances*, *Nova*, *Live from Lincoln Center*, and *Sesame Street*. Popular British imports included the sitcom *Upstairs, Downstairs*; Sir Kenneth Clark's series on the history of art, *Civilisation*; Jacob Bronowski's *The Ascent of Man*; and *Monty Python's Flying Circus*. These shows became popular PBS staples, leading to more of the same in later decades.

CLASSIC PBS

In 1973 the network's detailed coverage of the Senate Watergate hearings proved to be a boon for fund-raising. By that time, PBS had formed an effective fund-raising system, and regional stations were kept on the air partially through viewer support. In 1990 *The Civil War*, which aired on five consecutive nights, set an all-time ratings record for a series of limited length. During the 1990s PBS's most popular shows were the *National Geographic Specials*, the *MacNeil/Lehrer News Hour*, *This Old House*, *The Frugal Gourmet*, and the British import *Mystery*.

Two extended miniseries attracted particular attention to public television during the late 1970s and early 1980s. Both were British productions, and both pushed the envelope of content and permissiveness for television in general, proving compulsively watchable on a scale that no PBS programming had achieved thus far. *I, Claudius*, a thirteen-hour BBC drama that first aired in 1976, challenged the boundaries of what was acceptable not only on PBS but for television as a whole. Adapted from two novels by Robert Graves—*I, Claudius* (1934) and *Claudius the God* (1935)—the series chronicled in fairly explicit detail the political and sexual intrigues of the reigns of the four decadent Roman emperors who followed Julius Caesar. Told from the viewpoint of Claudius, a presumed idiot who ultimately became emperor, the violence and sexuality of the series made many PBS station executives uneasy, though none of them failed to air it. *I, Claudius* was one of the most popular entries in PBS's excellent *Masterpiece Theater* series.

In 1981 an elaborate eleven-episode adaptation of Evelyn Waugh's 1945 novel *Brideshead Revisited* emulated both the critical success and the audience ratings of *I, Claudius*. Produced by England's Granada Television International, the production was one of the most expensive British television series to date. The extended story followed an Oxford student who becomes emotionally involved in the life of the semidecadent upper classes of an England between world wars. It was filmed on location in opulent settings in England, Venice, and Malta. The series created controversy in its discreet but unselfconscious depiction of the homosexuality of one of the leading characters, Sebastian Flyte, and his intense involvement with the story's narrator, Charles Ryder.

I, Claudius and *Brideshead Revisited* pioneered a new genre of high-toned television and literary adaptation. Longer by far than the longest movies ever made, both productions (*Brideshead* especially) maintained the production values and prestige of quality filmmaking. Whereas ABC's popular success *Roots* had appeared as a ten-episode miniseries in 1977, the PBS broadcasts were the first time that classic works of literature were given their due in a format that finally did justice to the detail and temp of their source material. Nothing like either miniseries had been seen before, and their overwhelming popularity on American public television laid the groundwork for global acceptance of a new and somewhat rarefied genre of quality visual entertainment. The genre thrived on PBS, but the style also influenced actual moviemaking, such as the popular films of James Ivory, who adapted many of the works of E. M. Forster in a similar fashion, and several adaptations of the novels of Jane Austen and others.

CHILDREN'S PROGRAMMING

Another innovative PBS series inspired a number of spin-offs and indeed launched an entire industry: the popular and enduring children's show *Sesame Street*, with its cast of globally beloved characters, including Jim Henson's Muppets. The series, which premiered in November 1969 with an initial budget of only $8 million, has long been considered revolutionary within the genre of children's programs. It operates on the simple principle of teaching letters, numbers, and social concepts according to techniques that had already proved effective in selling consumer products to television audiences. *Sesame Street*'s original target audience was language-impaired preschool inner-city children. Thus the colorful and ethnically diverse characters (both human and Muppet) were often seen in drab urban settings uncharacteristic of children's shows.

Visual zap animation, an innovative instructional method, was pioneered on the show, and evaluative tests soon verified that *Sesame Street*'s formula of teaching letters and numbers though animation, paced at the attention-friendly duration of television commercials and augmented by the use of frequent repetition, was indeed an effective teaching method. The show later expanded from the teaching of educational basics to dealing with more complex issues such as the environment and racial understanding. With the 1984 death of actor Will Lee, who played Mr. Hooper, one of the show's leading characters, the subjects of death and dying were raised for what was probably the first time on a children's television program. *Sesame Street* remains *the* most innovative end product of the venerable educational TV system, and as such it has changed the face and techniques of children's programming everywhere.

In 1990 the death of Jim Henson, who not only created the show's popular Muppet characters but lent his distinctive voice characterizations to several of them, left another void in the show, but his creations live on. The Muppets are one the show's most popular elements. Big Bird, Elmo, Cookie Monster, and the rest of the gang remain among the most recognized and exploited characters on television.

Children's programming proved so successful that in 2005, PBS, along with partners Sesame Workshop, Comcast, and HIT

Entertainment, founded a new network, PBS Kids Sprout. Sprout airs children's shows twenty-four hours a day, including PBS standards *Sesame Street*, *Barney & Friends*, *Bob the Builder*, *Calliou*, and *Thomas & Friends*, along with Sprout original shows such as *The Good Night Show* and *Sunny Side up Show*.

POLITICS AND FUNDING

In spite of its popular successes, PBS has seldom been without its opponents since Lyndon Johnson signed the Public Broadcasting Act that created the Corporation for Public Broadcasting (CPB) in 1967. Johnson suggested that he would also work out a long-range funding plan for public TV in the coming year, but his withdrawal from the 1968 presidential campaign crushed the hope of extended support. Within the context of public television, the ensuing Nixon administration is remembered for its attacks upon PBS as a "fourth network" and for repeated attempts to decentralize public television. Documents later released under the Freedom of Information Act verify that the aim of the Nixon White House was to shift control to individual stations, believing that they produce more conservative programming. In 1972 Nixon vetoed CPB's authorization bill, but after several key members, including the chairman, president, and director of television of CPB, resigned, the president signed a bill authorizing public broadcast funding for 1973.

The affair made public television executives aware that their stations were vulnerable to political pressure. It was also clear that the medium needed to develop a new, decentralized method for distributing production funds and to look for new sources of funding, particularly from the private sector. As a result, PBS turned more aggressively toward corporate underwriting, initially from major oil companies, as a new source of program funding. This move led to Exxon's sponsorship of the *Great Performances* series, which aired such programming as *Brideshead Revisited*.

Congressional Democrats have been traditional supporters of public television, and the Carter administration was relatively hospitable to PBS, which prospered during Carter's term. However, Ronald Reagan's election in 1981, just as public TV was becoming a viable alternative to commercial television, occasioned renewed political opposition. During the Reagan years, some stations came to believe they could survive only by airing commercials. Reagan's drastic budget cuts resulted in FCC approval for experimentation with a form of commercial advertising on public television. Although this was termed *enhanced underwriting*, it meant that "logos or slogans that identify—but do not promote or compare—trade names, and product and service listings" were made permissible on public television, and they have remained so.

In 1992 public television came under attack from a coalition of conservative groups led by the Heritage Foundation. The attack was timed to coincide with a period when Congress was considering the reauthorization of public broadcast funding, and the Heritage Foundation simultaneously distributed "Making Public Television Public," a widely quoted report that actually called for the privatization of public television. (One concept espoused was the selling of CBP to private companies, which would "clean up the public television mess.") The outcome, at least in the short run, was that a Democratic-controlled Congress passed the reauthorization bill, but with some qualifications. To many, the 1992 debate was merely a reprise of ground covered in the Nixon and Reagan years, although as William Hoynes writes in *Public Television for Sale*, it occurred within a "post–Cold War climate that celebrated the market in a quasireligious manner."

CONTINUING STRUGGLES AND TRIUMPHS

The issue of funding for public television took on new urgency in 2011 as the Obama administration and Republicans in Congress battled it out over budget issues, threatening to shut down the government. By that time there were 349 public television stations operating in the United States under the authority of 173 licenses issued to community organizations, universities, and local and state governments. Although federal funding accounts for only 15 percent of overall funding, it remains an essential ingredient in keeping public television on the air. The remainder of funding is derived from member fees, businesses, foundations, grants, and donations. Because CPB does not originate funding, it must purchase programs from suppliers such as WGBH Boston, WNET New York, Sesame Workshop, historian Ken Burns, and American Public Television. After the terrorist attacks on the United States on September 11, 2001, and the subsequent creation of the Department of Homeland Security, public television has been involved in the endeavor to create a digital emergency service that is designed to reach 100 percent of American homes in case of a catastrophic emergency.

The frequent periods of airtime devoted to lengthy but necessary fund-raising campaigns that occur regularly on all public television and radio stations throughout the year sometimes chafe even the most dedicated supporters of regional PBS. Some of these campaigns offer audience members the opportunity to appear "on the air" as the vital phone-answering staff for the call-ins from donors or to see their friends and neighbors become temporary TV personalities on their favorite PBS channel in a kind of throwback to the older and more audience-friendly days of early local and regional television. But as its fund-raising campaigns have proved increasingly successful, PBS has continued to air compelling and popular programs, including Ken Burn's documentaries and the series *Downtown Abbey*.

E. B. White once commented on the television medium:

> I think television should be the counterpart of the literary essay, should arouse our dreams, satisfy our hunger for beauty, take us on journeys, enable us to participate in events, present great drama and music, explore the sea and the sky and the woods and the hills. It should be our Lyceum, our Chautauqua, our Minsky's, and our Camelot. It should state and clarify the social dilemma and the political pickle.

While still far from perfect, and while still evolving and often in harm's way, public television has come the closest of anything yet in the pervasive and much maligned medium in attempting to fulfill White's ideals.

Ross Care

SEE ALSO: Barney and Friends; Brideshead Revisited; *Burns, Ken; Cold War; Ford Motor Company; Henson, Jim; Lehrer, Tom;* Masterpiece Theatre; Monty Python's Flying Circus; *The Muppets;* National Geographic; *9/11; Reagan, Ronald;* Roots; Sesame Street; *Sitcom; Television; Television Anchors;* Upstairs, Downstairs; *Vietnam; Watergate; World War II.*

BIBLIOGRAPHY

Brown, Les. *Les Brown's Encyclopedia of Television*, 3rd ed. Detroit, MI: Visible Ink, 1992.

Calabrese, Andrew, and Colin Sparks, eds. *Toward a Political Economy of Culture: Capitalism and Communication in the Twenty-First Century*. Lanham, MD: Rowman and Littlefield, 2004.

Cambridge, Vibert C. *Immigration, Diversity, and Broadcasting in the United States, 1990–2001*. Athens: Ohio University Press, 2005.

Hoynes, William. *Public Television for Sale: Media, the Market, and the Public Sphere*. Boulder, CO: Westview Press, 1994.

Macy, John W., Jr. *To Irrigate a Wasteland: The Struggle to Shape a Public Television System in the United States*. Berkeley: University of California Press, 1974.

Miller, Carolyn Handler. *Illustrated T.V. Dictionary*. New York: Harvey House, 1980.

Moyers, Bill. *Moyers on Democracy*. New York: Doubleday, 2008.

"Public Television Funding." *Congressional Digest* 90, no. 5 (2011).

Stewart, David C. *The PBS Companion: A History of Public Television*. New York: TV Books, 1999.

Puente, Tito *(1923–2000)*

No individual performer contributed more to the popularity of Latin music in the United States than the legendary Tito Puente. A musician, an arranger, a composer, a bandleader, and a five-time Grammy winner, the internationally acclaimed "King of Latin Music" moved audiences around the world to the beat of *cha-cha-chas, mambos*, and *pachangas*. Best known as a virtuoso of the timbales, Puente was also an accomplished pianist with a degree from the prestigious Juilliard School of Music.

Over the course of his remarkable career, which spanned nearly sixty years, he produced more than 100 albums. He was featured in numerous television sitcoms, commercials, music shows, and motion pictures (including *Radio Days*, 1987, and *The Mambo Kings*, 1992). The recipient of the Smithsonian Medal and three honorary doctorates, Puente was nominated eight times for Grammy Awards (more than any other Latin music artist). His name, which means "bridge" in Spanish, truly captures his achievements—for Puente's music reached across generational, national, and racial boundaries.

Born April 20, 1923, in New York City to Puerto Rican parents, Ernesto Antonio Puente Jr. grew up in Spanish Harlem to the sounds of Afro-Cuban and jazz music. By 1949 the successful fusion of these influences produced one of his first crossover hit songs, "Abaniquito," and fueled the mambo craze of the 1950s. As one of the famed mambo kings of the era, Puente consistently earned top billing at New York's Palladium Ballroom, a *nuyorican* club that served as the cradle of what is now called *salsa*. Jazz greats such as Dizzy Gillespie, Charlie Parker, and Woody Herman often showed up to jam with the mostly Cuban and Puerto Rican musicians appearing nightly at the Palladium.

Always in tune with the tempo of his day, Puente contributed to the various Latin music trends of the 1950s and 1960s, first appealing to the early popularity of the *cha cha cha*, then releasing several hits in the *pachanga* style that became the rage. In the late 1960s, when an R&B/Latin fusion called *boogaloo* emerged as the latest dance music craze, Puente kept up with the times and obliged his audiences, despite his professed dislike of the form. During those years Puente recorded and performed with numerous other Latin music stars, including "Queen of Salsa" Celia Cruz, La Lupe, Santos Colon, Machito, Mongo Santamaria, Mario Bauza, and Xavier Cugat. He also played with Gillespie and would pay tribute to the jazz master in a 1994 concert event at the Apollo Theater.

Puente's "Oye Como Va" and "Para los Rumberos," first recorded in the early 1960s, were later adapted and released by Carlos Santana, introducing audiences in the 1970s to a new synthesis of rock and Latin music. The overwhelming popularity of Santana's remakes led to a joint concert in 1977 and revitalized an interest in Latin music among a new generation of concert-goers. By 1979, when President Jimmy Carter invited him to play at the White House in honor of Hispanic Heritage month, Puente had achieved world-class status.

Puente's musical talent and warm, outgoing personality made him a favorite among young and old. He was featured on the popular television sitcom *The Cosby Show*, in a Coca-Cola commercial, and even a 1995 episode of *The Simpsons*. Burger King used Puente's tune "I Like It like That" in its ads, and he hosted his own show on Spanish-language television. At the closing ceremony of the 1996 Olympic games in Atlanta, Georgia, Puente joined B. B. King, Wynton Marsalis, Stevie Wonder, and Gloria Estefan in an extraordinary finale. According to *Time* correspondent Mark Coatney, the group "whipped up an ever-growing conga line that threatened to spill into the streets." Puente's joyous participation in this event helped to rekindle everyone's spirits and proved that Latin music had truly achieved international recognition.

Puente died on May 31, 2000, and was posthumously awarded the Grammy Lifetime Achievement Award in 2003.

Myra Mendible

SEE ALSO: *Apollo Theater;* The Cosby Show*; Gillespie, Dizzy; Grammy Awards; Herman, Woody; King, B. B.; Parker, Charlie; Rhythm and Blues; Rock and Roll; Salsa Music;* The Simpsons*; Sitcom; Television; Wonder, Stevie.*

BIBLIOGRAPHY

Bourgin, Suzanne M. *Contemporary Musicians: Profiles of the People in Music*. Detroit, MI: Gale Research, 1995.

Loza, Steven Joseph. *Tito Puente and the Making of Latin Music*. Urbana: University of Illinois Press, 1999.

McNeese, Tim. *Tito Puente*. New York: Chelsea House, 2008.

Pulp Fiction

Crime drama is given stylish and original treatment in American director Quentin Tarantino's 1994 film *Pulp Fiction*. In his take on the genre there is an easy interplay between the mundane and the brutal. Told with visual panache and unconventional dialogue, three stories of the Los Angeles underworld interweave in a complex structure.

The tales were written separately, with two of them completed years before the film was conceived. In the first story,

Pulp Fiction. *John Travolta, left, and Uma Thurman dance the twist in a famous scene from* Pulp Fiction. MIRAMAX/BUENA VISTA/THE KOBAL COLLECTION.

two professional hit men, Jules (Samuel L. Jackson) and Vincent (John Travolta), kill some young men who have stolen a briefcase containing something of great beauty and value from gang boss Marcellus Wallace (Ving Rhames). The routine job becomes a life-changing incident for Jules when one of the young men shoots repeatedly at Jules and Vincent from across the small room, but every shot misses. Jules takes this miracle as a sign from God. The job is further complicated when Vincent creates a literal and figurative mess by accidentally blowing out their informant's brains in the backseat of the car.

The second story begins when Wallace asks Vincent to take out his wife, Mia (Uma Thurman), and show her a good time while he is away. After dinner and a dance contest, Vincent and Mia return to the Wallace home, where Mia overdoses on Vincent's powerful heroin and almost dies. In the third story, Wallace pays an aging fighter, Butch (Bruce Willis), to take a dive. Instead, Butch wins the fight and attempts to flee the country before Wallace can have him killed. In addition to these three stories, the film begins and ends with a framing incident of a husband-and-wife team of small-time crooks deciding to hold up the restaurant where Jules and Vincent are having breakfast. The incident takes place chronologically between stories one and two.

The seemingly unrelated stories all tie together in a highly unconventional plot. The structure of the film is not only nonchronological, but there are also repeated actions and parallel actions. A single viewing of the film is a powerful experience, but subsequent viewings are also rewarding, as more of the subtleties and complexities of the film become apparent. It often takes more than one viewing to become comfortable with the film's blending of the horrifying and the oddly funny; not every watcher is prepared to find dark humor in scenes that involve scooping skull fragments off of the upholstery, homosexual rape, or a family heirloom hidden for years in a rectum. The film is an unpredictable mix of the lurid and the absurd, told in dialogue that is alternately hip, mundane, or intriguingly odd.

The dialogue in *Pulp Fiction* does more than simply advance the plot. Tarantino avoids the typical gangster stereotypes by giving his thugs distinctive speech patterns and quirky conversations that bring the characters to life. No two characters in the film speak alike. Mr. Wolf (Harvey Keitel), the professional problem solver who comes in to take care of Vincent and Jules's mess, speaks in clipped, efficient sentences. Jules freely spices his erudite vocabulary with the harshest profanity, and just before putting a bullet into his target he likes to give a dramatic and frightening recitation of Ezekiel 25:17. Although the dialogue often meanders, just like real conversation, it is still memorable. On the way to make the hit on the college boys, Vincent explains to Jules that at the Paris McDonald's a Quarter Pounder is called a Royale with cheese. It is just the type of inane conversation that goes on between two coworkers passing the time during the morning commute.

Pulp Fiction's style and originality did not go unnoticed in the film community. At the Cannes Film Festival, the film won the Palm d'Or. *Pulp Fiction* revitalized the career of Travolta, making him one of the hottest stars in Hollywood for the next several years. Travolta garnered Academy Award, Golden Globe, and Screen Actors Guild nominations for best actor. The film was nominated for seven Academy Awards, including best picture, but only Roger Avary and Tarantino won for best original screenplay. *Pulp Fiction* established Tarantino as a major player in Hollywood.

Randy Duncan

SEE ALSO: *Academy Awards; Keitel, Harvey; Tarantino, Quentin; Travolta, John.*

BIBLIOGRAPHY

Clarkson, Wensley. *Quentin Tarantino: Shooting from the Hip.* Woodstock, NY: Overlook Press, 1995.

Dawson, Jeff. *Quentin Tarantino: The Cinema of Cool.* New York: Applause, 1995.

Jami, Bernard. *Quentin Tarantino: The Man and His Movies.* New York: HarperPerennial, 1995.

Tarantino, Quentin. *Pulp Fiction: A Quentin Tarantino Screenplay.* New York: Hyperion, 1994.

Woods, Paul. *King Pulp: The Wild World of Quentin Tarantino.* London: Plexus, 1998.

Pulp Magazines

Pulp magazines were a cheap form of popular entertainment that emerged just before the dawn of the twentieth century, grew to immense popularity during the 1930s, and withered away by the early 1950s. Sold for five to twenty-five cents apiece and filled with sensational action stories, the pulps appealed primarily to the middle class and educated lower class but drew avid readers from every strata of society. As pulp publisher Henry Steeger notes in the preface to Tony Goodstone's *The Pulps* (1970), "the names of Harry Truman, President of the United States, and Al Capone, lowest figure of the underworld, graced our subscription lists at the same time."

Beneath the garish and lurid covers, the rough-edged pages (made from the cheapest wood pulp) were often filled with hastily written purple prose. Yet a few of the pulp magazines boasted genuinely fine writing, and many contained crude but powerful storytelling that shaped American popular culture. The pulps provided proving grounds for some of the twentieth century's most popular authors and introduced fictional heroes who became household names.

The pulp magazines grew from a nineteenth-century tradition of stories for the masses that began with religious chapbooks warning against "the pernicious effects of dram drinking" and other vices. These small paperbacks were peddled on street corners by hawkers, or chapmen. Although the stories of innocent young girls seduced into lives of alcohol and prostitution were meant to be cautionary tales, some buyers no doubt read them more for titillation than moral inspiration. The chapbooks created an appetite for fiction that was satisfied for a time by serialized tales in the weekly story papers that emerged midcentury.

In 1860 the publishing house of Beadle & Adams began publishing entire novels in a small paperback format that became known as a dime novel (although many of them actually sold for five cents). Once the format proved successful, Street & Smith, which had been in the weekly fiction business since the 1850s, started its own line of dime novels. Street & Smith soon had two very popular dime novel series that would have direct links to the pulps: *Nick Carter Weekly* featured a clean-cut young detective who was a master of disguise, and Edward Zane Carroll Judson, writing under the pen name Ned Buntline, elaborated on the exploits of the real-life William Cody in *Buffalo Bill Weekly.* However, the story papers and "nickel weeklies" did not disappear, and at the end of the nineteenth century, sensational popular fiction existed in a variety of formats.

THE MAN WHO STARTED IT ALL

Frank A. Munsey is generally considered to be the father of pulp magazines. In 1882 he launched *Golden Argosy*, a weekly story magazine for children. Over the next decade Munsey modified the magazine in a number of ways. He changed the content to all fiction, targeted it for an older audience, switched to cheap wood-pulp paper, and shortened the name. By 1896 Munsey had transformed *Argosy* into the first pulp magazine.

Famed writer Stephen Crane was one of the early contributors to the magazine. As the turn of the century approached, *Argosy* was selling half a million copies per month. Munsey added *The All-Story Magazine* in 1905, followed by *Cavalier Weekly* in 1908. With the publication of the 1912 story "Under the Moons of Mars," *All-Story* introduced Edgar Rice Burroughs, whose work ensured the popularity of the pulps and left an indelible mark on popular culture. Later that same year, *All-Story* published Burroughs's "Tarzan of the Apes."

In 1913 Burroughs began his Pellucidar series. After the *All-Story* editor repeatedly quibbled about rate of payment and rejected the sequel to the first Tarzan story, Burroughs began sending his work to other pulp magazines. *All-Story* fell on hard times and was combined first with *Cavalier* and then with *Argosy.* In its 1919 incarnation as *All-Story Weekly*, the magazine published Johnston McCulley's first Zorro story, "The Curse of Capistrano." Munsey's magazines were creating cultural icons, but they were also facing stiff market competition.

Once again, Street & Smith shifted to a format pioneered by other publishers and soon dominated the field. It began with *Popular Magazine* in 1903 and *Top Notch* in 1910. Street & Smith steadily expanded its offerings until it was one of the largest and most successful publishers of pulp magazines. Soon dozens of other publishers were trying to copy its success. At the end of World War I, only a few dozen pulps were being published; in the midst of the Great Depression, there would be several hundred.

By the 1920s general interest, or family, pulp gave way to specialized pulp. At the height of the pulps in the 1930s, there seemed to be a magazine for every interest: horror, sports, exploitative "spicy" topics, gangsters, romance, cowboys, and trains. There was even a magazine titled *Zeppelin Stories.* Because profit margins were small, publishers constantly shuffled their offerings and followed new trends. If a title started to lose readers, it was dropped immediately and a new genre was tried. The history of the pulps is littered with esoteric and short-lived magazines.

DETECTIVE PULPS

Street & Smith created the first successful specialized pulp magazine in 1915 when it converted its dime novel *Nick Carter Weekly* into the pulp magazine *Detective Story Magazine* (which was supposedly edited by "Nick Carter"). Police sleuths and private detectives had been a staple in other popular fiction formats, and the pulps initially offered nothing new in this genre.

In 1920, however, H. L. Mencken and George Jean Nathan (who published pulps only to subsidize their literary magazine, *The Smart Set*) began *The Black Mask*. The magazine published general adventure fiction at first, but within a few years, a distinctive style began to emerge. First there was Carroll John Daly's brutally tough Race Williams; next there was Dashiell Hammett's world-weary and often violent Continental Op. Employing terse dialogue, nuanced characters, and realistic settings, Hammett began to develop the new style of detective story that would become known as hard-boiled fiction.

When Joseph T. Shaw took over as editor in 1926, he sought more writers who could produce work in the Hammett tradition. Shaw made his greatest find in 1933, publishing "Blackmailers Don't Shoot," the first work of detective fiction by Raymond Chandler. Chandler's tough guys, who followed their own code and dealt their own justice in a harsh world, helped define hard-boiled fiction.

Black Mask was the most significant of the detective pulps, but it was certainly not the only entry in the field. The "Black Mask School" was perpetuated, and even refined, in the pages of *Detective Fiction Weekly*, *Dime Detective*, *Thrilling Detective*, *Ten Detective Aces*, and others. The detective pulps also launched many significant authors in addition to Hammett and Chandler. Erle Stanley Gardner was one of the most prolific and popular of the detective pulp writers.

As with most genres, the detective pulps had "spicy" versions, which mixed healthy doses of sex with the detection. Most notable among these was *Spicy Detective Stories*, featuring the erotic adventures of Hollywood private eye Dan Turner, written by Robert Leslie Bellem,. An altogether different tradition in detective fiction, the "weird menace," began in *Dime Mystery Magazine*. With covers that often combined the ghoulish and sadistic, *Dime Mystery* and its spawn offered stories of "impossible" crimes that seemed to be caused by the supernatural but were eventually revealed by the detective to have a rational solution and a human culprit. (Oddly enough, the *Scooby-Doo* cartoons seem to be a direct descendent of this subgenre.)

IN RIDES THE WESTERN

The Western, a staple of dime novels, came to pulp magazines when Street & Smith converted its *Buffalo Bill Weekly* dime novel series into *Western Story Magazine*. With a loyal audience already in place for tales of gunfights, wars with Native Americans, and hairbreadth escapes, the leading Western pulps, such as *Far West*, *Western Story*, and *Ranch Romances*, easily sold millions of copies per month.

Gradually, the pulp Westerns deviated from the blood-and-thunder style of the dime novels as more pulp writers began to emulate the more restrained and polished style of best-selling novelists in the genre, such as Owen Wister and Zane Grey (who had a number of his novels serialized in the pulps). Louis L'Amour was among the new breed of Western writers. In creating characters such as Hondo, L'Amour began to crystallize the Western hero. The most popular author in this genre was Frederick Faust, who wrote under numerous pseudonyms but became best known as Max Brand. Whereas some Western pulp writers strove for gritty realism, Brand elevated the cowboy to a figure of mythical proportions—this character could stand shoulder-to-shoulder in the popular culture pantheon with the fantastic heroes of the adventure or single-character pulps.

THE HEYDAY OF SCIENCE FICTION

More than any other popular genre, science fiction owes a great debt to the pulp magazines. Jules Verne, H. G. Wells, and others had planted the seeds in the previous century, but the true golden age of science fiction flowered in the pulp magazines of the 1920s and 1930s. The "scientific romances" of Edgar Rice Burroughs and his imitators had been appearing in pulp magazines for more than a decade, but it was not until an immigrant with a love of science got into publishing that the pulps provided an outlet for true science fiction.

Hugo Gernsback immigrated to the United States from Luxembourg in 1904 and immediately became involved with the new technology of radio. He began publishing a magazine, the *Electrical Experimenter*, that was devoted to his new interest. By 1919 Gernsback had expanded the scope of his magazine and changed the name to *Science and Inventions*. He had also begun including stories of what he called "scientifiction." In 1923 he produced an all-scientifiction issue with six stories, and reader response was enthusiastic.

In 1926 Gernsback debuted *Amazing Stories*, the first magazine devoted solely to science fiction. Although it was not until 1933—and after a change of publishers—that the magazine became standard pulp size, *Amazing Stories* is considered the genre's first pulp. By August 1928 Gernsback's magazine was publishing landmark science fiction novels, such as E. E. "Doc" Smith's first installment of the *Skylark* series and Philip Francis Nolan's "Armageddon, 2419 A.D.," the first Anthony "Buck" Rogers story.

Gernsback did more than anyone to establish science fiction as a distinct genre, earning the title of "father of science fiction." Yet much of what *Amazing Stories* published tended toward space opera, and Gernsback never quite realized the dream of teaching readers hard science through the stories in his magazine. It was John W. Campbell, editor of *Astounding Stories* (started in 1930), who truly championed hard science and ushered in the golden age of science fiction. Campbell demanded high-quality fiction based on believable extrapolations of hard science. He also discovered and nurtured many of the authors who would set the standards for science fiction writing, including Isaac Asimov, Arthur C. Clarke, Lester del Rey, and Robert Heinlein. There were plenty of other science fiction pulps on the stands over the years, but *Amazing Stories* and *Astounding Stories* were what defined the future of the genre.

FANTASY FICTION

Weird Tales, launched in 1923, was aptly subtitled *The Unique Magazine* and warrants consideration in a category all by itself. The magazine provided an outlet for some of the earliest and most outré work of Clark Ashton Smith, Robert Bloch, Ray Bradbury, Fritz Lieber, and other notable authors. Tennessee Williams's first published work, "The Vengeance of Nitocris," was in *Weird Tales*. However, the writers who did the most to sustain the magazine during its first decade were H. P. Lovecraft and Robert E. Howard. Lovecraft specialized in tales of slithering ancient horrors; his most enduring contributions are his creation of the Cthulhu Mythos, about the indescribably ancient and horrific beings that exist in the dark infinity outside humankind's perception, and the fictional grimoire of forbidden lore, the Necronomicon. In relentlessly vigorous prose, Howard chronicled the adventures of many a brawny and brutal hero, but his best-known creation is Conan of Cimmeria.

Although never a consistently profitable magazine, *Weird Tales* was published for 279 issues and was one of the last pulps to grace the newsstands when it finally ceased publication in 1954. Other pulps, such as *Strange Tales*, *Unknown*, and *Fantastic Adventures*, emerged to compete with *Weird Tales* in the fantasy market, but none managed to match the wonderful strangeness of the original.

THE "HERO PULP"

The greatest boon to the sales of pulp magazines was the advent of the single-character pulp, or the "hero pulp." Recurring heroes such as Tarzan and Zorro had been appearing in pulp magazines for years, but Street & Smith published *The Shadow, A Detective Magazine* in 1931, and the Shadow became the first character to appear in a magazine created specifically for his adventures. It did not take long for the Shadow's success to be noticed, and the next wave of characters seemed to hit all at once. *The Phantom Detective*, *Doc Savage*, *G-8 and His Battle Aces*, and *The Spider*—the four longest-running hero pulps next to *The Shadow*—all appeared in 1933.

These and other single-character pulps had a direct influence on the superhero comic books that appeared in the late 1930s and early 1940s. Some of the Superman mythos seems to come directly from Doc Savage: they are both named Clark, each hero has a female cousin nearly as remarkable as himself, and each has a secret arctic getaway referred to as a Fortress of Solitude. Although Doc Savage has no true powers, he is often referred to as a superman.

Perhaps no superhero has inherited more from his pulp ancestors than Batman. His costume and vigilante crusade are reminiscent of Zorro, and his modus operandi of prowling the night and striking fear in criminals is borrowed from the Shadow. Like Doc Savage, Batman is a normal human who has, through years of hard work, honed his mind and body to perfection.

GONE BUT NOT FORGOTTEN

A number of forces converged to bring an end to pulp magazines, including the immense popularity of progeny such as Superman and Batman. By the early 1940s these magazines faced stiff competition from comic books. The comic-book heroes were flashier, and a number of pulp publishers converted to this new medium when it proved profitable. Additionally, World War II brought about paper shortages, though a new format, the paperback book, managed to emerge. It offered pulp-type content, featuring authors such as Mickey Spillane, in a more convenient format and at the same price.

After the war, paperback publishing boomed and pulp magazines faded away. By the middle of the following decade, the pulps were all but gone, with only a few of the science fiction and mystery titles continuing in digest format. The tradition of the hero pulp lives on in comic books and paperback adventure series.

As products, the pulps proved ephemeral. Of the thousands of different magazines and characters that existed, most have been forgotten by everyone except a handful of collectors and historians. More copies of the cheaply made magazines crumble to dust each day, yet they have shaped every genre of popular fiction—their influence can be seen in every hero of film, television, and paperback. Pulp magazines wound up being the wellspring of the American mythology.

Randy Duncan

SEE ALSO: Argosy*;* Astounding Science Fiction*; Batman;* Black Mask*; Brand, Max; Buck Rogers; Burroughs, Edgar Rice; Chandler, Raymond; Detective Fiction; Dime Novels; Doc Savage; Gernsback, Hugo; Lovecraft, H. P.; Mencken, H. L.; Paperbacks; Science Fiction Publishing; The Shadow; Street and Smith; Superman; Tarzan;* Weird Tales*; The Western; Zorro.*

BIBLIOGRAPHY

Del Rey, Lester. *The World of Science Fiction, 1926—1976: The History of a Subculture.* New York: Ballantine Books, 1979.

Goodstone, Tony. *The Pulps: Fifty Years of American Popular Culture.* New York: Chelsea House, 1970.

Goulart, Ron. *An Informal History of the Pulp Magazine.* New York: Ace Books, 1973.

Goulart, Ron. *The Dime Detectives.* New York: Mysterious Press, 1988.

Sampson, Robert. *Deadly Excitements: Shadows and Phantoms.* Bowling Green, OH: Bowling Green State University Popular Press, 1989.

Server, Lee. *Encyclopedia of Pulp Fiction Writers.* New York: Facts On File, 2002.

The Punisher

The Punisher is a superhero character appearing in Marvel comic books. Created in 1974 by Gerry Conway, the Punisher is a costumed vigilante—something of a comic-book answer to *Death Wish.* He is Frank Castle, a Vietnam veteran who embarks on a solemn war against crime after his family is murdered by gangsters. Clad in a black costume emblazoned with a skull and crossbones, he punishes the guilty whom the law is either unable or unwilling to convict.

After a decade as a recurring character in various Marvel titles, the Punisher won his own series in 1986. The vigilante superhero found a large and receptive audience at the height of the Reagan-Rambo era and became one of the most popular comic books of the late 1980s and early 1990s. The series has gone through several relaunches, including one in 2011 that attempted to freshen the concept by revealing how other characters viewed the antihero. The Punisher has also appeared in two feature-length films: *The Punisher* (2004) and *Punisher: War Zone* (2008).

Bradford Wright

SEE ALSO: *Comic Books; Marvel Comics; Rambo; Reagan, Ronald; Vietnam.*

BIBLIOGRAPHY

Daniels, Les. *Marvel: Five Fabulous Decades of the World's Greatest Comics.* New York: Harry N. Abrams, 1991.

Rhodes, Shirrel. *Comic Books.* New York: Peter Lang, 2008.

Punk

In the early 1970s a radical youth culture called "punk" emerged out of the larger rock-and-roll scene and quickly developed its own music, attire, and ideology. For many listeners, the Sex Pistols remain the most famous of the early punk bands; their music, like all punk rock, was aggressive, fast, and loud. Punk attire is characterized by dark clothes and outlandish costumes and ornamentation, such as colored hair and earrings and bracelets made from assembled items (the quintessential punk earring was a safety pin). Punk ideology is explicitly at odds with mainstream society and rails against contemporary civilization, which is seen as sterile and banal. Punk is heavily critical of existing political, economic, and cultural institutions yet is ambivalent about creating alternatives.

The punk movement enjoyed its peak during the late 1970s and early 1980s, with major musical and cultural scenes emerging in London, New York, Los Angeles, and Washington, D.C., as well as in smaller cities throughout the United States and England. Although punk lost popularity during the mid-1980s, it survived in various forms in the ensuing years, and by the late 1990s a new generation of punk followers had emerged, along with new favorite bands, fashions, and political and cultural beliefs.

AN ALTERNATIVE TO MAINSTREAM ROCK

The earliest forms of punk rock developed in the 1960s. In the United States, bands such as the Count Five, the Seeds, and the Sonics began playing a raw new form of rock and roll, one rooted in crude guitar riffs and suggestive lyrics. At the same time, British bands such as the Kinks and the Troggs developed a similar style, deliberately distorting the sounds of their instruments to create a more immediate and emotionally powerful sound. By decade's end, bands such as the MC5 and the Stooges had begun to incorporate the raw energy of this new sound into their stage performances, shocking audiences with their loud, volatile playing style, as well as their occasionally lascivious behavior.

At around the same time, New York band the Velvet Underground began to play a similarly harsh, experimental type of rock and roll, with lyrics that offered commentaries about life outside mainstream society. By the early 1970s the New York Dolls had amassed a cult of loyal followers, blending a discordant and aggressive musical style with a transgressive and sexually charged stage presence, with the members typically performing in drag. Historically, the bands from this era are sometimes categorized by the label "protopunk."

The Sex Pistols. *Johnny Rotten leads an updated version of the Sex Pistols, the first punk band to come out of Britain in the 1970s, at a performance in 1996.* PATTI OUDERKIRK/CONTRIBUTOR/WIREIMAGE/GETTY IMAGES.

The first group to be widely regarded as a true punk rock band was the Ramones. Formed in 1974, the Ramones gained a following around New York City by stripping rock down to its bare essentials and playing with near-anarchic energy. Their first album, *Ramones* (1976), featured a string of songs, most shorter than two minutes, including "Blitzkrieg Bop" and "Now I Wanna Sniff Some Glue." The album became a minor hit in the United States and a major hit in England, where the energetic rock played by the Ramones, the Voidoids, and the Dead Boys inspired a new generation of musicians that had become disenchanted with mainstream rock and roll. During these years, the hub of New York punk revolved primarily around an East Village club, CBGB, where such bands as the Talking Heads, Blondie, and Television all launched their careers.

Although punk was a relatively minor sensation in the United States, it quickly gained widespread popularity in the United Kingdom. The first British punk band was the Sex Pistols, which in the three short years of its existence largely created the ideal of the punk rock band. Led by singer Johnny Rotten (formerly John Lydon) and bassist Sid Vicious and managed by Malcolm McLaren, the Sex Pistols took the music scene by storm when they began playing in 1975, singing about anarchy, abortion, and fascism in some of the most violent live shows and recordings ever heard. The band alienated several recording labels and frightened the establishment, but they also encouraged the rapid growth of the punk scene in England and sparked the creation of such bands as the Clash, the Damned, the Buzzcocks, and others.

Punk made a very visible, shocking, and memorable impact on the public. With the drug-related death of Sid Vicious in 1979 and the demise of several punk bands, some proclaimed that punk was a short-lived fad that had come to an end. In fact, rumors of punk's death were unfounded, and many bands set about to defend the true meaning of punk and to extend its musical influence. The most direct development from early punk is the hardcore punk movement that developed during the 1980s, foremost in the United States, but also in England, France, Italy, and other countries. The style was best represented by such bands as the Dead Kennedys, Social Distortion, the Misfits, and Upright Citizens. As the 1980s progressed, other bands began to echo the influence of punk, including Hüsker Dü, the Replacements, Sonic Youth, and the Minutemen, among others. Though punk purists considered the movement's peak years to be between 1975 and 1980, the punk ethos clearly lived on.

DEFINED BY ITS ALTERNATIVE STYLE

Musically, rock and roll provided an important foundation for punk, as youths who came of age in the 1970s and 1980s were well acquainted with rock bands such as the Beatles, the Rolling Stones, and Led Zeppelin. Many punk bands learned music by playing other people's songs, and it was commonplace among young punks, and even well-known bands, to release cover songs. The Dickies, for example, played fast but melodic versions of Led Zeppelin's "Communication Breakdown" and the Moody Blues' "Nights in White Satin." Bands often performed cover versions of older songs that had historical significance or that made a particularly salient political point. Generation X, for example, performed a cover version of John Lennon's "Gimme Some Truth." While cover songs often signaled respect for past music, they could also represent an ironic comment on or critique of rock and roll. Although cover songs were common, punk ideology derided cover bands that did not play original songs for a lack of creativity.

Despite the powerful influence of rock, punk music differs significantly from its predecessor. Punk songs are generally short, fast, and loud and place increased emphasis on distorted guitars. Many punk bands use "power" or bar chords, and speed is often emphasized over intricacy. The musical skills of punk musicians are often rudimentary, and this lack of virtuosity is connected to an ideology that anyone can write and play songs. Fairly simple songs with basic four-four drum beats are common, and many punk bands form with friends picking up instruments and learning as they play. Punk's minimalist three-chord approach and shouted vocals stand in clear opposition to the melodic singing of earlier styles.

Punk music developed "scenes" centered on bands, clubs, and fans in a particular area, such as Manchester and London, England. The Damned, Stiff Little Fingers, the Jam, and Sham 69 were particularly influential, as were the Gang of Four, the Mekons, and the Delta 5 from Leeds, England. In the United States, the Los Angeles scene produced such bands as Black Flag, Fear, the Germs, X, and the Circle Jerks. Two documentaries—*The Decline of Western Civilization* (1981) and *Another State of Mind* (1984)—document the lives of various L.A. punk bands both onstage and off. The Dead Kennedys (San Francisco); the Teen Idols, State of Alert (S.O.A.), and the Bad Brains (all Washington, D.C.); and Hüsker Dü (Minneapolis) were all especially important early punk bands.

Punk was always about more than music, however. For both fans and musicians punk amounted to a kind of lifestyle. From the beginning, punk haircuts and clothing stood in stark contrast to the appearance of rock and rollers. As Dick Hebdige describes in *Subculture: The Meaning of Style*, punks rebelled by wearing ripped clothing, black leather, and assembling cultural icons as decoration. Mohawk haircuts, dyed hair, or extremely short cropped haircuts distinguished punks from the typically long-haired rockers. Hardcore attire followed directly from punk, although it tended to be more subdued. Dark clothes, black leather jackets, ripped jeans, sneakers, or boots (especially Doc Martens) were common; the outlandish costumes of punk—bright clothes and colored hair—were often toned down.

Many hardcore fans simply wore jeans, a T-shirt (often with a band insignia), and sneakers. In some sense this was a rebellion against the mainstream co-optation of punk dress, but it was also an attempt to get beyond an antifashion style that was not only a lot of work but made punks subject to verbal, and occasionally physical, harassment. Less dramatic attire allowed hardcore punks to move more easily between mainstream and alternative cultures. Thus, hardcore, while characterized by a louder and more aggressive music, began a tendency back to more mainstream attire.

ROOTED IN RADICAL POLITICAL VIEWS

From its beginnings, punk offered a radical critique of society and was noted for its unique ideological characteristics; however, it never presented a coherent philosophy but rather a series of related critiques. Punks were particularly hostile to authority and questioned rules and rule makers. Rather than focusing simply on politics in the conventional sense, punk challenged the patterns and norms of contemporary social relations. As Hebdige writes, punk "signified chaos at every level."

The politics of everyday life were most central to punk, and lyrics question social rules and relationships. Many lyrics were centered on love, relationships, jobs, and so on, but punks put a radical spin on such issues. They aimed to shock and offend and were particularly anti-romantic in their sentiments. Love was frequently referred to only in sexual terms and often quite graphically, as in the Dead Boys' "Caught with the Meat in Your Mouth." Some punks used Nazi images and ornaments in their outfits and made callous reference to such tragedies as the Holocaust in such songs as "Belsen Was a Gas." Such practices generally reflected an attempt to use images in an ironic sense to question conventional meanings. Furthermore, punks were by and large anti-Nazi and antifascist and have frequently espoused left-wing and humanitarian concerns.

Political issues were important for many in the hardcore punk scene as well. War, social inequality, and capitalism were common topics of punk lyrics. *MaximumRocknRoll*, one of the foremost hardcore fanzines, covered these and other topics in its columns, letters, and interviews. Leftist, anarchist, and communist leanings were prevalent as punks expressed concerns about politics, the military, censorship, corporate crime, and other issues. The band Millions of Dead Cops (MDC) attacked government and police authority. MDC also railed against corporate capitalism, calling a McDonald's hamburger a "corporate deathburger." Although a wide range of political views emerged from the hardcore movement, most of these political statements were rudimentary, as few had worked out the complexities of the many issues they discussed. Typical of a punk political critique was a catch phrase such as "Reagan sucks."

In spite of its political underpinnings, punk tended to be very cynical regarding direct activism and emphasized chaos rather than concerted action. While for some punks this meant an attempt to avoid politics or just to have fun, for others this critique represented an emphasis on social or personal politics rather than large-scale political concerns. Many emphasized personal politics and promoted difference as a value; in the early 1980s, the Big Boys sang: "I want to be different / I want to make you see / I want to make you wonder / Is it you or is it me?" Adherence to the local scene for its own sake was important, as punks tried to establish a core set of values that set punk off from mainstream society. Bands such as Reagan Youth, Minor Threat, Youth of Today, and Youth Brigade promoted youth power as an ideology opposed to conventional adult married and working life.

Anger was also a common characteristic of punk lyrics. Henry Rollins of Black Flag yelled: "Everybody just get away / I'm gonna boil over inside today / They say things are gonna get better / All I know is they fuckin' better." Void growled: "I'm so fucking filled with hate / I just need to decapitate." Boredom is also a common complaint, as Tony of the Adolescents sang: "We're just a wrecking crew / Bored boys with nothing to do." Punks launched critiques against hippies and consumerist yuppies alike: the Teen Idles sang "Deadhead deadhead / Take another toke deadhead / You're a lousy joke." "Die yuppie scum" was also a common punk mantra.

STRUGGLES WITH ITS OWN EXCESSES

Whereas many punks were critical of "hippie burnouts," drug use was a pervasive element of punk culture and a symbol of punk excess. Indeed, punk lore has tended to glorify some of the more outrageous drug-influenced behavior of punk rock icons. Scott Asheton, in *Please Kill Me*, recounts a story about Iggy Pop: "He was walking down the street and he finally just collapsed. It was from massive amounts of drugs—I mean, you can't take acid and Quaaludes at the same time, it just doesn't work." Similarly, in *Please Kill Me*, one person describes the night of the death of Sid Vicious's girlfriend Nancy Spungen:

> Nancy was stoned. She was stoned and she was bragging. She's talking in that fucking cockney accent, you know, being Mrs. Sid Vicious. But it wasn't much of a party because Sid was passed out. Sid did not look like he was going to get up. He wasn't moving.
>
> I said, "What's wrong with Sid?" Someone said, "Oh, he just ate about thirty Tuinals." I said, "Oh, he's going to be fun tonight."

The deaths of Vicious and Spungen (the subject of the movie *Sid and Nancy*, 1986) were particularly vivid reminders of the presence of drug use and violence in the punk scene. Many other drug-related deaths occurred among punks, particularly in connection with heroin use.

In response to frequent cases of addiction and overdose and in the face of legal restrictions, some punks rejected the use of drugs. The Washington, D.C., straight-edge scene—opposed to drinking, drugs, and casual sex—developed alongside the refusal of club owners to let underage kids into shows. As a compromise, underage kids were allowed in but were marked with X's on their hands to signify that they couldn't buy alcohol. The kids took this would-be stigma and turned it into a symbol of positive self-identification.

Punk identity was strengthened by the social networks that developed to organize concerts, start 'zines, and spread ideas. Bands and fans established ties across the country (as well as through much of the world) through which they could share common interests, book shows, or find a needed place to sleep. Many punk musicians, ignored by major record labels, produced their own music on independent labels such as Dischord, SST, Touch and Go, and SubPop. Punk was particularly critical of the rock-and-roll establishment. Whereas rock began as a nonconformist youth culture, punks voiced opposition to the cult of rock stardom and the large stadium concerts that clearly separated the audience from musicians. Punk, by contrast, was premised on the idea that anyone could start a band. Punks were also critical of major record labels and large-scale industry in general and espoused a "do-it-yourself" philosophy that emphasized independent action and personal creativity.

INTO THE NEW CENTURY

Centered primarily around music, the punk movement was an important development in the youth culture of the late 1970s and remained an identifiable element in youth culture into the twenty-first century. Punk appealed to young people because of its aggressive and fast musical style; its purposefully shocking visual impact; and its ideological emphasis on chaos, nonconformity, and radical criticism. Punk rock's role as an ideological, musical, and stylistic critique of modern society continued to resonate with new generations of fans, a number of who emulated the movement's do-it-yourself mentality by starting their own bands. Meanwhile, punk expanded its global influence, emerging as a form of protest against political oppression in such diverse countries as Russia, Indonesia, and Burma.

By the mid-1990s punk rock had begun to show signs of entering the mainstream, as bands such as Green Day, Blink-182, and the Offspring began to blend the speed and intensity of old-school punk with the polish and radio-friendly sensibility of popular music. Appropriately, this new iteration of the punk genre came to be known as "pop punk"—although detractors had other names for it, including "faux punk." A turning point in the movement's growing popularity came in 2004, with the release of Green Day's *American Idiot.* A harsh critique of the of the George W. Bush presidency, the album rose to number one on the Billboard 200, while introducing the punk sound to a broad range of new listeners. As evidence of its widespread appeal, the album was adapted into a Broadway show in 2010.

Even as Green Day achieved crossover popularity, lesser-known punk rock bands continued to proliferate both in the United States and abroad, playing venues in small cities and towns, producing their own publicity materials, and frequently recording their own music. Indeed, with the rapid improvement of digital technology, twenty-first-century bands had greater power to embody the do-it-yourself ethos than their predecessors, as it became easier and cheaper to record, produce, and distribute music than ever before. In a world where discovering unconventional sounds and fashions was as easy as connecting to the Internet, the punk movement clearly remained a vital alternative to mainstream culture.

Perry Grossman

SEE ALSO: *Blink-182; Blondie; Doc Martens; Green Day; Hippies; Led Zeppelin; Pop, Iggy; The Ramones; Rock and Roll; The Rolling Stones; The Sex Pistols; The Velvet Underground; Yuppies.*

BIBLIOGRAPHY

Frith, Simon. *Sound Effects: Youth, Leisure and the Politics of Rock 'n' Roll.* New York: Pantheon Books. 1981.

Gardner, Elysa. "'American Idiot' Elevates Hope above Nihilism." *USA Today*, April 21 , 2010.

Harris, John. "Punk Rock . . . Alive and Kicking in a Repressive State Near You." *Guardian* (London), March 17, 2012.

Hebdige, Dick. *Subculture: The Meaning of Style.* London: Routledge, 1991.

Herman, Andrew. "You're in Suspicion: Punk and the Secret Passion Play of White Noise." *Canadian Journal of Political and Social Theory* 14 (1990): 47–67.

Heylin, Clinton. *From the Velvets to the Voidoids: A Pre-Punk History for a Post-Punk World.* New York: Penguin, 1993.

Laing, Dave. *OneChord Wonders: Power and Meaning in Punk Rock.* Philadelphia: Open University Press, 1985.

Marcus, Greil. *Lipstick Traces: A Secret History of the Twentieth Century.* Cambridge, MA: Harvard University Press, 1989.

McNeil, Legs, and Gillian McCain. *Please Kill Me: The Uncensored Oral History of Punk.* New York: Grove Press, 1996.

Savage, John. *England's Dreaming: Anarchy, Sex Pistols, Punk Rock, and Beyond.* New York: St. Martin's Press, 1992.

Punk'd

Punk'd is a reality TV series created by Jason Goldberg and Ashton Kutcher that premiered on MTV in 2002. Hosted by Kutcher, the hidden-camera show pulls pranks on various celebrities, allowing tension to escalate until Kutcher or another celebrity host intervenes with the catchphrase, "You just got punk'd!" Since the show's debut, the term *punk'd* has been defined by UrbanDictionary.com as "being fooled, tricked, or made the butt of a practical joke." Although the show was similar to earlier TV sensations such as *Candid Camera* (1960–1967), *Super Bloopers & Practical Jokes* (1984), and *Foul-Ups, Bleeps & Blunders* (1984–1985), it differed in that all pranks involved celebrities who were unaware they were being set up for ridicule.

While he was host, Kutcher regularly insisted that the show would end after its second season, but this was a lie stemming from his desire to continually fool celebrities into believing his ruses. The list of celebrities pranked reads like a list of who's who in sports, film, and music: Jessica Alba, "Stone Cold" Steve Austin, Simon Cowell, Seth Green, Katie Holmes, Shaquille O'Neal, Britney Spears, Usher, and Shaun White, to name a few. After eight seasons, the series ended in 2007 with "The First Annual Punk'd Awards" episode, in which past celebrity clips were highlighted and given awards for categories such as "Best Destruction of Private Property" and "Man Tear Award."

The most sensational celebrity victim by far was Justin Timberlake, whose segment on the series premiere made number three on *Time* magazine's "32 Epic Moments of Reality-TV History" list. When fake IRS agents showed up at his door threatening to repossess his house, cars, dogs, and all of his belongings for owing $900,000 in back taxes, Timberlake called his mom and broke down crying before being told he had been punk'd. Timberlake returned to help prank Kelly Osbourne several episodes later and eventually got his revenge on Kutcher by parodying him on a 2003 episode of *Saturday Night Live.* Another notable moment of the series was when *Scrubs* star Zach Braff got into a fistfight with a young vandal for spray-painting his brand-new car before he was told it was a prank. The footage of the fight was cut, but the incident vividly showed just how wrong things could go even in a controlled setting.

Punk'd has sparked multiple international versions in countries including Iceland, Japan, Norway, and the Philippines. It has also sparked numerous YouTube parodies as well as more famous versions such as Lance Krall's *Trick'd*, Jimmy Fallon's *Sheen'd*, and Mad TV's "Kenny Rogers Punk'd," with the country music star swilling Jack Daniels and botching his attempts to prank fake celebrities. *Punk'd* returned to MTV in March 2012 after a five-year hiatus, with Kutcher as producer and new celebrity hosts, including Justin Bieber and Miley Cyrus, and veteran host Dax Shepard.

Ron Horton

SEE ALSO: *Bieber, Justin; Cable TV;* Candid Camera*; Celebrity; Cyrus, Miley / Hannah Montana; Kutcher, Ashton; Movie Stars; MTV; O'Neal, Shaquille; Reality Television; Rogers, Kenny;* Saturday Night Live*; Spears, Britney; Television; White, Shaun; YouTube.*

BIBLIOGRAPHY

Adalian, Josef. "MTV Bringing Back *Punk'd*, with Host Justin Bieber." *Vulture*, October 5, 2010.

Dumenco, Simon. "Punk'd Rocker." *New York Magazine*, November 3, 2003.

"Punk'd." MTV.com. Accessed May 2012. Available from http://

www.mtv.com/shows/punkd/series.jhtml?xrs=googlekw_punkdma

Strecker, Erin. "Ashton Kutcher Headed Back to 'Punk'd.'" *EW*, May 17, 2012.

Webley, Kayla. "32 Epic Moments in Reality-TV History: *Punk'd*: Justin Timberlake Cries." Time Entertainment. Accessed May 2012. Available from http://entertainment.time.com/2011/04/08/32-epic-moments-in-reality-tv-history/#punkd-justin-timberlake-cries

Pynchon, Thomas *(1937–)*

Though a complicated author who has written only seven novels in forty-six years, Thomas Pynchon has remained a figure who has captured the imagination of a wider public and has avoided the academic and literary communities who revere him. His use of popular culture in his fiction, along with other such "unliterary" subjects as science, has had a highly influential effect on modern fiction. Pynchon, however, is also known to many who have never read his work as an author who has maintained an unheard of level of anonymity in a literary culture that thrives on self-promotion.

ACADEMIC RECEPTION

Thomas Pynchon was born on May 8, 1937, in Glen Cove, Long Island, New York, into a prosperous family with an American heritage dating back to the early seventeenth century. He studied at Cornell University, served a two-year stint in the navy, and worked in Seattle for Boeing Aircraft Corporation. From the late 1950s to the early 1960s, he published a number of short stories and began work on his first novel, *V.*, published in 1963. *The Crying of Lot 49* was published in 1966, and *Gravity's Rainbow* (1973) was selected by the judges for the Pulitzer Prize for Fiction. The judges were overruled, however, by the Pulitzer advisory board, whose members called the sprawling and bawdy book, with a cast of more than 400 characters, "unreadable," "turgid," "overwritten," and "obscene." In 1990 the much-awaited *Vineland* came out to mixed reviews. The reception of Pynchon's 1997 novel *Mason & Dixon* was far more positive. In the first decade of the 2000s he published two additional novels, *Against the Day* (2006) and *Inherent Vice* (2009), though they received less attention than his previous books.

Pynchon's work has received wide acclaim not only among the literary media and the academic fraternity but also among readers outside these fields who are drawn to his use of science and philosophy and his use of science fiction and other popular genres. Over his career, his very dense, extensively researched prose has taken him across many periods and many places, studying the motivation and circumstances behind the excesses of empire and the forces of institution and rationalization at the center of Western society. Pynchon uses the "languages" of popular fiction, comics, cinema, and television. *V.* is obviously influenced by the British tradition of spy and adventure fiction; *The Crying of Lot 49* by the detective novel; *Gravity's Rainbow* by spy and war fiction—not to mention a plethora of cinema genres and the comic—and *Vineland* is laced with metaphors surrounding rerun television—from *The Brady Bunch* to *CHiPs*—and the blockbuster movies of the age, such as the *Star Wars* trilogy. Even *Mason & Dixon* is partly a product of the genre of historical romance. Pynchon uses codes, knowledge, and language to both show their worth and show that anything with a structure can be integrated into rationalized and institutionalized control in order to manipulate and exploit. Ironically, nowhere is this more clear than in the academic reception to his work, where interpreting his wide frames of reference has become an industry in itself.

TRACKING THE MYSTERY

Although Pynchon may be relatively unread compared to some of the popular writers he adapts in his own writing, he has a broader presence in the popular imagination. Since successfully evading a *Time* photographer attempting to take his picture in Mexico in 1963, Pynchon has become famous for maintaining his privacy. In the years following the success of *Gravity's Rainbow*, he avoided television interviews, lecture tours, and literary prize ceremonies (even when he won prizes); any knowledge of his whereabouts became increasingly valuable and scarce.

It was considered something of a scoop in 1974 when *New York* magazine was able to show a 20-year-old photo. *Playboy* magazine printed an article in 1977 by a friend of Pynchon's from Cornell, and over the years various magazines and newspapers have run articles by individuals who claim to have run into him: from reporters attempting to track him down to pundits peddling theories he is anyone from J. D. Salinger to the Unabomber. In the 1980s a series of letters written by a supposed bag lady named Wanda Tinasky appeared in a Northern California newspaper, and Pynchon scholars began to suspect they were the work of the reclusive author. The letters were collected and published in 1996 under the title *The Letters of Wanda Tinasky*. Whether Pynchon is indeed Tinasky remains a matter of great debate, although Pynchon has vigorously denied it.

Considering the number of websites that Pynchon-mania has engendered—sharing information on everything the media says of Pynchon as well as attempting to detail and decipher his work—the writer appears more a phenomenon than a mere novelist. Clearly, his mixture of intellectual extravagance and biographical frugality has created a fascinated audience larger than his prose alone could muster. In 1996 *New York* magazine finally tracked Pynchon down to a neighborhood in Manhattan. Surprisingly, in 2004, Pynchon performed two cameos in the animated series *The Simpsons*, mocking his own elusive self-image. Though he frequently publishes reviews and essays, he rarely produces public statements. When writer Ian McEwan was accused of plagiarism in 2006, however, Pynchon wrote a letter in support of the writer, which was printed in the *Daily Telegraph*.

The ability to blend subject matters from so-called "high art" and "low culture," science and literature, and contemporary politics and history may in the 2010s almost appear a necessity in the budding "great novelist." Pynchon, however, has been doing this since 1963 while maintaining a political agenda that denounces empire and slavery in all its racial, economic, and political manifestations. His fierce protection of his privacy is probably both a personal matter and a reflection of his distrust of authority, patently obvious in all his work. Whatever the reasons, Pynchon's wariness of creating a public persona has inadvertently created one for him: a much more intriguing one than most media-friendly writers have achieved.

Kyle Smith

SEE ALSO: *Best Sellers;* The Brady Bunch*; Celebrity; Comics; Detective Fiction; The* New York Times*;* Playboy*; Romance Novels;* Star Wars*; Television;* Time.

BIBLIOGRAPHY

Bloom, Harold, and Dave Kress, eds. *Thomas Pynchon*. New York: Chelsea House Publishers, 2003.

Factor, T. R., ed. *The Letters of Wanda Tinasky*. Portland, OR: vers libre press, 1996.

Maltby, Paul. *Dissident Postmodernists: Barthelme, Coover, Pynchon*. Philadelphia: University of Pennsylvania Press, 1991.

Weisenburger, Steven. *A "Gravity's Rainbow" Companion*. Athens: University of Georgia Press, 1988.

Quayle, Dan *(1947–)*

Forty-fourth U.S. vice president James Danforth Quayle was a figure of mild controversy from the time he was announced as running mate through his term (1989–1993) with President George H. W. Bush. On the summer day in 1988 when Republican presidential nominee Bush declared his choice for a running mate, it was difficult to assess who was more surprised—the journalists covering the convention, Bush's advisers, or the junior senator from Indiana himself.

Quayle was born on February 4, 1947, in Indianapolis, Indiana. After graduating from DePauw University in Greencastle, Indiana, in 1969, he attended Indiana University Law School. He was elected to the House of Representatives in 1976 with a campaign emphasizing conservative issues and was reelected in 1978. In 1980 he was elected to the Senate and was reelected six years later. During his tenure he was identified as a spokesman for the New Right of the conservative movement. He had married Marilyn Tucker in 1972 and was the father of three children.

VICE PRESIDENTIAL RACE

Bush selected Quayle as a running mate for several reasons. First, it was thought that Quayle, who bore a slight resemblance to actor Robert Redford, might help Bush with the gender gap that the polls were warning him about, as Bush was far more popular among men than women. Second, Quayle was politically to the right of the moderate Bush, and his selection might help to reassure conservative Republicans, who had never found Bush a kindred spirit. Third, Quayle provided the geographic balance that the ticket needed: Bush had roots in both the Northeast and Southwest and believed that some connection to the Midwest would be helpful in the election. Finally, Quayle was part of the baby boomer generation, and Bush adviser Lee Atwater was convinced that this group would prove crucial to the campaign.

Upon being introduced as Bush's choice for a running mate, Quayle was immediately the subject of a media feeding frenzy. As with most modern conventions, the Republican National Convention of 1988 was dull; Bush's nomination had been a foregone conclusion for months, leaving the assembled journalists with little of consequence to cover—until Bush gave them Quayle. The Indiana senator was not well known outside his home state, but the reporters quickly made up for lost time. Quayle's life and record were under the national media microscope within hours, and it did not take long for the blemishes to appear.

CRITICISM DURING THE CAMPAIGN

One criticism, for example, centered on Quayle's academic record. Professors at DePauw remembered Quayle as an indifferent student, more interested in golf and fraternity life than his political science courses. A story about a golfing trip that Quayle had taken to Florida a few years earlier also drew critics' attention. Apparently, he had stayed at a rented house with two other men and Paula Parkinson, a beautiful Washington lobbyist of reputedly easy virtue. But most damaging was the account of Quayle's military service. A strong supporter of U.S. involvement in Vietnam, Quayle had nonetheless joined the Indiana National Guard instead of a unit more likely to see combat. Further, some said that Quayle's influential family had pulled strings to get him into the guard ahead of other applicants.

Unused to the national spotlight, Quayle became flustered easily and tended to be sloppy about details, sometimes contradicting himself from one interview to the next. Bush's staff helped Quayle work out acceptable answers to the questions about his grades, marital fidelity, and patriotism, but considerable damage had already been done to the young senator's credibility. Many people, both in the news media and among the public, had developed the impression that Quayle was an intellectual lightweight who had benefited greatly from his family's money and connections. Privately, there were some in the Bush camp who shared that assessment, but Bush's choice had been made, so damage control became the order of the day.

It was decided that Quayle would spend most of the campaign in small towns, away from the major media markets and among audiences who shared his conservative values. This strategy worked well, but it could not protect Quayle from the national exposure of a debate between him and the Democrats' vice presidential candidate, Senator Lloyd Bentsen of Texas. Quayle worked hard in preparation for the debate, and he committed no major gaffes, but he appeared nervous and did, at one point, give Bentsen an opening for a devastating retort. In response to a question about his limited experience in the U.S. Senate, Quayle compared his term of service with that of John F. Kennedy. Bentsen, in response, shook his head, saying, "I served with Jack Kennedy. I knew Jack Kennedy. Jack Kennedy was a friend of mine." Then, with a scornful look at Quayle, he concluded, "Senator, you're no Jack Kennedy."

Despite all the controversy, Bush and Quayle were elected. But election results notwithstanding, Quayle had become a national joke. He was a favorite topic in the nightly monologues delivered by Johnny Carson, David Letterman, and others. One joke, for example, went: "Have you heard about the new Dan Quayle savings bond? It has no interest and no maturity." Unfortunately for Quayle, he was often his own worst enemy.

While it must be admitted that one of his mistakes received more media attention than a slip by other public figures, Quayle managed to misspeak on a regular basis. It was even possible to buy videotapes containing footage of the vice president's flubs.

THE 1992 CAMPAIGN

During the 1992 campaign, Quayle staked out a position on the family values issue by publicly criticizing the TV series *Murphy Brown*, in which the lead character, played by Candice Bergen, has a baby out of wedlock. "Fathers are important," Quayle declared, "and shows like *Murphy Brown* are sending the wrong message." But Quayle's ethos was such that few were inclined to take him seriously. A few nights later Letterman described the controversy on his show, then sneered to the camera, "Vice President Quayle, sir, Murphy Brown is a fictional character!" When the new season of *Murphy Brown* began a few months later, the entire first episode was devoted to making fun of Quayle.

As the 1992 political race became tighter, Bush considered asking Quayle to step down but decided against it for fear of appearing unappreciative of Quayle's loyalty. The Bush-Quayle ticket lost to Bill Clinton and Al Gore, and Quayle disappeared from the limelight. He continued to act as a spokesman for conservative issues and published a best-selling memoir, *Standing Firm*, in 1994. That book was followed by two others—*The American Family: Discovering the Values That Make Us Strong* (1996) and *Worth Fighting For* (1999)—which were less successful. Beginning in the late 1990s Quayle served on a number of executive boards of multinational corporations, private equity firms, and banks. He initially declared his intent to seek the Republican Party presidential nomination in 2000 but soon withdrew and gave his support to George W. Bush. In late 2011 he endorsed Republican politician Mitt Romney for the 2012 presidential race.

Justin Gustainis

SEE ALSO: *Bergen, Candice;* Bush v. Gore *(2000); Carson, Johnny; Letterman, David; Media Feeding Frenzies;* Murphy Brown*; Redford, Robert; Vietnam.*

BIBLIOGRAPHY

Goldman, Peter, Tom Mathews, and the *Newsweek* Special Election Team. *The Quest for the Presidency 1988.* New York: Simon & Schuster, 1989.

Quayle, Dan. *Standing Firm: A Vice-Presidential Memoir.* New York: HarperCollins, 1994.

Quayle, Dan. *Worth Fighting For.* Nashville, TN: Word Publishing, 1999.

Quayle, Dan, and Diane Medved. *The American Family: Discovering the Values That Make Us Strong.* New York: HarperCollins, 1996.

Queenan, Joe. *Imperial Caddy: The Rise of Dan Quayle in America and the Decline and Fall of Practically Everything Else.* New York: Hyperion, 1992.

Queen, Ellery

Ellery Queen was the pseudonym of writers Manfred B. Lee (1905–1971) and his cousin Frederic Dannay (1905–1982) and

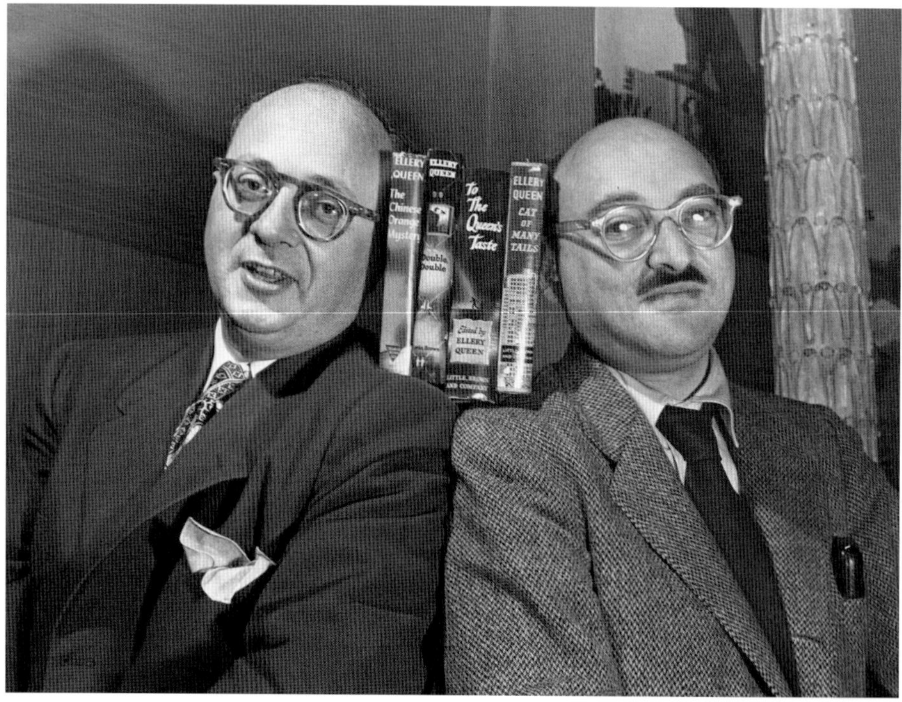

Ellery Queen Authors Manfred Lee and Frederic Dannay. *Cousins Manfred B. Lee, left, and Frederic Dannay were the authors behind the Ellery Queen mystery novel series.* © **BETTMANN/CORBIS.**

the name of the main character of their popular mystery novel series. Ellery Queen was also probably the most popular American mystery novelist of the golden era of detective fiction, from the 1920s to the 1940s. The cousins (particularly Dannay) also did much to preserve and promote the mystery short-story form. They produced the long-running *Ellery Queen's Mystery Magazine*, edited short-story anthologies that promoted short fiction as a viable mystery vehicle, and avidly collected short-form mystery fiction. As fellow mystery writer Anthony Boucher (1911–1968) is often quoted as saying, "Ellery Queen is the American Detective Story."

The cousins grew up together in New York and tried their hands at various careers in adulthood. In the late 1920s, Lee and Dannay (real names Manford Lepofsky and Daniel Nathan) decided to try writing a mystery novel in response to a contest cosponsored by *McClure's* magazine and publisher Frederick A. Stokes. They chose the name Ellery Queen for their author, and, reasoning that mystery readers are better at remembering names of characters than names of authors, they decided to give their detective the same name. They submitted their story and were told they had won the contest, but then the magazine went bankrupt and changed hands, after which the prize was awarded to someone else. Stokes still wanted to publish the book, however, and *The Roman Hat Mystery* (1929) was the first Ellery Queen novel. The early Queen novels were notable for titles that followed the same formula—"The Adjective-of-Nationality Noun Mystery"—such as *The Chinese Orange Mystery*.

After several successful Queen novels, the cousins decided to create another character and pseudonym, and the Barnaby Ross series was born. The detective in this series was a deaf former Shakespearean actor named Drury Lane. This series, which began with *The Tragedy of X*, survived through only four books.

In 1939 Lee and Dannay launched the first Ellery Queen radio series. The Queen mystery shows became a popular fixture on the radio. Subsequently three different television series were produced from 1950 to 1959, none very successfully. Later a critically acclaimed series starring Jim Hutton premiered in 1975, but the ratings were not good and the show was canceled. The show's producers later had more success as the creators of the long-running show *Murder, She Wrote*, starring Angela Lansbury.

Queen was not any more successful as a motion picture character. There were several Ellery Queen films beginning in 1935 and continuing with a series of films in the 1940s, starring Ralph Bellamy as Ellery. Other motion pictures were made in the 1960s and 1970s, all of them forgettable. None of the films was considered very good, although the Bellamy series did have a following.

In 1938 Dannay started *Challenge to the Reader*, the first of many anthologies edited as Ellery Queen. In 1941 *Ellery Queen's Mystery Magazine* was launched, and it remains the most successful magazine of its type. Also in 1941, Dannay published the anthology *101 Years' Entertainment*, considered the definitive anthology of short mystery fiction of its time. Dannay was principally responsible for the magazine and the anthologies, while Lee devoted more of his time to the radio show.

The cousins were also among the founding members of the Mystery Writers of America, the organization that annually presents the Edgar Allan Poe Awards—the "Edgars." They themselves won a Special Edgar in 1950, a Grand Master Edgar in 1961, and another Special Edgar in 1969.

Ellery Queen continued to produce novels and short stories throughout the 1950s and 1960s, with the last book, *A Fine and Private Place*, appearing in 1971. Lee died that year, and Dannay briefly considered continuing the series with another writing partner. He later rejected the idea. Dannay did, however, continue to produce anthologies, and he personally edited the magazine until his death in 1982.

Ellery Queen novels are still widely read by fans of older mystery fiction, and they certainly influenced many mystery writers of today. However, it is probably from the *Ellery Queen Mystery Magazine* that most people recognize the name. The magazine continues to be the most popular and enduring of its kind and is considered a valuable training ground for future mystery novelists.

Jill A. Gregg

SEE ALSO: *Detective Fiction;* Murder, She Wrote.

BIBLIOGRAPHY

Herbert, Rosemary, and Dennis Lehane. *Whodunit?: A Who's Who in Crime and Mystery Writing*. Oxford, UK: Oxford University Press, 2003.

Nevins, Francis M. *Royal Bloodline: Ellery Queen, Author and Detective*. Bowling Green, OH: Bowling Green University Popular Press, 1974.

Nevins, Francis M., and Ray Stanich. *The Sound of Detection*. Madison, IN: Brownstone Books, 1983.

Queen for a Day

Queen for a Day, a popular afternoon network television program from 1956 to 1964, originated on radio in 1945. Running five days a week during its peak years, this program featured four or five women chosen from a studio audience. Each woman competed by presenting her hard-luck story to persuade the audience that she was in the most dire straits. The audience selected the "queen" for each day by applause that was recorded on an applause meter. The winner was adorned with a sable-collared velvet robe, given a scepter, and crowned by the host, Jack Bailey, who loudly proclaimed, "I now pronounce you—Queen for a Day!" The queen was then showered with an array of prizes, such as appliances, furs, and jewelry—all donated by the show's sponsors in exchange for commercial consideration.

With its obvious Cinderella fantasy, this show added a royal twist to the rags-to-riches myth linked to the American Dream. The show's producers encouraged this comparison by using an opening format in which Bailey pointed at the camera and yelled, "Would *you* like to be queen for a day?" The audience would respond with a resounding "Yes!"

First broadcast on National Broadcasting Company (NBC) Radio in 1945, with Dud Williamson as the original host, the program debuted on NBC Television in 1956. In 1960 it moved to American Broadcasting Company (ABC) Television, where it remained until its demise in 1964. Expanded from thirty to forty-five minutes during its peak years, the show reached a daily audience of about thirteen million and commanded advertising rates of $4,000 per commercial minute. Its longevity of almost twenty years attests to the show's popularity with the mass audiences of both radio and television. Because *Queen for a*

Day was a live show, only a few kinescope recordings remain as historical records of the program.

Queen for a Day was frequently described by critics as a vulgar exploitation of the helpless female contestants' miserable conditions sandwiched in between commercial advertising. They pointed out that the show excluded unattractive or inarticulate women and contestants who needed more assistance than brand-name merchandise could provide, such as legal or medical counseling. The program was also criticized for rewarding the losers with minor consolation prizes, such as hosiery or toasters. "Sure, *Queen* was vulgar and sleazy and filled with bathos and bad taste," the former producer Howard Blake wrote in 1966, as quoted in *The New York Times Encyclopedia of Television* (1978). "That was why it was so successful. It was exactly what the general public wanted."

In answering the critics who pointed to the women as victims of a sleazy entertainment production, Blake's retort cynically reflects on the American consumerism of the 1950s, as quoted in *The Ultimate Television Book* (1977):

> Everybody was on the make—we on the show, NBC and later ABC, the sponsors and the suppliers of gifts. And how about all the down-on-their-luck women who we used to further our money-grubbing ends? Weren't they all on the make? Weren't they all after something for anything? Weren't they willing to wash their dirty linen on coast-to-coast TV for a chance at big money, for a chance to ride in our chauffeured Cadillac for the free tour of Disneyland and the Hollywood nightclubs? What about one of the most common wishes they turned in? "I'd like to pay back my mother for all the wonderful things she's done for me." The women who made that wish didn't want to pay back their mothers at all. They wanted *us* to.

While Blake's comments have been widely quoted, some scholars in the late twentieth century began to take a less critical attitude toward the program. Rather than categorically dismissing millions of women as tasteless and on the make, they argued that the show was popular in part because women were the centers of attention and were given a voice at a time when men dominated the public domain, including the airwaves, and when women were expected to keep their private miseries to themselves.

Mary Lou Nemanic

SEE ALSO: *Game Shows; Radio; Television.*

BIBLIOGRAPHY

Brown, Les. *The New York Times Encyclopedia of Television*. New York: Times Books, 1978.

Cassidy, Marsha. *What Women Watched: Daytime Television in the 1950s*. Austin: University of Texas Press, 2005.

DeLong, Thomas A. *Quiz Craze: America's Infatuation with Game Shows*. New York: Praeger, 1991.

Fabe, Maxene. *TV Game Shows*. Garden City, NY: Dolphin Books, 1979.

Fireman, Judy, ed. *TV Book: The Ultimate Television Book*. New York: Workman Publishing Company, 1977.

Scheiner, Georganne. "Would You Like to Be Queen for a Day?: Finding a Working Class Voice in American Television of the 1950s." *Historical Journal of Film, Radio and Television* 23, no. 4 (2003).

Queen Latifah *(1970?–)*

Rapper and actress Queen Latifah challenges the male-dominated stereotype of the urban music style known as rap by using it to address issues such as female power and the discrimination against women. Throughout her career as an entertainer, she has advanced the cause of female empowerment, speaking with particular eloquence about the plight of black women.

Born Dana Owens in Newark, New Jersey, Queen Latifah began her musical career singing in a choir. As a teenager in the 1980s, she became interested in rap, then an emerging genre, and formed an all-girl rap group called Ladies Fresh. Queen Latifah's professional career began while she was still in high school when she rocketed to the top with her first full-length album, *All Hail the Queen* (1989) and became the first female solo rap artist to have a gold record. Before Queen Latifah, women in rap were rare and not taken very seriously, but *All Hail the Queen* demonstrated that women could rhyme and beat box with the best of them. Rap, through its style and content, tends to address oppression, racism, economics, lack of adequate access to the legal and medical systems, inadequate public education, and the need for revolution on all fronts. Queen Latifah added sexism to the mix.

In some sense Queen Latifah's persona can be described as androgynous, for it combines both masculine and feminine traits. Her chosen moniker, which means "delicate" or "sensitive" in Arabic, almost contradicts her musical persona, which is strong, independent, and ready to challenge any rapper—male or female—while still maintaining her womanhood. On her first album, which was nominated for a Grammy, is a track that critics have called hip-hop's first "womanist anthem." "Ladies First" deploys a call-and-response pattern performed with British female rapper Monie Love, contesting sexism in the rap music world: "Some think that we can't flow / Stereotypes they got to go / I'm gonna mess around and flip the scene into reverse / With what? / With a little touch of ladies first." The follow-up album *Nature of a Sista'* (1991) made Queen Latifah, swathed in African prints and wearing a homemade crown, one of the most recognizable figures in American culture.

Queen Latifah has continued her pro-woman stance throughout her career, tackling issues that divide the African American community along gender lines, such as domestic violence, sexual harassment, and a lack of respect for women. Her 1994 single "U.N.I.T.Y.," included on the 1993 album *Black Reign*, earned Queen Latifah her first Grammy Award (for Best Rap Solo Performance). Since then, she has released four more albums—*Order in the Court* (1998), *The Dana Owens Album* (2004), *Trav'lin Light* (2007), and *Persona* (2009). In 2006 she became the first rap star to be awarded a star on the Hollywood Walk of Fame.

As the influence of rap and hip-hop culture expanded to other forms of popular culture, Queen Latifah began applying her talents to television and film. On television she starred on the Fox series *Living Single* between 1993 and 1998 and had her own syndicated daytime talk show, *The Queen Latifah Show*, between 1999 and 2001. In film Queen Latifah was recognized by the Independent Spirit Awards for her role in *Set It Off* (1996) as Cleo, one of the first overt depictions of an African American lesbian in a big-budget Hollywood production. She was nominated for an Oscar and won a Screen Actors Guild award for her role as "Mama" Morton in *Chicago* (2002), and she subsequently had leading roles in *Bringing Down the House* (2003), *Beauty Shop* (2005), *Hairspray* (2007), *The Secret Life of Bees* (2008), and *Joyful Noise* (2012).

In addition to her artistic accomplishments, Queen Latifah has engaged in a number of business endeavors, serving as a spokesperson for CoverGirl, Curvation women's lingerie, Pizza Hut, and Weight Watchers, as well as developing a perfume line called Queen. She has also written two books that are part memoir, part motivational text, titled *Ladies First: Revelations of a Strong Woman* (1999) and *Put on Your Crown* (2010).

Mary Lou Nemanic

SEE ALSO: *Daytime Talk Shows; Feminism; Grammy Awards; Hip-Hop; Hollywood; Lesbianism; Sexual Harassment; Television.*

BIBLIOGRAPHY

Queen Latifah, and Karen Hunter. *Ladies First: Revelations of a Strong Woman.* New York: HarperCollins, 1999.

Queen Latifah, and Samantha Marshall. *Put on Your Crown: Life-Changing Moments on the Way to Queendom.* New York: Grand Central Publishing, 2010.

Queer Eye for the Straight Guy

Queer Eye for the Straight Guy is a reality television show that aired on the Bravo cable network from 2003 to 2007. It featured Ted Allen, Kyan Douglas, Thom Filicia, Carson Kressley, and Jai Rodriguez, five gay men who are experts in food and wine, grooming, design, fashion, and culture. In each episode, they educate and remake an unstylish heterosexual man. The concept played on the long-held, though unsubstantiated, belief that homosexual men are inherently more fashionable than heterosexual men. This presumption, the sometimes unflattering stereotype of gay men propagated by the show, and the mere presence of openly gay men on television, provoked outcry from both conservatives and liberals, all of which served to make *Queer Eye for the Straight Guy* a true cultural phenomenon.

Openly gay producers David Collins and Michael Williams and their straight business partner David Metzler created *Queer Eye for the Straight Guy*, and Bravo aggressively promoted it. Billboards in major metropolitan areas and print ads heralded the coming makeover show, which premiered on July 15, 2003. It was immediately a smash hit. The first episodes earned the twenty-three-year-old Bravo network it most-watched debut ever. At the start of the third season, the name of the show was abbreviated to simply *Queer Eye*.

Each episode focuses on one man who wants to be made over in order to impress his family, friends, or most often a woman. The quintet of gay men rehabilitate the man's wardrobe, grooming habits, cooking skills, home organization, and social interactions through shopping outings and demonstrations. They then show their guest how to prepare for a special event, such as a date, and then the guest prepares on his own, while the five hosts watch on closed-circuit television to critique his performance. Throughout the culminating event, viewers are treated to a running commentary by the hosts, who then offer closing advice to their made-over subject.

The show quickly became popular, earning more than three million viewers at its peak in September of its first season. *Queer Eye* won the 2004 Emmy Award for Outstanding Reality Program, as well as the 2004 and 2005 GLAAD (Gay & Lesbian Alliance against Defamation) Media Award for Outstanding Reality Program. The "Fab Five," as the hosts came to be called, became cultural icons in both gay and straight communities, frequently appearing on daytime talk shows. Cast member and breakout star Kressley was named one of *Instinct* magazine's Leading Men of 2004. "Design Doctor" Filicia became a spokesperson for home furnishing store Pier 1 Imports. Merchandising also helped drive the popularity of the cast with a soundtrack, an advice book, and DVDs, all released under the *Queer Eye* moniker. In 2005 a spin-off show, *Queer Eye for the Straight Girl*, premiered on Bravo to a less favorable reception.

Although *Queer Eye* generally represent gay men positively, the show caused a stir on both sides of the political spectrum. Conservatives were disturbed by the seeming onslaught of pro-gay images in popular culture, through shows such as *Queer Eye* and the sitcom *Will & Grace* (1998–2006). However, petitions and condemnations failed to get *Queer Eye* canceled due to its overwhelming popularity and its strong showing in ratings. The gay community was not entirely pleased with the show either. Some felt that it promoted a generalized and stereotypical view of homosexual men that did not accurately represent the diversity within the gay community. This critique was tempered by the perception that an important barrier had been broken for gays on television, regardless of the generalizations the show might make about gay culture.

Perhaps a truer mark of a show's fame is the moment others lampoon it. Television network Comedy Central parodied the hit reality show with *Straight Plan for the Gay Man.* Producers also attempted to adapt the show for other countries but with less success. The phenomenon lost steam almost as quickly as it had rocketed to fame. Viewership dropped precipitously in the second season, and Bravo canceled the show in 2007 after five seasons on air. Nevertheless, when it first aired, *Queer Eye* was a unique concept in television, and its success indicates that American culture was more accepting of diverse lifestyles. While its premise that gay men are more chic than straight men is still up for debate, *Queer Eye* brought the gay and lesbian communities into American homes in a fun and friendly way.

Jill Gregg Clever

SEE ALSO: *Advertising; Billboards; Emmy Awards; Gay Men; Metrosexual; Reality Television; Television;* Will & Grace.

BIBLIOGRAPHY

Allen, Ted; Kyan Douglas; Thom Filicia; et al. *Queer Eye for the Straight Guy: The Fab 5's Guide to Looking Better, Cooking Better, Dressing Better, Behaving Better, and Living Better.* New York: Clarkson Potter, 2004.

Fonesca, Nicholas. "They're Here! They're Queer! And They Don't Like Your End Tables." *Entertainment Weekly*, August 8, 2003.

Queer Nation

Formed in March 1990, Queer Nation is an activist organization founded in New York City by four men, all of whom had been victims of anti-gay violence. Its goal was to be a grassroots, direct-action response to the invisibility of homosexuality in American culture and expressions of homophobic prejudice, using tactics proven effective by the AIDS (Acquired Immune Deficiency Syndrome) Coalition to Unleash Power (ACT UP). It espoused the idea of "outing" persons whose homosexuality was not public knowledge, a concept whose radical nature drew objections from more moderate gay rights organizations. Even its name reflected a defiantly marginal identity, reclaiming a common epithet and reworking it into a newly proud badge, most visible in its trademark slogan of "We're here, we're queer, get used to it."

Robert Ridinger

SEE ALSO: *AIDS; Gay and Lesbian Press; Gay Liberation Movement; Gay Men; Outing.*

BIBLIOGRAPHY

Bronski, Michael. *A Queer History of the United States*. Boston: Beacon Press, 2011.

Slagle, R. Anthony. "In Defense of Queer Nation: From Identity Politics to a Politics of Difference." *Western Journal of Communication* 59, (Spring 1995): 85–102.

Quiz Show Scandals

In 1958, while television was in its infancy, Americans were still innocent about the medium's predilection for sacrificing veracity in favor of entertainment. Particularly popular with the viewing public were television quiz shows, which had big money and high ratings and were subject to the whims of sponsors; these aspects combined to corrupt the quiz shows. The more charismatic and telegenic contestants were supplied with answers, while other contestants were told to miss questions intentionally. Shows were so scripted that producers told contestants when to wring their hands or mop their brows. A series of tie games was often fabricated as a way to build suspense and to keep viewers tuning in each week. Contestants, enamored with their newfound fame and prize money, were more than willing to go along with the charade. Finally, a series of revelations in the press from disgruntled former contestants led to a congressional investigation in 1959—the results of which shook the confidence of viewers. The rigged contests marred an otherwise innocent era in America, prefiguring the large-scale lies that surrounded Vietnam and Watergate.

RISE OF THE QUIZ SHOWS

The most popular of the quiz shows, *The $64,000 Question*, was modeled after its radio predecessor, *The $64 Question*. *The $64,000 Question* debuted in 1955, after a 1954 Supreme Court ruling paved the way for high-stakes quiz shows by eliminating jackpot-type quizzes from the category of gambling. However, no specific laws existed to regulate television game shows in the wake of the high court's ruling. Quiz shows were immediately and wildly popular: in August 1955 approximately 47 million viewers tuned in to watch *The $64,000 Question*.

Americans watched these shows because of the big prize money and their "spontaneous" and "unpredictable" nature. The prosperity of the 1950s gave rise to the American Dream, as Americans sought to acquire the material goods, homes, and good-paying jobs that were denied to their Depression-era parents. The quiz shows were a reflection of the new materialism. The 1957–1958 television season featured 22 network quiz shows, broadcast live and mainly during prime time. The most popular shows were those that featured contestants competing for unlimited cash prizes. Some contestants amassed winnings of more than $100,000, a large sum for the pre-inflationary dollar. Contestants included future celebrities like television actress Patty Duke and popular psychologist Dr. Joyce Brothers. Picked by producers to fail, Brothers beat the system by studying so extensively that she won her prize money legitimately.

One former contestant, Antoinette DuBarry Hillman, described a typical screening session that the producers of *Dotto* used to coach contestants. At the time the highest-rated daytime quiz show, *Dotto* required players to answer questions and then identify a puzzle in which drawings of famous people were gradually revealed. In Kent Anderson's *Television Fraud* (1978), Hillman recalled:

> Actually the first day I was on the show (the screener) asked me in the preliminary thing how I would recognize Victor Borge. Then when I got on the show and was answering the questions, I got my first clue (for the emerging dot connections) and it was Danish. I didn't think much about that. Then the second clue was a musician. How many Danish musicians do you know? . . . Finally I had to give in and say Victor Borge. I was right and I won. When I went off stage I popped over to Mr. Green (the screener) and started to thank him, and he said hush, hush, hush.

In his defense, Edward Jurist, the producer of *Dotto*, complained in his 1959 testimony before Congress that the world of information was so vast that "you cannot ask random questions of people and have a show. You simply have failure, failure, failure, and that does not make for entertainment."

SPONSORSHIP DEMANDS

One major flaw with the quiz shows was that they were created around one sponsor. One company would act as a show's sole advertiser and would use the sponsorship to its advantage by exerting its influence on the show's production. The stakes involving the quiz shows were as high for the networks and the sponsors as they presumably were for the contestants. For instance, *Twenty-One*'s sponsor, Geritol, advertised as "a relief for tired blood," saw annual sales jump by an average of $3 million a year during the years 1957 and 1958, when the show was being televised. After the scandal erupted and *Twenty-One* was canceled, Geritol's sales fell back to pre–quiz show levels.

Twenty-One, one of the most popular of the quiz shows, featured two competitors in isolation booths who were required to answer questions on any given topic. Questions were rated by difficulty from one to eleven. The first contestant to reach a score of twenty-one without a tie won, and each player's score was concealed from the other until one of them reached twenty-one. The show was not immediately popular after its debut on September 12, 1956, and the show's producers, Jack Barry and Dan Enright, were under pressure to improve its ratings. "*Twenty-One*," wrote Walter Karp in *American Heritage* in 1989, "needed talking encyclopedias and human almanacs." The knowledge required was so broad and expert that initial contests ended in 0-0 ties.

Twenty-One recruited Herbert Stempel, a short, awkward New Yorker from Forrest Hills who had a photographic memory, to represent the underdog figure of the "average man." Viewers soon began watching to see if he could continue winning for one more week. Despite his considerable knowledge, Stempel was enlisted to help fix the show. Stempel was told how to dress and how to get his hair cut, and he was rehearsed with questions that would appear on-air. In his testimony to Congress in 1959, Stempel stated that producer Enright visited him at home to go through questions and answers. "After having done this," Stempel attested, "he very, very bluntly sat back and said with a smile, 'How would you like to win $25,000?' I had been a poor boy all my life, and I was sort of overjoyed." However, Stempel was not a photogenic man; viewers could see him visibly sweating during the telecast. Geritol felt that Stempel did not project the right image, and new contestants were sought in order to attract bigger audiences.

CHARLES VAN DOREN

Enter Charles Van Doren, an instructor at Columbia University, whose father, Mark Van Doren, was a Pulitzer Prize–winning poet. Van Doren possessed a cool, WASP-like detachment and was attractive as well: "He was very American," wrote Joseph Epstein, who knew Van Doren, in the December 1944 issue of *Commentary*. "He looked as if he could have played on our Davis Cup tennis team. . . . Mothers, it was said, saw him as the answer to Elvis Presley." The antipodal contestants played a series of staged ties that delivered big ratings, until Stempel was told by producers to take a dive, giving the wrong response to a question to which he genuinely knew the correct answer. Van Doren continued as reigning champion for fifteen weeks.

For his part, Van Doren was told that the riggings were common practice and that the shows were mere entertainment. Karp quotes Van Doren's statement that producer Al Freedman convinced him with "the fact that by appearing on a nationally televised program, I would be doing a great service to the intellectual life, to teachers and to education in general, by increasing public respect for the work of the mind through my performances."

Stempel had grown accustomed to minor celebrity status and felt betrayed by Enright, who in turn considered Stempel to be an ingrate. The disgruntled contestant took his "defeat" in hard fashion and began seeing a psychiatrist. Stempel tried to tell anybody he could about the fraud, including the newspapers, which were reluctant to print his charges, fearing a libel suit. Enright produced a statement, signed by Stempel, that denied Stempel had been coached in any way while on the program. Stempel continued trying to get someone to listen to his story; meanwhile, his nemesis, Van Doren, was being featured on the covers of *Life* and *Time*.

THE SCANDAL BREAKS

Stempel was not the only former contestant to come forward. One of them, the Reverend Charles E. "Stoney" Jackson Jr., was an unwitting participant in the frauds. After going public with his charges, Jackson discovered that the quiz shows were highly regarded indeed, for he could not even convince his own congregation of the misdeeds of the shows. Another contestant on *Dotto*, Edward Hilgemeier Jr., produced a page from a winner's crib sheet. Hilgemeier refused an initial $500 settlement from the show, which then accused him of trying to blackmail the network. Eventually, a reporter convinced him to accept hush money in order to obtain evidence of the show's corruption. Hilgemeier assented, and left a copy of his affidavit to the Federal Communications Commission at Colgate-Palmolive, *Dotto*'s sponsor. Rumors began appearing in print of the quiz show's misdeeds, and *Dotto* was canceled in August 1958.

Reaction to the revelations was disbelief. As early as April 1957, *Look* magazine published accounts that claimed the shows were controlled by selecting more or less difficult questions, but argued that "no TV quiz shows are fixed in the sense of being dishonest." Of three polls that appeared shortly after the revelations, the most emphatic response was from the 65 percent of respondents who answered in the affirmative to the following statement: "These practices are very wrong and should be stopped immediately, but you can't condemn all of television because of them." Americans liked their new TV sets, and they were not going to let one segment of programming taint the overall "experience" of watching television. Some were more alarmed by the public's apathy or cynicism than they were by the fixed shows. In the end, the cynicism on the part of Americans may have been justified, since the only people who were legally punished were contestants—not the producers of the shows.

The New York District Attorney's Office announced its investigation of *Dotto* on August 25, 1958. Three days later, two New York newspapers published Stempel's allegations, which were once considered to be the products of a hysterical, raving maniac. Enright produced a tape recording of a conversation between himself and Stempel that included the revelations that Stempel had received psychiatric help, and that he owed gambling debts to a bookmaker. Stempel claimed that part of the tape was altered. After nine months of testimony, the grand jury's report was expunged by the presiding judge "to protect the dubious reputations of the not-so-innocent." Anderson quotes District Attorney Frank Hogan in 1959 as saying, "The very essence of the quiz program's appeal lies in its implied representation of honesty. Were it generally understood that these programs do not present honest tests of the contestants' knowledge and intellectual skills, they would be utterly ineffectual in acquiring the public's 'time.'"

FEDERAL INVESTIGATION

In 1959 Oren Harris (a Democrat representing Arkansas) announced a House of Representatives investigation committee, which convened on October 6. During testimony by quiz show contestants, former *Twenty-One* contestant James Snodgrass produced letters that he sent to himself by registered mail. Snodgrass's letters correctly predicted the outcome of the televised proceedings: "According to the plan I am to miss the first question, specifically the lines by Emily Dickinson. I've been told to answer Ralph Waldo Emerson. I have decided not to 'take the fall' but to answer the question correctly." It was also revealed that, of the 150 witnesses called before the New York grand jury, 100 committed perjury under oath. According to Epstein, when it was suggested to the committee that Van Doren—who by his own testimony was the "principal symbol" of the corruption—be spared the exposure of testifying, one member replied, "It would be like playing *Hamlet* without Hamlet."

In response to the investigation, the networks swiftly canceled the quiz shows during the 1958–1959 season. Van Doren lost his job as an assistant professor. President Eisenhower signed a bill in 1960 that declared illegal any contest or game with intent to deceive the audience. People in television began working to get the networks to acquire or produce their programs *before* lining up advertisers. The lasting effect on the quiz shows was a change within their fundamental nature. They returned to television as "game shows," free from any negative associations with the old shows. The overall effect of the scandals, wrote Olaf Hoerschelmann in *Museum of Broadcast Communications Encyclopedia of Television* (1997), was that they "undermined the legitimacy of high cultural values that quiz shows—the term and the genre—embodied. Thus, the new name, 'game shows,' removed the genre from certain cultural assumptions and instead created associations with the less sensitive concepts of play and leisure." By the late 1980s, thirty years after the scandal, game shows were more likely to present contests with questions requiring everyday knowledge, rather than expert knowledge.

LASTING EFFECTS

The quiz show scandals have been used to interpret, with varying degrees of plausibility, the downfall of innocence in America. Some blamed them for laying the groundwork for future deceptions involving Vietnam and Watergate. Others saw the scandals as a precursor to the 1960 Nixon/Kennedy presidential debates, in which the telegenic man (Kennedy) won again. In essence, a discussion of the quiz shows is a discussion about American naïveté toward a new medium, not the complete shakedown of national innocence; it is dubious that there was such an innocence in the first place. Breathless assertions that Van Doren's televised intellectual ability was the American answer to Soviet Russia's *Sputnik* launch showed that people made far too much out of the quiz shows during their broadcast.

The view from the 1990s, as expressed by John Leo in a 1994 piece in *U.S. News & World Report*, was that the Van Doren/Stempel pairing exploited stereotypes of class and race by featuring "the elegant high WASP from a family of famous scholars versus the underachieving and volatile Jewish nerd from Queens." *Quiz Show*, the 1994 movie directed by Robert Redford, successfully highlighted this angle. However, the movie's docudrama presentation yielded to making changes of fact in order to enhance dramatic effect. The movie ignored the newspapers, the district attorney, and the grand jury by making bureaucrat Richard Goodwin the singular force behind the exposure of Van Doren. Although widely regarded as a well-made movie, the irony had come full circle: television, represented by *Los Angeles Times* TV critic Howard Rosenberg, got to stand on the high moral ground for a change. "How ironic," the *U.S. News & World Report* quotes Rosenberg, "that a movie so judgmental about the TV industry's dishonesty in the 1950s should itself play so fast and loose with the truth for the sake of putting on a good show."

Television's "high ground" is still not solid. One of the reasons the quiz show scandals remain instructive is that television retains the use of deception: it routinely employs dramatic reenactments of crimes, talk-show guests who are rehearsed before tapings, and staged consumer product safety tests. In the beginning, people believed that television was inherently trustworthy and factual. The quiz shows shattered such beliefs, and showed that television was fictional, engineered, and manipulative rather than innocent or natural. This is perhaps the longest-lasting effect of the quiz show scandals upon television: they at once uncovered and reinforced the notion that television was solely designed to entertain. Any subsequent successful television show that is inventive, creative, or educational *and* entertaining is regarded as a curious anomaly.

Daryl Umberger

SEE ALSO: *Brothers, Dr. Joyce; Game Shows; Redford, Robert;* The $64,000 Question*; Television; Vietnam; Watergate.*

BIBLIOGRAPHY

Anderson, Kent. *Television Fraud: The History and Implications of the Quiz Show Scandals.* Westport, CT: Greenwood Press, 1978.

Diamond, Edwin, and Ellen Hume. *Quiz Show: Television Betrayals Past and Present.* Washington, DC: Annenberg Washington Program in Communications Policy Studies, Northwestern University, 1994.

Epstein, Joseph. "Redford's Van Doren & Mine." *Commentary*, December 1994, 40–46.

Frank, Reuven. "'Quiz Show' Follies." *New Leader*, September 12, 1994, 18–19.

Gould, Jack, and Lewis L. Gould. *Watching Television Come of Age: The* New York Times *Review.* Austin: University of Texas Press, 2002.

Hoerschelmann, Olaf. "Quiz and Game Shows." In *Museum of Broadcast Communications Encyclopedia of Television*, ed. Horace Newcomb. Chicago: Fitzroy Dearborn Publishers, 1997.

Karp, Walter. "The Quiz Show Scandal." *American Heritage*, May/June 1989, 76–88.

Leo, John. "Faking It in 'Quiz Show.'" *U.S. News & World Report*, October 17, 1994, 24.

Stone, J., and T. Yohn. *Prime Time Misdemeanors: Investigating the 1950s TV Quiz Scandal—A D.A.'s Account.* New Brunswick, NJ: Rutgers University Press, 1992.

QVC

SEE: *Home Shopping Network/QVC.*

Race Music

Prior to the emergence of rhythm and blues as a musical genre in the 1940s, *race music* and *race records* were terms used to categorize practically all types of African American music. Race records were the first examples of popular music recorded by and marketed to black Americans. Reflecting the segregated status of American society and culture, race records were separate catalogs of black music. Prior to the 1940s, African Americans were scarcely represented on radio, and live performances were largely limited to segregated venues. Race music and records, therefore, were also the primary medium for African American musical expression during the 1920s and 1930s. An estimated 15,000 titles were released on race records during this period—approximately 10,000 blues, 3,250 jazz, and 1,750 gospel songs. Race records are significant historical documents of early twentieth-century African American music and have been and remain influential to artists, audiences, and scholars alike. Most twentieth-century white, popular music—especially rock and roll and country—has roots in race music, in particular jazz, swing, and blues.

THE ORIGINS OF RACE MUSIC

The terms *race music* and *race records* had conflicting meanings. In one respect, they were indicative of segregation in the 1920s. Race records were separated from the recordings of white musicians and were based solely on the race of the artists. On the other hand, the terms represented an emerging awareness by the recording industry of African American audiences. The term *race* was not pejorative; in fact, it was "symbolic of black pride, militancy, and solidarity in the 1920s, and it was generally favored over *colored* or *Negro* by African American city dwellers," notes scholar William Barlow in his article in *Split Image: African Americans in the Mass Media*. The term *race records* first appeared in the *Chicago Defender*, an African American newspaper, within an advertisement in 1922.

Race music and records resulted from the concentrated commercialization of American popular music beginning in the early twentieth century. In 1920 Mamie Smith, a female African American singer little known outside of vaudeville, recorded the song "Crazy Blues" for the small OKeh record label. The record unexpectedly sold more than 100,000 copies by the end of the year and turned the nascent recording industry's attention to African American artists and audiences.

The early 1920s were a period of declining revenues for the recording industry, and race records emerged in part as a way of expanding the consumer market for recorded music. The two dominant record companies, Victor and Columbia, had seen their status erode dramatically. Victor's sales had fallen from $51 million, and Columbia's had declined from $7 million to $4.5 million in the period of 1921 to 1925. The combined impact of radio and competition from new labels were catalysts for the emergence of race records. The onset of commercial radio broadcasts in the early 1920s impacted the recording industry's dominant position as the gatekeeper of recorded music. Prior to a lawsuit in 1919, the two dominant recording companies controlled the patents for phonograph record production. Following this lawsuit, however, the industry was opened to competition. Many of the new record labels that emerged, such as OKeh, Paramount, and Gennett, would be instrumental in the development and production of race records.

The production of race records was a more profitable endeavor than the recording of white artists. As in other endeavors, African American artists were paid less than their white counterparts for recording sessions and were often exploited. Artists' ignorance of copyright law and the lack of an independent accounting body to track sales allowed industry personnel to grossly underpay or waive royalty monies. Bessie Smith, "the queen of the blues," recorded more than 160 songs for Columbia and never received royalty payments in the ten years she recorded for the company. Folk blues artists, such as Blind Lemon Jefferson and Son House, were also more profitable to record because their songs could be copyrighted. Unlike their urban peers, folk blues artists' songs generally had not been published, thus record companies could make money off the published songs in addition to sales of records. Once published, songs became commodities, and any future recordings would result in royalty payments to the publisher. This practice has remained widespread throughout the twentieth and twenty-first centuries.

With few exceptions, the labels that produced race records were white owned and controlled. One significant exception was Black Swan, formed in 1921 by Harry Pace, W. C. Handy's former partner, as a division of Pace Phonography. Musician and arranger Fletcher Henderson was retained as musical director and recording manager. In 1924, largely due to a lack of sustained financial success, Black Swan sold its catalog to Paramount. Paramount also had a connection to the other major African American–owned label of this time, Black Patti. Black Patti was started in 1927 by J. "Mayo" Williams, an African American who was recording director for the Paramount label. While employed there, Williams started the label with money from disgruntled Paramount vice president E. J. Barrett and Richard Gennett, brother of Gennett Records owner Harry Gennett. After releasing approximately fifty records, Black Patti folded in less than a year.

Other African American-owned labels included Sunshine and Merrit. Overall, the race labels constituted a small minority in the context of race record production during this period. Segregation and racism, combined with only fleeting access to capital, technology, and distribution—which were almost exclusively controlled by whites—placed the African American labels at a disadvantage and ultimately contributed to their quick demise.

JAZZ AND BLUES

Race music and records in the 1920s were characterized by the popularity of two significant genres of music and the dominance of three race record labels. In particular, jazz and blues became part of the American musical idiom in the 1920s, popularized in large part through recordings released on Columbia, Paramount, and OKeh. Jazz, the dominant American indigenous popular music, emerged from the New Orleans area to become national, and eventually international, in popularity and practice. For example, Joe "King" Oliver was a seminal figure in jazz, and his band featured Louis Armstrong. Oliver's Creole Jazz Band came out of New Orleans and was a mainstay in several Chicago clubs; the group recorded some of the earliest and most influential jazz records for the Gennett label. Likewise, Jelly Roll Morton, an influential pianist from New Orleans, recorded groundbreaking songs for the Gennett label.

The blues emerged from diverse regions of the American South and Southwest and had urban and rural progenitors. In the urban North, the vaudeville blues became popular in the early 1920s, especially following the success of Mamie Smith's 1920 recording. Female blues artists in particular were quite successful during the early 1920s. Artists such as Alberta Hunter, who recorded for Paramount, and Sean Martin had a large following through their recordings. The folk blues, with origins in the rural South, became popular in the latter half of the 1920s. Artists such as Texan Blind Lemon Jefferson, who recorded more than seventy-five songs for Paramount between 1926 and 1929, were popular with audiences and would influence later generations of blues artists. Other folk blues artists of note who recorded during this period were Mississippians Charley Patton—also known as "The Masked Marvel"—and Son House; both recorded for Paramount.

THE DEPRESSION

During the 1930s the commercial success and expansion of race music and records were impacted by the Great Depression. While sales of race records had reached $100 million in 1927, they had fallen drastically to $6 million in 1933. In response, the record companies dropped their record prices from an average of seventy-five cents in the 1920s to thirty-five cents in the 1930s. Until the mid-1930s few new songs were released, and virtually no new race recordings were made; instead the industry rereleased titles and songs that had been previously unreleased.

Following the repeal of Prohibition in 1933, the demand for live music increased. And in the late 1930s the emergence of the jukebox stimulated sales of records. Three race record labels dominated the production of recordings in the 1930s and reflected the impact of the Depression on the music industry: Columbia, RCA-Victor (whose race label was Bluebird), and Decca. Columbia, which had acquired OKeh in 1926, was profitable until 1938, at which time it was sold to CBS. The RCA-Victor label had emerged from RCA's purchase of Victor in 1929. Decca, a new entry into the race market, was a subsidiary of London-based Decca.

Race music was also expanded around this time by the popularity of swing. Swing grew out of big band jazz ensembles in the 1920s. Unlike the jazz bands of the 1920s, however, swing was more often arranged and scored, instead of improvised, and used reed instruments as well as the brass instruments that dominated earlier jazz. Swing in the 1930s was epitomized by the Fletcher Henderson Band, which featured Louis Armstrong on trumpet, Coleman Hawkins on tenor saxophone, and arranger Don Redman. Other notable swing bands during this period included Chick Webb's band, which had vocalist Ella Fitzgerald; Jimmie Lunceford's Band; Duke Ellington's Orchestra; Count Basie's Orchestra; and Cab Calloway's Orchestra. Despite the economic downturn, the 1930s were a creative period for race music.

THE DECLINE OF RACE RECORDS

During the 1940s race records as a distinctly separate catalog of recordings waned due to several factors. America's entry into World War II curtailed the production and consumption of recorded music. In 1942 the government rationed shellac, a key component in the manufacture of record discs, which limited the number of releases. Likewise in 1942, the American Federation of Music announced a ban on all recording, and as a result the studios were closed for two years. Following the war and the lifting of the recording ban, recording resumed with verve, but the industry concentrated on mass-market sales and neglected their race catalogs. Small labels that emphasized African American music emerged in the Midwest and South and challenged the status of the major labels.

Significantly, these labels—such as Chess, King, and Vee-Jay—did not use the nomenclature *race records*. Race music during this period was greatly expanded. While blues and jazz titles were still being recorded and released, a diversity of styles, collectively known as "rhythm and blues," began to coalesce. Although race music was still largely produced for and consumed by black audiences, the segregated status of the music and recordings was declining.

In the late twentieth century, scholars and historians began to recognize the need to honor and preserve the history of African American music, including race music. In 1999 an organization was formed to establish the Museum of African American Music, which, when completed, will be affiliated with the Smithsonian Institution.

Matthew A. Killmeier

SEE ALSO: *Armstrong, Louis; Basie, Count; Blues; Calloway, Cab; Ellington, Duke; Fitzgerald, Ella; Gospel Music; Hawkins, Coleman; Henderson, Fletcher; Jazz; Morton, Jelly Roll; New Orleans Rhythm and Blues; Rhythm and Blues; Webb, Chick.*

BIBLIOGRAPHY

Barlow, William. "Cashing In: 1900–1939." In *Split Image: African Americans in the Mass Media*, ed. Jannette L. Dates and William Barlow. Washington, DC: Howard University Press, 1990.

Dixon, Robert M. W., and John Godrich. *Recording the Blues.* New York: Stein & Day, 1970.

Dixon, Robert M. W.; John Godrich; and Howard Rye. *Blues*

and Gospel Records 1890–1943. New York: Oxford University Press, 1997.

Foreman, Ronald Clifford, Jr. "Jazz and Race Records, 1920–32: Their Origins and Their Significance for the Record Industry and Society." PhD diss., University of Illinois, 1968.

Kennedy, Rick. *Jelly Roll, Bix, and Hoagy: Gennett Studios and the Birth of Recorded Jazz.* Bloomington: Indiana University Press, 1994.

Oliver, Paul. *Songsters and Saints: Vocal Traditions on Race Records.* New York: Cambridge University Press, 1984.

Ramsey, Guthrie P., Jr. *Race Music: Black Cultures from Bebop to Hip-Hop.* Music of the African Diaspora, 7. Berkeley: University of California Press, 2004.

Russell, Tony. *Blacks, Whites, and Blues.* New York: Stein & Day, 1970.

Southern, Eileen. *The Music of Black Americans: A History,* 3rd ed. New York: W. W. Norton, 1997.

Race Riots

Although baseball, Mom's apple pie, and the Fourth of July are known as staples in the American cultural fabric, race riots have become similarly associated with the United States. They have been a constant throughout the nation's history. In many ways racial warfare has taken on a life and a culture of its own.

A 1906 riot in Atlanta, Georgia, set the stage for the majority of later attacks by whites on African Americans. The conflict erupted on September 22, when approximately 10,000 whites, angry at allegations that black men had assaulted white women, "beat every black person they found on the streets of the city." The violence occurred at a time when African Americans had begun to assert themselves, shedding an image of compliancy. The death toll was between twelve and twenty-five. Two years later a similar attack occurred in Springfield, Illinois.

World War I ushered in a new era of racial conflict. African Americans began migrating to urban areas in search of better social and economic conditions. The immediate postwar period was a powder keg as white GIs returned home to find a "New Negro" emerging. The first World War I–related riot occurred in East St. Louis, Illinois, in 1917; it left forty African Americans dead at the hands of white attackers. The riot foreshadowed the notorious "Red Summer of 1919," when twenty-five cities witnessed racial conflict that ended in 100 fatalities and another 1,000 wounded. The most dramatic riot of 1919 was in Chicago, where an incident at a Lake Michigan beach touched off thirteen days of rioting that led to the deaths of fifteen whites and twenty-three blacks. In 1921 Tulsa, Oklahoma, was the scene of a race "war" after whites destroyed more than $1 million worth of black-owned property.

The World War II period was a watershed in the history of race riots in the United States. Whereas the previous conflicts had been initiated by whites, these new outbreaks were fueled

Detroit Race Riots, July 1967. *Police attempt to control a crowd gathered in the street after race riots in Detroit, Michigan, in July 1967.* AP IMAGES.

by both black and white frustration. The most notorious World War II riot occurred in Detroit, Michigan, in 1943. Twenty-five blacks and nine whites died in what was largely a battle over jobs and housing. The all-white Detroit Police Department was responsible for the majority of black deaths.

After World War II a second great migration brought more than three million African Americans from the South to the urban North and West. The "Promised Land" turned out to be an illusion. Greeted with poor housing, unequal police protection, de facto school segregation, and employment discrimination, black migrants felt increasingly thwarted. As conditions continued to worsen in the mid-1960s, African Americans took their battle to the streets, destroying white property in hopes of drawing attention to their plight. In 1964 Harlem, Chicago, and Philadelphia were the scene of incidents that left more than 100 citizens dead. When the black enclave of Watts in Los Angeles erupted a year later, the toll was thirty-four deaths and approximately $200 million in property damage. In all, the 35,000 active rioters caused 1,000 injuries, but the riot also highlighted the conditions faced by the urban poor.

Racial disturbances peaked in the United States in 1967. Serious riots occurred in Newark, New Jersey, and Detroit, causing twenty-six and forty deaths, respectively. Most were at the hands of white policemen who valued white property over black lives. More than thirty other cities also experienced outbreaks, as black northerners took out their frustrations on white property. Martin Luther King Jr.'s assassination on the night of April 4, 1968, triggered similar riots in more than 110 cities.

The decades of the 1970s and 1980s witnessed a decline in rioting. In 1992, however, Americans were jolted out of a short-term complacency by the Rodney King riots in Los Angeles. King was brutally beaten by at least four white officers from the Los Angeles Police Department in March 1991. A nearby resident videotaped the incident, and within hours the images were broadcast throughout the world. The officers were indicted, but in the all-white suburb of Simi Valley, they were acquitted of police brutality by a jury composed of eleven whites and one Hispanic. The verdict touched off several days of rioting that resulted in more than 50 deaths, 4,000 arrests, and $500 million in property damage. The most infamous image of the riot was of Reginald Denny, a white truck driver who was pulled from his truck in a black neighborhood and beaten nearly to death. At the height of the violence, King pleaded on television, "Can't we all just get along?" Sadly, the answer has proved to be no. In the decades since 1991, incidents as diverse as police brutality, neo-Nazi rallies, and power struggles between rival gangs have sparked recurring interracial crises in cities across the country.

Leonard N. Moore

SEE ALSO: *Gangs; King, Martin Luther, Jr.; King, Rodney; World War I; World War II.*

BIBLIOGRAPHY

Hersey, John. *The Algiers Motel Incident.* New York: Alfred A. Knopf, 1968.

Hirsch, James S. *Riot and Remembrance: America's Worst Race Riot and Its Legacy.* New York: Mariner, 2003.

Horne, Gerald. *The Fire This Time: The Watts Riot and the 1960s.* Charlottesville: University Press of Virginia, 1995.

Madigan, Tim. *The Burning: Massacre, Destruction, and the Tulsa Race Riot of 1921.* New York: Thomas Dunne Books, 2001.

Sugrue, Thomas. *Origins of the Urban Crisis.* Princeton, NJ: Princeton University Press, 1996.

Kerner Commission, United States. *Report of the National Advisory Commission on Civil Disorders.* New York: Bantam, 1968.

Radio

A medium from relatively humble beginnings, radio was the basis of an electronic revolution that shaped American culture during the mid-twentieth century. Guglielmo Marconi, a young Italian inventor, pioneered wireless telegraphy in September 1895 when he transmitted a message to his brother, who was out of sight beyond a hill. By 1906 U.S. inventor Lee De Forest had greatly increased the potential of Marconi's work by developing a three-electrode vacuum-tube amplifier that made modern radio broadcasts possible. From the early 1920s to the mid-1950s radio both recorded and influenced popular culture in a way that no other medium had. It forever changed the way information and entertainment were disseminated and paved the way for television.

BEGINNINGS

Westinghouse engineer Frank Conrad created the first modern radio station in 1920 when he set up KDKA in East Pittsburgh, Pennsylvania, and began sending out programs "over the ether," in the parlance of the day. On November 2 KDKA broadcast the results of the Warren G. Harding–James M. Cox presidential election. However, at the time only about 5,000 Americans had radio receivers, so the broadcast went largely unnoticed. As Susan Smulyan writes in *Selling Radio*, the problem was that "when the first radio station began in 1920, no one knew how to make money from broadcasting."

A number of groups realized that radio could be a powerful and important medium, which resulted in a battle for control of the airwaves. One faction, spearheaded primarily by educators, believed that radio could help enrich people's lives. These advocates wanted a government-funded national radio program that would be largely informational and educational. However, they would have to wait until 1967, when President Lyndon B. Johnson signed the Public Broadcasting Act into law, creating the noncommercial National Public Radio.

In the 1920s consumers were not ready to pay for information and entertainment, so the question remained, who would pay for radio? In 1922 New York radio station WEAF—which would later become WNBC—solved the funding dilemma when it aired the first paid radio commercials. Although advertisers were initially unconvinced as to radio's ability to sell products, they eventually realized its effectiveness in reaching people in their homes.

Accordingly, WEAF's commercialization set into motion private control of U.S. public airwaves. In a now famous quote, De Forest responded to radio's commercialization by asking, "What have you done with my child? You have sent him out on the street in rags of ragtime to collect money from all and sundry. You have made of him a laughing stock of intelligence, surely a stench in the nostrils of the gods of the ionosphere."

The concept of selling time for advertisements had immense ramifications as radio broadcasters pioneered the format and structure of media advertising used in television and on the Internet.

EARLY FORMAT

Before the Great Depression began, radio had established a core of music, news, and entertainment programming. Of the three, music and news programming were predominant because they were the cheapest to produce. (Entertainment programming would not enter its golden age until the early 1930s.) At the time, there were two ways of presenting music: either by playing records or by broadcasting musicians as they played live in a studio, concert hall, or hotel ballroom. Integration of musical numbers into complex variety shows would not occur for several years. News broadcasts and issue-based discussion shows flourished because of their immediacy. Sports events such as the World Series and news such as the infamous Scopes Monkey Trial, which Chicago station WGN broadcast live, united Americans around their radios.

Radio networks began appearing in the late 1920s. NBC was established in 1926 and CBS, in 1927. Perhaps the most important effect of these networks was their nationalization of the medium. As networks bought up local stations, which became known as "affiliates," regional shows gave way to uniform national shows. Concurrently, radios were becoming common in American homes. By the early 1930s approximately 90 percent of Americans had at least one radio in their homes. As a result, American regionalism began to disappear at an accelerated rate, contributing to the twentieth-century homogenization of American culture.

THE GOLDEN AGE

By the early 1930s listeners had grown bored with a steady menu of music, news, and talk. Many craved escape from the hard reality of the Depression. Broadcasters responded by diversifying their programming and broadcasting shows in many genres, including Westerns, detective shows, dramas, soap operas, comedies, romances, and variety shows. Americans danced to the latest rhythms, played by bandleaders who broadcast live from hotel ballrooms, or gathered around their sets on Sunday morning to hear prominent preachers and choirs.

Many radio shows were serialized. Each week, fans could follow the ongoing adventures of their favorite characters. *Amos 'n' Andy* (1928–1960), for example, was an overwhelming success, with movie theaters stopping films to play the program so that people could listen to it. *The Lone Ranger* (1933–1954), which was on the air for twenty-one years, was another noteworthy example. Likewise, *The Jack Benny Program* (1932–1955) enjoyed a twenty-three-year run. As programmers realized that to achieve immediate success national shows needed national celebrities, ex-vaudevillians such as comedians Jack Benny and Fred Allen, family act the Marx Brothers, and comedy duo George Burns and Gracie Allen were natural broadcast stars.

The domestic sphere exercised a profound influence on radio programming with the rise of the soap opera in the 1930s. Programs such as *Clara, Lu, and Em*; *Painted Dreams*; and *Today's Children* catered to female listeners, and the shows proved to be a lucrative market for sponsors wishing to court female consumers. By 1941 women's serials dominated the radio between 10:00 a.m. and 6:00 p.m.

Radio provided a medium for playing out America's race dynamics. The famous Joe Louis and Max Schmeling fights exemplified the racial tensions that existed at the time. Over 70 million listeners tuned in to hear the second bout in 1938 when the African American Louis knocked out Schmeling in the first round. Although African Americans were portrayed in the *Amos 'n' Andy* program, it was not until 1948 that scripts tailored to African American radio audiences began to be written. In 1979 Jesse B. Blayton purchased and started the first black-owned radio station, WERD in Atlanta. Initially, the segregated airwaves mimicked the cultural practices in the United States, but black radio served as a guiding voice during the civil rights movement, eventually helping to desegregate the medium.

Conversely, in the early 1930s, entertainment's brightest lights—Hollywood movie stars—were reluctant to appear on radio. Most studios, and many stars, believed that appearing on radio would lessen actors' cinematic appeal. Nevertheless, radio loved the movies, and most stations ran movie reviews. Syndicated radio gossip columnists such as Louella Parsons and Walter Winchell often focused on Hollywood figures. Studios eventually realized that radio exposure for stars meant increased box office revenues.

By the early 1940s Hollywood actors, including Humphrey Bogart, Katharine Hepburn, Jimmy Stewart, James Cagney, and Clark Gable, routinely participated in radio reenactments of their films. A number of actors who got their start in radio, such as Don Ameche, Richard Widmark, Agnes Moorehead, and Art Carney, also appeared in films. When the stars of radio appeared on the big screen and their fans finally got a visual image to accompany the voice, the fascination with the celebrity world increased greatly. As TV became more popular, actors and actresses found radio to be a convenient way to prolong their careers as well as serve as a spring board into television.

Perhaps the most vivid example of radio's cultural influence is actor and director Orson Welles's October 30, 1938, adaptation of author H. G. Wells's *The War of the Worlds*. The real-time broadcast of a Martian invasion, though intended purely as dramatic fiction, convinced many listeners that Earth was indeed under attack. Although the show ran an opening explanation, many who tuned in late were panicked to hear the words, "Ladies and gentlemen, we interrupt our program of dance music to bring you a special bulletin from the Intercontinental Radio News."

WORLD WAR II

As radio entertainment became more diversified during the 1930s, news also was transformed. A new type of reporter, the broadcast journalist, emerged. Previously, newscasters had simply read the news. Broadcast journalists instead gave live coverage of developing stories and often gave on-air appraisals of news stories as they happened. Live broadcasts of social and political events played an important role in shaping Americans' sense of national unity as the country entered World War II. Unlike during World War I, the public was keenly aware of the buildup to the conflict.

As the popularity of radio grew, political leaders realized its importance as a means of disseminating their ideology. European dictators Benito Mussolini and Adolf Hitler routinely gave live broadcasts of their impassioned speeches. Perhaps the most fervent ideologue on U.S. radio in the late 1930s was Father Charles E. Coughlin, the radio priest of Royal Oak, Michigan, who commanded an audience of millions with tirades that became increasingly anti-Semitic and pro-Franco.

Perhaps no U.S. leader used radio as effectively as President Franklin Delano Roosevelt. Beginning in 1933 until his death in 1945, he delivered his message to Americans through a series of live radio speeches. He called some of them fireside chats because of their personal quality. Each began with the phrase "My dear friends" and contained a careful explanation of his policies and programs. Radio helped cement in the minds of Americans Rooseveltian phrases such as "the only thing we have to fear is fear itself" (from his inauguration) and "a date which will live infamy" (from his speech to Congress after the bombing of Pearl Harbor).

Perhaps the most memorable broadcasts of the war were broadcaster Edward R. Murrow's reports during the London blitz of 1940, which helped to solidify U.S. public opinion on behalf of the Allies. As the war proceeded, and despite strict censorship restrictions, other broadcast journalists reported from military hot spots. The U.S. government took advantage of the medium's immediacy, using radio to communicate with the nation.

THE RISE OF FM

Although radio continued to enjoy tremendous popularity in the early 1950s, it never regained the significance it had during the war. Producers scrambled to institute peacetime programming that could match the heady wartime broadcasts. Traditional formats began to lose popularity, but radio was slow to change. The Cold War atmosphere of fear limited media experimentation as producers became afraid of being labeled as subversive or communist.

Concurrently, television was gaining a firm hold in American homes. Many of the shows long broadcast on the radio transitioned to television. By 1960 radio's golden age had ended, though the medium remained an important cultural influence. The rise of FM radio stations in the 1960s propelled rock and roll to a popularity unequaled by any other musical genre. FM stations had better sound quality than AM stations and came in stereo. Disc jockeys took advantage of their newfound freedom to experiment with the FM dial as free-form radio. Whereas radio news had chronicled the cultural events of the 1930s, 1940s, and 1950s, rock-and-roll radio became the soundtrack for the cultural revolution of the 1960s and early 1970s.

Stations began to create round-the-clock programming for specific musical formats, such as rock and roll, Top 40, classical, rhythm and blues, or jazz. In the 1990s talk radio enjoyed a resurgence, especially on the AM dial, with figures as diverse as conservative host Rush Limbaugh, advice columnist Dr. Laura Schlessinger, and shock jock Howard Stern.

DIGITAL RADIO

By the late 1990s broadcasters had begun digitizing their content to broadcast to almost anywhere in the world. With the advent of the Internet, anyone with a computer and a microphone could be a broadcaster. By the first decade of the 2000s most major radio stations offered simultaneous Internet streams of their programming. Users created thousands of new, low-budget radio stations using Internet radio services such as Live365, Rhapsody, Pandora, and Last.FM. Listeners could tune in, or stream, Internet stations by using an assortment of web-enabled devices, such as smartphones and digital music players.

Digital radio effectively removed one of the medium's biggest hindrances—small broadcast ranges. Satellite radio services, such as Sirius and XM, which transmit the same stations to all of their subscribers, greatly increased the number of options for die-hard radio enthusiasts. In exchange for a subscription fee and for purchasing a satellite-enabled receiver, satellite services offer listeners commercial-free and uncensored content. Stern, for example, made a high-profile move to Sirius in 2006, citing increased censorship and frequent, hefty fines from the Federal Communications Commission. Other multimedia superstars have followed suit, including musician Bob Dylan, talk show host Oprah Winfrey, homemaking guru Martha Stewart, and actress Rosie O'Donnell. In 2008 Sirius and XM merged, and by 2011 the new company boasted more than twenty-one million subscribers.

Although radio's golden age lasted only forty years, its legacy continues to permeate the digital age. From pioneering the first advertising spots to making news and entertainment immediately accessible, radio laid the groundwork for the development of mass media. Its unique contributions to American culture include uniting the country and inspiring the national imagination in a way no medium has done before or since.

Robert C. Sickels

SEE ALSO: *Advertising; Advice Columns; Benny, Jack; Big Bands; Bogart, Humphrey; Burns, George, and Gracie Allen; Cagney, James; Cold War; Communism; Consumerism; Coughlin, Father Charles E.; Daytime Talk Shows; Disc Jockeys; Dylan, Bob; Gable, Clark; Gossip Columns; The Great Depression; Hepburn, Katharine; The Internet; Jazz; Limbaugh, Rush; The Lone Ranger; The Marx Brothers; Movie Stars; Murrow, Edward R.; O'Donnell, Rosie; Radio Drama; Rhythm and Blues; Rock and Roll; Satellite Radio; Schlessinger, Dr. Laura; Scopes Monkey Trial; Shock Radio; Smartphones; Soap Operas; Stern, Howard; Stewart, Jimmy; Stewart, Martha; Talk Radio; Television; Top 40; Vaudeville;* War of the Worlds; *Welles, Orson; The Western; Winchell, Walter; Winfrey, Oprah; World Series; World War I; World War II.*

BIBLIOGRAPHY

Bray, John. *The Communications Miracle: The Telecommunication Pioneers from Morse to the Information Superhighway.* New York: Plenum Press, 1995.

Hilmes, Michele. *Radio Voices: American Broadcasting, 1922–1952.* Minneapolis: University of Minnesota Press, 1997.

Hilmes, Michele, and Jason Loviglio, eds. *Radio Reader: Essays in the Cultural History of Radio.* New York: Routledge, 2002.

Keith, Michael C. *The Radio Station: Broadcast, Satellite and Internet*, 8th ed. Oxford, UK: Focal Press, 2010.

Ladd, Jim. *Radio Waves: Life and Revolution on the FM Dial.* New York: St. Martin's Press, 1991.

MacDonald, Fred J. *Don't Touch That Dial!: Radio Programming in American Life, 1920–1960.* Chicago: Nelson-Hall, 1979.

Maltin, Leonard. *The Great American Broadcast: A Celebration of Radio's Golden Age.* New York: Dutton, 1997.

Nachman, Gerald. *Raised on Radio.* New York: Pantheon Books, 1998.

Regal, Brian. *Radio: The Life Story of a Technology.* Westport, CT: Greenwood Press, 2005.

Ryan, Thomas. *American Hit Radio: A History of Popular Singles from 1955 to the Present.* Rocklin, CA: Prima Publishing, 1996.

Smulyan, Susan. *Selling Radio: The Commercialization of American Broadcasting, 1920–1934.* Washington, DC: Smithsonian Institution Press, 1994.

Urban, George R. *Radio Free Europe and the Pursuit of Democracy: My War within the Cold War.* New Haven, CT: Yale University Press, 1997.

Radio Drama

Before the advent of television in the late 1940s, radio was the most popular mass medium in America. During a golden age that lasted from 1929 through World War II, radio's comedy-variety, soap opera, and drama programs were a part of the daily lives of most Americans. Unlike movies, radio brought mass entertainment directly into the home, and stars such as Jack Benny, Gracie Allen, and Orson Welles became familiar presences within the family's private space.

For the first time, listeners across the country planned their schedules around programs and personalities; for example, movie theaters were forced to pipe in the popular *Amos 'n' Andy* program in 1929 because so many people did not want to leave their homes and miss hearing it. Radio programs functioned as tools of assimilation for many people, defining "American" identities through voices. Radio nationalized ethnic, class, and regional accents, creating recognizable blueprints for how *black, Irish, rich,* and *rural* were supposed to sound. As radio historian Michele Hilmes writes in *Radio Voices: American Broadcasting, 1922–1952,* "In speaking to us as a nation during a crucial period of time [radio] helped to shape our cultural consciousness and define us as a people."

APPEALING TO THE MASSES

Radio drama emerged in the late 1920s with the formation of national networks and the subsequent commercialization of the industry. In the Radio Act of 1927, the U.S. government endorsed commercial over government ownership of radio by favoring the networks in allocating wavelengths. Because national networks provided advertisers with the opportunity to sell their products to a large audience, the government's decision ensured the dominance of mass culture over high culture and educational programming on radio.

In order to appeal to this mass audience (especially to women, whom they recognized as the primary consumers within the household), advertisers relied on personalities and programs that seemed to have popular appeal. Throughout the 1920s music and talk radio had been radio's primary fare, but in 1929 NBC began daily broadcasts of a minstrel act that had become quite popular in the Midwest, *Amos 'n' Andy.* It was the network's first attempt at a fictional serial program, and radio was never the same. The tremendous popularity of *Amos 'n' Andy* convinced advertisers that audiences wanted more narrative programs, and *radio drama,* the common inclusive term for radio fiction programs, began to take up more and more network time.

The evolution of radio drama is rooted in the tension between the advertisers and the networks. To make the most

Radio Drama Players. *Actors rehearse a radio drama in a studio in 1925.* © SCHENECTADY MUSEUM; HALL OF ELECTRICAL HISTORY FOUNDATION/CORBIS.

money and attract the broadest audience, programs had to appeal to the masses without alienating the middle-class family audience. Thus, advertisers took a new "lowbrow" approach to advertising, developing programs that emphasized the most pleasurable and stimulating aspects of popular culture, such as "gag" humor and "shocking" stories. At the time, mass culture was associated primarily with the working class and the street culture of recent immigrants. Moviemakers and vaudeville entrepreneurs had worked hard to attract a middle-class family audience by toning down their bawdier aspects, but the dominance of mass culture on radio was still a cause for concern among the middle class.

It was the responsibility of the networks to maintain cultural standards in order to keep their licenses; they had to avoid public attacks from the morality-minded who worried about the effects of low-culture programming on society. To avoid criticism—and hence, maintain their monopoly (and their profits)—networks developed two different kinds of radio drama: popular drama, produced by advertisers, and commercial-free "prestige" drama, produced and sustained by the networks to appease their critics. Although these two forms developed separately, they had each begun to take on aspects of one another by the end of the 1930s, blurring the line between popular and high culture.

POPULAR DRAMA

Popular radio drama drew on a variety of mass-culture forms, including pulp fiction, comic strips, and vaudeville. Pulp fiction anthologies of short stories had become immensely popular in the United States from the 1890s to the 1920s with the development of cheap printing techniques and national distribution systems. The "pulps" were usually first printed in magazines, and they offered audiences the predictable satisfactions of standard genres: romance, Western, crime, detective mystery, and horror. Pulp fiction had been the major source of advertising before radio; with the advent of radio drama, advertisers were able to simply shift their sponsorships to a different medium.

Pulp fiction genres became well known on radio: programs such as *The Shadow*, *Gangbusters*, and *Gunsmoke* were developed from mystery, crime, and Western pulp fiction, respectively. Romance genres aimed primarily at women were soon segregated into daytime and became popularly known as soap operas because soap companies sponsored them. Comic strips were also popular sources for radio programs, particularly children's serials such as *Little Orphan Annie*. When radio took over these forms, it made them more dramatic. The crime-fighting Shadow, for example, became much more a man of action than he had been in print form, and the constant sound of riot guns in the "real-life" crime show *Gangbusters* produced complaints from parents who charged that the guns frightened their children.

Certainly the most successful of radio's popular programs were comedy-variety shows. In the early 1930s, as the Great Depression put more and more vaudeville theaters out of business, vaudeville players made increasing use of radio and became the medium's biggest stars. These programs combined vaudeville "gag" humor with nightclub performance, linking the different sections together through one central personality and continuing, familiar stock characters. *The Jack Benny Show* was the most popular of such programs, running from 1932 until 1955; Benny starred as the miserly, childish, vain star of a radio program called *The Jack Benny Show*. Like other popular comedy-variety programs, such as *The Edgar Bergen and Charlie McCarthy Show* and *The Bob Hope Show*, *The Jack Benny Show* relied on ethnic and gender stereotypes widely used in vaudeville. In some ways, however, radio programs differed from vaudeville. Whereas vaudeville shows were much more fragmented and often adapted to local tastes, radio comedy-variety offered audiences a more predictable narrative structure and consistent characters in order to foster familiarity between the players and listeners. Programs that attempted to be more spontaneous or have a more satirical edge either failed to attract a significant audience or, such as comedian Fred Allen's show, were streamlined to fit the Benny formula.

PRESTIGE DRAMA

While popular drama garnered much higher ratings than prestige drama, the latter had a significant impact on the evolution of radio drama because of its technical and artistic innovations. Because prestige drama did not have the constraints of commercial sponsorship, its producers could experiment with sound effects, acting styles, language, and traditional narrative structure. Programs such as the *Radio Guild* adapted classical plays for radio audiences, while *The Columbia Workshop* produced original scripts created for radio by some of the country's best-known writers, including Archibald MacLeish, William Saroyan, and Dorothy Parker.

The most famous name associated with radio prestige drama is Orson Welles, whose 1938 adaptation of H. G. Wells's *The War of the Worlds* caused a nationwide panic. Welles's *Mercury Theatre of the Air* program featured radio's first repertory theater, and Welles was the first prestige drama auteur, serving as writer, director, and leading player in most of the program's productions. He was also known for his imaginative use of the medium; *The War of the Worlds* was so convincing in part because Welles borrowed techniques from radio news programs, giving his program the semblance of a news broadcast. Throughout the 1930s and 1940s, he continued to do radio work in both sustaining and sponsored programs, but his name was always linked to "high culture," although he often used material from more popular sources. For every dramatization of *A Tale of Two Cities*, Welles offered a *Dracula* or a *Sherlock Holmes*.

Two other famous names associated with prestige drama are writer-directors Norman Corwin and Arch Oboler. Corwin, who worked for CBS, pushed the boundaries of the radio drama form, developing new genres such as radio opera (musical-documentary-dramas) and adapting poetic works such as Walt Whitman's *Leaves of Grass* and Edgar Lee Masters's *Spoon River Anthology* for radio. Oboler, who worked for NBC, focused on realist drama and psychological horror. He is best known for his *Arch Oboler's Plays* series and his original scripts for the horror series *Lights Out*. Oboler's work often explored the supernatural, taking his listeners into settings where they could not ordinarily go; his characters were haunted by ghosts, buried alive, or made bargains with the devil. Whereas Corwin's work focused on language, Oboler's exploited radio's potential to unnerve. The war interrupted Oboler's and Corwin's experiments, and like other radio writers, they turned their attention to patriotic themes. While prestige dramas were never again given the airtime they enjoyed in the late 1930s, the influence of these dramatists became more obvious in commercial drama during and after the war.

SUSPENSE

One of the most popular radio genres of the 1940s was suspense. Programs such as *Suspense*, *Inner Sanctum*, and *Mystery in the Air* were very much products of the radio drama that proceeded them. Unlike most radio genres that originated in pulp fiction, suspense programs shared with prestige dramas a reliance on scripts produced originally for radio. They also used several of the techniques of prestige radio programs, including first-person narration and interior monologue, psychological complexity, dreams and fantasy, and a preoccupation with the supernatural. Like Oboler's plays, they foregrounded psychological horror, but their context in an uncertain postwar America meant that certain subjects, such as wartime traumas and sexual tension, came to the fore.

The most famous radio play is the *Suspense* offering "Sorry, Wrong Number" (1943), written by Lucille Fletcher and starring Agnes Moorehead. The play focuses on an invalid wife who overhears a murder plot on the phone and does not realize until the last few moments that she is the intended victim. The success of this program influenced radio dramas throughout the 1940s; plots continued to emphasize mistrust between the sexes and feature bizarre, often graphic violence.

THE IMPACT OF TECHNOLOGY

As television came to dominate the postwar era in the late 1940s and early 1950s, radio drama faded in significance and popularity. Furthermore, the rise of the disc jockey in the 1950s ensured the resurgence of popular music as the medium's dominant entertainment. Radio drama's lasting influence is most obvious in the content and structure of television programming, which lifted its stars and genres directly from radio fiction. However, commercialized radio was distinct from television in its greater acknowledgment of ethnic and class differences. Although both television and radio served to homogenize U.S. culture, much of radio's mass-culture programming remained rooted in the humor and worldview of the nation's underclass. Television's fiction programs moved away from the culture of the urban masses to appeal primarily to middle-class nuclear families.

In spite of television's dominance, nostalgia for radio drama has never completely gone away, and thanks to technological innovations, the genre—now often called audio drama—is enjoying a slight resurgence. Artists are recording dramatizations once again. In 2010 Sue Zizza, a sound-effects expert who teaches at New York University, estimated that some 300 audio dramatists are active in the United States. Most of the shows they produce will never be broadcast over the radio, but they can be downloaded from the Internet as podcasts. Perhaps this latest wave of technology will manage to rescue the art form that television nearly killed.

Allison McCracken

SEE ALSO: The Amos 'n' Andy Show*; Benny, Jack; Burns, George, and Gracie Allen; Comics; Corwin, Norman; Detective Fiction; Disc Jockeys; The Great Depression;* Gunsmoke*; Hope, Bob;* Inner Sanctum *Mysteries; Little Orphan Annie; Parker, Dorothy; Pulp Magazines; Radio; The Shadow; Soap Operas; Talk Radio; Television; Vaudeville;* War of the Worlds*; Welles, Orson; The Western.*

BIBLIOGRAPHY

Crook, Tim. *Radio Drama*. London: Routledge, 1999.

Hand, Richard J., and Mary Traynor. *The Radio Drama Handbook: Audio Drama in Context and Practice*. New York: Continuum, 2011.

Hilmes, Michele. *Radio Voices: American Broadcasting*. Minneapolis: University of Minnesota Press, 1997.

Lewis, Peter, ed. *Radio Drama*. New York: Longman Group, 1981.

Lipsitz, George. *Time Passages: Collective Memory and American Popular Culture*. Minneapolis: University of Minnesota Press, 1990.

MacDonald, J. Fred. *Don't Touch That Dial!: Radio Programming in American Life, 1920–1960*. Chicago: Nelson-Hall, 1979.

Radiohead

One of the most commercially successful and critically acclaimed bands of the 1990s and early in the first decade of the 2000s, Radiohead initially called itself On a Friday when the band formed in 1985 on the campus of Abingdon School, a prep school for boys in Oxfordshire, United Kingdom. The lineup consisted of brothers Colin and Jonny Greenwood, Ed O'Brien, Phil Selway, and Thom Yorke. On a Friday played intermittently throughout the late 1980s but had difficulty rehearsing and creating new material after 1987, when all of the members save Greenwood graduated from Abingdon and attended university. In 1991 when the four older members had finished college and were again able to meet regularly, the band achieved a greater level of continuity and cohesion. Success soon followed, as On a Friday quickly distinguished itself with a series of tight live shows that drew the attention of producers scouting new talent in the vibrant Thames Valley independent music scene. After signing a six-album deal with EMI, the band changed its name to Radiohead—after the title of track six ("Radio Head") on Talking Heads' *True Stories* album—at the request of the record company.

Radiohead's debut album, *Pablo Honey* (1993), was universally panned in the United Kingdom, and all of its major singles—"Creep," "Anyone Can Play Guitar," and "Stop Whispering"—fell flat with critics and listeners, who dismissed the group as a safe, dull-sounding version of Nirvana. "Creep," however, climbed all the way to number two on U.S. alternative charts and was rereleased in the United Kingdom in 1993 to widespread critical and popular acclaim. In keeping with the trends of the time, "Creep" was a grungy, swelling rock song with self-deprecating lyrics, the most famous of which went "I wish I was special / But I'm a creep." Fueled by a hit single getting regular airplay, sales of *Pablo Honey* suddenly skyrocketed, and the tour promoting the album unexpectedly stretched into a second year.

With the release of the follow-up album *The Bends* (1995), front man Yorke emerged as a cryptic, disenchanted leader whose caustic lyrics and terse, distorted sound pushed the band away from convention. On "My Iron Lung," the first single, Yorke sang, "This is our new song / Just like the last one / A total waste of time / My iron lung." After a slow start *The Bends* found favor with critics and fans alike and was eventually ranked at 110 on *Rolling Stone*'s list of the greatest albums of all time. Unlike its predecessors, *OK Computer* (1997) was an immediate success, debuting at number one in the United Kingdom and featuring the singles "Karma Police" and "Paranoid Android," which were an instant hit with fans.

The band's next album, *Kid A* (2000), dispensed with many of the conventions of contemporary popular rock music, including the verse-chorus-verse formula and traditional guitar-bass-and-drums instrumentation, and it resolutely broke the band out of the Britpop and grunge scenes that it had long been trying to leave behind. *Rolling Stone* named the album the best of the decade for doing nothing less than "rebuilding rock itself." *Amnesiac*, which was released the next year, cemented Radiohead's reputation as a dour and difficult band that was still palatable to the masses. On 2003's *Hail to the Thief*, another commercial success, Radiohead returned to a more guitar-based sound.

In 2007 the band experimented with a new method of distribution, releasing *In Rainbows* independently online and allowing fans to name their own price for it. The first major release to be put out in this way, *In Rainbows* was an important experiment not only for the band but also for many other recording artists, who were looking for a profitable way to promote and distribute material without the help of a major label. While Radiohead's exact system was not widely mimicked, its example suggested a model for survival in the face of plummeting CD sales due to online file sharing. Though the album's release was novel, the music itself was conventional, representing a step back toward "pop melodies and proper instruments," as the British music magazine *NME* put it. For its eighth album, 2011's *The King of Limbs*, Radiohead dropped its pay-what-you-want model and instead released the album in various formats for various fixed prices. The album received many positive reviews and sold well, but it failed to meet critics' and fans' lofty expectations.

Ted McDermott

SEE ALSO: *Alternative Rock; Compact Discs; File Sharing; Grunge; MP3; Napster; Nirvana; Rock and Roll; Talking Heads.*

BIBLIOGRAPHY

Footman, Tim. *Radiohead: Welcome to the Machine: "OK Computer" and the Death of the Classic Rock Album.* Surrey, UK: Chrome Dreams, 2007.

Kot, Greg. Review of *OK Computer. Chicago Tribune*, July 4, 1997.

Ross, Alex. "The Searchers: Radiohead's Unquiet Revolution." *New Yorker*, August 20, 2001.

Radner, Gilda *(1946–1989)*

Gilda Radner, with her mass of seemingly untamable curly hair and striking ability to use her voice for comic effect, will be best remembered as one of the original "Not Ready for Prime Time Players" who starred in *Saturday Night Live* (1975–), a television series that became a hit with young adults despite its late time slot. She stayed with the series for five years, during which time she parodied many celebrities (most memorably, Barbara Walters) and created several of her own characters, such as news commentators Roseanne Roseannadanna and Emily Litella. Radner married actor Gene Wilder in 1984. She died of ovarian cancer in 1989. After her death, Wilder became active in raising cancer awareness.

Denise Lowe

SEE ALSO: *Cancer;* Saturday Night Live*; Walters, Barbara.*

BIBLIOGRAPHY

Cader, Michael, ed. Saturday Night Live: *The First Twenty Years.* Boston: Houghton Mifflin, 1994.

Zweibel, Alan. *Bunny, Bunny: Gilda Radner, a Sort of Romantic Comedy.* New York: Applause Books, 1997.

Rado, James

SEE: *Ragni, Gerome, and James Rado.*

Raft, George *(1895–1980)*

Screen actor George Raft's greatest and most lasting contribution to the film industry was in creating the cliché image of the caring and compassionate gangster who was more victim than victimizer. He may be more famous, however, for turning down star-making roles that all went to Humphrey Bogart than for any of the parts he did play. Raft was offered the leads in *High Sierra*, *The Maltese Falcon*, and *Casablanca;* he turned down each one only to be quickly eclipsed by Bogart, who until then had been struggling to make a name for himself in Hollywood.

Raft's acting career was based on the premise that as a former gangster himself (he was friends with racketeer Owney Madden and at one time aspired to be a big shot in Madden's liquor mob), he would excel at playing one. He preferred playing outwardly tough, brutal men who were revealed to be not as cold and heartless as they pretended to be. He was very concerned with how crime was portrayed on-screen and would insist on stipulations in his contract about how his character could treat women and children, how knowledgeable about the crime scene his character was, and what his idea of crime was—Raft refused to play an out-and-out rat.

Raft was born in New York City in 1895 and brought up in the Hell's Kitchen area. As a young man, he boxed and became a dancer and dance hall gigolo (dance partner for pay). He then began to get parts in stage shows such as *City Chap*, *Gay Paree*, *Palm Beach Nights*, and *No Foolin'*. Heading to Los Angeles, Raft was discovered at the Brown Derby restaurant by director Rowland Brown, who gave him a bit part in *Quick Millions*. His most notable parts were in *Taxi!* (1932); *Scarface* (1932), as the coin-flipping best friend of Tony Camonte, the main character; *Each Dawn I Die* (1939), as an idealistic gang leader who learns honesty from a fellow inmate played by James Cagney; and *Dancers in the Dark* (1932), as a murderer.

Thinking they had found another romantic leading man like Rudolph Valentino, Paramount signed Raft to a contract and starred him in lackluster features, then suspended him after he refused to appear in *The Story of Temple Drake* (1933), a film about a ruthless bootlegger who turns a sultry southern belle into his sex slave. While he had a few tough-guy parts, he did his best work at Paramount as a dancer starring with Carole

Lombard in *Bolero* (1934) and *Rumba* (1935). Raft also objected to his role in *Souls at Sea* (1937) and went on suspension until his part was more sympathetically written. The gambit paid off, and he earned an Oscar nomination for his work as a likable, romantic tough guy with a sinister slave-trading past who spends most of his time romancing Olympe Bradna's character. Throughout the story, his character is encouraged to be good by his idealistic buddy, played by Gary Cooper, resulting in his character's eventual redemption.

By the end of the 1930s, Paramount let Raft go, and Warner Brothers made a bid for his services, teaming him with Cagney and Bogart in such pictures as *Each Dawn I Die* and *They Drive by Night* (1940). Raft refused to appear in *South of Suez* (1940), and, as Bogart's star had now risen brightly, the studio was quite willing to let Raft go. From there, he drifted from one minor part to another, appearing mostly in forgettable "B" movies from United Artists or RKO. He finally got a couple of good parts in *Black Widow* (1954) and *Rogue Cop* (1954), but they did not get enough exposure to reestablish him as a star. He appeared in the television series *I'm the Law* in 1953 and took a cameo role in *Around the World in 80 Days* (1956).

Nevertheless, director Billy Wilder remembered Raft and cast him as gangster "Spats" Baxter in the comedy classic *Some Like It Hot* (1959) with Marilyn Monroe, Tony Curtis, and Jack Lemmon. He made another cameo appearance in *Ocean's Eleven* (1960), the first Rat Pack film, and was given parts in Jerry Lewis's *Ladies' Man* (1961) and *The Patsy* (1964). In 1965 Raft was indicted for income tax evasion and could have spent the rest of his life behind bars, but the court proved merciful and the case did not go to trial. From there Raft traveled to Europe and made a few disastrous comedies, from a high in *Casino Royale* (1967) to a low in Otto Preminger's *Skidoo* (1968). Unable to get work, he spent his declining years watching television until his death in 1980.

Dennis Fischer

SEE ALSO: *"B" Movies; Bogart, Humphrey; Cagney, James;* Casablanca*; Cooper, Gary; Hollywood; James Bond Films; Lewis, Jerry;* The Maltese Falcon*; Monroe, Marilyn; Preminger, Otto;* Some Like It Hot*; United Artists; Valentino, Rudolph; Wilder, Billy.*

BIBLIOGRAPHY

Neibaur, James L. *Tough Guy: The American Movie Macho.* Jefferson, NC: McFarland, 1989.

Shipman, David. *The Great Movie Stars: The Golden Years.* New York: Bonanza Books, 1970.

Thompson, David. *A Biographical Dictionary of Film*, 3rd ed. New York: Knopf, 1994.

Wallace, Stone. *George Raft.* Albany, GA: BearManor Media, 2008.

Yablonsky, Lewis. *George Raft.* New York: McGraw-Hill, 1974.

Raggedy Ann and Raggedy Andy

Raggedy Ann is the central character in a series of children's books about dolls that come alive when their owners are away. She made her official debut in 1918 in *Raggedy Ann Stories* by author and illustrator Johnny Gruelle. Based on a rag doll that the author's daughter carried around, Raggedy Ann dolls were mass produced to accompany the nearly 1,000 stories Gruelle wrote before his death in 1938.

Raggedy Andy, Raggedy Ann's rag-doll brother, was introduced in 1920 in *The Raggedy Andy Stories.* Raggedy Ann's image, with her black shoe-button eyes, red yarn hair, white pinafore, and scalloped pantaloons over red-and-white-striped legs, has remained surprisingly intact over the years and has been featured in an array of children's toys, clothing, furnishings, and other products. Although Gruelle produced a series of forty books about Raggedy Ann and she appeared in cartoons, the dolls remain the most popular Raggedy Ann collectibles.

John Barton Gruelle, the son of a painter, was born in 1880. He grew up in Indianapolis, Indiana, and later illustrated stories and drew cartoons for several newspapers. In 1910 he won first prize in a comic drawing contest sponsored by the *New York Herald* with a story about an elf named Mr. Twee Deedle. The full-color cartoon was syndicated as a full-page feature. Gruelle also wrote and illustrated children's stories for popular magazines, and in 1914 he received his first book commission, a set of illustrations for a volume of Grimm's fairy tales.

The idea for Raggedy Ann came from Gruelle's daughter, Marcella, who was devoted to an old rag doll that had belonged to Gruelle's mother. Resurrected from the attic and given a new face and name, the first Raggedy Ann doll was Marcella's companion throughout an illness that ended in her death in 1916. The initial adventures of Raggedy Ann were stories Gruelle told to amuse and distract his bedridden daughter.

In 1915 Gruelle applied for a patent on Raggedy Ann. He made a dozen prototype dolls, although accounts differ as to whether the idea for Raggedy Ann's manufacture came from Gruelle or the P. F. Volland Company of Chicago, with whom he had a book contract. The dolls and stories were produced simultaneously and became instantly successful.

In the time-honored tradition of little brothers, Raggedy Andy came along two years later, though he never acquired the central status of his sister, remaining a secondary character. Nevertheless, Raggedy Ann's popularity is attributable, in part, to him and the cast of other characters—the Scotsman Uncle Clem, Beloved Belindy, Percy the Policeman—who were kept at the forefront of consumer consciousness by a plethora of books (Gruelle wrote a sequel, or two, every year). Unlike high-priced porcelain dolls with exclusive wardrobes, Raggedy Ann and her coterie had a homespun quality that was deliberately preserved in their manufacture. The dolls could even be made at home, beginning in the 1940s when McCall's Pattern Company marketed an authorized pattern to reproduce Raggedy Ann and Andy.

While never enjoying great critical acclaim, the Raggedy Ann book series greatly appealed to its young audience through Gruelle's soft line drawings and full-page, color illustrations. Gruelle used his talents as a cartoonist to imbue the dolls, whose faces never changed, with a full range of expression and attitudes. The narratives—romping adventures usually involving peril and a cheerful resolution, out of sight of the "real-for-sure folks"—are set in an innocent and somewhat dated world. Nevertheless, Gruelle had insight into the way children think. He used repetition and naming devices consistent with children's language patterns and filled his stories with tiny creatures, delicious foods, and fun games. Through his stories, he created an internally consistent, vicarious world.

No discussion of Raggedy Ann would be complete without revealing her secret: She wears the words "I Love You" stamped over her heart. According to Gruelle's stories, she fell into a bucket of paint one day and the person who restuffed her sewed a candy heart with the motto "I Love You" onto her chest. A household presence for the greater part of the twentieth century, Raggedy Ann was a classic American character produced with Gruelle's gifts as an author and illustrator.

Karen Hovde

SEE ALSO: McCall's Magazine*; Toys.*

BIBLIOGRAPHY

Gruelle, Johnny. *Raggedy Ann & Andy: A Read-Aloud Treasury.* New York: Little Simon, 2005.

Hall, Patricia. *Johnny Gruelle, Creator of Raggedy Ann and Andy.* Gretna, LA: Pelican, 1993.

Williams, Martin. "Some Remarks on Raggedy Ann and Johnny Gruelle." *Children's Literature* 3 (1974): 140–146.

Raging Bull

When *Raging Bull,* Martin Scorsese's biopic of 1940s-era middleweight boxing champion Jake LaMotta, premiered in November 1980, critics and audiences alike hailed it as a masterpiece. The film's expressionistic black-and-white photography, its lyrical realism, and Robert De Niro's stunning performance as LaMotta give it an expressive power of great magnitude. The amazing physical transformation De Niro underwent—adding an estimated 60 pounds of fat to his slender frame to portray the older, bloated LaMotta—also make it the most extreme example of method acting in filmmaking. De Niro garnered the Oscar for Best Actor, and Thelma Schoonmaker won for Best Film Editing. However, some critics, most notably Pauline Kael of the *New Yorker* magazine, were uncomfortable with the film, wondering if LaMotta—a violent, troubled, wife-abusing lout—was worthy of the spiritual transformation Scorsese attributed to him.

Scorsese undertook the film at a time of crisis in his career. His previous feature, *New York, New York* (1977), had been a critical and commercial bomb. Scorsese was so demoralized by its failure that he embarked on a debauch of epic length, resulting in his 1978 hospitalization. While visiting Scorsese in the hospital, De Niro—who had been lobbying to adapt LaMotta's memoir, *Raging Bull: My Story* (1970), for over four years—once again broached the subject with his friend and collaborator.

The picture Scorsese envisioned would be a meditation on the Catholic themes that had inspired his best work of the 1970s: redemption, alienation, morality, and guilt. It would be at once a wholly personal work and a revision of the 1940s-era movies he had loved as a child. It is the tension generated between the formal aspects of the picture—the stylized black-and-white photography, at times documentary-like in execution—and the subject matter that gives *Raging Bull* its almost hallucinatory ferocity. "What De Niro does in this picture isn't acting, exactly," wrote Kael, who, for the most part, took a pejorative view of the film's excesses. "Though it may at some level be awesome, it definitely isn't pleasurable." She is right. In fact, De Niro's portrayal is so harrowing that every moment he is on-screen is excruciatingly tense.

THE STORY

De Niro's LaMotta is violent, self-centered, and egotistical, a man possessed by uncontrollable paranoia. And like his sobriquet, "The Bronx Bull," LaMotta is bullish. However, as the film begins in medias res, the audience never learns the reasons for LaMotta's obstinate behavior, only that it is his fatal flaw, the chink in his armor. Because of his intransigence in dealing with a local mob boss, he is unable to gain a shot at the title for several years. Only after acquiescing to mob demands to throw a fight does he get his chance at the championship. In his final boxing match—against his old nemesis, Sugar Ray Robinson—LaMotta is virtually crucified on the ropes, taking a brutal beating while refusing to go down. With his face reduced to a bleeding pulp, he taunts the victor, chanting in an almost infantile manner, "You never got me down, Ray."

Retired in Florida, LaMotta has become an obese parody of himself, presiding over a Miami nightclub where he introduces the acts with a crass version of suave nightclub patter. Indeed, things fall apart: his long-suffering wife leaves him, and he is

Raging Bull. *Robert De Niro played the self-destructive boxer Jake LaMotta in* Raging Bull. ARTISTS/THE KOBAL COLLECTION.

eventually arrested on a morals charge. In a pivotal scene, he retrieves his championship belt, attacking it with a hammer to dislodge the gems he needs for bail money, mindlessly deforming the belt as he has destroyed his life. Finally, locked in solitary confinement, LaMotta reaches a spiritual crisis, attacking his confinement, banging his head against the wall, kicking and punching it in anger and frustration, his body half in shadow and half in light. "Why, you're so stupid, an animal," he screams. Finally he collapses, sobbing, "I wasn't that bad." As he cries, a piece of his sleeve catches a beam of light in the darkened cell. It is one of Scorsese's most transcendent moments, perfectly blending religious metaphor with film language.

The film closes as it begins, with LaMotta, now a nightclub entertainer, practicing Marlon Brando's "I coulda been a contender" speech from *On the Waterfront* in front of his dressing-room mirror. He has achieved a measure of peace. Something is now apparent that was not clear in the first scene, when LaMotta appeared a figure of ridicule, butchering William Shakespeare with his ludicrous Bronx accent: looking at his face in the mirror, he says, "Let's face it, it was you, it was you."

UNIVERSAL THEMES

Scorsese told an interviewer at the time of *Raging Bull*'s release that "those who think it's a boxing picture would be out of their minds. It's brutal, sure, but it is a brutality that could take place not only in the boxing ring, but in the bedroom or in an office." Because the film speaks on the level of the universal craving for redemption, its brilliance affects one in a visceral way. As a child, Scorsese had been "taught to hate the sin, but love the sinner." Perhaps no other film so complexly embodies this basic philosophy.

Raging Bull is the culmination of one of several cycles in Scorsese's work—it is preoccupied with, in the words of Paul Schrader, "the sense of guilt, redemption by blood, and moral purpose." For Scorsese, filming it seemed to have a salutary effect, resolving the moral conflicts that permeate *Mean Streets* (1973) and *Taxi Driver* (1976). Despite some critics' initial discomfort with *Raging Bull*, it is now considered a classic and is listed in the National Film Registry. Rumors of a sequel have circulated since 2006, but Scorsese has vowed not be involved in such a project, saying that he already has explored this territory.

Michael J. Baers

SEE ALSO: *Boxing; De Niro, Robert; LaMotta, Jake;* Mean Streets; *Robinson, Sugar Ray; Scorsese, Martin;* Taxi Driver.

BIBLIOGRAPHY

Connelly, Marie Katheryn. *Martin Scorsese: An Analysis of His Feature Films, with a Filmography of His Entire Directorial Career.* Jefferson, NC: McFarland, 1993.

Dougan, Andy. *Martin Scorsese Close Up: The Making of His Movies.* London: Orion, 1997.

Ehrenstein, David. *The Scorsese Picture: The Art and Life of Martin Scorsese.* New York: Carol Publishing Group, 1992.

Evans, Mike. *The Making of "Raging Bull."* London: Unanimous, 2006.

Ferrante, Leonard. *Redemption in the Narrative Films of Martin Scorsese.* Ann Arbor, MI: UMI Dissertation Services, 1994.

Hayes, Kevin. *Martin Scorsese's "Raging Bull."* New York: Cambridge University Press, 2005.

Kael, Pauline. *New Yorker*, December 1980.

Kellman, Steven, ed. *Perspectives on Raging Bull.* New York: G. K. Hall, 1994.

Kelly, Mary Pat. *Martin Scorsese: A Journey.* New York: Thunder's Mouth Press, 1991.

Keyser, Lester J., ed. *Twayne's Filmmakers Series: Martin Scorsese.* New York: Twayne, 1992.

Thompson, David, and Ian Christie, eds. *Scorsese on Scorsese.* London: Faber and Faber, 1989.

Weiss, Marion. *Martin Scorsese: A Guide to References and Resources.* Boston: G. K. Hall, 1987.

Ragni, Gerome, and James Rado

The collaborative theatrical team of Gerome Ragni (1935–1991) and James Rado (1932–) created *Hair* (1968), the first rock musical on Broadway. *Hair* was a milestone for musical theater as an art form: experimental in nature, controversial in its subject matter and presentation. It was the first Broadway show to display totally nude performers and to have a truly racially integrated cast. Supported by composer Galt MacDermot's rock music score, *Hair* celebrated the 1960s hippie lifestyle and examined the concerns of America's youth at that time—antiwar beliefs, sexual freedom, drug use, and the search for community. Though the show remained Ragni and Rado's only major success, it was a substantial one. *Hair* became wildly popular—even spawning a film version a decade later (1979) as well as Broadway revivals in 1977, 2004, 2009, and 2011—and became the only show that fully embodied the youthful energy of the 1960s.

Brian Granger

SEE ALSO: *Broadway;* Hair; *Hippies; The Musical; Rock and Roll; Sexual Revolution; Vietnam.*

BIBLIOGRAPHY

Davis, Lorrie, and Rachel Gallagher. *Letting Down My Hair: Two Years with the Love Rock Tribe—From Dawning to Downing of Aquarius.* New York: Arthur Fields Books, 1973.

Grode, Eric. *"Hair": The Story of the Show That Defined a Generation.* Philadelphia: Running Press, 2010.

Horn, Barbara Lee. *The Age of "Hair": Evolution and Impact of Broadway's First Rock Musical.* New York: Greenwood Press, 1991.

Raiders of the Lost Ark

While on vacation in Hawaii in 1977, filmmakers Steven Spielberg and George Lucas came up with a movie idea based on the serials they had loved as children: an adventure set in exotic locales with cliffhangers every second. Recalled Spielberg: "I wondered why they didn't make movies like that anymore. I still wanted to see them." Apparently, so did millions of Americans, as *Raiders of the Lost Ark* (1981), the fruit of the filmmakers' labors, grossed more than $200 million domestically in its first box-office run and reestablished the adventure genre in U.S. film.

With Spielberg as director and Lucas as executive producer, *Raiders of the Lost Ark* follows the adventures of Indiana Jones (played by burgeoning screen icon Harrison Ford), a mild-mannered, bespectacled archaeology professor who leads a double life as a whip-wielding swashbuckler who hunts down ancient treasures and prevents them from falling into the wrong hands, generally those of profit-seekers. Jones's adversaries in this particular episode, set in the 1930s, are Nazis in search of the Ark of the Covenant, allegedly once the storehouse for the Ten Commandments. The Nazis wanted the Ark because they believe possession of such an ancient treasure would serve as a rallying point for nationalistic pride. Jones and his partner, Marion (Karen Allen), venture across the globe in search of the Ark, all the while avoiding the Nazis' best attempts on their lives. The movie climaxes with a fantastic showdown between the two sides over the prized treasure.

With its exotic locations and thrill-a-second story line, *Raiders of the Lost Ark* brought adventure back to American cinema. The "B"-movie adventure story had been out of style since the 1940s, and only in the James Bond films of British cinema could plots be found that were remotely adventure based. In making *Raiders of the Lost Ark*, Spielberg and Lucas attempted to do away with the quintessentially British adventure narrative and restore to the action film the uniquely American flavor of such 1930s and 1940s serials as *Commando Cody* and *Don Winslow of the Coast Guard.*

In addition to being resoundingly popular with audiences, *Raiders of the Lost Ark* was a hit with critics, earning Oscars for film editing, visual effects, sound, and art direction. It also ushered in a new era of American action movies, as the 1980s and 1990s gave rise to a host of adventure serials, not the least of which were the two *Raiders of the Lost Ark* sequels: *Indiana Jones and the Temple of Doom* (1984) and *Indiana Jones and the Last Crusade* (1989), also starring Ford. The much-later sequel *Indiana Jones and the Kingdom of the Crystal Skull* (2008), which reunites Ford with his costar Allen from the first film and gives them a teenage son, was less popular. Lucas also produced the TV series *The Young Indiana Jones Chronicles* (1992–1993), which portrays the early life of the fictional hero and pits him in adventures with figures throughout history. Lucas followed with four made-for-TV movies that aired between 1994 and 1996. There have also been several computer and video games based on *Raiders of the Lost Ark*, as well as adventure novels for both kids and adults.

An unintended consequence of *Raiders of the Lost Ark* was a renewed interest in the profession of archaeology. With series such as *Mysteries of the Pyramids*, the Discovery Channel and the Arts & Entertainment Television Network maintained the public's fascination with the exotic and fantastic image of archaeology presented by *Raiders of the Lost Ark*. However, much to the chagrin of savants in the field, *Raiders of the Lost Ark* created a less than accurate portrait of professional fieldwork, in which the spoon, not the bullwhip, is the tool of choice. More than a few starry-eyed youngsters have been surprised to learn that the field is not as exciting as the movies make it out to be.

Scott Tribble

SEE ALSO: *Academy Awards; "B" Movies; Blockbusters; Ford, Harrison; James Bond Films; Lucas, George; Made-for-Television Movies; Spielberg, Steven; Television; Video Games.*

BIBLIOGRAPHY

Cotta, Mark, and Shinji Hata. *From "Star Wars" to "Indiana Jones": The Best of the Lucasfilm Archives.* San Francisco: Chronicle Books, 1994.

McBride, Joseph. *Steven Spielberg: A Biography.* New York: Simon & Schuster, 1997.

Rinzler, J. W., and Laurent Bouzereau. *The Complete Making of "Indiana Jones": The Definitive Story behind All Four Films.* New York: Del Rey, 2008.

Taylor, Philip M. *Steven Spielberg: The Man, His Movies, and Their Meaning.* New York: Continuum Publishing, 1992.

Williams, Stephen. *Fantastic Archaeology.* Philadelphia: University of Pennsylvania Press, 1991.

Rainey, Gertrude "Ma" *(1886–1939)*

Gertrude "Ma" Rainey is called the mother of the blues. Born Gertrude Pridgett in Columbus, Georgia, on April 26, 1886, Rainey was the first woman known to sing the blues, combining country blues simplicity with more urban styles. Her accompanists included Louis Armstrong and Fletcher Henderson. More commonly, however, her accompaniment consisted of an old-style jug or a washboard band.

Rainey began her entertainment career when she was still a teenager. At fourteen she started singing in front of audiences, and not long after, she was touring with the Rabbit Foot Minstrels. It is commonly held that while touring with the Minstrels, she taught Bessie Smith. Rainey is given credit for being the first woman to bring the blues into the popular entertainment of her day—vaudeville, minstrel, and tent shows. In 1904 she married Will "Pa" Rainey, an elderly entrepreneur from the minstrel circuit and, thus, got the name by which she became famous. She and her husband had an act billed as "Rainey and Rainey, Assassinators of the Blues."

During the 1910s and 1920s, Ma Rainey became a solo act and the foremost proponent of the blues style. She was the most rural of the classic blues singers, drawing most of her support from a southern audience. She picked up a number of other nicknames, including the "Paramount Wildcat" (for Paramount Records) and "Gold Necklace Woman of the Blues" (for the necklace of gold coins that she always wore when she performed). She earned for the blues its reputation as "low-down music"—her open bisexuality did a great deal to foster that standing.

Rainey's advertisement for the notorious 1928 record "Prove It on Me" featured her in a man's outfit coming on to two women. The lyrics were similarly challenging: "Wear my clothes just like a fan / Talk to gals just like any old man / 'Cause they say I do it, ain't nobody caught me / Sure got to prove it on me." The song confirmed Rainey's independent image and her advocacy of women's issues. Rainey practiced what she preached and controlled her own career; she was famous for her business acumen and always carried a trunk full of money.

In 1923 the thirty-eight-year-old Rainey began recording for Paramount Records. She recorded more than 100 sides in her six years at Paramount, including "C. C. Rider" and "Ma Rainey's Black Bottom." However, male blues singers soon began to surpass female blues singers in popularity as the blues in general went into a decline. Rainey's last recording was in 1928, but she continued to perform until 1935, when she left the

Ma Rainey. Gertrude "Ma" Rainey poses with her band in 1923, the year she began recording for Paramount Records. FRANK DRIGGS COLLECTION/CONTRIBUTOR/ARCHIVE PHOTOS/GETTY IMAGES.

circuit and went back home to Columbus, where she ran two theaters until she died in 1939 of heart failure.

Rainey followed the path of other blues singers by returning to the church in her later years. She became active in the Congregation of Friendship Baptist Church, joining her brother, who was a deacon there. In 1983 Rainey was posthumously inducted into the Blues Foundation's Hall of Fame. The Rock and Roll Hall of Fame followed suit in 1990, citing her as an early influence on rock and roll. In 1994 the U.S. Postal Service honored her with a stamp.

Frank A. Salamone

SEE ALSO: *Armstrong, Lance; Armstrong, Louis; Blues; Henderson, Fletcher; Minstrel Shows; Rock and Roll; Smith, Bessie; Vaudeville.*

BIBLIOGRAPHY

Davis, Angela. *Blues Legacies and Black Feminism: Gertrude "Ma" Rainey, Bessie Smith, and Billie Holiday.* New York: Pantheon Books, 1998.

Lieb, Sandra. *Mother of the Blues: A Study of Ma Rainey.* Amherst: University of Massachusetts Press, 1981.

Nadel, Alan. *August Wilson: Completing the Twentieth-Century Cycle.* Iowa City: University of Iowa Press, 2010.

Stewart-Baxter, Derrick. *Ma Rainey and the Classic Blues Singers.* New York: Stein & Day, 1970.

Rains, Claude *(1889–1967)*

The words *unique actor* and *consummate professional* are overused in the entertainment industry, but they describe perfectly Claude Rains, an exceptional character actor of the Golden Age of moviemaking in Hollywood during the 1930s and 1940s. Rains is known for his subtle nuances in style, his perfect diction, and his mellifluous voice as he skillfully created memorable characters on stage, screen, television, and radio for nearly fifty years.

Of the more than fifty movies Rains made from 1933 to 1965, he is most remembered for his unforgettable performances as the mad chemist in *The Invisible Man* (1933), the smoothly corrupt senator foiled by Jimmy Stewart in Frank Capra's *Mr. Smith Goes to Washington* (1939), the sympathetic and pitiful (yet villainous) betrayed husband of Ingrid Bergman in Alfred

Hitchcock's *Notorious* (1946), and the charmingly corrupt Vichy police official who joins Humphrey Bogart to fight for freedom at the end of *Casablanca* (1942). Few Americans know, however, that the British-born Rains was an eminent stage actor both in London and with the renowned Theatre Guild in New York before he entered motion pictures.

OVERCOMING CHALLENGES

Even though Rains was not particularly good looking and at 5 feet, 6 inches was rather short, he possessed a commanding air, a seemingly inbred impeccable manner, and a sly humor, all of which resulted in a presence more imposing than his slight physical build implied. His acting suggested suaveness with just a hint of wickedness, but it was his elocution and husky-toned, velvety voice that became his trademark. Rains could combine words, subtle gestures, and emphatic pauses with perfect timing.

His speech and style were all the more remarkable given that he was born into abject poverty in London's slums during the late Victorian era and lived a rather Dickensian childhood on the streets. Until well into his teens, Rains suffered a serious speech defect and also spoke in a strong Cockney dialect. In his book *Particular Pleasures*, writer J. B. Priestley says this about the actor's persona: "I can imagine an American filmgoer, seeing Claude Rains . . . as an autocrat or smooth villain, feeling certain that here was a man who must have left an aristocratic landed family . . . to amuse himself making films. Rains had that air [of refinement]."

Rains began his career at age ten as a callboy in the British theater and was encouraged to take voice lessons and overcome his speech problems. His self-discipline and responsible attitude were noticed by theater owners, and in an unprecedented manner, he eventually became stage manager. In this way he learned every aspect of theatrical production, including effective acting.

***Claude Rains in* The Invisible Man.** *Claude Rains, left, stars as the title character and Gloria Stuart as his fiancée in the 1933 film* The Invisible Man. FPG/ARCHIVE PHOTOS/GETTY IMAGES.

In 1915 Rains served with the British army in France, where he suffered the ill effects of the Germans' use of mustard gas. Although his vocal cords were damaged, he astonished doctors when, ironically, he recovered with a much deeper and unusual voice. In 1919 he returned to the London stage as an actor and performed in diverse plays penned by talents ranging from George Bernard Shaw to Luigi Pirandello and was noticed by critics for his exceptional ability. Prominent writers were highly complimentary; Graham Greene described the actor's interpretations as brilliant: "Mr. Rains' low husky voice, his power of investing even commonplace dialogue with smoldering conviction, is remarkable. . . . He can catch, as no one else can, the bitter distrust of the world, religious in its intensity." Rains arrived in the United States in 1927 with a touring company and decided to remain in the country, becoming a naturalized citizen in 1938. By the early 1930s he was one of the leading star actors with the Theatre Guild.

FROM THEATER TO HOLLYWOOD

Initially Rains avoided films, and he especially refrained from making silent movies. The Great Depression, however, forced him, and many other actors, to leave the theater for Hollywood. In 1933 he accepted the lead role in Universal's *The Invisible Man*, a film directed by his old theater friend James Whale, who insisted on Rains for the part. Whale recognized the power of the actor's extraordinary voice, which was essential since the actor's face was completely covered during the entire film. Rains made three movies in 1934 and 1935, impressing studio heads, and by 1936 Jack Warner had offered the actor a contract, recognizing that he had the ability "to do anything and do it well." The relationship lasted ten years.

While most film admirers saw Rains as a reflection of the characters he portrayed—self-assured, cunning, devious, well educated, polished, and urbane—in reality he was none of these things. He was an extremely honest, entirely self-taught, shy, reserved man who lived quite simply but who always felt very insecure and frightened. Rains's persona of sophistication was self-created, and in his acting he never used his own personality, as did many film stars, such as Cary Grant and Gary Cooper. Above all Rains rarely duplicated his characters and with equal aplomb could be a heavenly messenger (*Here Comes Mr. Jordan*, 1941) or the devil himself (*Angel on My Shoulder*, 1946), a wise and shrewd Caesar (*Caesar and Cleopatra*, 1945) or a naive cuckold to Bette Davis (*Mr. Skeffington*, 1944). Davis considered Rains the greatest actor she ever worked with, and they were friends for many years. Rains made two other popular films with her—as the kindly and understanding psychiatrist in *Now, Voyager* (1942) and as an egotistical, brilliant, but mean-spirited composer in *Deception* (1946).

Rains displayed an inherent intelligence in his characterizations that enabled him to overcome a shallow script or trite dialogue in many films. Producers and directors knew his broad range and his box-office popularity, and they frequently enlarged or built in roles for him. Even when his part was small, though, Rains's presence was commanding, and he made a powerful impression, such as his portrayal of the mysterious Dr. Tower in *Kings Row* (1942).

Rains could suggest thoughts without words, but when he did speak, his tone revealed, without affectation, the complexity of his character or set the mood for the scene. He was often labeled a "villain" simply because in some parts he implied intrigue and exuded an element of cunning. He used his unique voice to intimidate, suggest, or seduce an audience by controlling the pitch, volume, and innuendo, and his timing was impeccable. Perhaps Rains's uniqueness was that he could "put on" a complex personality as easily as other actors use makeup or costumes. This ability is especially apparent in his suggestive "effete" portrayal of Prince John in *The Adventures of Robin Hood* (1938). Often his characters seemed to border between being scrupulous and unscrupulous, and while scheming, not necessarily evil; these qualities are particularly evident in Rains's performance as the wily police captain in *Casablanca*. Although Rains was nominated four times for an Academy Award, he never won the honor.

LATER CAREER

At age sixty-two and after a nearly twenty-year absence, Rains returned to the New York stage in 1951 in Sidney Kingsley's *Darkness at Noon*, playing an old Bolshevik during the Stalinist purge trials. For his remarkable and astonishing portrayal, he won every award the theater world bestows. During the 1950s he attempted a few plays but found critical success only in T. S. Eliot's *The Confidential Clerk* (1954). Rains also acted in many early prominent television shows, such as *Judgment at Nuremburg*, and appeared in a musical version of *The Pied Piper*, along with several Alfred Hitchcock episodes.

Sadly, by 1960 his voice had begun to fail, along with his health, circumstances that were apparent in his portrayal of the devious British official in David Lean's *Lawrence of Arabia* (1962). Rains's last film role was as King Herod in *The Greatest Story Ever Told* (1965), of which one reviewer wrote, "After you've seen Rains in the first twenty minutes of the film, you can leave the theatre."

In the early 1960s, Rains married for a sixth time and moved to New Hampshire, but within a few years his wife died of cancer. Old, quite ill, and alone, he remained isolated in his home until his death in May 1967. His friend Davis best summed up Rains's artistry when she stated during an interview that "an actor of his technique and style was irreplaceable; we shall not see his kind again."

Toby Irene Cohen

SEE ALSO: *Bergman, Ingrid; Bogart, Humphrey; Capra, Frank;* Casablanca*; Cooper, Gary; Davis, Bette; Grant, Cary; The Great Depression; Hitchcock, Alfred;* Invisible Man*;* Lawrence of Arabia*;* Mr. Smith Goes to Washington*; Stewart, Jimmy.*

BIBLIOGRAPHY

Behlmer, Rudy. *Inside Warner Bros. (1935–1951)*. New York: Simon & Schuster, 1985.

Harmetz, Aljean. *Round Up the Usual Suspects: The Making of* Casablanca. New York: Hyperion, 1992.

Mank, Greg. *The Hollywood Hissables*. Metuchen, NJ: Scarecrow Press, 1989.

Mordden, Ethan. *The Hollywood Studios*. New York: Alfred A. Knopf, 1988.

Priestley, J. B. *Particular Pleasures: Being a Personal Record of Some Varied Arts and Many Different Artists*. New York: Stein & Day, 1975.

Skal, David J., and Jessica Rains. *Claude Rains: An Actor's Voice*. Lexington: University Press of Kentucky, 2008.

Raitt, Bonnie *(1949–)*

Although she is one of rock and roll's most enduring stars, Bonnie Raitt has always been more concerned with musical integrity and social activism than with easy fame. The daughter of Broadway musical star John Raitt, she was raised in Los Angeles in a politically active Quaker household. She began playing guitar at age twelve but only began to pursue a musical career while she attended Radcliffe College, playing at Cambridge, Massachusetts, blues clubs. Becoming a dedicated student of Massachusetts African American musical traditions, Raitt dropped out of college to sign with Warner Brothers and released her first album in 1971. Her virtuoso guitar playing and appealing voice made her—a white woman performing classic black blues—a critical darling.

Raitt devoted as much time to political activism as to music. She struggled with alcoholism, and by the early 1980s her career began to wane. Raitt became sober in the mid-1980s, and in 1989 she released *Nick of Time*. At age forty, after almost twenty years of being overlooked by commercial audiences, Raitt was an overnight success, winning four Grammys and establishing herself as one of the music industry's most successful artists.

In the 1990s and the first decade of the 2000s Raitt continued to eschew formulaic pop albums in favor of work that reflects her musical heritage and political beliefs. In 2005 she released the well-received *Souls Alike*, then took a seven-year hiatus. During this time Raitt continued her political activism: she was involved in NukeFree.org in 2007 as well as a number of organizations advocating social justice, environmental responsibility, music education, and other causes. In 2012 she released *Slipstream*, her first album since *Souls Alike*. Raitt also founded her own record label, Redwing Records, and launched a tour with her old bandmates. Even on tour the activist in Raitt did not rest—she raised funds in partnership with the Guacamole Fund, a charity supporting environmental causes and social justice.

Victoria Price

SEE ALSO: *Blues; Broadway; Environmentalism; Grammy Awards; The Musical; Rock and Roll.*

BIBLIOGRAPHY

Bego, Mark. *Bonnie Raitt: Just in the Nick of Time*. New York: Birch Lane Press, 1995.

Bego, Mark. *Bonnie Raitt: Still in the Nick of Time*. New York: Cooper Square Press, 2003.

Rambo

One of the best-known and most popular fictional characters of the 1980s, Rambo was introduced in David Morrell's 1972 novel *First Blood* with the words, "His name was Rambo, and he was just some nothing kid for all anybody knew, standing by the pump of a gas station at the outskirts of Madison,

Rambo. *Sylvester Stallone, left, as Rambo, exacts revenge against Brian Dennehy's Sheriff William Teasle in* First Blood, *the first Rambo film.* CAROLCO/THE KOBAL COLLECTION.

Kentucky." Rambo's popularity was due especially to the series of films based on the character, especially the second movie, *Rambo: First Blood Part II* (1985), in which the hero, played by Sylvester Stallone, symbolically "wins" the Vietnam War. After the humiliation of Vietnam; the disgust over Watergate; and the one-term presidency of the somber, soul-searching Jimmy Carter, America was ready for a change in the 1980s. Throughout that decade, both President Ronald Reagan and Rambo proclaimed the same message: America is back!

THE NOVEL VS. THE FILM

In the novel, Rambo bears little resemblance to Stallone, as the character is barely out of his teens. He is only six months removed from Vietnam, where he served with the elite Special Forces, was captured by the Viet Cong, escaped, and went a little mad in the process. He has let his hair and beard grow and now hitchhikes aimlessly around the country. In Madison, Kentucky, Rambo runs afoul of the local sheriff, who arrests him for vagrancy. While being forcibly shaved at the local jail, Rambo has a flashback to the war. In a panic, he kills one deputy, wounds another, and escapes to the nearby wilderness.

Rambo is soon the focus of a manhunt by a posse of men who have no idea what kind of tiger they have by the tail. His hard-won guerrilla skills allow him both to avoid capture and to inflict heavy casualties upon his pursuers. The National Guard is eventually brought in but is no match for the former Green Beret. Many deaths later, Rambo kills his enemy, the sheriff, before being shot dead himself by his former Special Forces commander, Captain Trautman.

The novel was moderately successful, but the story was not filmed until 1981, as *First Blood*, and a number of changes were made before Stallone would take on the lead role. The biggest was in the behavior of Rambo. In the film, he is still a Special Forces veteran of Vietnam, but his use of survival skills is much more restrained. In the novel, Rambo kills his pursuers with no thought of mercy; for him, it is war. Stallone's Rambo is kinder and gentler. He wounds many people but kills no one directly, and the one death attributable to him is an accident. Clearly, this revision stems from a desire to have Rambo conform more closely to the mold of the "good guy" hero, whereas his literary incarnation is more of an antihero. The character alterations may also explain why, unlike in the novel, the film version of Rambo lives to fight another day.

RAMBO: FIRST BLOOD PART II

Rambo: First Blood Part II burst upon America's movie screens in May 1985. Rambo is released from prison to undertake a mission for the CIA. Satellite photos suggest that Americans are still being held prisoner in Vietnam, and Rambo is to sneak in through the jungle to find out for certain. The tone of the movie is set early when Trautman, Rambo's former commander, comes to retrieve him from prison and explain the mission. Rambo asks, "Do we get to win this time?" Trautman's reply: "This time it's up to you."

Once in Vietnam, Rambo is betrayed by the CIA, captured by the Vietnamese, and tortured by their Russian "advisers." Refusing to break under torture, he escapes, arms himself, and proceeds to slaughter every Vietnamese and Russian soldier in the vicinity. In an interesting reversal of America's role in the Vietnam War, Rambo is now the wily guerrilla, using stealth, guile, and primitive weapons (a knife and longbow) against a large force of well-armed enemies.

The film was a huge international success, earning more than $150 million in its U.S. theatrical release alone. Even Reagan praised it. For some, however, that was a problem: the character of Rambo seemed to represent the kind of kill-the-commies machismo that had involved the country in Vietnam in the first place—an attitude that also could be said to typify most U.S. foreign policy in the Reagan years.

RAMBO III

The next sequel, *Rambo III* (1988), was one of the most expensive movies ever made up to that time. Some estimates put the film's budget at a whopping $63 million, with about a quarter of that going to Stallone. In this incarnation, Rambo is seeking tranquillity in a Thai monastery when he is visited by his mentor, Trautman. The Green Beret colonel has been given a dangerous assignment: to help Afghan guerrillas fight the Soviet invaders of their country. Trautman asks Rambo to come to Afghanistan with him, but Rambo is tired of war and declines. Trautman undertakes the mission alone and is captured by the evil Russians. When Rambo learns of his friend's plight, he vows to rescue him. Reaching Afghanistan, Rambo finds Trautman and frees him, and the two then mow down the Russians in an orgy of grunts, explosions, and automatic weapons fire.

To the surprise of many, *Rambo III* actually lost money, at least in its U.S. release. One reason was its immense budget, but the "Rambo formula" also appeared to be growing stale, and the Soviet invasion of Afghanistan lacked the kind of emotional resonance for Americans that could be found in the second film's refighting of the Vietnam War.

RAMBO LIVES ON

Rambo also saw action as a Saturday-morning cartoon character, battling such enemies as Russian spies, Arab terrorists, and evil American punk rockers. A number of toy companies were licensed to produce action figures of Rambo and his foes, as well as plastic guns and knives modeled after the weapons used by Stallone's character in the films.

The fourth installment in the film franchise, titled simply *Rambo*, appeared in 2008. Set in the middle of the first decade of the 2000s, the film opens when the former soldier is hired to rescue missionaries who have been captured by a vicious Burmese military group. With 226 deaths, *Rambo* continues the franchise's tradition of violence. The film received mixed reviews from both critics and audiences. Detractors were appalled by the level of violence and critical of Stallone's wooden acting. Those who liked the movie, however, praised Stallone, claiming that the actor's portrayal of the aging Rambo was on par with Clint Eastwood's depiction of William Munny, a senior outlaw in the highly regarded Western *Unforgiven* (1992). *Rambo* was banned in Myanmar (Burma) because the government claimed the movie supported the cause of the country's freedom fighters.

Justin Gustainis

SEE ALSO: *Blockbusters; Reagan, Ronald; Stallone, Sylvester;* Unforgiven*; Vietnam; War Movies.*

BIBLIOGRAPHY

Greenberg, Harvey R. "Dangerous Recuperations: *Red Dawn, Rambo*, and the New Decaturism." *Journal of Popular Film and Television* 15, no. 2 (1987): 60–70.

Jeffords, Susan. *Hard Bodies: Hollywood Masculinity in the Reagan Era.* New Brunswick, NJ: Rutgers University Press, 1993.

Morrell, David. *First Blood.* New York: M. Evans, 1972.

Walsh, Jeffrey, and James Aulich, eds. *Vietnam Images: War and Representation.* Hampshire, UK: Macmillan Press, 1989.

The Ramones

Generally regarded as the forefathers of the punk rock movement, the Ramones—Joey, Dee Dee, Johnny, and Tommy—formed in Forest Hills, New York, in 1974. Their influence was felt overseas after several future members of Britain's leading punk acts witnessed the Ramones' 1976 tour of England. Many Americans, though, were not sure whether the band was a joke. Their uniforms of ripped denim and biker jackets along with their use of the same surname ("Ramon" was a pseudonym used by Paul McCartney when he was with the Beatles) poked fun at the pomposity that infected rock during the 1970s.

Joey Ramone recalled to Matt Diehl in *Rolling Stone* in 1997 that "1976 was the height of disco and corporate rock, and we were like nobody else." When other groups were recording songs that lasted the length of an LP's entire side, the Ramones' first album clocked in at thirty minutes, with many songs lasting a mere two minutes. The songs' short length was part of the same minimalist, no-frills technique that characterized the band's career-long discipline and consistency. A Ramones show in the 1990s was pretty much the same show as one in the 1970s, and this consistency helped the band outlast most of its punk peers.

MUSIC

The Ramones were signed in 1975 by Sire Records, an independent American label that had a heavy roster of punk and new wave acts, including the Replacements and the Talking Heads. Their first release, *Ramones* (1976), contained short, energetic songs that used three chords and shunned existing rock conventions like guitar solos. The combination of surf music and fast rhythm guitar was initially abrasive, something the band undoubtedly knew and capitalized on by recording an actual chain saw to introduce "Chain Saw." Songs like "Beat on the Brat" and "Blitzkrieg Bop" contain elements of aggression and conquest, but these fueled a campaign to overtake the music industry, not one that advocated street violence.

By the time *Rocket to Russia* was released in 1977, the group's cartoonish persona was established; the "joke" band that people thought would fall into obscurity did not. As many of rock's superstars clung to a leftover 1960s mysticism, the Ramones' records featured cretins, pinheads, lobotomies, and shock treatment. On a more serious level these elements of fun served to repudiate 1960s hippie culture. The Ramones recaptured the short and simple aesthetic that rock music had abandoned and revived the generation gap all in the same stroke.

Road to Ruin (1978) introduced the group's first lineup change. Tommy, the Ramones' drummer and coproducer, gave up performing to produce records; he was replaced by Marky Ramone. *Road to Ruin* included a cover from the British Invasion period and—surprise—a ballad called "Questioningly." The group then starred in the 1979 movie *Rock 'n' Roll High School*, which fairly represented their just-dumb-fun ethos.

The Ramones' last recording was *Adios Amigos* (1995). They left fans with thirteen original albums and a number of live recordings and retrospectives. Throughout their career the Ramones' style remained largely intact, with the occasional incorporation of metal and psychedelia. Lyrically, the band expanded into topical subjects, as in 1986's "Bonzo Goes to Bitburg," a reference to Ronald Reagan's ill-advised trip to a German war cemetery. The song was retitled "My Brain Is Hanging Upside Down" for its release on *Animal Boy* (1986).

IMAGE

The Ramones characterized the complex nature of punk while exposing the contradictions within rock and roll itself. Their music, lyrics, and image were drawn entirely from popular culture. Some critics, especially those who tried to legitimize rock music to a broader audience, dismissed the Ramones as lowbrow entertainment. These writers missed the point—or forgot—that rock derives a large part of its validity by standing in opposition to mainstream culture. Reminding people of this, the Ramones were put in the position of initiating a conservative artistic reaction within the punk movement, a movement that was perceived by many as a radical threat. Even among their songs the group expressed seemingly contradictory ideas: the group that recorded "Bonzo Goes to Bitburg" later recorded a pro–National Rifle Association song called "Scattergun."

The Ramones' cartoonish image masked their conceptual nature, which Talking Heads bassist Tina Weymouth commented on in 1990 interview for *Rolling Stone*: "What set the Ramones apart from all the hardcore bands that came later was their discipline. They chose to be primitive." Their spontaneous do-it-yourself style made them a mass-scale influence in rock. They launched the development of punk, but they also emboldened musicians outside the realm of punk. Once young musicians realized that forming a band did not require anyone's blessing, local club scenes emerged and independent record labels developed. In the commercially conservative climate of the music business in the late 1970s, the Ramones' appearance showed others that it was possible to work outside an often hostile music industry.

Joey, Dee Dee, Johnny, and Tommy Ramone appeared together for the last time for a signing at Virgin Megastore in New York City on July 20, 1999; within five years three of the founding members had died. Joey died April 15, 2001, after a struggle with lymphoma; Dee Dee died of a heroin overdose on June 5, 2002; and Johnny died of prostate cancer on September 15, 2004. The Ramones were inducted into the Rock and Roll Hall of Fame in 2002 and received a Grammy Lifetime Achievement Award in 2011.

Daryl Umberger

SEE ALSO: *The Beatles; British Invasion; Disco; Grammy Awards; Hippies; McCartney, Paul; New Wave Music; Pop Music; Punk; Reagan, Ronald; The Replacements; Talking Heads.*

BIBLIOGRAPHY

Bessman, Jim. *Ramones: An American Band.* New York: St. Martin's Press, 1993.

Diehl, Matt. "The Making of Ramones' Ramones." *Rolling Stone*, May 15, 1997, 80.

Eddy, Chuck. "The Ramones." *Rolling Stone*, September 20, 1990, 78–81.

Gaines, Donna. "My Life with the Ramones." *Village Voice*, January 16, 1996.

Ramone, Dee Dee, and Veronica Kofman. *Poison Heart: Surviving the Ramones.* Wembley, UK: Firefly, 1997.

Schinder, Scott, and Andy Schwartz. *Icons of Rock: An Encyclopedia of the Legends Who Changed Music Forever.* Westport, CT: Greenwood Press, 2008.

Ranch House

One of many new residential designs that proliferated after World War II, the ranch house emerged during the largest housing boom in U.S. history. The boom followed a hiatus in home building that occurred during the Great Depression, which marked the decline of older architectural styles such as the bungalow. Unlike the designs made popular at the turn of the twentieth century, post–World War II designs incorporated public discourse about the role of the modern home. Magazines such as *Ladies' Home Journal* linked surveys of home owners with ideas of architects and designers, arguing that the modern home should pair the latest building technology with the needs of the modern family. The discourse, led by Dr. Benjamin Spock, suggested that the design of a home greatly influenced family life.

As early as 1940, the ranch house became linked to the new ideal of the American family. Its simple, informal features—the one-story structure, low-pitched eaves, and expansive picture windows—were fused with the easygoing lifestyle associated with the Southwest and West Coast. Although the design did not dominate the ranches of western prairie states (which cared little about architecture), the form resembled western ranch houses of the 1880s. More directly, it derived from architect Frank Lloyd Wright's prairie and Usonian houses.

Over time the design evolved, and the size and complexity of the floor plans increased. The modest ranch became a sprawling, highly articulated ranch rambler, which had split and bi-level variations. All of the designs were structured on the same three basic zones: bedroom, family living and entertaining, and garage with adjoining hobby area. The center of the home was the living zone, which was strikingly open to give it a free-flowing feel. Although the house appeared from the exterior to be a single story, inside the zones stretched into main and lower floors, making it seem large even on a small lot, an attractive feature for developers.

As the most ubiquitous home design after 1950, the ranch house helped to define American family life and structure. The dominance of the living zone, which served as a multipurpose area and composed the heart of the home, dovetailed with the life of leisure many middle-class Americans were enjoying. The design was conducive to television viewing, as a television set could be placed in the living room and viewed from the other areas in the same zone. Although purchasers associated the form with heritage, status, and respectability, functionality was never far from their minds.

Brian Black

SEE ALSO: *Bok, Edward; Catalog Houses; Leisure Time; Spock, Dr. Benjamin; Suburbia; Television; World War II.*

BIBLIOGRAPHY

Clark, Clifford Edward, Jr. *The American Family Home, 1800–1960.* Chapel Hill: University of North Carolina Press, 1986.

Gregory, Daniel Platt. *Cliff May and the Modern Ranch House.* New York: Rizzoli, 2008.

Samon, Katherine. *The Ranch House Style.* New York: Clarkson Potter, 2003.

Wright, Gwendolyn. *Building the Dream: A Social History of Housing in America.* Cambridge, MA: MIT Press, 1983.

Rand, Ayn

SEE: *Objectivism/Ayn Rand.*

Rand, Sally *(1904–1979)*

Sally Rand was best known for her sexually provocative dance that featured the use of ostrich feather fans. She introduced this dance at the 1933 Chicago World's Fair and supplemented it with a bubble dance in 1934. Eventually she made her form of erotic movement more acceptable to mainstream audiences than striptease had been.

Coming to her calling following stints as a chorine (chorus girl), vaudeville performer, circus acrobat, and Hollywood film star, Rand thought of herself as a "terpsichorean artiste" rather than a stripper or an exotic dancer. While her act was controversial enough during the 1930s through the mid-1960s to earn her an arrest for indecency, there was considerable debate about whether she actually wore a body stocking or was naked underneath her feathers. Ultimately Rand was adept at creating the illusion of nudity while cavorting tastefully under blue or pink lights to the music of Frédéric Chopin and Claude Debussy. She performed into her seventies.

Frederick J. Augustyn Jr.

SEE ALSO: *Century of Progress (Chicago, 1933); Circus; Hollywood; Strip Joints/Striptease; Vaudeville.*

BIBLIOGRAPHY

Carskadon, T. R. "Sally Rand Dances to the Rescue." *American Mercury* 35 (1935): 355–58.

Ganz, Cheryl R. *The 1933 Chicago World's Fair: A Century of Progress.* Urbana: University of Illinois Press, 2008.

Ragan, David. *Who's Who in Hollywood, 1900–1976.* New Rochelle, NY: Arlington House, 1976.

Rand, Sally. "Bubbles Become Big Business." *Review of Reviews* 91 (1935): 40–41.

Rap

Rap is a genre of music (directly related to hip-hop) that emerged in 1970s New York City; both forms are derived from early African and Jamaican poetry. The term *rap* stems from hip-hop emcees, called rappers, who sang rhyming lyrics over music. Rap is heavily influenced by earlier African American musical forms, including blues, funk, and jazz, as well as by disc jockeys in Jamaica who "toasted," or talked over, the music they played.

EARLY RAP

Early rap music focused on basic rhymes, evolving over time in part due to pioneers such as Kool Moe Dee, Rakim, and Guru. Much like scholarly writers and poets, rap artists use metaphors and similes to heighten their work's theme. Over the years, rap artists continued to build upon these methods, but not without paying tribute, or "props," to their predecessors by name or through the use of allusion. As rap evolved, the new style went beyond simple poetry techniques, employing internal rhyme, syncopation, and a style unique to each artist. Contemporary rappers such as Jay-Z, Snoop Dogg, Kanye West, and Wu-Tang Clan all pay tribute to pioneers such as the Notorious B.I.G., Slick Rick, and Rakim through sampling beats, covering songs, or recycling lyrics.

This new evolution of rap relied heavily on creativity to continually create fresh lyrics, which led to the art of "freestyling," or making up lyrics on the spot. Freestyle rappers take turns rhyming back and forth, taunting and insulting one another, in what is called a "battle rap." While these battles generally end when participants leave the stage, some hip-hop feuds run much deeper. Former N.W.A members Dr. Dre and Eazy-E openly threatened each other on their respective albums, and the rivalry between Tupac Shakur and Notorious B.I.G. sparked an East Coast/West Coast feud that allegedly played a role in both of their murders in 1997. As of 2012 both homicides remain unsolved, a testament to the "don't snitch" gang code and its effect on rap culture.

GANGSTA RAP

Two early rap groups that emerged in the 1980s, Public Enemy and N.W.A (Niggaz with Attitude), are prime examples of the diversity of the rap genre. Public Enemy's Chuck D looked to the greater world for musical inspiration, adopting Malcolm X's mantra, "By any means necessary." Public Enemy's albums include images reminiscent of the Black Panther Party, and the band's logo was a human silhouette inside the crosshairs of a rifle scope. The group sought global political reform with songs such as "Don't Believe the Hype" (1988) and "Fight the Power" (1989), blaming corrupt governmental systems with preventing African Americans from succeeding. N.W.A., whose members included rap icons Dr. Dre, Eazy-E, and Ice Cube, were deemed "gangsta rappers." They focused on their Los Angeles neighborhood of Compton for artistic inspiration and glorified the gang lifestyle with songs including "Dopeman" (1987) and "F--- tha Police" (1988). Front man Eazy-E openly admitted starting his record label with profits earned from dealing cocaine. Both groups garnered heavy media criticism for promoting violence and endorsing crime.

Other gangsta rap songs, such as 1992's "187" by Snoop Dogg and "Cop Killer" by Ice-T, promoted violence against police, creating even more negative press. In 1987 Ice-T's album *Rhyme Pays* was the first to receive a Parental Advisory Label for explicit content. While not all rap music is associated with felonious activities, some of its origins derive from underground gang culture and prison life. The baggy clothing and sagging pants of the gangsta rap culture can be attributed to the loose-fitting outfits and lack of belts found in prison. Some musical forms, such as beatboxing with the mouth and lips and drumming on the chest or legs, stem from the lack of instruments in the penal system. Whereas some individuals have learned rap in prison, others have become famous and have later been incarcerated—Lil Wayne (weapons charges), Notorious B.I.G. (drugs), and Shakur (sexual assault).

RAP IN OTHER GENRES

TV shows such as *Yo! MTV Raps* (1988) and BET's *Rap City* (1989) brought hip-hop and rap to a worldwide audience. Early movies that starred rap artists include *Boyz n the Hood* (1991), *Colors* (1988), and *New Jack City* (1991) and described the perils of inner-city life, gang culture, and the drug trade. Later films, such as *8 Mile* (2002), *Get Rich or Die Tryin'* (2005), and *Notorious* (2009), were more biopic—urban fairy tales recounting the lives of Eminem, 50 Cent, and Notorious B.I.G., respectively. These artists credit rap with helping them escape drugs and crime, although their lyrics still glorify that lifestyle. Rap artists often preach violence, endorse materialism, flaunt wealth, and boast fame, but this showmanship is generally more for the marketing purpose of promoting album sales.

As of 2012, rap had crossed into all genres of music, including rock, pop, punk, soul, and even country. In 1986 Run-DMC teamed up with Aerosmith to perform a rap hybrid of the group's hit song "Walk This Way," which topped both rap and rock charts. Reverend Run went on to perform the song again in 2011 on *Sesame Street* with Elmo, changing the title to "Hop This Way." Another group responsible for this crossover was the Beastie Boys, an all-white New York rock/rap hybrid band. The release of their 1986 album *License to ILL* proved that rap music was not just a product of African American culture. Growing up in New York, the group rhymed about what they knew: areas around Brooklyn and Manhattan and the culture of the Big Apple. They opened the door for later groups such as Rage against the Machine, Kid Rock, and the Red Hot Chili Peppers, who followed suit by blending rap stylings with other musical forms, such as punk, country, and funk. The boundaries between hip-hop and rap have blurred considerably over the years, with many artists creating songs in both genres.

INTO THE MAINSTREAM

As rap evolved, TV sitcoms such as *The Fresh Prince of Bel-Air* (1990–1996) brought the genre out of the inner city and into suburban living rooms. Rapper-turned-actor Will Smith plays a street-savvy Philadelphia teenager who moves in with his straitlaced wealthy California relatives. Smith won the first Grammy for Best Rap Performance (1989), and he went on to become a respected Hollywood "A"-list actor, starring in such films as *Independence Day* (1996), *Men in Black* (1997), *Ali* (2001), and *The Pursuit of Happyness* (2006); he earned Oscar nominations for Best Actor for the latter two movies. Public Enemy's Flavor Flav became famous as a reality television star on shows such as VH1's *The Surreal Life* (200) and *Strange Love* (2005), where he met and courted Sylvester Stallone's ex-wife, Brigitte Nielsen. This blending of culture has continued over the years, such as on Dr. Dre's 2001 album, *The Chronic 2001*, which featured white rapper Eminem. Director James Toback addressed the phenomenon of African American rap culture's influence over a predominately white, suburban America in his 1999 film *Black and White*. Starring actors Ben Stiller, Brooke Shields, and Robert Downey Jr., along with members of the Wu-Tang Clan, Mike Tyson, and rapper Sticky Fingaz, the movie vividly depicts both the benefits and pitfalls of two cultures colliding.

As rap music has evolved from a culturally isolated phenomenon into mainstream suburban culture, rappers have gone from community pariahs to role models, with "Cop Killer" Ice-T playing a police detective on *Law & Order: SVU* (1999–); ex-drug dealer 50 Cent helping to fight hunger in Africa, and former assault defendant Sean "P. Diddy" Combs hosting multiple reality shows. Although gang violence is still a major issue in the world today, in the case of rap music, society is now able to draw a line between fiction and reality. *New York Times* writer Jon Pareles commented on this phenomenon in a 1990 article:

> Gangster rappers write rhymes about inner-city violence, sometimes as cautionary tales, sometimes as fantasies and sometimes as chronicles without comment. The genre also calls for a detailed put-down (with threats of violence) of anyone the rappers dislike. Gangster rap unnerves those outsiders who only hear aggressive, profane young black men talking about mayhem. Whether the raps are intelligent or juvenile, a threatening tone is at the style's core. But gangster rap, for all its first-person machismo, is not a simple or naive narrative form, and it's certainly not autobiography.

Ron Horton

SEE ALSO: *Academy Awards; Aerosmith; The Beastie Boys; Celebrity; Combs, Sean "P. Diddy"; Disc Jockeys; Downey, Robert, Jr.; Eminem; Gangs; Gangsta Rap; Grammy Awards; Hip-Hop; Hollywood; Jay-Z;* Law & Order: SVU*; MTV; Public Enemy; Reality Television; Run-DMC; Sagging; Sampling;* Sesame Street*; Shakur, Tupac; Sitcom; Smith, Will; Snoop Dogg; Stallone, Sylvester; Stiller, Ben; Tyson, Mike; West, Kanye.*

BIBLIOGRAPHY

Chang, Jeff. *Can't Stop Won't Stop: A History of the Hip-Hop Generation.* New York: Picador, 2005.

Kool Moe Dee. *There's a God on the Mic: The True 50 Greatest MCs.* Boston, MA: Da Capo Press, 2003.

Pareles, Jon. "Gangster Rap: Life and Music in the Combat Zone." *New York Times*, October 7, 1990.

Quinn, Eithne. *Nuthin' but a "G" Thang: The Culture and Commerce of Gangsta Rap.* New York: Columbia University Press, 2005.

Reeves, Marcus. *Somebody Scream! Rap Music's Rise . . .* New York: Faber & Faber, 2008.

Toop, David. *Rap Attack: African Rap to Global Hip Hop*, 3rd ed. London: Serpent's Tail, 2000.

The Rat Pack

SEE: *Martin, Dean; Sinatra, Frank.*

Rather, Dan *(1931–)*

Dan Rather, former CBS News anchorman, has spent more than sixty years as a journalist, forty-four of those years with CBS News. He started in his native Texas with the Associated Press, moving to the *Houston Chronicle* and then into local TV. His coverage of Hurricane Carla in 1961, including showing radar of the storm, brought him to the attention of CBS. (Rather never lost his love of hurricane coverage—when anchoring the *CBS Evening News*, he notably covered a Florida hurricane on the beachfront, clinging to a light pole for dear life as the hurricane blew in.)

RISE TO THE NATIONAL STAGE

CBS brought Rather to New York in 1962, then sent him to run the southern bureau, where he covered the civil rights movement. As head of the bureau, he was on the scene of the John F. Kennedy assassination in 1963 and was the first reporter to confirm that Kennedy was dead. Rather followed that with tours in foreign bureaus (including reporting from Vietnam); being beaten up on the floor of the 1968 Democratic National Convention in Chicago; and covering Watergate as a White House correspondent, famously wrangling with President Richard Nixon. After that, he joined the team at *60 Minutes* and used that platform to eventually outmaneuver fellow journalist Roger Mudd to succeed Walter Cronkite as anchor of the *CBS Evening News* on March 9, 1981.

Once Rather took over the anchor desk, he maintained CBS's number one newscast status, but soon CBS News dissolved into turmoil due to budget cuts and new owners, and the ratings slipped. Rather's expertise soon proved less noteworthy than the often bizarre happenings that occurred around him. His sign-off one week in 1986 was "courage"; he tended to use the vernacular of his Texas upbringing during broadcasts—including "that dog won't hunt" and "tight as a too-small bathing suit on a too-long ride back from the beach"—which became known as "Ratherisms." Rather allowed CBS to go to black for six minutes on September 11, 1987, when U.S. Open tennis ran too long, and he tangled on air with Vice President George H. W. Bush (this and his contentiousness with Nixon led to long-standing charges of "liberal bias" by conservatives).

Perhaps oddest was the October 4, 1986, physical assault on Rather by a man who inexplicably asked him, "What's the frequency, Kenneth?" (Later, during an appearance on *The Late Show with David Letterman*, Rather joined rock band R.E.M. in a performance of their song based on this incident.) While at the time Rather's account of the incident was doubted, his attacker was eventually identified as William Tager, who was convicted in 1994 of killing an NBC stagehand outside the *Today* show set.

From 1993 to 1995, Rather coanchored the *CBS Evening News* with Connie Chung, but the ratings did not improve and she was forced out; he subsequently trumpeted a "hard news" program. In 1998 he signed a contract to stay with CBS until 2003. By the end of his contract, *CBS Evening News* was in third place and there was much talk in and out of CBS of replacing him as the anchor. Rather himself did not show any inclination of leaving, but circumstances quickly changed. He was also the host of *60 Minutes II*, a midweek spin-off of *60 Minutes* that broke the Abu Ghraib scandal.

OUSTER FROM CBS

In another breaking story, on September 8, 2004, the program led with information that President George W. Bush had been unfit for duty and was suspended during his time with the Air National Guard. The incident had allegedly been covered up, despite many documents from the commanding officer of the base. These documents formed the basis of the story. Rather was not the reporter but read the story on air. Soon after the report aired, several right-wing bloggers focused on the typewritten documents used to back up the story, claiming that they were computer-created forgeries. Rather and his team stood behind the report, but the furor continued as experts began denying that they had authenticated the documents. Eventually CBS retracted the story, fired lead producer Mary Mapes, and forced out other staffers. Rather was pressured to leave his *CBS Evening News* job and return to the original *60 Minutes*. He left *CBS Evening News* on the anniversary of his first broadcast, March 9, 2005—a record twenty-four years. Bob Schieffer took over until CBS hired Katie Couric as the show's anchor.

Being "sent down" to *60 Minutes* did not work, as Rather was given few stories, and he left the network in the summer of 2006. In 2007 Rather sued CBS for breach of contract, claiming that the network had forced him out by giving him few stories on *60 Minutes* and that he was made a scapegoat for a story that he was not the reporter on (he also claimed that the story was correct). However, the $70 million breach of contract suit was dismissed and ultimately ended in 2010 when New York's highest court refused to hear it.

After he left CBS, Rather founded his own production company, News & Guts, and began appearing as anchor and managing editor of *Dan Rather Reports* on HDNet, a cable channel owned by Internet billionaire/Dallas Mavericks owner Mark Cuban. According to its description, the show "specializes in investigative journalism and international reporting." Rather has also made appearances on various news roundtable shows and on *The Daily Show with Jon Stewart*, even appearing in several skits.

Michele Lellouche

SEE ALSO: *Blogging; Cable TV; Civil Rights Movement; Cronkite, Walter; The Internet; Kennedy Assassination; Letterman, David; R.E.M.;* 60 Minutes*; Stewart, Jon; Television Anchors;* Today*; Vietnam; Watergate.*

BIBLIOGRAPHY

Goldberg, Robert, and Gerald Jay Goldberg. *Anchors: Brokaw, Jennings, Rather and the Evening News*. Secaucus, NJ: Carol Publishing Group, 1990.

Kurtz, Howard. "Dan Rather to Step Down at CBS." *Washington Post*, November 24, 2004.

Rather, Dan. *The Camera Never Blinks: Adventures of a TV Journalist*. New York: William Morrow, 1977.

Rather, Dan. *Deadlines and Datelines*. New York: Morrow, 1999.

Rather, Dan, and Mickey Herskowitz. *The Camera Never Blinks Twice: The Further Adventures of a Television Journalist*. New York: William Morrow, 1994.

Rather, Dan, and Peter Wyden. *I Remember*. Boston: Little, Brown, 1991.

Raves

At the simplest level, a rave is just a particular kind of dance party, often held in an impromptu location, usually featuring electronic music, and probably involving some amount of drug use, that was popular among young people in the late twentieth century. But rave was more than just a fad. Aspects of the rave scene have permanently influenced popular culture, especially the development of electronic music and the continuing evolution of movements focused on collective transformation.

Like the hippie movement of the 1960s or the disco scene of the 1970s, rave was an immersive experience designed to alter consciousness, as well as a social statement that rejects or critiques the norms of ordinary behavior. For some, rave had a spiritual aspect; for others, a tribal character, and for still others, a political component. Rave produced its own art form (the colorful flyers that announced rave locations), its own variety of social theater, and its own complex musical landscape, subdivided into subtle categories such as "acid house," "hardcore techno," "breakbeat," "trance," and "jungle."

In other words, rave was many things to many people. Although the rave scene is best known to the outside world through news reports and cultural commentaries in the late 1980s and early 1990s, the origin of rave goes back to the Beat movement of the 1950s, and its influence goes forward to "post-rave" versions of electronic dance culture. Rave is often thought of as a primarily British and American phenomenon, but iconic rave events took place in far-flung locations like the coast of India, the outback of Australia, and the island of Ibiza. Viewed in retrospect, rave culture can be seen to cut across boundaries of nationality, ethnicity, and sexual orientation, reflecting an eclectic assortment of influences, from urban-industrial to techno-pagan.

Throughout the history of rave and into its later evolutions, one element remained consistent: continuous dancing to an uninterrupted flow of electronic music. For many participants, the whole point of rave is to dance into a trancelike state, and electronic dance music is designed to provide a hypnotic, beat-driven sound environment. In its fundamental aspect, rave is related to traditional practices that use sound and music to alter consciousness. Familiar examples are the continuous "whirling" motion of Sufi dervishes and the ritual dances common to African and Native American cultures. Some traditional practices also include the use of euphoria-inducing substances, similar in effect to the popular rave drug MDMA, commonly known as Ecstasy.

The decline of rave occurred in part because drug use and other countercultural aspects of the original movement attracted condemnation from politicians and scrutiny from law enforcement. In addition, the "pure" rave culture of underground improvisation gave way to more structured events, and as elements of the rave scene became part of mainstream popular culture, its outlaw mystique subsided. At the same time, communal functions provided by rave were supplanted by the rise of Internet culture. Given such a rich historical context, social scientists have found much to study in connection with rave, including the dynamics of youth culture, the mainstream assimilation of alternative movements, and the continuing pursuit of transformative experience.

Cynthia Giles

SEE ALSO: *The Beat Generation; Consciousness Raising Groups; Disco; Hippies; The Internet; Social Dancing.*

BIBLIOGRAPHY

Reynolds, Simon. *Generation Ecstasy: Into the World of Techno and Rave Culture.* Boston: Little, Brown, 1998.

Sylvan, Robin. *Trance Formation: The Spiritual and Religious Dimensions of Global Rave Culture.* New York: Routledge, 2005.

Ray, Rachael *(1968–)*

Rachael Ray is a television personality and cookbook author who became known in the late twentieth century for her cooking shows on the Food Network. Critics decried her simplistic approach to cooking, while fans loved her easy recipes and Ray herself.

Ray was born on August 25, 1968, in Cape Cod, Massachusetts, where her family owned several restaurants. The family eventually relocated to northern New York to manage yet another restaurant. When she was in her twenties, she moved to New York City. She got a job working at Macy's candy counter and ultimately became manager of the fresh foods department.

After a mugging left her bruised and terrified, Ray moved back to upstate New York, where she managed several restaurants and bars at the famed Sagamore Resort. She then became the food buyer for Cowan & Lobel, a large gourmet market in Albany, New York, where she also created and taught a series of cooking classes to promote sales. The classes proved so popular that a local television station eventually hired her to do a weekly "30-Minute Meals" segment for the evening news.

In 2001 Ray signed her first contract with the Food Network, where she has had much success with several shows, including *30 Minute Meals with Rachael Ray* (2001–), which received the 2006 Daytime Emmy Award for Outstanding Service Show, and *Rachael's Vacation* (2008–2010). She also wrote many cookbooks, including *365: No Repeats, a Year of Deliciously Different Dinners* (2005) and *Rachael Ray's Look + Cook: 100 Can't-Miss Main Courses in Pictures* (2010).

Not everyone is a fan, however. Many prominent chefs disapprove of Ray's cooking philosophy and have not hesitated to say so. Chef Anthony Bourdain opines, "We KNOW she can't cook. She shrewdly tells us so. So . . . what is she selling us? Really? She's selling us satisfaction, the smug reassurance that mediocrity is quite enough." Ray, who has no formal culinary training, makes no apologies for her easy-to-prepare foods and shortcut techniques, and she freely admits, "I have no formal anything."

In the fall of 2006 Ray launched a new daytime talk show, *Rachael Ray*, on CBS. It deviates from her other shows by offering celebrity interviews and musical guests. It was an immediate hit, becoming the number one syndicated debut of the season and receiving praise from critics. *Newsweek* magazine declared that Ray was "the most down-to-earth TV star on the planet." *Rachael Ray* won both the 2008 and 2009 Daytime Emmy Award for Outstanding Talk Show. In January 2012 CBS renewed the show through the 2013–2014 season.

Ray used her success with television shows and cookbooks to launch other endeavors. In November 2006 *Every Day with Rachael Ray*, a lifestyle magazine, debuted. In 2007 she launched a nonprofit organization called Yum-o! (named after her go-to expression of culinary approval) to help children and their families develop healthier relationships with food. She also has a line of cookware and a line of all-natural dog food, Rachael Ray Nutrish, in honor of her own dog, Isaboo. A portion of the proceeds from Nutrish go to various animal rescue organizations.

Despite her critics, Ray refuses to alter her cooking philosophy or her style. She says, "Decide what it is that you are and then stay true to that thing. My brand is based very much on how I live my day-to-day life."

Jill Gregg Clever

SEE ALSO: *Cable TV; Celebrity Chefs; Daytime Talk Shows; Emmy Awards; Foodies; Macy's;* Newsweek; *Television.*

BIBLIOGRAPHY

Abrams, Dennis. *Rachael Ray: Food Entrepreneur.* New York: Chelsea House Publishers, 2009.

Harris, Paul. "Rachael Ray, the New Queen of US Cookery—and She Can't Bake." *Observer*, December 5, 2010. Accessed June 3, 2012. Available from http://www.guardian.co.uk/tv-and-radio/2010/dec/05/rachael-ray-us-tv-new-oprah

"How to Succeed in 2007: Rachael Ray." CNNMoney, 2006. Accessed June 3, 2012. Available from http://money.cnn.com/popups/2006/biz2/howtosucceed/3.html

Magee, C. Max. "Food Fight: Anthony Bourdain Slams Rachael Ray." Millions, February 2007. Accessed June 3, 2012. Available from http://www.themillions.com/2007/02/food-fight-anthony-bourdain-slams_09.html

"Rachael Ray." Food Network. Accessed June 3, 2012. Available from http://www.foodnetwork.com/rachael-ray/bio/index.html

"Rachael's Bio." Rachael Ray Show. Accessed June 3, 2012. Available from http://www.rachaelrayshow.com/show-info/rachaels-bio/

Reader's Digest

The desire to save time has been a force in American culture since colonial days. It took on added importance in the twentieth century, when businessmen sought to standardize the performance of the country's industrial sector. *Reader's Digest*, introduced in 1922, was another expression of the time-saving initiative, and it went on to become one of the most powerful vehicles for the printed word in world history. Published in a handy booklet form, *Reader's Digest* featured thirty-one articles, one for each day of the month, culled from leading magazines, with each "article of enduring value and interest, in condensed and permanent form," as the publication maintained. It lost its place as the best-selling U.S. consumer magazine in 2009 but remained the largest paid-circulation magazine in the world, reaching an estimated forty million people.

Reader's Digest did not introduce the concept of sampling from and condensing other publications. An American magazine called *Littell's Living Age* reprinted periodical articles in 1844. Almost fifty years later, *Literary Digest*, founded by Isaac Kauffman Funk of Funk & Wagnalls fame, capitalized upon the success of a British periodical, *Review of Reviews*, and presented condensations of articles from American, Canadian, and European publications. The highbrow *Literary Digest* achieved a circulation of more than one million by 1927, earning praise from *Time* magazine (another 1920s time-saving publication) as "one of the greatest publishing successes in history." However, *Literary Digest* fell out of the reading public's good graces in 1936 when it incorrectly predicted that Franklin D. Roosevelt would lose in a landslide in one of the first national presidential preference polls. The magazine failed the following year, not long after Roosevelt was inaugurated for the second of his record four terms.

THE EARLY YEARS

The less esoteric *Reader's Digest* was the brainchild of William Roy DeWitt Wallace (1889–1981), a Minnesota-born college dropout who, according to biographer Peter Canning, touted various "schemes and stunts" as a young man. While employed as a traveling salesman, Wallace would condense and memorize important facts from magazine articles on 3-by-5-inch slips of paper in an effort to impress customers. He suffered shrapnel injuries fighting in France in World War I, and during his recovery, he read a variety of popular magazines and practiced condensing their articles. His father, a college professor, lent him $300, which Wallace used in January 1920 to produce a sixty-four-page prototype issue of *Reader's Digest*, complete with articles from publications such as *Ladies' Home Journal*, *McClure's*, and *Vanity Fair*. Potential publishers—such as William Randolph Hearst—rejected the magazine's concept, calling it interesting but without any commercial promise because of an assumed limited audience and Wallace's determination not to have illustrations or advertisements detract from the reading material in his magazine.

While searching for a publisher, Wallace met feminist reformer Lila Acheson (1887–1984), who was not looking for a husband so much as a business partner in life. She encouraged Wallace to publish *Reader's Digest* himself and helped him advertise and process the first subscription orders. The two married in Pleasantville, New York, and with $5,000 in advance subscription orders, they established the Reader's Digest Association in the New York City suburb in 1921. Pleasantville remained the headquarters of the *Reader's Digest* empire until 2010, when it moved to New York City. The magazine was an immediate success, capitalizing on the self-education and self-confidence crazes that were then underway; a growing sense of national pride; and, of course, the constant desire of readers to save time.

Except for a signature line drawing of a woman within a circle on the front cover, *Reader's Digest* was issued without artwork or illustrations until 1939. A front-cover table of contents became a trademark for *Reader's Digest* until 1998, when it was moved inside the magazine and replaced by a photograph. The table of contents was placed on the cover again in 2008, and the back cover was sold to advertisers for the first time. A greater number of illustrations began appearing with articles in the 1970s, giving the magazine more visual appeal.

A NO-NONSENSE STYLE

The Wallaces were able to support their publication on circulation revenues alone until the 1950s, using their financial freedom to espouse populist causes that other magazines were less willing to discuss. When a survey revealed that 81 percent of readers preferred advertising over increased subscription costs, advertisements began appearing in April 1955. Tobacco advertisements, a mainstay for many publications, were never accepted, and the first liquor advertisement did not appear in *Reader's Digest* until 1979.

Wallace never surveyed readers about their article preferences. Until he and his wife turned over control of the magazine to senior editors during the 1970s, he selected the articles for condensation based on what interested him, though he was mindful of the need to appeal to a large audience of both sexes and all educational levels. In 1954 *Reader's Digest* business manager Albert Cole called the magazine "the greatest common denominator in communications we have." The topics were almost always universal: science and nature, morals, health, ordeals, education, biography, animals, lifestyle, sex, and humor. The contents remained remarkably similar over the years, including feature departments such as "My Most Unforgettable Character," "Humor in Uniform," "Campus Comedy," "Life in These United States," "Picturesque Speech," "News in Medicine," and "It Pays to Enrich Your Word Power." Occasionally, Wallace's personal tastes intruded. Often, articles were heartwarming and inspirational, involved personal success stories such as his own, or advocated a nondenominational Protestantism that was described as "muscular Christianity."

Poet Carl Sandburg once observed that *Reader's Digest* was "often as solemn as death and now and then funny as a barrel of monkeys." The Wallaces were criticized for their socially and politically conservative agenda, which chided labor, big government, and any form of political radicalism and all but openly endorsed the Republican Party. The magazine's staff even wrote articles for other publications, adhering to the Wallaces' conservative leanings, so that they could be reprinted in *Reader's Digest*. The magazine defended such "plants" as a means of providing proper editorial balance. *Reader's Digest* was also criticized for refusing to publish any letters to the editor, especially corrections or rebuttals. The editors maintained that the mail was usually evenly split, making letters unnecessary. Furthermore, *Reader's Digest* articles were shortened by as much as three-fourths, leading to complaints that the points of the originals were diluted or lost. Although conservative, the magazine did not shy away from controversy. Some *Reader's Digest* articles reported on medical or scientific breakthroughs years before details appeared in other publications. The magazine also published crusading articles on venereal disease, cigarette smoking, safe driving, conservation, and other populist-style issues.

A GLOBAL MISSION

From 5,000 copies of its first issue, the circulation of *Reader's Digest* soared for most of the twentieth century. The Wallaces kept circulation figures secret until 1936, but the number of copies exceeded 200,000 by 1930, more than one million by 1935, and nine million by 1950. In 1954 it was estimated that one out of every four families in the United States received the magazine. The domestic circulation peaked at more than seventeen million copies in 1984. The magazine's profits were enhanced by a series of foreign editions, beginning with Great Britain in 1938 and extending to fifty international editions published in twenty-one languages with a global circulation of more than 100 million. Along with Disney and other major American content providers, the magazine has been criticized for surreptitiously imposing American values on other cultures, especially during the Cold War years.

In 1934 Wallace added a condensed book section as a regular feature to the magazine, which led to a Reader's Digest Condensed Book Club in 1950. In 1965 he purchased Funk & Wagnalls, publisher of *Literary Digest*, and added its extensive line of encyclopedias, dictionaries, and reference works to his magazine's book publishing division. Records, movies, and videos were added, along with a direct-mail sweepstakes competition that landed the Reader's Digest Association in trouble with the Federal Trade Commission in 1983. The Wallaces' longstanding belief in the golden rule prompted them to fund the Reader's Digest Foundation, one of the greatest philanthropic institutions of its time. The foundation supported a variety of causes, including education, the arts, and major projects such as a new contemporary wing for New York City's Metropolitan Museum of Art and the effort to move Egypt's Abu Simbel temple up the Nile Valley to make way for the Aswan High Dam.

TRYING TO STAY RELEVANT

DeWitt Wallace died in 1981 followed by Lila in 1984. In the wake of their deaths, the Reader's Digest Association began to flounder. The association went public in 1990, but advertising losses, increased competition, and the aging of its core readership dogged *Reader's Digest* into the twenty-first century. The association reached an agreement with thirty-two states in 2001 to stop making deceptive claims for its sweepstakes; it would no longer claim that the millions of direct-mail recipients were each a "guaranteed winner," and recipients did not have to subscribe to the magazine to participate in the sweepstakes. The latter part of the agreement reduced circulation, and in 2007 the association was sold to Ripplewood Holdings LLC for $2.8 billion and debt. Two years later Ripplewood declared bankruptcy but emerged in part by selling the UK edition.

More recently, the magazine and its website have focused on health, food, and personal finance advice along with humor and spiritual stories. An iPad edition was added in 2011. In the United States, the publication also sponsored community campaigns such as "We Hear You America," "Do You Live in America's Most Interesting Town?" and a national contest based on its longtime "Word Power" column. "People have always turned to *Reader's Digest*," editor Liz Vaccariello said in 2011. "Who better than *Reader's Digest* to cut through the bureaucracy and red tape to help towns fund projects and to enhance community pride?"

Richard Junger

SEE ALSO: *Advertising; Hearst, William Randolph; Metropolitan Museum of Art; Muscular Christianity;* Vanity Fair.

BIBLIOGRAPHY

Canning, Peter. *American Dreamers: The Wallaces and "Reader's Digest": An Insider's Story*. New York: Simon & Schuster, 1996.

Christensen, Reo M. "Report on the *Reader's Digest*." *Columbia Journalism Review*, Winter 1965, 30–36.

Heidenry, John. *Theirs Was the Kingdom: Lila and DeWitt Wallace and the Story of the "Reader's Digest."* New York: W. W. Norton, 1993.

Mott, Frank Luther. *A History of American Magazines, 1885–*

1905. Cambridge, MA: Harvard University Press, 1957.

Peterson, Theodore. *Magazines in the Twentieth Century*. Urbana: University of Illinois Press, 1964.

Sharp, Joane P. *Condensing the Cold War: "Reader's Digest" and American Identity*. Minneapolis: University of Minnesota Press, 2000.

Wood, James Playsted. *Of Lasting Interest: The Story of the "Reader's Digest."* Garden City, NY: Doubleday, 1967.

Wood, James Playsted. *Magazines in the United States*. New York: The Ronald Press, 1971.

Reagan, Ronald *(1911–2004)*

Ronald Wilson Reagan—America's fortieth president (1981–1989), known variously as "Dutch," the "Teflon President," the "Great Communicator" and as the father of an economic system named after him (Reaganomics)—is one of the most controversial political figures of the twentieth century. In fact, an entire system of thought, appropriately called *Reaganism*, was coined to describe the effects of his policies, which were variously called a destructive social legacy or his repositioning of American optimism and strength at the forefront of world politics. In either case, one cannot underestimate the importance of Reagan's influence during the social and political upheavals of the 1980s and beyond.

Known for his communication skills and his ease with media, Reagan avoided the press in order to avoid controversy. His advisers reportedly lived in fear that he would say something unscripted and get himself, and them, in trouble with the media and the public. As president he told his advisers to reduce all memos to one page if they wanted them to be read. If former budget adviser David Stockman's account in *The Triumph of Politics: How the Reagan Revolution Failed* is to be believed, Reagan often made decisions on a multiple-choice basis without fully understanding the consequences of his actions. In *The Presidential Character*, James David Barber summarizes the memoirs written by Reagan advisers during his presidency as offering "a fairly consistent portrayal of presidential detachment and of chaotic administration led by an enigmatic monarch who reigned rather than ruled."

Ronald and Nancy Reagan. *Ronald Reagan, right, and his wife Nancy make an appearance at the Ronald Reagan Presidential Library and Museum, Simi Valley, California, in 1994.* **AP IMAGES.**

For modern conservatives, the Reagan era encompassed the golden years of American conservatism. Former Reagan speechwriter Peggy Noonan wrote in a 1998 column for *Time* magazine that Reagan "brought Big Government to its knees and stared down the Soviet Union." Conservative political candidates at all levels of government continue to call upon the Reagan legacy. Some scholars also insist that he continues to influence modern debates on political issues. Overall, liberals recall a less friendly picture of the Reagan years. The National Organization for Women, for instance, reminded women in a 2004 article in *National NOW Times* that "for women, minorities, and the poor, the Reagan years were the bad, old days."

GROWING UP

On February 6, 1911, Reagan was born to Nelle and John Reagan in Tampico, Illinois. Although Reagan recalls his younger years as idyllic, his family moved often, living on the fly in five different places in Dixon, four in Tampico, and two in Galesburg, Illinois. His family was involved in the religious revivals hitting Tampico at the time. Although his mother was a leader of church life in her area, his father displayed a destructive reliance upon alcohol. Reagan's acting skills and religious views were formed simultaneously in these early years as he acted in his mother's skits, dated his pastor's daughter for eight years, led the Easter sunrise service, and cleaned and worked at the church.

Reagan attended high school in Dixon and enrolled at Eureka College as a freshman in 1928. He was a fairly good student, studying just enough on the easiest courses to get by, but his brother Neil recalls that he displayed a skill for last-minute memorization. Reagan performed solidly at the guard position for the football team and became a lifeguard at Lowell Park from 1927 to 1932. While in college, Reagan performed in seven plays, lettered in two sports, and was a cheerleader for other sports. He also became president of both the booster club and the senate and spent time on the school paper and the yearbook, all while majoring in economics.

Upon graduation, Reagan became a radio sports announcer at WHO in Des Moines, Iowa. He was particularly associated with baseball but did not attend most of the games he called. Though he became wildly popular in Des Moines for his broadcasting, he worked from a telegraph relay, providing his listeners with improvised action and drama. Success as an announcer eventually landed him at the Warner Brothers studio in Hollywood. A screen test in 1937 won Reagan a contract, and during the next three decades he appeared in fifty-three films, becoming famous for his cool vocal command and grace under pressure.

Reagan was best known for playing Notre Dame football player George Gipp in the film *Knute Rockne, All American* (1940) and the reckless Drake McHugh in *Kings Row* (1942), a star vehicle that put Reagan firmly on the Hollywood map. He eventually married actress Jane Wyman, with whom he had two children, Maureen and Michael. The couple divorced, and

Reagan married his second wife, Nancy Davis, another Hollywood starlet, in 1952; the couple had two more children, Patricia and Ronald.

EARLY POLITICAL CAREER

By the late 1950s Reagan's political career was already under way. As president of the Screen Actors Guild he became embroiled in disputes over the issue of communism in the film industry. His political views shifted from liberal to conservative, though, in an ironic twist, Franklin D. Roosevelt was one of his heroes. Reagan toured the country as a television host, becoming a spokesman for conservatism and a company man for General Electric. He spent the next years delivering speeches to groups across the country, mostly in favor of business and conservative interests and against big government. His oratory was considered dazzling, and he was elected governor of California in 1966 by a margin of a million votes.

Reagan's terms as governor were marked by conflict and controversy. Although he ran as a candidate opposed to tax increases (a consideration that carried itself into his presidency), Reagan implemented the highest tax hike in California up to that time. He demanded the resignation of University of California at Berkeley Chancellor Clark Kerr during the free speech demonstrations of the late 1960s, positioning himself as the voice of moderation exasperated with "campus radicals" yet was lauded by the state for balancing the books. The early stirrings of Reaganism thus became evident during Reagan's stint as governor: a devotion to business interests (General Electric), hard-line stances against liberals seeking to expand social freedoms, the demonization of communism and the Soviet Union, concern over America's perceived moral disintegration, a delegation of power to the point where the executive's ultimate responsibility lay in his rhetorical influence over party constituents, and the entrenchment of governmental power and influence coupled with the oratorical promise of deregulation.

PRESIDENCY

Reagan won the Republican presidential nomination in 1980 and chose former Texas congressman and United Nations ambassador George H. W. Bush as his running mate. Because Bush was more ideologically in line with the rest of the Republican Party at the time, he was chosen to balance the ticket and pull in the traditional party vote. Heavily influenced by the theories of economist Milton Friedman, the "New Right" program of the minimalist state and the free-market economy adopted by Reagan Republicans hit Washington, D.C., by force. Primary among these policies was supply-side economics, which was called "voodoo economics" by Bush—before he became Reagan's vice president.

Reaganomics was a curious theory that relied upon the "trickle down" of revenue from the wealthy to the poor. This effect was supposed to occur as the rich spent more money, jump-starting the overall economy. To implement the plan Reagan signed into law tax breaks and benefits to the wealthy that continued long past his presidency. He linked tax breaks for the wealthy with drastic cutbacks in social spending. Hardest hit by these cuts were programs such as AFDC (Aid to Families with Dependent Children), commonly known as welfare, and Medicaid. Welfare recipients were castigated by the Republican Party as loafers who had been coddled by the oversized government Reagan campaigned against throughout his career.

Some observers believe that Reagan's most important political victories came in the arena of foreign policy. He came into power on the heels of a crisis involving Iranian seizure of the U.S. embassy and the taking of hostages. President Jimmy Carter had made freeing the hostages a major priority; when he failed to do so he came across as incompetent though he continued to negotiate with Iranian representatives until the eleventh hour. The hostages were ready to board a plane to freedom on January 20, 1981, Inauguration Day, but their release was delayed until minutes after Reagan was sworn in to prevent Carter from getting credit for freeing them.

As president, Reagan set about establishing relations with countries that Carter had battled over human rights abuses. He continued to rail against the Soviet Union and communism, as he had done throughout his Hollywood and California years, and increased defense spending became a major priority. One of his pet projects was the Strategic Defense Initiative, dubbed "Star Wars" by critics because it was seen as being as unrealistic as the events in the popular *Star Wars* movies. Reagan poured billions of U.S. tax dollars into the project until it was abandoned because it was unworkable.

IMAGE AND REALITY

Reagan implemented aggressive domestic policies against crime, drugs, and pornography. Although he championed a United States free from the dictates of oppressive government control, he used government to further his conservative social agenda, which included the banning of abortion, the reinstatement of school prayer, and the promotion of the nuclear heterosexual family. During the Reagan years, American prosperity and position increased, at least in theory. Some people have argued that Reagan was instrumental in the eventual fall of communism in the Soviet Union. The other side of the coin is that economic deregulation led to at least one major economic recession, a growth in the unemployment rate, and a stigmatization of citizens who relied upon social programs such as AFDC and Medicaid for assistance.

Reagan's punishing stances on social disintegration came back to haunt him during the infamous Iran-Contra hearings. Despite the fact that Reagan had become known as the "Teflon President" because no criticism stuck long enough to damage his popularity, he did not emerge from the scandal with his reputation totally intact. In 1986 a magazine in Beirut broke the story that the Reagan administration had been selling arms to Iran despite an embargo that had been in place since 1979. Further investigation revealed that when Congress refused to fund the anticommunist Contras in Nicaragua, Reagan bypassed Congress by using money from the secret arms deal with Iran to fund the Contras. During hearings, it became clear that Reagan was not always in charge of his own White House. Despite similarities to the Watergate scandal that had landed members of the Nixon administration in jail in the 1970s, those indicted in Iran-Contra were not imprisoned. As president, Bush pardoned the last of them in 1992 before leaving office.

Inconsistencies between reality and the persona that Reagan presented can be traced all the way back to his imaginative renderings of baseball games at which he was never present. Despite his failings, Reagan was particularly adept at oratory, and he managed to imbue the American public with a sense of relentless optimism, helping to rejuvenate nationalism within a country whose national character and trust in its government had been marred by upheavals at home that included battles over civil rights and women's rights, the sexual revolution, divisive stances on the Vietnam War, and a feeling of helplessness during the Iranian hostage situation.

POPULAR CULTURE

Although he was never more than a mediocre performer, Reagan brought his acting skills—his greatest asset—to the presidency. He became known as the "Great Communicator" despite the fact that he often avoided the press. He gave fewer press conferences than most modern presidents, but the label stuck. Reagan's conservatism and the liberal backlash against it were essential elements in the culture of the 1980s, which came to be associated with the Me Generation and an unchecked appetite for material greed.

In music, down-home heroes like Bruce Springsteen and John Mellencamp climbed the charts on the strength of their blue-collar, heartland lyrics. Yet the birth of rap and its vocal dissatisfaction with unfair treatment of minorities and the poor in the lyrics of groups such as Public Enemy, KRS-One, and Grandmaster Flash & the Furious Five also occurred in the Reagan era. Films moved toward blockbusters featuring hard-bodied, masculine heroes such as Sylvester Stallone, whose mythic Rambo was the de facto Reagan icon. Reagan frequently referred to himself as a movie hero; in political speeches he often told anecdotes that had actually occurred in films rather than in real life. He particularly identified with action-adventure characters played by Chuck Norris, Arnold Schwarzenegger, and Clint Eastwood. Reagan actually appropriated Eastwood's Dirty Harry line from the film *Sudden Impact*, "Go ahead, make my day," for a foreign policy speech.

Television reflected the Reagan era, especially the world of glitz and glamour. *Dynasty* (1981–1989) was one of the biggest hits of the 1980s, and *thirtysomething* (1987–1991) provided the yuppies (young urban professionals, who became the de facto Reaganite model constituents) with a forum for voicing their middle-class concerns. Further, the ultimate conflation of the entertainment industry and political sphere by the end of the Reagan era prefigured the rise in power of so-called tabloid talk shows, news programs (even twenty-four-hour news channels such as CNN and C-SPAN), reality television shows such as *Cops* (1989–), and an increasing influx of media attention on the personal lives of political figures (Nancy Reagan's alleged affair with Frank Sinatra, the Clarence Thomas–Anita Hill hearings, Gary Hart's indiscretions, and the Bill Clinton–Monica Lewinsky affair, among others). Politics and entertainment had finally reached the stage in their evolution where they became linked together. Reagan's persuasive use of the media in his policy implementation, as well as his economic deregulation, which allowed media monopolies to grow from film to publishing to sports and beyond, gave the media heretofore unrealized power that continues to expand with each technological innovation.

In his 1990 autobiography, *An American Life*, Reagan announced that he had been diagnosed with Alzheimer's disease, causing many Americans to wonder how long he had been suffering from the condition. He lived out much of the rest of his life in seclusion and died on June 5, 2004, leaving a lasting legacy for his party as well as his country.

Scott Thill

SEE ALSO: *Abortion; Anita Hill–Clarence Thomas Senate Hearings; Cheerleading; Civil Rights Movement; Communism; Daytime Talk Shows;* Dynasty*; Eastwood, Clint; Grandmaster Flash; Hollywood; Iran Contra; Lewinsky, Monica; Me Decade; Mellencamp, John; Movie Stars; National Organization for Women (NOW); Public Enemy; Radio; Rambo; Rap; Reality Television; Rockne, Knute; Schwarzenegger, Arnold; Sexual Revolution; Sinatra, Frank; Springsteen, Bruce; Stallone, Sylvester;* Star Wars*; Tabloid Television; Television;* Time*; Vietnam; Watergate; Yuppies.*

BIBLIOGRAPHY

Barber, James David. *The Presidential Character: Predicting Performance in the White House*. Englewood Cliffs, NJ: Prentice Hall, 1992.

Conley, Richard S., ed. *Reassessing the Reagan Presidency*. Lanham, MD: University Press of America, 2003.

Draper, Theodore. *A Very Thin Line: The Iran-Contra Affairs*. New York: Hill and Way, 1991.

Edel, Wilbur. *The Reagan Presidency: An Actor's Finest Performance*. New York: Hippocrene, 1992.

Feuer, Jane. *Seeing through the Eighties: Television and Reaganism*. Durham, NC: Duke University Press, 1995.

Hill, Dilys; Raymond Moore; and Phil Williams. *The Reagan Presidency: An Incomplete Revolution?* New York: St. Martin's Press, 1990.

Jeffords, Susan. *Hard Bodies: Hollywood Masculinity in the Reagan Era*. New Brunswick, NJ: Rutgers University Press, 1994.

Jordan, Chris. *Movies and the Reagan Presidency: Success and Ethics*. Westport, CT: Praeger, 2003.

Kengor, Paul, and Peter Schweizer. *The Reagan Presidency: Assessing the Man and His Legacy*. Lanham, MD: Rowman & Littlefield, 2005.

National Organization of Women. "Golden Glow of Reagan Legacy Lacks Luster for Feminists." *National NOW Times*, Fall 2004.

Noonan, Peggy. "Ronald Reagan." *Time*, April 13, 1998.

Schieffer, Bob, and Gary Paul Gates. *The Acting President*. New York: E. P. Dutton, 1989.

Stockman, David Alan. *The Triumph of Politics: How the Reagan Revolution Failed*. New York: Harper & Row, 1986.

Wills, Garry. *Reagan's America: Innocents at Home*. Garden City, NY: Doubleday, 1987.

The Real Housewives of . . .

The Real Housewives of . . . is a reality television franchise on the Bravo cable network that follows the lives of wealthy housewives in different sections of the country. Producer Scott Dunlop had always been fascinated with the wealthy middle-aged women in his gated community of Coto de Caza, California, and he thought they would make an excellent subject for a reality television series. *The Real Housewives of Orange County* premiered on the Bravo channel in 2006. As of 2012 there were five different U.S. spin-offs: *The Real Housewives of New York City*, *The Real Housewives of Atlanta*, *The Real Housewives of New Jersey*, *The Real Housewives of Beverly Hills*, and *The Real Housewives of Miami*. Mixing traditional, scripted storytelling with the candor and spontaneity of reality TV, *The Real Housewives of . . .* series drew approximately two million viewers per episode as of 2012.

The idea for the reality show arose from the success of the fictional ABC series *Desperate Housewives*, which had attracted a large audience and critical acclaim for its depiction of the troubled secret lives of women who inhabit a seemingly quaint American suburb. Unlike the women on *Desperate Housewives*, however, those portrayed on *The Real Housewives of . . .* shows do not necessarily live in precisely the same neighborhood and may not experience the high drama and extravagant misadventures that their fictional counterparts do. The cast of a *Real Housewives* show consists of friends and acquaintances who live in the same general area, typically within several miles of each other, and often have competing interests and ambitions. Over the course of a season, the women typically expose their petty vanities as well as more disconcerting vices that are more threatening to family life.

The spin-offs all follow the original's model. *The Real Housewives of DC*, which premiered in 2010 and ran for one season, was the only spin-off not to be renewed. *The Real Housewives of Athens* was the first international show in the franchise, and as of 2012 the series was poised to expand to Israel, France, and the United Kingdom.

The series has drawn the ire of social critics who claim that the show both objectifies women and also exposes their superficiality, greed, and narcissism. Critics have noted that in the context of the series, *housewife* becomes a term that is largely demeaning: the women are wealthy, obsessed with their looks, and materialistic. Television critic Carina Chocano observes that the women on the show "reliably engage in all kinds of confusing, contradictory, neo-housewife behavior" and argues that the series has "re-branded" the upper-middle-class housewife as a hopelessly shallow individual.

Isabel Istanders

SEE ALSO: *Cable TV;* Desperate Housewives*; Frankel, Bethenny;* The Real World*; Reality Television; Television.*

BIBLIOGRAPHY

Bravo Network. *The Real Housewives Tell It Like it Is*. San Francisco: Chronicle Books, 2011.

Chocano, Carina. "'Housewives,' Rebranded." *New York Times*, November 18, 2011.

David, Anna, ed. *Reality Matters: 19 Writers Come Clean about the Shows We Can't Stop Watching*. New York: HarperCollins, 2010.

Lee, Michael, and Leigh Moscowitz. "The 'Rich Bitch': Class and Gender on the *Real Housewives of New York City*. *Feminist Media Studies*, February 2012.

Maher, J. "What Do Women Watch? Tuning In to the Compulsory Heterosexual Channel." In *Reality TV: Remaking Television Culture*, ed. Susan Murray and Laura Ouellette. New York: New York University Press, 2004.

The Real World

The Real World, MTV's first "reality-based" television series, was launched in the fall of 1992 to immense critical and popular acclaim. Over the course of the ensuing twenty-seven seasons, it has transformed from a controversial experiment into a money-making franchise. Besides being the longest-running MTV program, it is also one of the longest-running reality programs in television history.

A pseudo-documentary, its concept—reiterated in the opening credits of each week's half-hour episode—is "This is the story of seven strangers, picked to live in a house, and have their lives taped, to see what happens when people stop being polite, and start getting real." The show's "strangers" are a diverse group of young people ages eighteen to twenty-five of various geographic, socioeconomic, religious, and sexual orientations, whom the producers carefully screen and assemble hoping for the most volatile—and therefore sensationally watchable—combination possible. According to producer Jon Murray, "the main point of the series is to tell the story of this group of kids. It's to show them getting involved with each other, learning from each other, sharing fears and dreams."

LIFE IN A FISHBOWL

To further ensure conflict, each season is set in a different city, state, or country to isolate the participants from friends and family—often for the first time in their lives. Already vulnerable then, the cast members must agree to allow themselves to be constantly video- and audiotaped by an arsenal of surveillance and hand-held cameras, as well as microphones hidden in every room, on each character, and in the phone. *The Real World* house for the season is usually large and colorful for television purposes, as the producers require that the housemates spend as much time at home as possible and disallow television, music, and other "distractions" that cause problems with the recording and inhibit social interaction.

To ensure some tension, bedrooms and bathrooms are coed. A Jacuzzi is provided, which seems to be in use day and night. There is also a constant supply of alcohol, which ensures the possibility of sex and arguments, as well as the drama that unfolds the morning after when the housemates deal with the aftermath of their drunken behavior. To add variety and further opportunities for conflict, producers began to require the participants to work together for a local business or do volunteer work. Partway through the season the housemates are also treated to a vacation in some exotic locale.

As the months in the house pass, allegiances and grudges are formed. The housemates are regularly filmed in direct-camera interviews about their feelings, their opinions, day-to-day incidents, and their changing attitudes toward their roommates. Murray contends that these interviews are held to clear up the narrative, not to create one. The "characters" are also expected to pay a weekly visit to the "confessional" room to air their feelings in private to a camera. Thus, *The Real World* has its antecedents in both cinema verité as well as direct cinema practices of the 1960s.

Once the months of filming are completed, the approximately 180,000 minutes of video are edited down to the 440 minutes of episodes that will compose the season; in other words, less than 1 percent of the actual filmed experience is aired. Footage of everyday activities such as reading, cooking, and cleaning are excised to focus on moments of conflict over philosophies, relationships, and the like.

The behavior in this "fishbowl" existence can turn ugly. In one episode of *Real World: Los Angeles*, abrasive stand-up comic David pulled the bedcovers off a scantily clad and laughing Tami. Tami later claimed that she had been "violated," and David was kicked off the show. In the 1994 San Francisco season, bike messenger Puck became infamous for his lack of hygiene and insensitive treatment of gay housemate Pedro Zamora, who was dying of AIDS. After Puck's removal from the house, Zamora's struggle with the disease and his on-screen marriage to his lover Sean further enhanced the show's popularity—and ratings. While many of the incidents that become the plotlines of an episode are significant, cast members also charge that focusing an episode on what they deem to be insignificant incidents tends to exaggerate their importance way out of proportion—a charge leveled by many subjects of documentary films.

RESULTING "CELEBRITY"

In addition, after each season begins airing and the respective casts are interviewed by the press, the first question often posed to them concerns whether they are being themselves or playing themselves. Though *Real World*-ers generally contend they quickly grew used to the constant surveillance, paradoxically they also agree that the cameras elevated the intensity of every encounter—so much so that MTV offers each cast free psychological counseling at the end of the taping as a means of recovering from the experience. Producer George Verschoor warns each cast at the outset:

> Once you get in this house, you are going to be challenged in ways you never thought of. Every move, every part of your past is going to be questioned. . . . So you'd better be ready to look in that mirror. Because when you do, you're going to see yourself—and not only what you think of yourself, but what others think of you . . . and then what a nation thinks of you.

Consequently, though they are not celebrities in the conventional sense, veterans of the show have found their "fifteen minutes of fame" through continual public recognition and occasionally harassment; the show's popularity, constant reruns, and updated reports on their respective activities never really allowing them to retire to anonymity. Some cast members have marketed their newfound fame into performing careers—models Jacinda Barrett and Eric Nies and even David "Puck" Rainey turning to acting, with Nies also doing a stint as the host of MTV's dance show *The Grind* and creating his own workout video.

SPIN-OFFS

The series' popularity also resulted in MTV expanding its slate of reality-based programming, including introducing the equally popular spin-off show *Road Rules* (1995–2007)—essentially "*The Real World*-in-a-Winnebago"—as five youths take an extensive, often international, road trip involving both thrills (skydiving, swimming with sharks) and chills (staying the night in a haunted house; milking snakes for venom).

In 1998 the spin-off *The Real World/Road Rules Challenge* (later *The Challenge*) pitted casts from different seasons of both shows against each other and, occasionally, outside participants to win a cash prize. As on TV's *Survivor*, the cast lives together in an exotic location and takes part in a series of physical challenges that result in members being voted off at regular intervals. Besides the stress of the physical competitions themselves, these "Challenges" become especially contentious due to the often-acrimonious relationships the respective contestants have developed with each other over the years.

Rick Moody

SEE ALSO: *AIDS; Cable TV; Celebrity; Gay and Lesbian Marriage; Gay Men; MTV; Reality Television;* Survivor; *Television.*

BIBLIOGRAPHY

Heigl, Alex. "Twelve Crucial Moments in the Evolution of MTV." Nerve, August 1, 2011. Accessed March 2012. Available from http://www.nerve.com/entertainment/evolved-mtv

Johnson, Hillary, and Nancy Rommelmann. *The Real "Real World."* New York: Melcher Media, 1995.

Patane, Joe. *Livin' in Joe's World.* New York: HarperPerennial, 1998.

"The Real World" Diaries. New York: Melcher Media, 1996.

Reality Television

Reality television shows are a loose genre of thematic shows and one-time episodes that have one unifying basis: they rely, in some fashion, on real, true, or unscripted events. The reality these shows present can take numerous forms, from *Candid Camera* in the late 1940s to the Loud family, who shared their lives with television audiences in 1973 on *An American Family*, to the behind-the-scenes struggles of *American Idol* thirty years later. The genre has become hugely diverse, both in the subject matter of the shows in question and the approaches taken for programming. Reality television embraces tabloid news in the form of programs such as *A Current Affair*; talk shows such as *The Jerry Springer Show*; "fly-on-the-wall" documentary-style shows such as *Pawn Stars*; and simple, cheap to make, candid video shows with titles beginning with phrases such as "World's Funniest" or "World's Most Shocking."

In the early twenty-first century, a new category of reality television show emerged in which real people were placed in artificial situations and recorded so their reactions could be observed by viewers in a kind of anthropological experiment. The phenomenon of reality television first gained momentum in the mid-1980s and quickly became a mainstay of TV schedules around the world.

THE BIRTH OF A GENRE

Television producers had explored using unscripted footage as far back as the 1940s, particularly in shows such as Allen Funt's *Candid Camera* in which people had pranks played on them while being filmed without their knowledge. However, before the 1980s, unscripted or partially scripted reality television was limited to a handful of game shows and a few "social experiment" shows.

In an article on reality television in the *New Yorker* in 2011, Kelefa Sanneh focused on *An American Family*, which was first broadcast on PBS in 1973. The show features the Louds, a family of seven from California who consented to be filmed for many months in 1971 and 1972, after which the footage was edited together into twelve episodes. The show was more controversial than expected. Not only did it show the collapse of Bill and Pat Loud's marriage, but their eldest son, Lance, told them he was gay and, in doing so, became the first openly gay person on American television. *An American Family* was a hit, but no similar show appeared until MTV's *The Real World* in 1992. In Britain a similar show called *The Family* aired in 1974. Featuring the Wilkins family, it is an early example of reality television shows crossing the Atlantic and an indication that the genre had cross-cultural appeal.

Reality television as a phenomenon grew out of the falling cost of home video equipment in the 1980s, the proliferation of TV channels—all of which needed cheap shows to fill schedules—and people's desire, going back to the earliest days of television, to be on TV. The arrival of low-cost, handheld video cameras meant that increasing numbers of people had video footage of street scenes, where crimes might be taking place, and of people and pets doing stupid things. Government agencies, including the police, also began to use video cameras to record their activities. Naturally, TV companies became interested in this "candid" footage, much of which could be acquired from viewers for nothing, and they worked out ways to make use of it. Tabloid news shows, including *Hard Copy*, which ran throughout the 1990s, used a lot of home video, including secretly taken videos of celebrities, to illustrate its stories.

CRIME AND COP SHOWS

Its entertainment value notwithstanding, reality television often presents itself as informative or of some social value. In 1989 the reality crime show *Cops* established a new form of reality TV by pulling together footage, filmed with handheld camcorders, of police officers pursuing criminals. Crime shows quickly became a significant part of TV schedules. Programs such as *Cops*, *America's Most Wanted*, and *Unsolved Mysteries* devoted themselves to exploring the world of crime and criminals. There were also many variants on police action car-chase shows, all of which used in-car footage to show poor driving or criminal behavior.

Reality crime shows present a central message regarding both crime and law and order, and through a careful construction of reality, they make their point quite effectively: crime is rampant, violent, and obvious to spot; criminals are villains; and the police and jails are America's best line of defense against these challenges to decent society. For example, *Cops* features "the men and women of law enforcement" and nightly ride-alongs with police from different parts of the country. *Cops* would appear on the surface to be the most realistic of these shows, as it does not have a narrator or host beyond the officers who offer background or context for the situations they encounter. However, in a 1993 article in *Harper's*, Debra Seagal reported that these shows often rely on stock footage, and producers spend a great deal of time constructing the "stories" that appear.

These programs also construct a version of reality through the narrative closure they attempt to provide. Resolution of events is preferred over unsolved crimes or escaped or unknown criminals, and reality television attempts to provide viewing audiences with this closure. The result is a view of law enforcement that is at odds with federal statistics on suspects apprehended and cases closed. For example, in *Entertaining Crime: Television Reality Programs*, Mary Beth Oliver and G. Blake Armstrong report that in a sample of reality-based programs, 61.5 percent of all crimes portrayed were depicted as solved, "as compared to FBI reports of an 18.0 percent arrest rate." Furthermore, the shows perpetuate the idea that minorities are more likely to engage in criminal activities. Oliver and Armstrong note that "the vast majority of African-American characters are cast in roles of criminal suspects where they are also shown as recipients of police aggression." And though shows such as *Cops* state that "all suspects are innocent until proven guilty in a court of law," researchers have found that most viewers believe the suspects apprehended are indeed guilty, otherwise the police would not have arrested them in the first place. Court TV, renamed "truTV" by Turner Entertainment in 2008, began by televising court proceedings, thus bringing the cop show format full circle. Its new tagline is "Not Reality. Actuality."

In addition to their low cost, reality crime shows are valuable to broadcasters for other reasons. For example, many of these shows do not contain temporal references, and so can be shown again and again in syndication, where the most profits can be made. Crime reality shows can also fill broadcast station owners' need to provide their viewing audience with public service programming, a requirement for maintaining their Federal Communications Commission (FCC) license. Because these shows are a somewhat ambiguous mix of news and documentary, station owners can claim they are fulfilling their obligation to air public service shows.

Shows such as *Cops* perpetuate the idea that criminals are one-dimensional villains, beyond redemption or reason, and therefore deserving of maximum sentences and harsh justice. In *Entertaining Crime: Television Reality Programs*, Gray Cavender writes that on shows such as *America's Most Wanted* and *Unsolved Mysteries*, "the night teems with drug dealers and satanists, and crazy, cold-blooded killers prowl the mean streets of cities and small towns. . . . Criminals are described in terms that connote physical ugliness. They are depicted as dangerous, depraved, unremorseful people." In other words, criminals are portrayed as caricatures and are depicted as fundamentally different from the audience and beyond redemption. This view of criminals as beyond reason—as "rotten to the core"—then legitimates strict crime control measures and idealizes justice as something wielded by a community to punish the bad apples that threaten the stability and life of the group.

SHOCK SHOWS

So-called shock shows are another popular form of reality television These draw together various types of amateur video, such as police surveillance footage, based on a particular theme. This first of these specials was *World's Most Dangerous Animals*, which appeared on the Fox network on January 25, 1996. The show collected film clips from nature documentaries, including an elephant stomping on a trainer and a bear attacking a woman. The show had a moral message that humanity was to blame for what had happened to these animals. *World's Most Dangerous Animals* spawned a series of successors—but without the pro-social message. In an interview with David Bauder, George Gerbner, a communications professor and scholar who studies violence on television, indicated that these shows "exploit the worst fears and nightmares of people." NBC executive Don Ohlmeyer called Fox's video of animal attacks "one step short of a snuff film."

Low production costs contribute in part to the survival of shows like these. Broadcast television has been in a long-term decline, steadily losing viewers to cable television and other sources of entertainment, notably online video services such as YouTube. This has led the networks to focus on smaller, more specific audience segments to appeal to advertisers (such as men aged eighteen to forty-nine) and has also led them to invest in low-cost programs. Typically drama and comedy series are quite expensive. For example, the science fiction program *Star Trek: Voyager* (1995–2001) cost approximately $1.5 million an episode, and the hospital drama *ER* (1994–2009) cost NBC $13 million per episode in 1998. In contrast, in its early days, *America's Most Wanted* cost $140,000 to $170,000 to produce one weekly half-hour episode. Thus, though they may not draw the same size audience, these shows are cheaper to produce and so can afford to generate smaller audiences and less advertising revenue.

GAME SHOWS

In the first decade of the twenty-first century, perhaps because television suddenly had to offer something that online video services couldn't—namely higher production values—reality game shows became popular. These ranged from "survival in the wilderness" shows such as *Survivor*, syndicated from a Swedish show *Expedition Robinson* in which contestants compete in tests of survival skills, to shows based on show business themes such as *Dancing with the Stars* and *American Idol*. The latter show, which is based on a British show with the same format, *Pop Idol*, first aired in 2002 and achieved the highest viewing figures for any show on American television in each of the eight following years.

The basic format of *American Idol* is that of a simple talent show. Performers go through auditions before being allowed to perform in front of the theatrically critical judges. Simon Cowell, British impresario and former *American Idol* judge, became famous in the United States for his sarcastic and dismissive comments. In a series of rounds the number of performers is reduced until they reach the finals, where they perform for a live studio audience. Over the years the production values and locations have become more expensive and ever larger. *American Idol* puts performers through a grueling test, but the prize is a record deal with a major label and almost guaranteed earnings of more than $1 million in the first year.

Many other similar talent shows exist, with variations such as ice dancing, ballroom dancing, and other kinds of performing. *America's Next Top Model* gave women the chance to compete to become exactly that. But the global reality game show giant *Big Brother* took a different approach, locking a group of carefully selected "contestants" in a closed compound and giving them assignments to complete. The idea behind *Big Brother*, which originated in the Netherlands in 1999, comes from George Orwell's book *1984*, which describes a society under constant surveillance. In the "Big Brother House," the inmates are observed at all times, and their interactions are discussed. Gossip and intrigue blossom as the inmates jostle not to be voted out by the outside audience.

By 2012 *Big Brother* was one of the world's largest TV show franchises, with seasons running in countries around the world. The psychological strains of being constantly observed make for challenging behavior among the contestants. However, there is also an element of gamesmanship in which contestants deliberately scandalize the audience to gain attention and, ultimately, fame.

Variations on the fly-on-the-wall style of *Big Brother* often include celebrities, such as *Celebrity Big Brother*. Many of these shows, which include *The Anna Nicole Show* (2002–2004) and *The Osbournes* (2002–2005), purport to show the lives of their subjects in reality documentary style. Others involve celebrities in difficult situations, including the British show *I'm a Celebrity, Get Me out of Here!* (2002) in which moderately famous people are made to do unpleasant things in the jungle, including eating bugs and handling various animals.

THE PARODIES

The appearance of *The Family* in Britain in 1974 also marked the beginning of a new form of comedy, based on parodying reality television. Within weeks of the show ending, *Monty Python's Flying Circus* produced a sketch called "The Most Awful Family in Britain," featuring the Garibaldi family of Worcestershire and a panel of judges deciding who should receive the award. The proliferation of fly-on-the-wall documentaries and tabloid news shows in the United States in the 1990s led to comedies such as *The Office* (2005), which parodies a fly-on-the-wall documentary about an office and its self-absorbed manager. *The Office* successfully made the transition from British to American television. Similarly the British political spoof documentary *The Thick of It* (2005) was remade in 2012, set in Washington, D.C., as *Veep*. Other more serious television dramas have also borrowed from reality television, such as HBO's *The Wire* (2002–2008), a gritty police drama set in Baltimore, Maryland, which often used shaky handheld footage to reinforce the realism of its imagery.

A DIVERSE GENRE

Reality television is one of the most diverse of all television genres. It ranges from fly-on-the-wall documentaries such as *Cops* and *Big Brother* to game shows, talent shows, and even home improvement shows. The number of activities given the reality TV treatment is almost limitless: photography, finding a job, cooking, learning to play sports, losing weight, and getting married, to name only a few. Always though it is the people involved who make these shows watchable, and nowhere was that more important than with reality talk shows such as *The Jerry Springer Show*, where dysfunctional families had fights on stage. In the first decade of the twenty-first century, reality television had to compete with online video services such as YouTube, where candid video of people doing humorous, stupid, or shocking things could be posted easily and cheaply. The move toward high production values in shows such as *American Idol* no doubt reflects this. Amateurs could not produce a talent show on such a scale or at such cost.

As popular as the genre is, the reality of reality TV is the fine line between what is real and what is not. Though many reality TV series are promoted as though all actions are spontaneous and "real," the fact remains that these shows have scriptwriters who create stories from the filmed material and editors who carefully select what viewers will and will not see. There have been a number of lawsuits filed against makers of reality TV shows by contestants who claimed the shows had fixed outcomes or otherwise manipulated situations. Among these shows are *Survivor*, *Temptation Island*, and *Joe Millionaire*.

Yet at the same time the "real world" worked its way into many other areas of television. Viewers voted for their favorites in talent shows, but they also increasingly provided video and photographic footage of newsworthy events, including the World Trade Center tragedy. The ubiquity of smartphones by 2010 made this trend all the more inevitable. Social networking sites such as Facebook and Twitter also brought "citizen journalists" to the fore. In 2011 Twitter ran an advertisement claiming to be "faster than earthquakes" in the sense that news of an earthquake coming could arrive via Twitter faster than the quake itself. In 2012 news channels including CNN often ran a "Twitter feed" alongside images during major news events, so that in the early twenty-first century, a great deal of what was on television could be said to have a grounding in "reality"—whatever that may be.

Mia Consalvo

SEE ALSO: *Advertising;* American Idol*;* America's Funniest Home Videos*; Cable TV;* Candid Camera*; Celebrity; CNN; Coming Out;* Dancing with the Stars*; Daytime Talk Shows; Divorce; DIY/Home Improvement; The Duggar Family;* ER*; Facebook; Game Shows; Gay Men; The Internet; Live Television;* Monty Python's Flying Circus*; MTV; The* New Yorker*;* The Office*; Osbourne, Ozzy;* The Osbournes*; Pets; Public Television (PBS);* The Real World*; Smartphones; Smith, Anna Nicole; Social Media; Springer, Jerry;* Star Trek*;* Survivor*; Syndication; Tabloid Television; Television; Twitter; Viral Videos;* The Wire*; World Trade Center; YouTube.*

BIBLIOGRAPHY

Bauder, David. "TV Turns to 'Local News on Steroids.'" *Daily News*, February 7, 1999, 19D.

Bauder, David. "90s Turbo-Charged 'Snuff Shows' All the Rage." *Daily Iowan*, February 9, 1999, 5A.

Boissard, Justine. "This Is Their Life." *UNESCO Courier*, October 1992, 14–16.

Fishman, Mark, and Gray Cavender, eds. *Entertaining Crime: Television Reality Programs*. New York: Aldine de Gruyter, 1998.

Pozner, Jennifer L. *Reality Bites Back: The Troubling Truth about Guilty Pleasure TV*. Berkeley, CA: Seal Press, 2010.

Sanneh, Kelefa. "The Reality Principle: The Rise and Rise of a Television Genre." *New Yorker*, May 9, 2011.

Seagal, Debra. "Tales from the Cutting-Room Floor." *Harper's Magazine*, November 1993, 50–57.

Rear Window

Rear Window (1954) is indisputably among director Alfred Hitchcock's masterpieces of suspense. It was first in his three-picture collaboration during the 1950s with actor James Stewart, who also starred in *The Man Who Knew Too Much* (1955) and *Vertigo* (1958). The films marked the flowering of Hitchcock's Technicolor period (he had ventured into color only twice previously, first for *Rope* in 1948, which also starred Stewart). *Rear Window* continues to be shown regularly on television and at retrospectives of Hitchcock's and Stewart's films and occasionally as a movie theater rerun. The film's popularity has endured, in part, because it never loses its suspense and intrigue, even with repeated viewings. It is a virtual master class in the concerns, obsessions, and techniques that distinguish Hitchcock's work from that of other filmmakers in the suspense thriller genre.

SCREENPLAY

Screenwriter John Michael Hayes, in close collaboration with Hitchcock, crafted the film's screenplay, tempering suspense with sadness, humor—both salty and sophisticated—and a rare nod to redemptive compassion. Hayes, who would write Hitchcock's next three films, worked from a novelette called *Window* by Cornell Woolrich (who also wrote under the pseudonym William Irish), whose fiction had, over the decades, provided fodder for countless "B"-movie thrillers and better film noirs, including Robert Siodmak's *Phantom Lady* (1944).

The plot of *Rear Window* is relatively simple: A news photographer (Stewart), having suffered an accident, has his left leg encased in a heavy plaster cast and is confined to a wheelchair in one room of his small city apartment. Bored and frustrated, he passes the time observing through a telephoto camera lens the occupants of the apartments across the building's courtyard. The hobby turns into a compulsion, and then a voyeuristic obsession, as the details of his neighbors' lives emerge. He grows convinced that one man (Raymond Burr) has murdered his wife and disposed of her body. The photographer's glamorous, society-girl fiancée (Grace Kelly), his down-to-earth nurse-housekeeper (Thelma Ritter), and his police detective buddy (Wendell Corey) are skeptical of his suspicions, though he eventually convinces the women, who become dangerously involved in investigating the mystery.

ACTING AND DIRECTION

Hitchcock enjoyed the challenges of filming in the confines of a single studio-bound set, as he did in *Lifeboat* (1944), *Rope*, and *Dial M for Murder* (1954). He chose to film *Rear Window* from the vantage of Stewart's character, never straying from the

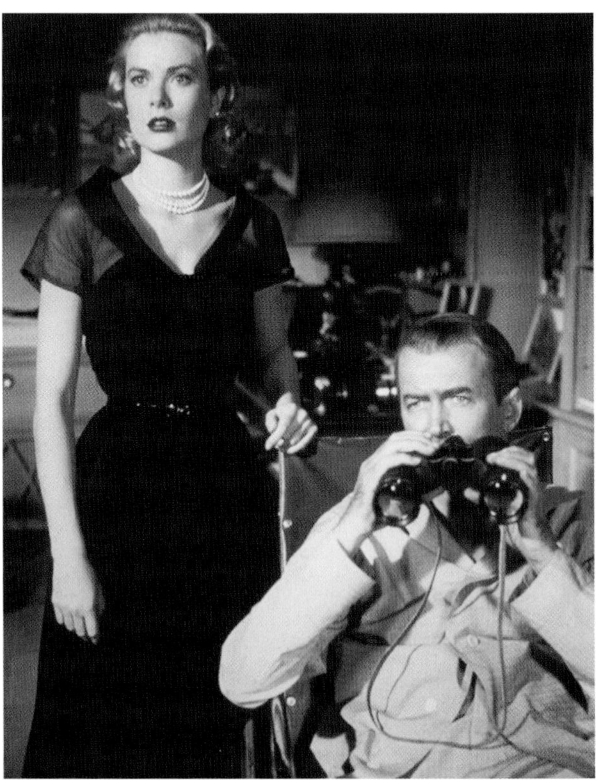

***Grace Kelly and James Stewart in* Rear Window.** *Grace Kelly, left, and James Stewart play a scene from* Rear Window. PARAMOUNT/THE KOBAL COLLECTION].

protagonist's apartment and showing the audience only what the protagonist himself sees. Stewart's character drives the film's action, though he is forced into a passive role as observer of the domestic dramas in the neighboring apartments—a role that the audience shares.

The task of populating the movie posed several problems to Hitchcock and his crew. In *The Celluloid Muse: Hollywood Directors Speak* (1969), the director tells authors Charles Higham and Joel Greenberg, "The set had to be pre-lit because it was such a tremendous job. We had thirty-one apartments, twelve of them fully furnished. The people moving around in them had microphones on, which you couldn't see at that distance, through which they received instructions." On a purely technical level, the challenge of filming a confined visual space necessitated the cinematic device of montage. The building blocks of *Rear Window* are the crosscuts between Stewart peering through his lens and the scenes he is watching across the courtyard. The same shot of Stewart could take on an entirely different meaning for the audience depending on whether Hitchcock preceded Stewart's reaction shot with one of a mother and child or one of an attractive blond disrobing.

In an interview with French filmmaker François Truffaut, published in *Hitchcock/Truffaut* (1985), Hitchcock explains the importance he had placed on the assorted vignettes of the neighbors: "What you see across the way is a group of little stories that . . . mirror a small universe." Truffaut responds that the neighbors' lives also have meaning for the protagonist and his fiancée: "All of the stories have a common denominator . . . love. James Stewart's problem is that he doesn't want to marry Grace Kelly. Everything he sees across the way has a bearing on love and marriage." In Woolrich's original story, the protagonist does not have a girlfriend, but Hitchcock and Hayes chose to use the secondary theme because it fueled sophisticated verbal sparring between the actors.

Hitchcock added further dimension to the film by cloaking Stewart's character in ambiguity. In an interview with the director, critics Ian Cameron and V. F. Perkins describe an argument they had about the film: "One of us says that a good deal of the suspense comes from one's not being sure whether James Stewart is right, whether he's making a fool of himself. The other says that you're meant to be certain that he's right and the suspense comes from whether he will prove it in time." Although Hitchcock espoused the latter perspective, the fact that the film builds suspense on several levels is a testament to its complex subtext.

On a deeper, more disturbing level, the film explores one of the director's recurring themes: the transference of guilt from villain to hero and from hero to audience. In his discussions with Truffaut, Hitchcock called the protagonist "a real Peeping Tom," noting that one critic complained, "*Rear Window* was a horrible film because the hero spent all of his time peeping out of the window," to which the director responded, "What's so horrible about that? Sure, he's a snooper, but aren't we all?" Through the protagonist's voyeurism, the film exposes the audience's own desire to hide in a darkened theater and watch dramas unfold.

LEGACY

Rear Window received four Academy Award nominations but failed to win in a bumper year for the film industry. (The same year, Best Actress favorite Judy Garland failed to win for *A Star Is Born* and *On the Waterfront* took home eight awards). Nevertheless, Hitchcock's tour de force is an exemplar on all fronts, from costume designer Edith Head's carefully crafted clothes and cinematographer Robert Burk's artistry to composer Franz Waxman's musical score and the impeccably chosen cast. A masterpiece of screenwriting and direction, the film is also a testament to the stature of Stewart who, in middle age, had matured into an actor of depth and subtlety. His performance proved he could play a dark, complex character, which he would reprise in *Vertigo* four years later.

In the 1990s Woolrich's story was remade for television, starring paralyzed actor Christopher Reeve. Not surprisingly, the movie failed to capture the rich subtexts of Hitchcock's version. In its technique and story elements, *Rear Window* exemplifies the director's best work and the depth of perspective that often eludes his imitators and continues to entertain audiences.

Preston Neal Jones

SEE ALSO: *Burr, Raymond; Hitchcock, Alfred; Kelly, Grace;* North by Northwest*; Stewart, Jimmy;* Vertigo.

BIBLIOGRAPHY

Belton, John, ed. *Alfred Hitchcock's* Rear Window. Cambridge, MA: Cambridge University Press, 2004.

Coe, Jonathan. *James Stewart, Leading Man.* London: Bloomsbury, 1994.

Higham, Charles, and Joel Greenberg. *The Celluloid Muse: Hollywood Directors Speak.* London: Angus & Robertson, 1969.

Hitchcock, Alfred, and François Truffaut. *Hitchcock/Truffaut.* New York: Simon & Schuster, 1985.

Nevins, Francis M. *Cornell Woolrich—First You Dream, Then You Die.* New York: Mysterious Press, 1988.

Sharff, Stefan. *The Art of Looking in Hitchcock's* Rear Window. New York: Limelight Editions, 1997.

Woolrich, Cornell. Rear Window *and Other Stories.* New York: Penguin Books, 1994.

Rebel without a Cause

Rebel without a Cause (1955) is Hollywood's best film about rebellious youth in the 1950s. Promoted as a story about why a kid from a "good" family would "tick . . . like a bomb," the film sympathetically presents an adolescent perspective on the rebelliousness of middle-class youth of the time. The film focuses on three frustrated teenagers who seek to form their own identities apart from the world and values of their parents and other adults from which they feel alienated. In his role as Jim Stark, James Dean presents the American archetype of the troubled and tormented teenager, and in so doing became a spokesperson for frustrated youth.

The Jim character is the insecure offspring of a domineering mother (Ann Doran) and henpecked father (Jim Backus), who seeks to find a place where his inner gentleness and love can be safely expressed. The other two teenagers include John Crawford (Sal Mineo)—called "Plato"—whose divorced parents have abandoned him, and Judy (Natalie Wood), who cannot understand why her father (William Hopper) seems to have withdrawn his love now that she is a young lady. The three meet at a police station at the beginning of the film, where Plato is brought in for drowning puppies, Judy for being out after curfew, and Jim for being drunk.

The juvenile offenders' officer, Ray Framek (Edward Platt), is the only sympathetic adult in the film, offering the teenagers a calm and considerate hearing. In contrast, both Judy's and Jim's parents seem confused by the needs of their teenagers and misunderstand or avoid their children's desires for comfort and guidance. Plato is cared for by a powerless black nanny (Marietta Canty).

A FOCUS ON TROUBLED TEENS

Director Nicholas Ray felt young people and their problems were important subject matters and regularly made movies that sympathized with outsiders. *Rebel* was adopted from his seventeen-page "The Blind Run," a series of images of troubled teens that lacked any real story. Taking his idea to Warner Brothers, Ray was asked to adapt a nonfiction book by Dr. Robert M. Lindner called *Rebel without a Cause: The Story of a Criminal Psychopath* into a script. Ray refused because he wanted to dramatize the problems of "normal" delinquents from "ordinary" families. The studio consented, and Ray's movie took Lindner's title but nothing else.

Leon Uris, Irving Shulman—the author of the first novel to deal with modern juvenile delinquency, *The Amboy Dukes* (1947)—and Stewart Stern all collaborated with Ray on the script. After Stern spent ten days in juvenile court passing himself off as a welfare worker and talking to various kids, he created a despairing script that convinced the studio that a film could be made from the project. *Rebel* is a modern-day version of *Peter Pan*, with three kids inventing a world of their own and expressing teen feelings about the nature of loneliness and love. The story also has a mythic feeling because the action is confined to a single day, recounting the happenings from dawn to dawn.

JAMES DEAN

Ray had already selected Dean for the role of Jim, and Dean had helped conceive many of the film's scenes. In playing Stark, he portrays the tensions of adolescence, bottling up his feelings to the point of explosion. *Rebel* captures the path Stark takes toward manhood, having him learn that he does not need violence to assert his power, that he can be brave, and that he can go against the pack and risk being unpopular as long as he is true to himself. Dean defined masculinity in a different way for his time, allowing the audience to see the undercurrent of sweetness in a character who longs for a world where people drop their bravado and treat each other gently.

To cast the supporting juvenile roles, Ray held two weeks of mass improvisations at an amphitheater on the Warner's backlot, where 300 boys were asked to run to the top of the bleachers and play King of the Mountain and other games. Ray cast not according to who was the winner but to the attitudes he could see expressed by the players as they competed. He considered Jeff Silver, Billy Gray, and even Dennis Hopper for the role of Plato, but Mineo expressed such enthusiasm as well as a facility for improvisation for the role that Ray was won over.

For Judy, the studio wanted a star and considered borrowing Debbie Reynolds from MGM (Metro-Goldwyn-Mayer), while Ray wanted Carroll Baker, consigning Wood to playing Judy's scheming friend. Wood badly wanted the part, and after being in a car accident with Hopper, when the police asked her for her parents' phone number, she supplied them with Ray's instead. She later told the director, "Nick, they called me a goddamn juvenile delinquent, now do I get the part?" She did, though Jack Warner initially complained about her delivery, resulting in Ray sending Wood to voice coach Nina Moise.

Censorship demands curtailed some of the violence in the film. There could not be any intention to kill, knives during the chase scene were to be replaced by bicycle chains that could not be whirled about, and there were to be no doubts about the innocent nature of cigarettes furtively palmed or Judy's chastity. Even so, when the movie opened in Great Britain, the British censor was so appalled at the chicken run, where teens watch as Buzz and Jim drive their cars over a cliff (originally over a crowded road, but changed to an empty seacoast at the studio's insistence), that he demanded six minutes of cuts and still gave the film an X rating.

Rebel without a Cause was released about four weeks after Dean's reckless demise in a car accident. The film received three Academy Award nominations—to Ray for Best Original Story, to Mineo for Best Supporting Actor, and to Wood for Best Supporting Actress—but won none of them. It was Ray's only film to be so honored. Dean, giving the finest performance of his career and one that would cement him forever in the public's imagination, was overlooked entirely, but the film unquestionably belongs to him and his portrayal of an anguished adolescent.

Dennis Fischer

SEE ALSO: *Academy Awards; Dean, James; The Fifties; Hopper, Dennis; MGM (Metro-Goldwyn-Mayer); Teenagers; Wood, Natalie.*

BIBLIOGRAPHY

Archer, Eugene. "Generations without a Cause." *Film Culture,* no. 7 (1956).

Eisenschitz, Bernard. *Nicholas Ray: An American Journey.* London: Faber & Faber, 1993.

Fox, Terry. "Nicholas Ray, without a Cause." *Village Voice,* July 9, 1979.

McVay, D. "Rebel without a Cause." *Films and Filming,* August 1977.

Rathgeb, Douglas L. *The Making of* Rebel without a Cause. Jefferson, NC: McFarland, 2004.

Steen, Mike. *Hollywood Speaks!: An Oral History.* New York: Putnam, 1974.

Recycling

Earth Day 1970 suggested to millions of Americans that environmental concern could be expressed locally. Through organized activities, many citizens found that they could actively improve the environment with their own hands. Communities responded by organizing ongoing efforts to alter wasteful patterns. Recycling would prove to be the most persistent of these grassroots efforts. Though trivialized by extremist environmentalists, trash and waste recycling now stands as the ultimate symbol of the American environmental consciousness.

Recycling grew out of a conservative impulse to reduce waste rather than as an expression of environmentalism. The ef-

Recycling Containers in New York City. *Recycling containers are part of the landscape at Union Square in New York City.* ELLEN MCKNIGHT/ALAMY.

fort to make worthwhile materials from waste can be traced throughout human society as an application of commonsense rationality. The term *recycling* became part of the American lexicon during wartime rationing, particularly during World War II. Scrap metals and other materials became resources to be collected and recycled into weaponry and other items to support the fighting overseas. But the public's enthusiasm for recycling did not last. Historians point to the conclusion of World War II and the commensurate growth in the U.S. middle class as defining points in the American "culture of consumption"—which reinforced carelessness, waste, and a demand for newness—that became prevalent in the 1950s but extended, in some form, through the end of the twentieth century.

The prodigious scale of American consumption quickly made the nation the most advanced and wasteful civilization in the world. It was only a matter of time before a backlash brought U.S. consumption patterns into question. As the 1960s counterculture imposed doubt on much of the "establishment," many Americans began to consider more carefully the patterns of their everyday lives. In the late 1960s and early 1970s this mindset was reinforced with a litany of examples—ranging from gas shortages to oil spills to toxic leaks—of Americans exploiting resources. Many began to call for a new ethic to guide everyday life, and Earth Day 1970 marked the symbolic start of a "greener" perspective.

Belittled by many environmentalists, recycling often seems like busywork for kids with little actual environmental benefit. Some critics claim that recycling actually stimulates consumption, which is counterproductive for environmentalists. However, the ubiquity of recycling suggests a significant shift in people's view of their place in nature. Environmental concerns such as overused landfills and excessive litter contributed to a new "ethic" within U.S. culture that began to value restraint, reuse, and living within limits.

Reusing products or creating useful byproducts from waste offered application of this new ethic while also offering new opportunity for economic profit and development. Green, or environmental, industries took form to facilitate and profit from this impulse, creating a significant growth portion of the American economy after the 1990s. Even more impressively, the grassroots desire to express an environmental commitment compelled middle-class Americans to make recycling part of an everyday effort. However, the consumptive momentum of the American economy in the twentieth century made it necessary for citizens to relearn the ethic to decrease waste, and often it was schools and children who fueled community efforts to recycle. By the end of the twentieth century many institutions and communities had made recycling a part of waste disposal service.

Most children born after the 1980s assume the "reduce, reuse, recycle" mantra has been part of the United States since its founding. In actuality it serves as a continuing ripple of the cultural and social impact of Earth Day 1970 and the effort of Americans to begin to live within limits.

Brian Black

SEE ALSO: *Consumerism; Earth Day; Environmentalism; World War II.*

BIBLIOGRAPHY

Melosi, Martin V. *Garbage in the Cities.* Pittsburgh, PA: University of Pittsburgh Press, 2004.

Melosi, Martin V. *The Sanitary City: Environmental Services in Urban American from Colonial Times to the Present.* Pittsburgh, PA: University of Pittsburgh Press, 2008.

Opie, John. *Nature's Nation: An Environmental History of the United States.* New York: Harcourt Brace, 1998.

Royte, Elizabeth. *Garbage Land: On the Secret Trail of Trash.* New York: Back Bay Books, 2006.

Strasser, Susan. *Waste and Want: A Social History of Trash.* New York: Holt, 2000.

Zimring, Carl. *Cash for Your Trash: Scrap Recycling in America.* New Brunswick, NJ: Rutgers University Press, 2005.

Red Scare

The Red Scare of 1919–1920 was the first, but not the last, widespread outbreak of anticommunist sentiment in U.S. history. In a national panic over alleged foreign-inspired subversion, people of varying political beliefs were termed "Reds" and became victims of public rage and government suppression. The culmination of these events was the arrest and deportation of hundreds of Americans—particularly immigrants—in the Palmer Raids of 1920.

BOLSHEVIK REVOLUTION

The event that initiated the Red Scare was the Bolshevik Revolution of November 1917 in Russia. Inspired by the writings of German philosopher Karl Marx, the Bolsheviks, under the leadership of Vladimir Lenin, believed that the revolution in Russia was the first in a chain of workers' revolutions that would spread throughout the world. In March 1919 the Bolsheviks founded the Communist International to coordinate communist parties worldwide and promote revolution abroad. Many Americans became fearful that, just as a small faction had seized power in Russia, so could a similar group take over the United States. Those under most suspicion were members of the Industrial Workers of the World (IWW), a syndicalist labor union, that had espoused revolution for the previous decade, and Bolshevik supporters who formed the Communist Labor Party and Communist Party of the USA in 1919.

The fear of a communist coup in the United States was fueled by a number of events. After World War I, the U.S. economy was in recession, living costs had risen, and many soldiers returned home to a country with high unemployment. In the summer of 1919, as blacks and whites competed for jobs, major race riots broke out in both the North and the South. Also labor unions, which had grown in size and influence during the war years, became involved in a number of major conflicts with employers. In 1919 alone, more than four million workers went on strike. There was a general strike in Seattle, Washington, in January and then a nationwide stoppage of steelworkers in September, both of which, employers alleged, were Bolshevik conspiracies. Worst of all, also in September, the Boston police force walked off the job, and Massachusetts governor Calvin Coolidge called out the state militia to replace the striking policemen and to stop incidents of looting.

In addition to economic distress and labor unrest, the public was further alarmed by a spate of bomb attacks on prominent figures in commerce and government. Although it was unclear who sent the bombs, newspapers and politicians blamed them on a communist conspiracy. In April 1919 the maid of U.S. senator Thomas R. Hardwick of Georgia had her hands blown off when she opened a package delivered to the senator's home. Several other mail bombs were detected that were addressed to other notable figures, including J. P. Morgan, John D. Rockefeller, and Supreme Court Justice Oliver Wendell Holmes Jr. In June 1919 Attorney General A. Mitchell Palmer was one of the targets of another series of attempted bombings. Consequently, Palmer organized a new general intelligence division within the Justice Department under the direction of J. Edgar Hoover, whose job it was to uncover the alleged conspiracy.

The panic over radicalism was chiefly directed at immigrants. Building on a tradition of nativism, many Americans came out of World War I inspired by a militant patriotism and a dislike of foreign influences. Many of the leading radicals were foreign-born, and newspapers and politicians portrayed anarchism, communism, and socialism as foreign ideologies. Moreover, many of the workers who went on strike in 1919 were recent immigrants from southern and eastern Europe. Opponents of labor, such as the newly formed American legion, labeled the strikes as un-American and claimed that radical immigrants were fomenting unrest.

Fear and hysteria mounted as the press, politicians, and pressure groups called for action against subversives. All across the nation, police broke up meetings of radical groups, raided their headquarters, and closed down their newspapers. In May 1919 the newly opened offices of the socialist paper the *New York Call* were ransacked by a mob and its workers hospitalized. On the weekend of November 7 and 8, 1919, federal agents raided the offices of the Union of Russian Workers in New York and arrested more than 200 of its members. A few days later in Centralia, Washington, an IWW hall was attacked by American Legionnaires, many of those inside were arrested in the fighting, and one was dragged from jail, castrated, and shot.

Also in 1919, socialist leader Victor Berger was elected to Congress from Milwaukee, Wisconsin, but the House of Representatives refused to allow him to serve his term. In April 1920 the New York State legislature expelled five elected socialist members. A number of liberal figures and organizations, such as Chicago settlement house worker and pacifist Jane Addams, the League of Women Voters, and the American Civil Liberties Union, also came under attack for their lack of patriotism.

PALMER RAIDS

The Red Scare reached a climax with the Palmer Raids of January 2, 1920. On the orders of Attorney General Palmer, about 10,000 people were arrested in thirty-three cities for their part in alleged subversion. In violation of people's constitutional rights, homes were searched, people who were arrested were held without bail, and foreigners were sent to Ellis Island to face deportation hearings without the aid of lawyers. Many of those arrested spent days or weeks in jail with no formal charges filed against them before they were released. Of those arrested, nearly 600 foreigners were ultimately deported.

After the Palmer Raids, the Red Scare quickly subsided. As labor unrest receded, the economy strengthened, bolshevism refused to take root anywhere outside Russia, and the American public became less concerned with subversion. The effects of the Red Scare, however, lingered. Throughout the 1920s reformers were afraid to speak openly, fearing that they would be labeled radical or anti-American. Americanization programs flourished as states sought to stamp out the foreign roots of this radicalism. Twentieth-century American radicalism never recovered from the Red Scare. The IWW was virtually destroyed, socialism's electoral strength declined, communism failed to grow, and radicalism was relegated to the margins of U.S. politics.

John F. Lyons

SEE ALSO: *Addams, Jane; Communism; Hoover, J. Edgar; The Rockefeller Family; World War I; World War II.*

BIBLIOGRAPHY

Murray, Robert K. *Red Scare: A Study in National Hysteria, 1919–1920.* Minneapolis: University of Minnesota Press, 1955.

Preston, William, Jr. *Aliens and Dissenters: Federal Suppression of Radicals, 1903–1933,* 2nd ed. Urbana: University of Illinois Press, 1994.

Schmidt, Regin. *Red Scare: FBI and the Origins of Anticommunism in the United States, 1919–1943.* Copenhagen: Museum Tusculanum Press, University of Copenhagen, 2000.

Redbook

Published continuously since 1903, when it was known as *The Red Book* magazine, this mass-circulation American monthly is now targeted toward young wives and mothers. *Red Book* is regarded in the media industry as one of the so-called Seven Sisters of women's service magazines, a badge shared with *Good Housekeeping, Ladies' Home Journal,* and *McCall's,* among others. But it was not until 1951 that its format was revamped to include its now-familiar mix of articles on contemporary living that, in its own words, "[help] young working mothers bring balance to a hectic life and focus on what matters most."

The Red Book was so named because, in the words of founding editor Trumbull White, "Red is the color of happiness." For the first several decades of its existence—many of them under the editorship of Edwin Balmer—the magazine was primarily a vehicle for short fiction. However, even Balmer realized that this format was becoming stale and unattractive to mass audiences, complaining that his publication seemed to appeal only to "the little old ladies in Kokomo." In 1951—following the lead of other periodicals that were redefining their images to appeal to the new post–World War II generation of younger, working women and mothers—the magazine metamorphosed into the *Redbook* that is still recognizable in the twenty-first century: a lifestyle publication with vivid four-color layouts; departments on child care, careers, intimacy, fashion, and homemaking; and thoughtful, sometimes controversial features on personal and social issues.

With Wade Nichols as editor, *Redbook* became "The Magazine for Young Adults," and its circulation soon increased to two million, doubling to 4.5 million by the end of the 1960s. By that decade *Redbook*'s editorial focus was considered generally more provocative and socially conscious than that of its sister publications, with frank articles that discussed feminism, social and cultural issues, and changing sexual mores. The readership had shifted from "the little old ladies in Kokomo" to a new generation of twenty- and thirty-something readers interested in child care and household tips but also in navigating their way in careers and marriages, the rules of which were being rewritten during a rather turbulent period of American history.

Despite several ownership changes during the 1970s and *Redbook*'s eventual acquisition by Hearst Magazines in 1982, the periodical continued its emphasis on contemporary issues. Editor-in-chief Kate White caused no little controversy when she selected for the December 1997 cover a photograph of actor Pierce Brosnan looking on as wife, Keely Shaye Smith, nurses their son, Dylan Thomas. The graphic cover was ultimately printed on newsstand copies only; a nonbreastfeeding version was supplied to the magazine's regular mail subscribers.

Lesley Jane Seymour took over as *Redbook*'s editor at the end of 1998, with promises to make over the publication. "My aim is to jazz up the magazine, make it more energetic and a little younger," she was quoted as saying. During the first decade of the 2000s two more editors tried to rejuvenate the publication, which was fighting to differentiate itself from the other women's service magazines. In 2001 Seymour was succeeded by Ellen Kunes, and in 2004 Stacy Morrison took over *Redbook*'s top job.

Morrison remained at the helm until family issues forced her to step down in 2010. Jill Herzig, who had spent the previous ten years working at *Glamour*, took over as editor-in-chief. During this time of transition, the magazine managed to hold fairly steady readership numbers. In 2011 *Redbook* had an audited circulation of 2.2 million. In 2012 Hearst's own website touted *Redbook* as "the total-life guide for every woman blazing her own path through adulthood and taking on new roles," one whose pages offer "a vibrant mix of just-for-her fashion and beauty coverage; get-stuff-done edit (from money and mealtime to health and home); thoughtful features on marriage, relationships, and family; and rich, affirming content to keep her connected to the part of herself that belongs to her and her alone."

Edward Moran

SEE ALSO: *Bok, Edward; Feminism;* Good Housekeeping*; Hearst, William Randolph;* McCall's Magazine*; World War II.*

BIBLIOGRAPHY

"*Redbook* 'Love Your Life.'" Hearst Corporation. Accessed March 2012. Available from http://www.hearst.com/magazines/redbook.php

Reed, David. *The Popular Magazine in Britain and the United States*. London: British Library, 1997.

Tebbel, John. *The American Magazine: A Compact History*. New York: Hawthorn Books, 1969.

Tebbel, John, and Mary Ellen Zuckerman. *The Magazine in America: 1741–1990*. New York: Oxford University Press, 1991.

Walker, Nancy A. *Women's Magazines, 1940–1960: Gender Roles and the Popular Press*. Bedford Series in History & Culture. Bedford, NY: Palgrave Macmillan, 1998.

Wood, James Playsted. *Magazines in the United States*. New York: Ronald Press, 1971.

Redding, Otis *(1941–1967)*

Hailing from Georgia, 1960s soul man Otis Redding exemplified the "Stax sound," named after the record company for which he recorded throughout his career as a solo artist. His grainy, emotive vocals backed by the raw but extremely tight house band (Booker T. and the MG's) created a sound that was much copied and was responsible for making Memphis-based Stax Records a major player in the 1960s rhythm-and-blues (R&B) market.

Earning a reputation as the penultimate showman and entertainer (rivaled only by fellow Georgian James Brown), Redding also became known both as an excellent interpreter (he covered the Rolling Stones' "Satisfaction" to great effect) and an exceptional songwriter (he wrote "Respect," which Aretha Franklin later popularized). Though most of his influence was confined to the R&B market, at the time of his death at age twenty-six, Redding was on the verge of crossing over to the pop market, which he later did with the posthumously released number one single, "(Sittin' on) The Dock of the Bay." It was with this song and his earlier crossover hits that Redding helped narrow the gulf between the pop and R&B markets during the 1960s.

Redding, who was born in Dawson, Georgia, and raised in Macon, was heavily influenced as a young man by the shouting of Little Richard and the more restrained gospel delivery of Sam Cooke. Beginning his career working in small clubs and recording a handful of singles as a Little Richard soundalike (such as "Shout Bamalama"), Redding joined Johnny Jenkins's band in the late 1950s. He would continue to work with Jenkins in an off-and-on fashion through the early 1960s. In 1962, when a recording session for Jenkins was going poorly, Redding stepped up to the microphone and used the studio band to record "These Arms of Mine," which hit the top twenty on the R&B charts and established Redding as a solo artist. But his career really did not take off until the mid-1960s when his cover of the Rolling Stones' "Satisfaction" and his own "I've Been Loving You Too Long," "Fa-Fa-Fa-Fa-Fa-Fa (Sad Song)," and "Respect" all became Top 40 hits.

His legendary sweat-drenched live shows on the so-called chitlin' circuit had already made him one of the most popular black solo artists of the 1960s among African American crowds, and his much-talked-about performance at the Monterey

International Pop Festival in 1967 helped bring him to the attention of a wider (read: white) audience. By 1967 Redding was not only on the verge of crossing over to the pop market in a big way but was expanding his artistic horizons dramatically and redefining what soul music could sound like in the process. "(Sittin' on) The Dock of the Bay" was the result of his experimentation, and it eventually went to number one on the Billboard pop charts, albeit posthumously. On December 10, 1967, Redding's plane went down near Madison, Wisconsin, killing Redding and four members of his backup band, Stax recording artists the Bar-Kays.

Kembrew McLeod

SEE ALSO: *Brown, James; Cooke, Sam; Franklin, Aretha; Little Richard; Rhythm and Blues; The Rolling Stones; Soul Music; Top 40.*

BIBLIOGRAPHY

Brown, Geoff. *Otis Redding: Try a Little Tenderness.* Edinburgh: Canongate, 2002.

Redford, Robert *(1937–)*

Robert Redford may very well be the last of the classic movie stars. With rugged good looks in the tradition of Clark Gable and Cary Grant, he has been a major leading man since he rocketed to fame in the role of the Sundance Kid in 1969's *Butch Cassidy and the Sundance Kid,* playing opposite another screen legend, Paul Newman. Throughout his fifty-plus-year career, which began on Broadway in 1959 in *Tall Story* and continued with his 1962 film debut in *War Hunt,* he has demonstrated an ability to portray American icons so memorably as to recreate them in his own image. Yet in other ways, Redford is rather an atypical movie star. Though not necessarily anti-Hollywood, he goes his own way both on-screen and off and is extremely selective about his film roles. His blond-haired, blue-eyed charisma made him the most popular actor in America in 1974, but his choices of screen roles were anything but glamorous.

BUCKING THE SYSTEM

In such films as *Downhill Racer* (1969), *The Candidate* (1972), *Jeremiah Johnson* (1972), and *The Way We Were* (1973), Redford portrays characters who question the prevailing political and social systems. *The Candidate,* for example, features him as a man running for the Senate on the basis of ethics and idealism who quickly learns that people care more about his appearance than his positions on real issues. Winning is what the game is about, he discovers. By the end of the film, the candidate discovers how to get himself elected but has no idea what he will do in office.

This theme is repeated in 1973's *The Way We Were,* in which he plays a "most likely to succeed" college athlete paired with Barbra Streisand's idealistic socialist in a marriage of opposites. As in *The Candidate,* Redford's character succeeds in life largely through appearances, connections, and an ability to say the right thing, even if it is meaningless. Thus, while he is living the American dream, he is also troubled by it.

Redford's characters during the early years of his career appear to be dichotomies: happy on the surface yet emanating a haunting emptiness. In *Jeremiah Johnson,* he steps out of the system all together by portraying a "frontier trapper" who cannot stand the restraints of society and is more at home in the wilderness. This film establishes the essential Redford character that dominates the films of his middle and later career. In a string of successful films beginning with *The Great Gatsby* in 1974 and continuing with *Three Days of the Condor* (1975), *All the President's Men* (1976), *Sneakers* (1992), and *Quiz Show* (1994), he takes decidedly mistrusting stances against the government, big business, cultural institutions (such as marriage), and the integrity of the media.

BEHIND THE SCENES

This attitude also typified his producing and directing efforts. By 1975 Redford had turned his production company, Wildwood Productions, into a major player in acquiring film properties, though it only picked projects that dealt with issues important to Redford. For example, the company acquired film rights to the best-selling book *All the President's Men,* which is about the Watergate investigation. The film won four Academy Awards. In 1980 Redford won the Academy Award for Best Director for *Ordinary People,* a brilliant dissection of the dark secrets haunting a well-to-do American family. He cast television's wholesome icon Mary Tyler Moore as the overbearingly neurotic mother who is haunted by the death of her son and blames it on the youngest sibling. In 1992 he continued his political themes by producing an award-winning documentary, *Incident at Oglala,* which investigates the persecution of a Native American by the FBI.

Redford is a passionate environmentalist and political activist who has genuine concerns about the quality of both life and art. He lobbied for the Clean Air Act of 1974, the Energy and the Conservation Act of 1976, and several opposition to strip-mining bills. Starting in 1976, he also took three years off from filmmaking to write a book, *The Outlaw Trail,* about the American West.

In 1980 he founded the Sundance Institute in Utah to promote the pure, idealistic side of filmmaking. Eschewing Hollywood, the institute aims to nurture young, independent film makers by creating an environment in which seasoned professionals can help beginners find their voices without the pressures of commercialism. An outgrowth of the Sundance Institute is an annual film festival dedicated to independent cinema. However, the festival was "discovered" by Hollywood executives desperate for new ideas in 1990, and a number of films screened there have subsequently been purchased and plunged into the mainstream cinema. While this has been financially beneficial for the artists involved, they rarely have gone on to experience the creative freedom in Hollywood that they enjoyed at Sundance. By the mid-1990s, the festival became a winter retreat for Hollywood executives. The products screened evolved from truly independent films devoid of big-name stars to Hollywood films using Hollywood talent.

THE MAN AND THE MYTH

Although he has had some setbacks, Redford has become one of only a few actors who can make his own choices. He has used his star power to produce and star in films that publicize his beliefs and his causes. Both his lifestyle and his motion pictures have become fully intertwined with the theme of the iconoclastic loner who takes on the establishment and lives life on his own terms. At the same time, most of his screen roles reflect his political and environmental views to such an extent that one may wonder if he could portray an unsympathetic character. He came close in 1990's *Havana*, in which he plays a Humphrey Bogart–like professional gambler who only looks out for himself. The film failed at the box office, perhaps because audiences were not used to seeing Redford in such a downbeat role. In 1998 Redford retreated to his traditional pro-environment, loner character in the successful *The Horse Whisperer*, but he broke with his off-Hollywood stance in his personal life by appearing on talk shows around the world to promote the film.

In the twenty-first century, Redford's work as both an actor and a director has received mixed reviews. *The Legend of Bagger Vance* (2000), which Redford directed, did well at the box office but was panned by critics. The following year, he starred with Brad Pitt in *Spy Game*, a thriller set primarily in China that grossed $143 million and received mostly positive reviews. Redford then directed and costarred with Meryl Streep and Tom Cruise in *Lions for Lambs* (2007), the story of an idealistic soldier who enlists to fight in Afghanistan at the urging of his professor. The movie was both a critical and commercial failure, but it was nevertheless quintessential Redford: he made it on his own terms.

Sandra Garcia-Myers

SEE ALSO: *Academy Awards; Best Sellers;* Butch Cassidy and the Sundance Kid*; Cruise, Tom; Environmentalism; Newman, Paul; Pitt, Brad; Streep, Meryl; Streisand, Barbra; Sundance Film Festival; Watergate.*

BIBLIOGRAPHY

Callan, Feeney Michael. *Robert Redford: The Biography*. New York: Knopf, 2011.

De Vries, Hillary. "Robert Redford: Why Does He Still Do It?" *Los Angeles Times Calendar*, December 9, 1990, 8.

Downing, David. *Robert Redford*. New York: St. Martin's Press, 1982.

Hanna, David. *Robert Redford: The Superstar Nobody Knows*. New York: A Leisure Book, 1975.

Redford, Robert. *The Outlaw Trail*. New York: Grossett & Dunlap, 1978.

Schoell, William, and Lawrence Quirk. *The Sundance Kid: A Biography of Robert Redford*. Dallas, TX: Taylor Trade Publishing, 2006.

Weiss, Michael J. "Redford Comes down from His Mountain." *Times* (London), September 14, 1984, 9.

Reed, Donna *(1921–1986)*

With *The Donna Reed Show* (1958–1966), actress Donna Reed was one of the most popular women of early television. She and her husband, Tony Owen, had created the show, which he also produced and in which she played a typical television housewife of the 1950s.

Reed began her career in the 1940s playing sweethearts and wives in movies, including the film classic *It's a Wonderful Life* (1946), in which she appeared opposite Jimmy Stewart. She eventually attempted to break out of good-girl roles by portraying a prostitute in *From Here to Eternity* (1953), for which she won an Academy Award. When the film industry did not provide her with other parts she wanted, Reed turned to the new medium of television, where she became a huge star. After *The Donna Reed Show* went off the air in the 1960s, she continued to act periodically until her death in 1986.

Jill A. Gregg

SEE ALSO: *Academy Awards;* From Here to Eternity*;* It's a Wonderful Life*; Movie Stars; Sitcom; Stewart, Jimmy.*

BIBLIOGRAPHY

Buhle, Paul, and Dave Wagner. *Hide in Plain Sight: The Hollywood Blacklistees in Film and Television, 1950–2002.* New York: Palgrave Macmillan, 2003.

Fultz, Jay. *In Search of Donna Reed*. Iowa City: University of Iowa Press, 1998.

Reed, Ishmael *(1938–)*

Ishmael Reed, regarded as one of the greatest satirists in America since Mark Twain, is also one of the best-known, multifaceted writers of the twentieth century; his titles include novelist, poet, publisher, playwright, literary critic, songwriter, jazz composer and player, editor, television producer, founder of the multicultural group Before Columbus Foundation and There City Cinema, and essayist. In 1967 he changed the American literary scene when he published *The Free-Lance Pallbearers*, a novel that set the tone and aesthetic for the eight novels, five collections of poetry, four essay books, and several anthologies that followed.

With a writing technique called Neo-HooDoo Aesthetic or Neo-HooDooism, a multicultural style based on voodoo and African-based religious beliefs, which he mixed with elements from other cultural traditions, Reed has consistently supported multiculturalism and argued for a multicultural society in the United States and the world over. Though literary critics have been baffled by his innovative techniques, which include combining several seemingly unrelated elements from different time periods into his writings—one novel, *Mumbo Jumbo* (1972), for example, contains photographs, drawings, footnotes, quotes, and a partial bibliography—he has been nationally and internationally recognized as the Charlie Parker of American fiction. In June 1998 Reed received a MacArthur Foundation Fellowship.

In the twenty-first century Reed continues to challenge American politics and popular culture by exposing the American media and their stereotypical representations of African Americans and other minority groups in the United States and around the world. This kind of writing is what he has called "Writin' Is Fightin'" or doing "intellectual combat." In *Mixing It Up: Taking on the Media Bullies and Other Reflections* (2008), *Barack Obama and the Jim Crow Media: The Return of the Nigger Breakers* (2010), and *Juice!* (2011), Reed likens the media to hyenas that prey on African Americans and other minorities and deliver them to the public as the preferred meal.

In *Mixing It Up* and *Barack Obama and the Return of the Jim Crow Media*, both collections of essays, Reed criticizes the media in general and exposes individual journalists and the kind of work they do in perpetuating the stereotypes about black Americans and other minorities. In *Mixing It Up*, Reed scolds the media (print and television), such as the *New York Times*, CNN, CBS, ABC, and Fox, for continually linking drugs with African Americans while ignoring the staggering drug problem in white America. Similarly, the media regularly report on the "pathologies" of black Americans while disregarding the "pathologies" in other groups. Just as he does not hesitate to criticize some feminists, such as Gloria Steinem when she charged Senator Barack Obama with being "mean" to Senator Hillary Clinton during the 2008 presidential campaign, so is he not afraid to criticize black public intellectuals such as Henry Louis Gates Jr., Michael Eric Dyson, or John McWhorter for being used by the media to chastise blacks or ridicule black culture. In *Mixing It Up*, Reed also celebrates African American writers such as Charles Chesnutt and August Wilson ("a Playwright of the Blues") and jazz icons such as Sonny Rollins, Miles Davis, Duke Ellington, and Parker.

As the title suggests, *Barack Obama and the Jim Crow Media* analyzes scurrilous propaganda against President Obama by all-white, male-dominated media and political pundits. Armed with statistics from a poll conducted by Daily Kos, Reed argues that Obama's main opponent is what he calls the "Jim Crow Media." Tracing the phenomenon to slavery times, when slave masters hired overseers such as Edward Covey to physically tame slaves such as Frederick Douglass, Reed lambastes the media and political pundits for using a repertoire of old stereotypes about blacks against the president. Though traditionally these "intellectual mercenaries" have been white, Reed points out that intellectuals such as Dinesh D'Souza are also overseers who endanger more minorities than the thugs who commit hate crimes insofar as minorities lack means to counter the attacks in the media. Reed also considers extremist conservative blacks to be overseers when the media use them to vilify Obama, during both the campaign and his presidency.

Another example of the media's bias against and obsession with the black male is the O. J. Simpson trial in the 1990s. In *Juice!*, a graphic novel starring Bear, Snakes, Rabbit, and Bat, Reed chastises the media for turning Simpson into a representative of the black man in America, in the sense that all black men are considered guilty by proxy. In the novel, America and the media are so obsessed with Simpson that they connect any issue to him, no matter how unrelated it might be. An astute writer in the African American trickster tradition, Reed shows this obsession with Simpson through Bear, a black cartoonist, whose own fascination with Simpson threatens to break his marriage and strains his relationship with his daughter, Hibiscus. He ultimately argues that, through propaganda, Hollywood and the media were capable of accomplishing what the jury in the criminal case was incapable of doing.

Pierre-Damien Mvuyekure

SEE ALSO: *Davis, Miles; Ellington, Duke; Jazz; Multiculturalism; Obama, Barack; Parker, Charlie; Simpson, O. J.; Steinem, Gloria.*

BIBLIOGRAPHY

Bruce, Dick, ed. *Conversations with Ishmael Reed.* Jackson: University Press of Mississippi, 1995.

McGee, Patrick. *Ishmael Reed and the Ends of Race.* New York: St. Martin's Press, 1997.

Mvuyekure, Pierre-Damien. *The "Dark Heathenism" of the American Novelist Ishmael Reed: African Voodoo as American Literary HooDoo.* New York: Edwin Mellen Press, 2007.

Reed, Ishmael. *Mumbo Jumbo.* New York: Atheneum, 1972.

Reed, Ishmael. *Writin' Is Fightin': Thirty-Seven Years of Boxing on Paper.* New York: Atheneum, 1988.

Reed, Ishmael, ed. *MultiAmerica: Essays on Cultural Wars and Cultural Peace.* New York: Viking, 1997.

Reed, Ishmael. *Barack Obama and the Jim Crow Media: The Return of the Nigger Breakers.* Montreal: Baraka Books, 2010.

Reed, Ishmael. *Juice!* Champaign, IL: Dalkey Archive Press, 2011.

Reed, Lou *(1942–)*

Both as a solo artist and as a member of the Velvet Underground, Lou Reed has had an extraordinary influence on the history of rock and roll. Musician and producer Brian Eno once observed that few people bought the Velvet Underground's albums when they were first released, but those who did formed their own bands.

THE VELVET UNDERGROUND

Born and raised on Long Island, New York, Reed attended Syracuse University before landing a position writing pop songs for Pickwick Records. There he met John Cale, a classically trained cellist who had played with the Dream Syndicate, La-Monte Young's avant-garde ensemble. In 1965 Cale and Reed formed a band, rounding out the lineup with guitarist Sterling Morrison, whom Reed had known from college, and drummer Angus MacLise, who was later replaced by Maureen "Mo" Tucker. After going through a variety of names, they finally settled on the Velvet Underground, the title of a pulp pornographic novel. The band's first show was less than auspicious: it was the opening act at a high school dance in Summit, New Jersey. The following year, the Velvets became the house band at The Factory, Andy Warhol's studio and performance space. Warhol convinced them to add Nico, a German actress and model, as a vocalist, and he signed them on to the Exploding Plastic Inevitable, his touring multimedia show.

Their first album, *The Velvet Underground and Nico* (1967), deals with topics that had been untouched up to that point in rock-and-roll history. "I'm Waiting for the Man" and "Heroin" are frank and even celebratory depictions of drug addiction, while the sadomasochistic themes of "Venus and Furs" would provide a model for many gothic bands of the 1980s and 1990s. Beyond the lyrics, however, the album is important for a number of reasons. The songs, all of which were written or cowritten by Reed, are deceptively simple (Reed once said he liked the fact that anyone could play them), and the musicianship is deliberately stripped down. Reed's vocals are often laconic, almost spoken, providing a model for singers such as Ric Ocasek of the Cars, Gordon Gano of the Violent Femmes, and Jonathan Richman. While the band acquired a reputation as both arty and dark, songs such as "I'll Be Your Mirror," "There She Goes Again," and "Femme Fatale" are straight-up pop offerings. That combination of a do-it-yourself attitude, artistic aspirations, and a strong pop sensibility would exert an enormous influence on the punk and independent music scenes of the late 1970s and 1980s.

While the Velvets' first release uses feedback and Cale's dissonant string arrangements as a kind of background noise, *White*

Light, White Heat (1968), the band's second album, is a relentless barrage of sound. Experimenting with various effects pedals for his guitar, Reed developed a style in which a squalling wall of feedback was overlaid on every song. It was a wildly different approach from the highly produced and orchestrated sounds that most rock bands of the 1960s had adopted. Even in the 1980s, *White Light, White Heat* remained influential, as bands such as the Gang of Four and the Jesus and Mary Chain incorporated a layer of feedback into their music.

GOING SOLO

Cale left the band after *White Light, White Heat*, and the Velvets recorded two more albums, *The Velvet Underground* (1969) and *Loaded* (1970), as well as unreleased sessions later issued as *VU* (1985), before Reed departed in 1970. While *The Velvet Underground* and *Loaded* at first did not reach even the less than impressive sales of the band's first two albums, they indicated the direction Reed's solo career would take. *Loaded* features "Sweet Jane" and "Rock and Roll," which are now among Reed's most famous songs.

After quitting the band, Reed took a day job as typist at his father's accounting firm and then released two albums in 1972: *Lou Reed* and *Transformer*. The latter was produced by David Bowie, who was an unapologetic Reed admirer. ("Queen Bitch," released on Bowie's 1971 album *Hunky Dory*, is an unmistakable tribute to the Velvets.) *Transformer* contains "Walk on the Wild Side," Reed's most popular song.

Reed was exceptionally prolific through the late 1990s, and although his work was often well received, few listeners believed it equaled what he did with the Velvet Underground or early in his solo career. In 1989 he reunited with Cale on *Songs for Drella*, an album of songs about Warhol, who had died two years earlier. In 1993 the original Velvet Underground reunited (minus Nico, who died in 1988) and played a brief reunion tour. Perhaps one of the oddest moments in Reed's career was when he played a thirty-five-minute set at the White House in 1998 at the request of Czech president Václav Havel, who had said Reed and the Velvets were important influences on the Czech underground that had fought against Soviet domination.

EXPLORING NEW GROUND

Though in his sixties in the first decade of the 2000s, Reed continued to record, perform, tour, and influence the music industry. In 2003 he released *The Raven*, a two-disc set that musically explores the works of Edgar Allan Poe and features collaborations with a number of performers, including actors Willem Dafoe and Steve Buscemi, Bowie, and jazz saxophonist Ornette Coleman.

In 2006 Reed adapted his 1973 album *Berlin* for the stage, creating a rock opera that was performed at St. Ann's Warehouse in Brooklyn, New York. Filmmaker Julian Schnabel, who served as set designer, recorded the performances and released the documentary movie *Berlin* (2007). Reed's *Metal Machine Music*, an experimental noise album, was poorly received upon its initial release in 1975, but he dug it out of the coffers and rereleased it. He also formed a new band, Metal Machine Trio, in 2008 with musicians Ulrich Krieger and Sarth Calhoun and launched a worldwide tour.

Reed is clearly not an artist to rest on his laurels and go quietly into retirement. He has continued to collaborate with other musicians, including the Killers, Gorillaz, and Laurie Anderson, whom he married in 2008. In 2011 he collaborated with the heavy metal band Metallica to produce the album *Lulu*. The album, which deviates from Metallica's traditional metal sound, upset some of the band's hard-core fans. Reed has also published several books of photography and appeared in films including *Arthur and the Revenge of Maltazard* (2009). He and Anderson, both dog lovers, put together "Music for Dogs," a concert specifically designed for a canine audience that was held in Australia in 2010. Indeed, Reed has grown from a rock legend into a true artist who is not afraid to stretch his limits.

Bill Freind

SEE ALSO: *Bowie, David; Indie Music; Punk; Rock and Roll; The Velvet Underground; Warhol, Andy.*

BIBLIOGRAPHY

Bockris, Victor. *Lou Reed: The Biography*. London: Hutchinson, 1994.

Bockris, Victor. *Transformer: The Lou Reed Story*. New York: Simon & Schuster, 1994.

Bockris, Victor, and Gerard Malanga. *Up-Tight: The Velvet Underground Story*. New York: Quill, 1983.

Doggett, Peter. *Lou Reed: Growing Up in Public*. New York: Omnibus Press, 1992.

McNeil, Legs, and Gillian McCain. *Please Kill Me: The Uncensored Oral History of Punk*. New York: Grove Press, 1996.

Roberts, Chris. *Lou Reed: Walk on the Wild Side: The Stories behind the Songs*. Milwaukee, WI: Hal Leonard, 2004.

Thompson, Dave. *Your Pretty Face Is Going to Hell: The Dangerous Glitter of David Bowie, Iggy Pop, and Lou Reed*. New York: Backbeat Books, 2009.

Reese, Pee Wee *(1918–1999)*

Known for his fine defensive play and leadership, shortstop Harold Henry "Pee Wee" Reese was the captain of the Brooklyn Dodgers baseball team in the 1940s and 1950s. The "Little Colonel" led Brooklyn to seven National League titles and a World Series victory in 1955. The intangibles Reese brought to the game earned him top-ten mention in Most Valuable Player voting eight times and induction into the Baseball Hall of Fame in 1984. In 1947 Reese gained attention off the field by befriending teammate Jackie Robinson, who was the first black baseball player allowed to play in the major leagues. His friendship with Robinson was instrumental in easing Robinson's acceptance among his Dodger teammates and major-league baseball. Reese's historic actions remain a symbol of social progress in American civil rights.

Nathan R. Meyer

SEE ALSO: *Baseball; The Brooklyn Dodgers; Robinson, Jackie; World Series.*

BIBLIOGRAPHY

Golenbock, Peter, and Paul Bacon. *Teammates*. San Diego, CA: Harcourt Brace Jovanovich, 1990.

Robinson, Jackie, and Michael G. Long. *First Class Citizenship: The Civil Rights Letters of Jackie Robinson.* New York: Times Books, 2007.

Wolpin, Stewart. *Bums No More! The Championship Season of the 1955 Brooklyn Dodgers.* New York: St. Martin's Press, 1995.

Reeves, Martha

SEE: *Martha and the Vandellas.*

Reeves, Steve *(1926–2000)*

From 1957 through 1968 Steve Reeves was able to parlay his bodybuilding success and classical good looks into a film career that, for a brief time, made him the highest-paid screen performer in Europe. Most of his films were "sword and sandal" spectaculars, made in Italy, that provided entertainment for his millions of fans around the world and served as an inspiration for later stars of action films, such as Sylvester Stallone and Arnold Schwarzenegger.

BUILDING HIS BODY

Reeves was born on a ranch outside the small town of Glasgow, Montana, and was not quite two years old when his father was killed in a farming accident. When Reeves was ten, he and his mother moved to Oakland, California, where the active youngster soon had a paper route and was developing his legendary calves by pedaling the rolling hills of his new hometown. Serendipity brought a teenage Reeves into contact with Ed Yarick, one of the most knowledgeable gym owners in the United States. Within two years Reeves's genetic gifts and Yarick's carefully designed programs had combined to produce a physique equaled by few men in the world at the time.

World War II interrupted Reeves's training for a time, but after fighting in the Philippines he returned to Yarick and began to train for competitive bodybuilding. His first national victory came in 1947, in the biggest contest of all in the United States—the A.A.U. Mr. America. As the holder of this prestigious title, he came to the attention of the media, which was drawn to the tall young man who looked, many said, like a living god.

HOLLYWOOD CALLING

One of the people who saw photos of Reeves was Hollywood's master of the epic, Cecil B. DeMille, who offered the young bodybuilder the role of Samson in an upcoming film. The one catch was that Reeves had to reduce his 216-pound weight to 200 pounds, a sacrifice he was unwilling to make, having trained so hard to build himself up, and he passed up the opportunity. However, he went to London in 1950 to compete for the world's most important physique title, Mr. Universe, won the contest, and began getting small roles onstage and in television. In 1954 the eccentric independent director of poverty row movies, Ed Wood, cast Reeves as a policeman in *Jail Bait,* and later that same year Reeves was given a much larger role in the musical *Athena.* In 1957 the daughter of Italian director Pietro Francisci saw *Athena* and suggested to her father that the big, handsome American would make a perfect lead for Francisci's upcoming Franco-Italian production of *Hercules.* Francisci saw Reeves, agreed with his daughter, and a deal was struck that launched Reeves into a series of mythological hero films that made both men wealthy.

A significant factor in the huge success of Reeves's first four European adventure films was the producer/promoter Joseph E. Levine, who took *Hercules* (1957), *Hercules Unchained* (1959), *Morgan the Pirate* (1960), and *The Thief of Baghdad* (1961), dubbed them into English, and premiered them internationally, not only using slick promotion and distribution methods but also instigating the publication of tie-in paperbacks and comic books. As a result, Reeves rapidly acquired massive marquee value and soon found himself in demand.

Unfortunately, however, the popularity of these "neoclassical" epics resulted in such a rash of Reeves films in a short time that his popularity began a steady decline in the early 1960s. *Hercules* opened in the United States in 1959, and by the summer of 1961 eight of his films had appeared in U.S. theaters. Eight films in twenty-four months was obviously too much for an American audience to take, and ticket sales fell off. He remained hugely popular in many overseas markets and continued to appear in films throughout the early 1960s. His last, and one of his personal favorites, was the 1969 *A Long Ride from Hell,* a late entry in a genre of violent Italian films dubbed "spaghetti Westerns." Ironically, Reeves had turned down the role that eventually went to Clint Eastwood in the movie that popularized spaghetti Westerns—Sergio Leone's *A Fistful of Dollars* (1964). With the success of the spaghetti Westerns, the costume epics in which Reeves had found fame and fortune were eclipsed and faded away as the men who made them turned to the new genre.

RETIREMENT

Over the years, the effects of the damage caused by a 1959 injury to Reeves's shoulder were exacerbated by the often dangerous stunts demanded by his action pictures—stunts that he did himself since, because of his unique build, no suitable stunt man could be found. Reeves prized his health, and as he mourned the early deaths of his friends Errol Flynn and Tyrone Power, he decided to retire while he was young and healthy enough to enjoy it. By 1970 Reeves, who had married Princess Aline Czartjarwicz in 1963, settled on a ranch in Southern California to raise Morgan horses.

In 1982 Reeves published a best-selling book, *Powerwalking,* in which he encouraged runners to slow down and save their knees, ankles, and hip joints. Instead, he advocated a form of fast walking using ankle and wrist weights as a safer and equally effective form of aerobic exercise. He was in many ways a pioneer in the field of exercise walking, and in the years since the publication of *Powerwalking,* millions of people have switched from running to walking.

For many years Reeves was an outspoken opponent of bodybuilding drugs, which were not used during the years in which he competed, and in 1995 he published *Building the Classic Physique—the Natural Way.* Reeves was diagnosed with lymphoma in early 2000 and died soon after, on May 1, 2000. Few historians would argue with the premise that no bodybuilder before or since Steve Reeves has ever had such a truly classic physique.

Jan and Terry Todd

SEE ALSO: *Bodybuilding; Celebrity; Comic Books; DeMille, Cecil B.; Eastwood, Clint; Flynn, Errol; Hollywood; Leone, Sergio; Movie Stars; Schwarzenegger, Arnold; Sex Symbol; Spaghetti Westerns; Stallone, Sylvester; Wood, Ed; World War II.*

BIBLIOGRAPHY

Reeves, Steve, and James A. Peterson. *Powerwalking.* Indianapolis, IN: Bobbs-Merrill, 1982.

Reeves, Steve; John Little; and Bob Wolff. *Building the Classic Physique: The Natural Way.* Calabasas, CA: Little-Wolff Group, 1995.

Reggae

Reggae is a broad term encompassing a related variety of musical styles that emerged from the island nation of Jamaica after 1960. These styles include ska, rock steady, reggae, and dancehall, all of which swept Jamaican music in distinct stylistic waves, one after the other, during the 1960s and 1970s. Musically, these styles share a common loping rhythm that accents the subsidiary beat.

Reggae, however, is many things to many people. It can be seen as merely another great Caribbean dance rhythm, but at the same time many of its songs have highly political overtones. It is also often associated with the Rastafarian religion, an ascetic, millenarian sect that originated in part in the back-to-Africa teachings of Marcus Garvey in the 1920s and 1930s. Since its arrival on the world scene after 1960, reggae and its associated musical styles have become immensely popular around the world. It is one of the world's first truly international musical forms, both in its origins and in its worldwide appeal.

BLEND OF STYLES

Reggae's origins come from a unique blend of Caribbean musical styles and American rhythm and blues from the 1950s. Prior to World War II, the most popular musical style in Jamaica was mento, which drew from Caribbean forms such as calypso, merengue, and rumba, as well as older African-derived folk styles. After World War II Jamaicans began to hear R&B music being broadcast from the United States, particularly from New Orleans. In comparison to the BBC-style official radio programming coming from within Jamaica, these R&B sounds were a breath of fresh air. Early American R&B pioneers such as Louis Jordan, Roscoe Gordon, and Fats Domino were immensely popular in Jamaica during the 1950s. These records were also promoted in Jamaica by sound-system operators who carried portable speakers and record players in their trucks, playing at parties and selling records.

As the classic phase of R&B music dried up in the late 1950s, Jamaicans turned to producing R&B-inspired music themselves. The first result of these efforts was ska, a hybrid of R&B and mento musical forms that featured shuffling rhythms, accented on the second and fourth beats; a chopped guitar or piano sound; and a loose horn section. Propelled by such groups as the Skatalites, the Ska Kings, the Soul Vendors, the Maytals, and Millie Small (whose song "My Boy Lollipop" was an international hit), ska became the dominant musical style in Jamaica after 1960. Much of this music was produced by new Jamaican-run studios, notably those of Coxsone Dodd, Duke Reid, and Prince Buster, all of whom were veterans of the sound-system circuit.

Jamaica's political independence from Great Britain in 1962 further strengthened the desire to produce all-Jamaican musical forms, and the dance rhythms of ska provided a soundtrack to the celebrations that accompanied independence. The era of ska's dominance lasted until about 1966, although

Steel Pulse. *Members of the reggae band Steel Pulse perform in 2011.* ANDY SHEPPARD/CONTRIBUTOR/REDFERNS/GETTY IMAGES.

the style continues to have adherents and practitioners, especially in the United States and Great Britain, where it was revived in the late 1970s.

By 1966, following American R&B's evolution into gospel-inspired soul music, the ska style gave way to slower rhythms called rock steady, after the Alton Ellis hit "Get Ready to Rock Steady." Other musicians, such as Heptone Lewis with "Take It Easy" and the Heptones with "Ting a Ling," contributed to the new rock-steady style. The music slowed down and the horns largely disappeared, replaced in dominance by a more melodic bass line. While rock steady was certainly dance music, it was not without its social commentary aspects: Desmond Dekker's "Shanty Town" commented on life in the ghetto communities around Kingston; the Ethiopians sang about the wave of strikes afflicting Jamaica in 1968 with their song "Everything Crash." As innovative as rock steady was in Jamaican music, combining sweeter melodies, lyrics worth listening to, and new rhythmic combinations, the rock-steady era lasted only until about 1969.

COALESCING INTO A MOVEMENT

Replacing rock steady was a new sound, reggae, a name that eventually would be applied to all Jamaican music. The exact meaning of the term is unclear, with some claiming it means "ragged" or "street rough." Others defined reggae as a general term referring to poor people who were suffering. For others it was simply a beat. Musically, reggae slowed the rock-steady beat down even further with a stronger bass driving the beat; a lopping, chopping guitar sound; and more rhythmic freedom for the drummer to play around the beat of the bass. Early reggae records, such as Toots and the Maytals' "Do the Reggay," blended elements of rock steady and reggae. Much of this new sound came from new producers, such as Lee Perry, Clancy Eccles, and Bunny Lee, who established their own studios in the late 1960s. Unable to hire established studio musicians, they turned to younger talents, such as Aston and Carlton Barrett and Leroy Wallace. These producers and musicians established the new reggae beat that soon became the most popular style in Jamaica, eclipsing both ska and rock steady.

Of all the various groups to emerge from the reggae sound, none had a greater impact than Bob Marley & the Wailers. Singer, songwriter, and guitarist Marley became the greatest reggae star ever, with an enduring international appeal. Born in 1945, Marley grew up in Trench Town, a rough slum in Kingston. He formed the Wailers with Peter Tosh and Bunny Livingston in 1960, and they made their first recordings in 1962. In the later 1960s Marley became an adherent of Rastafarianism. In 1972 they signed a recording contract with Chris Blackwell's Island Records. Blackwell gave Marley the money and artistic freedom to do largely as he pleased. What followed was a string of some of the most influential reggae recordings in the genre's history.

On albums such as *Catch a Fire* and early singles, Marley and the Wailers took on political, religious, and social topics, from ghetto conditions in "Trench Town Rock" and "Concrete Jungle" to Rastafarianism in "Natty Dread." Tosh and Livingston left the group in the early 1970s, but Marley continued on, releasing such reggae classics as "No Woman No Cry," "Get Up Stand Up," "Exodus," and "Them Belly Full (But We Hungry)." His 1975 album, *Live*, was a best-selling record that encapsulated the live power of Bob Marley & the Wailers' sound. Marley died of cancer in 1981 at thirty-six.

Along with the success of such reggae ambassadors as Marley and the Wailers during the 1970s, another event that made reggae an international cultural force was the release of the 1972 film *The Harder They Come*. This film, by white Jamaican filmmaker Perry Henzell, starred reggae singer Jimmy Cliff as a young street tough (or "rude boy," in Jamaican slang terms) who comes to Kingston, records a hit record, and then gets in trouble with the law. Although fictional, *The Harder They Come* was based on several years of research by Henzell on the culture that surrounded reggae music. The story of success, oppression, and rebellion hit a literal and figurative chord with young people around the world, awakening an interest in Jamaican music and culture that has never completely subsided. The soundtrack that accompanied it, which featured such stars as Cliff, the Melodians, the Maytals, and Dekker, introduced reggae music to millions around the world.

A FAR-REACHING LEGACY

By the early 1980s reggae was evolving once again. Disc jockeys (DJs) had always been important in Jamaican popular music, bringing music to the masses and sometimes acting as producers of reggae artists. DJs began to dominate Jamaican music in the late 1970s and early 1980s in a style that came to be known as dancehall. DJs such as Ranking Trevor, U Brown, and Trinity revived an earlier style from the 1960s, called toasting, that had DJs adding vocal effects or talking over instrumental tracks, creating an ad-hoc musical form. In the late 1970s these younger DJs began to record their own songs in the toasting style, which was dubbed dancehall. The dancehall style became the dominant musical form in reggae with such performers as Yellowman, Sugar Minott, and U Roy and had direct connections to the emerging rap and hip-hop style among African American performers in the United States in the early 1980s. The dancehall style continued to be the dominant form of reggae in the late 1990s.

Although the dancehall style now predominates, the earlier Jamaican musical forms continued through the 1980s and 1990s. The reggae style was by no means dead, and groups and artists such as Black Uhuru, Steel Pulse, Peter Tosh, Gregory Isaacs, Third World, and a host of other stars carried the reggae tradition forward. Ska enjoyed a revival in Britain in the late 1970s as young English musicians discovered the music through the many Jamaicans and West Indians living in London. Such groups as the Selector, Madness, the Specials, the Beat, and hundreds of others revived the ska sound, using its musical forms while often combining them with socially conscious lyrics that commented on life in Margaret Thatcher's Great Britain. The ska revival also infected the United States, and the style continued to draw a large cult following both in the United States and in Britain during the 1990s.

In addition to the enduring popularity of the quintessential reggae sound and message epitomized by Marley, adaptations and offshoots of the style can be heard throughout the world and in several other genres. Among popular music styles in the twenty-first century that owe their sound to the Jamaican genre are hip-hop mixing techniques; Raggamuffin, a more electronic-sounding style; and Reggaeton, which blends the reggae and Latin American influences. Subgenres developed in locations as disparate as Iceland, South Africa, and Thailand demonstrate the true internationality of this music and its lasting appeal.

Timothy Berg

SEE ALSO: *Disc Jockeys; Domino, Fats; Garvey, Marcus; Gospel Music; Hip-Hop; Jordan, Louis; Marley, Bob; Rhythm and Blues; Soul Music.*

BIBLIOGRAPHY

Barrow, Steve. *Tougher than Tough: The Story of Jamaican Music.* London: Island Records, 1993.

Bradley, Lloyd. *This Is Reggae Music: The Story of Jamaica's Music.* New York: Grove Press, 2001.

Chang, Kevin O'Brien, and Wayne Chen. *Reggae Routes: The Story of Jamaican Music.* Philadelphia: Temple University Press, 1998.

Manuel, Peter; Kenneth M. Bilby; and Michael D. Largey. *Caribbean Currents: Caribbean Music from Rumba to Reggae.* Philadelphia: Temple University Press, 1995.

Moskowitz, David. *Caribbean Popular Music: An Encyclopedia of Reggae, Mento, Ska, Rock Steady, and Dancehall.* Westport, CT: Greenwood Press, 2005.

Ward, Ed. "Reggae." In *The Rolling Stone Illustrated History of Rock & Roll*, ed. Jim Miller. New York: Rolling Stone Press, 1980.

White, Timothy. *Catch a Fire: The Life of Bob Marley.* New York: Owl Books, 1998.

Reiner, Carl *(1922–)*

Carl Reiner is among the most influential comedic actors, writers, directors, and producers of his generation. He has been associated with many of the brightest lights in American comedy during the post–World War II era, including Mel Brooks, Dick Van Dyke, and Steve Martin.

Reiner was born in the Bronx, New York, on March 20, 1922. During the Great Depression, he received his first taste of show business as a writer and an actor in a dramatic workshop sponsored by the Works Projects Administration (WPA). He was drafted into the U.S. Army during World War II and further developed his performing abilities while acting in a South Pacific service troupe directed by Shakespearean actor Maurice Evans.

After the war, Reiner was part of the first generation of writer-performers on the new medium of television. In 1950 he was signed to write and costar on the NBC variety series *Your Show of Shows* (1950–1954), starring Sid Caesar and Imogene Coca. Reiner appeared on-screen largely as a straight man to Caesar and Coca's antics. In the writers' room, he worked alongside such greats as Neil Simon, Joe Stein, and a young and maniacal Brooks. Reiner and Brooks developed a rapport for mad improvisation—Reiner would introduce Brooks as a Jewish pirate, for example, and Brooks would begin off-the-cuff dialogue. On one such occasion, Reiner asked Brooks about witnessing the Crucifixion; Brooks's persona became the genesis of his famous 2,000-Year-Old Man character. The pair developed the routine at show business parties during the 1950s, and on the advice of Steve Allen and George Burns, they recorded a best-selling album of the routine in 1960.

Reiner wrote the critically acclaimed autobiographical novel *Enter Laughing* in 1958, which Stein adapted into a hit Broadway play. Reiner realized that the story of his life—a young husband and father who wrote comedy—would make a good TV situation comedy. The idea eventually became *The Dick Van Dyke Show*, which debuted in 1961 and ran for five seasons. The series was a beautiful combination of physical shtick, verbal jousting, and ensemble acting, and it turned Van Dyke and costar Mary Tyler Moore into TV superstars. Reiner made guest appearances as Alan Brady, the demanding, vainglorious star for whom Van Dyke's character writes.

During the 1960s and 1970s Reiner branched out as a successful film director. His 1969 movie *The Comic* stars Van Dyke as a silent screen comedian. Reiner's next film was the cult classic *Where's Poppa?* (1970), a blissfully off-color farce with something to offend everyone (the film ends with the middle-aged protagonist about to go to bed with his aged mother). He directed the 1977 surprise hit, *"Oh, God!"*, starring Burns as the Almighty; the film was written by fellow Caesar alumnus Larry Gelbart, and its style echoes the 2,000-Year-Old Man routines. Reiner found his ideal film collaborator in Martin, a stand-up phenomenon, directing Martin's first starring role, *The Jerk* (1979), which grossed well over $100 million. They teamed up several more times, most famously on the 1984 hit *All of Me* (costarring Lily Tomlin).

By the 1990s Reiner was an elder statesman in the comedy genre. He reprised his Alan Brady character (and won an Emmy) in a 1995 episode of the popular *Mad about You* (1992–1999) sitcom. In 1998 he and Brooks recorded another 2,000-Year-Old Man album, for which they won a long overdue Grammy. "Thirty-nine years ago we were nominated for a Grammy and didn't win," Reiner said in his acceptance speech. "We can't wait another thirty-nine years."

Despite entering his eighties, Reiner kept working in the first decade of the 2000s. He became known to a younger audience via Steven Soderbergh's *Ocean's* films, in which he acted alongside such heartthrob actors as George Clooney, Brad Pitt, and Matt Damon. He also appeared in a number of television shows, both as a guest star and as a regular. He provided the voice of Sarmoti in the animated television series *Father of the Pride* in the middle of the decade and joined the cast of the sitcom *Hot in Cleveland*, starring fellow octogenarian Betty White, in 2010. Reiner also continued to write, publishing the humorous novel *NNNNN* in 2006.

Reiner married singer Estelle Lebost in 1943, and they had three children. The eldest is actor/director Rob Reiner, known for such films as *This Is Spinal Tap* (1984) and *A Few Good Men* (1992). Lebost is probably best remembered for one line: "I'll have what she's having," from the deli scene in son Rob's 1989 hit *When Harry Met Sally . . . .* She died in 2008.

Andrew Milner

SEE ALSO: *Allen, Steve; Brooks, Mel; Caesar, Sid; Coca, Imogene; Emmy Awards; Grammy Awards; Martin, Steve; Simon, Neil; Sitcom; Television; Van Dyke, Dick; White, Betty.*

BIBLIOGRAPHY

Reiner, Carl. *Enter Laughing.* New York: Simon & Schuster, 1958.

Reiner, Carl. *All Kinds of Love.* Secaucus, NJ: Carol Publishing, 1993.

Reiner, Carl. *Continue Laughing.* New York: Birch Lane Press, 1995.

Reiner, Carl. *How Paul Robeson Saved My Life and Other Mostly Happy Stories.* New York: Cliff Street, 1999.

Reiner, Carl. *My Anecdotal Life: A Memoir.* New York: St. Martin's Press, 2003.

Reiner, Carl. *Tell Me a Scary Story—But Not Too Scary!* New York: Little, Brown, 2003.

Reiner, Carl. *NNNNN.* New York: Simon & Schuster, 2006.

Reiner, Carl, and Mel Brooks. *The 2,000 Year Old Man in the Year 2000: The Book, Including How to Not Die and Other Good Tips.* New York: HarperCollins, 1997.

Reiner, Carl, and Mel Brooks. *The 2,000 Year Old Man Goes to School.* New York: HarperCollins, 2005.

Waldron, Vince. *The Official "Dick Van Dyke Show" Book.* New York: Hyperion, 1994.

Religious Right

Since the 1970s the Religious Right, also known as the Christian Right or the New Christian Right, has constituted a U.S. coalition of organizations and individuals with three major political goals: to engage Protestants in the political process, to bring Protestants into the Republican Party, and to elect social conservatives to public office. The movement, however, is not merely focused on elections. Broadly speaking, the Religious Right is made up of evangelical Christians who are socially, theologically, and economically conservative—although the coalition also has support from conservative Catholics and members of other religious groupings. The Religious Right's adherents are primarily, but not exclusively, white middle-class Americans who affirm their idea of family values, promote laissez-faire economics, and generally believe in a literal interpretation of the Bible. Best known for their positions on contemporary hot-button issues such as opposition to abortion, homosexuality, and removal of sanctioned prayer in public schools, members also tend to oppose high taxes and to reject expansion of welfare.

POLITICAL PROMINENCE

The rise of the Religious Right began in 1976, which was dubbed the "Year of the Evangelical" by *Time* magazine. The *New York Times* claimed that the blossoming evangelical movement was "the major religious force in America, both in numbers and impact," and Christian periodicals such as *Christianity Today* praised evangelicals for finally reaching cultural prominence. Americans elected Jimmy Carter, a Southern Baptist, to the White House, a sign to some that the self-indulgence of the 1960s was giving way to born-again Christian fervor. However, Carter was a middle-of-the-road Democrat who was far more tolerant of diversity in American culture than many of the outspoken evangelists and politicians who have since come to represent the Religious Right. His election was not so much the fruit of a proactive evangelical movement as the result of voters expressing frustration with a decade of Washington-based excesses, including unpopular Vietnam policies by the Democrats and the Watergate scandal by the Republicans.

Ronald Reagan, who ran for president in 1976, was determined to win the next election. He hired conservative pollster Richard Wirthin, who used a hierarchical values map to learn what positions successful candidates should take on hot-button issues. In 1980 Reagan espoused those positions to win votes away from Carter, and many conservative Christians who had helped to elect Carter in 1976 turned on him in 1980 in favor of the Republican Party. The election marked the beginning of the association between evangelical Christians and Republicanism. However, many liberal-leaning evangelicals have decried the conflation of the two terms.

The Religious Right remained influential through the end of the 1980s, until the movement was weakened by several events: a series of televangelist scandals; the failed 1988 presidential bid of televangelist Pat Robertson; the disbanding of preacher Jerry Falwell's Moral Majority; and Democratic electoral gains, including the recapture of the White House in 1992. The Christian Right responded by establishing influential new organizations such as the Christian Coalition and organizing voters on the local level. The efforts made conservative Christians an important voting bloc and fueled the Republican resurgence in 1994.

EVANGELICALISM IN AMERICA

The Religious Right draws some of its power from the historical forces that have shaped church-state relations in the United States for more than three centuries. The New England Puritans of the seventeenth century believed that they were founding a holy commonwealth and that they were entering into an explicit covenant with God. They thought that if they obeyed God's commands, they would be blessed, and if they disobeyed, they would be punished. Puritans saw their society as a city on a hill, a redeemer nation that the world should revere and imitate. This combination of covenantal thinking and sense of divine mission has shaped American Protestants' perceptions of themselves as custodians of U.S. culture.

Many of the nation's nineteenth-century social reformers were evangelical Christians. Leading revivalists preached the doctrine of perfectionism—the idea that Christians could and should lead holy lives. Evangelicals tended to be obsessed with shortcomings in personal piety and opposed such vices as alcohol, gambling, fornication, profanity, and dishonesty. Although these values helped to civilize the frontier and to encourage pioneers to lead sober and decent lives, social conservatism tended to cause some evangelicals to ignore larger issues such as political decision making; economic policies; and social ills like slavery, exploitation of workers, and poverty. Some were content to abide the rigid moralism that would come to characterize the Religious Right. Other antebellum evangelicals opposed slavery, and some founded many of the nation's most prominent institutions of higher learning.

By the mid-nineteenth century, the United States had become, more than at any other point in its history, a Christian republic. Evangelical, revivalist Protestantism was the dominant form of religious expression. Roman Catholics were excluded because of their supposed allegiance to the papacy (a foreign power), tolerance of alcohol use, and because of fears that poor Catholic immigrants would upset the social order. Church membership reached record levels, and Americans believed more than ever in their role as saviors of society. Buttressed by the support of wealthy businessmen, evangelists set out to improve the world through personal piety, public service, and reform.

Evangelicals pioneered scores of voluntary associations whose attention to single issues made them highly effective instruments of reform. Activists learned how to raise money, promote their enterprises, and continually add numbers to their ranks. Even women, who had long been marginalized in

American culture, found a voice through evangelism in the nineteenth century by forming the Woman's Christian Temperance Union in 1873. Most American colleges have evangelical roots, and Protestant clergymen were among the most influential American celebrities. In many ways Victorian America was the heyday of American evangelicalism, as it dominated much of American public life and grew exponentially.

THE RISE OF FUNDAMENTALISM

Starting in the second half of the nineteenth century, forces of industrialization, urbanization, and immigration interrupted the evangelical march to cultural preeminence. Subcultures divided by class, ethnicity, language, and religion replaced relative homogeneity and social cohesion. Expansive immigration from eastern and southern Europe brought Jews, Roman Catholics, and Orthodox Christians to North America, thus weakening Protestants' cultural influence. The growing secularism of urban America alarmed many in the country's leading Protestant denominations.

Darwinism and historical criticism of the Bible made traditional religious belief untenable for many more sophisticated Americans. Christian progressives such as Jane Addams and Toledo, Ohio, mayor Samuel "Golden Rule" Jones sought to address the social problems that accompanied growing industrialism, such as urban poverty, inadequate public housing, and political corruption. In response, they emphasized social service and created the Social Gospel movement, which began to eclipse evangelicalism's traditional emphasis on personal salvation.

Between 1870 and 1925, evangelicals divided into two warring camps: modernists and fundamentalists (though each branch had many gradations). Modernists adapted the Christian faith to modern science and to new biblical criticism. They espoused theistic evolution, which made room for Charles Darwin's theories and admitted that the earth was very old. Conceding that the Bible was often factually untrue and at times supernaturally naive, modernists focused instead on a social gospel that emphasized moral instruction and service to fellow humans.

Fundamentalists, on the other hand, rejected modernism in all its forms, arguing that the Bible was literally true in all its claims. They rejected evolution and any findings of modern science that questioned divine creation. They also eschewed politics, believing that concern for this world was of little importance. Urban revivalists such as Dwight L. Moody and Billy Sunday carried fundamentalist, old-time religion to millions of Americans, giving rise to what would later become known as the Old Christian Right.

After World War I fundamentalist leaders such as Sunday, William Jennings Bryan, and William Bell Riley championed the two leading causes of the Old Christian Right: prohibiting the sale of intoxicating liquor and banning the teaching of evolution in tax-supported public schools. By 1920 fundamentalism had become well organized and had made impressive gains. Leaders achieved a stunning moral victory in the passage of Prohibition. The movement had respectable intellectuals who defended the fundamentals of the faith, and a handful of southern states passed laws that banned the teaching of evolution in public schools.

By the early 1930s, however, the movement had disintegrated and had lost public credibility. Trouble began in 1925 with the trial of teacher John T. Scopes, who had been accused of teaching evolution in Dayton, Tennessee, where such lessons were prohibited. The event, swarming with national media, became one of the first news events broadcast live on radio. In the minds of Americans, the coverage cemented an image of fundamentalists as rural, uneducated, backward simpletons unwilling to embrace advances in science and technology—such a depiction was cruelly fostered by the commentary of newspaper columnist H. L. Mencken. Moreover, Prohibition was repealed in 1933, ending the fundamentalist dream of an America free from drunkenness and immorality.

RETRENCHING: 1930s–1960s

By the mid-1930s, modernists had taken control of the largest Protestant denominations as liberals opted for a more flexible faith that was free from fundamentalism's doctrinal rigor. As many northern denominations embraced modernity, the fundamentalist center of gravity shifted to the rural South, where Protestant conservatives stopped short of demanding social transformation. Southern evangelicals had traditionally been socially conservative, seeking to preserve the southern ideal against northern capitalistic encroachment. Evangelical Protestantism was now in the hands of social conservatives, a marriage that would grow stronger year by year.

Fundamentalists retreated into culturally conservative communities. Some were associated with the Ku Klux Klan in the 1920s and with segregation and anticommunism in the 1950s. The links between conservative Christianity and retrograde political movements hardened the image of fundamentalists as narrow-minded, bigoted, and backward looking—far removed from the image evangelical progressives had maintained a generation earlier. Thus, between 1930 and 1970, Americans paid little attention to conservative evangelical Protestants.

Because fundamentalists had lost control of the country's major Protestant denominations, they set out to create new organizations to preserve what they considered an unadulterated Christian message. Large, independent congregations sprouted up across the country, led by famous preachers such as Riley, John Roach Straton, Frank Norris, Carl McIntire, and "Fighting" Bob Shuler. Individuals and churches formed coalitions to increase their strength and effectiveness, most notably the World's Christian Fundamentals Association, the National Federation of Fundamentalists, and the Baptist Bible Union. In addition, fundamentalists established Bible colleges that favored Christian teaching and practical instruction over the liberal arts—such as Moody Bible Institute in Chicago, Bob Jones University in Bay County, Florida (later Greenville, South Carolina), and the Bible Institute of Los Angeles (BIOLA). Conservative evangelicals published newspapers and periodicals such as *King's Business*, *Christian Beacon*, and *Crusaders' Champion*. Evangelicals also moved into radio broadcasting as they attempted to spread the Christian message.

Before the 1960s southern Protestants' sympathies generally remained with the Democratic Party, which had reestablished white political dominance in the wake of Reconstruction. The popularity of New Deal social-welfare programs to eradicate poverty and assist farmers further strengthened this linkage. However, as evangelicals climbed the social and economic ladders, their affinity for liberal programs faded. A significant number of conservative evangelicals fled the Democratic Party in 1960 when it nominated John F. Kennedy, a Roman Catholic, for president.

At the same time, the civil rights movement began building steam, and Democratic efforts to end segregation pushed large numbers of racist evangelicals toward the Republican Party. Southern whites, who fifty years earlier had supported Bryan, a Democrat, now responded favorably to the presidential candidacies of Republicans Richard Nixon and Barry Goldwater and of Independent George Wallace. Although Carter won the White House in 1976, carrying most of the southern states, he did not win the majority of votes from white southern evangelicals. By the mid-1970s, most conservative Protestants were Republicans, turning on Carter en masse in 1980 in support of the ultraconservative Reagan.

CREATING THE NEW CHRISTIAN RIGHT

Scholars refer to the return of conservative Protestants to organized political action as the rise of the New Christian Right. During the 1950s and 1960s, American culture became more liberal. The U.S. Supreme Court under Earl Warren declared segregated schools unconstitutional in 1954 and upheld laws banning organized prayer in public schools in 1963. Also during this time, the space race led to federal intrusion in the public schools with an emphasis on science that sometimes went against fundamentalist teachings. The Warren court also progressively lifted prohibitions against books and movies that had been considered obscene. In 1960 the Food and Drug Administration approved use of the birth control pill, removing a barrier to nonmarital sex and infuriating religious conservatives. The 1973 U.S. Supreme Court decision *Roe v. Wade*, which legalized abortion, further exasperated the Religious Right.

Conservative reaction intensified in 1974 when a group of fundamentalists led by educators Mel and Norma Gabler and Alice Moore protested proposed public school textbooks in Kanawha County, West Virginia. They argued that the sex education curriculum was too explicit; that the science books pushed evolution at the expense of creation science; and that books with sexually explicit, negative, or morbid language were inappropriate for young people. A culture war developed as conservatives and liberals squared off over educational freedom, public school curricula, and issues of public decency. Religious and political conservatives from across the country offered support to the embattled Kanawha County fundamentalists. Paul Weyrich and James McKenna, founders of the Heritage Foundation, a fledgling conservative think tank in Washington, D.C., and others used the standoff to return the Religious Right to the limelight of American politics.

As the 1970s continued, conservative Protestants became prominent in American business, political, and social circles. Evangelist Billy Graham emerged as a celebrity through his well-organized crusades into U.S. cities, where he preached a born-again message. Graham rarely engaged in commentary on specific political issues and avoided personal scandal, becoming generally regarded as a middle-of-the-road pastor and unofficial chaplain to national political figures of both parties. (Earlier, Graham, along with Carl F. H. Henry, founded *Christianity Today* as a conservative counterpart to the progressive *Christian Century*.) Chuck Colson, one of Nixon's Watergate-era henchmen, publicly found Jesus and fought for an evangelical presence in American politics. Lawyer and activist Phyllis Schlafly led conservative Christians in a battle against feminism, lesbianism, and the Equal Rights Amendment. The belief that fundamentalist evangelical values should infuse all aspects of private and public life soon coalesced into several movements such as Christian Reconstructionism and Dominionism, led by figures like Francis Schaeffer and Rousas John Rushdoony.

UNITING POLITICS AND RELIGION

Political activists with little or no background in the Religious Right attempted to strengthen the Republican Party by building bridges between secular and religious conservatives. Leaders such as Howard Phillips of the Conservative Caucus. John "Terry" Dolan of the National Conservative Political Action Committee. Weyrich of the National Committee for the Survival of a Free Congress; and Richard Viguerie, a major fund-raiser for conservative causes, all attempted to woo both fundamentalist and evangelical Christians. In 1978 former missionary Robert Billings, assisted by Weyrich, formed the National Christian Action Coalition, the first national organization of the Christian Right. Televangelist Jerry Falwell followed suit by founding the Moral Majority, a conservative political action group, in 1979.

The basis for the new coalition was an all-out attack on big government as the major threat to traditional religious and economic values. In addition to traditional, anticommunist, probusiness, and antitax stances, conservative activists espoused the concerns of the Religious Right on feminism, homosexuality, school prayer, and sexual laxity, among others. Fundamentalist ministers who had long warned their constituents to avoid secular politics now encouraged them to ignore the division between the sacred and secular. They insisted that no area of human activity, including law and politics, should be outside of Christian influence. Falwell helped singer Anita Bryant in her crusade to repeal a gay-rights ordinance in Dade County, Florida. Billings, Focus on the Family founder James Dobson, and scores of other evangelicals battled the Internal Revenue Service (IRS) in 1978 when it attempted to remove tax-exempt status from those private Christian schools resisting desegregation.

Evangelical leaders embraced conservative political issues using a religious rationale. They justified increased defense spending as a way of keeping the world free for ongoing preaching of the gospel: support for the government of Taiwan was key because the United States was protecting Christian allies from the godless, communist Chinese. Governmental support for Israel was necessary because biblical prophecy demanded a unified and strong Israeli state. Now ideologically and institutionally viable, and savvy about electronic media such as television and radio, the Religious Right entered the 1980s stronger than before.

THE REAGAN ERA

Elected president in 1980, Reagan embraced the views of the Religious Right and pledged to work on its behalf. Among other gestures, he appointed antiabortion activist and evangelical Christian C. Everett Koop as U.S. surgeon general. (However, Koop frustrated many conservatives and delighted liberals when he took a strong, proactive, nonjudgmental stance on the AIDS crisis.) Republicans also regained control of the Senate in 1980 for the first time in a quarter century. Many credited the Religious Right with securing those congressional victories.

Throughout the decade, the Religious Right was constantly on the minds and lips of political commentators and electoral analysts. Falwell became the unofficial spokesperson for conservative Protestants, and Robertson's *700 Club* television show reached a record numbers of viewers by combining revivalist preaching with analysis of current events in a network news format. No one could ignore the Religious Right for its profound influence on local and national elections during the Reagan years. Approximately 25 percent of Americans self-reported to be "born again," forcing politicians to contend with conservative Christians as a key voting bloc.

SCANDALS

Beginning in 1987, a series of scandals involving prominent televangelists tarnished the image of religious conservatives, and the movement began to lose cohesion. First, preacher Oral Roberts brought ridicule upon himself by threatening that if his supporters did not contribute $8 million to save his City of Faith Hospital, then "God is going to call me home." Then Jim and Tammy Faye Bakker, heroes of the PTL television network and Heritage USA amusement park, found themselves embroiled in controversy. Journalists uncovered Jim's romantic tryst with former secretary Jessica Hahn and discovered that one of his colleagues had paid Hahn $250,000 in hush money. To make matters worse, IRS investigators charged Jim with tax evasion and fraud, exposing the Bakkers' mismanagement of financial contributions from loyal followers, which the Bakkers used to support their lavish lifestyle. Jim was sentenced to forty-five years in prison, though he was released on parole a few years later, and his wife, Tammy Faye, entered the Betty Ford Center to deal with a drug problem brought about by the stress.

Soon after, televangelist Jimmy Swaggart was caught in a seedy hotel room with a New Orleans prostitute, further humiliating the conservative Christian community and sowing seeds of dissension among constituents. Journalists and cultural critics heaped ridicule upon the Religious Right for its leaders' misdeeds, and the movement began to disintegrate politically. In 1988 Christian Right religious leaders were politically split during the Republican primary campaign: Falwell endorsed George H. W. Bush, while many others supported Jack Kemp and Bob Dole. Robertson, head of the multimillion-dollar Christian Broadcasting Network, campaigned for president and even made impressive showings in several early primaries (although he eventually withdrew from the race, unable to garner the full support of the Religious Right). Falwell disbanded the Moral Majority in 1989. Many commentators announced the death of the Religious Right in 1992 when Bill Clinton, a liberal, southern, pro-choice, pro–gay rights child of the 1960s, and nominal Baptist, took the White House.

CHANGING TACTICS: 1990s

The Republican congressional resurgence in 1994 revealed the obituary to be premature. The Religious Right helped to elect political conservatives to office, and Robertson's new organization, the Christian Coalition, was instrumental to the effort. Five years earlier, Robertson had formed the coalition as a grassroots conservative political organization independent of the structures of the Republican Party. Under the leadership of a young and vibrant activist Ralph Reed, the new organization no longer kowtowed to Republican presidents. Instead the coalition de-emphasized national politics and followed the principle that the real battles were in neighborhoods, school boards, city councils, and state legislatures. In other words, they accepted the dictum that all politics is local.

During the 1994 election, the Christian Coalition distributed thirty-five million voter guides and seventeen million congressional scorecards and made telephone calls to three million voters. In 1995 the organization added its support to the Republicans' Contract with America and penned its own Contract with the American Family. The fundamentalist contract called for religious equality, local control of education, school choice, protection of parental rights, family-friendly tax relief, eradication of pornography, privatization of the arts, and victims' rights. By 1995 the Christian Coalition had 1.6 million members and a budget of more than $25 million. The organization continued to educate conservative Christians about local political issues and candidates in a grassroots campaign to purify the United States.

During the 1990s, a group called the Promise Keepers also garnered national attention. Founded by University of Colorado football coach Bill McCartney and friend Dave Wardell, the Promise Keepers united large numbers of Christian men in stadium rallies across the country, asking them to recommit their lives to Christ and to reclaim their traditional role as head of the family. The group's mission was to be "a Christ-centered ministry dedicated to uniting men through vital relationships to become godly influences in their world." However, the organization came under fire from the National Organization for Women and Religious Left groups such as People of Faith, who claimed Promise Keepers was advancing a right-wing, antifeminist agenda to relegate women to traditional, submissive roles. The Promise Keepers denied affiliation with the Christian Coalition and any political motivation. In fact, this spiritual men's movement expanded the white Protestant image of the Religious Right by including Catholics and members of racial minorities in rallies.

THE NEW MILLENNIUM

Robertson resumed the presidency of the Christian Coalition after Reed's departure. In June 1999 the organization announced it was splitting into two separate organizations after the IRS revoked its tax-exempt status for engaging in political activities. Under the reorganization, Christian Coalition International focused on endorsing candidates and making political contributions, whereas the tax-exempt Christian Coalition of America continued to distribute its controversial voters' guides. The move was seen by critics as yet another example of the decline of the once-powerful organization.

During the 2012 presidential primary, former Republican senator Rick Santorum emerged as the standard bearer for the Religious Right. Santorum began engaging in what liberals called "the Republican war on women" as he announced that he was against both contraception and prenatal testing. At the same time, talk show host Rush Limbaugh, long a mouthpiece for the Religious Right, attacked a young law student for lobbying for her school's insurance to cover contraception, calling her a "slut" and a "prostitute." Members of the newly emergent Tea Party, who were elected to Congress in 2010 because of their extreme conservatism, unsuccessfully set out to shut down Planned Parenthood. Such failures led Michael Crowley of *Time* to suggest that the fervor of the Religious Right has never died but has only been "drowned" by issues such as the economy and health care.

Kurt W. Peterson

SEE ALSO: *Abortion; AIDS; Bakker, Jim, and Tammy Faye; Celebrity; Civil Rights Movement; Communism; Equal Rights Amendment; Feminism; Fundamentalism; Gambling; Gay and Lesbian Marriage; Gay Men; Graham, Billy; Ku Klux Klan; Lesbianism; Limbaugh, Rush; Megachurches; Modernism; Moral Majority; New Deal; Norris, Frank; Pornography;*

Prohibition; Protest Groups; Radio; Reagan, Ronald; Robertson, Pat; Scopes Monkey Trial; Sex Scandals; Sexual Revolution; Sunday, Billy; Swaggart, Jimmy; The Tea Party; Televangelism; Television; Watergate; World War I.

BIBLIOGRAPHY

Bartkowski, John P. *The Promise Keepers: Servants, Soldiers, and Godly Men.* New Brunswick, NJ: Rutgers University Press, 2004.

Bruce, Steve. *The Rise and Fall of the New Christian Right.* New York: Oxford University Press, 1988.

Carpenter, Joel. *Revive Us Again: The Reawakening of American Fundamentalism.* New York: Oxford University Press, 1997.

Christian Coalition. *Contract with the American Family.* Nashville, TN: Moorings, 1995.

Christian Coalition of America Official Website. Accessed April 2012. Available from http://www.cc.org

Diamond, Sara. *Spiritual Warfare: The Politics of the Christian Right.* Boston: South End Press, 1989.

Fetner, Tina. *How the Religious Right Shaped Lesbian and Gay Activism.* Minneapolis: University of Minnesota Press, 2008.

Flippen, J. Brooks. *Jimmy Carter, the Politics of Family, and the Rise of the Religious Right.* Athens: University of Georgia Press, 2011.

Hedges, Chris. *American Fascists: The Christian Right and the War on America.* New York: Free Press, 2007.

Lienesch, Michael. *Redeeming America: Piety and Politics in the New Christian Right.* Chapel Hill: University of North Carolina Press, 1993.

Lindlof, Thomas R. *Hollywood under Siege: Martin Scorsese, the Religious Right, and the Culture Wars.* Lexington: University of Kentucky Press, 2008.

Marsden, George. *Fundamentalism and American Culture.* New York: Oxford University Press, 1982.

Martin, William. *With God on Our Side: The Rise of the Religious Right in America.* New York: Broadway Books, 1996.

Menendez, Albert J. *Evangelicals at the Ballot Box.* New York: Prometheus Books, 1996.

Schulman, Bruce J., and Julian E. Zelizer, eds. *Rightward Bound: Making America Conservative in the 1970s.* Cambridge, MA: Harvard University Press, 2008.

Silk, Mark. *Spiritual Politics: Religion and America since World War II.* New York: Simon & Schuster, 1988.

Wallis, Jim. *The Great Awakening: Reviving Faith & Politics in a Post–Religious Right America.* New York: HarperOne, 2008.

R.E.M.

An alternative rock band perhaps most popular during the 1980s and 1990s, R.E.M. served up an eclectic mix of musical styles that included punk, rock, and even country and folk. Composed of lead singer Michael Stipe (1960–), guitarist Peter Buck (1956–), bassist Mike Mills (1958–), and drummer Bill Berry (1958–), R.E.M. had a homegrown feel to its music, with a jangly guitar sound that was reminiscent of the U.S. folk-rock band the Byrds. R.E.M.'s music also represented a link between the post-punk alternative music of the 1980s and punk forerunners Patti Smith (who appeared on 1996's *New Adventures in Hi-Fi*) and the Velvet Underground. According to *Rolling Stone* magazine, which selected the group as its 1992 Artist of the Year, R.E.M. ascended to "mainstream popularity without caving in to record-industry dictums or betraying its original college-radio constituency."

The group began the 1980s in Athens, Georgia, hometown to its members and a small college town with a vibrant and diverse music scene, one that rejected the southern rock establishment's sounds of barroom blues and boogie. Although R.E.M. recalled traditional U.S. songwriting forms, such as country and folk, the band was definitely shaped by 1977's punk scene. R.E.M.'s music had little to do with punk, but the do-it-yourself ethic of punk rock carried tremendous influence within the band. "You have to remember," said Buck, "growing up at the time I did, there wasn't anyone who made records like us. Rock & roll was full of super-rich guys that had mustaches and were ten years older than me."

Tiny HibTone Records released R.E.M.'s first single in 1981. Not a hit in conventional terms, "Radio Free Europe" still caused considerable excitement. Independent record labels had yet to become a mainstay in the United States, so the single's reach was nothing but astonishing. It almost single-handedly revitalized the U.S. independent recording scene. If the punk groups of 1977 showed Buck and Stipe that anyone could perform in a band, R.E.M. took things one step further by demonstrating that relative success could be attained without the support of a major record label. A year later the band signed with I.R.S. Records, a larger independent, and released an extended play single called "Chronic Town."

THE 1980s

R.E.M.'s first full-length release, *Murmur* (1983), displayed the group's melodic guitar and harmonies. Stipe's vague lyrics, emphasizing subtlety over abrasiveness, added to the band's idiosyncratic manner. Passionate, atmospheric, and pensive, *Murmur* defined R.E.M.'s sound and set the standard for alternative guitar pop. The follow-up, *Reckoning* (1984), had a clearer sound and used traditional song forms, like the country sound in "(Don't Go Back to) Rockville." The next two releases—*Fables of the Reconstruction* (1985) and *Life's Rich Pageant* (1986)—represented a transitional phase. *Fables of the Reconstruction* was depicted in the rock press as either an interesting experiment with dissonance and melody or an unfocused and meandering mess. Correspondingly, *Life's Rich Pageant* was viewed by some critics as the band's renewal—a return to melodic songs, augmented by powerful guitar riffs—while for others it was a stop on the way to the big time.

All doubts about the band were put to rest in 1987 with the succinct pop of the album *Document* and its hit single "The One I Love." What sounded at first to be a song of devotion was, on closer inspection, cloaked in spite. For years people wanted to know what Stipe was singing. When he was once asked if he would not like people to understand him, he replied, "I don't see any reason for it. I think music is way beyond rational thinking. It doesn't have to make any sense." Finally, R.E.M. delivered a clear mix with "The One I Love," another song whose meaning bypassed many listeners. By 1988 R.E.M. signed with Warner Brothers Records, becoming a major-label artist. The promise of a larger audience made some fans worry that the group would dilute its sound for a new mass audience.

R.E.M. *The original lineup of R.E.M. included, from left, Mike Mills, Michael Stipe, Peter Buck (bottom), and Bob Berry.* PAUL NATKIN/WIREIMAGE/GETTY IMAGES.

Die-hard fans, however, were not disappointed with the release of *Green* in 1988.

THE 1990s

Having allayed fans' fears, the group's next series of releases challenged the expectations of their audience. *Out of Time*, released in 1991, featured rapper KRS-One in "Radio Song" and then proceeded to use string arrangements for a large part of the album. *Automatic for the People* (1992) switched moods by being elegiac. In 1994 the group responded to the suicide of Kurt Cobain, lead singer of the grunge band Nirvana, as well as to the death of actor River Phoenix, with the furious electric guitar of *Monster*. Its next release, *New Adventures in Hi-Fi* (1996), had been recorded on the band's tour for *Monster*, during sound checks and live performances. That same tour witnessed a series of medical emergencies that affected three of the band's members, with Berry undergoing brain surgery, forcing his departure from the band.

THE EARLY 2000s

After Berry left the band, R.E.M. went through a period of reorganization but continued to record and tour with several different drummers. They released a few albums between 2000 and 2011, displaying a decidedly different style that Stipe, speaking of *Around the Sun* (2004), described as "primitive and howling." The albums were all relatively successful, with *Accelerate* (2008) receiving particular critical and popular success. In September 2011, to the surprise and dismay of R.E.M.'s numerous fans, the band announced on its website that it was breaking up, explaining that "all things must end, and we wanted to do it right, to do it our way." The last album R.E.M. released, a collection of songs over the tenure of the band titled *Part Lies, Part Heart, Part Truth, Part Garbage 1982–2011* was released in November 2011. The group was inducted into the Rock and Roll Hall of Fame in 2007.

By helping revitalize the independent recording industry as well as bolstering college radio and local music scenes, R.E.M. contributed to several shifts in American rock. The band's success from Athens and the achievements of singer Prince and the punk-rock band the Replacements from Minneapolis, Minnesota, signaled to young musicians that relocating to New York or Los Angeles was no longer a prerequisite to breaking into the music business. R.E.M.'s success with roots-based, traditional forms marked a major shift away from the Anglophilia of album-oriented rock to a more organic, indigenous perspective that reached its full development in grunge rock.

Daryl Umberger

SEE ALSO: *Alternative Rock; The Byrds; Country Music; Folk Music; Grunge; Nirvana; Pop Music; Prince; Punk; The Replacements; Smith, Patti.*

BIBLIOGRAPHY

Bowler, David, and Bryan Dray. *R.E.M.: From "Chronic Town" to "Monster."* Secaucus, NJ: Carol Publishing Group, 1995.

Buckley, David. *R.E.M. Fiction: An Alternate Biography.* London: Virgin, 2002.

Fletcher, Tony. *Remarks: The Story of R.E.M.* London: Omnibus, 1989.

Fricke, David. "R.E.M." *Rolling Stone*, November 15, 1990, 124–131.

Fricke, David. "Artist of the Year: R.E.M." *Rolling Stone*, March 5, 1992, 45–50.

Fricke, David. "Michael Stipe." *Rolling Stone*, October 15, 1992, 187–188.

Gray, Marcus. *It Crawled from the South: An R.E.M. Companion.* New York: Da Capo Press, 1993.

Greer, Jim. *R.E.M.: Behind the Mask.* Boston: Little, Brown, 1992.

McKinley, James C., Jr. "The End of R.E.M., and They Feel Fine." *New York Times*, September 21, 2011.

Sullivan, Denise. *Talk about the Passion: R.E.M., an Oral History.* Lancaster, PA: Underwood-Miller, 1994.

Remington, Frederic *(1861–1909)*

Largely recognized as one of the great artists of the Wild West, Frederic Remington led a life that mirrored, in many ways, those of his subjects. Capturing the last days of the exciting, vibrant western frontier, he completed nearly 3,000 works derived from working cowboys whose lifestyles were rapidly vanishing. He spent two years at the Yale School of Art and studied at the Art Students League of New York, after which, in the 1880s, he went to the American West, where he sketched, rode, and prospected in new territories. His traveling was to be his most practical on-the-job training. Commissioned by *Harper's Weekly* to provide drawings of the West for publication, the artist recorded the Sioux uprisings, Sitting Bull's murder, the capture of Geronimo, and the last great buffalo slaughter in the northern plains. During this time he continually published, wrote, and illustrated short stories from his experiences with the cavalry and western escapades.

Frederic Remington. The Cheyenne *is one of bronze several statues created by Frederic Remington, whose art depicted life in the American West in the late 1800s.* SISSIE BRIMBERG/CONTRIBUTOR/NATIONAL GEOGRAPHIC/GETTY IMAGES.

After watching Frederick Ruckstull in 1895, Remington decided to sculpt his cowboy subjects in motion. The clay models he made were then cast in bronze and became immediately successful, with his masterful ability to depict fine details, action, and characterizations. *Bronco Buster*, cast in 1895, depicting a bucking horse and a tenacious rider, became one of Remington's most identifiable works. Multiples were produced for the large audience that had been created through the popularity of his published prints and the art he had produced in *Colliers* and *Scribner's*. Since 1901 these drawings had appeared in full-color, double-page spreads, further increasing the demand for his oil paintings.

Remington's work had the ability to connect directly with a vast audience that was often suspicious of "high art," people who were conventionally moral and patriotic. He worked at a time when newspapers and magazines provided a new vehicle for making art available to a mass audience with an insatiable appetite for dramatic content. As the popularity of his work continued to rise, Remington began painting landscapes, broadened his enthusiasm for easel painting, and heightened the exacting demands of his technical standards. Extremely interested in fine detail and a connoisseur of draftsmanship, the artist remarked that he wanted to make his paintings "so you could feel the details instead of seeing them." Two of his most famous works, *Downing the Nigh Leader* (1907) and *Dash for the Timber* (1889), realistically show the action and drama of the Wild West.

Sparking even more interest in his work, in 1935, wealthy oilmen, including Amon Carter, Sid Richardson, and the Hogg brothers of Houston, became major collectors of Remington's art. They identified with the dynamics and energy in the trail-blazing cowboy and horse images, viewing them as similar to their "wildcat" attitudes in the oil business. Both the artist and the oilmen were enthused by active, physical movement and the championing of the "little guy." The value of Remington's work has continued to rise in recent years. For example, a posthumous cast of *Coming through the Rye* was sold in 1998 at Sotheby's in New York for more than $1 million.

In his appreciation of U.S. culture 100 years earlier, Remington made a significant contribution. His ambition and determination, combined with his position as part of the West's vanishing, romanticized last days, helped bring him wide recognition. The printing industry expanded his ability to reach a wide, general audience as well as important men, including Theodore Roosevelt, who believed in Remington's importance and approved of his efforts.

Cheryl McGrath

SEE ALSO: Harper's*;* Scribner's.

BIBLIOGRAPHY

Ballinger, James. *Frederic Remington.* New York: Harry N. Abrams, 1989.

Foxley, W. C. "Remington, Frederic." In *The Dictionary of Art,* vol. 26, 181–182. New York: Grove Dictionaries, 1996.

Hassrick, P. H. *Frederic Remington: Paintings, Drawings and Sculpture in the Amon Carter Museum and the Sid W. Richardson Foundation Collections.* Exhibition Catalog. Fort Worth, TX: Amon Carter Museum, 1974.

Marter, Joan. *The Grove Encyclopedia of American Art.* New York: Oxford University Press, 2011.

McCracken, H. *Frederic Remington, Artist of the Old West.* Philadelphia: Lippincott, 1947.

Mehlman, Robert. "Inexplicable Happenings." *Art Newspaper* 5 (1994), 26.

Samuels, P., and H. Samuels, eds. *The Collected Writings of Frederic Remington.* Garden City, NY: Doubleday, 1979.

Reno, Don *(1927–1984)*

A pioneer of bluegrass banjo playing, Don Reno had an instantly identifiable approach to the instrument that was widely admired but seldom imitated. After a brief stint with Bill Monroe in the late 1940s, Reno formed a highly productive partnership with guitarist-singer Red Smiley, and the two made well over 100 influential recordings in the 1950s and early 1960s. When Smiley's health failed, Reno took his tenor vocalizing and banjo style—an innovative blend of country and jazz chording and single-string, guitarlike picking—into a partnership with Bill Harrell. Reno followed that with a solo career that lasted until his death in 1984. Ironically, it was a casual, short-term studio partnership with Arthur Smith that produced one of Reno's most enduring and influential recordings, the original version of the widely known "Dueling Banjos" (1955).

Jon Weisberger

SEE ALSO: *Bluegrass; Monroe, Bill.*

BIBLIOGRAPHY

Carlin, Richard. *Folk.* New York: Facts On File, 2006.

Renoir, Jean *(1894–1979)*

A French filmmaker who created some thirty-seven films in the realist tradition during a forty-year career, Jean Renoir is regarded as a mentor to the French New Wave directors of the late 1950s and a mainstay of art films beloved by American cinephiles. The son of Impressionist painter Pierre-Auguste Renoir, he released his first film, *La Fille de l'eau,* in 1925 and his last, *Le Petit théâtre de Jean Renoir,* in 1970. Renoir treated complex issues of class and sexuality in his films, in which he created a sense of cinematic space through in-depth staging, location shooting, and camera work noted for its long, complex takes. These processes inflect such seminal works as *La Grande illusion* (1937; *Grand Illusion*), *La Bête humaine* (1938; *The Human Beast*), and *La Règle du jeu* (1939; *The Rules of the Game*). With the outbreak of World War II, he moved to Hollywood, where he made several films. He returned to France after the war. In 1975 Renoir received an honorary Academy Award for lifetime achievement.

Neal Baker

SEE ALSO: *World War I.*

BIBLIOGRAPHY

Cardullo, Bert, ed. *Jean Renoir: Interviews.* Jackson: University Press of Mississippi, 2005.

Faulkner, Christopher. *Jean Renoir: A Guide to References and Resources.* Boston: G. K. Hall, 1979.

O'Shaughnessy, Martin. *Jean Renoir.* Manchester, UK: Manchester University Press, 2000.

Renoir, Jean. *My Life and My Films.* New York: Atheneum, 1974.

Rent

Few could have foreseen the enormous impact Jonathan Larson's musical *Rent* would have on American musical theater when it was produced at the New York Theatre Workshop in 1996. Since its opening, the musical has won the Pulitzer Prize for Drama, Tony Awards, Obie Awards, the New York Drama Critics' Circle Award, and the Drama Desk Award. It also launched the careers of many of its original cast members, including Jesse L. Martin, Idina Menzel, and Taye Diggs. *Rent* has become the seventh-longest-running production in Broadway history and was adapted into a Hollywood film in 2005.

In *Rent,* author-composer-lyricist Larson combined a modern-day *La Bohème* adaptation with contemporary music and issues. He infused his plot with a statement about the HIV epidemic he saw ravaging the artistic community in New York in the late 1980s and early 1990s. "I am the kind of person that when I write my own work, I have something I need to say," Larson said. "It surprises me that in musicals, even plays today, sometimes I don't see what the impetus was, other than thinking it was a good smart idea or it could make them some money or something."

The story revolves around a group of destitute composers, directors, dancers, and junkies living in Manhattan's East Village who struggle with their inability to make art, to find love, and to pay their rent. In addition, the characters struggle with AIDS-related deaths in their artistic community. Despite these obstacles, the characters find a way to, in the words of one of the songs, "share love, give love, spread love." The songs "One Song Glory," "Out Tonight," "Without You," and "Seasons of Love" became instant Broadway hits as the musical spoke to a generation of musical theater fans who called themselves "RentHeads" and camped for hours outside the theater to see the production. The sung-through musical combines many different genres, including grunge, soul, rock, and cabaret.

Larson was not able to see his musical reach the heights of fame: on January 25, 1996, the night before previews began, Larson died of an aortic aneurysm in his Manhattan home. Three months later the show was transferred to the Nederlander Theatre, where it received critical and popular acclaim. The *New York Times* review of the original production concluded, "The show remains a sentimental triumph, and it will doubtless have, and deserves, a long and healthy run." The review was spot on: *Rent* has been performed in countless professional and university theaters since its original Broadway production and was revived in New York City at New World Stages in 2011.

Rent is credited with bridging the gap between musical theater and rock concerts. The musical's influences can be seen in many of the pop/rock musicals that have followed. Larson continues to be an inspiration for many young artists who—as Larson did—struggle to reconcile economic insecurity and artistic aspirations.

Michael Najjar

SEE ALSO: *AIDS; Broadway; Grunge; Hollywood; The Musical; Rock and Roll; Soul Music; Tony Awards.*

BIBLIOGRAPHY

Brantley, Ben. "Enter Singing: Young, Hopeful and Taking on the Big Time." *New York Times*, April 30, 1996.

Hischak, Thomas. "Rent." In *The Oxford Companion to the American Musical.* New York: Oxford University Press, 2008.

Istel, John. "I Have Something to Say: An Interview with Jonathan Larson by John Istel." In *The American Theatre Reader: Essays and Conversations from American Theatre Magazine.* New York: Theatre Communications Group, 2009.

Maslon, Laurence, and Michael Kantor. *Broadway: the American Musical.* New York: Bulfinch Press, 2004.

The Replacements

A Minneapolis, Minnesota, punk quartet that formed in 1979, the Replacements quickly gained notoriety for their inebriated, freewheeling live performances. After a few name changes and personnel adjustments, the band found a good fit with Paul Westerberg as lead vocalist; brothers Tommy and Bob Stinson on bass and guitar, respectively; and Chris Mars on drums. Verging on success in the mid-1980s, the group mocked rock's conventional marketing tools. Their video for "Bastards of Young," from the 1985 album *Tim*, was a three-and-a-half-minute close-up of a stereo speaker—not MTV friendly.

Over the years, Westerberg's songwriting demonstrated a newfound maturity. Beginning with "Hootenanny" (1983), the band incorporated styles that veered from punk into country, folk, and jazz. The Replacements pushed aside purists who regarded punk as a self-contained musical form closed to outside influence. Neither musically mainstream nor punk, the band had, as Westerberg sang in 1987, "One foot in the door / The other one in the gutter."

Rifts among the bandmates caused Bob Stinson and Mars to depart in the late 1980s as Westerberg exerted greater creative control. Steve Foley replaced Mars on drums, and Bob "Slim" Dunlap replaced Stinson on guitar. Yet, the group could not find a niche and disbanded in 1991. Nevertheless, they became a model for the guitar-pop bands that proliferated in the mid-1990s, when alternative music became mainstream.

Following the breakup, each of the band members pursued a solo career. After leaving in 1988, Bob Stinson formed a series of bands before his death in 1995. Tommy Stinson recorded two albums as a solo artist and continues to play bass with Guns N' Roses and Soul Asylum. Mars joined the supergroup Golden Smog with members of various other 1990s bands. He later released a solo album, demonstrating that his musical talents far exceeded just drumming. Westerberg has also released several solo albums, and many of his songs can be heard on television and film soundtracks.

During the 1990s and early in the first decade of the 2000s, the Replacements released several greatest hits albums, collections of previously recorded work, and reissues of remastered albums. Westerberg suggested in 2002 that the band might re-form, although the proposed reunion never happened. Westerberg, Mars, and Tommy Stinson came together in 2005 to record two new songs for a best-of compilation. In 2011 director Gorman Bechard released the film *Color Me Obsessed: A Film about the Replacements*, which featured commentary by musicians, music writers, and ordinary fans expounding on their love of the band and demonstrating the group's influence on popular music and culture.

Daryl Umberger

SEE ALSO: *Alternative Rock; Country Music; Electric Guitar; Folk Music; Jazz; MTV; Pop Music; Punk.*

BIBLIOGRAPHY

Mundy, Chris. "Achin' to Be Understood." *Rolling Stone*, June 24, 1993, 51–55.

Ressner, Jeffrey. "Replacements: A Band on the Verge." *Rolling Stone*, October 18, 1990, 32–33.

Wild, David. "Paul Westerberg." *Rolling Stone*, November 17, 1994, 106–107.

Retro Fashion

The term *retro* applies to stylistic trends in music, film, and fashion characterized by an iconic or kitschy use of the past. Stemming from the late-1960s concept of "retrochic" developed by the Parisian avant garde, retro fashion embraced the use of revival or period styles as examples of counterculture and alternative consumerism. Although retrochic was an impromptu style of antifashion in the 1990s, it has blossomed into a profitable, commercial style known by fashion critics as the nostalgia industry.

What distinguished retro fashion of the 1990s from older forms of revivalism was a cavalier and eclectic disregard for the past. Consumers used designs and styles without sentimentality or discrimination, and the aura of a past style inspired revelry more than reverence. Retro fashion thus became a form of pastiche, less concerned with historical context than with the fashionable and hip qualities of pastness.

There has been much critical and media debate on the topic of marketing the past within new regimes of style. Writer Fredric Jameson, in his book *The Cultural Turn: Selected Writings on the Postmodern, 1983–1998*, suggests that "in a world in which stylistic innovation is no longer possible, all that is left is to imitate dead styles." For critics such as Jameson, retro fashion offers a profound lack of invention. For others, it represents an ironic return to a past, giving the old a new and creative cachet.

Some have used the term *retro* to describe any type of pop-cultural kitsch. However, within the vintage clothing market, the difference between vintage and retro styles is a historical one. Retro fashion is commonly associated with kitsch of the 1960s, 1970s, and 1980s, whereas vintage fashion is more commonly associated with the pre–World War II era.

Within the music industry, the term *retro* has been used by radio stations, journalists, and marketing managers to categorize music linked to a particular moment or musical zeitgeist, principally disco and new wave. The music cognoscenti in Great Britain and the United States have used the term to describe the creative character of "Britpop" (exemplified by nineties rock groups Blur and Oasis, which evoked 1960s rock pioneers the Kinks and the Beatles, respectively). However, retro music is more widely associated with 1970s and 1980s pop groups such as ABBA and Duran Duran.

Retro films have been labeled as such because of their music. *Boogie Nights* (1997) and *The Wedding Singer* (1998) both display a self-conscious use of iconic style and sound in their evocation of the 1970s and 1980s, respectively. Both films illustrate a tendency in postmodern culture to understand the past through stylistic connotation—which Jameson describes as less 1970s, more 1970s-ness.

The fashion industry has embraced retro fashion perhaps more than any other industry. The popularity of stylistic nostalgia and the selling of vintage clothing and retrochic in the 1980s began, in part, as a response to consolidation of designer fashions such as Calvin Klein and Ralph Lauren. Vintage and retro clothing stores (London's American Retro opened in 1986) provided an alternative to international offerings of designer labels. The success of these stores influenced mainstream fashion, and in the 1990s both vintage and retro became distinguishable looks in Britain and the States. Matthew Rolston's portraits for *Vanity Fair, Rolling Stone*, and British *GQ* and *Vogue* illustrate these looks, using motifs of 1930s glamour photography and the style of 1940s Hollywood studio stills.

The retro aesthetic became mainstream with the comeback of 1970s flares, fly collars, and platform shoes in the 1990s. The media embraced the trend with the 1998 premier of the FOX television network sitcom *That '70s Show* (1998–2006) and a McDonald's advertising campaign urging consumers to "Get Back with Big Mac," with fashion and dance trends from the 1970s. In the first decade of the 2000s cable network HBO's *Sex and the City* (1998–2004) provided a blueprint for augmenting contemporary fashion with retro accents. Films such as *The Royal Tenenbaums* (2001), *Napoleon Dynamite* (2004), and *Superbad* (2007) cultivated a retro aesthetic by featuring clothing such as tracksuits, western snap shirts, hoodies, tennis dresses, and aviator sunglasses.

The rise of the hipster look facilitated the proliferation of vintage clothing stores across the United States. From New York to Portland, Oregon, secondhand clothing stores morphed into boutiques. Shops and online markets such as eBay and Etsy have been flooded with vintage clothes, from boots and dresses to hats and overcoats. Urban fashion, borrowing from punk, hip-hop, and bohemian styles, has combined retro elements, such as large glasses, cardigans, and netted skirts, in a variety of ways. In each case, the overall style continues to be one of playful pastness.

Paul Grainge

SEE ALSO: *ABBA; The Beatles; Consumerism; Disco; eBay; Hipsters; Kitsch; Klein, Calvin; Lauren, Ralph; McDonald's; New Wave Music; Pop Music; Postmodernism;* Rolling Stone*;* Sex and the City*;* Vanity Fair*;* Vogue*; World War II.*

BIBLIOGRAPHY

Davis, Angela Y. "Afro Images: Politics, Fashion, and Nostalgia." *Critical Inquiry* 21, no. 1 (1994): 37–45.

Greif, Mark. "The Sociology of the Hipster." *New York Times*, October 15, 2010.

Jameson, Fredric. *Postmodernism, or, The Cultural Logic of Late Capitalism*. London: Verso, 1991.

Jameson, Fredric. *The Cultural Turn: Selected Writings on the Postmodern, 1983–1998*. Verso: London, 1998.

Kammen, Michael. *Mystic Chords of Memory: The Transformation of Tradition in American Culture*. New York: Vintage, 1993.

Samuel, Raphael. *Theatres of Memory: Past and Present in Contemporary Culture*. London: Verso, 1994.

Reynolds, Simon. *Retromania: Pop Culture's Addiction to Its Own Past*. New York: Faber & Faber, 2011.

Reynolds, Burt *(1936–)*

A motion picture superstar of the late 1970s and early 1980s—thanks largely to his roles in the *Smokey and the Bandit* and *Cannonball Run* movies—the affable and charming Burt Reynolds was voted the number one box-office attraction five years in a row during this period and received nine People's Choice Awards for favorite motion picture actor and favorite all-around male entertainer. He also enjoyed a successful television career in series such as the Western *Gunsmoke*, the detective show *Dan August*, and the sitcom *Evening Shade*. Despite a much-publicized divorce from actress Loni Anderson that left him bankrupt, Reynolds bounced back in the late 1990s with an Oscar-nominated role in *Boogie Nights*.

With his dreams of a career in sports ended by a car accident, Reynolds headed to New York to break into acting and worked on Broadway. He soon landed a role on the TV series *Riverboat* (1959–1960), which led to a popular three-year stint on *Gunsmoke* (1962–1965), where he played the half-breed blacksmith Quint Asper. His husky good looks and muscular physique increased the number of female viewers and, in turn, caused the writers to contrive more opportunities for Quint to take off his shirt. Reynolds's popularity eventually led to his own short-lived detective show, *Dan August* (1970–1971).

Though he had been making a series of forgettable motion pictures since 1961—which Reynolds once explained "were the kind they show in prisons and airplanes, because nobody can leave"—his big movie break came in the widely praised *Deliverance* in 1972. In the story of a group of men on a river trip who run afoul of murderous backwoods yokels, Reynolds shined as the macho leader of the group who is seriously wounded early on and must bow to the ministrations of his insecure peers.

That same year, Reynolds agreed to appear nude in *Cosmopolitan* magazine, causing sales to soar. Simultaneously his private life also became increasingly public due to his involvement with a succession of women that included Kim Basinger, Candice Bergen, Catherine Deneuve, Farrah Fawcett, Sally Field, Sarah Miles, Cybill Shepherd, Dinah Shore, and Tammy Wynette.

Burt Reynolds. *Burt Reynolds as "Boss" Hogg takes a punch from Willie Nelson as Uncle Jesse in the 2005 movie* The Dukes of Hazzard. WARNER BROS./THE KOBAL COLLECTION/EMERSON, SAM.

Reynolds's increasing popularity paved the way for his late-1970s fame in a series of films designed to showcase his image as a cocky, carefree, and smooth-talking charmer who wooed women and bucked authority—*Smokey and the Bandit* (1977), *The Cannonball Run* (1981), and *Stroker Ace* (1983).

Though Reynolds occasionally attempted to branch out of this mold, the success of these "lame-brained action comedies directed by and costarring his pals"—as critic Roger Ebert characterized them—thwarted his efforts. (Intriguingly, Orson Welles once quipped that "Success is Burt Reynolds's only handicap.") Reynolds turned to directing with *The End* in 1978, a well-received black comedy about a man who learns he has a short time to live and determines to end his life. This was followed by the highly praised cop thriller *Sharky's Machine* (1981) and the comedy *Paternity* (1981), about a man who hires a woman to have his child.

Reynolds returned to television with the series *B. L. Stryker* in 1989 and on the sitcom *Evening Shade* from 1990 to 1994. His role as a small-town football coach won him an Emmy Award for Outstanding Lead Actor in a Comedy (1991) and a Golden Globe for Best Performance in a Television Comedy (1992). Reynolds also created and toured in the one-man stage shows *An Evening with Burt Reynolds* in 1991 and *My Life* in 1992.

Despite the breakup of his second marriage to Anderson (his first was to actress Judy Carne, the "sock-it-to-me" girl from TV's *Laugh-In*) and his subsequent declaration of bankruptcy in 1996, Reynolds returned to the big screen in 1997 with an acclaimed performance in *Boogie Nights* as a veteran porn film director serving as a father figure to new discovery Dirk Diggler (Mark Wahlberg). Despite losing the Best Supporting Actor Oscar to Robin Williams, Reynolds won the Golden Globe, the New York Film Critics' Circle Award, the Los Angeles Film Critics Association Award, and the National Society of Film Critics Award for what many critics described as an "outstanding" performance. This in turn led to further offers, including a three-picture production deal from Turner Network Television. High-profile roles in the 2005 remake of his 1974 hit *The Longest Yard* (opposite Adam Sandler, who played the role Reynolds originated), and as Boss Hogg in the movie remake of TV's *The Dukes of Hazzard* have alternated with occasional parts in series television.

Rick Moody

SEE ALSO: *Academy Awards; Bergen, Candice; Broadway; Celebrity; Celebrity Couples;* Cosmopolitan*; Divorce;* Dukes of Hazzard*; Emmy Awards; Fawcett, Farrah; Field, Sally;* Gunsmoke*; Hollywood;* Laugh-In*; Movie Stars; Shore, Dinah; Sitcom; Television; Welles, Orson; Williams, Robin; Wynette, Tammy.*

BIBLIOGRAPHY

Resnick, Sylvia Safran. *Burt Reynolds: An Unauthorized Biography*. New York: St. Martin's Press, 1983.

Reynolds, Burt. *My Life*. New York: Hyperion, 1994.

Smith, Lisa. *Burt Reynolds*. Palm Beach, FL: Magic Light Productions, 1994.

Streebeck, Nancy. *The Films of Burt Reynolds*. Secaucus, NJ: Citadel Press, 1982.

Whitley, Dianna. *Burt Reynolds: Portrait of a Superstar*. New York: Grosset & Dunlap, 1979.

Rhythm and Blues

Rhythm and blues was the urban popular black music of the 1940s and 1950s. Its antecedents were the jazz and blues of the 1930s, especially Kansas City jazz; in the 1960s it turned into soul. R&B, as it is often known, was the precursor and the vital center of rock and roll. It used small-group jazz instrumentation, centered on piano and saxophone as often as on guitar, and it moved in the direction of straightforward, danceable rhythms at the time when jazz was moving toward the more complex structures of bebop. Blending the emotional immediacy of the blues, the instrumental intensity of jazz, and the wit of black vaudeville, it became arguably the most irresistible of American musical forms.

SOCIAL AND TECHNOLOGICAL INFLUENCES

Billboard magazine first used the term *rhythm and blues* as the title for its black music charts in 1949, replacing the term *race music*. But more than the name was new. The postwar era had created an entirely original musical landscape, involving new black audiences, new black musical styles, and new musical markets that were being serviced by a new music business.

There were social and technological reasons for these changes. The black migration to Los Angeles; New York; Chicago; and Detroit, Michigan, with their healthy blue-collar economy of defense plants that then retooled to service the postwar economy, created a solid urban working class with some disposable income and a changed social dynamic. Black performers, meanwhile, had been hardest hit by the wartime demand for shellac in the defense industry, which had drastically cut back on the production of records and had made labels trim their rosters dramatically. But a war-created technology was about to open unprecedented possibilities for entrepreneurship in the music industry. The development of recording tape meant that anyone could have a recording studio, and the recording business was no longer in the hands of a few major companies. Thus, newly entrepreneurial musicians began producing music for a waiting audience.

MUSICAL INFLUENCES—JAZZ AND BLUES

The precursors of rhythm and blues came from the jazz and blues worlds, which were starting to come closer together in the 1930s. Singer-pianist Leroy Carr was the first of the delta blues singers to incorporate jazz influences and smooth urban stylings. Through the early 1930s until his death in 1935, Carr was one of the most influential figures in blues. Kansas City blues shouter Big Joe Turner created a solo style on a new instrument, the electric guitar. Jazzman Illinois Jacquet, in Lionel Hampton's 1941 recording "Flying Home," played a honking, emotionally charged tenor sax solo that became the model for rhythm-and-blues instrumentals.

The most important jazzman to enter rhythm and blues, however, was Louis Jordan, who virtually created "jump blues." Like so much of the music of the 1940s, jump blues came out of the driving dance music of Count Basie's great 1930s bands in such numbers as "One O'clock Jump" and "Jumpin' at the Woodside." Jordan adapted Basie's big band swing to small group instrumentation, with an emphatic 2/4 shuffle beat and brilliant comic showmanship derived from Cab Calloway and black vaudevillians. Jordan dominated the charts throughout the early 1940s.

NEW YORK AND LOS ANGELES

Jordan recorded on Decca. The new rhythm-and-blues performers of the 1940s, though, were a phenomenon of the new independent labels. Many of these labels were located in the entertainment centers of New York and Los Angeles, but others were regional. They tended to be run by entrepreneurs (more often than not white) who had businesses that serviced the black urban communities and who saw a hugely popular sound ripe for commercial exploitation. Each label contributed some facet of the developing rhythm-and-blues sound.

The earliest important indie label was Savoy. Founded in 1942 by Herman Lubinsky, a Newark, New Jersey, record store owner, Savoy was one of the few labels to specialize in both of the cutting-edge black musical styles of the 1940s: bebop and rhythm and blues. Apollo (founded in 1943), a New York label, and King (1944), a Cincinnati, Ohio, label that also recorded country singers, came along during the war years, but the real explosion of independents began in the postwar era.

Los Angeles in these years became a huge center for rhythm-and-blues recording. T-Bone Walker had settled in the city. The first breakout rhythm-and-blues single, "I Wonder," was recorded by Private Cecil Gant in a simple basement studio and released in 1944 on Gilt Edge Records, a short-lived LA indie. When "I Wonder" went to the top of the Billboard race charts, a number of labels sprang up to capitalize on the smooth, cool, Carr-derived LA blues style Gant had popularized. The most successful of these was Modern Records, which was to have its biggest success with a Walker disciple, B. B. King. Aladdin Records signed Charles Brown, who brought jazz-pop stylings reminiscent of Nat King Cole to R&B. Swingtime recorded Lowell Fulson, who combined the smooth LA sound with a Walker-influenced guitar style and a Brown-influenced singer-pianist who would later develop his own revolutionary style: Ray Charles.

NEW ORLEANS

The two most important postwar independent labels out of Los Angeles were Imperial and Specialty. Imperial, founded by record producer Lew Chudd in 1945, became a major player—and changed the face of rhythm and blues—when Chudd moved his talent search from Los Angeles to New Orleans and signed Fats Domino. Domino had some of the smooth style of the LA singers, but he also had the robust energy of Turner and the rollicking, quirky rhythm that grew up in the Caribbean seaport city of New Orleans. Imperial, which also recorded other New Orleans R&B performers such as Smiley Lewis and Guitar Slim, adopted the finest New Orleans session musicians—producer-arranger Dave Bartholomew and brilliant instrumentalists such as saxophonist Lee Allen and drummer Earl Palmer. Domino was also one of the first successful R&B artists to incorporate the influence of white country music. Generally, when discussing the fusion of rhythm and blues and country that produced rock and roll, music historians point to white singers such as Elvis Presley and Carl Perkins, but the real pioneers were Domino and, a few years later, Chuck Berry.

Other LA labels started to scout New Orleans for talent. Aladdin signed Shirley and Lee, whose 1950s hits such as "Feel So Good" and "Let the Good Times Roll" were a unique amalgam of the mature sexuality of the blues and the teenage sexuality of rock and roll. But the most important Los Angeles beachhead in New Orleans was established by Specialty Records' Art Rupe. Rupe, who started Specialty in 1946, had developed a successful small label, originally recording jump blues bands such as Joe Liggins and the Honeydrippers, then signing former Swingtime artist Percy Mayfield, a fine singer in the LA style and one of the twentieth century's greatest songwriters. Mayfield's first recording for Specialty in 1950 was his masterpiece, "Please Send Me Someone to Love."

In 1955 Rupe, excited by Imperial's New Orleans roster, sent producer Bumps Blackwell to scout for talent in New Orleans. Blackwell's first success was Lloyd Price, who hit with "Lawdy, Miss Clawdy," backed by Domino and Bartholomew, in 1952. Specialty had a hit in 1954 with Guitar Slim's "The Things I Used to Do" (with Charles). But the label's most significant performer, also signed and produced by Blackwell, was Little Richard. Richard had made a few marginally successful records for Peacock, a Houston, Texas–based indie owned by Don Robey, one of the few black entrepreneurs in the rhythm-and-blues business (romantic balladeer Johnny Ace recorded for Robey's Duke-Peacock, as did Big Mama Thornton and Bobby "Blue" Bland). With Blackwell he developed a new, over-the-top style. His first single, "Tutti Frutti," came out in 1955 and was one of the most important developments in the merging of rhythm and blues into rock and roll.

AUDIENCE

The major difference between rhythm and blues and rock and roll was that white teenagers, as well as blacks, listened to rock and roll. As a result, rock and roll was generally safer and more conservative. As Robert Palmer pointed out in his book *Baby, That Was Rock and Roll* (about Jerry Leiber and Mike Stoller), the theme of conflict between blacks and the surrounding white culture turned into the theme of conflict between teens and their parents. Little Richard was an exception to that rule. His songs were full of heavy sexual innuendo, and his performances held nothing back.

Specialty had a strong lineup of gospel singers along with its rhythm-and-blues line. One of its best gospel groups, the Soul Stirrers, had Sam Cooke as its lead singer. Cooke wanted to go into R&B, but Rupe, afraid of losing his gospel audience, forbade it. Cooke and Blackwell left the label together. Rupe hired Sonny Bono as his new chief talent scout, and Specialty lost its edge.

CHICAGO

Chess Records, begun in Chicago in 1947 by Leonard and Phil Chess, drew on a different musical style: the delta blues singers who had migrated north from Mississippi and electrified their sound. The Chicago audiences, like other postwar urban black audiences, were ready for something newer and livelier than the traditional blues they—or their parents—had left behind in the Mississippi delta. They wanted the big sound of jump blues and the loud, electric sound that could be heard in the nightclubs they frequented, but they were also still largely recent southern immigrants, and they wanted a more down-home sound. The musicians were ready to give the public what it wanted, but they were blues-based guitar and harmonica players, not jazz-based horn players. The most successful performers were the ones who could adapt the country blues style to the group configuration of jump. The best of these was Muddy Waters, who put together bands with such brilliant instrumentalists as Little Walter, Jimmy Rogers, Otis Spann, and Fred Below.

The Chess brothers were nightclub owners who realized that there was a record market for the music that was packing their clubs. Using the talent of brilliant producer/songwriter Willie Dixon, Chess Records began to sign the top Chicago rhythm-and-blues acts. Waters first recorded for Chess in 1950, singing traditional blues with only a bass accompaniment. These records were so successful that the Chess brothers were reluctant to change the formula, and it was not until 1950 that they let Waters record with his group. Waters was the prototype of the Chicago blues style; other successful Chess rhythm-and-blues acts were Howlin' Wolf and Little Walter. These artists did not cross over, at least not in the 1950s; their sales were to black audiences. But they were the most profound of influences on the British rockers of the 1960s and the guitar rock bands of the 1970s.

CROSSOVER

The first Chess rhythm-and-blues record that made an impact on what was to become the rock-and-roll market was "Rocket 88" by Jackie Brenston and Ike Turner. Produced in Memphis by Sam Phillips and leased to Chess, it inspired Phillips to go on experimenting with the sound that was to lead to Sun Records and Presley. The Chess artist who was to change the face of American music most profoundly, though, was Chuck Berry.

Berry, introduced to the Chess brothers by Waters, was a formidable musician who had absorbed the jump blues of Jordan, the jazz-guitar innovations of Charlie Christian, the Chicago rhythm and blues of Waters, and—as with Domino—country. Berry's first recording for Chess was "Maybellene" in 1955, and it was one of the key records to cross black rhythm and blues over to a white audience. Berry's style was so immediately accessible to the new rock-and-roll market that his hits, unlike Domino's or Little Richard's, were never taken away from him by white artists such as Pat Boone. Berry's gifts as a lyricist have led literary critics, as well as pop culture scholars, to hail him as one of the century's most significant writers. Because of Berry and other rhythm-and-blues artists who appealed to rock-and-roll audiences (Bo Diddley; Clarence "Frogman" Henry; and groups such as the Dells, the Flamingoes, and the Moonglows), Chess became one of the most influential independent R&B labels of the 1950s.

The most important label, though, was unquestionably Atlantic. Founded in 1947 by Ahmet and Nesuhi Ertegun and Herb Abramson, Atlantic came to dominate rhythm and blues and rock and roll. Atlantic's biggest drawback became its greatest strength. Since there was no blues tradition to speak of in New York, the Erteguns were more or less forced to invent one. Using a brilliant black producer, Jesse Stone, and musicians drawn from the jazz clubs on 52nd Street, they created a slick but bluesy sound that redefined American music. Atlantic's first major star was Ruth Brown, a jazz-pop singer who told Ahmet Ertegun when he signed her, "I don't like blues." But her pop-blues amalgam was perfectly suited to the hip New York audience and to the white teenagers who were starting to listen to rhythm and blues. She and LaVern Baker, signed in 1953, became the biggest female stars in R&B.

MUSICAL INFLUENCES—GOSPEL

The vocal harmony group style that came to be known as doo-wop found its most popular manifestation on Atlantic, with the Clovers, the Drifters, and the Coasters as the label's biggest stars. Doo-wop came from one of the oldest traditions of black music: harmony singing. In the early 1940s the main harmony purveyors were gospel groups and smooth pop groups, principally the Mills Brothers and the Ink Spots. The doo-wop groups modeled themselves after the smooth groups, but they had something of the rawness and the rocking rhythm of the gospel groups too.

The first important doo-wop group was the Orioles on Jubilee Records. Chess developed a significant doo-wop stable with the Dells, the Flamingoes, and the Moonglows. The Los Angeles scene produced the Penguins and the Platters. In New York record executives George Goldner and Morris Levy, on a succession of labels, recorded a number of classic doo-wop groups, the most famous being Frankie Lymon and the Teenagers.

The Clovers signed with Atlantic in 1951, and from their first recordings—Orioles-influenced harmonies with a stronger, more danceable beat—they were at the top of the charts. The Clovers had a strong career throughout the 1950s. The Drifters were signed by Atlantic in 1953 as a setting for the talents of Clyde McPhatter, whose gospel-tinged voice and erotic passion were the precursors of Cooke and the soul singers of the 1960s. McPhatter left the Drifters in 1955, but the group, with a series of other lead singers, continued into the 1960s. The Coasters, originally a West Coast group, were produced by songwriters Leiber and Stoller, two white men who began by writing blues and who became, along with Berry, the architects of the rock-and-roll sensibility. Berry, Leiber, and Stoller had always had a wider range to their writing than sexuality, which was the subject of most blues writing.

Atlantic signed and rejuvenated the careers of R&B pioneers Walker and Turner. But artistically the label's most important solo star was Charles, who had begun on the West Coast as a ballad singer in the Brown/Cole tradition. With Atlantic, Charles moved from the Cole piano trio model to a horn-driven band that was unlike Jordan's Tympany Five and created a gospel-influenced sound that remains one of the most powerful, original contributions to American music.

In the 1960s a new group of singers came to Atlantic. The first of these was Solomon Burke, signed to the label to replace the departing Charles. According to Burke, he refused to allow the label to promote him as a rhythm-and-blues singer because of his religious beliefs. The label had to come up with a new name for this new music, and it settled on *soul*, a name with religious overtones. Regardless of whether the story is true, the coming of Burke, Otis Redding, Aretha Franklin, and others signaled the beginning of a new musical era.

Rhythm and blues inspired rock and roll, soul, funk, hip-hop, and contemporary R&B. In *Rolling Stone* magazine's 2004 list of the 100 greatest artists of all time, six of the Top 10 are rhythm-and-blues musicians, including Berry, Little Richard, and Charles. The Rhythm & Blues Foundation was formed in 1988 with an initial donation by Atlantic Records founder Ahmet Ertegun in response to Ruth Brown's appeal for royalty reform. Though Atlantic Records had become known as "the House That Ruth Built," she had received little compensation because of exploitive royalty rates (royalties were as low as 2 percent, compared with the 20 percent paid to today's music stars) and had worked as a domestic and resorted to welfare to provide for her children. The foundation advocates for increased royalty rates on reissues and gives monetary awards to rhythm-and-blues musicians.

In 2004 Charles passed away, and the film *Ray* (2004), which earned Jamie Foxx an Academy Award in the title role, celebrated the life and legacy of this musical giant who resembled rhythm and blues itself, with solid roots of blues and gospel and strong branches into soul, rock and roll, jazz, and pop, all united in the enormous umbrella of R&B.

Tad Richards

SEE ALSO: *Academy Awards; Atlantic Records; Basie, Count; Berry, Chuck; Bland, Bobby "Blue"; Blues; Bono, Sonny; Calloway, Cab; Charles, Ray; Cole, Nat King; Cooke, Sam; Diddley, Bo; Domino, Fats; The Drifters; Foxx, Jamie; The Ink Spots; Jazz; Jordan, Louis; Kansas City Jazz; King, B. B.; Little Richard; Long-Playing Record; Mayfield, Percy; New Orleans Rhythm and Blues; Presley, Elvis; Rock and Roll; Sun Records; Turner, Ike and Tina; Vaudeville; Waters, Muddy; World War II.*

BIBLIOGRAPHY

Deffaa, Chip. *Blue Rhythms: Six Lives in Rhythm and Blues.* Urbana: University of Illinois Press, 1996.

George, Nelson. *The Death of Rhythm & Blues.* New York: Plume, 1988.

Gillett, Charlie. *Sound of the City.* New York: Pantheon, 1983.

Goosman, Stuart L. *Group Harmony: The Black Urban Roots of Rhythm & Blues.* Philadelphia: University of Pennsylvania Press, 2005.

Guralnick, Peter. *Sweet Soul Music: Rhythm and Blues and the Southern Dream of Freedom.* Boston: Little, Brown, 1999.

Otis, Johnny. *Upside Your Head! Rhythm and Blues on Central Avenue.* Hanover, NH: Wesleyan University Press, 1993.

Shaw, Arnold. *Black Popular Music in America.* New York: Schirmer Books, 1986.

Shaw, Arnold. *Honkers and Shouters: The Golden Years of Rhythm and Blues.* New York: Macmillan, 1986.

Ward, Brian. *Just My Soul Responding: Rhythm and Blues, Black Consciousness, and Race Relations.* Berkeley: University of California Press, 1998.

Wexler, Jerry, and David Ritz. *Rhythm and the Blues: A Life in American Music.* New York: St. Martin's Press, 1994.

Rice, Grantland *(1880–1954)*

Grantland Rice, arguably the best-known American sportswriter ever, was also one of the most highly regarded personally and professionally. Born in Murfreesboro, Tennessee, Rice attended Vanderbilt University and upon graduation began his journalism career with the *Nashville Daily News*. After stints at the *Atlanta Journal* and the *New York Evening Mail*, he finally landed at the *New York Tribune* (later the *Herald-Tribune*).

In 1930 his column, "The Sportlight," was nationally syndicated, strengthening his position as the "Voice of Sports." What separated his column from others were his writing style and choice of topics: a combination of sports news, gossip, and commentary. Since his death, the Football Writers Association of America has awarded the Grantland Rice Trophy each year to the team it considers the best in college football. In 2011 cable sports network ESPN launched a sports and popular culture website called Grantland.com in honor of the legendary sportswriter.

Lloyd Chiasson Jr.

SEE ALSO: *Cable TV; College Football; ESPN; Gossip Columns.*

BIBLIOGRAPHY

Fountain, Charles. *Sportswriter: The Life and Times of Grantland Rice.* New York: Oxford University Press, 1993.

Ham, Eldon L. *Broadcasting Baseball: A History of the National Pastime on Radio and Television.* Jefferson, NC: McFarland, 2011.

Inabinett, Mark. *Grantland Rice and His Heroes: The Sportswriter as Mythmaker in the 1920s.* Knoxville: University of Tennessee Press, 1994.

Rice, Jerry *(1962–)*

Jerry Rice is regarded as one of the greatest wide receivers in the history of the National Football League (NFL). After playing college football at Mississippi Valley State, he spent the majority of his NFL career with the San Francisco 49ers (1985–2000), helping them to be among the most dominant teams in the league. Rice retired after the 2004 season with virtually every noteworthy receiving record in the book, including career receptions (1,549) and career receiving yards (22,895).

In 1997 Rice's storybook career was put in jeopardy when he tore the anterior cruciate ligament in his left knee. Miraculously, he returned just three and a half months later in a Monday night game against the Denver Broncos. Unfortunately, Rice suffered a shattered kneecap and missed the rest of the season, but he was his old self again in 1998, racking up more than 1,000 receiving yards and leading the 49ers in receptions with eighty-two.

Though the 49ers offered Rice a retirement deal in 2000, he was not ready to quit the game. Instead, he signed with the Oakland Raiders. His playing time steadily dwindled, however, and he had a brief stint with the Seattle Seahawks in 2004 before retiring. The following year, Rice was inducted into the College Football Hall of Fame, and he was inducted into the Pro Football Hall of Fame in 2010.

Retirement did not slow Rice down—on the contrary, his fame spread beyond the realm of football. In 2006 he was a contestant on the popular network television show *Dancing with the Stars*, advancing to the finals. Rice also made guest appearances on such TV series as the drama *Law & Order: SVU* and the sitcom *Rules of Engagement*. In addition, he emerged as a popular corporate spokesperson, making TV commercials for companies such as Gatorade and Visa.

Rice also became active in charity work. He established the Jerry Rice 127 Foundation to raise funds to help children and supported a number of other charitable organizations, including the United Negro College Fund. A decade after he left the 49ers, the team retired his jersey number (80). By then, he had evolved from a football hero into a full-blown celebrity.

D. Byron Painter

SEE ALSO: *College Football;* Dancing with the Stars*;* Monday Night Football*; National Football League (NFL); The Oakland Raiders; Professional Football; Sports Heroes.*

BIBLIOGRAPHY

Bloom, Barry M. "I'm Not Invincible Anymore." *Sport*, September 1998, 76–80.

Evans, J. Edward. *Jerry Rice: Touchdown Talent.* Minneapolis, MN: Lerner, 1993.

Rice, Jerry, and Michael Silver. *Rice.* New York: St. Martin's Press, 1996.

Rice, Jerry, and Brian Curtis. *Go Long! My Journey beyond the Game and the Fame.* New York: Ballantine Books, 2007.

Rich, Charlie *(1932–1995)*

A versatile artist whose recording career spanned five decades and seven labels, Charlie Rich is primarily remembered for his 1970s country crossover megahits "Behind Closed Doors" and "The Most Beautiful Girl." Produced by Billy Sherrill, the architect of the crossover country sound, these two songs propelled a reluctant Rich into country music stardom. Despite his identification with country, Rich's music incorporated jazz, pop, rock, gospel, R&B, and soul, making him one eclectic country musician.

Born in Arkansas in 1932, Rich began his musical career as an enlisted man in the early 1950s, playing piano with a jazzy outfit called the Velvetones at the U.S. Air Force base in Oklahoma where he was stationed. After leaving the service in the mid-1950s, Rich farmed by day and worked as a supper-club pianist in Memphis, Tennessee, by night. Margaret Ann Rich, Charlie's wife, biggest fan, and sometime collaborator, took his tapes to Sun Records, Sam Phillips's legendary recording label, and the early musical home of Elvis Presley, Jerry Lee Lewis, Johnny Cash, and Carl Perkins. Phillips's associate Bill Justis liked the tapes, and Rich was signed to Sun, first as a session man and arranger and eventually as a recording artist. In 1960 Rich had his first Top 30 hit with "Lonely Weekends." Unable to score with any of his follow-up singles, his career stalled.

In 1964 Rich left Sun and signed with Groove, an RCA subsidiary, where he recorded several albums that were not commercial successes until they were reissued in the wake of his big 1970s hits. After Groove's demise in 1965, Rich signed with Smash/Mercury, where he had another Top 30 novelty hit with "Mohair Sam." Once again unable to follow up his hit, Rich switched labels again, signing with Hi Records in 1966, where he was unable to make any impression on the charts.

In 1967 Rich signed with Epic, and with Sherrill he recorded the body of work with which he became most closely identified. Sherrill's production style, which favored lush string arrangements and vocal choruses over the steel guitar and fiddle found in much recorded country music, was a great fit with Rich's soulful, sultry voice and supple phrasing. In his first five years at Epic, Rich had no commercial successes, but remarkably, the label stuck with him. Sherrill had some clout, having scored major hits for Epic with Tammy Wynette and David Houston, and Epic was probably sticking with Rich at Sherrill's insistence.

This persistence paid off in 1972 when "I Take It on Home" was a hit on the country charts. In 1973 "Behind Closed Doors" spent twelve weeks on the Top 40 chart, peaking at number fifteen, and "The Most Beautiful Girl" spent seventeen weeks on the same chart, and hit number one. For those breakthroughs, Rich was named the Country Music Association's (CMA's) Male Vocalist of the Year for 1973, and he won the Grammy for best male country vocal performance. In the wake of these successes, Rich's earlier labels began to rerelease the previously unsuccessful material in their vaults, and Rich continued to chart. In 1974 he was the CMA's Entertainer of the Year. After 1974, though the hits kept coming to a degree, Rich never again reached the commercial success of the early 1970s.

While Sun's Phillips called Rich the most talented musician he had ever worked with and the only one who had the potential to rival Presley, Rich seemed uncomfortable with his status as international sensation. His well-documented drinking problem and occasional erratic behavior (in 1975, while on national television presenting the CMA award to his successor for male vocalist of the year, Rich set fire to the piece of paper that revealed John Denver to be the winner) may be part of what kept him from becoming a superstar. In addition, Rich was always reluctant to do the kind of touring and personal appearances a performer is urged to do to maximize record sales, opting instead to spend time at home with Margaret Ann and their children. Perhaps it had something to do with the fact that commercial tastes dictated that he should temper his tendency for artistic experimentation in blending genres.

Rich left Epic for United Artists in 1978 and had a few country hits there. In 1980 he moved to Elektra and had some successes through 1981, when he went into semiretirement for a decade. In 1992 he reemerged to make his final album, a lovely, heart-wrenching, jazzy record called *Pictures and Paintings*. In the liner notes to Epic's *Feel Like Going Home: The Essential Charlie Rich*, Margaret Ann talks about *Pictures and Paintings*:

> That last album that he did I think was more representative of what he really was all about, because it was all different kinds of music—it was the music he loved, and he was really pleased about that. But I don't think he had any idea of the lives he touched. I'm sure he didn't. Because it was just always about the music. It wasn't about being famous. He never really cared a flip for that. In fact, he kind of ran from it. He just wanted to play music; that's all.

Charlie Rich died from a blood clot in 1995 while traveling through Louisiana with Margaret Ann.

Joyce Linehan

SEE ALSO: *Cash, Johnny; Country Music; Lewis, Jerry Lee; Presley, Elvis; Sun Records; Wynette, Tammy.*

BIBLIOGRAPHY

Bogdanov, Vladimir; Chris and Erlewine Woodstra; and Stephen Thomas, eds. *All Music Guide: The Definitive Guide to Popular Music*. San Francisco: Backbeat Books, 2001.

Guralnick, Peter. *The Lost Highway: Journeys and Arrivals of American Musicians*. Boston: D. R. Godine, 1979.

Richards, J(iles) P(erry)

SEE: *Big Bopper.*

Rigby, Cathy *(1952–)*

Though Cathy Rigby never won an Olympic medal, her plucky strength and vulnerability won the hearts of U.S. sports fans in the late 1960s and early 1970s, when she competed as a gymnast. At the 1968 Summer Olympics in Mexico City, "Little Cathy Rigby" was the media's darling, finishing sixteenth in the all-around competition, the best ranking ever for a U.S. female. She continued to compete internationally, becoming the first U.S. female to win a silver medal at the 1970 World Gymnastics Championships. In all, she won twelve medals in international competitions, eight of them gold. She was highly favored, by the U.S. press at least, to take the honors at the 1972 Summer Olympics in Munich until her aspirations were thwarted by the stress of public attention, bringing on eating disorders that jeopardized her health for some years to come. She was twenty when she retired from sports and past thirty before she began a new and surprisingly successful career on the stage.

Rigby was born in Los Alamitos, California, into a middle-class family. Her parents were protective of their daughter, whose health was poor as a child. At ten years of age, the small and lithe child discovered a talent for the trampoline and tumbling. Her father aggressively encouraged her newfound skills and hired a coach to push along her development. Rigby began to win gymnastic competitions, becoming especially well known for her expertise on the balance beam.

Rigby was just under five feet tall and weighed a slight ninety-two pounds, but her coach insisted that she needed to reduce even further. Plagued by insecurity and lack of self-confidence, Rigby soon became obsessed with her weight and the need to control it. She tried starvation diets and fasting, but it was difficult to compete without food. By the time of the 1972 Munich games, she had become bulimic. Having learned the technique from a teammate with similar worries, Rigby ate what she wished then forced herself to vomit, sometimes as often as six times a day.

Fighting dizziness and exhaustion caused by her bulimia, Rigby placed tenth at the 1972 Olympics, still higher than any American woman ever had. But the press called her performance "disappointing" and flocked to their new darling, Olga Korbut, who had eclipsed Rigby at the games. Disappointed, Rigby retired from the sport and married Tommy Mason, also a former athlete. They had two children, and Rigby forged a career doing sports commentary and commercials; still obsessed with being thin, she continued to force herself to vomit several times a day.

It was not until 1981 that Rigby began to face her eating disorder. Offered the role of Dorothy in a revival of *The Wizard*

Cathy Rigby as Peter Pan. *Olympic gymnast Cathy Rigby poses as her signature character, Peter Pan, 2011.* SLAVEN VLASIC/CONTRIBUTOR/WIREIMAGE/GETTY IMAGES.

of Oz, Rigby developed a new driving interest—the stage. Buoyed by the enthusiastic critical response to her acting and supported by a new friend, Tom McCoy, who would become her second husband, she finally defeated her eating disorder. She "came out" in the press as a bulimic and continued to tell her story in the hopes of helping other young women fight their self-destructive obsession with weight.

Soon Rigby found herself cast in other acting roles. She acted in several movies, among them *The Great Wallendas* (1978), a vehicle for her considerable gymnastic skills, and *Perfect Body* (1997), about the problem of eating disorders among young women athletes. Her trademark role, however, was Peter Pan, which she revived on Broadway on the thirty-fifth anniversary of the original production. Once again the American press was charmed by Rigby, and she received rave reviews for her performance in a role that Mary Martin, a Peter of the 1950s, had once said "you'd have to be an acrobat" to play.

It was not only her athletic ability that won her a Tony nomination, however, but also her spunky, upbeat acting style and her accomplished singing and dancing. When she first joined the cast of *Peter Pan*, the songs were prerecorded by another singer, but Rigby was determined to learn to perform them herself. She studied acting and singing with palpable success. "It's that athlete's obsessiveness," she said of training for her new career, "the need to prove yourself and work harder than anybody else. I think it's what helped me do well in the theater."

Rigby continued to perform regularly, including in the musicals *Annie Get Your Gun* and *South Pacific*, and she continued to play the boy who never grew up with the *Peter Pan* touring company. She also appeared in a video called *Faces of Recovery* (1988) about the dangers of eating disorders. Rigby's resilient career and the help she has offered those who come after her continue to make her a role model, not only for young athletes but for all young women seeking to discover their strengths and use them.

Tina Gianoulis

SEE ALSO: Annie Get Your Gun*; Broadway; Gymnastics; The Musical; Olympics;* South Pacific*;* The Wizard of Oz.

BIBLIOGRAPHY

Goodman, Mark. "Cathy Rigby, Flying High." *People Weekly*, May 6, 1991, 107.

Hoffman, Greg. "Little Big Woman: Catching Up with Cathy Rigby." *Woman Sports*, October 1980, 12.

Rigby, Cathy. "The Worst Day I Ever Had." *Sports Illustrated for Kids*, August 1994, 26.

Sherrow, Victoria. *Encyclopedia of Women and Sports*. Santa Barbara, CA: ABC-CLIO, 1996.

Riggs, Bobby *(1918–1995)*

In 1939 Bobby Riggs was the number-one-ranked tennis player in the world. He is perhaps best remembered, however, not as much for his skills as for his ill-fated "Battle of the Sexes" match with Billie Jean King at the Houston Astrodome in 1973.

Robert Larimore Riggs started tennis lessons when he was twelve years old, and six years later he was near the top in the U.S. tennis rankings. Throughout the 1930s and 1940s he continued to win countless titles as both an amateur and a professional player. Although he quit playing professional tennis in 1951, he stayed in shape and participated in senior events.

In 1973 the fifty-five-year-old Riggs, who called himself a "chauvinist pig," criticized women's tennis as mediocre and claimed that he could beat any woman despite his age. He challenged one of the top female competitor's of the time, Margaret Smith Court, to a match and easily won. Basking in his victory, Riggs next took on King in front of a national television audience of about fifty million people, during which he lost in three straight sets. King thought that her victory was more symbolic and psychological than athletic, and she hoped it would provide a springboard for women's athletics, which it ultimately did. The timing of her victory was also important; Title IX, which banned gender discrimination in education, had just passed.

D. Byron Painter

SEE ALSO: *King, Billie Jean; Television; Tennis.*

BIBLIOGRAPHY

King, Billie Jean. "My Favorite Chauvinist." *Sports Illustrated*, November 6, 1995, 118.

"Robert Larimore Riggs, American Tennis Champion and Braggart Male Chauvinist Died on October 25, Aged 77." *Economist*, November 4, 1995, 113.

Starr, Mark. "The Battle of the Sexes." *Newsweek*, September 21, 1998, 90.

Rihanna *(1988–)*

Sexy singing sensation Rihanna shot to stardom in 2005 with the release of her first hit, "Pon de Replay," when she was only seventeen years old. Her Caribbean-influenced musical style and sleek good looks, combined with a fiercely independent rebellious image, gave the singer almost immediate icon status in the world of popular music. Having already achieved fame through number one hits, platinum albums, and dramatic music videos, Rihanna gained unwanted notoriety in 2009 when she was beaten by her boyfriend, R&B singer Chris Brown, in a widely publicized incident of domestic violence. With characteristic determination, Rihanna drew on the experience to deepen and expand her music. She also overcame her reluctance to expose her private life and openly discussed the abuse in hopes of encouraging other young women to break the silence about their own abuse. In 2012 Rihanna and Brown collaborated musically again, causing controversy among fans and critics.

Robyn Rihanna Fenty was born in 1988 in the parish of St. Michael on the Caribbean island of Barbados. She grew up in a working-class family, the daughter of a black mother and a mixed-race father, and was often harassed in school because of her light skin. When she was still a child her parents separated, in part due to her father's problems with drugs and domestic violence, but her mother provided a loving home, and young Robyn was happy to help care for her younger brothers. Even as a young girl, she loved to sing and dreamed of becoming a star. By the time she was a teenager, she had begun performing with a singing group.

In 2003 she met music producers Evan Rogers and Carl Sturken, who helped her go to New York to make demos of her music. Her demo performances attracted the attention of another powerful producer, Jay-Z, the CEO of Def Jam Recordings. In 2005 he asked her to audition, and, within weeks, "Pon de Replay," was climbing the charts, followed soon after by her first album, *Music of the Sun*. Rihanna's sensuous island rhythms became an instant hit. Her second album, *A Girl Like Me*, released in 2006, launched two number one songs, "S.O.S." and "Unfaithful."

It was not only Rihanna's strong voice and reggae-influenced dance beat that made her a star but also her confidence and highly independent style. She put together a unique look combining street fashions with haute couture, and just before the photo shoot for the cover of her *Good Girl Gone Bad* album, without consulting agents or stylists, she cut off her long hair and dyed it black, creating a tough new look that set her apart from other female R&B performers. The dramatic new hairstyle became widely popular, as fans around the world asked hairdressers for "the Rihanna." "Umbrella," a single release from *Good Girl Gone Bad*, remained at number one on the Billboard charts for seven weeks.

In February 2009, the night before the fifty-first Grammy Awards, Rihanna was attacked and badly beaten by her boyfriend, singer/songwriter Chris Brown, as they were driving in Brown's car. Police photos of Rihanna's bruised face and details of the beating were leaked to the press and Internet, causing an uproar among fans and journalists. Distressed and humiliated, the singer retreated to Barbados to heal. As she recovered from the experience and its public aftermath, she turned her pain into her most personal album yet, *Rated R*, released in November 2009. *Rated R* showcased the singer's versatility with a mixture of genres and deep emotionality, from anger in the songs "G4L (Gangsta for Life)" and "Hard" to complex fear and loss in "Russian Roulette" and "The Last Song."

Rihanna, who set up the Believe Foundation in 2006 to help provide educational and medical supplies for at-risk children, had always felt a responsibility to her fans, and she soon overcame her personal embarrassment to talk about her experience with domestic violence. Though she ended her relationship with Brown (who received a five-year probation for the attack), she spoke of him with ambivalence and expressed hope that the incident would not damage his career. When a restraining order forbidding Brown to be near her threatened to prevent him from performing at awards shows she was attending, Rihanna amended the order to allow them to attend the same music industry functions. Many fans were horrified in 2012 when Rihanna apparently forgave Brown and collaborated with him on two songs, including the sexually explicit "Birthday Cake."

Rihanna has continued her successful career, releasing the albums *Loud* in 2010 and *Talk That Talk* in 2011. In 2012 she realized a longtime ambition to star in an action movie with the role of Petty Officer Cora "Weps" Raikes in the Peter Berg science fiction film *Battleship*.

Tina Gianoulis

SEE ALSO: *Grammy Awards; Hip-Hop; Jay-Z; Pop Music; Rhythm and Blues; Top 40.*

BIBLIOGRAPHY

Govan, Chloe. *Rihanna: Rebel Flower*. London: Omnibus Press, 2012.

Herrera, Monica. "The Happiness Project: With 'The Dark Moment' in Her Life behind her, Rihanna Embraces Fun, Sex Games and Fist-Pump-Worthy Beats on Her Stridently Upbeat New Album, *Loud*." *Billboard*, October 16, 2010, 18.

Oliver, Sarah. *Rihanna: The Only Girl in the World*. London: John Blake Publishing, 2012.

Sandell, Laurie. "Up-Close Woman of the Year 2009: Rihanna Back on Top." *Glamour*, November 2009, 238.

Riley, Pat *(1945–)*

National Basketball Association (NBA) coach Pat Riley is one of the most successful basketball coaches of all time, and his achievements have led him to become one of the country's most respected motivational speakers. After three years at the University of Kentucky, a mediocre nine-year professional playing career, and a two-year stint as a broadcaster, Riley became head coach of the Lakers during the 1981–1982 season. He instituted a fast-breaking style that became known as "Showtime"—a term that reflected his offense as well as his personal, media-savvy style. Riley coached the team to four NBA championships, and, through their battles with the Boston Celtics, helped the NBA become a top spectator sport. After leaving Los Angeles, Riley showed his coaching flexibility by instituting a defensive, slow-down style in taking both the New York Knicks and Miami Heat to the playoffs.

A three-time NBA Coach of the Year, Riley won his fifth NBA title as coach of the Heat in 2006. When he retired from coaching in 2008, he was the career leader for most playoff victories. After his retirement from coaching, Riley took over as the president of the Heat, where he was named 2011 NBA Executive of the Year after bringing LeBron James and Chris Bosh to the team.

Robert S. Brown

SEE ALSO: *Basketball; The Boston Celtics; The Los Angeles Lakers; National Basketball Association (NBA).*

BIBLIOGRAPHY

Riley, Pat. *Showtime: Inside the Lakers' Breakthrough Season*. New York: Warner Books, 1988.

Riley, Pat. *The Winner Within*. New York: Berkley Publishing Group, 1994.

"Top 10 Coaches in NBA History." NBA Encyclopedia. Accessed April 2012. Available from http://www.nba.com/history/top_10_coaches.html

Ringling Bros., Barnum & Bailey Circus

Two nineteenth-century American men, Phineas T. Barnum and James A. Bailey, largely defined the image of the circus—that of a spectacle of acrobats, animals, band music, clowns, and trapeze artists—that is now deeply embedded in American popular culture. In 1881 they merged their separate circuses into Barnum & Bailey's Circus, which crisscrossed the United States for decades, bringing the excitement of the Big Top to towns and cities from coast to coast. In 1919 the Barnum & Bailey Circus was merged with the Ringling Brothers Circus, which had purchased it in 1907 but ran it as a separate entity for twelve years. In the twenty-first century the Ringling Bros., Barnum & Bailey Circus continued to thrill thousands of children and adults nationwide.

THE TRAVELING SHOW

The first circuses to be seen in the United States were opened in 1793 in New York and Philadelphia by John Bill Ricketts, who specialized in riding horses through flaming hoops. These shows were performed in semipermanent structures, but as early as the 1840s traveling circuses on the Barnum & Bailey model moved slowly overland in their horse-drawn caravans, attracting excited, entertainment-starved crowds to their tents. The idea of presenting the circus in a tent is an American contribution, believed to have begun in 1825 with an itinerant show belonging to J. Purdy Brown. The custom evolved from small tents with a single ring and a few hundred seats to two rings in 1872 and three in 1881, calling for larger and larger canvas coliseums. The distinctive quarter poles, invented by former chemist Gilbert

The Ringling Bros., Barnum & Bailey Circus Grand Parade. *Performers ride elephants during the Grand Parade at the start of the 133rd edition of the Ringling Bros., Barnum & Bailey Circus in Boston, Massachusetts, in 2004.* AP IMAGES.

Spalding, that support the canvas roof in large areas between the central "king poles" and the side poles make it possible to cover much larger areas for spectators.

The idea of having a number of acts going on simultaneously in several rings is also an American innovation. In Europe there are many circuses, such as the famous one in Copenhagen, that were staged in a permanent building with a single ring. The nomadic U.S. circuses relied more and more on the railroads, and Ringling Bros., Barnum & Bailey at one time traversed the country in four trains, pulling a total of 107 seventy-foot railroad cars.

THE GREATEST SHOW ON EARTH

Circus impresario Phineas T. Barnum (1810–1891) was a flamboyant showman who bought a five-story marble museum in New York City in 1842 and transformed it into the American Museum, a carnival of live "freaks," theatrical tableaux, beauty contests, and other sensational attractions. In the first year he attracted thousands with such exhibits as the Feejee Mermaid, who wore the fake body of a fish; Siamese twins Chang and Eng; and Charles S. Stratton, a 25-inch-tall man whom he renamed General Tom Thumb. In 1850 he risked his entire fortune to bring Jenny Lind, a Swedish soprano he had never heard, to America for 150 concerts. The move paid off with huge returns.

With his rare talent for gaining publicity for his enterprises, Barnum became an international celebrity who called himself the "Prince of Humbugs." In 1871 he opened the extravaganza he called the "Greatest Show on Earth," combining traditional circus acts with a menagerie of caged animals and sideshows featuring both human and animal curiosities—alive and dead, real and bogus. There is no evidence he ever spoke or said the words, but Barnum has long been credited with the remark, "There's a sucker born every minute." Although he is not the sole originator of the present-day circus, Barnum made this popular theatrical form into a gigantic spectacle, drawing huge crowds to his famous attractions gathered from all parts of the world. The grand climax of Barnum's circus career was his purchase of Jumbo, an elephant weighing 6.5 tons. Barnum's sales pitch was so compelling that the huge pachyderm earned back his purchase price in one season under the Big Top.

MERGERS WITH BAILEY AND RINGLING

James Anthony Bailey (1847–1906) was much more retiring in personality than his partner, but his efficiency and astute sense of business combined well with Barnum's flamboyant salesmanship. Bailey had begun traveling with circuses as a boy and gradually worked up the ladder to managerial positions. In 1872 he became a partner in James E. Cooper's Circus, later called the Great International Circus after a lucrative tour of Australia, New Zealand, Java, and several South American countries. When it was renamed Cooper, Bailey & Company Circus in 1876, it was seen as a strong competitor to Barnum's Greatest Show on Earth, and in 1881 the two shows merged as Barnum & Bailey Circus. After Barnum's death in 1891, Bailey led the show on several successful tours of Europe and brought his circus to new levels of popularity in America, transporting it coast-to-coast on eighty-five railroad cars. His version of the greatest show on Earth boasted the largest traveling menagerie and displayed its spectacles in five rings as well as on stages. More than a thousand people were employed in the enterprise.

The Ringling Brothers of Baraboo, Wisconsin, had begun their tent shows in 1884 with the lengthy name "Ringling Bros. United Monster Shows, Great Double Circus, Royal European Menagerie, Museum, Caravan, and Congress of Trained Animals." In a short time Alf, Al, Charles, John, and Otto Ringling became known as the Kings of the Circus. Later, two other brothers, Henry and Gus, joined their ranks. By 1889 the show had a seating capacity of 4,000 under its Big Top and was playing cities and towns in the Midwest, charging fifty cents for adults and twenty-five cents for children. That same year they became the twelfth American circus to travel by rail. In 1907, after Bailey's death the previous year, the Ringling Brothers bought the Barnum & Bailey Circus for $400,000. They ran it as a separate entity until 1919, when their operations were combined into Ringling Bros., Barnum & Bailey, its present name.

STAR ATTRACTIONS

American circuses made important contributions to popular spectacle, including the traditional free morning parade down Main Street. Beginning usually at 11 a.m., a uniformed brass band would step out sharply, their instruments blaring a stirring march. Next would come a long procession of flag bearers, beautiful ladies on horseback, trapeze artists waving from brightly painted circus wagons, and clowns performing their well-choreographed high jinks. Cages of wild animals moved by in horse-drawn cages, followed by cowboys and Indians on horseback, Roman chariots, and a line of elephants marching trunk to tail in their characteristic shuffling gait. Last in the parade was always the steam calliope, with thirty-two steam whistles, operated by a keyboard, hissing smoke as well as high-pitched tunes such as "The Sidewalks of New York."

Many performers who appeared in the Barnum & Bailey Circus became star attractions, notably those who performed daring death-defying feats on the high wire or the flying trapeze. The Wallenda family, who came from Germany to join the circus in 1928, did acrobatics and rode bicycles on the high wire under the name the Flying Wallendas; they ultimately developed a stunt in which three bikes were balanced on the wire. In 1947 they began performing a seven-man pyramid, and in a tragic accident in 1962, two family members were killed in a fall and a third was paralyzed. Another acrobat, Con Colleano, the "Toreador of the Tight Wire," retained his popularity in America for decades, dancing a flamenco on the high wire. Lillian Leitzel, who came from a German circus family, thrilled audiences by performing 150 or more swingovers—pivoting on her shoulder socket like a pinwheel—while suspended by a rope looped around her right wrist. The petite star was fatally injured in 1931 when her rigging broke during her act. Aerialist Alfredo Codona, her husband, was the first to perform a triple aerial somersault from the high trapeze, and Tito Gaona later began performing the same act blindfolded.

Clowns, who came in a variety of makeup, wigs, and costumes, were always immensely popular as they packed themselves into a small vehicle or performed juggling or comic acrobatics. The best-known clown of all was Emmett Kelly, who played the sad-faced tramp "Weary Willie." Kelly joined the Ringling Bros., Barnum & Bailey Circus in the late 1930s and was a special favorite until he died in 1979 on the opening day of that year's circus season. He made his motion-picture debut in *The Greatest Show on Earth* (1952).

CIRCUS ANIMALS

Trained animals, both wild and domestic, were popular in circuses. One of the crowd favorites involved "liberty" horses, who performed intricate routines without rider or reins, guided only by visual or oral commands from the trainer. In 1897 Barnum & Bailey featured an act that used a record seventy liberty horses performing simultaneously in one ring. The traditional finale in most of the larger circuses was the Great Roman Hippodrome Races, demonstrating the ancient arts of chariot racing and riding horses while the equestrians were standing erect. Clyde Beatty, who appeared with Ringling Bros., Barnum & Bailey in 1934, used a whip and a handheld wooden chair to subdue as many as forty lions and tigers in a round cage in the center ring. He also performed with other dangerous animals, including leopards, pumas, hyenas, and bears. The Knie family of Switzerland also became well known in the United States for their training of such exotic animals as giraffes, polar bears, hippopotamuses, and rhinoceroses. Elephants were always popular, and Barnum & Bailey reportedly used as many as fifty of the huge animals in three-ring spectacles.

By the 1990s animal-rights activists were boycotting circuses around the world for their practice of using animals for mere spectacle, or for allegedly abusing the beasts. The allegations are denied by circuses, but the boycotts encouraged the development of new-wave "nonanimal" circuses, such as Le Cirque du Soleil of Montreal, which uses human performers exclusively. In 2011 the U.S. Department of Agriculture fined the Ringling Bros., Barnum & Bailey Circus $270,000 for mistreating elephants by using metal bull hooks to guide the animals and chaining their legs when they were not performing. Although the company paid the fine, it did not admit any wrongdoing and pointed to the elephant conservation center it runs in Florida as proof of its concern for animals.

THE MODERN CIRCUS

The circus passed out of the Ringling family's hands in 1967 when Irving Feld bought it, but he decided to retain the name Ringling Bros., Barnum & Bailey Circus. Mattel briefly owned the circus during the 1970s, but the Feld family bought it back in 1982. Today, it is headed by Irving Feld's son Kenneth.

Through the years the circus has remained one of the most enduring of America's popular entertainments, remaining in much the same format while modes of transportation and venues have changed. The canvas Big Top was generally abandoned after 167 people died in a disastrous circus-tent fire in Hartford, Connecticut, in 1944, and circuses moved into large indoor arenas. Despite this change, parents and grandparents can still accompany children to Ringling Bros., Barnum & Bailey Circuses with the confidence that the show will go on and be much as it was when they were children.

Benjamin Griffith

SEE ALSO: *Bicycling; Circus; Freak Shows.*

BIBLIOGRAPHY

Fenner, Mildred Sandison, and Wolcott Fenner. *The Circus, Lore and Legend.* Englewood Cliffs, NJ: Prentice-Hall, 1970.

Hammarstrom, David Lewis. *Behind the Big Top.* New York: Barnes & Noble, 1980.

Kirk, Rhina. *Circus Heroes and Heroines.* New York: Hammond, 1974.

MacVicar, Jamie. *The Advance Man: A Journey into the World of the Circus.* Albany, GA: Bear Manor Media, 2009.

O'Nan, Stewart. *The Circus Fire: A True Story of an American Tragedy.* New York: Doubleday, 2000.

Taylor, Robert Lewis. *Center Ring: The People of the Circus.* Garden City, NY: Doubleday, 1956.

Wallace, Irving. *The Fabulous Showman: The Life and Times of P. T. Barnum.* Norwalk, CT: Easton Press, 1990.

Ripken, Cal, Jr. *(1960–)*

During the 1990s "Iron Man" Cal Ripken Jr. was more responsible for the resurgent popularity of baseball than any other player. His pursuit of first-baseman Lou Gehrig's record for number of consecutive games played became the focus of national attention in 1995. Ripken's calm, good-natured, average-guy demeanor and clear understanding of his place in history made him a favorite of millions of baseball fans around the world.

Ripken was born August 24, 1960, in Havre de Grace, Maryland, and grew up in nearby Aberdeen. He attended Aberdeen High School, earning All-County and All-State honors. The Baltimore Orioles selected him in the second round (the forty-eighth overall pick) of the 1978 baseball draft. He quickly rose though the Orioles' minor-league system and was the starting third baseman of the 1982 the season, moving to shortstop in May of the same year. At the end of the season, he was voted American League Rookie of the Year. The next season, he became the American League's Most Valuable Player (MVP), and the Orioles won the World Series.

He continued to demonstrate his abilities as a player throughout the 1980s and early 1990s. In 1990 he compiled a string of ninety-five consecutive games without an error, setting a major-league record for shortstops. In the same year, he set records for fewest errors by a shortstop (three) and highest fielding percentage by a shortstop (.996). In 1991 he became the second player in major-league history to be named MVP, Major League Player of the Year (by the *Sporting News*, the Associated Press, and *Baseball Digest*), All-Star Game MVP, and Gold Glove winner in the same season (the other was shortstop Maury Wills in 1962). Ripken hit twenty or more home runs in ten consecutive seasons and led American League shortstops in fielding percentage for two years straight.

Anticipation that Ripken might break Gehrig's record did more than ensure the shortstop's place in baseball history. His playing streak was particularly important for baseball because of labor problems during the mid-1990s. Players went on strike in late 1994, resulting in the cancellation of the 1994 World Series. The strike continued into the start of the 1995 season, and fans became increasingly disillusioned with the players and the owners. When playing finally resumed, attendance for most teams was down 25 percent or more. Independent estimates put total lost revenue at nearly $700 million over the two-year span.

But Ripken's hunt for the record helped reverse waning interest. The shortstop had not missed a game since the 1982 season. On September 6, 1995, he played his 2,131st consecutive game, breaking Gehrig's record, set in 1939. Baseball fans around the world tuned in to watch Ripken play in the historic game. He capped off the record-breaking event by hitting the game-winning home run. The Associated Press and United Press International named him Male Athlete of the Year, the *Sporting News* named him Major League Player of the Year, and *Sports Illustrated* honored him as Sportsman of the Year.

Even after breaking Gehrig's record, Ripken continued to play every game of every season. In 1996 the streak reached 2,216 games, surpassing the world record for consecutive games played set by Sachio Kinugasa of Japan. In 1997 Ripken moved from shortstop to third base, but his streak continued until September 20, 1998, when he chose to sit out a game and the streak finally ended at 2,632. Ripken had played 502 more consecutive games than Gehrig and more than twice as many as the player in third place, Everett Scott.

Although the playing streak may be what most people remember about Ripken, who retired from baseball in 2001, he had many other important achievements. He was named to the Associated Press Major League All-Star Team six times, the American League All-Stars eighteen times, and the *Sporting News* American League All-Star Team seven times. He also received nine Silver Slugger Awards for the most productive offensive shortstop in baseball and two American League Gold Gloves at shortstop. He set records for fewest errors in a season by a shortstop (later tied by Omar Vizquel), most career home runs as a shortstop, and most consecutive games without an error (since surpassed by Mike Bordick of the Orioles in 2002). In 2007 he was elected to the Baseball Hall of Fame as one of the greatest players ever at his position.

Geoff Peterson

SEE ALSO: *Baseball; Gehrig, Lou; The* Sporting News*; Sports Heroes;* Sports Illustrated*; World Series.*

BIBLIOGRAPHY

Ripken, Cal, Jr., and Donald T. Phillips. *Get in the Game: 8 Elements of Perseverance That Make the Difference.* New York: Gotham, 2007.

Ripken, Cal, Jr.; Bill Ripken; and Larry Burke. *Play Baseball the Ripken Way: The Complete Illustrated Guide to the Fundamentals.* New York: Random House, 2004.

Rosenfeld, H. *Iron Man: The Cal Ripken, Jr., Story.* New York: St. Martin's Press, 1995.

Ripley's Believe It or Not!

Truths stranger than fiction have captivated writers for centuries. But for most twentieth-century Americans, the phrase "Believe it or not!" is indissolubly wedded to the name of Robert LeRoy Ripley, whose illustrated panel of wonders and curiosities was published in 200 newspapers across the United States. Although Ripley himself died in 1949, his famous brainchild continued to be produced by his successors into the 2010s.

Ripley's career might have been very different but for several strokes of luck. In 1907, as a teenager in Santa Rosa, California, he sold his first cartoon to the humor magazine *Life*. Later, while he was still a teen, his talent was recognized by a neighbor, Carol Ennis, who steered him to his first newspaper job with the *San Francisco Bulletin*.

BELIEVE IT OR NOT

Ripley's biggest break came after he moved to Manhattan and was hired as a sports cartoonist for the *New York Globe*. Casting about for ideas in a slow week, he decided to draw up a panel of surprising sports facts, heading it "Believe It or Not!" Reader response was overwhelmingly enthusiastic, and Ripley's editors urged him to do more in the same vein.

Ripley soon branched out beyond sports oddities to all of the world's wonders, and "Believe It or Not!" was in limited syndication, earning him a modest but respectable $10,000 annually by the end of 1927. He had moved to the *New York Post* in 1923, the same year he produced one of his most famous cartoons, in which he points out that "The Star-Spangled Banner" was not the national anthem because America had never officially designated one. As a result Congress was flooded with letters, resulting in the statutory adoption of the song in 1931. In 1929 Ripley was sought out by the head of King Features Syndicate, Joseph V. Connolly, who had been sent a laconic telegram from William Randolph Hearst saying "SIGN RIPLEY." Ripley signed, and his income immediately jumped tenfold; by the mid-1930s he was making $500,000 a year, enabling him to travel worldwide and to buy expensive properties on Long Island, New York, and in Florida.

Ripley's staff grew until he had dozens of paid assistants. One of his most loyal researchers was Norbert Pearlroth, who had been hired in the 1920s because he knew fourteen languages. Pearlroth became legendary at the New York Public Library reading room, where he could be seen nearly every day for more than fifty years, combing foreign journals for the unusual facts that were the feature's stock in trade. (Although Ripley left Pearlroth a surprisingly modest bequest when he died, the cartoonist had also put Pearlroth's son through school at his own expense.)

As long as Ripley could find an item in print somewhere, he considered it true. Hearing of a president of Mexico whose term had set a record for brevity (thirty-seven minutes from inauguration to assassination), Ripley set his research team scouring sources until, in the 9,832nd book checked, the desired documentation was found. Some of Ripley's eye-openers were

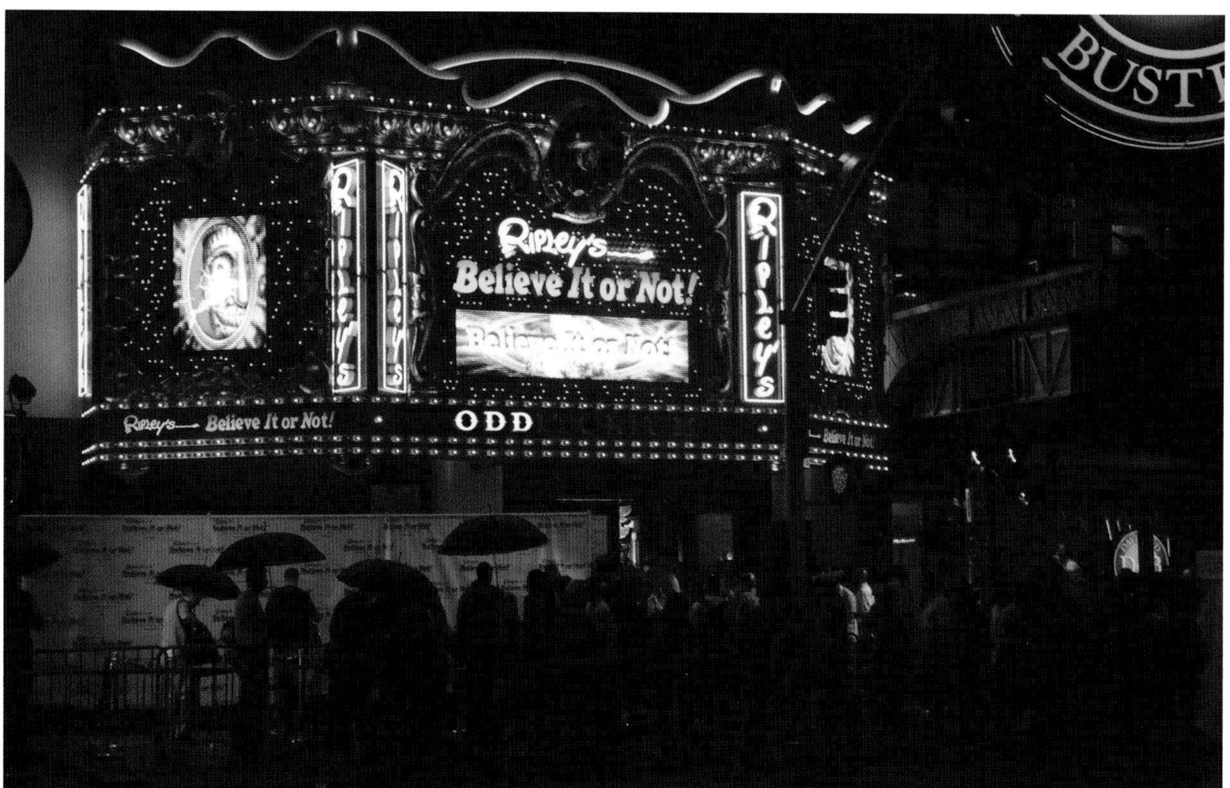

Ripley's Believe It! or Not in New York. *Fans wait to enter the Ripley's Believe It! or Not Times Square Odditorium in New York City in 2007.* BRAD BARKET/CONTRIBUTOR/GETTY IMAGES ENTERTAINMENT/GETTY IMAGES.

simply matters of deduction: based on an estimated birthrate plus the standard day's march for U.S. Army infantry units, Ripley came up with one of his most famous panels, the "Marching Chinese," which purported to demonstrate that if all the inhabitants of China were to begin marching four abreast past a given point, their numbers and birthrate were such that the column would never end.

Ripley's exoticism and ethnocentrism were comfortable bedfellows, and his account of a visit to India in the late 1920s—published in his first book for Simon & Schuster in 1929—is rife with contempt for Hinduism. On the other hand, he had great respect for Chinese civilization and artifacts, collecting the latter avidly, including a motorized junk—the pride of a motley flotilla that Ripley stored near his twenty-eight-room mansion on a private island named BION (located near Long Island). Like many self-made men of his era, Ripley tended to flaunt his wealth.

In addition to his newspaper feature and the books that anthologized it, Ripley went on radio in the 1930s, first as a feature on the *Collier Hour* in 1930 and then with his own show, with a succession of sponsors that included Standard Oil, Hudson Motors, General Foods, and Royal Crown Cola. Outmaneuvered for a World's Fair concession in 1939 by rival John Hix, who produced the panel "Strange as It Seems," Ripley simply opened up nearby with his "Odditorium."

RIPLEY ORGANIZATION CARRIES ON

After World War II Ripley also tried his hand at television, hosting his own show beginning on March 1, 1949. Unfortunately, three months later he was dead, having blacked out on the set of his show on May 24. He died of heart failure in a hospital bed several days later.

The Ripley organization, however, carried on almost seamlessly. The research team, including Pearlroth, continued to ferret out marvels, which were drawn in the Ripley style by Paul Frehm, whom Ripley had hired as an understudy when Frehm was illustrating ads for Borg-Warner. Frehm ran the organization until 1978, when his brother Walter, who had begun his career doing Paul's lettering, took control. In 1989 Walter Frehm retired and was succeeded by Don Wimmer, formerly a freelance artist with United Features Syndicate, which had acquired the rights to *Believe It or Not!* and was still distributing it to newspapers nationwide in 2012. A reality TV show based on the feature ran from 1982 to 1986, hosted by actor Jack Palance. A second version of the show, hosted by Dean Cain, ran on TBS from 2000 to 2003.

Ripley's Believe It or Not! continues to be operated under license in a number of U.S. cities, including Chicago and Orlando, Florida. Ripley's feature gave rise to numerous parodies as well, from a *MAD Magazine* spoof titled "Ripup's Believe It or Don't" to the National Lampoon's *True Facts: The Book*, a photo archive of funny roadside signs, and Kevin Goldstein's *The Leslie Frewin Book of Ridiculous Facts.*

In 2008 Ripley's Entertainment expanded its empire by acquiring Guinness World Records. As of 2012 the corporation ran thirty-one Believe It or Not! Odditoriums in eleven countries around the world, as well as five Guinness World Record Museums, three aquariums, and numerous other tourist attractions.

Nick Humez

SEE ALSO: *Advertising; Hearst, William Randolph;* Life; MAD Magazine; National Lampoon; *Radio; Reality Television; Syndication; Television; World War II; World's Fairs.*

BIBLIOGRAPHY

Bendel, John. *National Lampoon Presents True Facts: The Book.* Chicago: Contemporary Books, 1991.

Goldstein-Jackson, Kevin. *The Leslie Frewin Book of Ridiculous Facts.* London: Frewin, 1974.

Hansen, William, tr. *Phlegon of Tralles' Book of Marvels.* Exeter, UK: University of Exeter Press, 1996.

Priest, Josiah. *Wonders of Nature and Providence, Displayed.* Albany, NY: J. Priest, 1825.

Ripley, Robert Le Roy. *Ripley's Believe It or Not!* New York: Simon & Schuster, 1929.

Ripley, Robert Le Roy. *Ripley's 35th Anniversary Believe It or Not!* New York: Simon & Schuster, 1954.

Ripley's Believe It or Not! Book of Chance. New York: Coward, McCann & Geoghehan, 1982.

Sloan, Mark; Roger Manley; and Michelle Van Pargs, eds. *Dear Mr. Ripley: A Compendium of Curiosities from the Believe It or Not! Archives.* Boston: Little, Brown, 1993.

Tibballs, Geoff. *Ripley's Believe It or Not! Strikingly True.* Orlando, FL: Ripley Publishing, 2011.

Rivera, Chita *(1933–)*

One of musical theater's most durable personalities, Chita Rivera is revered as an actress, a singer, and a dancer. Her first major role was as Anita in *West Side Story* (1957). Other Broadway credits include *Bye Bye Birdie* (1960), *Chicago* (1975), *The Rink* (1984), and *Kiss of the Spider Woman* (1993). She has received numerous accolades for her work, including Tony Awards for *The Rink* and *Kiss of the Spider Woman;* the Drama Desk Award for *The Rink;* and top honors at the 1996 Helen Hayes Awards for contributions to theater. Her film credits include *Sweet Charity* (1969) and *Pippin* (1981).

In the first decade of the 2000s she appeared on the TV show *Will & Grace* and in the hit movie *Chicago* (2002). She was selected for the Kennedy Center Honors in 2002 and was awarded the Presidential Medal of Freedom in 2009. Possessing a voice with a wide dynamic and timbral range, Rivera's talent and charisma both as a singer and a dancer have allowed her to enjoy a successful and diverse stage career for more than fifty years.

William A. Everett

SEE ALSO: *Broadway; Tony Awards;* West Side Story; Will & Grace.

BIBLIOGRAPHY

Henderson, Robert. "Theatre: Chita Rivera: My Broadway." *Fuse.* Accessed October 24, 2011. Available from http://www.fusemagazine.com.au/index.php/whats-on/canberra/1757-chita-rivera-my-broadway

Sandla, Robert. "Chita Rivera: Now Is the Gleam in the Eye." *Dance Magazine* 68, no. 2 (1994): 76–81.

Telgen, Diane, and Jim Kamp, eds. *Latinas! Women of Achievement.* Detroit, MI: Visible Ink Press, 1996.

Rivera, Diego *(1886–1957)*

Probably more than the work of any other visual artist, Diego Rivera's murals and paintings are representative and emblematic of Mexico's history and culture. A man of his times, Rivera used a language very much his own to express his conception of the world. Through the use of figures representing his socialist ideology and others that went against his beliefs, Rivera created his compositions following simple horizontal and vertical lines. His murals, balanced in terms of color, form, and composition, offer us a peaceful world, static and inert yet filled with the energy of the search for a just and better world.

Born in Guanajuato, Mexico, Rivera began his art studies at the age of ten. Three years later his father insisted that he enroll in a military college, but Diego lasted only two weeks, repelled by the regimented training. He then enrolled in regular classes at the Academy of San Carlos in Mexico City. His first exhibit took place in 1906 at the academy. A year later he took his first trip abroad, one of many to come, traveling to Spain to study and forming friendships with leading members of the Spanish avant-garde. A couple of years later he traveled to Paris, France, and Brugge, Belgium, and studied with several painters, exhibiting his work at the Société des artistes indépendants. In 1910 he returned to Mexico.

On his many trips to Europe, Rivera exhibited at numerous galleries, salons, and studios. In 1913 his work showed a transition to cubism, yet he was also executing drawings in the style of Jean-Auguste-Dominique Ingres and paintings and pencil studies inspired by Paul Cézanne. Several years later he became obsessed with the sensuous quality of paintings by Pierre-Auguste Renoir and traveled to Italy to study Renaissance art. Finally, in 1921 Rivera returned to Mexico and saw his country with new eyes, as a foreigner, the way painter Paul Gauguin had seen Tahiti. With his new outlook, Rivera began his long trajectory of mural painting for public buildings, schools, museums, and chapels. His figures became more and more indigenous, his themes political and social. A reevaluation and dignification of the Indian and the workers of the world would, over the years, turn into a longing for the recovery of a better everyday life for these majorities.

In 1922 Rivera joined the Mexican Communist Party and in 1927 traveled to the Soviet Union to participate in the celebrations of the tenth anniversary of the October Revolution. The Soviets recognized him as a great Communist artist whose art was dedicated to the public and the masses. In 1929 Rivera married Frida Kahlo, a union that lasted, on and off, until her death in 1954. Rivera and Kahlo, a painter in her own right, became a fashionable and much-talked-about couple in Mexico and abroad, their extramarital affairs and frequent separations the material of gossip columnists and art lovers alike.

Rivera was expelled from the Communist Party in 1929, and a year later he arrived in San Francisco to paint two murals for the California School of Fine Arts. He also painted twenty-seven murals depicting automotive history for the Detroit Institute of Arts (1932–1933) and in 1933 began work on a mural commissioned by Nelson A. Rockefeller for the RCA Building in New York City. Depicting the Soviet May Day celebrations and a portrait of Vladimir Lenin, *Man at the Crossroads* provoked a series of pro and con demonstrations. When Rivera refused to cover Lenin's face with the portrait of an unknown individual, the mural was destroyed and covered with canvas painted to match the adjoining blank wall. Rivera later reproduced the work at the Palace of Fine Arts in Mexico City.

In 1937 Communist theorist-in-exile Leon Trotsky found asylum in Mexico, and Rivera became his host. In 1939, however, Rivera broke off with Trotsky after several personal and political arguments. Around this time Rivera's painting career escalated to the point where he spent most of his time traveling and working. His political trajectory also moved from one end of the spectrum to the other.

In 1954 Rivera participated in the demonstrations in support of fallen Guatemalan president Jacobo Árbenz. Kahlo died that same year, and Rivera was reinstated into the Communist Party. Three years later, on November 24, 1957, Rivera died of heart failure in his San Angel studio and was buried, against his wishes, in the Rotonda de los Hombres Ilustres (Rotunda of Illustrious Men, now known as the Rotunda of Illustrious Persons) at the Panteón Civil de Dolores (Civilian Pantheon of Sorrows) cemetery in Mexico City.

Beatriz Badikian

SEE ALSO: *Communism; The Rockefeller Family.*

BIBLIOGRAPHY

Bloch, Lucienne. "On Location with Diego Rivera." *Art in America*, February 1986, 102–123.

Herner de Larrea, Irene. *Diego Rivera's Mural at the Rockefeller Center.* Mexico City: Edicupes, S.A. de C.V., 1990.

Kettenman, Andrea. *Diego Rivera (1886–1957): A Revolutionary Spirit in Modern Art.* New York: Taschen, 1997.

Woronoff, Kristen. *Frida Kahlo: Mexican Painter.* Detroit, MI: Blackbirch Press, 2002.

Rivera, Geraldo *(1943–)*

In 1987 Geraldo Miguel Rivera became the first Hispanic American to host a nationally syndicated talk show. In his personal life and media career, he has experienced roller-coaster-like highs and lows. After growing up on the mean streets of New York City, he received some of the most distinguished awards for broadcast journalism—only to suffer a tarnished reputation for pandering to the masses as an exponent of trashy television.

Born to a Puerto Rican father and a Jewish American mother, Rivera studied at the University of Arizona and Brooklyn Law School. He received a law degree from the prestigious University of Pennsylvania Law School and a degree in journalism from the equally prestigious Columbia University. As such, he was one of the best-prepared and most intellectual broadcast and investigative journalists of his generation.

He began his journalistic career as a reporter for WABC-TV in New York in 1970. Later he served as a reporter, producer, and host for various television news and entertainment shows. In 1971 he became the first Hispanic to win the New York State

Associated Press Broadcaster Association Award, for his investigative series "Drug Crisis in East Harlem." He also became the first Hispanic to be named Broadcaster of the Year in 1972 and 1974. One of the original team of reporters on the early show *Good Morning America* (1975–), he later served a seven-year stint on the evening news program *20/20* (1978–). In all he has won one Peabody Award and ten Emmy Awards for distinguished broadcast journalism.

In 1987 he became host of the sensationalized *The Geraldo Rivera Show* (1987–1998), which fit squarely into the "trash TV" genre. He was heavily involved in the coverage of the investigation and murder trial of former football player O. J. Simpson. Nevertheless, in the late 1990s, he was one of the most visible and successful Hispanics in media and entertainment. He hosted a nightly news commentary show for the CNBC network and produced and starred in NBC network broadcast specials. He is often best remembered for an NBC special in which he was to break into one of mobster Al Capone's long-lost treasure vaults on live television. He became a laughingstock when the vault turned out to be empty—one of live television's greatest fiascoes.

Since, Rivera has tried to exhibit a more serious and sober approach to his coverage and discussions of national topics. He won the Robert F. Kennedy Journalism Award for his documentary, *Women in Prison*, in 2000. Following the terrorist attacks of 9/11, in an effort to win back the respect that he had lost, he left his job with CNBC and signed on as an investigative journalist with Fox News Channel to cover the war in Afghanistan. Two years later he launched the investigative series *Geraldo at Large* (2003–).

His endeavor to return to legitimate reporting has met with controversy. In his first year on the air, he claimed to have witnessed a friendly fire incident in Afghanistan when he was actually 300 miles away at the time it occurred. In 2003 American government officials expelled him from Iraq after he drew a crude map in the sand to illustrate the location of the 101st Airborne during a broadcast for Fox News. Two years later he ran afoul of the *New York Times* during coverage of Hurricane Katrina. The newspaper reported that Rivera had nudged a rescue worker aside in order to be shown on camera assisting a woman in a wheelchair down some steps. When he threatened to sue, the *Times* grudgingly acknowledged that the reference was symbolic rather than literal, insisting that Rivera was insinuating himself into Katrina coverage.

Controversy followed him into the 2010s. Following the death of terrorist Osama bin Laden in 2011, Rivera mistakenly said, "Obama is dead. I don't care"—although he immediately corrected himself. In March 2012 he again raised public ire over his insinuations that Trayvon Martin, the unarmed seventeen-year-old African American slain by a neighborhood watch member, was partially responsible for his own death because he wore a hooded sweatshirt. Rivera subsequently apologized to Martin's parents for his remarks. Despite his numerous faux pas, he has managed to maintain a significant viewership.

Nicolás Kanellos

SEE ALSO: *Capone, Al; Daytime Talk Shows; Emmy Awards; Fox News Channel; Hurricane Katrina; The* New York Times*; 9/11; Obama, Barack; Simpson, O. J.; Simpson Trial;* 20/20*; War in Afghanistan.*

BIBLIOGRAPHY

Kanellos, Nicolás. *Hispanic American Almanac*, 2nd ed. Detroit, MI: Gale, 1997.

Meier, Matt S. *Notable Latino Americans: A Biographical Dictionary*. Westport, CT: Greenwood Press, 1997.

Tardiff, Joseph T., and L. Mpho Mabunda, eds. *Dictionary of Hispanic Biography*. Detroit, MI: Gale, 1996.

Timberg, Bernard. *Television Talk: A History of the TV Talk Show*. Austin, TX: University of Texas Press, 2002.

Rivers, Joan *(1933–)*

Funnywoman Joan Rivers is known as a pioneer of contemporary stand-up comedy. In the 1960s and 1970s her bold, bitchy, self-deprecating humor broke new ground for female comics. Like shock comic Lenny Bruce, whose outrageous routines set the tone for a new wave of comedy in the 1960s, Rivers's bravura

Joan Rivers. *Joan Rivers's edgy brand of self-deprecating comedy, as well as her work as a producer, talk-show host, fashion commentator, and jewelry designer, has made her a household name.* BECK STARR/CONTRIBUTOR/FILMMAGIC/GETTY IMAGES.

flew in the face of acceptable female behavior, paving the way for future generations of tough-talking, straight-shooting comediennes.

EARLY LIFE

The daughter of a successful doctor and his hardworking wife, Joan Molinsky was born on June 8, 1933, in Brooklyn, New York. A smart girl, Rivers earned grades good enough to get her into competitive Barnard College. After graduating with honors and a degree in English, she worked as a publicist for Lord & Taylor.

Her dream was to become an actress, however, so she auditioned for agents all over Manhattan. Time after time she was turned away. As she described it, "They told me I had everything needed to be a star, except for looks and talent. After hearing such moving responses, I would wander back to the receptionist and make jokes to cover the hurt I was feeling. And the receptionists began to tell their bosses that I was funny." Finally one of the agents offered her a gig at a small stand-up comedy club.

BREAKING NEW GROUND

In the 1950s and early 1960s, comediennes were few and far between. Fanny Brice was dead, and the only other women making a living doing stand-up were Phyllis Diller and Totie Fields. Rivers's humor was edgy, raunchy, and often unladylike. But she was funny and determined to succeed.

For almost seven years, the overweight Jewish girl from Brooklyn tried to make it in stand-up. She slogged away at small clubs all over the East Coast, even using the name Pepper January before permanently becoming Joan Rivers. In the early 1960s she started working at Greenwich Village coffee shops, telling jokes that pushed the limits of the acceptable. As she later wrote, "I was not unaware of my gender. In a routine about how I got into show business, I used to say: 'How do I get booked? My talent? No, I just go into the agent's office and say, "Hi, I'm Joan Rivers and I put out."'"

In the late 1960s most women did not say the things Rivers would, at least in public. None other than Rivers dare quip that when she had her baby, she screamed for twenty-three hours straight—and that was just during conception. Certainly no white woman would have come onstage after the audience had applauded a black male singer's performance and say, "I'm so glad you loved my husband." She remarked, "Critics felt that such jokes entitled me to another line of work, perhaps in a delicatessen."

Yet, as she was being panned, Bruce was being praised for his shocking comedy. One day he came to see her show and sent her a note backstage. He wrote, "You're right, they're wrong." Encouraged, she stuck with it. In 1965 her big chance finally came: she was booked on *The Tonight Show Starring Johnny Carson* (1962–1992). Her routine was a hit, and she continued to be asked back on the program.

PUBLIC SUCCESS, PERSONAL TRAGEDY

Rivers frequently joked that her marriage prospects were so grim that her mother hung out a sign that said, "Last girl before thruway." Her marriage to the erudite, Oxford-educated Edgar Rosenberg was a loving, happy union of twenty-two years. Rosenberg, who also was Rivers's manager, was her biggest supporter. With his encouragement she became a Las Vegas headliner; an actress; a movie director (1978's *Rabbit Test*); and in 1983 *The Tonight Show*'s sole guest host, filling in for Carson every third week. The now petite blond became a household name, and her bitchy, self-deprecating humor, once reviled by critics, was now imitated by young women hoping to follow in her footsteps. Her signature line "Can we talk?" became ubiquitous.

Although Rosenberg was sometimes the butt of her jokes, their marriage was stronger than ever. Despite suffering a heart attack in 1984, he orchestrated her move to a show on the new Fox network, which would be in direct competition with *The Tonight Show*. The move provoked Carson's wrath, and with low ratings, *The Late Show with Joan Rivers* floundered. In 1987, after less than a year on the air, she left the show and *The Late Show* was canceled. Rosenberg was distraught and took the blame for the failure. Suffering from chemical depression brought on by his heart medication, he committed suicide a few months later.

A devastated Rivers and her daughter, Melissa, were left nearly broke. A few weeks later Rivers's agent canceled her contract, saying that no one would book a comedienne whose husband had just died—too unfunny. She slowly crept back into show business, doing gigs at tiny comedy clubs and appearing as the center square on *The New Hollywood Squares* (1986–1989). A year later she was asked to read for a small part in playwright Neil Simon's *Broadway Bound* (1987). She leapt at the chance, not only winning the part but also wowing critics.

RETURN TO THE SPOTLIGHT

Rivers found her way back in front of a national audience with her syndicated daytime talk show, for which she won a 1990 Emmy Award for Best Talk Show Host. In the mid-1990s, however, she decided to give up the program to perform in a Broadway play she had written about Bruce's mother. *Sally Marr . . . and Her Escorts* (1994) was a critical success but closed due to financial difficulties. When Rivers's popular jewelry business fell apart at the same time, she once again found her life in pieces.

But she bounced back. After reconciling a difficult estrangement from daughter Melissa in the wake of Edgar's death, Rivers and Melissa played themselves in an NBC TV movie called *Tears and Laughter: The Joan and Melissa Rivers Story* (1994). The mother-daughter duo began appearing regularly on the E! network, providing commentary on the Oscars and other major awards shows. A popular author, Rivers has written three top-selling books, *Enter Talking* (1986); *Still Talking* (1995); and *Bouncing Back* (1997), a humorous self-help memoir.

In 2009 Rivers and Melissa were contestants on NBC's reality television show *The Apprentice* (2004–). Despite threatening to walk off the show midseason when Melissa was "fired," Rivers went on to win the competition, helping to raise more than $150 million for God's Love We Deliver, a meal-delivery charity. The following year, she was the subject of a feature-length documentary, *Joan Rivers: A Piece of Work* (2010), which explores her past while following her through a year in her life. She and Melissa also debuted a reality television show, *Joan & Melissa: Joan Knows Best*, on the WE network in January 2011. The series mixes real events (including the infidelity of Melissa's longtime partner, Jason) with guest appearances from stars such as comedienne Carol Burnett.

Like her comedic predecessor, Brice, Rivers has survived tragedy through humor. Her petite, ladylike appearance notwithstanding, she remains a tough-talking, funny woman from Brooklyn. Alternately panned and praised, she and her unflinching ability to tell it like it is broke long-standing taboos and paved the way for other brash women such as comic actresses Roseanne, Ellen DeGeneres, and Rosie O'Donnell.

Victoria Price

SEE ALSO: The Apprentice; *Brice, Fanny; Broadway; Bruce, Lenny; Burnett, Carol; Cable TV; Carson, Johnny; Daytime Talk Shows; DeGeneres, Ellen; Depression; Diller, Phyllis; Emmy Awards; Greenwich Village;* Hollywood Squares; *Las Vegas; Made-for-Television Movies; O'Donnell, Rosie; Reality Television;* Roseanne; *Simon, Neil; Stand-Up Comedy; Suicide; Television;* The Tonight Show.

BIBLIOGRAPHY

Bellafante, Ginia. "Joan in Full Throat." *Time*, May 16, 1994.

Rivers, Joan. *Bouncing Back*. New York: HarperCollins, 1997.

Rivers, Joan. "How I Triumphed over Tough Times." *McCall's*, April 1997.

Rizzuto, Phil *(1917–2007)*

Phil Rizzuto, New York Yankees shortstop and later the team's colorful television and radio announcer, gave new meaning to the exclamation "Holy cow!" The wiry New York native debuted with the Yankees in 1941 and, except for a three-year stint in the navy during World War II, made the baseball team his lifelong career. A keystone of the team's defense in the 1940s and 1950s, he was voted the American League Most Valuable Player in 1950 and inducted into the National Baseball Hall of Fame in 1994.

"The Scooter," as he was known, became an announcer for the Yankees after retiring as a player in 1956, bringing his tremendous personal warmth to the broadcast booth. He appealed to fans not only with his enthusiasm and insider's knowledge but also with his rambling anecdotes, amusing commentary, and descriptions of the Italian delicacies he consumed with colleagues in the booth. His *cri de cow*—used to describe everything from bad calls to violent rainstorms to grand slams—was used in a rock song by Meat Loaf, "Paradise by the Dashboard Light" (1977), and served as the title of a book of his on-air musings translated into free verse, *O Holy Cow! The Selected Verse of Phil Rizzuto* (1993). Rizzuto retired from broadcasting in 1996. After some years of declining health, he died on August 13, 2007.

Daniel Lindley

SEE ALSO: *Baseball; Major League Baseball; The New York Yankees; Sports Heroes.*

BIBLIOGRAPHY

DeVito, Carlo. *Scooter: The Biography of Phil Rizzuto*. Chicago: Triumph Books, 2009.

Halberstam, David. *Summer of '49*. New York: William Morrow, 1989.

Kelley, Brent. *Baseball Stars of the 1950s*. Jefferson, NC: McFarland, 1993.

Peyer, Tom, and Hart Seely, eds. *O Holy Cow! The Selected Verse of Phil Rizzuto*. Hopewell, NJ: Ecco Press, 1993.

Road Rage

As American roadways became increasingly congested in the 1980s and 1990s, drivers began to experience, either as aggressors or victims, a new phenomenon called "road rage." Reports of violence and shootings provoked by incidental breeches of driving etiquette caused an escalating level of paranoia surrounding driving. News headlines such as these started popping up: "Five-Year-Old Victim of Road-Rage Shootout," "Father Charged with 'Road Rage' Killing of Son," and "Ugly Increase in Acts of Freeway Fury." While the shootings made the biggest splashes in the news, road rage could be characterized by any display of aggression by a driver, including verbal abuse, tailgating, hand gestures, intimidating stares, or violence. The American Automobile Association (AAA) reported in 1997 that incidents of "aggressive driving" in which an "angry or impatient driver tries to kill or injure another driver after a traffic dispute [have] risen by 51 percent since 1990."

The term *road rage*, coined in 1988, is derived from "roid rage," which refers to sudden, violent outbursts in people taking steroids. As the violence spread, some observers called road rage an "epidemic." A 1996 poll indicated that aggressive driving concerned people more than drunk driving. In 1998 the U.S. Department of Transportation listed aggressive driving as one of the top three highway-safety concerns.

Sandra Ball-Rokeach, who launched the Media and Injury Prevention Program at the University of Southern California in 1991, explained that "aggressive driving is now the most common way of driving. It's not just a few crazies, it's a subculture of driving." In focus groups set up by her organization, two-thirds of drivers said they reacted to frustrating situations aggressively, and almost half admitted to deliberately braking suddenly, pulling close to another car, or driving in some other potentially dangerous way. By 1997 nearly 90 percent of motorists had experienced road rage incidents during the previous twelve months, while 60 percent admitted to losing their temper behind the wheel, according to a survey released by AAA. The most common examples of road rage include verbal abuse, hand gestures, and driving in an intimidating manner.

THE IMPLICATIONS

Reports of extreme incidences of road rage have made drivers acutely aware of their vulnerability, which leads to increased anxiety. Furthermore, when drivers feel provoked, their cars are self-contained places where they can engage in confrontations without the tense proximity of face-to-face interactions. The concern about the ease with which drivers could be provoked gave birth in the 1990s to a group of so-called road rage experts who began examining the roots of the phenomenon. John Larson, a psychiatrist at Yale University, linked certain car models to specific forms of aggressive driving behavior, saying, "BMWs, pickup trucks, sports cars, or off-road vehicles may be given aggressive motivations; thus aggressive drivers react to the 'personality' they associate with the make and model of the vehicle, not the person inside it." Arnold Nerenberg, a clinical psychologist in Whittier, California, and an expert on road rage, cited evolution as one cause. "This competitiveness on the road is similar to what you see in all social mammals," he theorized. "There is this 'I will not let you get ahead of me [mentality].'"

Leon James, a professor of psychology at the University of Hawaii who began researching driving behavior in 1997, defines road rage as a cultural problem, not an individual mental problem, because U.S. culture condones the expression of hostility when people feel wronged. He proposed that drivers should use "emotional intelligence skills" when upset by another driver. Instead of being intent on teaching the other driver a lesson, he advocated that drivers should choose to back out of an escalating conflict. Doing so, he suggested, would help drivers develop peaceful attitudes.

The righteous indignation often found at the core of hostile outbursts by drivers may be fostered by other elements in American culture. Talk shows encouraging emotional venting, such as *The Jerry Springer Show*—as well as the cultural obsession with the self, as indicated by the popularity of confessional and self-help books—promote Americans' concern for their own problems. Furthermore, technological advances such as the Internet, e-mail, and fast food have helped nurture expectations of convenience. Americans' affection for their automobiles may be the ultimate representation of their cultural obsession with convenience and the self. Sometimes purchased as an ego boost, cars allow people to feel as if they have control over their lives and environments while providing them with the convenience of self-determined travel. However, crowded roadways impede their ability to reach their destinations.

PREVENTIVE MEASURES

A study of fifty metropolitan areas by the Federal Highway Administration in the 1990s found each area clogged during rush hour. The study also predicted that congestion would subsequently spread to unspoiled locations. As the suburban sprawl across the United States continued in the 1990s, road rage appeared to be unstoppable, especially when automobiles remained Americans' preferred mode of travel. Advocates of safer roads continued to lobby for ways to ease traffic congestion through mass transit and better urban planning.

In 1997 government reports revealed that road rage was responsible for two-thirds of 41,000 fatalities from automobile accidents. Most incidents of road rage involved in those fatalities dealt with speeding, one motorist cutting off another, or a driver following too closely. By 2011 the number of road rage incidents had declined in response to greater public awareness, stricter enforcement in some areas, and targeted training for individuals involved in aggressive driving incidents. However, the AAA Foundation for Traffic Safety reported that 56 percent of all fatal car crashes still involved some form of aggressive driving.

Around 90 percent of Americans admit to feeling threatened by other drivers. Experts such as Barry Glassner suggest that the whole issue of road rage was overblown because it was easier to identify road rage as a major social problem than to deal with the issues that created an environment where it could flourish. In June 2006 journalist Richard Schlesinger told CBS News that road rage may be a result of a medical condition called intermittent explosive disorder, which causes as many as sixteen million Americans to lose control of their own behavior on a periodic basis. Twenty-first-century drivers have learned that a defensive approach behind the wheel and not giving in to anger are the best ways to avoid a confrontation that might escalate into road rage.

Sharon Yablon

SEE ALSO: *Automobile; Highway System; Suburbia.*

BIBLIOGRAPHY

Adair, Michael. *Hey! You're Driving Me Crazy! The Definitive Guide to Handling the Stress and Anxiety of Driving.* Crystal Lake, IL: A. B. Publishing, 1996.

Altman, Kyoko. "'Road Rage' Runs Rampant in High-Stress U.S. Society." CNN, July 18, 1997. Accessed June 1999. Available from http://www.cnn.com/US/9707/18/aggresive.driving/index.html

Fumento, Michael. "'Road Rage' versus Reality." *Atlantic Monthly*, August 1998, 12–17.

Gest, Emily. "Driven Mad." *New York Daily News*, October 19, 1997.

Glassner, Barry. "Still Fearful after All These Years." *Chronicle of Higher Education*, January 17, 2010.

Gordon, Larry, and Tom Gorman. "Inland Empire Leads in Fatal Road Rage." *Los Angeles Times*, March 9, 1999.

Ladd, Brian. *Autophobia: Love and Hate in the Automotive Age.* Chicago: University of Chicago Press, 2008.

Moffatt, Gregory K. *A Violent Heart: Understanding Aggressive Individuals.* New York: Praeger, 2002.

Smith, Euclid O. *When Culture and Biology Collide: Why We Are Stressed, Depressed, and Self Obsessed.* New Brunswick, NJ: Rutgers University Press, 2002.

Twitchell, James B. *Preposterous Violence: Fables of Aggression in Modern Culture.* New York: Oxford University Press, 1989.

Vest, Jason; Warren Cohen; and Mike Thapp. "Road Rage." *U.S. News & World Report*, June 2, 1997.

Road Runner and Wile E. Coyote

The Road Runner and Coyote cartoons have endured since 1949, when legendary director Chuck Jones and storyboard artist Michael Maltese created Wile E. Coyote and the Road Runner for the Warner Brothers cartoon short "Fast and Furry-Ous." The cartoon established a formula that has continued to entertain audiences for more than sixty years. The hungry Coyote ("Carnivorous Vulgaris") chases the truly wily Road Runner ("Accelleratii Incredibus") across the desert Southwest. In escalating frustration, the Coyote resorts to using a boomerang, a rocket, a boulder, jet-propelled tennis shoes, and the first in a long line of Acme products doomed to failure—the Acme Super Outfit. Each scheme backfires, leaving the Coyote on the wrong end of a boulder, falling off a cliff, or simply exploding.

As Jones recalls in *Chuck Reducks*, studio management, fearful that no one would like the cartoon duo, was reluctant to allow Jones and Maltese to create any more Coyote and Road Runner cartoons. Although it was three years before the release of the second cartoon, "Beep, Beep," Wile E. Coyote and the Road Runner proved so popular that they appeared in thirty-five cartoons together by 1966, with one, "Beep Prepared," nominated for an Academy Award in 1961. The timeless premise and comedy of these cartoons was common to many successful cartoons produced in the 1940s and 1950s: the bungling predator simply cannot outwit his smarter or just plain luckier prey.

Such classic pairing as Bugs Bunny and Elmer Fudd (Warner Brothers), Sylvester and Tweety (Warner Brothers), and Tom and Jerry (MGM Studios) thrived on this idea. What set the Coyote and Road Runner cartoons apart was the uniqueness of the characters themselves.

COYOTE'S FOLLY

The Road Runner may be one of the most irritating foes any cartoon character has faced. While Bugs, Tweety, and Jerry often display ingenuity, the Road Runner is comparatively oblivious. In the first cartoon the swift bird displays more aggression, going out of his way to irritate the Coyote. At one point, with the Coyote close on his tail, the Road Runner even looks concerned. In subsequent cartoons, as the Coyote's efforts escalate, the Road Runner generally does not seem to even notice his foe. The Road Runner does on occasion take deliberate steps to avoid a trap, but, more commonly, with nothing more than a "beep, beep" and a flick of his tongue, the Road Runner eats the birdseed without setting off traps, runs through rock walls, and stops short at the edges of cliffs while the Coyote goes toppling over.

It is Wile E. Coyote himself who creates the primary appeal of these cartoons. While other predators plow ahead, the Coyote plans, diagrams, and builds. As the cartoons progress and the Coyote's schemes become more and more violent, culminating in a plan involving dynamite or dropping a piano on the Road Runner, the audience realizes that the Coyote's quest is no longer about hunger. With the Coyote, the chase eventually becomes a matter of his wounded pride. Mute, communicating only through the occasional handheld sign or yelp of pain, his expressive face conveys emotions from cunning to frustration to confusion to fear and back again. He frequently addresses the audience, holding signs that say "Egad" or throwing a sly look toward the camera. Audiences see the effort the Coyote puts into his plans and his doomed hope, making it somehow funnier when his plans do not work.

More than anything, the characteristic that truly distinguishes the Coyote is his inability to learn from his mistakes. Despite his diagrams, his schemes fail in often surprising ways. The rocket does not take off, it just explodes; the boulder falls backward off the catapult; and the jet-propelled sneakers send him off a cliff. The Coyote often averts one mishap only to find another. When he gets his Acme Bat-Man's Outfit to work only moments before hitting the ground, he smashes into a rock wall. The Coyote faithfully uses Acme products even though, again and again, the explosives, the magnetic birdseed, and the rocket-powered roller skates do not work. The Coyote is surprisingly human in his dogged attempt to attain a goal that does not seem to be meant for him. When audiences laugh at the Coyote, it is part slapstick humor and part catharsis, part visual and part mental. People see themselves in the Coyote's continually frustrated attempts to achieve his goal, but they do not seem to have it quite as bad as the poor Coyote.

ADDITIONAL CARTOONS

The Road Runner appeared only with the Coyote. The Coyote proved to be so popular a character, however, he appeared in other Warner Brothers cartoons. Most notable is a series with Bugs Bunny. In these cartoons the Coyote is somewhat snooty and introduces himself as "Wile E. Coyote, Genius." Of course, in spite of being a genius, he cannot outwit the likes of Bugs Bunny. The Coyote also doubled as a red-nosed wolf, Ralph, in a series of cartoons with Sam the Sheepdog. Again he simply cannot seem to catch his dinner. The Coyote is ever the doomed schemer.

Cartoons featuring Wile E. Coyote and the Road Runner first appeared as "curtain-raisers" in theaters, eventually moving to television. In September 1966 *The Road Runner Show*, a repackaged version of the older cartoons, premiered in the CBS Saturday morning lineup. From the 1960s through today, the Road Runner and Coyote cartoons have been a staple of children's programming, running on the networks as well as cable stations such as TNT and the Cartoon Network.

Adrienne Furness

SEE ALSO: *Bugs Bunny; Saturday Morning Cartoons; Tweety Pie and Sylvester.*

BIBLIOGRAPHY

Barrier, J. Michael. *Hollywood Cartoons: American Animation in Its Golden Age*. Oxford: Oxford University Press, 1999.

Friedwald, Will, and Jerry Beck. *The Warner Brothers Cartoons.* Metuchen, NJ: Scarecrow Press, 1981.

Jones, Chuck. *Chuck Reducks: Drawing from the Fun Side of Life.* New York: Warner Books, 1996.

Lenburg, Jeff. *The Encyclopedia of Animated Cartoons.* New York: Facts On File, 1991.

Woolery, George W. *Children's Television: The First Thirty-Five Years, 1946–1981: Part 1: Animated Cartoon Series.* Metuchen, NJ: Scarecrow Press, 1983.

Robbins, Tom *(1936–)*

Novelist Tom Robbins, one of the foremost writers of 1970s and 1980s counterculture, joined writers Kurt Vonnegut Jr. and Robert Pirsig as the gurus of the youth market. His novels wittily debunked the powers that be and challenged conceptions of normalcy, earning him a following of college student groupies. His novels' trademarks are episodic, nonlinear structures that mimic psychedelic LSD trips; casts of eccentric characters with such names as Bonanza Jellybean and Marx Marvelous; plots that center on the quest for the meaning of life; a flamboyant style characterized by over-the-top metaphors and absurd images; and an optimistic philosophy based on Eastern mysticism, quantum physics, antimaterialism, feminism, and above all playfulness.

Robbins grew up in Virginia and was raised to be a southern gentleman, although two years at Washington and Lee University convinced him that he did not fit the mold. In the 1950s he hitchhiked across the country and was drafted into the military, serving in the air force in Korea. After the war he earned a degree from the Richmond Professional Institute and started a career as a newspaper arts critic. He fled the conservative South in 1962 and settled in the Seattle, Washington, area, where he still lives.

During the 1960s he began to experiment with LSD, which he told author Steven Dougherty ranks "right up there with the microscope and the telescope as an instrument of exploration." When he began to publish his novels, he was already a prominent figure of countercultural Seattle and New York. His first book, *Another Roadside Attraction* (1971), landed him on the national scene when it came out in paperback in 1973. Its popularity fueled by word of mouth, the novel became an instant cult favorite on college campuses. In the book, a group of eccentrics discover Christ's mummified body, bring it to a hot dog stand called Capt. Kendrick Memorial Hot Dog Wildlife Preserve, and try to disprove Christianity. The book repudiates the authority of Christianity and offers Eastern religion as a healthier alternative.

His second book, *Even Cowgirls Get the Blues* (1976), is his most popular. Within four years it sold 1.3 million copies. It tells the story of Sissy Hankshaw, a beautiful woman who learns to live with her socially unacceptable oversized thumbs by becoming the best hitchhiker in the country. She ends up at a South Dakota ranch run by cowgirl feminists, where a Japanese hermit helps show her why Americans must reach back to their spiritual roots in pantheism, which is characterized by feminine receptivity rather than masculine aggression. The book struck a chord with readers who had grown disillusioned with America's materialist and patriarchal society. In 1993, after years of failed deals, the novel was finally made into a film, starring Uma Thurman and directed by Gus Van Sant. The story was adapted for the stage in 2008.

Robbins's next novel, *Still Life with Woodpecker* (1980), a love story about a terrorist and a princess who escape their assailants through the image of the desert on a pack of Camel cigarettes, gained him popularity with a new generation of college students. However, critics were growing tired of his style and playfulness, believing him unwilling to grow up and accept the status quo. *Jitterbug Perfume* (1984), an elaborate novel loosely centered on the search for immortality, likewise landed on best-seller lists. The reviews also improved.

His next two novels, *Skinny Legs and All* (1990), which features inanimate, everyday objects as characters, and *Half Asleep in Frog Pajamas* (1994), which is told entirely in the second person, employ his trademark style but with dark themes. He followed these works with *Fierce Invalids Home from Hot Climates* (2000); *Villa Incognito* (2003); *Wild Ducks Flying Backward* (2005); and *B Is for Beer* (2009), a children's book about the alcoholic beverage. During the 1990s critics observed that he became more serious in his depiction of greed, religious fundamentalism, and destruction of the environment, turning off some readers. Some have said that his style and message have lost their appeal for a generation of readers and critics who have outgrown their attraction to absurdity and countercultural ethics. But for Robbins, critiquing the culture he lives in is not a fad but his life's work. He states his goal as a writer is to help change human consciousness: "We are in this life to enlarge the soul, liberate the spirit, and light up the brain."

Anne Boyd

SEE ALSO: *Beer; Best Sellers; Feminism; Fundamentalism; LSD; Paperbacks; Vonnegut, Kurt, Jr.*

BIBLIOGRAPHY

Dougherty, Steven. "Cowgirls May Get the Blues, but Not Tom Robbins, Who Pours It on in *Jitterbug Perfume*." *People Weekly*, April 1, 1985, 123–124.

Hoyser, Catherine E., and Lorena Laura Stookey. *Tom Robbins: A Critical Companion*. Westport, CT: Greenwood Press, 1997.

O'Connell, Nicholas. *At the Field's End: Interviews with Twenty Pacific Northwest Writers*. Seattle, WA: Madrona Publishers, 1987.

Purdon, Liam O., and Beef Torrey, eds. *Conversations with Tom Robbins*. Jackson: University Press of Mississippi, 2010.

Siegel, Mark. *Tom Robbins*. Boise, ID: Boise State University Press, 1980.

Roberts, Jake "The Snake" *(1955–)*

Part of a professional wrestling family, Jake Roberts (born Aurelian Smith Jr.) was known for bringing a pet snake into the ring and for inventing the wrestling finishing hold called "the DDT." Roberts started wrestling in 1975 but achieved his greatest success after entering the World Wrestling Federation (WWF) in 1986. Although never the star of the promotion, his interview skills, ring psychology, and pet snake gimmick kept him near the top of the card. Roberts left the WWF after Wrestlemania VIII in 1992 for a brief stint in World Championship Wrestling (WCW). After leaving WCW, he announced he had been "born again" and appeared on Christian TV stations to talk about his battles with substance abuse.

Roberts's 1996 comeback in the WWF was most notable for his loss to Stone Cold Steve Austin in a match that helped Austin win over WWF fans. Roberts left the WWF in 1997 and appeared on the independent wrestling circuit. In 1999 he was one of the subjects of the 1999 documentary *Beyond the Mat*. In the film, Roberts appears on camera while under the influence of drugs. As of 2011 Roberts had yet to be inducted into the WWF (now WWE) Hall of Fame.

Patrick Jones

SEE ALSO: *Sports Heroes; Television; World Wrestling Federation.*

BIBLIOGRAPHY

Beyond the Mat. DVD. Directed by Barry W. Blaustein. Universal City, CA: Universal Studios, 1999.

Lentz, Harris M. *Biographical Dictionary of Professional Wrestling*. Jefferson, NC: McFarland, 1997.

Roberts, Julia *(1967–)*

Julia Roberts shot to stardom in 1989 with her role as a slightly tarnished girl next door in the romantic comedy *Pretty Woman*. As Vivian Ward, a disarmingly innocent hooker who captures the libido and, eventually, the heart of a handsome millionaire (played by Richard Gere), the tall redhead with the impossibly wide smile became America's sweetheart. By the end of the twentieth century, she was the highest-paid female actress of her generation, earning $20 million per picture.

Roberts's unique charm lies in her ability to portray both the all-American fresh-faced ingenue and the alluring sex symbol, but this quality has also proven detrimental to the search for roles that are both commercially successful and artistically satisfying. Although she has taken on serious dramatic parts throughout her career, her most successful roles have been leads in other romantic comedies, notably *Notting Hill* (1999), where

Julia Roberts. *Julia Roberts starred in the movie adaptation of the popular novel* Eat, Pray, Love *in 2010.* COLUMBIA PICTURES/THE KOBAL COLLECTION.

she was paired with British actor Hugh Grant. Despite a 2001 Oscar win for the drama *Erin Brockovich*, Roberts sometimes seems destined to be forever remembered as the hooker with a heart of gold.

The youngest sister of actor Eric Roberts, she began her career in 1986 with a minor role in a film starring her brother, soon followed by a leading role in *Mystic Pizza* (1988). At age twenty two, Roberts received her first Oscar nomination for her role as a dying southern belle in the popular tearjerker *Steel Magnolias* (1989). A year later an Oscar nomination for Best Actress for *Pretty Woman* plunged Roberts into the full glare of the public eye, turning her private life into fodder for the sensationalist press. A string of romantic relationships with other well-known actors and a failed marriage to singer Lyle Lovett perpetuated the public's interest in her.

Roberts, like other comedic actresses of her generation, has struggled to dissociate her image from the romantic roles that made her famous. Although the remarkable box-office performances of the comedies *Notting Hill* and *My Best Friend's Wedding* (1997) indicate that audiences love to see her in romantic roles, the actress has repeatedly tried to branch out over the course of her career. In the 1990s her attempts to take nonromantic roles were generally unsuccessful. Performances in suspense films such as *Flatliners* (1990), *Sleeping with the Enemy* (1991), and *The Pelican Brief* (1993) were sound but met with only moderate acclaim, whereas Roberts's dramatic roles in Neil Jordan's *Michael Collins* (1996) and Stephen Frears's *Mary Reilly* (1996) were seen as lackluster.

This perception of Roberts changed when she took on the title role in the 2000 true-life drama *Erin Brockovich*, the story of a lone female lawyer who goes up against a large energy company. Since winning the Best Actress Oscar for this role, Roberts has worked steadily, taking on roles in such blockbusters as *Ocean's Eleven* (2001), *Full Frontal* (2002), and *Ocean's Twelve* (2004), as well as in more serious films: she played a 1950s professor in the women's lib flick *Mona Lisa Smile* (2003) and a maverick politician's friend in *Charlie Wilson's War* (2007). She also starred in romantic films including *Valentine's Day* (2010) and *Eat Pray Love* (2010), an adaptation of Elizabeth Gilbert's best-selling 2006 novel.

Through two pregnancies and the birth of three children (her first pregnancy resulted in twins), Roberts has continued to work as an actress and a producer, taking her first stage role in 2006's *Three Days of Rain*. She also stars as the evil stepmother/queen in *Mirror Mirror* (2012), an adaptation of the fairy tale "Snow White."

Sara Martin

SEE ALSO: *Academy Awards; Best Sellers; Blockbusters; Celebrity; Celebrity Couples; Divorce; Gere, Richard; Hollywood; Movie Stars; Sex Symbol;* Snow White and the Seven Dwarfs.

BIBLIOGRAPHY

Bego, Mark, and Nicholas Maier. *Julia Roberts: America's Sweetheart*. Boca Raton, FL: American Media, 2003.

Connelly, C. "Nobody's Fool." *Premiere*, December 1993, 70–73.

Joyce, Aileen. *Julia: The Untold Story of America's Pretty Woman*. New York: Pinnacle Books, 1993.

McInerney, Jay. "I'm 5'9" with a Famous Smile." *Harper's Bazaar*, September 1995, 400–405.

Schneller, J. "Barefoot Girl with Cheek." *Gentlemen's Quarterly*, February 1991, 158–165.

Sessums, K. "The Crown Julia." *Vanity Fair*, October 1993, 234–241.

Roberts, Nora *(1950–)*

Author Nora Roberts is one of the most prolific novelists of all time, with an output of more than 200 books, 400 million copies in print as of 2009, and more than 100 appearances on the *New York Times* best-seller list. A popular writer who specializes in paperback romances such as *Carnal Innocence* (1992), *Born in Shame* (1996), and *Chasing Fire* (2011), she broke into publishing in 1979 as a twenty-nine-year-old housewife. She turned to writing to avoid becoming stir crazy during a snowstorm that confined her to the house for a week. The experience played a major role in shaping her research and writing style, which does not depend on firsthand knowledge of the world she writes about. In fact, most of her research is performed on the Internet. "I know they say write what you know," she told *Publishers Weekly* in 1998, "but I write about what I want to know."

Her "category romances," as she terms them, rely less on reality and fully fleshed-out plots than on idealized characters and romanticized settings. She views her works as appealing to readers on an emotional level, evoking memories of first loves, bitter losses, and quiet romances. She cites readers' identification with her characters, rather than escapism, as the reason for her novels' continued popularity. Ten of her books were adapted into TV movies in the first decades of the 2000s, eight of which were produced by the women-centric Lifetime channel. Called "America's most popular novelist" by the *New Yorker*, Roberts is a founding member and inaugural inductee into the Romance Writers Hall of Fame and has earned an esteemed place among not only her fans but also her peers.

Sandra Garcia-Myers

SEE ALSO: *Cable TV; The Internet; The* New York Times*; The* New Yorker*; Paperbacks; Romance Novels.*

BIBLIOGRAPHY

Collins, Lauren. "Real Romance: How Nora Roberts Became America's Most Popular Novelist." *New Yorker*, June 22, 2009, 60.

Quinn, Judy. "Nora Roberts: A Celebration of Emotion." *Publishers Weekly*, February 23, 1998, 46.

Tichemer, Louise. "Drive, Discipline, and Desire." *Writer's Digest*, February, 1997, 25.

Robertson, Oscar *(1938–)*

Although now almost unknown to many younger basketball fans, Oscar Robertson ranks among the greatest players in the history of the sport. Red Auerbach, longtime Boston Celtic coach and general manager, called the "Big O" one of the most versatile and complete players he had ever seen. Fellow Hall of Fame member and Celtic guard John Havlicek simply stated, "Oscar was the best player I ever played against." Robertson was an unstoppable offensive force who could also pass, rebound, and play tenacious defense. At 6'5" and 220 pounds, he was the prototype of the modern "big" point guard, paving the way for more recent big players who have excelled at the position, such as Earvin "Magic" Johnson and Anfernee "Penny" Hardaway. Robertson is one of only seven guards to have ever won the National Basketball Association (NBA) Most Valuable Player (MVP) Award, along with Bob Cousy, Magic Johnson, Michael Jordan, and others.

While a collegiate player at the University of Cincinnati (1957–1960), Robertson was both a three-time National Player of the Year and three-time national scoring champion, leading the Bearcats to two appearances in the National Collegiate Athletic Association (NCAA) Final Four (1959 and 1960). He is one of only three players to have scored more than 900 points in three different seasons as a collegiate player and ranks eighth all-time on the NCAA career scoring list with 2,973 points (33.8 points per game). Prior to his collegiate career, Robertson was a two-time "Mr. Basketball" in Indiana and led Crispus Attucks High School of Indianapolis to two state championships. The capstone of his amateur career came in 1960, when Robertson was cocaptain with Jerry West of the U.S. Olympic basketball team, a group that easily won the gold medal at the games in Rome. That team is considered by many basketball experts to be among the most talented amateur teams in the history of the sport.

In 1960 Robertson was drafted by the Cincinnati Royals of the NBA and began a fourteen-year professional career that ranks among the most prolific and successful of all time. In 1961 he was voted Rookie of the Year and won the first of his three All-Star Game MVP awards. In 1964 Robertson won the league MVP. But his greatest individual accomplishment may have come in his second season (1961–1962), when he averaged a triple double for the entire season (30.8 points, 11.4 assists, and 12.5 rebounds per game). This achievement is undoubtedly his most legendary among basketball players and fans. Many modern players are lucky to attain a triple double in an individual game, let alone for an entire season, and Robertson's feat has yet to be duplicated after fifty years. Robertson was also a member of the All Star squad twelve of his fourteen seasons in the NBA.

Following the 1969–1970 season, Robertson was traded by the financially strapped Royals to the Milwaukee Bucks, where he teamed up with a young Lew Alcindor (later known as Kareem Abdul-Jabbar) to win the NBA title in 1971. Following a second appearance in the NBA Finals in 1974, Robertson retired from the league as the highest scoring guard of all time, with 26,710 points. At the time of his retirement he was also the all-time career assists leader and had made more free throws than any player in NBA history. Additionally, Robertson was an outspoken leader of the National Basketball Players Association and is credited with helping to bring free agency to the league in the 1970s. Robertson was inducted into the Naismith Memorial Basketball Hall of Fame in 1979.

Since his retirement as a player, Robertson has been a community and business leader in Cincinnati, working in both the land development and political arenas to bring economic and civic improvements to lower-income neighborhoods throughout the city. In 1997, at the age of fifty-eight, he displayed his character and love for his family by donating a kidney to his daughter, who was suffering from severe kidney failure. For his many contributions to the community, his friends, and family, Robertson is among the most beloved citizens that both Cincinnati and the broader basketball community have ever known.

G. Allen Finchum

SEE ALSO: *Abdul-Jabbar, Kareem; Auerbach, Red; Basketball; The Boston Celtics; Havlicek, John; Johnson, Earvin "Magic"; Jordan, Michael; National Basketball Association (NBA); Olympics; Russell, Bill; West, Jerry.*

BIBLIOGRAPHY

Cohen, Joel H. *Oscar Robertson.* New York: Rosen, 2001.

Dickey, Glenn. *The History of Professional Basketball since 1986.* Briarcliff Manor, NY: Stein & Day, 1982.

Sachare, Alex. *100 Greatest Basketball Players of All Time.* New York: Pocket Books, 1997.

Robertson, Pat *(1930–)*

The son of a Democratic U.S. senator from Virginia, Pat Robertson turned from a career in the law to one in religion and made himself one of the most influential and enigmatic leaders of the so-called Christian Right during the Reagan era of the 1980s and beyond. As founder of the Christian Coalition and as its president from 1989 to 1997, Robertson helped galvanize millions of evangelical Christians toward greater participation in the political process and has himself made a run for the White House.

Raised in the Southern Baptist tradition, Robertson graduated magna cum laude from Washington and Lee University in 1950. After serving as a marine corps officer during the Korean conflict, he returned to his education, receiving a JD from Yale Law School in 1955. Failures in an early business venture and his unsuccessful attempts to pass the New York bar exam helped steer him back toward his religious roots. He attended a theological seminary, graduating with a bachelor of divinity, and worked for a time with the mostly black inner-city poor in Brooklyn, New York, before returning to Virginia, where he was ordained a Southern Baptist minister in 1959.

Pat Robertson. *Pat Robertson, host of* The 700 Club, *is known for taking the lead to involve conservative Christians in the political process.* AP IMAGES.

MEDIA EMPIRE

Robertson demonstrated the intensely entrepreneurial side of his character in 1961 when he started operating WYAH, a television station in Virginia that became the first in the nation primarily devoted to religious programming. From this single station he launched what would become a veritable communications empire: the Christian Broadcasting Network (CBN), offshoots of which grew to include a relief agency; cable television holdings; the American Center for Law and Justice, which specializes in First Amendment cases; and Regent University, which came to call itself "America's premier Christian graduate school."

The flagship program of his network was *The 700 Club*, which Robertson hosted from 1966. His success both behind and before the camera led many conservative Christians to promote Robertson's involvement in U.S. politics. Though he at first thought political organizing was inconsistent with his clerical calling, he had a change of heart by the 1980s when he began to organize mobilization efforts such as a 1980 "Washington for Jesus" rally and his own Freedom Council (1981–1986). In 1984 he changed his party affiliation to Republican. When presented in 1987 with what was purported to be a petition of some 3.3 million names urging him to run for office, he resigned his church offices and launched a campaign for the 1988 Republican presidential nomination. Despite early successes in some primaries, Robertson's candidacy was decisively rejected by "Super Tuesday" in March of that year, even by many members of conservative Christian churches.

INVOLVEMENT WITH CHRISTIAN COALITION

Undaunted by his electoral failure, Robertson returned to the idea of grassroots organizing. In 1989 he founded and became the first president of the Christian Coalition, an organization whose mission was to represent evangelical opinion to government bodies, protest anti-Christian bias in public life, train leaders, and develop policies—all while being careful not to lose its tax-exempt status by supporting partisan candidates. The Christian Coalition proved very successful in enunciating the social agenda of the Religious Right in the United States. With a national membership well in excess of a million, the group raised the political profile of a hitherto-marginalized section of the population. Mirroring the Republican Party's "Contract with America," the Christian Coalition advanced its "Contract with the American Family," which was trumpeted as "A Bold Plan to Strengthen the Family and Restore Common-Sense Values." Many attributed the GOP's triumphs in 1996 congressional races to the efforts of Robertson and his branch of the Religious Right.

Robertson astonished the media world in 1997 when, on the same day he resigned the presidency of the Christian Coalition, he sold his International Family Entertainment corporation to Rupert Murdoch, a media mogul whose television and newspaper holdings had often been criticized for taking the low moral road. Robertson tried to assuage criticism by promising that the hundreds of millions of dollars the sale had generated would go toward a new global television evangelism campaign as well as to enhance the endowment of Regent University. Part of the deal with Murdoch's Fox Kids Worldwide was that *The 700 Club* would continue to be aired by the new entity and that CBN itself would remain independent.

Robertson remains a figure who defies easy characterization. For many on the political Left, he is—as described by writer Robert Boston—"the most dangerous man in America" due to his stance on such social issues as homosexuality and the role of women. Those who valued the country's multicultural heritage reacted with horror to Robertson's suggestion that only devout Christians and Jews were fit to hold public office. Other liberals decried his proposals to abolish the Corporation for Public Broadcasting and the National Endowment for the Arts. Robertson's hopes of restoring prayer to public schools and reestablishing the United States as a "Christian nation" seemed an affront to the constitutional separation of church and state and drew the ire of the Jewish Anti-Defamation League.

Robertson is neither a backwoods fundamentalist nor a one-dimensional Elmer Gantry. He is well educated, well off, and well connected, with two American presidents on his family tree, and his pragmatism has made him an enormously successful businessman. His particular brand of charismatic theology, moreover, is opposed by many right-wing Christians who are uneasy about his claim to receiving divinely inspired "words of knowledge" and his belief that even the faithful will suffer from a premillennial period of tribulation before the final coming of Christ. During the 1988 primaries, for example, Robertson's bid for the Republican nomination drew less support from members attending conservative Baptist churches than it did from other white voters. Despite the criticism he has received from some American Jewish groups, he is a leading defender of the State of Israel, which he sees in the context of biblical end-times prophecies.

For a time Robertson resumed the presidency of the Christian Coalition after the departure of Ralph Reed; he also presided over the reorganization of the group into two entities—Christian Coalition International and Christian Coalition of America—in the wake of a 1999 IRS ruling that revoked its tax-exempt status. He continues to be active in business, media, and social advocacy of issues favored by the Christian right. His capacity for stirring outrage continues to attract media attention. He seemed to attribute the 9/11 attacks in 2001 and Hurricane Katrina in 2005 to divine retribution against Americans for their permissive lifestyles; he blamed the 2010 Haiti earthquakes on a 1791 pact with the devil. He offended many fellow Christians with the suggestion that it was morally permissible to divorce a spouse with Alzheimer's disease and with revelations of financial dealings with African dictator Charles Taylor of Liberia.

Gerry Bowler

SEE ALSO: *Cable TV; Divorce; Feminism; Gay Liberation Movement; Hurricane Katrina; Multiculturalism; 9/11; Public Television (PBS); Reagan, Ronald; Religious Right; Television; World Trade Center.*

BIBLIOGRAPHY

Boston, Robert. *The Most Dangerous Man in America?: Pat Robertson and the Rise of the Christian Coalition.* Amherst, NY: Prometheus Books, 1996.

Christian Coalition of America Official Website. Accessed April 2012. Available from http://www.cc.org

Foege, Alec. *The Empire That God Built: Inside Pat Robertson's Media Machine.* New York: John Wiley, 1996.

Robertson, Pat. *America's Dates with Destiny.* Nashville, TN: Thomas Nelson, 1986.

Robertson, Pat. *The Secret Kingdom: Your Path to Peace, Love, and Financial Security.* Nashville, TN: Word Publishing, 1992.

Watson, Justin. *The Christian Coalition: Dreams of Restoration, Demands for Recognition.* New York: St. Martin's Press, 1997.

Robeson, Paul *(1898–1976)*

Paul Robeson must be counted among the most broadly talented men ever born in the United States, but the fact that he was also a "Negro" in a society that could not easily accept exceptional skills in one of his race regularly limited his opportunities to demonstrate his talents. That he accomplished so much in so many public arenas despite the restrictions he faced remains especially remarkable. At times Robeson was probably the most famous and controversial black man in America, often

Paul Robeson as Othello. *Paul Robeson performs as Othello opposite Mary Ure as Desdemona in 1959.* HULTON ARCHIVE/STRINGER/GETTY IMAGES.

simultaneously; in retrospect, his long and complex public career marks some of the high and low points in American race relations during the twentieth century.

SCHOLAR, ATHLETE, AND ACTOR

Although Robeson frequently faced racism and, eventually, political intolerance, he nevertheless excelled in whatever field he entered: he was an excellent scholar, an all-American athlete, a riveting stage and screen actor, a spellbinding orator, and one of America's most powerful folk singers. Born and raised in New Jersey, Robeson acted, sang, and delivered speeches in high school before entering Rutgers University, where he then triumphed in several sports, was elected to Phi Beta Kappa in his junior year, and addressed his graduating class as valedictorian.

While attending Columbia University Law School, Robeson played professional football with the Akron Pros and made his professional stage debut. Recognizing the barriers facing black lawyers, he concentrated on his theatrical career after graduation, accepting lead roles in Eugene O'Neill's *All God's Chillun Got Wings* and *The Emperor Jones* in 1924. In the same year Robeson made his screen debut in the independent film *Body and Soul* (directed by African American Oscar Micheaux), signaling his career-long attempt to address both mainstream and minority audiences.

By 1925 Robeson was frequently recording and singing in concert, as if no single entertainment form could contain his talents; by 1929 he could easily fill both London's Royal Albert Hall and New York's Carnegie Hall. In 1928 he was added to the cast of Jerome Kern and Oscar Hammerstein's *Show Boat*, beginning his indelible association with the pseudospiritual "Ol' Man River," originally a cry of resignation that he eventually reformed in concert as a defiant protest song. By the time the watershed musical was filmed in 1936, Robeson's fame demanded that his small but crucial role be filled out with additional songs provided by the show's composers. Robeson and his wife, Eslanda, appeared in the experimental film *Borderline* in 1930, and in 1933 *The Emperor Jones* was adapted as Robeson's first talkie. In 1930 he had also opened in London to rave reviews as William Shakespeare's Othello, a role that, along with O'Neill's Brutus Jones and *Show Boat*'s Joe, he would often reprise in later years.

POLITICAL ACTIVISM

As early as 1933 Robeson had become involved with leftist organizations and causes, and his direct involvement with international politics intensified as he continued to act, sing, and make films. Traveling extensively in the late 1930s, he supported the Republicans in Spain fighting Francisco Franco's Fascists; sang for dozens of working-class organizations; denounced racial discrimination in every form; and regularly defended the Soviet Union, even after the signing of the Nazi-Soviet Nonaggression Pact in 1939.

Although a number of Robeson's films from this period—including *Song of Freedom* (1936), *Jericho* (1937), *Big Fella* (1937), and *The Proud Valley* (1940)—tacitly supported his political views and growing attachment to Africa, others, such as *Sanders of the River* (1934) and *King Solomon's Mines* (1937), placed him uncomfortably in the role of the exotic native within nostalgic colonialist fantasies. After appearing as an ignorant sharecropper in *Tales of Manhattan* (1942), Robeson announced his rejection of Hollywood films. Almost all of his films, whether produced in Hollywood or Europe, betray their uncertainty about how to depict a charismatic black man in entertainment directed at white audiences, so that even Robeson's apparent strengths were usually qualified. As Richard Dyer argues in *Heavenly Bodies: Film Stars and Society*, in his films "Robeson was taken to embody a set of specifically black qualities—naturalness, primitiveness, simplicity, and others—that were equally valued and similarly evoked, but for different reasons, by whites and blacks."

A high point in Robeson's singing career came in late 1940, when he sang "Ballad for Americans" on the radio. Once recorded, the patriotic piece became one of his best-known numbers. While performing the "Ballad" at the Hollywood Bowl, Robeson set an attendance record by drawing a crowd of 30,000 listeners.

Following World War II, Robeson regularly drew attention to the restrictions preventing African American achievement in the United States, leading the Crusade against Lynching to Washington and meeting with President Harry Truman in 1946. In 1949 two Robeson concerts held in Peekskill, New York, were disrupted by riots, and in the following year the State Department refused to issue Robeson a passport to travel outside of the United States, a restriction that would not be lifted until 1956. This resulted in such bizarre circumstances as his singing to 40,000 listeners across the Canadian border in 1952. Declining health and persistent suspicions regarding Robeson's earlier communist and Soviet affiliations prevented him from participating fully in the prominent civil rights struggles of the 1960s, but his last decade was marked by a number of awards and affirmations that would have been unthinkable only a decade earlier, including the renaming of a number of Rutgers University buildings after the school's prominent alumnus. When Robeson died in the first month of the American bicentennial, more than 5,000 people attended his funeral.

Although by any measure a remarkable individual, Robeson was fated to represent his race even when his views clashed with those of many other African Americans. Often he was a proud and willing representative of black America, but the persistent demand that he stand for others also exceeded his control, forcing Robeson to carry an impossible symbolic weight. In the long run, the dignity with which he bore the burden of America's racial heritage far outweighs his—or anyone else's—inability to fully contain the varied meanings of blackness in and beyond Robeson's lifetime.

Corey K. Creekmur

SEE ALSO: *Civil Rights Movement; Communism; Harlem Renaissance; Kern, Jerome; Lynching; McCarthyism; O'Neill, Eugene; Rodgers and Hammerstein;* Show Boat.

BIBLIOGRAPHY

Brown, Lloyd L. *The Young Paul Robeson: On My Journey Now.* Boulder, CO: Westview Press, 1996.

Duberman, Martin B. *Paul Robeson: A Biography.* New York: Knopf, 1988.

Dyer, Richard. *Heavenly Bodies: Film Stars and Society.* New York: St. Martin's, 1986.

Robeson, Eslanda Goode. *Paul Robeson: Negro.* New York: Harper & Brothers, 1930.

Robeson, Paul. *Here I Stand.* Boston: Beacon Press, 1971.

Robeson, Paul, and Philip S. Foner, ed. *Paul Robeson Speaks: Writings, Speeches, Interviews, 1918–1974.* New York: Brunner/Mazel, 1978.

Robeson, Susan. *The Whole World in His Hands: A Pictorial Biography of Paul Robeson.* Secaucus, NJ: Citadel Press, 1981.

Stewart, Jeffrey C., ed. *Paul Robeson: Artist and Citizen.* New Brunswick, NJ: Rutgers University Press, 1998.

Robinson, Edward G. *(1893–1973)*

Actor Edward G. Robinson remains inextricably linked with the establishment in the early 1930s of a new, popular, and influential genre in the cinema: the Warner Brothers Pictures gangster movie. The films reflected an era overshadowed by the Great Depression, Prohibition, and the reign of notorious Chicago mobster Al Capone; expanded into hard-hitting social-conscience dramas; and progressed to film noir in the 1940s with Humphrey Bogart at the center of the Warner contribution. This significant strand in film history dates from *Little Caesar* (1931), which enhanced the reputation of Warner Brothers, unleashed a torrent of similar films—established the producer credentials of Darryl F. Zanuck and Hal Wallis and the reputation of director Mervyn LeRoy—and made Robinson into a huge star.

Robinson was a man of many contradictions. Despite his world-famous screen image as a crude gangster, in the course of his career he demonstrated his artistry and versatility many times over, segueing from mobsters to blue-collar workers, businessmen, and detectives. Offscreen he was a highly cultured person who, over the course of a lifetime, managed to amass two art collections of museum quality. He preferred working in the theater and reluctantly turned to movies when the Depression hit, the switch making him an instant sensation as a gangster in *Little Caesar*, which then led to a long and successful career—even though he claimed never to enjoy the piecemeal process of filming. Despite his stardom, he avoided the trappings of celebrity, yet, like many prominent Hollywood citizens of liberal bent, he ran afoul of the House Committee on Un-American Activities (HUAC)—a misfortune that he met by returning triumphantly to the stage. His last years were spent as one of cinema's elder statesmen, gracing films from science fiction to melodrama with his innate dignity and now-vintage craft.

U.S. ARRIVAL

Born in Bucharest in 1893, Emanuel Goldenberg arrived with his Romanian Jewish family in the United States when he was ten years old. The child was fluent in multiple languages, none of them English, but he quickly picked up the language from his young classmates and from the Shakespearean actors whose performances thrilled him from his vantage point in the top balcony. He was involved with school plays and eventually chose a theatrical career. It was while training at the American Academy of Dramatic Arts that Emanuel became Edward G. Robinson. His short stature and thick features gave him no hope of ever becoming a leading man, but he was still determined to become a successful actor. After a stint in the navy during World War I that interrupted his progress, he returned to begin a career on the New York stage, appearing in numerous plays.

LITTLE CAESAR

Robinson appeared in his first film, *The Bright Shawl*, in 1923 and did not make another until *The Hole in the Wall* (1929). He went to Hollywood to play a gangster in *A Lady to Love* (1930), based on Sidney Howard's play *They Knew What They Wanted*, and made four more films that year. One of them was *The Widow from Chicago*, in which he played a Prohibition beer racketeer. It was his first film for Warner Brothers, which went on to cast him in the title role in the film version of W. R. Burnett's gangster novel, *Little Caesar* (inspired by the career of Capone). In director LeRoy's fast-moving film, the stocky, diminutive New York actor electrified audiences, whether sneering, shooting, or uttering one of cinema's most well-remembered curtain lines: "Mother of mercy, is this the end of Rico?" For years thereafter, all a comedian had to do was clench an imaginary cigar and sneer, "Nyah," for the audience to recognize his impression of Robinson's iconic mobster. Well into the 1940s and 1950s, comics and animated cartoons were caricaturing Robinson's "Rico" face and mannerisms. (Late in his life, Robinson himself jokingly closed off a TV commercial by imitating that famous "Nyah.")

TOUGH GUY ROLES

Throughout the 1930s Robinson, along with James Cagney and Bogart, made up a triumvirate of Warner Brothers' preeminent tough guys. Not content to become stereotyped, however, Robinson sought other roles as often as he could, going so far as to satirize himself in John Ford's *The Whole Town's Talking* (1935), playing a milquetoast office clerk mistaken for a public enemy. He was a fight manager in Michael Curtiz's *Kid Galahad* (1937), the chief investigating G-man in *Confessions of a Nazi Spy* (1939), and the doctor who discovered the cure for syphilis in the biopic *Dr. Ehrlich's Magic Bullet* (1940)—his personal favorite. During and after World War II, Robinson excelled at portraying both the lighter and darker facets of the American businessman, from the insurance investigator in Billy Wilder's classic *Double Indemnity* (1944) to the war profiteer getting his comeuppance in *All My Sons* (1948), from Arthur Miller's somber play. In two classic Fritz Lang noirs, *The Woman in the Window* (1944) and *Scarlet Street* (1945), Robinson personified to perfection the mild-mannered Everyman caught in a grim web of fate.

MCCARTHYISM

The McCarthy era could well have seemed to Robinson a real-life evocation of Lang's dark vision. Never openly accused of disloyalty yet unable to find work, Robinson made no less than four humiliating appearances at HUAC before his career could resume in full. Ironically, the lack of Hollywood opportunities drove Robinson into a triumphant return to stage acting in Arthur Koestler's anticommunist drama *Darkness at Noon* (1951). He was forced back into gangster mode in a handful of second-league films, but 1956 saw him in the star-filled lineup of Cecil B. DeMille's remake of *The Ten Commandments* and marked his successful Broadway starring role in Paddy Chayefsky's *Middle of the Night*. But 1956 was unfortunately also the year of Robinson's divorce, after nearly three decades of marriage, from Gladys Lloyd, the terms of which forced the actor (and amateur painter) to sell off his precious art collection.

Eventually, Robinson amassed a second art collection equally as distinguished as his first and enjoyed a second marriage with Jane Adler. In 1973 the eighty-year-old veteran filmed his last part, a death scene in *Soylent Green* (1973), in which Sol, an old man, submits himself to euthanasia while bidding farewell to images of a beautiful world. Within a few months Robinson, the revered artistic tough guy, was dead of cancer. In his last days he had been informed that he would be receiving an honorary Academy Award—his first. His widow accepted it for him.

Preston Neal Jones

SEE ALSO: *Academy Awards; Bogart, Humphrey; Broadway; Cagney, James; Chayefsky, Paddy; DeMille, Cecil B.;* Double Indemnity*; Film Noir; Ford, John; Lang, Fritz; McCarthyism; Miller, Arthur;* The Ten Commandments*; Wilder, Billy; Zanuck, Darryl F.*

BIBLIOGRAPHY

Gansberg, Alan L. *Little Caesar: A Biography of Edward G. Robinson.* Lanham, MD: Scarecrow Press, 2004.

McDowall, Roddy. *Double Exposure.* New York: Delacorte Press, 1966.

McGilligan, Patrick. *Fritz Lang: The Nature of the Beast.* New York: St. Martin's Press, 1997.

Robinson, Edward G., and Leonard Spigelgass. *All My Yesterdays.* New York: Hawthorn, 1973.

Shay, Don. *Conversations.* Albuquerque, NM: Kaleidoscope Press, 1969.

Robinson, Frank *(1935–)*

In the Cleveland Indians' first win of the 1975 season, the team's new manager, Frank Robinson, achieved the distinction of entering his own name in the lineup and hitting a home run. A standout ballplayer for more than two decades, Robinson is perhaps equally remembered for being Major League Baseball's first black manager. As the only major leaguer to win the Most Valuable Player (MVP) Award in each league (1961 in the National League with the Cincinnati Reds, 1966 in the American League with the Baltimore Orioles), Robinson was one of those rare players who combined power, an excellent batting average, base-stealing ability, and solid defense. When he retired as a player in 1976 to focus solely on managing, his 586 home runs were fourth on the all-time list. Although his managerial career was somewhat less successful, he displayed the same level of intensity he had as a player.

A STAR PLAYER

Robinson was signed by the Reds out of McClymonds High School in Oakland, California, in 1953. Three years later he began his major-league career as an unknown twenty-year-old outfielder. By season's end, however, he had established himself as a star, tying the rookie record of thirty-eight home runs. In 1947 another Robinson—Jackie—had paved the way for the first generation of black ballplayers, which included Roy Campanella and Larry Doby. Thus, when Frank Robinson began his major-league career in 1956 (the same year Jackie played his final season), blacks had been in major-league baseball for less than a decade. Robinson, Willie Mays (1951–1973), Hank Aaron (1954–1976), Ernie Banks (1953–1971), and Bob Gibson (1959–75) were part of a remarkable second generation of black players.

In his nine years in Cincinnati, Robinson was a perennial All-Star who struck fear into opposing pitchers with his bat and played the game aggressively in the field and on the base paths. He led the 1961 Reds to their first pennant in twenty-one years, winning the National League MVP Award with a .323 batting average and thirty-seven home runs. His follow-up season was equally spectacular, as Robinson achieved new career highs in runs (134), hits (208), doubles (51), home runs (39), runs batted in (136), and batting average (.342). After the 1965 season, however, the Reds' front office judged Robinson to be an "old thirty" and traded him to the Orioles. The deal proved to be a boon for the Orioles, who captured their first world championship in 1966 with Robinson leading the way. That year Robinson won baseball's coveted Triple Crown by leading the American League in home runs (49), runs batted in (122), and batting average (.316) en route to another MVP award.

The Orioles went on to win another three American League pennants (1969–1971) and a second World Series title (1970) during Robinson's six seasons in Baltimore. The team's biggest strength was pitching, though Robinson, third baseman Brooks Robinson, and first baseman Boog Powell provided plenty of offense. Back in the National League with the Los Angeles Dodgers in 1972, Robinson appeared to be slowing down. However, when he was traded to the California Angels in 1973, his career was extended by the American League's adoption that year of the designated hitter rule, which enabled older players such as Robinson to hit while not having to play the field.

BREAKING INTO MANAGING

Robinson was hired as the team's player-manager in 1975, breaking another color barrier in baseball. Midway through the 1977 season, a year after hanging up his spikes as a player, he also became the first black major-league manager to be fired. He experienced modest success at the helm of the San Francisco Giants from 1981 through 1984 but failed to lead them to a playoff berth. Perhaps his most painful year as a manager was 1988, when he was hired by the Orioles after the team lost its first six games. Unfortunately for Robinson and for Orioles fans, the team continued its losing streak, setting a league record with twenty-one losses in a row on its way to a last-place finish. The next year was considerably more successful: the Orioles finished only two games behind the first-place Toronto Blue Jays in the American League East Division, resulting in the American League Manager of the Year Award for Robinson.

Robinson continued at the helm of the Orioles until 1991, but like many former stars who have tried managing, he did not enjoy the success he had as a player. After not managing for a decade, he returned to the dugout in 2002 with the Montreal Expos. The team moved to Washington, D.C., in 2005 and changed its name to the Nationals, and Robinson continued as manager through 2006.

Throughout his managerial career, Robinson was outspoken about racial issues in baseball, calling attention to the underrepresentation of blacks in front-office positions. In 1982 he was elected to the National Baseball Hall of Fame on the first ballot. Robinson received another honor in 2005 when he was given the Presidential Medal of Freedom. In presenting him with the award, President George W. Bush noted, "In the game we love, few names will ever command as much respect and esteem as the name of Frank Robinson."

Kevin O'Connor

SEE ALSO: *Aaron, Hank; Baseball; Doby, Larry; Gibson, Bob; Major League Baseball; Mays, Willie; Robinson, Jackie; Sports Heroes; World Series.*

BIBLIOGRAPHY

Robinson, Frank, and Dave Anderson. *Frank: The First Year.* New York: Holt, Rinehart & Winston, 1976.

Robinson, Frank, and Al Silverman. *My Life in Baseball.* Garden City, NY: Doubleday, 1975.

Robinson, Frank, and Berry Stainback. *Extra Innings.* New York: McGraw-Hill, 1988.

Rosenthal, Ken. "Q&A: Frank Robinson." *Sporting News,* May 20, 1995, 44.

Thorn, John; Pete Palmer; and David Reuther, eds. *Total Baseball.* New York: Warner Books, 1989.

Robinson, Jackie *(1919–1972)*

When Jackie Robinson broke Major League Baseball's color barrier in 1947, he was both hailed as a hero and vilified as a traitor. So much attention was paid to the color of his skin that it took the public a little while to realize the scope of his talents. When they did, it only increased the animosity of those who were determined to keep America's national pastime an all-white bastion. Nevertheless, with his quiet dignity and brilliant athleticism, Robinson tore down the walls of bigotry, forever changing the course of American sports.

BASEBALL'S SLOW INTEGRATION

Although nineteenth-century baseball had fielded all-black teams and even featured a few black players on white teams, twentieth-century major-league baseball had steadfastly been a white-only sport. Black players found an outlet for the sport in various incarnations of the Negro Leagues throughout the first half of the twentieth century. These leagues were widely acclaimed among management, players, and fans of major-league baseball, both for the depth and scope of their talent as well as for the unique style of quick, tough, and athletic baseball that was played. Stars of the Negro Leagues such as catcher and slugger Josh Gibson, center fielder and brilliant base-runner Cool Papa Bell, and the extraordinary pitcher Satchel Paige were known to be as good or better than their white contemporaries such as Babe Ruth and Lou Gehrig. The only time they could play against these white players, however, was in rare exhibition games.

Although integration was often discussed by fans, owners, and players alike, not until the United States entered World War II in 1941 was there any real thought that it might happen. Major League Baseball's ranks were quickly decimated as players joined the armed services. Baseball's commissioner, Judge Kenesaw Mountain Landis, was adamant on the subject of integration: as long as he remained commissioner, Major League Baseball would remain all white. Nonetheless, as the war drew to a close and baseball's ranks remained depleted by the war, the subject continued to surface, and the stars of the Negro Leagues dared to hope that one day they would play in the majors.

Commissioner Landis's death, in 1944, brought a new commissioner, Albert Benjamin "Happy" Chandler, whose views on integration were diametrically opposed to those of his predecessor. Chandler said, "I'm for the Four Freedoms. If a black boy can make it in Okinawa and Guadalcanal, hell, he can make it in baseball." A secret vote held among club owners revealed, however, that all but one of them opposed integration—that person was Branch Rickey of the Brooklyn Dodgers.

A God-fearing, teetotaling Christian and a staunch Republican, Rickey had revolutionized Major League Baseball when he created the first farm system for the St. Louis Cardinals. He was now president, part owner, and general manager of the Dodgers, and he firmly believed that integration would not only be good for the country and for baseball but also would mean big business. All he needed was the right man for the job. That man, he ultimately decided, was Jackie Robinson.

ROBINSON'S EARLY YEARS

Jack Roosevelt Robinson was born on January 31, 1919, in Cairo, Georgia. When his father abandoned the family, Robinson's strong-willed mother, Mallie, moved her five children west

Jackie Robinson. *Jackie Robinson, the first African American to break the color barrier in the major leagues, played for the Brooklyn Dodgers from 1947 to 1956.* **PHOTO FILE/CONTRIBUTOR/MAJOR LEAGUE BASEBALL/GETTY IMAGES.**

to the predominately all-white town of Pasadena, California, where her half-brother was living. Although poor, Mallie found a way to provide her children with a good home and a solid education. She quickly realized that two of her sons were precocious young athletes. Mack excelled in track and field and would eventually earn a spot on the 1936 Olympic team, placing second to Jesse Owens in Berlin in the 200-meter dash.

Mallie's youngest son, Jackie, preferred team sports along with the jumping events in track and field. In high school he played baseball, basketball, tennis, and football. Following high school, he enrolled at Pasadena Junior College, where he devoted most of his energy to football, at which he excelled. After two years he was heavily recruited by many of the West Coast universities. Robinson chose the University of California at Los Angeles (UCLA), where he would become the first player to letter in four sports—football, basketball, track, and baseball.

When the United States entered World War II in 1941, so did Robinson. Black servicemen still faced extreme racial discrimination. Despite being a nationally recognized athlete, Robinson was no exception. He was eventually admitted to officer candidate school and obtained a commission as a second lieutenant. He continued to be hounded by racism, however, eventually being subjected to court-martial proceedings based on trumped-up charges. After Robinson was acquitted of the charges against him, he left the army in 1944 with an honorable discharge.

Robinson soon took a job playing baseball in the Negro Leagues. After a year of hitting .387 with the Monarchs, he was invited in 1945 to meet Rickey. In their now-legendary exchange, Rickey told Robinson that he needed not only a great black player to integrate Major League Baseball but also a great man—someone who would be able to stand up to the abuse he was sure to receive and have the guts not to fight back. After a few minutes of consideration, Robinson accepted Rickey's offer.

On October 23, 1945, Rickey announced that the Montreal Royals, Brooklyn's AAA farm team, had signed Robinson to a contract. Robinson spent the next season in Montreal, playing superb baseball, undergoing daily taunts and abuse from fans and players alike, and ultimately leading the Royals to victory in the Minor League World Series.

SUCCESS IN THE MAJORS

In 1947 Robinson was called up to the Brooklyn Dodgers, despite the opposition of some of the southern players on the team, who initially refused to have an African American teammate—but Rickey and Robinson were ready to make history. On April 15, 1947, 26,623 fans—more than half of whom were African American—turned up to watch Robinson play. Although the play in his first game was anticlimactic, the crowd was electrified, as crowds would be all season everywhere the Dodgers played. Robinson endured verbal abuse from fans and players alike; deliberate spikings from opposing teams; and even death threats aimed at his wife, Rachel, and their young son. Yet Robinson kept his promise to Rickey and never reacted. In the meantime, he brought a brilliant new style of baseball to the major leagues.

As Ken Burns writes:

> It was Robinson's style as much as his statistics or his color that made him a star; the fast, scrambling style of play Negro Leaguers called "tricky baseball" has been largely absent from the big leagues since Ty Cobb's day. Robinson brought it back, flustering pitchers by dancing off first base, even stealing home (something he would manage to accomplish nineteen times before he was through).

In just his first year in the majors, Robinson would be voted Rookie of the Year, hitting twelve home runs, stealing twenty-nine bases, and boasting a .297 average. He would also lead the Dodgers to a National League pennant.

With Robinson's success in the majors, the American League soon had their first African American player when the Cleveland Indians signed Larry Doby and then perhaps the greatest Negro League star of them all, Satchel Paige. More and more great African American players became baseball stars in the ensuing years, from the Giants' Willie Mays to the Cardinals' Curt Flood to the Braves' Hank Aaron. It was Robinson, however, who continued to symbolize the integration of America's national pastime. Nevertheless, Robinson was never content to be a mere figurehead. Rather, he became a team leader and a National League Most Valuable Player who, through his brilliant play, helped transform the once hapless Dodgers into a team of perennial contenders.

In 1955 the Dodgers won their eighth pennant. Seven times before they had entered the World Series as National League champions, and seven times they had lost. Although he was thirty-five years old, Robinson was still a terror on the base paths. His intimidating base running would help lead the Dodgers to their first World Series championship. A little more than a year later, after ten years in the major leagues, Robinson retired.

LIFE IN RETIREMENT

For the next seventeen years, until his death in 1972, Robinson lived an extraordinary yet difficult life. Nominated to the National Baseball Hall of Fame in 1962, his legend as a baseball star continued to grow. He used his fame to bring the public's attention to the African American struggle to end racial discrimination, becoming a staunch and outspoken supporter of the civil rights movement. Toward the end of his life, he struggled with illness and suffered the death of his eldest son. Robinson died in 1972, at age fifty-three. Eulogized by athletes, politicians, and presidents, Robinson was hailed as a hero—a courageous man, an outstanding athlete, and a trailblazer for humanity. In 1997 Major League Baseball honored Robinson by retiring his number, 42, forever.

In the early twenty-first century, the legacy of Robinson continues to grow, receiving recognition from organizations as diverse as the U.S. Postal Service and the UCLA Bruins baseball team. Many buildings bear his name, memorial statues and plaques attest to his impact, and on April 15 each year since 2007 major-league players observe Jackie Robinson Day by wearing the number 42 to commemorate the anniversary of Robinson's opening day. In 2005 Robinson was posthumously awarded a Congressional Gold Medal for his lasting influence on American culture.

Victoria Price

SEE ALSO: *Aaron, Hank; Baseball; Basketball; The Brooklyn Dodgers; Burns, Ken; Civil Rights Movement; Cobb, Ty; College Football; Doby, Larry; Gehrig, Lou; Major League Baseball; Mays, Willie; Negro Leagues; Olympics; Owens, Jesse;*

Paige, Satchel; Ruth, Babe; Sports Heroes; World Series; World War II.

BIBLIOGRAPHY

Eig, Jonathan. *Opening Day: The Story of Jackie Robinson's First Season*. New York: Simon & Schuster, 2007.

Falkner, David. *Great Time Coming: The Life of Jackie Robinson, from Baseball to Birmingham*. New York: Simon & Schuster, 1995.

Kahn, Roger. *The Boys of Summer*. New York: Harper Perennial, 1971.

Rampersand, Arnold. *Jackie Robinson: A Biography*. New York: Alfred A. Knopf, 1997.

Robinson, Jackie, and Alfred Duckett. *I Never Had It Made: An Autobiography of Jackie Robinson*. New York: Putnam, 1972.

Tygiel, Jules. *Baseball's Great Experiment: Jackie Robinson and His Legacy*. New York: Oxford University Press, 1983.

Ward, Geoffrey, and Ken Burns. *Baseball: An Illustrated History*. New York: Alfred A. Knopf, 1994.

Robinson, Smokey *(1940–)*

William "Smokey" Robinson did more to define the Motown sound than anyone except studio founder Berry Gordy. Involved in all facets of the operation—songwriter, producer, vice president, member of the quality-control board that approved or rejected every candidate for single release—Robinson somehow found time for a successful singing career, first as leader of the Miracles and then as a solo artist. Along the way, he set a standard for clever wordplay and smooth crooning that has rarely been equaled.

Robinson was born in Detroit, Michigan, on February 19, 1940. He put together his first vocal group, the Matadors, at the age of fourteen. They were a smooth doo-wop group in the tradition of the Five Satins or the Platters. In 1957 the Matadors became the Miracles, when original member Emerson Rogers went into the army and was replaced by his sister Claudette, who would later become Mrs. Smokey Robinson and retire from the group. From the start, Robinson had a hand in writing the group's material, as well as handling most of the leads with his pure, expressive tenor. He met Gordy in 1957, and together they wrote the Miracles' first local hit, "Got a Job," an answer to the Silhouettes' "Get a Job." When Gordy started his own Motown label with his modest songwriting royalties and a loan from his parents, the Miracles were one of the first acts he signed, and Motown's 1960 breakthrough hit was a Miracles tune written by Robinson—"Shop Around."

Robinson soon branched out into songwriting and production for other Motown artists. He wrote and produced nearly every hit single for the label's first bona fide star, Mary Wells, including her number one hit "My Guy." More than his early Miracles numbers, which were often simplistic, this song showed Robinson's genius at creating intelligent, moving music within the restrictions of the pop single format. He also wrote the first charting Supremes single, "Breathtaking Guy," though their incredible run of success came later with the Holland-Dozier-Holland writing/production team.

From 1963 to 1965, Motown grew at an unprecedented rate, and Robinson grew along with it. His hits with the Miracles included "Mickey's Monkey," "The Tracks of My Tears," "Going to a Go-Go," and "Ooo Baby Baby." He was also chief songwriter for the Temptations, giving them "The Way You Do the Things You Do," "My Girl," and "Get Ready." Robinson was demanding in the studio and often recorded dozens of takes of a track before he was satisfied, but his perfectionism resulted in many of the most well-crafted, memorable recordings of the 1960s. His catchy melodies, painstaking arrangements, and cliché-free love song lyrics influenced such 1960s giants as the Beatles, who covered his "You've Really Got a Hold on Me," and Bob Dylan, who once called Robinson "America's greatest living poet."

Robinson scored more hits in the late 1960s—"I Second That Emotion," "Baby Baby Don't Cry," and "The Tears of a Clown" (his first number one single as a performer)—but musical tastes were changing. The Temptations left Robinson behind, reaching new commercial heights with the psychedelic funk of producer Norman Whitfield. The Holland-Dozier-Holland team had left Motown, and flagship acts the Supremes and Four Tops were struggling. The tuneful precision exemplified by Motown at its peak had lost popularity to the rawer sounds of hard rock being incorporated by James Brown and Aretha Franklin.

After a number of lackluster albums, Robinson left the Miracles, but he was unable to resist the lure of recording, and regained chart success with the 1975 solo album *A Quiet Storm*, which adopted the long-song formats and thematic coherency of his former protégés Marvin Gaye and Stevie Wonder. Though he scored a number of hits in his second singing career, including "Cruisin'," "Being with You," and "Just to See Her," Robinson had nothing like his former influence over the pop scene. His key contribution came with the rapid maturity of the pop song in the early and mid-1960s, for which he is still respected and revered.

Robinson was inducted into the Rock and Roll Hall of Fame as a solo artist in 1987, received a Grammy Lifetime Achievement Award in 1999, and received the National Medal of Arts in 2002. He has performed on numerous late-night shows and award shows and acted as a mentor for the eighth season of *American Idol* in 2009.

David B. Wilson

SEE ALSO: American Idol; *The Beatles; Blues; Brown, James; Doo-wop Music; Dylan, Bob; Franklin, Aretha; Gaye, Marvin; Gordy, Berry; Grammy Awards; Motown; Pop Music; Rhythm and Blues; Rock and Roll; Ross, Diana, and the Supremes; The Temptations; Top 40; Wells, Mary; Wonder, Stevie.*

BIBLIOGRAPHY

Gulla, Bob. *Icons of R&B and Soul: An Encyclopedia of the Artists Who Revolutionized Rhythm.* Westport, CT: Greenwood Press, 2008.

Robinson, William "Smokey," and David Ritz. *Smokey: Inside My Life.* New York: Jove Books, 1990.

Robinson, Sugar Ray *(1921–1989)*

Sugar Ray Robinson's abilities and accomplishments made him the idol not only of a generation of boxing fans but of a genera-

LaMotta vs. Robinson. *Sugar Ray Robinson, right, lands an uppercut on champion Jake LaMotta on his way to winning the world middleweight title in 1951.* AP IMAGES.

tion of boxers as well. Muhammad Ali, for one, idolized Robinson. During the 1940s and 1950s, Robinson dominated boxing like no one else, sometimes on the front pages of the newspapers and always in the ring.

Born Walker Smith—and later nicknamed "Sugar" for his sweet-as-sugar style of fighting—he originally borrowed the identity of a friend named Ray Robinson in order to enter an amateur boxing tournament for which he was under the required age. Known in the ring for his raw athletic ability, refined boxing skill, and devastating punching power, Robinson was identifiable outside the ring by his handsome features and flashy pink Cadillac, both of which he sported all over New York City and especially in Harlem. In an era when most fighters did what they were told when they were told, Robinson remained independent, refusing to do business with organized crime and negotiating many of the contracts for his own fights by himself. His reputation as a tough negotiator is legendary, and the fact that he in effect managed his own career is part of his legacy as an American original.

Robinson began fighting professionally in 1940 and retired for the final time in 1965. Along the way he defeated a list of champions and near-champions that reads like a roll call of the Boxing Hall of Fame. At his best, as a welterweight (147 pounds), he was nearly invincible. As an older middleweight (160 pounds), he became a five-time champion. Nearly all the fighters who fought him and nearly all the fans who watched him fight insist that Robinson was the best ever. The great Jake LaMotta (of *Raging Bull* fame) managed one single victory against Robinson in six fights, and LaMotta outweighed him in many of their fights by up to 16 pounds. Because the only fighters able to compete with Robinson were fighters larger than him, writers began referring to Robinson as "pound for pound" the best fighter in the world. Indeed, by the time he completed his career, he was known as the greatest fighter, pound for pound, in the history of boxing. He out-boxed all the boxers and out-slugged all the sluggers. "Robinson could knock you out with either hand, while he was going backwards!" was the mantra of those who watched his career unfold.

The title *Pound for Pound* is not the only expression developed for the express purpose of describing the career of Robinson. The term *entourage*, widely used in the sporting world of the 1990s, was rather new to the boxing world when it was first used to describe the gang of hangers-on that surrounded Robinson. During the height of his career, after winning the middleweight title against LaMotta in 1951, Robinson and his entourage toured Europe for a year, living the good life. Along the way, however, he lost the title to an Englishman named Randy Turpin. Though Robinson got serious for the rematch and won back the title a few months later, it was becoming clear that interests other than boxing were beginning to occupy the time of the greatest fighter the world had ever seen. Sure enough, Robinson retired in 1952 to become a nightclub entertainer, doing song and dance acts—and not doing them very well.

By 1955 he was back in the ring, winning and losing the title three more times before finally hanging up his gloves for good at the age of forty-five—ancient for a boxer. Robinson occupies a niche similar to that of Babe Ruth or Michael Jordan, if not in popular culture, then at least in the history of sports. All three were thoroughly dominant during their sport's golden age, and all three represent the standard by which greatness in their sport is measured.

Robinson's greatness was acknowledged when the Associated Press named him its Fighter of the Century in 1999—and also proclaimed him both the greatest welterweight and middleweight boxer. In 2006 he was honored on a commemorative stamp by the U.S. Postal Service. Other boxers have paid him the ultimate homage by adopting his nickname, including Sugar Ray Leonard.

Max Kellerman

SEE ALSO: *Ali, Muhammad; Boxing; The Fifties; Jordan, Michael; LaMotta, Jake; Leonard, Sugar Ray; Mafia/Organized Crime;* Raging Bull*; Ruth, Babe; Sports Heroes.*

BIBLIOGRAPHY

Boyd, Herb, and Ray Robinson II. *Pound for Pound: A Biography of Sugar Ray Robinson.* New York: Amistad, 2005.

Haygood, Wil. *Sweet Thunder: The Life and Times of Sugar Ray Robinson.* New York: Alfred A. Knopf, 2009.

Robinson, Sugar Ray, and Dave Anderson. *Sugar Ray.* London: Putnam, 1970.

Schoor, Gene. *Sugar Ray Robinson.* New York: Greenberg, 1951.

Rock, Chris *(1965–)*

Comedian Chris Rock's blunt, honest commentary on sensitive topics such as racism, poverty, and drug abuse quickly gained him a wide following during the stand-up comedy boom of the late 1980s and has since elevated him to being one of the most popular and respected comedians in the world. While performing stand-up in New York City throughout the mid-1980s, Rock caught the attention of comic legend Eddie Murphy, who offered him a small role on *Beverly Hills Cop II* (1987), leading to another small part in the spoof *I'm Gonna Git You Sucka* (1988) and a slot on the sketch-comedy shows *Saturday Night Live* (1990–1993) and *In Living Color* (1993–1994). In 1991 he had a prominent role in the hit film *New Jack City* and released his first comedy album, *Born Suspect.* Such widespread exposure landed Rock his first starring role in a feature film, the hip-hop mockumentary *CB4* (1993).

Rock provided the voice for a series of Nike basketball shoe commercials starring Anfernee "Penny" Hardaway and continued to appear in films throughout the 1990s, including *Beverly Hills Ninja* (1997), *Doctor Dolittle* (1998), and *Lethal Weapon 4* (1998). He released the stand-up specials *Big Ass Jokes* (1994) and the Emmy Award–winning *Bring the Pain* (1996) on HBO, which subsequently offered him his own talk show, *The Chris Rock Show* (1997–2000). He also published a book of essays titled *Rock This!* (1997).

In the first decade of the 2000s, Rock provided voices for a number of animated films, including Steven Spielberg's *A.I. Artificial Intelligence* (2001), *Osmosis Jones* (2001), *Madagascar* (2005), and *Bee Movie* (2007), while enjoying the success of the massively popular stand-up specials *Bigger & Blacker* (1999) and *Never Scared* (2004).

In 2005 Rock hosted the Seventy-Seventh Academy Awards and began writing, producing, and narrating the autobiographical sitcom *Everybody Hates Chris* (2005–2009). He also wrote, directed, and starred in the film *I Think I Love My Wife* (2007), and his 2008 stand-up special, *Kill the Messenger*, won two Emmy Awards. In addition, his 2009 documentary about African American hair styles, *Good Hair*, won a Special Jury Prize at the Sundance Film Festival. In the 2010s Rock starred in a number of ensemble films, including *Death at a Funeral* (2010), *Grown Ups* (2010), and *What to Expect When You're Expecting* (2012).

Christian L. Pyle

SEE ALSO: *Academy Awards; Blaxploitation Films; Emmy Awards; Hip-Hop;* In Living Color*; Murphy, Eddie; Nike;* Saturday Night Live*; Spielberg, Steven; Stand-Up Comedy; Sundance Film Festival.*

BIBLIOGRAPHY

Blue, Rose, and Corinne J. Naden. *Chris Rock.* Philadelphia: Chelsea House, 2000.

Rock, Chris. *Rock This!* New York: Hyperion, 1997.

Todd, Anne M. *Chris Rock: Comedian and Actor.* New York: Chelsea House, 2006.

Rock and Roll

In the beginning, rock-and-roll music was a provocation, an affront to parents and proper citizens. As rock critic Jim Miller put it, "It was the music you loved to have them [parents] hate." The name itself was sexual, deriving from black slang for copulation. Dominated by a heavy back-beat and amplified guitars, the music was crude, raucous, easily accessible, and within a few years of its inception, tailored and marketed specifically to the young, now a consumer block of singular importance. And rock was inherently democratic. Any kid could muster up enough money for a guitar, and, gathering together three or four like-minded souls, start a band—many of the best groups were started in precisely this manner. But if the music itself was simple, its origins were not. In fact, rock and roll was the culmination of more than a century of musical cross-pollination between white and black, master and slave; a music born of miscegenation. It was in essence a post-modern medium, one of the first true products of the consumer society. With a whole array of gestures, attitudes, styles, inflections, and narratives, it was endlessly receptive to outside influences and was thus endlessly adaptable—a ground to receive all the narratives of youthful rebellion. Hence, it was far more contingent on history than other musical forms.

EARLY STAGES: 1950s

When parents first heard rock music in the 1950s, they heard only cacophony. They were unaware of the rich tradition behind rock and roll, that it was playing out a cultural evolution begun in slavery, a blending of musical and cultural forms—African and European, religious and secular—a syncretistic blending of two traditions of music. Prior to the Civil War, white minstrels began to copy the styles of the plantation orchestras, becoming the rage of Europe and America. These slave orchestras had learned a smattering of European dance tunes, which they combined with traditional African forms played on European instruments (not too dissimilar from the lutes and fiddles used by African griots—storytellers—of the Savannah), adapting their traditional music in ways both overt and clandestine, and thereby continuing a cultural heritage that had been in effect outlawed by the slaves' owners. By the time of rock's inception, this musical cross-fertilization had already occurred several times over, creating jazz, blues, gospel, western swing, and rhythm and blues.

These new musical forms—western swing, rhythm and blues, jump blues—proliferated in the years following World War II, the result of migrations out of the rural South and Southwest, as well as greater dissemination through radio and records. Many country musicians introduced blues tunes into their repertoire, while delta blues musicians adapted to urban nightclubs with electric guitars and small combo arrangements. In the Southwest, small combos and jazz orchestras were combining blues vocals and arrangements with raucous saxophones and a backbeat-heavy rhythm section that spread from its Texas-Oklahoma roots west to Los Angeles and San Francisco. The birth of rock, however, centers around Memphis and a few farsighted individuals. Sam Phillips moved to Memphis in 1945, lured by the black music that had been his lifelong passion. He set up Sun Studios, recording Beale Street blues musicians, moonlighting and engineering demos to make ends meet. In 1951 he recorded "Rocket 88" by Ike Turner. It became a number-one rhythm and blues hit and is considered by many to be the first rock-and-roll song. Phillips himself was not concerned with race, but he knew intuitively that all the music he recorded would remain "race" music until a white man recorded it. He boasted to friends that if he could find a white singer who sang like a black man, he would make them both rich.

Memphis was home to a particularly energetic urban blues movement and a magnet for poor blacks and whites seeking to escape the grinding poverty of the countryside. The Presley family was characteristic of this pattern, moving there from rural Mississippi after World War II. They lived in the federal housing (the best housing they had ever had), and the illiterate Vernon Presley got a job driving a truck. Their son majored in shop at Hume High School, where he was regularly beaten for his long hair and effeminate appearance, but despite these eccentricities, it was anticipated that he would follow in his father's marginal footsteps, working some menial job and perhaps playing music on the side.

Elvis Presley's genius lay in his capacity to absorb different influences. He watched *Rebel without a Cause* a dozen times, cultivating a James Dean sneer and memorizing whole pages of dialogue, and visited the late-night gospel revivals, absorbing the religious frenzy. He listened to the radio, to the black gospel stations and groundbreaking DJ Dewey Phillips on WHBQ. At a

DJ Alan Freed. *DJ Alan Freed brought rock and roll to the East Coast when he moved from Cleveland to New York in 1954.* **MICHAEL OCHS ARCHIVE/GETTY IMAGES.**

time when Memphis itself was thoroughly segregated, Phillips was one of the first DJs in the country with an integrated setlist, playing blues and country alongside each other, and his influence on Elvis was evident by the songs on the singer's first legendary Sun single—"I'm All Right, Mama," a blues by well-known delta transplant Arthur "Big Boy" Crudup, and bluegrasser Bill Monroe's country hit "Blue Moon of Kentucky." The bluesy "I'm All Right, Mama" was countrified, featuring a country-style guitar solo, while Monroe's classic was delivered with a rollicking back beat and a vocal delivery unlike any country singer; Presley sang with the fervor of the gospel musicians he loved to watch. This single 45, the culmination of two hundred years of musical cross-pollination, changed the music forever, and because Presley was white (an early radio interviewer made a point of asking what high school Elvis went to simply to prove that this was so), the entire nature of the music industry was stood on its head.

The music had arrived in the night, as it were. Like Dewey Phillips before him, DJ Alan Freed began mixing black and white artists on his late night show, *The Moondog Show*, after a Cleveland record store owner mentioned the droves of white teenagers buying black music at his store. Freed was soon promoting live rock events, drawing crowds well in excess of capacity, and alarming Cleveland's powers-that-be with integrated audiences and performers at a time when the city was largely segregated. "This unprecedented convergence of black and white," wrote cultural theorist Dick Hebdige, "so aggressively, so unashamedly proclaimed, attracted the inevitable controversy which centered on the predictable themes of race, sex, rebellion, etc., and which rapidly developed into a moral panic." Freed became a champion of scandal, an unashamed proponent for the young, and one of rock and roll's first martyrs, suffering legal harassment throughout his career and later an indictment in the payola scandal (he died sick and penniless in Palm Springs, California), but he was a crucial figure in its dissemination, especially when his 1954 move to WINS in New York blanketed the East Coast with rock-and-roll music.

CORPORATE PROFIT

Having seen the commercial potential of rock and roll, the large record companies were eager to profit from the craze but were not altogether enthusiastic about the music itself. Rock and roll was not respectable, nor proper; it was redolent of the kind of culture mainstream America had tried to keep at arm's length for years. Its growing popularity fed into middle-class anxiety that their children were being inextricably corrupted; a study on juvenile delinquency by a Dr. Walter B. Miller asserted among other things that the parental anxiety was not attributable to any increase in delinquency as much as to the adoption by middle-class youth of conduct formerly reserved to the working class; that is, the adoption of a whole array of slangs, styles, and attitudes—proletariat chic—that constituted rock and roll in its essence. Needless to say, the corporate record companies were uncomfortable with southern and black musicians alike. They were suspicious of rock, could not fathom it, and, as history will attest, did their utmost to tone it down whenever possible. Rock's original journeymen were replaced by sanitized teen idols—Bobby Rydell, Fabian, Frankie Avalon—scrubbed and polished little gems, carefully groomed for their role as sex symbols minus the sex. "It [the music] tended to become bowdlerized, drained of surplus eroticism, and any hint of anger or recrimination blown along the 'hot' lines was delicately refined into inoffensive nightclub sound," wrote Hebdige of jazz's mutation into swing. The same could be said of rock and roll in the late 1950s. There was pressure to cleanse the music of unwholesome (black or the more obvious poor southern musician) influences. Jerry Lee Lewis fell victim to this cultural sanitation, convicted by public opinion of incorrigible perversity after he married his underage teenage second cousin. His music was as heavily influenced by white Pentecostal ecstasy as by black gospel, but Lewis's very personal battle with sin made him an obvious target for the legions of decency. Chuck Berry was dispatched first through violation of the Mann Act, and then by internecine squabbles with the IRS that netted him several jail terms, but it was the infamous payola scandal (*payola* being a term for the bribery to which many small record companies resorted in order to get airplay) that broke the market power of small, independent labels and cleansed the airwaves for the sanitized dreck of the teen idols.

As it was, most of the original rock-and-rollers fell victim to a premature anachronism. Of all the pioneer musicians who carved rock and roll out of the musical wilderness, only Johnny Cash and Elvis survived the early 1960s as anything more than an oldies-but-goodies attraction. A list of these performers reads like a litany of bad luck and willful destruction: Buddy Holly, Ritchie Valens, and the Big Bopper dead in a plane crash, February 3, 1959; Chuck Berry and Jerry Lee Lewis, who found out too late that fame could not insulate them from the law; the flamboyant Little Richard, who traded in rock and roll for the Bible; Carl Perkins, destroyed by alcohol and drugs; rockabilly legend Eddie Cochran, killed in an automobile accident in England just after rock's first decade came to a close. Pioneering always exacts a heavy price on body and soul, and it would appear that bringing rock and roll into fruition turned out to be one of the more lethal endeavors in the creative history of the modern era.

BRITISH INVASION AND ROCK'S TRANSFORMATION

While the pioneering musicians' music and influence was being subsumed in the United States by teen idols, in Great Britain rock and roll was undergoing a parallel evolution that started where stateside rock left off. Vintage rock, blues, rhythm and blues, and country were originally brought over by American servicemen following World War II. For the British youth, it was a revelation, a welcome change from the threadbare music hall tradition of British jazz. The ensuing generation of British rock stars, from ardent blues revivalists to their pop-inflected cousins, all credit the importation of American music as being central to their musical evolution. The British heard rock and roll through a cultural scrim, a sensibility expertly attuned to picking up the subtleties of class differences. With its introduction, the music was formed amid a complex, invisible relationship between its roots in the working-class American South and the chronic dissatisfaction of the British working class, curtailed by the accident of birth from anything more meaningful than menial labor. The British absorbed blues and rock like holy writ, bringing to the music an insouciance born of desperation that had withered in American pop. The British groups that would emerge as vanguards of the new style—the Beatles, the Animals, the Rolling Stones, the Yardbirds, Them, the Dave Clark Five, not to mention a whole host of lesser names—introduced an enthusiasm for American forms that seemed fresh and vital. Incidentally, it caused near riots, panic in the streets, and all sorts of other commotion when it returned to American shores, capturing a new generation grown quite bored by Frankie Avalon, Annette Funicello, Connie Francis, and company.

The expropriation of rock by British artists had a profound effect on rock music and rock fashion, as if, seen through the alien lens of another culture, rock music was revealed as at once more complex and more immediate to American musicians. Many of the British musicians—John Lennon, Pete Townshend, Keith Richards, to name a few—were the products of the English art school system and took influences from the world of art, especially the pop artists and their preoccupation with the language of advertising and their enthusiasm for obliterating the traditional demarcation between high and low art. In fact, Townshend borrowed the idea of auto-destruction from a lecture by artist Gustave Metzke at Townshend's art school, Ealing. As Chris Charlesworth wrote shortly before that crucial year, 1967, "Pop music was no longer aimed directly at young fans who screamed at their idols, and neither was it looked upon by its creators as a disposable commodity, good for a quick run on the charts and little else." Rock strove to make statements and be considered as serious art. In the Beatles' single "A Day in the Life" (on *Sgt. Pepper's Lonely Hearts Club Band*), one can hear echoes of John Cage, Nam June Paik, and the whole current of high art. "How does the musician compose," wrote Dave Marsh, "when what's being heard is not the noise that the instrument and/or orchestra makes but the noise that the instrument and/or orchestra makes many times removed, on a piece of black plastic with a context of its own? This is what John Russell refers to as the 'element of exorcism' in pop, and it functions as effectively in a Who 45 as in an Oldenburg sculpture. . . . Thus were barriers—between art objects and everyday stuff, between the theory of avant-garde viewers and unaesthetic masses, between high culture and low, between respectability and trash—not simply eradicated but demolished."

The ecstatic communion of a Fillmore West concert (very similar to the ecstatic communion of the "holy rollers" who so influenced Elvis, Jerry Lee Lewis, and others) was a connection to rock's past, but rock music was fundamentally at odds with mainstream culture in a different way than in the 1950s. No longer was it a matter merely of social stigma or cultural chauvinism on the part of the dominant culture. "For performers like John Lennon, Bob Dylan, and Pete Townshend, Vegas and supper clubs, Hollywood movies and glittering television specials weren't a goal, they were a trap to avoid," wrote Marsh. "Very few of the post-Beatles performers courted the kind of respectability that Col. Tom Parker or Larry Parnes would have understood." For generational reasons and in large part because of the Vietnam War, which many rock performers viewed as symptomatic of a larger rot, the options that had satisfied previous generations of performers were no longer open to rock musicians. But as a music, rock was more dependent on the whole armature of consumer capitalism than any previous genre, and in the ensuing decade, these contradictions became glaringly apparent.

ROCK AND THE MARKETPLACE

Rock is a porous music; this is its value as a social glue and, like other essentially postmodern arts, also its weakness. It is wholly contingent on historical circumstance, not divorced from it, and with the end of the 1960s, rock would once again be in the position it had occupied in the early 1960s—a holding period until the next big thing came along. Early in the 1970s, 1960s rock had become but a vivid memory, with many of its best talents dead or in retirement: Jimi Hendrix, Janis Joplin, and Jim Morrison were dead; the Beatles had broken up. Those bands that remained intact could offer little more than a gesture of resistance (the gesture being an important figuration of the music—think of Pete Townshend's upstretched arm about to rip through his guitar strings, or Mick Jagger's effeminate stage persona, mincing and limp-wristed). Without the cohesion of the Vietnam War behind that rebellious, defiant gesture, it was employed as mere dramatic embellishment. It might be striking, but rock had become essentially hollow.

With nothing left to rebel against, rock devolved into specialized subgenres that bore only a passing resemblance to each other—heavy metal, the singer-songwriter, country rock, disco. The music was reflective of lifestyle choices as much as generational identity, and it no longer spoke to issues of class and youthful rebellion, except in the most base, degraded manner. The gentility of a Joni Mitchell listener bespoke sensitive college-educated professional; Fleetwood Mac and the Eagles, a relaxed middle-class hedonism—nonintellectual, but respectable; while the testosterone bluster of heavy metal—the music of choice for teenage boys and a certain type of blue-collar post-adolescent, hence its status as keeper of rock's rebellious flame—was critically derided. Critics might deride both disco and heavy metal, but appropriately enough, it was these two genres that transcended class distinctions in a similar manner to 1950s rock: as constituting a craze.

In the 1980s, rock, its fire stolen by the punks, appeared even more moribund. Its leading proponents were either aging or one of a variety of manufactured anonymous drones producing vapid, formulaic music not so dissimilar in content from the offerings of the teen idol years. Rock music had been assimilated, contained, and with the advent of MTV, entrenched in an "entertainment" industry to a far greater degree than ever before. Even punk, which had begun its life as a brutal caricature of consumer culture, insisting that rock must be *detourned*, as the French would say, led away from its intended signifier, was finally integrated into the mainstream fifteen years after the fact. One could see the commercial acceptance of bands such as Nirvana, Rancid, and Green Day as evidence of some final co-optation, or the stardom of Marilyn Manson as a final embrace and integration of the *other* (when all is familiar, nothing is strange) or as punk rock's final triumph. More likely, punk's popularity was proof that the gestures of youth rebellion, as they had been since James Dean, were implicitly exciting and thus easily marketed given the proper incentive, which is, if one is a record executive, to swallow one's revulsion all the way to the bank. Was rock finally a dead form, as safe and nonthreatening as swing music?

RETURN TO YOUTH CULTURE

The explosion of alternative rock music during the 1990s gave rise to a seemingly endless array of subgenres, and rock and roll appeared poised to remake itself once again; however, as the major record labels clamored to sign any band that had the "Seattle" sound, it looked as if mainstream rock was content with recycling sounds and aesthetics. The post-grunge and indie movements emerged from the overpopulated "alternative" umbrella as the two most commercially sustainable genres. Acts like Pavement, the Breeders, Fugazi, and Jane's Addiction experienced commercial success that was driven by large musical festivals such as Lollapalooza and Sasquatch. At times, driven more by the need for retailers to categorize the music than the actual differences in the sound, rock and roll seemed destined to become a mere shell of its once rebellious youth culture. Perhaps one of the most positive effects of the alternative and indie movements was a return to an overt political preoccupation in music. Many fans soured over the posturing of arena rock in the 1980s. Bands like Winger, Skid Row, and Mötley Crüe were known for their lavish stage shows and gimmicks more than for their music. The legendary tales of excess while on tour and the increased presence of corporate sponsors like Budweiser distorted the rock roll's antiestablishment image. Indie and alternative bands sought to take a larger control in the creative process and embraced the do-it-yourself ethic of punk rock. Additionally, the riot grrrl bands of the 1990s offered a compelling counter-narrative to the masculine and, at times, misogynist environment that pervaded every rock-and-roll scene. Like the grunge movement, however, riot grrrl was quickly coopted and misrepresented. For every Bikini Kill or the Coathangers, there were countless bands, like Spice Girls or Avril Lavigne, that mimicked the style and slogans of the riot grrrl aesthetic but were devoid of its substance.

With such theorizing, it is easy to lose sight of rock's essential nature as being anti-high-art, proletarian, and egalitarian. What was true in the 1950s—that rock in its fundamentals was easy to play, hence easily accessible—remains true in the present, though some rock music is indeed as difficult and as rigorous in composition as any classical music. But there is a possibility inherent in rock, a possibility inherent in all folk forms. The music is not owned by experts or specialists, but by the people; rock celebrates the potential of four kids getting together in a garage and playing. And as a legacy of rock's roots in slave music, where the slave master's strict prohibitions necessitated concealment, rock encodes within it a hidden corrosive message, a secret, a call to arms based on symbols and repetition discernible to anyone with a mind to decipher it, broadcasting its complaint despite the manipulations of record executives. "According to one theory," writes Lester Bangs, "punk rock goes back to Ritchie Valens's 'La Bamba.' Just consider Valens's three-chord mariachi squawkup in the light of 'Louie Louie' by the Kingsmen, then consider 'Louie Louie' in the light of 'You Really Got Me' by the Kinks, then 'You Really Got Me' in the light of 'No Fun' by the Stooges, then 'No Fun' in the light of 'Blitzkrieg Bop' by the Ramones, and finally note that 'Blitzkrieg Bop' sounds a lot like 'La Bamba.' There: twenty years of rock & roll history in three chords, played more primitively each time they are recycled."

The marketing success of post-grunge and crossover metal bands over saturated the market place with bands like Limp Bizkit and Papa Roach, who played venues that rivaled the 1980s glam metal bands. Garage rock offered a simpler, paired down sound. Bands like the White Stripes, Dávila 666, the Dirtbombs, and the Black Lips ushered what many hoped would be a further rekindling of rock and roll's fire. Many of the bands experienced critical and commercial success, and rock's ethic once again teetered in the precarious balance between market exploitation and creative integrity. In spite of capitalism's ability to absorb rock music into the marketplace, its storied history and intimate relationship with youth culture allowed for it to continually remake itself and to simultaneously exist as a subcultural force and as a lucrative business endeavor.

Michael Baers

SEE ALSO: *Advertising; Alternative Rock; Automobile; Avalon, Frankie; The Beatles; Berry, Chuck; Big Bopper; Bluegrass; Blues; Cash, Johnny; Celebrity; Consumerism; Dean, James; Disc Jockeys; Disco; Fabian; The Fifties; Fleetwood Mac; Francis, Connie; Freed, Alan "Moondog"; Funicello, Annette; Gospel Music; Green Day; Grunge; Heavy Metal; Hendrix, Jimi; Holly, Buddy; Hollywood; Jazz; Las Vegas; Leisure Time; Lennon, John; Lewis, Jerry Lee; Little Richard; Lollapalooza; Mitchell, Joni; Monroe, Bill; Movie Stars; MTV; Nirvana; Pop Art; Pop Music; Postmodernism; Presley, Elvis; Punk; Race Music; Radio; The Ramones;* Rebel without a Cause*; Rhythm and Blues;* Rolling Stone*; Rydell, Bobby; Slang; The Spice Girls; Sun Records; Teen Idols; Teenagers;* Them!*; Valens, Ritchie; Vietnam; The Who; World War II; The Yardbirds.*

BIBLIOGRAPHY

Arnold, Gina. *Route 666: On the Road to Nirvana.* New York: St. Martin's Press, 1993.

Arnold, Gina. *Kiss This: Punk in the Present Tense.* New York: St. Martin's Press, 1997.

Bangs, Lester. "Protopunk: The Garage Bands." *The Rolling Stone Illustrated History of Rock & Roll.* New York: Random House/Rolling Stone Press, 1980.

Bangs, Lester. *Psychotic Reactions and Carburetor Dung.* New York: Alfred A. Knopf, 1987.

Escott, Colin. *Sun Records: The Brief History of the Legendary Recording Label.* New York: Quick Fox, 1980.

Friedlander, Paul, with Peter Miller. *Rock and Roll: A Social History*, 2nd ed. Boulder, CO: Westview Press, 2006.

Gillett, Charlie. *The Sound of the City: The Rise of Rock and Roll.* New York: Pantheon, 1983.

Gilmore, Mikal. *Night Beat: A Shadow History of Rock & Roll.* New York: Doubleday, 1998.

Herman, Gary. *Rock 'n' Roll Babylon.* New York: Putnam, 1982.

Loder, Kurt. *Bat Chain Puller: Rock & Roll in the Age of Celebrity.* New York, St. Martin's Press, 1990.

Marcus, Greil. *Mystery Train: Images of Rock 'n' Roll Music.* New York: Dutton, 1975.

Marcus, Greil. *Stranded: Rock & Roll for a Desert Island.* New York: Knopf, 1979.

Marsh, Dave. *Before I Get Old: The Story of the Who.* New York: St. Martin's Press, 1983.

Miller, Jim, ed. *The Rolling Stone Illustrated History of Rock & Roll.* New York: Random House/Rolling Stone Press, 1980.

Palmer, Robert. *Rock 'n' Roll: An Unruly History.* New York: Harmony Books, 1995.

Young, Bob, and Mickey Moody. *Language of Rock & Roll.* London: Sidgwick & Jackson, 1989.

Rock Climbing

Once a chic pursuit for the wealthy and adventurous, rock climbing by the 1990s had come to embody a path toward greater self-fulfillment for the average person. Embraced by corporations and schools, rock climbing and the rope skills as sociated with it became tools to improve corporate teamwork and boost self-esteem in "at-risk" schoolchildren. An international audience watched skilled athletes scale dangerous rock faces in televised competitions. For the average person, the physical challenges offered by rock climbing were overshadowed by the mental strength participants could gain by learning the sport's skills even if they never stepped foot on an actual mountaintop.

TYPES OF ROCK CLIMBING

Essentially a subset of mountaineering, especially during the early part of the twentieth century, rock climbing involves scaling rock faces ranging in height from tens to thousands of feet in environments ranging from Southern California seawalls to Alaskan mountain faces. Mountain climbing became a popular sport among the British gentry during the nineteenth century, with most expeditions operating under the guise of scientific study. Not until the 1920s did people begin to climb rock faces simply for the sake of the climbing experience. Over the course of the twentieth century, rock climbing grew into a multifaceted sport that encompassed recreational climbing on crags and cliffs worldwide, difficult mountaineering, competitive sport climbing, and afternoons at the gym.

The sport of rock climbing has numerous subsets, all defined by the type of activity in which a climber engages; a rock climber may engage in some or all of them. The simplest form of rock climbing is known as bouldering, in which climbers work out problems in scaling or traversing boulders or small cliffs without protective ropes. Bouldering is generally considered to be training for climbing larger and more challenging rock faces, though some climbers, most notably John Gill, have focused solely on this often extremely difficult kind of climbing. Crag climbing consists of climbing rock faces anywhere from 75 feet (half of a standard climbing rope length) to 1,000 or more feet. Usually, climbing routes on crags take no more than a single day to climb. Routes that take longer than a day are considered "big wall" climbs. These are climbs in which climbers often spend multiple days on a rock face or may drop to the ground at night before climbing back up fixed ropes to the day's earlier high point.

During the 1980s, sport climbing, a type of crag climbing prevalent in France that involved extremely safe preplaced rope anchors on relatively short climbs, became popular on crags worldwide. This new climbing, with a focus almost exclusively on difficult gymnastic moves to gain the top, led into the sport of competitive climbing that moved off of natural rock walls and into gyms or prefabricated outdoor walls with resin "holds." In this arena, climbers were judged on speed, style, and the highest point reached on any given route (climbing routes are defined by which resin holds a climber may or may not use). Climbers who focused on bouldering, crag climbing, or big wall climbing tended to group together, cultivating an image as adventurers, social outcasts, or heroes, while sport climbers were seen as athletes; sport climbing's competitive nature differed sharply from the recreational enthusiasm of weekend rock-jocks or devoted big wall mountaineers.

Recreational climbing was generally seen as an outdoor activity more akin to hiking, backpacking, or nontechnical mountain climbing. Schools devoted to teaching outdoor skills appeared throughout the twentieth century. The two largest and most popular schools were Outward Bound, which started in Wales in 1941 to train young sailors to survive in lifeboats during World War II, and the National Outdoor Leadership School, which opened in Wyoming in 1965 and focused on leadership training and wilderness skills. During the last quarter of the century, attending these schools became a rite of passage for certain groups of generally affluent teenagers (and occasionally their parents during a midlife search for meaning or adventure). While rock climbing was not the singular focus of these programs, it was a central skill that students learned not only as a wilderness activity but also as a tool toward personal growth and maturity.

CONTEMPORARY ATTITUDES AND CONCERNS

By the 1980s, as the popularity of the sport spread and the growth of sport climbing made climbing safer and accessible to more people, rock climbing became not simply a recreational activity or a competitive sport but an avenue toward self-fulfillment. With the increasing development of indoor artificial facilities during the 1990s, a rhetoric of "facing one's fears" and increasing one's "mental fitness" emphasized climbing for the sake of mental well-being rather than for recreational purposes. Ropes courses were an offshoot of rock climbing combined with specific kinds of military training in which teams work to get groups or individuals through various climbing-oriented tasks, such as rope climbing, falls, or beam walking.

These courses were not training grounds for future climbing activities but rather focused on self-improvement and teamwork among the participants. The courses were especially popular among corporations who sent management teams there to learn skills they could apply to the contemporary corporate culture, particularly the teamwork approach of Total Quality Management. Ropes courses and rock-climbing activities also became popular as self-empowerment tools for people working with at-risk inner-city youths who had little experience beyond urban centers. By the end of the twentieth century, rock climbing had become both a form of recreation or sport and a personal empowerment tool.

In the first decade of the 2000s a climber named Aron Ralston came to epitomize the independence and self-sufficiency that many people associated with the sport. In April 2003 he went on a solo climb in Utah's Bluejohn Canyon and suffered a horrific accident. An 800-pound boulder shifted, smashing his hand and pinning him to the canyon wall. No one knew where he was. On the sixth day of being trapped, he decided he had to take drastic action to survive and amputated his own hand to free himself. Ralston's story was portrayed in the Academy Award–nominated film *127 Hours* (2010).

Other climbers contributed to the sport's popularity by bringing along photographers to publicize their feats. One of these was Dean Potter, who has made some spectacular free climbs, using only ropes as equipment. He has also generated controversy by climbing—and allegedly damaging—endangered formations such as Utah's Delicate Arch.

As rock climbing became increasingly popular, two closely related issues gained attention. One was a cultural concern: indigenous people have objected to having sites they view as sacred places scaled for recreational purposes. As one response to this issue, in 1995 the National Park Service instituted a new policy requesting that during the month of June, climbers voluntarily refrain from climbing the Devil's Tower National

Monument in Wyoming, which is sacred to many Plains tribes. June is an especially important month in their religious calendar. As of 2012 the voluntary ban remained in effect.

A second concern was the fear that rock climbing was causing damage to the environment, not only because of the use of invasive techniques like pitons and bolts that chipped and scarred the rock but also because of the introduction of so many people into a formerly pristine environment. Climbers have been known to damage fragile ecosystems by treading on plants; disturbing nests; and leaving behind litter, excrement, and equipment such as ropes. In response to this concern, many climbers have tried to educate themselves about the ecology of the regions they enter and have begun to practice "clean climbing" in which they use only available cracks and holds, thus reducing changes to the rock. In spite of this, some environmentalists still would like to see rock climbing banned altogether. If the sport continues its rapid gain in popularity, this debate is sure to continue.

Dan Moos

SEE ALSO: *Academy Awards; Environmentalism; Extreme Sports; National Parks.*

BIBLIOGRAPHY

Burbach, Matt. *Gym Climbing: Maximizing Your Indoor Experience.* Seattle, WA: Mountaineers Books, 2004.

Hattingh, Garth. *The Climber's Handbook.* London: New Holland Publishers, 1998.

Jones, Chris. *Climbing in North America.* Berkeley: University of California Press, 1976.

Luebben, Craig. *Rock Climbing: Mastering Basic Skills.* Seattle, WA: Mountaineers Books, 2004.

Ralston, Aron. *Between a Rock and a Hard Place.* New York: Atria Books, 2004.

Randall, Glenn. *Vertigo Games.* Sioux City, IA: W. R. Publications, 1983.

Roper, Steve, and Allen Steck. *Fifty Classic Climbs of North America.* San Francisco: Sierra Club Books, 1979.

The Rockefeller Family

During the seventy years between oil magnate John D. Rockefeller Sr.'s emergence as the richest man in the world at the turn of the twentieth century and grandson Nelson A. Rockefeller's service as the first U.S. vice president to be appointed, not elected, to that office (1974), the Rockefeller family stood as the very epitome of extraordinary wealth and influence, unrivaled in popular imagination until the emergence of Bill Gates in the 1990s. John D. Sr. at one time earned 2.5 percent of the entire national income. Proof of the Rockefeller family's pervasiveness and power came in the 1950s, when the Chock Full o' Nuts Coffee jingle that had originally run as "Better coffee Rockefeller's money can't buy" was altered to "Better coffee a millionaire's money can't buy" after the family objected to the allusion. The Rockefeller family executed enormous philanthropic efforts and acts of public service throughout the twentieth century as several generations of Rockefellers tried to demonstrate how a robber-baron aristocracy could justify its extraordinary wealth.

CONTRADICTIONS

When John D. Sr. (founder of Standard Oil) retired from his active business life at the company in the mid-1890s, he was earning an average of $10 million per year, at a time when the average American earned less than $10 per week. One of the two originators of the modern U.S. corporation—the other was Andrew Carnegie—John D. Sr. remained as aloof and secretive as he was before his ascent from utter poverty and as loyal to the fundamentalist Baptist pieties of his youth. He never bought a yacht, he never sought the treasures of Europe and other continents, and he never exhibited any undue passions for worldly pleasures. Despite glad tidings about his essential humility, the public could not decide what to make of him—just as in years to come, contemporaries of his descendants could not reach any firm conclusions about them.

On the one hand, John D. Sr. used his money primarily for charitable and educational purposes: to improve health care not only in America but worldwide, to finance great institutions of higher learning such as Spelman College and the University of Chicago, to improve education in the South, and to wipe out hookworm. John D. Jr. used the family's money to re-create Colonial Williamsburg and to assume quasi-governmental responsibilities in dealing with the scourge of "white slavery." John D. Sr.'s grandsons (the brothers) used family funds to help pay for the Museum of Modern Art and the Lincoln Center for the Performing Arts, which not only provided the masses with access to the arts but also raised American standing in the world community. All the Rockefellers, through grants by their foundations, helped catalyze significant advances in knowledge, particularly in medicine and in the sciences.

Its financial benefactions were not the only reasons for the wide respect the family enjoyed. John D. Sr. and his descendants symbolized the utter determination and boundless energy that made America a superpower. He had achieved his wealth and position by eliminating competitors so remorselessly that he enjoyed a virtual monopoly in oil production. Americans regarded him as a genius of private enterprise who demonstrated his superiority over his rivals so commendably that he fully deserved all the rewards of his marvelous organizational abilities. Paradoxically, John D. Sr. was also seen as the great American villain, a living, breathing dollar sign, a corrupter of railroads and legislators, the murderer of free enterprise in the oil industry, someone who declared individualism dead. He dealt in millions, saved in pennies, gave away dimes, and savored pettiness. Among examples cited of his miserliness was his directive to use one less drop of solder in the manufacture of each oil can.

On the positive side of the ledger, he and John D. Jr. deeply impressed the public with the sincerity of their religious beliefs. John D. Sr. tithed consistently, and even after he had begun his climb to fortune, he helped sweep Cleveland's Euclid Avenue Baptist Church. One of the monuments built by Rockefeller money in 1930, the Riverside Church in New York City, remains a contradictory symbol: it is at once a memorial to John

D. Sr.'s childhood religion and a bastion of the liberal Social Gospel theology that finds more sin in unbridled capitalism than in personal peccadilloes. John D. Jr., who saw to its building and the appointment of the liberal Harry Emerson Fosdick to its pulpit, was a more sensitive man who suffered from nervous disorders and had little interest in business—his main interest was Christian benevolence. John D. Jr. also collected Renaissance art and Ming dynasty porcelain. He explained to his father, "I have never squandered money on horses, yachts, automobiles, or other foolish extravagances. . . . This hobby [of collecting], while a costly one, is quiet and unostentatious and not sensational."

THE ROBBER BARON

Yet, even the charities of father and son and their claims of piety struck suspicious observers as nothing but covers for their insatiable need to dominate and to profit from duping the masses. The *New York Herald* commented, "The only thing Standard Oil lacks is a . . . twenty-five-thousand-dollar chaplain who would open their meetings with religious services." According to the *University of Chicago Magazine*, at the university's first commencement, John D. Sr. said, "The good Lord gave me my money," to which grateful students responded, "John D. Rockefeller, wonderful great man is he / Gives all his spare change to the U. of C."

Few criticisms of Rockefeller's tactics were as withering as muckraker Ida Tarbell's *The History of the Standard Oil Company* (1904). Rockefeller's defenders claimed that the writer's antagonism toward the titan sprang from her background as the fiercely independent daughter of an oil producer broken by Rockefeller. Nonetheless, her analysis of Standard Oil was masterful and would thereafter serve as a model for how to dissect a giant corporation. Readers almost invariably came to believe that Rockefeller (like Carnegie) had to be assigned responsibility for the labor strife that had begun to besiege the country in the early 1900s.

Congress's reaction to such anti-Rockefeller sentiment was not only to pass antitrust legislation but also to refuse to grant the Rockefeller Foundation a federal charter in 1913. A second development, which mightily stoked fires against the family, occurred after Woodrow Wilson appointed Frank Walsh, a prominent Kansas City trial attorney, as head of the U.S. Commission on Industrial Relations, an agency created to explore causes of industrial violence. Walsh turned commission hearings into lectures at which he declared that the family's huge philanthropic trusts were not only a "menace to the welfare of society" but also "attempts to present to the world, as handsome and admirable, an economic and industrial regime that draws its substance from the sweat and blood and tears of exploited and dispossessed humanity."

THE LUDLOW MASSACRE

When the commission met for the first time in the fall of 1913, strikes marked by violence had become commonplace. Possibly the worst took place in Ludlow, Colorado, in April 1914, where about 1,000 miners living in tents with their families struck Colorado Fuel and Iron, a Rockefeller-owned subsidiary. The company dug trenches around the tents, brought machine guns, employed a private army to guard its property, and persuaded Colorado's governor to call out National Guard units. Strikers acquired weapons, and guardsmen and workers fought a twelve-hour pitched battle, the Ludlow Massacre, during which several miners, two women, and eleven children were killed.

Walsh moved commission hearings to Denver, Colorado, and then back to Washington, D.C., where he called John D. Sr. as a witness. The magnate skillfully deflected Walsh's probing comments and questions. "Let the world wag," he advised John D. Jr., to whom he had already begun to transfer significant assets and authority over family philanthropic and business enterprises. But John D. Jr. had neither his father's studied calm nor his deep conviction of his own saintliness. He wilted under Walsh's ruthless examination, and his weak responses helped convince the public that the family was legally and morally guilty in the Ludlow incident. The manifest rise in public anger toward the family led John D. Sr. to hire a public relations counsel named Ivy Lee (recommended by John D. Jr.), and John D. Sr. began handing out dimes to passersby, a tactic said to increase his popularity. Still, bodyguards had to protect family members.

The most surprising development in the aftermath of Ludlow, however, was that John D. Jr. made one of the most abrupt turnabouts of any major capitalist in American history. After first defending Colorado Fuel and Iron, he toured the Ludlow site, ate with miners in their homes, and advised that improvements would be forthcoming. Thereafter, he received excellent press nationwide. John D. Jr.'s "transformation" distinguished him from his father, who did not relent.

THE NEXT GENERATIONS

There was no break with fundamentalist outlooks in the family's second generation. Like John D. Sr., John D. Jr. and his six children reserved Sundays for prayer, and the five boys and one girl were taught that careful accounts must be kept of money received and spent. Above all, as befit an imperial family, they received constant reminders that they were Rockefellers and that their wealth and good name were sacred trusts. The Rockefeller grandsons, John III, Nelson, Laurance, Winthrop, and David, tended to fall in line uncomplainingly with their father's and grandfather's strict rules. But Abby (Babs) kept sloppy accounts, smoked at age fifteen, drove recklessly, was ticketed repeatedly for speeding, and necked with her future husband in full view of servants. Winthrop's experiences with liquor and women became the stuff of tabloids; he became a cattle rancher who served as Republican governor of Arkansas in the late 1960s.

In the generation of the brothers, it would be Nelson, born on the founding grandfather's birthday, who not only had the most active and direct contact with the public but also exhibited some of John D. Sr.'s most pronounced characteristics. Everything Nelson did was strategic, and, like his grandfather, he demonstrated the relentless drive of the self-made go-getter and could not be hurried in his decisions. His brother David remarked, "He spent a lot of time in seeing where he wanted to go, and then developing a strategy to get there. In other words, things did not happen by accident in his life."

Nelson served four terms as governor of New York and unsuccessfully sought nomination as the Republican candidate for president three times. The public had problems deciding what to make of John D. Sr. and had to be persuaded after

Ludlow that John D. Jr. truly regretted what had happened. But Nelson's "anything is possible" behavior both confirmed and confused the public's perception of how the very rich behave. Nelson placed no limits on satisfying his demands for personal gratification. Whether in art, real estate, women, or building monuments to himself with public funds, he simply took whatever he wanted. And this was the basis for his political undoing. He was perceived as the mainstay of an eastern establishment of money and power, which contrasted unfavorably with "cloth coat" Republicans such as Barry Goldwater (in 1964) and Richard Nixon (in 1968 and 1972).

Succeeding generations of Rockefellers (the cousins followed the brothers) have not produced personalities who dominate headlines as the earlier ones, except for John D. IV (Jay), who went to West Virginia in 1964 as a VISTA volunteer and remained there, becoming its governor and a U.S. senator devoted to progressive causes, and his cousin Abby Aldrich, daughter of David, who came to be seen as the "hippie" of the family for her interest in environmentalism. She formed a company in the 1970s to import a Swedish composting toilet, the Clivus Multrum, and to educate Americans about the value of recycling—showing at least that the Rockefellers still had a knack for worthy endeavors with their traditional habits of thrift and shrewd business sense.

Milton Goldin

SEE ALSO: *Advertising; Environmentalism; Labor Unions; Lincoln Center for the Performing Arts.*

BIBLIOGRAPHY

Chernow, Ron. *Titan: The Life of John D. Rockefeller, Sr.* New York: Random House, 1998.

Collier, Peter, and David Horowitz. *The Rockefellers: An American Dynasty.* New York: Holt, Rinehart & Winston, 1976.

Reich, Cary. *The Life of Nelson A. Rockefeller: Worlds to Conquer, 1908–1958.* New York: Doubleday, 1996.

Rockefeller, David. *Memoirs.* New York: Random House Trade Paperbacks, 2003.

Sealander, Judith. *Private Wealth and Public Life: Foundation Philanthropy and the Reshaping of American Social Policy from the Progressive Era to the New Deal.* Baltimore, MD: Johns Hopkins University Press, 1997.

Tarbell, Ida M. *The History of the Standard Oil Company.* New York: McClure, Phillips, 1904.

The Rockettes

The most renowned chorus line in the world, the Rockettes engendered the American form of precision dancing and have remained the paramount practitioners of synchronized tap-dance routines ever since. A quintessential New York tourist attraction, seen by millions of spectators since their debut at Radio City Music Hall in 1932, the Rockettes spawned multitudinous imitations and made precision kick lines an established element of American entertainment culture—from amateur theatricals and school productions to Broadway and Hollywood musicals, Las Vegas extravaganzas, ice spectaculars, and half-time shows. The Rockettes are often recognized as epitomizing the "all-American girl," perhaps from a bygone era. They are beautiful but not overtly sexy; they move in unison but with a natural athleticism, not as automatons.

HISTORY

The Rockettes were the brainchild of Broadway dance director Russell Markert, who was inspired by the Tiller Girls, a precision dance troupe from England that he saw in the *Ziegfeld Follies* during the 1920s. Markert yearned to create an American counterpart of the British troupe, but with taller dancers, longer legs, and higher kicks. In 1925 Markert assembled a sixteen-member precision dance team, which he called the Missouri Rockets, for stage shows he was producing in St. Louis. The group enjoyed great popularity and soon began touring as the American Rockets. "Hide your daughters—here comes Markert" became a common phrase of the late 1920s as the choreographer scoured the land for suitable girls to join the ever-increasing number of dance troupes he was assembling to meet the growing demand for performances nationwide.

While rehearsing in New York for a Broadway appearance, one of Markert's troupes was observed by Samuel L. "Roxy" Rothafel, who invited them to perform in nightly shows at his Roxy Theatre for the six weeks before their Broadway opening. They were such a hit that Rothafel was reluctant to let them go, so Markert trained yet another group to continue performing at the Roxy. When it came time for the theater's big Easter show, Markert combined two groups into a new thirty-two-member troupe called the Roxyettes.

When Rothafel was asked to produce a gigantic stage spectacular for the opening of Rockefeller Center's Radio City Music Hall on December 27, 1932, he cast his Roxyettes as one of the featured attractions, along with the Flying Wallendas and modern dancer Martha Graham, among others. Unfortunately, the production was not a success, and by January 1933 the Music Hall decided to abandon full-evening variety shows and adopted what became its signature format—the showing of a first-run family film, accompanied by a live stage show. The only performers retained from the opening night production were the Roxyettes. In 1934 their name was changed to the Rockettes, and they became a regular institution at the famous Art Deco–style music hall. In 1937 the Rockettes were invited to represent the United States in an international dance festival at the Paris Exposition and won the grand prize. In accepting the award, the director of the Rockefeller Center, John D. Rockefeller Jr., said the Rockettes remind us that "the only way we can find success in any walk of life is in working for the group and not for personal aggrandizement."

The governing aesthetic principle of the Rockettes is uniformity. Although they range in height from 5 feet, 6 inches, to 5 feet, 10.5 inches, the illusion that they are all the same height is achieved by placing the tallest dancers in the center of the line and sloping downward. As director of the Rockettes from their inception until his retirement in 1971, Markert was criticized for his "whites-only" hiring policy. But he defended his actions by claiming that visual harmony is the backbone of precision dancing, explaining that was why he didn't even allow his Rockettes to get suntanned. (In 1988, for the first time, an African American dancer performed as a Rockette.) When auditioning his dancers Markert looked not only for women who could tap, turn, and kick with proficiency but who also could suppress their individuality to conform to the group dancing style. Although many Rockettes have spoken of the "high" they get while performing with the troupe on the magnificent music hall stage, others have found the experience mechanical, demeaning, and boring for anyone with creative inclinations.

The Rockettes have been elaborately costumed over the decades, appearing as everything from cowgirls, poodles, and daffodils to West Point cadets and astronauts, yet their routines are choreographically predictable, consisting of a series of tap-danced military drill formations and an obligatory kick-line finale. Unlike the Tiller Girls, who kicked only waist high, the Rockettes kick to eye level, straight front, and on the second beat, following a tiny two-footed preparatory jump on the downbeat. The troupe's most distinctive maneuver is the contagious toppling of the annual Christmas show's wooden soldiers: they fall backward one at a time, neatly collapsing like a row of dominoes.

By the 1970s as the music hall's G-rated films and wholesome variety shows grew out of step with the youth culture of the time, many viewed the Rockettes as kitsch. When, due to sagging box-office receipts, the famous showplace was scheduled to close on April 12, 1978, the Rockettes were instrumental in spearheading the successful efforts to save their home. In order to remain open, however, the music hall cut back to producing only three large-scale productions a year and began renting its space to presenters of rock concerts and other entertainment attractions. By the late 1990s the annual "Christmas Spectacular" remained the only vestige of the music hall's extravagant stage shows.

KEEPING STEP WITH THE TIMES

The Rockettes, however, have continued to perform there as well as at entertainment events worldwide. In 1983 their backstage lives were celebrated in the fictionalized ABC-TV movie *Legs*. They franchised in the 1990s, permitting cities such

Rockettes. *The Rockettes perform their famous precision kick-line in 2011.* CHARLES ESHELMAN/CONTRIBUTOR/WIREIMAGE/GETTY IMAGES.

as Las Vegas and Branson, Missouri, to form their own Rockette companies. In 2006 Linda Haberman became the first woman ever to serve as solo director and choreographer of the Radio City Rockettes and director of the music hall's "Christmas Spectacular." Under her leadership the iconic dance troupe began to display a higher level of dance technique and to perform a wider variety of dance styles.

Critics have opined that precision dancing continues to attract audiences because it conveys a reassuring sense of stability. Nevertheless, in an attempt to keep pace with the times and tastes of younger spectators, Haberman created fresh routines to "modernize" the Rockettes. For example, in "Humbugged: Rockettes to the Rescue," their new number for the 2011 Christmas show, the Rockettes appeared to be ensconced in a video game as their live, onstage dancing was merged with 3-D video images produced by state-of-the-art technology. In the rapidly changing techno world of the twenty-first century, the Rockettes and their simulators are reflecting the latest trends in visual culture while remaining familiar and comforting providers of popular entertainment.

Lisa Jo Sagolla

SEE ALSO: *Broadway; Christmas; Graham, Martha; Hollywood; Ice Shows; Las Vegas; Made-for-Television Movies; Movie Palaces; The Rockefeller Family; Tap Dancing; Video Games;* The Ziegfeld Follies.

BIBLIOGRAPHY

Jonas, Gerald. "From Innovation to High Camp: The Line at Radio City Music Hall." *New York Times Magazine*, November 12, 1967, 114–121.

Kourlas, Gia. "Rockettes, Rebooted for a New Era." *New York Times*, November 4, 2011, AR1.

Leavin, Paul. "Twenty-One Ways of Looking at the Rockettes." *Eddy* 8 (1976): 66–79.

Love, Judith Anne. *Thirty Thousand Kicks: What's It Like to Be a Rockette?* Hicksville, NY: Exposition Press, 1980.

Rockne, Knute *(1888–1931)*

The legend of Knute Rockne goes beyond football. Every school with an active athletic program has its share of sports legends—stories about great athletes and coaches of the past and the games that made them famous. The University of Notre Dame in South Bend, Indiana, is no exception; the school's athletic tradition has produced many legendary figures, especially from its Fighting Irish football team. The tale of Rockne, however, has transcended Notre Dame to become part of Americana.

Knute K. Rockne was born in Voss, Norway, on March 4, 1888. His family immigrated to the United States in 1893, settling in Chicago. Rockne entered the University of Notre Dame in 1910 and tried out for the football team—unsuccessfully. In that era, football was almost entirely a game of brute force, and Rockne was deemed neither large enough nor muscular enough. The following year, with the Irish under a different coach, Rockne made the team and played for three years, striving to make up in speed and guile what he lacked in size and strength.

Upon graduating in 1914, Rockne was immediately hired as assistant coach of Notre Dame's football team. During his four years in that position, he was credited with introducing two innovations into the game: the forward pass and the shift. In fact, Rockne probably did not invent these tactics (and never claimed that he had), but his teams were the first to integrate these new moves into their regular game plan. The use of the forward pass greatly increased the role of strategy in the game. The shift (lateral movement on the part of offensive players before the ball is snapped) allowed the offense to adapt to the defense's formation, and it made the game more exciting.

It was while he was assistant coach in 1916 that Rockne recruited a young man named George Gipp to the team. Gipp turned out to be the best athlete Rockne ever coached. When Rockne was appointed Notre Dame's head coach in 1918, Gipp was his star player. However, in his senior year, Gipp contracted pneumonia following a game. Despite hospitalization, his condition worsened, and, tragically, Gipp died on December 14, 1920.

But the story of Gipp did not end with his death. Years later, when a surprisingly mediocre Notre Dame team was trying to salvage a winning season by defeating football powerhouse Army, Rockne gave the locker-room speech that is the centerpiece of the Rockne legend. The team knew who Gipp was, but Rockne told them something they didn't know: Gipp's last words to his coach. According to Rockne, the dying Gipp had told him, "I've got to go, Rock. It's all right, I'm not afraid. Some time, Rock, when the team is up against it, when things are wrong and the breaks are beating the boys, tell them to go in there with all they've got and win just one for the Gipper. I don't know where I'll be then, Rock, but I'll know about it, and I'll be happy."

This sentimental story of Gipp's last wish may well have been fiction, but it worked for the Fighting Irish, who went on to defeat Army, the heavy favorites. It also became the key scene in the 1940 film about Rockne's life, *Knute Rockne, All American*. Pat O'Brien portrayed the great coach, and a young Ronald Reagan played Gipp. The role followed Reagan for the rest of his life. When he left movies for a career in politics, the Gipp nickname was revived by journalists, who sometimes referred to Reagan in print as "the Gipper." This led to "Win One for the Gipper" being used as a campaign slogan when Reagan ran for president in 1980. Reporters used the term occasionally during his presidency and afterward.

The skill and spirit of Rockne also resides in another enduring aspect of sports mythology that has passed into popular culture; it is arguably the most famous passage in American sports journalism. After another Rockne-coached Notre Dame team defeated Army on October 18, 1924, Grantland Rice wrote in the next day's edition of the *New York Herald Tribune*:

> Outlined against a blue-gray October sky, the Four Horsemen rode again. In dramatic lore they are known as Famine, Pestilence, Destruction and Death. These are only aliases. Their real names are: Stuhldreher,

> Miller, Crowly and Layden. They formed the crest of the South Bend cyclone before which another fighting Army team was swept over the precipice at the Polo Grounds this afternoon as 55,000 spectators peered down upon the bewildering panorama spread out on the green plain below.

Rockne's team was undefeated that season, one of five such triumphant seasons that he enjoyed during his thirteen years as Notre Dame's head coach. His overall record during that time was 105 wins, 12 losses, and 5 ties. Knute Rockne was killed in a plane crash on March 31, 1931.

Justin Gustainis

SEE ALSO: *College Football; Reagan, Ronald; Rice, Grantland.*

BIBLIOGRAPHY

Brondfield, Jerry. *Rockne: The Coach, the Man, the Legend.* New York: Random House, 1976.

Gekas, George. *Gipper: Life and Times of George Gipp.* South Bend, IN: And Books, 1987.

Sperber, Murray. *Shake Down the Thunder: The Creation of Notre Dame Football.* New York: Henry Holt, 1993.

Rockwell, Norman *(1894–1978)*

Despite his distinction as a popular painter of everyday life, for much of the twentieth century Norman Rockwell represented a point of controversy concerning the definition of art and the nature of American culture itself. Although a sizable public embraced the illustrator as America's greatest painter, others have reviled his work as vacuous commercial art depicting a highly restricted spectrum of the national makeup. Rockwell's prominence and the prevailing conception of advocates and critics alike—that his task was to represent America—largely issued from his long association with the popular magazine the *Saturday Evening Post.* Even when, in the last decades of his life, Rockwell undertook assignments challenging the conservative cultural values of the *Post*—values that were mistakenly ascribed to the illustrator as well—his apparently unself-conscious, realistic style remained out of step with contemporary artistic practices. By the end of the twentieth century, he was widely recognized as a highly successful illustrator though not as an artist, his name serving as a shorthand term for the values of small-town America that he so often depicted.

Rockwell himself enjoyed the pleasant irony that, his reputation notwithstanding, he was born—on February 3, 1894—in the paramount metropolis of New York City. Although his father's family had once held substantial wealth and his mother took great pride in an English aristocratic ancestry, by the time of Norman Percevel's birth, the family's fortune and status had both declined. Rockwell recalled growing up in modest circumstances and described episodes of acute embarrassment in the face of his own social indiscretions, which he thought bespoke his lower-middle-class background. His family remained respectably pious, to the extent that Rockwell and his younger brother were conscripted into the church choir by their parents. This religiosity, however, did not stick, and as an adult he would decline to attend church services.

In his autobiography, Rockwell describes a boyhood full of anxieties and punctuated by numerous unpleasant episodes. Among his friends he stood out as an awkward and pigeon-toed boy, his face dominated by large round eyeglasses that earned him the despised nickname "Mooney." He nonetheless participated in all the games and pranks of his neighborhood playmates, including, as he later recalled with contrition, incidents of bigoted name-calling. Urban encounters with indigent drunks and rancorous couples enhanced, by contrast, his cherished memories of summer trips away from the city. He would later characterize his early interest in drawing as a compensatory practice that won him admiration from his peers.

EARLY SUCCESS

As a high school freshman, Rockwell began taking weekly leave in order to attend the Chase School of Art, and in his

Norman Rockwell in His Studio. *Norman Rockwell works in his Stockbridge, Massachusetts, studio in 1973.* **AP IMAGES.**

sophomore year he left altogether, becoming a full-time student at the National Academy of Design at the age of sixteen. Finding the academy's program "stiff and scholarly," he enrolled at the Art Students League in New York in 1910. There he devoted himself to the study of the human figure and illustration under instructors George Bridgman and Thomas Fogarty.

Like his fellow students, Rockwell admired and identified with the work of prominent American illustrators such as Howard Pyle and Edward Austin Abbey, particularly their inspiring attention to historically accurate detail and compelling visual narratives. At the same time he esteemed the expressive qualities and technical virtuosity of painters ranging from Rembrandt and Johannes Vermeer to James Whistler and Pablo Picasso. Although modernist practices held little interest for Rockwell in his own art—excepting some brief experiments in the 1920s—neither he nor his peers saw much distinction between the fine arts and illustration. They did, however, disdain other, debased spheres of artistic practice.

Rockwell writes in his autobiography that he and his peers "signed our names in blood, swearing never to prostitute our art, never to do advertising jobs." However, the nature of the field of illustration itself was in transition, with the proliferation of cheap illustrated magazines (which needed advertisers who in turn needed illustrators), the increasing use of photography, and the demise of handsomely decorated books that had seen their zenith during the so-called golden age of illustration. Rockwell's own practice would soon include the production of successful and highly sought-after advertising illustrations.

His first inroads into a professional career included illustrating a didactic children's book called *Tell Me Why Stories.* Landing the position of contributing art director for *Boys' Life* in 1913, Rockwell soon developed a reputation as an illustrator for an emerging group of youth magazines. These popular magazines, including *St. Nicholas*, *American Boy*, and *Youth's Companion*, were intended to entertain white, middle-class adolescents and promote the same ideals of American citizenry embodied in the Boy Scouts and the Young Men's Christian Association movements. Yet Rockwell sought a more distinguished venue for his art.

THE *SATURDAY EVENING POST*

Working for the youth magazines, he was soon able to afford a succession of shared studios in New York City and then in New Rochelle, where his family took up residence in a boardinghouse. Despite his steady income, Rockwell aspired to see his work on the cover of what he considered "the greatest show window in America for an illustrator," the *Saturday Evening Post.* Setting his sights on the *Post*, he struggled to paint a sample image of a sophisticated society couple in the style of the Charles Dana Gibson but soon realized that his strength lay in genre scenes, realistically rendered pictures of everyday life. He presented the *Post* editors with two finished canvases depicting scenes of American boyhood and several similar sketches. All were approved, and within two months his first illustration for the *Saturday Evening Post* appeared on the cover of the issue for May 20, 1916. In his words, he "had arrived."

Having broken into the field of illustration for adult magazines, Rockwell was soon submitting work to *Life*, *Judge*, *Leslie's*, and the *Country Gentleman.* By the early 1920s he would gain substantial recognition and could be selective about his assignments, working only for the most prominent magazines.

Throughout Rockwell's forty-seven-year association with the *Post* as its most prominent cover illustrator, he continued to undertake a variety of assignments, including calendars, books, and advertisements. Among his best-known works are the annual Boy Scout calendars painted from 1924 to 1976 (he missed only two years), his illustrations for new editions of Mark Twain's *The Adventures of Tom Sawyer* (1936) and *Huckleberry Finn* (1940), and the long series of pencil-drawn advertisements for Massachusetts Mutual Life Insurance Company from 1950 to 1963. In 1943 the *Post* published his *Four Freedoms*—illustrating the essential principles declared by President Franklin Roosevelt—which soon became successful war bond posters. Each of these has in common the optimism and moral salubrity Rockwell depicted throughout his seven-decade career.

Still, it was his long-standing affiliation with the *Saturday Evening Post* that marked Rockwell's cultural reception. Between the World Wars and under editor George Horace Lorimer, the *Post* advanced illustration as a particularly American art. Illustration was characterized there as speaking a commonsense visual language, in opposition to modern art as a rarified and intellectualized foreign import. In short, illustration was wrapped in the magazine's conservative and isolationist positions on culture and politics. This legacy, combined with the *Post*'s pronounced decline and unsteady revival as a discredited voice of nostalgia during the 1960s and 1970s, left Rockwell himself as a representative of obsolescence.

In 1963 Rockwell left the *Post* and soon expanded his repertoire of themes to encompass explicitly controversial social issues. Until this time he had applied his high-detail realism to folksy scenes—usually witty, sometimes poignant—of what appeared to be everyday life in America. As critics would note, this image of the nation's people was generally restricted to white, middle-class, and heterosexual families. Rockwell later explained, in part, that longtime *Post* editor Lorimer had instructed him "never to show colored people except as servants." And so they appeared throughout the *Post* and Rockwell's oeuvre.

By contrast, Rockwell's work for *Look* magazine in the mid-1960s explored black-white race relations and the social turmoil that followed the civil rights movement and subsequent legislation. Best known of these is his 1964 image of Ruby Bridges escorted by U.S. Marshal's deputies as she integrated a white elementary school in New Orleans in 1960 (*Look*, January 14). Thus, it was only in the last decade and a half of his life that Rockwell's own liberal views might have become readily apparent to a broader public.

EFFORTS TO REASSESS HIS WORK

This late turn toward inclusive subject matter came packaged in Rockwell's brilliant, if familiar, realist style, which itself seemed antiprogressive to many art-scene observers. For them, Rockwell's illustrations, though technically accomplished, lacked artistic freedom, intellectual engagement, and creative insight. Still, he remained popular with a substantial portion of the American public. This disparity was played out when art critics dismissed a popular 1968 exhibition of his canvases at a New York City gallery, and again in 1972 on the occasion of a Rockwell retrospective held at the Brooklyn Museum. Any reconsideration of his aesthetic and historical significance proposed by these exhibitions was further stymied after 1969 by the apparent crass commercialism of an agreement permitting the Franklin Mint to produce versions of his well-known earlier images as porcelain figurines and silver coins.

Rockwell died on November 8, 1978, in Stockbridge, Massachusetts. His first marriage, which had followed the success of his earliest *Post* cover, ended in divorce in 1930. In that same year he met and married Mary Barstow, with whom he was to raise three sons, Jarvis, Thomas, and Peter. After Mary's death he was remarried once more, to Mary (Molly) Punderson. The most comprehensive collection of his works is found at the Norman Rockwell Museum at Stockbridge, to which he left many paintings and papers upon his death.

Notwithstanding the failure of earlier attempts to present a convincing reassessment of Rockwell, in the 1980s and 1990s he was reasserted as a significant cultural figure. Popular interest in his work hardly abated, as witnessed by the proliferation of Rockwell picture books. In the early 1980s a major fund-raising campaign to build a new home for the Norman Rockwell Museum in Stockbridge drew substantial support from a range of prominent political figures, indicating that with regard to Rockwell's reception, so-called traditional values might be severed from conservative politics. Decades after his death, Rockwell remains an iconic figure, his name serving as shorthand for idyllic values promoting family and community. These deeply nostalgic associations recall an America of the past, one imagined as modern, prosperous, homogeneous, and free of the social ills that continue to plague the United States.

Eric J. Segal

SEE ALSO: *Boy Scouts of America; Civil Rights Movement; Mass Market Magazine Revolution; The Saturday Evening Post; War Bonds.*

BIBLIOGRAPHY

Guptill, Arthur L. *Norman Rockwell, Illustrator.* New York: Watson-Guptill Publications, 1970.

Halpern, Richard. *Norman Rockwell: The Underside of Innocence.* Chicago: University of Chicago Press, 2006.

Marling, Karal Ann. *Norman Rockwell.* New York: Abrams, 1997.

Rockwell, Norman, and Thomas Rockwell. *My Adventures as an Illustrator.* Garden City, NY: Doubleday, 1960.

Segal, Eric. "Norman Rockwell and the Fashioning of American Masculinity." *Art Bulletin* 78, no. 4 (1996): 633–646.

Rocky

Rocky (1976) may not be the best sports film ever made, but for many it is the best loved. As much love story as boxing movie, this feel-good box-office smash launched Sylvester Stallone's career into the stratosphere, inspired countless imitations (some of which were the *Rocky* sequels), and provided America with a simple blue-collar hero at a time when nonheroes and antiheroes—in movies such as *One Flew over the Cuckoo's Nest* and *Dog Day Afternoon*—predominated on American movie screens. As Stallone told the *New York Times* at the time the film came out, "I've really had it with anti-this and anti-that. . . . I want to be remembered as a man of raging optimism, who believes in the American dream. . . . Where are all the heroes?"

SYLVESTER STALLONE

Much of the film's appeal stems from the fact that Rocky Balboa's succeeding-against-all-odds story is neatly paralleled by the succeeding-against-all-odds story of Stallone himself. The actor had been living in a seedy Hollywood apartment with his wife, his savings having dwindled to $106, when he wrote his script about the Italian Stallion. Producers Irwin Winkler and Robert Chartoff showed the script to United Artists, and the studio was sufficiently impressed to offer Stallone $75,000 for the script—then $125,000, then $350,000—so they could make the film starring Ryan O'Neal, Robert Redford, James Caan, or one of the other superstars of the day. Stallone, however, wanted the role for himself and, realizing that the story was about having faith in yourself and going the distance, he declined the offers, even though he was about to be evicted from his apartment and his wife was pregnant with their first child. When he finally got the chance to star in the film, it launched his career and the film went on to win the Academy Award for best picture of 1976, beating out such box-office and critical champs as *Network* and *All the President's Men.*

THE INSPIRATION: CHUCK WEPNER

Early in 1975, before Rocky Balboa existed in anyone's imagination, Chuck Wepner was, to many boxing fans, a joke. Living in Bayonne, New Jersey, he sold liquor by day and boxed at night. The thirty-five-year-old Wepner, who was ranked as the world's eighth-best heavyweight by *Ring* magazine, had been nicknamed "the Bayonne Bleeder" because of the 300-plus stitches he had accumulated on his face, mostly around his eyes. He was an unlikely boxer to be facing "the Greatest," Muhammad Ali, in the ring, but Ali was just looking for an easy fight as a warm-up for his next major heavyweight title bout. The fight was such a joke that oddsmakers did not even put out a betting line. The week before the fight, a reporter asked Ali if he thought of Wepner as representing white America in their upcoming bout. Ali rolled his eyes and said, "White America wouldn't pick *him*!" Ali called Wepner a "cinch," and someone else suggested that if Wepner was ranked eighth, then a punching bag must have been seventh.

This champ-vs.-chump fight was a joke to everyone—except, of course, to Wepner himself, who spent the two months leading up to the fight in the Catskill Mountains with his trainer and manager, training constantly. On March 24, 1975, the spectators who gathered in the Coliseum outside Cleveland were expecting Wepner to last three rounds at most, but, to everyone's amazement, Wepner hung in there round after round after round. At one point Ali's fist broke Wepner's nose. In round seven Ali opened a cut over Wepner's left eye, and reopened it in every round thereafter. Wepner's eye swelled shut to the point where he could no longer see Ali's powerful right jabs coming.

But in round nine Wepner brought the crowd to its feet when he knocked Ali down with a roundhouse right—only the fourth time in Ali's long illustrious career that he had been knocked down. When Wepner answered the bell beginning the fifteenth and final round, he became only the sixth Ali opponent to make it so far. Ali then slammed a powerful right into Wepner's bloody face, the barely conscious Wepner slumped against the ropes and, with nineteen seconds remaining in the fight, the referee stopped the bout and awarded Ali a TKO (technical knockout). Ali later said, "None of my fights was tougher than this one. There's not another human being in the world that can go fifteen rounds like that."

The spectators had been galvanized, not just in Cleveland but at pay-per-view venues across the country where the fight was carried on closed-circuit television. One of those spectators was Stallone, who had dipped into his $106 in savings to watch the fight at the Wiltern Theater in Los Angeles. Stallone had gone because "there's something about sweating that inspires me to write," and he certainly got his money's worth. According to Stallone, "That night, Rocky Balboa was born."

ROCKY

Stallone nurtured the idea for three months before churning out the script in three and a half days. He was reluctant to show his script to potential investors because he considered it a rough draft with a number of problems. In this early version, Rocky's trainer Mickey (played by Burgess Meredith in the film) was a racist, and opponent Apollo Creed (played by Carl Weathers) was much older. At the climax, when Rocky has Apollo on the ropes, Mickey's racism comes out in full force, and he screams at Rocky to kill his opponent. This angers Rocky, who then allows Apollo to land a punch so Rocky can take a dive, and Apollo wins. Rocky retires from fighting and uses his earnings from the fight to buy girlfriend Adrian (played by Talia Shire) a pet shop. In his next two drafts Stallone considered having Rocky win, but realized that this would not only be unbelievable, it would turn Rocky from a common man into a superhero. Cannily, Stallone opted for the ending that was eventually filmed, with Rocky losing the fight but "going the distance." For Stallone the film was not about winning, it was about courage; the opponent was not Apollo Creed, it was unrealized dreams and fear of failure.

Even though Stallone had refused United Artists' offer of $350,000, Winkler and Chartoff still thought the film might get backing with Stallone as the star if they could come up with a low-enough budget. They finally trimmed the budget to an extremely modest $1,750,000. United Artists executives felt even this was too high, considering the fact that they were not sure if Stallone had sufficient charisma to be a leading man or could be convincing as a boxer. They finally agreed to back the film if the budget were trimmed to an even $1,000,000, with Chartoff and Winkler paying for any budget overruns. The producers then proceeded to slash salaries in exchange for a percentage of the profits, agreed to take nothing up front, told Stallone he would get only $20,000 for his script and would have to act for union scale, found file footage of crowd scenes from actual fights to save having to hire extras, and scouted real locations to reduce the number of sets that had to be built. Stallone rewrote the scene where Rocky takes Adrian to a crowded skating rink for their first date, substituting a rink that is closed for Thanksgiving in order to save the cost of all those extras on skates. Director John G. Avildsen agreed to direct for one-half his usual $100,000 fee in exchange for a percentage of the film. For the five months before the cameras rolled, Stallone and Weathers trained together, and Stallone spent every spare moment jogging on the beach, doing pushups, studying fight films, and working out at a gym with a former fight trainer. The film was shot in twenty-eight days and came in $40,000 under budget.

RECEPTION OF *ROCKY*

The movie was a box-office and critical smash, with the public taking to heart this story of a Philadelphia lug who supplements his income by working as an enforcer for a loan shark but refuses to break thumbs, talks to his pet turtles Cuff and Link, trains at a slaughterhouse by pummeling sides of beef, and makes that triumphant run up the steps of the Philadelphia Museum of Art. *Rocky* received ten Academy Award nominations, and Stallone's nominations for both Best Actor and Best Screenplay marked only the third time in Oscar history that someone had received both nominations for the same film, previous nominees being Charlie Chaplin and Orson Welles. The film won for Best Picture, Best Director, and Best Film Editing. Following the movie men flocked to gyms in order to bulk up, drinking raw eggs became a passing fad, and a wave of films flooded out of Hollywood copying the *Rocky* formula, notably the *Karate Kid* films directed by Avildsen and the *Rocky* sequels.

When the first *Rocky* premiered, Stallone said he was planning two sequels: in the first, Rocky would attend night school, enter politics, and get elected mayor of Philadelphia; and in the second he would get framed by the political machine because of his honesty, get impeached, and return to the ring. After the phenomenal success of *Rocky*, however, Stallone and the producers realized that a fortune could be made by, in effect, remaking the first film, but climaxing it with a Rocky–Apollo Creed championship fight with Rocky winning. Stallone directed *Rocky II* (1979) and all involved made fortunes, but the film was a far cry from the original. Stallone then directed *Rocky III* (1982) and *Rocky IV* (1985), and Avildsen returned to direct *Rocky V* (1990), each film generally worse than the one before. Stallone felt that his input was ignored in *Rocky V* and returned to direct and star in the 2006 film *Rocky Balboa* (also known as *Rocky VI*), which depicts the retired and aging Rocky returning to the ring for one last round. The film was a surprise hit, garnering both critical and popular acclaim. Although the sequels are generally considered inferior, the original *Rocky* has held up over time, retaining enough of a reputation to have been selected by the American Film Institute as one of the hundred greatest films of the last hundred years.

Bob Sullivan

SEE ALSO: *Academy Awards; Ali, Muhammad; Boxing; Cult Films; Movie Stars;* One Flew over the Cuckoo's Nest*; Sports Heroes; Stallone, Sylvester; United Artists.*

BIBLIOGRAPHY

Daly, Marsha. *Sylvester Stallone.* New York: St. Martin's Press, 1986.

Rovin, Jeff. *Stallone! A Hero's Story.* New York: Pocket Books, 1985.

Stallone, Sylvester. *The Official Rocky Scrapbook.* New York: Grosset & Dunlap, 1977.

Wright, Adrian. *Sylvester Stallone: A Life in Film*. London: Robert Hale Limited, 1991.

Rocky and Bullwinkle

The 1990s saw a renaissance in American animation on television, as the phenomenal ratings success of *The Simpsons* prompted network executives to introduce a host of new cartoon series for adult audiences. The irreverent humor and satirical eye of these postmodern programs owed a great debt, however, to one of the pioneering shows of this genre, an animated series featuring a squirrel and a moose—Rocky and Bullwinkle. The series, which debuted as *Rocky and His Friends* and was later retitled *The Bullwinkle Show*, aired from 1959 to 1964, setting the standard for sophisticated cartoon whimsy.

Although the program followed the adventures of Bullwinkle J. Moose, a good-natured, if slightly dim, antlered mammal, and his resourceful cohort Rocky the Flying Squirrel, this was no ordinary cutesy animal cartoon. Episodes were leavened with generous helpings of topical humor, including Cold War satire in the form of Boris and Natasha, dastardly spies from a nebulous Eastern Bloc nation called Pottsylvania. In a typical series plotline, Boris and Natasha attempt to sabotage the U.S. economy by counterfeiting America's most indispensable currency, the cereal box top. "Serial" became an operative term for the show itself, as the story lines carried over from week to week in the manner of old-time adventure movies.

There were a number of additional segments of the program, including "The Adventures of Dudley Do-Right," about a stolid Mountie; "Fractured Fairy Tales," a send-up of the Brothers Grimm and company; and "Mr. Peabody's Improbable History," which followed the exploits of a pedantic pooch who can travel back in time to great moments in the past. All the elements of the show incorporated the same dry humor, reliance on puns, and disdain for the "fourth wall" separating the characters from the audience. The various elements of the show succeeded in keeping the attention of children and adults alike.

"*Bullwinkle* was a magnificent marriage of concept, writing, performing, and direction," observed June Foray in 1991. Foray would know, having served as the voice of Rocket J. Squirrel since the cartoon's inception. A one-time radio performer, she was hired for the cartoon series by Jay Ward, a Harvard Business School graduate who created Rocky and Bullwinkle in the late 1950s. Ward, who had no background in writing or animation, relied on a staff of creative types led by writer and vocal stylist Bill Scott, who became the voice of Bullwinkle J. Moose. Others who worked on the show included Allan Burns, a talented comedy writer who helped create *The Mary Tyler Moore Show* in the 1970s.

After concluding its original run of 156 episodes, *Rocky and Bullwinkle* appeared regularly in reruns until 1973. At that point, sophisticated animation sadly went out of style. The moose and squirrel popped up only sporadically in reruns on local stations for the next eighteen years. But this long fallow period was only the prelude to a grand *Bullwinkle* renaissance.

In 1991 six video tapes of classic Rocky and Bullwinkle episodes were released by Disney as *The Adventures of Rocky and Bullwinkle*. With the success of Fox's animated series *The Simpsons* fostering a renewed appreciation for edgy cartoon comedy, sales were brisk. Nostalgic baby boomers and their offspring gobbled up two million copies of the video cassettes in the first year of release. Even an ill-conceived 1992 live-action movie, *Boris and Natasha*, could not slow the moose's long march back to public favor. Cable television's Cartoon Network soon added *The Rocky and Bullwinkle Show* to its lineup of cartoon classics, and it quickly became one of the channel's most watched shows among teenagers, a notoriously hard-to-please demographic. To capitalize further on the cartoon's retro hipness, a handsome commemorative volume, *The Rocky and Bullwinkle Book*, reached bookstore shelves in 1996. The animated movie *The Adventures of Rocky & Bullwinkle* was released in 2000, but it received poor reviews and did badly at the box office.

Perhaps there was no greater indication of Rocky and Bullwinkle's return to the pinnacle of the pop-culture pantheon than their reinstatement to the front lines of the annual Macy's Thanksgiving Day Parade in New York City. The inflatable moose had disappeared from the parade after 1983, but in 1996 a new Bullwinkle balloon, redesigned with Rocky on his back, once again joined the likes of Bugs Bunny, Mighty Mouse, and Underdog. The pair were later replaced by Spider-Man and SpongeBob SquarePants, among other favorites in the cartoon world. However, for those who grew up with Rocky and Bullwinkle or discovered them in reruns, nothing could truly replace the inimitable pair.

Robert E. Schnakenberg

SEE ALSO: *Baby Boomers; Bugs Bunny; Disney (Walt Disney Company); Macy's;* The Mary Tyler Moore Show*;* The Simpsons*; Spider-Man; SpongeBob SquarePants; Television; Thanksgiving.*

BIBLIOGRAPHY

Chunovic, Louis. *The Rocky and Bullwinkle Book*. New York: Bantam Doubleday Dell, 1996.

Scott, Keith. *The Moose That Roared: The Story of Jay Ward, Bill Scott, a Flying Squirrel, and a Talking Moose*. New York: St Martin's Griffin, 2000.

The Rocky Horror Picture Show

The Rocky Horror Picture Show was not the first midnight movie, but it is arguably the most well known. With its rebellious blend of "B"-movie science fiction, horror, and a rock-and-roll soundtrack, *Rocky Horror* celebrates sexual difference. Inspiring viewers with the catch phrase, "Don't dream it, be it!" *Rocky Horror* earned its cult status in part through its transgressive nature. Its fans are legion, and since the film's release in 1975, *Rocky Horror* has developed into a full-fledged cult that has spawned its own cottage industry of merchandise and memorabilia. *Rocky Horror* has become synonymous with participatory cinema, and its history as a midnight feature helped define what it meant to be a cult film in the late twentieth century.

FROM ROCK MUSICAL TO MOVIE

The Rocky Horror Picture Show grew out of the fertile imagination of English actor Richard O'Brien, who wrote a rock musical titled *The Rocky Horror Show* over the course of six months

The Rocky Horror Picture Show. *Tim Curry, left, Barry Bostwick, and Susan Sarandon starred in the 1975 cult classic* The Rocky Horror Picture Show. **20TH CENTURY FOX/THE KOBAL COLLECTION.**

in 1972. O'Brien's play combined his appreciation for "B" movies and his love of science fiction within a story set in the fictional town of Denton, Ohio. After attending the wedding of two friends, nerdy sweethearts Brad Majors and Janet Weiss are caught up in the moment and decide to get married. En route to the home of Brad's former college professor, Dr. Everett V. Scott, the couple is deterred by inclement weather. Taking shelter in a roadside mansion, Brad and Janet encounter their host, Dr. Frank-N-Furter, a transvestite overseeing the annual convention of aliens from the planet Transylvania. Although Brad and Janet are less than charmed by the doctor, he insists that they remain in the mansion overnight to witness his ultimate scientific creation: the perfect male specimen.

In the course of their stay, Brad and Janet are seduced by Frank, and Janet in turn seduces the doctor's creation, Rocky Horror. Along the way the couple meets Riff Raff, the doctor's sidekick; his sister Magenta; and a groupie named Columbia. The next morning Brad's mentor comes to the mansion looking for his nephew Eddie, the former lover of Frank whose brain was used to create Rocky Horror and whose remains become the main dish in an elaborate last supper held at the mansion. In a grand finale Frank is overthrown as overseer of the Transylvanians, and Riff Raff and Magenta take over the group, blasting the mansion back to Transylvania and leaving Brad, Janet, and Dr. Scott to contemplate their experiences.

Premiering at a small theater in the Chelsea neighborhood of London in June 1973, *The Rocky Horror Show* was an instant success. The popularity of the musical, which starred the charismatic performer Tim Curry as Frank, made it necessary to move the production to successively larger theaters throughout London. After seeing one of these performances in 1974, U.S. movie producer Lou Adler (*Monterey Pop*, *Brewster McCloud*) struck a deal with O'Brien and fellow *Rocky Horror* producer Michael White that allowed Adler to bring the stage show to Los Angeles and eventually turn the musical into a feature-length film produced by Twentieth Century Fox.

After O'Brien's musical finished its ten-month run in Los Angeles, Curry returned to London with some of the other performers to shoot the film version at Bray Studios, the former home of the horror films made by Hammer Studios. The film, whose title was changed to *The Rocky Horror Picture Show*, was shot over the course of eight weeks by director Jim Sharman from a script cowritten by Sharman and O'Brien. Although some of the stage actors, such as Curry and O'Brien (Riff Raff), reprised their roles in the film version, actors Susan Sarandon and Barry Bostwick were brought in to play Janet and Brad. Patricia Quinn played Magenta both onstage and in the film, and her wet, red lips provide *Rocky Horror* with its seductive opening sequence as she mouths the words to the song, "Science Fiction/ Double Feature." As J. Hoberman and Jonathan Rosenbaum observe in *Midnight Movies*, this image of Quinn's salacious mouth lip-synching the lyrics sung on the accompanying soundtrack by O'Brien immediately introduces viewers to the tantalizing presence and overwhelming significance of bisexuality within *Rocky Horror*.

GAINING CULT STATUS

After a brief, unsuccessful run of the play on Broadway at the Belasco Theater, *Rocky Horror* the film previewed in California in the summer of 1975. Responses to preview screenings of the film were as negative as those leveled at the Broadway production, but Tim Deegan, the film's publicist, focused on the few viewers who were enthusiastic about the film and kept their responses in mind when promoting it. When it opened in Los Angeles in the early fall of 1975, *Rocky Horror* had little trouble filling the theater. Elsewhere in the country, however, the film did not fare as well. Inspired by the exhibition techniques used to promote George Romero's *Night of the Living Dead*, however, Deegan arranged to release the film in New York only at midnight and to keep it at the same theater for at least one month so the film could find its audience. As it turned out, word-of-mouth drew viewers to the theater, and the movie itself kept audiences coming back for repeat viewings—a defining characteristic of cult films.

Although it is difficult to pinpoint when audiences first began participating in the *Rocky Horror* experience, Hoberman and Rosenbaum suggest one of the earliest instances occurred in New York City in 1976, a few months after the film's release. Dubbed "counterpoint dialogue," this verbal interaction with the film began as a way to fill the awkward pauses between dialogue exchanges and to comment on the poorly written lines uttered by some of the characters. Soon repeat audiences were staging their own "shows" before the film's midnight screening and during the screening as well. Scripts were written by *Rocky Horror* fans containing counterpoint dialogue for the entire film, and directions for dancing the Time Warp (a dance sequence that occurs in the film) were passed out to audiences—a technique that had its roots in the stage show's early days.

Some fans began attending screenings dressed as the film's characters. Props were used as a kind of visual counterpoint to the film as well. During a screening of *Rocky Horror*, for instance, it is customary for audience members to throw rice at the screen during the wedding sequence. When Brad and Janet get caught in a storm, viewers open umbrellas in the theater or hold newspapers over their heads while other members of the audience fire water pistols into the crowd. Newcomers to the *Rocky Horror* film are called virgins, and their initiation into the experience is gleefully overseen by veterans who have attended the screenings many times over.

The cult surrounding *Rocky Horror* has continued to grow since the film's release in late 1975. Movies such as *Fame* (1980), which contains a sequence in which two characters attend a *Rocky Horror* screening, introduced mainstream audiences to a phenomenon that may have otherwise eluded them. During the 1980s in liberal arts classes throughout the country, scholars began to analyze and write about the cult of *Rocky Horror* and to discuss this cultural phenomenon in terms of religion, socialization, sexuality, and ritual. It is customary for the film to screen on college campuses, and this event serves as a kind of initiation into underground culture, sexual difference, and participatory cinema.

THE HORROR LIVES ON

For some hard-core *Rocky Horror* fans, the film's acceptance into mainstream society contradicts the very essence of what *Rocky Horror* represents. With its emphasis on unbridled sexuality and transgressive behavior, *Rocky Horror* has been described by Hoberman and Rosenbaum as an "adolescent initiation" that rearticulates the sexual politics of the 1960s. Its release to home video in 1990 struck some as counterproductive because so much of one's enjoyment in the film comes from watching it with an audience. Nonetheless, the video release proved successful enough to spawn a laser disc version in 1992, and in 1995, to celebrate the twentieth anniversary of the film's wide release, Fox Video unveiled a deluxe, remastered edit of the film. On an alternate audio track, the counterpoint dialogue of two Los Angeles–based audiences of *Rocky Horror* regulars can be heard. The inclusion of this separate audio track, carefully selected from the scores of *Rocky Horror* fan communities in existence, acknowledges the significant role the audience plays in the experience and success of *Rocky Horror*.

In 1981 O'Brien and Sharman reteamed to direct the sequel to *Rocky Horror*, titled *Shock Treatment*. In the film Brad (played by Cliff De Young) and Janet (Jessica Harper) are still married but are dissatisfied with their lives and one another. Their hometown has become a large television station, and citizens are either participants or viewers. Although *Shock Treatment* did not fare as well as its predecessor and disappointed many *Rocky Horror* fans, its plot recapitulates *Rocky Horror*'s original message, which encouraged viewers to lose their inhibitions and become participants rather than mere viewers of life. Even decades after its release, *Rocky Horror* continues to screen at midnight in theaters all around the globe and attract new generations of fans on a regular basis. It also continues to invade mainstream culture. In 2010 the television show *Glee* aired an episode in which the students put on a production of *Rocky Horror Picture Show*, and the program's cast later released an album of the music. The open text of *Rocky Horror*'s narrative allows viewers from a variety of cultural backgrounds to appreciate its campy spectacle. The film's ability to be read by audiences as both transgressive and recuperative, argues Barry K. Grant in his essay in *The Cult Film Experience: Beyond All Reason*, has contributed to *Rocky Horror*'s longevity.

Alison Macor

SEE ALSO: *"B" Movies; Broadway; Cult Films;* Glee; *Horror Movies; The Musical;* Night of the Living Dead; *Rock and Roll; Sarandon, Susan; Television.*

BIBLIOGRAPHY

Austin, Bruce A. "Portrait of a Cult Film Audience: *The Rocky Horror Picture Show.*" *Journal of Communications* 31 (1981): 450–465.

Evans, David, and Scott Michaels. *Rocky Horror: From Concept to Cult*. London: Sanctuary Publishing, 2002.

Grant, Barry K. "Science Fiction Double Feature: Ideology in the Cult Film." *The Cult Film Experience: Beyond All Reason*, ed. J. P. Telotte, 122–127. Austin: University of Texas Press, 1991.

Henkin, Bill. *The Rocky Horror Picture Show Book*. New York: Hawthorn Books, 1979.

Hoberman, J., and Jonathan Rosenbaum. *Midnight Movies*. New York: Da Capo Press, 1991.

Peary, Danny. *Cult Movies*. New York: Delta Books, 1981.

Piro, Sal. *Creatures of the Night: The Rocky Horror Experience*. Redford, MI: Stabur Press, 1990.

Weinstock, Jeffrey Andrew, ed. *Reading Rocky Horror: The Rocky Horror Picture Show and Popular Culture.* New York: Palgrave Macmillan, 2008.

Roddenberry, Gene *(1921–1991)*

Gene Roddenberry was the creator of a genuine cultural phenomenon: the *Star Trek* television series. It aired for three seasons between 1966 and 1969 before its cancellation but went on to thrive in syndication. The various *Star Trek* manifestations have included five live-action television series; one animated television series; eleven feature films; and countless novels, short stories, technical manuals, magazines and fanzines, comic books, fan conventions, and websites. There is even a *Star Trek*–inspired language: Klingon. Though Roddenberry died in 1991, the utopian future he envisioned continues to thrill millions of "Trekkies" or "Trekkers," as fans are known, via print, television, and cinema.

EARLY CAREER

Growing up in El Paso, Texas, as an isolated and sickly boy who sought temporary refuge from his unhappy circumstances in fantasy, Roddenberry discovered science fiction. Though he grew out of his youthful shell to embark on a varied and adventurous early career, he never lost his appreciation of the genre. After flying for the army and Pan Am, Roddenberry moved to Los Angeles to become a television writer in the 1950s. While working as a motorcycle policeman for the Los Angeles Police Department, he also wrote episodes for many respected TV series, such as *Dr. Kildare* (1961–1966), *Highway Patrol* (1955–1959), and *Naked City* (1958–1963), and became head writer for *Have Gun—Will Travel* (1957–1963).

In 1962 Roddenberry began writing one-hour pilots to sell as potential series and was the producer of the short-lived show *The Lieutenant* (1963–1964). When it became clear that *The Lieutenant* would not last longer than one season, Roddenberry turned to the science fiction genre for his next project. Tired of the constraints and timidity of American commercial television, he believed that science fiction was a way to covertly address social issues that sponsors, and hence networks, would otherwise shy away from.

Pursuing this idea, Roddenberry wrote a proposal for a series titled *Star Trek*, which, as every true fan knows, he described as a kind of "*Wagon Train* to the stars." He imagined a future in which a united Earth would work together with alien worlds to create a Federation, which would then dispatch giant starships throughout the galaxy "to boldly go where no man has gone before." The series would focus on the captain and crew of one starship (initially called *Yorktown* but later changed to *Enterprise*) during its five-year mission of exploration. To create limitless story potential, Roddenberry staffed his starship with hundreds of crew members; to save money, he emphasized that the series would use standing sets and visit only "Class M" (Earth-like) planets.

He submitted his proposal to MGM on March 11, 1964, and when they failed to respond, he took it to other Hollywood studios. Eventually, Desilu, a financially strapped studio looking for a hit series, signed Roddenberry to a three-year deal. His next step was to find a network for the show. CBS turned him down, but NBC agreed to give him $20,000 to write three stories, one of which would be chosen for development as a screenplay and pilot episode. Eventually, NBC chose "The Cage" (later changed to "The Menagerie") as the pilot for *Star Trek*.

STAR TREK

Filming on the pilot began December 12, 1964, and lasted for twelve days. The pilot introduced the characters of Captain Christopher Pike (played by Jeffrey Hunter), Vulcan officer Mr. Spock (Leonard Nimoy), and female executive officer Number One (Majel Barrett, who later married Roddenberry). The pilot cost $686,000 to make because of postproduction special effects and budget overruns and was eventually rejected by NBC as "too cerebral" for the television audience. However, the network took the unprecedented step of requesting another, more action-oriented pilot from Roddenberry. The second pilot, titled "Where No Man Has Gone Before," used a much different cast than the first and was accepted. The series was scheduled to begin in the fall of 1966, and after personally supervising the show's crucial first half season, Roddenberry became executive producer.

For the next three television seasons the series regulars included Captain James Kirk (William Shatner), First Officer Mr. Spock (Nimoy), Chief Medical Officer Leonard McCoy (DeForest Kelley), Chief Engineer Montgomery Scott (James Doohan), Helmsman Hikaru Sulu (George Takei), Communications Officer Uhuru (Nichelle Nichols), and Nurse Christine Chapel (Barrett). Ensign Pavel Chekov (Walter Koenig) was added to the show in the second season. The show's ratings were low, and NBC decided to cancel the next series, but Roddenberry capitalized on a tremendous outpouring of fan-mail support for the series' renewal in order to convince network executives to continue the show. However, when the network decided to place *Star Trek* in a late-night Friday time slot, which effectively meant killing the show's ratings once and for all, Roddenberry chose to distance himself from daily production, becoming executive producer again. At the end of the 1969 season the series was canceled.

Although he began developing other television and movie projects, most of which failed, Roddenberry was very much aware of the extremely enthusiastic following that grew around *Star Trek* in syndication. In 1972 he began working the *Star Trek* convention circuit, asking the Trekkers to write or call Hollywood executives in support of reviving the series. Paramount Studios and Roddenberry worked together over a period of years to bring back *Star Trek* as, alternately, a made-for-television movie, a series, and a low-budget theatrical movie, but none of the projects panned out.

BIG-SCREEN SUCCESS

Following the financial success of science fiction feature films such as *Star Wars* and *Close Encounters of the Third Kind* (both 1977), Paramount green-lighted a project that reunited the principals from the television cast and became *Star Trek: The Motion Picture* (1979). Roddenberry cowrote the screenplay and served as the film's producer. The finished product proved an expensive, effects-heavy disappointment, although it still earned more than $100 million—enough to justify a sequel.

With the sequels, Roddenberry fought a bitter but futile battle over what he saw as ideas designed to damage the franchise. In particular he objected to the death of Mr. Spock in the second film, the destruction of the *Enterprise* in the third, and the militaristic Federation of the sixth. Nonetheless, he continued as executive producer of the lucrative franchise, and in 1987 he created a spin-off television series, *Star Trek: The Next Generation*. The second series was set seventy-five years after the original and featured a fresh crew, led by Patrick Stewart's cerebral Captain Jean-Luc Picard, and a larger and faster starship, the *Enterprise D*. After a shaky start, *The Next Generation*, with Roddenberry as executive producer, became a bona fide hit during its third season and ran four more years until the cast graduated to their own feature films in 1994.

Roddenberry died of a heart attack shortly after attending a screening of *Star Trek VI: The Undiscovered Country* in late 1991. The success of *The Next Generation* films and the syndicated *Star Trek: Deep Space Nine* (1993–1999) and *Star Trek: Voyager* (1995–2001) series retained the popular appeal of the franchise for a number of years, until the cancellation of the series *Star Trek: Enterprise* in 2005 ended the eighteen-year stretch of Trek-inspired series and seemingly signaled "Star Trek exhaustion." However, the franchise warped back to life in 2009 with the financially and critically successful reboot, simply titled *Star Trek*, directed by J. J. Abrams.

With more sequels to come and perhaps another television series on the horizon, Roddenberry's film and television legacy continues into another generation. As for Roddenberry himself, the Space Foundation awarded him and his wife, Majel, with the Douglas S. Morrow Public Outreach Award, bestowed on the couple for promoting public enthusiasm for space exploration. The Television Academy Hall of Fame inducted Roddenberry in 2010. These awards are a testament to his vision and determination.

Phil Simpson

SEE ALSO: *Abrams, J. J.;* Close Encounters of the Third Kind*;* *Comic Books;* Dr. Kildare*; Hollywood; Made-for-Television Movies; MGM (Metro-Goldwyn-Mayer);* Star Trek*;* Star Trek: The Next Generation*;* Star Wars*; Television;* Wagon Train.

BIBLIOGRAPHY

Alexander, David. *"Star Trek" Creator: The Authorized Biography of Gene Roddenberry*. New York: Roc, 1994.

Engel, Joel. *Gene Roddenberry: The Myth and the Man behind "Star Trek."* New York: Hyperion, 1994.

Fern, Yvonne. *Inside the Mind of Gene Roddenberry: The Creator of "Star Trek."* London: HarperCollins, 1995.

Gross, Edward, and Mark Altman. *Great Birds of the Galaxy: Gene Roddenberry and the Creators of "Star Trek."* New York: Image, 1992.

Roddenberry, Gene, and Susan Sackett. *"Star Trek": The First 25 Years*. New York: Pocket Books, 1992.

Sackett, Susan. *Inside Trek: My Secret Life with "Star Trek" Creator Gene Roddenberry*. Tulsa, OK: Hawk Publishing Group, 2002.

Shatner, William, and Chris Kreski. *"Star Trek" Memories*. New York: HarperPaperbacks, 1994.

Shatner, William, and Chris Kreski. *"Star Trek" Movie Memories*. New York: HarperPaperbacks, 1995.

Van Hise, James. *The Man Who Created "Star Trek": Gene Roddenberry*. Las Vegas, NV: Pioneer, 1992.

Whitfield, Stephen E., and Gene Roddenberry. *The Making of "Star Trek."* New York: Ballantine, 1968.

Rodeo

Roping, riding, and bronco busting all form part of one of the oldest American spectator competitions, the rodeo. What began as a way for working cowboys to blow off steam has developed into a lucrative international skills competition replete with glitzy costumes, whooping audiences, and Broadway production values. Less violent than wrestling and even smellier than the circus, rodeo remains an enormously popular family entertainment option across the United States and Canada, but most especially in the Great Plains and the West.

THE HISTORY OF RODEO

Traditionally rodeo competition consists of eight events divided into two categories: rough stock and timed. In rough stock events, cowboys (or, in some instances, cowgirls) try to ride bucking horses or bulls for a specified length of time. The customary rough stock events are bareback bronco riding (or busting), saddled bronco riding, and bull riding.

In timed events, contestants must complete a certain task, such as roping a steer, within a required number of seconds. The five customary timed rodeo events are calf roping, steer wrestling, team roping, steer roping, and barrel racing. Traditionally, female competitors take part only in barrel racing, a precision equestrian event that involves riding a horse in a cloverleaf pattern around an array of barrels. The advent of all-female rodeos, however, has resulted in the easing of this restriction.

The word *rodeo* derives from the Spanish word *rodear*, meaning to encircle or surround. Spanish settlers in sixteenth-century Mexico used the word *rodeo* to refer to a cattle roundup. It did not attain its present-day meaning—that of a skills competition devoted to roundup events—until the late nineteenth century. At that time cowboys looked forward to the Fourth of July holiday (or Cowboy Christmas, as it was also called) as an opportunity not to grill up some burgers and set off some fireworks but to ride through town roping steers and corralling them in the public square. Eventually this activity was systematized into a form resembling today's organized rodeos.

A number of states—including Texas, Colorado, and Wyoming—take credit for being the birthplace of rodeo, though its true place of origin is unclear. Cheyenne, Wyoming, was the scene of one of the first tumultuous exhibitions, on Independence Day in 1872, when a band of cowboys thundered down its main drag on the backs of unruly steers. A short time later bronco busting was added to the mix, and thus began the diversification of activities that led to today's eight standard rodeo events.

Buffalo Bill Cody became one of the first impresarios of the rodeo during the 1880s. In 1883 Cody and others formed Buffalo Bill's Wild West, a traveling show that toured the United States and parts of Europe. The show included a mock battle with Native Americans and a demonstration of Cody's shooting skill. In addition, cowboys competed for prizes in the arenas of roping, riding, bronco busting, and bull riding. Cody used the term *rodeo* to sell these extravaganzas to a fascinated public. Sometimes as many as 1,000 cowboys participated.

By the 1890s rodeos had proliferated throughout the cattle-raising regions of the American West. Over time they spread to other areas of the country as well. Today rodeos are held in many parts of the United States, Canada, and Australia. The sport's continuing popularity can be credited to its increasing concentration on entertainment value, as a onetime leisure pursuit for cowboys grew into a multimillion-dollar entertainment extravaganza.

MODERN RODEO

Nowhere were the changes in rodeo more visible than in the contributions of its female participants. Though barred from competing in many of the events, women made significant contributions to the rodeo from its very beginnings. Female equestrian performers carved out a niche with their acrobatic feats, pleasing crowds with their ability to balance themselves on two horses as they traversed the arena. When allowed to take part in the more rough-and-tumble events, they invariably wowed spectators with their steer-roping and bronco-busting prowess.

Women achieved their most noticeable impact on rodeo, however, in the area of costuming. In the early days of motion pictures, many female rodeo performers found that winning rodeo championships was a surefire way to break into silent films, so they began wearing highly decorated outfits to attract the attention of talent scouts. Bright-colored leggings and red velvet skirts with embroidered hems eventually gave way to bold pants, silk blouses, and eye-catching neckerchiefs. Rodeo fans became so enamored with these costumes that they soon demanded the men wear them also—to the chagrin of the blue-jeaned and brown-shirted cowboys. Glitzy getups such as the one worn by Robert Redford in the 1979 film *The Electric Horseman* became de rigueur for the rodeo set, giving the sport a raucous game-show quality that turned off some purists while winning many new adherents nationwide. A grittier portrayal of rodeo was shown in the film *8 Seconds* (1994), starring Luke Perry; it told the true story of a bull rider who died at the height of his career.

Over the decades rodeo's new adherents turned up in some strange places. Prison rodeo was for many years a popular event in America's southern penitentiaries, but in recent years it has been deemed cruel and unusual—or at least politically incorrect. Angola Prison Rodeo, conducted annually at the Louisiana State Penitentiary in Angola, now stands as the only remaining competition of its kind.

With its incongruously festive atmosphere, prison rodeo features food booths and a fenced-in bazaar where inmates can sell their handicrafts. Many of the events are unique to Angola and only tangentially derived from rodeo. In fact, the activities of the Roman Coliseum may be a more apt antecedent. In one popular event, Convict Poker, four inmates sit at a table in the center of the arena and a bull is released. A perverse game of chicken ensues, in which the convict who remains seated longest wins. The showstopper of every prison rodeo is the Guts and Glory Challenge, in which an especially ferocious bull enters the ring with horns painted bright orange and a $100 chit attached to the front of its head. A group of inmates (whose typical salary for prison work is four cents an hour) are then given three minutes to subdue the beast long enough to retrieve the chit.

GAY RODEO

The gay and lesbian community has not remained immune from the charm of rodeo. The idea for a gay rodeo originated with Reno, Nevada, gay activist Phil Ragsdale in 1975. It was Ragsdale who decided that a rodeo for homosexuals might be a good way to raise money for the Muscular Dystrophy Association (MDA). At first Ragsdale was not able to find any ranchers willing to lease livestock for the spectacle, but eventually the animals were procured and the rodeo went on as scheduled. Crowds were sparse the first year, but Ragsdale opted to keep it as an annual event. The extravaganza became known as the National Reno Gay Rodeo and raised thousands of dollars for MDA over the first decade of its existence.

In fact, gay rodeo became so popular that it eventually spread to other localities—and other countries as well. In 1985 the International Gay Rodeo Association (IGRA) was formed with the express intention of "fostering of national and international amateur rodeo and other equestrian competition and related arts, crafts and activities which encourage the education on or preservation of 'Country/Western' lifestyle heritage." The group immediately ratified bylaws, approved events, and standardized rodeo rules, largely along the same lines as traditional rodeo. By 2012 the IGRA was composed of twenty-eight member associations representing twenty-six states, the District of Columbia, and five Canadian provinces.

Some of the biggest and best-attended rodeos in the United States include the National Western Stock Show in Denver, Colorado, which has been held for more than 100 years; the Caldwell Night Rodeo in Caldwell, Idaho, held since 1935; Dodge City Days in Dodge City, Kansas, which attracts more than 100,000 spectators; and the National Finals Rodeo in Las Vegas, Nevada, which is the final event in the annual professional rodeo circuit. As of spring 2012 the top money-earning professional bull riders were Justin McBride (more than $5 million), Guilherme Marchi (almost $4 million), and Chris Shivers (almost $4 million). For overall rodeo performance, Texan Trevor Brazile had won an astonishing nine all-around world titles from the Professional Rodeo Championship Association through 2011.

Robert E. Schnakenberg

SEE ALSO: *Circus; Cody, Buffalo Bill, and His Wild West Show; The Cowboy Look; Gay Men; Lesbianism; Traveling Carnivals; The Western.*

BIBLIOGRAPHY

Bernstein, Joel. *Wild Ride: The History and Lore of Rodeo.* Layton, UT: Gibbs Smith, 2007.

Coombs, Charles. *Let's Rodeo!* New York: Holt, Rinehart, & Winston, 1986.

Fredriksson, Kristine. *American Rodeo: From Buffalo Bill to Big Business.* College Station: Texas A&M University Press, 1985.

Jordan, Bob. *Rodeo History and Legends.* Montrose, CO: Rodeo Stuff, 1994.

Rattenbury, Richard C.; Ed Muno; and Larry Mahan. *Arena Legacy: The Heritage of American Rodeo.* Norman: University of Oklahoma Press, 2010.

Riske, Milt. *Those Magnificent Cowgirls: A History of the Rodeo Cowgirl.* Cheyenne: Wyoming Publications, 1983.

Westermeier, Clifford P. *Man, Beast, Dust: The Story of Rodeo.* Lincoln: University of Nebraska Press, 1987.

Woerner, Gail Hughbanks. *A Belly Full of Bedsprings: The History of Bronc Riding.* Austin, TX: Eakin Press, 1998.

Wooden, Wayne S., and Gavin Ehringer. *Rodeo in America: Wranglers, Roughstock, & Paydirt.* Lawrence: University Press of Kansas, 1996.

Rodgers, Jimmie *(1897–1933)*

Singer and musician Jimmie Rodgers, who rose to national fame through his recordings in the late 1920s and early 1930s, is profoundly connected to a uniquely American form of popular music—country. Since the 1950s he has been known as the father of country music to musicians and fans alike, and his records have continued to sell decades after his death, solidifying a national and international following that was still alive in the 1990s. Rodgers's unique amalgamation of folk, blues, popular, and hillbilly music disseminated previously marginal, regional styles to national and international audiences, and he was one of the first nationally recognized musicians to feature and popularize the guitar in his recordings.

Considered a "popular" or "hillbilly" artist in his lifetime, Rodgers was officially canonized as the father of country music at a memorial celebration in Meridian, Mississippi, in 1953, on the twentieth anniversary of his death. With tens of thousands of people in attendance, his songs were played by Hank Snow, Ernest Tubb, Webb Pierce, Bill Monroe, and Roy Acuff. In his lifetime, Rodgers's songs were covered by jazz bands and orchestras, while Gene Autry, the "singing cowboy," recorded many Rodgers songs in the 1930s. Tribute songs were recorded after his death by Autry and by Bradley Kincaid and Dwight Butcher. They have also been recorded by the likes of Woody Guthrie, Merle Haggard, the Blasters, and Snow. In 1961 Rodgers, Hank Williams, and Fred Rose were the first inductees into the Country Music Association Hall of Fame.

Born James Charles Rodgers in Pine Springs, Mississippi, Rodgers spent his formative years in and around the city of Meridian. Drawn to music at an early age, he won an amateur singing contest when he was twelve. In his early teens, Rodgers went to work on the railroad, where he picked up diverse musical styles, and traded songs with hobos, roustabouts, and rounders throughout the South and Southwest. However, he contracted tuberculosis in 1924, and the resultant health problems, coinciding with a decline in available work, forced Rodgers off the railroad in 1925. Over the next two years, he worked a handful of odd jobs to sustain his wife and young daughter while concentrating on music. In 1927 he auditioned and recorded for Victor in Bristol, Tennessee, in a session that was the first to capture the songs of the Carter Family, another foundational country act.

Although Rodgers was a uniquely radical figure in twentieth-century American popular music, his composition, lyrics, and life epitomize the prototypical country artist. His music featured African American blues stylings, nasal vocals, and a southern accent. His lyrics further emphasized his southern roots, drawing as they did on his difficult life experiences and his travels as a brakeman on the railroad. Many of his songs used the bawdy double entendres and sexual boasts that characterized African American blues of the period. Rodgers was deft at rendering the sentimental ("The Mystery of Number Five") as well as the blues ("In the Jailhouse Now"), and he did so with a simplicity and sincerity that touched the working-class audiences who were his biggest fans. His creative works mirrored his life most clearly when he sang about tuberculosis in such songs as "T.B. Blues" and "Whippin' That Old T.B." Although he was a national star on radio and records, he preferred to play live performances throughout small towns in the South and Southwest. Rodgers rubbed elbows with his fans whenever he had a chance.

While much of his music is an adaptation of the folk blues idiom, Rodgers's work is eclectic and resists simple categorization. He recorded with artists as diverse as the Carter Family, Louis Armstrong, the Louisville Jug Band, and Lani McIntire's Hawaiians during his short six-year recording career. Traveling with the railroad, Rodgers was likely exposed to African American folk blues, which he incorporated into his distinct style, and his interpretations of the blues often confused listeners about his race, leading one critic to characterize him as a "White Man Gone Black." Rodgers was an early "crossover" artist who was heard and admired by African American audiences and working- and middle-class whites alike. Unlike later white blues performers, Rodgers was respectful of the material, interpreting it rather than imitating black singers; as music scholar Tony Russell noted in *Blacks, Whites, and Blues*, some African American artists "may have even regarded him as an honorary Negro." Most of Rodgers's songs featured falsetto yodeling, which he termed "blue yodeling," a characteristic that further distinguished him from other musicians during his career, and he was known as "The Singing Brakeman" and "America's Blue Yodeler" during his lifetime.

Rodgers bridged the regional world of the nineteenth century and the global world of the twentieth century. He worked in vaudeville and in blackface minstrel shows, performed on radio, recorded more than 100 songs, and appeared in a movie short titled *The Singing Brakeman* in 1929. He played shows in conjunction with movies, headlined at the Earle Theater in Washington, D.C., toured with Will Rogers to raise money for victims of drought and the Great Depression, and played a plethora of small venues throughout the South. His best-known songs include "Blue Yodel (T for Texas)," "T.B. Blues," "Blue Yodel No. 9" (which features Louis Armstrong), and "Blue Yodel No. 8 (Muleskinner Blues)."

Although his health was progressively failing, Rodgers signed autographs, performed in country theaters, and continued to record until his untimely death at the age of thirty-five. He recorded his last songs just two days before his death.

Matthew A. Killmeier

SEE ALSO: *Armstrong, Louis; Autry, Gene; Blackface Minstrelsy; The Carter Family; Country Music; Folk Music; Guthrie, Woody; Haggard, Merle; Rhythm and Blues; Rogers, Will.*

BIBLIOGRAPHY

George-Warren, Holly. *Honky-Tonk Heroes and Hillbilly Angels: The Pioneers of Country and Western Music.* Boston: Houghton Mifflin, 2006.

Malone, Bill C. *Country Music, U.S.A.* Austin: University of Texas Press, 1985.

Paris, Mike, and Chris Comber. *Jimmie the Kid: The Life of Jimmie Rodgers.* London: Eddison Press, 1977.

Porterfield, Nolan. *Jimmie Rodgers: The Life and Times of America's Blue Yodeler.* Urbana: University of Illinois Press, 1992.

Rodgers, Carrie. *My Husband Jimmie Rodgers.* San Antonio, TX: Southern Literary Institute, 1935.

Russell, Tony. *Blacks, Whites, and Blues.* New York: Stein & Day, 1970.

Rodgers, Richard

SEE: *Rodgers and Hammerstein; Rodgers and Hart.*

Rodgers and Hammerstein

The collaboration of composer Richard Rodgers (1902–1979) and lyricist/librettist Oscar Hammerstein II (1895–1960) began in 1943 with their landmark musical *Oklahoma!* Each man had already enjoyed a long and impressive career in musical theater. Hammerstein had worked with some of the most famous composers writing for Broadway and Hollywood, including Vincent Youmans, Rudolf Friml, Sigmund Romberg, and George Gershwin, as well as—most notably—for Hammerstein's own colleague, Jerome Kern, with whom Hammerstein wrote the stunning *Show Boat* in 1927 and whose music Rodgers greatly admired. By 1943 Rodgers had written nearly thirty shows with his previous partner Lorenz Hart (1895–1943), including musicals, film versions of musicals, and original film music.

The Rodgers and Hammerstein partnership produced a series of critically and commercially acclaimed musicals, beginning with *Oklahoma!* and ending with *The Sound of Music* in 1959. Rodgers and Hammerstein also excelled in the business aspects of musical theater, establishing a music publishing company and producing the shows of other composers in addition to their own. However, it is their contribution to the evolution of musical theater—the genre's style and form—and the extraordinary number of highly touted shows they wrote together, that determines their unique place in musical theater history.

Rodgers and Hammerstein. *Richard Rodgers, left, and Oscar Hammerstein each had accomplished careers in musical theater before they began their collaboration in 1947.* EVENING STANDARD/STRINGER/HULTON ARCHIVE/GETTY IMAGES.

EARLY COLLABORATIONS

In the early 1940s Rodgers reluctantly began to contemplate working with a new lyricist. The shows he had written with Hart were popular and profitable and had spawned many durable hit songs, but Hart's drinking problems, poor health, and erratic working habits had become difficult to overcome. Nevertheless, Rodgers wanted to continue the relationship with his close friend and creative partner of twenty-five years, so he asked Hart to join him in a new project, turning Lynn Riggs's play *Green Grow the Lilacs* into a musical. Hart, who could write so compellingly about the darker sides of life, was not persuaded that this play provided good material for a musical and declined. Thus, requiring another collaborator for the new show, Rodgers turned to another old friend, Hammerstein.

Hammerstein brought a wealth of experience and theatrical wisdom to the endeavor. He was the grandson of opera impresario Oscar Hammerstein I, and both his father, William, and his uncle, Arthur Hammerstein, worked in show business. The well-established lyricist/librettist Otto Harbach had been Hammerstein's mentor, and the two became full-fledged colleagues in 1920. Throughout the 1920s Hammerstein shared lyricist's responsibilities with Harbach for several important shows: *Wildflower* (music by Youmans, 1923); *Rose-Marie* (music by Friml, 1924); *Sunny* (music by Kern, 1925); *Song of the Flame* (music by Gershwin and Herbert Stothart, 1925); and *The Desert Song* (music by Romberg, 1926). Then in 1927 Hammerstein and Kern wrote what many historians consider their masterpiece: *Show Boat.* In this work Kern and Hammerstein took American themes and musical idioms and infused them with a dramatic coherence and intensity that changed the landscape of musical theater.

Hammerstein's career seemed secure. He went on to write *The New Moon* with Romberg in 1928 and *Sweet Adeline* with Kern in 1929, but, surprisingly, the 1930s brought little of the recognition he had enjoyed in the 1920s. Although *Music in the Air* (1932) with Kern was well received, other shows did not prosper—not even *Very Warm for May* (1939), also with Kern, which included the much-recorded song "All the Things You Are." Hammerstein had worked steadily through the 1930s writing and directing some productions, but by the 1940s he needed a new challenge; that challenge appeared in the person of Richard Rodgers.

Rodgers had always been concerned with the integration of words and music—both the careful setting of text to music and the significance of the songs to the plot and character development of the whole work. When working with Hart, Rodgers usually wrote the music first, then collaborated with Hart on the lyrics. Even though he and Hart would discuss the libretto and how the musical numbers would fit, their songs could often easily and effectively be sung outside the context of the show. Many of these songs have become much-loved standards.

With Hammerstein, however, the creative process worked the opposite way. Hammerstein often labored over the lyrics for weeks. Rodgers then took the lyricist's carefully polished words and quickly produced the appropriate music to support the text. Working with Hammerstein brought a change to Rodgers's musical style. The typical thirty-two-bar forms of his earlier work became less predictable as the musical forms were altered to fit Hammerstein's lyrics, producing many songs that were so fundamental to the thrust of the show that they often carried plot or character development.

A WINNING FORMULA

Their first show—*Oklahoma!*—already clearly demonstrated Rodgers and Hammerstein's commitment to integrating lyrics, libretto, and music. Its incorporation of dance into the story continued a current in Rodgers's work, which had first appeared in *On Your Toes*, written with Hart in 1936 and choreographed by George Balanchine. The dances in *Oklahoma!* were choreographed by Agnes de Mille, whose ballet background imbued her work with a narrative quality. *Oklahoma!* opened on March 31, 1943—during the dreadful years of World War II—and ran for 2,212 performances.

Several elements coalesced to produce a hit like nothing Broadway had ever seen before: The story of frontier life and the Oklahoma land rush at the turn of the twentieth century was a perfect vehicle for Hammerstein's gift for fresh, simple poetry, and characters such as Ado Annie were treated with sympathetic humor. The musical was at once folksy ("Oh, What a Beautiful Morning"), romantic, and charming ("The Surrey with the Fringe on Top"), yet held hints of dark undercurrents as represented by the character of Jud Fry. The muscular, popular-dance and ballet-influenced choreography broke new ground, and Rodgers's sensitive score was witty ("I'm Just a Gal Who Cain't Say No"), rambunctious ("Everything's up to Date in Kansas City"), and soaringly romantic ("People Will Say We're in Love") as the context demanded. *Oklahoma!* held the record as the longest-running musical in Broadway history until 1961. In 1944 the show won a special Pulitzer Prize for Drama; touring companies presented it from October 1943 until May 1954, and revivals have been frequent. A film version appeared in 1955, and in 1993 the U.S. Postal Service issued a fiftieth-anniversary commemorative stamp.

Following the phenomenon of *Oklahoma!* Rodgers and Hammerstein continued to astound the musical theater world with a series of extraordinary shows. The first of these, *Carousel* (1945) was hugely successful and proved that *Oklahoma!* had been no mere flash in the pan. Rodgers and Hammerstein dominated the Broadway scene between 1945 and 1959. *South Pacific* (1949) brought them a second Pulitzer Prize for Drama (awarded in 1950) and was followed by *The King and I* (1951) and *The Sound of Music* (1959). All enjoyed long runs, critical recognition, and commercial success, and all were made into popular films. The preeminent composer/lyricist position that the partnership held ended with Hammerstein's death from cancer in 1960.

Rodgers continued to compose until his death in 1979, writing some of his own lyrics, but nothing in his later life equaled the sustained flood of musical and dramatic brilliance that he and Hammerstein had created together. Thanks to royalties and licensing fees from their celebrated catalog, Rodgers and Hammerstein ranked among *Forbes* magazine's top-earning deceased celebrities in 2009. The enduring quality and emotional resonance of their work is demonstrated by the countless high school, university, and Broadway productions of their classic musicals that persist well into the twenty-first century.

Ann Sears

SEE ALSO: *Balanchine, George; Ballet; Broadway; Cancer; Hollywood; Kern, Jerome; The Musical;* Oklahoma!*; Rodgers and Hart;* Show Boat*;* The Sound of Music*;* South Pacific*; World War II.*

BIBLIOGRAPHY

Citron, Stephen. *The Wordsmiths: Oscar Hammerstein and Alan Jay Lerner*. New York: Oxford University Press, 1995.

Ewen, David. *Richard Rodgers*. New York: Henry Holt, 1957.

Fordin, Hugh. *Getting to Know Him: A Biography of Oscar Hammerstein II*. New York: Ungar Publishing, 1977.

Green, Stanley. *The Rodgers and Hammerstein Story*. New York: John Day, 1963.

Hammerstein, Oscar, II. *Lyrics*. New York: Simon & Schuster, 1949.

Hischak, Thomas, ed. *The Rodgers and Hammerstein Encyclopedia*. Westport, CT: Greenwood Press, 2007.

Hyland, William G. *Richard Rodgers*. New Haven, CT: Yale University Press, 1998.

Mordden, Ethan. *Rodgers & Hammerstein*. New York: Harry N. Abrams, 1992.

Nolan, Frederick. *The Sound of Their Music*. New York: Walker, 1978.

Rodgers, Richard. *Musical Stages: An Autobiography*. New York: Random House, 1975.

Rodgers, Richard. *Letters to Dorothy, 1926–1937*. New York: New York Public Library, 1988.

Rodgers, Richard, and Oscar Hammerstein. *Six Plays*. New York: Random House, 1954.

Secrest, Meryle. *Somewhere for Me: A Biography of Richard Rodgers*. New York: Knopf, 2001.

Taylor, Deems. *Some Enchanted Evenings: The Story of Rodgers and Hammerstein*. New York: Harper and Brothers, 1953.

Rodgers and Hart

Composer Richard Rodgers (1902–1979) and lyricist/librettist Lorenz Hart (1895–1943) were among the most successful composer-lyricist teams during the golden age of American musical theater. From the beginning of a collaboration that began in 1925 and lasted until Hart's death in 1943, the two shared the goal of joining lyrics and music in a way that gave their work dramatic and emotional coherence. Their experiments in musical theater paved the way for Rodgers's later shows with Oscar Hammerstein II, such as *Oklahoma!* (1943) and *Carousel* (1945), in which the interactions between lyrics, libretto, music, and dance reached new levels. Rodgers and Hart's best-known shows are *The Boys from Syracuse* (1938), for which the songs "Falling in Love with Love" and "This Can't Be Love" were written, and *Pal Joey* (1940), highlighted by "Bewitched (Bothered and Bewildered)," one of their most popular tunes.

A DYNAMIC DUO

Both Rodgers and Hart were born in New York City, and both also had early interests in music and theater. Rodgers studied at Columbia University from 1919 to 1921 and then at the

Institute of Musical Art (later known as the Juilliard School of Music) from 1921 to 1923. He began writing for amateur musical theater productions while still a student, and in 1918 he met Hart, who was majoring in journalism at Columbia. Rodgers and Hart shared an interest in a style of writing that integrated words and music in an artistically successful manner. Rodgers's first published song, "Any Old Place with You," interpolated in *A Lonely Romeo* (1919), was a collaboration with Hart. They continued to work together and achieved success with 1925's *The Garrick Gaieties*, a revue that included the classic "Manhattan." By their show *A Connecticut Yankee* in 1927, Rodgers was much in demand as a Broadway composer, and Hart was acknowledged as an accomplished lyricist whose only serious competitor was Ira Gershwin.

From 1926 to 1930 the pair produced fourteen shows for both the New York and London stages, along with individual songs for other productions. Following the Wall Street crash in 1929, financing for musical theater in New York became difficult to obtain; thus, like many other Broadway composers and lyricists, Rodgers and Hart turned to Hollywood. From 1930 to 1934 they wrote songs and background music for many films, and they were memorably responsible for the score of the smash-hit *Love Me Tonight* (1932). Rodgers and Hart returned to New York in 1935 and unveiled a spate of new shows, including *On Your Toes* (1936), for which Rodgers wrote his first extensive orchestral music, the ballet score "Slaughter on Tenth Avenue." This ballet was George Balanchine's first choreography for a book musical, and its importance to the plot presaged "Dream Ballet," which would be so crucial in *Oklahoma!* The string of Rodgers and Hart hits continued with *Babes in Arms* (1937) *and The Boys from Syracuse.*

BREAKING NEW GROUND

With 1940's *Pal Joey*, they departed from conventional musical theater and explored much darker subject matter than Broadway was accustomed to staging. *Pal Joey* is based on John O'Hara's series of *New Yorker* stories about Joey Evans, an opportunistic, small-time entertainer. Joey gets a job at a nightclub, where he begins a relationship with fellow entertainer Linda English. When a wealthy older woman, Vera Simpson, notices Joey, he leaves Linda. Vera builds a glitzy nightclub, Chez Joey, for her lover, but soon she tires of him, ultimately leaving him for greener pastures. The best-known song from *Pal Joey* is "Bewitched (Bothered and Bewildered)," whose suggestive lyrics were shocking at the time. The show not only introduced adult themes and provocative lyrics to Broadway but also addressed a segment of American life that was unfamiliar to many in the audience. Although *Pal Joey* ran for 374 performances following its opening on December 25, 1940, critics were ambivalent about it. However, the revival in 1952 and the 1957 film starring Frank Sinatra were more successful, assuring *Pal Joey* a place in the pantheon of musical theater.

A SAD ENDING

In 1942 Rodgers and Hart wrote their final show together, *By Jupiter*, set in ancient Greece. Starring Ray Bolger, it had a run of 427 performances, the longest of any Rodgers and Hart Broadway collaboration. Rodgers attempted to interest Hart in one more project together, a musical adaptation of Lynn Riggs's play *Green Grow the Lilacs*, but Hart was unenthusiastic about the suitability of the material and declined to participate. His refusal coincided with the escalation of difficulties that had plagued their partnership for years—largely the consequence of Hart's futile and self-destructive battle with alcoholism—and the situation was now nearly impossible for Rodgers to manage.

Throughout their collaboration, Rodgers had usually composed the music before Hart wrote the lyrics. This approach served two purposes: (1) it enabled Rodgers to be prepared to work when Hart was available, and (2) having the music already written stimulated Hart's interest. As Hart's health deteriorated, however, his ability to keep appointments, appear at rehearsals, or revise material failed. He died only a few months after the show he turned down, *Green Grow the Lilacs*, opened under the new title of *Oklahoma!* on March 31, 1943, beginning an unprecedented run of 2,212 performances and a fruitful partnership for Rodgers with Hammerstein.

Rodgers and Hart created some of the most beloved American songs for their shows, such as "My Funny Valentine," "The Lady Is a Tramp," "Blue Moon," "Mountain Greenery," and "With a Song in My Heart." Written primarily in the thirty-two-measure form popular with Tin Pan Alley's songsmiths and often able to stand alone from the shows in which they originally appeared, their songs were recorded time and again over the years by top vocal artists. Their style combined Hart's witty lyrics, brilliant interior rhymes, and wry twists of meaning with Rodgers's expressive approach to harmony and his highly individualized rhythmic choices. Even though Rodgers and Hart's shows are infrequently revived, many of their songs are regarded as popular culture cornerstones.

Ann Sears

SEE ALSO: *Broadway; Hollywood; The Musical;* Oklahoma!*; Rodgers and Hammerstein; Sinatra, Frank.*

BIBLIOGRAPHY

Block, Geoffrey. *The Richard Rodgers Reader*. New York: Oxford University Press, 2006.

Hart, Dorothy, ed. *Thou Swell, Thou Witty: The Life and Lyrics of Lorenz Hart*. New York: Harper & Row, 1976.

Hart, Dorothy, and Robert Kimball, eds. *The Complete Lyrics of Lorenz Hart*. New York: Alfred A. Knopf, 1986.

Hischak, Thomas S. *Word Crazy: Broadway Lyricists from Cohan to Sondheim*. New York: Praeger, 1991.

Marx, Samuel, and Jan Clayton. *Rodgers and Hart: Bewitched, Bothered, and Bedeviled*. New York: Putnam, 1976.

Nolan, Frederick. *Lorenz Hart: A Poet on Broadway*. New York: Oxford University Press, 1994.

Rodgers, Richard. *Musical Stages: An Autobiography*. New York: Da Capo Press, 1995.

Rodman, Dennis *(1961–)*

One of the National Basketball Association's (NBA) top rebounders in history, a onetime Madonna paramour and cross-dresser to boot, Dennis Rodman remains one of the NBA's most eccentric players. He is second only to Wilt Chamberlain in winning seven consecutive rebounding crowns (1992–1998) despite being significantly shorter and lighter than Chamberlain. Yet Rodman's post-basketball celebrity career and erratic personal life may overshadow his truly legendary play. During the 1990s he made news headlines with stories of his hot-tempered antics on the court (such as head-butting referees), his unlikely romances (including dates with Madonna and his impromptu Las Vegas marriage to actress Carmen Electra), his ever-changing hair color, and later violent public disturbances that led to his checking into a rehab.

EARLY YEARS

Dennis Keith "The Worm" Rodman was born in Trenton, New Jersey, and grew up in Dallas's infamous Oak Cliff housing projects after his father abandoned the family early on. A gangly, small child, Rodman lived in the shadows of his two extremely tall older sisters, both of whom were adept with a basketball. In his autobiography *Bad as I Wanna Be* (1996), he describes growing up feeling invisible and clumsy. Everything changed in his late teens, however, when he grew more than a foot. He announces in his autobiography, "It was like I had a new body that knew how to do all this shit the old one didn't." At age twenty-one Rodman's new body transformed him from a nobody who stole wristwatches and worked the janitorial night shift at a local airport into a somebody who played basketball. After one year at Cooke County Junior College, where he stood out on the courts but failed academically, Rodman won a basketball scholarship in 1983 to Southeastern Oklahoma University, a National Association of Intercollegiate Athletes (NAIA, a National Collegiate Athletic Association [NCAA]–type organization for smaller schools). He averaged 26 points and 16 rebounds per game over his three years at Southeastern and twice led the NAIA in rebounds with 16.1 in 1985 and 17.8 in 1986. He was named All-American in his senior year. His profile was still fairly low, however, and the Detroit Pistons did not draft him until the second round; he was the 27th pick overall.

BASKETBALL SUCCESS AND STARDOM

Rodman arrived in Detroit in 1986 and formed an immediate friendship both with coach Chuck Daly and his teammates on the Pistons, led by Isiah Thomas. The team came to be known as the "Bad Boys" for their aggressive defensive style of play, with Rodman giving a reliable, important sixth-man contribution. The Pistons won the NBA Championship in both 1989 and 1990, and Rodman was named Defensive Player of the Year in 1990 and 1991. In 1992, his last year with the Pistons, he racked up what would be the first of seven consecutive rebounding titles. For the 43 games that Rodman started in the 1990 season, the Pistons went 39–4 and he averaged 18.7 rebounds per game (again, second only to Chamberlain's 19.2 rebounds per game in 1972). Rodman was named an All-Star in both 1990 and 1992.

When Daly retired in 1993 and team management made some choices Rodman did not agree with, he demanded a trade and was sent to the San Antonio Spurs. Rodman reacted emotionally to the breakup of the Pistons' championship group, and in February he was found asleep in his truck with a loaded gun. Despite his personal struggles, however, Rodman and center David Robinson became the first teammates to lead the league in rebounding and scoring, respectively, in the same season. The Rodman-Robinson-led team finished the season at 55–27 but lost in the first round of the playoffs. The following season the Spurs finished with the best record in the league at 62–20 but were knocked out of the playoffs in the conference finals. Although Rodman's defensive prowess gained him widespread respect, he became known for his bizarre hairstyles and eccentric behavior—coach Bob Hill actually kept him out of a playoff game against the Lakers after he removed his shoes on the sidelines.

Rodman maintained his reputation as the league's best rebounder and finally realized his ultimate dream in 1995: he was acquired by the Chicago Bulls and became a World Champion—a major component of the Bulls' three-part chemistry under coach Phil Jackson. During Rodman's three seasons with the Bulls, the team won three championships, and he continued to lead the league in rebounds. His behavior during this time became more erratic, however; in the 1996–1997 season he received a number of suspensions during the regular season and had limited playoff time due to his propensity to draw technical fouls. During one regular season game, Rodman's assault on a courtside photographer resulted in his paying $200,000 to settle the case.

He went on to play with the Los Angeles Lakers for the 1998–1999 season, but despite propelling the team to eleven consecutive wins, he was released after playing just twenty-three games. He was picked up by the Dallas Mavericks the following season but released after only twelve games. Rodman left the NBA to join the American Basketball Association's Long Beach Jam from 2003 to 2004, followed by a year with the Orange County Crush.

CELEBRITY LIFE BEYOND BASKETBALL

Despite these attempts to keep playing, Rodman's professional basketball career dwindled to an end. His life as a celebrity, however, remained in full swing, and Rodman was willing to try it all, including a stint as a part-time professional wrestler (1997–2000); producing his own TV show, *The Rodman World Tour* (1996); and starring in several reality TV shows, including ABC's *Celebrity Mole Yucatan* in 2004, for which he won the grand prize, and two UK celebrity shows: *Celebrity Big Brother* (the fourth version) and *Love Island*, both in 2006. Because of, or perhaps despite, his celebrity, Rodman eventually became a contestant on Donald Trump's second season of *Celebrity Apprentice*. He made it through the first few rounds but was ultimately fired in the fifth episode after his teammates accused him repeatedly of having a drinking problem. Rodman denied this, but he went from *Apprentice* to an outpatient rehab program and in 2010 appeared on *Celebrity Rehab with Dr. Drew* and its spin-off *Sober House* as part of his recovery. In 2011 Rodman hosted fiftieth birthday parties for himself around the globe, publicized via his website: http://www.dennisrodman.com/main. He also hosts parties, DJs, and takes on celebrity coaching gigs.

In his personal life, Rodman has repeatedly faced legal troubles: he was accused of rape in 2003, charged with slapping a waitress on the butt in 2006, and arrested for domestic abuse in 2008. Rodman's first wife, Annie, divorced him in 1993. His second, Carmen Electra, divorced him in 1999. Rodman married third wife Michelle in 2003, and they quickly became estranged and involved in an eight-year divorce battle. In 2008 Rodman was arrested on domestic abuse charges and did forty-five days of community service after pleading no contest. The couple finally agreed to completely divorce in 2012 but remained in court due to Michelle's claims that Rodman owed more than $800,000 in child support for the couple's two children and $50,000 in spousal support. Rodman's lawyers claimed the support filings were based on imaginary income and that he was both bankrupt and sick with alcohol addiction—a story Rodman himself repeatedly denied in the celebrity rags. Rodman reportedly also owed back taxes in Orange County for withdrawing some of his NBA pension funds to pay other debts.

Rodman was inducted into the Naismith Memorial Basketball Hall of Fame in 2011. In an unexpected and highly emotional acceptance speech, Rodman focused on his personal life, apologizing to family and friends for his behavior and citing former coaches Daly and Jackson as father figures. He also announced that director Penny Marshall, of *A League of Their Own* (1992) and *Awakenings* (1990) fame, was working on a documentary about his life.

Rodman has penned several autobiographies, including *Rebound: The Dennis Rodman Story* (1994), *Bad as I Wanna Be* (1996)—which sold more than 800,000 copies and spent 20 weeks on the *New York Times* best-seller list—*Walk on the Wild Side* (1997), and *I Should Be Dead by Now* (2005). He has tried his hand at acting in feature films such as *Double Team* with Jean-Claude Van Damme (1997), *Simon Sez* (1999), and *Cutaway* (2000).

Frederick Luis Aldama

SEE ALSO: The Apprentice; *Basketball; Celebrity; Chamberlain, Wilt; The Chicago Bulls; Divorce;* A League of Their Own; *The Los Angeles Lakers; National Basketball Association (NBA); Pinsky, Dr. Drew; Thomas, Isiah.*

BIBLIOGRAPHY

Bickley, Dan. *No Bull: The Unauthorized Biography of Dennis Rodman.* New York: St. Martin's Press, 1997.

Feinberg, Leslie. *Transgender Warriors: Making History from Joan of Arc to Dennis Rodman.* Boston: Beacon Press, 1996.

Rodman, Anicka, with Alexander Scott. *Worse than He Says He Is: White Girls Don't Bounce.* New York: Dove Books, 1997.

Rodman, Dennis, and Jack Isenhour. *I Should Be Dead by Now.* Champaign, IL: Sports Publishing LLC, 2005.

Rodman, Dennis, and Tim Keown. *Bad as I Wanna Be.* New York: Delacorte Press, 1996.

Rodman, Dennis, and Michael Silver. *Walk on the Wild Side.* New York: Delacorte Press, 1997.

Rodman, Dennis, with Pat Rich and Alan Steinberg. *Rebound: The Dennis Rodman Story.* New York: Crown, 1994.

Rodríguez, Chi Chi *(1935–)*

One of golf's all-time greats, Juan "Chi Chi" Rodríguez was the first Hispanic to become an international champion in golf. Born Juan Rodríguez in Río Piedras, Puerto Rico, on October 23, 1935, into an extremely impoverished family, Rodríguez found his way into golf as a caddy on the links that served Puerto Rico's booming tourist industry. His is one of the most famous Hispanic "rags to riches through sports" tales, his career earnings having passed the $3 million mark. Included among the important tournaments he won were the Denver Open (1963), Lucky Strike International Open (1964), Western Open (1964), Dorado Pro-Am (1965), Texas Open (1967), and Tallahassee Open (1979). As a member of the Senior PGA (Professional Golfers' Association) Tour, he won numerous tournaments, including the Silver Pages Classic (1987), GTE Northwest Classic (1987), and Sunwest Senior Classic (1990).

Nicolás Kanellos

SEE ALSO: *Golf.*

BIBLIOGRAPHY

Benson, Sonia, ed. *The Hispanic-American Almanac.* Detroit, MI: Gale, 2003.

Lapchick, Richard E. *100 Campeones: Latino Groundbreakers Who Paved the Way in Sport.* Morgantown, WV: Fitness Information Technology, 2010.

Rodríguez, Chi Chi, and John Anderson. *Chi Chi's Golf Games You Gotta Play.* Champaign, IL: Human Kinetics, 2003.

Roe v. Wade

In 1973 the Supreme Court of the United States handed down a 7–2 verdict in *Roe v. Wade* that would become arguably its most controversial decision of the twentieth century. Using the concept of privacy and the statute of due process, the court determined that the decision to end a pregnancy within its first three months was a constitutionally protected right. Beyond the first trimester, states were given the right to limit access to abortions. The verdict resulted in battle lines being drawn, and pro-choice and pro-life advocates, as they came to be known, have engaged in a decades-long struggle to dictate the reproductive rights of American women.

EARLY DEBATE

Before *Roe v. Wade* only three states and Washington, D.C., provided easy access to abortion. All other states had more restricted access. Public opinion on the procedure shifted, however, when prescription of the European sedative Thalidomide (used to treat morning sickness) proliferated among U.S. women in the 1960s and after an epidemic of German measles occurred, which resulted in a large number of babies born with serious birth defects. At the time, the only women able to end an unwanted or unhealthy pregnancy were those who could afford to travel to a state or foreign country where laws were less stringent. Desperate women often self-aborted or entrusted themselves to back-alley abortionists. Both practices frequently led to later health problems, sterility, or even death.

The year before *Roe v. Wade*, thirty-nine maternal deaths from illegal abortion were reported; prior to the use of penicillin that number was estimated closer to 1,500. Many pregnant women and health care professionals advocated for safe abortions by trained medical personnel as a right rather than a privilege, challenging state restrictions. Seven years before *Roe v. Wade*, the American Medical Association endorsed legal abortion.

Ten years before the decision in *Roe v. Wade*, the women's movement had gained momentum with the 1963 publication of National Organization for Women (NOW) cofounder Betty Friedan's *The Feminine Mystique*, which explored the unhappiness of American housewives of the era. The text initiated a "second wave" of feminism (the first having fought for equal voting and property rights) and led to a greater awareness of the social inequalities women suffered. Gaining control of reproduc-

Protest on* Roe v. Wade *Anniversary. *Pro-life demonstrators confront pro-choice counterparts outside the U.S. Supreme Court at a rally on the anniversary of the court's* Roe v. Wade *ruling in 2006.* KAREN BLEIER/AFP/GETTY IMAGES.

tive rights became hugely significant in the battle for equality, and a focus of Friedan's organization, NOW. Arguing that women should not have to become mothers against their will, the medical community and some religious groups, including the Episcopalian Church; several Jewish organizations; and the Presbyterian Church went on record as supporting the right to choose abortion.

THE CASE

The chief players in the *Roe v. Wade* case were a poor pregnant woman; two young, inexperienced lawyers; and a Supreme Court justice with a background in medical law. Norma McCorvey, who came to be known as "Jane Roe," claimed that she had been raped by a carnival worker in Augusta, Georgia, which would have allowed her to obtain a legal abortion; she later recanted the story. When McCorvey returned to her home state of Texas and attempted to obtain an abortion, she was denied. She consulted two young lawyers, Sarah Weddington and Linda Coffee, who were looking for a pregnant woman willing to serve as a test case to challenge restrictive abortion laws. By the time the case was heard before the Supreme Court, McCorvey had given birth and had put the baby up for adoption.

Weddington first argued for the right of Jane Roe (and by extension all pregnant women) to make decisions regarding her own body—in this case, to determine whether to give birth. Coffee served as a consultant but took a lesser role as the case progressed through legal channels. Although she was inexperienced, Weddington was a thorough researcher and a quick learner. When it was suggested that she shift her chief argument from equal protection to the right to privacy, she did so. This move was based on another landmark case, *Griswold v. Connecticut* (1965), which ruled that the use of contraceptives was legally protected because of individuals' right to privacy. The case was controversial not only because of its ruling but also because the majority opinion asserted that privacy was a constitutionally protected right, despite never being mentioned in the Bill of Rights. This established an important precedent for cases such as *Roe v. Wade*.

Harry Blackmun, a conservative Republican member of the Supreme Court, was assigned to write the majority opinion in the case. Based on available medical information that traced the development of the fetus, he devised the trimester system as a determinant for abortion decisions. Blackmun became a lifelong proponent of a woman's right to control her reproductive life, remaining true to his convictions even when the Supreme Court shifted to the Right.

From the day of the decision forward, *Roe v. Wade* incited strong emotions among both supporters and detractors. Feminists lauded the autonomy it gave to women, while the Religious Right began a battle to overturn it that would last for decades. Even though Congress managed to limit the right of poor women to obtain abortions with its passage of the Hyde Amendment in 1976 (the first law banning the use of federal funds for the procedure), the Supreme Court stood solidly behind its decision.

DILUTED BUT STILL STANDING

During the presidency of Ronald Reagan, the pro-life movement took on renewed energy. Throughout the 1980s political candidates turned their views on abortion into campaign slogans. Nominees' positions on this issue became the litmus test for their entry onto the federal judiciary, including the Supreme Court. In a 1989 decision the court weakened *Roe v. Wade* but did not overturn it: *Webster v. Reproductive Health Services* gave more control over abortion access to individual states and resulted in a number of restrictive laws, such as those passed in

Louisiana and Guam. State-by-state regulations varied wildly: "personhood" bills, which defined life as the moment of conception and therefore legally recognized abortion an act of murder, were proposed in many states, though as of 2012 none had yet ratified such bills. Some states mandated waiting periods or ultrasounds prior to undergoing the procedure. Other states recognized the federal law without any amendments.

Given the mood of the conservative Reagan/Bush court, scholars, political activists, and the legal community all predicted that *Roe v. Wade* would be overturned in the 1992 case *Planned Parenthood of Southeastern Pennsylvania v. Casey*. To the contrary, in that election-year decision, the Supreme Court reaffirmed *Roe v. Wade* but upheld restrictions such as informed consent and mandatory waiting periods. It rejected the requirement that married women notify their husbands before obtaining an abortion. Once the right to choose had been endorsed by the conservative court, the focus of the pro-life movement shifted to violent attacks on doctors and clinics that performed abortions. After a 1993 decision that, in effect, protected the attackers, the Supreme Court again changed position in 1994, upholding bans on blocking abortion clinics and on intimidating or injuring providers and patients.

Pro-life trends persisted throughout the 1990s and into the twenty-first century. Even McCorvey, who converted to Christianity in 1994, became a vocal pro-life supporter and publicly denounced her role in the case. Two memoirs, *I Am Roe* (1994) and *Won by Love* (1997) detail her conversion to Christianity and explain her change of opinion. She has been an activist for the pro-life movement since the late 1990s. In 2005 McCorvey unsuccessfully petitioned the U.S. Supreme Court to overturn its ruling on the basis that the abortion procedure is medically unsound. McCorvey is not alone in her activism. Each year on the anniversary of the ruling, hundreds of thousands of pro-life advocates congregate in Washington, D.C., at the March for Life rally to protest abortion. And in towns all across the United States, abortion opponents use horrifying visual images on billboards or posters to make their point.

Pro-choice and pro-life supporters have argued unfalteringly over the definition of personhood. Pro-choice advocates believe that a fetus is not a person according to the letter of the law. While some pro-life proponents, on the other hand, insist that from the moment of conception, a fetus is a living being and that its rights should be on par with those of the mother. Personhood is not the only basis for disagreement: the violation of personal liberty has often been cited by pro-choice supporters as a strike against overturning the Roe v. Wade decision, and the lack of constitutional underpinnings has been cited by pro-life supporters against the ruling. As the political debate raged on in courtrooms and outside clinics, between 2000 and 2005 the number of women obtaining abortions dropped from 1.3 million to 1.2 million. Public opinion also shifted. By 2009 51 percent of the public identified themselves as pro-life. In 2012 more than twenty states had abortion-related legislation in process, demonstrating that the issue was far from settled nearly forty years after the controversial verdict was handed down. Although *Roe v. Wade* continues to protect a woman's right to choose an abortion, there is little likelihood of ending the controversy that surrounds it.

Elizabeth Rholetter Purdy

SEE ALSO: *Abortion; Feminism; Obama, Barack; Reagan, Ronald; Religious Right.*

BIBLIOGRAPHY

Craig, Barbara Hinkson, and David M. O'Brien. *Abortion and American Politics.* Chatham, NJ: Chatham House Publishers, 1993.

Faux, Marian. Roe v. Wade: *The Untold Story of the Landmark Supreme Court Decision That Made Abortion Legal.* New York: New American Library, 1988.

Freedman, Lori. *Willing and Unable: Doctors' Constraints in Abortion Care.* Nashville, TN: Vanderbilt University Press, 2010.

Hull, N. E. H., and Peter Charles Hoffer. *The Abortion Rights Controversy in America.* Chapel Hill: University of North Carolina Press, 2004.

McCorvey, Norma. *I Am Roe: My Life,* Roe v. Wade, *and Freedom of Choice.* New York: HarperCollins, 1994.

McCorvey, Norma. *Won by Love: Norma McCorvey, Jane Roe of "Roe v. Wade," Speaks Out for the Unborn as She Shares Her New Conviction for Life.* Nashville, TN: T. Nelson, 1997.

Nossiff, Rosemary. "Abortion Policy before *Roe*: Grassroots and Interest-Group Mobilization." *Journal of Policy History* (2001): 463–78.

Reagan, Leslie J. *When Abortion Was a Crime: Women, Medicine, and Law in the United States, 1867–1973.* Berkeley: University of California Press, 1997.

Rose, Melody. *Abortion: A Documentary and Reference Guide.* Westport, CT: Greenwood Press, 2008.

Rogers, Ginger

SEE: *Astaire, Fred, and Ginger Rogers.*

Rogers, Kenny *(1938–)*

Born in Texas in 1938 and raised in one of the state's poorest federal housing projects, country singer Kenny Rogers grew up to become one of the most recognizable celebrities in the United States. Although variously a television and film actor, a photographer, an author, and a fast-food entrepreneur, Rogers secured a place in popular American culture mostly for his music.

Rogers began his first career, music, in the 1950s when he joined a singing group called the Scholars, which had local hits. He made his first national television appearance in 1958, when a solo hit on a local label, Carlton Records, became popular enough to land him an *American Bandstand* slot. In the late 1950s, he played bass in a jazz combo called the Bobby Doyle Three, and he made one record with them before being given a solo contract with Mercury. The arrangement proved short-lived and commercially fruitless.

When Mercury failed to renew his contract, Rogers joined the folk-pop group the New Christy Minstrels and stayed with them for a year. Together with other members of the group, he left to form the First Edition, with which he made his first significant national splash. The First Edition performed a mixed bag of styles, but the group scored a Top 10 hit for Reprise in 1968 with the psychedelic "Just Dropped in (To See What Condition My Condition Was In)." The group also had success with Mel Tillis's "Ruby Don't Take Your Love to Town," as well as "Reuben James," in which Rogers's country tendencies were becoming apparent. The group parlayed this and a few other minor hits into a prime-time television show in 1972. Rogers left the group in 1974, which broke up shortly after.

In 1975 Rogers signed with United Artists and released a number of records, achieving his first major number one smash hit with "Lucille" in 1977. It was also a big crossover success, peaking at number five on the pop charts. Thus began a run of massive crossover hits, including "The Gambler" in 1978, a song that spawned a series of made-for-television movies starring the singer. In the late 1970s Rogers teamed up with Dottie West for several successful duets, beginning a run of pairings in the early 1980s with such major female stars as Sheena Easton; Kim Carnes; and, memorably, Dolly Parton, with whom he duetted to a number one smash with the Bee Gees' "Islands in the Stream." He also had a hit with Lionel Richie's "Lady," further blurring the lines between country and pop.

Crossover successes such as those enjoyed by Rogers and a handful of other artists changed the course of the country music industry. Country artists were no longer satisfied to succeed solely in the country charts, and they began producing music with a sonic quality appropriate for Top 40 radio. The twangy steel guitars and fiddles of the Grand Ole Opry were widely forsaken in favor of the lusher "Nashville Sound," as pop success became both desirable and attainable.

In 1983 Rogers signed with RCA records, and though he had several number one country hits, his crossover appeal was starting to wane. When his contract came up for renewal in 1988, RCA opted out. Though he was no longer as looming a presence on the radio charts, he did appear in several television shows and continued to tour. He invested in the new country music mecca of Branson, Missouri, the Ozark Mountain resort where many older country stars built theaters in which to perform regularly. He also became involved in charity work and published two well-received books of his own photography. He diversified further into the fast-food business, lending his name to the Kenny Rogers Roasters franchise, which expanded to hundreds of outlets countrywide.

In 1996 Rogers twice moved into a new spot on the cultural radar. In January that year his album *Vote for Love* was the first release on "onQ" records, owned by the QVC cable shopping station. It was, of course, marketed exclusively through QVC. Then in November the television comedy *Seinfeld* produced a classic episode revolving around Kenny Rogers Roasters. In 1999 Rogers released the single "Buy Me a Rose," which topped the charts, and he also released the well-received album *Back to the Well* in 2003. Since then he has toured regularly and released several successful albums. With the rise of the genre of alt-country and the immense popularity of crossover artists such as Shania Twain and Taylor Swift, a new generation of listeners tuned into older country greats such as Rogers, bringing him into the limelight once again.

Joyce Linehan

SEE ALSO: *Country Music; Fast Food; Home Shopping Network/QVC; Made-for-Television Movies; Parton, Dolly; Pop Music; Top 40.*

BIBLIOGRAPHY

Hume, Martha. *Kenny Rogers: Gambler, Dreamer, Lover*. New York: New American Library, 1980.

Rogers, Roy *(1911–1998)*

Roy Rogers, with his horse, Trigger, came to prominence in the late 1930s and early 1940s, following closely in the footsteps of singing cowboy Gene Autry. Rogers's rise to stardom transformed the "singing cowboy" from an isolated phenomenon to a recognized movie genre, and his popular success, added to Autry's, brought screen stardom in turn to Tex Ritter, Jimmy Wakely, Monte Hale, Johnny Mack Brown, and others. None of them attained the iconic status of Rogers or Autry, but all of them contributed to the mythology of the straight-shooting, clean-living hero who is also sensitive enough, in a folksy, regular-guy sort of way, to pick up a guitar and sing a song or two.

The singing cowboy movie was—at least in retrospect—a natural phenomenon for the 1930s. The old West was only a generation or so removed from movie audiences, and the cowboy films or "B" Westerns (as opposed to the weightier Western as conceived by John Ford) spoke to the public's sense of nostalgia. Then, too, the arrival of sound in the cinema created a demand for music and singing, which dovetailed neatly with Rogers's style of Westerns, set in an increasingly stylized world not unlike the fanciful Ruritanian villages of light opera, which created a perfect backdrop for good-looking, guitar-playing, singing heroes.

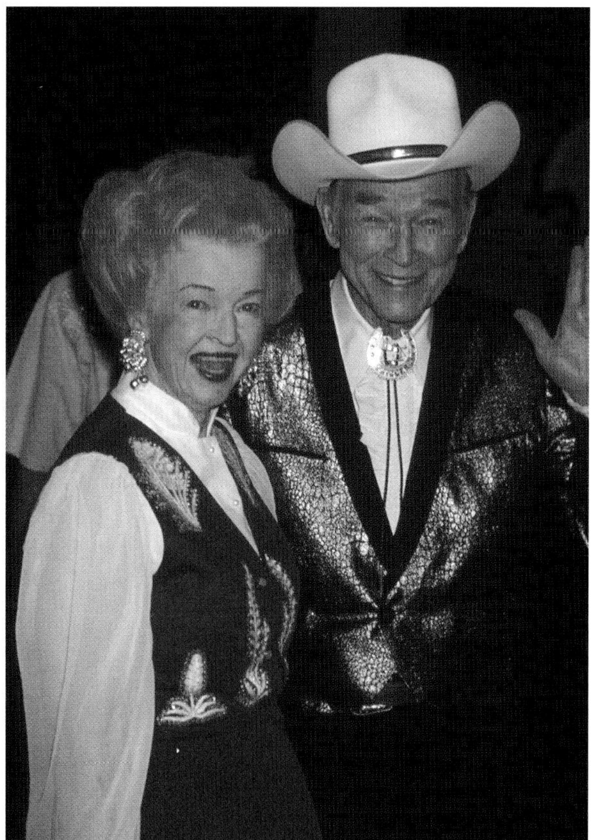

Roy Rogers. *Roy Rogers, right, known as the singing cowboy since his career began in the 1930s, appears with Dale Evans in 1995.* RON GALELLA, LTD./CONTRIBUTOR/WIREIMAGE/GETTY IMAGES.

EARLY CAREER

Unlike Autry, Rogers didn't have a western background, but he did come from a rural environment. Born Leonard Slye in Cincinnati, Ohio, he moved to California with his father, a migrant laborer, and worked as a fruit picker and truck driver; he also sang with a variety of country groups. In the California of the 1930s, country music was influenced by Hollywood pop and by Western swing, and Rogers (then using the name Dick Weston) was in groups with names like Uncle Tom Murray's Hollywood Hillbillies, the International Cowboys, and the O-Bar-O Cowboys.

In 1933, with Bob Nolan and Tim Spencer, he formed a group called the Pioneer Trio, which changed its name to the Sons of the Pioneers shortly thereafter. The Sons of the Pioneers was a harmony trio, more influenced by barbershop and contemporary jazz-flavored pop groups like the Modernaires than by any country music, but they had a unique sound and, in Nolan, the advantage of a brilliant songwriter ("Tumbling Tumbleweeds," "Cool Water"). They became an important influence on the country-and-western music that followed them. Rogers, in fact, is the only person to have been inducted into the Country Music Hall of Fame twice—once as a solo performer and once as a member of the Sons of the Pioneers.

Rogers broke into movies in the mid-1930s, playing bit parts in Westerns, first for Columbia Pictures and then for Republic, Autry's studio and the leading purveyor of "B" Westerns. His first starring role was in *Under Western Stars* (1938), and for the next five years he and Autry shared stardom at Republic, with Autry still considered the screen's "King of the Cowboys." When Autry went into the air force during World War II, Republic threw all the weight of its publicity machine behind Rogers, and his career really took off. From 1943 through 1954 he was listed by a theater owners' poll as the top Western star in Hollywood.

KING OF THE COWBOYS

In a genre characterized by stylization, Rogers was perhaps the most stylized of all, as evidenced by his colorful and distinctive outfits, designed by Nudie of Hollywood. Other cowboys had been associated with horses, from Tom Mix (Tony) to Autry (Champion), but no other cowboy had a horse as colorful and identifiable as Rogers's palomino, Trigger, billed as "the smartest horse in movies." Other cowboys had sidekicks, but none quite as colorful as Rogers's Gabby Hayes. Rogers inherited Autry's title of King of the Cowboys, and his wife, Dale Evans, whom he married in 1947, was dubbed the Queen of the West.

Rogers became a symbol of an idealized America in the spirit and style of Norman Rockwell's paintings. He represented the normality that Americans were seeking in the aftermath of the war years, but his films eventually proved too tame for later postwar audiences. His on-screen romances, generally with Evans, were shy and chaste, and his action sequences had a low violence quotient; he would shoot the gun out of the bad guy's hand, toss away his own, and subdue the baddie in a rousing but fair fist fight. To a generation that had seen the horrors of war, this was at first reassuring, then tame and corny, and Rogers's popularity waned, along with that of the "B" Western.

THE ROY ROGERS SHOW

A shrewd businessman, Rogers took his talents to television, aiming his initial show at younger audiences whose parents, the cowboy's former fans, enthusiastically encouraged their children to enjoy the innocent myths that Rogers perpetrated. *The Roy Rogers Show* debuted in 1951 and continued with first-run episodes until 1957, retaining the familiar style of Rogers's big-screen image. It was all there: Roy and Dale on their ranch, the Double R Bar; sidekick Pat Brady (formerly with the Sons of the Pioneers, replacing Hayes); wonder horse Trigger and faithful dog Bullet; and Dale's horse Buttermilk and Brady's jeep Nellybelle. The show's theme song, "Happy Trails" (by Evans, a skilled songwriter), remains a national catchphrase. Rogers's popularity through the 1950s was international, and of his more than 200 fan clubs—the one in London with over 50,000 members—was estimated to be the biggest such club for any performer anywhere on earth.

In 1962 Rogers and his wife cohosted a variety program, *The Roy Rogers and Dale Evans Show*, but most of his time after the late 1950s was given over to building a substantial business empire, which included ownership of a TV company, interests in thoroughbred horses, real estate, rodeo, and his well-known Roy Rogers fast-food chain. In 1967 he opened the Roy Rogers museum in Apple Valley, California. The most noteworthy display, among other Rogers memorabilia, was Trigger himself, stuffed and mounted in a rearing posture.

During the 1980s and 1990s Rogers made a singing comeback, recording solo and as a duet performer with Clint Black and others. Some said it was a publicity move to advertise his restaurant chains by reviving his image for a generation that didn't know who he was. Whether or not this was so, his legacy remained strong, with even Bruce Willis's character in *Die Hard* (1988) invoking Roy Rogers as his ideal of courage and decent values.

Tad Richards

SEE ALSO: *Autry, Gene; "B" Movies; Barbershop Quartets; Black, Clint; Country Music; The Cowboy Look; Fast Food; Ford, John; Hollywood; Jazz; Pop Music; Rockwell, Norman; Rodeo; Television; The Western; Willis, Bruce; World War II.*

BIBLIOGRAPHY

Kazanjian, Howard, and Chris Enss. *The Cowboy and the Senorita: A Biography of Roy Rogers and Dale Evans.* Guilford, CT: TwoDot, 2004.

Morris, Georgia, and Mark Pollard, eds. *Roy Rogers: King of the Cowboys.* San Francisco: Collins, 1994.

Phillips, Robert W. *Roy Rogers: A Biography, Radio History, Television Career Chronicle, Discography, Filmography, Comicography, Merchandising and Advertising History, Collectibles Description, Bibliography, and Index.* Jefferson, NC: McFarland, 1995.

Rogers, Roy; Dale Evans; and Carlton Stowers. *Happy Trails.* Waco, TX: Word Books, 1979.

Rogers, Roy; Dale Evans; Jane Stern; et al. *Happy Trails: Our Life Story.* New York: Simon & Schuster, 1994.

Rogers, Will *(1879–1935)*

Although he is seldom referenced in contemporary commentary these days, humorist Will Rogers's impact upon American culture was great and lasting. He made himself into the archetypal American Everyman, apparently baffled and outsmarted by the machinations of politicians and tycoons but, in reality, always managing to get the better of them through the shrewd and timely use of common sense and self-effacing humor. Some thirty-five years before Mort Sahl based his nightclub act on satirical observations of government officials, writer-actor-humorist Rogers told a joint session of Congress, "It's a pleasure to be here in Washington with all these other comedians. The only thing is, when *you* make a joke, it's a law! And when you make a law, it's a joke."

But Rogers was not so much a pioneer in the realm of political humor as he was an utterly unique character, whose wry and seemingly naive comments on American politics and society were so integral a part of his public persona that no entertainer could have modeled his act on Rogers's without being dismissed as a mere imitator. When Rogers, a lifelong Democrat ("No, I'm not a member of an organized political party. I'm a Democrat"), was introduced to Republican President Calvin Coolidge, he held out his hand and cocked his head to one side. "Pardon," he said, "Didn't catch the name." It was the only occasion on which Coolidge was seen to smile during the whole of his presidency.

Born William Penn Adair Rogers on November 4, 1879, on a ranch between Claremore and Oologah, in Oklahoma (then known as the Indian Nation), he became an expert rider and roper at a very early age. Both of Rogers's parents were part Cherokee. He received a very light formal education, admitting only to two years at Kemper Military Academy in Booneville, Missouri ("one year in the guardhouse and one in the fourth grade"). He left school for good in 1898 to become a cowboy in the Texas panhandle; from there drifted to Argentina; and eventually joined Texas Jack's Wild West Circus with a rope-trick act, making his first public appearance in Johannesburg, South Africa, during the Boer War (1899–1902).

When Rogers returned to the United States, he continued with his roping act, playing at county fairs and in vaudeville. Twirling his lariat, making fantastic shapes in the air, he would tell stories and jokes and began to introduce topical humor into his act. As his popularity increased, the humor became more and more important, and by the time his act reached the New York stage in 1905, the rope tricks had become props and punctuation for the jokes. Branching into musical comedy, he had his first taste of real fame: a starring role in the *Ziegfeld Follies* of 1916. His standard lead-in line, "All I know is what I read in the papers," became something of a signature and a ubiquitous phrase in the 1920s. The zenith of his New York stage career came in 1934 when he appeared in Eugene O'Neill's only comedy, *Ah, Wilderness!*

Rogers made his film debut in 1918, but it wasn't until the advent of sound that he became a popular box-office attraction, starring in such memorable John Ford features as *Judge Priest* (1934) and *Steamboat round the Bend* (1935). Meanwhile, he had begun a successful parallel career as a writer, at first of humorous books (*The Cowboy Philosopher on Prohibition* and *The Illiterate Digest*) and, from 1926 onward, as a syndicated columnist. He also conquered the new medium of radio as a commentator, and he had all of America laughing when he announced, "I don't know jokes; I just watch the government and report the facts." All of his brilliant gifts were tragically silenced in 1935 when, flying in Alaska with the noted aviator Wiley Post, the plane crashed and both men were killed.

Rogers left other political humorists with very little to do, and the field lay mostly fallow until the late 1950s when Mort Sahl revived political humor. Sahl did so from a very different point of view, commenting that "Will Rogers's act was that he was a country bumpkin up against clever sophisticates, whereas my situation is just the reverse."

Gerald Carpenter

SEE ALSO: *Ford, John; O'Neill, Eugene; Sahl, Mort; Vaudeville; The Western;* The Ziegfeld Follies.

BIBLIOGRAPHY

Alworth, E. Paul. *Will Rogers*. New York: Twayne Publishers, 1974.

Axtell, Margaret S. *Will Rogers Rode the Range*. Phoenix, AZ: Allied Printing, 1972.

Brown, William R. *Imagemaker: Will Rogers and the American Dream*. Columbia: University of Missouri Press, 1970.

Carter, Joseph H. *I Never Met a Man I Didn't Like: The Life and Writings of Will Rogers*. New York: Avon Books, 1991.

Robinson, Ray. *American Original: A Life of Will Rogers*. New York: Oxford University Press, 1996.

Rogers, Will. *Autobiography*, ed. Donald Day. Boston: Houghton Mifflin, 1949.

Rogers, Will. *The Papers of Will Rogers*, eds. Arthur Frank Wertheim and Barbara Bair. Norman: University of Oklahoma Press, 1996.

Yagoda, Ben. *Will Rogers: A Biography*. Norman: University of Oklahoma Press, 2000.

Rolle, Esther *(1920–1998)*

Emmy Award–winning Esther Rolle is best remembered as Florida Evans, the strong matriarch of the hit CBS television series *Good Times* (1974–1979). *Good Times* was a spin-off of Norman Lear's *Maude*, in which Rolle played Florida from 1972–1974. Florida was a feisty, sarcastic black maid employed by Bea Arthur's loud, white, middle-aged liberal Maude Findlay. On *Good Times* Florida was the female head of a lower-class family of five in the Chicago projects. At Rolle's insistence, hoping to present positive role models to black Americans, the family was not fatherless. Rolle left the series in 1977 reportedly feeling the story lines involving Jimmie Walker, who played her oldest son, were reinforcing negative stereotypes. Promised changes, she returned in 1978, but ratings had slipped and the show was canceled.

Rolle won three National Association for the Advancement of Colored People (NAACP) Image Awards throughout her career. She also appeared in numerous feature films. Rolle died in 1998 at the age of seventy-eight.

Joyce Linehan

SEE ALSO: *Arthur, Bea; Emmy Awards;* Good Times; *Lear, Norman; Leisure Time;* Maude; *Television.*

BIBLIOGRAPHY

Bogle, Donald. *Prime Time Blues: African Americans on Network Television*. New York: Farrar, Straus & Giroux, 2001.

Otfinoski, Steven. *African Americans in the Performing Arts*. New York: Facts On File, 2010.

Roller Coasters

Most everyone can remember the first time he or she rode a roller coaster and how it felt. People either love to ride them or not, but very few are indifferent to the bone-rattling structures that have become a popular pastime worldwide, ever since the first one—"Flying Mountains," developed in Russia in the fifteenth century—introduced the combination of fear and amusement. The engineering technology of roller coasters defies nature by allowing human beings to be catapulted at varying speeds every which way.

There were approximately 750 operating roller coasters in North America as of 2012, all competing in speed, architecture, and inventiveness. The progress of engineering has enabled coasters to travel backward or around inverted loops at alarming speeds (most average in the mid-60-miles-per-hour [mph] range), while riders can sometimes stand, be in the dark, or sit in chairlift-style trains with tracks that run along the top, while strapped tightly into their seats. Whether they are steel or wooden, roller coasters receive names that are always given careful thought, their purpose being to evoke a really good and scary ride (Colossus, Fireball, Cyclone, and the Superman are some examples). In the first decade of the 2000s there were about a dozen roller coaster clubs and organizations formed by people who share a similar enthusiasm and spend much of their leisure time engaging in lengthy critiques of coasters all over the world. There are even front seat and backseat enthusiasts who argue over which seat will elicit the most surprises and offer the best ride.

HOW ROLLER COASTERS WORK

The physics are relatively simple: roller coasters are powered by gravity (and operated by computers). As the train is pulled up the hill, potential energy is built up and then converted into kinetic energy once it begins its descent. Positive gravitational forces (g-forces) press riders into their seats at the bottom of a dip, whereas negative g-forces create a temporary sense of weightlessness that is pleasurable for some and nauseating for others. During the ride people experience a communal thrill of traveling at extreme speeds and heights while being in the open air.

Part of the fun of roller coasters is that they are scary, and there is a perverse delight people feel in being afraid, especially when they are (relatively) sure that nothing can go wrong. Some roller coasters have speed to offer (the best usually surpass 70 mph), the height of dips (225 feet, for example), or the frequency of the dips during a ride (a coaster in Texas boasts twenty additional drops, after the first one, which descends 137 feet). Most trains travel slowly up the track at the ride's beginning to allow the coaster to gain speed during its first plunge that will sustain it for the duration of the ride but also to build up the anticipation of riders as to what lies ahead (most likely the highest of many drops, loops, or speed). But some blast off instantly, gaining awesome speed in a short time (one popular roller coaster accelerates from 0 to 128 mph in just 3.5 seconds). Sometimes the real adventure, though, lies in a roller coaster's stature or age. A creaky, old wooden coaster, without fancy safety mechanisms, can hint at an impending derailment, as well as offer a truly jostling, loud ride.

The famous, rickety Cyclone in Coney Island, New York, helped to popularize the roller coaster in the United States at the beginning of the twentieth century. Coaster mythology has it that a mute man once rode it and spoke his very first words after riding it: "I feel sick." The coaster continues to frighten riders, who can never be sure if and when it will fall apart. In 1927 a nurse was stationed next to a coaster named the Cyclone in Crystal Beach, Ontario, just as a precaution, because of its 90-foot drop and hairpin turns. The Zippin Pippin in Liberty-

Roller Coasters. *Thrill-seekers ride Intimidator 305 roller coaster at Kings Dominion Amusement Park in Doswell, Virginia.* THE WASHINGTON POST/CONTRIBUTOR/GETTY IMAGES.

land, Memphis, was singer Elvis Presley's favorite amusement park ride. Apparently the King once rode it nonstop for hours when he rented out the park one night in 1977, just eight days before he died.

INCREASED THRILLS, HIGHER RISKS

There is always an element of uncertainty in riding these machines, and roller coasters have had their share of widely publicized mishaps. Sometimes the computers that run them fail. Cars have smashed into each other, safety lap bars have suddenly popped open during a ride, and trains have become uncoupled while climbing hills. In turn, riders have been thrown out of trains and suffered injuries that—combined with the speed, twists, and turns of roller coasters—can be very serious, if not fatal. An extensive study by the Associated Press found that the roller coaster industry was one in which blunders and bad judgment can abound.

There is constant competition for companies to design faster, bigger, and more awesome rides. In fact, new terms have been developed to distinguish categories of rides. A hypercoaster is one that reaches heights between 200 and 299 feet. One of the first was the Magnum XL-200 at Cedar Point in Ohio. It attains a maximum speed of 72 mph and has multiple hills, three tunnels, and a pretzel turnaround. A giga coaster reaches heights between 300 and 399 feet. As of 2012 there were only three in the world. One of those is the Intimidator at Kings Dominion in Doswell, Virginia. It has a maximum height of 305 feet, and its first drop of 300 feet causes it to reach speeds of 90 mph. A strata coaster is a complete circuit roller coaster with a height between 400 and 499 feet. The Kingda Ka at Six Flags in Jackson, New Jersey, is one such roller coaster. It has a drop of 418 feet and goes from 0 to 128 mph in 3.5 seconds.

For the companies that develop such monster roller coasters, the riders often serve as guinea pigs, testing the rides' safety when they first open. "It's hard sometimes on paper to anticipate those forces," said Robert Johnson, executive director of the Outdoor Amusement Business Association, a carnival trade group. "People aren't built the same. Some people can withstand forces differently than others. Any major new ride, it's a trial ride. It's a prototype. The first year is a trial year." There is a certain degree of misbehaving that goes on in parks with patrons (holding up their hands during a ride, for example), and that coupled with the fact that the industry is one of the least regulated and monitored in the country (there are no federal guidelines for the degree of gravitational forces that people can be subjected to), can produce more risks. But the knowledge that an occasional, injurious accident can occur does not stop enthusiasts from waiting in long lines to ride roller coasters.

Sharon Yablon

SEE ALSO: *Amusement Parks; Leisure Time; Traveling Carnivals.*

BIBLIOGRAPHY

Cartmell, Robert. *The Incredible Scream Machine: A History of the Roller Coaster.* Bowling Green, OH: Bowling Green State University Popular Press, 1987.

Costanza, Jared. Rideaccidents.com. Accessed May 2012. Available from http://www.rideaccidents.com

Silverstein, Herma. *Scream Machines: Roller Coasters Past, Present, and Future.* New York: Walker, 1986.

Throgmorton, Todd H. *Roller Coasters: United States and Canada.* Jefferson, NC: McFarland, 2009.

Urbanowicz, Steven J. *The Roller Coaster Lover's Companion: A Thrill-Seeker's Guide to the World's Best Coasters.* Secaucus, NJ: Carol Publishing, 1997.

Van Steenwyk, Elizabeth. *Behind the Scenes at the Amusement Park.* Niles, IL: A. Whitman, 1983.

Roller Derby

Roller derby—a team sport of fast, furious, and often violent action—first appeared in the mid-1930s. It was often compared to professional wrestling because the two popular culture spectacles shared many traits, including fixed finishes, story lines featuring heroes and villains, and an explosion of popularity due to early television coverage. Roller derby games take place on a banked oval track, where two squads of five skate around the track, with each team sending out "jammers" in front of the pack. Points are scored when jammers lap an opponent. As in rugby or football, other players act as "blockers," clearing the way for the jammer. The team with the most points wins—although, much like in wrestling, it's the action, not the outcome, that matters most.

While professional wrestling flourished in the 1980s thanks to cable television, roller derby did not enjoy a similar surge in popularity. Instead, it was the next big thing—the Internet—that led to the resurgence of roller derby in the first part of the twenty-first century. Unlike the earlier form of roller derby, which was controlled by one person and the outcomes were rigged, the new derby is a grassroots movement of real contests. While early roller derby featured both male and female skaters, the new derby is a female/feminist phenomenon. A large part of the roller derby audience has always been women, in part because the roller derby was almost the only sports activity prior to the 1970s where female athletes could be seen on television. In addition, the roller derby integrated very early, and many of the skaters were black or Hispanic—among them Ronnie Robinson, son of boxing great Sugar Ray Robinson

SPORTS ENTERTAINMENT

Inspired by long-distance bicycle races and dance marathons, Leo Seltzer invented roller derby in 1935. The original objective was an endurance race around the track, featuring teams of one man and one woman each who would circle the track thousands of times, skating up to eleven-and-a-half hours a day. While at that time it was a true athletic contest, it was also quite boring for the spectators. Similar to the development of professional wrestling, when roller derby introduced violent contact and shorter matches and began developing personality players, its popularity boomed.

Legend has it that writer Damon Runyon, after witnessing a fight between two female skaters in 1938, suggested that Seltzer turn roller derby into something akin to pro wrestling on skates, with "heroes" and "villains" acting out feuds and grudges. The most popular skaters were not necessarily the best athletes but rather the most charismatic characters, dramatic performers, and captivating interview subjects. The mix of speed and mayhem, coupled with cheap production costs, was perfect for early television, and roller derby was the most popular show on ABC during the network's infancy. While teams were based in many major U.S. cities, the Bay City Bombers in San Francisco became the game's iconic franchise. The popularity of the sport was such that in 1949 the playoffs of the National Roller Derby League sold out New York's Madison Square Garden for a week.

Seltzer's son Jerry took over the roller derby and in the mid-1950s moved the base of operations to Southern California, then to Northern California in 1958. The home team Bay Area Bombers achieved the most success. With stars such as Charlie O'Connell, Ann Calvello, and "The Blonde Bomber" Joanie Weston, the Bombers dominated the sport and Weston was the star of the show. In *Five Strides on the Banked Track: The Life and Times of the Roller Derby*, sportswriter Frank Deford describes Weston as "not only the best skater, but she clearly looks the part as well. With her bleached blond pigtails flowing out from beneath her shiny black pivot helmet, Joanie appeared like a brave Viking queen in full battle regalia."

With huge local shows that often outdrew those of the expanding Oakland Raiders football team in the early 1960s, the popularity of roller derby remained strong. The sport spread to more cities and to other countries and had ten full-time teams at its peak of popularity. Yet, in 1973, only two years after drawing a record 35,000 people to the Oakland Coliseum, Seltzer folded the league, selling out to a rival organization based out of Los Angeles called Roller Games. Roller Games was even more outlandish than roller derby and featured more gimmicks seen in professional wrestling, such as "death matches." The Roller Game league's Los Angeles T-Birds, which once featured a huge female skater with the number 747, was the most dominant team until Roller Games folded in 1975.

Like its cousin, professional wrestling, roller derby has often been labeled a "trash" sport, or "sports entertainment." Yet the popularity of roller derby found its way into mainstream popular culture. It was the subject of Jim Croce's song "Roller Derby Queen" from his 1973 best-selling album *Life and Times*. On the big screen, the film *Kansas City Bomber* (1972) featured Raquel Welch as a roller derby queen, while *Rollerball* (1975), starring James Caan, was a futuristic parable set in a society where an ultraviolent, roller-derby-like sport is used to give people an outlet for their antisocial feelings, thus becoming a popular mass pastime. *Rollerball* would be remade in 2002 featuring professional wrestling personality Paul Heyman.

The 1971 documentary *Derby* examined the sport, and a 1976 episode of *Charlie's Angels* centered on a murder at a roller derby game. In 1978 the TV series *Roller Girls* focused on the fictional Pittsburgh Pitts roller derby team. The show lasted only four episodes. In the meantime, numerous attempts at comebacks for the league were equally unsuccessful. The International Roller Derby League was formed in 1979 but appeared only in the Bay Area, and in 1986 a souped-up version of Roller Games that included "a wall of death" appeared on ESPN. It lasted less than a season.

REVIVAL

When roller derby icon Weston died suddenly in 1997, roller derby was thrust back into the news. After reading her obituary, TV executive Stephen Land was "inspired to get together with The Nashville Network (TNN) and make Weston's dream come true." Weston had also been featured in ESPN's Classic Sports Network show *Roller Super Stars*, which ran old tapes featuring the golden years of "The Blonde Bomber" and her teammates.

Another revival occurred in 1998 with Seltzer, as president of the World Skating League (WSL), again at the helm. The WSL put together six teams to produce *Roller Jams* for TNN. While the concept remained the same, the packaging was much different. Rather than roller skates, skaters in the new league donned inline skates and tight-fitting uniforms, and special effects and rock music were introduced to accompany the event. The late-1990s sport was faster and sexier than ever before, and Seltzer expressed the belief that the resurgence of pro wrestling in the 1990s, coupled with the wide attraction of inline skating, would put roller derby back on top for the twenty-first century. Despite his high hopes, however, the show lasted only one season. It seemed once again the sports entertainment spectacle was dead.

"DERBY GIRLS"

One of the early attractions of roller derby on TV was that it featured women as athletes. For years, roller derby, professional wrestling, and the Olympics were the only places fans could see female athletes compete on television. While men were often attracted to roller derby for the "catfights," for women, it represented something different. As Diane Williams wrote in an article for the *Nation*, "Sassy, strong and aggressive, 'derby girls' challenged traditional notions of acceptable female behavior through the male-dominated world of sports."

The idea of derby girls combined with other movements—in particular, punk rock and "third wave" feminism—led to a new roller derby. This new version took root in Austin, Texas, in the early part of the twenty-first century, and, according to Williams, married "an underground vibe with the fun of athletic competition in a blend of sport and spectacle that is as much fun to play as it is to watch." This version wouldn't be controlled by one person but instead became a grassroots movements spurred on by the Internet. With social media to send out the word (and video), roller derby spread like wildfire, as young women all over the world began to form teams. In the early 2010s there were more than 1,190 amateur leagues around the globe. Some matches are held in large stadiums seating thousands, while others take place in small venues.

Unlike the old roller derby, the new version is an authentic athletic contest. Some early elements remain, including the basic structure of the game. The new players adopt personae and skater names rife with pop culture allusions, sexual references, and outrageous puns. Like pro wrestlers, these skaters live the gimmick. Thanks in large part to these outlandish elements, roller derby soared back into the mainstream with a 2006 TV show *Rollergirls* on the A&E network and the 2007 documentary *Blood on the Flat Track: The Rise of the Rat City Rollergirls*. A huge burst in notoriety came with the 2009 movie *Whip It!*, directed by Drew Barrymore and starring Ellen Page as a skater for the Austin roller derby squad. It will be interesting to see if roller derby returns to its sports entertainment roots or if it can stay true to the new vision of sports, spectacle, and political statement.

Patrick Jones

SEE ALSO: *Cable TV;* Charlie's Angels*; ESPN; The Internet; Robinson, Sugar Ray; Social Media; Television; World Wrestling Federation.*

BIBLIOGRAPHY

Deford, Frank. *Five Strides on the Banked Track: The Life and Times of the Roller Derby*. Boston: Little, Brown, 1971.

La Gorce, Tammy. "With Names That Could Kill, Women Rev Up Roller Derby." *New York Times*, November 7, 2008, NJ6.

Leland, John. "Cruising for a Bruising." *Newsweek*, January 17, 1999, 50.

Mabe, Catherine. *Roller Derby: The History and All-Girl Revival of the Greatest Sport on Wheels*. Denver, CO: Speck Press, 2007.

Neale, Rick. "All-Female Roller Derby Elbows Its Way in as a Legitimate Sport." *USA Today*, June 24, 2008, F:3.

Werts, Diane. "What Goes around Comes around—Like Roller Derby." *Los Angeles Times*, January 8, 1999.

Williams, Diane. "Revolution on Eight Wheels." *Nation*, August 15–22, 2011, 18.

Rolling Stone

In 1967, with $7,500 lent to them by family and friends, Jann Wenner, a University of California at Berkeley student and aspiring rock journalist, and Ralph Gleason, a jazz critic for the *San Francisco Chronicle*, launched *Rolling Stone*. They put together the first issue, dated November 9, in a San Francisco loft lent to them by their printer. With the look of an underground newspaper, *Rolling Stone* targeted a young readership that was attuned to the counterculture. The new magazine never intended to follow the leads of popular magazines of the day, choosing instead to forge its own path. Its covers became icons in themselves, serving as cultural barometers for many Americans.

At different points in its history, the biweekly has been regarded as a daring antiestablishment voice or a slick mainstream commodity. The one constant has been the magazine's music coverage. *Rolling Stone* has always deemed rock and roll to be newsworthy, understanding from the beginning that musical preferences are often overtly political in nature. In fact, its coverage in the 1960s of rock helped to legitimize key elements of that decade's oppositional culture.

THE BEGINNING

Wenner was twenty years old when he started *Rolling Stone* as editor and publisher. Dropping out of college, he turned his attention to realizing his dream of getting to know his personal idols, who included Bob Dylan, John Lennon, and Mick Jagger. "*Rolling Stone* is not just about music," wrote Wenner in the inaugural issue, "but also about the things and attitudes that the music embraces." The magazine's name was taken from a song by blues legend Muddy Waters that borrows its title from an old proverb: "A rolling stone gathers no moss." *Rolling Stone*'s underground feel, with its newsprint paper and quarter-fold format, was the opposite of Wenner's intention. He wanted to make the magazine look as professional as possible, which was why it featured column rules and Times Roman type. Wenner, who derisively referred to "the hippie press," wanted to be as legitimate as *Time* magazine. Despite Wenner's efforts, outsiders saw *Rolling Stone* as being part of the counterculture movement, a perception that lasted into the 1970s.

The magazine took its slogan, "All the News That Fits," from the *New York Times*' "All the News That's Fit to Print." In addition to being a facetious swipe at the *Times*, it described the limitless space allotted to *Rolling Stone*'s writers. The magazine's focus on music as a newsworthy topic distinguished it from any other publication that came before it. Its interviews with musicians (and later, with actors, politicians, and other celebrities) went beyond the subject's personal likes and dislikes and probed the creative process. One of the magazine's early record critics, Greil Marcus, declared in Robert Anson's 1981 book *Gone Crazy and Back Again*: "I am no more capable of mulling over Elvis without thinking of Herman Melville, than I am of reading Jonathan Edwards without putting on Robert Johnson's records as background music."

FINDING A MARKET

After a fledgling debut issue that had a press run of 40,000 copies, 34,000 of which were returned, the magazine reached a circulation of 325,000 by 1974 and 1.25 million by 1998. Along the way, it dropped its quarter-fold format for a regular four-color tabloid style. In 1974, 16 percent of its readership was over twenty-five with a median age of twenty-one. By the end of the 1990s, however, that original audience was older, and many of the readers had become yuppies. Once a must-read for young Americans, *Rolling Stone* faced heavy competition from other music magazines by the 1990s, as well as from MTV.

Wenner, dubbed the "hip capitalist" by journalist Robert Draper, once offered an early subscription incentive of a free roach clip (to hold marijuana joints). Hip promotion aside, the magazine steadily gained a reputation for publishing "some remarkably good reportage," as even the stodgy *New York Times* admitted in 1973. Such recognition allowed *Rolling Stone* to gain a foothold in the competitive world of magazine publishing.

THE VOICE OF A GENERATION

Wenner's magazine thrived on reporting on cultural events of the late 1960s that were deemed relevant to its readers. While mainstream newspapers condemned the tribal goings-on at Woodstock in 1969, *Rolling Stone* reported that the festival crowd temporarily constituted New York State's third-largest city and successfully policed itself. When 1969's Altamont festival self-destructed into violence, *Rolling Stone* weighed in with the headline "Let It Bleed" and assigned blame to anyone even remotely involved with the festival. Its hard-hitting coverage of Altamont stood in sharp contrast to that of the establishment press, which lazily reported facts and figures such as the length of the traffic jam and offered estimates on the attendance without ever giving an inkling of the orgy of violence that had occurred.

The shootings of students protesting the Vietnam War at Kent State in 1970 provoked many members of *Rolling Stone*'s staff to steer the magazine toward coverage that was more political in nature. Wenner fought off the revolt and insisted the magazine remain focused on music, which resulted in several resignations. Maintaining the same editorial direction proved to be problematic because rock music was limping into the 1970s. Many of rock's legends from the 1960s, including Jimi Hendrix, Jim Morrison, Janis Joplin, and the Beatles, were either dead or defunct. As rock critic Jon Landau expressed in a 1974 book review in the *New York Times*, "Bob Dylan has lost much of his impact . . . the end of the Beatles as a group is now irreversible . . . there are no longer any superhumans to Joe us on."

TRANSFORMATIONS

Enter Hunter S. Thompson, the iconoclastic writer who became a celebrity through the magazine's pages. Thompson, the "Gonzo

Journalist," practiced a bombastic style of writing that pushed aside objectivity and forced him to enter the stories he covered. Thompson was a cultural outlaw. Open about his drug abuse and alcohol consumption, he crafted prose that could be keenly insightful on one page and babbling nonsense on the next. The man who once wrote that President Richard Nixon had "the integrity of a hyena and the style of a poison toad" managed to find himself with Nixon in the presidential limousine during the 1968 campaign. They talked about football. It was this kind of inconceivable situation that endeared Thompson to *Rolling Stone*'s readers. Issues that carried installments of his infamous book *Fear and Loathing in Las Vegas* (1972) sold out quickly. Soon Thompson was covering the 1972 presidential election for the magazine, which was beginning to display a unique ability to transfer rock-and-roll panache to more sober pursuits, such as literature and politics.

Rolling Stone quietly became a literate magazine that happened to cover music. More influential celebrities were granting lengthy interviews similar to those that had been popularized in *Playboy*. The magazine's literary credentials were further established by the contributions of authors Tom Wolfe and Truman Capote, and Richard Goodwin, a former speechwriter for John F. Kennedy, helped to give it political cachet. *Rolling Stone* won the 1970 National Magazine Award for its pieces on Altamont and Charles Manson. Now recognized for challenging its readers' assumptions, the magazine had the envious ability to cover stories in ways that major newspapers either could not or would not.

Rolling Stone's breakthrough came in 1975 after the publication was contacted by a San Francisco attorney who claimed that he had provided refuge for fugitive Patty Hearst, the kidnapped newspaper heiress. "The Inside Story," as the article was titled, scooped the major media outlets in what was among the most-covered events of the day. It was widely recognized that *Rolling Stone*'s Hearst story was the biggest journalistic coup since the *New York Times* had printed the Pentagon Papers five years earlier.

Perhaps the magazine's toughest critics were its readers and staff. Every decision, from changes in format to the kind of advertising that was accepted, was subjected to vigorous debate. According to Draper, it was simply that "*Rolling Stone*'s staffers wanted nothing so much as to set a good example for their peers." When the magazine came up short in that regard, readers were quick to accuse it of selling out. After *Rolling Stone*'s move to New York in 1977, the magazine's culture was altered. Bit by bit, the look and content shifted toward more market-driven concerns. By that time, Wenner had become eager to shake the magazine's hippie image in pursuit of mainstream success. The fragmented music scene and the aging readership helped to underscore the editorial drift that ensued. The magazine, once a haven for writers seeking an alternative outlet, was put in the unusual position of watching its writers defect to the mainstream press.

ADJUSTING TO A NEW ERA

"Few things sound less glamorous," proclaimed Louis Menand in a 1991 *New Republic* piece, "than 'the counterculture'—a term many people are likely to associate with Charles Manson." *Rolling Stone*'s constituency had changed. Other music magazines rose to prominence in the 1990s, such as *Spin* (alternative music) and *Vibe* (hip-hop/rap), and young people could now receive their music news without *Rolling Stone*. The magazine responded by beefing up its fashion and technology content. Out of touch with even its core topic, *Rolling Stone* gave covers to major rock acts from the previous decade, such as U2 and the Talking Heads.

By 2002, when *Rolling Stone* turned thirty-five years old, the magazine still had many of its original readers. That confirmed the notion among younger readers that it was of their parents' generation. The publications found itself in a difficult predicament. While magazines such as *Spin*, *Vibe*, and *Blender* offered specialized coverage, *Rolling Stone* attempted to court multiple generations and musical tastes. Its sales steadily declined in the twenty-first century as competition continued to increase and more people turned to the Internet for up-to-date information on the music scene.

Rolling Stone executives responded by redesigning the magazine, enhancing its music coverage, and running less-lengthy fare. The publications also revamped its website to include message boards and searchable archives. Its most successful move was a return to polemical journalism with the hiring of Matt Taibbi and Michael Hastings. The two journalists signaled renewed credibility and relevance for the magazine and inserted it squarely in the center of some of the biggest hot-button issues facing the United States.

Daryl Umberger

SEE ALSO: *Advertising; Altamont; The Beatles; Capote, Truman; Dylan, Bob; Hearst, Patty; Hendrix, Jimi; Hippies; Joplin, Janis; Kent State Massacre; Lennon, John; Manson, Charles; MTV;* Playboy*; Rock and Roll; Talking Heads; Thompson, Hunter S.; U2; Wolfe, Tom; Woodstock; Yuppies.*

BIBLIOGRAPHY

Anson, Robert Sam. *The Rise and Fall of the "Rolling Stone" Generation*. Garden City, NY: Doubleday, 1981.

Arnold, Martin. "'Rolling Stone' Is Still Gathering Readers, Revenue and Prestige." *New York Times*, October 22, 1973, 32.

"The Birth of 'Rolling Stone.'" *Rolling Stone*, July 12, 2007.

Draper, Robert. *"Rolling Stone" Magazine: The Uncensored History*. Garden City, NY: Doubleday, 1990.

Fine, Jon. "'Rolling Stone' Reinvents Itself." *Advertising Age*, August 26, 2002.

Granatstein, Lisa. "'RS' Rolls Out Fresher Look." *Mediaweek*, August 10, 1998, 6–7.

Menand, Louis. "Life in the Stone Age." *New Republic*, January 7, 1991, 38–44.

Nelson, Alix. "Review of *The Rolling Stone Reader*." *New York Times*, April 14, 1974, sec. 7, 19.

Seymour, Corey. "On the Cover of 'Rolling Stone': A Twenty-Fifth Anniversary Special." *Rolling Stone*, December 10, 1992, 147–154.

Woodward, Fred, ed. *"Rolling Stone": The Illustrated Portraits*. San Francisco: Chronicle Books, 2000.

The Rolling Stones

Whereas the Beatles and other exponents of the British Invasion served an updated version of rock and roll to the United States, the Rolling Stones emerged in 1963–1964 as the most prominent of the British acts that brought the African American musical form of blues to a young, white American audience. The group was at the peak of their musical and cultural significance at the end of the 1960s, when their violent lyrics and brooding blues-rock seemed to reflect the potentially cataclysmic clefts in American society. After the early 1970s, the Rolling Stones made very few musically or politically radical records, but their famous 1960s songs continue to resound.

THE ANTI-BEATLES

Mick Jagger and Keith Richards attended the same primary school in Dartford, England, during the late 1940s, but they lost touch until a legendary reunion at Dartford railway station in 1961, when Richards's interest was piqued by Jagger's selection of Chuck Berry records. Jagger and Richards soon began to play with slide guitar aficionado Brian Jones. The trio recruited jazz drummer Charlie Watts and bassist Bill Wyman. Jones named the fledgling group the Rolling Stones after a Muddy Waters song. In April 1963 aspiring pop-group manager Andrew Oldham saw the Stones at the Crawdaddy Club in Richmond, London. Oldham later reminisced: "I knew what I was looking at. It was sex."

Oldham negotiated the Stones' contract with Decca Records in early 1963. The group's earliest recorded songs were a compromise between expurgated rhythm and blues (R&B) and pop ballads intended to exploit the popularity of the Beatles. In early 1964, however, Oldham began to promote the Rolling Stones as the antithesis of the Fab Four, ordering the band to abandon their Beatle boots and leather waistcoats and to accentuate the slovenly, surly sexuality that he had seen have such an effect on audiences at their early Crawdaddy gigs. Oldham's propaganda included planting newspaper headlines such as "Would you let your daughter go with a Rolling Stone?"

When the Stones arrived for their first tour of the United States in June 1964, American newspapers fulminated that the "new Beatles" were a disgrace compared to the adorable, mop-topped originals. Old-school crooner Dean Martin made sneering references to the Stones' long hair during their appearance on *Hollywood Palace*. But hip American youths embraced the Stones, not least because the Beatles had been co-opted by their parents, and, as rock critic Lillian Roxon later noted, "No one had ever seen a white man move on stage the way Jagger moved."

The Rolling Stones' commercial appeal to young Americans was confirmed when the single "(I Can't Get No) Satisfaction," a sexually aggressive anthem of disillusionment with society, reached number one in June 1965. A run of similarly incendiary hit singles followed before the 1967 albums *Between the Buttons* and *Their Satanic Majesties Request*, a disastrous foray into fey Anglocentric psychedelia, revealed the extent to which the Stones had neglected their R&B influences during their immersion in the swinging London scene. Nevertheless, the Stones remained

The Rolling Stones. *The Rolling Stones lineup in 1978 included, from left, Ronnie Wood, Keith Richards, Mick Jagger, Charlie Watts, and Bill Wyman.* MICHAEL PUTLAND/GETTY IMAGES.

notorious during the Summer of Love. Jagger and Richards were busted for possession of drugs at the latter's English country home, and the June 1967 court case was a very public microcosm of the clash between traditional moral strictures and the liberalized youth culture burgeoning on both sides of the Atlantic.

THE BAND'S HEYDAY

In early 1968 "Jumpin' Jack Flash" was released, instigating an astonishing period during which the Stones harnessed sinister and salacious lyrics to an intense, rootsy sound. Their finest album, *Beggars Banquet*, released in late 1968, featured "Street Fighting Man," on which Jagger pondered his position as a figurehead for an imminent revolution, and "Sympathy for the Devil," an ironic ode to their own demonic image, which incorporated a topical reference to the murder of Bobby Kennedy. In June 1969 Jones was sacked and replaced by young blues virtuoso Mick Taylor. The following month Jones drowned in his swimming pool.

On *Let It Bleed* (1969), the Stones extended their devilish disquisition on violence in contemporary society on such songs as "Midnight Rambler" and "Gimme Shelter" ("Rape, murder, it's just a shot away"). In December 1969 the Stones headlined a free festival, organized in the spirit of Woodstock, at Altamont speedway in California. The Hells Angels were hired as bodyguards, and one of the gang, fueled by liquor and LSD, murdered a young black teenager while the Stones performed. In hindsight, "Gimme Shelter" (also the title of the Maysles brothers' brilliant tour film, which concluded with the horror of Altamont) seemed to have anticipated the nihilistic death knell of 1960s idealism.

Sticky Fingers (1971) was a prime piece of Americana, featuring "Brown Sugar," a typically scurrilous account of sex and slavery in Dixie. Though criticized at the time, *Exile on Main Street* (1972) has since been recognized as the influential apogee of the Rolling Stones' relationship with the American musical forms of country, blues, and soul. They adapted to the glam era with what biographer Philip Norman called the "mid-1970s high camp" of "It's Only Rock'N'Roll (But I Like It)" (1974). The song's title, however, was telling: creating musically innovative and culturally representative music was no longer the Rolling Stones' top priority. Jagger would later admit that after 1972 the group became "complacent." Instead the Stones became, along with Led Zeppelin, the archetypal early 1970s rock-and-roll circus, a touring cavalcade of sexual, chemical, and egotistical excess.

On *Some Girls* (1978), the band was somewhat reinvigorated by the influence and challenge of disco and punk, but the Glimmer Twins (as Jagger and Richards nicknamed themselves) were now more media celebrities than musicians. Jagger began reveling in his jet-set, high-society lifestyle, whereas Richards became infamous for his decline into heroin addiction.

AND THE BAND PLAYED ON

The group effectively split from 1986 to 1989 due to antagonism between Jagger and Richards. Wyman belatedly emerged as a target of tabloid opprobrium over his relationship with thirteen-year-old Mandy Smith. During the 1990s Jagger and Richards made millions from commercials: their seminal mid-1960s attack on consumerism was adapted to promote the "Satisfaction" provided by a particular chocolate bar, whereas the 1981 hit "Start Me Up" provided appropriate lyrics for the launch of Microsoft's Windows 95 computer program. The reunited Stones, minus the retired Wyman, continued to undertake extravagant world tours into the twenty-first century, during which a bewildering variety of official Stones merchandise was sold. Appropriately, Andy Warhol's lapping-tongue logo had become the massively reproduced signifier that the Rolling Stones' cultural significance had turned into just another commodity.

In 2005 the band released *A Bigger Bang*, and during the tour for that album acclaimed director Martin Scorsese shot concert footage that he produced into the film *Shine a Light* (2008). The Rolling Stones also did the halftime show at Super Bowl XL in 2006, performing three of their most famous songs: "Start Me Up," "Rough Justice," and "(I Can't Get No) Satisfaction." In 2010 a rerelease of their 1972 album *Exile on Main Street* once again topped the British charts. That same year Richards published a memoir, *Life*, in which he chronicled his life and career by drawing on old notebooks and diaries. He also leveled criticism at Jagger, whom he characterized as treating the rest of the band as "basically hirelings."

The long-standing hostility between Jagger and Richards played out again in 2012. In March of that year the band members all failed to attend a concert at Carnegie Hall given to honor their 50th anniversary, and observers thought that the rift between the stars might be one reason for their absence. In addition, rumors swirled that Richards's health was poor. In 2006 he suffered a head injury with long-term consequences, causing him to stop playing for a few years. An anniversary tour scheduled for 2012 was postponed because Richards admittedly felt too rusty to perform. Insiders questioned whether he was healthy enough for a worldwide tour, and longtime fans were left wondering if they had seen the last of the Stones.

Martyn Bone

SEE ALSO: *Altamont; The Beatles; Berry, Chuck; Blues; British Invasion; Hells Angels; Led Zeppelin; Lennon, John; Little Richard; McCartney, Paul; Pop Music; Rock and Roll; Stadium Concerts; Waters, Muddy; The Who.*

BIBLIOGRAPHY

Booth, Stanley. *The True Adventures of the Rolling Stones.* London: Heinemann, 1985.

Kent, Nick. *The Dark Stuff: Selected Writings on Rock Music 1972–1993.* London: Penguin, 1994.

Marion, Larry. *The Lost Rolling Stones Photographs: The Bob Bonis Archive, 1964–1966.* New York: It Books, 2010.

Norman, Philip. *The Stones.* London: Penguin, 1993.

Richards, Keith, and James Fox. *Life.* New York: Little, Brown, 2010.

Wells, Simon, and Getty Images. *The Rolling Stones: 365 Days.* New York: Harry N. Abrams, 2006.

Wyman, Bill, and Ray Coleman. *Stone Alone.* New York: Viking, 1990.

Romance Novels

Critics denounce romance novels as "mind candy" and are adamant about the intellect-eroding properties of these titles, which account for about half of all mass-market paperback sales.

The phenomenal sales figures seem only to intensify the attacks of those who claim the plots are simplistic and the characters flat. Some see these criticisms as a chauvinistic refusal to take seriously this popular literature, written and edited largely by women for a mostly female audience. But, traditionally, many of the genre's sternest critics have been other women who condemn romance novels as dangerously passive texts that encourage readers to find in the fictional world consolation for the fulfillment that a patriarchal culture denies them.

LITERARY ROOTS OF ROMANCE

Romance novels have always been frowned upon by champions of high culture, who value fiction for its originality and see formulaic romance novels as sentimental trash. More than a century ago, Mary Ann Evans called them "silly novels by lady novelists," distinguishing between this species of subliterature and her own, more serious fiction, published under the pseudonym George Eliot. Across the Atlantic Nathaniel Hawthorne complained bitterly of "that damned lot of scribbling women" whose novels outsold his own work. Despite the contempt with which denizens of "real literature" view the novels, the romance formula can claim roots deep in Western literary tradition. Mikhail Bakhtin's description of classical Greek romances (a male and female of marriageable age experience a mutual, passionate attraction; encounter obstacles that threaten their union; overcome the obstacles; and consummate their love within marriage) could as easily describe the latest romance to roll off Harlequin's presses.

Jane Austen's *Pride and Prejudice* has been called the greatest romantic novel of English literature. It, along with Austen's other novels, is entrenched in the literary canon, yet readers of romance novels claim Austen as one of their own. Although Austen would no doubt be shocked by the frank sexuality of many twenty-first-century romantic heroines, she would recognize the sensible, independent women and the arrogant males they humble as descendants of Elizabeth and Darcy. The most famous characters created by Emily and Charlotte Brontë also serve as inspiration for romance writers: Heathcliff, the dark and dangerous spirit who serves as hero and villain of the monumental *Wuthering Heights*; Jane Eyre, the plain heroine who wins with courage and integrity; and Rochester, the maimed hero who learns that true love conquers all, are stock characters in romance novels.

THE DOMESTIC NOVEL

Although the romance novel can claim legitimate kinship with works that have earned established places in the Western literary canon, the most direct precursor of popular romance novels is the "domestic novel" of the nineteenth century. Susan Warner's *The Wide, Wide World* (1851) defined the term *best seller*, and Maria Cummins's *The Lamplighter* (1854) was nearly as popular. These novels focused on the trials of a young heroine, often an orphan, who struggled to survive and cherished her independence but who ultimately married and surrendered her autonomy. These "scribbling women" recognized that most women could find economic security only within marriage. Yet, if marriage offered the young heroine salvation from economic deprivation, her love offered the hero salvation from an emotionally and spiritually barren life. In Augusta Jane Evans's *St. Elmo* (1867), beloved by generations of readers, the beautiful, virtuous Edna Earl capitulates to St. Elmo Murray, the Byronic hero complete with "piercing eyes" and "savage sneer," only after his reformation from hardened cynic to tender lover and Christian minister.

Writers such as the prolific Grace Livingston Hill continued this pattern of mutual redemption into the twentieth century. By the 1920s, however, Hill's strict religious tales were the exception. Women's magazines were enjoying enormous success; periodicals with a circulation of 128,621,000 per issue were flooding U.S. households. The top titles regularly included romance stories with predictable characters and plots and the requisite happy ending. These pre–World War II romances, still formulaic in many ways, had a new heroine, the "New Woman," eager for career success and unwilling to surrender her right to self-expression. These new novels extended the range of romance to reflect the wider experiences available to women in the twentieth century. Meanwhile, Georgette Heyer, only seventeen when she wrote her first novel, *The Black Moth*, was proving herself a worthy successor to Austen and founding a subgenre of the romance novel, the Regency.

Heyer, James Baldwin, and dozens of others continued to write what by the end of the twentieth century would be labeled "gentle romances" to distinguish their novels from the sexually explicit romances of the post-1960s era. In Great Britain, Mills and Boon was publishing books that were little more than modernizations of the nineteenth-century sentimental novels: an eighteen-year-old heroine saved from genteel poverty by an older, incredibly wealthy hero who raises her to the heights of luxury as she brings him to his knees in an acknowledgment of love's power. In 1949 Harlequin Enterprises, a Canadian company, began publishing Mills and Boon reprints for a North American audience. The venture was so successful that in 1957 Harlequin suspended publication of other genre fiction to focus exclusively on Mills and Boon romances. Around the same time another subgenre of romance was also experiencing a revival. Phyllis Whitney's *Thunder Heights* and Victoria Holt's *Mistress of Mellyn*, both published in 1960, sold more than a million copies, and by the end of the 1970s gothic romances (issued at a rate of thirty-five titles a month) were outselling every other form of genre fiction. But an unsolicited manuscript was about to change the romance scene to an unprecedented degree.

THE ROMANCE REVOLUTION

In 1972 Avon published *The Flame and the Flower*, a slush pile find by then-unknown Kathleen Woodiwiss. This historical romance, more than twice the length of the average gothic, featured conventional elements of popular romance—mature hero; young, virginal heroine; orphan in peril; forced marriage—but it also introduced explicit sex as part of the formula. Woodiwiss doubtless owed part of her success to timing; greater openness about female sexuality characterized the larger culture of the 1970s. However, Woodiwiss and those who followed her were able to incorporate this new openness within the conventional frame of a monogamous relationship that culminated in marriage. A generation of romance readers and writers date their love affair with the genre from their reading of a Woodiwiss novel.

But the "bodice rippers" had their detractors too. Vehement in their criticism were the feminists who deplored the rape scenes standard in the Woodiwiss-influenced historical romance novels. Some saw such scenes as fodder for those who claimed women wanted to be raped. Others saw the scenes as reflecting a culture in which violence against women was commonplace. But readers, as Janice Radway found in *Reading the Romance*, drew a sharp distinction between the hero's passion for the irresistible heroine that led to "forceful persuasion" and "true rape," which brutally dehumanized a woman. More than a decade after Radway's study, romance writers themselves argue that readers are capable of distinguishing between fiction and reality and that these attacks are mere prejudice against romance novels.

Jayne Ann Krentz, a Romance Writers of America Lifetime Achievement Award winner and an outspoken defender of the genre, points out that female predators who seduce passive males have long been a feature of male detective fiction with no public outcry. The controversy was never resolved, but rape scenarios became rarer by the early the 1980s, and the damsel with the ripped bodice, though still around, was replaced by the bare-chested, fantastically muscled hero as the cover model. Eventually the age of Fabio (the best known of the cover boys) also ended, and the clinches retreated to inside covers for a time.

THE VICTORY OF HARLEQUIN

While detractors and defenders were debating the violence in the new historical romances, readers just kept buying the books, and they were buying not only historical romances. Harlequin Enterprises merged with Mills and Boon in 1971 and began marketing contemporary romances in new outlets. Suddenly romance was everywhere. Women could buy romance novels in supermarkets, variety stores, airports, and drugstores. By the end of the decade Harlequin sales had increased 800 percent, and the company was distributing 168 million copies of its titles in ninety-eight countries. By the end of the twentieth century one in six mass paperbacks sold in North America was published by Harlequin.

Other publishing companies, eager to duplicate Harlequin's success, rushed into romance publishing. Dell, Fawcett, Warner, and Bantam introduced their own romance lines, but Harlequin's stiffest competition came from Simon & Schuster's Silhouette romances. Sexier romances were outselling the traditional, and imprints with such provocative names as Candlelight Ecstasy, Harlequin Temptation, and Silhouette Desire appeared. Promiscuity was unacceptable, and the relationships were love affairs that led to marriage, but graphic descriptions of love scenes became common in the "sensual romances."

By 1984 "the romance wars" were over. A year later Harlequin purchased Silhouette, and only Bantam's Loveswept line challenged Harlequin's absolute rule over series romance fiction. Loveswept ceased publication in 1998, only to resurrect digital-only titles in 2011. Romance novels had also become subjects of interest for mainstream publications as diverse as *Time*, *Forbes*, and *Psychology Today*. Scholars, too, were examining this phenomenally popular fiction, but most significant were the changes in the novels themselves—changes that accelerated in the next decade. The eighteen-year-old virgin did not disappear as heroine, but she became a rare species. In her place was an older heroine, often sexually experienced, who had meaningful work, female friends, and a sense of humor. The romantic hero was still handsome and usually wealthy, but he was now sensitive, expressive, and supportive of a woman's autonomy; the story line had become socially relevant. Although the love story was still primary and the happy ending still sacrosanct, single parents, alcoholism, infertility, divorce, and even homelessness were woven into plots.

HEROINES WHO "DO" AND HEROES WHO CHANGE DIAPERS

The romance audience was changing as well. By the 1990s romance readers saw themselves as mature women who could support themselves, think independently, and contribute to their communities. Though some critics continued to sneer at romance novels, others, including some feminist scholars, had broadened their ideas about women's experience. Those who had predicted the demise of romance novels had been proved wrong. *Dangerous Men and Adventurous Women*, a collection of essays written by romance writers about their craft, became the fastest-selling title in the history of the University of Pennsylvania Press. The idea these essays challenged most firmly was the stereotype of the passive heroine.

Judith Arnold, one of the contributors, describes the romance heroines of the 1990s: they "do"; "[they] take steps, hold opinions, and move forward into the world." Any random sampling of romance novels published after 1990 will support Arnold's contention. Heroines include teachers, lawyers, doctors, corporate executives, small business owners, architects, computer geniuses, builders, psychologists, artists, and country music singers. The romance heroine has not surrendered her place in the domestic world; she has merely added triumph in the public world. She can rescue herself and sometimes the hero as well. It is not a question of the heroine usurping the hero's role but of her proving the interdependence of their relationship.

The hero may have mixed emotions about this new balance of power, but he learns to accept it. Romantic heroes have always been skillful lovers and conquerors in the public realm, but modern heroes must prove their prowess outside the boardroom and the bedroom. They cook, clean, and change diapers, and this new image seems to hold true across subgenres.

THE PARANORMAL TREND

Well before *Twilight* became a phenomenon of pop culture, romance novels featuring vampires, shape shifters, and other paranormal protagonists were racking up sales. Many date the paranormal trend in romance to the popularity of *Buffy the Vampire Slayer*, a television series that ran from 1997 through 2003. Others see it as a response to 9/11 and attribute its continuing popularity to the economic crisis that began in late 2007. Christine Feehan's *Dark* series debuted in 1999, and in 2001 *Dark Fire*, the sixth novel in the vampire series, hit the *New York Times* best-seller list. As of 2012 the series included twenty-three books.

Soon authors established in other subgenres were writing paranormal romances. Nora Roberts, queen of the best-seller lists, had included paranormal elements in her category romances for years, but she added to her lists of number one best sellers with the *Circle* trilogy in 2006 and the *Sign of Seven* trilogy in 2007 and 2008. Christina Dodd, who had already found success as an author of historical and contemporary romances, gained new readers, beginning in 2007, with her shape-shifter series, *Darkness Chosen*, and a spin-off series, *The Chosen Ones*, beginning in 2009.

SMALL-TOWN ROMANCE

However significant the paranormal trend, it is only one of the changes in romance fiction that keep the genre evolving in the twenty-first century. Another trend during a time of security concerns and recession has been the contemporary small-town romance that focuses on community, family ties, and places where everybody not only knows the names of the hero and heroine but their secrets as well. Although small-town settings have long been a staple of romance fiction, the number of small-town series appearing on best-seller lists has definitely increased since 2000. Debbie Macomber's *Cedar Cove* books, a sweet romance series that began in 2001 and ended with book twelve in 2011, earned the prolific author her first number one title on the *New York Times* best-seller list. Robyn Carr introduced her *Virgin River* series in 2007, and as of 2012 the series included nineteen novels and two novellas. Dozens of other small-town romance series compete for readers' dollars.

EXTREME ROMANCE: EROTIC AND INSPIRATIONAL

Another change that the twenty-first century brought to romance novels was an increase in the popularity of both erotic and inspirational romance. The bedroom door that Woodiwiss and company opened in the 1970s was hanging by its hinges forty years later as mainstream romance fiction increased its sensuality level. As heat on the page led to hot sales, the temperature continued to increase, and erotic romance was born. The subgenre has the basic elements of all romance fiction: a focus on the relationship of the protagonists and a happy ending, but the love scenes are more plentiful and include details that are more vivid and graphic than those found in sexy romances. Subjects such as threesomes, bondage/discipline, S&M, and gay lit, which are typically taboo in mainstream romance, may be part of erotic romance.

Erotic romance was introduced by small presses, most notably Red Sage, which began publishing anthologies in 1995. E-publishers had even more freedom than small presses, and Ellora's Cave and Samhain became known for their erotic romances. Harlequin introduced its Blaze imprint in 2001 to promote hotter books, and by 2005 New York publishers were establishing imprints such as Kensington's Brava, Avon Red, and Berkley Heat. By the end of the decade erotic romance was so widely accepted that Pam Rosenthal's historical erotic romance, *The Edge of Impropriety*, was named one of the best romances of the year by *Library Journal*, a designation confirmed when it also won a Rita Award from the Romance Writers of America.

Romances at the other end of the sensuality continuum were also drawing larger audiences. Inspirational romance, often though not always Christian in orientation, is free of violence, profanity, and sex. Inspirational romance has been an annual Rita category since 1995 when Francine Rivers won the first of three awards for Best Inspirational. Rivers's *Redeeming Love*, a retelling of the Old Testament book of Hosea set in the 1850s gold rush in California, was recognized by the Evangelical Christian Publishers Association for having sold more than a million copies. *The Shunning* (1997) by Beverly Lewis started the trend for Amish fiction, or "bonnet rippers," a popular segment of inspirational romance, but like erotic romance, "inspys" can be found in a variety of subgenres and are no longer the sole province of Christian publishing houses.

ONLINE: REVIEWS AND COMMUNITIES

Because romance fiction was rarely reviewed by print review media other than romance-specific publications such as *Romantic Times*, the genre has traditionally depended upon word of mouth to introduce new books and new authors. Although some romance readers found a reading community locally among friends or through bookstores, others read in isolation. That began to change as early as the 1980s with bulletin boards, Usenet, and Listservs. The 1990s saw communities created around review sites such as the Romance Reader (founded in 1995) and All about Romance (founded in 1997). But when LiveJournal and blogger.com launched in 1999, offering a way for romance authors and readers with little or no technological knowledge to interact with one another, romance blogs proliferated, including Mrs. Giggles, widely known for her humorous, often scathing reviews, and Wendy the Super Librarian. Both attracted romance readers who read and commented on their blogs, but the powerhouses of romance bloggers opened their virtual doors a few years later.

In 2005 Candy Tan and Sarah Wendell invited the romance community to read their book reviews on Smart Bitches [Love] Trashy Books, promising "a website that reviews romance novels from a couple of smart bitches who will always give it to you straight." A large and active community developed, and the "Smart Bitches" became influential voices within the romance community. In 2009 they coauthored *Beyond Heaving Bosoms: The Smart Bitches Guide to Romance*—part mockery, part defense of the genre—which won reviews at such atypical spots as NPR and the *New York Times*. Dear Author, another blog for romance book reviews, was founded by Jane Little and a friend known simply as Jayne, in 2006. Many hundreds of other romance readers joined in the conversation, creating individual or group blogs that allowed them to rave, rant, or condemn with faint praise the books they were reading.

Author blogs and bulletin boards encouraged interaction between fans and authors at an unprecedented level. Group blogs were particularly popular. Among the first were the Whine Sisters and Squawk Radio. The Whine Sisters were founded by Sherri Browning Erwin, Kathleen Givens, and Julia London in 2004. Givens died in 2010, but as of 2012 Erwin and London were still blogging with the help of additional "sisters": Dee Davis, Jacquie D'Alessandro, Julie Kenner/J. K. Beck, and Kathleen O'Reilly.

Squawk Radio was founded in 2006 by six *New York Times* best-selling authors: Elizabeth Bevarly, Connie Brockway, Christina Dodd, Eloisa James, Lisa Kleypas, and Teresa Medeiros. The Squawkers developed one of the liveliest, most loyal communities in the blogosphere, but the blog has not been active since 2010. A later addition to romance bloggers was the industry blog, with sites such as Macmillan's Heroes and Heartbreakers, Pocket after Dark, and eHarlequin giving publishers a chance to interact with readers and hear their opinions on all things romance. Bulletin boards, both publisher sponsored, such as Avon's active board, and author sponsored, such as the one hosted by Susan Elizabeth Phillips, continued into the second decade of the twenty-first century.

ELECTRONIC PUBLISHING

Romance fiction entered the e-publishing world early. Ellora's Cave began selling original erotic romance, which the company dubbed "romantica," in 2000. Samhain began business in 2005. Both have since expanded their offerings beyond erotic romance, and both boast authors whose books have made national best-seller lists. Romance giant Harlequin launched Carina Press, a digital-only imprint in 2009. As dedicated e-book readers became more accessible in use and price, traditional publishers began releasing electronic versions of print titles. Romance readers and e-readers were a particularly good match, since electronic books were immediately available, eliminated book storage problems, and allowed readers who were embarrassed by the clinch covers to hide them.

In 2010 a breakout year for e-books, Jennifer Crusie, one of the genre's superstar authors, sold as many e-books as hardcover copies of *Maybe This Time*, her first solo novel in six years. St. Martin's Press, publisher of forty to fifty romance novels each year, announced that the e-editions of its romance titles equaled print books in popularity, and All Romance, an online romance bookstore said that sales had doubled over the previous year. The *New York Times* reported that, according to Bowker, a research organization for the publishing industry, romance became the fastest-growing segment of the e-reading market.

ROMANCE NOVELS IN ACADEMIA

A decade ago the idea that modern romance fiction was a suitable topic for academic study would have been laughable, but the twenty-first century has seen a significant change in the relationship between the romance novel and the academy. In 2003 the University of Pennsylvania Press published *A Natural History of the Romance Novel* by Pamela Regis. Regis defines the genre; posits eight "narrative elements" that characterize the genre; and provides a historical context that includes *Pamela* (1740–1741), *Pride and Prejudice* (1813), *Jane Eyre* (1847), *Framley Parsonage* (1860), and *A Room with a View* (1908). In 2006 Regis also joined a half dozen scholars with an interest in romance fiction in creating Teach Me Tonight, a popular blog that regularly examines romance fiction from a scholar's perspective.

Another signal of romance fiction's change in status came in 2009 when Princeton University hosted a scholarly conference "Love as the Practice of Freedom? Romance Fiction and American Culture" that included academics and romance authors. The International Association for the Study of Popular Romance was founded in 2009. The association launched an online, open-source journal, the *Journal of Popular Romance Studies*, a year later. The fourth international conference was held in Los Angeles in 2012.

The National Endowment for the Humanities joined with the Romance Writers of America and the Tavris Fund at Brandeis University/Women's Studies Research Center in 2010 to fund Laurie Kahn's Popular Romance Project. Kahn, an award-winning documentary filmmaker, explored the origins and influences of popular romance across media and across cultures from the ancient to the contemporary in a series of three films, an interactive website, an academic symposium, and a series of library programs, plus a traveling exhibit, organized by the American Library Association (ALA). The list of partners in Kahn's project included the Library of Congress Center for the Book, ALA, Center for History and New Media (George Mason University), and the International Association for the Study of Popular Romance.

The enduring success of romance novels can be attributed to a paradox. Romance novels remain true to an ancient formula, but they are constantly evolving. More than thirty years ago John Cawelti speculated that the women's movement would render the "moral fantasy" of the popular romance obsolete. But the romance novel has reshaped itself and thrived, as evidenced by the 2012 success of the erotic romance trilogy *Fifty Shades of Grey* by E. L. James, which topped the *New York Times* bestseller list with ten million copies sold in a mere six weeks. Originally written as fan fiction inspired by *Twilight*, *Fifty Shades of Grey* contains such explicit sex scenes—including those featuring both bondage and masochism—that it has been dubbed "mommy porn." The series is not without its critics, however, many of whom deride the titles for violence against women.

Wylene Rholetter

SEE ALSO: *Avon; Best Sellers; Blogging;* Buffy the Vampire Slayer*; Country Music; Detective Fiction; Divorce; Fabio; Feminism; Gay and Lesbian Press; Harlequin Romances; Leisure Time; The* New York Times*; 9/11; Paperbacks; Pornography; Public Libraries; Radio; Roberts, Nora; Television;* Twilight*; Vampires; World War II;* Wuthering Heights.

BIBLIOGRAPHY

Austen, Jane. *Pride and Prejudice*. New York: Knopf, 1991.

Bakhtin, M. M. *The Dialogic Imagination*. Austin: University of Texas Press, 1981.

Bosman, Julie. "Lusty Tales and Hot Sales: Romance Novels Thrive as E-Books." *New York Times*, December 8, 2010.

Cawelti, John G. *Adventure, Mystery, and Romance: Formula Stories as Art and Popular Culture*. Chicago: University of Chicago Press, 1976.

Fallon, Eileen. *Words of Love: A Complete Guide to Romance Fiction*. New York: Garland, 1984.

Freethy, Barbara. *The Sweetest Thing*. New York: Avon, 1999.

Frenier, Mariam Darce. *Good-Bye Heathcliff: Changing Heroes, Heroines, Roles, and Values in Women's Category Romances*. New York: Greenwood Press, 1988.

Goade, Sally, ed. *Empowerment versus Oppression: Twenty-First Century Views of Popular Romance Novels*. Newcastle, UK: Cambridge Scholars, 2007.

Heyer, Georgette. *These Old Shades*. London: Heinemann, 1926.

Heyer, Georgette. *The Grand Sophy*. London: Heinemann, 1950.

Heyer, Georgette. *Frederica*. London: Bodley Head, 1965.

Hill, Grace Livingston. *White Orchids*. New York: Zebra Books, 1994

Jensen, Margaret Ann. *Love's $weet Return: The Harlequin Story*. Bowling Green, OH: Bowling Green State University Popular Press, 1984.

Johnson, Victoria M. *All I Need to Know in Life I Learned from Romance Novels*. Santa Monica, CA: General Publishing Group, 1998.

Krentz, Jayne Ann, ed. *Dangerous Men and Adventurous Women: Romance Writers on the Appeal of Romance*. Philadelphia: University of Pennsylvania Press, 1992.

Mitchell, Karen S. "Ever After: Reading the Women Who Read (and Re-write) Romances." *Theater Topics* 6, no. 1 (1996): 51–69.

Modleski, Tania. *Loving with a Vengeance: Mass-Produced Fantasies for Women*. Hamden, CT: Archon Books, 1982.

Neal, Lynn S. *Romancing God: Evangelical Women and Inspirational Fiction*. Chapel Hill: University of North Carolina Press, 2006.

Phillips, Susan Elizabeth. *Lady Be Good.* New York: Avon, 1999.

Porter, Cheryl Anne. *From Here to Maternity. Love & Laughter.* New York: Harlequin, 1999.

Rabine, Leslie W. *Reading the Romantic Heroine: Text, History, Ideology.* Ann Arbor: University of Michigan Press, 1985.

Radway, Janice. *Reading the Romance: Women, Patriarchy, and Popular Literature.* Chapel Hill: University of North Carolina Press, 1984.

Regis, Pamela. *A Natural History of the Romance Novel.* Philadelphia: University of Pennsylvania Press, 2003.

Roberts, Nora. *The Perfect Neighbor.* New York: Silhouette Books, 1999.

Romance Writers of America. "Romance Literature Statistics: Overview." Accessed January 2012. Available from http://www.rwa.org/cs/the_romance_genre/romance_literature_statistics

Thurston, Carol. *The Romance Revolution: Erotic Novels for Women and the Quest for a New Sexual Identity.* Urbana: University of Illinois Press, 1987.

Woods, Sherryl. *The Unclaimed Baby.* New York: Silhouette Books, 1999.

Romero, Cesar *(1907–1994)*

Tall, urbane, and sleekly handsome, Cuban American actor Cesar Romero helped define the stereotypical "Latin lover" in more than 100 film and television appearances beginning in 1933. However, he made his biggest impact on American pop culture playing the outlandishly coifed Joker on television's *Batman* from 1966 to 1968. Outfitted in an over-the-top green fright wig and pasty white clown makeup (which took about an hour to apply), Romero mugged and cackled his way through the villainous part with unbridled relish. His campy capering clearly influenced Jack Nicholson's interpretation of the role in the 1989 film adaptation of the comic-book adventure. After hanging up his fright wig in 1968, Romero returned to playing elegant rogues on film and television. He died of a blood clot on New Year's Day in 1994 at the age of eighty-six.

Robert E. Schnakenberg

SEE ALSO: *Batman; Camp; Nicholson, Jack.*

BIBLIOGRAPHY

Eisner, Joel. *The Official* Batman *Batbook.* Chicago: Contemporary Books, 1986.

Hadleigh, Boze. *Hollywood Gays: Conversations with Cary Grant, Liberace, Tony Perkins, Paul Lynde, Cesar Romero, Brad Davis, Randolph Scott, James Coco, William Haines, David Lewis.* New York: Barricade Books, 1996.

Wise, James E., and Anne Collier Rehill. *Stars in Blue: Movie Actors in America's Sea Services.* Annapolis, MD: Naval Institute Press, 1997.

Ronco

SEE: *Popeil, Ron.*

Rooney, Mickey

SEE: *Andy Hardy.*

Roots

In 1976 African American author Alex Haley published *Roots: The Saga of an American Family*, in which he traces the history of his mother's family. The book begins in 1750 with Kunta Kinte, a young man who was captured in Africa by slavers and brought to the United States. Haley tells the story of Kinte's descendants through seven generations in America.

The book immediately captured the imaginations of both whites and blacks in the always racially uneasy United States. By February 1977 it was the number-one-selling book in the nation. *Roots* spent twenty weeks on the *New York Times* best-seller list, earned its author a Pulitzer Prize, and later that year was made into a television event: a twelve-hour miniseries that was broadcast over eight consecutive nights to more viewers than had watched any program in the history of television. One hundred and thirty million people watched some portion of *Roots*, drawn by its all-star cast and its moving drama. In 1979 the story continued with another hit miniseries, *Roots, the Next Generations.*

Starting with Kinte's traumatic capture and tracing an African American family through slavery, the Civil War, and the complex transition into freedom, *Roots* gave blacks something they had been lacking in American popular culture: a history with a human face. Though the days of slavery had been the subject of debate, bitterness, and defensiveness, *Roots* looked at slavery in a different way, as the life experience of real people, bringing the African American experience vividly to life in an epic tale of family continuity. Black faces were rare on television, and devoting so many prime-time hours to the story of a black family was a fairly radical concept. Though there were some complaints from whites that *Roots* villainized white people, many more whites were themselves captivated by the humanity of the story.

THE AUTHOR'S ROOTS

Haley was born in Ithaca, New York, in 1921. His father was a professor, the first of his family to attend college, and Haley's brothers followed his upwardly mobile track, becoming professionals themselves. Haley, however, sought something different, a search that led him to spend twenty years as a cook in the coast guard, where he honed his writing skills and earned extra money writing love letters for fellow crew members. After his retirement from the coast guard, he began his writing career in earnest with adventure stories published in *Reader's Digest*, the *Saturday Evening Post*, and *Playboy*. He landed a regular job writing interviews for *Playboy* and collaborated with civil rights activist Malcolm X to write *The Autobiography of Malcolm X.* Haley remained relatively obscure, however, until his grandmother's stories inspired him to begin researching his family history. The research took him twelve years and led him to the small African nation of Gambia, where he claimed to have found the village where his great-great-great-great-grandfather had lived before being captured into slavery.

With the publication of *Roots*, Haley became famous and *Roots* would dominate the rest of his career. He outlined another television special, *Roots: The Gift*, which he later wrote in book

Roots. *LeVar Burton, center, starred as Kunta Kinte, the African villager abducted and sold into slavery, in* Roots. WARNER BROS TV/ DAVID L. WOLPER PRODS./THE KOBAL COLLECTION.

form as *A Different Kind of Christmas*, and he continued his family research, spending several years tracing his father's family. He died in 1992, before he could write up the results of his work, leaving the Australian writer David Stevens to take over for him. Stevens wrote the epic *Queen*, which was also made into a television miniseries, but critics lambasted both the book and series as boring and derivative. The problems were just as likely the overworked miniseries format and a jaded new audience of readers and viewers. The topic of *Roots*, once innovative, had become old hat.

CRITICS

Writing the story of Kinte and his descendants Kizzy, Chicken George, and others, Haley blended history with fictional embellishments to create a writing genre he called "faction." Though *Roots* was published as nonfiction, its authenticity has always been questioned. Immediately upon its publication, novelists Harold Courlander (*The African*, 1967) and Margaret Walker (*Jubilee*, 1966) brought suits against Haley, accusing him of plagiarism. Walker's suit was dismissed, but Haley paid Courlander $650,000 in settlement, admitting that parts of his book "found their way" into *Roots*.

In 1997, as Haley's publisher Doubleday was preparing a twentieth-anniversary celebration for *Roots*, the British Broadcasting Company (BBC) released a documentary called *The Roots of Alex Haley*, pointing out the many controversies about the book. Along with the accusations of plagiarism, Haley had frequently been accused of making up many of the most important facts in the book, even his emotional meeting with the griot, or oral historian, in Gambia, who confirmed for him that Kinte was Haley's forefather. Haley's critics claim that his family cynically planned to set the beginning of the story in Gambia so that they could use the success of *Roots* to boost the family travel business, which arranged tours to Gambia. His supporters call this sort of criticism "literary lynching" and point out that it matters little whether or not the actual facts in the book are true. *Roots*, they say, contains a truth that is deeper than small details of fact, and it continues to resonate with readers and viewers on the basis of that deeper truth. Johns Hopkins historian Philip Curtin counseled those trying to disprove Haley's story: "You can't win," he advised, "You're fighting TV."

Roots has brought a steady stream of African American tourists to Gambia, seeking perhaps something of their own roots in the country from which Kinte was stolen. In June 1997 the country hosted the Roots Homecoming Festival to celebrate the connection between Africa and the descendants of slaves. Gambia, however, is a poor country, one of the smallest in Africa, with a population of just 1.2 million, and there are conflicting feelings about the fame that *Roots* has brought. Many Gambians are angry that Haley and his family did not share more of the profits from the books and television shows with their nation of origin, while the Haleys insist that adequate compensation was made.

LEGACY

Both a best-selling book and a record-breaking television production, *Roots* was remarkably influential as literature and entertainment. Though Haley did not invent the expression "tracing one's roots," he did introduce it into everyday parlance, bringing the idea of tracing one's heritage dramatically into the popular imagination. Since the publication of Haley's book, the word *roots* has become a sort of shorthand for the search for a personal history that will give meaning to modern struggles. After Haley's death, many of his possessions were auctioned off to pay debts on his estate, with the Pulitzer Prize Haley had won for *Roots* bringing $50,000. But the manuscript for *Roots* was not sold. Haley gave it to the University of Tennessee in 1991, a year before he died.

Ironically, the man who had impressed upon the nation the importance of gathering one's history together had much of his own history scattered upon his death. He left an enduring legacy, however—an affirmation that each family history is a drama of survival and endurance and an inspiration for people to seek out their own histories. Distinguished African American historian James Baldwin described the phenomenon this way: "*Roots* is a study of continuities, of consequences, of how a people perpetuate themselves, how each generation helps to doom, or helps to liberate, the coming one."

Tina Gianoulis

SEE ALSO: *Best Sellers; Civil Rights Movement; Haley, Alex; Made-for-Television Movies; Malcolm X; The* New York Times*;* Playboy*;* Reader's Digest*; The* Saturday Evening Post*; Television.*

BIBLIOGRAPHY

Fisher, Murray. "In Memoriam: Alex Haley." *Playboy*, July 1992, 161.

Gonzales, Doreen. *Alex Haley: Author of Roots.* Hillside, NJ: Enslow Publishers, 1994.

Reid, Calvin. "Fact or Fiction? Hoax Charges Still Dog *Roots* 20 Years On." *Publishers Weekly*, October 7, 1997, 16.

Smith, Vivian Backford, and Richard Mendelsohn. *Black and White in Colour.* Athens: Ohio University Press, 2007.

Rose, Pete *(1941–)*

Although ballplayer Pete Rose ended a twenty-six-year career with retirement in 1986, in the twenty-first century he was still actively at the center of controversy in the sport. The holder of several records, including major-league records for most career hits, games played, and at-bats, he was declared ineligible for the Baseball Hall of Fame because of allegations that he placed bets on games while both a player and a manager in the major leagues. His reputation as a player has also been thrown into question over the years, with some pundits contesting his abilities and arguing that, gambling charges aside, Rose never displayed the talent necessary to be considered for the Hall of Fame.

Rose started playing professional baseball in 1960 with the minor-league Geneva (New York) Red Legs. By 1963 he had reached the majors as a second baseman with the National League's Cincinnati Reds and was named Rookie of the Year. During his subsequent career as a player he broke one of baseball's seemingly unbreakable records, Ty Cobb's career record of 4,191 hits. Rose ended his career with 4,256 hits, 14,053 at-bats, 3,562 games played, and 3,215 singles—figures that remained unsurpassed more than twenty-five years after his retirement.

Although his career numbers are impressive, Rose was arguably more famous for his attitude on the baseball diamond. Known as "Charlie Hustle" among fans and fellow players, he was famed for his constant effort, headfirst slides, and incredibly competitive demeanor. His presence on the field seemed to energize the players around him, and his willingness to do anything to help his team win was apparent. It was also apparent that Rose was not the most physically gifted player in baseball, but he made up for his lack of physical abilities with an awesome show of determination and persistence that appealed to his fans. Many fans saw Rose as an "average guy" who was willing to give everything he had to win, and he actively encouraged this perception.

When Rose retired as a player in 1986, it was unanimously believed that he would be elected to the Baseball Hall of Fame. In 1989, however, everything changed. After months of investigation, Rose was fired from his job as Reds manager (a position he had held since 1984), permanently banned from baseball, and declared ineligible for the Hall of Fame by Commissioner Bart Giamatti. Giamatti concluded there was substantial and credible evidence that Rose had bet on baseball games, including those involving his own team, the Cincinnati Reds. After the disaster of the 1919 Black Sox scandal, baseball had established a zero-tolerance policy for gambling. In 1927 Commissioner Kenesaw Mountain Landis laid down the law that any player or manager who gambles on baseball would be banned from baseball for life. Although Rose initially denied the charges, he signed an agreement with Major League Baseball and accepted his de facto banishment from the sport.

Although there are many who call for Rose's election to the Hall of Fame, others argue that he was never Hall of Fame caliber. While it is true that he has sixty-five more hits than Cobb to his credit, it took Rose an extra 2,624 at-bats to get those sixty-five hits. He was never a great home-run hitter, base stealer, or fielder, and he did not drive in very many runs, given the number of times he came to the plate; nor did he score very many runs, given the number of times he was on base. In many ways, the argument for Rose's entrance into the Hall is based on his longevity and persistence rather than his abilities. Bill James, baseball's most famous statistician/historian, argued in 1986 that even at his peak Rose was only the ninety-seventh greatest player of all time, fanning the continuing debate that surrounds the player's reputation.

In addition to the controversies over his career, Rose encountered trouble with the federal government. He was fined $50,000 in 1990 and had to serve five months in prison for filing false tax returns that failed to declare his income from autograph signings, memorabilia sales, and gambling wins on horse racing. More than ten years later, in 2004, the IRS hit him with another million-dollar lien for unpaid taxes.

In 2004 Rose finally publically admitted, both in a television interview and in a new autobiography, that he had bet on baseball. He once again petitioned the commissioner for reinstatement, a request supported by legions of his fans who continue to call for his punishment to end. However, many people took a more cynical view of Rose's actions by pointing out that he stood to make a lot of money from a best-selling book and that his repentance was nicely timed to try to get him included on the Hall of Fame ballot before his eligibility expired in 2006. Whatever Rose's motives were, Major League Baseball did not reinstate him.

Geoff Peterson

SEE ALSO: *Baseball; Cobb, Ty; Gambling; Major League Baseball; Sports Heroes.*

BIBLIOGRAPHY

Reston, James. *Collision at Home Plate: The Lives of Pete Rose and Bart Giamatti.* New York: Edward Burlingame Books, 1991.

Rose, Pete, and Rick Hill. *My Prison without Bars.* Emmaus, PA: Rodale, 2004.

Rose, Pete, and Roger Kahn. *Pete Rose: My Story.* New York: Macmillan, 1989.

Rose, Pete, and Hal McCoy. *The Official Pete Rose Scrapbook.* New York: New American Library, 1985.

Sokolove, Michael Y. *Hustle: The Myth, Life, and Lies of Pete Rose.* New York: Simon & Schuster, 1990.

Rose Bowl

Long considered college football's premier postseason game, the Rose Bowl was first played on New Year's Day in 1902, when 8,500 fans watched Fielding H. Yost's Michigan "point-a-minute" Wolverines blank Stanford 49–0. The Tournament of Roses committee in Pasadena, California, was the driving force behind this first contest. However, disappointed by Stanford's performance, the committee decided to focus on events other than football, arranging chariot races and other proceedings over the next several years. As a result, fourteen years passed before a second Rose Bowl was held, with Washington State shutting out Brown—which was led by All-American halfback Fritz Pollard—14–0. Held continuously since 1916, the East-West classic was played in the Rose Bowl Stadium from 1923 onward; ultimately the capacity crowd surpassed 100,000.

HISTORY

The stature garnered by the Rose Bowl for both its participants and sponsors, along with the economic doldrums engendered by the Great Depression, led to the formation of additional postseason college games during the 1930s. Hoping for a financial windfall, boosters in the American South helped establish the Orange (1933), Sugar (1935), Sun (1936), and Cotton (1937) Bowls. Initially monetary rewards were lacking, but a series of additional bowls were created in the following decades. Indeed, by the 1990s analysts contended that the large number of such bowls enabled mediocre teams to play while detracting from the quality games.

Starting in 1947, when Illinois defeated the University of California at Los Angeles (UCLA) 45–14, the champions of the Western Conference battled one another. Over the years the Western Conference evolved into the Big Ten, and the Pacific Coast Conference evolved into the Pacific-12. By 1998 the two conferences agreed to join in the Bowl Alliance that sought to bring together the top pair of ranked teams in the country to determine an uncontested national champion. For the first eight years of this agreement, the championship games took the place of the Fiesta, Sugar, Orange, and Rose Bowls on a rotating basis. In 2006 the system was revised again so that the championship game did not replace one of the four bowl games but was held in addition to it, so that once every four years, two significant college football contests are held in the Rose Bowl. Traditionally the Rose Bowl game is held on New Year's Day, unless the holiday falls on a Sunday, in which case it is held on January 2.

MEMORABLE GAMES

Beginning with Michigan's undefeated 1901 team, nineteen squads that won Rose Bowls were proclaimed national champions. Two schools, Wallace Wade's Alabama and Pop Warner's Stanford, played to a 7–7 tie and were named cochampions following the 1926 season. Three competitors had already been named the best team in the country prior to their defeat in the Rose Bowl. Other Hall of Famers who guided teams to Pasadena included Notre Dame's Knute Rockne, Southern California's Howard Jones, Ohio State's Woody Hayes, and the University of Southern California's (USC) John McKay. Some of college football's legendary games were played in the Rose Bowl, such as the 27–10 shellacking in 1925 by Rockne's team, featuring its Four Horsemen backfield, of Stanford and fullback Ernie Nevers. In 1948 Fritz Crisler's great Michigan team—boasting a two-platoon system—destroyed USC 49–0, resulting in a second "final" Associated Press poll that placed the Wolverines at its top rather than Frank Leahy's unbeaten Notre Dame squad. In one of the most exciting finishes, Wisconsin, in 1963, roared from far behind but still fell to McKay's Trojans, 42–37. In 1968 USC, led by halfback and Most Valuable Player (MVP) O. J. Simpson, beat Indiana 14–3. The following year, notwithstanding an 80-yard touchdown scamper by Heisman trophy winner Simpson, USC's bid for a repeat national championship ended with a 27–16 Rose Bowl defeat at the hands of Hayes's Buckeyes.

The Bowl Championship Series (BCS) era has also seen memorable championship games take place at the Rose Bowl. In 2006 a dominating performance by quarterback Vince Young, who had 200 rushing yards, 267 passing yards, and three touchdowns—the last one scored with only nineteen seconds remaining on the clock—led Texas to a 41–38 victory over USC. In 2010 Alabama capped off an undefeated season by using a crushing defense and a powerful rushing tandem to beat Texas 37–21.

The amount of available television revenue has ensured that no scarcity of bowl games will result. Another source of cash for the BCS has been corporate sponsorship. For example, from 2004 to 2011, the Rose Bowl was officially known as "The Rose Bowl presented by Citi" because of a sponsorship deal. As a result of TV and corporate moneys, the bowls earn millions of dollars annually. Schools going to a bowl game receive a travel allowance—in 2011 that allowance was $2 million—and the rest of the money is divided among all the member schools in the conference. As revenues went up, so too did the costs of taking a team to a game such as the Rose Bowl, and by 2010 many participating universities actually sustained short-term losses because of such events. In the long term, however, going to a bowl game was still considered worth the expense because it increased the school's prestige, presumably leading to increased donations and easier recruitment of athletes.

Many bowl games, such as the one generally held on January 1 in Pasadena, are preceded by elaborate parades. Once again the most famous is the Tournament of Roses carried out in Pasadena, which involves scores of elaborately designed floats, richly covered with floral arrangements and plant-based materials. Marching bands, festively attired horses and riders, a grand marshal, and the Rose queen are prominently featured for both the gathered throng and large television audiences. The television presence of the Tournament of Roses parade followed by the Rose Bowl every New Year's Day has guaranteed both events a place in the American popular consciousness.

Robert C. Cottrell

SEE ALSO: *Advertising; College Football; The Great Depression; Leisure Time; Parades; Rockne, Knute; Simpson, O. J.; Sports Heroes; Television.*

BIBLIOGRAPHY

Hendrickson, Joe, and Maxwell Stiles. *The Tournament of Roses: A Pictorial History.* Los Angeles: Brooke House, 1971.

Hibner, John Charles. *The Rose Bowl, 1902–1929: A Game-by-Game History of Collegiate Football's Foremost Event, from Its Advent through Its Golden Era.* Jefferson, NC: McFarland, 1993.

Jones, Adam. *Rose Bowl Dreams: A Memoir of Faith, Family, and Football.* New York: St. Martin's Griffin, 2009.

McCallum, John Dennis. *Big Ten Football since 1895.* Radnor, PA: Chilton Books, 1976.

McCallum, John Dennis. *PAC 10 Football, the Rose Bowl Conference.* Seattle, WA: Writing Works, 1982.

Michelson, Herb, and Dave Newhouse. *Rose Bowl Football since 1902.* New York: Stein & Day, 1977.

Perrin, Tom. *Football: A College History.* Jefferson, NC: McFarland, 1987.

Roseanne

Consistently in the top ten in the Nielsen ratings, the sitcom *Roseanne* (1988–1997) had an unprecedented sociocultural influence on American television viewers. The series played a key role in revitalizing an ailing television genre by demonstrating that playing for laughs need not preclude intelligent, thought-provoking scripts. As with its contemporary *Cheers* (1982–1993), fine ensemble acting and even finer writing ensured this blue-collar sitcom's longevity.

A NEW KIND OF SITCOM

That the show actually reached the nation's television screens is as much a testament to a major shake-up in the world of American television as it is to the creative endeavors of those directly involved in its production. The 1980s brought a challenge to the power of the Big Three networks (CBS, NBC, and ABC), whose near monopoly of audience share dropped from 90 percent to 60 percent by decade's end. Shaken by the success of Rupert Murdoch's Fox network and by the rise of satellite and cable TV and VCR ownership, the networks were forced to take a long, hard look at their own output. One positive outcome of this reappraisal was the commissioning and purchase of innovative programs, often made by independent production companies such as Carsey-Werner, the creator of *Roseanne.* The challenge to the hegemony of the Big Three, then, undoubtedly helped reinvigorate the tired sitcom genre.

With *Roseanne*, viewers witnessed the return of the blue-collar family to their TV screens. The Conners, led by mother and father Roseanne and Dan Conner (played by Roseanne Barr and John Goodman), are subject to the stresses and strains of contemporary living. The small midwestern town of Lanford—the sitcom's fictional setting—is recession-hit for much of the series, and the family is unable to escape this context. In contrast to so many sitcoms, the domestic arena in *Roseanne* does not provide the Conners with a safe haven in a heartless world; rather, that harsh outside world frequently threatens to engulf the family as it staggers from one economic crisis to another. As a result, *Roseanne*'s literate comedy often takes on a clear sociopolitical dimension, attributable in large measure to the creative influence of the show's star, Barr, a successful stand-up comedienne.

Roseanne. *The Conner family on TV's* Roseanne *included, clockwise from left, Roseanne as the titular character, Sara Gilbert as Darlene, Alicia Goranson as Becky, John Goodman as Dan, and Michael Fishman as D. J.* CARSEY-WERNER/WIND DANCER PROD/ THE KOBAL COLLECTION.

The sassy humor of Barr's heavily autobiographical "trailer mom" monologues supplied the show's writers with a ready-made central character around which to build a variety of relationships. As the show's cocreator, Barr unquestionably stamped both her unique personality and her own agenda on the series, which pointedly shares her name. In response to an interviewer's query as to exactly how much of the real her was invested in the screen character, Barr observed, "That's me up there, [although] there's a deliberate choice of what to expose."

REAL-LIFE ISSUES

By the early 1990s, on the heels of a successful second season in which *Roseanne* took over the top slot in the ratings from *The Cosby Show* (1984–1992), Barr had gained complete creative control. In these early 1990s shows, an explicit political edge emerges, partly as a result of plots that focus on the workplace as much as the home. In one episode, Roseanne harasses a vote-canvassing congressional candidate, first when he calls on her at home and again when he turns up at her husband's failing motorbike shop. When the politician talks of attracting new businesses to Lanford, Roseanne presses him on how and why these companies would want to set up business in her hometown. Given a stock answer that points to the lure of tax incentives and inexpensive production costs, Roseanne pithily notes that the promise of cheap, deunionized labor and generous corporate-friendly tax breaks simply means that the ordinary working folk in her town will have to pay twice by making up the shortfall in taxation and then taking jobs at "scab" wages. In this same episode, the Conners' son, D. J., wins a regional spelling bee by correctly spelling the word *foreclosure*, while their inconsolable eldest daughter, Becky, discovers that there is no family college fund for her.

While *Roseanne*'s ancestry might appear traceable to early blue-collar sitcoms such as *The Honeymooners* (1955–1956), it arguably owes more of a debt to the uncompromising and occasionally uncomfortable humor of a show like *All in the Family* (1971–1979). It certainly does not have much in common with its anodyne immediate predecessors, such as *Family Ties* (1982–1989) or *The Cosby Show*. As Judine Mayerle points out in her essay in *Journal of Popular Culture*, the show simply does not look "television-ish," from the physical appearance, speech, and behavior of the characters themselves to the variety of cheaply furnished sets that make up the Conners' household and workplaces (diner, factory, garage). More significantly, the show consistently shuns the familiar sitcom narrative trajectory, which offers resolution in the form of a "warm hug," moral lesson, or sermon. Instead, *Roseanne* presents the viewer with a "slice of life" episodic structure more akin to a drama series, offering ongoing narratives that deny comedic closure since issues such as marital or financial difficulties cannot be neatly tied up in under half an hour. The fact that the Conner kids appear destined to follow in their parents' footsteps is often at the very core of the show's bittersweet humor, and such a recognition rests on a successful narrative carryover from episode to episode.

THE VIEWERS RESPOND

Both the plots and characterizations prompt a more complex set of audience responses to the adventures of the Conners, simply because on one important level, we laugh *with* instead of *at* them. The show avoids lazy stereotypes of ordinary, working Americans, and as a result Roseanne (who, for example, talks to her daughter, Darlene, about Sylvia Plath in one episode) and her family are played as sharp, intelligent, and funny. While life frequently deals them and their friends a losing hand, they remain defiant in defeat, their one-liners empowering them when few other options were available.

Roseanne spearheaded a revival of the satiric, blue-collar sitcom in the late 1980s, in the process bucking the trend for shows in which working-class characters were often represented as loud-mouthed bigots in the Archie Bunker mold. The show shares many traits with *The Simpsons*, started in 1989 and still running in 2012 after 500 episodes, and *Married . . . with Children* (1987–1997). Both of these programs offer conflict as opposed to resolution, mercilessly lampooning authority figures and unflinchingly pointing out America's failings.

Despite its early instances of a direct political agenda, David Marc's *Comic Visions: Television Comedy and American Culture* points out that *Roseanne* "len[t] itself more successfully to the politics of culture than the politics of labor." For example, the show stirred up the ire of conservatives because of its perceived failure to back traditional family values. Along with *Murphy Brown* (1988–1998), which Vice President Dan Quayle described as "socially disruptive" for its depiction of and failure to condemn single motherhood, *Roseanne* prompted complaints from pro-family groups about the prime-time representation of poor parenting, as displayed by the Conners. In his book *Hollywood vs. America*, Michael Medved quotes Ross Perot complaining that "if you watch Roseanne Barr on television you don't get a very good role model. . . . You and I didn't see that kind of stuff growing up." Backing Perot, Medved himself draws attention to an episode in which Roseanne takes Becky to her gynecologist for birth control pills. To Medved, this is an act of gross indecency and parental irresponsibility, tantamount to an active endorsement of teenage promiscuity:

> Roseanne's sister Jackie applauds the main character's willingness to facilitate the girl's sex life: "Isn't it great, Roseanne, that Becky has such a progressive, open-minded mom that she can talk to about that? " When Roseanne moans, "She's all grown up. . . . She doesn't need me anymore!" her sister reassures her: "Of course she needs you! She needs you to pay for her pills."

A LASTING IMPACT

The sheer variety of issues aired on *Roseanne* extended the range of subject matter deemed appropriate for future sitcoms. By tackling in a commonsense way such subjects as masturbation, lesbianism, same-sex marriage, teenage sex and pregnancy, abortion, drug use, unemployment, and familial abuse, *Roseanne* surely contributed to a healthy and responsible discourse on these previously taboo topics. Thus, in the case of the birth control episode, *Roseanne* points out that it is far better that Becky should avoid running the risk of an unwanted pregnancy or disease, particularly if she is going to "experiment" anyway.

However, the show limped on a season too long. In *Roseanne*'s ninth and final season, the Conners' multimillion-dollar lottery win deprives the show of its satiric engine, in that so much of the humor had emanated from its portrayal of real people facing real daily struggles with flashes of extraordinary wit. Yet *Roseanne* is remembered for an earthy, natural warmth and unabashed display of human imperfection that appealed to millions of viewers. The program fostered a level of audience identification and affection that flew in the face of much critical opprobrium.

This is not to say that *Roseanne* did not have fans among the critics who hand out awards. The show, as well as Barr herself, won numerous Golden Globe and Emmy Awards. In 2002 *TV Guide* ranked *Roseanne* thirty-fifth on its list of greatest TV shows of all time. In 2008 the cable network TV Land gave *Roseanne* its Innovator Award for a "show that carved our new territory, redefining elements of the genre and opening new pathways for others to follow."

Simon Philo

SEE ALSO: All in the Family*;* The Cosby Show*;* Family Ties*;* The Honeymooners*;* Married . . . with Children*;* Murphy Brown*;* The Simpsons*; Sitcom; Stand-Up Comedy; Television.*

BIBLIOGRAPHY

Angus, Ian H., and Sut Jhally, eds. *Cultural Politics in Contemporary America.* London: Routledge, 1989.

Barr, Roseanne. *Stand Up! My Life as a Woman.* New York: Harper & Row, 1989.

Barr, Roseanne. *Roseannearchy: Dispatches from the Nut Farm.* New York: Gallery Books, 2011.

Dutka, Elaine. "Slightly to the Left of Normal." *Time,* May 8, 1989, 82–83.

Marc, David. *Comic Visions: Television Comedy and American Culture.* Malden, MA: Blackwell, 1997.

Mayerle, Judine. "Roseanne—How Did You Get inside My House?: A Case Study of a Hit Blue-Collar Situation Comedy." *Journal of Popular Culture* 24, no. 4 (1991): 71–88.

Medved, Michael. *Hollywood vs. America: Popular Culture and the War on Traditional Values.* New York: HarperCollins, 1992.

Rowe, Kathleen. "Roseanne: Unruly Woman as Domestic Goddess." *Screen* 31, no. 4 (1990): 408–419.

Watson, Mary Ann. *Defining Visions: Television and the American Experience since 1945.* Orlando, FL: Harcourt Brace, 1998.

Rosemary's Baby

Rosemary's Baby, director Roman Polanski's 1968 film adaptation of Ira Levin's 1967 occult novel of the same name, remains as unsettling as when it was first released. Mia Farrow and John Cassavetes play a young couple who becomes part of a Manhattan devil cult's plan to impregnate Farrow with Satan's child. Ruth Gordon won the Oscar for Best Supporting Actress for her performance as a sinister neighbor whose husband makes Cassavetes a bargain he can't resist.

Instead of using graphic violence for shock value as many horror films do, Polanski employs a hallucinatory tone that vacillates between eerie and banal. Set in a creepy, old apartment building, the film questions neighborly friendliness and posits that home might be the most menacing place of all—ideas that continue to fascinate. Few films since have as skillfully used mood and character, rather than blood and violence, to convey horror.

Sharon Yablon

SEE ALSO: *Horror Movies.*

BIBLIOGRAPHY

Dimare, Philip C. *Movies in American History: An Encyclopedia.* Santa Barbara, CA: ABC-CLIO, 2011.

Levin, Ira. *Rosemary's Baby.* New York: Random House, 1967.

Ursini, James, and Alain Silver. *More Things than Are Dreamt Of: Masterpieces of Supernatural Horror—From Mary Shelley to Stephen King in Literature and Film.* New York: Limelight Editions, 1994.

Rosenberg, Julius and Ethel

In 1953 Julius and Ethel Rosenberg became the first Americans to be executed for espionage. Their convictions and executions were crucial factors in the intensification of the Cold War in America, which led to the phenomenon known as McCarthyism. Their guilt and the harshness of their sentences continue to be vigorously debated. The Rosenbergs have been viewed by leftist intellectuals as martyrs, conveniently sacrificed by an iniquitous United States in the name of anticommunism. They have been remembered for their deaths far more than for their lives and have been the subject of many books, articles, poems, plays, works of art, and documentaries.

A TRIAL FOR THE TIMES

Ethel (1915–1953; née Greenglass) and Julius (1918–1953) Rosenberg both hailed from the Lower East Side of Manhattan. Like many young Americans during the Great Depression, both became involved in leftist groups. They met at a union-sponsored party in 1936, and they were married in the summer of 1939. In 1943 they curtailed their official affiliation with the Communist Party.

The explosion of an atomic bomb by Russia in 1949 led to a search for spies in the American government, and it was discovered that David Greenglass, Ethel's brother, had passed secret information to Soviet agents. Greenglass implicated the Rosenbergs in his confession, prompting their arrest. Their trial lasted from March 6 through March 29, 1951, and after appeals, they were executed on June 19, 1953. A young Richard Nixon made a name for himself as the congressional investigator who originally uncovered the Rosenbergs' crime.

The Rosenberg case divided Americans, many of whom believed the couple was innocent. It also had a dramatic impact on U.S. leftists. In particular, it was a watershed event for the New York Jewish intellectuals who had become anti-Stalinist, pro-American Cold Warriors. They used the Rosenberg case to dissociate themselves from their previous radicalism at a time when such activity was construed as un-American. U.S. Jewish leaders feared that the case would increase anti-Semitism as the public drew a link between communism and the Jewishness of the Rosenbergs. Consequently, a great deal of effort was expended by liberal anticommunist organizations and anti-Stalinist intellectuals to dissociate Jews from the actions of the Rosenbergs.

A flurry of literary activity occurred that aimed to discredit the Rosenbergs and to prove the political loyalty of American Jewry. Liberal anticommunist Jewish intellectuals, in particular,

Rosenberg Espionage Trial. *Ethel (center left) and Julius Rosenberg (center right) attend their espionage trial in New York City in 1951.* AP IMAGES.

Leslie Fiedler and Robert Warshow, wrote vicious critiques of the Rosenbergs. This bloc supported the prosecution's case and argued for the couple's execution. Liberal anticommunists, in contrast, countered these attacks by accusing the prosecution of anti-Semitism. They pointed to the flimsiness of the evidence against the Rosenbergs and highlighted the plight of their two sons—Robert and Michael—who would be orphaned as a result of the government's actions.

THE CULTURAL FALLOUT

The image of the Rosenbergs as sacrificial lambs, martyred by a complex of Cold War interests, has entered American popular culture. One of the earliest appearances of the Rosenbergs-as-martyrs theme is Arthur Miller's *The Crucible* (1953). The initials of the central protagonists—John and Elizabeth—have been construed as representing Julius and Ethel. In the post-Rosenberg era, further texts have appeared. The Rosenbergs figure in Sylvia Plath's *The Bell Jar* (1966), E. L. Doctorow's *The Book of Daniel* (1971), and Robert Coover's *The Public Burning* (1977). Focusing on the idea of the Rosenbergs rather than the factual details of their lives and deaths, the latter two texts intersperse actual historical reality with fictional characterization in postmodern representations of the Rosenberg story. Other popular texts in which the Rosenbergs have appeared include John Updike's *Couples* (1968), Gore Vidal's *Myra Breckinridge* (1968), Howard Fast's *The Outsider* (1984), Joyce Carol Oates's *You Must Remember This* (1988), Don DeLillo's *Libra* (1988), and Tema Nason's *Ethel: A Fictional Autobiography* (1990).

The imagery of the Rosenbergs has been further extended in other media. In 1969 Donald Freed's multimedia play, *Inquest*, opened in Cleveland, Ohio. The play highlighted the sensitivity that the Rosenberg case still aroused: the presiding Judge Irving Kaufman contacted the Federal Bureau of Investigation to complain that the play represented politically threatening pro-communist propaganda. In 1991 Tony Kushner's two-part drama, *Angels in America*, was produced. Set in the era of Ronald Reagan's presidency, the Rosenbergs' prosecutor—Roy Cohn—figures prominently. Rosenberg iconography has also animated visual artists. In 1988 an exhibit titled "Unknown Secrets" opened under the auspices of the Rosenberg-Era Art Project. Some of the works memorialize the Rosenbergs as Jewish victims of American injustice with titles such as *Roy Judas Cohn*, *Remembering the Rosenbergs*, and Robert Arneson's *2 Fried Commie Jews*. Other works take a multimedia, postmodern approach that emphasizes the Cold War context of the Rosenbergs' death.

In 2008 Morton Sobell, who was convicted with the Rosenbergs, confessed to being a spy and implicated Julius. This renewed the controversy over the extent of the Rosenbergs' spying, with their orphaned children admitting finally that although their father may have done some limited spying, their mother was completely innocent and had been framed by her brother's testimony. Their deaths continue to stand for the paranoid McCarthyism and Cold War fears of America's past and, for some writers, a vision of its possible future.

Nathan Abrams

SEE ALSO: *Cold War; Communism; The Great Depression; McCarthyism.*

BIBLIOGRAPHY

Alman, Emily A., and David Alman. *Exoneration: The Trial of*

Julius and Ethel Rosenberg and Morton Sobell—Prosecutorial Deceptions, Suborned Perjuries, Anti-Semitism, and Precedent for Today's Unconstitutional Trials. Seattle, WA: Green Elms Press, 2010.

Carmichael, Virginia. *Framing History: The Rosenberg Story and the Cold War.* Minneapolis: University of Minnesota Press, 1993.

Garber, Marjorie, and Rebecca L. Walkowitz, eds. *Secret Agents: The Rosenberg Case, McCarthyism, and Fifties America.* New York: Routledge, 1995.

Hornblum, Allen M. *The Invisible Harry Gold: The Man Who Gave the Soviets the Atom Bomb.* New Haven, CT: Yale University Press, 2010.

Meeropol, Michael, ed. *The Rosenberg Letters: A Complete Edition of the Prison Correspondence of Julius and Ethel Rosenberg.* New York: Garland Publishing, 1994.

Meeropol, Robert. *An Execution in the Family: One Son's Journey.* New York: St. Martin's Press, 2003.

Meeropol, Robert, and Michael Meeropol. *We Are Your Sons, The Legacy of Ethel and Julius Rosenberg.* Urbana: University of Illinois Press, 1986.

Radosh, Ronald, and Joyce Milton. *The Rosenberg File.* New Haven, CT: Yale University Press, 1997.

Ross, Andrew. *No Respect: Intellectuals and Popular Culture.* New York: Routledge, 1989.

Ross, Diana, and the Supremes

Although their time in the spotlight lasted only six years, singing sensations Diana Ross and the Supremes quickly became the most successful female group in American popular music. During the height of their popularity, from 1964 to 1970, the black female trio brought producer Berry Gordy's fledgling Motown Records to international visibility through a string of successive number one pop hits. With their flashy gowns, coiffed hairdos, stylized choreography, and polished harmonies, the group helped define the Motown sound. Their crossover music reached diverse audiences, acting as a soundtrack for the civil rights movement. Offstage, internal conflict rocked the group, and in 1970 Ross left to embark on a solo career that would bring her to unprecedented levels of fame.

RISE TO STARDOM

Although the details of their history are somewhat contentious, the development of the Supremes dates back to Detroit, Michigan, in 1958. Originally named the Primettes, the group was created as a female counterpart to the Primes, a male vocal quartet that would eventually rocket to success as the Temptations. The Primettes consisted of sixteen-year-old Ross, then named Diane; fifteen-year-old Florence Ballard; sixteen-year-old Mary Wilson; and seventeen-year-old Betty McGlown. Ballard and Ross alternated lead vocals, and Wilson and McGlown mostly sang backup.

In their first year, the Primettes toured local venues and sock hops as the opening act for the Primes. By 1960 the teenage girls had already recorded their first single, which consisted of two songs, "Tears of Sorrow" and "Pretty Baby." Released on a small-time record label called LuPine, the single found little success or circulation outside their hometown of Detroit.

Eventually their professional demeanor and skill won them a first-place trophy in the 1960 Detroit/Windsor International Freedom Festival talent contest. There, the Primettes were spotted by a talent scout from Tamla Records (a division of the Motown Corporation), and the group secured an audition with the founder of Motown. Although they failed to catch Gordy's interest, the Primettes soon became regulars at Motown Studios, spending hours after school learning about the music business and singing backup vocals for known acts. When McGlown left the group to get married, she was quickly replaced by Barbara Martin.

The Primettes' diligence paid off in January 1961 when they were contractually signed to Motown. After some debate, the group was renamed the Supremes. Despite landing a record deal, the Supremes faced many obstacles. Soon after their first two singles failed to catch the public's attention, Martin left the group to attend to family life.

The group decided to continue as a trio, eventually touring the country as the opening act for the Motown Revue. Their first album, *Meet the Supremes* (1962), failed to make a splash. Still without a major hit, the Supremes performed strenuous hours for low pay despite being underage. Touring the South at the height of the civil rights movement, the young women witnessed firsthand incidents of racial prejudice.

A MATCH MADE IN MOTOWN

The turning point for the Supremes arrived in early 1963 when Gordy decided to pair the female trio with songwriting team Eddie and Brian Holland and Lamont Dozier, better known as Holland-Dozier-Holland. Gordy also made the contentious decision to make Ross the group's lead vocalist. Years later his decision proved to be a persistent thorn in the side of Wilson and Ballard.

The string of hits that followed was unprecedented and helped the burgeoning record label cross racial lines to reach a wide and diverse audience. The Supremes' first hit, "Where Did Our Love Go?" exemplified the infectious rhythm that was quickly becoming known as the Motown Sound. Sung by Ross in a sultry tone, the single reached number one on the pop and R&B charts in July 1964. The group's next two singles, "Baby Love" and "Come See about Me," also reached number one on the pop charts.

The Supremes' second album, *Where Did Our Love Go?* (1965), sold more than two million copies and remained on the pop charts for more than a year. After record-breaking tours of the United States and Europe, the Supremes became the first Motown act to appear on *The Ed Sullivan Show* (1948–1971), the most popular variety television show of the era. Surpassed in success only by British rock and rollers the Beatles, the Supremes were known as surefire hit makers. The group's new status meant that black popular music could reach audiences across color lines, propelling other Motown artists to visibility and boosting the label's revenue to levels never imagined. Although the entertainment industry had previously regarded black music as "race music," the Supremes' success demanded that African American music be integrated into American pop consciousness.

DISCORD AND REFORMULATION

As the trio continued to rack up number one hits with such songs as "Stop! in the Name of Love," changes within the group began to threaten its cohesiveness. In January 1966 Ross officially changed her name from Diane to Diana. To enhance their success, the girls were subjected to refinement and finishing through Motown's Artist Development Unit. Their new clean-cut image would eventually allow them to play sophisticated venues and nightclubs such as New York's Copacabana. As music critic Nelson George claims in *Where Did Our Love Go?: The Rise & Fall of the Motown Sound*, this turn of events would "change The Supremes from a diligent, rather juvenile trio into the epitome of upwardly mobile, adult bourgeois charm."

Although each Supreme altered her image, Ross in particular showed a knack for audience appeal, charisma, and spotlight performances. Around this time she began a romantic affair with Gordy, much to the consternation of Wilson and Ballard. Although the couple's relationship remained a public secret, Gordy would father Diana's first child, Rhonda, in 1971.

When Ballard left the group in 1967, she was replaced by Cindy Birdsong, who had previously been a member of Patti LaBelle and the Bluebelles. As a result, Gordy decided to change the name of the trio to Diana Ross and the Supremes in order to bring more focus to the lead singer. The group continued to release chart-topping hits such as "Love Child" and "I'm Livin' in Shame," which featured lyrics that leaned toward social commentary and reflected the turbulent changes of the era. Moreover, the Supremes began to diversify by starring in Motown's first TV productions and appearing on popular television shows.

By 1969, however, Ross announced her intentions to leave. After changing the face of popular music over the course of twelve years, the trio made a final, historic appearance on *The Ed Sullivan Show* in December 1969 and a final live performance in 1970. Their last single, "Someday We'll Be Together," proved a fitting tribute to a group ready to disband.

LIFE AFTER PARTING

The Supremes continued on, replacing lead singer Ross with Jean Terrell, but they never again reached the level of success they had found with Ross. As a Motown solo act, Ross quickly became the most popular black singer in pop or R&B, landing chart hits throughout the 1970s such as "Reach Out and Touch Somebody's Hand" and "Ain't No Mountain High Enough." After marrying publicist Bob Silberstein in 1971, she gained new levels of credibility and acceptance through her much-acclaimed film performance as Billie Holiday in *Lady Sings the Blues* (1972), for which she received an Oscar nomination. She also reunited with her costar, actor Billy Dee Williams, for the romantic film *Mahogany* (1975).

In the early 1970s she and Silberstein had two children, Tracee and Chudney, before divorcing in 1977. After taking a critical misstep with her performance in the film musical *The Wiz* (1978), she left the film business. In 1980 she decided to take greater control of her career by ending her contract with Motown Records. Her last record with the company was the platinum-selling *Diana* (1980), which spawned the hit singles "Upside Down," "I'm Coming Out," and "It's My Turn."

As her albums in the 1980s and 1990s became less commercially viable, she married Norwegian shipping magnate Arne Naess in 1985 and they had two children. In the late 1990s she continued to exemplify the same penchant for glamour and sophistication that she had demonstrated during her tenure with the Supremes, and she consistently produced work as a singer and an actress. In the first decade of the 2000s she added the TV singing contest *American Idol* (2002–) to her résumé, serving as a mentor to new singers, and continued to tour.

Diana Ross and the Supremes proved to be a lasting cultural force, paving the way for female R&B trios and quartets of the 1990s and the first decade of the 2000s such as TLC, En Vogue, and Destiny's Child. In 1981 *Dreamgirls*, a lavish Broadway musical, opened in New York, based in large part on the rise and fall of the Supremes, particularly the group's expulsion of Ballard, who died in 1976. The musical was nominated for thirteen Tony Awards in 1982, winning six. A film version was released in 2006, starring pop star Beyoncé Knowles and *American Idol* contestant Jennifer Hudson and making more explicit references to the story of the Supremes. Critically well received, the film was nominated for seven Academy Awards.

Although they only lasted six years in the limelight, Diana Ross and the Supremes left a lasting impression on American society and culture. The group transformed live R&B performance through their emphasis on professionalism and stylized choreography, helping make Ross the first African American international superstar. They also changed racial consciousness during a time of civil rights struggles and social upheaval.

Jason King

SEE ALSO: *Academy Awards;* American Idol*; The Beatles; Broadway; Civil Rights Movement; Girl Groups; Gordy, Berry; Knowles, Beyoncé; Motown; Pop Music; Race Music; Rhythm and Blues; Soul Music; Sullivan, Ed; Television; The Temptations; Tony Awards; Top 40.*

BIBLIOGRAPHY

Betrock, Alan. *Girl Groups: The Story of a Sound.* New York: Delilah, 1982.

Easlea, Daryl. *The Story of the Supremes.* London: V&A Publishing, 2008.

George, Nelson. *Where Did Our Love Go?: The Rise & Fall of the Motown Sound.* New York: St. Martin's Press, 1985.

Ribowsky, Mark. *The Supremes: A Saga of Motown Dreams, Success, and Betrayal.* Cambridge, MA: Da Capo Press, 2009.

Ross, Diana. *Secrets of a Sparrow.* New York: Villard, 1993.

Taraborrelli, J. Randy. *Call Her Miss Ross.* New York: Ballantine, 1989.

Taraborrelli, J. Randy. *Diana Ross: A Biography.* New York: Citadel, 2007.

Wilson, Mary. *Dreamgirl: My Life as a Supreme.* New York: St. Martin's Press, 1986.

Roswell Incident

The Roswell Incident—the alleged government cover-up of the recovery of a crashed flying saucer and the bodies of its crew at a site near Roswell, New Mexico, in 1947—has achieved worldwide notoriety as the strongest "proof" of extraterrestrial visitation.

On June 14, 1947, William "Mac" Brazel discovered a sizable amount of debris on the ranch he operated some 75 miles north of the town of Roswell. The material included a tangle of rubber strips, paper, sticks, and tinfoil. Brazel reported his findings to local authorities, which occasioned a minor cause célèbre in Roswell. The police ultimately referred the matter to the nearby Roswell Army Air Field. Base officers collected the debris from Brazel and shipped it to Wright-Patterson Air Force Base, where, after much analysis, it was determined to be the wreckage of a weather balloon.

The public accepted the story, and the case was closed for some forty years. In 1979 Jesse A. Marcel, a former base intelligence officer at Roswell Army Air Field, resurrected the episode in an interview with the *National Enquirer*. Marcel claimed that the wreckage at Roswell had not been of this earth. It had borne strange alien pictorial markings, and it could be neither dented nor burned. A number of civilian witnesses stepped forward to say that they had seen alien bodies among the wreckage. Ufologists Charles Moore and Stanton Friedman compiled these statements and, in 1980, with the help of well-known occult writer Charles Berlitz, published *The Roswell Incident*, which charged the government with conspiring to withhold the evidence of this alien visitation from the public.

In the 1980s and 1990s, the Roswell incident came to represent the foundation of faith in the UFO phenomenon for a growing community in the United States; Roswell offered the only known UFO case that involved physical evidence of any sort, and believers considered the incident a validation of their years of belief. A number of books published in the last two decades of the twentieth century explored further the government "cover-up," and thousands of letters poured in to Congress, demanding that the "truth" be revealed. Filmmakers and television producers capitalized on Roswell mania. The hit film *Independence Day* (1996) refigured the Roswell tale for its narrative, and the popular television series *The X-Files* routinely dealt with government conspiracies connected with alien visitations.

On July 5, 1997, the fiftieth anniversary of the government's seizure of the wreckage, nearly forty thousand people flocked to Roswell to pay homage to the crash site. They were undeterred by a 231-page government report, published one month earlier, that again asserted there had been no crashed flying saucer, no alien bodies, and no cover-up associated with the episode.

Scott Tribble

SEE ALSO: Independence Day*;* The National Enquirer*; UFOs (Unidentified Flying Objects);* The X-Files.

BIBLIOGRAPHY

Berlitz, Charles, and William L. Moore. *The Roswell Incident.* New York: Grosset & Dunlap, 1980.

Carey, Thomas J., and Donald R. Schmitt. *The Roswell Incident: An Eyewitness Account.* New York: Rosen, 2012.

Peebles, Curtis. *Watch the Skies! A Chronicle of the Flying Saucer Myth.* Washington, DC: Smithsonian Institution Press, 1994.

Saler, Benson; Charles A. Ziegler; and Charles B. Moore. *UFO Crash at Roswell: The Genesis of a Modern Myth.* Washington, DC: Smithsonian Institution Press, 1997.

Roundtree, Richard *(1942–)*

Born July 9, 1942, in New Rochelle, New York, ex-model Richard Roundtree established himself as one of Hollywood's first black action heroes in only his second feature film, *Shaft* (1971). Expertly directed by Gordon Parks and with an Oscar-nominated soundtrack by Isaac Hayes, *Shaft* (based on a novel by Ernest Tidyman) is probably the best representative of the genre of low-budget American movies known as "blaxploitation." Roundtree stars as a streetwise private eye who sets out to find the missing daughter of a Harlem, New York, gang lord. Two sequels, *Shaft's Big Score* (1972) and *Shaft in Africa* (1973), as well as a short-lived network television show, soon followed.

Over the years Roundtree has established himself as a popular character actor. His work numbers more than sixty movies and television miniseries, not to mention an album, *The Man from "Shaft"* (1972). Films include *Q: The Winged Serpent* (1982), *Seven* (1995), and *Original Gangstas* (1996). He has also had cameo appearances and short-lived roles in numerous television shows, including *413 Hope Street* (1997–1998), *The Closer* (2005–2012), and *Lincoln Heights* (2007–2009).

Steven Schneider

SEE ALSO: *Academy Awards; Blaxploitation Films; Hollywood;* Shaft*; Television.*

BIBLIOGRAPHY

James, Darius. *That's Blaxploitation!: Roots of the Baadasssss 'Tude (Rated X by an All-Whyte Jury).* New York: St. Martin's Griffin, 1995.

Tidyman, Ernest. *Shaft.* New York: Macmillan, 1970.

Rouse Company

Founded in 1939, the Rouse Company established a national reputation by building some of the first enclosed malls in the United States. In the 1970s and 1980s, the Rouse Company developed and managed a series of "festival marketplaces." These shopping malls featured entertainment and historically themed architecture and were widely credited with attracting crowds of consumers and new investment dollars to formerly blighted downtown commercial areas. In the ten years following the 1976 opening of its Faneuil Hall Marketplace in Boston, Rouse built such colorful retail complexes as South Street Seaport in New York; Harborplace in Baltimore, Maryland; Grand Avenue Mall in Milwaukee, Wisconsin; and Union Station in St. Louis, Missouri. It was a frenzy of development that some observers dubbed the "Rouse-ification" of the American city.

Typically such developments depended on extensive subsidies from city governments. Critics charged that Rouse projects failed to provide jobs for the urban poor, catered to the nostalgia of yuppie consumers with their use of stylized historical architecture, and squandered scarce public dollars better used elsewhere. Controversy continued to hound the Rouse Company until it was purchased in 2004 by General Growth Properties, which had designed the Ala Moana Center in Honolulu, Hawaii; Tysons Galleria in Washington, D.C.; Glendale Galleria in Los Angeles; and Water Tower Place in Chicago.

Steve Macek

SEE ALSO: *Consumerism; Malls; Yuppies.*

BIBLIOGRAPHY

Beck, Gregory. "Signs of Life: A New Lesson from Las Vegas." *Architectural Record*, June 2003.

Frieden, Bernard, and Lynne Sagalyn. *Downtown Inc.: How America Rebuilds Cities.* Cambridge, MA: MIT Press, 1989.

Sorkin, Michael, ed. *Variations on a Theme Park.* New York: Noonday Press, 1992.

Squires, Gregory, ed. *Unequal Partnerships: The Political Economy of Urban Redevelopment in Postwar America.* New Brunswick, NJ: Rutgers University Press, 1989.

Route 66

Though it no longer carries travelers across the nation the way it once did, Route 66 remains America's highway. "America's Main Street" spawned popular songs—"Get Your Kicks on Route 66"—and helped to define the culture of the American automobile in its heyday, the 1940s through the 1960s. Route 66 represented the "open road" and an escape from reality and nostalgia continues to imbue the road and road culture with symbolic significance.

CONNECTING AMERICA'S MAIN STREETS

From the outset, planners endowed U.S. 66 with a nationalistic goal: to connect the main streets of rural and urban communities along its course. Entrepreneurs Cyrus Avery of Tulsa, Oklahoma, and John Woodruff of Springfield, Missouri, originally conceived of a road to link Chicago to Los Angeles, but more than their efforts were needed to kick off such a massive road-building project. Legislation for public highways first appeared in 1916, but it was not until Congress enacted an even more comprehensive version of the act in 1925 that the government initiated the construction of a national highway. The numerical designation 66 was assigned to the Chicago-to-Los Angeles route in the summer of 1926. America's "main streets" now accessed one common "Main Street," Route 66.

As opposed to existing regional highways, which cut straight to their destination, Route 66 followed a meandering course that linked hundreds of surrounding rural communities to the metropolis of Chicago. Farmers shipping produce and trucking companies were some of the most frequent users of the road in its early days. The route from Chicago to the Pacific coast quickly dropped south toward the flat prairie lands and temperate climates that made Route 66 a favorite of truckers. But the road soon became beloved by more than truckers seeking the fastest route between cities.

In *The Grapes of Wrath* (1939), novelist John Steinbeck proclaimed U.S. Highway 66 the "Mother Road," for it came to stand for personal survival for the thousands of "Okies" who used the road to migrate to California to escape the despair of the Dust Bowl. Such cultural and social significance increased the road's legendary and mythic standing nationwide. With continuous paving completed in 1938, the road was ready to unlock a nation's dreams as well as its hopes.

The increased mobility made possible by the automobile and the expansion of leisure time for America's growing middle class helped draw ever more drivers to Route 66 after World War II. In such a time of change, relocation was very frequent—particularly to California, where many segments of the defense industry had mobilized during the war. These sensibilities were represented in the song of one such transient professional, former

Route 66. *The escape from reality embodied by the "open road" defined Route 66, and nostalgia continues to imbue the road and road culture with symbolic significance.* DAVID P. SMITH/SHUTTERSTOCK.COM.

Marine captain Bobby Troup, as he traveled west to begin playing with Tommy Dorsey's well-known band. "Get Your Kicks on Route 66," his song about his move, became a catch phrase for countless motorists. The popular recording was released in 1946 by Nat King Cole, only one week after Troup's arrival in Los Angeles. It became a "musical map" of the traveler's odyssey by listing the stops, the feel, and the aura of the road.

BUSTLING BUSINESS ON ROUTE 66

A unique "automobile culture" soon took shape along Route 66. Enterprising entrepreneurs met the needs of even the poorest travelers by building motels, gas stations, diners, and tourist attractions. Most Americans who drove the route preferred motels instead of hotels, because they provided ease of access to their car. Motels evolved from earlier features of the American roadside such as the auto camp and the tourist home. The auto camp had been an entirely informal development as townspeople along Route 66 roped off spaces in which travelers could camp for the night. An outgrowth of the auto camp and tourist home was the cabin camp (sometimes called cottages), which offered minimal comfort at affordable prices.

Gas stations were another new presence on the American landscape. Initially, "filling stations" consisted of a house with one or two gasoline pumps in front. With the addition of service bays the facilities began to grow. Finally, petroleum companies realized that entire structures could serve as advertisements if designed properly. Service stations were developed through regional prototypes and then dispersed across the country. The buildings were distinctive and clearly associated with a particular petroleum company.

Route 66 and the many points of interest along its length had become familiar landmarks by the time a new generation of postwar motorists hit the road in the 1960s. It was during this period that the television series *Route 66* (1960–1964), starring Martin Milner and George Maharis, brought Americans back to the route looking for new adventure. American youth romanticized the image of the road portrayed in the program and in the writings of authors such as Jack Kerouac. The "open road" became a symbol of new opportunities and unfettered living. Driving the route to California became for many a rite of passage into adulthood; for some adults, it became an opportunity to revisit one's youth. The leisure culture of the 1950s and 1960s thus defined itself around sites such as Route 66.

ROUTE 66 FALLS BY THE WAYSIDE

Ironically, such popularity also eroded the future of Route 66. The public cry for easy and rapid automobile travel soon led to improved highways, beginning in the 1950s. Under President Dwight D. Eisenhower, massive federal funding went into the construction of a national highway system. When Congress passed the Federal Aid Highway Act of 1956, Route 66 lost its figurative and literal meaning. It became an impractical mode of travel in contrast to the rapidly moving highways. Slowly, Route 66 was taken out of service—the signs removed and the roads taken over by individual states. By the 1970s, the "Mother Road" no longer existed.

Nostalgia, though, can do funny things to practicality. In the late twentieth century, preservationists reclaimed stretches of the road as a living museum about the evolution of tourist-targeted, roadside architecture. "The Main Street of America" has proven a great attraction, and Historic Route 66 signs now bind the disparate state routes to their common heritage. Route 66 thus brings together the nation's attraction to the automobile and the open road, and the opportunity to control one's own destiny, whether it be for a momentary escape or a lifetime move across the country. Many generations will likely continue to learn about the "kicks" a society got on a seemingly insignificant highway.

Brian Black

SEE ALSO: *Automobile; Cole, Nat King; Dorsey, Tommy;* The Grapes of Wrath*; Highway System.*

BIBLIOGRAPHY

Crump, Spencer. *Route 66: America's First Main Street*, 2nd ed. Corona del Mar, CA: Zeta Publishers, 1996.

Dedek, Peter B. *Hip to the Trip: A Cultural History of Route 66.* Albuquerque: University of New Mexico Press, 2007.

Kelly, Susan Croce; photographs by Quinta Scott. *Route 66: The Highway and Its People.* Norman: University of Oklahoma Press, 1988.

Snyder, Tom. *Route 66 Traveler's Guide and Roadside Companion.* New York: St. Martin's Press, 1995.

Rowan and Martin's Laugh-In

SEE: *Laugh-In.*

Royko, Mike *(1932–1997)*

Pulitzer Prize–winning journalist Mike Royko was born on September 19, 1932, in Chicago, the city in which he lived most of his life, and it was as a distinctively Chicagoan journalist that he earned nationwide fame. Royko's journalism awards included the Ernie Pyle Memorial Award, the Heywood Broun Award, the H. L. Mencken Award, the National Headliner Award, and the Pulitzer Prize for commentary; however, his readers did not need any award committees to tell them that Royko was a great journalist.

Royko had a sporadic formal education, dropping in and out of school. But at a young age he received another form of education by working for his father, Michael, a tavern owner, and by holding several other jobs. The last degree he earned came when he graduated from Central YMCA High School. Royko then joined the air force and was stationed near Seoul, South Korea, during the final months of the Korean War. While in the air force, he was transferred to O'Hare Field, Chicago. There he became editor of the base's newspaper. This was his inauguration into newspaper work.

Royko's first job as a civilian journalist was with the *Lincoln-Belmont Booster*. In 1959 he became a cub reporter for the *Chicago Daily News*, where he was promoted to a full-time columnist in January 1964. The *Daily News* closed down in 1978, but Royko got a columnist position at the *Chicago Sun-Times*, which was owned by the same company as the defunct *News*. In 1984 Royko left the *Sun-Times*, which had been purchased by Australian press baron Rupert Murdoch (whom he despised), for the rival *Chicago Tribune*. At all three papers, Royko wrote a column whose distinctive style set a new standard for journalistic commentary.

A COLUMN LIKE NO OTHER

Like other opinion journalists, Royko would comment about the news of the day; however, he would approach his topics with a commonsense perspective that often eluded fellow columnists. For instance, in an April 26, 1981, column, Royko dealt with a *Washington Post* reporter who had won the Pulitzer Prize for a story that turned out to be fake. The story claimed that a man was getting his girlfriend's eight-year-old son addicted to heroin. Other columnists were talking about how horrible it was that a journalist had faked a story, but Royko brought up a different issue: What if the fake story had actually been true? Royko argued that the *Post* should have reported the alleged dope pusher to the authorities, even though the reporter had claimed that she had promised the man confidentiality: "What would the *Post* have done if it had discovered that a congressman knew that an eight-year-old child was being murdered, but had given the killer his word he wouldn't reveal his identity? . . . What does [the publisher of the *Post*] have to say about her editors covering up the murder of an eight-year-old child?"

Royko often used his column to expose injustice. For example, a Royko column on December 10, 1973, described a Vietnam veteran whose face had been mutilated by an enemy rocket. The veteran, who was forced to take his food in liquid form, wanted surgery so that he would be able to eat solid foods. The veteran thought that the Veterans Administration (VA) should pay for the operation, but the VA said that the damage to his face was not a "service-connected disability." Royko discussed the VA's position as follows: "How can this surgery be for anything else but his 'service-connected disability'? Until he was hit by a rocket, [the veteran] had teeth. Now he has none. He had eyes. Now he has none. People could look at him. Now most of them turn away." The day after this column ran, Royko was able to report that the VA would pay the faceless veteran's medical expenses after all. "It shows how efficient a government agency can be—a year late—if its inefficiency is suddenly splashed across a newspaper."

Royko's columns also featured fictional characters who discussed matters of political or cultural importance. One such character, Slats Grobnik, was portrayed as a native of the same area of Chicago as Royko. A column on March 31, 1972, described the young Slats Grobnik's reason for not believing in Santa Claus: "Anybody who can get in and out of that many houses without being seen is going to take stuff, not leave it." Another piece of Slats Grobnik's wisdom (from a column on January 11, 1984): "Everybody says that work is so good for ya. Well, if work is supposed to be so great, how come they got to pay ya to do it?"

BEYOND THE NEWSPAPER

Royko published one book (apart from several collections of his columns). That book was the best seller *Boss*, which was published in 1971 during the reign of Chicago Mayor Richard J. Daley, whose career the book described. Royko described Daley as the political ruler of Chicago, a man who focused on developing the business district but who neglected the inner city. As portrayed by Royko, Daley was an honest man whose political machine was staffed by less than honest men. Royko said that Daley's "moral code" was: "Thou shalt not steal, but thou shalt not blow the whistle on anyone who does." While discussing how members of Daley's machine profited from certain shady deals, Royko reported (but did not claim credit for) a suggested change in Chicago's civic motto. According to the suggestion, the old motto, "Urbs in Horto" (City in a Garden), should be replaced with "Ubi Est Mea" ("Where's Mine?").

A 1981 movie, *Continental Divide*, featured a character based on Royko. The Royko character was played by the columnist's friend John Belushi, of which Royko noted: "As much as I like Belushi personally, I think the producers might have made a mistake in casting my part. I think Paul Newman would have been a better choice, although he's older than I am. And in appearance we're different because he has blue eyes and mine are brownish-green." Royko died in his native city on April 29, 1997, in Chicago's Memorial Hospital.

Eric Longley

SEE ALSO: *Belushi, John; Newman, Paul; The* Washington Post.

BIBLIOGRAPHY

Ciccone, F. Richard. *Royko: A Life in Print.* New York: Public Affairs, 2003.

Crimmins, Jerry. "Royko's Early Years." *Chicago Tribune*, May 4, 1997.

Crimmins, Jerry, and Rick Kogan. "'Quite Simply the Best': Legendary Columnist, the Voice of Chicago for Decades, Dies." *Chicago Tribune*, April 29, 1997.

Moe, Doug. *The World of Mike Royko.* Madison: University of Wisconsin Press, 1999.

Royko, Mike. *Up against It.* Chicago: Henry Regnery, 1967.

Royko, Mike. *I May Be Wrong, but I Doubt It.* Chicago: Henry Regnery, 1968.

Royko, Mike. *Boss: Richard J. Daley of Chicago.* New York: Signet, 1971.

Royko, Mike. *Slats Grobnik and Some Other Friends.* New York: Popular Library, 1976.

Royko, Mike. *Sez Who? Sez Me.* New York: E. P. Dutton, 1982.

Royko, Mike. *Like I Was Sayin' . . .* New York: E. P. Dutton, 1984.

Royko, Mike. *Dr. Kookie, You're Right!* New York: E. P. Dutton, 1989.

Royko, Mike, and Lois Wille. *One More Time: The Best of Mike Royko.* Chicago: University of Chicago Press, 1999.

Rubik's Cube

Rubik's Cube, the multicolor puzzle with only one solution and 43,252,003,274,489,856,000 possible combinations, baffled many a partygoer in the early 1980s, when it seized America's attention. The quintessential Reagan-era toy fad was actually a product of the 1970s, when Hungarian professor Erno Rubik came up with the idea as a way to stump his students. He was awarded a patent in 1976 and promptly licensed the product to the Ideal Toy Corporation. Cube fever soon began spreading across North America in the form of clubs, newsletters, and even a Saturday morning cartoon, *Rubik the Amazing Cube* (1983–1984). Once solved, however, a Rubik's Cube did not have many other uses, and the market for the multicolor mind game declined. However, it remained a part of popular culture and frequently appeared as a prop in movies and TV shows.

The colorful puzzle made a comeback in the first decade of the 2000s, and in 2009 *Time* magazine published an article on its success. As of that date, 350 million cubes had been sold since its introduction. The World Cube Association governs Rubik's Cube competitions around the world. Events include fastest time, fewest moves, and most successive blindfolded solves. As of 2011, the fastest officially recorded time was 5.66 seconds.

Robert E. Schnakenberg

SEE ALSO: *Board Games; Leisure Time; Saturday Morning Cartoons;* Time; *Toys.*

BIBLIOGRAPHY

Adams, William Lee. "The Rubik's Cube: A Puzzling Success." *Time*, January 28, 2009. Accessed April 2012. Available from http://www.time.com/time/magazine/article/0,9171,1874509,00.html

Rubik, Erno. *Rubik's Cubic Compendium*. New York: Oxford University Press, 1987.

Taylor, Don. *Mastering Rubik's Cube*. New York: Holt, Rinehart & Winston, 1981.

Rudolph the Red-Nosed Reindeer

"The most famous reindeer of all," Rudolph has become a vital part of Christmas lore for generations of children around the world, but few people recall the true genesis of the story. Fewer still would be able to explain how much the original Rudolph fable has been changed by the efforts of songwriters and animators through the decades since its 1939 conception. Yet such is the enduring popularity of this tale in its myriad forms that sociologist James Barnett declared Rudolph the twentieth-century Christmas symbol "most likely to become a lasting addition" to Christmas folklore.

RUDOLPH IS BORN

Rudolph the Red-Nosed Reindeer was the brainchild of Robert L. May, a thirty-five-year-old advertising copywriter for the Chicago-based Montgomery Ward department store. In 1939 he was commissioned by his supervisor to create an original Christmas story that the store could give away to shoppers at holiday time. May was tapped in part for his affinity for children's limericks, the form in which the first Rudolph iteration was written.

Drawing on his own childhood experiences (he had experienced ridicule because of his slight frame), May dreamed up a title character who was ostracized by his fellow reindeer because of his glowing red nose. For an alliterative name, he originally suggested Rollo, but this idea was rejected by the Montgomery Ward catalog department. After briefly considering Reginald, May finally settled on Rudolph as the moniker for his creation, a name reputedly arrived at with the help of his four-year-old daughter.

The first Rudolph booklet, with illustrations by Denver Gillen, was distributed to more than two million Montgomery Ward customers during the 1939 Christmas season. Although it was quite popular, it was not released again until 1946 due to wartime paper shortages, but by the end of that year, a total of six million copies had been distributed nationwide.

The story of *Rudolph the Red-Nosed Reindeer* that these initial customers enjoyed was quite different from the one that would be immortalized in later versions. In May's original poem, Rudolph is not one of Santa's reindeer—at least, not at first. He is an ordinary reindeer living with his family in an obscure village, and although he *is* ostracized by some of his companions for his glowing red nose, he maintains a positive self-image and has the loving support of his parents. He hooks up with Santa only after the corpulent gift-giver's reindeer team arrives at Rudolph's house one particularly foggy Christmas Eve. Upon noticing his beaming honker, Santa enlists Rudolph to lead his beleaguered team. Rudolph does so with great skill and bravery, prompting Santa to congratulate him upon the team's safe return with the words, "By *you* last night's journey was actually bossed. / Without you, I'm certain we'd all have been lost."

It was in this form that Rudolph first became an icon for wartime Christmas celebrants and a lucrative marketing tool for Montgomery Ward. It made little money for May, however, until 1947, when he persuaded Montgomery Ward president Sewell Avery to transfer the copyright to him.

THE NEXT GENERATION

With these rights secured, May set about building the next generation of Rudolphiana. In 1948 an eight-minute *Rudolph the Red-Nosed Reindeer* cartoon, directed by *Popeye* creator Max Fleisher, played in movie theaters nationwide. Two years later May commissioned his brother-in-law Johnny Marks to write a song based on the Rudolph character. The song, which glossed over many of the key details of May's original story, became an immense hit for vocalist Gene Autry, selling two million copies in 1949 and joining "White Christmas" in the pantheon of Yuletide standards. In 1952 a now-wealthy May quit his job at Montgomery Ward to manage the Rudolph business full time.

In 1964 the stop-motion animation house of Rankin and Bass produced a new *Rudolph the Red-Nosed Reindeer* TV special that solidified the legend—again in altered form—in the minds of baby boom viewers. In this new version, narrated by bearded songster Burl Ives, Rudolph is a sad, insecure creature rejected even by his status-conscious parents. The "other reindeer" who taunt him are no longer peers from his village but Santa's actual reindeer, who compete among themselves for the old man's favor. Even Santa himself seems a little ashamed of Rudolph's deformity, and it is only after Rudolph links up with a society of "misfit toys" and proves himself as the head of the sleigh team that he earns the respect of those around him.

This new iteration of the Rudolph legend was to prove almost as popular as the previous ones. In its own way, it was certainly more influential. The innovative stop-motion techniques devised by Rankin-Bass inspired a generation of animators, most prominent among them Tim Burton, who paid homage to Rudolph in his 1993 feature *The Nightmare before Christmas*. The hit movie *Toy Story* and the popular MTV series *Celebrity Death Match* both showed the influence of the Rankin-Bass *Rudolph* as well.

The 1964 *Rudolph the Red-Nosed Reindeer* special continues to generate huge television ratings for its annual holiday broadcast, and the Autry song recording, among many other renditions, is a staple of every radio station's Yuletide music programming. May's prototypical creation was commemorated in 1990 with the publication of a handsome facsimile edition—the first time the story had been offered for sale in its original form. Rudolph's fans have thus had many ways in which to appreciate this enduring icon of Americana.

Robert E. Schnakenberg

SEE ALSO: *Animated Films; Autry, Gene; Christmas; Ives, Burl; MTV; Popeye; Television;* Toy Story; *World War II.*

BIBLIOGRAPHY

Archibald, John J. "Rudolph's Tale Left Him Cold." *St. Louis Post-Dispatch.* December 6, 1989, 3E.

Barnett, James. *The American Christmas: A Study in National Culture.* Manchester, NH: Ayer Company Publishing, 1976.

Frankel, Stanley A. "The Story behind Rudolph the Red-Nosed Reindeer." *Good Housekeeping*, December 1989, 126.

Lillard, Margaret. "Rudolph Lit Up Creator's Career." *Los Angeles Times*, December 17, 1989, A7.

Lollar, Kevin. "Reginald the Red-Nosed Reindeer?" Gannett News Service, December 21, 1989.

Murphy, Cullen. "Rudolph Redux." *Atlantic Monthly*, August 1990, 18.

Walsh, Joseph J. *Were They Wise Men or Kings?: The Book of Christmas Questions.* Louisville, KY: Westminster John Knox Press, 2001.

Run-DMC

Queens, New York–based hip-hop artists Run-DMC and Jam Master Jay are responsible for revolutionizing hip-hop in two very important ways. First, during hip-hop's infancy as a recorded form, they changed the direction of recorded hip-hop by stripping it of all its "old school" aural fluff and cutting it down to its barest essentials: hard-core beats and rhymes. Their debut 1983 single, "It's Like That" with "B"-side "Sucker MCs," reflected the way hip-hop sounded as it was performed in local parks and nightclubs, and it laid a blueprint that most 1980s hip-hop artists followed. Second, Run-DMC is credited for almost single-handedly bringing hip-hop music to a wide-scale audience with their Aerosmith collaboration, "Walk This Way," a single that reached number four on the Billboard pop charts in 1986. Among other firsts, they were the first hip-hop artists to earn a gold record, a platinum record, and a multiplatinum record; the first to be featured on a *Rolling Stone* cover; and the first to have their videos regularly played on MTV.

A NEW SOUND

Run (Joseph Simmons, born November 14, 1964); DMC (Darryl McDaniels, born May 31, 1964); and their DJ, Jam Master Jay (Jason Mizell, January 21, 1965–October 30, 2002),were three black middle-class Hollis, Queens, high school kids who grew up listening to hip-hop in New York City parks. Run got his foot in the recording studio door because he was the brother of Russell Simmons, then-manager of hip-hop stars Kurtis Blow and Whodini (and soon-to-be cofounder of one of the most important hip-hop labels, Def Jam). Having rapped professionally since age twelve as "the son of Kurtis Blow," Run often boasted that he could make a record better than the older guys who dominated the early recorded hip-hop scene. Run even went so far as to dismiss those more lightweight records as "bulls---."

After continually bugging Russell Simmons, Run finally got his older brother to allow him and his two friends to cut a 12-inch single in 1983. Using just their voices and a drum machine (with light touches of synthesizer used to punctuate the rhythm), they essentially created hip-hop's first "new school" with "It's Like That" and especially "Sucker MCs." Rendering previous acts Grandmaster Flash & the Furious Five, the Cold Crush Brothers, Funky 4 + 1, and the Sugarhill Gang "old school," Run-DMC created a new sound that was truer to the way hip-hop sounded in its raw form when it was performed live with a DJ and one or more MCs. Theirs was also a harsher, more hard-core style, lacking the jazz grooves and lightness of earlier rap acts, paving the way for later groups and styles like Public Enemy and gangsta rap.

Run-DMC was also unusual in their vocal style, as they overlapped and finished lines for each other instead of trading verses back and forth. This new sound was extremely popular, and the group's 1984 self-titled debut album went gold. They followed it up with the platinum-selling *King of Rock* (1985) and multiplatinum *Raising Hell* (1986). Not only was their musical and vocal style different than that of their predecessors, the group set new clothing fads as well, performing in baggy

Run-DMC. *Left to right: Reverend Run, DMC, and Jam Master Jay.* © CHRIS CARROLL/CORBIS.

clothes, adidas sneakers (with the laces removed), and fedoras. Their success earned them an invitation to Bob Geldof's 1985 Live Aid concert, the only rap group to appear. Between albums, Run-DMC would also appear in the 1985 film *Krush Groove*, an account of Def Jam's early days, also featuring Kurtis Blow, L. L. Cool J., and the Beastie Boys.

CROSSOVER FAME

Although singles like "King of Rock" received significant airplay and Run-DMC was the first rap act to be shown on MTV, it was not until their collaboration with Aerosmith on a cover of that hard rock band's "Walk This Way" in 1986 that they truly reached the top. Run-DMC was familiar with the song only because they had rapped over the song's beat for years, but they had no idea who Aerosmith was; until they entered the studio with those veterans, they thought the name of the group was Toys in the Attic (the Aerosmith album from which "Walk This Way" came). The Run-DMC/Aerosmith collaboration smashed down walls between rock and hip-hop audiences, pleasing both crowds and making music history in the process. (This wasn't Run-DMC's first fusion of rock and rap; they had done it before, on 1984's "Rock Box" and 1985's "King of Rock.")

The Run-DMC album that contained "Walk This Way," *Raising Hell*, featured a number of popular songs, including "It's Tricky," "You Be Illin'," and "My Adidas," which not only became a Top 10 R&B single but also won the group a corporate sponsorship. The album reached number three on the Billboard charts and went platinum, selling more than three million copies—the highest-selling rap album up to that time. The collaboration was also credited by some with reviving Aerosmith's career.

By the late 1980s Run-DMC found themselves victims of the restless drive for innovation and freshness. After 1988's *Tougher than Leather*was critically panned and its accompanying film was a box-office disappointment, *Back from Hell* (1990) became the group's first album not to go gold, and Run-DMC was viewed as old-school has-beens. Although the band had a clean image, both McDaniels and Simmons were struggling with drug and alcohol problems, and Simmons was accused of rape (he was later cleared of the charge).

In the process of cleaning up, both became born-again Christians. Their subsequently released sixth album was the Christian-themed *Down with the King* (1993). The album entered the R&B charts at number one, but the group was busy with various ministry involvements—DMC was a deacon at his church, and Run had become an ordained minister, founding his own church in Harlem and starting a gospel and Christian-rap record label, REV RUN Records. The group remained active in the late 1990s, touring as well as performing in a popular 1998 Gap clothing television ad, but they still had not released a record of new rap material.

FINAL DAYS

Run-DMC put out a final album on Arista in 2001, *Crown Royal* featuring numerous appearances from musicians such as Kid Rock, Nas, Method Man, and Fred Durst, but the album had various obstacles, including a lack of involvement on DMC's part (he appears on only three songs) and problems with the album's release due to guest star rights issues—it ultimately did not do well. Despite the album's tepid performance, Run-DMC went out on tour with Aerosmith and was generally well received. Only weeks after the tour ended, Jam Master Jay was shot at his music studio in Queens. His murder has never been solved. Run and DMC officially disbanded the group after his death.

Run-DMC's first four albums were rereleased in 2005 with bonus tracks; write-ups from biographer Bill Adler and journalist Sacha Jenkins; and liner notes from such rap luminaries as Chuck D of Public Enemy, who calls *Raising Hell* "the greatest rap album ever recorded." Run-DMC was inducted into the Rock and Roll Hall of Fame in 2009, but the group refused to perform without Jam Master Jay.

BACK IN THE SPOTLIGHT

In the years since disbanding the group, both men have found themselves in the spotlight. In 2005, after family-reality success with *The Osbournes*, MTV began airing the new family-reality show *Run's House*, featuring Run, now known as Reverend Run; his wife, Justine; and their five children. Run also released a solo album in 2005, *Rev Run: Mind on the Road*. DMC had learned he was adopted while tour with Run-DMC in 1997. After years of searching, he finally located his biological mother—his search was filmed by VH-1 and aired as the documentary *DMC: My Adoption Journey* in 2006—the documentary won an Emmy Award. The experience led DMC to establish a foundation that supports an adoption camp for children. He also recorded a single with fellow adoptee Sarah McLachlan, "Just Like Me," in 2005.

Run-DMC remains disbanded, but both Rev Run and DMC make appearances in Ice-T's documentary film *Something from Nothing: The Art of Rap*, shown at the Sundance Film Festival in 2012.

Kembrew McLeod

SEE ALSO: *Aerosmith; The Beastie Boys; Disc Jockeys; Emmy Awards; Gangsta Rap; Grandmaster Flash; Hip-Hop; Ice-T; L. L. Cool J., MTV,* The Osbournes*; Pop Music; Public Enemy; Rap; Reality Television; Rhythm and Blues; Rock and Roll;* Rolling Stone*; Sundance Film Festival.*

BIBLIOGRAPHY

Adler, Bill. *Tougher than Leather: The Rise of Run-DMC: The Authorized Biography*. Los Angeles: Consafos Press, 2002.

Fernando, S. H., Jr. *The New Beats: Exploring the Music, Culture, and Attitudes of Hip-Hop*. New York: Doubleday, 1994.

Gueraseva, Stacy. *Def Jam, Inc.: Russell Simmons, Rick Rubin, and the Extraordinary Story of the World's Most Influential Hip-Hop Label*. New York: One World Books, 2005.

Ronin, Ro. *Raising Hell: The Reign, Ruin, and Redemption of Run-D.M.C. and Jam Master Jay*. New York: Amistad, 2005.

Rose, Tricia. *Black Noise: Rap Music and Black Culture in Contemporary America*. Middletown, CT: Wesleyan University Press, 1994.

Toop, David. *Rap Attack 2: African Rap to Global Hip-Hop*. London: Serpent's Tail, 1991.

Runyon, Damon *(1884–1946)*

Damon Runyon personified the spirit of Broadway in the Roaring Twenties. A renowned American journalist and sportswriter for three and a half decades, he is best remembered for the people he created in his popular short stories of New York during Prohibition—touts, bookies, gamblers, and gangsters and their molls, who frequented the glittering world of speakeasies and nightclubs. *Runyonesque* is a commonly used term, denoting a rough-talking person with a slightly shady purpose, a wisecracking Good Time Charley or grasping Miss Billy Perry.

Runyon's short-story collection, *Guys and Dolls* (1931), became a Tony Award–winning musical on Broadway and later a successful movie, starring Marlon Brando and Frank Sinatra, while his *Little Miss Marker* launched the screen career of child-actress Shirley Temple. Together with American journalist Walter Winchell and short-story writer Ring Lardner, Runyon presented a lively, humorous vision of Broadway during this era.

Joan Gajadhar
Jim Sinclair

SEE ALSO: *Brando, Marlon; Broadway; Lardner, Ring; Prohibition; Sinatra, Frank; Temple, Shirley; The Twenties; Winchell, Walter.*

BIBLIOGRAPHY

Clark, Tom. *The World of Damon Runyon.* New York: Harper & Row, 1978.

Mosedale, John. *The Men Who Invented Broadway.* New York: Richard Marek Publishers, 1981.

RuPaul *(1960–)*

In 1995 RuPaul Andre Charles became the first African American, disco-loving drag queen to secure a contract with a major cosmetics company, the Canadian M.A.C. In drag RuPaul was a stunning blond beauty, standing 6 feet, 7 inches tall in heels, who propagated an ethic of self-love and tolerance with a finger-wagging questioning of convention and self-promotion not seen since Andy Warhol. Projecting total comfort in his ever-changing identity, RuPaul's gentle warmth brought a new visibility to the world of drag and the lesbian, gay, bisexual, and transgender (LGBT) community in general.

Born in 1960 in San Diego, California, RuPaul was lip-synching to the Supremes by the age of five and was aware of his attraction to boys by the time he was twelve. His childhood was made difficult by his parents' painful divorce in 1967 and the poverty and neglect that followed, but he found comfort and affirmation in performing. In 1976 he moved in with his sister and her husband; he later moved with them to Atlanta, Georgia, where he attended the Northside School of the Performing Arts. In 1982 he appeared on television for the first time on a public access program called *The American Music Show*. His group, RuPaul and the U-Hauls, was a hit and began playing clubs in New York and Atlanta. But by 1984 the band had broken up, and RuPaul was a solo act, doing everything from recording to musical theater to nightclubs.

A fixture of the fashion and dance club scene in New York City by the late 1980s, RuPaul became a household name when his 1993 debut album, *Supermodel of the World*, earned three number one Billboard hits and received heavy airplay on cable music video channels and radio stations. In 1994 he teamed with Elton John to record "Don't Go Breaking My Heart" for John's *Duets* album. RuPaul hosted a morning drive-time show on New York City's top-rated WKTU-FM (1996–1997), several cable television specials, and a talk show on cable's VH1 music video channel (1996–1998). Addressing fashion, music, and current news issues, *The RuPaul Show* was a half hour of glitz, glamour, and infectious self-affirmation.

Between 1994 and 2012 RuPaul appeared in nineteen films, sometimes in drag, sometimes not. Some were sheer camp, such as the 2007 Mike Ruiz film *Starrbooty*, and others had more substantial gay themes, such as the 1995 Beeban Kidron production *To Wong Foo, Thanks for Everything! Julie Newmar*, in which he plays a drag queen named Rachael Tensions. His roles in *The Brady Bunch* (1995) and *A Very Brady Sequel* (1996) movies aptly combined the RuPaul neo-disco style with the retro-chic, tongue-in-cheek revival of the Brady franchise for a bit of cultural nostalgia that was very successful commercially. In 2000 he narrated the acclaimed Fenton Bailey/Randy Barbato documentary, *The Eyes of Tammy Faye*, an ironic choice because many recognize the heavily mascaraed Christian televangelist Bakker as something of an unintentional drag icon herself.

RuPaul also appeared on television in shows as widely varied as the USA network's *Walker, Texas Ranger* (1998) and LOGO's animated *Rick & Steve, the Happiest Gay Couple in the World* (2009). He also continued his recording career, releasing *RuPaul Red Hot* (2004), *Champion* (2009), and *Glamazon* (2011). In 2005 RuPaul, in conjunction with the offbeat marketing firm Two Sheps That Pass, introduced the RuPaul doll—possibly the first-ever cross-dressing action figure.

During the first decade of the 2000s, as queer activism resulted in higher visibility and more liberal policies about gays in the military and same-sex marriage, LGBT images went from being merely accepted in film and on television to qualifying as a genuine media trend. In 2003 *Queer Eye for the Straight Guy* debuted on the Bravo network, featuring a team of gay men advising their fashion-challenged brothers. In 2005 the LGBT-focused cable channel LOGO began broadcasting; it was the perfect home for RuPaul's lovable camp. In 2009 the network introduced *RuPaul's Drag Race*, a reality competition show that featured a group of hopefuls competing for drag superstardom. The first episode of the show's inaugural season challenged contestants to create the most glamorous outfits they could using only items from thrift shops and dollar stores. As *Drag Race* entered its second successful season, LOGO spun off the program to launch *RuPaul's Drag U*, another reality show where three women who feel the need for a change are invited to attend "Drag University." Three former *Drag Race* contestants give their "students" makeovers, which are then judged by a panel that includes the dean of drag, RuPaul.

Always straightforward about his identity as a cross-dressing gay man, RuPaul has made a significant contribution to the visibility of queers in popular culture. His gracious teasing persona has made gay culture unthreatening and acceptable to mainstream audiences. Faced from birth with the challenge of being a big, black gay man in a racist and homophobic society, RuPaul has learned the skill of defusing prejudice while unashamedly, even flagrantly, maintaining his identity with dignity, grace, and humor.

Tilney Marsh

SEE ALSO: *Bakker, Jim, and Tammy Faye;* The Brady Bunch*; Cable TV; Camp; Disco; Divorce; Drag; Gay and Lesbian Press; Gay Liberation Movement; Gay Men; John, Elton;* Queer Eye for the Straight Guy*; Radio; Television; Toys; Warhol, Andy.*

BIBLIOGRAPHY

Feinberg, Leslie. *Transgender Warriors: Making History from Joan of Arc to RuPaul.* Boston: Beacon Press, 1996.

Romanowski, Patricia, and Holly George-Warren, eds. *The New Rolling Stone Encyclopedia of Rock & Roll.* New York: Rolling Stone Press, 1995.

RuPaul. "Bio." Accessed April 2012. Available from http://www.rupaul.com/bio/index.shtml

RuPaul. *Lettin It All Hang Out.* New York: Hyperion, 1995.

Stransky, Tanner. "The Return of RuPaul." *Entertainment Weekly*, March 6, 2009, 62.

Rupp, Adolph *(1901–1977)*

Known as the "Baron of the Bluegrass," Adolph Rupp led the University of Kentucky basketball team to twenty-seven Southeastern Conference championships, a National Invitational Tournament championship, and four National Collegiate Athletic Association (NCAA) national championships (1948, 1949, 1951, and 1958) while compiling a record of 876–190 in his forty-one years as head coach. In 1951 three of his star players admitted to taking money to shave points in a 1949 game. The NCAA suspended the team for the 1952–1953 season and publicly reprimanded Rupp.

Rupp's all-white Wildcats squared off against the all-black Texas Western University in the 1966 National Championship game and lost, prompting Rupp to make some disparaging racist comments after the game. Soon after that season, all southern schools began to lift the unspoken ban on recruiting black athletes.

Jay Parrent

SEE ALSO: *Basketball; National Collegiate Athletic Association (NCAA).*

BIBLIOGRAPHY

Doyel, Greg. *Kentucky Wildcats: Where Have You Gone?* Champaign, IL: Sports Publishing, 2005.

Laudeman, Tev. *The Rupp Years—The University of Kentucky's Golden Era of Basketball.* Louisville, KY: *Courier Journal* and *Louisville Times*, 1972.

Rice, Russell. *Kentucky Basketball's Big Blue Machine.* Huntsville, AL: Strode Publishers, 1976.

Russell, Bill *(1934–)*

Between 1956 and 1969, in thirteen seasons as a professional basketball player, Bill Russell played on a record eleven National Basketball Association (NBA) championship teams for the Boston Celtics, serving as both player and coach on the final two. Although many believe that Michael Jordan was the best individual player in league history, that accolade often went to Russell prior to Jordan's ascent in the late 1980s through the 1990s. Russell is still widely recognized for his incredible winning record.

EARLY CAREER

Born in Monroe, Louisiana, in 1934, Russell moved with his family to the San Francisco area and played basketball, without great distinction, at McClymonds High School in Oakland, California. Despite his lack of success at the high school level, Russell was big enough and promising enough to earn a scholarship to the University of San Francisco. There he developed both physically and athletically and enjoyed an impressive career during which he and future Celtic teammate K. C. Jones led the team to two National Collegiate Athletic Association (NCAA) championships in 1955 and 1956. Russell averaged more than twenty points and twenty rebounds a game during his college career—one of a very select group of players ever to have done so. He joined the Celtics after helping the United States win a gold medal at the 1956 Olympic Games in Melbourne, Australia. Russell was initially drafted by the St. Louis Hawks, but Celtics coach Arnold "Red" Auerbach engineered a trade for Russell—the high-scoring Celtics sorely lacked a player who could rebound and play defense.

NBA CAREER

Russell's defensive ability, coupled with the team's already high-powered offense, proved the key to an unprecedented string of NBA championships for Boston. In his rookie season, the Celtics defeated the St. Louis Hawks for the league championship in 1956–1957, due largely to Russell's nineteen points and thirty-two rebounds in the decisive final game. Although the Celtics lost to the Hawks the following season, with Russell suffering a debilitating ankle injury in the opening moments of the third game of the championship series, the Celtics began a string of eight straight championships from 1958–1959 through 1965–1966.

The 6-foot, 9-inch Russell became the leading rebounder in Celtics' history and the second in NBA history after Wilt Chamberlain. His biggest innovation, however, was related to his ability as a shot blocker. He would patrol the area near the basket and wait for opposing players to drive for an attempted score. With impeccable timing, Russell would gently swat the ball away to a teammate, who would often take it to the other end of the court for an easy basket. Later, as an outspoken television announcer in the 1970s and 1980s, Russell would criticize players who blocked shots by violently knocking the ball out of bounds. This, according to Russell, was a form of showing off that offended his concept of team play. Unfortunately for Russell, the NBA did not begin keeping track of blocked shots until the 1973–1974 season, so his exact number of blocked shots is unknown.

Russell's career-long rivalry with Chamberlain, one of the greatest scorers in NBA history, epitomizes his commitment to team play. Although Chamberlain's scoring numbers were much higher (Russell never averaged more than nineteen points a game during the regular season, whereas Chamberlain averaged at least fifty on several occasions), Russell was famed for his ability to help his teammates, particularly in crucial game situations. Russell won five NBA Most Valuable Player Awards, an honor given to the player who most contributes to helping his team win. As Russell notes in his autobiography, *Second Wind*, "Star players have an enormous responsibility beyond their statistics—the responsibility to pick their team up and carry it. . . . I always thought that the most important measure of how good a game I'd played was how much better I'd made my teammates play."

During the 1966–1967 season, Russell was named the player-coach of the Celtics—becoming the first African American head coach in league history and the first African American to coach any major sport at the professional level. Although the Celtics lost to a powerful Philadelphia team in that season, Russell led the aging Celtics to consecutive championships in the 1967–1968 and 1968–1969 seasons. The 1969 championship was perhaps the team's most dramatic, as the Celtics, who had finished a mere fourth in their own division during the regular season, won a decisive game seven in Los Angeles to defeat a heavily favored Los Angeles Lakers team that included future Hall-of-Famers Chamberlain, Jerry West, and Elgin Baylor.

Russell retired after the 1968–1969 season and was elected to the Naismith Memorial Hall of Fame in 1974. He undertook stints as the coach and general manager of the Seattle SuperSonics from 1973 to 1977 and as coach of the Sacramento Kings in 1987–1988, neither of which approached his success as a player. Part of the problem was that the game had become more and more focused on individual stars since Russell's playing days, and players had a difficult time adjusting to the team style of play that Russell advocated. In addition, even Russell's admirers concede that he had little patience for detail and practice. As a player, notes former coach and close friend Auerbach in *On and off the Court*, Russell would put forth the minimum effort in practice, saving his energy for games. During his stint as player-coach of the Celtics, he would often sit on the bench and drink coffee and read a newspaper while the team practiced. Once the game started, however, Russell was always ready to play.

For his contributions to basketball and his advocacy of human rights—he had marched with Dr. Martin Luther King Jr. during the civil rights movement—Russell received the Medal of Freedom from President Barack Obama in 2010.

Jason George

SEE ALSO: *Auerbach, Red; Basketball; The Boston Celtics; Chamberlain, Wilt; Civil Rights Movement; Jordan, Michael; King, Martin Luther, Jr.; The Los Angeles Lakers; National Basketball Association (NBA); National Collegiate Athletic Association (NCAA); Obama, Barack; Olympics; Sports Heroes; Television; West, Jerry.*

BIBLIOGRAPHY

Auerbach, Arnold "Red," and Joe Fitzgerald. *On and off the Court.* New York: Macmillan, 1985.

"Bill Russell." NBA Encyclopedia Playoff Edition. Accessed March 2012. Available from http://www.nba.com/history/players/russell_bio.html

Fitzgerald, Joe. *That Championship Feeling: The Story of the Boston Celtics.* New York: Scribner, 1975.

Russell, Bill, and Alan Steinberg. *Red and Me: My Coach, My Lifelong Friend.* New York: Harper, 2009.

Russell, Bill, and Taylor Branch. *Second Wind: The Memoirs of an Opinionated Man.* New York: Random House, 1979.

Ryan, Bob. *The Boston Celtics: The History, Legends, and Images of America's Most Celebrated Team.* Reading, MA: Addison-Wesley, 1989.

Taylor, John. *The Rivalry: Bill Russell, Wilt Chamberlain, and the Golden Age of Basketball.* New York: Random House, 2005.

Russell, Jane *(1921–2011)*

It was voluptuous Jane Russell's cleavage that brought her to the attention of eccentric Hollywood producer Howard Hughes. It was the exposure of too much of said cleavage in the 1943 film *The Outlaw* that brought the censors down on Hughes and brought Russell an avalanche of publicity. But it was Russell's ability to both laugh at and rise above her sex-symbol status and prove herself a talented actress, a lovely singer, and a gifted comedienne that made her one of Hollywood's top stars during the 1950s.

THE ACTING BUG

Ernestine Jane Geraldine Russell was born on June 21, 1921, in Bemidji, Minnesota. The daughter of a former actress and a former army lieutenant, Russell moved to Southern California at nine months and it was there she grew up, a tall, fun-loving tomboy. The oldest of five children, and the only girl, she loved the outdoors and spent much of her time riding horses and climbing trees on her family's Van Nuys ranch. Even in high

Jane Russell. *Jane Russell was one of Hollywood's leading sex symbols in the 1940s and 1950s.* **SILVER SCREEN COLLECTION/CONTRIBUTOR/MOVIEPIX/GETTY IMAGES.**

school, Russell's rambunctious spirit was more self-evident than her study habits. But after graduation, her mother insisted that her tall, beautiful, raven-haired daughter go to finishing school. When Russell balked at the idea, they compromised on drama school. After all, when her daughter was born, Geraldine had named her Jane Russell because she thought the name would look good up in lights.

After graduating from high school, Russell started taking lessons at the Max Reinhardt School of Drama. But she missed classes more than she attended them and instead hung out at the bowling alley across the street. She dropped out, only to decide to enroll at Maria Ouspenskaya's School of Dramatic Arts. Bitten by the acting bug, Russell stuck with her studies, and six months later she was on her way to her first screen tests at Twentieth Century Fox and Warner Brothers. But nothing came of it except that Russell's desire to become an actress grew, as did her disappointment when no one else called for a screen test. At last, she realized that she was going to have to give up her dream and get a real job, which she did, working as a chiropodist's assistant.

THE OUTLAW

One day, out of the blue, her mother called to tell her that an agent had been calling every day. But Russell was no longer interested in pipe dreams. The agent persisted and finally got Russell on the phone, telling her that Hughes wanted to test her for a picture. The next day Russell was at the studio meeting with Howard Hawks, who would direct *The Outlaw* for Hughes. Russell's part in this Western was as a half-Irish, half-Mexican girl whose brother has been killed by Billy the Kid. She tries to kill the kid with a pitchfork but is raped by the outlaw in retribution. The nineteen-year-old's knockout figure and devil-may-care attitude may have won her the role, but she didn't care. She was now a working actress.

On the shoot in Arizona, national magazines such as *Look*, *Life*, and *Photoplay* photographed the new star in her costume of a low-cut peasant blouse and skirt. As Russell would later write, "My boobs were bulging out over the top of my blouse every time I picked up those pails. But I didn't know it until I saw myself on the covers and centerfolds of practically every magazine on the newsstands. . . . Those pictures came out for the next five years."

When Hawks walked off the set of *The Outlaw*, Hughes took over. The result was a film that the Hays Office censors took two years to approve, a film that critic Pauline Kael describes in *5001 Nights at the Movies* as:

> the definitive burlesque of cowtown dramas. . . . Jane Russell swings her bosom around and shows her love for frail, seedy Billy the Kid (Jack Buetel) by hitting him over the head with a coffeepot and putting sand in his water flasks when he is setting out across the desert. To reciprocate, he ties her up with wet thongs and leaves her out in the sun. Walter Huston and Thomas Mitchell provide a little relief from the amorous games.

But even after the 1943 San Francisco premiere, the film remained hung up in red tape and was not released nationwide until 1946, leaving Russell's dream of becoming a working actress seemingly hopelessly stalled. Hughes owned her contract and refused to lend her out to other studios. She was, however, famous. During World War II Russell was hailed as the "sexpot of the century," becoming one of the favorite pinup girls for American soldiers overseas.

STAGE AND SCREEN SUCCESS

Finally, after five years of inactivity, during which she married her high school sweetheart, football star Robert Waterfield, Hughes agreed to lend Russell out to make *Young Widow*, a teary war film. But the weepy widow role didn't suit her strengths, and it wasn't until 1948's *Paleface*, in which she starred opposite Bob Hope, playing the strong, sharpshooting straight woman to Hope's timid funny man, that she hit her stride.

When Hughes bought RKO the same year, Russell's career finally took off. She exhibited her singing and acting ability in *His Kind of Woman* (1951) and *Macao* (1952), both opposite frequent costar Robert Mitchum; her appeal as a dark, sexy, leading lady in *The Las Vegas Story* (1952); and her comic talent in two more 1952 films with Hope, *Road to Bali* and *Son of Paleface*. But it was 1953's *Gentlemen Prefer Blondes* that best showcased Russell. Starring opposite Marilyn Monroe, she gave what Leonard Maltin has called a "sly, knowing, comic performance," more than holding her own against the electric Monroe.

Russell remained an audience favorite in movies through the 1950s and 1960s. However, it wasn't until she took over for Elaine Stritch in the Broadway musical *Company* in 1970 that she found another vehicle suited to her many talents. Playing a blowsy, boozy broad, Russell showed off her ability to sing, dance, act, and have a laugh at her own expense. Though 1970s TV audiences will always associate Russell and her full figure with the many commercials she made touting the virtues of Playtex bras, she certainly proved herself to be more than the woman Hope once introduced as "the two and only Jane Russell." Beautiful, talented, and funny, Russell was that rare Hollywood sex symbol who was able to simultaneously laugh at herself and enjoy being the star that she was. Russell died on February 28, 2011, at the age of eighty-nine.

Victoria Price

SEE ALSO: *Advertising; Bra; Broadway; Celebrity;* Gentlemen Prefer Blondes*; Hawks, Howard; Hollywood; Hope, Bob; Hughes, Howard;* Life*; Mitchum, Robert; Monroe, Marilyn; Movie Stars; Sex Symbol; War Movies; The Western; World War II.*

BIBLIOGRAPHY

Kael, Pauline. *5001 Nights at the Movies*. New York: Henry Holt, 1991.

Microsoft Corporation. *Cinemania 96: The Best-Selling Interactive Guide to Movies and the Moviemakers*. Redmond, WA: Author, 1995.

Russell, Jane. *Jane Russell: An Autobiography*. New York: Franklin Watts, 1985.

Russell, Nipsey *(1918?–2005)*

With an air of grace and intelligence and an endless supply of original comic poems, comedian Nipsey Russell was one of the first African Americans to become a national television personality. Russell came to prominence in 1959 after a series of appearances on *The Tonight Show* with Jack Paar. He then surfaced on a long list of comedy, variety, and talk shows. His forte, however, was as a quiz show panelist. Known as "the poet laureate of television," he entertained with clever conversation and the recitation of his poems, which ranged in humor from silly to topical. His game show credits include *Masquerade Party* (1952–1960), *To Tell the Truth* (1956–1968), *Hollywood Squares* (1965–1982), and *Match Game 73* (1973–1982).

During the 1961–1962 television season, Russell played the character of Officer Anderson on *Car 54, Where Are You?*, a popular sitcom about police antics in the Bronx, New York. His big-screen credits are sparse, with his most memorable movie performance as the Tin Man in *The Wiz*, a 1978 black-cast musical version of *The Wizard of Oz*. Russell died on October 2, 2005.

Audrey E. Kupferberg

SEE ALSO: *Celebrity; Game Shows; Hollywood; Paar, Jack; Sitcom; Stand-Up Comedy; Television;* The Tonight Show.

BIBLIOGRAPHY

"Russell, Julius ("Nipsey")." In *The Scribner Encyclopedia of American Lives*, ed. by Arnold Markoe, Karen Markoe, and Kenneth T. Jackson. Detroit: Charles Scribner's Sons, 2007.

"Russell, Nipsey." In *Who's Who among African Americans*, 19th ed. Detroit: Gale, 2006.

"Russell, Nipsey 1924–2005." In *Contemporary Black Biography*, Vol. 66. Detroit: Gale, 2008.

Russell, Rosalind *(1907–1976)*

Rosalind Russell is best remembered for numerous roles in 1930s and 1940s comedies as high-powered career women (executives, judges, psychiatrists) caught between the problems of ambition and independence and the romantic notions of love and domesticity. Russell was allowed to dominate many of her scenes in these films, playing with power, verve, and perfect comic timing. Many of these scenes involved role reversal as well, questioning gender relationships and exemplifying the dilemmas facing women in the war period and beyond. But these roles were played out in the relatively safe haven of comedy and with the promise she would, in the last reel, settle down to domestic bliss with the right man.

Kyle Smith

SEE ALSO: *Feminism; Grant, Cary; Screwball Comedies.*

BIBLIOGRAPHY

Basinger, Jeanine. *A Woman's View: How Hollywood Spoke to Women, 1930–1960.* New York: Knof, 1993.

Dick, Bernard F. *Forever Mame: The Life of Rosalind Russell.* Jackson: University of Mississippi, 2006.

Russell, Rosalind, and Chris Chase. *Life Is a Banquet.* New York: Random House, 1977.

Ruth, Babe *(1895–1948)*

By most estimates, George Herman "Babe" Ruth was the greatest baseball player in the history of the game and easily the sport's most renowned and enduring symbol. His legendary power with the bat—many announcers still describe long home runs as Ruthian blasts—and his extravagant life off the field ensured his continuing fame. His prodigious slugging helped alter the way baseball is played, and his enormous visibility changed the public role and responsibilities of professional athletes. Through his success with the New York Yankees during the 1920s, Ruth helped establish baseball as the national pastime and his status as an international celebrity.

"A ROTTEN START IN LIFE"

Though Ruth was the most famous person in the United States at the time of his death—he was more recognizable to the public than film stars or U.S. presidents—his humble beginnings led him to conclude that he had "gotten a rotten start in life." Born on February 6, 1895, the son of second-generation German saloon proprietors, he grew up in the working-class harbor district of Baltimore, Maryland. Unsupervised during most of his childhood years, he spent his time on the street with the sons of longshoremen.

His refusal to attend school eventually led to his enrollment at St. Mary's Industrial School for Boys, a Roman Catholic

Babe Ruth. *Babe Ruth's prolific power dominated the major leagues in the 1920s and 1930s, effectively bringing an end to baseball's "dead ball" era of low-scoring, pitcher-dominated contests.* **PHOTO FILE/CONTRIBUTOR/ARCHIVE PHOTOS/GETTY IMAGES.**

protectory for orphans, delinquents, and poor children consigned there by the city. Later in life he would reminisce fondly on his days at St. Mary's. Even after he became the most highly paid player in the major leagues, he often bragged that he could make a tailored shirt, the trade he had learned as a youth at St. Mary's, in under twenty minutes.

Ruth gained a surrogate father at the school, Brother Matthias, the Xaverian priest who became his first instructor in the game of baseball. Ruth exhibited passion and talent from the beginning. The lanky left-hander, also an able student, became one of the finest pitching prospects in Baltimore by the age of fourteen. In 1914 Matthias helped him secure a tryout with International League team the Baltimore Orioles, a competitive minor-league franchise. Ruth's first contract as a professional baseball player stipulated a salary of $600 a year.

Ruth got his odd nickname early in his career with the Orioles. While speaking to a reporter about the team's new recruits, one of the coaches suggested that Ruth "is the biggest and most promising babe in the lot." Mistakenly thinking that Ruth's former home of St. Mary's was a refuge for foundlings and *babe* was a reference to that past, the reporter used the moniker and it stuck. Ruth's baseball acumen so impressed big-league scouts that his contract was purchased by the Boston Red Sox in July 1914. On the eleventh of that month, Ruth began his twenty-two-year major-league career, starting as a pitcher and winning his first game.

THE MAN WHO CHANGED BASEBALL

Ruth entered baseball at a time when the National and American Leagues (the two dominant, and still extant, professional associations in the United States) faced significant challenges to their supremacy. One threat was the creation of a rival organization, the Federal League, in 1914. Competition from the well-supported Federal League team in Baltimore, the Terrapins, had forced the owner of the struggling Orioles to sell Ruth and other top prospects. By competing for players, the Federal League also caused temporary inflation in the market value of athletes, a trend Ruth would single-handedly perpetuate throughout the 1920s.

Before he changed the game with his powerful batting style, baseball was played much differently. During the era of record-setting hitter Ty Cobb, from about 1900 to 1920, the league's best players specialized in hitting for a high average, bunting, stealing bases, and cultivating defensive skills. It was also the "dead ball" era, in which spitball-hurling pitchers dominated and home runs were a rarity. Rule changes and redesigned baseballs made the 1920s more favorable to batters, and power hitters, though rarely as prolific as Ruth, became common.

Ruth's transition from pitcher to hitter was gradual and ended during his final year in Boston. Though he was a fine pitcher (he won ninety-four games as a hurler and still holds World Series' pitching records from his time with the Red Sox), he became a full-time outfielder for the Red Sox the same year the baseball world was rocked by the Black Sox scandal, in which players from the Chicago White Sox accepted bribes in order to throw the World Series. Ruth did his part to return focus to the game by hitting twenty-nine home runs in 130 games, shattering the previous single-season record.

THE YANKEE YEARS

During the winter of 1919, Boston sold Ruth to the Yankees for a record $125,000. Although Ruth's statistical feats with the Yankees were immediately clear, his performance gradually affected the way baseball is played and watched. Though no player in the American League had topped sixteen home runs since the turn of the twentieth century, Ruth hit twenty-five or more in fifteen consecutive years, from 1919 to 1934, bettering fifty in four of the seasons. He set records not only for home runs but also for extra-base hits, runs batted in, runs scored, walks, and strikeouts.

With Ruth onboard, the Yankees continually set attendance records at home and on the road, making the American League easily the most famous sports franchise in the United States. At its opening in 1923, Yankee Stadium set an attendance record of 74,000 paying customers, an astounding number in an age before radio broadcasts had widened baseball's fan base. The stadium later became known as "The House That Ruth Built" (coincidentally its outfield wall was tailored to Ruth's home run swing). In 1927 he hit sixty home runs, and his Yankee club, after winning 110 games and the World Series, became known as the greatest baseball team of all time.

His most famous hit came during the 1932 World Series, though the story is steeped in the mythology that often surrounded him. During the third game, he allegedly called his home run against Charlie Root of the Chicago Cubs by pointing at the center field wall. As the story goes, he hit one over the fence just where he had pointed. Often repeated by reporters but rarely confirmed by Ruth, the tale, widely circulated after his retirement and death, only augments his legendary status. He finished his career with more World Series appearances than any other player, and his record of 714 career home runs remained unbroken until Atlanta Braves star Hank Aaron topped it in 1974.

His flamboyance off the field only added to his enormous fame. Newspapers carried daily reports of his legendary gluttony (it was rumored that he could consume up to eighteen hot dogs and a dozen bottles of soda at one sitting). His stomach problems during the 1925 season was called "The Bellyache Heard 'round the World." Toward the end of his career, his expanding waistline became a common concern of the press. His nightly debauchery was another popular topic (when the team traveled, he rarely returned to the hotel before five in the morning), and stories about his numerous love affairs caused trouble in both his marriages.

Perpetually unsatisfied with his contract, he frequently threatened to quit baseball in favor of boxing, Hollywood (he appeared in several films during his baseball days), or professional golf. A great lover of children, he visited hospitals and orphanages with astounding regularity. He also contributed time and money to a number of charitable organizations during his career.

LIFE AFTER BASEBALL

Ruth was honored in retirement by becoming one of the five original inductees to the National Baseball Hall of Fame in Cooperstown, New York. Even after retiring, he remained a public figure. He continued to champion a series of philanthropic causes through campaigns across the country. Acting as an ambassador for baseball, he traveled the globe, making successful tours of England, France, and Japan to increase the sport's popularity. Thirteen years after his retirement from professional baseball, he developed throat cancer, a result of years of incessant cigar smoking. His number, 3, was retired in 1948 at Yankee Stadium in front of 70,000 fans, before he died on August 16 of that year.

Throngs of supporters crowded New York's Fifth Avenue to catch a glimpse of Ruth's funeral cortege, and thousands later visited Yankee Stadium, where his body was displayed before burial. Given the unrivaled popularity of baseball during his playing days and his undisputed dominance, few other sports figures could have captivated the American public as he did. In 1999, more than fifty years after his death, ESPN named him the third-greatest North American athlete of the twentieth century after basketball legend Michael Jordan and boxing great Muhammad Ali.

The house where Babe was born in Baltimore has been operated as a museum since 1974. Over the course of its history, it has acquired many artifacts related to the famous slugger, some of which have been transferred to the Sports Legends Museum at Baltimore's Camden Yards ballpark. In 2005 the famous contract selling Ruth to the Yankees sold for just short of $1 million. The high demand for his memorabilia continues, another reminder of the indelible mark he left on American sports.

Peter Kalliney

SEE ALSO: *Aaron, Hank; Ali, Muhammad; Baseball; Black Sox Scandal; Boston Red Sox; Boxing; Celebrity; The Chicago Cubs; Cobb, Ty; Cooperstown, New York; Golf; Hollywood; Jordan, Michael; Major League Baseball; The New York Yankees; Sports Heroes; Tabloids.*

BIBLIOGRAPHY

Creamer, Robert. *Babe: The Legend Comes to Life*. New York: Simon & Schuster, 1992.

Meany, Tom. *Babe Ruth: The Big Moments of the Big Fellow*. New York: A. S. Barnes, 1947.

Montville, Leigh. *The Big Bam: The Life and Times of Babe Ruth*. New York: Doubleday, 2006.

Smelser, Marshall. *The Life That Ruth Built: A Biography*. New York: Quadrangle/New York Times Book Company, 1975.

Wagenheim, Kal. *Babe Ruth: His Life and Legend*. New York: Praeger, 1974.

Ruth, George Herman

SEE: *Ruth, Babe.*

RV

When technological innovation brought early twentieth-century Americans the liberating effects of the automobile, it also produced ancillary developments in terms of vacation, travel, and shelter. Long-distance auto travel led many Americans to use tents or lean-tos in roadside areas, but trailers and recreational vehicles (RVs) would not begin to appear until the 1920s. What began as haphazard homemade contraptions evolved into a major industry constructing lavish homes on wheels.

Following the model of the "gypsy kit," which was first marketed in 1909, manufacturers sold trailers and trucks that featured enclosed living areas. The liberation of the American traveler had reached a new level. RVs would become identified with complete autonomy because they represented fully transportable shelter. One of the first applications of the new RVs had little to do with the independence of the open road; instead the military made this form of temporary shelter part of many endeavors. During World War II, trailers replaced tents in the field, and on the domestic side, trailers served as overflow housing outside military bases.

As leisure time and road quality increased after World War II, many Americans began to purchase RVs for lengthy summer travel, particularly in the American West, where motels were rare. Tourist travel fed by the interstate highway system, which had been begun in the late 1950s, made even remote areas of the United States potential tourist destinations. Even infamous commercial sites, such as Wall Drug in South Dakota or South of the Border in South Carolina, could manufacture a tourist industry through excessive signage along interstates, leading travelers to such destinations as Mount Rushmore and the southern beaches. The popularity of RVs increased as new models—some with the towing vehicle incorporated into the design—appeared after 1950.

Many retirees found such mobility ideal; some even sold their homes in order to own an Airstream trailer or a Winnebago RV. The creation of Airstream led to one of the most distinctive cultures in the United States. The easily recognizable Airstream trailer campers have a bulletlike, metallic, industrial appearance that makes little claim to aesthetics. This utilitarian design, however, has attracted a huge number of appreciators, some organizing into clubs, such as the Vintage Airstream Club. The Wally Byam Foundation, which was named after Airstream's founder, declares that its purpose is to "support people-to-people understanding through trailer travel," and Airstreamers have led the way in transforming a form of travel into a culture of its own. With organized trips, called caravans, Airstreamers can be seen throughout the U.S. highway system.

RVs have actually had little to do with outdoor adventure and exploration. By the beginning of the twenty-first century, American families seeking outdoor exploration continued to use tents and hike into areas difficult—if not impossible—for the large-sized RVs to travel. RVs had instead become part of road tourism particularly for retired couples. RVs represent the pinnacle of American mobility, making it possible for Americans to remain "on the road" for as long as they like. This mobility has led Americans of many different ages to explore distant locations along the open road.

Brian Black

SEE ALSO: *Automobile; Camping; Highway System; Hiking; Leisure Time; Trailer Parks.*

BIBLIOGRAPHY

Edwards, Carlton M. *Homes for Travel and Living: The History and Development of the Recreation Vehicle and Mobile Industries*. East Lansing, MI: C. Edwards, 1977.

Farlow, Bill, and Sharlene Minshall. *Freedom Unlimited: The Fun and Facts of Fulltime RVing*, ed. Liz McGowen. Lake Forest, IL: Woodall Publishing, 1994.

Hart, John Fraser. *The Unknown World of the Mobile Home*. Baltimore, MD: Johns Hopkins University Press, 2002.

Hurley, Andrew. *Diners, Bowling Alleys, and Trailer Parks*. New York: Basic Books, 2002.

Pollard, Ted. *King of the Road: The Beginner's Guide to RV Travel.* Radnor, PA: Remington Press, 1993.

Wallis, Allan D. *Wheel Estate.* Baltimore, MD: Johns Hopkins University Press, 1997.

Ryan, Meg *(1961–)*

Born Margaret Mary Emily Anne Hyra on November 19, 1961, Meg Ryan began acting in her twenties while attending first the University of Connecticut and then New York University. After several small television and film roles, she received her first big break at the age of twenty-one, landing a long-term gig on the soap opera *As the World Turns.* She remained with the show, playing the beloved character Betsy Stewart, until 1984, when a part in the series *Wildside* led her to Los Angeles.

Ryan's first major film role was in the 1986 Tom Cruise hit *Top Gun,* where she played the wife, and then widow, of Anthony Edwards's fighter pilot "Goose." She followed up with a starring role opposite Billy Crystal in the Rob Reiner romantic comedy *When Harry Met Sally . . .* (1989), earning a Golden Globe nomination for her portrayal of neurotic but lovable Sally Albright, who eventually earns the love of Crystal's playboy with a heart of gold. The film includes a famous scene where Ryan, to the dismay of Crystal's character, fakes an orgasm at lunchtime in the middle of New York City's Katz's Delicatessen. After appearing in *The Doors* (1991) and *Prelude to a Kiss* (1992), Ryan had another huge success with *Sleepless in Seattle* (1993), a blockbuster hit that paired her with Tom Hanks. Ryan is effortlessly charming as a reporter who leaves her fiancé to track down the dream man she heard about on a radio show, searching for true love in the face of all obstacles.

Indeed, Ryan's all-American beauty and artless charm made her perfect for romantic comedy lead roles, playing good girls whose meld of innocence and persistence pay off—romantically and otherwise—in the end. *When Harry Met Sally . . .* and *Sleepless in Seattle* were followed by a series of other romances, some more popular—*You've Got Mail* (1998) and the time-travel flick *Kate & Leopold* (2001)—and some less so—*French Kiss* (1995) and *City of Angels* (1998)—all adding to Ryan's image as America's sweetheart. *You've Got Mail,* which reunited Ryan and Hanks, depicts a small bookstore owner angry about the chain that is trying to shut her shop down, never imagining that the sensitive guy she is falling in love with over e-mail is, in fact, the owner of the chain.

Frustrated by her wholesome image and tired of being typecast, Ryan attempted to leave her sunny persona behind, taking on more challenging roles in the 1990s. She played an alcoholic wife in *When a Man Loves a Woman* (1994) and a heroic Gulf War captain in *Courage under Fire* (1996). In the next decade she shocked audiences by appearing nude for the first time in the erotic thriller *In the Cut* (2003) followed by the lead role in *Against the Ropes* (2004), a biopic about Jackie Kallen, the first female American boxing manager. Ryan's performances in these more serious roles were generally panned by critics, and the films fared poorly at the box office. Nevertheless the actor was praised for her portrayal of a woman whose fight against breast cancer leads to a friendship with the much younger grandson of a neighbor in *In the Land of Women* (2007).

Ryan's uneven filmography reveals an underlying tension between movie audiences' preferences for her romantic roles and her own desire to play more interesting parts. In general, the handful of romantic comedies Ryan made during the late 1990s and the first decade of the 2000s—*French Kiss, You've Got Mail,* and *Kate & Leopold*—were much more successful than her other film roles and helped to keep her career alive through a number of box-office flops.

Perhaps partly due to having undergone plastic surgery early in the first decade of the 2000s and most likely due to her age, Ryan began to receive fewer roles later in the decade, and the films she did appear in were generally unsuccessful. Two of her 2008 films—*The Deal* and *My Mom's New Boyfriend*—went straight to DVD; *The Women* (2008), a remake of the 1939 film of the same title starring Ryan, Annette Bening, Debra Messing, and Jada Pinkett Smith as Manhattan socialites, was relatively successful at the box office but was viciously panned by critics. She made her directorial debut in 2011 with *Into the Beautiful.* Ryan also collected a number of production credits with Prufrock Pictures, the company she set up in 1994 with Twentieth Century Fox, though none of the movies was particularly successful; Prufrock was shut down in 2000.

Ryan was married for nearly ten years to actor Dennis Quaid, after reportedly refusing to marry him until he quit his drug habit. The couple broke up in 2000 and received a divorce in 2001. Since then Ryan has been linked with a number of high-profile male stars, most recently John Mellencamp, who separated from his wife in 2010. In 2006 Ryan adopted Daisy True, a fourteen-month-old Chinese girl.

Sara Martin

SEE ALSO: As the World Turns*; Blockbusters; Boxing; Celebrity; Celebrity Couples; The City of Angels; Cruise, Tom; Crystal, Billy; Divorce; The Doors; Gulf Wars; Hanks, Tom; Hollywood; Mellencamp, John; Movie Stars; Plastic Surgery; Radio; Soap Operas; Television.*

BIBLIOGRAPHY

Abramowitz, R. "Private Meg." *Premiere,* May 1996, 52–56.

Collins, A. F. "Faces of Meg." *Harper's Bazaar,* June 1994, 120–123.

Sessums, K. "Maximum Meg." *Vanity Fair,* May 1995, 104–111.

Ryan, Nolan *(1947–)*

Nolan Ryan was the greatest power pitcher of his era and certainly the greatest pitcher never to win the Cy Young Award. His blazing fastball (consistently measured in excess of 100 miles per hour) and intensity on the mound made him one of the most dominant pitchers in baseball history. His extraordinary work ethic and perseverance became legendary, and his ability to strike out opposing batters made him a role model for thousands of aspiring pitchers. Consigned to playing on mediocre teams for his entire career, Ryan still managed to win 324 games, throw seven no-hitters, and strike out more than 5,700 batters in his twenty-seven years in the majors.

Lynn Nolan Ryan Jr. was born January 31, 1947, in Refugio, Texas, the youngest of six children. He grew up playing Little League baseball under his father's coaching and later played in high school. It was in high school that a New York Mets scout saw him pitch and signed him to play rookie ball in Virginia.

Early in his career Ryan's flaming fastball caused many problems. Although he could throw the ball with astonishing velocity, he had little control over where it would actually go. This lack of control translated into a large number of walks and hit batters, and the Mets kept him pitching in middle relief for most of the time he was with the team. In 1969 Ryan made his first appearance in the World Series as a reliever, earning a save in game three.

Although he clearly had the arm to be a major-league pitcher, Ryan's poor control became an increasingly big problem for the Mets, and in 1971, after four years with the team, he was traded with three other players to the California Angels. It was with the Angels that Ryan began realizing his potential. As a member of the pitching rotation from 1972 to 1979, he threw four no-hitters, compiled a 138–121 won-lost record (far better than the team's overall winning percentage), and set the single-season strikeout record in 1973 with 383. Although he liked pitching for California, he wanted to return to his home state of Texas, and he signed a contract with the Houston Astros for the then-record-breaking sum of $1 million per year.

In Houston Ryan consistently ranked among the league leaders in strikeouts and pitched his record fifth no-hitter in 1981. In 1987 he became the first pitcher to lead the league in earned-run average and strikeouts without winning the Cy Young Award for pitching. This snub was probably due to his record of eight wins and sixteen losses, a consequence of the Astros' anemic offense. In 1988 the Astros asked Ryan, who was forty-one years old at the time, to take a pay cut, but he preferred to leave them rather than accept the cut and signed with the Texas Rangers.

With the Rangers, Ryan earned his 300th win, his 5,000th strikeout, and tossed his sixth and seventh no-hitters (no-hitters being previously unthinkable for a pitcher of his age). During his tenure with the Rangers, he finally gained recognition for his astounding achievements, with baseball fans and writers at last recognizing his phenomenal athleticism and perseverance as he approached the end of his career. His amazing conditioning regimen and natural physical gifts allowed Ryan to continue to pitch effectively well past the age of forty, and he reached the status of the "Grand Old Man" of the game of baseball.

The 1992 and 1993 seasons were full of injuries, and Ryan retired from the game he had served on the field for twenty-seven years. He was elected to the Baseball Hall of Fame in 1999, his first year of eligibility. His uniform numbers have been retired by the Angels, the Astros, and the Rangers. In 2008 he became the president of the Texas Rangers, and in 2010 he became a member of the ownership group that bought the team.

Geoff Peterson

SEE ALSO: *Baseball; Little League; Major League Baseball; The New York Mets; Sports Heroes; World Series; Young, Cy.*

BIBLIOGRAPHY

Goldman, Rob. *Once They Were Angels*. Champaign, IL: Sports Publishing, 2006.

Rolfe, John. *Nolan Ryan*. Boston: Little, Brown, 1992.

Ryan, Nolan, and Harvey Frommer. *Throwing Heat: The Autobiography of Nolan Ryan*. New York: Doubleday, 1988.

Ryan, Nolan; Harvey Frommer; and Jerry Jenkins. *Miracle Man: Nolan Ryan, the Autobiography*. Dallas, TX: Word Publishing, 1992.

Trujillo, Nick. *The Meaning of Nolan Ryan*. College Station: Texas A&M University Press, 1994.

Rydell, Bobby *(1942–)*

Boyishly handsome, with an infectious smile, teen idol Bobby Rydell seemed like the boy next door. Like fellow Philadelphians and musical heartthrobs Frankie Avalon and Fabian, Rydell catered to teenage desires. As the 1960s dawned, the music world wanted safe alternatives to the sexually explosive rock singer Elvis Presley. Still, Rydell stood out as a bona fide talent. A musical prodigy, he began playing drums at six, had a nightclub act at seven, and became a regular on a television amateur show at nine. He played drums with the group Rocco and the Saints, which boasted Avalon on trumpet, until he was approached about a singing career.

His hits, such as "Volare" and "Wild One," are marked by his smooth delivery. In his only major movie, *Bye Bye Birdie* (1963), however, he was eclipsed by the explosive talent of singer-actress Ann-Margret. In a nod to Rydell's influence during the early 1960s, the school in the 1978 musical *Grease* is named Rydell High. In the 1990s and the first decade of the 2000s Rydell played to former fans in solo oldies shows and as part of the trio the Golden Boys with Avalon and Fabian. Due to his declining health, however, Rydell suspended touring.

Pat H. Broeske

SEE ALSO: *Avalon, Frankie; Fabian; Pop Music; Presley, Elvis; Teen Idols.*

BIBLIOGRAPHY

Miller, Jim, ed. *The Rolling Stone Illustrated History of Rock & Roll*. New York: Random House, 1976.

Rydell, Bobby; Marya Saunders; and Bob Gaines. "Now That I'm of Age." *Family Weekly*, April 28, 1963, 4.

Ryder, Winona *(1971–)*

Actress Winona Ryder was born Winona Laura Horowitz in 1971 in rural Minnesota. After moving to California as a child, she spent her teen years in San Francisco, where she and her countercultural parents spent a year living in a commune. A socially awkward teenager, she decided she wanted to act and got a role in the film *Lucas* (1986) when she was fifteen years old. Her unique combination of precocious maturity and porcelain-skinned beauty soon brought her fame, and she appeared in nine films before the age of twenty.

Ryder's breakout role was in the movie *Beetlejuice* (1988), directed by Tim Burton. She plays a sullen goth teen who discovers that the Yuppie couple who previously lived in her new house are dead and now haunting it. The movie was successful at the box office, and critics praised Ryder's performance. Ryder went on to play the thirteen-year-old bride of rocker Jerry Lee

Lewis in *Great Balls of Fire!* (1989); a tortured teen whose boyfriend begins killing off the popular girls in their high school in the cult hit *Heathers* (1988); a solemn daughter charged with the care of her irresponsible, charming mother and morbid baby sister, while secretly dreaming of American normalcy in *Mermaids* (1990); and an unhappy adopted teenager fantasizing about her birth mother in *Welcome Home, Roxy Carmichael* (1990).

In 1990 Ryder teamed up again with Burton for *Edward Scissorhands*, a beautifully rendered fairy tale about a conventional young woman who falls in love with a young man who was the final project of an eccentric local inventor. The inventor dies before completing his work, leaving his robotic progeny with scissors for hands. During the making of the movie, Ryder began dating Johnny Depp, who played the mournful and soulful Edward. Depp, who was twenty-seven to Ryder's nineteen, famously had "Winona Forever" tattooed on his arm, only to have it altered to "Wino Forever" after their three-year relationship ended.

Young, fresh-faced, and slightly edgy, Ryder was the darling of Generation X viewers and became one of the few actresses of her generation to successfully make the transition from teen to adult roles. She appeared in ten films in the early 1990s. Her roles include Count Dracula's lover in *Bram Stoker's Dracula* (1992); a young woman who falls in love with a man her father disapproves of in *The House of the Spirits* (1993); an engaged socialite in *The Age of Innocence* (1993); a floundering college graduate in *Reality Bites* (1994); and the feisty tomboy Jo March in *Little Women* (1994). She received an Academy Award nomination for Best Supporting Actress for her performance in *The Age of Innocence* and a nomination for Best Actress for *Little Women*. Ryder undertook several high-profile but underwhelming film roles in the late 1990s, appearing in the film version of playwright Arthur Miller's play *The Crucible* (1996); the action movie *Alien: Resurrection* (1997); and the drama *Girl, Interrupted* (1999), based on Susanna Kaysen's best-selling memoir about her struggles with depression.

The next decade began brightly for Ryder. She starred in the romance *Autumn in New York*, which was released in 2000. Also in 2000 she received a star on the Hollywood Walk of Fame. Ryder was in the news again the next year but not for her acting chops. In December 2001 she was caught shoplifting several thousand dollars' worth of merchandise from Saks Fifth Avenue in Beverly Hills, California, and was arrested. After a trial, during which prosecutors accused Ryder of abusing prescription drugs, she was convicted of grand theft, shoplifting, and vandalism and was subsequently sentenced to three years' probation, 480 hours of community service, and nearly $4,000 in fines. She was also required to pay restitution to Saks Fifth Avenue in the amount of $6,355 and to attend mandatory drug and counseling sessions assigned by the court.

Ryder took a break from acting following her conviction. As the first decade of the 2000s neared its end, she began working again, appearing in the immensely successful *Star Trek*, a resurrection of the classic franchise with a new cast, in 2009; starring in a television biopic about the founder of Alcoholics Anonymous, titled *When Love Is Not Enough: The Lois Wilson Story* (2010); and costarring in the psychological thriller *Black Swan* (2010). Ryder received a Screen Actors Guild (SAG) Award nomination for her performance in *When Love Is Not Enough*.

S. K. Bane

SEE ALSO: *Academy Awards; Celebrity; Celebrity Couples; Depp, Johnny; Generation X; Hollywood; Lewis, Jerry Lee; Miller, Arthur; Saks Fifth Avenue;* Star Trek.

BIBLIOGRAPHY

Campbell, Duncan. "Show Trial." *Guardian*, November 8, 2002.

Cawley, Janet. "Little Woman, Big Career." *Biography*, June 1997, 24–29.

Editors of *US*. *Winona Ryder*. Boston: Little, Brown, 1997.

Siegel, Scott, and Barbara Siegel. *The Winona Ryder Scrapbook*. Secaucus, NJ: Carol Publishing, 1997.

Thompson, Dave. *Winona Ryder*. Dallas, TX: Taylor Publishing, 1996.

S

Safe Sex

Sex can be considered "safe" if it avoids the risk of one person infecting another with a sexually transmitted disease (STD). Some individuals and groups maintain that the only sex that is 100 percent safe is no sex—that is, abstinence from sex. But because STDs are usually passed on through bodily fluids (genital herpes is an exception, being transmitted by skin-to-skin contact), any form of sexual expression that avoids one partner's exposure to the bodily fluids of another can be reasonably described as safe. Although this definition would include such practices as mutual masturbation (once known as heavy petting), the most common contemporary definition of the term *safe sex* involves the use of a latex condom to avoid the spread of STDs; such devices have been shown to be 98 to 99 percent effective.

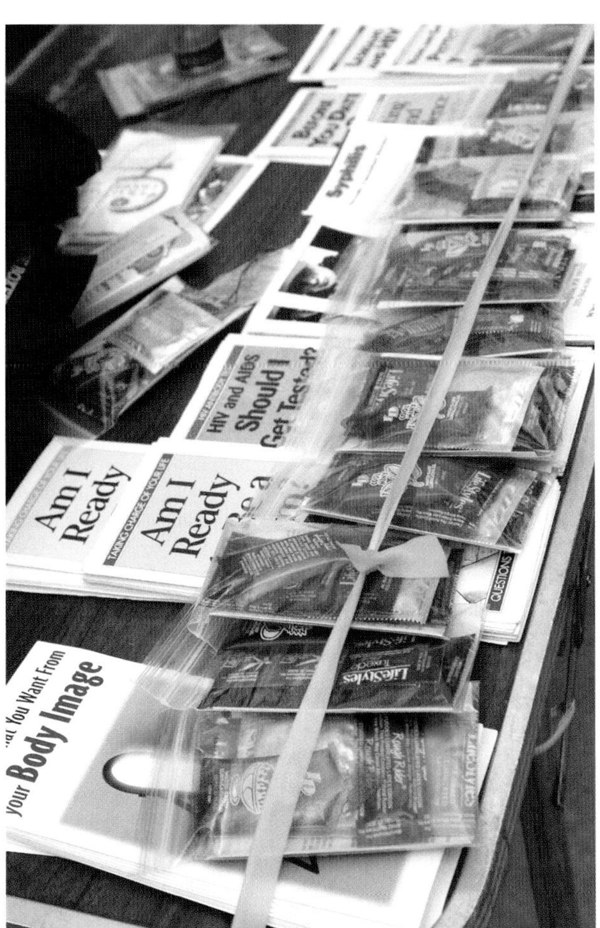

Safe Sex Information. *An information table at a rally outside the National STD Prevention Conference in 2004 includes packages of condoms and pamphlets about various safe-sex topics.* JEFF FUSCO/ GETTY IMAGES.

EARLY CAMPAIGNS

Safe sex is a vital necessity in the modern age and has been so ever since the 1980s, when medical science first identified the virus that causes AIDS (acquired immunodeficiency syndrome), a fatal disease with no known vaccine or cure. The Centers for Disease Control and Prevention (CDC) report that STDs constitute five of the ten most common infectious diseases reported in the United States: AIDS, syphilis, gonorrhea, hepatitis B, and chlamydia. Further, some twelve million new cases of STDs are reported in the United States every year.

One of the early efforts to increase public awareness of STDs in the age of AIDS was made by Otis R. Bowen, secretary for the U.S. Department of Health and Human Services during the Reagan administration. In a 1987 press conference, he claimed that "when a person has sex, they're not just having it with that partner, they're having it with everybody that partner had it with in the past ten years." Bowen's observation quickly made its way into the popular culture. It was picked up by the newsmagazines, appeared in public service advertisements, and even showed up in television dramas such as *L.A. Law*. In addition, Surgeon General C. Everett Koop, who also served under President Ronald Reagan, issued a nationwide report in 1987 that advocated the use of condoms to protect against the spread of HIV. Koop, a conservative evangelical Christian, was criticized by his fellow conservatives for his report, but he viewed AIDS as a public health issue rather than a moral one. An up-and-coming radio personality, Rush Limbaugh, parodied Koop's suggestion by placing a condom over his microphone, stating "This, my friends, is safe talk. You are protected from any evil because of this." Limbaugh further suggested that the 20 percent failure rate of condoms rendered them useless and that the only purpose they served was to generate profit.

On the lighter side, beginning in 1978 at University of California at Berkeley, and later adopted through the 1980s and 1990s by other college campuses, high schools, and health advocacy groups, National Condom Week employed humor to raise awareness about safe sex. Using slogans such as "Don't be silly, protect your willy" and "No glove, no love!" the campaign takes place during the week of Valentine's Day. In addition to schools, volunteers targeted bars, clubs, public parks, and street corners, distributing condom earrings, condom lollipops, and other accessories, as well as free condoms. Some have argued that such events only served to promote sexual activity, while organizers countered that in light of rising STDs and pregnancies, awareness and education were more realistic measures to take.

REPRESENTATIONS IN THE MEDIA

When it comes to depictions of sexual activity, however, television entertainment programs are contributors to the STD problem much more than they are part of the solution. A 1999 study by the Henry J. Kaiser Family Foundation showed that 67 percent of prime-time television programs contained verbal or visual references to sex, but only 10 percent made any mention of safe sex or contraception. Within the program sample studied, eighty-eight scenes were identified portraying or implying sexual intercourse, and not one contained any depiction or mention of safe sex. These results were consistent with similar studies performed in 1986, 1993, and 1996: there was considerable sexual activity portrayed on television but very little mention of STD prevention by any of the sexually involved characters.

There have been a few notable exceptions to this trend. In 1989 an episode of the situation comedy *Head of the Class* caused a stir when one of the characters, a teenage boy, asks his teacher whether he should have intercourse with his girlfriend. The teacher (portrayed by Howard Hesseman) advises the boy not to have sex but, if he must, to be sure to use a condom. In the late 1990s several WB network shows, including *Dawson's Creek* and *Felicity*, showed characters discussing sex with disease prevention raised as an issue; similar scenes also took place on the UPN network's popular show *Moesha*.

If discussion of condoms is rare in network television shows, until the 1990s it was unheard of in the advertising that paid for those programs. The networks were concerned that such advertisements would cause offense in the more conservative areas of the country and also that some advertisers of more conventional products would not wish to have their advertisements preceded or followed by a condom commercial. By 1999 Fox, NBC, and CBS accepted condom ads with limitations on tone, time of day, and message; ABC, UPN, and the WB began airing ads by 2005. Cable channels such as MTV, Comedy Central, BET, CNN, TNT, USA, and TBS agreed to air ads; however, the ads typically ran during the late-night programs.

Although the networks agreed to run the advertisements, there remained a high amount of controversy over what was considered to be proper advertising. In 2007 CBS and Fox refused to air an ad from Trojan's "Evolve" campaign, which showed a pig transform into an attractive male after he purchased a condom. The networks felt that such an ad focused on pregnancy prevention rather than disease prevention, and, therefore, it was not an appropriate ad to air at any time. Internet channels such as Hulu accepted condom ads without restrictions.

Local network affiliates, however, are allowed to accept condom advertisements, and several have done so. In August 1998 CBS affiliate stations in New York and Los Angeles broadcast condom advertisements for the first time. The advertisements were protested by the conservative American Family Association, but the stations continued to run them.

The networks have been more open to the airing of public service announcements (PSAs) for AIDS prevention, which often mention condoms. In 1994 the networks (along with many cable television channels) began broadcasting a series of PSAs sponsored by the CDC. Although Fox and NBC showed the six advertisements without alteration, ABC felt obliged to add this tagline to each: "Abstinence is the safest, but if you do have sex, latex condoms can protect you." CBS was willing to air five of the PSAs but drew the line at one that featured a counselor infected with AIDS and an 800 number to call for more information.

Just as concern about safe sex rarely shows up in television programs, it is also generally absent from the movies Americans watch. One exception was *Pretty Woman* (1990), in which prostitute Vivian Ward (played by Julia Roberts) offers a choice of condoms to her "date," Edward Lewis (Richard Gere). The 1997 sex farce *Booty Call* features two women's insistence on condom use by their men as a central plot element.

Condoms are also becoming more common in the last place where one might expect to find them—XXX adult films. In 1998 porn star Mark Wallice reportedly tested positive for HIV, the virus that causes AIDS. This is not unusual in itself, but it has been alleged that Wallice had tested positive more than a year earlier and had concealed that fact while continuing to have unprotected sex in films, apparently infecting several of his female costars in the process. Consequently, pornography shows a lot more latex; in fact, Los Angeles voted that condoms would be required in pornography filmed in the city starting in 2012.

Another unlikely source for safe sex advocacy was Kate Shindle, the 1997–1998 Miss America. Unlike her predecessors, who generally shied away from controversy, Shindle used her many public appearances to discuss AIDS and its prevention through safe sex practices. This caused the cancellation of some of her speaking engagements, but Shindle was undeterred, delivering her message in any venue where she could reach an audience. "To me," she said, "the most important thing is saving lives."

In 1998 MTV launched the "Staying Alive" initiative. Following the success of the initial documentary, "Staying Alive" grew into a worldwide foundation that offered grants and support to young people and organizations who worked on HIV/AIDS intervention. As sex education and safe sex practices increasingly became public concern, celebrities took part in the conversation. Such pop singers as Madonna and Lady Gaga routinely encouraged their fans to practice safe sex; Justin Bieber and the Jonas Brothers advocated abstinence.

POLITICS OF SAFE SEX

Although advertising and media representations of safe sex made some strides through the first decade of the twenty-first century, safe sex education for adolescents remained a highly politicized issue. Under the direction of President George W. Bush and his administration, the federal government instituted a series of policies that awarded funding in favor of abstinence-only education over comprehensive sex education. Funding for abstinence-only education began in 1996 as part of the Welfare Reform Act, which established $50 million in grants annually for programs that promoted abstinence as the accepted standard for adolescents. The Bush administration extended this to Community-Based Abstinence Education programs that allowed for school districts and community organizations to apply for funds. Funding for abstinence-based programs increased to close to $200 million a year by 2007.

Proponents of abstinence-based education were quick to point out that not only did it prevent disease and limit unwanted pregnancies, but it also provided moral instruction. Critics were quick to point out that studies indicated that abstinence-only programs actually failed to decrease teenage sexual activity. They suggested that comprehensive or abstinence-plus education adequately addressed the real life of teens as well as offered a curriculum that accounted for nonheterosexual relationships and alternatives to marriage. Numerous studies have been conducted on the effectiveness of abstinence-only education. The results vary depending on the organization conducting the study, but most analysts and organizations agreed that abstinence-only education was ineffective.

Following his election in 2008, President Barack Obama cut funding to abstinence programs; however, in 2010 a rider to the health care legislation restored $250 million to abstinence-based education. The debate between abstinence-only and comprehensive sex education illustrated the extent to which safe sex had become politicized. Drifting far from the public initiatives to prevent sexually transmitted diseases, the discussions took on increasingly moral tones.

Justin Gustainis

SEE ALSO: *Advertising; AIDS; Bieber, Justin; CNN; Condoms;* Dawson's Creek*; Gere, Richard; Hulu; The Jonas Brothers;* L.A. Law*; Lady Gaga; Madonna; Miss America Pageant; MTV; Obama, Barack; Pornography; Reagan, Ronald; Roberts, Julia; Television.*

BIBLIOGRAPHY

DiClimente, Ralph J., ed. *Adolescents and AIDS: A Generation in Jeopardy.* Newbury Park, CA: Sage Publications, 1992.

Edgar, Timothy; Mary Anne Fitzpatrick; and Vicki S. Freimuth, eds. *AIDS: A Communication Perspective.* Hillsdale, NJ: Lawrence Erlbaum Associates, 1992.

Irvine, Janice M. *Talk about Sex: The Battles over Sex Education in the United States.* Berkeley: University of California Press, 2002.

Lord, Alexandra M. *Condom Nation: The U.S. Government's Sex Education Campaign from World War I to the Internet.* Baltimore, MD: Johns Hopkins University Press, 2009.

Lowry, Dennis T., and Jon A. Shidler. "Prime Time TV Portrayals of Sex, 'Safe Sex' and AIDS: A Longitudinal Analysis." *Journalism Quarterly* 70, no. 3 (1993): 628–637.

Nourse, Alan E. *Teen Guide to Safe Sex.* New York: Franklin Watts, 1988.

Patton, Cindy. *Fatal Advice: How Safe-Sex Education Went Wrong.* Durham, NC: Duke University Press, 1996.

Peters, Brooks. *Terrific Sex in Fearful Times.* New York: St. Martin's Press, 1988.

Preston, John, and Glenn Swann. *Safe Sex: The Ultimate Erotic Guide.* New York: New American Library, 1986.

Scotti, Angelo T., and Thomas A. Moore. *Safe Sex: What Everyone Should Know about Sexually Transmitted Diseases.* New York: PaperJacks, 1987.

Sagan, Carl *(1934–1996)*

Of all the spokespeople for the space sciences active during the last three decades of the twentieth century, astronomer Carl Sagan was the most widely recognized and articulate. Through his accessible and instructive writings and their accompanying television programs, he earned a significant place in American culture and named one of the world's most frightening forebodings—that of annihilation by atomic weapons—as "nuclear winter."

POPULAR SCIENCE

Popular interest in astronomy and space travel in the United States exploded after the Soviet Union's launch of the first artificial satellite, *Sputnik*, on October 4, 1957. This unparalleled opportunity for the scientific community to provide public education continued for several decades. An entirely new genre of writing was born, involving prominent figures active in the American space effort, such as Wernher von Braun and the members of the newly formed astronaut corps, and science writers knowledgeable in the field. The discussion of the obvious political overtones of the so-called "space race" expanded to encompass humanity's place in the universe. Questions regarding the future uses of outer space assumed new importance in both American and worldwide consciousness.

Born in New York City on November 9, 1934, Sagan showed an interest in astronomy early in his life. He made the subject a career, completing doctoral work at the University of

Carl Sagan. *Carl Sagan's writings and television programs made the complex subjects of astrophysics and space travel accessible to general audiences.* MICKEY ADAIR/CONTRIBUTOR/HULTON ARCHIVE/GETTY IMAGES.

Chicago in 1960 and serving as a faculty member at the University of California at Berkeley, Harvard University, and the Smithsonian Institution before settling at Cornell University. His main research interests lay in planetary studies and the origin of life. Many of his writings were designed to educate the general public about these fields, a task into which he poured his heart and mind throughout his life.

His first popular work was the 1973 book about the search for extraterrestrial life and space travel, *The Cosmic Connection*. His studies in the origins of life and the development of intelligent awareness were the focus of his next work, *The Dragons of Eden* (1977), which won the Pulitzer Prize in 1978. After the publication of *Cosmos* (1980), written in conjunction with a series of thirteen programs widely broadcast on public television networks, the unassuming astronomer became a recognizable and familiar figure in the public mind of America and the world.

EARTH AND SPACE

The idea for the *Cosmos* project was born in 1976, when Sagan participated in the imaging team working on the Viking Lander's mission to Mars. Journalistic interest in the operation quickly waned once it became clear that the question of the presence of life on the planet remained unsettled. Sagan and B. Gentry Lee, director of data analysis and mission planning, decided to create a television production company whose goal was the communication of science in an accessible and inviting manner. The introduction to the book set forth the essential features of a personal and philosophical view of the space age: "The present epoch is a major crossroads for our civilization and perhaps for our species. Whatever road we take, our fate is indissolubly bound up with science." A lively respect for the intelligence of his audiences and an unfailing wonder at the infinite diversity of a patterned universe made Sagan the ideal voice for the project. He was able to provide a comprehensible perspective on the flood of new information becoming available from various space missions and orbiting instruments.

Sagan's research on the potential effects of nuclear weapons on Earth's biosphere is also evidence of his belief in science and its potential to determine the future of humanity. After the *Mariner 9* probe encountered a massive Martian dust storm in 1971, Sagan and other scientists produced the first comprehensive study of the impact of numerous megaton atomic weapon explosions on global climate and atmospheric factors. The researchers created models by analyzing the temperature fluctuations caused by synthesized available data. Sagan presented the grim results of these findings at the 1983 Conference on the Long-Term Worldwide Biological Consequences of Nuclear War held in Washington, D.C. It was here that he first publicly used the phrase "nuclear winter." A report of the conference was published as *The Cold and the Dark: The World after Nuclear War*.

HUMANITY'S FUTURE

Arguably, Sagan's most influential contribution was as head of the 1976 team that composed a message for extraterrestrials. It was sent with the *Voyager* spacecraft, an unmanned probe that ventured into deep space after its years-long mission through the solar system was completed. Rather than duplicate the aluminum plaques affixed to the earlier *Pioneer 10* and *11* probes, Sagan and his team created a long-playing record album containing both audio recordings and visual images gathered from diverse societies that, collectively, would enable extraterrestrial beings to gain a sense of human accomplishment. Among their many selections, the scientists included 118 pictures representing different aspects of human civilization and its world; greetings in fifty-five languages; music ranging from the Navajo Night Chant and Indian ragas to a Mozart aria; and recorded natural sounds, including the cry of a newborn infant. Sagan's motivation for sending this rich record was his belief that "no one sends such a message on such a journey, to other worlds and beings, without a positive passion for the future."

Until his death from cancer on December 20, 1996, Sagan continued to promote a clear and well-reasoned perspective on the wonders and complexities of space and on humanity's future aboard its "pale blue dot." His cultural legacy is an active intellectual presence in the world community. In 1997 a film was made from his 1985 science fiction novel *Contact*, in which humans successfully confirm the presence of other intelligent species in the universe. The movie brought the philosophical dialogue on humanity's relationship to space exploration to a mass audience.

Detailed biographies of his life have been published for all audiences, from elementary school students to professional astronomers, and his earlier works have been reprinted. His effective teaching example has inspired others to promote scientific literacy among the public, as evidenced in such programs as astrophysicist Neil deGrasse Tyson's *NOVA scienceNOW* and physicist Brian Greene's *NOVA: The Fabric of the Cosmos*. The Planetary Society, the Council of Scientific Society Presidents, and the American Astronomical Society have all established awards bearing Sagan's name. In 1997 his contributions to the series of planetary probes launched between 1960 and 1990 and his advocacy for the exploration of Mars were honored when the landing site for the Mars *Pathfinder* was named the Carl Sagan Memorial Station.

Robert Ridinger

SEE ALSO: *Apollo Missions; The Bomb; Cancer; Long-Playing Record; Public Television (PBS); Satellites; Smithsonian Institution;* Sputnik; *Television.*

BIBLIOGRAPHY

Davidson, Keay. *Carl Sagan: A Life*. New York: Wiley, 1999.

Ehrlich, Paul R., and Carl Sagan. *The Cold and the Dark: The World after Nuclear War*. New York: W. W. Norton, 1984.

Poundstone, William. *Carl Sagan: A Life in the Cosmos*. New York: Henry Holt, 1999.

Sagan, Carl. *Carl Sagan's Cosmic Connection: An Extraterrestrial Perspective*. New York: Doubleday, 1973.

Sagan, Carl. *The Dragons of Eden: Speculations on the Evolution of Human Intelligence*. New York: Random House, 1977.

Sagan, Carl. *Cosmos*. New York: Random House, 1980.

Sagan, Carl. *Pale Blue Dot: A Vision of the Human Future in Space*. New York: Random House, 1994.

Sagan, Carl; Frank Drake; and Ann Druyan. *Murmurs of Earth: The Voyager Interstellar Record*. New York: Ballantine Books, 1978.

Terzian, Yervant, and Elizabeth Bilson, eds. *Carl Sagan's Universe*. New York: Cambridge University Press, 1997.

Sagging

The sometimes controversial practice of wearing one's pants below one's waist (and exposing one's underwear) is known as "sagging." Its practitioners, called "saggers," tend to be young men, but some women have also adopted the style. The prevailing theory is that this trend got its start in prisons, where inmates walked around with droopy drawers after their belts were taken away to prevent suicide attempts. The look was first popularized by gangsta rap and hip-hop artists in the late 1980s, but the phenomenon has since spread to a variety of cultural groups, including skateboarders and snowboarders.

Whereas some see sagging as yet another passing fad in teens' ongoing search for stylistic self-expression, others see this exposure of underwear as indecent. Some have also expressed concern that sagging may be an indicator of a tendency toward violent or criminal behavior, pointing to the fact that some gang members wear this style. Debates over the trend have led some high schools to ban the look, and some communities have even passed laws to force all saggers to pull up their pants for good. Sagging is currently illegal in the towns of Delcambre and Mansfield, Louisiana: saggers can face fines or even jail time (attempts to pass a statewide ban in Louisiana have failed). In April 2012, an Alabama judge sentenced twenty-year-old LaMarcus D. Ramsey to three days in jail for wearing saggy pants to court.

The fact that saggers have been primarily African American has raised questions about some of the objections. The American Civil Liberties Union (ACLU) and the National Association for the Advancement of Colored People (NAACP) have said that laws against sagging target minorities and violate personal freedom.

That sagging has cemented a place in pop culture history was made evident in 2010, when during auditions for *American Idol* "General" Larry Platt performed a song called "Pants on the Ground," admonishing saggers to "get your pants off the ground!" Judge Simon Cowell accurately predicted the song's popularity, stating, "I have a horrible feeling that song could be a hit." As of April 2012, the song had more than eight million views on YouTube. Sagging itself may have declined somewhat in popularity, but the trend has proved it has staying power—at least for now.

Sarah Roggio

SEE ALSO: *Gangsta Rap; Hip-Hop; Rap; Skateboarding; Snowboarding; Teenagers.*

BIBLIOGRAPHY

"Are Saggy Pants Really a Threat to Flight Safety?" American Civil Liberties Union (ACLU), June 17, 2011. Accessed April 2012. Available from http://www.aclu.org/blog/criminal-law-reform-racial-justice/are-saggy-pants-really-threat-flight-safety

Associated Press. "Bill to Ban Sagging Pants Rejected." WWLTV, May 12, 2010. Accessed April 2012. Available from http://www.wwltv.com/news/Bill-to-ban-sagging-pants-rejected-93603674.html

"Buy a Belt! Alabama Judge Orders Man to Serve Three-Day Jail Sentence for Wearing Sagging Pants." *Daily Mail*, April 11, 2012.

"Green Day's Billie Joe Armstrong Kicked Off Plane for Saggy Pants." *US Weekly*, September 3, 2011.

Koppel, Niko. "Are Your Jeans Sagging? Go Directly to Jail." *New York Times*, August 30, 2007.

Mathis, Greg. "The Sad Truth about Saggin' Pants: Emulating Convicts Can Lead to Prison Mentality." *Ebony*, July 2008.

"What Is Sagging?" WiseGeek. Accessed April 2012. Available from http://www.wisegeek.com/what-is-sagging.htm

"Who Are Saggers?" WiseGeek. Accessed April 2012. Available from http://www.wisegeek.com/who-are-saggers.htm

Sahl, Mort *(1927–)*

Mort Sahl pioneered the type of biting satirical political humor that inspired so many other comics who came after him, from Lenny Bruce to Jay Leno. Appearing first in nightclubs during the late 1950s, Sahl did not follow earlier comics who told mother-in-law jokes or stuck to ribbing their show-business cronies. Instead, he adopted the style of jazz musicians who begin with a theme, are reminded of another idea, and then circle back to the original theme.

Sahl was born May 11, 1927, in Montreal but soon moved to Los Angeles, where his father eventually worked as a clerk for the Federal Bureau for Investigation. Sahl was a ROTC member in high school and was stationed, after being drafted, in Alaska. There, he got into trouble as editor of the base newspaper, *Poop from the Group*, and claimed to have served eighty-three days in a row on KP (kitchen police) as punishment. Nevertheless, Sahl claimed to have remained an establishment supporter, the same boy who won an American Legion Americanism Award. He served his country with pride, but as he drifted away from those values he turned to the comedy of satire.

It took time for Sahl's style of comedy to catch on. Audiences at first did not quite know what to make of him. He appeared onstage with a rolled-up newspaper. The paper held a crib sheet of topics and lines he wanted to follow. The owners of San Francisco's Hungry i comedy club believed in him and kept him working until fans came to appreciate the sweater-clad, hip comedian. Here was a man who dared chide President Dwight D. Eisenhower: "Eisenhower proved that we don't need a president," Sahl once said. Nothing was sacred to him, and he paraded his ability to expose others' foibles, wondering, "Is there any group I haven't offended yet?"

Sahl was one of the first comedians to do comedy records. In the late 1950s his recordings—such as 1958's *The Future Lies Ahead*—sold quite well, and his humor became familiar to many who never had the chance to see him in clubs. He set his sights on politicians especially, taking swipes at Eisenhower, Adlai Stevenson, and John F. Kennedy (even though he had once penned one-liners for the Kennedy campaign). Sahl once remarked, "Whoever the president is, I will attack him." But liberals who supported the jibes aimed at Eisenhower failed to appreciate the jokes made at Kennedy's expense, and this lack of fan appreciation, coupled with what Sahl complained was a blacklisting by entertainment executives sympathetic to Kennedy, sent his career into a sharp decline in the later 1960s.

Sahl soon became obsessed with Kennedy's assassination, and he felt it was his responsibility to educate the American public that the CIA was responsible for the president's death. Alienating his fans even further, his income dropped from about $400,000 a year to $17,000. He published an autobiography,

Heartland, in 1976, and in the 1980s earned a decent living by ghostwriting movies. Later that decade he staged a comeback of sorts, appearing in a one-man show on Broadway called simply *Mort Sahl on Broadway* and hosting the radio program *Publishers Weekly's between the Covers with Mort Sahl* on the ABC radio network beginning in 1995. While the comedian continues to perform and appear on political talk shows and late-night television shows, he has not found his foothold with younger generations. However, his lasting importance to American comedy can be seen in the way his satiric voice and unflinching critique of high-powered figures influenced the work of major political comedians of the 1990s and the first decade of the 2000s such as Stephen Colbert, Jon Stewart, and Bill Maher.

Frank A. Salamone

SEE ALSO: *Broadway; Bruce, Lenny; Colbert, Stephen; Kennedy Assassination; Leno, Jay; Radio; Stand-Up Comedy; Stewart, Jon; Television.*

BIBLIOGRAPHY

Disch, Thomas. "Mort Sahl on Broadway." *Nation*, November 14, 1987, 570.

Gross, Ken. "Not Going Gentle into That Good Night, Caustic Comic Mort Sahl Gears Up for a Broadway Comeback." *People*, October 12, 1987, 134–136.

Sahl, Mort. *Heartland.* New York: Harcourt, 1976.

Saks Fifth Avenue

The retail specialty store Saks Fifth Avenue stood as a symbol of American wealth and prestige for most of the twentieth century. The firm was founded in 1902 when Andrew Saks, a street peddler from Philadelphia, opened Saks & Company, a men's clothing shop in Washington, D.C. Andrew soon expanded his store operations to Richmond, Virginia; Indianapolis, Indiana; and New York City. For his New York store, he began actively courting the high-end retail market by stocking quality merchandise and offering first-class service. Upon Andrew's death in 1912, his son Horace became firm president and made a bid to become the premier specialty store for New York society. Saks buyers scoured the globe for unique and fashionable merchandise in order to build the store's reputation.

With the shift of New York retail uptown during the 1910s, it became apparent to Saks that for the firm to continue its fashionable reputation, it needed a more prestigious address than 34th Street near Herald Square. The firm entered negotiations to take over the site of the New York Democratic Club between 49th and 50th Streets on Fifth Avenue, but Saks lacked sufficient capital to meet Tammany Hall's asking price. Therefore, Horace agreed to merge his retail store chain with Gimbel Brothers department store, which operated stores in New York; Philadelphia; and Madison, Wisconsin. The resultant merger in 1923 created one of the earliest regional department store chains in the United States. Saks's old Herald Square store site was leased to Gimbels and combined with their existing store nearby, making it the largest department store in the world at that time.

The uptown store, christened Saks Fifth Avenue, opened in 1924 with great fanfare. Street windows displayed such luxurious items as raccoon coats and foot muffs for automobile travel. An electric-lighting system signaled chauffeurs when to pick up patrons. In an attempt to capitalize on the growing notoriety of the uptown store, Saks president Adam Long Gimbel decided to rename all the firm's outlets Saks Fifth Avenue, a stroke of marketing genius that conveyed the prestige of the address to every store. Gimbel undertook a branch store building program in 1926 designed to place Saks Fifth Avenues in carefully chosen locations in resort towns and prestigious residential areas in Chicago; Miami Beach, Florida; and Beverly Hills, California. Gimbel established several trademark services, including a gift-buying service for business executives, and Saks was the first retail store to have its own in-house fashion designer producing collections—Sophie Gimbel, wife of the president of Saks. The store's national reputation grew to such an extent that "very Saks Fifth Avenue" became a popular euphemism for posh style.

Bought out by Brown & Williamson Tobacco in 1973, Saks managed to weather a Securities and Exchange Commission accounting scandal and a failed merger in 1998. The early twenty-first century proved to be a time of great change for the company. In 2000 Saks launched an online store. Five years later, the company sold its northern department store group to Bon-Ton Stores and then set about selling Proffitt's and McRae's department stores to Belk Inc. In 2006 declining sales forced Saks to rethink the thrust of its marketing, which had been focused on selling tight, hip clothing to a young market. Attempting to reclaim its older, more traditional, customers, Saks changed its focus to classics such as those designed by Ellen Tracy. In addition to the Club Libby Lu specialty chain, Saks had trimmed its holdings to forty-six Saks stores in twenty-two states by 2012.

Stephanie Dyer

SEE ALSO: *Advertising; Department Stores; Online Shopping.*

BIBLIOGRAPHY

D'Innocenzio, Anne. "Saks Tries to Get Back on Track after a Couple of Wrong Turns." *Houston Chronicle*, September 17, 2006.

Harris, Leon. *Merchant Princes: An Intimate History of the Jewish Families Who Built the Great Department Stores.* New York: Harper & Row, 1979.

Hendrickson, Robert. *The Grand Emporiums: The Illustrated History of America's Great Department Stores.* New York: Stein & Day, 1979.

Leach, William. *Land of Desire: Merchants, Power, and the Rise of a New American Culture.* New York: Pantheon, 1993.

Martin, R. Brad. *Saks Incorporated: The Saks Story.* New York: Newcomen Society of the United States, 2003.

Sales, Soupy *(1926–2009)*

Comedian Soupy Sales built his reputation on the unlikely skill of pie throwing; he is reputed to have thrown 20,000 pies in a career that stretched from the 1950s into the 1990s. Sales, born Milton Supman, planted pies in the faces of some of America's most noted celebrities, including Frank Sinatra, Sammy Davis Jr., and Tony Curtis. The comedian appeared on local television variety shows for both children and adults in several major markets before taking the *Soupy Sales Show* national in the mid-

1960s. Sales, who delighted fans with his antics, went too far on New Year's Day in 1965 when he asked the children who watched his show to "go to Daddy's wallet and get those little green pieces of paper with pictures of George Washington on it and send them to me." They did, to the tune of $80,000, but the prank led to the show's brief suspension. Sales made frequent guest appearances on TV and in movies into the 1990s. He died on October 22, 2009, at the age of eighty-three.

Naomi Finkelstein

SEE ALSO: *Sinatra, Frank; Stand-up Comedy; Television.*

BIBLIOGRAPHY

Brooks, Tim, and Earle Marsh. *The Complete Directory of Prime Time Network and Cable TV Shows, 1946–Present*, 9th ed. New York: Ballantine, 2007.

Kiska, Tim. *From Soupy to Nuts! A History of Detroit Television.* Royal Oak, MI: Momentum Books, 2005.

Salsa Music

Salsa has transcended its humble beginnings to become a powerful influence on music and culture worldwide. A blend of African rhythms and European harmony born in Cuba and developed in New York City, it is a truly international music encapsulating the Latin American experience—and, you can dance to it.

AFRO-CUBAN ROOTS

Beginning in the sixteenth century, Spanish settlers brought Africans to Cuba to work as slaves, mostly on sugar and tobacco plantations. Afro-Cuban music grew from traditional West African musical forms and was replicated on homemade or Spanish instruments. Some elements stemming from African religious practice, including call-and-response singing and polyrhythms, remain dominant features of Afro-Cuban music today, and *santería*, a typically Cuban blend of African religions and Catholicism, is still a popular musical topic.

By the beginning of the twentieth century, Afro-Cuban music had taken three main forms: *son* (pronounced sewn), a popular dance music, has three contrasting rhythms; *rumba*, an informal street music, enthusiastic and improvised, typically uses just percussion and vocals; and *danzón*, derived from European dance forms, spotlights piano and flute. All three forms are distinguished by their use of the clave, a two-measure, five-beat syncopated rhythm played on small wooden sticks called claves. The music's impact was first felt beyond the island in the 1930s, when dance bands in the United States began to play rumba and mambo (an evolution of *danzón*). Soon thereafter, jazz pioneer Dizzy Gillespie incorporated Cuban elements into bebop, a combination Gillespie called "Cubop."

By the early 1960s rumba and mambo had become passé in the United States, at least among those who considered themselves too hip for the likes of Ricky Ricardo (Lucille Ball's husband on the *I Love Lucy* television show, played by Desi Arnaz, the leader of a Latin music band in his own right). At the same time many of Cuba's biggest talents moved to New York City, fleeing their country's leftist revolution—most notably Celia Cruz. These artists joined with young, predominantly Puerto Rican New Yorkers (Nuyoricans) to breathe new life into the city's Latin dance scene, dropping the traditional violins in favor of blaring, often dazzling, horn arrangements. Pianist and bandleader Eddie Palmieri was the first to bring the complex mozambique rhythm—developed in Cuba by Pello el Afrokán—to New York; he was also the foremost of a new generation of jazz-trained pianists, adding a new harmonic complexity to the music. By the late 1960s Fania Records, a label owned by Jerry Masucci, had signed most of the rising stars of the new Afro-Cuban music.

The genesis of the word *salsa* is unknown, but Masucci and Fania's musical director, Johnny Pacheco, relentlessly promoted its use. Many older Latin musicians and fans still bristle at the name, feeling that their cultural heritage is being reduced to a condiment, but it caught on and is now used—if grudgingly—by nearly all participants.

SALSA SUCCESS

Almost immediately, sales of salsa records went through the roof, and in the early 1970s there was a wealth of successful bands, making up in energy and swing what they lacked in technical polish and production values. The best-known musicians (many of them also bandleaders) of the genre included Palmieri; Cruz; Joe Bataan; Ray Barretto; Larry Harlow; Johnny Colón; and, most importantly, trombonist Willie Colón (no relation to Johnny). Raised in the Bronx, New York, Willie cut his first record, *El Malo* (1967), in his late teens with vocalist Héctor Lavoe and soon established a reputation as salsa's biggest hit maker. His orchestra moved beyond familiar romantic themes to depict the often harsh reality of New York's barrios in such songs as "Piraña," "Barrunto," and "Te Conozco." Colón refused to be limited to Masucci's vision, and he soon expanded his musical palette to include traditional Puerto Rican rhythms—*bomba* and *plena*—and Brazilian styles. Of the 1940s and 1950s generation of bandleaders, only the seemingly ageless percussion master Tito Puente remained prominent during this period.

Salsa's lyrics have been criticized for their sexist content, and aside from Cruz, the "queen of salsa," there have been very few female singers—and almost no female writers or arrangers—involved in the form. Central to Masucci's marketing plan was advertising salsa as a completely new style, and to this end he downplayed the music's Cuban origins, even though nearly everything Fania released—aside from merengue, which came from the Dominican Republic—was Afro-Cuban in character. Partly because of sour relations between the United States and Cuba, Masucci did not credit Cuban composers on Fania records, even when the majority of an album's tracks were covers of Cuban songs.

In the late 1970s Panamanian-born Rubén Blades brought a new level of lyrical sophistication to salsa. Both his love songs and his devastating political critiques borrowed the imagery and nuance of Latin American protest music (*nueva canción*, called *nueva trova* in Cuba) but brought them to a larger audience by blending them with driving dance rhythms. Blades came to prominence as the vocalist and main songwriter for Willie Colón, and their collaboration *Siembra* (1978) is the best-selling and probably the most critically praised salsa album of all time. Blades reached his solo peak a few years later with *Buscando América* (1984) and *Escenas* (1985). Thanks in part to his fluency in English, he made friends with many rock stars: his 1988 English-language release *Nothing but the Truth* features Sting, Lou Reed, and Elvis Costello, and he also recorded with Joe

Jackson and Jackson Browne. In the early 1990s Blades became better known for his character roles in Hollywood films, and in 1994 he put both entertainment careers on hold in favor of an unsuccessful run for president of Panama.

LATIN POP

Salsa was not incorporated into mainstream music in the United States in the way that reggae was, perhaps because of the language barrier. Even amateur ethnologists Paul Simon and Peter Gabriel, who made several forays into world music, largely avoided the genre: it was at once too close to home and too far away. Some New York pop artists, including Janis Ian and Patti LaBelle, recorded salsa tunes, but such efforts were few, and no one—traditionalist or imitator—hit the Top 40 with salsa. The best illustration of salsa's failure to cross over to English-speaking markets in the 1980s was that the Puerto Rican act best known to the U.S. public was not El Gran Combo or Willie Colón but Menudo, a prefab pretty-boy group with little connection to Afro-Cuban rhythms.

By the late 1980s Nuyorican youth were buying more high-energy dance music than salsa. Many of the old guard (such as Harlow and Barretto) had retired or faded into obscurity, while those who remained (Willie Colón among them) had trouble getting their records played. The film *Salsa!* (1988), starring former Menudo vocalist Robby Rosa, bombed. The singers who flourished in this environment were those with the slickest production, the least penchant for innovation, and absolutely no political message: for example, Jerry Rivera and Tito Nieves, "the Pavarotti of Salsa." Although salsa was still popular throughout Latin America—as demonstrated by the success of Colombia's Grupo Niche and Venezuela's Oscar D'León—the music stagnated in New York City, where the new hit makers were lightweight "Latin hip-hop" acts (such as Brenda K. Starr) that relied on static, preprogrammed beats and breathy, high-pitched vocals—the antithesis of salsa.

SALSA REVIVAL

In a backhanded way Latin hip-hop provided the impetus for salsa's revival in the mid-1990s. Marc Anthony and La India, two artists whose personalities and voices were too strong to be confined by Latin hip-hop's formulas, returned to the music of their childhoods, cutting albums with young producer and arranger Sergio George. George was unafraid to supplement traditional elements with innovative borrowings from funk, soul, and hip-hop; both artists' albums were unmistakably salsa, however, and they succeeded on those terms, reawakening critical and commercial interest in the genre. Anthony even made it to Broadway, along with Blades, appearing in Paul Simon's ill-fated musical *The Capeman* (1998).

At the same time, enormous Latin American immigration into many parts of the United States helped bring the music out of its traditional strongholds in New York; Miami, Florida; and California. Cuban-born pop singer Gloria Estefan also helped repopularize salsa with her tremendously successful album *Mi Tierra* (1993), which featured many top salsa artists. Ultimately, salsa outlived Latin hip-hop, and by 1997 Starr was attempting to revive her career with a disc of salsa tunes.

Meanwhile, back in Cuba, the most forward-thinking bands were beginning to incorporate elements of New York salsa into their music. NG La Banda's "Yo Necesito Una Amiga" was a perfect New York salsa ballad, and when it became a hit, other bands followed suit. By the mid-1990s all of the most popular Cuban bands—Los Van Van, Orquesta Revé, Irakere, Dan Den—had cut salsa numbers. Young sensation Manolín even dubbed himself "el Médico de la Salsa" (the doctor of salsa). The music had come full circle—a development Jerry Masucci had probably never imagined.

The 1990s revival of salsa continued into the next century, along with increased interest in Latino music and culture in general. The Latin Recording Academy, formed in 1997, began awarding Latin Grammy Awards in 2000. Anthony's third salsa album, *Contra la Corriente* (1997), was named on *Time* magazine's Top 10 list of pop albums of the year and made the cross-genre Billboard 200 list, which the singer did several more times in the ensuing decade, most often with Spanish-language albums. Cruz released a plethora of new recordings between 2000 and 2003, the year she died. Anthony starred with Jennifer Lopez in *El Cantante* (2006), a biopic about salsa great Lavoe. La India, dubbed "La Princesa de la Salsa," made the Billboard 200 with her ninth album, *Unica*, in 2010.

Fania records, whose recordings had been in storage and unavailable for years, was bought in 2005 by Emusica, a Miami company that instantly made plans for 300 reissues of the great salsa music of the label's heyday. In 2011 Anthony and Lopez began a talent search for Latino performers in twenty-one Latin American countries to create the television show *¡Q'Viva! The Chosen*, which debuted in 2012. The growing mainstream appeal of Latino music, especially in the hands of such stars as Anthony, suggests that Latin pop built a bridge that gradually reestablished salsa as an all-American genre.

David B. Wilson

SEE ALSO: *Arnaz, Desi; Ball, Lucille; Blades, Rubén; Boy Bands; Broadway; Browne, Jackson; Costello, Elvis; Funk; Gillespie, Dizzy; Grammy Awards; Hip-Hop; Hollywood;* I Love Lucy*; Latin Jazz; Lopez, Jennifer; Movie Stars; Pop Music; Puente, Tito; Reed, Lou; Reggae; Simon, Paul; Soul Music; Television;* Time*; Top 40.*

BIBLIOGRAPHY

Aparicio, Frances R. *Listening to Salsa: Gender, Latin Popular Music, and Puerto Rican Cultures.* Hanover, NH: Wesleyan University Press, 1998.

Gerard, Charley, and Marty Sheller. *Salsa! The Rhythm of Latin Music.* Tempe, AZ: White Cliffs Media, 1998.

Mauleón, Rebeca. *Salsa Guidebook for Piano and Ensemble.* Petaluma, CA: Sher Music, 1993.

Padura Fuentes, Leonardo. *Faces of Salsa: A Spoken History of the Music*, tr. Stephen J. Clark. Washington, DC: Smithsonian Books, 2003.

Rondón, César Miguel. *The Book of Salsa: A Chronicle of Urban Music from the Caribbean to New York City*, tr. Frances R. Aparicio and Jackie White. Chapel Hill: University of North Carolina Press, 2008.

Washburne, Christopher. *Sounding Salsa: Performing Latin Music in New York City.* Philadelphia: Temple University Press, 2008.

Waxer, Lise, ed. *Situating Salsa: Global Markets and Local Meanings in Latin Popular Music.* New York: Routledge, 2002.

Salt-n-Pepa

In 1986, at a time when hip-hop music was shunned by mainstream radio, Salt-n-Pepa broke through with their multi-platinum crossover debut, *Hot, Cool & Vicious.* Along with Run-DMC and the Beastie Boys, Salt-n-Pepa was among the first hip-hop groups to be heard on a wide scale outside American urban centers. The Queens, New York–based Salt-n-Pepa were the first all-female hip-hop group to gain commercial success in a genre dominated by men, opening doors for such female hip-hop artists as MC Lyte, Yo Yo, Foxy Brown, Lil' Kim, Lauryn Hill, Lady of Rage, Missy Elliott, Queen Latifah, Bahamadia, and Heather B. In a genre where the life of a hip-hop career is about one year, Salt-n-Pepa continued to have hits for more than a decade.

Formed in 1985 under the name Super Nature and later renamed Salt-n-Pepa, the group—which included Cheryl "Salt" James (now Wray), Sandy "Pepa" Denton, and their Sears department store coworker turned producer Hurby "Luv Bug" Azor—released a minor hit called "The Show Stoppa," an answer record to the Doug E. Fresh hit, "The Show." Super Nature's song reached number forty-six on the Billboard R&B singles chart, making enough of a splash for the group to perform in local New York clubs. The women changed the group's name to Salt-n-Pepa and added a DJ named Spinderella (Pamela Greene, who was later replaced by Deidre "Dee Dee" Roper). Salt-n-Pepa signed to the independent hip-hop label Next Plateau and released *Hot, Cool & Vicious* in 1986. The album sold successfully, with a number of singles doing well on the R&B charts, but it was not until a remix of "Push It" was released in 1987 that Salt-n-Pepa was launched into the mainstream of pop music.

In 1988 they released a relatively lackluster album, *A Salt with a Deadly Pepa,* which did well enough with the singles "Twist and Shout" and the EU collaboration, "Shake Your Thang." After facing the gendered charges of "selling out" and "going pop," they put out the Afrocentric-tinged *Black's Magic,* a commercial and artistic success with the number one rap chart song "Expression" and the Top 20 Billboard pop hit, "Let's Talk about Sex." For their fourth album, Salt-n-Pepa signed to the major label London and distanced themselves from their longtime producer Azor, whom the group felt imposed too much control. For instance, he got full songwriting credits on their first album, despite the women's assertions that they also contributed lyrics.

Very Necessary, released in 1993, was a massive hit—the biggest of their career. It spawned the Top 10 pop hits "Shoop" and "Whatta Man" and a lesser hit, "None of Your Business," and won the group a Grammy in 1995 for Best Rap Performance by a Duo or Group. Songs such as "Shoop" and "None of Your Business" exemplify the assertive female-centered sexuality that the group has cultivated since its earliest recordings, such as 1986's "Tramp." Group members successfully walked the line between engaging in a fun-loving sexual expression and being reduced to purely sexual objects, primarily because of their smart, in-your-face lyrics. For example, Salt-n-Pepa often engaged in dialogue with their sexist male peers in their songs, challenging traditional notions of femininity and sex-role double standards. In 1995 the group recorded the single "Ain't Nuthin' but a She Thing," the theme song of a documentary about women that aired on MTV in November 1995.

Having completely split with Azor and taken time off from their careers to raise their children, Salt-n-Pepa entered a new hip-hop era in which many more female hip-hop artists were gaining popularity. For a variety of reasons, including changing audience tastes and poor record company marketing, their 1997 album was generally considered a disappointment.

Salt-n-Pepa disbanded in 2000 when Wray abruptly decided to leave the band. This created a feud between the

Salt-n-Pepa. *Rappers Salt-n-Pepa, center and right, and their DJ Spinderella, left, pose in 1988.* MICHAEL OCHS ARCHIVES/GETTY IMAGES.

members, and their next appearance together was in 2005, when they were honored at VH-1's Hip Hop Honors. The group tentatively reformed in 2007, and the debut of their VH-1 reality show *The Salt-n-Pepa Show* allowed the two to finally air old grievances and overcome the sudden dissolution of the band. The show lasted two seasons. In 2007 Salt-n-Pepa was given a Billboard Hip Hop Founders Award. Although the band has never returned to the studio, Salt-n-Pepa continues to tour.

Kembrew McLeod

SEE ALSO: *The Beastie Boys; Hip-Hop; MTV; Pop Music; Queen Latifah; Radio; Reality Television; Rhythm and Blues; Run-DMC; Television; Top 40.*

BIBLIOGRAPHY

Fernando, S. H., Jr. *The New Beats: Exploring the Music, Culture, and Attitudes of Hip-Hop*. New York: Doubleday, 1994.

Rose, Tricia. *Black Noise: Rap Music and Black Culture in Contemporary America*. Hanover, NH: Wesleyan University Press, 1994.

Toop, David. *Rap Attack 2: African Rap to Global Hip-Hop*. London: Serpent's Tail, 1991.

Sam and Dave

Sam Moore and Dave Prater were perhaps the most exciting soul duo of the 1960s. Both got their start as gospel singers in Miami, Florida. After turning to secular music, they caught the attention of Atlantic Records coowner Jerry Wexler, who quickly signed them to a recording contract. Wexler wisely decided to "lend" them to Stax Records, the Memphis, Tennessee, soul label that was distributed by Atlantic. At Stax, they secured not only the label's formidable studio musicians but also the songwriting talents of David Porter and Isaac Hayes, who penned such hits as "Hold on! I'm Comin'" and "Soul Man."

Moore and Prater sometimes used vocal harmonies, but their more distinctive contribution was a call-and-response approach that stemmed from their roots in gospel music. Although the duo broke up in 1970, they performed together off and on until the end of 1981. Prater died in 1988. In 1992 Sam and Dave were inducted into the Rock and Roll Hall of Fame.

Bill Freind

SEE ALSO: *Atlantic Records; Gospel Music; Rock and Roll; Soul Music.*

BIBLIOGRAPHY

Bowman, Rob. *Soulsville, U.S.A.: The Story of Stax Records*. New York: Schirmer, 1997.

Sampling

Sampling is the practice of taking a small piece of prerecorded sound and inserting it into another recording. The practice's origin can be traced back to innovations in musical composition in the mid-twentieth century, and hip-hop DJs experimented with samples in the 1970s and 1980s. However, the technique did not truly enter popular culture until 1990, when rapper Vanilla Ice tacked a sample from the Queen/David Bowie song "Under Pressure" to the beginning of his smash hit "Ice Ice Baby." Although Vanilla Ice was successfully sued for copyright infringement, the practice nevertheless spread throughout mainstream music. Samples were at the heart of best-selling records produced by artists such as Moby and Fatboy Slim and have become commonplace in hip-hop and rap records.

The pioneers of the practice were the creators of "musique Concrete" in the 1940s. They used either tape recorders or record turntables to access the source sounds, which they then rerecorded and assembled with other recorded sounds to make new and experimental music. At the time, sampling was a complicated technical process that required specialized equipment and some skill in operating it.

The development of multitrack tape recording in the 1960s made it easier to rerecord on tape and opened the way for more musicians to use samples in the form of loops of tape. Multitrack recording allowed engineers to construct a perfect recording out of numerous versions (or takes) of a song, as flubbed parts could be easily replaced with better versions of them. It was a short, natural progression to begin inserting pieces of recordings from other songs into a track. In the 1970s DJs used two turntables (connected to a mixer) to access short pieces of music from spinning vinyl records and add it to their mix. Sampling became popular in disco, electronic dance music, and early hip-hop.

The introduction of digital recording in the 1980s made sampling much easier because digital recording was based on extremely rapid continuous sampling of the source sounds. The first digital samplers designed specifically to save and manipulate pieces of recorded sound were large and expensive. By the end of the decade, though, there were machines—such as the Akai S1000—that made sampling much more accessible. The results were soon heard in electronic dance and techno music. Digital sampling was also employed in drum machines that became popular in all genres of music in the 1980s and 1990s. Soon, music and spoken word samples were introduced into a wide range of popular music. When digital recording was incorporated in personal computers in the 1990s, sampling was brought within reach of millions of professional and amateur musicians. Recording software such as Pro Tools made it possible to make twenty-four-track recordings on a home computer and add samples to any song being recorded.

Popular music in the twenty-first century is full of samples. The ease with which one can access, rerecord, and manipulate digital samples has raised legal and moral issues about the ownership of source sounds. The first recombinant records that became hits, such as M/A/R/R/S's "Pump Up the Volume" in 1989 and "Ice Ice Baby," brought lawsuits claiming infringement of copyright. Even a few sampled drumbeats can be deemed as infringement, even though they might not sound anything like the original. As digital piracy has increased, stricter laws to protect copyright have been introduced. This has made gaining permission to employ samples essential in the music business.

Andre Millard

SEE ALSO: *Cassette Tape; Disc Jockeys; Disco; Hip-Hop; Pop Music; Rap; Vanilla Ice.*

BIBLIOGRAPHY

Alderman, John. *Sonic Boom: Napster, MP3 and the New Pioneers of Music.* Cambridge, MA: Perseus, 2001.

Kot, Greg. *Ripped: How the Wired Generation Revolutionized Music.* New York: Scribner, 2009.

Miller, Paul, ed. *Sound Unbound: Sampling Digital Music and Culture.* Cambridge, MA: MIT Press, 2008.

Sinnreich, Aram. *Mashed Up: Music Technology and the Rise of a Configurable Culture.* Amherst: University of Massachusetts Press, 2010.

Sandburg, Carl *(1878–1967)*

A maverick son of Swedish immigrant parents, Carl Sandburg became one of America's best-loved poets, as well as one of its most significant. He was also a journalist, storyteller, balladeer, and noted biographer of Abraham Lincoln. His literary works and journalistic writings became ingrained in popular American culture beginning during World War I through the Roaring Twenties and the Great Depression to the tumultuous times of World War II and its aftermath.

Part newspaperman, part poet, Sandburg reflected the lives of ordinary people caught up in current events, articulating his concerns through his writings in a career that spanned half a century. He wrote during a time of great industrial and social change. Across America, cities proliferated and grew, while rural populations were displaced from the land and European immigrants flooded the cities. Sandburg wrote in a broad, earthy style—and with honesty and perception—about the burgeoning urban life. Adopting a bold, free-verse style reminiscent of Walt Whitman, Sandburg spoke, not in poetically lyrical language, but in the slang and speech patterns of working people, the language of factory and sidewalk. In *A Profile of Twentieth Century American Poetry*, Roger Mitchell explains that "Sandburg wrote in the language of the people he described and in the belief that their lives mattered." Unlike many of his contemporaries, he looked only to America for his inspiration and celebrated the lives of its ordinary citizens.

Carl Sandburg. *Poet and Lincoln biographer Carl Sandburg poses at home in 1956.* AP IMAGES.

EARLY YEARS

Born in Galesburg, Illinois, in 1878, Sandburg grew up on the prairies of Illinois, left school at thirteen, and—in the wake of a depression—joined the homeless and unemployed in a journey across America. He worked as a laborer and lived as a hobo, sleeping in boxcars. In 1898 he returned to Galesburg and became a housepainter but soon after enlisted in the Sixth Illinois Infantry during the Spanish-American War. It was during his eight months' service in Cuba and Puerto Rico that Sandburg wrote in his journal of the hypocrisy and injustice of war and its effects on the ordinary soldiers, who were dying of heat, malaria, and dysentery without firing a shot in battle.

After the war he again returned to Galesburg, attended Lombard College, but left without a degree. He pursued journalistic work and become a staunch member of the Socialist Party, through which he met his future wife, Lillian (Paula) Steichen, sister of the great photographer, Edward Steichen. Paula, a university graduate, encouraged Sandburg in his writing, especially his poetry.

In 1916 Sandburg had his first real taste of success as a poet with the publication of the publicly acclaimed volume, *Chicago Poems* (1916); the title poem, "Chicago," attracted popular attention. In it, he describes the city as "stormy, husky, brawling . . . a crooked brutal place." He pictured the people of the city with a harsh reality: prostitutes, gangsters, and exploited factory workers and their families starving on low wages. Sandburg's Chicago, however, for all its coarseness and cruelty, was "alive . . . strong . . . cunning." The poet received negative reviews from critics, but encouraging mail from ordinary Americans proved that his works had their support. This situation prevailed more than once during his long and prolific career, but he had more success with *Cornhuskers* (1918) and *Smoke and Steel* (1920).

A CHAMPION FOR AMERICANS

Sandburg was a great storyteller, and his *Rootabaga Stories* (1922) were written for children. When he felt his old wanderlust during this period, he began touring the country as a lecturer and folksinger, accompanying himself on his guitar. He also collected folk songs and folk tales that he published as *American Songbag* (1927). Returning to poetry in "The People Yes" (1936), he expressed his belief in Americans at a time when they needed a champion. His hope for the future lay in the common people. In her biography of Sandburg, Penelope Niven suggests that, in the process, he became "the passionate champion of people who did not have the words or power to speak for themselves."

The historical writings of Sandburg were the most important twentieth-century factor in Abraham Lincoln's continuing popularity. In 1940 Sandburg received the Pulitzer

Prize for his four-volume biography, *Lincoln: The War Years*, published in 1939. For once Sandburg's critics were silenced by the immediate success of the massive work, in which he defines Lincoln as an ordinary person—no idealist, but a beleaguered man struggling to make the right decisions under pressure. Sandburg examines the inside of the government during a time of crisis in American history and reveals his faith in Lincoln as a representative of the American spirit of democracy. Together with his earlier two-volume biography, *Lincoln: the Prairie Years*, (1926), the word count outstripped that of the collected works of William Shakespeare.

Sandburg's total commitment to World War II led to his greatest undertaking, the novel *Remembrance Rock* (1948), which spans American experience from Plymouth Rock to World War II and beyond. The book was a labor of love for its author but was never acclaimed as a literary success. He was awarded a second Pulitzer Prize for his *Complete Poems* (1950), and in 1953 he wrote an autobiography, *Always the Young Strangers*. Niven describes Sandburg's life as "an odyssey into the American experience. He helped the American people discover their national identity through songs, poems and that mythical national hero, Abraham Lincoln."

Together with Robert Frost and William Carlos Williams, Sandburg stands as one of the greatest and best-loved poets of the twentieth century. He died on July 22, 1967, and his ashes were buried at his birthplace in Galesburg, beneath a granite boulder called Remembrance Rock.

Joan Gajadhar

SEE ALSO: *Frost, Robert; The Great Depression; The Twenties; World War I; World War II.*

BIBLIOGRAPHY

Mitchell, Roger. "Modernism Comes to American Poetry: 1908–1920." In *A Profile of Twentieth-Century American Poetry*, ed. Jack Myers and David Wojahn. Carbondale: Southern Illinois University Press, 1991.

Niven, Penelope. *Carl Sandburg: A Biography*. New York: Scribner, 1991.

Sandburg, Carl. *Chicago Poems*. New York: Henry Holt, 1916.

Yannella, Philip. *The Other Carl Sandburg*. Jackson: University Press of Mississippi, 1996.

Sanders, Barry *(1968–)*

While many people argue whether or not he was the best ever or even the best of his decade, Barry Sanders of the Detroit Lions was perhaps the most intriguing running back in the National Football League (NFL) during the 1990s. His productivity and his personality made him a star athlete during both his amateur and professional careers.

Because of his height (5 feet 8 inches), Sanders's high school football coaches rarely let him play in the running back position. When he was given the opportunity, however, his natural abilities, reflected in outstanding statistics, helped him gain a scholarship to Oklahoma State University. In 1988 he won the Heisman Trophy, awarded each year to the country's best college football player. The next year he was drafted by the Detroit Lions—as the third overall pick.

Sanders's consistent productivity on the football field was incredible; he averaged more than 100 rushing yards for every game in which he played. Despite never playing for a championship team, his remarkable on-the-field production—achieved through a combination of power, speed, and tremendous agility—made him an all-pro selection every year of his playing career and brought him many postseason awards, including being named the NFL's Most Valuable Player in 1997.

Yet, Sanders may be best known for his humility during an era of professional sports dominated by outspoken and self-absorbed players constantly trying to increase their wealth. According to Paul Attner of the *Sporting News*, Sanders preferred a lifestyle that was "neither flamboyant nor extravagant," which was why he consistently turned down lucrative endorsement opportunities. In the final game of one season, Sanders even took himself out of the game in the closing minutes despite being close to setting the season rushing record. He later explained that the personal achievement meant little to him, and he wanted to let his backup have a chance to play.

Accentuated by his quiet demeanor, the leadership, modesty, and family values exhibited by Sanders made him not just a great athlete but a uniquely humble superstar. Prior to the 1999 season, in a surprising move, Sanders retired from playing professional football for the Detroit Lions, claiming that he had lost his drive to play. Since his retirement, he has, unlike nearly all his contemporaries, remained away from the game and out of the media spotlight. He was inducted into the Pro Football Hall of Fame in 2004.

Randall McClure

SEE ALSO: *College Football; National Football League (NFL); Professional Football; Sports Heroes.*

BIBLIOGRAPHY

Attner, Paul. "Be Like Barry." *Sporting News*, September 7, 1998, 16–25.

Guss, Greg. "The Father, the Son, and the Holy Numbers." *Sport*, September 1998, 70–75.

Gutman, Bill. *Barry Sanders: Football's Rushing Champ*. Brookfield, CT: Millbrook Press, 1993.

Hinton, Ed. "Cut and Run." *Sports Illustrated*, December 5, 1994, 36–46.

Kavanagh, Jack. *Barry Sanders: Rocket Running Back*. Minneapolis, MN: Lerner Publications, 1994.

Sanders, Barry, and Mark McCormick. *Barry Sanders: Now You See Him*. Indianapolis, IN: B. Sanders in conjunction with Emmis Books, 2003.

Sandman

In 1989 a comic book hit the shelves that would change the way fans, critics, and even the indifferent would view the industry. Its title was *Sandman*, its hero Morpheus. At the height of its popularity, sales of *Sandman* rivaled, and frequently exceeded, those of individual *Superman* or *Batman* titles, the two reliable top sellers for its parent company, DC Comics. The series and its British author, Neil Gaiman, won praise from critics both within and without the comic-book industry; even

Norman Mailer hailed it as a literary achievement. Among its many awards, the most notable might be the World Fantasy Award, which no comic book had ever won before, and which—as a result of rule changes after *Sandman*'s win—no comic book is likely to win again.

The publication consistently sold over a million copies a year and remained one of the most stable modern titles in the speculators' market. The individual issues became so scarce and valuable that DC released collections of the issues in hardback to meet the demands of new readers. In 2006 new, oversized leatherbound *Absolute* editions were released with some retouching and recoloring with Gaiman's approval.

Sandman tells the story of a godlike being who is captured by a group of occultists. He frees himself in the first issue; the rest of the series continues to analyze a large diversity of issues, unafraid to tackle concepts that had previously been taboo for comic books.

UNPRECEDENTED POPULARITY

What is most astounding about *Sandman*'s success is that it was achieved in a fraction of the time it has generally taken other champions of the genre to reach high levels of popularity. *Sandman* ran for under a decade—a blink of an eye compared to *Superman*'s half-century or the *X-Men*'s thirty-plus years—and went to a voluntary grave at issue number 75. Within its pages Gaiman and a host of groundbreaking visual artists floated away from conventional comics with only the thinnest of umbilical cords connecting their work to the mainstream. "There's definitely a level on which *Sandman* is my creating a superhero I'd be happy writing," Gaiman has said. "One of the things I like best about Sandman is all the wonderful powers he has . . . and they really have nothing to do with anything. They don't get used much, because he doesn't go around doing things heroically." In fact, the title character—Morpheus, an enigmatic symbol of the realm of dreams—often appears only at the fringes of the tale. Because of the protagonist's unique perspective on reality and history, the stories can be told from nearly any point of view and at any point in human history.

The themes Gaiman chose also push the envelope. He reached an adult audience, a demographic that could not have been depended on before the 1980s, and crafted tales that featured homosexuals, alternate histories, unreliable narrators, and an intricately told story that began in the first issue and is explored from a multitude of angles. All this is done within stories structured with careful attention to good storytelling, and readers responded accordingly. "Very few people seem to turn around and say, 'This comic has lesbians in it,'" Gaiman reported. "What they tend to say is, 'This comic has really good people in it.'"

As one critic has pointed out, "Although Gaiman's talent shouldn't be downplayed, it should be noted that his breed of story owes some of its success to the mood of the times, an environment where stories of coincidence and unseen powers fill a nagging cultural need." Gaiman has often stressed that the conclusion of the story in issue 75 is the same story that begins, despite various digressions, in issue 1. In the first issue, Morpheus is stripped of his godhood and forced to reevaluate humanity precisely at the moment Generation X is questioning the bourgeois values it has been asked to accept from the generations before it.

EFFECT ON THE COMIC-BOOK INDUSTRY

What is perhaps most important to the field of popular culture is how *Sandman* affected the comic-book industry. Stanley Wiater and Stephen R. Bissette, in their *Comic Book Rebels*, say of Gaiman that he is "representative of a new order of creators. Cosmopolitan and nomadic, they successfully maintain their creative autonomy while demanding the respect of their chosen publishers through a clear sense of who they are, what they are worth, and a canny blend of independence and diplomacy."

This new breed of comic-book creators was revolutionary in that, for most of comic-book history, creators who worked for major publishers wrote within the bounds set by their editors and were divested of any right to influence the character created once the individual story was finished. Characters that proved popular would not reap rewards for the creator but instead for the publisher who owned the copyright through work-for-hire laws. *Sandman*, under what was almost exclusively Gaiman's guidance, became so popular that, as Wiater and Bissette note, "the first year of its run led to DC's granting a historically unprecedented (and retroactive) creative co-ownership and share of the character and title, including all licensing and foreign sales—rights and revenue DC had always denied creators."

Gaiman's creativity and sheer storytelling power seemed to increase with the continuing monetary rewards, and *Sandman*'s following swelled. Many retailers have credited *Sandman* with reaching female fans in a readership that had always been largely male. As the comic's fan base swelled, DC saw that there was a large market for comic books written for adults. and in 1993, a handful of years after *Sandman*'s debut, the company launched Vertigo, a new imprint that has since produced some of the comic-book world's most promising titles. *Preacher*, *Y: The Last Man*, and *Fables* in particular have enjoyed success through the high-profile creative atmosphere provided by Vertigo, and though *Sandman* finished its run in 1996, Vertigo guaranteed that its influence would continue well into the future.

Joe Sutliff Sanders

SEE ALSO: *Batman; Comic Books; DC Comics; Graphic Novels; Superman; The X-Men.*

BIBLIOGRAPHY

Rauch, Stephen. *Neil Gaiman's The Sandman and Joseph Campbell: In Search of the Modern Myth*. Holicong, PA: Wildside Press, 2003.

Wiater, Stanley, and Stephen R. Bissette. *Comic Book Rebels: Conversations with the Creators of the New Comics*. New York: Donald I. Fine, 1993.

Sandow, Eugen *(1867–1925)*

Although a native of Königsberg, Germany, Eugen Sandow left an indelible mark on American life. Born Friedrich Wilhelm Müller on April 2, 1867, he became one of the most popular and influential men of his age worldwide because of his activities that gave rise to the modern conceptualization of what we now term bodybuilding. Sandow traveled Europe as an acrobat, an artist's model, and a wrestler before achieving prominence in England as a strongman/physique artist in the latter stages of the nineteenth century.

Eugen Sandow. *Eugen Sandow was a leader in the "physical culture" movement at the turn of the twentieth century, a precursor to what is known today as bodybuilding.* © HULTON-DEUTSCH COLLECTION/CORBIS.

While Sandow's stage act consisted of the standard weightlifting feats of the era's strongmen, he achieved his greatest recognition for artistic physique posing, in which he displayed hitherto unseen muscular definition and vascularity. In contrast to the barrel-chested and pot-bellied weightlifters of the era, he popularized a new physical ideal that captured the imagination of men and women at the turn of the twentieth century. Appearing onstage in nothing but a pair of briefs or posing for physique photographs clad only in a fig leaf, Sandow offered an aesthetically appealing, scantily clad, sexualized physique that challenged the repressive conventions of the late Victorian age.

PHYSICAL CULTURE MOVEMENT LEADER

A leading figure of the late-nineteenth- and early-twentieth-century "physical culture" movement, Sandow became one of the most recognized and influential men of his generation. Far from being merely a strongman, or what later generations would term a sex symbol, he branched out into lecturing and publishing, penning five full-length books and innumerable pamphlets and brochures, as well as editing a physical culture publication, *Sandow's Magazine*, from 1898 to 1907. While not regarded as a leading academic in any sense, he espoused theories that were considered scientific, and he was respected for his practical knowledge of physiology and medicine.

Sandow's interplay with the scientific and medical authorities extended throughout his professional career. His system of weightlifting and physical fitness was endorsed by a great number of physicians, including blood pressure diagnostics pioneer Sir Lauder Brunton. In December 1892 Sandow's exhibition before army cadets was the subject of an article in the medical journal the *Lancet*. He was examined by Harvard professor and medical doctor Dudley Sargent, considered the "dean of American physical educators," and was judged to be "the most perfectly developed man in the world." Sargent then invited Sandow to lecture the students at Harvard, an offer that the strongman took up in 1902. He was also selected by the British Museum to represent the Caucasian race in the natural history branch's Races of the World exhibit. His crowning achievement in the field of medico-bodybuilding, however, came when he was named "Professor of Scientific and Physical Culture" to King George V in 1911.

POP CULTURE ICON

While cementing his reputation as a scientistic, if not scientific, entity, Sandow also advanced his career as a popular cultural icon. Having achieved widespread acclaim as a stage star touring the United States with impresario Florenz Ziegfeld Jr., he was invited by Thomas Edison to star in one of the inventor's Kinetoscope films. On March 10, 1894, Sandow waived his $250 appearance fee to shake the hand of Edison—who he considered "the greatest man of the age"—and to become the star of one of the first moving pictures. He later went on to star in big-screen shorts produced by Edison's rival, the American Mutoscope and Biograph Company.

Along with his on-screen exploits, Sandow continued to travel as a stage performer. He incorporated into his act a glass-case posing routine, whereby he would occupy a glass enclosure with a rotating pedestal, which allowed the audience a voyeuristic total view of the bodybuilder's physique. After touring Europe, the British Isles, and the United States, where he was a star attraction at the 1893 Columbian Exposition in Chicago, Sandow set out to take his brand of physical culture and his trademark physique to the rest of the world. In the first few years of the twentieth century, he toured Australia and New Zealand, preaching his sermon on bodybuilding, and embarked upon a grand tour of South Africa, India, China, Japan, Java, and Burma. He brought along an entire troupe of performing athletes and a tent that could comfortably accommodate 6,000 people for his exhibitions in areas lacking appropriate theatrical facilities.

While Sandow is noted for his own stage performances, he also organized the first major bodybuilding competition, the so-called Great Competition of 1901, in Great Britain. Gathering together the foremost British physique artists, he hosted a pageant where, together with sculptor Charles Lawes and Sherlock Holmes creator Sir Arthur Conan Doyle, he set about determining the most perfectly developed man in the British Isles. Before a capacity crowd of 15,000 spectators, Sandow put forth an exhibition the likes of which had never been seen. After a parade of athletes, marching to a musical composition written by Sandow, a performance by a boys' choir, wrestling, gymnastics, fencing, exercise displays, and an exhibition by the premier bodybuilder himself, bronze, silver, and gold statuettes of Sandow were given to those judged to have the three best physiques.

Though age began to take its toll on the athlete's musculature, Sandow was a very popular figure well into the early decades of the twentieth century. His likeness was used to sell numerous products, from exercisers and dime novels to cocoa and cigars, and he remained active in his adopted homeland of Great Britain through publishing and public speaking. While preparing for a lecture tour of Britain in 1925, he fell ill and was forced to cancel his plans. Hazy details surround his ailment, and when he died at the age of fifty-eight on October 14, 1925, newspaper accounts stated that he suffered a burst blood vessel in his brain after attempting to single-handedly pull an automobile out of a ditch. The story was questioned at the time and is still in question today. Sandow's biographer, David Chapman, speculates that the strongman's death may have been the result of an aortic aneurysm brought about by syphilis.

Nicholas Turse

SEE ALSO: *Bodybuilding; Doyle, Arthur Conan; Edison, Thomas Alva; Sex Symbol;* The Ziegfeld Follies.

BIBLIOGRAPHY

Budd, Michael A. *The Sculpture Machine: Physical Culture and Body Politics in the Age of Empire*. New York: New York University Press, 1997.

Chapman, David L. *Sandow the Magnificent: Eugen Sandow and the Beginnings of Bodybuilding*. Urbana: University of Illinois, 1994.

Daley, Caroline. *Leisure & Pleasure: Reshaping & Revealing the New Zealand Body 1900–1960*. Auckland, New Zealand: Auckland University Press, 2003.

Dutton, Kenneth R. *The Perfectible Body: The Western Ideal of Male Physical Development*. New York: Continuum, 1995.

Green, Harvey. *Fit for America: Health, Fitness, Sport and American Society*. New York: Pantheon Books, 1986.

Sanford and Son

The NBC television sitcom *Sanford and Son* was created by writer-director and independent producer Norman Lear, whose lengthy list of successful, award-winning, and sometimes provocative television programs revolutionized prime-time television during the 1970s. *Sanford and Son* chronicled the escapades of Fred G. Sanford, a cantankerous widower living with his thirty-something son, Lamont, played by Demond Wilson, in the Watts section of Los Angeles, California. *Sanford and Son* was the first program with African Americans in the leading roles to air on prime-time American television since the cancellation of *The Amos 'n' Andy Show* in 1953.

Airing from 1972 to 1977, *Sanford and Son* was the American version of a British program called *Steptoe & Son*, which featured the exploits of a Cockney father-and-son junkman team. In the starring role of *Sanford and Son* was veteran actor-comedian John Elroy Sanford, popularly known as Redd Foxx, whose bawdy recordings and racy nightclub routines had influenced generations of comics since the 1950s. Foxx was born in St. Louis, Missouri, and began his career in the late 1930s performing street acts. By the 1960s he was headlining in Las Vegas. In 1970 Foxx earned a role as an aging junk dealer in the motion picture *Cotton Comes to Harlem*. This portrayal brought him to the attention of Lear, who was casting his newest show, *Sanford and Son*.

In addition to its two stars—Foxx and Wilson—*Sanford and Son* featured a unique multiracial cast of regular and occasional characters who served as the butt of Sanford's often bigoted jokes and insults, including Bubba (Don Bexly), Smitty the cop (Hal Williams), Grady (Mayo Whitman), Julio (Gregory Sierra), Rollo (Nathaniel Taylor), and Ah Chew (Pat Morita). LaWanda Page played "evil and ugly" Aunt Esther, Fred's archenemy. Their constant bickering and put-downs of each other provided some of the funniest moments in the show. "I'm convinced that *Sanford and Son* shows middle class America a lot of what they need to know," Foxx said in a 1973 interview. "The show . . . doesn't drive home a lesson, but it can open up people's minds enough for them to see how stupid every kind of prejudice can be."

The feigned heart attack routine became a trademark of the series as Fred, pretending to have a heart attack, clasped his chest in mock pain and threatened to join his deceased wife, saying, "I'm coming to join you, Elizabeth!" Foxx's enormously funny portrayal quickly earned *Sanford and Son* a place among the top ten most-watched programs to air on NBC television.

In 1977 Foxx walked out on the production of his enormously successful show, complaining that the mostly white producers and writers had little regard or understanding of African American life. He lambasted the total absence of black writers or directors on the crew. Moreover, he was dissatisfied with his treatment as the star of the program. Believing that his efforts were not appreciated, he left NBC for his own variety show on ABC. The program barely lasted one season. After Foxx left *Sanford and Son*, a pseudo spin-off, *Sanford Arms*, proved unsuccessful and it too lasted only one season.

Pamala S. Deane

SEE ALSO: The Amos 'n' Andy Show*; Foxx, Redd; Lear, Norman; Sitcom; Television.*

BIBLIOGRAPHY

Barnouw, Erik. *Tube of Plenty*. Oxford, UK: Oxford University Press, 1982.

Brooks, Tim, and Earle Marsh. *The Complete Directory of Prime Time Network and Cable TV Shows, 1946–Present*, 6th ed. New York: Ballantine Books, 1995.

MacDonald, J. Fred. *Blacks and White TV: African Americans in Television since 1948*, 2nd ed. Chicago: Nelson-Hall Publishers, 1992.

Marc, David, and Robert J. Thompson. *Prime Time, Prime Movers: From "I Love Lucy" to "L.A. Law," America's Greatest TV Shows and People Who Created Them*. Boston: Little, Brown, 1992.

Robinson, Louie. "*Sanford and Son*: Redd Foxx and Demond Wilson Wake Up TV's Jaded Audience." *Ebony*, July 1972.

Tafoya, Eddie M. *Icons of African American Comedy*. Santa Barbara, CA: Greenwood Press, 2011.

Santana

Led by virtuoso guitarist Carlos Santana (1947–), the band Santana has been one of the most successful mainstream ethnic fusion acts in rock history, topping the charts since the 1960s with its signature blend of Latin and African sounds. Carlos Santana grew up to the distinctive mariachi sounds of his native Tijuana, Mexico. As a teenager in the 1950s, he became fascinated by the R&B and rock-and-roll sounds he heard on the radio. When he learned to play guitar he fused these disparate traditions into an exciting and unique sound that became his trademark.

In the mid-1960s Carlos moved to San Francisco, where he and other local musicians formed the Santana Blues Band, later shortened to Santana. The group—featuring Carlos (guitar), Gregg Rolie (vocals and keyboards), Dave Brown (bass), Mike Shrieve (drums), Armando Peraza (percussion and vocals), Mike Carabello (percussion), and José Areas (percussion)—first gained recognition in the same dance halls that hosted psychedelic rock groups of the era such as the Grateful Dead and Jefferson Airplane. Santana's blend of Latin and African sounds was ill suited to the acid rock scene, but the group's frenetic performances captivated hippie audiences across the Bay Area. Under the direction of concert promoter Bill Graham, Santana landed a spot at the Woodstock Festival in New York, where the band's tour de force performance lodged Santana in the mainstream consciousness before the group had even recorded an album.

Santana released its first album, *Evil Ways*, in 1969. The title track from that debut effort reached the Top 10—an unprecedented feat given the song's overt Latin sound. The group's 1970 single "Black Magic Woman" enjoyed similar mass appeal and pushed their second album, *Abraxas*, to the top of the charts for six weeks. *Santana III* (1971) likewise topped the charts and established Santana as a major force in the recording industry.

The band underwent frequent personnel changes during the remainder of the decade. Carlos brought drummer Buddy Miles and guitarist John McLaughlin into the fold while original vocalist Rolie, along with newer member Neil Schon, departed to form the highly successful band Journey. Despite their internal flux, Santana continued to release such stellar albums as *Amigos* (1976) and *Moonflower* (1977), as well as hit singles such as the group's 1977 cover of the Zombies' "She's Not There."

The band continued recording but more often than not Carlos's supporting cast was a revolving set of hired session musicians. Nevertheless, the group's signature sound remained intact and relevant. In 1987 the group took part in Rock and Roll Summit, the first joint American and Soviet rock concert in history, and seven years later Santana made a triumphant return to the Woodstock II anniversary concert in New York. In 1998 Santana—the original lineup—was inducted into the Rock and Roll Hall of Fame. By 2010 the band had earned eight Grammy Awards and three Latin Grammy Awards. In 2012 they began a two-year engagement at the House of Blues in Las Vegas, Nevada.

Carlos has also had a successful solo career. He achieved great commercial success with the release of *Supernatural* (1999). Featuring a litany of guest artists, including Rob Thomas of Matchbox Twenty, Eric Clapton, Cee Lo, and Dave Matthews, the album won multiple Grammy Awards and went fifteen times platinum. He followed this format on his next records, *Shaman* (2002) and *All That I Am* (2005). Although neither album experienced the success of *Supernatural*, the collaborations produced numerous radio singles, including "The Game of Love" with Michelle Branch and "Just Feel Better" with Steven Tyler. He performed the Oscar-winning song "Al Otro Lado del Rio" with Antonio Banderas at the 77th Academy Awards. With his renewed success, Santana launched the Supernatural Santana—A Trip through the Hits tour in 2009.

Carlos made headlines in 2011 when he criticized a decision by the National Academy of Recording Arts and Sciences to cut or consolidate several Latin music categories from the Grammy Awards. He claimed that the decision was racist since the academy did not cut categories for rock and country.

Scott Tribble

SEE ALSO: *Academy Awards; Clapton, Eric; Grammy Awards; The Grateful Dead; Hippies; Jefferson Airplane/Starship; Las Vegas; Latin Jazz; Mariachi Music; Psychedelia; Rhythm and Blues; Rock and Roll; Woodstock.*

BIBLIOGRAPHY

Shapiro, Marc. *Carlos Santana: Back on Top*. New York: St. Martin's Griffin, 2002.

Weinstein, Norman. *Carlos Santana: A Biography*. Santa Barbara, CA: ABC-CLIO, 2009.

Sarandon, Susan *(1946–)*

Susan Sarandon is an accomplished actress who began her long career when she was in her twenties. She got her first role in a movie when she accompanied her actor husband, Chris Sarandon, to an audition for the movie *Joe* (1970). While his audition was unsuccessful, she walked out with a small role. Several minor appearances in movies and extended stints on daytime television led to her first major role in the cult film *The Rocky Horror Picture Show* (1975). Sarandon then went on to play a number of erotic parts in movies such as *Pretty Baby* (1978) and *Atlantic City* (1980), both directed by Louis Malle, and *The Hunger* (1983), in which she has a lesbian love scene with actress Catherine Deneuve. Sarandon received her first Academy Award nomination for Best Actress for her performance in *Atlantic City* (1980).

Sarandon worked steadily through the 1980s, appearing in *Compromising Positions* (1985) and *The Witches of Eastwick* (1987). Her performance as a baseball groupie in *Bull Durham* (1988), a wildly successful retro baseball story, led to more high-profile roles. In the early 1990s Sarandon, now in her forties, became a household name for her portrayal of Louise in the massive blockbuster *Thelma & Louise*. Directed by Ridley Scott, the movie features two friends whose getaway weekend in a '66 Thunderbird becomes a cross-country road trip and crime spree after Louise shoots and kills a man trying to rape Thelma. Noted for its frank depiction of sexual violence and the reduced social roles of women, the movie was nominated for six Academy Awards, including a Best Actress nomination for Sarandon.

Throughout the 1990s Sarandon took on a number of high-profile roles, including a high-class drug dealer in *Light Sleeper* (1992); a mother searching for a cure for her child's rare disease in *Lorenzo's Oil* (1992); the beloved Marmee in a film adaptation of Louisa May Alcott's book, *Little Women* (1994); and a tough attorney in *The Client* (1994), and she received Academy Award nominations for Best Actress for *Lorenzo's Oil* and *The Client*. Sarandon received her fifth nomination for Best Actress, and her first Academy Award, for her performance as Sister Helen Prejean in *Dead Man Walking* (1996), the true story of the nun's visits to a death row inmate in the final days of his life. In the first decade of the 2000s Sarandon appeared in a number of less prominent films, including *Elizabethtown* (2005), *Romance & Cigarettes* (2005), and *The Lovely Bones* (2009).

Sarandon is an activist as well as an actress. She has championed progressive politics and been involved in a number of social and political causes since her teenage years, when she was arrested for participating in civil rights and antiwar protests. She actively uses her public profile to bring awareness to sensitive political issues, often focusing on opposition to violence and support of equal rights under the law. Over the years Sarandon has spoken out, marched, and raised money in support of reproductive rights, equal rights, and domestic programs to help the homeless and mentally ill; she has protested a succession of wars prosecuted by the United States and is an outspoken critic of nuclear weapons.

Sarandon became particularly notorious for her public opposition to the 1991 Persian Gulf War, an unpopular and controversial stance. She also notably used the 1993 Academy Awards ceremony to plea for aid and asylum for Haitian refugees. Sarandon's political activism is also evident in her film work. She starred in *Bob Roberts* (1992), a satire of political lobbyists, and she contributed to several documentary projects, including *And This Is What Democracy Looks Like* (2000), an account of the 1999 World Trade Organization meeting in Seattle.

Sarandon's marriage to Chris Sarandon lasted for twelve years, and, when it ended, she became adamantly opposed to marriage, telling an interviewer for *Cosmopolitan* magazine that "I no longer believe in marriage." After several long-term relationships, including liaisons with Malle and Italian director Franco Amurri, with whom she had a daughter in 1985, Sarandon had a twenty-three-year relationship with actor, writer, and director Tim Robbins. They have two sons. The couple split up in 2009.

Courtney Bennett

SEE ALSO: *Academy Awards; Civil Rights Movement;* Cosmopolitan*; Divorce;* The Rocky Horror Picture Show*; Scott, Ridley.*

BIBLIOGRAPHY

Blau, E. "Susan Sarandon's Roughest Role." *New York Times*, January 14, 1983.

Neuman, B. "Susan Sarandon: Lover, Lawyer, Marmee." *New York Times*, July 17, 1994.

Shapiro, Marc. *Susan Sarandon: Actress-Activist.* Amherst, NY: Prometheus Books, 2001.

Tucker, Betty Jo. *Susan Sarandon: A True Maverick.* Tucson, AZ: Hats Off Books, 2004.

Saratoga Springs

Throughout the twentieth and twenty-first centuries this upstate New York summer resort has jumbled together invalids, nouveau-riche social climbers, fastidious old-money sports people, and both hard-core and petty gamblers. A nineteenth-century health resort featuring carbonated waters, the village began promoting summer horse racing in 1863, and the Saratoga racetrack now holds the distinction of being the oldest racetrack still in existence in the United States. Saratoga's reputation as a distinctive American congeries was spread in such disparate novels as Edith Wharton's unfinished *The Buccaneers* (1938), Edna Ferber's *Saratoga Trunk* (1945; the movie version starred Gary Cooper and Ingrid Bergman), and E. L. Doctorow's *Billy Bathgate* (1989). The Kefauver investigation (1950) ended a century of public gaming, but the horse racing continues unabated and, unlike similar resorts, Saratoga underwent a popular renaissance during the 1970s. It continued to thrive in the 1990s as "the summer place to be," entertaining an appealingly raffish mix attracted to health, history, horses, and the Saratoga Performing Arts Center, which hosts an annual Saratoga Native American Festival and is also the summer venue for the New York City Ballet. Saratoga Springs boasted a 2010 population of 26,586.

Jon Sterngass

SEE ALSO: *Bergman, Ingrid; Cooper, Gary; Doctorow, E. L.; Gambling; Leisure Time; Wharton, Edith.*

BIBLIOGRAPHY

Andrews, Peter. *Saratoga: The Place and Its People.* New York: Harry Abrams, 1988.

Corbett, Theodore. *The Making of American Resorts: Saratoga Springs, Ballston Spa, and Lake George.* New Brunswick, NJ: Rutgers University Press, 2001.

Holmes, Timothy A., and Martha Stonequist. *Saratoga Springs: A Historical Portrait.* Charleston, SC: Arcadia, 2000.

Waller, George. *Saratoga: Saga of an Impious Era.* Englewood Cliffs, NJ: Prentice Hall, 1966.

Sarnoff, David *(1891–1971)*

A significant innovator in the field of communications, particularly in radio and television, David Sarnoff's influence is indelibly stamped on the cultural development of these media. In creating the National Broadcasting Company (NBC) as the first permanent network, he invented commercial broadcasting as we know it. Sarnoff clearly valued technology and foresaw uses for it beyond the understanding of his contemporaries. In doing so, he helped to propel television from the domain of experimentation to one of global status.

Sarnoff was born in Uzlian, near Minsk, in what is now Belarus. His family immigrated to New York in 1900, and the young Sarnoff was raised in Lower Manhattan's Hell's Kitchen district. In 1906 he was employed as an office worker by the Marconi Wireless Telegraph Company and soon after became a telegrapher. He was first noticed as the lone radioman to relay news from the sinking *Titanic* to the rest of the world. He advanced rapidly, and in 1915 presented his idea for a radio receiving set to the company.

In 1919, at the age of twenty-eight, Sarnoff became commercial manager of the Radio Corporation of America (RCA) when it absorbed Marconi. He contradicted the current thinking that radio had no application beyond military and corporate use by proposing the "radio music box," a home radio that could receive entertainment programming. Initially, the radio manufacturers financed programming production, but increasing costs led Sarnoff, together with General Electric (GE) and West-

David Sarnoff. *David Sarnoff launched the era of network broadcasting when he founded the National Broadcasting Company (NBC), the first advertiser-sponsored national radio network, in 1926.* BACHRACH/CONTRIBUTOR/ARCHIVE PHOTOS/GETTY IMAGES.

inghouse, to organize NBC as part of RCA in 1926. Thus, the first advertiser-sponsored national radio network was born, and radio was thereafter established as the medium for home entertainment.

In 1930 Sarnoff became president of RCA and, with radio firmly established, concentrated his energies on the development of television. He masterminded the independence of RCA from GE and Westinghouse and acquired the Victor Company as a manufacturing base for his assault on the television market. In 1939 he demonstrated television as a new industry at the World's Fair. The onset of World War II, however, caused a temporary hiatus in RCA's advance into television research. Once the war ended, Sarnoff turned back to marketing his new visual technology and spearheaded the development of color television. In 1947 he became chairman of the board of RCA.

Sarnoff was also an enthusiastic partner for governmental initiatives. Prior to World War II he had overseen RCA's total conversion to defense production, and during the war he offered his services to the military and was appointed General Dwight D. Eisenhower's chief of communications. He organized and coordinated all radio communications on the Western front, and in recognition of his services, he was named a brigadier general in the U.S. Army. Sarnoff's involvement with government projects did not end with the war. He was an energetic participant in the Cold War struggle against the Soviet Union; indeed, with the onset of the Cold War, his involvement with the government deepened as he submitted regular proposals to the administration for fighting communism. He also advised Radio Free Europe and Radio Liberation, whose staff members trained at NBC studios. At his suggestion, *Voice of America* adopted the sign-off, "This is the Voice of America, for freedom and peace." RCA also cooperated with the U.S. Information Agency to produce advertising that would sell its own products while also promoting America.

Sarnoff died in 1971, but he will be remembered by many as the "father of television." His faith in technology and his support for innovation led to the creation of modern radio and television commercial broadcasting in a manner and on a scale that his contemporaries could not have foreseen, and he has been immortalized by the communications industry.

Nathan Abrams

SEE ALSO: *Cold War; Radio; Television; World War II.*

BIBLIOGRAPHY

Barnouw, Erik. *The Image Empire: A History of Broadcasting in the United States, from 1953, Volume III.* New York: Oxford University Press, 1970.

Bilby, Kenneth W. *The General: David Sarnoff and the Rise of the Communications Industry.* New York: Harper & Row, 1986.

Lyons, Eugene. *David Sarnoff.* Pyramid Books, 1977.

Myers, Elisabeth P. *David Sarnoff: Radio and TV Boy.* Indianapolis, IN: Bobbs Merrill, 1972.

Noll, A. Michael. *Principles of Modern Communications Technology.* Boston: Artech House, 2001.

Sarnoff, David. *Looking Ahead: The Papers of David Sarnoff.* New York: McGraw-Hill, 1968.

Sasquatch

SEE: *Bigfoot.*

Sassoon, Vidal *(1928–2012)*

Home to fashion mecca Carnaby Street and rock-and-roll sensations the Beatles, London of the 1960s had another important claim to fame: hairstylist Vidal Sassoon. Perhaps no revolution was more important for women of the era than Sassoon's invention of the bob and other easy hairstyles, which freed ladies from weekly visits to the beauty parlor and from the stiff, heavy, fixed hairstyles of prior generations. Sassoon's new ideal of beauty was literally care free, and for most women his styles needed to be touched up only once a month.

His abiding principle was geometry, letting the hair move naturally, as typified by the hairstyles of the Beatles. Having freed women from the beauty parlor and nights of sleeping with curlers on their heads, Sassoon became emblematic of liberation and sensible, good health. He created the first worldwide chain of styling salons and an international line of hair-treatment products, also becoming a television talk show host and celebrity. A 2010 documentary film on his life and work, *Vidal Sassoon: The Movie*, tells the story of how he became a household name for spearheading the wash-and-wear revolution.

Richard Martin

BIBLIOGRAPHY

Fishman, Diane, and Marcia Powell. *Vidal Sassoon: Fifty Years Ahead*. New York: Rizzoli, 1993.

Sassoon, Vidal. *Vidal Sassoon: The Autobiography*. London: Macmillan, 2011.

Vidal Sassoon: The Movie. Directed by Craig Teper. DVD. Toronto: Phase 4 Films, 2010.

Sassy

Launched in 1988 in the midday heat of conservative Reagan America, *Sassy* was the first magazine aimed at teenage girls and young women to deal frankly with the fact that its readership—despite statutory rape laws, remaining cultural taboos against premarital sex, parental strictures, and limited access to adequate birth control—might indeed be engaging in sexual activity. Instead of addressing the topic of boys and physical attraction in moralistic tones, *Sassy*'s writers tried to provide a realistic viewpoint along with coherent, practical advice, and it forced its competition to do the same. "What *Sassy* did—to its everlasting shame or credit, depending on one's point of view—was to suggest not only that these teenage girls had sexual lives but that it was a proper editorial mission for a magazine to address their urgent informational needs about sex," write Kathleen L. Endres and Therese L. Lueck in *Women's Periodicals in the United States*. "Perhaps unsurprisingly," the authors continue, *Sassy* became "an immediate success with its teenage readers."

When *Sassy* debuted in early 1988, statistics indicated a population of 14 million young American women aged fourteen to nineteen, with only about 30 percent of that figure purchasing or reading the typical teen fare for females: *YM*, *Seventeen*, and *Teen*, all holdovers from a more virginal era. *Sassy*'s publishers also recognized the potential force of this captive audience in the realm of advertising dollars: because many teens were being raised in households with two working parents, a combination of guilt and affluence led to a greater "income" level for such young women. With their allowances and access to parental credit cards, they spent an average of $65 a week on clothes and cosmetics. Advertisers were excited at the prospect of reaching such a malleable demographic—buyers with vast leisure time and a desire to conform through consumerism.

Sassy was a knockoff of a successful Australian publication named *Dolly* but was toned down for its American readership. Key to its success was a young, iconoclastic editor to head it, and Fairfax, Ltd., the American branch of the Australian media company, found one in Jane Pratt, the twenty-four-year-old granddaughter of a onetime executive at Doubleday with a liberal arts degree and a documented wild streak. Pratt had grown up reading teen magazines and had some experience in the field at a few failed publications. Perhaps more importantly, she had undergone a rough time as a teen after being shipped off to an elite boarding school. She would later say the incident traumatized her so much that she would remain stuck at that age for the rest of her life.

Sassy set itself apart from its major competition in its very first issue in March 1988. Unlike *Seventeen*, which strove to impart a "good girl" ethos, *Sassy* offered readers the feature, "Losing Your Virginity: Read This before You Decide." Readers bought *Sassy* in droves. *Seventeen* and other magazines got hip to the competition and immediately drew up plans for redesign and refocus. *Sassy* also made media history by allowing ads for condoms. From the start the magazine was accused of encouraging young women to be boy crazy and engage in sexual activity, but a more careful reading of its articles showed them to be balanced and frank about the negative physical and emotional consequences of sexual activity.

Most adults seemed to have strong feelings against *Sassy*. Media pundits faulted it for its self-reflexive editorial content—it was not unusual for copy to incorporate penciled rejoinders from dissenting colleagues in the margins—and parents found it threatening, to say the least. In a 1992 *New York* magazine article about Pratt and the success of *Sassy*, *Seventeen* editor Midge Richardson Richardson—perhaps forgetting the perpetual raison d'être for teens in general—declared her competition "sometimes vulgar." She continued, "the politics are unabashedly liberal. The magazine also pokes fun at traditional values." Yet both *Seventeen* and *YM* immediately jazzed up their features and style to compete and become more "sassy." Meanwhile *Sassy*'s own ad campaign trumpeted the line "I'm too Sassy to read *Teen*."

From the start, however, *Sassy*'s critics seemed bent on silencing it. After only a few months on the newsstands, the magazine became the target of a well-organized boycott from the Moral Majority and Christian fundamentalist minister Jerry Falwell for what was deemed its promotion of promiscuity and alternative sexuality. A letter-writing campaign managed to scare off a few big advertisers, and Pratt and the staff writers began to tone down the sex features. Unrelated financial difficulties with Fairfax led to *Sassy*'s sale to Matilda Publications in 1989 (Matilda sold the magazine to Lang Communications in 1990), and though it still addressed teen sexuality, it attempted to bring its zingy style to a wider range of issues. In 1991, for instance, it ran articles explaining the Gulf War situation with such titles as "What Saddam Is Irked About."

Under Pratt's guidance, a *Sassy* for boys was launched in 1991 (titled *Dirt*). Pratt also landed her own television talk show on the Fox Network. Both eventually failed, and Pratt left *Sassy* to create another magazine, a sort of *Sassy* for the eighteen to thirty-four female demographic called *Jane*. In 1994 *Sassy* briefly halted publication because it had been losing money. In December of that year, Petersen Publishing, which owned rival magazine *Teen*, bought *Sassy* and restarted it with the aim of attracting a fifteen- to twenty-four-year-old readership. In 1996 *Sassy*'s run ended with the December 1996 issue, after which the magazine merged with *Teen*.

Carol Brennan

SEE ALSO: *Advertising; Condoms; Consumerism; Daytime Talk Shows; Gulf Wars; Moral Majority; The Pill; Reagan, Ronald; Safe Sex;* Seventeen*; Teen Idols; Teenagers; Television.*

BIBLIOGRAPHY

Carmody, Deirdre. "Reaching Teen-Agers, without Using a Phone." *New York Times*, January 18, 1993.

Daley, Suzanne. "Sassy: Like, You Know, for Kids." *New York Times*, April 11, 1988.

Endres, Kathleen L., and Therese L. Lueck, eds. "Sassy." In *Women's Periodicals in the United States: Consumer*

Magazines. Westport, CT: Greenwood Press, 1995.

Jesella, Kara, and Marisa Meltzer. *How Sassy Changed My Life: A Love Letter to the Greatest Teen Magazine of All Time.* New York: Faber & Faber, 2007.

Pratt, Jane, and Kelli Pryor. *For Real: The Uncensored Truth about America's Teenagers.* New York: Hyperion Books, 1995.

Smith, Dinitia. "Jane's World! Jane's World!" *New York,* May 25, 1992, 60–71.

Satellite Radio

Satellite radio is a kind of technology—but it is also an entertainment delivery system and a business platform. Although satellite radio was once expected to be an important component of the media landscape, implementation of the technology has faced challenges, and most attempts to commercialize the service have failed. By 2012 North America's SiriusXM was the only large-scale implementation with a substantial business and technology infrastructure. Other potential uses—in parts of the world underserved by conventional communications, for example—have generally not materialized, and the future of satellite radio remains unclear.

Conventional terrestrial radio sends out signals in two different forms (AM, or amplitude modulation, and FM, or frequency modulation) from land-based transmitters. AM and FM programming can be picked up for free by inexpensive, widely available receivers. The signals can travel only a certain distance, however, so in order for radio programming to reach a national audience, some kind of system is needed to relay the signal or to syndicate the same programs to stations in multiple areas. During the golden age of radio, from the 1920s through the 1950s, nationwide radio networks delivered entertainment and information to a very broad audience—but when television took over the airways, AM and FM radio stations became primarily local.

Fast-forward to the twenty-first century, when satellite radio can use orbital communication platforms to send signals over a wide geographic area. One benefit of satellite radio is that it can usually be heard in mountainous or rural areas where terrestrial radio cannot be picked up reliably. Another benefit is that satellite channels stay the same everywhere, so listeners on the road do not have to keep searching for new radio sources. Not surprisingly, however, it is much more expensive to send radio programming by satellite than by way of land-based transmitters—and creating the infrastructure for a satellite radio network requires a substantial investment of money and time. To make that investment worthwhile, satellite radio providers encrypt transmissions so they will be heard only on certain types of equipment, requiring users to purchase the required equipment and pay an ongoing fee to access the provider's exclusive set of radio channels.

This pay-to-listen model offers several benefits for users. While most terrestrial stations depend on advertising for revenue, subscriber fees enable satellite radio to deliver programming with few or no commercial interruptions. Satellite radio can also carry types of programming that terrestrial stations cannot. Because over-the-air stations broadcast unencrypted programming, they are subject to regulations that prevent public airways from carrying content that may be inappropriate for a general audience. Fee-based satellite channels, on the other hand, are generally not subject to the same limitations—so providers can sell access to programs that push past conventional limits.

The commercialization of satellite radio was driven primarily by two U.S.-based companies, XM and Sirius, both of which made extensive investments in technology, programming, and marketing during the first decade of the 2000s. Neither was able to gain a sufficient market advantage, however, and the two companies merged in 2008 to form SiriusXM. As of 2012 the composite company provided 135 channels of programming to more than twenty-one million subscribers, and its satellite receivers were available in most new automobiles. Although cars are the primary site of use for satellite radios, SiriusXM subscribers can access the same programming online, through portable devices such as tablets and smart phones, and via receivers designed for use in homes, boats, and RVs.

Cynthia Giles

SEE ALSO: *Advertising; Automobile; Consumerism; Radio; RVs; Smart Phones.*

BIBLIOGRAPHY

Pavlik, John V. *Media in the Digital Age.* New York: Columbia University Press, 2008.

Verklin, David, and Bernice Kanner. *Watch This, Listen Up, Click Here: Inside the 300 Billion Dollar Business behind the Media You Constantly Consume.* Hoboken, NJ: John Wiley, 2007.

Satellites

The term *satellite* describes any object that orbits around a larger body. Some satellites occur naturally, such as moons and comets. However, the term is commonly used to simply refer to artificial satellites, or objects placed in Earth's orbit through human action. Most such satellites are used for communications purposes. The launch of the *Telstar* satellite on July 10, 1962, heralded a new age for communications. Prior to *Telstar,* live television broadcasts had been confined within continental borders, hindered by the inability of television's high frequencies to bounce off the ionosphere. Although transatlantic telephone cables to Europe existed, as late as 1957 the system could accommodate a mere thirty-six calls at any one time. *Telstar* was designed as the first link in a vast network of satellites capable of relaying images and telephone calls around the globe.

While the Soviet Union's *Sputnik* thrust satellites onto the world stage, its faint chirping beeps served little purpose other than as a tracking signal. However, beyond the immense political ramifications, *Sputnik* proved that a manmade object could not only be placed into orbit but also could function in the hostile environment of space. The possibilities for satellites were far reaching—they could be distant sentinels tracking volatile weather formations, spies in the sky for the military, or communication repeater outposts.

AN AUSPICIOUS START

The concept of using satellites for communication purposes first appeared in an article penned by space visionary Arthur C. Clarke in October 1945. Titled "Extra-Terrestrial Relays," the article, published in the trade journal *Wireless World*, predicted three geostationary communication satellites would provide simultaneous worldwide radio broadcasts by 1995. Less than twenty years after the publication of this article, science fiction was well on its way to becoming scientific reality, with *Telstar* blazing the trail.

Realizing the potential of satellites, U.S. telecommunications giant AT&T (American Telephone & Telegraph) initiated funding for a project named Telstar in fall 1960. (AT&T coined the term *Telstar* by combining *telecommunications* and *star*.) This ambitious network of satellites was an expensive venture, but AT&T's monopoly status at that time allowed the company to simply pass research and operating costs to the consumer. AT&T even reimbursed the National Aeronautics and Space Administration (NASA) $3 million for the use of its Thor-Delta launch vehicle.

From its initial relay, *Telstar* electrified the world. For the first time an image generated on one side of the Atlantic Ocean could be instantly viewed on the other. The telecasting feat answered critics who questioned the practical applications of the Sputnik-induced space race. As a propaganda tool, *Telstar* bolstered America's sagging image as a technological innovator. The Soviets could claim the world's first artificial satellite, but its scientific value paled when compared to the technologically sophisticated instrument designed by American scientists.

EARLY TRANSMISSIONS

Reflecting Vice President Lyndon Johnson's assessment of Telstar as "another first in [the American] conquest of space," the first image telecast from 3,000 miles above Earth was an American flag waving in the foreground of AT&T's antenna tracking facility near Andover, Maine, on July 10, 1962. "America the Beautiful" and "The Star-Spangled Banner" acted as the musical score for the sequence. Although European tracking stations were unable to receive this broadcast, France was able to establish a link at 7:35 p.m. eastern time. The following evening, July 11, American television viewers were treated to their first live images of Europe courtesy of *Telstar*; they watched entertainer Yves Montand singing "La Chansonette."

Telstar was a technological wonder relaying both television signals and telephone calls, but its basic premise was flawed. *Telstar* was capable of transatlantic relay for a mere 102 minutes a day. In order to create a stable communications network AT&T estimated fifty to 120 Telstars would need to be placed into orbit. The geostationary concept of Clarke, in which a satellite is in synch with Earth's rotation at a height where it could cover more than 40 percent of the planet's surface, required only three satellites. On July 26, 1963, *Telstar* became obsolete as *Syncom II* became the first satellite to transmit from a synchronous orbit some 22,235 miles in space.

President John F. Kennedy looked to *Telstar* as an "outstanding example of the way in which government and business can cooperate in a most important field of human endeavor." *Telstar* benefited both the United States and AT&T greatly. The satellite restored America's image as a leader in technology, an image severely battered in the wake of a series of humiliating space firsts achieved by the Soviet Union. While geostationary communication satellites quickly eclipsed the Telstar network concept, subsequent satellites failed to achieve the public notoriety of *Telstar*.

A WAY OF LIFE

Satellites have largely receded from public awareness, but their increased presence in the stratosphere has enabled easy and unimpeded global communications, which many people take for granted. After the launch of *Telstar* and its successor, the geostationary *Syncom III*, in 1964, nations around the world endeavored to launch their own satellites. The space race fueled a worldwide fervor to participate—if not to dominate—in achieving technological advancements. This fervor pushed satellite technology to develop at a rapid pace throughout the 1960s and 1970s.

The most significant contribution of satellites to daily human life has been the ability to make long-distance phone calls. Communications satellites enabled locally made, hardwired calls to be uplinked to a station in orbit, transmitted across an ocean or a continent, and then downlinked in a similar system. Even the most remote locations have now become accessible through satellite phones, which can uplink directly from the device. Television broadcasting is another area in which satellite technology has made vast distances seem insignificant. Satellite television, which comes in several different formats—including direct-to-home or broadcast-to-networks systems—can broadcast live images from one part of the world to another and also services remote areas where ground-based transmission is limited or nonexistent. Satellite radio, Global Positioning Systems (GPS), and satellite Internet are other methods the private market has developed to capitalize on the capacity for far-reaching communications.

It is estimated that nearly 1,000 satellites orbit Earth. Russia and the United States hold the number one and two positions, respectively, for most satellites in use. In a world where making a transatlantic phone call has become a mundane experience, and where the prevalence of smartphones means that millions of people carry GPS technology in their pockets, many wonder how we survived without these advances. As corporations find new ways to employ satellites, we can be assured that they will continue to be an integral albeit largely unseen part of contemporary daily life.

Lori C. Walters

SEE ALSO: *AT&T; Cell Phones; Clarke, Arthur C.; GPS; The Internet; NASA; Radio; Smartphones;* Sputnik*; Telephone; Television.*

BIBLIOGRAPHY

Clarke, Arthur C. "Extra-Terrestrial Relays." *Wireless World*, October 1945, 305–308.

Findley, Rowe. "Telephone a Star." *National Geographic*, May 1962, 638–651.

Gavaghan, Helen. *Something New under the Sun: Satellites and the Beginning of the Space Age*. New York: Copernicus, 1998.

Whalen, David. *The Origins of Satellite Communications, 1945–1965*. Smithsonian History of Aviation and Spaceflight Series. Washington, DC: Smithsonian Institution Scholarly Press, 2002.

The *Saturday Evening Post*

Long before *Time* and *Newsweek* recapped the events of the world for millions of Americans, long before *Reader's Digest* and

Life condensed the news into words and pictures, the *Saturday Evening Post* was truly America's magazine. Born in earnest at the turn of the twentieth century, with roots in colonial America, the *Saturday Evening Post* quickly became required reading for anyone who wished to stay in touch with the issues that mattered in culture, politics, and the economy. The *Post*, as it became widely known, dominated the American magazine landscape for the first thirty years of the century, both in circulation and influence. In its heyday, it was the voice of American common-sense conservatism. The *Saturday Evening Post* ultimately faded along with that brand of conservatism, giving way to a less impressive contemporary incarnation of the publication. However, memories of the magazine's greatness live on through the classic Norman Rockwell *Post* covers that have become essential elements in Americana collections.

THE EARLY DAYS

The modern *Post* was born when magazine magnate Cyrus H. K. Curtis, who published the nation's leading magazine, *Ladies' Home Journal*, purchased it from Andrew Smythe in 1897 for $1,000. Curtis liked the magazine's pedigree. It claimed to be the oldest magazine in America, with ties to Benjamin Franklin. While some historians doubt that Franklin had anything to do with the publication, official *Post* history states that the magazine evolved from his four-page newspaper, the *Saturday Evening Post*, which he began publishing in 1821. In 1897 the content of the magazine had nothing to distinguish it particularly, but Curtis soon hired George Horace Lorimer to edit it. Lorimer, the son of a minister, arrived with a clear vision of how to pitch the magazine to the great middle class. He believed that such middle-class values as honesty, integrity, hard work, and self-reliance could be used to sustain the nation as it entered a new century. By retaining final say on every word that was printed in his magazine, Lorimer made sure that each issue echoed his vision for America, and he discovered that many readers agreed with his view.

The *Post*'s circulation reached one million per week in 1908, two million in 1913, and three million in 1937. Lorimer had devised what became known as the "*Post* formula," a mix that was equal parts business, public affairs, and romance spiced with sports, humor, illustrations, and cartoons. The magazine also published fiction, much of it serialized and of the romantic variety. Meanwhile, its nonfiction articles celebrated American achievement. The *Post* rarely opposed the status quo and seemed perfectly attuned to the tastes of the "average" American, as long as that American was white, from the middle class, and middle-aged. Rockwell, who began to illustrate covers for the *Post* in 1916, perfectly captured the tone of the magazine. While the contents remained largely the same for the better part of the 1910s, 1920s, and 1930s, so did the price. Until 1942 an issue cost just five cents. The stable price was a measure of the magazine's success, for it attracted so many advertisers eager to peddle their products before the *Post*'s readers that the publisher could cushion his readers from the rising costs of its production.

CONSERVATISM

Critics complained that the *Post* sugarcoated the rise of big business in America. Whereas other notable American magazines, such as *McClure's*, drew attention to the dangers posed by monopolistic corporations, the *Saturday Evening Post* generally applauded the effects of big business on the American landscape. As long as pro-business politicians were in office, Lorimer was convinced that his magazine would benefit. However, when the political and economic tide turned, Lorimer was accused of becoming a scold. It was not the stock market crash of 1929 that changed his mood, as he viewed it as a healthy correction to an economy that had grown dangerously speculative. Rather, it was the election of President Franklin Delano Roosevelt and his New Deal programs that turned Lorimer and the *Post* from advocates for the common-sense majority into the shrill voice of American conservatism.

Lorimer deplored Roosevelt's New Deal because he felt that what Americans needed to do most was tighten their belts and return to the "old values" he had long promoted in the *Post*. In opposing the New Deal, Lorimer "changed the Post from an organ of entertainment and enlightenment into a weapon of political warfare," writes magazine historian Theodore Peterson in *Magazines in the Twentieth Century* (1964). Lorimer's views were popular with many Americans, but fighting these battles took the steam out of the aging editor, who left the *Post* in 1937. At that time the magazine had its highest circulation ever, but it experienced a sharp decline during World War II in response to an unpopular isolationist stance and a nasty article on Jews. The *Post*, however, made a comeback during the postwar boom.

POSTWAR YEARS

The *Post* reached four million readers in 1949 and five million in 1955. While such continually increasing circulation figures might once have convinced both editors and advertisers that the publication was healthy, major changes in the increasingly competitive American magazine market put a spotlight on the *Post*'s tenuous position. Firstly, progressively sophisticated means of tracking magazine readership made it possible to determine precisely which demographics were likely to bring revenue to potential advertisers. The *Post*, with its aging readership, was no longer the best medium for carrying advertising. Secondly, the number of magazines on the market had exploded in the 1940s, and the arrival of television in the 1950s further heightened competition for the now-selective advertising dollar.

Hoping to return the *Post* to its former position as the leading medium for advertising in the United States, the Curtis Company experimented with a number of changes to the magazine's format and contents. However, the venerable *Saturday Evening Post* was losing so much money that it ceased publication in February 1969. Two years later the *Post* resumed publication with a new emphasis on health and medical technologies. The magazine paid particular attention to children's health, and its foundation even established the Children's Better Health Institute in 1976. Although it has never reclaimed its status as a major magazine, the *Post* continues to appear regularly, covering such topics as Social Security, education, and finance and regularly publishing fiction. It also has a presence on the Internet.

CHANGING TIMES

The *Saturday Evening Post* has been one of many contemporary American magazines struggling to attract enough readers and advertisers to survive, but during its heyday, it was a true phenomenon. According to Jan Cohn, author of *Creating America: George Horace Lorimer and the "Saturday Evening Post,"* "Despite the vast changes in American society between 1899 and 1936, what the *Post* achieved was the fullest expression of a broad American consensual view." The *Post* combined enthusiasm for the benefits of modern society, such technological developments and economic growth that introduced a wealth of new goods, with a healthy respect for the traditional American truths, such as reverence for hard work, a belief in honesty and sincerity, and a love of the home. It spoke in a language that calmed Americans during a time of dramatic social change. Even during the tumultuous 1920s, a period known for its crazes and flaming youth, the *Post* managed to contain the burgeoning energy of popular culture within its pages, publishing stories from Jazz Age icon F. Scott Fitzgerald, among other notable authors.

Anyone wishing to understand America during the first decades of the twentieth century must surely turn to the pages of the *Post*. It was a consensus magazine for a time when Americans believed that a consensus still existed. The magazine's demise is representative of changes in America, for it occurred amid the splintering of the country's identity that characterized the 1960s. No one magazine today could aspire to represent all Americans, but for a brief span, the *Post* truly was, as it often claimed to be, "America's magazine."

Tom Pendergast

SEE ALSO: *Advertising; Consumerism;* Life*; Mass Market Magazine Revolution; New Deal;* Newsweek*;* Reader's Digest*; Rockwell, Norman;* Time.

BIBLIOGRAPHY

Bigelow, Frederick S. *A Short History of the "Saturday Evening Post": "An American Institution" in Three Centuries.* Philadelphia: Curtis Publishing, 1936.

Cohn, Jan. *Creating America: George Horace Lorimer and the "Saturday Evening Post."* Pittsburgh, PA: University of Pittsburgh Press, 1989.

A Short History of the "Saturday Evening Post." Philadelphia: Curtis Publishing, 1953.

Damon-Moore, Helen. *Magazines for the Millions: Gender and Commerce in the "Ladies' Home Journal" and "Saturday Evening Post."* Albany: State University of New York, 1994.

Friedrich, Otto. *Decline and Fall.* New York: Harper & Row, 1970.

Mott, Frank L. *A History of American Magazines.* Cambridge, MA: Harvard University Press, 1957.

Tebbel, John. *George Horace Lorimer and the "Saturday Evening Post."* Garden City, NY: Doubleday, 1948.

Wood, James Playsted. *Magazines in the United States: Their Social and Economic Influence.* New York: Ronald Press, 1971.

Saturday Morning Cartoons

Saturday morning cartoons have been an integral part of the American television scene since the 1960s. Saturday morning is unlike any other time of the programming week in that the viewing audience is at its most monolithic. At no other time do so many stations broadcast such similar material for such an extended period, all to capture the same audience: children. Several generations of children have planned their weekends around the ritual of pouring huge bowls of sugar-saturated cereal and gathering around the television for the week's dose of animation. Almost from the beginning, the Saturday morning cartoon period was a dream come true for advertisers, which were able to promote products associated with cartoon characters to an undiscerning audience.

CRUSADER RABBIT

The earliest incarnation of the Saturday morning cartoon came about almost by accident. In 1949 producer Jerry Fairbanks sold NBC on the idea of a new series of cartoons developed especially for television. His product was a low-budget series titled *Crusader Rabbit* (1949–1952), created by Jay Ward and Alex Anderson. This simply animated program follows the adventures of an intrepid rabbit and his tiger sidekick. "I don't recall anything special about Saturday morning at that point except that the networks had some vague idea that they wanted programs for kids," Fairbanks says in Hal Erickson's *Television Cartoon Shows: An Illustrated Encyclopedia*.

The idea certainly had merit. According to Erickson, statistics going back to the radio years showed that the peak tune-in hours for children were between 10 a.m. and noon on Saturday morning and 4 p.m. to 6 p.m. on weekdays. *Crusader Rabbit* was the first cartoon created exclusively for television and the first to take advantage of this window to reach children. Prior to *Crusader Rabbit*, the only cartoons that had appeared on television were repackaged shorts originally created for the big screen. In order to keep costs down and constantly turn out new material, Ward and Anderson pared down *Crusader Rabbit* to its absolute bare essentials. Characters moved an average of once every four seconds and tended to stay in static poses.

HANNA-BARBERA

Crusader Rabbit did not trigger a deluge of morning cartoons. Television stations preferred to stay with the tried-and-true (and much less expensive) format of a live-action host holding court over a studio audience of children and plugging the sponsors' products. CBS, however, took a gamble and placed a well-known character, Mighty Mouse, on Saturday mornings in 1955. *Mighty Mouse Playhouse* ran for twelve highly successful seasons and further edged live-action shows out the door in favor of direct-to-television animation.

That same year, another important development occurred when William Hanna and Joseph Barbera, two talented MGM animators, took over the animation division of MGM, only to be shown the door in 1957. The pair soon set up its own animation studio and started turning out television animation, usually aimed toward prime-time or afternoon slots. Such shows as *Ruff and Reddy* (1957–1959, the studio's first effort), *The Jetsons* (1962–1963), and *The Flintstones* (1960–1966) were strong successes for the fledgling studio, but it was in the Saturday morning field that its cost-effective techniques made Hanna-Barbera an industry powerhouse.

In order to meet the huge time and work demands required to develop a half hour of animation every week, Hanna-Barbera, Ward, and other early television cartoon pioneers developed a wide array of cost-cutting techniques. Characters were often drawn with a minimum of motion; if characters were speaking, for example, only their mouths moved. Character design was also geared toward efficiency of action. Many Hanna-Barbera characters, such as those in *The Jetsons* and the seminal *Ruff and Reddy*, were designed with wide collars so that a head could be turned simply by flopping it on the collar.

In some cases, sharp writing made up for the deficiencies in animation. *The Jetsons* and *The Flintstones* were well known for their occasional double entendres. The characters on Ward's *The Rocky & Bullwinkle Show* (1959–1964, later titled *The Bullwinkle Show*) rely more on their sharp gags and jokes, which work on two levels, than the rough, sketchy animation that characterizes them. The Hanna-Barbera studio was not without its share of critics, many of whom felt that its quickie techniques cheapened all forms of animation. "Hanna-Barbera proved to the networks that by cutting corners (actually chunks), it was possible to make cartoons cheaply enough for television's needs," Mark Nardone says in *Television Cartoon Shows: An Illustrated Encyclopedia*.

SUPERHEROES AND LIVE ACTION

As the 1960s progressed, animation was increasingly seen as a children's medium. Consequently, animation was funneled away from the prime-time slots and into those on Saturday morning. The year 1966 marked an important turning point in the history of Saturday morning cartoons, as that was when all three major networks (ABC, CBS, and NBC) started to broadcast animation blocs on Saturday morning. The ongoing battle for the support of advertisers, the attention of children, and the money of their parents was waged in earnest. Prime-time animation, though not completely dead, was a flagging form.

Many comic-book characters jumped to Saturday morning cartoons. In the 1960s *Spider-Man*, *The Fantastic Four*, and *Iron Man* made their marks on Saturday morning, and *Superman*, *Aquaman*, *Batman*, and *Superfriends* followed in the 1970s. A revamped Spider-Man series, *Spider-Man and His Amazing Friends*, hit the airwaves in the 1980s, and the 1990s were a boom time with the likes of *Batman*, *Superman*, and *Spider-Man* revivals, *X-Men*, and *Silver Surfer*.

A recurring trend has been to produce live-action programs to compete with the animated stars on Saturday morning. Not surprisingly, the most successful of these have been similar to cartoons. *H.R. Pufnstuf*, first produced in 1969, and *Mighty Morphin Power Rangers*, which has aired in various incarnations since the 1990s, are live-action shows with liberal doses of garish color; surreal design; outlandish costumes; and fast-paced, cartoon-style plots. *Pee Wee's Playhouse* (1986–1991), which deposits comedian Pee Wee Herman into a surreal world of talking chairs, puppets, and wacky neighbors, was a particularly big hit. Of all the live-action shows, it most effectively replicates an animated world.

IMITATIONS AND ACCUSATIONS

An unusual side development of live-action Saturday morning television was the creation of animated programs based on (and sometimes voiced by) real celebrities. *The Beatles* (1965) was the first Saturday morning show to embrace this concept. In the ensuing decades, Kid 'n' Play, the New Kids on the Block, and the Jackson Five were only a few of the musical groups to follow in the footsteps of the Fab Four. Similarly, animated versions of live-action shows such as *Mork & Mindy*, *Laverne & Shirley*, *Punky Brewster*, and *Alf* have appeared on Saturday morning over the years.

Like most other forms of entertainment, Saturday morning cartoons exemplify the following truism: "Imitation is the sincerest form of flattery." When *The Smurfs*, featuring a band of friendly forest dwellers, premiered on NBC in 1981, it became one of the most successful animated shows ever. *The Smurfs*, which ran until 1990, is often credited with bringing renewed vigor to an art form that had slipped into a creative slump throughout the 1970s. Studios and broadcasters were encouraged to pay even greater attention to the Saturday morning market—everybody suddenly wanted a piece of the action. The many clones that followed, such as *The Care Bears* (1985–1988) and *My Little Pony* (1986–1987), further expounded on the themes of happiness and friendliness that made *The Smurfs* popular.

Saturday morning cartoons have made important and lasting changes to the landscape of American popular culture, including a subtle but irrevocable shift in the makeup of the week. Sunday may have been a day of rest, but Saturday became a day of entertainment. In a very real sense, Saturday emerged as an unofficial holiday, an event manufactured by advertisers and programmers to capitalize on a captive audience that was home from school with little to do except, perhaps, park in front of a television set.

Parent groups and government agencies expressed concern about the effect the saturation of Saturday morning cartoons might have on children. Violence was their prime concern. As far back as the 1950s, there were those who had expressed dismay at the alien-blasting antics of Space Ghost or Popeye's tendency to solve problems with a can of spinach and an act of violence. In fact, the majority of scholarly attention paid to television animation focused on the question of whether its violence was harmful to children. Additionally, parents and regulators feared the growing phenomenon of "half-hour commercials" disguised as cartoons whose purpose was to market toys and trinkets to children.

FORMAT CHANGES

Under pressure from many fronts over the course of the 1960s and 1970s, the networks imposed firm standards on themselves to avoid having the Federal Communications Commission (FCC) or some other regulatory agency do it for them. In 1969 the National Association of Broadcasters dictated that advertisements for toys based on a show would not be aired during that program. In other words, children watching *Spider-Man* would no longer be regaled with commercials entreating them to get their parents to run out and purchase products associated with the superhero. Violent acts were curtailed by the broadcasters themselves, as was any act that might encourage children at home to imitate their on-screen heroes. Such changes required rewriting and revisions; even old cartoon shorts rerun on Saturday morning were subject to the new slash-and-burn treatment, sometimes rendering them incoherent in the process.

In the late 1970s and early 1980s, some networks attempted to stem the tide by airing cartoons with social messages. Bill Cosby, producer and creator of *Fat Albert and the Cosby Kids* (1972–1979), was a particular proponent of educating children by building his stories around social messages. In most other programs, however, the lesson would come in the form of a short epilogue featuring characters breaking "the fourth wall" and speaking directly to children about an educational or moral issue. Erickson writes critically of this trend in *Television Cartoon Shows: An Illustrated Encyclopedia*: "While some of these prosocial bites came off with sincerity, most appeared to be hastily inserted with an eye-dropper and wedged in with a shoehorn—a fleeting conscious-stricken afterthought, or a forced apology, for *not* educating the viewers within the body of the program."

EDUCATIONAL PROGRAMMING

In the 1980s NBC took this one step further by placing popular live-action stars of the day in *One to Grow On*. The star would set up the morally tricky theme of an episode and help the young viewers to resolve it. In a similar vein, educational and religious programmers have sometimes tried to "draw in" viewers by offering programs that are disguised as typical cartoon fare. Such efforts have mostly fared poorly. Kids, after all, are savvy TV viewers.

Schoolhouse Rock! (1973–2000), a series of short lessons, was among the most successful attempts at educational programming on Saturday morning. Slowly but surely, the program inserted itself into popular culture. In the 1990s, a generation after *Schoolhouse Rock!* first bopped its way onto the scene, the program experienced a revival of sorts. *Schoolhouse Rock!* T-shirts and albums sold well, and many college students could still sing along to "Conjunction Junction, What's Your Function?" and "I'm Just a Bill, Sittin' Here on Capitol Hill."

MERCHANDISING

Possibly the most important economic impact of Saturday morning cartoons has been merchandising, which began in earnest in the late 1970s. There seemed to be no end to the ways animated characters could be displayed. Characters such as the Smurfs appeared on lunchboxes, clothes, shoes, party favors, napkins, and school supplies. And, of course, there were toys. For a successful cartoon, the potential seemed limitless.

The increasingly lucrative Saturday morning shows prompted a shift in the business dynamic of other creative forms. Many comic-book-based and animated movies began to be developed with an eye toward eventual Saturday morning success. The weekly adventures of the characters in *The Little Mermaid*, *Aladdin*, or *Wild C.A.T.s* could go a long way in raising the profiles of these brands.

A LASTING INFLUENCE

By the mid-1990s Saturday morning cartoons as they had been perceived for decades were on their way out. Following federal mandates to include three hours of educational programming per week, many networks replaced their animated programming with live-action series such as *Saved by the Bell* or weekend versions of the morning news programs *Today* and *The Early Show*. Cable channels such as Nickelodeon, Cartoon Network, and Disney Channel filled the cartoon void. Additionally, video games, the Internet, and DVDs provided children with a host of alternatives to Saturday morning cartoons. While cartoons have not lost their appeal to children, they are no longer relegated to a specific part of the day or week.

Nevertheless, the influence of Saturday morning cartoons should not be discounted. Thanks to the advertising and marketing blitzes that accompanied the cartoon takeover of Saturday morning, the characters border on the legendary for those who grew up watching them. Better than 90 percent of all Saturday morning cartoon characters have slipped into television oblivion—few people remember the Snorks or the Orbots. However, the characters that did resonate catapulted into the popular imagination in a manner normally reserved for music or film stars. Although the Saturday morning cartoon form suffered through slumps, turmoil, regulation, and change, it transformed the TV landscape.

Paul F. P. Pogue

SEE ALSO: *Advertising; Batman; The Beatles; Comic Books; Comics; Consumerism; Cosby, Bill;* The Fantastic Four*;* The Flintstones*; Hanna-Barbera; The Jackson Five;* Laverne and Shirley*; MGM (Metro-Goldwyn-Mayer);* Mork & Mindy*; The New Kids on the Block;* Pee-wee's Playhouse*;* Rocky and Bullwinkle*;* Schoolhouse Rock!*; Spider-Man; Superman; Television.*

BIBLIOGRAPHY

Barbera, Joseph. *My Life in 'Toons: From Flatbush to Bedrock in under a Century*. Atlanta, GA: Turner Publishing, 1994.

Burke, Timothy, and Kevin Burke. *Saturday Morning Fever*. New York: St. Martin's Griffin, 1999.

Cholodenke, Alan, ed. *The Illusion of Life*. Sydney: Power Publications, 1991.

Erickson, Hal. *Television Cartoon Shows: An Illustrated Encyclopedia, 1949–1993*. Jefferson, NC: McFarland, 1995.

Hanna, Bill, and Tom Ito. *A Cast of Friends*. Dallas, TX: Taylor Publishing, 1996.

Heraldson, Donald. *Creators of Life: A History of Animation*. New York: Drake Publishers, 1975.

Kanfer, Stefan. *Serious Business: The Art and Commerce of Animation in America from Betty Boop to "Toy Story."* New York: Scribner, 1997.

Minow, Newton N., and Craig L. LaMay. *Abandoned in the Wasteland: Children, Television, and the First Amendment*. New York: Hill and Wang, 1995.

Swan, Karen; Carla Meskill; and Steven DeMaio, eds. *Social Learning from Broadcast Television*. Cresskill, NJ: Hampton Press, 1998.

Woolery, George W. *Children's Television: The First Thirty-Five Years, 1946–1981*. Metuchen, NJ: Scarecrow Press, 1983–1985.

Saturday Night Fever

A film that captures the essence of the disco craze that flowered in the 1970s, *Saturday Night Fever* (1977) is arguably the quintessential document of an era that came, a decade later, to be one of the most ridiculed periods of the twentieth century. Supported by a best-selling movie soundtrack and John Travolta—an instantly iconic leading man—*Saturday Night Fever* survived the demise of 1970s cultural artifacts such as polyester, *Soul Train*, and KC and the Sunshine Band to become a cult classic. The film enjoyed a resurgence in popularity with the 1990s disco-culture renaissance that was heralded by films such as *Boogie Nights* (1997) and *The Last Days of Disco* (1998).

Based on a short story by Nik Cohn and directed by John Badham, *Saturday Night Fever* starred Donna Pescow, Karen Lynn Gorney, and Travolta as Tony Manero, an average Italian American working man by day and a disco demigod by night. The role rocketed Travolta to international stardom while making him as idolized a figure in America as Farrah Fawcett (a poster of whom Tony has on his bedroom wall in the film).

An overabundance of foggy, disco-ball dance scenes aside, *Saturday Night Fever* is as much a film about what some consider to be the frivolous, politically neutral disco scene of the 1970s as it is about long-standing class and cultural differences. Set in a lower-middle-class Catholic neighborhood of Brooklyn, New York, *Saturday Night Fever* traces Tony's struggle to attain a sense of self-worth in economically depressed, culturally conservative surroundings. The film opens with an aerial shot of the Manhattan skyline that moves across the Brooklyn Bridge in silence until, as the camera reaches Brooklyn itself, the throbbing sounds of the Bee Gees and the noise of traffic chime in as Tony struts down the streets of his neighborhood.

Raised by conservative, Catholic parents with a revered older brother who is a priest, Tony spends all of his free time and money perfecting his image for weekend appearances at the "2001-Odyssey" discotheque, where he excels as a dancer. Tony's function in his community can be likened to that of shaman, according to critic John Cooke in "Patterns of Shamanic Ritual in Popular Film." Neither a priest nor a medicine man, the shaman's function is to cure the sick in his community. On the dance floor, Tony commands ecstatic admiration from his peers and acts as a new type of spiritual savior in the face of Catholic conservatism. His dancing unites and lifts the spirits of his alienated, economically depressed community of peers. The power of his physical presence and prowess, combined with his confident "attitude" is graphically demonstrated in scenes where the crowd parts when Tony hits the dance floor; his friends cheer as he dances his solos. The bartender of the club even calls him Nureyev.

The film's opposition between the nonideological impact of the disco scene and the staunch, ideological power of the Catholic Church is underscored in the relationship between Tony and his brother, Frank. When Frank announces that he has lost his faith in religion and will leave the priesthood, Tony's own faith in his talent as a dancer and his belief in the regenerative space of the discotheque grows. After meeting Stephanie Mangano, an older woman from the neighborhood who is enamored with Manhattan and is in the process of refining her image, he begins to drift away from his group of friends. Stephanie, a local girl turned posh, presents the key to escape from his neighborhood along with entry into the upscale world of Manhattan, just over the bridge.

Travolta was a trained actor and dancer by the time he landed the role of Tony. He quit school at the age of sixteen to pursue acting; studied dance under Gene Kelly's brother, Fred Kelly; and had appeared in several stage productions, a popular television show (*Welcome Back, Kotter*, 1975–1979), and a major motion picture by the time he made *Saturday Night Fever*. He reprised his role as Tony in *Staying Alive* (1983), but the disco craze had faded and so had Travolta's luster. After a long period out of the limelight, Travolta returned to mainstream Hollywood cinema with a string of 1990s hit films, including *Pulp Fiction* (1994), *Phenomenon* (1996), and *Primary Colors* (1998).

Kristi M. Wilson

SEE ALSO: *The Bee Gees; Disco; Fawcett, Farrah; Hollywood;* Pulp Fiction*;* Soul Train*; Travolta, John;* Welcome Back, Kotter.

BIBLIOGRAPHY

Cohn, Nik. "Another Saturday Night." *Life* 8, no. 21 (1998): 48–49.

Cooke, John. "Patterns of Shamanic Ritual in Popular Film." *Literature/Film Quarterly* 12 (1984): 50–57.

Sautman, Francesca Canadé. "Women of the Shadows: Italian American Women, Ethnicity and Racism in American Cinema." *Differentia* 6–7 (1994): 219–246.

Tamburri, Anthony Julian; Paolo A. Giordano; and Fred L. Gardaphé, eds. *From the Margin: Writings in Italian Americana.* West Lafayette, IN: Purdue University Press, 1991.

Saturday Night Live

Saturday Night Live (*SNL*) is a late-night comedy television show that debuted on NBC in 1975. Challenging America's comic sensibilities with its outrageous and satirical skits, the show launched the careers of many of the brightest comedy performers America has ever known, including Chevy Chase, Gilda Radner, Jane Curtin, Eddie Murphy, Bill Murray, Adam Sandler, David Spade, Chris Rock, Tina Fey, Jimmy Fallon, Will Ferrell, Kristen Wiig, and Amy Poehler. Whether mocking current events on "Weekend Update," the show's longest-running recurring sketch, or impersonating politicians to ridicule their gaffes, *SNL* comedians are committed to scrutinizing (or skewering) the news of the moment. *SNL* is also famous for its fake commercials that pitch outrageous products and services, including mood-altering drugs for dogs, funeral homes that promise not to have sex with dead relatives, and a car that handles so smoothly one can perform a circumcision in the back seat while on a Sunday drive. The show also features of-the-moment musical talent usually not found on network television. In 2011 *SNL* began its thirty-seventh season, still airing at 11:30 p.m. on Saturday nights.

Producer Lorne Michaels first conceived of *SNL* as a reaction to the staid, prime-time comedy of American television. Inspired by Britain's *Monty Python's Flying Circus* (1969–1974), Michaels wanted to produce a comedy show that would break all the rules. He wanted to bring the dangerous energy evident in America's comedy clubs to a television industry that he instinctively distrusted. He was lucky to get the moribund 11:30 p.m. Saturday evening slot, and he began to create a comedy variety show. Michaels was constantly quoted as saying he knew the ingredients of the show but not the recipe.

Michaels scoured the underground comedy scene for his writers and performers and found many in Chicago's Second City comedy troupe. He established a repertory of actors, the so-called Not Ready for Prime Time Players, and a core of writers who were raised on television and ready to break its rules. They were all aware that few comedians with anything serious to say got to do so on network television, where humor was kept safe and orderly.

On October 11, 1975, *Saturday Night Live* debuted from NBC studio 8H in New York City's Rockefeller Center. From the first moment, with its trademark cold opening (no credits or titles), the audience knew something different had arrived on late-night television. In the first episode actor John Belushi plays an immigrant taking English lessons from a teacher played by Michael O'Donoghue. As the teacher is helping the immigrant learn how to say "I would like . . . to feed your fingertips . . . to the wolverines," he suddenly dies of a heart attack. A tremulous Chase, playing the stage manager, walks into camera shot, looks at the audience with a grin, and bellows, "Live from New York, it's Saturday Night!"

Saturday Night Live*'s Not Ready for Prime Time Players.* *The cast of* Saturday Night Live *in the show's second season included, from left, Laraine Newman, John Belushi, Jane Curtin, Bill Murray, Gilda Radner, Dan Aykroyd, and Garrett Morris.* NBC/NBCU PHOTO BANK VIA/GETTY IMAGES.

CHALLENGING NORMS

At first, the regular cast took a backseat to the guests. The exception in the first few episodes was Chase, who was originally hired as a writer. His suave, sophisticated looks and his recurring role as the anchor of the "Weekend Update" news parody segment soon set him apart from the rest of the cast. The others, Dan Aykroyd, Belushi, Curtin, Garrett Morris, Laraine Newman, and Radner, got their chance to shine in the third show, which was hosted by actor Rob Reiner. They all act resentful as Reiner acts dictatorial, and Belushi goes up to him onstage, dressed as a bumble bee, and announces:

> We didn't ask to be Bees. . . . But this is all [the writers] came up with for us. DO YOU THINK WE LIKE THIS? No, no, Mr. Reiner, we don't have any choice. . . . We're just a bunch of actors looking for a break, that's all! What do you WANT from us! Mr. Rob Reiner, Mr. Star! What did you expect? THE STING?

SNL was determined to challenge all the rules and norms of late-night comedy shows. Michaels himself stepped in front of the camera in April 1976 to offer the Beatles $3,000 to appear on the show and sing three songs. He later came back and upped the offer to $3,200. In November George Harrison showed up and tried to claim all the money for himself. Michaels again appeared to say that if it was up to him, Harrison could have the money, but NBC would not agree. When Paul McCartney appeared on the show in 1993, he and Michaels talk about the offer during the monologue.

The *SNL* cast went through numerous changes over the years. At the end of the first season, Chase departed for Hollywood. Murray joined the repertory, but it was Belushi who ended up star of the show with his manic weatherman, Samurai Warrior, and Joliet Jake Blues characters. In 1979 Belushi and Aykroyd left to make the movie *The Blues Brothers* (1980), followed at the end of the fifth season by Michaels and virtually the rest of his cast and writers. The season that followed, led by producer Jean Doumanian, saw the show fall in the ratings, and it is considered one of the worst in the show's history, but it also saw the debut of the brash young Murphy.

Murphy was only an occasional player for most of his first season on *SNL*. His big break came during a commentary he cowrote for "Weekend Update." He belted out "Yo, baby" with force, and he proceeded to steal the show as his character Raheem Abdul Muhammed. Murphy became the undeclared star, appearing in virtually every other "Weekend Update" segment for the rest of the season, and when new producer Dick Ebersol took over the show the next season, Murphy and Joe Piscopo were the only two cast members asked to stay.

MICHAELS RETURNS

Ebersol moved away from Michaels's repertory idea, hiring tried-and-true comics, such as Billy Crystal and Martin Short, to star as part of the cast for the 1984–1985 season, but they did not stay with the show for long. Crystal's impersonations of Sammy Davis Jr., Muhammad Ali, and John F. Kennedy delighted fans, but it was his parody of talk-show host Fernando Lamas that brought him the most laughs. Lamas's catchphrase "You look marvelous" became an ongoing Crystal gig, a single on the Billboard Hot 100, and the basis for the title of Crystal's

1985 stand-up album *Marvelous*. Short was most celebrated for his performances as Ed Grimley, a *Wheel of Fortune* game show fanatic. Grimley was a character Short originally created on *Second City Television* (1976), a Canadian television show run by an improv comedy group; the character has continued to appear in Short's work, from an animated series, *The Completely Mental Misadventures of Ed Grimley* (1988), to an appearance on *Let Freedom Hum: An Evening of Comedy Hosted by Martin Short* (2009).

In 1985 Michaels returned as executive producer. During his first season back, however, he brought in too many new faces, and the show failed to connect with audiences. Dropping all but three cast members to start the 1986–1987 season, Michaels stole an idea from an episode of the popular television show *Dallas* (1978–1991) that had aired a few weeks earlier, and Madonna led off *SNL*'s first episode of the season by announcing that the last season had all been a bad dream. Michaels proceeded to reinvent *SNL* as America's one true comedy factory, where new and untried performers and comedians could experiment with their art and in the process reinvent television comedy standards. He brought new comedians to the show, such as Dana Carvey, Chris Farley, Phil Hartman, Mike Myers, and Dennis Miller. In fact, Michaels continued to add to his repertory even when his actors stayed with the show, hiring more mainstream actors, such as Robert Downey Jr., Randy Quaid, and Joan Cusack.

Some suggested that Michaels decided to overstaff to protect himself should more of his stars head for Hollywood. Whatever the reason, the show overcame its legendary past to produce some of its most memorable moments: Carvey presented razor-sharp caricatures of President George H. W. Bush and businessman and presidential candidate Ross Perot, while Hartman responded with an uncanny President Bill Clinton and Miller revitalized "Weekend Update." Myers and Carvey brought the world into the basement of "Wayne's World," a skit about two slacker, metal-loving friends, airing a public access show about heavy metal.

Rock band Aerosmith came to the show as the musical guest in February 1990 and demanded to be included in a Wayne's World sketch. Two *Wayne's World* movies followed in 1992 and 1993. Farley also appeared in the *Wayne's World* movies but is better known for his role as motivational speaker Matt Foley, who "live[d] in a van, down by the river," and for his sketch with guest Patrick Swayze in which the two audition to be Chippendale's dancers, with the svelte Swayze losing out.

CAST CHANGES

SNL experienced a great deal of cast turnover in the 1990s. Many full-time cast members, such as Rock, Spade, Hartman, and Christopher Guest, decided to move on to Hollywood and other shows. Others, such as Sandler and Farley, were actually fired, while Janeane Garofalo, who departed midseason, reportedly left due to disagreements with the writers. Al Franken's fifteen-year run with the show ended when NBC president Fred Silverman refused Michaels's request to make Franken the show's next producer. Franken returned a few years later but then left in protest again after Norm MacDonald got the anchor role for "Weekend Update."

The 1990s also saw the arrival of many cast members who went on to become famous, such as Jimmy Fallon, Maya Rudolph, and Tracy Morgan. The "Weekend Update" segments anchored by Miller from 1985 to 1991, Kevin Nealon from 1991 to 1994, and MacDonald from 1994 to 1997 were highlights of their respective seasons and kept the show fresh and relevant, even when other sketches and recurring characters were fading. The 1990s also saw numerous *SNL* sketches become full-length movies, although the two *Wayne's World* movies are the only ones that were successful. *Coneheads* (1993), *It's Pat* (1994), *Stuart [Smalley] Saves His Family* (1995), *A Night at the Roxbury* (1998), *Superstar* (1999), as well as a reboot of the *Blues Brothers* with *Blues Brothers 2000* (1998), all met critical derision and only small showings at the box office.

In 1997 Tina Fey joined the writing cast, and Fey and Fallon became the first coanchors of "Weekend Update" in eighteen years; two years later Fey became the show's first female head writer. In 2001 Ferrell became the highest-paid member of the show, receiving $350,000 for the 2001–2002 season, which turned out to be his last. Ferrell's tenure at *SNL* features such gems as Craig the Cheerleader and fake commercials for the Dissing Your Dog Training Program. His impersonations of Alex Trebek, the host of the popular game show *Jeopardy!* (1984–), and James Lipton, the host of the talk show *Inside the Actors Studio* (1994–), were even funnier for how straight Ferrell played them.

Seth Meyers joined the cast in 2001 and became co–head writer in 2005. He became head writer when Fey left the show in 2006, and in late 2008 became the sole anchor of "Weekend Update." In 2011 Meyers received great acclaim for his performance in a sketch called "White House Correspondents' Dinner," in which he spoofed both President Barack Obama and businessman Donald Trump.

In 2008 Fey returned to the show as a guest, spoofing vice presidential candidate Sarah Palin, which earned her an Emmy Award and cemented the show's regained relevance in late-night comedy. Poehler, who joined the cast in 2001, also won an Emmy Award in 2008 for her work on *SNL*. Wiig, who joined the cast in 2005, was the first female cast member of *SNL* to ever be nominated for an Academy Award. She was nominated for cowriting the original screenplay for the movie *Bridesmaids* (2012).

GUEST HOSTS

Another popular feature of *SNL* is the guest host. Every show is hosted by a guest who may be an actor, musician, comedian, athlete, political figure, or a former cast member. As of 2012 actor Alec Baldwin had hosted a record sixteen times. Actor and comedian Steve Martin was close behind, with fifteen host appearances. In May 2010 actress Betty White became the oldest guest host, at age eighty-eight-and-a-half. She was invited to host after fans started a "Betty White to Host SNL" campaign on Facebook, sparked by her appearance in a Super Bowl ad for Snickers.

When singer and actor Justin Timberlake appeared on the show, he practically became an auxiliary cast member, starring in numerous skits and helping to launch some of *SNL*'s most memorable sketches of the first decade of the 2000s, including the original song "Dick in a Box" as well as a parody video of singer Beyoncé Knowles's "Single Ladies." He joins Baldwin and Martin in the "Five Timers Club," performers who have hosted or appeared as the musical guests at least five times. Actress Drew Barrymore has hosted five times, the most of any female.

SNL has aired for so long that it has been through three Writers Guild of America strikes, in 1981, 1988, and 2007–

2008. Many of its cast members were born after the show's inception in 1975. One cast member, Abby Elliott, is the child of a former cast member (Chris Elliott). When Darrell Hammond left the show after the 2008–2009 season, he had been with the show for fourteen years, the longest run of any repertory player. In addition to its thirty-two Emmy Awards and record 142 Emmy nominations, *SNL* has won two Peabody Awards and was inducted into the Broadcasting Hall of Fame in 2000.

John J. Doherty

SEE ALSO: *Academy Awards; Aerosmith; Ali, Muhammad; Baldwin, Alec; Belushi, John; The Blues Brothers; Chase, Chevy; Crystal, Billy; Downey, Robert, Jr.; Emmy Awards; Farley, Chris; Ferrell, Will; Fey, Tina; Hollywood;* Jeopardy!*; Madonna; Martin, Steve; Murphy, Eddie; Murray, Bill; Palin, Sarah; Radner, Gilda; Rock, Chris; Stand-Up Comedy; Television; Timberlake, Justin;* Wayne's World*; White, Betty.*

BIBLIOGRAPHY

Beatts, Anne, and John Head, eds. *Saturday Night Live.* New York: Avon Books, 1977.

Cader, Michael, ed. *"Saturday Night Live": The First Twenty Years.* New York: Houghton Mifflin 1994.

Hill, Doug, and Jeff Weingrad. *Saturday Night: A Backstage History of "Saturday Night Live."* New York: Beech Tree, 1986.

Miller, James A., and Tom Shales. *Live from New York: An Uncensored History of "Saturday Night Live" as Told by Its Stars, Writers and Guests.* Boston: Little, Brown, 2002.

Mohr, Jay. *Gasping for Airtime: Two Years in the Trenches of "Saturday Night Live."* New York: Hyperion, 2004.

Partridge, Marianne, ed. *"Rolling Stone" Visits "Saturday Night Live."* Garden City, NY: Dolphin Books, 1979.

Savage, Dan *(1964–)*

The genre of advice columns in American print and online media has traditionally taken the field of interpersonal relationships as its own, presenting nationally syndicated discussions of a wide variety of problems from writers of all ages. While sexuality would occasionally surface within such columns, frankly addressing sex-related questions was not the chief purpose of any of the mainstream writers who responded. An exception is the advice offered by the widely syndicated, openly gay writer and cultural observer Dan Savage.

Born in Chicago on October 7, 1964, Savage grew up within a large extended Catholic family, a fact that made his coming out as a gay man at age eighteen problematic. The death of his grandmother in 1970 and his parents' divorce in 1984 also impacted his views on the issues of family and monogamy in ways that would later emerge in his writing. After completing a degree at the University of Illinois in history and theater, he was working in Madison, Wisconsin, when he met Tim Keck, an editor of the popular satirical paper the *Onion*, who planned to open a new paper in the Seattle, Washington, area. Savage told him that it ought to have an advice column, and Keck invited him to write it. Despite his lack of writing experience, Savage wrote a sample entry, which marked the beginning of his long-running (and eventually internationally syndicated) column Savage Love, which premiered on September 23, 1991, in the Seattle alternative newspaper the *Stranger*.

After relocating to Seattle, Savage soon crafted a public voice that was at once humorous, sarcastic when needed, and uniquely based in the life experiences of an American gay man. His diverse readership quickly included both the straight and gay communities, who found his willingness to discuss explicitly sexual subjects challenging and refreshing. A selection of his columns appeared in book form in 1998, and in its introduction he offered the philosophy that because gay men were obliged to achieve an understanding of their sexuality through conscious research and questioning of roles and behaviors accepted as the norm by heterosexuals, this process made them more aware of the diversity of information available. The collection was followed by three books relating the experience of Savage and his partner successfully adopting their son (*The Kid*), their exploration of the idea of getting married (*The Commitment*), and an evaluation of contemporary American society's attitudes toward morality (*Skipping towards Gomorrah*).

In September 2010, following the nationally reported suicide of Billy Lucas, a gay teenager from Greenburg, Indiana, as a consequence of constant harassment and bullying, Savage and his partner, Terry Miller, created a video they titled *It Gets Better*, which they posted to the YouTube network. Its message was aimed at offering hope and counsel to young lesbian, gay, bisexual, and transgender (LGBT) people who were encountering prejudices, harassment, bullying, and emotional abuse that made them doubt their self-worth and sometimes led them to commit suicide. Savage's initial video generated a large number of responses from both within America and overseas and within a year had grown into an international movement with more than 30,000 user-generated videos posted to the It Gets Better website. On March 22, 2011, a sample of 100 of the essays sent in by contributors ranging from high school students to President Barack Obama was published as *It Gets Better: Coming Out, Overcoming Bullying, and Creating a Life Worth Living.* The proceeds from the book were designated to support charitable organizations working with LGBT youth such as the Trevor Project and GLSEN (the Gay, Lesbian and Straight Education Network).

Savage has also engaged in direct-action political activism, both in person and via his Internet column to stimulate dialogue on issues and candidates of concern to the LGBT community. He has frequently used his writing to challenge the statements and philosophies of antigay mainstream politicians (both liberal and conservative) and to question the effectiveness of established LGBT institutions such as pride parades. Among Savage's numerous political crusades, the 2003 "Google-bombing" of Rick Santorum is perhaps the most famous. In response to antigay remarks by Santorum, a prominent Republican who was at the time serving as a U.S. senator from Pennsylvania, Savage held a contest in which he invited participants to create a definition for the word *santorum*. Savage chose an especially crude response as the winner ("the frothy mixture of lube and fecal matter that is sometimes the by-product of anal sex") and posted it on a website (santorum.com) and a blog (*spreadingsantorum*), both of which ranked high for Google searches of the name Rick Santorum. When criticized for being vulgar, Savage typically responded that his joke was less offensive and damaging than Santorum's position on homosexuality.

Robert B. Ridinger

SEE ALSO: *Advice Columns; Alternative Press; Gay and Lesbian Marriage; Gay and Lesbian Press; Gay Liberation Movement; Gay Men; Google; The Internet; Obama, Barack; Social Media; Viral Videos; YouTube.*

BIBLIOGRAPHY

It Gets Better Project. Accessed May 23, 2012. Available from http://www.itgetsbetter.org

Savage, Dan. *Savage Love: Straight Answers from America's Most Popular Sex Columnist.* New York: Plume, 1998.

Savage , Dan. *The Kid: What Happened after My Boyfriend and I Decided to Go Get Pregnant.* London: Fusion, 2000.

Savage, Dan. *Skipping towards Gomorrah: The Seven Deadly Sins and the Pursuit of Happiness in America.* New York: Dutton, 2002.

Savage, Dan. *The Commitment: Love, Sex, Marriage, and My Family.* New York: Dutton, 2005.

Savage, Dan, and Terry Miller. *It Gets Better: Coming Out, Overcoming Bullying, and Creating a Life Worth Living.* New York: Dutton, 2011.

Savage, Randy "Macho Man" *(1952–2011)*

When Randy Savage (born Randy Poffo) died in an auto accident in May 2011, it was national news. In a *New York Times* obituary, Elizabeth Harris noted that Savage, "with his trademark sunglasses, bandannas and raspy voice was one of the most recognizable professional wrestlers of the 1980s and '90s as the character Macho Man." Like many wrestlers, Savage was a second-generation star, getting his start working for his father, Angelo Poffo, after failing to make the cut as a professional baseball player. After working around the United States in independent promotions, Savage entered the World Wrestling Federation (WWF) in 1985.

Although other wrestlers had been accompanied to the ring by a female valet, the pairing of Savage and his then real-life wife Miss Elizabeth—a "beauty and the beast" gimmick—pushed Savage to the top. With a manic ring style, outlandish wardrobe, and catchphrase of "Oh yea!," Savage quickly won over WWF fans. He was one of the first "bad guys" to be cheered, a trend that took off in the late 1990s with the success of antiheroes like "Stone Cold" Steve Austin. A feud with Hulk Hogan—started on NBC's *Main Event*—culminated in Hogan defeating Savage for the WWF title at Wrestlemania V in 1989. Like Hogan, Savage made public appearances on television talk shows. He also achieved success as the spokesperson for Slim Jim beef jerky. Savage lost a retirement match at Wrestlemania VII in 1991 but was soon back in the ring, including for a staged wedding to Elizabeth; their marriage ended in 1993.

In 1994 Savage left the WWF to join Hogan in World Championship Wrestling (WCW) as they resumed their feud, drawing a record gate for their *Halloween Havoc* pay-per-view match in 1996. Like many wrestlers who joined WCW, Savage enjoyed short-term success, winning championships and headlining pay-per-view bouts, but in the long run, WCW ruined many careers. After WCW folded in 2001, Savage was one of the few wrestlers Vince McMahon never invited to return. He enjoyed some mainstream success with a memorable turn as Bonesaw McGraw in the movie *Spider-Man* (2002), as well voice work in the animated movie *Bolt* (2008). After the death of Elizabeth in 2003, Savage all but disappeared from wrestling. As of early 2012 he has yet to be enshrined in the WWE Hall of Fame, but his remarkable ring presence will never be forgotten.

Patrick Jones

SEE ALSO: *Hogan, Hulk; Spider-Man; World Wrestling Federation.*

BIBLIOGRAPHY

Harris, Elizabeth. "Randy Savage, 58, Pro Wrestling's Macho Man, Dies." *New York Times*, May 21, 2011, A20.

Lentz, Harris M. *Biographical Dictionary of Professional Wrestling.* Jefferson, NC: McFarland, 1997.

Macho Madness: The Randy Savage Ultimate Collection. DVD. Stamford, CT: World Wrestling Entertainment, 2009.

Savoy Ballroom

The Savoy Ballroom was the most popular dance venue in Harlem, New York, enjoying a successful run from its opening in 1926 to 1956. The Lindy Hop, jitterbug jive, Rhumboogie, and the mambo were some of the many dance styles originated and refined at the Savoy. The Savoy was a veritable institution that featured the best of jazz bands, competitions, and dancers. It was also known for the "Battle of the Bands," or "cutting contest," between the Benny Goodman Orchestra and the Chick Webb Orchestra in 1937. Vocalist Ella Fitzgerald made her famous recording of "A-Tisket, A-Tasket" with the Chick Webb Orchestra, which was the Savoy's house band at the venue; Fitzgerald later led the band after Webb's untimely death. The big band jazz standard titled "Stompin' at the Savoy," was named after the ballroom.

Moe Gale (Moses Galewski, known as the great white father of Harlem), Charles Galewski, and Harlem real estate investor Charles Buchanan opened the Savoy Ballroom to the public on March 12, 1926. Buchanan served as the venue's manager. First marketed as "The World's Most Beautiful Ballroom" and later as "The Home of Happy Feet," the Savoy was situated on the second floor of a building that stretched for a whole block on Lenox Avenue between West 140th Street and West 141st Street in Harlem. Prior to the ballroom's opening, streetcar barns had occupied the site.

DANCERS' PARADISE

Also known as "The Track" because of its early use for dog racing, the Savoy was a dancer's paradise. The interior consisted of a large dance floor (approximately 200 by 50 feet), two bandstands, and a retractable stage. Marble stairs were sandwiched between mirrored walls. The springy dance floor bounced from the dancers' feet and was completely renovated every three years.

Different nights drew different clientele. Saturday night saw the largest crowds and was known as "square's night" to the regulars because there was not much room to dance. Tuesday was the night for serious dancers because there was plenty of floor space. Wednesday and Friday nights were reserved for social clubs and the like, while Thursday night was known as the "kitchen mechanics' night" since most of the patrons were domestics who had the night off. And on Sundays, dancers could compete in the "Opportunity Contest," where prizes were awarded for first and second place. Sunday night also attracted a number of celebrities. In addition to its large African American clientele, the Savoy encouraged and welcomed white dancers and spectators. "The lindy-hoppers at the Savoy even began to practice acrobatic routines, and to do absurd things for the entertainment of the whites. . . . The Harlem nights became show nights for the Nordics," observed poet Langston Hughes.

The Savoy was a place of intense and creative dance activity—new and old steps were refined and taken to new heights in response to the evolution of swing jazz and be-bop. When the Savoy opened in 1926, it instituted a policy forbidding sprightly dances such as the Charleston. Two muscular bouncers enforced the rule, but the dancers evaded the policy by creating a dance move called "the run," a swift step that allowed them to quickly escape the bouncers. Savoy dancers even adapted to the new and difficult-to-dance-to rhythms of be-bop, and the bands that played there likewise created new rhythms in response to the movement of the dancers. The Savoy dancers were known to add "air steps" to the Lindy, which later became known as the jitterbug. Dancers at the Savoy Ballroom were occasionally filmed and their dance steps shared so others could watch and learn the movements.

BIG BANDS

In its thirty years of existence, the Savoy featured a veritable who's who of jazz bands of the Swing Era. Some bandleaders were inherently associated with the Savoy because of their long residencies there. The first such band was the Charleston Bearcats, who opened the Savoy and later changed its name to the Savoy Bearcats. Fess Williams and His Royal Flush Orchestra and the Fletcher Henderson band also participated in the opening night ceremonies. By 1935 Webb and Fitzgerald played frequently at the Savoy, several years later becoming the house band and broadcasting nationally. Trumpeter and bandleader Erskine Hawkins achieved great popularity playing at the Savoy in the late 1930s and early 1940s, and he continued playing extended engagements through the 1950s. Another group that enjoyed a long association with the Savoy Ballroom was the Savoy Sultans, a swing band led by Al Cooper that was extremely popular with dancers and played a powerful swing later known as "jump." Benny Carter, Coleman Hawkins, Andy Kirk, and Glenn Miller, among many other bandleaders, played single engagements at the ballroom.

Webb's band has been inextricably linked to the Savoy Ballroom. In 1932 the band was renamed Chick Webb's Savoy Orchestra and began drawing record-breaking crowds. More than 4,600 patrons came to one breakfast dance. One of the band members, alto saxophonist Edgar Sampson, wrote "Stompin' at the Savoy," which became the ballroom's theme song. Sampson's "Stompin' at the Savoy," Eddie Durham's "Harlem Shout," and Sy Oliver's "Raggin' the Scale" and "For Dancers Only" set the riff instrumental formula for dozens of white swing bands, from Tommy Dorsey to Miller to Les Brown. "Stompin' at the Savoy" was a hit for the Benny Goodman band, and "Big John's Special," his encore for his Carnegie Hall performance, was reportedly named after the Savoy's doorman.

The ballroom usually employed two bands that played alternate sets and became famous for the battles of the bands. One band would spar with the other for the dancers' favor. The Savoy hosted a number of significant band battles during the Swing Era. One long-anticipated battle occurred in 1938 between the Savoy's house band and the Count Basie Band, with the Basie band receiving the longest applause. Nonetheless, Webb's band, on most occasions, won out in the battles.

Although the Savoy closed its doors in 1956, it was instrumental in the dissemination of swing dance and played an important role in the coalescence of popular dance and music.

Willie Collins

SEE ALSO: *Basie, Count; Big Bands; Brown, Les; Carnegie Hall; Dorsey, Tommy; Fitzgerald, Ella; Goodman, Benny; Harlem Renaissance; Hughes, Langston; Jazz; Miller, Glenn; Radio; Swing Dancing; Webb, Chick.*

BIBLIOGRAPHY

Fletcher, Tony. *All Hopped Up and Ready to Go: Music from the Streets of New York, 1927–77.* New York: W. W. Norton, 2009.

Kernfeld, Barry Dean, ed. *The New Grove Dictionary of Jazz.* New York: St. Martin's Press, 1994.

Wood, Ean. *Born to Swing.* London: Sanctuary Publishing, 1996.

Schindler's List

The highly anticipated film *Schindler's List*, directed by Steven Spielberg and based on a 1982 historical novel titled *Schindler's Ark* by Australian writer Thomas Keneally, premiered in December 1993. In a year that had also seen the opening of the Holocaust Museum in Washington, D.C., the film quickly became a cultural event. The public and many critics praised the film, which told a harrowing but inspirational tale of individual decency in response to the horrors of genocide. The $23 million film was also a box-office success, eventually earning more than $300 million worldwide, in spite of its black-and-white photography and three-hour-plus running time—normally considered audience deterrents. Given the epic film's high public profile and cross-cultural praise, it was not surprising that *Schindler's List* would go on to garner seven Academy Awards in 1994, winning for Best Picture and giving Spielberg his first Best Director honor from the Academy. In later years, the American Film Institute listed the film eighth on its list the "100 Best American Films," and the Library of Congress placed it in the National Film Registry in 2004.

It should be noted that a great many academic critics are troubled by certain aspects of Spielberg's treatment of such sensitive subject matter, particularly in regard to the film's sentimentalized conclusion, the portrayal of Jews as passive victims, and the perhaps inevitable trivializing of the Holocaust through traditional Hollywood narrative technique. However, even with the shortcomings, the film was generally acknowledged to be Spielberg's most mature, visually striking, and well-crafted work to date. Not even *Saving Private Ryan*, another Spielberg-directed World War II epic, which opened to general praise during the summer of 1998, has come close to capturing the cultural impact of *Schindler's List.*

BACKGROUND

The film and novel differ in dramatic emphasis and characterization but are both reasonably faithful to the details of the real-life

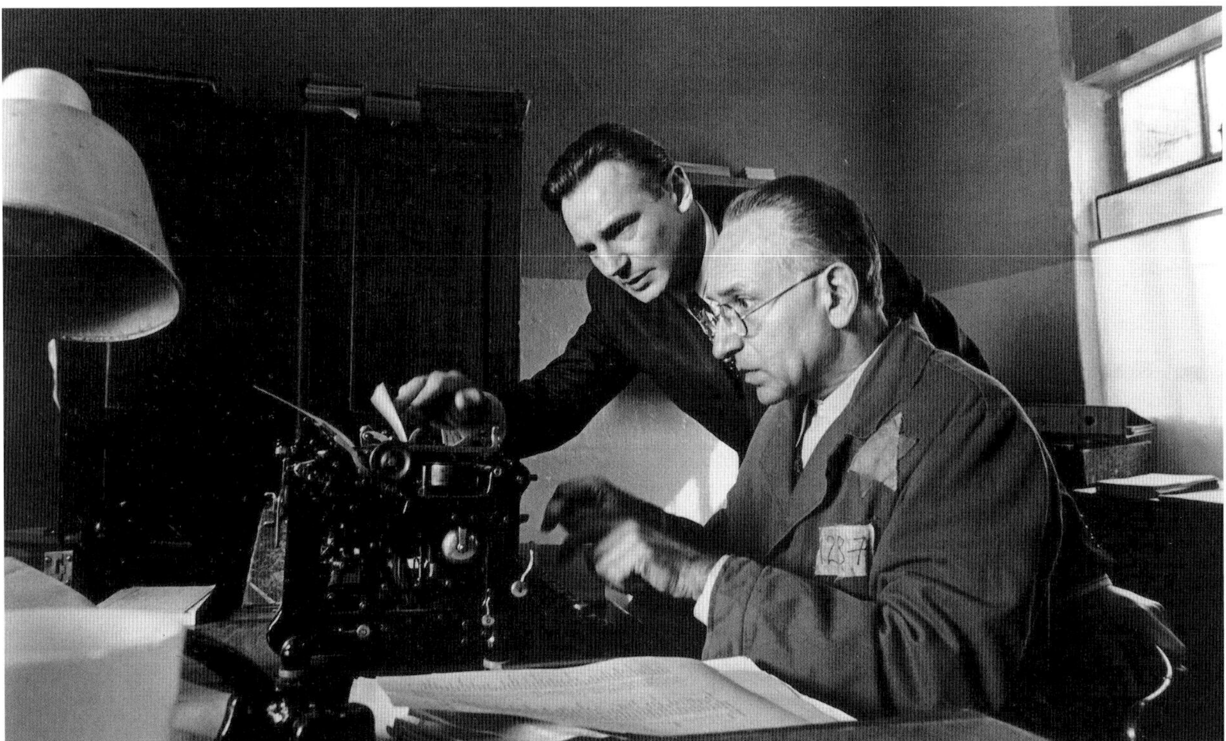

Schindler's List. *Ben Kingsley's Itzhak Stern, right, types a list of Jewish workers to be employed at a factory owned by Liam Neeson's Oskar Schindler in a scene from* Schindler's List. UNIVERSAL/THE KOBAL COLLECTION/JAMES, DAVID.

story of a Catholic-German entrepreneur named Oskar Schindler, who saved more than 1,000 Polish Jews from the Nazi death camps during World War II. As detailed in the novel, Schindler was born in 1908 in the Sudetenland, in an area that would later become Czechoslovakia. As he grew to manhood, Schindler quickly developed a reputation as a carouser and playboy—a reputation founded in reckless actions that even his early marriage in 1928 to a devoutly religious woman named Emilie did not stop. His parents were prosperous in their hometown of Zwittau until the family business, a farm implement factory, went bankrupt in 1935. At this point, the elder Schindler left his wife, and Oskar was forced to seek his living elsewhere. As a salesman and a member of both the Nazi Party and German military intelligence, he traveled alone to Kraków after the German military occupation of Poland in 1939. (This is the point at which Spielberg's adaptation of the novel begins.) In Kraków, Schindler bought an enamel factory that he then staffed with Jewish workers.

Shortly thereafter, the Germans forced the Jews of Kraków to move to a ghetto within the city and also built a forced labor camp named Plaszow outside the city. The extermination camp of Auschwitz began receiving Plaszow inmates during 1942. Throughout the escalating levels of Nazi persecution and brutality directed against Jews, Schindler was able to keep his well-treated Jewish workforce more or less intact, even after the Kraków ghetto was closed in 1943 and all Jews were forced into Plaszow, which was under the command of a ruthless man named Amon Goeth. Goeth and Schindler formed an unusual relationship: each exploiting the other for personal advantage but nevertheless reluctantly sharing some similarities of taste and lifestyle. (Spielberg emphasizes their duality of character throughout the middle portion of the film.)

Schindler's employees were able to work in his factory by day until 1944, when orders came to send all of Plaszow's Jews to Auschwitz. Through his close contacts with Goeth and others in the German military hierarchy, Schindler somehow managed to receive permission to relocate 1,000 Jewish workers to another camp in the relative safety of Czechoslovakia. In one of the most amazing episodes of the Schindler legend, he even retrieved a group of his female employees from Auschwitz, where their train had been mistakenly diverted. At the Czechoslovakian camp, Schindler provided a haven for another 200 or so escaped Jewish refugees. With the European war's end in May 1945, the "Nazi war profiteer" Schindler and his wife were forced to flee the camp ahead of its Russian liberators.

After the war Schindler moved from Austria to Argentina to West Germany, eventually leaving Emilie. He proved consistently unable to make any kind of living and in the end had to rely for daily survival on the financial largesse of the Jews he had protected during the war. He also visited Israel yearly, all expenses paid by Jewish organizations and individuals. Yad Vashem, the Holocaust memorial in Jerusalem, recognized Schindler as a Righteous Gentile in 1962. He died, perhaps predictably given his lifestyle, of liver failure in 1974 and was buried in a Catholic cemetery in Jerusalem.

MAKING THE MOVIE

The story of Schindler remained in relative obscurity until the early 1980s, when author Thomas Keneally published *Schindler's Ark*. The historical novel had its origins in a 1980 visit by Keneally to a luggage store in Los Angeles, where Keneally met and struck up a conversation with the store owner—a Jew who had been rescued by Schindler. Intrigued by the owner's dramatic tale, Keneally interviewed dozens of the *Schindlerjuden* (Schindler Jews) in several different countries and researched the relevant documents in Israel and Poland. After Keneally's book was published as *Schindler's List* in America, Universal Studios acquired it for development. Director Steven Spielberg, about to achieve yet another spectacular box-office success with *E.T. The Extra-Terrestrial*, read the book and was determined that he, too, when he felt he was a mature-enough filmmaker, would someday tell the story of Schindler.

Ten years passed, during which Spielberg alternated between taking on the project and passing it to others. Finally, in 1992, he believed the time was personally and historically right to begin active production on the film. He made several important and risky artistic decisions: to use black-and-white film, to shoot on location in Europe, to rely heavily on hand-held cameras, to select European extras, and to cast nonstars in the key roles (Liam Neeson as Schindler, Ben Kingsley as Schindler's Jewish accountant Stern, and Ralph Fiennes as Amon Goeth). In spite of Spielberg's determination to use authentic locations, some were unavailable: he had to painstakingly reconstruct the Plaszow camp, and when his request to film inside Auschwitz was denied by the World Jewish Congress, he and production designer Allan Starski built a chillingly convincing replica directly outside the grounds. After principal photography was finished, Michael Kahn edited the film to its three-and-a-half-hour running length, and longtime Spielberg collaborator John Williams composed the musical score.

The final result, released in theaters at the end of 1993, was generally well received and capped one of Spielberg's most personally and financially successful years ever. (Earlier that summer, his film *Jurassic Park* had earned nearly $360 million domestically.) Many critics reevaluated their previous dismissal of Spielberg as a skilled but trivial filmmaker. But more significant historically, with the profits from *Schindler's List*, Spielberg established two organizations: the Righteous Persons Foundation, dedicated to memorializing Gentile rescuers of Jews during World War II, and the Shoah Visual History Foundation, set up to record the first-hand accounts of Holocaust survivors before the passage of time silences their voices. Additionally, Spielberg financed several documentaries about the Holocaust, including *Anne Frank Remembered* (1995), *Lost Children of Berlin* (1996), and *The Lost Days* (1998).

Philip Simpson

SEE ALSO: *Academy Awards;* E.T. The Extra-Terrestrial*; Hollywood;* Jurassic Park*; Movie Stars; Spielberg, Steven; World War II.*

BIBLIOGRAPHY

Keneally, Thomas. *Schindler's List.* New York: Simon & Schuster, 1994.

Loshitzky, Yosefa, ed. *Spielberg's Holocaust: Critical Perspectives on Schindler's List.* Bloomington: Indiana University Press, 1997.

Morris, Nigel. *The Cinema of Steven Spielberg: Empire of Light.* London: Wallflower, 2007.

Palowski, Franciszek. *The Making of Schindler's List: Behind the Scenes of an Epic Film.* Secaucus, NJ: Carol Publishing Group, 1998.

Perry, George. *Steven Spielberg Close Up: The Making of His Movies.* New York: Thunder's Mouth Press, 1998.

Schlatter, George *(1932–)*

Television producer-writer-director George Schlatter's credits are impressive. He has produced special programming that has featured a Hall of Fame of entertainers, from Nat King Cole to Elton John, Frank Sinatra to Michael Jackson, Judy Garland to Bette Midler. He founded the American Comedy Awards, an annual televised event that spotlights the accomplishments of male and female comedians. Over the years he has earned more than two dozen Emmy nominations and a quartet of Emmy Awards.

Schlatter's greatest contribution to television, however, was as coexecutive producer (with Ed Friendly) of the initial—and funniest—seasons of *Rowan & Martin's Laugh-In. Laugh-In*, which aired from 1968 to 1973, was a fast-paced hour crammed with goofy, irreverent sketch comedy. While its often surreal sensibility evolved from Ernie Kovacs's pioneering television humor, *Laugh-In* itself altered the future of television comedy from the pacing of sitcom buffoonery to the structure and content of sketch comedy shows such as *Saturday Night Live.* The show also served as the launching pad for the careers of Goldie Hawn and Lily Tomlin.

Rob Edelman

SEE ALSO: *Cole, Nat King; Davis, Bette; Emmy Awards; Garland, Judy; Jackson, Michael; John, Elton; Kovacs, Ernie;* Laugh-In*;* Saturday Night Live*; Sinatra, Frank; Television; Tomlin, Lily.*

BIBLIOGRAPHY

"Schlatter, George." *Contemporary Theatre, Film and Television*, Vol. 7. Ed. Linda S. Hubbard and Owen O'Donnell. Detroit: Gale Research, 1989. 355–356.

Schlessinger, Dr. Laura *(1947–)*

With an estimated weekly listening audience of eighteen million, Dr. Laura Schlessinger ranked as the most popular talk radio personality of the late 1990s, surpassing even Rush Limbaugh and Howard Stern. An advocate of high ethical standards and personal accountability, Schlessinger—known to her fans as Dr. Laura—takes to the airwaves each weekday to offer her "never to be humble opinion" on various moral dilemmas. Employing her own brand of tough love, Schlessinger, an Orthodox Jew, often preaches to her callers, frequently chastising them for their behaviors and nagging them to mend their ways. She is alternately hailed for her stern morality and criticized for her intolerance of contrary viewpoints. Dr. Laura stands in opposition to everything from abortion to day care and has proposed that no one under the age of thirty should marry. She also frequently targets the gay community, calling homosexuality "a biological error." In August 2010 Schlessinger ignited a storm of controversy when she used the "N word" eleven times within five minutes while conversing with a caller.

TOUGH TALK AND IMPECCABLE TIMING

Dr. Laura's nationally syndicated radio program draws a large audience—approximately 8.25 million weekly listeners—despite assertions that her message is one of hate, punishment, and vengeance. For many years she also wrote a syndicated column, which ran in fifty-five newspapers nationwide. She has written numerous self-help books, many of which have topped best-seller lists, as well as several children's books. Her overwhelming popularity suggests that she is sending messages that at least some Americans are eager to hear. Many people, including Schlessinger, attribute her success to tough talk and impeccable timing.

The so-called Me Generation—composed of individuals born in the 1970s, 1980s, and 1990s (though most often associated with members of Generation Y)—describes individuals obsessed with material greed and the desire for instant gratification. Contrarily, Schlessinger offers a radically different message: one of personal responsibility. She challenges her listeners to improve their characters by employing a strong moral code when making decisions rather than relying on emotions. In a 1996 interview for *U.S. News & World Report* with Amy Bernstein, Schlessinger stated that between the 1960s and the 1990s Americans had "erected a monument to feelings and made them the vantage point from which to make decisions. That's dangerous." Instead, Schlessinger instructs her listeners to take responsibility for their actions by making rational choices and doing the morally correct thing, regardless of emotion.

Dr. Laura Schlessinger. *Dr. Laura Schlessinger's brand of no-nonsense advice put her show at the top of the talk-radio ratings in the 1990s.* ALEXANDRA WYMAN/STAFF/WIREIMAGE/GETTY IMAGES.

As strident as she sometimes sounds, her message is one that many Americans want to hear. Indeed, after witnessing numerous high-profile personal and political scandals, the American populace had grown tired of excuses. Instead the public craved integrity, commitment, candor, and conscience, which are keystones of Schlessinger's definition of character. Such characteristics also became part of a new counterculture that Americans appeared to be embracing. During the presidential elections of 1992 and 1996, "family values" were at the foundation of every campaign platform, indicating that Americans were anxious for a return to the simplicity of life symbolized by the 1950s.

In addition to her moral message, Schlessinger offers the idea that individuals have ultimate control of their lives, claiming that even physical addictions such as alcoholism are a matter of personal choice. According to Schlessinger a person can choose the direction his or her life will take by practicing self-restraint and religious faith. In a society where many people feel their lives are spinning out of control because violence appears commonplace and marriage is no longer a sacrament, hers is a message that portends to offer stability amid the chaos.

CRITICISM AND CONTROVERSY

However, for every American who has embraced Schlessinger's message, there is another who has rejected it. Her critics describe her as narrow-minded, self-righteous, and prudish, primarily due to her stances against live-in relationships, which she refers to inimically as "shacking up." She also opposes premarital sex, abortion (in most cases), and gossip. Charges of hypocrisy were leveled when nude pictures of Schlessinger, taken by a former lover, surfaced on the Internet. She regularly badgers listeners who engage in what she considers immoral behaviors, telling them to "grow up," "stop whining," or "quit cold turkey." Her detractors fault such advice for its harsh, black-and-white nature. Ironically, this is precisely the kind of advice that keeps other listeners rushing to their telephones. On average, nearly 50,000 callers vie for a moment on air with Dr. Laura, seeking her matter-of-fact opinions, regardless of how severe they might be.

The issue that has drawn the biggest fire, however, is Schlessinger's position on child care. As evidenced by her assertion following every commercial break that she is, first and foremost, "her kid's mom," children rank high on her agenda. She espouses the belief that once a child is born, a parent should put everything on hold, including careers, to stay home and care for that child. In most cases, she believes the at-home parent should be the mother, explaining that women are better and more natural nurturers, especially during a child's first few years. In Schlessinger's view, day-care centers are inadequate venues of child care, and she contends that they are largely to blame for delinquent, immoral, or irresponsible youths, who suffer from a lack of one-on-one time with their parents.

This view is criticized by many who say Schlessinger abuses her powerful position by placing unnecessary guilt on parents, especially working mothers, by demanding unhealthy amounts of self-sacrifice. Adding more fuel to the fire, Schlessinger has asserted that the feminist movement was responsible for breaking up families by encouraging women to put their own needs before those of their children.

"AMERICA'S MORAL COMPASS"?

In addition to their disenchantment with her message, detractors have tagged Schlessinger as both a fraud and a hypocrite. The fraud charge stems from her use of the prefix *doctor* on air. Although she does have a PhD, it is in physiology—not psychology, as many listeners assume. Schlessinger does have a postdoctoral certificate in marriage, family, and child counseling and did practice as a licensed counselor for twelve years, but critics worry that some callers have assumed her knowledge of psychotherapy to be more vast than it is. As for being a hypocrite, detractors cite nude photos taken of a twenty-something Schlessinger by a former lover, not to mention her extramarital affair with Lewis Bishop, whom she married in 1985. Schlessinger insists that the particulars of morality can always be debated, contending that her focus is on the lifelong struggle to be a person of character. Needless to say, Schlessinger's position as "America's moral compass" continues to inspire devotion, antipathy, and above all controversy wherever her message is heard.

As might be expected, the Gay and Lesbian Alliance against Defamation (GLAAD) has been among Schlessinger's most vocal opponents. Things came to a head in 2000 when plans were announced to give her a television talk show. In response to overwhelming protest, advertisers began bailing on the show. It premiered in September 2000 to low ratings. Schlessinger attempted to backtrack on some of her opinions to save her career, announcing that she was no longer an Orthodox Jew. By that time, however, she had lost much of her credibility. When the talk show was taken off the air a year later, it was ranked 132 in the Nielsen ratings.

In an August 2010 radio broadcast Schlessinger drew fire for using the word *nigger* several times during a conversation with a caller who phoned in seeking advice for dealing with rude comments about her interracial marriage. The program caused an uproar, and Schlessinger apologized the following day. She subsequently gave up her radio program, only to later sign a contract for a program with Sirius/XM radio. Exhibiting less religious fervor in her subsequent on-air time, Schlessinger continues to offer advice to some nine million listeners a week. Some professionals have come out soundly against what they refer to as her "blame the victim" mentality, insisting that it may do serious damage. A 2002 study of therapy patients revealed that the single most important factor in success was empathy on the part of a therapist, and Schlessinger seems to eschew such emotions.

Belinda S. Ray

SEE ALSO: *Abortion; Best Sellers; Feminism; Gay Liberation Movement; Gay Men; Generation X; Limbaugh, Rush; Radio; Satellite Radio; Sex Scandals; Shock Radio; Stern, Howard; Syndication; Talk Radio; Telephone; Television.*

BIBLIOGRAPHY

Arkowitz, Hal. "The 'Just Do It!' Trap." *Scientific American Mind* 21, no. 4 (2010): 64–65.

Bernstein, Amy. "Dr. Laura Schlessinger's Moral Health Show." *U.S. News & World Report*, April 29, 1996, 19.

Perls, Frederick S. *Ego, Hunger & Aggression: A Revision of Freud's Theory & Method*. Highland, NY: Gestalt Journal Press, 1992.

Salerno, Steve. *Sham: How the Self-Help Movement Made America Helpless*. New York: Crown Publishers, 2005.

Schlessinger, Laura C. *Ten Stupid Things Women Do to Mess Up Their Lives*. New York: HarperPerennial Library, 1995.

Schlessinger, Laura C. *How Could You Do That? The Abdication of Character, Courage and Conscience*. New York: HarperCollins, 1997.

Schlessinger, Laura C. *Ten Stupid Things Men Do to Mess Up Their Lives*. New York: HarperCollins, 1997.

Schlessinger, Laura C., and Stewart Vogel. *The Ten Commandments: The Significance of God's Laws in Everyday Life*. New York: HarperCollins, 1998.

Williams, Walter L., and Yolanda Retter. *Gay and Lesbian Rights in the United States: A Documentary History*. Westport, CT: Greenwood Press, 2003.

Schnabel, Julian *(1951–)*

Widely viewed as the "bad boy" of the 1980s New York art scene, Julian Schnabel seemed to rise to prominence from nowhere. After earning a bachelor of fine arts degree from the University of Houston, Schnabel toured Europe before returning home to New York City. On his journeys both stateside and abroad, Schnabel tackled many occupations, including cab driver and cook, while living a bohemian lifestyle. Once he began painting as a profession, Schnabel's talent for self-promotion propelled him into the limelight, and he quickly assumed a mythical status within the modern art world. During the 1990s and the first decade of the 2000s, Schnabel steered his prodigious creative energy into filmmaking, earning international renown with several critically acclaimed movies.

Enormous canvases filled with vibrant colors and bold strokes typify Schnabel's paintings. With his first exhibition at Mary Boone Gallery in 1979, which launched him into the New York art scene, he gathered a following for his unusual emotion-filled works. By the time he exhibited his work in a show jointly organized by Boone and Leo Castelli in 1981, he had become firmly established, and a clamoring for his neoexpressionist paintings created on and with remarkable surfaces ensued. Schnabel's signature works, both abstract and figurative, have as a base surface either black velvet or broken crockery. Filled with raw emotion, the paintings contain an underlying edge of brutality while still being suffused with energy. Schnabel claims that he's "aiming at an emotional state, a state that people can literally walk into and be engulfed by." Although his monstrous canvases have elements of collage, Schnabel's arrival as an artist signified the return of painting to an art scene that previously revolved around conceptual and minimalist art.

Schnabel's quick rise to popularity became representative of the money-driven 1980s. His notoriety exemplified the commercialization of the art world that related to the economic boom. Considered heroic, with his charismatic and somewhat eccentric personality—the artist reportedly worked in pajamas, slippers, and robe—Schnabel became a superstar in art. Controversially, his persona, carefully hyped, often outshone the artwork itself, which inspired debate by critics as to whether it actually held any artistic merit. To the art-buying public, Schnabel's was the work to own, and his exhibitions often sold out. A proficient artist who worked quickly, Schnabel once claimed to have sold more than sixty canvases in one year. Typifying the era, many critics judged Schnabel's success as an artist based on the incredible demand for his work. With the recession of the late 1980s and the stabilization of the economy in the 1990s, Schnabel's star faded somewhat.

Although Schnabel continued to paint successfully throughout the 1990s, he also explored other art forms. In 1996 he wrote and directed the movie *Basquiat*. The $3.3 million independent film related to the life and struggles of his friend and fellow artist Jean-Michel Basquiat. This proved to be a fairly triumphant endeavor, realizing some commercial and critical recognition and success. Schnabel's foray into the cinematic arena again proved his mastery at adapting to the current trends, and the addition of filmmaker to his persona further solidified his reputation as a modern artist.

Schnabel followed the success of *Basquiat* with *Before Night Falls* (2000), the story of homosexual Cuban poet and author Reinaldo Arenas and his struggles to escape persecution under the regime of Fidel Castro. Schnabel's next film, *The Diving Bell and the Butterfly* (2007), told the real-life saga of *Elle* magazine editor Jean-Dominique Bauby's struggle to retain his passion for life after suffering a devastating stroke. Among Schnabel's most celebrated films, *The Diving Bell and the Butterfly* earned the artist Best Director prize at the 2008 Cannes Film Festival as well as a nomination for the prestigious Palme d'Or for best film. Also in 2007 Schnabel directed *Berlin*, a documentary of Lou Reed's epic 2006 performance of his 1973 album of the same name.

In 2010 the Art Gallery of Ontario hosted a retrospective of Schnabel's artwork, the first major exhibition of his paintings since the late 1980s. That same year he directed *Miral*, the story of an orphaned Palestinian girl set against the backdrop of the Arab-Israeli conflict. In late 2011 the Museo Correr in Venice hosted an exhibition of forty Schnabel works that included pieces spanning his entire career.

Jennifer Jankauskas

SEE ALSO: *Conceptual Art; Gay Men; Minimalism; Reed, Lou.*

BIBLIOGRAPHY

Gopnik, Blake. "A Fired-Up Schnabel Gets Political." *Newsweek*, March 13, 2011.

McEvilley, Thomas, and Lisa Phillips. *Julian Schnabel: Paintings 1975–1987*. London: Whitechapel Art Gallery, 1987.

Schnabel, Julian. *C. V. J.: Nicknames of Maitre D's and Other Excerpts from Life*. New York: Random House, 1987.

Whyte, Murray. "Putting the Pieces Back Together." *Toronto Star*, September 2, 2010.

Schoolhouse Rock!

The *Schoolhouse Rock!* series of animated musical shorts, which ran on the ABC network on weekend mornings from 1973 to 1985, dazzled a generation of young viewers raised in front of the television. Vibrant, catchy, exuberant, fast-paced, and entertaining, the series was also educational and instructive about basic grammar, mathematics, science, and American history.

AN IDEA THAT ROCKED

David McCall, president of New York's McCaffrey and McCall advertising agency, conceived the series. He had observed that his young son had trouble learning his multiplication table but easily and happily recounted the lyrics and music of popular songs. Working with his agency colleagues, McCall commissioned some songs about mathematics and presented them to Michael Eisner, then vice president of children's programming at ABC (and future chairman of the Walt Disney Company), and Chuck Jones, famed for his Bugs Bunny, Daffy Duck, and Road Runner cartoons. ABC bought the series, and General Foods sponsored it. The first animated shorts, a series of songs with titles such as "Zero My Hero" and "Three Is the Magic Number," appeared in January 1973. The timing was perfect: in the early 1970s Saturday morning cartoons became an institution, and the networks were under pressure to run programming that was perceived as having social value. In addition, in 1974 the Federal Communications Commission (FCC) established guidelines for children's programming in an effort to improve their educational content. *Schoolhouse Rock!* satisfied on both counts.

Over the next twelve years ABC aired more than forty of these animated musical pieces, running as many as seven different spots in one weekend. The spots were broken into five subject areas: multiplication, grammar, American history, science, and computers. For the "Multiplication Rock" series, the creative team wrote songs concerning the multiplication products from zero to twelve (excluding one); "Grammar Rock" informed viewers of the parts of speech. "America Rock" was created for the American bicentennial in 1976, and its songs detailed the American Revolution, the Constitution, the westward expansion, racial diversity, and women's suffrage. Later series included "Science Rock" and "Scooter Computer & Mr. Chips."

The series won four Emmy Awards, making McCaffrey and McCall the first advertising agency ever to win the coveted television prize. Advertising art directors working at McCaffrey and McCall, as well as at the Young and Rubicam agency, created most of the designs, and many of the songs were penned by copy and jingle writers. The language of advertising drove the three-minute spots, which featured vivid images supported by a catchy tune and continuous repetition of a key message. As a method for teaching a generation raised on television, *Schoolhouse Rock!* was anticipated somewhat by the animated segments interspersed between live-action sequences on the Public Broadcasting Service's successful *Sesame Street* television program, which debuted a few years earlier. But in style, look, feel, and tone, the series was unique in children's programming.

The creative team that grew out of McCaffrey and McCall created all but a few of the original pieces during the 1970s. The design, colors, and lyrics of the spots were in tune with the aesthetic and the ethic of this era—more so than many of the Saturday morning cartoons and advertisements alongside which they ran. Visually they were more faithful to the work of underground comic-book artist R. Crumb and the Beatles movie *Yellow Submarine* (1968) than to cartoons by Walt Disney or Hanna-Barbera. The *Schoolhouse Rock!* images were bright, colorful, simple, and playfully psychedelic. The colors were earthy, the hip lyrics accessible and vernacular, and the jazzy music had a rock-and-roll edge. The tone was optimistic and the outlook diverse. The spots presumed that everyone was capable of learning simple mathematics and grammar and celebrated American history and civic life. The animated spots included refreshingly non-stereotyped people of color, a rarity in the medium.

Among the more renowned *Schoolhouse Rock!* pieces was "Conjunction Junction," which asked, "Conjunction junction, what's your function?" while a manic train conductor linked various colored boxcars as an illustration of the conjunction's grammatical role in "Hookin' up words and phrases and clauses." In another well-known spot, a young boy visiting the Capitol spots a "sad little scrap of paper" that turns out to be a bill under consideration by Congress. "Bill" pines to become a law and plaintively sings his predicament to the boy: "I know I'll be a law some day / At least I hope and pray that I will / But today I am still just a bill." Bill then musically explains to the boy the precise legislative process he must endure to become a law.

GENERATION X PUSHES FOR MORE ROCK

As the Reagan administration deregulated broadcasters' duties in the area of children's programming in the early 1980s, there was less pressure to include educational pieces during commercial air time. Production of *Schoolhouse Rock!* was discontinued in 1985, and ABC took the series off the air. However, in the early and mid-1990s, as the generation that was raised on *Schoolhouse Rock!* grew up to become Generation X, the series experienced a resurgence. College students led a national petition drive to bring it back on the air, and in 1993 ABC began rerunning the spots and commissioning new ones. That same year the musical stage show, *Schoolhouse Rock Live*, opened, eventually running on Broadway and across the country. The original songs were re-released on CD and in 1996 were also rerecorded by popular musicians of the day and released as *Schoolhouse Rock Rocks*. The animated spots themselves were released on video. An "Official Guide" was published by some of the creators in 1996, and *Schoolhouse Rock!* T-shirts and other popular paraphernalia began to appear.

In 1996 Walt Disney became the corporate owner of ABC and *Schoolhouse Rock!* The company released a thirtieth-anniversary two-disc DVD set in 2002. Ten years later the set was still among Amazon's top 100 sellers in children's videos. In 2008 Walt Disney Studios released *Schoolhouse Rock! The Election Collection* straight to DVD. It was a repackaging of previously recorded songs about history, government, money, and science. In 2009 Disney completed *Schoolhouse Rock!—Earth* in time for Earth Day; it featured songs about conservation, recycling, and biodiversity. *Schoolhouse Rock!* was not only one of the many inventive and original cultural phenomena of the 1970s but also unique as a cultural creation that a generation returned in force to retrieve.

Steven Kotok

SEE ALSO: *Advertising; The Beatles; Broadway; Bugs Bunny; Compact Discs; Crumb, Robert; Disney (Walt Disney Company); Earth Day; Emmy Awards; Environmentalism; Generation X; Hanna-Barbera; Multiculturalism; The Musical; Public Television (PBS); Reagan, Ronald; Road Runner and Wile E. Coyote; Rock and Roll; Saturday Morning Cartoons;* Sesame Street*; Television; T-Shirts.*

BIBLIOGRAPHY

Engstrom, Erika. "*Schoolhouse Rock!*: Cartoons as Education." *Journal of Popular Film and Television*, Fall 1995, 98–104.

Smith, Chris. *101 Albums That Changed Popular Music*. New York: Oxford University Press, 2009.

Yohe, Tom, and George Newall. *"Schoolhouse Rock!": The Official Guide*. Hyperion: New York, 1996.

Schwarzenegger, Arnold *(1947–)*

Born in Austria and naturalized as an American citizen in 1983, Arnold Schwarzenegger was one of the main Hollywood male icons of the 1980s and 1990s, a position he used as the basis for a successful political career in the early twenty-first century. Schwarzenegger—Arnie, as he is known to his fans—was able to use his spectacular body as a passport to fame, gaining celebrity in bodybuilding contests.

In 1967 Schwarzenegger won, for the first of five times, the title of Mr. Universe, the world's top bodybuilding distinction. During this time he started businesses in a number of areas, including real estate and diet products. The next phase in his rising career included film stardom, which he reached in the 1980s despite his limited acting skills. Established as both a Hollywood star and businessman, Schwarzenegger launched a political career and in 2003 became the governor of California, earning the nickname "Governator" after his trademark roles as the original Terminator in the popular movie series of the same name.

ACTING CAREER

Schwarzenegger's acting career began with a role as Hercules in a mediocre television film. His first memorable screen appearance was as himself in George Butler and Robert Fiori's documentary on bodybuilding contests, *Pumping Iron* (1977). Schwarzenegger achieved stardom, however, thanks to two roles he played in the 1980s. One was as Robert Howard's sword-

Arnold Schwarzenegger. *Arnold Schwarzenegger's time in the public eye has taken him from celebrity bodybuilder to actor to governor of California.* PABLO BLAZQUEZ DOMINGUEZ/CONTRIBUTOR/FILMMAGIC/GETTY IMAGES.

and-sorcery hero Conan in *Conan the Barbarian* (1982) and *Conan the Destroyer* (1984). The other was as the ultraviolent cyborg sent from the future to eliminate the mother of humankind's future leader in James Cameron's *The Terminator* (1984). A number of action films followed, including the box-office hits *Predator* (1987) and *Total Recall* (1990). In the same period, Schwarzenegger played leading roles in the Ivan Reitman comedies *Twins* (1988) and *Kindergarten Cop* (1990).

His next hit was the sequel to *The Terminator, Terminator 2* (1991). He also starred in a rather long list of interesting films, including *The Last Action Hero* (1993); *True Lies* (1994); *Eraser* (1996); and *Junior* (1994), in which he played a pregnant father. Schwarzenegger became Hollywood's best-paid villain with the role of Mr. Freeze in *Batman & Robin* (1997), for which he reaped $25 million. His last film roles before becoming governor of California were in the 2002 action thriller *Collateral Damage*, the third Terminator film *Terminator 3: Rise of the Machines* (2003), and as the voice of Prince Hapi in the animated film *Around the World in 80 Days* (2004).

Several factors contributed to Schwarzenegger's popularity as an actor. He is a self-made man in two senses—he has "made" his body and has "made" himself. He embodied health and heroism and was, no doubt, perceived as a father figure. Yet each aspect of his success is in itself ambiguous, even contradictory. His thick Austrian accent clashed with his roles as all-American hero. His harsh facial features—deeply set eyes, prominent cheekbones and jaw—somewhat mellowed by age have allowed him to play both heroes and villains. Few actors could have successfully transformed, as he did, the murderous first Terminator into the heroic fatherly Terminator of the sequel.

The capacity to cross the line between good and evil on the screen (and also that between comedy and the action film) seems also closely intertwined with his capacity to quickly overcome the failure of some of his films, such as *Jingle All the Way* (1996) and *Last Action Hero*. Schwarzenegger is, in short, a much more malleable, flexible star than he might seem at first glance. This characteristic may have helped him in his initial success and contributed to his subsequent political career.

GOVERNORSHIP

In 2003 efforts to recall the governor of California, Gray Davis, provided Schwarzenegger with an opportunity to transform his political interests into a surprisingly successful gubernatorial campaign. Schwarzenegger ran as a Republican, despite his marriage to Maria Shriver—niece to liberal stalwarts John F. Kennedy, Robert F. Kennedy, and Edward Kennedy. Following a campaign that many complained relied too heavily on his celebrity status and offered little by way of public policy, Schwarzenegger easily won with 48.5 percent of the vote, which was divided among a large field of candidates.

As governor, Schwarzenegger suffered embarrassment when four initiatives that he sponsored in a 2005 special election went down to defeat. Nevertheless, he completed Davis's term and was elected to a second term in 2006. In his second term, he moved away from his conservative heritage by supporting the passage of a state law that required a 25 percent reduction in greenhouse-gas emissions by 2020. Many observers saw this policy as one that reflected his true, centrist beliefs.

SCANDAL AND AFTERMATH

After his second term came to a close in early 2011, rumors of a long record of infidelity and sexual misconduct—first reported by the *Los Angeles Times* during his campaign in 2003—were revealed to be true. Schwarzenegger and Shriver abruptly ended their marriage of twenty-five years in May 2011, and a week later reports surfaced that he had secretly fathered a son with the couple's longtime housekeeper in 1997. Schwarzenegger had previously denied involvement in a number of other affairs, but he sheepishly admitted to fathering the boy and supporting the boy and his mother.

Although such foibles seemed to shut the door on his political career for good, Schwarzenegger continued to pursue his policy interests, including spearheading R20, a nonprofit organization promoting projects to minimize climate change. After the scandal, he temporarily retreated from the spotlight, though he took a small role in Sylvester Stallone's *The Expendables 2* (2012).

Sara Martin

SEE ALSO: *Bodybuilding; Dieting; Hollywood; Stallone, Sylvester;* The Terminator.

BIBLIOGRAPHY

Andrews, Nigel. *True Myths: The Life and Times of Arnold Schwarzenegger*. London: Bloomsbury, 1995.

Flynn, John. *The Films of Arnold Schwarzenegger*. New York: Citadel Press, 1996.

Halperin, Ian. *The Governator: From Muscle Beach to His Quest for the White House, the Improbable Rise of Arnold Schwarzenegger*. New York: William Morrow, 2010.

Jeffords, Susan. *Hard Bodies: Hollywood Masculinity in the Reagan Era*. New Brunswick, NJ: Rutgers University Press, 1994.

Krasniewicz, Louise, and Michael Blitz. *Arnold Schwarzenegger: A Biography*. Westport, CT: Greenwood Press, 2006.

Mathews, Joe. *The People's Machine: Arnold Schwarzenegger and the Rise of Blockbuster Democracy*. New York: Public Affairs, 2006.

Neale, Steve. "Masculinity as Spectacle: Reflections on Men and Mainstream Cinema." *Screen* 24, no. 6 (1983): 2–17.

Rafiq, Fiaz. *Arnold Schwarzenegger: Conversations*. Birmingham, UK: Health n Life, 2011.

Tasker, Yvonne. *Spectacular Bodies: Gender, Genre and the Action Cinema*. New York: Routledge, 1993.

Thomas, David. *Not Guilty: In Defence of the Modern Man*. London: Weidenfeld & Nicolson, 1993.

Science Fiction Publishing

Science fiction is a popular literary genre, abutting such fictional fields as techno-thrillers, fantasy, horror, and the "lost world" narratives of the early twentieth century. Less frequently it overlaps spy novels, mysteries, and romantic fiction; it occasionally even surfaces as "serious" literature. With varying degrees of success, science fiction narratives and themes have been translated into movies, television, radio dramas, comics, games, and (in one instance) opera. The genre has created or popularized such concepts as spaceflight, extraterrestrials, time travel, atomic war, genetic engineering, and ecological disaster. Science fiction mirrors the apprehensions and anticipations of an age; it is increasingly the product of a society that is concerned about the relationship between its continued existence and its dependence upon technological development and scientific knowledge beyond the comprehension of laypeople.

SCIENCE FICTION: THE EARLY YEARS

Those seeking a worthy pedigree for science fiction have found its ancestors in the works of H. G. Wells and Jules Verne, Mary Shelley's *Frankenstein*, Edmond Rostand's *Cyrano de Bergerac*, Edgar Allan Poe stories, and *The Golden Ass* of Lucius Apuleius. All were published in their time as ordinary literature without stigma. Modern science fiction, born of the "pulps" of the 1920s and 1930s, is the natural child of these classics, neglected and even despised by its legitimate relatives. Occasionally, however, a title would rise to prominence.

Imaginative stories—notably Edgar Rice Burroughs's tales of Tarzan and John Carter's adventures on Barsoom—had appeared for decades in magazines such as Frank Munsey's *All-Story*. However, in the 1920s fashion changed when general interest fiction magazines lost circulation to more narrowly focused publications, and the remaining readers demanded fiction with ever more conventional settings. Authors without name recognition were thus pushed toward genre magazines, which did not pay as well but accepted their stories without qualms. Readers with specialized tastes—for interplanetary sagas, plainly told detective yarns, and G-8 and his Battle Aces—also defected to the newer magazines, which in turn made the general interest publications even more conservative. Ultimately even Burroughs, Abraham Merritt, and Ray Cummings were banished to the pulps.

By early 1919 Street and Smith's *Thrill Book* already specialized in imaginative literature; it lasted for sixteen issues. *Weird Tales*, whose métier was blood-curdling fantasy, fared better, circulating from 1923 to 1954. By general agreement the first true science fiction magazine was Hugo Gernsback's *Amazing Stories*, which began in April 1926. (The publisher's name is commemorated today in the "Hugos," much-coveted awards presented annually at the official World Science Fiction Convention—a fan-dominated event that Gernsback himself helped institute.) Technically neither *Amazing Stories* nor the clones later started by Gernsback (*Science Wonder Stories, Air Wonder Stories*) began as pulp magazines, for they were printed on 8-inch-by-11-inch "bedsheet-size" paper instead of 7-inch-by-10-inch sheets.

BEGINNING OF THE PULPS

The Clayton chain's *Astounding Stories of Super-Science* earned the distinction of becoming the first science fiction pulp in January 1930. From the beginning, *Astounding* outdid its competitors, paying contributors more and establishing a steady, secure distribution. In addition, *Astounding* was better edited. Both Harry Bates (editor, 1930–1933)—who wrote the story that later became the movie *The Day the Earth Stood Still*—and F. Orlin Tremaine (editor, 1933–1937) were only adequate writers, but they excelled as editors who believed in the future of the new genre. Their pursuit of quality and encouragement of new writers secured better authors and better stories for *Astounding*, which helped the magazine build a higher circulation and become profitable more quickly than its rivals. These aspects aided *Astounding*'s return from the grave when the Clayton chain fell into bankruptcy in 1933 and the rapid rebuilding of its circulation after the Street and Smith takeover of the Clayton chain in 1933. As of 1998 the magazine was named *Analog Science Fiction and Fact* and was published by Dell Magazines.

Tremaine's handpicked successor, twenty-seven-year-old John W. Campbell Jr. (editor, 1937–1971), proved to be brilliant. A well-regarded but second-string author of super scientific romances (that he was also the author of the moody "Don A. Stuart" stories was generally unknown), Campbell quickly mastered the editorial skills of his mentor and moved on to shape the magazine's—and for a while, the field's—philosophy. Gernsback, mesmerized by turn-of-the-twentieth-century experimental science, had favored stories in which the narrative element was often little more than sugar coating around a core of semi-imaginable technological achievements. Campbell, better educated and an inveterate tinkerer, controversialist, and promoter of science fiction, placed equal emphasis on the science and the impact of science and technology upon human beings. Campbell was also a stern advocate of plots with logical consistency, many of which he devised himself and cast wholesale at his contributors in an unending series of letters that doubled as mini-lectures on writing style and technique.

The different emphasis did not make humanists of Campbell and his evolving school of authors, which included A. E. Van Vogt, Theodore Sturgeon, George O. Smith, C. L. Moore, Henry Kuttner, Robert Heinlein, L. Sprague de Camp, and Isaac Asimov. Pulp fiction was fast moving, easily comprehensible, and generally devoid of moral ambiguity; its readers were not disposed to look below the textual surface for deconstructive ironies, and if they had been, they would generally have been disappointed. At a penny a word, writers took no pains to be subtle; they seldom found time to do second drafts.

Fortunately, readers of science fiction were easily satisfied. They sought the affirmation of moral or ideological views rather than avant-garde literary values: that justice was obtainable in a corrupt society in the detective magazines, that courage and gentlemanly virtues coexisted in adventure tales. Science fiction magazines promised an expanding technological and technocratic future and provided ever more grandiose descriptions of action and scenery. Whether the readers sought "transcendence" or a "sense of wonder," this fiction had little to do with the private epiphanies that climaxed much "literary" fiction.

Moreover, pulp fiction was ephemeral. Some pulp authors cracked the book market for detective stories, but most writers' work perished as the yellowing, brittle pages of the magazines crumbled away. A handful of specialist reprint publishers—among them Gnome Books, Shasta, Fantasy Press, Prime Press, and Arkham House—appeared to publish imaginative fiction, but their print runs were small and their material limited. No one expected pulp science fiction to last through the ages, and no one expected to make a living writing it. As the 1930s and 1940s wore on, readers and writers of science fiction were increasingly isolated from the literary values that came to prominence with modernism.

EVOLUTION DURING THE POSTWAR YEARS

Defenders of science fiction's merits tend to point out certain masterpieces of the genre, works so carefully told not a comma seems misplaced, so heartbreakingly beautiful that it seems their readers must break into tears. Included among these masterpieces are *More than Human* (1953) by Theodore Sturgeon, *Childhood's End* (1953) by Arthur C. Clarke, *The Man in the High*

Castle (1962) by Philip K. Dick, *The Year of the Quiet Sun* (1970) by Wilson Tucker, and *Dying Inside* (1972) by Robert Silverberg. Advocates also list the utilitarianism offered by science fiction as a predictor of inventions used in the modern world—from Verne's Nautilus to Heinlein's waldoes—and the impact of those inventions on modern lives. Campbell predicted in his magazine that men would reach the moon by 1950 and that *Astounding* would be on sale there in 1955. Heinlein's projections, in a 1947 letter to the *Saturday Evening Post*, were only slightly paler, with a permanent base on the moon by 1962. But science fiction writers were not alone in contemplating how technology impacted modern lives, as *Collier's* and Walt Disney would demonstrate in the next decade. And science fiction writers had foretold both atomic energy and atomic weapons, which became a reality with the devastation of Hiroshima and Nagasaki.

Despite the reality of atomic energy and the promise of spaceflight, however, there was no great increase in science fiction's prestige in the immediate wake of the war. Much of the internal esprit de corps of Campbell's school had evaporated. The genre was aging, and its practitioners were retiring or moving on to other fields. By the early 1950s new authors had come to prominence; this later generation was often better trained in the sciences than their predecessors, more attuned to good prose, more sophisticated politically, and more reflective. By and large they labored in similar obscurity. Only Clarke would achieve a real reputation among the general public—and not until 1969—though 1980s filmgoers might recognize the names of Philip Dick and Frank Herbert.

A few things were different, however. Blessed with a good agent, Heinlein had found it possible in the late 1940s to sell short fiction to the *Saturday Evening Post*, becoming the first pulp science fiction writer to break that market. Later on Ray Bradbury also made it to the slicks, but for most science fiction authors such high-paying sales remained aspirations rather than reality until *Playboy* proved a receptive audience. Heinlein broke more new ground in 1947, when Scribner published his original *Rocket Ship Galileo*, a novel specifically aimed at teenagers. Throughout the 1950s he, Andre Norton, Fred Pohl, Jack Williamson, Lester del Rey, Isaac Asimov, and others would write for the juvenile market. Sales were not great, since the hardbound editions usually wound up in public libraries, and few were reprinted before the 1960s (Norton proved the exception), but the books were well read, allowing Heinlein to spread his pro-spaceflight "propaganda" and Asimov to describe the wonders of science to a new crop of readers.

Anthologies of science fiction stories also appeared after the war. Sales were good enough to encourage Simon & Schuster to bring out A. E. Van Vogt's *The World of A* in 1948. In 1949 Doubleday published Max Ehrlich's *The Big Eye*, Asimov's *Pebble in the Sky*, and Heinlein's *Waldo and Magic, Inc.* At last major publishers were willing to print science fiction between hard covers. Soon thereafter Ace Books and other soft-cover publishers were reprinting those editions and original material themselves. For science fiction writers who could break into this market, it was suddenly possible to tell a science fiction story for more than one or two cents a word; it was even possible to tell a story that would pay royalties for years afterward. One could actually make a living as a full-time writer.

But not everyone, for the book market was not large enough for all the magazine writers, and the publishers preferred novels to stories. As late as 1959 even Heinlein's story collections *The Menace from Earth* and *The Unpleasant Profession of Jonathan Hoag* were first printed in hardback by small press publisher Gnome Books, reaching a mass audience only later through paperback. In terms of volume, science fiction continued to be a magazine phenomenon through the late 1950s. The magazines were smaller than before, the paper of better quality, and the storytelling more sophisticated, but circulation figures were small. *Astounding* probably never sold more than 100,000 copies per issue (whereas *Playboy* had sales of two million by the end of decade, and the *Saturday Evening Post* boasted sales of more than five million). To make up for this, there were many magazines, twenty to thirty at a time, often no longer lived than mayflies, but all—if only briefly—were markets for aspiring writers.

The boom in American science fiction magazines peaked in 1953, with 174 issues of thirty-six magazines. Thereafter the number of magazines fell off slowly at first, then abruptly in 1958 when the American News Service folded. Twenty science fiction magazines ceased publication in 1958; sales of those that remained were cut in half. The survivors learned to rely on subscribers rather than newsstand sales. This brought stability but at a cost; the magazines became increasingly set in molds. Late 1950s issues of *Astounding* and *F&SF* sometimes seemed parodies of themselves in happier times, and, of course, without impulse buyers, total circulation figures did not increase. Like other publications, science fiction magazines also faced competition from television and the increasing volume of paperback books. These juggernauts were not to be defeated; a handful of magazines limp on today with stable (and small) lists of subscribers, but they are peripheral to the film and book markets. Most self-professed science fiction "fans" do not read them.

A full account of science fiction in the 1950s would be incomplete without mention of movies and television shows, from *Them!* (1954) to *Twilight Zone* (1959–1964). It is enough to note that Hollywood's version of science fiction was a separate art form, with strengths and weaknesses of its own, and that until the 1970s the influence ran one way: the movies used some themes of genre science fiction but had virtually no effect on magazine fiction and novels. A similar story could be told of the comics, except that *Superman* and *Flash Gordon* stayed closer to their literary roots.

THE SPACE AGE

It is surprising to note that science fiction did not appreciate any improvement in its respectability and sales figures with the advent of the Space Age in the late 1950s and 1960s—a mystery perhaps best explained by the notion that the general public does not want firsthand acquaintanceship with technology and is thoroughly suspicious of science's offerings. Certainly the general repute of scientists deteriorated as the 1960s wore on (as did that of most authority figures). Even that triumphant symbol of science fiction perspicaciousness—the first crewed flight to the moon in July 1969—failed to satisfy, as many Americans (49 percent according to one poll) disapproved of the Apollo program, and space exploration has languished ever since.

Instead, readers of science fiction (and many authors) turned to the field of heroic fantasy in extraordinary numbers, as exemplified by J. R. R. Tolkien's *Lord of the Rings* trilogy and the Conan tales of Robert E. Howard. The same authors often write both science fiction and fantasy, the same readers buy both genres (more or less, although fantasy is reputed to appeal more to women than does science fiction), and the same publishers print both, so distinguishing between them may be wasted effort. Fantasy's allure continues to increase, and its sales may now rival or even surpass those of traditional science fiction. The material generally runs low on literary merit (with some honorable exceptions, including C. J. Cherryh, Glen Cook, and Joel Rosenberg) but brims over with action, villainy, and schmaltz; admirers of Lord Dunsany and James Branch Cabell would be disappointed by the generally solemn mood. In tone and style this material is redolent of the pulps, without the 1930s touch of class consciousness—American fantasy readers turn up their noses at proletarian protagonists but adore heroic lords, ladies, and royalty.

In retrospect the science fiction of the 1960s looks very like what one might expect of science fiction published during that era. By 1950s standards, it was rebellious. Authors as diverse as Heinlein and Philip José Farmer chose sex as their subject matter (Farmer was more successful); others touched upon drugs (Herbert) and mysticism (Dick). English authors toyed with surrealism and the multiple-viewpoint characterization of John Dos Passos; these fifty-year-old literary techniques became renowned as a New Wave. Stylistic experimentation coincided frequently with opposition to the Vietnam War and enthusiasm for alternative lifestyles. In the 1970s Vietnam's fall made political argument pointless; authors perceived that the New Wave was on the ebb, wrote their "unprintable" stories for Harlan Ellison's *Dangerous Visions* series of anthologies, and moved on to cyperpunk and fast-paced militaristic sagas.

THRILLERS, HORROR NOVELS, AND BLOCKBUSTER FILMS

Meanwhile, the great American public moved on to horror fiction. Horror, one might think, is an offshoot of fantasy and might be expected to have the same sort of readership and perhaps the same authors. This has not been the case. To generalize, science fiction fans read fantasy and vice versa, and the same authors may write in both genres. Science fiction and fantasy readers, however, are not automatically fans of horror. In any event, they form only a small portion of the readership for horror; most horror readers are uninterested in science fiction and fantasy, and most horror writers are not linked to science fiction. This seems rather strange, because science fiction and fantasy elements are often prominent in horror works (consider Stephen King's *The Tommyknockers*), but the visceral appeal of the three genres is evidently quite different.

In the 1980s war novels, in the form of near-future technothrillers by Tom Clancy, Larry Bond, Stephen Coonts, and others, made a return to publishing prominence. As with horror, despite the apparent overlap with science fiction, high-tech military fiction is a separate market. It has proven impenetrable to science fiction authors—even to those who specialize in military science fiction.

Movie science fiction has passed through several phases, from low-budget "B" movies in the 1950s to studio-breaking spectaculars in the 1970s. In this last period, movies did influence the literary science fiction market: part of making these big-budget films profitable involved extramural marketing of all kinds, and the book publishers cooperated to the hilt, with novelizations of the scripts, cocktail table volumes showing off *The Art of "Star Wars,"* and the like. These in turn have created an audience for novels set in *Star Wars* settings, semifacetious nonfiction such as *The Physics of "Star Trek,"* autobiographies by some principal actors, and even series of novels by those actors (or with those actors' names on the covers). These spin-offs continued to be profitable into the twenty-first century, producing a slew of science fiction "readers" who seemed familiar with the literature primarily through movies and television. This is good news for publishers; whether the market for science fiction outside the *Star Wars–Star Trek* "Universes" has increased is another issue.

For all its claims to prescience, science fiction since World War II has been shaped by popular culture rather than the other way around. The atomic wars and mutants of the 1950s are obvious tokens of the Cold War and echo ambivalence about atomic energy. The mismanaged battles and angst-torn protagonists depicted in the military science fiction of the 1970s (most memorably Joe Haldeman's *The Forever War*) were parables of the Vietnam experience, and the comic-book heroics of soldiers in 1980s stories reflected the revival of American morale during the Reagan era. Sagas of pollution, overpopulation, and genetic engineering gone awry also draw more from day-to-day experience and commonplace observation than from esoteric scientific knowledge. Even the omnipresent computer and Internet have developed largely without anticipation by science fiction writers; technology evolves today at a faster pace than science fiction authors can accommodate in their stories. However, numerous science fiction stories, some of them quite dark, have articulated the social and cultural implications of computers and related technologies, such as robotics and artificial consciousness.

DECLINE OF SCIENCE FICTION

Conservatism has tended to be the norm in recent science fiction's treatment of lifestyles. Despite some claims, science fiction has never been a good medium for presenting feminist ideas, it has not advanced gay rights, and until the 1980s it had problems with multiculturalism. In the 1990s gay and lesbian characters could be used, but they tended to be in the background; non-European or non-American protagonists were equally unusual. A woman's viewpoint is sometimes used—ironically, male authors seem to do this with more skill. (Worthy of note is C. J. Cherryh's approach of using as protagonist a low-status, insecure male who in the climax must prove himself worthy of a domineering, high-status female love interest.) A similar lack of nerve is present in 1990s-vintage science fiction's treatment of political and economic topics, a rather surprising development given the political consciousness of most authors and the large number of stories dealing with socioeconomic trends in the 1950s and 1960s.

At the end of the 1990s genre science fiction seemed to be reaching exhaustion. Some magazines continued, notably *Analog, Isaac Asimov's*, and *F&SF*. In technique and literary quality, their material was not much different from the 1940s or 1950s vintages; the "Can Do!" spirit was much rarer.

In book publishing, after a slump in the early 1980s, the flow of both hardbacks and paperbacks continued unabated. Science fiction works tended to be profitable in a small way; they were seldom best sellers, but since modern technology made print runs of under 5,000 copies practical, that had not mattered. With the consolidation of the publishing industry in the 1990s, however, presumably to be paid for by concentration on best sellers and the ever-increasing importance of bookselling chains and "superstores," the situation changed. Desktop publishing gave rise to a new generation of small press operators.

A related trend was the almost universal rejection of over-the-transom manuscripts by major American publishers. It became very difficult for unagented writers to break into the commercial science fiction field and difficult even for established authors with mediocre sales to find their manuscripts considered, regardless of merit. This harmed the careers of European authors who had relied on American sales for the bulk of their income and probably made science fiction a more insular and parochial field in the 1990s than it was in the 1960s. The book market effectively adopted the star system; a relative handful of authors could hope to achieve success by being well known and well publicized, whereas others lingered in the shadows. A number of Old Guard authors died in the previous two decades, most notably Heinlein, Asimov, Clifford Simak, and Sturgeon. Authors of the later period—Poul Anderson, Hal Clement, Clarke, Gordon Dickson, Silverberg, Jack Vance—had reached their sixties or seventies and were declining in productivity. None of their possible successors seemed likely to reach the heights attained by Heinlein or Clarke.

Science fiction was ceasing to be a medium in which ordinary authors could make a living simply by writing. Publicity—in the form of frequent convention attendance, a Web page, negotiated advertising figures in book contracts, and ceaseless self-marketing—was a necessity for the modern author. It is likely that no shortage of authors will undergo such rigors; the question at hand is whether such a career is as rewarding as the "school teacher's" existence L. Sprague de Camp once saw as characteristic of science fiction writers.

Increasingly the fiction itself, as it attempted to fit itself to the realities of the modern world, seemed tired. The excitement of space travel and the expectation that technology may bring wonders to the world are no longer part of the science fiction writer's repertoire. Governments are unlikely to underwrite exploration or innovation, modern writers know, and thus books such as Michael Flynn's *Firestar* series and Anderson's *Harvest of Stars* show spaceflight as the product of gifted, obsessed entrepreneurs stamped from the mold of Ayn Rand's tycoons. Great inventions are now devised by misfits rather than heroic leaders; their impact on the world is often inadvertent and, more often than not, gruesome.

In science fiction of the 1990s, planetary pioneers are met by bureaucrats and pummeled by paperwork; it is hard to colonize new worlds, it is expensive, it is tedious, and it is about as adventurous as sidewalk superintending. In direct contrast to earlier science fiction, which proposed that the future was full of exciting possibility, much recent writing offers the thrilling prospect that the future will be glum and unrewarding. Undoubtedly this approach brings science fiction closer to serious literature, but it is not likely to increase readers or to inspire them with a sense of wonder.

SHIFTING PARADIGM

The first decade of the 2000s saw the introduction and proliferation of electronic reading devices and books. Traditional publishing was declared to be dying (some considered it already dead), and bookstores nationwide were closing at an alarming rate. Self-publishing and digital publishing were gaining in momentum, making new works and authors easily accessible to the reading public. This period saw a veritable explosion of online genre magazines. Some of these, like the short-lived (2000–2005) *Sci Fiction*, had big budgets and made a huge splash, publishing both award-winning new stories and "reprints" of classic older stories. Other publications, such as *Strange Horizons*, had more modest budgets (*Strange Horizons'* pay rate matches the rest of the pro magazine markets in the field) but have lasted longer, still publishing today. Most of the remaining new e-publications are closer in quality to fanzines, which have been part of science fiction's publishing landscape since the first fanzine was published in 1930. With advances in technology, much of the subject matter of science fiction works of the past was coming to fruition. As such, science fiction in this decade became less about the science and more about the human and humanity's relationship with science.

One example of this is the emergence of new subgenres with fantastic elements that appeal to different readerships, such as the paranormal romance. These are novels in which the plot is built around a romance but given new spark and challenges through the inclusion of science fiction elements such as time travel (for example, Audrey Niffenegger's 2003 *The Time Traveler's Wife* or fantastic elements like magic or vampirism (such as the wildly popular *Twilight* series). The phenomenal success of J. K. Rowling's Harry Potter series was followed with numerous young adult books or series containing fantastic elements, such as Suzanne Collins's *The Hunger Games* (2008).

As with all genres, science fiction fought to maintain relevance in the first decade of the 2000s. Its traditional categorical lumping with fantasy may have helped, as fantasy fiction gained in popularity and inched toward the mainstream. Some publishers pushed crossover titles—works that crossed various genres and were marked as mainstream fiction, whereas others looked for breakout authors in Europe and elsewhere. Hugely popular in Russia, author Sergei Lukyanenko's *Night Watch* fantasy series entered English-speaking markets, as did works by Finnish science fiction author Hannu Rajaniemi, French fantasy writer Pierre Pevel, and German fantasy writer Markus Heitz.

Numerous specialized presses have made a modest mark in science fiction publishing in the twenty-first century, often through publishing works in a specific tradition. For example, Hippocampus Press (founded in 1999) has republished works by authors in the Lovecraftian/Weird Tales lineage, such as Clark Ashton Smith, while Wheatland Press focuses on slipstream and magical realist works.

Although some considered electronic publishing to be the death knell for traditional publishing, others embraced it. It may not be surprising that a group of science fiction writers that included Ursula K. Le Guin made the leap to publish directly to two e-readers—the Amazon Kindle and the Sony e-reader—cutting out the traditional publishing house entirely. The Internet also presented opportunities for publishers and writers; Orion Publishing Group's science fiction and fantasy arm, Gollancz, launched the "SF Gateway" in 2011, a digital library offering thousands of books as well as information on authors, a discussion forum, and more. In such trying times it was clear that forward thinking, something that should come naturally to science fiction buffs, would be critical to survival. Contemporary authors like Cory Doctorow offer hints of what this might look like; Doctorow interweaves his science fiction activities with his work as a journalist, blogger, and culture critic. The result is a hybrid rather than pure science fiction, but it is influential far beyond the traditional confines of the science fiction field.

Mike Shupp

SEE ALSO: *Advertising; Agents;* Amazing Stories; *Amazon.com; Apollo Missions; Argosy; Asimov, Isaac; "B" Movies; Best Sellers; Bradbury, Ray; Burroughs, Edgar Rice; Clancy, Tom; Clarke, Arthur C.; Cold War; Comic Books;* The Day the

Earth Stood Still*; Detective Fiction; Dick, Philip K.; Disney (Walt Disney Company); Ellison, Harlan; E-Readers; Feminism; The Fifties;* Flash Gordon*; Frankenstein; Gay Liberation Movement; Gernsback, Hugo; Herbert, Frank; Hollywood; The Internet; King, Stephen; Le Guin, Ursula K.;* Lord of the Rings *Film Trilogy; Modernism; Multiculturalism;* Munsey's Magazine*; Objectivism/Ayn Rand; Paperbacks;* Playboy*; Pulp Magazines; Radio; Reagan, Ronald; The* Saturday Evening Post*;* Scribner's*;* Star Trek*;* Star Wars*; Street and Smith; Superman; Tarzan; Teenagers; Television;* Them!*; Tolkien, J. R. R.;* The Twilight Zone*; UFOs (Unidentified Flying Objects); Vietnam;* Weird Tales*; World War II.*

BIBLIOGRAPHY

Caroti, Simone. *The Generation Starship in Science Fiction: A Critical History, 1934–2001*. Jefferson, NC: McFarland, 2011.

Chapdelaine, Perry A., Sr.; Tony Chapdelaine; and George Hay, eds. *The John W. Campbell Letters, Vol. 1*. Franklin, TN: AC Projects, 1985.

Dallmann, Antje; Reinhard Isensee; and Philipp Kneis, eds. *Envisioning American Utopias: Fictions of Science and Politics in Literature and Visual Culture*. New York: Peter Lang, 2011.

Davenport, Basil, ed. *The Science Fiction Novel: Imagination and Social Criticism*. Chicago: Advent, 1959.

De Camp, L. Sprague, and Catherine C. de Camp. *Science Fiction Handbook*, rev. ed. Philadelphia: Owlswick Press, 1975.

Delany, Samuel R. *The Jewel-Hinged Jaw: Essays on Science Fiction*. New York: Berkley, 1977.

Heinlein, Robert. *Grumbles from the Grave*. New York: Del Rey Books, 1989.

Knight, Damon. *In Search of Wonder: Essays on Modern Science Fiction*. Chicago: Advent, 1956.

Malzberg, Barry N. *The Engines of the Night: Science Fiction in the Eighties*. Garden City, NY: Doubleday, 1982.

Panshin, Alexei, and Cory Panshin. *The World beyond the Hill: Science Fiction and the Quest for Transcendence*. Los Angeles: Jeremy P. Tarcher, 1989.

Platt, Charles. *Dream Makers: The Uncommon People Who Write Science Fiction*. New York: Berkley Books, 1980.

Pohl, Frederik. *The Way the Future Was: A Memoir*. New York: Del Rey Books, 1978.

Reid, Robin Anne, ed. *Women in Science Fiction and Fantasy*. Westport, CT: Greenwood Press, 2009.

Roberts, Adam. *The History of Science Fiction*. New York: Palgrave Macmillan, 2006.

Rogers, Alva. *A Requiem for Astounding*. Chicago: Advent, 1964.

Spinrad, Norman. *Science Fiction in the Real World*. Carbondale: Southern Illinois University Press, 1990.

Warren, Bill. *Keep Watching the Skies! American Science Fiction Movies of the Fifties*, 2 vols. Jefferson, NC: McFarland, 1982, 1986.

Scientific American

The reliable and readable scientific writing in *Scientific American* has instructed and entertained readers since the magazine's founding in 1845. Indeed, *Scientific American* occupies a unique position in the culture of science. Early readers felt an affinity for the magazine because of its personal contact with inventors. Clarifying patent procedures, the magazine's editors answered readers' questions, stimulated their creativity, and encouraged their ambitions. By being accessible to, and interactive with, its readers, the magazine had a significant impact on the development, understanding, and acceptance of science in America. Throughout its history, it has remained at the forefront in providing informative articles about current and emerging technology, covering the space age, the development of modern pharmaceuticals, and philosophical debates about science. Simply put, *Scientific American* has chronicled the inventive spirit of America.

PATENTS AND INVENTIONS: THE EARLY YEARS

The first issue of *Scientific American* was dated August 28, 1845, and the magazine appeared weekly until monthly editions began in November 1921. Inventor Rufus Porter created *Scientific American* in New York City. Experimenting with electrotyping, Porter produced a four-page periodical focusing on new inventions. The early *Scientific American* sold for $2 per copy and had the following subtitle: "The Advocate of Industry and Enterprise, and Journal of Mechanical and Other Improvements." At that time, unique technological achievements were forming American industry, and several magazines, such as the monthly *Journal of the Franklin Institute*, addressed the topics of patents and mechanics as applied to mining, transportation, and manufacturing.

Porter served as *Scientific American*'s editor until Munn & Company purchased the magazine in 1846. Orson Desaix Munn and Alfred Ely Beach, the son of *New York Sun* publisher and inventor Moses Y. Beach, jointly invested money in printing their first edition of *Scientific American* on July 23, 1846. They focused on providing information about patented inventions, including the official list of patents approved by the U.S. Patent Office.

Because so many hopeful inventors asked for help with the patenting process and laws, the partners created a patent agency. *Scientific American* described the models of inventions their clients brought them, among them Thomas Edison's 1877 phonograph. The thriving agency attracted such major inventors as Samuel F. B. Morse, Captain John Ericsson, and Elias Howe. The pages of *Scientific American* published a few lines about every invention the agency promoted, even obscure and unsuccessful ideas, thus revealing insights into the history of invention in the United States.

Expanding to eight pages, the September 26, 1846, *Scientific American* remarked that the editors strived to "furnish an acceptable family newspaper" and "give in brief and condensed form the most useful and interesting intelligence of passing events" while "avoiding the disgusting and pernicious details of crime." Although inventions dominated the news, information about other aspects of science were included. Circulation reached 10,000 subscribers by 1848, doubled to 20,000 in 1852, and hit 30,000 the next year. Whereas other scientific periodicals struggled for survival, *Scientific American* succeeded, merging with the *People's Journal* in 1854 to boost readership. Readers especially liked such features as Salem Howe Wales's letters from the 1855 Paris Exposition.

In July 1859 *Scientific American* began producing a new series of semiannual volumes. A Washington, D.C., bureau of

Munn & Company opened with Judge Charles Mason, a former commissioner of patents, acting as a legal adviser to inventors. During the Civil War the journal commented primarily on military inventions. After the war the editors improved the publication's appearance with engraved illustrations and larger pages, increasing the price per issue to $3. Additionally, *Scientific American*'s editorial and financial support for construction of an underground pneumatic tube 21 feet below Broadway in 1870 increased public curiosity both about inventions and the publication.

CONTINUED GROWTH

In 1885 Munn & Company founded the monthly *Scientific American: Architects' and Builders' Edition*, later known as *Scientific American Building Monthly*. Demand for specialized periodicals and the incentive to profit from increased advertising resulted in Munn & Company catering to business construction, and it hired architects to provide building plans featured in the magazines. By January 1905 the company was publishing the monthly *American Homes and Gardens* with the subtitle "New Series of *Scientific American Building Monthly*." (This magazine was absorbed by *House and Gardens* in September 1915.) The *Scientific American* house also published export and Spanish editions.

Scientific American featured many inventions and their applications years before the American public was familiar with those ideas—for example, horseless carriages were pictured, with plans for construction, half a century prior to the popularization of automobiles in America. Such major events as the Chicago World's Fair were also covered by *Scientific American*, and the magazine was the primary source of information for many industries. Promoting aviation, it chronicled the efforts of the Wright Brothers and sponsored monetary prizes for aerospace achievements. The editors were, however, critical of unscientific efforts and designs.

In 1911 *Scientific American* began publishing a "mid-month number" focusing on a specific topic, such as agricultural science or reviews of automobiles. The special issue featured a color cover, which the main magazine also adopted. The June 5, 1915, issue celebrated the publication's seventieth anniversary, and two years later the price rose to $4 an issue, with the format by then resembling popular magazines of the era in size and print. The 1919 printers' strike, however, resulted in the suspension of the weekly supplement. Declining circulation due to competitive specialized magazines caused *Scientific American* to become a monthly magazine in 1921 to save costs. Munn & Company changed its name to Scientific American Publishing Company, and the magazine stopped printing lists of patents. No longer primarily an inventor's magazine, it attempted to transmit scientific information to the American public as a popular science magazine. "It has been the constant aim of this journal to impress the fact that science is not inherently dull, heavy or abstruse," an editorial stated, "but that it is essentially fascinating, understandable, and full of undeniable charm."

STAYING POWER

In the post–World War II era, a revised *Scientific American* reached out to the segment of the community that was already scientifically literate and yearned to learn more. The modern *Scientific American* expanded in size and cost, had glossy covers and illustrations, and increased its circulation to hundreds of thousands of readers.

At the turn of the twenty-first century, with technology booming and the publishing industry declining, *Scientific American* doggedly marched ahead. German media giant Verlagsgruppe Georg von Holtzbrinck acquired the company in 1986, and some two decades later, in 2009, it became part of Holtzbrinck's consumer media division. Additionally in 2009, Mariette DiChristina was named editor-in-chief; she was the first female editor-in-chief, and eighth overall, in the magazine's history.

To maintain its relevance and attract new audiences, the magazine produced a television series, *Scientific American Frontiers*, that aired on public television stations nationwide from 1990 to 2005. Actor Alan Alda served as host. In 1996 it launched a website, linking readers to articles, the latest news, podcasts, and more. A second magazine, *Scientific American Mind*, entered circulation in 2004. The magazine covered such subjects as neuroscience and psychology. By 2012 *Scientific American* could brag that it was the oldest continuously published magazine in the nation and had a global readership that topped five million people. Aging, it seems, has agreed with *Scientific American*.

Elizabeth D. Schafer

SEE ALSO: *Alda, Alan; Automobile; Edison, Thomas Alva; World's Fairs.*

BIBLIOGRAPHY

Borut, Michael. "The *Scientific American* in Nineteenth Century America." PhD dissertation, New York University, 1977.

Burnham, John C. *How Superstition Won and Science Lost: Popularization of Science and Health in the United States.* New Brunswick, NJ: Rutgers University Press, 1987.

Mott, Frank Luther. *A History of American Magazines, Vol. 2, 1850–1865*. Cambridge, MA: Harvard University Press, 1938.

Scientific American. Accessed March 2012. Available from http://www.scientificamerican.com/

Scientology

SEE: *Hubbard, L. Ron.*

Scopes Monkey Trial

One of the most sensational court cases in twentieth-century America, what came to be called the Scopes Monkey Trial went infinitely beyond the boundaries of law and the courtroom to question the social, intellectual, and cultural values of America. The explosive and passionate conflicts instigated by the arguments in the case of the state of Tennessee versus public schoolteacher John T. Scopes in 1925 characterized the decade in which they took place. On one side stood those who emphasized secularism, science, new ideas and theories, and individual self-expression; on the other side stood religious dogma and traditionalism. Thus, there was a bitter division between those Americans who wanted change and the many others who clung to repressive notions of conformity, moral purity, and order.

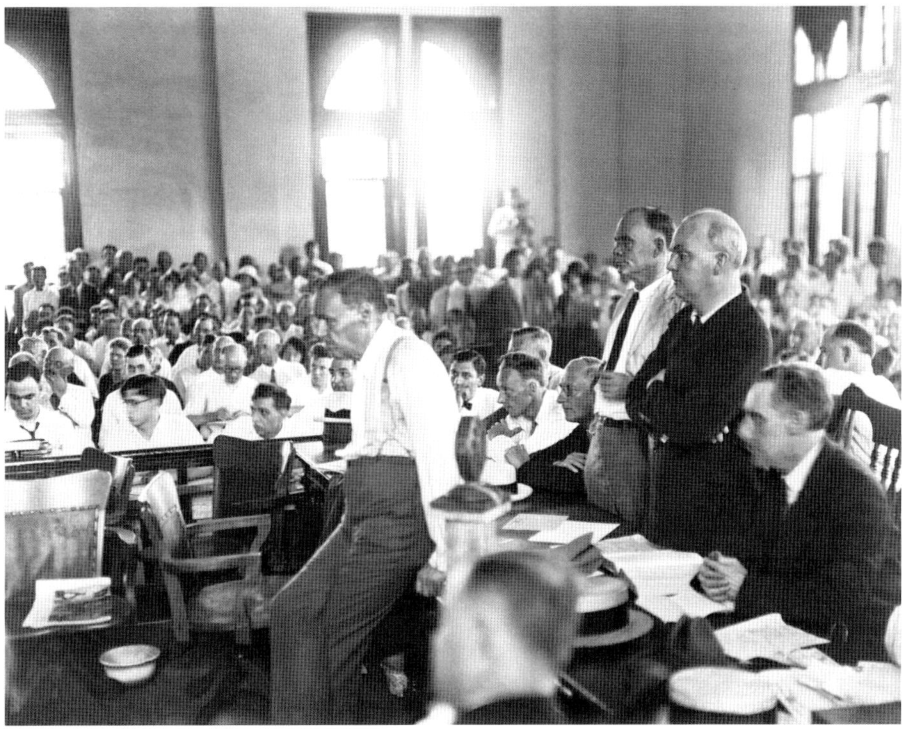

Scopes Monkey Trial. *Clarence Darrow leans against a table in the packed courtroom during the Scopes Monkey Trial in July 1925. Biology teacher John T. Scopes is seated to Darrow's right with his arms folded.* © BETTMANN/CORBIS.

The battleground for this conflict between new and old ideas was the public school system within which Scopes taught Charles Darwin's theory of evolution, which contradicted the Bible's interpretation of the origins of man. Although by the 1920s Darwin's principles were being taught in most American universities and public schools, the middle of the decade brought a concerted drive by religious fundamentalists to stop the teaching of evolution in the schools. School boards, individual schools, and many states in the South prohibited the teaching in public schools of any theory about the origins of human life that conflicted with the teachings of the Bible.

In 1925 the American Civil Liberties Union (ACLU) announced that it was willing to financially support anyone challenging a recently enacted Tennessee law that prohibited the teaching of Darwin in the state's schools. John T. Scopes, a twenty-five-year-old high school science teacher in Dayton, Tennessee, who taught evolution in his school biology class, accepted the ACLU's offer and agreed to stand as the defendant in a test case to challenge the law. On the initiative of Scopes's friend George Rappelyea, the teacher was reported to the police for breaking the new law, arrested, and sent for trial. A number of prominent legal counselors, led by the famous liberal trial lawyer Clarence Darrow, undertook the defense of Scopes. The prosecuting attorney was William Jennings Bryan, former secretary of state, three-time Democratic candidate for president, onetime Populist, and then leader of the new fundamentalist movement in Christianity.

During the summer of 1925, the Scopes Monkey Trial grabbed national and international headlines. Almost 1,000 people packed the Tennessee courtroom daily, and millions more listened to the proceedings—it was the first trial ever to be broadcast live on the radio. Judge John T. Raulston, a conservative Christian who started each day's court proceedings with a prayer, did not allow the defense to bring any expert scientific testimony about evolution. As a result, Darrow called prosecuting attorney Bryan, an expert on science and religion, as his only witness and systematically proceeded to humiliate him. With his probing questions, Darrow led Bryan to declare that a big fish had swallowed Jonah, that Eve was literally created from a piece of Adam's rib, and that in 2348 BCE the world was flooded and fish and animals escaped onto Noah's ark. The press mocked Bryan's literal interpretation of the Bible, thus undermining the fundamentalist cause.

At the conclusion of the hearings, Darrow asked the jury to return a verdict of guilty so the case might be appealed to the Tennessee Supreme Court, where he hoped the anti-Darwin law would be overturned. The jury, complying with Darrow's request, returned a verdict of guilty, and Judge Raulston fined Scopes $100. Publicly humiliated and exhausted, Bryan died just a few days after the trial. A year later, however, the decision of the Dayton court was overturned by the Tennessee Supreme Court on a technicality.

Although Scopes was convicted and the existing antievolution law remained on the Tennessee statute books, many Americans perceived the religious fundamentalist cause as the loser in the trial. The existing statutes banning Darwin's theories were never enforced, and evolution continued to be taught in the schools. Moreover, the need for the separation of theology from general education became even more firmly entrenched in the minds of many Americans. Everywhere, prayer and other religious activities were eventually abolished in the public schools.

The Scopes Monkey Trial, wearing only the thinnest of disguises in that the names of the place and the protagonists were changed, became the subject of Jerome Lawrence and Robert E. Lee's successful Broadway play *Inherit the Wind* (1956), which was turned into a film in 1960 with Spencer Tracy and Fredric March as Darrow and Bryan, respectively.

John F. Lyons

SEE ALSO: *Darrow, Clarence; Fundamentalism; Tracy, Spencer.*

BIBLIOGRAPHY

Conkin, Paul K. *When All the Gods Trembled: Darwinism, Scopes, and American Intellectuals.* Lanham, MD: Rowman & Littlefield, 1998.

Furniss, Norman F. *The Fundamentalist Controversy, 1918–1931.* New Haven, CT: Yale University Press, 1954.

Hansen, Ellen. *Evolution on Trial.* Lowell, MA: Discovery Enterprises, 1994.

Larson, Edward L. *Summer for the Gods: The Scopes Trial and America's Continuing Debate over Science and Religion.* New York: BasicBooks, 1997.

Scopes, John Thomas, and Tennessee County Court. *The World's Most Famous Court Trial: Tennessee Evolution Case.* Union, NJ: Lawbook Exchange, 1997.

Scorsese, Martin *(1942–)*

Martin Scorsese is one of the most significant American film directors of the late twentieth and early twenty-first centuries. He was among a select group of innovative, film school–educated young filmmakers, famously dubbed the Movie Brats, or the American New Wave, who began making a mark during the 1960s and went on to secure major reputations. By the 1990s Francis Ford Coppola, who had led the way for the Movie Brats, had become a venerable but unpredictable artist, veering dizzily between huge successes and dismal failures; George Lucas, the creator of *Star Wars,* was long entrenched in trailblazing technology; Brian De Palma was committed to a controversial, individualistic, and uneven course as a skillful specialist in screen violence; and Steven Spielberg reigned as the acknowledged master of the movie blockbuster. Scorsese, meanwhile, emerged as the most consistently powerful and provocative film director of his generation. His early films, such as *Taxi Driver* (1976), *Raging Bull* (1980), and *GoodFellas* (1990), are high-water marks in Hollywood cinema, while his later work, including *The Age of Innocence* (1993), *Gangs of New York* (2002), *The Aviator* (2004), and *Shutter Island* (2010), embrace a diversity of subject matter and style that confirms Scorsese's total command of his art.

Scorsese's own background provides the fertile soil in which his filmmaking ambitions take root. Born in New York to a first-generation Italian American family, he grew up in Manhattan's Little Italy, the setting of his first full-length features. A sickly child, often confined indoors because of asthma, he became addicted to movies at an early age. In the 1960s he abandoned ambitions to become a Catholic priest and joined the New York University film school, where he wrote and directed several award-winning shorts, including *The Big Shave* (1968), while ideas germinated for his first full-length feature, *Who's That Knocking at My Door* (1967).

Starring Harvey Keitel in his movie debut, *Who's That Knocking at My Door* tells the story of an Italian American man trapped by his working-class background and ever-present Catholic guilt. The low-budget film combines realistic street scenes with new wave techniques, such as long takes and hand-held shots, that reveal Scorsese's self-confessed enthusiasm for the European cinema of the time. He then hired himself out as supervising editor on *Woodstock* (1969) and *Elvis on Tour* (1972) and had a directorial breakthrough with *Boxcar Bertha* (1972), a Depression-era tale of Arkansas misfits who rob trains.

It was, however, *Mean Streets* (1973) that alerted critics and the movie industry to Scorsese's talent. Dealing with the life of streetwise youth and petty crime in Little Italy and starring Keitel, the movie pulsates with life (and a pounding rock soundtrack) in its depiction of friendship, betrayal, guilt, and casual violence. It also unleashes an electrifying Robert De Niro, an Italian American New York actor whose collaboration with Scorsese in later years resulted in a handful of major films on which Scorsese's reputation rests. After *Mean Streets* came the heavily contrasting *Alice Doesn't Live Here Anymore* (1974), a tough, contemporary slice-of-life take on the Hollywood "woman's weepie," for which Ellen Burstyn won an Academy Award for Best Actress.

Martin Scorsese. *Martin Scorsese displays the Golden Globe Award he won in 2012 as Best Director of* Hugo. STEVE GRANITZ/CONTRIBUTOR/WIREIMAGE/GETTY IMAGES.

TAXI DRIVER

In 1976 came the most completely realized example of Scorsese's particular vision of New York as a hell on Earth and the first of his unsurpassed major films with De Niro. Moving away from the bonding of brothers, friends, and hoods that characterize *Mean Streets, Taxi Driver* focuses on an alienated, disturbed loner, the taxi-driving Vietnam veteran, Travis Bickle, whose abhorrence of the antisocial behavior he encounters in the city sends him over the edge into psychopathic violence. Self-appointed to cleanse the city of its pimps, prostitutes, and other human detritus, Bickle embarks on a spree of organized savagery, calculated with impeccable logic from his point of view.

As Bickle, De Niro gives one of the best screen performances of his illustrious career, and he received a Best Actor Oscar nomination. A teenage Jodie Foster received an Oscar nomination for Best Supporting Actress for her portrayal as a drug-addicted whore. Composer Bernard Herrmann also received an Oscar nomination for Best Score. While the movie was nominated for an Academy Award for Best Picture, Scorsese was not nominated for Best Director. The omission demonstrated a gulf in appreciation for the director's work between the Hollywood powerbrokers who vote at Academy Award time and respected critics and serious moviegoers.

Scorsese and De Niro followed *Taxi Driver* with *New York, New York* (1977), a cynical musical in which De Niro, costarring with Liza Minnelli, plays a saxophonist. This movie was a box-office failure, as were two later excursions into ironic comedy, *King of Comedy* (1983), again with De Niro, and *After Hours* (1985). After making the "rockumentary" *The Last Waltz* (1978), Scorsese began the 1980s with *Raging Bull* (1980), which many consider to be his masterpiece.

Based on the autobiography of heavyweight boxer Jake LaMotta, *Raging Bull*—shot in black and white—reveals the interior as well as exterior violence of the fight profession and its deleterious effect on the life and relationships of its protagonist. With an astonishing and authentic Academy Award–winning performance by De Niro at its center, the movie lays bare the brutality of its subject matter, both in the ring (the fights are filmed with uncompromising accuracy, grace, and alternating speed) and out. It is full of rage, and the documentary style of the domestic scenes resonates with the verbal blows. The movie is enhanced by the editing of Thelma Schoonmaker, an integral fixture of Scorsese's team. Both Scorsese and the movie received Academy Award nominations.

A CONTROVERSIAL FILMMAKER

During the 1980s, continuing his attempts to vary his choice of material, Scorsese successfully entered more reliable commercial territory with *The Color of Money* (1986), a sequel to director Robert Rossen's classic, *The Hustler* (1961), and starring Tom Cruise and Paul Newman in a reprise of his original role. Scorsese triggered an international controversy with *The Last Temptation of Christ* (1988). Adapted by Paul Schrader from the novel of the same name by Nikos Kazantzakis, the movie presents Christ (Willem Dafoe) as a fallible human and victim of circumstance, who longs to escape his destiny and live the life of a normal man. Overlong and verbose but rich in ideas and striking photography by Michael Ballhaus, *The Last Temptation of Christ* suffered from prerelease condemnation, but Scorsese did receive an Academy Award nomination, and the movie continues to occupy a respected place in the canon of his work.

Scorsese next teamed up with directors Woody Allen and Coppola to direct the triptych anthology *New York Stories* (1989), after which came *GoodFellas* (1990) and *Cape Fear* (1991). Adapted by Scorsese and Nicholas Pileggi from the latter's book about real-life Mafia hood Henry Hill, *GoodFellas* joins *Taxi Driver* and *Raging Bull* as a Scorsese masterwork. Starring Ray Liotta and a galaxy of America's finest character actors, including De Niro and Joe Pesci, the film graphically depicts the criminal subculture in a masterful, complex blend of uncompromising violence and its influence on personal morality. *GoodFellas* dazzles with its technique and control, enthralls with its plot, and entertains with its relationships, wisecracks, threats, and performances. It received Academy Award nominations for Best Adapted Screenplay and Best Picture.

Cape Fear showcases Scorsese's technical expertise. This remake of the 1962 movie starring Robert Mitchum features De Niro, covered in full-body tattoos, as a convict released from prison and seeking sadistic vengeance against the lawyer who got him convicted. Although successful in its delivery of tension and menace, *Cape Fear* bludgeons its audience with shock tactics and conveys an unmistakable voyeuristic nastiness that many viewers found distasteful. The *New Yorker* called it Scorsese's "worst picture—an ugly, incoherent piece of work."

By the 1990s Scorsese had branched out into producing, as well as making occasional cameo acting appearances in his own movies and in movies made by others, including director Bertrand Tavernier's *'Round Midnight* (1986) and director Akira Kurosawa's *Dreams* (1990). Having acquired a reputation for tough, violent movies, Scorsese turned to a classic literary source to venture into his first period piece. The announcement that he would film Edith Wharton's stylish, scathing, and poignant Pulitzer Prize–winning novel *The Age of Innocence* (1920), a story about a love affair thwarted by the morals and manners of New York high society, was greeted with undisguised skepticism. A review of the movie in the *New York Times*, published before the movie's release, notes that much anticipation focused on how Scorsese, given his previous movies, "would adjust to the statelier rhythms of an atmosphere so rarefied that a woman crossing a party to talk to a man could throw the whole gathering into social shock."

Scorsese's *The Age of Innocence* (1993), set in the 1870s and starring Daniel Day-Lewis, Michelle Pfeiffer, Winona Ryder, and a starry supporting cast of British actors, turned out to be a dazzling adaptation, capturing the opulence, elegance, and disappointed passions in Wharton's novel with taste, style, and a sumptuous visual display.

AN ACADEMY AWARD

Scorsese's next movie, *Casino* (1995), turned out to be an overblown excursion back into *GoodFellas* territory, but *Kundun* (1997), signaled a return to higher ambition. In *Kundun* Scorsese makes the leap into another culture, philosophy, and place to recount the early years of the Dalai Lama in Tibet. He received another Best Director Oscar nomination for the movie.

Scorsese continued to work as a director, and films such as *Gangs of New York* (2002), a gangster movie set in nineteenth-century New York, and *The Aviator* (2004), a biopic of movie director and pioneering aviator Howard Hughes starring Leonardo DiCaprio, demonstrate his versatility and brilliance. In 2007 Scorsese finally won an Academy Award for Best Director for *The Departed* (2006), an action thriller adaptation of the Hong Kong movie *Infernal Affairs* (2002). Starring DiCaprio alongside Matt Damon, Jack Nicholson, and Mark Wahlberg, it was widely praised. The movie also won the Academy Award for Best Picture.

Shutter Island (2010), a mystery thriller set in a hospital for the criminally insane, stars DiCaprio and Emily Mortimer, who also starred in *Hugo* (2011). With *Hugo*, based on the children's book *The Invention of Hugo Cabret* by Brian Selznick, Scorsese embraces 3-D technology. A period fantasy set in 1930s Paris, *Hugo* was a great success, and it was nominated for Best Picture Academy Award. Scorsese received an Oscar nomination for Best Director.

Scorsese has also indulged in his passion for music, making music videos and, as a producer, a documentary about former Beatle George Harrison, *George Harrison: Living in the Material World* (2011). By the time he made *Hugo*, Scorsese was a major Hollywood figure, instantly recognizable on the red carpet at premieres and award ceremonies by his short stature, bushy eyebrows, and thick-rimmed spectacles.

Stephen Keane

SEE ALSO: *Academy Awards; Allen, Woody; The Beatles; Cruise, Tom; Damon, Matt; De Niro, Robert; DiCaprio, Leonardo; Foster, Jodie;* GoodFellas*; Hollywood; Hughes, Howard; Keitel, Harvey; LaMotta, Jake; Lucas, George; Minnelli, Liza; Mitchum, Robert; The* New York Times*; The* New Yorker*; Newman, Paul; Nicholson, Jack; Pfeiffer, Michelle;* Raging Bull*; Ryder, Winona; Spielberg, Steven;* Star Wars*;* Taxi Driver*; Wharton, Edith.*

BIBLIOGRAPHY

Child, Ben. "Martin Scorsese Considers Shooting All His Future Films in 3-D." *Guardian*, November 28, 2011. Accessed March 20, 2012. Available from http://www.guardian.co.uk/film/2011/nov/28/martin-scorsese-films-3d-hugo

Dougan, Andy. *Martin Scorsese—Close Up*. London: Orion, 1997.

Prose, Francine. "In 'Age of Innocence,' Eternal Questions." *New York Times*, September 12, 1993. Accessed March 19, 2012. Available from http://movies.nytimes.com/movie/review?res=9F0CEED81230F931A2575AC0A965958260

Pye, Michael, and Lynda Myles. *The Movie Brats: How the Film Generation Took over Hollywood*. New York: Holt, Rinehart and Winston, 1979.

Ryan, Michael, and Douglas Kellner. *Camera Politica: The Politics and Ideology of Contemporary Hollywood Film*. Bloomington: Indiana University Press, 1988.

Scorsese, Martin. *Scorsese on Scorsese*, ed. David Thompson and Ian Christie. London: Faber & Faber, 1996.

Scorsese, Martin, and Michael Henry Wilson. *A Personal Journey with Martin Scorsese through American Movies*. New York: Hyperion, 1997.

Scott, George C. *(1927–1999)*

At once a commanding presence on the screen and a subtly nuanced character actor, George C. Scott was a significant force in American theater, film, and television for almost forty years. A workmanlike actor who had always spread his focus among all of the available stages, Scott the man was almost as hard-boiled and sensitive as the characters he played. With little patience for fuss or pandering, he was never a publicity seeker; nonetheless, publicity sought him out, sometimes for his quietly principled stands but often simply because of his incredibly prolific career.

Born in Wise, Virginia, and raised in Detroit, Michigan, George Campbell Scott spent World War II in the Marine Corps. When he was discharged, he enrolled in journalism school at the University of Missouri on the GI Bill. He soon grew disenchanted with the idea of a writing career; "I discovered I had no talent for it," he said, "so I looked around for something else to do." While looking, he tried out for a college play and discovered where his talents really lay.

In 1957 Scott landed his first professional acting job in the New York Shakespeare Festival, performing in *Richard III*, *The Merchant of Venice*, and *As You Like It* over the course of the next few years. At almost the same moment, he began to get job offers on television, an exciting new medium that had just begun to burgeon with programs of serious theatrical merit. Scott starred in productions on such respected shows as *Hallmark Hall of Fame*, the *DuPont Show of the Month*, *Playhouse 90*, *Kraft Television Theatre*, and *Omnibus*. By 1959 the movie offers began to roll in. That year, Scott had major roles in *The Hanging Tree* and *Anatomy of a Murder*.

During the 1960s, Scott continued to perform with great vigor and flexibility on the Broadway stage, on television—in TV movies and in his own series (*East Side, West Side*, 1963–1964)—and in more than thirty motion pictures. A few of his best-known films from this period are *The Hustler*, with Paul Newman (1961); *Dr. Strangelove*, with Peter Sellers (1964); and *They Might Be Giants*, with Joanne Woodward (1971). Along with many great films, Scott also made his share of hack films, such as *Exorcist III* (1990), notable for little else than his august presence. His craggy face, imposing size, and trademark raspy growl might tend to typecast an actor with less skill and versatility, but Scott managed to play everything from tragedy to farce to rugged adventure. He also succeeded in portraying a widely diverse range of characters, from sleazy gangsters to tender grandpas, from an antisocial aging Huckleberry Finn (*The Boys of Autumn*, Broadway, 1986) to "Old Blood and Guts," the megalomaniacal General George Patton.

It is perhaps the character of Patton, in the 1970 film of the same name, that will remain as being most identified with Scott. The actor, who once called Patton "a once-in-a-lifetime part," read thirteen biographies of the famous general to prepare for the part. His portrayal of the controversial general is still recognized as a tour de force, and immortalized Patton in a way that the general's checkered military career did not. The other enduring legacy of the film is the famous incident when Scott refused his Best Actor Oscar for the role. Though he had been nominated for Academy Awards before, he had made very public his distaste for the Academy's voting methods and for the whole notion of competition among actors. He had announced his intention to refuse the Oscar if it was awarded to him, and, indeed, was home in bed when the award was announced. Scott's snub to the Academy was felt dramatically and is often still listed among memorable moments of the Oscars.

Scott himself felt a strong attachment to the character of Patton. Though he had, like many actors, agreed to appear in commercials, he had adamantly refused to trade on the likeness of himself as Patton. In 1986 he bought the rights to the general's memoirs and portrayed him again in a TV movie, *The Last Days of Patton.*

Scott's personal life contained as much drama as the roles he played, including a reputation for heavy drinking and abusive behavior toward women. Married five times, twice to actor Colleen Dewhurst, he also had a public and tempestuous affair with film star Ava Gardner during the 1960s. In 1972 he married actor Trish Van Devere, with whom he remained until his death on September 22, 1999, of an aneurysm. That night, the lights of New York's Broadway theaters dimmed for one minute to honor him.

Though he had never played the establishment game in Hollywood, Scott remained an admired and highly employable star. Throughout his life as a performer, he divided his time among television, film, and the Broadway stage, giving him a control and flexibility in his career that few actors have managed. He was nominated for a Tony for his performance in *Inherit the Wind* on Broadway in 1996 and appeared in a made-for-TV movie of the play the year he died. Though he disdained the destructive competition of the awards system, Scott would perhaps have appreciated the tribute to his eclectic and independent career that was part of the 2000 Academy Awards show.

Tina Gianoulis

SEE ALSO: *Academy Awards; Broadway;* Dr. Strangelove or: How I Learned to Stop Worrying and Love the Bomb*;* Hallmark Hall of Fame*;* Kraft Television Theatre*; Made-for-Television Movies; Newman, Paul;* Omnibus*;* Patton*;* Playhouse 90*; Sellers, Peter; Television; Tony Awards.*

BIBLIOGRAPHY

Grobel, Lawrence. "George C. Scott (Interview)." *Playboy,* December 1980, 81.

Harbinson, W. A. *George C. Scott.* New York: Pinnacle Books, 1977.

Sheward, David. *Rage and Glory: The Volatile Life and Career of George C. Scott.* Montclair, NJ: Applause Theatre & Cinema Books, 2008.

Scott, Randolph *(1903–1987)*

Probably more so than any other Western film star, Randolph Scott symbolized rugged individualism, unwavering honesty, and a gentleman quality seldom matched. As an actor, Scott was noted for his polite, civil manner in an industry filled with out-of-control egos and temper tantrums. A soft-spoken man with a rather passive screen presence, Scott made more than sixty pictures from 1932 to 1962, placing him within the ranks of Western film legends Gary Cooper and John Wayne.

Born in Orange, Virginia, in 1903 (some sources say 1898), George Randolph Scott attended Georgia Tech and the University of North Carolina to prepare for a career in textile engineering. After a brief stint working for his father's textile company in Charlotte, North Carolina, Scott moved to Hollywood to satisfy his growing interest in acting. He found work as an extra in several pictures and landed roles with local theater groups, including the Pasadena Playhouse. This exposure led to Paramount signing him to a seven-year contract. Although many of his early roles were bit parts, Scott received top billing from 1932 to 1935 in a popular series of nine Westerns based on Zane Grey stories. In seven of these films, Scott learned much about the acting process from director Henry Hathaway, a veteran filmmaker best known for directing John Wayne in *True Grit* (1969). Paramount used Scott in several non-Westerns as well, then in 1936, he was cast as James Fenimore Cooper's Leatherstocking hero, Hawkeye, in *The Last of the Mohicans.*

When Scott completed his Paramount contract in 1938, he signed nonexclusive contracts with Twentieth Century Fox and Universal. In 1938, Fox teamed him with Shirley Temple in *Rebecca of Sunnybrook Farm,* then cast him opposite Tyrone Power and Henry Fonda in the financially successful *Jesse James* in 1939. As he did throughout his career, Scott played the tall, handsome marshal who was bound by his honor in enforcing the law. The box-office success of *Jesse James* prompted a Fox sequel, *The Return of Frank James* (1940), and a flurry of other outlaw tales. *When the Daltons Rode* (1940) and *The Desperadoes* (1943) again featured Scott as a law-and-order hero reacting to the colorful exploits of the outlaws.

After paying his dues in numerous Western film supporting roles in the 1930s, Scott finally achieved stardom by the early 1940s and was teamed with some of Hollywood's leading actors. Warner Brothers signed him to play opposite Errol Flynn in *Virginia City* (1940), while Universal teamed him with John Wayne in *The Spoilers* (1942), but those were not as successful as his Westerns. Nor did Scott appear particularly comfortable playing a sword-wielding son of an English nobleman in the pirate movie *Captain Kidd.*

After World War II, Scott returned to the genre that suited him best—the Western. Except for three pictures, Scott's forty-two postwar films were all Westerns. During the next fifteen years, Scott averaged five Westerns every two years. His total of thirty-eight Westerns from 1946 to 1960 made Scott the most prolific Western star of his time. Unlike his acting counterparts Gary Cooper, Wayne, or Alan Ladd, Scott never made a critical or box-office hit. Instead, he relied on a steady stream of professionally made, action-packed, entertaining movies. In 1951, Scott revealed to a reporter his formula for making movies, saying that he looked for "a strong believable story with seventy-five percent outdoor action and twenty-five percent indoor. If you get any more of your picture indoors, you're in trouble."

Scott did some of his finest work in a series of Westerns he made in the 1950s and early 1960s with director Budd Boetticher. In such pictures as *Seven Men from Now* (1956), *Decision at Sundown* (1957), *Ride Lonesome* (1959), and *Comanche Station* (1960), Scott's presence filled the screen with courageous dignity and laconic stoicism in tales concerning redressing personal tragedy. In each of the films, Boetticher focused on a group of individuals reacting under stress, with Scott and a capable adversary inevitably facing a showdown.

Scott's final film before retiring is considered by critics to be perhaps his finest work—Sam Peckinpah's *Ride the High Country* (1962). In the movie, Joel McCrea was cast as the poor but honest former marshal who is hired to bring in a gold shipment from a mining camp. Scott played McCrea's longtime friend, also an ex-lawman, who hires on to help escort the gold shipment, but who intends to steal it. The theme of the displacement of aging frontier individualists by an encroaching civilization intrigued critics, and Western fans enjoyed watching Scott and McCrea work together. Between them, they had starred in eighty-seven Westerns since the early 1930s.

Following *Ride the High Country*, Scott retired from the movie industry, overseeing his considerable business investments in oil wells, real estate, and securities. By the time of his death in 1987, it was estimated that Scott's holdings were worth anywhere from $50 million to $100 million. But from a popular culture standpoint, Scott left behind more than substantial personal wealth—he left behind a body of work that helped define the rugged individualism theme of American Westerns and provided one of the more convincing portrayals of the frontier hero.

Dennis Russell

SEE ALSO: *Cooper, Gary; Flynn, Errol; Grey, Zane; Temple, Shirley; Wayne, John; The Western.*

BIBLIOGRAPHY

Crow, Jefferson Brim. *Randolph Scott: The Gentleman from Virginia; A Film Biography.* Carrollton, TX: Wind River Publishing, 1987.

Everson, William K. *A Pictorial History of the Western Film.* Secaucus, NJ: Citadel Press, 1969.

Eyles, Allen. *The Western.* South Brunswick, NJ: A. S. Barnes, 1975.

Fenin, George N., and William K. Everson. *The Western: From Silents to Cinerama.* New York: Bonanza Books, 1962.

Hitt, Jim. *The American West from Fiction (1823–1976) into Film (1909–1986).* Jefferson, NC: McFarland, 1990.

Nott, Robert. *Last of the Cowboy Heroes: The Westerns of Randolph Scott, Joel McCrea, and Audie Murphy.* Jefferson, NC: McFarland, 2005.

Scott, C. H., with historical assistance and editing by William C. Cline. *Whatever Happened to Randolph Scott?* Madison, NC: Empire Publishing, 1994.

Scott, Ridley *(1937–)*

Prolific movie director Ridley Scott got his start in British television and commercials before becoming one of the iconic filmmakers of the late twentieth and early twenty-first centuries. An imaginative artist and meticulous perfectionist, Scott has created memorable worlds in his films, as varied as an alien-ridden spaceship, a twelfth-century Jerusalem beset by Christians and Muslims, and a 1966 Thunderbird convertible containing two rebels racing across the American Southwest in search of freedom. Though his films have frequently been controversial, Scott has earned an indisputable place among the world's most respected directors.

Born in 1937 in South Shields near Newcastle upon Tyne in northern England, Ridley Scott is the son of Colonel Francis Percy Scott and Elizabeth Jean Scott and the brother of filmmaker Tony Scott. During his childhood, the family moved frequently as a consequence of Colonel Scott's military career, and Elizabeth took on much of the responsibility of caring for her children. Her strength and competence inspired her son's later penchant for powerful female leads in his films.

Scott studied at West Hartlepool College of Art and at London's Royal College of Art before getting a job as an art director with the BBC in 1966. He soon moved into directing, helming episodes of the popular British series *Z-Cars* and *The Informer*. Although he made his first short film, *Boy and Bicycle* starring his brother Tony, in 1965, Scott did not move directly from television into filmmaking. Instead he began making commercials, forming his own production company, Ridley Scott Associates (RSA), in 1967. Over the next decades, he honed his directing skills by creating thousands of commercials, many acclaimed for their lush special effects and subtle lighting style.

Even after he became a filmmaker, Scott continued his work in commercials, enjoying the challenge and immediacy of the short projects. Indeed, one of his best-known accomplishments is his creation of the Apple Macintosh commercial shown during the 1984 Super Bowl. Shown only once, and thus made even more powerful, the ad featured a gray-and-white society of beaten-down automatons watching a Big Brother–style dictator on a huge screen as a full-color female runner charges the screen and shatters it with a thrown hammer. *Advertising Age* named the stunning ad "Commercial of the Decade." In 1987 Scott joined his brother Tony in forming RSA USA, an American bureau of his advertising productions.

Scott was forty years old when he made his first feature film, *The Duellists*, which did not attract audiences even though it was visually beautiful and won the award for Best First Work at the Cannes Film Festival. His second film, the 1979 science fiction blockbuster *Alien*, was an enormous success that immediately established Scott as a dynamic and mesmerizing filmmaker and launched the career of Sigourney Weaver, who played the powerful female lead. *Blade Runner*, an enigmatic dystopian action movie, did not succeed with either critics or fans upon its release in 1982, but over time the film became a cult classic with a devoted following. Many critics would later consider *Blade Runner* to be one of the most influential science fiction films of all time. In 1992 Scott delighted devotees of the film by issuing a "director's cut" with significant changes from the original release, including the elimination of a happy ending that had been tacked on at the insistence of the producers.

Although Scott's work always inspired debate among critics, his next films, *Someone to Watch over Me* (1987) and *Black Rain* (1989) were well regarded. However, his 1991 feminist revenge/road-trip movie *Thelma and Louise* was a tour de force that provoked intense debate among critics and audiences and boosted the careers of cast members Susan Sarandon, Geena Davis, and Brad Pitt. It also earned Scott his first Oscar nomination for Best Director.

Scott directed fourteen films between 1991 and 2012, including the lush epic *1492: Conquest of Paradise* (1992) and the gritty and personal *Matchstick Men* (2003). The historical action picture *Gladiator* became one of the highest-grossing films of 2000 and won the Oscar for Best Picture, and the ambitious 2005 *Kingdom of Heaven* presented a uniquely broad view of the Crusades while drawing criticism from conservatives for being too pro-Muslim. In 2012 Scott reentered the world of scary science fiction with *Prometheus*, the long-awaited prequel to *Alien*.

Scott has also built a prolific career as a producer. In 1995 he and brother Tony, who died in August 2012, launched Scott Free Productions, which, besides producing Scott's own films, has backed numerous films and such innovative television programming as the CBS drama *The Good Wife*.

Tina Gianoulis

SEE ALSO: *Advertising; Alien; Apple Computer;* Blade Runner*; Blockbusters; Convertible; Feminism; Pitt, Brad; Sarandon, Susan; Television; Weaver, Sigourney.*

BIBLIOGRAPHY

Davis, Brian. "Ridley Scott: He Revolutionized TV Ads." *Adweek*, October 2, 1989, 54.

Erickson, Steve. "Blood and Sand: The Deliriously Epic Mind of Ridley Scott." *Los Angeles Magazine*, July 2005, 98.

Evans, Marlea. "Ridley Scott." *Back Stage* 30, no. 9 (1989): 6B.

Parrill, William B. *Ridley Scott: A Critical Filmography*. Jefferson, NC: McFarland, 2011.

Robb, Brian J. *Ridley Scott*. Harpenden, UK: Pocket Essentials, 2001.

Scream

Single-handedly resuscitating both the horror genre and the sagging career of director Wes Craven, *Scream*, the 1996 sleeper written by then-Hollywood neophyte Kevin Williamson, brought in a staggering $103 million at the box office and inaugurated a new wave of "teenie kill pics." Self-consciously flagging the hackneyed conventions of post-*Halloween* stalk-and-slash horror movies, *Scream* contrived to grip audiences by mixing genuine scares with affectionate spoofing. Originally titled *Scary Movie*, the name was changed amid concerns that viewers might think the film was a comedy. Beyond the startle effects and the self-parody, however, there lies in *Scream* a scathing critique of the way America's mass-media representations exploit tragedy for profit.

Scream 4. *The fourth installment of the* Scream *series was released in 2011.* DIMENSION FILMS/THE KOBAL COLLECTION.

DEVELOPMENT

After unsuccessful stints as an actor and as an assistant director of music videos, Williamson found his calling with *Scream*, only his second screenplay, which quickly sold to Dimension Films, the newly established "genre division" of Miramax. Craven signed on as director immediately upon reading it. Craven, whose past successes in the horror genre include *The Hills Have Eyes* (1977) and *A Nightmare on Elm Street* (1984), was at the time mired in a decade-long slump, having directed such duds as *A Vampire in Brooklyn* (1995) and *Shocker* (1989). Understandably bored with conventional slasher fare, he saw that Williamson's story had the potential to bring lapsed horror fans back to their seats while simultaneously initiating a new crop of enthusiasts. In fact, Craven's 1994 contribution to the *Nightmare on Elm Street* franchise, which he wrote as well as directed, can be seen as an ambitious, if underappreciated, attempt at generating just the kind of reflexive horror that would come to be *Scream*'s signature. With a $15 million budget, an experienced director, and an established star (Drew Barrymore) already attached, *Scream* attracted a bevy of gifted Gen-X actors eager to gain recognition in a popular genre.

THE PLOT

The intense ten-minute opening of *Scream* bears a striking resemblance to the award-winning prologue of *When a Stranger Calls* (1979). An anonymous caller raises the stakes of playing "slasher movie trivia" by threatening the lives of teenage cutie Casey Becker (Barrymore) and her incapacitated boyfriend unless she can answer such questions as "Who was the killer in *Friday the 13th*"? Like everyone else in *Scream*, Casey is familiar with the clichés of the horror film subgenre that began with *Halloween* in 1978. But only copious amounts of insider knowledge are enough to ensure one's survival in *Scream*, a paean to postmodern pastiche. Indeed, Casey fails the test and, unusually for a Hollywood film, the best-known actress in the film and the first character to be introduced does not make it past the opening scene. After Casey's death, the main story line emerges, centered on the efforts of Sidney Prescott (played with the appropriate mixture of sensibility and sex appeal by Neve Campbell) to avoid the murderous advances of a sadistic slasher film fanatic. "Ghostface " (or Mr. Ghostface) wields a very sharp knife and wears a mask appropriately inspired by Edvard Munch's masterpiece expressionist painting *The Scream*. With a nod to the traditional whodunit, the identity of Sidney's stalker is kept a secret until the movie's final scene, while each of her high school buddies exhibits just enough dubious behavior to qualify as a suspect. Only the timely intervention of dirt-seeking newshound Gale Weathers (Cox of sitcom *Friends* fame) saves Sidney, who is stunned to discover that her assailant is really a pair of male friends who revel in the motiveless nature of their crimes.

THEMES AND REFERENCES

Much has been made of *Scream*'s numerous slasher film references and its abundance of in-jokes. Linda Blair (the demon-possessed star of *The Exorcist*), Priscilla Pointer (*Carrie*), and Craven himself (playing a Freddy Krueger lookalike) all make uncredited cameos. One of the killers—Billy Loomis (Skeet Ulrich)—is named after the psychiatrist in *Halloween*, who is himself named after Janet Leigh's lover in *Psycho* (1960). And at one point, Sidney's friend mentions the director "Wes Carpenter," obviously referring to both Craven and *Halloween* director John Carpenter. At times, however, *Scream* goes beyond mere self-referentiality, approaching something closer to self-reflexivity. Not only do the characters exhibit insider knowledge about slasher films, but they also occasionally evince awareness of being in one. Thus, an unwitting victim pleads sarcastically, "Oh please don't kill me, Mr. Ghostface, I wanna be in the sequel!" And in response to Sidney's cry that "this is NOT a movie," Billy states, "Yes it is Sidney. It's all one big movie."

As noted by Isabel Pinedo, *Scream* breaks the "rules" of the traditional slasher in a variety of ways. There are two killers, for example, and two heroines, both of whom are sexually active. The victims are bright and articulate, even witty; the nerd survives; and the film ends with the killers' unambiguous deaths. Indeed, much of *Scream*'s effectiveness comes from the setting up and frustration of audience expectations and from a blurring of the already hazy line between real-life violence and violent entertainment. Tabloid news reporters in particular are singled out as insensitive instigators of mayhem; one such reporter asks Sidney "how it feels to be almost brutally butchered. How does it feel? People have a right to know!"

THE FRANCHISE

In a coup of self-marketing, Williamson had circulated his original script with short proposals for two potential sequels, and when Dimension Films signed on to the project, they agreed to produce the two follow-up films if the original was a hit. When *Scream* proved itself at the box office, production on the second movie commenced. Williamson and Craven teamed up for both *Scream 2* (1997) and *Scream 3* (2000), with lead actors Campbell, Cox, David Arquette, and Liev Schreiber reprising their roles. *Scream 2* took the self-reflexivity of its predecessor to new heights; there is a film within the film, for example, supposedly a fictionalized account of the "events" of the first film. Like its predecessor, *Scream 2* grossed more than $100 million at the box office. *Scream 3*, however, proved less successful—viewers were unenthusiastic and critics suggested that the film fell prey to the clichés of the genre that the first two films parodied. In 2011, fifteen years after the release of the original, *Scream 4* was released to lackluster critical reviews and little acclaim. Despite the return of Campbell, Cox, and Arquette, and of Williamson and Craven, the film was a box-office flop. While director Craven's contract for *Scream 4* contained a clause committing him to working on two more sequels, it remains unclear as to whether these films will ever be made.

Steven Schneider

SEE ALSO: Friday the 13th*;* Halloween*; Horror Movies;* Psycho*; Slasher Movies.*

BIBLIOGRAPHY

Muir, John Kenneth. *Wes Craven: The Art of Horror*. Jefferson, NC: McFarland, 2004.

Pinedo, Isabel. *Recreational Terror: Women and the Pleasures of Horror Film Viewing*. Albany: State University of New York Press, 1997.

Schneider, Steven. "Uncanny Realism and the Decline of the Modern Horror Film." *Paradoxa: Studies in World Literary Genres* 3, nos. 3–4 (1997): 417–428.

Williamson, Kevin. *Scream: A Screenplay*. New York: Hyperion, 1997.

Screwball Comedies

Born in the early 1930s, during the bleakest years of the Great Depression, the screwball comedy became a popular variation of the romantic comedy film. Although the leading characters were usually reconciled to the basic values of polite society by the story's end, most screwball comedies, up until that final reel, were irreverent toward the rich, big business, small-town life, government, and assorted other sacred cows, not the least of which was the institution of marriage. Among the unorthodox notions that these movies advocated were that marriage could be fun, that women and men were created equal, and that being bright and articulate was not necessarily a handicap for a woman. Screwballs were known for their witty, fast-paced dialogue and for choosing the silly romantic notion over the sentimental. While attempts have been made in most subsequent decades to revive the genre, for the most part the best screwball comedies remain the ones made more than seventy years ago.

ADVENT OF THE SCREWBALL

There were, from the early 1930s to the mid-1940s, more than 200 screwball films, almost all of them dedicated to the celebration of eccentric, unconventional behavior and attitudes and the proposition that life could be a lot of fun in spite of war and a fouled-up economy. These movies frequently offered smart, savvy reinterpretations of such classic folktale plots as *Beauty and the Beast*; *Sleeping Beauty*; and, most especially, *Cinderella*. Although the plots always dealt with romance, the focal couple might also find themselves involved, while trying to pursue the path of true love, with kidnapping, election campaigns, scandals, runaway leopards, shipwreck, amnesia, divorce, murder, seeming adultery, and all sorts of impersonations.

Of the considerable number of actors and actresses who tried their hands at the screwball category, there were several who displayed a true knack for the genre and appeared in quite a few successful titles. Among the top women were Rosalind Russell, Carole Lombard, Jean Arthur, Claudette Colbert, Myrna Loy, and Irene Dunne. Top men included Cary Grant, Joel McCrea, Melvyn Douglas, Fred MacMurray, and William Powell. It was not just the madcap heiresses, masquerading shop girls, and disinherited playboys who behaved in wild and eccentric ways. A majority of the films were peopled with a wide variety of odd and outrageous minor characters. Anybody from a rural judge to a Park Avenue cabdriver to a nightclub torch singer might turn out to be a world-class screwball. Frequently falling into this category were Alice Brady, Charlie Ruggles, Eugene Pallette, Eve Arden, Mischa Auer, Una Merkel, Robert Benchley, William Demarest, Franklin Pangborn, Billie Burke, and Luis Alberni. Many of these gifted character actors appeared so frequently in this sort of film that they give the impression they must have been permanent residents of a special screwball world. Ralph

Bellamy was the ablest portrayer of an essential screwball movie type: the attractive but flawed suitor who is never going to win the leading lady.

GOLDEN ERA

Movies with most of the essential screwball ingredients started to show up on the screen in 1932, notably *Trouble in Paradise*. Set in Venice, it dealt with a pair of thieves, played by Miriam Hopkins and Herbert Marshall, who set out to fleece wealthy Kay Francis. Directed by Ernst Lubitsch from a script by Samson Raphaelson, it also made use of several actors who would become part of the screwball stock company throughout the 1930s and into the 1940s—Ruggles, Edward Everett Horton, and Robert Greig (who specialized in playing the grouchy butler and worked with everybody from the Marx Brothers to Veronica Lake). The following year saw such films as *Bombshell*, which featured Jean Harlow, aided by the energetic Lee Tracy, in a very funny burlesque version of what looked a lot like her own life as a movie star.

Things picked up even more in 1934. Probably the most important screwball comedy was Frank Capra's *It Happened One Night*, scripted by Robert Riskin. Colbert was the runaway heiress who ends up taking a very strenuous cross-country bus trip with salty reporter Clark Gable. Backing them up were portly Walter Connolly, an expert at irascibility, and Roscoe Karns. The film swept the Oscars and put Columbia Pictures firmly in the screwball business for the rest of the decade. Also released in 1934 was *The Thin Man*, adapted from the Dashiell Hammett novel and briskly directed by W. S. Van Dyke. Extremely appealing as the wisecracking husband-and-wife detective team, Myrna Loy and William Powell went on to make five more movies about Nick and Nora Charles as well as several very good non-mystery screwball comedies, including *I Love You Again* (1940) and *Libeled Lady* (1936).

A moderately successful Broadway playwright before going to Hollywood, Preston Sturges started writing comedy screenplays in the mid-1930s. His adaptation of *The Good Fairy* changed the Ferenc Molnár play completely, turning it into an effective screwball comedy set in Vienna. William Wyler directed and Margaret Sullavan and Herbert Marshall starred in this variation of the Cinderella story that has orphan Sullavan instrumental in changing the fortunes of struggling attorney Marshall; character actors included Frank Morgan and Reginald Owen. Sturges's *Easy Living* came out in 1937, with Mitchell Leisen directing. Another cockeyed Cinderella story, it has working girl Jean Arthur being mistaken for the mistress of Wall Street tycoon Edward Arnold. Ray Milland is the young man who falls in love with the transformed Arthur. Demarest and Pangborn are in the cast, and Alberni gives a bravura performance as the English-mangling, hyperactive manager of a faltering ritzy hotel who offers Arthur a luxury suite because he thinks it will influence Arnold.

END OF THE GENRE

In 1940 Paramount Pictures offered Sturges the opportunity to direct, and he proceeded to turn out an impressive string of successful comedies at a rapid rate. They included *The Great McGinty* (1940), with Brian Donlevy; *The Lady Eve* (1941), with Barbara Stanwyck and Henry Fonda; *The Palm Beach Story* (1942), with McCrea and Colbert; *Sullivan's Travels* (1941), with McCrea and Lake; and *The Miracle of Morgan's Creek* (1944), with Eddie Bracken and Betty Hutton. Sturges's comedies had a headlong pace, bright dialogue, social satire, eccentrics, curmudgeons, fatheads, and generous helpings of broad slapstick. He gathered around him a group of gifted comedy actors who appeared in nearly every one of his films. These included Greig, Demarest, Pangborn, Raymond Walburn, Al Bridge, and Eric Blore.

Leisen, working with various writers, provided a string of other screwball comedies. Among them were *Hands across the Table* (1935), with Lombard, MacMurray, and Bellamy—as the fellow who does not get the girl—and *Take a Letter, Darling* (1942), with MacMurray as a very reluctant male secretary to Russell. He also directed, from a script by Charles Brackett and Billy Wilder, the quintessential screwball Cinderella movie of the period, *Midnight* (1939). Colbert is a gold-digging chorus girl stranded in Paris, and she ends up impersonating a countess. Don Ameche is a cab driver who falls in love with her, and John Barrymore and Mary Astor are also on hand.

The performer several critics and historians consider perhaps the best comedienne of these years always thought of herself as a serious actress and a singer. Irene Dunne had to be coerced into taking the starring role in the 1936 comedy *Theodora Goes Wild* at Columbia Pictures. Cast opposite Melvyn Douglas, she plays a quiet small-town young woman who writes a racy best seller under a pen name. The transformation she undergoes after meeting and falling in love with Douglas, and then realizing that he is even less liberated than she is, forms the basis for the story. Dunne had, in the words of historian James Harvey, "the acutest kind of self-awareness. . . . Where Lombard seems driven and distrait, Dunne seems intoxicated, magical, high-flying. . . . Dunne doesn't just see the joke—she is radiant with it, possessed by it and glowing with it. Nobody does this so completely or to quite the same degree."

The next year Dunne appeared in Leo McCarey's *The Awful Truth*, which has been called "the definitive screwball comedy." It is about infidelity, love, trust, and the inevitability of some relationships. Cary Grant, who originally did not want the part, plays opposite her and establishes the style of characterization he used for much of his subsequent career. Bellamy does one of his most memorable turns as the loser of the girl and, for good measure, the dog who played Asta in the *Thin Man* movies appears as the pet over whom the divorcing Dunne and Grant get into a custody battle. As in *Theodora*, Dunne gets to cause considerable embarrassment for the object of her affection by impersonating a different sort of woman, this time Grant's vulgar, and fictitious, sister. She made a few more comedies, including the equally successful *My Favorite Wife*, again with Grant, in 1940.

Standouts on the long list of other screwball comedies include *Nothing Sacred* (1937), with Lombard, Connolly, and Fredric March; *My Man Godfrey* (1936), with Lombard and Powell; *Bringing Up Baby* (1938), with Katharine Hepburn and Grant, which would eventually become one of the most referenced comedies in film history; *Bachelor Mother* (1939), with Ginger Rogers and David Niven; *Ninotchka* (1939), with Melvyn Douglas and, of all people, Greta Garbo; *His Girl Friday* (1940), with Grant and Russell and directed by Howard Hawks; *The Major and the Minor* (1942), with Ginger Rogers and Ray Milland—the first film directed by Billy Wilder; and *The More the Merrier* (1943), with Arthur, McCrea and Charles Coburn.

ROMANTIC COMEDY VS. SCREWBALL COMEDY

While the mad rush toward the screwball comedy petered out in the late 1940s, directors Hawks and Wilder would continue to explore the genre well into the 1950s and 1960s. Hawks's early screwball films such as *His Girl Friday* may have fit more succinctly into the screwball era, but *Man's Favorite Sport?* (1964) contained significant screwball elements as well: a man who purports to be a world-class fisherman while never having fished a day in his life is forced to prove himself in a fishing contest by the more savvy female character—a quintessentially screwball plotline. After great success with *The Major and the Minor*, Wilder continued to pursue screwball-type plots, dialogue, and characters in films such as *Some Like It Hot* (1959), whose various farcical plot elements and mix-ups can make sense only in a screwball context; and *One, Two, Three* (1961), in which the actors were reportedly told to take their dialogue "100 miles an hour on the curves, 140 miles an hour on the straight."

True screwball comedies manage to create just the right balance between goofiness and reality. Peter Bogdanovich called *Bringing Up Baby* the "wildest, most outrageously funny talking picture I had ever seen," and many critics have suggested his 1972 film *What's up, Doc?* is nothing less than a remake of the former. Regardless of whether it is an homage or an outright copy, it certainly hits all the screwball highlights: at least one truly eccentric character, a one-sided romance with an unwitting fiancée off to the side, a chase, fast witty dialogue, physical comedy, and the favoring of silliness over romance. Another movie many critics consider a deliberate homage to the screwball is Neil Simon's *Seems Like Old Times* (1980), starring Goldie Hawn and Charles Grodin. Hawn is obviously perfect for the screwball leading lady—and indeed you could argue that many of Hawn's movies come very close to classic screwball style, including *Overboard* (1987), in which the rich socialite is fooled into thinking she is married to her carpenter, played by Hawn's longtime companion Kurt Russell.

One reason the screwball style may have fallen out of fashion is the class element: the classic screwball often had a mismatch between a rich heroine and a man of lower social (and economic class) or vice versa. As the disparity between the very rich and the very poor becomes wider and wider, the majority of Hollywood films focus on the more mundane middle-class (albeit failing to recognize that many Americans fall far lower on that middle-class rung than is often publicly acknowledged). This class element is one reason the original *Arthur* (1981), with Dudley Moore as the rich drunk who falls in love with a poor young woman, would likely qualify as a screwball—not to mention the blatant eccentricities of Moore's character. Michael Hoffman's 1991 farce *Soapdish*—with Sally Field, Whoopi Goldberg, Kevin Kline, and Robert Downey Jr. all giving truly comedic performances—is another example of a modern film that remains true to screwball characteristics: mistaken identity, rich versus poor, romantic entanglements, eccentric characters, and situations so over the top they are only believable within the confines of the movie. *The Hudsucker Proxy* (1994), with its scam, undercover sleuthing, and rapid-fire line delivery, and *Flirting with Disaster* (1996), with its multiple mistaken identifications, eccentric characters, and wildly farcical subplots, are two other modern candidates.

While many more modern comedies contain a screwball element here and there, those comedies have come to become known as "romantic" rather than "screwball" because of the presence of only one (or lack of any) of the following: truly eccentric characters, farcical situations, witty repartee, a class element, and an emphasis on comedy over coupling. In other words, while a movie such as *Four Weddings and a Funeral* (1994) may contain some eccentric characters (Fiona's brother, for example, or even Fiona), the final emphasis is sentimental: love conquers all.

When it comes time for a resolution, contemporary comedy films choose the romantic over the screwball, but perhaps that is what the modern audience needs. However, the films of Adam Sandler and Ben Stiller point to a resuscitation of the screwball genre. Sandler's *Happy Gilmore* (1996), *Mr. Deeds* (2002), and *50 First Dates* (2004) all share many of the same traits and plot devices of the screwball comedy and push the bounds of traditional romantic comedies. In *Happy Gilmore* he portrays an aspiring hockey star who lacks the ability to skate but possesses a powerful slapshot. Through pure chance, he stumbles into the exclusive world of professional golf, where he meets and falls in love with the tour's head of public relations, Virginia Venit (Julie Bowen). Through her tutelage, Gilmore represses his anger and goes on to win the tournament.

Mr. Deeds, a loose remake of *Mr. Deeds Goes to Town* (1936), features Sandler as the unlikely heir to a media conglomerate. The film twists and turns around the on-again, off-again relationship between Deeds and reporter Babe Bennett, ending with the two married in a small town. In *50 First Dates* the womanizing Sandler is faced with the short-term memory loss of Drew Barrymore. Although each of the films celebrates the "love conquers all" motif, the use of chance, class, and eccentric characters positions them more as hybrids of the genre.

Similarly, Stiller's comedic films seem to redefine screwball comedies in a contemporary context. *There's Something about Mary* (1998) follows Stiller's character, Ted Stroehmann, as he tries to reconnect with his high school prom date, Mary Jenson, played by Cameron Diaz. Throughout the film it is revealed the Mary has an unnameable quality about her over which numerous suitors obsess. In 2004's *Along Came Polly*, Polly Prince (played by Jennifer Aniston) pulls Stiller's character, Reuben Feffer, a risk-assessment expert, out from his risk-free lifestyle into a more carefree and spontaneous existence. Stiller's characters must let go of their inhibitions in order to function in a chaotic world.

While Stiller's films are at times formulaic, the witty and fast-paced banter coupled with elements of slapstick and scatological humor serve to reinvent the screwball comedy. He employs new ways to play on class dynamics by creating an outsider who is confined by impotent rage, by repositioning the female role to be immensely important to the salvation of the lead character but also the catalyst for much of the comedy, and by finding new ways to create zany yet grounded characters. While purists will undoubtedly say that the era of screwball comedies is over, Sandler and Stiller, in particular, have introduced new ways to reveal romantic comedies' indebtedness to their screwball cousin.

Ron Goulart

SEE ALSO: *Academy Awards; Astaire, Fred, and Ginger Rogers; Barrymore, John; Benchley, Robert;* Bringing Up Baby; *Broadway; Capra, Frank; Colbert, Claudette; Douglas, Melvyn; Downey, Robert, Jr.; Dunne, Irene; Field, Sally; Fonda, Henry; Gable, Clark; Garbo, Greta; Goldberg, Whoopi; Grant, Cary;*

The Great Depression; Hammett, Dashiell; Harlow, Jean; Hawks, Howard; Hepburn, Katharine; Hollywood; Lake, Veronica; Lombard, Carole; Loy, Myrna; MacMurray, Fred; Marx, Groucho; The Marx Brothers; Movie Stars; Powell, William; Russell, Rosalind; Simon, Neil; Some Like It Hot*; Stanwyck, Barbara; Stiller, Ben; Sturges, Preston; Wilder, Billy.*

BIBLIOGRAPHY

Basinger, Jeanine. *A Woman's View.* New York: Alfred A. Knopf, 1993.

Harvey, James. *Romantic Comedy.* New York: Alfred A. Knopf, 1987.

Kendall, Elizabeth. *The Runaway Bride.* New York: Alfred A. Knopf, 1990.

Landay, Lori. *Madcaps, Screwballs, and Con Women: The Female Trickster in American Culture.* Philadelphia: University of Pennsylvania Press, 1998

Scribner's

In their heyday *Scribner's Monthly* (1870–1881) and *Scribner's Magazine* (1887–1939) gave their largely middle-class readerships beautiful illustrations and outstanding popular fiction and nonfiction. *Scribner's Monthly* was named for New York publisher Charles Scribner, who founded it with attorney Roswell C. Smith and Dr. Josiah Gilbert Holland, a writer of moral tales and poems scorned by critics but popular with young Americans. From the start, the men imbued the magazine with their shared Christian outlook, giving it a religious tone that was rare among general interest periodicals. Part of the stated mission of *Scribner's* was to extend art and literature to readers outside big cities. Promising that the publications would be "profusely illustrated," Holland proposed it as a "democratic form of literature" for people who lacked time for books. After Scribner died in 1871, Holland became the magazine's guiding light. He emphasized a sort of moderate Christianity, favoring temperance but not prohibition, for instance. "Orthodoxy saves nobody; Christian love and Christian character save everybody," he wrote.

Spurred by advancements in printing, engraving, and other facets of production, the number of American magazines nearly doubled to 1,200 in the five years after the Civil War. Intended as competition for two older, high-quality rivals, *Harper's Monthly* and the *Atlantic Monthly*, *Scribner's* published more nonfiction than both. Early on it worked to capture the attention of the public through a combination of eye-catching illustrations and articles on a variety of subjects. Many of these subjects were chosen to appeal to women; the magazine published a good deal of sentimental fiction and poetry, as well as nonfiction articles on children, gardening, fashion, and the like.

CHANGING DIRECTIONS

Holland and his assistant editor, Richard Watson Gilder, gradually took a more daring tack later in the 1870s. Walt Whitman's sensual poems offended Holland, and the editor often disparaged them in print and even rejected a poem he submitted for publication. Nevertheless, Holland published an article that described Whitman as one of America's leading poets (although "too anatomical and malodorous"), making *Scribner's* one of the first conventional magazines to recognize him as a great American poet. The magazine also began printing more realistic fiction, including stories by Henry James and Bret Harte. John Muir contributed nature pieces. Illustrators included artists such as Winslow Homer. Circulation rose steadily, and by 1878 *Scribner's* was earning a solid profit. It owed part of its financial success to accepting nonliterary advertisements. (*Scribner's* was among the first well-respected magazines to adopt this policy.)

Following a dispute with Charles Scribner's Sons, the editors and part owners of *Scribner's* separated from the publishing firm in 1881 and changed the magazine's name to the *Century Illustrated Monthly.* Holland died after editing just one issue. Gilder took over as editor and led the *Century* to even greater success than its predecessor had enjoyed, nearly doubling its circulation in the 1880s with retrospectives on the Civil War written by leading participants such as William T. Sherman and Ulysses Grant. The *Century* continued to flourish until 1900, when it began a long, slow decline brought on partly by competition from muckraking magazines. By 1930, when it had cut back to quarterly publication with a circulation of just 20,000, it was merged with *Forum* magazine and its name disappeared.

A NEW *SCRIBNER'S*

Charles Scribner's Sons had started *Scribner's Magazine* in 1887. Under its first editor, Edward L. Burlingame, the new *Scribner's* continued its namesake's tradition of publishing fine illustrations and articles. Burlingame gained an early advantage over his main competitors, *Harper's*, the *Atlantic*, and the *Century*, by offering the new *Scribner's* at twenty-five cents an issue, or $3 a year, compared to the standard thirty-five cents an issue or $4 a year. Publishing works by writers such as Stephen Crane and Rudyard Kipling helped the magazine to overtake its rivals in the 1890s. *Scribner's* continued to publish nonfiction articles on social issues such as labor unrest and urban poverty by relatively unknown writers such as Charles Francis Adams ("The Prevention of Railroad Strikes") and Jacob A. Riis ("How the Other Half Lives").

Also in the 1890s, the magazine weathered a severe economic depression and challenges from new and cheaper competitors such as *McClure's*. For the most part, *Scribner's* disdained the muckraking stance common in many magazines of the early twentieth century. It continued to concentrate on art, running lavishly illustrated articles with outstanding full-color pictures by artists such as N. C. Wyeth. The magazine also printed outstanding fiction as well as popular travel and adventure features, including a number of articles by Theodore Roosevelt describing his exploits in Africa, South America, and elsewhere. The magazine published fiction by Edith Wharton, Ernest Hemingway, John Galsworthy, and Thomas Wolfe. It reached its peak circulation of more than 200,000 around 1911 and began to decline thereafter.

GONE BUT NOT FORGOTTEN

Dogged by its old-fashioned appearance and the onset of the Great Depression, *Scribner's* suffered a severe slump in the 1930s. Alfred Dashiell, who became editor in 1930, attempted to revive its sagging fortunes by running more Left-leaning political articles intended to appeal to young intellectuals. He also continued the magazine's strong literary tradition, publishing stories by Sherwood Anderson, Langston Hughes, Erskine Caldwell, William Saroyan, William Faulkner, and F. Scott Fitzgerald. Nevertheless, he lost many longtime readers and did not replace them with new ones. By the time he resigned in 1936 to take a job at *Reader's Digest*, circulation had fallen from 70,000 to 40,000.

Harlan Logan, an English professor and magazine analyst, became editor in 1936 and redesigned and enlivened the magazine. Although he doubled circulation and cut financial losses, his efforts fell short of what was needed, and *Scribner's* ceased publication in May 1939. *Esquire* acquired its subscriber list, and the title was merged with that of another magazine. The resulting *Scribner's Commentator* met an inglorious death in 1942. Without the Internet, *Scribner's* might have faded into total obscurity, but a number of websites have made old issues of the magazine available to twenty-first century audiences who want a glimpse of history, literature, and culture in the early twentieth century.

Daniel Lindley

SEE ALSO: *Anderson, Sherwood;* Atlantic Monthly*; Caldwell, Erskine;* Esquire*; Faulkner, William; Fitzgerald, F. Scott;* Harper's*; Hemingway, Ernest; Hughes, Langston; Mass Market Magazine Revolution; Muckraking; Wharton, Edith.*

BIBLIOGRAPHY

John, Arthur. *The Best Years of the Century: Richard Watson Gilder, "Scribner's Monthly," and "Century Magazine," 1870–1909.* Urbana: University of Illinois Press, 1981.

"Making of America: *Scribner's Monthly.*" Cornell University. Accessed March 2012. Available from http://digital.library.cornell.edu/s/scmo/index.html

Mott, Frank Luther. *A History of American Magazines: 1885–1905.* Cambridge, MA: Harvard University Press, 1957.

Noonan, Mark J. *Reading the "Century Illustrated Monthly" Magazine: American Literature and Culture, 1870–1893.* Kent, OH: Kent State University, 2010.

Peterson, Theodore. *Magazines in the Twentieth Century.* Urbana: University of Illinois Press, 1964.

Tebbel, John. *The American Magazine: A Compact History.* New York: Hawthorn Books, 1969.

Scruggs, Earl *(1924–2012)*

An enormously influential musician, North Carolina native Earl Scruggs rescued the five-string banjo from its fate as a country comedian's instrument, moving it into the realm of virtuosity through his work with Bill Monroe's Blue Grass Boys and with his own band, the Foggy Mountain Boys, in the 1940s, 1950s, and 1960s. Scruggs's work became familiar to television audiences after he wrote "The Ballad of Jed Clampett," the theme for the popular series *The Beverly Hillbillies* (1962–1971). Though he did not invent the three-finger picking style known as Scruggs-style picking, he refined, developed, and popularized it as a backing and solo approach, winning enthusiastic fans worldwide and earning comparisons to great classical music instrumentalists.

In 1969 he left the Foggy Mountain Boys to work with his sons in the Earl Scruggs Revue, bringing a fusion of bluegrass, country, and rock to U.S. audiences, especially on college campuses. Thanks to the soundtrack for the movie *Bonnie and Clyde* (1967), his "Foggy Mountain Breakdown" (1949) is one of the best-known bluegrass numbers. He retired from the music scene in the late twentieth century due to ill health, but after heart bypass surgery and a hip replacement, he began recording and touring again. In 2001 he recorded his first album in seventeen years, *Earl Scruggs and Friends*, which featured music icons Johnny Cash, Don Henley, Elton John, Melissa Etheridge, and Sting. Scruggs died at age eighty-eight on March 28, 2012.

Jon Weisberger

SEE ALSO: The Beverly Hillbillies*; Bluegrass;* Bonnie and Clyde*; Cash, Johnny; Country Music; The Foggy Mountain Boys; John, Elton; Monroe, Bill; Rock and Roll.*

BIBLIOGRAPHY

Goldsmith, Thomas, ed. *The Bluegrass Reader.* Urbana: University of Illinois Press, 2004.

Kochman, Marilyn, ed. *The Big Book of Bluegrass.* New York: W. Morrow, 1984.

Price, Deborah Evans. "Bluegrass Great Earl Scruggs Calls on 'Friends' for All-Star MCA Album." *Billboard*, September 1, 2001, 36–37.

Scully, Vin *(1927–)*

Known as the "Voice of the Dodgers," Vin Scully is one of the top sportscasters in American history. In addition to his more than sixty years as a play-by-play announcer for the Brooklyn and then Los Angeles Dodgers, Scully announced play-by-play for the World Series, All-Star games, *Game of the Week*, National Football League (NFL) games, and Professional Golfers' Association (PGA) Tour events, exposing his mellifluous vocal stylings to viewers from coast to coast. Scully joined the Dodgers' broadcast team in 1950, just a year after graduating from Fordham University. Under the tutelage of legendary sportscaster Red Barber, he developed a warm, personable on-air style that perfectly suited the national pastime. His vivid descriptions of such events as Sandy Koufax's perfect game in 1965 and Kirk Gibson's dramatic home run in the 1988 World Series remain iconic moments in baseball play-by-play.

In 1998 Scully retired from national broadcasting to concentrate solely on broadcasting for the Dodgers. All told, he called twenty-five World Series and twelve All-Star games over the course of his career. One evening in 2010, Scully suffered what doctors later diagnosed as a vasovagal episode; he stood up too fast, got dizzy, fainted, and fell, hitting his head. Eighty-two-year-old Scully was back in the broadcast booth just days later. When asked by a reporter if doctors had recommended any restrictions on his activities, he replied, "I'm supposed to cut back on dangling participles and I'm not allowed to split an infinitive for at least another week, but otherwise, no," according to Jim Peltz, writing for the *Los Angeles Times*. In 2012 Scully began his sixty-third year as an announcer with the Dodgers, working part time.

Robert E. Schnakenberg

SEE ALSO: *Barber, Red; Baseball; The Brooklyn Dodgers; Golf; Koufax, Sandy; National Football League (NFL); World Series.*

BIBLIOGRAPHY

Peltz, Jim. "Vin Scully 'Embarrassed over All the Fuss.'" *Los Angeles Times*, March 21, 2010. Accessed April 7, 2012. Available from http://articles.latimes.com/2010/mar/21/sports/la-sp-dodgers-fyi-20100322

Smith, Curt. *The Storytellers: From Mel Allen to Bob Costas: Sixty Years of Baseball Tales from the Broadcast Booth*. New York: Macmillan, 1995.

Smith, Curt. *Pull Up a Chair: The Vin Scully Story*. Dulles, VA: Potomac Books, 2009.

Seals, Son *(1942–2004)*

One of the strongest live performers to work Chicago's blues circuit, Son Seals brought a new energy to the scene as many of the older musicians were beginning to slow down. Seals was at the forefront of a generation of young guitar players who carried on the traditions of Muddy Waters, Sonny Boy Williamson, and Howlin' Wolf.

Born in 1942 in Osceola, Arkansas, Seals grew up in the back room of his father's juke joint, the Dipsy Doodle, an arrangement that exposed him to blues at an early age. He took up drums and began playing live at age thirteen with artists such as Williamson, Robert Nighthawk, Earl Hooker, and Albert King during the mid-1960s.

Seals moved to Chicago in 1971. By 1972 he had formed his own group as a guitarist and a year later recorded his debut album, *The Son Seals Blues Band*, for Alligator Records. His follow-up album, *Midnight Sun* (1976), received widespread acclaim. Upon its release, the *New York Times* called Seals "the most exciting young blues guitarist and singer in years." He recorded six more albums for Alligator through 1996.

His later years were inundated by various health issues—Seals was shot in the jaw by his wife during a domestic disturbance in January 1997, the first of two such instances. In 1999 he lost a leg due to diabetes and only recorded one more album, 2000's *Lettin Go*. He did, however, continue to tour and remained a top draw in Chicago's clubs. The jam-band Phish often invited Seals on tour with them, and their cover of his hit "Funky Bitch" was a staple of their live show.

Alligator issued a retrospective of Seals's career, *Deluxe Edition*, in 2002. Seals died in Chicago on December 20, 2004, from diabetes complications. He was survived by fourteen children. A video biography *A Journey through the Blues: The Son Seals Story* was released in 2007.

Jon Klinkowitz

SEE ALSO: *Blues; Howlin' Wolf; Waters, Muddy.*

BIBLIOGRAPHY

Corbett, John. "Son Seals." *Down Beat*, February 1995, 52.

Poses, Jonathan. "Son Seals Blues Band." *Down Beat*, March 1984, 50.

Search for Tomorrow

Producer Roy Winsor developed *Search for Tomorrow* and proved that the soap opera could succeed on television. The CBS serial, which debuted on September 3, 1951, reflected the concerns of the United States in the postwar era by focusing on a widowed heroine, Joanne Tate (played for all thirty-five years by Mary Stuart), who struggled with issues of marriage and children. Jo was the problem solver for the town of Henderson, counseling friends and neighbors, especially the comic Bergmans (Larry Haines and Melba Rae). Later story lines centered on Jo's children and the exotic adventures of a new family, the Sentells.

Search for Tomorrow moved to NBC in 1982 and, a year later, presented the first live show on daytime in seventeen years (the tape was reportedly stolen). In the mid-1980s the entire community of Henderson was flooded, and surviving citizens were forced to live in the same building. The final episode of *Search for Tomorrow* was broadcast on December 26, 1986, and in the last scene Jo was asked for what she was searching. She responded, "Tomorrow. I can't wait."

Ron Simon

SEE ALSO: *Soap Operas; Television.*

BIBLIOGRAPHY

The Museum of Television & Radio. *Worlds without End: The Art and History of the Soap Opera*. New York: Abrams, 1997.

Schemering, Christopher. *The Soap Opera Encyclopedia*. New York: Ballantine Books, 1985.

Stahl, B. "Mary Stuart's Soap Opera Problems." *TV Guide*, November 19, 1960, 17–19.

Stuart, Mary. *Both of Me*. New York: Doubleday, 1980.

The Searchers

Since its release in 1956, American director John Ford's Western *The Searchers* has become one of the most controversial films in Hollywood history. At the center of the dispute is the character Ethan Edwards, played by John Wayne in what many consider his finest performance. Throughout the film Edwards pursues a band of Native Americans who killed his brother's family and captured the daughters, one of whom, Debbie (Natalie Wood), is still alive. Many film scholars, particularly during the late 1980s and early 1990s, have attacked Ford's shabby treatment of American Indians, which is perhaps most vividly evidenced in the reactionary persona of Edwards.

Despite its critics, *The Searchers* remains a hugely influential film. It is often cited as a seminal influence by filmmakers as diverse as those of the French New Wave and the American directors who came of age in the late 1960s and early 1970s—most notably Martin Scorsese, Francis Ford Coppola, and Brian De Palma. And in Edwards filmmakers found a model for the semi-psychopathic antihero so often present in films since the late 1960s.

Robert C. Sickels

SEE ALSO: *Ford, John; Hollywood; Scorsese, Martin; Wayne, John; The Western; Wood, Natalie.*

BIBLIOGRAPHY

Courtney, Susan. "Looking for (Race and Gender) Trouble in

Monument Valley." *Qui Parle* 6, no. 2 (1993): 97–130.

Lehman, Peter. "Texas 1868/America 1956: *The Searchers*." In *Close Viewings: A New Anthology of Film Criticism*. Tallahassee: Florida State University Press, 1990.

Nolley, Ken. "John Ford and the Hollywood Indian." *Film & History* 23, nos. 1–4 (1993): 44–56.

Skerry, Philip J. "What Makes a Man to Wander? Ethan Edwards of John Ford's *The Searchers*." *New Orleans Review* 18, no. 4 (1991): 86–91.

Stoehr, Kevin L., and Michael C. Connolly, eds. *John Ford in Focus: Essays on the Filmmaker's Life and Work*. Jefferson, NC: McFarland, 2008.

Sears Roebuck Catalog

Known affectionately as "a department store in a book," "the farmer's wishbook," and the "farmer's Bible," the Sears Roebuck mail-order catalog, while not the first of its kind in retail merchandising, was certainly the most famous and the one that inspired the most imitations.

Mail-order catalogs are similar to print magazines. Instead of presenting articles on various subjects, however, they feature merchandise that a store offers for sale. While their size and design differ, catalogs all have pictures of the products for sale, accompanied by descriptions and prices. Although the first publication resembling a mail-order catalog was supposedly a mail circular distributed by inventor and publisher Benjamin Franklin in 1744, modern versions became popular in America during the 1870s. Merchant Aaron Montgomery Ward established the modern mail-order industry in 1872, selling his wares, selected primarily for the needs of farming families, through the mail.

Sears, Roebuck & Company Catalog. *The cover of an early Sears, Roebuck & Company catalog touts the retailer as the "Cheapest Supply House on Earth."* AP IMAGES.

In 1886 Richard W. Sears founded the R. W. Sears Watch Company in Minneapolis, Minnesota, and sold watches by mail using a catalog that featured only watches. In 1887 he moved his business to Chicago and hired Alvah C. Roebuck, a watch repairman. Sears realized that farmers in rural America were a huge untapped market and soon the company offered everything a farmer and his family could possibly need. In 1893 the name of the company became Sears, Roebuck and Co., and in 1894 the company's rapidly growing catalog reached more than 700 pages and offered more than 6,000 products for sale.

The early years of the Sears, Roebuck catalog were significant in bringing a largely urban and mass-manufactured way of life to rural areas that had previously been relatively isolated from metropolitan goods and culture. In 1897 the company distributed 318,000 copies of its catalog in the Midwest; by 1908 it was shipping 3.6 million copies. Sears's drawings and product descriptions helped sell the company's goods, through the mail, to customers far away. The success of mail-order businesses was aided by new products and services offered by the U.S. Post Office, such as prestamped penny postcards in 1873, rural free delivery in 1896, and parcel post in 1913. Both Sears and Ward took advantage of them, remaining mail-order competitors well into the twentieth century. Sears shrewdly published a catalog smaller than Ward's so that it would sit on top of his rival's book in the family home.

As historian Thomas Schlereth points out in the book *Consuming Visions: Accumulation and Display of Goods in America, 1880–1920*, "with the spread of mail-order merchandising, many rural people who had lived, to a large extent, on a barter or an extended credit system now became immersed in a money economy." Rural merchants, feeling their businesses threatened, decried the use of mail-order catalogs, trying to convince local townspeople that the merchandise offered within was inferior and its delivery unreliable. But Sears allayed people's fears, establishing the company's "Satisfaction guaranteed or your money back!" policy.

Catalogs changed rural life in other ways as well. Farmers were no longer completely reliant on the food that they grew themselves or procured from local produce merchants. Instead, they could purchase prepackaged food through the mail. The catalogs also presented middle-class styles and tastes and made them accessible to everyone in the country. Further, families often used catalogs as educational tools: children practiced their math by computing the total price of orders, became literate by reading the endless product descriptions, and learned geography by studying the maps inside.

In 1946 the Grolier Club, a distinguished organization of book lovers in New York, selected the Sears catalog as one of the 100 most influential books in America. By the 1970s Sears was distributing sixty-five million copies of its main catalog—by then a familiar adjunct to Sears retail sales floors—along with an additional 250 million tabloid catalogs per year. The 1897 catalog has even been successfully reprinted, a testament to its endurance as a cultural icon and as a source of American nostalgia.

The Sears catalog is perhaps most significant in having established the viability of mail-order trade, no longer requiring face-to-face interaction between buyer and seller. Thousands of other catalogs appeared during the twentieth century, including those selling clothing, jewelry, gourmet food, plants, herbs, and art supplies. The mail-order catalog paved the way for television shopping channels, such as QVC and the Home Shopping Network, and online shopping on commercial websites. While Sears, Roebuck and Co. stopped publishing its main catalog in 1993, it continues to publish its smaller specialized catalogs, such as the Christmas Wish Book.

Wendy Woloson

SEE ALSO: *Advertising; Cable TV; Catalog Houses; Consumerism; Home Shopping Network/QVC; The Internet; Postcards.*

BIBLIOGRAPHY

Cohn, David L. *The Good Old Days: A History of American Morals and Manners as Seen through the Sears, Roebuck Catalogues 1905 to the Present.* New York: Simon & Schuster, 1940.

Schlereth, Thomas J. "Country Stores, County Fairs, and Mail-Order Catalogues: Consumption in Rural America." In *Consuming Visions: Accumulation and Display of Goods in America, 1880–1920*, ed. Simon J. Bronner. New York: Norton, 1989.

Thornton, Rosemary. *The Houses That Sears Built.* Alton, IL: Gentle Beam Publications, 2004.

Weil, Gordon L. *Sears, Roebuck, U.S.A.: The Great American Catalogue Store and How It Grew.* New York: Stein & Day, 1977.

Sears Tower

The Willis Tower (formerly known as the Sears Tower) looms over downtown Chicago, an unmistakable symbol of the city's pride in its heritage as the birthplace of a uniquely American creation, the modern skyscraper. Built in 1974 to a height of 1,450 feet, the Sears Tower succeeded the twin towers of the World Trade Center as the world's tallest building and held that title until 1996. The building was designed by the distinguished and world-famous firm of architects Skidmore, Owings & Merrill, to serve as the corporate headquarters for Sears Roebuck and Company. Its architectural style, while incorporating significant engineering advances, reflects the impersonal glass boxes of the 1950s and 1960s rather than looking forward to the more idiosyncratic towers of the 1980s and 1990s.

Despite its prominence, the building was nearly half vacant for the first decade of its existence. Sears began moving out in 1992, and by the end of the decade, ownership of the building had changed hands twice. The tower was considered by many to be a prime terrorist target after the attack on the World Trade Center in 2001, and in fact the FBI arrested a group of American men plotting to destroy the building in 2006. Three years later a London-based insurance brokerage, Willis Group Holdings, purchased the property and renamed it the Willis Tower.

Though large and impressive, the building never quite captured the hearts of Chicagoans in the same way as the city's John Hancock Center. Nevertheless, the Willis Tower epitomizes the bustling prairie metropolis that Carl Sandburg called the "City of Big Shoulders."

Dale Allen Gyure

SEE ALSO: *9/11; Sandburg, Carl; Sears Roebuck Catalog; Skyscrapers; World Trade Center.*

BIBLIOGRAPHY

Douglas, George H. *Skyscrapers: A Social History of the Very Tall Building in America.* Jefferson, NC: McFarland, 1996.

Khan, Yasmin Sabina. *Engineering Architecture: The Vision of Fazlur R. Khan.* New York: W. W. Norton Books, 2004.

Pridmore, Jay. *Sears Tower: A Building Book from the Chicago Architecture Foundation.* Rohnert Park, CA: Pomegranate Communications, 2002.

SeaWorld

In the highly competitive amusement industry, SeaWorld Adventure Parks have attempted to provide visitors with a greater understanding of marine life. Opened in 1964, the original SeaWorld was soon purchased by Anheuser-Busch and expanded into the late 1990s to include parks in Florida, California, and Ohio. Unlike Disneyland and other amusement parks, SeaWorld uses environmental education, spectacle, and science to create an experience that appeals to tourists. However, many critics will never be comfortable with the basic premise of SeaWorld: the forced performance of captive animals.

The spectacle of SeaWorld is centered on orca shows; the most famous orca is Shamu. With an environmental experience that brings to mind *Wild Kingdom* and *Jacques Cousteau*, SeaWorld enables tourists to appreciate nature in a tradition that places humans in control. SeaWorld serves as a figurehead for green consumerism. "SeaWorld," Susan Davis notes in her cultural analysis of the theme parks, *Spectacular Nature*, "is not so much a substitute for nature as an opinion about it, an attempt to convince a broad public that nature is going to be all right." But Davis contends, "SeaWorld represents an enormous contradiction. Using living animals, captive seas, and flourishing landscapes, the theme park has organized the subtle and contradictory cultural meanings of nature into a machine for mass consumption."

Criticism of SeaWorld's capture of sea animals was renewed with the release of the award-winning documentary film *The Cove* (2009), which accused the park of obtaining dolphins in drive hunts. Although inconclusive, this episode demonstrates that due to its unique attraction, SeaWorld will never completely escape criticism for the fact that it relies on captive animals—regardless of how they are acquired.

Brian Black

SEE ALSO: *Amusement Parks; Cousteau, Jacques; Disney (Walt Disney Company); Environmentalism;* Wild Kingdom.

BIBLIOGRAPHY

Davis, Susan G. *Spectacular Nature: Corporate Culture and the*

Sea World Experience. Berkeley: University of California Press, 1997.

Francis, Daniel. *Operation Orca*. Madeira Park, BC: Harbour Books, 2007.

Nibert, David Alan. *Animal Rights/Human Rights*. Lanham, MD: Rowman & Littlefield, 2002.

Second City

The Second City theater company of Chicago has set the standard for improvisational comedy since the early 1960s, and no single institution has made a greater impact on the development of American comedy since. The comedy troupe has produced a stellar array of improvisational and stand-up comedians, actors, writers, and directors who have had a profound influence on comedy worldwide.

THE ROOTS OF SECOND CITY

The troupe's roots go back to the progressive campus of the University of Chicago in 1951, where a group of performers and writers began presenting plays. After two years the group migrated from the university's South Side campus to a North Side converted chop suey house, pooled their resources, and launched the Playwrights Theatre Club, which produced twenty-five plays over the next two years. When the fire department ordered extensive remodeling, the club broke apart, forming two new groups: the Compass Players, an improvisational troupe that played nightclubs around Chicago, and the Studebaker Theater Company, which presented repertory theater in a 1,200-seat house in the Loop area. Members oscillated back and forth between these two new companies until, a year later, both of them also broke up.

Three former members of the group (or groups)—Mike Nichols, Elaine May, and Shelley Berman—rapidly achieved individual national recognition. Berman became a successful stand-up comedian and recording star, while Nichols and May played nightclubs across the country, were a hit on Broadway, and produced several smash comedy albums. They parted ways in 1961, with May going on to work variously as an actress, a writer, and a director, and Nichols forging a major directing career on Broadway and in Hollywood. The comedy background of each was evident in films such as Nichols's *The Graduate* (1967) and May's *A New Leaf* (1971). Meanwhile, the other members of the original group kept in touch, dreaming of reuniting. Their dream came true in 1959 when they obtained use of a defunct Chinese laundry building on the edge of Old Town, which they converted into a coffeehouse.

THE CAST

Taking their name from a derisive article about Chicago written by A. J. Liebling for the *New Yorker*, Second City opened in December 1959 to dazzling reviews and continued to perform into the 2010s, delighting audiences and training successive generations of comics. Among Second City alumni are several who reached national recognition as cast members of *Saturday Night Live*, including John Belushi, Bill Murray, Dan Aykroyd, Gilda Radner, Martin Short, Mike Myers, Chris Farley, James Belushi, Tim Kazurinsky, Mary Gross, Robin Duke, and Tina Fey. Stand-up comics who started at Second City include Robert Klein, David Steinberg, and Joan Rivers and the comedy teams of Stiller and Meara and Burns and Schreiber.

Film actors who got their start improvising at this coffeehouse include Alan Arkin (*The In-Laws*), Jane Alexander (*The Great White Hope*), Barbara Harris (*Family Plot*), Ron Liebman (*Slaughterhouse-Five*), and Severn Darden (*The President's Analyst*). Television actors include Ed Asner and Valerie Harper (*The Mary Tyler Moore Show*, then *Lou Grant* and *Rhoda*, respectively), Shelley Long and George Wendt (*Cheers*), Linda Lavin (*Alice*), Dan Castellaneta (the voice of Homer Simpson), Fred Willard (*Fernwood 2Night*), Peter Boyle (*Everybody Loves Raymond*), Bob Odenkirk (*Mr. Show*), David Rasche (*Sledge Hammer!*), Stephen Colbert (*The Daily Show with Jon Stewart* and *The Colbert Report*), Steve Carell (*The Office*), and Jane Lynch (*Glee*). Directors include Paul Mazursky (*Bob & Carol & Ted & Alice, Moscow on the Hudson*), Betty Thomas (*The Brady Bunch Movie, Private Parts*), indie favorite Henry Jaglom (*Eating, Babyfever*), and actor/director/writer Alan Alda (*M*A*S*H, Sweet Liberty*).

ON TELEVISION

Apart from its reputation as the most fertile breeding ground for American comics, Second City is best known for the most consistently hilarious sketch comedy show in television history, *SCTV*. In 1976, when the members of the Toronto company of Second City were searching for something to satirize on a proposed television show, they hit upon the perfect topic: television itself. Regulars John Candy, Joe Flaherty, Eugene Levy, Andrea Martin, Rick Moranis, Catherine O'Hara, Harold Ramis, Martin Short, and Dave Thomas week after week acted as various members of the staff of *SCTV*, the call letters for the fictional Second City television station, serving Melonville. The station was owned by wheelchair-bound Guy Caballero (Flaherty), with Moe Green (Ramis) as the station manager—until he was kidnapped by the Leutonian Liberation Front and Edith Prickley (Martin) took over.

Other staffers included Monster Chiller Horror Theatre host Count Floyd (Flaherty), exercise show host Johnny Larue (Candy), Bob and Doug McKenzie (Moranis and Thomas) with their Great White North, pitchmen Tex and Edna Boil (Thomas and Martin), the polka-playing Schmenge Brothers (Candy and Levy) and Ed Grimley (Short)—not to mention cleaning woman Perini Scleroso (Martin) and porn salesman Harry, the Guy with the Snake on His Face (Candy). The show ran for seven years and produced 185 episodes, starting on Canada's Global television and in syndication in the United States, then moving to NBC and finally to Cinemax.

All the show's stars moved on to success in other projects. Candy became a film star (*Uncle Buck* and *Planes, Trains & Automobiles*), as did Short (*Innerspace*, *¡Three Amigos!*) and Moranis (*Little Shop of Horrors*; *Honey, I Shrunk the Kids*). O'Hara appeared in films (*Beetlejuice*, *Home Alone*), and Martin did both films (*Club Paradise*) and television (*Kate & Allie*). Ramis directed *Caddyshack*, *National Lampoon's Vacation*, and *Groundhog Day*. Thomas directed and costarred in the McKenzie Brothers movie *Strange Brew* and was a regular on *Grace under Fire*. Levy had a supporting role in the *American Pie* film franchise, and created the children's show *Maniac Mansion*—starring Joe Flaherty, who also appeared in the cult TV series *Freaks and Geeks*.

The original Second City troupe continues in Chicago, supporting national touring companies and training new generations of improvisational actors. "In a changing society," writes Second City chronicler Donna McCrohan, "The Second City is a constant, no less committed to quality theater than in 1959." In December 2009 the comedy troupe celebrated its fiftieth anniversary with a performance featuring many of its notable alumni.

Bob Sullivan

SEE ALSO: *Asner, Ed; Aykroyd, Dan; Belushi, John; Cable TV;* Cheers*; Colbert, Stephen; Farley, Chris; Fey, Tina;* Glee*;* The Graduate*; Long, Shelley;* The Mary Tyler Moore Show*;* M*A*S*H*; Murray, Bill;* National Lampoon*; The* New Yorker*; Nichols, Mike, and Elaine May;* The Office*; Radner, Gilda;* Saturday Night Live*; Sitcom; Stand-Up Comedy; Television.*

BIBLIOGRAPHY

Coleman, Janet. *The Compass: The Improvisational Theatre That Revolutionized American Comedy*. Chicago: University of Chicago Press, 1990.

Libera, Anne. *The Second City Almanac of Improvisation*. Evanston, IL: Northwestern University Press, 2004.

McCrohan, Donna. *The Second City: A Backstage History of Comedy's Hottest Troupe*. New York: Putnam Publishing Group, 1987.

Patinkin, Sheldon. *The Second City: Backstage at the World's Greatest Comedy Theater*. Naperville, IL: Sourcebooks, 2000.

Sweet, Jeffrey. *Something Wonderful Right Away*. New York: Limelight, 1987.

Thomas, Dave. *SCTV: Behind the Scenes*. Toronto: McClelland & Stewart, 1996.

Thomas, Mike. *The Second City Unscripted: Revolution and Revelation at the World-Famous Comedy Theater*. New York: Villard Books, 2009.

Second Life

In 2003 Linden Lab released a virtual reality computer software system called Second Life. Users can download a free software viewer onto their computers, allowing them to access a virtual world, or grid, through programmable avatars (physical representations of the users). Unlike online games such as *World of Warcraft*, there is no plot or directed game play; instead, users, called residents, visit the world to socialize, explore virtual environments, build and trade virtual property, or participate in activities such as bingo.

From the start, Second Life's virtual reality has been customizable, which seems to be the reason for its popularity. Avatars can be designed to appear as humans, animals, or anything else. Participants make clothing with the system's Linden scripting language or buy kits to design features for their characters. Essentially, users can become better versions of themselves. Residents can also purchase land, allowing them to build their own custom realms for others to visit. The Linden uses three-dimensional modeling so that objects and buildings look more real.

Linden dollars, an in-world currency traded at an exchange rate for U.S. dollars or other currencies, allow a virtual economy to develop within the Second Life reality. Some residents set up in-world shops to sell scripted items such as furniture for people's online homes. Since Linden dollars have a direct relationship with real-life money, people are able to earn real dollars with virtual products. As reports spread of users making substantial incomes from virtual sales, more people downloaded the program to see what all the media hype was about.

As Second Life became more popular, various businesses set up virtual stores or displays to allow people to interact with their brands. Coca-Cola and the ice cream maker Ben & Jerry's have been just two of the many companies to market to residents. Several universities also set up sections of Second Life for students, some for advertising and others for online classes, with a professor using an avatar to lecture to online students. Some events, including author lectures and press conferences, were staged online to show the potential of the technology.

Eventually, the simulation faced the real-world problems of human nature. Some residents reported being harassed by others in the virtual world. This harassment, known as griefing, became a serious issue. In addition, the computer servers frequently could not handle the number of viewer programs running simultaneously. Backgrounds and avatars would refuse to load or purchased items would disappear, making interactions difficult. The computer issues worried some advertisers, and a few high-profile events were disrupted by griefers, including a press conference that found itself covered by flying penises. These concerns slowed the spread of offline businesses setting up shop within the simulated environment.

One of the more controversial uses for Second Life is online sexual activity. There are certain areas of the virtual world that can be entered only by avatars whose users are over eighteen years old. In these sections, users program their avatars to appear nude, mimic sexual behavior on screen, and use chat and instant message systems to talk to each other about sexual matters. Discussions about the suitability of such online locations for young people and the impact of online relationships on the real world became commonplace.

When Second Life began, gambling was allowed, but Linden Lab eventually banned it. This created a panic among some users who lost money when online banks crashed. Linden Lab also cracked down on the proliferation of user-operated banks. The online economy took another serious hit as residents lost Linden dollars from failed banks. "When virtual environments first started, they were viewed as libertarian dreams with no interference," Behnam Dayanim, a specialist in Internet law, told the *Wall Street Journal* in 2008. "As companies that sponsor these environments become more accountable to investors or regulators, they are starting to encounter real-world limitations."

Most people use Second Life with a free account, although purchases of land and other products bring some income to the makers of the game. The height of Second Life's popularity was 2008 and 2009; an average of 62,000 people logged onto the system at any given time in 2009. Numbers have declined since then, and much less attention has been paid to the system in the media.

Still, many users remain. Some continue to build and sell virtual items for real money, while others simply explore the virtual environment. Second Life is ultimately a creative expression for people, both at their best and at their worst, with all the real-world difficulties that come from interactions with others. The difference is, in Second Life the person you are arguing with may appear to be a purple unicorn.

Kim Keeline

SEE ALSO: *Computer Games; The Internet; Online Gaming; Video Games.*

BIBLIOGRAPHY

Boellstorff, Tom. *Coming of Age in Second Life: An Anthropologist Explores the Virtually Human.* Princeton NJ: Princeton University Press, 2010.

Reiss, Spencer. "Virtual Economics." *Technology Review,* December 2005.

Robbins, Sarah, and Mark Bell. *Second Life for Dummies.* Hoboken, NJ: John Wiley, 2008.

Sidel, Robin. "Cheer Up, Ben: Your Economy Isn't as Bad as This One." *Wall Street Journal,* January 2008.

"Virtual World, Real Emotions: Relationships in Second Life." CNN, December 12, 2008. Accessed May 2012. Available from http://edition.cnn.com/2008/LIVING/12/12/second.life.relationship.irpt/index.html

Sedaris, Amy *(1961–)*

Amy Sedaris is an American actress and author known for her irreverent and unconventional sense of humor. She has appeared in numerous movies and television shows in both supporting and starring roles. Sedaris's popular books combine instructions on crafting and entertaining with heavy comedic touches unlike any other books of their kind.

The fourth of six children, Amy Louise Sedaris was born March 29, 1961, in Endicott, New York. Her father, an IBM engineer, was transferred to Raleigh, North Carolina, where Sedaris spent her childhood. One of her brothers, David Sedaris, is a popular, well-respected writer and humorist known for his essays and short stories. Amy Sedaris was an energetic, mischievous child who studied people so she could pretend to be them. In his book *Me Talk Pretty One Day*, David writes, "[Amy's] fondness for transformation began at an early age and has developed into something closely resembling a multiple personality disorder. . . . 'And who are we today?' my mother used to ask, leading to Amy's 'Who don't you want me to be?'" This penchant for disguises has become a part of her acting repertoire, and she said in an interview, "I need a costume to be convinced that I'm somebody else. Otherwise, it's just me. It's just Amy saying lines. I haven't really become somebody else. And what's the fun in that?"

Sedaris's career in entertainment and comedy began with a move to Chicago, where she eventually joined the legendary Second City comedy group. There she met future collaborators Stephen Colbert and Paul Dinello. The group later starred in the Comedy Central sketch series *Exit 57* from 1995 to 1996. The show was short-lived but critically acclaimed. After its cancellation, the trio worked to develop a new series. Starring Sedaris, *Strangers with Candy* aired on the Comedy Central network from 1999 to 2000.

In the series, Sedaris portrayed forty-six-year-old high school dropout Jerri Blank, who describes herself as a "boozer, a user, and a loser." A sometimes-recovering drug addict and prostitute, Blank had dropped out of high school to pursue a life of less-than-noble pursuits. The show details her attempts to return to and finish high school. Plots for *Strangers with Candy* were outlandish and often pushed boundaries. Modeled like an after-school special, the show included traditional story lines of pregnancy, drug use, and family issues—but with a dark sensibility and decidedly adult twist. Sedaris fully embraced role, making the show a cult favorite. She has also said that she uses Blank's character as a starting point for other roles.

After the run of the show, ideas for a feature film were discussed. Eventually, a *Strangers with Candy* movie was released in 2006. While not a major commercial success, it was popular among fans of the show. Colbert and Dinello reprised their roles from the television series; however, the film made only a reported $2.3 million at the box office. Despite this, Sedaris has had a successful career as a voice actor in successful films such as *Chicken Little* (2005), *Shrek the Third* (2007), and *Puss in Boots* (2011). Additional film credits include *Elf* (2003), *Jennifer's Body* (2009), and *The Best and the Brightest* (2010).

Since *Exit 57*, Sedaris has been a guest star in episodic television for a number of years. She played recurring roles on several popular programs in the late 1990s and the first decade of the 2000s, including *Sex and the City*, *Ed*, and *Just Shoot Me*. Well-known for her ditzy, flirty rapport with hosts, she has also appeared frequently on late-night television programs. David Letterman's Worldwide Pants production company was even involved with the making of the *Strangers with Candy* film. On these late-night shows, Sedaris frequently discusses her imaginary boyfriends or pets and displays a new craft she is working on, to the delight of the audience.

A frequent character in her brother David's writing, Sedaris has collaborated with him on plays and other projects under the working name the "Talent Family." Some of their more successful collaborations include *Stump the Host*, *Stitches*, and *The Book of Liz*. She worked with Colbert and Dinello on the novel *Wigfield: The Can Do Town That Just May Not*, published in 2003. The novel tells the story of a town facing imminent annihilation due to the upcoming destruction of an important dam in the area.

Sedaris has enjoyed craft making, baking, and other homemaking activities since her youth, when she was part of the Girl Scouts. She operated a successful cupcake and cheese ball business from her apartment for several years. These activities provided ample material for her books on hospitality and crafts. In *I Like You: Hospitality under the Influence*, published in 2006, Sedaris shares recipes and ideas about how to throw the perfect party for any occasion. Her follow up in 2010, *Simple Times: Crafts for Poor People*, gave similar treatment to the art of crafting with the familiar Sedaris charisma and comedic approach.

A woman who is not afraid to wear a fat suit in public or appear in a magazine looking like she has been beaten up, Sedaris continues to push comedic boundaries. As Eric Spitznagel wrote for *Believer* in 2004, "While most comedy writers get their laughs by pointing out a character's flaws, Sedaris actually embraces them. She truly likes these people, and that somehow makes it easier to laugh at them." It is this quality of embracing flaws that Sedaris's fans find most endearing.

Jay Parrent

SEE ALSO: *Cable TV; Colbert, Stephen; Girl Scouts; Letterman, David; Second City; Sedaris, David;* Shrek; *Television.*

BIBLIOGRAPHY

Sedaris, Amy. *I Like You: Hospitality under the Influence*. New York: Warner Books, 2006.

Sedaris, Amy. *Simple Times: Crafts for Poor People*. New York: Grand Central Publishing, 2010.

Sedaris, David. *Me Talk Pretty One Day*. New York: Little, Brown, 2000.

Spitznagel, Eric. "Amy Sedaris." *Believer*, March 2004.

Sedaris, David *(1956–)*

Humorist David Sedaris is best known for his autobiographical essays, which he has read aloud on the Public Radio International series *This American Life* (1995–) and has published in best-selling collections such as *Me Talk Pretty One Day* (2000) and *Dress Your Family in Corduroy and Denim* (2004). His writing is known for its focus on human foibles and on the absurdity of life. Sedaris often employs humor to explore dysfunction and to broach taboo subjects. His work has been translated into twenty-five languages, and in 2008 there were more than seven million copies of his books in print.

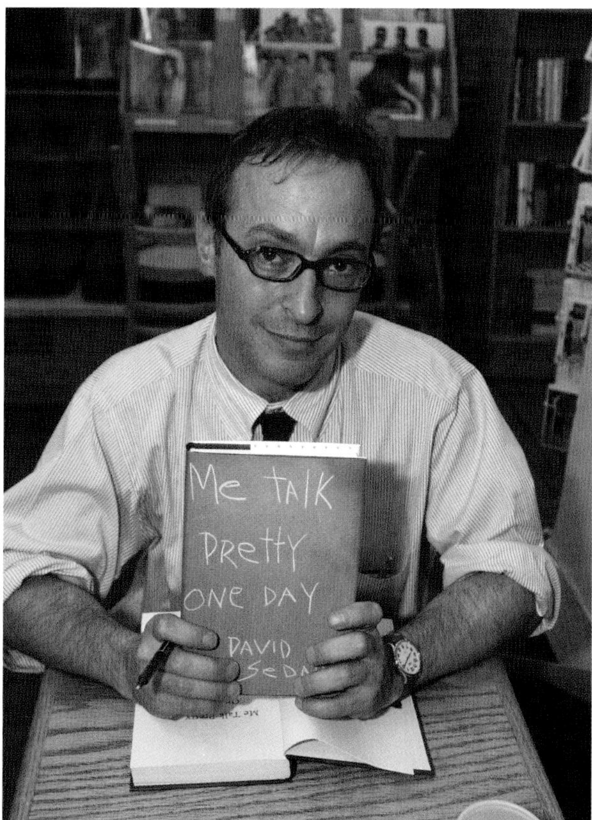

David Sedaris. *David Sedaris signs copies of his book* Me Talk Pretty One Day *at a bookstore in New York City in 2000.* CHRIS HONDROS/GETTY IMAGES.

Born in 1956 in Johnson City, New York, Sedaris took a conventional educational path until he dropped out of college in 1977. He spent much of the next fifteen years battling drug addiction and working odd jobs. Eventually, he decided to go back to college, and he became a performance artist, reading entries from his diary to live audiences. Public radio producer Ira Glass attended one of Sedaris's readings and in 1992 asked the author to read a holiday essay on the air. Sedaris read "The SantaLand Diaries," a story about working as a Macy's Christmas elf, and the comic tale was a hit with listeners.

Sedaris became a frequent contributor to Glass's newly created series *This American Life*. Sedaris's distinct and quiet voice, often at odds with the antic subject matter of his work, worked well on the radio. His first book, *Barrel Fever: Stories and Essays* (1994), became popular for its frank and often outrageous depictions of gay men. Sedaris became a regular magazine contributor, publishing essays in *Esquire*, *GQ*, and the *New Yorker*, many of which were compiled in *Naked* (1997) and *Holidays on Ice* (1997). Both collections were well received by critics and Sedaris's growing readership.

Much of the author's early work centers on his childhood and his family, including his grandmother, parents, and five siblings. Sedaris depicts an unconventional childhood, recounting his father's odd and graphic cautionary tales, his and his sisters' discovery of a pornographic novel, and his mother locking the kids out of the house one snowy day. He also mines his odd jobs and adventures during early adulthood to great effect, including his experiences hitchhiking and working in a psychiatric hospital. He has become known particularly for holiday stories, such as fan favorite "Six to Eight Black Men," which is about Dutch Christmas traditions.

He achieved national fame with *Me Talk Pretty One Day* (2000), most notably with the title essay, which features a hilarious account of the author's suffering at the hands of a dictatorial French teacher. The book marked a change in Sedaris's subject matter, and he began focusing more on the present, particularly on his efforts to adjust to a new life with his partner, Hugh, after they move to France. *When You Are Engulfed in Flames* (2008) chronicles the few months he spent in Japan trying to quit smoking. *Squirrel Seeks Chipmunk: A Modest Bestiary* (2010) marks his first book of entirely fictional stories.

Live readings and performances have always been part of Sedaris's work. He regularly tours and performs readings in the United States and overseas. He often shares a mix of published work and works in progress, making notes based on the audience's reactions during his readings. He also has written numerous plays with sister and comedic actress Amy Sedaris, including the Obie-winning *One Woman Shoe* (1995) and *Stump the Host* (1993). He also has created a stage adaptation of "The SantaLand Diaries."

In 2007 Sedaris became a subject of debate when writer Alex Heard published the article "This American Lie" in *New Republic* magazine. Heard fact-checked essays from Sedaris's books and found that the writer had fabricated and embellished events, a claim Sedaris does not deny. Heard went further, suggesting that Sedaris owed his subjects apologies and that his essays should not be considered nonfiction. Writers in the *Washington Post* and *Boston Globe* defended Sedaris's work, and the *New Yorker* verified that his many essays for the magazine had undergone a rigorous fact-checking process before publication. Sedaris has stated that he has always been open about exaggerating events for the sake of humor and that he regularly points out obvious fabrications in his work. Ultimately, the debate has not affected his popularity or presence on nonfiction best-seller lists.

Sedaris has been nominated for two Grammy Awards in the same year, for Best Spoken Word Album for the audio production of *Dress Your Family* and for Best Comedy Album (*David Sedaris: Live at Carnegie Hall*, 2003). *Time* magazine declared him Humorist of the Year in 2001, and the same year he won a Thurber Prize for American Humor for *Me Talk Pretty*. His success has created a path to fame for other performers featured on *This American Life*, such as writer Sarah Vowell and comedian Mike Birbiglia. Sedaris's essays, particularly the Christmas-themed ones, have become perennial favorites, and his live readings are often sold-out events.

Adrienne Furness

SEE ALSO: *Christmas;* Esquire; *Fake Memoirs; Gay Men; Grammy Awards;* New Republic; *The* New Yorker; *Performance Art; Radio; Sedaris, Amy.*

BIBLIOGRAPHY

"David Sedaris." In *Gale Biography in Context*. Detroit, MI: Gale, 2010.

Heard, Alex. "This American Lie." *New Republic*, March 19, 2007.

Lyall, Sarah. "David Sedaris Talks Funny: But Is It Real?" *New York Times*, June 6, 2008.

Sedona, Arizona

The small town of Sedona in northern Arizona had a marked influence on late twentieth-century American religious culture. Characterized by its red rocks and boasting a population of about 10,000 people in 2010, Sedona is the New Age capital of the world. It is home to UFO enthusiasts, New Religious movements, New Age philosophers, and devotees of paranormal phenomena. Located in the high desert 120 miles north of Phoenix, Sedona is on the edge of the Colorado Plateau, surrounded by a landscape of hellfire cliffs, buttes, and spires, and enjoys a climate that is described as near perfect. Tourism and a thriving community of artists form its economic base. That more people do not live there is a surprise.

Like most western tourist towns, Sedona is really two places: one where more than four million tourists a year stop to gawk and buy crystals; the other where the real Sedonians live. In popular imagination, however, Sedona is one place, where new churches form—some to die, others to thrive—to worship some alien deity or to follow Native American shamanism or Eastern mythology. It is the Mecca of the New Age, where people flock to change their lives and the place of Gabriel of Sedona, who *Dateline NBC* suggested was a fraudulent guru.

Sedona did not always have such a reputation. When the nearby Cline Library of Northern Arizona University began collecting materials relating to Sedona in 1992, little enough could be found to fill one box. Six years later, the collection had overflowed to 18 linear feet of ephemera on the Sedona experience. Things changed for Sedona when psychic Page Bryant announced the discovery of seven vortexes, or natural power

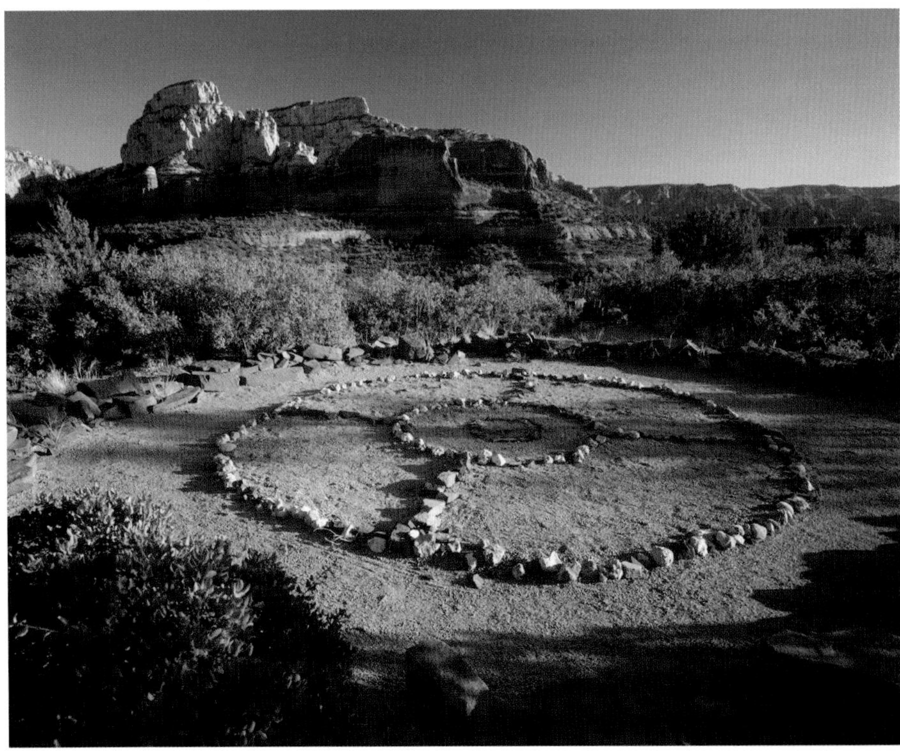

Medicine Wheel in Sedona, Arizona. *A medicine wheel lies in the shadow of the rock formations in Sedona, Arizona, which is a center of New Age activity.* © GEORGE H.H. HUEY/CORBIS.

spots, of psychic energy. Many today feel that the Sedona area contains the highest concentration of key lines, power centers, and vortexes in the world. These vortexes are said to be wells of natural power emanating from deep within the Earth that, some believe, act as a beacon for intergalactic travelers. People can also heighten their psychic awareness through the vortexes and are able to see beyond this dimension into others. The surrounding hellfire landscape of the place encourages these mystical musings, quests for circles of power, and the communing with spirits or aliens.

Hikers in the wilderness have reported suffering from inexplicable fatigue and have recounted tales of 3-foot-tall "rock people," mysterious rumblings beneath the ground, and floating balls of light. Some have also been confronted by dark-suited secret agents, the "Men in Black," who are said to guard the UFO base beneath Secret Mountain.

The area is also the home of many Native American cultures. Scattered throughout the landscape are ruins and wonderfully preserved examples of prehistoric artwork. Until the late 1800s the Yavapai Apache lived in the canyons; before them were the Sinagua and other ancient peoples, or Anasazi. All left their indelible marks on the landscape that spiritualists believe was a result of the magnetic attraction of the vortexes. The descendants of these people, however, believe otherwise and are concerned that Sedona's popularity is endangering their own sacred sites.

Many New Age businesses thrive in the Sedona area, which encompasses the nearby communities of Oak Creek, Cottonwood, and Jerome. In Sedona alone, some eighty businesses cater to spiritual needs. These businesses include publishers, retailers, and so forth, but there are also many holistic health practitioners, psychic readers, channelers, Sacred Earth tour guides, and others who service the demands of the town's ever-growing New Age reputation.

In 2006 a wildfire began 2 miles from Sedona, but it was contained before it damaged the community. However, it did burn some 4,300 acres of land.

John J. Doherty

SEE ALSO: *New Age Spirituality; UFOs (Unidentified Flying Objects).*

BIBLIOGRAPHY

Dannelley, Richard. *Sedona Power Spot, Vortex, and Medicine Wheel Guide.* Sedona, AZ: Vortex Society, 1991.

Johnson, Hoyt. *What's the Name of that Rock?* Sedona, AZ: Sedona Magazine, 1994.

Lee, Ilchi. *The Call of Sedona: Journey of the Heart.* Sedona, AZ: Best Life Media, 2011.

Mann, Nicholas R. *Sedona—Sacred Earth, Ancient Lore, Modern Myths: A Guide to the Red Rock Country.* Prescott, AZ: ZIVAH Publishers, 1991.

"Official Tourism Site for Sedona." Accessed March 12, 2012. Available from http://www.sedona.net

Seduction of the Innocent

In 1948 Dr. Fredric Wertham, a respected New York psychiatrist, began a campaign against comic books. Wertham, the author of two books on the causes of violence, argued in *Collier's* and the *Saturday Review of Literature* that comic books, particularly crime comics, corrupted young minds and contributed to juvenile delinquency. His conclusions were based on his work with juvenile delinquents, who reported that comics showed them how to commit crimes, and on his examination of the violence and sex depicted in comics. Wertham's work on the subject culminated in his 1954 book, *Seduction of the Innocent.* The campaign he spearheaded led to the formation of many committees against comics as well as to mass burnings of comics, Senate hearings, and the formation of the Comics Code Authority (CCA). The word *Werthamite* came to mean "censor," and for decades after Wertham and his book were notorious among comic-book fans and professionals.

In the 1940s comic books were a popular form of entertainment for both children and adults. The adult readership was particularly important after World War II, when many men took up reading comics in the service, largely because the slim magazines could be read quickly and were easily carried rolled up in a pocket. Perhaps to appeal to these older readers, comic-book publishers introduced dozens of crime and horror titles after the war, which often depicted gruesome acts of cruelty.

In *Seduction of the Innocent,* Wertham writes, "the most subtle and pervading effect of crime comics on children can be summarized in a single phrase: moral disarmament." In crime comics, he argues, the reader is often asked to identify with a criminal on the run from the law. Even though the criminal is usually captured or killed at the story's end, the stories romanticize a violent and immoral life outside the law. The outlaw protagonist "lives like a hero until the very end, and even then he often dies like a hero, in a burst of gun fire and violence."

Wertham did not find the "good guys" of comic books to be any more wholesome. Superman, for example, seemed to embody the fascist idea of a master race that got its way by force: "The superman conceit gives boys and girls the feeling that ruthless go-getting based on physical strength or the power of weapons or machines is the desirable way to behave." Batman and Wonder Woman, Wertham argues, promoted homosexuality because they had child sidekicks of the same gender. He describes the home life of Batman and Robin as "a wish dream of two homosexuals living together." Wonder Woman represents "the cruel, 'phallic' woman," a poor role model for girls because she emphasized power and independence rather than nurturance. Wertham also discovered sadomasochism and other variant sexualities in crime and adventure comics. He titled one of his chapters after a young patient's exclamation, "I want to be a sex maniac!"

Stirred by the outcry against comics that Wertham's charges created, the U.S. Senate put the comics industry on trial. In 1950 a Senate subcommittee chaired by Estes Kefauver found no evidence that linked crime comics to juvenile delinquency. Undaunted, Wertham and others continued to agitate for further government inquiry. In 1954 the Senate Judiciary Subcommittee on Juvenile Delinquency investigated comics again. The committee's verdict was that comics needed to be cleaned up and that the comic-book industry should police itself. Publishers were already moving in that direction.

In 1948, fearing government censorship, many of the leading comic-book publishers formed the Association of Comics Magazine Publishers to establish standards of decency for their publications. Because their efforts at self-censorship were ineffective and failed to convince their critics, these publishers created the Comics Code Authority (CCA), an independent board, to evaluate every story before publication. For decades after, most comic books sold in the United States bore a CCA stamp of approval on their covers.

One lasting effect of this era is that by the end of the twentieth century, comics were still considered by most Americans to be children's entertainment and to be incapable of conveying substantial artistic content. While countries such as Italy, France, and Japan have developed sophisticated varieties of comics for adult readers, American comics have remained marginalized. The attitude that comics are "bad for you"—the intellectual equivalent of junk food—has lingered.

Christian L. Pyle

SEE ALSO: *Batman; Comic Books; Comics; Comics Code Authority; Gay Men; Wertham, Fredric; Wonder Woman; World War II.*

BIBLIOGRAPHY

Barker, Martin. *A Haunt of Fears: The Strange History of the British Horror Comics Campaign.* London: Pluto Press, 1984.

Benton, Mike. *Crime Comics: The Illustrated History.* Dallas, TX: Taylor Publishing, 1993.

Gilbert, James. *A Cycle of Outrage: America's Reaction to the Juvenile Delinquent in the 1950s.* New York: Oxford University Press, 1986.

Wertham, Fredric. *Seduction of the Innocent.* New York: Rinehart, 1954.

West, Mark I. *Children, Culture, and Controversy.* Hamden, CT: Archon Books, 1988.

Seeger, Pete *(1919–)*

American singer and composer Pete Seeger was quite simply the foremost popularizer of American folk music of the twentieth century. While others engaged in fieldwork or labored in dusty archives, Seeger recorded more than 100 albums over a half century of performing. An evangelizer with an inborn sensitivity to crowd techniques, Seeger excelled in concert and had few musical peers in working a crowd. An intimate, casual, and charming performer, he often successfully invited his audience to sing along with him. The stringbean performer, bent over his long-necked five-string banjo and dressed in an old work shirt and denims, completely reshaped American musical taste in folk, topical, and protest music. Seeger's banjo read, "This machine surrounds hate and forces it to surrender," and if some segments of America reviled him as a communist sympathizer, others perceived him as standing for peace, equality, and decency in a troubled world. Seeger formed a bridge from the folk song revival of the 1940s, across the political repression of the 1950s, to the folk/protest scene of the 1960s. A gifted storyteller and musical historian, his influence on American music is incalculable.

Seeger was born in New York City in 1919, the son of a violinist mother and musicologist father, both on the faculty of the Juilliard School of Music. His uncle was the war poet Alan Seeger (who wrote "Rendezvous with Death"); his sister, Peggy, became an accomplished singer and songwriter and married British folk-legend Ewan MacColl; and his brother, Mike, made a career as one of the foremost proponents of banjo music. Seeger learned banjo, ukulele, and guitar by his teens. He received a scholarship to Harvard in 1936 (the same class as John F. Kennedy) but left in 1938 due to disinterest and poor grades. He journeyed through the United States, collecting songs, meeting Woody Guthrie and Huddie Ledbetter (Leadbelly), and working with noted folk archivist and field recorder Alan Lomax.

THE ALMANAC SINGERS AND THE WEAVERS

In 1940 Seeger organized the Almanac Singers with Lee Hays and Mill Lampell. Guthrie joined the group the next year, and they recorded an album, *Talking Union.* Seeger's zeal for labor organizing was nearly religious, as evidenced on the album's title track, and the group often performed antiwar songs for left-wing audiences and organizations. After Pearl Harbor, the Almanac Singers emphasized their patriotism ("The Sinking of the Reuben James"), and Seeger served in World War II entertaining American troops by singing folk songs. In 1944 he helped create People's Songs Inc. (PSI), which formed a national network of folk music that eventually boasted more than 2,000 members. In 1948 he toured with the anti–Cold War presidential candidate Henry Wallace, but PSI drew more interest from the

Pete Seeger. *Pete Seeger performs at the 2011 Newport Folk Festival.* DOUGLAS MASON/CONTRIBUTOR/GETTY IMAGES ENTERTAINMENT/GETTY IMAGES.

FBI than labor unions, and it eventually went bankrupt in 1949.

At the low point of his fortunes in 1948, Seeger joined with Hays, Ronnie Gilbert, and Fred Hellerman to form the Weavers. Despite their unpopular leftward leanings (they were present at the Peekskill "anticommunist" riot of September 1949), the Weavers not only helped to revive national interest in folk music, but they also enjoyed astonishing commercial success. Their second single, "Goodnight Irene" (1950), backed with Leadbelly's cover of the Israeli song "Tzena, Tzena, Tzena," went to the top of the pop charts and sold more than two million copies, a phenomenal amount for 1950. They followed with other hits that became (re)established in the American folk tradition, including "Kisses Sweeter than Wine" (1950) and, in 1951, "On Top of Old Smoky," "So Long It's Been Good to Know You," "Wimoweh (The Lion Sleeps Tonight)," and "Rock Island Line." Concert promoters and the media blacklisted the group in 1952 because of their political views and associations, and the Weavers all but disappeared. Seeger left the group to go solo in 1958 after opposing their participation in a cigarette commercial.

Always active in left-wing politics, Seeger refused to answer questions when investigated by the House Un-American Activities Committee (HUAC) in 1955, although he never invoked the Fifth Amendment. He was indicted in 1956, convicted in 1961 on ten counts of contempt of Congress, and sentenced to an astounding ten years in jail. The U.S. Court of Appeals dismissed all charges against Seeger on a technicality, the very same week in 1962 that the cover version of his song "Where Have All the Flowers Gone" hit the Top 40.

REVIVAL

In 1958 the success of the Kingston Trio touched off an enormous five-year folk music revival. Seeger's music was "rediscovered," and his career once again ascended. In 1962 the group Peter, Paul, and Mary made a hit out of "If I Had a Hammer," a song Seeger cowrote during his Weavers' days. The Byrds covered "The Bells of Rhymney" and eventually had a huge number one hit with "Turn! Turn! Turn!" (1965), a biblical passage from Ecclesiastes that Seeger had set to music. In 1964 commercial radio listeners heard Seeger's voice for the first time in more than a decade when his version of Malvina Reynolds's "Little Boxes" became a minor hit.

Since the 1940s Seeger had been one of the guiding lights of the folk magazine *Sing Out!* (still in circulation, with nearly 20,000 subscribers), and in 1961 he helped Sis Cunningham and Gordon Friesen found *Broadside*, a bulletin of topical songs that helped stimulate the careers of singer-songwriters such as Bob Dylan, Phil Ochs, Tom Paxton, and Eric Andersen.

Paradoxically, Seeger had become a semipopular success despite being one of the most picketed and blacklisted singers in American history. In 1962 ABC television refused to let him perform on the folk music show *Hootenanny*, resulting in a boycott that tore the folk community in half. The incident hurt him commercially but only served to reinforce his standing as a martyr for freedom of speech. By the mid-1960s Seeger had become a cultural hero through his outspoken commitment to the antiwar and civil rights struggles. He was involved in several civil rights campaigns from 1962 through 1965, and he helped popularize the anthem "We Shall Overcome" with mainstream audiences. Even supporters had felt that Seeger's belief that music could transform society was hopelessly naive, but—for a moment—it all seemed to be coming true. This period of his greatest influence is wonderfully captured on the recording of his concert at Carnegie Hall in June 1963.

LIVING LEGEND

Then it all fell apart. The folk-topical song revival came to a crashing halt at the Newport Folk Festival in 1965, when Dylan appeared with electric accompaniment. Seeger, who distrusted electric music as inauthentic, was crestfallen, and he literally tried to pull the plug on the amplifiers. He fought on, however, despite Dylan's defection, the crumbling of the civil rights movement, and the escalation of the war in Asia. His anti–Vietnam War ballad, "Waist Deep in the Big Muddy" (1967), became a classic of the 1960s, and he dusted off a series of antiwar ballads he had performed with the Almanac Singers a generation before. His disdain for wealth and worldly vanities seemed hopelessly outdated in an indulgent age, but his moral rectitude still inspired, or infuriated, vast numbers of Americans.

In the 1970s Seeger mirrored the cultural movement away from mass politics to localism and community control. He became particularly interested in ecology, cofounding the organization Clearwater, dedicated to the cleanup and revival of the Hudson River. Through sheer tenacity, he had become a living legend, more frequently parodied than banned. Critics from all over the spectrum praised his life's work, and the grandchildren of his original listeners attended his concerts.

Seeger widely influenced countless performers, and his instructional books and records inspired generations of self-taught musicians and folksingers. He always believed there was something in the best music to inform, stir, rally, direct, or cause social and personal interaction. His moral earnestness often overflowed into self-righteousness, but both friends and foes conceded his indomitability. Perhaps his optimism was often naive, but his music helped unionize workers, inspired Americans to revere their own musical traditions, encouraged civil rights and antiwar activists, and helped clean up a river. In his case, at least, one person could make a difference, and the United States became a better place for his having lived in it.

Seeger has won innumerable musical awards over the decades, including two Grammy Awards (1996 and 2008), a Grammy Lifetime Achievement Award (1993), and a National Medal of Arts (1994), as well as several honors for his social justice work, including the Eugene V. Debs Award (1979) and the Letelier-Moffitt Human Rights Award (1986). He was inducted into the Rock and Roll Hall of Fame in 1996. In 2006 Bruce Springsteen released *We Shall Overcome: The Seeger Sessions*, an album on which Springsteen covers thirteen of Seeger's songs. Seeger's influence on modern American musical and activism is perhaps best illustrated by his appearance at the end of Barack Obama's inauguration celebration in 2009, where he, Springsteen, and Seeger's grandson performed "This Land Is Your Land" while a crowd of thousands sang along.

Jon Sterngass

SEE ALSO: *The Byrds; Carnegie Hall; Civil Rights Movement; Communism; Dylan, Bob; Electric Guitar; Folk Music; Grammy Awards; Guthrie, Woody; Hippies; The Kingston Trio; Labor Unions; Leadbelly; McCarthyism; Newport Jazz and Folk Festivals; Obama, Barack; Ochs, Phil; Peter, Paul, and Mary; Protest Groups; Rock and Roll; Springsteen, Bruce; Television; Vietnam; The Weavers; World War II.*

BIBLIOGRAPHY

Cantwell, Robert. *When We Were Good: The Folk Revival.* Cambridge, MA: Harvard University Press, 1996.

Dunaway, David King. *How Can I Keep from Singing: Pete Seeger.* New York: McGraw-Hill, 1981.

Seeger, Pete. *Where Have All the Flowers Gone: A Singer's Stories, Songs, Seeds, Robberies.* Bethlehem, PA: Sing Out, 1993.

Seeger, Pete, and Jo Metcalf Schwartz. *The Incompleat Folksinger.* New York: Simon & Schuster, 1972.

Segway

By the time the Segway was unveiled in 2001, the hype surrounding it had reached a fever pitch. A two-wheeled self-balancing electric scooter invented by Dean Kamen, the Segway was claimed by Steve Jobs to be "as big a deal as the PC" and "maybe bigger than the Internet" by venture capitalist John Doerr. Understandably, audiences were surprised and underwhelmed by what seemed like a simple battery-powered scooter. While the Segway may not have lived up to the world's expectations, it has found some limited use.

An inventor and advocate of science and technology, Kamen had previously invented a wheelchair that could climb stairs and the first drug infusion pump. In 1999 journalist Steve Kemper began a book titled *Code Name Ginger* or *Reinventing the Wheel,* detailing the invention, development, and financing of Kamen's newest project, codenamed "Ginger" or "IT." Kemper did not specify the product's function in his book proposal, which was leaked before "Ginger" was officially revealed. This caused a great deal of excitement since the media and the public did not know what the actual invention was. Numerous publications speculated "IT" was everything from a jet pack to an antigravity device. The animated television sitcom *South Park* even produced a spoof of "IT." Due to the media hype, the public was shocked when the Segway made its debut on *Good Morning America.*

Despite the public's disappointment, the Segway was actually a revolutionary invention, using gyroscopic technology to right itself. A person stands on a platform and leans slightly forward or back, causing the machine to roll forward or stop, respectively. The original had a dial on the handlebars, which caused one wheel to slow, initiating a turn, but later versions require a slight lean to make a turn. The design "mimics the human body's ability to maintain its balance," without brakes or even an engine. Kamen sees the future as filled with "empowered pedestrians" rather than cars. He designed the Segway's system to run on very little electricity, making it a cheap and reliable transport perfect for city living.

Unfortunately, the scooter immediately faced challenges to its acceptance. People feared that riding it on sidewalks would endanger pedestrians, and there were doubts that it was safe on roads. This was something that Kamen and his design team had not considered until very late into production. These concerns caused many cities and countries around the world to ban it except on private property.

Another downside of the Segway was the price tag. Costing about $5,000, the machine was unaffordable for many people, except the wealthy who purchased it only as a toy. It was eventually used in some cities for jobs that require patrols, such as mall cops, police, or postal workers. As a novelty, many cities offer Segway tours of historic areas.

Initially Segway owners formed clubs, held annual conventions to support the scooter, and played Segway polo. However, the enthusiasm over the invention has begun to wane, with more and more clubs disbanding. People known for their Segway ownership include Steve Wozniak, one of the founders of Apple Computers, and Adam Savage, the star of the television show *Mythbusters.* Perhaps the initial hype and letdown over its release worked against it, but Kamen has not let this get him down. He still believes it will "be to the car what the car was to the horse and buggy."

Kim Keeline

SEE ALSO: *Automobile;* South Park.

BIBLIOGRAPHY

Corkill, Edan. "Will Segway Sci-Fi Ever Be Everyday Fact?" *Japan Times,* November 15, 2009.

Heilemann, John. "Reinventing the Wheel." *Time,* December 2, 2001.

Higginbotham, Adam. "Dean Kamen: Part Man, Part Machine." *Telegraph,* October 27, 2008.

Kemper, Steve. *Code Name Ginger: The Story behind Segway and Dean Kamen's Quest to Invent a New World.* Boston: Harvard Business School Press, 2003.

Seinfeld

Seinfeld, a weekly situation comedy that aired on NBC from 1990 to 1998, was the highest-rated show on American television during much of its production run. The series marked the revival of a comic subgenre that had originated on radio and was then adapted for early television by such stars as iconic Jack Benny and the team of George Burns and Gracie Allen. In the contemporary sitcom, Jerry Seinfeld plays a stand-up comic bearing the name Jerry Seinfeld who, the audience is led to believe, closely resembles the real Jerry Seinfeld, but who is nonetheless a distinct character. In the first three seasons, each episode begins with Seinfeld doing a standup routine, and the show that follows enacts the joke or observation (usually a funny remark about why casual romantic relationships fail) he has made in the stand-up performance. The show returns to the stand-up act in the middle and then closes with Seinfeld onstage once again telling a joke, either finishing up the one he introduced at the start of the show or saying something else related to how the plot of the episode has been resolved.

The fictional Jerry is an upper-middle-class Jewish New Yorker with a Manhattan apartment, a trio of offbeat friends, a career, an active sex life, and several other recognizable trappings of a contemporary successful American. While Jerry and the others—Elaine, George, and Kramer—appear to be close friends and spend a lot of time together, they are habitually cruel and insensitive to each other and to the outsiders they meet, in venal, seemingly inconsequential ways. On the final episode of the series, the main characters are jailed for exhibiting nothing but selfishness and brutal indifference to the rest of the world over the course of the show's nine-year run.

SOURCES OF SEINFELD'S HUMOR

Like Benny and Burns before him, Seinfeld uses the combination of the opening and closing nightclub scenes that frame the

Seinfeld. *The characters of* Seinfeld, *played by, from left, Julia Louis-Dreyfus, Jerry Seinfeld, Michael Richards, and Jason Alexander, play a scene in the fictional Jerry's apartment.* NBC TV/THE KOBAL COLLECTION].

show and the prolonged sketch that makes up the heart of the episode to address the audience in two distinct ways. When he tells the jokes as a comic, he addresses the audience in the second person and comes across as an "everyman," an average, single American who is bemused by the many reasons why most people, including himself, cannot find the right mate.

However, in the comic sketch, Jerry is not quite "one of us." This is emphasized by the slight differences between him and his three friends. Though no one in the group holds a steady job, Jerry is the only one who does not need the work. He is, after all, a famous comedian. While all of them fail in romance, Jerry has not failed professionally, and, perhaps because of this, he seems to be able to brush aside his failures, even if they bother him for a short time. Unlike the nightclub performer, the character in the skits is, in many ways, unlikable. He is a sarcastic, wisecracking cynic who lives just beyond the reach of the emotional pain most people are vulnerable to. Benny and Burns did not go to such lengths to make the characters they played so distinct and unlikable to the viewing audience. Seinfeld, on the other hand, uses the combination of George, Elaine, and Kramer to maintain the connection to middle-class America. Throughout the show's run audiences were perhaps most responsive to Kramer, a tall, thin character with wild hair who tempers Jerry's cynicism each episode with an array of physical humor that keeps the mood of the show light.

Seinfeld borrows heavily from the Jewish American comic tradition, most notably the schlemiel/schlimazel routine, which puts two unlucky people (but people who are unlucky in very different ways) in an everyday situation, with humorous results. The schlemiel is unlucky in the sense that he brings misfortune on others, while the schlimazel always has bad things happen to him. In the most common vaudeville rendering of this routine, the schlemiel, due to a misunderstanding or because his is tripped over something, spills soup in the schlimazel's lap.

The writers of *Seinfeld* came up with numerous, highly sophisticated variations on this trope. In a typical episode, Kramer plays the schlemiel and George, a short, balding middle-aged man with few prospects, plays the schlimazel. The show starts with each embarking on a quest, Kramer for one of life's simple pleasures like a ripe mango or a better way to take a shower, and George, for a lasting relationship. Their paths cross in the middle of the show, and by the end Kramer gets what he wants but ruins everything for George. In one famous episode, Kramer becomes obsessed with Cuban cigars. George, meanwhile, has started dating the perfect woman. When she invites George to come to her father's cabin, George talks her into letting him bring his friends. At the cabin, Kramer finds a box of Cuban cigars. Everything goes well, but as they are leaving Kramer inadvertently throws a lit cigar in a wastebasket and burns down the cabin.

While that may be enough to bring the schlemiel/schlimazel routine to a close (the soup has been spilled, so to speak), the writers of Seinfeld unfailingly add something extra to the sketch. In this particular case, when George's girlfriend goes through the wreckage of the burned cabin, she discovers love letters her father has received from another man—the famous American short-story writer John Cheever, as fate would have it. The conclusion to the episode may seem extraneous to the plot, but it is actually important to sustaining Kramer's character throughout the series. By having a larger crisis emerge from the fire, Kramer is never made accountable for his gaffe, since everyone's attention is diverted from the loss of property as they help George's girlfriend cope with the fallout from her father's secret. Kramer, meanwhile, walks away with a clean conscience.

JERRY AND ELAINE

Jerry and Elaine Benes (Julia Louis-Dreyfus), the other two members of the quartet, sometimes engage in the same routine, playing the farce out between themselves or with one of the other two. More often, however, they contribute tangentially to the antics and bring sexual tension to the show. Their coexistence amounts to a humorous examination of the popular question about whether former lovers can truly be friends. As the story goes, Jerry and Elaine had dated and broken up before the series started. They now help each other get dates and take turns serving as sounding boards when the other has endured a breakup. Sometimes they help each other get out of relationships. Both are hopelessly shallow but fail in romance for opposite reasons: Jerry because he has been misunderstood, and Elaine usually because she tries too hard to get someone who is out of her league.

In one famous episode about personal hygiene, Jerry thinks he has finally found someone who meets his persnickety, neurotic standards. The episode ends on an evening the couple has decided to spend apart. While stopped at a red light, Jerry scratches his face. As it happens, his girlfriend stops next to him, and from her vantage point it appears that Jerry is picking his nose. She drives off in a huff, quite obviously aghast, leaving Jerry with no hope of explaining himself and recovering her affection.

For her part, Elaine is a diva, or would like to be a diva, except that she knows she lacks the superficial qualities—the striking good looks along with the grace and elegance—that would make highly desirable men fall all over her. That does not keep her from trying to land an attractive, rich man, though. Over the course of the series, she works at a succession of jobs for neurotic and borderline psychotic men who derive much of their pleasure in life from being her boss. Whereas Jerry is doomed to be misunderstood, Elaine's foolishly high standards cause her to cast aside a host of "regular guy" suitors, for various trivial reasons—one because he has ugly feet, another because he has an obnoxious laugh.

"ABOUT NOTHING"

While the show aired for nine seasons, *Seinfeld* did not become a hit until season four, which opens with Jerry, the character, being asked by network executives to create his own television show. Stumped, he goes to his friends for help, and he does not land on anything until George finally suggests a show about nothing. With no other alternative, he takes the idea back to the executives, who are surprisingly receptive. The series sustained this story arc throughout the entire season and reduced Jerry's stand-up appearances to two—one at the beginning and one at the end. The series won three Emmys at the end of season four, including Outstanding Writing in a Comedy Series and its only Emmy for Best Comedy Series. More tellingly, lead writer Larry David drew comparisons to Nobel laureate Samuel Beckett, whose "Waiting for Godot" is a stark yet hilarious and absurd play depicting four characters who do essentially nothing while they wait for something important, or meaningful, to happen to them

Airing Thursday evenings at nine, the most coveted spot in network television at the time, Seinfeld continued to be a staple in American homes for each of its last five seasons. The schlemiel/schlimazel routine was repeated over and over again, sustaining the laughs and the ratings all the way until it went off the air. In fact, perhaps the only noticeable change came in season eight, after David had left, when the producers dropped Seinfeld's opening and closing monologues. More than seventy-five million viewers tuned into the much-awaited final episode in 1998, a send-off that was nearly on par with the conclusions to *M*A*S*H* and *Cheers* in previous decades.

JERRY AFTER *SEINFELD*

During the course of *Seinfeld*, Jerry Seinfeld appeared to be much like his alter ego. However, his life took a completely different direction in 1999 when he married Jessica Sklar. The couple now have a daughter, Sascha, and two sons, Julian and Shepherd (Pepper). Since the end of *Seinfeld*, the comedian has kept a relatively low profile, appearing on television infrequently. He has, however, returned to stand-up comedy, frequently using his family as a topic of humor. He wrote a children's book (*Halloween*) in 2002 and penned the screenplay for *Bee Movie* (2007), in which he voices Barry B. Benson. For a man who spent nine years in a show "about nothing," Seinfeld's life has become increasingly about the things that matter most to Americans.

In 2009 the HBO comedy *Curb Your Enthusiasm*—in which Larry David plays a fictional version of himself—paid tribute to *Seinfeld* with a pseudo-reunion of cast members. Their appearance gave fans a glimpse of what life was like for the *Seinfeld* characters after the cameras stopped rolling. Elaine had given birth to Jerry's baby, and George had invented iToilet, a successful app for the iPhone. Mention was made of the scandal that erupted when Michael Richards made racist remarks during a stand-up comedy routine in 2006.

David Marc

SEE ALSO: *Benny, Jack; Burns, George, and Gracie Allen; Celebrity; Emmy Awards; Sitcom; Stand-Up Comedy; Television.*

BIBLIOGRAPHY

Cagle, Jess. "Jerry Seinfeld Goes Back to Work." *Time*, September 26, 2007.

Dunne, Michael. *Intertextual Encounters in American Fiction, Film, and Popular Culture.* Bowling Green, OH: Bowling Green State University Popular Press, 2001.

Irwin, William. *"Seinfeld" and Philosophy: A Book about Everything and Nothing.* Chicago: Open Court, 1999.

Museum of Television and Radio. *Stand-Up Comedians on Television.* New York: Abrams, 1996.

Seinfeld, Jerry. *Sein Off: The Final Days of "Seinfeld."* New York: HarperEntertainment, 1998.

Tracy, Kathleen. *Jerry Seinfeld: The Entire Domain.* Secaucus, NJ: Carol Publishing, 1998.

Selena *(1971–1995)*

Singer Selena Quintanilla-Perez's life was short but dynamic. She began her career at the age of five and was murdered just a month short of her twenty-fourth birthday. Raised in the bicultural world of southern Texas, she brought a flamboyant new face to Tejano, the Tex-Mex fusion music she performed. More significantly, she instilled a new kind of pride and ambition in the young Latina women who were her fans. Though her future as an entertainer and businesswoman will forever remain a question mark, her death itself gave Anglo American society a new perspective on the twenty-eight million of its fellow citizens who make up the Latino community in the United States.

BORN TO PERFORM

Selena was born on April 16, 1971, in Lake Jackson, Texas. Her father, Abraham, a musician and restaurateur, put together a family band that played the traditional Tejano music of the Texas borderland. By the time she was five, Selena was performing regularly with Los Dinos (the guys), performing at parties, weddings, and bars throughout Texas. Her strong, clear voice and personable interpretations captivated audiences, and by the time she was nine, the band had been renamed Selena y los Dinos and she had been chosen as the Tejano Music Awards' Female Entertainer of the Year. She would claim that award for each of the next eight years.

Once discovered by a major Latin music record label at the Tejano Music Awards, Selena was on her way to becoming a star. She was wildly popular with Latino audiences, especially young women, who looked to her as a role model. Raised a strict Jehovah's Witness, she embodied a "clean," moral lifestyle. At the same time, she exuded vitality and sexuality onstage, wearing revealing costumes such as a rhinestone-studded brassiere. Selena embodied a fusion of cultures, and it was her unabashed expression of all of her differing selves that prompted many Latinos to identify with her.

THE HISTORY OF TEJANO

To fully appreciate Selena's contribution to American culture, it is necessary to understand the Tejano music tradition. In the early 1900s Czech and German immigrants brought their accordions and polka beats to the southern Texas border towns where they settled. That music was blended with the traditional Mexican style to form something called *conjunto*. In the 1930s and 1940s migrant workers who were returning from fields in the north brought with them big band sounds that were then mixed with the *conjunto* of *la frontera* (the border). This new music was called Tejano, which is Spanish for "Texan" and is the same word used to describe the Mexican American people of Texas. Like the Latino people, Tejano music has continued to grow and change as it has been exposed to new influences. By the time Selena brought her own voice to Tejano, it carried flavors of rap, rhythm and blues, country, and rock, as well as the traditional Mexican sound and the polka beat.

Like Tejano music, Selena herself was that uniquely American product—the fusion of cultures. Raised speaking only English, she learned Spanish songs phonetically and had only begun to learn the Spanish language months before her death. Though in part the obedient and submissive Latina daughter, she had definite plans for herself. In at least two important instances, she defied her controlling father, first by marrying fellow band member Chris Perez and then by using her skills at costume design to open a clothing boutique, Selena, Etc. She had ambitions to become a crossover artist, and many music critics, comparing her to Madonna and Marilyn Monroe, believe she could have succeeded.

A TRAGIC END

Before these ambitions could be put to the test, Selena was shot by a trusted friend and employee. Yolanda Saldivar was president of Selena's fan club when the two met and became friends. When Selena's clothing boutique required more time than she had to spare, she hired Saldivar to manage it for her. In March 1995, however, Selena began to suspect Saldivar of stealing money. When Selena confronted her, Saldivar shot and killed her in the parking lot of a motel in Corpus Christi, Texas. Though Saldivar always insisted the shooting was an accident, she was convicted of murder and sentenced to life in prison. The Latino community across the Southwest, reeling with pain and outrage, followed *el juicio de Selena* (the Selena trial) closely, demanding punishment for the woman who had killed the golden girl.

In death, Selena achieved her goal of making it as a crossover artist. Before her murder, she had won a Grammy for Best Mexican-American Performance. Her album *Amor Prohibido* had sold 500,000 copies, and she had performed in Houston's Astrodome to a crowd of 61,041. Those are impressive achievements to be sure, but they pale compared to her posthumous numbers. Just months after her death, her posthumously released album *Dreaming of You* debuted at number one on the Billboard Top 200 and sold more than five million copies. Her songs received play on Anglo radio stations, and a feature film and a television movie were made about her life and death. The former, *Selena* (1997), was released in two versions—one with Spanish subtitles—and starred Jennifer Lopez; the latter, *E! True Hollywood Story: The Selena Murder Trial*, aired in 1996.

HER SPIRIT LIVES ON

Perhaps Selena's greatest achievement, however, was making Anglo America take notice of its Latino counterpart. Though there are close to thirty million American Latinos, possessing more than $300 billion in purchasing power, media and corporations often ignore them. After Selena's death, she became something of a folk hero in the Latino American community. Her face appeared everywhere—from street murals to bank checks—and hundreds of babies in Texas and California were named after her.

The media responded to this surge of grief in unprecedented ways. *People* magazine not only released a special southwest edition with Selena's death as the cover story, but it also followed up with a tribute issue, only the third such publication in the magazine's history, and continued to reach out to Latino readers with *People en Español*. During Saldivar's trial, *TV Guide* published a bilingual edition for the first time in its history, with English and Spanish versions of an article about *el juicio de Selena*.

Had Selena lived, she might not have achieved such massive crossover fame. Certainly it would not have come without conflict and controversy. Few Latin music performers have succeeded on the Anglo music scene, and those who do break through often alienate their Latin audiences by leaving too much of their roots behind them. Though her life was cut tragically short, Selena Quintanilla-Perez remains *una de nosotros* (one of us) to her Latino community, and she unquestionably opened the door for a wider awareness and appreciation of the Latin pop music she loved.

Tina Gianoulis

SEE ALSO: *Lopez, Jennifer; Made-for-Television Movies; Madonna; Monroe, Marilyn; Pop Music; Tejano Music.*

BIBLIOGRAPHY

Arraras, Maria Celeste. *Selena's Secret: The Revealing Story behind Her Tragic Death.* New York: Simon & Schuster, 1997.

Patoski, Joe Nick. *Selena: Como la flor.* Boston: Little, Brown, 1996.

Valdez, Carlos. *Justice for Selena: The State versus Yolanda Saldivar.* Victoria, BC: Trafford, 2005.

Wheeler, Jill C. *Selena: The Queen of Tejano.* Edina, MN: Abdo and Daughters, 1996.

Seles, Monica *(1973–)*

Yugoslavian-born Monica Seles burst onto the women's professional tennis scene in 1988 at the tender age of fifteen and made it all the way to number one in the world within just two years. Easily recognizable because of her powerful two-handed groundstrokes and her loud grunting during points, Seles relished her role as a young female sports celebrity and role model. Between January 1991 and January 1993, she won seven of eight Grand Slam tournaments. In April 1993, when she was well on her way to becoming the most dominant women's tennis player of all time, a deranged Steffi Graf supporter stabbed her in the left shoulder while she was resting between matches during a tournament in Germany. Her attacker never served a day in prison for his crime. The attack on Seles focused public attention on the danger that obsessed fans pose to pro athletes.

Seles made a comeback in 1995 after an arduous twenty-seven month recuperation period. To the delight of her fans and the astonishment of her peers, she was a winner in her very first tournament back. An eighth Grand Slam victory soon followed. However, Seles never recovered her earlier drive. She began gaining weight and suffered an injury to her right foot. In 2008 she retired from tennis. Seles has chronicled her road back to good health in *Getting a Grip* (2009). She has become involved in women's issues and finds time to follow passions that include architecture, photography, and jewelry design.

Steven Schneider

SEE ALSO: *Sports Heroes; Tennis.*

BIBLIOGRAPHY

Layden, Joseph. *Return of a Champion: The Monica Seles Story.* New York: St. Martin's Press, 1996.

Seles, Monica. *Getting a Grip.* New York: Penguin Group, 2009.

Seles, Monica, and Nancy Ann Richardson. *Monica: My Journey from Fear to Victory.* New York: HarperCollins, 1996.

Wertheim, Jon. "Monica Seles." *Sports Illustrated*, July 13, 2009, 2.

Woolum, Janet, ed. *Outstanding Women Athletes and How They Influenced Sports.* Phoenix, AZ: Oryx Press, 1998.

Sellers, Peter *(1925–1980)*

Born in London to parents who were professional performers in the music halls, Peter Sellers became one of Britain's foremost comic actors of radio, film, and television in the 1950s and 1960s. Famous for his impeccable comedic timing, his improvisational skills, and his ability to switch from one character to another, Sellers appeared in films as diverse as *The Ladykillers* (1955), *Lolita* (1962), and *Dr. Strangelove* (1964). He made more than fifty feature films in his relatively short career in Hollywood and in Britain. But it was the Pink Panther series that both confirmed his versatility as an actor and raised him to the status of international superstar. Since his death in 1980, several biographies of Sellers have been published, and the actor has gained notoriety for his unpredictable behavior and the excesses of his life as a movie star.

Sellers spent the last couple of years of World War II in the Royal Air Force, where he infuriated high-ranking senior officers by impersonating their voices. After the war he tried to build a career as a drummer, but after an audition at the Windmill Theatre in London, he became a comedian instead. In the late 1940s Sellers established himself as a comedian and impressionist on BBC radio, working first on *Showtime*, a program that encouraged new talent. Later, he became a regular BBC "voice man," impersonating well-known personalities on a show called *Ray's a Laugh.*

In 1951, when he began working with Michael Bentine, Spike Milligan, and Harry Secombe on a radio show called *Crazy People*, later to become known as *The Goon Show*, Sellers's comic talent began to blossom. The anarchic, surrealistic humor of "The Goons" marked a significant break with the comedy that had gone before and paved the way for the comic style of *Monty Python's Flying Circus* and the "alternative" comedy of the 1980s and 1990s. It was from working with "The Goons" that Sellers was able to move into films, having his first major success with the British-made *The Ladykillers*, in which he worked alongside Alec Guinness and Margaret Rutherford. It was inevitable that he would eventually move to Hollywood, where he made the Pink Panther series of films for which he is, arguably, best known.

PINK PANTHER

Five original Pink Panther movies were made, featuring Sellers as Inspector Clouseau, the endearingly clumsy and incompetent French detective. The first film, *The Pink Panther*, appeared in 1963, followed by *A Shot in the Dark* (1964), *The Return of the Pink Panther* (1975), *The Pink Panther Strikes Again* (1976), and *Revenge of the Pink Panther* (1978). All the films focus on Clouseau's earnest efforts to solve bizarre, trivial, even nonexistent mysteries with a maximum of fuss and melodramatic intrigue. The humor, as with much of Sellers's work, is based on language and voices. Clouseau's comic accent, his inability to understand or pronounce English words, and his attempts to cover up his mistakes with elaborate explanations, satirize our often misplaced respect for authorities of all kinds. A sixth Pink Panther film, *Trail of the Pink Panther*, was made in 1982, after Sellers's death. This final, ill-advised outing for the bumbling detective contains no original material involving him, being constructed from outtakes from the five earlier films.

Away from comic acting, Sellers excelled in two movies directed by Stanley Kubrick: *Lolita* (1962), where he played the menacing, dangerous sadist Clare Quilty, and *Dr. Strangelove or: How I Learned to Stop Worrying and Love the Bomb* (1964), embodying three lead roles and largely improvising his way to an Oscar nomination. After suffering a major heart attack in 1964, his performances, though occasionally brilliant, were no longer as consistent as they had been, and the films to which he contributed in the late 1960s and the 1970s varied in their quality and their success at the box office.

PERSONAL STRUGGLES

Roger Lewis's 1994 biography of Sellers, *The Life and Death of Peter Sellers*, points to his chaotic private life and dramatic mood swings as part of the reason for the inconsistency of his later work. Throughout the 1960s and 1970s, Sellers's behavior became increasingly unpredictable: he was a drug abuser, became self-destructively obsessed with people, and could be generous and dangerously violent by turns. He married four times, to Anne Howe, Britt Ekland, Miranda Quarry, and Lynne Frederick, respectively, and was known to be sexually promiscuous. While he was a comic actor of extraordinary abilities, Sellers was also a vain, self-centered man who enjoyed, and was ultimately let down by, his fame.

Lewis's biography draws loose connections between Sellers's on-screen persona and the private man, suggesting that the megalomania that made his performances so exacting spilled over into his private life. The book became a play, premiering in Australia in 1998, and then a movie *The Life and Death of Peter Sellers* in 2004. Peter Evans, an earlier, more reserved, biographer, confirms this connection between Sellers's personality and his work when he suggests that such was his immersion in whatever role he was playing, Sellers had practically no personality of his own.

Sellers died from a heart attack in July 1980. However difficult or unpleasant he could be as a man, most of those who worked with him agree that as an actor, he has left a legacy of comic performance and innovation that is among the most rewarding of his generation.

Chris Routledge

SEE ALSO: *Celebrity;* Dr. Strangelove or: How I Learned to Stop Worrying and Love the Bomb*; Hollywood; Kubrick, Stanley;* Lolita*;* Monty Python's Flying Circus*; Movie Stars; Radio; Screwball Comedies; Television; World War II.*

BIBLIOGRAPHY

Evans, Peter. *Peter Sellers: The Mask behind the Mask*. London: Severn House, 1981.

Lewis, Roger. *The Life and Death of Peter Sellers*. London: Century, 1994.

Rigelsford, Adrian. *Peter Sellers: A Celebration*. London: Virgin, 1997.

Sikov, Ed. *Mr. Strangelove: A Biography of Peter Sellers*. New York: Hyperion, 2002.

Walker, Alexander. *Peter Sellers: The Authorized Biography*. London: Weidenfeld & Nicholson, 1981.

Selznick, David O. *(1902–1965)*

David Selznick's production of *Gone with the Wind* (1939) is enough to secure his place in history, but his influence extends well beyond that classic. Other blockbuster movies he produced include *David Copperfield* (1935), *A Star Is Born* (1937), and *Rebecca* (1940).

Selznick worked for his father's motion picture company, Lewis J. Selznick Productions, until it was forced into bankruptcy in 1923. The first feature he produced was *Roulette* in 1924. Selznick joined Metro-Goldwyn-Mayer (MGM) in 1926 as a script reader and assistant story editor. After rapidly rising to supervisor of production, he was fired because of disagreements with the production head, Irving Thalberg.

Paramount Pictures made Selznick its head of production in 1927, but after the Depression forced salary cuts, he moved to RKO Radio Pictures in 1931 as the studio's boss. While there, Selznick personally oversaw such productions as *A Bill of Divorcement* (1932) and *Little Women* (1933), both starring Katharine Hepburn.

When MGM decided to spread Thalberg's production duties around because of his ill health, Louis B. Mayer was able to lure Selznick back to the studio. Because Selznick had married Mayer's daughter Irene in 1930, his return to MGM sparked the following saying: "The son-in-law also rises." Intent on bringing pictures to the screen that were more prestigious, Selznick produced hits such as *Dinner at Eight* (1933) and *Anna Karenina* (1935). In the former picture, Selznick defied conventional wisdom and cast stars in every major role instead of hiring just one big-name actor. Those performers—Marie Dressler, Jean Harlow, and John Barrymore—helped the movie become a blockbuster.

In 1936 Selznick again left MGM to become an independent producer, founding Selznick International Pictures. His first film was the highly successful *A Star Is Born* (1937). Of course, his most memorable creation is *Gone with the Wind*. The film was fraught with production difficulties—for example, six different directors were used, and Selznick had to give up the distribution rights to MGM to get Clark Gable as the male lead. The making of the movie sparked quite a buzz in Hollywood and beyond. Selznick's search for an actress to play Scarlett O'Hara created a national sensation, as young women everywhere auditioned for the role. Ultimately, the film was a triumph: it won ten Oscars and remains extremely popular. Selznick followed *Gone with the Wind* with the classic *Rebecca* (1940), which was directed by Alfred Hitchcock and won the Oscar for Best Picture.

After a massive tax debt forced his company onto the auction block, Selznick formed a new studio, David Selznick Productions. Selznick became more of a talent scout than a producer, and one of his most notable projects was Jennifer Jones, who won an Oscar for *Song of Bernadette* (1943). While he was not responsible for discovering Jones, he fell in love with her and did his best to make her a superstar. He produced many films starring her, the most successful of which was *Duel in the Sun* (1946).

When Selznick and Jones were married in 1949, he virtually gave up his status as an independent producer and became more of a Svengali to her. Some of Jones's pictures, such as *A Farewell to Arms* (1957), did fairly well, but Selznick became something of a joke because of his obsession with her. He continued to work in Hollywood, though he faded into the background until his death in 1965. Nevertheless, the name David O. Selznick has a prominent place in motion picture history. He was a big-time independent producer at a time when such people were rare.

Jill A. Gregg

SEE ALSO: *Barrymore, John; Gable, Clark;* Gone with the Wind*; Harlow, Jean; Hepburn, Katharine; Hitchcock, Alfred; Jones, Jennifer; MGM (Metro-Goldwyn-Mayer).*

BIBLIOGRAPHY

Haver, Ronald. *David O. Selznick's Hollywood.* New York: Knopf, 1980.

Leff, Leonard J. *Hitchcock and Selznick: The Rich and Strange Collaboration of Alfred Hitchcock and David O. Selznick in Hollywood.* Berkeley: University of California Press, 1999.

Selznick, David O. *Memo from David O. Selznick.* New York: Modern Library, 2000.

Thomson, David. *Showman: The Life of David O. Selznick.* New York: Knopf, 1992.

Sennett, Mack *(1880–1960)*

In February 1914 Mack Sennett's Keystone company released a comedy called *Kid Auto Races at Venice*, in which a young English vaudevillian who had recently joined Sennett's company of comedians appeared briefly in a battered suit of morning clothes and top hat. His name was Charlie Chaplin, and the cameo gave birth to the most famous comedic creation in cinema history, "The Tramp."

The very name Mack Sennett resonates with images of early pioneering Hollywood, when rickety, makeshift "studios" sprang up in dusty streets, and directors in plus-fours and caps cranked out one- and two-reel silent movies with primitive equipment. It was an era both rough and romantic, the earliest days of the Dream Factory when maids and chauffeurs, waitresses, shop girls, and street sweepers flocked to find fortune, and when fame too often fell victim to scandal in the hothouse atmosphere of the closed film community. It was a time, too, when comedy, brilliantly suited to the technical limitations of the early silent screen, reached a peak of public popularity with stars such as "Madcap" Mabel Normand, Roscoe "Fatty" Arbuckle, Ford Sterling, and Chester Conklin. It was to the acumen, imagination, and energy of Sennett, who entered legend and history as the "King of Comedy," that they owed their rise.

Born Michael Sinnott in Danville, Quebec, Sennett harbored unfulfilled ambitions to become an opera singer. At age twenty-two he was working as a laborer in Massachusetts when a chance meeting with actress Marie Dressler led him to New York, where he was introduced to producer David Belasco. Ignoring Belasco's advice to go home, Sennett embarked on a minor stage career in burlesque and musicals until 1908 when he talked himself into film work at the Biograph studios in Manhattan. He graduated from supporting roles to leads, costarring with many top leading ladies of the day, including Florence Lawrence (the "Biograph Girl"), Mary Pickford, and the irrepressible Mabel Normand, who played a profound role in both his professional and personal life for many years. To gain education in the filmmaking process, Sennett had D. W. Griffith direct many of his films at Biograph; he also wrote some scripts for Griffith. Driven by curiosity and a desire to learn, Sennett was directing shorts at the studio by 1910.

FORMING KEYSTONE

In 1912 Sennett, now an experienced director with a pronounced facility for comedy, formed his Keystone company in California, with former bookies Charles Bauman and Adam Kessel acting as his business partners. Several of his Biograph colleagues joined him, notably Normand, the most gifted comedienne of her time. The first Keystone program, released in September 1912, consisted of two split-reel comedies—*Cohen Collects a Debt* and *The Water Nymph*—prototypes for the unrestrained style that became the keystone trademark. Thereafter Sennett, something of a slave driver, worked at a furious pace, turning out a reel of comedy per week, and rapidly became the foremost purveyor of filmed comedy in America.

The earliest Keystone movies were crude, haphazard affairs, largely improvised from the flimsiest of scripts, but they had enormous physical gusto and hilarious sight gags, a stable of major comic acting talents, and Sennett's impeccable sense of timing and skillful editing to control the finished product. Gradually as the company expanded both its roster of actors, the length of its films, and its prodigious output, the frenzied, freewheeling custard-pie-in-the-face-slapstick farce that was its trademark gave way to more carefully considered and controlled material, and the general chaos that prevailed was subjected to better organization.

Within two years Sennett's Keystone Kops (or "Cops"), a bunch of inept, accident-prone policemen, were a national American institution in films that poked irreverent fun at the guardians of law and order; a little later they were joined by the famous Mack Sennett Bathing Beauties, a lineup of dizzy "sexpots" from whom several successful early female stars emerged in due course. In January 1914 Chaplin arrived, a total newcomer to film, at the invitation of Sennett, who had seen him onstage in Fred Karno's traveling vaudeville company.

Chaplin stayed almost a year before being lured to Essanay by big money and more artistic freedom, but he made thirty-five films at Keystone, establishing himself not only as a star actor and creator of the Tramp, but also as a writer and director. He made several with Normand, and their partnership and his tenure with Sennett concluded with the six-reel *Tillie's Punctured Romance* (1914). Directed by Sennett, the film was unusual in that Chaplin and Normand played second fiddle to a star (Dressler) and was historically important for being the first feature-length comedy (approximately ninety minutes) to have been made anywhere in the world, exceeding the running time of any previous comic film by two-thirds.

Sennett, dedicated to an ever-increasing production schedule and to the editing process, as well as to retaining final say over each and every film, hired several other directors to come in and make them. To the Kops and the Bathing Beauties, he added the Kid Komedies series for children, predating Hal Roach's famous Our Gang series by nearly ten years. In 1915, however, Keystone was absorbed into the new Triangle Film Corporation, which—with Sennett joining directors Griffith and Thomas Ince—could now boast a triumvirate of the American silent screen's most famous filmmaking names.

Keystone retained autonomy within Triangle and benefited from larger budgets. Their productions became more polished, and their material more varied, with slapstick no longer the sole product. Humor was broadened to include what would now be called situation comedy, and a series of romantic comedies were made that provided star vehicles for the young Gloria Swanson. For all its seeming advantages, however, Triangle failed to live up to expectation, and in 1917—at the cost of relinquishing the Keystone title—Sennett (following the example of Griffith and

Ince) broke away and formed Mack Sennett Comedies, his own company releasing first through Paramount and later Associate Producers and First National.

Living up to its name, the company continued to make two-reel comedies but also produced several features, some showcasing Normand and comic Ben Turpin. Then in 1923 Sennett entered an association with Pathe that saw out the silent era. It was here that, continuing his gift for recognizing and nurturing talent, Sennett launched the career of the great comedian Harry Langdon in a series of shorts. Throughout his career, Sennett adhered to assembly-line discipline and prodigious working hours, but to work for him as a writer or director was tantamount to attending a graduate school in how to make films. He hired Frank Capra to write gags for Langdon, and when the comedian left Sennett he took Capra with him.

END OF HIS REIGN

The coming of sound toppled Sennett from his throne as the King of Comedy, though he continued producing and directing for some years. He made low-budget shorts for the Educational studio and produced some comedy shorts with W. C. Fields and a series of musical shorts with Bing Crosby for Paramount in 1932. At Educational he directed *The Timid Young Man* (1935), a short starring Buster Keaton (the only time they worked together), before retiring back to Canada, broke and alone. Normand, dogged by scandal and disillusioned by her long and stormy affair with Sennett, which failed to lead to marriage, married actor Lew Cody in 1926 and had died of drug abuse and tuberculosis by 1930, at the age of thirty-five. Their relationship is the subject of Jerry Herman's nostalgic musical, *Mack and Mabel*, first performed on Broadway in 1974 with Robert Preston and Bernadette Peters.

In 1937 Sennett received a special Academy Award "to the master of fun, discoverer of stars, sympathetic, kindly, understanding comedy genius . . . for his lasting contribution to the comedy technique of the screen, the basic principles of which are as important today as when they were first put into practice." Sennett, the self-proclaimed King of Comedy, wrote his autobiography under that title in 1954 and died on November 5, 1960, in Woodland Hills, California.

Peter C. Holloran

SEE ALSO: *Academy Awards; Arbuckle, Fatty; Broadway; Capra, Frank; Celebrity; Celebrity Couples; Chaplin, Charlie; Crosby, Bing; Fields, W. C.; Griffith, D. W.; Hollywood; Keaton, Buster; The Keystone Kops;* Our Gang*; Peters, Bernadette; Pickford, Mary; Silent Movies; Vaudeville.*

BIBLIOGRAPHY

Lahue, Kalton C. *Mack Sennett's Keystone: The Man, the Myth, and the Comedies*. South Brunswick, NJ: A. S. Barnes, 1971.

Sennett, Mack. *King of Comedy*. Garden City, NY: Doubleday, 1954.

Sherk, Warren M., ed. *The Films of Mack Sennett*. Lanham, MD: Scarecrow Press, 1998.

Walker, Brent. *Mack Sennett's Fun Factory*. Jefferson, NC: McFarland, 2010.

Serial Killers

During the late twentieth and early twenty-first centuries, the threat of serial and mass murder was a topic of great popular and academic interest in America. While there is no murder "epidemic," as hyperbolic writers and law-enforcement officials often claimed in the mid-1980s, the apprehension of high-profile serial killers, such as David Berkowitz, Ted Bundy, John Wayne Gacy, and Henry Lee Lucas, and an upswing in mass shootings in places such as schoolyards, post offices, and college campuses served to bring the problem to the attention of the public. The apprehension of other high-profile killers, such as Gary Ridgway, the Green River Killer, in 2001 and Dennis Rader, the BTK Killer, in 2005 has consistently kept the phenomenon in the public eye.

In a capitalistic mass-media age in which sensational news stories increase ratings and sell advertising time, the "random" killer (especially the serial murderer) provides good source material. He also inspires generations of fiction writers, who simultaneously view him not only as an artistic metaphor for any number of social ills but as a guaranteed moneymaker. Literally thousands of fiction and nonfiction ("true crime") novels and films centered on multiple killers have grossed hundreds of millions of dollars in America alone.

One of the most recognizable of these is the Academy Award–winning movie *The Silence of the Lambs*, which is based on a best-selling novel by Thomas Harris. Harris, in turn, was inspired to create his memorable work of fiction by his research into the lives of real-life serial killers and the law-enforcement agents and profilers who pursue them. Most of the well-known fictional stories that feature serial and/or mass murder, then, are contemporary morality plays in which evil, murdering villains threaten the social fabric but are eventually caught by heroic law enforcement. The reality of serial and mass murder, however, is much more complicated.

HISTORY AND DEFINITIONS

Multiple homicide, whether called "serial murder" or "mass murder," has always been a part of human history. The most notorious practitioners of multicide include Gilles de Rais, Countess Elizabeth Bathory, Jack the Ripper, Belle Gunness, Carl Panzram, Albert Fish, Earle Nelson, Peter Kurten, Ed Gein, Albert DeSalvo, Ian Brady and Myra Hindley, Edmund Kemper, Juan Corona, David Berkowitz, Ted Bundy, John Wayne Gacy, Peter Sutcliffe, Angelo Buono, Kenneth Bianchi, Dean Corll, Wayne Henley, Henry Lucas, Ottis Toole, Richard Ramirez, Joel Rifkin, Danny Rolling, Dennis Nilsen, Jeffrey Dahmer, Andrei Chikatilo, and Aileen Wuornos. *Serial murder*, however, has existed only, in the strictest sense, after Federal Bureau of Investigation (FBI) agent Robert Ressler coined the term and the American mass media disseminated it throughout the culture during the 1980s. Before *serial murder* as a sobriquet came into vogue, the phenomenon in question was usually called "lust murder" or "mass murder" and included a variety of multiple-homicide crimes. In criminological jargon, serial murder and mass murder usually refer to two disparate concepts. Complicating matters further, there are many "subspecies" of serial murderers and mass murderers. All of them must be distinguished from other varieties of multiple killers, such as paid hit men or state-sanctioned assassins, executioners, and torturers.

Serial murder is most commonly defined as the commission of three or more murders over time by the same killer, with a hiatus between each murder. The victims may or may not be known to the killer, but more often than not the social class any one victim represents to the killer is more important than the victim's identity. The fact that victims are often unknown to the

FINAL ★ ★ ★ **DAILY NEWS** Cloudy, showers, 85. Cloudy tonight, 60s. Sunny tomorrow. Details, page 79.

Vol. 59. No. 39 New York, Wednesday, August 10, 1977 Price: 20 cents

WANTED

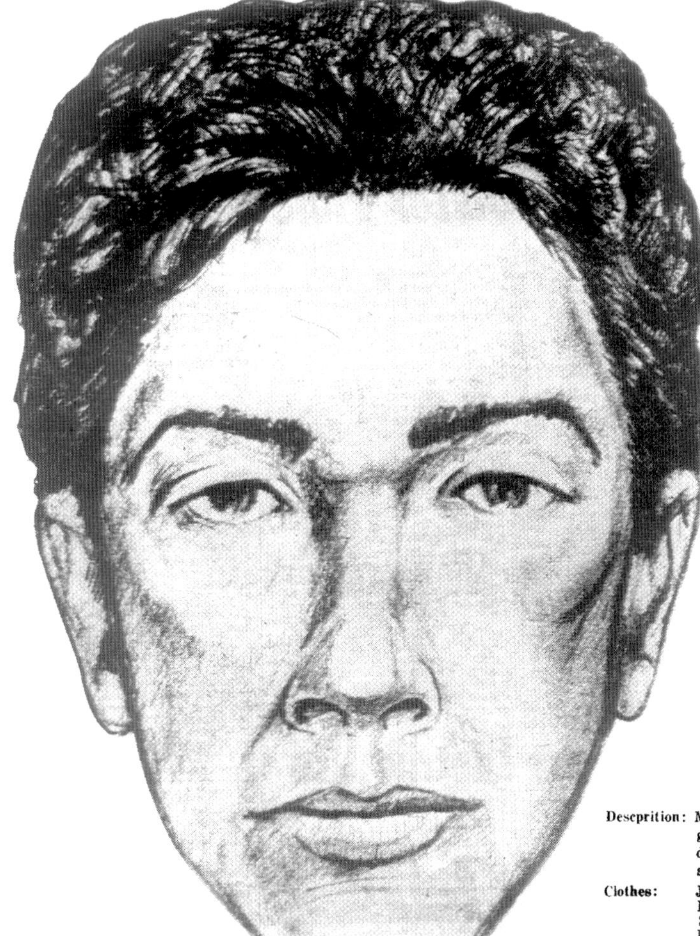

Son of Sam

This is new sketch released by police hunting for Son of Sam. Drawing is based on descriptions by witnesses to shootings of Stacy Moskowitz and Robert Violante and previous shootings.

Stories on page 3

Descprition: Male, whti,e 25 to 32, 5′8″-5′9″, 165-175 lbs, good athletic type build, clean shaven, dark almond-shaped eyes, dark wavy hair, sensuous mouth, high cheekbones.

Clothes: Jacket—blue denim
Pants—blue denim, slightly flared
Shirt—bluish grey Qiana with small kidney-shaped design spaced 3″ apart
Shoes—blue denim with narrow white band.

Notify special homicide task force at 109th Precinct with information on suspect: Call 961-9613 or 844-0999.

Son of Sam Sketch. *The front page of the August 10, 1977, edition of the* New York Daily News *is devoted to a sketch of the serial killer referred to as Son of Sam.* NY DAILY NEWS ARCHIVE/GETTY IMAGES.

killer prior to the murder leads many people to call serial murder "irrational" or "evil." In most cases, no comprehensible motive exists for the crimes, and the murders do not seem to provide the killer with any clearly understood, tangible benefits.

According to serial murder expert Elliott Leyton, the serial-killer category most definitely does not include those who kill repeatedly for profit or for governments. These killers are performing murder for someone else rather than as a significant act for themselves. The motive is basically rational and readily apparent. By contrast, the serial killer, while not without certain aspirations of his own, works according to a more esoteric agenda that observers often find inscrutable. This leads them to consider him *insane*, *psychotic*, or *schizophrenic*, psychiatric terms that all denote a severe and socially crippling disjunction between reality and perception. These terms do not fit most serial killers. The serial killer only appears nonrational because he operates from, as criminologists Ronald M. Holmes and James De Burger explain in their book *Serial Murder*, "intrinsic motive systems . . . that originate within the individual; they govern and structure the serial killer's homicidal behavior."

CHARACTERISTICS

The vast majority of known serial killers are male, and the vast majority of their victims are female, a fact that understandably leads many to conclude that serial murder is synonymous with sexual murder; however, this is not strictly the case. In August 1985 the *FBI Law Enforcement Bulletin* published a series of articles (expanded to a book-length study titled *Sexual Homicide* in 1988) in which primary offender characteristics are listed. The data were compiled from lengthy interviews with thirty-six incarcerated serial murderers, all of them male. Most writers on the fact and fiction of serial murder, even those critical of law enforcement claims and methods, have been drawing on this specific set of FBI conclusions ever since, so the study is crucial to any analysis of the popular culture's portrayal of the "typical" serial murderer.

According to the report, he is usually a white male between twenty-five and thirty-five years old. Generally he is at the height of his physical powers, a fact that not only serves him in the practical matter of overpowering victims but also empowers him in the public arena. His strength and apparent potency (and of course, choice of victims) render him an effective media monster. He is also likely to be an eldest son or an only child and of average or above-average intelligence. His childhood may have been marked by incidents of sexual or physical abuse, and his parents may be divorced or flagrantly unfaithful to one another. He usually possesses a strong belief that he is more intelligent and privileged than ordinary people and thus exempted from the social restrictions that govern the masses. This belief grows only stronger when he is confronted by evidence to the contrary. No safe predictions can be made about his economic origins, but according to Leyton, serial murder in the modern era is more a crime of the middle classes than of the lower or upper ranges of the socioeconomic hierarchy.

It should be noted that while males are overwhelmingly responsible for most serial murders and mass murders, there are more female multicides than commonly believed. A partial list of female American multiple killers alone includes Susan Denise Atkins, Patricia Krenwrinkel, Charlene Gallego, Belle Gunness, Nannie Doss, Martha Beck, Carol Bundy, Dorothea Puente, Priscilla Ford, Amy Archer-Gilligan, Anna Hahn, Mary Eleanor Smith, Jane Toppan, Genene Jones, Judy Neeley, and Debra Brown. The most famous female multicide of all is Hungarian countess Elizabeth Bathory, who with a coterie of female disciples imprisoned and murdered hundreds of women in her castle in the early 1600s.

MASS MURDERERS

Not all privately conceived acts of multiple homicide qualify as serial murders. Scholars now generally agree that mass murder forms a separate category. James Alan Fox and Jack Levin, professors at the College of Criminal Justice at Northeastern University, point out that mass murderers are generally caught at or near the crime scene and that the crime is of horrific proportions but relatively short duration. Unlike serial killers, who typically target strangers and traumatize a community over an extended period, the mass murderer plans one ultraviolent assault upon victims who, more often than not, are known to him.

Mass murderers can be depressed people who kill their entire family before committing suicide, but more commonly they are those who violently retaliate against a specific group or class of people because of a real or imagined grievance, such as a disgruntled employee gunning down supervisors and coworkers at work. Racism or sexism also often motivates this kind of killer, as was the case with James Huberty, who killed twenty-one people in California because of an obsessive hatred of Hispanics, and Marc Lepine, who killed fourteen women at the University of Montreal because he blamed feminists for his romantic and professional difficulties.

Massacres in public places, such as restaurants, schoolyards, post offices, and commuter trains, typically involve one heavily armed killer who kills as many people as he can. However, the massacre is a one-time-only event that often ends in the death of the killer either by his own hand or by the police. Charles Whitman, who opened fire on students from the University of Texas Tower in 1966, is a well-known example of this kind of mass murderer. He killed thirteen people and wounded thirty-two before police shot him to death. Other examples are Eric Harris and Dylan Klebold, who shot to death a teacher and twelve fellow students before killing themselves at Columbine High School in 1999, and Seung-Hui Cho, who killed thirty-two people and then himself on the campus of Virginia Tech in 2007.

SPREE KILLERS

The spree killer occupies an intermediate position between the mass murderer and the serial murderer, although it should be noted that some authorities see no real distinction between spree killing, mass murder, and serial murder. The spree killer does not operate in secret like the serial killer, but neither does he lay siege to one specific locale until law enforcement stops him. Instead, he often drives cross-country, more often than not with a companion or two, murdering randomly and noisily until he is captured or killed. His weapon of choice is a gun, as opposed to the serial killer's more intimate knife. He makes little or no effort to cover his tracks; instead, he exults in the sheer nihilism of destruction and relies on brute mobility to keep him free as long as possible. His crimes are very visible but generally of short duration because of their high profile.

During the 1950s, for example, embittered garbageman Charles Starkweather and his young girlfriend, Caril Fugate, rampaged across the Midwest, killing eleven people before they were captured, arousing a nation to new heights of paranoia concerning the dangers of juvenile delinquency. The conspicuousness of the spree killer contrasts significantly with the serial killer, who wishes to remain undetected for a period of time, at least in identity if not in deed.

The United States has been producing more of these sensational criminals in the late twentieth and early twenty-first centuries than other industrialized nations. Sociologists point to many possible explanations. One of the most compelling is that the American cult of individuality has always prized violence (particularly for males) as a quick response to frustration. The simple outlaw on the lam from the maddening complexities of communal, multicultural existence remains a heroic American icon. For many, if not most, violence is more attractive as a form of immediate gratification than the intangible results of long-term, peaceful political activism.

In spite of the public rhetoric condemning violence, Americans have traditionally accepted even extreme levels of group and individual violence alike as appropriate responses to conditions perceived as intolerable. The hugely influential study, *The Subculture of Violence* (1967), by criminologist Marvin E. Wolfgang and clinician Franco Ferracuti, analyzes how it is possible for people within a culture to embrace some of its general values while denying, deemphasizing, or inversing others and yet remain within that culture. For many segments of the American public, violence is regarded as a perfectly legitimate form of social expression and problem solving, dependent upon and framed in terms of prevailing local conditions even as it is decried by the supposedly overriding social discourse.

The serial killers and mass murderers of America are no exception or aberration in this sense. Their fantasies of murder and revenge are constructed from accessible cultural symbols recognizable to others. If such killers were truly alien to us, as facile notions of evil and deviance insist, then their motives would not be comprehensible. Indeed, many insist that serial murder is incomprehensible. While such exclusionary approaches are undeniably comforting, the unsettling observation must be made that serial murder is clearly rooted in our consensual reality and discourse. Its manifestation and shape obviously relies on the contemporary values, norms, and beliefs it seeks to overturn or, perversely enough, to uphold.

In medieval Europe multiple killers were perceived as, and often believed themselves to be, vampires or werewolves; in modern America, they are perceived as demonically possessed monsters or formerly abused children, depending on the observer's sociopolitical orientation. The only commonality easily discerned about multiple murderers from century to century and country to country is their monstrous outcast status.

In ancient legend and contemporary fiction, they lurk on the fringes of civilization, attack the vulnerable, then retreat back into the wilderness until a hero (usually an amateur or professional detective) can find and destroy them. After this ritual expurgation of the murderous exile, people can reassume their complacency until the next time. In the interval, however, narrative myths keep alive the awareness that somewhere out there, the monsters grow hungry. The names and details may change from one generation's folklore to the next, but the basic plot remains the same.

Philip L. Simpson

SEE ALSO: *Bundy, Ted; Dahmer, Jeffrey; FBI (Federal Bureau of Investigation);* The Silence of the Lambs; *Vampires.*

BIBLIOGRAPHY

Caputi, Jane. *The Age of Sex Crime*. Bowling Green, OH: Bowling Green State University Popular Press, 1987.

Douglas, John, and Mark Olshaker. *Mind Hunter: Inside the FBI's Elite Serial Crime Unit*. New York: Scribner, 1995.

Douglas, John, and Mark Olshaker. *Journey into Darkness*. New York: Pocket, 1997.

Fox, James Alan, and Jack Levin. *Overkill: Mass Murder and Serial Killing Exposed*. New York: Dell, 1996.

Hickey, Eric W. *Serial Murderers and Their Victims*. Pacific Grove, CA: Brooks/Cole Publishing, 1991.

Holmes, Ronald M., and James De Burger. *Serial Murder*. Newbury Park, CA: Sage Publications, 1988.

Holmes, Ronald M., and Stephen T. Holmes. *Murder in America*. Newbury Park, CA: Sage Publications, 1994.

Jenkins, Philip. *Using Murder: The Social Construction of Serial Homicide*. New York: Aldine de Gruyter, 1994.

Keppel, Robert D., and William J. Birnes. *Signature Killers*. New York: Pocket, 1997.

Leyton, Elliott. *Hunting Humans: Inside the Minds of Mass Murderers*. New York: Pocket, 1988.

Norris, Joel. *Serial Killers: The Growing Menace*. New York: Doubleday, 1988.

Ressler, Robert; Ann W. Burgess; Roger L. Depue, et al. *FBI Law Enforcement Bulletin* 54, no. 8 (1985): 2–31.

Ressler, Robert K.; Ann W. Burgess; and John E. Douglas. *Sexual Homicide: Patterns and Motives*. Lexington, MA: Lexington Books, 1988.

Ressler, Robert K., and Tom Shachtman. *Whoever Fights Monsters*. New York: St. Martin's, 1992.

Schechter, Harold, and David Everitt. *The A to Z Encyclopedia of Serial Killers*. New York: Pocket, 1996.

Schmid, David. *Natural Born Celebrities: Serial Killers in American Culture*. Chicago: University of Chicago Press, 2005.

Seltzer, Mark. *Serial Killers: Death and Life in America's Wound Culture*. New York: Routledge, 1998.

Tithecott, Richard. *Of Men and Monsters: Jeffrey Dahmer and the Construction of the Serial Killer*. Madison: University of Wisconsin Press, 1997.

Vronsky, Peter. *Serial Killers: The Method and Madness of Monsters*. New York: Berkley Books, 2004.

Wilson, Colin, and Damon Wilson. *The Killers among Us: Motives behind Their Madness*. New York: Warner, 1996.

Serling, Rod *(1924–1975)*

Best known as the host of television's *The Twilight Zone*, Rod Serling was a prolific author of live teleplays and television scripts who did much to raise the artistic bar of a fledgling medium in the 1950s and 1960s. With contemporaries such as Paddy Chayefsky and Reginald Rose, Serling found television a reprobate cousin to film and theater and left it a respected forum for expression.

Born Rodman Edward Serling on Christmas Day in 1924, he grew up in the sleepy university town of Binghamton in upstate New York. He served in the army during World War II, seeing combat action in the Philippines. Hospitalized with multiple shrapnel wounds, Serling sought an outlet for his pent-up emotions. "I was bitter about everything and at loose ends when I got out of the service," he later recalled. "I think I turned to writing to get it off my chest."

START IN TELEVISION

After he returned from the war, Serling began selling radio scripts to programs in New York City. When television's growing popularity created a demand for writers, he moved on to that medium. In four years of freelancing, Serling saw seventy-one of his teleplays produced, but none approached the quality of his seventy-second. "Patterns," a powerful drama about internecine warfare within the halls of a major corporation, aired on *Kraft Television Theatre* on January 12, 1955. It earned Serling the first of six Emmy Awards and provided his big break.

The glowing reviews of "Patterns" made Serling one of the hottest commodities in the entertainment industry. "I found I could sell everything I had—and I did," he said later. Some of his scripts were brilliant. The harrowing boxing drama "Requiem for a Heavyweight" became a live television classic, for example. Others should have remained buried in the author's desk drawer. All of them bore the trademark Serling attributes of moral probity and social concern.

Those social concerns occasionally got Serling into trouble with jittery advertisers and network censors, however, and as a defiant defender of free expression, he bristled at every change to his work. In one instance, the word *lucky* was stricken from one of Serling's scripts because the sponsor, a tobacco company, did not want viewers to be reminded of Lucky Strike cigarettes. That was harmless compared to what CBS did to his drama "A Town Has Turned to Dust." An outspoken progressive on civil rights issues, Serling had penned a script based on the case of Emmett Till, a black teenager who was lynched for allegedly whistling at a white woman. The network, afraid that the show would outrage viewers in the South, changed the setting from present-day Mississippi to Mexico in the 1870s. Other racially charged story elements were likewise toned down. Of his original script, the author lamented, "They chopped it up like a roomful of butchers at work on a steer."

In part because of his desire to make an end run around the television censors, Serling turned his creative energies in 1959 away from live drama. He envisioned a weekly half-hour fantasy anthology series that could address philosophical and political topics in an oblique way. Intrigued at the prospect of signing up one of television's most respected writers, CBS green-lighted the project, which Serling christened *The Twilight Zone*. He was given total artistic control along with the title of executive producer.

THE TWILIGHT ZONE

The Twilight Zone debuted on October 2, 1959, to generally positive reviews. Literate and highly entertaining, the show raised the science fiction/fantasy genre to a new level of artistic quality. True to Serling's concept, many of the stories used sci-fi trappings to speak to contemporary social issues such as racism, cultural conformity, and Cold War paranoia. For actors, the series relied on a dizzying repertory company of seasoned character players and up-and-comers. Serling himself joined their ranks by serving as on-camera host and narrator. His bizarre persona—clenched teeth and gravelly monotone, crisp Kuppenheimer suits, and the eternally cupped cigarette—made him seem like some kind of celestial undertaker beamed in to viewers' homes once a week for their edification and enjoyment.

In addition to hosting and serving as executive producer, Serling wrote ninety-two of *Twilight Zone*'s 156 episodes over the course of five seasons. He contributed some of the show's most memorable teleplays, including "Eye of the Beholder," which explored relative perceptions of beauty through the eyes of a "disfigured" young woman. Unfortunately, the demands on Serling's time and concentration also forced him to write quickly and sloppily. Many of the show's worst installments—and its often preachy and moralizing tone—bore his imprimatur as well.

With the occasional critical brickbat, however, came the fame and recognition due to the unmistakable face and voice of a successful network television series. Serling collected numerous awards for his work on *The Twilight Zone*, including another Emmy. After the series was canceled in 1964, he went back to writing dramatic teleplays for anthology shows. In 1968 he wrote the first three drafts of the screenplay for the film *Planet of the Apes*. His verbose, purple style still can be heard in the finished film, voiced with delicious pomposity by the perfectly cast Charlton Heston.

Lured back to series television in 1970, Serling lent his name and visage to *Night Gallery*, a *Twilight Zone*-esque anthology that ran for two seasons on NBC. Although he penned some exceptional episodes, he became frustrated with the network's vision of the show as, in his words, "Mannix in a cemetery." He even suffered the indignity of having several of his own scripts rejected for insufficiently frightening content. Contractually bound to serve as host, the humiliated fantasist desultorily went through his paces until the show's cancellation. Three years later he died following complications of heart bypass surgery. To the end, he remained committed to the integrity of his work and the vision of a higher standard of televised entertainment.

Robert E. Schnakenberg

SEE ALSO: *Civil Rights Movement; Heston, Charlton;* Kraft Television Theatre*; Live Television;* Planet of the Apes*;* Playhouse 90*; Television;* The Twilight Zone.

BIBLIOGRAPHY

Brode, Douglas, and Carol Serling. *Rod Serling and* The Twilight Zone: *The 50th Anniversary Tribute.* Fort Lee, NJ: Barricade, 2009.

Feldman, Leslie Dale. *Spaceships and Politics: The Political Theory of Rod Serling.* Lanham, MD: Lexington Books, 2010.

Sander, Gordon F. *Serling: The Rise and Twilight of Television's Last Angry Man.* New York: Dutton, 1992.

Zicree, Marc Scott. *The* Twilight Zone *Companion.* New York: Bantam, 1982.

Sesame Street

Broadcast on more than 300 Public Broadcasting Service (PBS) stations and in more than 140 countries around the world,

Sesame Street is a widely acclaimed children's television program that celebrated its fortieth anniversary in 2009. The show holds the record for the longest-running children's series in American history. It has won more than 100 of the top awards in its field, including 109 Emmy Awards, 2 Peabody Awards, 9 Grammy Awards, 4 Parent's Choice Awards, and the Action for Children's Television Special Achievement Award. The Television Critics Association recognized the show for Outstanding Achievement in Children's Programming in 2001 and again in 2011.

Created by Joan Ganz Cooney for the Children's Television Network to provide educational material to inner-city kids, *Sesame Street* has endured by remaining true to its initial goals while changing with the times. It survived the deaths of Will Lee, who played Mr. Hooper, one of its major characters, and of Jim Henson, its creative force, who made his Muppet characters, including Kermit the Frog, Big Bird, and Cookie Monster, some of the most familiar faces in American popular culture. Other characters have come and gone, and actors have been replaced over the years, but *Sesame Street* remains an important element in the lives of American children.

CREATION AND DEVELOPMENT

The originators of *Sesame Street* spent several years culling the expertise they needed from relevant fields to present a show that would educate and entertain at the same time. The show is geared toward a viewing culture in which the typical child spends more than 5,000 hours watching television before entering first grade—and 19,000 hours by his or her high school graduation. According to Cooney, none of the people involved in the beginning realized that *Sesame Street* would become an icon of popular culture and a family to which generations of children would belong. From the beginning *Sesame Street* employed techniques that had been successful in commercials by presenting educational material in the form of fast-paced, highly visual, and oft-repeated commercials. Children who watched the show quickly learned the alphabet, numbers, concepts, and relationships through repetition. The songs sung daily on *Sesame Street* became part of the repertoire of preschoolers and parents alike for the same reason.

The producers of the show develop a specific curriculum for each season aimed at imparting key information and concepts. For example, in its twenty-ninth season the show sought to teach social concepts such as acceptance, cooperation, tolerance, conflict resolution, birth, love, and marriage; practical skills such as addition, computers, drawing, geography, and history; and social awareness of such issues as cultural diversity, handicaps, Native Americans, Hispanic Americans, and Chinese Americans. Following the terrorist attacks of September 11, 2001, *Sesame Street* focused on children's fears, with the

Sesame Street. *The characters of* Sesame Street *have been entertaining and educating preschoolers since 1969.* JOHN LAMPARSKI/CONTRIBUTOR/WIREIMAGE/GETTY IMAGES.

neighborhood in the show experiencing fires, the loss of loved ones, and bullying. In response to national concerns about increasing childhood obesity, in 2006 producers changed the diet of Cookie Monster, who announced that cookies were only meant to be occasional treats. Cauliflower, cantaloupe, and carrots, on the other hand, were good choices for everyday food.

CAST

The adults who appeared on *Sesame Street* at its outset won their roles by auditioning before real kids who chose only the actors with whom they felt comfortable; many of them have remained with the show for many years. Adults were chosen to represent specific role models for young children. The character Maria, played by Sonia Manzano, joined *Sesame Street* in 1969 as a young teenager who worked at the lending library. She grew up on the show, married Luis (Emilio Delgado), and had a baby, teaching children about love, marriage, and birth along the way. Bob McGrath, a member of the original cast, has continued to provide stability as children grew up and watched the show with their own children.

Gordon, played by Roscoe Orman since 1974, was already married to Susan (Loretta Long) when the show began. Later they adopted a son and taught children about adoption. In response to concerns of the National Organization for Women (NOW) that the character of Susan had become a negative role model for young girls, Susan became a public-health nurse. From the show's inception until his death in 1982, Mr. Hooper (Will Lee) ran the neighborhood store, representing the ideal grandfather as he served up love, comfort, and cookies. *Sesame Street* used Lee's death to help children recognize the importance of memories when someone they love dies and to understand that death is real and final. Other adults have been added to the show, including Buffy Sainte-Marie, a Native American folksinger; comedienne Ruth Buzzi, who uses magical objects in her thrift shop to tell stories to children in the studio and at home; and dancer Savion Glover, who entertains and teaches with music.

Guest stars have been a staple of *Sesame Street* since its inception. Actor Noah Wyle noted that the most exciting thing about being a guest star was being able to meet his idol, Big Bird. A classic moment in television occurred when a plethora of guest stars, including Paul Simon, Jane Curtin, Barbara Walters, and Danny DeVito, implored Ernie to "put down the duckie if you want to play the saxophone." They referred, of course, to Ernie's tendency to clutch his rubber duckie the way that Linus clutches his blanket in the *Peanuts* cartoons.

MUPPETS

The creative genius of Jim Henson gave birth to the Muppets, some of the best-loved children's characters of all time. Henson had brought the Muppet named Rowlf to national attention on *The Jimmy Dean Show* and was hired to do a series of commercials with his appealing inventions, which were a combination of marionettes and puppets. The first Muppets were simple pieces of cloth that came alive under Henson's hand; though today's Muppets are more elaborate, the secret of how they are made is still closely guarded. Originally, the Muppets were not meant to interact with the adults on *Sesame Street*, but tests revealed that young children paid more attention when their favorite Muppets were on-screen. This allowed the show's producers to use the Muppets as surrogate children.

Big Bird, operated by Caroll Spinney, is the epitome of a child with the best of intentions who is often confused and who constantly makes mistakes. One of the central plots on *Sesame Street* concerned the friendship of Big Bird and Mr. Snuffleupagus, who was thought by the whole neighborhood to be a figment of Big Bird's imagination for more than a decade. One of the best-loved Muppets, Kermit the Frog, appeared on the show for only a short time. In the early days Kermit served as a roving reporter, attempting to discover the truth behind various tales and usually becoming an unwitting part of the story. Henson chose to remove Kermit from *Sesame Street* because he had appeared in commercials before the show aired. Kermit went on to star in *The Muppet Show* and a series of movies, including a 2011 movie in which the Muppets set out to save their theater from a greedy oil tycoon.

Bert and Ernie, the *Odd Couple* of *Sesame Street*, have demonstrated the give and take of friendship through four decades of manipulation on the part of Ernie and gullibility on the part of Bert. Grover, on the other hand, is bright and patient and is always ready to share his wisdom by teaching concepts and relationships. Oscar the Grouch, with his irascible personality, teaches children that some people use gruffness to hide a heart of gold. Cookie Monster allows children to laugh at the selfishness that they sense is part of their own personalities. Perhaps the favorite of the newer Muppets is Elmo, who represents the sweet, gentle, and trusting child. In the 1990s Elmo frequently visited *The Rosie O'Donnell Show* as a welcomed guest, saying whatever came to mind and expressing his affection through frequent kisses, just as many small children do. Indeed, with some help from O'Donnell, the Tickle Me Elmo doll became the top-selling toy of 1996.

It is impossible to say whether *Sesame Street* would have succeeded without the Muppets, but no one would argue that the show has endured in great part because of their charm and originality and because of the hard work of those who manipulate them. In addition to Spinney, who plays Big Bird and Oscar the Grouch, Frank Oz played Bert, Grover, and Cookie Monster for more than thirty years. Bert and Grover have been played since 1997 and 2002, respectively, by Eric Jacobson, while the role of Cookie Monster is played by David Rudman. Kevin Clash is the puppeteer who plays Elmo, in addition to the character Baby Natasha.

CRITICISM

During its more than forty-year run, *Sesame Street* has not escaped criticism. Some studies have demonstrated that television stunts imagination or turns out restless and ill-informed students. Such studies also suggest that kids who grow up watching *Sesame Street* expect school to be like the show: colorful, fast-paced, and entertaining. In contrast, many teachers and parents agreed with a 1988 report that found that watching television may nurture attention-focusing capabilities and self-control while promoting teacher-student responses. Students who watched *Sesame Street* and its sister show for older children, *The Electric Company*, were found to be more proficient in basic skills.

At times in *Sesame Street*'s history, right-wing critics have demanded that the show be removed from the air because the close relationship of Muppets Ernie and Bert suggests that they are gay. Conservatives who deplore the use of tax money to fund public television have used this alleged relationship as support for cutting all funds to public television stations and to the

National Endowment for the Arts. In 2011 gay rights advocates launched an online campaign to have Bert and Ernie marry on the show. The producers responded that Bert and Ernie are puppets and therefore do not have a sexual orientation.

Elizabeth Rholetter Purdy

SEE ALSO: *Emmy Awards; Grammy Awards; Henson, Jim; The Muppets; National Organization for Women (NOW); O'Donnell, Rosie;* Peanuts*; Public Television (PBS); Simon, Paul; Television; Walters, Barbara.*

BIBLIOGRAPHY

Borgenicht, David, and Children's Television Workshop. Sesame Street *Unpaved: Scripts, Stories, Secrets, and Songs.* New York: Hyperion, 1998.

Davis, Michael. *Street Gang: The Complete History of* Sesame Street. New York: Viking, 2008.

Frye, Karen Hill. *Television's* Sesame Street*: An Experiment in Early Education.* Los Angeles: Center for Afro-American Studies, University of California, 1972.

Lesser, Gerald S. *Children and Television: Lessons from* Sesame Street. New York: Random House, 1974.

Morrow, R. W. Sesame Street *and the Reform of Children's Television.* Baltimore, MD: Johns Hopkins University Press, 2006.

Polsky, Richard M., and Aspen Program on Communications and Society. *Getting to* Sesame Street*: Origins of the Children's Television Workshop.* New York: Praeger, 1974.

Seven Days in May

Released in 1964, *Seven Days in May*, directed by John Frankenheimer, is a political thriller based on the 1962 Fletcher Knebel and Charles W. Bailey II novel of the same title. Addressing the issue of nuclear disarmament treaties at the height of the Cold War, *Seven Days in May* tells of a coup by U.S. military leaders in response to American participation in such a disarmament treaty. Fueled by a combination of patriotism and megalomania, Chairman of the Joint Chiefs of Staff General James Mattoon Scott, played by Burt Lancaster, plots to "save" the United States from the president of the United States, the person who signed the treaty. Black-and-white cinematography adds to the film's tense dialogue provided by screenwriter Rod Serling. Kirk Douglas, Fredric March, and Ava Gardner also star.

Lori C. Walters

SEE ALSO: *Cold War; Gardner, Ava; Lancaster, Burt; Serling, Rod.*

BIBLIOGRAPHY

Kabatchnik, Amnon. *Blood on the Stage, 1950–1975: Milestone Plays of Crime, Mystery, and Detection.* Lanham, MD: Scarecrow Press, 2011.

Knebel, Fletcher, and Charles W. Bailey II. *Seven Days in May.* New York: Harper & Row, 1964.

The Seven Year Itch

Released in 1955, *The Seven Year Itch* represents the epitome of actress Marilyn Monroe's popular screen persona as the naive and sexually appealing blond. Directed by Billy Wilder and based on the play of the same name by George Axelrod, the film centers on the supposed tendency of men married for seven years to seek extramarital affairs. One hot New York summer, while his wife is vacationing in Maine, a middle-aged publisher (Tom Ewell) considers just such an affair with his pretty, young neighbor (Monroe). In the end, however, he chooses to remain faithful and leaves to join his wife. The film features several humorous sexual fantasy sequences and the famous image of Monroe exposing her shapely legs as she stands over a subway vent in a billowy white dress.

Scott W. Hoffman

SEE ALSO: *Monroe, Marilyn; Sex Symbol; Wilder, Billy.*

BIBLIOGRAPHY

Conway, Michael, and Mark Ricci. *The Complete Films of Marilyn Monroe.* New York: Carol Publishing Group, 1994.

Spoto, Donald. *Marilyn Monroe.* Barcelona: Debolsillo, 2009.

Zolotow, Maurice. *Billy Wilder in Hollywood.* New York: Limelight Editions, 1992.

Seventeen

Seventeen magazine debuted on newsstands in September 1944, forever changing the media and consumer market for teenage girls. Although it was not the first magazine to appeal to young adults, it was the first devoted entirely to girls and the first to successfully reach a large teenage audience. The colorful cover promised "Young fashions and beauty, movies and music, ideas and people." Sections like "What You Wear," "How You Look and Feel," "Getting Along in the World," "Your Mind," and "Having Fun" offered a world of advertising, shopping, and advice in the voice of a big sister.

From the beginning, *Seventeen* was remarkably popular. All 400,000 copies of the first issue sold out in six days. By February 1947, the magazine's circulation exceeded one million, and by July 1949 more than 2.5 million copies were sold each month. The circular's success continued for decades, despite stiff competition and an increasingly specialized market. *Seventeen* continues to be widely read, appearing in multiple formats including print, online, and mobile.

THE EMERGING TEENAGE MARKET

The concept for *Seventeen* emerged in 1944 when Walter Annenberg of Triangle Publications decided to overhaul a lackluster movie magazine named *Stardom*. Helen Valentine, the promotional director at *Mademoiselle*, agreed to serve as the new editor-in-chief, rechristening the magazine after Booth Tarkington's novel *Seventeen* in order to appeal to the target group of thirteen- to eighteen-year-olds. Although the bulk of the magazine focused on fashion and beauty, Valentine insisted on treating teenage girls' emotional and intellectual needs with sincerity and respect. She wanted to teach them about the world and their role in it as responsible citizens—in addition to helping them to choose their first lipstick and to survive their first dates.

In the mid-1940s advertisers, manufacturers, and media producers were only beginning to recognize the economic importance of the teenage market. Young adults began to look for guidance and entertainment in magazines, movies, and music. The decreasing presence of teenagers in the full-time work force, along with growing high school attendance, helped to divide teenagers and adults and create a new teen consumer identity. With growing access to disposable income, especially in the years following World War II, teen girls were poised for a magazine that addressed them directly.

In order to capitalize on teen girls as a distinct consumer group, *Seventeen*'s promotional staff created an advisory board to encourage age-appropriate ad placement and to unite advertising and editorial content. The magazine rejected ads for dark red nail polish or shoes with spiked heels and discouraged copy with heavy slang, preferring to advertise a "wholesome" teenage girl who dressed neatly and conservatively for high school and dates. Triangle Publications supported the effort with a lavish promotional campaign and by cultivating the image of a prototypical teenage girl dubbed "Teena."

CONTENT FOR GIRLS

From its inception, *Seventeen* was primarily devoted to fashion and beauty, encouraging girls to learn to fix their hair; shape or enhance their bodies; wear appropriate clothing; attract boys; and throw the perfect party. However, it also ran articles that addressed politics, voting, the United Nations, postwar inflation, and atomic energy. Book reviews encouraged readers to learn about community forums, the World Youth Conference, and college and career options for young women. Letters to the editor showed that readers took the political articles seriously and wanted more coverage of these important issues.

As the median age of marriage dropped during the postwar years, one of *Seventeen*'s editorial messages—not to marry young—increasingly came into conflict with its advertising. A proliferation of wedding-related ads for engagement rings, hope chests, silver, linen, china, and carpets showed dreamy-eyed young women in new homes posing with their handsome husbands or sitting on their bedroom floors collecting china or silver in anticipation of their wedding day. Yet, the magazine continued to present a variety of options, both for readers who married right out of high school and for those headed to college or work.

In 1951 Valentine was fired as editor-in-chief. Although *Seventeen* retained its basic structure, it moved away from topics of responsible citizenship to focus on advertising. "What You Wear," "How You Look and Feel," "Home Food and Doings," and "Having Fun" became noticeably longer and by the mid-1950s constituted the majority of the magazine.

FEMINISM AND THE LATE TWENTIETH CENTURY

During the feminist movement of the 1960s and 1970s, the magazine's focus shifted once more—this time toward themes of self-development and independence. Articles on prejudice, the Peace Corps, new careers in science, and teen Democrats and Republicans joined the well of features on clothing, beauty, and domestic talents. The magazine's thirtieth anniversary issue heralded new opportunities that had opened up for teenage girls since the 1940s, proclaiming that discrimination based on sex no longer existed in the workplace.

The conservatism of the 1980s marked a return to more domestic and traditionally feminine content and a decline in articles encouraging self-development. Although other magazines had tried to copy *Seventeen*'s formula, it was not until *Sassy* entered the market in the late 1980s that serious competition emerged. *Sassy* was provocative and imitated the language of its readers. Other competitors such as *Young Miss* emphasized boys and sex. Although *Seventeen*'s content changed to keep pace with the industry, the magazine maintained its focus on fashion, beauty, relationships, school, and entertainment, though it never regained its emphasis on politics, current events, and civic consumerism.

For the magazine's fiftieth anniversary, the editorial staff reflected on half a century of *Seventeen*, declaring that teenagers at the end of the century no longer looked to adults for information, guidance, and taste. Modern teens were more focused on their peers and more likely to reject direct advice than the teenagers of the 1940s. Contemporary issues, such as gun violence, AIDS, and homelessness, personally affected readers, who were constantly exposed to adult topics, violence, and sexuality, whether in their own lives or in talk shows, news, and movies.

Seventeen continues to be a fashion and beauty magazine that addresses teenage girls' interpersonal concerns about boys, family, and friends. The publication leads the Hearst Teen Network of online, mobile, and print content alongside other teen magazines such as *CosmoGirl* and *Mis Quince*. Although it has many competitors, *Seventeen* retains its central role in identifying teenage girls as a distinct and important consumer market.

Kelly Schrum

SEE ALSO: *Advertising; Consumerism;* Cosmopolitan*; Feminism;* Sassy*; Tarkington, Booth; Teenagers.*

BIBLIOGRAPHY

Budgeon, Shelley, and Dawn H. Currie. "From Feminism to Postfeminism: Women's Liberation in Fashion Magazines." *Women's Studies International Forum* 18, no. 2 (1995): 173 186.

McCracken, Ellen. *Decoding Women's Magazines: From* Mademoiselle*to* Ms. New York: St. Martin's Press, 1993.

Peirce, Kate. "A Feminist Theoretical Perspective on the Socialization of Teenage Girls through *Seventeen* Magazine." *Sex Roles* 23, nos. 9/10 (1990): 491–500.

Schlenker, Jennifer A.; Sandra L. Caron; and William A. Halteman. "A Feminist Analysis of *Seventeen* Magazine: Content Analysis from 1945 to 1995." *Sex Roles* 38, nos. 1/2 (1998): 135–149.

Schrum, Kelly. "'Teena Means Business': Teenage Girls' Culture and *Seventeen* Magazine, 1944–1950." In *Delinquents and Debutantes: Twentieth-Century American Girls' Cultures*, ed. Sherrie A. Inness. New York: New York University Press, 1998.

Schrum, Kelly. *Some Wore Bobby Sox: The Emergence of Teenage Girls' Culture, 1920–1945.* New York: Palgrave Macmillan, 2006.

"Seventeen: A Unique Case Study." *Tide*, April 15, 1945.

Sex and the City

HBO's popular TV series *Sex and the City*, which aired from 1998 to 2004, was a commercial and critical hit. A show about the wildly complex romantic lives of four pre-middle-aged female New Yorkers, it gave audiences a welcome dose of glamour, wisecracking comedy, and pathos, as well as a frank view of modern sexuality. It was nominated for dozens of Emmy and Golden Globe Awards, and in 2007 *Time* magazine dubbed it one of the 100 best series ever.

Sarah Jessica Parker played the show's protagonist, Carrie Bradshaw, a cigarette-smoking, gum-cracking, neurotic Everywoman. Like Candace Bushnell, whose autobiographical book of the same name provided the show's template, Bradshaw writes a popular weekly newspaper column that explores sex, relationships, and romance. The fodder for her writing comes mostly from her experiences and from those of her close female friends. Charlotte (Kristin Davis) is a preppy art dealer who steadfastly pursues the dream of true romance. Miranda (Cynthia Nixon) is a tough lawyer conflicted about love and an accidental pregnancy. Those two often collide with Samantha (Kim Cattrall), who treats sex as nothing more than a form of recreation.

The show began by asking whether women could have sex with the same emotional detachment as men. It explored this question through the lives of women who felt pressure to marry and reproduce. Through travails both sardonic and harrowing—impotency, sexually transmitted diseases, younger lovers, complicated fetishes, and breast cancer—the friends always have each other and their girl talk. This talk constitutes much of the show, as the characters try to make sense of their seemingly endless big city dating misadventures while drinking cosmopolitans and extolling the merits of designer clothes and shoes.

Two loves dominate Carrie's story. The first is "Mr. Big" (Chris Noth), a throwback to the unattainable heroes of romance novels. Wealthy Big is emotionally remote, even while he cheats on a young wife with Carrie. The other major player is Aidan (John Corbett), a laidback furniture maker who seems too accommodating; naturally, Carrie has trouble committing to him. Otherwise, new lovers pop up every few episodes—musicians, politicians, writers, and other New York types.

But *Sex and the City* is about more than sex. The friends try to find ways to pursue not just men but also professional success, and career struggles always loom large. As Carrie wrangles her "little" column into a successful book, Miranda, Samantha, and their gay male friend Stanford (Willie Garson) toughen up to get ahead, while Charlotte gives up her job for a troubled marriage.

The series' end spawned two feature-length films for theaters. Loyal viewers looked forward to more of the zingy banter and engrossing romance of the television show but instead were given a movie that seemed dark and pessimistic. It began with Big abandoning Carrie at the altar. Though they do wed in the end—thanks to a Cinderella moment involving a shoe—the tone overall was depressed. When the second feature film was announced, it corrected for this glumness and declared itself to be about sparkle. It put the characters in one glittery outfit after another and brought them to Abu Dhabi on a business and pleasure trip. Though things begin to fall apart when Carrie runs into old flame Aidan again, this proves good in the end, as it puts the zing back in her still-strong, long-term relationship with Big. Unlike the first film, the second film was largely lambasted by critics and performed less favorably in U.S. theaters. Loyal fans, however, supported the film, and it proved to be an international success.

The show's popularity derived, at least in part, from its willingness to acknowledge the difficulties (especially for women) of maturing in a youth-oriented culture and from the characters' ability to remain fabulous at any age. While some critics worry about the effect of glamorized sexual activity on viewers, *Sex and the City* has endured and the franchise remains a cultural touchstone all over the world. Its frank discussions about sex and relationships opened the door for shows such as HBO's *Girls* (2012–) to explore in more detail the contradictory bonds that develop in friendships. The program also provided a framework that allowed for fashion and consumption to exist playfully alongside female agency and independence. *Sex and the City* took on relevant issues such as infertility, discrimination, and single motherhood that most shows either avoided or glossed over, and since its debut has pushed the media to portray the lives of women in a more honest light, but not necessarily with the melodramatic tones of the Hallmark or Lifetime channels.

Susann Cokal

SEE ALSO: *Cable TV; Emmy Awards;* Sex and the Single Girl*; Sitcom; Television;* Time.

BIBLIOGRAPHY

Akass, Kim, and Janet McCabe, eds. *Reading "Sex and the City."* New York: St. Martin's Press, 2004.

Bushnell, Candace. *Sex and the City*. New York: Grand Central Publishing. 1997.

Wignall, Alice. "Can a Feminist Really Love *Sex and the City*?" *Guardian*, April 15, 2008.

Sex and the Single Girl

When Helen Gurley Brown's candid primer *Sex and the Single Girl* was published in 1962, both its provocative title and its spirited tips on men, money, and morals caused a sensation. It became one of the best-selling books of the year and went on to international success in translation as well. Overnight its author became a media sensation, and just a few years later Brown would practically be handed a magazine of her own—*Cosmopolitan*—to remake according to the *Sex and the Single Girl* principles.

Sex and the Single Girl was published only two years after the oral contraceptive pill appeared on the market in the United States. Though there were tens of millions of unmarried women in the country, conventional attitudes in the media—with the exception of *Playboy*—largely assumed that women did not engage in premarital sexual relations. If they did they were usually shown to suffer degradation, unwanted pregnancy, or social ostracism as a result. Magazines for young women typically featured articles that recommended "saying no" as a strategy to avoid a man's sexual advances while on a date. Brides were generally expected to be virgins, and abortion was still illegal in most states.

Belying her glamour-girl persona, Brown was actually of humble origins. A native of the Ozarks, she could not afford college and so learned how to type and got a job as a secretary. Eventually she became an advertising copywriter, and by 1959 (also the year of her marriage to film producer David Brown) she was the highest-paid woman in advertising on the West Coast. Wishing to write a book, Brown heeded the advice of her

Sex and the Single Girl. *Helen Gurley Brown caused a stir with the 1962 publication of* Sex and the Single Girl, *in which the author offered young women advice on entertaining, dating, and sex.* SUSAN WOOD/GETTY IMAGES/CONTRIBUTOR/HULTON ARCHIVE/GETTY IMAGES.

husband: "Write what you know." And so Brown began pounding out chapters for a primer on single life for young women.

Sex and the Single Girl offers tips on decorating, on making one's way through more affluent social circles, and for looking stylish on a budget. Throughout its pages is this message: being single is fun, and there's a whole world of men out there ready to flatter their dates. Brown cautions readers against interrupting a man when he is telling a story, and she advises them to conveniently "forget" to wear some of their lingerie on a date and to wow guests at chic little dinner parties with "champagne peach"—a peeled peach in a pilsner glass with bubbly poured over. In the book's recipe for stuffed lobster tails, Brown begins the preliminaries with the helpful hint to "ask that nice gentleman behind the counter to scoop out the lobster meat and then put it back in the tail." She even gives tips for investing in the stock market.

But most significantly, Brown wrote both frankly and coyly about sex. She claimed that single women probably enjoyed far more exciting and satisfying sex lives than married women. The text treats married people and their attitudes toward single women rather scathingly. A modern unmarried woman, declares Brown, "is so driven by herself and her well-meaning but addle-pated friends to become married that her whole existence seems to be an apology for *not* being married." Elsewhere Brown theorizes that "the single woman, far from being a creature to be pitied and patronized, is emerging as the newest glamour girl of our times." In one of the last chapters, "The Affair: From Beginning to End," Brown writes of several different reasons a woman might engage in an affair—even with a married man.

The book was an immediate best seller. Not surprisingly it incited a huge outcry from conservatives—it was an era when U.S. courts were still battling over Henry Miller's *Tropic of Cancer*, a novel that had been legally banned for explicit sexual content since the 1930s. Later Brown would also become an easy target for angry feminists, who accused her of objectifying women and encouraging them to see themselves only as sexual creatures.

But *Sex and the Single Girl* was a hit nonetheless and had sold more than 100,000 copies by April 1963. Brown began to appear often on television and radio, and she wrote three other books, including *Sex and the Office*, which actually caused even more of a stir. In it she set forth explicit guidelines for a woman to make herself indispensable to her boss. Some newspapers refused to run advertisements for it. Warner Brothers bought the rights to her first book for $200,000, which was the highest amount ever paid for a nonfiction title at that time. The resulting film (1964) was less a documentary than a comic tale, starring Natalie Wood as a marriage counselor with a PhD who is the author of a best-selling book for single women.

Brown and her husband came up with the idea for a magazine, *Femme*, which would bring the *Single Girl* attitude to readers on a monthly basis. They were unable to secure funding for a launch, but in early 1965 Brown was hired by the Hearst Corporation to revitalize *Cosmopolitan*, a moribund magazine that was trying to target a readership of single, fun-loving women. By Brown's retirement in 1997, it had become one of the most successful mass-market magazines for women in publishing history.

Carol Brennan

SEE ALSO: *Abortion; Best Sellers;* Cosmopolitan*; Feminism; The Pill;* Playboy*; Radio; Sexual Revolution; Television; Wood, Natalie.*

BIBLIOGRAPHY

Alexander, Shana. "Singular Girl's Success." *Life*, March 1, 1963.

Collins, Glenn. "At 60, Helen Gurley Brown Talks about Life and Love." *New York Times*, September 19, 1982, 68.

Ferguson, Marjorie. *Forever Feminine: Women's Magazines and the Cult of Femininity*. London: Heinemann, 1982.

Lippert, Barbara. "Gurley Show." *Mediaweek*, March 4, 1996, MR40.

"Meat Loaf, Anyone?" *Newsweek*, August 31, 1964, 53.

Roberts, Roxanne. "The Oldest Living Cosmo Girl." *Washington Post*, January 31, 1996, D1.

"Sex and the Editor." *Time*, March 26, 1965, 40.

"Sex, the Single Girl and a Magazine." *New York Times*, March 17, 1965.

"What Price the Single Girl?" *Esquire*, October 1964, 108–109.

sex, lies and videotape

The film *sex, lies and videotape* has entered the annals of movie history on several counts. A low-budget, independent film, it was a surprise hit that captured the popular imagination with its provocative examination of sexuality at the height of the AIDS crisis. The movie follows the lives of four people in contemporary Baton Rouge, Louisiana: a dissatisfied and possibly frigid housewife, Ann; her unfaithful husband, yuppie lawyer John; her rebellious sister, Cynthia, John's sexually voracious lover; and a sensitive drifter named Graham, an old fraternity brother of John's who is troubled by his dishonest past and only able to gratify himself sexually by watching videotapes he has made of women talking about their sex lives and fantasies. Graham's videotape sessions with Cynthia and Ann help to expose the lies and secrets festering among the characters.

Winner of the Audience Award at its January 1989 debut at the Sundance Film Festival, *sex, lies and videotape* soared to international acclaim at the Cannes Film Festival that summer, where it garnered the top prize, the Palme d'Or, for its twenty-six-year-old novice writer-director, Steven Soderbergh. Released in August 1989 by Miramax Films, who had purchased the rights from Soderbergh for just $1.2 million, *sex, lies and videotape* achieved commercial success unprecedented for the independent market, grossing $25 million in the United States and $100 million worldwide. The movie launched the estimable career of Soderbergh, who has since directed such blockbusters as *Erin Brockovich* (2000) and the Academy Award–winning *Traffic* (2000). The film marked a critical breakthrough as well for actors Andie MacDowell (Ann), Peter Gallagher (John), and James Spader (Palme d'Or winner for his portrayal of Graham) and introduced Laura San Giacomo (Cynthia) in her first feature role.

Even more important to movie history, *sex, lies and videotape* revolutionized the film industry, proving that independent productions could compete with the major Hollywood studios. The movie propelled the 1990s boom in indie filmmaking, with Miramax's promotion of sophisticated art films and niche-driven distribution strategy serving as the template. In a 2009 essay commemorating the twenty-fifth anniversary of Sundance, *Los Angeles Times* critic Chris Lee noted that *sex, lies and videotape* "inspired a generation of underground moviemakers, opened Hollywood's eyes to the commercial viability of indie movies and established Sundance as America's vanguard showcase for quality cutting-edge film." In 2006 the U.S. Library of Congress named *sex, lies and videotape* to the National Film Registry.

Janet Mullane

SEE ALSO: *Academy Awards; AIDS; Soderbergh, Steven; Sundance Film Festival.*

BIBLIOGRAPHY

Biskind, Peter. *Down and Dirty Pictures: Miramax, Sundance, and the Rise of Independent Film*. New York: Simon & Schuster, 2004.

Corliss, Richard. "Top 10 Sundance Hits." *Time*, January 17, 2011.

Lee, Chris. "Sundance Film Festival Got a Boost from *sex, lies and videotape*." *Los Angeles Times*, January 15, 2009.

Newman, Michael A. *Indie: An American Film Culture*. New York: Columbia University Press, 2011.

The Sex Pistols

One of the most influential bands in rock-and-roll history, the Sex Pistols helped launch and craft the first wave of England's punk rock movement in the late 1970s. Although the band existed for just over two years and released only one studio album, *Never Mind the Bollocks, Here's the Sex Pistols* (1977), the reputation of its live shows, its antiauthoritarian lyrics, and its highly publicized crass behavior tapped into and exploited the rough, unadulterated chaos of London's disaffected youth subculture.

The group's beginnings can be traced back to the Strand, which formed in 1972 and featured future Sex Pistols guitarist Steve Jones and drummer Paul Cook. By 1975 Malcolm McLaren, coowner of the boutique Sex in London's Kings Road and onetime manager of the New York Dolls, assumed management responsibilities of the band, ushering it through several lineup and name changes. Glen Matlock was brought on to play bass guitar, and in August of that year John Lydon joined the group. Lydon's poor dental hygiene birthed the name Johnny Rotten; soon after, McClaren pushed the group toward its final name change. After deliberating over a dozen choices, they decided on the Sex Pistols and played their first gig at St. Martin's College on November 6, 1975. Reportedly, they covered songs by the Monkees, the Who, and the New York Dolls, but in a sign of things to come they were booted off the stage before they could perform original material.

FIRST RECORDINGS

The band signed with EMI and released their first single, "Anarchy in the U.K.," in November 1976. One of the most iconic punk rock songs to date, "Anarchy" served as a virtual call to arms, pushing all the right angst-ridden buttons into a final scream to "Destroy!" EMI soon realized that it had more than it could handle in the Sex Pistols. During an infamous live appearance on the Bill Grundy show, a television show aired in London, Jones and Rotten uttered profanities numerous times, landing them on the front page of the tabloids. EMI dropped the band in January 1977.

Matlock was replaced by Sid Vicious (born John Simon Ritchie) in early 1977. Vicious was brought on more for his attitude and persona than for his musical ability. His ripped T-shirts, spiky hair, and leather jacket became staples of punk rock fashion. Although he learned some basic bass chords, his lack of skills was a running joke between band members and their fans. Shortly after Vicious joined the group, the Pistols signed with A&M Records, but the release of "God Save the Queen," their second single, was hampered by several factors relating to the band's violent behavior on a visit to the offices of A&M and in a brawl with another band. A&M severed the contract and destroyed 25,000 unreleased copies of the record. The Sex Pistols were subsequently signed by Virgin Records and faced a different problem there. Record plant employees refused to produce their record because they found the lyrics so offensive. Released during Queen Elizabeth II's Silver Jubilee, the single was banned by the BBC and almost every radio station in the United Kingdom.

In October 1977 they released their only studio LP, "Never Mind the Bollocks." The LP, which included four previously released hit singles, topped the album charts despite being banned by the major retailers Boots, W. H. Smith, and Woolworths. The ban was not much of a surprise, owing to the album's controversial title and the explicit lyrics. The band embarked on a supporting tour in the United Kingdom and followed up with a tour of the United States in 1978. The tour was mired in dysfunction. Vicious, suffering from heroin addiction and withdrawal, attacked fans and photographers; Rotten became increasingly disillusioned with the band and disgusted by Vicious's antics. The band played its final show in San Francisco.

Distancing himself from the band, Lydon dropped the name Johnny Rotten and formed Public Image Limited, experiencing commercial and critical success with 1979's *Metal Box*. Vicious moved to New York with Nancy Spungen and attempted to launch a solo career. The two shared a tumultuous and mutually abusive relationship. On October 12, 1978, Spungen was found dead from a knife wound, leading to the arrest of Vicious. He was released on bail, but he was arrested for physically assaulting Patti Smith's brother, Todd, in December of that year. He was released on February 1, 1979. Vicious died of a heroin overdose in the early morning after celebrating his release.

The band never reunited before Vicious died. McLaren spearheaded the release and recording of *The Great Rock and Roll Swindle* in 1979, piecing together recordings from Vicious, Cook, Jones, and replacement vocalist Ronald Biggs. Initially the remaining members were embroiled in legal proceedings concerning royalties and ownership of the band's material. Animosity lingered for a time, but the original four members reunited in 1996 for a brief tour.

Though the Sex Pistols were short-lived and only produced one album, the band's importance has been widely recognized. The Sex Pistols were, wrote John Rockwell in a 1977 *New York Times* article, "the best-known young band in the land. But those who know them don't necessarily understand them or like them. . . . The public's anger . . . has reached a point now that most concert halls and clubs refuse to book the band, the BBC won't play Sex Pistols records and most record stores won't stock them." But, he added, "their songs have a strength and individuality, both in the words in the music, that sets them above nearly every other so-called punk band."

Rolling Stone ranked them fifty-eighth in its 2005 list of "The Immortals," with Billie Joe Armstrong writing that their sole album "punched a huge hole in everything that was bullshit about rock music, and everything that was going wrong with the world, too. No one else has had that kind of impact with one album." Two years earlier *Rolling Stone* had ranked "Never Mind the Bollocks" forty-first in its list of the top 500 albums of all time, calling the record "the Sermon on the Mount of English punk."

The Sex Pistols were inducted into the Rock and Roll Hall of Fame in 2006, with that organization noting that "the group's stature" continued to grow long after its breakup and had strongly influenced many later, more commercially successful groups such as the Clash and Green Day. They "shocked and upend[ed] the music industry, reclaiming by force of will a place within it for those who were young, restless, bored and angry." True to form, the remaining band members refused to attend their induction ceremony.

Jeff Merron

SEE ALSO: *Dime Stores/Woolworth's; Green Day; The Monkees; Punk; Rock and Roll; Smith, Patti; The Who.*

BIBLIOGRAPHY

Armstrong, Billie Joe. "The Immortals: 58—The Sex Pistols." *Rolling Stone*, April 21, 2005.

Blashill, Pat; Anthony De Curtis; Ben Edmonds; et al. "The 500 Greatest Albums of All Time." *Rolling Stone*, December 11, 2003.

Hilburn, Robert. "The Sex Pistols: Second Thoughts." *Los Angeles Times*, March 24, 1979, B9.

Laing, Dave. *One Chord Wonders: Power and Meaning in Punk Rock*. London: Open University, 1985.

Rockwell, John. "The Sex Pistols—A Fired-Up Rock Band." *New York Times*, August 7, 1977, D16.

Savage, Jon. *England's Dreaming: Anarchy, Sex Pistols, Punk Rock, and Beyond*, rev. ed. New York: St. Martin's Griffin, 2001.

Sex Scandals

Scandals motivated by human sexuality have always been with us. From the Old Testament and those lustful Greek deities to the modern tabloids that obsessively monitor the erotic misadventures of celebrities and politicians, the sexual Achilles' heel of the human race has provided hot copy through the ages. Scandal has been defined as "grave loss of or injury to reputation" resulting from actual (or suspected) violation of morality, ethics, propriety, or law. Sex, deceit, bribery, power, excess, and fame are the key elements of most scandals. And, of course, it all has to be exposed in some publicized, often lurid fashion. As George C. Kohn notes in *The New Encyclopedia of American Scandal*: "There has to be some extra element as well—something untoward, shocking, or reprehensible to the public." Kohn might also add that there should be something infinitely fascinating.

THE WORLD OF ENTERTAINMENT

Artists and entertainers have always been considered innately scandalous, and in the early twentieth century, movies and sex became inextricably linked. In 1921 Roscoe "Fatty" Arbuckle,

Hollywood's most popular silent-era comedian, threw a party to celebrate his new $3 million contract. The three-day affair resulted in the death of a starlet, Virginia Rappe, who suffered a ruptured bladder and died three days later as a result of a questionable sexual encounter with the 266-pound Arbuckle. The comedian was charged with Rappe's rape and murder and became a symbol of all that appeared morally offensive in early Hollywood. Though he was acquitted, public opinion remained against him. His contract was canceled, his films banned, and he was no longer cast in Hollywood productions. By 1933 both Hollywood and the public had either forgiven Arbuckle or forgotten about the sordid incident, and he managed a comeback. However, just hours after completing his first film in over a decade, he died in his sleep of a heart attack in a New York hotel room.

William Randolph Hearst and actress Marion Davies indulged in a longtime affair that was only partially shielded by the newspaper mogul's wealth and power. The married Hearst became infatuated with Davies in the early 1920s. She became his mistress, and he relentlessly promoted her movie career. Hearst and Davies became the subject of an unresolved scandal when director Thomas Harper Ince died on the Hearst yacht in 1924. Though the final verdict was death by "heart attack due to acute indigestion," rumors of foul play persisted, including one that Ince had been accidentally shot in a fit of Hearst jealousy aimed at Charlie Chaplin. After the incident, the Hearst-Davies relationship continued. It was later fictionalized by Orson Welles in *Citizen Kane*, a 1941 film that enraged Hearst, though he was unable to suppress it with his vast media empire.

EVANGELISM, THE INTERNET, AND MORE SCANDALS

Sinclair Lewis explored the relationship between sex and evangelism in his famous novel *Elmer Gantry* (1926). Several decades later, in the 1980s, fiction became fact in a scandal involving evangelist Jim Bakker, who founded the PTL Television Network. With wife Tammy Faye, Bakker became embroiled in a lurid affair encompassing everything from embezzlement to wife swapping and homosexuality. The scandal was motivated by Bakker's brief extramarital liaison with Jessica Hahn and his ensuing attempt to bribe her into silence. Bakker was eventually forced to yield control of his lucrative empire to Jerry Falwell, and in 1987 Bakker was dismissed from serving as a minister in the Assemblies of God Church. The scandal did not subside even after he went to prison, as the tabloids gleefully continued to report on his alleged affair with a male inmate.

With the arrival of video sharing on the Internet in the twenty-first century, celebrity sex scandals became even more prurient. Suddenly, the "sex tapes" of celebrities were leaked online and viewed by millions. Hotel heiress Paris Hilton was among the first to be embroiled in such a scandal, but as the twenty-first century progressed, numerous singers, actors, and other celebrities found their careers briefly boosted by the "accidental" releases of video footage of them having sex.

SEX AND POLITICS

Political sex scandals are among the most time honored. In their book *One Nation under Sex* (2011), Larry Flynt and David Eisenbach explore the sexual adventures of major U.S. political figures, arguing that while these scandals have often been seen as damaging, or at least compromising to high political offices, they have been behind some of the most momentous events in history. The authors contend, for example, that Benjamin Franklin gained access to French government officials by sleeping with important women and, thus, persuaded France to support the Americans in the Revolutionary War. The highest office in the United States has not been immune to lurid affairs. In modern times, presidents such as Woodrow Wilson (who married his mistress) and Dwight D. Eisenhower (whose affair with his wartime driver, Kay Summersby, led to his falling out with Senator Joseph McCarthy in the 1950s) have succumbed to their desires.

JFK

John Fitzgerald Kennedy (JFK) was informally known as the "playboy" president, but his extracurricular sex life was carefully suppressed to maintain his well-publicized family image. His erotic exploits commenced while he was still a senator, and the first affair to endanger his presidency was with twenty-six-year-old playgirl Judy Campbell. Campbell, also known as Judith Exner, was also involved with Chicago mafia boss Salvatore "Sam" Giancana. Campbell eventually asserted that Kennedy had encouraged her sexual relationship with Giancana and used her as a courier to pass intelligence and money to the mob boss, with some of the funds being used to buy votes for Kennedy in the 1960 presidential election. In 1962 FBI chief J. Edgar Hoover, noted for his knowledge of Kennedy's sexual habits, lunched with the president, and the affair with Campbell came to an end shortly thereafter.

The affairs both JFK and his brother Bobby Kennedy had with Hollywood star Marilyn Monroe have continued to provoke speculation. These liaisons were cast into history by Monroe's sudden death in 1962, officially ruled a suicide, but rumors have persisted that she was murdered, either by mafia hit men or U.S. intelligence operatives. One investigator claimed that Bobby Kennedy and Monroe shared angry words shortly before her death when Kennedy, fearing public scandal, attempted to end the affair. However, key evidence vanished in the immediate wake of her death, and the truth may never be known.

The assassination of JFK in 1963 threw a sanctified shroud over any scandalous revelations for more than a decade. Thus, the American public was considerably jolted when, in 1975, word first leaked out concerning Campbell and Kennedy's other affairs. Kennedy's final involvement was with a Washington socialite, Mary Pinchot Meyer. The affair might have remained a secret if not for the bizarre fact that Meyer was murdered only eleven months after Kennedy's assassination and their relationship was revealed during the investigation.

MORE POLITICAL INTRIGUE

Of the later controversies surrounding the Kennedy family, the most publicized was a 1969 incident in which Senator Edward Kennedy's secretary, Mary Jo Kopechne, was killed when the car he was driving careened off a bridge on Chappaquiddick Island in Massachusetts. Kennedy did not report the fatal accident until the following morning, arousing suspicion of an illicit affair between the two. Kennedy pleaded guilty to leaving the scene of an accident, and after his driver's license was suspended and he was handed a two-month suspended jail sentence, local authorities closed the case. It was, however, reopened by the Massachusetts federal district attorney. No one was indicted in the closed inquest in October 1969, and while Kennedy won reelection to the Senate in 1970, the incident haunted him in his future failed bids to be president.

Almost twenty years later, Gary Hart was a leading contender for the 1988 Democratic presidential nomination. However, accusations of an extramarital affair with actress and model Donna Rice became an overriding campaign issue and thwarted his candidacy. The Hart affair also featured a backlash against the scandal mongering of the press, particularly the *Miami Herald*, which launched an aggressive investigation that included a secret stakeout of Hart's Washington town house. Though no proof of adultery was unearthed, the damage had been done. Before withdrawing from the race, Hart made the startling but true comment that if elected, he would not "be the first adulterer in the White House."

THE MONICA LEWINSKY AFFAIR

The twentieth century closed with the most graphically documented sex scandal in American history: the affair between President Bill Clinton and White House intern Monica Lewinsky, which dominated the American political landscape in 1998 and 1999. Lewinsky, twenty-seven years Clinton's junior, alleged that she and the president had been involved in a sexual relationship. The subsequent investigation was state-of-the-art, involving DNA testing and forensics, phone tapping, the Internet, and new buzzwords such as *censure-plus*. It was accompanied by reams of newspaper copy and an overload of TV coverage, not to mention a voluminous outpouring of commentary from a passionately divided American public. Further allegations of sexual harassment from other women threatened to derail Clinton's presidency.

Clinton was made to declare publicly the extent of his involvement with Lewinsky, but he did so in ways that led to accusations of perjury with convoluted explanations that included this famous defense: "It depends on what the meaning of the word *is* is." In contrast to the Kennedy affairs, the public was spared no detail of the Clinton incident, to the point where articles began popping up that counseled parents on how to explain the explicit revelations to their children.

After a prolonged investigation, a terse item appeared in the "Milestones" department of *Time* magazine's February 22, 1999, issue: "Acquitted, William Jefferson Clinton, 52, of perjury and obstruction-of-justice charges; by the U.S. Senate; in Washington (see cover story)." The headline of the cover story, however, took a deeper dive into the matter, reading, "How the Scandal Was Good for America." After the official verdict, a public consensus seemed to emerge indicating that while many people remained disapproving of Clinton's morals, most were satisfied with his performance as president and happy with the state of the American economy. With the support of his wife, Hillary, Clinton managed to rescue his reputation.

After the Clinton affair, it seemed that political sex scandals could go no further. That, however, has not been the case—the relationship between sex and power continues. Furthermore, it still has the power to destroy political careers. In 2011 a sex scandal once again impacted American politics, when Herman Cain, a candidate for the Republican presidential nomination, withdrew from the race in the face of sexual harassment allegations. Both Cain and his wife denied the charges, but again, the damage had been done.

THE CATHOLIC CHURCH

While political and show-business sex scandals have usually involved consenting adults, those that enveloped the Catholic Church in the first decade of the twenty-first century did not. The abuse of minors by Catholic priests was initially uncovered in the 1980s. However, it was not until 2001 that large-scale lawsuits alleging sex abuse by priests were filed—abuse that had been covered up by senior clergy. This was not the type of sex scandal that was beloved by tabloid editors. The abuse of children touched a raw nerve.

Over the following decade, thousands of cases emerged, mostly in the United States and Ireland, though dioceses around the world were implicated. At first, the church tried to downplay the abuse, claiming that the number of incidents was no greater than in other organizations. By 2002, however, around $1 billion had been spent on lawsuits, and widespread abuse going back many decades had been uncovered. Among the ramifications, the Catholic Church became more vigilant, making considerable efforts to provide a safer environment for children, in particular by removing abusers from contact with young people and by working with law enforcement and other agencies rather than dealing with allegations itself.

Ross Care

SEE ALSO: *Arbuckle, Fatty; Bakker, Jim, and Tammy Faye; Celebrity; Celebrity Couples;* Citizen Kane*; Evangelism; Hearst, William Randolph; Hilton, Paris; Hollywood; Hoover, J. Edgar; Lewinsky, Monica; Lewis, Sinclair; Mafia/Organized Crime; Media Feeding Frenzies; Monroe, Marilyn; Tabloids.*

BIBLIOGRAPHY

Brown, Peter Harry, and Patte B. Barham. *Marilyn: The Last Take.* New York: Dutton, 1992.

Canin, Ethan. "The Talk of the Town." *New Yorker*, October 5, 1998, 32–39.

Flynt, Larry, and David Eisenbach. *One Nation under Sex: How the Private Lives of Presidents, First Ladies, and Their Lovers Changed the Course of American History.* New York: Palgrave Macmillan, 2011.

Gibbs, Nancy. "Nightmare's End. Yes, It Was Wretched, and We're Glad to Wake Up. But Even Bad Dreams Can Serve Useful Purposes." *Time*, February 22, 1999, 32–37.

Gordon, William A. *The Ultimate Hollywood Tour Book: The Incomparable Guide to Movie Stars' Homes, Movie and TV Locations, Scandals, Murders, Suicides, and All the Famous Tourist Sites.* El Toro, CA: North Ridge Books, 1998.

Hersh, Seymour M. *The Dark Side of Camelot.* Boston: Little, Brown, 1997.

Kohn George C. *Encyclopedia of American Scandal from ABSCAM to the Zenger Case.* New York: Facts On File, 1989.

Lord, Lewis. "Jefferson Knew Value of Silence with Press." *U.S. News & World Report*, November 16, 1998, 66.

Miller, Hope Ridings. *Scandals in the Highest Office Facts and Fiction in the Private Lives of Our Presidents.* New York: Random House, 1973.

Wallace, Irving; Amy Wallace; David Wallechinsky; et al. *The Intimate Sex Lives of Famous People.* New York: Delacorte Press, 1981.

Sex Symbol

Sex symbols are celebrity women and men who are considered outstanding for their physical attractiveness and also represent physical and sexual archetypes. The sex symbol is, for the most part, a product of the movies, which have offered a dizzying variety of images to American audiences over the decades: the Vamp; the Red-Hot Mama; the Gold Digger; the Exotic Other; the Girl (and Guy) Next Door; the Femme Fatale, the Strong, Silent Type; the Sex Bomb; the Sex Kitten; the Latin Lover; the Matinee Idol; the Punk; and the Hunk, among many others. Such characterizations are important parts of every generation's relationship with the movies and with mass culture, but the golden age of the sex symbol was the 1950s, when the term was first used, and the 1960s. In this period, women such as Marilyn Monroe and Brigitte Bardot and men such as Marlon Brando and Elvis Presley pushed the boundaries of sexual behavior in popular entertainment.

Before films became popular entertainment in the 1910s, attractive models having particular standards of "desirability" were only seen in popular magazines in the form of the Gibson Girl and Gibson Guy illustrations. However, once Americans were able to attend films, it was possible for millions to see the same kinds of women and men being held up as models of beauty and sensuality on the silver screen. Over the years, practically the only threads of commonality to be found throughout the various manifestations of the movie sex symbol have been racial and ethnic. In the twentieth century, Hollywood sex symbols were almost always white, of northern or western European heritage, and American. There were, of course, convenient exceptions, real or invented. Rudolph Valentino, the "Latin Lover," was Italian, while Theda Bara, the woman who became known as "the Vamp," was billed as the daughter of an Arabian prince. In fact, she was the daughter of a European Jewish immigrants.

THE SILENT ERA

Bara was one of the first modern sex symbols. Born Theodosia Goodman in Ohio, she appeared as a vampire woman—hence, her nickname "the Vamp,"—in the 1915 film *A Fool There Was.* In contrast to the prevailing and desexualized image of wholesome European American womanhood embodied by Mary Pickford, Bara's Vamp embodied a dark, exotic, and foreign sensuality. This kind of sexuality was appropriated by some of the black blues divas of the 1920s, such as Bessie Smith, Sippie Wallace, and Ma Rainey, and inspired the sexually liberated "flappers" of that decade.

In later films such as *The Vixen* (1916) and *The She-Devil* (1918), Bara's Vamp entraps men with her sexual wiles only to be punished in the end for transgressing gender roles. Bara's career in film was short-lived—she retired in 1921—and much of her identity as a sex symbol was invented. She was almost thirty when she made her first film, though she claimed to be twenty-five, and her "Arabian" origins were a fabrication by the Fox publicity department. Nevertheless, the figure of the Vamp that she pioneered has remained important in American film.

In the 1920s, when the androgynous flapper look was in vogue, Mae West, with her unfashionably curvaceous figure and unapologetic bawdiness, offered the Red-Hot Mama as a counterpoint to the more popular ingenue or girl-next-door image of stars such as Clara Bow. Known for her humorous quips and innuendo ("Come up sometime and see me?"; "What're you doin', honey? Makin' love or takin' inventory?"); for styling one of her characters as "Lady Lou, one of the finest women whoever walked the streets"; and even for being jailed for obscenity in 1926, West both exuded sexuality and contained it through humor. She played the Red-Hot-Mama role well into her eighties. Sexual transgressiveness has also been a part of West's camp appeal to gay men, especially with her role in the 1970 film adaptation of Gore Vidal's *Myra Breckinridge*, a romp in polymorphous sexuality.

THE 1930s

In the Depression-ravaged 1930s, Hollywood crafted the Gold Digger in the person of Jean Harlow. Harlow's platinum-blond hair and wisecracking persona set her in the tradition of West, but her brassy, open sensuality seemed disconcerting from the mouth of a sweet-looking young woman who was "out to make a killing" in more ways than one. "Would you be shocked if I changed into something more comfortable?" she asks in *Hell's Angels* (1930). The Hays Production Code, which set rules for the depiction of sexuality in the movies in the 1930s, is often seen in part as a response to Harlow's unabashed sensuality.

The other major sex symbol archetype of the 1930s was represented by Swedish actress Greta Garbo, the Exotic Other. Interest in Garbo seemed to stem mainly from the fact that she was foreign, different, and could therefore be made to symbolize whatever the viewer desired. Always carefully made up and glamorous, Garbo exuded a melancholy persona that seemed designed to draw viewers into her personal torment. When, in *Grand Hotel* (1932), she utters her famous line about wanting to be left alone, audiences responded to her faintly mysterious Swedish accent and swooned over her noble, classy, and discreet suffering. On-screen, male characters want her, but she always wants the wrong men. Her allure for American audiences was so great that after she retired from acting in 1941, she remained the object of cultish obsession. Don McPherson and Louise Brody fuel this myth in their profile of Garbo in *Leading Ladies: Photographs from the Kobal Collection*, claiming that she "remained an enigmatic and unreachable phenomenon. . . . It is not so much a face as a shadow of one, suggested by isolated glimpses and memories, inscrutable and austere."

WORLD WAR II

World War II ushered in the era of the sex symbol as a pinup, the suggestive photos that graced lockers, military barracks, and the nose cones of airplanes in all theaters of war. Actresses who had made their reputations before the war, including Betty Grable, Rita Hayworth, Jane Russell, Veronica Lake, and Lana Turner, were suddenly in great demand in "pinup" form, usually as images characterizing the sex roles for which they were known. The two most popular wartime versions were the wholesome Girl Next Door (personified by Grable) and the Femmes Fatale (Hayworth, Russell, Lake, Turner). The stylized poses of these actresses—the most famous being that of Grable in shorts and high heels, showing off her cleavage and million-dollar gams—offered a femininity that seemed to be missing at home, where wives and girlfriends were working in factories. They provided reminders of the peacetime normality that had women filling traditional roles. If Grable's look was that of the "good girl," the pinups of Hayworth, Russell, and Turner smoldered openly. These women's provocative poses promised a sexuality just out of reach and a vision of American womanhood worth fighting for.

World War II had a profound effect on the representation and symbolization of sexuality in general. The term *bombshell* entered the American lexicon as a reference to the openly sexual woman, pointing not only to her power over men but also to her potential for destroying those same men, as well as herself. A woman's sexuality, according to this logic, was dangerous, in need of containment, lest the hapless male end up obliterated by the sex bomb. Coming partly from the portrayals of hard-boiled Femmes Fatales in the popular 1940s-era movies from the film noir genre and partly from an anxiety over destabilized gender roles during wartime, the association of a woman's sexuality with danger continued to linger in American popular culture. This same threatening sexuality led to the naming of the bikini bathing suit after the Bikini Atoll on which nuclear weapons were tested in the 1940s and 1950s, and the voguish slang word *atomic* was used to describe a desirable woman.

THE MONROE ERA

The most famous sex symbol of the 1950s was Monroe, an Ingenue-cum-Sex Bomb who oozed sexuality but seemed never to recognize it. Her on-screen persona, that of the breathy, innocent girl, provided a welcome return to clear gender roles, to a kind of idyllic sexual past. She is not attired in a sexless coverall like the wartime factory workers. Rather than work, she prefers to marry a millionaire, and once married, she has no intentions of chewing him up and spitting him out like a Gold Digger or a Femme Fatale. She wants true love, too, in a reassuring return to "lost" femininity.

In his book *Marilyn Monroe: The Biography*, Donald Spoto explains that she represented "the post-war ideal of the American girl, soft, transparently needy, worshipful of men, naïve, offering sex without demands." Beyond the film persona, Monroe herself often wanted to be "taken seriously," marrying the American dramatist Arthur Miller and seeking more challenging film roles, but she never managed to separate herself from her Sex Bomb image. At times, she became a parody of herself, such as with her famous birthday serenade to her sometimes lover, President John F. Kennedy.

Latching on to Monroe's huge popularity, other studios tried to create their own Sex Bombs. American actresses such as Mamie Van Doren, Jayne Mansfield, and Kim Novak and foreigners such as Bardot, Sophia Loren, and Gina Lollobrigida were cast in roles emphasizing their sexual power. Still, no others quite reached the stratospheric heights of Monroe in popular consciousness. Monroe and the other Sex Bombs represented one version of womanhood in the 1950s, promising a kind of power in sensuality. Doris Day offered another: smart, sporty, and a perpetual virgin. If Monroe was the kind of girl men lusted after to scratch their seven-year itch, Day was the not-so-dumb blond, the kind of girl men married.

Monroe's influence in the 1950s went beyond her carefully managed Hollywood sensuality. In 1953, the year she appeared in *Gentlemen Prefer Blondes*, she was featured on the cover of the very first issue of Hugh Hefner's *Playboy* magazine. The nude photographs came from a photo shoot in 1949, before she was famous, and Monroe had already won public sympathy by admitting she did the work because she was broke. Both Mansfield and Novak appeared in*Playboy* during the 1950s and 1960s, adding to their status as sex symbols and rewarding an "adult" male audience in ways that were impossible in their mainstream movie appearances.

THE 1960s AND 1970s

Monroe's death from a drug overdose in 1962 was for many people evidence of the perils of unrestrained female sexuality and its tragic consequences. It showed that the sexually liberated woman was desperately unhappy and a danger to herself. Thus, the 1960s offered up a range of sex symbols who seemed designed to counter the overkill of the 1950s-era Sex Bomb. Women such as Julie Christie, Twiggy, and Jean Shrimpton were a different sort of sexy. Pretty in a healthy (Christie) or a waifish (Twiggy and Shrimpton) way, these actresses and models were, as Sheila Rowbotham describes them in *A Century of Women*, "descendants of Doris Day . . . adapted to an era when virginity was no longer feasible or fashionable." Even stars who seemed closer to the Sex Bomb role—Jane Fonda, Raquel Welch, Faye Dunaway—were, in the end, very much a part of the youthful, no-nonsense image of the Icon.

By the 1970s—perhaps because attitudes about sex had become more relaxed in mainstream society or because women had begun to find new roles for themselves—female sex symbols combined almost cartoonish physical attractiveness with improbable practical skills. The rooms of many teenage boys were decorated with posters of Farrah Fawcett, Cheryl Tiegs, and other "all-American" women (blond, blue-eyed, fair-skinned) posing semiprovocatively in swimsuits. However, while television shows such as *Charlie's Angels* (1976–1981), *Three's Company* (1976–1984), and *The New Adventures of Wonder Woman* (1975–1979) promote various revisions of the sex symbols from decades past, much of the action in these programs involves the stars physically fighting, and beating, men.

The women of *Charlie's Angels*—Fawcett, Cheryl Ladd, and Jaclyn Smith—are smart and resourceful but who also happen to look lovely in the revealing outfits their crime-fighting efforts seem to require. In *Three's Company*, Suzanne Somers offers a return to the Ingenue-Sex Bomb. She is blond, sweet, and not too bright, and her antics, comic misunderstandings, tight blouses, and short shorts are among the show's main attractions. Lynda Carter's Wonder Woman is a street-savvy superhero who just so happens to fight crime wearing a strapless, red, white, and blue bathing suit and go-go boots. The 1960s and 1970s also marked the introduction of nonwhite sex symbols into American popular culture, such as Pam Grier, the African American star of the early 1970s blaxpoitation films.

THE 1980s AND 1990s

Changing standards in film, particularly the introduction of more female nudity and explicit sexual content, may have contributed to the shift away from sex symbols as such. The female sex symbol's mystique is, after all, predicated in part on her mystery, on the audience's desire to know more about her.

Sex symbols of the 1980s and 1990s seemed to be reinventions of past models. Elvira, Mistress of the Dark, harkened back to the Vamp with her dark clothing, ample cleavage, and promises of gothic intrigue. The Red-Hot Mama was reborn in Bette Midler, whose stage performances as "the Divine Miss M" depicted her as the reincarnation of West's brassy, wisecracking dame who knew a thing or two about sex and wasn't afraid to say so. The Femme Fatale was personified by Kathleen Turner and Sharon Stone, among others—women who used their sexual wiles to manipulate and even destroy the men they claimed to love. Cindy Crawford and Claudia Schiffer seemed to combine their roles as exotic fashion models with that of the down-to-earth gal to play the role of the Girl Next Door. No-nonsense talk-show pals one minute and hot-and-sultry catwalk models the next, they offered both public and supposedly private visions of what that girl would be like. Kate Moss, particularly in her Calvin Klein advertisements, assumed the role of the Waifish Icon, seemingly vulnerable and desirable at once. Pop singer Madonna developed a series of onstage personae that both exploited these archetypes and challenged their validity as representations of female sexuality and identity.

MALE SEX SYMBOLS

Although the female sex symbol has dominated American popular culture, male sex symbols have existed alongside them—from Valentino in the days of silent cinema to Humphrey Bogart, Cary Grant, and Frank Sinatra in the mid-twentieth century to Brad Pitt, George Clooney, and Daniel Craig in the twenty-first century. The Matinee Idol has been the primary manifestation of the male sex symbol. Actors such as Grant, Clark Gable, and Rock Hudson captivated moviegoers during their heydays with their suave masculinity, classic good looks, and promises of economic security. The 1950s also saw the introduction of the male sex symbol as Bad Boy. Both Elvis Presley and James Dean played this role when their shaking hips, brooding looks, and sullen demeanors made young girls swoon and parents worry. Good-looking stars of the 1960s such as Paul Newman, Robert Redford, and Warren Beatty combined the Matinee Idol with the Bad Boy, often playing the parts of criminals or outsiders with "hearts of gold," notably Redford and Newman in *Butch Cassidy and the Sundance Kid* (1969) and Beatty in *Bonnie and Clyde* (1967).

In the 1970s the Sex Machine arrived on the scene. Burt Reynolds posed nude in *Cosmopolitan* in 1972, while *Playgirl* magazine, featuring nude men, was introduced in 1973 as a "counterpoint" to *Playboy*, attracting a readership of women and gay men. Singers such as Tom Jones found that their female fans threw underwear at them during live shows. As with female sex symbols, the first nonwhite male sex symbols appeared during the 1970s, particularly as a result of blaxploitation films such as *Shaft* (1971), whose theme song promises that its star, Richard Roundtree, is a "sex machine with all the chicks," and *Dolemite* (1975), starring Rudy Ray Moore. These stars embodied the Sex Machine role, turning women on-screen into putty with their sexual prowess and doing the same to fans in the audience. This particular vision also partook of cultural folklore and stereotype about the virility of black males. Other male sex symbols of the 1970s assumed a James Bond–type image of a man as suave and sexually irresistible.

In the 1980s and 1990s, male sex symbols included Richard Gere, Harrison Ford, Tom Cruise, Johnny Depp, Leonardo DiCaprio, and Mark Wahlberg. Like their female counterparts, they combined elements of various manifestations of the sex symbols of generations past to create their screen personae.

THE CONTEMPORARY SEX SYMBOL

As the twenty-first century began, a new kind of celebrity culture had taken hold, in which people from outside the usual Hollywood and old media spheres could become famous and, in their own ways, sex symbols. Paris Hilton, a multimillionaire hotel heiress whose sex tape was leaked online in 2003, became the subject of tabloid fantasies overnight. Meanwhile, the global media fixated on the off-field exploits of certain desirable athletes. Perhaps the most notable of these is David Beckham, a British soccer player who is also famous as a model. Beckham appeared tattooed and shirtless in an ad for H&M underwear during the 2012 Super Bowl.

In the early twenty-first century, Hollywood and the music industry retained the power to create sex symbols as a way of selling their products, but there is a sense that individuals are less important than they were in the era of Monroe and Dean. Singers such as Rihanna and Katy Perry and movie stars such as Christian Bale and Scarlett Johansson may have taken on the sex symbol mantle, but changing attitudes toward sex, the ubiquitous mass media, and the possibilities for self-promotion offered by the Internet have diminished the value of sex symbols in the twenty-first century.

Deborah M. Mix

SEE ALSO: *Bara, Theda; Beatty, Warren; Blaxploitation Films; Bogart, Humphrey;* Bonnie and Clyde*; Brando, Marlon;* Butch Cassidy and the Sundance Kid*; Celebrity;* Charlie's Angels*; Clooney, George; Crawford, Cindy; Cruise, Tom; Day, Doris; Dean, James; Depp, Johnny; DiCaprio, Leonardo; Fawcett, Farrah; Film Noir; Fonda, Jane; Ford, Harrison; Gable, Clark; Garbo, Greta; Gere, Richard; Grable, Betty; Grant, Cary; Grier, Pam; Harlow, Jean; Hayworth, Rita; Hilton, Paris; Hudson, Rock; The Internet; Jones, Tom; Madonna; Mansfield, Jayne; Midler, Bette; Monroe, Marilyn; Moss, Kate; Newman, Paul; Novak, Kim; Perry, Katy; Pitt, Brad;* Playboy*;* Playgirl*; Presley, Elvis; Redford, Robert; Reynolds, Burt; Rihanna; Roundtree, Richard; Russell, Jane; Sex Scandals; Sexual Revolution;* Shaft*; Sinatra, Frank; Television;* Three's Company*; Turner, Lana; Twiggy; Valentino, Rudolph; West, Mae.*

BIBLIOGRAPHY

Da, Lottie, and Jan Alexander. *Bad Girls of the Silver Screen.* New York: Carroll and Graf, 1989.

MacPherson, Don, and Louise Brody. *Leading Ladies: Photographs from the Kobal Collection.* New York: St. Martin's Press, 1986.

Norman, Barry. *The Story of Hollywood.* New York: New American Library, 1988.

Rowbotham, Sheila. *A Century of Women.* New York: Penguin, 1997.

Shipman, David. *The Story of Cinema.* New York: St. Martin's Press, 1982.

Spoto, Donald. *Marilyn Monroe: The Biography.* London: Arrow Books, 1994.

Sexting

Sexting (a combination of the words *sex* and *texting*) is the act of sending explicit photographs and/or texts via cell phones or the Internet. Teens make up the majority of sexters, though adults also sext. The practice typically occurs between people who know each other, but anonymous, or location-based, sexting is sometimes used to seek out sexual partners in a given proximity.

Humans have long used available technologies to enhance, extend, or experiment with sex. In their essay in *Sexual Addic-*

tion & Compulsivity, researchers Robert Weiss and Charles P. Samenow characterize sexting as part of a wave of increased sexual access in the digital age. Recent digital predecessors to sexting include bulletin boards (BBS) and newsgroups; chat rooms; webcams; and porn, classified, and prostitution sites. Sexting is often considered to be distinct from previous forms because the original message can be easily replicated and forwarded. People sext for a variety of reasons, such as to enhance their popularity, bully, increase intimacy, or experiment.

Teens who sext enter murky legal territory. For example, Vermont lawmakers passed a bill in 2009 to legalize the consensual exchange of graphic images between people ages thirteen to eighteen so that sexting would be dealt with in juvenile courts and the offenders would not be subject to sex offender registry requirements. In other states, such as Ohio, Illinois, and Nebraska, sexting is a misdemeanor and convicted sexters are not subject to sex offender registration.

Within the adult population, sexting has been associated with infidelity due to several high-profile cases, such as those of professional golfer Tiger Woods and U.S. Representative Anthony Weiner. In 2009 more than a dozen women stated that they had engaged in extramarital affairs with Woods, and many produced sexts as evidence. Weiner used Twitter to send sexually explicit texts and photos to women other than his wife. However, not all sexts are intertwined with illicit affairs. Oprah Winfrey, the popular talk show host and billionaire executive, has advocated for relationship expert Michael Fiore's "Text the Romance Back" program, the purpose of which is to use texting to reinvigorate romances.

Due to the relative newness of sexting, long-term studies on it do not yet exist, though several are ongoing. Responses to sexting in popular culture range from nonchalance to the feeling that it should be regarded as a criminal act. Many experts are unconvinced that sexting is a true epidemic. In fact, articles have been written that portray the backlash against sexting as more of an epidemic of fuzzy math and moral panic.

Dayna Goldstein

SEE ALSO: *Cell Phones; The Internet; Sex Scandals; Smartphones; Texting; Twitter; Winfrey, Oprah; Woods, Tiger.*

BIBLIOGRAPHY

Bialik, Carl. "Which Is Epidemic—Sexting or Worrying about It?" *Wall Street Journal*, April 8, 2009.

Lumby, Catherine, and Nina Funnell. "Between Heat and Light: The Opportunity in Moral Panics. *Crime, Media, Culture*, December 2011, 277–291.

Weiss, Robert, and Charles P. Samenow. "Smart Phones, Social Networking, Sexting and Problematic Sexual Behaviors—A Call for Research." *Sexual Addiction & Compulsivity*, 17, no. 4 (2010). Accessed May 2012. Available from http://www.tandfonline.com/doi/full/10.1080/10720162.2010.532079

Sexual Harassment

In the 1990s sexual harassment became a highly visible part of American pop culture. Anita Hill testified in a televised U.S. Senate hearing in 1991 that Supreme Court nominee Clarence Thomas had sexually harassed her when she worked for him in the early 1980s at the Equal Employment Opportunity Commission. Thomas was confirmed, but by a very close vote of 52–48. Some of the senators who voted in favor of his confirmation were defeated for reelection in 1992. In 1994 Paula Jones accused President Bill Clinton of sexually harassing her when he was governor of Arkansas and she was an employee of the state. Jones's lawsuit was dismissed in 1998, but a deposition President Clinton gave about his relationship with Monica Lewinsky, a former White House intern, triggered an investigation by independent counsel Kenneth Starr that resulted in Starr recommending to Congress that the president be impeached.

THE DEFINITION

Sexual harassment is defined as unwelcome sexual advances and requests for sexual favors. Other verbal or physical conduct of a sexual nature constitutes sexual harassment when submission or rejection of this conduct explicitly or implicitly affects an individual's employment; unreasonably interferes with an individual's work performance; or creates an intimidating, hostile, or offensive work environment. The two types of harassment are quid pro quo and hostile environment. Quid pro quo, or "this for that," exists when an employee's supervisor or a person of higher employment rank demands sexual favors from a subordinate in exchange for tangible job benefits. Hostile environment, or environmental harassment, is a pattern of intimidating, hostile, or offensive behavior that affects the person being harassed.

Federal laws on sexual harassment have existed since Congress passed Title VII of the 1964 Civil Rights Act and Title IX of the 1972 Education Amendments. Title VII prohibits sex discrimination in employment; sexual harassment is considered a form of sex discrimination. Title IX prohibits sex discrimination in education. The laws began to have effect when in 1980, and again in 1988, the Equal Employment Opportunity Commission issued guidelines to define sexual harassment.

KEY SUPREME COURT DECISIONS

The courts have defined sexual harassment more precisely and have been involved in resolving key issues. In 1986, in *Meritor Savings Bank v. Vinson*, the Supreme Court ruled that quid pro quo sexual harassment was a form of sex discrimination under Title VII. In the *Meritor* case, the Supreme Court made an important distinction, affirming that a victim may comply voluntarily with sexually harassing behavior but may not welcome it. If it is unwelcome, it is sexual harassment. The *Meritor* case also set a precedent because it established employer liability for acts of sexual harassment committed by its employees. The court ruled that quid pro quo and environmental harassment are two distinct claims but that they can, and often do, occur at the same time. It is necessary, however, to distinguish between these points when employer liability is being determined; the employer is always liable in quid pro quo harassment but may not always be liable in hostile environment cases.

In education, the Supreme Court significantly expanded protection for student victims in *Christine Franklin, Petitioner v. Gwinnett County Public Schools and William Prescott* on February 26, 1992. For the first time, students had the right to win monetary damages from schools that receive federal funds. This decision provided strong motivation for schools to engage in proactive strategies to prevent sexual harassment. An area of

Paula Jones Arrives for Deposition. *Paula Jones, woman on right, is swarmed by reporters as she arrives to give a deposition in her sexual harassment lawsuit against President Bill Clinton in January 1998.* HARRY HAMBURG/NY DAILY NEWS ARCHIVE/GETTY IMAGES.

ongoing concern is the presence of sexual harassment within the pervasive problem of bullying in American society.

On November 9, 1993, the Supreme Court ruled in *Harris v. Forklift Systems* that harassing conduct need not seriously affect an employee's psychological well-being or cause the plaintiff to suffer injury. On March 4, 1998, the court ruled again, in *Oncale v. Sundowner Offshore Services*, that same-sex harassment in the workplace violates federal law. In 2009 in *Crawford v. Nashville*, the court extended protection from retaliation to employees who merely cooperate with an internal probe.

The Hill-Thomas hearings led to more legislation. On November 21, 1991, titles I, II, and III of the 1991 Civil Rights Act were passed. Title I expands the rights of sexual harassment victims to enable them to collect monetary damages. Title II, commonly referred to as the "Glass Ceiling Act of 1991," encourages corporate practices and policies that promote opportunities for, and eliminate artificial barriers to, the advancement of women and minorities into higher-level positions. Title III focuses on fair employment practices and covers employees of the House of Representatives, Senate, and Executive Office of the President.

MILITARY INCIDENTS

The military faced the issue of sexual harassment in September 1991 when the "Tailhook" scandal became public. A female navy helicopter pilot, Lieutenant Paula Coughlin, complained to Rear Admiral John Snyder that she had been physically and indecently assaulted on September 7, 1991, by a group of naval officers at the 1991 Tailhook Symposium at the Las Vegas Hilton in Nevada. Rear Admiral Duvall M. "Mac" Williams was requested to open an investigation, which was initiated on October 11, 1991. Snyder was relieved of his command for dealing inappropriately with Coughlin's complaint. On February 7, 1994, Coughlin resigned from the navy, saying her departure was the result of the retaliation she had experienced due to her complaint.

Coughlin filed civil lawsuits against the Tailhook Association and the Las Vegas Hilton. She settled with the Tailhook Association for $400,000 before the trial began. On October 28, 1994, a jury in Las Vegas decided that the Las Vegas Hilton Hotel was negligent because it had failed to provide adequate security during the 1991 Tailhook Convention. The jury awarded Coughlin $1.7 million in damages. On October 31, 1994, the jury ordered the Las Vegas Hilton and its parent company to pay Coughlin $5 million in punitive damages for a total award of $6.7 million, an amount later reduced to $5.3 million.

In November 1996 the U.S. Army brought charges of rape and sexual harassment against military trainers at the Army Ordnance Center at Aberdeen Proving Ground, Maryland. According to the Pentagon, there were more than a dozen victims, all of whom were female soldiers in their second eight weeks of training. The army charged twelve staff members of Aberdeen with sex crimes ranging from inappropriate sexual comments to rape. In September 1997, the army issued a report acknowledging that sexual harassment and discrimination were prevalent.

THE POLITICAL ARENA

The Jones case broke legal ground when the Supreme Court ruled that a sitting president can be sued for actions that occurred before he or she took office and that the case can proceed while the president is still in office. The case went forward and depositions were taken, including a deposition from President Clinton in January 1998 that questioned whether he had engaged in sexual relations with Lewinsky. In March 1998 judge Susan Webber Wright ruled that Lewinsky was "not essential to the core issues" of Jones's case and ordered all evidence related to Lewinsky to be excluded from the proceedings. Judge Wright dismissed the Jones's lawsuit on April 1, 1998.

However, President Clinton's legal troubles did not end with the dismissal of Jones's lawsuit. While under oath during his deposition in the Jones's case, he denied having sexual relations with Lewinsky. Starr requested and received permission to investigate whether the president had lied under oath. After a seven-month investigation, Starr reported to Congress that there were possible grounds for impeachment. The House voted to impeach the president, and the Senate conducted the trial to decide whether to remove him from office. The Senate vote fell far short of the two-thirds majority needed to remove him.

Since Clinton left office in 2001, other politicians have been involved in sexual harassment scandals. For example, Herman Cain was a contender for the 2012 Republican presidential nomination until reports surfaced that two sexual harassment cases had been brought against him when he was the head of the National Restaurant Association in the 1990s. The ensuing scandal prompted Cain to suspend his presidential campaign.

CELEBRITY SCANDALS

Celebrities have also been the subjects of sexual harassment cases, including one involving Isiah Thomas, who was head coach and general manager of the National Basketball Association's New York Knicks. In October 2007 Thomas and Madison Square Garden (owner of the Knicks) were found guilty of sexually harassing Anucha Browne Sanders. Madison Square Garden was ordered to pay Sanders $6 million for condoning a hostile work environment and $2.6 million for retaliation. Madison Square Garden chairman James Dolan was ordered to pay $3 million for harassing Sanders and firing her from her $260,000-a-year job out of spite.

Bill O'Reilly, host of *The O'Reilly Factor* on the Fox News Channel, was accused of sexual harassment by Andrea Mackris, a producer for the network, in 2004. Mackris filed a lawsuit alleging O'Reilly had made a series of explicit phone calls to her, advised her to use a vibrator, and told her about his sexual fantasies involving her. O'Reilly filed a lawsuit accusing Mackris and her lawyer of trying to extort $60 million in hush money to make the case go away. The case was settled out of court in October 2004. While the terms of the settlement were not disclosed, the *New York Daily News*, citing unidentified sources, reported that O'Reilly had agreed to pay Mackris anywhere from $2 million to $10 million.

Social networking and text messaging have had growing roles in sexual harassment cases. When Brett Favre was the quarterback for the National Football League's New York Jets in 2008, he text-messaged a massage therapist employed by the team suggesting that she and another therapist have a sexual encounter with him. The two therapists filed a sexual harassment complaint against Favre in a New York court on January 2011. In May 2011 Congressman Anthony Weiner used Twitter to send a photo of himself in his underwear to at least six women. The photo wound up going viral on the Internet. While no sexual harassment case was filed against Weiner, he resigned from Congress on June 16 of that year.

Sexual harassment in America has evolved from a behavior without a name to a precisely defined legal and highly visible social transgression. It is pervasive and impacts people in all walks of life.

Rosemarie Skaine

SEE ALSO: *Anita Hill–Clarence Thomas Senate Hearings; Lewinsky, Monica; O'Reilly, Bill; Sex Scandals; Sexting; Starr, Kenneth; Thomas, Isiah.*

BIBLIOGRAPHY

Farley, Lin. *Sexual Shake Down: Sexual Harassment of Women on the Job.* New York: McGraw-Hill, 1978.

MacKinnon, Catharine A. *Sexual Harassment of Working Women: A Case of Sex Discrimination.* New Haven, CT: Yale University Press, 1979.

Skaine, Rosemarie. *Power and Gender: Issues in Sexual Dominance and Harassment.* Jefferson, NC: McFarland, 1996.

Skaine, Rosemarie. *Women at War: Gender Issues of Americans in Combat.* Jefferson, NC: McFarland, 1998.

Starr, Kenneth. *The Starr Report: The Independent Counsel's Complete Report to Congress on the Investigation of President Clinton.* New York: Pocket Books, 1998.

Strauss, Susan. *Sexual Harassment and Bullying: A Guide to Keeping Kids Safe and Holding Schools Accountable.* Lanham, MD: Rowman & Littlefield, 2011.

Vander Schaaf, Derek J. *Tailhook 91, Part 1—Review of the Navy Investigations.* Washington, DC: Department of Defense, Office of the Inspector General, 1992.

Sexual Revolution

Reports of a "sexual revolution" first appeared in the media in the mid-1960s, identifying a number of trends and developments throughout American society. Midway through the decade, the popularity of rock music; the increased use among youths of marijuana, hallucinogenics such as LSD, and other drugs; widespread public displays of nudity; and a new openness about sexuality contributed to the awareness of a radical cultural change.

Public interest in sex had been growing since the late 1940s, and the number of novels, magazine articles, and advice books on the subject grew to epic proportions. Already in the 1950s, several novels that had previously been banned because of their sexual explicitness—such as D. H. Lawrence's *Lady Chatterley's Lover* (1928) and Henry Miller's *Tropic of Cancer* (1934)—began to be published in the United States. Advice books such as *Sex and the Single Girl* (1962) by *Cosmopolitan* editor Helen Gurley Brown and *The Sensuous Woman* (1969) by Joan Garrity rolled off the presses.

Betty Friedan's *The Feminine Mystique* (1963) initiated the revival of feminism and stimulated the discussion of sex and gender roles. Popular sociologists such as Vance Packard in *The Sexual Wilderness: The Contemporary Upheaval in Male-Female Relationships* (1968) explored the interplay of both feminism and the sexual revolution. In 1966 Drs. William Masters and Virginia Johnson published the first of their scientific studies, *Human Sexual Response*. Sexually explicit pulp novels (such as Jacqueline Susann's *Valley of the Dolls*, 1966) and movies (such as *I Am Curious (Yellow)*, 1967) attempted to satisfy the public's growing hunger for the vicarious experience of sex. By the 1970s, newspapers with names such as *Screw*, offering sexual information, personal ads, and sexually explicit photos and art, were available on street corners in larger American cities. These cultural developments demonstrated an increased public interest in sex and suggested that sexual behavior was undergoing changes as well.

A DEFINITION

What *sexual revolution* means, when it began (if it did), to whom it applied, and what changes it wrought are highly contested subjects. According to sociologists, there is no doubt that the pattern of sexual partnering underwent a significant change in the 1960s, and it was this shift away from monogamy that is usually signified by the term *sexual revolution*. However, the revolution that emerged in the 1960s was as much about attitude as conduct.

Changes in the way people thought about sexuality and gender roles stimulated new modes of behavior that were not always measured by increased sexual activity. For example, women entered marriage with greater sexual experience and confidence than in the past. As a result, there was an increased demand for sexual satisfaction in marriage. This contributed to the growth of a market for books and magazine articles about how to improve one's sex life, as well as a greater demand for marriage manuals and counselors. It may have also led to an increase in divorces, which reinforced the likelihood that these estranged couples would have other sexual partners in their lifetimes. These developments also challenged the double standard, which permitted men to engage in sexual activity outside their marriages but harshly stigmatized women who did so. In the end, there was both increased frustration and greater freedom. Friedan's *The Feminine Mystique* capitalized on precisely these developments—thus, the emergence of feminism and women's rights overlapped with and were intertwined with the developments later labeled "the sexual revolution."

BACKGROUND

The sexual revolution as it emerged in the 1960s was the historical culmination of processes that began during World War II. The term *revolution* usually implies something that occurs rapidly and dramatically. However, the time frame of the sexual revolution is much longer. In terms of longevity, it most resembles the Industrial Revolution, which was the transition in the eighteenth and nineteenth centuries from an agricultural society to one built on new technologies and industrial production. The sexual revolution was an immense and contradictory process, often not very obvious and stretching over two generations. It radically altered the sex/gender system, as anthropologist Gayle Rubin has called the system that translates biological capacities into the cultural and social patterns that constitute our lives as gendered and sexual human beings.

The sexual revolution started as a result of three major cultural forces: first, the explosion of youth culture and the thirst for sexual experiences before marriage by young men and women; second, the emergence of feminism and the women's movement at the end of the 1960s; and third, the gay liberation movement's dramatic Stonewall rebellion in 1969, in which homosexuals in New York City demonstrated against the police. However, the sexual revolution also provoked a profound and powerful counterrevolution: the emergence of the religious fundamentalist right, which continues to wage its battle.

During World War II, the mobilization of men for the armed services and the recruitment of female factory workers initiated a profound shift in social relations in the United States. Young men and women left the havens of their families and lived among other people, far from parental guidance. Most of these men and women were in their late teens and twenties and were entering their most sexually active stages. Furthermore, they were usually unmarried. This generation had grown up during the Great Depression and was heavily influenced by the exuberant and freewheeling nature of swing—a cultural explosion roughly analogous to the rock culture of the 1960s. Throughout the war years, young men and women—in constant motion and under the uncertainty and stress of the military conflict—engaged in sexual relations with each other outside of marriage and other constraining contexts.

THE KINSEY REPORTS

Recognition of the sexual revolution dawned slowly after the war. The publication of Alfred Kinsey's two groundbreaking volumes on human sexuality, *Sexual Behavior in the Human Male* (1948) and *Sexual Behavior in the Human Female* (1953), probably exerted greater influence on modern conceptions of sexuality than any works since Sigmund Freud's. Moral outrage and professional hypocrisy greeted the reports, but few Americans remained immune to a new awareness of sexual behavior.

Kinsey was so struck by the extraordinary extent of individual variations in sexual behavior that he argued that any attempt to establish uniform standards was both impracticable and unjust. He believed that his discovery of the widespread deviations from accepted standards showed that attempts to regulate sexual behavior were doomed to failure, and "the only proper sexual policy was no policy at all." The Kinsey reports were not based on the generation that experienced the postwar sexual revolution—rather, they focused on the inter-war generations. Although much of his data would later be discredited due to its reliance on prison-population males (represented in his research as the average male), the reports came to symbolize the idea of a sexual revolution in the popular American consciousness.

SOCIAL TRENDS

Most of what we mean by sexual revolution refers to nonmarital sexual activity. By the early 1960s, shifts had begun to take place along several fronts that consolidated the sexual revolution. One of the most important was that young men and women engaged in their first acts of sexual intercourse at increasingly younger ages. The impact of earlier sexual experimentation was reinforced by a trend in which people were married at later ages. Thus, young men and women had more time to garner sexual experience before entering into long-term monogamous relationships. In addition, the growing number of marriages resulting in divorce provided another opportunity for men and, to a lesser degree, women to engage in nonmonogamous sexual activity. The bottom line was that the generation born between 1935 and 1945 experienced sexual activity with a larger number of sexual partners than most men and women born earlier.

Furthermore, increased technology in and better access to birth control methods made it easier for women to engage in sex without the risk of unwanted pregnancy. In 1960, an oral contraceptive pill became commercially available. Political developments, such as the emergence of the women's movement, also encouraged women to reject the double standard and to postpone marriage. In the wake of the women's movement, the gay liberation movement emerged in 1969. It sought to combat the stigma attached to homosexuality, promoting a self-acceptance of homosexuality that significantly contributed to the sexual revolution. For example, lesbians and gay men organized dances, meetings in coffeehouses, and other activities in order to facilitate social and sexual contact.

If the Kinsey reports were the first shot fired in the sexual revolution, the research of Masters and Johnson was an ambiguous resolution to some of the issues that had been raised. *Human Sexual Response* (1966) was the first volume they published, followed by *Human Sexual Inadequacy* (1970); both books are based on laboratory observations of sexual behavior and became the basis of a therapeutic practice devoted to sexual dysfunction. Their work also exemplified the sexual egalitarianism of the 1960s—not only in their working relationship but also in the image of sexual relations that they project in their books. Masters and Johnson stressed the importance of the *quality* of sexual activity, though they made the couple—rather than the unattached individual—the preferred unit of analysis and therapy. They did not discuss improving the quality of sex for those men and women who engaged in casual (nonmarital) sex—in other words, their research ignored the very definition of the sexual revolution.

THE PEAK OF THE REVOLUTION

By the late 1960s, social institutions emerged to facilitate nonmarital sexual relationships. Singles bars opened, and there was a proliferation in major cities of alternative newspapers that printed personal ads of people looking for sexual partners. Swinging, or mate swapping, also became a practice within certain social circles. Swingers clubs emerged, and couples interested in swapping mates took out ads in the alternative publications. The proportion of the population that participated in the new swinging and singles scenes was relatively small, but it was widely publicized. The dilemmas of sophisticated sexual experiments such as swinging are satirized in movies such as *Bob & Carol & Ted & Alice* (1969) and *Shampoo* (1975). Movies such as *Looking for Mr. Goodbar* (1977) depict the vulnerabilities and anxieties of young women regarding these trends, and *Cruising* (1980) is a police thriller set in the gay world of men engaged in endless and desperate hunts for sex.

Another sign of the sexual revolution was the increased availability of sexually explicit books, magazines, and films. In 1967, the U.S. Congress set up a Commission on Pornography and Obscenity to define pornography and obscenity, provide guidelines for their regulation, and assess their significance in American society. The commission's report concluded that there was no evidence that exposure to explicit sexual materials led to any criminal or deviant behavior among youth and adults. In the 1980s, this report was criticized by both conservatives and some feminists and was countered by a commission formed by the administration of President Ronald Reagan.

BACKLASH

By the late 1970s, the sexual revolution encountered a number of obstacles. One was the growing opposition of conservative and religious groups to the new gender roles and forms of sexual conduct that appeared during the peak years of the sexual revolution (1964–1977): nonmarital and youth sex, birth control, abortion, and homosexuality. Conservatives established new organizations, elected political representatives, and passed legislation to promote a more sexually conservative agenda. These battles continue to take place. What many commentators call "the culture wars" are, in part, an extension of the sexual revolution.

The sexual revolution was also thwarted by sexually transmitted diseases (STDs) such as gonorrhea, syphilis, genital warts, genital herpes, and hepatitis B. Starting in the late 1970s, a number of reports focused on STDs—both *Time* and *Newsweek*, for example, addressed the issue with cover stories. AIDS, discovered in 1981, has had the most devastatingly profound effect. An AIDS epidemic among gay men in the early 1980s caused a major crisis in the sexual politics of the gay community. Medical researchers and gay leaders struggled to find ways of stopping the epidemic without completely excluding all sexual activity. Eventually, gay activists promoted the idea of "safer sex," by which gay men could use condoms without transmitting the virus (HIV) that causes AIDS. Safer sex was adopted by public health educators and AIDS activists as the basis for HIV prevention, and it, along with traditional public health programs, has significantly reduced the spread of all STDs.

THE POLITICAL ANGLE

Another aspect of the sexual revolution—beyond the ideas of sexual mores, feminism, and gay rights—was the emphasis in the 1960s on challenging the status quo on political grounds. Some social commentators view the 1965 Supreme Court ruling *Griswold v. Connecticut* as an important step in the revolution. The lawsuit started as an attempt by the state of Connecticut to ban the use of contraceptives, but the Supreme Court ruled by a 7–2 margin that this violated the "fundamental" right to privacy (marital and otherwise) of citizens. This ruling on the right to privacy became one of the deciding factors in the landmark 1973 case *Roe v. Wade*, which effectively legalized abortion in the United States. Conservatives and religious fundamentalists say these decisions encourage the idea of promiscuity without consequences. Feminists counter that both birth control and the right to have an abortion simply give women the same kind of sexual autonomy that biology granted males.

Conservative opposition to the sexual revolution has played a critical role in remaking American politics. In the first two decades of the 2000s, the rights of women and homosexuals have again become a hot topic. As states begin to legalize same-sex marriage, conservatives have revisited the argument that sexual love should be about procreation. Whereas the Religious Right's earlier stance focused more on reinforcing contempt for homosexuality as an abomination against God and abortion as a direct attack on the nuclear family, it has shifted its focus to promote the notions that homosexuality is an illness requiring treatment, abstinence is the best prevention against both pregnancy and STDs, and sex is only good and moral within the framework of a heterosexual Christian marriage.

Social conservatives have begun to oppose sex education of any kind in public schools; the Vatican has publicly criticized

New York City's mandatory sex-ed program; Congress has had public hearings on whether hormonal birth control should be covered by health insurance policies, fifty years after the pill became commercially available; and the Religious Right has campaigned to recognize life as beginning at conception, an idea that, if voted into law, would effectively make all forms of birth control illegal. While this so-called Republican War on Women rages on in the headlines, and programs that do not cite abstinence as a birth-control method fail to receive government funding (something that went into effect under President George W. Bush), pharmacies report an increased demand for sexual health products. For example, erectile dysfunction drugs such as Viagra, introduced by Pfizer in 1998, have become staples.

Cultural and political changes resulting from the sexual revolution continue to evolve. The sexual revolution of post–World War II America changed sexual and gender roles permanently, and the question of whether the government has the right to police what happens in the bedroom remains open for discussion.

Jeffrey Escoffier

SEE ALSO: *Abortion; AIDS; Alternative Press; Divorce; Feminism; Gay and Lesbian Press; Gay Liberation Movement; Kinsey, Dr. Alfred C.; Lesbianism; Masters and Johnson; The Pill; Pornography;* Roe v. Wade*; Safe Sex; Singles Bars; Stonewall Rebellion; Swinging; Viagra; World War II.*

BIBLIOGRAPHY

Cohen, Nancy L. *Delirium: How the Sexual Counterrevolution Is Polarizing America.* Berkeley, CA: Counterpoint, 2012.

Collins, Gail. *When Everything Changed: The Amazing Journey of American Women from 1960 to the Present.* New York: Little, Brown, 2009.

Costello, John. *Love, Sex, and War: Changing Values, 1939–45.* London: Collins, 1985.

D'Emilio, John, and Estelle Freedman. *Intimate Matters: A History of Sexuality in America.* Chicago: University of Chicago Press, 1997.

Escoffier, Jeffrey. *American Homo: Community and Perversity.* Berkeley: University of California Press, 1998.

Heidenry, John. *What Wild Ecstasy: The Rise and Fall of the Sexual Revolution.* New York: Simon & Schuster, 1997.

Herzog, Dagmar. *Sex in Crisis: The New Sexual Revolution and the Future of American Politics.* New York: Basic Books, 2008.

May, Elaine Tyler. *America + The Pill: A History of Promise, Peril, and Liberation.* New York: Basic Books, 2010.

Michael, Robert T.; John H. Gagnon; Edward O. Laumann; et al. *Sex in America: A Definitive Survey.* New York: Warner Books, 1995.

Page, Cristina. *How the Pro-Choice Movement Saved America: Freedom, Politics, and the War on Sex.* New York: Basic Books, 2006.

Petersen, James R. *The Century of Sex:* Playboy*'s History of the Sexual Revolution, 1900–1999.* New York: Grove Press, 1999.

Seidman, Steven. *Embattled Eros: Sexual Politics and Ethics in Contemporary America.* New York: Routledge, 1992.

Smith, Raymond A. *The Politics of Sexuality: A Documentary and Reference Guide.* Santa Barbara, CA: Greenwood Press, 2010.

Ullman, Sharon R. *Sex Seen: The Emergence of Modern Sexuality in America.* Berkeley: University of California Press, 1997.

Watkins, Elizabeth Siegel. *On the Pill: A Social History of Oral Contraceptives, 1950–1970.* Baltimore, MD: Johns Hopkins University Press, 1998.

The Shadow

For eighteen years, from 1931 to 1949, The Shadow, an unrelenting defender of justice, appeared as the title character in 325 novel-length adventures in *The Shadow* magazine, making it the first and most important of the character, or hero, pulps. A prototypical figure named The Shadow had appeared on radio even earlier, on the *Detective Story Hour*, but the fully evolved character is best remembered for the radio series that ran from 1937 to 1954, with episodes punctuated by such memorable phrases as "Who knows what evil lurks in the hearts of men? The Shadow knows!" and "The weed of crime bears bitter fruit. Crime does not pay. The Shadow knows!"

THE SHADOW IS BORN

The creation of the character named The Shadow is appropriately shrouded in mystery. Although no actual link has been established between the two characters, a seeming prototype of The Shadow appeared in the February 1929 issue of Street and Smith's *Fame and Fortune*. In that story a character named Compton Moore, with glittering eyes and a mocking laugh, donned a green shroud to fight evil as The Shadow. Whether by imitation or coincidence, when pulp publishers Street and Smith sponsored *Detective Story Hour*, a radio dramatization of stories from its *Detective Story Magazine*, The Shadow was portrayed as the show's narrator, voiced by James La Curto, complete with that familiar haunting laugh.

To get a copyright on its accidental creation and meet what seemed to be a growing demand, Street and Smith quickly created a new pulp magazine, *The Shadow, a Detective Magazine.* John Nanovic, who would a few years later create the Doc Savage character, served as editor for the first twelve years. Journalist and amateur magician Walter Gibson was hired to turn the name and the laugh into a character. In just a few weeks Gibson produced *The Living Shadow*, the first of the 325 novels that the magazine would publish over the next eighteen years. The stories were all attributed to the house name of Maxwell Grant, and Gibson did not write all of them. He did, however, write an astounding 282 of the novels, including the first 112 stories that firmly established the character. When the magazine went from quarterly to a twice-monthly publication, Gibson simply picked up his pace and produced two complete novels a month.

In the first story The Shadow is a mysterious presence who works through Harry Vincent and his other operatives. It took a few issues before The Shadow himself was in the center of the action, but the basic look and ambiance was established at an early stage. On the first page of the first story, The Shadow, an ominous figure in a long black coat, seems to materialize out of the thick fog, with only his hawk nose and piercing eyes visible beneath his broad-brimmed felt hat. When The Shadow does go into action, he does so with an automatic pistol spitting death from each hand.

THE SHADOW GROWS

As Gibson fleshed out the mythos, The Shadow acquired scores of agents in addition to right-hand man Vincent. Chief among them were cab driver Moe Shrevitz; gangster Cliff Marsland; reporter Clyde Burke; and the mysterious Burbank, who coordinates communications between The Shadow and his cadre of agents. Another operative, would-be love interest Margo Lane, originated on the radio program but was eventually added to the pulp stories. The Shadow's most interesting relationship is with Lamont Cranston, a wealthy playboy whose guise The Shadow sometimes assumes when Cranston is traveling abroad. The 1937 novel *The Shadow Unmasks* reveals the fact that The Shadow is really World War I flying ace and former spy Kent Allard, although some later novels call even this identity into doubt. When The Shadow appeared in other media, his background was simplified—he *was* Lamont Cranston, though he was not so in the original pulps. The final novel in the series, *The Whispering Eyes*, appeared in 1949.

Within a decade after his creation, The Shadow had captured the popular imagination. "As intensely exploited as Tarzan, The Shadow sold wrist watches, coloring books, disguise and fingerprint kits, sheet music, Better Little Books, comic books, and a succession of nearly worthless moving pictures," recounts Robert Sampson, author of *Deadly Excitements*. In 1937 The Shadow returned to radio, not only as narrator but also as the lead character, voiced for the first year by Orson Welles. The radio series portrayed The Shadow as less dark and deadly, relying more on his newfound hypnotic powers than on his twin automatics. The show was immensely popular, lasting until 1954.

The 1937 feature film, *The Shadow Strikes*, was based on the radio program, and there was a film serial in 1940 that starred Victor Jory. Some of the later Shadow films are almost domestic comedies, in which the hero is beset with more trouble from his jealous wife than from the villain. The 1994 film starring Alec Baldwin returns to the dark pulp roots for inspiration, pitting The Shadow against his greatest pulp nemesis, Shiwan Khan. The opening scene of the film is even reminiscent of the first chapter of *The Living Shadow*.

The Shadow had a long and varied life in comic books. Street and Smith published the first of them. Even though Gibson wrote the scripts for the first six years, The Shadow appeared quite differently in the comic-book version than in the pulps. Since the radio show had become more popular than the pulp magazine, Gibson was pressured to conform to the radio concept. From 1938 to 1942 Ledger Syndicate distributed a *Shadow* comic strip by Gibson and Vernon Greene, and in the 1960s Archie Comics published a series featuring The Shadow. One of the most faithful comic-book adaptations was the series published by DC Comics from 1973 to 1975.

Randy Duncan

SEE ALSO: *Archie Comics; Baldwin, Alec; DC Comics; Detective Fiction; Pulp Magazines; Radio; Street and Smith.*

BIBLIOGRAPHY

Goodstone, Tony. *The Pulps: Fifty Years of American Popular Culture.* New York: Bonanza Books, 1970.

Goulart, Ron. *An Informal History of the Pulp Magazine.* New York: Ace Books, 1973.

Murray, Will. *The Duende History of the Shadow Magazine.* Greenwood, MA: Odyssey Press, 1980.

Sampson, Robert. *Deadly Excitements: Shadows and Phantoms.* Bowling Green, OH: Bowling Green State University Popular Press, 1989.

Shimeld, Thomas J., and Robert W. Gibson. *Walter B. Gibson and the Shadow.* Jefferson, NC: McFarland, 2005.

"What Evil Lurked?" *Comics Collector*, Summer 1984, 33–42.

Shaft

Directed by Gordon Parks and starring Richard Roundtree as itinerant black detective John Shaft, MGM's hugely successful *Shaft* (1971) helped initiate Hollywood's blaxploitation craze, a series of cheaply made and sensational films that featured provocative ethnic protagonists and proved to be extremely lucrative. Although John Shaft was a proud and raw revision of the typical Hollywood African American hero, he did little to aid the real-life cause of racial harmony and understanding.

BLAXPLOITATION IN THE 1970s

When Melvin Van Peebles's independently produced *Sweet Sweetback's Baadasssss Song* (1971) made $10 million in profits, the aging Hollywood studios took notice. They saw that Van

Richard Roundtree as Shaft. *Richard Roundtree starred as action hero John Shaft in the 1972 film, ushering in the era of the blaxploitation film.* SILVER SCREEN COLLECTION/CONTRIBUTOR/MOVIEPIX/GETTY IMAGES.

Peebles had successfully targeted a widely ignored box-office patronage. Three social factors combined to create a new public taste for ethnic "badasses" such as Sweetback and Shaft. First, the rise of the civil rights and Black Power movements fostered an appreciation for the intelligent, capable, and righteous African American who triumphed in his attack on the white establishment. Second, the white flight to the suburbs contributed to a revised racial demographic in city centers such as Chicago; Detroit, Michigan; and Atlanta, Georgia, where downtown cinemas now catered primarily to middle- and working-class African Americans. Third, in the late 1960s, Hollywood's long-standing policy of self-censorship gave way to a more liberal rating system that offered mainstream film a new outlet for what had been previously considered uncomfortably blatant expressions of African American sexuality and anger.

Not as openly revolutionary as the X-rated *Sweet Sweetback*, whose title character escapes white justice after a virulent spree of fornication and murder, *Shaft* tapped into popular feelings of racial tension as it revised the standard Hollywood hard-boiled detective with an R-rated ghetto flavor that tweaked but never attempted to topple the status quo. With *Shaft*, in the words of African American film historian Ed Guerrero, "Hollywood's formula for the 'new' filmic representation of blacks began to crystallize."

THE PLOT

The film itself revolves around private detective John Shaft's rude but shrewd negotiation of a triple threat. Hired to free the kidnapped daughter of "Bumpy Jonas," a dubious black mob boss, Shaft tangles with the white racist police who attempt to reduce him to a slavish errand boy, navigates the race-complicated grudges between black and white organized crime, and uses the revolutionary fervor of militant but ultimately doomed black urban youth. Roundtree's performance as the indefatigable private detective subtly revises many of the best hard-boiled moments of Sam Spade and Philip Marlowe. Like Humphrey Bogart in *The Maltese Falcon* (1941), Shaft overpowers an attacker in his own office and taunts both his employers and the police. However, he also makes deft use of his ethnic appearance when he masquerades as a servile bartending "boy" in order to foil two white assassins. Finally, *Shaft*'s dramatic climactic assault on the hired guns in a seedy inner-city hotel references both the war film and the Western in its calculated, paramilitary strike on a fortified outpost of white evil.

Shaft's sexual escapades, boldly aestheticized by Park's disco-energized cinematography and Isaac Hayes's funky grooves, further define his prowess as a thoroughly masculine black badass. While Shaft shares his most romantic liaisons with a comely African American woman, he also asserts his manhood by picking up random white women in a local bar. His postcoital pillow talk with his regular black partner is tender, but his biracial one-night stand ends coldly. As Shaft ignores and insults his nameless white lover the following morning, she labels him decidedly "shitty." This brief exchange between the black hero and his white bedfellow powerfully informs the film's finale, when Shaft mimics the angry white woman's insult as a climactic joke on a white establishment cop. Subtly taunting but never openly attacking the racial hierarchy in which he survives, Shaft ends the film disappearing into the city after having effectively "screwed" all his white antagonists.

THE AFTERMATH OF *SHAFT*

Aside from two fair sequels, *Shaft's Big Score!* (1972) and *Shaft in Africa* (1973), Roundtree's depiction of the sexy, truculent black male spawned an often bizarre series of blaxploitation rip-offs and pretenders. Some of these heroes, such as *Super Fly*'s Youngblood Priest (1972) and *The Harder They Come*'s Ivan Martin (1972), offer some psychological depth. Most, however, are grotesque, ultraviolent perversions of black sexuality. In films such as *Welcome Home, Brother Charles* (1975), black male pride and defiance are reduced to crude arrogance, degrading sexual stunts, and brutal vengeance. Hollywood also marketed the feminine side of blaxploitation through female Shafts such as Pam Grier and Tamara Dobson. Films such as *Coffy* (1973), *Foxy Brown* (1974), and *Cleopatra Jones and the Casino of Gold* (1975) advertise a shapely, violent black heroine whose arrogant appeal centers on ample doses of ethnic attitude and T&A.

Shaft, however, could only take the new image of the African American male hero so far. In *Black Film as a Signifying Practice*, Gladstone Yearwood writes that "films such as *Shaft*, *Superfly*, and *Cooley High* attempt to subvert, or at least question, the dominant tradition in the cinema, but they are effectively harnessed by it in their usage of the Hollywood model as the basis for the development of black heroes." *Shaft* was originally conceived and scripted for a white actor, but MGM altered its project for an inner-city African American audience in order to test drive a new narrative formula in which the black wins and survives for profitable sequels. Roundtree received a mere $13,000 for his starring role in the first film, and the majority of *Shaft*'s profits wound up in the wallets of MGM's white executives.

COMMERCIALIZATION

Exemplifying the studios' new drive toward customized saturation marketing, *Shaft*'s success with an African American urban audience resulted in a wave of diversified product tie-ins. In addition to the more than $10 million in profits from the film's first year of release and Hayes's Oscar-winning, platinum-selling soundtrack, MGM capitalized on the popularity of John Shaft's refusal to bow to the man through a merchandising storm that B. J. Mason detailed in *Ebony* as a plague of *Shaft* "suits, watches, belts and sunglasses, leather coats, decals, sweatshirts and night shirts, beach towels, posters, after shave lotion and cologne." Beginning with *Shaft*, Hollywood's cheap and sly appropriation of the racial tensions in America's metropolitan centers became the basis for a parade of crude fantasies and commercial gimmicks revolving around predominantly brutal and misogynistic black heroes who rule the ghetto but would never garner Sidney Poitier's invitation to dinner.

In 2000 a sequel of sorts was released by Paramount. The new version of *Shaft* starred Samuel L. Jackson as John Shaft, the nephew of the original Shaft. The film was directed by John Singleton, known for the 1991 film *Boyz n the Hood* about growing up in South Central Los Angeles. For Singleton, making a *Shaft* film was a dream come true, but it did not fare as well at the box office as the studio had hoped, so plans for a sequel were squelched.

Daniel Yezbick

SEE ALSO: *Academy Awards; Blaxploitation Films; Civil Rights Movement; Grier, Pam; Hollywood;* The Maltese Falcon*; MGM (Metro-Goldwyn-Mayer); Roundtree, Richard.*

BIBLIOGRAPHY

Guerrero, Ed. *Framing Blackness.* Philadelphia: Temple University Press, 1993.

Henry, Matthew. "He Is a 'Bad Mother*$%@!#': 'Shaft' and Contemporary Black Masculinity." *African American Review* 38, no. 1: 119–126.

James, Darius. *That's Blaxploitation: Roots of the Baadassss 'Tude (Rated X by an All-Whyte Jury).* New York: St. Martin's Press, 1995.

Mason, B. J. "The New Films: Culture or Con Game?" *Ebony,* December 1972, 68.

Riley, Clayton. "Shaft Can Do Everything—I Can Do Nothing." *New York Times,* August 13, 1972.

Yearwood, Gladstone. "The Hero in Black Film." *Wide Angle* 5, no. 2 (1983): 32–50.

Shakur, Tupac *(1971–1996)*

Rapper, film actor, and poet Tupac "Amaru" Shakur, also known as "2Pac," was one of the most influential and successful rappers of the 1990s. Shakur's rap career was launched when he appeared in the Digital Underground's "Same Song" video in 1991. After the video aired, rap fans across America were asking who the young man was in the African outfit with beads streaming down his chest like an African king. Critic Armond White notes in *Rebel for the Hell of It: The Life of Tupac Shakur* (1997) that it was after his appearance in the Digital Underground video that Shakur "first realized the thrill of putting a rhyme on tape and getting it to the public."

2PACKALYPSE NOW

As a solo artist Shakur burst onto the rap scene with *2Pacalypse Now* (1991), a thirteen-track album that changed the face of rap music. In this album Shakur used his poetic power to tell those stories from the streets and the ghetto that the mainstream media refused to talk about, including the plight of black males and other African Americans, police brutality, and poverty. In the rap song "Rebel of the Underground," Shakur foreshadows his own conflict with the police/media by arguing that they cannot stand the reign of a man like him "who goes against the grain." In the song, not only does he characterize himself as "cold as the devil" and "straight out of the underground," but he calls himself "the lyrical lunatic, the maniac MC" and asserts that "the most dangerous weapon" is "an educated black man."

Themes of police brutality, black-on-black crimes, the American Dream deferred, black males in America, and African American struggle and survival permeate songs like "Trapped," "Soulja's Story," "I Don't Give a Fuck," and "Words of Wisdom." While in "I Don't Give a Fuck" and "Soulja's Story" Shakur raps that he does not care about the police and other American officials and institutions who oppress African Americans, in "Words of Wisdom" he charges America with the "crime of rape, murder, and assault" for "suppressing and punishing" his people. Additionally, he accuses America of falsifying black history and of falsely imprisoning black males by keeping them "trapped in the projects." He concludes the song by warning America that it reaps what it sows and that he is "2Pacalypse, America's nightmare."

The rough side and revolutionary stance of *2Pacalypse Now* led music and popular culture critics to mistakenly label Shakur a *gangsta rapper* and his music *gangsta rap*, thus blaming the messenger for the message. For example, when a young man in Texas shot a state trooper and his attorney alleged that he was listening to *2Pacalypse Now* at the time, Vice President Dan Quayle was widely reported as saying, "There's no reason for a record like this to be released. It has no place in society." Tupac mocked Quayle's words on his second album.

THE CODE OF THUG LIFE

Critics who labeled Shakur a gangsta rapper and called him controversial and confused failed to understand his code of *thug life*. The term is an acronym—one that Shakur had tattooed across his chest—for "The Hate U Gave Lil' Infants Fucks Everybody," a clear message to the community. In Candace Sandy and Dawn Marie Daniels's unauthorized biography *How Long Will They Mourn Me?* Shakur is quoted as saying that although he diagnosed thug life, he did not create it. He established the thug life movement with the help of Mutulu Shakur, his stepfather, and created a twenty-six-rule code for it.

In *Tupac Shakur: The Life and Times of an American Icon*, Tayanna Lee McQuillar and Freddie Lee Johnson confirm the existence of the code of thug life. Some of the tenets of the code include the directive that members must know their enemies, civilians must be protected, senseless brutality and rape must stop, and harm to children will not be tolerated. Yet it is clear that this was not the perspective that the media and mainstream Americans understood. For them, Shakur's thug life was just more gangsta rap.

Moreover, critics failed to realize that Shakur's music always contained two sides: a tough side bristling with the realities of the ghetto life and a didactic side endowed with positive messages. Such was the case with "Brenda's Got a Baby" from *2Pacalypse Now*, one of Shakur's best-known rap songs. The song describes the carelessness of a cousin who impregnates Brenda; the ignorance of Brenda, who tries to throw the baby in a garbage can; and the callousness of a community that fails to realize that Brenda's plight affects them all.

Strictly 4 My N.I.G.G.A.Z. (1993), Shakur's second album, contains a song called "Keep Ya Head Up," in which he both criticizes some black men for their misogyny, sexism, and irresponsibility and advises black women to keep their heads up no matter what the situation is. Shakur showed his softer side yet again on *Me against the World* (1995) with "Dear Mama," a tribute to his mother, Afeni Shakur. Autobiographical in nature, "Dear Mama" chronicles the Black Panther days of Afeni and how she struggled to keep her family together. In the song, Shakur reminisces about the stress he caused a mother trying to raise him while struggling with drugs and how, in the absence of a father, he turned to the streets in search of love and fame.

In 1996 the music scene changed when Shakur became the first rapper to release a double album, *All Eyez on Me*; it reached number one on the rhythm-and-blues and pop charts and was certified multiplatinum within months. Through the late 1990s *All Eyez on Me* remained the best-selling rap album of all time. The most notable and famous song on the album was "California Love," a song that, according to White, "certifies a level of achievement, of rap triumph, and American commercial bliss." White goes on to say that Dr. Dre and Shakur create "a sense of belonging that neglects rap protest, preferring an affirmation that is vaguely patriotic." Shakur's other work includes two posthumous albums, *Makaveli the Don Killuminati: The 7 Day*

Theory (1996) and the double album *R U Still Down? [Remember Me]* (1997).

FILM CAREER

Shakur starred in six films in five years: *Juice* (1992), *Poetic Justice* (1993), *Above the Rim* (1994), *Bullet* (1996), *Gridlock'd* (1997), and *Gang Related* (1997). Except for *Poetic Justice*, a romantic comedy that also starred Janet Jackson, the films seem like they could have been written from Shakur's song lyrics. The roles that were offered to Shakur all furthered his image as a gangsta rapper, whereas in his life Shakur was known as a reserved, sensitive, and well-learned person. In its October/ November 2011 issue, *Vibe* magazine devoted an entire article, "Tupac: Menace to Hollywood," to Shakur's acting legacy and Hollywood typecasting. In the article, Allen Hughes, who directed *Menace II Society* (1993), asserts, "In real life, Tupac was a very demure person. He was not that thug dude, at all. He was very thoughtful, sensitive, well-read, well-studied, book smart, fell in love very easily with everyone and everything."

In 1993 writer/director John Singleton called Shakur to star in *Poetic Justice* after Ice Cube declined the role. Convinced that Shakur was the next Denzel Washington, Singleton originally wrote the lead role in the film *Higher Learning* (1995) for him, but the role went to Omar Epps when Shakur got in trouble with the law in New York City. In 1996 Singleton told Shakur that he had written a script called *Baby Boy* (2001)—and with it, a role that could earn Shakur an Oscar. It was a role that never came to fruition because Shakur was shot and killed on September 13, 1996.

Years after his death Shakur has become a legend, and his legacy keeps growing, not only through his music, poetry, and film but also through the growing body of literature published about his life and work. Shakur's influence can be seen in the work of rap artists such as DMX, 50 Cent, Jay-Z, Ja-Rule, and Eminem, and his legacy includes the Tupac Amaru Shakur Foundation, created by Afeni, and the Tupac Amaru Shakur Center for the Arts in Stone Mountain, Georgia. Young people around the United States flock to the center and the camp to study creative arts and to receive leadership training.

Pierre-Damien Mvuyekure

SEE ALSO: *Academy Awards; Black Panthers; Eminem; Gangsta Rap; Jackson, Janet; Jay-Z; Pop Music; Quayle, Dan; Rap; Rhythm and Blues; Washington, Denzel.*

BIBLIOGRAPHY

Alexander, Frank, and Heidi Siegmund Cuda. *Got Your Back: The Life of a Bodyguard in the Hardcore World of Gangsta Rap*. New York: St. Martin's Press, 1998.

Dyson, Michael Eric. *Holler if You Hear Me: Searching for Tupac Shakur*. New York: Basic Civitas Books, 2001.

McQuiller, Tayanna Lee, and Freddie Lee Johnson. *Tupac Shakur: The Life and Times of an American Icon*. Cambridge, MA: Da Capo Press, 2010.

Monjauze, Molly, ed. *Tupac Remembered: Bearing Witness to a Life and Legacy*. San Francisco: Chronicle Books, 2008.

Sandy, Candace, and Dawn Marie Daniels. *How Long Will They Mourn Me?: The Life and Legacy of Tupac Shakur*. New York: One World/Random House, 2006.

Scott, Cathy. *The Killing of Tupac Shakur*. Las Vegas, NV: Huntington Press, 1997.

"Tupac: Menace to Hollywood." *Vibe*, October/November 2011.

Vibe magazine editors. *Tupac Amaru Shakur, 1971–1996*. New York: Crown Publishers, 1997.

West, Michael O.; William G. Martin; and Fanon Che Wilkins, eds. *From Toussaint to Tupac: The Black International since the Age of Revolution*. Chapel Hill: University of North Carolina Press, 2009.

White, Armond. *Rebel for the Hell of It: The Life of Tupac Shakur*. New York: Thunder's Mouth Press, 1997.

Shane

In 1945 Jack Schaefer, an editor and reporter for the *Norfolk Virginian-Pilot*, wrote and published the story "Rider from Nowhere" in *Argosy* magazine. Houghton Mifflin released a revised and expanded version of the story as *Shane* in 1949. Based somewhat on the Johnson County War in Wyoming in the early 1890s, the story was Schaefer's attempt to reduce the legend of the West to its basic components and, at the same time, elevate it to the level of Homeric mythology. *Shane* remains a simple tale of a mysterious stranger who descends into the valley in the midst of a conflict. Choosing sides, he removes his godly raiment (metaphorically) to mingle with the common people. He crosses a body of water to challenge the enemy and then, after again donning his godly clothes, recrosses the body of water to vanquish the enemy before ascending from the valley into the night. The novel, which has been published in more than thirty languages, has sold more than six million copies in dozens of editions. The movie rendition remains the ultimate statement of the legend of the American West.

THE BOOK'S PLOT

At the start of the novel, young Bob Starrett watches the lone rider make his way slowly across the valley toward the cluster of small farms. "Call me Shane," he said. He was from Arkansas. At 15 he had left his Arkansas home to wander. He did not say where. Bob's parents, Joe and Marian Starrett, invite Shane to stay on with them as a farm hand. There is something about him, something mysterious and terrifying, but Joe senses they have nothing to fear. "He's dangerous, all right . . . but not to us."

The West is changing. The frontier is gone. Homesteaders are fencing off the land in 80- and 160-acre lots. But old ways die hard. The Fletcher brothers, owners of the biggest ranch in the valley, have recently contracted with the army to supply them with beef, and they need the range land. This precipitates a conflict between the Fletchers and the farmers that leads to several confrontations. Joe Starrett, the strongest-willed of the farmers, becomes their leader, and Shane, sensing the danger of the growing tension, supports Starrett and the farmers.

Shane humiliates the Fletcher cowhands in two initial bouts. The first is a fistfight with Chris, a man he admires, in which he breaks the man's arm. In the second, a barroom brawl at Grafton's Saloon, Shane and Starrett soundly defeat a group of cowhands. In the days following the brawl, young Bob notices a growing restlessness in Shane, a gradual loss of the serenity that had come over him after he hired on. Fletcher's response to the brawl is to call for a hired gun, Stark Wilson, to come to the valley as their enforcer. When Wilson instigates a face-off with Ernie Wright and then kills him before Ernie can clear his holster, Shane knows that the conflict has gone far beyond what the farmers could manage. He decides that the time has come to act. "You seem to know a lot about that kind of dirty business," says one of the farmers. "I do," responds Shane.

Fletcher and Joe Starrett arrange a meeting. But Shane, knowing that it is a trap, knocks Joe unconscious and goes to Grafton's alone, followed by Bob. Shane kills Wilson and Fletcher in a gunfight. Then he rides out of town, but not out of memory, as the stories of Shane are told and retold for years after in the valley.

THE MOVIE

The 1953 film version was produced and directed by George Stevens for Paramount. Alan Ladd played Shane, Van Heflin and Jean Arthur played Joe and Marian, and Brandon De Wilde played little Joey Starrett. Jack Palance portrayed Wilson, and the Ryker brothers, Rufus and Morgan, were played by Emile Meyer and John Dierkes.

In this beautifully filmed movie, the basic elements of Schaefer's story are presented as a mythological tale set in the West. The simple American theme of good triumphing over evil, and the more complex themes of unstated love, the virtue of economic progress, and the inexorable progress of the order of civilization superseding the chaos of the frontier, unfold beneath the dominating peaks of the Grand Tetons.

As the movie begins, a lone rider descends into the valley. As a stag bends to drink from a stream and then raises his head, the rider is framed by the antlers as he advances slowly toward little Joey, who is watching him. The audience knows immediately that this is no ordinary drifter. Where is he from? "Here and there." Where is he going? "Someplace I've never been." He learns of the conflict between the homesteaders and the Rykers, who own the largest cattle ranch in the valley. The Rykers want the range opened up and the fences torn down. They are standing in the way of progress. The old ways of open-range ranching and cattle drives are inefficient in the face of feed lots and fenced-off farming. Shane, in a melancholy surrender to changing times, sees his world coming to an end. The open range is gone. The presence of women and children in abundance requires the banishment of guns and the violent way of life in which he flourished. Reluctantly, he sheds the buckskins of the trail and adopts the drab homespun of the farmer, becoming Starrett's farmhand.

Marian, who watched him ride up, is immediately taken by this handsome Apollo who stands in stark contrast to her dull, dependable husband, Joe. Although she is committed to her family and the farm, she is in love with Shane, as he is with her. Their love, however, is unfulfilled passion, chivalric and pure. This upholds Shane's heroic stature and sets him apart from ordinary men. Little Joey is mesmerized by Shane and his obvious proficiency with guns. He loves his parents, seeks their advice and counsel, and obeys their directives. But he worships Shane. Shane is a fantasy hero, a little boy's dream.

In the confrontations with Ryker's men, Shane at first backs down. This makes some of the farmers question his dependability. To counter this perception, Shane picks a fight with Chris Calloway, the ranch hand who first challenged him. The fight turns into a brawl in which Joe and Shane defeat a large group of Ryker's men. Ryker, rebuffed angrily when he offers to hire Shane, responds by sending for Wilson, an evil gunfighter. Played by Palance as a morose, soft-spoken, calculating killer, Wilson personifies evil. As he strolls into the darkened saloon, a dog gets up and walks away, adding an exclamation point to this evil presence. Wilson baits and then kills Torrey, one of the farmers. This prompts an attempt at negotiation between Starrett and Ryker, but Shane is worried that the confab is a setup, that Joe will be killed. Shane then knocks Joe unconscious and rides to meet Wilson at the saloon. In a beautifully choreographed scene underlined by Loyal Griggs's point-of-view photography, Shane kills Wilson and both Ryker brothers in a poetic replay of Wilson's murder of Torrey.

In keeping with the innocent-eye narrative of the novel, the film is presented from little Joey's point of view. Many of the scenes were filmed in low-angle camera shots, as if the audience were viewing the action from Joey's level. Joey is presented as an observer in most pivotal scenes, and as such, Ladd is filmed in a manner that depicts Shane as a godlike figure, looming over the action of the story.

THE LEGEND

Both the novel and the film succeed in transforming the Western legend into a pure and simple tale of the triumph of good over evil. Shane is presented as an incongruous hero, out of his element, in desperate search for a new existence. His world is ending. He tries farming, but he cannot change what is. He appears hopelessly out of place in the family scenes and in the burial scene. He is forced to revert to an existence he realizes cannot exist anymore. He is an ambiguous hero who desires to eliminate violence and killing from the valley, but he must kill to accomplish his objective. Then he must leave the valley. "There is no living with a killing," he tells Joey, "It's a brand."

Shane's desperate struggle to escape his past thus ends tragically. In order to save the lifestyle he sought to embrace, he is forced to revert to his past life. "I tried and it didn't work for me," he explains to Joey. As Shane rides off, Joey begs him not to go. "Shane, come back!" he yells into the night. It is a plaintive cry for a return of his lost innocence, of his fantasy hero, and of his hero's way of life. Before civilization came to the West, life was simple and predictable, pure and unambiguous. Personal honor and the law of the gun marked the difference between right and wrong. In the final analysis, *Shane* appeals to that nostalgic longing in urban society for a time long past, when life's options remained open, where men were dominant, and where ethical gray areas did not exist. The invocation of a person's moral code was abrupt and final.

This is a towering, landmark Western film. It is the final statement of the legend of the West, reduced to its simplest components and elevated to the status of myth. Yet it is also flawed. It is slow and pretentious; it is studied and self-conscious. It lacks spontaneity. At times, the understated dialogue and suggested themes of unfulfilled love, hero worship, male bonding, and the adherence to moral codes seem stagey and lacking in vitality. But these are trivial points. After *Shane*, the Hollywood Western became less and less viable as a genre and, except for *The Searchers* (1956), it remains unmatched in stature or influence by any later Western films.

The Academy of Motion Picture Arts and Sciences nominated *Shane* for Best Picture, Best Director, and Best Writing (screen adaptation by A. B. Guthrie). Brandon De Wilde and Jack Palance were both nominated for Best Supporting

Actor. Loyal Griggs won an Oscar for his superb color photography. *Shane* was remade by Malpaso Productions in 1985 as *Pale Rider*, starring Clint Eastwood as a lonely preacher riding in to help a group of miners. It is a gritty film and in places almost a frame-by-frame clone of the original. It marked Eastwood's return to the Western genre after a nine-year absence.

James R. Belpedio

SEE ALSO: *Academy Awards; Eastwood, Clint; Ladd, Alan; The Western.*

BIBLIOGRAPHY

Cawelti, John G. *The Six-Gun Mystique*. Bowling Green, OH: Bowling Green University Popular Press, 1971.

Hine, Robert V. *The American West: An Interpretive History*, 2nd ed. Boston: Little, Brown, 1984.

Petri, Bruce Humleker. "A Theory of American Film: The Films and Techniques of George Stevens." PhD dissertation. Harvard University, 1974.

Schaefer, Jack. *Shane*. Boston: Houghton Mifflin, 1949.

Slotkin, Richard. *Gunfighter Nation: The Myth of the Frontier in Twentieth-Century America*. New York: Atheneum, 1992.

Shaw, Artie *(1910–2004)*

One of the three great clarinet-playing band leaders of the twentieth century, along with Benny Goodman and Woody Herman, Artie Shaw was also an experimental leader during the big band era. Born Arthur Arshawsky in New York City, he played in dance bands while in high school and turned professional at age fifteen, eventually freelancing in recording studios. In 1935 he played jazz backed by a string quartet and formed a big band that included a string section. Two years later, returning to traditional instrumentation, he recorded his first big hit, Cole Porter's "Begin the Beguine." In 1939 he abandoned his band and went to Mexico.

After frequent stops and starts in the music business, Shaw published his autobiography in 1952 and played briefly with a new combo called the Gramercy Five before a final retirement. He was married eight times to a bevy of beauties that included screen stars Ava Gardner and Lana Turner. In 2004 the Recording Academy honored Shaw with a Grammy Lifetime Achievement Award shortly before his diabetes-related death later that same year. His lasting legacy is the pursuit of innovative sounds, evinced by his interest in combining classical music and jazz stylings and by his experimentations with bebop. He will also be remembered for his pure and indisputable talent.

Benjamin Griffith

SEE ALSO: *Big Bands; Gardner, Ava; Goodman, Benny; Grammy Awards; Herman, Woody; Jazz; Porter, Cole; Swing Dancing; Turner, Lana.*

BIBLIOGRAPHY

Balliett, Whitney. *American Musicians*. New York: Oxford University Press, 1986.

Nolan, Tom. *Three Chords for Beauty's Sake: The Life of Artie Shaw*. New York: W. W. Norton, 2010.

Shaw, Artie. *The Trouble with Cinderella*. New York: Farrar, Straus & Young, 1952.

Shaw, Artie. *I Love You, I Hate You, Drop Dead: Variations on a Theme*. New York: Barricade Books, 1997.

Simon, George T. *The Big Bands*. New York: Macmillan, 1974.

Simosko, Vladimir. *Artie Shaw: A Musical Biography and Discography*. Lanham, MD: Scarecrow Press, 2000.

Shawn, Ted *(1891–1972)*

Ted Shawn is regarded as the father of American modern dance. Born Edwin Meyers Shawn, he began dancing as a form of physical therapy for paralysis. He recovered and became a partner and husband to dancer Ruth St. Denis, who was famous for her religious solo dances. The couple formed a pioneering dance company and training school called Denishawn in 1915, which toured across the United States and the world. Shawn often explored Christian and other world religious themes, and he was the first American choreographer to combine nudity with movement.

After leaving Denishawn, he created the first all-male dance troupe in America, called simply Men Dancers, and Jacob's Pillow, an international dance festival and training center in Massachusetts. Shawn was responsible for establishing dance as a legitimate career for men in the United States, inspiring generations of dancers and choreographers.

Brian Granger

SEE ALSO: *Denishawn; Modern Dance; St. Denis, Ruth.*

BIBLIOGRAPHY

Harbin, Billy J.; Kim Marra; and Robert A. Schanke. *The Gay & Lesbian Theatrical Legacy*. Ann Arbor: University of Michigan Press, 2005.

Shawn, Ted. *One Thousand and One Night Stands*. Garden City, NY: Doubleday, 1960.

Sherman, Jane, and Barton Mumaw. *Barton Mumaw, Dancer: From Denishawn to Jacob's Pillow and Beyond*. New York: Dance Horizons, 1986.

Terry, Walter. *Ted Shawn, Father of American Dance: A Biography*. New York: Dial Press, 1976.

She Wore a Yellow Ribbon

Director John Ford's *She Wore a Yellow Ribbon* (1949) is the first color feature film shot in Monument Valley, Arizona, and the second of three films Ford made about the 7th Cavalry—the other two are *Fort Apache* (1948) and *Rio Grande* (1950). Collectively these films are known as the "Cavalry Trilogy." Set in the American Southwest in 1876, *She Wore a Yellow Ribbon* revolves around Captain Nathan Brittles (played by John Wayne), an aging officer leading a final patrol before retirement. Due to its gung-ho glorification of the concept of Manifest Destiny, the film is best known as a reflection of mainstream America's post–World War II optimism.

Robert C. Sickels

SEE ALSO: *Ford, John; Wayne, John; The Western.*

BIBLIOGRAPHY

Darby, William. *John Ford's Westerns: A Thematic Analysis, with a Filmography*. Jefferson, NC: McFarland, 2006.

Nolley, Ken. "Printing the Legend in the Age of MX: Reconsidering Ford's Military Trilogy." *Film/Literature Quarterly* 14, no. 2 (1986): 82–88.

Place, J. A. *The Western Films of John Ford*. Secaucus, NJ: Citadel Press, 1977.

Stowell, Peter. *John Ford*. Boston: Twayne Publishers, 1986.

Westbrook, Max. "The Night John Wayne Danced with Shirley Temple." *Western American Literature* 25, no. 2 (1990): 157–167.

Sheldon, Sidney *(1917–2007)*

By the time he wrote his first book at age fifty-three, Sidney Sheldon had already had a substantial impact on popular culture via the creation of successful screenplays and television series, but his subsequent career as a novelist far eclipsed all that preceded it. Along with such rivals as Irving Wallace, Jacqueline Susann, Harold Robbins, and Judith Krantz, Sheldon dominated the best-seller lists by producing fast-moving tales of sex and power among the jet set, such as *Bloodline*, *The Other Side of Midnight*, and *A Stranger in the Mirror*. As with these other authors, Sheldon's popularity with the public was in inverse proportion to his standing with literary critics. Unfazed by the critics' disapproval of his efforts, Sheldon created tales that enthralled readers and—bringing his career full circle—often found a second life dramatized as feature films or television miniseries.

EARLY LIFE AND HOLLYWOOD CAREER

Born in Chicago in 1917, Sheldon entered Northwestern University on a scholarship in 1935, but the economic hardships of the Depression soon forced him to drop out. He journeyed to Manhattan in hopes of becoming a songwriter, and when that did not pan out he tried the other coast, where he had better luck. On the strength of the story sense displayed in his sample précis of John Steinbeck's *Of Mice and Men*, Sheldon was hired as a reader by Universal Studios. He had managed to break into screenwriting on a modest basis when World War II broke out, but Sheldon's service proved only a brief interruption, and he was quickly discharged for medical reasons.

Sidney Sheldon. *After a notable career as a writer for movies and television, Sidney Sheldon wrote his first novel at age fifty-three.* JON SOOHOO/CONTRIBUTOR/WIREIMAGE/GETTY IMAGES.

After some ventures into writing musicals and comedies for the New York stage, Sheldon returned to Hollywood. His acclaim as a scriptwriter was capped by the Oscar he won for the screenplay of *The Bachelor and the Bobby Soxer* (1947), a romantic comedy starring Cary Grant, Myrna Loy, and Shirley Temple. The following year, Sheldon collaborated with Frances Goodrich and Albert Hackett on the script for the highly successful MGM musical, Irving Berlin's *Easter Parade*, the only film to unite Judy Garland and Fred Astaire. That script earned the Screen Writers Guild Award for best musical of the year, as did Sheldon's adaptation of Berlin's *Annie Get Your Gun* in 1950.

Other frothy Hollywood vehicles in which Sheldon was involved as writer or producer include *You're Never Too Young* and *Pardners* (1955 and 1956, respectively, both starring Dean Martin and Jerry Lewis), Cole Porter's *Anything Goes* (1956, with Bing Crosby), and *Dream Wife* (1953, starring Cary Grant, and Sheldon's debut as a director). In the late 1950s, he made a second assault on Broadway, which proved more successful than his first. He collaborated with Herbert and Dorothy Fields and David Shaw on the 1959 Gwen Verdon vehicle, *Redhead*, which earned four Tony Awards, including best musical.

TELEVISION CAREER

Following less than stellar work on other shows and movies, Sheldon transferred to the medium of television, where he created and produced two memorable situation comedies for two different networks. ABC premiered Sheldon's *The Patty Duke Show* in 1963. The young actress, most famed for her portrayal of Helen Keller in the serious drama *The Miracle Worker*, played identical cousins, one from America and one from Scotland, who often exchanged identities in Sheldon's frivolous plots. That series ran for three seasons.

Even more successful for Sheldon was his NBC series *I Dream of Jeannie*, starring Barbara Eden as a sweet-natured but naive genie and Larry Hagman as the befuddled astronaut for whom she performs her magic. Debuting in 1965, the show initially ran for five years and has been rerunning ever since, spawning further *Jeannie* TV movies and commercials. A generation of Americans can probably, if asked, sing the entire lyrics of these two sitcoms' theme songs as readily, if not more so, than they could sing Berlin's "Easter Parade." Sheldon's 1970s ABC series *Hart to Hart* was another ratings winner, starring Robert Wagner and Stefanie Powers as wealthy married sleuths in the romantic comedic tradition of Nick and Nora Charles.

NOVELS

Looking for new worlds to conquer and anxious to create characterizations with more depth than afforded by most TV or film scripts, Sheldon tried his hand at writing novels. His first effort, *The Naked Face* (1970), was a suspense tale about a psychoanalyst who discovers that someone wants him dead.

Although it was not a great success in its first printing, *Naked Face* was followed by Sheldon's first blockbuster success, *The Other Side of Midnight* (1974). This rags-to-riches story of a woman's vengeance catapulted Sheldon to the best-seller lists, where he remained with each successive book. (Thanks to his later volumes, his initially moribund *Naked Face* became a steady seller in reprints.) *Midnight* brought Sheldon a movie sale, but not, unfortunately, a successful movie. The same pattern was repeated with other Sheldon best sellers, such as *Bloodline* (1977). Consequently, he elected to write and produce his own adaptation of *Rage of Angels* (1980), among others. Whatever the outcome of these adaptations, however, the hardworking Sheldon took pride in the success of the novels themselves.

At the age of eighty, on the eve of the publication of his fifteenth novel, *The Best Laid Plans* (1997), the author described his working methods to the *Los Angeles Times*: "I dictate everything to a secretary and she transcribes it. I'll do up to fifty pages a day, but when I get those pages, I'll do a dozen to fifteen total rewrites before I ever let my publisher see them." At last count, according to Guinness World Records, Sheldon is the most translated author in the world, with books in fifty-one languages in 180 countries. He continued to write well into his eighties. His final novel, *Are You Afraid of the Dark?* appeared in 2004 and was followed by a memoir titled *The Other Side of Me*, which addresses his struggles with bipolar disorder. Sheldon died on January 30, 2007, at the age of eighty-nine.

Preston Neal Jones

SEE ALSO: Annie Get Your Gun*; Astaire, Fred, and Ginger Rogers; Berlin, Irving; Broadway; Crosby, Bing; Garland, Judy; Grant, Cary;* I Dream of Jeannie*; Krantz, Judith; Lewis, Jerry; Loy, Myrna; Martin, Dean; MGM (Metro-Goldwyn-Mayer); The Musical; Porter, Cole; Sitcom; Susann, Jacqueline; Temple, Shirley.*

BIBLIOGRAPHY

Sheldon, Sidney. *The Other Side of Midnight.* New York: Morrow, 1973.

Sheldon, Sidney. *A Stranger in the Mirror.* New York: Morrow, 1976.

Sheldon, Sidney. *Master of the Game.* New York: Morrow, 1982.

Sheldon, Sidney. *Three Complete Novels: Bloodline; A Stranger in the Mirror; The Naked Face.* New York: Wings Books, 1992.

Sheldon, Sidney. *The Other Side of Me.* New York: Warner Books, 2005.

Shepard, Sam *(1943–)*

Sam Shepard is a serious and distinguished playwright whose work is admired by critics and audiences internationally. In addition, he has tried his hand at film directing. He is, however, most widely known as a movie actor, notably in *The Right Stuff* (1983), writer-director Philip Kaufman's tribute to the Mercury astronauts. His portrayal of Chuck Yeager earned him an Oscar nomination for Best Supporting Actor.

Shepard's stage and screen persona is as the strong and silent type. Tall, slim, cleft-chinned, and good-looking, he has numerous screen credits besides *The Right Stuff*, including *Crimes of the Heart* (1986), *Steel Magnolias* (1989), and *Thunderheart* (1992). He also starred with Jessica Lange, his offscreen partner for many years and the mother of some of his children, in *Frances* (1982) and *Country* (1984).

Shepard's primary cultural contribution, however, has been as a playwright. The structure of his dramatic language has received close critical attention from directors and scholars, who, as author Stephen J. Bottoms puts it in *The Theatre of Sam Shepard: States of Crises*, have tried to discover "how it is that his strange language and stage imagery so often seem to lodge themselves in the spectators imagination with such peculiar force." Shepard earned Obie Awards for three one-act plays early in his career in the 1960s, the New York Drama Critics' Circle Best Play Award for *A Lie of the Mind* (1985), and the Pulitzer Prize for Drama for his play *Buried Child* (1978).

Born Samuel Shepard Rogers IV on November 5, 1943, in Mount Sheridan, Illinois, he endured an "army brat" childhood until his family eventually settled in California. Shepard became interested in theater early, joining a church dramatic group, and later became a playwright-in-residence at the Magic Theatre in San Francisco. He moved to New York in the 1960s and began working on off-off-Broadway as a writer and an actor with such experimental groups as the La MaMa Experimental Theatre Club. Shepard was also closely associated with Manhattan's Theatre Genesis. The origin of his unique dramatic language can be traced to this early period and his subsequent move to London in 1971. The music scene in Greenwich Village, New York; the fragmented, improvisational nature of jazz; and the driving, electrified sound of rock and roll influenced the tone, structure, and characters of his initial theatrical experiments. Shepard's plays do not conform to the established dramatic style of Arthur Miller or Tennessee Williams but instead take an original language-based approach that has become his trademark.

HITTING HIS THEATRICAL STRIDE

Eschewing both realism and conventional exposition, character conflicts and inner meaning in Shepard's plays are expressed through his use of syntax, imagery, and rhythm. In the preface to *Angel City* (1976), Shepard wrote a "Note to the Actors," revealing how music influences characterization. "Instead of the idea of a 'whole character' with logical motives behind his behavior which the actor submerges himself into," he explains, "[the actor] should consider [himself] a fractured whole with bits and pieces of characters flying off the central theme. In other words, more in terms of collage construction or jazz improvisation." Although he staged nearly twenty plays in New York City between 1964 and 1971, drug addiction and a troubled affair with rock musician Patti Smith prompted a move to England, where he remained until 1974.

Of his major plays, only the rock star/status struggle drama *The Tooth of Crime* (1972) was written and first produced in London, yet Shepard's brief departure from American culture significantly influenced his work. In an interview conducted in England in 1974, he explained that "it wasn't until I came to England that I found out what it means to be an American. Nothing really makes sense when you're there, but the more distant you are from it, the more implications of what you grew up with start to emerge." His background in America became the subject of what many critics have termed a "family tetralogy," made up of *Curse of the Starving Class* (1976), *Buried Child*, *True West* (1980), and *Fool for Love* (1983). Although these works, all among his most major, deal with the psychological dysfunction of the American family, Shepard has remained an artist who resists traditional genre classification, mixing comic absurdism with a hint of the sinister.

WRITING STYLE

Shepard is an actor writing for actors whose powerful language links him to a renowned tradition of American playwrights. Yet it is precisely this language, which is uniquely his own, that also separates his work from that of his predecessors. Actor Joyce Aaron, who originated many of the female roles in Shepard's early plays, concurs, stating: "Sam is a recorder of the authentic American voice. He starts from a certain perception of daily life, and then transforms that into a specific voice—a voice with its own rhythms and shifting consciousness, its unique, particular curve or leap. . . . That is part of the theatrical challenge and wonder of speaking Sam's language."

Shepard wrote the screenplay for Wim Wenders's *Paris, Texas* (1984); adapted *Fool for Love* (1985) to the screen and starred in it; and wrote an original screenplay, *Far North* (1988), which starred Lange and also marked his none-too-successful film directing debut. Throughout the 1990s he starred in a number of television and Hollywood films, including mainstream successes *The Pelican Brief* (1993), *All the Pretty Horses* (2000), and *Black Hawk Down* (2001). During these years he did little writing, but he picked up the pen in earnest again in the first decade of the 2000s with a renewed interest in politics, addressing what he refers to as "Republican fascism" in *The God of Hell* (2004).

Since then, Shepard has balanced playwriting with smaller screen roles, including an acclaimed turn in Jim Sheridan's *Brothers* (2009). The following year he published his first collection of short fiction, *Day out of Days*. On a personal note, he and Lange announced in 2011 that their long and intensely private relationship had ended nearly two years earlier. Professionally, Shepard has built a legacy that is sure to endure. He became a member of the American Academy of Arts and Letters in 1986 and was inducted into the Theatre Hall of Fame in 1994.

John A. Price

SEE ALSO: *Broadway; Celebrity Couples; Miller, Arthur; Smith, Patti; Williams, Tennessee.*

BIBLIOGRAPHY

Bloom, Harold. *Sam Shepard*. Broomall, PA: Chelsea House Publishers, 2003.

Bottoms, Stephen J. *The Theatre of Sam Shepard: States of Crises*. Cambridge, UK: Cambridge University Press, 1998.

DeRose, David J. *Sam Shepard*. New York: Twayne, 1992.

Marranca, Bonnie, ed. *American Dreams: The Imagination of Sam Shepard*. New York: Performing Arts Journal Publications, 1981.

Wade, Leslie A. *Sam Shepard and the American Theatre*. Westport, CT: Greenwood Press, 1997.

Sherman, Cindy *(1954–)*

To some extent, Cindy Sherman has achieved cult status in the art world. With her ability to transform herself into various subjects, she uses her photography as a way to confront and explore the representations of women in society; additionally, she challenges ideas about appearance. Sherman burst upon the art scene with the showing of her first series, the black-and-white photographs in the *Untitled Film Stills* (1977–1980). Immediately recognized for her new way of approaching photography while promoting a feminist viewpoint, Sherman has generated a large following and prompted much discussion about many issues. Her images cross the boundaries of several genres, yet her photographs essentially deal with the ideas of exhibitionism, voyeurism, and the portrayal of women. Her theatrical works employ both art theories and critical issues and actively engage critics, collectors, museums, and the general public.

UPBRINGING AND STYLE DEVELOPMENT

For an artist who so quickly became successful with her sometimes surreal and horrific characters, Sherman had a simple upbringing. The youngest of five children, she was born on January 19, 1954, in Glen Ridge, New Jersey. Not long after her birth, Sherman's father, an engineer, and her mother, a school teacher, moved the family to Huntington Beach, Long Island, where she grew up. For fun, Sherman would dress up in her mother's and grandmother's clothes, but she was not trying to be "pretty"—even at an early age, Sherman was trying to create new characters. As an adult, she continued a form of "dress-up," shopping at secondhand stores to find clothing and props to enhance the characters that she would develop in front of a mirror. This element of her personality would directly feed into later images.

While studying painting at Buffalo State College, State University of New York, Sherman often produced self-portraits. She found difficulty expressing some of her ideas in this medium, however, and turned to photography. Failing her first photography class due to troubles with the technical aspects, Sherman began focusing on ideas rather than technology; this finally produced some success. Sherman's friend, artist Robert Longo, suggested that she incorporate her dress-up sessions into her artwork. It was then that Sherman found her niche; it provided her with a way to assert her ideas about the roles and depiction of women. Sherman graduated with a BA in 1976 and received a National Endowment for the Arts grant the next year. The money gave her the resources to move into New York City and helped finance her first project.

EARLY WORK

Appropriating ideas and images from film noir and movies of the 1950s and 1960s, Sherman's *Untitled Film Stills* carries nostalgic overtones. She uses herself as a model to portray and identify stereotypical roles of women, such as the femme fatale, housewife, and innocent office girl. The photographs are not self-portraits but are studies of characters that Sherman invented. For each image, she dressed up and applied makeup to change or obscure some of her facial features, thus creating a new character. She feels that her face becomes a canvas. *Untitled Film Stills* is a series of essays influenced by the media. Sherman adapts the messages promoted in the media regarding the universal archetypes of women and holds them up for scrutiny, a focus she has maintained in her more recent works. She persists in questioning how the structuring of identity relates to society's visions of womanhood.

Continuing to examine mass media, Sherman began to use her constructed identities exclusively in color images, delving into the emotions and situations of her representations. Her artwork of the early 1980s deals with portrayals of women in the porn and fashion industries. Commissioned to make fashion images for several designers, boutiques, fashion houses, and magazines, she created unglamorous images that directly contrast with most fashion photographs. The delineation between commercial photography and fine art becomes blurred in Sherman's work. Her photographs for the 1994–1995 Comme des Garçons collections directly challenge the idea of what fashion photography should be.

AN INCREASED INTEREST IN MANIPULATION

She has also imbued her works with social commentary, referencing the psychological and emotional toll brought on by conforming to society's ideals. Sherman reveals and highlights internal pathos in her *Fairy Tales* and *Disaster* images (1985–1989). These horrific and grotesque images portray the dark side of fairy tales. The subject matter of the photographs becomes less concerned with identities invented by Sherman. In these works, she begins to remove herself from the images in a blatant way—unrecognizable aspects of her body are often found in the photographs.

In *History Portraits* (1988–1990), Sherman adapted elements from several famous paintings and combined them to create parodies of historical images and icons. She photographed herself with exaggerated makeup, costumes, and props. The characterizations take on specific identities: the Madonna and Bacchus, for example. After this series, Sherman removed her body from the images completely. By manipulating dolls and interchangeable body parts ordered from a medical supply magazine, she created strange still-life tableaux in her *Sex Pictures* (1992). This series proved to be controversial, as many critics felt it was pornographic. The work, however, surpasses pornography; the clinical approach that Sherman employed removes any erotic overtones and infuses the images with an artificiality. The images were a reaction to censorship issues stirred by the definition of obscenity and pornography that the National Endowment for the Arts used in its grant-award process in the 1990s.

Despite the controversy, Sherman's work continued to receive critical acclaim. In 1995 she was awarded a MacArthur Fellowship (colloquially known as a Genius Award), which provides the recipient with $500,000. The following year New York's Museum of Modern Art (MOMA) cemented Sherman's place in the history of art photography by purchasing a complete set of *Untitled Film Stills* for a reported $1 million. However, critical acceptance did not stop Sherman's experimental process. *Horror and Surrealist Pictures* (1994–1996) continues the use of masks and objects, which become almost indiscernible due to photographic techniques such as double exposure. These color-saturated images again refer to the inner psychological and emotional elements that constitute identity.

In 1997 Sherman made her directorial debut with the horror movie *Office Killer*, a black comedy about a group of female coworkers that stars Carol Kane, Molly Ringwald, and Jeanne Tripplehorn. The film was Sherman's least successful venture to date, mocked for an illogical plot and flat dialogue, although some critics saw merit in the visual style and cinematography.

GOING DIGITAL

In her 2003–2004 project *Clowns*, Sherman made the move into digital technology, manipulating the scale of the figures and the background while still employing her usual cavalcade of makeup, wigs, and costumes. This series explores the underlying pathos behind a seemingly cheerful exterior, the sense that clowns are sad underneath while also being, in her own words, "psychotically, hysterically happy." In these pictures, Sherman underscores the ambivalence with which clowns are often received, particularly by children.

Her work in the fashion world continued, and in 2006 she designed a series of ads for Marc Jacobs that were then photographed by Juergen Teller rather than Sherman herself. She was the photographer, however, on her next fashion project, a six-image series of middle-aged fashion victims for Balenciaga. This drove the focus of her 2008 project *Socialites*, in which she appears as older society women. These wall-length digital photos suggest the marginalization of the older female, of the aging society matron whose power is slipping away.

CONTINUING TO EVOLVE

In addition to her photography and fashion work, Sherman has been exploring other media: in 2008 she did costume design for dance choreographer Stephen Petronio; in 2010 she tried her hand at jewelry design on a project with Anna Hu; and in 2011 she was the inspiration for MAC Cosmetics' fall line. A major retrospective of Sherman's work opened at MOMA in 2012—it was the first comprehensive display of her work since 1997. The show included more than 170 photographs, including recent work such as an 18-foot-high photomural with life-sized images of Sherman posing in historical costumes.

In all of her images, Sherman plays off of existing elements in mass media culture. She finds inspiration in movies, fairy tales, fashion, and books. Using components from these groups in exaggerated forms, she presents her ideas as new representations that attack and transcend universal stereotypes.

Jennifer Jankauskas

SEE ALSO: *Feminism; Film Noir.*

BIBLIOGRAPHY

Cruz, Amanda; Elizabeth A. T. Smith; and Amelia Jones. *Cindy Sherman: Retrospective*. London: Thames and Hudson, 1997.

Fuku, Noriko. "A Woman of Parts." *Art in America*, June 1997, 85, 125.

Krauss, Rosalind E. *Cindy Sherman, 1975–1993*. New York: Rizzoli, 1993.

Respini, Eva; Johanna Burton; Cindy Sherman; et al. *Cindy Sherman*. New York: Museum of Modern Art, 2012.

The Shirelles

In 1961 four young African American women known as the Shirelles—original members: Doris Kenner Jackson (1941–2000), Addie "Micki" Harris (1940–1982), Beverly Lee (1941–), and Shirley Alston Reeves (1941–)—ushered in the girl group era with the Gerry Goffin–Carole King composition "Will You Love Me Tomorrow?" Released on Scepter Records, the song reached number one on the Billboard pop charts.

The first all-female act to reach the number one position, the Shirelles demonstrated that girl groups could be commercially successful, challenging the music industry's prejudice against female rhythm-and-blues groups. Subsequent hits that made the Top 10 included "Baby, It's You" (later recorded by the Beatles) and "Dedicated to the One I Love." After "Soldier Boy" was released in 1962, the group's popularity began to diminish. At the time, they were competing with other girl groups, and their label had turned its attention to new artists, including Dionne Warwick. The Shirelles disbanded in the late 1960s; decades later, original members of the group teamed with new singers to play oldies revival shows. In 1996 the Shirelles were inducted into the Rock and Roll Hall of Fame.

Anna Hunt Graves

SEE ALSO: *The Beatles; Girl Groups; King, Carole; Pop Music; Rhythm and Blues.*

BIBLIOGRAPHY

Betrock, Alan. *Girl Groups: The Story of a Sound.* New York: Delilah Books, 1982.

Gaar, Gillian G. *She's a Rebel: The History of Women in Rock and Roll.* Seattle, WA: Seal Press, 1992.

Warwick, Jacqueline C. *Girl Groups, Girl Culture: Popular Music and Identity in the 1960s.* New York: Routledge, 2007.

Shirer, William L. *(1904–1993)*

A globe-trotting newspaperman and author of several major works of fiction and history, William L. Shirer is best known for his pioneering work as a radio newscaster during Europe's march toward World War II. From Germany's forcible union with Austria and the Czech crisis of 1938 to the Nuremberg war crimes trials in 1945, Shirer spanned the Atlantic and kept Americans informed of the aggressive intentions of Adolf Hitler and the dynamics of Nazism in his memorable *European News Round-Up* broadcasts. By the time he left CBS radio in 1947, he had helped lay the foundation for modern international news broadcasting and achieved, with his "Fall of France" report, one of the biggest on-air scoops in history.

Shirer began his career as a foreign correspondent in 1925 when he joined the Paris office of the *Chicago Tribune.* Before moving to the newspaper's Central European Bureau in Vienna in 1929, he had the opportunity to cover Charles Lindbergh's famous oceanic flight and the sessions of the League of Nations. During 1930 and 1931 Shirer traveled the breadth of India with Mohandas Gandhi and reported on the activities of Gandhi's civil disobedience movement. Shirer returned to Paris in January 1934 after a skiing accident robbed him of part of his eyesight, and he secured a position with the *New York Herald.* He was Universal News Service's Berlin correspondent from August 1934 until the organization was disbanded by William Randolph Hearst in 1937.

REPORTING HOSTILITIES

Shirer did not remain unemployed for long. When Edward R. Murrow (chief of CBS's European staff) recognized Shirer's vast experience covering European affairs and his facility with the German and French languages, he asked Shirer to open the network's office in Vienna and arrange for the broadcasts of its correspondents there. At first Shirer was to act only in an administrative capacity, because his voice was considered inadequate for extensive broadcasts. But when the German army moved into Austria on March 12, 1938, in an effort to achieve *Anschluss* (union) between the two states, Shirer was given a rare opportunity.

As soldiers swarmed through the streets of Vienna, he managed to locate a microphone. However, when he tried to deliver his account, he was forced out of the studio at bayonet-point. Undeterred, Shirer hopped the first flight to London and made his uncensored broadcast there over the network's 117-station hookup. The next day, March 13, CBS news director Paul White charged Shirer with making the arrangements for the first international multiple pickup broadcast, in which a succession of correspondents at various strategic points across the continent would go on the air and provide their own perspective on the crisis. Because this type of direct broadcast had never been done before, Shirer was compelled to improvise.

In the few hours before airtime, he located the relevant personnel and ensured their access to shortwave facilities. In order that all scheduled sources could be heard within the time allotted for the broadcast, and in the absence of any cueing system or feedback device, Shirer instructed his correspondents to time their words precisely and to go on the air blind. The success achieved with this first *European News Round-Up* guaranteed it a regular spot in the nightly newscasts of the war period. In many ways, it established the pattern for international coverage later found on television.

As a result of his *Anschluss* performance, CBS made Shirer one of its regular newscasters. In September 1938 he was the man-on-the-scene during the Czech crisis. As Hitler's conflict with the Czech government over the fate of the Sudetenland threatened to precipitate a major European war, millions of Americans anxiously tuned in to Shirer's nightly five-minute broadcasts from Prague. When the führer set his sights on Poland in September 1939, Shirer covered the impending crisis from the main vantage point of Berlin itself. On the first day of war, September 1, Shirer captivated listeners with his report of an air raid alarm while it was in progress.

BIGGEST SCOOP

Reporting from the Nazi capital offered distinct opportunities but also had significant drawbacks. Shirer's accounts of German life and strategy during wartime had to pass three rigorous censors prior to airtime, and the approved script could be read only in the presence of official observers from the propaganda office. Shirer used his ingenuity to mitigate the effects of such adulteration. Listeners became sensitive to the way he expressed his true feelings by his ironic sense of humor, sarcastic tone, and use of peculiarly American phrasing and slang that academically trained German censors could not comprehend. In May 1940 Shirer became one of a handful of correspondents allowed to accompany the German army during its conquest of France and one of the few to broadcast reports from occupied Paris.

The *Wehrmacht*'s (armed forces') advance was so swift that, by the end of the campaign, CBS had lost all contact with Shirer. When he finally reached a transmitter on June 22, he achieved one of the greatest scoops in the history of American broadcasting. Most correspondents had believed the Franco-German armistice would be signed in Berlin, and they took up positions there. Learning the actual location would be a railroad car in the Compiègne Forest (where the Germans had been forced to capitulate to the French in 1918), Shirer was able to arrive there in time to witness the spectacle and relay his account several hours before any other reporter.

In December 1940 the burden of German censorship became intolerable, and Shirer ceased his "This Is Berlin" broadcasts. He returned to the United States, embarked upon a vigorous lecture tour, and became technical adviser for the wartime film *Passport to Bordeaux*. While continuing to analyze the news for CBS, he published an uncensored account of the story behind his on-the-spot broadcast from Germany in *Berlin Diary: Journal of a Foreign Correspondent, 1934–41*. In 1941 his book became a best seller, and the Headliner's Club honored him with an award for "excellence in radio reporting."

In 1945 he returned to Germany as CBS's chief European correspondent to cover the Nuremberg war crimes trials and made it back in time to cover the opening of the United Nations in San Francisco. In 1946 Shirer received the Peabody Award for his "outstanding interpretation of the news." The following year he resigned from CBS after an objectivity dispute with Murrow.

Shirer served briefly as a commentator for the Mutual Broadcasting System from 1947 to 1949 but was blacklisted and forced to retire from broadcasting in the early 1950s because of his links with the Hollywood Ten. Thereafter Shirer sustained himself through his lectures and prolific writings. He wrote substantial articles for *Life*, *Harper's*, and *Collier's*, and the fictionalized biographies *Traitor* (1950) and *Stranger Go Home* (1954). He produced *End of a Berlin Diary* (1947) as a sequel to his earlier historical work and authored five additional books based on his experience as a correspondent: *Midcentury Journey* (1952), *The Collapse of the Third Republic* (1969), *Twentieth-Century Journey* (1976), *The Nightmare Years* (1984), and *A Native's Return* (1990). His most well-known literary achievement, *The Rise and Fall of the Third Reich*, was published in 1959, after five years of scrutinizing rare Nazi state documents and private memoirs. The work received the National Book Award in 1961. Shirer died in December 1993 in his home state of Massachusetts.

Robert J. Brown

SEE ALSO: *Blacklisting; Hearst, William Randolph; The Hollywood Ten; Murrow, Edward R.; Radio; World War II.*

BIBLIOGRAPHY

Brown, Robert J. *Manipulating the Ether: The Power of Broadcast Radio in Thirties America*. Jefferson, NC: McFarland, 1998.

Cloud, Stanley, and Lynne Olson. *The Murrow Boys: Pioneers on the Front Lines of Broadcast Journalism*. Boston: Houghton Mifflin, 1996.

Hohenberg, John. *Foreign Correspondence: The Great Reporters and Their Times*. New York: Columbia University Press, 1964.

Shirer, William L. *Berlin Diary: The Journal of a Foreign Correspondent, 1934–41*. New York: Popular Library, 1941.

Shirer, William L. *The Rise and Fall of the Third Reich: A History of Nazi Germany*. New York: Simon & Schuster, 1959.

Wick, Steve. *The Long Night: William L. Shirer and* The Rise and Fall of the Third Reich. New York: Palgrave Macmillan, 2011.

Shock Radio

The bane of the Federal Communications Commission (FCC), shock radio exploded on the American scene in the closing decades of the twentieth century. Some hailed this format as a refreshing example of free speech at work—its very outrageousness standing as proof that any message could be disseminated over America's airwaves if there was an audience willing to receive it. Others decried the success of shock radio as a sign of the coarsening of the nation's popular culture and pointed to its origins in broadcast hate speech as evidence of its secretly poisonous nature.

BEGINNINGS

Shock radio has a thousand fathers (all of them illegitimate, its detractors might add). From the mid-1920s to the 1940s, Father Charles Coughlin spewed anti-Semitic, pro-Nazi, and crypto-fascist venom to an audience of millions via his national radio program. The so-called father of hate radio was one of the first broadcasters to divine the nexus between controversial opinions and a large and avid listenership. Coughlin also established a pattern followed by other successful radio hosts of leaping into other media. He started his own newsletter, *Social Justice*, to disseminate his views. When Franklin Roosevelt dared him to run for president in 1936, Coughlin did so, as the head of the xenophobic National Union for Social Justice (Union) Party. However, America's involvement in World War II dealt a severe blow to the vituperative priest, whose tirades against "international Jewry" began to take on a seditious connotation for a nation committed to the struggle against fascism.

After Coughlin and his imitators departed the airwaves, American talk radio largely slept through the serene 1950s. The advent of rock and roll presented the only challenge to the heterodoxy of somnambulant Top 40 fare being offered up on a local and national basis. That all started to change in the 1960s, when big-city markets began to buzz with the controversial opinions of hosts such as Joe Pyne. Working out of KABC in Los Angeles, America's first all-talk station, Pyne was one of the first radio hosts to fuse conversation, confrontation, and conservatism in an effort to boost ratings. He once famously directed a caller to "go gargle with razor blades." Pyne's right-wing rants continued in the political tradition of Father Coughlin, a path many subsequent shock jocks followed as well. Others, by contrast, opted to depoliticize their programs in an effort to move beyond an audience of like-minded adherents while still maintaining a high shock value.

EXPANSION AND REDEFINITION

WNBC in New York became the proving ground for the wave of shock radio hosts in the late 1970s. Two DJs in particular, Don Imus and Howard Stern, helped to perfect the form that each later rode to an even higher level of popularity. Imus, a former marine and onetime rhythm-and-blues performer, was among the first to devote the bulk of his show to outrageous, scatological, and offensive humor. He often started a conversation with a female guest by asking what she was wearing. Inquiries into breast size and sexual history invariably followed. There was also an abundance of anticlerical material, as personified by Imus's popular "Rev. Billy Sol Hargus" character, a lapsed minister whose riffs Imus later expanded into a best-selling book and comedy album. All of this chatter was accompanied by a cacophony of quacking noises and sound effects that became standard fare for the shock radio genre. A peanut gallery of sidekicks and joke suppliers was always on hand to prop up the host when his alcohol and cocaine addictions rendered him unfit to broadcast, which was often.

Playing second fiddle to Imus in those heady days was Stern, a gangly Long Island, New York, native who at first merely aped the "I-Man's" high-volume shtick but later outstripped him in influence. Stern's daily program took Imus's audacious sex chatter to its logical extreme. Anchored around a running commentary on the news of the day, *The Howard Stern Show* also featured mock game show segments such as "Guess the Jew," in which callers would try to pick the Semite from a group of three celebrities. Stern's own sexual obsessions, such as lesbianism and the size of his own sex organ, were also given copious attention. "Conversations" with guests such as Jessica Hahn, the former Playboy bunny who had been involved in a sex scandal with televangelist Jim Bakker, often devolved into simulated sex acts or on-air stripteases. Despite constant scrutiny by the FCC, Stern managed to remain on the air and even exported his show to markets across the country. By the early 1990s he was dubbing himself the "King of All Media."

RISING IN POPULARITY

During the 1980s, thanks largely to Stern, "shock" became a hot format among radio programmers. Every city, it seemed, had its "morning zoo" crew dedicated to keeping alive the art of the prank phone call. Some of these shows were fairly tame, never straying far from the standard repertoire of "big boob" and dumb politician jokes. Others ventured dangerously far into the minefield of racial and sexual humor. Two St. Louis, Missouri, DJs, Steve Shannon and D. C. Chymes, shocked themselves out of their jobs in 1993 when they accused a caller of "acting like a nigger." The incident sparked a massive protest by the National Association for the Advancement of Colored People and the Urban League and illustrated the perils of on-air confrontation, but most hosts had a better understanding of where their bread was buttered. Even the nascent sports radio format was not immune to the allure of shock. Jim Rome, a host at 690-AM in Los Angeles, was one of the first to bring the arts of insult and confrontation to the job of covering professional athletics. His daily four-hour "smack-talking" session proved highly successful and inspired a slew of imitators.

In the 1990s, shock radio reached the apex of its influence. However, in all but taking over the talk radio airwaves, it became a genre increasingly hard to define. Politically oriented hosts such as Rush Limbaugh and New York City's conservative firebrand Bob Grant argued that their purpose was not to shock but to inform and rally support for their viewpoints. Their critics on the other side of the ideological aisle rejected this claim and dismissed their output as "hate radio." Stern and his many imitators treated politics as a mere lark, subservient to their primary mission to titillate and break taboos. Imus, who had blazed the trail in this arena, largely forsook such adolescent shenanigans altogether in his later career. His daily forum, *Imus in the Morning*, originating out of WFAN in New York beginning in 1988, took on an increasingly topical tone. The phone calls to seminude women were replaced by conversations with U.S. senators and political commentators such as Jeff Greenfield and Tim Russert.

A POLITICAL BENT

Whatever its format, shock radio's influence on the American pop cultural landscape has been undeniable. The new and improved Imus became something of a cult figure with the C-SPAN crowd after a well-publicized interview with then-presidential candidate Bill Clinton during the New York Democratic primary in 1992. In 1993 *Imus in the Morning* entered national syndication. Within three years, it was airing on more than eighty stations across the country, and the I-Man's daily audience was estimated at ten million. Not unexpectedly, Imus later squandered much of his newfound political capital in 1996 during a speech at the annual Radio and Television Correspondents dinner in Washington, D.C., calling now-President Clinton a "pot-smoking weasel" to his face. Still, his brand of shock continued to sell around the country. A 1999 *Newsweek* cover featuring the grizzled shock jock had the following headline: "The Importance of Being Imus."

Stern was even more successful. The era of political correctness gave an additional impetus to his transgressive brand of comedy. His listeners were among the most loyal and dedicated in the medium, often prank-calling TV phone-in shows to drop the name of their leader. Stern briefly stood for election as governor of New York in 1994, but he realized his extreme brand of libertarian politics was too idiosyncratic for both liberals and conservatives and quickly withdrew. Instead, he published a best-selling autobiography, *Private Parts* (1993), and starred in a movie adaptation of the same name (1997) that was well received by critics. By adding a weekly national television show in 1998, Stern came close to living up to the King of All Media label he had applied to himself. His meteoric rise in stature, like that of Imus, cemented shock radio's place at the forefront of American popular culture as the twentieth century ended.

In the twenty-first century, shock radio faced stricter regulations. Following a "wardrobe malfunction" during Super Bowl XXXVIII's halftime show in 2004, when Janet Jackson's top slipped down and part of her breast was exposed, the FCC launched the Broadcast Indecency Enforcement Act of 2005, which increased fines for violations on public airwaves and caused station owners and managers to more tightly monitor content. Already a transgressor of multiple FCC rules, Stern signed with Sirius Satellite Radio following the approval of the act, a move that allowed him to circumvent the new content laws. He was able to continue his program unabated, and his new format surpassed initial subscriber targets.

CONTINUED CONTROVERSY

In 2007 Imus fell victim to more than the indecency standards. During a conversation about an upcoming National Collegiate Athletic Association (NCAA) women's basketball game between Rutgers and Tennessee, Imus referred to the Rutgers females as "nappy-headed hos." Media Matters for America, a liberal watchdog group, alerted journalists and civil rights and women's groups. As a result of the public outcry and a loss of advertisers, Imus was suspended from MSNBC and CBS canceled his show. Imus returned to the airwaves in 2007 with a syndicated show on Citadel Media and later signed a contract with Fox Business Network. He was again engulfed in controversy in June 2008 when he connected race with the legal troubles of Adam Jones, an African American National Football League cornerback. This time, however, no disciplinary action resulted. Imus was diagnosed with cancer in 2009.

In 2012 Limbaugh wound up in hot water for incendiary comments about Sandra Fluke, a Georgetown University law student. Testifying before Democrats in the House of Representatives, Fluke had argued that health insurers ought to cover women's contraceptive costs. Limbaugh responded by calling Fluke a "slut" and a "prostitute." A loss of advertising followed, though there was no disciplinary action. It was the latest in a long line of incidents on shock radio, where controversy goes with the territory.

Robert E. Schnakenberg

SEE ALSO: *Coughlin, Father Charles E.; Jackson, Janet; Limbaugh, Rush; Radio; Stern, Howard; Super Bowl.*

BIBLIOGRAPHY

Adubato, Steve. *You Are the Brand.* New Brunswick, NJ: Rutgers University Press, 2011.

Allen, Steve. *Vulgarians at the Gate: Trash TV and Raunch Radio: Raising the Standards of Pop Culture.* Amherst, NY: Prometheus Books, 2001.

Hall, Ann C., and Mardia J. Bishop. *Pop-Porn: Pornography in American Culture.* Westport, CT: Praeger, 2007.

Kosova, Weston. "The Power That Was." *Newsweek,* April 23, 2007.

Reed, Jim. *Everything Imus.* Secaucus, NJ: Carol Publishing, 1999.

Stern, Howard. *Private Parts.* New York: Pocket Books, 1996.

Shore, Dinah *(1917–1994)*

A sultry-voiced pop singer with southern charm, Dinah Shore recorded seventy-five hit records between 1940 and 1955. After a modest career in the movies, Shore found her niche in television, making her debut in 1951 as the cheery host of a fifteen-minute variety show, which aired twice a week. She became even more popular with *The Dinah Shore Chevy Show* (1956–1963), singing the jingle "See the USA in your Chevrolet" and smacking a signature sign-off kiss to the audience. Like another of that era's television singers, Kate Smith, Shore quickly became a national institution.

Born in Winchester, Tennessee, Shore graduated from Vanderbilt University with a degree in sociology. Moving to New York City after graduation, she sang on radio with Frank Sinatra—who nicknamed her Magnolia Blossom—and tried out unsuccessfully as a vocalist for several top dance bands. Eddie Cantor's daughters heard her singing on WNEW, and she successfully auditioned for Cantor's radio show, which had been a career springboard for singers Deanna Durbin, Margaret Whiting, and Bobby Breen. Within weeks of her debut she had a Columbia recording contract, and Cantor put up $750 of his own money to buy her the rights to the song, "Yes, My Darling Daughter," which became her first hit. By the end of 1940, she was voted Outstanding New Star of the Year by 600 radio editors.

Shore made her movie debut in the Cantor musical *Thank Your Lucky Stars,* perhaps best remembered for a decision made by Warner Brothers' makeup artists to lighten Shore's dark hair to an off-blond color. Samuel Goldwyn chose her to costar in Danny Kaye's 1944 debut film, a GI comedy, *Up in Arms,* in which she introduced two Harold Arlen songs, "Now I Know" and "Tess's Torch Song." In the few movies that followed (*Belle of the Yukon, Follow the Boys, Till the Clouds Roll By,* and *Aaron Slick from Punkin Crick*), Shore was featured in guest-singing spots or given minor roles. "I bombed as a movie star," she candidly admitted, but she soon became a superstar on television.

Shore's warm, friendly manner with her top-name guest stars made her one of the few women to achieve a major success as a variety-series host, and the *Chevy Show* ran for seven seasons as a highlight of NBC's Sunday night schedule. The program allowed Shore to display a variety of talents in skits and production numbers, in addition to singing such perennial favorites as "Blues in the Night," "I'll Walk Alone," and "Buttons and Bows." In 1961 NBC moved her to Friday nights to give a new Western show, *Bonanza,* the Sunday slot, but her popularity continued.

During her years on television, Shore received ten Emmy Awards and was regularly named to the list of the nation's most admired women. Making the transition from variety show to talk show host, she continued to win fans with *Dinah's Place* (1970–1974), *Dinah and Her Friends* (1979–1984), and *A Conversation with Dinah* (1989–1991).

In the early 1970s, Shore's six-year romance with Burt Reynolds, who was almost twenty years her junior, made big news in the tabloids. A UPI reporter called it "one of the most tastefully handled Hollywood love affairs in recent memory." Both Reynolds and Shore openly conversed about it on talk shows and saw no problem with the age difference. They remained good friends after the breakup, and he often appeared on her television shows.

In 1981, at the age of sixty-four, Shore boldly signed a contract for a series of live stage performances, her first in more than thirty years. Although accustomed to television cue cards, she was able, after a few rehearsals, to remember all her new lyrics and arrangements, and the shows went smoothly. During her last years she was an avid tennis player and golfer, also sponsoring a tournament on the Ladies Professional Golf Association Tour.

Benjamin Griffith

SEE ALSO: *Big Bands; Cantor, Eddie; Celebrity; Celebrity Couples; Durbin, Deanna; Goldwyn, Samuel; Golf; Hollywood; Kaye, Danny; Reynolds, Burt; Sinatra, Frank; Smith, Kate; Television; Whiting, Margaret.*

BIBLIOGRAPHY

Brooks, Tim, and Earle Marsh. *The Complete Directory to Prime Time Network and Cable TV Shows: 1946 to Present,* 6th ed. New York: Ballantine, 1995.

Hemming, Roy, and David Hajdu. *Discovering Great Singers of Classic Pop.* New York: Newmarket, 1991.

Inman, David. *The TV Encyclopedia.* New York: Perigee, 1991.

Shorter, Frank *(1947–)*

Often credited with having spurred the running boom of the 1970s, Frank Shorter was one of America's greatest Olympic performers. He is best remembered for his victory in the marathon during the ill-starred games in Munich in 1972 and for his runner-up finish four years later in Montreal. The Munich games were marred by the terrorism meted out against Israeli athletes, but they are also recalled for swimmer Mark Spitz's unprecedented seven gold medals and Shorter's long-distance triumph. On the day of the marathon, September 10, 1972, *Runner's World* later contended "distance running was changed forever . . . transformed from the cult exercise of an eccentric breed of skinny men into what would become for many a way of life."

OLYMPIC FEATS

An international television audience watched as the tousle-haired Shorter, born in Munich in 1947—his father was an American army physician stationed in Germany after the war—and a graduate of Yale University, held the lead from the 15-kilometer marker. Days earlier, Shorter had finished fifth in the 10,000-meter race. On entering the stadium near the close of the marathon, he was stunned to encounter jeering and booing, which was intended for a prankster who had landed on the track a short while earlier. Shorter went on to best the Belgian Karel Lismont, who had never lost a marathon previously. "Five seconds beyond the finish line it hit me what I'd done," Shorter, who often ran 140 miles a week, remembered. "I don't have to do it again for a while." The marathon, he reasoned, "is a battle against slowing down."

Four years later in Montreal, Shorter, by then a graduate of the University of Florida School of Law and an associate with French & Stone in Boulder, Colorado, was favored to repeat and thereby duplicate the feat of Ethiopia's Abebe Bikila. Shorter, however, was defeated by the little known East German Waldermar Cierpinski, who established an Olympic record. When he passed the front-running Shorter, Cierpinski later reflected, "I did so, and looked right into the eyes of the man who was my idol as a marathon runner. I knew all about him. And yet I could tell by the return glance that he didn't know much, if anything, about me. The psychological advantage was mine."

Shorter's Olympic accomplishments followed earlier victories in the 1969 National Collegiate Athletic Association (NCAA) 6-mile run, the 10,000-meter race in the 1970 U.S.-USSR dual meet in Leningrad, the 1970 Amateur Athletic Union (AAU) outdoor 3-mile and 6-mile events, the 1971 AAU 6-mile run, and the 1971 Pan-American Games 10,000-meter race and the marathon. From 1970 to 1973 he was also the AAU cross-country champion. Shorter eventually won a record four Fukoka marathons. In 1972 he received the Sullivan Award, given annually to the nation's top amateur athlete, but by 1979 serious foot and back injuries sorely hampered his track performances.

RUNNING ADVOCATE

Shorter is a member of the National Track & Field Hall of Fame and the Olympic Hall of Fame. He has served as a television sports commentator for track-and-field performances and founded Frank Shorter Running Gear, headquartered in Colorado. But among his greatest achievements is his success at challenging the false separation between amateur and professional track-and-field performers, thus ushering in "a new cooperative climate between athletes, sponsors and federations," according to *Runner's World*.

Shorter's Olympic feats, including the first victory in the marathon by an American in sixty-four years, helped to trigger a running boom in the United States. (Instrumental, too, were the early successes and later nearly epochal failures in the 1968 and 1972 Olympic Games by world-record-holding miler Jim Ryun, Dr. Kenneth Cooper's championing of aerobic conditioning, and James F. Fixx's and Joe Henderson's writings extolling running.) By 1970 two million Americans were jogging regularly, according to a Gallup poll. Following Shorter's triumph, road racing became more popular in the United States, thanks to favorable media coverage and corporate sponsorships. For a time, under-the-table expense payments were often delivered, as the lines between amateur and professional athletes continued to narrow.

By 1980 the United States reportedly boasted thirty million runners, while by 1997 *Runner's World* suggested a second running boom was occurring. This one tended to be less competitive, "more individual- and family-centered, more health- and fitness-oriented, more 'set your own goals and choose your own pace.'" Shorter's contribution to one of late-twentieth-century America's most ubiquitous fitness crazes renders him a significant figure in U.S. popular culture.

Shorter made another significant contribution to U.S. athletics by founding the U.S. Anti-Doping Agency in 2000 and serving as its chairman until 2003. He testified before Congress during the hearings into steroid abuse in Major League Baseball in 2005, and he continued to act as an advocate for drug-free sports after that. Speaking of the need for testing that is independent of the control of sports leagues, he says, "You can't make money on something and police it." Forty years after his stunning marathon victory at Munich, Shorter is fighting for a different kind of long-term win.

Robert C. Cottrell

SEE ALSO: *Baseball; Boston Marathon; Olympics; Spitz, Mark; Sports Heroes.*

BIBLIOGRAPHY

Bloom, Marc. "Olympic Flashback: Shorter in the Long Run." *Runner's World*, February 1992, 20.

Bloom, Marc. "Frankly Speaking." *Runner's World*, September 1997, 57–58.

Bloom, Marc. "The Second Boom." *Runner's World*, November 1997, 66–72.

Cooper, Pamela. *The American Marathon*. Syracuse, NY: Syracuse University Press, 1998.

Espy, Richard. *The Politics of the Olympic Games*. Berkeley: University of California Press, 1979.

Krise, Raymond, and Bill Squires. *Fast Tracks: The History of Distance Running since 884 B.C.* Brattleboro, VT: Stephen Greene Press, 1982.

Lovett, Charlie. *Olympic Marathon: A Centennial History of the Games' Most Storied Race*. Westport, CT: Praeger, 1997.

Shainberg, Lawrence. "The Obsessiveness of the Long-Distance Runner." *New York Times Magazine*, February 25, 1973, 28, 30–34.

Shorter, Frank, and Marc Bloom. *Olympic Gold: A Runner's Life and Times*. Boston: Houghton Mifflin, 1984.

Shorter, Frank, and Marc Bloom. *Frank Shorter's Running for Peak Performance*. New York: DK Adult, 2005.

Wallechinsky, David. *The Complete Book of the Summer Olympics*. Boston: Little, Brown, 1996.

Show Boat

Show Boat (1927), Jerome Kern and Oscar Hammerstein II's immortal tale of life on the Mississippi River from the 1880s to the 1920s, was one of the landmark works of the American musical theater. It not only contained a cavalcade of songs that included "Ol' Man River," "Can't Help Lovin' Dat Man," "Make Believe," and "You Are Love," but it also helped propel the American musical theater forward with its serious libretto and a musical score that was wedded to the dramatic content.

PLOTLINES

Based on Edna Ferber's 1926 novel of life on the Mississippi River, Hammerstein's libretto focuses on Magnolia (Nola) Hawks, impressionable daughter of Cap'n Andy Hawks—owner of the showboat *Cotton Blossom*—and his domineering wife, Parthy. Nola falls in love at first sight with Gaylord Ravenal, a river gambler. They marry and move to Chicago, where their daughter, Kim, is born. Gaylord loses all his money and deserts his family. The musical ends in 1927, years later, with a reunion of Nola, Gaylord, and Kim on the *Cotton Blossom*.

Show Boat. *Kathryn Grayson as Magnolia Hawks, right, falls in love with Howard Keel as charming gambler Gaylord Ravenal in* Show Boat. MGM/THE KOBAL COLLECTION.

Secondary plots and characters are of great importance in the show. Julie, the mixed-race actress, is forced to leave the *Cotton Blossom* when her racial background is exposed. In the second act Julie sacrifices her career for Nola, who, destitute, auditions to sing at the Trocadero Club. Joe and Queenie, an African American couple who live on the *Cotton Blossom*, provide continuity as the personifications of wisdom and the joy of life through numbers such as Joe's "Ol' Man River" and the couple's "Ah Still Suits Me," written for the 1936 film and interpolated into some of the show's subsequent revivals. Frank and Ellie embody the essence of musical comedy with their farcical antics. In Ellie's "Life upon the Wicked Stage," the comic actress describes her profession to her adoring fans.

THE MUSIC

Show Boat's musical score contains a substantial number of songs that entered the canon of American popular music. Considered the most operatic of Kern's scores, the music in *Show Boat* elevated the standard of popular song. The show's numbers became defining works in the musical theater repertoire. In *Show Boat*, characters are defined through their music. The relationship of Nola and Gaylord develops from the fantasy world of "Make Believe" to overt expression in "You Are Love" and "Why Do I Love You?"; Julie's torch song, "Bill" (written in 1918 for *Oh, Lady, Lady!* but cut from the show), became a classic of the genre; and "Can't Help Lovin' Dat Man," with its opening line "Fish gotta swim, birds gotta fly," emerged as a standard romantic ballad.

Show Boat became an institution in American musical theater because of its skillful integration of operetta, realistic drama, and musical comedy. The fantasy world of the operetta is captured through the show's numerous waltzes. The credo of operetta, "Make Believe" (though not a waltz), is the title of one of the musical's early numbers. The fantasy world of the operetta is represented by the showboat and its theatrical escapism. The real world is manifested through the Chicago scenes—the World's Fair, Gaylord's gambling and desertion, and the plights of Julie and Nola. The real world enters the *Cotton Blossom* in the miscegenation scene, where Julie and her husband, Steve, are forced to leave the showboat. Musical comedy elements appear in the characters of Ellie and Frank, whose music is decidedly Tin Pan Alley in style. The integration of these diverse musical styles accounts for *Show Boat*'s importance and popularity.

The musical score of *Show Boat* is integrated with the show's dramatic narrative. Music does not exist solely for its own sake—its purpose is to enhance the drama. The standard was set and groundwork was laid for a more serious approach to the Broadway musical. Characters could no longer waltz their way out of difficulty as the tragedy of real life entered the popular musical theater. Kern and Hammerstein did give in to the Broadway tradition of a happy ending, however. Ferber's novel does not include the final scene of reconciliation between Nola and Gaylord.

SHOW BOAT'S SUCCESS

Show Boat, produced by Florenz Ziegfeld, opened at the Ziegfeld Theatre in New York on December 27, 1927. Howard Marsh and Norma Terris played the lead roles of Nola and

Gaylord. Helen Morgan created her legendary role of Julie, and Jules Bledsoe was the first Joe. The show ran for 572 performances, making it the second-longest running Broadway musical of the 1920s.

Show Boat has continued to be successful on both stage and screen. Numerous revivals included Ziegfeld's in 1932, Kern and Hammerstein's 1946 production, the Musical Theater of Lincoln Center's 1966 version, and Hal Prince's lavish treatment that opened in Toronto in 1993 and in New York the following year. Three film versions of *Show Boat* were created: a 1929 part-talkie, a 1936 adaptation with Irene Dunne and Allan Jones, and the 1951 classic with Kathryn Grayson and Howard Keel.

In 1988 EMI released what it claimed to be "the first ever complete recording" of *Show Boat*. Under the direction of John McGlinn, it features opera singers Frederica von Stade, Jerry Hadley, Teresa Stratas, and Bruce Hubbard in the principal roles, thus emphasizing the work's operatic qualities. Music that was cut from the show during its pre-Broadway tryout and songs written for film versions and revivals are included on the recording.

Show Boat is a classic American musical. Its memorable score and its integration of plot and music display a high level of crafting on the part of its creators. The combination of realism and fantasy inherent in the story ensures that *Show Boat* will continue to delight audiences for generations to come.

William A. Everett

SEE ALSO: *Broadway; Kern, Jerome; The Musical; Rodgers and Hammerstein.*

BIBLIOGRAPHY

Block, Geoffrey. "The Broadway Canon from *Show Boat* to *West Side Story* and the European Operatic Ideal." *Journal of Musicology* 11 (1993): 525–544.

Block, Geoffrey. *Some Enchanted Evenings: The Broadway Musical from* Show Boat *to Sondheim*. New York: Oxford University Press, 1997.

Citron, Stephen. *The Wordsmiths: Oscar Hammerstein II and Alan Jay Lerner*. New York: Oxford University Press, 1995.

Kreuger, Miles. Show Boat: *The Story of a Classic American Musical*. New York: Da Capo Press, 1990.

Mordenn, Ethan. "'Show Boat' Crosses Over." *New Yorker*, July 3, 1989, 79–93.

Shrek

In 2001 *Shrek* set box-office records, garnered the first Academy Award for Best Animated Feature, and started an entertainment franchise that expanded to include three more films and two holiday television specials, along with video games, comic books, and even a Broadway musical. The common denominator in all these manifestations is an irreverent attitude toward the typical themes and characters of traditional fairy tales. *Shrek* and its sequels have achieved popular success by combining child-friendly fun with tongue-in-cheek humor that appeals to adult audiences.

The character Shrek is a green ogre, originally created by artist William Steig in his 1990 picture book, *Shrek!* Ogres are fictional beings, usually depicted in folktales as large, ill-tempered, and unattractive. In the first film, which was loosely based on Steig's book, Shrek is a cranky, swamp-dwelling loner whose solitary life is disrupted by the arrival of various fairy-tale characters exiled by the villainous Lord Farquaad. The plot revolves around Farquaad's plan to marry the beautiful—but unexpectedly feisty—Princess Fiona. No one knows that Fiona is under a curse that turns her into an ogress every night. Fiona and Shrek fall in love, are parted by misunderstanding, and reunited. When they kiss, Fiona's curse is lifted in a surprising way: she turns into a full-time ogre. The two marry and leave for a romantic honeymoon.

The essential story of this first film is Shrek's transformation through love and Fiona's discovery of her true self. Along the way, Shrek shares adventures with his sassy new friend Donkey, and much fun is made of clichéd fairy-tale characters and plots, including Snow White, Cinderella, and the Three Little Pigs. The film also parodies an assortment of popular movies, including *Taxi Driver* (1976), *Star Wars* (1977), and *Crouching Tiger, Hidden Dragon* (2000). This general formula is reused for *Shrek 2* (2004), in which the happy couple pays a humorously complicated visit to Fiona's parents, the king and queen of Far Far Away, and in *Shrek the Third* (2007), in which the king dies and Shrek must take his place temporarily.

By the beginning of *Shrek Forever After* (2010), Shrek and Fiona have triplets, but family life is making Shrek feel cranky again. It is only after magically experiencing a world in which he never lived that Shrek learns to appreciate his good fortune. *Shrek 2* can be viewed as a comic remake of *Guess Who's Coming to Dinner* (a groundbreaking 1967 film about interracial marriage), and *Shrek Forever After* echoes the 1946 classic *It's a Wonderful Life*. *Shrek the Third* draws on literary sources, playfully mixing up bits of William Shakespeare with a pastiche of Arthurian romance.

Part of *Shrek*'s appeal—especially for adults—comes from the deflation of conventional plot elements (such as rescuing distressed damsels or transforming beast to beauty with a kiss) and familiar characters. In the *Shrek* world, famed heroes are really villains or weaklings, for example, and pretty princesses prove to be anything but demure. This strategy of turning fairy-tale elements upside down often creates genuine humor, but in the view of some commentators, it may occasionally go too far. Even the widely praised first movie includes controversial scenes, such as the torture of the Gingerbread Man, and has sparked debate about whether the film promotes female empowerment or reinforces traditional gender stereotypes. By *Shrek the Third*, the balance between fun and meanness may have tipped in a negative direction, with a vengeful Prince Charming killed off after attempting to murder the future King Arthur. This installment of the series was the least-liked by critics, who generally felt it lacked the originality and emotional engagement of the first two films. Nevertheless, it was a success at the box office, and the next *Shrek* film drew more positive reviews.

Shrek became the first big hit for newly established DreamWorks Animation, and the film is generally viewed as a lampoon of the romanticized, sanitized fairy-tale world of the Disney classics. By introducing references to contemporary culture and integrating songs from pop music, DreamWorks modernized the fairy tale and developed a signature approach that can be seen in its other successful features—including the *Madagascar* and *Kung Fu Panda* series, as well as the 2011 Shrek spin-off, *Puss in*

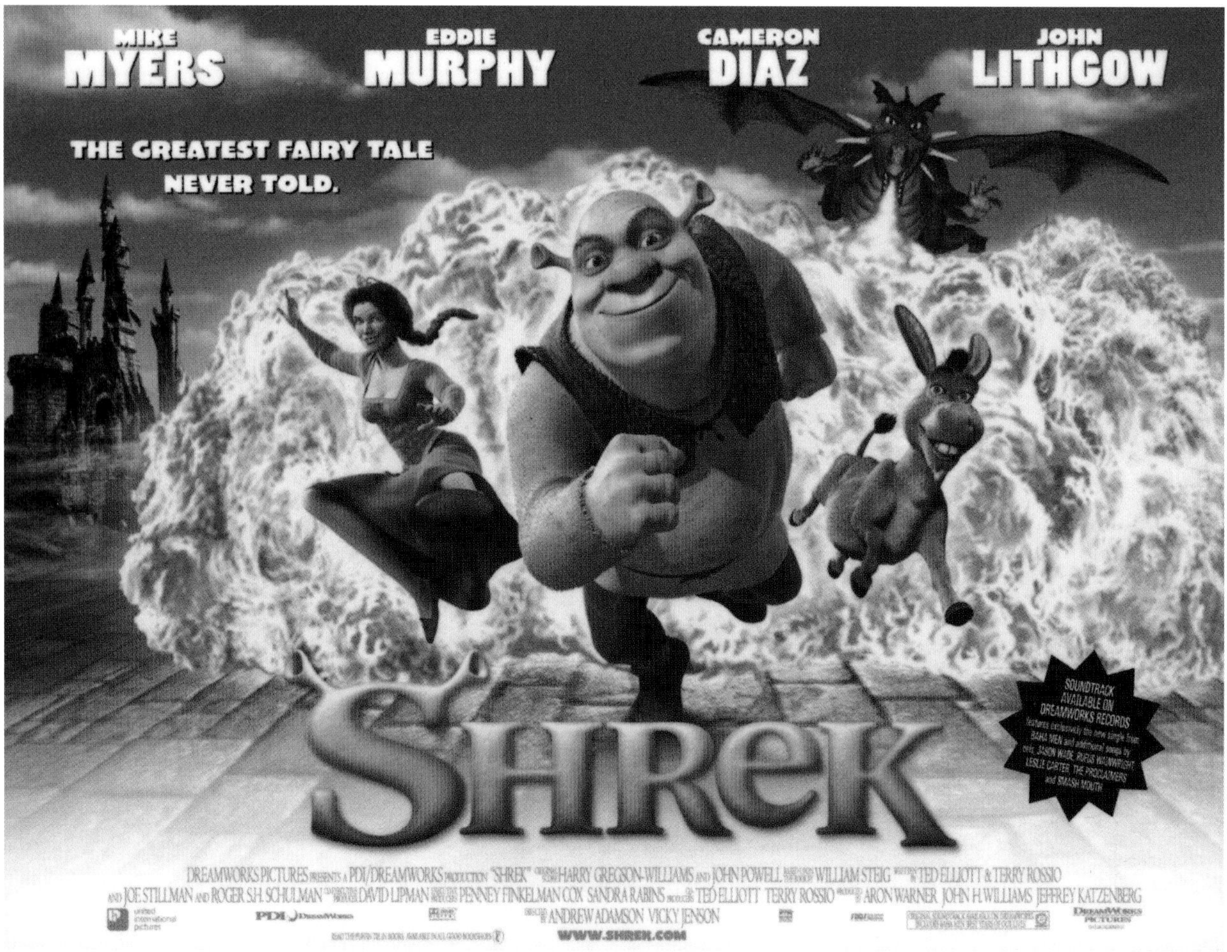

Shrek. *A movie poster casts the original* Shrek *in 2001 as "the greatest fairy tale never told."* DREAMWORKS LLC/THE KOBAL COLLECTION.

Boots. Although five *Shrek* films were originally planned, DreamWorks decided that *Shrek Forever After* would be the final installment, noting that it made a fitting conclusion for Shrek's personal journey. Widely recognized as a trendsetting influence on the animation industry, by 2012 the *Shrek* franchise ranked as the fifth-highest-grossing film series of all time.

Cynthia Giles

SEE ALSO: *Academy Awards; Animated Films; Broadway; Comic Books;* Crouching Tiger, Hidden Dragon*; Disney (Walt Disney Company);* It's a Wonderful Life*; Murphy, Eddie; The Musical; Pop Music;* Star Wars*;* Taxi Driver*; Video Games.*

BIBLIOGRAPHY

Booker, M. K. *Disney, Pixar, and the Hidden Messages of Children's Films*. Santa Barbara, CA: Praeger, 2010.

Hopkins, John. *Shrek: From the Swamp to the Screen*. New York: Harry N. Abrams, 2004.

McCooey, David, and Maria Takolander. "You Can't Say No to the Beauty and the Beast: *Shrek* and Ideology." *Papers: Explorations into Children's Literature* 15, no. 1 (2005): 5.

Zipes, Jack D. *Happily Ever After: Fairy Tales, Children, and the Culture Industry*. London: Routledge, 1997.

Shula, Don *(1930–)*

Don Shula retired as the winningest coach in National Football League (NFL) history. Born on January 4, 1930, in Grand River, Ohio, Shula started his professional football career as a defensive back with the Cleveland Browns in 1951. He also played for the Baltimore Colts from 1953 to 1956 and the Washington Redskins in 1957.

Shula is best known for his thirty-three seasons as a head coach, eight with the Baltimore Colts (1963–1969) and twenty-five with the Miami Dolphins (1970–1995). His teams compiled a record of 347–173–6, and they reached the playoffs twenty times. Shula took the Colts to the Super Bowl in 1969 and the Dolphins in 1972, 1973, 1974, 1983, and 1985. He is also the only coach in NFL history to record an undefeated year in the regular season and the postseason, capped when his 1972–1973 Dolphins beat the Washington Redskins 14–7 in Super Bowl VII.

After several disappointing seasons, Shula stepped down as head coach of the Miami Dolphins on January 5, 1996. He was elected in his first year of eligibility to the Pro Football Hall of Fame.

Daniel Bernardi

SEE ALSO: *National Football League (NFL); Professional Football; Super Bowl.*

BIBLIOGRAPHY

Brown, Jody. *Don Shula: Countdown to Supremacy.* New York: Leisure Press, 1983.

Harvey, Walter. *Football's Most Wanted II.* Dulles, VA: Potomac Books, 2006.

Shula, Don, and Ken Blanchard. *Everyone's a Coach: You Can Inspire Anyone to Be a Winner.* New York: Harper Business, 1995.

Stein, R. Conrad. *Don Shula: Football's Winningest Coach.* Chicago: Children's Press, 1994.

Shulman, Max *(1919–1988)*

Popular American humorist Max Shulman is best known for *The Many Loves of Dobie Gillis,* a CBS television sitcom he created from his volume of short stories of the same name. The television series, for which Shulman was also a writer, ran from 1959 to 1963 and starred Dwayne Hickman as Dobie and Bob Denver as his good friend Maynard G. Krebs. *Dobie Gillis* was one of the first television shows to focus on the lives of teenagers.

Shulman began writing seriously while he attended the University of Minnesota. After graduation, he served in the U.S. Army Air Corps during World War II. During this time he published comic novels concerning college students, civilians during the war, and the difficulties of adjusting to peacetime. Some of his early works include *Barefoot Boy with Cheek* (1943), *The Feather Merchants* (1944), and *The Zebra Derby* (1946). The Dobie Gillis stories were collected in 1951.

Shulman adapted his first novel into an unsuccessful musical in 1947 but coauthored the Broadway hit *The Tender Trap* seven years later. In 1957 he published a novel titled *Rally round the Flag, Boys!,* about the establishment of a missile base next to a complacent commuter town in Connecticut; Paul Newman, Joanne Woodward, and Joan Collins starred in the film adaptation. Shulman was also a Metro-Goldwyn-Mayer (MGM) screenwriter for a brief period, during which time he wrote three comedies in 1953, including *The Affairs of Dobie Gillis,* starring Debbie Reynolds.

Later in life Shulman was less productive, writing little after the mid-1960s. Of note during this time, however, he co-wrote the screenplay for *House Calls* (1978), a film starring Walter Matthau and Glenda Jackson, and was cocreator of the television series of the same name a year later.

David Lonergan

SEE ALSO: *Broadway; Dobie Gillis; MGM (Metro-Goldwyn-Mayer); Newman, Paul; Sitcom; Television; World War II.*

BIBLIOGRAPHY

Shulman, Max. *The Many Loves of Dobie Gillis: Eleven Campus Stories.* Garden City, NY: Doubleday, 1951.

Super, John C. *The Fifties in America.* Pasadena, CA: Salem Press, 2005.

SIDS (Sudden Infant Death Syndrome)

Of all the fears associated with early parenthood, none is greater than the possibility of an infant's unexplainable and sudden death. Sudden infant death syndrome (SIDS) poses such a threat to seemingly healthy babies of all socioeconomic and racial backgrounds under one year old. Officially defined and named at a 1969 international conference on causes of sudden death in infants, SIDS has been a political and medical controversy ever since. Although researchers had linked a lower risk of SIDS to babies sleeping on their backs and a higher risk of SIDS to babies exposed to secondhand smoke, SIDS remained the leading cause of postnatal mortality from 1980 to 1994. Heightening the fears surrounding SIDS, controversy rose in late 1997 when an article in *Pediatrics* stated that some SIDS-attributed deaths were caused by child abuse and again in 1998 when a large German study linked SIDS with cytomegalovirus (CMV), a virus that is common in AIDS patients.

In the first decade of the 2000s researchers were investigating the relationship that apnea (brief cessations of breathing), bradycardia (slow heart rates), and other abnormalities might have with SIDS. The research was so promising that scientists hoped that tests would eventually be developed to identify high-risk babies. Until such time as that could take place, experts recommended that parents continue with the earlier guidelines and also do the following: breastfeed babies, give them pacifiers, avoid bed-sharing between adults and infants, avoid exposing infants to respiratory infections, and keep the crib in an adult's bedroom until the baby reaches six months of age. Such advice seemed to make a substantial difference; from 1983 to 2004 the rate of SIDS fell by nearly two-thirds, from 1.46 per 1,000 live births to 0.51.

Tova Stabin

SEE ALSO: *AIDS; Cigarettes.*

BIBLIOGRAPHY

Bergman, Abraham B.; J. Bruce Beckwith; and C. George Ray, eds. *Sudden Infant Death Syndrome: Proceedings of the Second International Conference on Causes of Sudden Death in Infants.* Seattle: University of Washington Press, 1970.

Guntheroth, Warren G. *Crib Death: The Sudden Infant Death Syndrome,* 3rd ed. Armonk, NY: Futura Publishing, 1995.

Horchler, Joani Nelson, and Robin Rice. *SIDS & Infant Death Survival Guide: Information and Comfort for Grieving Family & Friends & Professionals Who Seek to Help Them,* 3rd ed. Hyattsville, MD: SIDS Educational Services, 2003.

Siegel, Bugsy *(1906–1947)*

Benjamin "Bugsy" Siegel is remembered as the visionary mobster who first recognized the enormous moneymaking potential of the legalized gambling oasis of Las Vegas, Nevada, and who oversaw the construction of the town's first lavish casino and hotel, the Flamingo, in the mid-1940s. Like his close associates Meyer Lansky and Lucky Luciano, Siegel began his underworld career as a street hoodlum on New York's Lower East Side. While still in his teens, Siegel, along with Lansky, formed the Bug-Meyer Mob. Specializing in protection rackets, gambling, and auto theft, Siegel quickly gained a reputation as a brutal hit man and worked alongside Lansky in the formation of Murder Inc., the enforcement arm of the New York syndicate.

In the mid-1930s Siegel moved to California, where he worked to expand organized crime operations chiefly in gambling and drug smuggling and renewed his acquaintance with movie actor George Raft, a childhood friend. Through Raft, Siegel (who longed for a movie career himself) gained contacts in the film industry and was linked romantically with several actresses, including Wendy Barrie and, most notably, the mob courier Virginia Hill. When the Flamingo failed to bring the promised quick return on their $6 million investment, Luciano and his syndicate associates demanded Siegel settle his debt. Siegel refused and was subsequently shot and killed while he sat in the living room of his Beverly Hills mansion in June 1947.

During the ensuing decades of the twentieth century, Siegel's vision was fully realized as Las Vegas became the chief gambling center of the United States and a favorite location for mob investment. While Siegel himself never found success in Hollywood, several films have traced his career, including *Neon Empire*, a cable television movie that aired in 1989, and the star-studded 1991 biographical feature *Bugsy*, directed by Barry Levinson, in which Siegel and Hill were portrayed by Warren Beatty and Annette Bening, respectively.

Laurie DiMauro

SEE ALSO: *Beatty, Warren; Gambling; Lansky, Meyer; Las Vegas; Luciano, Lucky; Mafia/Organized Crime; Raft, George.*

BIBLIOGRAPHY

Buntin, John. *L.A. Noir: The Struggle for the Soul of America's Most Seductive City*. New York: Three Rivers Press, 2009.

Dorigo, Joe. *Mafia*. Secaucus, NJ: Chartwell Books, 1992.

Jennings, Dean Southern. *We Only Kill Each Other: The Life and Bad Times of Bugsy Siegel*. Englewood Cliffs, NJ: Prentice-Hall, 1967.

Nash, Jay Robert. *Encyclopedia of World Crime*, vol. IV. Wilmette, IL: CrimeBooks, 1990.

Nash, Jay Robert. *World Encyclopedia of Organized Crime*. New York: Da Capo Press, 1993.

Sifakis, Carl. *The Encyclopedia of American Crime*. New York: Smithmark, 1992.

Wilen, John. "New LV Hotel-Casino Named in Honor of Bugsy Siegel." *Las Vegas Sun*, June 26, 1998.

The Silence of the Lambs

The film *The Silence of the Lambs*, directed by Jonathan Demme and starring Jodie Foster and Anthony Hopkins, was released in the winter of 1991 to substantial financial and critical success. The film is based on a 1988 novel by Thomas Harris, which in turn is a sequel to Harris's 1981 best seller on similarly themed material, *Red Dragon*.

Both novel and film focus on the strange emotional and intellectual connection between a female FBI Academy student, Clarice Starling, and an imprisoned serial killer, Dr. Hannibal "The Cannibal" Lecter. The two work together to apprehend another serial killer, known in the tabloid press as "Buffalo Bill," before he can kill his next female victim. The film version not only introduced Dr. Lecter into the ranks of popular culture villains but garnered the top five Oscars during the Academy Awards in 1992. The film won for Best Picture, Best Actor (Hopkins), Best Actress (Foster), and Best Adapted Screenplay (Ted Tally).

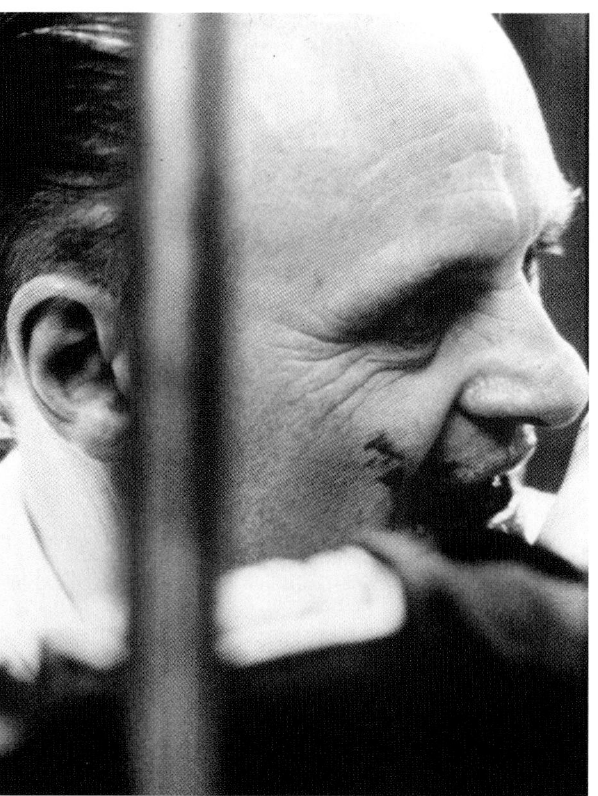

***Anthony Hopkins in* The Silence of the Lambs.** *Anthony Hopkins starred as Hannibal "The Cannibal" Lecter in the 1991 thriller* The Silence of the Lambs. ORION/THE KOBAL COLLECTION/REGAN, KEN.

A sequel and prequel to the movie were released in the first decade of the 2000s: *Hannibal* (2001) and *Red Dragon* (2002). Neither attained the critical or popular success of the original film. The next decade went in a new direction when a musical theater parody of the film called *Silence! The Musical* debuted, and won the NYC Fringe's Best Musical Award, Time Magazine Top Ten, and a Best Musical at the Off Broadway Alliance Awards.

Philip Simpson

SEE ALSO: *Academy Awards; FBI (Federal Bureau of Investigation); Foster, Jodie; Serial Killers.*

BIBLIOGRAPHY

Gire, Dann. "*Silence of the Lambs*: Anthony Hopkins on Hannibal Lecter." *Cinefantastique*, October 1992, 108–109.

Harris, Thomas. *The Silence of the Lambs*. New York: St. Martin's Press, 1988.

O'Brien, Daniel. *The Hannibal Files: The Unauthorized Guide to the Hannibal Lecter Trilogy*. London: Reynolds & Hearns, 2001.

Persons, Dan. "*Silence of the Lambs*: The Making of Director Jonathan Demme's Instant Horror Classic, a Chiller for the '90s." *Cinefantastique*, February 1992, 16–38.

Persons, Dan. "*Silence of the Lambs.*" *Cinefantastique*, October 1992, 106–111.

Silent Movies

At the advent of the twentieth century, the United States stood as the most prosperous nation in the world. William McKinley was well regarded as president, photographs replaced illustrations in newspapers, and coal was the fuel of choice. There was a strange amalgamation of old and new: horse and buggy and the automobile, covered wagon and locomotive. In Europe, modern art eschewed realism for the abstract, as Sigmund Freud challenged the way people thought about behavior. For those who could indulge in such pleasures, there were the phonograph, the theater, and vaudeville entertainments. Yet by 1895 a new curiosity emerged that would slowly but surely inflict profound, controversial, and sometimes curious changes in the moral sensibilities, cultural life, and social order of human society. That new curiosity was the moving picture.

The moving picture was never intended to be silent but was envisioned by American inventor Thomas Edison as visual accompaniment to his earlier phonograph. It wasn't until the late 1920s, however, that "talkies" would be technologically and economically viable. The first three decades of film, therefore, would be the history of the silent movie.

To the average viewer, the silent movie may appear to represent little more than dusty vestiges of a bygone era, featuring story lines with little in common with current issues and production values that pale in comparison to the slick look of contemporary cinema. Yet the silent film can evoke more than nostalgia. The story of silent film offers a history of the brand-new industry of movie making as it struggled to overcome the forces of public opinion and censorship, differentiate its products, and create styles of filmmaking that would survive generations.

Beyond industry and economics, it is during the period of the silent movie that we see the first glimpses of the film medium as an art form; the surviving collection of silent pictures, produced in both the United States and abroad, include some of the finest creative achievements in cinematic history. Far from being primitive, a number of silent pictures are today considered marvels, with high levels of technological innovation achieved by their producers (including color and special effects), long before the advent of computers, portable power tools, and motion picture capture and morphing.

Moreover, the era of silent moving pictures has left behind a fascinating record of the biases and prejudices, fads and fixations, taboos and preoccupations of human history during the late nineteenth and early twentieth centuries—and not just in the documentary or fact film but also in the perhaps thousands of shorts, one and two reelers, and feature films produced between 1896 and 1927.

THE GENESIS OF FILM

The history of the early development of the moving picture, from its origins as 1870s series photography to the American studio system, is long and convoluted and has no single point of origin. Moreover, the history of the invention of the moving picture is associated with a great deal of myth and lore.

The Great Train Robbery, *1903*. The Great Train Robbery, *one of the first film narratives, was only twelve minutes long.* EDISON/THE KOBAL COLLECTION.

Americans commonly attribute the invention of the moving picture to the pioneering efforts of Edison, the flawed genius noted for his patents for electric light, storage batteries, the phonograph, and the telegraph. Contrary to common belief, the birth of the moving picture was not the genius of a single originator but of a kind of competition between inventors in Britain, France, Germany, and the United States. It was in Edison's West Orange, New Jersey, laboratory, however, that the genesis of the U.S. film industry was nurtured through its embryonic stages. In 1893 Edison patented the kinetoscope, an early movie projector, and in a makeshift studio called the Black Maria the next year, he and his associates produced the earliest American silent pictures.

Soon after the initial discoveries of Edison and his rivals, the moving picture quickly arose as a phenomenal success. Perhaps thousands of small-time businesspeople from all backgrounds and ethnic constituencies competed to enjoy the profit-making potential of the newest novelty. Moreover, notes David Cook in his *History of Narrative Film*, the new medium of film moved quickly "toward becoming a mass medium with the then-unimaginable power to communicate without print or speech."

By the turn of the twentieth century, Kinetoscope "shorts" attempted to satisfy a quickly growing audience fascinated with the moving picture. The nickelodeon boom (a period known as "nickel madness") saw the growth of film-showing storefronts from a mere handful in 1904 to nearly 10,000 in less than five years. Almost overnight, any available space was converted to a movie theater. The moving picture evolved from a sideshow and filler for vaudeville to an entertainment by itself. Recordings of "entertaining or amusing subjects," as noted in one catalog, comprised short films such as *That Chinese Laundry*, *The Dancing Bears*, and *The Gaiety Girls Dancing*, featuring comedy, skits, and other brief performances. The storytelling possibilities of film were all but lost on early filmmakers. Yet whether novelty, filler, or short, as the popularity of this new form of entertainment arose, so did public concern.

EARLY MORALITY CONCERNS

Similar to contemporary debates about film content and effects on society, the emergence of the moving picture as a popular form of entertainment caused an increasing measure of public disapproval. Daniel Czitrom documents early public concern about the movies in *Media and the American Mind*, noting that unlike the near "unanimous praise" afforded the introduction of the telegraph, "the motion picture confronted the accepted standards of culture itself." Film emerged during a time when a glimpse of a woman's bare ankle was considered by some to be obscene. To be sure, there were many early film shorts containing material of an adult nature. *Serpentine Dance* (1895), produced by the Edison Co., was banned because the brief film included titillating glimpses of the female performer's undergarments. Content wasn't the only concern, however. "Indeed," notes Charles Champlin in an article on the film production code for *American Film*, "it was the instant and immense popularity of the movies that stirred the first fears of their corrupting and inciting power." The culture war had begun.

As all and sundry flocked to the local store theater to take in the latest short, worried cultural traditionalists and moralists debated the effects of motion pictures on society. "At the turn of the century," notes Janet Staiger in her book on sex and the early cinema, "people argued about what should and should not be said or shown during the first years of the American cinema." The people to whom she refers include the upper classes and cultural and moral elite, who felt themselves to be responsible for the maintenance of public culture and morals and for the governance of the middle and working classes.

To a punctilious Gilded Age society with Victorian moral sensibilities, a knowing glance, a leer, a glimpse of a woman's undergarment, and anything resembling burlesque could be considered inappropriate or outright obscene. In 1896 the seconds-long Edison short *The Kiss* created quite a stir. There, in grainy black and white, were stage actors May Erwin and John Rice bound together in a long and loving caress. Many were shocked at what they deemed a brazen lack of morality in this brief exhibition.

It was not only film content that worried moralists but also the nature of the audiences that flocked to the theaters and the circumstances of exhibition. The patrons of theater stores included members of all ethnic constituencies as well as the lower and working classes. Some felt that this opportunity for races and classes of people to commingle could have potentially disastrous effects on the social structure. Moreover, the places where store theaters were located were considered indecorous, including amusement parks, penny arcades, dance halls, and pubs. A woman's reputation could suffer were she seen in such questionable establishments. Sanctioned censorship occurred in 1907 in Chicago, where the first ordinances preventing the "exhibition of obscene and immoral pictures" were established. The film industry in America would escape its first decade with only a mild scolding and a bit of self-regulation, including the 1909 National Board of Censorship. Yet the die was cast, and in subsequent decades, the cries for regulation of the pictures would grow more strident.

FROM IMAGES TO STORIES

The very earliest silent motion pictures were not full-fledged stories, notes Cook, but "unmediated glimpses of real action as it unfolded before the camera." French film entrepreneur Louis Lumière was said to have wandered the streets and set up his portable camera before any scene that happened to take his fancy, creating what the French called *actualités*. These brief glimpses of unmanipulated life fascinated viewers because nothing like them had ever been seen before. It is said that during the film screening of a train pulling into a station, panicked audience members rushed from their seats to get out of harm's way (*The Arrival of a Train at the Station*, 1895). In America, surviving film-as-record include glimpses of San Francisco before and after the earthquake and fire in 1906, a peek inside a turn-of-the-twentieth-century factory, footage of the Spanish-American War, and the inauguration (in 1897) and funeral (in 1901) of President McKinley. Although mostly staged for the camera, silent shorts were produced as fillers and teasers for vaudeville, leaving behind a rare peek at Gilded Age theatrical performance and popular entertainment.

Quickly, the moving picture began to evolve into its next phase: storytelling. Film pioneers such as Georges Méliès, Ferdinand Zecca, Émile Cohl, D. W. Griffith, and countless others contributed to the development and refinement of film narrative. In the United States, it is Edwin S. Porter whose name is strongly connected with creation of the true film story and who is often afforded much of the credit for the birth of narrative film.

Porter, a protégé of Edison, began his filmmaking career in Edison's labs turning out *actualités* and one-shot film shorts. His

The Life of an American Fireman and *The Great Train Robbery* (both 1903) are seen as the earliest true film narratives produced in the United States. The latter was a popular sensation. Although only twelve minutes in length, the building of suspense and the development of action captivated an audience used to static shots of a single scene. Porter also directed *The Ex-Convict* (1904) and *The Kleptomaniac* (1905). It is interesting to note that these were more than simply stories for entertainment's sake; they also reflected prevailing social values. The message movie was born.

RELIANCE ON MYTHS AND STEREOTYPES

Porter's *Uncle Tom's Cabin* (1903) is considered one of the longest and most expensive American movies produced at the time. Running less than fifteen minutes, it would be the first of many adaptations of the 1852 Harriet Beecher Stowe abolitionist classic. Edward Campbell has documented filmdom's romance with various American myths, noting, "significant was the wedding of film with historical myths that were uniquely American . . . story lines which would rapidly grow to be among the most beloved, the Western and the Old South romance." As the length of the silent movie increased, so did the story possibilities. Filmmakers and the writers of scenarios turned to many sources for material, including literature, legend, lore, and stereotypes.

A striking element in film shorts and early narratives is America's painful legacy of racism and bigotry. Early film audiences didn't need to ask why an Indian craved whiskey or a black man was a thief. "Racial stereotypes," note Thomas W. Bohn and Richard L. Stromgren in *Light and Shadows*, "served the formula film because they provided the motivation or helped trigger conflict without the need of complex explanations." Early filmmakers relied heavily upon rather egregious ethnic typecasting in their depictions of African American life and culture, Native Americans, and recent immigrants. Contributors to the book *Unspeakable Images: Ethnicity and the American Cinema* document the inclusion of "pilfering, lazy blacks, dumb Irish maids, unscrupulously savvy Jewish storekeepers, [and] naive Yankee farmers" as the subjects of short subjects and ethnic-based comedies. The racial stereotyping evident in early film didn't suddenly evolve with the medium but emerged from predominant ideas about race and class communicated through literature, sociological studies, vaudeville, and cultural artifacts such as advertisements.

Ruthless and sinister Asian gangsters, whooping savage Indians, and superstitious "coon" characters were common fare in shorts; popular film series; and, later, full-length features. "The Mexican bandits were clearly the most vile," notes Allen Woll in *The Latin Image in American Film*. "They robbed, murdered, plundered, raped, cheated, gambled, lied and displayed virtually every vice that could be shown on the screen." It took a combination of complaints and World War I (which provided new villains) to "end the derogatory portrayals." In 1915 Cecil B. DeMille produced the highly successful *The Cheat*. In this story, a white socialite takes out a loan with a rich but lecherous and evil Asian man, who viciously brands her with a hot iron when she can't repay him. Black Americans were viciously lampooned and portrayed as ignorant, ridiculous, and animal-like on the covers of sheet music and advertisements. These same depictions quickly found their way into silent pictures. Early titles (often featuring whites in blackface) included the popular Rastus series about an ignorant black thief, and the Sambo comedies. "The pages were thick with chicken thieves and crapshooters," notes film historian Thomas Cripps in *Slow Fade to Black*, "one catalogue urging its wares because 'these darkies of the 'Old Virginny' type.'"

The year 1900 saw the largest influx of immigrants to the United States ever, and many native-born Americans were distrustful if not outright hostile toward foreigners. Wars, revolution in Russia, anarchy, and fear of communism led some Americans to view foreigners as warmongers and blame them for the often squalid conditions that were the reality in urban centers with high immigrant populations. Early on, foreigners were often used as the butt of jokes in such titles as *How Bridget Served the Salad Undressed* (1898); *A Bucket of Cream Ale*; and *Murphy's Wake*, a film that earned the outrage of Irish movie patrons because of its stereotypes of the Irish as drunkards.

THE FILMS BECOME LONGER

By the early 1910s film shorts and one reelers would expand to multiple reels that later came to be known as "features." The rise of the longer-length film was significant in that it helped to make motion pictures respectable for middle-class patrons. Longer films could more resemble legitimate theater, and classic plays and novels could now be adapted for film.

Silent features expanded to several reels with more defined story lines, creative editing techniques, crosscutting, and innovative use of camera angles (some discovered accidentally). The popularity and success of the feature was in large part caused by the success of Italian-produced spectacles, which transfixed and delighted American audiences. These include Enrico Guazzoni's 1913 *Quo Vadis?* and Giovanni Pastrone's twelve-reel masterpiece *Cabiria* (1914). *Cabiria*, more than two hours long, featured elaborately constructed sets, intricately designed costumes, and unique camerawork, dazzling the American moviegoing public and influencing American directors such as Griffith and DeMille. Soon, nickel madness gave way to feature madness.

D. W. GRIFFITH

David Wark Griffith was one of the earliest American filmmakers to realize, perhaps by accident, the dramatic potential of the cinema and its persuasive power over an audience. A failed actor, he turned to directing pictures for the Biograph Company in 1908. Regarded as the master of melodrama, he refined techniques already in use and created new styles of editing, photography, montage, camera movement, and placement—precursors to the emerging classical Hollywood style. With his ensemble of silent film luminaries (including Mary Pickford, Lillian Gish, Lionel Barrymore, and Blanche Sweet), he all but perfected the potboiler and chase-scene story and also adapted the serious work of William Shakespeare, Leo Tolstoy, and Edgar Allan Poe. He approached his work with an energy, style, and innovation that worried investors while it fascinated and delighted audiences.

Although he enjoyed a respectable career in film, Griffith's name will be forever associated with the notoriety surrounding his film adaption of the Civil War novel *The Clansman*. *The Birth of a Nation* was released in 1915 to much fanfare. It was widely hailed by most, including President Woodrow Wilson. Yet the film's scenes of racial violence, including sexually depraved black villains and hooded Ku Klux Klan heroes, were not lost on everyone. In 1915 the Boston branch of the National Association for the Advancement of Colored People (NAACP) led the way in organized protest of the film's patently racist message. The group was one of many that sought to have the film banned altogether, producing a forty-seven-page pamphlet, supported with endorsements by leading public figures. Black citizens picketed and protested. In some places where the film was shown, race riots broke out. Wilson was forced to recant his earlier praise. The film was banned in some states.

Griffith, a southerner and the son of a Confederate officer, was surprised, perplexed, and insulted by the criticism of the film. As far as he was concerned, the film was based on a true and accurate portrayal of history. Black citizens knew better, realizing that such pejorative propaganda could only cause more lynchings and distrust and heighten racial tensions. Griffith responded with a pamphlet on free speech and countered with his epic production *Intolerance* (1916). Though one could argue about the overall effectiveness of the campaign against this highly successful and groundbreaking silent film, the incident was one of many in a long history of organized protests staged by pressure groups against the images in American cinema.

"RACE MOVIES"

With so much dissension over the early film industry's disparaging depictions of black life and culture, it is not surprising that a number of enterprising film entrepreneurs attempted to fill the void with independently produced "race movies"—feature films with predominantly African American casts intended for African American audiences. Race movies, which evolved in large part as a response to *The Birth of a Nation*, provided black audiences a sometimes telling glimpse of how they saw themselves and their world. Some race movies were the products of white producers, such as Richard Norman's Norman Film Manufacturing Company, which produced features starring black cowboy Bill Pickett.

Though there were perhaps hundreds of independent African American filmmakers, of particular mention is Oscar Micheaux. Like Edison, he was only mildly interested in the cinematic possibilities of the film medium. Micheaux was a businessman who wrote, produced, directed, and distributed his own pictures from 1919 to 1948. His subject matter varied widely, but he seemed particularly interested in melodramatic interpretations of personal events in his life. His scenarios included interracial romance, race and color consciousness, lynching, failed marriages, the black bourgeoisie, and class issues. Most of his work was derived from his own novels, and he was known for his penurious approach to filmmaking. Notes Richard Gehr for *American Film*, Micheaux "translated standard Western, gangster, and melodramatic fare to a black context, something unique, if only in the form of his own rough-hewn, self-taught technique." Not surprisingly, his surviving work has an unfinished look—an odd amalgamation of bad acting, thin story lines, and sometimes nonsensical editing.

Yet the significance of Micheaux and his contemporaries is not aesthetic value. Their films provided work for many black artists and filled the void for a people desperately seeking an improved image. Although the scripts may not have always been perfect and the production values lacking, in race movies African Americans could be doctors, lawyers, police officers, entertainers, and otherwise contributing members of society. Micheaux produced approximately twenty silent films between 1919 and 1929, including *The Homesteader* (1919), *Body and Soul* (1925; featuring Paul Robeson in his first film role), *Within Our Gates* (1920), and *The Exile* (1931).

BIG BUSINESS

In the 1910s the American film industry evolved from a scientific oddity to an important big business. In *The Hollywood Studio System*, Douglas Gomery, a scholar of the economic history of the film industry, notes that "the former system of film sales 'by the foot' was soon replaced with the star system, a finely tuned network of national and international distribution, and the 'run-zone-clearance' system of little exhibition." Fights over patents and the eventual monopolistic ownership of the means of production, distribution, and exhibition helped to change the structure of the film industry to one that came to be dominated by a handful of very powerful companies, including the Famous Players-Lasky Company (later Paramount), the Goldwyn Picture Corporation, Universal, and the Twentieth Century Fox Film Corporation. Film production shifted to the West Coast to escape patent litigation and unpredictable weather.

Early on the names of the performers and directors of a film were not publicized. It didn't take long, however, for the newly organized studios to exploit the profit potential of "star power." By 1916 Mary Pickford, nicknamed "America's Sweetheart," earned thousands of dollars weekly and the adoration of millions of fans; Theda Bara became the first screen vamp, and Clara Bow the "It" Girl. The faces of Lon Chaney, John Barrymore, little Jackie Coogan, Rudolph Valentino, and a young Swedish newcomer named Greta Garbo would grace the covers of fan magazines. Striking was the swift development of the new industry. Notes Czitrom, "of all the facets of motion picture history, none is so stunning as the extraordinarily rapid growth in the audience during the brief period between 1915 and 1918." As Europeans mobilized for war, the American motion picture industry became an important, legitimate, and powerful facet of American industry.

FEMALE FILM PIONEERS

While film history books have most often chronicled the "great men" of the movies, a number of women managed to carve out respectable filmmaking careers in the new male-dominated industry. Alice Guy Blaché (also known as Alice Guy) was probably the first woman film director, directing nearly 200 films between 1897 and 1920. Born in Paris, by 1910 she used her own money to organize the Solax Film Company. Her mission, notes Ally Acker in *Reel Women*, was to "cater films specific to American tastes and acted in by American artists." Among her American films were *The Vampire* (1915), *The Heart of a Painted Woman* (1915), and *When You and I Were Young* (1917).

Former teenage actress Ida May Park was one of several prominent women directors employed at Universal Studios during the late 1910s. Dorothy Arzner began as a script girl during the silent film era and continued on a respectable career as a director of women's pictures well into the 1940s. Similar was the career of Virginia Van Upp, a former assistant, screenwriter, producer, director, and executive producer and one of few early film women who would later crash the glass ceiling of a major film studio. Also notable are the contributions of women who wrote hundreds of scenarios and screenplays for the early silent pictures. Respected women writers such as Grace Cunard, June Mathis, Frances Marion, Julia Crawford Ivers, and Anita Loos created or contributed to the scripts for such films as *Ben Hur* (1907), *The Four Horsemen of Apocalypse* (1921), *The Sheik* (1921), and *Tom Sawyer* (1917).

THE STUDIO SYSTEM

Although some filmmakers continued the style for years to come, the decade of the 1920s would be the final decade that the silent movie would be a viable, profit-making mode of production. The film industry in the United States began to organize itself into what would become known as the American studio system. Though the reasons for this development are many, the evolution of the studio system is often attributed to the success of producer Thomas Ince. Ince's legacy to film history was not the production of a classic film. He was no cinema-auteur, nor did he enjoy a long reign as a mogul of a major studio. His contribution was the institution of production conventions, including his absolute control over screenplays, shooting script content, and editing. His Inceville Studio served as a model for the efficient and cost-effective running of a motion picture factory. Under his guidance, directors had to adhere to tight budgets and preapproved schedules. Moreover, he required that scripts not emerge extemporaneously from the muse of a director but be finished products that contained lines of dialogue. The power of the individual would diminish greatly. Variations of Ince's model would soon dominate U.S. film production.

Soon cash would overpower creativity. Film became industry, and filmmaking was business. American film studios evolved into factories for the large-scale production of mass entertainment. Filmmakers developed conventions and formulas: frequently used devices and techniques that were cheap, economical, easily recognizable, and easy to re-create over and over. Formulas allowed producers to remain within tried-and-true patterns; they helped keep costs contained as the same sets, props, and costumes could be used more than once. Early mass-produced films quickly began to appear very much alike, with the director's task being to create an illusion of variety (keeping well within, of course, the tight economic boundaries that would ensure profit margins). Among other things, producers in the 1920s quickly tried to capitalize on whatever fad, controversy, or preoccupation had caught the imagination of the public: "cycle filmmaking" was born. It is estimated that between 1920 and 1927, nearly 100 films apiece were produced about cars, aviation, and chorus girls, three of the decade's more popular subjects.

Filmmaking strategies in the 1920s also included the development of genres or distinctive categories of films, the continued exploitation of types and stereotypes, the homogenization of cultures, and the creation and propagation of a mythical and filmic view of manners and morals. The process of standardization that occurred in silent filmmaking in America had a profound effect on film structure and determined the images and stories audiences would see in the movies for generations to come.

The emerging Hollywood formula film came to include such tried-and-true conventions as stories with a linear plot (a clearly defined beginning, middle, and "happy" ending), a focus on one or two central characters with clearly defined goals, and in general a style that didn't call much attention to itself. Moreover, a high premium was placed on the conventions of genre (Western, gangster, women's picture) and the film's entertainment value. It was at this time that many of the more endearing, popular, and successful American film genres would emerge.

EARLY FILM GENRES

With its emphasis on wide open spaces, firearms, exciting action, clear delineation of heroes and villains, and Native American stereotypes, the Western emerged as one of the most popular and enduring genres in American filmmaking. Western formulas included the "myth of the West" stories; Western epics such as *The Iron Horse* (1924); and the Western star vehicle, which included the popular films of William S. Hart, such as *The Gun Fighter* (1917) and *The Covered Wagon* (1923), and films featuring Tom Mix, Buck Jones, and Hoot Gibson.

The virile planter bedecked in a white suit; the ever-present mint julep; frail white womanhood (whose existence never included a day of work); and happy and contented darkie slaves who profited from the benevolence and care of the overseer—these were some of the conventions of "plantation tales." "The movies of the Antebellum South," notes Campbell, "with their increasingly familiar settings and character types . . . reinforced an image shaped cinematically since 1903."

The suave, dashing, acrobatic, athletic, swashbuckling hero of the action-adventure film also found popularity in the silent film, as popularized by screen star Douglas Fairbanks Sr. His films, including *The Three Musketeers* (1921), *Robin Hood* (1922), *Q, Son of Zorro* (1925), and *The Black Pirate* (1926), helped to establish a new kind of filmmaking with a flow and tempo, dynamic editing, and a building of action scenes still evident in contemporary action-adventure films.

SILENT SCREEN COMEDY

Although film as a visual medium was perfectly suited for physical gags and comic mime, the potential for true comedy went unrecognized by early filmmakers. At first, some directors copied the popular style of trick photography pioneered by Méliès in France, but a true comic style had yet to be identified. By 1913 an amalgamation of foreign and American performers and producers came to create what has been described as American filmmaking's most enduring contribution to the history of film—that of silent screen comedy.

Mack Sennett was a Canadian who became head of the Keystone Company in 1912. He is the originator of silent slapstick comedy, high-action films signified by their purely visual acrobatic humor, including pie-throwing, cliff-hangers, auto chases, explosions, and last-minute rescues. He is notable for his creation of the zany Keystone Cops and is responsible for discovering comedy greats Fatty Arbuckle, Ben Turpin, and Charles Chaplin. Between 1913 and 1935 he produced thousands of one- and two-reel films and features, helping to fine-tune a new screen genre in a way that no one ever had done before.

America's favorite comics also included Harry Langdon and Buster Keaton, whose deadpan countenance never changed even as he struggled to hang onto a moving locomotive; Harold Lloyd with his wide-rim glasses, dangling precariously from the hands of a clock suspended over a busy street in a "comedy of thrills"; and Stan Laurel and Oliver Hardy, who continued their successful careers into the sound era.

CHAPLIN

By far the most celebrated figure in silent filmmaking was Chaplin, an English vaudevillian who made his first appearance in the United States in a 1913 film by Keystone Studios' producer

Sennett. A master of the art of mime, he developed a unique style of humor that exploited the connection between comedy and tragedy—a style that was in sharp contrast to the average Sennett picture. He developed his famous persona the "Little Tramp" while still working for Sennett. In 1919 he formed a partnership with three of the more powerful names in film—Pickford, Fairbanks, and Griffith—that they called the United Artists Corporation. There Chaplin produced *A Woman of Paris* (1923) and his signature film, *The Gold Rush* (1925), where in a classic scene he serves up a boiled boot and devours it like a gourmet meal. The success of this film and others caused him to become the most popular, highest-paid, and most successful figure in film history. "During the silent era," notes Charles Silver for *American Film*, "[Chaplin] was regarded as an indisputable genius by nearly everyone who cared about movies in any remotely serious matter." Chaplin continued to produce silent or near-silent pictures well after the evolution of sound in film.

THE JAZZ AGE AND FILM

The exigencies of World War I and the launching of the industrial age helped to melt away Victorian-age ideals in American society. Women cut their hair and donned short dresses for a night of dancing to the sultry sounds of black jazz artists such as Louis Armstrong and Bessie Smith. Former taboos such as divorce were discussed more freely. For some, it was an exhilarating time when the champagne flowed and the party was endless. It is not surprising that this prevailing mood was depicted on Hollywood film screens. Divorce, adultery, sex, drinking, and drugs were treated openly in the same medium that once gasped at the sight of a woman's bare ankle. Valentino resonated a smoldering, on-screen sexuality in films such as *Blood and Sand* (1922), while a young Garbo made her U.S. film debut in *Torrent* (1926).

Dark clouds formed on the Hollywood horizon, however, as a series of scandals rocked the film world. First, there was Chaplin's highly publicized divorce in 1920. Then Pickford was accused of bigamy for her liaison with Fairbanks (while still married to Owen Moore). Arbuckle, one of the country's more cherished comic figures, was falsely implicated in the brutal rape and death of a young starlet during a party that was described as wild, drunken, and orgiastic. The lurid details of the crime were widely exploited in the press, and even though he was cleared of charges, Arbuckle's career was over. In 1923 actor Wallace Reid, positioned as an "all-American boy" type, was found dead of a drug overdose. Director William Desmond Taylor was found murdered, and the two women film stars he was involved with (Mabel Normand and Mary Miles Minter) were implicated in the crime that was never solved. Notes Champlin in an article on the Taylor murder for *American Film*, "all were seen as proof that Hollywood, on and off screen, was an affront to decent men and women everywhere."

The public outcry was tremendous. Some called for government legislation of the film industry. To stave off government regulation, the industry once again turned to self-regulation. It hired a conservative Presbyterian elder named William Hays to head its trade association, the Motion Picture Producers and Distributors of America. Among other things, a list humorously referred to as *Don't's and Be Carefuls* was published to serve as a kind of guideline for producers. In truth, the Hays Office was ineffectual, possibly even corrupt. But the die was cast. Censorship of the movies was reality. As silent pictures evolved into sound, a much more stringent and limiting form of censorship would emerge that would influence filmmaking for decades to come.

EUROPEAN FILMS

As American movies were fitted into formulas, shrouded in conventions, and stamped out in an assembly-line process, the artistic potential of the medium continued to emerge. It was during the era of silent filmmaking that some of greatest artistic achievements in film were produced. Nowhere was the film-as-art movement more evident than in Europe. Emerging from the rubble of World War I, German expressionists, Soviet revolutionaries, and French artists and intellectuals sought freedom from the conventions, behaviors, and structures of the former world order. The roots of the phenomenon can be attributed to artistic movements then in vogue and the influence of American directors such as Griffith. European filmmakers were particularly interested in the "visual potential" of the medium. They experimented freely with makeshift mobile cameras, bold new editing techniques, and revolutionary optical effects such as masks, superimpositions, and dissolves. Soon, film production in 1920s Europe would pose the strongest competition ever to the growing Hollywood machine.

In Germany, the art movement known as expressionism first became important in painting around 1910 and was later adapted to theater and literature. The motto of filmmakers who adapted the expressionist style was "the film image must become graphic art." Expressionist artists tended to distort or exaggerate natural appearances in order to create a reflection of an inner world. The stylistic techniques of *schauerfilme* (films of fantasy and horror), notes Cook, included extreme stylization—such as a "moving expressionist woodcut." The effect was heavily dependent upon mise-en-scène, including geometrically stylized sets and nightmarishly distorted decor, actors with heavy makeup moving in jerky or slow motion, chiaroscuro (or Rembrandt) lighting, and unusual camera work.

In addition to the prominent expressionist artists hired to design and paint film sets, important German filmmakers and screenwriters include Carl Mayer, who cowrote the screenplay for *The Cabinet of Dr. Caligari* (1920); F. W. Murnau, with *Nosferatu, a Symphony of Horrors* (1922); and Fritz Lang, with *Dr. Mabuse: The Gambler* (1922) and *Metropolis* (1927). So prominent and striking were the works of these men that Hollywood felt compelled to lure many of them away to produce films for American movie screens.

In Denmark, notes Cook, Carl Dreyer concerned himself with "communicating with the audience's soul" in his monumental *The Passion of Joan of Arc* (1928), which featured Renee Falconetti, who cropped her hair and wore no makeup for the role. In sharp contrast to America's straightforward approach, Dreyer's directing technique emphasized close-ups that could relay Joan's "spiritual agony."

It was the success of French silent filmmaking, however, that perhaps posed the most competition for America. Between 1919 and 1929 film artists in France developed a style that offered interesting alternatives to the classical Hollywood style. Film, felt the French, should owe nothing to literature or theater but instead serve as an occasion for the artist to express feelings. After surviving near destruction during World War I, the French film industry rose like a phoenix to produce some of the finest silent motion pictures in the history of film. Of particular mention is the work of Abel Gance and his production of the epic

Napoleon (1927). Notes Cook, "Cameras were carried at arm's length, attached to swings, strapped to a horse's back and sent into the air in balloons." Gance used three cameras during the shooting and introduced the earliest use of wide-screen effects.

"Of all arts, for us cinema is the most important," stated Russian revolutionary Vladimir Lenin. Probably the most striking and influential of all the European styles to emerge during the period is the film-editing technique that came to be known as Soviet montage. Sergei Eisenstein is possibly the most famous filmmaker to emerge from the silent period. He was a Marxist intellectual and a veteran of the abortive 1905 revolution who saw film as a mass medium designed to appeal to and educate millions of illiterate Russian peasants. His *The Battleship Potemkin* (1925) is considered by some to be one of the most influential films ever made and is even today the focus of analysis and marvel. Eisenstein's stylistic techniques represented a sharp contrast to the style of American pictures.

Eisenstein communicated primarily by means of emotion. He highlighted no individual protagonist (large groups could form a collective hero), used everyday people instead of professional actors, and promoted documentary reality in his use of photography. Most significantly, he pioneered a new editing technique, one based on psychological stimulation rather than narrative logic. As opposed to the seamless or invisible editing that signified American films, Eisenstein used a juxtaposition of shots to create a concept and/or emotion. He felt that to create the maximum effect (a jolt for the viewer), shots should not fit together perfectly but create a montage of "shock stimuli."

The reality of a second European war would curtail the short-lived triumph of film production in Europe. A host of European actors, performers, designers, and directors made the transition to the sound stages of Hollywood, with varying degrees of success. Although no one style would have a profound effect on the American film industry, the influence of montage editing, crosscutting, wide screen, and mosaic narrative would inspire generations of filmmakers on both continents for generations to come.

More than merely a repository of the past, the era of the silent movie represents nearly three decades of sex and scandal, art and angst, sin and censorship, and crime and comedy. In the United States, from the Gilded Age to the Jazz Age, the silent picture has left behind striking images of American society as it swelled to include the recently manumitted and the hundreds of thousands of immigrants from many nations who appeared on its shores. From the Black Maria to motion picture palaces, from seconds-long shorts to feature-length spectacles, from film-by-the-foot to multinational business, the silent film helped create new and profitable forms of commerce, forms which continued on in the guise of the talking film, which has dominated the industry ever since. A combination of myth proffering, image building, and empire construction, the legacy of the silent film still endures and remains a vital and potent facet of human cultural history.

Pamala S. Deane

SEE ALSO: *Arbuckle, Fatty; Armstrong, Louis; Bara, Theda; Barrymore, John;* The Birth of a Nation*; Blackface Minstrelsy; Bow, Clara; Chaplin, Charlie; DeMille, Cecil B.; Edison, Thomas Alva; Fairbanks, Douglas, Sr.; Fan Magazines; Garbo, Greta; Gish, Lillian; Goldwyn, Samuel;* The Great Train Robbery*; Griffith, D. W.; Hollywood; Keaton, Buster; The Keystone Kops; Ku Klux Klan; Lang, Fritz; Laurel and Hardy; Mix, Tom; Nickelodeons; Pickford, Mary; Robeson, Paul; Sex Scandals; Smith, Bessie; Studio System; The Twenties; United Artists; Valentino, Rudolph; The Western; World War I.*

BIBLIOGRAPHY

Acker, Ally. *Reel Women: Pioneers of the Cinema, 1896 to the Present.* New York: Continuum, 1991.

Bogle, Donald. *Blacks in American Films and Television: An Encyclopedia.* New York: Garland Publishing, 1988.

Bohn, Thomas W., and Richard L. Stromgren. *Light and Shadows: A History of Motion Pictures*, 3rd ed. Mountain View, CA: Mayfield, 1987.

Campbell, Edward D. C. *The Celluloid South: Hollywood and the Southern Myth.* Knoxville: University of Tennessee Press, 1981.

Champlin, Charles. "What Will H. Hays Begat: Fifty Years since His Code Office Ruled Hollywood." *American Film* 6, no. 1 (1980).

Cohen, Paula Marantz. *Silent Film and the Triumph of the American Myth.* New York: Oxford University Press, 2001.

Cook, David A. *A History of Narrative Film.* New York: Norton, 1981.

Cripps, Thomas. *Slow Fade to Black: The Negro in American Film, 1900–1942.* New York: Oxford University Press, 1977.

Czitrom, Daniel J. *Media and the American Mind: From Morse to McLuhan.* Chapel Hill: University of North Carolina Press, 1982.

Friedman, Lester D., ed. *Unspeakable Images: Ethnicity and the American Cinema.* Urbana: University of Illinois Press, 1991.

Gehr, Richard. "One-Man Show." *American Film* 16, no. 5 (1991): 34–39.

Gomery, Douglas. *The Hollywood Studio System.* New York: St. Martin's, 1986.

Kobel, Peter, and Library of Congress. *Silent Movies: The Birth of Film and the Triumph of Movie Culture.* New York: Little, Brown, 2007.

Miller, Randall M., ed. *The Kaleidoscopic Lens: How Hollywood Views Ethnic Groups.* Englewood, NJ: Ozer, 1980.

Richards, Larry. *African American Films through 1959: A Comprehensive, Illustrated Filmography.* Jefferson, NC: McFarland, 1998.

Silver, Charles. "Chaplin Redux." *American Film*, September 1984.

Sobchack, Thomas, and Vivian C. Sobchack. *An Introduction to Film*, 2nd ed. Boston: Little, Brown, 1987.

Staiger, Janet. *Bad Women: Regulating Sexuality in Early American Cinema.* Minneapolis: University of Minnesota Press, 1995.

Woll, Allen L. *The Latin Image in American Film.* Los Angeles: University of California, 1977.

The Silver Surfer

The Silver Surfer, a Marvel comic-book superhero, was created by Stan Lee and Jack Kirby in the mid-1960s. The Surfer is a noble alien endowed with the "power cosmic" as he travels throughout the universe on a surfboard championing good over evil. During the late 1960s the Surfer's comic book became unusually "adult" in tone as the character became a vehicle for Lee's existentialist musings and commentary on the failures of human civilization.

The Surfer won a sizable cult following, especially among college students. But it was too small to support the series, which was canceled after only a few years. Nevertheless, Lee's ambitious writing influenced young creators seeking to "make a statement" even in a medium widely dismissed as ephemeral by the mainstream public. And the Surfer's audience later grew; Marvel revived the character's series in 1986, and it remained a popular title into the twenty-first century. The character also appeared in the *Silver Surfer* television show (1998–1999); *The Super Hero Squad Show* (which began airing on television in 2009); and the movie *Fantastic 4: Rise of the Silver Surfer* (2007).

Bradford Wright

SEE ALSO: *Comic Books;* The Fantastic Four*; Lee, Stan; Marvel Comics.*

BIBLIOGRAPHY

Daniels, Les. *Marvel: Five Fabulous Decades of the World's Greatest Comics.* New York: Harry N. Abrams, 1991.

Dougall, Alastair, ed. *The Marvel Comics Encyclopedia*, rev. ed. New York: DK Publishing, 2009.

Lee, Stan. *Origins of Marvel Comics.* New York: Simon & Schuster, 1974.

Silverman, Sarah *(1970–)*

By the time she was twenty-two, comedian Sarah Silverman was already writing for, and performing on, *Saturday Night Live.* First appearing onstage at age twelve, Silverman has built a career on deftly crafting jokes that can be construed as incredibly offensive but, at their heart, cast light on what offends—in particular, racism. Silverman, who is Jewish—culturally, but not in any religious sense—has said that she trades on her background in her comedy by playing the stereotypical Jewish American Princess conceit.

After studying at New York University for a year, she dropped out to focus on her stand-up career. Silverman was already a comedy club circuit regular when she appeared a few years later on an episode of the Fox show *Comic Strip Live.* Shortly after seeing this appearance, the producers of *Saturday Night Live* (*SNL*) invited her to write and perform for the 1993–1994 season, only to fire her at the end of the season. Silverman went on to play bit parts in various television comedies, including *Mr. Show* and *The Larry Sanders Show*, where her character lampooned her experiences working on *SNL*. She also appeared in two episodes of *Star Trek: Voyager*. In 1998 Silverman transitioned from television shows to small roles in films, including *Overnight Delivery* and *There's Something about Mary*. She continued to occasionally appear in films, such as *The School of Rock* (2003) and *Rent* (2005), but she mainly stuck to television comedy.

While a guest on *Late Night with Conan O'Brien* in 2001, Silverman cemented her role as provocateur when she used a derogatory term to refer to Asian Americans. She was immediately attacked by Guy Aoki, head of the Media Action Network for Asian Americans. The show's network apologized, but Silverman did not. Instead she explained that the joke was "about racism, not a racist joke" and, in what she called a "well-thought-out, with-all-my-heart letter," apologized to Aoki for hurting his feelings.

The controversy, and Silverman's handling of it, gave an extra dimension of intelligence and fearlessness to her public persona. She capitalized on this in 2005, appearing with dozens of comedians in the movie *The Aristocrats*, a documentary about a singular joke commonly told privately among comedians and discussed at length in the movie. Also in 2005 *Jesus Is Magic* was released. A film of Silverman's current comedy routine, it showcases her repertoire of sexually explicit humor dealing with any number of topics normally considered taboo. The film was well received by critics and fans.

Her career in television late in the first decade of the 2000s became more substantial. She earned an Emmy nomination for a performance on *Monk* (2002–2009), and started her own show, *The Sarah Silverman Program* (2007–2010), which starred her and her real-life sister Laura (an actress). Typical for Silverman, the show was either critically acclaimed or reviled. One critic judged it "a juvenile, crude, and wholly irreverent exercise." But Tim Goodman of the *San Francisco Chronicle* wrote, "Sarah Silverman . . . has delivered an offbeat gem."

In 2009 she published her first book, *Eat, Pray, Fart*, which garnered little attention, and continued to act on film (*Peep World* [2010]) and television (*The Good Wife* [2009–]). Her second book, a memoir titled *The Bedwetter: Stories of Courage, Redemption, and Pee* (2010), received generally good reviews. It also gave readers a glimpse into another side of Silverman that showed her to be more than the sum of the parts of her public comic persona. As Silverman told Kate Fillion in an interview for *Maclean's*, "I want to do things that don't meet the audience's expectations of me."

Daniel Coffey

SEE ALSO: *Cable TV; Celebrity; Emmy Awards; Kimmel, Jimmy;* The Larry Sanders Show*; O'Brien, Conan;* Rent*;* Saturday Night Live*; Stand-Up Comedy;* Star Trek*; Television.*

BIBLIOGRAPHY

Fillion, Kate. "Sarah Silverman Talks to Kate Fillion." *Maclean's*, October 22, 2007, 13–14.

Lewis, Paul. "Beyond Empathy: Sarah Silverman and the Limits of Comedy." *Tikkun*, September/October 2007, 88–89.

Thorpe, David. "Is America Ready for Sarah Silverman? The Raunchy, Rising Comedy Star Has Audiences Asking, Should I Be Laughing at This?" *Jewish Daily Forward*, January 3, 2003.

Wortham, Jenna. "Shooting Star." *Bust*, October/November 2008, 42–47.

Simon, Neil *(1927–)*

Since the early 1960s, Broadway has almost never been without a Neil Simon hit play, which has earned the prolific New Yorker the title of the world's most commercially successful playwright. In his earlier work, with such hits as *The Odd Couple* and *The*

Sunshine Boys, Simon garnered a reputation for churning out charming comedies that were virtually guaranteed long Broadway runs. But in his later work, including the 1980s bittersweet autobiographical trilogy composed of *Brighton Beach Memoirs*, *Biloxi Blues*, and *Broadway Bound*, Simon conclusively proved that he was capable of more than light comedy. In the early 1990s, when his *Lost in Yonkers* earned four Tony Awards and the prestigious Pulitzer Prize, the transformation of Simon from Broadway wonder to "serious author" was complete. With plays that both bespeak and laugh at the human condition, Simon is one of the world's best-loved playwrights and a fixture of American popular culture.

Born Marvin Neil Simon in the Bronx, New York, on July 4, 1927, America's greatest living comedic playwright was raised in a troubled Depression-era household, which would ultimately provide the inspiration for much of his future work. Growing up with a father who frequently abandoned his family and a mother for whom young Neil felt a great sense of responsibility, the boy looked up to his older brother, Danny, who would become his most important influence. With eight years between them, Simon idolized his older brother, who had dropped out of high school to become a comedy writer. Danny Simon, about whom Woody Allen would later say, "Everything I learned about comedy, I learned from Danny Simon," was a comic genius. But so, as it turned out, was his younger brother, whom Danny nicknamed Doc because of Simon's childhood infatuation with a toy medical set. By the time Doc was sixteen, the two brothers had begun working together.

Neil Simon. *A string of hit plays beginning in the 1960s made Neil Simon the world's most commercially successful playwright.* JIM SPELLMAN/CONTRIBUTOR/WIREIMAGE/GETTY IMAGES.

During the early 1950s, in what would come to be known as the Golden Age of Television, Danny and Doc Simon were staff writers for such classic programs as Sid Caesar's *Your Show of Shows* and Phil Silvers's *The Sergeant Bilko Show*. Although the Simon brothers wrote almost exclusively for the small screen, one of their sketches did make it to Broadway in the 1956 revue *New Faces*, starring Maggie Smith.

PLAYWRIGHT BEGINNINGS

After working with his brother for many years, Simon went out on his own. But as the quality of the shows for which he wrote gradually began to dwindle, Simon began dreaming of writing for the theater. He began his first play when he was thirty years old. Almost two years and twenty-two drafts later, *Come Blow Your Horn*, based on Simon's family and, specifically, the relationship between Neil and Danny, opened on Broadway in 1961. Although the initial reviews were lukewarm, audiences loved it, and it played 677 performances.

Thus was Simon's career as a playwright launched. His next effort was the book for a 1962 Cy Coleman–Carolyn Leigh musical called *Little Me*, a vehicle for Caesar, for whom Simon had previously written. A year later *Barefoot in the Park*, directed by first-timer Mike Nichols and starring Elizabeth Ashley and Robert Redford, opened at the Biltmore. Although the play would go on to become a huge success, running for more than 1,500 performances, Simon was greeted with the dual-edged reviews that would forever plague him. Howard Taubman of the *New York Times* wrote that "Mr. Simon evidently has no aspirations except to be diverting, and he achieves those with the dash of a highly skilled writer."

Two years later, Simon followed up with his second unqualified hit, *The Odd Couple* (1965), starring Walter Matthau and Jack Lemmon, for which he won the Tony Award for Best Author. By 1966, with *Barefoot in the Park* still running, Simon, who had also written the book for the 1966 Bob Fosse musical *Sweet Charity*, was now earning approximately $20,000 a week as a playwright. Not yet forty years old, he was already the most commercially successful playwright in the world.

AND THE HITS KEPT COMING

Throughout the 1960s, Simon continued to write hit after hit, including *Star Spangled Girl* (1966), *Plaza Suite* (1968), *Promises, Promises* (1968), and *The Last of the Red Hot Lovers* (1969). Despite this string of successes, he was regularly attacked by critics for glib comedy and commercialism. And so he set out to write his first "serious play." *The Gingerbread Lady* opened in 1970; *The Prisoner of Second Avenue* followed a year later. Both were successful, but still critical recognition continued to elude him. Then, in 1973, tragedy struck when his wife of twenty years and the mother of his two daughters, Joan Baim Simon, died of cancer. Always a prolific writer, Simon struggled through Joan's illness while writing *The Sunshine Boys*, a play about aging vaudevillians, which would open at the end of 1973.

By the early 1970s, Simon had written ten Broadway plays that had grossed more than $30 million. He had also written three books for musicals, and still he continued to work, rarely going a day without writing.

The same year his wife died, Simon married actress Marsha Mason, an Academy Award–nominated actress and the star of

Simon's 1973 play, *The Good Doctor.* Not long thereafter, the couple moved to Hollywood, where they soon became popular members of the film community. Although Simon had written a number of screenplays based on his Broadway hits—*Barefoot in the Park, The Odd Couple, Plaza Suite*—he soon began to write exclusively for films, usually creating vehicles in which Mason starred. *The Goodbye Girl* (1977), *Chapter Two* (1979), and *Only When I Laugh* (1981) earned Mason three Academy Award nominations for Best Actress. Simon himself was nominated for four Oscars for screenwriting. But his heart was still in the theater, and so he continued to write for Broadway, where in 1976 his *California Suite* opened—a play that the *New York Times*'s Clive Barnes called "*Plaza Suite* gone West."

AUTOBIOGRAPHICAL TRILOGY

Throughout his career, Simon's material continued to be inspired by the people in his life. In the early 1980s he embarked on a trilogy that would chronicle his younger years. The first play, *Brighton Beach Memoirs*, opened on Broadway in 1983, with Matthew Broderick playing Simon's alter ego, Eugene. Highlighting the trials and tribulations of a Brooklyn family struggling through the Depression, *Brighton Beach Memoirs* was awarded Best Play by the New York Drama Critics' Circle. It ran for more than 1,500 performances at the Alvin—the theater was renamed the Neil Simon Theatre in honor of the playwright.

Also in 1983, Simon and Mason were divorced. Two years later he returned to Broadway with *Biloxi Blues*, the second play in his autobiographical trilogy. This time, Simon was awarded the Tony for Best Play. Broderick returned to Broadway as Eugene, undergoing army basic training during World War II. It would be one more year before the third play of the trilogy, *Broadway Bound*, would find it its way to the New York stage.

At the end of the 1980s, Simon was still plagued by a reputation for writing frivolous comedic works. Thus, it came as a wonderful kind of redemption when his 1991 play, *Lost in Yonkers*, received not only four Tony Awards, including Best Play, but also the coveted Pulitzer Prize. Because Simon had long been decried as a "popular" playwright, he had never expected to win the prestigious Pulitzer. Finally, after years of commercial success, he had been accepted into the pantheon of America's great playwrights.

Throughout the 1990s and the first decade of the 2000s, Simon continued to write, although his Broadway hits were fewer and farther between. With plays appearing on the London stage and even off-Broadway, he focused his energies on reworking *Jake's Women* and writing *The Goodbye Girl* for the stage. He also penned two autobiographies—*Rewrites: A Memoir* (1996) and *The Play Goes On: A Memoir* (1997)—that draw connections between his writing life and his personal life, with particular attention to the death of his first wife in 1973. Although Simon is not the prolific playwright he once was, he still remains one of the theater's most recognizable figures.

A Pulitzer Prize–, New York Drama Critics' Circle–, and Tony Award–winning playwright and an Academy Award–nominated screenwriter, Simon is one of the icons of twentieth-century film and theater—a man whose comic view of American life has helped to shape popular culture. For his contributions to the American comedy tradition, he was awarded the 2006 Mark Twain Prize for American Humor.

Victoria Price

SEE ALSO: *Academy Awards; Allen, Woody; Broadway; Caesar, Sid; Cancer; Fosse, Bob; Hollywood;* The Odd Couple; *Redford, Robert; Television; Tony Awards;* Your Show of Shows.

BIBLIOGRAPHY

Brown, Gene. *Show Time: A Chronology of Broadway and the Theatre from Its Beginnings to the Present.* New York: Macmillan, 1997.

Koprince, Susan Fehrenbacher. *Understanding Neil Simon.* Columbia: University of South Carolina Press, 2002.

Simon, Neil. *Rewrites: A Memoir.* New York: Simon & Schuster, 1996.

Simon, Neil. *The Play Goes On: A Memoir.* New York: Simon & Schuster, 1997.

Simon, Paul *(1941–)*

As one half of the 1960s folk-rock team Simon and Garfunkel, Paul Simon's place in pop music history as a first-rate songwriter was sealed. But after Simon's split with his partner in 1970, this Newark, New Jersey–born musician went on to distinguish himself not only as a veteran songwriter with a substantial body of work but also as a performer who experimented with a variety of musical genres. Throughout his career as a solo artist, Simon has incorporated salsa, jazz, reggae, gospel, doo-wop, Caribbean, South African, and Brazilian music into his finely crafted pop songs. One of his most well-known works, the Grammy-winning album *Graceland* (1986), drew both protest and praise for his use of South African musicians during the height of apartheid. Simon's music-making method is also interesting for the questions of cultural identity and appropriation that it raises.

Although Simon had experimented with a variety of styles that strayed from Simon and Garfunkel's poetic folk-rock formula when he was part of that duo ("Cecilia" and "Bridge over Troubled Water" [both 1970], for example), Simon's first post-breakup solo record was more eclectic. The Latino music influence was evident on that 1972 self-titled album's cut "Me and Julio down by the Schoolyard," and the Caribbean-flavored song "Mother and Child Reunion," which was recorded in Jamaica. His even more varied second album, *There Goes Rhymin' Simon* (1973), was recorded at the Muscle Shoals Studio, where dozens of classic soul records were made. It contained a Dixieland number, "Mardi Gras," mixed in with songs such as "Tenderness" and "Loves Me Like a Rock," which featured the gospel-like vocals of the Dixie Hummingbirds. The rest of his albums have followed this precedent (excepting the more sober 1975 album *Still Crazy after All These Years*), with each one charting new musical paths that Simon explored, culminating in 1986's Grammy-winning world music fusion album, *Graceland.*

Graceland is chock full of Simon's consistently good pop songs, but it has also sparked many debates surrounding the political and cultural implications of a white American working with black South Africans under apartheid. While the South African vocal group Ladysmith Black Mambazo and other native musicians contributed to the "sound" of the songs, *Graceland*'s songs were all written by Simon himself. This is significant from an intellectual property vantage, but also from the standpoint of identity politics. Simon could legally "capture" indigenous forms of music and make them his own, and, as a famous white

American artist, he also had the power to mediate the representation of black South Africans. The critical discourse that surrounds *Graceland* can also apply both to a critique of Simon's frequent use of "exotic" music throughout his career and to the Western music industry's and consumers' relationship with world music.

Throughout his solo career Simon has occasionally rejoined Garfunkel, once for a George McGovern fund-raiser for the 1972 election and later during a free Central Park concert for an estimated half-million fans. Further, Garfunkel intermittently joined Simon onstage as a guest at his concerts, and the two worked together on the single "My Little Town," which was featured both on Simon's *Still Crazy after All These Years* and Garfunkel's *Breakaway* (1975) albums. The duo toured together several more times while each pursued his own career.

The late 1990s were a dismal time for Simon's independent work. It was an era in which he was heavily involved financially and creatively in a failed musical, *The Capeman* (1998), and he released his only album not to reach the Billboard Top 40, *Songs from the Capeman* (1997). Simon was restored to favorable popular opinion after a successful North American tour with Bob Dylan in 1999 and a well-received Grammy-nominated album, *You're the One* (2000). The singer continues to perform frequently, including a 2011 world tour; has made several television appearances; has published a book of lyrics; and remains active in philanthropic endeavors promoting children's health and music education. A seminal figure in shaping contemporary American music, Simon shows no sign of slowing down.

Kembrew McLeod

SEE ALSO: *Doo-wop Music; Dylan, Bob; Folk Music; Grammy Awards; Jazz; Pop Music; Salsa Music; Simon and Garfunkel; Top 40.*

BIBLIOGRAPHY

Eliot, Marc. *Paul Simon: A Life*. Hoboken, NJ: Wiley, 2010.

Humphries, Patrick. *The Boy in the Bubble: A Biography of Paul Simon*. London: New English Library, 1990.

Jackson, Laura. *Paul Simon: The Definitive Biography of the Legendary Singer/Songwriter*. New York: Citadel, 2004.

Luftig, Stacey. *The Paul Simon Companion: Four Decades of Commentary*. New York: Schirmer Books, 1997.

Simon and Garfunkel

Simon and Garfunkel, the legendary folk-rock duo from the 1960s, were among the first groups to emphasize poetry in their lyrics, demonstrating that such complexity could enhance pop music. Along with the Byrds and a handful of other artists, they also led the way in melding acoustic folk instrumentation with the sounds associated with rock and roll: electric guitar, electric bass, and drums. Significantly and symbolically, Simon and Garfunkel's songs are featured prominently in the Mike Nichols film *The Graduate* (1967), a coming-of-age story for the 1960s generation starring Dustin Hoffman. Taken as a whole, their albums—*Wednesday Morning, 3 A.M.* (1964), *Sounds of Silence* (1966), *Parsley, Sage, Rosemary and Thyme* (1966), *Bookends* (1968), *The Graduate* soundtrack, and *Bridge over Troubled Water* (1970)—provide an eloquent and moving soundtrack to the turbulent second half of the 1960s.

RISING TO FAME

The duo, made up of Paul Simon (1941–) and Art Garfunkel (1941–), met at their elementary school in Forest Hills, New York, and soon realized that they could harmonize to the doo-wop songs that were popular on the radio. Soon the two began singing some of the many songs Simon was writing, and when they were both sixteen, they recorded "Hey Schoolgirl." This Everly Brothers–inspired song was released as a single on the independent label Big Records under the name Tom & Jerry, and it sold respectably, reaching the Billboard Top 50. The two continued to work with each other intermittently throughout the late 1950s and early 1960s, though they primarily remained solo artists during this time. Garfunkel recorded as Artie Garr, while Simon had modest chart success as a member of Tico and the Triumphs ("Motorcycle" briefly appeared at number ninety-nine on the charts in 1962) and as Jerry Landis ("The Lone Teen Ranger" topped off at ninety-seven in 1963).

The two reunited in 1964, playing in coffeehouses in New York's Greenwich Village and recording the album *Wednesday Morning, 3 A.M.*, which sold poorly. They split up again, with Simon going to England to eke out a living by performing live and recording his first solo album. While he was away, folk-rock producer Tom Wilson added electric bass, electric guitar, and drums to an obscure track from *Wednesday Morning, 3 A.M.* titled "The Sound of Silence," which wound up going to the top of the Billboard pop singles chart in 1965. Hearing of his unexpected overnight success, Simon promptly returned to the States for a promotional tour and to record the duo's second album, which is primarily made up of songs from his UK solo effort. That second album, *Sounds of Silence*, contains the popular remixed version of "The Sound of Silence" and another Top 40 hit, "I Am a Rock." The success of their subsequent albums made Simon and Garfunkel among the most beloved musical artists of the 1960s, and Simon's complex poetry influenced a number of other imitators.

Because Simon was not a prolific writer (most of the material contained on their first three albums was written between 1962 and 1965), the songs came more slowly near the end of the duo's career. This, along with the pair's increasing inability to get along, was one of the major reasons Simon and Garfunkel's final album, *Bridge over Troubled Water*, took two years to record. This, however, was their most popular album, containing their most complex and varied material, from the genre dabbling of "Cecilia" and "El Condor Pasa" to the symphonic grandiosity of the title track, all of which were Top 40 hits.

POST-BREAKUP

Since their breakup in 1970, Simon and Garfunkel have played together for many live performances and even attempted to record a new album. These reunions, however, have been punctuated by long periods of estrangement. Their first reunion was at a 1972 fund-raiser for presidential candidate George McGovern. A 1981 free concert in New York City's Central Park yielded the album *The Concert in Central Park* and sparked a world tour. Throughout the 1990s and into the twenty-first century, their relationship has followed a similar pattern: they have reunited for public appearances on important occasions, such as for their induction into the Rock and Roll Hall of Fame in 1990 and their Grammy Lifetime Achievement Award in 2003, and the overwhelmingly positive receptions have sometimes prompted a series of performance dates or a tour. During this time, several live albums have been released, including *Live from New York City: 1967* (2002) and *Live 1969* (2007), both of which contain unreleased studio songs in addition to the live recordings.

Simon and Garfunkel's crossover success with *The Graduate* soundtrack cemented their legacy. Despite releasing only five studio albums, the duo remains prominent in popular culture. Numerous television shows, films, and musicians make reference to Simon and Garfunkel or reappropriate their iconic songs. For example, two of their songs, "The Sound of Silence" and "The 59th Street Bridge Song (Feelin' Groovy)," have been parodied on the animated television series *The Simpsons*. Films such as 1993's *Wayne's World 2*, 2003's *Old School*, and 2005's *Rumor Has It . . .* pay homage to the *The Graduate* with selections from Simon and Garfunkel's soundtrack. There are numerous covers of their songs, notably Bob Dylan's version of "The Boxer" and Elvis Presley's rendering of "Bridge over Troubled Water." Marked by their impeccable harmonies and penetrating lyrics, Simon and Garfunkel stand out as one of the greatest American musical acts of the twentieth century.

Kembrew McLeod

SEE ALSO: *The Byrds; Doo-wop Music; Dylan, Bob; The Everly Brothers; Folk Music;* The Graduate*; Greenwich Village; Hoffman, Dustin; Pop Music; Presley, Elvis; Rock and Roll; Simon, Paul;* The Simpsons*; Top 40;* Wayne's World.

BIBLIOGRAPHY

Charlesworth, Chris. *The Complete Guide to the Music of Paul Simon and Simon and Garfunkel.* New York: Omnibus Press, 1997.

Kingston, Victoria. *Simon and Garfunkel: The Definitive Biography.* London: Sidgwick & Jackson, 1996.

Kingston, Victoria. *Simon and Garfunkel: A Biography.* New York: Fromm, 2000.

Morella, Joseph, and Patricia Barey. *Simon and Garfunkel: Old Friends, a Dual Biography.* London: Robert Hale, 1992.

Simpson, Jessica *(1980–)*

Born July 10, 1980, singer and actress Jessica Simpson grew up in Richardson, Texas. The daughter of a psychologist/youth minister, Simpson sang gospel music in church from an early age before turning her focus to popular music and country. While in her teens she made a vow to practice abstinence until her wedding, and her wholesome image made her a role model for young girls and a highly marketable figure for the entertainment industry. Simpson found initial fame in music and film but has since become a successful businesswoman in the world of fashion and merchandising.

As a child Simpson discovered her love of music by singing in a Baptist choir at a church where her father, Joe, worked as a youth minister. In 1992 she auditioned for *The New Mickey Mouse Club* and made the finals with future stars Britney Spears, Christina Aguilera, and Justin Timberlake. After failing to be named to the cast, Simpson returned to the gospel circuit and eventually signed with the small gospel label Proclaim Records. Her first album *Jessica*, completed as the company succumbed to bankruptcy, enjoyed a small pressing financed by her grandmother. The album eventually made its way to Tommy Mottola, head of Columbia Music.

Impressed by Simpson's style, Mottola immediately signed her to his label. Simpson then dropped out of high school and released her first Columbia album, *Sweet Kisses* (1999), which contained her first hit single, "I Wanna Love You Forever." The album eventually went double platinum, and Simpson became a sensation on the strength of her perceived innocence and girl-next-door looks. She gained wider exposure when her second single, "Did You Ever Love Somebody," appeared on the teen drama *Dawson's Creek* (1998–2003). Her second album, *Irresistible* (2001), also found popular success, with the eponymous single surpassing her previous offerings on the Billboard charts.

On October 26, 2002, Simpson married singer Nick Lachey, formerly of the boy band 98 Degrees. The couple became reality stars in 2003 with the MTV show *Newlyweds: Nick and Jessica* (2003–2005). The program drew a wide audience and made Simpson a household name, due in part to some of her nonsensical comments (in particular an exchange in which she questions whether Chicken of the Sea is actually tuna or chicken), which led some critics to question her intelligence. Simpson later told *Seventeen* magazine, "I think there is a difference between ditzy and dumb. Dumb is just not knowing. Ditzy is having the courage to ask!" Simpsons's third album, *In This Skin* (2003, rereleased in 2004) contained a number of songs that sought to counter her airhead image. She and Lachey later appeared in a widely panned variety show called *The Nick & Jessica Variety Hour* (2004). Simpson also published a book about her experience marrying Lachey, *I Do: Achieving Your Dream Wedding*, in 2004. The couple would go on to separate in 2005; their divorce was finalized in 2006.

During this period Simpson also embarked on an acting career, with several appearances on the sitcom *That '70s Show* early in the first decade of the 2000s, and in 2005 she starred in the film adaptation of *The Dukes of Hazzard*, playing the role of the voluptuous Daisy Duke. She also provided a cover of the Nancy Sinatra hit "These Boots Are Made for Walking" for the film soundtrack and later included the track on her 2006 album *A Public Affair*. The album, however, did not perform well, nor did her second or third films, *Employee of the Month* (2006) and *Blonde Ambition* (2008).

She returned to her home state of Texas and had a brief, high-profile relationship with Dallas Cowboys quarterback Tony Romo and released the country album *Do You Know* in 2008. The single "Come on Over" debuted at number forty-one on the Billboard country charts, but Simpson faced criticism for her decision to switch from pop to country, and Sony Nashville released her from her contract in 2009. Simpson then returned to reality television with *Jessica Simpson: The Price of Beauty* (2010), which explores the meaning of beauty to women in other countries.

As Simpson's music career continued to decline, she began to focus her efforts on her budding fashion ventures. Inspired by the success of her 2004 line of edible perfumes and lip glosses, Simpson later added hair and beauty products, which are sold through the Home Shopping Network. She went on to develop a wide range of clothing and accessories under the enormously successful Jessica Simpson Collection (JSC) brand, which announced the addition of a maternity and toddler line for 2012. Also in 2012 Simpson began serving as a mentor/judge on the NBC competition show *Fashion Star*.

Simpson enjoys success on many fronts but also faces criticism for her choices. Becoming a tabloid darling after her separation from Lachey, Simpson faces unending scrutiny when it comes to her romantic life and personal appearance. While dating Romo, she was blamed for the Dallas Cowboys' loss in the 2008 National Football League (NFL) playoffs. And in 2011 she was the subject of a series of vicious tabloid articles detailing her weight gain while pregnant with her and fiancé Eric Johnson's daughter, Maxwell, who was born on May 1, 2012. Like the numerous other setbacks and career downturns she has experienced, Simpson took the criticism in stride and turned it into a lucrative business opportunity, announcing a $4 million contract to serve as a Weight Watchers spokesperson just weeks after the birth of her daughter.

Linda Martindale

SEE ALSO: *Aguilera, Christina; Boy Bands; Country Music; The Dallas Cowboys;* Dawson's Creek*; Dieting; Divorce;* Dukes of Hazzard*; Gospel Music; Home Shopping Network/QVC;* The Mickey Mouse Club*; MTV; National Football League (NFL); Pop Music; Reality Television;* Seventeen*; Sitcom; Spears, Britney; Tabloids; Teenagers; Television; Timberlake, Justin.*

BIBLIOGRAPHY

Adams, Michelle M. *Jessica Simpson*. Hockessin, DE: Mitchell Lane Publishers, 2008.

Elyse, Nicole, and Shannon McCarthy. "Simpson, Jessica." In *Contemporary Musicians*, vol. 52, ed. Angela Pilchak. Detroit, MI: Gale, 2005.

Jessica Simpson Official Site. Accessed March 2012. Available from http://www.jessicasimpson.com/

Larocca, Amy. "The $1 Billion Girl; Jessica Simpson Is Laughing All the Way to the Fashion Bank." *New York Magazine*, February 21, 2011.

Simpson, O. J. *(1947–)*

O. J. Simpson was one of America's top college and professional football players in the late 1960s and 1970s, but since the 1990s he has been remembered not for his gridiron exploits but for his role as the defendant in one of the most celebrated murder trials of the twentieth century. Accused of the 1994 slayings of his ex-wife, Nicole Brown Simpson, and her friend Ron Goldman, Simpson was brought to trial in Los Angeles in a case that attracted enormous media attention because of his earlier sports celebrity status and because of his race. From Simpson's arrest until his eventual acquittal and beyond, his case has divided Americans along racial lines, with most blacks believing in his innocence and most whites convinced that he is guilty.

Prior to these sorry events, Orenthal James Simpson was one of America's most beloved sports heroes. In the late 1960s he was a college gridiron idol and Heisman Trophy winner. In the 1970s he starred in the National Football League (NFL) and earned a reputation as one of the greatest running backs in the history of college and professional football.

EARLY ATHLETIC EXCELLENCE

Simpson, a cousin of Chicago Cubs baseball player Ernie Banks, was born July 9, 1947, in San Francisco. At age two he was diagnosed with rickets; he wore leg braces for three years to treat the condition. In 1960, when he was thirteen, Simpson joined the Persian Warriors, a San Francisco–based street gang. Upon his entry into the Pro Football Hall of Fame in 1985, Simpson's mother, Eunice, observed, "I didn't really think he'd turn out the way he did, but he always said you'd read about him in the papers someday, and my oldest daughter would always say, 'In the police report.'"

Athletics eventually consumed Simpson's life, and he realized he had a special talent for carrying a football. He earned national attention in 1967 and 1968 during two varsity seasons as star rusher at the University of Southern California (USC). Most famously, in his senior year he was handed the ball forty times in USC's game against the University of California at Los Angeles (UCLA), during which he ran for 205 yards. He also set a National Collegiate Athletic Association (NCAA) record with 355 carries in a season, and his total of 1,709 yards gained was another NCAA milestone. Simpson earned All-American honors both years and topped off his college career by winning the 1968 Heisman Trophy. In 1983 he was elected to the College Football Hall of Fame. John McKay, Simpson's USC coach, once observed, "Simpson was not only the greatest player I ever had—he was the greatest player anyone ever had."

NFL CAREER

Simpson was the number one draft pick of the NFL Buffalo Bills. He played for the Bills from 1969 through 1977, during which time he rushed for 10,183 yards on 2,123 carries. In 1972 he gained more than 1,000 rushing yards for the first time and was named American Football Conference (AFC) Player of the Year. The following season he set a single-game NFL rushing record with 250 yards ground out against the New England Patriots. In the season finale, in which the Bills faced the New York Jets, Simpson ran for 200 yards, allowing him to finish the season with 2,003 yards (in 332 attempts) and become the first player in league history to amass 2,000-plus rushing yards in a single season. It was Simpson's greatest year as a pro, and he was named the NFL's Most Valuable Player.

Simpson enjoyed several other solid years with the Bills, along with one more superior campaign: 1975, in which he rushed for 1,817 yards, set an NFL record for touchdowns in a season with twenty-three, and was named the AFC's Most Valuable Player. While he was with the Bills Simpson played in the NFL Pro Bowl on six occasions, in 1969 and from 1972 to 1976. In 1978 the aging runner, disheartened that the Bills had failed to reach the Super Bowl during his career, requested a trade to a West Coast team. He was traded to the San Francisco 49ers and retired the following year after rushing for an additional 1,053 yards on 281 carries. In addition to his election to the Pro Football Hall of Fame, he was named to the NFL's 75th Anniversary Team.

Simpson's friendly smile, movie-star looks, and extroverted personality allowed him to become a media fixture who appealed to a cross-section of Americans. While still starring on the gridiron, he established himself as an actor. While at USC, he played a student on TV's *Dragnet 1967* (1968); in 1973 he appeared as himself in "The Big Game," an episode of *Here's Lucy*. While playing for the Bills, he debuted on the big screen in *The Klansman* (1974) and *The Towering Inferno* (1974) and went on to appear in *The Cassandra Crossing* (1976), *Capricorn One* (1977), and three *Naked Gun* comedies (1988, 1991, and 1994), in addition to spots on several television series and made-for-TV movies.

MURDER TRIAL AND AFTERMATH

Simpson remained in the public eye as an actor, as a football broadcaster on ABC and NBC, and most famously as a Hertz Rent-a-Car spokesperson who could be seen dashing through airline terminals in TV commercials. Just before the Nicole Brown Simpson–Ron Goldman murders, Simpson had starred in *Frogmen* (1994), a TV series pilot, and the third *Naked Gun* feature, *Naked Gun 33 1/3: The Final Insult.* His post-gridiron popularity and marketability permanently vanished when he was accused of the killings. Though Simpson was acquitted of the murders after a widely televised criminal trial, just two years later, in 1997, a civil jury unanimously found him responsible for the wrongful death of Goldman; he was also found liable for committing criminal battery against both Goldman and Brown Simpson, whose families were awarded $33.5 million in damages. To meet this obligation, in 1999 Simpson sold his Heisman Trophy for a reported sum of $230,000. While that money was awarded to the Goldman family, across the years Simpson has paid only a small fraction of the total judgment.

Simpson settled in Florida but steadfastly refused to fade from the limelight. He derived income from his NFL pension and by signing autographs at sports memorabilia shows, and photos occasionally surfaced in the media of a smiling Simpson on the golf course. In 2001 he was charged with burglary and criminal battery during an altercation with a motorist; he went on trial but was found innocent of all charges.

Facing mounting financial troubles, Simpson attempted to derive income by writing *If I Did It,* a book in which he offers a hypothetical scenario describing how he would have murdered Brown Simpson and Goldman. A massive public outcry resulted in the cancellation of *If I Did It* before it was published, and a federal bankruptcy court turned the rights to the book over to the Goldman family. The book was finally published in 2007 with a modified title: *If I Did It: The Confessions of the Killer.* The word *If* was obscured on the covers of the various editions of the book to make the title appear at first glance to be *I Did It: The Confessions of the Killer.* Simpson was not cited as the author. Highlighted instead was the inclusion of commentary by the Goldman family.

In 2007 Simpson was detained by police after he and several accomplices broke into a Las Vegas, Nevada, hotel room and stole hundreds of collectible souvenirs from his athletic career. The charges he faced included conspiracy to commit a crime, conspiracy to commit kidnapping, conspiracy to commit robbery, and burglary while in possession of a deadly weapon. Simpson claimed that two sports memorabilia dealers had stolen the items from him, and he was merely retrieving stolen property. He went on trial for the crime, and in October 2008 was found guilty on all counts. He was sentenced to thirty-three years in prison, which included a minimum of nine years behind bars without parole. He began serving his sentence at the Lovelock Correctional Center in Nevada.

In 2008 Mike Gilbert published a book, *How I Helped O. J. Get Away with Murder: The Shocking Inside Story of Violence, Loyalty, Regret, and Remorse,* in which he alleged that Simpson had acknowledged his guilt to him several weeks after his acquittal. On the book's cover, Gilbert is described as a "former sports agent and confidant to O. J. Simpson." In response to the allegations, Simpson's representatives asserted that the tome was loaded with falsehoods.

Rob Edelman

SEE ALSO: *The Chicago Cubs; College Football;* Dragnet*; Gangs; Hollywood; Made-for-Television Movies; National Collegiate Athletic Association (NCAA); National Football League (NFL); Professional Football; Simpson Trial; Super Bowl; Television.*

BIBLIOGRAPHY

Baker, Jim. *O. J. Simpson's Most Memorable Games.* New York: Putnam, 1978.

Barbieri, Paula. *The Other Woman: My Years with O. J. Simpson: A Story of Love, Trust, and Betrayal.* Boston: Little, Brown, 1997.

Cerasini, Marc. *O. J. Simpson: American Hero, American Tragedy.* New York: Windsor, 1994.

Davis, Don. *Fallen Hero.* New York: St. Martin's Press, 1994.

Devaney, John. *O. J. Simpson: Football's Greatest Runner.* New York: Warner Books, 1974.

Gilbert, Mike. *How I Helped O. J. Get Away with Murder: The Shocking Inside Story of Violence, Loyalty, Regret, and Remorse.* Washington, DC: Regnery, 2008.

Gutman, Bill. *O. J.* New York: Grosset & Dunlap, 1974.

Hayslett, Jerrianne. *Anatomy of a Trial: Public Loss, Lessons Learned from "The People vs. O. J. Simpson."* Columbia: University of Missouri Press, 2008.

Simpson, O. J.; Dominick Dunne; and Pablo F. Fenjves. *If I Did It: Confessions of the Killer.* New York: Beaufort Books, 2007.

Simpson Trial

On the night of June 12, 1994, Nicole Brown Simpson and her friend Ronald Lyle Goldman were viciously stabbed to death outside the former's town house in Brentwood, California. The murders immediately received an extraordinary amount of media coverage because Nicole Brown Simpson was the ex-wife of former football star, minor film star, and celebrity pitchman O. J. Simpson. O. J. Simpson came under immediate suspicion in the murders, was briefly questioned by detectives assigned to the case, and formally notified four days later of his impending arrest on double homicide charges. Rather than surrender, however, Simpson left behind a maudlin note for the media, which some construed to be a suicide note, and took off with his friend A. C. Cowlings in Cowlings's white Bronco. After a few hours of uncertainty and suspense, police cars located the white Bronco on a Los Angeles freeway and began pursuing it in what the media, televising the dramatic event to a spellbound worldwide audience, quickly dubbed a "low-speed chase." In contrast to the public animosity that would soon make Simpson a social outcast, hundreds of people lined the freeway overpasses above the bizarre procession and waved handwritten signs of support for the "Juice." The strangest chase in the Los Angeles Police Department (LAPD) history ended at Simpson's estate in Rockingham, where he was quietly placed under arrest, out of camera range of the circling news helicopters, and taken to the Los Angeles County Jail.

O. J. Simpson Trial. O. J. Simpson tries on a leather glove connected the murders of Nicole Brown Simpson and Ronald Goldman during testimony in his murder trial in 1995. LEE CELANO/CONTRIBUTOR/WIREIMAGE/GETTY IMAGES.

Eighteen months later, Simpson, acquitted of all charges, would again be escorted home by the LAPD, but this time to the jeers and contempt of his neighbors and the scorn of much of white America. The reaction to Simpson's acquittal, as well as belief in his ultimate innocence or guilt, was and still is sharply divided along racial lines, with African Americans tending to support Simpson and white Americans ostracizing him. The process by which Simpson became legally vindicated but socially exiled indicated the force of the mass media in late twentieth-century America and anticipated any number of media-driven news sensations into the new century.

MEDIA OBSESSION

The spectacle of the Bronco chase was only a hint of the media obsession to come regarding the Simpson case. All of the major figures involved in the investigation and trial procedures would become celebrities in their own right, courted by the media and in many cases given multimillion-dollar book deals. The preliminary hearing and the trial were televised in whole or in part by the major networks, and night after night the cable news stations, such as CNN and MSNBC, devoted hours of often-heated analysis from mostly obscure legal pundits to the day's legal developments. (Some of these legal pundits, such as Roger Cossack and Greta Van Susteren, soon gained their own regular cable shows, and much later some of the Simpson trial veterans, such as Johnnie Cochran and Marcia Clark, ironically became pundits themselves.) Millions of viewers across the United States followed the television proceedings throughout the day, and millions more watched the nighttime trial summaries, commentary, and analysis. The wall-to-wall coverage and the high ratings ensured that future extended real-life dramas, such as the 1998 national sex scandal involving President Bill Clinton and a young White House former intern Monica Lewinsky, would receive the same exhaustive treatment from the media.

SIMPSON'S HISTORY

Simpson was formally arraigned on June 20, 1994, entering a plea of not guilty. Thus far, public opinion seemed to have more or less reserved judgment on Simpson's guilt, but all of that began to change on June 22. That was the day that the district attorney's office leaked to the media a tape of a frantic 911 call made by Nicole Simpson back in October 1993. In that tape, Nicole tearfully pleads for help as an enraged Simpson shouts and swears in the background. The contrast between the chilling tape and Simpson's genial public persona could not have been more striking, and many students of the case point to the release of the tape as the beginning of the public shift of opinion against Simpson. Two other instances of domestic violence in the Simpson household then received widespread media play: a 1985 incident that resulted in no formal charges, and a 1989 incident in which Simpson was charged but eventually pleaded "no contest." On the basis of such abusive incidents, the District Attorney's Office, under the leadership of D.A. Gil Garcetti, began formulating its theory of the murders: that O. J. Simpson, already a violent wife-batterer, had killed Nicole and her friend Goldman out of jealousy and rage. Thus began a public debate between various experts as to whether Simpson fit the "profile" of an abuser-turned-murderer.

Contrary to most expectations, the prosecution's emphasis on domestic violence eventually proved to be a losing strategy. What ultimately carried the day for Simpson was a defense that compellingly argued that a combination of LAPD malfeasance (evidence planting and tampering) and crime lab incompetence (evidence contamination) had conspired to make an innocent man look guilty. Central to this defense strategy was the ambiguous figure of Detective Mark Fuhrman, one of the original investigating detectives at the crime scene. Fuhrman was in some ways a star witness for the prosecution: movie-star striking in appearance and unwaveringly methodical in crime-scene investigation. According to some sources, however, Fuhrman had a reputation as a racist who allegedly targeted black suspects for brutal treatment. Problematically for Fourth Amendment advocates, Fuhrman had also entered Simpson's Rockingham estate on the night of the murders without a warrant, ostensibly because he and fellow detectives Tom Lange, Philip Vannatter, and Ronald Phillips—having just come from one bloody crime scene—feared for Simpson's safety and did not consider him a suspect. (Judge Lance Ito later characterized Vannatter's version of this story as demonstrating "reckless disregard for the truth.") Fuhrman provided a convenient way for defense lawyers to negate one of the most damning bits of evidence against Simpson: a bloody leather glove found by Fuhrman at Simpson's Rockingham home that matched one left behind at the crime scene. The defense theory, which was formulated early on and never so much explicitly stated in court as implied, was that racist Fuhrman, alone behind Simpson's house, had motive and opportunity to plant the bloody glove, surreptitiously lifted from the crime scene, and thus make the case against Simpson ironclad. Such a theory had undeniable resonance in racially troubled Los Angeles, which still remembered all too clearly the deadly riots that followed the 1991 acquittal of four LAPD officers charged with beating African American motorist Rodney King.

THE ATTORNEYS

It would be some months before the defense could square off against Fuhrman and the LAPD in open court. In July 1994 at the preliminary hearing, Judge Kathleen Kennedy-Powell found that there was enough evidence for Simpson to stand trial. A few weeks later, Judge Ito became the trial judge. Jury selection began in September and continued into November. The jury was predominantly African American, a fact that would later cause much controversy. The attorneys who represented Simpson, some of them nationally famous, became hyperbolically known in the media as "The Dream Team." Simpson's team of lawyers at various times included F. Lee Bailey, Bob Blazier, Shawn Chapman, Johnnie Cochran, Alan Dershowitz, Carl Douglas, Robert Kardashian, Ralph Lotkin, Peter Neufeld, Barry Scheck, Robert Shapiro, Skip Taft, and Bill Thompson. Shapiro first organized Simpson's defense. Later, the locally famous African American lawyer Cochran joined the defense team and eventually became its lead attorney after public disputes between Shapiro and Bailey caused a severe rift in strategy. Against this team were arrayed some forty full-time prosecutors, of which Marcia Clark and Chris Darden (an African American) became the most visible advocates for the people's case.

Clark and Darden delivered opening arguments in the case of *The People v. O. J. Simpson* on January 24, 1995. The trial lasted for nine months, during which the rapt television audiences witnessed many defining moments, some of high drama and others of low comedy, that have since passed into legal lore. A partial list of those moments includes Nicole's sister Denise crying on the stand as she described Simpson's contemptuous and abusive behavior toward Nicole; the jury field trip to Simpson's elaborately staged Rockingham estate; the cross-examination of Detective Fuhrman by Bailey, in which Fuhrman unwisely denied using the word *nigger* in the previous ten years; the befuddled demeanor and tortured vocabulary of Kato Kaelin, a houseguest of Simpson's who had been with Simpson on the night of the murders; the rigorous cross-examination of LAPD criminalist Dennis Fung by Scheck, in which Fung admitted to numerous errors in processing the crime scene; the horrendous decision by prosecutor Darden for Simpson to try on the killer's leather gloves, which apparently did not fit, in front of the jury; the defense team's first courtroom suggestions that evidence may have planted by the LAPD in order to frame Simpson; the playing to the jury of tapes which conclusively refuted Fuhrman's contention that he had never said "nigger" in the past ten years; Fuhrman's subsequent pleading of the Fifth Amendment as to whether he had planted evidence in the case; the calling of two sinister-looking mob informants to impeach the testimony of one of the case's detectives; Simpson's in-court assertion to Judge Ito that "I did not, could not, and would not commit this crime"; and Clark's impassioned rebuttal to the defense's closing arguments.

ACQUITTAL

By far the most dramatic days of the trial were October 2 and 3, when the jury deliberated the case for only four hours before reaching a verdict. Judge Ito decided to delay the announcement of the verdict until the following day, thus allowing one full night of feverish pundit speculation as to the outcome. On the morning of October 3, 1995, as much of the nation halted work to watch the suspenseful reading of the verdict, Simpson was found not guilty of the murders of Nicole Brown Simpson and Ronald Lyle Goldman.

Television viewers across the nation saw news video of white audiences stunned by the news and black audiences rejoicing. Official reaction was primarily that of disbelief. A visibly stunned Garcetti and his lead prosecutors held a post-verdict press conference, during which Darden was reduced to tears. Public reaction depended very much on the race of those being asked. Polls taken in the days and weeks after the verdict confirmed that people's views of the verdict tended to break down along racial lines. The voices of the white establishment press, including those of highly visible network news anchors, swiftly grew in protest against the African American jury that, it was implied, freed Simpson for reasons of racial solidarity. Subtly racist criticism was also leveled against Asian American Judge Ito for not having kept tighter control of his courtroom.

THE CIVIL CASE

The white backlash against the jury and its verdict grew only stronger over the coming months, eventually reaching its crescendo in the wrongful-death civil trial that grew out of a suit earlier filed against Simpson by Fred Goldman, the father of Ron. Fred Goldman had been a highly visible spokesman for his slain son during the criminal trial. The lead lawyer for the plaintiff was Daniel Petrocelli; Simpson's lead lawyer in the civil trial was Robert Baker. The civil trial began on September 17, 1996, in Santa Monica. In contrast to the first trial, the civil trial was not televised, and Simpson himself took the stand to testify. On the evening of February 4, 1997, in another media spectacle that threatened to overshadow President Clinton's annual State of the Union address, a predominantly white jury found Simpson liable for the wrongful deaths of Nicole Brown Simpson and Ron Goldman and assessed combined compensatory and punitive damages of $33 million. Just as the first trial's verdict was roundly condemned by the establishment press, the second verdict was hailed as a triumph of justice. O. J. Simpson was forced to sell his Rockingham estate but, as of this writing, has paid very little of the judgment.

AFTER THE TRIALS

Simpson later attempted to publish a supposedly fictional first-person account of the murders titled *If I Did It*, but following a public outcry the publisher declined to publish. The Goldman family, awarded the publishing rights to satisfy in part the unpaid legal judgment from the civil trial, renamed the book *If I Did It: Confessions of the Killer* and published it in 2007. Simpson landed in further legal trouble with an arrest for battery in Miami in 2001, for which he was acquitted. His luck ran out with his arrest for robbery and a host of other charges for breaking into a hotel room with some other men in Las Vegas to take sports memorabilia that Simpson claimed belonged to him. In 2008 Simpson was convicted of all charges and sentenced to thirty-three years in prison in Nevada. If this incarceration was viewed by some as belated justice for his earlier acquittal for murder, the memory of the "Trial of the Century" in 1995 satisfies few. Many people remain convinced that Simpson legally if not financially got away with murder, while others are equally convinced that institutional racism and police malevolence allowed the real murderer(s) to escape justice.

Philip L. Simpson

SEE ALSO: *King, Rodney; Media Feeding Frenzies; Simpson, O. J.*

BIBLIOGRAPHY

Bosco, Joseph. *A Problem of Evidence: How the Prosecution Freed O. J. Simpson.* New York: William Morrow, 1996.

Bugliosi, Vincent. *Outrage.* New York: W. W. Norton, 1996.

Clark, Marcia, and Teresa Carpenter. *Without a Doubt.* New York: Viking Press, 1997.

Cochran, Johnnie L., and Tim Rutten. *Journey to Justice.* New York: Ballantine, 1996.

Cooley, Armanda; Carrie Bess; and Marsha Rubin-Jackson; as told to Tom Byrnes and Mike Walker. *Madam Foreman.* Beverly Hills, CA: Dove Books, 1995.

Darden, Christopher A., with Jess Walter. *In Contempt.* New York: Regan Books, 1996.

Dershowitz, Alan M. *Reasonable Doubts.* New York: Simon & Schuster, 1996.

Elias, Tom, and Dennis Schatzman. *The Simpson Trial in Black and White.* Los Angeles: General Publishing Group, 1996.

Freed, Donald, and Raymond P. Briggs. *Killing Time: The First Full Investigation.* New York: Macmillan, 1996.

Fuhrman, Mark. *Murder in Brentwood.* Washington, DC: Regnery Publishing, 1997.

Gibbs, Jewelle Taylor. *Race and Justice: Rodney King and O. J. Simpson in a House Divided.* San Francisco: Jossey-Bass, 1996.

Gilbert, Mike. *How I Helped O. J. Simpson Get Away with Murder.* Washington, DC: Regnery Publishing, 2008.

Goldberg, Hank M. *The Prosecution Responds.* Secaucus, NJ: Birch Lane Press, 1996.

The Goldman Family. *If I Did It: Confessions of the Killer.* New York: Beaufort Books, 2007.

Kennedy, Tracy; Judith Kennedy; and Alan Abrahamson. *Mistrial of the Century.* Beverly Hills, CA: Dove Books, 1995.

Knox, Michael, with Mike Walker. *The Private Diary of an O. J. Juror.* Beverly Hills, CA: Dove Books, 1995.

Lange, Tom, and Philip Vannatter, as told to Dan E. Moldea. *Evidence Dismissed.* New York: Pocket Books, 1997.

Morrison, Toni, and Claudia Brodsky Lacour, eds. *Birth of a Nation 'hood: Gaze, Script, and Spectacle in the O. J. Simpson Case.* New York: Pantheon, 1997.

Petrocelli, Daniel M., and Peter Knobler. *Triumph of Justice: Closing the Book on the Simpson Saga.* New York: Crown, 1998.

Roberts, Peter. *OJ: 101 Theories, Conspiracies, & Alibis.* Diamond Bar, CA: Goldtree Press, 1995.

Schiller, Lawrence, and James Willwerth. *American Tragedy: The Uncensored Story of the Simpson Defense.* New York: Avon, 1997.

Shapiro, Robert L., with Larkin Warren. *The Search for Justice.* New York: Warner, 1996.

Simpson, O. J. *I Want to Tell You.* Boston: Little, Brown, 1995.

Singular, Stephen. *Legacy of Deception.* Beverly Hills, CA: Dove Books, 1995.

Toobin, Jeffrey. *The Run of His Life: The People v. O. J. Simpson.* New York: Simon & Schuster, 1997.

Uelmen, Gerald F. *Lessons from the Trial: The People v. O. J. Simpson.* Kansas City, MO: Andrews and McMeel, 1996.

The Simpsons

The family situation comedy has long been a staple of American entertainment, and no family brings together more of the foibles and saving graces of the family than *The Simpsons*, which has aired on the Fox network since 1989, making it the longest-running sitcom and animated series in American television history. Part *Honeymooners*, part *All in the Family*, the animated Simpson family, crudely drawn with bright yellow skin and outlandish stylized hair, have represented the flailing attempts of human beings to keep up with twentieth-century life and the social and technological changes of the early twenty-first century. Far from being a cartoon show for children only, *The Simpsons* deals with adult and teenage issues as well as world events. At the same time, the show is full of enough visual goofiness to keep the attention of children.

THE SIMPSONS OF SPRINGFIELD, USA

Homer, the dad, works, between doughnut breaks, as a safety inspector at the Springfield nuclear power plant, where he was once replaced during a strike by a brick placed on a lever. Homer has a taste for just about anything remotely edible, washed down with Duff Beer, which he prefers to drink on the sofa in front of the television or at the local bar, Moe's. Homer is always on the lookout for a free lunch, or at least a piece of lint-covered candy behind the sofa cushion. Marge, Homer's better half, sports a towering blue beehive and is the sensible anchor of the family. She has what Homer lacks in both common sense and moral fiber, and though she struggles to stay a step ahead of the damage her family wreaks, she loves them all like—well, like a mother.

The Simpsons Movie. *The characters of television's long-running* The Simpsons *hit the big screen in 2007.* 20TH CENTURY FOX/THE KOBAL COLLECTION/GROENING, MATT.

Bart is the demon spawn of Homer and Marge. From his first word—"Cowabunga!"—Bart has faced the world with an irreverent attitude. There is no scheme too depraved for Bart to consider, no mischief too evil to undertake. He is, however, only in the third grade, so once in a while even Bart finds himself in over his head. Lisa, in second grade, is the middle child and must have received her genes solely from Marge's pool. Lisa is a prodigy and, therefore, somewhat of a misfit in the Simpson family. She loves school and learning and plays saxophone like a professional, using its sweet tones to voice her own angst—a sensitive soul trapped in a crude wasteland. However, her Simpson side does show through now and then, and she always gets a laugh out of *Itchy and Scratchy*, the ultraviolent cartoon show she and Bart love.

Maggie, the baby, has uttered only one word, "Daddy." For the most part, she makes sucking noises while nursing her "Neglecto" brand pacifier, but she shows signs of becoming a true Simpson. When her pacifier is taken away by a brutish day-care worker, Maggie organizes the other babies in a *Great Escape*-style caper to retrieve their contraband "binkies." And, despite her tender age, she has already been responsible for a murder attempt on Homer's boss.

The supporting cast of *The Simpsons* represents a colorful assortment of characters, many of whom play against their stereotype to create a commentary on the wide variation among modern U.S. citizenry: Moe, the hard-boiled bartender, who secretly reads to children while weeping over *Little Women*; Waylon Smithers, the closeted gay administrative assistant, who harbors a not-so-secret yen for his boss, power plant owner, Mr. Burns; Apu, the Kwik-E-Mart owner, who has a Hindu shrine and a shotgun behind the cash register; Krusty the Clown, who had to leave behind his orthodox Jewish family and career as a cantor to follow his calling to make little children laugh and to make a fortune from licensing his name. Though clearly stereotyped, each character contains surprising quirks and changes that make audiences laugh but that are also surprisingly realistic and reassuring in an ever more complex society.

Each week *The Simpsons* begins with a long opening sequence. The afternoon whistle blows, and Homer packs up to leave work. He does not notice that one of the glowing radioactive bars he has been handling falls into his jacket and follows him home. At school, Bart finishes his daily punishment: writing 1,000 times on the blackboard "I will not . . . " (" . . . waste chalk," " . . . instigate murder," etc.). Marge finishes shopping; Lisa blows a blues riff on her saxophone as she leaves band practice. The family reunites in the modern archetypal spot—plopped on the sofa in front of the television.

WIDESPREAD APPEAL

There is much that speaks to American families in the silliness of *The Simpsons*, and the show appeals to all ages. Adult viewers approaching middle age recognize themselves caricatured in the Simpsons and their friends, from disillusion with dead-end jobs, to children they cannot handle, to fear of nuclear radiation, to the love and warmth they experience in life despite it all. The quirky, innovative animation contains visual jokes, some very subtle, that spoof all aspects of American life and culture, from consumerism to baby boomer political values. The light vehicle of animated comedy allows exploration of many normally taboo topics. While network live-action sitcoms have only recently warmed to gay characters, *The Simpsons* has been a long-time favorite with gay audiences because it has featured not only gay story lines but also a recurring gay character, Smithers, whose crush on the evil Mr. Burns is not always as hopeless as it looks. *The Simpsons*' forward-looking themes and all-ages appeal has earned it countless awards, a star on the Hollywood Walk of Fame, and the title of best television show of the twentieth century from *Time* magazine.

Matt Groening is the cartoonist who created the Simpsons, though the television series is produced by an army of writers, animators, and voice actors. Groening, who draws an alternative comic strip called "Life in Hell," first created the Simpsons for short animated spots in 1986 on *The Tracey Ullman Show* (1987–1990). He named the characters after his own family, except for Bart, who started life as "Matt" but was soon changed to an anagram of "brat." The bright-yellow family quickly captured an audience of its own, and, as Groening says, "The phenomenon has gone beyond my wildest dreams—and my wildest nightmares." Their first full-length show was a Christmas special in 1989, called *Simpsons Roasting on an Open Fire*, followed by a half-hour weekly series in January. By the end of 1990, *The Simpsons* was the highest-rated show on the Fox network and was widely syndicated.

"I try not to let anything in our culture be either too high or too low for me," Groening has said, and his work on *The Simpsons* bears this out. With a leftist, alternative point of view, Groening has created a palatable critique of American values, combining sophisticated humor with goofy cartoon slapstick. A husband and father himself, his skewering of the family is incisive yet loving. Episodes of *The Simpsons* often parody popular movies, movements, and public figures. The perennial mayor of Springfield, for example, speaks with a Kennedy-like Boston accent, and one episode revolves around his attempt to cover up the misdeeds of his spoiled, dissolute nephew. For one vacation, the family goes to a crassly commercial beer theme park, Duff Gardens, which shamelessly promotes alcoholism. Director John Waters guest stars on another episode, as a gay character, John, who Homer initially likes until he finds out that John is gay. Angriest about being fooled, he sputters, "He should at least have the good taste to mince around and let everyone know that he's that way!"

Not to be outdone by Krusty the Clown, Groening is unapologetic about licensing products with the Simpson name. Dozens of products carry pictures of the bright-yellow crew. *The Simpsons Comics Extravaganza* put the family in print, along with *Maggie Simpson's Alphabet Book* and *Counting Book*, and there have been Simpsons video games and even a record, *The Simpsons Sing the Blues* (1990). In the early 1990s a single cel of Groening's animation sold at Christie's famous art auction house for $24,200. The 2007 feature film *The Simpsons Movie* grossed more than $525 million worldwide and initiated a new wave of merchandising possibilities, with action figure and video game sales bolstered by promotions by Ben & Jerry's, Burger King, and 7-Eleven. The latter even converted several of its stores in the United States and Canada into Kwik-E-Marts, complete with items sold at the fictional store such as Squishees and KrustyO's cereal.

In its twenty-third season as of 2012, *The Simpsons* was briefly in danger of cancellation in 2011 due to a dispute between the show's voice actors and Fox executives, who wanted to cut production costs by 30 percent. Cooler heads prevailed, however, and the show was renewed through 2014, when its twenty-fifth season would air. Even in the face of increased competition from a new generation of animated shows, from

South Park (1997–) to *Family Guy* (1999–), *The Simpsons* maintains its appeal simply because it is hilarious entertainment; it is packed with cultural satire and is full of throw-away visual references. The show pulls the audience into its in-jokes, not requiring too much effort, but rewards a little mental exertion with hidden layers of meaning. Then, just when the viewer seems to find real depth, *The Simpsons* refuses to be predictable and dissolves into old-fashioned buffoonery. Its cartoon format gives the show that touch of fantasy, which makes it the perfect vehicle for cataloging the stuff of real life.

Tina Gianoulis

SEE ALSO: All in the Family*; Animated Films; Burger King; Comics; Emmy Awards; Groening, Matt;* The Honeymooners*; Sitcom;* South Park*; Television;* Time*; Waters, John.*

BIBLIOGRAPHY

Gray, Jonathan. *Watching with "The Simpsons": Television, Parody, and Intertextuality.* New York: Routledge, 2006.

Groening, Matt. *Matt Groening's Cartooning with "The Simpsons."* New York: HarperPerennial, 1993.

Groening, Matt; Ray Richmond; and Antonia Coffman, eds. *"The Simpsons": A Complete Guide to Our Favorite Family.* New York: HarperPerennial, 1997.

Harris, Jessica. "Check Him Out, Man! (Simpson's Creator Matt Groening)." *National Geographic World,* July 1994, 8–9.

Irwin, William; Mark T. Conard; and Aeon J. Skoble. *"The Simpsons" and Philosophy: The D'oh! of Homer.* Chicago: Open Court, 2001.

"The Odyssey of Homer." *Entertainment Weekly,* March 12, 1993, 84.

Ortved, John. *"The Simpsons": An Uncensored, Unauthorized History.* New York: Faber & Faber, 2009.

Turner, Chris. *Planet Simpson: How a Cartoon Masterpiece Documented an Era and Defined a Generation.* Toronto: Random House, 2004.

Waltonen, Karma, and Denise Du Vernay. *"The Simpsons" in the Classroom: Embiggening the Learning Experience with the Wisdom of Springfield.* Jefferson, NC: McFarland, 2010.

Sinatra, Frank *(1915–1998)*

Singer and actor Frank Sinatra was, by most accounts, the greatest entertainer of his time, known to his legions of fans as "the Voice" during the twentieth century. But his life intersected with worlds beyond show business—with both left- and right-wing politics, with the underworld, and with the celebrity culture of a postwar United States. An exceedingly complex man, Sinatra articulated in his songs the romantic dreams and existential longings of his generation. His music and life had a Shakespearean ages of man arc—from the callow youth of "I Fall in Love Too Easily" to the world-weary maturity of "In the Wee Small Hours" and, ultimately, to the triumphant patriarch of "My Way." But above everything, Sinatra will be remembered, in the words of Pete Hamill, as "a genuine artist, and his work will endure as long as men and women can hear, and ponder, and feel."

Frank Sinatra and Teen Fans. *Frank Sinatra signs autographs while standing on a ladder amid a crowd of young fans in 1943.* GENE LESTER/GETTY IMAGES.

During a career that spanned almost sixty years, Sinatra exploited the technology of the twentieth century to define and transform his public persona. He received major breaks in his early career when he was heard over the radio by bandleaders seeking a vocalist. During the 1940s his voice seemed to caress the microphone in concert, and Sinatra created a sexual awakening, some say mass hypnotism, among adolescent girls.

More than anyone else during the 1950s, Sinatra conceived the long-playing record as a vehicle of personal expression for a mature artist. His more than sixty movies yielded a multitude of Sinatras to contemplate: the joyous song-and-dance man of *Anchors Aweigh* (1945) and *On the Town* (1949); the brooding, doomed loner of *From Here to Eternity* (1953) and *The Manchurian Candidate* (1962); and the suave hipster of *Pal Joey* (1957) and *Ocean's 11* (1960). Sinatra's final project, *Duets*, produced by recording wizard Phil Ramone in the early 1990s, used digital fiber optics to create electronic pairings with a new generation of performers and resulted in one of his best-selling albums of all time.

EARLY CAREER

Sinatra's upbringing reflected the immigrant world of an urban United States. He was born in rough-and-tumble Hoboken, New Jersey, on December 12, 1915. The only child of a hard-working Sicilian household, Sinatra had big dreams to cross the Hudson River and discover his fortune in New York City. He dabbled in sportswriting and engineering before finding his calling at a Bing Crosby concert in the mid-1930s. Determined to become a singer, he polished his act at church suppers and firemen's socials. In September 1935 he and several local musicians made their radio debut as the Hoboken Four on *Major Bowes' Original Amateur Hour*. Host Edward Bowes took a liking to the boys, and they began to tour with one of his traveling companies. After immediate success proved elusive, Sinatra went solo.

Frank Sinatra, the Chairman of the Board. *Frank Sinatra performs in the late 1960s.* MARTIN MILLS/GETTY IMAGES.

The ambitious Sinatra did everything he could to nurture his talent. He appeared on local radio with little compensation to attract any type of attention. He undertook voice lessons, which he would continue throughout his career. And, most importantly, he sang publicly, notably at the Rustic Cabin, a small North Jersey roadhouse. His persistence achieved what every singer of his era desired—a featured vocalist spot in a big band. Harry James, a former trumpeter for Benny Goodman, heard Sinatra broadcast from the roadhouse and signed him to his first contract in June 1939. James's new orchestra spotlighted the confident Sinatra, especially on "All or Nothing at All," one of the first big band recordings to feature a vocalist from start to finish.

At the end of 1939 Sinatra was lured away by a more prominent bandleader, Tommy Dorsey. Inspired by Dorsey's trombone playing, Sinatra crafted a distinctive singing style, gliding from note to note without a semblance of breath. Sinatra's apprenticeship with the band lasted three years, and his recordings of "I'll Never Smile Again," "I'll Be Seeing You," and "This Love of Mine" established the boy vocalist as a star in his own right. Sinatra's ascent anticipated the dominance of the singer in postwar popular music.

TEENAGE FANS

Beginning in late 1942 Sinatra took control of his destiny, the first of many such moves throughout his mature years. After rancorous negotiations, he left Dorsey, leading the way for featured vocalists to make it as soloists. His debut performance at the Paramount Theatre on the last day of 1942 created a riotous sensation as thousands of teenage girls, known as the bobby-soxers, swooned (a publicist's description that caught on) at the skinny crooner in a bow tie. Amateur psychologists debated this ardent popularity: did he signify wartime degeneracy, or did he bring out the maternal instinct in adolescents? Whatever the reason, Sinatra became a regular on *Your Hit Parade*, network radio's most popular show on Saturday night.

Critics also analyzed the unique communication that Sinatra had with his audience. E. J. Kahn, in one of the first major articles on the Sinatra phenomenon, stated for the *New Yorker* that, while singing, Sinatra "stares with shattering intensity into the eyes of one trembling disciple after another." His intimacy with the microphone and personalization of the lyrics involved his listeners in a sexual experience. He learned how to transmit powerful emotions through his songs by studying the haunted textures of Billie Holiday. And, in the best jazz tradition, he also liked to come up with innovative ways to treat musical phrases.

Sinatra strove to completely identify with the music in the recording studio. He teamed up with Dorsey arranger Axel

Stordahl to produce introspective ballads for Columbia Records throughout the 1940s. Stordahl's lush strings complemented the soulful rapture of Sinatra's baritone. Between 1943 and 1946 he had seventeen top singles, including his first Columbia recording, the tender "Close to You," and the more upbeat "Saturday Night (Is the Loneliest Night in the Week)," which had special meaning for women whose lovers were away fighting in Europe.

BRANCHING OUT

Sinatra made his first movie appearances as a Dorsey vocalist in *Las Vegas Nights* (1941) and *Ships Ahoy* (1942). The hysteria surrounding his personal appearances in the early 1940s led to a contract with MGM (Metro-Goldwyn-Mayer) in 1944. Gene Kelly became his mentor and teacher, and he was groomed for energetic, splashy musicals. He starred as a nerdy, shy sailor in *Anchors Aweigh*; a show-business-crazed New Yorker in *It Happened in Brooklyn* (1947); and a baseball-playing, tap-dancing vaudevillian in *Take Me out to the Ball Game* (1949) with Kelly. But Sinatra quickly outgrew this manufactured image of cheerfulness and frivolity.

Since his boyhood, Sinatra was immersed in Democratic politics. His mother was a party ward organizer, and her only child became a crusader for racial tolerance. Sinatra and his Hoboken sweetheart, Nancy, whom he had married in 1939, named their son Franklin after President Franklin D. Roosevelt, for whom the singer had campaigned vigorously. In 1946 Sinatra had received a special Academy Award for the short *The House I Live In*, an outspoken attack on religious and ethnic bigotry. But in the late 1940s, when the political mood of a Cold War United States was shifting rightward, Sinatra was lambasted as a communist sympathizer and fellow traveler as well as criticized for his trip to Havana, Cuba, to meet syndicate boss Lucky Luciano. Questions about his connection to the underworld, especially as the quintessential nightclub and Las Vegas performer, bedeviled the Italian American entertainer the rest of his career, begetting a nasty feud with the press over personal privacy.

By 1950 Sinatra's public and personal worlds had collapsed. As the United States began celebrating economic prosperity and organizational conformity, Sinatra's record sales slumped, and MGM dropped him from their galaxy of stars. His private indiscretions had become fodder for the gossip columns, and the singer was crucified for a tumultuous affair with movie goddess Ava Gardner, which disintegrated his marriage. Sinatra also failed to conquer the new medium of the home—television, in the early 1950s—as his first series was widely assailed by the critics. The city girls, who had idolized the singer during the war years, were now busy raising families in the suburbs; Sinatra appeared to be a relic.

MAKING A COMEBACK

Sinatra's comeback, receiving a 1954 Oscar for his portrayal of the downtrodden Maggio in *From Here to Eternity*, has been the stuff of legend. What was more remarkable was the entire transformation of the Sinatra persona. No longer would he be the sensitive balladeer who spoke directly to a woman's heart. He became a man's man, the one who hoped for swinging times but was often left anguished at the bar alone. His image in the movies was toughened. He played a psychopathic presidential assassin in *Suddenly* (1954), an agonized heroin addict in *The Man with the Golden Arm* (1955), and a disillusioned writer in *Some Came Running* (1958). He also brought a maturity to his musical roles: as the cynical reporter in *High Society* (1956), where he performed a rousing "Well Did You Evah?" with his inspiration, Crosby, and as the ultimate heel in *Pal Joey* (1957), where he took delight in his crucial number, "The Lady Is a Tramp."

In 1953 Sinatra signed with Capitol Records and, collaborating with arranger/conductor Nelson Riddle, orchestrated an entirely new sound for his mature self. They pioneered the concept album, which in a suite of songs focused on one aspect of adult love. Riddle, a former trombonist, brought a pulsating rhythm to the records, helping to define Sinatra's new swinging style. Sinatra adapted a variety of roles to articulate a deeper understanding of romance: the bold sensualist in *Song for Swingin' Lovers* (1956); the tender, intimate companion of *Close to You* (1957); and the gloomy, introspective loner in *Only the Lonely* (1958). Sinatra also hooked up with arrangers Gordon Jenkins and Billy May to explore other masks: the intense and tortured romantic (Jenkins's *Where Are You?* [1957] and *No One Cares* [1959]) and the raucous swinger (May's *Come Fly Me* [1958] and *Come Dance with Me!* [1959]). In the studio Sinatra incarnated each role; he was the ultimate method singer.

From 1953 to 1962 Sinatra recorded seventeen albums for Capitol and exploited the dramatic possibilities of the long-playing 12-inch disc. He was at his most expressive as an interpretative artist, and these recordings constitute a treasury of U.S. popular song. Many songs were carefully selected from the golden age of the Broadway musical, and Sinatra's readings plumb the emotional depths of the lyrics. A majority of his meticulously rehearsed versions are considered definitive, including "I've Got a Crush on You" (George and Ira Gershwin); "I've Got You under My Skin" (Cole Porter); "One for My Baby" (Harold Arlen and Johnny Mercer); and "I Wish I Were in Love Again (Richard Rodgers and Lorenz Hart). Sinatra always paid tribute to the songwriting art by announcing in concert the name of the composer before each song. During the Capitol years he also returned to the charts with singles produced for quick recognition and consumption, most notably "Learnin' the Blues," "All the Way," and "Witchcraft." By the end of the 1950s Sinatra was again the most prominent performer in the United States.

THE RAT PACK

During the next decade Sinatra reconfigured his identity once again. He formed his own record company, Reprise, in 1960. (He sold the company to Warner Brothers in 1963, retaining a one-third interest.) He became the embodiment of a middle-aged swinging playboy with the release of *Ring-a-Ding Ding!* (1960) and *Swing along with Me* (1961). He surrounded himself with hard-drinking and high-living friends, called by the press the Rat Pack, whose members included Dean Martin, Sammy Davis Jr., Peter Lawford, and Joey Bishop. The Rats, nicknamed the Summit by the leader, were headquartered in Las Vegas, where Sinatra was established as the premier performer and an owner of the Sands Hotel. Reveling in tuxedos until daybreak, they were, and for some will always be, the epitome of cool.

Sinatra and his pals promulgated a hedonistic philosophy of swagger and style. An outgrowth of Humphrey Bogart's inner circle, they campaigned for the equally fun-loving John F. Kennedy in 1960, with Sinatra supervising the inaugural gala. The Rat Pack made lighthearted slapdash movies, including *Ocean's 11* (1960), *Sergeants 3* (1962), and *Robin and the 7*

Hoods (1964). With the assassination of Kennedy, who publicly snubbed Sinatra in 1962 because of his mob associations, and the popularity of the Beatles, the Rat Pack seemed tired and out of touch by the middle of the decade. And once again, Sinatra reinvented himself.

In 1965, when he was fifty years old, he contemplated his life and profession. He released *September of My Years*, one of his most personal works, a touching musical reflection on the joys and anguishes of his younger years. Later that year he also compiled and narrated a retrospective album, *A Man and His Music*, which surveyed his career in thirty-two songs. Both projects received the Grammy Award for Album of the Year in successive years, anointing Sinatra as elder statesman of the industry. Personally, Sinatra was still a playboy, marrying actress Mia Farrow, almost thirty years his junior.

A Man and His Music also inspired a television special, which marked Sinatra's triumphant return to the medium. His two previous weekly series had fizzled, both perhaps succumbing to Sinatra's unwillingness to rehearse outside the recording studio. His most noteworthy performances had been one-time-only engagements: as the stage manager in a musical adaptation of *Our Town* (which yielded the hit single "Love and Marriage") and as host of a "Welcome Home, Elvis" extravaganza, in which the two former teen idols joined for an incomparable duet. The 1965 special was acclaimed "the television musical of the season," receiving an Emmy Award for Outstanding Program. Sinatra continued to produce and star in television specials, almost on an annual basis, making sure he remained a force in contemporary music.

During the 1950s Sinatra dismissed rock and roll as music "sung, played, and written for the most part by cretinous goons." By the late 1960s he had accommodated many diverse sounds in his repertoire. Adapting to changing fashions, he recorded songs composed by Jimmy Webb, Stevie Wonder, Paul Simon, and George Harrison. One of his most advantageous collaborations was with the Brazilian samba stylist Antonio Carlos Jobim. Sinatra discovered unexpected pleasures in the soft and delicate rhythms of the bossa nova. This embrace of a new beat also provided several popular hits, including "Strangers in the Night," winner of the Grammy Award for Record of the Year; "That's Life," Sinatra at his bluesiest; and "Something Stupid," a duet with his eldest daughter, Nancy. In 1969 he adapted a French ballad, "Mon Habitude," with English lyrics by Paul Anka, and crafted one of his signature songs, "My Way."

RETURN AFTER RETIREMENT

Tired of the investigations into his private life, Sinatra announced his retirement from show business in June 1971. He made yet another comeback two years later with the album and TV special, *Ol' Blue Eyes Is Back* (1973), engendering another show business moniker. He was most frequently nicknamed the Chairman of the Board, referring to his pervasive presence in all aspects of the entertainment industry. Although his professional life slowed down, especially after his marriage to Barbara Marx in 1976, Sinatra still made artistic waves. He delivered a classic reading of Stephen Sondheim's innovative "Send in the Clowns," a staple of his concerts during the 1970s. In 1980 he released his most ambitious undertaking, *Trilogy: Past, Present & Future*, three discs that showed off both the swinging and serious facets of his artistry. Sinatra recorded for *Trilogy* yet another defining song, "Theme from New York, New York," which became a showstopper in performance.

In movies Sinatra was most comfortable as a hard-boiled, aging sleuth, a role he began in *The Detective* (1968) and further explored in the television movie *Contract on Cherry Street* (1977) and his final starring theatrical role in *The First Deadly Sin* (1980). In 1987 *The Manchurian Candidate*, featuring Sinatra's most complex role as a brainwashed soldier, was rereleased, twenty-five years after its premiere. There was a renewed appreciation for Sinatra's acting skills, especially in challenging material.

Like many in his generation, Sinatra's politics drifted toward the Right as he got older. Becoming an ardent Republican during the Vietnam era (though still a registered Democrat), he campaigned aggressively for Ronald Reagan in 1980. Victorious again, as twenty years before, he produced the presidential inaugural gala. He was appointed to the President's Committee on the Arts and the Humanities and was awarded the Kennedy Center Honor for Lifetime Achievement (1983) and the Presidential Medal of Freedom (1985), the highest civilian recognition in the United States. He still received millions of dollars for concert performances around the world, including a controversial appearance in Sun City, South Africa.

Sinatra's personal life was always riddled with contradictions. His generosity to friends was legendary, as was his vicious feuds with targeted members of the press. Back in 1947 he publicly attacked one of his critics, Lee Mortimer, and was ordered to pay a substantial fine. Although his friendship with Chicago mobster Sam Giancana cost him a gambling license in the 1960s, he still associated with the underworld throughout his career, including a 1976 infamous photograph backstage at the Westchester Premier Theater with Mafia boss Carlo Gambino and Jimmy (the Weasel) Fratianno. Many unauthorized biographies focused on these unsavory aspects of Sinatra's volatile temperament, most significantly the best-selling *His Way* (1986), by Kitty Kelley. Even the 1992 authorized miniseries *Sinatra*, produced by youngest daughter Tina, did not shy away from controversies, portraying Sinatra's relationship with Giancana (played by Rod Steiger).

FINAL YEARS

Sinatra remained a permanent fixture and influence on the U.S. popular culture landscape even in his twilight years. Although his 1988 reunion tour with Davis and Martin dissipated when the latter lost interest, the Rat Pack were embraced as the arbiters of hip by the twenty-something generation in the 1990s. At the age of seventy-seven Sinatra made another recording comeback as his *Duets* album unexpectedly sold several million copies. Although his partners were not in the same studio and were electronically overdubbed, Sinatra was heard singing with stars from other musical fields, including international personalities Julio Iglesias and Charles Aznavour; from the jazz and soul front, Aretha Franklin, Luther Vandross, and Anita Baker; and from his own genre, Barbra Streisand and Tony Bennett. Rocker Bono of U2, another duettist, grandiloquently presented Sinatra with the 1994 Grammy Legend Award, enshrining him as the Big Bang of Pop. Sinatra's eightieth-birthday special also featured a wide array of celebrants, including rappers Salt-n-Pepa and rock superstars Bruce Springsteen and Bob Dylan. Sinatra himself toured rigorously well into his seventies, before giving his last concert in February 1995.

Sinatra's death on May 14, 1998, eclipsed one of television's most heavily promoted events, the final episode of *Seinfeld*. Every corner of news, from print to cyberspace, was awash in memorial tributes. As David Hadju of *Entertainment Weekly* pointed out, "No American since JFK (the Sinatra of Presidents) seemed to have received such a grand media memorial, effusive in its praise of his talent and celebratory in its recollection of his life."

Sinatra was selected as one of *Time* magazine's 100 Most Influential People of the 20th Century. His influence continued into the succeeding century as musical entertainers such as Harry Connick Jr. and Michael Bublé kept his spirit alive. In 2009 choreographer Twyla Tharp assembled his songs into a dance performance, which played in numerous cities. The next year the reality television series *American Idol* presented a special evening devoted to Sinatra, in which all the contestants were required to sing his songs. Sales of Sinatra's recordings continued to do well into the digital era, with much archival material being released for the first time.

The one quality that Sinatra strove for in his nearly 1,300 commercially available recordings and his many different incarnations was honesty. Each song was the personal expression of a deeply felt moment. There was no separating the incomparable singer from the intimate experience of the lyric. Like many other supremely gifted artists, his life did not always live up to the ideals of his art. But, as *New York Times* critic John Rockwell noted, "no singer of our time has better invested the widest range of emotion in his music than Frank Sinatra."

Ron Simon

SEE ALSO: *Academy Awards; Anka, Paul; The Beatles; Bennett, Tony; Big Bands; Blues; Bogart, Humphrey; Broadway; Crosby, Bing; Dorsey, Tommy; Dylan, Bob; Franklin, Aretha;* From Here to Eternity*; Gardner, Ava; Goodman, Benny; Grammy Awards; Holiday, Billie; Hollywood; Jazz; Kelly, Gene; Kennedy Assassination; Las Vegas; Luciano, Lucky; Mafia/Organized Crime;* The Manchurian Candidate*; Martin, Dean; MGM (Metro-Goldwyn-Mayer); The Musical; The* New Yorker*; Pop Music; Porter, Cole; Presley, Elvis; Radio; Reagan, Ronald; Rock and Roll; Rodgers and Hart; Salt-n-Pepa;* Seinfeld*; Simon, Paul; Sondheim, Stephen; Soul Music; Springsteen, Bruce; Streisand, Barbra; Television; Tharp, Twyla;* Time*; U2; Vietnam; Wonder, Stevie;* Your Hit Parade.

BIBLIOGRAPHY

Douglas-Home, Robin. *Sinatra*. New York: Grosset & Dunlap, 1962.

Friedwald, Will. *Sinatra! The Song Is You*. New York: Da Capo Press, 1997.

Granata, Charles. *Sessions with Sinatra: Frank Sinatra and the Art of Recording*. Chicago: Chicago Review Press, 2003.

Hamill, Pete. *Why Sinatra Matters*. Boston: Little, Brown, 1998.

Kahn, E. J. *The Voice: The Story of an American Phenomenon*. New York: Harper & Brothers, 1947.

Kaplan, James. *Frank: The Voice*. New York: Doubleday Books, 2010.

Kelley, Kitty. *His Way*. New York: Bantam, 1986.

Lahr, John. *Sinatra: The Artist and the Man*. New York: Random House, 1997.

Levy, Shawn. *Rat Pack Confidential*. New York: Doubleday, 1998.

O'Brien, Ed, and Scott Sayers. *Sinatra: The Man and His Music*. Austin, TX: TSD Press, 1992.

Petkov, Steven, and Leonard Mustazza, eds. *The Frank Sinatra Reader*. New York: Oxford University Press, 1995.

Pignone, Charles. *The Sinatra Treasures: Intimate Photos, Mementos, and Music from the Sinatra Family Collection*. New York: Bulfinch, 2004.

Rockwell, John. *Sinatra: An American Classic*. New York: Rolling Stone Press, 1984.

Shaw, Arnold. *Sinatra: Twentieth-Century Romantic*. New York: Holt, Rinehart and Winston, 1968.

Sinatra, Nancy. *Frank Sinatra, My Father*. New York: Pocket Books, 1985.

Sinatra, Nancy. *Frank Sinatra: An American Legend*. Santa Monica, CA: General Publishing Group, 1995.

Taraborrelli, J. Randy. *Sinatra: Behind the Legend*. Secaucus, NJ: Carol Publishing, 1997.

Vare, Ethlie Ann, ed. *Legend: Frank Sinatra and the American Dream*. New York: Boulevard Books, 1995.

Wilson, Earl. *Sinatra: An Unauthorized Biography*. New York: Macmillan, 1976.

Zehme, Bill. *The Way You Wear Your Hat*. New York: HarperCollins, 1997.

Sinbad *(1956–)*

A popular African American television comic actor of the 1980s and 1990s, Sinbad, whose real name was David Adkins, offered wholesome, family-oriented entertainment for children and adults alike. The legitimate heir to Bill Cosby's clean-cut comic style, he broke barriers at mainstream studios such as Disney by starring in youth-oriented feature films with predominately white casts, including *Houseguest* (1995) and *First Kid* (1996).

Sinbad first entered mainstream culture as a dorm director, Walter Oakes, on the Cosby-produced NBC sitcom *A Different World* (1987–1993). It was this role that catapulted him into living rooms across the nation. Following the show's run, he gained further notoriety as host of *It's Showtime at the Apollo*, where his improvisational storytelling on topics such as hair weaves, parenting, and divorce helped to make him one of the most widely recognized comedians in the United States.

Born in Benton Harbor, Michigan, on November 10, 1956, he was the son of Baptist minister Reverend Donald Adkins and his wife, Louise. The future funnyman was raised in a household in which a high value was placed on morals, personal responsibility, and God. Rejecting both alcohol and drugs throughout his life, Sinbad took seriously his job as a role model—challenging the need for vulgar language in his performances with the oft-quoted maxim: "If my kids can't watch it, I can't do it."

Tall in stature—he reached 6 foot, 5 inches in adulthood—the comedian grew up feeling "big and goofy" and saw himself as something of an outsider. Luckily, his size was of use in pursuing his first love: basketball. He won an athletic scholarship to the University of Denver but found himself particularly isolated on the largely white campus, where he became increasingly militant during the Black Power era of the 1970s. Never one to play by the rules, he surprised his peers by quitting college just short of a diploma. After dropping out he signed up with the U.S. Air Force, where he soon discovered his true calling during a talent contest. Arriving at a steadfast decision to pursue comedy, he got himself discharged from the service—as legend has it—by walking off duty in his underwear.

CAREER HIGHLIGHTS

In 1983, embarking on what he called his Poverty Tour, the future Sinbad crossed the country by Greyhound bus, performing stand-up routines in small-town clubs and hitching rides with members of his audience. The grueling schedule paid off. By the mid-1980s the comedian's first big break came through repeated appearances on *Star Search*. With his brightly colored hair (dyed every shade from gold to red to platinum blond) and feather earrings in both ears, the budding talent had made an impression. This look would later be replaced by a more straitlaced image with a shaved head, but the original look certainly got him noticed in showbiz. He relocated to Los Angeles and was cast as Redd Foxx's foster son on ABC television's *The Redd Foxx Show* (1986).

Like his mentor, Cosby, Sinbad consistently challenged stereotypical images in Hollywood film and television productions. On *Houseguest*, for example, he refused to do humor that he termed "very broad and anatomical." During production on his short-lived sitcom, *The Sinbad Show* (1993), which aired on the Fox network, the star's arguments with producers and executives were legendary, as he struggled to represent his character, a black single father, in a positive light. His vehemence was possibly due in part to his own recent divorce and new life as a single parent. His efforts to portray contemporary African Americans positively, however, garnered him several NAACP Image Awards.

In 1990 Sinbad hosted his own HBO comedy special, *Sinbad: Brain Damaged*. The show was so successful that three more followed. In 1997 he joined the flurry of black-oriented, late-night talk shows when he was asked to take over hosting duties on *Vibe* (1997–1998). It was a time when competition was stiff for the genre: *The Keenen Ivory Wayans Show* (1997–1998) ran neck-and-neck with *Vibe* before being replaced by Magic Johnson's *The Magic Hour* (1998). But Sinbad had also cohosted, with singer Stephen Bishop, another late-night variety show ten years earlier called *Keep on Cruisin'* (1987).

EXPANDING INFLUENCE

At the close of the 1990s, Sinbad expanded his influence beyond the world of entertainment and became a pioneer advocate for technology, particularly among inner-city youth. A computer buff who was known to chat online for hours, he served on an advisory council at Howard University and as a spokesperson for the National Action Council for Minorities in Engineering. In the latter capacity he lectured to millions of kids about the importance of math and science in a technologically advanced world. Sinbad also participated in the first annual ThinkQuest Internet competition—along with actor and director Ron Howard; Nobel-laureate physicist Kenneth Wilson; and Gene Sperling, adviser to President Bill Clinton—in which more than $1 million in scholarships and cash prizes were awarded to students, teachers, and schools across the country. In 1996 Sinbad accompanied First Lady Hillary Rodham Clinton to Bosnia to provide comic relief for U.S. peacekeeping forces stationed there and throughout Europe.

Although Sinbad was no longer a household name in the 2010s, the comedian remained active professionally. Comedy DVDs, cameo appearances on popular television shows, emcee responsibilities, and reality TV competitions kept him busy. Despite filing for Chapter 7 bankruptcy in 2009, he maintained a positive and proactive attitude; a 2011 reality television show, *Sinbad: It's Just Family*, endeavored to document the Adkins family life and Sinbad's attempts to make it back on top. Love him or hate him, Sinbad has left a lasting mark on African American comedians through his family-friendly and always affirmative humor.

Kristal Brent Zook

SEE ALSO: *Cosby, Bill; Disney (Walt Disney Company); Foxx, Redd; Greyhound Buses; Hairstyles; Hollywood; Howard, Ron; Johnson, Earvin "Magic"; Reality Television; Sitcom; Stand-Up Comedy; Television; The Wayans Family.*

BIBLIOGRAPHY

Littleton, Darryl. *Black Comedians on Black Comedy: How African-Americans Taught Us to Laugh*. New York: Applause Books, 2006.

Lovece, Frank. "When Sinbad Says No Offense, He Means It." *Newsday*, January 10, 1995, B3.

Sinbad, and David Ritz. *Sinbad's Guide to Life (Because I Know Everything)*. New York: Bantam Books, 1997.

Watkins, Mel. *On the Real Side: Laughing, Lying, and Signifying*. New York: Touchstone, 1994.

Sinclair, Upton *(1878–1968)*

American novelist Upton Sinclair is most famous for his 1906 novel *The Jungle* and the reforms to which it gave rise. Sinclair was a muckraker—so dubbed by President Theodore Roosevelt, who regarded them as a nuisance—one of a group of journalists who were relentless in their exposure of corruption in American business and government.

Sinclair intended his book, set in the Chicago meat-packing industry, to arouse support for the plight of immigrant laborers. In it, he exposed the political machinations of the Democratic and Republican parties and put forward the Socialist Party as the only trustworthy organization. Instead, however, *The Jungle* triggered public outrage at the malfeasance of the meat packers, who did not care that much of their processed meat was adulterated with dirt, dung, poisoned rats, and the odd human body part.

Roosevelt apparently read Sinclair's book and dispatched officials to investigate the industry; they confirmed the veracity of the novel's account. The president, after threatening to release the report, was able to force through the 1906 Meat Inspection Act in order to regulate the industry. The act brought the meat packers under the regulatory arm of the government; however, the government was unable to adequately enforce the rules. Moreover, bigger firms were able to meet the government's requirements, whereas many smaller firms could not, so the act effectively increased the strength of big business—certainly not Sinclair's intended outcome. At the time, Sinclair joked, "I aimed at the public's heart and by accident I hit it in the stomach."

The Jungle was Sinclair's sole best seller, but he went on to publish a series of similarly themed novels, including *Oil!* (1927), about the Teapot Dome scandal of President Warren Harding's administration. He also wrote *Boston* (1928), which details the trial and execution of Nicola Sacco and Bartolomeo Vanzetti, two Italian American radicals convicted and executed for robbery and murder, a cause célèbre of 1927. In 1940 Sinclair began a series of eleven novels with a contemporary setting featuring an antifascist hero, Lanny Budd. He placed Budd in the action of all major events of his time.

In 1933 Sinclair established and led the End Poverty in California (EPIC) campaign. His solution to Depression-era unemployment was for the state to rent unused land and factories so the unemployed could grow their own food and produce clothing and furniture. In August 1934 he easily won the Democratic primary race for governor. Conservative Democrats then aligned with the anti–New Deal Republican Governor Frank Merriman to defeat Sinclair in the November election. The campaign was marked by an excessive amount of anti-Sinclair material, which included fake newsreels showing hoboes descending on California and accusations of communism.

By the end of the twentieth century, *The Jungle* was still in print but not included in college anthologies of American literature. EPIC generally has been treated either as a political anomaly produced by the Depression or as an aside to Franklin D. Roosevelt's New Deal.

Ian Gordon

SEE ALSO: *The Great Depression; Muckraking.*

BIBLIOGRAPHY

Mitchell, Greg. *The Campaign of the Century: Upton Sinclair's Race for Governor of California and the Birth of Media Politics*. New York: Random House, 1992.

Scott, Ivan. *Upton Sinclair, the Forgotten Socialist*. Lewiston, NY: Mellen Press, 1997.

Sinclair, Upton. *I, Candidate for Governor: And How I Got Licked*. New York: Farrar & Rinehart, 1935.

Sinclair, Upton. *The Jungle: The Uncensored Original Edition*. Tucson, AZ: See Sharp Press, 2003.

Singer, Isaac Bashevis *(1904–1991)*

Isaac Bashevis Singer is considered by many to be the greatest post–World War II author of Yiddish literature. Born on July 21, 1904, in Leoncin, Poland, to a Hasidic rabbi and a pious mother, Singer began his writing career with *Globus*, a literary magazine in Warsaw, which serialized his first novel, *Satan in Goray* (1932) in 1934. The next year Singer moved to the United States, where he began writing for the Yiddish-language newspaper the *Jewish Daily Forward*, which also serialized his fiction. He became a naturalized citizen in 1943.

In 1966 he published *Zlateh the Goat*, the first of several well-received children's books, and in 1978 he received the Nobel Prize in Literature. Several of his novels were made into movies, including *The Magician of Lublin* (1960) and *Enemies: A Love Story* (1972). His short story "Yentl, the Yeshiva Boy" is the basis of the movie musical *Yentl* (1983), starring Barbra Streisand. Singer died on July 24, 1991, after a series of strokes.

Bennett Lovett-Graff

SEE ALSO: *Streisand, Barbra; World War II.*

BIBLIOGRAPHY

Farrell, Grace, ed. *Isaac Bashevis Singer: Conversations*. Jackson: University Press of Mississippi, 1992.

Farrell, Grace. *Critical Essays on Isaac Bashevis Singer*. New York: Hall, 1996.

Hadda, Janet. *Isaac Bashevis Singer: A Life*. New York: Oxford University Press, 1997.

Lee, Grace Farrell. *From Exile to Redemption: The Fiction of Isaac Bashevis Singer*. Carbondale: Southern Illinois University Press, 1987.

Miller, David Neal. *Fear of Fiction: Narrative Strategies in the Works of Isaac Bashevis Singer*. Albany: State University of New York Press, 1985.

Singin' in the Rain

Codirected by dancer Gene Kelly and Stanley Donen, *Singin' in the Rain* epitomizes how the musical works as Hollywood genre, studio (MGM) product, and instrument of American popular culture. Produced in 1952, the movie's narrative, scripted by Broadway writers Betty Comden and Adolph Green, is set in the 1920s, when viable sound synchronization spawned the "talkie," forcing universal adoption of sound and the invention of the musical. *Singin' in the Rain* is a parody of the backstage musical and the biopic; it playfully mocks the trials of the early studio system and the egos of its silent film stars being tutored to speak and perform in sound pictures.

The movie pays homage to the musical's classical form, tracing its roots from vaudeville to its influence on film. Kelly plays Don Lockwood, who rises from variety shows to the silver screen with dance partner Cosmo Brown (Donald O'Connor). Within the musical's formula of narrative-inspired production numbers and romance, Don guides the object of his desire, Kathy Selden (Debbie Reynolds), into the emotional effects of song and dance.

It is the Hollywood kiss, that staple of romantic resolution, which seals the attraction between Don and Kathy, then prompts Don to begin "singin' in the rain." Critic Jane Feuer, in *Film Genre Reader II*, dubs this outburst into song and dance "the myth of spontaneity" common to the musical genre. Kelly's athletic free spirit in the "Singin' in the Rain" number celebrates the individual male at play within the American neighborhood. In this liberating, public site, Don moves his feet skillfully through rain with umbrella as ballast, gets soaked and loves it, and is chided by a local cop and shrugs it off. His "gotta dance" compulsion not only drives *Rain*'s theme-song number as if coming from the streets as well as his heart, but it also inspires Don to move instinctively into the full-blown artistry and seduction of Cyd Charisse's enigmatic dance/love object in the "Broadway Melody Ballet" fantasy.

In *The American Film Musical*, critic Rick Altman calls this device of courtship through dance the male's "loving lesson." In the film's major dance suite, the "Broadway Melody Ballet," the sexual connotations of Don's earlier loving lesson with the neophyte Kathy are projected as a fantasy danced with an "other" woman (Charisse). In the course of the suite, Charisse's vamp transforms into bride, then ethereal "angel," then back to

Singin' in the Rain. *Gene Kelly dances in the iconic scene featuring the title song in* Singin' in the Rain. MGM/THE KOBAL COLLECTION/HUBBELL, EDDIE.

vamp willingly controlled by gangster "hoods." Only dance itself safely permits this eruption of coded sex and this evocation of American culture's darker forces.

These forces, inflected in *Rain* as fantasy, are made central in Charles Vidor's *Love Me or Leave Me* (1955). A biopic of another order, the film is based on singer Ruth Etting's successful career and dark personal life in the 1920s and her marriage to a petty gangster whose possessiveness turns into rape on their wedding night. Domestic melodrama delineates the couple's fraught relationship, with musical numbers playing out of, and off, the drama. In *Rain*, Don's loving protection of the amber-voiced Kathy from the wily, tin-eared silent star Lina Lamont (Jean Hagen) is without social threat, whereas *Love Me or Leave Me*'s foregrounding of obsessive male control is made tough by its basis in melodrama. In Stanley Kubrick's *A Clockwork Orange* (1971), the darkly parodic "Singin' in the Rain" song and dance by Alex (Malcolm McDowell) in the act of torturing a woman makes a cold ritual of violence, a major ideological reach from the original source, *Rain*, but closer to *Love Me or Leave Me*.

In his television special, *You Must Remember This* (1994), Canadian figure skater Kurt Browning's skilled athletic homage restores to family entertainment *Rain*'s 1950s classicism and the nostalgia of Kelly's muscular dancer's persona. Browning's faithful re-creation of Kelly's "Singin' in the Rain" number—complete with rain-covered ice surface, lookalike set, and original soundtrack of Kelly's singing and tapping—circulates a memory of the film, specifically a myth of wholesomeness for popular culture of the 1990s. Figure skating's popularity has grown as its imitative performers, tour shows, and television specials have adopted elements of the production number established and conventionalized by the Hollywood musical, including costuming, lighting, familiar theme songs, dance-step choreography, tributes to screen and pop music stars, and the loving lesson evident in pairs and dance skating.

The impulse to act out in song-and-dance form reveals the gears of social engineering adapted by the Hollywood musical to produce and to promote show-musical culture as a vital ingredient of American popular culture. *Singin' in the Rain* reveals the seams of this process, much as it enfolds audiences into its veiled pleasures.

Joan Nicks

SEE ALSO: *Broadway;* A Clockwork Orange*; Hollywood; Kelly, Gene; MGM (Metro-Goldwyn-Mayer); Movie Stars; The Musical; Pop Music; Silent Movies; Skating; Vaudeville.*

BIBLIOGRAPHY

Altman, Rick. *The American Film Musical.* Bloomington: Indiana University Press, 1987.

Croce, Arlene. "Dance in Film." In *Cinema: A Critical Dictionary: The Major Film-makers*, ed. Richard Roud. New York: Viking Press, 1980.

Feuer, Jane. "The Self-Reflexive Musical and the Myth of Entertainment." In *Film Genre Reader II*, ed. Barry Keith Grant. Austin: University of Texas Press, 1995.

Hess, Earl J., and Pratibha A. Dabholkar. Singin' in the Rain: *The Making of an American Masterpiece.* Lawrence: University Press of Kansas, 2009.

Maltby, Richard. *Hollywood Cinema: An Introduction.* Cambridge, MA: Blackwell Publishers, 1995.

Singles Bars

Singles bars flourished in the 1970s, reflecting the sweeping changes that followed the Sexual Revolution and the attempted passage of the Equal Rights Movement. Commonly referred to as "meat markets," singles bars acted as an open setting in which men and women felt free to engage one another. Statistics cited by sociologist Nancy Netting revealed that by 1980 the rate of premarital sexual intercourse for American college-age women equaled the rate for college-age men. This was a significant change, as studies showed that the rate for women having premarital intercourse between 1930 and 1965 was 30 percent lower than that of men. One change that resulted from all of these factors was that bar patrons were no longer exclusively male.

THE SINGLES SCENE

Singles bars have a popular image as hotbeds of frenzied, sexual activity, but there is some evidence to suggest that this presumption may be somewhat exaggerated. Despite the promiscuous conduct that many assume occurs, the singles scene operates upon some rather traditional gender roles: men initiate contact, and women flirt as passive objects of desire. By pursuing a female in this environment, the male places his self-assessment at risk, since "rejection may signify that he has miscalculated and is less desirable than he had assumed," concluded a 1991 ethnographic study of singles bars. Another study, published by two psychologists in 1978, found that men avoid the most attractive women because they fear rejection. The study also found that attractive women responded just as positively to researchers as unattractive women. In this respect, the study concluded, "men's anxieties about attractive women may be unfounded."

If a conversation is struck, the talk is likely to be about generalities, wrote Jamie James in *Rolling Stone* in 1979:

> They talk about the weather, football (year-round), the latest big murder trial ("Do you think he's guilty?" "Of course he's guilty. But he'll get off"). They talk about everything but what's on their minds. The clincher comes in its own good time: "This place is so noisy I can hardly hear you. Listen, my place is just a few blocks away."

The 1991 study showed that the micro-order of the singles bar is a fragile one and can fracture when the male "presses forward, failing to accept (the female's) rejection and the chance to save face." The female's rejection can take the form of a polite refusal; a rejection not final ("maybe some other time"); or an excuse, such as "I'm married," "I have a boyfriend," or "I can't dance in these shoes." Fracturing occurs when the male insults the female to "even the score" or by ignoring her suggestion and continuing his pursuit. When this occurs, the ethnologists noted changes in the female's demeanor through a stiff posture or sharper tone: "concern with softening the blow is jettisoned for the overriding concern of extricating oneself from the situation."

Faced with excusing oneself, what could possibly serve as refuge in a noisy singles bar? The study noted:

> The most common refuge for escape from unsolicited encounters appeared to be the women's restroom. One of the authors tested this observation by remarking to a queue of women in a restroom that she

> guessed she wasn't the only one avoiding a man. She was answered by an affirmative nod by a number of women. . . . Women can plan future strategies to avoid male approaches or escape from the necessity of performing these strategies through retreat into an all-female world.

The need to parry male advances is one explanation for findings that show that most women are usually accompanied by at least one other woman at the bars. An element of danger exists in encountering people who are strangers. This risk was portrayed in the sensational 1975 novel *Looking for Mr. Goodbar*, in which a single woman picks up a stranger in a bar, only to be murdered in her own apartment. "Everybody who hangs out in these places is acutely aware of the intrinsic creepiness of the (singles) scene," explained a woman to James. "It's sort of demeaning, but there has to be some way for us to meet, you know." The one commonly acknowledged taboo among singles is "never go to bed with a stranger."

ALTERNATIVES

Although singles bars remained one way for singles to meet, other alternatives appeared in the 1980s. Those who desired more control used the screening process of a matchmaking service or did their own screening through newspaper personal ads. More adventurous singles opted for singles cruises, a marketing device that successfully contributed to the boom in cruise-ship trips during the 1990s. After AIDS became a serious concern during the 1980s, screening and refraining from risky sexual activity became important for health reasons. In a survey conducted at a college in British Columbia, Canada, the number of students who reported having one-night stands decreased by more than 50 percent between 1980 and 1990.

Concern for personal safety was one reason for the rapid increase in popularity that online dating sites gained during the first decade of the 2000s. Most such sites offer matching services and ways to screen one's contacts. Through e-mail or other forms of online communications, singles can get to know one another gradually before meeting face to face—perhaps even in a bar. By 2010 surveys were reporting that some 30 percent of Americans met their new romantic partners online. For some groups—such as singles who were middle-aged or older—the percentage of couples meeting online was even higher. For people in college or in their twenties, the bar scene remained popular, but most other Americans had moved on to other ways of finding a soul mate.

Daryl Umberger

SEE ALSO: *AIDS; Equal Rights Amendment; The Internet; Online Dating; Safe Sex; Sexual Revolution.*

BIBLIOGRAPHY

Cory, Christopher T. "The Seven-Second Singles Scene." *Psychology Today*, December 1978, 32.

James, Jamie. "Houston after Dark." *Rolling Stone*, May 31, 1979, 35–40.

Netting, Nancy S. "Sexuality in Youth Culture: Identity and Change." *Adolescence*, Winter 1992, 961–976.

Page, Susan. *If I'm So Wonderful, Why Am I Still Single?: Ten Strategies That Will Change Your Love Life Forever*, rev. ed. New York: Three Rivers Press, 2002

Rossner, Judith. *Looking for Mr. Goodbar*. New York: Simon & Schuster, 1975.

Snow, David A.; Cherylon Robinson; and Patricia L. McCall. "'Cooling Out' Men in Singles Bars and Nightclubs: Observations on the Interpersonal Survival Strategies of Women in Public Places." *Journal of Contemporary Ethnography*, January 1991, 423–449.

Spradley, J. P., and J. Mann. *The Cocktail Waitress: Woman's Work in a Man's World*. New York: Wiley, 1975.

Wuethrich, B. "Evolutionists Pick Up on One-Night Stands." *Science News*, July 3, 1993, 6.

Sirk, Douglas *(1900–1987)*

Born Claus Detlef Sierk in Germany to Danish parents, filmmaker Douglas Sirk fled Nazi Germany for the United States, where he later directed some of the largest-grossing melodramas of the 1950s, such as *All I Desire* (1953), *Magnificent Obsession* (1954), *All That Heaven Allows* (1955), *There's Always Tomorrow* (1955), *Written on the Wind* (1956), and *Imitation of Life* (1959). These movies were clearly marketed as "adult films" whose social concerns such as class and race relations justified the graphic, voyeuristic displays of upper-class lifestyle, psychological malaise, sex (Rock Hudson starred in eight of Sirk's movies as the quintessential American heterosexual male), and murder. Considered by critics in turn as subversive critiques of family values and of 1950s sexual repression or as products celebrating the consumerist ideologies of the decade, by the late twentieth century Sirk's melodramas had come to be regarded, in Barbara Klinger's words, "as 'camp,' as outdated forms that exuded artifice in everything from narrative structure to depiction of romance."

Luca Prono

SEE ALSO: *Camp; Hudson, Rock.*

BIBLIOGRAPHY

Byars, Jackie. *All That Heaven Allows: Re-reading Gender in 1950s Melodrama*. Chapel Hill: University of North Carolina Press, 1991.

Harvey, James. *Movie Love in the Fifties*. New York: Knopf, 2001.

Klinger, Barbara. *Melodrama and Meaning: History, Culture, and the Films of Douglas Sirk*. Bloomington: Indiana University Press, 1994.

Mulvey, Laura. *Visual and Other Pleasures*. Bloomington: Indiana University Press, 1989.

Sirk, Douglas, and Jon Halliday. *Sirk on Sirk: Interviews with Jon Halliday*. New York: Viking Press, 1972.

Siskel and Ebert

In the late twentieth century, Gene Siskel (1946–1999) and Roger Ebert (1942–) were to film criticism what Steve Jobs and Bill Gates were to personal computers. Although often disagreeing with each other, they popularized a formerly stuffy discipline

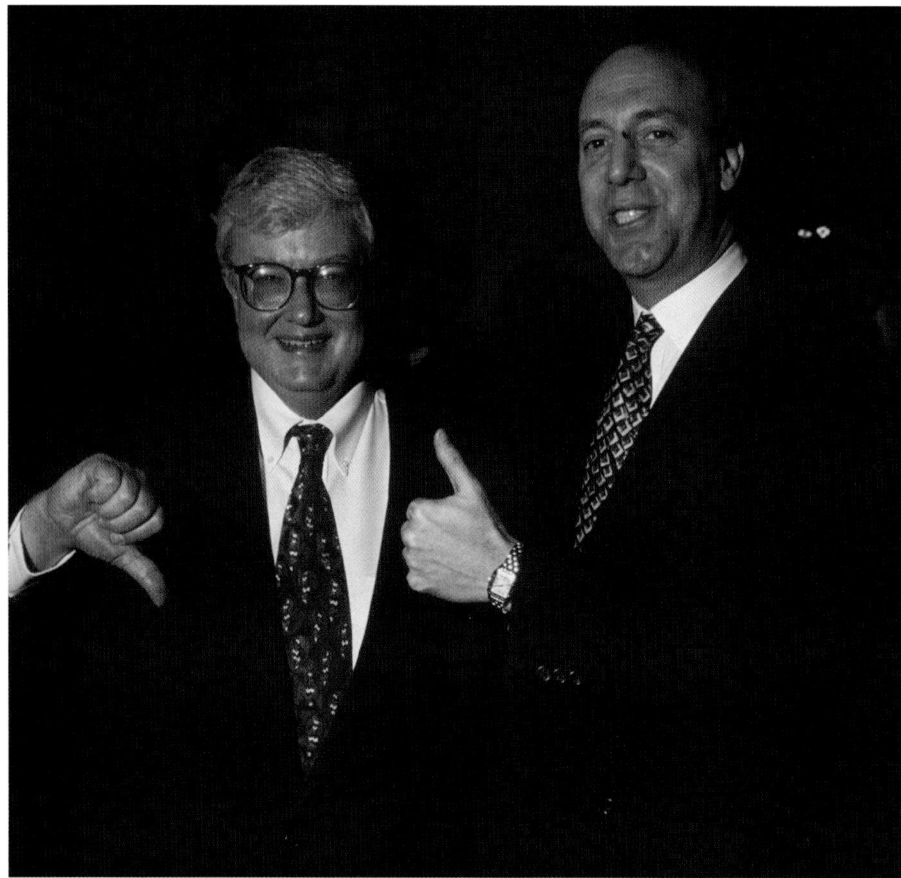

Siskel and Ebert. *Roger Ebert, left, and Gene Siskel demonstrate their trademark thumbs down/thumbs up rating system, which made movie criticism accessible to mainstream audiences.* RON GALELLA, LTD./CONTRIBUTOR/GETTY IMAGES.

and made it accessible to the masses. Long after Bosley Crowther, Pauline Kael, and other highbrow critics made reviewing movies an art form, Siskel and Ebert's nationally syndicated television program turned it into a spectator sport.

Siskel and Ebert established their critical credentials writing for rival Chicago newspapers, the *Chicago Tribune* and *Chicago Sun-Times*, respectively. They began their strange odyssey together in 1975, when producers at the Chicago-based PBS station WTTW invited them to cohost a weekly film review program. Though initially reluctant, the two men were persuaded that their mutual hostility might make for good television. The series began its run under the name *Opening Soon at a Theater near You* and was wisely retitled *Sneak Previews*.

The show's low budget allowed the hosts to do little more than air a succession of clips and bicker about the latest theatrical releases, which they then rated with a "thumbs up" or "thumbs down" in the old gladiatorial tradition. To everyone's surprise, *Sneak Previews* became a huge local hit and was broadcast nationally beginning in 1978. It quickly became the highest-rated series in PBS history.

On the surface, the show's appeal lay in the bar-stool simplicity of its premise: two guys sitting around arguing about the merits of the latest crop of movies. However, the clash of personalities allowed viewers to feel as if they were eavesdropping on a private argument. Siskel was arguably the more intellectual of the two. Lean and birdlike, he combed the few thin wisps of hair he had left over the bare crown of his head. Ebert was the people's favorite, a beefy failed screenwriter who amazingly chose not to expunge his name from the credits of the soft-core porn turkey *Beyond the Valley of the Dolls* (1970). Together they were like oil and water, soon referred to nationwide as "the bald one" and "the fat one."

In 1982 Siskel and Ebert outgrew PBS and moved their show into commercial syndication, retitling it *At the Movies*. Along the way, the show lost some of its ramshackle charm. The "Dog of the Week," a feature honoring the week's worst low-budget film release, was replaced by the "Stinker of the Week" and was later scrapped entirely. New segments were created to highlight home-video releases, a sop to the program's new bourgeois commercial audience. *At the Movies* went through a second, tortuous retitling to *Siskel & Ebert & the Movies* before settling on the prosaic *Siskel & Ebert* in 1989.

With increased popularity came greatly enhanced power. Woody Allen and Eddie Murphy were just two of the stars who railed publicly about the pair's ability to sink a picture with a bad review. On the flipside, the encomium "two thumbs up from Siskel and Ebert" soon became prized by publicists all over Hollywood. When Siskel and Ebert gave their stamp of approval to more outré fare (both loved 1994's *Pulp Fiction*, for example), it was as if mainstream America had been granted permission to check out the film. Their critical criteria—they both put great emphasis on the likability of characters—influenced many mainstream reviewers, as did their show's format (they spawned a slew of imitators). Siskel and Ebert became late-night talk show mainstays and frequent targets of parodies, such as *In Living Color*'s cheeky "Men on Film."

Both men continued their newspaper writing, while Ebert also enjoyed a profitable sideline as the nominal writer of an annual movie reference guide. In 1998 Siskel underwent an emergency brain operation to remove an unspecified growth, but he vowed to return to television quickly so that Ebert would not receive too much airtime. He emerged only slightly worse for wear, his hopeless comb-over an apparent casualty of surgery and his cognitive skills only slightly diminished. In February 1999, however, Siskel died at age fifty-three from complications linked to his brain tumor.

After Siskel's death, Ebert went on with the show, partnering with *Chicago Sun-Times* film critic Richard Roeper. In 2005, as a tribute to his long career, Ebert was given a star on Hollywood's Walk of Fame. A year later he had surgery to treat cancer of the thyroid and was left unable to speak. Despite this setback, Ebert continued his newspaper work as a movie critic and also took to writing online, in particular on his blog and the social networking service Twitter. Using custom voice software, Ebert returned to broadcasting in 2011 with the show *Ebert Presents: At the Movies*.

Robert E. Schnakenberg

SEE ALSO: *Allen, Woody;* In Living Color*; Murphy, Eddie; Public Television (PBS);* Pulp Fiction*; Television.*

BIBLIOGRAPHY

Bernstein, Fred. "Tough! Tender! Gritty! Evocative! Gene Siskel and Roger Ebert Live to Dissect Films—and Each Other." *People Weekly*, August 20, 1984.

Ebert, Roger. *Roger Ebert's Book of Film*. New York: W. W. Norton, 1996.

Roger Ebert. Accessed March 2012. Available from http://rogerebert.com

Sister Souljah *(1964–)*

Black female rapper Sister Souljah, born Lisa Williamson, made national headlines in 1992 in the wake of the Los Angeles riots when she asked an interviewer, "If black people kill black people every day, why not have a week and kill white people?" The interview, in support of her album *360 Degrees of Power*, gained national attention when 1992 Democratic presidential candidate Bill Clinton, in order to attract the conservative white vote, condemned her remarks while addressing Jesse Jackson's Rainbow Coalition. Political analysts suggested that this criticism of Sister Souljah in front of an all-black gathering was responsible for Clinton attracting a sizable number of white southern voters. Although the media attention increased sales of her disappointing album, it was not enough to energize her rap career. The New York City native turned to writing with her 1995 quasiautobiography, *No Disrespect*, which focused on black male/female relationships. Since then, she has published three novels—*The Coldest Winter Ever* (1999), *Midnight: A Gangster Love Story* (2008), and *Midnight and the Meaning of Love* (2011).

Leonard Nathaniel Moore

SEE ALSO: *Jackson, Jesse; Race Riots; Rap.*

BIBLIOGRAPHY

Drew, Bernard A. *100 Most Popular African American Authors: Biographical Sketches and Bibliographies*. Westport, CT: Libraries Unlimited, 2007.

Sister Souljah. *No Disrespect*. New York: Time Warner, 1995.

Sitcom

Sitcom is the moniker for the situation comedy, a form of television programming generally thirty minutes in length and consisting, in writer's jargon, of an opening teaser, two acts, and a closing tag. Currently, a sitcom contains about twenty minutes of program sandwiched between advertisements, public service announcements, and station IDs. The situation comedy derives its name from the fact that each episode involves the antics of regular characters who find themselves in a humorous "situation."

The history of the television sitcom dovetails that of the radio situation comedy. Soon after its invention, the medium of radio evolved from experimental, often amateur-produced stunts to organized formats that included music performances, news, talk, drama, public affairs, and situation comedy. The most notable sitcom from this period was *The Amos 'n' Andy Show*, which originated on WMAQ Radio in Chicago in 1928 and went on to become the longest-running radio program in American history. The *The Amos 'n' Andy Show* prefaced the creation of other successful programs, including *Fibber McGee and Molly*, *The George Burns and Gracie Allen Show*, and *Beulah*. All of these shows eventually made the transition to the new medium of television.

From the earliest days of TV situation comedies to the present, the characters, themes, and plots have consisted of little more than fantasies sprung from the fertile minds of their creators. The genre has provided a compelling portrait of the American landscape throughout periods of plenty, recession, and great societal upheaval. Evolving notions about sex; fashion; child rearing; government; war; and the changing status of African Americans, gays, and women have all been fodder for the producers and writers of the episodic comedy. In fact, it is the episodic comedy, with its humorous take on life, weekly format, and regular characters, that has most soundly presented the taboos, preoccupations, prejudices, obsessions, fads, and fixations of American society—not only by what has been shown on the small screen but also by what has been omitted.

A FLEDGLING FORM

In his book *Tube of Plenty*, media scholar Erik Barnouw traces the unfolding of two circumstances that played key roles in the success of the sitcom as a programming format. Very early television shows were broadcast live. A viable form of videotape recording had not yet been introduced, and film was considered an unnecessary expense. The programs that were preserved for rebroadcast were kinescope reproductions of poor quality. In 1951 Lucille Ball and her husband, Desi Arnaz, used several thousand dollars of their own money to produce a pilot television program based on her successful radio show, *My Favorite*

All in the Family. All in the Family *starred, from left, Jean Stapleton as Edith Bunker, Carroll O'Connor as Archie Bunker, Sally Struthers as Gloria Bunker-Stivic, and Rob Reiner as Michael "Meathead" Stivic.* CBS-TV/THE KOBAL COLLECTION.

Husband. Ball's show, *I Love Lucy,* was shot employing a three-camera process and using film, providing high-quality prints that could be broadcast repeatedly and at previously designated times. Additionally, Ball's decision to shoot her show in Hollywood hastened the migration of television production from the live studios of New York to the motion picture soundstages of Hollywood. The show was filmed before a live audience, an innovation that did not catch on with other sitcoms until nearly the 1970s. *I Love Lucy,* which ran until 1961, enjoyed six full seasons as the most-watched program in the nation.

Another important development was the partnership forged between motion pictures and television. At first, the film industry regarded TV as a competitor and refused to allow feature films to be aired on television or movie stars to make appearances on the small screen. Eventually, film studios such as Paramount and Walt Disney began a dialogue with television executives, and the partnerships that were forged drastically altered the course of prime-time TV. Motion picture studios began to produce filmed programming for network television, including sitcoms such as *Father Knows Best* (1954–1960), which was produced by Columbia Pictures. By the end of the 1950s, the golden age of television, with its variety shows and live-broadcast anthology dramatic series, had begun to fade. For better or for worse, a new era was about to begin featuring formulaic fare, including the situation comedy.

LIGHTWEIGHT OFFERINGS

Sitcoms of the 1950s are signified by their vanilla suburbs, emphasis on hearth and home, and nonthreatening humor. Outside of the occasional light reference to a social issue, such as teenage smoking, the characters on *The Aldrich Family* (1949–1953), *Make Room for Daddy* (1953–1965), *Lassie* (1954–1974), and *Father Knows Best* exist in worlds that are generally far removed from the harsh realities of the day, including poverty, the threat posed by atomic weapons, and segregation. By the 1960s—as America increased its presence in Vietnam, civil rights tensions heightened to a boiling point, and Premier Nikita Khrushchev of the Soviet Union aimed Cuban-based missiles at the United States—television viewers found solace in the hayseed humor of sitcoms such as *The Beverly Hillbillies* (1962–1971), *Petticoat Junction* (1963–1970), and *The Andy Griffith Show* (1960–1968). Moreover, "idiot sitcoms" such as *My Favorite Martian* (1963–1966), *Bewitched* (1964–1972), *The Flying Nun* (1967–1970), and *Gilligan's Island* (1964–1967) had viewership ratings in the top ten.

The 1970s brought changes that were striking and often provocative. In 1969 Robert D. Wood became president of CBS. Robert Slater claims in his book *This Is . . . CBS* that Wood will be remembered for his "extensive overhaul" of CBS's programming strategy—one that significantly changed the flavor of prime-time American television. Since the 1950s CBS had been the undisputed ratings leader. The network retained its top ranking with a strong lineup that included both new shows and long-running programs that audiences watched loyally, such as Western dramas and *The Ed Sullivan Show.* Slater notes, however, that with the great popularity of programs such as *The Beverly Hillbillies* and *Green Acres* (1965–1971), CBS was jokingly referred to as "the Hillbilly Network." Bigger threats than stereotyping loomed over CBS, though.

The business side of television had changed a great deal since the days of General Foods' sponsorship of *The Aldrich Family.* Programming had slowly evolved from sponsor-owned, sponsor-controlled shows to the selling of "spots" (thirty- and sixty-second commercial messages) to many sponsors. Moreover, a new concept was being addressed by programming executives in the conference rooms of the major networks: demographics. Now it was no longer enough for a program to attract the widest possible audience. It also had to attract the *right* audience, that being viewers with enough disposable income to spend on an advertiser's products. CBS's loyal but aging and fixed-income audience lacked the sophistication and spending power that advertisers coveted. Advertisers were eager to attract a younger demographic, specifically one that was made up of viewers between the ages of twenty-five and forty-nine. In *Tube of Plenty*, Barnouw writes, "Older viewers were not big spenders. Programs now tended to survive to the extent that they served the demographic requirements of sponsors." It was clear to Wood and CBS executive William S. Paley that if the network simply rested on its laurels, it would soon lose rating points and, in turn, all-important advertising dollars.

SOCIAL UPHEAVAL

Not only had the television industry changed, so had life in America. The 1960s were a period of great social and cultural upheaval. Americans had witnessed the assassinations of President John F. Kennedy, his brother Robert, and civil rights activist Martin Luther King Jr. The nightly news brought grim footage of the death and destruction of the Vietnam War to American living rooms. Civil rights protestors were doused with fire hoses and attacked with dogs. Student activists created a new American Left. College campuses, draft cards, and cities burned. Consequently, many people in the television industry believed that programming needed to reflect the ideals and interests of the contemporary culture and include social issues and themes more appealing and relevant to a young, educated audience.

Wood initiated a clean sweep of CBS's programming. Successful programs such as *Green Acres*, *The Ed Sullivan Show*, and *The Beverly Hillbillies* were canceled. Also banished were old favorites such as *Here's Lucy* (1968–1974), *Gunsmoke* (1955–1975), and *The Red Skelton Hour* (1951–1971). Independent producer Norman Lear purchased the rights to a hit British television show called *Till Death Do Us Part*. In the American version, now called *All in the Family* (1971–1979), he cast veteran actor Carroll O'Connor as the loud-mouthed bigot Archie Bunker. The program delivered themes never before seen by a TV audience, with scripts featuring crude racial epithets and verbal sparring. In January 1971 CBS launched the program "with trepidation," Barnouw notes. *All in the Family* was not an instant hit, but within about a year, it became the most-watched and talked-about sitcom in America.

More importantly, the program's success bred a slew of other provocative offerings, including *The Jeffersons* (1975–1985), *Maude* (1972–1978), and *Good Times* (1974–1979). *Good Times*, featuring a predominantly African American cast, depicts the lives of a family eking out a precarious existence in a Chicago housing project. Suburban street crime, muggings, unemployment, evictions, black empowerment, and criticism of the government are frequent and resounding themes. *Sanford and Son* (1972–1977), with a multiracial cast, is propelled by the irreverent and topical humor of the star, Redd Foxx, as the owner of a junkyard. *M*A*S*H* (1972–1983) proved to be the most successful of these topical programs. Set during the Korean War, it was created by veteran writer Larry Gelbart and based on the hit movie of the same name (1970). All of these programs were considered *relevant* in that they feature characters of various races, creeds, religions, and political bents and tackle such formerly taboo subject matter as interracial marriage, birth control, and racism.

Of course, not all sitcoms took this route, especially entering the 1980s, when the conservative Ronald Reagan became president. Programs such as *Happy Days* (1974–1984), *Laverne & Shirley* (1976–1983), *Three's Company* (1977–1984), and *Mork & Mindy* (1978–1982) hark back to a more vanilla brand of humor.

SITCOMS AND WOMEN

To the consternation of traditionalists, the women's liberation movement in America unfolded on prime-time TV screens. In early sitcoms, the concerns of the model stay-at-home mom are relegated mostly to household issues. Although Lucy (*I Love Lucy*), June Cleaver (*Leave It to Beaver*, 1957–1963), and Margaret Anderson (*Father Knows Best*) may occasionally assert their authority, these moments occur safely within the minor vicissitudes of family life. Single women with jobs in early sitcoms are generally secretaries or assistants of some other sort. In *Comic Visions*, David Marc describes the long-suffering career-oriented woman who "worked for a living in lieu of marriage, which was valorized as the principal or 'real' goal of any woman." Early comedies featuring single, working women include *Our Miss Brooks* (1952–1956), *The Dick Van Dyke Show* (1961–1966), and *Private Secretary* (1953–1957).

The evolution of *The Doris Day Show* (1968–1973) offers an interesting glimpse at the sitcom's portrayal of the changing status of women America. In the first season of the show, Day is a recent widower with two sons who returns to her rural roots to live with her father. By the second season, Day is a secretary working for the editor of a magazine. In the third season, she has moved to San Francisco and is not just a secretary but also an independent writer. By the fourth and final season, she is a strong single woman and independent writer—her life as a mother, secretary, and daughter is all but forgotten.

In *That Girl* (1966–1971), meanwhile, Marlo Thomas portrays a young, independent woman trying to make it as an actress in New York. Some critics regard her Ann Marie character, with her comical antics and zany behavior, as little more than an extension of Lucy. Moreover, she is often rescued by her understanding boyfriend or doting father. Unlike the long-suffering TV career women of earlier television, however, Ann Marie works hard at building a viable career—she is not simply marking time until her wedding day.

The sitcom *Julia* (1968–1971) is noteworthy, too, in that it also features a working professional woman and single mom. Additionally, the lead character, Julia, is African American. "Respectably widowed" and a nurse, Julia and her polite young son Corey live quietly in a safe and accepting world, successfully negotiating the minor challenges of life—far removed, it seems, from the harsh realities that existed in many African American communities at the time.

MARY RICHARDS AND MURPHY BROWN

The women's liberation movement brought more than freedom from bras and Victorian conventions. It shook up long-held and cherished assumptions about women and sex, gender, marriage, family life, respect, and equal opportunity in jobs and pay. Perhaps the most celebrated in the vein of early sitcoms featuring liberated women is the *Mary Tyler Moore Show* (1970–1977).

Mary Richards is a career woman employed as an associate producer at a Minneapolis, Minnesota, television station. Her survival does not depend on the support and benevolence of a father figure, steady man, or supportive family. She has a Jewish friend named Rhoda and, in a twist on the previously established sitcom scenario, together they often joke about—and not in an envious way—the life of the married woman. Mary's suitably gruff boss has personal problems and sometimes drinks too much, but they develop a unique affection for each other. Moreover, Mary maintains a close but platonic relationship with a male coworker. Now sitcom men and women could be friends without the compulsory romantic relationship. The *Mary Tyler Moore Show* "transcended the model moms" of earlier TV, "replaced the widowed career-women role and remade the ambitious, eligible single woman 'on-the-make,'" notes Marc in *Comic Visions*. This, he adds, was "a watershed event in American television."

Still, few people would have predicted the later triumph of *Murphy Brown* (1988–1998). Murphy, played by Candice Bergen, is a television journalist and single woman who becomes pregnant but shows little inclination to marry the father and settle into a life of domesticity. In 1992 Vice President Dan Quayle led the attack on this highly popular sitcom, saying that the idea of an unmarried woman becoming a mother was unacceptable for prime-time television. As noted liberally in American newspapers, he regarded the entire affair as "an attack on family values."

THE SITCOM FAMILY

Indeed, the television sitcom has endured its fair share of blame for exacerbating the social problems that have plagued American society over the decades. From the homogenous suburban life of *Leave It to Beaver* to the social realism of *Good Times*, many critics have pondered the effects of television comedy on the most sacred of American institutions: the family. In her book *Prime Time Families*, Ella Taylor describes the early TV sitcom family as "harmonious, well-oiled building blocks of a benignly conceived American society founded in affluence and consensus." The Cleavers of *Leave It to Beaver* do not raise their voices in anger, use bad words, or suffer from intestinal gas. Sex, ethnic issues, and alcoholics are all missing from the mix. Dad is happily, gainfully employed, and Mom is always there (usually in the kitchen) when needed.

Sitcom families of the 1990s, on the other hand, tend to feature dopey dads, absentee parents, grandparents who have sex, and moms whose behavior is borderline sadistic. The flawless persona of Jim Anderson (*Father Knows Best*) has evolved into parents whose flaws are clearly apparent. In an article titled "Father Knows Squat," Megan Rosenfeld of the *Washington Post* notes, "Parents are one of the few remaining groups that are regularly ridiculed, caricatured and marginalized on television. Ask a typical viewer to describe how parents are portrayed on most shows and the answer is: stupid."

THE COSBY SHOW

The 1980s saw the emergence of the baby boomer audience, the youngish, upscale professionals favored by advertisers that snatched up commercial time for programs such as *Cheers* (1982–1993). For a time, nighttime soaps and realistic crime dramas displaced sitcoms as viewer favorites, but the decade is also noteworthy for a family-oriented comedy that featured a predominantly African American cast and became one of the biggest hits ever. Using ratings as a measure, seemingly everyone watched *The Cosby Show* (1984–1992).

Jack Curry, in an article for *American Film*, explained the significance of a hit comedy to a television network: In addition to "delivering its own night," it was used as a "promotional base for other series." It was also used to "troubleshoot," assisting with "ratings battles" wherever needed. No sitcom of the 1980s "had the impact and the acclaim of NBC's *The Cosby Show*," which became a cash cow. Noted John Lippman in the *Wall Street Journal*, "*The Cosby Show*, for example, has generated nearly $900 million in revenue since it was sold into syndication in the late 1980s." Indeed, far from being little more than mindless entertainment, the television sitcom had attained major stature.

THE ISSUE OF RACE

Long before the success of *The Cosby Show* could even be imagined, the sitcom contributed mightily to the dialogue about race in America. In 1950 Ethel Waters took up the title role in the popular sitcom *Beulah*, which ran until 1952. The show, which concerns the life of a lovable housekeeper working for the Henderson family, was described by the *New York Times* as such: "The story of one of those southern jewels who turns out corn bread and greens and generally manages the household made the transition to television . . . but on the whole the opening installment suffered from a trite story and was regrettably stereotyped in concept." After three seasons (and three different dissatisfied actresses in the title role), *Beulah* was canceled.

However, the level of resentment that took *Beulah* off the air barely approached that surrounding *The Amos 'n' Andy Show* (1951–1953). The Beulah character, although an obvious stereotype, is at least well-mannered and speaks intelligible English, but *Amos 'n' Andy*—with its shady low-life characters, malapropisms, and ethnic humor—caused a great deal of divisiveness within the African American community. Some organs of the black press campaigned against the show, contributing to its eventual cancellation.

Twenty years would pass before another network would feature a sitcom with a predominately African American cast. By the 1980s, however, viewers of all races were enjoying the comical antics of the African American characters in comedies such as *The Hughleys* (1998–2000), *Roc* (1991–1994), *The Fresh Prince of Bel-Air* (1990–1996), and *Family Matters* (1989–1998). African Americans and other people of color have become fixtures in sitcoms, including those produced for cable networks by independent producers such as Tyler Perry. Malcolm Jamal-Warner, who played Cosby's son Theo on *The Cosby Show*, is all grown up with his own wife and family on the BET network's *Reed between the Lines* (2011–).

Still, some critics believe there is much work to be done on the racial front. Loretha Jones, president of original programming at BET and developer of *Reed between the Lines*, told the Associated Press in 2011 that television lacks shows that include "a diverse class of black characters." Tracee Ellis Ross, who stars opposite Jamal-Warner in the show, believes that TV viewers long for programs that, like *The Cosby Show*, instill "good moral values in their children."

ROSEANNE

Whereas *Cosby* features the lives of a professional, educated, upwardly mobile family, another sitcom from the 1980s, *Roseanne* (1988–1997), had a major influence by taking the opposite route. Like a mom in the 1950s, Roseanne Conner cleans house, washes clothes, and makes meatloaf for dinner. The similarities to 1950s-style domesticity end there, though.

Roseanne is "she who must be obeyed." She spars (verbally and physically) with her occasionally employed and promiscuous younger sister. Roseanne's own mother drinks too much and, at one point, thinks she is gay. Her boss is indeed gay, as is a female friend who takes Roseanne for a night of dancing at a gay bar. Whereas Lucy and Desi could not share a bed, Dan and Roseanne Conner openly discuss the particulars of their sex life. Over the years, Roseanne's oldest daughter elopes with a mechanic; her college-enrolled daughter is discovered living with her boyfriend; her pubescent son D. J. suffers the embarrassment of getting an erection in math class; and the electricity in her home is cut off because of nonpayment. The Conners refer to themselves as "white trash."

Indeed, given such grimness, it is surprising the show is so funny and was so successful. It enjoyed top ratings for most of its nearly ten-year run and was at least partially responsible for the success of other shows centered on quarrelsome, dysfunctional families, such as *Married . . . with Children* (1987–1997) and *The Simpsons* (1989–).

THE 1990s

Some of the most popular sitcoms from the 1990s feature self-absorbed young professionals who sip expensive coffee as they drown in angst of their own making. The period also brought forth a rise in "literate humor." Rife with references to such concepts as existentialism, shows such as *Frasier* (1993—2004) were created to appeal to upscale audiences with graduate degrees, people who, like the characters Frasier and Niles, had "advanced" cultural tastes.

Slowly, the depiction of gay characters became less controversial and more routine. On the comedy *Ellen* (1994–1998), the character Ellen (played by Ellen DeGeneres) comes out, announcing to the world on an open mike that she is indeed gay. Now the lives of everyday gay Americans could be fodder for the pens of comedy writers. *Will & Grace* (1998–2006) features the hilarious antics of a handsome and well-appointed gay man; his best female friend (who is straight); his best gay male friend; and the rich, quirky, alcohol- and pills-reliant straight married woman who hangs out with them. The sight gags and "gay" humor traverse a range of topics, from Will's attempts to find a decent boyfriend to Grace having to fend off the occasional sexual harassment of her married female friend.

SEINFELD

Of the sitcoms during this period, *Seinfeld* (1990–1998) merits particular mention, due to its unique and quirky cast, irreverent humor, and the fact that it was billed as a show about nothing. Set in New York City, the program follows the lives of the fictional comedian Jerry Seinfeld, his three closest friends (Elaine, George, and Kramer), their families, and an odd assortment of other characters. In an example of art imitating life, the show even parodies itself, with several episodes following Jerry's attempts to produce a sitcom about himself on the same network, NBC, as the real *Seinfeld* aired. The group explores former TV taboos and other "touchy" subject matter, such as a chef who neglects to wash his hands after using the toilet, sperm counts, and the size of a man's genitals after a swim. In one episode, the group makes bets to see who can hold off masturbating the longest. There are ugly babies, cancer scares, bras for men, scary bar mitzvahs, lesbian weddings, and stolen lobsters.

The program was so profitable for NBC that Seinfeld (the actor) was eventually paid $1 million per episode. The cost of advertising on an episode during the 1997–1998 season was $700,000 for a thirty-second spot; the price for the program's final episode was $1.5 million for thirty seconds. The *Wall Street Journal* noted in 1998 that the $1 million-per-episode syndication fee that the TBS cable network paid for *Seinfeld* was "one of the richest rerun deals in cable history." The *Seattle Times* reported, "The program is poised to become the first television show to generate more than $1 billion in syndication revenues."

THE TWENTY-FIRST CENTURY

The exorbitant fees connected with producing shows such as *Seinfeld* caused them to be become less desirable to networks during the economic downturns of the first decade of the 2000s. Networks began to favor documentary-style, single-camera comedies such as *30 Rock* (2006–), which were cheaper to make.

After a period of some decline—due, in part, to the popularity of more cost-effective reality programming and the lack of innovation by producers who relied too heavily on tried-and-true formulas—the sitcom experienced a comeback as the decade progressed. Some social commentators believe that in tough economic times, like those in the first decade of the 2000s, viewers would rather laugh than watch, say, a depressing crime drama. Sitcom offerings during this period ran the gamut from the corny and formulaic to the innovative. The scenarios are diverse, ranging from the comic machinations of married gay men with an adopted child (*Modern Family*, which premiered in 2009) to an obsessive-compulsive theoretical physicist and his band of nerdy friends (*The Big Bang Theory*, 2007–).

Despite competition from other genres, the ever-changing tastes of television viewers, and the advent of seemingly countless cable TV offerings, the sitcom has managed to survive and thrive in the sixty-plus years since *I Love Lucy* hit the airwaves. The episodic comedy has ushered America through recessions, economic booms, wars, civil unrest, and conservative and liberal presidencies. It has challenged ideas about sex, morals, reproduction, and fashion and has endured mergers and takeovers within the industry, endless controversies, unflattering scholarly assessments, and censorship. In other words, the sitcom is America's most durable form of television entertainment.

Pamala S. Deane

SEE ALSO: *Advertising;* All in the Family; The Amos 'n' Andy Show; The Andy Griffith Show; *Arnaz, Desi; Baby Boomers; Ball, Lucille;* Beulah; The Beverly Hillbillies; Bewitched; Cheers; *Civil Rights Movement;* The Cosby Show; *DeGeneres, Ellen;* Family Matters; Father Knows Best; *Feminism;* Fibber McGee and Molly; The Flying Nun; Frasier; Gilligan's Island; Good Times; Happy Days; I Love Lucy; The Jeffersons; *Lassie;* Laverne and Shirley; *Lear, Norman;* Leave It to Beaver; Married . . . with Children; The Mary Tyler Moore Show; M*A*S*H; Maude; Modern Family; Mork & Mindy; Murphy Brown; *Radio; Reality Television;* Roseanne; Sanford and Son; Seinfeld; The Simpsons; *Television;* 30 Rock; Three's Company; Will & Grace.

BIBLIOGRAPHY

"'Amos 'n' Andy' Protest Rocks Radio, TV Industry." *Afro-American*, July 21, 1951.

Arney, June. "Ads on Last *Seinfeld* Outscore Super Bowl." *Baltimore Sun*, May 14, 1998.

Barnouw, Erik. *Tube of Plenty: The Evolution of American Television*. New York: Oxford University Press, 1982.

Blair, Iain. "The Producers of *News Radio*, *Family Matters* . . . Discuss the Serious Business of Sitcoms." *Film & Video*, April 1996.

Bogle, Donald. *Blacks in American Films and Television: An Encyclopedia*. New York: Garland Publishers, 1988.

Brooks, Tim, and Earle Marsh. *The Complete Directory to Prime Time Network and Cable TV Shows: 1946–Present*, 9th ed. New York: Ballantine, 2007.

Carson, Tom. "The Great Fox Chase." *American Film*, June 1989.

Carter, Bill. "In a Gloomy Economy, TV Sitcoms Are Making a Comeback." *New York Times*, October 24, 2011.

Curry, Jack. "The Cloning of *Cosby*." *American Film*, October 1986.

Ely, Melvin Patrick. *The Adventures of "Amos 'n' Andy": A Social History of an American Phenomenon*. New York: Free Press, 1991.

Gilbert, James. *Another Chance: Postwar America 1945–1985*. Chicago: Dorsey Press, 1986.

Gross, Lynne Schaefer. *Telecommunications: An Introduction to Electronic Media*. Madison, WI: Brown and Benchmark Publishers, 1997.

Huff, Richard. "What Will Be the Total Take for *Seinfeld*? Billions and Billions." *Seattle Times*, May 15, 1998.

Lichter, S. Robert; Linda Lichter; and Stanley Rothman. *Prime Time: How TV Portrays American Culture*. Washington, DC: Regnery Publishing, 1994.

MacDonald, J. Fred. *Blacks and White TV: Afro-Americans in Television since 1948*. Chicago: Nelson-Hall Publishers, 1983.

Marc, David. *Comic Visions: Television Comedy & American Culture*. Malden, MA: Blackwell Publishers, 1997.

Marc, David, and Robert J. Thompson. *Prime Time, Prime Movers: From "I Love Lucy" to "L.A. Law," America's Greatest TV Shows and People Who Created Them*. Boston: Little, Brown, 1992.

Mayer, Martin. "Summing up the Seventies: Television." *American Film*, December 1979.

Moss, Linda. "A Laughing Matter: Cable Makes Serious Play for Scripted Comedy Success." *Multichannel News*, February 27, 2006.

"*Reed between the Lines* Fills BET's Positive Gap." Associated Press, October 20, 2011.

Singer, Dorothy; J. L. Singer; and D. M. Zuckerman. "What Every Parent Should Know about Television." *American Film*, January–February 1981.

Slater, Robert. *This . . . Is CBS: A Chronicle of 60 Years*. Englewood Cliffs, NJ: Prentice Hall, 1988.

Taylor, Ella. *Prime-Time Families: Television Culture in Postwar America*. Berkeley: University of California Press, 1989.

"Television Tykes: Series Contemplates Effect on Children." *Columbus Dispatch*, July 18, 1997.

Umstead, R. Thomas. "Laughing Matters: With a Dearth of Comedy on Broadcast, Cable Tickles Viewers with New Sitcoms." *Multichannel News*, November 9, 2009.

The Six Million Dollar Man

After hitting the airwaves as a made-for-TV movie in 1973, *The Six Million Dollar Man* became a weekly hour-long series that ran from 1974 to 1978 on ABC. The show stars Lee Majors as Colonel Steve Austin, an astronaut who suffers serious injuries from the crash of an experimental craft and is rebuilt into a bionic man by the government. Austin receives bionic legs, a bionic arm, and bionic eye. His new parts give him super strength, speed, and vision, which he utilizes in his work for the Office of Strategic Investigation (OSI). His superior is Oscar Goldman (Richard Anderson), and his doctor is the scientist Rudy Wells (Allan Oppenheimer and later Martin E. Brooks).

Austin faces a variety of foes, including spies, a rogue bionic man, Bigfoot (a robot created by aliens), and fembots (lethal androids). In most of the episodes, Austin works as a secret agent. When the Austin character achieved superhero status among young television viewers, the show's producers imitated comic-book hero plots with spin-offs and a "bionic family." Austin's love interest, Jaime Sommers (Lindsay Wagner) "dies," only to be brought back the next season. This led to the spin-off *The Bionic Women* (1976–1978), involving a bionic boy and Sommers's bionic dog, a German shepherd named Max. The two shows shared a supporting cast, and Majors and Wagner crossed over onto each other's programs.

The Six Million Dollar Man lasted longer than several other super-spy shows that appeared around the same time (*The Invisible Man*, 1975–1976; *Gemini Man*, 1976). At one point, it was even the top-rated program in America. *The Six Million Dollar Man* enjoyed a healthy run in syndication both in the United States and internationally and was broadcast on cable television into the late 1990s. Majors and Wagner also appeared in several bionic-themed movie specials that aired in the late 1980s and early 1990s. (These movies introduce another bionic man—Austin's son—and a bionic girl.)

Based on the 1972 novel *Cyborg* by Martin Caidin, the television series made the terms *bionics* and *cybernetics* familiar to America's general population, especially its youth. Caidin served as technical adviser to the show. The *The Six Million Dollar Man* spawned other forms of popular culture. Novels, especially those aimed at young adults, were written based on episodes and characters from the series. Austin was given in his own comic-book series (produced by Charlton Comics), and a *Six Million Dollar Man* action figure and lunchbox hit the marketplace. In addition, Dusty Springfield recorded the show's theme song. Parodies also appeared. For example, the Bionic Watermelon debuted on *The Captain and Tennille* TV show, and a children's joke book was titled *The Bionic Banana*.

The show's opening sequence, showing Austin's near-fatal crash, produced the following popular catchphrases: "He's breaking up! He's breaking up!" and "We can rebuild him; we have the technology. . . . We can make him better than he was before." Pretending to be bionic was easy thanks to the show's low-budget special effects. Every bionic act on the program is done in slow motion and is accompanied by a distinctive sound effect that kids imitated in backyards and on playgrounds across America.

Besides being a fun to say on the playground, the show's opening statement about "[making] him better than he was before" reflected an American attitude toward technology. The country had only recently put a man on the moon, and most Americans saw technology as a remedy to any problem. *The Six*

Million Dollar Man played right into this belief. However, while technology solves many problems on the show, it is also a source of power for the villains—killer robots and Venus probes are Austin's biggest challenges. Furthermore, Austin's human qualities play as big a role as his bionic parts in helping him triumph over his mechanical foes.

The show also expresses a view that government agencies exist to protect the population. OSI is concerned with doing good and is mostly benign in its practices. This stands in stark contrast to the way government is portrayed in later science fiction shows, such *The X-Files* (1993–2002).

P. Andrew Miller

SEE ALSO: *Comic Books; Science Fiction Publishing;* The X-Files.

BIBLIOGRAPHY

Cohen, Joel. *"The Six Million Dollar Man" and "The Bionic Woman."* New York: Scholastic Book Services, 1976.

Philips, Mark, and Frank Garcia. *Science Fiction Television Series*. Jefferson, NC: McFarland, 1996.

16 and Pregnant

A reality television program that premiered on the MTV network on June 11, 2009, *16 and Pregnant* addresses the loaded issue of teen pregnancy in contemporary America. In its first three seasons the show presented the stories of thirty-five high-school girls dealing with the difficulties and issues of teenage pregnancy. A typical episode follows one girl through the last five months of her pregnancy and the first few months after the baby is born, narrating her decision to keep the child or put him or her up for adoption, how she tells her family and friends, and the decisions she makes about how she will care for the child. Produced in a documentary format, the show provides footage of each pregnant teen's life interspersed with interviews with her, with the father of the child, and with her friends and family. Each season ends with a reunion episode hosted by celebrity psychiatrist and sexual health counselor Dr. Drew Pinsky, in which the families featured during the season meet to discuss what has happened in their lives since the events that occurred on the show. *16 and Pregnant* was an immediate success and inspired a spin-off series titled *Teen Mom*, which first aired on MTV on December 8, 2009, and followed the lives of teen mothers and their children in the first few years of motherhood.

16 and Pregnant received a great deal of media attention because it tackles the difficult and controversial issue of teen pregnancy. The creator of the show, Lauren Dolgen, said that the show was intended to raise awareness about teen pregnancy and the difficulties and pressures of raising a child. While some critics applauded it for bringing the issue to the forefront on a major television network, others have suggested that it glorifies the issue of teen pregnancy. The show was criticized because it features largely poor teenagers who mature over the course of an episode, and some commentators argued that this narrative arc makes motherhood appear to be an important learning experience. On the other hand, a number of commentators say that because the show is explicit about the physical and psychological difficulties of pregnancy and motherhood, and because it points out the opportunities these young women lose, it disparages young women who are sexually active.

The show has also been also criticized because, although it features several girls who choose to give up their babies for adoption, it does not show anyone who decides to have an abortion. MTV responded to this criticism by producing an hour-long special titled *No Easy Decision*, featuring season two's Markai Durham and hosted by Pinsky. In this special, which aired on December 28, 2010, Durham, who says she was initially antiabortion, chooses to end a second pregnancy. The show also received negative media attention because a number of the girls became tabloid stars, and one featured couple, Ebony Jackson-Rendon and Joshua Rendon, was arrested for drug possession and mistreatment of their child in September 2011.

Jenny Ludwig

SEE ALSO: *Abortion; Cable TV; MTV; Reality Television; Tabloids; Teenagers; Television.*

BIBLIOGRAPHY

Bellafante, Ginia. "Real Life Is Like *Juno*, Except Maybe the Dialogue." *New York Times*, June 11, 2009. Accessed May 2012. Available from http://www.nytimes.com/2009/06/11/arts/television/11sixteen.html?_r=1

Dolgen. Lauren. "Why I Created MTV's *16 and Pregnant*." CNN Entertainment, May 4, 2011. Accessed May 2012. Available from http://articles.cnn.com/2011-05-04/entertainment/teen.mom.dolgen_1_teen-pregnancy-teen-mom-teen-mothers?_s=PM:SHOWBIZ

Page, Christina. "16 & Pregnant & Having an Abortion." Huffington Post, January 21, 2012. Accessed May 2012. Available from http://www.huffingtonpost.com/cristina-page/16-pregnant-having-an-abo_b_1220490.html

Seltzer, Sarah. "MTV's *16 and Pregnant* Exploits Teen Moms but Addresses Abortion with Dignity." *Washington Post*, December 30, 2010. Accessed May 2012. Available from http://www.washingtonpost.com/wp-dyn/content/article/2010/12/30/AR2010123001953.html

The Sixth Sense

In an increasingly overhyped industry, the film *The Sixth Sense* was that rarest of things, a surprise hit. The cerebral thriller was released with little fanfare in the summer of 1999 and stimulated enough word-of-mouth publicity to make it the second-highest grossing film of the year. A cult favorite with teenage audiences, who often saw it several times, the film had a broad appeal thanks to sensitive performances from its lead actors and a stunning twist at the end. For years after the film's run, those who saw it would be chilled by the whispered line "I see dead people."

Written and directed by M. Night Shyamalan, *The Sixth Sense* tells the story of Malcolm Crowe, a child psychologist (played by Bruce Willis) who is attacked by a disgruntled former patient (Donnie Wahlberg as Vincent Grey) who shoots Crowe and then kills himself. Later, recovering and trying to pick up the pieces of his life, Crowe begins treatment with a disturbed and lonely nine-year-old (Haley Joel Osment as Cole Sear) who confides to the therapist that he sees the dead all around him. Though disturbed by his deteriorating relationship with his wife (they barely speak any more), Crowe helps Cole discover the reason he is haunted by the dead—they need him to help them take care of unfinished business so they can move on. Crowe also helps Cole heal his relationship with his mother (Toni Collette as Lynn Sear) before going home to his wife. Once there, he—and the audience—discover the secret underlying the film: Crowe himself died when Vincent shot him and his work with Cole has been helping him come to terms with it and move on.

Director Manoj Night Shyamalan, the son of two doctors, was born in 1970 in India and raised in Pennsylvania. A movie fan from a young age, he was given a Super 8 camera when he was a child and made forty-five short films by the time he was fifteen. *The Sixth Sense* was his third feature film. He made careful choices in the casting of the film, surprising many with his selection of action film star Willis for the lead role. Shyamalan was confident in Willis's ability to give an understated performance, however, and Willis's popularity gave the film a boost with audiences. Osment was also acclaimed in the difficult role of Cole, and Australian actor Collette brought subtlety to Cole's anguished mother.

Though the film's reviews were mixed, audiences fell in love with *The Sixth Sense*, and it earned People's Choice Awards for Favorite Motion Picture, Favorite Dramatic Motion Picture, and Favorite Actor for Willis.

Tina Gianoulis

SEE ALSO: *Cult Films; Willis, Bruce.*

BIBLIOGRAPHY

Bamberger, Michael. *The Man Who Heard Voices: or, How M. Night Shyamalan Risked His Career on a Fairy Tale.* New York: Gotham, 2006.

Lavik, Erlend. "Narrative Structure in *The Sixth Sense*: A New Twist in 'Twist Movies'?" *Velvet Light Trap* 58 (2006): 55.

Malanowski, Jamie. "A Director with a Sense of Where He's Going." *New York Times*, March 12, 2000, 2A.

Weinstock, Jeffrey Andrews, ed. *Critical Approaches to the Films of M. Night Shyamalan: Spoiler Warnings.* New York: Palgrave Macmillan, 2010.

60 Minutes

Before the emergence of prime-time network newsmagazine programs such as *20/20*, *Primetime Live*, and *Dateline*, and before the era of round-the-clock cable news on CNN, MSNBC, and Fox News Channel, the CBS newsmagazine *60 Minutes* was unchallenged as television's premiere news program. From its initial broadcast on September 24, 1968, *60 Minutes* pioneered the "magazine format" of television journalism, which allowed it to run a mixture of hard news, investigative reports, personality profiles, and light feature pieces. Its prominence enabled it to feature candid stories on the most powerful world leaders, distinguished artists, and crafty villains of the past four decades. Although it was not a ratings sensation during its first several seasons, by the mid-1970s *60 Minutes* had become the most prestigious, most watched, and most imitated news program on television.

INNOVATION

Don Hewitt, the longtime executive producer of *60 Minutes*, created the program after he was fired in 1964 from his position as producer of *The CBS Evening News with Walter Cronkite*. Before his dismissal, he had become a key behind-the-scenes player at CBS News. Hewitt had directed Edward R. Murrow's *See It Now* programs in the 1950s, including the first live coast-to-coast hookup in November 1951, which depicted the simultaneously broadcast images of the Brooklyn Bridge and the Golden Gate Bridge. In 1960 he produced and directed the nation's first televised presidential debate, between John F. Kennedy and Richard Nixon. Hewitt was also remembered for such technical achievements as the invention of cue cards, the development of subtitles to identify people and places on-screen, the creation of the "double projector" system to enable smoother editing, and the coining of the term *anchorman*.

After a dispute with Fred Friendly, president of CBS News, Hewitt was relegated to the network's lowly documentary division. In describing his attempts to revive the little-watched, moribund format, he said, "Sometime in 1967 it dawned on me that if we split those public affairs hours into three parts to deal with the viewers' short attention span . . . and come up with personal journalism in which a reporter takes the viewer along with him on the story, I was willing to bet that we could take informational programming out of the ratings cellar."

Hewitt presented his newly fashioned documentary program in the guise of a newsmagazine such as *Time* or *Newsweek*. Each week his chief correspondents would present several stories on a wide variety of topics. A brief concluding segment in the early years, titled "Point Counterpoint," consisted of debates between liberal and conservative columnists Shana Alexander and James Kilpatrick. In 1978 writer Andy Rooney assumed this segment to present his own brand of short, humorous commentary. Each portion of the program was separated by an image of a ticking stopwatch, which became the show's symbol.

By the late 1970s *60 Minutes*, with its concept of stories presented in a "Hollywood style" that emphasized attractively packaged factual events, had become one of most popular shows on television. In 1979 it was the highest-rated television program of the season—a distinction that no other news show had ever attained. Its great popular success made *60 Minutes* one of the most profitable programs in TV history. Costing only about half the price of an hour-long entertainment show while commanding the same rates for commercials, the show earned CBS enormous sums of money from what had been the least watched type of network program. Much of the show's appeal was based on its increasingly hard-hitting investigative reports. Presented mainly by aggressive correspondents Mike Wallace and Dan Rather, the reports exposed a number of frauds and abuses, including the sale of phony passports, kickbacks in the Medicaid business, and mislabeling in the meatpacking industry. Reporter Morley Safer commented on the show's ability to get dishonest businessmen and scam artists on camera by saying, "A crook doesn't believe he's made it as a crook until he's been on *60 Minutes*."

An examination of the personalities, issues, lifestyles, and major events covered on *60 Minutes* provides a remarkable window into the United States from the late 1960s onward. Hewitt created a format that has allowed for a varied presentation of ideas that have shaped the post-Vietnam era. He and his able correspondents, led by Wallace, revealed to the networks that factual, documentary programming could be highly successful both in terms of journalism and ratings. Their success led to a proliferation of other television newsmagazines from the 1990s into the twenty-first century.

CORRESPONDENTS

The show's greatest strength long derived from its correspondents and their choice of stories. In the 1980s and 1990s correspondents such as Harry Reasoner, Ed Bradley, Diane Sawyer, Steve Kroft, and Lesley Stahl were able to deliver insightful pieces within the show's potpourri format. A reporter might speak from a war zone one week, then interview movie stars or pool hustlers the next. The correspondents were not bound to the studio but free to report from the field, supported by a team that would include six producers, a cameraperson, an assistant, a soundperson, and an electrician. Hewitt's focus on "personality journalism" allowed each correspondent's characteristics to shine through. Wallace was seen to embody the image of the tough reporter, for example, whereas Safer projected a more elegant image.

Of all the journalists associated with *60 Minutes*, none is as strongly identified with the program as Wallace. His intense reporter's image came only after a long and varied career. He was a radio performer in the 1940s and appeared as an actor on popular shows such as *Sky King*, *The Lone Ranger*, *The Green Hornet*, and *Ma Perkins*. After moving to television in 1949, he hosted a variety of talk, interview, and game shows. Following the 1962 death of his son Peter in a climbing accident, Wallace decided to become a straight newsman. He possessed a direct, often abrasive, style that was well suited for the show's confrontational format. He was generally regarded as the most fearless reporter in the business and was unafraid to ask the most provocative questions even of friends.

Wallace announced his retirement from *60 Minutes* in 2006, after thirty-eight years with the program. He continued with the network as a "Correspondent Emeritus" until 2008. His final segment on the program was an interview with retired baseball star Roger Clemens. Hewitt had begun to reduce his role on the program in 2002, when viewership began to decline.

60 Minutes. *The principles on* Sixty Minutes *in the early 1990s included, clockwise from top left, Steve Kroft, Ed Bradley, Morley Safer, and producer Don Hewitt, Mike Wallace, Lesley Stahl, and Andy Rooney.* CBS PHOTO ARCHIVE/CONTRIBUTOR/CBS/GETTY IMAGES.

He remained at CBS until his death in 2009. Commentator Rooney made his final appearance on the program on October 2, 2011. He died one month later at age ninety-two. As the program continued into the second decade of the twenty-first century, active correspondents included Safer, Kroft, Stahl, Bob Simon, Anderson Cooper, Lara Logan, Scott Pelley, and Byron Pitts.

CRITICISM AND OUTLOOK

Although it has long been considered television's most distinguished news program, *60 Minutes* has not been without its critics or controversies. Some claimed it practiced "ambush journalism" by editing its massive amounts of interview footage to distort the positions of some of its subjects. Others have complained that the many offscreen producers do the majority of the reporting, whereas the on-air correspondents merely provide each story's narration. In the 1990s Rooney was temporarily suspended for a supposedly racist remark. Other low moments in the program's long history include its being duped in 1972 by a forged diary of industrialist Howard Hughes and, most seriously, its being forced to delay an exposé on the tobacco industry owing to the network's fears of litigation. Despite these problems, *60 Minutes* remains a respected program that is trusted by viewers in Middle America. From 1999 to 2005 CBS aired a second weekly installment of the series titled *60 Minutes II*. Beginning in 2011 another spin-off—*60 Minutes on CNBC*—offered updated business reports and unaired footage from original broadcasts.

Charles Coletta

SEE ALSO: *Cable TV; CNN; Cronkite, Walter;* Dateline*; Fox News Channel; Golden Gate Bridge; Hughes, Howard; The Lone Ranger;* Ma Perkins*; Murrow, Edward R.;* Newsweek*; Rather, Dan; Television; Television Anchors;* Time*; 20/20; Vietnam.*

BIBLIOGRAPHY

Coffey, Frank. *60 Minutes: 25 Years of Television's Finest Hour.* Los Angeles: General Publishing, 1993.

Hewitt, Don. *Minute by Minute.* New York: Random House, 1985.

Hewitt, Don. *Tell Me a Story: Fifty Years and "60 Minutes" in Television.* New York: Public Affairs, 2002.

The $64,000 Question

During the 1950s, game shows were television's most popular fare, and *The $64,000 Question* (1955–1958) was unquestionably America's favorite game show. Every Sunday night, the country came to a stop as millions of households tuned in to watch. The premise behind the show was brilliant—in addition to a profession or vocation, many people have hobbies or avocations about which they are remarkably well informed. The show featured contestants with specialized knowledge of a subject unrelated to his or her profession, such as a jockey who was an art expert, or a psychologist—the young Dr. Joyce Brothers, who became famous because of the show—who loved prize fighting. Players entered an isolation booth and answered questions, working their way up each week to the final "$64,000 Question."

Unbeknownst to viewers and, indeed, some of the contestants, however, the producers of the show were giving answers to the more charismatic players. A few years later, *The $64,000 Question* came under scrutiny during the investigation by the U.S. Congress known as the "Quiz Show Scandal." When the public learned the truth about the fixed quiz shows, game shows fell out of favor for years and the U.S. television audience adopted a cynicism that has permeated popular culture ever since.

Victoria Price

SEE ALSO: *Brothers, Dr. Joyce; Game Shows; Quiz Show Scandals.*

BIBLIOGRAPHY

DeLong, Thomas A. *Quiz Craze: America's Infatuation with Game Shows.* New York: Praeger, 1991.

Holms, John Pynchon, and Ernest Wood. *The TV Game Show Almanac.* Radnor, PA: Chilton, 1995.

Newcomb, Horace, et al. *Encyclopedia of Television.* Chicago: Fitzroy Dearborn, 2004.

Skaggs, Ricky *(1954–)*

A musical veteran by the age of eighteen, Ricky Skaggs parlayed his early bluegrass prominence and an apprenticeship with Emmylou Harris's country-rock Hot Band into a residency atop the country charts in the early 1980s. In fact, *Billboard* magazine included him on its list of the top artists of the 1980s. Skaggs created a modern sound out of traditional elements of bluegrass and country that earned him widespread acclaim and respect even after the rise of the "new country" format shut him (and others like him) out of country radio in the early 1990s. Undaunted, he roared back into the limelight in 1997 with *Bluegrass Rules!*—a return to his roots that was the first traditional bluegrass album to break onto the country charts.

Born in the remote hills of eastern Kentucky in 1954, Skaggs began his music career at age five, playing mandolin and fiddle with his parents' semiprofessional band. In 1970 he and partner Keith Whitley were taken under the wing of bluegrass pioneer Ralph Stanley, with whom they toured and recorded for several years. While Whitley continued to work with Stanley through much of the 1970s, Skaggs left to take a short-term job with the Country Gentlemen before joining J. D. Crowe and the New South in 1974. Though his tenure with Crowe was brief, it was exceedingly influential because the band toured widely, including playing in Japan. The group also made one of the most significant bluegrass albums ever, a self-titled release for Rounder Records in 1975. When Skaggs departed from the New South, he and fellow alumnus Jerry Douglas formed Boone Creek, another influential act that combined traditional bluegrass with a more modern, rock-influenced sound.

GOING SOLO

Following the breakup of Boone Creek, Skaggs went to work for Harris, then a frequent presence at the top of the country music charts. As a member of the Hot Band, he both influenced and was influenced by Harris, bringing bluegrass sounds into her material while honing his skills as an electric guitar picker and developing an appreciation for the application of rock beats and accents to traditional country material. A 1979 solo album,

Ricky Skaggs. *Ricky Skaggs's return to his bluegrass roots after a string of chart-topping country hits in the 1980s was welcomed by enthusiasts of the genre.* MINDY SMALL/CONTRIBUTOR/FILMMAGIC/GETTY IMAGES.

Sweet Temptation, made while he was still with Harris, shows Skaggs in the process of turning these lessons into a catchy, distinctive sound that melds his influences and experiences into something new. When a single from the album, "I'll Take the Blame," garnered airplay on country radio, he plunged into a solo country music career, signing with Epic Records and producing *Waiting for the Sun to Shine* (1981).

Skaggs's first single from the album, "Don't Get above Your Raisin'," hit the Top 20, and then he had a number one song with an updated version of Flatt and Scruggs' "Crying My Heart out over You." From then until 1986, Skaggs was never absent from the upper end of the country charts, scoring fifteen consecutive Top 10 hits, most of which reached the top spot. His winning formula proved to be a combination of modern-sounding remakes of country and bluegrass classics ("I Don't Care," "I Wouldn't Change You if I Could," "Don't Cheat in Our Hometown," "Uncle Pen") and well-crafted country rockers by younger, sophisticated writers, all delivered by a supremely talented band of musicians, many with bluegrass backgrounds ("Heartbroke," "Highway 40 Blues").

These achievements brought Skaggs considerable acclaim, and legendary guitarist/producer Chet Atkins credited him with "single-handedly" saving country music. He was flooded with honors, including membership in the Grand Ole Opry (at the time of his induction, he was one of the youngest entertainers ever to join the cast), seven awards from the Country Music Association, and three Grammys. Though he continued to make occasional guest appearances with bluegrass acts in concert and on record, the 1980s saw Skaggs take up what seemed to be a permanent residence in the world of country music.

DOWN, THEN UP AGAIN

By the end of the 1980s, however, Skaggs's releases were no longer topping the charts. Some critics attributed the decline to stagnation and the diminishing quality of his material, while others took note of changes in country radio, which was turning toward a variety of broader rock influences. Whatever the cause, his only number one recording after 1986 was "Lovin' Only Me," (1989), and by 1988 most of his singles were failing to reach the Top 20. Though he continued to maintain a high profile at the Opry and on cable television's The Nashville Network, hosting a well-received concert series on the latter in the mid-1990s, mutual dissatisfaction between Skaggs and his label found him making a jump to Atlantic Records, for which he made two albums—*Solid Ground* (1995) and *Life Is a Journey* (1997)—that were favorably received by critics but not by mainstream country radio.

Shortly after the release of the second Atlantic album, Skaggs experienced a resurgence by returning to his traditional bluegrass roots. He recorded an album of standards, *Bluegrass Rules!* which earned him a sixth Grammy and was named the International Bluegrass Music Association Album of the Year. Not by coincidence, the shift came at a time when the death of bluegrass's founder, Bill Monroe, had prompted concern about the future of the genre. Skaggs was as well positioned as anyone to contribute to its survival, and the marketing strategy for the album bypassed commercial radio and focused on reaching listeners directly through broad-ranging tours, televised appearances, and savvy use of the Internet.

PLAYING ON

By the end of the decade, Skaggs was proclaiming his permanent commitment to bluegrass, which pleased his legions of fans. He had started Skaggs Family Records in 1997 and used it to turn out award-winning albums such as *Ancient Tones* (1999) and *History of the Future* (2001). In 2003 he released *Soldier of the Cross, Live at the Charleston Music Hall* and *Big Mon: The Songs of Bill Monroe*. That same year, Skaggs teamed with Earl Scruggs and Doc Watson for *The Three Pickers. Brand New Strings* followed in 2005, and two years later *Instrumentals* debuted at number one on the bluegrass charts.

Skaggs then released *Salt of the Earth and Honoring the Fathers of Bluegrass: Tribute to 1946 and 1947* (2008) and *Ricky Skaggs Solo: Songs My Dad Loved* (2010), on which he plays every instrument and sings every vocal part. In 2011 he returned to the blending of country and bluegrass for which he is best known with the release of *Country Hits Bluegrass Style*.

Jon Weisberger

SEE ALSO: *Atkins, Chet; Bluegrass; Country Music;* Grand Ole Opry*; Monroe, Bill; Scruggs, Earl.*

BIBLIOGRAPHY

Goldsmith, Thomas, ed. *The Bluegrass Reader*. Urbana: University of Illinois Press, 2004.

"Ricky Skaggs." Country Music Television. Accessed March 2012. Available from http://www.cmt.com/artists/az/skaggs_ricky/artist.jhtml

"Ricky Skaggs." Grand Ole Opry. Accessed March 2012. Available from http://www.opry.com/artists/s/Skaggs_Ricky.html

"Ricky Skaggs." Skaggs Family Records. Accessed March 2012. Available from http://www.skaggsfamilyrecords.com/index.htm?id=12253

Skateboarding

Invented in the 1950s by Southern California surfers seeking a way to surf without waves, skateboarding has itself experienced several waves of popularity. Skateboarding was universally outlawed in the 1960s because it was perceived as dangerous, but it enjoyed a revival in the 1970s and another in the 1980s, helped along by Marty McFly, the skateboarding hero of the *Back to the Future* movies. Since the 1990s skateboarding has once again flourished, not only as a popular "extreme" sport but also as a business that generates $500 million annually. Perhaps because it was spawned by the surfer culture, skateboarding has always had a rebel image, and this may explain its renewals of popularity among youth.

SKATEBOARDING CULTURE

In the 1950s, bored surfers attached composite roller skate wheels to pivoting axles and put them on the front and back of a wooden plank. The pivoting action helped with the steering of the board, which was maneuvered much like a surfboard on the water by changing the position of the feet and shifting one's weight. In 1973 the old-fashioned metal wheels were replaced by those from newer roller skates that were made of polyurethane. The new wheels gave the board stability, a smoother ride, and greater traction.

Modern boards are made with scientific precision—often at small specialty companies run by skaters—with lighter, more durable decks (the board itself); neoprene wheels; and lightweight tempered trucks (the pivoting axle assembly). Selling at $100 apiece or more, skateboards are efficient vehicles both for transportation and for the flamboyant tricks that skaters refer to as "grabbing air."

Unlike surfers, skateboarders need nothing but the streets and concrete structures to hone their skills, and they have nothing but those hard surfaces to break their falls. Thus, skateboarding has attracted tough, independent, and rebellious types who have created their own subculture. Skateboarders, who call themselves "thrashers" or "shredders," are largely self-taught. They have their own lingo, clothing style, competitions, publications, and websites.

Thrasher, a radical "zine," and *Transworld Skateboarding*, a slightly more clean-cut publication, are two of the most successful skateboarding magazines. Each has a circulation of well over 150,000. Skateboarding also spawned its own music genre, with a similarly wild image. Groups with names such as Agression and Stinkbug record their "speed metal" music on small labels devoted to "skate rock." One skate rock disc jockey, Skatemaster Tate, describes the music vividly: "It's punk rock and skating rolled up in a ball of confusion and screaming down the alley in a gutter."

Since skateboarding is often done by groups of teenagers on urban and suburban streets, parking garages, empty swimming pools, and the like, skaters are often subject to hostility from the citizenry and law-enforcement officials. Cities have taken two basic approaches in controlling the thrashers: banning skateboarding or developing special parks devoted to the sport. Banning skating is usually unsuccessful simply because breaking the rules is as much a part of the rebellious street sport as wheelies and spins.

SKATE PARKS AND STARS

Skateboard parks offer a compromise that is often at least partially successful. Parks such as the Louisville Extreme Park in Kentucky and the Venice Skatepark in Los Angeles attract hundreds of skaters who show off their tricks on specially constructed ramps and half-pipes. Several skate-park design companies have emerged, such as Team Pain in Winter Springs, Florida, and Grindline in Seattle, Washington. These companies combine engineering with a love of skateboarding so that shredders in communities throughout the country can have state-of-the-art bowls and grinding rails. Some skaters, however, feel that skating is by right a street sport and that relegating it to special parks robs it of its rebel cachet. This antipathy between thrashers and the law resulted in the most widely known skateboarding slogan, seen on bumper stickers nationwide, "Skateboarding is not a crime."

If skateboarding has a superstar, he is Tony "The Birdman" Hawk. Born in 1968 in San Diego, California, Hawk started skateboarding at the age of nine and went professional at fourteen. His relentless style, gravity-defying tricks, and record-breaking number of wins made Hawk a champion and helped skateboarding become a world-class sport. Even after his retirement in 1999, Hawk remains one of the best-known names in skating, with his own line of boards and clothing and a series of Tony Hawk's Pro Skater video games. In 2001 his status as a pop culture icon was confirmed when he appeared on the Fox network's satirical animated show *The Simpsons*, playing opposite that other skateboarding bad boy, Bart Simpson.

Another professional skater, Stacy Peralta, has used his own experiences to preserve skateboard history on film. His 2001 documentary *Dogtown and Zboys* uses archival footage of the Zephyr skateboard team to capture the exhilaration of the early days of the sport in its Southern California birthplace. His second film, *Bones Brigade: An Autobiography* (2012), continues the historical journey into the 1980s and 1990s.

Skateboarding, with more than eleven million participants early in the twenty-first century, has become well entrenched as a flamboyant mode of transportation and expression for youth. Competitions such as the Maloof Money Cup and ESPN's X Games offer both male and female thrashers chances to win cash and medals in events such as downhill, street, and park skating. Though often considered dangerous, skateboarding has far fewer reported injuries than soccer, baseball, and basketball, and many skaters, in addition to the mandatory baggy T-shirt and baggier shorts, now sport kneepads, wrist guards, and helmets. Perhaps the injury statistics are best kept secret from older generations, however, to avoid ruining a perfectly good rebellious outlet.

Tina Gianoulis

SEE ALSO: Back to the Future*; ESPN; Extreme Sports; Leisure Time; Punk;* The Simpsons*; Suburbia; X Games.*

BIBLIOGRAPHY

Cocks, Jay. "The Irresistible Lure of Grabbing Air." *Time*, June 6, 1988, 90.

Evans, Jeremy, and Graham Morecroft. *Skateboarding*. New York: Crestwood House, 1993.

Fried-Cassorla, Albert. *The Ultimate Skateboard Book*. Philadelphia: Running Press, 1988.

Greenfeld, Karl Taro. "Killer Profits in Velcro Valley." *Time*, January 25, 1999, 50.

Hawk, Tony, and Sean Mortimer. *Hawk: Occupation Skateboarder*. New York: Regan Books, 2000.

Thatcher, Kevin J.; Brian Brannon; and Bryce Kanights. *Thrasher: The Radical Skateboard Book*. New York: Random House, 1992.

Thrasher. Accessed April 20, 2012. Available from http://www.thrashermagazine.com

Skating

From its ninth-century, northern European origins as a means for hunting and traveling on ice, skating has been explored for its leisure possibilities. By the time that iron skates—or *schaats*, as their sixteenth-century Dutch inventors called them—had replaced their wooden or bone predecessors, their transformation to recreational usage was well under way. This can be seen in some of Pieter Brueghel's sixteenth-century paintings of peasants skating on the canals of Belgium and the Netherlands, activities that were made famous in Hans Christian Andersen's fairy tales of Denmark. Not so long after iron blades were invented, skates that could snap on to the sole and heel of boots were being manufactured by the Acme Skate Company in Halifax, Nova Scotia. These skates were electroplated in nickel or gold for the wealthy to carry around in expensive carrying cases.

FIGURE SKATING GAINS POPULARITY

It may be the numerous variations on ice skating that explains its growing popularity today. There is short- and long-track speedskating, barrel jumping, and pairs and figure skating. Originally a sport for the Dutch common folk, speedskating was initially made popular in the Winter Olympics as a sport that involved packs of skaters racing in laps over different distances on a track. The current objective of speedskating is to get around an oval track as quickly as possible (although some of speedskating's most popular races are marathons set on the canals of the Netherlands). Barrel jumping, a common variation of speedskating, was especially popular around the turn of the twentieth century. Skaters, set side-by-side on the ice, would skate as fast as they could and try to jump over as many barrels as possible. Without a doubt, however, it is figure skating—and specifically Sonja Henie's white skates and short skirts in the Olympics of 1928, 1932, and 1936—that commanded the world's attention. Henie's jumps and spins so captured the public imagination that ice skating began to evoke images of talented individuals, alone or in pairs, performing highly technical actions in nearly perfect union with music and all toward the goal of "a clean skate."

Henie was one of the most successful figure skaters ever, maintaining a public skating career for more than forty years. Born in Oslo, Norway, on April 8, 1912, she began skating when she was six years old. At the age of eleven she competed in the Olympics. In 1927 she won the world amateur championship for women, holding that title for ten consecutive years. She won three gold medals in the Winter Olympics of 1928, 1932, and 1936. Trained in ballet, Henie incorporated some of its maneuvers into female figure skating; she was largely responsible for converting a predictable series of colorless exercises into a spectacular and popular exhibition.

After having caught the attention of Americans at the 1930 World Championships in New York, she turned professional after her Olympic triumph in 1936, toured Europe and the Americas as the star of the *Hollywood Ice Revue*, and for a time (1951–1952) she acted as producer of her ice shows. In 1936 she signed with Twentieth Century Fox and starred in ten popular films including *One in a Million* (1936), *Thin Ice* (1937), and *Wintertime* (1943). From 1937 to 1945 she was one of the leading box-office attractions in the motion-picture industry, and she died in 1969 with a fortune estimated at $47 million.

SKATING ON TELEVISION

Since Henie's time, her status as celebrity has been replicated by other female figure skaters. Peggy Fleming, Dorothy Hamill, Katarina Witt, and Kristi Yamaguchi have loomed larger than male figure skaters in the public imagination, paying for this privilege by almost always being cast, as Jane Feuer explains in her essay in *Women on Ice*, as the "wounded bird, a child, or a fairy tale princess." This embodiment of grace has traditionally belied the athleticism necessary to perform the necessary jumps, loops, and spirals that mark elite amateur and professional figure skating careers. The move away from, and reinterpretations of, vestigial images of femaleness and maleness marked figure skating's skyrocketing popularity in the 1990s. The new figure skating was a media-conscious, entertainment-driven form that thrived in the age of tabloid TV. Although part of the tabloidization of skating is attributable to the death of compulsory figures and endless speculation about whom Witt was dating, the current connection between skating and the tabloids owes much of its origin to the disgraceful but unforgettable Tonya Harding and Nancy Kerrigan scrum.

The rivalry between "trailer trash" Harding and "ice princess" Kerrigan, the subsequent scandal in which Harding was found complicit in her ex-husband's assault on Kerrigan at the 1994 U.S. National Championships, and the controversial representation of the two women on the U.S. women's team at the 1994 Lillehammer Winter Olympics are integral in the current popularity of figure skating. Almost 50 percent of U.S. homes with television sets were tuned into the primetime telecasts of the women's figure skating competition, making it the sixth most popular television program ever.

From that point, figure skating increased its allure. Figure skating in the 1990s became a form of public spectacle, the extension of skating beyond competitions such as the Olympics to myriad touring ice shows and pseudo-competitions that appeared regularly on prime-time television. The change was most telling in men's skating, where competitors were acclaimed by fans for their masculine rather than artistic qualities—thus world champion Elvis Stojko performed as a motocross bike-driving, karate-fighting, arm-pumping, quadruple-toe-loop-jumping super male. More telling were the young members of the audience who hooted and hollered as Philippe Candeloro took off his shirt amid squeals of pleasure.

Skating's new popularity was revealed in very full arenas in cities where double axles are more traditionally associated with truckers, not skaters. It was revealed on TV, where the airwaves featured Fox Television's *Rock 'n' Roll Skating Championship* and professional championships on CBS. There were also television specials hosted by individual skaters (Kurt Browning's *You Must Remember This* was considered the best). Finally, rock-and-roll-like touring such as Campbell Soups' *Tour of World Figure Skating Champions* (televised by CBS as *Artistry on Ice*) ensured complete saturation.

CHANGES IN SKATING

Figure skating was rocked by a different kind of scandal at the 2002 Winter Olympics in Salt Lake City, Utah. During the pairs competition, the Canadian pair of Jamie Salé and David Pelletier skated a flawless long program, while the Russian pair, Yelena Berezhnaya and Anton Sikharulidze, made several mistakes, yet the Russians received the gold medal. Afterward, a French judge admitted that a behind-the-scenes deal had been made to trade votes in two events: the top vote for the Russian pair in exchange for a top vote for the French ice-dancing pair. The International Skating Union decided to award the Canadian pairs skaters gold medals but did not revoke the medals received by the Russians.

This black eye to the popular sport prompted swift reform. The International Skating Union (ISU) developed a new judging system that went into effect in 2005. No longer would skaters be rated on a single scale with 6.0 as a perfect score. Instead, each element in their program would have a base value, from which a set number of points could be added or subtracted to indicate the quality of execution. In addition to the technical score, skaters were given points for skating skills, transitions, performance/execution, choreography/composition, and interpretation. Skaters were no longer to be ranked against each other; their resulting numeric scores would determine their final position. Although skating fans found the new system confusing—scores at a major competitions typically range into the 200s and include decimal points—the ISU felt certain that the new system was more fair than the one it replaced.

During the late 1990s and into the first decade of the 2000s, figure skaters placed increasing emphasis on athleticism. Japanese skater Shizuka Arakawa won the women's gold medal at the 2006 Winter Olympics by combining artistry with an astonishing eleven jumps, five of them triples. In contrast, American Michelle Kwan—almost universally acknowledged as one of the most elegant and artistic skaters in the history of the sport—never won an Olympic gold medal despite her nine U.S. titles. Even though she was the favorite in at least two Olympics, she lost the most coveted prize to younger girls who were better jumpers. For example, in 2002 Kwan lost to sixteen-year-old American Sarah Hughes, who landed an unprecedented seven triple jumps.

On the men's side, whereas quadruple jumps were once considered an anomaly, by the first decade of the 2000s men were expected to perform at least one in their routine. In fact, controversy broke out at the 2010 Olympics when American Evan Lysacek became the first male figure skater since 1994 to win the gold medal without having a quadruple jump in his long program; his most complex combination was a triple Lutz to triple toe loop. Many observers felt the top prize should have gone to defending champion Yevgeny Plushenko, who pulled off the more difficult combination of a quad followed by a triple. However, Lysacek's overall performance was more polished, and he racked up more points with his fancy footwork and overall artistry. His victory demonstrated that perhaps the new judging system provided a more complete overall assessment.

From 1989 to 2006 the United States Figure Skating Association membership jumped from 64,000 to 196,000. It is speculated that 35 percent of the audience for figure skating may be male. According to some marketers, figure skating ranks as the sixth most popular televised sport. The prime-time coverage of skating in the 2010 Olympics captured, on average, 13.4 percent of televisions in the United States. In other words, figure skating may have merely completed its compulsory and long programs while its more exciting and even more popular short program awaits.

Robert VanWynsberghe

SEE ALSO: *Fleming, Peggy; Hamill, Dorothy; Hamill, Dorothy; Ice Shows; Kwan, Michelle; Olympics; Sports Heroes.*

BIBLIOGRAPHY

Baughman, Cynthia, ed. *Women on Ice: Feminist Essays on the Tonya Harding/Nancy Kerrigan Spectacle.* New York: Routledge, 1995.

Milton, Steve. *Skate: 100 Years of Figure Skating.* North Pomfret, VT: Trafalgar Square, 1996.

Senft, Jean Riley. *Triumph on Ice: The New World of Figure Skating.* Vancouver: Greystone Books, 2011.

Shivers, Jay S., and Lee J. deLisle. *The Story of Leisure: Context, Concepts, and Current Controversy.* Windsor, IL: Human Kinetics, 1997.

Skelton, Red *(1913–1997)*

One of television's most popular comedians, Red Skelton is fondly remembered for *The Red Skelton Show*, which ran on NBC from 1951 to 1953, and then on CBS from 1953 to 1970 (with a brief return to NBC for the 1970–1971 season). A very likable personality and gifted pantomimist, Skelton also starred

Red Skelton. *Red Skelton, left, poses with Lucille Ball after she presented him with the Governors Award at the Emmy Awards in 1986.* AP IMAGES.

in a series of comedy films and had a career filled with contradictions. In *The Great Movie Comedians*, Ross Wetzsteon writes:

> [Skelton was] a mime whose greatest success was on the radio. A folk humorist in the years when American entertainment was becoming urban. A vulgar knockabout at a time when American comedy was becoming sophisticated and verbal. A naive ne'er-do-well in the age of the self-conscious schlemiel. Red Skelton's career is a study in how to miss every trend that comes down the pike.

Skelton was born Richard Bernard Skelton in 1913, the son of a clown with the Haggenback and Wallace circus. His father died before he was born, and he grew up in punishing poverty. Active in show business from the age of ten, Skelton trained in stock companies, tent shows, burlesque, and vaudeville. In the 1930s he stumbled upon a formula for finding humor in people's idiosyncrasies and displaying his gift for pantomime, developing his famous routine on the different ways people dunked their doughnuts—he later performed this bit for a two-reel short, *The Broadway Buckaroo*. Skelton developed much of this material with the help of his wife, Edna, who served as his manager, writer, and foil for many years.

MOVIE CAREER

Skelton started his film career in 1938 when RKO hired him to perform some of his vaudeville routines for *Having a Wonderful Time*. In the film Skelton plays Itchy Faulkner, the entertainment director of a resort camp in the Catskill Mountains, performing a routine about the different ways people walk up a flight of stairs. RKO, however, expressed no continued interest in his services. In 1940 Metro-Goldwyn-Mayer (MGM) assigned Skelton to appear as comedy relief in *Flight Command* and two Dr. Kildare films, but his first starring role and real breakthrough came when he got the lead role of Wally Benton, also known as the radio comic "The Fox," who solves mysteries in a remake of *Whistling in the Dark* (1941). Ace comedy writer Nat Perrin added a bounty of snappy lines for Skelton, and a brief series of *Whistling* films was launched. Although this series, which included *Whistling in Dixie* (1942) and *Whistling in Brooklyn* (1943), was not wildly funny, it was unpretentious and diverting and represents Skelton's best film work.

Despite its resources, MGM had difficulty figuring out how to present Skelton, often relegating the new star to more minor comedy relief roles. He was given brief routines in a number of elaborate MGM productions, including *Neptune's Daughter* (1949), *Three Little Words* (1950), *Texas Carnival* (1951), and *Lovely to Look At* (1952). He was most notable in *Bathing Beauty* (1944), where he performed a routine about a woman getting up in the morning, and *Ziegfeld Follies* (1946), where his Guzzler's Gin routine was rechristened "When Television Comes" and represented the comic highlight of this kitchen-sink film.

During his radio series from 1941 until 1953, Skelton developed the characters he is most noted for, including Junior (the Mean Widdle Kid), Freddie the Freeloader, Clem Kadiddlehopper, George Appleby, Sheriff Deadeye, Willie Lump Lump, Cauliflower McPugg, Cookie the Sailor, San Fernando Red, and Bolivar Shagnasty.

Skelton served for a time in the army, and his return vehicles at MGM proved unfunny flops (*The Show-off*, 1946, and *Merton of the Movies*, 1947). One of his better efforts, Vincente Minnelli's *I Dood It* (1943), is loosely based on Buster Keaton's MGM film *Spite Marriage* (1929). Skelton developed a good relationship with the out-of-work and underutilized Keaton, who supplied him with advice about comedy and worked with Skelton on some of his better efforts, notably *A Southern Yankee* (1948) and *The Yellow Cab Man* (1950), both of which credited former Keaton director Edward Sedgwick as "comedy consultant" to keep the resistant front office from getting suspicious. Keaton pinpointed a problem with *A Southern Yankee* right away, noting that when the film began, Skelton, who plays a bumbling northern spy down South, acted like an imbecile and alienated the audience. The scenes were reshot to tone down his nutty behavior. Keaton also contributed the classic gag where Skelton wears a uniform that is half Union and half Confederate, strolling between the two sides to cheers until the charade is discovered.

In *The Yellow Cab Man*, which features a classic routine about Skelton's first day driving a cab, he plays a would-be inventor of unbreakable glass and other "safety" devices. Skelton was also lent to Columbia for *The Fuller Brush Man* (1948), where he plays a door-to-door salesperson who becomes involved in a murder. This film was successful enough to spawn a follow-up, *The Fuller Brush Girl* (1950), starring Lucille Ball, in which Skelton makes a brief appearance. One of his most memorable quips occurred on the occasion of Columbia head Harry Cohn's death. When someone remarked on the large number of people who turned out for the hated studio head's funeral, Skelton returned, "If you give the people what they want, they'll come out."

Skelton's remaining film comedies proved rather lackluster. His final film role involved a series of comedy sketches—miming various aviation pioneers—at the beginning of *Those Magnificent Men in Their Flying Machines* (1965).

MOVE TO TELEVISION

Skelton's true medium turned out to be television. One of his earliest writers was legendary television host Johnny Carson, who got his first on-camera big break when Skelton knocked himself unconscious one day during rehearsal. Carson was quickly summoned to fill in, and CBS liked his appearance enough to offer him his own show in 1955.

Skelton was an inveterate ad libber, much to the consternation of his guest stars, who expected him to follow the script (Tim Burton's movie *Ed Wood* [1994] captures the confusion of Bela Lugosi when he appeared on the show). Skelton delighted in getting his guest stars to break up on camera. The rock band the Rolling Stones made one of their earliest television appearances on Skelton's show.

As his professional life was soaring, however, his personal life turned grim. His nine-year-old son Richard Jr. died of leukemia, and his second wife tried to commit suicide. Skelton's work became more maudlin, and he began losing his audience. He spent his declining years painting a large series of clown faces, which were sold in art galleries across the country. These paintings proved enormously lucrative. Skelton died from pneumonia in 1997 at his home in Rancho Mirage, California.

With his television episodes rarely revived, Skelton is in danger of being forgotten, which is a pity because he was a talented comic with a genuinely inspired gift of mimicry. His gifts put him in the same league as Marcel Marceau. One of the most popular comics of the 1940s and 1950s, he was awarded a Golden Globe for Best Television Series in 1959 and received a Cecil B. DeMille Golden Globe years later, as well as a Governors Award from the Emmys in honor of his contributions.

Dennis Fischer

SEE ALSO: *Ball, Lucille; Burlesque; Carson, Johnny;* Dr. Kildare*; Emmy Awards; Keaton, Buster; Lugosi, Bela; MGM (Metro-Goldwyn-Mayer); The Rolling Stones; Vaudeville;* The Ziegfeld Follies.

BIBLIOGRAPHY

Hyatt, Wesley. *A Critical History of Television's* The Red Skelton Show, *1951–1971*. Jefferson, NC: McFarland, 2004.

Maltin, Leonard. *The Great Movie Comedians: from Charlie Chaplin to Woody Allen*. New York: Crown Publishers, 1978.

Siegel, Scott, and Barbara Siegel. *American Film Comedy*. New York: Prentice Hall, 1994.

Skype

The voice-over-Internet-protocol (VoIP) service known as Skype is one of the most popular and longest-running applications for making phone and video calls over the Web. With more than 650 million registered users and up to forty million people using the service at any given time, Skype is the largest computer-based phone service in the world. It allows users to make free voice or video calls to others signed in to the service and can even connect with traditional landlines around the world for a small fee. Since its inception, its popularity has grown as profits for traditional long-distance telephone providers have declined.

Skype was founded in 2003 by Niklas Zennström of Sweden and Janus Friis of Denmark, who had previously owned the peer-to-peer file sharing service KaZaA. Zennström and Friis then adapted the peer-to-peer functionality of KaZaA, essentially creating a network out of users' computers and allowing users to share files and information without connecting to a central server. The free service provided users in even the most remote locations to make voice calls and to instant message one other without the potential disruptions that are introduced when the signal is routed through a third-party server. The popular Skype-Out service—enabling Skype users to call traditional landline and mobile phone numbers for a small fee—was launched in July 2004. Within two years Skype had fifty-four million active users in more than 200 different countries, and in October 2005 the Internet auction company eBay purchased Skype for more than $2.5 billion. Two months later Skype 2.0, which allowed users with webcams to make video calls to one other, was introduced.

As Skype continued to grow in popularity throughout the middle of the first decade of the 2000s, a number of computer and mobile phone manufacturers, such as Dell, Panasonic, Intel, and Packard Bell, began incorporating the software into their products. The company discontinued its free SkypeOut calling in late 2006, offering instead a subscription pricing plan that was significantly cheaper than most long-distance calling plans and that still allowed for free Skype-to-Skype calls. A number of new features were then introduced that targeted Skype's potential as a communications tool for small businesses, including a premium subscription plan for unlimited SkypeOut calls and the ability to transfer files using Skype's instant-messaging service. Tensions between Skype and eBay grew throughout 2007 and 2008, with eBay announcing that it had overvalued the company by around $1 billion and Zennström and Friis departing amid disappointing growth numbers and increasing connectivity issues.

In February 2008 eBay executives appointed Josh Silverman, former CEO of the eBay-owned website Shopping.com, as Skype's new chief executive. Silverman refocused Skype's development on the incredibly popular video-calling service and its business-oriented aspects, such as conference calling, and discontinued a number of underperforming or unpopular features of the program. In March 2009 Skype released an iPhone application that offered free Skype-to-Skype voice and video calls, instant messaging, and inexpensive SkypeOut calls over a wireless Wi-Fi network. The app was incredibly popular, with more than one million downloads in the first thirty-six hours of availability, and a similar application for Android phones appeared in late 2010. Despite Silverman's successful leadership of the company, eBay decided to sell its majority stake, transferring around 70 percent of the company to a group of several different investors (including Zennström and Friis, who acquired a 14 percent stake) for $2 billion in September 2009.

Between 2009 and 2010 Skype's user base grew from 397 million to 560 million, and its revenues grew by around 25 percent to more than $406 million in the first half of 2010 alone. These figures were bolstered by an updated version of the iPhone application, released in May 2010, which made voice and video calls over third-generation (3G) networks possible, essentially permitting users to bypass their minute limitations by making calls over a mobile signal provided by their cellular service. This move drew the ire of a number of mobile carriers, and many chose to block any calls made over 3G networks.

Skype then began exploring the possibility of entering the stock market as a publicly owned company and filed for an initial public offering (IPO) with the Securities and Exchange Commission (SEC) in August 2010, though the company later announced that the IPO would be delayed until 2011. In October 2010 Skype released Skype 5.0, which allowed up to four users to participate in the same video call and which also integrated Skype calling into users' Facebook pages. The former Cisco vice president Tony Bates took over as CEO of Skype in October 2010.

In May 2011 the technology behemoth Microsoft raised eyebrows in the tech community by purchasing Skype for $8.5 billion, a monumental jump from the $2.5 billion valuation of the company just two years prior and Microsoft's largest purchase ever. While Microsoft already offered a range of instant-messaging and video-conferencing software, many suggested that the company viewed Skype as a potential add-on for such Microsoft devices as the Xbox 360 and various Windows-based mobile phones. (A Windows phone Skype app was released in April 2012.) Although Microsoft Skype continued to encounter resistance from mobile carriers in the 2010s, the service sustained its gradual growth, with the company announcing that it had broken its own usage record by logging 41.5 million concurrent users on April 23, 2012.

Jacob Schmitt

SEE ALSO: *Cell Phones; Chatting; Community Media; eBay; Facebook; The Internet; Microsoft; Smartphones; Social Media; Telephone.*

BIBLIOGRAPHY

Abdulezer, Loren; Susan Abdulezer; and Howard Dammond. *Skype for Dummies*. Hoboken, NJ: Wiley, 2007.

Gough, Michael. *Skype Me!: From Single User to Small Enterprise and Beyond*. Rockland, MA: Syngress, 2006.

Huang, Te-Yuan. "Could Skype Be More Satisfying? A QoE-Centric Study of the FEC Mechanism in an Internet-Scale VoIP System." *IEEE Network* 24, no. 2 (2010): 42–28.

Maney, Kevin. "Skype: The Inside Story of the Boffo $8.5 Million Deal." *Fortune*, July 25, 2011.

Max, Harry, and Taylor Ray. *Skype: The Definitive Guide*. Indianapolis, IN: Que, 2006.

Vitaliev, Vitali, and Kris Sangani. "Inside Skype." *Engineering & Technology* 5, no. 6 (2010): 28–29.

Skyscrapers

The skyscraper is a uniquely American invention that came to symbolize the cultural and economic predominance of the United States in the twentieth century. With the invention of the elevator in 1859 and the development of new building materials and techniques, tall buildings have been occupying the heart of American cities since the late nineteenth century. They are both soaring examples of technological capability and symbols of deeper concerns. As architectural historian Carol Willis writes in *Form Follows Finance: Skyscrapers and Skylines in New York and Chicago*, "Skyscrapers are the ultimate architecture of capitalism. The first blueprint for every tall building is a balance sheet of estimated costs and returns." The modern city, center of economic activity and capital of culture, is unimaginable without skyscrapers.

Although the definition of what qualifies as a skyscraper has changed over the years as construction technologies improve, the inherent elements remain the same as they were more than a century ago—a tall building of stacked, repetitive office spaces (and sometimes retail and residential spaces) located in an urban setting. In 1900 the Park Row Building in New York City was, at 391 feet and thirty stories, the tallest building in the world. Today it would be dwarfed in most large cities. In 1997 the twin 1,476-foot Petronas Towers were completed in Kuala Lumpur, Malaysia, surpassing the Sears Tower (later renamed the Willis Tower) of Chicago as the tallest occupied building in the world. By 2010 the 2,717-foot Burj Khalifa in Dubai, United Arab Emirates, dwarfed all existing buildings. By that time, twenty-two of the twenty-five tallest skyscrapers in the world stood in Asia or the Middle East, demonstrating the emerging economic power of these regions in the early twenty-first century and the global exportation of American cultural symbols and economic models.

Skyscrapers. *Skyscrapers dot New York City's Manhattan skyline at night.* SONGQUAN DENG/SHUTTERSTOCK.COM.

DEVELOPMENT OF THE SKYSCRAPER

The century-long evolution of the skyscraper from five-story building to 2,000-foot-plus pinnacle was influenced by many factors. In addition to the invention of the passenger elevator by Elisha Graves Otis in the 1850s, two other important influences were the development of steel framing by William Le Baron Jenney of Chicago in the 1880s and the escalation of real estate prices in downtown areas. Other factors included stylistic trends, legislation concerning building height restrictions, and civic competition (mainly between New York City and Chicago). The first identifiable skyscrapers appeared in Chicago in the 1880s. Masonry buildings, in which stone walls carry the weight of the building, were approaching the limits of their weight-bearing capacity. The sixteen-story Monadnock Building (1891) in Chicago remains the tallest masonry building in the world; because of the load created by this height, the walls of the building are 6 feet thick at the base. By the time of its completion, however, a totally new generation of Chicago-style skyscraper construction was in progress. This change was being led by Louis Sullivan, who wrote a famous essay in 1896 titled "The Tall Office Building Artistically Considered."

With the invention of steel-frame construction, in which a lightweight steel skeleton is covered by a masonry skin, buildings could rise higher and provide more interior space than before while more nearly expressing the spirit of the industrial age. Tall buildings soon appeared in New York City and other cities. As downtown real estate became more expensive, the only logical solution was to build upward. The steel-frame building and its derivatives proved indispensable in the development of the twentieth-century American city.

Skyscrapers embody many things, including technical achievement, economic prosperity, urban congestion, and civic and corporate pride. The extent to which the skyscraper has become an American icon demonstrates how corporate capitalism has come to represent the United States to the rest of the world. Tall buildings as recognizable urban symbols appear in countless movies and television shows, and they have been the subject of paintings, poems, and musical compositions. The Empire State Building (New York City), the world's tallest building for four decades (1931–1972), is one of the most famous silhouettes in the world.

IMAGE OF THE SKYSCRAPER

Skyscrapers provide an instantaneous means of identification in the modern world; they can be used as shorthand for the anonymous twentieth-first-century city. Individual buildings such as the Empire State Building (1931), Willis Tower (1974; Chicago) and Transamerica Pyramid (1972; San Francisco) stand as prominent civic symbols and tourist attractions. One of the most daring and atypical skyscraper designs was never realized: the visionary 1930s proposal by Frank Lloyd Wright for a mile-high skyscraper called "The Illinois."

Tall buildings also serve as advertising for corporations. In the early 1900s corporate capitalists discovered that the skyscraper was a more effective advertisement than any billboard, newspaper, or magazine ad. Beginning with the striking neo-Gothic Woolworth Building (New York City)—designed by Cass Gilbert and the world's tallest building at the time of its completion in 1913—skyscrapers have become indelibly linked with top companies in the United States. Prominent examples of the tall building as corporate symbol include the Gothic-style Chicago Tribune Tower (1922); the American Art Deco Chrysler Building (1930, New York City); two International-style skyscrapers, the Seagrams Building (1958, New York City) and the John Hancock Center (1968, Chicago); and the postmodern AT&T Building (1984, New York City).

The skyscraper form proved so popular that it was also applied outside the business world. The Nebraska State Capitol, designed by Bertram Goodhue and completed in 1932, combined a two-story base with a soaring 400-foot tower that copies the setback style of New York City skyscrapers. The United Nations Secretariat Building (1950), designed by Le Corbusier and the 860–880 Lakeshore Drive Apartments (1951–1952) designed by Ludwig Mies van der Rohe are typical examples of a European high modernist interpretation of an originally American architectural form. These buildings helped pave the way for the international style "glass boxes" typically seen in mid-Manhattan and elsewhere, a style that would become pervasive in the 1950s and 1960s in many other American and European cities.

Following the terrorist attacks on the World Trade Center in New York City on September 11, 2001, many observers believed that the era of skyscrapers had ended. Safety concerns were raised about tall buildings, leading politicians and developers to question whether such buildings already in the planning or early construction stages should be completed. Interest in new skyscraper construction proved resilient, however, and high-rise construction soon began to make a comeback. The interest was led in part both by the attention surrounding construction plans for the World Trade Center site and by inventive new skyscraper designs in China as a result of its embrace of state capitalism. This situation demonstrated that, among their other functions, skyscrapers are an index to the economic health of a society.

In the early twenty-first century, almost every U.S. city of moderate size has at least one tall building—even where real estate prices do not justify it. The skyscraper is a technological and economic solution to an urban problem that has been transformed into a status symbol for cities and developers alike. Because it fulfills so many functions, the skyscraper has proven to be the typical building type for the modern urban world.

Dale Allen Gyure

SEE ALSO: *Advertising; AT&T; Billboards; Chrysler Building; Dime Stores/Woolworth's; Empire State Building; 9/11; Postmodernism; Sears Tower; World Trade Center.*

BIBLIOGRAPHY

Douglas, George H. *Skyscrapers: A Social History of the Very Tall Building in America.* Jefferson, NC: McFarland, 1996.

Dupré, Judith. *Skyscrapers.* New York: Black Dog & Leventhal Publishers, 1996.

Goldberger, Paul. *The Skyscraper.* New York: Alfred A. Knopf, 1992.

Huxtable, Ada Louise. *The Tall Building Artistically Reconsidered.* New York: Pantheon, 1984.

Van Leeuwen, Thomas A. P. *The Skyward Trend of Thought.* The Hague: AHA Books, 1986.

Willis, Carol. *Form Follows Finance: Skyscrapers and Skylines in New York and Chicago.* New York: Princeton Architectural Press, 1995.

Schleier, Merrill. *Skyscraper Cinema: Architecture and Gender in American Film.* Minneapolis: University of Minnesota Press, 2009.

Slaney, Mary Decker *(1958–)*

Mary Decker Slaney, the first woman to win the prestigious Jesse Owens track-and-field award, was one of the greatest mid-distance runners in the United States. She won both the 1,500 and 3,000 meters at the 1983 World Championships in Helsinki, setting thirty-six American and seventeen world records in competitions between 1983 and 1985. Slaney's career began at age eleven. She ran her first marathon when she was twelve and set her first world record at fourteen. Although she managed to remain competitive into her late thirties, Slaney's career was blighted by injuries, most famously at the 1984 Los Angeles Olympics, when she collided with Zola Budd and injured her hip. Though she qualified for four Olympics and competed in three (the U.S. team did not attend the 1980 games in Moscow), Slaney never managed to win an Olympic medal.

After a successful comeback in 1996 at age thirty-eight, Slaney tested positive for high levels of testosterone in 1997. Her name was cleared the following year, when the test was shown to be inaccurate when applied to older women. In 1999, hoping to return to full fitness, Slaney had a series of surgeries to repair stress fractures. Although her legs and feet were operated on more than thirty times, she was unable to return to competitive running.

John R. Deitrick

SEE ALSO: *Olympics; Owens, Jesse.*

BIBLIOGRAPHY

Cherry, Gene. "Even after All the Pain, the Surgery and the Heartbreak, Mary Slaney Still Wants to Run." Reuters, July 28, 2009. Accessed February 2012. Available from http://in.reuters.com/article/2009/07/28/idINIndia-41362720090728

Kardong, Don. "Bright Speed." *Runner's World*, July 1997, 86–90.

Slang

Slang is unconventional, hard-hitting, metaphorical language that is colloquial, sometimes vulgar, and always innovative—nothing registers change in cultural thought faster or more dramatically than slang. Lexicologist Stuart Berg Flexner defines slang more precisely as "the body of words and expressions frequently used by or intelligible to a rather large portion of the general American public, but not accepted as good, formal usage by the majority." Linguists Lars Andersson and Peter Trudgill, however, claim there is no good definition of slang and quote the poet Carl Sandburg: "Slang is a language that rolls up its sleeves, spits on its hands, and goes to work." Although linguists make no value judgments on levels of language, the general public seldom views slang without passion. It is seen as either a harbinger of hope and change (particularly among the young) or as a threat to what is perceived as "proper" language and society.

SLANG'S MANY SOURCES

Informal and spoken rather than formal and written, slang is not the same as dialect, nor is it equal to swearing, although it may take on a vulgar edge, and it often evokes negative attitudes. Characterized by its ability to startle, slang falls below the "neutral register" of daily speech: terms such as *whore, ho, tart*, and *slagheap* for the neutral *prostitute*, for example. Perhaps most importantly, slang changes its identity according to who is speaking. What is slang to one is not to another, depending on one's educational, economic, or social position, and even according to location and generation. Slang is generated from any number of specific language and discourse communities or subgroups: jazz musicians, college students, narcotics addicts, immigrants, the military, show business, street gangs, etc., and more recently, computer geeks. (Even the term *geek* has taken on new meaning, changing from a term of derision to a proudly assumed label. The term now signals someone highly skilled rather than someone who is inept.) From each of these sometimes overlapping groups comes specific terms that identify practices and behaviors particular to their members.

Distinct lifestyle choices fuel the need to find a language to name evolving social behaviors and thought, which often challenge more established cultural codes. *Mallie*, a term unimaginable prior to the rise of American shopping malls, refers to a person (usually young) who frequents shopping malls for socialization and entertainment. Although most slang is generated by male speakers, the rise of feminism has spawned a female slang or "girl talk," showing the degree to which ideas about gender are changing. Because slang is spoken rather than written, it lacks the status of standard written English. Once slang terms appear in dictionaries, they are seen as having gained currency and, therefore, fuller entrance into the culture. Until then, slang is fully accessible only to insiders of particular subgroups.

SHIFTS IN SLANG OVER TIME

Slang also changes over time, and either disappears quickly or becomes fully integrated into the language. Few, if any, would now recognize the word *knucker*, which originated in the criminal world of the mid-1880s, but most would understand its current incarnation, *pickpocket*, which comes from late-eighteenth-century criminal slang. Drug slang changes quickly, in part so that drug dealers can more easily spot undercover agents. *Phone, bike*, and *bus*, once slang versions of the more formal *telephone, bicycle*, and *omnibus*, have now all but replaced the original terms. Most slang coinages are local in both time and place; much of it, like other cultural phenomena, originates in such large cities as New York or London and fans out to distant towns and cities.

The exact origin of slang is not known, although given the nature of language as a living, changing entity, it is probably as old as language itself. Andersson and Trudgill identify Aristophanes, the fifth-century BCE Greek playwright, as the first writer to use slang. The Roman writers Plautus, Horace, Juvenal, and Petronius also employed slang for stylistic purposes, and William Shakespeare used slang in his plays. During the nineteenth and twentieth centuries, underworld criminal societies became rich and potent sources of slang, some of which is reflected in early detective fiction by such writers as Wilkie Collins and Agatha Christie.

What differentiates slang from other categories of speech (such as jargon or argot) is one's reasons for using it. In *Slang, Today and Yesterday*, Eric Partridge identifies several reasons for using slang, including the desire to be different, novel, or picturesque; to enrich the language; to engage in playfulness; to identify one's self with a certain school, trade, or social class; to reduce or disperse the pomposity or excessive seriousness of an occasion; or to be secret. Slang is always used self-consciously, with a desire to create a particular identity. One might say (but not write) affectionately, "Sweetheart, you da cat's meow," or "Yo—what's happenin'?"

In the twentieth century, the development of slang has paralleled the rise of dominant cultural movements throughout the decades. The 1920s left its mark with jazz, women's rights, and the rise of the machine, creating such terms as *flapper* (a female dancer in a short skirt), *percolate* (to run smoothly), and *ciggy* (cigarette). The 1930s contributed *dehorn*, a hobo word for bootleg whiskey or denatured alcohol, and such railroad slang as *groundhog*, meaning a train's brake operator. The 1940s was the decade of the military with such coinages as *peashooter*, from World War II army air force pilots to denote a fighter pilot or plane, and the word *buddy* (meaning "pal"), which was heavily used by American GIs during World War II and took on a particularly sentimental connotation. This term later evolved into several variations such as *ace boon* or *ace buddy* in the black community. The 1950s beatnik generation revived 1930s jive talk and used such enduring slang phrases as "cool it" to mean "relax," and such colorful phrases as "cool as a Christian with aces wired" to signify someone who is tranquilly confident.

By the 1960s political unrest resulted in the use of such words as *dove* and *hawk*, which by the 1980s became accepted terms for antiwar advocates and the military, respectively. The youth culture (or "NOW generation") coined such phrases as "where it's at" to signify being up to date, and also used the term *groady* (with variations *grotty* and *groddy*) to denote anything that was disgusting, nasty, or repellent. Often this was followed by the phrase "to the max" for emphasis. The 1970s drug scene left numerous terms, such as *crack* for a type of cocaine and *narc* for an undercover narcotics agent.

During the 1990s the rise in reliance on computers created not only a whole new way of life but also a language to describe it, although this resulted in a computer jargon rather than a computer slang. Nonetheless, such terms as *PC* (personal computer) and *e-mail* (electronic mail) were not even thought of prior to the development and widespread use of personal computers. By the end of the 1990s, the term *Y2K* was commonly used to signify "the year 2000." The terms *millennium bug* and *Y2K*, which were incorporated into the dictionary, referenced anticipated problems (that never arose) stemming from the inability of existing computer programs to recognize dates beyond the year 1999.

During the first decade of the twenty-first century, the language continued to import lexical items from the computer industry and the rise of cell phones and handheld devices. The emergence of smaller and less expensive computers promoted a major shift in the exchange of ideas and the spread of information, creating a worldwide discourse community based on personal computing and cell phone use. An entirely new international vocabulary developed, shorthand for sharing news and information, that spread quickly throughout the world. Initially the domain of younger people, cell phones and social networking grew exponentially, creating with them entirely new verb forms, such as *texting, Facebooking*, and *tweeting*. As the demand for, and use of, instant communication has grown, such terms have found their way into mainstream national and international media, contributing to radical social change in the Middle East and causing traditional news outlets to embrace the new media. These rapid developments in technology bear witness to the impact of new cultural phenomena on language change.

DOCUMENTING EVER-CHANGING SLANG

While slang itself always reflects contemporary trends of thought, the practice of recording slang in Anglo-American dictionaries goes back more than 200 years. The British antiquarian Francis Grose published *A Classical Dictionary of the Vulgar Tongue* in 1785, the first known lexicon of slang. Grose's work went through several editions and remained the seminal work in the field until John C. Hotten's *A Dictionary of Modern Slang, Cant, and Vulgar Words* was published in 1859. From the late nineteenth century through the early twentieth century, several dictionaries of slang were produced, but it was not until 1937, when Partridge published the landmark *A Dictionary of Slang and Unconventional English*, that slang gained respectability. This text was enlarged and reprinted several times through the 1980s and remains one of the best resources available. Also significant was Harold Wentworth and Stuart Berg Flexner's *Dictionary of American Slang*, published in 1960.

Since then, numerous dictionaries of slang have appeared. The titles of these texts alone trace the degree to which slang has become more accepted by the general public; by the late 1990s slang was viewed with an increasing degree of amusement, as illustrated in such playful titles as *Juba to Jive: A Dictionary of African-American Slang*. As public sentiment moved toward a greater sense of multiculturalism during the 1990s and the first decades of the new millennium, slang enjoyed increased acceptance, although with a recognition of its lower than standard status in the language.

Lolly Ockerstrom

SEE ALSO: *Christie, Agatha; E-mail; Facebook; Gangs; Multiculturalism; Sandburg, Carl; Texting; Twitter; World War II.*

BIBLIOGRAPHY

Andersson, Lars, and Peter Trudgill. "Slang." In *Bad Language*. Cambridge, MA: Basil Blackwell, 1990.

Chapman, Robert L., ed. *New Dictionary of American Slang*. New York: Harper & Row, 1986.

Flexner, Stuart Berg. "Preface to the Dictionary of American Slang." In *New Dictionary of American Slang*. New York: Harper & Row, 1986.

Kovecses, Zoltan. *American English: An Introduction*. Peterborough, ON: Broadview Press, 2000.

Lewin, Esther, and Albert E. Lewin. *The Thesaurus of Slang*. New York: Facts On File, 1994.

Major, Clarence, ed. *Juba to Jive: A Dictionary of African-American Slang*. New York: Penguin Books, 1994.

Partridge, Eric. *Slang, Today and Yesterday*, 2nd ed. London: Routledge, 1935.

Partridge, Eric. *A Dictionary of Slang and Unconventional English*. London: Routledge & Kegan Paul, 1937.

Rawson, Hugh. *Wicked Words: A Treasury of Curses, Insults, Put-Downs, and Other Formerly Unprintable Terms from Anglo Saxon Times to the Present*. New York: Crown Trade Paperback, 1989.

Spears, Richard A., ed. *Slang and Euphemism: A Dictionary of Oaths, Curses, Insults, Ethnic Slurs, Sexual Slang and Metaphor, Drug Talk, Homosexual Lingo and Related Matters*. New York: Signet, 1991.

Wentworth, Harold, and Stuart Berg Flexner, eds. *Dictionary of American Slang*. New York: Thomas Y. Crowell, 1960.

Slasher Movies

With the possible exception of the hard-core porn flick, no modern film genre has managed to achieve quite the level of commercial success in spite (or because) of its inherent controversy as has the slasher movie. Otherwise known as the "stalker," "dead babysitter," or "teenie-kill" pic, the "slasher" label has been adopted by most fans and critics to designate the entries in a voluminous collection of remarkably similar post-1960 horror films. In these movies, isolated psychotic males, often masked or at least hidden from view, are pitted against one or more young men and women (especially the latter) whose looks, personalities, or promiscuities serve to trigger recollections of some past trauma in the killer's mind, thereby unleashing his seemingly boundless psychosexual fury.

Although the precise formula of the slasher movie varies depending on one's initial characterization, the genre's exploration (at times its exploitation) of some or all of the following themes has remained strikingly consistent through the years: male-upon-female voyeurism, gender confusion and sexual perversion, the spectacle of murder, the efficacy of female self-defense, the substitution of violent killing for sexual gratification, and the utter inability of traditional authority figures to eliminate a communal threat. Vilified by feminists for supposedly promoting misogynistic messages and targeted for censorship by outraged parents and lawmakers, the slasher movie has

Texas Chainsaw Massacre. *A poster advertises the 1974 release of* Texas Chainsaw Massacre. VORTEX-HENKEL-HOOPER/BRYANSTON/THE KOBAL COLLECTION.

been treated as unworthy of critical discussion by most mainstream academics, presumably because of its "low-culture" status. In recent years, however, the progressive potential of a genre once dismissed as "violent pornography" has been examined by film theorists as well as cultural historians.

ORIGINS

The slasher has its roots in two 1960 films, Alfred Hitchcock's *Psycho* and Michael Powell's *Peeping Tom*. Although the former movie has since received immeasurably more critical and commercial attention than the latter, together they are responsible for establishing many of the slasher's primary generic elements. These elements include an "explanation" of the killer's motive in quasi-psychoanalytic terms; a figuring of the main victim as a sexually transgressive female; and a focus on intimate assault with sharp, phallic, penetrating implements. It is tempting to read the subsequent history of the slasher as little more than elaborations on the themes introduced in these two films.

Like *Psycho* before it, Tobe Hooper's *The Texas Chainsaw Massacre* (1974) took for inspiration the monstrous crimes of necrophilic serial killer Ed Gein. Unlike *Psycho*, however, Hooper's film emphasizes gore and bodily carnage, thereby situating itself within the tradition of Herschell Gordon Lewis's notorious "splatter" films, *Blood Feast* (1963) and *The Wizard of Gore* (1970). *The Texas Chainsaw Massacre* also contributed two important elements of its own to the slasher movie formula: a group of adolescent victims who are picked off one by one and a "final girl" who undergoes a lengthy, terrifying ordeal in the film's second half, only to come out alive at the end.

Although John Carpenter's *Halloween* (1978) eschewed the gore of *The Texas Chainsaw Massacre* in favor of impressively subtle startle effects, it kept the latter film's youthful victims and made its final girl (Jamie Lee Curtis, daughter of *Psycho* star Janet Leigh) even more aggressive and self-reliant. The unprecedented commercial success of this movie ensured its place at the head of the "stalker cycle" class; between 1978 and 1981, no fewer than 11 *Halloween*-inspired slashers were made (including *Friday the 13th*, *Prom Night*, *Terror Train*, and *Graduation Day*), all structural, if not quite stylistic, copies of the original. In these movies the predator-prey theme takes on unprecedented importance, as does the emphasis on "creative" murders and a reliance on camera shots taken from the killer's point of view. To what extent this camerawork forces viewer identification with the killer, however, remains an open question.

Despite the final girl's ever-increasing strength and ferocity—as exemplified by Ripley (Sigourney Weaver) in the *Alien* series of outer-space slashers—public debate over the genre's antisocial consequences only intensified in the 1980s. Representatives from numerous states, citing hastily acquired and somewhat dubious "empirical evidence" for support, complained of a direct cause-and-effect relationship between the depiction of graphic violence in films such as *Friday the 13th* and the increase in violent crimes perpetrated by youths. In 1984 the Video Recordings Act passed through Britain's Parliament on the heels of an effort to restrict the consumption of arbitrarily designated "video nasties" (the vast majority of which were slashers). By 1989 bills were passed in Colorado, Missouri, Ohio, and Texas granting local prosecutors the power to decide which videos cross the line of "excessive violence" and so cannot be rented to persons under age eighteen without parental permission.

It is arguable that at least some of this negative attention was unnecessary, even self-defeating. By 1986 the slasher movie was in a state of decline, primarily because of an overreliance on convention and a glut of predictable entries. But just like its best-known psychopaths, Michael Myers and Jason Voorhees, the slasher would rise from the dead. *Fatal Attraction* (1987), *Pacific Heights* (1990), and especially the Oscar Award–winning *Silence of the Lambs* (1991)—the so-called yuppie slashers—brought a heretofore unimagined respectability to the genre. And with the appearance of self-consciously reflexive slashers such as *Scream* (1996), *Scream 2* (1997), and *Halloween H20* (1998) came a whole new range of convention-bending possibilities.

REMAKES

At the turn of the millennium, filmmakers drew on the nostalgia of the late 1990s slashers to produce a range of remakes (Marcus Nispel's *The Texas Chainsaw Massacre* [2003] and *Friday the 13th* [2009], Rob Zombie's *Halloween* [2007], Glen Morgan's *Black Christmas* [2006], Dennis Iliadis's *The Last House on the Left* [2009], Alexandre Aja's *The Hills Have Eyes* [2006], and Samuel Bayer's *A Nightmare on Elm Street* [2010]), sequels (*Scream 3* [2000] and *Scream 4* [2011], *Halloween: Resurrection* [2002], *Jason X* [2002], and *Seed of Chucky* [2004]) and novelty crossovers or 3-D experiments (*Freddy vs. Jason* [2003], *Night of the Living Dead 3-D* [2006], and *My Bloody Valentine 3-D* [2009]). In the middle of the decade, James Wan's runaway hit *Saw* (2004) initiated a new wave of incredibly gory films based on the capture and excruciating torture of a group of victims. Dubbed "torture porn" by film critics, this new wave of meticulous, ultraviolent slashers includes seven different *Saw* films (2004–2010), the *Hostel* trilogy (2005–2011), and one-off films like *The Human Centipede* (2010) and *The Cabin in the Woods* (2011). While critics raised the familiar complaints of misogyny, exploitation, and gratuitous violence in response to the rise of the "torture porn" genre, it undoubtedly helped to revive an industry that, at the turn of the twenty-first century, had little to offer fans other than tedious remakes and sequels to favorite films from the slasher heyday of the late 1980s.

One thing is clear: no easy answer to the question why slasher movies have proven so popular exists. Whether they enforce conservative values by demonstrating "the inefficacy of sexual freedom" (Vera Dika), promote tolerance by "constitut[ing] a visible adjustment in the terms of gender representations" (Carol Clover), or further a feminist agenda by "articulating the legitimacy of female rage in the face of male aggression" (Isabel Pinedo), it can hardly be denied that these films appeal to different audiences at different times and for different reasons or that they will continue to engender heated debate in homes, classrooms, and courtrooms.

Steven Schneider

SEE ALSO: *Academy Awards;* Alien*;* Cult Films*;* Fatal Attraction*;* Friday the 13th*;* Halloween*; Hitchcock, Alfred; Horror Movies;* Night of the Living Dead*; Pornography;* Psycho*;* Scream*;* The Silence of the Lambs*; Weaver, Sigourney.*

BIBLIOGRAPHY

Barker, Martin, ed. *The Video Nasties: Freedom and Censorship in the Media*. London: Pluto, 1984.

Clover, Carol J. *Men, Women, and Chain Saws: Gender in the Modern Horror Film*. Princeton, NJ: Princeton University Press, 1992.

Dika, Vera. "The Stalker Film, 1978–81." In *American Horrors: Essays on the Modern American Horror Film*, ed. Gregory Waller, 86–101. Urbana: University of Illinois Press, 1987.

Fahy, Thomas R. *The Philosophy of Horror*. Lexington: University Press of Kentucky, 2010.

Hantke, Steffen. *American Horror Film: The Genre at the Turn of the Millennium*. Jackson: University Press of Mississippi, 2010.

Harper, Jim. *Legacy of Blood: A Comprehensive Guide to Slasher Movies*. Manchester, UK: Critical Vision, 2004.

Nowell, Richard. *Blood Money: A History of the First Teen Slasher Film Cycle*. New York: Continuum, 2010.

Pinedo, Isabel. " . . . And Then She Killed Him: Women and Violence in the Slasher Film." In *Recreational Terror: Women and the Pleasures of Horror Film Viewing*, 69–95. Albany: State University of New York Press, 1997.

Rockoff, Adam. *Going to Pieces: The Rise and Fall of the Slasher Film, 1978–1986*. Jefferson, NC: McFarland, 2002.

Schneider, Steven. "Uncanny Realism and the Decline of the Modern Horror Film." *Paradoxa: Studies in World Literary Genres* 3, nos. 3–4 (1997): 417–428.

Slinky

Since its introduction to the public at Gimbels department store in Philadelphia in 1945, the Slinky has been one of the best-selling toys in the United States. A simple, steel spring developed by Richard James, a naval engineer who was trying to produce an anti-vibration device for ship instruments, the Slinky has become one of the most widely recognized toys, with more than 300 million sold by the time of its sixtieth anniversary. When James and his wife, Betty, first demonstrated the Slinky's rhythmical step-by-step movement at Gimbels, they sold their entire lot of 400 Slinkys in ninety minutes. The Slinky has been inducted into the National Toy Hall of Fame and included on the Toy Industry Association's "Century of Toys List."

In addition to playing with Slinkys, innovative Americans have used them as pecan-picking devices, envelope holders, light fixtures, and makeshift radio antennae. Beginning in 1962, children watching television have heard the Slinky jingle with its famous lines, "It's Slinky, it's Slinky, for fun it's a wonderful toy / It's Slinky, it's Slinky, it's fun for a girl and a boy." In addition to being featured in television commercials, the Slinky has appeared in the films *Hairspray* (1988) and *Ace Ventura: When Nature Calls* (1995) and—as Slinky Dog, a leading animated character—in the *Toy Story* movies (1995, 1999, and 2010). A variety of Slinky models have been manufactured, including a large brightly colored plastic model for younger children and an $80 gold Slinky sold by the elite retailer Neiman Marcus. The original steel model sold in 1945 for $1. Fifty years later, in 1995, the same model (changed only by having its ends crimped for safety) sold for a mere $1.99. Its low price helped lead to its presence, at one time or another, in the vast majority of American homes.

Sharon Brown

SEE ALSO: *Leisure Time;* Toy Story*; Toys.*

BIBLIOGRAPHY

The National Toy Hall of Fame. "Slinky." Accessed November 21, 2011. Available from http://www.toyhalloffame.org/toys/slinky

Panati, Charles. *Extraordinary Origins of Everyday Things*. New York: Harper & Row, 1987.

Slumdog Millionaire

Slumdog Millionaire (2008) is an Academy Award–winning film based on the debut novel of Indian writer and diplomat Vikas Swarup. Simon Beaufoy, screenwriter for *The Full Monty* (1997) and *Salmon Fishing in the Yemen* (2012), adapted the novel for the screen. Directed by Danny Boyle (codirected in India by Loveleen Tandan), the film is an epic tale that combines a set of Dickensian characters—namely innocent orphans dogged by sinister, if slightly cartoonish, villains—with Bollywood conventions, such as ensemble song and dance numbers and a host of contrived chance encounters that advance the plot. The movie won eight Academy Awards, including Best Picture, Best Director, and Best Screenplay; seven awards from the British Academy of Film and Television Arts, again including Best Film; and four Golden Globes, including Best Drama. Despite such widespread acclaim, the film was not without its detractors. Protests in India raged around what many saw as the derogatory attitude implicit in the use of the word *slumdog*, and the intellectual elite labeled the film "middlebrow" and charged Beaufoy, Boyle, and company with oversimplifying the complexities of Indian culture.

The movie recounts the life of Jamal Malik, played by British actor Dev Patel, an orphan from the slums of Mumbai who wins a large sum of money by correctly answering questions on India's most popular quiz show, the Indian version of *Who Wants to Be a Millionaire*. The ability of an uneducated street kid to answer such questions raises suspicions in some quarters, and the night before Jamal is to return to answer the big-money question, he is arrested and interrogated in a brutal fashion by Mumbai policemen who accuse him of cheating. As he explains how he knew the answers to the questions, his life is revealed in a series of flashbacks that show the horrors of his past with his brother Salim and another street urchin, Latika (played as a teen by Freida Pinto). Jamal's past includes abject poverty, homelessness, crime, and torture, but his relationship with Latika is an abiding source of joy. The story is a mix of true crime, adventure, and romance.

As numerous reviewers have noted, the picaresque structure and the triumph of the underdog hero who overcomes tremendous odds in a social setting designed to make his survival nearly impossible are reminiscent of the novels of Charles Dickens. The pure-hearted hero who prevails; the reunion of siblings; the pursuit of love; the evil villains; and, of course, the musical finale are all Bollywood tropes. The combination led to diametrically different interpretations from critics. A *USA Today* reviewer praised the mix of fairy-tale fantasy and disturbing realism and found the movie both universal and essentially Indian. A writer for *Cineaste*, a quarterly periodical about the art and politics of film, agreed on the Dickens–Bollywood mix but found the film lacking in genuine Dickensian sensibilities and dated in its Bollywood tribute. Furthermore, he declared the image of India in *Slumdog Millionaire* a false one, dumbed down for an audience who prefers the comfortably fake to the uncomfortably real.

The general public worldwide championed the view of the *USA Today* critic. The movie grossed more than $140 million at the North American box office and another $30 million-plus in DVD sales. It was also successful in Europe, Australia, and Japan, particularly after its Oscar wins. Worldwide, the film grossed more than $377 million. But the movie's success story, like its protagonist's, is one of triumph against the odds. In May 2008 Warner Independent Pictures, the company that owned the North American rights to the movie, was shut down, and Warner Brothers, skeptical of the commercial appeal of *Slumdog Millionaire*, considered skipping a theatrical release and sending the film straight to DVD. Film history would be different had Fox Searchlight Pictures, the mini-studio behind hits such as *Little Miss Sunshine* and *Juno*, not bought 50 percent interest in *Slumdog Millionaire* and agreed to handle distribution in the United States. The movie became Fox Searchlight's highest-grossing film, a happy ending for the studio and all those connected to the movie.

North American success did not translate well to Indian audiences, however, who are well known for preferring the movies of their own nation's filmmakers to Hollywood's offerings. *Slumdog Millionaire* enjoyed a large debut there, but Indian moviegoers seeking escapist fare found the tale of slum children familiar and unappealing. National pride played a role as well, leading some to reject the film on the grounds that it was "poverty porn" and "slum voyeurism." Slum dwellers also protested, displaying banners that read "I AM NOT A DOG." One slum leader in Patna went so far as to sue the movie's Indian cast and crew for offending slum dwellers. There have also been charges that the slum children hired as actors in the movie were exploited by the filmmakers. Boyle, along with all others involved in the film's production, vehemently denies that the young actors were treated unfairly in any way. As for the title, Boyle insists that it is a term coined from *slum* and *underdog* and is intended as an affirmation of the character's resilient spirit and eventual triumph.

Pulitzer Prize–winning journalist Katherine Boo was among those who found Boyle's depiction of life in India's poor communities misleading and irresponsible. Her nonfiction work *Behind the Beautiful Forevers; Life, Death, and Hope in a Mumbai Undercity* documents the experience of Abdul, a teenage waste collector who lives in an indigent community near the Mumbai International Airport, just as Jamal does in Boyle's film. Unlike Jamal, however, Abdul will not get out of the slum by making a fortune on a game show. Nonetheless, in Boo's starker slum the people do not require Jamal's outrageous luck to make a good life for themselves.

Wylene Rholetter

SEE ALSO: *Academy Awards; Hollywood;* Who Wants to Be a Millionaire.

BIBLIOGRAPHY

Boo, Katherine. *Behind the Beautiful Forevers: Life, Death, and Hope in a Mumbai Undercity.* New York: Random House, 2012.

Corliss, Richard. "From Slumdog to Top Dog." *Time*, January 29, 2009.

Koehler, Robert. "Slumdog Millionaire." *Cineaste*, Spring 2009, 75.

Puig, Claudia. "Epic *Slumdog Millionaire* Is Pricelessly Original." *USA Today*, November 14, 2008.

Travers, Peter. "Slumdog Millionaire." *Rolling Stone*, November 13, 2008.

Sly and the Family Stone

At their apogee, Sly and the Family Stone made music that broke racial and commercial barriers, combining soul, rhythm-and-blues (R&B), doo-wop, white rock, and British Invasion influences into an ineluctably delicious package that slithered and grooved and, at times, shouted from radios and turntables across America. For its time, the group's personnel was no less remarkable: an integrated, multigender lineup in which the musicians switched instruments and roles with a fluidity as snaky as the band's trademark syncopated backbeat. Emerging in 1968, Sly and the Family Stone filled a vacuum in the musical landscape, presaging a whole new form of funk with their musical cross-pollination and incandescent live shows.

SYLVESTER STEWART

Sylvester Stewart, the guiding force behind this musical potpourri, was born in Texas and grew up in Vallejo, California, a tough town in the San Francisco Bay Area. As a child, Stewart sang in church choirs, playing music with his siblings and learning guitar, piano, and organ, among other instruments. By all accounts, he was already something of a wunderkind by the time he met up with radio personality Tom Donahue and was hired as resident producer for Donahue's Autumn Records label. Stewart produced much of the mid-1960s San Francisco rock music, crafting albums for groups such as the Beau Brummels, the Mojo Men, and the Vejtables. However, he was an imperious presence in the studio, a notorious perfectionist, and by the time the acid-rock groups began to beat a path to Autumn Records' doorstep, he decided he had more important things to do besides marshal stoned musicians. (He allegedly forced Grace Slick and the Great Society through 200 takes, resulting in exactly one completed song.) Stewart took a DJ job at a local black radio station, where, always iconoclastic, he interspersed Beatles and Bob Dylan tracks among the regular Stax-Volt and Motown fare.

THE LATE 1960s

"The pop scene was then at a turning point," writes Dave Marsh in *The "Rolling Stone" Illustrated History of Rock and Roll.* "Both Soul and Rock were trapped—the former by its own conventions, the latter by its increasing solemnity as it pursued High Art. Sensing a gap, Sly moved to fill it with his characteristic mixture of calculation, conviction, and dumb luck." He had formed a bar band and was regularly plying his trade with what would become the nucleus of Sly and the Family Stone while hunting for a record label. His first effort for Columbia, *A Whole New Thing* (1967), was praised by critics but a commercial failure. Nevertheless, Columbia was interested enough to give him a second chance.

Through the rest of the decade, Sly and the Family Stone registered an impressive list of hit singles, music as mold breaking as it was danceable, with an ideological twist: part populist, part utopian hippie. In songs such as "Dance to the Music" (1968), "Everyday People" (1968), "Everybody Is a Star" (1969), and "You Can Make It if You Try" (1969), Sly and the Family Stone preached a message of total reconciliation, expressing, in the words of Marsh, "the sentiments of the Haight and the hopes of the ghetto."

Onstage, the band dressed like psychedelic peacocks, sporting fringes, satin shirts, leathers, and bangles. Musically, there were role reversals, epiphanies, and surprises. The women played instruments, the men sang, the whites grooved, the blacks freaked out. The result was a revelation and a call to arms; when Sly sang "I Want to Take You Higher"—as he did for a half million people at Woodstock in the summer of 1969—audiences believed him.

THE 1970s

However, being a spokesperson for inner-racial unity is a tough act, and like Jimi Hendrix before him, Stewart was resistant to become swept up in the internecine squabbles between the New Left and Black Power groups. There were other problems too. As one of the highest-paid performers in the business, Stewart succumbed to the excesses of stardom. He began missing shows, his behavior became more eccentric, and no new music was forthcoming, although his progeny were filling the charts with their versions of Sly's Whole New Thing. When he broke his silence late in 1971 with *There's a Riot Goin' On*, he took his formula and stood it on its head. It is an abstract, introspective album that shies away from declamations, acknowledging instead the bitter realities of racial inequity—utopia turned dystopic. It was the perfect soundtrack for the waning of ideals from the 1960s, a brilliant synthesis of despair. If the album's success was any measure—it rose to number one on the charts and generated three hit singles—Stewart had once again hit the mark.

There's a Riot Goin' On was a tour de force, but it was also a blind alley. Apparently, Stewart was unable to extricate himself from this self-created musical cul-de-sac. As the 1970s progressed, his musical output diminished significantly. A 1976 *Jet* magazine article reported Stewart had gone broke. Rumors abounded that he had spiraled into addiction-fueled seclusion, living alone in his mansion without a telephone or much to eat. In 1979 he released *Back on the Right Track*, but it was an aberration. The silence continued.

TROUBLED TIMES

Stewart was plagued by legal and financial problems through the 1990s and into the first decade of the 2000s, and while he appeared for a tribute to the band at the Grammys in 2006, he remained reclusive. The 2008 documentary *Coming Back for More*, following fan and director Willem Alkema's search for and discovery of Stewart, depicts the aging singer living in drug squalor in a trailer. Although he has appeared more frequently in public since the documentary was released, Stewart's 2011 album *I'm Back! Family and Friends*, his first musical offering in decades, featured only three new tracks and was panned by critics.

In the dialectic of creativity, Stewart's career followed a predictable arc from synthesis to innovation to decline, but if he

Sly and the Family Stone. *The members of Sly and the Family Stone in 1968 included, from left, Rosie Stone, Larry Graham, Sly Stone, Freddie Stone, Gregg Errico, Jerry Martini, and Cynthia Robinson.* MICHAEL OCHS ARCHIVES/GETTY IMAGES.

could only go so far, he left in his wake a legion of imitators that kept his vision very much in evidence. Established soul groups let their hair down and started turning out records with a pointed political subtext. Sly and the Family Stone's slinky drum beats, slapped bass lines (a technique Stone bassist Larry Graham is credited with inventing), and minimalist keyboard arrangements were responsible for the evolution of funk and disco. Furthermore, the sartorial splendor—rhinestones, leathers, gold lame—that was the band's trademark was embellished by everyone from George Clinton to Earth, Wind and Fire. In their music and flamboyance, artists ranging from Rick James to Prince have paid homage to Sly and the Family Stone. Indeed, these disparate artists sprang from the Sly and the Family Stone template, and as Marsh writes, "No one has gone past them."

Michael Baers

SEE ALSO: *British Invasion; Disco; Doo-wop Music; Funk; Prince; Rhythm and Blues; Rock and Roll; Woodstock.*

BIBLIOGRAPHY

Miller, Jim, ed. *The "Rolling Stone" Illustrated History of Rock and Roll.* New York: Random House/Rolling Stone Press, 1980.

Reed, Ishmael, ed. *19 Necromancers from Now.* New York: Doubleday, 1970.

Smartphones

A smartphone is a mobile phone that has a display screen and a variety of other features, including personal information-management systems and a computer operating system (OS) that allows users to perform a variety of functions. Popular applications include cameras, GPS navigation units, Internet browsers, e-mail, games, music, and video. The most recent smartphones usually have high-resolution touchscreens that allow users to type messages and do Web searches with the touch of a finger. The computers within the phones can access and download high-speed data by way of Wi-Fi and mobile broadband.

The first smartphone prototype was the IBM Simon, designed in 1992 as a concept product for COMDEX, the computer industry trade show held annually in Las Vegas, Nevada. Released to the public in 1993 and sold by BellSouth, the Simon was the first phone to offer a calendar, address book, world clock, calculator, note pad, e-mail client, games, and the ability to send and receive faxes. Instead of pressing the physical buttons featured on earlier mobile phones, owners could use their fingers to input telephone numbers on a touchscreen, or they could use a stylus to create faxes and memos. Then, in 2000, the touchscreen Ericsson R380 became the first mobile phone released and marketed specifically as a "smartphone." It was the first phone to implement a mobile OS, using Nokia's Symbian platform. Soon after, nearly all smartphones employed a mobile OS manufactured by companies such as Apple, Google, Microsoft, Nokia, Research in Motion (RIM), and Linux. From there, innovations in smartphone technology appeared in rapid succession.

In early 2001, Palm, Inc., released its Kyocera 6035. The first widely purchased smartphone in the United States, the 6035 integrated the features of a personal digital assistant (PDA) with Palm's new Palm OS mobile platform. Following the 6035's success, Palm released the Treo, which was the first phone available to the public to feature a full QWERTY keyboard. Phone maker RIM began its domination of the business market in 2002 with the release of the BlackBerry smartphone, which appealed to professionals with its secure e-mail client. By 2009 the BlackBerry had secured a customer base of about 32 million subscribers for RIM.

The smartphone market changed in January 2007 when the Apple computer company announced the impending release of its iPhone. Using its best-selling MP3 music device, the iPod touch, as a prototype, Apple promised customers a new phone experience. For the iPhone, Apple adapted the Mac computer OS into a mobile platform called iOS. The iPhone was distinguished by its use of only a large, multi-touch screen that responded to fingers instead of older input methods such as stylus, keyboard, or keypad. The mobile Web version of the browser Safari built into iOS was hailed by *Ars Technica* as "far superior" to anything else offered at the time, and its e-mail client featured a sleeker interface than the dominant BlackBerry's. Most importantly, the iPhone's integrated iTunes software and store made it easy to move music and video content onto the phone.

Released in June 2008, the second-generation iPhone allowed users to install third-party software applications, known as "apps," directly onto the phone via iTunes. While apps had been available for other phones, Apple allowed users to download them over Wi-Fi and third-generation (3G) connections rather than physical connection to a computer, as most smartphones at the time required. In 2009 alone, apps sales accounted for $769 million of Apple's revenue. The popularity of apps and of games such as Angry Birds gave rise to the sardonic catchprase, "There's an app for that."

Meanwhile Google had moved into the phone market in late 2007, partnering with the Open Handset Alliance to develop the Android OS. The system was free for use by any carrier and could be modified to suit their needs, thanks to its open-source platform. Google created its own phone brand, but most Android phones were produced by established phone manufacturers such as Samsung and HTC. Its free, open-source platform appealed to consumers who resented Apple's exorbitant pricing and monolithic control. As Android rose in popularity, spurred by the release of dozens of phones utilizing its OS, a sense of competition arose between Apple and Android devotees.

With Android joining the apps craze and releasing Android Market in 2008, the two computer giants soon dominated the smartphone market, overtaking BlackBerry's and Palm's systems. Microsoft tried to gain traction by replacing its mobile CE system with the entirely new and positively reviewed Windows Phone OS, which featured Windows' new Metro interface, but Microsoft fell far behind in the market. As of 2011 the most common mobile OSs were Google's Android, Nokia's Symbian, and Apple's iOS.

By the end of 2011 smartphones accounted for 44 percent of the U.S. mobile-phone market and seemed to be changing not only the way people communicated, but national and global culture as a whole. Unrest in the Middle East in 2011, known as the Arab Spring, was fueled in part by the ability of protesters to take high-quality photos and videos on smartphones and upload them to Facebook and Twitter without use of a computer.

Mobile phone operating systems were beginning to influence computer OSs. Microsoft announced that the Metro interface would be part of its forthcoming Windows 8 and that it would begin to integrate its computers, tablets, and phones into a common ecosystem. Apple brought elements of iOS back into its desktop system OSX for the Lion release. By 2012 the future of computing looked more and more like it would be driven by mobile innovation. The prevalence of smartphone technology had led to extensive wireless Internet access, the rise of digital social networks, a new app economy, and an overhaul in the way people communicated, shopped, and worked.

Michele Lellouche

SEE ALSO: *Apple Computer; BlackBerry; Cell Phones; E-mail; E-Readers; IBM (International Business Machines); The Internet; Sexting; Telephone; Texting.*

BIBLIOGRAPHY

Arthur, Charles. "The History of Smartphones: Timeline." *Guardian*, January. 24, 2012.

Cheng, Jacqui. "iPhone in Depth: The *Ars* Review." *ArsTechnica*, July 9, 2007.

Grobart, Sam, and Ian Austen. "The BlackBerry, Trying to Avoid the Hall of Fallen Giants." *New York Times*, January 28, 2012.

King, Rachel. "Almost Half of U.S. Mobile Users Own Smartphones, Survey Says." *ZDNet.com/Blog*, September 1, 2011. Accessed June 2012. Available from http://www.zdnet.com/blog/btl/almost-half-of-us-mobile-users-own-smartphones-survey-says/57067

McLaughlin, Kevin. "BlackBerry Users Call for RIM to Rethink Service." *CRN.com/News*, December 17, 2009. Accessed June 2012. Available from http://www.crn.com/news/mobility/222002587/blackberry-users-call-for-rim-to-rethink-service.htm;jsessionid=TDs-9s3DeXwdSYUHg4YH3A**.ecappj01

Reed, Brad. "A Brief History of Smartphones." *PCWorld*, June 18, 2010. Accessed June 2012. Available from http://www.pcworld.com/article/199243/a_brief_history_of_smartphones.html

Schneidawind, J. "Big Blue Unveiling." *USA Today*, November. 23, 1992.

Smith, Anna Nicole *(1967–2007)*

Known for her larger-than-life persona, Anna Nicole Smith rose to fame as *Playboy*'s 1993 Playmate of the Year but is best known as a subject of tabloid journalism. Portrayed alternately as "white trash," a "dumb blond," or a "gold digger," Smith became a spectacle who was judged more than admired.

Smith's humble beginnings fed her public persona. She was born Vickie Lynn Hogan in Mexia, Texas, in 1967. While still in her teens she had a child, Daniel, and was married for a short time. Smith then became a topless dancer and attempted to find modeling work. She attracted the attention of Howard Marshall II, a wealthy patron of the club where she danced. The 1994 wedding of the twenty-six-year-old Playmate and the eighty-nine-year-old billionaire attracted intense speculation. In his 2005 essay in *Feminist Review*, Jeffrey A. Brown suggested that the fact that Smith was "depicted as [a] simple-minded seductress who used her cartoonish sexuality to swindle an old man out of his hard-earned fortune reflects the American belief that capital, and thus class standing, must be appropriately earned."

Smith's brash personality and penchant for revealing clothing guaranteed media attention. Although some commentators praised her confidence and embraced her as an alternative image of beauty, most treatments of her were derogatory and judgmental. In October 1994 she sued *New York Magazine* after a photo of her squatting in a revealing miniskirt and eating from a bag of junk food appeared on its cover under the headline "White Trash Nation." Smith claimed she had been misled about the magazine's intentions and that the particular photo had not been intended for publication. The controversial image contributed to the perception of Smith as someone who lacked taste and was unable to control her appetites, whether for food or for sex.

After her husband's death in 1995, Smith became embroiled in litigation over his fortune, eventually taking her case to the U.S. Supreme Court. The American public watched with fascination as Smith battled her husband's children for access to his money, struggled with her weight, and attempted to revive her career. In 2002 E! Entertainment capitalized on Smith's notoriety with a reality show about her life. As its tagline, "It's not meant to be funny. It just is," suggests, the show repeatedly poked fun at its star's perceived lack of intelligence.

After her show ended in 2004, Smith garnered attention for increasingly erratic behavior. Scrutiny intensified in 2006 when she announced she was pregnant and gave birth to a daughter, Dannielynn. Three days after Dannielynn's birth, Smith's son died of a drug overdose. Smith became increasingly despondent, and in February 2007, following months of legal controversy concerning Dannielynn's paternity, she died from an overdose of prescription drugs.

Even after her death, Smith remains a controversial figure. She is viewed by some as victim of both class and gender bias and by others as a cunning opportunist. For scholars such as Brown, Smith is a cautionary figure, whose public vilification serves as a warning to those who fail to submit to social expectations.

Greta Gard

SEE ALSO: Playboy; *Reality Television; Strip Joints/Striptease; Supermodels.*

BIBLIOGRAPHY

Brown, Jeffrey A. "Class and Feminine Excess: The Strange Case of Anna Nicole Smith." *Feminist Review* 81 (2005): 74–94.

Long, Rob. "The Story of Anna Nicole: A Typical American Second Act." *National Review*, March 19, 2007, 33–34.

Thomas, Evan; Catharine Skipp; and Carmen Gentile. "Anna Nicole's Tabloid Odyssey." *Newsweek*, February 19, 2007, 50–53.

Smith, Bessie *(1894–1937)*

Elizabeth "Bessie" Smith was born in Chattanooga, Tennessee, and became known as the "empress of the blues." She began her career with Chappelle's Rabbit Foot Minstrels, starring Ma Rainey, who taught Smith the art of blues singing. Smith developed her own style of powerful and theatrical blues with a jazz orientation, which became the accepted classic blues style. Her first recording, "Down Hearted Blues" (1923), sold 780,000 copies in the first six months. She recorded until 1933, toured extensively with her troupe, the Liberty Belles, and appeared in the film *St. Louis Blues* (1929). Smith died while on tour in Mississippi when her car was hit by a truck and run off the road.

Charles J. Shindo

SEE ALSO: *Jazz; Rainey, Gertrude "Ma"; Rhythm and Blues.*

BIBLIOGRAPHY

Albertson, Chris. *Bessie*. New York: Stein & Day, 1972.

Manera, Alexandria. *Bessie Smith*. Chicago: Raintree, 2003.

Smith, Dean *(1931–)*

North Carolina's Dean Smith retired after the 1997 season as the all-time winningest head coach in college basketball. Smith's 879 wins over thirty-six years surpassed legendary Kentucky coach Adolph Rupp by three games (the record was broken a decade later by Bobby Knight). For twenty-seven consecutive years, Smith's squads won twenty or more games, and they captured two national titles along the way.

Smith coached some of the game's best players during his years at North Carolina, including Billy Cunningham, James Worthy, Mitch Kupchak, and Michael Jordan. He also saw many of his assistant coaches go on to become head coaches, including Roy Williams and Larry Brown. But the achievement of which Smith is most proud is the fact that 97 percent of his players graduated with a degree. In the 1980s and 1990s, as college hoops came to seem ever more glamorous under the bright lights of increasing television coverage, Smith represented the finest values of amateur athleticism.

D. Byron Painter

SEE ALSO: *Basketball; Jordan, Michael; Knight, Bobby; National Basketball Association (NBA); National Collegiate Athletic Association (NCAA); Rupp, Adolph.*

BIBLIOGRAPHY

Chansky, Art, and Michael Jordan. *The Dean's List: A Celebration of Tar Heel Basketball and Dean Smith*. New York: Warner Books, 1997.

Price, S. L. *Far Afield: A Sportswriting Odyssey*. Guilford, CT: Lyons Press, 2007.

Wolff, Alexander. "Fanfare for an Uncommon Man." *Sports Illustrated*, December 22, 1997, 32–43.

Wolff, Alexander. "Dean Smith Unplugged." *Sports Illustrated*, December 22, 1997, 50–55.

Wulf, Steve. "Tears for the Tar Heels: North Carolina Coach Dean Smith Takes Himself out of the Game for Which He Has Done So Much." *Time*, October 20, 1997, 93.

Smith, Kate *(1909–1986)*

Kate Smith was known as "the First Lady of Radio," and with good reason. She starred on network radio from 1931 to 1947, always opening her show with her theme song, "When the Moon Comes over the Mountain." The lyrics of this song were adapted from a poem Smith had written as a teenager to celebrate her native Shenandoah Mountain region. She is most closely linked to Irving Berlin's "God Bless America," which she introduced on Armistice Day in 1938. Berlin was so pleased with her treatment of the song that he granted her exclusive rights to sing it on radio in the late 1930s. Moving to television in later years, Smith continued to be a popular entertainer, prompting pop music critics Roy Hemming and David Hajdu to write in *Discovering Great Singers of Classic Pop* (1991): "For at least five decades, Kate Smith ranked close to apple pie, baseball, and the Statue of Liberty among America's best-loved and most instantly recognized symbols."

Smith became a household name within a month of her radio show's debut on her twenty-second birthday on May 1, 1931. The long-running program, originally called *The A&P Bandwagon*, provided the first radio appearances for such show-business luminaries as Greta Garbo, John Barrymore, Bert Lahr, and Mary Boland. Comedians on their way to the top, including Henny Youngman and the duo Abbott and Costello, were also first brought to national attention on her show.

Kate Smith. *Kate Smith first performed Irving Berlin's "God Bless America" in 1938, and it quickly became her signature tune.* HULTON ARCHIVE/STRINGER/ARCHIVE PHOTOS/GETTY IMAGES.

FROM MAIN STREET TO BROADWAY

Smith's homespun, small-town image flowed naturally out of her upbringing. Her birthplace was the small town of Greenville, Virginia, and she was originally billed on radio as "the Songbird of the South." As a child, she began singing in church services, and her talent was evident. During World War I an eight-year old Smith sang at Liberty Loan rallies, where she was once introduced to President Woodrow Wilson.

After the war Smith entered amateur contests in the Washington, D.C., area and aspired to a career behind the footlights. Her family, fearing that her increasing girth would make her the target of taunts in a theatrical career, insisted that she study nursing. However, Smith found that she was unhappy as a nursing student, and when she was sixteen she tried out some song routines in Washington vaudeville houses and then headed for New York City.

While waiting her turn in an amateur contest, she saw a young dancer bring down the house doing the Charleston and became convinced that, despite her bulk, she could do the vigorous, hip-wiggling dance herself. She worked it into her closing number and won a standing ovation. The show's headliner, Broadway star Eddie Dowling, hired her for a small part in a new musical, *Honeymoon Lane* (1926), in which she sang "Half a Moon" and danced the Charleston. The review in the *New York Times* read: "*Honeymoon Lane* is Colorful & Lavish; Kate Smith, 250-pound Blues Singer, a Hit."

A RADIO STAR

Several other Broadway shows followed. Made up in blackface, she sang "Hallelujah" in Vincent Youman's *Hit the Deck* (1927). In George White's *Flying High* (1930), she played star Bert Lahr's mail-order bride and suffered his relentless jibes about her size. Every performance she heard him say, "When she sits down, it's like a dirigible coming in for a landing."

After the show closed, she made her radio debut on Rudy Vallee's variety show, attracting the attention of Columbia Records executive Ted Collins, who offered her a recording contract and became her personal manager. Collins secured an eleven-week run for Smith at a vaudeville institution, the Palace Theatre in New York, as well as a contract with CBS for a fifteen-minute network radio show four nights a week. The show became an instant success that only grew in popularity over the next sixteen years. By 1933—during the Great Depression, no less—Smith was making $3,000 a week, the highest salary of any woman in radio.

During World War II Smith traveled over a half million miles to entertain the troops, and she sold more than $600 million in war bonds. Her recording of "God Bless America" sold thousands of copies, and following the lead of Berlin, she gave all her royalties to the Boy Scouts and Girl Scouts.

TELEVISION AND BEYOND

Smith moved to television in 1950, hosting a daytime variety show aimed mainly at housewives. When her popularity waned in the 1960s, Collins stepped in. Noting that Judy Garland's career had been rekindled by a famous concert, Collins arranged for Smith to appear at Carnegie Hall in 1963. The concert spurred a new RCA recording contract and numerous guest appearances on television. When Collins died in 1964, Smith stopped performing.

Her career was revived again starting in the early 1970s—this time, in a curious way—when the Philadelphia Flyers hockey team discovered that they always won when her rendition of "God Bless America" preceded the game. The team made her its official team sweetheart. In addition, she was a guest on TV shows hosted by Ed Sullivan, Jackie Gleason, Dean Martin, and the Smothers Brothers.

In the mid-1970s Smith embarked on a major national tour, but it was interrupted in Lincoln, Nebraska, and ultimately canceled when she became ill. Severe diabetes made her a virtual recluse for the next ten years. In 1982 she was awarded the U.S. Medal of Freedom by President Ronald Reagan. George T. Simon, former editor of *Metronome*, observed, "From 1931 onward, Kate Smith did indeed seem to personify the country—idealistic, generous, home-spun, sentimental, emotional, and proud."

Benjamin Griffith

SEE ALSO: *Abbott and Costello; Barrymore, John; Berlin, Irving; Boy Scouts of America; Broadway; Garbo, Greta; Girl Scouts; Lahr, Bert; The Musical; Radio; Television; Vaudeville; War Bonds; Youngman, Henny.*

BIBLIOGRAPHY

Hayes, Richard K. *Kate Smith: A Biography*. Jefferson, NC: McFarland, 1995.

Hemming, Roy, and David Hajdu. *Discovering Great Singers of Classic Pop*. New York: Newmarket, 1991.

Lackmann, Ronald. *Same Time . . . Same Station: An A–Z Guide to Radio from Jack Benny to Howard Stern*. New York: Facts On File, 1996.

Pitts, Michael R. *Kate Smith: A Bio-bibliography*. New York: Greenwood Press, 1988.

Smith, Patti *(1946–)*

Patti Smith made her mark in disparate artistic worlds, with a canon of studio albums starting with *Horses* (1975), several books of poetry, and a world-renowned performing style that led to her nickname "the queen of punk." As she once said, her music is "three chord rock merged with the power of the word."

Smith was born in Chicago but raised in rural Woodbury, New Jersey, the eldest of Grant and Beverly Smith's four children. Isolated and sickly as a child, Smith was encouraged to be creative by her mother and lived an intense imaginary life in games with her siblings and, as she grew older, in her writing, which was informed by the work of Arthur Rimbaud, Bob Dylan, James Brown, and the Rolling Stones. A literate punk icon in the 1970s, Smith achieved her greatest success with the single "Because the Night," off her album *Easter* (1978). In 1979 she left performing, opting to start a family in suburban Detroit, Michigan, with her husband Fred Smith, formerly the guitarist for MC5 and the leader of Sonic Rendezvous Band.

In 1994 Smith lost her husband, her brother Todd, and her longtime friend and former lover Robert Mapplethorpe to untimely deaths. She slowly returned to performing and publishing with a book of poems, *Early Work* (1994), and the albums *Gone Again* (1996) and *Peace and Noise* (1997). Her output increased in the first decade of the 2000s, as she released three albums in steady succession: *Gung Ho* (2000), *Trampin'* (2004), and *Twelve* (2007). She also wrote an acclaimed memoir, *Just Kids*, which chronicles the beginning of her relationship with Mapplethorpe as they learned about New York City together in the summer of 1969. It won the 2010 National Book Award for nonfiction.

Smith has earned a number of other honors over the years, including induction into the Rock and Roll Hall of Fame in 2007. Perhaps the single greatest tribute to her influence on American culture, however, is that she was chosen as the last performer to take the stage at the legendary punk rock club CBGB, playing a three-and-a-half-hour concert on October 16, 2006, before the doors of the venue closed forever.

Celia White

SEE ALSO: *Brown, James; Dylan, Bob; Mapplethorpe, Robert; Punk; Rock and Roll; The Rolling Stones.*

BIBLIOGRAPHY

Johnstone, Nick. *Patti Smith: A Biography*. London: Omnibus Press, 1997.

Roach, Dusty. *Patti Smith: Rock and Roll Madonna*. South Bend, IN: And Books, 1979.

Smith, Patti. *Early Work, 1970–1979*. New York: W. W. Norton, 1994.

Smith, Patti. *Patti Smith Complete: Lyrics, Reflections and Notes for the Future*. New York: Doubleday, 1998.

Smith, Patti. *Just Kids*. New York: Ecco Press, 2010.

Smith, Rosamond

SEE: *Oates, Joyce Carol.*

Smith, Will *(1968–)*

Beneath his trademark charm and affability, Will Smith is a disciplined and dedicated professional who built his career as an "A"-list actor with hard work and careful planning. A popular rap star whose albums had made more than a million dollars by the time he was eighteen, Smith moved seamlessly into television and then into films, where he became a box-office powerhouse. In addition to being one of Hollywood's most dependably bankable leading men, Smith is also one of its most stable, a committed family man who proudly supports his children's budding acting careers.

Willard Christopher Smith II was born in 1968 in Philadelphia, one of four children of Willard and Caroline Smith. Though his parents separated when he was thirteen, they both remained present in his life. His father was a disciplinarian who taught his children persistence and responsibility, lessons Smith later credited for giving him the drive to succeed. Raised in the largely black neighborhood of West Philadelphia and schooled in both a primarily white Catholic elementary school and a mostly black high school, Smith learned early how to communicate across the racial divide. He used that knowledge to create a rap music style that was accessible to both urban black and suburban white teenagers. An excellent student, Smith turned down a Massachusetts Institute of Technology scholarship in computer science in order to pursue his music career.

FINDING SUCCESS

West Philadelphia has a rich musical heritage, and young Will began to create the rapid-fire rhymes of rap by the time he was thirteen. With musical partner "Jazzy Jeff" Townes, Smith, using the name "The Fresh Prince," became first a popular local celebrity, then a national recording star with such hits as "Parents Just Don't Understand" (1988). DJ Jazzy Jeff and the Fresh Prince released five albums, *Rock the House* (1987), *He's the DJ, I'm the Rapper* (1988), *And in This Corner . . .* (1989), *Homebase* (1991), and *Code Red* (1993). Smith's playful vitality and impish charm attracted the attention of producer Quincy Jones, who approached the young rapper with the offer of his own television show. *The Fresh Prince of Bel-Air*, which premiered on NBC in 1990, highlighted the adventures of a cheeky young teenager named Will Smith who comes from Philadelphia to live with his wealthy relatives in the ritzy Los Angeles suburb of Bel-Air.

The Fresh Prince was frothy entertainment, and Smith was a novice actor, but his cocky sweetness appealed to audiences, and by 1993 the show had risen to number fourteen in the Nielsen ratings with general audiences and number one with black audiences. Smith tackled his lack of experience with typical determination by taking acting classes and studying videos of successful comic actors. Anxious to work in films, he carefully planned the next steps of his career, starting slowly with a small part in the 1992 Marc Rocco film *Where the Day Takes You*. He followed that with a scene-stealing role in the 1993 comedy *Made in America*, in which he began to prove his abilities as an actor.

Smith's next role as a gay con artist in the 1993 film *Six Degrees of Separation* was a departure from his appealing comic persona. He gave a riveting performance and proved that he could carry a lead role with confidence, though his refusal to do a scripted same-sex kissing scene gained some notice. He followed in 1995 with the Michael Bay film *Bad Boys*, a police-buddy comedy that introduced Smith to the action genre that would make him a superstar. His next films, both science fiction/action blockbusters, were *Independence Day*, directed by Roland Emmerich in 1996, and *Men in Black*, made by Barry Sonnenfeld in 1997. Smith's easygoing but steadfast heroes delighted audiences and helped make *Independence Day* and *Men in Black* among the highest-grossing films up to that point.

DEVELOPING VERSATILITY

Following a career plan of exploring and developing new facets of his skills, Smith followed the cartoonish *Men in Black* with the more cerebral Tony Scott thriller *Enemy of the State* (1998). In 2001 he stepped away from action altogether to take on the challenging role of boxing champ Muhammad Ali in Michael Mann's *Ali*, a stunning tour-de-force performance for which he received a Best Actor Academy Award nomination.

Smith continued to make comedies, including the sequels *Men in Black II* (2002) and *Bad Boys II* (2003), before tackling a series of more serious films, beginning with *The Pursuit of Happyness* in 2006. In a role that drew upon his own fierce love for his children, Smith plays an unemployed and homeless father struggling to care for his son while he rebuilds his life. The film was acclaimed internationally, and Smith received his second Oscar nomination for Best Actor.

Alongside his dynamic acting career, Smith has maintained a stable and committed family life. During the *Fresh Prince* years he was married to Sheree Zampino (1992–1995), and the two had a son, Willard III, nicknamed Trey. In 1997 he married actor Jada Pinkett, and they have two children, Jaden and Willow. Both have begun their own acting careers and have costarred with their famous father: Jaden in *The Pursuit of Happyness* and Willow in the dystopian science fiction thriller *I Am Legend* (2007). Trey appeared with his father in a music video titled "Just the Two of Us" in 1998.

Tina Gianoulis

SEE ALSO: *Academy Awards; Ali, Muhammad; Blockbusters; Celebrity; Celebrity Couples; Disc Jockeys; Hollywood; Movie Stars; Rap; Sitcom; Television.*

BIBLIOGRAPHY

Iannucci, Lisa M. *Will Smith: A Biography*. Santa Barbara, CA: Greenwood Press, 2010.

Koehler, Robert. "No Grasp beyond His Reach: For Smith, Finding a Comfort Zone as an Actor Means It's Time to Move On." *Variety*, December 15, 2008, S4.

Rhodes, Joe. "Iron Will." *Premiere*, November 1998, 90.

Schoemer, Karen. "His Future's So Bright . . . " *Newsweek*, July 7, 1997, 63.

Talley, Lori. "Will to Power: How a Fresh-Faced Philly Rapper Became One of America's Best and Biggest Actors." *Back Stage West*, January 17, 2002, 1.

Smithsonian Institution

Established by an Act of Congress in 1846 with the bequest of English scientist James Smithson, the Smithsonian Institution is a research center that holds some 100 million artifacts and specimens in nineteen museums and galleries. The mission of the Smithsonian includes public education, national service, and scholarship in the arts, sciences, history, and culture. Artifacts held by the Smithsonian include the Wright Brothers' 1903 Flyer, the Hope Diamond (one of the world's largest deep blue diamonds), the Star-Spangled Banner, Judy Garland's red slippers from *The Wizard of Oz* (1939), Harrison Ford's fedora and leather jacket from *Raiders of the Lost Ark* (1981), and Archie Bunker's chair and Fonzie's leather jacket from the television shows *All in the Family* (1971–1979) and *Happy Days* (1974–1984), respectively. Duke Ellington's papers are housed in the Smithsonian, and the institution also owns the Folkways Records back catalog.

Museums and galleries of the Smithsonian include the National Air and Space Museum, the National Museum of American History, the National Museum of African Art, the National Museum of Natural History, the Smithsonian American Art Museum, and the National Portrait Gallery, all of which are in Washington, D.C. The Smithsonian-run Cooper-Hewitt National Design Museum is in New York City, while the National Museum of the American Indian has locations in both Washington, D.C., and New York City. The Smithsonian is also responsible for the National Zoo and a number of scientific research institutes.

Many of the museums are located on the Mall in Washington, and a visit to the capital seems to require an obligatory visit to at least one of these buildings. From April through October the various Washington locales of the Smithsonian are packed with visitors. One summer highlight is the Festival of Folklife, which explores the diversity of American and world cultures and takes place on the Mall in late June and early July.

In 1970 the Smithsonian launched its own magazine, *Smithsonian*, which carries general readership articles on the arts, the environment, sciences, and popular culture. The magazine has a readership approaching eight million. Another magazine, *Air & Space/Smithsonian*, was created as an extension of the Smithsonian Institution's National Air and Space Museum. It examines the culture of aviation and space. The institution's website is another avenue for educating the American public, with online access to the Smithsonian encyclopedia, collections, and exhibitions, as well as to the magazines' archives.

In the 1990s the Smithsonian engendered considerable controversy with its exhibition *The West as America* at the National Museum of American Art and its *Enola Gay* exhibition at the National Air and Space Museum to mark the fiftieth anniversary of the atomic bombing of Hiroshima and Nagasaki. These exhibitions questioned received versions of history, and the outrage generated broad public debates about history, culture, and the role of academics and museums.

The Smithsonian has continued to make headlines through exhibits such as Subhankar Banerjee's 2003 photographic essay on the Arctic National Wildlife Refuge. *Seasons of Life & Land* raised questions about global climate change. Due to political controversy over the issue, the exhibit was temporarily removed and heavily edited to reflect a more neutral stance on the causes and effects of climate change. But not all of the headlines were controversial. The 2009 film *Night at the Museum: Battle of the Smithsonian*, starring comedian Ben Stiller, captured the imaginations of children so well that the Smithsonian initiated a treasure-hunt activity inspired by the film's plot.

The Smithsonian Institution is a repository of American cultural artifacts. Its purview encompasses nineteen museums, nine research facilities, and more than 150 affiliated museums. As has always been the case, entrance to many of the Smithsonian museums is free; in 2011 the number of visitors to its various locations totaled more than twenty-eight million. The diversity of its collections and activities places it at the center of public understanding of American history and culture.

Ian Gordon

SEE ALSO: All in the Family*; The Bomb; Ellington, Duke; Ford, Harrison; Garland, Judy;* Happy Days*;* Raiders of the Lost Ark*; Stiller, Ben; Washington Monument;* The Wizard of Oz*; World War II.*

BIBLIOGRAPHY

America's Smithsonian: Celebrating 150 Years. Washington, DC: Smithsonian Institution Press, 1996.

Conaway, James. *The Smithsonian: 150 Years of Adventure, Discovery, and Wonder*. Washington, DC: Smithsonian Institution Press, 1995.

Fink, Lois Marie. *A History of the Smithsonian American Art Museum: The Intersection of Art, Science, and Bureaucracy*. Amherst: University of Massachusetts Press, 2007.

"History and the Public: What Can We Handle? A Roundtable about History after the *Enola Gay* Controversy." *Journal of American History* 82, no. 3 (1995): 1029–1144.

Smits, Jimmy *(1955–)*

Emmy Award–winning television, film, and stage actor Jimmy Smits is one of a handful of highly visible Hispanic actors. A cofounder of the National Hispanic Foundation for the Arts, an organization whose mission is to establish opportunities for Hispanic Americans in entertainment, Smits has used his popularity and fame—both of which derive in part from his stunning good looks—to publicize the cause of Hispanics and other minority groups in the entertainment industry. An elegant and truthful actor with a persona that combines charm, sex appeal, and vulnerability with a steely inner core, Smits carved a place for himself as an American cultural icon when he was cast in Steven Bochco's landmark television ensemble drama series, *L.A. Law* (1986–1994) and reached an even higher profile as detective Bobby Simone in Bochco's hard-hitting cop series, *NYPD Blue* (1994–1998).

Born in Brooklyn, New York, on July 9, 1955, to a Puerto Rican mother and a South American (Suriname) father, Smits was raised mostly in Brooklyn. While attending school at Thomas Jefferson High, he made the championship football team but quit playing to become the star of the school's drama club. He went to Brooklyn College where he got a BA in education and worked for a while as a teacher before becoming a student again, earning his master's degree in theater arts from Cornell in 1982. After graduating he traveled around the country working in repertory theater until 1984 when he made his television debut in the pilot episode of *Miami Vice*. The experience was short-lived: Smits was cast as Don Johnson's partner, and his character was killed in the course of the episode.

EARLY CAREER

In 1986 Smits landed the role of Victor Sifuentes, Hispanic public defender turned corporate litigator, in Bochco's critically acclaimed and wildly successful—the number of law school applications in the United States increased dramatically at the height of the show's popularity—*L.A. Law* on NBC. The role of Sifuentes catapulted Smits into stardom, and he became a heartthrob and sex symbol much as George Clooney did in *ER* a few years later. He was nominated for a Best Supporting Actor Emmy every year, finally winning it in 1990, but left the show in 1991 to pursue opportunities on the big screen. However, with the exception of his costarring appearance alongside Jane Fonda and Gregory Peck as a smoldering Mexican soldier in *Old Gringo* (1989) and a role in the 1995 Chicano family drama *My Family, Mi Familia*—both critically respected but commercially unspectacular features—he made only a handful of forgettable films.

Bochco and ABC came to the rescue in 1994 when Smits joined *NYPD Blue* in its second season, playing detective Bobby Simone. For the next five years, he delivered an elegant, understated portrayal of a quietly complex character in perfect counterpoint to the explosive acting of Dennis Franz as Simone's troubled, sometimes bigoted partner, Andy Sipowicz. The gritty cop drama was controversial from the outset because of its coarse language and explicit sexual content, and during its first season many network affiliates refused to carry it. Despite (or maybe because of) this, it was an almost immediate ratings success, as were its sometimes ambiguous lead characters, multidimensional and complex, following a trend already set in other cop series such as *Homicide: Life on the Street* (1993–1999) and *Law & Order* (1990–2010). Smits was thoroughly convincing as an introspective widower who joins the 15th Precinct after months of tending to his dying wife and who raises homing pigeons as a hobby. However, the fact that Simone was conceived as being of French-Portuguese rather than Hispanic descent drew some criticism, emphasized by the fact that the only Hispanic officer was played by an actor of Italian heritage (Nicholas Turturro).

In 1998, with his contract up for renewal, Smits decided to leave *NYPD Blue* in search of fresh challenges. The challenge to the program in finding a way to write him out resulted in a sequence of tense and tear-jerking episodes in which Simone succumbs to previously undetected heart disease. This turn of events in the plot all but dominated the 1998 series and tested Smits's acting abilities. He passed with flying colors. Smits, who Bochco said was the solid, subtle character needed to balance Franz's Sipowicz, was nominated every year for his performance on the show, and Franz won four times during that period. In 1999 Smits won the HOLA Award for Excellence from the Hispanic Organization of Latin Actors.

ONGOING SUCCESS

In 2004 Smits joined the cast of *The West Wing* (1999–2006) for its final two seasons, playing Matthew Vincente Santos, a young senator with two children who wins a presidential campaign against more established politicians by proclaiming a message of hope. Prescient *West Wing* writers did indeed consult a Barack Obama staffer after his impressive 2004 Democratic National Convention address and modeled Smits's character after the real future president. In 2007 Smits starred as Cuban American family businessman Alex Vega in *Cane*, which he also coproduced but which was canceled by CBS. Smits was nominated for an Emmy Award for his performance as Assistant District Attorney Miguel Prado in *Dexter* (2008).

Smits has said he does not see a boundary between television and film and that it is normal for actors to bounce back and forth in search of good roles, though at least one critic has commented that his movie persona tends to be too nice and uncomplicated to be realistic or memorable on the big screen. Smits continues to pair television and film acting, playing Ruben Santiago Sr. in the television movie *Lackawanna Blues* (2005), Daniel Avila in the film *The Jane Austen Book Club* (2007), and Paco in the well-reviewed film *Mother and Child* (2009). He also returned to the stage for two New York Shakespeare Festival performances—*Twelfth Night* in 2002 and *Much Ado about Nothing* in 2004—and starred in *God of Carnage* on Broadway in 2009 and 2010. Speaking in a 1998 *Los Angeles Times* interview with Yvette Doss, Smits said, "The representation of Latinos in the media today is abysmal." His work continues to combat the stereotyped portrayal of Latinos in the media and performing arts.

Joyce Linehan

SEE ALSO: *Bochco, Steven; Clooney, George; Emmy Awards;* ER*; Fonda, Jane;* L.A. Law*; Made-for-Television Movies;* Miami Vice*;* My Family, Mi Familia*;* NYPD Blue*; Obama, Barack; Peck, Gregory; Sex Symbol; Television.*

BIBLIOGRAPHY

Cole, Melanie. *Jimmy Smits*. Childs, MD: Mitchell Lane, 1998.

Doss, Yvette C. "Latino Awards Battle Stereotypes." *Los Angeles Times*, June 4, 1998.

Smoothies

The *Oxford English Dictionary* records 1977 as the first use of the word *smoothie* to refer to a drink consisting of fruit "pureed with milk, yogurt, or ice cream." History suggests that the drink, if not the term, is considerably older. According to some sources, the origin of the smoothie can be found in South America and Latin America, where an abundant supply of exotic fruits and an understanding of the benefits of fresh fruit have long made juice drinks popular. Health food stores on the West Coast began selling pureed fruit drinks as early as the 1930s.

It was not until the 1960s, however, that smoothies gained widespread popularity in the United States. An interest in the Zen macrobiotic diet was common among hippies of that period, and retail health restaurants offered smoothies to cater to the demand, particularly in California. But the largest chain developed in the Southeast. Steve Kuhnau, founder of Smoothie King, a privately owned company based in Louisiana, claims to have developed the first nutritional smoothie in 1967 in an effort to find a high-energy drink compatible with his own allergies. In 1973 he opened a health food store where he sold smoothies, and in 1987 Smoothie King was trademarked and incorporated. Two years later, Kuhnau opened the first franchise in New Orleans. As of 2012 there were more than 600 Smoothie King stores in the United States and abroad.

By the time Smoothie King incorporated, smoothie chains were developing across the United States, a pattern that persisted throughout the 1980s and 1990s. The drinks fit the needs of the wave of fitness-conscious Americans who wanted healthful food with the convenience and ease of fast food. Jamba Juice was the largest of several chains that developed in the 1990s as smoothie shops opened in strip malls and on college campuses across the United States. Jamba Juice founder Kirk Perron, a cyclist who wanted a replenishing energy drink after taxing rides, focused on fruit juice concoctions. He opened his first store, the Juice Club, in 1990. In 2012 Jamba Juice, a public company with more than 700 stores in the United States, is part of the success story of the multibillion-dollar smoothie industry.

By the twenty-first century, the smoothie had moved beyond health food shops and national chains into coffee and ice cream franchises, convenience stores, and fast-food restaurants. Nutritionists began to caution consumers that the healthful smoothie could sometimes prove an unhealthful choice. While smoothies could offer low-calorie, healthful options rich in vitamins, minerals, antioxidants, and dietary fiber, many smoothies contain high-calorie, low-nutrient ingredients. Depending on ingredients and serving size, a smoothie may contain from 100 calories to more than 1,000.

Wylene Rholetter

SEE ALSO: *Energy Drinks; Fast Food; Hippies; Malls.*

BIBLIOGRAPHY

Brown, Ellen. *The Complete Idiot's Guide to Smoothies*. New York: Alpha Books, 2005.

Liebman, Bonnie, and Jayne Hurley. "5 Overrated & Underrated Foods." *Nutrition Action Health Letter* 37, no. 4 (2010): 8–11.

Titus, Don. *Smoothies! The Original Smoothie Book*, vol. 2. Chino Hills, CA: Juice Gallery Multimedia, 2004.

The Smothers Brothers

Comedy-singing team the Smothers Brothers has been entertaining audiences onstage; on record albums; and, most famously, on television for more than fifty years. "Mom always liked you best!" stuttering, slow-witted comic dunce Tom Smothers on guitar would complain to his supercilious, smooth-talking, straight-man brother Dick on bass as they both crooned folk songs and engaged in comic banter, often with pointed political overtones. During the late 1960s the Smothers Brothers' penchant for political satire resulted in one of the most celebrated and infamous cases of television censorship. The brothers battled their network, CBS, over the antiwar and countercultural content of their top-rated variety series, *The Smothers Brothers Comedy Hour*—a precursor of later shows featuring political comedy, such as *Saturday Night Live*. Attempting to bring some of the political and social turmoil of the era into prime time, the Smothers Brothers discovered the limits set by American commercial television in the 1960s for controversial material in entertainment. Their variety show, with its ongoing battles against network censorship, become a flash point of debate about the role of popular entertainment in the process of social change.

EARLY YEARS

Nothing much in the Smothers's background would indicate that they would become rebels against the system. Tom and Dick, born, respectively, in 1937 and 1939, were sons of West Pointer Thomas Bolyn Smothers Jr., who died in a prisoner-of-war camp during World War II. The boys were raised by their mother and stepfather in Redondo Beach, California. Their comic career began while students at San Jose State College, where they found themselves working the burgeoning folk circuit of college clubs, blending accomplished folk singing with eminently clean-cut comedy.

Their first big break into television came in 1961 when Jack Paar introduced them to a national audience on his show. A few years later CBS gave the Smothers their first television series. Running for only one season, 1965–1966, *The Smothers Brothers Show* featured Tom and Dick in a situation comedy. Similar to other contemporary "magical" shows—for example, *My Mother the Car*, *My Favorite Martian*, and *Bewitched*—the Smothers's series had Tom as an apprentice angel who made life difficult for his mortal brother, Dick. The series failed, but CBS remained committed to finding a more appropriate vehicle for the Smothers Brothers' talents.

Debuting on Sunday night in February 1967, *The Smothers Brothers Comedy Hour*, a variety show, found itself in an unenviable position scheduled opposite the long-standing, top-rated NBC stalwart *Bonanza*. CBS's strategy for the *Comedy Hour* was to attract a younger, more urbane audience than was traditionally drawn to the rival network's horse opera. The gambit worked. *The Smothers Brothers Comedy Hour* cracked the top twenty Nielsen ratings in its first two years on the air, in its second year helping to dislodge *Bonanza* from its three-year run as the number-one-ranked series in the country.

In its first season, the series played things fairly safe. The brothers attempted to appeal both to the burgeoning generation of disaffected and politicized baby boomers as well as to their parents. According to *Time* magazine, the Smothers were "hippies with haircuts." The show featured countercultural bands such as Buffalo Springfield singing its anthem of youthful

Smothers Brothers. *Tom, left, and Dick Smothers perform their trademark music and comedy routine in 2004.* ROB HILL/CONTRIBUTOR/FILMMAGIC/GETTY IMAGES.

paranoia and alienation, "For What It's Worth," and also middle-of-the-road Jim Nabors singing "The Impossible Dream." Like Ed Sullivan in his show, the Smothers Brothers in theirs balanced the tastes and sensibilities of the increasingly polarized generations.

CONTROVERSY BEGINS

Controversy and censorship started to plague the series beginning most notably following the *Comedy Hour*'s second season premiere, aired on September 10, 1967. The Smothers had invited folksinger Pete Seeger as a special guest. While the network expressed no qualms about having the previously blacklisted performer appear on the airwaves, CBS balked at a song Seeger proposed to sing: "Waist Deep in the Big Muddy." The song was an allegory about Vietnam and contained the following lyrics, which CBS found unacceptable: "But every time I read the papers / That old feelin' comes on / We're waist deep in the Big Muddy / And the big fool says to push on."

The network disapproved of the disrespectful reference to the president as a fool and, further, felt political material such as this had no place on an entertainment show. The performance was summarily censored. The network's action led to an avalanche of public criticism of the network's high-handed action. CBS eventually relented and allowed Seeger to pay another visit to the show later in the season, when he was permitted to sing the song in its entirety.

Emboldened by the show's popularity, Tom began pushing for more confrontational and cutting-edge material. Despite his slow-witted stage persona, he was both highly intelligent and increasingly aligned with antiestablishment youth politics. He was also the major creative force behind the series. Pushing the envelope of political satire, sexual innuendo, and matters of taste, Tom dared CBS to censor his show. The network responded, and the battle was on.

Many of the flaps between the show and the censors involved material that now seems benign. CBS objected to a sketch about sex education: the words *sex* and *sex education* were unacceptable. The network also objected to a sketch about censorship in which Tom and guest star Elaine May played motion picture censors at work objecting to the use of the word *breast* in a sequence. Says censor Elaine: "I think the word *breast* should be cut out of the dinner scene. I think that *breast* is a relatively tasteless thing to say while you're eating." CBS censors were not amused and blue penciled the entire sketch.

The network was also uneasy with a recurring character on the show, Goldie O'Keefe, a kooky hippie whose comedy revolved around celebratory references to hallucinogenics. In a recurring sketch, a parody of advice shows for housewives titled "Share a Little Tea with Goldie," the character proclaimed, "A lot of you ladies have written in asking when I'm on. . . . Ladies, I'm on as often as possible and I highly recommend it." Some of the marijuana and LSD references evaded censorship as the elderly guardians of taste did not understand that *Goldie*, *tea*, and *Keefe* were drug code words. Comedian David Steinberg created consternation for the network as well with a series of sacrilegious sermonettes. The network began demanding that the Smothers make preview copies of their episodes available for affiliated stations to review—a completely unprecedented move by any network.

CONFRONTATIONS ESCALATE

The most infamous run-ins with the network involved the Smothers's increasingly unapologetic antiestablishment political material. In their third season premiere in September 1968, CBS balked at letting guest star Harry Belafonte do a song criticizing the police and institutional violence meted out to youthful demonstrators at the Chicago Democratic convention the previous month. The number included lyrics such as "Tell all the population / We're havin' a confrontation / Let it be known freedom's gone / And the country's not our own" to images of police rioting against unarmed demonstrators. The network axed the entire number and, to add insult to injury, sold the five minutes' worth of airtime to the Republican Party for a Nixon-Agnew campaign ad. Tom refused to submit his name for Emmy consideration as a writer for fear the network's issues with him would hurt the show's chances; the show did win the Emmy for Outstanding Writing Achievement in Comedy Variety in 1969.

The escalating confrontations between Tom and the network eventually came to a head. In April 1969, with a few weeks yet to go in the television season, Robert D. Wood, president of CBS television, informed Tom by wire that the brothers were fired. The ostensible reason was that the Smothers had not delivered an acceptable broadcast tape in time for preview by network censors and affiliated stations. The unprecedented forced removal of a television series from a network schedule led to public uproar. Tom attempted to launch a free speech campaign in Washington, D.C., to force the network to relent, but to no avail. The Smothers eventually filed a lawsuit against the network for wrongful dismissal. They won, but it was a Pyrrhic victory, as *The Smothers Brothers Comedy Hour* would not be revived for twenty years.

In the meantime, the brothers continued to turn up on the broadcast dial. A year after being kicked off of CBS, ABC gave them a summer variety series. The wind was out of Tom's sails, however, and the series was not picked up in the fall. In January 1975 NBC gave the brothers a try with yet another variety series, but that one also did not last the full season. The brothers continued touring in their highly successful stage concerts and were frequent guests on various television shows.

Then, nearly twenty years after being booted off CBS's airwaves, the network invited the brothers back to do a *Smothers Brothers Comedy Hour* special in 1988. The special brought back the familiar stage set and many of the show's supporting players, such as Leigh French as O'Keefe, Pat Paulsen, and Bob Einstein as Officer Judy. The special was a big enough hit that CBS agreed to bring *The Smothers Brothers Comedy Hour* back in the regular season. O'Keefe was now a yuppie, and political commentary tended to focus on American intervention in Central America. Tom also introduced his alter ego, the Zen-like, silent "master of Yo," the "Yo-Yo Man." The revived *Comedy Hour* was moderately successful but did not result in a second season.

After more than fifty years in show business, the Smothers Brothers continue to tour extensively and very successfully throughout North America, playing more than 100 shows a year. The brothers have continued to dabble in acting throughout the years, appearing as guest stars on various television shows and in small roles in movies. *The Smothers Brothers Comedy Hour* remains their most important popular cultural achievement, and they have been honored by numerous organizations. The Museum of Television and Radio produced a retrospective on their work; they were given a star on the Hollywood Walk of Fame; they have received honorary doctorate degrees from San Jose University; and the Boston Comedy Festival presented them with a Lifetime Achievement Award. In 2002 Maureen Muldaur directed the documentary film *Smothered*, detailing the brothers' fight against censorship at CBS and their wrongful termination. The film features interviews not only with the brothers but also with singer Joan Baez, actors Jack Benny and Steve Martin, writer-director Rob Reiner, and others. In 2008 Martin presented Tom with a Commemorative Writing Emmy for his contributions in 1968.

The Smothers Brothers Comedy Hour was enormously influential on future comics and television shows that attempted to bring political satire to the television, *Saturday Night Live* being the most noteworthy legacy of the Smothers's groundbreaking work. Bill Maher of the late night *Politically Incorrect* talk-comedy series has also credited the *Comedy Hour* with inspiring his approach to political satire. *Saturday Night Live* alum Dennis Miller's show on HBO also owes much to the Smothers Brothers' example. Notable, however, is that all of these shows have aired either outside prime time or on cable and specialty channels: thirty years after *The Smothers Brothers Comedy Hour*, it would appear that sophisticated political satire and comedy is still not ready for prime time.

Aniko Bodroghkozy

SEE ALSO: *Baez, Joan; Belafonte, Harry; Benny, Jack;* Bewitched*;* Bonanza*; Buffalo Springfield; Emmy Awards; Hippies; Hollywood; LSD; Marijuana; Martin, Steve; Nichols, Mike, and Elaine May; Paar, Jack; Paulsen, Pat;* Saturday Night Live*; Seeger, Pete; Television;* Time*; Vietnam; World War II.*

BIBLIOGRAPHY

Bianculli, David. *Dangerously Funny: The Uncensored Story of "The Smothers Brothers Comedy Hour."* New York: Simon & Schuster, 2009.

Bodroghkozy, Aniko. "*The Smothers Brothers Comedy Hour* and the Youth Rebellion." In *The Revolution Wasn't Televised: Sixties Television and Social Conflict*, ed. Lynn Spigel and Michael Curtin, 201–219. New York: Routledge, 1997.

Carr, Steven Allen. "On the Edge of Tastelessness: CBS, the Smothers Brothers, and the Struggle for Control." *Cinema Journal* 31, no. 4 (1992): 3–24.

Hendra, Tony. "Death by Committee." In *Going Too Far*, 202–226. Garden City, NY: Doubleday, 1987.

Mertz, Robert. "The Smothered Brothers." In *CBS: Reflections in a Bloodshot Eye*, 293–305. Chicago: Playboy Press, 1975.

Spector, Bert. "A Clash of Cultures: The Smothers Brothers vs. CBS Television." In *American History, American Television*, ed. John E. O'Connor. New York: Frederick Ungar, 1983.

Snapple

Snapple's unique name was coined in the 1970s to capture the "snappy" flavor of a carbonated apple drink created by entrepreneurs Leonard Marsh, Hyman Golden, and Arnold Greenburg. Over the next several decades, their original line of fruity drinks expanded to include dozens of products, including a variety of flavored teas. Innovative marketing strategies made Snapple one of the most widely recognized beverage brands in the United States, especially after the drink was mentioned in episodes of the 1990s situation comedy *Seinfeld*. Since then, Snapple has been featured on shows such as *30 Rock*, *Celebrity Apprentice*, and *The Amazing Race*. The product is also known for its collectible bottle caps, which feature trivia-style "real facts."

Snapple was certainly a success story, but after its founders sold out in 1992, the company changed hands several times—hitting some highs and lows along the way. In 2003 Snapple began partnering with New York City to provide more healthful drinks in public schools and city vending machines. The company ran into criticism, however, over its use of high-fructose corn syrup, and in 2009 Snapple products switched to real sugar.

Cynthia Giles

SEE ALSO: *Advertising;* The Apprentice*;* Seinfeld*;* 30 Rock.

BIBLIOGRAPHY

Haig, Matt. *Brand Failures: The Truth about the 100 Biggest Branding Mistakes of All Time*. London: Kogan Page, 2011.

Wood, Sandy, and Kara Kovalchik. *The Snapple Aptitude Test*. New York: Broadway Books, 2006.

Sneakers

SEE: *Tennis Shoes/Sneakers.*

Snoop Dogg *(1971–)*

Perhaps the most recognized performer of the gangsta rap tradition, Snoop Doggy Dogg emerged in 1993 with *Doggystyle*, a commercially successful debut album on controversial Death Row/Interscope Records. As notorious for his violent and explicit lyrics as for his popularization of the suffix *-izzle*, Snoop Doggy Dogg became a central target of political censorship and attack soon after his appearance on the rap scene. Despite his initial commercial success, the rapper's career began to flounder after gangsta rap fell out of favor in the late 1990s. By 1998 Snoop Doggy Dogg had changed his name to Snoop Dogg, switched music labels, and toned down his graphic and controversial act in an effort to maintain his status in the industry.

EARLY YEARS

Cordozar Calvin Broadus was nicknamed "Snoop" as a child (after the *Peanuts* character Snoopy) and raised in an urban

Snoop Dog. *Snoop Dogg, a legend of the West Coast hip-hop scene who rose to fame in the 1990s at the height of gangsta rap, performs in concert 2011.* **JONATHAN LEIBSON/CONTRIBUTOR/FILMMAGIC/ GETTY IMAGES.**

ghetto in California, suffering through a childhood of harsh social realities. One month after his high school graduation, the soon-to-be rap star was arrested on drug charges and spent the next three years in and out of jail on three separate charges related to drug possession.

Following his release from jail, Snoop Dogg began to hone his skills as a rapper and shopped a demo tape of his work around his hometown. He was introduced to Dr. Dre, a key member of the controversial rap group N.W.A. Dre invited the young rapper to make a cameo appearance on his song "Deep Cover" (1992), which reached number one on the rap charts. Snoop then was invited to appear on Dre's critically acclaimed solo album *The Chronic* (1992), and the young rapper's performances became legendary in the hip-hop community. Their rapping duet on the song "Nuthin' but a 'G' Thang" launched the single into the Top 5 on the pop charts, establishing hard-core rap as crossover music. Snoop Dogg's unique rap style—aggressive but melodic, nasal and "cool"—created an instant buzz on the streets. After he appeared on several major magazine covers, the widespread anticipation for his solo project seemed unprecedented in the history of rap music.

Nothing could prepare the young rapper for the attention he received with his debut, *Doggystyle*. The album sold 800,000 copies in its first week and debuted at number one on the Billboard charts. With his lanky, 6-foot, 4-inch frame and his long, braided hair, Snoop Dogg presented an image of black masculinity that hadn't been seen before. To his fans the rapper appeared slightly effeminate but also menacing and hard-core.

Through his realistic, graphic lyrics about living in the ghetto, Snoop Dogg helped bring to public attention the form of hip-hop known as gangsta rap. In this musical form rappers portray themselves as instruments of menace and terror in order to shed light on the problems of youth living in the harsh social realities of urban ghettos. The success of *Doggystyle* also helped establish the West Coast as a viable center for the production of rap music.

GANGSTA RAP

Snoop Dogg's success was a double-edged sword. Along with the Death Row record label and the label's head, Suge Knight, he came under the scrutiny of a number of politicians and critics for the glorification of violence and criminality, explicit language, and promotion of hustler and pimp lifestyles. Moreover, Snoop Dogg's legal troubles and his portrayal of criminality also seemed to spill into his personal life: three months before *Doggystyle* was released, Snoop Dogg was charged as an accomplice in the shooting death of a young black man.

After receiving the legal services of O. J. Simpson trial lawyer Johnnie Cochran, Snoop Dogg was acquitted in 1996. His brush with the law only boosted his credibility among his fans, as they witnessed his personal life blend into his art. As a result his soundtrack for the short film *Murder Was the Case* (1994) sold more than two million copies. By the mid-1990s Snoop Dogg had also became one of the leading proponents of an escalating and highly publicized war of words between East Coast and West Coast rappers.

As gangsta rap began to weaken in its cultural power, Snoop Dogg's career likewise suffered. In 1996 Death Row Records buckled under massive censorship from political conservatives, and as the year wore on the hip-hop community was devastated by the shooting deaths of two of the genre's biggest stars, Tupac Shakur and Notorious B.I.G., as well as the incarceration of Knight. Snoop Dogg was unprepared to respond to the changing culture, and his next album, *Tha Doggfather* (1996), received poor critical reviews and limited commercial attention.

To increase his bad fortune, the rapper was then sued by Knight's wife, who also acted as Snoop Dogg's manager, for millions of dollars in unpaid management fees. As Time Warner sold its share of Interscope Records to MCA, Snoop Dogg found his musical home of Death Row Records in serious disrepair and public disrepute. Yet the record company continued to claim that the rapper contractually owed it another six albums. He responded with the commercially unreleased single "Death Row Is Bitches."

In 1997 Snoop Dogg played the Lollapalooza music festival, an unusual step for a hard-core rapper, and critics suggested it was an attempt to move toward a calmer, crossover aesthetic. In 1998 Louisiana's No Limit Records label, run by emerging hip-hop entrepreneur and rapper Master P, entered into a deal with Death Row Records to release Snoop Dogg from future responsibilities. After having sold seven million albums in six years, his first two albums with No Limit—*Da Game Is to Be Sold Not to Be Told* (1998) and *No Limit Top Dogg* (1999)—both reached number one on the Billboard hip-hop charts. He also branched into acting, appearing in bit parts in the straight-to-video movie *The Game of Life* (1998) and in the feature film *Half-Baked* (1998), and he decided to drop "Doggy" from his name to distance himself from his association with the gangsta rap idiom he had helped popularize.

BROADENING HORIZONS

While continuing to make rap albums at a steady rate, Snoop Dogg began to branch out, directing the pornographic film *Snoop Dogg's Doggystyle* (2001), which was produced by *Hustler*, and writing the autobiography *Tha Doggfather* (1999). He also appeared in guest roles in various films and television shows, including the animated *The PJs* (1999–2001) and *King of the Hill* (1997–2010); cable series *The L Word* (2004–2009), *Weeds* (2005–), *Entourage* (2004–2011), and *Monk* (2002–2009); and small parts in *Training Day* (2001) and *Starsky and Hutch* (2004). For many of these roles Snoop Dogg was cast as a character; in others, he played himself, as he did for three appearances on *One Life to Live* (2008–2010).

In 2002 Snoop Dogg joined with MTV to create the sketch comedy show *Doggy Fizzle Televizzle* (2002–2003), which featured the rapper playing numerous characters, as well as inviting other artists for guest performances and interviews. This was followed in 2007 by *Snoop Dogg's Father Hood* (2007–2009), a family reality show on E! featuring Snoop Dogg; his wife, Shante; and their kids, Corde, Cordell, and Cori. In 2009 MTV hosted another Snoop Dogg variety show, *Dogg after Dark* with celebrity interviews and musical performances.

Snoop Dogg began recording for Geffen in 2004 with the album *R&G (Rhythm & Gangsta): The Masterpiece* and the first single "Drop It Like It's Hot" (featuring Pharrell) was his first number one song. In addition to hosting various other rappers and singers on his own albums, Snoop Dogg has made guest appearances on albums by rappers such as Ice Cube, Tha Dogg Pound, and Coolio. In 2007 he released the song "It's the D.O.G." as a ringtone prior to releasing it as a single; he was the first artist to do so.

As Snoop Dogg continues to release rap albums and make film and television appearances, he continues to run into trouble. He was charged with sexually assaulting a woman at a taping of *Jimmy Kimmel Live* in 2003, and he was taken into custody in London after causing a ruckus at the airport. He was subsequently banned from flying British Airways and from entering the United Kingdom altogether. In 2006 he was arrested for marijuana and/or gun possession numerous times. The rapper was scheduled to appear at the 2007 MTV Australia Music Video Awards but was banned from entering the country due to his prior criminal convictions.

In 2010 Snoop Dogg made a guest appearance on Katy Perry's single "California Girls," which stayed at number one on the charts for six weeks. He then released his eleventh studio album, *Doggumentary* (2011), featuring numerous guest collaborators, from T. Pain, R. Kelly, and Kanye West to country star Willie Nelson. In addition to releasing his solo album, Snoop Dogg partnered with young up-and-comer Wiz Khalifa to put out a movie, *Mac & Devin Go to High School*, a Cheech and Chong–type comedy, along with a collaborative soundtrack that included the single "Young, Wild & Free," another Top 10 hit for the rapper.

Snoop Dogg has embraced digital technology and is known to be an avaricious Twitter user—he appeared in Twitter's five-year anniversary video explaining that he follows Martha Stewart's tweets "because she keeps it stuttered and buttered, baked and flaked, and she love to wake and bake with the big Snoop Dogg." He instituted Puff Puff Pass Tuesdays (named after the 2006 Mekhi Phifer–directed stoner movie), during which he releases exclusive video and audio content to his Twitter followers, and he often hosts Twitter trivia contests and gives backstage passes to the winners.

Jason King

SEE ALSO: *Cable TV; Gangsta Rap; Hip-Hop;* Hustler*; Lollapalooza; MTV; Nelson, Willie;* Peanuts*; Perry, Katy; Rap; Reality Television; Shakur, Tupac; Simpson Trial;* Starsky and Hutch*; Stewart, Martha; Top 40; Twitter;* Weeds*; West, Kanye.*

BIBLIOGRAPHY

Powell, Kevin. "Hot Dogg." *Vibe* 1, no. 1 (1993): 51–55.

Ro, Ronin. *Have Gun Will Travel: The Spectacular Rise and Violent Fall of Death Row Records.* New York: Doubleday, 1998.

Snow White and the Seven Dwarfs

Though criticized for the implied message that every girl needs a "prince" to rescue her, Walt Disney's first animated feature, *Snow White and the Seven Dwarfs*, remains a classic. Premiering in 1937, the movie tells a simple story. Snow White escapes the murderous Queen and finds refuge with the Seven Dwarfs (Doc, Bashful, Sleepy, Sneezy, Happy, Grumpy, and Dopey). Learning she is alive, the Queen disguises herself and tricks Snow White into eating a poisoned apple. She apparently dies, but a handsome prince wakes her with a kiss. Many reviewers complained that the human characters were wooden, but the film broke ground in animation. The illusion of depth in the forest scenes and details such as rain splashing on the ground had never been previously seen. The movie proved that animation had a place in the realm of feature films, and it paved the way for later Disney movies. A restored version of the movie was released in 1993. The American Film Institute named *Snow White and the Seven Dwarfs* to its list of the top 100 films in 1997 and again in 2007.

P. Andrew Miller

SEE ALSO: *Animated Films; Disney (Walt Disney Company).*

BIBLIOGRAPHY

Gabler, Neal. *Walt Disney: The Triumph of the American Imagination.* New York: Knopf, 2006.

Holliss, Richard, and Brian Sibley. *Walt Disney's "Snow White and the Seven Dwarfs" and the Making of the Classic Film.* New York: Simon & Schuster, 1987.

Krause, Martin F.; Linda Witkowski; and Stephen H. Ison. *Walt Disney's "Snow White and the Seven Dwarfs."* New York: Hyperion, 1995.

Maltin, Leonard. *The Disney Films.* New York: Crown Publishers, 1973.

Snowboarding

Snowboarding is a popular sport that involves riding a flat, ski-like board with bindings on snow-covered inclines in a stance similar to surfing or skateboarding. While it is impossible to specifically date the sport's beginning, several events stand out in the evolution of snowboarding. In 1939 the first patented snowboard, called a "Bunker," was created in Illinois by brothers Gunnar and Harvey Burgeson with Vern Wicklund. The "Bunker" was never mass-produced, however, so the commercialization of snowboarding is attributed to an inventor named Sherman Poppen from Muskegon, Michigan.

Poppen created the "Snurfer" in 1965 for his daughter Wendy by binding two skis together and nailing a string to the tip for steering. The craze caught on, and between 1966 and 1980 Poppen sold more than a half-million "Snurfers." Although the invention was viewed as little more than a children's toy, it sparked the imaginations of early snowboard pioneers who had already been devising a way to bring the movements of surfing and skateboarding to the medium of snow.

In 1972 Dimitrije Milovich's commercially produced "Winterstick," designed for ski mountain terrain, gained national exposure in publications such as *Newsweek*, *Playboy*, and *Powder*. In 1977 skateboard designers Chuck Barfoot and Tom Sims began mass-producing the "Flying Yellow Banana," or "Skiboard," designed specifically for powder conditions. In 1980 Jake Burton revolutionized snowboard design by using ski technology, with a highly durable thermoplastic P Tex base, metal edges, and plastic bindings for support.

As the 1980s progressed, snowboarding began to establish itself in the world of sports with the advent of competitions and media coverage via magazines, television, and movies. The first National Snow Surfing Championships, held in 1982 at Suicide Six in Vermont, was covered in the magazine *Sports Illustrated* and on national TV shows such as *Good Morning America*. By 1985 this event had become known as the U.S. Open. That same year saw the publication of *International Snowboarder Magazine*, dedicated solely to the sport of snowboarding, as well as a scene in the James Bond film *A View to a Kill* in which the suave secret agent rides a snowboard.

Despite this seeming acceptance of the sport in the mid-1980s, snowboarding was still either limited to certain ski runs or banned altogether at more than 90 percent of American resorts. Snowboarders were viewed by the general populous as rebels, drug users, and fringe dwellers. There existed a certain rivalry between skiers and snowboarders: old guard vs. new school.

In 1990 the ISF (International Snowboarding Federation) became the regulatory association for all snowboard competitions worldwide. Most contests were held in either a traditional ski slalom format or a freestyle/halfpipe format. As more contests were organized, corporate endorsements and sponsorships became commonplace among competitors.

Shortly after Molson Golden's 1994 commercial featuring snowboarders aired nationally on *Monday Night Football*, snowboarding was adopted as an Olympic sport. During the first 1998 Olympic snowboard competition in Nagano, Japan, Canadian snowboarder Ross Rebagliati tested positive for trace amounts of marijuana after winning the gold medal. Although contested, his medal was not taken away, but this scandal upheld the popular view of the day that snowboarders were little more than troublemakers.

Over the next decade, snowboarding grew from its infancy at the periphery of the sports world into adulthood and global acceptance. New competitions like the Winter X Games in 1997 aired in 198 countries on ABC Sports and ESPN, making extreme sports accessible to mainstream society. Younger generations saw that they too could push the boundaries of the sport to become future competitors. A new, youthful breed of professional athletes such as Terje Haakonsen, Craig Kelly, and Shaun Palmer paved the way for a generation of future snowboarders including a wave of female competitors like Tina Basich and Victoria Jealouse.

By the end of the new millennium's first decade, there were hundreds of snowboarding companies, and there were likely to be as many snowboarders as skiers at any given resort worldwide. In 2011 the most talented, popular rider was Shaun White, a young professional boarder deemed "The Flying Tomato" for his long, red locks. Ross Rebagliati sums up the sport's impact on contemporary culture in his description of White: "Shaun White on the cover of *Rolling Stone* [is] solid proof that the snowboarding stars of today have achieved the same status as rock stars."

From fringe life to front page, snowboarding brought extreme to mainstream, forever changing the face of professional sports.

Ron Horton

SEE ALSO: *ESPN; James Bond Films;* Monday Night Football*;* Rolling Stone*;* Sports Illustrated*; White, Shaun; X Games.*

BIBLIOGRAPHY

Fry, John. *The Story of Modern Skiing*. Hanover, NH: University of New England Press, 2006.

Howe, Susanna. *Sick: A Cultural History of Snowboarding*. New York: St. Martin's Griffin, 1998.

Rebagliati, Ross. *Off the Chain: An Insider's History of Snowboarding*. Vancouver, BC: Greystone Books, 2009.

Snuggie

The Snuggie is a full-body, long-sleeved fleece garment that resembles a bathrobe worn backward. Allstar Marketing Group debuted the blue, unisex Snuggie in October 2008, and it soon became available in custom, designer, and children's styles. A Snuggie for dogs was even introduced. Similar products, such as the Slanket and Freedom Blanket, were available, but the Snuggie's infomercial sparked a cult following. In the commercial, people knit, eat popcorn, read, perform chores, and even attend sporting events while wearing their Snuggies. Allstar president Scott Boilen explains the famous commercial: "We were definitely in on the joke. . . . Do we expect a family to wear these to a football game? No. . . . Certain products transcend advertising and become an indelible part of popular culture."

As of 2012, the Snuggie had hundreds of Facebook fan sites and YouTube parodies. The Associated Press described the product as the "ultimate kitsch gift," and it has been discussed or worn on television by, among others, Jimmy Fallon, Matt Lauer, Jay Leno, and Oprah Winfrey. The Snuggie has also been featured in nationwide pub crawls and New York fashion shows.

Ron Horton

SEE ALSO: *Advertising; Consumerism; Facebook; Leno, Jay; Winfrey, Oprah; YouTube.*

BIBLIOGRAPHY

Schmidt, Mackenzie. "2009, The Year of the Snuggie." *Village Voice*, December 21, 2009. Accessed May 2012. Available from http://blogs.villagevoice.com/runninscared/2009/12/2009_year_of_th.php

Soap Operas

In the 1930s companies such as Procter & Gamble sought sponsorship of daily radio programming targeted to homemakers, who controlled the purse strings for cleaning and other household product purchases. Daytime serial dramas soon answered this call, focusing melodramatically on women, multigenerational families, and romantic intrigue in live, fifteen-minute shows. Although derogatory at first, the term *soap opera* became the genre's customary designation. After making the transition to television, soap operas were eventually adapted for prime-time and worldwide audiences, making their mark as a highly influential genre. In the early twenty-first century, however, the original form of the soap opera waned in popularity.

The first soap opera, *Painted Dreams*, was developed in 1931 for WGN radio in Chicago by Irna Phillips, who would go on to become the most prolific creator of soap operas for both radio and television. The program aired without specific product association until content changes were made to accommodate Montgomery Ward & Co., the show's first sponsor. Phillips employed the same enticements to secure advertisers for her other serials, and the genre's characteristic sponsor ties were established.

Luke and Laura Wed. *Thirty million viewers tuned in to watch the wedding of Luke and Laura on* General Hospital *in 1981.* ABC-TV/THE KOBAL COLLECTION.

Phillips's *Today's Children* (1932), sponsored first by General Foods and later by Pillsbury, evolved into the first network soap opera when NBC began airing it nationwide in 1933. Understanding that women often performed their domestic chores while listening to radio and were, consequently, all the more inclined to buy and use merchandise that was casually promoted within a program, Procter & Gamble (P&G) made advertising on soap operas central in its marketing campaigns and promoted its products on programs such as *Ma Perkins* (1933), *The O'Neills* (1935), *The Guiding Light* (1937), and *Kitty Keene* (1937).

Once television became a feature of the domestic landscape after World War II, soap operas gradually faded from radio and took up residence on the small screen. *The Guiding Light* (1952), a Phillips creation, ran simultaneously on both media for several years (its name changed to just *Guiding Light* in 1975). While radio soaps shifted to tape before transitioning, television soaps were, until the late 1950s, presented live. The decade saw myriad TV soaps begin and end abruptly, but several in addition to *The Guiding Light*—including *Search for Tomorrow* (1951), created by Agnes Nixon and Roy Winsor; *Love of Life* (1951), created by Winsor; and *As the World Turns* (1956), created by Phillips—exhibited staying power. As a by-product of the shift to television, an extra measure of redundancy and backstory exposition was added to the soap opera formula in order to accommodate viewers' tendency to step away from the screen in attending to their household tasks. When added to the genre's open, serial form, this element further ingrained feminine domesticity into the very fabric of the soap opera.

The ability of soap operas to target the preferred audience of women, ages eighteen to forty-nine, was unmatched. Younger viewers became hooked on the shows by watching them with their mothers after school, during the summer, and on holidays, and advertisers counted on them to become loyal viewers into adulthood. With the lucrative, baby boom generation coming of age beginning in the late 1950s, soap opera producers geared up to capture a new crop of female consumers.

LURING BABY BOOMERS

When *As the World Turns* (CBS) featured the elopement of teenagers Penny Hughes and Jeff Baker in 1957, the strategy of the summer story line was inaugurated. From then on soap operas made special efforts to highlight and write for younger characters during the summer months when students were out of school and likely to be watching. New soaps with new angles also attempted to snare young viewers. The gothic soap opera *Dark Shadows* (1966) emerged on ABC in the mid-1960s to beguile a largely cult audience with vampires, witches, and werewolves for half a decade. Additionally, by the end of the 1960s, most soap operas had expanded from fifteen minutes to thirty minutes.

The summer story line became more of a year-round prospect in the 1970s, as *All My Children* (1970), created by Nixon, on ABC and *The Young and the Restless* (1973), created by Lee Phillip Bell and William J. Bell, on CBS were devised with baby boomers in mind. Meanwhile, in 1975 NBC's *Another World* (1964), a cocreation of Phillips and William Bell, became the first soap opera to expand to sixty minutes.

In 1981 *General Hospital* (1963), created by Doris, Frank, and Jim Hursley, made daytime ratings history when more than thirty million people tuned in to watch Luke Spencer (Anthony Geary) and Laura Baldwin (Genie Francis), two of the show's most popular characters, get married. Luke and Laura were the first soap opera "supercouple," and after their wedding episode, supercouples began appearing on other soap operas, such as Bo (Peter Reckell) and Hope (Kristian Alfonso) on NBC's *Days of Our Lives* (1965), created by Phillips, Ted Corday, and Alan Chase.

In the 1970s and 1980s soap operas addressed taboo topics as an integral part of a campaign to lure baby boomer viewers. The rape of Holly (Maureen Garrett) by her husband, Roger Thorpe (Michael Zaslow), was the groundbreaking issue on *Guiding Light* in 1979. The writers who penned it, Jerome and Bridget Dobson, followed with a similar story on *As the World Turns*, where *General Hospital*'s former scribe, Douglas Marland, eventually took the reins and conceived socially conscious tales about bulimia, incest, and homosexuality. *Another World*, which tackled addiction, abortion, and alcoholism under the leadership of Phillips, William Bell, and later, Harding Lemay, went on to offer the first AIDS story in the late 1980s.

As much as they tried, soap operas that were caught behind the curve during the youth boom soon experienced downturns in popularity, and many never completely recovered. *Search for Tomorrow* switched from CBS to NBC before going under in 1986. *Guiding Light*, *Another World*, and *As the World Turns* also struggled with their aging viewers. The 1980s saw short-lived efforts to reach other demographics with NBC's *Generations* (1989), targeted primarily to African Americans, and Christian Broadcasting Network's *Another Life* (1981) geared to Christian viewers.

Soap operas underwent another change in the 1970s and 1980s: they debuted in prime time. Although *Peyton Place* (1964–1969) on ABC had attempted such a temporal shift in the 1960s, it was not until *Dallas* (1978–1991), headed by the infamous J. R. Ewing (Larry Hagman), that the idea finally caught on. *Dallas* became immensely popular, enduring for a decade and gaining worldwide appeal. When a 1980 season-ending cliffhanger left viewers wondering "Who shot J. R.?" massive, global speculation ensued. CBS later added other serial sagas to its prime-time lineup, including *Knots Landing* (1979–1993), a *Dallas* spin-off, and *Falcon Crest* (1981–1990).

But it was *Dynasty* (1981–1989) that answered the challenge for ABC, resonating narcissism and opulence of the 1980s and dishing up vixen Alexis Carrington (Joan Collins). Moreover, other nighttime formats began exhibiting seriality and other soap opera conventions as the genre's influence was seen in domestic dramas such as *thirtysomething* (1987–1991); law enforcement, legal, and medical shows such as *Hill Street Blues* (1981–1987), *L.A. Law* (1986–1994), and *St. Elsewhere* (1982–1988); and dramedies such as *Moonlighting* (1985–1989).

ATTRACTING THE MTV GENERATION

By the 1980s academic study of daytime soap operas had evolved from statistical surveys and content analyses to critical reviews of soap opera texts and the potential identifications of viewing subjects. Despite their denigration in the larger culture, soaps were found to provide central female characters through whom women in the audience might seek affirmation. Although some scholars found many aspects of these representations lacking, the genre's serial form, its emphasis on and elevation of the domestic sphere, and its focus on feminine subjects were considered by most to be positive and noteworthy traits.

As the 1990s loomed, soaps began to undergo a period of transition, seeking to retain their audience of baby boomers while attracting the younger MTV generation. NBC's *Santa Barbara* (1984–1993), created by Jerome and Bridget Dobson, took a lesson from *Dynasty* and delivered camp postmodernism to daytime. While proving a huge success overseas, the soap failed to capture the domestic demographics the network was hoping for, and NBC canceled it within a decade. *All My Children*'s devilish diva, Erica Kane, and the actress playing her, Susan Lucci, became household names, as multiple marriages for Erica and multiple Emmy Award losses for Lucci were grist for the publicity mill.

In the late 1980s another Agnes Nixon soap, *One Life to Live* (1968–2012) on ABC, endeavored to replicate *General Hospital*'s winning fantasy adventures. With former movie producer Linda Gottlieb and mystery novelist Michael Malone, the program shifted to hard-hitting realism in the 1990s. Stories involved the town of Llanview's homophobic response to a gay teen, Billy Douglas (Ryan Phillippe), and the brutal gang rape of a college student by three fraternity brothers led by Todd Manning (Roger Howarth). Controversy ensued when Howarth's charisma with fans led the writers to orchestrate Todd's redemption, much to the chagrin of Howarth, who found himself braving screams of "rape me, Todd," from overly ardent admirers. Later *All My Children* produced a homophobia story of its own about a popular teacher who nearly loses his job after revealing his homosexuality during a classroom lecture.

General Hospital adopted a similar tone of verisimilitude during this period, largely as a result of head writer Claire Labine's heart-wrenching tales of a child's tragic death, her gift of a healthy organ to an ailing cousin, and a middle-aged woman's battle with breast cancer. Labine's most significant decision was to have teenager Robin Scorpio (Kimberly McCullough) contract AIDS by engaging in unprotected sex with her boyfriend, who subsequently dies of the dreaded disease. These dark stories garnered *General Hospital* critical acclaim but endangered the program's healthy ratings, as the incoming generation of fans seemed more stimulated by fantasy and escape than by tragedy and catharsis.

Meanwhile, it was NBC's long-running *Days of Our Lives*, under the leadership of executive producer Corday and innovative writer James E. Reilly, that appeared to discover the key to unlocking the devotion of a new generation of viewers. Taking a lead from *Dark Shadows*, Reilly conjured up gothic fantasy scenarios, camp supervillains, never-ending supertriangles, and bizarre sagas involving premature burial and demon possession. This latter escapade required the soap's most beloved diva, Marlena Evans (Deidre Hall), to levitate and morph into wild animals. Although many longtime fans disliked the program's drastic change, teens rushed aboard. While *The Young and the Restless* gained and retained the number one spot in ratings during the late 1980s and 1990s, warranting the addition of *The Bold and the Beautiful* (1987–) to CBS's lineup, *Days of Our Lives* mounted a serious challenge to this ratings leader and at one point surpassed it in terms of demographics—the advertisers' target group of younger women.

YOUTHIFICATION

Days of Our Lives was very influential in the 1990s, with many programs emulating it. Even more than during the baby boom influx, "youthification" became the order of the day. Multigenerational and baby boom–centered soap operas had become scarce in prime time, with only NBC's *Sisters* (1991–1996) breaking out as an instance of both. Most remarkable were producer Aaron Spelling's groundbreaking creations for Fox: *Beverly Hills, 90210* (1990–2000) and *Melrose Place* (1992–1999), which demonstrated that it was possible for soaps to focus almost exclusively on younger characters and be successful in prime time. Late in the decade *Party of Five* (1994–2000) on Fox and *Dawson's Creek* (1998–2003) on the WB extended this trend. Some daytime executives hoped they could corner the youth market in similar fashion.

With the children of the baby boom generation, the millennials, lying in wait and nearly as numerous as their parents, there appeared to be no turning back. Although some had predicted that boomers would dominate the culture for several decades, the trajectory of soap operas responding to the advertisers' increasing concern with demographics, as opposed to household ratings, portended otherwise. In the new millennium, a few new youth-oriented soaps appeared in prime time, such as *The O.C.* (2003–2007) on Fox and *One Tree Hill* (2003–) on the CW, but soapy dramas such as *Mad Men* (2007–) on AMC, *Grey's Anatomy* (2005–) on ABC, *The Good Wife* (2009–) on CBS, *Friday Night Lights* (2006–) on NBC, and *Revenge* (2011–) on ABC were otherwise the mainstay. These tended to resolve one or two story lines in each episode in order to retain busy, less loyal audience members who might become frustrated and stop watching if they missed two many episodes.

Meanwhile, in the late 1990s and beyond, networks continued their youthification of daytime dramas. NBC made *Days of Our Lives* its standard bearer and pressured its only other soap, the struggling *Another World*, to thin much of its over-forty cast, while adopting a decidedly more outrageous tone. Those steps were not enough, and in the summer of 1999 NBC canceled the show. The network also picked up Spelling's first daytime offering, the virtually unigenerational *Sunset Beach* (1997–1999), which lasted only two years. It was replaced by *Passions* (1999–2008), developed by *Days of Our Lives* alum Reilly. Over on ABC, *All My Children* adopted hard-hitting stories about younger characters, and in 2000 revealed that Erica's teenage daughter, Bianca Montgomery (Eden Riegel), was a lesbian. On CBS *As the World Turns* and *Guiding Light* also underwent casting changes, letting many of its veterans go while hiring young, inexperienced performers. *Guiding Light* also began featuring otherworldly stories, including an especially controversial one in which popular diva Reva Shayne (Kim Zimmer) was cloned.

DECLINING VIEWERSHIP

Starting in 2000 daytime soap operas realized an overall decline in viewership, and between 2007 and 2012 several daytime soaps were canceled due to flagging ratings, including *Passions*, *Guiding Light*, *As the World Turns*, *All My Children*, and *One Life to Live*. Part of the reason for poor ratings is the plethora of tabloid news shows, talk shows, and reality shows that have taken over daytime television, drawing viewers away from soaps. The fact that more and more women are in the workforce and that teens and twentysomethings are more attracted to social networking and other new media also has had an impact. Although many working women record their soaps, advertisers are reluctant to spend money on commercials that viewers are likely to fast-forward through and not watch. Still, avid soap fans have become more active and, indeed, interactive, in the digital age. They have joined Internet communities to discuss the latest story lines, root for their favorite characters, and share information about soap stars.

Despite their attempts to capture succeeding generations of viewers with controversial and outlandish subject matter, daytime soaps persist in their essential conservatism. White actors still outnumbered minority actors, and mixed-race romantic relationships were few. Serious romances between older women and men under forty remain uncommon. Moreover, while soaps depict women in career roles, the workplace continues to serve as a stage upon which women fought with one another over men.

With its ongoing focus on human relationships, the soap opera has forever impacted prime-time genres from drama to news to reality and has adapted to a plethora of international cultures, producing the more naturalistic, British variety epitomized by *EastEnders* (1985–); shorter-term Latin American *telenovelas* such as the much-imitated Colombian offering *Yo Soy Betty, La Fea* (I am Betty the ugly) (1999–2001); and a plethora of other serials emanating from India to Australia. Lampooned in movies (*Soapdish*, 1991; *Tootsie*, 1982) and television (*Mary Hartman, Mary Hartman*, 1976–1978; *Soap*, 1977–1981; *The Carol Burnett Show*, 1967–1978) and recognized around the world, the soap opera has secured its place as a fundamental influence on the panoply of popular culture.

Christine Scodari

SEE ALSO: *Advertising; AIDS;* All My Children*;* Another World*;* As the World Turns*; Baby Boomers;* Beverly Hills, 90210*;* Dallas*;* Dark Shadows*;* Dawson's Creek*;* Days of Our Lives*;* Dynasty*;* General Hospital*;* Grey's Anatomy*;* Guiding Light*;* Hill Street Blues*; The Internet;* Knots Landing*;* L.A. Law*;* Mad Men*;* Mary Hartman, Mary Hartman*;* Moonlighting*; MTV; Nixon, Agnes; Peyton Place; Phillips, Irna; Radio; Radio Drama;* Search for Tomorrow*; Simpson, O. J.;* The Sopranos*; Spelling, Aaron;* St. Elsewhere*; Television;* Tootsie*; 24; World War II;* The Young and the Restless.

BIBLIOGRAPHY

Allen, Robert C. *Speaking of Soap Operas.* Chapel Hill: University of North Carolina Press, 1985.

Blumenthal, Dannielle. *Women and Soap Opera: A Cultural Feminist Perspective.* Westport, CT: Praeger, 1997.

Cassata, Mary, and Thomas Skill. *Life on Daytime Television.* Norwood, NJ: Ablex, 1983.

Ford, Sam; Abigail De Kosnik; and C. Lee Harrington, eds. *The Survival of Soap Opera: Transformations for a New Media Era.* Jackson: University Press of Mississippi, 2011.

Liebes, Tamar, and Elihu Katz. *The Export of Meaning: Cross-Cultural Readings of* Dallas. New York: Oxford University Press, 1990.

Modleski, Tania. *Loving with a Vengeance: Mass-Produced Fantasies for Women.* Hamden, CT: Archon, 1982.

Mumford, Laura Stempel. *Love and Ideology in the Afternoon: Soap Opera, Women, and Television Genre*. Bloomington: Indiana University Press, 1995.

Museum of Television and Radio. *Worlds without End: The Art and History of the Soap Opera*. New York: Abrams, 1997.

Scodari, Christine. *Serial Monogamy: Soap Opera, Lifespan, and the Gendered Politics of Fantasy*. Cresskill, NJ: Hampton Press, 2004.

Waggett, Gerard J. *Soap Opera Encyclopedia*. New York: Harper Paperbacks, 1997.

Soccer

Soccer in the United States is in a strangely paradoxical position. It is the world's most popular sport (although not under that name), yet it has never managed to gain much of a spectator footing in the United States. It may be virtually ignored on television as a spectator sport, but by the late 1990s it had become one of the country's biggest participatory forms of leisure activity. Nonetheless, many Americans are still ignorant not only of the rules of the world's most popular game but also of their country's own soccer history.

SOCCER COMES TO AMERICA

The origins of soccer in the United States are obscure. Folklore suggests that the Pilgrim fathers discovered the American Indians playing a form of the game along the Massachusetts coastline. However, in the seventeenth century British immigrants imported into America the game that developed into association football (soccer) around the world in the nineteenth century; there is documentation of the game as early as 1609. The game was an early folk pastime played mainly in the streets and open squares. By the 1820s soccer was a violent, unorganized, and casual game played almost exclusively on college campuses. The first intercollegiate soccer match took place in 1869 between Princeton and Rutgers. Schoolboys established the first organized soccer club, the Oneidas of Boston, in 1862. They played on Boston Common and were undefeated for several years.

At this point it looked as if soccer would develop in the United States. British expatriates had exported soccer around the world, and many immigrants from the British Isles arrived in the United States, bringing the game with them. Harvard, however, had other ideas. In an attempt to distinguish itself from the other Ivy League colleges, Harvard adopted rules similar to those developed by rugby football. Because Harvard was a leader in physical education during the nineteenth century and because other colleges did not want to lose such prestigious competition, they adopted rugby rules. This set of rules subsequently became the basis for the innovation of American football. Football was then highlighted as a uniquely American sport, while soccer was deemed the game of immigrants, particularly as it was played by the new arrivals from southern Europe.

Nonetheless, soccer did not die out in America. In 1884 the American Football Association was organized in Newark, New Jersey. In 1885 the United States played its first "international" against Canada, one of the first soccer games to be played outside the British Isles. The U.S. soccer team participated in the 1904 Olympic games in St. Louis, Missouri, and in 1914 the United States Football Association (USFA) was granted full membership in the Fédération Internationale de Football Association (FIFA), the governing body of world soccer. In 1916 the USFA team traveled to Sweden and Norway. It played its first international match on foreign soil on August 20, defeating Sweden 3–0. When the first World Cup competition was organized in 1930, the United States was one of thirteen nations to compete. U.S. team member Bert Patenaude was the first player to score three goals in a single World Cup game. The highlight of the USFA's international games, however, was in the 1950 World Cup, when the team defeated England 1–0. Some consider this game the biggest upset ever in international soccer.

SOCCER IN THE TWENTIETH CENTURY

Soccer in the United States underwent many incarnations during the twentieth century. In 1923 the world's first indoor soccer league was organized in Boston. In 1958 the International Soccer League was set up. It was composed of top teams from Europe, South America, and the United States, holding its first championship tournament in 1959. The league survived for a decade as a testing ground for soccer as a spectator sport in the United States. In 1967 two more soccer leagues were established: the United Soccer Association (USA) and the National Professional Soccer League. At the end of the year, these leagues were merged at the request of FIFA, forming the North American Soccer League (NASL). This newly established professional league had eighteen teams by 1974, and it achieved a major success by signing the world's greatest footballer, Pelé, in 1975. Professional soccer as a spectator sport finally appeared to have taken root in the United States in 1977, when a seven-game contract was signed with national television. The NASL eventually collapsed, however, because of a combination of highly paid foreign stars, a failure to develop the game at the grassroots level, the withdrawal of its sponsors, and falling gate receipts.

Indoor soccer appeared to carry the torch for those organizers hoping to capture a fan following with its small arena surface, faster-paced action, and higher game scores. While there have been several indoor professional leagues, the Major Indoor Soccer League (MISL) has been the preeminent league in three different incarnations: 1978–1992, 2001–2007, and 2008–present. Attendance that seldom surpassed 8,000 per game led to the failure of the first two runs of the MISL, and the U.S. Indoor Soccer Association sanctions tournaments and championships for adult and youth teams nationwide.

Soccer was revitalized once again during the early 1990s. It became an increasingly common option for youth sports, in part because it is seen as safer to play than American football. In fact, the growing popularity of the sport led to the new expression "soccer mom," used to describe suburban mothers who drive their children to sports practices and other activities. From 1990 to 2010 the number of high school students playing soccer more than doubled to 730,000 athletes. The number of college teams for both men and women also increased substantially.

At the adult level, in 1994 the United States hosted the World Cup for the first time. Around 3.5 million fans filled the stadia and broke all previous attendance records. For the first time in sixty-four years the U.S. team progressed beyond the first round, eventually losing a creditable 1–0 to the team from Brazil. On the back of the World Cup, the United States Soccer Federation set up Major League Soccer (MLS), promising a blend of homegrown talent, imported foreign stars, and audiences of 14,000 per game.

The World Cup had proven that Americans could both play and watch soccer. Major investment in the sport, from companies such as Nike, has also boosted the popularity of soccer among Americans. In the United States soccer is now played by both sexes and is a major participatory activity. Indeed, the U.S. women's team has won four Olympic gold medals (1996, 2004, 2008, 2012) and won the World Cup in 1999. The men's team, however, has not fared as well. At the 1998 World Cup in France, they went out during the first round. The lowest point came when they were defeated 3–1 by Iran, a team that had never previously appeared in the World Cup final. The team did better in 2002 and 2010 but, as of 2012, has never made it past the quarterfinals. Women's Professional Soccer formed in 2007 and began playing in 2009; as of 2012 the league had five franchises.

SOCCER IN THE TWENTY-FIRST CENTURY

Despite the formation of domestic soccer leagues and international successes, soccer is somehow still not universally recognized as an American sport. Unlike football and baseball, it is considered not an American invention but a sport of immigrants. Undoubtedly soccer has suffered from its lack of prime-time television coverage. Television sports schedules are virtually monopolized by the "big three": football, baseball, and basketball. This lack of exposure has continued to hinder soccer's development at the professional level while overshadowing its thriving grassroots existence at a participatory level. Until soccer's television and earning power match that of the big three, the sport will continue to remain in their shadows. The main hope for soccer in the United States seems to come from the young fans playing the sport (as it becomes popular among children) and the increasingly large immigrant population in America, especially from Mexico and Latin America, where *futbol* has widespread appeal.

There may be signs that soccer is gaining ground in the United States. The explosion of sports-dedicated television stations, particularly on cable networks such as the Fox Soccer Network and the Spanish-speaking GolTV, has allowed more soccer programming to reach viewers, and the U.S. fan base seems slowly to be growing. Disney-owned ESPN and ABC began airing UEFA European Championship matches in 2000 and continue to have broadcast rights through 2016. ESPN also acquired the rights to English Premier League matches and to the Spanish La Liga in 2009, subsequently adding German Bundesliga and Italian Serie A coverage to its Internet-based ESPN3 Network. The English Premier League offers American fans the opportunity to see such U.S. World Cup performers as Tim Howard; Brad Freidel; Clint Dempsey, who became the first American to score a hat trick in a Premier League game for Fulham in 2012; and Landon Donovan, when he has been lent from the L.A. Galaxy.

The 2010 World Cup final between the Netherlands and Spain attracted a record number of U.S. viewers: 15.5 million viewers in English and an additional 8.8 million viewers in Spanish. This number was actually higher than the number of viewers for the previous year's baseball World Series. MLS has been offering more star appeal by signing prominent international players, such as David Beckham and Thierry Henry. Beckham's marriage to Victoria Adams (aka Posh Spice), a former member of the popular music group "Spice Girls," has helped to make him a familiar American media figure with his move to MLS's L.A. Galaxy. In another ploy to attract fans, MLS has invited such international teams as Manchester United—a member of the Premier League—to visit the United States for exhibition games against MLS teams. Manchester United is perhaps the most famous team in the world and has won twelve titles since the Premier League formed in 1992.

As one sign of soccer's growing appeal, more Americans have begun wearing international soccer jerseys, particularly those from Premier League teams and from Spain's La Liga, which includes Real Madrid and Barcelona. One reason for Barcelona's popularity may be that it boasts the star Lionel Messi, an Argentine who was named the FIFA world player of the year from 2009 to 2011. With the growing availability of soccer broadcasts come increased chances to see such flashy international players as Messi, and these opportunities can only boost soccer's popularity in the United States.

Nathan Abrams

SEE ALSO: *College Football; Nike; Pelé; The Spice Girls; Sports Heroes; World Cup.*

BIBLIOGRAPHY

Abrams, Nathan D. "Inhibited but Not 'Crowded Out': The Strange Fate of Soccer in the United States." *International Journal of the History of Sport* 12, no. 3 (1995): 1–17.

Foulds, Sam, and Paul Harris. *America's Soccer Heritage: A History of the Game.* Manhattan Beach, CA: Soccer for Americans, 1979.

Manzo, J. T. "A Ball in the Grass: An Exploratory Look at Soccer in the United States." *Sport Place* 1 (1987): 30–38.

Markovits, Andrei S. "The Other 'American Exceptionalism': Why Is There No Soccer in the United States?" *International Journal of the History of Sport* 7, no. 2 (1990): 230–264.

Miller, Rory, and Liz Crolley, eds. *Football in the Americas: Fútbol, Futebol, Soccer.* London: Institute for the Study of the Americas, 2007.

Sugden, John. "USA and the World Cup: American Nativism and the Rejection of the People's Game." In *Hosts and Champions: Soccer Cultures, National Identities and the USA World Cup*, ed. John Sugden and Alan Tomlinson. Aldershot, UK: Arena, 1994.

Waldstein, David, and Stephen Wagg. "UnAmerican Activity? Football in U.S. and Canadian Society." In *Giving the Game Away: Football, Politics and Culture on Five Continents*, ed. Stephen Wagg. London: Leicester University Press, 1995.

Wangerin, David. *Soccer in a Football World: The Story of America's Forgotten Game.* Philadelphia: Temple University Press, 2008.

Social Dancing

Social dancing refers to all those forms of dance that are recreational and public. It is not a professional form of dance, except for exhibition dancing or teaching, nor a form of theatrical dancing, such as ballet, modern dance, tap dancing, or flamenco, although such forms of art and entertainment incorporate steps and gestures from social dance. In American society almost everyone has some sort of relationship to social dancing. Many people participate with great intensity in social dance activities for a period of their lives. In preindustrial societies and working-class communities, social dancing has often been a group activity, but by the end of the twentieth century, social dancing in many parts of the world was primarily a form of couples dancing.

EARLY SOCIAL DANCING

Folk dancing is the earliest form of social dancing. Most folk dancing is a group activity and often includes only a single sex. A common folk dance form is the European round dance, which is for both men and women. The dancers are linked in a circle by holding hands or holding the arms and shoulders or the waist belts of the other dancers. Couples dancing where a man and woman hold each in their arms is a late development in folk dancing and probably originated as courtship or wedding dances. Folk dances have often existed in a dialectical relationship with court dancing. Folk dances were usually codified by "dancing masters" when they were introduced to the aristocratic courts so that the dances could be taught more easily.

English country dances were exported to France, where they were codified and introduced into French aristocratic circles. Known as the *contredanse*, they were group dances in which the people dancing formed circles and lines to make an elaborate shape through which members of the court could thread. In the minuet, a related dance form, couples danced as part of the group. These early ballroom dances were grouped together under the title of cotillion and quadrille. Elite ballroom dancing of this sort was destroyed by the French Revolution.

After the French Revolution, the waltz swept across Europe; it was considered a "popular" democratic dance—the dance of the rising middle classes. Social dance moved out of the ballroom of the aristocratic court into public dance halls and "assembly rooms." Paris had, in the period following the revolution, more than 700 dance halls. The waltz was also the first dance of urban life. It was the first example of the "closed couple" dance—the dance partners faced one another and were in intimate physical contact. Because of that and the dance's whirling and the intoxicating effect of its three-quarter time, it was thought to be vulgar and lascivious. The waltz was introduced to the United States in the early nineteenth century. It remained the dominant form of social dance in Europe—where it culminated in the Viennese waltzes of Johann Strauss—and in North America. Other dances that emerged rivaled it for short periods but did not displace it until late in the nineteenth century.

FROM RAGTIME TO THE TWIST

At the end of the twentieth century in the United States, most forms of social dance were hybrid dance forms descended from European and African musical and dance traditions. During the eighteenth and nineteenth centuries, most of the social dances that Americans participated in were imported from Europe, but since the beginning of the twentieth century, American popular forms of social dance have originated in or were primarily influenced by African American music and dance styles. Even the many forms of Latin dancing that have also been popular—from the tango to the samba to salsa—are cross acculturations of African and Hispanic musical traditions.

The emergence of ragtime in the 1890s revolutionized social dancing in the United States. Composed by black musicians as piano music to be played in saloons, bars, brothels, and cafés, ragtime was rarely written down or recorded. The first identifiable style of jazz, ragtime comes from *ragged music*, also known as syncopation, where the musical stress is on an unaccented beat and then held over until the next beat. The most famous ragtime composer in the early twentieth century was Scott Joplin. His pieces "Maple Leaf Rag" and "The Entertainer" were among the most popular compositions of the day. Ragtime radically changed American dance styles. Before it there was an emphasis on learning complicated steps and the pleasure in movement. After ragtime the main impetus of social dancing was the music's rhythm and the impulse that it gave to dancing.

The one-step—called so because one step was taken to each beat of the music with a constant tempo—was the first kind of dancing done to ragtime. The one-step spawned a series of other one-step dances accompanied by different arm and body gestures: the turkey trot involved flapping one's arms like a turkey; the grizzly bear included lurching like a bear; and so on with the bunny hug, the shiver, and the Boston dip. Vernon and Irene Castle, a world-famous husband-and-wife team, adapted the one-step as the Castle Walk and popularized it across the country, commanding huge fees for performing ballroom dances in exhibitions, cafés, and theaters.

The one-step and the other new dances were much simpler—they undercut the social distinction to be gained by ballroom dancing lessons. Anyone could learn them by observation in an evening of dancing. One English observer noted that "all you have to do is grab hold of the nearest lady, grasp her very tightly, push her shoulders down a bit, and then wiggle about as much like a slippery slush as you possibly can." Many new dances also allowed much closer physical contact between the couple, in part because they were somewhat slower than the waltz or the polka.

One offshoot from these early one-steps was the two-step, which is basically a marching step with interpolated skips. Neither the one-step nor the two-step had the major impact of later dance styles on American recreational dancing. The two-step was originally danced to the popular marches of John Philip Sousa. Ragtime, Dixieland jazz, and later swing offered rhythmically complex musical frameworks for more sophisticated dance forms. With the revival in popularity of country music in the late twentieth century, the two-step survived as country dancing primarily as a line dance incorporating open couples.

The next dance to sweep the country was the fox-trot; its invention was the most significant development in social dancing until the 1960s. Incorporating some aspects of the one-step and other new dances, the fox-trot was more enjoyable to dance because its combination of quick and slow steps allowed greater variety and flexibility than the monotonous one-step. Most ballroom dances that followed—the shimmy, Black Bottom, and Charleston—were variations on the fox-trot.

After ragtime, jazz became the dominant idiom of urban dance music and popular song up until the 1950s. The popularity of the fox-trot and its centrality to ballroom dancing was instrumental to the infusion of jazz into mainstream American popular music. The big dance bands of the 1920s and 1930s were the vehicle for the most popular and exciting dance vogue in the era before rock and roll—swing and all the dances that grew out of it, such as the jitterbug, Lindy Hop, and jive.

Rock and roll, a new style of music that emerged in the late 1950s and a synthesis of blues, rhythm, and country music, was a popular form of dance music. Songs such as "Shake, Rattle and Roll" and "Rock around the Clock" typified both this new music as well as a dance style. Couples continued to dance the jitterbug to early rock and roll. Then in the early 1960s Chubby Checker recorded a dance song called "The Twist." In this dance, which swept across the United States, partners shook their shoulders and swiveled their hips but did not touch. Although enthusiasm for it faded within a year or two, popular social dance was decisively changed. Coordinated couples dancing was a thing of the past. After the twist, social dancing was characterized by dancers standing in one place, making small foot movements (somewhat resembling the motion of putting out a cigarette). The focus was no longer on footwork so much as on the motion of the arms and upper body. Dance partners hardly touched one another, but they usually maintained eye contact. Some people danced alone on a crowded dance floor.

AFRO-LATIN SOCIAL DANCING

Less influential than the dance forms that emerged from jazz, rock and roll, soul, and hip-hop, although still highly visible at times, were Afro-Latin dances such as the tango, rumba, samba, mambo, cha-cha, and salsa. First to arrive was the tango, creating a huge dance craze in 1913 and 1914. The tango traveled back and forth throughout the nineteenth century between Europe and Latin America; it passed through Japan in the 1940s. In the course of these movements, the tango was modified by black and Creole influences being transformed once more in the brothels and cafés of Buenos Aires in the 1930s and 1940s. Popular at the end of the twentieth century, the tango has enjoyed several revivals throughout the years.

Rumba music is popular throughout the Caribbean countries of Jamaica, Haiti, and Cuba. The rumba as a dance migrated to the United States from Cuba, where it was a sex pantomime danced extremely fast with exaggerated hip movements and very aggressively led by the male partner. The music is played with a staccato beat. The samba, a Brazilian dance form first performed by blacks at carnival time and other holidays, is a difficult dance because of its speed and because its steps are taken on a quarter of a beat with a rocking motion. It was introduced to the United States by Fred Astaire and Dolores Del Rio in the 1933 movie *Flying down to Rio*, where they danced the ballroom version of the samba, the carioca. The "Brazilian Bombshell," as movie star Carmen Miranda was known, popularized the samba's rhythms in her movies.

Mambo is a voodoo term in Haiti, although as a dance it was created among upper-class Cubans for the ballroom. To some extent it evolved from the rumba, although it is more difficult and danced fairly fast with jitterbug-like acrobatics and jerky staccato rhythm. The difficulties of the mambo led to the creation of the cha-cha, a simpler and easier dance, which resembled a much slower version of the mambo. In the United States the cha-cha has been the most popular Latin dance since the 1950s, although in the 1990s the mambo, tango, and salsa eclipsed the cha-cha. Salsa, a Puerto Rican dance, steadily gained in popularity in the last decade of the twentieth century.

SOCIAL DANCING IN THE 1970s AND BEYOND

In the 1970s new dance forms emerged that revived close couples dancing as well as a greater stress on footwork and coordination than did dances that came on the heels of the twist. The hustle and its close cousin, disco, grew up among the black and Puerto Rican bars and dance clubs in New York City. *Saturday Night Fever* (1977), starring John Travolta, had an immense impact on the popularity of disco dancing. Disco spurred an exhibition-style dancing, emphasizing improvisation and individual expression—the dancer becoming almost a soloist or choreographer. The hustle (and disco) closely resembles the Lindy except that disco music does not have the rhythmic swing of big band music. Instead, the hustle consists of dancing three beats against the music's four beats. One variation of the hustle was the "Good Foot" popularized by soul singer James Brown in his 1969 hit song, "Get on the Good Foot," which he performed in an acrobatic style. The "Good Foot" pointed toward break dancing.

Hip-hop as a musical style emerged in opposition to the increasing commercialization of disco, funk, and soul. It came out of New York, Los Angeles, and Chicago. This new style was created by DJs (disc jockeys) in dance clubs, who blended, scratched, and intercut music from different tracks, thus creating a new musical form. Break dancing, or breaking, emerged as a dance form in response to a number of new developments. The DJs melding of percussion breaks from two identical records and playing the breaks over and over again generated opportunities for dancers to perform their gymnastic dance routines. Some break dancing routines were derived from the miming of robotlike actions, inspired by the character of Robot on the popular 1970s TV program *Soul Train.*

It also resulted from the incorporation of moves from martial arts, especially kung fu and capoeira, the Brazilian dance-like martial art. In some cases this also transformed violent conflict between gangs into dance competitions. Break dancing requires great skill and acrobatic abilities and was popularized by the 1983 movie *Flashdance.*

Hip-hop musical culture has continued to generate variations on break dancing, such as popping, uprock, house, and bebop (a swinglike revival).The most significant dance style to emerge in the first decade of the twenty-first century was krumping. A freestyle street dance characterized by fast-paced, energetic, and exaggerated movements of the head, legs, and feet, it evolved from a hip-hop offshoot called "clowning." David LaChapelle's 2005 documentary *Rize* documents the clown and krumping subculture of Los Angeles, where the dance style first surfaced. Krump dancing is allied with turf dancing, which first developed in Oakland, California, in 2002. Turf dancing is organized around dance battles and focuses more on storytelling and the creation of optical illusions. Krumping is more freestyle, while turfing relies on improvisatory and sophisticated dance moves including popping, locking, and miming. Both styles evolved from and play out within the culture of hip-hop.

Jeffrey Escoffier

SEE ALSO: *Astaire, Fred, and Ginger Rogers; Ballet; Big Bands; Brown, James; Castle, Vernon and Irene; Checker, Chubby; Country Music; Disc Jockeys; Disco; Dixieland; Flashdance Style; Hip-Hop; Martial Arts; Modern Dance; Salsa Music;* Saturday Night Fever*;* Soul Train*; Sousa, John Philip; Tap Dancing; Travolta, John.*

BIBLIOGRAPHY

Giordano, Ralph G. *Social Dancing in America: A History and a*

Reference. Volume 1, Fair Terpsichore to the Ghost Dance, 1607–1900. Volume 2, Lindy Hop to Hip Hop, 1901–2000. Westport, CT: Greenwood Press, 2006.

Hager, Steven. *Hip Hop: The Illustrated History of Break Dancing, Rap Music, and Graffiti.* New York: St. Martin's Press, 1984.

Hazzard-Gordon, Katrina. *Jookin': The Rise of Social Dance Formations in African-American Culture.* Philadelphia: Temple University Press, 1990.

Social Media

Though the definition remains somewhat in flux, the term *social media* is broadly defined as electronic platforms or channels that allow people to communicate and share content. Most social media attract users with technologies that facilitate a variety of online relationships. Social media can be divided into several categories, including social networking, blogs, social news, content sites, and collaboration-based sites. These have allowed people not only to develop an online identity and reputation but also to form virtual communities by sharing information through such sites as Facebook, Twitter, Bebo, Pinterest, YouTube, Wikipedia, and LinkedIn. Although information can be protected, most social media operate as public forums, presenting content or promoting individual users to a larger audience. Some operate in real time, like human conversation, and others preserve some of their content, like mail. Few charge for their basic services, depending on advertising or other forms of revenue. Early-twenty-first century social media have altered the nature of human interaction, but they have also been criticized for reducing traditional face-to-face, personal relationships between family and friends to more distant, ethereal connections.

EARLY FORMS OF SOCIAL MEDIA

Social media actually existed before the invention of the Internet. President Abraham Lincoln used the telegraph to send an early version of e-mail—more recently nicknamed "T-mail"—to his generals and operatives during the Civil War. After the war, telegraph operators used abbreviations and symbolic jargon expressed in Morse code to communicate socially. Many telephone customers in the first half of the twentieth century had party lines, a single shared landline that allowed users to listen surreptitiously to the conversations of other users or to converse without dialing a number. Party lines even played a role in the 1959 movie *Pillow Talk* with Doris Day and Rock Hudson. IBM debuted another early version of e-mail, called Radiotype, at the 1939 New York World's Fair. Using shortwave radio, Radiotype transmitted written messages from one electric typewriter to another. It was widely used by the U.S. Army throughout World War II.

Touchtone telephones were introduced in 1963 and presented to the public at the 1964 New York World's Fair. "Techies," including a young Steve Jobs and Steve Wozniak, created electronic devices nicknamed blueboxes that imitated the telephone tones, and they used them to conduct unpaid conference or group calls with fellow techies in the early 1970s, a social medium called "phreaking." Citizens band (CB) radios allowed users to socialize anonymously over short distances via public airwaves, especially while driving. With the birth of the Internet, early e-mail networks such as ARPANET and BITNET and personal computer programs such as cc:Mail and Eudora made the mass transmission of electronic messages possible. Computerized bulletin board systems (BBS) offered message boards and chat rooms for multiple users as early as 1979.

Web-page designer Darcy DiNucci envisioned twenty-first-century social media in 1999. Labeling her vision Web 2.0, she predicted that the Internet would evolve from a static, one-way means of communication, like a printed page, to a flexible two-way "transport mechanism, the ether through which interactivity happens." The social media website SixDegrees.com had appeared two years earlier, providing an opportunity for users to share messages based on six degrees of connectivity. The site attracted millions of users before it was sold in 2000. Ryze.com appeared the following year as a professional social media site, allowing business and technology workers to network. Blogs, user-friendly software that allows users to post and share Internet content, first appeared in the early 1990s. Although DiNucci coined the term, Web 2.0 gained more traction in 2004 when O'Reilly Media held the first Web 2.0 conference.

FRIENDSTER, MYSPACE, FACEBOOK, AND YOUTUBE

Friendster was the first digital social medium to attract widespread public attention. Founded as a dating website by programmer Jonathan Abrams in 2002, its name was the merging of the word *friend* with *Napster*, a peer-to-peer file-sharing site that had been convicted of violating copyright law the previous year. Friendster had more than three million users within months. "It helped us into a computer sugar coma," a *Rolling Stone* reporter observed in 2003, "Friendster is the hotel where you can check out but never leave." Abrams refused a $30 million offer from Google to sell the site in 2003, considered one of the greatest Silicon Valley business blunders. As it grew in users, the site failed to keep up technologically. Toward the end of the first decade of the 2000s, Friendster boasted 115 million users, mostly in Asia, and it became a social gaming site in 2009.

Allegiance to a particular site was short-lived in the early years of digital social media. For example, Friendster was surpassed in users by MySpace in 2004. Founded by several employees of eUniverse, a Los Angeles Internet company with Friendster accounts, it grew quickly by capitalizing on user familiarity with the somewhat similar Friendster platform. It was purchased by Rupert Murdoch's News Corporation in 2005 for $580 million and was the most visited social networking site in the world until overtaken by Facebook. MySpace did not require users to identify themselves but was less customized than Facebook and did not have features such as the latter's "Profile" and "Wall."

Facebook had its roots in the 2003 site Facemash, which compared photographs of female college students. Created by Harvard University sophomore Mark Zuckerberg, "thefacebook" (which was renamed Facebook in 2005) was originally restricted to college students. It added high school students and other defined groups until by 2006 it was open to anyone thirteen or older. It grew in users from around one million in 2004 to become the leading site based on unique monthly visitors in 2008. The site broadened its user base in 2009 by adding interactive game applications. More than 50 percent of the American population ages twelve and over had a Facebook account by April 2011, and it reached its one trillion page view mark that year, making it the most visited website in history.

Words such as *facebooking* and *unfriend* entered the English language due to the site.

By March 2012, Facebook had 901 million active users. "Timeline" was introduced as a user interface in 2012, designed to follow users literally from cradle to grave. "I've found long-lost friends and made a couple new ones," an Associated Press reporter observed of social media like Myspace and Facebook in 2009, "But I've also never felt more distracted, and I don't like that."

YouTube, the preeminent video social medium, debuted in 2005. Founded by Chad Hurley, Steve Chen, and Jawed Karim as a site for users to share videos, it was purchased by Google in 2006 for $1.65 billion and gained notoriety in 2009 when Iranian protesters uploaded a video of a young woman being shot to death by a militiaman. The video quickly went "viral," meaning that it was copied and linked to other sites around the world, helping create support for the protesters. YouTube tags and channels allow viewers to search videos for subjects or types, but the site lacked the exacting search function of print media sites. Flickr, founded in 2004, allowed users to share and store still images and video.

Beyond social network sites, location-based social media proliferated following the introduction of the first Apple iPhone in 2007. Envisioned in 2006 as a platform for inconsequential bursts of information, Twitter went from 60,000 tweets (individual 140-character messages) per day in 2006 to more than 340 million tweets per day in 2012, quickly becoming one of the most-utilized social media platforms. Twitter has offered its users the opportunity to participate in real-time conversations on a range of topics, including sporting events, presidential debates, and natural disasters. The compact messages have been used to organize protests, break news stories, and coordinate emergency response teams.

FourSquare allowed smartphone users to interact by awarding points and badges for visiting various locations beginning in 2009. The same year, Blippy appeared as a site allowing users to track and compare purchases. SubMate was created in 2010 to facilitate communication between subway passengers in large cities, and Highlight, introduced in 2012, allows users to locate and communicate with nearby Facebook friends.

POLITICAL AND PERSONAL IMPACT

Social media have been lauded for their positive impact on global politics. Portions of the 2011 Middle Eastern uprisings were made possible by Twitter, Facebook, and YouTube, especially in Tunisia, Egypt, and Libya. The American Occupy Wall Street movement was driven in part by the emergence of online social media communities. Psychologists point to the chance for users to express themselves on social media sites, providing educational and social growth opportunities. Social media allow constant contact over great distances, making it easier to unite people with common interests and to reunite with absent friends or family members. Also facilitating autonomy and space for individual expression and growth, social media provide a convergence of consumers and high-powered technology as never seen before.

Social media have created unanticipated problems as well. High school students have discovered that MySpace and Facebook can provide revealing information to college and university admissions officers engaging in a practice known as online snooping, and prospective employers have used social media to obtain information not available on resumes or in interviews with potential employees. Although sites say they do not track ethnicity or similar personal information, in practice users with common backgrounds tend to gravitate toward each other, and their "friends" can be used to provide information unwittingly. Constant contact with social media can build relationships but also inflame them. Criminal activities such as stalking, hazing, sexual predation, and bullying have been linked to social media.

Perhaps the greatest challenge for social media involves user privacy. Sites such as Facebook use tracking programs to gather and preserve personal user information, and more recent technologies such as Google Analytics have created a new profession known as marketing technology in order to take advantage of what is called "non-personally identifiable information" (NPII). Web searches, Web purchases, online viewing choices, and related information are aggregated and sold to online marketers, presumably for life. More and more employers are ferreting out information about potential employees from Facebook and other social media sites. Responding to these threats to personal privacy, President Barack Obama's administration established the Privacy Bill of Rights in 2012. An attempt to protect user information through federal regulation, the privacy agreement specifies what information can and cannot be accessed from the Internet.

As the popularity of social media continues to grow, it is likely that more rules will follow. Speaking to both the private and public sector, President Obama has argued that "American consumers can't wait longer for clear rules of the road that ensure their personal information is safe online." Although some concerns remain, social media have accelerated the rate at which information is made available to the global community and have provided a way for people to interact in that community.

Richard Junger

SEE ALSO: *Apple Computer; Blogging; CB Radio; Day, Doris; Facebook; Google; GPS; Hudson, Rock; IBM (International Business Machines); The Internet; Napster; Obama, Barack; Smartphones; Telephone; Twitter; YouTube.*

BIBLIOGRAPHY

Aaker, Jennifer Lynn; Andy Smith; and Carlye Adler. *The Dragonfly Effect: Quick, Effective, and Powerful Ways to Use Social Media to Drive Social Change.* San Francisco: Jossey-Bass, 2010.

Boyd, Danah M., and Nicole B. Ellison. "Social Network Sites: Definition, History, and Scholarship." *Journal of Computer-Mediated Communication* 13, no. 1 (2007).

Bryfonski, Dedria. *The Global Impact of Social Media.* Detroit, MI: Greenhaven Press, 2012.

DiNucci, Darcy. "Design and New Media: Fragmented Future—Web Development Faces a Process of Mitosis, Mutation, and Natural Selection." *Print* 53, no. 4 (1999): 32.

Irvine, Martha. "Social Networking Sites Take Off." *Deseret News,* December 31, 2009.

Mitchell, Patrick. "A Space of Their Own." *Children's Voice,* May/June 2008, 25.

Partridge, Kenneth. *Social Networking.* New York: H.W. Wilson, 2011.

Soda Fountains

The classic American soda fountain was defined as much by its atmosphere as by what it served. Light, cool, and airy places furnished with marble-topped counters and tables, shining mirrors, and sparkling glass-and-chrome serving dishes, soda fountains began springing up in the early nineteenth century and kept essentially the same formula until the 1950s. The bill of fare was simple: carbonated beverages and, later, ice cream and combinations thereof. In the heyday of the soda fountain (roughly 1890–1940) one could order a tempting variety of dishes, from an ice-cream soda (soda water and ice cream) to an ice-cream sundae (ice cream topped with nuts and a chocolate or fruit sauce) to a plain soda (carbonated water mixed with fruit syrup).

Bubbly mineral water from natural springs has long been thought to have therapeutic qualities. After chemists figured out how to make artificially carbonated water, apothecaries and eventually drugstores featured it as one of their many curatives. In 1770 a Swede named Bergman produced artificially carbonated water, and by 1806 Professor Benjamin Silliman of Yale was manufacturing bottled water in New Haven, Connecticut. Early in the nineteenth century druggists began carbonating water in their basements, installing a readily accessible spigot on the first floor to serve customers. Before long the local literati started gathering at drugstores, making them common meeting places and establishing the soda as a social beverage.

In 1832 John Matthews of New York City invented the first compact soda-water machine and dispenser unit, which popularized the drink and gave tavern owners their first stiff competition. Six years later Eugene Roussel, a Philadelphia perfume maker, combined fruit syrups with carbonated water, making the first flavored sodas, including orange, cherry, lemon, teaberry, ginger, peach, and root beer.

The ice-cream soda was not invented until about 1874, at the Franklin Institute Exposition in Philadelphia, when Robert M. Green, a soft drinks vendor, ran out of cream and substituted ice cream in his drinks. This new libation quickly became a national institution. By 1876, helped along by the Centennial Exposition's 30-foot-high fountain, soda fountains replaced ice-cream saloons as fashionable places for the elite to patronize and see the wonders of technology at work. By 1900 common brands sold at soda fountains included Hires Rootbeer, Moxie, Dr. Pepper, and Coca-Cola, the "great national temperance drink."

Prohibition greatly increased the popularity of the soda fountain. By the 1920s the improvement of refrigeration allowed soda fountains to serve meals, and they were incorporated into department stores, luncheonettes, grocery stores, tobacco shops, and five-and-dime stores. While they were popular with all Americans, teenagers frequented soda fountains the most. Soda jerks, named for the way they jerked the handles used to extract fruit syrups from the pumps, worked behind the counter making the sometimes complicated concoctions for the patrons—anything from a Brown Cow to a Bonnie Belle Cream to a Catawba Frappe. Usually good-looking men, soda jerks were a popular attraction to their customers and even had their own lingo. For example, "shoot (or hang) an honest" meant a cherry coke, "one sweet" or "pull one" referred to milk, "Adam and Eve on a raft" translated as two eggs on toast, a "ninety-five" described someone trying to get away without paying, and "thirteen!" warned that the boss was around.

A familiar icon in popular culture, the soda fountain has appeared in plays and movies: People drank strawberry sodas at

Teens at a Soda Fountain. *A clerk serves a group of teenagers at a soda fountain in 1945.* HULTON ARCHIVE/GETTY IMAGES.

the fountain in *Our Town*. It appears as the place of courtship in the 1919 movie *True Heart Susie*. Mickey Rooney and Judy Garland flirt over sodas in the 1938 film *Love Finds Andy Hardy*. The legendary soda fountain at Schwab's drugstore in Hollywood, California, was supposedly the place where young hopefuls went to get noticed by the film industry; legend has it that Lana Turner was "discovered" there in 1937.

The golden age of the soda fountain stretched from the end of the nineteenth century to the early 1940s. During World War II soda jerks got drafted, sugar was rationed, manufacturers of soda equipment had to retool for the war effort, and fountain operators saw larger profits in goods like cosmetics and nylon stockings. After the war there was a brief resurgence in soda fountains, but the business was never as popular as it had been earlier in the century. Americans turned to ready-made food and began motoring to the new fast-food restaurants that sprouted up along the nation's highways, spelling the demise of the time-consuming ice-cream soda and its attendant institution, the soda fountain. One of the last department stores to operate some soda fountains was Woolworth's, but the company closed all of its U.S. locations in 1997.

Wendy Woloson

SEE ALSO: *Coca-Cola; Department Stores; Dime Stores/Woolworth's; Diners; Fast Food; Garland, Judy; Ice Cream Cone; Nylon; Pepsi-Cola; Prohibition; Teenagers; Turner, Lana; World War II.*

BIBLIOGRAPHY

Dickson, Paul. *The Great American Ice Cream Book*. New York: Atheneum, 1972.

Funderburg, Anne Cooper. *Sundae Best: A History of Soda Fountains*. Madison: University of Wisconsin Press, 2001.

Jonas, Susan, and Marilyn Nissenson. *Going, Going, Gone: Vanishing Americana*. San Francisco: Chronicle Books, 1994.

Morrison, Joseph L. "The Soda Fountain." *American Heritage*, August 1962, 10–19.

Riordan, John Lancaster. "Soda Fountain Lingo." *California Folklore Quarterly* 4 (1945): 50–57.

Schwartz, David M. "Life Was Sweeter, and More Innocent in Our Soda Days." *Smithsonian* 17 (1986).

Soderbergh, Steven *(1963–)*

Steven Soderbergh is an American film director, screenwriter, and producer known not only for his low-budget art films but also for commercial successes such as *Erin Brockovich*, *Traffic*, and *Ocean's Eleven*. Soderbergh's first film, *sex, lies and videotape*, won the prestigious Palme d'Or at the Cannes Film Festival in 1989 and marked a turning point in the history of independent filmmaking. During the next decade, however, he struggled to find his own creative balance, making a succession of offbeat, often controversial films that included *Kafka* (1991), *Schizopolis* (1996), and *The Limey* (1999). Although some of these early works were well regarded by critics, it was not until *Erin Brockovich* and *Traffic* debuted in 2000 that Soderbergh once again succeeded in combining provocative content with popular appeal. Both films garnered Academy Awards, establishing Soderbergh as one of the most influential figures in Hollywood. In the years following, he has continued to explore the creative possibilities of filmmaking and has delivered audience pleasers such as the *Ocean's* trilogy (2001–2007) and *Contagion* (2011).

Born in 1963 in Atlanta, Georgia, Soderbergh grew up in Charlottesville, Virginia, then moved to Baton Rouge, Louisiana, when his father became dean of education at Louisiana State University. He attended the university's laboratory school, where he discovered filmmaking. The attraction was so strong that after finishing his secondary education, Soderbergh headed to Los Angeles in search of a film career. After a series of odd jobs in the industry, he returned to Baton Rouge and found his first success directing music videos. Then, on the way to Los Angeles for a second try, Soderbergh wrote the script for *sex, lies and videotape*. He found modest funding for the project and went back home to film the brilliant account of sexual deception that made him the youngest director ever to win the highest prize at Cannes.

The success of Soderbergh's low-budget debut attracted new interest to independent filmmaking and brought a flood of attention to the young director, who found himself confronting the challenge of inflated expectations. Although some of his cinematic efforts during the 1990s were critically praised, some were fairly criticized, and none was commercially successful. Nevertheless, they provided Soderbergh with an opportunity to hone his skills and to expand his base of industry contacts. In 1998 he scored a modest success with the stylish crime romance *Out of Sight*, which earned two Oscar nominations and reestablished his reputation.

Though known to the public primarily as a director, Soderbergh is widely admired in the film community for his range of skills. On several projects he served not only as director but as writer, cinematographer (under the name Peter Andrews), or editor (under the name Mary Ann Bernard). He took on all four roles for his 2002 science fiction film *Solaris*. Soderbergh is also a highly regarded producer, bringing to the screen a series of successful films that includes *Pleasantville* (1998), *Confessions of a Dangerous Mind* (2002), *Syriana* (2005), *Good Night and Good Luck* (2005), and *Michael Clayton* (2007). In several of these projects he partnered with George Clooney, who has been a frequent star in Soderbergh films. Other recurring collaborators include Julia Roberts, Matt Damon, and Catherine Zeta-Jones.

At first glance Soderbergh's films may seem to have few common elements, but there are several unifying characteristics found throughout his work. In his biography of Soderbergh, Aaron Baker points out that almost every Soderbergh film features an alienated main character and makes a statement on some issue—for example, political repression, environmental degradation, or economic inequality. Although his films often focus on crime and may include violence, they also offer thoughtful philosophical explorations. In *The Philosophy of Steven Soderbergh*, a collection of essays edited by R. B. Palmer and Steven Sanders, scholars discuss topics such as "the nature of reality in *Solaris*; the heritage of Enlightenment thought in *Schizopolis*; guilt, punishment, and redemption in *The Limey*; altruism in *Erin Brockovich*; truth, knowledge, and ethics in *sex, lies and videotape*; and Kantian ethics, performance, and agency in *Traffic* and the *Ocean's* trilogy."

Many of Soderbergh's films either remake or strongly reference film classics, and several critics have characterized his work as blending the exuberance of American crime drama with the stylized introspection of European art cinema. Although the

European influence is most evident in his smaller films, it is also visible in the discontinuous editing and fatalistic tone of large-scale works such as *Traffic* and *Contagion*. Overall, Soderbergh's career has been marked by experimentation with varied forms and ideas as well as an ability to explore disturbing aspects of the human condition while entertaining audiences with masterful filmmaking.

Cynthia Giles

SEE ALSO: *Academy Awards; Clooney, George; Damon, Matt; Hollywood; Roberts, Julia;* sex, lies and videotape.

BIBLIOGRAPHY

Baker, Aaron. *Steven Soderbergh*. Urbana: University of Illinois Press, 2011.

Palmer, R. B., and Steven Sanders. *The Philosophy of Steven Soderbergh*. Lexington: University Press of Kentucky, 2011.

Soderbergh, Steven, and Anthony Kaufman. *Steven Soderbergh: Interviews*. Jackson: University Press of Mississippi, 2002.

Soldier Field

Dedicated as a memorial to World War I soldiers, the colonnaded stadium known as Soldier Field has served as a cultural mecca for Chicago residents, hosting professional sports, presidential visits, religious events, and concerts. The architectural firm Holabird & Roche was awarded the commission for the stadium in 1919. Construction on the stadium (originally known as Grant Park Stadium) began in 1922, and it was dedicated in November 1925.

Though a centerpiece of Chicago's waterfront, Soldier Field fell victim to disuse and poor maintenance. Talks were initiated in the 1950s to bring a professional baseball team to the stadium, but it was not until 1971 that it found a permanent resident in the Chicago Bears of the National Football League (NFL). Plans for demolishing, revamping, or possibly doming the stadium continued until 1983, when the structure was placed on the National Register of Historic Places. In 1994 Soldier Field played host to the opening ceremonies of the World Cup soccer competition.

The building—with its classic columns and precast concrete resembling slabs of stone—was a familiar sight along the shore of Lake Michigan. It was also an anomaly in the NFL as the league's smallest stadium. Despite its status on the National Register of Historic Places, Soldier Field underwent a long-awaited renovation starting in 2001, consisting of a new stadium within the old colonnaded exterior that featured updates such as huge video screens and a better sound system. The new Soldier Field opened in 2003 to weak reviews and was christened the "Spaceship on Soldier Field" because the new portion of the bowl resembles a flying saucer. In 2006 Soldier Field was removed from the National Register of Historic Places because the changes had compromised the stadium's original character.

In addition to Bears games, the renovated stadium has hosted high-profile rock acts, including U2. During the 2011 football season, the Chicago Park District, which manages the facility for the Bears, came under intense criticism because of the poor condition of the grass playing field. The Bears suffered a public relations disaster in the preseason when they had to cancel their annual family night for fans because of fears that the loose sod would jeopardize player safety. New sod was installed before the regular season started, but at the end of the 2011 season, NFL players still rated Soldier Field's surface as the third worst in the league.

Michael A. Lutes

SEE ALSO: *The Chicago Bears; National Football League (NFL); Professional Football; Stadium Concerts; U2; World Cup.*

BIBLIOGRAPHY

Bruegmann, Robert. *Holabird Roche Holabird Root: An Illustrated Catalogue of Works*. New York: Garland, 1991.

Ford, T. A. Liam. *Soldier Field: A Stadium and Its City*. Chicago: University of Chicago Press, 2009.

Peterson, Paul Michael. *Chicago's Soldier Field*. Charleston, SC: Arcadia Publishing, 2007.

Some Like It Hot

Some Like It Hot, a critically acclaimed farcical romp produced by United Artists and directed by Billy Wilder, premiered at Loew's Capitol Theatre on Broadway in 1959. Set in Chicago in the 1920s, the film stars Tony Curtis as Joe and Jack Lemmon as Jerry, two hapless musicians who are pursued by gangsters when they witness the St. Valentine's Day Massacre. Joe and Jerry decide to disguise themselves as Josephine and Geraldine, respectively, and join a female band headed for Florida. (Actually, Jerry takes to his new role quickly, spontaneously introducing himself as Daphne.)

On the southbound train the pair befriend Sugar Kane, played by Marilyn Monroe, and begin competing for her affections. It turns out that Sugar is on the run as well, fleeing the string of saxophone players who have loved and left her. In Florida Joe woos Sugar by masquerading as a millionaire, and Daphne is courted by Osgood (Joe E. Brown), who is indeed a millionaire. Interestingly, Jerry Lewis was asked to play the role that went to Lemmon, who never let Lewis forget that he had made a mistake. On holidays Lemmon sent Lewis candy and roses with a card reading, "Thanks for being an idiot."

By the time *Some Like It Hot* was released, Wilder had already become an established auteur. Reviews of the movie compare his sophisticated comedy to that of Ernst Lubitsch and refer to the Wilder touch. The director enjoyed a great deal of control over the production of the film. By the end of the 1950s, few films were being shot in black and white, partly because Hollywood was competing with television for viewers. Wilder, however, felt that Lemmon and Curtis would look too garish in color and convinced the studio that he was right.

Some Like It Hot marked Monroe's emergence from semiretirement. She had made twenty-one films between 1950 and 1956, only one in 1957, and none in 1958. She was married to playwright Arthur Miller and pregnant with his child during filming, but she suffered a miscarriage shortly after. She had long since earned the reputation of being extremely difficult to work with, showing up late, drinking on the set, stumbling over lines, and consulting with her drama coach constantly.

Wilder is the only director ever to work with Monroe more

than once (the other film was *The Seven Year Itch* [1955]), and afterward he was extremely critical of her unprofessionalism. According to Carl Rollyson in *Marilyn Monroe: A Life of the Actress*, "He had been cautious with the press during filming, but shortly afterwards he allowed his disgust with her to show. She had seldom worked a full day on the set, and because of her the production had gone several weeks past its scheduled end and had exceeded its budget by about half a million dollars. He took his revenge in a series of sarcastic statements." For example, Wilder suggested that the Screen Directors Guild should give him a Purple Heart for casting her in two of his films, and he said that he was too old and too rich to ever go through such an ordeal again.

According to film legend, Curtis also spoke of Monroe contemptuously, describing their love scene as "like kissing Hitler." He later insisted that he never made that statement. In the final film, however, the ensemble acting of the cast was considered superb. According to Bernard F. Dick, "It would not be hyperbole to call *Some Like It Hot* a comic masterpiece. It has the classic comic plot of disguise, deception, and intrigue where a single complication generates a series of subplots the way a single pebble creates concentric ripples in a pool." He continues, "*Some Like It Hot* also possesses a quality found in the best comedies—a sense of humanity and an attitude of compassion for the lunatics and lovers who play the fool for our sake." In 2000 the American Film Institute named *Some Like It Hot* the funniest film of all time, outranking such perennial favorites as *Tootsie*, *Blazing Saddles*, *Duck Soup*, *Annie Hall*, and *The Graduate*.

Jeanne Hall

SEE ALSO: Annie Hall*;* Duck Soup*;* The Graduate*; Hollywood; Lewis, Jerry; Lubitsch, Ernst; Monroe, Marilyn; Movie Stars; Raft, George;* The Seven Year Itch*; Television; Wilder, Billy.*

BIBLIOGRAPHY

Dick, Bernard F. *Billy Wilder*. New York: Da Capo Press, 1996.

Dyer, Richard. *Heavenly Bodies*. New York: St. Martin's Press, 1986.

French, Brandon. *On the Verge of Revolt: Women in American Films of the Fifties*. New York: Frederick Ungar Publishing, 1978.

Haskell, Molly. *From Reverence to Rape: The Treatment of Women in the Movies*. New York: Penguin Books, 1974.

Horton, Robert, ed. *Billy Wilder: Interviews*. Jackson: University Press of Mississippi, 2011.

Palmer, R. Barton, ed. *Larger than Life: Movie Stars of the 1950s*. New Brunswick, NJ: Rutgers University Press, 2010.

Rollyson, Carl E. *Marilyn Monroe: A Life of the Actress*. Ann Arbor, MI: UMI Research Press, 1986.

Straayer, Chris. "Redressing the 'Natural': The Temporary Transvestite Film." *Wide Angle* 14, no. 1 (1992): 36–55.

Sondheim, Stephen *(1930–)*

Stephen Sondheim is one of the most important creative personalities in American musical theater. Like George M. Cohan and Cole Porter before him, he is a rare songster who creates both words and music. Sondheim and his shows have almost a cult following because of their sophisticated topics, music, and approaches. He is a composer who creates unique works, yet each bears his unmistakable imprint. His most popular song, "Send in the Clowns" (1973), has been recorded by numerous singers worldwide.

Sondheim was born on March 22, 1930, into an affluent New York family and began his musical studies at very young age. He graduated from Williams College with a music degree and then continued his composition studies with Milton Babbitt, a pioneer in computer-generated music. Sondheim began his career as a composer of musicals in the 1950s with *Saturday Night* (1955), a show that was not staged until 1997. He also wrote incidental music for the play *Girls of Summer* (1956). Sondheim's first commercial success was as librettist for *West Side Story* (1957), which was nominated for a Tony Award for best musical. With music by Leonard Bernstein, Sondheim penned the words to such immortal songs as "Maria," "Tonight," "America," "One Hand, One Heart," "I Feel Pretty," and "Somewhere."

Sondheim's next major project was *Gypsy* (1959). He was to write both the words and music before the star of the show, Ethel Merman, demanded a more experienced composer. So Sondheim created the lyrics, while Jule Styne wrote the music. The show was a hit and nominated for the Tony Award for best musical. Songs in *Gypsy* include "Let Me Entertain You," "Everything's Coming Up Roses," "Wherever We Go," and "Rose's Turn."

The first show to appear on Broadway for which Sondheim penned both the words and music was *A Funny Thing Happened on the Way to the Forum* (1962). Based on the plays of Plautus, the fast-moving musical farce includes such songs as "Comedy Tonight" and "Everybody Ought to Have a Maid." The plot features Pseudolus, a slave who must go through a series of hilarious adventures in order to gain his freedom. Zero Mostel received rave reviews for his performance as Pseudolus in the original production. The show won Tony Awards for best musical and best producer (Hal Prince). It was revived on Broadway in 1972 with Phil Silvers in the lead role and again in 1996 with Nathan Lane. A number of original songs were dropped for the 1966 film version, starring Zero Mostel and Phil Silvers.

Following *A Funny Thing Happened on the Way to the Forum*, Sondheim worked on *Anyone Can Whistle* (1964) and *Do I Hear a Waltz?* (1965). *Anyone Can Whistle*, a musical about corrupt city officials, played only one week on Broadway. Its cast album, made after the show closed, gained cult status. Sondheim was the lyricist for *Do I Hear a Waltz?*, and Richard Rodgers wrote the music. The show is about the experiences of an American tourist in Venice and, like its immediate predecessor, was a commercial failure.

THE 1970s

Sondheim's work during the 1970s began with two concept musicals, *Company* (1970) and *Follies* (1971). Both shows revolve around a central theme. *Company* features five New York couples and their mutual bachelor friend, while *Follies* centers on four people in their early fifties who attend a reunion and reflect on earlier times. *Company* includes the songs "Being Alive," "You Could Drive a Person Crazy," "Another Hundred People," and "Barcelona." The show won the New York Drama Critics' Circle Award for best musical and six Tony Awards, including best musical, best score, and best lyrics. *Follies*, with a fifty-member cast and a twenty-two-number score, includes "Who's That

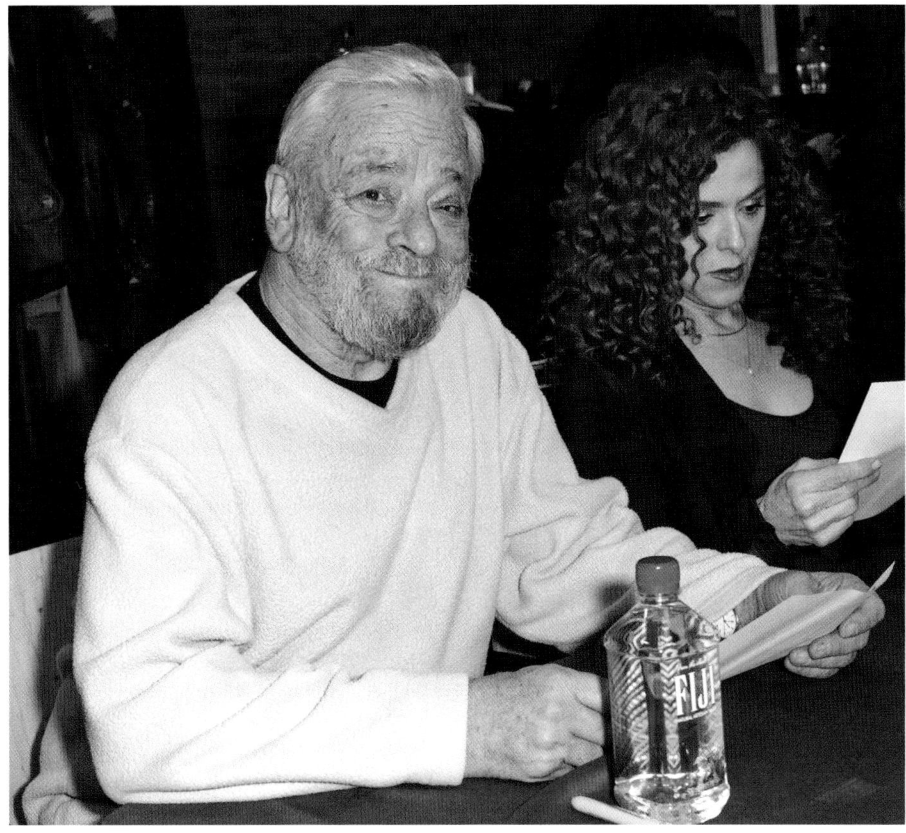

Stephen Sondheim. *Stephen Sondheim (left), with Bernadette Peters, promotes the release of a new album of music from* Follies, *one of his many smash-hit musicals, in 2011.* D DIPASUPIL/CONTRIBUTOR/WIREIMAGE/GETTY IMAGES.

Woman?" "I'm Still Here," and myriad pastiche songs in the styles of earlier Broadway composers. Although *Follies* won the New York Drama Critics' Circle Award for best musical and seven Tony Awards, it closed after 522 performances, losing its $800,000 investment. A revival of *Follies* appeared in 1987.

Sondheim next wrote the music and lyrics for *A Little Night Music* (1973), which is based on the 1955 film *Sommarnattens leende* (Smiles of a summer night), directed by Ingmar Bergman. Set in Sweden at the turn of the twentieth century, the plot deals with the complicated romantic world of the aging actress Desiree Arnfeldt; her former lover, the lawyer Fredrik Egerman; his child-bride, Anne; and their circle of acquaintances. Glynis Johns and Len Cariou starred in the original Broadway production, while Elizabeth Taylor and Cariou appeared in the 1977 film. *A Little Night Music* is entirely in three-quarter time (or multiples thereof), the meter of a waltz, a musical symbol of nostalgia. The show has a number of memorable songs, including "A Weekend in the Country," "Night Waltz," and "Remember." But the show's most unforgettable number is "Send in the Clowns," Desiree's nostalgic soliloquy.

The Frogs (1974) is one of Sondheim's most curious experiments. Created as incidental music for a Yale Repertory Theatre production of Burt Shevelove's English adaptation of the Greek play of the same name, Sondheim's score was first performed in the swimming pool at Yale University. The score avoids traditional musical theater idioms and contains fiendishly difficult choral writing. Without the experience of writing *The Frogs*, the innovation that Sondheim demonstrates in *Pacific Overtures* (1976) may not have been possible. Sondheim wrote new songs for the 2004 Broadway revival starring Nathan Lane.

Pacific Overtures is one of the most singular shows in the repertory of the American musical theater. Japanese history, from the arrival of Commodore Perry in 1856 to the late twentieth century, is told in the style of traditional Japanese Kabuki theater. The all-male, all-Asian cast performs songs, such as "Chrysanthemum Tea," "Please Hello," and "The Advantages of Floating in the Middle of the Sea." Despite its striking originality (or perhaps because of it), *Pacific Overtures* closed after 193 performances, losing all of its $500,000 budget.

Always wanting to expand the boundaries of musical theater, Sondheim chose the macabre tale of a murderous barber as the basis for *Sweeney Todd, the Demon Barber of Fleet Street* (1979). The title character, swearing revenge on a judge for the demise of his family and murdering everyone who sits in his barber chair, enters into a business partnership with Mrs. Lovett, the owner of a pie shop who has difficulty finding meat for her pies. The pair find a practical, but macabre, solution to both of their problems. Among the most memorable numbers are "Not While I'm Around," "Epiphany," "A Little Priest," "God, That's Good," "Pretty Women," and "Johanna." The show garnered eight Tony Awards, including best musical, best score, and best book. Angela Lansbury and Len Cariou starred in the original Broadway production.

THE 1980s AND 1990s

The 1980s did not start out well for Sondheim. His show, *Merrily We Roll Along* (1981) ran for only sixteen performances on Broadway. Like *Anyone Can Whistle, Merrily We Roll Along* lived beyond its Broadway run through the success of its cast album. *Sunday in the Park with George* (1984) did much better. It revealed yet another approach to Sondheim's efforts to expand the musical theater. Based on the book of the same name by James Lapine, it deals with issues of creativity and the power of art. Mandy Patinkin and Bernadette Peters starred in the original production. The show won the 1985 Pulitzer Prize for Drama. Among the numbers in its intriguingly intricate score are "Finishing the Hat" and "Move On."

Sondheim ventured into the world of fairy tales for his next show, *Into the Woods* (1987). The stories of Cinderella, Jack and the Beanstalk, Little Red Riding Hood, Snow White, and Rapunzel are fused into a tale about a baker and his wife, who live under the curse of a witch. In order to break the curse, the baker and his wife must secure an item from each of the fairy tales. All ends well at the end of the first act. In the second act the widow of the giant in Jack and the Beanstalk demands revenge, and the characters must join together in order to defeat her. Songs include "Into the Woods," "Agony," "Giants in the Sky," "No One Is Alone," and "Children Will Listen." Peters, Joanna Gleason, and Chip Zien starred in the original Broadway production.

At the beginning of the 1990s, Sondheim returned to the darker side of the human experience with *Assassins* (1991). All of the major characters are people who tried, either successfully or unsuccessfully, to assassinate American presidents. From the opening chorus, "Everybody's Got the Right to Be Happy," to the final scene at the Texas School Book Depository, these "antiheroes" of American society each present the motives behind their actions. In 1994 Sondheim turned to love for *Passion* (1994), based on the French film *Passione d'amore*. The show is about the love triangle of a military officer, his beautiful young lover, and an invalid who captures his soul. The story is presented in a rhapsodic manner with a seamless blend of music and dialogue. Songs include "Happiness," "I Wish I Could Forget You," and "No One Has Ever Loved Me."

THE TWENTY-FIRST CENTURY

In the twenty-first century, numerous Broadway revivals of Sondheim's shows were mounted, including *Into the Woods* (2002), *Assassins* (2004), *The Frogs* (2004), *Pacific Overtures* (2004), *Sweeney Todd* (2005), *Company* (2006), *Sunday in the Park with George* (2006), and *A Little Night Music* (2009). A film version of *Sweeney Todd: The Demon Barber of Fleet Street*, starring Johnny Depp and Helena Bonham Carter, appeared in 2007.

In addition to original shows, several stage compilations of Sondheim songs have appeared in London and New York, including *Side by Side by Sondheim* (1976), *A Stephen Sondheim Evening* (also known as *You're Gonna Love Tomorrow*, 1983), and *Putting It Together* (1992). Sondheim has also written music and lyrics for movies. Among his film credits are *The Seven Per-Cent Solution* (1976), *Reds* (1981), and *Dick Tracy* (1990). The song "Sooner or Later" from *Dick Tracy*, performed by Madonna in the film, earned Sondheim an Academy Award for Best Original Song. Sondheim's only television work was an episode of *ABC Stage 67* (1966) called "Evening Primrose," starring Anthony Perkins.

Sondheim is one of the most original creators for the musical theater, and he expands boundaries not only through his choice of subject matter (in which he often challenges the audience to extremes) but also in his handling of musical form and structure. Songs are intrinsically joined together in his shows and are likewise bound to particular characters. Through live performances, video releases, and recordings, Sondheim's music is enjoyed around the world.

William A. Everett

SEE ALSO: *Academy Awards; Bergman, Ingmar; Bernstein, Leonard; Broadway; Cohan, George M.; Depp, Johnny; Dick Tracy; Madonna; Patinkin, Mandy; Peters, Bernadette; Porter, Cole; Prince, Hal; Rodgers and Hammerstein; Rodgers and Hart; Taylor, Elizabeth; Tony Awards;* West Side Story.

BIBLIOGRAPHY

Banfield, Stephen. *Sondheim's Broadway Musicals*. Ann Arbor: University of Michigan Press, 1993.

Bristow, Eugene K., and J. Kevin Butler. "Company, About Face! The Show That Revolutionized the American Musical." *American Music* 5, no. 3 (1987): 241–254.

Fraser, Barbara Meares. "The Dream Shattered: America's Seventies Musicals." *Journal of American Culture* 12, no. 3 (1989): 31–37.

Gordon, Joanne. *Art Isn't Easy: The Theater of Stephen Sondheim*, rev. ed. New York: Da Capo, 1992.

Gottfried, Martin. *Sondheim*. New York: Abrams, 1993.

Herbert, Trevor. "Sondheim's Technique." *Contemporary Music Review* 5 (1989): 199–214.

Horowitz, Mark Eden. *Sondheim on Music: Minor Details and Major Decisions*, 2nd ed. Lanham, MD: Scarecrow, 2010.

Martin, George Whitney. "On the Verge of Opera: Stephen Sondheim." *Opera Quarterly* 6, no. 3 (1989): 76–85.

Mollin, Alfred. "Mayhem and Morality in *Sweeney Todd*." *American Music* 9, no. 4 (1991): 405–417.

Secrest, Meryle. *Stephen Sondheim: A Life*. New York: Knopf, 1998.

Sondheim, Stephen. *Finishing the Hat: Collected Lyrics (1954–1981) with Attendant Comments, Principles, Heresies, Grudges, Whines and Anecdotes*. New York: Knopf, 2010.

Sondheim, Stephen. *Look, I Made a Hat: Collected Lyrics (1981–2011) with Attendant Comments, Amplifications, Dogmas, Harangues, Digressions, Anecdotes and Miscellany*. New York: Knopf, 2011.

Swayne, Steve. *How Sondheim Found His Sound*. Ann Arbor: University of Michigan Press, 2005.

Zadan, Craig. *Sondheim & Company*. New York: Da Capo, 1994.

Sonny and Cher

SEE: *Bono, Sonny; Cher.*

The Sopranos

The Sopranos is a critically acclaimed television drama that aired on the HBO cable channel from 1999 to 2007. Starring James Gandolfini as New Jersey mob boss Tony Soprano, the show brought a depth and complexity to television not previously seen by viewing audiences. *The Sopranos* garnered twenty-one Emmy Awards and five Golden Globe Awards, and many critics, including writers for the *New Yorker* and *Vanity Fair*, praised the drama as one of the best shows ever produced, citing its nuanced character portrayals and its deft interweaving of multiple story lines.

The creator and head writer of *The Sopranos*, David Chase, based the show partly on his experiences growing up in New Jersey and partly on a famous real-life organized-crime family. He initially envisioned a movie about a mobster, who sees a psychiatrist because of issues with his mother. He adapted his script into a television series to evade the one-note nature of the original concept.

The main character in the *The Sopranos* is Tony Soprano, who spends his days weeding out traitors, juggling the needs of his wife and children against those of his mistresses and cohorts, seeking out business opportunities, and ordering hits, all while attending therapy to come to terms with his own unhappy childhood and cope with job-related anxiety. He describes himself as a "sad clown," but few would recognize him as such. He wields a gun as liberally as his hero, Gary Cooper and clings to outdated gender roles, yet he faces a contemporary-style neurotic crisis, including panic attacks and fever dreams.

Much of Soprano's business takes place at Satriale's, a butcher shop, and at Bada Bing, a strip club operated by loyal Silvio (played by Steve Van Zandt). Soprano's closest associates include Paulie Walnuts, Big Pussy, Bobby Bacala, Ralphie Cifaretto, Furio Giunta, Vito Spatafore, and Cousin Tony Blundetto. Their jostling for position keeps the organization in constant upheaval. Meanwhile, Soprano grooms his nephew, Christopher (Michael Imperioli), to be his successor.

External conflict arises from the rival Aprile crime family, with whom Soprano establishes an uneasy truce. For example, Richie Aprile is first engaged to and then killed by Soprano's wild-child sister, Janice (Aida Turturro). This type of turnaround is common. By the end of the series, nearly every major character outside the immediate Soprano family has been killed off as Soprano's chaotic attempts at organization inevitably implode.

Some critics argue that women are the real powers controlling Soprano's actions, although others see that interpretation as forced and far-fetched. The series begins with Soprano waiting to see his psychiatrist, Jennifer Melfi (Lorraine Bracco), to whom he is immediately attracted. She wants to focus on his issues with his mother (Nancy Marchand), a harpy who nags Soprano constantly. Melfi's work with Soprano is necessarily circumscribed. She would have to report any violent crimes that he tells her about, so they speak in euphemisms. Soprano romantically pursues Melfi throughout the series. His efforts are by turns shy and assertive, and he eventually arouses her interest in him as "a dangerous alpha male."

Despite his hefty, hairy body and crude manners, Soprano attracts women who appear to genuinely care about him or who become intoxicated by his power. Chief among them is his wife, Carmela (Edie Falco). Carmela's feelings for him are conflicted: she is jealous and angry by his obvious affairs, but her strong Catholic faith will not let her leave him. During confession, she admits to feeling guilt over what her family does. She has crushes on "good" men and even has an affair, but consummation is always threatened by her potential partner's fear of her husband.

The Sopranos. *HBO's successful crime drama* The Sopranos *starred, from left, Tony Sirico, Steve Van Zandt, James Gandolfini, Michael Imperioli, and Vincent Pastore as New Jersey mobsters.* HBO/THE KOBAL COLLECTION/NESTE, ANTHONY.

A late-series separation is short-lived; Soprano is as forceful with Carmela as he is with his avowed enemies. Soprano, meanwhile, often steps outside his marriage, much to his mistresses' detriment. A Russian girlfriend attempts suicide, and another lover kills herself. He mistreats and hurts all of them.

"You have to understand that your father means well," Carmela reassures their daughter, Meadow (Jamie-Lynn Sigler), early on in the series. "He's given his life . . . for us." Meadow and her brother, Anthony Junior, represent the couple's aspiration to give their children more options than they enjoy in their literally life-or-death marriage. Meadow escapes to Columbia University and decides to become a lawyer—a "good" one—but even she is tempted by a romance with one of the Apriles.

Conspiracies against Soprano run as rampant as his suspicions. Betrayals come from every direction, and Soprano methodically eliminates his enemies. He shoots Big Pussy for informing against him. He guns down Cousin Tony, albeit with a tear in his eye. When Christopher's girlfriend, Adriana (Drea de Matteo), becomes an FBI informant, Soprano orders Silvio to execute her.

The final season is a bloodbath, beginning with a shot that lands Soprano in a coma. As he recovers, one character after another meets his or her end, as rival organizations clean house. Among the victims are Silvio; Bobby; and Vito, who has finally acknowledged his homosexuality. Soprano himself smothers drug-addicted Christopher.

The final episode of the series itself is controversial. The Soprano family gathers slowly in a diner, where every other patron seems to have an eye on them. Then, Meadow walks in, and the screen goes black: the episode is over. Viewers are left with only a black screen and silence. It is testimony to the lasting impact of the series that fans continue to debate the meaning of the ending and the fate of the Sopranos, just as film and television producers keep trying to emulate the intricacy and psychological sophistication of one of the most influential series in television history.

Susann Cokal

SEE ALSO: *Cooper, Gary; Emmy Awards; Mafia/Organized Crime; The* New Yorker*; Television;* Vanity Fair.

BIBLIOGRAPHY

Fahy, Thomas, ed. *Considering David Chase: Essays on "The Rockford Files," "Northern Exposure," and "The Sopranos."* Jefferson, NC: McFarland, 2008.

Kashner, Sam. "The Family Hour: An Oral History of *The Sopranos.*" *Vanity Fair*, April 2012, 212–228.

Martin, Brett. *"The Sopranos": The Book: The Complete Collector's Edition.* New York: Time Home Entertainment, 2007.

Sosa, Sammy *(1968–)*

Born in the Dominican Republic, outfielder Sammy Sosa became a baseball sensation almost overnight with the Chicago Cubs in 1998 when he was named the National League Most Valuable Player after battling St. Louis Cardinals slugger Mark McGwire for the single-season home run record. Roger Maris's thirty-seven-year-old record was broken twice, by McGwire's seventy homers and Sosa's sixty-six. Sosa had hit twenty home runs in June of that season, the most ever by a player in a single month. Furthermore, his 158 runs batted in were the fourth-highest total in National League history. His impressive statistics helped the Cubs reach the playoffs for only the third time since 1945.

Despite being constantly followed by the media during his homer chase with McGwire, Sosa maintained his charm and easygoing manner and helped contribute to a renewal of America's faith in its national pastime, which had fallen out of favor due to a work stoppage in 1994 that wiped out the playoffs. In 1999 Sosa hit sixty-three home runs, becoming the first player in major-league history to reach the sixty mark in back-to-back years.

In the first decade of the 2000s, however, Sosa's reputation started to unravel. In 2003 he was ejected from a game when his bat shattered and it was discovered to be "corked." (A piece of cork had been inserted into the bat, something that is against the rules because it is believed to make the baseball fly farther.) Sosa dismissed the incident as an innocent accident, saying that the bat was supposed to be used only for batting practice to give fans a show. Many skeptics, however, began to wonder if his records were tainted.

In 2005 a slumping Sosa was traded from the Cubs to the Baltimore Orioles. That same year he was called to testify before the U.S. Congress, which was investigating the use of illegal performance-enhancing drugs (PEDs), such as steroids, in baseball. Sosa swore under oath that he had "never taken illegal performance-enhancing drugs." However, rumors had swirled about him for some time because of his sudden improvement as a slugger and his suspicious loss of bulk once testing became a regular procedure in baseball. In 2006 he did not play for any team, but he returned in 2007 for one last season with the Texas Rangers, his original club.

In 2009 the *New York Times* leaked test results from 2003, and the story claimed that Sosa had been one of 104 players to test positively for PEDs. The results were supposed to have been confidential. The story fueled speculation that Sosa might be charged with perjury for his testimony before Congress, but no charges were ever brought. As one lawyer noted, the outfielder had been careful to say he had used no illegal drugs rather than no drugs at all; at the time, steroids were legal in Sosa's home country, where he presumably used them. Even though Sosa retired with 609 home runs, a milestone reached by only a handful of players, his reputation was in tatters, and no one—except perhaps Sosa himself—expected that the once-beloved ballplayer would ever be elected to the National Baseball Hall of Fame.

Matt Kerr

SEE ALSO: *Baseball; The Chicago Cubs; Major League Baseball; McGwire, Mark.*

BIBLIOGRAPHY

Canseco, Jose. *Juiced: Wild Times, Rampant 'Roids, Smash Hits, and How Baseball Got Big.* New York: Regan Books, 2005.

Preller, James. *McGwire & Sosa: A Season to Remember.* New York: Aladdin Paperbacks, 1998.

Sammy's Season. Lincolnwood, IL: Contemporary Books, 1998.

Smith, Gary. "The Race Is On." *Sports Illustrated*, September 21, 1998.

Sosa, Sammy, and Marcos Bretón. *Sosa: An Autobiography*. New York: Grand Central Publishing, 2000.

Soul Music

Soul music emerged in the late 1950s and early 1960s as one of the most distinctive forms in the history of American popular music. For black Americans especially, soul music defined the 1960s, offering a cultural soundtrack to the civil rights movement and the larger awakening of black consciousness and pride. Soul hits dominated the charts during that decade, but defining exactly what soul was proved no easy task, even for some of its greatest artists.

Wilson Pickett defined soul as "nothin' but a feelin'," while Don Covay said, "For a singer, soul is total vocal freedom." Aretha Franklin explained, "Soul to me is a feeling, a lot of depth and being able to bring to the surface that which is happening inside. . . . It's just the emotion, the way it affects other people." Elements of the genre live on, but the classic period of soul music was from about 1960 to 1975. Alongside jazz, soul music is one of America's most original contributions to world culture.

BEGINNINGS

If defining soul music is difficult, identifying its origins is not. Soul music emerged during the 1950s as a cross between rhythm and blues and gospel music. The genre combined the Saturday-night sinner and the Sunday-morning repentant into one person or one song, just as they existed in real life. In combining the R&B themes with gospel elements (call-and-response singing, close harmonies, and themes of celebration, loss, and longing), early soul artists often secularized gospel tunes by changing key words: the gospel song "Talkin' 'bout Jesus" became "Talkin' 'bout You"; "This Little Light of Mine" became "This Little Girl of Mine"; "I've Got a Savior" became "I Got a Woman."

Ray Charles. *Ray Charles, performing in 2003, is considered the first artist to bring secularized gospel music into the mainstream, blending it with a rhythm and blues sound to create soul music.* TOM BRIGLIA/CONTRIBUTOR/FILMMAGIC/GETTY IMAGES.

This transition reflected changes occurring in the black community after World War II as more and more black Americans moved from the rural South to the urban North. Early arrivals in the North had created R&B music in the mid-1940s as an expression of the new realities of life in these urban neighborhoods. Later, as more southern blacks poured into these communities, they brought with them elements of southern gospel music. Both musical forms coexisted as separate expressions of black life. They soon crossed, however, producing what became soul music.

The acknowledged father of this cross was Ray Charles. All of the secularized gospel songs just mentioned were hits for Charles in the mid-1950s. Born in 1930 in Albany, Georgia, Charles moved to Seattle, Washington, as a teenager and emerged in the late 1940s as a Nat King Cole–style crooner playing local clubs such as the Rocking Chair and the Black and Tan. There he caught the attention of Swingtime Records, one of the early black-owned R&B recording companies, and he released a number of blues and Cole-inspired tunes, among them "Kissa Me Baby" and "Confession Blues." Moving to Atlantic Records in 1952, Charles began developing an earthier style that he picked up working with blues musicians Guitar Slim and Lowell Fulson. At Atlantic, he began to combine blues elements with gospel stylings he had picked up as a child in Georgia.

That style became the basis for soul music and during the 1950s provided Charles with a string of hits, including "Lonely Avenue"; "I Got a Woman"; "Hallelujah I Love Her So"; and perhaps his biggest hit, "What'd I Say," which combined a gospel call-and-response segment between Charles and his backup singers, the Raelettes, moans that could easily have come from either the bedroom or the pulpit, and a driving R&B band.

Following close on Charles's heels was Sam Cooke, who had come to prominence as the lead singer of the gospel group the Soul Stirrers before developing a more pop-oriented soul style that brought him such hits as "You Send Me," "Twistin' the Night Away," and "Bring It on Home to Me." Jackie Wilson similarly had started out in a vocal group, the Dominoes, before forging a driving pop-soul style with such songs as "Reet Petite," "Lonely Teardrops," and "Baby Workout." While Charles's music maintained a close connection with the raw elements of R&B music, Wilson and Cooke moved the R&B and gospel marriage closer to the realm of pop.

It took three record companies to bring soul into the mainstream. They were Atlantic Records in New York City; Motown Records in Detroit, Michigan; and Stax/Volt Records in Memphis, Tennessee. While numerous smaller labels made invaluable contributions to soul music, these three labels were responsible for some of the most explosive soul music of the 1950s and 1960s. Most of the major talents in soul music, with some very notable exceptions, were on these three record labels. And, while there were major individual talents on each label roster, each company managed to build a unique sound that identified each artist with his or her particular label.

ATLANTIC RECORDS AND ARETHA FRANKLIN

In 1947 Herb Abramson and Ahmet Ertegun formed Atlantic Records, which became one of the dominant independent record labels in R&B in the 1950s through successes with such artists as Ruth Brown, Charles, Joe Turner, LaVern Baker, and the Clovers. With the early success of Charles, Atlantic moved even further into soul music. In the early to mid-1960s, Atlantic had soul hits with the Drifters' "Up on the Roof," "This Magic Moment," and "Save the Last Dance for Me"; Ben E. King's "Stand by Me" and "Spanish Harlem"; Percy Sledge's "When a Man Loves a Woman"; Wilson Pickett's "Land of 1000 Dances," "Mustang Sally," and "Funky Broadway"; Don Covay's "Seesaw"; and Solomon Burke's "Just out of Reach." Atlantic's major sound innovation was to bring soul "uptown" with a more polished, professional sound accomplished by adding string arrangements and by using professional Brill Building songwriters.

Atlantic's biggest success, however, came in 1967 with the discovery of singer Aretha Franklin. Franklin was the perfect embodiment of soul music, combining a strong background in church music (her father, the Reverend C. L. Franklin, was the well-known minister of the New Bethel Baptist Church in Detroit) with the depth of feeling and style required to take her gospel training to the secular music world. She had first signed with Columbia Records in the early 1960s, where she attempted to become a pop-soul singer in the Sam Cooke style. Her records in this vein fared poorly, and when her contract with Columbia expired in 1966, producer Jerry Wexler signed her to Atlantic. There, Wexler took Franklin to Rick Hall's Fame Studios in Muscle Shoals, Alabama, which was developing a reputation as a hotbed of soul music, a place where the all-important *feeling* necessary in soul music seemed to come out more readily. Franklin remade her sound, letting her gospel roots come out.

She debuted on Atlantic in 1967 with the album *I Never Loved a Man the Way I Love You*, which went to number two on the album charts that year. Both the title song and Franklin's cover of Otis Redding's "Respect" reached number one. The album also contained "Do Right Woman—Do Right Man"; "Baby, Baby, Baby"; and "Save Me," all of which have become soul classics. Franklin released two more records in the space of a year, unleashing such hits as "Baby I Love You," "Chain of Fools," and the smash "(You Make Me Feel Like) A Natural Woman," a Top 10 hit on both the pop and R&B charts. These releases earned Franklin the undisputed title of the "Queen of Soul" and cemented Atlantic as the home of some of the most powerful soul music ever produced.

MOTOWN: THE SOUND OF YOUNG AMERICA

Songwriter, producer, and one-time record shop owner Berry Gordy Jr. founded Motown Records in 1959 in a simple white bungalow at 2648 West Grand Boulevard in Detroit. Drawing on Charles's innovations in fusing R&B and gospel styles, Gordy successfully wrote and produced songs for Jackie Wilson ("Lonely Teardrops") and Barrett Strong ("Money") during the late 1950s. In 1959 Gordy moved from independent producing (where he would lease songs to other labels) and began his own label, Tamla, which later became part of Motown.

At Motown, Gordy put together a songwriting-producing-recording formula that would sell more singles by the end of the 1960s than any other company. He did this with what resembled assembly-line production; Gordy referred to his role as "quality control." First, he assembled a team of crack songwriters and producers, including Smokey Robinson and the team of Brian Holland, Lamont Dozier, and Eddie Holland, who wrote hit after hit. Next, Gordy put together a house band that included Benny Benjamin on drums, Joe Messina on guitar, James Jamerson on bass, Earl Van Dyke on keyboards, and other regulars. Together, the songwriting-production teams and house band established a signature style that was unmistakable. Then, drawing from the rich local talent of Detroit, Gordy assembled or signed vocal groups or individual singers to record the songs.

Part of Gordy's gift lay in transforming raw street talent into a polished musical product, which he did using this assembly-line process and his eye for promising young talent, calling Motown the "Sound of Young America." Motown's roster of stars included the Supremes ("Baby Love," "You Can't Hurry Love," "Love Child"), Marvin Gaye ("I Heard It through the Grapevine," "Pride and Joy"), the Four Tops ("Standing in the Shadows of Love," "Bernadette," "Reach Out I'll Be There"), the Temptations ("My Girl," "Ain't Too Proud to Beg"), Mary Wells ("My Guy"), Martha and the Vandellas, Smokey Robinson and the Miracles ("I Second That Emotion," "The Tracks of My Tears"), the Marvelettes, Junior Walker and the All Stars, Stevie Wonder ("Uptight," "Signed, Sealed, Delivered, I'm Yours," "For Once in My Life"), and Gladys Knight and the Pips. Motown's nationwide success with this formula lay in the ability of its music to resonate in both the black and white communities, and many of the aforementioned hits topped both the R&B and pop charts throughout the 1960s. From the very beginning, for commercial reasons or otherwise, Gordy followed an integrationist approach, and his success pushed the soul music created at Motown closer and closer to the larger pop realm.

Although Gordy's formula was responsible for most of Motown's success, in the later 1960s and early 1970s, a few of his early artists began to break out of the Motown formula, maturing musically to create very personal, signature styles all their own. The two most prominent and unique were Gaye and Wonder. Gaye broke out of the Motown mold in a decisive way with the topical album *What's Going On* in 1971: both its title track and "What's Happening Brother" addressed the war in Vietnam, "Mercy Mercy Me" the environment, and "Inner City Blues" the urban crisis in America's ghetto communities.

Wonder became a musical force unto himself with a string of important albums in the early 1970s on which he wrote and sang all of the songs and played most of the instruments. Included in albums such as *Innervisions*, *Talking Book*, *Fulfillingness First Finale*, *Music of My Mind*, and his double-album opus *Songs in the Key of Life*, Wonder scored huge hits with such songs as "You Are the Sunshine of My Life," "Isn't She Lovely," "I Wish," and "Superstition." His songs also often took a topical turn, such as "Living for the City" and "Village Ghetto Land" on urban problems and "Too High" on drug addiction. "Higher Ground" was an exhortation for black self-empowerment, and "You Haven't Done Nothin'" a larger critique of the white power structure.

The classic Motown era ended after 1971 when Gordy moved the company to Los Angeles and gave up direct hands-on control over studio production. With those changes, the trademark sound disintegrated.

STAX RECORDS AND SOUTHERN SOUL

If Atlantic and Motown defined soul in the urban North, Memphis's Stax/Volt Records, during its classic period from 1960 to 1968, virtually defined southern soul, a sound at once relaxed and easy yet filled with musical tension and as easily recognizable as the Motown sound. Jim Stewart and his sister Estelle Axton founded Satellite Records in 1959, changing the name to Stax by 1961 (Volt Records was a later subsidiary), and began to record local black musicians, eventually establishing a studio in an old Memphis movie theater. Among their first recording artists were local DJ Rufus Thomas and his daughter Carla.

Carla Thomas scored an early hit in 1960 with "Gee Whiz," which reached the Top 10 on both the R&B and pop charts. Stax's next hit was "Last Night," an instrumental number by the Mar-Keys that featured a unique combination of organ, guitar, and horns that would become the hallmark of Stax/Volt's sound. Although not quite as tightly run as Motown, Stax/Volt did employ some of the same techniques. The instrumental band Booker T. and the MG's became in essence Stax's house band in addition to scoring numerous hits on its own, such as "Green Onions" and "Time Is Tight." Stax also benefited from a core group of songwriters and producers, most prominent among them David Porter and Isaac Hayes, who wrote many of Stax's great hits, including "Hold On! I'm Comin'" and "Soul Man" by Sam and Dave and "B-A-B-Y" by Thomas.

A number of Stax/Volt's stars were also writers, including Eddie Floyd, who cowrote his own hits "Knock on Wood" and "Raise Your Hand," among others. Even more prolific was MG guitarist Steve Cropper, who, in addition to playing guitar on many Stax/Volt records, also cowrote many songs with other Stax/Volt artists, including the best-selling Stax/Volt single of all time, "(Sittin' on) The Dock of the Bay," with Otis Redding. Like Franklin at Atlantic, Redding was far and away Stax/Volt's greatest star and one of the most distinctive soul singers ever, with a powerful, raw, emotional style that seemed to wring every bit of feeling from every note of a song. A prolific songwriter as well, Redding had some of Stax/Volt's biggest hits, including "Respect," "Try a Little Tenderness," "These Arms of Mine," "Mr. Pitiful," "The Happy Song (Dum-Dum)," and dozens of others before his untimely death in a plane crash in December 1967.

Stax/Volt continued after the death of Redding, but things were never quite the same. Despite a number of hits in the 1968–1972 period, Stax declined with the dissolution of Booker T. and the MG's and the loss of its deal with Atlantic Records, which had given Atlantic distribution rights to Stax's recordings since the early 1960s. With the breakup of that deal, Atlantic took Stax's biggest sellers, the Redding and Sam and Dave catalogs, which were in many ways the heart of the Stax/Volt empire. These problems slowly eroded Stax's signature style, and the company declared bankruptcy in 1975.

BEYOND SOUL

Outside the three major soul record labels, James Brown emerged as an early R&B-soul singer in the mid-1950s, with such hits as "Please, Please, Please" and "Try Me." He scored more hits in the early 1960s, but his heyday came later in the decade when he diverged from more standard soul forms to fashion his own brand of soul/funk, a harder-driving, more intense and powerful sound that came through on such songs as "Cold Sweat," "Papa's Got a Brand New Bag," "Get up (I Feel like Being a) Sex Machine," and "I Got You (I Feel Good)." During the heyday of Black Power, Brown also made powerful statement songs, including "Say It Loud—I'm Black and I'm Proud"; "I Don't Want Nobody to Give Me Nothing (Open up the Door I'll Get It Myself)"; "Get up, Get into It, and Get Involved"; and "Soul Power." Brown's stylistic innovations in soul music influenced the development of both funk music in the 1970s and rap music in the 1980s.

Although great soul artists such as Al Green, the Staple Singers, Curtis Mayfield, Marvin Gaye, Stevie Wonder, and many others continued to record soul music, the classic soul era ended in the mid-1970s as black music fragmented into such styles as disco and funk, which emphasized dance rhythms over well-crafted singing and songwriting. The great record labels that had acted as important conduits for soul music had moved in other directions as well. Atlantic moved more toward rock acts, Motown left for Los Angeles, and Stax/Volt fell apart in financial trouble. In terms of style, the connection to gospel music that was such a hallmark of soul became less influential in black music generally, and soul evolved into a more homogenous sound known as urban contemporary music. Soul was always an adaptable musical form, however, and in the 1980s the genre began to blend with smooth jazz, disco, and other styles.

Neo-soul emerged in the late 1990s as a reaction to the heavily produced, synthetic sound of much mainstream music of the time. The term itself was invented by Kedar Massenburg, who hoped to develop a new category of soul as a marketing move for Motown Records. By then the growing popularity of hip-hop and synth-pop in the 1980s had caused a decline in soul as a commercial force. At the same time, R&B became a more diverse musical form, through the work of experimenters such as Prince and Terence Trent D'Arby. Perhaps because they were already working with a musical style that was from elsewhere, British artists such as Soul II Soul and Lisa Stansfield are credited with developing the blend of styles from different eras that defines what later became known as neo soul.

In particular, during the early 1990s British musician Omar Lye-Fook began making R&B-influenced soul that moved away from the heavily produced, synthetic sound of much mainstream music of the time. This move back to "real" instruments and voices was a feature of music by artists such as D'Angelo, whose album *Brown Sugar* was neo-soul's breakthrough work; Lauryn Hill; and Maxwell. The value of the term *neo-soul* is much disputed, but the music it describes, which is vocally driven, with simple production values, was influential for several years at the turn of the twenty-first century, blending synthesized sounds with voice and traditional instruments in a more organic way than before.

Reaching its peak around 2000, neo-soul produced several major artists, including Erykah Badu, Q-Tip, and Alicia Keys. Perhaps because many neo-soul performers wrote political, and often uncommercial, songs, or perhaps because the music itself was predisposed to be experimental, neo-soul declined from its mainstream high point after about 2003. In the second decade of the twenty-first century, singers such as Cee-Lo, Keys, and Leela James ensured that the influence of soul on mainstream music remains strong.

Timothy Berg

SEE ALSO: *Atlantic Records; Blues; Booker T. and the MG's; Brill Building; Brown, James; Charles, Ray; Civil Rights Movement; Cole, Nat King; Cooke, Sam; Disco; The Drifters;*

Franklin, Aretha; Gaye, Marvin; Gordy, Berry; Gospel Music; Green, Al; Hip-Hop; Jazz; Martha and the Vandellas; Mayfield, Curtis; Motown; Pop Music; Redding, Otis; Rhythm and Blues; Robinson, Smokey; Ross, Diana, and the Supremes; Sam and Dave; The Temptations; Walker, Junior, and the All-Stars; Wonder, Stevie; World War II.

BIBLIOGRAPHY

George, Nelson. *The Death of Rhythm & Blues.* New York: Pantheon, 1988.

Guralnick, Peter. *Sweet Soul Music: Rhythm and Blues and the Southern Dream of Freedom.* New York: Harper & Row, 1986.

Haralambos, Michael. *Right On: From Blues to Soul in Black America.* New York: Drake Publishers, 1975.

Hirshey, Gerri. *Nowhere to Run: The Story of Soul Music.* New York: Times Books, 1984.

Kot, Greg. "A Fresh Collective Soul?" *Chicago Tribune*, March 19, 2000.

Miller, Jim, ed. *The Rolling Stone Illustrated History of Rock & Roll.* New York: Random House/Rolling Stone Press, 1980.

Shaw, Arnold. *The World of Soul: Black America's Contribution to the Pop Music Scene.* New York: Cowles, 1970.

Szatmary, David P. *Rockin' in Time: A Social History of Rock-and-Roll.* Englewood Cliffs, NJ: Prentice Hall, 1991.

Various Artists. *Atlantic Rhythm and Blues: 1947–1974.* New York: Atlantic Recording Corporation, 1985.

Various Artists. *The Complete Stax/Volt Singles, 1959–1968.* New York: Atlantic Recording Corporation, 1991.

Various Artists. *Hitsville U.S.A.: The Motown Singles Collection, 1959–1971.* Detroit, MI: Motown Records, 1992.

Various Artists. *Beg, Scream, and Shout!: The Big Ol' Box of '60s Soul.* Los Angeles: Rhino Records, 1997.

Werner, Craig Hansen. *A Change Is Gonna Come: Music, Race & the Soul of America.* Ann Arbor: University of Michigan Press, 2006.

Soul Train

Since 1970 fans have been grooving every week to America's top soul and R&B hits on a televised boogie down called *Soul Train.* Known as "the black *American Bandstand,*" the syndicated dance party proved to be more than just a musical showcase: It established an African American presence on television at a time when such representation was almost nonexistent.

Created and hosted for twenty-three years by Don Cornelius, a former Chicago disc jockey with a silky, measured baritone, *Soul Train* was conceived around the notion of "soul music going from city to city as a train would." The program relied on a sequence of stock elements that gave it an air of familiarity. Its distinctive squealing "Soooulll Traaain" opening, devised by a DJ friend of the host, has remained unchanged since 1970. Each week Cornelius opened the show by promising viewers that they could "bet your last money it's gonna be a stone gas, honey." A series of musical performances followed, with the camera alternating between the lip-synching band and the gyrating denizens on the dance floor. Occasionally stopping to banter with his musical guests, Cornelius closed each program by wishing his viewers "love, peace, and soul!"

The show was a first of its kind on mainstream American television, a weekly forum for the best in African American rhythm and blues. "It was trailblazing," observed J. R. Reynolds, R&B editor of *Billboard* magazine, "not in terms of being a dance music show, but in terms of R&B being offered a platform on a consistent basis." In its heyday during the 1970s, *Soul Train* was able to attract some of the top names in the entertainment industry. Guests on the first national telecast were Gladys Knight and the Pips. Performers who made regular appearances included Barry White, Marvin Gaye, Aretha Franklin, and James Brown. Several of the dancers, including Jody Watley, Rosie Perez, and Fred "Rerun" Berry, went on to have show business careers of their own. *Soul Train* programs from the 1970s even became popular staples of Japanese TV in the 1990s.

In the 1980s, with the advent of rap, *Soul Train* began taking on a hip-hop orientation. The appearance of the politically charged rap group Public Enemy was a sure sign that the torch had been passed to a new generation of African American musicians. Through it all, Cornelius continued to beam beatifically and tout his program as "the hippest trip on television."

The transition from trailblazing series to revered television institution did not diminish the show's impact. Young people of all races continued to watch *Soul Train* for tips on dress and personal style. "*Soul Train* showed a generation what it meant to be cool," declared Todd Boyd, assistant professor of critical studies at the University of Southern California's School of Cinema-Television. In the 1990s the show became a cultural touchstone for the African American artistic community, cropping up in movies such as Spike Lee's *Crooklyn* and the Hughes brothers' *Dead Presidents. Soul Train* also had a wider pop-cultural influence, as exemplified by *Soul Trek,* a 1992 comic-book parody that placed the affable Cornelius in command of the U.S.S. *Enterprise.*

Cornelius served as host of *Soul Train* until 1993, when he assumed the role of "host emeritus," introducing a new guest emcee every week for several years, and then drafting comedian Mystro Clark (1997–1999), actor Shemar Moore (1999–2003), and actor Dorian Gregory (2003–2006) to host the show. Cornelius himself graduated from independent producer to partner with the Tribune Entertainment, the show's distributor. In 1995 he was inducted into the Broadcasting & Cable Hall of Fame.

Despite the show's success, however, Cornelius continued to have difficulty getting exposure from TV stations. Even in cities with large African American populations such as Cleveland, Ohio, and St. Louis, Missouri, *Soul Train* continued to air at irregular times well into the 1990s. Moreover, after Cornelius left, the show's popularity began to falter, despite the introduction of well-known entertainers to take over the hosting role. Production halted in 2006, although *Soul Train* continues to air in syndication. Cornelius's own life ended in tragedy—after a highly publicized domestic-abuse charge and conviction in 2009, he took his own life on February 1, 2012, possibly as a result of early-onset Alzheimer's disease.

Soul Train holds a spot in television history as the longest-running program that was originally produced for first-run syndication. Although originally created by African Americans for young black viewers, it has grown to attract a much larger and more diverse audience. "I've been a fan for a long time!" gushed President Bill Clinton on the *Soul Train* 25th Anniversary Special in 1995. Despite Cornelius's later troubles, his death was mourned by generations of viewers across the United States and the world. He left behind a grand legacy—the television show that popularized black culture from the mid-twentieth century into the twenty-first century and stands as a historical archive of the development of American popular culture.

Robert E. Schnakenberg

SEE ALSO: American Bandstand; *Brown, James; Franklin, Aretha; Gaye, Marvin; Hip-Hop; Lee, Spike; Public Enemy; Rap; Rhythm and Blues; Soul Music; Syndication; Television; White, Barry.*

BIBLIOGRAPHY

Dean, Chuck. "*Soul Train* Rolls into Its 25th Year; Get Don with Your Bad Self." *Entertainment Weekly*, March 17, 1995.

Elber, Lynn. "Don Cornelius Reflects on *Soul Train*, His 'Little Dance Show.'" *Minneapolis Star Tribune*, August 11, 1995.

McKinley, James C., Jr. "Don Cornelius, *Soul Train* Creator, Is Dead at 75." *New York Times*, February 1, 2012.

Moody, Lori. "Durable *Soul Train* Is Pop History in the Making." *Minneapolis Star Tribune*, November 22, 1995.

"Soul Train Still Chugging down the Track." *Michigan Chronicle*, June 17, 1997.

The Sound of Music

The Sound of Music, one of the longest-running Broadway musical of the 1960s, marked the last collaboration between composer Richard Rodgers (1902–1979) and lyricist/librettist Oscar Hammerstein II (1895–1960). After the work was completed, Hammerstein died of cancer. Based partially on Maria Von Trapp's autobiography, *The Story of the Trapp Family Singers* (1949), and the German film *Die Trapp familie* (1956), the show was written for Mary Martin, who had already appeared as Nellie in Rodgers and Hammerstein's musical *South Pacific* (1949). Like many other Rodgers and Hammerstein productions, *The Sound of Music* includes a remarkable number of popular songs: "The Sound of Music," "My Favorite Things," "Climb Ev'ry Mountain," "Do-Re-Mi," and "Edelweiss."

The setting for *The Sound of Music* is Salzburg, Austria, where Maria, a postulant at Nonnberg Abbey, is too free-spirited to accept the discipline of the order and frequently escapes to the mountains. Thus, the Mother Abbess arranges for Maria to work as a governess for the wealthy, aristocratic Captain George Von Trapp—a widower with seven children. By adding music and outdoor expeditions to the children's normally disciplined schedule, Maria wins the children's hearts. Although Captain Von Trapp is engaged to an elegant socialite, Elsa Schraeder, he falls in love with Maria and eventually marries her. However, it is 1938, and the Von Trapps' married life is quickly disrupted by Nazi Germany's annexation of Austria. As fate would have it, the family has become well known as an amateur singing group. After a final appearance at a local contest, the family manages to escape and cross the mountains on foot to Switzerland. The first romance of Von Trapp's oldest daughter, Liesl, unfortunately with a young Nazi, provides a bittersweet subplot.

The Sound of Music was originally the idea of director Vincent J. Donehue with Martin's husband, Richard Halliday, and Leland Hayward producing. Howard Lindsay and Russel Crouse adapted Maria Von Trapp's book. Rodgers and Hammerstein were approached to write only one song but ended up doing the entire score and lyrics, as well as coproducing the show. *The Sound of Music* opened at the Lunt-Fontanne Theatre on November 16, 1959, and ran for 1,443 performances. There have been several successful revivals since its original run, including on Broadway in 1998 and in London from 2006 to 2009.

In 1965 Twentieth Century Fox released a film version starring Julie Andrews as Maria and Christopher Plummer as Captain Von Trapp. With a young, exuberant Andrews singing one of Rodgers and Hammerstein's most accessible scores and spectacular cinematic views of the Alps and Salzburg, *The Sound of Music* garnered ten Oscar nominations and won in five categories: Best Picture, Best Director (Robert Wise), Best Adapted Score, Best Film Editing, and Best Sound. The film also won awards from the Directors Guild of America, the Golden Globes (Best Actress in a Musical Comedy), and the National Board of Review. It was the top box-office draw from 1966 through 1969, and it has remained one of the most popular films ever made.

In the late 1990s a new phenomenon was born: the singalong *Sound of Music*, in which audiences attend showings of the movie and sing the songs aloud. These events take place across Europe, in major cities around the United States, and even in Japan and Australia. One cannot help but think that the music-loving Maria von Trapp would approve.

Ann Sears

SEE ALSO: *Academy Awards; Broadway; The Musical; Rodgers and Hammerstein.*

BIBLIOGRAPHY

Carr, Charmian, and Jean A. S. Strauss. *Forever Liesl: A Memoir of "The Sound of Music."* New York: Viking Adult/Penguin, 2000.

Fordin, Hugh. *Getting to Know Him: A Biography of Oscar Hammerstein II.* New York: Da Capo Press, 1995.

Green, Stanley. *Encyclopaedia of the Musical Film*. New York: Oxford University Press, 1981.

Green, Stanley, and Cary Ginell. *Broadway Musicals Show by Show*, 7th ed. Milwaukee, WI: Applause Theatre & Cinema Books, 2011.

Rodgers, Richard. *Musical Stages: An Autobiography*. New York: Da Capo Press, 1995.

Trapp, Agathe von. *Memories before and after "The Sound of Music": An Autobiography*. New York: Harper Perennial, 2010.

Trapp, Maria Augusta. *The Story of the Trapp Family Singers*. New York: J. B. Lippincott Company, 1949.

Sousa, John Philip *(1854–1932)*

Known as the "March King," John Philip Sousa created more than 100 marches that reflected the optimism, patriotism, and military prowess of the United States during the late nineteenth and early twentieth centuries. Sousa was called the "Dickens of Music" and "Knight of the Baton." He described himself as a "Salesman of Americanism, globetrotter, and musician."

Sousa was born on November 6, 1854, in Washington, D.C., to John Antonio and Maria Elisabeth (Trinkhaus) Sousa.

John Philip Sousa. *John Philip Sousa conducts the United States Marine Band in 1890.* KEYSTONE/STRINGER/HULTON ARCHIVE/GETTY IMAGES.

His father played a trombone for the U.S. Marine Band. Musically gifted at a young age, Sousa studied at a local conservatory and was inspired by Civil War marches he heard during his boyhood. At age thirteen he considered joining a circus band; instead, his father enlisted him in the U.S. Marine Band.

By the summer of 1872 Sousa conducted and played in orchestras in Washington, D.C., and began composing music. His first published composition was "Moonlight on the Potomac Waltzes." Sousa's early work reveals a unique style that would ultimately gain him international distinction. Touring as orchestra conductor for various companies, he performed as a violinist during the Philadelphia Centennial Exhibition in 1876. He composed his first comic opera, *The Smugglers* (1879), for a Philadelphia choir.

On September 30, 1880, Sousa became conductor of the U.S. Marine Band. Under his leadership the band improved in quality from a mediocre ensemble into a superb group. Sousa's exacting standards enabled the band to achieve international fame for its spirited style, and it soon became the model for other bands to emulate. Sousa led the U.S. Marine Band on national and international tours while composing music such as "Semper Fidelis" (1888).

In the spring of 1892 Sousa resigned from the marines to create a concert band of civilians. He assembled talented musicians and staged his band's first concert on September 26, 1892, in Plainfield, New Jersey. The band's programming was a unique blend of instrumentalists, a soprano vocalist, and violinist. "In dynamics, I have never heard any orchestra that could touch us," Sousa told *Music* magazine in 1899. His band appeared throughout the United States and traveled to Europe, including an around-the-world trip from 1910 to 1911. Sousa and his band enhanced the image of American culture in Europe, proving that American musicians were not inferior to European performers.

Sousa constantly composed new music for his band, such as "The Stars and Stripes Forever" (1896), which later was designated the official march of the United States. Some critics believe that this composition alone secured Sousa's acclaimed status as a composer. A patriotic and emotional musician, Sousa sought to create music that was assertive and energetic—just as the United States was militarily at the turn of the twentieth century. He wanted his music to make people proud to be Americans. During the Spanish-American War, Sousa was musical director of the VI Army Corps and prepared a pageant, *The Trooping of the Colors.*

THE PIED PIPER OF PATRIOTISM

Nicknamed the "Pied Piper of Patriotism," Sousa thought a march should "make goose pimples chase each other up and down your spine." He stressed that marches should be characterized by simplicity with a steady, stimulating rhythm. Sousa's marches reflect the country's spirit of optimism, and his driving, pulsating tunes emphasize the strength of the country. His martial music standardized the march form and became popular classics. In addition to his music, Sousa developed a new instrument, the Sousaphone, which resembles a tuba. He also devoted time to protecting composers' rights. He coined the term *canned music* in 1906 when he protested the phonograph industry's practice of recording music without compensating composers.

During World War I Sousa joined the U.S. Naval Reserve as a lieutenant, directing the Great Lakes Naval Training Station Band, which toured the country to raise millions of dollars in Liberty Loan drives. Sousa was a familiar figure, wearing his uniform and carrying his sword at the head of parades. After the war he toured with his band, promoted music education, and testified to Congress about composers' rights. His dramatic performances reinforced his reputation as a showman.

Choosing entertainment over education, he vowed to give audiences the music that they wanted. His band played in remote parts of the United States, where people had never before heard a symphony orchestra. Town dignitaries declared "Sousa Day" when the band arrived, and performances were often standing room only. Sousa performed music that people appreciated while also making unfamiliar music, such as early jazz, accessible to them. In this way he influenced Americans' musical tastes. He often invited the audiences to sing along with the band.

SOUSA EVERYWHERE

The American public's interest in bands peaked between 1890 and 1910, and Sousa helped to disseminate band music. Before televisions, radios, and movies, instruments provided entertainment in homes, and people played Sousa pieces, especially popular dance songs. The July 4, 1898, issue of *Musical Courier* commented, "go where you may, you hear Sousa, always Sousa. . . . It is Sousa in the band, Sousa in the orchestra, Sousa in the phonograph, Sousa in the hand organ, Sousa in the music box, Sousa everywhere." Sousa became a household name, and at one time he was the best-known musician in America. Vaudeville comedians imitated him, and towns hosted public celebrations for his birthday. He also received many honors and medals.

Although he refused to perform on the radio because he preferred interacting with live audiences, Sousa was convinced to broadcast concert series in 1929 and 1931 because of overwhelming public demand. He especially focused on encouraging young musicians. He accepted invitations to help amateur bands and supported the school music movement and the National Music Camp at Interlochen, Michigan. Every year John Philip Sousa awards are given by high school band directors to talented band members. The John Philip Sousa foundation recognizes excellent high school, college, and community bands.

LEGACY

Sousa died on March 6, 1932, after a rehearsal at Reading, Pennsylvania. The last piece he conducted was "The Stars and Stripes Forever." The U.S. Marine Band played "Semper Fidelis" during his funeral procession. Buried at Congressional Cemetery in Washington, D.C., Sousa's gravestone is carved with a bar from "The Stars and Stripes Forever." His music library was donated to the University of Illinois.

Sousa's contributions have been acknowledged in popular culture in the years since his death. The movie *Stars and Stripes Forever* (also called *Marching Along*) premiered in 1952 with Clifton Webb playing Sousa, though Sousa's family and band members criticized the movie's inaccuracies. In 1957 George Balanchine choreographed the ballet *Stars and Stripes*, and the Public Broadcasting Service televised the documentary *If You Knew Sousa* in 1993. In 1997 Sousa was immortalized when the U.S. Postal Service issued a thirty-two-cent stamp, "The Stars and Stripes Forever!" to celebrate the centennial of his most famous march.

Elizabeth D. Schafer

SEE ALSO: *Balanchine, George; Big Bands; The Musical; World War I.*

BIBLIOGRAPHY

Berger, Kenneth Walter. *The March King and His Band: The Story of John Philip Sousa.* New York: Exposition Press, 1957.

Bierley, Paul E. *John Philip Sousa: American Phenomenon*, 2nd ed. New York: Appleton-Century-Crofts, 1973.

Bierley, Paul E. *The Works of John Philip Sousa.* Columbus, OH: Integrity Press, 1984.

Bierley, Paul E. *The Incredible Band of John Philip Sousa.* Urbana: University of Illinois Press, 2006.

Heslip, Malcolm. *Nostalgic Happenings in the Three Bands of John Philip Sousa*, rev. ed. Westerville, OH: Integrity Press, 1992.

Newsom, Jon, ed. *Perspectives on John Philip Sousa.* Washington, DC: Library of Congress, 1983.

Sousa, John Philip. *A Book of Instruction for the Field-Trumpet and Drum: Together with the Trumpet and Drum Signals Now in Use in the Army, Navy, and Marine Corps of the United States.* Cleveland, OH: Ludwig Music Publishing Company, 1985.

Sousa, John Philip, and Paul E. Bierley. *Marching Along: Recollections of Men, Women and Music.* Westerville, OH: Integrity Press, 1994.

South Beach Diet

SEE: *Low-Carb Diets.*

South Pacific

With Mary Martin and Ezio Pinza in the lead roles, the musical *South Pacific* opened at the Majestic Theatre in New York on April 7, 1949, and ran for 1,925 performances. It was the fifth collaboration between composer Richard Rodgers (1902–1979) and lyricist/librettist Oscar Hammerstein II (1895–1960), following *Oklahoma!* (1943), *Carousel* and *State Fair* (1945), and *Allegro* (1947). The phenomenal success of *Oklahoma!* and *Carousel* had made Rodgers and Hammerstein the dominant figures in American musical theater, and *South Pacific* only enhanced their reputation.

Director Joshua Logan suggested that Rodgers and Hammerstein base a musical theater production on one of the short stories from James Michener's *Tales of the South Pacific*, winner of a 1948 Pulitzer Prize. They decided to combine two stories, "Fo' Dolla'" and "Our Heroine," and the resulting musical went on to win Rodgers and Hammerstein their second Pulitzer Prize in a decade (the first was for *Oklahoma!* in 1944). *South Pacific* marked Martin's first Rodgers and Hammerstein show, and it was the Broadway debut for Metropolitan basso Pinza. Coproduced and directed by Logan, *South Pacific*, like *Oklahoma!*, yielded a remarkable number of songs that became popular apart from the show: "Some Enchanted Evening," "There Is Nothin' Like a Dame," "Bali Ha'i," "I'm Gonna Wash That Man Right Outa My Hair," "A Wonderful Guy," and "Younger than Springtime." A film version, also directed by Logan, was released by Twentieth Century Fox in 1958, starring Mitzi Gaynor, Rossano Brazzi, Ray Walston, Juanita Hall, and France Nuyen.

The story takes place in the islands of the South Pacific during World War II, as two very different romantic couples face similar obstacles to their happiness together. First, French plantation owner Emile de Becque and young navy nurse Nellie Forbush from Arkansas fall in love. When Nellie encounters his children from a deceased Polynesian wife, she reconsiders married life with him. Meanwhile, Lieutenant Joe Cable from Philadelphia has a brief romance with Liat, a native girl, but like Nellie, he wonders how he can explain the racial issues to his family back home. De Becque and Cable go on a secret mission behind Japanese lines. Cable is killed, but de Becque returns to find Nellie transformed. She has faced her racism and realized that the children are fellow human beings whom she has already begun to love.

Commenting on social issues through music was a pattern in Rodgers and Hammerstein's work from the beginning of their partnership. The issue of racism had rarely been addressed directly onstage in musical theater, with the exception of the revolutionary *Show Boat* (1927), whose book and lyrics, not coincidentally, were also written by Hammerstein. *South Pacific* meets Caucasian-versus-Asian racial prejudice head on through the stories of its main characters and through the song "You've Got to Be Carefully Taught to Hate." This approach to social justice continues in later Rodgers and Hammerstein shows; for example, there are gender and racial issues in *The King and I* (1951), conflicts between generations and cultures in *Flower Drum Song* (1958), and issues of freedom and patriotism in *The Sound of Music* (1959).

The initial touring company of *South Pacific* traveled for five years. The musical was revived at Lincoln Center in 1967 and staged by the New York City Opera in 1987. The popular film version of 1958 was shot in Fiji and Hawaii, but the colored filters that change lighting effects from scene to scene detract from the scenic beauty and the glorious music. Nonetheless, the film has kept the musical before the public, and *South Pacific* remains a perennial favorite with amateur theater groups around the world.

In 2001 ABC aired a made-for-television movie of the musical starring Glenn Close in the role of Nellie, and it received generally positive reviews for its acting and its beautiful production. In 2008 the musical returned to Broadway for a highly acclaimed two-and-a-half year revival. A television version of that production aired on PBS in 2010.

Ann Sears

SEE ALSO: *Broadway; Made-for-Television Movies; Michener, James; The Musical;* Oklahoma!*; Rodgers and Hammerstein;* Show Boat*;* The Sound of Music.

BIBLIOGRAPHY

Fordin, Hugh. *Getting to Know Him: A Biography of Oscar Hammerstein II.* New York: Ungar Publishing, 1977.

Green, Stanley. *Encyclopaedia of the Musical Film.* New York: Oxford University Press, 1981.

Green, Stanley. *Broadway Musicals Show by Show.* Milwaukee, WI: Hal Leonard Publishing, 1990.

Hyland, William G. *Richard Rodgers.* New Haven, CT: Yale University Press, 1998.

May, Stephen J. *Michener's South Pacific.* Gainesville: University Press of Florida, 2011.

Michener, James. *Tales of the South Pacific.* New York: Macmillan, 1947.

Mordden, Ethan. *Rodgers & Hammerstein.* New York: Harry N. Abrams, 1992.

Rodgers, Richard. *Musical Stages: An Autobiography.* New York: Random House, 1975.

Taylor, Deems. *Some Enchanted Evenings: The Story of Rodgers and Hammerstein.* New York: Harper and Brothers, 1953.

South Park

Trey Parker and Matt Stone's animated comedy *South Park* premiered on Comedy Central in August 1997 to rave reviews and harsh criticism, both of which have persisted for the long-running show. The program follows four young boys: Stan Marsh, Kyle Broflovski, Eric Cartman, and Kenny McCormick, and the citizens of the small, mountain town of South Park, Colorado. *South Park* evolved from a small short, "The Spirit of Christmas: Jesus vs. Frosty," that Parker and Stone created while attending the University of Colorado at Boulder. With funding from Brian Graden, then an executive at Fox, the two re-created the short, which erupted across the Internet. It is reported that George Clooney helped spread the episode by making copies for his friends, and the viral video eventually crossed the screen of Doug Herzog, then president of Comedy Central.

South Park was an immediate success, becoming Comedy Central's highest-rated program. While the show is about children and its crude cutout animation style appeals to young audiences, *South Park* is aimed at adults and carries a TV-MA rating. The episode titles from the first season—"Cartman Gets an Anal Probe," "Big Gay Al's Big Gay Boat Ride," and "Cartman's Mom Is a Dirty Slut," for example—signaled from the start that *South Park* aimed to be more provocative and vulgar than *The Simpsons* (1989–) and *Beavis and Butt-Head* (1993–1997, 2011–), its groundbreaking predecessors.

By 1997 *The Simpsons* and *Beavis and Butt-Head* had established a precedent for animated series aimed at adult audiences, but Parker and Stone distinguished *South Park* by offering stories that were far more vulgar than anything uttered by teenage miscreants Beavis and Butt-Head and more violent than any event the Simpsons encountered in Springfield. Stan, Kyle, Cartman, Kenny, and the other residents of South Park—adults and children alike—swear constantly, but there are surprising moments of naïveté, for example Stan's tendency to vomit from sheer nervousness whenever he sees his girlfriend. The show is wickedly and often darkly funny, and its creators consider almost nothing taboo: in "Starvin' Marvin," for instance, Parker and Stone mock the motivations and effectiveness of philanthropy by having the boys donate to a charity in the hope of getting a sports watch; they wind up getting a starving African child instead. And at least once during each episode, Kenny dies a horrible death, leaving one of the others to lament, "You killed Kenny! You bastards!"

In spite of detractors who have called the show childish, crude, and unsophisticated, *South Park* has won multiple Emmy Awards for Outstanding Animated Program. Throughout its run the show has grown more refined, focusing on satire and current events. One of its Emmy-winning episodes, the three-part "Imaginationland" (2007), takes aim at the U.S. war on terror by having Islamic terrorists hold hostage all the imaginary creatures humans have dreamed up. The episode "Make Love, Not Warcraft" (2006) satirizes the world of online gaming when the boys decide to play *World of Warcraft* online.

South Park has courted controversy throughout its run and never shied away from current events. In the June 2001 episode "It Hits the Fan," the word *shit* or *shitty* is uttered uncensored 162 times, unleashing the knights of Broadcast Standards and Practices. In its first episode after the attacks of September 11, "Osama bin Laden Has Farty Pants" (2001), the show depicts the town covered in American flags but juxtaposes it against a parallel town in Afghanistan that is ravaged by bombs.

A number of celebrities have been parodied on the show, with little backlash. Isaac Hayes, the voice of Chef, left the show after the episode "Trapped in the Closet" criticized Scientology. The very next episode, Chef is portrayed as brainwashed with spliced recordings of previous shows used for his voice. The creators also received a great deal of attention for depicting the prophet Muhammad in an early episode and then going out of their way to comment on not being allowed to do so again in later episodes. In a town where Jesus has his own cable access show, Parker and Stone consider nothing sacred.

OFF THE SMALL SCREEN

Music has played a central role in *South Park* from the start, with episodes often incorporating fairly sophisticated musical numbers. The first soundtrack album, *Chef Aid: The South Park Album* (1998), includes songs sung by the characters as well as performances by such artists as Ozzy Osbourne and Elton John. The popularity of the episode "Mr. Hankey the Christmas Poo" in the show's first season inspired the release of a Christmas CD, *Mr. Hankey's Christmas Classics* (1999). That same year saw the release of a feature film, *South Park: Bigger, Longer & Uncut*, which prompted another soundtrack album. The film's signature song, "Blame Canada," was nominated for an Academy Award for Best Original Song.

Part parody and part satire, *South Park: Bigger, Longer & Uncut* primarily targeted censorship and theories on media-influenced behavior. The film revolves around the boys sneaking into an R-rated film, *Asses on Fire*, starring the Canadian comedy-duo Terrence and Philip. The boys repeat the profane language that they hear in the movie, and Kenny and Cartman reenact the fart-lighting scene, which eventually leads to Kenny's death. Kyle's mom, Sheila, forms Mothers against Canada and kidnaps the duo, resulting in a hostage crisis and war between Canada and the United States. The film lampoons Disney movies, including *Beauty and the Beast* (1991), *The Little Mermaid* (1989), and *The Hunchback of Notre Dame* (1996), by twisting their promotional pop songs into criticisms of small-town life, hero worship, and childhood innocence.

The film's R rating allowed Parker and Stone to employ their usual vulgar plot devices while the myriad show-tune-inspired songs added further levity to the film's message. Like the television series, the movie generated plenty of controversy. From the outset, Parker and Stone battled with Paramount and the Motion Picture Association of America over how the film would be promoted and what rating it would receive. In addition to its Academy Award nomination for Best Original Song, the film received awards from the New York Film Critics Association, Los Angeles Film Critics Association, and MTV. The film also set a Guinness world record for the most swearing in an animated film.

Parker and Stone's success has led them to other opportunities, including the film *Team America: World Police* (2004) and their work writing the Tony-winning musical *The Book of Mormon* (2011). They continue to be deeply involved in every aspect of *South Park*—writing, directing, and voicing its main characters—and their influence can be seen in an increasing number of animated programs aimed at adults.

Adrienne Furness

SEE ALSO: *Academy Awards;* Beavis and Butt-Head*; Cable TV; Disney (Walt Disney Company); John, Elton; MTV; Osbourne, Ozzy;* The Simpsons*; Television.*

BIBLIOGRAPHY

Gardner, Elysa. "It's Back to School for *South Park* Creators." *USA Today*, October 3, 2011, D6.

Johnson-Woods, Toni. *Blame Canada!: "South Park" and Contemporary Culture*. New York: Continuum International, 2007.

Marin, Rick; T. Trent Gegax; Debra Rosenberg; et al. "*South Park*: The Rude Tube." *Newsweek*, March 23, 1998, 56–62.

Southern, Terry *(1924–1995)*

Texas-born writer Terry Southern is best remembered for the wildly written satires—usually featuring a *Candide*-esque heroine—that earned him acclaim in the early 1960s. Southern also cut a swath through the film world in the 1960s. He garnered Academy Award nominations for his screenwriting on *Dr. Strangelove or: How I Learned to Stop Worrying and Love the Bomb* (1964) and *Easy Rider* (1969), films that helped define the rebelliousness and paranoia of that era. By all accounts, however, Southern's exposure to Hollywood had a debilitating effect on him.

His fictional output slowed to a trickle by 1970, and what he did publish belied the promise of his early work. Silent for the next two decades, he published *Texas Summer* in 1992, a poorly received autobiographical novel. When he died, he left behind more than forty unproduced screenplays and an unpublished spoof of Virgin Records titled *Virgin*. Although many found his work to be sophomoric, Southern had a special gift for unmasking hypocrisy, and for a while in the 1960s he was among the funniest writers on the scene.

Michael Baers

SEE ALSO: Dr. Strangelove or: How I Learned to Stop Worrying and Love the Bomb*;* Easy Rider.

BIBLIOGRAPHY

Gerber, Gail, and Tom Lisanti. *Trippin' with Terry Southern: What I Think I Remember*. Jefferson, NC: McFarland, 2009.

Murray, D. M. "Candy Christian as a Pop-Art Daisy Miller." *Journal of Popular Culture* 5 (1971): 340–348.

Silva, Edward T. "From *Candide* to *Candy*: Love's Labor Lost."

Journal of Popular Culture 8 (1975): 783–791.

"Terry Southern." In *Dictionary of Literary Biography*, vol. 2. *American Novelists since World War II*, ed. by Jeffrey Helterman and Richard Layman. Detroit, MI: Gale Research Company, 1978.

Spacek, Sissy *(1949–)*

Elizabeth Mary "Sissy" Spacek spent her childhood in Texas before moving to New York City in her late teens to pursue a singing career. Though she spent several years playing in coffee shops in Lower Manhattan, supporting herself through modeling gigs, her only recorded song—a ballad critiquing John Lennon and Yoko Ono's nude cover for the 1968 album *Unfinished Music No. 1: Two Virgins*—was a commercial failure.

During her early years in New York, Spacek fell in with Andy Warhol's hip Lower Manhattan Factory crowd and was cast in her first nonspeaking role in Warhol acolyte Paul Morrissey's *Trash* (1970). Her waiflike features and innocent mien captured the attention of director Terrence Malick, who cast her as the female lead in the melancholic Americana film ballad *Badlands* (1973). The first of several roles in which the actress would portray disturbed yet sympathetic teens, the film saw Spacek's Holly and her boyfriend (played by Martin Sheen) traveling across the bleak land of the American West after Sheen's character murders Holly's father for forbidding their relationship.

Playing Holly in *Badlands* led to the part that made Spacek famous—the title role in Brian De Palma's 1976 adaptation of the 1974 Stephen King novel *Carrie*. In the film, tormented telekinetic high schooler Carrie White is bullied by her classmates and by her mother (Piper Laurie); Spacek's tour-de-force performance resulted in her first Oscar nomination. She went on to work with director Alan Rudolph in *Welcome to L.A.* (1977) and Robert Altman in *Three Women* (1977).

Spacek won her first Oscar for her portrayal of Loretta Lynn in *Coal Miner's Daughter* (1979). Selected for the part by Lynn herself, Spacek did all of her own singing for the movie and was also nominated for a Grammy Award for the soundtrack. Although only twenty-nine during the filming of *Coal Miner's Daughter*, she portrayed Lynn over the course of twenty years—from thirteen-year-old mother to battered wife to rising star and drug addict—cementing her uncanny ability to play nearly any age.

Spacek earned two more Oscar nominations in the early 1980s for her portrayals of an American woman who disappears in an unnamed South American country in Costa-Gavras's *Missing* (1982) and a wife who attempts to save the family farm in *The River* (1984). Later in the decade she took a break from acting to raise her two daughters. Although she returned to acting in the 1990s—receiving an Oscar nomination for her portrayal of a southern women who has an affair with a young black man in *Crimes of the Heart* (1986) and taking on a prominent cameo as the wife of Jim Garrison (Kevin Costner) in Oliver Stone's 1991 blockbuster *JFK*—she appeared in fewer films overall during that decade, supplementing those roles with a scattering of small comedic and television appearances.

At the end of the 1990s Spacek took on larger film roles. In the psychological thriller *Affliction* (1997), she played the girlfriend of a small-town sheriff (Nick Nolte) who is afraid that what his buddy has identified as a self-inflicted hunting accident is really murder. She appeared in David Lynch's *The Straight Story* (1999), the true story of estranged brothers Alvin and Lyle Straight. Despite their not having spoken in decades, when Alvin hears of his brother's illness, he drives his tractor from Iowa to Wisconsin to renew their friendship. Spacek, a longtime friend of Lynch, played Alvin's mentally challenged daughter, Rose, to great acclaim. She received another Oscar nomination for the role of Ruth Fowler, a tightly wound, unpleasant music teacher in a high school in small-town Maine whose marriage begins to disintegrate in the aftermath of her son's violent death, in the independent release *In the Bedroom* (2001).

Spacek has continued to work steadily throughout the first decade of the 2000s and the 2010s, appearing in such films as *A Home at the End of the World* (2004), *The Ring Two* (2005), *Lake City* (2008), and *The Help* (2011). For the latter, a critically acclaimed adaptation of Kathryn Stockett's 2009 novel of the same name about black maids working in the American South in the 1960s, Spacek was included in the 2011 Hollywood Film Award for Ensemble of the Year. She has appeared in a number of television films and was nominated for an Emmy in 2010 for her stint playing a lobbyist on the HBO drama *Big Love*. In 2011 Spacek was honored with a star on the Walk of Fame in Hollywood. She has written a biography titled *My Extraordinary Ordinary Life* (2012).

Robyn Karney

SEE ALSO: *Academy Awards; Altman, Robert; Costner, Kevin; Emmy Awards; Grammy Awards; Hollywood; Horror Movies;* JFK*; King, Stephen; Lennon, John; Lynch, David; Lynn, Loretta; Stone, Oliver; Warhol, Andy.*

BIBLIOGRAPHY

Ayers, Carrie. *The Sissy Spacek Handbook: Everything You Need to Know about Sissy Spacek*. New York: Lightning Source, 2010.

Emerson, Mark, and Eugene E. Pfaff. *Country Girl: The Life of Sissy Spacek*. New York: St. Martin's Press, 1988.

Spacek, Sissy, and Maryanne Vollers. *My Extraordinary Ordinary Life*. New York: Hyperion, 2012.

Spaghetti Westerns

Spaghetti Westerns were hyperviolent, low-budget genre films made in Europe by European (usually Italian) studios in the 1960s and 1970s. The more than 500 films, many forgettable, used European crews, writers, directors, and for the most part actors. Location shooting often took place in Spain, parts of which resemble the geography of the American Southwest.

The spaghetti Western shot its way into mainstream American culture in 1964 with the release of *A Fistful of Dollars*, directed by Sergio Leone and starring a little-known American actor named Clint Eastwood. Eastwood plays the Man with No Name, an amoral bounty hunter with a lightning-fast draw. The film was immensely popular in the United States and around the world and led to the production of two sequels: *For a Few Dollars More* (1965) and *The Good, the Bad, and the Ugly* (1966). Two other Leone films were also successful in the United States: the lavish, sprawling 1969 epic *Once upon a Time in the West*—

starring Charles Bronson, Jason Robards, Claudia Cardinale, and a cast-against-type Henry Fonda playing a ruthless killer—and *Duck, You Sucker*, also known as *A Fistful of Dynamite* (1971), which paired James Coburn with Rod Steiger.

Spaghetti Westerns had several stylistic elements in common. They were often very violent (for their time) and did not flinch from portraying brutal beatings, rape, and the murder of women and children. The films were usually made cheaply, and their production values showed it (exceptions were *The Good, the Bad, and the Ugly* and *Once upon a Time in the West*, both of which had large budgets for production). Further, as the supporting actors (and sometimes the stars) of spaghetti Westerns were usually Italian, most of the speaking parts had to be dubbed for release outside Italy (in some cases, limited budgets made for sloppy dubbing and unintentionally hilarious results).

Finally, the films often made use of tight close-up shots, which meant that the actors, even bit players, tended to have interesting (if not always handsome) faces. This photographic technique was especially common in scenes leading to a showdown: the camera would alternate between the two (or more) characters who were preparing to duel, with the close-ups growing increasingly tight until only the eyes could be seen. Then the tension would be broken as the gunmen drew and fired. This trademark motif was labeled by some critics the "squint and shoot" style of cinematography.

The musical scores for spaghetti Westerns tended to be moody and atmospheric. The best-known composer to work in the genre was Ennio Morricone, who went on to write music for a variety of other films. Morricone's scores for Leone constitute some of the best-known movie music of the 1960s and early 1970s. In addition to traditional instruments, he made use of bells, jangling spurs, whistling, and a mouth harp to create a distinctive, and much-imitated, sound.

An attempt was made to revive the genre in 1998, when Turner Network Television produced and broadcast a made-for-cable homage called *A Dollar for the Dead*, starring Emilio Estevez as yet another Man with No Name.

Justin Gustainis

SEE ALSO: *Eastwood, Clint;* A Fistful of Dollars*;* The Good, the Bad, and the Ugly*; Leone, Sergio; The Western.*

BIBLIOGRAPHY

Frayling, Christopher. *Spaghetti Westerns: Cowboys and Europeans from Karl May to Sergio Leone*. London: I. B. Taurus, 2006.

Fridlund, Bert. *The Spaghetti Western: A Thematic Analysis.* Jefferson, NC: McFarland, 2006.

Weisser, Thomas. *Spaghetti Westerns: The Good, the Bad, and the Violent*. Jefferson, NC: McFarland, 1992.

Spalding, Albert G. *(1850–1915)*

After fully dedicating his career to baseball in 1871, Albert Goodwill Spalding went on to become pro baseball's first recorded 200-game winner, dividing his time between the Boston Red Stockings and the Chicago White Stockings. As first captain/manager and later as president/owner of the White Stockings, Spalding helped mold Chicago into the baseball dynasty of the 1880s. Yet it was as an owner that Spalding had his greatest cultural impact.

In 1876 he helped found the National League and became its president in 1901. Through such actions he was key in establishing baseball as a viable and acceptable commercial enterprise. Spalding helped solidify professional baseball as a business. In addition to his baseball duties, he and his brother opened their first sporting goods store in Chicago in 1876, the beginning of the Spalding sporting goods enterprise.

Paul O'Hara

SEE ALSO: *Baseball; Boston Red Sox; Sports Heroes.*

BIBLIOGRAPHY

Bartlett, Arthur Charles. *Baseball and Mr. Spalding: The History and Romance of Baseball.* New York: Farrar, Straus & Young, 1951.

Lamster, Mark. *Spalding's World Tour: The Epic Adventure That Took Baseball around the Globe—and Made It America's Game.* New York: Public Affairs, 2006.

Levine, Peter. *A. G. Spalding and the Rise of Baseball: The Promise of American Sport.* New York: Oxford University Press, 1985.

Spartacus

Spartacus (1960) represents the pinnacle of the epic film trend that included spectaculars such as *Ben Hur* (1959), *Cleopatra* (1963), and *The Fall of the Roman Empire* (1964). It is considered the first truly intelligent epic, but its director, the highly acclaimed Stanley Kubrick, largely disowned it. Kubrick took the assignment, partially as a way of escaping the ill-fated *One-Eyed Jacks* (1961) project he was working on with Marlon Brando. (Brando himself then took over direction and went heavily overbudget with the film.)

Kubrick was belatedly brought aboard by *Spartacus* producer-star Kirk Douglas, who was impressed with their classic collaboration on *Paths of Glory* (1957). The original director, Anthony Mann, resigned after just a week's worth of shooting, completing only the opening scenes at the rock quarry. Kubrick picked up the project from scenes of the gladiator school on.

Kubrick objected to the script for *Spartacus* on the grounds that it was dumb and rarely faithful to what is known about the actual Spartacus. In reality, the former slave twice led his victorious slave army to the northern borders of Italy and could have easily gotten out of the country, but instead he led his army back to pillage Roman cities. Rather than exploring the question of why Spartacus chose to do this or whether the intentions of the rebellion changed—whether Spartacus lost the control of his followers who became more interested in the spoils of war rather than in freedom—writer Dalton Trumbo's script simply has Spartacus prevented from escaping by a silly contrivance in which a pirate leader (played by Herbert Lom) reneges on a deal to take the slave army away in his ships.

Nor did Spartacus die by crucifixion, as the film depicts. He was actually killed in battle and hacked into pieces on the battlefield. Six thousand of his followers, however, were later

Spartacus. *Kirk Douglas starred as the title character and leader of a Roman slave revolt in the 1960 epic* Spartacus. SILVER SCREEN COLLECTION/CONTRIBUTOR/MOVIEPIX/GETTY IMAGES.

crucified along the Appian Way. As a director-for-hire, Kubrick discovered he had to bow to the wishes of his producer.

FILM ORIGINS

Spartacus came to be because producer Eddie Lewis brought the Howard Fast novel to the attention of Douglas, who, seeing its potential to become a popular epic, optioned the book. He hoped to interest United Artists in the film, but the studio was planning its own version of the tale called *The Gladiators*, which was to be directed by Martin Ritt and star Yul Brynner and Anthony Quinn with a script by Abe Polonsky. Fast was given first crack at adapting the material into a screenplay, but he had a political ax to grind, apparent in his script, which was thus quickly rejected. Douglas needed somebody who could write both well and fast, and so he pitched the project to blacklisted writer Trumbo, who agreed to write the script under the name Sam Jackson.

Needing some high-powered talent to convince a studio to back the film, Douglas approached Laurence Olivier, Charles Laughton, and Peter Ustinov. Olivier expressed interest in both starring and directing the film, but he then committed to appearing in *Coriolanus* in Stratford-on-Avon and consented to taking the role of Crassus, provided the part was improved. Laughton did not care for the material but needed the money and so agreed to appear as Gracchus, the rotund Republican senator who opposes Crassus. Ustinov was eager to play the role of an ingratiating middleman for once (he usually had played kings or peasants) and had suggestions for improving his part. Universal agreed to undertake the film.

Douglas wanted Ingrid Bergman to play his love interest, Varinia, but she turned it down as being "too bloody." Jean Simmons wanted the role, but Douglas preferred a foreigner who was not British. Jeanne Moreau refused to leave a play she was in to take the part. Douglas thought German actress Sabina Bethmann had the right look and hired her for the part, despite her thick accent. She was sent to be coached by blacklist victim Jeff Corey.

ENTER KUBRICK

Spartacus began with Mann as director on January 27, 1959, when he filmed the mine sequence in Death Valley. When the production started filming the sequences at the gladiator school, it started to fall apart. Universal pushed for Mann's replacement, so Douglas paid him off and asked for Kubrick to come in. Universal was against hiring the thirty-year-old maverick director, but with the clock already running up large expenses, they capitulated, and filming resumed under Kubrick on February 16.

Kubrick immediately realized that the inexpressive Bethmann was not going to work out and decided to test her powers of improvisation by telling her that she had just lost the part in the movie. Rather than reacting emotionally, the actress froze and thereby ensured her departure from the production. Simmons was quickly summoned to take her place. Shortly after, however, she had emergency surgery and could not work for more than a month, so the production had to shoot around her.

One of Kubrick's innovations was to film the scene where Varinia serves food to the gladiator trainees without dialogue, using only Alex North's music to make his point, and thereby improving the scene. Indeed, the scenes in the gladiatorial school are some of the best in the film, especially those where Marcellus (Charles McGraw) uses Spartacus to demonstrate where to maim or kill one's opponent. In another notable scene, Draba (Woody Strode), because of an idle whim by two Roman ladies, is forced to fight Spartacus in the ring, but the Ethiopian chooses to attack Crassus at the cost of his own life rather than kill a fellow slave.

Tony Curtis begged to be put in the film, and so a part was written for him. He played Antoninus, a sensitive young man who becomes like a son to Spartacus and is forced to fight him to the death at the end of the film. Curtis severed his Achilles tendon and had to spend some time in a wheelchair. Even Douglas became sick. Because of all the delays, the film went months over schedule and 250 percent over budget.

At one point Douglas, Lewis, and Kubrick got into a discussion over who should get the writing credit on the film. Lewis did not feel right taking credit for Trumbo's work, and Douglas was uneasy about crediting the film to a Sam Jackson who did not really exist. Kubrick put forth the suggestion that he be given credit for the script. Revolted, Douglas decided to break the blacklist by crediting Trumbo and summoning him to the studio. (Soon afterward, Otto Preminger announced that Trumbo would be credited on *Exodus* as well, and other blacklisted artists started to find employment again.) One of the most significant accomplishments brought about by the film was this breaking of the blacklist, considered a risky move at the time.

Kubrick's rough assemblage of the film was not well received. Trumbo wrote a lengthy critique, detailing the changes made and what he felt was wrong with them. Douglas agreed and declared that the film would have to be restructured and a battle scene added (originally, the battle was just to have been suggested). Visual design consultant Saul Bass was hired to design the battle sequence and noted that scenes of preparation for the battle helped build up more excitement than the actual battle itself. The Spanish government lent its army to play the Roman army, and the scenes were shot in Spain. The budget rose to $12 million.

AN EPIC RELEASE

Finally, *Spartacus* was ready for release. The American Legion sent a letter to 17,000 local posts demanding a boycott of the film because of Trumbo's involvement. Hedda Hopper joined the fray, attacking the film's use of "communist" writers. Still, despite its shortcomings, the film stands as one of the best of the Roman screen epics. Ustinov won an Academy Award for Best Supporting Actor for his role as Batiatus, the conniving purveyor of slaves.

In 1988 *Spartacus* was restored and rereleased to theaters in all its glory. Kubrick, although he had never expressed a fondness for the film, was involved in carefully reediting the film, adding numerous snippets that had been trimmed previously. One of the most significant additions was the scene where the bisexual Crassus attempts to seduce Antoninus while Antoninus is bathing him by asking Antoninus if he eats oysters and snails, explaining that it is a matter of appetites rather than morals. Crassus then proceeds to compare himself to Rome, expounding, "No nation can withstand Rome. No man can withstand her. And how much less—a boy. There's only one way to deal with Rome, Antoninus. You must serve her. You must abase yourself before her. You must grovel at her feet. You must love her."

The footage for the scene was located, but not the original soundtrack. Curtis agreed to revoice his part, but Olivier was dead, and so Anthony Hopkins imitated Olivier's vocal inflections in order to restore this scene that had so outraged the censors of the 1960s. The scene does add to the film's portrait of Crassus as a self-serving manipulator obsessed with asserting his power and authority.

Dennis Fischer

SEE ALSO: *Bergman, Ingrid; Blacklisting; Brando, Marlon; Brynner, Yul;* Cleopatra*; The Hollywood Ten; Kubrick, Stanley; McCarthyism; Olivier, Laurence; Preminger, Otto.*

BIBLIOGRAPHY

Baxter, John. *Stanley Kubrick: A Biography*. New York: Carroll & Graf Publishers, 1997.

Ciment, Michel. *Kubrick*. Paris: Calmann-Levy, 1980.

Douglas, Kirk. *The Ragman's Son: An Autobiography*. London: Simon & Schuster, 1988.

Duncan, Paul. *Stanley Kubrick: Visual Poet 1928–1999*. Cologne, Germany: Taschen, 2003.

Harris, W. V. "Spartacus." In *Past Imperfect: History According to the Movies*, ed. Mark C. Carnes. New York: Henry Holt, 1995.

Kagan, Norman. *The Cinema of Stanley Kubrick*. New York: Continuum, 1994.

Monaco, James. *The Films of Stanley Kubrick*. New York: New School Department of Film, 1974.

Nelson, Thomas Alan. *Kubrick: Inside a Film Artist's Maze*. Bloomington: Indiana University Press, 1982.

Walker, Alexander. *Stanley Kubrick Directs*. New York: Harcourt, Brace Jovanovich, 1971.

Spawn

Todd McFarlane's *Spawn* comic book changed the dynamics of the comic-book industry in the 1990s. *Spawn* set sales records, helped an upstart company become a major publisher, and enticed the top talents in the industry to leave Marvel and DC to make their fortunes with creator-owned properties.

In the late 1980s McFarlane gained some notoriety as a comic-book artist for his work on Marvel Comics' *Incredible Hulk* title. At the time "hot" artists drove comic-book sales, and when McFarlane moved to penciling *Amazing Spider-Man*, it quickly became Marvel's best-selling book. In 1990 Marvel created a new *Spider-Man* title for McFarlane to write, pencil, and ink. It immediately became their top-selling monthly, and the first issue sold an incredible two and a half million copies. McFarlane began to wonder why, if he was so popular, he needed to do work-for-hire on a character that someone else owned.

Born of this thinking, McFarlane formed a partnership with a few of Marvel's other popular young artists in 1992. Together they founded Image Comics in order to publish creator-owned comic books and reap the full rewards of their popularity. For the first few years Image Comics, true to its name, proved to be more flash than substance. When McFarlane came up with *Spawn*, however, it proved to be the backbone of the company. Unlike the majority of Image books, *Spawn* was consistently published on time and, thus, enjoyed consistently high sales. The first issue sold 1.7 million copies, far outstripping the circulation of any other independent comic book. For decades Marvel and DC had so dominated the industry that any comic not published by one of the "big two" was considered "independent." By its second year Image Comics had such a high volume of sales that the industry press began to suggest the possibility of "the big three," and by 1996 Image, albeit briefly, surpassed DC to become number two in market share.

McFarlane proved to have the best head for business of the young Image artists and was aggressive in marketing his characters. *Spawn* became a multimillion-dollar industry. By 1993 there was a "Spawnmobile" super-competition funny car touring with car shows, and Mattel was selling a "Spawnmobile" Hot Wheel. A comics industry trade magazine, *Hero Illustrated*, named McFarlane the "Most Important Person in Comics," and in 1995, with New Line Cinema's McFarlane-scripted live-action *Spawn* movie in preproduction (it was released in 1997), he signed contracts for a *Spawn* animated series on HBO. Also in 1995 Sony began developing a *Spawn* video game, a *Spawn* board game was in stores, Halloween costumes were licensed, and McFarlane Toys brought out a new line of action figures. Somehow, McFarlane found time to keep producing a new *Spawn* comic book each month, remaining number one in industry-wide sales for a fourth year in a row. Both the sales and the marketing frenzy then began waning somewhat, but in the space of four years McFarlane had become one of the wealthiest people in the comic-book industry.

The name and face of McFarlane's main character were borrowed from his real-life friend Al Simmons, who became somewhat of a minor celebrity on the comic convention circuit. The fictional Al Simmons is a principled but efficient killer for a mysterious branch of the government. When he begins to question the orders of his commander, Jason Wynn, he is burned to death with laser weapons by two of his fellow agents. Sent to hell for the bloody deeds he has committed, Simmons becomes a pawn of the Dark Lord Malebolgia, who needs just such a soldier to lead hell's army in the final battle against heaven. For a chance to return to earth to see his family again and take revenge on Wynn, Simmons forfeits his soul and agrees to become Malebolgia's general. Simmons's horribly burned body is reanimated, and he returns to earth as a grotesque but incredibly powerful hell spawn.

Spawn is clothed in a symbiotic uniform and wields hell-born energy that is seemingly capable of anything that he can imagine. Yet, once this energy is fully expended, Simmons will have to return to hell to fulfill the rest of his bargain. As Spawn regains memories of his former life, he begins following his own agenda and using his powers against the forces of evil. He lives with homeless people in a Bowery alley and becomes their defender. He watches over his family, and his love for his wife begins healing him spiritually. However, he is constantly plagued by his "guardian demon," The Clown, whose task is to keep Spawn from straying too far from hell's path.

Spawn provides savage, gory adolescent fantasy with sexy images; McFarlane has admitted that much of the success of his book is probably due to his ability to draw a "really cool looking cape." As other "hot" artists migrated to Image, or copied the Image style, there was an ascendancy of what comics pioneer Will Eisner refers to as "wallpaper comics," filled with splash pages, double-page spreads, and bravura artwork but not much story. In a medium that already stressed the visual over the verbal, the success of *Spawn* and other "wallpaper" comic books further diminished the role of the writer.

Randy Duncan

SEE ALSO: *Comic Books; DC Comics; Marvel Comics.*

BIBLIOGRAPHY

Jones, Gerard, and Will Jacobs. *The Comic Book Heroes*. Rocklin, CA: Prima Publishing, 1997.

Malloy, Alex G., ed. *Comic Book Artists*. Radnor, PA: Wallace-Homestead Book Company, 1993.

Spears, Britney *(1981–)*

Britney Jean Spears was born December 2, 1981, in Kentwood, Louisiana, to Lynne and James Spears. She has two siblings, Bryan and Jamie Lynn. Spears grew up performing in church and in school and spending summers in New York at the Off Broadway Dance Center and at the Professional Performing Arts School. In 1991 she landed the role of lead understudy in the off-Broadway play *Ruthless*.

In 1992 Spears appeared on the television show *Star Search* (1983–1995), and in 1993 she joined the cast of the television show *The All New Mickey Mouse Club* (1989–1995) and remained with the show until it ended in 1995. In 1997 Spears signed a recording contract with Jive Records, which sent her on a tour of shopping malls, where her stage presence and unique dance moves made her an instant sensation. In January 1999 Jive released Spears's first album, *. . . Baby, One More Time*, which debuted at number one on the Billboard music charts. In April she appeared on the cover of *Rolling Stone* in a bra and panties, sparking controversy. In the article that accompanies the cover photo, Steven Daly writes, "[Spears] stands today as the latest model of a classic product: the unneurotic pop star who performs her duties with vaudevillian pluck and spokesmodel charm." Interviewed for the article, Spears admitted, "I want to be big all around the world."

Spears's next three albums, *Oops! . . . I Did It Again* (2000), *Britney* (2001), and *In the Zone* (2003), all debuted at number one on the charts. In 2008 *Entertainment Weekly* magazine named *Britney* number ninety-seven on its list of the "100 Best Albums from 1983 to 2008." In 2009 National Public Radio included *In the Zone* on its list of the "50 Most Important Recordings of the Decade." In early 2005 Spears won the 2004 Grammy Award for Best Dance Recording for her song "Toxic" from *In the Zone*.

In 2003 Spears performed the opening number at the MTV Music Awards with Christina Aguilera and Madonna, shocking fans by engaging in an onstage kiss on the mouth with Madonna. She surprised her fans again in 2004 by marrying her childhood friend Jason Alexander on New Year's Eve in Las Vegas. The marriage ended in annulment fifty-five hours later. Six months later she became engaged to dancer Kevin Federline. The couple filmed themselves throughout their courtship and engagement, and their home movies aired as a five-episode miniseries on the UPN network as *Britney and Kevin: Chaotic* in 2005.

Spears then took a break from recording and performing to start a family and gave birth to Sean Preston Federline on September 14, 2005. Shortly after, tabloid pictures surfaced of Spears driving with the child on her lap and another of her almost falling while holding him with a drink in her hand. While Spears blamed these incidents on the paparazzi, they set the tone for future perceptions of her parenting skills. In 2006 she appeared nude on the cover of *Harper's Bazaar* magazine while six months pregnant with her second son, Jayden James Federline, who was born September 12.

OUT OF CONTROL

In November 2006 Spears filed for divorce from Federline, and shortly thereafter, her life began to spiral out of control. Pictures surfaced of her partying with celebrity Paris Hilton and actress Lindsay Lohan and flashing her bare crotch. She had all of her hair shaved off in a Los Angeles salon, and she menacingly beat on a car driven by paparazzi with an umbrella.

In February 2007 Spears entered the Promises Malibu Alcohol and Drug Rehab Treatment Facility in Southern California and checked out a month later after successfully completing its program. She did not disclose her reasons for seeking treatment. In July 2007 Spears's divorce from Federline became final, and she and her ex-husband shared joint custody of their sons. Her personal problems continued, however, and in October 2007 Federline obtained full custody of their children.

Also in October 2007 Jive released Spears's fifth album, *Blackout*. It debuted at number two, but this success was short-lived, as her performance at the 2007 MTV Video Awards received terrible reviews. On January 3, 2008, she locked herself in a bathroom and refused to give her sons to Federline's representatives. Police intervened, determining that she was under the influence of controlled substances; her mother then arranged to have her hospitalized, and she was placed on a mental health evaluation hold. Spears lost custody of her sons and then control of her assets when a court put her estate into temporary conservatorship, placing her father and attorney Andrew Wallet in charge of her millions.

BACK ON TRACK

After her release from the hospital, Spears began rebuilding her image and her life, working out a visitation schedule to see her sons with Federline, who continued to retain full custody. *Circus* (2008), her sixth studio album, entered the charts at number one, making her the first female artist to have five albums debut at the top of the charts. Jive released her seventh studio album, *Femme Fatale*, in 2011, and that same year she received the coveted Michael Jackson Video Vanguard Award at the MTV Video Music Awards. In December 2011 Spears became engaged to longtime friend and former manager Jason Trawick.

Spears has appeared in movies, including *Austin Powers: Goldmember* (2002) and *Crossroads* (2002), and in several television shows, such as *Saturday Night Live* (1975–), *Will & Grace* (1998–2006), *How I Met Your Mother* (2005–), *The Simpsons* (1989–), *Punk'd* (2003–2007), and *Glee* (2009–). She endorses many products, including Britney's Dance Beat video game, a Candies' clothing line, and several Elizabeth Arden fragrances. In 2002 *Forbes* magazine deemed her "the world's most powerful celebrity," and *People* magazine named her one of the fifty most beautiful people in the world. Spears has a star on the Hollywood Walk of Fame and several Guinness World Records for her music and celebrity. There are also multiple parodies of her songs on YouTube and entire episodes of the television show *South Park* (1997–) devoted to her.

Since her very public breakdown, Spears has managed to stay out of the tabloids and continues to keep her home life and career on track. In an article on the Huffington Post website, Cathleen Falsani explains, "Spears' personal tragedy and public dismantling became a twisted form of entertainment. . . . Collectively, we placed her on a pedestal, knocked her off, picked her back up and set her back upon it. Only time will tell whether that cruel cycle will repeat itself."

Ron Horton

SEE ALSO: *Aguilera, Christina; Arden, Elizabeth; Broadway; Celebrity; Disney (Walt Disney Company); Divorce;* Entertainment Weekly*; * Glee*; Grammy Awards;* Harper's*; Hilton, Paris; Hollywood; Jackson, Michael; Lohan, Lindsay; Madonna;* The Mickey Mouse Club*; MTV;* People*; Pop Music;* Rolling Stone*;* Saturday Night Live*;* The Simpsons*;* South Park*; Top 40;* Will & Grace*; YouTube.*

BIBLIOGRAPHY

Daly, Steven. "Britney Spears Teen Queen." *Rolling Stone*, April 15, 1999.

Dennis, Steve. *Britney: Inside the Dream; The Biography.* London: HarperCollins, 2009.

Falsani, Cathleen. "Consuming Britney: Oops We Did It Again." HuffingtonPost, April 5, 2011. Accessed May 30, 2012. Available from http://www.huffingtonpost.com/cathleen-falsani/consuming-britney-oops-we_b_843294.html

Hall, Dennis. "Spears' Space: The Play of Innocence and Experience in the Bare-Midriff Fashion. *Journal of Popular Culture* 39, no. 6 (2006): 1025–1034.

Heard, Christopher. *Britney Spears: Little Girl Lost.* East Montreal: Transit Publishing, 2010.

Lowe, Melanie. "Colliding Feminisms: Britney Spears, 'Tweens,' and the Politics of Reception." *Popular Music and Society* 26, no. 2 (2003): 123–140.

Smit, Christopher M. *The Exile of Britney Spears: A Tale of Twenty-First Century Consumption.* Chicago: University of Chicago Press, 2011.

Spears, Britney, and Lynne Spears. *Britney Spears' Heart to Heart.* New York: Three Rivers Press, 2000.

Special Olympics

The first International Special Olympics took place at Chicago's Soldier Field in July 1968. Before this event, there were no ways for mentally disabled children to compete in sporting events. With the help of the Joseph P. Kennedy Jr. Foundation and the thousands of volunteers who organize the Special Olympics, such opportunities now abound. Eunice Kennedy Shriver was the guiding force in developing this tradition, in which participants compete locally, regionally, and internationally in games based on the Greek Olympics.

Traditionally, athletic avenues were closed to many mentally disabled children because popular theory held that they did not need physical activity. As early as 1963, however, a movement was afoot to change this perception. The Kennedy Foundation, in conjunction with the American Alliance for Health, Physical Education, and Recreation, began work to provide a physical fitness program for the mentally disabled. In addition, President Dwight D. Eisenhower had established the President's Council for Physical Fitness and Sports, and by 1967, after considerable study by different organizations, it was determined that a lack of opportunity, not a lack of ability, was the major reason for the thwarted physical development of mentally disabled children.

In 1968 members of the Chicago Park District organized a track-and-field meet for mentally disabled children based on the Greek Olympics. When letters were sent to representatives from the individual states inviting them to join, the responses were mixed. Reasons for not participating included the idea that promoting physical activity among the mentally disabled would be a waste of time and effort. Nearly half the states opted out of the first Special Olympics. Unwilling to give in to negative feedback, however, several states, as well as Canada, pressed on. The Kennedy Foundation donated $25,000, and the games were staged at Soldier Field as planned.

At a press conference shortly after the first International Special Olympics, Shriver reiterated the mission of the games: to provide all mentally disabled children a chance to participate in athletic events. She also pledged $75,000 in support on behalf of the Kennedy Foundation to build the Special Olympics program. This seed money allowed communities across the United States to take part in the Special Olympics. Because the response to the first Special Olympics was so positive, Senator Edward Kennedy announced the formation of Special Olympics Inc. and named Shriver its president. The new foundation's purpose was to provide the means for all mentally disabled citizens to have access to physical fitness programs.

The Special Olympics are divided into winter and summer games with both team and individual competitions. Each Special

Olympics—the winter and summer games—is held every two years, just like the regular Olympics. Anyone ranging in age from eight to seventeen and with an IQ of seventy-five or below is eligible to compete free of charge. One thousand children from twenty-six states and Canada participated in the first International Special Olympics in 1968. In 1970 all fifty states, the District of Columbia, and Canada had Special Olympics organizations and directors, and the event had grown to 3,200 participants by 1975. At the turn of the twenty-first century, approximately 7,000 athletes from 150 countries were participating in the 19 sports at the Special Olympics, generating a need for 35,000 volunteers.

However, this growth did not come without controversy. In the 1980s and 1990s the Special Olympics came under intense scrutiny by mental health professionals who questioned the games and their benefits. Critics had reservations about the value of segregating the mentally handicapped from mainstream athletic events, and they were also concerned that the games were becoming overly competitive. In response, Special Olympics organizers emphasized the positive physical, mental, and emotional achievements of the athletes.

Despite the debate, the movement continued to gain worldwide support. In 1988 the International Olympic Committee officially recognized and endorsed the Special Olympics. In the late 1990s the movement adopted an initiative called Healthy Athletes to provide health care services to Special Olympics athletes. Furthermore, President George W. Bush signed the Special Olympics Sport and Empowerment Act in 2004 to provide funding for the Special Olympics in the United States.

By 2008 the Special Olympics organization was made up of nearly three million athletes from more than 180 countries. Not even the death in 2009 of the Special Olympics' greatest advocate, Shriver, could slow the expansion of the movement. The motto of the Special Olympics states, "Let me win, but if I cannot win, let me be brave in the attempt." It sums up the attitude and accomplishments of both the organizers and participants throughout the forty-plus years of the Special Olympics.

Kimberley H. Kidd

SEE ALSO: *Olympics; Soldier Field.*

BIBLIOGRAPHY

Dinn, Sheila. *Hearts of Gold: A Celebration of Special Olympics and Its Heroes.* Woodbridge, CT: Blackbirch Press, 1996.

Haskins, James. *A New Kind of Joy: The Story of the Special Olympics.* New York: Doubleday, 1976.

Klein, Tovah, and Gilman E. Zigler. "Special Olympics: An Evaluation by Professionals and Parents." *Mental Retardation* 3, no. 1 (1993): 15–23.

Spector, Phil *(1940–)*

As the developer of a style of production so lush it was dubbed "the wall of sound," Phil Spector was arguably the most influential record producer in the history of popular music. From the late 1950s through the early 1960s, Spector, along with his arranger, Jack Nitzsche, produced a sound characterized by complex arrangements of strings, horns, and percussion. Although that sound is most evident in pop songs by the Ronettes, the Crystals, and the Righteous Brothers, all of whom recorded for Spector's label, he also produced a variety of other performers. The Beatles enlisted his skills in the studio, and Spector also produced solo efforts by John Lennon and George Harrison. Acts as diverse as the Ramones and Leonard Cohen worked with him, and Bruce Springsteen cited him as a major influence on his own music.

When he was seventeen, Spector wrote "To Know Him Is to Love Him," which became a number one single for his band the Teddy Bears. It was the beginning of an impressive songwriting career, but Spector's real achievements were in the studio. He learned the craft of production under Lee Hazlewood, who had given Duane Eddy his trademark guitar sound through a variety of techniques, including manipulating tape speeds and recording in an empty grain elevator. Spector left California for New York City, ostensibly in hopes of securing a position at the United Nations, but within a few months he had cowritten "Spanish Harlem" with Jerry Leiber, half of the songwriting team of Leiber and Stoller. The song would become a hit for Ben E. King.

Spector also began producing prominent performers such as LaVern Baker, Ruth Brown, and Gene Pitney, but his most original and influential work came after he established Philles Records. Although he originally had three partners, Spector became sole owner when he was only twenty-one; he was also a millionaire. The Crystals' "He's a Rebel" was the label's first hit and is generally regarded as the first "wall of sound" song. It's worth noting that the phrase is something of a misnomer: although Spector employed an extraordinary number of musicians, and although the primitive technology of the time required an extensive use of overdubbing, the instruments remain surprisingly distinct. That is certainly a result of Spector's obsessiveness in the studio. According to one story, Spector once listened to the same note for twelve hours, trying to determine whether it needed to be rerecorded. Although that tale is probably apocryphal, it is undeniable that he worked with a vastly higher degree of attention than most other producers of the time.

Labels usually worked on a variety of singles simultaneously in an attempt to get a hit single. Spector, however, focused his energies on one single at a time, and that approach proved extraordinarily successful. Songs such as the Ronettes' "Be My Baby" and the Righteous Brothers' "You've Lost That Lovin' Feeling" are some of the most recognizable hits of the 1960s, and Spector's collection of Christmas songs, *A Christmas Gift for You*, remains an exceptionally popular holiday album.

Spector shut down Philles Records in 1966. Some have claimed that he did so because Ike and Tina Turner's "River Deep, Mountain High" failed to achieve the success he had expected. A more likely explanation is that he recognized the music industry had changed fundamentally. The increasingly corporate nature of record distribution pushed independent labels to the margins; additionally, listeners began to favor full-length albums instead of singles. Spector no doubt understood that those shifts worked against his emphasis on the hit song. Ironically, however, other changes showed just how deeply Spector had influenced contemporary music. Although the Beach Boys had been known for their hit singles, in 1966 they released *Pet Sounds*, an album of complex and highly orchestrated pop songs that showed a clear debt to the wall of sound. The following year, the Beatles issued *Sergeant Pepper's Lonely Hearts Club Band*; in part a response to *Pet Sounds*, it also bore the hallmarks of Spector's work.

Despite his undeniable genius, Spector's megalomania and eccentricities became so infamous that fewer artists sought his talents in the 1980s and 1990s. At the same time, Spector became reclusive, showing little interest in searching out new acts to produce. In 1996 a short-lived collaboration with Céline Dion ended amid rumors that Spector had been impossible to work with in the studio.

While Spector's musical star waned after the 1960s, he returned to headlines in 2003 when actress Lana Clarkson was discovered dead of a gunshot wound in his California mansion. Spector was accused of the crime, and a high-profile court case ensued, making him a household name. In 2007 the case first went to trial and, although it ended in a hung jury, the proceedings were televised, publicizing Spector's history of violent interactions with women. When the case was retried in 2009, he was found guilty and remanded to the California State Prison System, where he was to serve nineteen years to life.

Bill Freind

SEE ALSO: *The Beach Boys; The Beatles; Eddy, Duane; Lennon, John; Pop Music; The Ramones; Springsteen, Bruce; Top 40; Turner, Ike and Tina.*

BIBLIOGRAPHY

Brown, Mick. *Tearing Down the Wall of Sound: The Rise and Fall of Phil Spector*. New York: Vintage, 2008.

Puterbaugh, Parke. "The Wall of Sound." *Rolling Stone*, August 23, 1990, 113–14.

Ribowsky, Mark. *He's a Rebel: Phil Spector: Rock & Roll's Legendary Producer*. New York: Da Capo Press, 2007.

Wolfe, Tom. *The Kandy-Kolored Tangerine-Flake Streamline Baby*. New York: Farrar, Straus & Giroux, 1965.

Spelling, Aaron *(1923–2006)*

The most successful producer in the history of television, Aaron Spelling began his career in the 1950s with writer/producer credits on such classic early TV fare as *Zane Grey Theater* (1956–1961) and *Playhouse 90* (1956–1961). At the time of his death in 2006, he had more than 3,000 productions to his credit, including audience favorites such as *The Mod Squad* (1968–1973), *Charlie's Angels* (1976–1981), *The Love Boat* (1977–1986), *Fantasy Island* (1977–1984), *Dynasty* (1981–1989), *Family* (1976–1980), *Beverly Hills, 90210* (1990–2000), *Melrose Place* (1992–1999), *Dawson's Creek* (1998–2003), *7th Heaven* (1996–2007), and *Charmed* (1998–2006)). Interspersed with these series were critically acclaimed television miniseries such as *Day One* (1989) and Spelling's only Emmy winner, *And the Band Played On* (1993).

Despite his success, Spelling was never a favorite of the critics. "There is good and there is bad Spelling," a *Washington Post* TV critic stated in a 1996 *Los Angeles Times Magazine* article, "but there is never great Spelling, only degrees of terribleness." Yet even his harshest detractors agreed that the producer had an uncanny knack for knowing what the public wanted to see. During the 1980s it was his *Dynasty*, a clone of the popular CBS hit *Dallas* (1978–1991), that propelled ABC to the top of the ratings. During the 1990s, his *Beverly Hills, 90210* and *Melrose Place* helped transform the fledgling Fox network into a major player, and he performed the same feat for the WB Television Network with *Felicity* (1998–2002).

THE RIGHT TIME AND PLACE

Spelling's background was remarkably similar to those of many legendary pioneers in both television and motion pictures. He was the youngest of five children born to struggling immigrant parents in Dallas, Texas. After an acting stint in *Gunsmoke* (1955–1975), he approached the producers of the Western anthology *Zane Grey Theater* with an idea for the host's segments on the show and was given an assignment to write it on a continuing basis for $100 per week. The spots were so successful that he was approached by producer Martin Manulis, who wanted to do a Western story on his *Playhouse 90* and offered Spelling the chance to write it. The resulting episode, "The Last Man," was so popular that Twentieth Century Fox optioned it as a feature film project within forty-eight hours of its airing.

The experience of writing the film version convinced Spelling that his rightful place was on television. Chided by his superiors for writing too quickly, he completed the screenplay, which was released as *One Foot in Hell* (1960), and returned to television, where he went to work for Four Star Productions and made a name for himself with his creative speed. At one point during the late 1950s, he was producing seven shows at once, highlighted by *Johnny Ringo* (1959–1960), *Alcoa Presents* (1959–1961), and *The June Allyson Show* (1959–1961).

As Spelling's TV career began to take off in the 1960s, his forte became his ability to capture the mood of the American public: *Burke's Law* (1963–1966) coincided with the detective and spy craze spurred by the James Bond films on the big screen, and *The Mod Squad* combined the timeless police genre with a teenage-rebels-seeking-social-justice motif that captured the unrest of a turbulent decade. Although some of his work was open to accusations of being derivative and less than cutting

Aaron Spelling. *Aaron Spelling, left, with wife Candy, created several of the most popular television shows of the 1970s and 1980s.* MICHAEL CAULFIELD/STAFF/WIREIMAGE/GETTY IMAGES.

edge, Spelling always managed to imbue his shows with qualities that differentiated them from their predecessors through unpredictable plot devices and eccentric characters.

A WINNING FORMULA

It was during the 1960s that Spelling developed his defining vision. He decided that his role was to present the audience with the vision of itself it most wanted to see. In most cases, this meant putting together a glossy, idealized version of Southern California. The public, he reasoned, was fascinated with the trials and tribulations of the wealthy, particularly problems that could not be solved by money, such as unrequited love, legal entanglements, and incurable diseases. During the next three decades, he packaged and exported the Southern California lifestyle.

In the 1970s he captured the viewers' interest in sex and titillation with *Charlie's Angels*, which combines crime-fighting action with glamorous women and lots of skin. Although the show is based in Los Angeles, its action routinely stretches to Palm Springs, California, and Las Vegas, Nevada—anywhere sex can be combined with wealth and glamour. In the 1980s Spelling took his formula even further with *Dynasty* and its spin-off, *The Colbys* (1985–1987), which present life among the wealthy in less black-and-white terms. Unlike *Charlie's Angels*, there are no clear-cut heroes. Even viewers who hated the rich and famous enjoyed these show—it was simply fun to watch the characters strive to do each other in.

By the end of the 1980s, Spelling's star began to dim. The emergence of the sitcom (*The Cosby Show* and *Cheers*) and the public's growing fascination with the gritty realism found in programs such as Steven Bochco's *Hill Street Blues* signaled trends that Spelling was slow to pick up on. In 1989, to headlines announcing "Spelling Dynasty Over," ABC canceled the show, *Dynasty*, that had taken it to the top of the ratings. Two of Spelling's medical dramas, ABC's *HeartBeat* and NBC's *Nightingales*, were also canceled that year. Suddenly, Spelling was unable to sell any of his one-hour programs, prompting him to admit to the *Los Angeles Times*, "I can honestly say that I don't know what the networks want anymore."

STAGING A COMEBACK

Within a year, however, he was back on top with the iconic drama *Beverly Hills, 90210*, which helped put Fox on the map. He followed with the successful spin-off *Melrose Place*, proving once and for all that that he was a master at combining money, glamour, and the Southern California lifestyle into an unforgettable package. His knowledge of the youth market paid big dividends in the mid-1990s with such popular shows as *7th Heaven*, *Dawson's Creek*, *Charmed*, and *Felicity*. With these programs, he reworked his traditional formula, incorporating more realistic casts of characters and putting them in areas of the country besides California.

Often photographed smoking his signature pipe, Spelling was diagnosed with and treated for oral cancer in 2001. Five years later, the prolific producer died of complications from a stroke. His memory was honored by some of his most infamous starlets at the Emmys the following August. While his shows may not have been critical successes, audiences gathered around their television sets religiously to live vicariously through the sumptuous, action-packed, and emotionally tumultuous worlds he had crafted. The reboots in the first decade of the 2000s of *Beverly Hills, 90210*, titled simply *90210*, and the short-lived *Melrose Place* carried on Spelling's tradition of depicting the exploits of wealthy and beautiful people in glamorous locales, a combination that continues to mesmerize Americans.

Sandra Garcia-Myers

SEE ALSO: Beverly Hills, 90210*;* Charlie's Angels*;* Dawson's Creek*;* Dynasty*; Emmy Awards;* Fantasy Island*;* Gunsmoke*;* The Love Boat*;* Playhouse 90*; Television; The Western.*

BIBLIOGRAPHY

"Aaron Spelling." *Daily Variety*, Special Issue. November 17, 1995.

Archambault, Dennis. *Producers Interviews*. Los Angeles: USC School of Cinema-Television, 1989.

De Vries, Hillary. "He's Made TV What It Is Today." *Los Angeles Times Magazine*, September 8, 1996, 17.

Finke, Nikki. "Can Spelling Cast His Spell Again?" *Los Angeles Times Calendar*, March 26, 1989, 3.

Idato, Michael. "The Great Escape." *Sydney Morning Herald*. September 19, 2005.

Spelling, Aaron, and Graham, Jefferson. *Aaron Spelling: A Prime-Time Life*. New York: St. Martin's Press, 1996.

Wild, David. *The Official "Melrose Place" Companion*. New York: Harper Perennial, 1995.

The Spice Girls

After half a decade of alternative rock ruling the music scene with its angst-ridden authenticity, Britain's Spice Girls came along in 1996 and—seemingly within five minutes after the release of their debut single, "Wannabe,"—helped change the direction of mainstream pop. While their explosion happened on a smaller scale than those of Madonna, Prince, and Michael Jackson, the Spice Girls nevertheless left a noticeable crater in the pop culture landscape that was still evident by the turn of the twenty-first century. Alternative demigods Nirvana and Pearl Jam had wiped away the superficial spectacle that was pop music in the late 1980s and early 1990s, but the Spice Girls made being shallow fun and cool again, paving the way for a number of other commercially successful soul/dance-influenced, good-looking boy and girl bands.

The Spice Girls were made up of five young women who were chosen to be in the group after auditioning in 1993. In this way, they were similar to many of the "manufactured" girl groups of the early 1960s, though the comparisons end there. Writing or cowriting many of their songs, publicly acting fiercely independent, and ultimately firing their original manager, these women were no mere puppets. Although they were not revolutionaries, instead existing very much as sexily dressed commodities, they did manage to bring the fire-and-brimstone rhetoric of the pro-woman punk rock movement to pubescent and prepubescent girls. Depending on one's perspective, this was either a calculated marketing strategy or a positive, empowering move.

Early on, the girls carved out very specific identities for themselves: Ginger Spice (Geri Halliwell), Scary Spice (Melanie Brown), Posh Spice (Victoria Adams), Sporty Spice (Melanie

Chisholm), and Baby Spice (Emma Bunton). This made the group more distinctive, and with the help of a number of catchy singles ("Wannabe," "Say You'll Be There" and "2 Become 1"), they were one of the top-selling acts in the world by the end of 1997. They seemed to be everywhere, with Pepsi commercials and a slew of Top 40 singles. Many critics dismissed them as an overexposed fad that wouldn't last another year. Their second album, *Spiceworld*, released in late 1997, was considered a flop, even though it went multiplatinum. However, the critical and commercial success of the feature film they released that same year, *Spice World*, and their subsequent sold-out world tour enabled them to prove their detractors wrong.

The departure of Halliwell at the beginning of the American leg of their world tour in 1998 similarly did not keep the group down and certainly did not discourage fans from attending their concerts. In 2000 they released their third album, *Forever*, which was slow to climb the charts and spurred the remaining band members to pursue solo careers. Thus, the book was closed on Spicemania.

As time passes, each former member of the Spice Girls has carved out a niche for herself. Halliwell found success as a solo artist, and in 2008 she also became a best-selling children's book author with the publication of *Ugenia Lavender*. Brown competed on the popular program *Dancing with the Stars* in 2007, and she is also recognized as the star of a reality show, *Mel B: It's a Scary World*. Victoria Adams is now famous as Victoria Beckham, having married international soccer superstar David Beckham in 1997. Following poor sales of her debut album, *Victoria Beckham* (2001), she focused on her family, though she has built a career designing her own fashion line. Chisholm has released several albums, including 2011's *The Sea*, and holds the record for the most number one hits in the United Kingdom written by a woman. Though Bunton recorded three albums and several singles, she found her true calling as a radio disc jockey and a reality television judge for the UK competition shows *Dancing on Ice* and *Don't Stop Believing*.

On June 28, 2007, the women joined together at London's O2 Arena to announce a reunion tour, "The Return of the Spice Girls." Including seventeen concerts in London, the entire international tour sold out. During the tour the group made several television appearances and released a single, "Headlines (Friendship Never Ends)." The group disbanded again following the tour, but rumors persisted that it would come together again.

On the surface, the Spice Girls seemed as plastic as Barbie dolls, just as artificial as the numerous dance-pop groups that preceded them before the alternative rock explosion. However, debates over their authenticity seemed moot when thousands of energized young girls were chanting "Girl power," the group's slogan, at concerts. The Spice Girls were certainly not as complex as female-centered artists such as Ani DiFranco and Bikini Kill, but at their best, they provided a jolt of self-esteem for millions of followers.

Kembrew McLeod

SEE ALSO: Dancing with the Stars*; Disc Jockeys; Girl Groups; Pop Music; Radio; Reality Television; Top 40.*

BIBLIOGRAPHY

Aplin, Rebecca. *Spice Girls: Giving You Everything*. London: UFO Music, 1997.

Fitzgerald, Muff. *Spiced Up!: My Mad Year with the Spice Girls*. London: Hodder & Stoughton, 1998.

Golden, Anna Louise. *Spice Girls: The Uncensored Story behind Pop's Biggest Phenomenon*. New York: Ballantine Books, 1997.

McGibbon, Rob. *Spice Power: The Inside Story*. London: Boxtree, 1997.

Shore, Nancy. *The Spice Girls*. Philadelphia: Chelsea House, 1998.

Sinclair, David. *Wannabe: How the Spice Girls Reinvented Pop Fame*. London: Omnibus Press, 2004.

Spider-Man

Spider-Man, a character appearing in Marvel comic books beginning in 1962, ranks not only as Marvel's most popular superhero but also as one of the most instantly recognizable comic-book characters of all. Of the many superheroes to appear over the years, only Superman and perhaps Batman have had a greater impact on the history and fortunes of the comic-book industry. And no other comic-book character has more perfectly realized the adolescent angst and male fantasies at the heart of the modern superhero genre.

MARVEL COMICS

With innovative characters like the Fantastic Four and the Incredible Hulk, Marvel, in the 1960s, pioneered the formula for superheroes who evinced such human failings as jealousy, insecurity, and alienation. This stood them in sharp contrast to the impossibly noble and stiff superheroes offered by competitors like DC Comics. Marvel's formula would attract an expanding fan base throughout the 1960s and beyond, ultimately making it the preeminent comic-book company.

Although Spider-Man was not the first of the new Marvel superheroes, he was the true archetype of the Marvel formula. In a calculated stab at the teenage market, which had dwindled since the institution of the Comics Code in 1954, writer-editor Stan Lee set out to create a superhero who was himself an adolescent—one who had to wrestle with his own insecurities and personal difficulties as often as he had to fight the bad guys. This superhero, in Lee's words, "would lose out as often as he'd win—in fact, more often." Lee bypassed his chief artist Jack Kirby and chose Steve Ditko to illustrate the concept, feeling that Ditko's own offbeat style was more appropriate for such an odd character as Spider-Man. The premise was so unusual, in fact, that Lee chose to debut Spider-Man in the fifteenth and final issue of *Amazing Fantasy*, a series slated for cancellation.

THE CHARACTER

The July 1962 issue of that title introduced readers to Peter Parker, a shy, bespectacled teenager ridiculed by his classmates for his social awkwardness and his love of science. One day, while attending an exhibit on radioactivity, Peter is bitten by a spider that, unbeknownst to him, has just been irradiated. Later, Peter discovers that somehow the radioactive spider's bite has transferred its power to him. Now possessing superhuman speed and agility, the ability to cling to walls, and the proportionate strength of a spider, Peter designs himself a pair of web-shooters attached to his wrists, tailors a costume to conceal his identity, and becomes Spider-Man.

Spider-Man. *The second installment of Raimi's* Spider-Man *movie series starred Tobey Maguire as Peter Parker/Spider-Man and Alfred Molina as Dr. Otto Octavius/Doc Ock.* MARVEL/SONY PICTURES/THE KOBAL COLLECTION/SONY PICTURES.

What came next in the originating story set the character apart from his costumed predecessors. Instead of swearing an altruistic oath to aid humanity, Peter sets out to cash in on his new powers. Why, after all, should he do anything for a society that has done nothing but ostracize him? He cares only for his Aunt May and Uncle Ben, who have raised him since the death of his parents. So selfish is his pursuit of fortune and glory that Spider-Man refuses to come to the aid of a policeman who fails to apprehend an escaping burglar. Then one night, Peter comes home to discover that his beloved Uncle Ben has been murdered. As Spider-Man, he pursues the killer, only to discover that it is the very same criminal whom he had earlier neglected to stop. The shocking revelation that his self-interest has indirectly led to the death of his uncle forces Spider-Man to accept the role that fate has forced upon him. He learns that "with great power there must also come great responsibility." It is this painful lesson that would form the guiding principle and tragic quality of his life as a superhero.

It is difficult to conceive of a more perfect origin story for a comic-book superhero. Lee and Ditko created a hero instantly relevant to the many shy, lonely, and disoriented adolescents who read comic books at a time when anxieties over the perils of atomic energy prevailed in the culture. Young people had a new superhero—one they could truly claim as their own. But Spider-Man's story imparted an important moral message as well. Although inclined to be a loner, Spider-Man was compelled by tragedy to enlist in a cause. This call to commitment proved to be a watchword not only for Spider-Man but also for the discontented baby boomers who mobilized their numbers in the service of political, social, and cultural change. In this important respect, Spider-Man meshed effortlessly with the currents then shaping 1960s youth culture.

THE AMAZING SPIDER-MAN

Spider-Man immediately became Marvel's most popular superhero—a distinction that he has held ever since. Responding to overwhelmingly positive reader mail, Lee in 1963 launched the character in his own series, *The Amazing Spider-Man*, which remained in circulation in the early 2010s. Spider-Man's commercial success fueled Marvel's mid-1960s superhero revival and set the company on the course toward becoming the industry leader.

Lee quite ingeniously billed Spider-Man as "the superhero who could be you." Peter lived at home with his Aunt May, whose motherly doting was a constant source of inconvenience, as he had to fabricate explanations for the late nights and extended absences that Spider-Man's lifestyle demanded. His high school and college life figured prominently into the stories, as did his job as a photographer for the cranky publisher J. Jonah Jameson's *Daily Bugle*. His perennial money problems and romantic travails with high school sweetheart Liz Allen, coworker Betty Brant, and college flames Gwen Stacy and Mary Jane Watson became an integral part of what was arguably the first comic-book soap opera. Spider-Man's good-natured wisecracking, irreverence for authority, and self-deprecating humor made him an especially endearing antihero to the young. Although he battled a colorful array of middle-aged villains, including Dr. Octopus, the Green Goblin, and the Vulture, Spider-Man was himself branded an outlaw by the press, the police, and other sources of adult authority who always seemed to suspect and misunderstand the hero's motives and actions.

GROWING POPULARITY

Spider-Man's popularity only grew over the following decades with a proliferation of licensed products, several Saturday-morning television cartoon series, and a long-running syndicated newspaper strip. In keeping with industry trends, Spider-Man's stories became increasingly sophisticated during the 1970s and 1980s. Three notable issues in 1971 defied the Comics Code Authority by dealing explicitly with the subject of drug abuse. The controversy over the antidrug stories led immediately to the liberalization of the Comics Code. Mindful of the fact that Spider-Man was especially popular among the youngest comic-book readers, Marvel has tended to keep the series rather squarely within the boundaries of mainstream cultural acceptability.

Several new comic-book titles featuring the hero increased his presence in the market to near saturation during the late 1980s and 1990s. The proliferation of the *Spider-Man* series and crossover stories prompted a number of fans to charge that Marvel was over-marketing their favorite hero at the expense of coherent stories, but this controversy did little to diminish his standing among general comic-book readers.

AT THE CINEMA

Spider-Man became a major movie franchise in the first decade of the 2000s, reintroducing the character to new generations of fans. After being trapped in development and production for more than two decades, the film *Spider-Man*, directed by Sam Raimi, was released to great critical and popular acclaim in 2002, grossing $100 million in ticket sales on the weekend it opened. Stars Tobey Maguire as the shy Peter Parker and Kirsten Dunst as Mary Jane received particularly high praise. The sequels *Spider-Man 2* (2004) and *Spider-Man 3* (2007) were fairly successful, but Sony Pictures decided to continue the series with a new lead actor (Andrew Garfield) and director (Marc Webb) for *The Amazing Spider-Man*, released in 2012.

Of all the superheroes, it is Spider-Man who most completely epitomizes the ideal of the comic-book superhero for people raised since the 1960s. As a personification of adolescent anxieties and fantasies, Spider-Man truly deserves his status as the quintessential modern comic-book superhero.

Bradford W. Wright

SEE ALSO: *Broadway; Comic Books; Comics Code Authority; DC Comics;* The Fantastic Four*; Hollywood; The Incredible Hulk; Kirby, Jack; Lee, Stan; Marvel Comics; Movie Stars; Saturday Morning Cartoons; Superman; Teenagers; Television.*

BIBLIOGRAPHY

Daniels, Les. *Marvel Comics: Five Fabulous Decades of the World's Greatest Comics*. New York: Harry N. Abrams, 1991.

The Essential Spider-Man, Vol. 1. New York: Marvel Comics, 1996.

Jacobs, Will, and Gerard Jones. *The Comic Book Heroes*. Rocklin, CA: Prima Publishing, 1997.

Lee, Stan. *Origins of Marvel Comics*. New York: Simon & Schuster, 1974.

Spiegelman, Art

SEE: *Maus.*

Spielberg, Steven *(1946–)*

In 1975 director Steven Spielberg made a splash in the movie industry when he came out with *Jaws*, the blockbuster that helped launch not only his career but also a new era in Hollywood. By the early twenty-first century, he was one of the most successful directors and producers in the history of Hollywood. His movies, including *E.T. The Extra-Terrestrial* (1982), *Jurassic Park* (1993), *Saving Private Ryan* (1998), and *War Horse* (2011), were often viewed as not only masterpieces of storytelling but also technological triumphs. He won many awards, including two Academy Awards for Best Director, for *Schindler's List* (1993) and *Saving Private Ryan*.

Steven Allan Spielberg was born on December 18, 1946, in Cincinnati, Ohio. His youth—displaced from Ohio to New Jersey to Arizona to California; obsessed with movies, television, and comic books; bullied by anti-Semites; and culminating in his parents' divorce—perhaps formed the subtext of many of his films. Crucial to his success was his ability to invest the horror, science fiction, and other Hollywood genres he continually recycled with the emotional force of his childhood obsessions. His early family difficulties, for example, might have provided raw material for a filmography crammed with broken homes; abandoned children; and wayward, would-be, or substitute fathers.

EARLY CAREER

Spielberg started making amateur films at the age of ten. He made the amateur 8-millimeter sci-fi feature *Firelight* in 1964, when he was sixteen years old. Rejected from the prestigious film schools at the University of Southern California and the University of California at Los Angeles, he attended California State College at Long Beach. While contemporaries such as George Lucas, Francis Ford Coppola, and Martin Scorsese became the first film school generation, Spielberg was essentially self-taught, spending three days a week during college hanging around the Universal lot, observing and hobnobbing. His last amateur film, the short *Amblin'* (1968), won him a directing contract at Universal, prompting the *Hollywood Reporter* to call him the youngest filmmaker ever contracted to a major studio. For the next five years he directed television programs such as *Night Gallery*, *Marcus Welby, M.D.*, and *Columbo*.

Spielberg's professional feature debut, the made-for-television road thriller *Duel* (1971), made an international splash, prompting *Los Angeles Times* television critic Cecil Smith to remark, "Steve Spielberg is really the *wunderkind* of the film business." Reviewing Spielberg's first theatrical film, *The Sugarland Express*, in 1974, critic Pauline Kael wrote, "The director, Steven Spielberg, is twenty-six; I can't tell if he has any mind, or even a strong personality . . . but he has a knack for bringing out young actors, and a sense of composition and movement that almost any director might envy. . . . He could be that rarity among directors—a born entertainer."

Spielberg was responsible for making some of the highest-grossing films of his era. *Jaws*, essentially a horror film starring a huge mechanical shark, was so successful that it helped transform the whole U.S. film industry from the post-studio dispersion of the 1960s to the blockbuster mentality of the 1980s. It also marked Spielberg's debut as an impresario of cutting-edge special effects.

POPULAR MOVIES

In *Close Encounters of the Third Kind* (1977), Spielberg transformed the 1950s movie alien from a monster into a saint. Author Ray Bradbury called it a religious film; French director Jean Renoir called it poetry. The more nakedly commercial *Raiders of the Lost Ark* (1981), which won the best director award from the Academy of Science Fiction, Fantasy and Horror Films in 1982, and its sequels (1984, 2008) repopularized the adventure serial. With *E.T.*, a fairy tale about a boy's friendship with an alien stranded on Earth, Spielberg made one of the most cherished films of its time. The movie made him a celebrity in his own right and even garnered him a United Nations Peace Medal. Spielberg's influence on U.S. culture in this period cannot be overestimated. Indiana Jones, E.T., and the shark became durable icons, helping to transform the national Zeitgeist from the turbulence of the 1960s to the high-tech nostalgia of the 1980s.

In 1985 Spielberg attempted to break away from the kind of genre-dominated filmmaking that had previously defined his career. *The Color Purple* (1985) was his first feature entirely about people (no car chases, sharks, or aliens). He took a huge risk in tackling Alice Walker's historical novel of black female liberation, and the results were ambiguous. While successful with mainstream U.S. viewers and critics, *The Color Purple* was the first in a series of serious Spielberg films that later came to include *Schindler's List*, *Amistad* (1997), and *War Horse*. These drew criticism for substituting sentimentality for an honest engagement with historical and political realities. The apparently perfect marriage between art and commerce that Spielberg had attained in his earlier genre films began to founder. *Empire of the Sun* (1987), *Always* (1989), and *Hook* (1991) met with mixed reviews.

In 1993 Spielberg regained commercial and critical success. First came another box-office smash, *Jurassic Park*, a return to the horror genre, with slick computer-generated imagery (CGI) of dinosaurs instead of a mechanical shark. Then came *Schindler's List*, a self-consciously European-style Holocaust film in black and white that won seven Academy Awards, including Best Picture and Spielberg's first for Best Director. This alternating pattern repeated with two films in 1997: a *Jurassic Park* sequel and *Amistad*, the true story of a maritime slave revolt. *Saving Private Ryan* (1998) was both a commercial and critical success, grossing more than $30 million in its opening weekend.

STYLE OF FILMS

Spielberg's films displayed a striking degree of thematic and stylistic unity, celebrating childlike wonder and the resilience of the human spirit. His movies were diverse in subject matter but fell into three main strands: adventure, science fiction, and historical drama. In Spielberg's world the highest ideal was childlike innocence—embodied by children themselves, endangered by monsters and villains, defended by heroes, reclaimed by grown men, and often symbolized by flying. Human relationships in his films were based on the model of the broken and mended family. Emotions tended to the extremes of terror and wonder. Stylistically, Spielberg's talent for visual composition was unsurpassed. With his embrace of high technology, his blending of genre and art cinema traditions, his prodigious quotation of other films, and his increasing concern with themes of vision and artifice, his often violent movies were tempered with a quiet optimism about the human capacity for redemption.

One of Spielberg's strengths was his ability to direct convincing large-scale adventure scenes, as in *War of the Worlds* (2005) and the Indiana Jones series, as well as more intimate, thoughtful moments, as in *The Color Purple* and *The Terminal* (2004). He showed technological mastery and a command of simple storytelling. Beginning in the early 1990s with the remarkable animated dinosaurs in *Jurassic Park*, he was at the forefront of seamlessly merging live action with CGI in movies such as the Philip K. Dick sci-fi thriller *Minority Report* and in the uplifting World War I drama *War Horse*. In *The Adventures of Tintin: The Secret of the Unicorn* (2011), he branched out into animation; this was also his first movie to be filmed digitally.

OTHER INTERESTS

While Spielberg's directorial career alone would guarantee him a place in the history of popular culture, he also made his mark as a film producer, with more than 130 movies to his name in that role. He formed the production company Amblin Entertainment in 1984, producing or executive producing films such as *Gremlins* (1984), *Back to the Future* (1985), *An American Tail* (1986), and *Who Framed Roger Rabbit* (1988), as well as television series such as *Tiny Toon Adventures* and *ER*.

In 1994 Spielberg launched both DreamWorks and the Survivors of the Shoah Visual History Foundation. DreamWorks SKG, cofounded with film executive Jeffrey Katzenberg and music mogul David Geffen, was the first new major Hollywood studio since the 1930s. With *Schindler's List* Spielberg publicly reclaimed his Jewish heritage and proclaimed his civic ideals. Seeded with $6 million from his *Schindler's List* earnings, the Shoah Foundation set out to videotape 50,000 testimonies by Holocaust survivors around the world, to catalog them, and to make them available for research and education via a sophisticated interactive computer system.

Thematically, economically, and ideologically, Spielberg's truest predecessor is Walt Disney. For many Spielberg represents Hollywood at its most entertaining, spectacular best. For others, when his movies are not being sentimental and manipulative, they are little more than theme park thrill rides. Spielberg has proclaimed a liberal political agenda, yet he has been accused of promoting a conservative, paternalistic attitude. Although the new Hollywood he helped create is often viewed as the embodiment of corporate greed and cynical marketing, as one of the most successful film directors of all time, Spielberg is at least able to use Hollywood's reach and power to promote causes and tell important stories.

Joshua Hirsch

SEE ALSO: *Academy Awards; Animated Films; Bradbury, Ray;* Columbo*; Dick, Philip K.; Disney (Walt Disney Company);* E.T. The Extra-Terrestrial*; Hollywood; Horror Movies;* Jaws*;* Jurassic Park*; Lucas, George; Made-for-Television Movies;* Marcus Welby, M.D.*; Movie Stars;* Raiders of the Lost Ark*;* Schindler's List*; Scorsese, Martin; Television; Walker, Alice; War Movies;* War of the Worlds.

BIBLIOGRAPHY

Brode, Douglas. *The Films of Steven Spielberg*. New York: Citadel, 1995.

Buckland, Warren. *Directed by Steven Spielberg: Poetics of the Contemporary Hollywood Blockbuster*. London: Continuum, 2006.

Freer, Ian. *The Complete Spielberg*. London: Virgin Books, 2001.

Friedman, Lester D., and Brent Notbohm, eds. *Steven Spielberg: Interviews*. Jackson: University Press of Mississippi, 2000.

Kael, Pauline. *For Keeps*. New York: Dutton, 1994.

Loshitzky, Yosefa, ed. *Spielberg's Holocaust: Critical Perspectives on "Schindler's List."* Bloomington: Indiana University Press, 1997.

McBride, Joseph. *Steven Spielberg: A Biography*. New York: Simon & Schuster, 1997.

Spillane, Mickey *(1918–2006)*

Mickey Spillane is one of the best-selling writers of the twentieth century—and of all time. The content of the books themselves and the two fictional heroes for which he is best known have been widely reviled for Spillane's portrayal of extreme violence, sexual excess, and right-wing bigotry. Whatever the opinions of his critics, from the 1940s Spillane proved himself to be a talented comic-book writer; an author of prize-winning books for children and young adults; and, through his Mike Hammer series, a key player in the history of the hard-boiled detective novel. The Mystery Writers of America awarded him a Grand Master Award in 1995.

Frank Michael Morrison Spillane was born in Brooklyn, New York, and brought up by working-class parents during the Depression. He began publishing stories in the pulp magazines soon after graduating from high school and, after dropping out of college and frustrated with his sales job, eventually ended up working on comic books. He was particularly successful, producing three times the output of other writers and devising a new, more efficient method of composition. When the war intervened, Spillane became a fighter pilot instructor and afterward found that comic books were no longer popular enough to provide a reliable source of income. This led him to write his first novel and create the New York-based detective, Mike Hammer.

The first Mike Hammer novel, *I, the Jury*, was published in 1947 and is a landmark in the development of private-eye fiction. Famously, in this novel, Hammer discovers that his lover is the killer he has been pursuing. When she tries to save herself by seducing him, Hammer shoots her and leaves her to die. The underlying moral logic of this (that the villain must be punished at whatever cost to the hero) is no different from Sam Spade's turning Brigid O'Shaughnessy over to the police in Dashiell Hammett's *The Maltese Falcon* (1930). However, Spillane's novel represents a significant shift from public to private justice. Spade investigates but does not punish crime. Hammer is investigator, judge, jury, and executioner.

Spillane's other series hero, the spy Tiger Mann, is also successful in his use of violence to solve problems. Mann differs in very little other than name from Hammer and appears to have been written in response to successful spy stories, including Ian Fleming's James Bond novels in the 1950s and 1960s.

After publishing seven novels between 1947 and 1952, Spillane seemed to respond to criticism of his portrayal of sex and violence by producing none for the next nine years, although he continued to write and publish short stories during this period. When he began publishing novels again in 1961, the violence, and particularly the link between sex and violence, was hardly diminished. Over time, Spillane's reputation with critics has gradually improved and he became respected as one of the most influential mystery writers of the late twentieth century. After producing more than thirty adult novels, including thirteen Mike Hammer adventures and four in the Tiger Mann spy series, he surprised critics by publishing a novel for children and young adults, *The Day the Sea Rolled Back* (1979), which won a Junior Guild Literary Award.

Spillane was always heavily involved in promoting his work. He appeared as Hammer on film and on the covers of some of the later novels and read his work on audio recordings. He made numerous talk show and game show appearances during the 1970s and even appeared as a parody of Hammer in television commercials for Miller Lite beer. Somewhat notoriously, his second wife, Sherri, posed nude for the dust jackets of *The Erection Set* (1972) and *The Last Cop Out* (1973). Despite this, Spillane was throughout his life a rather private man, and his desire for publicity is perhaps summed up in a comment he made, quoted in *One Lonely Knight*: "Hell, I'm not an author, I'm a writer. I've got to make a living, somehow." He published his last novel, *Something's Down There* in 2003 and died from cancer in 2006. He left many unfinished projects, seven of which have been completed by his friend Max Allan Collins.

Chris Routledge

SEE ALSO: *Best Sellers; Detective Fiction; Fleming, Ian; Hard-Boiled Detective Fiction;* The Maltese Falcon*; Miller Beer; Pulp Magazines.*

BIBLIOGRAPHY

Cawelti, John G. *Adventure, Mystery, and Romance: Formula Stories as Art and Popular Culture*. Chicago: University of Chicago Press, 1976.

Collins, Max Allan, and James L. Traylor. *One Lonely Knight: Mickey Spillane's Mike Hammer*. Bowling Green, OH: Bowling Green State University Popular Press, 1984.

Palmer, Jerry. *Thrillers: Genesis and Structure of a Popular Genre*. New York: St. Martin's Press, 1979.

Severo, Richard. "Mickey Spillane, 88, Critic-Proof Writer of Pulpy Mike Hammer Novels, Dies." *New York Times*, July 18, 2006.

Symons, Julian. *Bloody Murder: From the Detective Story to the Crime Novel*. New York: Viking, 1985.

Van Dover, J. Kenneth. *Murder in the Millions: Erle Stanley Gardner, Mickey Spillane, Ian Fleming*. New York: Frederick Ungar, 1984.

Spin

Just as a tennis player puts spin on the ball in order to influence the direction of its bounce, public figures (especially politicians) try to "spin" events so as to favorably influence coverage by the news media. The first uses of the term *spin* in this context date to the U.S. elections of 1984, and the term *spin doctor*, meaning a press secretary, publicist, campaign manager, or other surrogate adept at dealing with the press, entered the popular lexicon around 1990. Given the plethora of news outlets and their undeniable power to influence public opinion, the concept of spin control has become more prevalent.

Political campaigns are prime occasions for the exercise of spin control, because everything that occurs, short of the final vote count, is open to interpretation. The candidate who placed second in a primary, for example, might spin the result as a moral victory or a sign of gathering momentum. The candidate in third place might assert that the result is acceptable, considering the limited time and money that was spent in the state. The fourth-place candidate may claim to have gained valuable experience and name recognition that might bode well for future primary contests.

One aspect of campaigns that is especially amenable to spin is the political debate, because it lacks clear criteria for victory and the television audience is not made up of trained debate judges. As a result, the opinions of media pundits can have a great influence on public perceptions of the outcome. This is well illustrated by Gerald Ford's remark about the status of Poland during a 1976 televised debate against Jimmy Carter. In response to an earlier statement by Carter, Ford claimed that Poland was not under the domination of the Soviet Union. Opinion polls conducted immediately after the debate showed that a significant portion of the audience thought Ford had done well. However, by the next day, after the news media had made much of Ford's gaffe about Poland, many viewers apparently decided that Carter was the debate's clear winner. Occasions like this have convinced political professionals of the necessity of effective spin control.

WARTIME JOURNALISM

Wartime provides another instance of the usefulness of spin, especially in the post–Vietnam War era. It is virtually doctrine at the highest levels of the U.S. armed forces that the news media "lost" the Vietnam War for America by writing and broadcasting stories that undermined the public's will to win. News stories about human rights abuses by the South Vietnamese government, atrocities allegedly committed by U.S. troops, and the effects upon civilians of indiscriminate bombing of North Vietnam—along with vivid images of dead, dying, and horribly disfigured American troops—are believed by the Pentagon to have convinced many citizens that the war was not winnable.

This does not mean spin control was absent during the Vietnam War. It was, in fact, widely attempted by politicians at home and by the Military Assistance Command in Vietnam. However, the official spin on the war lost effectiveness as the conflict dragged on. President Lyndon Johnson, whose Vietnam policies had enjoyed wide support in 1964, was alleged to have developed a "credibility gap" concerning the war by 1967—a euphemism for the belief that Johnson had been caught lying. In Vietnam, military public information officers held daily press briefings in Saigon at 5 p.m. Over time, many journalists grew so cynical about the official spin on the war that they began to refer to the briefings as the "Five O'Clock Follies." Fed up with the official line, many reporters went off on their own and, in the process, sometimes uncovered stories embarrassing to both the U.S. military and its commander in chief.

Having learned what it saw as the public-relations lesson of Vietnam, the Pentagon has since taken careful and comprehensive steps to ensure that media coverage of military conflicts receive the proper spin. The new policy involves the close supervision of reporters in combat zones, restriction of journalists from "sensitive" areas, and frequent official briefings to ensure that journalists receive the military's version of events. This approach was followed successfully by the military in Grenada (1984) and Panama (1990). However, the crowning achievement in military spin control probably came in the Persian Gulf War in 1990 and 1991. In the Saudi Arabia staging area for coalition forces, correspondents were forbidden to travel on their own; instead, battlefield news gathering was permitted only by a closely supervised "pool" of reporters while the others were left behind. Then the journalists would be brought back to the press area to brief their colleagues. Military briefings during the Gulf War were much more effective as spin than the Five O'Clock Follies, as the carefully scripted briefings created the desired impression of the coalition's invincibility.

CONTEMPORARY SPIN

A more recent spin initiative began in the spring of 1998, when stories began to surface alleging that President Bill Clinton had engaged in a sexual relationship with a young White House intern named Monica Lewinsky. The Clinton White House, especially press secretary Mike McCurry, tried hard to spin the story into something innocuous. Observing McCurry at work over a long period, writer Howard Kurtz derived some of the press secretary's spin strategies. These included: (1) Do not let television break a scandal. If it is inevitable, leak it to the print media, which tend to provide more nuance and are seen by considerably fewer people. (2) Do not let Senate committees break scandals either. Beat them to the punch by informing the media yourself, providing your own "spin" in the process. (3) Leak favorable but boring stories to one media outlet as an "exclusive"—chances are, it will be grateful enough to give the story a positive spin.

Spin has become even more prevalent through radio talk shows, Internet blogs, and twenty-four-hour cable news channels. In response to increased competition and public cynicism, and through marketing wizardry, each network has attempted to convey that it is the most objective and trusted source for news. Most notably, cable's Fox News Channel's slogan "Fair & Balanced," coupled with *The O'Reilly Factor*'s "No Spin Zone," purports to offer unbiased reporting of information. Fox News Channel uses an array of graphics to present its news, which sparked cable news outlets such as MSNBC to follow suit. In addition to aggressive presentations, the news channels pepper their broadcasts with polarizing and charismatic personalities such as Bill O'Reilly (Fox), Sean Hannity (Fox), Rachel Maddow (MSNBC), and Keith Olbermann (formerly of MSNBC).

NETWORK BIAS

Although these networks claim to remain objective, they have had accusations of bias leveled against them by media watchdog groups and, not surprisingly, each other. At worst, the commentators have been characterized as mouthpieces for the political agendas of the networks. Radio talk-show host Rush Limbaugh has based his career on challenging the perceived liberal bias in the media and routinely champions conservative causes. O'Reilly has advocated for unbiased media coverage, but his critics often charge him with supporting Republican causes, in particular the invasion of Iraq in 2003. Maddow has provided a daily one-hour block of progressive media coverage that challenges Fox's spin, but in doing so, she has been criticized for shilling for liberal causes such as health care reform and same-sex marriage.

In one sense, the political ideologies of the media outlets have fueled their coverage, but at the same time, the various channels have attempted to veil their agendas by throwing stones at those of their rivals. Spin doctors massage every political development, working out of "spin rooms" and visiting media outlets. However, despite the public's reported mistrust of spin, the major news outlets have experienced increased ratings and the pundits have authored best-selling books.

Justin Gustainis

SEE ALSO: *Fox News Channel; Gulf Wars; Lewinsky, Monica; Limbaugh, Rush; Networks; O'Reilly, Bill; Television; Television Anchors; Vietnam.*

BIBLIOGRAPHY

Burton, Bob. *Inside Spin: The Dark Underbelly of the PR Industry*. Crows Nest, Australia: Allen & Unwin, 2007.

Ewen, Stewart. *PR: The Social History of Spin*. New York: Basic Books, 1996.

Kurtz, Howard. *Spin Cycle: Inside the Clinton Propaganda Machine*. New York: Free Press, 1998.

Maltese, John Anthony. *Spin Control: The White House Office of Communications and the Management of Presidential News*. Chapel Hill: University of North Carolina Press, 1994.

McChesney, Robert Waterman. *The Political Economy of Media: Enduring Issues, Emerging Dilemmas*. New York: Monthly Review Press, 2008.

Partington, Alan. *The Linguistics of Political Argument: The Spin-Doctor and the Wolf-Pack at the White House*. New York: Routledge, 2002.

Press, Bill. *Spin This! All the Ways We Don't Tell the Truth*. New York: Pocket Books, 2002.

Sellers, Patrick J. *Cycles of Spin: Strategic Communication in the U.S. Congress*. New York: Cambridge University Press, 2009.

Spinal Tap

When Rob Reiner's film directorial debut, *This Is Spinal Tap*, premiered in 1984, the self-dubbed "rockumentary" about the comeback tour of a fictionalized rock-and-roll band called Spinal Tap was hailed by Vincent Canby of the *New York Times* as "one of the brightest, funniest American film parodies to come along since 'Airplane!'" while Janet Maslin of the *New York Times* said "it stays so wickedly close to the subject that it is very nearly indistinguishable from the real thing." *This Is Spinal Tap* has had a devoted fan base ever since, including innumerable musicians as well as filmmakers. As *Newsweek*'s Jennie Yabroff reflected in 2009, it "made mockumentaries the art form of our time. It also made life hell for every struggling hair-metal band."

Reiner's costars and cowriters Christopher Guest, Michael McKean, and Harry Shearer—three friends with prior experience in acting and guerrilla comedy—found inspiration in rock documentaries such as the Rolling Stones' tour diary *Gimme Shelter* (1970) and the Bob Dylan tribute *Don't Look Back* (1967). They were also following a growing tradition of mockumentaries including news-parodying sketches on *Saturday Night Live* (1975–) and films such as Woody Allen's *Zelig* (1983) and *Take the Money and Run* (1969)—about the career of an inept bank robber.

Before *This Is Spinal Tap*, Reiner had achieved fame playing Michael "Meathead" Stivic, Archie Bunker's son-in-law, on Norman Lear's hit sitcom *All in the Family* (1971–1978). In the film he plays interviewer and filmmaker Marty DiBergi, who follows the band on its promotional U.S. tour. McKean plays lead guitarist David St. Hubbins (named for "the patron saint of quality footwear"), while Guest plays his guitar-collecting best friend Nigel Tufnel. Shearer is drug-dazed bassist Derek Smalls, and David Kaff is the slightly creepy keyboardist Viv Savage, who claims that he can eschew rock and roll as long as there's still sex and drugs.

The movie's jokes and sight gags satirize nearly every aspect of the music industry, including the often bizarre and untimely deaths of band members. One of the recurring jokes is that the band cannot keep the same drummer. One dies from a gardening accident, while another chokes on a friend's vomit. A third drummer self-combusts in the middle of a show and is replaced with no comment. Doing a Yoko Ono turn, David's obnoxious and clueless girlfriend Jeanine Pettibone (June Chadwick) tells him that his larynx is fat and schedules the tour according to astrology.

The band hits rock bottom when they desperately attempt to perform free-form jazz and end up playing a gym-floor gig at an air force base. For many struggling and successful bands, the

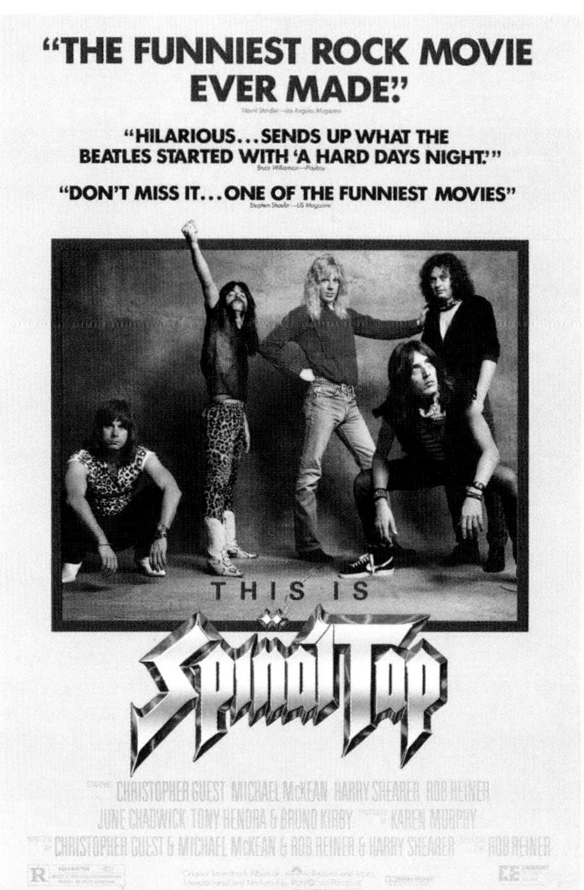

This Is Spinal Tap *Movie Poster*. This Is Spinal Tap *uses the "mockumentary" format as a comic send-up of not only self-indulgent, self-important rock stars, but of the music industry as a whole.* SPINAL TAP PRODUCTION/THE KOBAL COLLECTION.

film hit too close to home. Bands such as Aerosmith, Metallica, and Van Halen found many of the touring scenes to be eerily similar to their own experiences. The pathetic nature of the band and its blind naïveté led to *Spinal Tap* being used as a derogatory term applied to inept bands that overcultivated their bad-boy image and took themselves too seriously.

After *This Is Spinal Tap* Reiner directed several box-office hits, including *Stand by Me* (1986), *The Princess Bride* (1987), *When Harry Met Sally* (1989), and *A Few Good Men* (1992). Guest has developed a strong cult following for his acclaimed mockumentaries, including *Waiting for Guffman* (1996) and *Best in Show* (2000), which satirize community theater actors and dog trainers, respectively. In a surprising turn, Spinal Tap has become real. Guest, Shearer, and McKean have toured and released albums together, including *Break Like the Wind* (1992) and *Back from the Dead* (2009).

Although critics praised the film, *This Is Spinal Tap* didn't develop a cultlike following until it was released on video. Since then it has been named one of the best movies of all time by the *New York Times*, *Entertainment Weekly*, and *Empire* magazine. In 2002 the Library of Congress selected the film to be preserved in the National Film Registry, and on November 11, 2011, fans of the movie organized Nigel Tufnel Day, celebrating the famous scene in which Tufnel demonstrates the power of his amplifier by explaining that its volume dial "goes to 11."

Stephen P. Davis

SEE ALSO: *Aerosmith;* Airplane!*;* All in the Family*; Allen, Woody; The Beatles; Cult Films; Dylan, Bob; Guest, Christopher; Heavy Metal; Lear, Norman; Mockumentaries; R.E.M.; Rock and Roll; The Rolling Stones;* Saturday Night Live*;* The Simpsons*; Van Halen.*

BIBLIOGRAPHY

French, Karl, ed. *"This Is Spinal Tap": Official Companion.* New York: Bloomsbury, 2000.

Spiritualists

SEE: *Psychics.*

Spitz, Mark *(1950–)*

The first person ever to win seven gold medals in a single Olympics, U.S. swimmer Mark Spitz became part American hero and part controversial commodity. With his black mustache and movie-star looks, Spitz dominated his sport in the 1972 Olympics in Munich and retired to find even greater fame as the first big-time pitchman for corporate America. In addition to a total of eleven medals during his Olympic career, he earned a reported $5 million in endorsements.

Spitz began training at an early age, and by the age of eight he was already swimming in competitions. Searching for a better training environment for Spitz, the family relocated to California. He received encouragement and training from both his father, Arnold, and three legendary coaches—Sherm Chavoor, Doc Counsilman, and George Haines—during the course of his career. Known for his self-confidence, Spitz was not always popular with his teammates but continued to train for both team and individual competitions.

By the 1968 Summer Olympics in Mexico City, the outspoken Spitz had already made a name for himself as a cocky, self-assured young man. In the days before the games, he boasted that he would take home six gold medals. His prediction fell far short—he won only two gold medals, as well as a silver medal and a bronze. Disappointed but undaunted, Spitz returned home to train with the Indiana University swim team in preparation for the 1972 Olympics in Munich.

Spitz had matured as both an athlete and a person by 1972. His personal appearances lacked the boastful predictions of 1968, and he seemed more focused on his goal of winning as many medals as possible. His determination paid off. Over eight days he won seven gold medals (and set seven world records), an achievement that remained unsurpassed throughout the rest of the twentieth century. Even amid horrifying terrorism during the Munich games—in which nine members of the Israeli team, a West German police officer, and five Arab terrorists were killed—Spitz's were celebrated.

Spitz's popularity did not wane following the 1972 Olympics. He returned home a hero, with endorsement contracts and even a popular poster commemorating his achievements soon following. Garnering a contract from the William Morris Agency, Spitz promoted a wide range of items, from swimwear and pool accessories to milk, razors, and hair dryers. In addition to his endorsements, he made numerous television appearances with such stars as Sonny and Cher and Bob Hope.

By current standards, Spitz's success in the advertising world was somewhat limited. Lacking the agents and the public relations experts employed by today's athletes, he did not receive the guidance he needed to maximize his endorsement potential.

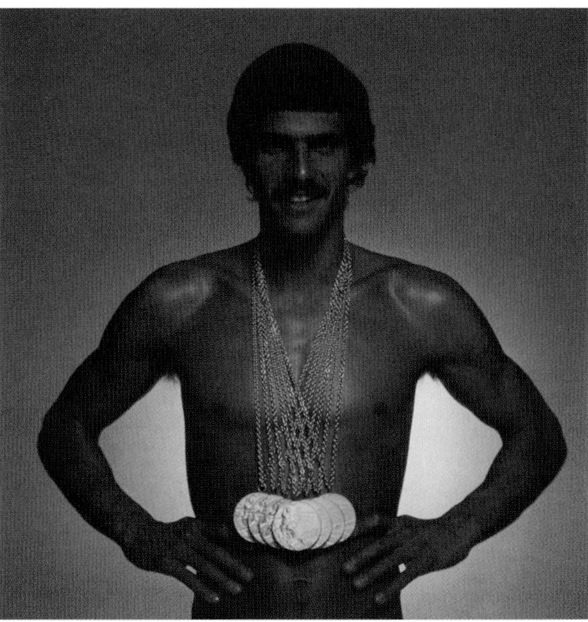

Mark Spitz. *Mark Spitz poses with the seven gold medals he won at the 1972 Olympic Games in Munich, Germany.* TERRY O'NEILL/ CONTRIBUTOR/GETTY IMAGES.

He was considered "too quiet" by some detractors and was criticized for his apparent stiff appearance on camera. Though it seems strange in the current endorsement world, where major athletes appear virtually everywhere, he was also chided for pitching too many products. Nevertheless, Spitz paved the way for these modern-day athletes, and after all the hoopla subsided, he opted for a life mostly outside the spotlight. Spitz went on to pursue a variety of interests, including real-estate investments, sailing, speaking engagements, and appearances at swimming events.

When he retired from swimming at age twenty-two shortly after the 1972 Olympics, Spitz had set twenty-six world and twenty-four national individual records. He was inducted into the International Swimming Hall of Fame as an Honor Swimmer in 1977. In the 1990s Spitz decided to make a comeback at age forty-one, but his attempt to qualify in the 100-meter butterfly for the 1992 Olympics fell short, and he retired again. However, this setback did not dampen his love of the sport or his active participation in it. At the 1998 World Championships in Perth, Australia, he proposed the creation of a position dealing with the problem of performance-enhancing drugs used by swimmers.

At the 2008 Olympics in Beijing, Spitz's Olympic record of seven gold medals was eclipsed by Michael Phelps, who won eight. That gave Phelps a total of fourteen Olympic gold medals, counting the six he had won four years earlier in Athens, so he also surpassed Spitz on that front. The Olympic Committee did not ask Spitz to attend the Beijing Olympics, and he felt snubbed. However, in interviews after the games, he took the high road and praised Phelps for his performance. Decades after his rise to fame in Munich, Spitz remains a national hero and a shining star in the Olympic firmament. He is considered one of the greatest Olympians of all time.

Kimberley H. Kidd

SEE ALSO: *Advertising; Olympics; Phelps, Michael; Sports Heroes; Swimming Pools.*

BIBLIOGRAPHY

Foster, Richard J. *Mark Spitz: The Extraordinary Life of an Olympic Champion.* Santa Monica, CA: Santa Monica Press, 2008.

Noden, Merrell. "Catching up with . . . Swimming Champion Mark Spitz." *Sports Illustrated*, August 4, 1997.

Reed, Susan, and Lorenzo Benet. "Superswimmer Mark Spitz." *People*, January 15, 1990.

Spitz, Mark, and Alan LeMond. *The Mark Spitz Complete Book of Swimming.* New York: Thomas Y. Crowell, 1976.

Spock, Dr. Benjamin *(1903–1998)*

By introducing new child-rearing techniques that contradicted those practiced for hundreds of years, pediatrician Benjamin McLane Spock changed the way generations of parents raised their children. Through his practice, books, and articles in numerous child-rearing magazines, he taught parents to trust their common sense, instinct, and unique bond with their children. As North America's foremost pediatrician and parenting authority for more than fifty years, he witnessed firsthand the results of his recommendations. Without being an ideologue or professing to be a guru, he used his liberal views on child rearing to pioneer or reinforce new directions in education.

Dr. Benjamin Spock. *Dr. Benjamin Spock introduced a novel approach to raising and educating children when his book* Baby and Child Care *was first published in 1946. The book has since sold millions of copies and has been translated into dozens of languages.* AP IMAGES.

His best-known work, *The Common Sense Book of Baby and Child Care* (1946; later retitled *Baby and Child Care*) has been printed in forty-two languages and has sold more than fifty million copies around the world. During the post–World War II baby boom, the book became the predominant how-to guide for parents. Spock embraced the flexibility he asked of parents by adapting his basic volume to changes in society, expanding and revising it several times during his lifetime. By the end of the twentieth century, virtually all parents with young children in the United States had grown up within the child-rearing and educational framework advised by Spock. Though parts of *Baby and Child Care* have been criticized as fostering overpermissiveness, the book remains one of the most influential works on parenting.

EARLY LIFE AND CAREER

Born on May 2, 1903, in New Haven, Connecticut, Spock attended Yale University and was a member of the crew team that won a gold medal for the United States in the 1924 Olympics. After completing his studies in 1925, he moved to Columbia University to earn his MD. In his spare time, he studied at the New York Psychoanalytic Institute, and in 1927 he married Jane Cheney, with whom he had two sons, Michael and John. A doctor and a teacher, he simultaneously maintained a private practice in New York City and taught pediatrics at Cornell University.

During World War II he served as a psychiatrist in the U.S. Naval Reserve Medical Corps, and in 1946 he was discharged as a lieutenant commander. The same year, *Baby and Child Care* was published, revolutionizing centuries of parenting traditions. Since the Middle Ages, children raised within Western tradition had been considered trainees who should be taught to obey specific rules. Feeding was restricted to specific hours, and toilet training had to be done according to specific principles and at precise ages. The rules applied to all children regardless of individual differences. The traditional approach, still widely practiced in some European contexts and in highly socialized countries in Asia, runs counter to the advice Spock gave to the parents of baby boomers. "I wanted to be supportive of parents rather than to scold them," he said. He explained that he "set out very deliberately to counteract some of the rigidities of pediatric tradition, particularly in infant feeding."

POSTWAR AMERICA

As the war ended, the joys of reuniting with returning veterans and the resultant baby boom spurred a celebration of life. In 1945, 2,873,000 babies were born in the United States; the next year the number increased by 20 percent to nearly 3,500,000. By 1954 the figure had reached 4,000,000, remaining high through 1964, the last year of the baby boom. The sheer number of babies born gave tremendous weight to Spock's writings and teachings.

Influenced by Enlightenment thinkers such as Frenchman Jean-Jacques Rousseau (1712–1778), Spock's romantic vision of humans as fundamentally good was welcomed in the postwar climate. Spock found willing readers in veterans who had experienced cruelty, savagery, and crimes against humanity during the war. Parents wanted to turn their backs on misery and despair, needing to believe that the world was good, life could get better, and the future was wide open. Gone were the rigid discipline and sacrifice of the war effort and the rationing of sugar, bananas, meat, cigarettes, butter, chocolate, and gasoline. Americans could rejoice in their lives and their new prosperity.

Spock emphasized what may have been obvious to some parents (especially those with multiple children) but not to authors of books on parenting: There are enormous differences between individual babies. These differences are important and should be taken into account. Parents need to be flexible and to avoid worrying constantly about spoiling children. Spock also set out to dispel myths about what was good or bad for children. For example, when he began practicing pediatrics, bananas were considered hazardous to a young child's health and castor oil was praised as a cure-all. Thus, his first book dealt with what he saw as persistent mistakes in child rearing.

CRITICISM AND ACCUSATIONS OF RADICALISM

After the war, Spock taught psychiatry at the University of Minnesota, which he left in 1951 to join the University of Pittsburgh as a professor of child development. In 1955 he joined the faculty at Case Western Reserve University. In addition to his paradigm-shifting views on child rearing, he is remembered for his increasing liberalism in the years following the war. Although he had always opposed the proliferation of nuclear weapons, the cause became his passion in the 1960s. When President John F. Kennedy alluded to the possibility of using nuclear weapons during the Cuban missile crisis of 1962, Spock and the National Committee for Sane Nuclear Policy took out a full-page ad in the *New York Times* denouncing the president.

After Spock retired from academia, he devoted his time to antiwar and antinuclear activities. By 1967 he was under investigation for aiding draft evaders, and in 1968 he was indicted and sentenced to two years in prison, although an appeals court later overturned his conviction. In 1972 he ran for president on the People's Party ticket, advocating nuclear disarmament, free university education and health care, and the legalization of abortion and marijuana. He won 80,000 votes.

A few years later, he and his wife divorced after forty-eight years of marriage, and he married feminist activist Mary Morgan. As a result of his activism and liberal views, he was criticized for preaching permissiveness and was held responsible for a "Spock-marked" generation of hippies. Vice President Spiro Agnew accused him of corrupting the youth of America, but Spock took credit for having only a "mild influence." Contrary to the claims of his critics, he had always been a firm believer in sound, responsible parental authority. "Respect children because . . . they deserve respect, and they'll grow up to be better people," he said. "But . . . ask for respect from your children, ask for cooperation, ask for politeness. Give your children firm leadership."

PUBLICATIONS AND LEGACY

Spock's enormous influence exemplified the changes in U.S. society. The traditional way of handling child-rearing practices had been by word of mouth or through confidential, direct information passed from doctor or nurse to parent. Such practices continued but did not satisfy Americans' needs in an age of mass media. To reach new audiences, Spock wrote or collaborated on thirteen books. With his second wife, Mary, he wrote an autobiography, *Spock on Spock*, published in 1989. In his work he confessed that as a father he often found it hard to put his theories on child rearing into practice, regretting that he had been a cold father.

For more than thirty years, he wrote columns in mass-market publications such as *Ladies' Home Journal* and *Redbook*, and he was a contributing editor to *Parenting* magazine from 1992 until his death. The editors of *Parenting* mourned his death by saying, "We will miss his common sense approach to parenting and his dedication to raising healthy, happy children." When he died at age ninety-four at his home in San Diego, California, with his family by his side, he left behind a strong legacy.

Despite the changes in U.S. society, his basic message had remained the same: "Don't take too seriously all that the neighbors say. Don't be overawed by what the experts say. Trust yourself, you know more than you think you know." His was a deeply humanist message, which stated that real values are always individual and the only valid judgments are those made by responsible individuals.

Henri Parette

SEE ALSO: *Abortion; Baby Boomers; The Draft; Marijuana; Protest Groups;* Redbook*; World War II.*

BIBLIOGRAPHY

Bloom, Lynn Z. *Doctor Spock: Biography of a Conservative Radical.* Indianapolis, IN: Bobbs-Merrill, 1972.

Caulfield, Rick. "'Trust Yourself': Revisiting Benjamin Spock." *Early Childhood Education Journal* 26, no. 4 (1999): 263–265.

Foley, Michael S., ed. *Dear Dr. Spock: Letters about the Vietnam War to America's Favorite Baby Doctor.* New York: New York University Press, 2005.

Kaye, Judith. *The Life of Benjamin Spock.* New York: Twenty-First Century Books, 1993.

Maier, Thomas. *Dr. Spock: An American Life.* New York: Harcourt Brace, 1998.

Parry, Manon. "Benjamin Spock: Pediatrician and Antiwar Activist." *American Journal of Public Health* 101 (2011): 802–803.

Petigny, Alan Cecil. *The Permissive Society, 1941–1965.* New York: Cambridge University Press, 2009.

Spock, Benjamin, and Mary Morgan. *Spock on Spock: A Memoir of Growing up with the Century.* New York: Pantheon Books, 1989.

Spock, Benjamin, and Stephen J. Parker. *Dr. Spock's Baby and Child Care*, 7th ed. New York: Dutton, 1998.

SpongeBob SquarePants

SpongeBob SquarePants is the title character of an animated TV series (1999–) and its spin-off movies, video games, books, and merchandise ranging from backpacks and toothbrushes to Lego sets. Created by Stephen Hillenburg, *SpongeBob SquarePants* is one of the longest-running cartoons on television. With its eleven-minute episodes and longer specials produced for Nickelodeon and translated into dozens of languages, it is also one of the world's most-watched television shows.

A yellow kitchen sponge, SpongeBob (voiced by Tom Kenny) cuts an unlikely figure in his red tie, white shirt, white socks, black dress shoes, and starched pants that are rectangular rather than actually square. His implausibly large face—round eyes, buck teeth, disarmingly wide grin, freckled cheeks, and protruding nose—occupies most of his 4-inch frame, from which extend arms and legs that are toothpick-thin except when SpongeBob becomes a wrestler, for example, or gets "ripped" as a fake bodybuilder.

Although SpongeBob has an almost eternally cheerful disposition, he cries torrents after losing a contest or a promotion at the Krusty Krab restaurant, where he is a dependably energetic fry cook. But whether he is sweating for minimum wage, helping a friend, or exploring the slum of Rock Bottom, SpongeBob's resilient optimism has always been the key to his popularity as a character. This trait remained unchanged despite other changes to the show after Hillenburg handed over control of his undersea kingdom to Paul Tibbitt in 2004; both are now credited as executive producers.

SpongeBob loves his motley crew of friends, although his childlike excitability and carelessness can also curse them, especially his oft-harried neighbor Squidward Tentacles (voiced by Rodger Bumpass), a cranky squid who can seldom relax at home with his clarinet. SpongeBob's best friend is Patrick Star (Bill Fagerbakke), a Bermuda-shorts-donning starfish who is perennially dumbfounded by SpongeBob's antics. Most of their adventures are set in the undersea city of Bikini Bottom, where SpongeBob's roomy pineapple sits near Squidward's imposing moai (Easter Island carved figure) and Patrick's weather-vane-topped rock.

Other seaworthy companions include SpongeBob's meowing pet snail, Gary; his often sweet and always greedy boss, Mr. Krabs (voiced by Clancy Brown); and the squirrel Sandy Cheeks (Carolyn Lawrence), a scientist whose flower-festooned spacesuit allows her full access to Bikini Bottom. On the darker side, Sheldon Plankton (voiced by Mr. Lawrence) is a diminutive, one-eyed schemer who owns the Chum Bucket, which is across the street from the Krusty Krab and is its main rival for business.

Hillenburg first created a talking sea sponge in an educational comic strip while pursuing marine biology. After switching to the study of animation and working on the series *Rocko's Modern Life*, he developed *SpongeBob SquarePants* as an alternative to more cynical "adult" cartoons such as *South Park*. However, the ghost of Nickelodeon's cartoon show *Ren and Stimpy* seems to possess *SpongeBob* in the show's penchant for grotesque close-ups of bloodshot eyes, popping veins, pectoral muscles, and body hair.

Despite its predilection for good-natured jibes rather than deep social critique, *SpongeBob* is not without its critics and detractors. Peter Keepnews of the *New York Times* wrote of the show: "The phenomenon that is 'SpongeBob SquarePants' is a little like the prose of James Joyce or the music of Sun Ra: there are those who love it with a deep, intense passion, and those who just don't get it." Conservative commentator James Dobson falls into the latter camp. In 2005 he alleged that the show encourages tolerance of homosexuality. Rumors then circulated that SpongeBob was gay, despite Hillenburg's elucidation that his sponge was "almost asexual," as well as the cartoon world's long tradition of gender ambiguity, including the famously cross-dressing Bugs Bunny. On the other side of the critical divide, film critic Roger Ebert has written approvingly of the "fast-paced and goofy" show, arguing that it "involves SpongeBob's determination to amount to something in this world."

One measure of the show's cultural influence is the long list of celebrities who have lined up to voice supporting characters or make cameos, including Johnny Depp, Alec Baldwin, David Bowie, Tina Fey, Will Ferrell, and Robin Williams. Another indicator is the millions of viewers who watch the show weekly, even after researchers claimed in 2011 that *SpongeBob*'s frenetic pace was detrimental to the attention spans of young children.

Stephen P. Davis

SEE ALSO: *Animated Films; Baldwin, Alec; Bowie, David; Depp, Johnny; Ferrell, Will; Fey, Tina; Saturday Morning Cartoons;* South Park*; Television; Williams, Robin.*

BIBLIOGRAPHY

Banks, Steven, and Gregg Schigiel (illustrator). *SpongeBob Exposed! The Insider's Guide to SpongeBob SquarePants.* New York: Simon Spotlight/Nickelodeon, 2004.

Harriman, Steven (aka Steven Spruill). *Absorbing SpongeBob: Ten Ways to Squeeze More Happiness out of Life.* New York: Berkley Trade, 2005.

Neuwirth, Allan. *Makin' Toons: Inside the Most Popular*

Animated TV Shows and Movies. New York: Allworth Communications, 2003.

Sport Utility Vehicles (SUVs)

The SUV, or sport utility vehicle, earned its name for its ability to transport people and their gear to outdoor recreation areas. The SUV has been available to drivers in the United States since the end of World War II, but its heyday was in the 1980s and 1990s, when baby boomers discovered that the more luxurious models were a sporty and practical alternative to the family sedan, minivan, or station wagon. Even though the majority of SUVs rarely leave the pavement, many owners like the fact that the SUV can be taken off-road, while safety-conscious drivers appreciate its handling on snow and ice.

The first SUVs in the United States were surplus military Jeeps converted to meet the needs of the civilian market at the end of World War II. They became popular with consumers who sought escape from wartime rationing and the deprivation of the Great Depression. The supply of surplus military Jeeps did not last long, however, and in 1945 the Willys-Overland company began to produce models specifically for the civilian market. Ranchers, farmers, hunters, and campers appreciated their affordability and the improved handling of four-wheel drive. The early SUVs did not compete with passenger automobiles because they lacked the space to carry both people and luggage and handled like the trucks on which they were based.

Although International Harvester manufactured the Travelall and the Scout and Jeep brought out the Jeep Wagoneer, the first dedicated sport utility vehicle from a major manufacturer was the Ford Bronco, introduced in 1966 and followed in 1969 by the Chevy Blazer and GMC Jimmy. These relatively compact SUVs were joined in 1973 by the Suburban, which was marketed by both Chevrolet and GMC and came with a choice of two- or four-wheel drive. (An earlier version of the Suburban, which appeared in the 1930s, was a delivery truck, not a true SUV.) The Suburban was the largest SUV available, offering unprecedented interior spaciousness and towing capacity.

The energy crisis of the 1970s brought numerous changes to U.S. driving habits. Gasoline shortages, long lines at the pumps, and pressure from public figures, including President Jimmy Carter, caused many Americans to abandon their gas-guzzling muscle cars for a more socially responsible alternative. Many drivers chose either small European or Japanese cars; others discovered the versatility of imported trucks. But there was always a need for vehicles that could tow a boat or trailer. In 1983 both General Motors (GM) and Ford offered alternatives to the imports: smaller versions of the Blazer and the Jimmy from GM and the Bronco II from Ford. By the early 1980s SUVs accounted for 2 percent of all vehicle sales in the United States, and their drivers were very different from those who had purchased converted military jeeps. Instead of wanting a vehicle for off-road use, the new generation of SUV owners included a high percentage of women who wanted an alternative to the station wagon and later to the minivan.

Attempting to appeal to these diverse drivers, manufacturers offered more amenities, including more horsepower, sophisticated sound systems, better handling, and the ability to "shift on the fly" (the ability to change while driving from two-wheel drive to four-wheel drive). Manufacturers also began offering a variety of sizes, from the tiny subcompact Suzuki Sidekick (which weighed under 3,000 pounds and towed a modest 1,500 pounds) to the behemoths of the SUV set, the Chevrolet and GMC Suburbans, weighing over two tons and able to tow 10,000 pounds. By 1998 about one in every eight vehicles sold in the United States was an SUV.

Enthusiasm for SUVs was dampened briefly in 1996 when Consumers Union, publishers of *Consumer Reports*, petitioned the National Highway Traffic Safety Administration (NHTSA) to investigate findings that the Isuzu Trooper and the Acura SLX placed occupants at a higher risk for rollovers. Other studies, including those by NHTSA, came to different conclusions, finding that the additional size and weight of SUVs made them safer than passenger automobiles. Nonetheless, many manufacturers aggressively addressed the perceived threat by warning consumers to modify the way they drove SUVs.

While SUVs have gained popularity with consumers, they are not popular with everyone. Groups like the Sierra Club and Friends of the Earth criticize SUVs for their impact on the environment. Classified as light trucks under federal rules, SUVs must meet less stringent fuel and emission standards than passenger automobiles. Because they can also go off-road, they can inflict greater damage on the environment. In addition, their higher ground clearance means that they can inflict costly damage on smaller cars. As a result, some insurance companies have raised their liability rates on SUVs.

Sales of SUVs continued strong at the end of the 1990s because they provided both a sporty feel and the ability to transport everything from boats and trailers to Labrador retrievers and a gaggle of schoolchildren and their gear. Luxury SUVs built by Lexus, Mercedes, Acura, and Volkswagen offered spacious interiors and comfortable amenities. More fun than the sedans and station wagons that baby boomers remembered from their childhoods and more versatile than their chief competitor, the minivan, SUVs (many with designer labels, such as the Orvis Edition Jeep Grand Cherokee and the Eddie Bauer Ford Explorer) offered American drivers both more practicality and more panache than their ancestors, the Jeeps and Land Rovers of the post–World War II years.

After 2000 the traditional heavy, often truck-based SUVs began to give way to a new category called crossover vehicles, which often looked much like conventional midsize SUVs but were structurally based on a chassis derived from passenger cars. As a result, these crossover vehicles were lighter and handled better than their predecessors, with fuel economy typically somewhere between a car and an SUV. While traditional SUVs are usually four-wheel drive, the crossovers are often front-wheel drive (like the passenger cars on which they are based), though all-wheel drive is a popular option. Nearly every manufacturer offers some form of crossover and many of the major brands have entire lineups of crossovers in various sizes and shapes.

Carol A. Senf
James Farlow

SEE ALSO: *Baby Boomers; Consumerism; Ford Motor Company; General Motors; Jeep; Suburbia.*

BIBLIOGRAPHY

DeLong, Brad. *4-Wheel Freedom: The Art of Off-Road Driving.* Boulder, CO: Paladin Press, 1996.

Jacobs, David H. *Sport Utility Vehicles: The Off-Road Revolution.* New York: Todtri Productions, 1998.

The *Sporting News*

Once widely known as the "the Bible of Baseball," the *Sporting News* helped to expand the popularity of America's pastime in the first half of the twentieth century, before coverage of the sport was saturated by daily newspapers, radio, and television. A weekly newspaper, the *Sporting News* provided in-depth coverage of baseball that reflected its close connections to the game's inner circles and thoroughly informed its readers. For many years, the tagline "The Base Ball Paper of the World" ran on the paper's front-page masthead.

Indeed, the *Sporting News* considered itself to be the keeper of the flame. "*The Sporting News*'s coverage of baseball issues, ranging from the reserve clause and the farm system to night baseball, radio, and the major leagues' color barrier, represents more than an incidental source of information about baseball," G. Edward White writes in his book *Creating the National Pastime: Baseball Transforms Itself 1903–1953.* "*The Sporting News* was consistently traditionalist to the point of being reactionary about most innovations in the game, although it made an effort to give a fair-minded presentation of most issues."

BASEBALL BASEBALL
The Sporting News
THE BASE BALL PAPER OF THE WORLD
VOLUME 143, NUMBER 12 — ST. LOUIS, APRIL 17, 1957 — PRICE: TWENTY-FIVE CENTS

Kubek, Rodgers Tabbed as Top Rookies

Experts' Nod Goes to Yank, Giant Flashes

of Cardinals, Pizarro of Braves Other Standouts

By DAN DANIEL
NEW YORK, N. Y.

As the major league clubs went into the pennant races, their rosters gave evidence of the unusual difficulty faced by newcomers this spring in breaking into experienced lineups.

This was due partly to the fact that the new cutdown rule, forcing clubs to trim their rosters to

(CONTINUED ON PAGE 4, COL. 1)

The **Sporting News, *1957.*** *The* Sporting News *covers the start of the major league baseball season in its April 17, 1957, issue.* SPORTING NEWS ARCHIVE/SPORTING NEWS/GETTY IMAGES.

EARLY YEARS

Sporting News was owned and operated by the Spink family from 1886 to 1977. Its founder, Al Spink, was a St. Louis, Missouri, promoter interested in horse racing and the theater in addition to baseball. When Al suffered a financial setback, he enticed his brother, Charlie, to leave his homestead in the Dakotas and take over the fledging newspaper. In its early years, the *Sporting News* covered horse racing and the theater as well as baseball, boxing, hunting, track, and cycling. In the early 1900s, however, Charlie set the editorial direction that would distinguish the publication for decades to come—the paper would cover only baseball.

Sporting News had a circulation of a meager 3,000 readers at the turn of the twentieth century, and Charlie hoped to capture more readers by establishing editorial positions that stood for the good of the game, positions that sometimes contrasted with those of team owners. Perhaps the paper's most controversial stance was to support Ban Johnson in his 1901 quest to establish the American League as a second major league to the National League. "The success of these crusades, combined with the changing nature of baseball, helped to consolidate the paper's editorial position," Stanley Frank wrote in his 1942 *Saturday Evening Post* article "Bible of Baseball."

Sparse advertising revenue in the early years led Charlie to contract with correspondents rather than hire permanent writers for much of the paper's content. Born out of frugality, the correspondent system became one of the paper's great strengths, giving readers the insight of a local scribe who witnessed the action and conversed with the participants as opposed to the basic details of wire reports. The correspondent system was especially important to the paper's extensive coverage of the minor leagues, a hallmark of its Bible of Baseball reputation. *Sporting News* was the only publication that touched on all facets of baseball, covering the up-and-coming players in the minor leagues in addition to the big leagues. Another hallmark of the *Sporting News* was its printing of box scores from games in both the major and minor leagues.

THE LAST WORD ON BASEBALL

When Charlie died in 1914, his son, J. G. Taylor Spink, took over as publisher. During his forty-eight-year tenure, he cemented the publication's place in baseball journalism. In his *Saturday Evening Post* article, Frank described Taylor as "the game's unofficial conscience, historian, watchdog and worshipper; and happily, he has made a nice piece of change in these public-spirited roles." Taylor piloted the *Sporting News* as baseball emerged as the nation's favorite spectator sport in the 1920s and 1930s, campaigning for progressive policies to improve the game and keep it honest following the 1919 Black Sox scandal. Two of his innovations had lasting impacts on baseball. In 1925 he introduced the *Sporting News* annual major-league all-star team, selecting the best players at each position. This was the precursor to an actual game among all-stars that began in 1933. In the late 1920s the *Sporting News* also picked the most valuable players in each major league, buttoning up the haphazard approaches previously used to bestow this honor. This led to the establishment of today's selection of Most Valuable Player by a vote of the Baseball Writers' Association of America.

While Taylor was said to have his finger on the pulse of baseball, critics of the *Sporting News* contended that its views were slanted toward the sport's powers, as the paper initially resisted integration (and virtually ignored the Negro Leagues), night baseball, and radio broadcasts. "Despite its traditional bias," White notes in *Creating the National Pastime*, "*The Sporting News* had a sense of when changes were on the verge of taking place in baseball."

In 1942 the *Sporting News* took over from Spalding the publication of baseball's annual *Official Record Book and Guide*. This furthered its influence on the game and spurred it into even greater publication pursuits. World War II also hastened a change of direction for the publication. Restricted advertising revenues during this period forced Spink to abandon the newspaper's baseball-only coverage, as it expanded into football, basketball, and hockey.

STEADY DECLINE

When Taylor died in 1962, his son, C. C. Johnson Spink, assumed the helm. In the 1960s Johnson further expanded coverage into golf, tennis, and auto racing. With no children to transfer the business to, Johnson sold it to the Times-Mirror Company in 1977 for $18 million.

The paper remained a force in baseball through the 1950s, but it diminished thereafter. Daily newspapers had significantly improved the quality and volume of baseball-related material following World War II, and television offered faster transmission of information. While the paper no longer exerted the influence it once had in baseball, its legacy was set in stone in 1962 when the J. G. Taylor Spink Award was established to honor outstanding writers in the National Baseball Hall of Fame.

The shifting media landscape of the late 1990s and the first decade of the 2000s further eroded the paper's significance. Many fans began to obtain their sports information from websites and from the cable juggernaut ESPN. In 2001 it was purchased by Vulcan Inc., which in turn sold the paper—by then called simply *Sporting News*—to American City Business Journals five years later. In 2006 the newspaper went from a weekly to a biweekly, and in 2011 it became a monthly. On the digital side, however, *Sporting News* developed a strong Internet presence by taking over the sports-information pages for AOL.

Charlie Bevis

SEE ALSO: *Baseball; Black Sox Scandal; ESPN; The Internet; Major League Baseball; Negro Leagues.*

BIBLIOGRAPHY

Frank, Stanley. "Bible of Baseball." *Saturday Evening Post*, June 20, 1942, 9–10.

Reidenbaugh, Lowell. *"The Sporting News": First Hundred Years 1886–1986*. St. Louis, MO: Sporting News Publishing Company, 1985.

Reidenbaugh, Lowell; Joe Hoppel; and Mike Nahrstedt, eds. *"The Sporting News" Selects Baseball's 50 Greatest Games*. St. Louis, MO: Sporting News Publishing Company, 1986.

White, G. Edward. *Creating the National Pastime: Baseball Transforms Itself 1903–1953*. Princeton, NJ: Princeton University Press, 1996.

Sports Heroes

Americans look to their sporting heroes to be models of courage, discipline, strong character, and success; those perceived to be breaking the rules of the game are stereotyped as villains. In the age of 24/7 media coverage, the public scrutinizes their heroes' off-field conduct nearly as much as their on-field performance. In addition to winning the physical contest, the hero must negotiate other conflicts: the technicalities of the game's rules, overcoming physical pain, and negotiating the pitfalls of private self-doubt. This accounts for the American notion that sports, in addition to building physical skills, also builds moral character. Therefore, the sports hero often transcends the athletic arena, as Robert Lipsyte and Peter Levine state in *Idols of the Game*: "Because their lives helped, in part, to shape our values, habits, and, arguably, the content of our character, no full understanding of America is possible without an understanding of its sports idols."

MEDIA MAKE HEROES

Developments in communications technologies throughout the twentieth century and into the twenty-first century changed the sports they broadcast. The rise of radio transformed local hero athletes into national icons. As television began reaching a wider audience, the expanded broadcasting of events created an insatiable need to find and promote heroes. Televised sports created a shared experience, in which national audiences participated in their heroes' victory or defeat, or bore witness to an athlete's sportsmanship or misconduct. "The most outstanding [athletes]," writes John Izod in a 1996 article in *Journal of Sport and Social Issues*, "become media personalities, and as such they reveal their hopes and fears, as well as their thoughts about their game to the viewer." The proliferation of statistics in modern-day sport has helped create an overabundance of sports heroes. Stats such as "most career home runs" or "career average rushing yards per carry" help the transfixed fan distinguish a pantheon of great athletes emanating from the television factory.

According to sociologist Orrin Klapp, author of the 1949 study "Hero Worship in America," the emotional behavior of hero worship encompasses "popular homage, familiarity, possessiveness, curiosity, identification, and imitation." Fans identify with their heroes by adopting their uniforms, mannerisms, and even their style. As an ad from the 1920s proclaimed: "A Spalding Swimming Suit won't teach you to swim. But it will make you *feel* like an Olympic champion." Following the 1969 Super Bowl triumph of the New York Jets, fans began wearing sideburns in emulation of pro quarterback Joe Namath. The veneration bestowed upon the sports hero often creates demigods, as this 1969 piece on Namath from *Esquire* demonstrates: "Once in a generation, more or less, a chosen figure detaches himself from the social matrix and swims into mythology, hovering somewhere near the center of the universe, organizing in himself our attention, monopolizing our hopes and fears, intruding on our dreams, compelling our hearts to beat as his."

The sports hero is at once distant, placed in high esteem, and the subject of intense personal interest. This intense curiosity sometimes turns into a possessive need to learn more about the hero. Boxer Jack Dempsey described fans who forced themselves into his dressing room: "They want to look at your eyes and your ears to see how badly you may have been injured. They want to pick up a word here or a gesture there which, later on, they can relay, magnified, to their own little public. I have always regarded these curious fans in a tolerant, even friendly way." By the 1990s superstars such as Michael Jordan could scarcely venture forth in public for fear they would be crushed by the onslaught of fan interest.

SPORTS HEROES OF THE GOLDEN AGE

The genesis for the American sports hero can be traced back to the 1920s—often referred to as the Golden Age of American Sports. The 1926 Jack Dempsey–Gene Tunney bout in Philadelphia attracted a paying audience of 120,757—at that time, the largest ever. Dempsey was boxing's main draw, but each sport boasted its own titan: baseball had Babe Ruth, football had Knute Rockne, tennis had Helen Wills, golf had Bobby Jones, and so on.

The most towering object of hero worship during the 1920s was aviator Charles Lindbergh. Like sports heroes, Lindbergh performed a colorful feat that received tremendous admiration. "Lindbergh," writes Klapp about the aviator's overnight recognition following his transatlantic flight, "was literally jerked upward in status and in his vertical ascent became almost a demigod." Americans' hero worship of Lindbergh literally set the tone for later fan behavior. This story about Lindbergh in Klapp's study could be in reference to any celebrity of the twentieth century: "A respectable-looking woman of middle age came up to Lindbergh, at dinner in a New York hotel, and tried to look into his mouth to see whether he was eating 'green beans or green peas.'"

In a similar fashion, Ruth's home-run-hitting feats captured the popular imagination. Prior to Ruth, the game of baseball was played in a methodical fashion, by stringing together a series of singles in order to achieve runs. Ruth's powerful swats produced runs instantly, in grand fashion. "Ruth was like the movie stars of the time who were discovered overnight," noted sports historian Benjamin Rader in a 1998 article in *Christian Science Monitor*. "Their seemingly effortless rise to fame and fortune was so unlike the arduous work of a bureaucrat or an assembly line worker."

By the 1920s the subjects of popular biographies shifted from "idols of production"—politicians or captains of industry—to the "idols of consumption," or sporting and entertainment heroes. These new heroic tales, writes Mark Dyreson in *Sport in America*, were "every bit as didactic as a tale about Horatio Alger" that describe the triumphs of heroes "who succeeded against the odds, not simply because they got the breaks, but because of their adherence to the traditional values of perseverance, hard work and clean living."

For decades following the rise of the sports hero, those enshrined in the public spotlight basked in the uncritical admiration of the media and fans alike. It wasn't that the private exploits of such heroes as baseball's Mickey Mantle and Ted Williams, basketball's Bill Russell, and football's Jim Brown were exempt from scrutiny; rather, it was that they were judged first and foremost on their public acts, and their private lives remained private. As the century wore on, however, a serious debate about what constitutes a true hero emerged among fans, the media, and athletes. Whereas the heroes of the 1920s were lionized for committing a specific feat that captured the public's imagination, by the 1990s the sports hero was asked to behave as a "role model" whose personal conduct was as important as his or her athletic feats.

SPORTS HEROES AS ROLE MODELS

Perhaps the figure that best marks this change was New York Yankees great Mickey Mantle. The Oklahoman who broke Ruth's record for home runs in a World Series in 1964 joined the Yankees during the 1950s. This was a decade of conflicting demands for those who were coming of age, writes Michael Anderson in a 1996 article in the *New York Times*: "Their best was never good enough. . . . Only by overachieving could they live up to their parents, those grimly stoic survivors of war and want." Mantle—as the old athletic cliché goes—lived hard and played hard, and few faulted him for it. Once he left the game of baseball, he was no longer able to outplay others on the field so he seemed to try to outdrink them. In 1994 Mantle publicly admitted his alcoholism and did his best to become a socially responsible role model, imploring others to avoid his mistakes. He also underwent a failed liver transplant and urged others to sign organ donor cards. "I have thought about trying to define what a hero is," wrote Mantle's son David, shortly after his father's death. "Dad was one throughout his baseball career, and a different kind at the end of his life."

In the 1980s and 1990s, as the private lives of all celebrities (even political celebrities) came under increasing scrutiny, it was no longer enough for sports figures to swat a baseball the farthest or catch a game-winning touchdown pass: they were increasingly sought after to set examples for the young. After sports fans witnessed several player strikes and watched well-paid athletes land in drug abuse clinics, many yearned for an Edenic time when athletes were clean-cut role models. This was a mythic notion, however: as Ruth was attaining his legendary status on the baseball field, he was also womanizing, drinking, and ignoring his poor physical condition. Sociologist Charles Payne in a 1993 *Newsweek* article sums up this mistaken notion of innocence before the advent of big-money sports: "If you were to go through baseball's or football's Hall of Fame, you're not going to come up with a bunch of choirboys."

Athletes themselves disagree over their obligation to lead exemplary private lives. In the same 1993 *Newsweek* article, basketball star Charles Barkley, in his typically forthcoming manner, declared, "I'm not paid to be a role model. I'm paid to wreak havoc on the basketball court." Karl Malone, another basketball great, openly disagreed with Barkley, stating, "We don't choose to be role models, we are chosen." Fans, devoted as they may be, had become hardened to the complaints of multimillionaire pro athletes. Sports columnist Phil Mushnick, speaking for many fans, has said, "Funny how big shots accept all the trappings of role modeldom—especially the residual commercial cash—before they renounce their broader responsibilities to society."

Although it is true that not every athlete deserves role-model status, critics inflate the debate somewhat by failing to recognize that children have the capacity to distinguish between real-life heroes and daydream ones. As one twelve-year-old told *Sports Illustrated for Kids* in 1995, if his sports hero were to "mess up" then "he wouldn't be my favorite player anymore. I would sell all his cards. I have about 65 of them, and I'd give them away." An enduring piece of baseball lore holds that after "Shoeless" Joe Jackson was implicated in the 1919 Black Sox Scandal, a young boy stopped him on the courthouse steps and plaintively called to the fallen hero, "Say it ain't so, Joe!" It is possible that the adults are the ones who have changed, not the kids.

HEROES WITH FEET OF CLAY

Americans learned to look for their heroes' faults, even while they were in the process of exalting them. In 1993 Michael Jordan, who is generally acknowledged as the greatest basketball player ever, was reported to have lost a substantial amount of money while gambling and was subjected to months of media attention and a brief dip in his popularity. A few years later, in the midst of 1998's home-run-record chase, record-setter Mark McGwire was spotted with a legal performance-enhancing drug (PED) sitting in his locker, prompting one editorial from St. Louis to proclaim: "There probably aren't going to be any heroes anymore. The media won't let us have them." Yet it is the media that has helped create the impossible dilemma that confronts the sports hero.

On the one hand, members of the media feed athletes a steady diet of adulation beginning in college and increasing exponentially once they reach a professional level. However, after being told for years that he or she can do no wrong, the hero is then subjected to equally intense scrutiny aimed at uncovering faults and weaknesses. Wrote a St. Louis paper after McGwire's legal steroid was reported, "In an oftentimes desperate attempt to get the story no one else has, the media look behind closed doors . . . to come up with something that might taint the reputation of an otherwise unblemished character." Ironically, even this defense proved to be premature, as McGwire became embroiled in the PED investigation that rocked baseball in the first decade of the 2000s. The achievements of McGwire, his home-run rival Sammy Sosa, Barry Bonds, and dozens of other players are now widely believed to be tainted because of the use of steroids and other PEDs.

Even though time after time sports heroes prove that they are, after all, only human, Americans continue to build up idols only to watch them fall from grace. Perhaps no one illustrates this phenomenon better than golfer Tiger Woods. Identified as a prodigious talent at an early age, Woods became a hero not just to American sports fans but to people around the world due in part to his mixed heritage; his mother is Thai and his father African American. From 1996 through 2009 he was the most dominant player on the Professional Golfers' Association (PGA) Tour and, with fourteen victories in the majors by 2009, seemed to be on track to break Jack Nicklaus's record of eighteen. In addition to his natural gifts, Woods was known as a relentless worker, and he seemed to be an upstanding citizen. His 2008 U.S. Open victory epitomized everything that people loved about him; during play, he damaged his knee, which was recovering from an earlier surgery, and yet he managed to win the tournament despite limping, grunting with pain, and struggling with a leg that buckled under the strain of his swing.

In addition to his winning performances, Woods seemed to have everything anyone could want—incredible wealth, a beautiful wife, and two young children. Then everything fell apart. After a family argument led to a one-car accident involving Woods, the news came out that he had been having multiple extramarital affairs for years. In the wake of enormous public disapproval, he took a leave of absence from the sport. He was unable to salvage his marriage, and when he returned to golf, his game had disappeared too—at least temporarily. Once again, America learned that if a sports hero seems too good to be true, quite possibly he is.

When sports heroes are accused of breaking the law, their fans can have trouble accepting that their hero may be badly flawed. In 1994 crowds gathered along a California freeway and watched on national TV to witness ex-football star O. J. Simpson engage police in a car chase as a suicidal fugitive. Like fans urging on a self-destructive rock star, the crowd implored him to run—as if he still carried the football. When Simpson was arrested and tried for the murder of his ex-wife, Nicole Brown Simpson, and her friend Ron Goldman, many made pronouncements like "I can't believe he did it." Tom Verducci of *Sports Illustrated* commented that "it sounded as if half of America lived next door to Simpson."

WOMEN AS SPORTS HEROES

Not all athletes have a choice about whether to act as a role model or not. Some, by virtue of their gender, race, or ethnicity, found that they had no choice but to perform to higher expectations in order to earn the same adulation. Early on, female athletes—such as Babe Didrikson, the winner of three track-and-field medals at the 1932 Los Angeles Olympics—found that their exploits were not viewed with the same legitimacy reserved for their male counterparts. "America has lionized the male athlete to the female athlete's disadvantage," write Lipsyte and Levine. "There is a definite misogynist streak in the sensibility of the big-time locker room and its boys-will-be-boys rationale."

By the 1990s women were still fighting against media images that trivialized female athletic accomplishments—this despite the fact that, in 1991, women outspent men in the purchase of athletic shoes and apparel, and more women participated in sports and fitness than did men. In 1994 athletic shoemaker Nike ran an ad depicting a female volleyball player lying on satin sheets in her underwear. CBS Sports, in 1996, suspended a golf commentator for characterizing professional female golfers as lesbians and opining that women with "big boobs" were less able to play the sport.

By the first decade of the 2000s women were getting more recognition for their accomplishments in the athletic arena. For example, Pat Summitt, coach of the University of Tennessee's Lady Vols basketball team, became a hero to many when she became the winningest coach in the history of National Collegiate Athletic Association (NCAA) basketball—and again when she told the public that she had been diagnosed with Alzheimer's disease but intended to keep working as long as possible. Yet female athletes still struggle to overcome a lack of respect and cases of subtle—and not-so-subtle—sexism. For example, in the tennis world, even a widely admired champion like Maria Sharapova gets routinely criticized for grunting during play, while equally vocal male players are given a pass. (Sharapova, it's important to point out, gets as much attention for her beauty as she does for her skill on the court. She has multiple modeling contracts and is viewed as a sex symbol by many.) Some female athletes have responded by fighting the double standards head on. For example, Venus Williams—who achieved iconic status for winning twenty-one Grand Slam titles in singles and doubles—took on the tennis establishment and worked for years to achieve equal prize money for women.

REPRESENTING A LARGER GROUP

Sports heroes have often been used as an avenue for disenfranchised groups to participate in an American life that was otherwise closed to them—politically, economically, or socially. Race is a prime example. It can be hard for twenty-first-century Americans, who take the achievements of African American athletes like Woods and Williams for granted, to understand the significance of boxer Joe Louis in the late 1930s and 1940s. Louis is generally regarded as the first African American national hero, and, as Lipsyte and Levine reconstruct it: "Louis was out there representing all black people in those bitter days when most colleges admitted few if any blacks, when college-educated blacks were lucky to get jobs as railroad waiters, when even the Army was segregated." American athletic heroes of ethnic minority bear the similar weight of carrying the hopes of millions. Unlike many of their parents, second-generation Americans had the time to devote to leisure and recreation, and sports heroes began serving as important role models.

The best example of a single athlete representing the aspirations of an entire people was Jackie Robinson, the first African American major-league baseball player. On the field, and off, Robinson was subject to racial slurs, hate mail, and death threats; once, in Philadelphia, his Brooklyn Dodger teammates were refused admittance into a hotel because of his presence on the team. Robinson was an integral symbol of the African American struggle against discrimination in the pre–civil rights era. The enormous burden placed on his shoulders is palpable in this passage by sportswriter Jimmy Cannon, written in 1947 as Robinson was just entering the majors: "In the clubhouse Robinson is a stranger. The Dodgers are polite and courteous with him, but it is obvious he is isolated by those with whom he plays. . . . Robinson never is part of the jovial and aimless banter of the locker room. He is the loneliest man I have ever seen in sports."

Sports heroes often represent as much about the larger social milieu as they do about themselves: "Independent of their own intentions and beliefs—sometimes even counter to those intentions and beliefs—idols can be co-opted to represent both the dominant culture and the concerns and interests of outsiders," write Lypsite and Levine. Every so often, though, a dominant figure emerges in sport to renew the fan's emotional involvement with sports that, according to Rader, "encourages a kind of primitive solidarity among the population despite our diverse backgrounds. Our society has many forces that pull it apart. . . . [Sports] is a tie that binds."

Daryl Umberger

SEE ALSO: *Advertising; Baseball; Black Sox Scandal; Bonds, Barry; Boxing; The Brooklyn Dodgers; Brown, Jim; Celebrity; Civil Rights Movement; Dempsey, Jack; Didrikson, Babe; Divorce;* Esquire*; Feminism; Gehrig, Lou; Golf; Hockey; Jackson, "Shoeless" Joe; Jones, Bobby; Jordan, Michael; Lindbergh, Charles; Louis, Joe; Mantle, Mickey; McGwire, Mark; Media Feeding Frenzies; Namath, Joe; National Basketball Association (NBA); National Collegiate Athletic Association (NCAA); National Football League (NFL);* Newsweek*; Nicklaus, Jack; Nike; Olympics; Professional Football; Radio; Robinson, Jackie; Rockne, Knute; Russell, Bill; Ruth, Babe; Simpson, O. J.;* Sports Illustrated*; Super Bowl; Television; Tennis; Williams, Ted; Williams, Venus and Serena; Woods, Tiger.*

BIBLIOGRAPHY

Anderson, Michael. "Like a Colossus." *New York Times*, April 7, 1996, sec. 7, 12.

"Batting Down a Hero." *St. Louis Business Journal*, August 30, 1998, 58.

"The Demi-God." *Esquire*, October 1969, 103–113.

Dyreson, Mark. "The Emergence of Consumer Culture and the Transformation of Physical Culture: American Sport in the 1920s." In *Sport in America: From Wicked Amusement to National Obsession*, ed. David K. Wiggins. Champaign, IL: Human Kinetics, 1995.

Fainaru-Wada, Mark, and Lance Williams. *Game of Shadows: Barry Bonds, BALCO, and the Steroids Scandal That Rocked Professional Sports*. New York: Gotham Books, 2006.

Fimrite, Ron. "A Sad Tale of Self-Loathing: Mickey Mantle Was Striving to Exorcise His Personal Demons When Death Intervened." *Sports Illustrated*, November 25, 1996, 10.

Gelman, David, and Sudarsan Raghavan. "I'm Not a Role Model." *Newsweek*, June 27, 1993, 56–57.

Izod, John. "Television Sport and the Sacrificial Hero." *Journal of Sport and Social Issues* 20 (1996): 173–193.

Klapp, Orrin E. "Hero Worship in America." *American Sociological Review* 14, no. 1 (1949): 53–62.

Lipsyte, Robert, and Peter Levine. *Idols of the Game: A Sporting History of the American Century*. Atlanta, GA: Turner Publishing, 1995.

Lopiano, Donna. "Women Athletes Deserve Respect from the Media." *USA Today Magazine*, March 1996, 74–76.

Lusetich, Robert. *Unplayable: An Inside Account of Tiger's Most Tumultuous Season*. New York: Atria Books, 2010.

Nack, William. "The Breakthrough." *Sports Illustrated*, May 5, 1997, 56–65.

Rader, Benjamin. "A Ball and a Bat: Exclamation Point of Our Time: The Home Run Mystique Involves the Power of One Dramatic Blast to Pull a People Together." *Christian Science Monitor*, October 1, 1998, 11.

"Role Models: What Kids and Athletes Say." *Sports Illustrated for Kids*, September 1995, 26–27.

Teitelbaum, Stanley H. *Sports Heroes, Fallen Idols*. Lincoln: University of Nebraska Press, 2005.

Verducci, Tom. "The Hero Trap." *Sports Illustrated*, July 11, 1994, 88.

Williams, Peter. *Sports Immortals: Deifying the American Athlete*. Bowling Green, OH: Bowling Green State University Popular Press, 1994.

Sports Illustrated

Using a blend of groundbreaking photography and revolutionary writing, *Sports Illustrated* changed the way spectator sports fit into American culture during the 1960s and 1970s. A weekly magazine devoted solely to athletics, *Sports Illustrated* contributed, along with television, to the evolution of sports from a pleasant diversion to a big business that spews out multimillion-dollar player salaries. The magazine's influence also transcended sports, as its annual midwinter swimsuit issue became a phenomenon and created lasting changes in the modeling industry. "*Sports Illustrated* served as a counterbalance to the persistent hype of television, offering a way for new and educated fans to put the endless rounds of games and matches into a meaningful context," Michael MacCambridge observes in his book *The Franchise*. "It made an art out of in-depth reporting on those games, and thereby made the games themselves more important to more Americans."

THE SPORTS MAGAZINE PROTOTYPE

Henry Luce, the founder of Time Inc. and publisher of *Time* and *Life*, conceived the idea for *Sports Illustrated*. Though he was not much of a sports fan, he saw the potential for a weekly sports magazine based on the increased leisure time of the burgeoning postwar middle class, a large percentage of which was migrating to the suburbs. Against the advice of his aides, who thought the idea folly, Luce launched *Sports Illustrated* on August 16, 1954. Initially, the magazine covered an eclectic assortment of pursuits—big-game hunting, yachting, horse racing, dog shows, and fishing, along with cooking, fashion, and travel—in addition to more traditional sports such as baseball, football, and boxing.

The magazine was positioned as a "class" magazine, much like the *New Yorker*, with sophisticated, intelligent, and critical writing that did not pander. However, it attracted neither readers nor advertisers in large numbers early on. The magazine began to fulfill its promise with the installation of Andre Laguerre as managing editor in 1960. Laguerre, a cosmopolitan and urbane native of France, had a keen appreciation of good writing. He focused the magazine on the four major team sports (baseball, football, basketball, and hockey) plus boxing, golf, and tennis. Fishing, which had ranked fourth among all sports in articles per year in the magazine's third year, was number thirteen by 1963.

Laguerre hired two writers who would forever change the face of sports journalism: Dan Jenkins and Frank Deford. They gave readers insight and analysis unavailable elsewhere and helped *SI*, as the magazine is often called, to create a new approach to sportswriting. MacCambridge describes the *SI* style as "not just reporting or covering an event, but distilling it, capturing its essence and presenting it in a compressed, lyrical image of deadline literature and photojournalism."

UNPRECEDENTED GROWTH

SI became part of the nation's weekly routine. Millions watched the games on the weekend, then waited for *SI* to arrive in their mailboxes on Thursday or Friday to tell them what had really happened behind the scenes. To many sports fans, *SI* was the final word—an event wasn't real until it had been ratified in the pages of the magazine. From its initial subscriber base of 350,000 in 1954, circulation grew to one million readers in 1960, two million in the mid-1970s, and three million in the mid-1980s before topping out at nearly 3.5 million in the late 1980s.

As James Michener explains in his book *Sports in America* (1976), "*SI* has become the bible of the industry, and it has done so because it appreciated from the start the facts that faced printed journalism in the age of television: don't give the scores, give the inside stories behind the scores. And deal openly with those topics which men in saloons talk about in whispers." Besides covering the ongoing sports seasons, the magazine took on hard subjects, as exemplified by Jack Olsen's 1968 series on the exploitation of the black athlete, "The Black Athlete—A Shameful Story." In the late 1960s *SI* also published series about the growing threat of drugs in sports, women's rights in athletics, and the electronic revolution in sports.

THE COVERS

In addition to great writers, Laguerre hired two photographers, Neil Leifer and Walter Iooss, who transformed the nature and art of sports photography. Leifer and Iooss shot many of the *SI* covers in the 1960s. As *SI* continually pushed the technological limits in color photography printing, Leifer and Iooss captured on film the very essence of a weekend sports event. Laguerre thus merged the best color photography with cutting-edge analysis to expand the *SI* influence. In 1965 Leifer shot one of the most famous sports photos of all time: Muhammad Ali standing over a prostrate Sonny Liston with Ali's fist angrily imploring Liston off the canvas and three faces—mouths agape—seen between his legs.

If athletes appeared on the cover of *Sports Illustrated*, it somehow enhanced their legitimacy. Sports fans framed *SI* covers for keepsakes, beginning with that of the first issue in 1954, Milwaukee Braves third baseman Eddie Mathews. On the downside, being on the *SI* cover also became identified as a jinx. The first incident occurred shortly after the release of the January 31, 1955, issue. The cover featured skier Jill Kinmont, who then fell in a ski race and was paralyzed below the neck. In the ensuing years, numerous athletes and teams suffered setbacks after being on the cover.

THE SWIMSUIT ISSUE

In 1964 Laguerre pioneered the swimsuit issue. The original concept was a "sunshine issue" in the bleak winter days of late January. It was designed to bridge the gap between the New Year's Day college bowl games and the start of baseball spring training in early March. What might have been just a single article blossomed into an annual event, with major hype surrounding the release of the issue. It brightened the winter for some people but angered others. The swimsuit issue went "from moral outrage to hallowed tradition in only one generation," Deford wrote in a 1989 article, "How It All Began."

Laguerre tapped Jule Campbell to take charge of the swimsuit issue. After fashion model Babette March graced the initial cover, Campbell used unknown women because they had looks that were more "natural" and "healthy." As the issue gained popularity, Campbell blended known faces with her "healthy" look. She even used the models' names in photo captions, providing a degree of identity that fashion magazines did not offer at the time. This helped to accelerate the career of Cheryl Tiegs, who appeared on the cover of the 1970 swimsuit issue and, some say, helped to usher in the supermodel era. Other famous models that appeared on the cover of the swimsuit issue early in their careers were Christie Brinkley (1979), Elle MacPherson (1986), Kathy Ireland (1989), Tyra Banks (1996), and Brooklyn Decker (2010).

THE INFLUENCE OF CHERYL TIEGS

As the issue's swimsuits became skimpier, the battle cry changed from the moral corruption of youth to sexism. "Women should stop screaming about that one issue and start screaming that *Sports Illustrated* doesn't carry enough women's sports. That's what's sexist," tennis star Billie Jean King said. The debate came to a head with the 1978 issue, when Iooss photographed Tiegs wearing a fishnet swimsuit. When dry, the suit was sensual but not revealing in the upper-body area. Tiegs, however, had dipped into the water, and the wetness created an exceptionally provocative photo that left nothing to the viewer's imagination. The picture caused a furor, eliciting the most letters and canceled subscriptions in the history of the swimsuit issue.

It was a defining moment for both the swimsuit issue and the supermodel industry. "If there was any doubt before that modeling was, like everything else, about to lose its virginity (or illusion of virginity) in the 70s, the January 1978 *Sports Il-*

lustrated swimsuit issue put an end to it," Stephen Fried writes in *Thing of Beauty*. "The uproar caused by one picture of Cheryl Tiegs reinforced the new truth that the way straight men perceived fashion models would determine the future of the business." In the Michael Gross book *Model: The Ugly Business of Beautiful Women*, Tiegs says, "It's a sweet little picture, that's it." Gross goes on to write, "But in fact, it was a major coup, adding the powerful appeal of the pinup picture to modeling's arsenal of promotional gimmicks."

CHANGING TIMES

As the swimsuit issue took on a life of its own, *SI* stepped up the marketing of it in the mid-1980s by introducing the swimsuit calendar and touting the models on the talk-show circuit. The 1986 issue with MacPherson on the cover sold 1.2 million copies at the newsstand, up from 300,000 in 1983. The twenty-fifth-anniversary issue in 1989 sold 2.7 million single copies, but newsstand sales had slumped back to 1986 levels by 1996, a reflection of the changing dynamic in sports journalism and print media in general.

The creation of ESPN and other round-the-clock media in the 1980s made the magazine's original mission less compelling. Its influence began to wane as sports fans no longer depended on the magazine to explain what had happened a few days before—a plethora of television highlight shows and the Internet had already done so. Following the 1989 merger of Time with Warner, *SI* moved away from its writing mission and began to pursue a strategy to "extend the brand." Videos and calendars were hawked in crass television advertisements, as were magazine subscriptions (for example, *This awesome [item] is free with your one-year subscription to* Sports Illustrated, *which includes the swimsuit issue!*). Spin-off magazines were also introduced: *Sports Illustrated Kids*, *Sports Illustrated Women*, and *Sports Illustrated on Campus*. *SI* also publishes an annual titled *Sports Illustrated Almanac*.

By the 1990s *Sports Illustrated* was as well known, if not more so, for its swimsuit issue, free videos, and clothing line as it was for the writing and photography that had made it famous in the first place. A website affiliated with CNN was also launched, giving the brand an Internet presence. Meanwhile, the magazine rolls on, even as other print publications fold because of competition from other media. In 2011 *SI* had an audited circulation of more than 3.1 million. The numbers do not lie: an army of loyal readers still treasures the arrival of *Sports Illustrated* in the mail each week.

Charlie Bevis

SEE ALSO: *Ali, Muhammad; Banks, Tyra; Baseball; Basketball; Boxing; College Football; ESPN; Golf; Hockey; The Internet; King, Billie Jean; Leisure Time;* Life; *Luce, Henry; The* New Yorker*; Professional Football; Sports Heroes; Supermodels; Tennis;* Time.

BIBLIOGRAPHY

Deford, Frank. "How It All Began." *Sports Illustrated*, February 1989, 38–46.

Fleder, Rob, ed. *Sports Illustrated 50: The Anniversary Book.* New York: Sports Illustrated, 2004.

Fried, Stephen. *Thing of Beauty: The Tragedy of Supermodel Gia.* New York: Pocket Books, 1993.

Gross, Michael. *Model: The Ugly Business of Beautiful Women.* New York: W. Morrow, 1995.

MacCambridge, Michael. *The Franchise: A History of Sports Illustrated Magazine.* New York: Hyperion, 1997.

Michener, James A. *Sports in America.* New York: Random House, 1976.

Spring Break

Each year, as the cold and gray of winter gives way to the bright new green of spring, human beings also experience an influx of energy: hopeful; youthful; and, at least partly, sexual. Psychologists explain this phenomenon with a variety of theories, but all agree that spring fever is normal and fairly universal. For the past seven decades U.S. college students have celebrated this vernal reawakening with a unique ritual called spring break, which involves travel to a sunny beachside resort to participate in drunken revelry and sexual debauchery. Though people of all ages, races, and classes may feel the urge to head somewhere sunny and warm as spring approaches, it is the fairly well-off, mostly white full-time students at four-year colleges and universities who have created the famous phenomenon of spring break, celebrated in movies, television, and police blotters.

Traditionally, college spring vacations are scheduled sometime between the first Saturday in March and Easter Sunday in April. Students converge on the most fashionable spot in which they can afford to go, often cramming fifteen to twenty people in a motel room to limit expenses. Local bars cater to partying students, offering drink specials and rowdy entertainment such as belly flop, hot body, and wet T-shirt contests, designed to appeal to the young and inebriated. Vacationers sport T-shirts with spirited slogans such as "Party Naked" and "University of Heineken." Crowds of tourists become a nightmare for local police, snarling traffic, littering, and vandalizing the streets of resort towns. Many spring breaks have turned literally riotous, resulting in destruction of property and arrests. Cleaning up after spring break becomes a major expense for cities that draw large numbers of students, though the money the students pour into a community during those first weeks of spring tends to offset the disadvantages.

THE TRADITION BEGINS

In 1936 the swim coach at Colgate University in Hamilton, New York, unwittingly began a tradition when he brought a few members of his swim team to train at the Casino Pool by the beach in Fort Lauderdale, Florida. The experiment was so successful that the entire team returned for Christmas vacation. In 1938 Fort Lauderdale continued to attract students as the Casino Pool hosted the first College Coaches' Swim Forum and the famous Elbo Room opened in the Seabreeze Hotel. By 1946, in spite of wartime travel restrictions, Fort Lauderdale had become a regular destination for college students on spring vacation. Fifteen thousand student revelers came in 1953, and in 1954, 20,000 arrived and started another spring break tradition: trouble with the police. That year eight students were arrested for disorderly conduct and two for public indecency. Two were killed in drunk-driving incidents.

Time magazine reported on the phenomenon in 1959, and the next year a new film solidified Fort Lauderdale as spring break capital of the United States. *Where the Boys Are* (1960),

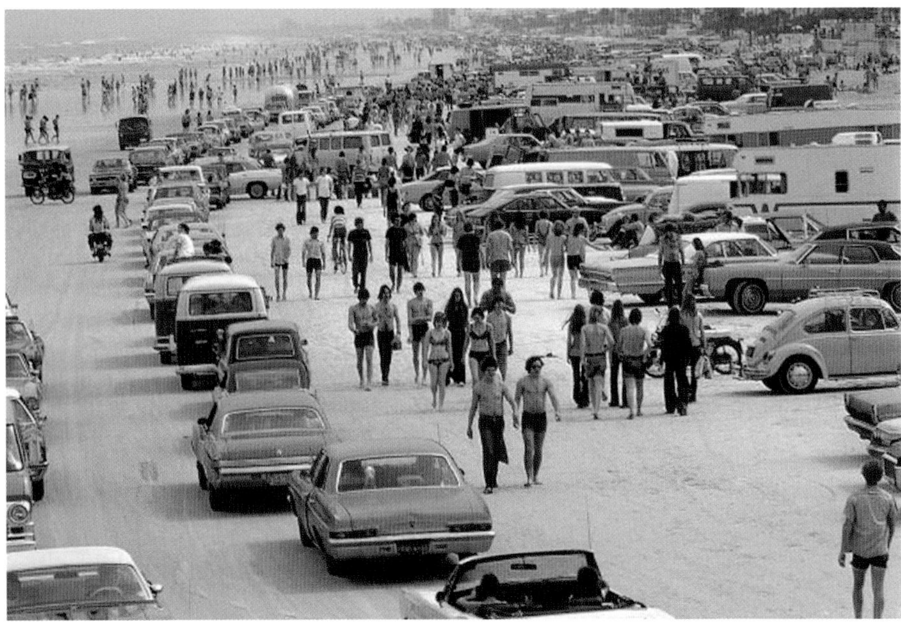

Spring Break, 1972. *College students and their cars line the shore of Daytona Beach during spring break in 1972.* © JAMES L. AMOS/CORBIS.

starring Connie Francis, Paula Prentiss, and Yvette Mimieux, was the film version of a 1958 novel by Glendon Swarthout. It describes the adventures of three young college women seeking independence, fun, and romance on spring vacation in Fort Lauderdale. The film, with its clean-cut adventure and obligatory cautionary tale of the tragic end of the girl who went too far, became an icon of the spring break experience. Along with the beach party movies of Frankie Avalon and Annette Funicello, *Where the Boys Are* advertised a beach vacation culture that many students were eager to emulate. By 1961, 50,000 of them flocked to Fort Lauderdale to find it.

In 1963 *Palm Springs Weekend*, starring Connie Stevens and Troy Donahue, advertised Palm Springs, California, as another mecca for students. By the late 1960s Florida's Daytona Beach was actively promoting itself as a spring break destination, trying to lure students and their dollars away from Fort Lauderdale. One hundred thousand students responded and converged on Daytona Beach.

EXPANDING SPRING BREAK DESTINATIONS

The self-indulgent 1980s were peak years for the hedonistic spring revels. In 1983 the film *Spring Break* was released, with Tom Cruise and Shelley Long, and *Where the Boys Are* was remade in 1984. In 1985 spring break in Fort Lauderdale reached its height as 350,000 students crammed into the city. Fort Lauderdale, however, had had enough. By erecting barricades between the beach and the streets and enforcing room-occupancy rules and alcohol laws, the city managed to reduce its spring break tourism numbers back to 20,000 by 1989. Of those, 2,400 were arrested. By the 2010s Fort Lauderdale had a new convention center; a performing arts center; and a new, more sophisticated image as a family-friendly year-round resort destination, relinquishing its title of spring break capital to Daytona Beach. By the turn of the twenty-first century, Daytona too was trying to find ways to manage the rowdy crowds without alienating the tourist dollars.

By the end of the 2010s spring break vacation spots were much more varied, though there were still hot spots that attract hundreds of thousands of visitors. Panama City, Florida, hosted 550,000 student tourists in 2005, and little South Padre Island, Texas, which has a resident population of just more than 1,000, attracted 10,000 to 15,000 vacationers a day during spring break 2004. California also welcomed its share of visitors, especially in San Diego and Palm Springs. Ski vacations became more and more popular, and destinations such as Colorado's Vail and Steamboat Springs and California's Lake Tahoe were flooded with students looking for both ski and après-ski adventures. Foreign travel had an appeal as well, not the least of which was a drinking age of eighteen in Mexico, the Bahamas, and Canada. Even in the United States many resort towns resisted enforcing laws such as the drinking age that might drive tourists away.

Many businesses not specifically related to the tourist trade also took advantage of the huge audiences drawn to spring break meccas. Daytona Beach hosted ExpoAmerica, a giant trade show with high-tech exhibits designed to appeal to modern students. Both CBS and MTV offered extensive spring break special telecasts from spots such as Daytona and San Diego to bring the festivities to those who had to stay at home. Some businesses even tried to recruit employees among the crowds of student vacationers, though some reported difficulties finding sober prospects.

REVELRY ALTERNATIVES

Each generation added its own personality to the celebration of spring break. Crazy Gregg, the manager of the venerable Fort Lauderdale institution called the Button, explained in 1986:

> Basically, we've had three different generations here. In the '50s, the kids were more mellow and conservative, not blatant. In the late '60s and early '70s, they

> weren't gung ho or rah-rah. They didn't seem to want to have fun. When we played 'God Bless America,' they booed us. But now the pendulum has swung completely around. They enjoy themselves to the hilt. The morality is looser. Golly, I saw a guy walk through the hotel stark naked. They wouldn't have done that 15 or 20 years ago.

The 1990s brought other influences to the spring break phenomenon. A sharpened awareness of the problems of alcoholism resulted in a marked decrease in the glorification of drink at resort destinations. While there continued to be a high level of consumption, liquor and beer company advertisements began to advise caution and adherence to drinking age laws, where a decade earlier they might have focused only on the fun and excitement of drinking. The first decade of the 2000s saw a trend toward extreme pre-spring-break dieting and anorexia in young women determined to fit into ever smaller bikinis for their beach vacations.

While drunkenness and promiscuity were still staples of the traditional spring break, by the turn of the twenty-first century another kind of spring break had taken hold with socially concerned students throughout the country. Pioneering this trend was the Break Away program at Vanderbilt University in Nashville, Tennessee. Started in 1991, Break Away is a national network that arranges what it terms "alternative spring break" for students who would rather volunteer in soup kitchens, homeless shelters, and other community programs than spend a week getting drunk and having casual sex.

In its first year the Break Away network served 2,500 students in forty colleges nationwide. By the late 1990s it had arranged volunteer work for close to 15,000 students in 350 colleges. In 2007 Break Away relocated to Atlanta, Georgia, where it continued to work with the Hands On Network volunteer service. A number of other colleges and universities from throughout the United States developed alternative spring break programs, arranging for students to spend vacation time working on poverty relief, gang intervention, ecology, and other social issues.

Spring break came of age in the 1950s and 1960s when students needed a hedonistic outlet from a repressive society. Perhaps in the pleasure-seeking culture of the twenty-first century, what young people really seek is an escape from self-indulgence.

Tina Gianoulis

SEE ALSO: *Avalon, Frankie; Cruise, Tom; Funicello, Annette; Long, Shelley; T-Shirts.*

BIBLIOGRAPHY

Break Away, the Alternative Break Connection. Accessed March 20, 2012. Available from http://www.alternativebreaks2012.org/about/

Flanagan, William P., and Diana Merelman. "Spring Break Alert." *Forbes*, February 24, 1997, 188.

Kalogerakis, George. "How to Win Friends . . . and Throw Up on People." *Esquire*, April 1992, 82.

Waldrop, Judith. "Spring Break." *American Demographics*, March 1993, 52.

Springer, Jerry *(1944–)*

Jerry Springer has taken the talk show genre to a new level and placed himself at the helm of public controversy. *The Jerry Springer Show* combines drama and sensationalism in a way that some people find hilarious. Since its debut in 1991, the show's outrageous style and often perverse topics either strongly entice or profusely offend individuals. The show not only allows but also encourages brawls between its guests, egged on by Springer's audience of adoring fans, who repeatedly chant, "Jerry, Jerry, Jerry!" Guests vent antagonistic emotions that often result in physical fights, quelled at the last minute by clean-cut, beefy bouncers.

Before becoming a talk show host, Springer, who has a law degree from Northwestern University, had a brief political career as the mayor of Cincinnati in the 1970s and worked as a news anchorman and commentator in Cincinnati in the 1980s, during which time he won seven Emmys. Yet when a Chicago television station in the 1990s hired him, an anchorwoman promptly resigned in disgust, calling him "the poster child for the worst television has to offer."

EXPLAINING THE PHENOMENON

Talk shows serve different purposes, acting as informal, supportive forums for topics or as battlegrounds for guests engaging in controversy. With the growing interest that some people have in hearing titillating, personal, and sometimes shocking details about others' lives, formats of shows such as Springer's swiftly veered toward the sensational. The trend began on the *Ricki Lake Show* (1993), when producers began encouraging confrontations among guests. The success of that format spawned imitators and paved the way for an expanding group of individuals and groups opposed to what has been labeled "trash TV."

The Jerry Springer Show took the sensationalism one step further and became the first talk show to include physical confrontation on a regular basis. The show's swift rise in ratings and the popularity of its host confirmed that many people find the show entertaining. Critics maintain that people watch the show for the same reasons they drive slowly by traffic accidents. Because *The Jerry Springer Show* often deals with such outrageous and often hopeless problems, some experts contend that people viewing it tend to feel better about their own lives.

SHOW VIOLENCE

Guests on the show are often marginalized people who have been socialized to solve their problems through physical conflict. The regularity of the fights on the show prompted speculation into whether they are staged with out-of-work actors. It is highly likely that guests are chosen for their willingness to engage in outrageous behavior once the cameras start to roll. Because of the nature of the show's topics and the often consistent personality traits of its guests, it came to be known as a humorous "white trash" sensation.

Springer says that he encourages guests to be as outrageous as possible, but he defends his show against charges of exploitation, stating that his critics are "elitists" who only want to see beautiful or rich people discussing their problems on television. However, poverty should not be an excuse for extreme inappropriate behavior, such as mothers sleeping with their twelve-year-old daughter's ex-boyfriends (a show topic). Other topics include a family of strippers, and possibly the most perverse in all of talk show history—bestiality.

Even though the appearance of brawling guests was consistent, not every topic on the show has shock value. For example, Springer also featured interracial couples facing disapproval from their families. And at the end of every show, Springer offers a brief epitaph, his "Final Thought," that portends to function as the show's "moral" thermometer. After an episode on cheating lovers, for example, he counseled viewers that it is unhealthy to pursue someone who does not want you and encourages guests to work on raising self-esteem.

Springer is most certainly an enigma and a man of contradictions. As the "ringmaster" of his exhibitionist show, he maintains a relatively private life. He is an active voice and fund raiser for various charities. He also has country music aspirations. "It struck me that the subjects of country songs and talk shows are very similar," he said and released a music CD. He has even impersonated Elvis Presley. Springer starred in the 1998 film *Ringmaster* (also the title of his autobiography).

POP CULTURE REFERENCES

In the twenty-first century, *The Jerry Springer Show* inspired an opera, which arrived on Broadway in 2008. Reviewing *Jerry Springer: The Opera* for *New York*, Jeremy McCarter cautioned that "once you get past the jolly fun of chicks with dicks and a potty-mouthed Jesus," the production simply did not really work. Another direct spin-off from the television show, which is in equally questionable taste, is a drinking game connected to the Party Central website in which participants take a drink every time a "Jerry-ism" occurs on the show. The term *Jerry-ism* refers to the sayings and outrageous behaviors that regularly occur on the show, such as when Springer warns a guest, "Don't even go there," a fight breaks out, a member of the Ku Klux Klan appears, or a curse word is bleeped out.

Scholars of the twenty-first century continue to debate the popularity of Springer's show. Even though Jill Jones has called it "the ultimate forum for publicly displayed depravity," she insists the show is simply a continuation of the American tendency toward shaming that began with the Puritans who, like contemporary audiences, were obsessed with indecency.

Sharon Yablon

SEE ALSO: *Daytime Talk Shows; Freak Shows; Lake, Ricki; Television.*

BIBLIOGRAPHY

Allen, Steve. *Vulgarians at the Gate: Trash TV and Raunch Radio: Raising the Standards of Popular Culture.* Amherst, NY: Prometheus Books, 2001.

Collins, James. "Talking Trash." *Time*, March 30, 1998, 63–66.

Gamson, Joshua. *Freaks Talk Back: Tabloid Talk Shows and Sexual Nonconformity.* Chicago: University of Chicago Press, 1998.

Jones, Jill. "Hags and Whores: American Sin and Shaming from Salem to Springer." *Journal of American Culture* 32, no. 2 (2009): 146–154.

McCarter, Jeremy. "The Two Americas." *New York*, February 11, 2008, 65.

Scott, Gini Graham. *Can We Talk? The Power and Influence of Talk Shows.* New York: Insight Books, 1996.

Springer, Jerry, and Laura Morton. *Ringmaster!* New York: St. Martin's Press, 1998.

Timberg, Bernard M. *Television Talk: A History of the TV Talk Show.* Austin: University of Texas Press, 2002.

Springsteen, Bruce *(1949–)*

Singer Bruce Springsteen has placed himself in a lineage of folk and popular musicians, including Woody Guthrie and Bob Dylan, who have sought to effect social change. An acclaimed songwriter and energetic performer, Springsteen spent his early years singing in New Jersey bars, garnered a sizable commercial audience by 1975, and achieved superstar status with the release of his album *Born in the U.S.A.* (1984). His tremendous popularity, combined with his own ambition for success, opened his music to interpretations that seemed to conflict with his populist lyrics. Anxious to ride the bandwagon of his success, politicians and pundits appropriated his image to support their own perspectives. In much of the work that followed *Born in the U.S.A.*, however, Springsteen made a self-conscious effort to elucidate a liberal cultural politics.

Bruce Springsteen. *Bruce Springsteen performs on his home turf of Asbury Park, New Jersey, in 2012.* TAYLOR HILL/CONTRIBUTOR/FILMMAGIC/GETTY IMAGES.

Born in Freehold, New Jersey, on September 23, 1949, Springsteen grew up in an austere working-class household. Uninterested in school, he was fascinated by Elvis Presley's 1957 performance on *The Ed Sullivan Show* and began to imagine that rock and roll might provide a ticket out of his socioeconomic situation. After leading several bands in the late 1960s, Springsteen was performing acoustic shows in Greenwich Village when he auditioned for the legendary Columbia Records talent scout John Hammond in 1972. "The kid absolutely knocked me out," recalled Hammond, who billed the guitarist as the successor to Dylan, another of his discoveries.

EARLY CAREER

Springsteen's first two albums, *Greetings from Asbury Park, N.J.* (1973) and *The Wild, the Innocent, and the E Street Shuffle* (1973), chronicled the culture of New York City streets and Jersey boardwalks in a familiar Dylanesque style. Despite lackluster sales figures, Springsteen enjoyed a warm critical reception and began to establish a loyal following along the eastern seaboard. Backed by the E Street Band, he was renowned for electrifying performances that often went on longer than three hours.

Springsteen's tremendous energy caught the eye of former *Rolling Stone* critic Jon Landau, whose enthusiastic review of a 1974 concert transformed the singer's career. "I saw the rock and roll future," writes Landau in *The Real Paper*, "and its name is Bruce Springsteen." Columbia enlisted this hyperbole to launch a marketing blitz for *Born to Run* (1975), which landed Springsteen on the covers of the October 27, 1975, issues of *Time* and *Newsweek*. The album was both a critical and commercial triumph, attaining platinum status within four months.

Springsteen's career stalled, however, when he became entangled in a legal battle with manager Mike Appel. In 1976 the two filed countersuits involving copyrights and royalty payments. Appel won a court injunction that prohibited Springsteen from recording a new album with Landau, who became the musician's manager when the dispute ended a year later.

The hiatus was intellectually productive for Springsteen. At Landau's urging, he read the works of Flannery O'Connor and John Steinbeck and watched the films of John Ford and Sergio Leone. Inspired in part by Steinbeck's *Grapes of Wrath* (1939) and Ford's 1940 adaptation of it, *Darkness on the Edge of Town* (1978) marked a turning point in Springsteen's career. While *Born to Run* expressed a longing to escape the rigors of working-class life, *Darkness* explored the human costs of social and economic injustices.

SUCCESS IN THE 1980s

This change in perspective compelled Springsteen to develop a political consciousness. Following the 1979 Three Mile Island nuclear power station accident in Pennsylvania, he headlined several shows for Musicians United for Safe Energy, an antinuclear power consortium that included Bonnie Raitt and Jackson Browne. Two years later he staged a benefit for the Vietnam Veterans' Association, asking the audience to help heal the physical and psychological wounds inflicted on the soldiers who fought the country's most unpopular war.

Meanwhile, Springsteen's double album, *The River* (1980), soared to number one on the Billboard chart and produced "Hungry Heart," his first Top 10 hit. *The River* not only treated familiar topics of cars and girls but also revealed Springsteen's burgeoning interest in both traditional music and social issues. Earlier in his career he had begun to listen to classic country recordings as well as the Folkways Records' *Anthology of American Folk Music* (1952). Based on Hank Williams's "Long Gone Lonesome Blues," the album's title track was a particularly moving ballad about two teenagers who have a child, marry, and watch their dreams evaporate in the face of economic uncertainty. Springsteen later identified this song as a breakthrough in his writing.

In November 1980 Springsteen acquired a copy of Joe Klein's *Woody Guthrie: A Life* (1980). Impressed with Guthrie's artistry and political commitments, he began to cover the folksinger's "This Land Is Your Land" (1940) in his concerts. Guthrie's influence was palpable on *Nebraska* (1982), a largely acoustic and remarkably uncommercial album that Springsteen recorded in his home. Sparse guitars, wailing harmonicas, and somber vocals guided listeners through a desolate, deprived landscape where individuals committed acts of desperation, ranging from petty crimes to mass murders. Greil Marcus describes *Nebraska* as "the most convincing statement of resistance and refusal that Ronald Reagan's U.S.A. has yet elicited." *Rolling Stone*, one of Springsteen's staunchest supporters, called it his "bravest" album, a work that solidified his reputation as a performer who cared more about artistic integrity than commercial success.

BORN IN THE U.S.A.

The validity of such observations was complicated when Springsteen attained unimagined fame and fortune in 1984. *Born in the U.S.A.* sold more than twenty million copies; generated seven Top 10 singles; fueled a worldwide stadium tour (1984–1985); and, with the aid of the music video, introduced the singer to a younger generation. This success, which Springsteen actively cultivated and obviously enjoyed, clouded his politics. Unlike most of the album's songs, which eschewed the bleak realities of *Nebraska*, "Born in the U.S.A." told the story of an unemployed Vietnam veteran who lost his brother in the war. The lyrics clearly questioned the morality of war as well as the country's treatment of its veterans, yet much of Springsteen's audience misconstrued his intentions. The ringing melody and the exuberant chorus of "Born in the U.S.A." led listeners to interpret it as a jingoistic celebration of U.S. militarism. Moreover, the working-class woes that Springsteen expressed were lost in the celebration of his own success story.

POLITICAL CONTROVERSY

Politicians scrambled to claim Springsteen as their own. Syndicated columnist George Will lauded him for both his optimism and the work ethic he demonstrated in his four-hour shows. Will's enthusiasm convinced Reagan to invoke the musician during a campaign stop in New Jersey. "America's future rests in the message of hope in songs of a man so many young Americans admire: New Jersey's own Bruce Springsteen," remarked the president. "And helping you make those dreams come true is what this job of mine is all about." Springsteen's antiwar song conflicted with Reagan's aggressive military policies, but the president's appropriation confused the musician's intentions. The song was further obscured by Sylvester Stallone's *Rambo: First Blood Part II* (1985), a film that sought to redeem the performance of the United States in Vietnam. Soon after its release, major newspapers dubbed Springsteen, whose muscle-bound body resembled Stallone's, the Rambo of Rock.

Springsteen was not an innocent bystander in this process. The Los Angeles Summer Olympic Games and the presidential election made 1984 a year for stars and stripes, a fact he exploited by placing the flag on the album cover and using it as a backdrop to his concert stage. Moreover, as his detested sobriquet "the Boss" suggests, he projected a commanding masculine presence that made it difficult to separate him from the hard-nosed aggression and conservatism that both Reagan and Rambo represented. But if Springsteen capitalized on the resurgence in U.S. patriotism, he made an effort to clarify his politics. At a Pittsburgh, Pennsylvania, concert, he dedicated "Johnny 99," a song about an unemployed autoworker, to the president.

In 1986 Springsteen documented his concert legend with the release *Live/1975–1985*, a forty-song compendium that used long introductory speeches to "The River" and a rendition of musician Edwin Starr's "War" to express his disapproval of U.S. military policy. He continued to articulate liberal viewpoints following the release of *Tunnel of Love* (1987), a collection inspired by his failing marriage to actress Julianne Phillips. In 1988 he underscored his connection to Guthrie by recording ballads about homelessness for the tribute album *A Vision Shared*. More importantly, he headlined Amnesty International's Human Rights Now! Tour, where he criticized the economic apartheid that existed in the United States.

THE 1990s

After divorcing Phillips and breaking up the E Street Band in 1989, Springsteen entered a period of depression and took a sojourn from cultural politics. Like *Tunnel*, *Human Touch* and *Lucky Town* (both released in 1992) explored the dynamics of gender relationships, celebrating his subsequent marriage to former band member Patti Scialfa and the birth of their children. Disappointing sales prompted many critics to question Springsteen's viability in a changing market, but success returned when he reembraced social issues in "Streets of Philadelphia." Written for Jonathan Demme's motion picture *Philadelphia* (1993) about an AIDS (acquired immunodeficiency syndrome) patient, the composition won an Academy Award. Two years later Springsteen earned his second Oscar nomination with "Dead Man Walking" from the movie of the same name starring Sean Penn and Susan Sarandon.

Springsteen reconvened the E Street Band to record four new songs for *Greatest Hits* (1995) but promptly returned to solo work. *The Ghost of Tom Joad* (1995) reasserted his connection to Steinbeck, Ford, and Guthrie: Joad was the protagonist of *Grapes of Wrath* and the subject of a lengthy Guthrie ballad. Following in the footsteps of its cultural predecessors, the folk-styled album explored the plight of the underclass and identified injustices endured by Mexican immigrants. To ensure that his political intentions were understood, Springsteen embarked on an acoustic tour during which he performed his most socially engaged songs and explained the meaning of and inspiration for his lyrics. He reiterated his politics on a 1996 edition of *60 Minutes*, where he criticized the policies of the Reagan–George H. W. Bush years and urged his audience to promote values of human welfare rather than individualism.

THE TWENTY-FIRST CENTURY

While Springsteen's star seemed to be fading in the late 1990s, he came back with a vengeance in the new century. After reuniting the E Street Band for an immensely successful reunion tour in 1999, he returned to the studio in the wake of the September 11, 2001, terrorist attacks against the United States, releasing *The Rising* in 2002. The first studio album recorded with the full band in nearly twenty years, a number of the songs on *The Rising* were inspired by conversations Springsteen had with the families of victims who had been particular fans of his music. It was a critical and popular success, with both album and title song rising to the top of the charts. The follow-up album, *Devils and Dust* (2005), whose title song addresses a soldier's experience of the Iraq War, reached headlines when the Starbucks coffeehouse chain refused a cobranding deal because Springsteen spoke out against corporate policies and politics. Since then, he released *We Shall Overcome: The Seeger Sessions* (2006), based on the work of folk musician and activist Pete Seeger; *Magic* (2007); *Working on a Dream* (2009); and *Wrecking Ball* (2012).

In the twenty-first century, having won innumerable Grammy Awards and other honors, such as being inducted into the Rock and Roll Hall of Fame, Springsteen remained one of the most influential and politically engaged performers in popular music. Particularly in the first decade of the new century, he began to intervene more actively in national politics, supporting John Kerry in the 2004 presidential race and Barack Obama in 2008. As a result, his song "The Rising" was broadcast over the loudspeakers just after Obama's victory speech in Chicago's Grant Park, and he was featured at the Obama inaugural ceremony in 2009, performing "The Rising" and, in duet with Seeger, Guthrie's anthem "This Land Is Your Land."

Bryan Garman

SEE ALSO: *Academy Awards; AIDS; Browne, Jackson; Country Music; Dylan, Bob; Folk Music; Ford, John; Grammy Awards; Greenwich Village; Guthrie, Woody; Leone, Sergio; Obama, Barack; O'Connor, Flannery; Olympics; Presley, Elvis; Raitt, Bonnie; Rock and Roll;* Rolling Stone*; Sarandon, Susan; Seeger, Pete; Stadium Concerts; Stallone, Sylvester; Steinbeck, John; Sullivan, Ed; Williams, Hank, Sr.*

BIBLIOGRAPHY

Eliot, Marc, and Mike Appel. *Down Thunder Road: The Making of Bruce Springsteen*. New York: Simon & Schuster, 1992.

Cullen, Jim. *Born in the U.S.A.: Bruce Springsteen and the American Tradition*. New York: HarperCollins, 1997.

Garman, Bryan. "The Ghost of History: Woody Guthrie, Bruce Springsteen, and the Hurt Song." *Popular Music and Society* 20, no. 2 (1996): 69–120.

Marsh, Dave. *Glory Days: Bruce Springsteen in the 1980s*. New York: Pantheon, 1987.

Marsh, Dave. *Bruce Springsteen: Two Hearts: The Definitive Biography, 1972–2003*. New York: Routledge, 2004.

Sprinkle, Annie *(1954–)*

American performance artist Annie Sprinkle (born Ellen Steinberg) made her mark as one of the preeminent practitioners of the art form in the 1980s with her one-woman show "Post-Porn Modernist." Sprinkle, who began her career as a prostitute in a massage parlor before acting in more than 200 adult films and videos in the 1970s and 1980s, was a controversial face for the performance art movement. Described in a British broadsheet newspaper in 1999 as "porn-queen-turned-new-age-sex-goddess," Sprinkle's onstage antics invoked the wrath of conservatives, who used her work, along with that of certain others, as a weapon for the argument to cut funding to the National Endowment for the Arts. Although allying her work to the feminist cause, she has also offended mainstream feminists. Her controversial exhibition, which aimed to demystify the female body and encourage sex as a spiritual act, included simulating oral sex, performing masturbation, and inviting audience members to inspect her cervix.

Despite the notoriously explicit nature of her art, Sprinkle's life since the 1990s has been far more mainstream. After receiving a BFA from the School of Visual Arts in 1986, she went on to get a degree in human sexuality from the San Francisco–based Institute for Advanced Study in Human Sexuality in 1992. In the 1990s and the first decade of the 2000s, Sprinkle and her wife, Beth Stephens, began exploring "ecosexuality" or "sexecology," a doctrine that brings together sexuality and awareness of the environment. Taking this concept to the extreme to both raise awareness of environmental concerns and introduce issues of sexuality into the ecology movement, Sprinkle and Stephens have produced a number of art projects promoting ecosexuality, including a series of "weddings" to the earth, moon, sky, and other natural entities.

Geri Speace

SEE ALSO: *Performance Art; Pornography.*

BIBLIOGRAPHY

Juno, Andrea, and V. Vale. *Angry Women.* San Francisco: RE/SEARCH Publications, 1991.

Sprinkle, Annie. "Some of My Performances in Retrospect." *Art Journal* 56, no. 4 (1997): 68–70.

Sprinkle, Annie. *Hardcore from the Heart: The Pleasures, Profits, and Politics of Sex in Performance.* New York: Continuum International Publishing Group, 2001.

Spurlock, Morgan

SEE: *Super Size Me.*

Sputnik

A thin plume of orange rising into the Soviet sky on October 4, 1957, carried humankind's first artificial satellite. This 22-inch, 184-pound, beeping sphere called *Sputnik* (fellow traveler) marked the beginning of a new chapter in the Cold War, in which national prestige would be measured by a race in space. An incredible technological achievement that all of humanity should have cheered, the flight of *Sputnik 1* and its successors (launched through 1961) was transformed into intense political propaganda. For the Soviets, a supposedly technologically backward nation, *Sputnik* produced national pride; for the United States, which had been helplessly watching its own puny Vanguard rockets fizzle and blow up on the launch pad, the flight enhanced fears of the growing Red Menace. While the satellite fell from orbit in January 1958, the word *Sputnik* became embedded in the American lexicon, symbolizing a period when the United States realized space exploration would not be a wholly American enterprise.

The International Geophysical Year (IGY), a period of worldwide scientific study from July 1957 to December 1958, prompted U.S. efforts to develop satellites. President Dwight Eisenhower announced that the United States would orbit a scientific package—Project Vanguard—during the IGY with an anticipated launch date in March 1958. Unlike Soviet Premier Nikita Khrushchev, the administration failed to foresee the propaganda coup of placing the first humanmade object into space. *Sputnik* captured headlines around the world, and the Soviet News agency TASS boasted how the people of a Socialist society had turned dreams into reality.

A CHALLENGE TO U.S. SUPREMACY

Noted atomic weapons pioneer Edward Teller professed, "America has lost a battle more important and greater than Pearl Harbor." Following the revelations of the Rosenberg trial, McCarthy hearings, the fall of mainland China to a Red Mao, conflict in Korea, and the revolt in Hungary, *Sputnik* only added to fears among Americans of the Red Menace. Eisenhower sought to alleviate anxiety by reminding the nation that U.S. satellite efforts had not been conducted as a race with other nations. Not only was the Vanguard rocket on schedule, but it

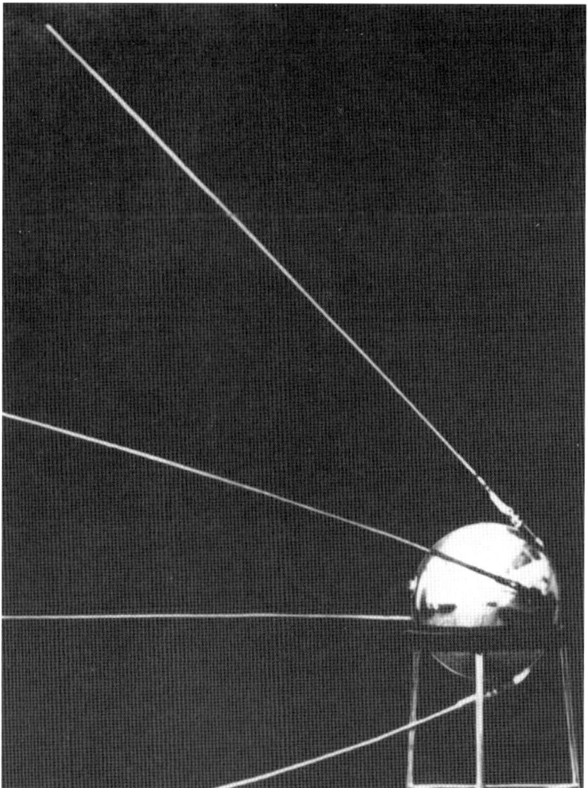

Sputnik. Sputnik 1, *the first artificial satellite, is displayed shortly before its launch on October 4, 1957, which marked the start of the space race between the USSR and the United States.* HULTON ARCHIVE/STRINGER/ARCHIVE PHOTOS/GETTY IMAGES.

would also make serious contributions to science; *Sputnik*, on the other hand, did little more than transmit its location. Such reassurances did little to calm the citizenry, as a blanket of paranoia and insecurity unfurled across the nation.

The role of the United States as the leader in science and technology was being directly challenged. Before *Sputnik*, there was a widespread belief among Americans that the Soviets were far behind the United States in such areas and that they relied on espionage rather than originality. Had such smugness bred mental stagnation among Americans? Senator Styles Bridges declared, "The time has clearly come to be less concerned with the depth on the new broadloom rug or the height of the tail fin of the car and to be more prepared to shed blood, sweat and tears if this country and the free world are to survive."

A second *Sputnik* was launched in less than a month, on November 3, which increased America's anxiety. *Sputnik 2* weighed an incredible 1,100 pounds and contained a living passenger, a dog named Laika. Clearly, any booster capable of such feats had to possess a massive thrust capacity. This brought to light fears that the Soviets were on the verge of perfecting the first intercontinental ballistic missile (ICBM) and with it nuclear warheads that could rain down upon the United States at any given moment.

THE RACE IS ON

Attempting to bolster national pride domestically and the image of the United States abroad, the White House ordered an acceleration of Vanguard's timetable by four months to attempt a December 1957 launch. With the nation's eyes transfixed on Cape Canaveral, the pencil-like Vanguard rocket rose four feet, dropped, and burst into flames. The Soviet United Nations delegation promptly inquired if the United States desired to enlist rocketry aid under its program of technical assistance to backward nations.

The United States did successfully launch the thirty-one-pound *Explorer 1* on January 31, 1958. In May, the Soviets launched *Sputnik 3*, which carried the first space laboratory and used solar energy to power its instruments and transmitters. *Sputnik 5* through *Sputnik 10* (four of which carried dogs) were launched in 1960 and 1961; these were working models of the spacecraft that carried Yury Alekseyevich Gagarin, the first human passenger, into space in 1961.

Politically, the impact of *Sputnik* within the United States was far-reaching. In Washington, D.C., critics charged that the president's policy of fiscal responsibility hindered the military's ability to develop ICBMs. Senate majority leader Lyndon Baines Johnson opened a subcommittee of the Senate Armed Services Committee to review the nation's missile and space programs. Eisenhower succumbed to such pressures, increasing defense dollars allocated for missiles. To ensure the peaceful exploration of space, the president called for the creation of a civilian space agency. The National Aeronautics and Space Act of 1958 formally established the National Aeronautics and Space Administration (NASA). Through NASA, the nation set forth to combat the Soviets in this new arena of the Cold War called the space race. Because some critics charged the U.S. educational system with not stressing the same fundamentals in science and mathematics as the Soviet system, the National Defense Education Act allocated nearly $1 billion to increase science, mathematics, and foreign languages in elementary, secondary, and collegiate education. American school children needed to be as versed in algebra formulas as they were in baseball batting averages if the United States hoped to surpass *Sputnik*.

While average Americans found themselves terrified by *Sputnik*, it became a phenomenon filtering into their everyday lives. *Sputnik* watching became a popular evening event. Broadcast in a frequency range that amateur shortwave radio operators could receive, the beeps of *Sputnik* were as familiar to many families as the "Ballad of Davy Crockett." Toy stores found their shelves lined with *Sputnik*-inspired toys. David Glover wrote and published the song "Go! Sputnik Boogie." Bartenders concocted *Sputnik*-themed cocktails—with vodka as a primary ingredient, naturally.

Lori C. Walters

SEE ALSO: *Cold War; The Fifties; NASA.*

BIBLIOGRAPHY

Clowse, Barbara Barksdale. *Brainpower for the Cold War: The Sputnik Crisis and National Defense Education Act of 1958.* Westport, CT: Greenwood Press, 1981.

Dickson, Paul. *Sputnik: The Shock of the Century.* New York: Walker & Company, 2001.

Divine, Robert A. *The Sputnik Challenge.* New York: Oxford University Press, 1993.

Harford, James. *Korolev.* New York: Wiley, 1997.

Killian, James Rhyne. *Sputnik, Scientists and Eisenhower: A Memoir of the First Special Assistant to the President for Science and Technology.* Cambridge, MA: MIT Press, 1977.

McDougall, Walter A. *The Heavens and the Earth: A Political History of the Space Age.* New York: Basic Books, 1985.

St. Denis, Ruth *(1879–1968)*

Ruth St. Denis was an American dancer and choreographer who influenced nearly every phase of dance in the United States in the early twentieth century. Born Ruth Dennis in Newark, New Jersey, in 1879, she began her dance career as a teenager and later took the stage name Ruth St. Denis. She traveled extensively, performing on the vaudeville circuit in the United States and using her visits abroad to learn about the dances of other countries.

St. Denis was the first to present Eastern dance forms and themes to American audiences, developing a nationwide acceptance of Eastern art. She performed her first dance work, *Radha*, in New York in 1906 after studying Hindu art and philosophy. With her husband and dance partner, Ted Shawn, she created the Denishawn School of Dancing, with studios in Los Angeles and New York, and the Denishawn Dancers, a popular performing company. St. Denis and Shawn profoundly influenced modern dance through their schools, the first organized centers for dance experiment in the United States. In 1931 they separated, both professionally and personally.

St. Denis is remembered for her teachings and often religious choreographic works that helped establish modern dance as a serious artistic genre for later generations. A dancer of considerable power and beauty, she was a great inspiration to her three most accomplished students: Martha Graham, Doris Humphrey, and Charles Weidman, who all went on to become legendary modern dance figures themselves. St. Denis continued to perform into the 1960s and died of a stroke at age eighty-nine in July 1968.

Brian Granger

SEE ALSO: *Denishawn; Graham, Martha; Modern Dance; Shawn, Ted; Vaudeville.*

BIBLIOGRAPHY

Dils, Ann, and Ann Cooper Albright, eds. *Moving History/Dancing Cultures: A Dance History Reader.* Middletown, CT: Wesleyan University Press, 2001.

Shelton, Suzanne. *Divine Dancer: A Biography of Ruth St. Denis.* Garden City, NY: Doubleday, 1981.

Sherman, Jane. *The Drama of Denishawn Dance.* Middletown, CT: Wesleyan University Press, 1979.

St. Denis, Ruth. *Ruth St. Denis, an Unfinished Life: An Autobiography.* New York: Harper & Bros., 1939.

St. Elsewhere

Medical dramas such as *Dr. Kildare*, *Medical Center*, *Chicago Hope*, *ER*, and *Grey's Anatomy* have long been one of the most popular television show formats. Of the many programs that have presented the issues surrounding major medical institutions, few—if any—have been more unique, ambitious, and unpredictable than *St. Elsewhere*. The series, which ran on NBC from 1982 to 1988, focuses on the lives of the doctors, nurses, and patients at St. Eligius, an inner-city Boston teaching hospital. Each episode offers a realistic look at the fallibility of doctors, the stresses of being hospitalized, and the ethical dilemmas inherent in the practice of medicine. Mixed in with the often-tragic story lines are oblique in-jokes, subtle bawdy humor, and countless intertextual references to other works of popular culture. Although the series often struggled with mediocre ratings, its strong appeal to the demographically important baby boomer and upscale urban professional audiences allowed the idiosyncratic show to remain on the air. After its surreal final episode, *St. Elsewhere* was widely hailed as one of television's most literate and original programs.

The term *St. Elsewhere* is derived from medical school jargon for a hospital that serves as a dumping ground for patients not wanted by more prestigious medical facilities. Unlike its namesake, however, the series had a distinguished pedigree. Joshua Brand (1950–) and John Falsey (1951–), staff writers on the basketball series *The White Shadow*, were inspired to create the series after hearing of a friend's experiences as an intern at the Cleveland Clinic. They assembled a core group of young producers and writers, including Bruce Paltrow (1943–2002), Mark Tinker (1951–), John Masius (1950–), and Tom Fontana (1951–), who crafted a program distinctly different from previous medical dramas featuring noble and perfect physicians. Their stories present flawed doctors trying, and often failing, to provide the best medical care in less than ideal circumstances. The show's narrative center is held by three veteran physicians: Daniel Auschlander, a liver specialist played by Norman Lloyd (1951–) who ironically is himself stricken with liver cancer; widowed chief of staff Donald Westphall, performed by Ed Flanders (1934–1995); and Mark Craig, a brilliant and heartless heart surgeon acted by William Daniels (1927–). They are surrounded by many young residents confronting their own problems.

That the series is set in a large, decaying urban institution; features a large and diverse cast; and continues plots over a number of episodes caused many critics to often and aptly compare it to *Hill Street Blues*. Similar to the police drama, *St. Elsewhere* exhibits an intense realism that is evident in its willingness to frankly address such issues as breast cancer, rape, infertility, impotence, and addiction. A 1983 episode features one of network television's first dramatic presentations of the AIDS (acquired immunodeficiency syndrome) crisis. To heighten the sense of reality, the writers routinely placed their main characters in life-threatening situations they did not always survive. Over the years main characters left the show through such means as committing suicide, being murdered, going to prison, and contracting fatal diseases. Howie Mandel (1955–), who played a resident, reflected that the characters were as vulnerable as real people: "I could get hit by a car and killed on my way to work and so could Fiscus (Mandel's character). You always felt they could've killed anybody off. It wasn't past what they would do on *St. Elsewhere.*"

The harshly realistic tone of the series was tempered by the writers' willingness to experiment with its form and their frequent use of black humor and pop culture references. The obnoxious patient Mrs. Hufnagel is at St. Eligius for an entire season only to die in a freak accident when her hospital bed folds up on her. Another recurring patient, the amnesiac John Doe number six, becomes convinced he is Mary Richards from *The Mary Tyler Moore Show*. For that episode the writers included dozens of references to the classic series and other MTM Enterprises productions. A highlight is a scene in a psych ward featuring actor Jack Riley (1935–) as "Mr. Carlin," his neurotic character from *The Bob Newhart Show*. Episodes that depart from the show's usual format include one doctor's journey to heaven, where he meets God, and another that is structured like the play *Our Town*. Robert J. Thompson, director of the Bleier Center for Television and Popular Culture at Syracuse University, writes in his 1997 book *Television's Second Golden Age*, "More than any other series in the history of American television, *St. Elsewhere* rewarded the attentive viewer."

Careful viewers were aware of the writers' affinity for placing dirty but subtle jokes in many episodes. The most infamous was one of the first references to oral sex on network television. While dictating a novel Dr. Craig says: "She came in from the garden, cheeks flushed, arms filled with flowers. I sat playing the Wurlitzer. She said wistfully, 'Where would you like these?' I smiled. 'Put roses on the piano and tulips on the organ.'" Such hidden gags were a bonus for active viewers. The series' final episode itself contains dozens of references to other programs throughout television history. In its final moments the writers offered devoted viewers a great surprise as it is revealed that the hospital is only a model within a snow globe. The entire series had sprung from the imagination of Westphall's autistic son.

Few television programs can claim to be as thoroughly dramatic, humorous, and inventive as *St. Elsewhere*. The writers showed respect for their audience's intelligence on a weekly basis and revealed that network television can provide a level of sophistication beyond mere mindless entertainment. Furthermore, the constant intertextual references demonstrate that television possesses a rich heritage that can be drawn from by capable artists. Although it may not have been high in the ratings, the series stands as a high point in television history that has rarely been matched by other series.

Charles Coletta

SEE ALSO: Grey's Anatomy; Hill Street Blues; Northern Exposure.

BIBLIOGRAPHY

Bianculli, David. *Dictionary of Teleliteracy*. New York: Continuum, 1996.

Thompson, Robert J. *Television's Second Golden Age*. Syracuse, NY: Syracuse University Press, 1997.

Stadium Concerts

In the 1970s stadiums became the main venues for performances of popular music. From country and rock-and-roll stars to more traditional performers such as Frank Sinatra and Barbra Streisand, top acts attracted anywhere from 20,000 to 100,000 people to their shows. Rock—with its communal aspect and amped-up volume—was particularly suited for large arenas. Rock musicians looked to the stadium as a way to play in front of the most people and, thus, earn the most money. Rock's dominance on the concert circuit continued into the 1990s. Of the twenty top-grossing North American concert tours between 1985 and 1994 (with an average gross of $55 million over forty-two cities), nearly all were by rock artists. By the twenty-first century, a wider variety of musicians were embarking on major tours; in 2011, for example, the top concerts also included country, rap, and pop acts, though rockers still reigned supreme.

1960s

The first stadium rock concert was in 1965, when the Beatles performed in New York's Shea Stadium to 55,000 screaming fans. Newspaper reports treated the concert as a curious aberration. The *New York Times* referred to the fans' "immature lungs," which produced a "magnificent and terrifying voice," and quoted a policewoman who called the audience members "psychos." The Shea Stadium concert, for which the Beatles earned more than $160,000 for twenty-eight minutes of work, prefigured rock's commercial power.

By 1967 outdoor rock festivals began attracting audiences on an even larger scale. The Monterey Pop Festival in 1967 drew more than 50,000 people, while the 1969 Woodstock festival attracted more than 400,000. Many of these festivals, however, were plagued by major problems. Promoters were often corrupt or inept, and violence was a looming threat that was realized at Altamont Speedway in Northern California, where a fan was killed during a Rolling Stones concert. In ensuing years, concert promoters—by virtue of having to coordinate forty-city tours—had no choice but to improve, though violence always remained a possibility.

At the beginning of the 1970s, concerts still lacked polish—for example, bands such as the Rolling Stones and Led Zeppelin would routinely arrive an hour or more late. The Jefferson Airplane's Paul Kantner, quoted by Bill Graham and Robert Greenfield in *Bill Graham Presents*, expresses the attitude toward performing in rock's pre-stadium era: "A show was not just a performance. . . . A show was a whole social something-or-other. Bonfire ceremony or something. After we played, we wanted to go out and hustle girls. Get drunk and party, come back and play another set, go out and party again, and pretty soon dawn was there. To break that up was business." The move toward the stadiums was inevitable, however, as rock artists commanded greater receipts. Madison Square Garden and venues like it "could not have had an artist play there unless the artist said they wanted to," writes Graham and Greenfield, who add that, at the time, they thought stadiums "should just be for . . . Roller Derby and boxing."

1970s

In the 1970s, declared *Rolling Stone* magazine, "there was no unifying presence in rock . . . and no artist whose latest record had to be heard by every fan and musician. By the time the decade began, rock was entertainment; in fact, it was well on its way to being the entertainment industry." Soon performers were using special effects such as pyrotechnics or laser light shows. Professionalism had become the norm, as the stadium concert gave birth to one of rock's biggest clichés: the audience ritual of requesting an encore by holding up flaming cigarette lighters. If the outdoor festivals were characterized by their freeform nature, then the stadium concert was defined by its ritualistic showmanship.

Holding the attention of 20,000 (or more) people at a time was a serious challenge, but the rock star was well armed. Any given tour might include several buses, a couple of trailer rigs, and a road crew (roadies) to set up and dismantle increasingly elaborate stages. Furthermore, stacks of speakers could unleash 120 decibels of sound, which helped to nullify the poor acoustics of many stadiums.

The dark side to such mass gatherings—when part of the audience was drinking, drugging, or both—was security concerns. The "stage rush," in which people in the front rows pushed forward toward the stage, sometimes threatened performers. At other times, the concert frenzy could produce tragedy, such as the December 1979 Who concert at the Riverfront Coliseum in Cincinnati, Ohio. A swell of 7,000 people crashed through two open banks of doors, resulting in eleven deaths. The practice known as "festival seating," in which there were no reserved seats and concertgoers rushed into the stadium to stake their claims, was held to blame.

1980s

By the late 1980s, rock and country artists used stadium concerts to voice their social concerns. Stadium-sized benefits of this period included Farm Aid—which helped to provide financial relief to America's farmers—and the Conspiracy of Hope Tour for Amnesty International. The biggest undertaking of this nature was the Live Aid shows, which took place simultaneously in Philadelphia and London on July 13, 1985. Between one and a half and two billion people worldwide watched the televised concerts, and more than $100 million was raised for African famine relief.

1990S AND BEYOND

Tours for individual groups grew to comparable proportions. The top two touring acts of 1994, the Rolling Stones and Pink Floyd, grossed $121 million and $103 million, respectively. In 2011 the top-grossing act, U2, earned $293 million playing in venues such as the 50,000-seat Angel Stadium in the Los Angeles area. Stadiums with capacities of 20,000 seats, which had been the big prizes in the 1970s, were now second-tier venues when superstar groups hit the road.

Daryl Umberger

SEE ALSO: *Altamont; The Beatles; Farm Aid; Jefferson Airplane/Starship; Led Zeppelin; Pink Floyd; Rock and Roll; The Rolling Stones; U2; The Who; Woodstock.*

BIBLIOGRAPHY

Coleman, Mark. "The Revival of Conscience." *Rolling Stone*, November 15, 1990, 69–73.

Coleman, Ray. *The Man Who Made the Beatles: An Intimate Biography of Brian Epstein.* New York: McGraw-Hill, 1989.

Famighetti, Robert, ed. *The World Almanac and Book of Facts, 1996.* Mahwah, NJ: World Almanac, 1995.

Graham, Bill, and Robert Greenfield. *Bill Graham Presents: My Life Inside Rock and Out.* New York: Doubleday, 1992.

Grushkin, Paul, and Elton John. *The Art of Classic Rock: Rock Memorabilia, Tour Posters, and Merchandise.* New York: Collins Design, 2010.

Mayer, Allan J., and Jon Lowell. "Cincinnati Stampede." *Newsweek*, December 17, 1979, 52–53.

Neely, Kim. "Music versus Muscle: Is Concert Security a Necessary Evil? And How Much Is Too Much?" *Rolling Stone*, April 15, 1993, 15–17.

Russell, Ethan A., and Gerard Van der Leun. *Let It Bleed: The Rolling Stones, Altamont, and the End of the Sixties.* New York: Springboard Press, 2009.

Schumach, Murray. "Shrieks of 55,000 Accompany Beatles." *New York Times*, August 16, 1965.

"The Seventies." *Rolling Stone*, September 20, 1990.

Stagecoach

The critically acclaimed classic film, *Stagecoach* (1939), not only helped to revive the "A"-movie Western, which had been out of favor since the release of the first talkie in 1926, but it also cemented director John Ford's reputation as one of America's greatest filmmakers. *Stagecoach* is also the movie that catapulted actor John Wayne into stardom. Based on Ernest Haycox's short story "Stage to Lordsburg," the film is about the adventures of nine people on a stagecoach trip through Indian country. It explores the tensions and relationships that develop during the trip.

TRADITIONAL WESTERN CHARACTERS

Even though it's considered a classic, *Stagecoach* shares many similarities with "B"-movie Westerns. Its characters are standard clichés from any number of low-grade cowboy flicks: Ringo Kid (John Wayne), the young outlaw bent on revenge; Dallas (Claire Trevor), the prostitute with a heart of gold; Josiah Boone

Stagecoach. *A scene from* Stagecoach *features stars Claire Trevor as Dallas and John Wayne as Ringo Kid.* UNITED ARTISTS/THE KOBAL COLLECTION.

(Thomas Mitchell), the drunken doctor; Gatewood (Benton Churchill), the pompous banker; Hatfield (John Carradine), the chivalrous gambler; Lucy Mallory (Louise Platt), the pregnant wife of a cavalry officer; and Peacock (Donald Meek), the timid whiskey drummer. Also along for the ride are Buck the driver (Andy Devine) and Curley Wilcox (George Bancroft), a marshal who provides protection for the passengers. The plot is not particularly original, and there are chases and shootouts that are typical Western fare.

Despite its "B"-movie attributes, *Stagecoach* excels in character development, and, more importantly, it presented a clear social vision to 1939 movie audiences mired in the Great Depression. Primary to this vision was the idea of community. The stagecoach, carrying people of diverse backgrounds and traveling alone in the savage wilderness of Indian country, represents a microcosm of civilized society. The people onboard work through their differences to form a cohesive unit (with one notable exception), and the driving force behind their union is crisis. The premature birth of Lucy's baby forces Dr. Boone to sober up, brings Dallas and Lucy together, and draws sympathy from the others. Similarly, the climactic (if not slightly stereotypical) Indian-stagecoach chase requires these disparate elements to join forces to repel the common foe.

The message was clear for contemporary audiences, who were facing a different sort of crisis: the best way to persevere through hard times is to band together and fight. Ford was no utopian idealist, however. Once the danger had passed, and the stagecoach reached Lordsburg (an ironic name, considering the amount of gambling, prostitution, and gunplay that took place there), the people on the stagecoach went their separate ways. Clearly, such a community could only exist in extraordinary times.

Ford's community is not all-inclusive, however. Significantly, Gatewood is left out, as if he has no role in society. Depression-era audiences, which largely blamed bankers for the decade's ills, found in Gatewood a figure richly deserving of their scorn. While others try to help Lucy after she gives birth, Gatewood impatiently demands that the stagecoach continue its trip. He is notably absent in the chase scene, remaining invisible inside the moving stagecoach, while the others desperately fire at the marauding Indians from the windows. Gatewood presents an alternative social vision, which is roundly rejected. The other passengers are noticeably bored when he demands that bankers be free from government inspection and proclaims that America needs a "businessman for president." Their disinterest is a swipe at the conservative Republican administrations of the 1920s and is an implicit nod of support for the more liberal Franklin D. Roosevelt and his New Deal. At the film's end, Gatewood is revealed to be a thief and is dragged off in handcuffs.

IDEAL TYPES

Ford extended his vision beyond this call for community and used *Stagecoach* to present a largely traditionalist idea of the perfect man and woman. The heroic men of *Stagecoach* are tough and rugged problem solvers who are not afraid to use weapons to defend themselves and their civilization from outside threats. Fainthearted men like Peacock are lampooned and exposed as effeminate. "I've had five children," Peacock notes when Lucy is in labor. "I mean," he notes, "my dear wife has." Throughout the movie, Peacock, doing his best impression of a disapproving nurse, tries to dissuade the alcoholic Dr. Boone from imbibing. Women, conversely, are most sympathetic when acting as mothers. The cold and aloof Lucy becomes a much more likable character once she has her baby, and Ringo first expresses his feelings for Dallas after he admires her as she holds Lucy's baby. These ideal types are as important to the film's message as its presentation of a society in crisis; to weather times of trouble, a community needs to be made up of the right kind of people.

Stagecoach struck a chord with both critics and audiences. The *New York Times* hailed the film as "a noble horse opera" and declared it "a beautiful sight to see." *Variety* called *Stagecoach* a "sweeping and powerful drama" and enthusiastically lauded its "photographic grandeur." The film packed movie theaters and won Academy Awards for Best Supporting Actor (Thomas Mitchell) and Best Score.

Stagecoach was Ford's first Western since he directed *3 Bad Men* (1926), and it was his first talkie Western (he made forty-three silent Westerns). He would go on to make many more Westerns, including *Fort Apache* (1948), *She Wore a Yellow Ribbon* (1949), and *The Man Who Shot Liberty Valance* (1962), all of which starred Wayne. Many people, however, consider *Stagecoach* to be Ford's best Western.

David B. Welky

SEE ALSO: *Academy Awards; "B" Movies; Ford, John; The Great Depression;* The Man Who Shot Liberty Valance*; New Deal; The* New York Times*;* She Wore a Yellow Ribbon*; Silent Movies; Wayne, John; The Western.*

BIBLIOGRAPHY

Bergman, Andrew. *We're in the Money: Depression America and Its Films*. New York: New York University Press, 1971.

Davis, Ronald L. *John Ford: Hollywood's Old Master*. Norman: University of Oklahoma Press, 1995.

Ford, Dan. *Pappy: The Life of John Ford*. Englewood Cliffs, NJ: Prentice-Hall, 1979.

Gallagher, Tag. *John Ford: The Man and His Films*. Berkeley: University of California Press, 1986.

Levy, Bill. *John Ford: A Bio-bibliography*. Westport, CT: Greenwood Press, 1998.

Roberts, Randy, and James S. Olson. *John Wayne: American*. New York: Free Press, 1995.

Stagg, Amos Alonzo *(1862–1965)*

Amos Alonzo Stagg, the charismatic "Grand Old Man" of college football, was one of the sport's immortal leaders and innovative strategists. Stagg coached on the college level for an astounding fifty-seven seasons. He started out at Springfield College in Massachusetts and in 1892 became head football coach and associate professor of physical culture at the University of Chicago, where he enjoyed the lengthy coaching tenure of forty years. After retiring from the Big Ten school in 1932, he headed the football program at the College of the Pacific in Stockton, California, through 1946.

Stagg was born in West Orange, New Jersey, and attended Yale University, where he participated in several sports. In 1886 he pitched Yale to a victory over Harvard to win the college baseball championship. He also played end on the football team, coached by Walter Camp, and made the 1889 All-America squad. It was under Camp's peerless guidance that he became a student of the game. Stagg, who originally wished to become a minister, also developed the conviction that within football there existed the positive force with which to mold men's characters. This concept, which he adhered to with evangelical zeal, was to become one of the cornerstones of his football philosophy.

At the University of Chicago, Stagg became the nation's initial tenured football coach, as well as his era's most imaginative, enterprising, and dominant athletic mentor. His on-field innovations ranged from the "ends back" flying wedge formation to end-around plays and hidden-ball plays (in which he had his runners hide the pigskin under their jerseys). He instituted the modern T-formation and the flea-flicker pass and was the first coach to spotlight the forward pass in his team's offense. He also was fabled for devising forceful defenses. The one he employed against the powerful Harold "Red" Grange of Illinois resulted in a 21–21 tie in 1924 and a moral victory for his underdog Maroons.

Stagg was the first coach to organize scrimmage games. In order to decrease injuries during practice, he devised the tackling dummy. He also was the first to add numbers to the jerseys worn by his players. As a coach, Stagg was noted for his intensity. Occasionally, he would even suit up and illustrate for his players the way he wished them to block and tackle. "No coach ever won a game by what he knows," he observed. "It's what his players have learned."

Stagg coached in the era in which professional football first emerged and was in its infancy. As his University of Chicago football program became renowned nationwide, he seized on the idea to commercialize the sport. In this regard, he and the university's president, William Rainey Harper, served to transform football from an intercollegiate pastime to a high-profile, moneymaking industry. In their wake, for better or worse, universities came to be defined by the success or failure of their football programs. Stagg also was a crafty recruiter of athletic talent. In 1902 he established the University of Chicago interscholastic, a national track-and-field tournament for high school students—an event that served to acquaint him with the country's top scholastic athletes, whom he then could entice to enter his athletic program.

At the University of Chicago, Stagg amassed a 268–141 record and earned six Big Ten conference titles, along with a tie for a seventh crown. Upon his retirement in 1932 at the age of seventy—when his football program was in the process of deteriorating—he moved on to coach at the College of the Pacific. At the end of the decade, the University of Chicago decided to close down its varsity football program. However, its unofficial demise came in 1938, when it was blanked 32–0 by a rising football power from California: Stagg's College of the Pacific team.

Stagg was eighty-four years old when he retired from the College of the Pacific in 1946. Incredibly, the following year, he became an assistant coach at Susquehanna College in Selinsgrove, Pennsylvania, working under his son, Amos Alonzo Stagg Jr. The younger Stagg coached at Susquehanna between 1935 and 1954; his father remained at the school for six seasons. Stagg Sr. did not officially retire until 1960, when he was ninety-eight years old. During his career he guided his teams to 314 victories, which ranks third among major college coaches, behind Glenn "Pop" Warner's 319 wins and Paul "Bear" Bryant's 323. (Division I-AA Grambling's Eddie Robinson is the all-time National Collegiate Athletic Association (NCAA) leader, with 408.)

Stagg was the first individual inducted into the College Football Hall of Fame as both a player and a coach and was cited as coach of the all-time Big Ten team. Across the land, high schools and athletic facilities are named for him, including those at the schools in which he coached. Each year the American Football Coaches Association hands out the Amos Alonzo Stagg Award, honoring "the individual, group or institution whose services have been outstanding in the advancement of the best interests of football."

Rob Edelman

SEE ALSO: *Bryant, Paul "Bear"; College Football.*

BIBLIOGRAPHY

Considine, Bob. *The Unreconstructed Amateur: A Pictorial Biography of Amos Alonzo Stagg.* San Francisco: Amos Alonzo Stagg Foundation, 1962.

Lester, Robin. *Stagg's University: The Rise, Decline & Fall of Big-Time Football at Chicago.* Urbana: University of Illinois Press, 1999.

Lucia, Ellis. *Mr. Football: Amos Alonzo Stagg.* South Brunswick, NJ: A. S. Barnes, 1970.

Stallone, Sylvester *(1946–)*

The most pervasive action star of the 1970s and the 1980s, Sylvester Stallone became renowned for his depictions of inarticulate, larger-than-life heroes, most notably the lovable pugilist Rocky Balboa and the alienated Vietnam War veteran John Rambo. A creative dynamo, he wrote, directed, or produced many of the movies in which he appeared. He also became a favorite target of critics, who took aim at the overt sentimentality of the formulaic *Rocky* sequels and at the revisionist politics of the *Rambo* series. Yet Stallone triumphed with audiences to become one of the biggest movie stars in the world.

Not coincidentally, the Hollywood anomaly rose to fame in the shadow of the Watergate scandal. Amid the cynicism of the 1970s, moviegoers flocked to *Rocky*, the uplifting 1976 saga of the Philadelphia southpaw, also known as the Italian Stallion, who inadvertently gets a shot at the title. The sleeper hit made its screenwriter-star the year's most talked-about talent.

AN UNDERDOG STORY

Like his character Rocky Balboa, whose saga was underscored by the line "his whole life was a million-to-one shot," Michael Sylvester Stallone was an unlikely contender for success. A native of Hell's Kitchen, New York, he was born with droopy eyes and slurred speech, the result of a forceps injury. His childhood and adolescence were troubled; growing up in a broken home, he had behavioral problems that resulted in frequent expulsion. By the age of fifteen, he had attended roughly a dozen schools. He was a good athlete, and after graduating from a high school for troubled youth, he won a scholarship to the American College in Switzerland. He then studied dramatics at the University of Miami and was just a few credits shy of graduating when he moved to New York.

Sylvester Stallone. *Sylvester Stallone served as both director and star of the 2010 film* The Expendables. MILENNIUM FILMS/THE KOBAL COLLECTION.

Stallone once described his earliest efforts in show business as "off the wall." Indeed, he costarred in the 1970 soft-core adult movie, *A Party at Kitty and Studs*, which was later re-released as *The Italian Stallion*, and he appeared nude in several off-off-Broadway plays. In 1974 he made his mainstream movie debut in *The Lords of Flatbush*, a 1950s-era look at Brooklyn buddies who form a gang. Roles in *Capone*, Woody Allen's *Bananas*, and *Death Race 2000* followed, but his career remained in stasis.

Stallone was thirty years old with a pregnant wife and $106 in the bank when he happened to see a closed-circuit prize fight between Muhammad Ali and Chuck Wepner, a long shot who thrilled the crowd by holding his own. Over the next three days, he wrote his screenplay about Rocky Balboa, who squares off against champion Apollo Creed. By the fight's end, Rocky has not only won respect but also the love of the shy, bespectacled Adrian, who works in a pet shop. The producers, Irwin Winkler and Robert Chartoff, initially envisioned the script as a vehicle for a leading actor such as Robert Redford or Al Pacino, but Stallone refused to sell it unless he could also star.

THE FIRST OF ITS KIND

Filmed over twenty-eight days for $960,000, *Rocky* became the year's top-grossing movie and won the Academy Award for Best Picture. Its ten nominations also included those for Best Actor and Best Original Screenplay, putting Stallone in prestigious company—at that time the dual honor had previously been bestowed only on Charlie Chaplin for *The Great Dictator* and Orson Welles for *Citizen Kane*. Of his watershed movie Stallone once said, "It was never a script about boxing. It was always about a man simply fighting for his dignity. People require symbols of humanity and heroism."

With its prolonged training sequences and publicity about Stallone's own bodybuilding regimen, *Rocky* also evoked the benefits of health and fitness, foreshadowing the fitness movement of the 1980s. Much of the Stallone oeuvre has celebrated physicality. The five *Rocky* movies have all included a rigorous workout sequence. With their loving close-ups of the title character's rippling pectorals and abs, the four *Rambo* movies (1982, 1985, 1988, and 2008) are as much a paean to the body beautiful as they are about the adventures of a modern-day warrior. Moreover, it was under Stallone's supervision that actor John Travolta resculpted his body to sinewy perfection for the 1983 movie *Staying Alive*, which Stallone directed, cowrote, and coproduced.

Stallone has said that as a teenager he was inspired to body build after watching the gladiator movies of Steve Reeves; doubtless, teenagers of the 1970s and 1980s were similarly inspired by Stallone. His fixation on body image persisted into Stallone's later years and even proved to be a source of controversy in 2007, when the star was caught in Australia with prohibited human growth hormones—a supplement that had supposed "fountain-of-youth" benefits.

Stallone's movies certainly impacted the action-adventure arena—particularly *Rambo: First Blood Part II*, the 1985 sequel to *First Blood* (1982). In fact, *Rambo II* (as it was also called) redefined the genre, using elements that became staples of action-adventure films. Among them are a visceral style, minimal dialogue, a ticking clock that gives the protagonist limited time to carry out his covert mission, and the scenes of the hero readying for war. Because the plot took the disenchanted veteran back to Vietnam to rescue forgotten American prisoners of war and because Rambo asks, "Sir, do we get to win this time?" critics and commentators assailed the movie for rewriting history. They also took personal aim at the star-cowriter, noting that, like John Wayne, also famed for his patriotic alter egos, Stallone had managed to elude real-life military service. *Rambo* proved critic-proof, however, touching a responsive chord that transcended language and cultural barriers.

A ROCKY TRANSITION

Stallone—or "Sly," as he is called—shrewdly parlayed his 1980s-era power into deals that included creative control and the highest salaries of the day. His celebrity was further amplified by his colorful personal life, which has included a string of public romances and marital woes. In the 1990s, however, as the action arena sought new directions, his career waned. He tried playing against type in several comedies that failed. More successful, though, was his turn as a paunchy, lonely sheriff in the 1997 crime drama *Cop Land*. It was widely publicized that Stallone had gained 40 pounds for the role. It seemed, however, that the career, not the man, needed redefinition; many of Stallone's late 1990s and first decade of the 2000s films were met with little enthusiasm.

Although Stallone's career had stalled in transition, there was no denying his charisma and star quality or the crowd-pleasing appeal of his most famous creations, *Rocky* and *Rambo*. In 2006 he returned to *Rocky* series for the sixth time with *Rocky Balboa*, and in 2008 he revisited the *Rambo* story line for a fourth installment. While neither of the sequels was embraced with the excitement of the originals, both were well received by fans and critics alike. Among his other successful ventures was the 2010 film *The Expendables*, for which Stallone is credited as lead actor, writer, and director. The star-packed action film marked his best opening box-office numbers and has perhaps set the multitalented star up for yet another successful franchise run.

Pat H. Broeske

SEE ALSO: *Academy Awards; Ali, Muhammad; Allen, Woody; Blockbusters; Bodybuilding; Boxing; Capone, Al; Chaplin, Charlie;* Citizen Kane*; Hollywood; Movie Stars; Pacino, Al; Pornography; Rambo; Redford, Robert; Reeves, Steve;* Rocky*; Travolta, John; Vietnam; Watergate; Wayne, John; Welles, Orson.*

BIBLIOGRAPHY

Broeske, Pat H. "Sly Stallone's Rocky Road." *Washington Post*, May 22, 1985, F1, F4.

Broeske, Pat H. "The Curious Evolution of John Rambo." *Los Angeles Times*, October 27, 1985, 32–38.

Daly, Marsha. *Sylvester Stallone: An Illustrated Life*. New York: St. Martin Press, 1984.

Rovin, Jeff. *Stallone! A Hero's Story*. New York: Pocket Books, 1985.

Sackett, Susan. *The Hollywood Reporter Book of Box Office Hits*. New York: Billboard Books, 1990.

Sanello, Frank. *Stallone: A Rocky Life*. Edinburgh: Mainstream Publishing, 1998.

Stand and Deliver

Stand and Deliver (1988) is a movie about mathematics—yes, mathematics. It also features a most unusual movie hero: an educator. Yet this independently produced drama is as riveting and satisfying as the most cleverly plotted, edge-of-your-seat thriller. It is the fact-based story of Jaime Escalante, a math teacher in an East Los Angeles barrio high school, brought brilliantly to life by Hispanic actor Edward James Olmos in an Oscar-nominated performance. Engaging, affecting, and inspirational, the film gave Escalante's philosophy and methods wide popular exposure, exercising a positive influence on American attitudes to education culture among those who saw it.

Jaime Escalante transformed a classroom of potential dropouts into calculus wizards, and *Stand and Deliver* shows how he did it. In so doing, the film's title takes on extra resonance. The phrase "stand and deliver" (originally a military term) has come to define how a person—any person—is capable of succeeding if he or she works hard, stands tall, and presents him or herself positively and intelligently. On-screen, the bespectacled educator's nondescript, slightly paunchy appearance in no way obscures his extreme intensity and his dedication to his job, and he wins the attention of his charges by the sheer force of his enthusiasm for his subject and his ability to communicate it.

Several of Escalante's students start off as underachievers. A few are nice enough youngsters but are destined never to progress beyond serving fast food or stocking shelves in a supermarket. Others are Hispanic "dead-end kids," macho punks with boulder-sized chips on their shoulders. Under Escalante's patient and gifted tutelage, eighteen students learn the intricacies of calculus and take an extremely difficult advanced placement exam. Each and every one passes the test. However, the story of *Stand and Deliver* begins only when this success is tainted by a charge of cheating, leading to an invalidation of the test results.

Stand and Deliver (the prerelease title was *Walking on Water*) is a multithemed film, at once a tale of institutional racism and false accusation and an allegory of how an individual can accomplish a task through sheer willpower. In its most incisive scenes, director Ramón Menéndez, who wrote the script with Tom Musca, tellingly conveys how youthful minds and spirits can be dulled by parents who quash their children's natural eagerness for knowledge. Ultimately, it is Escalante, always aware of the pressures in their lives, who pushes, manipulates, cajoles, and hustles the kids—and gets results.

At the heart of *Stand and Deliver* is the wonderfully lively and expressive acting of Olmos. His performance is crammed with keenly observed inflections and mannerisms. As Olmos explained while promoting the film prior to its release:

> When we see a film like *Rocky*, we see an Anglo in a boxing ring. I'd say about 98 per cent of us, black, white or Hispanic, will never step in a boxing ring. But imagine how people must feel when they see a film set in a classroom—a place where everybody has been. Everyone has at one point or another sat behind a desk, and everyone knows that calculus is hard. But in this movie, you realize that calculus really isn't that hard—if you have an exceptional teacher.

Most of the real-life Escalante's calculus prodigies went on to complete college. When the film was released, several were in graduate school, and one had even joined Escalante as a colleague. "You can get anything you want in this country, as long as you are willing to pay the price and the price is right," Escalante declared, nine years after his story was told on-screen. "You don't get anything unless you work for it." He also stressed that schools alone cannot be responsible for educating children, noting that he prescribes the "Three Ts" to parents: Tell your kid, 'I love you'; touch your kid; and time. "It is important to devote time to your kid. The best investment you can make in your kid is time."

Escalante, who was a fervent advocate of English-only education for Hispanics, moved to his native Bolivia in 2001 and taught at the Universidad del Valle in Cochabamba, his wife's hometown. By the end of the decade, he was battling bladder cancer and returned to California. He died on March 30, 2010.

Rob Edelman

SEE ALSO: *Academy Awards; Bilingual Education; Olmos, Edward James.*

BIBLIOGRAPHY

Byers, Ann. *Jaime Escalante: Sensational Teacher*. Springfield, NJ: Enslow Publishers, 1996.

Mathews, Jay. *Escalante: The Best Teacher in America*. New York: Holt, 1988.

Standardized Testing

Despite a long-standing tradition in many cultures around the world, standardized testing remains a topic of heated debate in education circles. While some say it fosters teaching to the test, others say it helps establish baseline standards for students and teachers. For most Americans, such testing begins in kindergarten and continues through college.

Administered and scored in a consistent or "standard" manner, standardized tests offer educators a way to assess a student's level of achievement relative to his or her peers. In the United States students are given a variety of standardized tests by the time they reach high school, which often consist of multiple-choice, essay, and true-false questions. The tests are sometimes taken with pencil and paper and other times administered by a computer and are generally scored by a computer to reduce the margin of error. However, essay questions are graded by a trained professional using a rubric. Because schools across the country vary greatly in teaching style, student demographics, and socioeconomic factors, standardized assessment serves to offer an equitable measure of aptitude, though critics of the method argue that the racial and ethnic disparities in test scores are a result of tests being designed for white middle-class students whose native language is English.

KINDERGARTEN THROUGH UNIVERSITY

At the beginning of the twentieth century, standardized testing was developed as a way to bar racial and ethnic minorities from colleges and the U.S. military. The tests were skewed, asking questions that only white-middle class Americans would know and poor immigrants with few or no English skills could not answer. In 1917 the Army Mental Tests were developed, which imposed quotas on immigrants entering the United States.

Since then standardized tests have evolved to measure the performance of students in the classroom in order to help them succeed. At the elementary-school level, students take a variety of assessments, including the Iowa Test of Basic Skills and STAR Early Literacy assessment. The two required exams are the National Assessment of Educational Progress (NAEP) and a state-specific assessment. A congressionally mandated test developed in 1964 and administered by the National Center for Education Statistics, NAEP tests fourth, eighth, and twelfth graders in a variety of subjects, including reading, writing, arithmetic, U.S. history, civics, and music. Tests are scored around demographics such as socioeconomic status, gender, and race rather than individual test takers or schools. State achievement tests are required by the No Child Left Behind Act (NCLB), and each state must administer an assessment in basic subjects such as arithmetic, reading, and writing in order to receive federal funding. Passed in 2001 during George W. Bush's presidency, NCLB was a hot-button issue and has continued to fuel controversy. Proponents argued that the goal was to improve the quality of education by tying performance to funding and increasing instruction of the core academic subjects: science, math, reading, and writing. However, critics point out that states can create their own tests and make them easier to improve the states' scores. Also, many schools have decreased the amount of art, music, language, and history instruction in order to spend more time on core subjects.

High school students are also required to take NAEP and a state-produced assessment and must take either the SAT (formerly the Scholastic Aptitude Test) or the ACT (originally American College Testing) in order to apply for college. Taken by over 1.6 million students in 2011, the SAT was developed in 1926 for use in college admissions and tests students in three subjects: mathematics, critical reading, and writing. In 1959 the ACT was created as a competitor to the SAT, consisting of English, Mathematics, Science Reasoning, and Reading and Writing categories. Students can also take the Advanced Placement (AP) exams. Developed to help students skip introductory classes when they enroll in college, AP exams are graded on a scale of 1 to 5, and students with a score of at least 3 or 4 are eligible for college credit in that subject. There are concerns that high school students should be concentrating on high school rather than college-level coursework, and over half of students who take the AP exam are white, indicating that the coursework required before taking the test may not be accessible to minorities.

At the college level, standardized tests become more degree specific. The MCAT (Medical College Admissions Test) contains curriculum-based questions on biology, chemistry, and physics, while the LSAT (Law School Admissions Test) assesses the reading comprehension, logical, and verbal reasoning skills of prospective law students. Also, the GRE (Graduate Record Examination) and GMAT (Graduate Management Admissions Test) are given to students applying to graduate-level programs.

VARIOUS FORMATS

Many tests contain some combination of math and verbal questions (analogies, sentence completions, and critical reading passages), while others includeanalytic questions. Program-specific assessments such the MCAT include curriculum-based questions All standardized tests used to be taken with a pencil and paper. However, by the 1990s, the GRE and GMAT were administered only by computer, in a format called "computer adaptive testing," or CAT. The CAT format redefines *standardized* as the computer program adapts each time the examinee gets a question right or wrong by following correct answers with more difficult questions and incorrect responses with easier questions. It is therefore possible that no two test takers will take the exact same standardized test.

IMPLICATIONS

Standardized testing has become a controversial issue in the twenty-first century as high school students struggle to get into good colleges. Student loans are linked to test scores, and by 2012 many graduating students have found themselves graduating with a significant amount of debt and no job. As college admissions to elite schools have gotten more competitive and student loans have become linked to standardized test scores, some parents have started to track their kids' educational future at the elementary-school level.

A sharp critique leveled against standardized testing is the degree to which it encourages "teaching to the test." Another contention is that scores correlate with the income and education of the tester's parents. College Board data show that those taking the SAT can expect to score about thirty points higher for every $10,000 in their parents' yearly income. For many years the median score for African Americans on the SAT has been 200 points below that of whites, and females have traditionally scored thirty-five points lower on the math sections than males. In 1996 SAT scores were "recentered" to address the implications of various scoring disparities and create a better distribution of scores around the test's numerical midpoint. This boosted the average scores for groups like African Americans and Hispanics.

Advocates of standardized testing argue that rather than grades which are assigned by individual teachers and can include personal bias, these assessment results can be empirically documented. This makes the scores more reliable when trying to compare students at the same grade-level or age nationwide. They also argue that test scores hold schools and teachers more accountable for student performance and give teachers valuable information, showing them where students need help so teachers can alter their teaching style in order to help students achieve success.

Karen Lurie

SEE ALSO: *Ivy League.*

BIBLIOGRAPHY

Berry, Barnett. *Teaching 2030: What We Must Do for Our Students and Our Public Schools: Now and in the Future.* New York: Teachers College Press, 2011.

Finkel, Ed. "Gearing Up for the New Assessment: The Next Generation of Standardized Testing Will Focus on Critical Thinking Skills." *District Administration* 46, no. 7 (2010).

Lemann, Nicholas. *The Big Test: The Secret History of the American Meritocracy.* New York: Farrar, Straus & Giroux, 1999.

Lewin, Tamar. "Math Scores Show No Gap for Girls, Study Finds." *New York Times,* July 25, 2008.

Murray, David W. "The War against Testing." *Commentary,* September 1998, 34.

Phelps, Richard P., Herbert J. Valberg, and J. E. Stone. *Kill the Messenger: The War on Standardized Testing.* Piscataway, NJ: Transaction Publishers, 2005.

Smith, Andrew Lee. "A Study of the Relationship between School Culture and Standardized Test Scores." Boca Raton, FL: Dissertation.com, 2006.

Stecher, Brian M., Laura Hamilton, and Steven P. Klein. *Making Sense of Test-based Accountability in Education.* San Diego: Rand Publishing, 2002.

United States Department of Education. "Race to the Top Fund." Accessed March 2012. Available from http://www2.ed.gov/programs/racetothetop/index.html

Wiliam, Dylan. "Standardized Testing and School Accountability." *Educational Psychologist* 45, no. 2 (2010).

Zenderland, Leila. *Measuring Minds: Henry Herbert Goddard and the Origins of American Intelligence Testing.* New York: Cambridge University Press, 1998.

Stand-Up Comedy

Born in the smoky halls of turn-of-the-twentieth-century vaudeville and thrust into mainstream American culture by the advent of radio and television, stand-up comedy is the entertainment industry's most accurate social thermometer. From Milton Berle to Ellen DeGeneres, comics have used the power of laughter to challenge Americans to face the controversial issues of the day, whether they involve sex, government, or religion. A good routine can turn the most tragic headlines into a gut-wrenching guffaw. Sometimes comics go too far for a laugh; sometimes they are the only ones brave enough to point out hypocrisy and social injustice.

VAUDEVILLE DAYS

The profession developed long before the discovery of electricity. Court jesters performed the first stand-up routines in medieval times. Elements of stand-up also pervaded William Shakespeare's work in the form of a fool providing the audience with a dose of comic relief. Nineteenth-century American humorists such as Mark Twain did their work on paper. The twentieth century ushered in the age of performance. Vaudeville, a precur-

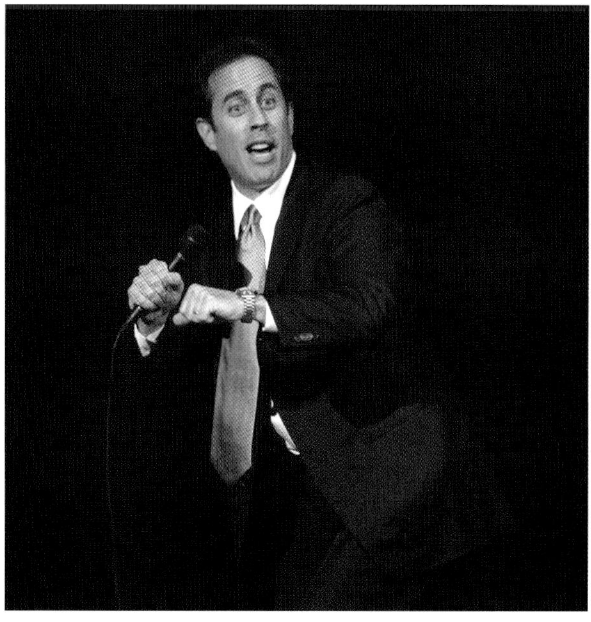

Jerry Seinfeld Performs. *Jerry Seinfeld performs his stand-up routine at Carnegie Hall in 2001.* KMAZUR/WIREIMAGE/GETTY IMAGES.

sor to the television variety show, provided a stage for the first generation of stand-up comedians such as Bob Hope, Jack Benny, George Burns and Gracie Allen, and Bud Abbott and Lou Costello.

In Oscar Hammerstein's Victoria Theatre, opened in Times Square in 1899, or the Palace Theatre, opened on Broadway and 47th Street in 1913, you could find singing women (Sophie Tucker, Nora Bayes, Elsie Janis), monologists (Berle, Julius Tannen), the earliest comedy teams (Burns and Allen), and an assortment of freak acts. This was nothing like the high-profile comedy showcases that would come later in the century, filled with Hollywood agents and television scouts. These variety shows were for the masses, which is why the young Berle, the brilliant monologist, might find himself on the same stage as the Armless Lutz Brothers, who could assemble a car with only their feet.

The foundations of stand-up were laid in the age of vaudeville, with terms such as the *one-liner* and *straight man* entering the lexicon. Comics also developed different styles, deciding whether to space out laughs, build elaborate routines, or just deliver the punch lines. Legendary society columnist Walter Winchell dubbed Henny Youngman the "King of the One-Liners." Youngman relied on vivid imagery in his jokes. "If a joke is too hard to visualize . . . then what the hell good is it?" he asked in his autobiography, *Take My Life, Please!* "I tell easy jokes where people don't have to think." His clear and concise one-liners continue to amuse: "I'm so old that when I order a three-minute egg here, they make me pay up front" or "A guy came up to me and said he'd bet me fifty dollars that I was dead. I was afraid to take the bet."

Burns and Allen became the first great comedy team. Making their debut in Newark, New Jersey, Burns cast himself as the joke man, with Allen delivering the straight lines. A funny thing happened: Allen got all the laughs. Burns rewrote the show and made himself the straight man. With the new formula, the couple continued to get laughs for years. One example of how Burns highlighted Allen's humor follows:

GRACIE: Where do you keep your money?

GEORGE: In the bank.

GRACIE: What interest do you get?

GEORGE: Four percent.

GRACIE: Ha! I get eight.

GEORGE: You get eight?

GRACIE: I keep it in two banks.

The vaudeville generation made a natural transition to the next stage of stand-up: radio and television. Burns and Allen debuted on radio in 1932 with *The Adventures of Gracie* (later renamed *Burns and Allen* [1932–1950]) and then moved to television with *The George Burns and Gracie Allen Show* in 1950 for another eight years. On the small screen, Burns would often talk to the viewing audience, dropping all pretenses that the program they were watching was in fact reality. Called "breaking the fourth wall," this method would be practiced years later by another former stand-up, Garry Shandling, in the 1980s.

Berle became known as "Mr. Television" because of his popular variety show, *The Texaco Star Theater*, which ran from 1948 to 1956. Abbott and Costello, before trying television and the big screen, debuted their famous "Who's on First?" routine on radio in 1938. As the people of vaudeville moved to radio, film, and television, these new media soon eclipsed vaudeville, which disappeared by the 1940s.

THE NIGHTCLUB CIRCUIT

Without the vaudeville stage to help hone their acts, stand-up comedians turned to strip clubs and the growing nightclub circuit. The new clubs proved fertile ground for comedians such as Bob Newhart, Woody Allen, Bill Cosby, and Lenny Bruce. No longer forced to shout over a rowdy audience riled by dancing girls or fish-swallowing Swedes, comics could develop stories for their acts in the more controlled atmosphere of these new venues. While one-liners still ruled many acts, younger comics worked to draw the audience into a "bit" that might run for twenty minutes—about the same amount of time it took Youngman to blast through a few dozen punch lines.

At the forefront of the movement stood Bruce, the comic philosopher. One of the first truly controversial stand-ups, he used vivid, sometimes obscene, language and sexually charged subject matter. Unlike comics who used profanity and went "blue" for cheap laughs, Bruce's monologues spoke to the simmering social war, the contrast between the emerging hipster cool and the prosperous, conservative, postwar America. At the time, communists—in Asia and in Hollywood—were under attack, and Pat Boone, the five-cent hamburger, and nondescript but affordable subdivisions were embraced. Into this cultural milieu came Bruce—a barely concealed heroin addict—with his thirst for controversial talk about race, censorship, and sex. "Show me the average sex maniac, the one who takes your eight-year-old, schtupps her in the parking lot, and then kills her, and I'll show you a guy who's had a good religious upbringing," went one of his routines. "You see, he saw his father or mother always telling his sister to cover up her body when she was only six years old, and so he figured, one day I'm going to find out what it is she's covering, and if it's as dirty as my father says I'll kill it."

Allen benefited from the nightclub scene as much as Bruce did. Though he went on to become one of stand-up's greatest success stories, Allen would never have made it in the vaudeville era. His quiet delivery with its intentional half-stutter would have been drowned out after the first few rows of a burlesque hall. In a nightclub world he was a headliner, known for his satiric stories and willingness to poke fun at himself, using his noodly, bookish physique to his advantage. Onstage Allen carved out a niche as the lovable schlemiel, an intellectual comic who referenced philosophers, shrinks, and college. He would tell long stories, presented as autobiographical. But somewhere before the punch line, an absurd twist would let the audience in on the tall tale; their comedic confessor was in fact a master yarn spinner.

Not interested in radio, and frustrated by the constraints of television, many among Allen's generation tapped into the growing comedy album industry. The 1960s and 1970s were a golden age for the comedy record, starting with Newhart's million-selling 1960 release *The Button-Down Mind of Bob Newhart*. For racier comics—George Carlin, Richard Pryor, and Eddie Murphy, in particular—comedy records would prove invaluable, enabling them to use hot material that would either not be allowed on television or have to be softened for the viewing audience.

PUSHING BOUNDARIES

Sparked by the general loosening of social rules brought on by the sexual revolution and youth-oriented civil rights and antiwar movements, stand-up comedy continued to push boundaries in the 1970s. Stuffy network executives were often tested or outright mocked, as in Carlin's famous "seven words you can never say on television." Female comics also began to get more stage time, in particular Lily Tomlin, Gilda Radner, and Joan Rivers. It was not until the 1980s, when Roseanne Barr (briefly Arnold when she was married) developed a successful sitcom out of her stage act, that female comics made a true mark in the male-dominated industry. *Saturday Night Live*, created in 1975, offered exposure to stand-up comics such as Carlin, Pryor, and Steve Martin, who served as guest hosts.

The 1970s generation included two of the more important comedians in Pryor and Andy Kaufman. Pryor grew up in a poor, black neighborhood; Kaufman was white and from Long Island. But they shared a thirst for original and unpredictable behavior, both onstage and off, leaving audiences and critics wondering where the act ended and reality began.

Kaufman did not just tell jokes. He wrestled with women onstage; slipped into a bad toupee to play the lounge lizard, Tony Clifton; and, according to legend, read *The Great Gatsby* in its entirety to an audience in Iowa. (On another occasion, after being asked to stop reading, Kaufman agreed and instead put on a record—of him reading *The Great Gatsby*.) He had the talent to succeed with more conventional fare: his "Foreign Man" character was adapted as Latka Gravas for the popular television series *Taxi*; his Elvis impersonation was so hilarious the pop band R.E.M. centered its 1992 Kaufman tribute, "Man on the Moon," around it.

But Kaufman preferred to push his act into performance art territory. On *Late Night with David Letterman*, he and professional wrestler Jerry Lawler appeared to get into a genuine argument, ending with Lawler slapping the comedian off his chair. The Clifton routine could run for a half hour, with Kaufman—as Clifton—growing angry at the suggestion that he was simply doing an impression. "Listen, folks, what I'm doing up here—that's how I make my living," Clifton would yell. "I don't have to take this kind of crap!" For several years he became so consumed by professional wrestling that his friend, comedian Robin Williams, noticed during lunch that Kaufman was wearing trunks under his clothing. When Kaufman died of cancer in 1984, many wondered whether it was the ultimate put-on.

Pryor was equally unpredictable. The most important black comics who preceded him, Cosby and Flip Wilson, tended to be nonconfrontational and television-ready. Dick Gregory's biting routines were political instead of personal and less effective in the postactivist climate of the 1970s. Pryor was unique in that he based his act on common black experience in America. He grew up poor, in a world of pimps, wife beaters, and poolroom hustlers.

Even as he became one of Hollywood's most bankable comic stars, Pryor remained erratic, cursing, yelling, and storming off the stage when he did not feel right. On *The Tonight Show*, he suggested to the studio audience: "If you want to do anything—if you're black and still here in America—get a gun and go to South Africa and kill some white people." He also bared his soul. In 1980, after setting himself on fire while free-basing cocaine, Pryor worked it into his routine. His red-hot stage show paved the way for the generation of black comics that would include Murphy, Martin Lawrence, and Chris Rock. His sexually oriented material also led to the one-dimensional smut routine of Andrew Dice Clay.

THE BOOM YEARS

The success of the late 1970s and early 1980s comics led to a boom in the stand-up business. Clubs opened, comedy specials were produced for cable television, John Belushi and Dan Aykroyd's Blues Brothers act toured the country playing rhythm and blues, and Sam Kinison's manic rerecording of "Wild Thing" climbed the Billboard charts. But, in the 1990s, the inevitable crash came when headliners moved on to television or films and left behind a glut of second- and third-rate comedians. Nearly 5,000 comedians were listed by *Comedy USA*, the bible of stand-up comedy, in the mid-1990s, and there were fewer stages for them to work: the 450 clubs registered in 1991 had dwindled to 350 by the middle of the decade.

The scene was unforgiving, as described by Neil Strauss of the *New York Times* in 1999: "The bottom rung of the comedy ladder can be uglier, crueler and more demeaning than in any other line of entertainment—be it actor, model, musician, writer or clown. Sexism and racism run rampant, club-owners ask struggling comedians to scrape gum off the bottom of tables to get a booking, competition between comics is fierce, and newcomers have to pay to perform."

In a way, stand-up comedy had returned to the days of vaudeville, when Burns and Allen were competing against acrobats or dancing dwarfs. And the sheer volume of comics led to an important development: the rise of the alternative stand-up scene. At places such as the Velveeta Room in Austin, Texas, comics did not dare trot out stand-up's war horses—jokes about mothers-in-law, terrible airplane flights, or the single life. With an audience packed mainly with other comics, the performers retired well-worn bits for fresher, more experimental material. That could be, as Strauss noted, a struggling comic delivering her monologue with her pants at her ankles or a male comic acting out how a cat feels.

As the comedy club declined in the late 1990s, stand-up grew even more pervasive. Bill Maher's *Politically Incorrect*, which featured four different roundtable guests each night, was hailed as one of the freshest TV talk shows. Books by Dennis Miller, Paul Reiser, and Martin—among others—climbed the *New York Times* best-seller list. Even CBS news, launching the *60 Minutes II* newsmagazine, chose a Boston stand-up, Jimmy Tingle, to offer a commentary at the end of each program. Jerry Seinfeld, after deciding to retire his groundbreaking television sitcom, took his stand-up routine back on the road.

The first decade of the 2000s saw a wide range of comedic styles being performed. Louis C.K. specialized in routines that articulated the things that most parents and spouses did not dare to say, such as "I want to throw my baby in the trash." DeGeneres perfected a quirky observational humor that was often gentler than the usual stand-up fare. In contrast, Jon Stewart delivered scathing political satire, and Ricky Gervais lampooned the entertainment industry, going so far as to shock the celebrity audience with his needling remarks during his stint as host of the Golden Globes in 2011.

The proliferation of cable stations, which were generally more permissive than the networks, gave comedians new places to perform besides clubs. Some stations were dedicated to comedy, most notably Comedy Central. Featuring shows such as

"Premium Blend," which styled its format on a condensed stand-up routine, the network helped launch the careers of Demetri Martin, Mitch Hedberg, Daniel Tosh, and Dane Cook.

Martin's style involved a bit of prop-comic antics mixed with Steven Wright's deadpan delivery. Using a large sketch pad and musical instruments, he typically offered a colorful examination of a single theme, such as power, money, and love. Tosh made his career by pushing the envelope of political correctness. At times seemingly misogynist or homophobic, his observational humor relied on stereotypes and was the foundation of his highly successful stand-up routines and TV show, *Tosh.0*. Cook's storytelling and physical humor retained hints of Williams and established himself as one of the most successful comedians of his generation. Well-established performers such as David Cross and Dave Chappelle continued performing stand-up in addition to, and in spite of, their enormous TV success. Comedy specials helped move stand-up comics from dark clubs into living rooms, and sketch comedy shows provided the perfect foil to promote their various stand-up tours and records.

Not much changed on the front lines, however. In comedy clubs all across America, managers continued to strain to make money on unknowns. Drink minimums kept crowds unruly and joke-hungry. Entertainers exposed themselves, under the glare of the klieg light, defended by only a microphone and every rage, fear, and insecurity that might be cashed in for a laugh. It had been this way since Berle's day, and there was never a shortage of young comics vying for that chance to deliver the perfect punch line. Because, as Steve Allen wrote in his book, *Funny People*, "Without laughter, life on our planet would be intolerable."

Geoff Edgers

SEE ALSO: *Abbott and Costello; Allen, Steve; Allen, Woody; Aykroyd, Dan; Belushi, John; Benny, Jack; Berle, Milton; The Blues Brothers; Boone, Pat; Broadway; Bruce, Lenny; Burns, George, and Gracie Allen; Cable TV; Carlin, George; Carson, Johnny; Chappelle, Dave; Cosby, Bill; DeGeneres, Ellen; Gervais, Ricky; Hollywood; Hope, Bob;* It's Garry Shandling's Show*; Kaufman, Andy; Kinison, Sam; Letterman, David; Martin, Steve; Murphy, Eddie; Newhart, Bob; Presley, Elvis; Pryor, Richard; Radio; Radner, Gilda; R.E.M.; Rivers, Joan; Rock, Chris;* Roseanne*;* Saturday Night Live*;* Seinfeld*;* Taxi*; Television; Tomlin, Lily;* The Tonight Show*; Vaudeville; Williams, Robin; Wilson, Flip; Winchell, Walter; Youngman, Henny.*

BIBLIOGRAPHY

Allen, Steve. *Funny People*. New York: Stein & Day, 1981.

Bruce, Lenny. *How to Talk Dirty and Influence People*. New York: Simon & Schuster, 1992.

Gottfried, Martin. *George Burns and the Hundred-Year Dash*. New York: Simon & Schuster, 1996.

Knoedelseder, William. *I'm Dying up Here: Heartbreak and High Times in Stand-Up Comedy's Golden Era*. New York: Public Affairs, 2009.

Leno, Jay, and Bill Zehme. *Leading with My Chin*. New York: HarperCollins, 1996.

Pryor, Richard, and Todd Gold. *Pryor Convictions and Other Life Sentences*. New York: Pantheon Books, 1995.

Slide, Anthony. *The Encyclopedia of Vaudeville*. Westport, CT: Greenwood Press, 1994.

Tafoya, Eddie. *The Legacy of the Wisecrack: Stand-Up Comedy as the Great American Literary Form*. Boca Raton, FL: Brown-Walker Press, 2009.

Youngman, Henny, and Neal Karlen. *Take My Life, Please!* New York: William Morrow, 1991.

Zoglin, Richard. *Comedy at the Edge: How Stand-Up in the 1970s Changed America*. New York: Bloomsbury USA, 2008.

The Stanley Brothers

During the late 1940s the Stanley Brothers (Carter, 1925–1966, and Ralph, 1927–) and their band, the Clinch Mountain Boys, helped establish bluegrass—as Bill Monroe's new style came to be known—as a musical genre. According to folklorist Neil Rosenberg, their 1948 recording of "Molly and Tenbrooks"—featuring Darrell "Pee Wee" Lambert, a tenor singer and mandolin player like Monroe—offers the first proof that Monroe's sound was being copied by other groups. Merging the old-time sound of traditional mountain music, haunting vocal harmonies, and bluegrass instrumentation, the early recordings of the Stanley Brothers have become bluegrass classics.

When lead singer Carter Stanley died in 1966, Ralph took control of the group. He revitalized the band with new members (including Keith Whitley and Ricky Skaggs during the 1970s), and over the next decades they developed and maintained a following among bluegrass and traditional folk fans that continued into the early twenty-first century. Stanley's music gained a wider audience after it was featured in the Coen brothers' film *O Brother, Where Art Thou?* (2000), for which he won his first Grammy Award.

Anna Hunt Graves

SEE ALSO: *Bluegrass; Coen, Joel and Ethan; Monroe, Bill.*

BIBLIOGRAPHY

Artis, Bob. *Bluegrass*. New York: Hawthorn Books, 1975.

Rosenberg, Neil V. *Bluegrass: A History*. Urbana: University of Illinois Press, 1985.

Stanwyck, Barbara *(1907–1990)*

From her modest beginnings as a Broadway chorus girl named Ruby Stevens, Barbara Stanwyck forged a long and versatile career as one of Hollywood's strongest female stars. Her breakthrough performance occurred in 1930's *Ladies of Leisure*, directed by Frank Capra, who said her emotionally charged acting could "grab your heart and tear it to pieces." In her earliest roles she epitomized the self-sacrificing woman, culminating in her title part in the 1937 woman's picture *Stella Dallas*.

The 1940s transformed her into a sexy, ruthless femme fatale. She played the movies' first woman to murder for no reason nobler than avarice in the 1944 seminal film noir *Double Indemnity*. Unlike Bette Davis and Joan Crawford, her peers in melodrama, Stanwyck also made an impression as a comedienne in such canonical romantic comedies as 1941's *Ball of Fire* and

The Lady Eve. Her image, on-screen and off, as a tough, independent woman overcoming a hardscrabble childhood is her legacy.

Elizabeth Haas

SEE ALSO: *Broadway; Capra, Frank; Crawford, Joan; Davis, Bette;* Double Indemnity; *Film Noir; Hollywood; Screwball Comedies.*

BIBLIOGRAPHY

DiOrio, Al. *Barbara Stanwyck: A Biography*. New York: Coward-McCann, 1983.

Madsen, Axel. *Stanwyck: A Biography*. New York: HarperCollins, 1995.

Wayne, Jane Ellen. *The Life and Loves of Barbara Stanwyck*. London: JR, 2009.

Star System

With the rise of the Hollywood film industry in the 1920s and thereafter, the world came to recognize that fame, like American automobiles or hot dogs, could also be manufactured and successfully marketed. In a democratic, nominally classless culture, where "personality" provided a vehicle for upward mobility, it came to be increasingly understood that personality required manufacturing and regular maintenance. As a mass movie audience, the anonymous public also began to recognize that many of the most notable people in the world were manufactured, like the movies featuring their close-up faces, in a semi-mythic place called Hollywood. Carefully crafted to complement the technical components of the entertainment industry, the "star system" focused attention of the public onto idealized "picture personalities" that simultaneously embodied familiar social types and represented privileged individuality for their fans.

While American show business, exemplified by early impresarios like P. T. Barnum, Florenz Ziegfeld, and "Buffalo Bill" Cody, had relied upon the promotion of featured "players" throughout the nineteenth century, the construction of a regulated system for the production and promotion of Hollywood stars was designed along the industrial model pioneered by Henry Ford and his Detroit, Michigan, assembly lines. Commercial cinema did not have stars in its early years, not until film producers, perhaps goaded by audiences, came to understand the commercial appeal of specific actors.

BEGINNINGS

Among the first "stars" so identified were Charlie Chaplin, Lillian Gish, Mary Pickford, Douglas Fairbanks Sr., Rudolph Valentino, and Clara Bow. As Hollywood's financial and cultural power grew, it came to heavily depend upon the distinctive charisma of specific actors to promote its product to an adoring audience. Working behind the scenes from the mid-1920s through the 1950s, the Hollywood star system relied on a coordination of working parts that both imitated and rivaled Ford's efficient factories: dance and singing lessons; careful decisions about names, makeup, hair, and clothing; the posing of glamour photographs; carefully chosen publicity appearances; and constructed gossip. Using these tools, the major film studios groomed and marketed their most visible products, the stars whose weekly secular worship sold millions of tickets, fan magazines, and tie-in consumer goods.

Beginning with *Motion Picture* in 1911 and dominated by the long-running *Photoplay*, fan magazines provided the public's key link to the "real lives" of their favorite actors; the construction of an offscreen image for its contract players thus became just as important for the studios as the tailoring of a specific star's screen persona. Fans were hungry for information on the "real" Clark Gable or the "actual" Joan Crawford that supplemented their film roles, and so the star system negotiated a careful balance of identification and adoration. Stars like Judy Garland and Mickey Rooney were kids "just like us" whom fans knew they would never really be.

The underlying tension between studio-controlled information about stars and less-regulated gossip occasionally surfaced when major stars were caught in scandals that threatened to create wide gaps between their on-screen and offscreen images. Shocking trials—featuring beloved comedians such as Chaplin (1943 and 1944) and Roscoe "Fatty" Arbuckle (1921 and 1922) and widespread rumors about the sex lives of Bow or Valentino—redefined the star system's promotional work as crisis management until the industry adoption of the Production Code allowed the studios to fully enforce "morality" clauses in actors' contracts. As far as the film studios were concerned, there was a direct relationship between a star's public behavior and his or her box-office receipt, so controlling the image of contract players was an economic imperative, even if it appeared under the guise of moral guardianship. Only in later decades would serious ethical questions be raised about, for instance, a film studio arranging dates and even a sham marriage for Rock Hudson so that his legions of female fans might not suspect that he was, in fact, a homosexual.

Of course, as a capitalist structure well aware of the quick gratifications of mass culture, the star system also demanded a regular selection of fresh products, so new names and new faces were constantly put before the public even as the careers of older stars were retooled as long as the public showed interest in them. While some stars, like Mae West, Boris Karloff, or John Wayne, were narrowly defined by their iconic star personae, other stars were transformed in attempts to attract changing audiences and reflect shifting fashions. Popular child stars such as Elizabeth Taylor or Shirley Temple were or were not successfully redefined for adult roles as they grew up, and performers once closely associated with one genre were reconceptualized for others: the 1930s boy singer Dick Powell reemerged as a screen tough guy in the 1940s, and Barbara Stanwyck moved with relative ease from women's melodramas and screwball comedies in the 1930s into 1950s Westerns.

DECLINE

The Hollywood star system began to weaken as the studio system itself lost prestige and power in the 1950s, especially after a number of major stars, including Burt Lancaster and Kirk Douglas, declared themselves "independent" by forming their own production companies. In other cases, a star's contracts with studios, once long term and binding, were redrawn as short-term, profit-sharing deals that linked an actor's salary directly to the success of a specific film. In 1950 James Stewart received a percentage of the profits of his hit Western *Winchester '73*, dramatically revising the industry's understanding of a star's earning potential.

As stars, along with their personal agents and talent agencies, became increasingly responsible for their own public images and career choices, the control over performers once secured within the studio hierarchy had clearly shifted. By the 1980s the old Hollywood concept of the "star vehicle," a film specifically tailored to the image and talents of its leading player, was again fully active, but only a handful of stars called the shots that determined which major films were produced and promoted. The self-styled moguls of the studio era had been displaced by their former puppets, the "talent" whose survival skills now included, most significantly, a keen business sense.

MODERN STAR SYSTEM

Certainly a contemporary "celebrity system" remains visible in the small army surrounding any major celebrity: agents, publicists, managers, and personal assistants all work to secure film projects, recording deals, promotional endorsements, talk-show appearances, and cameo roles for their employers. The earlier star system, however, has merged into a much larger "culture of celebrity" that extends massive fame not only to film stars and professional athletes or pop musicians but also to the legions of "minor celebrities" necessary to regularly replenish television talk shows, fashion catwalks, award presentations, and "special guest" appearances on weekly sitcoms. The pop artist Andy Warhol's notorious designation of previously unknown figures as "superstars" and his famous allotment of fifteen minutes of fame to everyone in a media-saturated world perhaps signaled the real end of any remaining purpose for a coherent "system" that was once constructed to transform mere mortals into minor gods and goddesses.

Although the traditional star system of Hollywood may have disappeared, the stars have persevered through special-effect-laden blockbusters and fascinations with the director. As the media pried deeper into the personal lives of stars, the line between their on-screen and offscreen personae blurred, and audiences were not only fascinated by movie characters but also the media-generated personality of the actors. Stars remained the top draw for movies, but they were hardly the biggest player in the game. The myriad talent agencies that blossomed since the 1970s gained more sway throughout the 1980s, 1990s, and into the twenty-first century. Agencies developed elaborate marketing campaigns that linked the star and image with a role. "A"-list stars such as Julia Roberts, Tom Hanks, Brad Pitt, and Will Smith were packaged with directors and producers, then linked to projects. Films like the *Men in Black* franchise received the green light when it paired actors Will Smith and Tommy Lee Jones with director Barry Sonnenfeld. HBO's hit series *Entourage* relied heavily on this phenomenon, as it depicted the rise of an "unknown" into a megastar.

Packaging films gave studios some insurance that they would see a profit, since a certain actor or group of actors would likely attract a consistent fan base. This, however, provided the star with more economic pull, and studios acquiesced to agencies and stars making changes to the script and selecting costars. Most notably, however, the agency-based system allowed for stars to operate like free agents. No longer tied to a single studio, they were able to select which project to work on regardless of which studio sat behind the movie. The switch of focus from the studio to the star provided the star with more negotiating power, allowing for the fee to be based on box-office sales and merchandising profits.

Despite the actors' increased power, the tastes of the audience still dictate how long a star's career will last. Coupled with their public image, stars can quickly fall from their pedestals. Mel Gibson, for example, commanded high fees for his movies, but after a series of racist and sexist tirades, his public image was so tainted that his image became a liability and he was summarily dropped by talent agency William Morris Endeavor Entertainment. As a brand, a star's success goes well beyond the confines of the screen and has become increasingly dependent upon his or her personal marketing strategies.

Corey K. Creekmur

SEE ALSO: American Idol*; Arbuckle, Fatty; Bow, Clara; Chaplin, Charlie; Cody, Buffalo Bill, and His Wild West Show; Crawford, Joan; Fairbanks, Douglas, Sr.; Ford, Henry; Gable, Clark; Garland, Judy; Gish, Lillian; Hanks, Tom; Hudson, Rock; Lancaster, Burt; Pickford, Mary; Pitt, Brad; Roberts, Julia; Smith, Will; Stewart, Jimmy; Studio System; Taylor, Elizabeth; Temple, Shirley; Valentino, Rudolph; Warhol, Andy.*

BIBLIOGRAPHY

Basinger, Jeanine. *The Star Machine.* New York: Vintage, 2009.

DeCordova, Richard. *Picture Personalities: The Emergence of the Star System in America.* Urbana: University of Illinois Press, 1990.

Dyer, Richard. *Heavenly Bodies: Film Stars and Society.* London: Macmillan, 1986.

Dyer, Richard. *Stars.* London: British Film Institute, 1998.

Fowles, Jib. *Starstruck: Celebrity Performers and the American Public.* Washington, DC: Smithsonian Institution, 1992.

Gamson, Joshua. *Claims to Fame: Celebrity in Contemporary America.* Berkeley: University of California Press, 1994.

Marshall, P. David. *Celebrity and Power: Fame in Contemporary Culture.* Minneapolis: University of Minnesota Press, 1997.

McDonald, Paul. *The Star System: Hollywood's Production of Popular Identities.* London: Wallflower Press, 2000.

Morin, Edgar. *The Stars.* New York: Grove Press, 1960.

Piazza, Jo. *Celebrity Inc.: How Famous People Make Money.* New York: Open Road Integrated Media, 2011.

Schickel, Richard. *Intimate Strangers: The Culture of Celebrity.* Garden City, NY: Doubleday, 1985.

Walker, Alexander. *Stardom: The Hollywood Phenomenon.* New York: Stein & Day, 1970.

Star Trek

Star Trek began as a science fiction television series, originally conceived by writer-producer Gene Roddenberry (1921–1991) in the early 1960s. Airing on NBC from the fall of 1966 through the spring of 1969, *Star Trek* episodes chronicled the adventures of the twenty-third-century starship *Enterprise*, serving the interplanetary Federation on a five-year mission to "explore strange new worlds" and "boldly go where no man has gone before." The show has since become a worldwide science fiction and pop culture phenomenon. Several other TV series followed, featuring different characters and set in different time periods. In addition, the series was the precursor to a popular movie franchise, novels, comic books, fanzines, clubs, conventions, board games, video games, and memorabilia.

THE ORIGINAL SHOW

Initially assembled at Desilu Studios, the first *Star Trek* series took shape with significant help from the actors, all of whom were participating in a new and important shift in television content. Captain James T. Kirk (played by William Shatner) was the young, handsome leader of the mission, the youngest captain in the history of Starfleet. Though occasionally headstrong and impetuous, and with a weakness for beautiful women of all races (and all species), he was an inspiring and resourceful leader.

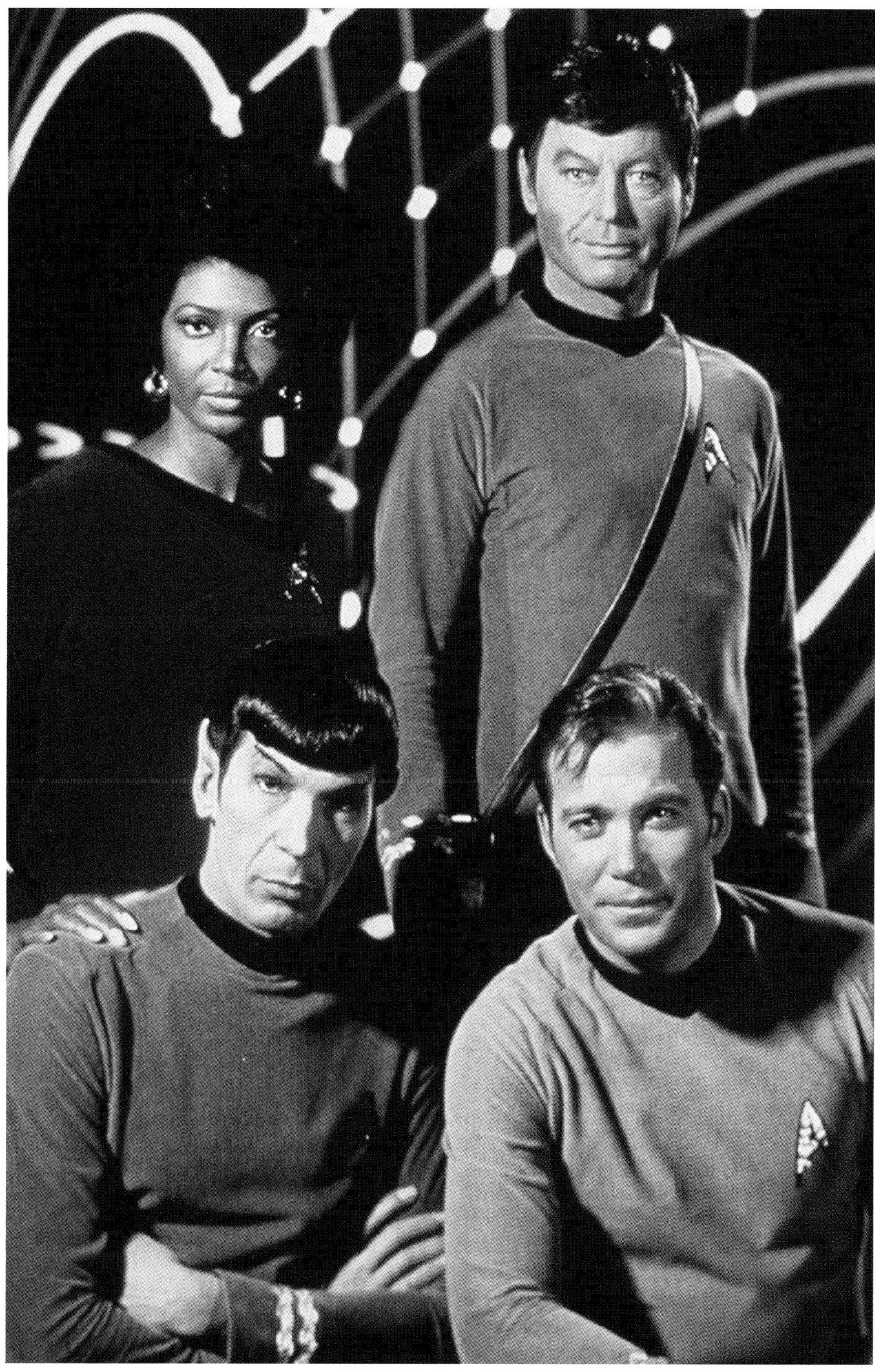

Star Trek. *The cast of the original* Start Trek *television series included, clockwise from upper left, Nichelle Nichols, DeForest Kelley, William Shatner, and Leonard Nimoy.* **PARAMOUNT TELEVISION/ THE KOBAL COLLECTION.**

Rivaling Kirk in popularity was Mr. Spock (Leonard Nimoy), a native of the planet Vulcan, where emotions are suppressed in an attempt to achieve complete objective logic. Spock's tapered eyebrows and pointed ears were at once sinister and fascinating, like a hybrid between a devil and an elf. Spock was particularly interesting because he was half human; though raised as a Vulcan, he was torn between the rigors of logic and the irrational pull of friendship and love. The third major character was Dr. "Bones" McCoy (DeForest Kelley), a curmudgeonly and quick-tempered older man. He had little patience for the impossible idealism that often accompanied Kirk's confidence and even less patience for the self-importance that often accompanied Spock's self-restraint.

The other prominent members of the original *Enterprise* crew were a deliberate mixture of races and nationalities, as Roddenberry felt an accurate vision of the future must depict humanity as having transcended ethnic and political strife. Montgomery Scott (James Doohan), nicknamed Scotty, was the ship's Scottish engineer; he could push the ship beyond its limits and work miracle repairs. The Japanese Lieutenant Sulu (George Takei) and the Russian Ensign Chekov (Walter Koenig) were the ship's helmsmen. The African Lieutenant Uhura (Nichelle Nichols) was the communications officer.

Star Trek was originally conceived as a rather dark and serious show, but it quickly became much more than that and incorporated tragedy, comedy, mystery, romance, action, and adventure. One of the most popular humorous episodes was "The Trouble with Tribbles," during which some members of the *Enterprise* crew purchase cute, round, fur-covered creatures known as tribbles from an intergalactic merchant, only to discover that the creatures multiply at a rate fast enough to threaten to engulf the entire ship. Often voted the best all-time episode was "The City on the Edge of Forever," a time-travel drama written by Harlan Ellison and costarring Joan Collins. In this heartrending episode, Kirk is forced to choose between saving the life of the woman he loves or forever altering the natural course of history. Other popular episodes feature the *Enterprise* in conflict with the Federation's redoubtable alien enemies, the warlike Klingons and the scheming Romulans.

SOCIAL COMMENTARY

The original*Star Trek* series was justly famous for its social commentary. A few episodes, including "A Private Little War," offer thinly veiled criticism of Vietnam by showing the problems of getting involved in other nations' internal struggles. Indeed, Starfleet's Prime Directive is that no technologically advanced society may interfere with the normal development of a more primitive society. Other episodes promote racial harmony and equality; the exciting "Let That Be Your Last Battlefield" episode shows a planet of racists engaged in a futile and self-destructive war. A few episodes, including "A Way to Eden," critique the communal counterculture: intergalactic hippie types are seen spoiled by drugs or foolishly deluded into thinking that they will find a perfect paradise. Overall the show was upbeat, suggesting that many of the problems of twentieth-century Earth would ultimately be solved. The later *Star Trek* series also included social commentary, examining issues such as overpopulation, environmentalism, homelessness, drug abuse, bisexuality, and religious fanaticism.

The original *Star Trek* was also remarkable for its breaking of television taboos. The show's setting in the future allowed it to get away with content that would have been unacceptable in a real life show. Many episodes feature scantily clad men and women, often in thin and flimsy outfits that seem about to fall off entirely; but, as many of these men and women were robots or aliens, the network censors allowed them on the show. *Star Trek* was also historic in condoning interracial (or even interspecies) love. The "Plato's Stepchildren" episode, which aired in November 1968, features the first interracial kiss on U.S. television.

Over the years the original *Star Trek* series furnished its fans with a multitude of inside jokes. Drinking games developed during which fans took one drink every time the show's most famous motifs were repeated. Common occurrences in the show included the ship's teleporting transporter breaking down; red-shirted security officers dying at the hands of evil aliens; Kirk finding a way to talk attractive female aliens into bed; Uhuru tapping the microphone in her ear to get better reception across the light-years; Spock and his fellow Vulcans greeting each other with mystic hand signals and with the words, "Live long and prosper"; McCoy examining a dead body and sadly saying to the captain, "He's dead, Jim"; and, after a successful mission, Kirk requesting, "Beam me up, Scotty." Yet all these jokes, along with the occasional silly looking sets and ham-acting, became a source of endearment rather than derision.

THE SHOW'S FAILURE

Despite the tremendous efforts of everyone involved with the show, and despite the high cost of close to $200,000 per episode, media critics considered the show a failure. Worse still, after some initially high Nielsen ratings, the show's popularity began to decline. Although fan mail increased week after week, the number of viewers appeared to be dwindling. NBC came close to canceling the show after the first season but relented after being deluged by letters written during a save *Star Trek* campaign organized by prominent science fiction writers. The show's second season, however, still failed to capture high ratings. Again the program was nearly canceled, but another save *Star Trek* campaign, this time organized by fans, saved it. The third season was the show's last, but the total of seventy-nine episodes were enough to allow syndication.

In syndication *Star Trek* became an immediate hit. Fanzines and fan clubs proliferated, and the first Star Trek convention took place in January 1972 in New York City. In response to this burgeoning popularity, NBC revived the show as an animated series, featuring the original actors as the voices of their characters. Unfortunately, although the animated show featured stories as complex as the live-action series, it was mistakenly aired for young viewers on Saturday mornings. It was canceled after a brief twenty-two-episode run from the fall of 1973 to the winter of 1974. Plans for a second television series were progressing, but, after the spectacular success of the movie *Star Wars* in 1977, *Star Trek*'s new owner Paramount decided to make the show into a movie. *Star Trek: The Motion Picture* (directed by Robert Wise) hit theaters in 1979, and while it was not well liked by critics or hard-core fans (mostly because of its extravagant special effects and emphasis on concept over character), the picture drew tremendous crowds and was a financial success.

MOVIE FRANCHISE

Star Trek movies have since hit theaters regularly every few years. *Star Trek II: The Wrath of Khan* (1982, directed by Nicholas

Meyer) was an action-packed adventure costarring Ricardo Montalban and Kirstie Alley; it became both a critical and popular success despite the death of Mr. Spock in the film's final scenes. *Star Trek III: The Search for Spock* (1984, directed by Nimoy) was another all-around success; the *Enterprise* is lost, but Spock is resurrected. *Star Trek IV: The Voyage Home* (1986, directed by Nimoy) time-warps the crew back to 1980s San Francisco in search of a pair of humpback whales and became the most successful *Star Trek* film of all. *Star Trek V: The Final Frontier* (1989, directed by Shatner) gives the crew a rebuilt *Enterprise* and sends them in search of an evil alien whom they mistake as God; the movie also purposefully suggests that the characters are perhaps getting too old to be adventuring in outer space. *Star Trek VI: The Undiscovered Country* (1991, directed by Meyer), in which the Klingons and the Federation make peace, was the last film to feature the original cast.

Star Trek: Generations (1994, directed by David Carson) portrays the death of Kirk; it was also the first film to feature the second generation of *Star Trek* characters from the already successful *Next Generation* television show. *Star Trek: First Contact* (1996, directed by Jonathan Frakes) is a multilayered time-travel film showing Earth's first contact with an alien race. And *Star Trek: Insurrection* (1998, directed by Frakes) portrays a power struggle over a beautiful pleasure-planet. In the tenth movie, *Star Trek: Nemesis* (2002), it appeared the franchise had run its course. Movie critic Roger Ebert gave it just two stars and describes it as an experience in which "gradually it occurs to me that 'Star Trek' is over for me." There followed a break of seven years, at the end of which *Star Trek* (2009) brought back the original characters, albeit played by a new, young cast. A box-office and critical success, the movie won an Academy Award for best makeup and had two other nominations.

NEW TV SHOWS

The success of the first *Star Trek* movies inspired Paramount to produce a second television series, *Star Trek: The Next Generation*, set twenty-one years after the first. The new show, which ran from 1987 to 1994, took a more contemplative and peaceful approach to its episodes; there was less action but more science and more diplomacy. Computer-generated special effects added further breadth. As with the original series, however, a prime appeal of the second series was the emphasis on character. With families and couples onboard a much larger starship, the show had a balanced group feel. Captain Jean-Luc Picard (played by Patrick Stewart) was mature and dignified, while First Officer Riker (Jonathan Frakes) was suave and sturdy. Klingon security officer Worf (Michael Dorn) was often torn between his hereditary codes of honor and his duties serving the Federation, while android Lieutenant Data (Brent Spiner) struggled to compare his thoughts and his emotions with those of human beings.

Other major characters included the empathetic Counselor Troi (Marina Sirtis), the young engineer Geordi La Forge (LeVar Burton), and the doctor Beverly Crusher (Gates McFadden). Some episodes featured Dr. Crusher's son Wesley (Wil Wheaton), the Ukrainian security officer Tasha Yar (Denise Crosby), and the 500-year-old Guinan (Whoopi Goldberg). Like the original series, *The Next Generation* offered fans a great variety of shows ranging from the lighthearted to the serious. Popular episodes feature the Romulans (now a major enemy of the Federation); the Borg (frightening and hostile aliens who resemble a cross between insects and robots); and the nearly omnipotent alien Q (John de Lancie), who enjoys teasing the earnest but helpless humans.

After seven seasons *The Next Generation* was replaced by a new show, *Star Trek: Deep Space Nine* (created largely by Rick Berman and debuting in 1993), whose characters inhabit a space station rather than a spaceship. The station is precariously situated at the edge of the Federation near an intergalactic wormhole through which all manner of alien spaceships frequently pass. Besides accommodating their alien visitors, the Deep Space Nine crew faces the challenge of a conflict raging in their sector between the empire of the Cardassians (reptilian Federation adversaries) and the inhabitants of the planet Bajor.

In later shows the crew faces the threat of the hostile Jem-'Hadar alien troops and their masters in the Dominion. The look and mood of the show is darker than in the earlier shows, but the optimistic vision remains. The characters include widower Captain Benjamin Sisko (Avery Brooks) and his son Jake (Cirroc Lofton), the Bajoran first officer Kira (Nana Visitor), the unscrupulous merchant Quark (Armin Shimerman), the symbiont-hosting alien Dax (Terry Farrell), and the shape-shifting officer Odo (René Auberjonois). As in the earlier shows, the Deep Space Nine crew is a harmonious mixture of peoples: Sisko is black; the ship's doctor (Siddig El Fadil) is Arab; the operations officer (Colm Meaney) is Irish; and the botanist (Rosalind Chao) is Japanese.

With *Deep Space Nine* still intended to run a full six or seven seasons, in 1995 yet another *Star Trek* TV series debuted, titled *Star Trek: Voyager* (also created largely by Berman). In this series USS *Voyager* is lost light-years from the Federation and must find its way home. The *Voyager* crew must also deal with internal Federation rebels known as the Maquis, some of whom serve on the Voyager bridge. As with the preceding series, there is not only an underlying sense of optimism about the future but also a broad variety of episodes that deal with serious subjects, such as personal versus professional loyalties, legitimate versus illegitimate forms of authority, foreign (or alien) codes of ethics, and the loss of families and loved ones. *Star Trek: Voyager* was itself replaced in 2001 by the fifth incarnation of the series, named *Enterprise* (subsequently renamed *Star Trek: Enterprise*). Set a decade before the formation of the Federation, the series ran until 2005.

IMPACT ON CULTURE

Star Trek had a deep and lasting impact on U.S. popular culture, an impact that resonated far beyond the Trekkies who attended conventions dressed in costumes from the shows and spoke Klingon to one another. The stars of the original *Star Trek* series were featured as the subjects of biographical articles, books, and documentaries. Under pressure from *Star Trek* fans, NASA even named its prototype space shuttle *Enterprise* in tribute to the show. World-renowned physicist Stephen Hawking appeared on a *Next Generation* episode, as did Mae Jemison, the first African American woman in space. *Star Trek* television shows were seen around the world, while *Star Trek* novels were almost guaranteed best sellers.

In addition, there were many websites devoted to the series, and the mythology of the show inspired real technology. For example, flip phones such as the Motorola Razr early in the first decade of the 2000s bore a striking resemblance to *Star Trek*'s Handheld Communicator devices, online translation services (including Google's, which for a while translated into Klingon, among other languages) resembled the show's Universal Translator, and an app for Apple's iPad turned the twenty-first-century tablet computer into the Personal Access Display Device used in the *Next Generation* series.

Star Trek's successes were often attributed to the deep and compelling characters, the charismatic actors, the intelligent themes and plots of individual shows, the consistency of the future technologies and devices, and the believability of the future universe. Perhaps one of the most important reasons for its success, however, was the show's positive vision of the future. *Star Trek* television shows and movies offered inspiration and hope for a world dealing with crime, homelessness, ethnic strife, and AIDS. It was a vision that emerged from the idealistic 1960s. Despite the show faltering in the early twenty-first century, the *Star Trek* culture and its millions of devotees remained a powerful force in the popular imagination.

Dave Goldweber

SEE ALSO: *Academy Awards; AIDS; Ellison, Harlan; Goldberg, Whoopi; Google; Hippies; Hollywood; iPad; Roddenberry, Gene; Siskel and Ebert;* Star Trek: The Next Generation*;* Star Wars*; Television; Video Games; Vietnam.*

BIBLIOGRAPHY

Asherman, Allan, and Kevin Ryan, eds. *The "Star Trek" Compendium*. New York: Pocket, 1993.

Bertolucci, Jeff. "Star Trek Tech We Use Today (Almost)." *PC-World*, May 5, 2009.

Bjorklund, Edi. "Women and *Star Trek* Fandom." *Minerva* 4, no. 2 (1986): 16–65.

Blair, Karin. "Sex and *Star Trek*." *Science-Fiction Studies* 10, no. 2 (1983): 292–297.

Dillard, J. M. *"Star Trek": Where No One Has Gone Before*. New York: Pocket, 1996.

Ebert, Roger. "*Star Trek: Nemesis*." *Chicago Sun-Times*, December 13, 2002.

Harrison, Taylor; Sarah Projansky; Kent Ono; et al., eds. *Enterprise Zones: Critical Positions on "Star Trek."* Boulder, CO: Westview Press, 1996.

Jindra, Michael. "*Star Trek* Fandom as a Religious Phenomenon." *Sociology of Religion* 55, no. 1 (1994): 27–51.

Okuda, Michael, and Denise Okuda. *The "Star Trek" Encyclopedia: A Reference Guide to the Future*, rev. ed. New York: Pocket Books, 1999.

Reeves-Stevens, Garfield, and Judith Reeves-Stevens. *The Art of "Star Trek": Thirty Years of Creating the Future*. New York: Pocket, 1997.

Richards, Thomas. *The Meaning of "Star Trek."* New York: Doubleday, 1997.

Shatner, William, and Chris Kreski. *"Star Trek" Memories*. New York: HarperCollins, 1994.

Solow, Herbert F., and Robert H. Justman. *Inside "Star Trek": The Real Story*. New York: Pocket, 1997.

Tipton, Scott. *"Star Trek" Vault: 40 Years from the Archives*. London: Aurum Press, 2011.

Worland, Rick. "Captain Kirk: Cold Warrior." *Journal of Popular Film and Television* 16, no. 3 (1988): 109–117.

Star Trek: The Next Generation

Despite the cancellation of the original *Star Trek* series (1966–1969), the success of the show in reruns and a subsequent series of feature films starring the original cast resulted in Gene Roddenberry's creation of a new series, *Star Trek: The Next Generation* in the fall of 1987. An immediate ratings hit, the show drew an average of twenty million weekly viewers during the course of its seven-year run (1987–1994) and also proved a critical success—winning eighteen Emmy Awards, as well as earning an Emmy nomination for Best Dramatic Series.

Much like the original series, *TNG* (*The Next Generation*) followed the exploits of an *Enterprise* crew—led by the indomitable Captain Jean-Luc Picard (Patrick Stewart)—to "explore new worlds." However, instead of planning to go "where no *man* has gone before," this Trek promised to go "where no *one* has gone before"—reflecting the decade of changes in society's view of gender and race. Female crew members such as medical officer Dr. Beverly Crusher (Gates McFadden) and psychological counselor Deanna Troi (Marina Sirtis) were featured in story lines involving their struggles with leadership as well as romance. *TNG*'s crew was also composed of multiple species including chief security officer Worf (Michael Dorn)—a member of the former arch enemy Klingons—who struggled with his loyalties to Starfleet. Similarly, android officer Data (Brent Spiner) often had difficulty assimilating into human culture. The series also dealt with physical disabilities, portraying the blindness of chief engineer Geordi La Forge (LeVar Burton) as both a disability but also an advantage depending on the situation.

In the process of "exploring new life," the crew must learn to deal politically, socially, and even romantically with the various species they encounter, which also involves interaction with new enemies. The malevolent Q (played by John de Lancie), believed that humans—and, by extension, their allies—should be destroyed for its "savage" behavior. His character reappears throughout the series in the guise of various crew members to create dissension and test the crew's commitment to peace. The "Borg," an interconnected robotic entity, proves to be the crew's most threatening adversary. Warning that "resistance is futile"—and already controlling much of the universe—their objective is to abduct individuals and make them a part of their collective unemotional and mechanical "perfection."

At the end of its last season, the crew made the transition into the feature film franchise. *Star Trek Generations* (1994) affected a passing of the torch, as Captain Picard joins forces with *Star Trek*'s Captain Kirk (William Shatner) to fight an intergalactic threat that results in Kirk's death. The subsequent *Star Trek: First Contact* (1996) has Picard and his crew traveling back in time to prevent the Borg from altering the future of Earth. In *Star Trek: Insurrection* (1998), Picard initiates an open rebellion against the Federation of Planets upon learning of its plot against the inhabitants of a unique planet. The final movie in the series, *Star Trek: Nemesis* (2002), finds the crew of the *Enterprise* struggling to thwart a Romulan attack on Earth and, in the process, pits Picard against his clone, Shinzon. The success of *Star Trek: The Next Generation* also led to three other franchise TV series—*Star Trek: Deep Space Nine* (1993–1999); *Star Trek: Voyager* (1995–2001); and a prequel to the original series, *Enterprise* (2001–2005).

Linda Martindale

SEE ALSO: *Emmy Awards; Multiculturalism; Roddenberry, Gene;* Star Trek*; Syndication; Television.*

BIBLIOGRAPHY

Nemecek, Larry. *"Star Trek: The Next Generation" Companion.* New York: Simon & Schuster, 2003.

Okuda, Michael, and Denise Okuda. *The "Star Trek" Encyclopedia: A Reference Guide to the Future*, rev ed. New York: Pocket Books. 1999.

Roberts, Robin. *Sexual Generations: "Star Trek: The Next Generation" and Gender.* Urbana: University of Illinois Press, 1999.

Roberts, Wess, and Bill Ross. *Make It So: Leadership Lessons from "Star Trek: The Next Generation."* New York: Simon & Schuster, 1995.

Sternbach, Rick, and Michael Okuda. *"Star Trek: The Next Generation": Technical Manual.* New York: Pocket Books, 1991.

Star Wars

The *Star Wars* saga is not merely one of the movie industry's most important series—it is also one of the most lucrative. The *Star Wars* phenomenon includes the original film, two sequels, and a trilogy of prequels, as well as a host of books, several animated series, a range of games, numerous awards, and more toys and merchandising tie-ins than was once thought imaginable. *Star Wars* has had a significant impact on American popular culture, from iconic characters to everyday sayings, to music, video games, books, and the evolution of Hollywood. The *Star Wars* movies are remarkable films, but the *Stars Wars* industry has permeated popular culture in an unprecedented fashion—and after thirty-five years shows no sign of slowing down.

THE MOVIES

The core of the *Star Wars* experience is the six movies. *Star Wars* was released May 25, 1977—it was later retitled *Star Wars Episode IV: A New Hope.* Its success led to two sequels: *Star Wars Episode V: The Empire Strikes Back* (1980) and *Star Wars Episode VI: Return of the Jedi* (1983). Although the films were generally advertised by their subtitles, the opening scrawl of each movie disclosed its episode numbers, placing it in the larger context of the story. After a sixteen-year hiatus from the *Star Wars* universe, creator George Lucas came back to the story line and created three prequels, *Star Wars Episode I: The Phantom Menace* (1999), *Star Wars Episode II: Attack of the Clones* (2002), and *Star Wars Episode III: Revenge of the Sith* (2005).

The original *Star Wars* movies are often described by critics as "corny" or "hokey" and as having childishly simplistic plots, but these plots have nevertheless taken hold of popular culture in an amazing fashion. The overall story has the simplicity of a myth: rebel forces do battle with an evil empire led by a cruel emperor; his enforcer, Darth Vader; and an army of hauntingly white-clad robots called Stormtroopers. *A New Hope* helped pioneer the genre pastiche, in which several classical movie genres are combined in one movie. The original trilogy was science fiction, a Western, a war film, and a quasi-mystical epic all at once. Fundamentally, however, "A New Hope," as well as its two sequels, were coming-of-age stories that chronicled the emotional and psychological development of Luke Skywalker,

Star Wars. *Cocky outlaw Han Solo, played by Harrison Ford, faces off against Jabba the Hutt in the original* Star Wars *movie in 1977.* LUCASFILM/20TH CENTURY FOX/THE KOBAL COLLECTION.

who, under the instruction of gurus, acquired the discipline and courage required to harness the power within him and confront the evil forces threatening to take over the universe. He is joined in this quest by a host of memorable characters, including Princess Leia, Han Solo, Obi-Wan Kenobi, and Chewbacca the Wookiee. Tagging along are the lovable robots C-3PO and R2-D2.

MERCHANDISING

The *Star Wars* saga is one of the most successful movie franchises of all time. Together the films rank third in total worldwide box-office revenue, and by 2010 it was estimated that the six movies had earned $4.4 billion. Combining the box-office take with the value of merchandising, *Star Wars* is the most profitable movie franchise in history. The marketing of *Star Wars* as not just a movie but a brand has had a lasting impact on the business of making movies.

Prior to *Star Wars*, merchandising was used only to help promote a movie and rarely lasted after the movie had finished its run. But *Star Wars* merchandising became a business unto itself and produced the most important licensing properties in history. The commercialization of *Star Wars* can be seen everywhere, from action figures to comic books to bank checks; there are even multiple *Star Wars*–branded versions of Monopoly, Trivial Pursuit, and Battleship. In 1996 *Star Wars* action figures were the best-selling toy for boys and the second overall best seller after Barbie. By the late 1990s sales of *Star Wars* merchandise exceeded $1 billion in a single year.

Even three decades after the original movie, the popularity of *Star Wars* toys has not ebbed. *Star Wars*–themed products run the gamut from dishes to snowboards and everything else imaginable. The LEGO Corporation has built a near empire of *Star Wars* products, including traditional building sets featuring the characters, ships, and planets of the movies; a host of video games; a number of animated films; and several *Star Wars* Minilands at LEGOLAND theme parks. The first of these parks, which opened in Carlsbad, California, in 2011, includes more than 2,000 separate LEGO models depicting seven of the most famous scenes from the six films—making the *Star Wars* universe as accessible as a family outing or even a vacation. The culture of *Star Wars* is transmitted in no small part through merchandise from one generation to another to an extent that no movie franchise has ever reached.

The popularity of and long-term interest in *Star Wars* merchandise have given rise to a substantial collectors industry. With the high-level demand for original-run *Star Wars* toys, values have skyrocketed. This has created a veritable growth industry of conventions, books, and websites dedicated to *Star Wars* collectibles. The demand and hoped-for return on investment have led many stores to limit the number of any one item that can be purchased by customers.

STAR WARS IN PRINT

The popularity of *Star Wars* can also be seen in the hundreds of books, graphic novels, and comic books that have been produced over the decades. In 1991 science fiction writer Timothy Zahn published *Heir to the Empire*, the first in a series of books based upon the *Star Wars* movies. It surprised the publishing world by reaching number one on the *New York Times* hardcover fiction best-seller list. Marketers quickly discovered a new generation of fans who had never seen the movies in theaters but were nevertheless obsessed with *Star Wars*. Many of the books published since *Heir to the Empire* have reached the *New York Times* best-seller list. The books have in one respect mirrored the real world: as the first generation of fans, now parents, take their children to see the theatrical rerelease of *Star Wars*, several of the books have mirrored that experience by creating entire series written for young children.

Writers have expanded the *Star Wars* universe dramatically; for example, the popular *Lost Tribe of the Sith* series takes place thousands of years prior to events depicted in *Star Wars Episode IV: A New Hope*. Other books and movies have spun off characters found in the films. One set of books focused on the adventures of Lando Calrissian; another depicted the adventures of the children of Han Solo and Princess Leia. Hundreds of books are set in the *Star Wars* universe or have been influenced by worlds created by Lucas.

SCREENS BIG AND SMALL

Books are not the only medium in which *Star Wars*–themed products have been aimed at young fans. The made-for-TV movies *The Ewok Adventure: Caravan of Courage* (1984) and *Ewoks: The Battle for Endor* (1985) benefited greatly from the splendid special effects provided by Lucas's Industrial Light & Magic, providing a rare treat for television viewers. Both were considered superior fare for television and were released in theaters abroad. The popularity of the two Ewok movies among children led to two half-hour animated adventure series: *Ewoks* (later renamed *The All New Ewoks*, 1985–1987) and *The Ewoks and Droids Adventure Hour* (1985–1986). Equally enticing to fans, though apparently poorly executed (according to Lucas), was the Steven Binder–directed *Star Wars Holiday Special* (1978). Having little to do with the film's production, Lucas was unhappy with the results—film critic and author David Hofstede called it "the worst two hours of television ever." The special aired only once on CBS, and Lucas has vowed to never allow its release again.

LucasArts, Lucas's development company, has produced several cartoons based on the *Star Wars* universe. Its first attempt, *Star Wars: Clone Wars* (2003–2005) lacked the cutting-edge technology that so many fans had become accustomed to and therefore was not a commercial success. In 2008, drawing upon advances in computer-generated imagery (CGI) animation, Lucasfilm Animation created an animated film, *Star Wars: The Clone Wars*, which has been adapted as a successful television series of the same name. Not only did the spin-offs demonstrate the appeal of a plethora of characters created by Lucas, but they also further ingrained the *Star Wars* myth into the cultural consciousness of fans old and new.

Star Wars merchandising kept pace with technology as LucasArts created several games designed for early gaming systems and personal computers. Among the most popular of these games were *X-Wing* (1993), which was the best-selling personal computer game of the year; *Rebel Assault II: The Hidden Empire* (1995); and *Dark Forces* (1995). In the late 1990s LucasArts became one of the top producers of video games in the United States. As Lucas did in the film industry, LucasArts has pushed the outer limits of the possible in computer games.

WIDE-RANGING INFLUENCE

Composer John Williams wrote the theme music for all six *Star Wars* films. His efforts earned him both an Oscar and a Golden

Globe in 1978. Williams's scores for the double trilogy, especially the "Main Title" theme and the recurring "The Imperial March (Darth Vader's Theme)" are undoubtedly some of the most identifiable pieces of film music ever created. Sound in general plays an important role in the *Star Wars* films. In the minds of many people the sound of Darth Vader's artificially enhanced breathing is automatically connected to foreboding danger, in much the same way that the theme music to films such as *Psycho* and *Friday the 13th* connote coming horror.

The most obvious influence *Star Wars* has had in the political arena was its use as a linguistic device in the debate over the Strategic Defense Initiative (SDI). In an unrehearsed speech that took many foreign policy analysts by surprise, on March 23, 1983, President Ronald Reagan announced a goal of rendering nuclear weapons "impotent and obsolete" by constructing a space-based defense system as part of the SDI. Shortly after Reagan's speech, Senator Ted Kennedy derided SDI as a *Star Wars* fantasy that was reckless, costly, and technologically unfeasible.

The resources generated by the success of the *Star Wars* saga allowed for the growth in scope and technology of Lucas-owned ventures, including Industrial Light & Magic, Skywalker Sound (THX), and Graphics Group (a division of Lucasfilm that was purchased by Steve Jobs and later became Pixar Animated Studios). This growth in special effects revolutionized the movie industry and brought science fiction into the mainstream. Without *Star Wars* a range of movies—of all genres—that employed sophisticated CGI in their creation might never have been made. The resulting explosion in popularity of science fiction productions even led to the creation of the Sci-Fi Channel (now known as SyFy) in 1992.

The *Star Wars* phenomena has become a part of Hollywood legend, and a host of other popular shows draw upon aspects of the saga that have permeated the cultural milieu. This is seen particularly in references to *Star Wars* characters, scenes, and story lines in other works. Mel Brooks's *Spaceballs* (1987) features a protagonist named Lord Dark Helmet. *Independence Day* (1996) paid homage Luke Skywalker's famous attack run through the Death Star's trench, replacing Tie fighters and X-Wings with F-18s and alien fighters.

The sheer number of *Star Wars* references in popular television mirrors the saga's penetration in society. The hit sitcom *Friends* had an episode revolving around the slave costume worn by Princess Leia in *Return of the Jedi*. The animated television series *Family Guy* did a set of episodes in parody of the original *Star Wars* movies: "Blue Harvest" (2007); "Something, Something, Something, Dark Side" (2009); and "It's a Trap!" (2010)—the last being a reference to Admiral Ackbar's famous warning in *Return of the Jedi*. One of the primary characters in the long-running sitcom *That '70s Show* is a huge *Star Wars* fan.

CULTURAL SIGNIFICANCE

The individual-against-state theme of *Star Wars* is qualified by its solemnly spiritual individualism. With the mysticism of the Force, a plot device that Lucas had not originally intended to be a centerpiece of the series, *Star Wars* conveys the values of faith over reason and simplicity over complexity. It is a force that binds, connects, and guides the universe, gives meaning to life, and stresses the important of faith. As religious traditionalism has grown in American society since the late 1970s, so has nonreligious spirituality; this has led to the formation in a number of English-speaking countries of a new quasi-religion: Jedi. This movement, which may be libertarian but is definitely not libertine, counted more than 400,000 members among its ranks in the United Kingdom alone—at least those who listed "Jedi" or "Jediism" as their religion on the 2001 census.

As a cultural phenomenon, *Star Wars* has consistently grown and spread for nearly four decades and shows no sign of slowing down. Every year there are new additions to the *Star Wars* universe, and the creative forces at Lucasfilm have been adept at incorporating the latest technological and media developments into the *Star Wars* franchise. With the commercial success of themed products, a loyal and growing fan base, and an entire universe to explore, *Star Wars* will remain a force in popular culture for the foreseeable future.

Craig T. Cobane
Nicholas A. Damask

SEE ALSO: *Academy Awards; Barbie; Best Sellers; Brooks, Mel; CGI; Comic Books; Ford, Harrison;* Friday the 13th*;* Friends*; Graphic Novels; Hollywood; The Internet; Legos; Lucas, George; Made-for-Television Movies; Monopoly; The* New York Times*;* Psycho*; Sitcom;* Star Wars *Episodes I–III: The Prequel Trilogy; Toys; Trivial Pursuit; Video Games; War Movies; The Western.*

BIBLIOGRAPHY

Bailey, T. J. *Devising a Dream: A Book of "Star Wars" Facts and Production Timeline.* Louisville, KY: Wasteland Press, 2005.

Brooker, Will. *Using the Force: Creativity, Community, and "Star Wars" Fans.* London: Continuum, 2002.

Champlin, Charles. *George Lucas: The Creative Impulse.* New York: Harry N. Abrams, 1997.

Decker, Kevin S., and Jason T. Eberl. *"Star Wars" and Philosophy: More Powerful than You Can Possibly Imagine.* Chicago: Open Court Publishing, 2005.

Edwards, Ted. *The Unauthorized "Star Wars" Compendium: The Complete Guide to the Movies, Comic Books, Novels, and More.* Boston: Little, Brown, 1999.

Gordon, Andrew. "*Star Wars*: A Myth for Our Time." *Literature/Film Quarterly* 6, no. 4 (1978): 314–326.

Jenkins, Garry. *Empire Building: The Remarkable Real-Life Story of "Star Wars."* Secaucus, NJ: Carol Publishing Group, 1999.

Kaminski, Michael. *The Secret History of "Star Wars."* Kingston, ON: Legacy Books Press, 2008.

Kapell, Matthew Wilhelm, and John Shelton Lawrence. *Finding the Force of the "Star Wars" Franchise.* New York: Peter Lang, 2006.

Rinzler, J. W. *The Making of "Star Wars."* New York: Ballantine, 2007.

Star Wars Episodes I–III: The Prequel Trilogy

After the release of *Return of the Jedi* in May 1983, the cultural phenomenon that was *Star Wars* seemingly reached its end. Darth Vader had been redeemed in death, Luke Skywalker and the rebel alliance were triumphant, and Han Solo and Princess Leia were destined to be progenitors of new generations of Jedi. Series creator George Lucas proclaimed he would not be making any more *Star Wars* films. A remarkable journey that had begun in 1977 with the unexpected box-office smash *Star Wars* (later retitled *Star Wars Episode IV: A New Hope*) was apparently over.

Yet the success in the early 1990s of novelist Timothy Zahn's three *Star Wars* novels, written as sequels to the original films, helped persuade Lucas that perhaps the time had come to revisit the *Star Wars* universe. Also influencing Lucas was the remarkable technological advances that had been made in computer-generated imagery (CGI) in film, evidenced in such visually sensational films as *Terminator 2* (1991) and *Jurassic Park* (1993).

Therefore, in 1993 Lucas set the world of fandom afire with his announcement that he would be working on a *Star Wars* prequel trilogy. During the prequel development process, Lucas returned to the original trilogy, gave the films a CGI revamp, restored some cut scenes, otherwise altered or extended existing scenes to correct continuity errors, and rereleased each film theatrically in 1997 in honor of the original film's twentieth anniversary. While a generation of fans was delighted to see the films back on the big screen, for nostalgic reasons and to introduce their own children to the saga, many objected to the directorial revisions to the originals, which had such an impact on them years before. This backlash was nothing compared to what divided fandom after the release of the first new *Star Wars* film in more than two decades: *Star Wars Episode I: The Phantom Menace* (1999). *Star Wars Episode II: Attack of the Clones* (2002) and *Star Wars Episode III: Revenge of the Sith* (2005) completed the prequel trilogy. The relative merits and flaws of the prequel trilogy compared to the original trilogy will no doubt be endlessly debated by generations of fans.

ORIGINS

The prequels grew out of the increasingly elaborate backstory that Lucas created during the writing of the first *Star Wars* film during the early 1970s. While *Star Wars* was developed as a more or less standalone film, in which Darth Vader was not Luke's father and Princess Leia was not Luke's sister, Lucas did have enough material for more stories. So with the success of the first film, he set out to make the first sequel of an indeterminate number of films. While Anakin Skywalker (originally Starkiller) was not Darth Vader in Lucas's backstory, Lucas changed his mind during the drafting process of *The Empire Strikes Back*. With that one unexpected deviation, his new direction of two trilogies, the first one being the Anakin Skywalker backstory and how he became Darth Vader, was solidified. However, it took many more years for the prequels to be produced.

THE STORIES

In *Star Wars Episode I: The Phantom Menace*, the Galactic Republic is engaged in a trade dispute with the Trade Federation. Federation ships blockade the planet of Naboo. As the film progresses, the major figures of the prequel trilogy are introduced: the Jedi knight Qui-Gon Jinn; his apprentice, Obi-Wan Kenobi; the Sith Lord, Darth Sidious, who has secretly ordered the invasion of Naboo by a droid army; Darth Maul, Sidious's lethal apprentice; the Gungan exile, Jar Jar Binks; Queen Amidala and her handmaid, Padmé; the astromech droid R2-D2; nine-year-old slave child Anakin Skywalker, whom Qui-Gon believes may be the "chosen one" spoken of in Jedi prophecy, destined to return balance to the Force; Anakin's home-built protocol droid, C-3PO; Yoda, the ancient Jedi master; Mace Windu, a powerful member of the Jedi Council; and the oily and secretive Senator Palpatine, who is attempting to bring a no-confidence vote against the republic's supreme chancellor in order to supplant him.

Eventually, Padmé shows herself to be the real queen; the other "queen" has been a decoy. The battle for Naboo climaxes on three fronts. Padmé and Jar Jar win the Gungans to their side to face down the Trade Federation's invading droid army; Anakin pilots a starship to destroy the droid control ship in orbit; and Qui-Gon and Obi-Wan engage in an extended light saber duel with Darth Maul that ends in both Qui-Gon's and Maul's deaths. The battle won, Obi-Wan, now a full Jedi knight, successfully persuades the Jedi Council to take on Anakin as his apprentice.

Star Wars Episode II: Attack of the Clones picks up ten years after the events depicted in *The Phantom Menace*. A separatist movement led by Count Dooku has spread across the galaxy and engulfed the republic in near-civil war. Against this backdrop Anakin stands as the spirited and occasionally defiant apprentice to master Obi-Wan. Following an assassination attempt on Padmé's life, Anakin is assigned to protect her while Obi-Wan investigates who has ordered the attempt. Obi-Wan discovers that a secret clone army is being manufactured for the republic to aid the Jedi in battling Dooku's droid army. The clones have been created from the DNA of bounty hunter Jango Fett; Fett also has a son named Boba. Dooku, operating from a secret fortress on the remote planet of Geonosis, captures Obi-Wan.

Meanwhile, Anakin finds that his mother has been kidnapped and killed by a tribe of Sandpeople on Tatooine. Enraged, he kills the entire tribe, including women and children. In another example of his emotional extremes, he becomes Padmé's ardent suitor as the plot progresses, in defiance of the Jedi code against strong emotional attachment. Padmé, bound by her own duties to the people of Naboo, rebuffs his advances initially. However, as they face death by execution on Geonosis, Padmé declares her love for him.

Just as matters look darkest for Obi-Wan, Padmé, and Anakin, Yoda arrives with the republic's clone army and clashes with Dooku's droid army in a spectacular battle. During the battle, Obi-Wan, Anakin, and Yoda cross light sabers with Dooku. Anakin loses his arm during the duel and Dooku escapes to rendezvous with Darth Sidious. The film ends with Anakin and Padmé's secret wedding on Naboo.

Star Wars Episode III: Revenge of the Sith is set three years after the beginning of the clone wars as Anakin and Obi-Wan rescue the kidnapped Chancellor Palpatine from the malevolent droid leader General Grievous. During the rescue Anakin confronts and kills Dooku at Palpatine's behest. Upon return to the capital planet of Coruscant, Palpatine exploits Anakin's prophetic fear for Padmé and their unborn child as well as Anakin's growing resentment for being shut out of the Jedi Council to eventually turn Anakin to the dark side of the Force. Thus corrupted, Anakin kills master Mace Windu. In the duel with Windu, Palpatine is hideously disfigured, but the clever politician turns even that to his advantage by persuading the Senate to abdicate its authority and proclaim him galactic emperor to combat the supposed treachery of the Jedi.

Palpatine's "Order 66," dispatched throughout the galaxy, leads to the extermination of nearly every Jedi as "enemies of the state." Only Yoda and Obi-Wan escape this fate. Anakin, now renamed Darth Vader as Sidious's new apprentice, murders every Jedi in the temple and flies to the lava planet of Mustafar to kill the remaining separatists. Padmé and Obi-Wan confront Anakin on Mustafar. Following an epic light saber battle with Obi-Wan, Anakin is left for dead, dismembered and cruelly burned at the edge of a lava flow. The emperor takes him to a medical center, where Anakin is transformed into the sinister black-clad and helmeted figure of episodes IV through VI. Obi-Wan escapes the planet with Padmé. She dies giving birth to twins, Luke and Leia. Obi-Wan and Yoda send the twins into hiding—Leia on the planet of Alderaan and Luke on the planet of Tatooine.

CRITICAL AND AUDIENCE RECEPTION

Vastly hyped by the time of its release, *The Phantom Menace* debuted to decidedly mixed critical reviews and widespread fan vituperation. Critics pointed to the film's flat characters and Byzantine political backstory as detriments. Many reserved their most strident criticisms for the character of Jar Jar Binks, whose Jamaican-styled accent led some to call him a blatantly racist caricature. Other characters in the film also received the same criticism, particularly the Trade Federation's Asian-accented Neimoidians and Anakin's owner, Watto, whom some believed embodied offensive Jewish stereotypes.

Fans seemed just as incensed by the film's introduction of midi-chlorians: microscopic organisms in the body that are linked to the Force. Many fans simply could not accept that to be "strong in the Force" meant that one had a higher concentration of midi-chlorians. In spite of the backlash, however, *The Phantom Menace* became 1999's most financially successful movie. It earned more than $900 million in its initial run domestically and internationally, and its 3-D release in February 2012 pushed the film's box-office totals over the $1 billion mark. It remains the most financially successful *Star Wars* movie of all.

Three years after the first film's release, *Attack of the Clones* was released. It, too, divided critics and fans. Many detractors pointed to wooden dialogue, especially in the courtship and love scenes between Anakin and Padmé. Actor Hayden Christensen, who plays Anakin, suffered more than his fair share of criticism for what some called a stiff performance. While its domestic and international box-office take of nearly $650 million could not by any means be deemed a failure, the film nevertheless suffered by comparison with the totals of the first prequel and was outperformed by other films, such as *The Lord of the Rings: The Two Towers*, during its year of release. It is considered to be the least financially (and critically) successful of the six *Star Wars* films.

The last prequel, *Revenge of the Sith*, opened in 2005. While critics still complained of Lucas's by-now-signature wooden dialogue, the film's dark story line of Anakin's tragic fall received much better reviews than the other two prequels, making it the most critically successful of the three. Some even compared it favorably to *Episode V: The Empire Strikes Back*, widely regarded as the best (and up to this point, the darkest) of the entire series. The film broke many financial records and ultimately grossed approximately $850 million, making it 2005's most successful film.

SIGNIFICANCE

Whatever else may be said of the prequels, they clearly bear the stamp of Lucas's unique vision of the *Star Wars* saga as action/adventure serial with science fiction trappings and historical allusions combined with quasi-religious Eastern and Western philosophy. The prequels clearly mirror (perhaps even subvert) the characters, events, themes, and imagery of the first trilogy. If the original series is about redemption, the prequel trilogy is about damnation and tragedy. In the more politically minded prequels, Palpatine's Hitleresque rise to power parallels Anakin's fall as a result of a Faustian alliance with Palpatine. Lucas's vision of Anakin's descent is both timeless and timely, given its obvious references to a simplistic worldview of good and evil that gripped the United States following 9/11. The prequels have much to say that is unsettling about the original trilogy that gave rise to them and about the culture that has greeted them with such enthusiastic ambivalence.

Philip L. Simpson

SEE ALSO: *Blockbusters; CGI; Ford, Harrison;* Jurassic Park*;* Lord of the Rings *Film Trilogy; Lucas, George; 9/11;* Star Wars*;* The Terminator.

BIBLIOGRAPHY

Bowen, Jonathan L. *Anticipation: The Real Life Story of "Star Wars: Episode I—The Phantom Menace."* New York: iUniverse, 2005.

Hearn, Marcus. *The Cinema of George Lucas*. New York: Harry N. Abrams, 2005.

Kaminski, Michael. *The Secret History of "Star Wars."* Kingston, ON: Legacy Books Press, 2008.

Pollock, Dale. *Skywalking: The Life and Films of George Lucas*, rev. ed. New York: Da Capo Press, 1999.

Rinzler, Jonathan W. *The Making of "Star Wars Episode III—Revenge of the Sith."* New York: Del Rey, 2005.

Starbucks

A chain of retail coffee outlets that offer fresh specialty drinks and beans to go, the Seattle, Washington–based company Starbucks expanded across the globe at a quick pace during the 1990s and the first decade of the 2000s, becoming the largest coffee chain in the world. Because of Starbucks, the U.S. public became familiar with the Italian-originated words *latte* and *barista* when discussing complex coffee beverages and the food-service professionals who make them.

SEATTLE ORIGINS

Starbucks's corporate origins date back to 1971, but the company did not really begin its march to massive success until 1986. That year a Starbucks executive, Howard Schultz, created a coffeehouse in Seattle to serve upscale espresso drinks. He called it Il Giornale and modeled it on the coffee-imbibing locales ubiquitous to Italian cities. The following year Schultz put financing together and bought out Starbucks's two original founders, who had little faith in his attempt to introduce European-style coffee and its corresponding coffee culture.

Starbucks was a hit in Seattle, however, and the company soon began expanding down the Pacific Coast. Exporting the concept to Chicago in the early 1990s was equally successful, and forays into the Northeast and Canada were also lucrative.

The trade journal *Restaurants & Institutions*, naming Starbucks as its Changemaker for 1995, explained that "with ethnic influences shaping the American palate, consumers demand more from everything they consume. . . . Along comes Starbucks with a flavor profile stronger than many Americans had ever experienced."

With a featured coffee of the day and a variety of espresso, cappuccino, and latte drinks priced from $1.15 to $3.15, Starbucks became a morning stop for urban commuters in major U.S. cities and a hangout for the home-office-bound and stroller-mom brigade of the more affluent suburbs. In some urban spots the coffee outlet was so successful that the company simply opened up a second Starbucks across the street.

By 1998 Starbucks was the number one roaster and retailer of specialty coffee in the United States, closing in on its goal of 2,000 stores by 2000, expanding into Asian markets, and introducing bottled beverages and packaged beans in supermarkets. Yet it was the actual Starbucks space that attracted both devotees and disparagers. The stores were carefully designed to look just slightly cutting edge and modern in their fixtures and fabrics; the lighting was subdued and ambient. Sociologists term such locales a "third place"—neither work nor home, but a neighborhood spot where it is okay to sit alone, offering the chance of running into old friends or making new ones. "I don't think Starbucks' success has that much to do with coffee," urban sociologist Peter Katz tells *Seattle Weekly*'s Bruce Barcott. "Starbucks is selling community."

REASONS FOR SUCCESS

Katz and other academics have contemplated Starbucks's success and increasing ubiquity and cite certain elements in North American culture and demographics as key factors. First was the importance of the private sphere in U.S. life and, because of it, a lack of designed community spaces. The predominance of suburban living spaces led, in turn, to too much isolation. Economic considerations also contributed to Starbucks's empire: by the 1990s the workplace no longer offered the security and stabilized socialization of the past, and more of the U.S. public had opted to work at home. Coupled with the extreme transientness of North American culture in general, these factors engendered this longing for just such a third place.

Furthermore, coffeehouse culture allowed, to a certain extent, people from different social and belief strata to mix and fulfilled a post-Yuppie era desire to appear sophisticated and European. It also allowed more straitlaced personality types to participate in what had been the coffeehouse culture pre-Starbucks, when such places were frequented by artists, college students, and the underemployed. "Square America needs a hangout too," observes the *Seattle Weekly*'s Barcott. "Starbucks joins the concept of the coffeehouse with mainstream America's demand for brand-name assurance." Locating the stores near or even inside mega-bookstores such as Barnes & Noble or Borders created what Barcott calls the "upscale leisure ghetto."

Yet anti-Starbucks sentiment was strong, especially among the original slacker coffeehouse crowd. Stores under construction were sometimes vandalized, there were websites that railed against McLatte, and National Public Radio host Ira Glass spoke of the common bond uniting his audience as "a fear of Starbucks."

EXPANSION AND GROWING PAINS

The anti-Starbucks crowd was greatly outnumbered by the chain's devotees, however, and in the first decade of the 2000s Starbucks continued its global dominance. In just five years, from 2000 to 2005, the company expanded from some 3,500 stores to more than 10,000. Still, it was not all smooth sailing. The U.S. recession made consumers think twice about shelling out for espresso drinks, and there was a backlash against the perhaps too rapid expansion of the chain. The homey, community-oriented feel of the coffeehouses was replaced by a mass market, fast-food undercurrent. Sales declined, and the stock price fell by more than half by the end of Starbuck's 2008 fiscal year.

Schultz, who had stepped down as chief executive officer in 2000, returned to Starbucks in 2008 to try to turn the company around. Some 600 underperforming shops in the United States were closed, and the company sought innovation, including the introduction of VIA, an instant coffee it had worked on for decades to perfect, to lure consumers. In 2011 the company launched a rebranding campaign, complete with a new logo designed to convey the idea that Starbucks was more than just a coffee company.

Starbucks might have been mainstream and commonplace in the United States, but there were still plenty of countries that could not get enough of the coffee chain. International expansion played a key role in the company's growth strategy, and by the close of 2011 it had a presence in more than fifty-five countries. The company planned to expand even further in the twenty-first century.

Revenues in 2010 and 2011 were strong, and sales continued to grow. Rather than remaining content with its past accomplishments, Starbucks continued to offer new products and ideas. The company jumped into the coffee pod revolution with K-Cups for Keurig coffeemakers, and it began experimenting with serving beer and wine at some of its stores. By the end of 2011 Starbucks had more than 17,000 stores all over the world and continued to make strides to remain relevant.

Carol Brennan

SEE ALSO: *Advertising; Coffee; Consumerism; Fast Food; Yuppies.*

BIBLIOGRAPHY

Barcott, Bruce. "Starbucks Nation." *Seattle Weekly*, February 19, 1997.

Behar, Howard, and Janet Goldstein. *It's Not about the Coffee: Leadership Principles from a Life at Starbucks.* New York: Portfolio, 2007.

Kugiya, Hugo. "Seattle's Coffee King." *Seattle Times Pacific Magazine*, December 15, 1996.

McDowell, Bill. "The Bean Counters." *Restaurants & Institutions*, December 15, 1995.

McDowell, Bill. "Starbucks Is Ground Zero in Today's Coffee Culture." *Advertising Age*, December 9, 1996, 1, 49.

Michelli, Joseph A. *The Starbucks Experience*. New York: McGraw, 2007.

Schultz, Howard, and Dori Jones Yang. *Pour Your Heart into It: How Starbucks Built a Company One Cup at a Time.* New York: Hyperion, 1997.

Schultz, Howard, and Joanne Gordon. *Onward: How Starbucks Fought for Its Life without Losing Its Soul.* New York: Rodale, 2011.

Starr, Bart *(1934–)*

When Bart Starr retired from the Green Bay Packers in 1971, he was the winningest quarterback in the history of professional football. For sixteen seasons he directed the Packers to six Western Division titles, five World Championships, and two Super Bowl victories. He won the National Football League's (NFL) Most Valuable Player award in 1966, made four Pro Bowl teams, and won the league passing title three times.

Even though he was the talented starting quarterback of the NFL's best team during the decade that saw football become America's number one sport, Starr, who had a humble personality, was initially overshadowed by more outspoken Packers, such as Ray Nitschke, Paul Hornung, and coach Vince Lombardi. Starr's stature rose, however, as the Packers evolved from a running to a passing team during their championship run. Teammates and fans recognized the balance his cool personality offered the intense Packers. Like other admired Americans at the time, such as actor Gary Cooper and President Dwight D. Eisenhower, Starr's public persona sprang from a dependable, appealing toughness and self-effacing gentility.

Bart Starr. *Bart Starr (number 15), who led the Green Bay Packers to five World Championships and two Super Bowl wins, is considered one of the most efficient quarterbacks in NFL history.* VERNON BIEVER/CONTRIBUTOR/GETTY IMAGES SPORT/GETTY IMAGES.

Born in Montgomery, Alabama, on January 9, 1934, Bryan Bartlett Starr struggled through his playing days in high school and college. Although he was not a high school star and was considered too shy to be an effective starting quarterback, his career at the University of Alabama began well. As a freshman, he was All-SEC (Southeastern Conference) and started in the 1953 Orange Bowl, which Alabama won 61–6. Due to injuries and a coaching change, however, Starr rode the bench his final two years.

At the urging of Starr's former coach at Alabama, the Green Bay Packers selected Starr in the seventeenth round of the 1956 NFL draft. For his first four seasons, he alternated at quarterback, and observers voiced concerns that Starr's arm was weak and that he was too passive and nice to develop the presence necessary for a championship quarterback. When Lombardi became head coach of the Packers in 1959, he, too, shared in that assessment, and like Starr's previous coaches, he badgered the quarterback to assert himself. In time, however, Lombardi recognized that Starr's future depended upon quiet encouragement instead of public humiliation, and he changed his approach. Starr responded, embracing Lombardi's single-minded will to succeed and dogged preparation for games.

Starr's liabilities—his quiet focus and selflessness—became advantages for the team, which needed a firm but unassuming presence to counter Lombardi's tumultuous personality. By mid-1961 Starr was the starter for good. "Everything I am as a man and a football player I owe to Vince Lombardi," Starr later told *Sport* magazine. "He is the man who taught me everything I know about football, about leadership, about life. He took a kid and made a man out of him, with his example, with his faith."

Starr developed into an inspiring leader and one of the most efficient passers in the history of football. A clever quarterback who expertly read defenses and studied game films year-round, he set NFL records for the lowest percentage of passes intercepted in a season (1.2 percent), the fewest interceptions in a season (three), and the highest passing completion percentage in a career (57.4 percent). In 1964 and 1965 he threw a record 294 passes without interception.

Starr came to symbolize the clutch player, creating a model for later NFL quarterbacks such as Terry Bradshaw and Joe Montana. His postseason quarterback rating set records as the highest in NFL history. In six NFL championship games he threw eleven touchdowns but only one interception. Starr made big plays too. He engineered "The Drive" in the final moments of the 1967 NFL Championship game against the Dallas Cowboys. One of the most famous series in the history of professional football, The Drive culminated in Starr's quarterback sneak behind Jerry Kramer to give the Packers the victory in the game later known as the "Ice Bowl."

Throughout all his successes and his failures, such as his disappointing nine years as head coach of the Packers from 1974 to 1983, Starr remained hardworking and retained his likable, modest personality. After coaching, he remained in Green Bay, setting up businesses in Wisconsin and in his home state of Alabama and working for charitable causes. To many, Starr will always be the sturdy conscience behind the Green Bay Packers dynasty.

Alexander Shashko

SEE ALSO: *Bradshaw, Terry; College Football; Cooper, Gary; The Dallas Cowboys; The Green Bay Packers; Lombardi, Vince;*

Montana, Joe; National Football League (NFL); Professional Football.

BIBLIOGRAPHY

Devaney, John. *Bart Starr.* New York: Scholastic, 1967.

Gruver, Ed. *The Ice Bowl: The Cold Truth about Football's Most Unforgettable Game.* Ithaca, NY: McBooks Press, 1998.

Gulbrandsen, Don. *Green Bay Packers: The Complete Illustrated History.* Minneapolis, MN: MVP Books, 2011.

Starr, Bart, and Murray Olderman. *Starr.* New York: Morrow, 1987.

Starr, Kenneth *(1946–)*

Kenneth Starr will be remembered in the popular imagination as the soft-spoken but tenacious Republican special prosecutor locked in mortal combat with Democratic president William Jefferson Clinton and his White House. Starr, a former federal appeals court judge and solicitor general under President George H. W. Bush, was appointed as independent counsel by Attorney General Janet Reno in 1994 to investigate allegations of wrongdoing by then-Arkansas governor Clinton; his wife, Hillary Rodham Clinton; and their various business and personal associates. Starr's investigation, which began as an attempt to ascertain if the president and First Lady had illegally benefited from a land deal in Arkansas, culminated in the referral of a controversial report to the U.S. House of Representatives regarding President Clinton's affair with a twenty-one-year-old White House intern, Monica Lewinsky. The story of the affair and the legal clash between Starr and Clinton dominated the media during 1998 and throughout 1999.

From the beginning of his investigation, Starr was accused of partisan bias and conflict of interest, particularly in representing tobacco companies for his law firm Kirkland & Ellis and nearly filing a Supreme Court brief in support of Paula Jones's sexual harassment suit against Clinton. The charges against Starr intensified when the Lewinsky story broke in January 1998. Though Starr had received permission from a three-judge panel and the attorney general to expand his Whitewater investigation to include the Lewinsky matter, critics took issue with some of the Office of the Independent Counsel's legal tactics, such as its wiring of Pentagon employee Linda Tripp to record Lewinsky, its justification for expanding the investigation, and its subpoenaing of sympathetic witnesses such as Betty Currie (the president's personal secretary) and Lewinsky's mother.

Starr, seemingly unheedful of his public relations problems even as the president's approval ratings climbed, pressed forward with his grand jury investigation throughout the first half of 1998. For months the president stood by his initial denial of having had "sexual relations" with Lewinsky, but testifying before Starr's grand jury on August 17, the president reluctantly admitted to at least some details of what he called an "inappropriate relationship."

The Starr Report, submitted to Congress on September 9, 1998, and quickly released to the American public both on the Internet and through various publications, was widely criticized not only for its omission of most matters relating to the original Whitewater investigation but also its explicitness in detailing specific sexual encounters between Clinton and Lewinsky. Starr's office and its defenders argued that the detail was unfortunate but necessary to prove that the president had obstructed justice and committed perjury in a deposition in the Jones sexual harassment case against him and again later before the grand jury investigating the matter. The referral went to the House Judiciary Committee, charged with the task of debating and drawing up articles of impeachment against the president. Starr himself appeared before the committee to defend his office's investigation and the report.

Following often acrimonious debate between Republicans and Democrats in the Judiciary Committee, President Clinton was formally impeached on December 19, 1998, on a mostly party-line vote by the full House on two charges of obstructing justice and committing perjury before a federal grand jury—only the second such presidential impeachment in U.S. history. The resulting Senate trial began on January 7, 1999, and ended on February 12, 2000, with the defeat, again largely along partisan lines, of both charges.

In the aftermath of the Clinton impeachment, Starr eventually resigned as special prosecutor and returned to private appellate practice at Kirkland & Ellis. He served as visiting professor at New York University and the George Mason University School of Law. In 2004 he accepted a position as dean of Pepperdine University School of Law, a position he had once declined during his tenure as special prosecutor as a perceived conflict of interest. In his role as a private litigator, he took on several high-profile cases, among them a class-action lawsuit against the Bipartisan Campaign Reform Act of 2002 (the McCain-Feingold Act) as well as lawsuits on behalf of the *Juneau School Board in Morse v. Frederick* in 2004, on behalf of the Blackwater security firm in the deaths of four unarmed civilians in Iraq in 2004, and on behalf of supporters of the controversial Proposition 8 (the California Marriage Protection Act) before the California Supreme Court in 2009. In 2010 Starr accepted the presidency of Baylor University.

With the benefit of some distance from the impeachment drama, he has publicly expressed regret that he was named by the Department of Justice as the special prosecutor in the Clinton case.

Philip L. Simpson

SEE ALSO: *Lewinsky, Monica; Sex Scandals.*

BIBLIOGRAPHY

Baker, Peter. *The Breach: Inside the Impeachment and Trial of William Jefferson Clinton.* New York: Scribner, 2000.

Bugliosi, Vincent. *No Island of Sanity: Paula Jones v. Bill Clinton: The Supreme Court on Trial.* New York: Ballantine, 1998.

Carville, James. *. . . And the Horse He Rode in On: The People v. Kenneth Starr.* New York: Simon & Schuster, 1998.

Clinton, Bill. *My Life.* New York: Alfred A. Knopf, 2004.

Conason, Joe, and Gene Lyons. *The Hunting of the President: The Ten-Year Campaign to Destroy Bill and Hillary Clinton.* New York: Thomas Dunne Books, 2000.

Coulter, Ann. *High Crimes and Misdemeanors: The Case against Bill Clinton.* Washington, DC: Regnery, 1998.

Dershowitz, Alan. *Sexual McCarthyism: Clinton, Starr, and the Emerging Constitutional Crisis.* New York: Basic Books, 1998.

Drew, Elizabeth. *On the Edge: The Clinton Presidency.* New

York: Simon & Schuster, 1994.

Kurtz, Howard. *Spin Cycle: How the White House and the Media Manipulate the News.* New York: Simon & Schuster, 1998.

The Starr Report: The Findings of Independent Counsel Kenneth W. Starr on President Clinton and the Lewinsky Affair. New York: PublicAffairs, 1998.

Starr, Kenneth. *The Starr Report: The Evidence*, ed. Phil Kuntz. New York: Pocket Books, 1998.

Stewart, James B. *Bloodsport: The President and His Adversaries.* London: Touchstone, 1997.

Starsky and Hutch

The police show *Starsky and Hutch* (1975–1979) brought violence on television to the forefront of national debate in the 1970s. Shot in Los Angeles but set in a city that is never named, *Starsky and Hutch* was known for car chases and shootouts the likes of which had not been previously seen on TV. The show starred dark-haired Paul Michael Glaser as the wisecracking, street-smart David Starsky and blue-eyed blond David Soul as the educated, soft-spoken Ken "Hutch" Hutchinson. Each episode the two undercover police officers come in contact with big-city criminals, drug dealers, prostitutes, mobsters, cultists, and murderers and manage to catch the bad guys in less than sixty minutes while wearing skin-tight bell-bottom pants. Drawing inspiration from hit movies such as *The French Connection* (1971), *Starsky and Hutch* always requires a car chase to capture the criminal, courtesy of Starsky's prize possession, the "red tomato," a 1974 Ford Torino with a white racing stripe.

When the show debuted on ABC in 1975, much was written about the chemistry between the two lead actors. *Starsky and Hutch* was one of the first shows in which men could be friends and openly care about each other. Young, hip, and bachelors, these two plainclothes detectives are as vulnerable as they are tough. Their relationship has sensitive qualities that make the duo a far cry from the cardboard Joe Fridays and Mike Stones that preceded them on television. For example, they are not afraid to hug each other.

The show also featured blaxploitation film star Antonio Fargas as the flamboyant Huggy Bear, a con man who moonlights as a police informant and has the fashion sense of a pimp. Starsky and Hutch's boss is Captain Harold Dobey (Bernie Hamilton). A member of the old guard, Captain Dobey often butts heads with his two new-breed detectives about the manner in which police work should be done. The gruff but lovable Dobey provides a glimpse at what would later become a staple in many television cop dramas: the almost one-dimensional African American police boss. The use of an African American actor as the supervisor in these kinds of dramas became trendy in the 1990s, with the likes of *Homicide*'s Lieutenant Al Giardello, *NYPD Blue*'s Lieutenant Arthur Fancy, and *Law and Order*'s Lieutenant Anita Van Buren.

William Blinn created *Starsky and Hutch.* Aaron Spelling and Leonard Goldberg acted as executive producers and produced ninety-two episodes before the show's run ended. Glaser and Soul directed several episodes themselves, which was unusual for actors at the time. In subsequent decades, the practice of actors also performing directing and producing duties would become more commonplace.

Starsky and Hutch's influence can be seen in TV cop shows in which the partners have close relationships. However, the good-looking hipster cops are descendants of television's *The Mod Squad* (1968–1973), and they are part of a post-*Serpico* (1973) spate of police narratives, including *Baretta* (1975–1978) and *Toma* (1973–1974), which depict law enforcement's battle with the dark side of America, the crime-ridden urban landscape. The contentious relationship these detectives have with their superior has become a staple in cop dramas. Although the violence in *Starsky and Hutch* was shocking in 1975, it seems tame by later standards.

In the late 1990s, though it had been off the air for nearly two decades and had not been particularly popular in syndication, *Starsky and Hutch* surfaced in a rather odd way. An August 18, 1997, *New York Times* article by Amy Harmon about fan fiction, an Internet phenomenon in which fans write and post new episodes of shows, mentions *Starsky and Hutch* as a favorite in the "slash" genre. In slash fan fiction, the sexual orientation of the main characters has been changed, and website pages about the homoerotic exploits of Starsky and Hutch abound.

In 2004 a tongue-in-cheek comedy based on the two detectives, *Starsky & Hutch*, hit movie theaters, starring Ben Stiller as Starsky and Owen Wilson as Hutch. Although it received decent reviews, the film was not a big box-office draw.

Joyce Linehan

SEE ALSO: *Bellbottoms; Blaxploitation Films;* The French Connection*;* Law & Order: SVU*;* The Mod Squad*;* NYPD Blue*; Spelling, Aaron; Stiller, Ben; Syndication; Television.*

BIBLIOGRAPHY

Blinn, William. *Starsky & Hutch.* New York: Ballantine Books, 1975.

Oldenburg, Ann. "Starsky and Hutch, Both Originals and Replicas." *USA Today*, March 5, 2004, p. 10e.

State Fairs

A reflection of American life and its diverse people and interests, state fairs featuring exhibits, rides, shows, and food have been popular since the mid-1800s and became an American tradition in the 1900s. The pride, nostalgia, and entertainment that make up a state fair experience have transcended political, social, and economic changes that the United States faced during the twentieth century. State fairs have come to represent a nostalgic, old-fashioned form of family entertainment that emphasizes state and national pride, agricultural roots, and good times.

THE EVOLUTION OF STATE FAIRS

Fairs have existed for centuries and can even be dated back to ancient Mesopotamia in 3000 BCE. Modern American fairs grew out of an 1807 idea by Elkanah Watson, a banker and farmer in Pittsfield, Massachusetts. He decided that the best way to convince other farmers to raise sheep was to show them his own animals. The townspeople were so impressed with Watson's idea that they gathered together to form the first Berkshire Cattle Show in 1810. Although many people were concerned about attending a nonreligious celebration, Watson convinced the people of New England that the show was an acceptable event for upstanding citizens because of its importance to the business of farming and its educational value. Throughout the next decade the show expanded to include men's and women's manufacturing exhibits, a parade, and a dance. The fair quickly spread throughout the United States, and by the time of the Civil War, agricultural societies in twenty-five states were holding annual fairs.

With the success of county and local agricultural fairs, state governments quickly realized that fairs could be used to highlight the growth and achievements of their states. New York held its first state fair in September 1841, and several states in the Midwest quickly followed its example. State fairs were among the first places in the nation where people could see electric lights, automobiles, solar homes, and dozens of other modern inventions. Railroads contributed to the popularity of state fairs by allowing people to travel quickly and cheaply. Some railroads even provided discounts for exhibitors and families going to the fair. People attended the early state fairs in overwhelming numbers and still do: More than 2.6 million people attended the 2010 Texas State Fair, which is the largest state fair. Second was Minnesota, with attendance of nearly 1.8 million that same year.

State fairs attempt to feature the most appealing aspects of their respective states. Each year people who have made a difference, such as sports heroes, celebrities, teachers, and activists are chosen to be recognized at the state fair. In cooperation with the state wildlife bureau, many state fairs offer an area showcasing native birds and animals. Prominent businesses, churches, and social organizations also highlight their achievements. Each organization is given a booth in which it can introduce people to its work. Visitors shopping for certain items are offered a large selection, while those who are just browsing are introduced to many new and exciting people and goods that they may not have known existed. Agriculture continues to be a vital component of state fairs in the twenty-first century, with exhibits of farm machinery and tools common. Competitions for crops and farm animals remain much the same as in the nineteenth century, except that advances in technology have allowed for stronger and healthier crops and livestock.

WHAT TO DO AT FAIRS

Young people are an important part of the state fair experience. Their presence allows older people to recall their own experiences at fairs past, and their participation helps to forge a new bond between the young and the old that often does not exist the rest of the year. High school marching bands come from around the state to play at the fair. Youth groups such as the 4-H, Future Farmers of America, and Girl and Boy Scouts hold competitions for raising animals, cooking, sewing, woodworking, citizenship, art, and gardening. Beginning in the 1970s, many young people who participated in state fairs were far removed from the rural farm setting of the traditional fairgoers. Encouraged by their parents' fond memories, young people living in urban and suburban areas often will concentrate on home manufacturing areas or raising small animals.

Mechanical rides became common at state fairs in the years following their introduction at the 1893 World's Columbian Exposition in Chicago. The Ferris wheel, first introduced there, became a hit at state fairs around the nation and remained popular into the twentieth-first century. In the first decade of the 2000s a state fair would not be complete without a diverse and abundant selection of rides for people of all ages. The Bumper Cars, the Himalaya, and the Scrambler are just a few of the rides that have kept Americans returning to the state fair since the 1950s. State fair rides are popular with teenagers and have been romanticized as the starting place for many first dates.

Sideshows featuring multiheaded people or animals, bearded women, and extra-human contortionists were once part of the novelty of discovery that made up the fair. Since the 1970s, however, sideshows have declined in popularity and presence at state fairs, either because of an effort to provide "wholesome" entertainment for families or simply due to lack of interest. Nonetheless, sideshows remain part of the nostalgic image of state fairs.

Food is an essential part of the state fair experience. French fries, coney dogs, Polish sausage, cotton candy, and apple pie fill the air with a smell that only a state fair can create. Many people look forward to fair-specific specialties, including deep-fried foods such as funnel cakes and food on a stick such as corn dogs. State fairs often offer specialty items that are made with locally grown ingredients, while other foods highlight the ethnic diversity of the state. It is common for a single state fair to have food from dozens of countries around the world—Mexican, Greek, Chinese, Polish, and German are especially popular.

Since the 1950s, state fairs have offered shows featuring popular musical groups of many different styles—rock, Christian, blues, folk, gospel, and even some classical. Country music is usually the most popular, however. In the 1980s and 1990s, country musicians Alabama, Willie Nelson, and Garth Brooks sold out shows at state fairs around the country. In 2011, country stars such as Randy Travis and Brad Paisley appeared on stage at various state fairs. While big names such as these do attract crowds, other sorts of shows such as rodeos, exhibition sporting events, and magic shows are also popular and can sometimes attract crowds as large as those for concerts.

Angela O'Neal

SEE ALSO: *Alabama; Boy Scouts of America; Brooks, Garth; Country Music; Girl Scouts; Hot Dogs; Marching Bands; Nelson, Willie; World's Fairs.*

BIBLIOGRAPHY

Alter, Judy. *Meet Me at the Fair.* New York: Franklin Watts, 1997.

Auger, Helen. *The Book of Fairs.* New York: Harcourt, Brace, 1939.

Braden, Donna. *Leisure and Entertainment in America.* Detroit, MI: Wayne State University Press, 1988.

Koutsky, Kathryn Strand, and Linda Koutsky. *Minnesota State Fair: An Illustrated History.* Minneapolis, MN: Coffee House Press, 2007.

Perl, Lila. *America Goes to the Fair: All about State and County Fairs in the USA.* New York: William Morrow, 1974.

Rydell, Robert W. *All the World's a Fair.* Chicago: University of Chicago Press, 1984.

Staubach, Roger *(1942–)*

In his eleven-year career with the Dallas Cowboys (1969–1979), quarterback Roger Staubach frequently engaged in last-second heroics to help his team to two Super Bowl victories and four National Football Conference (NFC) titles.

A native of Cincinnati, Ohio, Staubach played quarterback for the U.S. Naval Academy, where he won the 1963 Heisman Trophy, awarded to the top player in college football each season. Staubach was drafted by the Cowboys in the tenth round of the 1964 National Football League (NFL) draft, but he served in the navy for four years before beginning his professional career.

Staubach joined the Cowboys in 1969 and played sparingly during his first several seasons, when Dallas coach Tom Landry was using Craig Morton as the team's starting quarterback. In 1971 Dallas had suffered a disappointing 16–13 loss to the Baltimore Colts in Super Bowl V, and the following season Landry decided that he would give Staubach the opportunity to compete for the job of starting quarterback. At the end of preseason, Landry decided to alternate Staubach and Morton at the position during 1971–1972, a strategy that did not work out particularly well, as the team lacked cohesion in the early part of the regular season. In midseason Landry made Staubach the starter, and the quarterback responded by leading the Cowboys to Super Bowl VI. The Cowboys defeated the Miami Dolphins by a score of 24–3, and Staubach earned the Most Valuable Player Award, completing twelve out of the nineteen passes he attempted, for 119 yards and two touchdowns.

Roger Staubach. *Roger Staubach was quarterback of the Dallas Cowboys for eleven seasons, leading the team to two Super Bowl victories.* GEORGE LONG/CONTRIBUTOR/GETTY IMAGES SPORT/ GETTY IMAGES.

Staubach had little chance to savor his success, unfortunately, for he badly separated his right shoulder in a game the following preseason, requiring surgery and causing him to miss much of the 1972 regular season. His injury came while he tried to fight through several defenders in an attempt to score, a style unlike that of most other quarterbacks, who in that era generally tried as hard as possible to avoid physical contact on the playing field.

Staubach was able to return later that season, however, and he delivered a playoff performance that defined much of the rest of his career and earned him the title "Captain Comeback." He entered a first-round game against the San Francisco 49ers with his team trailing at the end of the third quarter and the 49ers already beginning their celebration. Captain Comeback made sure the celebration was premature: he led the Cowboys to two dramatic touchdowns in the last two minutes and an improbable come-from-behind 30–28 victory. Despite Staubach's heroics, the Cowboys lost that season's NFC title game 26–3 to the Washington Redskins.

The Cowboys reached the Super Bowl three times in the late 1970s with Staubach at quarterback. Twice, in Super Bowls X and XIII, they lost to Pittsburgh teams that are considered by many to be among the greatest of all time. However, the Cowboys defeated the Denver Broncos in Super Bowl XII in 1978 by a 27–10 margin, giving Staubach his second Super Bowl victory. In that game, he threw a 45-yard touchdown pass in the third quarter to give the Cowboys an insurmountable 20–3 lead. During this period, the Cowboys came to be known as "America's Team."

Staubach retired following the 1979 season, despite the fact that, at age thirty-seven, he was still playing at a very high level. He cited a desire to spend more time with his family, a declining enthusiasm for football, and concern over the possibility of permanent injuries, as he had already suffered numerous concussions and a variety of other physical problems as a result of his tenacious style of play.

In spite of his own history of concussions—Staubach has said he experienced twenty during his playing days—he is not a fan of recent football rules changes to promote player safety. In a 2010 interview, he described watching a game in which officials called two roughing-the-passer penalties for plays against Peyton Manning and awarded 15 yards to the Colts for each penalty. Staubach said, "I'm thinking, 'I don't ever remember having one of those.' It's kind of a wussy game, really, in a way."

Staubach was enshrined in the Professional Football Hall of Fame in Canton, Ohio, in 1985. He led the NFL in passing during four of his eleven seasons and was an All-NFC selection five times during his career. Captain Comeback also managed to lead the Cowboys to twenty-three come-from-behind victories in the fourth period, cementing his nickname.

The famous quarterback's competitive spirit led him into a new venture in the first decade of the 2000s. In 2003 Staubach and Troy Aikman, another former Cowboys quarterback, went into partnership to form a NASCAR racing team. In 2007 their team was purchased by executives with the Arizona Diamondbacks, making Staubach and Aikman minority owners.

Jason George

SEE ALSO: *College Football; The Dallas Cowboys; Landry, Tom; National Football League (NFL); Professional Football; Sports Heroes; Super Bowl.*

BIBLIOGRAPHY

"Hall of Famers: Roger Staubach." Pro Football Hall of Fame. Accessed April 2012. Available from http://www.profootballhof.com/hof/member.aspx?PlayerId=201

St. John, Bob. *The Landry Legend: Grace under Pressure.* Dallas, TX: Word Books, 1989.

Staubach, Roger, and Frank Luksa. *Time Enough to Win.* Waco, TX: Word Books, 1980.

Stowers, Carlton; Drew Pearson; and Jim Dent. *Staubach: Portrait of the Brightest Star.* Chicago: Triumph Books, 2010.

Steamboat Willie

Premiering in 1928, *Steamboat Willie* was the first of Disney's Mickey Mouse cartoons to feature sound, which helped to launch the character's phenomenal career. Unlike other cartoons of the time, where sound served simply as a background to the action, both music and sound effects were essential to the film's structure and visual rhythm. The clever animal concert (in which Mickey plays a cow's teeth like a xylophone and transforms a nursing sow into a bagpipe) illustrates Disney's ability to successfully blend sight and sound, so that neither element dominates the other. It also anticipates the complex musical sequences, featured in later films such as *Fantasia*, which transformed the art of animation and became key to Disney's financial success.

Scott W. Hoffman

SEE ALSO: *Animated Films; Disney (Walt Disney Company);* Fantasia.

BIBLIOGRAPHY

Barrier, Michael. *The Animated Man: A Life of Walt Disney.* Berkeley: University of California Press, 2007.

Maltin, Leonard. *Of Mice and Magic: A History of American Animated Cartoons.* New York: McGraw-Hill, 1980.

Schickel, Richard. *The Disney Version: The Life, Times, Art and Commerce of Walt Disney.* New York: Simon & Schuster, 1968.

Watts, Steven. *The Magic Kingdom: Walt Disney and the American Way of Life.* New York: Houghton Mifflin, 1997.

Steel Curtain

The Steel Curtain was the name given to the defensive line of the Pittsburgh Steelers football team during their glory days in the 1970s. L. C. Greenwood, Ernie Holmes, "Mean" Joe Greene, and Dwight White, the four members of the Steel Curtain, routinely dominated the opposition, crushing running backs and sacking quarterbacks. Although the Steelers defensive unit as a whole was one of the greatest of all time, the Steel Curtain was a particular focus of public attention. Greene, the leader of the Steel Curtain and two-time NFL Defensive Player of the Year, was also a media celebrity in his own right. He appeared in one of the most famous soft drink advertisements in television history. The ad featured Greene trading his football jersey to a small child in exchange for a bottle of Coca-Cola.

Geoff Peterson

SEE ALSO: *Advertising; Coca-Cola;* Monday Night Football*; The Pittsburgh Steelers; Professional Football; Sports Heroes.*

BIBLIOGRAPHY

Bouchette, Ed. *The Pittsburgh Steelers.* New York: St. Martin's Press, 1994.

Freedman, Lew. *Pittsburgh Steelers: The Complete Illustrated History.* Minneapolis, MN: MBI Publishing, 2009.

Livingston, Pat. *The Pittsburgh Steelers: A Pictorial History.* Virginia Beach, VA: Jordan, 1980.

Steffens, Lincoln *(1866–1936)*

At the beginning of the twentieth century, when corruption in city government ran rampant in large American cities, one of the original muckrakers—so named by Theodore Roosevelt for their aggressive journalistic tactics in investigating controversial stories—was Lincoln Steffens. Steffens hounded corrupt city officials all across the United States. He faced numerous death threats and stood up to local political machines in many cities, including Pittsburgh, New York City, and Minneapolis.

His first effort at a story came in Philadelphia, where he compared the local extortionists' control of the city voting to that of the disenfranchisement of African Americans in the South. He wrote in *McClure's* magazine, "The honest citizens of Philadelphia have no more rights at the polls than the Negroes of the South." Over the course of his career, Steffens's muckraking led to the indictment of eighteen municipal legislators in St. Louis and the ouster of twenty corrupt city councilmen in Chicago. Through the journalistic ideology of muckraking, Steffens challenged the way in which city business was done and set a standard many others would follow.

Lincoln Steffens was born in 1866 in San Francisco. He failed his first attempt at the entrance exam to the University of California at Berkeley. On his second try he succeeded and graduated in 1889 with a degree in philosophy. In 1891 Steffens moved to Paris and married Josephine Bontecou. He returned to New York City in 1892 after landing a job with the *New York Evening Post.* He later became managing editor of *McClure's*, joining muckrakers such as Ida Tarbell and Ray Stannard Baker. In a nationwide publication, Steffens exposed corrupt city officials, who often received and gave bribes, and bought and sold privilege at all levels. He published six articles on corruption in local city governments, and these articles formed the hallmark on city reform for the next half-century. The six articles were published together in a book in 1904. *Shame of the Cities* quickly became a best seller and stood out for its prose and style.

Steffens's public call for the end of democracy led to a permanent split with *McClure's*. In 1906 he became co-owner of *American* magazine but sold his shares in 1907, after a little more than a year. By 1910 Steffens had become disillusioned with muckraking and concerned himself with the radical revolutionaries in Mexico. This involvement led him to become even more skeptical of capitalism.

In 1917 he traveled to the Soviet Union and proclaimed himself a Marxist. At the conclusion of World War I, Steffens attended the 1919 Paris Peace Conference at Versailles. After leaving Paris, he returned to the United States and embarked on a cross-country tour promoting the Bolshevik Revolution. By late 1921 Steffens was pressured out of America with the onset of the first Red Scare. He first returned to Paris then later moved to Italy, where he wrote his autobiography in 1931. *The Autobiography of Lincoln Steffens* and its theme of an intellectual reformer turned revolutionary appealed to many readers during the Great Depression. The book, with its witty, charming, and compassionate narrative, sold well in the United States and laid the groundwork for autobiographical style for years to come.

Steffens moved back to the United States in 1927 and died in 1936 in Carmel, California. He is buried in San Francisco. Steffens's life will be remembered for many achievements in journalism. He helped end city corruption, published two popular books nearly thirty years apart, and became the first truly revolutionary American journalist. With the decline of the newspaper industry and the rise of Internet news reporting in the twenty-first century, many new works have come out to support the use of journalism to expose injustices. Two recent biographies of Steffens have emphasized the importance of his journalistic activities in reflection on the current state of the profession.

Scott Stabler

SEE ALSO: *Baker, Ray Stannard; Muckraking; Sinclair, Upton; Tarbell, Ida.*

BIBLIOGRAPHY

Bausum, Ann. *Muckrakers: How Ida Tarbell, Upton Sinclair, and Lincoln Steffens Helped Expose Scandal, Inspire Reform, and Invent Investigative Journalism.* Washington, DC: National Geographic, 2007.

Connery, Thomas, ed. *A Sourcebook of American Literary Journalism: Representative Writers in an Emerging Genre.* New York: Greenwood Press, 1992.

Hartshorn, Peter. *I Have Seen the Future: A Life of Lincoln Steffens.* Berkeley, CA: Counterpoint, 2011.

Kaplan, Justin. *Lincoln Steffens: A Biography.* New York: Simon & Schuster, 2004.

Palermo, Patrick. *Lincoln Steffens.* Boston: Twayne Publishers, 1978.

Steffens, Lincoln. *Shame of the Cities.* New York: McClure, Phillips, 1904.

Steffens, Lincoln. *The Autobiography of Lincoln Steffens.* New York: Harcourt, Brace, 1931.

Stinson, Robert. *Lincoln Steffens.* New York: F. Ungar Publishing, 1979.

Steinbeck, John *(1902–1968)*

A native Californian, writer John Steinbeck built his career on stories based primarily in Northern and central California, around his hometown of Salinas. Best known for the novels *Of Mice and Men* (1937), *The Grapes of Wrath* (1939), and *East of Eden* (1952), along with numerous short stories, Steinbeck also published nonfiction, plays, and screenplays. He was awarded the Pulitzer Prize for *The Grapes of Wrath*, and in 1962 he received the Nobel Prize in Literature. Steinbeck's works are widely read and have been the subject of many motion pictures.

Born John Ernest Steinbeck in the fertile valley of Salinas, inland from Monterey Bay, Steinbeck grew up in an environment caught between the transition from farming and ranching to the "respectable culture" of universities and businesspeople. His parents were middle-class citizens of Salinas (his father served as Monterey County treasurer and his mother was a schoolteacher), but Steinbeck himself often worked as a laborer on nearby farms. Attending Stanford University, he took courses in English and marine biology but left without completing his degree, having made the decision to try to make a living at writing, first in New York and then back in California.

His early works—*Cup of Gold* (1929), *The Pastures of Heaven* (1932), and *To a God Unknown* (1933)—went largely unnoticed until the publication of *Tortilla Flats* (1935), which describes the exploits of a group of *paisanos* (Mexican Americans) living in Monterey. Steinbeck's reputation as an advocate for farm labor organization began with the publication of *In Dubious Battle* (1936), which recounts the efforts of farm labor organizers during a fruit pickers' strike. His next work, *Of Mice and Men* (1937), was first conceived as a stage play and was produced simultaneously as a play and a novel. The play received the Drama Critics' Circle Award, and the novel, the compelling story of two itinerant farm hands, firmly established Steinbeck as a major California writer.

John Steinbeck. *John Steinbeck was awarded both the Pulitzer Prize and the Nobel Prize in Literature during a writing career that helped establish a distinct American literary style.* FRED STEIN ARCHIVE/CONTRIBUTOR/ARCHIVE PHOTOS/GETTY IMAGES.

Steinbeck's most acclaimed work, *The Grapes of Wrath* (1939), has become a classic work of the Depression era. The book was awarded the Pulitzer Prize in 1940, in addition to being made into a classic motion picture by John Ford that same year. Following the success of *The Grapes of Wrath*, Steinbeck concentrated on nonfiction works such as *Sea of Cortez* (with Edward F. Ricketts, 1941) and *Bombs Away: The Story of a Bomber Team* (1942). During World War II he worked as a war correspondent; his articles were published collectively as *Once There Was a War* in 1958. He returned to fiction with *Cannery Row* (1945); *Sweet Thursday* (1954); *The Red Pony* (1945); *The Pearl* (1947); and his most ambitious novel, *East of Eden* (1952), which tells the stories of three generations of the Trask family, focusing on the conflict between two brothers.

In the 1960s Steinbeck once again returned to nonfiction with *Travels with Charley in Search of America* (1962) and *America and Americans* (1966). In addition to having many of his works adapted for the screen, including *Of Mice and Men* (1939 and 1992), *The Grapes of Wrath* (1940), *Tortilla Flats* (1942), *The Moon Is Down* (1943), *The Pearl* (1947), *The Red Pony* (1949), *East of Eden* (1955), and *Cannery Row* (1982), Steinbeck wrote several original screenplays, including Alfred Hitchcock's *Lifeboat* (1944) and Elia Kazan's *Viva Zapata!* (1952).

In his acceptance speech for the Nobel Prize, Steinbeck described his belief in the power of literature to improve the condition of humankind: "I hold that a writer who does not passionately believe in the perfectibility of man has no dedication nor any membership in literature." The realism of his writing, along with the intensity of his belief in the transformative power of literature, has helped develop an American literary style, which influenced the protest writings, both literary and musical, of the late 1950s and 1960s.

Charles J. Shindo

SEE ALSO: *Fonda, Henry; Ford, John;* The Grapes of Wrath*; Hitchcock, Alfred.*

BIBLIOGRAPHY

Benson, Jackson J. *The True Adventures of John Steinbeck, Writer*. New York: Viking, 1984.

Bloom, Harold. *John Steinbeck*. New York: Bloom's Literary Criticism, 2008.

Davis, Robert. *Steinbeck: A Collection of Critical Essays*. Englewood Cliffs, NJ: Prentice-Hall, 1972.

Fensch, Thomas. *Conversations with John Steinbeck*. Jackson: University of Mississippi Press, 1988.

Lisca, Peter. *John Steinbeck: Nature and Myth*. New York: Thomas Y. Crowell, 1978.

Steinbeck, Elaine, and Robert Wallsten, eds. *Steinbeck: A Life in Letters*. New York: Penguin, 1975.

Steinbeck, John. *The Portable Steinbeck*, ed. Pascal Covici. New York: Viking, 1946.

Steinberg, Saul *(1914–1999)*

Best known for the hundreds of enigmatic, captionless drawings and frequent covers he contributed to the highbrow *New Yorker* magazine from 1941 on, the Romanian-born, world-traveled Saul Steinberg employed in his long career an eclectic range of media and styles that are rarely straightforward and frequently attest to his literary and philosophical musings. Steinberg often incorporated the likes of unintelligible calligraphy, watercolor, rubber stamps, tracings, thumbprints, graph paper, and collage into his pen-and-ink drawings for books and magazines. Recurring themes have included the relationships among abstract concepts, as in "Ship of State" (1959), and places he has known, such as "Bleecker Street" (1971), in which a parade of street characters are rendered in dozens of cartoon styles. Few artists have so successfully blurred the line between popular and high art.

Craig Bunch

SEE ALSO: *The* New Yorker*; Pop Art.*

BIBLIOGRAPHY

Blechman, R. O. *Attention, Mr. Steinberg: My Encounters with Saul Steinberg*. Washington, DC: Shoemaker & Hoard, 2004.

Steinberg, Saul, and Harold Rosenberg. *Saul Steinberg*. New York: Alfred A. Knopf in association with the Whitney Museum of American Art, 1978.

Steinbrenner, George *(1930–2010)*

The word *controversial* preceded George Steinbrenner's name from the time the multimillionaire shipbuilder from Cleveland, Ohio, became the principal owner of the New York Yankees in 1973. Considered to be the driving force behind baseball's escalating salary structure in the late 1970s and 1980s, Steinbrenner was loathed for his frequent criticism of his players and managers while also credited with bringing winning baseball back to New York City. Never one to shy away from the media limelight, he had a brash personality that often overshadowed his team's play on the field.

BUYING THE YANKEES

With his father's retirement from the family shipping business in 1963, George M. Steinbrenner III, a former football player for Ohio State University, was called upon to take over the company. Steinbrenner took the millions he made in business and returned to the sports world, attempting in the early 1970s to acquire the Cleveland Indians. When that deal fell through, his attention turned to the floundering Yankees, at that time owned by CBS. In 1973 CBS sold the team to a syndicate headed by Steinbrenner for about $10 million. Although he had vowed not to take a prominent role in running the club, the new Yankees president soon became one of the most controversial owners in the game.

After a decade of disappointing seasons, the Yankees quickly became competitive again under the new ownership, finishing a close second to the Baltimore Orioles in the American League East Division in 1974, winning the American League pennant in 1976, and garnering World Series titles in 1977 and 1978. Through a series of shrewd trades and large free-agent contracts, "Boss" Steinbrenner had definitely brought winning baseball back to New York. He was defined by headline-grabbing moves such as the one he made on New Year's Eve 1974, when he signed American League Cy Young Award winner Jim "Catfish" Hunter to a five-year contract worth an estimated (and unprecedented) $3.75 million. He followed that in later years by giving huge contracts to sluggers such as Reggie Jackson and Dave Winfield.

THE BRONX ZOO

Although he was successful on the baseball diamond during his first decade with the Yankees, Steinbrenner was beset off of it with legal battles and feuds with managers and players. In 1974 baseball's commissioner, Bowie Kuhn, barred Steinbrenner from serving as Yankees president for one season for having made illegal contributions to President Richard Nixon's campaign two years earlier. Steinbrenner's tempestuous relationship with his managers began with the resignation of longtime manager Ralph Houk after the 1973 season. Over the next twenty years, he made eighteen more managerial moves. His most turbulent relationship was with former Yankees second baseman Billy Martin, who was first hired as the team's manager in 1975 and first fired in 1978. The hiring/firing sequence was repeated four more times before Martin's last ouster in 1988. After being dismissed as manager sixteen games into the 1985 season, Yogi Berra, a former star catcher with the team and a fan favorite, vowed never to set foot in Yankee Stadium again as long as Steinbrenner was in charge.

George Steinbrenner. *George Steinbrenner earned his fortune in the shipbuilding business, but he is best known for his tenure as the outspoken, controversial owner of the New York Yankees.* JAMIE MCCARTHY/STAFF/WIREIMAGE/GETTY IMAGES.

The clubhouse was a whirl of controversy in the 1970s and 1980s. As Yankees third baseman Graig Nettles recalled, "When I was a little boy, I wanted to be a baseball player and join the circus. With the Yankees, I've accomplished both." Egos clashed with the arrival of highly paid free agents. Jackson, an outfielder signed to a record-setting free-agent contract in 1977, made himself unwelcome to his Yankees teammates when he brazenly announced, "I'm the straw that stirs the drink." Though Jackson was dubbed "Mr. October" for his World Series heroics, his five years with the Yankees were marked by a love-hate relationship with Steinbrenner. Many players felt animosity toward Steinbrenner because he frequently called them out in public, such as when he apologized to the city of New York after the team's poor performance in the 1981 World Series.

OUT AND IN

Steinbrenner's ownership of the Yankees reached a nadir in 1990: following a decade of steady decline, the team finished in last place for the first time since 1966. That year, Steinbrenner once again found himself embroiled in controversy when Commissioner Fay Vincent learned that he had paid professional gambler Howard Spira $40,000 to dig up damaging information on Winfield, a player with whom the Yankees owner had feuded for nine seasons. Steinbrenner had unfavorably compared the millionaire outfielder to Jackson with the demeaning moniker "Mr. May." On July 30, 1990, Steinbrenner agreed to resign permanently as general managing partner of the Yankees due to his violation of "the best interests of baseball" rule.

Steinbrenner's campaign to have himself reinstated came to fruition in July 1992, when the outgoing Vincent lifted the ban, effective March 1, 1993. The seasons that followed were among the most placid and successful of the Steinbrenner era. He appeared to defer more often to his front-office staff, giving it more breathing room. In the strike-plagued year of 1994, the Yankees finished in first place for the first time since 1981. Two years later, under the calm leadership of manager Joe Torre, they staged an unlikely come-from-behind World Series victory over the defending-champion Atlanta Braves.

However, Steinbrenner's greatest success came in 1998, when the Yankees astounded the baseball world by winning 114 games en route to their second world championship in three years. What made this team different from the rowdy crews from the 1970s was that the players actually seemed to actually like each other and their visibly mellowed owner appeared content to avoid controversy. For once, Steinbrenner remained silent while the accomplishments of the team itself received most of the attention.

In July 2010 Steinbrenner died at the age of eighty. At that time, the Yankees, in whom he had originally invested $8.8 million, were worth more than $3 billion. During his thirty-seven years as owner, the Yankees won eleven pennants and seven World Series. Steinbrenner understood that he was an atypical boss and even agreed to pose as Napoleon on a *Sports Illustrated* cover on March 1, 1993. Comparing him to a man who had set out to rule the world was a stroke of genius. After all, in his early days, Steinbrenner was all about ruling the world he had carved out for himself, and he had little patience with anyone who stood in his way.

Kevin O'Connor

SEE ALSO: *Baseball; Berra, Yogi; Jackson, Reggie; Major League Baseball; The New York Yankees.*

BIBLIOGRAPHY

Cassuto, Leonard, and Stephen Partridge. *The Cambridge Companion to Baseball.* New York: Cambridge University Press, 2011.

Hoffer, Richard. "Bye George, You Got It." *Sports Illustrated,* July 26, 2010.

Jacobson, Steve. *The Best Team Money Could Buy: The Turmoil and Triumph of the 1977 Yankees.* New York: Atheneum, 1978.

Kahn, Roger. *October Men: Reggie Jackson, George Steinbrenner, Billy Martin, and the Yankees' Miraculous Finish in 1978.* Orlando, FL: Harcourt, 2003.

Lyle, Sparky, and Peter Golenbock. *The Bronx Zoo.* New York: Crown, 1979.

Madden, Bill, and Moss Klein. *Damned Yankees: A No-Holds-Barred Account of Life with "Boss" Steinbrenner.* New York: Warner, 1991.

Preston, Joseph G. *Major League Baseball in the 1970s: A Modern Game Emerges.* Jefferson, NC: McFarland, 2004.

Schaap, Dick. *Steinbrenner!* New York: Putnam, 1982.

Steinem, Gloria *(1934–)*

American feminist and journalist Gloria Steinem is perhaps the most visible representative of the women's rights movement, an effort that resulted in immeasurable effects in contemporary society. She is perhaps best known for cofounding the groundbreaking women's magazine *Ms.* in the early 1970s and for being heavily involved in spearheading the drive to ratify the Equal Rights Amendment, which, although never adopted, was a major factor in legislation on such issues as equal pay, pregnancy discrimination, and educational funding for female athletes. It also generated a maelstrom of dialogue on the topic and contributed to a new consciousness for women in America. Although more radical feminists have criticized Steinem for having too much of a middle-class approach to the struggle, some noted that her mainstream persona helped make women's rights accessible to a greater number of women.

Steinem was born March 25, 1934, in Toledo, Ohio, to Leo and Ruth (Nunevillar) Steinem. Her parents divorced when she was young, leaving her mother—who had already been prone to nervous breakdowns—extremely depressed. Steinem spent much of her youth caring for her incapacitated mother,

Gloria Steinem. *Gloria Steinem addresses delegates at the Democratic National Convention in 1972.* JOHN OLSON/TIME LIFE PICTURES/GETTY IMAGES.

who enriched her daughter by exposing her to literature and instilling a deep respect for others. In high school, Steinem moved to Washington, D.C., to live with her older sister, Suzanne, then went on to attend Smith College. After graduating magna cum laude in 1956, Steinem earned a fellowship to study in India, where she learned of the nonviolent philosophy of Mohandas K. Gandhi.

EARLY ACTIVISM

Steinem returned to the United States and aspired to a career in journalism. In 1960 she began writing for periodicals, and in 1963 she went undercover as a Playboy "bunny," a cocktail waitress in the famous men's club, to write a wry exposé detailing the degradation that female employees were forced to undergo. By the late 1960s, she had begun to emerge as a serious journalist. She was tapped to produce a weekly political column for the newly launched *New York* magazine. Brimming with advocacy and pleas for activism, her pieces tackled subjects ranging from the fight to free Angela Davis to support of Cesar Chavez and the United Farm Workers to backing author Norman Mailer in his bid for mayor of New York City. However, she was not considered a leader in the women's movement until 1969, when she produced the article "After Black Power, Women's Liberation" following a meeting of a group called the Redstockings that addressed the issue of abortion.

RISE TO PROMINENCE

After 1969 Steinem rose to acclaim as a leader within the women's rights movement. Less abrasive and more attractive than Betty Friedan, who is credited with founding the second wave of the movement, Steinem was an obvious choice as its spokesperson. Appearing regularly in the media, she was articulate and humorous, thus endearing many to the cause. She appeared in stark contrast to the Far Left feminists of the day, who quickly earned derision and ridicule from much of the press for their Marxist views and lesbian orientation.

In July 1971, Steinem joined Friedan, Bella Abzug, and Shirley Chisholm to found the National Women's Political Caucus, which encouraged and supported women running for public office. Also that year, she cofounded *Ms.*, a magazine by, for, and about women. The first full issue was published in January 1972 and sold out its print run of 300,000 in just over a week. By the summer of 1972 it had become a monthly magazine, financed by Warner Communications. Beginning in 1979 it operated as a nonprofit organization.

As she gained prominence, Steinem faced opposition from various radical feminist camps because her views did not always agree with theirs. In addition, men from both the conservative and liberal camps were threatened by her attacks on male power as well as by her feminist stance on issues such as pornography, which she opposes as degrading to women. In addition, the Redstockings began accusing Steinem in the mid-1970s of working for the CIA in the 1950s. She had briefly been employed with a liberal student group after college that was funded by the agency but maintained that she was not aware of the ties.

EQUAL RIGHTS AMENDMENT

Meanwhile, the Equal Rights Amendment (ERA)—a proposed amendment to the U.S. Constitution—was introduced and approved by both houses of Congress in 1972. It simply stated that "equality of rights shall not be denied or abridged by the United States or any state on account of sex." Due to the efforts of antifeminists and the widespread scare that granting women constitutional equality would signal the end of the American family, the ERA was ratified by only thirty-five states, three short of the number needed. In response to changing societal and legal norms, more and more women began entering the workforce, thus empowering themselves economically. It became illegal to discriminate against and sexually harass women, and states began passing laws that made it illegal for men to rape or beat their wives. As recently as the early 1960s, classified ads for jobs were segregated by sex; that practice was outlawed by the Civil Rights Act of 1964, which banned employment discrimination on the basis of sex. Though women still may not have achieved the full status of men in American business and politics, the effects of the women's movement on society has been enormous.

Into the 1980s, Steinem continued to urge for more fairness in the treatment of women. She championed the concept of equal pay for equal work. Despite laws that ban the practice, in reality, women have never been paid equal wages for equal work. Steinem also began shifting her focus from mainly financial and job-related issues to a more humanistic approach, hoping to encourage a world where gender lines are not so strictly defined. Pushing for men to accept more of the responsibility of child-rearing and domestic duties, she espoused that men and women should be less bound by traditional roles in order to make their lives more well-rounded. In 1983 Steinem published a well-received collection of essays, *Outrageous Acts and Everyday Rebellions*.

Steinem also stayed involved with *Ms.*, but in 1987 Australian company John Fairfax Ltd. bought the magazine, and readership fell drastically. The legendary publication was in dire straits. In 1990 *Ms.* returned without paid advertising. For the first of the new issues, Steinem wrote a scathing commentary on the control that advertisers exercised over editorial operations of women's magazines. In 1994 she released a new set of essays, *Moving beyond Words*, and continued to stand as the leading spokesperson for feminist activism in America.

Because of her repeated insistence that women did not need men in their lives to make them happy or complete, in 2000 Steinem shocked and outraged many fellow feminists when she married David Bale, a South African environmental and animal rights activist and the father of actor Christian Bale. After he became ill, she nursed him until his death from brain cancer in 2003.

Steinem contends that the fight for women's rights is still far from over. In addition to issues involving U.S. women, she focuses on global issues such as genital mutilation, which is still prevalent in developing countries and is a leading factor in high rates of maternal and childhood mortality. She also continues to write and speak on women's issues.

Geri Speace

SEE ALSO: *Chavez, Cesar; Equal Rights Amendment; Feminism; Mailer, Norman;* Ms.*;* Playboy.

BIBLIOGRAPHY

Brokaw, Tom. *Boom! Voices of the Sixties: Personal Reflections on the '60s and Today*. New York: Random House, 2007.

Gloria: In Her Own Words. Directed by Peter Kunhardt. DVD. New York: HBO, 2011.

Gorney, Cynthia. "Gloria: At 61, Steinem Wants Straight Talk, More Fun, and a New Congress." *Mother Jones*, November–December 1995, 22.

Hass, Nancy. "Gloria Steinem Still Wants More." *Newsweek*, August 15, 2011.

Steinem, Gloria. *Outrageous Acts and Everyday Rebellions*. New York: Holt, Rinehart, and Winston, 1983.

Winokur, L. A. "Gloria Steinem." *Progressive*, June 1995, 34–37.

Stengel, Casey *(1890–1975)*

Baseball legend Casey Stengel spent fifty-five years in baseball as both player and manager. He is best remembered for managing the highly successful New York Yankees and the highly unsuccessful New York Mets. While his management skills sustained his career, his outrageous use of the English language gained him equal fame.

He was born Charles Dillon Stengel in Kansas City, Kansas, and began playing semiprofessional baseball while in high school, where he was known as "Dutch" because of his German ancestry. An outfielder, he played with different minor-league teams before joining the Brooklyn Dodgers in 1912. It was there he acquired the nickname "K. C." because he was from Kansas City, a nickname that soon eased into "Casey," after the poem *Casey at the Bat*. After Brooklyn, he played major-league ball for the Pittsburgh Pirates (1918–1919, with time out for the U.S. Navy), Philadelphia Phillies (1920–1921), New York Giants (1921–1923, where in 1923 he batted .339 and won two World Series games with two home runs), and the Boston Braves (1924–1925). He ended his playing career as a player-manager for the minor-league Toledo (Ohio) Mud Hens.

Stengel was a jokester and a fighter and was thrown out of many games both as a player and a manager. For one of his early pranks, he stepped back from the plate, doffed his hat, and out flew a sparrow. The fans loved his antics. Stengel was also famous for his "Stengelese," with statements such as "I've always heard it couldn't be done, but sometimes it don't always work." Yet he could be succinct and telling: when he married his wife in 1924, he said of himself in the third person, "It is the best catch he ever made in his career." He said of Willie Mays, who played in a notoriously windy Candlestick Park in San Francisco, "If a typhoon is blowing, he catches the ball." Sometimes he could describe someone in a phrase: a nervous batter had "jelly leg," bad players were "road apples," rookies were "green peas," and a player who didn't carouse was a "milkshake drinker."

From 1934 to 1948 Stengel managed the Dodgers, Boston Braves, Milwaukee Brewers, Kansas City Blues, and Oakland Oaks. The Stengel legend began in October 1948 when he was named manager of the Yankees. In his first year as manager, the Yankees beat the Dodgers in the World Series and went on to win six more out of ten appearances under Stengel, thus being the team to beat in the 1950s. Stengel managed outstanding players such as Joe DiMaggio, Billy Martin, Yogi Berra, and Mickey Mantle. His critics said that anyone with that kind of talent playing for him could win, and many wouldn't give him credit for his knowledge of baseball and players. "Ability," Stengel once said, "is the art of getting credit for all the home runs someone else hits." His ability ran out when the Yankees lost the World Series to the Pirates in 1960 and he was fired, although the public story was that he was stepping aside as part of a youth movement at the Yankees. A bitter seventy-year-old Stengel quipped, "I'll never make the mistake of being seventy again."

Stengel was down but not out. A year later he was the manager of the expansion National League New York Mets, a team he was to call the "Amazin' Mets." What was amazing was that they ever took the field. In his four seasons as manager, the team never played better than .327. Stengel once said, "The only thing worse than a Mets game was a Mets doubleheader" and "Without losers, where would the winners be?" However, because they were bad, they were endearing and drew a better crowd than their cross-town rivals, the Yankees, viewed by many as an elitist team.

A broken hip finished Stengel's managing career. He retired one month after turning seventy-five. He was inducted into the National Baseball Hall of Fame on a fast-track vote. The honor was obviously important to him, for afterward he signed his letters "Casey Stengel, N.Y. Mets & Hall of Famer." Stengel died the day after the 1975 season ended.

R. Thomas Berner

SEE ALSO: *Baseball; Berra, Yogi; DiMaggio, Joe; Major League Baseball; Mantle, Mickey; The New York Mets; The New York Yankees.*

BIBLIOGRAPHY

Bak, Richard. *Casey Stengel: A Splendid Baseball Life*. Dallas, TX: Taylor Publishing, 1997.

Baseball Digest 33, no. 8 (1974).

Berkow, Ira, and Jim Kaplan. *The Gospel According to Casey*. New York: St. Martin's Press, 1992.

Creamer, Robert W. *Stengel: His Life and Times*. New York: Simon & Schuster, 1984.

Durso, Joseph. *Casey: The Life and Legend of Charles Dillon Stengel*. Englewood Cliffs, NJ: Prentice-Hall, 1967.

Steppenwolf

With landmark power-chord anthems such as "Born to Be Wild," the popular late-1960s band Steppenwolf coined the phrase for the bombastic, fast-paced genre it created: heavy metal, one of the most popular musical styles of the late twentieth century. The group came to prominence in 1969, when "Born to Be Wild" was featured in the opening sequence of the landmark film *Easy Rider* (1969). The song became a call to arms for a generation of rebellious youth, and its reference to "heavy metal thunder" became the tagline for the new musical style. "Born to Be Wild" ultimately reached number two on the Billboard singles chart. By 1999 the song had appeared in more than sixty films and television programs.

Steppenwolf's founder and lead vocalist John Kay was born Joachim Krauledat in East Germany in 1944, where he grew up listening to an Armed Forces Radio playlist that featured American blues-rock artists such as Chuck Berry and Little Richard. Immigrating to Toronto in the early 1960s, Kay joined a local blues band known as the Sparrows. After attempts to record with the Sparrows for Columbia Records, Kay left the group, relocating to New York and later to San Francisco. In 1967 he formed Steppenwolf, named after the novel by Hermann Hesse. The band featured guitarist Michael Monarch, keyboard player Goldy McJohn, drummer Jerry Edmonton, and bass player Rushton Moreve, later replaced by Nick St. Nicholas.

Steppenwolf's eponymous debut album, released in 1968, belied some of Kay's blues influences as well as the group's ties to the Bay Area psychedelic scene. However, it was the fierce power-chord stomp "Born to Be Wild" that captured the counterculture's imagination. Steppenwolf largely forsook its blues influences to hone this tough hard rock sound on its next two albums, *The Second* (1968) and *At Your Birthday Party* (1969). The albums spawned two Top 10 hits, "Magic Carpet Ride" and "Rock Me," as well as a host of heavy metal classics such as "Move Over" and "Hey Lawdy Mama." The band reached its creative peak in 1969 with the release of *Monster*, a concept album based on Kay's jaundiced view of contemporary America. *Monster* featured newcomers Larry Byrom on guitar and St. Nicholas on bass, both former members of the band called T.I.M.E.

Constrained by the pressure of making music for bikers and frustrated by continued personnel turnover, Kay disbanded Steppenwolf in 1972. After a less than successful solo career, Kay reconstituted the band in 1980 with longtime writing partner Michael Wilk on keyboards and bass and, beginning in 1984, Ron Hurst on drums. This most recent incarnation of Steppenwolf had produced several albums as of 2012—including a twenty-fifth-anniversary compilation and the concert record *Live at Louisville* (2004)—but none had enjoyed the commercial success of the group's 1960s hits. In 2007 the band gave what it termed its "farewell concert," although it has performed a few small shows since then.

The success of the heavy metal genre that the group spawned as well as the continued popularity of "Born to Be Wild" have ensured Steppenwolf's legacy in rock history. The band toured well into the first decade of the 2000s, headlining numerous "oldies" shows and selling out concerts throughout the country. In 1996 Kay was inducted into the Canadian Academy of Recording Arts and Sciences (CARAS) Hall of Fame.

Scott Tribble

SEE ALSO: Easy Rider*; Heavy Metal; Psychedelia; Rock and Roll.*

BIBLIOGRAPHY

The Billboard Encyclopedia of Music. Cincinnati, OH: 1998.

Kay, John, and John Einarson. *Magic Carpet Ride: The Autobiography of John Kay and Steppenwolf.* Kingston, ON: Quarry Press, 1994.

Popoff, Martin. *The Top 500 Heavy Metal Songs of All Time*. Toronto: ECW Press, 2002.

Stepping

Stepping (sometimes called step dancing) is a percussive style of dance that is not done to music. Rather, the dancers' bodies provide the "music" as they clap, stomp their feet, and slap their hands against their arms, chests, and legs to create a hard, driving beat. Dancers work as one to establish the rhythm through these movements and their verbal call-and-response with the dance leader.

A decades-old tradition in African American sororities and fraternities, stepping originated as a ritualized expression of allegiance to one's sister- or brotherhood. As stepping culture has grown over the decades, group identity has remained at the heart of its ethos and its style. Stepping draws from African and Caribbean folk traditions but also includes elements of tap dance, marching, gymnastics, break dancing, and hip-hop choreography. Author and researcher Elizabeth Fine explains, "There are a lot of different streams coming in to what we think of as stepping, and it's always evolving and taking in new styles."

Stepping experienced a surge in popularity in the United States at the end of the twentieth century, as many schools, churches, and community organizations began to sponsor stepping teams and clubs, seeking to harness the dynamism and positivity of the dance form to build fitness, self-esteem, and social bonds among young people. (Dancers sometimes step solo, but it is more often a group activity.)

The dance style has gained increased visibility through the efforts of Washington, D.C.–based Step Afrika!, which was founded in 1994 as the world's first professional step dance company. At the same time, amateur team stepping competitions have proliferated at both local and national levels. BET (Black Entertainment Television) often airs short step shows, and in 2009 the Coca-Cola Company introduced the Sprite Step-Off, billing it as the largest national step competition in history. The influence of stepping can be seen in music videos and Broadway productions. Since the late 1980s, step has also been featured in a number of movies, including *School Daze* (1988), *Mac and Me* (1988), *Drumline* (2002), *Stomp the Yard* (2007), and *How She Move* (2008).

Stepping is still widely practiced on college campuses and is increasingly being embraced by other cultures. As Latino and Asian American fraternities and sororities take up the form, they are infusing step with distinctive elements of their own musical heritage. Latino dancers, for example, often add bachata, salsa, or merengue rhythms to their routines.

Kerri Kennedy

SEE ALSO: *Broadway; Coca-Cola; Gymnastics; Hip-Hop; Marching Bands; Modern Dance; Social Dancing; Tap Dancing.*

BIBLIOGRAPHY

Fine, Elizabeth. *Soulstepping: African American Step Shows*. Chicago: University of Illinois Press, 2003.

Malone, Jacqui. *Steppin on the Blues*. Chicago: University of Illinois Press, 1996.

Step Afrika! Accessed May 2012. Available from http://www.stepafrika.org/

Stereographs

SEE: *Stereoscopes.*

Stereoscopes

Stereoscopy—creating three-dimensional (3-D) visual experiences from two-dimensional materials—informed nearly every visual medium of the modern age: art, photography, cinema, television, and newspapers. In the nineteenth century the marriage of stereoscopy, photography, and industrial production resulted in the first photographic mass media: the Victorian stereoscope. Popular from 1850 to 1920, the stereoscope answered desires for greater realism in visual representation, while its popular, yet intimate, visual experience prefigured visual media such as cinema and television. Eventually overshadowed by cinema and later electronic visual technologies, the optical principles of the stereoscope grounded many popular visual entertainments of the twentieth century: View-Master viewers, 3-D cinema and comic books, and Magic Eye stereograms.

The Victorian stereoscope was part of a general trend in the nineteenth century toward more realistic visual representations, mass-produced for an emergent commodity culture. It has been long known that two-dimensional representations, such as drawing and painting, are a poor imitation of human visual experiences. Paintings present but a single image, whereas in normal binocular vision the two different images received by each eye are synthesized by the brain into a single image, allowing the perception of depth and spatial relationships.

In 1832 British physicist Charles Wheatstone invented a device—the reflecting stereoscope—which induced normal binocular vision using prepared imagery. He created two drawings of an object that mimicked the slightly different perspective two eyes have of a single scene. By using mirrors, the reflecting stereoscope channeled vision so that only one of the drawings could be seen by each eye. The viewer's brain combined the two images into a single stereoscopic image with qualities similar to that of unaided vision. It was soon discovered that stereo-photographs could be prepared for Wheatstone's device by simultaneously taking two photographs with a double-lensed camera. If the imagery was properly prepared, the visual effects of solidity, depth, and realism were unparalleled.

Wheatstone's awkward device was merely a scientific curiosity until modified by William Brewster in 1849. Brewster's lenticular stereoscope, a small box outfitted with lenses and a slot to hold stereographic imagery, debuted in 1851 at London's Great International Exhibition. Although the interest of Queen Victoria ensured immediate popularity, early photographic technologies hampered broad circulation. In the 1840s Wheatstone's device used daguerreotypes and calotypes, but only after the 1851 introduction of glass-plate negatives could stereo-photographs be mass-produced. With cheap viewers and abundant imagery, stereoscopic viewing came within reach of a broad middle-class audience, fulfilling the London Stereoscopic Company's motto "A Stereoscope in Every Home."

MASS APPEAL

Popularity depended on a plentiful supply of imagery in the form of stereographs, also called stereocards or stereoviews. Generally, stereographs were 4-by-7-inch rectangular cards with two stereo-photographs pasted side-by-side. The photographer's, or more commonly publisher's, imprint and a short caption might be shown on the front, with a longer text on the reverse. Later thematic boxed sets were accompanied by maps and an explanatory guidebook. Because the overall size and shape of the stereograph was dictated by the stereoscope (similar to later standardized mass media like cassette tapes or CDs), stereographic publishers anticipated consumer desire and sought market niches through aesthetic innovation. Collectors attest to the bewildering diversity of stereographs: examples are known with tintype, daguerreotype, ambrotype, and lithographic images, which are pasted on paper, cardstock, glass, and porcelain mounts. Usually a stereograph can be dated to within a few years based solely on physical details.

Initially, stereographs were produced by lone figures who often took the photograph, processed the film, assembled the stereograph, and sold it to tourists. Stereo-photographers included the obscure and the famous; William Henry Jackson, Carleton Watkins, Timothy O'Sullivan, Eadweard Muybridge, and Matthew Brady are better-known producers. Historian William Culp Darrah estimated that between 1860 and 1890, as many as 12,000 stereo-photographers took between 3.5 million and 4.5 million individual images, which were printed on upward of 400 million stereographs. In the later nineteenth century, large factories churned out thousands of stereographs a day using assembly-line methods. Stereographs were sold at tourist spots, from storefronts, through mail-order catalogs, and door to door. Production gradually consolidated until, in 1921, the Keystone View Company was the sole purveyor of stereographs in the United States.

If the invention and early developments of stereoscopy belonged to Europeans, the phenomenon attained its greatest success in America. Stereoscopes were known in the United States from the early 1850s. In 1854 the Langenheim Brothers of Philadelphia became the first large-scale retailers of stereoscopic equipment. Between 1859 and 1863 noted essayist Oliver Wendell Holmes promoted the stereoscope in three enthusiastic articles in the *Atlantic Monthly*. Holmes also designed a simple handheld wooden stereoscope, improved and marketed by Boston photographer J. L. Bates. Stereo-photography was central to convincing skeptical East Coast audiences of the wonders of the American West, as well as conveying in realistic detail the horrors of the Civil and Spanish-American Wars.

By delivering news of the world in visual form, stereographs were roughly analogous to cinematic newsreels and television. Stereographs were a way to travel the world and experience its events from the security of one's armchair. Subjects included cities, famous places, tourist destinations and resorts, portraits of famous people, fine artworks, modes of transportation, international expositions, wars, natural disasters, aftermaths of fires and earthquakes, erotica and pornography, and educational and scientific matter. One card showed the full moon, which when viewed through a stereoscope showed every crater and mountain with a degree of detailed relief unattainable using even a telescope. Similar to early narrative silent film, a short series of stereographs could present a comedy or morality play.

Subject matter accommodated and anticipated the taste of the white Euro-American middle class, its primary consumer. Racial and social stereotyping was prevalent, especially in images of Native and African Americans, urban immigrants, and colonized peoples in Africa and Asia. Collecting, trading, organizing, viewing, and sharing stereocards was a prominent family pastime. Home filing cabinets for stereographs allowed collectors to construct a personal visual cartography of the world, infinite in its variety and endlessly malleable in form.

With the emergence of cinema, and especially after the 1920s, the stereoscope became largely an educational tool and later a children's toy. Tru-Vue stereoscopic filmstrips (from the 1920s through the 1950s) and the better-known View-Master system introduced at the 1939 New York World's Fair employed a similar optical apparatus. View-Master reels held ten translucent celluloid stereoscopic images on a thin plastic disk that was inserted into a lightweight View-Master viewer. Translucent celluloid imitated the luminescence of cinematic projections, injecting new life into an old gadget. View-Master contracted with Walt Disney studios to publish its popular animated films as View-Master reels, suggesting a growing audience among children. In the 1980s View-Master viewers appeared in the shape of popular children's animated characters such as Mickey Mouse, Casper the Ghost, Big Bird, Batman, and Tweety Bird.

MOVIES, COMIC BOOKS, AND BEYOND

Three-dimensional cinema of the early 1950s briefly revived adult interest in three-dimensional viewing. Broadcast television had reduced theater attendance, and to attract viewers, Hollywood introduced Natural Vision, or 3-D movies. Between 1952 and 1954 Hollywood produced more than seventy 3-D movies, beginning with *Bwana Devil* (1952) and the most famous being Alfred Hitchcock's *Dial M for Murder* (1954). To see a movie in 3-D, moviegoers wore special throwaway glasses with one red and one blue lens that permitted each eye to perceive only certain parts of a color-polarized film. The process had been known since the mid-nineteenth century, and a few monochromatic 3-D films were made in the 1920s and 1930s. Due to technical limitations and the uncomfortable glasses, the novelty was short-lived. It was briefly reintroduced in early 1980s horror flicks and television broadcasts and in panoramic IMAX 3-D movies of the 1990s. The early twenty-first century has also seen a resurgence in 3-D movies, especially in animated and comic-book-hero films.

Hollywood's flirtation with 3-D heralded the first comic book in 3-D, by Norman Maurer and Joe Kubert: *Three Dimension Comics* (1953), featuring Mighty Mouse. The comics are viewed with the same glasses as in 3-D cinema. The necessity of hand-drawing limited early 3-D comics to bicolor images, but after the 1970s limited polychromy was possible using computer-drafting technologies. Three-dimensional comics continue to appear sporadically, engaging some venerable talents of comic arts such as Ray Zone, Jack Kirby, and Wally Wood.

Beginning in the 1990s, computer-generated Magic Eye stereograms put a new twist on traditional stereoscopic viewing. Based on the theories of Bela Julesz and Christopher Tyler, Magic Eye artists employed a sophisticated computer algorithm that manipulated images at the pixel level, disguising simple stereoscopic images within another unrelated pattern. By free viewing (seeing a stereoscopic image without a stereoscope), the hidden image emerges from the generic background. Between 1992 and 1995 Magic Eye sold twenty-five million books in twenty-six languages worldwide, and in 1994 Magic Eye syndicated a weekly image to more than 200 newspapers.

By the late 1990s computerized flight simulators, high-altitude surveillance photography, and weapon targeting systems employed stereoscopic science. Using stereo-photography, NASA's Pathfinder Mission (1997) produced interactive topographical maps of Mars. For its report on the Mars mission, *National Geographic* featured some of the 3-D images from the Pathfinder Mission and included a pair of 3-D glasses to view them. Gradually, this technology has become available to a broader consumer culture through holographic and virtual-reality devices. Amateur and professional interest in stereoscopy has been accompanied by intense collecting of antique stereoviewers and stereoscopic imagery. There are regional, national, and international associations; a magazine devoted to the topic, *Stereo World*; and numerous websites. Although Victorian stereographs have become the province of antiquarians and museums, the desire to see in 3-D remains of unfailing interest to a popular audience.

Michael J. Murphy

SEE ALSO: *Animated Films;* Atlantic Monthly*; Batman; Comic Books; Disney (Walt Disney Company); Hitchcock, Alfred; Kirby, Jack; New 3-D; Television; Tweety Pie and Sylvester.*

BIBLIOGRAPHY

Darrah, William C. *The World of Stereographs.* Nashville, TN: Land Yacht Press, 1997.

Earle, Edward W., ed. *Points of View: The Stereograph in America: A Cultural History.* Rochester, NY: Visual Studies Workshop Press, 1979.

Grossman, Marc; Rachel Cooper; and N. E. Thing Enterprises. *Magic Eye: The 3D Guide.* Kansas City, MO: Andrews McMeel, 1995.

Higham, Charles. *Hollywood at Sunset.* New York: Saturday Review Press, 1972.

Jones, John. *Wonders of the Stereoscope.* New York: Knopf, 1976.

Nelson, M. Alexandra. "Dots of Illusion." *Popular Science,* September 1994, 56–59.

Newcott, William R. "Return to Mars." *National Geographic,* August 1998, 2.

Sell, MaryAnn, and Wolfgang Sell. *View-Master Viewers: An Illustrated History.* Borger, Netherlands: 3-D Book Productions, 1994.

Terrell, Maria S., and Robert E. Terrell. "Behind the Scenes of a Random Dot Stereogram." *American Mathematical Monthly,* October 1994, 715–724.

Waldsmith, John S. *Stereo Views: An Illustrated History and Price Guide.* Iola, WI: Krause Publications, 2002.

Wing, Paul. *Stereoscopes: The First One Hundred Years.* Nashua, NH: Transition, 1996.

Zone, Ray. *Stereoscopic Cinema and the Origins of 3-D Film, 1838–1952.* Lexington: University Press of Kentucky, 2007.

Zone, Ray. *The 3-D Zone.* Accessed November 2011. Available from http://www.ray3dzone.com

Stern, Howard *(1954–)*

One of the most popular and enduring talents in late-twentieth- and early-twenty-first-century radio, Howard Stern evokes the kind of controversy that you wouldn't expect from a typical celebrity. Stern, however, is not a typical celebrity. The audience for his nationally broadcast morning show numbers in the millions, and it is composed mostly of men, ages twenty-five to fifty-four, who listen religiously. A typical morning on the *Howard Stern Show* might include discussions on sex, lesbianism, race relations, lawyers, the latest tabloid stories, or flatulence. His radio show transcends the bounds of good taste and has tested the limits of radio broadcasting codes and regulations for more than thirty years.

Howard Stern's First Satellite Radio Broadcast. *Howard Stern broadcasts his first show on Sirius Satellite Radio from the network's studios at in New York City on January 9, 2006.* GETTY IMAGES.

Stern has been called the "poet laureate of urban American white trash" and the funniest man on radio. He cites as his major influence Lenny Bruce, another comedian with a highly critical view of moral standards.

EARLY LIFE AND CAREER

Howard Allen Stern was born on January 12, 1954, in the Queens borough of New York City. His father, Ben, was an engineer at a Manhattan radio station and was hard on his only son, frequently calling him a "moron." Stern describes his mother, Ray, as an overprotective woman who thought that her son would grow up to be sensitive if he played with puppets. The idea backfired, however, when little Howard put on X-rated puppet shows for his friends in his parents' basement.

Stern graduated from high school in 1972 and enrolled at Boston University, where he pursued a degree in communications. After graduating in 1976, he started working for WRNW-AM in Briarcliff, New York, as an afternoon disc jockey (DJ) and eventually took over several other duties. It was at WRNW that Stern realized he would have to be funnier than normal DJs if he wanted to be a success. His first antics on the air included bizarre commercial spots complete with weird sound effects and off-color calls to the business owners.

Stern lasted about two years at WRNW before moving to Hartford, Connecticut, to work for WCCC. Further honing his comedic technique, he experimented with on-air gags such as the "Cadaverathon" for the Yale and Harvard medical schools, which were purported to lack corpses for their students. Another event was his "To Hell with Shell" campaign aimed at gas companies and the long lines at the pumps during the late-1970s fuel shortage. Routines like these got him noticed by WWWW-FM in Detroit, a rock station that took him on in 1979. More irreverent gags and sketches followed, including a bra-burning demonstration in support of the Equal Rights Amendment and a raunchy daily piece in which a dominatrix would call in and give the weather forecast. Then, literally overnight, WWWW changed its format to country and Stern left.

In 1978 Stern married his college sweetheart, Alison Berns, a social worker. Stern tested the strength of his marriage by making it the subject of frequent on-air conversations. When his wife miscarried their first child, Stern did a sketch on it, a call from God himself who denigrated him for not being able to reproduce. The consequences were disastrous—the gag hurt his wife severely. Reaching a point where nothing was sacred on his show, Stern would even make fun of his wife's clients and their odd behavioral habits.

Stern apologized for such antics in his first book, *Private Parts* (1993), and insists that he is a family-oriented man. He and Alison had three children, all girls, before parting ways in 1999 and finalizing their divorce in 2001. In 2000 Stern began a long-term relationship with model Beth Ostrosky, who later became the cohost of *Casino Cinema*. The two married on October 3, 2008.

In 1981 Stern began working for WWDC-FM in Washington, D.C. Building a base for his morning show, he persuaded his supervisors to hire Fred Norris, a comedy writer with whom he worked in Hartford. Though Stern jokes that Norris does nothing for the show, Norris's part is a large one, doing voices, sound effects, and bogus recordings of celebrity voices. It was at WWDC that Stern first met Robin Quivers, who has been his news anchor ever since. Quivers, a Baltimore, Maryland, native, had her reservations about working with Stern at first, but she was clearly impressed with his spontaneous, unrehearsed style.

In February 1982 Stern pulled what may have been his most outrageous stunt when, in the wake of the crash of Air Florida Flight 90 into the 14th Street Bridge, he called the airline and asked how much a one-way ticket to the bridge would cost. The call offended many listeners, though Stern claimed he was expressing his own outrage against the flight crew that allowed the plane to take off without the wings being deiced. Shortly thereafter Stern was fired from DC-101 (though not for the prank call—he was fired for referring to station management as "scumbags").

STERN TAKES ON NEW YORK

Stern was quickly hired to work for WNBC-AM, fulfilling his dream of working in New York City. But he found himself in frequent disagreements with his superiors at the station. In order to control his antics, NBC executives would often write new rules and regulations for him to follow. Stern usually refused and was suspended several times before he was fired in September 1985. It wasn't long before a competing New York station, WXRK-FM (K-Rock), picked him up. The station promised Stern no restrictions in running his show. Stern brought along Quivers, Norris, Gary Dell'Abate, a former producer for NBC and the show's punching bag, and his chief comedy artist, Jackie "The Jokeman" Martling, who did a large part of the show's writing. One addition to his crew of regulars was "Stuttering" John Melendez, whose speech impediment was put to use by Stern. He believed that no one would turn down an interview with a stutterer, even one who asked rude questions.

Only months after starting at K-Rock, Stern was given the chance to move his show to the coveted morning slot, in direct competition with fellow "shock jock" Don Imus. Stern prized the rivalry with Imus, who remained the whipping boy for Stern and his crew into the 1990s. In 1986 Stern completed his objective, surpassing Imus in the ratings. To celebrate the event, Stern organized a mock funeral at Rockefeller Center.

In 1990 Stern launched the TV version of the *Howard Stern Show* on WWOR-TV in New York. The program was a visual rendition of his radio show but was ultimately canceled because of budget setbacks. *The Howard Stern Interview* followed but also didn't last. In 1994 the E! network began broadcasting a thirty-minute simulcast of his radio show, using several stationary cameras placed in the radio studio. In August 1998 Stern launched yet another talk show, called *The Howard Stern Radio Show*, which aired directly opposite *Saturday Night Live*.

Stern's book *Private Parts* is mostly a memoir of events in his childhood and broadcasting career, and it became the fastest-selling item in the history of its publisher, Simon & Schuster. The book saw a resurgence in sales in 1995 when Stern released his second book, *Miss America*, which featured Stern himself on the cover in drag. *Private Parts* was made into a feature film in 1997. Stern supposedly rejected multiple scripts before settling on what he thought was the best representation of his book. The film received positive reviews and is mostly a tribute to his relationship with his (now ex-) wife, Alison. A very funny and surprisingly touching film, it reenacts many of the sketches that marked his early career. It also gives more insight into his partnership with Quivers and their undying friendship.

Though his radio show has brought him millions of fans, he has had one consistent enemy throughout his career: the Federal Communications Commission (FCC). Radio station owner Infinity Broadcasting was fined $600,000 in 1992 after Stern boasted about masturbating to pictures of Aunt Jemima and having rough sex with Michelle Pfeiffer. It was not the first but only the most dramatic in a series of inquiries, reprimands, and fines aimed at Stern since 1986. Stern alleged that the FCC had a personal vendetta against him and told *Rolling Stone* that he'll never win against the powerful government organization "because they're bureaucrats . . . they've got all the time in the world and they're going to sit there and just wear me down."

In March 2001 Stern's head writer, Jackie Martling, left the show amicably. The circumstances of his departure were not heavily publicized. His replacement, Artie Lang, joined the crew officially in October of the same year after sitting in on the show for several months. Lang's long-time fandom of the show is generally cited as the deciding factor in Stern hiring him.

MOVE TO SATELLITE

Perhaps the biggest shift in Stern's recent career has been his departure from "terrestrial" radio for satellite radio, a medium that Stern felt would allow him more creative freedom. He announced the finalization of a lucrative contract with Sirius Satellite Radio in October 2004. Stern cited increased restrictive control of his show by his station, WXRK, in the aftermath of the Super Bowl XXXVIII (2004) halftime show incident (during which Janet Jackson's bare breast was exposed on camera) among his reasons for leaving. On Sirius (which merged in 2008 with XM to form SiriusXM), he would not be subjected to regulation by his old enemy, the FCC. The show was launched on January 9, 2006, on two Sirius channels, *Howard 100* and *Howard 101*.

Tom Trinchera

SEE ALSO: *Bruce, Lenny; Divorce; Radio; Satellite Radio; Shock Radio; Television.*

BIBLIOGRAPHY

Cegielski, Jim. *The Howard Stern Book: An Unauthorized, Unabashed, Uncensored Fan's Guide*. Secaucus, NJ: Carol Publishing Group, 1994.

Colford, Paul D. *Howard Stern, King of All Media: The Unauthorized Biography*. New York: St. Martin's Press, 1996.

Kunen, James S. "Howard Stern: New York's Mad-Dog Deejay May Be the Mouth of the '80s." *People Weekly*, October 22, 1984.

Lucaire, Luigi. *Howard Stern, A to Z: The Stern Fanatic's Guide to the King of All Media*. New York: St. Martin's Press, 1997.

Marin, Rick. "Man or Mouth: The *Rolling Stone* Interview with

Howard Stern." *Rolling Stone*, February 10, 1994.

Menell, Jeff. *Howard Stern: Big Mouth*. New York: Windsor, 1993.

Mintzer, Richard. *Howard Stern: A Biography*. Santa Barbara, CA: Greenwood Press, 2010.

Remnick, David. "The Accidental Anarchist." *New Yorker*, March 10, 1997.

Stern, Howard. *Private Parts*. New York: Simon & Schuster, 1993.

Stern, Howard. *Miss America*. New York: ReganBooks, 1995.

Stetson Hat

When Philadelphia hat maker John B. Stetson went west in 1860 to cure his tuberculosis, he worked the gold rush at Pikes Peak, Colorado, where he designed a hat for working in the hot sun and for keeping off the rain. Stetson returned to Philadelphia to mass-produce the "Boss of the Plains" hat, made of tan felt with a wide brim and high crown. Worn by presidents, Buffalo Bill Cody, and the Texas Rangers, the hat became a symbol of the West. Stetson widened their production to include other styles and eventually other products (including cologne), but Stetson felt hats remained the majority of the company's sales.

Over time, Stetson and the "Boss" hat became synonymous with, simply, a cowboy hat. However, the original Boss design bears slight resemblance to the typical cowboy hat known in the early twenty-first century. Legend has it that the curved brim and dimpled top of currently fashionable cowboy hats developed from the wear and tear inflicted on the "Boss" hats while breaking them in. Other influences have also helped shape the hat into what it is today, but the essential construction has not changed since its 1865 inception. Despite the decline of the American ranching and cowboy traditions at the beginning of the twenty-first century, Stetson hats remain an American icon and can still be seen in popular culture and on the heads of many men and women.

S. Naomi Finkelstein

SEE ALSO: *Cody, Buffalo Bill, and His Wild West Show; Retro Fashion.*

BIBLIOGRAPHY

Reynolds, William, and Ritch Rand. *The Cowboy Hat Book*. Layton, UT: Gibbs Smith, 2003.

Snyder, Jeffrey. *Stetson Hats & the John B. Stetson Company: 1865–1970*. Atglen, PA: Schiffer Publishing, 1997.

Stetson Hat Company. *The Stetson Century 1865–1965*. St. Louis, MO: Stetson Hat Company, 1965.

Stevens, Ray *(1939–)*

Originally best known for his novelty songs, country music singer-songwriter Ray Stevens grew into a conservative political satirist. Although the tone of his songs changed over his career of more than fifty years, Stevens maintains his cultural relevance through his wit and perseverance.

Born Harry Ray Ragsdale on January 24, 1939, Stevens started recording music in 1957. His career began with the 1961 hit "Jeremiah Peabody's Poly Unsaturated Quick Dissolving Fast Acting Pleasant Tasting Green and Purple Pills." The following year, he had an even bigger success with "Ahab the Arab," an off-the-wall saga of a camel driver, complete with sound effects. Stevens went on to score hit records with more traditional songs, but he continued to find success through parody and humor. He spoofed Tarzan and rock and roll at the same time in "Gitarzan," streaking (a 1970s public nakedness fad) in "The Streak," and 1980s televangelism with "Would Jesus Wear a Rolex?"

Stevens displayed a talent for sophisticated musical humor when he transformed the jazz standard "Misty" into a bluegrass romp. He also had a way with sentimental country in his 1970 chart-topper, "Everything Is Beautiful." Both works garnered him Grammy Awards. During the 1980s the success that Stevens had as a traditional country artist waned as he released strictly comedy albums. Although his singles did not chart as high as they once had, he had staying power on the charts, and he appeared on *Hee Haw* and other television variety shows.

During the 1990s Stevens branched out into other media. Emboldened by the success of his live shows, he began to sell videos of the shows to his audiences. He also became one of the leaders in music marketing with his aggressive and successful television mail-order promotions of his music videos. After surviving a bout with prostate cancer in 1999, Stevens returned to performing, and in early 2002 he released "Osama Yo' Mama."

In 2007 Stevens began to release music and music videos via his website. Capitalizing on its success, he then began placing his music videos on YouTube. In early 2010 he released "We the People," a music video critique of health care reform, and it proved to be extremely popular on YouTube, receiving millions of views. He followed up with a CD/DVD collection by the same name, featuring additional political songs and videos. Another political music video by Stevens that achieved great success on YouTube was "Come to the USA," a satire on immigration reform.

In 2009 Stevens was inducted into the Christian Music Hall of Fame, and—maintaining his identification as a country artist—he was honored in 2010 by the Country Music Hall of Fame. In 2011 Stevens embarked upon a tour during which he appeared on numerous radio programs. Never one to miss an opportunity for self-promotion, he took full advantage of his time on the air by offering his opinions on current events while also plugging his new projects. The following year Stevens issued *The Encyclopedia of Recorded Comedy Music*, a nine-CD compilation of comedy songs featuring both his hits and those of other artists.

Tad Richards

SEE ALSO: *Bluegrass; Facebook; Grammy Awards;* Hee Haw; *Jazz; Radio; Rock and Roll; Social Media; Streaking; Tarzan; Televangelism; Twitter; Videos; YouTube.*

BIBLIOGRAPHY

Cooper, Lee. "It's Still Rock and Roll to Me: Reflections on the Evolution of Popular Music and Rock Scholarship." *Popular Music and Society* 21, no. 1 (1997): 101–108.

Cusic, Don. "Comedy and Humor in Country Music." *Journal of American Culture* 16, no. 2 (1993): 45–50.

Roy, Don. "Ray Stevens." *The Encyclopedia of Country Music*, ed. Paul Kingsbury. New York: Oxford University Press, 1998.

Wadhams, Wayne. "The Funny Men: Novelty Records, Ray Stevens, 'Ahab the Arab' (1962)." In *Inside the Hits: The Seduction of a Rock and Roll Generation.* Boston: Berklee Press, 2001.

Stewart, Jimmy *(1908–1997)*

One of the most universally recognized and beloved movie stars of the twentieth century, iconic actor Jimmy Stewart enjoyed a prolific career that spanned six decades, from the 1930s to the 1980s, as well as many filmmaking genres, from comedy to serious drama, from the dark Westerns of the 1950s to the brilliant suspense of Alfred Hitchcock. No matter what part Stewart played, audiences responded to the gangly, good-looking actor, believing that underneath it all, he was always a good man, as his "aw shucks" personality endeared him to fans around the world.

Born in the small town of Indiana, Pennsylvania, to Elizabeth and Alexander Stewart, James Maitland Stewart was raised in a loving middle-class home. His father was the proprietor of the local J. M. Stewart Hardware Store (which would later become famous as the home of his son's Academy Award, which was housed in the store window for many years), and by all accounts Stewart had a happy and normal childhood. Upon graduation from high school, he decided, with encouragement from his very practical father, to study civil engineering and architecture at Princeton University, from which he graduated in 1932 with honors. While at college, however, he became involved in the theater group, the Triangle Club, and met fellow student (and future director) Joshua Logan. After graduation Logan invited Stewart to join the University Players, his summer stock theater company in Massachusetts.

Jimmy Stewart. *Jimmy Stewart poses with the honorary Oscar awarded to him in 1985 for his achievements during his fifty-year career.* MAUREEN DONALDSON/CONTRIBUTOR/ARCHIVE PHOTOS/ GETTY IMAGES.

FROM STAGE TO SCREEN

After making his professional debut with the Players, Stewart abandoned architecture forever, much to his parents' displeasure. He eventually moved to Broadway to appear in the production *Carry Nation* (1932), which was not successful. His next role, however, was in *Goodbye Again* (1932), a play he had appeared in while in Massachusetts. This production was a hit, earning Stewart excellent notices, and by 1934 he was working steadily. Producer/director Guthrie McClintic, husband of stage actress Katharine Cornell, hired him to appear in the play *Yellow Jack* (1934), for which he again received rave reviews. It was during this production that Stewart also appeared in his first motion picture, a small uncredited role in *Art Trouble* (1934).

In 1935, while Stewart was visiting his family, he received an offer from Metro-Goldwyn-Mayer (MGM) to appear in a small role in *Murder Man*, starring Spencer Tracy. MGM signed him to a standard contract and put him in several productions, but his first real break came when an old friend from his University Player days, actress Margaret Sullavan, insisted on him as her costar in *Next Time We Love* (1936). A second break came when Stewart played opposite Eleanor Powell in *Born to Dance* (1936), where he introduced the Cole Porter song "Easy to Love." While his singing was unremarkable, *Born to Dance* was one of the biggest hits of the year.

STAR POWER

It was a film released in 1939 that finally made Stewart a major star. He had worked with director Frank Capra previously on the classic comedy *You Can't Take It with You* (1938). When Capra needed a leading man for his new picture, *Mr. Smith Goes to Washington*, he wanted no one else for the role of the idealistic young man thrust into the corrupt world of Washington politics. The film and Stewart were a sensation, although many political figures at the time denounced the implication that the U.S. government might contain corrupt elements. For his performance, Stewart won the New York Film Critics Circle Award for best actor. He was also nominated for an Academy Award but was a surprising loser to Robert Donat in *Goodbye, Mr. Chips*. The following year he costarred with Katharine Hepburn and Cary Grant in *The Philadelphia Story* and took home an Oscar for that performance, though many felt it was a consolation prize for *Mr. Smith*.

In 1941 America entered World War II, which put a temporary hold on Stewart's Hollywood career. He was one of the very first movie stars to enlist in the military, earning a distinguished record as an air force pilot and commander and becoming one of the highest-ranking officers in the U.S. Auxiliary Air Force, rising to the rank of colonel.

For his first film project after the war, Stewart chose to work with Capra again. *It's a Wonderful Life* (1946) is now considered a classic and a Christmas staple, but when it was originally released, neither audiences nor critics particularly cared for it. Capra and Stewart were disappointed with the reception the picture received, and both maintained in later years that it was their favorite film.

The late 1940s saw many changes in Stewart's life. First, at the age of forty-one, he married Gloria McLean and became an instant father to Gloria's children from a previous marriage. He also decided that his career needed to take a different direction. This led to two successful collaborations each with directors Anthony Mann and Alfred Hitchcock. The results were some of Stewart's darkest and most critically acclaimed works—*Winchester 73* (1950) and *Broken Arrow* (1950) with Mann, and *Rear Window* (1954) and *Vertigo* (1958) with Hitchcock. The latter is considered by many to be Stewart's finest performance and Hitchcock's masterpiece.

After the 1950s Stewart continued to do film work, although good roles became less frequent. By the 1970s he had turned to television, appearing in two short-lived television series, *The Jimmy Stewart Show* (1971–1972) and *Hawkins* (1973–1974). He also did several made-for-television movies, such as *Mr. Krueger's Christmas* in 1980 and *Right of Way* with Bette Davis in 1983. In 1980 he received the American Film Institute's Lifetime Achievement Award. His last film performance was as the voice of the gunfighting dog, Wylie Burp, in *An American Tail: Fievel Goes West* (1991). Stewart continued to be active until the death of his wife, Gloria, in 1994. His health began failing soon after, and he died in 1997.

Stewart will long be remembered as exemplifying the best of America. His heroic roles and his devotion to his family made Americans feel he was a part of their own family, making him one of the best-loved figures of twentieth-century American popular culture.

Jill A. Gregg

SEE ALSO: *Academy Awards; Broadway; Capra, Frank; Community Theater; Davis, Bette; Film Noir; Grant, Cary; Hepburn, Katharine; Hitchcock, Alfred; Hollywood;* It's a Wonderful Life*; Made-for-Television Movies; MGM (Metro-Goldwyn-Mayer); Movie Stars;* Mr. Smith Goes to Washington*;* The Philadelphia Story*; Porter, Cole;* Rear Window*; Tracy, Spencer;* Vertigo*; World War II.*

BIBLIOGRAPHY

Coe, Jonathan. *Jimmy Stewart: A Wonderful Life.* New York: Arcade, 1994.

Dewey, Donald. *James Stewart: A Biography.* Atlanta, GA: Turner Publications, 1996

Fishgall, Gary. *Pieces of Time: The Life of James Stewart.* New York: Scribner, 1997.

Pickard, Roy. *James Stewart: The Hollywood Years.* London: Hale, 1992.

Quirk, Lawrence J. *James Stewart: Behind the Scenes of a Wonderful Life.* New York: Applause Books, 1997.

Robbins, Jhan. *Everybody's Man: A Biography of Jimmy Stewart.* New York: Putnam, 1985.

Smith, Starr. *Jimmy Stewart: Bomber Pilot.* St. Paul, MN: Zenith Press, 2006.

Stewart, Jon *(1962–)*

Jon Stewart was a comedian and perennial talk-show guest host in 1999 when he got the job of anchoring Comedy Central's satiric news program *The Daily Show. The Daily Show with Jon Stewart* proved to be the perfect vehicle for Stewart's dry humor and trademark self-deprecating delivery. He not only spurred the show to higher ratings, but he also became the spokes-mensch for a liberal population tired of a news media that did not reflect their perspectives. Through comedy as subtle as a raised eyebrow and as blatant as a whoopee cushion, Stewart made the news interesting and earned the trust of his audience. In the process, he became much more than just a funnyman. Though he is resolutely humble, describing his role as that of "dancing monkey," Stewart takes his position as comic gadfly very seriously. A surprising number of others have taken him seriously as well—Stewart may be one of the first comedians to be studied by political scholars for his impact on contemporary political discourse.

Stewart was born Jonathan Stuart Leibowitz in 1962 in New York City and grew up in Lawrenceville, New Jersey. He attended the College of William and Mary in Virginia, where his good-natured humor resulted in the establishment of an annual "Leibo award" for the funniest male soccer player. After graduation he returned to New York, where he worked tending bar and honing his stand-up skills in local comedy clubs, chang-

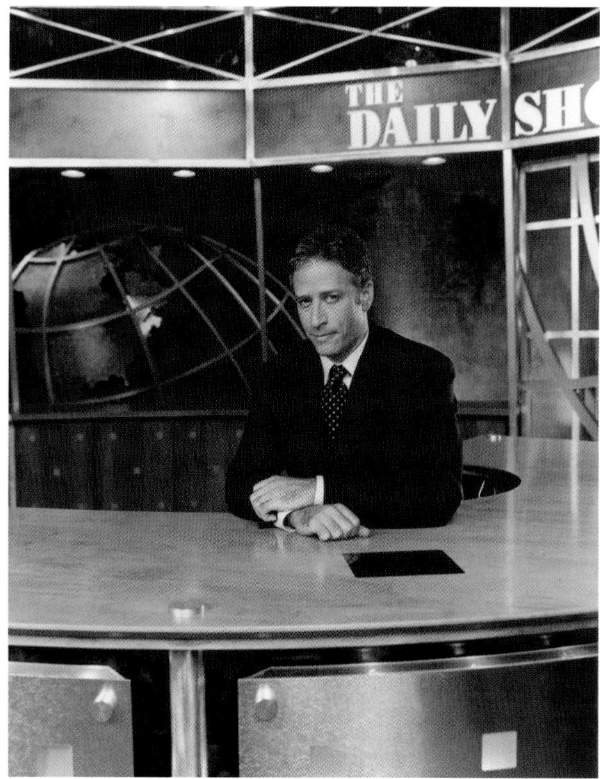

Jon Stewart. *Jon Stewart took over as host of* The Daily Show *in 1999.* COMEDY CENT/MAD COW PROD/THE KOBAL COLLECTION.

ing his last name to Stewart. His first regular stand-up gig was a late-night slot at Manhattan's famous Comedy Cellar in 1989, which led to his first television job as host of Comedy Central's *Short Attention Span Theater*, a collection of film clips and skits.

Stewart's amiable patter and natural spontaneity drew the attention of MTV, which offered him his own late-night talk show in 1993. In 1994 Paramount launched an hour-long syndicated version of the rambunctious *Jon Stewart Show*, but it never found a consistent audience and was canceled in 1995. Stewart spent the next few years on a variety of projects, guest hosting for Tom Snyder on CBS's *Late, Late Show* and playing a guest host on the talk show parody *The Larry Sanders Show*. In the late 1990s Stewart had small roles in several movies, and in 1999 he published a well-received book of comic essays, *Naked Pictures of Famous People*.

In 1998 Comedy Central approached him with an offer—Craig Kilborn, host of the satiric news report *The Daily Show*, was leaving, and the network wanted Stewart to replace him. They offered him an attractive four-year contract to serve as host, writer, and executive producer. Stewart, tired of guest-hosting, readily agreed. He stepped into the host/anchor position in January 1999. The news-spoof format of the show and Stewart's sad-eyed ironic persona seemed made for each other. By March the show was pulling in its largest audience ever.

The Daily Show with Jon Stewart preserved the show's liberal bent and its familiar format—current headlines with comic commentary at the beginning, followed by skits and a celebrity interview. Stewart soon put his own brand on each segment. His skillful interviewing style drew interesting commentary from guests from both the Left and the Right, whom he probed with humor and persistence. He had an unsettling technique of exposing disinformation by showing news clips of the interviewee's own words contradicting their later statements, but Stewart himself was never harsh or disrespectful.

In 2000 *The Daily Show* team took to the road to cover the Republican and Democratic conventions in what Stewart described as "a fake news organization covering a fake news event." The resulting series of telecasts, titled *Indecision 2000*, received a Peabody Award. In 2004 he published his second book, *America (The Book): A Citizen's Guide to Democracy Inaction*. In a 2007 poll, Stewart turned up fourth on a list of Americans' most respected journalists. In 2005 and 2007 he was tapped to host the Academy Awards ceremony.

In his work on *The Daily Show*, Stewart found a venue for expressing something deeper than comedy. In 2010, disgusted with the adversarial discourse he felt was promoted by conservative news organizations like Fox News, he and fellow comic news pundit Stephen Colbert hosted the Rally to Restore Sanity in Washington, D.C., suggesting that participants bring signs with a measured tone such as, "I disagree with you, but I'm pretty sure you're not Hitler." The tongue-in-cheek demonstration drew 200,000 people, more than twice as many as a previous right-wing Rally to Restore America.

By 2012 *The Daily Show* had won sixteen Emmy Awards and had a devoted audience of more than 2.3 million viewers. Stewart's fans get more than a laugh from his show; in a climate of agenda-driven news networks, many liberal viewers say *The Daily Show*'s satirical reports are their best source of information about current events. This has proved to be perhaps Stewart's most important contribution to the contemporary political scene: the use of comic critique to expose the myth of objectivity and challenge the inadequacy of the mainstream news media. Though some analysts have expressed concern that *The Daily Show*'s mocking tone may have increased cynicism and apathy in its liberal viewers, others have seen the show as the herald of a new honesty in political discourse.

Tina Gianoulis

SEE ALSO: *Academy Awards; Cable TV; Celebrity; Colbert, Stephen; Emmy Awards; Hollywood;* The Larry Sanders Show*; MTV; Stand-Up Comedy; Television.*

BIBLIOGRAPHY

Cassino, Dan, and Yesemin Besen-Cassino. *Consuming Politics: Jon Stewart, Branding, and the Youth Vote in America*. Madison, NJ: Fairleigh Dickinson University Press, 2009.

Erickson, Steve. "The News Hound." *Los Angeles Magazine*, January 2012, 68.

Hamm, Theodore. *The New Blue Media: How Michael Moore, MoveOn.org, Jon Stewart and Company Are Transforming Progressive Politics*. New York: New Press, 2008.

Junod, Tom. "Jon Stewart and the Burden of History." *Esquire*, October 2011, 151.

McConville, Jim. "Jon Stewart: Building His Own House at Comedy Central." *Electronic Media*, January 25, 1999, 38.

Morris, Jonathan. "*The Daily Show with Jon Stewart* and Audience Attitude Change during the 2004 Party Conventions." *Political Behavior* 31, no. 16 (2009): 79–102.

Scherer, Randy. *Jon Stewart*. Farmington Hills, MI: Lucent Books, 2011.

Stewart, Martha *(1941–)*

Martha Stewart, born August 3, 1941, in Jersey City, New Jersey, has made her name synonymous with contemporary American homemaking. Throughout her career, which has spanned more than thirty years, Stewart has offered advice on cooking, entertaining, and home decorating. Known for sophistication and country living, she launched a media empire in 1997, Martha Stewart Omnimedia, featuring books, magazines, and retail products. Her entrepreneurial success embodied the American dream, until 2004, when she was convicted of lying to federal authorities about her knowledge of the stock scandal surrounding the pharmaceutical company ImClone. Although many analysts and pundits predicted that Stewart and her empire would fall, upon her release from prison in 2005 she restored her public image as well as her company's financial status. Her successes and failures may haunt her, but Stewart continues to be one of the most powerful and prominent names in the cooking and home decor industries.

Born to Eddie and Martha Kostyra, Stewart received much of her training in cooking and sewing from her mother and in canning from her grandmother. After graduating from Barnard College with a degree in European and architectural history, she married Andrew Stewart in 1961. She gave birth to the couple's only child, daughter Alexis, in 1965. During the early years of her marriage, Stewart worked on Wall Street as a stockbroker for Monness, Williams and Sidel, where she learned the inner workings of the financial world. Leaving Wall Street to move to the countryside with her husband in 1972, Stewart undertook renovating the Turkey Hill farmhouse. In 1976 in the basement of her home, she started a catering business, the Uncatered Affair, with her friend Norma Collier. The partnership dissolved within six months after Collier accused Stewart of taking jobs without her knowledge. Stewart continued to cater on her own and briefly managed the Market Basket, selling bakery and dinner items at a local mall. In 1977, after a dispute with the owners, she left the mall and started her own business.

Soon after, Stewart's husband hired her to cater a book-release party, where he introduced her to Alan Mirken of Crown Publishing. Impressed by her catering abilities, Mirken enlisted Stewart for a cookbook. Her first book, *Entertaining* (1982), which was ghostwritten by Elizabeth Hawes, features pictorials and recipes from Stewart's events. She quickly followed this success with numerous other works, including *Martha Stewart's Quick Cook* (1983), *Weddings* (1987), and *Martha Stewart's Christmas* (1989) for Clarkson Potter Publishing. Stewart expanded her writing to newspaper and magazine columns and made appearances on *The Oprah Winfrey Show* and *Larry King Live*. While she found success in the business world, her marriage ended in divorce in 1989.

In 1990 Stewart partnered with Time Publishing Ventures on the magazine *Martha Stewart Living* and developed a half-hour version for television in 1993. Her repeated appearances on *The Early Show* on CBS expanded her fame, earning her the title "the guru of homemaking." With her business partner Sharon Patrick, she secured funding for all of her merchandising and business ventures, including television and print, successfully consolidating her brand under Martha Stewart Living Omnimedia in 1997. That same year, Stewart launched a website and a mail-order catalog. The company went public on October 19, 1999, enjoying a successful launch on Wall Street. She served as CEO until 2003 and expanded the company to include a variety of goods, such as sheets, towels, and kitchen utensils.

At various points in her career, Stewart has experienced problems resulting from judgment errors. Early in her career, she was accused of selling precooked food out of a store and faced issues with a health inspector. As a stockbroker, she frequently offered advice that lost her clients money. In 2002, however, she faced her greatest challenge. An investigation of her stock broker, Peter Bacanovic, revealed that Stewart had received insider trader information and avoided a significant financial loss when she sold her ImClone stock. She was indicted in 2003 on charges of securities fraud and obstruction of justice and was sentenced to prison for five months at a minimum-security prison in Alderson, West Virginia. After her release on March 4, 2005, she served an additional five months of house arrest and wore an electronic monitoring device.

Post-prison sentence, Stewart mounted a comeback. She resumed her role as CEO of Omnimedia, expanded her retail catalog for Kmart, and returned to daytime TV. She signed lucrative contracts with the high-end flooring company FLOR Inc., the E. J. Gallo Winery, Costco, and Wal-Mart. Having teamed with Sherwin Williams (2001–2007) and Lowe's (2007–2009) on house paint, Stewart moved to Home Depot in 2009. Marketing everything from lawn furniture to dishes through such chains as Macy's and Kmart, Stewart has established a brand name associated with mid- to high-priced merchandise.

In early 2012 Stewart announced a deal with J. C. Penney, leading Macy's to rethink its involvement with her brand. Still viable in the home arena, her company constantly developed items sold exclusively in these outlets. With multiple lines coexisting in the medium and high price ranges, some critics question overexposure of the brand. Additionally, Stewart has lost some of her audience and influence to the Food Network stars. The emergence of flamboyant food celebrities such as Rachael Ray and Paula Deen pressured Stewart at once to continually reinvent and relocate herself. In 2012 Hallmark canceled *The Martha Stewart Show*, but Stewart quickly found a new home on PBS with *Martha Stewart's Cooking School* and continued to produce *Emeril's Table* for her protégé Emeril Lagasse.

Linda Martindale

SEE ALSO: *DIY/Home Improvement; Foodies; Kmart; Macy's; Ray, Rachael; Reality Television; Television.*

BIBLIOGRAPHY

Byron, Christopher. *Martha Inc.: The Incredible Story of Martha Stewart Living Omnimedia.* New York: Wiley, 2002.

"Martha Stewart." Martha Stewart Living Omnimedia. Accessed March 2012. Available from http://www.marthastewart.com/

Price, Joann F. *Martha Stewart: A Biography.* Westport, CT: Greenwood Press, 2007.

Stickball

Stickball refers to a form of baseball developed to accommodate play on streets and sidewalks. A janitor's mop handle is the preferred bat, and a pink rubber ball—known as a "Spaulding" or "Spauldeen"—is considered to be the best ball. The ball is pitched or bounced toward the hitter; sewers and chalk markings are used for bases; and a hit may be played off of fire escapes, cars, stoops, or any other urban obstacle.

Stickball traces its origins to eighteenth-century English games such as old cat, rounders, and town ball, although some sources trace it back to games played by Plains Indians. As of the 2010s stickball is still played in its purest form in summer leagues in New York City and exists in some form in most American cities. Other versions are known as Strikeout, Fast Pitch, Corkball, Bottle Caps, and Fuzzball and are played with a wide range of bats and balls, sometimes against walls with painted strike zones. Stickball and its variations offer players the chance to use basic baseball skills without requiring full teams of players; expensive gloves or bats; or the rarest of all urban commodities, an open stretch of grass. In 2010 the game was featured in the PBS documentary *New York Street Games.*

Colby Vargas

SEE ALSO: *Baseball; Leisure Time.*

BIBLIOGRAPHY

Ravielli, Anthony. *What Are Street Games?* New York: Atheneum, 1981.

Schindler, Steven. *Sewer Balls.* Los Angeles: Elevated Press, 1998.

Vignola, Ray; Dennis Vignola; and Tim Haggerty. *New York City Street Games/Includes Chalk Ball Bottlecaps.* Berkeley, CA: Mig Communications, 1994.

Wirth, Cliff. *Stickball, Streetcars, and Saturday Matinees: Illustrated Memories*. Greendale, WI: Reiman Publications, 1995.

Stiller, Ben *(1965–)*

Actor, director, writer, and producer Ben Stiller was quite literally born into the entertainment industry. The child of performers, Stiller grew up immersed in the world of television and began making his own films when he was ten. His adult career has been marked by savagely daffy comedies in which he often plays perennially frustrated characters. His darkly ironic comic sensibility resonated deeply with the media-saturated offspring of the baby boom generation, and Stiller became one of the most popular comic actors of the turn of the twenty-first century. His real love, however, is directing, where his best efforts have been incisive spoofs of celebrity and media that manage to combine satire with a real affection for his pop culture targets.

Benjamin Edward Stiller was born in 1965 in New York City. His parents, Jerry Stiller and Anne Meara, had separate careers as actors and writers, as well as working together as the comedy team Stiller and Meara. Their careers were flourishing during the 1960s when their children, Amy and Ben, were born, and both youngsters grew up surrounded by entertainers and mesmerized by television. Ben received his first Super 8 movie camera at the age of ten and immediately began making films starring his sister. The same year, Stiller's parents sent him to a therapist, thinking it might help him to deal with his unconventional upbringing.

However, Stiller survived his celebrity childhood quite happily and set his sights on a career in entertainment. He attended the University of California at Los Angeles (UCLA) for less than a year before leaving to pursue his acting career. A return to New York in 1985 led to a part in a Tony Award–winning production of John Guare's play *House of Blue Leaves*. Soon after, he got small roles on a number of television shows and parts in Steven Spielberg's *Empire of the Sun* in 1987 and David Anspaugh's *Fresh Horses* in 1988.

HIS CAREER TAKES OFF

In 1987 Stiller wrote and filmed a comic skit satirizing Martin Scorsese's 1986 film *The Color of Money* and sold it to *Saturday Night Live* (*SNL*). This led to a five-week stint as a writer for *SNL*. He was hired for a six-episode sketch series on MTV in 1990, and in 1992 joined the Fox network for *The Ben Stiller Show*, another sketch-comedy series. The series showcased Stiller's skill for trenchant pop culture satire and boosted the careers of a number of promising comics, including Janeane Garofalo, Andy Dick, and Bob Odenkirk. In spite of enthusiastic reviews from critics, Fox canceled the show after only twelve episodes.

In 1994 Stiller directed and starred in his first full-length feature, *Reality Bites*, about a group of college graduates coming to terms with adulthood. In typical Stiller style, the film centers on a young filmmaker working on a documentary about her friends. Though *Reality Bites* did not do well at the box office, many critics saw it as a defining film for the post–baby boomer generation.

Stiller's next directorial effort was the 1996 comedy/thriller *The Cable Guy*, which starred Jim Carrey. In this satirical look at a media-driven culture, popular comic actor Carrey plays a sociopathic cable repairman warped by a lonely childhood spent watching television. Again critics were impressed by Stiller's work, but the public did not support the film. More successful was his appearance in David O. Russell's 1996 comedy *Flirting with Disaster*.

WIDESPREAD POPULARITY

Stiller's breakthrough role as an actor came in the 1998 "gross-out" comedy *There's Something about Mary*, directed by Bobby and Peter Farrelly. In a film that intentionally broke all taboos of good taste, Stiller developed one of his trademark characterizations—the hapless doofus beleaguered by circumstance—and his popularity skyrocketed. Though he played a more serious role as drug-addicted comedy writer Jerry Stahl in *Permanent Midnight* (1998), it was his frustrated mensch persona that gained him his most loyal audience. In 2000 he costarred with film icon Robert De Niro in *Meet the Parents*, which led to two sequels, *Meet the Fockers* (2004)—the highest-grossing film of his career—and *Little Fockers* (2010). Stiller did similar turns as the sad-sack night watchman in the 2006 comedy *Night at the Museum* and its 2009 sequel, *Night at the Museum: Battle of the Smithsonian*.

Another of Stiller's classic comic personae is the self-absorbed egotist, sometimes obliviously harmless (such as in 2001's *Zoolander*, a send-up of the world of high fashion, which Stiller also directed), and sometimes arrogant and angry (as in 2004's *Dodgeball: A True Underdog Story*, where he plays an unscrupulous fitness guru). In 2008 Stiller returned to the fertile ground of spoofing Hollywood pretentions with *Tropic Thunder*, which he directed and cowrote with Justin Theroux, as well as starring in a lead role. *Tropic Thunder* tells the story of a big-budget action movie being filmed on location by a crew of actors so clueless they do not realize when the danger becomes real. Though the edgy script offended some, critics praised it and applauded its skewering of artificial Hollywood values.

Returning to his roots in 2010, Stiller began producing, and frequently directing episodes of, a new Yahoo! comedy Web series for his parents. *Stiller and Meara: A Show about Everything* showcases the older Stiller generation reprising old bits and creating new comic commentary.

Tina Gianoulis

SEE ALSO: *Broadway; Cable TV; Celebrity; Celebrity Couples; De Niro, Robert; Generation X; The Internet; Movie Stars;* Saturday Night Live*; Spielberg, Steven; Stand-Up Comedy; Stiller and Meara; Television; Tony Awards.*

BIBLIOGRAPHY

Ansen, David. "Ben Stiller Made $40 Million Last Year to Act Silly. But Let's Get Serious. What He Really Wants to Do Is Direct." *Newsweek*, August 11, 2008, 54.

Denby, David. "The Contender." *New Yorker*, January 24, 2005, 99.

McCarthy, Ellen. "Ben Stiller Isn't Funny. Or So He Says." *Washington Post*, December 22, 2006, WW 27.

Mitchell, Sean. "What Makes Him Run? Ben Stiller Seems to Be Showing Up Just about Everywhere, with *Mary* His Biggest Hit So Far. But Don't Write Him off as Just Another Comic Actor." *Los Angeles Times*, September 13, 1998, 22.

Verini, Bob. "The Everyman Inside: Ben Stiller's Characters

Zing from Dumb and Dumber to Sharp Wit and Wisdom." *Daily Variety*, November 12, 2008, A2.

Stiller and Meara

Since the mid-1900s, the comedy team of Stiller and Meara—5-foot-4-inch Jewish actor Jerry Stiller and his 5-foot-6-inch Irish-Catholic wife Anne Meara—have been best known for wringing laughter out of improvisational situations, appearing thirty-six times on *The Ed Sullivan Show* in the 1950s and 1960s. They have also acted on Broadway—separately and as a team—and have each starred in a number of television sitcoms and motion pictures. Jerry's role as George Costanza's short-fused father on *Seinfeld* in the late 1990s sent his revitalized career to a higher level, leading to further work on Broadway and in network television commercials. In the first decade of the 2000s Stiller was a regular cast member on the TV show *King of Queens* (1998–2007), a program that Meara occasionally appeared on as a guest. In recent years Stiller and Meara have perhaps been better known as the parents of talented writer-director-actor Ben Stiller and actress Amy Stiller.

Both born in New York City, Jerry Stiller and Anne Meara were stage-struck in their teens. When they met in the early 1950s at an agent's office in Manhattan, Stiller had already acted in a number of plays, including *Peter Pan* with Veronica Lake. The pair signed with a comedy improv group, the Compass Players in St. Louis, Missouri, and set out on their own as a "boy-girl" act in comedy clubs. They appeared first in a small Greenwich Village club, then moved to the popular Blue Angel, followed shortly by bookings into other major nightclubs and guest spots on television. The first comedy sketch they wrote was called "Jonah," with Meara playing a TV news reporter and Stiller an older Miami Beach man who had been swallowed by a whale.

They were married in 1954 at a time when Jewish-Catholic marriages raised eyebrows. Stiller explains: "But when I met Anne, nobody of my own background wanted to marry me. I was an actor, and an actor had no credentials. Anne was an actress, and she had no credentials either. What brought us together was unconditional love." They were also attracted to each other's comic talent and offbeat humor. Besides performing onstage, the couple wrote and performed radio commercials. The best known of these—a commercial for an obscure wine called Blue Nun—increased the product's sales overnight.

Honing her talents by writing comedy routines and commercials, Meara has become a successful playwright. Her comedy, *After-Play*, had a long run on Broadway as well as in major cities coast to coast. She and Stiller starred in the comedy about two New York couples, the Shredmans and the Gutemans, having dinner and many drinks and tossing around hundreds of witty one-liners after seeing a Broadway play they reviewed in total disagreement.

The couple has also enjoyed a varied career in films. Meara has appeared in a variety of movies, including *Night at the Museum* (2006) with son Ben. Other films include *Like Mike* (2002), *The Daytrippers* (1996), and *The Search for One-Eye Jimmy* (1994). Stiller has appeared in dozens of movies, ranging from *The Taking of Pelham One Two Three* (1974) and *Airport 1975* (1974) to the more recent *A Rat's Tale* (1997) and *The Heartbreak Kid* (2007), which starred Ben.

The comedy team has appeared in a variety of television sitcoms, both together and separately. They were regulars on *The Paul Lynde Show* in the 1970s and made numerous guest appearances as a couple on *Love, American Style*; *The Courtship of Eddie's Father*; and *The Love Boat*. Stiller was a regular on two sitcoms in the late 1980s, *Tattinger's* and *Nick and Hillary*, in addition to *The King of Queens* and *Seinfeld*. Meara was a regular on such popular sitcoms as *Rhoda* (1976–1977), *Archie Bunker's Place* (1979–1982), and *ALF* (1987–1989), as well as having guest appearances on shows such as *Sex and the City* (2002–2004) and *Law and Order: Special Victims Unit* (2004).

Benjamin Griffith

SEE ALSO: *Broadway; Greenwich Village; Lake, Veronica;* The Love Boat*;* Seinfeld*;* Sex and the City*; Sitcom; Stand-Up Comedy; Stiller, Ben; Sullivan, Ed; Television.*

BIBLIOGRAPHY

Inman, David. *The TV Encyclopedia*. New York: Perigee, 1991.

Marc, David. *Comic Visions: Television Comedy in American Culture*. New York: Blackwell, 1997.

Schleier, Curt. "Jerry Stiller's Youth in Brooklyn Set Stage for Lifetime of Laughs." *Jewish Bulletin of Northern California*, March 20, 1998.

Stiller, Jerry. *Married to Laughter: A Love Story Featuring Anne Meara*. New York: Simon & Schuster, 2001.

Waldron, Vince. *Classic Sitcoms: A Celebration of the Best in Prime-Time Comedy*. New York: Silman Jam, 1998.

Stine, R. L. *(1943–)*

In just over a decade, R. L. Stine went from being an obscure humor-magazine editor to the biggest name in books for youths. Though his achievement is sometimes discounted as a fluke, Stine found a formula and tapped an audience that brought him unprecedented success. Many attribute his success to the great entertainment his books provide kids. Like Stephen King, to whom Stine is often compared, Stine knows how to tell a story. He knows how to keep readers interested and involved and, most importantly, how to satisfy them. Stine is not creating well-rounded characters; he is not using symbolism, metaphor, or any of the tricks of the trade in his writing. Instead, he practices the tricks of his own trade: that of entertaining people with "cheap thrills." He uses humor, roller-coaster plots, suspenseful chapter endings, gross-outs, credible kids' dialogue, recognizable if stereotypical characters, cliffhangers and red herrings, and a bare-bones style that gets to the point: to scare his readers. He is not interested in educating, enlightening, or informing; he is only interested in entertaining kids by terrifying them with gruesome, plot-twisting, scary thrillers.

CHILDHOOD AND EARLY CAREER

Robert Lawrence Stine began telling and writing scary stories when he was growing up in Columbus, Ohio. He learned that he could be entertaining by telling stories such as those he shared with his brother as they tried to go to sleep at night. Stine began writing when he was nine years old after he found an old typewriter that he began to use. He wrote and illustrated his own magazines throughout his school years, then was the editor of the Ohio State University humor magazine, the *Sundial*, during his college years.

After a brief stint as a social studies teacher, Stine moved from Ohio to New York to break into the writing business. After a series of short-lived jobs writing for fan magazines and trade industry publications, he landed a job at Scholastic. Within a few years he had moved from a staff writer to editor of the youth humor magazine *Bananas*. While he was editing *Bananas*, he was writing joke books such as *How to Be Funny* and *The Beast Handbook*. Soon after *Bananas* folded, Stine was downsized at Scholastic and began freelancing full-time, turning out more joke books, penning numerous *Choose Your Own Adventure*-style multiple story line books, writing a television show, and even writing bubble gum cards and coloring books.

THE GOOSEBUMPS SERIES

Stine's first financial success came in the late 1980s with the Fear Street series for teens. About this time he also helped create a new successful television series, *Eureeka's Castle* (1989–1995). Stine then developed an idea for another scary series, this one to be aimed at younger kids. The series would still have scares and dangers, but no blood, no guts, no bullets, and no guns. In these books Stine played up the humor—another of his strengths—while playing down the violence.

R. L. Stine. *R. L. Stine, whose* Goosebumps *books were popular among young readers in the 1990s, began writing scary stories when he was a child.* MIKE COPPOLA/CONTRIBUTOR/FILMMAGIC/GETTY IMAGES.

He launched the Goosebumps book series for upper elementary/middle school kids in 1992. Edited by his wife, Jane, and packaged through her company Parachute Press, Goosebumps quickly became the most popular children's book series of all time. By the late 1990s there were 180 Goosebumps titles in print in more thirty languages. The sales figures for Goosebumps products were also impressive, and the *Goosebumps* television show (1995–1998) was a top-rated program and a centerpiece in the Saturday morning schedule of the Fox network for many years. *Goosebumps* prime-time and after-school specials had high viewer ratings as well. Videos based on the shows sold more than one million copies, and the first CD-ROM based on the books, *Escape from Horrorland*, was a big seller. Disney cashed in with a Goosebumps Horror Land at its Metro Goldwyn Mayer Studios site in Florida.

In his autobiography *It Came from Ohio*, Stine writes that he saw an advertisement in *TV Guide* to promote horror films which read, "It's *goosebumps* week." Inspired by the word, he was off and running, turning out *Welcome to Dead House*, the first title of series, in ten days. The next books were *Stay Out of the Basement* and *Monster Blood*. Like the Fear Street series before it, Goosebumps was a series without a central set of characters, and in this case, not even a central location. There was nothing even remotely like Goosebumps on the market: it was a brand-new field.

With their easy availability through Scholastic book clubs, the growing number of mega bookstores, and discount stores such as Wal-Mart, Goosebumps books soon began selling well. By the sixth title, *Let's Get Invisible!*, Goosebumps cracked *Publishers Weekly*'s children's best-seller chart. The books received a boost in visibility when *USA Today* began its own best-seller list in 1994. Unlike other rankings that did not include paperbacks or children's books—or if they did include them, they did not compare their sales to adult best sellers—the premise of *USA Today* was: a book is a book is a book. The list in *USA Today* showed that books in the Goosebumps series were outselling even adult authors such as Michael Crichton.

By early 1997 Scholastic, the publisher of Stine's Goosebumps books, began to see a decline in sales of the series, in particular the older titles. "The kids got tired of them," Mr. Stine said simply. "There were too many of them out there." Nevertheless, the Goosebumps brand name was still going strong, appearing on fast-food drink cups, snack foods, calendars, and clothing. According to Deb Forte, then president of Scholastic Media, Goosebumps was the first book-based multimedia brand. The decline in Goosebumps sales led to conflict between Scholastic and Parachute Press, however. By the end of 1997, Scholastic had stopped paying advances to Parachute, which then filed suit. The suit was settled in 2003 with Scholastic paying $9.65 million for the rights to existing and future titles in the series.

LATER DEVELOPMENTS

Stine continued his prolific writing, producing dozens of new titles, in particular thrillers aimed at boys. In the process he spun off new series such as Mostly Ghostly and Nightmare Room. In 2004 he wrote a new adult novel, *Eye Candy*, which like his first adult novel, *Superstitious* (1995), was a suspenseful thriller. The following year Stine started the book series Rotten School, which was written to be funny and not scary. By 2008

Scholastic and Stine launched a new Goosebumps franchise called Goosebumps Horrorland. Despite the word *horror* in the title, Stine told a *New York Times* reporter that "I don't really want to terrify kids," he said. "I want them to have a really good time reading."

Because of Goosebumps, Stine went from hack writer to celebrity in just a few months, yet Stine told *People* that "No one over fourteen has ever heard of me." By the early twenty-first century, however, there were few people with any significant contact with kids who had not heard of R. L. Stine. As author Stephen King noted in *Entertainment Weekly* while laying at Stine's feet the groundwork for the success of the Harry Potter books: "He's largely unknown and uncredited . . . but of course, John the Baptist never got the same press as Jesus either." The huge sales of adult writers such as James Patterson and Dan Brown follow the Stine formula of short chapters, cliffhanger endings, and plot-heavy books. For years, Stine made reading cool for kids by making it something most kids, especially boys, did not think it could be: fun and easy to do.

Patrick Jones

SEE ALSO: *Disney (Walt Disney Company); King, Stephen; Videos.*

BIBLIOGRAPHY

Jones, Patrick. *What's So Scary about R. L. Stine?* Lanham, MD: Scarecrow Press, 1998.

Rorke, Robert. "Scare Tactics: By Giving Children Goosebumps, R. L. Stine Cultivated a Devoted Readership." *Publishers Weekly*, June 17, 2005, 36+.

Santow, Dan, and Toby Kahn. "The Scarier the Better." *People Weekly*, November 14, 1994, 115.

Silver, Marc. "Horrors! It's R. L. Stine!" *U.S. News & World Report*, October 15, 1995, 95.

Stelter, Brian. "*Goosebumps* Rises from the Literary Grave." *New York Times*, March 25, 2008.

Stine, R. L. "Why Kids Love to Get *Goosebumps*." *TV Guide*, October 28, 1995, 24.

Stine, R. L., and Joe Arthur. *It Came from Ohio!: My Life as a Writer*. New York: Scholastic, 1997.

West, Diana. "The Horror of R. L. Stine." *Weekly Standard*, September 25, 1995, 42–45.

Stock Market Crashes

Information about the stock market fills American daily newspapers and television reports. With so many Americans belonging to pension plans and other long-term investment programs, stock market shifts touch more people now than ever before. When the stock market is on the rise, everyone views it is a positive signal; investments are increasing in value, and a bullish market must mean the economy is good. Yet what are the repercussions when the stock market goes sour? What happens to American society and culture when the stock market falters or even crashes? In order to evaluate the full social and cultural implications of market crashes, an understanding of the 1929 crash and subsequent Great Depression is necessary. For it was the 1929 crash that has left a permanent mark on American society. That crash led to important policy changes and basically defined the terminology and standards by which the United States would judge future market shifts.

1929 CRASH

The 1920s had been very good economic times for most Americans. By 1929 production and employment were high, wages were increasing, and prices were stable; there were more middle-class Americans than ever before. American capitalism was in a lively phase, and business was good. Yet while most of the American public did not understand the nuances of the stock market, they did understand there was a lot of speculation and many "get-rich-quick" schemes. In fact, rich and well-connected investors were buying stocks with little or no money down. There was also a feeling throughout the nation that these speculative designs were immoral and might soon lead to severe economic problems.

Still, by the summer of 1929 the stock market boom was a dominant topic of conversation. The bull market not only dominated the news, but it also dominated the culture. At any posh party was an investment broker willing to tell his rich friends what to do. Everybody seemed to be a stock market expert, and many regular investors were looking to make a quick fortune. According to historian Frederick Lewis Allen, as quoted in economist John Kenneth Galbraith's book *The Great Crash 1929*:

> The rich man's chauffeur drove with his ears laid back to catch the news of an impending move in Bethlehem Steel; he held fifty shares himself. . . . The window-cleaner at the broker's office paused to watch the ticker. . . . [I was told of] a broker's valet who made nearly a quarter of a million in the market, of a trained nurse who cleaned up thirty thousand following the tips given her by grateful patients, and of a Wyoming cattleman, thirty miles from the nearest railroad, who bought or sold a thousand shares a day.

Then came the famous stock market crash. At first it seemed like it might be just another downturn. Most assumed the market would just right itself as it had done on earlier occasions. On October 24, 1929, the day now called Black Thursday, however, thirteen million shares were traded, and many of America's key businesses, including RCA and Westinghouse, lost nearly half their value. It is a day in which millions lost all of their money, savings, and hope. By 11 a.m. there was a wild scramble to sell, but few buyers. Prices continued to drop as crowds began to form around brokerage houses throughout cities all over the nation. That day, suicides had already begun, as eleven well-known speculators killed themselves. There was a last-ditch effort by some key bankers to prop up the market, but that worked only for several days.

Then came October 29, a day in which more than sixteen million shares were dumped. The holes the bankers had closed opened wide. One precocious messenger boy at the stock exchange decided to bid a dollar for a block of stocks and he actually got them. No bankers were around to bale the market out, for they were all broke too.

EFFECTS OF THE GREAT DEPRESSION

The stock market never righted itself, and for a variety of reasons a severe depression ensued. By 1932 unemployment had reached 25 percent—it had been 3 percent in 1929. The gross national product fell to 56.7 percent of its 1929 level. Farm prices fell 60 percent from 1929 to 1932, and between 1930 and 1933 more than 5,500 banks closed. In addition, the suicide rate climbed

30 percent between 1929 and 1932. This Great Depression lasted from 1929 to 1941, ending only when the United States began to prepare for World War II.

The Great Depression had a lasting effect on several generations of Americans. Even after World War II ended, many assumed the Depression would resume. The conservative culture of the 1950s, marked by its lack of dissent and need for social acceptance, can be traced back to that 1929 Depression. By 1950 many American families feared another economic crash and remained uncomfortable with economic expansion, credit, and cheap loans. It is accurate to say that the generation of Americans who lived through the 1929 crash and the subsequent economic downturn never forgot it. It was those Americans who continued to make the crash and Great Depression part of American culture and lore.

Evidence shows that the American people and its government, from 1945 to about 1973, were indeed influenced by the Depression in several ways. First was the belief that both the federal budget and family budgets should be balanced. On the federal level, the budget deficit did not begin in earnest until 1980. On the personal level, families only purchased major household items when they could pay cash. There was little or no credit for most Americans, as debt was considered a poor judgment at best and even immoral to some. Second, people saved more money in the post-Depression years. Savings reached a peak during the 1950s as the American public still worried about economic downturns. The belief in society was that if families stayed out of debt and saved their money, they could survive another serious economic downturn.

Personal economic paradigms, however, began to change in the United States—along with everything else—during the 1960s. First, the federal government began to spend more than it took in. This started during the Vietnam War, and although the deficit never reached 1980 levels, the mere fact deficits existed provided a startling change in economic policy. Second, as the economy boomed during the 1960s, more and more consumer spending was needed to keep the economy vigorous. Because of this, more credit cards and cheap loans were issued, and people were actually encouraged to spend more than they earned. Business leaders argued that spending was good for the economy while too much savings was counterproductive—saving too much money would slow economic growth and cost American jobs. Third, going in debt did not seem immoral to the new generation of Americans who did not remember the Depression. The youth of the 1960s and 1970s only heard stories about the Great Depression but had not faced the economic challenges of their parents and grandparents. These new consumers wanted to purchase goods and did not want to wait until they had the cash. Consumer credit and personal debt began to soar.

Clearly, since 1929 the effects of stock market dips have changed with generational perceptions. Market downturns in the late 1940s and early 1950s were met by citizens who lived through the Depression. Their survival tactics during these periods included increased savings and earning extra income and, in rural areas, growing and selling their own food and produce. Those were all lessons learned from earlier times; the key during an economic downturn was not to borrow or increase your debt.

The new generation of consumers that came of age in the early 1970s, however, viewed the economy in a much different way. When the market dipped in the 1970s, people actually spent more, went into debt, did not save, and assumed they would make up the difference when the economy rebounded. To these baby boomers coming of age, the market would always right itself and debt was not an immoral thing.

LATER CRASHES

There have been crashes since 1929, and each time the stock market falls, the 1929 terminology permeates newspapers and other media outlets. However, the crashes that have occurred since 1929 have not had the same economic, social, or cultural effects because the salience of the Great Crash has disappeared. In 1987 there was a stock market crash reminiscent to the 1929 fall. Several brokerage houses collapsed, thousands of investors lost money, and the Dow Jones industrial stocks fell 22.6 percent. This time, however, things did right themselves relatively quickly. Fearing the economic repercussions of the 1987 crash, the Federal Reserve Board, the White House, and Congress acted swiftly. Passing legislation to right the economy was not considered in 1929 because politicians believed it more prudent not to tinker with the free market system. A major result of the 1929 crash was that the government began to take an active role in times of economic downturn by enacting fiscal and monetary policy changes.

In 1998 the stock market again fell precipitously. Investment portfolios declined, but it seemed to cause little panic and few economic worries. Again, the federal government and Federal Reserve Board offered policy alterations, and the market recovered in a short period of time. Those most adversely affected by the 1998 crash were small nations with strong economic ties to the United States. The American economy, with fiscal and monetary policy changes, was able to weather market fluctuations, but many smaller nations were hurt when the American economy went into a tailspin, even if for a short period of time.

With fewer and fewer people who remembered the 1929 crash still living in the early twenty-first century, fears about stock market crashes were blunted. In 1929 many American economic and business structures were still weak and could not handle the crash, yet because of the 1929 crash American banks, businesses, and policy makers grew prepared for problems and made the necessary adjustments. In every crash after 1929, the market rebounded and subsequent recessions or depressions were avoided.

However, because the 1929 crash had such dire economic consequences, it remained an important social and cultural event—even if its economic significance had lost salience. Drops in the current market are always compared with 1929 declines. Unemployment rates, productivity figures, and other economic data are generally contrasted with 1929 figures, and post-crash Depression stories are still part of American popular culture. There are many tales about those who lived through the Depression and in later years refused to put their money in banks, opting instead to place all their savings in mattresses or freezers. Although more enlightened economic policies have made it possible to more easily survive a stock market crash, the 1929 calamity and its aftermath will forever be the standard against which Americans measure economic and social problems.

ECONOMIC CRISIS OF 2007

The "Great Recession" of 2007 was something different. Unlike the 1929 economic collapse, it was not initiated by a stock market crash. This global collapse centered more on real estate and housing, equities, and food and oil prices. Risky loans and inflated asset prices started the panic in late 2007, which was exacerbated when several major financial houses dissolved. As housing prices quickly fell, many large and well-established investment and commercial banks in the United States and Europe suffered huge losses and faced bankruptcy. As this recession continued, it was not the stock market that was the primary focus.

It is possible that if the global recession that started in 2007 continues for a considerable length of time, it could replace the 1929 stock market crash as the cultural standard by which citizens look at economic downturns. It may be that the United States will no longer view stock market crashes as the benchmark—but will look at other criteria such as food prices, housing foreclosures, and loan defaults.

David E. Woodard

SEE ALSO: *Bank Failures/Subprime Mortgages; Credit Cards; The Great Depression; The Great Recession; Housing Market Bubble.*

BIBLIOGRAPHY

Brinkley, Alan. *The End of Reform: New Deal Liberalism in Recession and War.* New York: Knopf, 1995.

Cohan, William. *Money and Power: How Goldman Sachs Came to Rule the World.* New York: Doubleday, 2011.

Galbraith, John Kenneth. *The Great Crash 1929.* Boston: Houghton Mifflin, 1955.

Krugman, Paul. *The Return of Depression Economics and the Crisis of 2008.* New York: W. W. Norton, 2009.

Leuchtenburg, William. *The Perils of Prosperity, 1914–1932.* Chicago: University of Chicago Press, 1968.

Lewis, Michael. *The Big Short: Inside the Doomsday Machine.* New York: W. W. Norton, 2010

Nash, Gerald D. *The Crucial Era: The Great Depression and World War II, 1929–1945.* New York: St. Martin's Press, 1992.

Stock-Car Racing

Each year, from February through November, there is a stock-car race somewhere in America, with tracks drawing up to 150,000 racing fans, eager to watch their favorite drivers zoom around the oval tracks in cars much like their own automobiles. From humble beginnings in a farmer's field in the mid-1930s, stock-car racing has become so popular nationwide that its television ratings are second only to the National Football League, and top drivers make millions of dollars a year from

NASCAR Daytona 500. *An aerial view of the track at Daytona International Speedway shows the start of the 2011 Daytona 500.* AP IMAGES.

racing and advertising endorsements. When Matt Kenseth won the opening race of the 2012 season at Daytona Beach, Florida, he collected more than $1.5 million.

MOONSHINE RUNNERS TO STOCK CARS

The earliest stock-car racers got their training by transporting moonshine whiskey over the dusty roads of Appalachia in the dead of night, outrunning the revenuers by driving flat out in dangerous conditions. These moonshine runners were part of a legend, later to be etched in the public mind by a movie, *Thunder Road* (1958), starring Robert Mitchum. In the mid-1930s, the drivers began arguing about who was fastest, and a race was set up in a quarter-mile dirt track carved out of a farmer's field near Stockbridge, Georgia. Unpublicized, the first race drew about fifty people, but after that thousands began showing up for the race, and the moonshiners began to collect cash prizes that surpassed their pay for nocturnal whiskey runs.

Among these early drivers were the Flock brothers—Tim, Bob, and Fonty—whose uncle owned one of the biggest stills in Georgia, and Junior Johnson, whose father had the largest moonshine operation in Wilkes County, North Carolina. Johnson, a legend in his own time, was featured in 1965 in a famous *Esquire* article by Tom Wolfe—"The Last American Hero is Junior Johnson—Yes!"—that was made into a movie. Unbeatable on the dirt tracks, Junior had his own special style of accelerating through the turns by cocking his steering wheel hard left and fishtailing the rear end of the car. Other drivers, who slowed their cars on turns and tried catching up on the straightaways, had little chance.

At about the time the Georgia farmer was carving a racetrack out of a cornfield, an auto mechanic and weekend dirt-track race driver named William Henry "Bill" France was beginning a journey that would eventually make him the pioneer and prime mover of organized stock-car racing. He moved to Daytona Beach, where Sir Malcolm Campbell made annual visits to attempt new land-speed records with his racing car "Bluebird." In 1935 France watched as Campbell made his last runs at Daytona before moving his operation to the less windy conditions of the Bonneville Salt Flats in Utah. To continue attracting speed-minded tourists to Daytona Beach, the city fathers organized beach races, with little success.

In 1938 they recruited the personable France, whose gasoline station was a hangout for drivers and mechanics, to organize the races. A natural promoter, France signed up drivers, gathered prizes from local merchants, and set his race for July 4. More than 4,500 spectators showed up, each paying fifty cents a ticket. France and his financial backers split $200 in profits, and the young promoter started planning a beach race for Labor Day. By the following year, attendance was sharply up and ticket prices had doubled to a dollar. His races were a roaring success, but World War II brought a temporary end to his operation.

THE BIRTH OF NASCAR

When he returned to the Daytona track after the war, France started the National Championship Stock Car Circuit (NCSCC) to sponsor monthly races, with a winner's fund and a cumulative point system to reward the circuit's champion driver. NCSCC's inaugural year in 1947 was a great success, with Fonty Flock declared national champion. France's next bold step came in December of that year when he invited the most influential members of the stock-car clan to a meeting in Daytona. He addressed thirty-five of his colleagues, urging them to "unite all stock car racing under one set of rules, with national point standings whereby only one driver could be crowned National Champion." He urged consistent, enforceable rules concerning the modification of cars, insisting that the races admit only standard cars that could be bought at automobile dealerships. After a brief debate, the group supported such an organization and named France president. The National Association for Stock Car Auto Racing (NASCAR) was incorporated on February 15, 1948, and a technical committee wrote rules to promote fair competition and provide for the safety of drivers and spectators.

Another important figure in stock-car racing history is Harold Brasington, who brought to reality his dream of building a 1.25-mile paved speedway in his hometown of Darlington, South Carolina, and hosting the first 500-mile race for stock cars, the South's version of the Indianapolis 500. France, in his second year of sanctioning races with his newly formed NASCAR, was called in to recruit drivers for the inaugural Southern 500 on Labor Day 1950. Expecting to attract perhaps 5,000 paying customers to the 9,000-seat stadium, Brasington and France were astounded when 25,000 people showed up. Tickets were sold for the infield, and the fans saw Johnny Mantz win the first Southern 500 driving a 1950 Plymouth with an average speed of 76 miles per hour, going the distance without a change of tires. By 1955 the Darlington track, known to racing fans as "the Granddaddy of them all," was attracting a maximum of 75,000 fans to the annual race, and the crowds remain that size every year. Brasington's dream succeeded beyond all expectation.

Another event that boosted NASCAR to national prominence came in 1951 when the Detroit Chamber of Commerce called on France to organize an automobile race as part of the Motor City's 250th anniversary celebration. France chose a 1-mile dirt racetrack in the Michigan State Fairgrounds and planned a race for stock cars that would run 250 miles, one for each year of the city's age. He also asked all the automobile manufacturers to enter at least one car in the race, and fifteen agreed. On August 12, a crowd of 16,500 racing fans filled the track for the Motor City 250, and they saw fifty-nine cars in a close, exciting race, with the lead changing fourteen times. The winner was undecided until the last lap, when Tommy Thompson, in a 1951 Chrysler, out-foxed Joe Eubanks in a 1950 Oldsmobile 88.

BREAKTHROUGHS IN RACING

The Motor City 250 enabled France to make two important breakthroughs: stock-car racing, a sport bred in the South, became accepted in the North, and automakers in Detroit, Michigan, became convinced that this popular sport could be good for a corporation's bottom line. Corporate sponsorships immediately began to bolster NASCAR's profits and winners' purses, and companies such as Chevrolet, Ford, Goodyear, and Unocal began partnerships that have enhanced more than fifty years of NASCAR's history. Before these sponsorships, race drivers could hardly earn enough in prizes to keep their cars in tires; in the Motor City race, the first three cars won $5,000, $2,000, and $1,000, with the next seven making a few hundred dollars and the other fifty-two cars only $25 or $50. By the first decade of the 2000s, winners' purses had escalated so much that the top drivers made unheard-of sums; in 2010 Dale Earnhardt Jr. earned $29 million, while Jeff Gordon earned $25 million.

However, racing costs have spiraled too. In 2011 driver Kenny Wallace estimated it took a minimum of $100,000 a race to maintain a top twenty team. Costs included leasing the engine at an average of $30,000 a week, paying more than $40,000 a week for tires, and shelling out some $11,000 in travel expenses.

To move NASCAR into the modern era, France risked his entire fortune to build the plush Daytona International Speedway, a 2.5-mile oval designed for high speeds with sweeping turns banked at 31 degrees. Fireball Roberts, a popular 1960s driver, said you could "flat-foot it all the way." Lee Petty, father of Richard and winner of the first Daytona 500, said there was not a driver there who was not "scared" of the steeply banked track. "We had never raced on a track like that before." It all added to the mystique of the race, and the fans came in droves. In 1959 there were 42,000, and today the grandstands at Daytona for the annual opening event of the NASCAR season hold about 140,000. This success led to other major tracks, and construction on super speedways in Atlanta, Georgia; Charlotte, North Carolina; and Hanford, California, started in 1960. In 1969 France lapped the field again with the building of the spectacular Talladega, Alabama, track—2.66 miles long and a lane wider than Daytona—which took the sport to a new level, with cars racing three abreast at higher speeds than ever before. It was at Talladega that Bill Elliott drove the fastest lap in the NASCAR books: 212 miles per hour.

One of the reasons for NASCAR's continued success has been the "consistent, enforceable rules" that France had envisioned for governing the sport. He always believed that it was close, side-by-side racing that drew the fans, and to preserve fair competition NASCAR showed no favoritism. Whether the rule violator was a champion or a rising star, the penalty was consistent. Seven-time Winston Cup champion Richard Petty was caught with an illegal engine in 1983 and fined $35,000. Gordon was the series leader and eventual Winston Cup champ in 1995 when his team was fined $60,000 for using an unapproved wheel hub. Such strict inspection had begun in the very first "Strictly Stock Car" race in 1949, when Glenn Dunnaway crossed the finish line first but was disqualified when a postrace inspector discovered a wedge had been placed in the rear suspension to stiffen the springs and improve handling—a trick long known by moonshine runners.

NASCAR IN THE TWENTY-FIRST CENTURY

In the 2010s NASCAR sanctioned more than 1,500 events a year at more than 100 racetracks across the United States. More than three million people attend these events, which are watched by millions more on television. The premier series is the Sprint Cup Series, featuring the top drivers and cars that are factory-supported by several manufacturers. Second is the Nationwide Series, a training ground for Sprint Cup drivers of the future. Also popular is the Craftsman Truck Series, which features American-made trucks in twenty-five races a year. NASCAR sponsors international series in Canada and Mexico. In addition, there are regional and local series, a grassroots level of racing on dozens of tracks across the United States.

On February 7, 1999, a stock-car race driver came in second in the ARCA 200 at Daytona after having taken four years off to give birth to two children and start an interior design business. The driver was Shawna Robinson, who walked away from racing in 1995 after five seasons in the Busch Grand National Series, in which she became the first woman to win a NASCAR national series race. From its beginning, stock-car racing has changed with the times while continuing to give its fans thrills and surprises.

In 1999 NASCAR reached a television deal with Fox Sports/FX and NBC Sports/TNT. The consistent TV exposure caused the sport's popularity to soar. For example, viewership for the Daytona 500 increased to 18.7 million in 2002, a 48 percent increase in ten years. In 2003 NASCAR announced that Brian France would replace his father as CEO and chairman of the board. At the start of 2004, a new format for determining the champions of the premier series was introduced.

In the 2010s the ever-competitive drivers discovered a new technique to help them win: tandem driving, also known as two-car drafting. Two drivers would circle the track together, then one would go ahead, breaking the airflow, while the second would follow behind, pushing the leader's rear bumper to make him go faster. After a few laps, the cars would have to switch positions to prevent the rear car from overheating. Cooperation and communication was key to the maneuver—with the end result that one driver agrees not to go all out to win the race. Fans objected vociferously to the development because it reduced the competitiveness of the sport. For the beginning of 2012, NASCAR decreed some changes to the cars to make the practice more dangerous to execute; however, drivers continued to work in partnership. The future of tandem driving remains uncertain.

Benjamin Griffith

SEE ALSO: *Daytona 500; Drag Racing; Indianapolis 500; Mitchum, Robert; Petty, Richard; Wolfe, Tom.*

BIBLIOGRAPHY

Bechtel, Mark. *He Crashed Me So I Crashed Him Back: The True Story of the Year the King, Jaws, Earnhardt, and the Rest of NASCAR's Feudin', Fightin' Good Ol' Boys Put Stock Car Racing on the Map*. New York: Little, Brown, 2010.

Bledsoe, Jerry. *The World's Number One, Flat-Out, All-Time Great, Stock Car Racing Book*. Garden City, NY: Doubleday, 1975.

Hagstrom, Robert G. *The NASCAR Way: The Business That Drives the Sport*. New York: Wiley, 1998.

Howell, Mark D. *From Moonshine to Madison Avenue: A Cultural History of the NASCAR Winston Cup Series*. Bowling Green, OH: Bowling Green State University Popular Press, 1997.

Thompson, Neal. *Driving with the Devil: Southern Moonshine, Detroit Wheels, and the Birth of NASCAR*. New York: Crown, 2006.

Stockton, "Pudgy" *(1917–2006)*

"Pudgy" Stockton was a weight lifter, an acrobat, a columnist, and a business owner. She inspired thousands of women to join gyms and take up weight training in the 1940s and early 1950s in much the same way that John Grimek ushered in the modern era of men's bodybuilding. Before Stockton, there were a few professional women weight lifters, but they were generally massively proportioned women who unintentionally helped perpetuate the myth that weight training made women large and unattractive. Stockton, with her glowing skin, shining hair, miraculous curves, and amazing strength, changed public perception. At the end of the Great Depression, she became emblematic of the new type of woman needed to win World War II. Competent, feminine, and strong yet still traditionally sexy, Stockton became the media darling of Muscle Beach and famous around the world.

"Pudgy" Stockton was born Abbye Eville on August 11, 1917, and moved to Santa Monica, California, in 1924. She was called "Pudgy" as a small child by her father and the name stuck, even though she grew to 5 feet, 2 inches tall and about 115 pounds. She began seeing Les Stockton, a student at the University of California at Los Angeles (UCLA), during her senior year of high school. Their favorite date was to go to the beach and practice gymnastics. In 1941 they married.

The beach where the Stocktons liked to go was Muscle Beach, a section of Santa Monica Beach, located south of the Santa Monica Pier in Santa Monica. The area was established in 1939 with a simple platform and was extremely popular in the 1940s and 1950s with tumblers, acrobats, weight lifters, and bodybuilders. The Stocktons, who performed acrobatic and gymnastic feats with their friend Bruce Conner at football game half-time shows and other venues as the Three Aces, practiced their act at Muscle Beach, helping to draw other gymnasts, adagio dancers, and hand balancers. Thousands of spectators soon joined them. The media also gathered at Muscle Beach and quickly capitalized on "Pudgy" Stockton's rare combination of strength, physical beauty, and charisma.

Life, *Pic*, and *Laff*, the top pictorial magazines of the era, included her in photo essays, and two newsreels, *Whatta Build* and *Muscle Town USA*, also featured her. She appeared in ads for the Ritamine Vitamin Company and the Universal Camera Company in the late 1930s, and, by her own count, she was on the cover of forty-two magazines from around the world by the end of the 1940s. Her costume was a two-piece bathing suit that she originally created by combining men's swim trunks with a bra because the one-piece bathing suits of the time were too confining for her stunts. One of her stunts was to hold her 185-pound husband upside down above her head.

In 1944 Stockton began writing a regular women's training column, called Barbelles, in *Strength & Health* magazine, the most influential fitness magazine in the world at the time. For the next ten years, in article after article, Stockton encouraged weight training for women, explaining that it enhances a woman's figure and makes any woman a better athlete. As proof, she included photographs of herself and other women who trained with weights. Stockton also publicized, and helped organize, the first weight-lifting contest for women to be sanctioned by the Amateur Athletic Union, a nonprofit, multisport organization that promotes amateur sports and physical fitness. That first contest was held February 28, 1947, at the Southwest Arena in Los Angeles. Stockton entered the contest, of course, and pressed 100 pounds, snatched 105 pounds, and clean and jerked 135 pounds.

In 1948 Stockton entered another contest, the Miss Physical Culture Venus Contest, held by fitness magazine *Physical Culture*, and she won. Also in 1948 Stockton and her husband opened a women's gym in Los Angeles, and for the next several decades she offered instruction in her own gym and in others in the Los Angeles area, preaching her message of the benefits of weight training for women.

Stockton's influence on women's bodybuilding and weight training was enormous. Every woman bodybuilder who puts on a swimsuit and steps up on the posing dais, every woman weight lifter who strains under a clean and jerk, and every woman power lifter who fights through the pull of a heavy dead lift owes a debt of gratitude to Stockton, whose personal example helped make these modern sports possible. Her great and enduring gift to the world of bodybuilding was the living proof that muscles could be feminine, womanly strength could be an asset, and that working out was fun.

In 2004 Stockton's husband, Les, died at the age of eighty-seven after a long battle with melanoma. Stockton died two years later of complications from Alzheimer's disease. She was eighty-eight years old. The Stocktons are survived by their daughter, Laura.

Jan Todd

SEE ALSO: *Bodybuilding; Feminism; The Great Depression; Grimek, John;* Life; *Muscle Beach; World War II.*

BIBLIOGRAPHY

Chapman, David L. *Venus with Biceps: A Pictorial History of Muscular Women*. Vancouver, BC: Arsenal Pulp Press, 2010.

Chowder, Ken. "Muscle Beach." *Smithsonian*, November 29, 1998, 124–137.

Kolata, Gina. *Ultimate Fitness: The Quest for Truth about Health and Exercise*. New York: Farrar, Straus & Giroux, 2003.

Malin, Jo. *My Life at the Gym: Feminist Perspectives on Community through the Body*. Albany: State University of New York Press, 2010.

Matzer, Marla. "The Venus of Muscle Beach." *Los Angeles Times Magazine*, February 22, 1998, 20–22.

Rose, Marla Matzer. *Muscle Beach: Where the Best Bodies in the World Started a Fitness Revolution*. New York: St. Martin's Griffin, 2001.

Todd, Jan. "The Legacy of Pudgy Stockton." *Iron Game History* 2, no. 1 (1992): 5–7.

Stokowski, Leopold *(1882–1977)*

A brilliant symphony orchestra conductor and arranger of classical music, Leopold Antoni Stanislaw Stokowski achieved his greatest fame as conductor of the Philadelphia Orchestra, beginning in 1912. His statuesque physique, flowing hair, and theatrical temperament came to symbolize for generations of Americans—and for other conductors—how the musical directors of symphony orchestras should look and behave. Stokowski was especially admired and respected for creating an ensemble with so unique a sound that the Philadelphia Orchestra was considered by many musicians to be the greatest in the world. Celebrity eventually entered his personal life when he married heiress Gloria Vanderbilt.

In the 1930s Hollywood beckoned and Stokowski appeared with singer Deanna Durbin in films that were merely vehicles for their talents. The exception was Walt Disney's *Fantasia*, in which animation was blended with Stokowski conducting superb renditions of works by classical composers. The films reinforced Stokowski's image, allowing millions to see him in action.

Milton Goldin

SEE ALSO: *Disney (Walt Disney Company); Durbin, Deanna;* Fantasia*; Hollywood.*

BIBLIOGRAPHY

Daniel, Oliver. *Stokowski: A Counterpoint of View*. New York: Dodd, Mead, 1982.

Smith, Rollin. *Stokowski and the Organ*. Hillsdale, NY: Pendragon Press, 2004.

Stone, Irving *(1903–1989)*

Irving Stone was a prolific, best-selling author whose entertaining biographical novels and "biohistories" have proved far more popular with readers than with scholars or critics. He is best known for works that, in the words of Marcus Cunliffe in the *New York Times Book Review*, citing the epigram from one of Stone's books, are pleasing to people "who like to have their history . . . 'a little embellished with fiction.'"

By far his two most memorable works are a pair of books that offer monumental, sweeping accounts of the lives of two world-class artists: *Lust for Life: A Novel of Vincent van Gogh* (1934) and *The Agony and the Ecstasy: A Novel of Michelangelo* (1961). Stone also wrote a series of popular fictionalized histories of American First Families: *The President's Lady* (1951), about Andrew and Rachel Jackson; *Love Is Eternal* (1954), about Abraham and Mary Lincoln; and *Those Who Love* (1965), about John and Abigail Adams. American political radicals figured in some of Stone's other works, such as *Sailor on Horseback: The Biography of Jack London* (1938), a book that, in translation, was immensely popular in the Soviet Union; *Clarence Darrow for the Defense* (1941); and *Adversary in the House* (1947), an account of socialist labor leader Eugene V. Debs.

Stone, who took his last name from his stepfather, was born Irving Tennenbaum in San Francisco on July 14, 1903, to Charles and Pauline Rosenberg Tennenbaum. As a child he was a self-described "hopeless bookworm" who was inspired to be a writer after devouring the works of Jack London, Frank Norris, Sherwood Anderson, and Gertrude Atherton. In order to continue his education after high school, Stone took a variety of odd jobs to work his way through the University of California, including saxophone player, fruit picker, meat packer, and hotel clerk. He majored in political science, graduating with honors in 1923, and taught economics at the University of Southern California while working toward his master's degree in economics there.

He soon abandoned his academic career, however, to indulge his passion for writing. With ambitions to be a dramatist, he moved to Paris, where he wrote seventeen plays in one year but sold none. While in Paris he saw an exhibit of Vincent van Gogh's paintings that forever changed his career direction. "It was the single most compelling emotional experience of my life," he later said and immediately embarked on extensive research into the life of the nineteenth-century postimpressionist painter. After rejection by more than a dozen publishers, during which time Stone supported himself by writing pulp-fiction detective stories, his van Gogh biography was finally published in 1934, as *Lust for Life*, and quickly became a best-selling book. (It would later be made into a popular film starring Kirk Douglas.)

Stone made one more foray into playwriting, but when his Broadway drama, *Truly Valiant*, closed after one performance in 1936, he realized he had no talent for the medium. From then on he devoted himself exclusively to biographical subjects with the help of his new bride, Jean Factor, who collaborated with him as an editor and a cowriter. Among the works they jointly edited was *Dear Theo* (1937), based on the correspondence between Vincent van Gogh and his brother. Several of the biographies Stone wrote over the next ten years were favorable portraits of progressive political figures admired by their author, including London, Darrow, and Debs. Another book, *Earl Warren* (1948), featured the then-California governor and future chief justice of the U.S. Supreme Court. In the 1950s Stone began using the term *biohistory* to describe his works, such as *Men to Match My Mountains* (1956), a fictionalized narrative of the settling of the American West written for Doubleday's Mainstream of America series.

Turning his attention next to the life of Michelangelo, Stone commissioned the first complete translation of the Renaissance artist's letters into English and spent more than two years living in Italy, near sites significant to his subject. The result, *The Agony and the Ecstasy* (1961), sold several million copies, was made into a motion picture starring Charlton Heston, and earned Stone decorations from the Italian government. Stone and his wife subsequently edited 600 of the letters into *I, Michelangelo, Sculptor* (1962), a first-person portrait. That year also saw the publication of *Lincoln: A Contemporary Portrait*, which Stone edited with historian Allan Nevins. Other subjects for his works included Charles Darwin (*The Origin*, 1980) and Sigmund Freud (*The Passions of the Mind*, 1971).

In a century in which popular culture appropriated politics, art, literature, and history, Stone was a preeminent purveyor of the accessible mainstream biography. He died on August 26, 1989.

Edward Moran

SEE ALSO: *Anderson, Sherwood; Best Sellers; Darrow, Clarence; Debs, Eugene V.; Freud, Sigmund; Heston, Charlton; London, Jack; Norris, Frank;* Pulp Fiction.

BIBLIOGRAPHY

Cunliffe, Marcus. "John and Abigail's Road to the White House." *New York Times Book Review*, November 7, 1965, 56.

International Celebrity Register, vol. 1. New York: Celebrity Register, 1959.

Stone, Irving. *Lust for Life: A Novel of Vincent van Gogh*. New York: Longmans Green, 1934.

Stone, Irving. *Love Is Eternal*. New York: Doubleday, 1954.

Stone, Irving. *Men to Match My Mountains*. New York: Doubleday, 1956.

Stone, Irving. *The Agony and the Ecstasy: A Novel of Michelangelo*. New York: Doubleday, 1961.

Stone, Irving. *I, Michelangelo, Sculptor*. New York: Doubleday, 1962.

Stone, Irving. *An Irving Stone Reader*. New York: Doubleday, 1963.

Stone, Irving. *The Passions of the Mind: A Novel of Sigmund Freud*. New York: Doubleday, 1971.

Stone, Irving. *The Origin*. New York: Doubleday, 1980.

Stone, Irving, and Jean Stone, eds. *Dear Theo.* New York: Houghton Mifflin, 1937.

Stone, Oliver *(1946–)*

Since the mid-1970s Oliver Stone has been involved in writing, directing, and producing films in a wide range of styles and genres. Most of his work has been critically and commercially successful, but since the 1980s it has also been controversial. Films such as *Salvador* and *Platoon,* both released in 1986, criticize U.S. government policy over El Salvador and Vietnam, sidestepping the prevailing confident patriotic mood to deal with the effects of war in a realistic and thoughtful way. In the 1990s films such as *Natural Born Killers* (1994), in which two young lovers travel around New Mexico, killing as they go, led to further accusations of exploitation and gratuitous violence. Since *Salvador,* the subject matter of Stone's films has ranged from political conspiracy in *JFK* (1991) and *Nixon* (1995) to war and its cultural effects in *Platoon* (1986) and *Born on the Fourth of July* (1989) to rock biopic in *The Doors* (1991). With their roots in the "New Cinema" of Hollywood at the end of the 1960s, Stone's films contain a blend of realism, social documentary, and political inquiry, which has made him a difficult but important commentator on American culture in the late twentieth century.

Oliver Stone. *Oliver Stone's films are known as much for their visual style as their politically charged, often controversial points of view.* DESIREE NAVARRO/CONTRIBUTOR/WIREIMAGE/GETTY IMAGES.

EARLY CAREER

After spells teaching English and later fighting in Vietnam in the 1960s, Stone returned from the war in 1968 to study film at New York University. Like many other directors of his generation, he benefited from the new graduate programs in film history, theory, and production that appeared in the 1960s. Film schools at the University of California at Los Angeles and New York University, among others, produced directors and writers such as Francis Ford Coppola, Brian De Palma, and Martin Scorsese, many of whose films, like Stone's, have been among the most influential of the 1970s, 1980s, and 1990s.

Stone began his filmmaking career as the writer, director, and editor of a horror film, *Seizure* (1974), and won his first Academy Award for Best Adapted Screenplay in 1979 for *Midnight Express.* In the early 1980s he had his most success as a screenwriter, taking writing credits for *Conan the Barbarian* (1982) and *Scarface* (1983). He also worked as a producer for the television series *Wild Palms* (1993) and for many of his own films as well as for films such as *The Joy Luck Club* (1993) and *Reversal of Fortune* (1990). Additionally, he acted, making appearances as a reporter in *Born on the Fourth of July,* as a professor in *The Doors,* and as a financial trader in his 1987 film *Wall Street.*

FILM TECHNIQUES

Graduates of the film schools have often become known for their technical skill and mastery of visual effects, and Stone is no exception. His best-known visual technique is the use of a variety of different types of film stock to present different viewpoints. In films such as *JFK* and *Natural Born Killers,* he also used news and amateur film, mixed in with "made" footage, to reconstruct events and give them an authentic appearance. Since the late 1980s the mixing of images using digital techniques has become much cheaper and easier, and other directors—such as Stone's contemporary Steven Spielberg, also a film school graduate—have used the technique to good effect, for example, in *Schindler's List* (1993). While Spielberg tends to blend "real" and "made" footage to create a continuous visual quality, Stone plays on the different textures of such formats as Super 8, 35-millimeter, and video to disrupt the flow of the narrative and make the viewer's position less secure.

A PLATOON OF WAR FILMS

Salvador was Stone's first major success as a film director. Based on the experiences of Richard Boyle, a journalist in El Salvador from 1980 to 1981, the film portrays the Salvadoran government's violent suppression of opposition and is deeply critical of American support for the right-wing regime. *Platoon* takes a similarly realistic approach in representing the war in Vietnam. The film won four Academy Awards, including Best Picture and Best Director, and marks the beginning of Stone's rise as an influential director and producer. Following *Platoon,* other Vietnam-related films found success; these included *Full Metal Jacket* (Stanley Kubrick, 1987) and *Good Morning, Vietnam* (Barry Levinson, 1987). As David Cook points out in *A History of Narrative Film,* however, the fashion for films about Vietnam did not only include sensitive treatments of modern warfare; *Platoon* came along around the same time as more exploitative films such as *Born American* (Renny Harlin, 1986) and *Rambo: First Blood Part II* (George Pan Cosmatos, 1985).

Stone's second Vietnam film, *Born on the Fourth of July*, contains some combat footage but concentrates on the cultural issues of the treatment of war veterans—in particular, those like Ron Kovic, whose injuries made them an embarrassment to military authorities and the general public. Having dealt with Vietnam from the point of view of soldiers in combat in *Platoon* and of veterans in *Born on the Fourth of July*, Stone considered the experience of war from the other side in *Heaven & Earth* (1993). This film describes the war from the viewpoint of a Vietnamese peasant woman who experiences the fighting as a child and later marries an American soldier.

Stone is not only known for his efforts to represent war in more realistic ways and from the point of view of its victims; he is also known as a shrewd social and cultural commentator. In the late 1980s, for example, films such as *Wall Street* (1987) and *Talk Radio* (1988) dealt with concerns about the financial markets, greed, and the media's manipulation of celebrities and its audience. In 1991 *The Doors* appeared as a film portrait of the rock band and its charismatic singer, Jim Morrison. Although the portrait of Morrison is a fan's account, the film is ruthless in its treatment of drug and rock culture.

JFK AND SUBSEQUENT FILMS

Since the early 1990s Stone's trademark technique of switching between film stocks, as well as using handheld cameras and natural lighting, has made watching his films a more directly engaging experience. The disorienting effect of the unstable camera involves the viewer in the unfolding scene in ways that are not possible with more formal styles of filmmaking. Perhaps his most important film, *JFK* (1991) relies on such techniques to make telling comments on the creation of myths by the media and government. Dealing with the assassination of President Kennedy in November 1963, the film revives the 1967 theory of New Orleans District Attorney Jim Garrison that Kennedy could not have been shot by Lee Harvey Oswald, as the Warren Commission had determined. Following the release of the film, Stone was attacked for having rewritten the facts about the assassination. Critics pointed to the way in which the famous amateur film of the killing had been enhanced and manipulated to prove Garrison's theory, but Stone was also criticized for his speculation about plots against Kennedy in the security forces and government.

Despite the opinions of critics, *JFK* was a success with audiences, prompting a run on books about the Kennedy assassination and eventually putting pressure on Congress to release records of the Warren Commission through a special act in 1992. Perhaps because of the controversy, *JFK* did not receive an Oscar for Best Picture or Best Director, but Stone did receive a Golden Globe Award for Best Director.

JFK was significant for its technical effects as well as the public response it triggered, and *Natural Born Killers*, perhaps Stone's most vilified film, takes the techniques learned in making *JFK* still further. The movie includes animation and other electronic imaging methods, as well as live action shots on several different film stocks, with the effect that the images themselves, as well as the subject matter, bombard the viewer relentlessly. Cook speculates that the film is Stone's response to the media's treatment of *JFK*. *Natural Born Killers* exposes the hypocrisy of a media that criticized him for twisting the truth yet makes a fortune goading the public to ever greater voyeuristic excesses. Certainly the murderous couple in Stone's film is presented in such a way as to make their acts of violence fascinating rather than repellent. Manipulating the viewer, even though it admits to doing so, *Natural Born Killers* speculates about how much more manipulative the supposedly objective media might be.

As a director and producer, Stone has always chosen dramatic, often controversial subjects. His biopics, such as *The Doors*; *Nixon*; and *Alexander* (2004), about the ancient king of Macedonia, tend to have a broad cultural sweep, which has led to accusations of historical inaccuracy and excessive melodrama. Stone favors dramatizations of significant historical moments or events, and his projects since the start of the twenty-first century have increasingly dealt with contemporary issues, as illustrated by *World Trade Center* (2006), which addresses the events of September 11, 2001, and *W* (2008), a biopic of President George W. Bush. In 2010, in the wake of the global financial crisis of 2008, Stone's film *Wall Street: Money Never Sleeps* revives Gordon Gekko, the malevolent corporate raider Stone invented for his 1987 movie *Wall Street*. In both films Gekko is played by Michael Douglas, and the material hints at Stone's previously sharp critique of unfettered corporate greed, but neither the script nor the performances match up to the earlier film.

Many of Stone's films look at the way individuals are controlled and used by bigger organizations. As a result he has often found himself in opposition to current thinking and has been described as a dissident by his supporters. Like those of many directors who came through the film schools in the 1960s, his films have a reputation for provoking strong emotional responses in audiences. Perhaps for this reason films such as *JFK* and *Natural Born Killers* have sometimes received harsh treatment at the hands of their critics. Stone's main achievement as a film director, however, has been his contribution to the valuable tradition of socially challenging independent filmmaking that began in the 1960s with directors such as Arthur Penn, Sam Peckinpah, and Stanley Kubrick.

Chris Routledge

SEE ALSO: *Academy Awards; Celebrity; Hollywood; Horror Movies;* JFK*; Kennedy Assassination; Kubrick, Stanley; Movie Stars;* Natural Born Killers*; 9/11;* Platoon*; Rambo; Rock and Roll;* Schindler's List*; Scorsese, Martin; Spielberg, Steven; Vietnam; War Movies; World Trade Center.*

BIBLIOGRAPHY

Cook, David A. *A History of Narrative Film.* New York: W. W. Norton, 1996.

Kagan, Norman. *The Cinema of Oliver Stone.* New York: Continuum, 1995.

Kunz, Don. *The Films of Oliver Stone.* Lanham, MD: Scarecrow Press, 1997.

Riordan, James. *Stone: The Controversies, Excesses, and Exploits of a Radical Filmmaker.* New York: Hyperion, 1995.

Toplin, Robert Brent. *Oliver Stone's USA: Film, History, and Controversy.* Lawrence: University Press of Kansas, 2000.

Stonewall Rebellion

In the early hours of June 28, 1969, patrons of a gay men's bar in Greenwich Village and their allies in the street vigorously resisted a routine police raid. The event, which has been described as "the hairpin drop heard around the world" and as one of those "specific sparks that ignites protest," was both timely and inevitable. It came about during an era of cultural and social ferment, after years of efforts on the part of homosexuals to gain a public voice and legitimate place in U.S. society. The Stonewall Rebellion became a "metaphor for emergence, visibility and pride," one that publicly affirmed the identity of a people burdened with a tradition of invisibility and abuse.

RISE OF HOMOSEXUAL MILITANCY

A variety of factors—including modernity, changes in cultural and sexual mores, and a politicized environment—have been identified as supporting the development of urban homosexual subcultures and subsequently a homosexual movement. In New York City the geographic and cultural setting for these radical changes was established in the bohemian, avant-garde atmosphere that began developing in Greenwich Village during the 1940s. Significant influences included the Beat culture, pop art, psychedelics, the New American Cinema, off-Broadway theater, and the activist folk music scene. In short, the area was an incubator for oppositional attitudes toward convention and traditional authority; these attitudes spread across the country.

Cultural critic Daniel Harris has proposed that "diva worship," among male homosexuals, was another factor that unwittingly contributed to gay militancy. Because gay males had no other gay positive images, many projected themselves either into the tragic and resilient Judy Garland ("the ultimate bellwether of the docile gay masses") or the "invincible personae" portrayed by the likes of Joan Crawford and Bette Davis. In short, homosexuals "recycled the refuse of popular culture and reconstituted it into an energizing force."

Homosexual militancy was also nurtured by the politicized atmosphere of the time. Since the 1950s, Mattachine, ONE, and Daughters of Bilitis had publicly advocated for respect and civil rights for homosexuals. In the 1960s the activities and gains of the civil rights movement and other social movements also promoted a new sense of hope and assertiveness among politicized homosexuals.

For some gay men, the death of Garland a few days before the Stonewall uprising symbolically transformed the stereotype of the quiet, suffering homosexual. Activist Alkarim Jivani observed that "Garland had been the archetypal gay icon because she represented bravery through adversity, but that bravery was characterized by a passive stoicism. With the death of Judy Garland, that image of the gay man died."

Meanwhile, for those who identified with the battling, invincible divas, the moment of truth was fast approaching. According to one report, the day of Garland's funeral was "sweltering and humid, and that night there was a full moon." Vito Russo, who later wrote a book (*The Celluloid Closet*) on homosexual themes in U.S. films, recalled that "I was in a foul mood that night because of the funeral." Ira Kushner, who was fifteen at the time, remembers standing outside the Stonewall as part of a crowd that had gathered to honor Garland. Then the police arrived.

EVENTS UNFOLD

At first the police arrested some of the younger men standing outside, and then the officers went into the bar. As the patrons were roughly hustled out of the bar, it was those most used to confrontations with the police (drag queens, street people, students, and a few butches) who were in the vanguard of the resistance. Drag queen Rey "Sylvia Lee" Rivera recalled that "that night, everything clicked." Rivera and some of the people he knew were already involved in other social movements. He told himself, "Great, now it's my time. I'm out there being a revolutionary for everybody else, now it's time to do my own thing for my own people," according to Eric Marcus's book *Making History*. In the midst of the Vietnam War, the civil rights movement, counterculture, student and women's movements, patrons of the Stonewall bar refused to go quietly into the police van.

There are also reports that, as the tension increased, a well-placed spark was contributed by a butch in drag. She had been visiting a male friend in the bar. When the police pulled her out of the bar and into a police car, she struggled. When she was hit, the audience exploded. Coins (symbolizing the bribes paid to the police by the bars), an uprooted parking meter, bottles, fists, and insults flew. Queens engaged in campy street theater that included sexual repartee aimed at the police and a chorus line singing "We are the Stonewall girls. . . . " The bar was set on fire, the police called for reinforcements, and the melee escalated into a riot. Although this was not the first time that homosexuals had resisted police abuse, this time there were significant political consequences.

While moderate homosexuals condemned the violence, more radical activists used the event as an organizing opportunity. In New York the event galvanized those sympathetic to confrontation politics. By July these activists had coalesced into the cogender Gay Liberation Front (GLF), a name that suggested solidarity with Third World resistance movements, such as the National Liberation Front in Vietnam. Across the United States, scores of groups with the same name sprang up. GLF was the first of many homosexual activist groups of that era, most of which were politically at odds with one another. What these groups did have in common was a radical commitment to the civil rights of homosexuals. The groups were loosely connected into a network known as the Gay Liberation Movement. By 1973 there were more than 800 gay and lesbian groups and organizations in the United States.

MEDIA REACTION

Main Street U.S.A. took little notice of the Stonewall event. News of the riot was buried in the back pages of the *New York Times*. Other mass market publications such as *Life*, *Newsweek*, *Time*, and *Harper's*, which had previously published sympathetic articles about homosexuals, also failed to recognize the importance of the event. While the mainstream press missed the significance of Stonewall, the homosexual press, which was politically moderate, treated the riot with ambivalence. The *Advocate*, a national gay male publication, published several reports, and one writer wondered if "the spark" set off by Stonewall would endure. The *Ladder*, a national lesbian publication, gave the event two pages of coverage, but the article did not appear until October 1969.

After Stonewall, coverage of homosexual issues in the mainstream media increased significantly. In October 1969 *Time* magazine featured the "Homosexual Movement" as a main story. *The Reader's Guide to Periodical Literature*, an index to popular magazines, listed nine entries on "sex perversion" in 1950, the year in which the first homophile organization (Mattachine) was founded. By 1970 *The Reader's Guide* listed thirty items under "homosexuality" and one under "lesbianism."

AFTERMATH

Gradually, the story of Stonewall came to occupy a central position in the folklore and chronology of U.S. gay and lesbian history. It remains so even in the face of claims that it was but one significant event in a long history of individual and collective resistance that spans 400 years of U.S. history. According Martin Duberman's account of Stonewall, the event simply "gave meaning and coherence to a struggle that was already underway." To many, however, the special appeal of the Stonewall Rebellion is based on it being a defiant and defining moment that took place during an era filled with similar moments. As in the Boston Tea Party, the use of confrontation radicalized a movement that had, up to that time, relied on documents and discourse.

Since 1970 lesbians and gays in cities across the United States have held annual gay pride parades and rallies to commemorate the event. There have been significant turnouts in San Francisco, New York, Los Angeles, and Chicago. Unlike the celebrations of other marginalized groups, gay pride memorializes the public emergence of a people and a movement that are still outside the equal protection of the law and are widely unwelcome at the diverse cultural table of this nation.

Stonewall signifies a dividing line between the brave but understandably more conservative efforts of homophile groups founded during the McCarthy era; those of liminal 1960s groups like the Society for Individual Rights in San Francisco and the Homosexual Action League in Philadelphia; and radical homosexual activists, many of whom had gained organizing skills and new political perspectives in other civil rights movements. The title of a well-known documentary film on gay and lesbian history, *Before Stonewall* (1979), suggests that the event was a radical departure from the homophile era. For those who subscribed to the new liberation ethos, assimilation and dissimulation were out. Instead, they were inspired by slogans like "gay is good" and "out of the closets and into the streets." For these lesbians, gay men, and other "sexual outlaws," Stonewall was a watershed event, one that galvanized them into radical activism on behalf of an historically despised group. For a specific generation of activists, the event "became the symbol of an oppressed and invisible minority at last demanding its place in the sun," according to Wayne Dynes in the *Encyclopedia of Homosexuality.*

Yolanda Retter

SEE ALSO: The Advocate*; The Beat Generation; Civil Rights Movement; Crawford, Joan; Davis, Bette; Folk Music; Garland, Judy; Gay Liberation Movement; Gay Men; Greenwich Village; Lesbianism; McCarthyism; Psychedelia.*

BIBLIOGRAPHY

Duberman, Martin. *Stonewall.* New York: Plume, 1994.

Dynes, Wayne, ed. *Encyclopedia of Homosexuality.* New York: Garland, 1990.

Harris, Daniel. "The Death of Camp: Gay Men and Hollywood Diva Worship, from Reverence to Ridicule." *Salmagundi*, Fall 1996, 166–191.

Hertel, Shareen, and Kathryn Libal, eds. *Human Rights in the United States: Beyond Exceptionalism.* Cambridge, UK: Cambridge University Press, 2011.

Marcus, Eric. *Making History: The Struggle for Gay and Lesbian Equal Rights, 1945–1990.* New York: HarperCollins Publishers, 1992.

Stout, Rex *(1886–1975)*

Detective novelist Rex Stout is best remembered for creating eccentric crime solver Nero Wolfe and his assistant, Archie Goodwin, a duo who appeared in more than fifty books over four decades beginning in the mid-1930s. Wolfe and Goodwin quickly endeared themselves to readers—not only for their adeptness at solving crimes but also for their trenchant comments on American life, war, big business, and politics. Wolfe—the puffing, grunting, Montenegro-born heavyweight gumshoe with a fondness for food and growing orchids—was introduced in 1934 with the publication of *Fer de Lance.* A steady stream of Nero Wolfe books followed, to the point where the character became better known than his creator.

Often compared by literary critics to Sherlock Holmes and Dr. Watson, Wolfe and Goodwin play complementary roles in Stout's fiction. Detective work for Wolfe is a business, and his

Rex Stout. *Rex Stout is best known for creating the fictional detective character Nero Wolfe in 1934.* **AP IMAGES.**

clients are charged handsomely for his services, allowing the investigator the means to indulge his penchant for orchids and food. Goodwin, like Watson, is the legman, the hard-boiled detective who satirically narrates the events in the story. He is dispatched to do all the detective work that Wolfe refuses to do. Wolfe is portrayed by his partner as being partly human and partly godlike, with an arrogantly expressed intellect; he has a gourmand's appetite and is an orchid grower extraordinaire. Goodwin treats clients, cops, women, and murderers with the same degree of wit and reality he applies to Wolfe. Singly they would be engaging, but together they form a brilliant partnership that brought a new and humorous touch to detective fiction.

Another character in the Nero Wolfe series, Inspector L. T. Cramer, NYPD, is described by George Dove in his 1982 book *The Police Procedural* as probably the most familiar policeman in classic detective fiction. Cramer's feelings toward Wolfe move from skepticism to open hostility to open admiration within the space of a single novel.

Rex Todhunter Stout was born in Noblesville, Indiana, in 1886, the sixth of nine children to John and Lucetta Todhunter Stout, who were Quakers. The family later moved to Kansas, where, by the age of nine, Stout was an academic prodigy, especially in mathematics. He attended the University of Kansas but did not complete a degree, leaving to enlist in the U.S. Navy, in which he served as a yeoman on President Theodore Roosevelt's yacht. When Stout returned to civilian life in 1908, he began working as a bookkeeper. He devised a system of school banking that netted him a considerable fortune, making possible a trip to Paris and an opportunity to write. Among his early freelance articles was one in which he purported to analyze the palm prints he personally obtained from President William Howard Taft.

Stout turned out three novels before *Fer de Lance* that were critically acclaimed but did not achieve the popularity of his later Nero Wolfe books. In his private life, he was outspoken, first against Nazism and later against the use of nuclear weapons. In 1941 he served as emcee of the radio program *Speaking of Liberty*, and during World War II he wrote propaganda and volunteered for the Fight for Freedom organization.

In Stout's Nero Wolfe series, the detective solves crimes from his brownstone on New York's 35th Street, adhering to a schedule regardless of murderers with guns, bombs in guest rooms, or clients with problems. In *The League of Frightened Men* (1935), Goodwin suggests that Wolfe step out into the street in front of the house to bring his powers to bear on a cabdriver who is an important witness. "Out?" Wolfe exclaims, looking at Goodwin in horror. When Goodwin explains that his employer would not even have to step off the curb, the unflappably cool Wolfe replies, "I don't know, Archie, why you persist in trying to badger me into frantic sorties." Wolfe does, however, leave the house on occasion to attend orchid shows, as in *Some Buried Caesar* (1938), or to be incarcerated in the local jail, as in *A Family Affair* (1973).

In Stout's novels, character and dialogue are more important than plot. Goodwin is always dashing around—even falling in love—while Wolfe is defined as a slightly comic but always impressive figure, even if only for his sheer bulk. Weighing a full seventh of a ton, Wolfe can cross his legs only with great difficulty, when he finds a chair strong enough to support his body, that is. Goodwin takes great delight in his observations of Wolfe's movements and habits, his glasses of beer, the way he tends to his collection of 10,000 orchids, or his method of entering a room. Stout summed up the appeal of his characters thusly:

> You know goddam well why, of all kinds of stories, the detective story is the most popular. It supports, more than any other kind of story, man's favorite myth, that he's *Homo sapien*, the rational animal. And of course the poor son-of-a-bitch isn't a rational animal at all—I think the most important function of the brain is thinking up reasons for the decisions his emotions have made. Detective stories support that myth.

Joan Gajadhar

SEE ALSO: *Detective Fiction; Doyle, Arthur Conan; Hard-Boiled Detective Fiction.*

BIBLIOGRAPHY

Dove, George. *The Police Procedural*. Bowling Green, OH: Bowling Green University Press, 1982.

Keating, H. R. F. *Crime and Mystery, the 100 Best Books*. New York: Carroll and Graf, 1987.

Stout, Rex. *Fer de Lance*. New York: Farrar and Rinehart, 1934.

Stout, Rex. *The League of Frightened Men*. New York: Bantam Books, 1935.

"Stout, Rex." In *World Authors 1900–1950*. New York: H.W. Wilson, 1996.

Symons, Julian. *Bloody Murder: From the Detective Story to the Crime Novel, a History*. London: Faber & Faber, 1972.

Strait, George *(1952–)*

When George Strait burst onto the national scene in 1981 he was identified with a movement in country music known as "new traditionalism," a return by young country artists to old country styles. Pop music had come to dominate the country charts during the 1970s, and Strait, along with Ricky Skaggs, Randy Travis, and others, was among the dissenters. Before long, Strait went on to become one of music's most commercially successful recording and touring artists. He has been fondly dubbed the "King of Country" and "King George" and is considered a living legend.

SINGER

Born in Poteet and raised in Pearsall, Texas, Strait and his brother lived with their father, a junior high school math teacher and part-time rancher. A true Texas cowboy, Strait helped out on the family ranch. Growing up, he ignored country music in favor of the pop music of the British Invasion of the 1960s, as did many of his peers. In high school Strait played in a number of garage bands. After graduation, he eloped with Norma, his high school sweetheart, and after a short flirtation with college, joined the army in 1971. It was while he was stationed in Hawaii that he began performing country music, as a singer in a band on the base.

Strait finished his military service in 1975 and returned to Texas to study agriculture at Southwest Texas State University. It was there that he formed the Ace in the Hole Band, which became a big regional draw. The group released a couple of records on the Dallas-based D Records label and made several trips to Nashville, Tennessee, though they failed to draw the attention of anyone in the music industry there. Erv Woolsey, a Texas club owner and former record promotions executive, saw the band one night and took an interest. In 1980 Woolsey convinced MCA to sign Strait and eventually became and remained his manager.

Strait's first single was released in the spring of 1981 and reached the Top 10. His 1982 offering "Fool Hearted Memory" was his first number one single, and since then he has had an amazing string of chart successes, including more than eighty Top 10 country singles. Every album he has released since 1981's *Strait Country* has been certified gold or platinum, and he holds more than twenty records for concert attendance across the United States. In 1992 Strait made his silver-screen debut with a starring role in the film *Pure Country*, and in 2010 he returned to the big screen to star in the follow-up film *Pure Country 2: The Gift*.

Though country music has become increasingly more pop since the 1980s, Strait seldom strays too far from Texas honky-tonk and the shuffle beat of western swing. He has successfully negotiated the line between commercial and traditional for several decades. His glitter-free cowboy-hat-and-denim fashion style has helped to spawn a legion of faceless "hat acts" in country music over the years, but Strait has an understated and elegant presence, existing in stark contrast to the bombastic style of Garth Brooks, one of country music's other giant male country superstars. Strait is a song stylist, greatly influenced by Merle Haggard, known for his subtle phrasing and supple vocals. His style is evocative of such classic country singers as Lefty Frizzell and Ray Price. Strait says he learned to sound like Haggard and George Jones because he began as a singer for a local Texas cover band and "people want you to sound like the records."

SONGWRITER

Though he excelled at song selection, for much of his career Strait was not a songwriter. Nearly three decades in, that changed when he cowrote three songs for his thirty-eighth studio album, *Twang* (2009), and seven songs for his thirty-ninth album, *Here for a Good Time* (2011). Both albums were sturdily reviewed and, in addition to ranking at number one on the country charts, reached number one and number three, respectively, on the Billboard 200 cross-genre chart. The title track from *Here for a Good Time*, one of the seven cowritten by Strait, peaked at number two on the country singles chart, becoming his eighty-fifth Top 10 song. Strait's cowriters are Dean Dillon and Strait's own son Bubba, who he says inspired him to return to songwriting, something he dabbled in early on in a career that took off the year Bubba was born.

Still going strong three decades later, Strait was named one of the top artists of the year by *Billboard* magazine in 2011. He had recently set a milestone, unprecedented on any Billboard chart, of thirty consecutive years on the Top 10 songs list, and he holds the record for the most number one hit singles in any genre in the history of music. He has had more platinum and multiplatinum albums (an album is certified platinum when it sells one million copies) than any country singer in history and ranks third across music genres, out-certified by only Elvis Presley and the Beatles; Strait has reached platinum or multiplatinum status with more than thirty-three. Top among them is his four-disc box set *Strait out of the Box*, which was released in September 1995 and by the following spring had already become one of the five best-selling box sets in popular music history.

Strait has won twenty-two Country Music Association (CMA) Awards and nineteen Academy of Country Music (ACM) Awards, including Artist of the Decade in 2009. His thirty-seventh album, *Troubadour* (2008), earned him a Grammy for Best Country Album. He holds the records for the most ACM and CMA wins and nominations. In 2010 *Billboard* named him the top country artist of the last twenty-five years. He has won the CMA Vocalist of the Year Award five times in two different decades and the CMA Album of the Year Award five times over three decades. In 2003 he received the National Medal of Art from President George W. Bush, and in 2007 he was inducted into the Country Music Hall of Fame.

With his classic new traditional country sound, his loyalty to tried-and-true honky-tonk and lonesome cowboy ballads, his unpretentious style, and his straightforward authenticity, Strait offers his fans country music they can depend on in a smooth baritone cadence. Reviewers have commented that Strait's success proves that fans like a country singer who sticks to his old-time roots. When asked about his success, he replied, "It just continues to be one heck of a ride that I'm enjoying every minute of. Long live country music!"

Joyce Linehan

SEE ALSO: *Brooks, Garth; Country Music; Frizzell, Lefty; Grammy Awards; Haggard, Merle; Jones, George; Skaggs, Ricky.*

BIBLIOGRAPHY

Bego, Mark. *George Strait: The Story of Country's Living Legends.* New York: Kensington Books, 1997.

Cantwell, David, and Dave Marsh. *George Strait.* New York: Boulevard Books, 1996.

Sgammato, Jo. *Keepin' It Country: The George Strait Story.* New York: Ballantine Books, 1998.

Teutsch, Austin. *King George: The Triumphs and Tragedies in the Life of George Strait.* Austin, TX: Golden Touch Press/JRAB, 2010.

Stratemeyer, Edward *(1862–1930)*

It seems ironic that America's most prolific creator of juvenile popular fiction is a man whose name is hardly known. Edward Stratemeyer revolutionized the world of children's writing by adapting it to the methods of mass production. His Stratemeyer Syndicate, founded at the turn of the twentieth century, hired ghostwriters to develop hundreds of stories based on Stratemeyer's outlines. From this "fiction factory," as some have called it, came such durable American heroes as the Bobbsey Twins, Tom Swift, the Hardy Boys, and Nancy Drew.

Born in New Jersey in 1862 to German immigrants, Stratemeyer grew up admiring the rags-to-riches stories of Horatio Alger and aspired to write similar books. In fact, the progress of his career is reminiscent of an Alger plot. Although he did not quite start in rags, Stratemeyer eventually obtained riches by steadily climbing the ranks of the professional fiction writer's business. As a child, he had a small printing press that he used to print and distribute copies of his own stories. As a young adult he sold several small pieces, for small sums, to various papers. But his first important sale came in 1889 when the popular *Golden Days* story paper bought "Victor Horton's Idea" for the substantial sum of $75.

Encouraged by this success, Stratemeyer spent the following years publishing widely, using both his own name and several pseudonyms. In addition to selling serials to story papers, he branched out to writing dime novels and became a regular contributor to the various publications owned by Street and Smith, the premier publisher of popular fiction in its day. In 1893 Stratemeyer became an editor at *Good News*, a Street and Smith publication, while also supplying it with original material.

During his years as a writer and editor of dime novels and story papers, Stratemeyer learned principles he would later apply to his own syndicate. He saw, for example, the value of establishing "house names" as pseudonyms, for this allowed several authors to work interchangeably on a series without disrupting the public's relationship with the "author." He also saw that copyright holders earned the greatest financial rewards: an author could be hired at a flat rate to produce a story, but the copyright holder could print and reprint that story at will and reap the benefits indefinitely.

Stratemeyer steadily steered his career toward the more respectable world of hardcover fiction. In 1894 he began recycling some of his former story-paper serials as complete books, shaping the volumes into series. The thrifty system of recycling, renaming, and reworking would become a hallmark of Stratemeyer's operations, influencing his own work and that of the Syndicate for years after his death. In 1898 Stratemeyer enjoyed his first great success with hardcover fiction. He had been circulating a war-themed manuscript just as the Spanish-American War broke out. The publishers reviewing the manuscript asked Stratemeyer to revise it, incorporating the news of Commodore George Dewey's naval victory in the Philippines. The result, *Under Dewey at Manila*, became an immediate best seller, initiating one of Stratemeyer's many series on historical and military themes.

THE STRATEMEYER SYNDICATE FORMULA

In 1899 Stratemeyer launched his watershed series, The Rover Boys, under the name Arthur M. Winfield. He later claimed to have chosen this pseudonym for its cryptic symbolism: Arthur stood for "author," and Winfield represented his desire to win in his field. The initial "M" stood for the number of books he hoped to sell—first "a thousand" (as the Roman numeral for 1,000) and then "a million," depending on when he was asked. The Rover Boys series was an enormous success and was the first series to exemplify what later became the Stratemeyer Syndicate formula: the extraordinary adventures of average teenage heroes, with lots of action and excitement driving the plot.

Despite his early training in the blood-and-thunder milieu of dime novels, Stratemeyer kept his hardcover fiction for youngsters clean and wholesome. After 1900 his work for story papers and dime novel houses diminished, as he focused more attention on his own series books. Within a few years he had several series going at once and decided that an assembly-line approach would be a more efficient method for producing the quantity of material he had in mind.

The Stratemeyer Syndicate, begun in 1905, employed the methods Stratemeyer had learned earlier in his career. He devised plots and titles for stories, then hired ghostwriters to flesh out the skeletons, making them sign agreements not to reveal their identities. His hired hands were other dime novel authors like himself, some of whom he had known at Street and Smith, as well as journalists and other professionals skilled in turning out high quantity on tight deadlines. His most important employee was his friend Howard Garis, who would later become famous in his own right as the author of the Uncle Wiggily stories. Garis wrote several series for Stratemeyer, with Tom Swift being the most famous. Howard's wife, Lilian, also a children's writer, contributed volumes to the Syndicate's Bobbsey Twins series and others.

Not all of Stratemeyer's properties were for children. He repackaged dime novels from his early career as fare for young adult readers. Moreover, he functioned as a literary agent who purchased manuscripts from other writers and had them published under various house pseudonyms. A handful of his properties were written for the adult fiction market, such as a series of mysteries written by "Chester K. Steele." But children's series were the backbone of the Stratemeyer Syndicate, and their themes were wide ranging, covering school stories, Westerns, mysteries, sports, career stories, and other genres. The popularity of these books was enormous. The catalogs of Cupples & Leon and Grosset & Dunlap, two of his main publishers, were laden with syndicate fare—though, thanks to the pseudonyms, young readers were unaware that all of the books they were devouring came from the same source.

CRITICS

Stratemeyer's near monopoly of the children's series market brought him some unwelcome scrutiny. Franklin K. Mathiews, librarian for the Boy Scouts of America, published a scathing article in *Outlook* magazine in 1914, "Blowing Out the Boys' Brains." In it, Mathiews asserts that sensationalist series books, marked by rapid-fire plots, absurd coincidences, multiple cliff-hangers, and a total lack of character development, damaged boys' imaginations by overstimulation, thus ruining them for the subtleties of better literature.

There was a degree of sense in Mathiews's complaints, and educators and librarians around the country took up the cry. Stratemeyer's success, however, was never seriously compromised; children loved his books and could afford to buy them themselves. However, through the decades there remained a strain of protest against the vapidity and sensationalism of series books. At the same time the books were not working in a vacuum. They were part of a general trend, catering to the same appetite for speed and superficiality that would later be fulfilled by television. Despite disapproval from the more educated segments of the population, children craved this style of entertainment, and the great demand called for an equally great supply.

DEATH AND LEGACY

In the spring of 1930 Stratemeyer succumbed to pneumonia; he died at age sixty-seven. After attempting unsuccessfully to find a buyer for the syndicate, Stratemeyer's daughters, Harriet Stratemeyer Adams and Edna Stratemeyer, assumed operation of the family business. The sisters trimmed the business down considerably, killing off nearly its whole line of series. They kept only the proven cash cows, including Nancy Drew and the Hardy Boys, among a few others. A few new series were begun during the Depression, but the syndicate remained a much more conservative and narrowly focused business than it had been during Edward Stratemeyer's tenure. By 1940 the syndicate was producing only nine series—a steep decline from the fourteen it had produced in 1935.

In 1942 Edna married and moved away, leaving Harriet as the active partner. Her strategy for success involved maximizing the value of the syndicate's back catalog. She resurrected old series in reprint editions with new publishers and signed deals to have her characters translated into foreign languages and other media. Former best seller *Bomba the Jungle Boy* benefited from this treatment, as he became the hero of a string of "B" movies (1949–1952) and a reprint series of books, both of which were released in other countries as well as in the United States.

In 1954 Harriet Adams revitalized the Tom Swift legacy by launching the Tom Swift Jr. series, based on the original hero's son. Guided by talented ghostwriter James Lawrence, this series became a major latter-day success for the syndicate. Other new series were attempted during the following years, but the only other substantial hit was The Happy Hollisters (1953–1970), written by syndicate partner Andrew Svenson.

Adams's most controversial decision came in 1959, when she launched a project to revise and rewrite all the volumes in the Hardy Boys and Nancy Drew series, as well as many of the Bobbsey Twins. Her decision was prompted primarily by concerns that modern children were impatient with the now old-fashioned texts of the original books. A further motivation came from complaints the syndicate received about the insulting portrayals of ethnic characters. Not only had the syndicate historically tended to cast minorities as villains, but early ghostwriters often used ethnic stereotypes as sources of humor. Adams responded to both concerns with one remedy, gradually replacing original books with new versions that were shorter, thoroughly modern, and (relatively) stereotype-free. The revisions were mere shadows of their former glory, however, as much of the books' charm and style had been erased.

CHANGE IN PUBLISHERS

Another controversy erupted in 1979 when Adams changed publishers. Dissatisfied with the practices of Grosset & Dunlap, her primary publishers for nearly fifty years, Adams signed a contract with Simon & Schuster. Grosset sued, and the litigation put the famous syndicate series at the center of a well-publicized custody battle. The case was decided in favor of the syndicate, and Simon & Schuster brought out new versions of Nancy Drew, Tom Swift, the Hardy Boys, and the Bobbsey Twins.

Adams died in 1982, and her partners sold the business to Simon & Schuster two years later. Throughout the 1980s and 1990s the publishers continued to work with their properties in much the same way the syndicate had, hiring ghostwriters and swearing them to secrecy. Despite efforts to revitalize Tom Swift and the Bobbsey Twins, both series were discontinued in the early 1990s, but Nancy Drew and the Hardy Boys continued and even expanded into a variety of spin-off series.

Simon & Schuster's greatest service to the Stratemeyer Syndicate came with its donation of nearly all of the syndicate's paperwork to the New York Public Library. This collection of records, which opened to the public in September 1998, dates from the earliest years of Stratemeyer's career and forms the largest single location for research into the syndicate's history. During the 1990s an increasing number of scholars noted the massive influence of the Stratemeyer Syndicate, not only as the single largest contributor to children's popular fiction in the twentieth century but also as a model of a publishing phenomenon. Reaching several generations of American readers, the products of the Stratemeyer Syndicate have had an incalculable effect on America's consciousness.

Ilana Nash

SEE ALSO: *The Bobbsey Twins; Boy Scouts of America; Dime Novels; The Great Depression; The Hardy Boys; Nancy Drew; Street and Smith; Tom Swift Series.*

BIBLIOGRAPHY

Billman, Carol. *The Secret of the Stratemeyer Syndicate: Nancy Drew, the Hardy Boys and the Million Dollar Fiction Factory.* New York: Ungar, 1986.

Dizer, John T. *Tom Swift & Company: "Boys' Books" by Stratemeyer and Others.* Jefferson, NC: McFarland, 1982.

Garis, Roger. *My Father Was Uncle Wiggily.* New York: McGraw-Hill, 1966.

Johnson, Deidre. *Stratemeyer Pseudonyms and Series Books: An Annotated Checklist of Stratemeyer and Stratemeyer Syndicate Publications.* Westport, CT: Greenwood Press, 1982.

Johnson, Deidre. *Edward Stratemeyer and the Stratemeyer Syndicate.* New York: Twayne, 1993.

Lange, Brenda. *Edward Stratemeyer.* Philadelphia: Chelsea House, 2004.

Stratemeyer Syndicate

SEE: *Stratemeyer, Edward.*

Stratton-Porter, Gene *(1863–1924)*

Gene Stratton-Porter was an author, a photographer, and an illustrator whose prolific output of romance-spiced nature writing was received enthusiastically by middle-class Americans in the early 1900s. Her books have been through multiple editions, and the most popular of these sold millions of copies in the years leading up to and encompassing World War I.

Stratton-Porter's novels have not endured on the basis of their literary merit. Even at the height of her popularity, many critics were not fond of her work, which they considered to be formulaic and unrealistic. Rather, the broad appeal of Stratton-Porter's fiction can be traced to her unique and seemingly effortless ability to foster the vicarious involvement of the reader in a naturalistic drama: the hatching of moths, the nesting of birds, the gurgling of a swamp, or the whispering of woodland. Nature writing was already an established and successful genre when Stratton-Porter came along, led by authors such as John Burroughs, Ernest Thompson Seton, and John Muir. She added her own twist, tempering the nature message with enough romantic fiction to engage the reader.

Stratton-Porter wrote what she knew best. Born Geneva Stratton in Wabash County, Indiana, as the youngest of twelve children, she spent long, unsupervised hours in rapt contemplation of the plant and wildlife that abounded. When her family moved into town when she was eleven, she brought along her collection of pet birds. Her marriage in 1886 to Charles Darwin Porter and the birth of her only daughter, Jeannette, two years later kept Stratton-Porter occupied with domestic concerns, but the family's move to Geneva, Indiana, in 1888 placed her adjacent to a unique setting: Limberlost Swamp. Here, in the kind of personal metamorphosis characteristic of her future book plots, she became the Bird Woman. Bored with the social boundaries of being a small-town housewife—and spurred by the need to illustrate some writing projects on bird life with a camera she had fatefully received as a gift—Stratton-Porter took to the swamp.

The long field hours and her bird studies, at which she became increasingly proficient, provided not only the raw material for her nonfiction but also the experiences, observations, and characters (from her interactions with farmers, loggers, and other people around the swamp) for her fiction. Her first book, *The Song of the Cardinal* (1903), illustrated with her own photographs and detailing the life of a cardinal and its mate, was received well, albeit by a small audience.

Stratton-Porter decided to try her hand at a second book—this time, with a human love story running through her naturalistic setting—and *Freckles* (1904) set the stage for the rest of her career. While publishers were initially concerned about the predominating natural world in her work, her insistence that it remain, and her subsequent sales numbers, won the day. The novels *Freckles*, *A Girl of the Limberlost* (1909), *Laddie* (1913), and *Michael O'Halloran* (1915) achieved best-seller status. Recognizing that her fiction produced better sales than her works on natural history, Stratton-Porter arranged with her publishers to alternate between nonfiction and novels. *What I Have Done with Birds* (1907) and *Moths of the Limberlost* (1912) represent the best of her nonfiction, which tends to be lavishly produced and includes her own photographic illustrations accompanied by text written in a descriptive, informal style. This presentation, while impressive in its detail, appealed more to nature lovers than naturalists and contributed to her being recognized as a novelist rather than for her substantial contributions to photography and studies on bird behavior.

Stratton-Porter's literary career also benefited from timing. First, she came along at a period when nature writing was in style. Second, her primary theme—overcoming personal obstacles through faith, trust, and hard work in a peaceful atmosphere brought upon by an interaction with nature—connected with an American public that read fiction voraciously and sought pleasant diversions from the urban grind and the grim realities of World War I.

Stratton-Porter's profile was further raised by the proliferation of women's magazines. She had regularly contributed articles to publications such as *Outing* and *Recreation*, but in 1921 she was approached by *McCall's* and was offered an editorial page. "Gene Stratton-Porter's Page" gave her a powerful forum for disseminating her message of positive thinking and right living. In addition, her poems and serializations of her novels appeared in *Good Housekeeping*.

Not surprisingly, Stratton-Porter's success drew the attention of Hollywood. She had moved from Indiana to California in 1920 and had initially contracted with filmmaker Thomas Inca, whose motto was "Clean Pictures for Clean People." Dissatisfied with the results of the first project, *Michael O'Halloran*, and by now a very wealthy and determined woman, Stratton-Porter established her own production company. Ultimately, seven of her novels were made into films.

In 1924 Stratton-Porter died in an automobile accident. Her novels are no longer sought out by mainstream readers, but they are still on the shelves of public and academic libraries, especially *Freckles*. The author and her audience were made for each other—her work provided a gentle reflection of American mores and desires in the first part of the twentieth century.

Karen Hovde

SEE ALSO: *Best Sellers;* McCall's Magazine.

BIBLIOGRAPHY

Long, Judith Reick. *Gene Stratton-Porter, Novelist and Naturalist*. Indianapolis: Indiana Historical Society, 1990.

Richards, Bertrand F. *Gene Stratton-Porter*. Boston: Twayne, 1980.

Satterwhite, Emily. *Dear Appalachia: Readers, Identity, and Popular Fiction since 1878*. Lexington: University Press of Kentucky, 2011.

Trosky, Susan M., and Donna Olendorf, eds. *Contemporary Authors*, vol. 137. Detroit, MI: Gale Research, 1992.

Strawberry, Darryl *(1962–)*

Darryl Strawberry's life reads like a soap opera. This major-league outfielder was the first pick overall in the 1980 free-agent draft, selected by the New York Mets. Without a doubt, he possessed the raw talent that could have earned him a spot in the National Baseball Hall of Fame, but his erratic career was a textbook case of overindulgence resulting in underachievement.

Professionally speaking, Strawberry's best years were the late 1980s; between the 1987 and 1990 seasons, he respectively belted 39, 29, and 37 homers. Although he was entrenched as a slugger-hero for the Mets, he never blossomed into national superstardom. Furthermore, he earned as much publicity for drinking, drugs, and marital and tax problems as he did for his on-the-field play. By the 1990s he had evolved into an injury-prone underachiever. A low point came in 1993, when he hit a measly .140 in thirty-two games for the Los Angeles Dodgers. In the mid-1990s, however, an older, humbled Strawberry was resurrected by the New York Yankees. Although he did not complain that he was relegated to part-time status, he spent most of 1997 on the disabled list.

Near the end of the 1998 season, as the Yanks were on their way to a record-breaking 125-win campaign, Strawberry faced the biggest challenge of his life when he was diagnosed with colon cancer. He immediately underwent surgery, during which a cancerous tumor and 24 inches of his colon were removed; the disease also was discovered in a lymph node, requiring that he undergo chemotherapy. But his troubles were not all linked to his health. In 1999 Strawberry was arrested for possessing a small amount of cocaine and propositioning a policewoman posing as a prostitute. After pleading no contest, he was sentenced to eighteen months of probation and suspended from baseball for 120 days; he retired from the sport at the end of the season.

The next few years saw Strawberry undergoing additional cancer-related surgery; he also was involved in further brushes with the law and spent time in drug-treatment centers—and in jail. But his post-baseball life has had an upside, as he has worked as an instructor for the New York Mets and as a pre- and post-game analyst on *SportsNet New York*. He also founded a charity, the Darryl Strawberry Foundation, which advocates for children with autism.

Rob Edelman

SEE ALSO: *Baseball; Cancer; Cocaine/Crack; Live Television; Major League Baseball; The New York Mets; The New York Yankees; Television.*

BIBLIOGRAPHY

Karlen, Neal. *Slouching toward Fargo: A Two-Year Saga of Sinners and St. Paul Saints at the Bottom of the Bush Leagues with Bill Murray, Darryl Strawberry, Dakota Sadie and Me.* New York: Spike, 1999.

Klapisch, Bob. *High and Tight: The Rise and Fall of Dwight Gooden and Darryl Strawberry.* New York: Villard Books, 1996.

Saxon, Walt. *Darryl Strawberry.* New York: Dell, 1985.

Sokolove, Michael Y. *The Ticket Out: Darryl Strawberry & the Boys of Crenshaw.* New York: Simon & Schuster, 2004.

Strawberry, Darryl, and Art Rust Jr. *Darryl.* New York: Bantam Books, 1992.

Strawberry, Darryl, and John Strausbaugh. *Straw: Finding My Way.* New York: Ecco, 2009.

Streaking

Streaking, the practice of running naked through a public gathering, has been around for many years, but it attained full-fledged craze status only in the 1970s when, it seemed, all manner of strange behavior was soaring into public consciousness. Some historians have tagged Lady Godiva as the world's first streaker, but she rode—not ran—while deliberately concealing her nudity under her long, flowing hair. Not to be confused with simple nudism, streaking is an inherently exhibitionist act and thus the perfect public gesture for an exhibitionist age.

The spring of 1974 represented the high moment of modern streaking. In March of that year, the University of Missouri endured a mass streaking by more than 600 students. The nude collegians paraded past the campus's Ionic columns as a crowd estimated at 1,500 watched and cheered. In April hayseed comedian Ray Stevens's single "The Streak" rocketed to number one on the pop charts. "He ain't rude. He ain't rude. He's just in the mood to run in the nude," crooned Stevens of the eponymous nudist. Full national exposure came that same month. During the broadcast of the Academy Awards ceremony, streaker Robert Opal shocked the crowd of Hollywood swells by letting it fly during David Niven's introduction of Elizabeth Taylor. "The only way he could get a laugh was by showing his shortcomings," quipped an unruffled Niven. Undeterred, the thirty-three-year-old streaker managed to extract his full fifteen minutes of fame from the situation. As a result of the Oscar publicity, he pursued a brief career as a stand-up comic and was hired as a "guest streaker" for Hollywood parties. When the streaking craze died down, Opal moved to San Francisco, where he was found murdered in 1979.

Not surprisingly, academics and opinion writers tried to explain the streaking craze. In 1974 a psychology professor at the University of South Carolina conducted one of the first studies on the phenomenon. After much research, he concluded that the average male streaker was "a tall Protestant male weighing 170 pounds with a B grade average [who] dated regularly, came from a town with a population less than 50,000 and a family where the father is a business or professional man and the mother is a housewife." Female streakers, the study found, "tended to be small, 5 feet 3 inches and 117 pounds."

Others tried a more sociological approach. At the low end, streaking was dismissed as little more than an outrageous fad on the order of swallowing goldfish or packing phone booths. At the high end, it was touted as a lifestyle choice, a nonviolent form of protest, and even a type of therapy. E. Paul Bindrim, the so-called father of nude psychotherapy, coached more than 3,000 people through their first experience of public nudity. Explaining his philosophy to the *Los Angeles Times*, Bindrim declared: "Clothing is kind of a mask. So there are reasons to think if you remove clothing, you get a freer atmosphere where people would talk more openly."

When streaking became a national craze, Bindrim wrote an op-ed piece for the *Los Angeles Times* in which he commented more specifically on the trend. "Streaking is healthy, and I predict that it is here to stay," he wrote. "It may change form, but its essential ingredient, the tacit sanctioning of public nudity, will remain. . . . Running is the only aspect of streaking that will die out." Belying Bindrim's prediction, scampering in the nude enjoyed something of a revival in the 1990s. It even briefly gained front-page status again when it invaded the pristine world of lawn tennis. In 1996 Melissa Johnson, a twenty-three-year-old London student, streaked across Centre Court moments before the men's Wimbledon final. The topless woman, wearing only a tiny maid's apron, pranced momentarily in front of finalists Richard Krajicek and MaliVai Washington as they posed near the net for photographs. She was quickly escorted off the court by two policemen as both players and most of the 14,000 fans broke into laughter.

As Bill Kirkpatrick suggests, by the twenty-first century, streaking had taken its place alongside hula-hoops and pet rocks as an innocuous passing fad. It seems as if the fad will never totally fade into the past, however. Most streakers in the twenty-first century have exposed themselves at sporting events that range from the British World Open to the World Snooker Championship. In the United States, Mark Roberts streaked onto the field during the 2004 Super Bowl. He was tackled and held by Patriots linebacker Matt Chatham until the police arrived to arrest him. The event achieved less publicity than it might have because of the flashing of Janet Jackson's nude breast during the same Super Bowl. The latter "mishap" became international news.

Robert E. Schnakenberg

SEE ALSO: *Academy Awards; Hollywood; Hula Hoop; Jackson, Janet; Pet Rocks; Super Bowl; Taylor, Elizabeth; Wimbledon.*

BIBLIOGRAPHY

Kirkpatrick, Bill. "'It Beats Rocks and Tear Gas': Streaking and Cultural Politics in the Post-Vietnam Era." *Journal of Popular Culture* 43, no. 5 (2010).

Long, A. Mark, and Jim Fee. *Bad Fads.* Toronto: ECW Press, 2002.

Pleasant, George. *The Joy of Streaking*. New York: Ballantine, 1974.

Streep, Meryl *(1949–)*

Considered by many to be *the* actress of her generation, Meryl Streep remains in a class by herself in terms of critical acclaim and career longevity. Her career spans more than thirty years and more than forty feature films. Known primarily for her heavy dramatic movie roles as neurotic or obsessed characters—many of which have required her to assume an accent—Streep is extremely versatile and has successfully performed in a variety of roles in the movies and on television.

Streep grew up in an affluent family in New Jersey. Drawn to athletics, she was a swimmer who later became a cheerleader in high school. She then attended the exclusive Vassar College, where she became obsessed with both literature and acting. One of her many leading roles at Vassar was in the play *Miss Julie*. In addition to acting, Streep worked behind the scenes in designing lighting and costumes, sang with a musical group, and served as vice president of her sophomore class.

Meryl Streep. *Meryl Streep's critically acclaimed body of work has earned her numerous awards and honors, including three Best Actress Oscars.* JEFFREY MAYER/CONTRIBUTOR/WIREIMAGE/GETTY IMAGES.

After graduating from Vassar with a bachelor of fine arts, Streep entered Yale School of Drama, where she played approximately forty roles during her three years there. After graduating in 1975 with a master of fine arts, she won major roles at the Public Theater in New York and at the New York Shakespeare Festival. She made her Broadway debut in *Trelawny of the "Wells"* and won rave reviews and a Tony Award nomination for her performance in *27 Wagons Full of Cotton*.

Streep's first film role was in *Julia*, which was released in 1977. She then gave an Emmy Award–winning performance in the highly praised 1978 TV miniseries *Holocaust* and an Academy Award–nominated performance in *The Deer Hunter* (1978), opposite Robert De Niro. Streep then costarred in *Kramer vs. Kramer* (1979) with Dustin Hoffman and won an Academy Award for Best Supporting Actress for her portrayal of Joanna, a neglected wife who abandons her family.

In the 1980s Streep starred in a string of high-profile films, earning Academy Award nominations for her performances in *The French Lieutenant's Woman* (1981), *Sophie's Choice* (1982), *Silkwood* (1983), *Out of Africa* (1985), *Ironweed* (1987), and *A Cry in the Dark* (1988). Only one of the nominations, however, resulted in an Oscar win, for her lead actress role as a tortured Polish concentration camp survivor in *Sophie's Choice*. Seeking a break from so many heavy, character-driven roles, Streep also starred in the 1989 comedy *She-Devil*.

In the 1990s Streep continued to produce many fine performances, earning Academy Award nominations for *Postcards from the Edge* (1990), *The Bridges of Madison County* (1995), *One True Thing* (1998), and *Music of the Heart* (1999). In a surprise move, she accepted the demanding role of a white-water rafting guide and performed her own stunts in the action thriller *The River Wild* (1994).

Streep has worked with nearly every director and every leading man of note, all of whom praise her talents. Sydney Pollack, who directed her in *Out of Africa*, claimed that not only is Streep capable of becoming "a totally new human being," but she is also able to effectively communicate her character's struggles to the audience. Alan J. Pakula, who directed Streep in *Sophie's Choice*, once commented, "If there's a heaven for directors, it would be to direct Meryl Streep your whole life."

MORE HIGH-PROFILE ROLES

After acclaimed roles in *Adaptation* (2002), for which she earned her thirteenth Academy Award nomination, and *The Hours* (2002), Streep played multiple roles in the television miniseries *Angels in America* (2003). In *The Devil Wears Prada* (2006), she is the mercilessly demanding fashion magazine editor Miranda Priestly. The movie was a critical success, and Streep won numerous awards and an Academy Award nomination. It also proved to be her biggest box-office success, grossing more than $300 million worldwide. Her unlikely casting in *Mamma Mia!* (2008), a film adaptation of the Broadway musical based on the songs of pop group ABBA, was an even bigger success. Streep plays Donna, a carefree single mother who is preparing for her daughter's wedding. The daughter, without Donna's knowledge, invites the three men who might be her father to the wedding. They all attend, surprising Donna, and funny, awkward, and touching moments ensue. The movie was a worldwide hit, grossing more than $600 million.

Streep's continuing success led to even more high-profile roles, such as the renowned chief Julia Child in the hit *Julie &*

Julia (2009), and British prime minister Margaret Thatcher in *The Iron Lady* (2011). Streep received Academy Award nominations for both roles and won for her performance as Thatcher.

Throughout her career, Streep has been nominated for and received many awards in addition to Academy Awards. In 1998 she received the first Bette Davis Lifetime Achievement Award. Presented by the Bette Davis Foundation, a nonprofit organization that awards scholarships to aspiring actors and actresses, the award recognizes an acting career that "distinctly parallels the high professional standards set by Bette Davis." Also in 1998 she received a star on the famous Hollywood Walk of Fame. In 2004 Streep received the AFI Life Achievement Award, presented by the American Film Institute (AFI) to honor "an individual whose career in motion pictures or television has greatly contributed to the enrichment of American culture."

In addition to being an actress, Streep is a political activist. She has hosted and narrated television specials championing the rights of women and children, literacy, and ecological issues. She not only testified in Congress against the use of pesticides but also organized Mothers and Others, an antipesticide organization.

Known for avoiding Hollywood glitz, Streep is fiercely defensive of her private life. She lives in the hills of northwestern Connecticut on a secluded 89-acre estate with a 47-acre private lake. Married since 1978 to sculptor Don Gummer, Streep is the mother of four children and claims "even my decisions about what films I make are predicated on the fact that I think about how my children will view them." Considering herself a mother first and an actor second, she often takes her family with her on location. In 1989 the National Mother's Day Committee, a nonprofit organization that recognizes "exceptional women for successfully building their careers, nurturing their families and helping improve the lives of others," honored Streep with an Outstanding Mother Award.

Rick Moody

SEE ALSO: *ABBA; Academy Awards;* The Bridges of Madison County*; Broadway; Celebrity; Child, Julia; De Niro, Robert;* The Deer Hunter*; Emmy Awards; Hoffman, Dustin; Hollywood;* Mamma Mia!*; Movie Stars; Television; Tony Awards.*

BIBLIOGRAPHY

Maychick, Diana. *Meryl Streep: The Reluctant Superstar*. New York: St. Martin's Press, 1985.

Woods, Vicki. "Meryl Streep: Force of Nature." *Vogue*, January 2012.

Street and Smith

One of America's oldest publishing houses, Street and Smith helped to ensure the spread of mass literacy in the United States. Producing inexpensive books and periodicals, Street and Smith was long known for its dime novels, pulp fiction, popular magazines, and comic books. Featured prominently were the tales of Jesse James, Buffalo Bill, Nick Carter, Frank Merriwell, and the Shadow. Noteworthy authors included Edward Z. C. Judson, Horatio Alger Jr., and Gilbert M. Patten, while reprints of Rudyard Kipling, Sir Arthur Conan Doyle, Robert Louis Stevenson, and Victor Hugo abounded.

In the 1850s Street and Smith began producing dime novels, soon becoming the most successful publisher in the field, surpassing even Beadle and Adams, Munro, and Tousey. As one commentator quipped, "Munros [*sic*] to the left of them, Tousey to right of them, Street and Smith behind them, Onward they blood-and-thundered." Beginning in 1859 many of Street and Smith's serialized novels appeared in the *New York Weekly*, recently purchased by Francis S. Street and Francis S. Smith.

From the mid-nineteenth century onward, Street and Smith helped shape the image of the American hero, while moving from dime novels—which frequently sold for a nickel—to pulp fiction. Real-life individuals with antiheroic qualities, such as the outlaw Jesse James and the Western adventurer Buffalo Bill, were presented in a glorified light. Alger's *Ragged Dick*, whose protagonist was a former bootblack turned bank clerk, helped to reinforce a belief in self-reliance and individualism as America entered an era of rapid modernization. Detective Nick Carter, who first appeared in the *New York Weekly* in 1886, was a more cerebral figure: "He was a master of disguise, and could so transform himself that even old Sim (his father) could not recognize him. And his intellect, naturally keen as a razor blade, had been incredibly sharpened by the judicious cultivation of the astute old man." In 1896 Patten offered Frank Merriwell, a genius of an athletic stripe who invariably bested his competitors—but always did so honorably—in the pages of *Tip-Top Weekly*. Thus, the Street and Smith heroes included men of the Wild West, city lads and slickers, and athletes, in a period when urbanization and industrialization were transforming the national landscape.

Street and Smith was known for its pulp fiction, which was initiated by Frank Munsey's *Argosy* at the close of the nineteenth century, supplanting dime novels and story papers. In *The Unembarrassed Muse*, Russell Nye contends that Street and Smith's *New Buffalo Bill Weekly*, published in 1912, was "the last genuine dime novel." After that, the demand was for pulp fiction. Pulp magazines, most of the general adventure variety, thrived, and Street and Smith contributed *Detective Story* (1915), *Western Story* (1919), and *Love Story* (1921). Created by a young woman, Amita Fairgrieve, *Love Story* began as a quarterly but ended up as a weekly. By 1938 *Love Story* had produced a score of imitators, including *True Love Stories*, *Pocket Love*, *Romantic Range*, and *Real Love*.

Selling as many as ten million copies by the 1930s, the pulps suffered from heightened production charges during the following decade. The death knell of pulp magazines was sounded by radio, television, and twenty-five-cent paperback books. Along with other publishers, Street and Smith began emphasizing publications that garnered large advertising budgets.

Street and Smith was known for far more than its pulp, producing periodicals such as *Popular Magazine*, which began in 1903 as a quarterly intended "for boys and 'Old Boys'" but soon became an action, adventure, and outdoors semimonthly. With a circulation of nearly a quarter of a million, *Popular Magazine* was published until 1928. Upton Sinclair contributed to the publication, as did such top pulp authors as B. M. Bower, H. H. Knibbs, and Rex Beach. Appearing in 1937, *Pic* began printing risqué photographs of young women while posing questions such as, "Do White Men Go Berserk in the Tropics?" With World War II coming to a close, *Pic* became a more respectable men's magazine, with its circulation surpassing the 600,000 mark; mounting costs, however, doomed it. By the late 1940s Street and Smith had closed its last pulp and a series of comic books, opting to highlight slick periodicals such as *Charm*, *Mademoiselle*, and *Living for Young Homemakers*. *Mademoiselle*, which targeted women between the ages of seventeen and thirty, had been introduced in 1935.

Quentin Reynolds referred to Street and Smith as "a fiction factory," while contending that the company had long thrived because of its diversity and readiness to discard increasingly unpopular publications. Family control of Street and Smith terminated in 1959 when the company was purchased by Condé Nast Publications, reportedly for $4 million and stock options. Among the magazines acquired were *Charm*, *Living for Young Homemakers*, *Astounding Science Fiction*, *Air Progress*, and *Hobbies for Young Men*.

Robert C. Cottrell

SEE ALSO: Argosy; Astounding Science Fiction; *Cody, Buffalo Bill, and His Wild West Show; Detective Fiction; Dime Novels; Pulp Magazines.*

BIBLIOGRAPHY

Mott, Frank Luther. *A History of American Magazines 1885–1905*. Cambridge, MA: Harvard University Press, 1957.

Mott, Frank Luther. *A History of American Magazines 1865–1885*. Cambridge, MA: Harvard University Press, 1967.

Murdoch, David Hamilton. *The American West: The Invention of a Myth*. Reno: University of Nevada Press, 2001.

Noel, Mary. *Villains Galore: The Heyday of the Popular Story Weekly*. New York: Macmillan, 1954.

Nye, Russell. *The Unembarrassed Muse: The Popular Arts in America*. New York: Dial Press, 1971

Peterson, Theodore. *Magazines in the Twentieth Century*. Urbana: University of Illinois Press, 1964.

Reynolds, Quentin. *The Fiction Factory, or from Pulp Row to Quality Street*. New York: Random House, 1955.

Smith, Henry Nash. *Virgin Land: The American West as Symbol and Myth*. Cambridge, MA: Harvard University Press, 1970.

Tebbel, John, and Mary Ellen Zuckerman. *The Magazine in America 1741–1990*. New York: Oxford University Press, 1991.

A Streetcar Named Desire

According to Brooks Atkinson, the major theater critic of the mid-twentieth century, Tennessee Williams's urban tragedy, *A Streetcar Named Desire*, was "a modern masterpiece" that "took Broadway by storm." Considered by many to be the finest drama of America's finest postwar playwright, *A Streetcar Named Desire* made an indelible impression on American culture. Under the muscular direction of Elia Kazan, the incendiary play, which won the Pulitzer Prize in 1948, was the follow-up to Williams's 1944 debut, *The Glass Menagerie*; but whereas the earlier play was primarily a meditative memory piece, *Streetcar* is rife with activity. Its melodramatic structure, however, is never allowed to eclipse the emotional and atmospheric authenticity of the play. It is particularly revered for its multifaceted characterizations; its rich dialogue, which is masterful in its lyricism as well as its use of working-class vernacular; and the role it played in popularizing a new, naturalistic style of American acting, known colloquially as the "The Method."

PLOT SUMMARY

Streetcar depicts domestic strife. At the start of the play, an unmarried, thirtyish, out-of-work schoolteacher, Blanche DuBois, arrives at the home of her younger sister, Stella. Since both young women were reared in the lap of luxury on a lush Mississippi homeplace called Belle Reve, the cultivated Blanche is somewhat shocked to find Stella living in rather squalid conditions in the French Quarter of New Orleans, Louisiana. More troubling to Blanche is her sister's marriage to a loutish, "common" ex-serviceman named Stanley Kowalski. For her part, Stella is dismayed to learn that Belle Reve was forfeited to creditors under Blanche's watch. Clearly, both sisters have lost their social and economic footing, but while Stella is perfectly content in her rough-hewn but passionate marriage, Blanche is dispossessed, one step away from poverty.

The play recounts Blanche's efforts to adapt to her new circumstances with her dignity and sanity intact and documents her poignant attempts to conceal her advancing age, her professional failure, and her highly sexual nature from those who might judge her harshly. "A woman's charm is fifty-percent illusion," Blanche confides to Stella, and Stella indulges her fragile sister, encouraging Blanche's blossoming courtship with Stanley's gentle coworker, Mitch. But Stanley ultimately becomes

A Streetcar Named Desire. *Vivien Leigh, left, and Marlon Brando starred in the 1951 movie adaptation of* A Streetcar Named Desire. WARNER BROS./HANDOUT/MOVIEPIX/GETTY IMAGES.

Blanche's destroyer, tearing away her tissue of lies and insulting her fine sensibilities. "I've been on to you from the start," he bellows to her at *Streetcar*'s climax. His subsequent rape of Blanche causes what scholar Harold Bloom calls "a psychic rending" that is enough to nudge Blanche into madness. In the end, bound for a state asylum, Blanche leaves the home of her merciless brother-in-law and disbelieving sister, a lovely but broken spirit in an inhumane world. Her destruction is so complete that some critics, Kenneth Tynan for one, have read the play as a comment on the decline of civilization, the trampling of man's finer instincts by the implacable brutality of the modern world.

STREETCAR IN POPULAR CULTURE

Several of the play's lines have found an affectionate place in the American vocabulary. Stanley's anguished, full-throated cry, "Stella, STELLAAAA!" has become something of a cultural touchstone, and Blanche's lilting final line, "I have always depended on the kindness of strangers," has endured as her rather ironic motto, as it uses a genteel euphemism for sexual promiscuity to reconcile Blanche's poetic frailty with her more desperate animal behavior. These lines have been both imitated as homage to Williams's play and lampooned for their melodrama.

Though Blanche is the role of greater complexity and sympathy, both major characters continue to live in the cultural imagination. Blanche's mix of cultivation, hysteria, and tragedy makes her an unforgettable creation, while Stanley, "the exuberantly macho American Pole," in Ronald Hayman's felicitous description, has been accorded iconic status. Much of this stature is no doubt due to the role's close identification with Marlon Brando, for rarely has an actor taken possession of a role so effectively and completely. Many actresses have triumphed as Blanche ("a relatively imperishable creature of the stage," according to Williams), not only Jessica Tandy in the original production, but Vivien Leigh in the 1951 film version, and in the 1990s, Jessica Lange onstage and on television.

As for Stanley, Brando's remains the definitive interpretation. His Stanley is cunning, explosive, and overtly sexual, and the ways in which the actor communicated character through his body language was startlingly modern to 1947 audiences, a living advertisement for the Method and the acting school that advanced it, Lee Strasberg's Actors Studio. It is ironic that in early drafts of the play this emblem of machismo appeared as a considerably more androgynous figure. According to *New Republic* writer Geoffrey O'Brien, the final product in the form of Brando—grunting and sweating with exhibitionistic virility—"proposed a different way for men to be. Talking was small part of it."

After originating the role on Broadway, Brando revived his performance for the acclaimed 1951 film, which was also directed by Kazan. Original Broadway cast members Kim Hunter (Stella) and Karl Malden (Mitch) re-created their supporting roles, carrying off Academy Awards for their efforts. Oscars were also awarded to the film for Best Picture and to Leigh as Best Actress; oddly, only Brando was passed over (he won three years later for the Kazan-directed *On the Waterfront*).

The great success of the Kazan movie adaptation has deterred any subsequent attempts to film the play as a feature. However, television producers have proven more intrepid; prior to the 1995 version that starred Lange and Alec Baldwin, Ann-Margret and Treat Williams filled the shoes of Blanche and Stanley for a 1984 TV movie, and the play continues to be performed at both the amateur and professional levels all over the world. Notable revivals include a 2005 run on Broadway, an all-black production at Pace University in 2009, and British and Australian productions in 2009 that both boasted A-list casts. Composer Andre Previn based an opera on the play and debuted it at the San Francisco Opera House in 1998 (Previn's *Streetcar* was also broadcast on public television that year), further attesting to the enduring legacy of Williams's masterpiece.

Drew Limsky

SEE ALSO: *Academy Awards; Baldwin, Alec; Brando, Marlon; Broadway; Williams, Tennessee.*

BIBLIOGRAPHY

Bloom, Harold. *Tennessee Williams's "A Streetcar Named Desire": Modern Critical Interpretations.* New York: Chelsea House, 1988.

Hayman, Ronald. *Tennessee Williams: Everyone Else Is an Audience.* New Haven, CT: Yale University Press, 1993.

Leverich, Lyle. *Tom: The Unknown Tennessee Williams.* New York: Crown, 1995.

Manso, Peter. *Brando: The Biography.* New York: Hyperion, 1994.

O'Brien, Geoffrey. Review of *Brando: Songs My Mother Taught Me*, by Marlon Brando, and *Brando: The Biography*, by Peter Manso. In *New Republic*, December 5, 1994, 35.

Staggs, Sam. *When Blanche Met Brando: The Scandalous Story of "A Streetcar Named Desire."* St. Martin's Griffin, 2006.

Williams, Tennessee. *A Streetcar Named Desire.* New York: Signet, 1947.

Williams, Tennessee. *Memoirs.* New York: Bantam, 1976.

Streisand, Barbra *(1942–)*

Barbra Streisand is an accomplished and respected singer, actress, director, producer, screenwriter, and activist, who has elicited extreme reactions from fans and critics. Either adored or detested, the Streisand persona has, almost from the beginning, been larger than life. Although she has often been confused, frightened, and angered by both the homage and the vitriol heaped upon her, Streisand is a strong personality, a productive artist, and a phenomenon in the entertainment industry.

Streisand was born Barbara Joan Streisand in Brooklyn, New York, in 1942 to Jewish working-class parents. Her father died when she was fifteen months old, and her mother remarried within a few years to an emotionally abusive man, who her mother described as "allergic to children." Streisand's mother was undemonstrative, calling her daughter "ugly" and ridiculing her aspirations to be an actress. Streisand, however, was undeterred, and as a young girl she sang in the halls of her Flatbush apartment building, learning to appreciate the sound of her own voice as it echoed off the walls. As a teenager she began taking acting lessons and haunting the theaters and clubs of Manhattan's Greenwich Village, seeking an entrance to the stage.

Streisand moved to Greenwich Village in 1960. Although she wanted to become an actress, friends who heard her sing

Barbra Streisand. *Barbra Streisand has gained both fans and detractors for her powerful singing style, choice of acting roles, and strong celebrity persona.* BARBRA STREISAND © DOUGLAS KIRKLAND/CORBIS.

encouraged her to enter talent night at a local club, and soon she embarked on a career as a cabaret singer, dropping the middle *a* from her first name so that it would stand out. Her vibrant soprano soon won Streisand a loyal local audience, made up of mostly gay men. Working in Greenwich Village, she also met the drag queens who performed in the clubs and learned from them the campy flamboyance of the diva, which she used to cover her insecurity onstage.

Streisand's big break came when she was cast as the frumpy Miss Marmelstein in the 1962 show *I Can Get It for You Wholesale*. Making the most of the small part, Streisand impressed critics and audiences alike, and when she sang her one song, she stopped the show. The following year, she released her first album, *The Barbra Streisand Album*, for which she won the Grammy Award for Album of the Year and the Grammy Award for Best Vocal Performance, Female.

In 1964 Streisand was cast in the leading role of the new play *Funny Girl*, playing comic and singer Fanny Brice. The role could have been written for her: Brice is a Jewish girl, who is not conventionally pretty but has a powerful talent and an intense will to succeed. The play was a success, and Streisand became a star overnight. She appeared on the covers of *Time* and *Life* magazines and on television. In 1965 *My Name Is Barbra*, the first of many Streisand television specials, aired on CBS. It was nominated for six Emmy Awards and won five.

MORE GRAMMYS AND AN ACADEMY AWARD

Streisand's voice has always been her most dependable asset. Most comfortable singing show tunes and popular classics, she has sung everything from Christmas carols to rock and roll. Since 1964 she has sold more than 140 million records worldwide. Thirty-one of her albums debuted on the Billboard Top 10, and thirty have sold one million copies, more than anyone except Elvis Presley. Her 2009 album *Love Is the Answer* became her ninth number one on the Billboard Top 200, more than any other artist.

Streisand won eight Grammy Awards from 1963 to 1986 and received the Grammy Legend Award in 1992 and the Grammy Lifetime Achievement Award in 1995. But she never lost her insecurity about performing onstage, and after she received death threats before a concert in New York's Central Park in 1967, she stopped giving public concerts for almost thirty years. In 1993 she finally returned to the stage, launching what she called her last concert tour. Streisand, however, gained a new poise and confidence in front of live audiences and continued to perform to sold-out crowds throughout the 1990s and the first decade of the 2000s, including her Timeless tour in 2000 and the Streisand: Live in Concert 2006 tour in 2006.

As an actress, Streisand's work has been less universally acclaimed. After starring in the movie *Funny Girl* (1968), for which she won an Academy Award for Best Actress (she tied with Katharine Hepburn, who received one for *The Lion in Winter*), Streisand went on to make many films; some were successes, such as *The Way We Were* in 1973, and some were failures, such as *The Main Event* in 1979. Many, such as *A Star Is Born* (1976), were critical flops but did well at the box office, proving the loyalty of Streisand's fans. In later years she tried her hand at comedy, appearing in the moderately successful *Meet the Fockers* (2004) and its sequel, *Little Fockers* (2010).

In 1983 Streisand became the first woman to cowrite, direct, produce, and star in a feature film. The movie, *Yentl*, tells the story of a Jewish girl in eighteenth-century Russia who disguises herself as a boy so that she can go to school. At that time girls were forbidden to attend school. The project was close to Streisand's heart, and she was hurt and angered by the mixed critical reception and by the complete lack of Academy Award nominations for the movie. She went on to direct and produce other films, but her work continued to be ignored by the Academy of Motion Picture Arts and Sciences. Even when *The Prince of Tides* (1991), a movie that she produced, directed, and starred in, was nominated for Best Picture, she did not receive the nomination for Best Director (traditionally, directors of Best Picture nominees are also recognized).

The motion picture establishment and many critics have been hard on Streisand. Even audiences have been polarized, some loving her ethnic looks and Brooklyn accent, others finding her ugly and abrasive. Her reputation in Hollywood ranges from hardworking perfectionist to neurotic narcissist. She has defended herself against accusations of egotism by citing the sexism of the Hollywood system. "A man is forceful," she says, "a woman is pushy. . . . He's assertive—she's aggressive. He strategizes—she manipulates."

THE STREISAND PERSONA

As a young singer, Streisand displayed raw emotion, ineffectively masked by awkward brashness and affected diva mannerisms, and she touched a chord with audiences. Fans identified with her endearing insecurity, respected her refusal to surgically alter her prominent nose or lose her accent, and admired her drive to succeed and be respected. Streisand's response to the adoration of her fans is complex. Stunned and overwhelmed by her sudden popularity after starring in the play *Funny Girl*, she called the crowds that mobbed the stage door "the crazies," and she would slip out alternate exits to avoid them. As she matured and achieved the success she sought, Streisand became more polished. She treats her fans with respect but remains aloof. Her fans, who have seen her progress flamboyantly through five decades of fashion and ideology, seem to welcome each transformation.

Streisand has many gay fans, and she has never tried to distance herself from them. She cheerfully acknowledges the connection, joking onstage about being outdone by a group of Barbra drag queens and even hiring a Barbra impersonator to fool her friends at a party. She has raised money for AIDS research, made a television movie about the career of lesbian coast guard officer Margarethe Cammermeyer, and spearheaded a celebrity boycott of Colorado after antigay legislation passed there.

Politically liberal and wealthy, Streisand created the Streisand Foundation in 1986 to distribute funds to support causes such as civil rights, AIDS, and the environment. During the presidency of Bill Clinton from 1993 to 2001, Streisand was a frequent visitor to Washington and an active fund-raiser for the Democratic Party. In 2011 she was honored for her service work at the Grammy Awards ceremony as the MusiCares Person of the Year.

While Streisand keeps her private life private, it is known that she was married to actor Elliott Gould from 1963 to 1971. They have one son, Jason. After her divorce from Gould, Streisand dated a number of celebrities, including hairdresser Jon Peters and Canadian prime minister Pierre Trudeau. In 1998, at the age of fifty-six, she married actor James Brolin, who was fifty-eight. He asked her to marry him five times before she finally said yes. The wedding was held on Streisand's oceanfront estate in Malibu, California.

Streisand's career, like her persona, has often been controversial, and while she has not always lived up to the expectations of critics or fans, she accomplished what she intended to from the beginning: she became a star. In an interview for a 1966 issue of *Look* magazine, Streisand admitted, "I always knew I would be famous. . . . I was never contented. . . . I wanted to prove to the world that they shouldn't make fun of me."

Tina Gianoulis

SEE ALSO: *Academy Awards; AIDS; The Beatles; Broadway; Emmy Awards; Gay Men; Grammy Awards; Greenwich Village;* Life; *Presley, Elvis;* Time.

BIBLIOGRAPHY

Edwards, Anne. *Streisand: A Biography*. Boston: Little, Brown, 1997.

Grein, Paul. "Barbra Streisand: The Way She Is, Part Two." Grammy.com, February 11, 2011. Accessed April 5, 2012. Available from http://www.grammy.com/news/barbra-streisand-2011-musicares-person-of-the-year-0

Kimbrell, James. *Barbra—An Actress Who Sings*, ed. Cheri Kimbrell. Boston: Branden Publishing, 1992.

Riese, Randall. *Her Name Is Barbra*. Secaucus, NJ: Carol Publishing Group, 1993.

Streisand, Barbra. "The Artist as Citizen." *New Perspective Quarterly* 12, no. 2 (1995): 36.

Streisand, Barbra. *My Passion for Design*. New York: Viking Adult, 2010.

Strip Joints/Striptease

Strip joints typically feature females engaging in provocative dance and titillating disrobing for a predominantly male clientele. Although some strip joints cater to females with male strippers (like the Chippendales), in general, a common reaction among women to male stripping is laughter, or nervous laughter, rather than sexual arousal. Antecedents of the modern striptease include the auletrides of ancient Greece, geishas of Japan, belly dancers of Arabia, and a variety of singing and dancing "strumpets" found throughout history.

HISTORICAL ROOTS

Virtually all animal, bird, and fish species engage in conscious display to stimulate sexual excitement and attraction as part of mating rituals. However, Gypsy Rose Lee, probably the most famous stripper in American history, warned that displaying human flesh must always be "hinted at rather than hollered about." By its very nature, striptease adds simultaneous disrobing to dance. Striptease costumes are often linked to specific areas of culture, including religion (the nun's habit and crucifix), sexual taboos (the schoolgirl uniform and anklet socks), hunting fetishes (feathers and animal skins), and socioeconomic symbols (jewels and furs). As a stripper slowly removes her clothes, flaunting mores and taboos and gradually revealing her nudity, the goal is to stimulate sexual arousal in her audience.

Female breasts have been the primary historic focus of striptease. According to Desmond Morris in *The Naked Ape*, the appeal of the breast is probably associated with the imprinting of the female breast on the male during early childhood, resulting in a permanent sexual reflex behavior, in addition to the human erect posture and face-to-face copulation in which the female breast substitutes for the buttocks, which is the primary sexual stimulus of all other primates.

AMERICAN STRIP

Classical dancers wearing diaphanous gowns and flashing calves were viewed as both titillating and scandalous in their day, but modern techniques of titillation and tease were perfected in the 1860 music halls of Paris and London. After World War I, risqué nudity became commonplace in the cabarets of Berlin, the reviews of Paris, and the nightclubs of the New York Bowery, where the term *striptease* was first used. With the introduction of jazz and more liberal lifestyles, burlesque reached its peak in the United States in the 1920s. American burlesque was dominated by the Ziegfeld, Schubert, and Minsky families. It was also the age in which burlesque entertainer Lee rose to prominence. A self-styled intellectual entertainer, she took America by storm and found herself hobnobbing with the rich and famous. She was frequently imitated by less successful strippers.

In the 1930s politicians began to outlaw strip joints and rein in some of the so-called depravity of the Jazz Age. However, by the mid-twentieth century, in response to changes wrought by the sexual revolution and civil rights, woman's rights, and free speech movements, striptease had become more mainstream and had moved into the discotheques, theater districts, cinemas, and adult entertainment districts in most cities worldwide. As striptease became more widespread, it influenced popular dance by introducing sensual and erotic body movements.

In the late twentieth century, striptease evolved from titillating dance into more radical show routines, lap dances, performance art exhibitions, and sex shows. In the show routine, the striptease is continued to full nudity and to a full exhibition of the vagina, often with simulated or actual masturbation by the dancer. In the lap dance (and table dance) simulated sex acts are performed on the male observer as the dancer gyrates in extremely close proximity to the observer's body. In the sex show, two or more performers engage in simulated or actual sex acts and copulation for the voyeuristic enjoyment of observers. Some criticize performance art exhibitions for seeking to exploit state and federal grants for arts funding and to avoid zoning restrictions by claiming to exhibit a more artistic and aesthetic rendition of many of the same acts performed in show routines and lap dances.

PLACE IN SOCIETY

The strip joint, and its historic antecedents, have served a variety of social functions. The venue has maintained gender separation, providing a males-only retreat where affairs of business, politics, and sport may be conducted. This function was highly criticized by feminists who demanded access to those affairs. The strip joint also has provided an outlet for the male libido. Lewis Berg and Robert Street offer a warning typical of the times in their 1953 marriage manual *Sex: Methods and Manners*: "A woman should realize that all normal men are sexually responsive to the exposure of the female body. This is particularly true where strange women are concerned, since the male perpetually seeks variety. It accounts for the popularity of burlesque and girl shows in general, and for exhibitions of the 'strip-tease,' bubble-dance, and fan-dance character. Few husbands, if any, are totally indifferent to these attractions."

Striptease has offered lucrative wages for female performers. Although some strippers lack the education, skills, or enthusiasm for other employment, research has shown that there are also skilled and educated women who abandon traditional careers for higher-paying and less demanding careers in striptease. Some strippers even remain active into middle age.

Offering unconditional sexual stimulation, the striptease artist has functioned as a surrogate lover for men who fear rejection in the postfeminist social world. The striptease offers genuine entertainment and a ration of female companionship for males in military camps and other isolated locations away from opportunities for social interaction with females. Despite the contributions of strip joints and strippers, they are relegated to low social status. Indeed, the strip joint is occasionally a front for prostitution, substance abuse, gambling, and other illegal activities, as shown by the Bada Bing! strip club in the television show *The Sopranos* (1999–2007). To limit their impact on the larger society, many communities try to restrict strip joints to certain locations safely away from schools and churches.

Striptease has been used as a symbol of both feminism and antifeminism. It represents the female right to self-expression and control of her body, but it also symbolizes the male chauvinistic exploitation of women as purely sexual objects for entertainment. Some feminists argue that many strip joints are simply houses of prostitution masquerading as entertainment venues.

Gordon Neal Diem

SEE ALSO: *Burlesque; Feminism; Jazz; Lee, Gypsy Rose; Sexual Revolution;* The Sopranos*; Vaudeville.*

BIBLIOGRAPHY

Allison, Anne. *Nightwork: Sexuality, Pleasure, and Corporate Masculinity in a Tokyo Hostess Club.* Chicago: University of Chicago Press, 1994.

Berg, Lewis, and Robert Street. *Sex: Methods and Manners.* New York: McBride, 1953.

Gray, Francine du Plessix. "Dirty Dancing." *New Yorker*, February 28, 2005, 86–89.

Grussendorf, Christine. "Stripping as a System of Prostitution." *Off Our Backs* 32, no. 112 (2002): 34–40.

Jarrett, Lucinda. *Stripping in Time: A History of Erotic Dancing.* San Francisco: HarperCollins, 1997.

Langner, Laurence. *The Importance of Wearing Clothes.* New York: Hastings House, 1959.

Morris, Desmond. *The Naked Ape: A Zoologist's Study of the Human Animal.* New York: McGraw-Hill, 1967.

Schweitzer, Dahlia. "The Art of Spectacle and Transgression." *Journal of Popular Culture* 34, no. 1 (2000): 65–75.

Scott, David Alexander. *Behind the G-String: An Exploration of the Stripper's Image, Her Person, and Her Meaning.* Jefferson, NC: McFarland, 1996.

Wilson, Robert Anton. *The Book of the Breast.* Chicago: Playboy Press, 1994.

Zeidman, Irving. *The American Burlesque Show.* New York: Hawthorn Books, 1967.

Stuart, Marty *(1958–)*

Beneath a rock-and-roll hairdo that makes donning a cowboy hat impossible and with a collection of flamboyant jackets that would have made Liberace jealous, Marty Stuart emerged in the 1980s as a talented country instrumentalist—he plays both guitar and mandolin—songwriter, and performer. Born in Philadelphia, Mississippi, in 1958, Stuart first picked up a mandolin at the age of five, and at thirteen he was playing the instrument with legendary bluegrass guitarist Lester Flatt. After Flatt's death in 1979, Stuart signed on as a guitarist with one of his all-time heroes, country music great Johnny Cash and remained with Cash's band for six years before leaving in 1986 to begin a solo career. Stuart has also performed with such stars as Bill Monroe, Bob Dylan, the Everly Brothers, Willie Nelson, guitarist Doc Watson, Billy Joel, Neil Young, fiddler Vassar Clements, and Emmylou Harris. Songs penned by Stuart have been recorded by Harris as well as Wynonna Judd, George Strait, and Buck Owens.

GOING SOLO

Stuart produced his first solo album, *Busy Bee Cafe*, in 1982 while still a member of Cash's band. For this album, he enlisted the help of fellow pickers such as guitarists Doc Watson and Cash, dobroist Jerry Douglas, and banjo sensation Carl Jackson, catching the eye of CBS Records, which signed him on and produced *Marty Stuart* four years later. In 1989, with his first MCA effort, *Hillbilly Rock*, Stuart caught fire with country music listeners in a big way. His "hillbilly music—with a thump!" as he called it, had fans clamoring for more, and he served it up on the 1991 release *Tempted*. The album allowed Stuart to focus on his own distinct style, especially in its best-known single, "Burn Me Down," which had a long run on country radio.

This One's Gonna Hurt You (1992), Stuart's first gold record, was driven up the charts by the momentum of *Tempted* and the celebrated "No Hats" tour he made with fellow country artist Travis Tritt. The album blends the best of bluegrass, delta blues, and 1950s rockabilly with honky-tonk swing, ringing gospel harmonies and some gutsy guitar work. One of its most popular cuts, "The Whiskey Ain't Workin' Anymore"—sung with fellow "No-Hatter" Tritt—earned Stuart a Grammy Award, his first Country Music Association Award, and three BMI songwriter awards. In 1992 he was also inducted as a member of Nashville's Grand Ole Opry, the "high church" of country music.

The kudos heaped on *This One's Gonna Hurt You* made it a tough act for Stuart to follow, and he postponed release of his seventh album, *Love and Luck* (1994), until he could get the mix of songs just right. Other albums made in the 1990s, including his popular *The Marty Party Hit Pack* (1995), provide a musical panorama of country influences that all come together under the musicianship of Stuart and his ever-changing four-star lineup of collaborators, among them bluegrass fiddler Stuart Duncan, country vocalists Vince Gill, guitarist Ricky Skaggs, and banjoist Béla Fleck.

NEW TRADITIONAL COUNTRY

Throughout his career in country music, Stuart has consistently striven to keep alive the musical traditions of old-time country. In 1992, the same year he released his first gold album, *This One's Gonna Hurt You*, he also released two new traditional country albums—the bluegrass *Once upon a Time* (1992) and *Let There Be Country* (1992), which he recorded in the late 1980s but which Columbia did not release because it did not think traditional country music would sell. Stuart's chart successes convinced them otherwise, but many reviewers later wondered why Columbia had failed to notice the fan base for country music that celebrates its roots. Quoted in the *New York Times* in 2006, Stuart said, "For me, the 90's were about fame, fortune and hillbilly stardom. And there's nothing wrong with that, that's always welcome. But the roots just kept calling." His 1999 album *The Pilgrim* was an ambitious new traditional country "opry," as Stuart called it, featuring bluegrass, gospel, honky-tonk, country rock, and guest stars Harris and Cash. Stuart told the *New York Times*, "With that record, I realized that I can chase radio or I can go to my death honorably. There's the heart, and there's the chart."

CULTURAL ARTIFACTS

As one of country music's leading historians and archivists, Stuart keeps alive its songs and sounds and also its cultural artifacts. He has collected more than 20,000 items of memorabilia, and his mentors and experiences through the years are captured in his photography, which he shares in books: *Pilgrims: Sinners, Saints, and Prophets* (1999) and *Country Music: The Masters* (2008). He shares his memorabilia and artifacts in exhibits, such as "Sparkle & Twang: Marty Stuart's American Musical Odyssey," which opened at the Tennessee State Museum in 2007, then traveled to other sites such as the Autry National Center in Los Angeles in 2009. The exhibit boasts performance costumes, handwritten lyrics, unpublished photographs, and instruments belonging to country legends such as Patsy Cline, Cash, and Hank Williams Sr. Stuart says, "I made it my mission to save the historic relics of country music, not just because they were things I loved, but to preserve them as cultural artifacts."

Stuart likens his career to the tours he used to make with the Sullivans, a family of bluegrass gospel singers, during the 1980s, calling it "a mission" and "a crusade for hillbilly music." His tour bus is modeled on the one used by honky-tonker Ernest Tubb. He plays country-rock pioneer Clarence White's 1954 Fender Telecaster, owns several Martins that belonged to Williams Sr. and Flatt, and in 2004 Yvonne and Mavis Staples unwittingly helped him put two very public DUIs and the drinking that caused them behind him when they gave him their father "Pops" Staples's Fender Jazzmaster guitar. Stuart told National Public Radio, "They said 'Pops' would want you to have this. . . . It was like being thrown a life preserver." Inspired by that honor, Stuart finished his Delta gospel album, *Soul's Chapel* (2005), and went on to create the rest of what he calls his "Church House Trilogy"—*Badlands: Ballads of the Lakota* (2005) and a bluegrass album, *Live at the Ryman* (2006).

Stuart lent his talents to the soundtrack for *All the Pretty Horses* in 2000. He later released *Country Music* (2003), recorded with his then newly formed band the Fabulous Superlatives, and *Compadres* (2007), a compilation of his duets with such performers as Flatt, Cash, B. B. King, the Staples Singers, Loretta Lynn, and Merle Haggard. In 2008 he released *Cool Country Favorites*, another tribute to traditional country, and that same year "The

Marty Stuart Show" began airing on RFD-TV. He was well reviewed in 2010 for *Ghost Train: The Studio B Sessions* (2010). It includes "Hangman," a song that Stuart wrote with Cash shortly before Cash died, and "I Run to You," a duet with his wife, country singer Connie Smith. Stuart was twelve years old when he first met her. He told his mother he would marry Smith someday, and some twenty-five years later, he did. Although Stuart has been awarded five Grammy Awards, he has made a lot of music that does not get radio airplay. In 2010 he partnered with Davis-Kidd Booksellers in Nashville to give greater exposure to traditional country music by curating a collection of what he considers "the essentials" of country music, titled "Marty Stuart's the Art of Country Music."

Pamela L. Shelton

SEE ALSO: *Bluegrass; Cash, Johnny; Cline, Patsy; Country Music; Dylan, Bob; The Everly Brothers; Flatt, Lester; Gospel Music; Grammy Awards;* Grand Ole Opry*; Haggard, Merle; King, B. B.; Liberace; Lynn, Loretta; Monroe, Bill; Nelson, Willie; Owens, Buck; Rock and Roll; Skaggs, Ricky; Strait, George; Williams, Hank, Sr.; Young, Neil.*

BIBLIOGRAPHY

Barnard, Russell D., ed. *The Comprehensive Country Music Encyclopedia.* New York: Times Books, 1994.

Country: The Music and the Musicians: From the Beginnings to the '90s. New York: Abbeville Press, 1994.

Stambler, Irwin, and Grelun Landon. *Country Music: The Encyclopedia*, 3rd ed. New York: St. Martin's Press, 2000.

Stuckey's

A stop at Stuckey's was a staple of many 1950s and 1960s road trips. Located along America's highways, the turquoise-roofed buildings offered weary travelers gas, food, and souvenirs; clean restrooms; and refreshing air-conditioning. But perhaps the main reason Americans stopped in at Stuckey's was to sample their famous Pecan Log Rolls.

The 1950s marked the first time in American history when families were able to travel throughout the United States. These benefits came about due to the post–World War II economic boom and the availability of leisure time afforded workers in the new American corporate structure. This freedom was also greatly enhanced by the introduction of the interstate highway system in 1956. Highways had a tremendous impact on American life. Average annual driving increased by 400 percent, and shopping centers, suburbs, drive-in movies, gas stations, and fast-food establishments entered the popular culture.

As people traveled cross-country on these new 41,000 miles of roads, they needed gas, restrooms, and places to eat—that is where Stuckey's came in. Vacationing by car became the American way after the war, and Stuckey's was an important part of that experience. Stuckey's establishments were especially prevalent in the South and western United States. In the 1950s and 1960s they seemed to be everywhere. Stuckey's billboards lined the interstate: "Pecan Log Rolls, 4 for $1 with Gas Fill-up."

Stuckey's opened its first store in 1934 when Williamson and Ethyl Stuckey began selling their family pecan candy to motorists in Georgia. After some success they opened other stores along busy highways in Georgia and Florida, and began including gasoline pumps, restaurants, and souvenirs along with their famous Pecan Log Roll candy. While the Pecan Log Rolls might have been its most significant contribution to America's sweet tooth, Stuckey's also distinguished itself with other items. Souvenirs such as rubber snakes; T-shirts; novelty cigarette lighters; state salt-and-pepper shakers; and, more recently, anything with Elvis Presley on it, gave Stuckey's a lasting place in the hearts and minds of traveling Americans during the 1950s and 1960s.

By the mid-1960s Stuckey's enjoyed a virtual monopoly on American highways. The company hit its peak in the early 1970s, with 360 Stuckey's stores in thirty-one states. But monopolies do not last forever, and things began to change. Fast-food chains such as McDonald's and Dairy Queen saw a golden opportunity to increase their business with highway travelers. Soon even those fast-food giants faced competition from such gas station/convenience store chains as Super America. By the late 1970s cheap air fares made long-distance traveling by car less common. New highways were also replacing some of the older routes, and many Stuckey's were left on less traveled roads. Consequently the number of Stuckey's began to fall in the late 1970s.

In 1985 W. S. Stuckey Jr. tried to reinvigorate the store by mixing some well-known brand names with traditional Stuckey's merchandise. More recently Stuckey's has entered into partnerships with other fast-food chains, including Dairy Queen and Citgo, to sell Stuckey's candies and souvenirs at those businesses. Stuckey's has also replaced its turquoise roof and old pecan shop look with a more contemporary facade and logo.

Stuckey's no longer rules the roadsides of America. At the start of the twenty-first century, Stuckey's operated just over fifty establishments. However, the chain still sells thousands of its Pecan Log Rolls and souvenir salt-and-pepper shakers. And, perhaps just as important, Stuckey's will always serve as a fond memory of the 1950s and 1960s road trip experience.

David E. Woodard

SEE ALSO: *Air Travel; Automobile; Drive-In Theater; Fast Food; The Fifties; Gas Stations; Highway System; Leisure Time; McDonald's; Presley, Elvis; Suburbia; T-Shirts.*

BIBLIOGRAPHY

"About Stuckey's." Accessed January 7, 2012. Available from http://stuckeys.com/about.php

Andrews, Greg. "Stuckey's Staples and Souvenirs Still Draw Traveling Customers." *Indianapolis Star/News*, January 24, 1998.

Caruso, Dale. "Stuckey's: Pecan Log Roll and Coffee Make a Comeback." *American Reporter*, February 17, 1998.

Jakle, John A., and Keith A. Sculle. *Fast Food: Roadside Restaurants in the Automobile Age.* Baltimore, MD: Johns Hopkins University Press, 2002.

Kaszynski, William. *The American Highway: The History and Culture of Roads in the United States.* Jefferson, NC: McFarland, 2000.

Student Demonstrations

Colleges and universities have historically been centers of political dissent. Perhaps because university students are in a rarefied state of independence, suspended between parental control and the mundane responsibilities of adult life, perhaps because the very nature of university education inspires students to form opinions and to take those opinions seriously, students have frequently been leaders in movements for social change. As early as the fourth century CE, throughout the Middle Ages, and continuing into the modern era, university students have protested against politics and policies they find distasteful.

The 1960s—shorthand for an era that began in the 1950s and continued into the 1970s—marked a time of massive social upheaval. African Americans began to organize to fight the state-supported racism that oppressed them. Women and gays began to question the social order that kept them subservient and invisible. There was open dissent about government policies, particularly regarding the undeclared war in Vietnam. Citizens began to mistrust the government officials they had always been told knew best. And at the core of each of these growing movements were the energetic, angry challenges of the student movements, both in the United States and around the world.

Though media representations of the student protest movements of the 1960s may be content with showing long-haired demonstrators waving flowers at police, the fact is that many complex political movements evolved in the 1960s. Some students were deeply involved in these movements, while others were simply swept up in their wake. The 1960s really began with the formation of two radical student organizations that would exemplify major waves of student activity of the era: the Student Nonviolent Coordinating Committee (SNCC, pronounced "snick") and Students for a Democratic Society (SDS).

CIVIL RIGHTS MOVEMENT

SNCC was formed in 1960 with the support of a major civil rights organization, the Southern Christian Leadership Conference, to give a voice to young black civil rights activists who were impatient with the careful tactics of their elders. Almost immediately, SNCC took a more radical approach to the fight for civil rights, though it maintained a commitment to nonviolence. SNCC organized demonstrations, became involved in the Freedom Rides campaign to desegregate southern buses, and worked to reform voting laws. In one of its most successful demonstrations, SNCC was instrumental in organizing the Freedom Summer of 1964, when busloads of mostly white students from the North went to the South, where they lived with black families and did extensive organizing, from teaching in the Freedom Schools to registering black voters. Besides the extraordinary accomplishment of public education and outreach, the Freedom Summer played a large part in the passage of the United States Voting Rights Act.

By 1966, impatient with continued prejudice and discrimination, the membership of SNCC grew increasingly radical. Members such as Stokely Carmichael and H. Rap Brown embodied this change of attitude. New catchphrases became "Black Power!" and "Violence is as American as cherry pie." SNCC joined with another new organization for young black militants, the Black Panther Party, and demonstrations were no longer peaceful sit-ins but rather were angry, threatening near-riots. The Black Panther Party began to look outside the United States for support, to countries such as Cuba, for whom revolution was more than a symbol.

Students for a Democratic Society President. *Mark Rudd, center, president of Students for a Democratic Society, addresses students at Columbia University in 1968.* HULTON ARCHIVE/GETTY IMAGES.

The Students for a Democratic Society (SDS), formed in 1960, put out its famous statement of purpose, the Port Huron Statement, in 1962. Drafted at a national meeting of SDS in Port Huron, Michigan, the statement began, "We are people of this generation, bred in at least modest comfort, housed now in universities, looking uncomfortably to the world we inherit." The statement was an indictment of modern American values and called for students to demand a truly "participatory democracy" and to fight against social injustice and materialistic capitalism. In 1963, in an effort to act on this statement, SDS formed the Economic Research and Action Project to put participatory democracy into practice. In the summer of 1964, some 125 SDS organizers attempted political organizing among the urban poor in various cities across the country. But it was its mobilization against the Vietnam War for which SDS is best remembered.

By the mid-1960s, television broadcasts of wartime violence and American casualties were causing doubt among many Americans as to the rationale behind the war, and the greatest doubters of all were college students of draft age and their friends. Demonstrations against the war sprang up on college and university campuses everywhere, some at military recruiting offices, some at Reserve Officers' Training Corps (ROTC) buildings—anywhere that held some connection to the war. On April 17, 1965, SDS organized the first of several mass demonstrations against the Vietnam War in Washington, D.C. Fifteen thousand demonstrators joined them. In November SDS cosponsored another demonstration, drawing 30,000 antiwar protesters.

FROM NONVIOLENCE TO MILITANCY

Like SNCC, SDS members grew impatient with the slowness of governmental response to their impassioned protests, and the group became more militant. By the time more than 700 demonstrators were arrested at an SDS protest at Columbia University in 1968, the organization was already beginning to metamorphose into the fiercely militant Weathermen. In 1969 the Weathermen organized the Days of Rage, consisting of violent protest and rioting in Chicago. Eventually, radical members formed the Weather Underground, which considered itself a guerrilla warfare group. The Weather Underground, which continued to be active until 1977, took responsibility for twelve bombings and released twenty-two political communiqués plus a book, *Prairie Fire*. While many radicals later disavowed their militant stands, many others, including SDS's Bernadette Dohrn, stand behind their youthful politics and continue to work on the Left for social change.

Most students were not members of any group, but a large number felt strongly about the social and political issues that motivated the organizations. Raised by a generation that had been largely unquestioningly patriotic, the students of the 1960s questioned everything their parents and their government told them. They began to feel they had been lied to, that the privilege they enjoyed was tainted because it came at the expense of people of color both at home and in Vietnam. Most of all, they did not want themselves or their friends to kill or be killed in Vietnam defending the lie. Following the pattern of such groups as SNCC and SDS, student demonstrations of the early 1960s were largely peaceful rallies and marches, with the occasional teach-in about the war or sit-in in a controversial building on campus.

Unfortunately, university administrations and campus police did not understand how to deal with such challenges to their authority and often responded by attempting to clamp down with tighter control, which usually resulted in greater and more violent rebellion. Along with antiwar protests, "student power" movements developed as students insisted on having a voice in the way their schools were run. The free speech movement (FSM) at the University of California at Berkeley began when the university attempted to ban student political organization on campus. When campus police tried to arrest a student distributing civil rights literature, 3,000 students sat down, immobilizing the police car, until beaten back by police with clubs. The FSM continued to protest the university policy, resulting in the occupation of Sproul Hall on campus on December 2, 1964, and the arrest of almost 800 students.

Though large universities, such as Berkeley and Columbia, are famous for dramatic student demonstrations, the wave of protest was nationwide and affected a broad spectrum of colleges. Buildings were occupied and even bombed at institutions from Washington University in St. Louis to the College of William and Mary in Virginia. Student organizers reasoned that since they were fighting to save lives, both American and Vietnamese, damage to mere property was imminently justified.

Perhaps the most famous example of overreaction to student protest occurred at Ohio's Kent State University in May 1970. Following an announcement by President Richard Nixon of a new escalation in the war, students across the United States rose up in a series of angry protests. The National Guard was called out to control crowds of demonstrators at Kent State, not an unusual practice for frustrated administrators. With little training in handling crowds, overwrought guardsmen fired into the crowd, killing four students and setting off a fresh wave of outraged protests. Ten days later, a similar incident at Jackson State University in Mississippi caused the deaths of two students and wounding of nine others. Though these incidents provoked public horror, little investigation was done, and the guardsmen involved were never punished.

THE REBELLIOUS GENERATION

While American students were organizing demonstrations across the United States, students in France, Japan, England, Spain, Czechoslovakia, and other countries around the world were also rising up in protest against university or government policies. May and June 1968, a turbulent year in the United States, saw a nationwide strike of students and workers in France. One of the differences between demonstrations in the United States and those in many other countries, especially in France, was that the European students often allied themselves with labor, protesting in conjunction with working people. In the United States, many working-class people viewed protesting students with angry suspicion, as privileged brats who despised their achievements and denigrated their flag. Though some American students sought alliances with working people, others referred to them derisively as "hard-hats" and saw them as the enemy, the arms and voices of unthinking patriotism that supported the state lie and the materialistic American dream. These stereotypes—the wealthy, downwardly mobile, foul-mouthed hippie and the "America, love it or leave it" narrow-minded hard-hat—often prevented communication between students and laborers that might have revealed their common interests.

There was some truth to the rebel stereotype. Counterculture young men did wear their hair long, both because it was fashionable and to challenge the authority that insisted they cut it. Young women wore their hair long and straight too, eschewed makeup and bras, and often did not shave their legs. Both sexes wore clothes that were casual to the point of raggedness. These styles were adopted by the youth of the 1960s, along with a direct mode of speech liberally peppered with profanity, partially as a reaction against the careful facades of propriety so important to their parents' generation and partially to conform with the careful facade of impropriety so necessary to the rebel generation. There was a culture of protest and, along with its mandated style of dress and speech, it had its own literature and music. Radicals read Richard Wright's *Native Son*, Eldridge Cleaver's *Ice and Fire*, and Angela Davis's speeches in the *Guardian*. They listened to rock music that was specifically political, such as Buffalo Springfield's "For What It's Worth" and Country Joe and the Fish's "I'm-Fixin'-to-Die Rag," or to music filled with a raw and painful passion, as in the music of Janis Joplin and the Doors.

SDS activist Tom Hayden later described the achievements of his generation grandly: "We ended a war, toppled two presidents, desegregated the South, broke other barriers of discrimination." While some former protesters of the 1960s might be more jaded as to the long-lasting effects of their efforts, there is no doubt that the idealistic energy of the youth of that period did change history. President Nixon later admitted that fears of heightened protest limited his escalation of the war in Vietnam. While racial discrimination clearly still exists in the United States, state-sanctioned segregation no longer does. Shortly after the dramatic demonstrations of 1968, both France and the United States lowered their voting age to eighteen. The Green Party in Germany continues to fight for the causes that German youth demonstrated for in the 1960s. For a period of a few years, the hippies and activists of the New Left felt sure they could change the world, and that passion is perhaps their greatest legacy.

THE SPIRIT OF PROTEST CONTINUES

Student protests continue around the world, with each generation defining its style and its issues. A politically conservative era in the United States during the 1980s saw a backlash to the activism of the previous decades, causing frustrated radical leader Abbie Hoffman to complain that college campuses had become "hotbeds of rest." Students in other countries, however, continued to mount massive campaigns of protest, such as the prodemocracy movement in China that ended in the massacre of hundreds of student demonstrators in Beijing's Tiananmen Square in 1989, and the antiapartheid demonstrations in South Africa. By the end of the 1980s, U.S. students also began large demonstrations against apartheid, demanding that their institutions divest funds from the white South African regime.

Opposition to wars in Afghanistan and Iraq drew students into the streets once more during the 1990s and early twenty-first century, and many began to protest a larger pattern of economic globalization that they saw as unjust. This new analysis broke down some of the polarization between students and labor, as students, along with protesting budget cuts in education, began to demonstrate for better pay for college clerical and maintenance workers.

At the end of 2010 a wave of protests swept many countries of North Africa and the Middle East. Dubbed the Arab Spring, these protests continued into 2012, largely led by university students and graduates driven to despair and militancy by political repression and lack of economic opportunity. U.S. students were inspired by the Arab Spring protests, which were widely publicized in the press and by social media. Joining together with labor, the poor, and other disenfranchised groups, these students created the Occupy movement for economic justice, setting up protest encampments on campuses and in economic centers, beginning in 2011 with New York's Wall Street. These protests became such a significant part of U.S. culture that *Time* magazine named "The Protester" its Person of the Year for 2011.

Tina Gianoulis

SEE ALSO: *Black Panthers; Buffalo Springfield; Civil Rights Movement; The Doors; Free Speech Movement; Freedom Rides; Gulf Wars; Hippies; Hoffman, Abbie; Joplin, Janis; Kent State Massacre; Protest Groups; Students for a Democratic Society (SDS); Vietnam; War in Afghanistan; The Weathermen; Wright, Richard.*

BIBLIOGRAPHY

De Groot, Gerard J. "Reagan's Rise." *History Today* 45, no. 9 (1995): 31.

De Groot, Gerard J. *Student Protest: The Sixties and After.* New York: Addison Wesley Longman, 1998.

Kerns, Ann. *Who Will Shout if Not Us? Student Activists and the Tiananmen Square Protest.* Minneapolis, MN: Twenty First Century Books, 2011.

Koning, Hans. *Nineteen Sixty Eight: A Personal Report.* New York: W. W. Norton, 1987.

Miller, James. *Democracy Is in the Streets: From Port Huron to the Siege of Chicago.* New York: Simon & Schuster, 1987.

What Is Occupy? Inside the Global Movement. New York: Time Books, 2011.

Students for a Democratic Society (SDS)

Students for a Democratic Society (SDS) was one of the largest and most militant organizations to oppose the Vietnam War. It grew from a small group of young socialists to an organization of more than 100,000 members, with chapters on some 350 college campuses. The small Student League for Industrial Democracy became Students for a Democratic Society in 1960, and 1962 saw the publication of its Port Huron Statement, a manifesto critiquing American society and proposing student activism as a solution to the problems identified. The document was circulated widely, causing student interest in SDS to grow significantly.

In 1964 some SDS chapters organized demonstrations against the growing American involvement in Vietnam. As the war intensified, so did SDS opposition, including attacks on Reserve Officers' Training Corp (ROTC) programs, the occupying of campus buildings, and student strikes. Media coverage of these protest activities tended to focus not only on the most disruptive and violent acts but also on the most radical SDS spokespeople. The coverage was to the group's disadvantage—it tended to attract the most politically extreme young people (thus radicalizing SDS even further), and it gave the impression to middle-class Americans that SDS consisted entirely of violent would-be revolutionaries.

In 1968 SDS participated in the demonstrations at the Democratic National Convention in Chicago. SDS president Tom Hayden was one of the Chicago Seven who were later tried on federal charges of conspiracy to riot. In 1969 internal dissension caused SDS to self-destruct, leaving only a core of its most radicalized members, who soon began to call themselves the Weathermen. In 2006 some students reached out to the members of the original SDS and a new group was formed under the same name, focused on ending the wars in Iraq and Afghanistan and working for "student rights."

Justin Gustainis

SEE ALSO: *The Chicago Seven; Protest Groups; Student Demonstrations; Vietnam.*

BIBLIOGRAPHY

Committee on Internal Security and U.S. House of Representatives. *Anatomy of a Revolutionary Movement: "Students for a Democratic Society."* Washington, DC: University Press of the Pacific, 2005.

Gilbert, David. *SDS/WUO, Students for a Democratic Society and the Weather Underground Organisation.* Montreal: Abraham Guillen Press, 2002.

Gitlin, Todd. *The Whole World Is Watching: Mass Media in the Making & Unmaking of the New Left.* Berkeley: University of California Press, 1980.

Miller, James. *Democracy Is in the Streets: From Port Huron to the Siege of Chicago.* New York: Simon & Schuster, 1987.

Pekar, Harvey; Paul Buhle; and Gary Dumm. *Students for a Democratic Society: A Graphic History.* New York: Hill and Wang, 2009.

Sale, Kirkpatrick. *SDS.* New York: Random House, 1973.

Studio 54

A legendary New York nightclub, Studio 54 was infamous for its sexual licentiousness (nudity on the dance floor, topless busboys, a unique gay/straight clientele mix) and an eclectic/elitist door policy that integrated the beautiful, the eccentric, and a vast array of celebrities (the Jaggers, Andy Warhol, Liza Minnelli, Michael Jackson, and so on). Studio 54 was opened in April 1977 by Steve Rubell and Ian Schrager; early in 1980 they were both sent to prison for tax evasion. Ownership then changed hands twice before the nightclub finally closed in March 1986. Immortalized, in a fictional form, in the films *Studio 54* (1998) and *The Last Days of Disco* (1998), Studio 54 has come to symbolize a historical transition point: from the freedom and hedonism of the 1970s into the yuppie elitism and self-destructiveness of the 1980s.

Glyn Davis

SEE ALSO: *Celebrity; Celebrity Couples; Gay Men; Jackson, Michael; Leisure Time; Minnelli, Liza; Sexual Revolution; Warhol, Andy; Yuppies.*

BIBLIOGRAPHY

Buckland, Fiona. *Impossible Dance Club Culture and Queer World-Making.* Middletown, CT: Wesleyan University Press, 2002.

Haden-Guest, Anthony. *The Last Party: Studio 54, Disco, and the Culture of the Night.* New York: William Morrow, 1997.

Studio One

Although it had its genesis as a radio program, *Studio One* became the longest-running anthology drama series of the "Golden Age of Television," with more than 450 live teleplays on CBS from 1948 through 1958, and earned a reputation as a visual innovator in broadcast storytelling. A product of television's infancy, the series disseminated drama of a high order, bringing classical works and serious "one-off" plays to a wide popular audience and sowing the seeds for a generation of Hollywood writers and directors to learn their craft on the small screen. While other series were known for psychological realism, *Studio One*, under its first producer, Worthington Miner, explored the technical and stylistic potentials of the medium.

Miner thought with his eyes, focusing on a highly inventive, visual mode of storytelling. For him, *Studio One* existed somewhere between live drama and film. It was a "live performance staged for multiple cameras." Whereas most dramatic series efficiently relayed a live performance using a static three-camera set-up, the camera movement was an integral part of the *Studio One* performance. The actors were positioned and choreographed so they could be shot through apertures in the scenery, and flying walls were employed. Elaborate physical productions filled the studio above Grand Central Terminal, and in the first two years of the show, Miner himself created thirty-nine of the forty-four live productions, employing techniques that kept audiences constantly attentive.

In a modern-dress production of William Shakespeare's *Julius Caesar* during the first season, for example, Miner moved the camera in extremely tight for a close-up of the eyes of one of the conspirators, while the actor's prerecorded voice played over the live close-up. In this attempt to reveal thought, Miner jumped inside the character's mind, using methods that both unnerved and excited viewers. For *Battleship Bismarck*, the producer used inventive camera angles, tight groupings, and quick, live-camera cuts in place of post-production editing—he often used long, shallow sets that allowed him to shoot from sharp angles. He also employed arresting lighting techniques for outdoor scenes, as in *Macbeth*, which starred Charlton Heston, one of the show's regular performers. This array of technical and stylistic devices created a specific form of visual storytelling appropriate for the infant medium.

These innovations were vital to the success of the program. Most outstanding dramatic material was already under option to Hollywood, which was not about to share it with an upstart medium that was perceived as a threat to the livelihood of the film industry. In addition, the film studios argued that kinescopes (a film of the image from the picture tube), which were broadcast later in markets other than New York, violated their rights to certain properties. Also, there were not yet seasoned television writers, and television could not afford to hire established stage or screen dramatists. Consequently, Miner not only adapted plays from the great classical canon and other work in the public domain, but also drew on lesser Broadway vehicles and short stories.

In 1953 Felix Jackson became producer of *Studio One* and began his stewardship with a critically acclaimed production of

George Orwell's *1984*. He established an emphasis on original drama, most notably with Reginald Rose's *12 Angry Men*, but despite these and other successes (including *The Defender*), many of the works from the mid-1950s were "kitchen sink" dramas, stories of ordinary people dealing with a range of ordinary domestic and emotional problems. Larger social and political themes were largely left untouched. In spite of high ratings, sponsors and advertising agencies were generally unhappy with the commonplace locales and stories, feeling that they were sabotaging the implicit fantasies and dreams of consumerism presented in their commercials. CBS and Westinghouse demanded that Rose's *Thunder on Sycamore Street*, based on an actual incident involving a black family moving into a white neighborhood, be altered. Fearing for the sensibilities of southern affiliates and their white viewers, producers made the black protagonist an ex-convict. Rose partially managed to subvert this revision by withholding this information until the very end of the show. As Erik Barnouw noted in *Tube of Plenty: The Evolution of American Television*, viewers responded with their own predilections, and the sponsors and network discovered that they had unwittingly presented the type of controversy they had hoped to avoid.

Actress Betty Furness began doing the commercials during the first year's telecasts and continued to do so for the remainder of the program's life on the air. Her live demonstrations of Westinghouse's household appliances made her the most famous and recognized spokesperson in American television.

The shift to Hollywood and film allowed the networks and sponsors to create something with production values more like those of feature films. Intimate, minimalist settings and the "marvelous world of the ordinary" were on their way out. Filmed productions for television had the potential for an economic afterlife in syndication, while action-oriented genres, especially Westerns, could be churned out quickly on film. Sponsors were relieved of the worry of approving a new set of characters and a potentially problematic script each week—they, and their audiences, could happily identify with a few ongoing characters and personalities instead. In 1957 the amount of prime-time programming originating on the West Coast rose to nearly 71 percent. *Studio One in Hollywood* premiered in January 1958, broadcasting live. It was off the air by September.

Louis Scheeder

SEE ALSO: *Advertising; Broadway; Heston, Charlton; Hollywood; Television.*

BIBLIOGRAPHY

Barnouw, Erik. *Tube of Plenty: The Evolution of American Television*. New York: Oxford University Press, 1975.

Stempel, Tom. *Storytellers to the Nation: A History of American Television Writing*. Syracuse, NY: Syracuse University Press, 1996.

Studio System

The term *studio system* refers to the process of producing and distributing films that dominated Hollywood from the late-1920s to the early-1950s. In this system large motion picture studios filmed on massive dedicated production facilities or lots to which they had exclusive access (employing a cast and production staff under very strict long-term contracts) and then released the films in theater chains that the studio controlled either through ownership or exclusive contractual obligation. The bulk of this period, lasting from the introduction of sound in the film industry in 1927 to the Supreme Court ruling that weakened the studio system in 1948, is often referred to as the "Golden Age of Hollywood."

During the Golden Age there were eight "major studios": Fox Film Corporation (later Twentieth Century Fox), Loew's Incorporated (owner of America's largest theater circuit and parent company to Metro-Goldwyn-Mayer), Paramount Pictures, RKO Radio Pictures, Warner Brothers, Universal Pictures, Columbia Pictures, and United Artists. The control exercised by each studio varied from complete vertical integration to loose contractual obligation. United Artists, for instance, owned a few theaters and had two dedicated production lots but functioned primarily as a financial backer and distributor for independent producers.

THE FOUNDATION OF AN EMPIRE

In 1903, when a cousin of Adolph Zukor, a young Hungarian immigrant who had made a small fortune in the fur business, came to him for a loan to open an arcade of electric novelties and "peep" machines, the usually cautious businessman saw great money-making possibilities. Zukor had an advantage that the purveyors of these machines lacked: from his years in the fur business, he had become adept at judging the market. At the time, films were only beginning to be shown on large screens. Their more common form was the peep machine, by which a brief film, such as *The Great Train Robbery* (1903), could be viewed for a nickel. Based on the popularity of these short films, Zukor and another partner in the business, Marcus Loew, saw the commercial potential of movie theaters. Zucker also perceived the potential market for longer films—"canned" theater, as it was called, a revolutionary idea for its time. Believing that movies could both entertain and edify, Zuckor obtained the rights for an hour-and-a-half French film, *Les Amours de la reine Élisabeth* (1912), starring Sarah Bernhardt, which became an instant success.

Across America, a similar narrative was being played out among ambitious young men like Zukor who were in touch with the desires of their audiences and willing to go out on a limb to satisfy their only half-formulated desires. Nickelodeons were popular in the immigrant community and subsequently were viewed as somewhat disreputable by established businessmen, precisely because of that popularity. These new young entrepreneurs, who had no such qualms, made a killing and then, in their efforts to satisfy the viewing public, began producing films of their own. At the time, Thomas Edison had put together a trust of older, more established film producers and distributors, with the intent of enforcing the patent payments he held on film equipment. Incensed, the upstart film producers waged a covert war on the Edison Trust. Many of them fled to Los Angeles, beyond the long arm of Edison. Coincidentally, the sunny, clement weather in Los Angeles was also conducive to filmmaking.

CLOSING THE RANKS

In the 1910s a period of consolidation occurred, resulting in several large conglomerates that both produced and distributed the films and owned the theaters. Thus, the major Hollywood

Movie Industry Pioneers. *From left, movie studio heads and industry pioneers Jesse Lasky, Adolph Zukor, Samuel Goldwyn, Cecil B. DeMille, and Albert Kaufman posing together circa 1916.* JOHN FLOREA/TIME LIFE PICTURES/GETTY IMAGES.

studios were born. By the mid-1920s a distinct pecking order existed in Hollywood between the smaller, poverty-row studios and the powerful conglomerates such as Paramount (Zukor's company), Universal, RKO, Twentieth Century Fox, and Metro-Goldwyn-Mayer (MGM). With the coming of sound film in the late 1920s, filmmakers had realized Zukor's ambition of "canned" theater. Paramount; MGM; Universal; Twentieth Century Fox; and, to a lesser extent, Warner Brothers and Columbia vied for supremacy in this period. Each established a distinctive style and stable of stars that in many ways reflected the personality and conceit of its boss. MGM, for example, had exclusive contracts with Greta Garbo, Joan Crawford, Buster Keaton, Clark Gable, Jean Harlow, and Spencer Tracy for most of the 1920s and 1930s.

Propelled by sound and the popularity of films during the Depression, the studios found themselves shaping the entertainment of an entire nation. Many studio heads took their roles as cultural arbiters seriously and crafted their pictures to fit a certain image. Zukor had a penchant for "quality" entertainment, scouring the European continent for artists and presenting his finds in lavish period pieces wholly devoid of any concern for realpolitik.

Louis B. Mayer, who as a result of luck and business cunning had finessed himself into heading the conglomeration of three rival companies, was preoccupied with family values. He perceived himself as a patriarch at the head of an enormous extended family (the studio) and, by extension, the viewing public. Mayer had refused to allow his two daughters to go to college for fear they might acquire subversive ideas, and he evinced the same concern for the viewing public as a whole. As could be expected from such a man, the pictures MGM made were wholesome things, and in the 1930s Mickey Rooney and his Andy Hardy movies and wholesome sporting epics were examples of the good, clean fun that predominated at MGM.

Universal and Twentieth Century Fox had both found early success in silent pictures but were unable to adapt as readily. Universal, outside of its classic 1930s horror movies and a few lavish production pieces, merely weathered the storm. It was Columbia and Warner Brothers, both marginal upstarts, that adapted best to the changing current of American life, Warner with fast-paced, starkly lit gangster films and Columbia with breezy, wise-cracking screwball comedies.

OVERWHELMING SUCCESS

Film succeeded so far beyond the studio presidents' dreams that they were soon involved in a continental search to expand the talent pool. Agents and scouts were sent scurrying across Europe to lure directors, technicians, and actors to Hollywood. Ernst Lubitsch and Erich von Stroheim came early, impressed by the technical innovations in American films. Fritz Lang came later, a refugee from Adolf Hitler's Germany, as were an increasing number of novelists, playwrights, musicians, artists, and composers who, while playing only a marginal role, enlivened the atmosphere considerably.

New York was not immune to studio agents' incursions either. Throughout the 1930s novelists and playwrights lit out west after the brass ring. Some, such as F. Scott Fitzgerald and Dorothy Parker, were feted and cajoled into writing for pictures and, in turn, reacted with derision. Others, such as William Faulkner and Raymond Chandler, were failed authors who relied on Hollywood to sustain them. Nathanael West, whose books had sold as poorly as Faulkner's, found an audience when he penned *Day of the Locust* (1939), which offered a brutally honest, if cynical, take on Hollywood in the 1930s.

In 1939, the year *Gone with the Wind* and *The Wizard of Oz* were released, film was the nation's eleventh-largest industry, with studios turning out some 500 new movies each year. A decade later, however, the major studios were losing money, and the influence of films was slipping, superseded by a pesky rival, television. The House Un-American Activities Committee hearings investigating communist influences in Hollywood further reduced any lingering sensations of omnipotence among the studio heads, who were forced to blacklist some of their most notable talent.

What damaged the studios most, however, was the success of an antitrust suit in the Supreme Court in 1948. Investigations of the studios' monopolistic practices dated back to 1920, when the consolidation of production and distribution had effectively squeezed out all but a few independents and spurred the studios to build enormous temples to themselves with their ornate theaters. Practices such as block booking (a system of selling multiple films to a theater as a unit) and blind selling (an element of the system involving the purchase of unseen films) enabled studios to cram a slew of mediocre films down the throats of theater owners to have access to the one film they wanted to show. By 1948 the Justice Department had finally drawn a line in the sand. RKO was the first to cave in, followed in short order by Loew's and then the other majors. Hollywood would never recover.

END OF AN ERA

The studio system these men created to sustain their visions lasted from the mid-1910s to the early 1950s. By the mid-1950s control of many majors had reverted to Wall Street, and the studio heads had either retired or were summarily fired by their newly established board of directors. The rise of television brought increased pressure on the studios to turn a profit. Initially the studios attempted a number of gimmicks, such 3-D and smell-o-vision. Many of the studios had already sold portions of their back catalog to television, which, in turn, began running movies during their prime-time slots. Box-office sales plummeted under the new competition coupled with the lower number of movies being released each year. The financial losses opened up the major studios for a series of corporate acquisitions throughout the 1960s.

In 1962 MCA purchased Universal, followed by Gulf Western acquiring Paramount in 1966, and Transamerica bought United Artists in 1967. Both Warner Brothers and MGM attempted to outlast the economic downturn by restructuring their corporate entities but eventually landed in the hands of Kinney National and Kirk Kerkorian, respectively. Abandoning low budget films, the studios turned to marketing blockbusters similar to *The Sound of Music* (1965).

Jaws (1975) ushered in an enhanced business model that rejuvenated the industry. Nationwide advertising campaigns and well-timed summer releases became the new trend. Movies like *Star Wars* (1977) and *Superman* (1978) set box-office records and were accompanied by merchandising efforts that spawned toys, television series, soundtracks, and, eventually, sequels. The new model steamed through the 1980s, taking advantage of technologies like video games and cable television. Additionally, Hollywood returned to a somewhat modified star system. Based on the success of *Star Wars*, Harrison Ford helped launch the highly profitable *Indiana Jones* (1981) franchise.

In the 1990s and the first decade of the 2000s, studios were transformed from film producers into distributors. The original studio powerhouses, along with Disney, grew into large conglomerates that primarily provided financial and distribution support to smaller, independent companies. The new corporate structures enabled Time Warner, Viacom, Comcast, Disney, News Corp., and Sony to dominate the market share of the film industry. For a short time, companies such as Lionsgate and MGM competed with the major companies, seemingly signaling the rise of an independent filmmaking market. However, these independent production companies were steadily acquired by the major conglomerates.

In the 1990s Time Warner purchased New Line Cinema and Castle Rock Entertainment. Meanwhile, Disney bought Miramax in 1993 and Pixar in 2006. Although studios including Summit Entertainment (now part of Lionsgate) experienced great commercial success with films such as *Twilight* (2008), the major studios established greater control of the market through merchandising and advertising revenues. Corporations such as DreamWorks and the Weinstein Company leveraged some influence through commercially successful films, but the overwhelming power of the transnational media conglomerates forced the independents to rely upon them for distribution.

Michael Baers

SEE ALSO: *Blacklisting; Chandler, Raymond; DeMille, Cecil B.; Edison, Thomas Alva; Faulkner, William; Fitzgerald, F. Scott; Goldwyn, Samuel;* Gone with the Wind*; The Great Depression;* The Great Train Robbery*; Hollywood; Lang, Fritz; Lubitsch, Ernst; Mayer, Louis B.; MGM (Metro-Goldwyn-Mayer); Movie Palaces; Nickelodeons; Parker, Dorothy; Screwball Comedies;* The Sound of Music*; Television;* Twilight*;* The Wizard of Oz.

BIBLIOGRAPHY

Anderson, Christopher. *Hollywood TV: The Studio System in the Fifties*. Austin: University of Texas Press, 1994.

Davis, Ronald L. *The Glamour Factory*. Dallas, TX: Southern Methodist University Press, 1993.

Friedrich, Otto. *City of Nets*. New York: Harper & Row, 1986.

Gabler, Neal. *An Empire of Their Own*. New York: Crown, 1988.

Gomery, Douglas. *The Hollywood Studio System: A History*. London: British Film Institute, 2008.

McDonald, Paul, and Janet Wasko, eds. *The Contemporary Hollywood Film Industry*. Malden, MA: Blackwell, 2008.

Mordden, Ethan. *The Hollywood Studios: House Style in the Golden Age of Movies*. New York: Knopf, 1988.

Schatz, Thomas. *The Genius of the System: Hollywood Filmmaking in the Studio Era*. New York: Pantheon, 1988.

Sturges, Preston *(1898–1959)*

In 1929, after a childhood abroad, a stint in the army, and a turn as an inventor creating kiss-proof lipstick, Chicago native Preston Sturges staged his first Broadway play. From that nearly accidental debut, he fashioned a career in Hollywood's Golden Age that film critic Andrew Sarris calls "one of the most brilliant and most bizarre bursts of creation in the history of the American cinema."

Hired as a writer in 1932, Sturges became, in 1940, the first screenplay author to direct his own script when he penned and directed *Christmas in July* and Academy Award–winner *The Great McGinty*. By 1944 he had secured his lasting legacy with signature romantic comedies: *The Lady Eve* and *Sullivan's Travels* (both 1941), *The Palm Beach Story* (1942), and *The Miracle of Morgan's Creek* (1944). Sturges was hailed for his brilliance in studio publicity and for his movies' eccentric, visionary critiques of American society.

Elizabeth Haas

SEE ALSO: *Academy Awards; Broadway; Hollywood; Screwball Comedies; Stanwyck, Barbara.*

BIBLIOGRAPHY

Harvey, James. *Romantic Comedy in Hollywood from Lubitsch to Sturges*. New York: A. A. Knopf, 1987.

Jacobs, Diane. *Christmas in July: The Life and Art of Preston Sturges*. Berkeley: University of California Press, 1992.

Pirolini, Alessandro. *The Cinema of Preston Sturges: A Critical Study*. Jefferson, NC: McFarland, 2010.

Rozgonyi, Jay. *Preston Sturges's Vision of America: Critical Analyses of Fourteen Films*. Jefferson, NC: McFarland, 1995.

Sturges, Preston. *Preston Sturges*, adapted and edited by Sandy Sturges. New York: Simon & Schuster, 1990.

Styron, William *(1925–2006)*

The few published novels of William Styron have won major literary awards, received tremendous popular attention, and been the subject of controversy. The author was best known for infusing his works with dysfunctional, tragic characters and dark subjects.

Styron was born on June 11, 1925, in Newport News, Virginia. He graduated from Duke University in North Carolina in 1947 and then traveled in Europe. Styron's two best-known novels, *The Confessions of Nat Turner* (1967) and *Sophie's Choice* (1979), deal with a U.S. slave rebellion and the Holocaust, respectively. *The Confessions of Nat Turner*, based on a documented revolt by slaves in Virginia's Tidewater area in 1831, won the Pulitzer Prize in 1968, yet sparked much hostile criticism from black writers and critics. Many charged Styron with historical falsification, while others believed it was unconscionable for a white novelist to presume to enter the mind of a black slave.

National Book Award winner *Sophie's Choice* is set in post–World War II Brooklyn, New York, and recounts the story of an Auschwitz concentration camp survivor who is plagued by horrible memories and caught in a turbulent love relationship. It was turned into a much acclaimed film released in 1982 and was also made into an opera in 2002. Styron chronicled his battle with depression in the well-received *Darkness Visible: A Memoir of Madness* (1990).

Styron died on November 1, 2006, from complications of pneumonia. Three collections of his work, including short stories, letters, and personal essays, were published posthumously between 2008 and 2009.

James Schiff

SEE ALSO: *Best Sellers; Depression; World War II.*

BIBLIOGRAPHY

Casciato, Arthur D., and James L. W. West III, eds. *Critical Essays on William Styron*. Boston: G.K. Hall, 1982.

Clarke, John Henrik, ed. *William Styron's Nat Turner: Ten Black Writers Respond*. Boston: Beacon Press, 1968.

Coale, Samuel Chase. *William Styron Revisited*. Boston: Twayne, 1991.

Styron, Alexandria. *Reading My Father: A Memoir*. New York: Scribner, 2011.

West, James L. W., III, ed. *Conversations with William Styron*. Jackson: University Press of Mississippi, 1985.

West, James L. W., III, ed. *William Styron: A Life*. New York: Random House, 1998.